Features

115th Edition
Statistical Abstract of the United States 1995

The National Data Book

U.S. Department of Commerce
Ronald H. Brown, Secretary
David J. Barram, Deputy Secretary

Economics and Statistics Administration
Everett M. Ehrlich, Under Secretary for Economic Affairs

Bureau of the Census
Martha Farnsworth Riche, Director

BERNAN PRESS
Lanham, Maryland

Economics and Statistics Administration
Everett M. Ehrlich, Under Secretary for Economic Affairs

BUREAU OF THE CENSUS
Martha Farnsworth Riche, Director
Harry A. Scarr, Deputy Director
Philip L. Sparks, Assistant Director for Communications

DATA USER SERVICES DIVISION
Richard L. Bitzer, Acting Chief

Acknowledgments

Glenn W. King, Chief, Statistical Compendia Staff, was responsible for general supervision and compilation of this volume. **Lars B. Johanson** was responsible for technical supervision and coordination. Assisting in the research and analytical phases of assigned sections and in the developmental aspects of new tables were **Rosemary E. Clark**, **Edward C. Jagers** and **David J. Fleck. Geraldine W. Blackburn** provided primary editorial assistance. Other editorial assistance was rendered by **Linda Beard**, **Patricia S. Lancaster**, **Catherine Lavender**, and **Joyce Mori**.

The staff of the Administrative and Publications Services Division, **Walter C. Odom**, Chief, performed publication planning, editorial review, design, composition, and printing planning and procurement. **Patricia Heiston,** assisted by **Gloria Davis,** provided publication coordination and editing. **Shirley A. Clark** provided design and graphics services, and **Richard Kersey** provided printing services.

The cooperation of many contributors to this volume is gratefully acknowledged. This year we want to especially acknowledge the assistance of many staff members at the International Trade Administration in the Department of Commerce and the help of **John J. Bistay** and **Rebecca A. Krafft** in the creation of our new section, "Industrial Outlook." The source note below each table credits the various government and private agencies which have collaborated in furnishing information for the **Statistical Abstract**. In a few instances, contributors have requested that their data be designated as subject to copyright restrictions, as indicated in the source notes to the tables affected. Permission to use copyright material should be obtained directly from the copyright owner.

Library of Congress Card No. 4–18089

SUGGESTED CITATION

U.S. Bureau of the Census, *Statistical Abstract of the United States: 1995*
(115th edition.) Washington, DC, 1995

Printed in the United States of America on acid-free paper

Bernan Press
4611-F Assembly Drive
Lanham, MD 20706 - 4391
(800) 274-4447
e-mail: info@kraus.com

ISBN: 0-89059-050-8
ISSN: 1063-1690

The *Statistical Abstract of the United States*, published since 1878, is the standard summary of statistics on the social, political, and economic organization of the United States. It is designed to serve as a convenient volume for statistical reference and as a guide to other statistical publications and sources.

The continuing importance of the *Statistical Abstract* has prompted Bernan Press to publish this quality edition. Any volume that receives such constant attention must be of the highest quality in order to withstand the rigors of many searches. This edition is printed on acid-free paper of increased weight, and has been Smyth-sewn into a durable cloth binding, two valuable modifications for librarians and frequent users.

The most obvious improvement, however, is the enlargement of every figure, table, and page. With this new edition, the *Statistical Abstract* is easier than ever to use.

Organization

This volume includes a selection of data from many statistical publications, both government and private. Publications cited as sources usually contain additional statistical detail and more comprehensive discussions of definitions and concepts than can be presented in these pages. Data not available in publications issued by the contributing agency but obtained from unpublished records are identified in the source notes as "unpublished data"; in general, more information on these tables may be obtained from the source.

Except as indicated, figures are for the United States as presently constituted. Although emphasis in the *Statistical Abstract* is primarily given to national data, many tables present data for regions and individual States, and a smaller number offer information on metropolitan areas and cities. Appendix II, Metropolitan Area Concepts and Components, presents explanatory text, a complete current listing, and population data for metropolitan statistical areas (MSAs), primary metropolitan statistical areas (PMSAs), and the consolidated metropolitan statistical areas (CMSAs). Table 43 in Section 1 presents selected population characteristics for MSAs with populations of 250,000 or more. Statistics for the Commonwealth of Puerto Rico and for outlying areas of the United States are included in many State tables, and are supplemented by information in Section 29. Additional information for States, cities, counties, metropolitan areas, and other geographic units, as well as historical data, are available in various supplements to the *Abstract* (see inside back cover).

Changes in this edition

As many of our users may know, the very popular *U.S. Industrial Outlook* no longer is being published by the Commerce Department's International Trade Administration (ITA). The loss of the data series contained in the *Outlook* has been of concern to many of our users. With the help of the ITA staff, this edition presents in section 31 updates of 92 data series previously published in the *Outlook*. These "Trends" tables will be updated in future editions of the *Abstract*. To help accommodate these extra pages for this section, the front matter "State Rankings" have been eliminated. These will be available separately in the fall and as a section on the CD-ROM version of the book.

Seventy-six new tables have been introduced throughout the other sections of the *Abstract*. These include many from the 1992 Economic and Agriculture Censuses. Other topics include estimates of undocumented immigrants, use of computers, bond ratings for States and cities, union membership by State, net worth, mutual funds, and home-ownership rates. (See Appendix VI, pp. 990-992, for a complete list of new tables introduced in this edition.)

Statistics in this edition are generally for the most recent year or period available by spring 1995. Each year almost 1,500 tables and charts are reviewed and evaluated; new tables and charts of current interest are added; continuing series are updated; and less timely data are condensed or eliminated. Text notes and appendices are revised as appropriate.

Historical statistics

Specific head-note references in this *Abstract* link many tables to earlier data shown in *Historical Statistics of the United States, Colonial Times to 1970*. (See Appendix IV, pp. 985 and 986.) Further information on this publication is printed on the inside back cover.

Statistics for States and metropolitan areas

Data for States, metropolitan areas, and central cities may be found in detail in the *County and City Extra*, an annual publication from Bernan Press which provides the most current data on a wide range of statistical categories.

Statistical reliability and responsibility

The contents of this volume were taken from many sources. All data from either censuses and surveys or from administrative records are subject to error arising from a number of factors: sampling variability (for statistics based on samples); reporting errors in the data for individual units; incomplete coverage; imputation and processing errors; and non-response. (See also Appendix III, pp. 970-984.) The Bureau of the Census cannot accept responsibility for the accuracy or limitations of the data presented here, other than that which it personally collects. The responsibility for selection of the material and its proper presentation, however, rests with the Bureau.

Bernan Press is responsible solely for the format and appearance of this reprint. With the exception of the changes noted in this preface, this publication has been reproduced in its entirety from the original edition issued by the Bureau of the Census. As the publisher of this enlarged print edition of the *Statistical Abstract*, Bernan Press cannot be held accountable for the content of tables which have been compiled by the Bureau of the Census, or by the private agencies which Census has selected to provide particular figures and information.

For additional information on data presented

Please consult the source publications available in local libraries or write to the agency indicated in the source notes. Write to the Bureau of the Census only if it is cited as the source.

Suggestions and comments

Users of the *Statistical Abstract* and its supplements are urged to make their data needs known for consideration in planning future editions. Suggestions and comments for improving coverage and presentation of data should be sent to the Director, U.S. Bureau of the Census, Washington, DC 20233.

Comments particular to this enlarged print edition should be sent to The Editors, Bernan Press, 4611-F Assembly Drive, Lanham, MD 20706-4391. All comments will be carefully reviewed for the purpose of future editions.

Acknowledgments

Bernan Press would like to thank the private organizations who kindly granted permission to include copyrighted data in this volume. We are certain the generosity of these businesses and institutions will be greatly appreciated by the users of the *Statistical Abstract*.

We also thank Mr. Glenn King, Chief of Statistical Compendia Staff at the Census Bureau, for his patient assistance. Due credit should be given to all of the Statistical Compendia personnel, and we direct the reader's attention to the preceding list of acknowledgments, printed on page iv of this edition.

In the future, Bernan Press will continue to publish quality editions of the most frequently used government publications, while adding to our own list of original reference titles. Information on this or any other Bernan Press publication can be obtained by calling Customer Relations at (800) 274-4447.

We hope this volume proves a valuable addition to your personal or public collection, and we look forward to the continued service of your information needs.

Contents

vii

[Numbers following subjects are page numbers]

Page

viii   Contents

APPROXIMATE CONVERSION MEASURES

[For assistance on metric usage, call or write the Office of Metric Programs, U.S. Department of Commerce, Washington, DC 20230 (301-975-3690)]

Symbol	When you know conventional	Multiply by	To find metric	Symbol
in	inch	2.54	centimeter	cm
ft	foot	30.48	centimeter	cm
yd	yard	0.91	meter	m
mi	mile	1.61	kilometer	km
in^2	square inch	6.45	square centimeter	cm^2
ft^2	square foot	0.09	square meter	m^2
yd^2	square yard	0.84	square meter	m^2
mi^2	square mile	2.59	square kilometer	km^2
	acre	0.41	hectare	ha
oz	ounce [1]	28.35	gram	g
lb	pound [1]	.45	kilograms	kg
oz (troy)	ounce [2]	31.10	gram	g
	short ton (2,000 lbs)	0.91	metric ton	t
	long ton (2,240 lbs)	1.02	metric ton	t
fl oz	fluid ounce	29.57	milliliter	mL
c	cup	0.24	liter	L
pt	pint	0.47	liter	L
qt	quart	0.95	liter	L
gal	gallon	3.78	liter	L
ft^3	cubic foot	0.03	cubic meter	m^3
yd^3	cubic yard	0.76	cubic meter	m^3
F	degrees Fahrenheit (subtract 32)	0.55	degrees Celsius	C

Symbol	When you know metric	Multiply by	To find conventional	Symbol
cm	centimeter	0.39	inch	in
cm	centimeter	0.33	foot	ft
m	meter	1.09	yard	yd
km	kilometer	0.62	mile	mi
cm^2	square centimeter	0.15	square inch	in^2
m^2	square meter	10.76	square foot	ft^2
m^2	square meter	1.20	square yard	yd^2
km^2	square kilometer	0.39	square mile	mi^2
ha	hectare	2.47	acre	
g	gram	.035	ounce [1]	oz
kg	kilogram	2.21	pounds	lb^1
g	gram	.032	ounce [2]	oz (troy)
t	metric ton	1.10	short ton (2,000 lbs)	
t	metric ton	0.98	long ton (2,240 lbs)	
mL	milliliter	0.03	fluid ounce	fl oz
L	liter	4.24	cup	c
L	liter	2.13	pint (liquid)	pt
L	liter	1.05	quart (liquid)	qt
L	liter	0.26	gallon	gal
m^3	cubic meter	35.32	cubic foot	ft^3
m^3	cubic meter	1.32	cubic yard	yd^3
C	degrees Celsius	1.80	degrees Fahrenheit (after subtracting 32)	F

[1] For weighing ordinary commodities.   [2] For weighing precious metals, jewels, etc.

Example of table structure:
No. 598. State and Local Government Retirement Systems—
Beneficiaries and Finances: 1980 to 1991

[In millions of dollars, except as indicated. For fiscal years closed during the 12 months ending June 30]

YEAR AND LEVEL OF GOVERNMENT	Number of beneficiaries (1,000)	RECEIPTS					BENEFITS AND WITHDRAWALS			Cash and security holdings
		Total	Employee contributions	Government contributions		Earnings on investments	Total	Benefits	Withdrawals	
				State	Local					
1980: All systems	(NA)	37,313	6,466	7,581	9,951	13,315	14,008	12,207	1,801	185,226
State-administered . . .	(NA)	28,603	5,285	7,399	5,611	10,308	10,257	8,809	1,448	144,682
Locally administered . .	(NA)	8,710	1,180	181	4,340	3,008	3,752	3,399	353	40,544
1985: All systems	3,378	71,411	9,468	12,227	15,170	34,546	24,413	21,999	2,414	374,433
State-administered . . .	2,661	55,960	7,901	11,976	8,944	27,139	18,230	16,183	2,047	296,951
Locally administered . .	716	15,451	1,567	251	6,226	7,407	6,183	5,816	367	77,481
1990: All systems	4,026	111,339	13,853	13,994	18,583	64,907	38,396	35,966	2,430	703,772
State-administered . . .	3,232	89,162	11,648	13,964	11,538	52,012	29,603	27,562	2,041	565,641
Locally administered . .	794	22,177	2,205	32	7,045	12,895	8,793	8,404	389	138,131
1991: All systems	4,179	108,240	16,268	14,473	18,691	58,808	42,028	39,421	2,607	783,405
State-administered . . .	3,357	85,576	12,563	14,455	11,553	47,006	32,323	30,167	2,156	630,551
Locally administered . .	822	22,664	3,705	18	7,138	11,803	9,706	9,255	451	152,854

NA Not available.

Source: U.S. Bureau of the Census, *Finances of Employee-Retirement Systems of State and Local Governments*, series GF, No. 2, annual.

Headnotes immediately below table titles provide information important for correct interpretation or evaluation of the table as a whole or for a major segment of it.

Footnotes below the bottom rule of tables give information relating to specific items or figures within the table.

Unit indicators show the *specified quantities* in which data items are presented. They are used for two primary reasons. Sometimes data are not available in absolute form and are estimates (as in the case of many surveys). In other cases we round the numbers in order to save space to show more data, as in the case above.

EXAMPLES OF UNIT INDICATOR INTERPRETATION FROM TABLE 598

Year	Item	Unit Indicator	Number shown	Multiplier
1991	Beneficiaries	Thousands	4,179	1,000
1991	Receipts	$ Millions	108,240	1,000,000

To Determine the Figure it Is Necessary to Multiply the Number Shown by the Unit Indicator:
Beneficiaries = 4,179 * 1,000 or 4,179,000 (over 4 million).
Receipts = 108,240 * 1,000,000 or 108,240,000,000 (over 108 billion).

When a table presents data with more than one unit indicator, they are found in the headnotes and column headings (shown above), spanner (table 53), stub (table 76), or unit column (table 75). When the data in a table are shown in the same unit indicator, it is shown in boldface as the first part of the headnote (table 2). If no unit indicator is shown, data presented are in absolute form (table 1).

Heavy vertical rules are used to separate independent sections of a table, as shown above, or in tables where the stub is continued into one or more additional columns (table 4).

Averages. An average is a single number or value that is often used to represent the "typical value" of a group of numbers. It is regarded as a measure of "location" or "central tendency" of a group of numbers.

The *arithmetic mean* is the type of average used most frequently. It is derived by summing the individual item values of a particular group and dividing the total by the number of items. The arithmetic mean is often referred to as simply the "mean" or "average."

The *median* of a group of numbers is the middle number or value when each item in the group is arranged according to size (lowest to highest or visa versa); it generally has the same number of items above it as well as below it. If there is an even number if items in the group, the median is taken to be the average of the two middle numbers.

Per capita (or per person) quantities. A per capita figure represents an average computed for every person in a specified group (or population). It is derived by taking the total for an item (such as income, taxes, or retail sales) and dividing it by the number of persons in the specified population.

Index numbers. An index number is the measure of difference or change, usually expressed as a percent, relating one quantity (the variable) of a specified kind to another quantity of the same kind. Index numbers are widely used to express changes in prices over periods of time but may also be used to express differences between related subjects for a single point in time.

To compute a price index, a base year or period is selected. The base year price (of the commodity or service) is then designated as the base or reference price to which the prices for other years or periods are related. Many price indexes use the year 1982 as the base year; in tables this is shown as "1982=100". A method of expressing the price relationship is: The price of a set of one or more items for a related year (e.g. 1990) **divided by** the price of the same set of items for the base year (e.g. 1982). The result multiplied by 100 provides the index number. When 100 is subtracted from the index number, the result equals the percent change in price from the base year.

Average annual percent change. Unless otherwise stated in the *Abstract* (as in Section 1, Population), average annual percent change is computed by use of a *compound interest formula.* This formula assumes that the rate of change is constant throughout a specified compounding period (one year for average annual rates of change). The formula is similar to that used to compute the balance of a savings account which receives compound interest. According to this formula, at the end of a compounding period the amount of accrued change (e.g. school enrollment or bank interest) is added to the amount which existed at the beginning the period. As a result, over time (e.g., with each year or quarter), the same rate of change is applied to a larger and larger figure.

The *exponential formula,* which is based on continuous compounding, is often used to measure population change. It is preferred by population experts because they view population and population-related subjects as changing without interruption, ever ongoing. Both exponential and compound interest formulas assume a constant rate of change. The former, however, applies the amount of change continuously to the base rather than at the end of each compounding period. When the average annual rates are small

(e.g., less than 5 percent) both formulas give virtually the same results. For an explanation of these two formulas as they relate to population, see U.S. Bureau of the Census, *The Methods and Materials of Demography,* vol. 2, 3d printing (rev.), 1975, pp. 372-381.

Current and constant dollars. Statistics in some tables in a number of sections are expressed in both current and constant dollars (see, for example, table 713 in section 14). Current dollar figures reflect actual prices or costs prevailing during the specified year(s). Constant dollar figures are estimates representing an effort to remove the effects of price changes from statistical series reported in dollar terms. In general, constant dollar series are derived by dividing current dollar estimates by the appropriate price index for the appropriate period (for example, the Consumer Price Index). The result is a series as it would presumably exist if prices were the same throughout, as in the base year—in other words as if the dollar had constant purchasing power. Any changes in this constant dollar series would reflect only changes in real volume of output, income, expenditures, or other measure.

Explanation of Symbols:

The following symbols, used in the tables throughout this book, are explained in condensed form in footnotes to the tables where they appear:

- Represents zero or rounds to less than half the unit of measurement shown.

B Base figure too small to meet statistical standards for reliability of a derived figure.

D Figure withheld to avoid disclosure pertaining to a specific organization or individual.

NA Data not enumerated, tabulated, or otherwise available separately.

NS Percent change irrelevant or insignificant.

S Figure does not meet publication standards for reasons other than that covered by symbol B, above.

X Figure not applicable because column heading and stub line make entry impossible, absurd, or meaningless.

Z Entry would amount to less than half the unit of measurement shown.

In many tables, details will not add to the totals shown because of rounding.

Telephone Contacts List

To help *Abstract* users find more data and information about statistical publications, we are issuing this list of contacts for Federal agencies with major statistical programs. The intent is to give a single, first-contact point-of-entry for users of statistics. These agencies will provide general information on their statistical programs and publications, as well as specific information on how to order their publications.

Executive Office of the President

Office of Management and Budget

Administrator
Office of Information and Regulatory Affairs
Office of Management and Budget
Washington, DC 20503
Information: 202-395-3000
Publications: 202-395-7332

Department of Agriculture

Economic Research Service

Research Support and Training Branch
U.S. Department of Agriculture
Room 110
1301 New York Ave., N.W.
Washington, DC 20005-4788
Information and Publications: 202-219-0515

National Agricultural Statistics Service

National Agricultural Statistics Service
U.S. Department of Agriculture
14th St. and Independence Ave., S.W.
Washington, DC 20250
Information Hotline: 1-800-727-9540

Department of Commerce

U.S. Department of Commerce
Room 5056 Main Commerce
14th St. and Constitution Ave., N.W.
Washington, DC 20230
Newsroom: 202-482-5007

Bureau of the Census

Customer Services Branch
Bureau of the Census
U.S. Department of Commerce
Washington, DC 20233
Information and Publications: 301-457-4100

Bureau of Economic Analysis

Current Business Analysis Division, BE-53
Bureau of Economic Analysis
U.S. Department of Commerce
Washington, DC 20230
Information and Publications: 202-606-9900

Department of Commerce —Con.

International Trade Administration

Trade Statistics Division
International Trade Administration
Room 2814 B
U.S. Department of Commerce
Washington, DC 20230
Information and Publications: 202-482-2185

National Oceanic and Atmospheric Administration

National Oceanic and Atmospheric Administration Library
U.S. Department of Commerce
1315 East-West Highway
2nd Floor
Silver Spring MD 20910
Library: 301-713-2600

Department of Defense

Department of Defense

Office of the Assistant to the Secretary of Defense (Public Affairs)
Attention: Directorate for Public Correspondence
The Pentagon, 1E794
Washington, DC 20301-1400
Information: 703-697-5737

Department of Education

Office of Information Services

Statistical Information Office
U.S. Department of Education
555 New Jersey Ave., N.W.
Washington, DC 20208-5641
Information and Publications:
1-800-424-1616

Department of Energy

Energy Information Administration

National Energy Information Center
Energy Information Administration
U.S. Department of Energy
Washington, DC 20585
Information and Publications: 202-586-8800

Department of Health and Human Services

Health Resources and Services Administration

Administrator for Health Resources and Services
Health Resources and Services Administration
U.S. Department of Health and Human Services
5600 Fishers Lane
Room 14-45
Rockville, MD 20857
Publications: 301-443-2086

Substance Abuse Mental Health Services Administration

U.S. Department of Health and Human Services
5600 Fishers Lane
Room 12C105
Rockville, MD 20857
Information: 301-443-0365
Publications: 1-800-729-6686

Centers for Disease Control

Office of Information
Centers for Disease Control
21600 Clifton Road, N.E.
Atlanta, GA 30333
Public Inquiries: 404-639-3534

Health Care Financing Administration

Office of Public Affairs
Health Care Financing Administration
U.S. Department of Health and Human Services
Room 428H, Humphrey Building
200 Independence Ave., S.W.
Washington, DC 20201
Media Relations: 202-690-6145

National Center for Health Statistics

Scientific and Technical Information Branch
National Center for Health Statistics
U.S. Department of Health and Human Services
6525 Belcrest Rd. Rm. 1064
Hyattsville, MD 20782
Information and Publications: 301-436-8500

Social Security Administration

Publications Staff
Office of Research and Statistics
Social Security Administration
U.S. Department of Health and Human Services
Van Ness Centre, Room 209
4301 Connecticut Ave., N.W.
Washington, DC 20008
Information and Publications: 202-282-7138

Department of Housing and Urban Development

Assistant Secretary for Community Planning and Development

Office of the Assistant Secretary for Community Planning and Development
U.S. Department of Housing and Urban Development
451 7th St., S.W.
Washington, DC 20410-0555
Information: 202-708-2690
Publications: 1-800-245-2691

Department of the Interior

Bureau of Mines

Office of Public Information
Bureau of Mines
U.S. Department of the Interior
Washington, DC 20241
Information: 202-501-9649
Publications: 202-501-9757

Geological Survey

Public Inquiries Office
Geological Survey
U.S. Department of the Interior
507 National Center
Reston, VA 22092
Information and Publications: 703-648-6892

Department of Justice

Bureau of Justice Statistics

Statistics Division
Bureau of Justice Statistics
U.S. Department of Justice
633 Indiana Ave., N.W.
Washington, DC 20531
Information and Publications: 202-307-6100

National Criminal Justice Reference Service

Box 6000
Rockville, MD 20850
Information and Publications: 301-251-5500
Publications: 1-800-732-3277

Federal Bureau of Investigation

National Crime Information Center
Federal Bureau of Investigation
U.S. Department of Justice
9th St. and Pennsylvania Ave., N.W.
Washington, DC 20535
Information and Publications: 202-324-3691
Publications: 202-324-5343

Immigration and Naturalization Service

Statistics Branch
Immigration and Naturalization Service
U.S. Department of Justice
425 I St., N.W.
Washington, DC 20536
Attention: Tariff Bldg. Rm. 235
Information and Publications: 202-376-3066

Department of Labor

Bureau of Labor Statistics

Office of Publications and Information
Services
Bureau of Labor Statistics
U.S. Department of Labor
441 G St., N.W., Room 2831A
Washington, DC 20212
Information and Publications: 202-606-7828

Employment and Training Administration

Office of Public Information
Employment and Training Administration
U.S. Department of Labor
200 Constitution Ave., N.W., Room N4700
Information and Publications: 202-219-6871

Department of Transportation

Federal Aviation Administration

Public Inquiry Center
APA 200
Federal Aviation Administration
U.S. Department of Transportation
800 Independence Ave., S.W.
Washington, DC 20591
Information and Publications: 202-267-3484

Federal Highway Administration

Office of Public Affairs
Federal Highway Administration
U.S. Department of Transportation
400 7th St., S.W.
Washington, DC 20590
Information: 202-366-0660

National Highway Traffic Safety Administration

Office of Public Affairs
National Highway Traffic Safety
Administration
U.S. Department of Transportation
400 7th St., S.W.
Washington, DC 20590
Information: 202-366-0123
Publications: 202-366-2588

Department of the Treasury

Internal Revenue Service

Statistics of Income Division
Internal Revenue Service
U.S. Department of the Treasury
P.O. Box 2608
Washington, DC 20013
Information and Publications: 202-874-0410

Department of Veterans Affairs

Department of Veterans Affairs

Office of Public Affairs
Department of Veterans Affairs
810 Vermont Ave., N.W.
Washington, DC 20420
Information: 202-273-5700

Independent Agencies

Environmental Protection Agency

Public Information Center, Rm. 3404
Environmental Protection Agency
401 M St., S.W.
Washington, DC 20460
Information: 202-260-2080

Federal Reserve Board

Division of Research and Statistics
Federal Reserve Board
Washington, DC 20551
Information: 202-452-3301

National Science Foundation

Office of Public Information
National Science Foundation
4201 Wilson Boulevard.
Arlington Virginia 22230
Information: 703-306-1234
Publications: 703-306-1130

Securities and Exchange Commission

Office of Public Affairs
Securities and Exchange Commission
450 5th St., N.W.
Washington, DC 20549
Information: 202-942-0020
Publications: 202-942-4040

Population

This section presents statistics on the growth, distribution, and characteristics of the U.S. population. The principal source of these data is the Bureau of the Census, which conducts a decennial census of population, a monthly population survey, a program of population estimates and projections, and a number of other periodic surveys relating to population characteristics. For a list of relevant publications, see the Guide to Sources of Statistics in Appendix I.

Decennial censuses.—The U.S. Constitution provides for a census of the population every 10 years, primarily to establish a basis for apportionment of members of the House of Representatives among the States. For over a century after the first census in 1790, the census organization was a temporary one, created only for each decennial census. In 1902, the Bureau of the Census was established as a permanent Federal agency, responsible for enumerating the population and also for compiling statistics on other subjects.

The census of population is a complete count. That is, an attempt is made to account for every person, for each person's residence, and for other characteristics (sex, age, family relationships, etc.). Since the 1940 census, in addition to the complete count information, some data have been obtained from representative samples of the population. In the 1990 census, variable sampling rates were employed. For most of the country, one in every six households (about 17 percent) received the long form or sample questionnaire; in governmental units estimated to have fewer than 2,500 inhabitants, every other household (50 percent) received the sample questionnaire to enhance the reliability of sample data for small areas. Exact agreement is not to be expected between sample data and the complete census count. Sample data may be used with confidence where large numbers are involved and assumed to indicate trends and relationships where small numbers are involved.

Census data presented here have not been adjusted for underenumeration.

In Brief

Total population, 1994	260 million
Northeast	*20%*
Midwest	*24%*
South	*35%*
West	*22%*
Total households, 1994	97 million
One-person households	*24%*

Results from the evaluation program for the 1990 census indicate that the overall national undercount was between 1 and 2 percent – the estimate from the Post Enumeration Survey (PES) was 1.6 percent and the estimate from Demographic Analysis (DA) was 1.8 percent. Both the PES and DA estimates show disproportionately high undercounts for some demographic groups. For example, the PES estimates of percent net undercount for Blacks (4.4 percent), Hispanics (5.0 percent), and American Indians (4.5 percent) were higher than the estimated undercount of non-Hispanic whites (0.7 percent). Historical DA estimates demonstrate that the overall undercount rate in the census has declined significantly over the past 50 years (from an estimated 5.4 percent in 1940 to 1.8 percent in 1990), yet the undercount of Blacks has remained disproportionately high.

Current Population Survey (CPS).—This is a monthly nationwide survey of a scientifically selected sample representing the noninstitutional civilian population. The sample is located in 729 areas comprising 1,973 counties, independent cities, and minor civil divisions with coverage in every State and the District of Columbia and is subject to sampling error. At the present time, about 60,000 occupied households are eligible for interview every month; of these between 4 and 5 percent are, for various reasons, unavailable for interview.

While the primary purpose of the CPS is to obtain monthly statistics on the labor force, it also serves as a vehicle for inquiries on other subjects. Using CPS data, the Bureau issues a series of publications under the general title of *Current Population Reports*, which cover population characteristics (P20), consumer income (P60), special studies (P23), and other topics.

Estimates of population characteristics based on the CPS will not agree with the counts from the census because the CPS and the census use different procedures for collecting and processing the data for racial groups, the Hispanic population, and other topics. Caution should also be used when comparing estimates for various years because of the periodic introduction of changes into the CPS. Beginning in January 1994, a number of changes were introduced into the CPS that effect all data comparisons with prior years. These changes include the results of a major redesign of the survey questionnaire and collection methodology and the introduction of 1990 census population controls, adjusted for the estimated undercount. This change in population controls had relatively little impact on derived measures such as means, medians, and percent distribution, but did have a significant impact on levels.

Population estimates and projections.— National population estimates are derived by using decennial census data as benchmarks and data available from various agencies as follows: Births and deaths (National Center for Health Statistics); immigrants (Immigration and Naturalization Service); Armed Forces (Department of Defense and Department of Transportation); net movement between Puerto Rico and the U.S. mainland (Puerto Rico Planning Board); and Federal employees abroad (Office of Personnel Management and Department of Defense). Estimates for States and smaller areas are based on data series such as births and deaths, school statistics from State departments of education and parochial school systems, and Federal income tax returns. These estimates contain estimated emigration of 222,000 per year since 1980 and net undocumented immigration of 225,000 per year.

Data for the population by age for April 1, 1990 (shown in tables 14, 21, and 23) are modified counts. The review of de-

tailed 1990 information indicated that respondents tended to provide their age as of the date of completion of the questionnaire, not their age as of April 1, 1990. In addition, there may have been a tendency for respondents to round up their age if they were close to having a birthday. A detailed explanation of the age modification procedure appears in 1990 Census of Population and Housing Data Paper Listing (CPH–L–74).

Population estimates and projections are published in the P25 series of *Current Population Reports*. These estimates and projections are generally consistent with official decennial census figures and do not reflect the amount of estimated census underenumeration. However, these estimates and projections by race have been modified and are not comparable to the census race categories (see section below under "race"). For details on methodology, see the sources cited below the individual tables.

The population projections for States, by single year of age, sex, race, and Hispanic origin prepared for July 1, 1993 to 2020 use the cohort–component method. This method requires separate assumptions for each component of population change: births, deaths, internal migration, and international migration. These components are produced and refined using various administrative records and census distributions. State estimates for 1992 are the starting points for these projections which are consistent with the national projections reported in the U.S. Bureau of the Census, *Current Population Reports*, series P25–1104. The four series of projections (see table 35) are based on different internal migration assumptions: 1) Series A, is the preferred series model and uses State–to-State migration observed from 1975-76 through 1991-92; 2) Series B, the economic model, uses the Bureau of Economic Analysis employment projections; 3) Series C, the floating mean model, is the mean of the n most recent years for the n-th projection year; and 4) Series D, is the zero net internal migration assumption.

Immigration.—The principal source of immigration data is the *Statistical Yearbook of the Immigration and Naturalization Service*, published annually by the

Immigration and Naturalization Service (INS), a unit of the Department of Justice. Immigration statistics are prepared from entry visas and change of immigration status forms. Immigrants are aliens admitted for legal permanent residence in the United States. The procedures for admission depend on whether the alien is residing inside or outside the United States at the time of application for permanent residence. Eligible aliens residing outside the United States are issued immigrant visas by the U.S. Department of State. Eligible aliens residing in the United States are allowed to change their status from temporary to permanent residence at INS district offices. The category, immigrant, includes persons who may have entered the United States as nonimmigrants or refugees, but who subsequently changed their status to that of a permanent resident. Nonresident aliens admitted to the United States for a temporary period are nonimmigrants (tables 7 and 432). Refugees are considered nonimmigrants when initially admitted into the United States, but are not included in nonimmigrant admission data. A refugee is any person who is outside his or her country of nationality who is unable or unwilling to return to that country because of persecution or a well-founded fear of persecution.

U.S. immigration law gives preferential immigration status to aliens who are related to certain U.S. citizens or legal permanent residents, aliens with needed job skills, or aliens who qualify as refugees. Immigration to the United States can be divided into two general categories: (1) those subject to the annual worldwide limitation, and (2) those exempt from it. The Immigration Act of 1990 established major revisions in the numerical limits and preference system regulating legal immigration. The numerical limits are imposed on visas issued and not on admissions. The maximum number of visas allowed to be issued under the preference categories in 1993 was 393,690— 232,483 for family-sponsored immigrants and 161,207 for employment-based immigrants. There are nine categories among which the family-sponsored and employment-based immigrant visas are distributed, beginning in fiscal year 1991. The family-sponsored preferences are based on the

alien's relationship with a U.S. citizen or legal permanent resident (see table 6). The employment-based preferences are: 1) priority workers (persons of extraordinary ability, outstanding professors and researchers, and certain multinational executives and managers); 2) professionals with advanced degrees or aliens with exceptional ability; 3) skilled workers, professionals without advanced degrees, and needed unskilled workers; 4) special immigrants; and 5) employment creation immigrants (investors). Within the overall limitations the per-country limit for independent countries is set to 7 percent of the total family-sponsored and employment-based limits, while dependent areas are limited to two percent of the total. The 1993 limit allowed no more than 27,558 preference visas for any independent country and 7,320 for any dependency. Those exempt from the worldwide limitation include immediate relatives of U.S. citizens, refugees and asylees adjusting to permanent residence, and other various classes of special immigrants (see table 6).

The Refugee Act of 1980, effective April 1, 1980, provides for a uniform admission procedure for refugees of all countries, based on the United Nations' definition of refugees. Authorized admission ceilings are set annually by the President in consultation with Congress. After one year of residence in the United States, refugees are eligible for immigrant status.

The Immigration Reform and Control Act of 1986 (IRCA) allows two groups of illegal aliens to become temporary and then permanent residents of the United States: aliens who have been in the United States unlawfully since January 1, 1982 (legalization applicants), and aliens who were employed in seasonal agricultural work for a minimum period of time (Special Agricultural Worker (SAW) applicants). The application period for temporary residency for legalization applicants began on May 5, 1987, and ended on May 4, 1988, while the application period for SAW applicants began on June 1, 1987, and ended on November 30, 1988. Legalization applicants became eligible for permanent residence beginning in fiscal year 1989. Beginning 1989 immigrant data include temporary residents who were granted permanent residence under the legalization program of IRCA.

Metropolitan Areas (MA's).—The general concept of a metropolitan area is one of a core area containing a large population nucleus, together with adjacent communities that have a high degree of social and economic integration with that core. Metropolitan statistical areas (MSA's), consolidated metropolitan statistical areas (CMSA's), and primary metropolitan statistical areas (PMSA's) are defined by the Office of Management and Budget (OMB) as a standard for Federal agencies in the preparation and publication of statistics relating to metropolitan areas. The entire territory of the United States is classified as metropolitan (inside MSA's or CMSA's) or nonmetropolitan (outside MSA's or CMSA's). MSA's, CMSA's, and PMSA's are defined in terms of entire counties except in New England, where the definitions are in terms of cities and towns. The OMB also defines New England County Metropolitan Areas (NECMA's) which are county-based alternatives to the MSA's and CMSA's in the six New England States. From time to time, new MA's are created and the boundaries of others change. As a result, data for MA's over time may not be comparable and the analysis of historical trends must be made cautiously. For descriptive details and a listing of titles and components of MA's, see Appendix II.

Urban and rural.—According to the 1990 census definition, the urban population comprises all persons living in (a) places of 2,500 or more inhabitants incorporated as cities, villages, boroughs (except in Alaska and New York), and towns (except in the New England States, New York, and Wisconsin), but excluding those persons living in the rural portions of extended cities (places with low population density in one or more large parts of their area); (b) census designated places (previously termed unincorporated) of 2,500 or more inhabitants; and (c) other territory, incorporated or unincorporated, included in urbanized areas. An urbanized area comprises one or more places and the adjacent densely settled surrounding territory that together have a minimum population of 50,000 persons. In all definitions, the population not classified as urban constitutes the rural population

Residence.—In determining residence, the Bureau of the Census counts each person as an inhabitant of a usual place of residence (i.e., the place where one usually lives and sleeps). While this place is not necessarily a person's legal residence or voting residence, the use of these different bases of classification would produce the same results in the vast majority of cases.

Race.—The Bureau of the Census collects and publishes racial statistics as outlined in Statistical Policy Directive No. 15 issued by the U.S. Office of Management and Budget. This directive provides standards on ethnic and racial categories for statistical reporting to be used by all Federal agencies. According to the directive, the basic racial categories are American Indian or Alaska Native, Asian or Pacific Islander, Black, and White. (The directive identifies Hispanic origin as an ethnicity.) The concept of race the Bureau of the Census uses reflects self-identification by respondents; that is the individual's perception of his/her racial identity. The concept is not intended to reflect any biological or anthropological definition. Although the Bureau of the Census adheres to the overall guidelines of Directive No. 15, it recognizes that there are persons who do not identify with a specific racial group. The 1990 census race question includes an "Other race" category with provisions for a write-in entry. Furthermore, the Bureau of the Census recognizes that the categories of the race item include both racial and national origin or socio-cultural groups.

Differences between the 1990 census and earlier censuses affect the comparability of data for certain racial groups and American Indian tribes. The lack of comparability is due to changes in the way some respondents reported their race as well as changes in 1990 census procedures related to the racial classification. (For a fuller explanation, see *1990 Census of Population, Volume I, General Population Characteristics* (1990 CP-1).)

Data for the population by race for April 1, 1990 (shown in tables 12, 13, 18, 19, 21, and 23) are modified counts and are not comparable to the 1990 census race categories. These numbers were computed using 1990 census data by race which had been modified to be consistent with the race categories used in the reporting of vital statistics by the U.S. National Center for Health Statistics. A detailed explanation of the race modification procedure appears in 1990 Census of Population and Housing Data Paper Listing (CPH-L-74).

In the CPS and other household sample surveys in which data are obtained through personal interview, respondents are asked to classify their race as: (1) White, (2) Black, (3) American Indian, Aleut, or Eskimo, or (4) Asian or Pacific Islander. The procedures for classifying persons of mixed races who could not provide a single response to the race question are generally similar to those used in the census.

Hispanic population.—In the 1990 census, the Bureau of the Census collected data on the Hispanic origin population in the United States by using a self-identification question. Persons of Spanish/Hispanic origin are those who classified themselves in one of the specific Hispanic origin categories listed on the questionnaire—Mexican, Puerto Rican, Cuban, or Other Spanish/Hispanic origin. The difference between the 1980 and the 1990 questionnaire was that in the 1980 census, a Hispanic origin question was used with prelisted categories for the largest Spanish origin groups and a residual Other Spanish/Hispanic category. For the 1990 census the questionnaire was modified by adding a space for the respondent to write-in the entry for the Other Spanish/Hispanic category. It should be noted that Hispanic persons may be of any race.

In the CPS information on Hispanic persons is gathered by using a self-identification question. Persons classify themselves in one of the Hispanic categories in response to the question: "What is the origin or descent of each person in this household?" Hispanic persons in the CPS are persons who report themselves as Mexican-American, Chicano, Mexican, Puerto Rican, Cuban, Central or South American (Spanish countries), or other Hispanic origin.

Nativity.—The native population consists of all persons born in the United States, Puerto Rico, or an outlying area of the United States. It also includes persons born at sea or in a foreign country who have at least one American parent. All others are classified as "foreign born."

Mobility status.—The U.S. population is classified according to mobility status on the basis of a comparison between the place of residence of each individual at the time of the survey or census and the place of residence at a specified earlier date. Nonmovers are all persons who were living in the same house or apartment at the end of the period as at the beginning of the period. Movers are all persons who were living in a different house at the end of the period from that in which they were living at the beginning of the period. Movers from abroad include all persons, either citizens or aliens, whose place of residence was outside the United States at the beginning of the period; that is, in Puerto Rico, an outlying area under the jurisdiction of the United States, or a foreign country.

Living arrangements.—Living arrangements refer to residency in households or in group quarters. A "household" comprises all persons who occupy a "housing unit," that is, a house, an apartment or other group of rooms, or a single room that constitutes "separate living quarters." A household includes the related family members and all the unrelated persons, if any, such as lodgers, foster children, wards, or employees who share the housing unit. A person living alone or a group of unrelated persons sharing the same housing unit is also counted as a household. See text, section 25, Construction and Housing, for definition of housing unit.

All persons not living in households are classified as living in group quarters. These individuals may be institutionalized, e.g., under care or custody in juvenile facilities, jails, correctional centers, hospitals, or rest homes; or they may be residents in college dormitories, military barracks, rooming houses, etc. (see table 82).

Householder.—The householder is the first adult household member listed on the questionnaire. The instructions call for listing first the person (or one of the persons) in whose name the home is owned or rented. If a home is owned or rented jointly by a married couple, either the husband or the wife may be listed first. Prior to 1980, the husband was always considered the household head (householder) in married-couple households.

Family.—The term "family" refers to a group of two or more persons related by birth, marriage, or adoption and residing together in a household. A family includes among its members the householder.

Subfamily.—A subfamily consists of a married couple and their children, if any, or one parent with one or more never-married children under 18 years old living in a household. Subfamilies are divided into "related" and "unrelated" subfamilies. A related subfamily is related to, but does not include, the householder. Members of a related subfamily are also members of the family with whom they live. The number of related subfamilies, therefore, is not included in the count of families. An unrelated subfamily may include persons such as guests, lodgers, or resident employees and their spouses and/or children; none of whom is related to the householder.

Married couple.—A "married couple" is defined as a husband and wife living together in the same household, with or without children and other relatives.

Unrelated individuals.—"Unrelated individuals" are persons (other than inmates of institutions) who are not members of families or subfamilies.

Secondary individuals.—Secondary individuals are persons of any age who reside in a household, but are not related to the householder (except unrelated subfamily members). Persons who reside in group quarters are also secondary individuals. Examples of a secondary individual include (1) a guest, partner, roommate, or resident employee; (2) a foster child; or (3) a person residing in a rooming house, a halfway house, staff quarters at a hospital, or other type of group quarters.

Statistical reliability.—For a discussion of statistical collection and estimation, sampling procedures, and measures of statistical reliability applicable to Census Bureau data, see Appendix III.

Historical statistics.—Tabular headnotes provide cross-references, where applicable, to Historical Statistics of the United States, Colonial Times to 1970. See Appendix IV.

Figure 1.1
Projected Percent Change in State Populations: 1990 to 2000

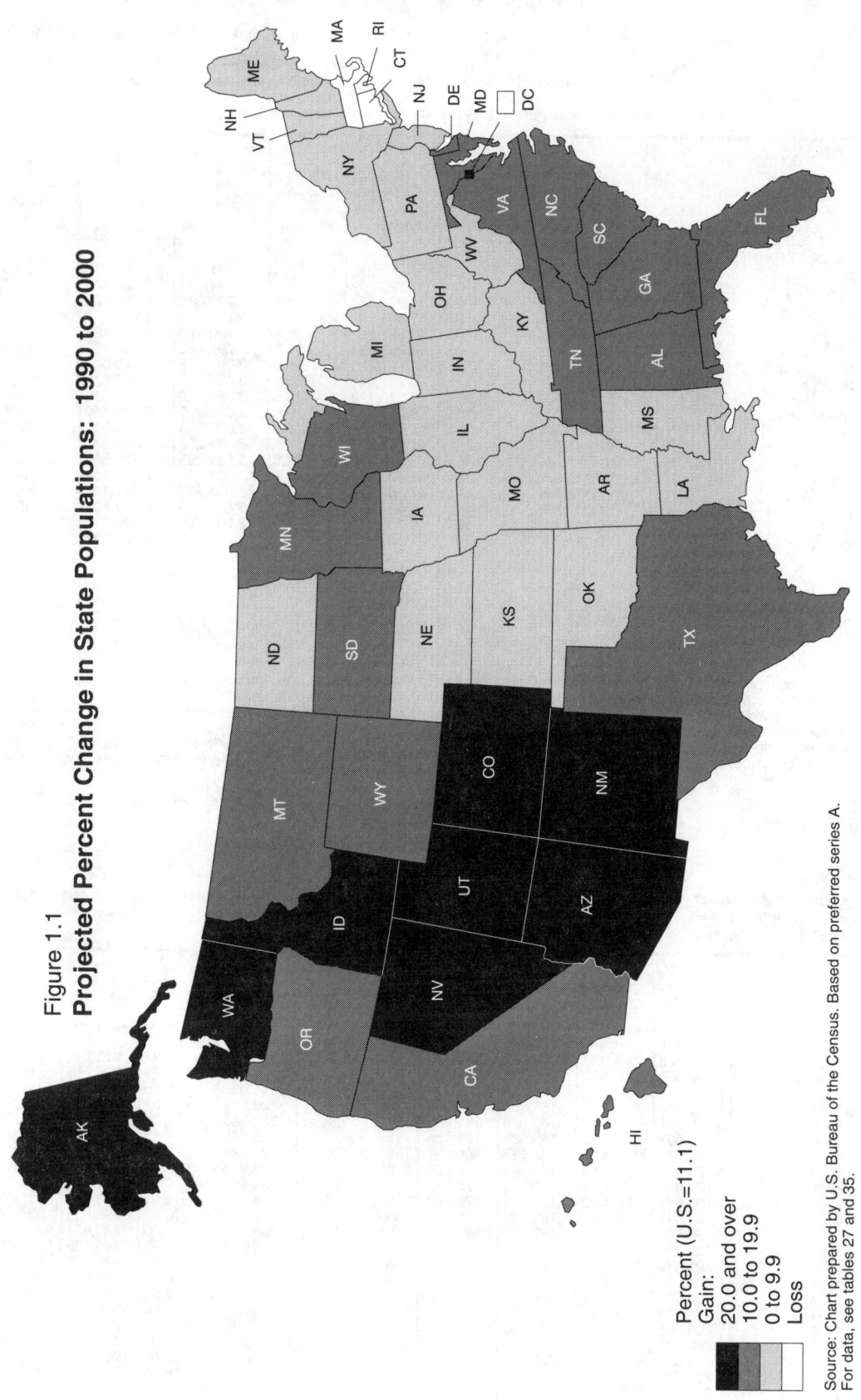

Percent (U.S.=11.1)
Gain:

20.0 and over

10.0 to 19.9

0 to 9.9

Loss

Source: Chart prepared by U.S. Bureau of the Census. Based on preferred series A.
For data, see tables 27 and 35.

Population

No. 1. Population and Area: 1790 to 1990

[Area figures represent area on indicated date including in some cases considerable areas not then organized or settled, and not covered by the census. Total area figures for 1790 to 1970 have been recalculated on the basis of the remeasurement of States and counties for the 1980 census, but not on the basis of the 1990 census. The land and water area figures for past censuses have not been adjusted and are not strictly comparable with the total area data for comparable dates because the land areas were derived from different base data, and these values are known to have changed with the construction of reservoirs, draining of lakes, etc. Density figures are based on land area measurements as reported in earlier censuses]

| | RESIDENT POPULATION | | | | AREA (square miles) | | |
| CENSUS DATE | Number | Per square mile of land area | Increase over preceding census | | Total | Land | Water |
			Number	Percent			
CONTERMINOUS U.S. [1]							
1790 (Aug. 2)	3,929,214	4.5	(X)	(X)	891,364	864,746	24,065
1800 (Aug. 4)	5,308,483	6.1	1,379,269	35.1	891,364	864,746	24,065
1810 (Aug. 6)	7,239,881	4.3	1,931,398	36.4	1,722,685	1,681,828	34,175
1820 (Aug. 7)	9,638,453	5.5	2,398,572	33.1	1,792,552	1,749,462	38,544
1830 (June 1)	12,866,020	7.4	3,227,567	33.5	1,792,552	1,749,462	38,544
1840 (June 1)	17,069,453	9.8	4,203,433	32.7	1,792,552	1,749,462	38,544
1850 (June 1)	23,191,876	7.9	6,122,423	35.9	2,991,655	2,940,042	52,705
1860 (June 1)	31,443,321	10.6	8,251,445	35.6	3,021,295	2,969,640	52,747
1870 (June 1)	[2]39,818,449	[2]13.4	8,375,128	26.6	3,021,295	2,969,640	52,747
1880 (June 1)	50,155,783	16.9	10,337,334	26.0	3,021,295	2,969,640	52,747
1890 (June 1)	62,947,714	21.2	12,791,931	25.5	3,021,295	2,969,640	52,747
1900 (June 1)	75,994,575	25.6	13,046,861	20.7	3,021,295	2,969,834	52,553
1910 (Apr. 15)	91,972,266	31.0	15,977,691	21.0	3,021,295	2,969,565	52,822
1920 (Jan. 1)	105,710,620	35.6	13,738,354	14.9	3,021,295	2,969,451	52,936
1930 (Apr. 1)	122,775,046	41.2	17,064,426	16.1	3,021,295	2,977,128	45,259
1940 (Apr. 1)	131,669,275	44.2	8,894,229	7.2	3,021,295	2,977,128	45,259
1950 (Apr. 1)	150,697,361	50.7	19,028,086	14.5	3,021,295	2,974,726	47,661
1960 (Apr. 1)	178,464,236	60.1	27,766,875	18.4	3,021,295	2,968,054	54,207
UNITED STATES							
1950 (Apr. 1)	151,325,798	42.6	19,161,229	14.5	3,618,770	3,552,206	63,005
1960 (Apr. 1)	179,323,175	50.6	27,997,377	18.5	3,618,770	3,540,911	74,212
1970 (Apr. 1)	[3]203,302,031	[3]57.4	23,978,856	13.4	3,618,770	[3]3,540,023	[3]78,444
1980 (Apr. 1)	[4]226,542,199	64.0	23,240,168	11.4	[6]3,717,796	[6]3,536,278	[6][7]181,518
1990 (Apr. 1)	[5]248,718,291	70.3	22,176,092	9.8		3,539,289	79,481

X Not applicable.   [1] Excludes Alaska and Hawaii.   [2] Revised to include adjustments for underenumeration in southern States; unrevised number is 38,558,371 (13.0 per square mile).   [3] Figures corrected after 1970 final reports were issued.   [4] Total population count has been revised since the 1980 census publications. Numbers by age, race, Hispanic origin, and sex have not been corrected.   [5] The April 1, 1990, census count includes count resolution corrections processed through March 1994, and does not include adjustments for census coverage errors.   [6] Data reflect corrections made after publication of the results.   [7] Comprises Great Lakes, inland, and coastal water. Data for prior years cover inland water only. For further explanation, see table 361.

Source: U.S. Bureau of the Census, *1990 Census of Population and Housing, Population and Housing Unit Counts* (CPH-2); and unpublished data.

No. 2. Population: 1950 to 1994

[**In thousands, except percent.** Estimates as of **July 1**. Total population includes Armed Forces abroad; civilian population excludes Armed Forces. For basis of estimates, see text, section 1. See also *Historical Statistics, Colonial Times to 1970*, series A 6-8]

| YEAR | TOTAL | | Resident population | Civilian population | YEAR | TOTAL | | Resident population | Civilian population |
	Population	Percent change				Population	Percent change		
1950	152,271	(X)	151,868	150,790	1973	211,909	0.96	211,357	209,600
1951	154,878	1.71	153,982	151,599	1974	213,854	0.92	213,342	211,636
1952	157,553	1.73	156,393	153,892	1975	215,973	0.99	215,465	213,789
1953	160,184	1.67	158,956	156,595	1976	218,035	0.95	217,563	215,894
1954	163,026	1.77	161,884	159,695	1977	220,239	1.01	219,760	218,106
1955	165,931	1.78	165,069	162,967	1978	222,585	1.06	222,095	220,467
1956	168,903	1.79	168,088	166,055	1979	225,055	1.11	224,567	222,969
1957	171,984	1.82	171,187	169,110	1980	227,726	1.19	227,225	225,621
1958	174,882	1.68	174,149	172,226	1981	229,966	0.98	229,466	227,818
1959	177,830	1.69	177,135	175,277	1982	232,188	0.97	231,664	229,995
1960	180,671	1.60	179,979	178,140	1983	234,307	0.91	233,792	232,097
1961	183,691	1.67	182,992	181,143	1984	236,348	0.87	235,825	234,110
1962	186,538	1.55	185,771	183,677	1985	238,466	0.90	237,924	236,219
1963	189,242	1.45	188,483	186,493	1986	240,651	0.92	240,133	238,412
1964	191,889	1.40	191,141	189,141	1987	242,804	0.89	242,289	240,550
1965	194,303	1.26	193,526	191,605	1988	245,021	0.91	244,499	242,817
1966	196,560	1.16	195,576	193,420	1989	247,342	0.95	246,819	245,131
1967	198,712	1.09	197,457	195,264	1990	249,911	1.04	249,402	247,762
1968	200,706	1.00	199,399	197,113	1991	252,643	1.09	252,131	250,520
1969	202,677	0.98	201,385	199,145	1992	255,407	1.09	255,028	253,443
1970	205,052	1.17	203,984	201,895	1993	258,120	1.06	257,783	256,311
1971	207,661	1.27	206,827	204,866	1994	260,651	0.98	260,341	258,932
1972	209,896	1.08	209,284	207,511					

X Not applicable.

Source: U.S. Bureau of the Census, *Current Population Reports*, P25-1045 and P25-1126.

No. 3. Resident Population Projections: 1995 to 2050

[**In thousands**. As of **July 1**. Each series shown assumes middle levels of fertility, life expectancy, and net immigration unless otherwise specified. Middle level components are shown in footnote 1]

YEAR	Middle series [1]	Lowest series [2]	Highest series [3]	FERTILITY		LIFE EXPECTANCY		NET IMMIGRATION	
				Low	High	Low	High	Low	High
1995	263,434	262,051	264,715	263,218	263,661	263,238	263,587	262,461	264,334
1996	266,096	263,905	268,138	265,730	266,486	265,795	266,333	264,569	267,510
1997	268,702	265,647	271,568	268,159	269,289	268,278	269,039	266,608	270,642
1998	271,258	267,281	275,011	270,510	272,074	270,692	271,710	268,584	273,736
1999	273,769	268,816	278,472	272,790	274,849	273,044	274,352	270,502	276,798
2000	276,241	270,259	281,957	275,004	277,618	275,341	276,970	272,370	279,832
2005	288,286	276,316	299,941	285,341	291,687	286,204	289,893	281,230	294,847
2010	300,431	281,180	319,536	295,014	306,876	296,775	303,115	289,969	310,179
2015	313,116	285,680	340,794	304,744	323,322	307,564	317,037	299,078	326,220
2020	325,942	289,553	363,213	314,281	340,512	318,164	331,271	308,158	342,572
2025	338,338	292,092	386,595	322,935	358,130	327,988	345,299	316,609	358,687
2030	349,993	292,902	410,991	330,290	376,130	336,732	358,859	324,111	374,268
2040	371,505	290,351	463,579	341,584	414,144	351,769	384,846	336,797	404,142
2050	392,031	285,502	522,098	350,233	456,471	366,036	409,960	348,032	433,501

[1] Ultimate total fertility rate = 2,150; life expectancy in 2050 = 82.6 years; and annual net immigration = 880,000. These are middle level assumptions. For explanation of total fertility rate; see headnote, table 91.　　[2] Ultimate total fertility rate = 1,892; life expectancy in 2050 = 75.3 years; and annual net immigration = 350,000. These are lowest level assumptions.　　[3] Ultimate total fertility rate = 2,622; life expectancy in 2050 = 87.5 years; and annual net immigration = 1,370,000. These are highest level assumptions.

Source: U.S. Bureau of the Census, *Current Population Reports*, P25-1104.

No. 4. Components of Population Change, 1980 to 1993, and Projections, 1994 to 2050

[Resident population. The estimates prior to 1990 are consistent with the original 1990 census count of 248,709,873. Starting with 1990, estimates reflect the revised April 1, 1990, census count of 248,718,291 which includes count resolution corrections processed through March 1994, and does not include adjustments for coverage errors]

| YEAR | Popula-tion at start of period (1,000) | TOTAL (Jan. 1-Dec. 31) | | | | | RATE PER 1,000 MIDYEAR POPULATION | | | |
| | | Net increase [1] | | Natural increase | | Net migra-tion [3] (1,000) | Net growth rate [1] | Natural increase | | Net migra-tion [3] |
		Total (1,000)	Per-cent [2]	Births (1,000)	Deaths (1,000)			Birth rate	Death rate	
1980 [4]	226,546	1,900	0.8	2,743	1,463	724	11.1	16.0	8.6	4.2
1981	228,446	2,200	1.0	3,629	1,978	690	9.6	15.8	8.6	3.0
1982	230,645	2,157	0.9	3,681	1,975	595	9.3	15.9	8.5	2.6
1983	232,803	2,066	0.9	3,639	2,019	592	8.8	15.6	8.6	2.5
1984	234,868	2,070	0.9	3,669	2,039	589	8.8	15.6	8.6	2.5
1985	236,938	2,171	0.9	3,761	2,086	649	9.1	15.8	8.8	2.7
1986	239,109	2,158	0.9	3,757	2,105	661	9.0	15.6	8.8	2.8
1987	241,267	2,195	0.9	3,809	2,123	666	9.1	15.7	8.8	2.7
1988	243,462	2,243	0.9	3,910	2,168	662	9.2	16.0	8.9	2.7
1989	245,705	2,438	1.0	4,041	2,150	712	9.9	16.4	8.7	2.9
1990	248,143	2,537	1.0	4,148	2,155	[5]576	10.2	16.6	8.6	[5]2.3
1991	250,680	2,935	1.2	4,111	2,170	[5]994	11.6	16.3	8.6	[5]3.9
1992	253,615	2,901	1.1	4,065	2,176	1,012	11.4	15.9	8.5	4.0
1993	256,516	2,651	1.0	4,039	2,268	880	10.3	15.7	8.8	3.4
PROJECTIONS [6]										
1994	259,319	2,754	1.1	4,055	2,181	880	10.6	15.6	8.4	3.4
1995	262,073	2,693	1.0	4,024	2,211	880	10.2	15.3	8.4	3.3
1996	264,765	2,634	1.0	3,995	2,241	880	9.9	15.0	8.4	3.3
1997	267,399	2,581	1.0	3,971	2,270	880	9.6	14.8	8.4	3.3
1998	269,980	2,533	0.9	3,953	2,300	880	9.3	14.6	8.5	3.2
1999	272,513	2,492	0.9	3,941	2,329	880	9.1	14.4	8.5	3.2
2000	275,005	2,458	0.9	3,934	2,357	880	8.9	14.2	8.5	3.2
2005	287,092	2,391	0.8	3,990	2,479	880	8.3	13.8	8.6	3.1
2010	299,194	2,486	0.8	4,207	2,601	880	8.3	14.0	8.7	2.9
2015	311,833	2,570	0.8	4,420	2,730	880	8.2	14.1	8.7	2.8
2020	324,668	2,539	0.8	4,543	2,884	880	7.8	13.9	8.8	2.7
2025	337,126	2,408	0.7	4,607	3,079	880	7.1	13.6	9.1	2.6
2030	348,858	2,257	0.6	4,690	3,313	880	6.4	13.4	9.5	2.5
2040	370,466	2,074	0.6	4,989	3,795	880	5.6	13.4	10.2	2.4
2050	391,000	2,067	0.5	5,250	4,064	880	5.3	13.4	10.4	2.2

[1] Prior to April 1, 1990, includes "error of closure" (the amount necessary to make the components of change add to the net change between censuses), for which figures are not shown separately.　　[2] Percent of population at beginning of period. [3] Covers net international migration and movement of Armed Forces, federally affiliated civilian citizens, and their dependents. [4] Data are for period April 1 to December 31.　　[5] Data reflect movement of Armed Forces due to the Gulf War.　　[6] Based on middle series of assumptions. See footnote 1, table 3.

Source: U.S. Bureau of the Census, *Current Population Reports*, P25-1095 and P25-1104; and unpublished data.

No. 5. Immigration: 1901 to 1993

[In thousands, except rate. For fiscal years ending in year shown ; see text, section 9. For definition of immigrants, see text, section 1. Data represent immigrants admitted. Rates based on Bureau of the Census estimates as of July 1 for resident population through 1929, and for total population thereafter (excluding Alaska and Hawaii prior to 1959). See also *Historical Statistics, Colonial Times to 1970*, series C 89]

PERIOD	Number	Rate [1]	YEAR	Number	Rate [1]
1901 to 1910	8,795	10.4	1980	531	2.3
1911 to 1920	5,736	5.7	1985	570	2.4
1921 to 1930	4,107	3.5	1986	602	2.5
1931 to 1940	528	0.4	1987	602	2.5
1941 to 1950	1,035	0.7	1988	643	2.6
1951 to 1960	2,515	1.5	1989 [2]	1,091	4.4
1961 to 1970	3,322	1.7	1990 [2]	1,536	6.1
1971 to 1980	4,493	2.1	1991 [2]	1,827	7.2
1981 to 1990	7,338	3.1	1992 [2]	974	3.8
1991 to 1993	3,705	4.8	1993 [2]	904	3.5

[1] Annual rate per 1,000 U.S. population. Rate computed by dividing sum of annual immigration totals by sum of annual U.S. population totals for same number of years.   [2] Includes persons who were granted permanent residence under the legalization program of the Immigration Reform and Control Act of 1986.

Source: U.S. Immigration and Naturalization Service, *Statistical Yearbook*, annual.

No. 6. Immigrants Admitted, by Class of Admission: 1980 to 1993

[For fiscal year ending September 30. For definition of immigrants, see text, section 1. See also *Historical Statistics, Colonial Times to 1970*, series C 143-157]

CLASS OF ADMISSION	1980	1985	1990	1991	1992	1993
Immigrants, total	**530,639**	**570,009**	**1,536,483**	**1,827,167**	**973,977**	**904,292**
New arrivals	339,355	356,365	435,729	443,107	511,769	536,294
Adjustments	191,284	213,644	1,100,754	1,384,060	462,208	367,998
Preference immigrants, total	264,367	266,703	272,742	275,613	329,321	373,788
Family-sponsored immigrants, total	216,856	213,257	214,550	216,088	213,123	226,776
Unmarried sons/daughters of U.S. citizens and their children	5,668	9,319	15,861	15,385	12,486	12,819
Spouses, unmarried sons/daughters of alien residents, and their children	110,269	114,997	107,686	110,126	118,247	128,308
Married sons/daughters of U.S. citizens [1]	10,752	18,460	26,751	27,115	22,195	23,385
Brothers or sisters of U.S. citizens [1]	90,167	70,481	64,252	63,462	60,195	62,264
Employment-based immigrants, total	47,511	53,446	58,192	59,525	116,198	147,012
Priority workers [1]	(X)	(X)	(X)	(X)	5,456	21,114
Professionals with advanced degrees [1]	(X)	(X)	(X)	(X)	58,401	29,468
Skilled workers, professionals, unskilled workers [1]	(X)	(X)	(X)	(X)	47,568	87,689
Special immigrants [1]	3,142	2,551	4,463	4,576	4,063	8,158
Employment creation [1]	(X)	(X)	(X)	(X)	59	583
Professional or highly skilled immigrants [1] [2]	18,583	24,905	26,546	27,748	340	(X)
Needed skilled or unskilled workers [1] [2]	25,786	25,990	27,183	27,201	311	(X)
Immediate relatives	157,743	204,368	231,680	237,103	235,484	255,059
Spouses of U.S. citizens	96,854	129,790	125,426	125,397	128,396	145,843
Children of U.S. citizens	27,207	35,592	46,065	48,130	42,324	46,788
Orphans	5,139	9,286	7,088	9,008	6,536	7,348
Parents of U.S. citizens	33,682	38,986	60,189	63,576	64,764	62,428
Refugees and asylees	88,057	95,040	97,364	139,079	117,037	127,343
Cuban Refugee Act, Nov. 1966	6,021	14,288	5,730	5,486	5,365	6,976
Indochinese Refugee Act, Oct. 1977	22,497	166	33	22	29	24
Refugee-Parolee Act, Oct. 1978	46,058	3,766	153	69	82	53
Asylees, Refugee Act of 1980	1,250	5,000	4,937	22,664	10,658	11,804
Refugees, Refugee Act of 1980	(X)	71,820	86,511	110,838	100,902	108,486
Other refugees	12,231	-	-	-	1	-
Other immigrants	20,472	3,898	934,697	1,175,372	292,135	148,102
Children born abroad to resident aliens or subsequent to issuance of visa	4,059	3,508	2,630	2,516	2,116	2,030
Diversity Programs [3]	(X)	(X)	29,161	22,070	36,348	33,468
Amerasians (P.L. 100-202) [4]	(X)	(X)	13,059	16,010	17,253	11,116
Immigration Reform and Control Act of 1986 legalization adjustments	(X)	(X)	880,372	1,123,162	163,342	24,278
Legalization dependents [5]	(X)	(X)	(X)	(X)	52,272	55,344
Other	16,413	390	9,475	11,614	20,804	21,866

- Represents zero.   X Not applicable.   [1] Includes spouses and children.   [2] Category was eliminated in 1992 by the Immigration Act of 1990.   [3] Includes categories of immigrants admitted under three laws intended to diversify immigration: P.L. 99-603, P.L. 100-658, and P.L. 101-649.   [4] Under Public Law 100-202, Amerasians are aliens born in Vietnam between January 1, 1962, and January 1, 1976, who were fathered by U.S. citizens.   [5] Spouses and children of persons granted permanent resident status under provisions of the Immigration Reform and Control Act of 1986.

Source: U.S. Immigration and Naturalization Service, *Statistical Yearbook*, annual.

No. 7. Nonimmigrants Admitted, by Class of Admission: 1985 to 1993

[In thousands, except as noted. For fiscal years ending Sept. 30; see text, section 9. Nonimmigrants are nonresident aliens (non-U.S. citizens) admitted to the United States for a temporary period. Excluded are border crossers, crewmen, and insular travelers. See also *Historical Statistics, Colonial Times to 1970*, series C 149-157]

CLASS OF ADMISSION	1985	1987	1988	1989	1990	1991	1992	1993
Nonimmigrants [1]	9,540	12,273	14,592	16,145	17,574	18,963	20,794	21,447
Temporary visitors, total	8,405	11,019	13,197	14,667	16,080	17,386	19,238	19,862
For pleasure	6,609	8,887	10,821	12,115	13,418	14,734	16,450	16,900
For business	1,797	2,132	2,376	2,553	2,661	2,652	2,788	2,962
Transit aliens [2]	237	264	299	293	306	364	346	337
Foreign government officials [3]	90	92	99	102	97	98	103	102
Treaty traders and investors [3]	97	114	126	140	148	155	152	145
Students [3]	286	289	338	361	355	314	275	291
Representatives to international organizations [3]	57	57	59	61	61	64	70	73
Temporary workers and trainees [4]	88	114	133	165	174	205	217	224
Registered nurses [5]	(X)	(X)	(X)	(X)	(X)	1	7	6
Specialty occupations [6]	(X)	(X)	(X)	(X)	(X)	117	110	93
Workers of distinguished merit or ability [7]	47	66	78	90	100	(X)	(X)	(X)
Performing services unavailable in U.S.	25	29	33	47	36	40	34	31
U.S.-Canada Free-Trade Agreement [8]	(X)	(X)	(X)	3	5	8	13	17
Spouses and children of workers and trainees	13	16	20	24	29	35	41	42
Representatives of foreign information media [3]	17	18	22	21	20	21	22	21
Exchange visitors [3]	141	183	203	217	215	224	232	240
NATO officials [3]	8	7	9	9	8	9	9	9
Fiances(ees) of U.S. citizens [9]	8	7	7	7	7	8	9	9
Intracompany transferees [3]	107	107	102	101	103	113	121	132
Parolees [10]	64	63	95	107	90	127	137	124
Refugees	68	67	80	101	110	100	123	113

X Not applicable.   [1] Includes nonimmigrants whose class of admission is unknown.   [2] Includes foreign government officials and their spouses and (unmarried minor or dependent) children, in transit.   [3] Includes spouses and children.   [4] Includes other classes of admission, not shown separately.   [5] Entries began October 1, 1990 (fiscal year 1991). Data for fiscal year 1991 are underreported; an unknown number of H1A entries were counted as H1B entries.   [6] Prior to October 1, 1991 (fiscal year 1992), H1B entries were termed "Distinguished merit or ability." Data for fiscal year 1991 are overreported; an unknown number of H1A entries were counted as H1B entries.   [7] Beginning 1992, as a result of the Immigration Act of 1990, the existing temporary worker and trainee classes of admission have been revised and new worker classes have been created.   [8] Entries under the U.S.-Canada Free Trade Agreement began in January 1989.   [9] Includes children of fiances(ees) of U.S. citizens.   [10] Aliens allowed to enter the United States for a temporary period of time on emergency conditions or when the entry is determined to be in the public interest (e.g., witness in court).

No. 8. Immigrants, by Country of Birth: 1971 to 1993

[In thousands. For fiscal years ending in year shown; see text, section 9. For definition of immigrants, see text, section 1]

COUNTRY OF BIRTH	1971-80, total	1981-90, total	1991-92, total	1993	COUNTRY OF BIRTH	1971-80, total	1981-90, total	1991-92, total	1993
All countries	4,493.3	7,338.1	2,801.1	904.3	Philippines	360.2	495.3	124.6	63.5
Europe [1]	801.3	705.6	280.6	158.3	Syria	13.3	20.6	5.8	2.9
France	17.8	23.1	5.7	2.9	Thailand	44.1	64.4	14.5	6.7
Germany	66.0	70.1	16.4	7.3	Turkey	18.6	20.9	5.0	2.2
Greece	93.7	29.1	3.9	1.9	Vietnam	179.7	401.4	133.0	59.6
Ireland	14.1	32.8	17.0	13.6	**North America** [1]	1,645.0	3,125.0	1,595.0	301.4
Italy	130.1	32.9	5.2	2.5	Canada	114.8	119.2	28.7	17.2
Poland	43.6	97.4	44.7	27.8	Mexico	637.2	1,653.3	1,160.0	126.6
Portugal	104.5	40.0	7.3	2.1	Caribbean [1]	759.8	892.7	237.6	99.4
Romania	17.5	38.9	14.6	5.6	Barbados	20.9	17.4	2.6	1.2
Soviet Union, former [2]	43.2	84.0	100.6	58.6	Cuba	276.8	159.2	22.1	13.7
Armenia	(NA)	(NA)	(NA)	6.3	Dominican Republic	148.0	251.8	83.4	45.4
Azerbaijan	(NA)	(NA)	(NA)	2.9	Haiti	58.7	140.2	58.5	10.1
Belarus	(NA)	(NA)	(NA)	4.7	Jamaica	142.0	213.8	42.7	17.2
Moldova	(NA)	(NA)	(NA)	2.6	Trinidad and Tobago	61.8	39.5	15.4	6.6
Russia	(NA)	(NA)	(NA)	12.1	Central America [1]	132.4	458.7	168.7	58.2
Ukraine	(NA)	(NA)	(NA)	18.3	El Salvador	34.4	214.6	73.5	26.8
Uzbekistan	(NA)	(NA)	(NA)	2.7	Guatemala	25.6	87.9	36.0	11.9
Spain	30.0	15.8	3.5	1.4	Honduras	17.2	49.5	18.0	7.3
United Kingdom	123.5	142.1	33.9	18.8	Nicaragua	13.0	44.1	26.8	7.1
Yugoslavia	42.1	19.2	5.3	2.8	Panama	22.7	29.0	7.0	2.7
Asia [1]	1,633.8	2,817.4	715.5	358.0	**South America** [1]	284.4	455.9	135.2	53.9
Bangladesh	(NA)	15.2	14.4	3.3	Argentina	25.1	25.7	7.8	2.8
Cambodia	8.4	116.6	5.8	1.6	Brazil	13.7	23.7	12.9	4.6
China	[3]202.5	[3]388.8	71.9	65.6	Chile	17.6	23.4	4.8	1.8
Taiwan	([3])	([3])	29.6	14.3	Colombia	77.6	124.4	32.9	12.8
Hong Kong	47.5	63.0	20.9	9.2	Ecuador	50.2	56.0	17.2	7.3
India	176.8	261.9	81.8	40.1	Guyana	47.5	95.4	20.7	8.4
Iran	46.2	154.8	32.8	14.8	Peru	29.1	64.4	26.1	10.4
Iraq	23.4	19.6	5.6	4.1	**Africa** [1]	91.5	192.3	63.3	27.8
Israel	26.6	36.3	9.3	4.5	Egypt	25.5	31.4	9.2	3.6
Japan	47.9	43.2	16.1	6.9	Ethiopia	(NA)	27.2	9.7	5.3
Jordan	29.6	32.6	8.3	4.7	Ghana	(NA)	14.9	5.2	1.6
Korea	272.0	338.8	45.9	18.0	Nigeria	8.8	35.3	12.5	4.4
Laos	22.6	145.6	18.6	7.3	Other countries [4]	37.3	41.9	11.5	4.9
Lebanon	33.8	41.6	11.8	5.5					
Pakistan	31.2	61.3	30.6	8.9					

NA Not available.   [1] Includes countries not shown separately.   [2] Includes other republics and unknown republics, not shown separately.   [3] Data for Taiwan included with China.   [4] Includes Australia, New Zealand, and unknown countries.

Source of tables 7 and 8: U.S. Immigration and Naturalization Service, *Statistical Yearbook*, annual; and releases.

No. 9. Immigrants Admitted as Permanent Residents Under Refugee Acts, by Country of Birth: 1971 to 1993

[For fiscal years ending in year shown; see text, section 9. Covers immigrants who were allowed to enter the United States under 1953 Refugee Relief Act and later acts; Hungarian parolees under July 1958 Act; refugee-escapee parolees under July 1960 Act; conditional entries by refugees under Oct. 1965 Act; Cuban parolees under Nov. 1966 Act; beginning 1978, Indochina refugees under Act of Oct. 1977; beginning 1980, refugee-parolees under the Act of Oct. 1978, and asylees under the Act of March 1980; and beginning 1981 refugees under the Act of March 1980]

COUNTRY OF BIRTH	1971-80, total	1981-90, total	1991-92, total	1993	COUNTRY OF BIRTH	1971-80, total	1981-90, total	1991-92, total	1993
Total	539,447	1,013,620	256,116	127,343	China [3]	13,760	7,928	1,519	1,154
Europe [1]	71,858	155,512	105,667	53,195	Hong Kong	3,468	1,916	268	90
Bulgaria	1,238	1,197	873	303	Iran	364	46,773	11,608	3,875
Czechoslovakia	3,646	8,204	978	119	Iraq	6,851	7,540	558	1,856
Hungary	4,358	4,942	1,046	80	Laos	21,690	142,964	17,153	6,547
Poland	5,882	33,889	5,717	731	Philippines	216	3,403	470	122
Romania	6,812	29,798	9,247	3,654	Syria	1,336	2,145	348	115
Soviet Union, former [2]	31,309	72,306	85,055	45,900	Thailand	1,241	30,259	7,651	3,724
Armenia	(NA)	(NA)	(NA)	329	Vietnam	150,266	324,453	53,698	30,249
Azerbaijan	(NA)	(NA)	(NA)	2,790	North America [1]	252,633	121,840	37,279	15,926
Belarus	(NA)	(NA)	(NA)	4,480	Cuba	251,514	113,367	17,872	11,603
Moldova	(NA)	(NA)	(NA)	2,546	El Salvador	45	1,383	1,992	811
Russia	(NA)	(NA)	(NA)	8,965	Guatemala	(NA)	(NA)	(NA)	210
Ukraine	(NA)	(NA)	(NA)	16,977	Nicaragua	36	5,590	15,901	2,892
Uzbekistan	(NA)	(NA)	(NA)	2,475	Panama	(NA)	(NA)	243	81
Spain	5,317	736	146	37	South America [1]	1,244	1,976	762	461
Yugoslavia	11,297	324	124	77	Venezuela	(NA)	(NA)	(NA)	135
Asia [1]	210,683	712,092	103,184	51,783	Africa [1]	2,991	22,149	9,211	5,944
Afghanistan	542	22,946	4,182	2,233	Ethiopia	1,307	18,542	6,850	3,682
Cambodia	7,739	114,064	4,245	808	Other	38	51	13	34

NA Not available.   [1] Includes other countries, not shown separately.   [2] Includes other republics and unknown republics, not shown separately.   [3] Includes Taiwan.

Source: U.S. Immigration and Naturalization Service, *Statistical Yearbook,* annual; and releases.

No. 10. Estimated Undocumented Immigrants, by Selected States and Countries of Origin: 1992 and 1994

[In thousands. The ranges of estimates supplied by the Bureau of the Census represent indicators of magnitude which the Bureau believes is responsive to the inherent uncertainty in the assumptions underlying these estimates. The Census indicators are the results of applying 3 calculated percent distributions to two national estimates of the undocumented population. The 3 percent distributions by State are based on: (1) an average between the number of undocumented immigrants by State included in the 1980 census and of the number of legalization applicants by State produced by the Immigration Reform and Control Act (IRCA) of 1986; (2) the number of undocumented immigrants by State estimated by the Immigration and Naturalization Service (INS); and (3) the number of foreign born noncitizens by State counted in the 1990 census. The figures supplied by INS are based on estimates of illegal immigrant population who established residence in the United States before 1982 and did not legalize under IRCA and annual estimates of the number of persons who enter surreptitiously across land borders and nonimmigrant overstays who established residence here during the 1982 to 1992 period. The estimates for each country were distributed to States by INS based on U.S. residence pattern of each country's total number of applicants for legalization under IRCA]

STATE	BUREAU OF THE CENSUS ESTIMATES, 1994		INS estimates, Oct. 1992	COUNTRY	INS estimates, Oct. 1992
	Low	High			
United States, total [1]	3,500	4,000	3,379	Total [1]	3,379
California	1,321	1,784	1,441	Mexico	1,321
New York	462	539	449	El Salvador	327
Texas	300	427	357	Guatemala	129
Florida	243	385	322	Canada	97
Illinois	157	225	176	Poland	91
New Jersey	98	168	116	Philippines	90
Massachusetts	42	106	45	Haiti	88
Arizona	50	68	57	Bahamas, The	71
Maryland	29	63	27	Nicaragua	68
Virginia	37	63	35	Italy	67
Washington	32	59	30	Honduras	61
Michigan	10	53	(NA)	Colombia	59
Pennsylvania	15	51	18	Ecuador	45
Connecticut	13	46	15	Jamaica	42
Georgia	29	36	28	Dominican Republic	40
Ohio	7	36	(NA)	Trinidad & Tobago	39
Colorado	22	29	22	Ireland	36
Oregon	21	27	20	Portugal	31
Hawaii	4	25	(NA)	Pakistan	30
New Mexico	14	25	19	India	28

NA Not available.   [1] Includes other States and countries not shown separately.

Source: U.S. Bureau of the Census, "Illustrative Ranges of the Distribution of Undocumented Immigrants by State" by Edward W. Fernandez and J. Gregory Robinson, *Technical Working Paper* No. 8, October 1994; and U.S. Immigration and Naturalization Service, *Statistical Yearbook,* annual.

No. 11. Immigrants Admitted, by Leading Country of Birth and State: 1993

[**For year ending September 30.** For definition of immigrants, see text, section 1]

REGION, DIVISION, AND STATE	Total [1]	Mexico	China	Philip-pines	Vietnam	Soviet Union	Dominican Republic	India	Poland
U.S. [2]	904,292	126,561	65,578	63,457	59,614	58,571	45,420	40,121	27,846
Northeast	260,413	2,883	22,693	10,999	7,063	23,096	35,296	13,157	13,241
N.E.	41,955	290	4,310	908	2,730	3,956	3,126	1,697	2,295
ME	838	7	85	53	97	57	13	18	16
NH	1,263	19	150	49	90	76	69	78	17
VT	709	6	83	9	157	45	1	27	4
MA	25,011	99	3,002	425	1,915	2,691	2,233	907	682
RI	3,168	23	227	86	17	343	581	43	86
CT	10,966	136	763	286	454	744	229	624	1,490
M.A	218,458	2,593	18,383	10,091	4,333	19,140	32,170	11,460	10,946
NY	151,209	1,911	13,958	4,905	1,759	14,345	26,799	5,338	6,517
NJ	50,285	462	2,548	4,637	937	1,875	5,176	4,725	3,887
PA	16,964	220	1,877	549	1,637	2,920	195	1,397	542
Midwest	103,124	11,669	11,206	4,936	6,094	8,074	191	7,634	11,879
E.N.C	82,067	10,304	8,210	4,125	2,431	5,980	170	6,793	11,691
OH	10,703	151	1,846	414	481	1,866	23	877	192
IN	4,539	486	929	200	182	248	10	406	104
IL	46,744	8,911	3,170	2,842	923	2,381	86	3,991	10,651
MI	14,913	400	1,574	497	729	1,195	46	1,283	615
WI	5,168	356	691	172	116	290	5	236	129
W.N.C	21,057	1,365	2,996	811	3,663	2,094	21	841	188
MN	7,438	192	911	201	812	942	5	236	77
IA	2,626	186	495	95	661	110	6	89	26
MO	4,644	182	792	274	810	497	7	271	41
ND	601	13	59	21	105	106	-	16	6
SD	543	7	35	38	44	95	1	18	8
NE	1,980	225	252	65	615	157	-	58	16
KS	3,225	560	452	117	616	187	2	153	14
South	204,534	36,289	12,854	8,336	14,082	4,887	2,955	9,221	1,322
S.A.	119,502	3,415	7,001	5,419	6,341	3,519	2,812	5,139	1,052
DE	1,132	53	152	64	13	37	12	129	11
MD	16,899	187	1,730	1,007	666	933	213	1,291	120
DC	3,608	33	239	123	453	57	159	46	8
VA	16,451	278	1,133	1,390	1,300	525	80	958	78
WV	689	19	113	60	41	8	8	101	1
NC	6,892	341	849	290	749	261	23	526	62
SC	2,195	66	276	186	136	70	16	198	23
GA	10,213	606	937	369	1,599	515	51	752	77
FL	61,423	1,832	1,572	1,930	1,384	1,113	2,250	1,138	672
E.S.C	9,673	296	1,369	486	1,018	452	10	852	71
KY	2,182	73	334	127	245	164	4	131	13
TN	4,287	125	473	177	457	217	3	332	42
AL	2,298	67	378	88	226	64	2	303	5
MS	906	31	184	94	90	7	1	86	11
W.S.C	75,359	32,578	4,484	2,431	6,723	916	133	3,230	199
AR	1,312	115	150	95	129	25	-	84	3
LA	3,725	116	411	165	846	60	26	160	10
OK	2,942	574	317	140	575	23	4	178	12
TX	67,380	31,773	3,606	2,031	5,173	808	103	2,808	174
West	323,491	75,622	18,681	36,453	32,360	22,514	201	10,063	1,404
Mountain	29,190	10,305	2,191	1,581	2,284	1,327	42	748	240
MT	509	12	75	41	7	47	-	10	2
ID	1,270	494	132	50	73	81	-	17	8
WY	263	36	53	13	-	6	2	6	1
CO	6,650	1,688	638	239	651	594	6	144	101
NM	3,409	2,010	167	88	229	39	3	90	9
AZ	9,778	4,719	416	345	808	269	9	290	71
UT	3,266	297	546	82	395	255	9	103	27
NV	4,045	1,049	164	723	121	36	13	88	21
Pacific	294,301	65,317	16,490	34,872	30,076	21,187	159	9,315	1,164
WA	17,147	1,108	1,313	1,834	3,080	2,678	5	426	179
OR	7,250	901	676	341	1,070	1,527	8	161	33
CA	260,090	63,221	13,700	27,614	25,429	16,886	126	8,674	888
AK	1,286	48	56	411	16	76	18	26	61
HI	8,528	39	745	4,672	481	20	2	28	3

- Represents zero.   [1] Includes other countries, not shown separately.   [2] Includes Guam, Puerto Rico, Northern Mariana Islands, Virgin Islands, and other or unknown areas not shown separately.

Source: U.S. Immigration and Naturalization Service, *Statistical Yearbook,* annual.

No. 12. Resident Population—Selected Characteristics, 1790 to 1994, and Projections, 1995 to 2050

[**In thousands**. See also *Historical Statistics, Colonial Times to 1970*, series A 73-81 and A 143-149]

DATE	SEX		RACE					Hispanic origin [1]
					Other			
	Male	Female	White	Black	Total	American Indians and Alaska Natives	Asian and Pacific Islanders	
1790 (Aug. 2) [2]	(NA)	(NA)	3,172	757	(NA)	(NA)	(NA)	(NA)
1800 (Aug. 4) [2]	(NA)	(NA)	4,306	1,002	(NA)	(NA)	(NA)	(NA)
1850 (June 1) [2]	11,838	11,354	19,553	3,639	(NA)	(NA)	(NA)	(NA)
1900 (June 1) [2]	38,816	37,178	66,809	8,834	351	(NA)	(NA)	(NA)
1910 (Apr. 15) [2]	47,332	44,640	81,732	9,828	413	(NA)	(NA)	(NA)
1920 (Jan. 1) [2]	53,900	51,810	94,821	10,463	427	(NA)	(NA)	(NA)
1930 (Apr. 1) [2]	62,137	60,638	110,287	11,891	597	(NA)	(NA)	(NA)
1940 (Apr. 1) [2]	66,062	65,608	118,215	12,866	589	(NA)	(NA)	(NA)
1950 (Apr. 1) [2]	74,833	75,864	134,942	15,042	713	(NA)	(NA)	(NA)
1950 (Apr. 1)....	75,187	76,139	135,150	15,045	1,131	(NA)	(NA)	(NA)
1960 (Apr. 1) [3]	88,331	90,992	158,832	18,872	1,620	(NA)	(NA)	(NA)
1970 (Apr. 1) [3]	98,926	104,309	178,098	22,581	2,557	(NA)	(NA)	(NA)
1980 (Apr. 1) [4][5]	110,053	116,493	194,713	26,683	5,150	1,420	3,729	14,609
1990 (Apr. 1) [4][6]	121,244	127,474	208,710	30,486	9,523	2,065	7,458	22,354
1991 (July 1) [7]	122,947	129,184	211,015	31,111	10,006	2,107	7,899	23,381
1992 (July 1) [7]	124,430	130,597	212,953	31,659	10,415	2,142	8,273	24,270
1993 (July 1) [7]	125,800	131,983	214,789	32,180	10,814	2,177	8,637	25,191
1994 (July 1) [7]	127,076	133,265	216,470	32,672	11,199	2,210	8,989	26,077
1995 (July 1) [8]	128,685	134,749	218,334	33,117	11,982	2,226	9,756	26,798
2000 (July 1) [8]	135,101	141,140	226,267	35,469	14,505	2,380	12,125	31,166
2005 (July 1) [8]	141,121	147,165	233,343	37,793	17,151	2,543	14,608	35,702
2010 (July 1) [8]	147,187	153,245	240,297	40,224	19,910	2,719	17,191	40,525
2015 (July 1) [8]	153,517	159,599	247,542	42,797	22,777	2,904	19,873	45,719
2020 (July 1) [8]	159,897	166,045	254,791	45,409	25,743	3,090	22,653	51,217
2025 (July 1) [8]	166,012	172,326	261,531	48,005	28,802	3,278	25,524	56,927
2050 (July 1) [8]	192,098	199,933	285,591	61,586	44,854	4,346	40,508	88,071

NA Not available. [1] Persons of Hispanic origin may be of any race. [2] Excludes Alaska and Hawaii. [3] The revised 1970 resident population count is 203,302,031; which incorporates changes due to errors found after tabulations were completed. The race and sex data shown here reflect the official 1970 census count. [4] The race data shown have been modified; see text, section 1, for explanation. [5] See footnote 4, table 1. [6] The April 1, 1990, census count (248,718,291) includes count resolution corrections processed through March 1994 and does not include adjustments for census coverage errors. [7] Estimated. [8] Middle series projection; see table 3.

No. 13. Resident Population Characteristics—Percent Distribution and Median Age, 1850 to 1994, and Projections, 1995 to 2050

[**In percent, except as indicated**. For definition of median, see Guide to Tabular Presentation]

DATE	SEX		RACE			Hispanic origin [1]	Median age (years)
	Male	Female	White	Black	Other		
1850 (June 1) [2]	51.0	49.0	84.3	15.7	(NA)	(NA)	18.9
1900 (June 1) [2]	51.1	48.9	87.9	11.6	0.5	(NA)	22.9
1910 (Apr. 15) [2]	51.5	48.5	88.9	10.7	0.4	(NA)	24.1
1920 (Jan. 1) [2]	51.0	49.0	89.7	9.9	0.4	(NA)	25.3
1930 (Apr. 1) [2]	50.6	49.4	89.8	9.7	0.5	(NA)	26.4
1940 (Apr. 1) [2]	50.2	49.8	89.8	9.8	0.4	(NA)	29.0
1950 (Apr. 1) [2]	49.7	50.3	89.5	10.0	0.5	(NA)	30.2
1950 (Apr. 1).	49.7	50.3	89.3	9.9	0.7	(NA)	30.2
1960 (Apr. 1).	49.3	50.7	88.6	10.5	0.9	(NA)	29.5
1970 (Apr. 1).	48.7	51.3	87.6	11.1	1.3	(NA)	28.0
1980 (Apr. 1) [3][4]	48.6	51.4	85.9	11.8	2.3	6.4	30.0
1990 (Apr. 1) [3][5]	48.7	51.3	83.9	12.3	3.8	9.0	32.8
1991 (July 1) [6]	48.8	51.2	83.7	12.3	4.0	9.3	33.1
1992 (July 1) [6]	48.8	51.2	83.5	12.4	4.1	9.5	33.4
1993 (July 1) [6]	48.8	51.2	83.3	12.5	4.2	9.8	33.7
1994 (July 1) [6]	48.8	51.2	83.1	12.5	4.3	10.0	34.0
1995 (July 1) [7]	48.8	51.2	82.9	12.6	4.5	10.2	34.0
2000 (July 1) [7]	48.9	51.1	81.9	12.8	5.3	11.3	35.5
2025 (July 1) [7]	49.1	50.9	77.3	14.2	8.5	16.8	38.1
2050 (July 1) [7]	49.0	51.0	72.8	15.7	11.4	22.5	39.0

NA Not available. [1] Persons of Hispanic origin may be of any race. [2] Excludes Alaska and Hawaii. [3] The race data shown have been modified; see text, section 1 for explanation. [4] See footnote 4, table 1. [5] See footnote 6, table 12. [6] Estimated. [7] Middle series projection; see table 3.

Source of tables 12 and 13: U.S. Bureau of the Census, *U.S. Census of Population: 1940*, vol. II, part 1, and vol. IV, part 1; *1950*, vol. II, part 1; *1960*, vol. I, part 1; *1970*, vol. I, part B; *Current Population Reports*, P25-1095 and P25-1104; and unpublished data.

No. 14. Resident Population, by Age and Sex: 1970 to 1994

[In thousands, except as indicated. 1970, 1980, and 1990 data are enumerated population as of April 1; data for other years are estimated population as of July 1. Excludes Armed Forces overseas. For definition of median, see Guide to Tabular Presentation. See also Historical Statistics, Colonial Times to 1970, series A119-134]

YEAR AND SEX	Total, all years	Under 5 years	5-9 years	10-14 years	15-19 years	20-24 years	25-29 years	30-34 years	35-39 years	40-44 years	45-49 years	50-54 years	55-59 years	60-64 years	65-74 years	75-84 years	85 years and over	5-13 years	14-17 years	18-24 years	Median age (yr.)
1970, total [1]	**203,235**	**17,163**	**19,969**	**20,804**	**19,084**	**16,383**	**13,486**	**11,437**	**11,113**	**11,988**	**12,124**	**11,111**	**9,979**	**8,623**	**12,443**	**6,122**	**1,408**	**36,675**	**15,851**	**23,714**	**28.0**
Male	98,926	8,750	10,175	10,598	9,641	7,925	6,626	5,599	5,416	5,823	5,855	5,351	4,769	4,030	5,440	2,437	489	18,687	8,069	11,583	26.8
Female	104,309	8,413	9,794	10,206	9,443	8,458	6,859	5,838	5,697	6,166	6,269	5,759	5,210	4,593	7,002	3,684	919	17,987	7,782	12,131	29.3
1980, total [2]	**226,546**	**16,348**	**16,700**	**18,242**	**21,168**	**21,319**	**19,521**	**17,561**	**13,965**	**11,669**	**11,090**	**11,710**	**11,615**	**10,088**	**15,581**	**7,729**	**2,240**	**31,159**	**16,247**	**30,022**	**30.0**
Male	110,053	8,362	8,539	9,316	10,755	10,663	9,705	8,677	6,862	5,708	5,388	5,621	5,482	4,670	6,757	2,867	682	15,923	8,298	15,054	28.8
Female	116,493	7,986	8,161	8,926	10,413	10,655	9,816	8,884	7,104	5,961	5,702	6,089	6,133	5,418	8,824	4,862	1,559	15,237	7,950	14,969	31.3
1981, total	229,466	16,893	16,060	18,300	20,541	21,663	20,169	18,731	14,366	12,028	10,985	11,595	11,554	10,359	15,890	7,982	2,349	30,711	15,609	30,245	30.3
1982, total	231,664	17,228	15,958	18,145	19,962	21,682	20,704	18,714	15,566	12,464	11,011	11,414	11,463	10,567	16,147	8,203	2,437	30,528	15,057	30,162	30.5
1983, total	233,792	17,547	16,053	17,869	19,388	21,632	21,141	19,067	16,117	13,150	11,201	11,155	11,457	10,655	16,414	8,429	2,518	30,279	14,740	29,922	30.8
1984, total	235,825	17,695	16,338	17,450	18,931	21,529	21,459	19,503	16,867	13,636	11,429	10,957	11,352	10,803	16,626	8,656	2,595	30,062	14,725	29,461	31.1
1985, total	237,924	17,842	16,665	17,027	18,727	21,265	21,671	20,025	17,604	14,087	11,606	10,854	11,229	10,906	16,858	8,890	2,667	29,893	14,888	28,902	31.4
1986, total	240,133	17,963	17,098	16,474	18,813	20,744	21,893	20,479	18,611	14,398	11,878	10,781	11,135	10,859	17,137	9,129	2,742	30,078	14,824	28,227	31.7
1987, total	242,289	18,052	17,430	16,377	18,698	20,192	21,857	20,984	18,619	15,608	12,294	10,802	10,968	10,783	17,426	9,376	2,823	30,502	14,502	27,694	32.0
1988, total	244,499	18,195	17,759	16,496	18,496	19,655	21,739	21,391	18,993	16,188	12,954	10,995	10,722	10,791	17,626	9,612	2,885	31,028	14,023	27,356	32.3
1989, total	246,819	18,508	17,917	16,797	18,133	19,258	21,560	21,676	19,455	16,960	13,421	11,212	10,534	10,707	17,864	9,850	2,968	31,413	13,536	27,156	32.6
1990, total [3]	**248,718**	**18,757**	**18,035**	**17,060**	**17,886**	**19,135**	**21,328**	**21,833**	**19,846**	**17,589**	**13,744**	**11,313**	**10,487**	**10,625**	**18,046**	**10,012**	**3,022**	**31,826**	**13,340**	**26,950**	**32.8**
Male	121,244	9,599	9,232	8,739	9,175	9,744	10,703	10,862	9,834	8,677	6,739	5,493	5,008	4,947	7,907	3,745	841	16,295	6,857	13,738	31.6
Female	127,474	9,158	8,803	8,322	8,711	9,391	10,625	10,971	10,012	8,912	7,004	5,820	5,479	5,679	10,139	6,267	2,180	15,532	6,482	13,212	34.0
1991, total	252,131	19,195	18,236	17,667	17,185	19,168	20,732	22,158	20,517	18,758	14,097	11,648	10,423	10,584	18,275	10,311	3,179	32,496	13,419	26,341	33.1
1992, total	255,028	19,501	18,354	18,098	17,099	19,050	20,179	22,251	21,082	18,801	15,358	12,055	10,485	10,444	18,451	10,527	3,294	33,008	13,653	25,939	33.4
1993, total	257,783	19,691	18,529	18,521	17,267	18,762	19,625	22,251	21,587	19,197	15,931	12,727	10,680	10,242	18,640	10,720	3,413	33,491	13,928	25,661	33.7
1994, total	**260,341**	**19,727**	**18,859**	**18,753**	**17,616**	**18,326**	**19,177**	**22,177**	**21,961**	**19,699**	**16,679**	**13,191**	**10,936**	**10,082**	**18,712**	**10,925**	**3,522**	**33,863**	**14,428**	**25,263**	**34.0**
Male	127,076	10,094	9,657	9,602	9,036	9,311	9,619	11,058	10,920	9,728	8,181	6,410	5,244	4,740	8,290	4,206	980	17,339	7,412	12,856	32.9
Female	133,265	9,633	9,201	9,150	8,580	9,015	9,558	11,119	11,040	9,970	8,498	6,781	5,692	5,342	10,422	6,719	2,542	16,524	7,016	12,407	35.2
Percent:																					
1970 [2]	100.0	8.4	9.8	10.2	9.4	8.1	6.6	5.6	5.5	5.9	6.0	5.5	4.9	4.2	6.1	3.0	0.7	18.0	7.8	11.7	(X)
1980 [2]	100.0	7.2	7.4	8.1	9.3	9.4	8.6	7.8	6.2	5.2	4.9	5.2	5.1	4.5	6.9	3.4	1.0	13.8	7.2	13.3	(X)
1990 [3]	100.0	7.5	7.3	6.9	7.2	7.7	8.6	8.8	8.0	7.1	5.5	4.5	4.2	4.3	7.3	4.0	1.2	12.8	5.4	10.8	(X)
1994	**100.0**	**7.6**	**7.2**	**7.2**	**6.8**	**7.0**	**7.4**	**8.5**	**8.4**	**7.6**	**6.4**	**5.1**	**4.2**	**3.9**	**7.2**	**4.2**	**1.4**	**13.0**	**5.5**	**9.7**	**(X)**
Male	100.0	7.9	7.6	7.6	7.1	7.3	7.6	8.7	8.6	7.7	6.4	5.0	4.1	3.7	6.5	3.3	0.8	13.6	5.8	10.1	(X)
Female	100.0	7.2	6.9	6.9	6.4	6.8	7.2	8.3	8.3	7.5	6.4	5.1	4.3	4.0	7.8	5.0	1.9	12.4	5.3	9.3	(X)

X Not applicable. [1] Official count. The revised 1970 resident population count is 203,302,031; the difference of 66,733 is due to errors found after release of the official series. [2] See footnote 4, table 1.
[3] The data shown have been modified from the official 1990 census counts. See text, section 1, for explanation. The April 1, 1990, census count (248,718,291) includes count resolution corrections processed through March 1994 and does not include adjustments for census coverage errors.

Source: U.S. Bureau of the Census, Current Population Reports, P25-917 and P25-1095; and Population Paper Listing 21.

No. 15. Ratio of Males to Females, by Age Group, 1950 to 1994, and Projections, 2000 and 2025

[Number of males per 100 females. Total resident population]

AGE	1950 (Apr. 1)	1960 (Apr. 1)	1970 (Apr. 1)	1980 (Apr. 1)	1990 [1] (Apr. 1)	1994 (July 1)	PROJECTIONS [2] 2000 (July 1)	2025 (July 1)
All ages........	98.6	97.1	94.8	94.5	95.1	95.4	95.7	96.3
Under 14 years	103.7	103.4	103.9	104.6	104.9	104.9	105.2	105.4
14 to 24 years	98.2	98.7	98.7	101.9	104.6	104.4	104.4	104.7
25 to 44 years	96.4	95.7	95.5	97.4	98.9	99.1	99.1	98.6
45 to 64 years	100.1	95.7	91.6	90.7	92.5	93.4	94.1	94.2
65 years and over....	89.6	82.8	72.1	67.6	67.2	68.5	70.5	82.0

[1] The April 1, 1990, census count (248,718,291) includes count resolution corrections processed through March 1994, and does not include adjustments for census coverage errors.   [2] Middle series projections; see table 3.

Source: U.S. Bureau of the Census, *U.S. Census of Population: 1950*, vol. II, part 1; *1960*, vol. I, part 1; *1970*, vol. I, part B; *Current Population Reports*, P25-1095 and P25-1104; and unpublished data.

No. 16. Resident Population, by Sex and Age: 1994

[In thousands, except as indicated. As of July 1. For derivation of estimates, see text, section 1]

AGE	Total	Male	Female	AGE	Total	Male	Female
Total	260,341	127,076	133,265	43 yrs. old	3,716	1,825	1,891
				44 yrs. old	3,825	1,897	1,927
Under 5 yrs. old	19,727	10,094	9,633	45 to 49 yrs. old	16,679	8,181	8,498
Under 1 yr. old	3,870	1,981	1,889	45 yrs. old	3,659	1,801	1,858
1 yr. old.........	3,878	1,985	1,893	46 yrs. old	3,550	1,743	1,807
2 yrs. old	3,956	2,023	1,933	47 yrs. old	3,843	1,886	1,957
3 yrs. old	3,990	2,041	1,949	48 yrs. old	2,652	1,292	1,360
4 yrs. old	4,032	2,064	1,968	49 yrs. old	2,974	1,458	1,517
5 to 9 yrs. old	18,859	9,657	9,201	50 to 54 yrs. old	13,191	6,410	6,781
5 yrs. old	3,884	1,989	1,894	50 yrs. old	2,890	1,409	1,481
6 yrs. old	3,792	1,940	1,852	51 yrs. old	2,931	1,430	1,502
7 yrs. old	3,747	1,917	1,830	52 yrs. old	2,549	1,238	1,312
8 yrs. old	3,595	1,841	1,754	53 yrs. old	2,440	1,182	1,258
9 yrs. old	3,841	1,969	1,872	54 yrs. old	2,381	1,152	1,229
				55 to 59 yrs. old	10,936	5,244	5,692
10 to 14 yrs. old	18,753	9,602	9,150	55 yrs. old	2,283	1,099	1,184
10 yrs. old	3,744	1,920	1,824	56 yrs. old	2,281	1,095	1,185
11 yrs. old	3,770	1,931	1,840	57 yrs. old	2,178	1,043	1,134
12 yrs. old	3,768	1,927	1,841	58 yrs. old	2,021	966	1,055
13 yrs. old	3,722	1,903	1,818	59 yrs. old	2,173	1,041	1,132
14 yrs. old	3,748	1,921	1,828	60 to 64 yrs. old	10,082	4,740	5,342
15 to 19 yrs. old	17,616	9,036	8,580	60 yrs. old	1,981	934	1,046
15 yrs. old	3,602	1,848	1,754	61 yrs. old	1,953	923	1,030
16 yrs. old	3,515	1,808	1,707	62 yrs. old	1,965	921	1,044
17 yrs. old	3,562	1,836	1,727	63 yrs. old	2,065	971	1,094
18 yrs. old	3,349	1,714	1,635	64 yrs. old	2,118	990	1,128
19 yrs. old	3,588	1,831	1,757	65 to 69 yrs. old	9,970	4,500	5,471
20 to 24 yrs. old	18,326	9,311	9,015	65 yrs. old	2,059	948	1,111
20 yrs. old	3,480	1,776	1,704	66 yrs. old	2,071	948	1,124
21 yrs. old	3,492	1,782	1,710	67 yrs. old	2,003	905	1,098
22 yrs. old	3,605	1,835	1,770	68 yrs. old	1,897	845	1,052
23 yrs. old	3,839	1,943	1,897	69 yrs. old	1,940	854	1,086
24 yrs. old	3,910	1,976	1,934	70 to 74 yrs. old	8,741	3,790	4,951
25 to 29 yrs. old	19,177	9,619	9,558	70 yrs. old	1,875	824	1,051
25 yrs. old	3,756	1,894	1,862	71 yrs. old	1,801	786	1,015
26 yrs. old	3,680	1,846	1,834	72 yrs. old	1,811	791	1,020
27 yrs. old	3,778	1,894	1,884	73 yrs. old	1,695	729	966
28 yrs. old	3,674	1,837	1,837	74 yrs. old	1,559	659	899
29 yrs. old	4,289	2,147	2,142	75 to 79 yrs. old	6,574	2,655	3,919
				75 yrs. old	1,473	614	859
30 to 34 yrs. old	22,177	11,058	11,119	76 yrs. old	1,369	563	806
30 yrs. old	4,354	2,173	2,181	77 yrs. old	1,294	524	770
31 yrs. old	4,332	2,160	2,172	78 yrs. old	1,254	496	758
32 yrs. old	4,431	2,209	2,222	79 yrs. old	1,184	459	725
33 yrs. old	4,433	2,201	2,232	80 to 84 yrs. old	4,351	1,550	2,801
34 yrs. old	4,626	2,315	2,311	80 yrs. old	1,048	393	655
35 to 39 yrs. old	21,961	10,920	11,040	81 yrs. old	966	352	614
35 yrs. old	4,523	2,253	2,270	82 yrs. old	855	306	549
36 yrs. old	4,439	2,208	2,231	83 yrs. old	784	268	516
37 yrs. old	4,472	2,223	2,248	84 yrs. old	699	232	467
38 yrs. old	4,055	2,007	2,048	85 to 89 yrs. old	2,274	686	1,588
39 yrs. old	4,472	2,229	2,243	90 to 94 yrs. old	948	235	713
40 to 44 yrs. old	19,699	9,728	9,970	95 to 99 yrs. old	249	50	199
40 yrs. old	4,223	2,090	2,133	100 yrs. old and over..	50	9	41
41 yrs. old	4,013	1,979	2,033	Median age (yr.)......	34.0	32.9	35.2
42 yrs. old	3,922	1,936	1,986				

Source: U.S. Bureau of the Census, Population Paper Listing 21.

No. 17. Resident Population Projections, by Age and Sex: 1995 to 2050

[In thousands, except as indicated. As of July. See headnote, table 3]

YEAR	Total	Under 5 years	5 to 13 years	14 to 17 years	18 to 24 years	25 to 34 years	35 to 44 years	45 to 54 years	55 to 64 years	65 to 74 years	75 to 84 years	85 years and over
TOTAL												
Lowest series:												
1995	262,051	19,892	34,140	14,519	25,281	41,435	42,023	30,142	21,166	18,881	11,023	3,547
2000	270,259	18,034	35,869	15,564	25,306	37,286	44,565	35,813	23,370	18,217	12,132	4,101
2005	276,316	16,951	34,668	16,542	27,309	35,121	41,898	40,475	28,203	17,984	12,600	4,564
2010	281,180	16,653	32,100	16,425	29,005	35,934	37,703	42,833	33,422	19,933	12,115	5,055
2020	289,553	17,336	31,272	14,404	26,764	40,218	36,362	36,228	39,890	28,513	13,439	5,127
2025	292,092	17,036	31,916	14,356	25,447	39,427	38,788	34,137	37,395	32,090	16,309	5,191
2030	292,902	16,519	31,773	14,792	25,260	36,593	40,553	34,921	33,656	33,800	19,228	5,808
2040	290,351	16,202	30,299	14,537	26,092	35,429	36,957	38,921	32,508	28,486	22,691	8,229
2050	285,502	16,250	30,174	13,986	24,920	36,106	35,791	35,443	36,185	27,665	19,088	9,894
Middle series:												
1995	263,434	20,181	34,262	14,591	25,465	41,670	42,150	30,224	21,241	18,963	11,087	3,598
2000	276,241	19,431	36,547	15,811	25,911	38,237	45,123	36,170	23,690	18,551	12,438	4,333
2005	288,286	19,333	36,843	16,947	28,238	36,792	43,075	41,219	28,870	18,623	13,265	5,082
2010	300,431	20,017	36,213	17,388	30,220	38,179	39,659	44,099	34,552	20,978	13,157	5,969
2020	325,942	21,957	38,701	17,119	30,456	43,553	39,662	38,885	42,262	30,910	15,480	6,959
2025	338,338	22,372	40,455	17,897	30,585	44,299	42,590	37,534	40,455	35,361	19,274	7,515
2030	349,993	22,689	41,528	18,820	31,802	43,572	45,040	38,936	37,429	37,984	23,348	8,843
2040	371,505	23,978	43,069	19,747	34,510	46,127	45,134	44,224	37,701	33,968	29,206	13,840
2050	392,031	25,382	45,742	20,630	35,710	49,462	47,739	44,337	42,920	34,628	26,588	18,893
Highest series:												
1995	264,715	20,470	34,380	14,659	25,643	41,907	42,294	30,295	21,295	19,008	11,139	3,626
2000	281,957	20,938	37,206	16,045	26,498	39,198	45,797	36,501	23,910	18,733	12,649	4,483
2005	299,941	22,076	39,099	17,333	29,131	38,444	44,443	41,979	29,311	18,990	13,687	5,445
2010	319,536	24,108	40,756	18,331	31,383	40,358	41,772	45,470	35,322	21,586	13,805	6,644
2020	363,213	27,960	47,760	20,174	34,302	46,735	43,000	41,674	44,162	32,313	16,729	8,405
2025	386,595	29,602	51,206	22,094	36,274	49,102	46,380	41,010	43,047	37,396	21,058	9,427
2030	410,991	31,472	54,296	23,745	39,423	50,832	49,467	42,984	40,729	40,776	25,855	11,410
2040	463,579	36,246	61,516	26,653	44,998	58,392	53,705	49,454	42,279	38,127	33,472	18,736
2050	522,098	41,404	70,680	30,400	50,494	65,872	61,394	53,662	48,751	40,095	32,028	27,318
MALE (middle series)												
1995	128,685	10,344	17,556	7,503	12,958	20,835	20,911	14,777	10,101	8,420	4,274	1,005
2000	135,101	9,958	18,738	8,129	13,177	19,059	22,425	17,692	11,321	8,385	4,980	1,238
2005	141,121	9,908	18,895	8,716	14,360	18,301	21,372	20,193	13,842	8,559	5,463	1,512
2010	147,187	10,262	18,575	8,949	15,382	18,991	19,620	21,631	16,603	9,744	5,574	1,855
2020	159,897	11,263	19,866	8,816	15,513	21,703	19,601	18,989	20,414	14,561	6,874	2,297
2025	166,012	11,476	20,765	9,216	15,578	22,084	21,062	18,301	19,519	16,755	8,693	2,561
2030	171,690	11,635	21,312	9,691	16,197	21,721	22,294	18,988	18,008	18,081	10,643	3,122
2040	182,049	12,289	22,091	10,161	17,571	22,998	22,361	21,597	18,125	16,174	13,566	5,116
2050	192,098	13,008	23,460	10,614	18,181	24,675	23,681	21,690	20,696	16,552	12,446	7,094
FEMALE (middle series)												
1995	134,749	9,837	16,707	7,087	12,507	20,835	21,238	15,447	11,140	10,544	6,814	2,593
2000	141,140	9,473	17,811	7,681	12,734	19,178	22,697	18,477	12,369	10,166	7,458	3,095
2005	147,165	9,425	17,948	8,230	13,878	18,491	21,702	21,028	15,027	10,065	7,802	3,570
2010	153,245	9,756	17,637	8,438	14,839	19,188	20,038	22,468	17,949	11,235	7,583	4,114
2020	166,045	10,693	18,835	8,303	14,943	21,849	20,060	19,896	21,848	16,348	8,606	4,662
2025	172,326	10,896	19,689	8,680	15,007	22,216	21,528	19,232	20,936	18,606	10,581	4,954
2030	178,303	11,054	20,216	9,131	15,606	21,851	22,746	19,947	19,421	19,903	12,705	5,721
2040	189,456	11,689	20,978	9,585	16,939	23,129	22,773	22,627	19,576	17,794	15,640	8,724
2050	199,933	12,374	22,282	10,016	17,530	24,787	24,057	22,647	22,224	18,076	14,141	11,799
PERCENT DISTRIBUTION (middle series)												
1995	100.0	7.7	13.0	5.4	10.1	16.6	15.7	10.8	8.2	7.2	4.1	1.3
2000	100.0	7.0	13.2	5.7	9.4	13.8	16.3	13.1	8.6	6.7	4.5	1.6
2005	100.0	6.7	12.8	5.9	9.8	12.8	14.9	14.3	10.0	6.5	4.6	1.8
2010	100.0	6.7	12.1	5.8	10.1	12.7	13.2	14.7	11.5	7.0	4.4	2.0
2020	100.0	6.7	11.9	5.3	9.3	13.4	12.2	11.9	13.0	9.5	4.7	2.1
2025	100.0	6.6	12.0	5.3	9.0	13.1	12.6	11.1	12.0	10.5	5.7	2.2
2030	100.0	6.5	11.9	5.4	9.1	12.4	12.9	11.1	10.7	10.9	6.7	2.5
2040	100.0	6.5	11.6	5.3	9.3	12.4	12.1	11.9	10.1	9.1	7.9	3.7
2050	100.0	6.5	11.7	5.3	9.1	12.6	12.2	11.3	10.9	8.8	6.8	4.8

Source: U.S. Bureau of the Census, Current Population Reports, P25-1104.

No. 18. Resident Population, by Race, 1980 to 1994, and Projections, 1995 to 2050

[**In thousands, except as indicated**. As of **July**, except as indicated. These data are consistent with the 1980 and 1990 decennial enumerations and have been modified from the official census counts; see text, section 1, for explanation. See headnote, table 3]

YEAR	Total	White	Black	American Indian, Eskimo, Aleut	Asian, Pacific Islander
1980 (April) [1]	226,546	194,713	26,683	1,420	3,729
1980	227,225	195,185	26,771	1,433	3,837
1981	229,466	196,635	27,133	1,483	4,214
1982	231,664	198,037	27,508	1,537	4,581
1983	233,792	199,420	27,867	1,596	4,909
1984	235,825	200,708	28,212	1,656	5,249
1985	237,924	202,031	28,569	1,718	5,606
1986	240,133	203,430	28,942	1,783	5,978
1987	242,289	204,770	29,325	1,851	6,343
1988	244,499	206,129	29,723	1,923	6,724
1989	246,819	207,540	30,143	2,001	7,134
1990 (April) [2]	248,718	208,710	30,486	2,065	7,458
1990	249,402	209,180	30,599	2,073	7,550
1991	252,131	211,015	31,111	2,107	7,899
1992	255,028	212,953	31,659	2,142	8,273
1993	257,783	214,789	32,180	2,177	8,637
1994	260,341	216,470	32,672	2,210	8,989
PROJECTIONS					
Lowest series:					
1995	262,051	217,381	32,954	2,222	9,493
2000	270,259	222,143	34,715	2,354	11,047
2005	276,316	225,080	36,175	2,480	12,581
2010	281,180	227,026	37,456	2,604	14,094
2020	289,553	229,790	39,735	2,837	17,191
2030	292,902	228,386	41,161	3,029	20,326
2040	290,351	222,048	41,828	3,191	23,284
2050	285,502	214,054	42,026	3,323	26,099
Middle series:					
1995	263,434	218,334	33,117	2,226	9,756
2000	276,241	226,267	35,469	2,380	12,125
2005	288,286	233,343	37,793	2,543	14,608
2010	300,431	240,297	40,224	2,719	17,191
2020	325,942	254,791	45,409	3,090	22,653
2030	349,993	267,457	50,596	3,473	28,467
2040	371,505	277,232	55,917	3,894	34,461
2050	392,031	285,591	61,586	4,346	40,508
Highest series:					
1995	264,715	219,210	33,274	2,228	10,002
2000	281,957	230,232	36,195	2,390	13,140
2005	299,941	241,516	39,314	2,569	16,541
2010	319,536	253,813	42,751	2,773	20,200
2020	363,213	281,304	50,475	3,223	28,212
2030	410,991	310,917	59,073	3,729	37,271
2040	463,579	342,960	68,767	4,336	47,516
2050	522,098	378,408	79,722	5,039	58,930
PERCENT DISTRIBUTION					
Middle series:					
1995	100.0	82.9	12.6	0.8	3.7
2000	100.0	81.9	12.8	0.9	4.4
2005	100.0	80.9	13.1	0.9	5.1
2010	100.0	80.0	13.4	0.9	5.7
2020	100.0	78.2	13.9	0.9	7.0
2030	100.0	76.4	14.5	1.0	8.1
2040	100.0	74.6	15.1	1.0	9.3
2050	100.0	72.8	15.7	1.1	10.3
PERCENT CHANGE (middle series)					
1995-2000	4.9	3.6	7.1	6.9	24.3
2000-2010	8.8	6.2	13.4	14.2	41.8
2010-2020	8.5	6.0	12.9	13.6	31.8
2020-2030	7.4	5.0	11.4	12.4	25.7
2030-2040	6.1	3.7	10.5	12.1	21.1
2040-2050	5.5	3.0	10.1	11.6	17.5

[1] See footnote 4, table 1.   [2] The April 1, 1990, census count (248,718,291) includes count resolution corrections processed through March 1994 and does not include adjustments for census coverage errors.

Source: U.S. Bureau of the Census, *Current Population Reports*, P25-1095 and P25-1104; and Population Paper Listing 21.

No. 19. Resident Population, by Hispanic Origin Status, 1980 to 1994, and Projections, 1995 to 2050

[**In thousands, except as indicated**. As of **July**, except as indicated. These data are consistent with the 1980 and 1990 decennial enumerations and have been modified from the official census counts; see text, section 1, for explanation. See headnote, table 3. Minus sign (-) indicates decrease]

YEAR	Total	Hispanic origin [1]	NOT OF HISPANIC ORIGIN			
			White	Black	American Indian, Eskimo, Aleut	Asian, Pacific Islander
1980 (April) [2]	226,546	14,609	180,906	26,142	1,326	3,563
1980	227,225	14,869	181,140	26,215	1,336	3,665
1981	229,466	15,560	181,974	26,532	1,377	4,022
1982	231,664	16,240	182,782	26,856	1,420	4,367
1983	233,792	16,935	183,561	27,159	1,466	4,671
1984	235,825	17,640	184,243	27,444	1,512	4,986
1985	237,924	18,368	184,945	27,738	1,558	5,315
1986	240,133	19,154	185,678	28,040	1,606	5,655
1987	242,289	19,946	186,353	28,351	1,654	5,985
1988	244,499	20,786	187,012	28,669	1,703	6,329
1989	246,819	21,648	187,713	29,005	1,755	6,698
1990 (April) [3]	248,718	22,354	188,306	29,275	1,796	6,988
1990	249,402	22,549	188,601	29,374	1,802	7,076
1991	252,131	23,381	189,690	29,825	1,829	7,406
1992	255,028	24,270	190,830	30,310	1,856	7,761
1993	257,783	25,191	191,841	30,764	1,882	8,105
1994	260,341	26,077	192,727	31,192	1,907	8,438
PROJECTIONS						
Lowest series:						
1995	262,051	26,402	193,295	31,514	1,924	8,915
2000	270,259	29,473	195,240	33,112	2,033	10,400
2005	276,316	32,373	195,520	34,419	2,137	11,867
2010	281,180	35,223	194,860	35,547	2,237	13,311
2020	289,553	41,235	192,130	37,503	2,424	16,261
2030	292,902	47,049	185,402	38,624	2,576	19,250
2040	290,351	52,450	174,123	39,009	2,704	22,066
2050	285,502	57,643	161,382	38,933	2,807	24,738
Middle series:						
1995	263,434	26,798	193,900	31,648	1,927	9,161
2000	276,241	31,166	197,872	33,741	2,055	11,407
2005	288,286	35,702	200,842	35,793	2,190	13,759
2010	300,431	40,525	203,441	37,930	2,336	16,199
2020	325,942	51,217	208,280	42,459	2,641	21,345
2030	349,993	62,810	210,480	46,934	2,960	26,810
2040	371,505	75,130	209,148	51,489	3,314	32,424
2050	392,031	88,071	205,849	56,346	3,701	38,064
Highest series:						
1995	264,715	27,150	194,465	31,779	1,929	9,392
2000	281,957	32,699	200,482	34,354	2,063	12,359
2005	299,941	38,767	206,306	37,089	2,210	15,569
2010	319,536	45,494	212,559	40,094	2,376	19,013
2020	363,213	61,104	226,025	46,813	2,741	26,530
2030	410,991	79,684	238,947	54,209	3,154	34,998
2040	463,579	101,872	251,077	62,453	3,647	44,529
2050	522,098	128,255	262,855	71,675	4,221	55,093
PERCENT DISTRIBUTION						
Middle series:						
1995	100.0	10.2	73.6	12.0	0.7	3.5
2000	100.0	11.3	71.6	12.2	0.7	4.1
2005	100.0	12.4	69.7	12.4	0.8	4.8
2010	100.0	13.5	67.7	12.6	0.8	5.4
2020	100.0	15.7	63.9	13.0	0.8	6.5
2030	100.0	17.9	60.1	13.4	0.8	7.7
2040	100.0	20.2	56.3	13.9	0.9	8.7
2050	100.0	22.5	52.5	14.4	0.9	9.7
PERCENT CHANGE (middle series)						
1995-2000	4.9	16.3	2.0	6.6	6.6	24.5
2000-2010	8.8	30.0	2.8	12.4	13.7	42.0
2010-2020	8.5	26.4	2.4	11.9	13.1	31.8
2020-2030	7.4	22.6	1.1	10.5	12.1	25.6
2030-2040	6.1	19.6	-0.6	9.7	12.0	20.9
2040-2050	5.5	17.2	-1.6	9.4	11.7	17.4

[1] Persons of Hispanic origin may be of any race.   [2] See footnote 4, table 1.   [3] The April 1, 1990, census count (248,718,291) includes count resolution corrections processed through March 1994 and does not include adjustments for census coverage errors.

Source: U.S. Bureau of the Census, *Current Population Reports*, P25-1095 and P25-1104; and Population Paper Listing 21.

No. 20. Components of Population Change, by Race and Hispanic Origin, 1990 to 1993, and Projections, 1995 and 2000

[The April 1, 1990, census count (248,718,291) includes count resolution corrections processed through March 1994 and does not include adjustments for census coverage errors]

YEAR	Population at start of period (1,000)	TOTAL (Jan. 1-Dec. 31)					RATE PER 1,000 MIDYEAR POPULATION			
		Net increase [1]		Natural increase		Net migra-tion [3] (1,000)	Net growth rate [1]	Natural increase		Net migra-tion rate [3]
		Total (1,000)	Per-cent [2]	Births (1,000)	Deaths (1,000)			Birth rate	Death rate	
WHITE										
1990	208,376	1,669	0.8	3,265	1,860	[4]306	8.0	15.6	8.9	[4]1.5
1991	210,046	1,966	0.9	3,241	1,869	[4]594	9.3	15.4	8.9	[4]2.8
1992	212,012	1,949	0.9	3,202	1,874	621	9.2	15.0	8.8	2.9
1993	213,961	1,757	0.8	3,169	1,950	539	8.2	14.8	9.1	2.5
Projections:[5]										
1995.	217,460	1,718	0.8	3,128	1,892	482	7.9	14.3	8.7	2.2
2000.	225,520	1,478	0.7	2,992	1,997	482	6.5	13.2	8.8	2.1
BLACK										
1990	30,377	440	1.4	692	266	[4]27	14.4	22.6	8.7	[4]0.9
1991	30,817	581	1.9	683	270	[4]168	18.7	21.9	8.7	[4]5.4
1992	31,398	541	1.7	674	269	136	17.1	21.3	8.5	4.3
1993	31,939	502	1.6	673	282	111	15.6	20.9	8.8	3.5
Projections:[5]										
1995.	32,874	483	1.5	685	283	81	14.6	20.7	8.5	2.4
2000.	35,238	463	1.3	695	313	81	13.0	19.6	8.8	2.3
AMERICAN INDIAN, ESKIMO, ALEUT										
1990	2,044	45	2.2	42	8	[4]1	21.8	20.1	4.1	[4]0.6
1991	2,089	35	1.7	39	9	[4]5	16.6	18.4	4.1	[4]2.3
1992	2,124	36	1.7	39	9	5	16.7	18.4	4.2	2.5
1993	2,160	34	1.6	40	11	5	15.5	18.2	4.9	2.1
Projections:[5]										
1995.	2,211	30	1.4	40	10	-	13.7	17.9	4.4	0.1
2000.	2,364	31	1.3	42	11	-	13.2	17.7	4.6	0.1
ASIAN, PACIFIC ISLANDER										
1990	7,345	382	5.2	149	21	[4]242	50.6	19.8	2.7	[4]32.0
1991	7,727	353	4.6	148	22	[4]227	44.7	18.8	2.8	[4]28.7
1992	8,080	376	4.6	150	24	249	45.4	18.2	2.9	30.1
1993	8,456	358	4.2	157	25	226	41.4	18.2	2.9	26.1
Projections:[5]										
1995.	9,527	461	4.8	170	26	317	47.2	17.5	2.7	32.5
2000.	11,883	486	4.1	205	36	317	40.1	16.9	2.9	26.1
HISPANIC ORIGIN [6]										
1990	22,122	847	3.8	595	84	[4]292	37.6	26.4	3.7	[4]12.9
1991	22,969	841	3.7	628	85	[4]298	36.0	26.8	3.6	[4]12.8
1992	23,810	913	3.8	646	87	354	37.6	26.6	3.6	14.6
1993	24,723	913	3.7	659	94	348	36.2	26.2	3.7	13.8
Projections:[5]										
1995.	26,368	862	3.3	639	100	322	32.1	23.8	3.7	12.0
2000.	30,723	888	2.9	690	125	322	28.5	22.1	4.0	10.3
WHITE, NON-HISPANIC										
1990	188,160	929	0.5	2,720	1,782	[4]52	4.9	14.4	9.4	[4]0.3
1991	189,089	1,211	0.6	2,667	1,790	[4]334	6.4	14.1	9.4	[4]1.8
1992	190,300	1,132	0.6	2,611	1,793	314	5.9	13.7	9.4	1.6
1993	191,432	938	0.5	2,566	1,864	236	4.9	13.4	9.7	1.2
Projections:[5]										
1995.	193,416	936	0.5	2,544	1,800	193	4.8	13.1	9.3	1.0
2000.	197,525	674	0.3	2,363	1,882	193	3.4	11.9	9.5	1.0
BLACK, NON-HISPANIC										
1990	29,191	372	1.3	659	262	[4]-	12.7	22.4	8.9	[4]-
1991	29,562	522	1.8	646	265	[4]140	17.5	21.7	8.9	[4]4.7
1992	30,084	474	1.6	636	265	102	15.6	21.0	8.7	3.4
1993	30,558	436	1.4	635	277	78	14.2	20.6	9.0	2.5
Projections:[5]										
1995.	31,430	432	1.4	649	278	61	13.7	20.5	8.8	1.9
2000.	33,536	410	1.2	655	307	61	12.1	19.4	9.1	1.8

- Represents or rounds to zero.   [1] Prior to April 1, 1990, includes "error of closure" (the amount necessary to make the components of change add to the net change between censuses), for which figures are not shown separately.   [2] Percent of population at beginning of period.   [3] Covers net international migration and movement of Armed Forces, federally affiliated civilian citizens, and their dependents.   [4] Data reflect movement of Armed Forces due to the Gulf War.   [5] Based on middle series of assumptions. See footnote 1, table 3.   [6] Persons of Hispanic origin may be of any race.

Source: U.S. Bureau of the Census, *Current Population Reports*, P25-1104; and Population Paper Listing 21.

No. 21. Resident Population, by Age and Race: 1980 to 1994

[In thousands, except percent. As of April, except 1994 as of July. See headnote, table 18 and, for 1980 data, footnote 4, table 1]

YEAR, SEX, AND RACE	Total, all years	Under 5 years	5-9 years	10-14 years	15-19 years	20-24 years	25-29 years	30-34 years	35-39 years	40-44 years	45-49 years	50-54 years	55-59 years	60-64 years	65-74 years	75-84 years	85 years and over	5-13 years	14-17 years	18-24 years
ALL RACES																				
1980[1]	226,546	16,348	16,700	18,242	21,168	21,319	19,521	17,561	13,965	11,669	11,090	11,710	11,615	10,088	15,581	7,729	2,240	31,159	16,247	30,022
1990[1]	248,718	18,757	18,035	17,060	17,886	19,135	21,328	21,833	19,846	17,589	13,744	11,313	10,487	10,625	18,046	10,012	3,022	31,826	13,340	26,950
1994	260,341	19,727	18,859	18,753	17,616	18,326	19,177	22,177	21,961	19,699	16,679	13,191	10,936	10,082	18,712	10,925	3,522	33,863	14,428	25,263
Male	127,076	10,094	9,657	9,602	9,036	9,311	9,619	11,058	10,920	9,728	8,181	6,410	5,244	4,740	8,290	4,206	980	17,339	7,412	12,856
Female	133,265	9,633	9,201	9,150	8,580	9,015	9,558	11,119	11,040	9,970	8,498	6,781	5,692	5,342	10,422	6,719	2,542	16,524	7,016	12,407
WHITE																				
1980[1]	194,713	13,414	13,717	15,095	17,681	18,072	16,658	15,157	12,122	10,110	9,693	10,360	10,394	9,078	14,045	7,057	2,060	25,692	13,491	25,381
1990[1]	208,710	14,960	14,502	13,670	14,354	15,640	17,638	18,190	16,652	15,001	11,826	9,744	9,131	9,381	16,175	9,085	2,761	25,557	10,664	21,946
1994	216,470	15,592	14,997	14,921	14,035	14,722	15,593	18,292	18,237	16,516	14,249	11,355	9,436	8,773	16,631	9,911	3,209	26,947	11,459	20,269
Male	106,139	7,995	7,695	7,661	7,222	7,527	7,894	9,218	9,165	8,250	7,064	5,572	4,573	4,172	7,419	3,827	885	13,829	5,902	10,373
Female	110,331	7,597	7,302	7,260	6,814	7,195	7,699	9,074	9,072	8,266	7,185	5,782	4,863	4,601	9,213	6,084	2,324	13,118	5,557	9,896
BLACK																				
1980[1]	26,683	2,459	2,509	2,691	3,007	2,749	2,342	1,904	1,469	1,260	1,150	1,135	1,041	874	1,344	588	159	4,628	2,380	3,948
1990[1]	30,486	2,939	2,711	2,629	2,715	2,656	2,780	2,718	2,360	1,882	1,413	1,178	1,041	972	1,498	772	223	4,838	2,056	3,818
1994	32,672	3,119	2,939	2,864	2,733	2,668	2,619	2,837	2,733	2,308	1,740	1,340	1,110	984	1,600	815	265	5,214	2,259	3,730
Male	15,491	1,581	1,491	1,452	1,385	1,313	1,250	1,330	1,280	1,069	793	602	487	424	665	295	76	2,644	1,150	1,846
Female	17,181	1,538	1,448	1,412	1,349	1,355	1,369	1,507	1,453	1,239	946	738	623	560	935	521	188	2,571	1,109	1,884
AMERICAN INDIAN, ESKIMO, ALEUT																				
1980[1]	1,420	149	147	156	170	149	125	107	84	69	58	52	45	34	48	21	6	270	136	216
1990[1]	2,065	220	209	197	191	179	188	181	157	132	99	79	64	53	73	34	9	368	151	257
1994	2,210	212	223	229	193	187	178	187	174	151	120	91	71	57	83	40	14	407	167	259
Male	1,094	108	113	116	98	96	92	93	85	73	58	43	34	26	37	16	4	207	85	132
Female	1,116	105	109	113	95	91	87	94	88	78	62	47	37	30	46	24	9	200	82	126
ASIAN, PACIFIC ISLANDER																				
1980[1]	3,729	326	328	300	310	349	396	393	291	230	188	163	135	101	143	63	15	570	239	478
1990[1]	7,458	638	612	564	626	661	722	745	678	574	405	312	252	220	300	122	29	1,063	469	930
1994	8,989	804	700	739	655	750	787	861	816	723	571	406	318	268	398	159	34	1,294	543	1,005
Male	4,352	411	358	374	332	375	383	417	390	336	266	192	150	117	170	69	14	659	276	505
Female	4,637	393	342	365	323	374	404	444	426	388	306	214	168	151	228	90	21	636	267	501
PERCENT																				
Total, 1994	100.0	7.6	7.2	7.2	6.8	7.0	7.4	8.5	8.4	7.6	6.4	5.1	4.2	3.9	7.2	4.2	1.4	13.0	5.5	9.7
White	100.0	7.2	6.9	6.9	6.5	6.8	7.2	8.5	8.4	7.6	6.6	5.2	4.4	4.1	7.7	4.6	1.5	12.4	5.3	9.4
Black	100.0	9.5	9.0	8.8	8.4	8.2	8.0	8.7	8.4	7.1	5.3	4.1	3.4	3.0	4.9	2.5	0.8	16.0	6.9	11.4
American Indian, Eskimo, Aleut	100.0	9.6	10.1	10.4	8.7	8.5	8.1	8.5	7.9	6.8	5.4	4.1	3.2	2.6	3.7	1.8	0.6	18.4	7.5	11.7
Asian, Pacific Islander	100.0	8.9	7.8	8.2	7.3	8.3	8.8	9.6	9.1	8.0	6.4	4.5	3.5	3.0	4.4	1.8	0.4	14.4	6.0	11.2

[1] The April 1, 1990, census count (248,718,291) includes count resolution corrections processed through March 1994, and does not include adjustments for census coverage errors.

Source: U.S. Bureau of the Census, *Current Population Reports*, P25-1095; and Population Paper Listing 21.

No. 22. Resident Population, by Race, Hispanic Origin, and Single Years of Age: 1994

[**In thousands, except as indicated**. As of **July 1**. Resident population. For derivation of estimates, see text, section 1]

| AGE | Total | RACE | | | | Hispanic origin [1] | NOT OF HISPANIC ORIGIN | | | |
		White	Black	American Indian, Eskimo, Aleut	Asian, Pacific Islander		White	Black	American Indian, Eskimo, Aleut	Asian, Pacific Islander
Total	260,341	216,470	32,672	2,210	8,989	26,077	192,727	31,192	1,907	8,438
Under 5 yrs. old . .	19,727	15,592	3,119	212	804	3,096	12,764	2,945	179	743
Under 1 yr. old .	3,870	3,041	619	42	168	643	2,453	583	35	156
1 yr. old	3,878	3,060	616	41	161	631	2,482	581	35	149
2 yrs. old	3,956	3,132	619	41	163	636	2,550	584	35	151
3 yrs. old	3,990	3,163	623	42	163	608	2,607	589	35	151
4 yrs. old	4,032	3,195	642	47	148	577	2,672	608	39	136
5-9 yrs. old	18,859	14,997	2,939	223	700	2,527	12,707	2,791	188	646
5 yrs. old	3,884	3,063	630	47	144	537	2,578	598	39	132
6 yrs. old	3,792	3,011	595	45	141	523	2,538	564	38	130
7 yrs. old	3,747	2,985	582	43	136	500	2,532	552	37	126
8 yrs. old	3,595	2,874	544	43	135	475	2,443	517	36	124
9 yrs. old	3,841	3,063	588	45	144	492	2,617	560	38	134
10-14 yrs. old	18,753	14,921	2,864	229	739	2,355	12,783	2,733	195	686
10 yrs. old	3,744	2,984	567	46	147	480	2,548	541	39	136
11 yrs. old	3,770	3,010	566	46	148	480	2,574	540	39	138
12 yrs. old	3,768	2,994	580	46	149	468	2,570	553	39	138
13 yrs. old	3,722	2,962	562	47	151	469	2,536	537	40	140
14 yrs. old	3,748	2,971	588	45	145	458	2,555	562	39	134
15-19 yrs. old	17,616	14,035	2,733	193	655	2,198	12,033	2,610	166	609
15 yrs. old	3,602	2,849	572	43	138	439	2,452	547	37	128
16 yrs. old	3,515	2,802	544	40	129	436	2,405	520	34	120
17 yrs. old	3,562	2,837	555	39	131	441	2,436	530	33	122
18 yrs. old	3,349	2,677	515	35	122	428	2,287	491	30	114
19 yrs. old	3,588	2,870	547	37	133	455	2,454	523	31	124
20-24 yrs. old	18,326	14,722	2,668	187	750	2,338	12,592	2,539	159	697
20 yrs. old	3,480	2,781	529	36	135	447	2,372	504	31	126
21 yrs. old	3,492	2,778	533	37	144	461	2,357	508	31	135
22 yrs. old	3,605	2,891	528	37	149	457	2,474	503	32	139
23 yrs. old	3,839	3,094	547	39	159	481	2,658	521	33	147
24 yrs. old	3,910	3,178	531	39	163	492	2,731	504	33	151
25-29 yrs. old	19,177	15,593	2,619	178	787	2,483	13,338	2,475	149	731
25 yrs. old	3,756	3,060	501	36	158	489	2,617	474	31	146
26 yrs. old	3,680	2,984	508	35	153	486	2,542	480	29	142
27 yrs. old	3,778	3,076	513	35	154	497	2,624	485	30	143
28 yrs. old	3,674	2,990	503	33	148	480	2,553	475	28	138
29 yrs. old	4,289	3,483	594	38	174	531	3,002	562	32	162
30-34 yrs. old	22,177	18,292	2,837	187	861	2,460	16,056	2,693	159	809
30 yrs. old	4,354	3,573	573	37	171	517	3,103	543	32	160
31 yrs. old	4,332	3,563	558	37	174	503	3,106	528	32	164
32 yrs. old	4,431	3,663	563	37	169	480	3,226	535	32	158
33 yrs. old	4,433	3,677	550	36	170	484	3,236	522	31	160
34 yrs. old	4,626	3,817	594	38	178	476	3,385	565	33	167
35-39 yrs. old	21,961	18,237	2,733	174	816	2,060	16,371	2,608	150	772
35 yrs. old	4,523	3,743	571	37	171	445	3,340	545	32	162
36 yrs. old	4,439	3,696	545	35	163	427	3,309	520	30	154
37 yrs. old	4,472	3,713	560	35	164	410	3,342	535	30	155
38 yrs. old	4,055	3,375	497	32	152	378	3,032	474	27	144
39 yrs. old	4,472	3,710	560	35	167	400	3,348	535	30	158
40-44 yrs. old	19,699	16,516	2,308	151	723	1,632	15,038	2,210	133	687
40 yrs. old	4,223	3,528	507	33	155	361	3,201	485	29	147
41 yrs. old	4,013	3,366	464	32	151	341	3,057	443	28	144
42 yrs. old	3,922	3,303	452	30	138	317	3,015	433	26	131
43 yrs. old	3,716	3,103	438	30	146	309	2,823	419	26	139
44 yrs. old	3,825	3,217	448	27	133	303	2,942	429	24	127

See footnotes at end of table.

No. 22. Resident Population, by Race, Hispanic Origin, and Single Years of Age: 1994—Continued

[See headnote, page 22]

AGE	Total	RACE				Hispanic origin [1]	NOT OF HISPANIC ORIGIN			
		White	Black	American Indian, Eskimo, Aleut	Asian, Pacific Islander		White	Black	American Indian, Eskimo, Aleut	Asian, Pacific Islander
45-49 yrs. old	16,679	14,249	1,740	120	571	1,230	13,130	1,669	107	544
45 yrs. old	3,659	3,096	407	26	130	278	2,844	391	23	124
46 yrs. old	3,550	3,036	369	25	120	259	2,800	354	22	114
47 yrs. old	3,843	3,322	375	26	120	258	3,088	360	23	115
48 yrs. old	2,652	2,269	267	20	96	213	2,074	255	18	92
49 yrs. old	2,974	2,525	322	22	105	222	2,323	309	20	100
50-54 yrs. old	13,191	11,355	1,340	91	406	913	10,522	1,287	82	387
50 yrs. old	2,890	2,483	293	21	93	204	2,298	282	19	88
51 yrs. old	2,931	2,549	278	19	85	195	2,371	267	17	81
52 yrs. old	2,549	2,191	263	18	78	174	2,032	253	16	74
53 yrs. old	2,440	2,099	250	17	75	172	1,941	240	15	72
54 yrs. old	2,381	2,033	256	17	76	167	1,880	246	15	72
55-59 yrs. old	10,936	9,436	1,110	71	318	738	8,760	1,069	64	304
55 yrs. old	2,283	1,950	246	16	71	157	1,808	237	14	67
56 yrs. old	2,281	1,966	234	15	66	154	1,825	226	13	63
57 yrs. old	2,178	1,876	224	14	64	147	1,742	215	13	62
58 yrs. old	2,021	1,758	195	12	56	137	1,632	187	11	54
59 yrs. old	2,173	1,886	212	14	61	144	1,754	204	13	59
60-64 yrs. old	10,082	8,773	984	57	268	616	8,208	950	51	257
60 yrs. old	1,981	1,714	198	12	56	128	1,597	191	11	54
61 yrs. old	1,953	1,693	194	12	54	123	1,581	187	11	52
62 yrs. old	1,965	1,705	196	11	53	118	1,597	189	10	50
63 yrs. old	2,065	1,810	192	11	52	125	1,695	185	10	50
64 yrs. old	2,118	1,850	204	11	54	123	1,737	197	10	51
65-69 yrs. old	9,970	8,792	906	47	226	521	8,312	878	42	217
65 yrs. old	2,059	1,796	202	10	50	116	1,689	196	9	48
66 yrs. old	2,071	1,822	193	10	47	111	1,720	187	9	45
67 yrs. old	2,003	1,765	184	9	45	103	1,670	179	8	43
68 yrs. old	1,897	1,678	168	9	43	96	1,589	163	8	41
69 yrs. old	1,940	1,730	159	9	42	94	1,643	155	8	40
70-74 yrs. old	8,741	7,840	694	36	171	383	7,485	676	33	164
70 yrs. old	1,875	1,674	153	8	40	88	1,592	149	8	38
71 yrs. old	1,801	1,611	146	8	37	83	1,534	142	7	36
72 yrs. old	1,811	1,630	138	8	35	77	1,558	135	7	34
73 yrs. old	1,695	1,527	130	7	31	71	1,461	127	6	30
74 yrs. old	1,559	1,398	127	6	28	63	1,340	123	5	27
75-79 yrs. old	6,574	5,949	499	24	102	243	5,724	487	23	98
75 yrs. old	1,473	1,326	117	6	24	56	1,274	114	5	23
76 yrs. old	1,369	1,243	101	5	21	51	1,196	98	5	20
77 yrs. old	1,294	1,173	96	5	20	47	1,130	94	4	19
78 yrs. old	1,254	1,139	92	5	19	46	1,097	90	4	18
79 yrs. old	1,184	1,068	94	4	18	44	1,028	91	4	17
80-84 yrs. old	4,351	3,962	316	16	57	162	3,810	309	15	54
80 yrs. old	1,048	953	77	4	14	39	917	75	4	14
81 yrs. old	966	878	72	4	12	36	844	70	3	12
82 yrs. old	855	783	58	3	11	32	753	57	3	10
83 yrs. old	784	716	55	3	10	30	688	54	3	10
84 yrs. old	699	633	54	3	9	25	609	53	2	9
85-89 yrs. old	2,274	2,083	161	8	22	80	2,008	158	8	21
90-94 yrs. old	948	859	77	4	8	32	828	76	4	8
95-99 yrs. old	249	225	20	1	3	8	218	20	1	3
100 yrs. old and over	50	42	7	-	1	2	40	7	-	1
Median age (yr.) . .	34.0	35.0	29.0	26.7	30.4	26.1	33.2	29.1	27.2	30.7

- Represents or rounds to zero.   [1] Persons of Hispanic origin may be of any race.

Source: U.S. Bureau of the Census, unpublished data.

No. 23. Resident Population, by Age and Hispanic Origin: 1980 to 1994

[In thousands, except percent. As of April, except 1994 as of July. See headnote, table 18 and, for 1980 data, footnote 4, table 1. Hispanic persons may be of any race]

YEAR AND SEX	Total, all years	Under 5 years	5-9 years	10-14 years	15-19 years	20-24 years	25-29 years	30-34 years	35-39 years	40-44 years	45-49 years	50-54 years	55-59 years	60-64 years	65-74 years	75-84 years	85 years and over	5-13 years	14-17 years	18-24 years
HISPANIC ORIGIN																				
1980	14,609	1,663	1,537	1,475	1,606	1,586	1,376	1,129	854	712	622	564	454	321	457	203	49	2,715	1,251	2,240
1990 †	22,354	2,467	2,178	1,989	2,085	2,320	2,337	2,045	1,642	1,276	936	750	633	550	715	340	91	3,782	1,574	3,215
1994	26,077	3,096	2,527	2,355	2,198	2,338	2,483	2,460	2,060	1,632	1,230	913	738	616	904	405	122	4,424	1,773	3,221
Male	13,219	1,583	1,292	1,202	1,128	1,245	1,334	1,291	1,058	818	603	438	348	285	398	155	40	2,260	910	1,698
Female	12,857	1,513	1,235	1,153	1,070	1,093	1,149	1,168	1,002	814	627	475	390	332	506	250	82	2,164	864	1,523
NON-HISPANIC WHITE																				
1980	180,906	11,842	12,262	13,703	16,166	16,574	15,358	14,091	11,315	9,437	9,104	9,824	9,963	8,775	13,614	6,863	2,014	23,126	12,313	23,267
1990 †	188,306	12,721	12,516	11,854	12,450	13,524	15,508	16,331	15,162	13,839	10,971	9,057	8,548	8,872	15,511	8,767	2,675	22,106	9,224	19,014
1994	192,727	12,764	12,707	12,783	12,033	12,592	13,338	16,056	16,371	15,038	13,130	10,522	8,760	8,208	15,797	9,534	3,094	22,935	9,847	17,333
Male	94,091	6,549	6,525	6,569	6,193	6,390	6,680	8,042	8,206	7,508	6,514	5,172	4,254	3,910	7,049	3,682	847	11,780	5,075	8,822
Female	98,636	6,215	6,183	6,214	5,840	6,202	6,657	8,014	8,165	7,529	6,615	5,350	4,507	4,298	8,748	5,852	2,247	11,155	4,772	8,511
BLACK																				
1980	26,142	2,399	2,455	2,635	2,944	2,689	2,292	1,865	1,438	1,233	1,127	1,114	1,024	861	1,327	582	157	4,530	2,331	3,862
1990 †	29,275	2,798	2,596	2,525	2,605	2,528	2,650	2,601	2,265	1,811	1,362	1,138	1,008	945	1,465	758	219	4,638	1,975	3,642
1994	31,192	2,945	2,791	2,733	2,610	2,539	2,475	2,693	2,608	2,210	1,669	1,287	1,069	950	1,554	797	260	4,962	2,159	3,553
Male	14,748	1,492	1,415	1,385	1,322	1,246	1,175	1,255	1,215	1,020	759	577	468	409	646	288	75	2,514	1,098	1,755
Female	16,444	1,453	1,376	1,348	1,289	1,293	1,301	1,438	1,393	1,190	910	710	601	541	908	509	185	2,448	1,061	1,798
AMERICAN INDIAN, ESKIMO, ALEUT																				
1980	1,326	136	135	145	158	138	116	100	79	66	55	49	43	32	46	20	6	249	127	199
1990 †	1,796	185	179	170	165	151	160	156	138	117	90	72	58	48	68	31	9	316	131	217
1994	1,907	179	188	195	166	159	149	159	150	133	107	82	64	51	75	37	13	344	143	221
Male	938	91	96	99	84	81	75	78	73	64	51	51	39	24	34	15	4	175	72	112
Female	969	89	92	96	82	78	74	81	77	69	55	43	34	27	42	22	9	169	70	109
ASIAN, PACIFIC ISLANDER																				
1980	3,563	308	311	285	294	332	378	376	279	221	182	158	131	98	136	60	14	540	226	455
1990 †	6,988	586	566	522	581	612	673	700	640	545	384	297	240	210	287	116	27	983	436	862
1994	8,438	743	646	686	609	697	731	809	772	687	544	387	304	257	381	152	32	1,197	505	936
Male	4,080	380	330	347	309	348	354	391	368	318	253	184	143	112	163	66	13	609	257	469
Female	4,358	363	316	339	300	349	377	418	404	369	292	204	161	145	218	86	20	588	248	467
1994, PERCENT																				
Hispanic origin	100.0	11.9	9.7	9.0	8.4	9.0	9.5	9.4	7.9	6.3	4.7	3.5	2.8	2.4	3.5	1.6	0.5	17.0	6.8	12.4
Non-Hispanic:																				
White	100.0	6.6	6.6	6.6	6.2	6.5	6.9	8.3	8.5	7.8	6.8	5.5	4.5	4.3	8.2	4.9	1.6	11.9	5.1	9.0
Black	100.0	9.4	8.9	8.8	8.4	8.1	7.9	8.6	8.4	7.1	5.4	4.1	3.4	3.0	5.0	2.6	0.8	15.9	6.9	11.4
American Indian, Eskimo, Aleut	100.0	9.4	9.8	10.2	8.7	8.4	7.8	8.3	7.9	6.9	5.6	4.3	3.4	2.7	3.9	2.0	0.7	18.0	7.5	11.6
Asian, Pacific Islander	100.0	8.8	7.7	8.1	7.2	8.3	8.7	9.6	9.1	8.1	6.5	4.6	3.6	3.0	4.5	1.8	0.4	14.2	6.0	11.1

† The April 1, 1990, census count (248,718,291) includes count resolution corrections processed through March 1994 and does not include adjustments for census coverage errors.

Source: U.S. Bureau of the Census, *Current Population Reports*, P25-1095; and Population Paper Listing 21.

No. 24. Projections of Resident Population, by Age, Sex, and Race: 1995 to 2025

[As of **July 1**. Data are for middle series; for assumptions, see table 3]

AGE, SEX, AND RACE	POPULATION (1,000)					PERCENT DISTRIBUTION		
	1995	2000	2005	2010	2025	2000	2010	2025
Total	**263,434**	**276,241**	**288,286**	**300,431**	**338,338**	**100.0**	**100.0**	**100.0**
Under 5 years old	20,181	19,431	19,333	20,017	22,372	7.0	6.7	6.6
5 to 13 years old	34,262	36,547	36,843	36,213	40,455	13.2	12.1	12.0
14 to 17 years old	14,591	15,811	16,947	17,388	17,897	5.7	5.8	5.3
18 to 24 years old	25,465	25,911	28,238	30,220	30,585	9.4	10.1	9.0
25 to 34 years old	41,670	38,237	36,792	38,179	44,299	13.8	12.7	13.1
35 to 44 years old	42,150	45,123	43,075	39,659	42,590	16.3	13.2	12.6
45 to 54 years old	30,224	36,170	41,219	44,099	37,534	13.1	14.7	11.1
55 to 64 years old	21,241	23,690	28,870	34,552	40,455	8.6	11.5	12.0
65 to 74 years old	18,963	18,551	18,623	20,978	35,361	6.7	7.0	10.5
75 to 84 years old	11,087	12,438	13,265	13,157	19,274	4.5	4.4	5.7
85 years old and over	3,598	4,333	5,082	5,969	7,515	1.6	2.0	2.2
Male	128,685	135,101	141,121	147,187	166,012	48.9	49.0	49.1
Female	134,749	141,140	147,165	153,245	172,326	51.1	51.0	50.9
White, total	**218,334**	**226,267**	**233,343**	**240,297**	**261,531**	**100.0**	**100.0**	**100.0**
Under 5 years old	15,841	14,945	14,587	14,893	16,117	6.6	6.2	6.2
5 to 13 years old	27,167	28,534	28,244	27,184	29,258	12.6	11.3	11.2
14 to 17 years old	11,544	12,409	13,078	13,203	12,874	5.5	5.5	4.9
18 to 24 years old	20,339	20,477	22,149	23,396	22,396	9.0	9.7	8.6
25 to 34 years old	34,027	30,534	28,900	29,715	33,202	13.5	12.4	12.7
35 to 44 years old	35,081	37,139	34,879	31,394	32,634	16.4	13.1	12.5
45 to 54 years old	25,852	30,535	34,313	36,330	29,259	13.5	15.1	11.2
55 to 64 years old	18,355	20,339	24,688	29,213	32,913	9.0	12.2	12.6
65 to 74 years old	16,822	16,220	16,058	17,998	29,634	7.2	7.5	11.3
75 to 84 years old	10,035	11,219	11,866	11,612	16,726	5.0	4.8	6.4
85 years old and over	3,271	3,917	4,581	5,357	6,518	1.7	2.2	2.5
Male	107,140	111,245	114,911	118,505	129,322	49.2	49.3	49.4
Female	111,195	115,022	118,433	121,792	132,209	50.8	50.7	50.6
Black, total	**33,117**	**35,469**	**37,793**	**40,224**	**48,005**	**100.0**	**100.0**	**100.0**
Under 5 years old	3,243	3,214	3,310	3,518	4,102	9.1	8.7	8.5
5 to 13 years old	5,285	5,836	6,025	6,114	7,238	16.5	15.2	15.1
14 to 17 years old	2,285	2,431	2,741	2,842	3,182	6.9	7.1	6.6
18 to 24 years old	3,764	3,900	4,222	4,687	5,140	11.0	11.7	10.7
25 to 34 years old	5,475	5,235	5,176	5,409	6,698	14.8	13.4	14.0
35 to 44 years old	5,088	5,610	5,506	5,268	5,933	15.8	13.1	12.4
45 to 54 years old	3,122	3,954	4,811	5,297	4,956	11.1	13.2	10.3
55 to 64 years old	2,124	2,370	2,880	3,654	4,858	6.7	9.1	10.1
65 to 74 years old	1,629	1,686	1,772	1,997	3,815	4.8	5.0	7.9
75 to 84 years old	835	907	981	1,025	1,547	2.6	2.5	3.2
85 years old and over	268	326	367	413	535	0.9	1.0	1.1
Male	15,697	16,802	17,886	19,027	22,713	47.4	47.3	47.3
Female	17,420	18,667	19,906	21,197	25,291	52.6	52.7	52.7
American Indian, Eskimo, Aleut, total	**2,226**	**2,380**	**2,543**	**2,719**	**3,278**	**100.0**	**100.0**	**100.0**
Under 5 years old	222	215	231	252	287	9.0	9.3	8.8
5 to 13 years old	410	428	420	435	533	18.0	16.0	16.3
14 to 17 years old	167	192	210	198	243	8.1	7.3	7.4
18 to 24 years old	256	271	312	342	364	11.4	12.6	11.1
25 to 34 years old	364	356	363	399	473	15.0	14.7	14.4
35 to 44 years old	327	352	345	340	432	14.8	12.5	13.2
45 to 54 years old	212	256	294	317	313	10.8	11.7	9.5
55 to 64 years old	129	149	180	218	268	6.3	8.0	8.2
65 to 74 years old	84	90	102	118	202	3.8	4.3	6.2
75 to 84 years old	41	50	58	63	104	2.1	2.3	3.2
85 years old and over	14	21	28	36	59	0.9	1.3	1.8
Male	1,103	1,177	1,256	1,342	1,614	49.5	49.4	49.2
Female	1,123	1,203	1,287	1,377	1,664	50.5	50.6	50.8
Asian, Pacific Islander, total	**9,756**	**12,125**	**14,608**	**17,191**	**25,524**	**100.0**	**100.0**	**100.0**
Under 5 years old	876	1,056	1,205	1,354	1,866	8.7	7.9	7.3
5 to 13 years old	1,400	1,751	2,153	2,479	3,425	14.4	14.4	13.4
14 to 17 years old	594	779	918	1,143	1,600	6.4	6.6	6.3
18 to 24 years old	1,105	1,262	1,553	1,795	2,685	10.4	10.4	10.5
25 to 34 years old	1,805	2,112	2,353	2,656	3,927	17.4	15.4	15.4
35 to 44 years old	1,655	2,023	2,344	2,657	3,591	16.7	15.5	14.1
45 to 54 years old	1,038	1,425	1,802	2,155	3,005	11.8	12.5	11.8
55 to 64 years old	633	833	1,120	1,468	2,417	6.9	8.5	9.5
65 to 74 years old	429	555	692	864	1,710	4.6	5.0	6.7
75 to 84 years old	178	261	360	458	897	2.2	2.7	3.5
85 years old and over	44	69	106	163	402	0.6	0.9	1.6
Male	4,745	5,877	7,068	8,312	12,363	48.5	48.4	48.4
Female	5,011	6,248	7,540	8,878	13,161	51.5	51.6	51.6

Source: U.S. Bureau of the Census, *Current Population Reports*, P25-1104.

No. 25. Projections of Hispanic and Non-Hispanic Populations, by Age and Sex: 1995 to 2025

[As of **July 1**. Resident population. Data are for middle series; for assumptions, see table 3]

AGE AND SEX	POPULATION (1,000)					PERCENT DISTRIBUTION		
	1995	2000	2005	2010	2025	2000	2010	2025
Hispanic origin, total [1]	**26,798**	**31,166**	**35,702**	**40,525**	**56,927**	**100.0**	**100.0**	**100.0**
Under 5 years old	3,090	3,293	3,579	3,983	5,337	10.6	9.8	9.4
5 to 13 years old	4,560	5,542	6,196	6,651	9,020	17.8	16.4	15.8
14 to 17 years old	1,817	2,102	2,582	2,909	3,750	6.7	7.2	6.6
18 to 24 years old	3,204	3,547	4,070	4,863	6,300	11.4	12.0	11.1
25 to 34 years old	5,021	5,145	5,301	5,834	8,464	16.5	14.4	14.9
35 to 44 years old	3,894	4,830	5,396	5,519	7,043	15.5	13.6	12.4
45 to 54 years old	2,274	3,046	3,930	4,828	5,668	9.8	11.9	10.0
55 to 64 years old	1,407	1,734	2,281	3,020	5,266	5.6	7.5	9.3
65 to 74 years old	955	1,137	1,333	1,637	3,609	3.6	4.0	6.3
75 to 84 years old	436	586	767	914	1,744	1.9	2.3	3.1
85 years old and over	141	203	267	367	725	0.7	0.9	1.3
Male	13,610	15,777	18,022	20,410	28,531	50.6	50.4	50.1
Female	13,188	15,388	17,679	20,115	28,396	49.4	49.6	49.9
Non-Hispanic White, total	**193,900**	**197,872**	**200,842**	**203,441**	**209,863**	**100.0**	**100.0**	**100.0**
Under 5 years old	13,020	11,936	11,326	11,273	11,267	6.0	5.5	5.4
5 to 13 years old	23,032	23,506	22,605	21,141	21,096	11.9	10.4	10.1
14 to 17 years old	9,892	10,507	10,751	10,564	9,494	5.3	5.2	4.5
18 to 24 years old	17,413	17,245	18,458	19,001	16,691	8.7	9.3	8.0
25 to 34 years old	29,455	25,852	24,077	24,421	25,531	13.1	12.0	12.2
35 to 44 years old	31,542	32,741	29,965	26,370	26,262	16.5	13.0	12.5
45 to 54 years old	23,777	27,760	30,735	31,928	24,094	14.0	15.7	11.5
55 to 64 years old	17,064	18,751	22,605	26,459	28,104	9.5	13.0	13.4
65 to 74 years old	15,938	15,174	14,837	16,503	26,348	7.7	8.1	12.6
75 to 84 years old	9,629	10,674	11,153	10,768	15,129	5.4	5.3	7.2
85 years old and over	3,138	3,726	4,331	5,013	5,846	1.9	2.5	2.8
Male	94,716	96,846	98,472	99,903	103,362	48.9	49.1	49.3
Female	99,184	101,025	102,370	103,538	106,501	51.1	50.9	50.7
Non-Hispanic Black, total	**31,648**	**33,741**	**35,793**	**37,930**	**44,705**	**100.0**	**100.0**	**100.0**
Under 5 years old	3,076	3,033	3,109	3,289	3,790	9.0	8.7	8.5
5 to 13 years old	5,027	5,519	5,678	5,735	6,704	16.4	15.1	15.0
14 to 17 years old	2,187	2,312	2,587	2,676	2,955	6.9	7.1	6.6
18 to 24 years old	3,593	3,705	3,990	4,400	4,769	11.0	11.6	10.7
25 to 34 years old	5,196	4,953	4,886	5,084	6,214	14.7	13.4	13.9
35 to 44 years old	4,863	5,338	5,207	4,967	5,526	15.8	13.1	12.4
45 to 54 years old	2,996	3,781	4,584	5,023	4,647	11.2	13.2	10.4
55 to 64 years old	2,049	2,274	2,752	3,480	4,561	6.7	9.2	10.2
65 to 74 years old	1,583	1,626	1,698	1,903	3,593	4.8	5.0	8.0
75 to 84 years old	814	880	945	978	1,447	2.6	2.6	3.2
85 years old and over	263	319	356	397	500	0.9	1.0	1.1
Male	14,958	15,939	16,891	17,890	21,089	47.2	47.2	47.2
Female	16,689	17,802	18,901	20,040	23,616	52.8	52.8	52.8
Non-Hispanic American Indian, Eskimo, Aleut, total	**1,927**	**2,055**	**2,190**	**2,336**	**2,796**	**100.0**	**100.0**	**100.0**
Under 5 years old	188	185	198	214	246	9.0	9.2	8.8
5 to 13 years old	347	361	359	372	453	17.6	15.9	16.2
14 to 17 years old	144	164	176	170	205	8.0	7.3	7.3
18 to 24 years old	222	232	265	286	310	11.3	12.2	11.1
25 to 34 years old	310	304	313	341	403	14.8	14.6	14.4
35 to 44 years old	284	302	293	290	363	14.7	12.4	13.0
45 to 54 years old	189	225	255	272	269	10.9	11.6	9.6
55 to 64 years old	117	134	161	191	226	6.5	8.2	8.1
65 to 74 years old	76	82	91	106	174	4.0	4.5	6.2
75 to 84 years old	38	46	53	58	92	2.2	2.5	3.3
85 years old and over	13	20	27	34	55	1.0	1.5	2.0
Male	948	1,010	1,075	1,146	1,370	49.1	49.1	49.0
Female	979	1,045	1,115	1,190	1,426	50.9	50.9	51.0
Non-Hispanic Asian, Pacific Islander, total	**9,161**	**11,407**	**13,759**	**16,199**	**24,046**	**100.0**	**100.0**	**100.0**
Under 5 years old	807	984	1,122	1,258	1,732	8.6	7.8	7.2
5 to 13 years old	1,295	1,617	2,006	2,314	3,184	14.2	14.3	13.2
14 to 17 years old	552	727	850	1,070	1,492	6.4	6.6	6.2
18 to 24 years old	1,034	1,181	1,454	1,670	2,515	10.4	10.3	10.5
25 to 34 years old	1,688	1,983	2,215	2,499	3,687	17.4	15.4	15.3
35 to 44 years old	1,567	1,914	2,214	2,513	3,394	16.8	15.5	14.1
45 to 54 years old	988	1,357	1,715	2,048	2,857	11.9	12.6	11.9
55 to 64 years old	604	795	1,071	1,403	2,298	7.0	8.7	9.6
65 to 74 years old	412	532	663	829	1,637	4.7	5.1	6.8
75 to 84 years old	170	251	346	441	861	2.2	2.7	3.6
85 years old and over	42	66	102	157	389	0.6	1.0	1.6
Male	4,453	5,529	6,660	7,838	11,660	48.5	48.4	48.5
Female	4,708	5,879	7,099	8,361	12,386	51.5	51.6	51.5

[1] Persons of Hispanic origin may be of any race.

Source: U.S. Bureau of the Census, *Current Population Reports*, P25-1104.

No. 26. Centers of Population: 1790 to 1990

[Prior to 1960, excludes Alaska and Hawaii. The median center is located at the intersection of two median lines, a north–south line constructed so that half of the Nation's population lives east and half lives west of it, and an east–west line selected so that half of the Nation's population lives north and half lives south of it. The mean center of population is that point at which an imaginary flat, weightless, and rigid map of the United States would balance if weights of identical value were placed on it so that each weight represented the location of one person on the date of the census]

| YEAR | MEDIAN CENTER | | MEAN CENTER | | |
	Latitude-N	Longitude-W	Latitude-N	Longitude-W	Approximate location
1790 (August 2)	(NA)	(NA)	39 16 30	76 11 12	In Kent County, MD, 23 miles E of Baltimore, MD
1850 (June 1) ..	(NA)	(NA)	38 59 00	81 19 00	In Wirt County, WV, 23 miles SE of Parkersburg, WV[1]
1900 (June 1) ..	40 03 32	84 49 01	39 09 36	85 48 54	In Bartholomew County, IN, 6 miles SE of Columbus, IN
1950 (April 1) ...	40 00 12	84 56 51	38 50 21	88 09 33	In Richland County, IL, 8 miles NNW of Olney, IL
1960 (April 1) ...	39 56 25	85 16 60	38 35 58	88 12 35	In Clinton County, IL, 6.5 miles NW of Centralia, IL
1970 (April 1) ...	39 47 43	85 31 43	38 27 47	89 42 22	In St. Clair County, IL, 5.0 miles ESE of Mascoutah, IL
1980 (April 1) ...	39 18 60	86 08 15	38 08 13	90 34 26	In Jefferson County, MO, .25 mile W of DeSoto, MO
1990 (April 1) ...	38 57 55	86 31 53	37 52 20	91 12 55	In Crawford County, MO, 10 miles SE of Steelville, MO

NA Not available. [1]West Virginia was set off from Virginia, Dec. 31, 1862, and admitted as a State, June 19, 1863.

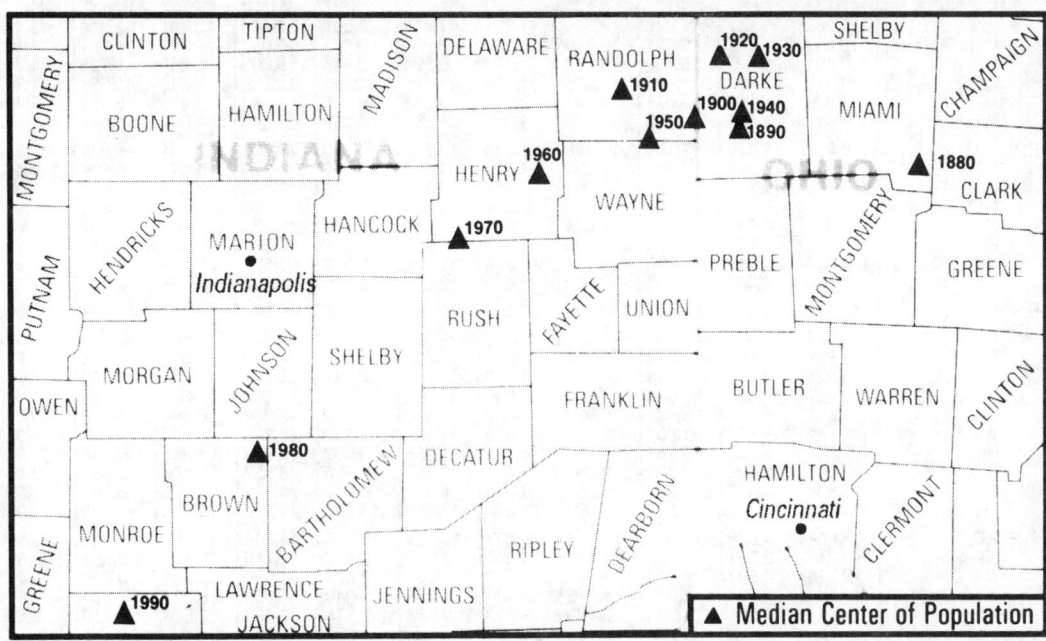

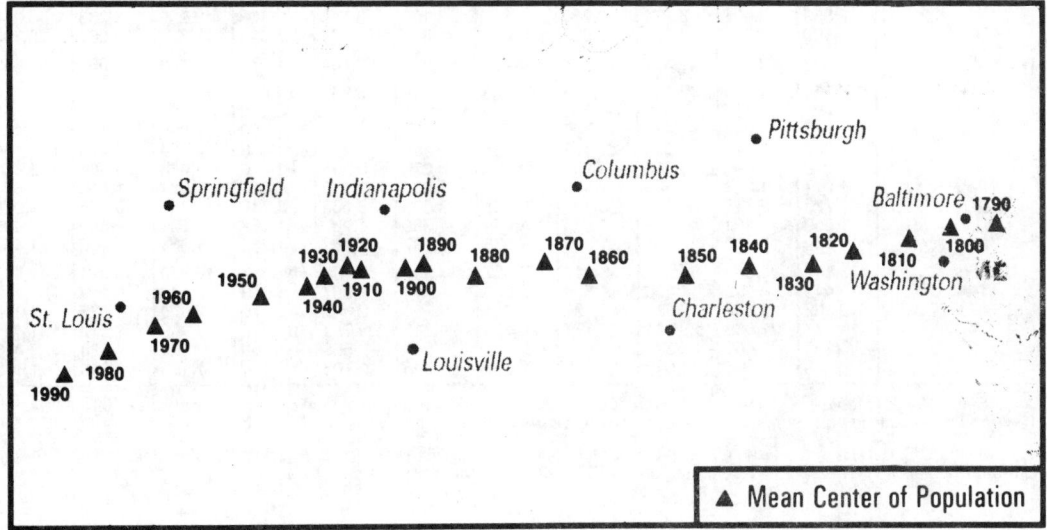

Source: U.S. Bureau of the Census, *1990 Census of Population and Housing, Population and Housing Unit Counts, United States* (1990 CPH-2-1).

Population

No. 27. Resident Population—States: 1970 to 1994

[**In thousands**. As of **July 1;** except **1970, 1980, and 1990**, as of **April 1**. Insofar as possible, population shown for all years is that of present area of State. See *Historical Statistics, Colonial Times to 1970*, series A 172, for population by regions, and A 195 for population by States]

REGION, DIVISION, AND STATE	1970	1980 [1]	1985	1987	1988	1989	1990 [2]	1991	1992	1993	1994
U.S.	203,302	226,546	237,924	242,289	244,499	246,819	248,718	252,131	255,028	257,783	260,341
Northeast	49,061	49,135	49,869	50,302	50,584	50,757	50,811	50,964	51,100	51,277	51,396
N.E.	11,848	12,348	12,741	12,951	13,085	13,182	13,207	13,209	13,203	13,235	13,270
ME	994	1,125	1,163	1,185	1,204	1,220	1,228	1,237	1,237	1,240	1,240
NH	738	921	997	1,054	1,083	1,105	1,109	1,108	1,114	1,124	1,137
VT	445	511	530	540	550	558	563	568	571	576	580
MA	5,689	5,737	5,881	5,935	5,980	6,015	6,016	6,002	5,999	6,018	6,041
RI	950	947	969	990	996	1,001	1,003	1,004	1,002	1,000	997
CT	3,032	3,108	3,201	3,247	3,272	3,283	3,287	3,291	3,279	3,278	3,275
M.A	37,213	36,787	37,128	37,350	37,499	37,575	37,604	37,755	37,897	38,042	38,125
NY	18,241	17,558	17,792	17,869	17,941	17,983	17,991	18,041	18,095	18,153	18,169
NJ	7,171	7,365	7,566	7,671	7,712	7,726	7,730	7,767	7,813	7,859	7,904
PA	11,801	11,864	11,771	11,811	11,846	11,866	11,883	11,947	11,990	12,030	12,052
Midwest	56,589	58,866	58,820	59,018	59,254	59,468	59,669	60,178	60,628	61,038	61,394
E.N.C	40,262	41,682	41,418	41,590	41,721	41,873	42,009	42,380	42,687	42,956	43,184
OH	10,657	10,798	10,735	10,760	10,799	10,829	10,847	10,932	11,005	11,061	11,102
IN	5,195	5,490	5,459	5,473	5,492	5,524	5,544	5,603	5,652	5,706	5,752
IL	11,110	11,427	11,400	11,391	11,390	11,410	11,431	11,525	11,610	11,686	11,752
MI	8,882	9,262	9,076	9,187	9,218	9,253	9,295	9,370	9,423	9,460	9,496
WI	4,418	4,706	4,748	4,778	4,822	4,857	4,892	4,949	4,997	5,044	5,082
W.N.C	16,327	17,183	17,402	17,428	17,533	17,595	17,660	17,798	17,941	18,082	18,210
MN	3,806	4,076	4,184	4,235	4,296	4,338	4,376	4,429	4,474	4,524	4,567
IA	2,825	2,914	2,830	2,767	2,768	2,771	2,777	2,792	2,808	2,821	2,829
MO	4,678	4,917	5,000	5,057	5,082	5,096	5,117	5,158	5,193	5,235	5,278
ND	618	653	677	661	655	646	639	634	635	637	638
SD	666	691	698	696	698	697	696	702	709	716	721
NE	1,485	1,570	1,585	1,567	1,571	1,575	1,578	1,592	1,604	1,613	1,623
KS	2,249	2,364	2,427	2,445	2,462	2,473	2,478	2,492	2,518	2,535	2,554
South	62,812	75,372	81,409	83,208	83,890	84,700	85,454	86,911	88,153	89,417	90,692
S.A.	30,678	36,959	40,159	41,619	42,318	43,008	43,571	44,441	45,094	45,737	46,398
DE	548	594	618	637	648	658	666	680	690	698	706
MD	3,924	4,217	4,413	4,566	4,658	4,727	4,781	4,859	4,914	4,958	5,006
DC	757	638	635	637	630	624	607	594	586	579	570
VA.	4,651	5,347	5,715	5,932	6,037	6,120	6,189	6,287	6,389	6,473	6,552
WV	1,744	1,950	1,907	1,858	1,830	1,807	1,793	1,799	1,807	1,818	1,822
NC	5,084	5,882	6,254	6,404	6,481	6,565	6,632	6,752	6,838	6,952	7,070
SC	2,591	3,122	3,303	3,381	3,412	3,457	3,486	3,557	3,595	3,630	3,664
GA	4,588	5,463	5,963	6,208	6,316	6,411	6,478	6,624	6,765	6,902	7,055
FL.	6,791	9,746	11,351	11,997	12,306	12,638	12,938	13,288	13,510	13,726	13,953
E.S.C	12,808	14,666	14,971	15,070	15,107	15,136	15,180	15,346	15,517	15,709	15,890
KY	3,221	3,661	3,695	3,683	3,680	3,677	3,687	3,715	3,753	3,794	3,827
TN	3,926	4,591	4,715	4,783	4,822	4,854	4,877	4,950	5,021	5,094	5,175
AL.	3,444	3,894	3,973	4,015	4,024	4,030	4,040	4,087	4,131	4,181	4,219
MS	2,217	2,521	2,588	2,589	2,580	2,574	2,575	2,594	2,613	2,640	2,669
W.S.C	19,326	23,747	26,279	26,518	26,466	26,556	26,703	27,124	27,542	27,971	28,404
AR	1,923	2,286	2,327	2,342	2,343	2,346	2,351	2,371	2,395	2,426	2,453
LA	3,645	4,206	4,408	4,344	4,289	4,253	4,220	4,241	4,273	4,290	4,315
OK	2,559	3,025	3,271	3,210	3,167	3,150	3,146	3,168	3,206	3,233	3,258
TX	11,199	14,229	16,273	16,622	16,667	16,807	16,986	17,344	17,667	18,022	18,378
West	34,838	43,172	47,827	49,762	50,770	51,894	52,784	54,078	55,146	56,051	56,859
Mountain.	8,289	11,373	12,741	13,145	13,303	13,498	13,659	14,021	14,376	14,777	15,214
MT	694	787	822	805	800	800	799	808	823	841	856
ID	713	944	994	985	986	994	1,007	1,039	1,066	1,100	1,133
WY	332	470	500	477	465	458	454	458	464	470	476
CO	2,210	2,890	3,209	3,260	3,262	3,276	3,294	3,370	3,463	3,564	3,656
NM	1,017	1,303	1,438	1,479	1,490	1,504	1,515	1,547	1,581	1,616	1,654
AZ.	1,775	2,718	3,184	3,437	3,535	3,622	3,665	3,747	3,835	3,945	4,075
UT	1,059	1,461	1,643	1,678	1,689	1,706	1,723	1,767	1,811	1,860	1,908
NV	489	800	951	1,023	1,075	1,137	1,202	1,285	1,331	1,382	1,457
Pacific	26,549	31,800	35,086	36,617	37,467	38,397	39,125	40,057	40,770	41,274	41,645
WA	3,413	4,132	4,400	4,532	4,640	4,746	4,867	5,018	5,146	5,259	5,343
OR	2,092	2,633	2,673	2,701	2,741	2,791	2,842	2,920	2,975	3,035	3,086
CA	19,971	23,668	26,441	27,777	28,464	29,218	29,758	30,416	30,909	31,217	31,431
AK	303	402	532	539	542	547	550	569	587	598	606
HI	770	965	1,040	1,068	1,080	1,095	1,108	1,134	1,153	1,166	1,179

[1] See footnote 4, table 1.   [2] The April 1, 1990, census counts include count resolution corrections processed through March 1994 and do not include adjustments for census coverage errors.

Source: U.S. Bureau of the Census, *1990 Census of Population and Housing, Population and Housing Unit Counts* (CPH-2); *Current Population Reports*, P25-1106; press release CB94-204; and unpublished data.

No. 28. State Population—Rank, Percent Change, and Population Density: 1970 to 1994

[As of **April 1**, except **1994**, as of **July 1**. For area figures of States, see table 361. Minus sign (-) indicates decrease. See *Historical Statistics, Colonial Times to 1970*, series A 197]

REGION, DIVISION, AND STATE	RANK				PERCENT CHANGE			POPULATION PER SQ. MILE OF LAND AREA [1]	
	1970	1980	1990	1994	1970-80	1980-90	1990-94	1970	1994
U.S.	(X)	(X)	(X)	(X)	11.4	9.8	4.7	57.5	73.6
Northeast	(X)	(X)	(X)	(X)	0.2	3.4	1.2	302.3	316.7
N.E.	(X)	(X)	(X)	(X)	4.2	6.9	0.5	188.6	211.3
ME	38	38	38	39	13.2	9.1	1.0	32.2	40.2
NH	41	42	40	41	24.8	20.5	2.5	82.2	126.7
VT.	48	48	48	49	15.0	10.0	3.1	48.1	62.7
MA	10	11	13	13	0.8	4.9	0.4	725.8	770.7
RI	39	40	43	43	-0.3	5.9	-0.7	908.8	953.8
CT	24	25	27	27	2.5	5.8	-0.4	625.8	676.0
M.A	(X)	(X)	(X)	(X)	-1.1	2.2	1.4	374.1	383.3
NY	2	2	2	3	-3.7	2.5	1.0	386.3	384.7
NJ	8	9	9	9	2.7	5.0	2.2	966.6	1,065.4
PA.	3	4	5	5	0.5	0.2	1.4	263.3	268.9
Midwest	(X)	(X)	(X)	(X)	4.0	1.4	2.9	75.3	81.7
E.N.C	(X)	(X)	(X)	(X)	3.5	0.8	2.8	165.3	177.3
OH	6	6	7	7	1.3	0.5	2.4	260.2	271.1
IN	11	12	14	14	5.7	1.0	3.8	144.8	160.4
IL	5	5	6	6	2.8	(Z)	2.8	199.9	211.4
MI	7	8	8	8	4.3	0.4	2.2	156.3	167.2
WI	16	16	16	18	6.5	4.0	3.9	81.3	93.6
W.N.C	(X)	(X)	(X)	(X)	5.2	2.8	3.1	32.1	35.8
MN	19	21	20	20	7.1	7.4	4.4	47.8	57.4
IA	25	27	30	30	3.1	-4.7	1.9	50.6	50.6
MO	13	15	15	16	5.1	4.1	3.1	67.9	76.6
ND	45	46	47	47	5.7	-2.1	-0.1	9.0	9.2
SD	44	45	45	45	3.7	0.8	3.6	8.8	9.5
NE	35	35	36	37	5.7	0.5	2.8	19.3	21.1
KS	28	32	32	32	5.1	4.8	3.1	27.5	31.2
South.	(X)	(X)	(X)	(X)	20.0	13.4	6.1	72.1	104.1
S.A.	(X)	(X)	(X)	(X)	20.5	17.9	6.5	115.2	174.3
DE	46	47	46	46	8.4	12.1	6.0	280.4	361.3
MD	18	18	19	19	7.5	13.4	4.7	401.4	512.1
DC	(X)	(X)	(X)	(X)	-15.6	-4.9	-6.1	12,404.4	9,347.1
VA.	14	14	12	12	14.9	15.8	5.9	117.5	165.5
WV	34	34	34	35	11.8	-8.0	1.6	72.4	75.6
NC	12	10	10	10	15.7	12.8	6.6	104.4	145.1
SC	26	24	25	25	20.5	11.7	5.1	86.0	121.7
GA.	15	13	11	11	19.1	18.6	8.9	79.2	121.8
FL.	9	7	4	4	43.5	32.7	7.8	125.8	258.4
E.S.C	(X)	(X)	(X)	(X)	14.5	3.5	4.7	71.7	89.0
KY	23	23	23	24	13.7	0.7	3.8	81.1	96.3
TN	17	17	17	17	16.9	6.2	6.1	95.2	125.6
AL.	21	22	22	22	13.1	3.8	4.4	67.9	83.1
MS	29	31	31	31	13.7	2.2	3.6	47.3	56.9
W.S.C	(X)	(X)	(X)	(X)	22.9	12.5	6.4	45.3	66.6
AR	32	33	33	33	18.9	2.8	4.3	36.9	47.1
LA.	20	19	21	21	15.4	0.3	2.2	83.7	99.0
OK	27	26	28	28	18.2	4.0	3.6	37.3	47.4
TX.	4	3	3	2	27.1	19.4	8.2	42.8	70.2
West	(X)	(X)	(X)	(X)	23.9	22.3	7.7	19.9	32.5
Mountain.	(X)	(X)	(X)	(X)	37.2	20.1	11.4	9.7	17.8
MT	43	44	44	44	13.3	1.6	7.1	4.8	5.9
ID	42	41	42	42	32.4	6.6	12.5	8.6	13.7
WY	49	49	50	50	41.3	-3.4	4.9	3.4	4.9
CO	30	28	26	26	30.8	14.0	11.0	21.3	35.2
NM	37	37	37	36	28.1	16.2	9.1	8.4	13.6
AZ.	33	29	24	23	53.1	34.9	11.2	15.6	35.9
UT	36	36	35	34	37.9	17.9	10.7	12.9	23.2
NV	47	43	39	38	63.8	50.1	21.2	4.5	13.3
Pacific	(X)	(X)	(X)	(X)	19.8	23.0	6.4	29.7	46.5
WA	22	20	18	15	21.1	17.8	9.8	51.3	80.2
OR	31	30	29	29	25.9	7.9	8.6	21.8	32.1
CA	1	1	1	1	18.5	25.7	5.6	128.0	201.5
AK	50	50	49	48	32.8	36.9	10.2	0.5	1.1
HI	40	39	41	40	25.3	14.9	6.3	119.9	183.5

X Not applicable.   Z Less than 0.5 percent.   [1] Persons per square mile were calculated on the basis of land area data from the 1990 census.

Source: U.S. Bureau of the Census, *1990 Census of Population and Housing, Population and Housing Unit Counts* (CPH-2); and *Current Population Reports*, P25, forthcoming report.

Population

No. 29. Components of Population Change—States: 1990 to 1994

[In thousands, except percent. Covers period April 1, 1990, to July 1, 1994]

REGION, DIVISION, AND STATE	NET CHANGE, 1990-94		Births	Deaths	NET MOVEMENT FROM ABROAD		Net domestic migration	Residual change [1]
	Number	Percent			International migration	Federal U.S. citizen		
United States . . .	**11,623**	**4.7**	**17,298**	**9,352**	**3,258**	**419**	**-**	**-**
Northeast.	**585**	**1.2**	**3,250**	**2,042**	**799**	**24**	**−1,439**	**−6**
New England	**63**	**0.5**	**809**	**498**	**111**	**9**	**−365**	**−3**
Maine	12	1.0	68	48	3	2	−12	-
New Hampshire. . . .	28	2.5	69	36	4	-	−10	-
Vermont.	17	3.1	33	20	2	-	2	-
Massachusetts	25	0.4	372	232	67	3	−184	−1
Rhode Island	−7	−0.7	62	40	6	1	−35	−1
Connecticut	−12	−0.4	204	121	30	3	−126	−2
Middle Atlantic	**522**	**1.4**	**2,441**	**1,544**	**688**	**15**	**−1,075**	**−3**
New York	178	1.0	1,234	714	476	9	−826	−1
New Jersey	174	2.2	508	303	162	4	−197	-
Pennsylvania	170	1.4	698	528	50	3	−52	−2
Midwest.	**1,725**	**2.9**	**3,902**	**2,330**	**348**	**32**	**−226**	**−1**
East North Central. . .	**1,175**	**2.8**	**2,786**	**1,620**	**292**	**14**	**−295**	**−1**
Ohio	255	2.4	691	430	29	3	−36	−2
Indiana	208	3.8	360	217	12	1	52	-
Illinois	321	2.8	817	446	188	7	−245	−0
Michigan	201	2.2	617	343	50	2	−125	1
Wisconsin	190	3.9	302	185	13	-	60	-
West North Central . .	**550**	**3.1**	**1,116**	**710**	**57**	**18**	**69**	**1**
Minnesota	192	4.4	281	152	19	1	43	-
Iowa	52	1.9	163	117	6	-	-	−1
Missouri.	161	3.1	327	221	13	4	37	-
North Dakota	−1	−0.1	37	26	2	2	−17	-
South Dakota	25	3.6	47	35	1	2	10	1
Nebraska	44	2.8	100	63	5	3	−1	-
Kansas	76	3.1	160	97	10	7	−3	-
South	**5,238**	**6.1**	**5,908**	**3,301**	**749**	**225**	**1,652**	**6**
South Atlantic.	**2,827**	**6.5**	**2,907**	**1,722**	**398**	**152**	**1,085**	**5**
Delaware	40	6.0	45	26	4	1	16	-
Maryland	226	4.7	334	167	54	11	−8	1
District of Columbia .	−37	−6.1	48	29	14	2	−71	-
Virginia	362	5.9	413	206	60	49	45	2
West Virginia	29	1.6	94	87	2	-	20	−0
North Carolina.	437	6.6	437	256	19	29	208	-
South Carolina	178	5.1	242	128	6	15	44	-
Georgia	577	8.9	471	224	33	19	277	1
Florida.	1,015	7.8	823	597	207	26	554	1
East South Central . .	**710**	**4.7**	**988**	**631**	**25**	**23**	**306**	**−1**
Kentucky	140	3.8	227	152	6	8	51	-
Tennessee	298	6.1	314	198	11	5	166	−1
Alabama	178	4.4	265	171	6	5	74	-
Mississippi	94	3.6	182	109	3	4	14	-
West South Central . .	**1,701**	**6.4**	**2,012**	**948**	**325**	**50**	**261**	**2**
Arkansas	102	4.3	149	109	3	2	58	−1
Louisiana	95	2.2	301	163	10	7	−60	-
Oklahoma	112	3.6	204	133	9	8	24	-
Texas	1,392	8.2	1,358	543	303	33	239	2
West	**4,075**	**7.7**	**4,239**	**1,678**	**1,361**	**138**	**14**	**1**
Mountain	**1,555**	**11.4**	**1,040**	**442**	**109**	**29**	**814**	**5**
Montana	57	7.1	49	30	1	1	36	-
Idaho	126	12.5	73	34	5	1	81	-
Wyoming	22	4.9	28	14	1	1	6	-
Colorado	361	11.0	229	97	22	11	194	1
New Mexico	138	9.1	118	47	15	4	48	-
Arizona	410	11.2	292	133	40	6	202	2
Utah	185	10.7	156	42	9	2	60	1
Nevada	255	21.2	94	45	15	2	187	1
Pacific	**2,519**	**6.4**	**3,199**	**1,236**	**1,252**	**109**	**−799**	**−5**
Washington	476	9.8	338	164	48	15	239	1
Oregon	244	8.6	179	111	21	1	153	1
California	1,672	5.6	2,549	922	1,150	71	−1,169	−6
Alaska	56	10.2	49	9	4	7	5	-
Hawaii	70	6.3	84	30	28	15	−27	-

- Represents or rounds to zero. [1] The residual is the effect of national controls on subnational estimates. It is the difference between the implementation of the national estimates model and the county/State estimates model.

Source: U.S. Bureau of the Census, unpublished data.

No. 30. U.S. Resident Population, by Region and Division: 1960 to 1994

[As of **April 1**; except **1985** and **1994**, as of **July 1**. For composition of divisions, see table 27]

REGION AND DIVISION	POPULATION (millions)						PERCENT DISTRIBUTION					
	1960	1970	1980	1985	1990	1994	1960	1970	1980	1985	1990	1994
United States.....	179.3	203.3	226.5	237.9	248.7	260.3	100.0	100.0	100.0	100.0	100.0	100.0
Northeast	44.7	49.1	49.1	49.9	50.8	51.4	24.9	24.1	21.7	21.0	20.4	19.7
New England	10.5	11.8	12.3	12.7	13.2	13.3	5.9	5.8	5.5	5.4	5.3	5.1
Middle Atlantic	34.2	37.2	36.8	37.1	37.6	38.1	19.1	18.3	16.2	15.6	15.1	14.6
Midwest	51.6	56.6	58.9	58.8	59.7	61.4	28.8	27.8	26.0	24.7	24.0	23.6
East North Central ...	36.2	40.3	41.7	41.4	42.0	43.2	20.2	19.8	18.4	17.4	16.9	16.6
West North Central ...	15.4	16.3	17.2	17.4	17.7	18.2	8.6	8.0	7.6	7.3	7.1	7.0
South.............	55.0	62.8	75.4	81.4	85.5	90.7	30.7	30.9	33.3	34.2	34.4	34.8
South Atlantic.......	26.0	30.7	37.0	40.2	43.6	46.4	14.5	15.1	16.3	16.9	17.5	17.8
East South Central ...	12.1	12.8	14.7	15.0	15.2	15.9	6.7	6.3	6.5	6.3	6.1	6.1
West South Central ...	17.0	19.3	23.7	26.3	26.7	28.4	9.5	9.5	10.5	11.0	10.7	10.9
West	28.1	34.8	43.2	47.8	52.8	56.9	15.6	17.1	19.1	20.1	21.2	21.8
Mountain...........	6.9	8.3	11.4	12.7	13.7	15.2	3.8	4.1	5.0	5.4	5.5	5.8
Pacific	21.2	26.5	31.8	35.1	39.1	41.6	11.8	13.1	14.0	14.7	15.7	16.0

Source: U.S. Bureau of the Census, *1990 Census of Population and Housing, Population and Housing Unit Counts* (CPH-2); and unpublished data.

No. 31. Resident Population, by Region, Race, and Hispanic Origin: 1990

[As of **April 1**. For composition of regions, see table 27]

RACE AND HISPANIC ORIGIN	POPULATION (1,000)					PERCENT DISTRIBUTION				
	United States	North-east	Midwest	South	West	United States	North-east	Midwest	South	West
Total............	248,710	50,809	59,669	85,446	52,786	100.0	20.4	24.0	34.4	21.2
White...............	199,686	42,069	52,018	65,582	40,017	100.0	21.1	26.0	32.8	20.0
Black...............	29,986	5,613	5,716	15,829	2,828	100.0	18.7	19.1	52.8	9.4
American Indian, Eskimo,										
Aleut	1,959	125	338	563	933	100.0	6.4	17.2	28.7	47.6
American Indian......	1,878	122	334	557	866	100.0	6.5	17.8	29.7	46.1
Eskimo............	57	2	2	3	51	100.0	2.9	3.5	4.9	88.8
Aleut	24	2	2	3	17	100.0	8.1	8.1	11.5	72.3
Asian or Pacific Islander ..	7,274	1,335	768	1,122	4,048	100.0	18.4	10.6	15.4	55.7
Chinese	1,645	445	133	204	863	100.0	27.0	8.1	12.4	52.4
Filipino	1,407	143	113	159	991	100.0	10.2	8.1	11.3	70.5
Japanese	848	74	63	67	643	100.0	8.8	7.5	7.9	75.9
Asian Indian	815	285	146	196	189	100.0	35.0	17.9	24.0	23.1
Korean	799	182	109	153	355	100.0	22.8	13.7	19.2	44.4
Vietnamese.........	615	61	52	169	334	100.0	9.8	8.5	27.4	54.3
Laotian...........	149	16	28	29	76	100.0	10.7	18.6	19.6	51.0
Cambodian	147	30	13	19	85	100.0	20.5	8.8	13.1	57.7
Thai.............	91	12	13	24	43	100.0	12.9	14.2	26.0	46.8
Hmong...........	90	2	37	2	50	100.0	1.9	41.3	1.8	55.0
Pakistani..........	81	28	15	22	17	100.0	34.3	18.9	26.5	20.4
Hawaiian..........	211	4	6	12	189	100.0	2.0	2.6	5.8	89.6
Samoan	63	2	2	4	55	100.0	2.4	3.6	6.4	87.6
Guamanian	49	4	3	8	34	100.0	7.3	6.4	16.8	69.5
Other Asian or Pacific										
Islander	263	49	34	54	126	100.0	18.6	12.9	20.5	48.0
Other races	9,805	1,667	829	2,350	4,960	100.0	17.0	8.5	24.0	50.6
Hispanic origin [1]	22,354	3,754	1,727	6,767	10,106	100.0	16.8	7.7	30.3	45.2
Mexican	13,496	175	1,153	4,344	7,824	100.0	1.3	8.5	32.2	58.0
Puerto Rican	2,728	1,872	258	406	192	100.0	68.6	9.4	14.9	7.0
Cuban	1,044	184	37	735	88	100.0	17.6	3.5	70.5	8.5
Other Hispanic.......	5,086	1,524	279	1,282	2,002	100.0	30.0	5.5	25.2	39.4
Not of Hispanic origin	226,356	47,055	57,942	78,679	42,680	100.0	20.8	25.6	34.8	18.9

[1] Persons of Hispanic origin may be of any race.

Source: U.S. Bureau of the Census, *1990 Census of Population, General Population Characteristics, United States* (CP-1-1).

No. 32. Annual Inmigration, Outmigration, and Net Migration for Regions: 1980 to 1993

[In thousands. As of March. For persons 1 year old and over. Excludes members of the Armed Forces except those living off post or with their families on post. Based on Current Population Survey; see text, section 1, and Appendix III. For composition of regions, see table 27. Minus sign (-) indicates net outmigration]

PERIOD	North-east	Mid-west	South	West	PERIOD	North-east	Mid-west	South	West
1980-81: Inmigrants	464	650	1,377	871	**1989-90**: Inmigrants	461	908	1,428	964
Outmigrants	706	1,056	890	710	Outmigrants	758	1,024	1,198	781
Net internal migration	-242	-406	487	161	Net internal migration	-297	-116	230	183
Movers from abroad	207	180	412	514	Movers from abroad	328	169	500	562
Net migration	-35	-226	899	675	Net migration	30	53	730	745
1984-85: Inmigrants	482	842	1,329	994	**1990-91**: Inmigrants	346	782	1,421	835
Outmigrants	691	1,053	1,169	734	Outmigrants	932	797	987	668
Net internal migration	-209	-211	160	260	Net internal migration	-585	-15	433	167
Movers from abroad	228	168	532	499	Movers from abroad	209	208	351	617
Net migration	19	-43	692	759	Net migration	-376	193	784	784
1985-86: Inmigrants	502	1,011	1,355	910	**1991-92**: Inmigrants	409	816	1,305	755
Outmigrants	752	996	1,320	710	Outmigrants	701	878	1,081	626
Net internal migration	-250	15	35	200	Net internal migration	-292	-62	224	129
Movers from abroad	198	158	342	502	Movers from abroad	255	175	383	442
Net migration	-52	173	377	702	Net migration	-37	113	607	571
1986-87: Inmigrants	398	858	1,374	916	**1992-93**:				
Outmigrants	732	969	1,095	750	Total inmigrants	313	841	1,145	769
Net internal migration	-334	-111	279	166	From Northeast	(X)	131	412	104
Movers from abroad	214	193	277	458	From Midwest	48	(X)	360	199
Net migration	-120	82	556	624	From South	203	375	(X)	466
1987-88: Inmigrants	430	715	1,338	613	From West	62	335	373	(X)
Outmigrants	671	818	886	721	Total outmigrants	647	608	1,044	770
Net internal migration	-241	-103	452	-108	To Northeast	(X)	48	203	62
Movers from abroad	261	146	414	379	To Midwest	131	(X)	375	335
Net migration	20	43	866	271	To South	412	360	(X)	373
1988-89: Inmigrants	370	777	1,318	791	To West	104	199	466	(X)
Outmigrants	714	703	1,071	637	Net internal migration	-334	233	101	-1
Net internal migration	-344	74	247	154	Movers from abroad	230	198	513	364
Movers from abroad	292	170	375	629	Net migration	-104	431	614	363
Net migration	-52	244	622	783					

X Not applicable.

Source: U.S. Bureau of the Census, Current Population Reports, P20-481, and earlier reports.

No. 33. Mobility Status of the Population, by Selected Characteristics: 1980 to 1993

[As of March. For persons 1 year old and over. Excludes members of the Armed Forces except those living off post or with their families on post. Based on Current Population Survey; see text, section 1, and Appendix III. For composition of regions, see table 27]

MOBILITY PERIOD, AGE, AND REGION	Total (1,000)	PERCENT DISTRIBUTION						
		Non-movers	Movers (different house in United States)					Movers from abroad
			Total	Same county	Different county			
					Total	Same State	Different State	
1980-81	221,641	83	17	10	6	3	3	1
1985-86	232,998	82	18	11	7	4	3	1
1989-90	242,208	82	17	11	7	3	3	1
1990-91	244,884	83	16	10	6	3	3	1
1991-92	247,380	83	17	11	6	3	3	1
1992-93, total	**250,210**	**83**	**16**	**11**	**6**	**3**	**3**	**1**
1 to 4 years old	15,802	77	22	15	7	4	3	(Z)
5 to 9 years old	18,727	83	17	11	5	3	3	1
10 to 14 years old	18,427	86	13	9	4	2	2	1
15 to 19 years old	16,627	83	17	11	5	3	2	1
20 to 24 years old	17,802	64	35	22	13	7	6	1
25 to 29 years old	19,603	69	30	20	10	6	4	1
30 to 44 years old	62,603	83	17	11	6	3	3	1
45 to 64 years old	49,750	91	9	6	4	2	2	(Z)
65 to 74 years old	18,362	94	6	3	3	1	1	(Z)
75 to 84 years old	9,917	95	5	3	2	1	1	(Z)
85 years old and over	2,590	94	6	4	3	1	1	(Z)
Northeast	50,003	89	10	7	4	2	2	1
Midwest	60,031	84	16	10	6	3	3	(Z)
South	86,107	82	18	11	7	4	3	1
West	54,068	79	20	14	6	3	3	1

Z Less than 0.5 percent.

Source: U.S. Bureau of the Census, Current Population Reports, P20-481.

No. 34. Resident Population, by Age and State: 1994

[In thousands, except percent. As of **July 1**. Includes Armed Forces stationed in area. See text, section 1, for basis of estimates. See *Historical Statistics, Colonial Times to 1970*, series A 204-209 for decennial census data]

REGION, DIVISION, AND STATE	Total	Under 5 years	5 to 17 years	18 to 24 years	25 to 34 years	35 to 44 years	45 to 54 years	55 to 64 years	65 to 74 years	75 to 84 years	85 years and over	Percent 65 years and over
U.S.	260,341	19,727	48,291	25,263	41,354	41,659	29,871	21,018	18,712	10,925	3,522	12.7
Northeast . .	51,396	3,681	8,853	4,711	8,224	8,265	6,077	4,347	4,037	2,411	790	14.1
N.E	13,270	921	2,274	1,216	2,212	2,182	1,565	1,053	1,007	626	216	13.9
ME. . . .	1,240	78	228	115	183	210	150	104	95	57	20	13.9
NH. . . .	1,137	80	212	100	190	203	134	83	76	44	16	11.9
VT	580	38	108	57	88	102	72	45	39	23	8	12.1
MA. . . .	6,041	423	1,001	566	1,058	972	699	473	460	288	101	14.1
RI	997	71	169	97	161	157	109	77	84	53	18	15.6
CT	3,275	231	557	281	531	538	401	271	253	159	53	14.2
M.A	38,125	2,760	6,579	3,495	6,012	6,082	4,512	3,295	3,030	1,785	575	14.1
NY	18,169	1,382	3,129	1,702	2,987	2,875	2,147	1,552	1,341	784	268	13.2
NJ	7,904	579	1,352	688	1,264	1,301	966	676	612	356	109	13.6
PA	12,052	799	2,099	1,105	1,760	1,906	1,399	1,066	1,077	644	197	15.9
Midwest . . .	61,394	4,444	11,699	5,940	9,370	9,796	6,992	5,046	4,456	2,716	935	13.2
E.N.C. . . .	43,184	3,157	8,125	4,213	6,665	6,926	4,972	3,557	3,118	1,847	604	12.9
OH. . . .	11,102	784	2,070	1,079	1,673	1,773	1,287	945	850	486	155	13.4
IN	5,752	407	1,066	591	878	919	674	483	413	241	80	12.8
IL.	11,752	915	2,168	1,128	1,886	1,878	1,341	955	818	499	164	12.6
MI	9,496	701	1,824	932	1,457	1,539	1,101	762	673	385	121	12.4
WI	5,082	350	997	483	771	817	570	412	364	236	84	13.4
W.N.C . . .	18,210	1,287	3,574	1,727	2,705	2,871	2,020	1,489	1,338	869	331	13.9
MN. . . .	4,567	327	914	416	723	757	511	348	300	198	75	12.5
IA. . . .	2,829	188	541	274	393	434	316	246	226	152	59	15.4
MO. . . .	5,278	376	1,003	498	792	816	600	448	405	249	91	14.1
ND. . . .	638	43	129	66	90	99	66	52	47	34	13	14.7
SD. . . .	721	54	154	70	97	108	73	58	55	36	14	14.7
NE. . . .	1,623	116	326	158	232	253	176	133	119	79	32	14.1
KS. . . .	2,554	184	506	247	378	403	278	203	187	120	47	13.9
South	90,692	6,780	16,824	9,076	14,283	14,285	10,440	7,468	6,614	3,749	1,167	12.7
S.A	46,398	3,345	8,107	4,457	7,475	7,383	5,429	3,872	3,651	2,065	616	13.6
DE. . . .	706	51	124	68	120	114	81	58	54	27	8	12.7
MD. . . .	5,006	379	884	441	876	861	616	391	330	175	55	11.2
DC. . . .	570	43	76	58	114	91	65	46	43	25	9	13.5
VA	6,552	469	1,134	670	1,135	1,098	804	517	426	229	70	11.1
WV	1,822	108	321	190	235	286	225	176	160	92	28	15.4
NC. . . .	7,070	510	1,246	733	1,143	1,119	834	599	521	280	83	12.5
SC. . . .	3,664	274	678	394	576	576	430	301	262	135	38	11.9
GA. . . .	7,055	549	1,344	729	1,207	1,161	830	527	413	228	69	10.1
FL	13,953	962	2,300	1,174	2,069	2,077	1,543	1,256	1,441	873	257	18.4
E.S.C. . . .	15,890	1,135	2,966	1,668	2,388	2,464	1,862	1,374	1,156	662	213	12.8
KY	3,827	261	709	400	577	604	455	333	278	159	52	12.8
TN	5,175	366	931	518	799	822	630	452	375	215	69	12.7
AL. . . .	4,219	302	778	446	631	648	491	371	317	179	56	13.1
MS. . . .	2,669	207	549	304	382	390	287	219	187	109	36	12.5
W.S.C . . .	28,404	2,306	5,751	2,952	4,420	4,438	3,148	2,222	1,807	1,022	338	11.1
AR. . . .	2,453	172	468	247	343	357	284	219	199	124	40	14.8
LA. . . .	4,315	337	898	458	642	663	476	347	287	157	50	11.4
OK. . . .	3,258	237	643	328	459	489	374	285	244	147	52	13.6
TX	18,378	1,559	3,742	1,919	2,975	2,929	2,014	1,371	1,078	594	196	10.2
West	56,859	4,816	10,915	5,536	9,478	9,313	6,362	4,157	3,604	2,049	629	11.0
Mountain .	15,214	1,229	3,139	1,503	2,294	2,431	1,713	1,180	1,001	561	164	11.3
MT. . . .	856	59	179	80	106	141	104	74	62	40	12	13.3
ID. . . .	1,133	87	252	120	149	177	127	89	72	46	14	11.6
WY. . . .	476	33	104	49	60	82	57	39	30	17	5	11.1
CO. . . .	3,656	270	700	344	575	660	453	286	212	117	39	10.1
NM. . . .	1,654	140	358	162	238	261	183	131	106	58	17	11.0
AZ. . . .	4,075	344	795	392	633	612	436	317	317	180	49	13.4
UT	1,908	181	491	232	283	261	173	118	96	56	17	8.8
NV	1,457	115	261	124	250	238	179	126	106	48	10	11.3
Pacific . . .	41,645	3,587	7,776	4,033	7,184	6,883	4,649	2,977	2,603	1,488	466	10.9
WA. . . .	5,343	394	1,014	492	845	929	649	402	345	208	65	11.6
OR. . . .	3,086	209	574	278	440	528	386	249	232	145	45	13.7
CA. . . .	31,431	2,833	5,844	3,085	5,615	5,109	3,403	2,195	1,921	1,084	342	10.6
AK. . . .	606	56	136	61	98	118	73	37	19	7	2	4.6
HI	1,179	95	209	116	186	199	138	94	86	43	12	12.1

Source: U.S. Bureau of the Census, unpublished data.

Population

No. 35. State Population Projections: 1995 to 2010

[**In thousands**. As of **July 1**. Series A, B, C, and D reflect different interstate migration assumptions. Series A is the preferred series model. For explanation of methodology, see text, section 1]

REGION, DIVISION, AND STATE	SERIES A			SERIES B			SERIES C			SERIES D		
	1995	2000	2010	1995	2000	2010	1995	2000	2010	1995	2000	2010
U.S. ...	263,437	276,242	300,430	263,437	276,242	300,431	263,435	276,239	300,431	263,435	276,239	300,430
Northeast . . .	51,441	51,884	53,301	52,123	53,210	55,102	51,465	52,329	54,225	52,507	54,582	58,183
N.E.	13,198	13,216	13,755	13,601	14,025	14,785	13,213	13,507	14,212	13,523	13,996	14,751
ME	1,236	1,240	1,309	1,276	1,323	1,413	1,242	1,288	1,375	1,250	1,270	1,300
NH	1,132	1,165	1,280	1,183	1,274	1,429	1,128	1,204	1,350	1,133	1,163	1,207
VT	579	592	623	593	623	675	580	605	644	581	596	620
MA	5,976	5,950	6,097	6,133	6,254	6,495	5,974	6,032	6,249	6,159	6,401	6,785
RI	1,001	998	1,034	1,031	1,060	1,115	1,004	1,022	1,072	1,029	1,065	1,126
CT	3,274	3,271	3,412	3,385	3,491	3,658	3,285	3,356	3,522	3,371	3,501	3,713
M.A.	38,243	38,668	39,546	38,522	39,185	40,317	38,252	38,822	40,013	38,984	40,586	43,432
NY	18,178	18,237	18,546	18,319	18,504	18,856	18,184	18,321	18,799	18,795	19,838	21,761
NJ	7,931	8,135	8,562	8,005	8,267	8,681	7,926	8,165	8,677	8,040	8,413	9,075
PA	12,134	12,296	12,438	12,198	12,414	12,780	12,142	12,336	12,537	12,149	12,335	12,596
Midwest	61,993	63,836	66,333	61,469	62,610	64,953	61,989	63,664	65,982	62,068	64,075	67,716
E.N.C	43,610	44,806	46,259	43,258	44,013	45,506	43,620	44,769	46,242	43,753	45,220	47,805
OH	11,203	11,453	11,659	11,103	11,238	11,500	11,203	11,430	11,661	11,209	11,479	11,913
IN	5,820	6,045	6,286	5,766	5,922	6,212	5,821	6,032	6,274	5,771	5,929	6,187
IL	11,853	12,168	12,652	11,770	11,974	12,424	11,855	12,153	12,621	11,991	12,533	13,541
MI . . .	9,575	9,759	10,033	9,512	9,614	9,803	9,584	9,826	10,160	9,682	10,040	10,666
WI	5,159	5,381	5,629	5,107	5,265	5,567	5,157	5,328	5,526	5,100	5,239	5,498
W.N.C	18,383	19,030	20,074	18,211	18,597	19,447	18,369	18,895	19,740	18,315	18,855	19,911
MN	4,619	4,824	5,127	4,581	4,733	5,020	4,618	4,814	5,096	4,591	4,756	5,068
IA	2,861	2,930	2,981	2,834	2,867	2,946	2,859	2,885	2,868	2,851	2,912	3,032
MO	5,286	5,437	5,760	5,241	5,313	5,489	5,289	5,459	5,788	5,279	5,406	5,638
ND	637	643	676	634	633	642	634	622	626	647	663	698
SD	735	770	815	720	737	781	732	750	786	725	749	805
NE	1,644	1,704	1,793	1,626	1,660	1,742	1,644	1,681	1,734	1,635	1,680	1,773
KS	2,601	2,722	2,922	2,575	2,654	2,827	2,593	2,684	2,842	2,587	2,689	2,897
South	91,728	97,244	107,385	91,387	96,576	106,120	91,705	96,931	106,852	90,684	94,503	101,445
S.A	47,019	50,005	55,321	46,988	50,015	55,422	47,070	50,517	56,737	46,257	48,004	50,976
DE	718	759	815	715	757	834	719	770	850	705	727	758
MD	5,078	5,322	5,782	5,081	5,334	5,762	5,089	5,420	6,008	5,081	5,334	5,763
DC	559	537	577	564	545	545	559	549	584	608	640	697
VA	6,646	7,048	7,728	6,645	7,060	7,760	6,644	7,106	7,902	6,570	6,854	7,318
WV	1,824	1,840	1,842	1,812	1,811	1,827	1,819	1,783	1,720	1,820	1,830	1,835
NC	7,150	7,617	8,341	7,130	7,588	8,416	7,143	7,616	8,455	6,980	7,169	7,438
SC	3,732	3,932	4,311	3,727	3,924	4,287	3,743	3,976	4,378	3,688	3,808	3,998
GA	7,102	7,637	8,553	7,120	7,678	8,679	7,097	7,664	8,732	6,954	7,249	7,758
FL	14,210	15,313	17,372	14,194	15,318	17,312	14,257	15,633	18,108	13,851	14,393	15,411
E.S.C	16,019	16,762	17,941	15,844	16,357	17,412	15,997	16,633	17,697	15,823	16,252	16,962
KY	3,851	3,989	4,160	3,803	3,883	4,050	3,842	3,927	4,046	3,819	3,913	4,064
TN	5,228	5,538	6,007	5,166	5,399	5,857	5,221	5,513	5,980	5,108	5,222	5,392
AL	4,274	4,485	4,856	4,228	4,375	4,677	4,272	4,471	4,818	4,225	4,357	4,580
MS	2,666	2,750	2,918	2,647	2,700	2,828	2,662	2,722	2,853	2,671	2,760	2,926
W.S.C	28,690	30,477	34,123	28,555	30,204	33,286	28,638	29,781	32,418	28,604	30,247	33,507
AR	2,468	2,578	2,782	2,456	2,557	2,751	2,462	2,546	2,716	2,434	2,489	2,592
LA	4,359	4,478	4,808	4,334	4,424	4,604	4,346	4,343	4,471	4,407	4,592	4,947
OK	3,271	3,382	3,683	3,265	3,366	3,578	3,262	3,259	3,352	3,267	3,353	3,524
TX	18,592	20,039	22,850	18,500	19,857	22,353	18,568	19,633	21,879	18,496	19,813	22,444
West.	58,275	63,278	73,411	58,458	63,846	74,256	58,276	63,315	73,372	58,176	63,079	73,086
Mountain . .	15,384	16,890	19,093	15,142	16,339	18,625	15,323	16,391	18,331	14,902	15,718	17,359
MT	862	920	996	851	894	993	855	867	899	837	859	906
ID	1,156	1,290	1,454	1,117	1,200	1,373	1,152	1,229	1,335	1,101	1,158	1,282
WY	487	522	596	484	512	571	484	483	491	477	495	534
CO	3,710	4,059	4,494	3,663	3,957	4,477	3,683	3,851	4,183	3,575	3,729	4,000
NM	1,676	1,823	2,082	1,658	1,780	2,005	1,670	1,776	2,009	1,641	1,737	1,939
AZ	4,072	4,437	5,074	4,024	4,320	4,891	4,051	4,404	5,136	3,978	4,201	4,645
UT	1,944	2,148	2,462	1,914	2,079	2,413	1,936	2,063	2,294	1,910	2,076	2,442
NV	1,477	1,691	1,935	1,431	1,597	1,902	1,492	1,718	1,984	1,383	1,463	1,611
Pacific. . . .	42,891	46,388	54,318	43,316	47,507	55,631	42,953	46,924	55,041	43,274	47,361	55,727
WA	5,497	6,070	7,025	5,453	6,025	7,087	5,504	6,054	6,898	5,295	5,539	6,005
OR	3,141	3,404	3,876	3,105	3,340	3,812	3,147	3,396	3,753	3,045	3,151	3,360
CA	32,398	34,888	41,085	32,892	36,062	42,255	32,450	35,490	42,075	33,097	36,689	44,076
AK	634	699	781	642	732	880	631	658	754	618	666	769
HI	1,221	1,327	1,551	1,224	1,348	1,597	1,221	1,326	1,561	1,219	1,316	1,517

Source: U.S. Bureau of the Census, *Current Population Reports*, series P25-1111.

No. 36. Population Projections, by Age—States: 1995 to 2010

[**In thousands**. As of **July 1**. Data shown are for series A, the preferred series model; for explanation of methodology, see text, section 1]

REGION, DIVISION, AND STATE	UNDER 18 YEARS			18 TO 44 YEARS			45 TO 64 YEARS			65 YEARS AND OVER		
	1995	2000	2010	1995	2000	2010	1995	2000	2010	1995	2000	2010
U.S.......	69,036	71,789	73,619	109,288	109,274	108,058	51,468	59,860	78,651	33,655	35,324	40,099
Northeast.......	12,593	12,801	12,326	21,056	20,069	18,912	10,523	11,711	14,465	7,272	7,304	7,597
N.E	3,187	3,191	3,045	5,503	5,154	4,902	2,667	3,018	3,830	1,842	1,853	1,977
ME.........	303	294	286	504	477	458	257	294	375	172	175	191
NH.........	288	288	285	482	464	457	228	273	372	135	141	165
VT.........	148	149	146	245	235	228	116	135	167	70	72	82
MA.........	1,418	1,420	1,317	2,530	2,358	2,226	1,184	1,329	1,672	844	842	881
RI.........	238	237	227	414	387	368	195	223	286	154	151	153
CT.........	792	803	784	1,328	1,233	1,165	687	764	958	467	472	505
M.A	9,406	9,610	9,281	15,553	14,915	14,010	7,856	8,693	10,635	5,430	5,451	5,620
NY.........	4,539	4,611	4,439	7,505	7,143	6,735	3,717	4,058	4,846	2,417	2,426	2,525
NJ.........	1,951	2,047	2,051	3,232	3,121	2,972	1,658	1,854	2,348	1,091	1,112	1,192
PA.........	2,916	2,952	2,791	4,816	4,651	4,303	2,481	2,781	3,441	1,922	1,913	1,903
Midwest.........	16,356	16,593	16,340	25,355	25,095	23,799	12,103	13,784	17,282	8,179	8,369	8,912
E.N.C.........	11,458	11,665	11,467	17,951	17,676	16,660	8,574	9,711	12,035	5,628	5,755	6,097
OH.........	2,873	2,891	2,778	4,567	4,483	4,159	2,253	2,532	3,103	1,509	1,547	1,618
IN.........	1,509	1,550	1,534	2,412	2,409	2,278	1,154	1,314	1,636	745	772	836
IL.........	3,126	3,206	3,198	4,930	4,857	4,640	2,303	2,592	3,225	1,496	1,513	1,589
MI.........	2,583	2,635	2,621	3,932	3,802	3,569	1,871	2,112	2,567	1,189	1,211	1,278
WI.........	1,367	1,383	1,336	2,110	2,125	2,014	993	1,161	1,504	689	712	776
W.N.C.........	4,898	4,928	4,873	7,404	7,419	7,139	3,529	4,073	5,247	2,551	2,614	2,815
MN.........	1,243	1,254	1,225	1,921	1,930	1,849	875	1,038	1,370	578	602	683
IA.........	743	736	705	1,125	1,128	1,061	556	627	767	438	439	449
MO.........	1,376	1,381	1,371	2,107	2,090	2,006	1,055	1,197	1,546	749	769	837
ND.........	170	164	163	259	254	250	115	133	170	93	94	93
SD.........	211	216	218	285	292	284	132	155	203	105	107	111
NE.........	449	452	448	656	663	649	309	354	447	231	236	248
KS.........	706	725	743	1,051	1,062	1,040	487	569	744	357	367	394
South.........	23,875	24,901	25,688	37,959	38,346	37,992	18,090	21,274	28,647	11,809	12,724	15,055
S.A	11,618	12,217	12,505	19,316	19,402	19,107	9,547	11,255	15,148	6,539	7,130	8,559
DE.........	182	191	193	302	305	295	142	164	214	92	99	113
MD.........	1,317	1,405	1,453	2,159	2,124	2,077	1,033	1,192	1,551	568	602	701
DC.........	109	99	102	263	248	261	112	117	142	76	73	72
VA.........	1,654	1,745	1,780	2,907	2,923	2,879	1,343	1,576	2,101	742	803	967
WV.........	432	425	406	724	703	642	389	434	514	280	277	280
NC.........	1,758	1,862	1,879	3,023	3,045	2,978	1,462	1,713	2,284	908	997	1,199
SC.........	980	1,013	1,036	1,569	1,570	1,548	740	867	1,152	443	481	575
GA.........	1,909	2,030	2,125	3,080	3,153	3,161	1,387	1,656	2,269	726	798	998
FL.........	3,277	3,447	3,531	5,289	5,331	5,266	2,939	3,536	4,921	2,704	3,000	3,654
E.S.C.........	4,157	4,275	4,305	6,574	6,606	6,352	3,232	3,714	4,824	2,058	2,167	2,459
KY.........	983	996	982	1,598	1,594	1,490	779	890	1,125	491	509	563
TN.........	1,295	1,343	1,343	2,173	2,209	2,151	1,090	1,269	1,674	671	717	839
AL.........	1,125	1,183	1,233	1,732	1,736	1,691	858	975	1,264	560	591	667
MS.........	754	753	747	1,071	1,067	1,020	505	580	761	336	350	390
W.S.C.........	8,100	8,409	8,878	12,069	12,338	12,533	5,311	6,305	8,675	3,212	3,427	4,037
AR.........	643	657	661	953	960	927	504	578	758	368	383	436
LA.........	1,251	1,247	1,282	1,803	1,792	1,766	808	925	1,195	498	515	565
OK.........	870	875	900	1,313	1,314	1,312	648	739	969	441	454	502
TX.........	5,336	5,630	6,035	8,000	8,272	8,528	3,351	4,063	5,753	1,905	2,075	2,534
West.........	16,212	17,494	19,265	24,918	25,764	27,355	10,752	13,091	18,257	6,395	6,927	8,535
Mountain......	4,376	4,690	4,967	6,410	6,770	6,919	2,848	3,503	4,847	1,750	1,924	2,362
MT.........	233	242	250	343	356	357	172	203	260	114	117	130
ID.........	344	373	396	466	512	526	211	262	360	133	143	172
WY.........	141	145	162	207	218	235	89	108	144	51	51	54
CO.........	972	1,037	1,054	1,645	1,722	1,728	717	885	1,198	376	415	514
NM.........	500	540	588	679	705	734	311	374	515	185	204	247
AZ.........	1,127	1,213	1,281	1,629	1,673	1,705	759	927	1,305	558	623	783
UT.........	684	723	800	803	882	928	286	356	504	172	188	230
NV.........	375	417	436	638	702	706	303	388	561	161	183	232
Pacific........	11,836	12,804	14,298	18,508	18,994	20,436	7,904	9,588	13,410	4,645	5,003	6,173
WA.........	1,461	1,589	1,712	2,336	2,464	2,589	1,070	1,342	1,888	631	675	836
OR.........	811	869	945	1,279	1,328	1,400	631	773	1,026	421	434	504
CA.........	9,048	9,779	11,008	14,061	14,327	15,494	5,867	7,077	9,978	3,422	3,704	4,605
AK.........	201	221	239	300	319	342	105	129	163	28	31	38
HI.........	315	346	394	532	556	611	231	267	355	143	159	190

Source: U.S. Bureau of the Census, *Current Population Reports*, series P25-1111.

No. 37. Population Projections, by Race—States: 1995 to 2010

[**In thousands**. As of **July 1**. Data shown are for series A, the preferred series model; for explanation of methodology, see text, section 1]

REGION, DIVISION, AND STATE	WHITE			BLACK			AMERICAN INDIAN, ESKIMO, ALEUT			ASIAN, PACIFIC ISLANDER		
	1995	2000	2010	1995	2000	2010	1995	2000	2010	1995	2000	2010
U.S.	218,333	226,268	240,293	33,118	35,475	40,227	2,229	2,382	2,718	9,756	12,121	17,188
Northeast.	43,381	43,218	43,268	6,263	6,570	7,267	118	108	98	1,678	1,989	2,669
N.E	12,183	12,120	12,408	691	718	810	32	31	31	291	348	506
ME	1,217	1,220	1,283	5	5	5	6	6	6	8	9	14
NH	1,109	1,137	1,236	7	8	10	2	3	3	14	18	31
VT	570	582	609	2	3	4	2	2	2	4	5	9
MA	5,445	5,373	5,387	340	352	393	11	10	10	180	215	307
RI	927	917	933	44	46	51	4	4	4	25	31	46
CT	2,915	2,891	2,960	293	304	347	7	6	6	60	70	99
M.A	31,198	31,098	30,860	5,572	5,852	6,457	86	77	67	1,387	1,641	2,163
NY	14,025	13,819	13,542	3,249	3,391	3,705	57	50	43	846	977	1,257
NJ	6,405	6,445	6,526	1,156	1,242	1,434	14	13	11	356	435	591
PA	10,768	10,834	10,792	1,167	1,219	1,318	15	14	13	185	229	315
Midwest.	54,306	55,391	56,441	6,249	6,689	7,526	382	411	460	1,055	1,345	1,900
E.N.C	37,392	38,006	38,350	5,277	5,653	6,379	165	170	174	776	976	1,354
OH	9,806	9,943	9,948	1,253	1,335	1,483	22	22	22	122	152	206
IN	5,275	5,444	5,587	476	514	582	14	15	15	55	72	102
IL	9,603	9,713	9,801	1,843	1,957	2,181	23	22	21	383	476	648
MI	7,958	8,000	7,979	1,417	1,520	1,737	61	63	64	140	176	253
WI	4,750	4,906	5,035	288	327	396	45	48	52	76	100	145
W.N.C.	16,914	17,385	18,091	972	1,036	1,147	217	241	286	279	369	546
MN	4,344	4,498	4,699	104	111	122	58	64	74	113	151	232
IA	2,763	2,816	2,841	57	65	78	8	8	8	33	41	53
MO	4,629	4,737	4,970	581	609	664	20	20	21	56	72	105
ND	600	601	622	4	4	5	28	31	37	5	7	11
SD	663	685	702	3	4	4	62	74	97	5	7	11
NE	1,550	1,598	1,669	64	69	76	14	15	16	17	22	31
KS	2,365	2,450	2,588	159	174	198	27	29	33	50	69	103
South	72,121	75,813	82,386	17,378	18,708	21,297	606	630	677	1,624	2,094	3,024
S.A	35,962	37,772	40,805	9,960	10,868	12,615	185	194	208	911	1,173	1,691
DE	570	589	603	132	149	181	3	3	3	14	18	28
MD	3,500	3,546	3,631	1,368	1,514	1,776	13	13	14	196	249	361
DC	178	176	195	369	349	365	1	1	1	11	12	16
VA	5,127	5,367	5,743	1,284	1,391	1,592	15	15	15	220	275	378
WV	1,756	1,770	1,768	54	53	50	3	3	3	11	14	20
NC	5,378	5,682	6,125	1,594	1,715	1,916	90	98	109	88	123	190
SC	2,561	2,677	2,902	1,131	1,207	1,344	9	9	9	31	39	56
GA	5,025	5,346	5,857	1,955	2,139	2,485	13	12	12	109	140	199
FL	11,867	12,619	13,981	2,073	2,351	2,906	38	40	42	231	303	443
E.S.C	12,690	13,231	14,042	3,166	3,331	3,634	44	45	46	120	155	219
KY	3,535	3,646	3,769	286	307	345	6	6	6	24	30	40
TN	4,327	4,563	4,899	845	905	1,014	11	11	11	46	59	83
AL	3,140	3,284	3,529	1,083	1,139	1,243	18	18	19	33	44	65
MS	1,688	1,738	1,845	952	980	1,032	9	10	10	17	22	31
W.S.C.	23,469	24,810	27,539	4,252	4,509	5,048	377	391	423	593	766	1,114
AR	2,047	2,139	2,311	386	395	412	15	17	18	20	27	41
LA	2,909	2,953	3,119	1,371	1,427	1,550	19	19	20	60	78	119
OK	2,699	2,770	2,979	244	251	269	276	290	320	52	71	115
TX	15,814	16,948	19,130	2,251	2,436	2,817	67	65	65	461	590	839
West	48,525	51,846	58,198	3,228	3,508	4,137	1,123	1,233	1,483	5,399	6,693	9,595
Mountain . . .	14,004	15,248	16,974	436	485	556	589	669	818	354	490	748
MT	798	847	908	2	2	3	55	62	74	6	8	12
ID	1,118	1,242	1,392	5	6	8	18	21	24	15	21	31
WY	467	498	564	4	5	5	12	14	17	4	6	9
CO	3,431	3,733	4,090	156	174	200	34	36	38	89	117	166
NM	1,460	1,574	1,760	32	33	35	159	181	231	25	35	56
AZ	3,606	3,894	4,379	123	131	143	251	285	348	91	127	204
UT	1,843	2,017	2,272	14	16	18	33	39	50	54	77	122
NV	1,281	1,443	1,609	100	118	144	27	31	36	70	99	148
Pacific	34,521	36,598	41,224	2,792	3,023	3,581	534	564	665	5,045	6,203	8,847
WA	4,915	5,360	6,071	164	174	187	101	112	131	318	424	635
OR	2,929	3,139	3,508	54	60	70	47	52	60	111	153	238
CA	25,701	26,987	30,357	2,512	2,719	3,245	277	276	314	3,908	4,906	7,169
AK	477	516	543	26	28	29	102	116	150	29	39	59
HI	499	596	745	36	42	50	7	8	10	679	681	746

Source: U.S. Bureau of the Census, *Current Population Reports*, series P25-1111.

No. 38. Population Projections, by Hispanic Origin Status—States: 1995 to 2010

[**In thousands**. As of **July 1**. Data shown are for series A, the preferred series model; for explanation of methodology, see text, section 1. Persons of Hispanic origin may be of any race]

REGION, DIVISION, AND STATE	HISPANIC ORIGIN			NOT OF HISPANIC ORIGIN		
	1995	2000	2010	1995	2000	2010
U.S	26,797	31,164	40,526	236,640	245,078	259,904
Northeast.	4,251	4,690	5,559	47,190	47,194	47,742
N.E	684	796	1,035	12,514	12,420	12,720
ME	9	11	15	1,227	1,229	1,294
NH	13	16	24	1,119	1,149	1,256
VT	4	5	8	575	587	615
MA	342	394	510	5,634	5,556	5,587
RI	58	70	95	943	928	939
CT	258	300	383	3,016	2,971	3,029
M.A	3,567	3,894	4,524	34,676	34,774	35,022
NY	2,372	2,498	2,750	15,806	15,739	15,796
NJ	898	1,037	1,287	7,033	7,098	7,275
PA	297	359	487	11,837	11,937	11,951
Midwest.	2,103	2,479	3,284	59,890	61,357	63,049
E.N.C	1,738	2,037	2,683	41,872	42,769	43,576
OH	170	201	268	11,033	11,252	11,391
IN	122	145	197	5,698	5,900	6,089
IL	1,086	1,264	1,643	10,767	10,904	11,009
MI	242	283	375	9,333	9,476	9,658
WI	118	144	200	5,041	5,237	5,429
W.N.C.	365	442	601	18,018	18,588	19,473
MN	68	83	116	4,551	4,741	5,011
IA	45	56	75	2,816	2,874	2,906
MO	71	82	108	5,215	5,355	5,652
ND	5	6	8	632	637	668
SD	7	9	11	728	761	804
NE	53	67	93	1,591	1,637	1,700
KS	116	139	190	2,485	2,583	2,732
South	8,259	9,752	12,944	83,469	87,492	94,441
S.A	2,645	3,166	4,316	44,374	46,839	51,005
DE	22	28	39	696	731	776
MD	158	188	248	4,920	5,134	5,534
DC	30	29	32	529	508	545
VA	193	228	308	6,453	6,820	7,420
WV	10	12	16	1,814	1,828	1,826
NC	100	123	167	7,050	7,494	8,174
SC	40	49	67	3,692	3,883	4,244
GA	144	176	237	6,958	7,461	8,316
FL	1,948	2,333	3,202	12,262	12,980	14,170
E.S.C	112	132	176	15,907	16,630	17,765
KY	23	26	34	3,828	3,963	4,126
TN	42	51	67	5,186	5,487	5,940
AL	29	35	49	4,245	4,450	4,807
MS	18	20	26	2,648	2,730	2,892
W.S.C.	5,502	6,454	8,452	23,188	24,023	25,671
AR	27	33	44	2,441	2,545	2,738
LA	109	124	154	4,250	4,354	4,654
OK	106	124	160	3,165	3,258	3,523
TX	5,260	6,173	8,094	13,332	13,866	14,756
West	12,184	14,243	18,739	46,091	49,035	54,672
Mountain . . .	2,471	2,945	3,954	12,913	13,945	15,139
MT	15	17	22	847	903	974
ID	74	95	138	1,082	1,195	1,316
WY	31	36	45	456	486	551
CO	511	595	771	3,199	3,464	3,723
NM	686	792	1,024	990	1,031	1,058
AZ	853	1,019	1,382	3,219	3,418	3,692
UT	106	127	170	1,838	2,021	2,292
NV	195	264	402	1,282	1,427	1,533
Pacific	9,713	11,298	14,785	33,178	35,090	39,533
WA	291	368	526	5,206	5,702	6,499
OR	151	189	265	2,990	3,215	3,611
CA	9,143	10,584	13,775	23,255	24,304	27,310
AK	22	26	33	612	673	748
HI	106	131	186	1,115	1,196	1,365

Source: U.S. Bureau of the Census, *Current Population Reports*, series P25-1111.

No. 39. Population in Coastal Counties: 1960 to 1994

[Enumerated population as of **April 1**, except as indicated. Areas as defined by U.S. National Oceanic and Atmospheric Agency, 1992. Covers 672 counties and equivalent areas with at least 15 percent of their land area either in a coastal watershed (drainage area) or in a coastal cataloging unit (a coastal area between watersheds)]

| YEAR | Total | COUNTIES IN COASTAL REGIONS | | | | | Balance of United States |
		Total	Atlantic	Gulf of Mexico	Great Lakes	Pacific	
Land area, 1990 (1,000 sq. mi.)	3,536	888	148	114	115	510	2,649
POPULATION							
1960 (mil.)......................	179.3	94.5	44.5	8.4	23.7	17.9	84.8
1970 (mil.)......................	203.3	110.0	51.1	10.0	26.0	22.8	93.3
1980 (mil.)......................	226.5	119.8	53.7	13.1	26.0	27.0	106.7
1990 (mil.)......................	248.7	133.4	59.0	15.2	25.9	33.2	115.3
1994 (July 1)(mil.).................	260.3	138.5	60.7	16.3	26.4	35.1	121.8
1960 (percent)	100	53	25	5	14	10	47
1970 (percent)	100	54	25	5	13	11	46
1980 (percent)	100	53	24	6	11	12	47
1990 (percent)	100	54	24	6	10	13	46
1994 (July 1)(percent)	100	53	23	6	10	13	47

Source: U.S. Bureau of the Census, *U.S. Census of Population: 1960* and *1970; 1980 Census of Population*, vol. 1, chapter A (PC80-1-A-1), *U.S. Summary; 1990 Census of Population and Housing* (CPH1); and unpublished data.

No. 40. Metropolitan and Nonmetropolitan Area Population: 1970 to 1992

[As of **April 1**, except **1992**, as of **July 1**. Data exclude Puerto Rico. Metropolitan areas are as defined by U.S. Office of Management and Budget as of year shown, except as noted]

| ITEM | 1970 | 1980 [1] (SMSA's) | MSA's AND CMSA's [2] | | |
			1980	1990	1992
Metropolitan areas: Number of areas	243	318	269	269	269
Population (1,000)...................	139,480	169,431	176,983	197,824	203,273
Percent change over previous year shown ..	[3]23.6	21.5	(X)	11.8	2.8
Percent of total U.S. population	68.6	74.8	78.1	79.5	79.7
Land area, percent of U.S. land area	10.9	16.0	19.1	19.1	19.1
Nonmetropolitan areas, population (1,000)	63,822	57,115	49,560	50,886	51,804

X Not applicable.   [1] SMSA=standard metropolitan statistical area. Areas are as defined June 30, 1981.   [2] Areas are as defined July 1, 1994.   [3] Percent change from 1960.

Source: U.S. Bureau of the Census, *U.S. Census of Population: 1970; 1990 Census of Population and Housing, Supplementary Reports, Metropolitan Areas as Defined by the Office of Management and Budget, June 30, 1993* (1990 CPH-S-1-1); *1990 Census of Population and Housing, Population and Housing Unit Counts* (CPH-2-26); Population Paper Listing 3; and unpublished data.

No. 41. Number and Population of Metropolitan Areas, by Population Size-Class in 1990: 1980 and 1990

[As of **April 1**. Data exclude Puerto Rico. CMSA=consolidated metropolitan statistical area. MSA=metropolitan statistical area. PMSA=primary metropolitan statistical area. Areas are as defined by U.S. Office of Management and Budget, July 1, 1994. For area definitions, see Appendix II. See also *Historical Statistics, Colonial Times to 1970*, series A 264-275]

| LEVEL AND POPULATION SIZE-CLASS OF METROPOLITAN AREA IN **1990** | CMSA's AND MSA's | | | | MSA's AND PMSA's | | |
| | Number, **1990** | Population, **1980** (mil.) | Population, 1990 | | Number, **1990** | Population, 1990 | |
			Total (mil.)	Percent in each class		Total (mil.)	Percent in each class
Total, all metropolitan areas . . .	**269**	**177.0**	**197.8**	**100**	**324**	**197.8**	**100**
Level A (1,000,000 or more)........	40	118.7	132.9	67	51	118.7	60
2,500,000 or more	15	84.3	94.1	48	13	58.2	29
1,000,000 to 2,499,999	25	34.4	38.8	20	38	60.5	31
Level B (250,000 to 999,999)	96	41.2	46.4	23	119	56.9	29
500,000 to 999,999	33	21.4	24.3	12	41	29.4	15
250,000 to 499,999	63	19.8	22.0	11	78	27.5	14
Level C (100,000 to 249,999)	110	15.2	16.6	8	130	20.1	10
Level D (less than 100,000)	23	1.9	2.0	1	24	2.1	1

Source: U.S. Bureau of the Census, *1980 Census of Population, Supplementary Report, Metropolitan Statistical Areas* (PC80-S1-18); *1990 Census of Population and Housing, Supplementary Reports, Metropolitan Areas as Defined by the Office of Management and Budget, June 30, 1993*, (1990 CPH-S-1-1); and *1990 Census of Population and Housing, Population and Housing Unit Counts* (CPH-2-26).

No. 42. Metropolitan and Nonmetropolitan Population—States: 1980 to 1992

[As of **April 1**, except **1992**, as of **July**. Metropolitan refers to 251 metropolitan statistical areas and 18 consolidated metropolitan statistical areas as defined by U.S. Office of Management and Budget, July 1, 1994; nonmetropolitan is the area outside metropolitan areas; see Appendix II. Minus sign (-) indicates decrease]

REGION, DIVISION, AND STATE	METROPOLITAN POPULATION						NONMETROPOLITAN POPULATION					
	Total (1,000)			Percent change, 1980-92	Percent of State		Total (1,000)			Percent change, 1980-92	Percent of State	
	1980	1990	1992		1980	1992	1980	1990	1992		1980	1992
U.S.	176,983	197,824	203,273	14.9	78.1	79.7	49,560	50,886	51,804	4.5	21.9	20.3
Northeast ..	44,047	45,455	45,698	3.7	89.6	89.4	5,090	5,354	5,423	6.5	10.4	10.6
N.E	10,470	11,127	11,095	6.0	84.8	84.1	1,878	2,080	2,101	11.8	15.2	15.9
ME....	405	443	441	9.0	36.0	35.7	721	785	795	10.4	64.0	64.3
NH....	535	659	662	23.8	58.1	59.4	386	450	453	17.4	41.9	40.6
VT....	133	152	154	15.9	26.0	27.0	378	411	417	10.2	74.0	73.0
MA....	5,530	5,788	5,763	4.2	96.4	96.2	207	229	230	11.2	3.6	3.8
RI	886	938	937	5.8	93.5	93.6	61	65	64	5.1	6.5	6.4
CT....	2,982	3,148	3,138	5.2	96.0	95.7	126	140	141	12.1	4.0	4.3
M.A.....	33,576	34,328	34,603	3.1	91.3	91.2	3,212	3,274	3,322	3.4	8.7	8.8
NY....	16,144	16,515	16,613	2.9	91.9	91.7	1,414	1,475	1,497	5.9	8.1	8.3
NJ....	7,365	7,730	7,820	6.2	100.0	100.0	(X)	(X)	(X)	(X)	(X)	(X)
PA....	10,067	10,083	10,170	1.0	84.8	84.8	1,798	1,799	1,825	1.5	15.2	15.2
Midwest ..	42,557	43,691	44,522	4.6	72.3	73.4	16,310	15,978	16,117	-1.2	27.7	26.6
E.N.C..	33,031	33,391	33,976	2.9	79.2	79.5	8,652	8,618	8,743	1.1	20.8	20.5
OH....	8,791	8,826	8,966	2.0	81.4	81.3	2,007	2,021	2,056	2.4	18.6	18.7
IN	3,885	3,962	4,052	4.3	70.8	71.6	1,605	1,582	1,606	(Z)	29.2	28.4
IL....	9,461	9,574	9,757	3.1	82.8	84.0	1,967	1,857	1,856	-5.6	17.2	16.0
MI	7,719	7,698	7,799	1.0	83.3	82.7	1,543	1,598	1,635	5.9	16.7	17.3
WI	3,176	3,331	3,402	7.1	67.5	68.1	1,530	1,561	1,591	4.0	32.5	31.9
W.N.C.	9,526	10,300	10,546	10.7	55.4	58.8	7,658	7,360	7,374	-3.7	44.6	41.2
MN....	2,674	3,011	3,096	15.8	65.6	69.3	1,402	1,364	1,372	-2.2	34.4	30.7
IA....	1,198	1,200	1,228	2.5	41.1	43.8	1,716	1,577	1,575	-8.2	58.9	56.2
MO....	3,314	3,491	3,543	6.9	67.4	68.3	1,603	1,626	1,647	2.8	32.6	31.7
ND....	234	257	263	12.4	35.9	41.6	418	381	371	-11.4	64.1	58.4
SD....	194	221	231	19.1	28.0	32.6	497	475	478	-3.9	72.0	67.4
NE....	728	787	809	11.1	46.4	50.6	842	791	791	-6.0	53.6	49.4
KS....	1,184	1,333	1,374	16.1	50.1	54.6	1,180	1,145	1,141	-3.3	49.9	45.4
South	53,724	63,190	65,564	22.0	71.3	74.3	21,643	22,256	22,621	4.5	28.7	25.7
S.A.....	28,226	34,294	35,599	26.1	76.4	78.9	8,732	9,273	9,493	8.7	23.6	21.1
DE....	496	553	571	15.1	83.5	82.7	98	113	120	22.3	16.5	17.3
MD....	3,920	4,439	4,563	16.4	93.0	92.8	297	343	354	19.1	7.0	7.2
DC....	638	607	585	-8.3	100.0	100.0	(X)	(X)	(X)	(X)	(X)	(X)
VA....	3,966	4,773	4,954	24.9	74.2	77.5	1,381	1,414	1,440	4.3	25.8	22.5
WV....	796	748	756	-5.0	40.8	41.8	1,155	1,045	1,053	-8.8	59.2	58.2
NC....	3,749	4,376	4,535	21.0	63.8	66.3	2,131	2,253	2,301	8.0	36.2	33.7
SC....	2,114	2,423	2,514	18.9	67.8	69.8	1,006	1,064	1,089	8.2	32.2	30.2
GA....	3,507	4,352	4,587	30.8	64.2	67.7	1,956	2,127	2,186	11.8	35.8	32.3
FL....	9,039	12,023	12,532	38.7	92.7	93.0	708	915	950	34.2	7.3	7.0
E.S.C...	8,147	8,662	8,916	9.4	55.5	57.4	6,519	6,515	6,615	1.5	44.5	42.6
KY....	1,735	1,780	1,820	4.9	47.4	48.5	1,925	1,906	1,934	0.5	52.6	51.5
TN....	3,045	3,298	3,404	11.8	66.3	67.7	1,546	1,579	1,621	4.9	33.7	32.3
AL....	2,560	2,710	2,788	8.9	65.7	67.4	1,334	1,331	1,349	1.1	34.3	32.6
MS....	806	874	904	12.2	32.0	34.6	1,715	1,699	1,711	-0.2	68.0	65.4
W.S.C ...	17,351	20,235	21,048	21.3	73.1	76.4	6,392	6,468	6,513	1.9	26.9	23.6
AR....	963	1,040	1,071	11.2	42.1	44.7	1,323	1,311	1,323	(Z)	57.9	55.3
LA....	3,125	3,160	3,210	2.7	74.3	75.0	1,082	1,060	1,069	-1.2	25.7	25.0
OK....	1,724	1,870	1,927	11.7	57.0	60.1	1,301	1,276	1,278	-1.8	43.0	39.9
TX....	11,539	14,166	14,840	28.6	81.1	83.9	2,686	2,821	2,842	5.8	18.9	16.1
West......	36,655	45,487	47,490	29.6	84.9	86.1	6,516	7,299	7,643	17.3	15.1	13.9
Mountain .	7,645	9,605	10,155	32.8	67.2	70.6	3,726	4,054	4,225	13.4	32.8	29.4
MT....	189	191	197	4.6	24.0	24.0	598	608	625	4.5	76.0	76.0
ID	257	296	320	24.4	27.2	30.0	687	711	746	8.6	72.8	70.0
WY....	141	134	138	-1.8	29.9	29.7	329	319	327	-0.7	70.1	70.3
CO....	2,326	2,686	2,832	21.7	80.5	81.8	563	608	632	12.3	19.5	18.2
NM....	675	842	886	31.3	51.8	56.0	628	673	696	10.7	48.2	44.0
AZ....	2,264	3,106	3,244	43.3	83.3	84.7	453	559	588	29.9	16.7	15.3
UT....	1,128	1,336	1,403	24.4	77.2	77.5	333	387	408	22.6	22.8	22.5
NV....	666	1,014	1,134	70.3	83.2	84.8	135	188	203	50.5	16.8	15.2
Pacific ...	29,010	35,882	37,335	28.7	91.2	91.6	2,790	3,245	3,418	22.5	8.8	8.4
WA....	3,366	4,036	4,270	26.8	81.5	83.0	766	830	873	14.0	18.5	17.0
OR....	1,799	1,985	2,081	15.7	68.3	70.0	834	858	890	6.7	31.7	30.0
CA....	22,907	28,799	29,875	30.4	96.8	96.7	760	961	1,021	34.3	3.2	3.3
AK	174	226	246	41.0	43.4	41.8	227	324	342	50.3	56.6	58.2
HI	763	836	863	13.2	79.0	74.7	202	272	293	44.8	21.0	25.3

X Not applicable.   Z Less than 0.05 percent.

Source: U.S. Bureau of the Census, *1990 Census of Population and Housing, Supplementary Reports, Metropolitan Areas as Defined by the Office of Management and Budget, June 30, 1993,* (1990 CPH-S-1-1); *1990 Census of Population and Housing, Population and Housing Unit Counts* (CPH-2-26); and unpublished data.

Population

No. 43. Large Metropolitan Areas—Population: 1980 to 1994

[In thousands, except percent. As of April 1, except as noted. Covers 18 consolidated metropolitan statistical areas (CMSA's), their 73 component primary metropolitan statistical areas (PMSA's), and the remaining 121 MSA's with 250,000 and over population in 1994 as defined by the U.S. Office of Management and Budget as of July 1, 1994. For definitions and components of all MA's and population of NECMA's (New England County Metropolitan Areas), see Appendix II. Minus sign (-) indicates decrease]

METROPOLITAN AREA	1980	1990 [1]	1991 (July)	1992 (July)	1993 (July)	1994 (July)	PERCENT CHANGE 1980-90	PERCENT CHANGE 1990-94
Albany-Schenectady-Troy, NY MSA	825	862	869	872	874	875	4.5	1.6
Albuquerque, NM MSA	485	589	602	616	630	646	21.4	9.6
Allentown-Bethlehem-Easton, PA MSA	551	595	602	606	609	612	8.0	2.8
Anchorage, AK MSA	174	226	235	246	250	254	29.8	12.1
Appleton-Oshkosh-Neenah, WI MSA	291	315	320	324	329	332	8.2	5.4
Atlanta, GA MSA	2,233	2,960	3,054	3,135	3,229	3,331	32.5	12.6
Augusta-Aiken, GA-SC MSA	363	415	430	443	444	448	14.2	8.0
Austin-San Marcos, TX MSA	585	846	873	900	932	964	44.6	13.9
Bakersfield, CA MSA	403	545	571	588	600	609	35.2	11.8
Baton Rouge, LA MSA	494	528	537	546	553	558	6.9	5.7
Beaumont-Port Arthur, TX MSA	373	361	366	369	372	373	-3.2	3.2
Biloxi-Gulfport-Pascagoula, MS MSA	300	312	316	323	330	339	4.1	8.6
Binghamton, NY MSA	263	264	265	266	264	262	0.4	-1.0
Birmingham, AL MSA	815	840	849	856	865	872	3.0	3.8
Boise City, ID MSA	257	296	310	320	334	348	15.2	17.5
Boston-Worcester-Lawrence, MA-NH-ME-CT CMSA	5,122	[2]5,455	(NA)	5,439	(NA)	(NA)	6.5	(NA)
Boston, MA-NH PMSA	3,149	[2]3,228	(NA)	3,211	(NA)	(NA)	2.5	(NA)
Brockton, MA PMSA	225	[2]236	(NA)	236	(NA)	(NA)	5.1	(NA)
Fitchburg-Leominster, MA PMSA	125	[2]138	(NA)	137	(NA)	(NA)	10.5	(NA)
Lawrence, MA-NH PMSA	298	[2]353	(NA)	357	(NA)	(NA)	18.4	(NA)
Lowell, MA-NH PMSA	249	[2]281	(NA)	283	(NA)	(NA)	12.5	(NA)
Manchester, NH PMSA	146	[2]174	(NA)	175	(NA)	(NA)	18.9	(NA)
Nashua, NH PMSA	134	[2]168	(NA)	171	(NA)	(NA)	25.4	(NA)
New Bedford, MA PMSA	167	[2]176	(NA)	173	(NA)	(NA)	5.4	(NA)
Portsmouth-Rochester, NH-ME PMSA	189	[2]223	(NA)	219	(NA)	(NA)	18.0	(NA)
Worcester, MA-CT PMSA	439	[2]478	(NA)	477	(NA)	(NA)	8.9	(NA)
Brownsville-Harlingen-San Benito, TX MSA	210	260	270	279	291	300	24.0	15.2
Buffalo-Niagara Falls, NY MSA	1,243	1,189	1,192	1,193	1,192	1,189	-4.3	-
Canton-Massillon, OH MSA	404	394	397	399	401	402	-2.6	2.1
Charleston-North Charleston, SC MSA	430	507	523	527	526	522	17.8	3.0
Charleston, WV MSA	270	250	251	253	254	255	-7.1	1.7
Charlotte-Gastonia-Rock Hill, NC-SC MSA	971	1,162	1,192	1,210	1,234	1,260	19.6	8.5
Chattanooga, TN-GA MSA	418	424	428	430	435	439	1.6	3.5
Chicago-Gary-Kenosha, IL-IN-WI CMSA	8,115	8,240	8,326	8,400	8,466	8,527	1.5	3.5
Chicago, IL PMSA	7,246	7,411	7,486	7,552	7,612	7,668	2.3	3.5
Gary, IN PMSA	643	605	611	614	617	620	-5.9	2.5
Kankakee, IL PMSA	103	96	98	99	100	101	-6.5	5.2
Kenosha, WI PMSA	123	128	132	134	136	138	4.1	7.5
Cincinnati-Hamilton, OH-KY-IN CMSA	1,726	1,818	1,843	1,862	1,881	1,894	5.3	4.2
Cincinnati, OH-KY-IN PMSA	1,468	1,526	1,544	1,558	1,572	1,581	4.0	3.6
Hamilton-Middletown, OH PMSA	259	291	299	304	309	313	12.6	7.3
Cleveland-Akron, OH CMSA	2,938	2,860	2,874	2,887	2,894	2,899	-2.7	1.4
Akron, OH PMSA	660	658	664	668	673	677	-0.4	2.9
Cleveland-Lorain-Elyria, OH PMSA	2,278	2,202	2,211	2,219	2,221	2,222	-3.3	0.9
Colorado Springs, CO MSA	309	397	404	421	435	452	28.3	14.0
Columbia, SC MSA	410	454	465	471	480	486	10.7	7.1
Columbus, GA-AL MSA	255	261	260	270	271	274	2.4	5.1
Columbus, OH MSA	1,214	1,345	1,371	1,391	1,409	1,423	10.8	5.8
Corpus Christi, TX MSA	326	350	356	361	369	376	7.3	7.4
Dallas-Fort Worth, TX CMSA	3,046	4,037	4,139	4,207	4,279	4,362	32.5	8.1
Dallas, TX PMSA	2,055	2,676	2,742	2,790	2,844	2,898	30.2	8.3
Fort Worth-Arlington, TX PMSA	991	1,361	1,397	1,417	1,435	1,464	37.4	7.6
Davenport-Moline-Rock Island, IA-IL MSA	385	351	354	357	357	358	-8.8	2.0
Dayton-Springfield, OH MSA	942	951	956	959	959	956	1.0	0.5
Daytona Beach, FL MSA	270	399	414	423	432	440	48.1	10.3
Denver-Boulder-Greeley, CO CMSA	1,742	1,980	2,029	2,088	2,146	2,190	13.7	10.6
Boulder-Longmont, CO PMSA	190	225	231	238	244	250	18.8	10.8
Denver, CO PMSA	1,429	1,623	1,664	1,714	1,762	1,796	13.6	10.7
Greeley, CO PMSA	123	132	134	136	140	144	6.8	9.3
Des Moines, IA MSA	368	393	400	406	412	416	6.9	6.0
Detroit-Ann Arbor-Flint, MI CMSA	5,293	5,187	5,215	5,236	5,246	5,255	-2.0	1.3
Ann Arbor, MI PMSA	455	490	498	504	509	515	7.7	5.1
Detroit, MI PMSA	4,388	4,267	4,285	4,299	4,304	4,307	-2.8	0.9
Flint, MI PMSA	450	430	432	432	433	433	-4.4	0.7
El Paso, TX MSA	480	592	613	628	647	665	23.3	12.4
Erie, PA MSA	280	276	278	279	280	280	-1.5	1.7
Eugene-Springfield, OR MSA	275	283	288	291	295	299	2.8	5.7
Evansville-Henderson, IN-KY MSA	276	279	281	283	285	287	1.0	2.7
Fayetteville, NC MSA	247	275	278	278	285	287	11.1	4.6
Fort Myers-Cape Coral, FL MSA	205	335	347	353	359	367	63.3	9.6
Fort Pierce-Port St. Lucie, FL MSA	151	251	261	266	272	278	66.1	10.8
Fort Wayne, IN MSA	445	456	460	463	466	469	2.6	2.8
Fresno, CA MSA	578	756	785	805	823	835	30.8	10.5

See footnotes at end of table.

No. 43. Metropolitan Areas—Population: 1980 to 1994—Continued

[See headnote, page 40]

METROPOLITAN AREA	1980	1990 [1]	1991 (July)	1992 (July)	1993 (July)	1994 (July)	PERCENT CHANGE	
							1980-90	1990-94
Grand Rapids-Muskegon-Holland, MI MSA	841	938	954	964	974	985	11.5	5.0
Greensboro—Winston-Salem—High Point, NC MSA	951	1,050	1,066	1,078	1,092	1,107	10.5	5.4
Greenville-Spartanburg-Anderson, SC MSA	744	831	843	852	862	873	11.6	5.2
Harrisburg-Lebanon-Carlisle, PA MSA	556	588	596	601	605	610	5.7	3.7
Hartford, CT MSA	1,081	[2]1,158	(NA)	1,156	(NA)	(NA)	7.1	(NA)
Hickory-Morganton, NC MSA	270	292	296	298	302	306	8.1	4.6
Honolulu, HI MSA	763	836	849	861	867	874	9.7	4.6
Houston-Galveston-Brazoria, TX CMSA	3,118	3,731	3,854	3,950	4,028	4,099	19.6	9.9
Brazoria, TX PMSA	170	192	199	203	207	212	13.0	10.3
Galveston-Texas City, TX PMSA	196	217	223	227	232	235	11.1	8.0
Houston, TX PMSA	2,753	3,322	3,433	3,520	3,589	3,653	20.7	10.0
Huntington-Ashland, WV-KY-OH MSA	336	313	314	315	316	316	-7.1	1.2
Huntsville, AL MSA	243	293	300	307	314	316	20.6	7.9
Indianapolis, IN MSA	1,306	1,380	1,406	1,424	1,443	1,462	5.7	5.9
Jackson, MS MSA	362	395	399	404	407	412	9.2	4.2
Jacksonville, FL MSA	722	907	931	950	962	972	25.5	7.2
Johnson City-Kingsport-Bristol, TN-VA MSA	434	436	440	444	448	451	0.6	3.3
Kalamazoo-Battle Creek, MI MSA	421	429	433	436	440	443	2.1	3.1
Kansas City, MO-KS MSA	1,449	1,583	1,601	1,614	1,631	1,647	9.2	4.1
Killeen-Temple, TX MSA	215	255	251	255	269	287	19.0	12.5
Knoxville, TN MSA	546	586	598	610	620	631	7.2	7.7
Lafayette, LA MSA	331	345	349	353	358	361	4.3	4.7
Lakeland-Winter Haven, FL MSA	322	405	413	419	423	430	26.0	6.0
Lancaster, PA MSA	362	423	430	434	439	443	16.7	4.7
Lansing-East Lansing, MI MSA	420	433	436	436	436	436	3.1	0.8
Las Vegas, NV-AZ MSA	528	853	927	966	1,010	1,076	61.5	26.2
Lexington, KY MSA	371	406	413	419	426	431	9.4	6.1
Little Rock-North Little Rock, AR MSA	474	513	519	525	533	538	8.1	4.8
Los Angeles-Riverside-Orange County, CA CMSA	11,498	14,532	14,823	15,063	15,210	15,302	26.4	5.3
Los Angeles-Long Beach, CA PMSA	7,477	8,863	8,960	9,068	9,134	9,150	18.5	3.2
Orange County, CA PMSA	1,933	2,411	2,447	2,486	2,515	2,543	24.7	5.5
Riverside-San Bernardino, CA PMSA	1,558	2,589	2,739	2,823	2,867	2,907	66.1	12.3
Ventura, CA PMSA	529	669	677	687	694	703	26.4	5.0
Louisville, KY-IN MSA	954	949	958	966	974	981	-0.5	3.4
Macon, GA MSA	273	291	295	298	303	307	6.6	5.6
Madison, WI MSA	324	367	375	380	386	390	13.5	6.3
McAllen-Edinburg-Mission, TX MSA	283	384	402	421	443	461	35.4	20.2
Melbourne-Titusville-Palm Bay, FL MSA	273	399	415	425	436	443	46.2	11.2
Memphis, TN-AR-MS MSA	939	1,007	1,021	1,032	1,042	1,056	7.3	4.8
Miami-Fort Lauderdale, FL CMSA	2,644	3,193	3,266	3,317	3,354	3,408	20.8	6.7
Fort Lauderdale, FL PMSA	1,018	1,256	1,288	1,311	1,351	1,383	23.3	10.2
Miami, FL PMSA	1,626	1,937	1,978	2,006	2,003	2,025	19.2	4.5
Milwaukee-Racine, WI CMSA	1,570	1,607	1,620	1,629	1,634	1,637	2.4	1.9
Milwaukee-Waukesha, WI PMSA	1,397	1,432	1,443	1,450	1,454	1,456	2.5	1.6
Racine, WI PMSA	173	175	178	179	180	182	1.1	3.8
Minneapolis-St. Paul, MN-WI MSA	2,198	2,539	2,582	2,617	2,655	2,688	15.5	5.9
Mobile, AL MSA	444	477	485	494	505	512	7.5	7.4
Modesto, CA MSA	266	371	386	395	402	407	39.3	9.8
Montgomery, AL MSA	273	293	298	302	307	312	7.3	6.7
Nashville, TN MSA	851	985	1,003	1,022	1,044	1,070	15.8	8.6
New London-Norwich, CT-RI MSA	273	[2]291	(NA)	284	(NA)	(NA)	6.5	(NA)
New Orleans, LA MSA	1,304	1,285	1,290	1,299	1,304	1,309	-1.5	1.8
New York-Northern New Jersey-Long Island, NY-NJ-CT-PA CMSA	18,906	[2]19,550	(NA)	(NA)	(NA)	(NA)	3.4	(NA)
Bergen-Passaic, NJ PMSA	1,293	1,279	1,282	1,290	1,298	1,304	-1.1	2.0
Bridgeport, CT PMSA	439	[2]444	(NA)	443	(NA)	(NA)	1.2	(NA)
Danbury, CT PMSA	175	[2]194	(NA)	196	(NA)	(NA)	10.3	(NA)
Dutchess County, NY PMSA	245	259	261	263	263	261	5.9	0.8
Jersey City, NJ PMSA	557	553	553	553	553	552	-0.7	-0.1
Middlesex-Somerset-Hunterdon, NJ PMSA	886	1,020	1,031	1,044	1,057	1,069	15.1	4.8
Monmouth-Ocean, NJ PMSA	849	986	998	1,010	1,023	1,035	16.1	4.9
Nassau-Suffolk, NY PMSA	2,606	2,609	2,617	2,631	2,643	2,651	0.1	1.6
New Haven-Meriden, CT PMSA	500	[2]530	(NA)	527	(NA)	(NA)	5.9	(NA)
New York, NY PMSA	8,275	8,547	8,538	8,545	8,573	8,584	3.3	0.4
Newark, NJ PMSA	1,964	1,916	1,915	1,921	1,929	1,934	-2.4	0.9
Newburgh, NY-PA PMSA	278	336	343	348	353	356	20.8	6.1
Stamford-Norwalk, CT PMSA	326	[2]330	(NA)	331	(NA)	(NA)	1.3	(NA)
Trenton, NJ PMSA	308	326	327	327	329	329	5.8	1.1
Waterbury, CT PMSA	205	[2]222	(NA)	222	(NA)	(NA)	8.1	(NA)
Norfolk-Virginia Beach-Newport News, VA-NC MSA	1,201	1,445	1,463	1,496	1,514	1,529	20.3	5.9
Oklahoma City, OK MSA	861	959	969	982	996	1,007	11.4	5.1
Omaha, NE-IA MSA	605	640	649	656	658	663	5.6	3.6
Orlando, FL MSA	805	1,225	1,275	1,303	1,334	1,361	52.2	11.2
Pensacola, FL MSA	290	344	352	360	365	371	18.9	7.7
Peoria-Pekin, IL MSA	366	339	342	343	343	344	-7.3	1.3

See footnotes at end of table.

Population

No. 43. Metropolitan Areas—Population: 1980 to 1994—Continued

[See headnote, page 40]

METROPOLITAN AREA	1980	1990 [1]	1991 (July)	1992 (July)	1993 (July)	1994 (July)	PERCENT CHANGE 1980-90	PERCENT CHANGE 1990-94
Philadelphia-Wilmington-Atlantic City, PA-NJ-DE-MD CMSA	5,649	5,893	5,916	5,928	5,941	5,957	4.3	1.1
Atlantic-Cape May, NJ PMSA	276	319	324	327	328	330	15.6	3.3
Philadelphia, PA-NJ PMSA	4,781	4,922	4,930	4,933	4,940	4,949	2.9	0.5
Vineland-Millville-Bridgeton, NJ PMSA	133	138	139	139	139	139	3.9	0.5
Wilmington-Newark, DE-MD PMSA	459	513	523	529	534	539	11.9	5.0
Phoenix-Mesa, AZ MSA	1,600	2,238	2,285	2,333	2,392	2,473	39.9	10.5
Pittsburgh, PA MSA	2,571	2,395	2,399	2,405	2,407	2,402	−6.9	0.3
Portland-Salem, OR-WA CMSA	1,584	1,793	1,857	1,899	1,944	1,982	13.3	10.5
Portland-Vancouver, OR-WA PMSA	1,334	1,515	1,571	1,606	1,644	1,676	13.6	10.6
Salem, OR PMSA	250	278	286	293	300	306	11.3	10.0
Providence-Fall River-Warwick, RI-MA MSA	1,077	[2]1,134	(NA)	1,131	(NA)	(NA)	5.4	(NA)
Provo-Orem, UT MSA	218	264	269	276	283	291	20.9	10.4
Raleigh-Durham-Chapel Hill, NC MSA	665	858	888	911	938	965	29.1	12.4
Reading, PA MSA	313	337	341	343	346	348	7.7	3.3
Reno, NV MSA	194	255	262	268	275	283	31.5	11.1
Richmond-Petersburg, VA MSA	761	866	880	894	906	917	13.7	5.9
Rochester, NY MSA	1,031	1,062	1,072	1,082	1,089	1,090	3.1	2.6
Rockford, IL MSA	326	330	336	339	343	347	1.2	5.2
Sacramento-Yolo, CA CMSA	1,100	1,481	1,538	1,561	1,576	1,588	34.7	7.2
Sacramento, CA PMSA	986	1,340	1,395	1,416	1,431	1,441	35.8	7.6
Yolo, CA PMSA	113	141	143	145	146	146	24.6	3.7
Saginaw-Bay City-Midland, MI MSA	422	399	401	402	403	402	−5.3	0.7
St. Louis, MO-IL MSA	2,414	2,492	2,508	2,516	2,528	2,536	3.2	1.8
Salinas, CA MSA	290	356	363	369	366	352	22.5	−1.1
Salt Lake City-Ogden, UT MSA	910	1,072	1,100	1,127	1,154	1,178	17.8	9.9
San Antonio, TX MSA	1,089	1,325	1,349	1,377	1,407	1,437	21.7	8.5
San Diego, CA MSA	1,862	2,498	2,556	2,602	2,612	2,632	34.2	5.4
San Francisco-Oakland-San Jose, CA CMSA	5,368	6,250	6,335	6,410	6,469	6,513	16.4	4.2
Oakland, CA PMSA	1,762	2,080	2,117	2,148	2,169	2,182	18.1	4.9
San Francisco, CA PMSA	1,489	1,604	1,614	1,626	1,638	1,646	7.7	2.6
San Jose, CA PMSA	1,295	1,498	1,511	1,528	1,544	1,557	15.6	4.0
Santa Cruz-Watsonville, CA PMSA	188	230	229	231	233	235	22.1	2.3
Santa Rosa, CA PMSA	300	388	397	403	406	410	29.5	5.7
Vallejo-Fairfield-Napa, CA PMSA	334	450	467	474	479	483	34.6	7.2
Santa Barbara-Santa Maria-Lompoc, CA MSA	299	370	374	377	378	380	23.7	2.9
Sarasota-Bradenton, FL MSA	351	489	501	504	510	518	39.6	5.8
Savannah, GA MSA	231	258	262	267	272	276	11.8	6.9
Scranton—Wilkes-Barre—Hazleton, PA MSA	659	639	640	640	639	637	−3.2	−0.2
Seattle-Tacoma-Bremerton, WA CMSA	2,409	2,970	3,057	3,132	3,189	3,225	23.3	8.6
Bremerton, WA PMSA	147	190	200	211	215	220	28.9	16.2
Olympia, WA PMSA	124	161	170	177	183	187	29.8	16.1
Seattle-Bellevue-Everett, WA PMSA	1,652	2,033	2,082	2,125	2,159	2,180	23.1	7.2
Tacoma, WA PMSA	486	586	605	620	632	638	20.7	8.9
Shreveport-Bossier City, LA MSA	377	376	373	374	377	378	−0.1	0.5
South Bend, IN MSA	242	247	249	251	253	255	2.2	3.4
Spokane, WA MSA	342	361	372	382	391	396	5.7	9.6
Springfield, MO MSA	228	264	270	276	282	289	15.9	9.3
Springfield, MA MSA	570	[2]588	(NA)	584	(NA)	(NA)	3.2	(NA)
Stockton-Lodi, CA MSA	347	481	495	504	511	518	38.4	7.8
Syracuse, NY MSA	723	742	749	752	755	754	2.7	1.6
Tallahassee, FL MSA	190	234	240	245	250	253	22.7	8.5
Tampa-St. Petersburg-Clearwater, FL MSA	1,614	2,068	2,101	2,117	2,137	2,157	28.2	4.3
Toledo, OH MSA	617	614	614	614	614	614	−0.4	-
Tucson, AZ MSA	531	667	676	692	710	732	25.5	9.7
Tulsa, OK MSA	657	709	721	730	738	743	7.9	4.8
Utica-Rome, NY MSA	320	317	319	319	318	316	−1.1	−0.1
Visalia-Tulare-Porterville, CA MSA	246	312	323	331	338	343	26.9	10.0
Washington-Baltimore, DC-MD-VA-WV CMSA	5,791	6,726	6,829	6,912	6,986	7,059	16.2	4.9
Baltimore, MD PMSA	2,199	2,382	2,412	2,430	2,444	2,458	8.3	3.2
Hagerstown, MD PMSA	113	121	124	125	126	127	7.3	4.3
Washington, DC-MD-VA-WV PMSA	3,478	4,223	4,293	4,357	4,416	4,474	21.4	5.9
West Palm Beach-Boca Raton, FL MSA	577	864	890	909	932	955	49.7	10.5
Wichita, KS MSA	442	485	492	500	505	507	9.7	4.4
York, PA MSA	313	340	345	350	354	358	8.5	5.4
Youngstown-Warren, OH MSA	645	601	603	605	605	604	−6.8	0.5

- Represents or rounds to zero.   NA Not available. [1] The April 1, 1990, census count includes count resolution corrections processed through March 1994, and does not include adjustments for census coverage errors.   [2] Uncorrected census counts.

Source: U.S. Bureau of the Census, unpublished data.

No. 44. Urban and Rural Population, 1960 to 1990, and by State, 1990

[**In thousands, except percent**. As of **April 1**. Resident population]

REGION, DIVISION, AND STATE	Total	URBAN		Rural	REGION, DIVISION, AND STATE	Total	URBAN		Rural
		Number	Percent				Number	Percent	
1960	179,323	125,269	69.9	54,054	MD	4,781	3,888	81.3	893
1970	[1]203,212	149,647	73.6	53,565	DC	607	607	100.0	-
1980	[2]226,546	167,051	73.7	59,495	VA	6,187	4,293	69.4	1,894
1990, total .	**248,710**	**187,053**	**75.2**	**61,656**	WV	1,793	648	36.1	1,145
Northeast.	**50,809**	**40,092**	**78.9**	**10,717**	NC	6,629	3,338	50.4	3,291
N.E	**13,207**	**9,829**	**74.4**	**3,378**	SC	3,487	1,905	54.6	1,581
ME	1,228	548	44.6	680	GA	6,478	4,097	63.2	2,381
NH	1,109	566	51.0	544	FL	12,938	10,967	84.8	1,971
VT	563	181	32.2	382	**E.S.C . . . . .**	**15,176**	**8,531**	**56.2**	**6,646**
MA	6,016	5,070	84.3	947	KY	3,685	1,910	51.8	1,775
RI	1,003	863	86.0	140	TN	4,877	2,970	60.9	1,907
CT	3,287	2,602	79.1	686	AL	4,041	2,440	60.4	1,601
M.A	**37,602**	**30,263**	**80.5**	**7,340**	MS	2,573	1,211	47.1	1,362
NY	17,990	15,164	84.3	2,826	**W.S.C . . . . .**	**26,703**	**19,894**	**74.5**	**6,808**
NJ	7,730	6,910	89.4	820	AR	2,351	1,258	53.5	1,093
PA	11,882	8,188	68.9	3,693	LA	4,220	2,872	68.1	1,348
Midwest.	**59,669**	**42,774**	**71.7**	**16,894**	OK	3,146	2,130	67.7	1,015
E.N.C	**42,009**	**31,074**	**74.0**	**10,935**	TX	16,987	13,635	80.3	3,352
OH	10,847	8,039	74.1	2,808	**West . . . .**	**52,786**	**45,531**	**86.3**	**7,255**
IN	5,544	3,598	64.9	1,946	**Mountain . . .**	**13,659**	**10,881**	**79.7**	**2,777**
IL	11,431	9,669	84.6	1,762	MT	799	420	52.5	379
MI	9,295	6,556	70.5	2,739	ID	1,007	578	57.4	429
WI	4,892	3,212	65.7	1,680	WY	454	295	65.0	159
W.N.C	**17,660**	**11,700**	**66.3**	**5,959**	CO	3,294	2,716	82.4	579
MN	4,375	3,056	69.9	1,319	NM	1,515	1,106	73.0	409
IA	2,777	1,683	60.6	1,094	AZ	3,665	3,207	87.5	458
MO	5,117	3,516	68.7	1,601	UT	1,723	1,499	87.0	224
ND	639	340	53.3	298	NV	1,202	1,061	88.3	140
SD	696	348	50.0	348	**Pacific . . . . .**	**39,127**	**34,650**	**88.6**	**4,477**
NE	1,578	1,044	66.1	534	WA	4,867	3,718	76.4	1,149
KS	2,478	1,713	69.1	765	OR	2,842	2,003	70.5	839
South	**85,446**	**58,656**	**68.6**	**26,790**	CA	29,760	27,571	92.6	2,189
S.A	**43,567**	**30,231**	**69.4**	**13,336**	AK	550	371	67.5	179
DE	666	487	73.0	180	HI	1,108	986	89.0	122

- Represents zero.   [1] The revised 1970 resident population count is 203,302,031; which incorporates changes due to errors found after tabulations were completed.   [2] Total population count has been revised since the 1980 census publications to 226,542,203.

Source: U.S. Bureau of the Census, *1990 Census of Population and Housing, Population and Housing Unit Counts* (1990 CPH-2).

No. 45. Incorporated Places, by Population Size: 1970 to 1992

POPULATION SIZE	NUMBER OF INCORPORATED PLACES				POPULATION (mil.)				PERCENT OF TOTAL			
	1970	1980	1990	1992	1970	1980	1990	1992	1970	1980	1990	1992
Total	**18,666**	**19,097**	**19,262**	**19,262**	**131.9**	**140.3**	**152.9**	**156.8**	**100.0**	**100.0**	**100.0**	**100.0**
1,000,000 or more. . . .	6	6	8	9	18.8	17.5	20.0	21.0	14.2	12.5	13.0	13.4
500,000 to 999,999 . . .	20	16	15	14	13.0	10.9	10.1	9.2	9.8	7.8	6.6	5.9
250,000 to 499,999 . . .	30	33	41	41	10.5	11.8	14.2	14.9	7.9	8.4	9.3	9.5
100,000 to 249,999 . . .	97	114	131	135	13.9	16.6	19.1	19.9	10.5	11.8	12.5	12.7
50,000 to 99,999	232	250	309	325	16.2	17.6	21.2	22.4	12.2	12.3	13.9	14.3
25,000 to 49,999	455	526	567	578	15.7	18.4	20.0	20.3	11.9	13.1	13.0	13.0
10,000 to 24,999	1,127	1,260	1,290	1,320	17.6	19.8	20.3	20.8	13.3	14.1	13.3	13.3
Under 10,000	16,699	16,892	16,901	16,840	26.4	28.0	28.2	28.3	20.0	20.0	18.4	18.1

Source: U.S. Bureau of the Census, *Census of Population: 1970, 1980,* and *1990,* vol. I and unpublished data.

No. 46. Cities With 100,000 or More Inhabitants in 1992—Population, 1980 to 1992, and Land Area, 1990

[**Population**: As of **April 1**; except **1992**, as of **July 1**. Data refer to boundaries in effect on January 1, 1990. Minus sign (-) indicates decrease]

CITY	1980, total (1,000)	POPULATION								Land area, 1990 (square miles)
		1990						1992		
		Total (1,000)	Percent—					Total (1,000)	Rank	Percent change, 1990-92	
			Black	American Indian, Eskimo, Aleut	Asian, Pacific Islander	His-panic [1]					
Abilene, TX	98	107	7.0	0.4	1.3	15.5		108	179	1.4	103.1
Akron, OH	237	223	24.5	0.3	1.2	0.7		224	73	0.3	62.2
Albuquerque, NM	332	385	3.0	3.0	1.7	34.5		398	36	3.6	132.2
Alexandria, VA	103	111	21.9	0.3	4.2	9.7		113	169	1.8	15.3
Allentown, PA	104	105	5.0	0.2	1.3	11.7		106	186	1.3	17.7
Amarillo, TX	149	158	6.0	0.8	1.9	14.7		161	112	2.2	87.9
Anaheim, CA	219	266	2.5	0.5	9.4	31.4		274	58	2.9	44.3
Anchorage, AK	174	226	6.4	6.4	4.8	4.1		246	65	8.6	1,697.6
Ann Arbor, MI	108	110	9.0	0.4	7.7	2.6		110	176	0.2	25.9
Arlington, TX	160	262	8.4	0.5	3.9	8.9		276	57	5.4	93.0
Atlanta, GA	425	394	67.1	0.1	0.9	1.9		395	37	0.2	131.8
Aurora, CO	159	222	11.4	0.6	3.8	6.6		240	66	7.9	132.5
Aurora, IL	81	100	11.9	0.2	1.3	23.0		106	190	6.4	33.5
Austin, TX	346	466	12.4	0.4	3.0	23.0		492	25	5.7	217.8
Bakersfield, CA	106	175	9.4	1.1	3.6	20.5		188	88	7.5	91.8
Baltimore, MD	787	736	59.2	0.3	1.1	1.0		726	14	-1.3	80.8
Baton Rouge, LA	220	220	43.9	0.1	1.7	1.6		225	72	2.4	73.9
Beaumont, TX	118	114	41.3	0.2	1.7	4.3		115	161	1.0	80.1
Berkeley, CA	103	103	18.8	0.6	14.8	8.4		101	198	-1.6	10.5
Birmingham, AL	284	266	63.3	0.1	0.6	(Z)		265	63	-0.4	148.5
Boise City, ID	102	126	0.6	0.6	1.6	2.7		136	141	7.8	46.1
Boston, MA	563	574	25.6	0.3	5.3	10.8		552	20	-3.9	48.4
Bridgeport, CT	143	142	26.6	0.3	2.3	26.5		137	138	-3.3	16.0
Brownsville, TX	85	99	0.2	0.1	0.3	90.1		106	191	6.9	27.9
Buffalo, NY	358	328	30.7	0.8	1.0	4.9		323	50	-1.5	40.6
Cedar Rapids, IA	110	109	2.9	0.2	1.0	1.1		112	173	2.7	53.5
Chandler, AZ	30	91	2.6	1.2	2.4	17.3		100	200	10.6	47.6
Charlotte, NC	315	396	31.8	0.4	1.8	1.4		416	34	5.1	174.3
Chattanooga, TN	170	152	33.7	0.2	1.0	0.6		153	116	0.3	118.4
Chesapeake, VA	114	152	27.4	0.3	1.2	1.3		166	106	9.2	340.7
Chicago, IL	3,005	2,784	39.1	0.3	3.7	19.6		2,768	3	-0.5	227.2
Chula Vista, CA	84	135	4.6	0.6	8.9	37.3		145	123	7.1	29.0
Cincinnati, OH	385	364	37.9	0.2	1.1	0.7		364	46	0.1	77.2
Cleveland, OH	574	506	46.6	0.3	1.0	4.6		503	23	-0.6	77.0
Colorado Springs, CO	215	281	7.0	0.8	2.4	9.1		296	53	5.2	183.2
Columbus, GA [2]	169	179	38.1	0.3	1.4	3.0		186	92	4.0	216.1
Columbus, OH	565	633	22.6	0.2	2.4	1.1		643	16	1.6	190.9
Concord, CA	104	111	2.4	0.7	8.7	11.5		113	171	1.2	29.5
Corpus Christi, TX	232	257	4.8	0.4	0.9	50.4		266	62	3.5	135.0
Dallas, TX	905	1,007	29.5	0.5	2.2	20.9		1,022	7	1.6	342.4
Dayton, OH	194	182	40.4	0.2	0.6	0.7		183	95	0.6	55.0
Denver, CO	493	468	12.8	1.2	2.4	23.0		484	27	3.5	153.3
Des Moines, IA	191	193	7.1	0.4	2.4	2.4		195	82	0.7	75.3
Detroit, MI	1,203	1,028	75.7	0.4	0.8	2.8		1,012	9	-1.5	138.7
Durham, NC	101	137	45.7	0.2	2.0	1.2		141	128	3.2	69.3
Elizabeth, NJ	106	110	19.8	0.3	2.7	39.1		108	180	-1.9	12.3
El Monte, CA	79	106	1.0	0.6	11.8	72.5		107	184	0.7	9.5
El Paso, TX	425	515	3.4	0.4	1.2	69.0		544	21	5.5	245.4
Erie, PA	119	109	12.0	0.2	0.5	2.4		109	177	0.5	22.0
Escondido, CA	64	109	1.5	0.8	3.7	23.4		113	168	4.2	35.6
Eugene, OR	106	113	1.3	0.9	3.5	2.7		116	160	2.9	38.0
Evansville, IN	130	126	9.5	0.2	0.6	0.6		128	154	1.0	40.7
Flint, MI	160	141	47.9	0.7	0.5	2.9		139	133	-1.0	33.8
Fort Lauderdale, FL	153	149	28.1	0.2	0.9	7.2		149	117	-0.6	31.4
Fort Wayne, IN	172	173	16.7	0.3	1.0	2.7		174	101	0.4	62.7
Fort Worth, TX	385	448	22.0	0.4	2.0	19.5		454	28	1.5	281.1
Fremont, CA	132	173	3.8	0.7	19.4	13.3		179	96	3.4	77.0
Fresno, CA	217	354	8.3	1.1	12.5	29.9		376	40	6.2	99.1
Fullerton, CA	102	114	2.2	0.5	12.2	21.3		115	162	1.2	22.1
Garden Grove, CA	123	143	1.5	0.6	20.5	23.5		146	119	2.0	17.9
Garland, TX	139	181	8.9	0.5	4.5	11.6		191	86	5.8	57.3
Gary, IN	152	117	80.6	0.2	0.2	5.7		117	158	(Z)	50.2
Glendale, AZ	97	148	3.0	0.9	2.1	15.5		156	113	5.4	52.2
Glendale, CA	139	180	1.3	0.3	14.1	21.0		178	97	-1.3	30.6
Grand Prairie, TX	71	100	9.7	0.8	3.0	20.5		104	193	4.9	68.5
Grand Rapids, MI	182	189	18.5	0.8	1.1	5.0		191	85	1.1	44.3
Green Bay, WI	88	96	0.5	2.5	2.3	1.1		100	199	4.1	43.8
Greensboro, NC	156	184	33.9	0.5	1.4	1.0		190	87	3.5	79.8

See footnotes at end of table.

No. 46. Cities With 100,000 or More Inhabitants in 1992—Population, 1980 to 1992, and Land Area, 1990—Continued

[See headnote, p. 44]

CITY	1980, total (1,000)	POPULATION								Land area, 1990 (square miles)
		1990					1992			
		Total (1,000)	Percent—				Total (1,000)	Rank	Per-cent change, 1990-92	
			Black	American Indian, Eskimo, Aleut	Asian, Pacific Islander	His-panic [1]				
Hampton, VA	123	134	38.9	0.3	1.7	2.0	137	136	2.4	51.8
Hartford, CT	136	140	38.9	0.3	1.4	31.6	132	144	−5.5	17.3
Hayward, CA	94	111	9.8	1.0	15.5	23.9	115	163	3.3	43.5
Hialeah, FL	145	188	1.9	0.1	0.5	87.6	192	84	2.0	19.2
Hollywood, FL [3]	121	122	8.5	0.2	1.3	11.9	122	151	(Z)	27.3
Honolulu, HI [3]	365	377	1.3	0.3	70.5	4.6	371	43	1.7	85.7
Houston, TX	1,595	1,631	28.1	0.3	4.1	27.6	1,690	4	3.7	539.9
Huntington Beach, CA	171	182	0.9	0.6	8.3	11.2	185	93	1.9	26.4
Huntsville, AL	143	160	24.4	0.5	2.1	1.2	163	109	2.2	164.4
Independence, MO	112	112	1.4	0.6	1.0	2.0	113	170	0.4	78.2
Indianapolis, IN [2]	701	731	22.6	0.2	0.9	1.1	747	12	2.1	361.7
Inglewood, CA	94	110	51.9	0.4	2.5	38.5	111	174	1.7	9.2
Irvine, CA	62	110	1.8	0.2	18.1	6.3	119	153	8.2	42.3
Irving, TX	110	155	7.5	0.6	4.6	16.3	161	111	4.0	67.6
Jackson, MS	203	197	55.7	0.1	0.5	0.4	196	80	−0.2	109.0
Jacksonville, FL [2]	541	635	25.2	0.3	1.9	2.6	661	15	4.1	758.7
Jersey City, NJ	224	229	29.7	0.3	11.4	24.2	229	71	(Z)	14.9
Kansas City, KS	161	150	29.3	0.7	1.2	7.1	147	118	−2.2	107.8
Kansas City, MO	448	435	29.6	0.5	1.2	3.9	432	32	−0.8	311.5
Knoxville, TN	175	165	15.8	0.2	1.0	0.7	167	105	1.3	77.2
Lakewood, CO	114	126	1.0	0.7	1.9	9.1	126	148	−0.4	40.8
Lancaster, CA	48	97	7.4	0.9	3.7	15.2	106	188	9.1	88.8
Lansing, MI	130	127	18.6	1.0	1.8	7.9	127	147	−0.5	33.9
Laredo, TX	91	123	0.1	0.2	0.4	93.9	137	139	11.1	32.9
Las Vegas, NV	165	258	11.4	0.9	3.6	12.5	296	54	14.4	83.3
Lexington-Fayette, KY	204	225	13.4	0.2	1.6	1.1	233	70	3.2	284.5
Lincoln, NE	172	192	2.4	0.6	1.7	2.0	197	78	2.9	63.3
Little Rock, AR	159	176	34.0	0.3	0.9	0.8	177	99	0.6	102.9
Livonia, MI	105	101	0.3	0.2	1.3	1.3	101	197	0.5	35.7
Long Beach, CA	361	429	13.7	0.6	13.6	23.6	439	31	2.2	50.0
Los Angeles, CA	2,969	3,485	14.0	0.5	9.8	39.9	3,490	2	0.1	469.3
Louisville, KY	299	269	29.7	0.2	0.7	0.7	271	59	0.7	62.1
Lubbock, TX	174	186	8.6	0.3	1.4	22.5	188	89	0.9	104.1
Macon, GA	117	107	52.2	0.1	0.4	0.6	107	183	0.6	47.9
Madison, WI	171	191	4.2	0.4	3.9	2.0	195	81	2.0	57.8
Memphis, TN	646	610	54.8	0.2	0.8	0.7	610	18	(-Z)	256.0
Mesa, AZ	152	288	1.9	1.0	1.5	10.9	297	52	3.0	108.6
Mesquite, TX	67	101	5.8	0.5	2.6	8.8	108	178	6.7	42.8
Miami, FL	347	359	27.4	0.2	0.6	62.5	367	44	2.4	35.6
Milwaukee, WI	636	628	30.5	0.9	1.9	6.3	617	17	−1.8	96.1
Minneapolis, MN	371	368	13.0	3.3	4.3	2.1	363	47	−1.5	54.9
Mobile, AL	200	196	38.9	0.2	1.0	1.0	202	77	2.9	118.0
Modesto, CA	107	165	2.7	1.0	7.9	16.3	172	103	4.6	30.2
Montgomery, AL	178	187	42.3	0.2	0.7	0.8	192	83	2.7	135.0
Moreno Valley, CA [2]	([4])	119	13.8	0.7	6.6	22.9	132	143	11.2	49.1
Nashville-Davidson, TN [2]	456	488	24.3	0.2	1.4	0.9	495	24	1.4	473.3
Newark, NJ	329	275	58.5	0.2	1.2	26.1	268	61	−2.7	23.8
New Haven, CT	126	130	36.1	0.3	2.4	13.2	124	150	−5.0	18.9
New Orleans, LA	558	497	61.9	0.2	1.9	3.5	490	26	−1.5	180.6
Newport News, VA	145	170	33.6	0.3	2.3	2.8	177	98	4.3	68.3
New York, NY	7,072	7,323	28.7	0.4	7.0	24.4	7,312	1	−0.1	308.9
Bronx Borough	1,169	1,204	37.3	0.5	3.0	43.5	1,195	(X)	−0.8	42.0
Brooklyn Borough	2,231	2,301	37.9	0.3	4.8	20.1	2,286	(X)	−0.6	70.5
Manhattan Borough	1,428	1,488	22.0	0.4	7.4	26.0	1,489	(X)	0.1	28.4
Queens Borough	1,891	1,952	21.7	0.4	12.2	19.5	1,951	(X)	(-Z)	109.4
Staten Island Borough	352	379	8.1	0.2	4.5	8.0	391	(X)	3.2	58.6
Norfolk, VA	267	261	39.1	0.4	2.6	2.9	254	64	−2.9	53.8
Oakland, CA	339	372	43.9	0.6	14.8	13.9	373	42	0.3	56.1
Oceanside, CA	77	128	7.9	0.7	6.1	22.6	140	131	8.8	40.7
Oklahoma City, OK	404	445	16.0	4.2	2.4	5.0	454	29	2.1	608.2
Omaha, NE	314	336	13.1	0.7	1.0	3.1	340	48	1.2	100.6
Ontario, CA	89	133	7.3	0.7	3.9	41.7	139	134	4.4	36.7
Orange, CA	91	111	1.4	0.5	7.9	22.8	114	167	2.7	23.3
Orlando, FL	128	165	26.9	0.3	1.6	8.7	174	100	5.8	67.3
Overland Park, KS	82	112	1.8	0.3	1.9	2.0	119	154	6.7	55.7
Oxnard, CA	108	142	5.2	0.8	8.6	54.4	145	121	1.8	24.4
Pasadena, CA	118	132	19.0	0.4	8.1	27.3	133	142	0.8	23.0
Pasadena, TX	113	119	1.0	0.5	1.6	28.8	125	149	5.1	43.8
Paterson, NJ	138	141	36.0	0.3	1.4	41.0	139	132	−1.1	8.4
Peoria, IL	124	114	20.9	0.2	1.7	1.6	114	165	0.4	40.9
Philadelphia, PA	1,688	1,586	39.9	0.2	2.7	5.6	1,553	5	−2.1	135.1
Phoenix, AZ	790	983	5.2	1.9	1.7	20.0	1,012	8	2.9	419.9
Pittsburgh, PA	424	370	25.8	0.2	1.6	0.9	367	45	−0.8	55.6

See footnotes at end of table.

No. 46. Cities With 100,000 or More Inhabitants in 1992—Population, 1980 to 1992, and Land Area, 1990—Continued

[See headnote, p. 44]

CITY	1980, total (1,000)	POPULATION 1990 Total (1,000)	1990 Percent— Black	American Indian, Eskimo, Aleut	Asian, Pacific Islander	His-panic [1]	1992 Total (1,000)	1992 Rank	1992 Per-cent change, 1990-92	Land area, 1990 (square miles)
Plano, TX	72	129	4.1	0.3	4.0	6.2	142	126	10.4	66.2
Pomona, CA	93	132	14.4	0.6	6.7	51.3	140	129	6.6	22.8
Portland, OR	368	437	7.7	1.2	5.3	3.2	445	30	1.9	124.7
Portsmouth, VA	105	104	47.3	0.3	0.8	1.3	104	194	0.4	33.1
Providence, RI	157	161	14.8	0.9	5.9	15.5	155	114	-3.3	18.5
Raleigh, NC	150	208	27.6	0.3	2.5	1.4	221	74	6.0	88.1
Rancho Cucamonga, CA	55	101	5.9	0.6	5.4	20.0	111	175	9.6	37.8
Reno, NV	101	134	2.9	1.4	4.9	11.1	140	130	4.5	57.5
Richmond, VA	219	203	55.2	0.2	0.9	0.9	202	76	-0.4	60.1
Riverside, CA	171	227	7.4	0.8	5.2	26.0	239	67	5.3	77.7
Rochester, NY	242	232	31.5	0.5	1.8	8.7	234	69	1.1	35.8
Rockford, IL	140	139	15.0	0.3	1.5	4.2	142	127	1.6	45.0
Sacramento, CA	276	369	15.3	1.2	15.0	16.2	383	39	3.6	96.3
St. Louis, MO	453	397	47.5	0.2	0.9	1.3	384	38	-3.3	61.9
St. Paul, MN	270	272	7.4	1.4	7.1	4.2	268	60	-1.5	52.8
St. Petersburg, FL	239	239	19.6	0.2	1.7	2.6	235	68	-1.4	59.2
Salem, OR	89	108	1.5	1.6	2.4	6.1	112	172	4.0	41.5
Salinas, CA	80	109	3.0	0.9	8.1	50.6	115	164	5.5	18.6
Salt Lake City, UT	163	160	1.7	1.6	4.7	9.7	166	107	3.7	109.0
San Antonio, TX	786	936	7.0	0.4	1.1	55.6	966	10	3.3	333.0
San Bernardino, CA	119	164	16.0	1.0	4.0	34.6	172	102	5.0	55.1
San Diego, CA	876	1,111	9.4	0.6	11.8	20.7	1,149	6	3.4	324.0
San Francisco, CA	679	724	10.9	0.5	29.1	13.9	729	13	0.7	46.7
San Jose, CA	629	782	4.7	0.7	19.5	26.6	801	11	2.4	171.3
Santa Ana, CA	204	294	2.6	0.5	9.7	65.2	288	55	-1.9	27.1
Santa Clarita, CA	([4])	111	1.5	0.6	4.2	13.4	119	155	7.3	40.5
Santa Rosa, CA	83	113	1.8	1.2	3.4	9.5	117	159	2.9	33.7
Savannah, GA	142	138	51.3	0.2	1.1	1.4	139	135	1.0	62.6
Scottsdale, AZ	89	130	0.8	0.6	1.2	4.8	137	137	5.3	184.4
Seattle, WA	494	516	10.1	1.4	11.8	3.6	520	22	0.6	83.9
Shreveport, LA	206	199	44.8	0.2	0.5	1.1	197	79	-0.9	98.6
Simi Valley, CA	78	100	1.5	0.6	5.5	12.7	104	196	3.6	33.0
Sioux Falls, SD	81	101	0.7	1.6	0.7	0.6	106	192	4.8	45.1
South Bend, IN	110	106	20.9	0.4	0.9	3.4	106	189	0.4	36.4
Spokane, WA	171	177	1.9	2.0	2.1	2.1	187	90	5.8	55.9
Springfield, IL	100	105	13.0	0.2	1.0	0.8	106	187	1.1	42.5
Springfield, MA	152	157	19.2	0.2	1.0	16.9	153	115	-2.2	32.1
Springfield, MO	133	140	2.5	0.7	0.9	1.0	145	120	3.5	68.0
Stamford, CT	102	108	17.8	0.1	2.6	9.8	108	181	-0.4	37.7
Sterling Heights, MI	109	118	0.4	0.2	2.9	1.1	118	157	0.4	36.6
Stockton, CA	150	211	9.6	1.0	22.8	25.0	220	75	4.1	52.6
Sunnyvale, CA	107	117	3.4	0.5	19.3	13.2	118	156	1.0	21.9
Syracuse, NY	170	164	20.3	1.3	2.2	2.9	163	110	-0.6	25.1
Tacoma, WA	159	177	11.4	2.0	6.9	3.8	184	94	4.1	48.0
Tallahassee, FL	82	125	29.1	0.2	1.8	3.0	130	145	4.5	63.3
Tampa, FL	272	280	25.0	0.3	1.4	15.0	285	56	1.7	108.7
Tempe, AZ	107	142	3.2	1.3	4.1	10.9	142	125	0.2	39.5
Thousand Oaks, CA	77	104	1.2	0.4	4.8	9.6	108	182	3.0	49.6
Toledo, OH	355	333	19.7	0.3	1.0	4.0	329	49	-1.1	80.6
Topeka, KS	119	120	10.6	1.3	0.8	5.8	120	152	0.3	55.2
Torrance, CA	130	133	1.5	0.4	21.9	10.1	136	140	1.9	20.5
Tucson, AZ	331	405	4.3	1.6	2.2	29.3	415	35	2.4	156.3
Tulsa, OK	361	367	13.6	4.7	1.4	2.6	375	41	2.2	183.5
Vallejo, CA	80	109	21.2	0.7	23.0	10.8	114	166	4.1	30.2
Virginia Beach, VA	262	393	13.9	0.4	4.3	3.1	417	33	6.1	248.3
Waco, TX	101	104	23.1	0.3	0.9	16.3	104	195	0.4	75.8
Warren, MI	161	145	0.7	0.5	1.3	1.1	142	124	-1.7	34.3
Washington, DC	638	607	65.8	0.2	1.8	5.4	585	19	-3.6	61.4
Waterbury, CT	103	109	13.0	0.3	0.7	13.4	107	185	-1.9	28.6
Wichita, KS	280	304	11.3	1.2	2.6	5.0	312	51	2.5	115.1
Winston-Salem, NC	132	143	39.3	0.2	0.8	0.9	145	122	0.9	71.1
Worcester, MA	162	170	4.5	0.3	2.8	9.6	163	108	-3.7	37.6
Yonkers, NY	195	188	14.1	0.2	3.0	16.7	186	91	-1.1	18.1

X Not applicable.   Z Less than .05 percent.   [1] Hispanic persons may be of any race.   [2] Represents the portion of a consolidated city that is not within one or more separately incorporated places.   [3] The population shown in this table is for the census designated place (CDP); the 1990 census population for the City and County of Honolulu is 836,231.   [4] Not incorporated.

Source: U.S. Bureau of the Census, *1980 Census of Population*, vol. 1, chapters A and B; *1990 Census of Population and Housing, Population and Housing Unit Counts*, (CPH-2); and press release CB94-15.

No. 47. Population 65 Years Old and Over, by Age Group and Sex, 1980 to 1994, and Projections, 2000

[As of **April**, except **1994** and **2000**, as of **July**. Projection based on middle series, see table 3]

AGE GROUP AND SEX	NUMBER (1,000)				PERCENT DISTRIBUTION			
	1980	1990[1]	1994	2000, proj.	1980	1990[1]	1994	2000, proj.
Persons 65 yrs. and over	**25,549**	**31,080**	**33,158**	**35,322**	**100.0**	**100.0**	**100.0**	**100.0**
65 to 69 years old	8,782	10,066	9,970	9,594	34.3	32.4	30.1	27.2
70 to 74 years old	6,798	7,980	8,741	8,957	26.6	25.7	26.4	25.4
75 to 79 years old	4,794	6,103	6,574	7,507	18.8	19.6	19.8	21.3
80 to 84 years old	2,935	3,909	4,351	4,931	11.5	12.6	13.1	14.0
85 years old and over	2,240	3,022	3,522	4,333	8.8	9.7	10.6	12.3
Males, 65 yrs. and over.........	10,305	12,493	13,475	14,603	100.0	100.0	100.0	100.0
65 to 69 years old..............	3,903	4,508	4,500	4,420	37.8	36.1	33.4	30.3
70 to 74 years old..............	2,854	3,399	3,790	3,965	27.7	27.2	28.1	27.2
75 to 79 years old..............	1,848	2,389	2,655	3,138	18.0	19.1	19.7	21.5
80 to 84 years old..............	1,019	1,356	1,550	1,842	9.9	10.9	11.5	12.6
85 years old and over	682	841	980	1,238	6.6	6.7	7.3	8.5
Females, 65 yrs. and over........	15,245	18,587	19,683	20,719	100.0	100.0	100.0	100.0
65 to 69 years old..............	4,880	5,558	5,471	5,173	31.9	29.9	27.8	25.0
70 to 74 years old..............	3,945	4,580	4,951	4,993	25.9	24.6	25.2	24.1
75 to 79 years old..............	2,946	3,714	3,919	4,369	19.3	20.0	19.9	21.1
80 to 84 years old..............	1,916	2,553	2,801	3,089	12.6	13.7	14.2	14.9
85 years old and over	1,559	2,180	2,542	3,095	10.3	11.7	12.9	14.9

[1] The April 1, 1990, census count (248,718,291) includes count resolution corrections processed through March 1994, and does not include adjustments for census coverage errors.

Source: U.S. Bureau of the Census, *Current Population Reports*, P25-1095 and P25-1104; and Population Paper Listing 21.

No. 48. Persons 65 Years Old and Over—Characteristics, by Sex: 1980 to 1994

[As of **March, except as noted.** Covers civilian noninstitutional population. See headnote, table 49]

CHARACTERISTIC	TOTAL				MALE				FEMALE			
	1980	1985	1990	1994	1980	1985	1990	1994	1980	1985	1990	1994
Total [1] (million)	**24.2**	**26.8**	**29.6**	**30.8**	**9.9**	**11.0**	**12.3**	**12.7**	**14.2**	**15.8**	**17.2**	**18.0**
White (million)	21.9	24.2	26.5	27.6	9.0	9.9	11.0	11.5	12.9	14.3	15.4	16.1
Black (million)	2.0	2.2	2.5	2.5	0.8	0.9	1.0	1.0	1.2	1.3	1.5	1.5
Percent below poverty level [2]	15.2	12.4	11.4	12.2	11.1	8.7	7.8	7.9	17.9	15.0	13.9	15.2
PERCENT DISTRIBUTION												
Marital status:												
Single..................	5.5	5.2	4.6	4.5	4.9	5.3	4.2	4.7	5.9	5.1	4.9	4.3
Married.................	55.4	55.2	56.1	57.0	78.0	77.2	76.5	77.2	39.5	39.9	41.4	42.8
Spouse present...........	53.6	53.4	54.1	55.1	76.1	75.0	74.2	75.1	37.9	38.3	39.7	41.0
Spouse absent	1.8	1.8	2.0	1.9	1.9	2.2	2.3	2.1	1.7	1.6	1.7	1.8
Widowed................	35.7	35.6	34.2	32.9	13.5	13.8	14.2	13.1	51.2	50.7	48.6	46.9
Divorced................	3.5	4.0	5.0	5.6	3.6	3.7	5.0	5.0	3.4	4.3	5.1	6.0
Family status:												
In families [3]	67.6	67.3	66.7	67.5	83.0	82.4	81.9	81.3	56.8	56.7	55.8	57.8
Nonfamily householders.........	31.2	31.1	31.9	31.2	15.7	15.4	16.6	17.1	42.0	42.1	42.8	41.1
Secondary individuals	1.2	1.6	1.4	1.3	1.3	2.2	1.5	1.6	1.1	1.1	1.4	1.1
Living arrangements:												
Living in household	99.8	99.6	99.7	99.9	99.9	99.5	99.9	99.9	99.7	99.6	99.5	99.8
Living alone	30.3	30.2	31.0	30.2	14.9	14.7	15.7	16.0	41.0	41.1	42.0	40.2
Spouse present...........	53.6	53.4	54.1	55.1	76.1	75.0	74.3	75.1	37.9	38.3	39.7	41.0
Living with someone else	15.9	15.9	14.6	14.6	8.9	9.8	9.9	8.8	20.8	20.2	17.8	18.6
Not in household [4]	0.2	0.4	0.3	0.1	0.1	0.5	0.1	0.1	0.3	0.4	0.5	0.2
Years of school completed:												
8 years or less	43.1	35.4	28.5	[5]22.3	45.3	37.2	30.0	[5]23.3	41.6	34.1	27.5	[5]21.5
1 to 3 years of high school	16.2	16.5	16.1	[5]15.4	15.5	15.7	15.7	[5]14.4	16.7	17.0	16.4	[5]16.0
4 years of high school	24.0	29.0	32.9	[6]34.1	21.4	26.4	29.0	[6]29.3	25.8	30.7	35.6	[6]37.6
1 to 3 years of college	8.2	9.8	10.9	[7]15.8	7.5	9.1	10.8	[7]16.4	8.6	10.3	11.0	[7]15.3
4 years or more of college	8.6	9.4	11.6	[8]12.5	10.3	11.5	14.5	[8]16.7	7.4	8.0	9.5	[8]9.5
Labor force participation: [9]												
Employed	12.2	10.4	11.5	11.9	18.4	15.3	15.9	16.2	7.8	7.0	8.4	8.8
Unemployed	0.4	0.3	0.4	0.5	0.6	0.5	0.5	0.7	0.3	0.2	0.3	0.4
Not in labor force	87.5	89.2	88.1	87.6	81.0	84.2	83.6	83.1	91.9	92.7	91.3	90.8

[1] Includes other races, not shown separately. [2] Poverty status based on income in preceding year. [3] Excludes those living in unrelated subfamilies. [4] In group quarters other than institutions. [5] Represents those who completed ninth to twelfth grade, but have no high school diploma. [6] High school graduate. [7] Some college or associate degree. [8] Bachelor's or advanced degree. [9] Annual averages of monthly figures. Source: U.S. Bureau of Labor Statistics, *Employment and Earnings*, January issues. Data beginning 1994 not directly comparable with earlier years. See text, section 13, and February 1994 issue of *Employment and Earnings*.

Source: Except as noted, U.S. Bureau of the Census, *Current Population Reports*, P20-450, and earlier reports; P60-188; and unpublished data.

No. 49. Social and Economic Characteristics of the White and Black Populations: 1980 to 1994

[As of **March, except labor force status, annual average**. Excludes members of Armed Forces except those living off post or with their families on post. Data for 1980 and 1990 are based on 1980 census population controls; 1994 data based on 1990 census population controls. Based on Current Population Survey; see text, section 1, and Appendix III]

CHARACTERISTIC	NUMBER (1,000)						PERCENT DISTRIBUTION			
	White			Black			White		Black	
	1980	1990	1994	1980	1990	1994	1980	1994	1980	1994
Total persons	**191,905**	**206,983**	**215,221**	**26,033**	**30,392**	**33,040**	**100.0**	**100.0**	**100.0**	**100.0**
Under 5 years old	13,307	15,161	16,055	2,444	2,932	3,357	6.9	7.5	9.4	10.2
5 to 14 years old	28,828	28,405	30,391	5,190	5,546	6,183	15.0	14.1	19.9	18.7
15 to 44 years old	88,570	96,656	97,917	12,247	14,660	15,907	46.2	45.5	47.0	48.1
45 to 64 years old	39,302	40,282	43,278	4,112	4,766	5,082	20.5	20.1	15.8	15.4
65 years old and over	21,898	26,479	27,580	2,040	2,487	2,510	11.4	12.8	7.8	7.6
YEARS OF SCHOOL COMPLETED										
Persons 25 years old and over	**114,763**	**134,687**	**139,760**	**12,927**	**16,751**	**18,103**	**100.0**	**100.0**	**100.0**	**100.0**
Elementary: 0 to 8 years	18,739	14,131	11,796	3,559	2,701	1,860	16.3	8.4	27.5	10.3
High school: 1 to 3 years	15,064	14,080	[1]13,340	2,748	2,969	[1]3,048	13.1	[1]9.5	21.3	[1]16.8
4 years	43,149	52,449	[2]48,236	3,980	6,239	[2]6,549	37.6	[2]34.5	30.8	[2]36.2
College: 1 to 3 years	17,350	24,350	[3]34,331	1,618	2,952	[3]4,310	15.1	[3]24.6	12.5	[3]23.8
4 years or more	20,460	29,677	[4]32,057	1,024	1,890	[4]2,337	17.8	[4]22.9	7.9	[4]12.9
LABOR FORCE STATUS [5]										
Civilians 16 years old and over	**146,122**	**160,415**	**165,555**	**17,824**	**21,300**	**22,879**	**100.0**	**100.0**	**100.0**	**100.0**
Civilian labor force	93,600	107,177	111,082	10,865	13,493	14,502	64.1	67.1	61.0	63.4
Employed	87,715	102,087	105,190	9,313	11,966	12,835	60.0	63.5	52.2	56.1
Unemployed	5,884	5,091	5,892	1,553	1,527	1,666	4.0	3.6	8.7	7.3
Unemployment rate [6]	6.3	4.7	5.3	14.3	11.3	11.5	(X)	(X)	(X)	(X)
Not in labor force	52,523	53,237	54,473	6,959	7,808	8,377	35.9	32.9	39.0	36.6
FAMILY TYPE										
Total families	**52,243**	**56,590**	**57,870**	**6,184**	**7,470**	**7,989**	**100.0**	**100.0**	**100.0**	**100.0**
With own children [7]	26,474	26,718	27,624	3,820	4,378	4,794	50.7	47.7	61.8	60.0
Married couple	44,751	46,981	47,443	3,433	3,750	3,714	85.7	82.0	55.5	46.5
With own children [7]	22,415	21,579	21,874	1,927	1,972	1,925	42.9	37.8	31.2	24.1
Female householder, no spouse present	6,052	7,306	8,130	2,495	3,275	3,825	11.6	14.0	40.3	47.9
With own children [7]	3,558	4,199	4,742	1,793	2,232	2,630	6.8	8.2	29.0	32.9
Male householder, no spouse present	1,441	2,303	2,297	256	446	450	2.8	4.0	4.1	5.6
With own children [7]	500	939	1,008	99	173	238	1.0	1.7	1.6	3.0
FAMILY INCOME IN PREVIOUS YEAR IN CONSTANT (1993) DOLLARS										
Total families	**52,243**	**56,590**	**57,870**	**6,184**	**7,470**	**7,989**	**100.0**	**100.0**	**100.0**	**100.0**
Less than $5,000	908	1,188	1,432	405	665	856	1.7	2.5	6.5	10.7
$5,000 to $9,999	2,110	2,264	2,765	872	964	1,205	4.0	4.8	14.1	15.1
$10,000 to $14,999	3,097	3,339	3,818	787	896	911	5.9	6.6	12.7	11.4
$15,000 to $24,999	7,906	7,923	8,756	1,326	1,389	1,485	15.1	15.1	21.4	18.6
$25,000 to $34,999	7,963	8,262	8,719	871	1,031	1,093	15.2	15.1	14.1	13.7
$35,000 to $49,999	12,244	11,318	10,865	972	1,091	1,035	23.4	18.8	15.7	13.0
$50,000 or more	18,015	22,296	21,515	952	1,434	1,404	34.5	37.2	15.3	17.6
Median income (dol.) [8]	39,911	41,922	39,308	22,601	23,550	21,548	(X)	(X)	(X)	(X)
Families below poverty level [9]	3,581	4,409	5,452	1,722	2,077	2,499	6.9	9.4	27.8	31.3
Persons below poverty level [9]	17,214	20,785	26,226	8,050	9,302	10,877	9.0	12.2	31.0	33.1
HOUSING TENURE										
Total occupied units	**70,766**	**80,163**	**82,387**	**8,586**	**10,486**	**11,281**	**100.0**	**100.0**	**100.0**	**100.0**
Owner-occupied	49,913	54,094	55,879	4,173	4,445	4,791	70.5	67.8	48.6	42.5
Renter-occupied	19,581	24,685	24,955	4,257	5,862	6,268	27.7	30.3	49.6	55.6
No cash rent	1,272	1,384	1,553	156	178	222	1.8	1.9	1.8	2.0

X Not applicable.　[1] Represents those who completed ninth to twelfth grade, but have no high school diploma.　[2] High school graduate.　[3] Some college or associate degree.　[4] Bachelor's or advanced degree.　[5] Source: U.S. Bureau of Labor Statistics, *Employment and Earnings*, January issues. Data beginning 1994 not directly comparable with earlier years. See text, section 13, and February 1994 issue of *Employment and Earnings*.　[6] Total unemployment as percent of civilian labor force.　[7] Children under 18 years old.　[8] For definition of median, see Guide to Tabular Presentation.　[9] For explanation of poverty level, see text, section 14.

Source: Except as noted, U.S. Bureau of the Census, *Current Population Reports*, P20-480, and earlier reports; P60-188; and unpublished data.

No. 50. Social and Economic Characteristics of the Asian and Pacific Islander Population: 1990 and 1994

[As of **March**. Excludes members of Armed Forces except those living off post or with their families on post. Data for 1990 are based on 1980 census population controls; 1994 data are based on 1990 census population controls. Based on Current Population Survey; see text, section 1, and Appendix III]

CHARACTERISTIC	NUMBER (1,000)		PERCENT DISTRIBUTION	
	1990	1994	1990	1994
Total persons	**6,679**	**7,444**	**100.0**	**100.0**
Under 5 years old	602	584	9.0	7.8
5 to 14 years old	1,112	1,165	16.6	15.7
15 to 44 years old	3,345	3,838	50.1	51.6
45 to 64 years old	1,155	1,355	17.3	18.2
65 years old and over	465	503	7.0	6.8
YEARS OF SCHOOL COMPLETED				
Persons 25 years old and over	**3,961**	**4,545**	**100.0**	**100.0**
Elementary: 0 to 8 years	543	444	13.7	9.8
High school: 1 to 3 years	234	[1]248	5.9	[1]5.5
4 years	1,038	[2]1,115	26.2	[2]24.5
College: 1 to 3 years	568	[3]866	14.3	[3]19.1
4 years or more	1,578	[4]1,872	39.9	[4]41.2
LABOR FORCE STATUS [5]				
Civilians 16 years old and over	**4,849**	**5,562**	**100.0**	**100.0**
Civilian labor force	3,216	3,540	66.3	63.7
Employed	3,079	3,310	63.5	59.5
Unemployed	136	230	2.8	4.1
Unemployment rate [6]	4.2	6.5	(X)	(X)
Not in labor force	1,634	2,022	33.7	36.3
FAMILY TYPE				
Total families	**1,531**	**1,737**	**100.0**	**100.0**
Married couple	1,256	1,426	82.1	82.1
Female householder, no spouse present	188	232	12.3	13.4
Male householder, no spouse present	86	79	5.6	4.6
FAMILY INCOME IN PREVIOUS YEAR IN CONSTANT (1993) DOLLARS				
Total families	**1,531**	**1,737**	**100.0**	**100.0**
Less than $5,000	(NA)	72	(NA)	4.2
$5,000 to $9,999	(NA)	107	(NA)	6.1
$10,000 to $14,999	(NA)	114	(NA)	6.6
$15,000 to $24,999	(NA)	220	(NA)	12.7
$25,000 to $34,999	(NA)	195	(NA)	11.3
$35,000 to $49,999	(NA)	243	(NA)	14.0
$50,000 or more	(NA)	784	(NA)	45.2
Median income [7]	47,021	44,456	(X)	(X)
Families below poverty level [8]	182	235	11.9	13.5
Persons below poverty level [8]	939	1,134	14.1	15.3
HOUSING TENURE				
Total occupied units	**1,988**	**2,233**	**100.0**	**100.0**
Owner-occupied	977	1,154	49.1	51.7
Renter-occupied	982	1,055	49.4	47.2
No cash rent	30	25	1.5	1.1

NA Not available. X Not applicable. [1] Represents those who completed ninth to twelfth grade, but have no high school diploma. [2] High school graduate. [3] Some college or associate degree. [4] Bachelor's or advanced degree. [5] Data beginning 1994 not directly comparable with earlier years. See text, section 14. [6] Total unemployment as percent of civilian labor force. [7] For definition of median, see Guide to Tabular Presentation. [8] For explanation of poverty level, see text, section 14.

Source: U.S. Bureau of the Census, *Current Population Reports*, P20-459; and unpublished data.

No. 51. Population Living on Selected Reservations and Trust Lands and American Indian Tribes With 10,000 or More American Indians: 1990

[As of April]

RESERVATION AND TRUST LANDS WITH 5,000 OR MORE AMERICAN INDIANS, ESKIMOS, AND ALEUTS	Total popula-tion	AMERICAN INDIANS, ESKIMOS, ALEUTS		AMERICAN INDIAN TRIBE	Number	Percent distri-bution
		Number	Percent of total			
All reservation and trust lands	**808,163**	**437,431**	**54.1**	**American Indian population, total** [2]	**1,878,285**	**100.0**
Navajo and Trust Lands,				Cherokee	308,132	16.4
AZ-NM-UT.	148,451	143,405	96.6	Navajo	219,198	11.7
Pine Ridge and Trust Lands,				Chippewa	103,826	5.5
NE-SD	12,215	11,182	91.5	Sioux [3]	103,255	5.5
Fort Apache, AZ.	10,394	9,825	94.5	Choctaw.	82,299	4.4
Gila River, AZ	9,540	9,116	95.6	Pueblo	52,939	2.8
Papago, AZ.	8,730	8,480	97.1	Apache	50,051	2.7
Rosebud and Trust Lands,				Iroquois [4]	49,038	2.6
SD.	9,696	8,043	83.0	Lumbee	48,444	2.6
San Carlos, AZ	7,294	7,110	97.5	Creek.	43,550	2.3
Zuni Pueblo, AZ-NM	7,412	7,073	95.4	Blackfoot	32,234	1.7
Hopi and Trust Lands, AZ . . .	7,360	7,061	95.9	Canadian and Latin American. .	22,379	1.2
Blackfeet, MT.	8,549	7,025	82.2	Chickasaw	20,631	1.1
Turtle Mountain and				Potawatomi [4]	16,763	0.9
Trust Lands, ND-SD	7,106	6,772	95.3	Tohono O'Odham	16,041	0.9
Yakima and Trust Lands, WA .	27,668	6,307	22.8	Pima	14,431	0.8
				Tlingit.	13,925	0.7
Osage, OK [1]	41,645	6,161	14.8	Seminole	13,797	0.7
Fort Peck, MT	10,595	5,782	54.6	Alaskan Athabaskans	13,738	0.7
Wind River, WY	21,851	5,676	26.0	Cheyenne.	11,456	0.6
Eastern Cherokee, NC	6,527	5,388	82.5	Comanche	11,322	0.6
Flathead, MT.	21,259	5,130	24.1	Paiute	11,142	0.6
Cheyenne River, SD	7,743	5,100	65.9	Puget Sound Salish	10,246	0.5

[1] The Osage Reservation is coextensive with Osage County. Data shown for the reservation are for the entire reservation.　[2] Includes other American Indian tribes, not shown separately.　[3] Any entry with the spelling "Siouan" was miscoded to Sioux in North Carolina.　[4] Reporting and/or processing problems have affected the data for this tribe.
Source: U.S. Bureau of the Census, *1990 Census of Population, General Population Characteristics, American Indian and Alaska Native Areas* (CP-1-1A); and press release CB92-244.

No. 52. Social and Economic Characteristics of the American Indian Population: 1990

[**As of April**. Based on a sample and subject to sampling variability]

CHARACTERISTIC	American Indian, total [1]	Chero-kee	Navajo	Sioux [2]	Chip-pewa	Choctaw	Pueblo	Apache	Iro-quois [3]	Lumbee
Total persons	**1,937,391**	**369,035**	**225,298**	**107,321**	**105,988**	**86,231**	**55,330**	**53,330**	**52,557**	**50,888**
Percent under 5 years old	9.7	6.3	13.6	12.3	10.3	8.2	10.3	10.2	8.1	8.3
Percent 18 years old and over .	65.8	73.3	57.7	60.0	64.0	68.8	64.2	64.7	71.1	66.2
Percent 65 years old and over .	5.9	7.2	4.6	4.4	4.7	8.0	5.8	3.4	6.7	5.6
EDUCATIONAL ATTAINMENT										
Persons 25 years old and over	1,040,955	229,231	100,594	51,014	54,804	49,128	28,597	27,717	30,882	27,343
Percent high school graduates or higher.	65.6	68.2	51.0	69.7	69.7	70.3	71.5	63.8	71.9	51.6
Percent bachelor's degree or higher	9.4	11.1	4.5	8.9	8.2	13.3	7.3	6.9	11.3	9.4
FAMILY TYPE										
Total families	449,281	98,610	44,845	22,669	25,077	21,856	11,825	12,314	12,988	12,650
Percent distribution:										
Married couple.	65.8	73.1	61.1	54.2	58.4	75.2	61.2	66.9	67.5	68.5
Female householder, no spouse present	26.2	20.8	28.6	36.0	33.1	20.0	29.2	24.7	25.5	23.9
Male householder, no spouse present	8.0	6.1	10.3	9.8	8.5	4.8	9.6	8.4	7.0	7.6
INCOME IN 1989										
Median family (dol.) [4]	21,619	24,907	13,940	16,525	20,249	24,467	19,845	19,690	27,025	23,934
Median household (dol.) [4]	19,900	21,922	12,817	15,611	18,801	21,640	19,097	18,484	23,460	21,708
Per capita (dol.).	8,284	10,469	4,788	6,508	7,777	9,463	6,679	7,271	10,568	8,625
Families below poverty level [5] .	122,237	19,100	21,204	8,939	7,814	4,347	3,691	3,913	2,249	2,554
Percent below poverty level .	27.2	19.4	47.3	39.4	31.2	19.9	31.2	31.8	17.3	20.2
Persons below poverty level [5] .	585,273	79,271	107,526	45,658	35,231	19,453	17,981	19,246	10,253	10,966
Percent below poverty level .	31.2	22.0	48.8	44.4	34.3	23.0	33.2	37.5	20.1	22.1

[1] Includes other American Indian tribes not shown separately.　[2] Any entry with the spelling "Siouan" was miscoded to Sioux in North Carolina.　[3] Reporting and/or processing problems have affected the data for this tribe.　[4] For definition of median, see Guide to Tabular Presentation.　[5] For explanation of poverty level, see text, section 14.
Source: U.S. Bureau of the Census, *1990 Census of Population, Characteristics of American Indians by Tribe and Language*, 1990 CP-3-7.

No. 53. Social and Economic Characteristics of the Hispanic Population: 1993

[As of March, except labor force status, annual average. Excludes members of the Armed Forces except those living off post or with their families on post. Based on Current Population Survey; see text, section 1, and Appendix III]

CHARACTERISTIC	NUMBER (1,000)						PERCENT DISTRIBUTION					
	His-panic, total	Mexi-can	Puer-to Rican	Cuban	Cen-tral and South Amer-ican	Other His-panic	His-panic, total	Mexi-can	Puer-to Rican	Cuban	Cen-tral and South Amer-ican	Other His-panic
Total persons........	22,752	14,628	2,402	1,071	3,052	1,598	100.0	100.0	100.0	100.0	100.0	100.0
Under 5 years old.........	2,523	1,787	251	49	304	133	11.1	12.2	10.4	4.6	10.0	8.3
5 to 14 years old	4,207	2,939	496	85	461	226	18.5	20.1	20.6	7.9	15.1	14.1
15 to 44 years old.........	11,529	7,447	1,162	429	1,732	759	50.7	50.9	48.4	40.1	56.7	47.5
45 to 64 years old.........	3,271	1,844	355	291	438	344	14.4	12.6	14.8	27.2	14.3	21.5
65 years old and over	1,222	612	138	218	119	135	5.4	4.2	5.7	20.3	3.9	8.4
EDUCATIONAL ATTAINMENT												
Persons 25 years old and over	12,100	7,198	1,280	818	1,776	1,029	100.0	100.0	100.0	100.0	100.0	100.0
High school graduate or higher...............	6,424	3,324	766	508	1,117	709	53.1	46.2	59.8	62.1	62.9	68.9
Bachelor's degree or higher ...	1,090	428	103	135	269	155	9.0	5.9	8.0	16.5	15.1	15.1
LABOR FORCE STATUS [1]												
Civilians 16 years old and over	15,753	9,693	1,676	927	(NA)	(NA)	100.0	100.0	100.0	100.0	(NA)	(NA)
Civilian labor force	10,377	6,499	950	554	(NA)	(NA)	65.9	67.0	56.7	59.8	(NA)	(NA)
Employed.............	9,272	5,805	828	511	(NA)	(NA)	58.9	59.9	49.4	55.1	(NA)	(NA)
Unemployed..........	1,104	693	122	43	(NA)	(NA)	7.0	7.1	7.3	4.6	(NA)	(NA)
Unemployment rate [2] ...	10.6	10.7	12.8	7.8	(NA)	(NA)	(X)	(X)	(X)	(X)	(NA)	(NA)
Not in labor force	5,377	3,194	725	373	(NA)	(NA)	34.1	33.0	43.3	40.2	(NA)	(NA)
FAMILY TYPE												
Total families	5,318	3,210	653	309	751	395	100.0	100.0	100.0	100.0	100.0	100.0
Married couple	3,674	2,320	349	235	510	261	69.1	72.3	53.4	76.1	67.9	66.0
Female householder, no spouse present........	1,238	622	264	56	186	110	23.3	19.4	40.5	18.2	24.7	27.7
Male householder, no spouse present........	407	269	40	18	56	25	7.7	8.4	6.2	5.7	7.4	6.3
FAMILY INCOME IN 1992												
Total families	5,318	3,210	653	309	751	395	100.0	100.0	100.0	100.0	100.0	100
Less than $5,000	320	178	60	14	45	23	6.0	5.5	9.2	4.5	6.0	5.8
$5,000 to $9,999	620	338	123	23	85	50	11.7	10.5	18.8	7.4	11.3	12.7
$10,000 to $14,999	671	423	70	29	116	32	12.6	13.2	10.7	9.4	15.4	8.1
$15,000 to $24,999	1,152	740	140	61	142	71	21.7	23.1	21.4	19.7	18.9	18.0
$25,000 to $34,999	865	550	89	47	124	53	16.3	17.1	13.6	15.2	16.5	13.4
$35,000 to $49,999	802	503	77	50	104	66	15.1	15.7	11.8	16.2	13.8	16.7
$50,000 or more..........	889	478	96	85	133	98	16.7	14.9	14.7	27.5	17.7	24.8
Median income (dol.) [3]......	23,912	23,714	20,301	31,015	23,649	28,562	(X)	(X)	(X)	(X)	(X)	(X)
Families below poverty level [4].	1,395	847	212	47	203	86	26.2	26.4	32.5	15.4	27.0	21.7
Persons below poverty level [4].	6,655	4,404	874	194	815	368	29.3	30.1	36.5	18.1	26.7	23.1
HOUSING TENURE												
Total occupied units ...	6,626	3,869	841	405	937	574	100.0	100.0	100.0	100.0	100.0	100.0
Owner-occupied	2,654	1,708	197	215	239	294	40.0	44.2	23.4	53.0	25.6	51.2
Renter-occupied [5].........	3,973	2,160	644	191	697	280	60.0	55.8	76.6	47.2	74.4	48.8

NA Not available.   X Not applicable.   [1] Source: U.S. Bureau of Labor Statistics, *Employment and Earnings*, January 1994.
[2] Total unemployment as percent of civilian labor force.   [3] For definition of median, see Guide to Tabular Presentation.   [4] For explanation of poverty level, see text, section 14.   [5] Includes no cash rent.

Source: Except as noted, U.S. Bureau of the Census, *Current Population Reports*, P20-475.

No. 54. Native and Foreign-Born Population, by Place of Birth: 1920 to 1990

[**In thousands, except percent**. Beginning 1950, data are based on a sample from the census; for details, see text, section 1. See source for sampling variability. See also *Historical Statistics, Colonial Times to 1970,* series C 1-10]

YEAR	Total popula-tion	NATIVE POPULATION						FOREIGN BORN	
		Total	Born in State of resi-dence	Born in other States	State of birth not reported	Born in outlying areas [1]	Born abroad or at sea of American parents	Number	Percent of total population
1920	105,711	91,790	71,071	20,274	314	38	93	13,921	13.2
1930	122,775	108,571	82,678	25,388	238	136	131	14,204	11.6
1940	131,669	120,074	92,610	26,906	280	157	122	11,595	8.8
1950	150,216	139,869	102,788	35,284	1,370	330	96	10,347	6.9
1960	178,467	168,806	118,802	44,264	4,526	817	397	9,661	5.4
1970	203,194	193,454	131,296	51,659	8,882	873	744	9,740	4.8
1980	226,546	212,466	144,871	65,452	(NA)	1,088	1,055	14,080	6.2
1990	248,710	228,943	153,685	72,011	(NA)	1,382	1,864	19,767	7.9

NA Not available.   [1] 1920-50, includes Alaska and Hawaii. Includes Puerto Rico.

No. 55. Foreign-Born Population, by Place of Birth: 1990

[**In percent, except as indicated**. As of **April 1**. Based on a sample and subject to sampling variability, see text, section 1]

PLACE OF BIRTH	Number (1,000)	Percent entered between **1980-90**	Percent 65 years old and over	EDUCATION [1]		OCCUPATION OF EMPLOYED PERSONS [3]			Median household income in **1989** (dol.)
				High school gradu-ates	College gradu-ates [2]	Profes-sional specialty	Service occupa-tions	Opera-tors, fabrica-tors laborers	
Total [4]	**19,767**	**43.8**	**13.6**	**58.8**	**20.4**	**12.3**	**18.1**	**18.6**	**28,314**
Europe [5]	4,017	17.9	31.4	63.5	18.0	15.4	14.5	12.8	30,892
France	119	29.4	18.6	82.0	31.9	21.6	15.8	6.1	33,165
Germany	712	11.2	27.3	75.9	19.1	16.3	13.3	8.8	30,652
Greece	177	12.8	18.8	50.0	14.8	10.8	22.7	11.9	33,500
Hungary	110	11.9	40.1	65.6	22.2	20.2	9.9	11.0	30,060
Ireland	170	19.4	35.1	63.9	14.6	17.1	19.5	8.8	31,562
Italy	581	6.4	40.2	39.3	8.6	8.5	17.2	18.3	29,369
Poland	388	30.0	39.4	58.1	16.3	11.9	18.1	19.7	26,948
Portugal	210	21.6	12.7	32.1	4.6	3.9	14.0	35.9	35,053
United Kingdom	640	24.1	26.6	81.3	23.1	20.8	10.6	5.8	34,339
Yugoslavia	142	15.8	25.3	52.6	13.7	10.6	18.6	18.8	32,352
Soviet Union [6]	334	39.4	40.5	64.0	27.1	20.1	11.9	11.0	19,125
Asia [5]	4,979	56.1	7.1	75.8	38.4	18.9	14.8	12.5	35,318
Cambodia	119	85.8	3.4	35.4	5.5	5.5	18.7	29.2	19,728
China	530	53.5	17.9	60.6	30.9	16.9	24.5	16.1	30,597
Hong Kong	147	44.3	1.9	83.3	46.8	22.5	12.2	7.2	42,033
India	450	55.7	3.9	87.2	64.9	34.0	6.2	8.5	48,320
Iran	211	49.6	6.1	86.7	50.6	24.0	9.3	6.3	35,836
Japan	290	52.7	6.2	86.4	35.0	17.6	16.9	7.4	34,999
Korea	568	56.1	5.3	80.1	34.4	13.3	15.0	13.0	30,147
Laos	172	76.4	3.5	37.8	5.1	4.4	15.5	41.1	19,671
Philippines	913	49.0	10.4	82.5	43.0	18.0	16.8	10.7	45,419
Taiwan	244	65.4	2.4	91.6	62.2	28.7	10.3	4.0	38,966
Thailand	107	55.7	1.1	74.1	33.2	14.2	26.6	14.4	31,815
Vietnam	543	61.8	3.3	58.9	15.9	10.7	15.6	20.8	30,039
Canada	745	16.6	33.7	72.6	22.1	21.1	9.5	8.3	30,186
Mexico	4,298	49.9	4.9	24.3	3.5	2.6	21.0	32.2	21,926
Caribbean [5]	1,938	40.4	12.0	56.9	13.6	10.5	21.4	17.8	26,621
Cuba	737	25.5	21.1	54.1	15.6	10.9	13.2	18.0	27,292
Dominican Republic. . .	348	53.1	5.0	41.7	7.5	5.2	23.0	31.0	19,996
Haiti	225	58.9	4.3	57.6	11.8	9.1	33.9	20.5	25,454
Jamaica	334	46.3	7.8	67.9	14.9	13.2	26.4	11.2	30,599
Trinidad and Tobago . .	116	40.1	5.7	74.1	15.6	12.9	22.2	9.4	30,236
Central America [5]	1,134	67.4	4.1	45.7	8.5	4.5	29.8	24.3	24,509
El Salvador	465	75.2	2.6	32.7	4.6	2.4	34.1	26.8	23,533
Guatemala.	226	68.3	2.7	37.5	5.8	3.3	31.3	27.6	24,362
Honduras	109	65.6	4.1	49.2	8.3	4.5	29.8	23.7	21,947
Nicaragua	169	74.0	4.6	58.8	14.6	5.0	23.2	24.2	24,944
South America [5]	1,037	52.1	5.6	71.3	20.0	11.4	21.0	17.9	31,129
Colombia.	286	51.2	5.0	66.8	15.5	8.8	22.1	21.4	29,139
Ecuador	143	43.3	5.8	60.3	11.8	6.9	19.5	26.8	30,615
Guyana.	121	60.3	6.3	69.5	15.8	11.6	19.1	12.8	34,243
Peru	144	60.8	5.2	78.6	21.0	10.0	24.1	18.5	30,465
Africa.	364	59.3	4.1	87.9	47.1	22.1	16.4	11.7	30,907
Oceania	104	46.1	11.0	77.0	24.2	18.0	15.8	11.2	35,067

[1] For persons 25 years old and over.   [2] Bachelor's or advanced degree.   [3] For persons 16 years old and over.   [4] Includes persons whose place of birth was not reported.   [5] Includes other areas not shown separately.   [6] The former Soviet Union is now referred to as the following geopolitical entities: Armenia, Azerbaijan, Belarus, Georgia, Kazakhstan, Kyrgyzstan, Moldova, Russia, Tajikistan, Turkmenistan, Ukraine, and Uzbekistan.

Source of tables 54 and 55: U.S. Bureau of the Census, *1970 Census of Population,* vol. II, PC(2)-2A; 1990 Census of Population and Housing Listing (1990 CPH-L-98 and 1990 CPH-L-121) and *1990 Census of Population, The Foreign-Born Population in the United States* (1990 CP-3-1).

No. 56. Population, by Selected Ancestry Group and Region: 1990

[As of **April 1**. Covers persons who reported single and multiple ancestry groups. Persons who reported a multiple ancestry group may be included in more than one category. Major classifications of ancestry groups do not represent strict geographic or cultural definitions. Based on a sample and subject to sampling variability; see text, section 1]

ANCESTRY GROUP	Total (1,000)	PERCENT DISTRIBUTION, BY REGION				ANCESTRY GROUP	Total (1,000)	PERCENT DISTRIBUTION, BY REGION			
		North-east	Mid-west	South	West			North-east	Mid-west	South	West
European: [1]						Central & South America [2]					
Austrian	865	38	21	19	22	and Spain:					
British.	1,119	17	18	39	26	Cuban	860	18	3	69	9
Croatian	544	21	43	20	16	Dominican. . . .	506	86	1	10	2
Czech	1,296	10	52	22	16	Hispanic	1,113	13	6	31	50
Danish	1,635	9	34	12	45	Mexican	11,587	1	9	33	57
Dutch	6,227	16	34	29	21	Puerto Rican . .	1,955	66	11	15	8
English	32,652	18	22	35	25	Salvadoran . . .	499	13	2	23	62
European	467	14	17	31	39	Spanish	2,024	16	8	30	45
Finnish	659	14	47	11	27	West Indian: [1]					
French	10,321	26	26	29	20	Jamaican	435	59	5	31	6
German	57,947	17	39	25	19						
Greek.	1,110	37	23	21	19	Asia:					
Hungarian	1,582	36	32	17	16	Asian Indian . .	570	32	19	26	24
Irish	38,736	24	25	33	17	Chinese	1,505	25	8	12	55
Italian.	14,665	51	17	17	15	Filipino	1,451	10	9	13	68
Lithuanian	812	43	28	16	13	Japanese	1,005	9	8	11	72
Norwegian. . . .	3,869	6	52	10	33	Korean	837	22	14	20	44
Polish.	9,366	37	37	15	11	Vietnamese . . .	536	9	8	28	54
Portuguese . . .	1,153	49	3	8	41						
Russian	2,953	44	16	18	22	North America:					
Scandinavian. .	679	8	33	15	45	Acadian/Cajun .	668	1	2	91	5
Scotch-Irish . . .	5,618	14	19	47	20	Afro-American .	23,777	15	21	54	10
Scottish	5,394	20	21	33	26	American Indian	8,708	9	22	47	23
Slovak	1,883	40	34	14	11	American	12,396	10	18	61	11
Swedish	4,681	14	40	14	32	Canadian	550	34	18	21	28
Swiss.	1,045	16	36	17	30	French Canadian	2,167	45	20	20	15
Ukrainian	741	51	22	14	13	United States. .	644	16	18	53	13
Welsh.	2,034	22	24	27	27	White	1,800	7	13	53	28
Yugoslavian. . .	258	23	28	12	37						

[1] Non-Hispanic groups. [2] Hispanic groups.

Source: U.S. Bureau of the Census, *1990 Census of Population, Supplementary Reports, Detailed Ancestry Groups for States* (1990 CP-S-1-2).

No. 57. Persons Speaking a Language Other Than English at Home, by Age and Language: 1990

[As of **April**. Based on a sample and subject to sampling variability]

AGE GROUP AND LANGUAGE SPOKEN AT HOME	Persons who speak language (1,000)	Percent who speak English less than "very well"	LANGUAGE	Persons, 5 years old and over who speak language (1,000)
Persons 5 years old and over	230,446	(X)	Speak only English	198,601
Speak only English.	198,601	(X)	Spanish.	17,339
Speak other language	31,845	43.9	French	1,702
Speak Spanish or Spanish Creole	17,345	47.9	German	1,547
Speak Asian or Pacific Island language. .	4,472	54.1	Italian	1,309
Speak other language	10,028	32.4	Chinese	1,249
			Tagalog	843
Persons 5 to 17 years old	45,342	(X)	Polish	723
Speak only English.	39,020	(X)	Korean	626
Speak other language	6,323	37.8	Vietnamese	507
Speak Spanish or Spanish Creole	4,168	39.3	Portuguese	430
Speak Asian or Pacific Island language. .	816	44.2	Japanese.	428
Speak other language	1,340	29.2	Greek	388
			Arabic	355
Persons 18 to 64 years old	153,908	(X)	Hindi (Urdu)	331
Speak only English.	132,200	(X)	Russian	242
Speak other language	21,708	45.1	Yiddish	213
Speak Spanish or Spanish Creole	12,121	49.6	Thai (Laotian)	206
Speak Asian or Pacific Island language. .	3,301	54.7	Persian	202
Speak other language	6,286	31.4	French Creole.	188
			Armenian	150
Persons 65 years old and over	31,195	(X)	Navaho	149
Speak only English.	27,381	(X)	Hungarian	148
Speak other language	3,814	47.2	Hebrew	144
Speak Spanish or Spanish Creole	1,057	62.3	Dutch	143
Speak Asian or Pacific Island language. .	355	72.0	Mon-Khmer (Cambodian) . . .	127
Speak other language	2,402	36.9	Gujarathi	102

X Not applicable.

Source: U.S. Bureau of the Census, *1990 Census of Population and Housing Data Paper Listing* (CPH-L-133); and Summary Tape File 3C.

No. 58. Marital Status of the Population, by Sex, Race, and Hispanic Origin: 1970 to 1994

[In millions, except percent. As of March, except as noted. Persons 18 years old and over. Excludes members of Armed Forces except those living off post or with their families on post. Except as noted, based on Current Population Survey, see text, section 1, and Appendix III. See *Historical Statistics, Colonial Times to 1970,* series A 160-171, for decennial data]

MARITAL STATUS, RACE, AND HISPANIC ORIGIN	TOTAL				MALE				FEMALE			
	1970	1980	1990	1994	1970	1980	1990	1994	1970	1980	1990	1994
Total [1]	**132.5**	**159.5**	**181.8**	**190.0**	**62.5**	**75.7**	**86.9**	**91.2**	**70.0**	**83.8**	**95.0**	**98.8**
Never married	21.4	32.3	40.4	44.2	11.8	18.0	22.4	24.7	9.6	14.3	17.9	19.5
Married	95.0	104.6	112.6	115.1	47.1	51.8	55.8	57.0	47.9	52.8	56.7	58.1
Widowed	11.8	12.7	13.8	13.3	2.1	2.0	2.3	2.2	9.7	10.8	11.5	11.1
Divorced	4.3	9.9	15.1	17.4	1.6	3.9	6.3	7.2	2.7	6.0	8.8	10.1
Percent of total	100.0	100.0	100.0	100.0	100.0	100.0	100.0	100.0	100.0	100.0	100.0	100.0
Never married	16.2	20.3	22.2	23.3	18.9	23.8	25.8	27.1	13.7	17.1	18.9	19.7
Married	71.7	65.5	61.9	60.6	75.3	68.4	64.3	62.5	68.5	63.0	59.7	58.8
Widowed	8.9	8.0	7.6	7.0	3.3	2.6	2.7	2.4	13.9	12.8	12.1	11.2
Divorced	3.2	6.2	8.3	9.2	2.5	5.2	7.2	7.9	3.9	7.1	9.3	10.2
Percent standardized for age: [2]												
Never married	14.1	16.5	20.6	23.7	16.5	18.7	23.3	27.8	12.1	14.5	18.2	19.7
Married	74.2	69.3	63.7	60.9	77.6	72.9	66.5	61.9	70.8	65.9	61.2	59.8
Widowed	8.3	7.6	6.9	6.2	3.3	2.7	2.7	2.3	13.0	12.1	10.8	9.9
Divorced	3.4	6.6	8.7	9.3	2.6	5.6	7.6	8.0	4.1	7.6	9.8	10.6
White, total	**118.2**	**139.5**	**155.5**	**160.3**	**55.9**	**66.7**	**74.8**	**77.6**	**62.2**	**72.8**	**80.6**	**82.6**
Never married	18.4	26.4	31.6	33.5	10.2	15.0	18.0	19.3	8.2	11.4	13.6	14.2
Married	85.8	93.8	99.5	100.9	42.7	46.7	49.5	50.2	43.1	47.1	49.9	50.7
Widowed	10.3	10.9	11.7	11.3	1.7	1.6	1.9	1.9	8.6	9.3	9.8	9.4
Divorced	3.7	8.3	12.6	14.5	1.3	3.4	5.4	6.2	2.3	5.0	7.3	8.3
Percent of total	100.0	100.0	100.0	100.0	100.0	100.0	100.0	100.0	100.0	100.0	100.0	100.0
Never married	15.6	18.9	20.3	20.9	18.2	22.5	24.1	24.9	13.2	15.7	16.9	17.1
Married	72.6	67.2	64.0	62.9	76.3	70.0	66.2	64.6	69.3	64.7	61.9	61.4
Widowed	8.7	7.8	7.5	7.1	3.1	2.5	2.6	2.4	13.8	12.8	12.2	11.4
Divorced	3.1	6.0	8.1	9.1	2.4	5.0	7.2	8.0	3.8	6.8	9.0	10.1
Black, total	**13.0**	**16.6**	**20.3**	**21.8**	**5.9**	**7.4**	**9.1**	**9.8**	**7.1**	**9.2**	**11.2**	**12.0**
Never married	2.7	5.1	7.1	8.5	1.4	2.5	3.5	4.1	1.2	2.5	3.6	4.3
Married	8.3	8.5	9.3	9.3	3.9	4.1	4.5	4.5	4.4	4.5	4.8	4.9
Widowed	1.4	1.6	1.7	1.6	0.3	0.3	0.3	0.3	1.1	1.3	1.4	1.3
Divorced	0.6	1.4	2.1	2.3	0.2	0.5	0.8	0.9	0.4	0.9	1.3	1.5
Percent of total	100.0	100.0	100.0	100.0	100.0	100.0	100.0	100.0	100.0	100.0	100.0	100.0
Never married	20.6	30.5	35.1	38.9	24.3	34.3	38.4	42.4	17.4	27.4	32.5	36.2
Married	64.1	51.4	45.8	42.8	66.9	54.6	49.2	45.9	61.7	48.7	43.0	40.4
Widowed	11.0	9.8	8.5	7.4	5.2	4.2	3.7	3.0	15.8	14.3	12.4	11.0
Divorced	4.4	8.4	10.6	10.8	3.6	7.0	8.8	8.7	5.0	9.5	12.0	12.4
Hispanic, [3] **total**	**5.1**	**7.9**	**13.6**	**17.1**	**2.4**	**3.8**	**6.7**	**8.6**	**2.6**	**4.1**	**6.8**	**8.5**
Never married	0.9	1.9	3.7	5.1	0.5	1.0	2.2	3.0	0.4	0.9	1.5	2.1
Married	3.6	5.2	8.4	10.0	1.8	2.5	4.1	4.8	1.8	2.6	4.3	5.1
Widowed	0.3	0.4	0.5	0.8	0.1	0.1	0.1	0.2	0.2	0.3	0.4	0.6
Divorced	0.2	0.5	1.0	1.3	0.1	0.2	0.4	0.5	0.1	0.3	0.6	0.7
Percent of total	100.0	100.0	100.0	100.0	100.0	100.0	100.0	100.0	100.0	100.0	100.0	100.0
Never married	18.6	24.1	27.2	29.8	21.2	27.3	32.1	35.4	16.2	21.1	22.5	24.2
Married	71.8	65.6	61.7	58.3	73.8	67.1	60.9	56.4	70.0	64.3	62.4	60.2
Widowed	5.6	4.4	4.0	4.4	2.3	1.6	1.5	2.0	8.7	7.1	6.5	6.9
Divorced	3.9	5.8	7.0	7.5	2.7	4.0	5.5	6.2	5.1	7.6	8.5	8.7

[1] Includes persons of other races, not shown separately.   [2] 1960 age distribution used as standard; standardization improves comparability over time by removing effects of changes in age distribution of population.   [3] Hispanic persons may be of any race. 1970 data as of April and based on census.

Source: U.S. Bureau of the Census, *1970 Census of Population,* vol. I, part 1, and *Current Population Reports,* P20-450, and earlier reports; and unpublished data.

No. 59. Marital Status of the Population, by Sex and Age: 1994

[As of **March. Persons 18 years old and over.** Excludes members of Armed Forces except those living off post or with their families on post. Based on Current Population Survey; see text, section 1, and Appendix III. See *Historical Statistics, Colonial Times to 1970,* series A 160-171, for decennial census data]

SEX AND AGE	NUMBER OF PERSONS (1,000)					PERCENT DISTRIBUTION				
	Total	Single	Married	Widowed	Divorced	Total	Single	Married	Widowed	Divorced
Male	**91,222**	**24,727**	**57,028**	**2,221**	**7,245**	**100.0**	**27.1**	**62.5**	**2.4**	**7.9**
18 to 19 years old. . . .	3,462	3,375	80	2	5	100.0	97.5	2.3	0.1	0.1
20 to 24 years old. . . .	9,221	7,469	1,658	5	89	100.0	81.0	18.0	0.1	1.0
25 to 29 years old. . . .	9,765	4,910	4,422	9	424	100.0	50.3	45.3	0.1	4.3
30 to 34 years old. . . .	11,108	3,298	6,940	6	864	100.0	29.7	62.5	0.1	7.8
35 to 39 years old. . . .	10,892	2,094	7,603	31	1,164	100.0	19.2	69.8	0.3	10.7
40 to 44 years old. . . .	9,651	1,255	7,104	31	1,262	100.0	13.0	73.6	0.3	13.1
45 to 54 years old. . . .	14,454	1,185	11,362	137	1,770	100.0	8.2	78.6	0.9	12.2
55 to 64 years old. . . .	9,933	539	8,034	327	1,033	100.0	5.4	80.9	3.3	10.4
65 to 74 years old. . . .	7,924	390	6,353	695	486	100.0	4.9	80.2	8.8	6.1
75 years old and over .	4,812	211	3,471	980	150	100.0	4.4	72.1	20.4	3.1
Female.	**98,765**	**19,458**	**58,113**	**11,073**	**10,120**	**100.0**	**19.7**	**58.8**	**11.2**	**10.2**
18 to 19 years old. . . .	3,454	3,152	278	3	21	100.0	91.3	8.0	0.1	0.6
20 to 24 years old. . . .	9,338	6,162	2,931	11	234	100.0	66.0	31.4	0.1	2.5
25 to 29 years old. . . .	9,861	3,476	5,689	29	667	100.0	35.2	57.7	0.3	6.8
30 to 34 years old. . . .	11,212	2,228	7,703	80	1,202	100.0	19.9	68.7	0.7	10.7
35 to 39 years old. . . .	11,078	1,420	7,959	135	1,563	100.0	12.8	71.8	1.2	14.1
40 to 44 years old. . . .	9,906	909	7,358	146	1,492	100.0	9.2	74.3	1.5	15.1
45 to 54 years old. . . .	15,068	892	10,977	705	2,494	100.0	5.9	72.8	4.7	16.6
55 to 64 years old. . . .	10,805	440	7,500	1,501	1,364	100.0	4.1	69.4	13.9	12.6
65 to 74 years old. . . .	10,163	386	5,520	3,476	781	100.0	3.8	54.3	34.2	7.7
75 years old and over .	7,880	393	2,199	4,986	302	100.0	5.0	27.9	63.3	3.8

No. 60. Unmarried Couples, by Selected Characteristics: 1970 to 1994

[**In thousands**. As of **March**. An "unmarried couple" is two unrelated adults of the opposite sex sharing the same household. See headnote, table 65]

PRESENCE OF CHILDREN AND AGE OF HOUSEHOLDER	1970	1980	1985	1990	1994
Unmarried couples, total.	**523**	**1,589**	**1,983**	**2,856**	**3,661**
No children under 15 years old	327	1,159	1,380	1,966	2,391
Some children under 15 years old	196	431	603	891	1,270
Under 25 years old.	55	411	425	596	772
25 to 44 years old	103	837	1,203	1,775	2,169
45 to 64 years old	186	221	239	358	537
65 years old and over	178	119	116	127	183

No. 61. Married Couples of Same or Mixed Races and Origins: 1970 to 1994

[**In thousands**. As of **March, except as noted. Persons 15 years old and over**. Persons of Hispanic origin may be of any race. Except as noted, based on Current Population Survey; see headnote, table 65]

RACE AND ORIGIN OF SPOUSES	1970 [1]	1980	1990	1994
Married couples, total.	**44,598**	**49,714**	**53,256**	**54,251**
RACE				
Same race couples.	43,922	48,264	50,889	51,204
White/White.	40,578	44,910	47,202	47,606
Black/Black	3,344	3,354	3,687	3,598
Interracial couples	310	651	964	1,283
Black/White	65	167	211	296
Black husband/White wife	41	122	150	196
White husband/Black wife	24	45	61	100
White/other race [2]	233	450	720	909
Black/other race [2]	12	34	33	78
All other couples [2]	366	799	1,401	1,764
HISPANIC ORIGIN				
Hispanic/Hispanic.	1,368	1,906	3,085	3,755
Hispanic/other origin (not Hispanic)	584	891	1,193	1,283
All other couples (not of Hispanic origin). . .	42,645	46,917	48,979	49,212

[1] As of April and based on Census of Population.   [2] Excluding White and Black.

Source of tables 59-61: U.S. Bureau of the Census, *Current Population Reports*, P20-450, and earlier reports; and unpublished data.

Population

No. 62. Living Arrangements of Persons 15 Years Old and Over, by Selected Characteristics: 1994

[As of **March**. Based on Current Population Survey which includes members of Armed Forces living off post or with families on post, but excludes other Armed Forces; see text, section 1, and Appendix III]

AGE AND SEX	Total (1,000)	ALL RACES [1] Percent living—				WHITE PERSONS PERCENT LIVING—			BLACK PERSONS PERCENT LIVING—		
		Alone	With spouse	With other relatives	With non-relatives	Alone	With spouse	With other relatives	Alone	With spouse	With other relatives
Total	**200,800**	**12**	**54**	**27**	**7**	**12**	**57**	**24**	**12**	**32**	**48**
15 to 19 years old	17,730	1	2	93	4	1	2	93	-	1	96
20 to 24 years old	18,559	5	22	56	16	6	25	53	4	12	75
25 to 34 years old	41,946	9	55	25	12	9	59	20	9	30	50
35 to 44 years old	41,527	8	67	17	7	8	71	14	11	41	39
45 to 54 years old	29,522	10	72	13	5	10	74	11	13	49	31
55 to 64 years old	20,737	14	72	10	4	14	74	9	21	49	23
65 years old and over	30,779	30	55	12	2	30	56	11	31	41	24
65 to 74 years old	18,087	23	64	11	2	23	66	9	27	46	22
75 years old and over . .	12,692	40	43	15	2	41	44	13	37	34	27
Male	**96,768**	**10**	**56**	**25**	**9**	**10**	**59**	**23**	**11**	**36**	**41**
15 to 19 years old	9,008	1	1	95	4	1	1	95	-	1	96
20 to 24 years old	9,221	6	17	60	17	6	18	58	3	10	74
25 to 34 years old	20,873	11	51	23	15	11	54	20	11	30	41
35 to 44 years old	20,543	10	67	13	9	10	70	11	14	45	27
45 to 54 years old	14,454	10	75	9	6	10	77	7	13	56	21
55 to 64 years old	9,933	10	78	7	5	10	80	6	17	61	12
65 years old and over	12,736	16	75	6	3	16	76	6	19	63	12
65 to 74 years old	7,924	13	78	6	3	13	79	5	16	65	10
75 years old and over . .	4,812	21	70	7	2	21	71	6	23	59	16
Female	**104,032**	**14**	**52**	**29**	**6**	**14**	**56**	**25**	**13**	**29**	**54**
15 to 19 years old	8,722	1	3	91	5	1	4	90	1	1	96
20 to 24 years old	9,338	5	28	52	15	5	31	48	4	13	76
25 to 34 years old	21,073	7	58	26	9	7	63	21	8	29	57
35 to 44 years old	20,984	7	68	21	5	6	72	17	9	38	48
45 to 54 years old	15,068	10	68	17	4	10	72	14	14	43	39
55 to 64 years old	10,805	18	66	14	2	17	69	11	25	40	32
65 years old and over	18,043	40	41	17	2	41	42	15	39	28	32
65 to 74 years old	10,163	31	52	15	2	31	55	12	35	33	30
75 years old and over . .	7,880	52	26	20	2	53	27	18	46	19	34

- Represents or rounds to zero.   [1] Includes other races not shown separately.

Source: U.S. Bureau of the Census, unpublished data.

No. 63. Living Arrangements of Young Adults: 1970 to 1994

[**1970** and **1980**, as of **April**. Beginning **1985**, as of **March** and based on Current Population Survey, see headnote, table 62]

LIVING ARRANGEMENTS AND SEX	PERSONS 18 TO 24 YEARS OLD					PERSONS 25 TO 34 YEARS OLD				
	1970	1980	1985	1990	1994	1970	1980	1985	1990	1994
Total (1,000)	**22,357**	**29,122**	**27,844**	**25,310**	**25,475**	**24,566**	**36,796**	**40,857**	**43,240**	**41,946**
Percent distribution:										
Child of householder [1]	47	48	54	53	53	8	9	11	12	12
Family householder or spouse . . .	38	29	24	22	21	83	72	68	65	62
Nonfamily householder	5	10	8	9	9	5	12	13	13	13
Other	10	13	14	16	17	4	7	9	11	13
Male (1,000)	**10,398**	**14,278**	**13,695**	**12,450**	**12,683**	**11,929**	**18,107**	**20,184**	**21,462**	**20,873**
Percent distribution:										
Child of householder [1]	54	54	60	58	60	10	11	13	15	16
Family householder or spouse . . .	30	21	16	15	14	79	66	60	56	53
Nonfamily householder	5	11	10	10	10	7	15	16	16	16
Other	10	13	14	17	17	5	8	11	13	16
Female (1,000)	**11,959**	**14,844**	**14,149**	**12,860**	**12,792**	**12,637**	**18,689**	**20,673**	**21,779**	**21,073**
Percent distribution:										
Child of householder [1]	41	43	48	48	46	7	7	8	8	9
Family householder or spouse . . .	45	36	32	30	29	86	78	76	73	71
Nonfamily householder	4	8	7	8	8	4	9	10	10	10
Other	10	13	13	15	17	4	6	7	9	10

[1] Includes unmarried college students living in dormitories.

Source: U.S. Bureau of the Census, *1970* and *1980 Census of Population*, PC(2)-4B and *Current Population Reports*, P20-410 and P20-450; and unpublished data.

No. 64. Householder and Marital Status of Population, 15 Years Old and Over: 1994

[**In thousands**. As of **March**. See headnote, table 65]

HOUSEHOLDER AND MARITAL STATUS	Total, 15 yrs. and over	MALE					FEMALE				
		Total [1]	20 to 24 years	25 to 44 years	45 to 64 years	65 yr. and over	Total [1]	20 to 24 years	25 to 44 years	45 to 64 years	65 yr. and over
Total persons	200,800	96,768	9,221	41,416	24,387	12,736	104,032	9,338	42,057	25,873	18,043
Householder	97,107	62,264	2,564	28,296	20,161	11,075	34,842	2,162	13,715	8,864	9,732
Never married	15,249	7,324	1,320	4,570	890	415	7,924	1,583	4,557	938	547
Married, spouse present	53,171	46,889	1,179	20,674	16,486	8,511	6,282	316	3,389	1,802	736
Married, spouse absent	4,608	1,607	30	835	527	214	3,001	150	1,734	837	261
Widowed	11,339	1,821	2	55	324	1,441	9,518	4	325	1,966	7,221
Divorced	12,740	4,622	32	2,163	1,933	494	8,118	109	3,711	3,321	967
Not householder	103,693	34,504	6,657	13,121	4,227	1,662	69,190	7,175	28,342	17,008	8,311
Never married	39,624	22,904	6,149	6,987	834	185	16,720	4,579	3,478	395	232
Married, spouse present	55,352	7,372	367	3,753	2,148	1,053	47,980	2,306	23,146	15,636	6,655
Married, spouse absent	2,122	1,199	82	806	236	48	923	159	441	201	68
Widowed	1,956	401	4	22	139	234	1,555	7	67	240	1,241
Divorced	4,639	2,628	56	1,550	869	142	2,011	125	1,213	537	115

[1] Includes 15 to 19 year olds.

Source: U.S. Bureau of the Census, unpublished data.

No. 65. Households, Families, Subfamilies, Married Couples, and Unrelated Individuals: 1960 to 1994

[**In thousands, except as indicated.** As of **March**. Based on Current Population Survey; includes members of Armed Forces living off post or with their families on post, but excludes all other members of Armed Forces; see text, section 1, and Appendix III. For definition of terms, see text, section 1. Minus sign (-) indicates decrease. See also *Historical Statistics, Colonial Times to 1970,* series A 288-319]

TYPE OF UNIT	1960	1970	1975	1980	1985	1990	1993	1994	PERCENT CHANGE		
									1970-80	1980-90	1990-94
Households	52,799	63,401	71,120	80,776	86,789	93,347	96,391	97,107	27	16	4
Average size	3.33	3.14	2.94	2.76	2.69	2.63	2.63	2.67	(X)	(X)	(X)
Family households	44,905	51,456	55,563	59,550	62,706	66,090	68,144	68,490	16	11	4
Married couple	39,254	44,728	46,951	49,112	50,350	52,317	53,171	53,171	10	7	2
Male householder [1]	1,228	1,228	1,485	1,733	2,228	2,884	3,026	2,913	41	66	1
Female householder [1]	4,422	5,500	7,127	8,705	10,129	10,890	11,947	12,406	58	25	14
Nonfamily households	7,895	11,945	15,557	21,226	24,082	27,257	28,247	28,617	78	28	5
Male householder	2,716	4,063	5,912	8,807	10,114	11,606	12,254	12,462	117	32	7
Female householder	5,179	7,882	9,645	12,419	13,968	15,651	15,993	16,155	58	26	3
One person	6,896	10,851	13,939	18,296	20,602	22,999	23,642	23,611	69	26	3
Families	45,111	51,586	55,712	59,550	62,706	66,090	68,144	68,490	15	11	4
Average size	3.67	3.58	3.42	3.29	3.23	3.17	3.16	3.20	(X)	(X)	(X)
Married couple	39,329	44,755	46,971	49,112	50,350	52,317	53,171	53,171	10	7	2
Male householder [1]	1,275	1,239	1,499	1,733	2,228	2,884	3,026	2,913	40	66	1
Female householder [1]	4,507	5,591	7,242	8,705	10,129	10,890	11,947	12,406	56	25	14
Unrelated subfamilies	207	130	149	360	526	534	708	716	177	48	34
Married couple	75	27	20	20	46	68	83	66	(B)	(B)	(B)
Male reference persons [1]	47	11	14	36	85	45	68	78	(B)	(B)	(B)
Female reference persons [1]	85	91	115	304	395	421	557	571	234	39	36
Related subfamilies	1,514	1,150	1,349	1,150	2,228	2,403	2,671	2,813	-	109	17
Married couple	871	617	576	582	719	871	945	1,014	-6	50	16
Father-child [1]	115	48	69	54	116	153	170	164	(B)	(B)	7
Mother-child [1]	528	484	705	512	1,392	1,378	1,556	1,636	6	169	19
Married couples	40,200	45,373	47,547	49,714	51,114	53,256	54,199	54,251	10	7	2
With own household	39,254	44,728	46,951	49,112	50,350	52,317	53,171	53,171	10	7	2
Without own household	946	645	596	602	764	939	1,028	1,080	-7	56	15
Percent without	2.4	1.4	1.3	1.2	1.5	1.8	1.9	2.0	(X)	(X)	(X)
Unrelated individuals	11,092	14,988	19,100	26,426	30,518	35,384	37,006	38,469	76	34	9
Nonfamily householders	7,895	11,945	15,557	21,226	24,082	27,257	28,247	28,617	78	28	5
Secondary individuals	3,198	3,043	3,543	5,200	6,436	8,127	8,759	9,852	71	56	21
Male	1,746	1,631	2,087	3,006	3,743	4,711	5,169	5,892	84	57	25
Female	1,451	1,412	1,456	2,194	2,693	3,416	3,589	3,961	55	56	16

- Represents or rounds to zero.   B Not shown; base less than 75,000.   X Not applicable.   [1] No spouse present.

Source: U.S. Bureau of the Census, *Current Population Reports*, P20-477 and unpublished data.

No. 66. Households, 1980 to 1994, and Persons in Households, 1994, by Type of Household and Presence of Children

[As of **March**. Based on Current Population Survey; see headnote, table 65]

TYPE OF HOUSEHOLD AND PRESENCE OF CHILDREN	HOUSEHOLDS					PERSONS IN HOUSEHOLDS, 1994		Persons per house-hold, 1994
	Number (1,000)			Percent distribution		Num-ber (1,000)	Percent distribu-tion	
	1980	1990	1994	1980	1994			
Total households	80,776	93,347	97,107	100	100	259,507	100	2.67
Family households	59,550	66,090	68,490	74	71	223,364	86	3.26
With own children under 18.	31,022	32,289	34,018	38	35	134,492	52	3.95
Without own children under 18.	28,528	33,801	34,471	35	35	88,872	34	2.58
Married couple family.	49,112	52,317	53,171	61	55	174,519	67	3.28
With own children under 18.	24,961	24,537	25,058	31	26	105,121	41	4.20
Without own children under 18.	24,151	27,780	28,113	30	29	69,398	27	2.47
Male householder, no spouse present. . .	1,733	2,884	2,913	2	3	9,226	4	3.17
With own children under 18.	616	1,153	1,314	1	1	4,416	2	3.36
Without own children under 18.	1,117	1,731	1,599	1	2	4,810	2	3.01
Female householder, no spouse present.	8,705	10,890	12,406	11	13	39,619	15	3.19
With own children under 18.	5,445	6,599	7,647	7	8	24,955	10	3.26
Without own children under 18.	3,261	4,290	4,759	4	5	14,664	6	3.08
Nonfamily households.	21,226	27,257	28,617	26	29	36,143	14	1.26
Living alone	18,296	22,999	23,611	23	24	23,611	9	1.00
Male householder	8,807	11,606	12,462	11	13	17,208	7	1.38
Living alone	6,966	9,049	9,440	9	10	9,440	4	1.00
Female householder	12,419	15,651	16,155	15	17	18,935	7	1.17
Living alone	11,330	13,950	14,171	14	15	14,171	5	1.00

Source: U.S. Bureau of the Census, *Current Population Reports*, P20-447, and earlier reports; and unpublished data.

No. 67. Household Characteristics, by Type of Household: 1994

[As of **March**. Based on Current Population Survey; see headnote, table 65. For composition of regions, see table 27]

CHARACTERISTIC	NUMBER OF HOUSEHOLDS (1,000)					PERCENT DISTRIBUTION				
	Total	Family households			Non-family house-holds	Total	Family households			Non-family house-holds
		Total [1]	Married couple	Female house-holder [2]			Total [1]	Married couple	Female house-holder [2]	
Total	97,107	68,490	53,171	12,406	28,617	100	100	100	100	100
Age of householder:										
15 to 24 years old.	5,265	2,998	1,573	1,121	2,266	5	4	3	9	8
25 to 29 years old.	8,472	5,733	4,021	1,346	2,739	9	8	8	11	10
30 to 34 years old.	11,245	8,512	6,351	1,765	2,733	12	12	12	14	10
35 to 44 years old.	22,293	17,803	13,691	3,370	4,490	23	26	26	27	16
45 to 54 years old.	16,837	13,278	10,724	2,093	3,559	17	19	20	17	12
55 to 64 years old.	12,188	8,950	7,565	1,123	3,237	13	13	14	9	11
65 to 74 years old.	11,639	7,237	6,061	953	4,402	12	11	11	8	15
75 years old and over	9,168	3,977	3,186	634	5,191	9	6	6	5	18
Region:										
Northeast	19,470	13,455	10,328	2,573	6,016	20	20	19	21	21
Midwest	23,385	16,208	12,677	2,862	7,176	24	24	24	23	25
South	33,904	24,430	18,766	4,680	9,474	35	36	35	38	33
West.	20,347	14,396	11,401	2,291	5,951	21	21	21	18	21
Size of household:										
One person	23,611	(X)	(X)	(X)	23,611	24	(X)	(X)	(X)	83
Two persons	31,211	27,268	20,816	5,165	3,943	32	40	39	42	14
Three persons	16,898	16,196	11,565	3,777	702	17	24	22	30	2
Four persons	15,073	14,828	12,377	2,022	245	16	22	23	16	1
Five persons	6,749	6,673	5,610	841	77	7	10	11	7	(Z)
Six persons	2,186	2,165	1,781	324	21	2	3	3	3	(Z)
Seven persons or more . . .	1,379	1,360	1,021	276	19	1	2	2	2	(Z)
Marital status of householder:										
Never married (single)	15,249	4,340	(X)	3,298	10,908	16	6	(X)	27	38
Married, spouse present. . .	53,171	53,171	53,171	(X)	(X)	55	78	100	(X)	(X)
Married, spouse absent. . .	4,608	2,612	(X)	2,208	1,996	5	4	(X)	18	7
Widowed.	11,339	2,830	(X)	2,421	8,509	12	4	(X)	20	30
Divorced	12,740	5,537	(X)	4,479	7,203	13	8	(X)	36	25
Tenure:										
Owner occupied	62,374	48,730	41,779	5,385	13,644	64	71	79	43	48
Renter occupied	34,732	19,760	11,392	7,021	14,973	36	29	21	57	52

X Not applicable. Z Less than 0.5 percent. [1] Includes male householder, no spouse present. [2] No spouse present.

Source: U.S. Bureau of the Census, *Current Population Reports*, unpublished data.

No. 68. Households, by Age of Householder and Size of Household: 1970 to 1994

[As of **March**. Based on Current Population Survey; see headnote, table 65. See also *Historical Statistics, Colonial Times to 1970*, series A 335-349]

AGE OF HOUSEHOLDER AND SIZE OF HOUSEHOLD	1970	1975	1980	1985	1990	1994 Total [1]	1994 White	1994 Black	1994 His-panic [2]
NUMBER (mil.)									
Total	**63.4**	**71.1**	**80.8**	**86.8**	**93.3**	**97.1**	**82.4**	**11.3**	**7.4**
Age of householder:									
15 to 24 years old [3]	4.4	5.8	6.6	5.4	5.1	5.3	4.2	0.8	0.6
25 to 29 years old	6.1	7.8	9.3	9.6	9.4	8.5	6.9	1.2	0.9
30 to 34 years old	5.6	7.1	9.3	10.4	11.0	11.2	9.2	1.5	1.2
35 to 44 years old	11.8	11.9	14.0	17.5	20.6	22.3	18.5	2.8	1.9
45 to 54 years old	12.2	12.9	12.7	12.6	14.5	16.8	14.3	1.9	1.2
55 to 64 years old	10.8	11.3	12.5	13.1	12.5	12.2	10.6	1.3	0.8
65 to 74 years old	7.7	8.9	10.1	10.9	11.7	11.6	10.3	1.1	0.5
75 years old and over	4.8	5.4	6.4	7.3	8.4	9.2	8.4	0.7	0.3
One person	10.9	13.9	18.3	20.6	23.0	23.6	20.2	2.8	1.1
Male	3.5	4.9	7.0	7.9	9.0	9.4	8.0	1.1	0.5
Female	7.3	9.0	11.3	12.7	14.0	14.2	12.2	1.7	0.6
Two persons	18.3	21.8	25.3	27.4	30.1	31.2	27.5	2.9	1.7
Three persons	10.9	12.4	14.1	15.5	16.1	16.9	14.0	2.3	1.4
Four persons	10.0	11.1	12.7	13.6	14.5	15.1	12.6	1.8	1.4
Five persons	6.5	6.4	6.1	6.1	6.2	6.7	5.5	0.9	1.0
Six persons	3.5	3.1	2.5	2.3	2.1	2.2	1.7	0.4	0.4
Seven persons or more	3.2	2.5	1.8	1.3	1.3	1.4	1.0	0.3	0.4
PERCENT DISTRIBUTION									
Total	**100**	**100**	**100**	**100**	**100**	**100**	**100**	**100**	**100**
Age of householder:									
15 to 24 years old [3]	7	8	8	6	6	5	5	7	8
25 to 29 years old	10	11	12	11	10	9	8	11	12
30 to 34 years old	9	10	12	12	12	12	11	13	16
35 to 44 years old	19	17	17	20	22	23	22	25	26
45 to 54 years old	20	18	16	15	16	17	17	17	16
55 to 64 years old	17	16	16	15	13	13	13	12	11
65 to 74 years old	12	13	13	13	13	12	13	10	7
75 years old and over	8	8	8	8	9	9	10	6	4
One person	17	20	23	24	25	24	25	25	15
Male	6	7	9	9	10	10	10	10	7
Female	12	13	14	15	15	15	15	15	8
Two persons	29	31	31	32	32	32	33	26	23
Three persons	17	17	18	18	17	17	17	20	19
Four persons	16	16	16	16	16	16	15	16	19
Five persons	10	9	8	7	7	7	7	8	14
Six persons	6	4	3	3	2	2	2	4	5
Seven persons or more	5	4	2	2	1	1	1	3	5

[1] Includes other races, not shown separately.   [2] Hispanic persons may be of any race.   [3] 1970 and 1975, persons 14 to 24 years old.

Source: U.S. Bureau of the Census, *Current Population Reports*, P20-447, and earlier reports; and unpublished data.

No. 69. Households—States: 1980 to 1994

[As of **April 1**, except **beginning 1991**, as of **July 1**. Minus sign (-) indicates decrease]

REGION, DIVISION, AND STATE	NUMBER (1,000)					1994		PERCENT CHANGE		PERSONS PER HOUSEHOLD		
	1980	1990	1991	1992	1993	Total	Householder 65 yrs. and over	1980-90	1990-94	1980	1990	1994
U.S.	80,390	91,946	93,183	94,652	95,335	95,946	20,876	14.4	4.4	2.75	2.63	2.64
Northeast ..	17,471	18,873	18,964	19,092	19,067	19,045	4,506	8.0	0.9	2.74	2.61	2.62
N.E	4,362	4,943	4,961	4,987	4,980	4,980	1,142	13.3	0.8	2.74	2.58	2.58
ME....	395	465	471	474	475	474	108	17.7	2.0	2.75	2.56	2.54
NH....	323	411	413	417	419	424	83	27.1	3.0	2.75	2.62	2.61
VT....	178	211	214	217	219	220	44	18.1	4.6	2.75	2.57	2.54
MA...	2,033	2,247	2,250	2,263	2,262	2,265	528	10.5	0.8	2.72	2.58	2.57
RI	339	378	379	380	377	374	96	11.6	-1.1	2.70	2.55	2.57
CT	1,094	1,230	1,234	1,235	1,228	1,222	283	12.5	-0.7	2.76	2.59	2.60
M.A	13,109	13,930	14,003	14,106	14,087	14,065	3,364	6.3	1.0	2.74	2.62	2.64
NY	6,340	6,639	6,662	6,703	6,689	6,669	1,494	4.7	0.4	2.70	2.63	2.64
NJ	2,549	2,795	2,812	2,839	2,839	2,845	659	9.7	1.8	2.84	2.70	2.72
PA	4,220	4,496	4,529	4,564	4,559	4,551	1,211	6.5	1.2	2.74	2.57	2.57
Midwest ...	20,859	22,317	22,543	22,818	22,893	22,937	5,156	7.0	2.8	2.75	2.60	2.61
E.N.C....	14,654	15,597	15,776	15,970	16,021	16,051	3,539	6.4	2.9	2.78	2.63	2.62
OH....	3,834	4,088	4,135	4,181	4,189	4,190	949	6.6	2.5	2.76	2.59	2.59
IN....	1,927	2,065	2,102	2,133	2,149	2,161	470	7.2	4.6	2.77	2.61	2.59
IL.....	4,045	4,202	4,243	4,291	4,301	4,308	936	3.9	2.5	2.76	2.65	2.66
MI	3,195	3,419	3,454	3,496	3,498	3,502	754	7.0	2.4	2.84	2.66	2.65
WI	1,652	1,822	1,842	1,869	1,883	1,890	430	10.3	3.7	2.77	2.61	2.62
W.N.C	6,205	6,720	6,767	6,848	6,872	6,886	1,617	8.3	2.5	2.68	2.55	2.57
MN....	1,445	1,648	1,667	1,689	1,702	1,711	362	14.0	3.8	2.74	2.58	2.60
IA.....	1,053	1,064	1,069	1,083	1,084	1,082	277	1.1	1.6	2.68	2.52	2.52
MO....	1,793	1,961	1,976	1,996	2,002	2,008	478	9.4	2.4	2.67	2.53	2.56
ND....	228	241	240	242	242	241	60	5.8	0.2	2.75	2.55	2.54
SD....	243	259	260	263	264	265	68	6.8	2.1	2.74	2.59	2.63
NE....	571	602	606	614	614	614	147	5.4	2.0	2.66	2.54	2.56
KS....	872	945	948	961	964	966	225	8.3	2.2	2.62	2.53	2.56
South	26,486	31,821	32,376	32,976	33,342	33,713	7,325	20.1	5.9	2.77	2.61	2.62
S.A	13,160	16,502	16,826	17,149	17,331	17,530	3,970	25.4	6.2	2.73	2.56	2.58
DE....	207	247	253	258	262	264	56	19.5	6.8	2.79	2.61	2.59
MD....	1,461	1,749	1,778	1,807	1,818	1,831	344	19.7	4.7	2.82	2.67	2.67
DC....	253	250	247	245	242	237	51	-1.4	-5.2	2.40	2.26	2.24
VA....	1,863	2,292	2,333	2,384	2,413	2,439	453	23.0	6.4	2.77	2.61	2.60
WV....	686	689	696	703	705	705	188	0.3	2.4	2.79	2.55	2.53
NC....	2,043	2,517	2,566	2,608	2,641	2,679	566	23.2	6.4	2.78	2.54	2.55
SC....	1,030	1,258	1,292	1,313	1,325	1,337	280	22.1	6.3	2.93	2.68	2.66
GA....	1,872	2,366	2,425	2,488	2,531	2,581	451	26.4	9.1	2.84	2.66	2.67
FL	3,744	5,135	5,236	5,341	5,393	5,456	1,581	37.1	6.3	2.55	2.46	2.50
E.S.C....	5,051	5,652	5,743	5,832	5,886	5,938	1,328	11.9	5.1	2.83	2.62	2.61
KY	1,263	1,380	1,398	1,418	1,431	1,440	321	9.2	4.3	2.82	2.60	2.59
TN	1,619	1,854	1,887	1,921	1,942	1,966	424	14.5	6.0	2.77	2.56	2.57
AL	1,342	1,507	1,533	1,558	1,573	1,583	363	12.3	5.1	2.84	2.62	2.61
MS....	827	911	925	934	941	949	221	10.2	4.2	2.97	2.75	2.74
W.S.C ...	8,276	9,667	9,807	9,996	10,124	10,245	2,027	16.8	6.0	2.80	2.69	2.71
AR	816	891	899	910	919	927	235	9.2	4.0	2.74	2.57	2.58
LA	1,412	1,499	1,514	1,534	1,538	1,543	321	6.2	2.9	2.91	2.74	2.72
OK....	1,119	1,206	1,211	1,229	1,234	1,236	288	7.8	2.5	2.62	2.53	2.56
TX	4,929	6,071	6,183	6,322	6,433	6,539	1,184	23.2	7.7	2.82	2.73	2.75
West......	15,574	18,935	19,300	19,765	20,033	20,251	3,889	21.6	6.9	2.71	2.72	2.74
Mountain .	3,986	5,033	5,151	5,303	5,433	5,574	1,092	26.3	10.7	2.79	2.65	2.68
MT....	284	306	309	315	321	325	73	7.9	6.1	2.70	2.53	2.56
ID....	324	361	372	384	395	405	84	11.3	12.2	2.85	2.73	2.75
WY....	166	169	170	174	176	178	34	1.9	5.3	2.78	2.63	2.62
CO....	1,061	1,282	1,306	1,348	1,386	1,417	234	20.8	10.5	2.65	2.51	2.52
NM....	441	543	553	568	577	587	116	22.9	8.1	2.90	2.74	2.77
AZ	957	1,369	1,390	1,429	1,461	1,503	340	43.0	9.8	2.79	2.62	2.66
UT	449	537	553	571	585	599	107	19.8	11.6	3.20	3.15	3.13
NV	304	466	496	516	532	560	102	53.2	20.1	2.59	2.53	2.56
Pacific...	11,587	13,902	14,149	14,462	14,600	14,677	2,798	20.0	5.6	2.68	2.74	2.77
WA....	1,541	1,872	1,922	1,977	2,018	2,042	391	21.5	9.1	2.61	2.53	2.56
OR....	992	1,103	1,130	1,156	1,178	1,195	267	11.3	8.3	2.60	2.52	2.53
CA	8,630	10,381	10,536	10,752	10,821	10,850	2,042	20.3	4.5	2.68	2.79	2.83
AK	131	189	194	202	206	208	17	43.7	10.3	2.93	2.80	2.81
HI	294	356	367	375	378	381	81	21.2	7.1	3.15	3.01	2.99

Source: U.S. Bureau of the Census, *1980 Census of Population*, vol. 1, chapter B; *1990 Census of Population, General Population Characteristics, United States* (1990 CP-1-1); and unpublished data.

No. 70. Family and Nonfamily Households, by Race, Hispanic Origin, and Type: 1970 to 1994

[As of **March**, except as noted. Based on Current Population Survey, except as noted; see headnote, table 65. See also *Historical Statistics, Colonial Times to 1970*, series A 292-295 and A 320-334]

RACE, HISPANIC ORIGIN, AND TYPE	NUMBER (1,000)					PERCENT DISTRIBUTION				
	1970	1980	1985	1990	1994	1970	1980	1985	1990	1994
TOTAL HOUSEHOLDS										
Total [1]	**63,401**	**80,776**	**86,789**	**93,347**	**97,107**	100	100	100	100	100
White	56,602	70,766	75,328	80,163	82,387	89	88	87	86	85
Black	6,223	8,586	9,480	10,486	11,281	10	11	11	11	12
Hispanic [2]	2,303	3,684	4,883	5,933	7,362	4	5	6	6	8
FAMILY HOUSEHOLDS										
White, total	**46,166**	**52,243**	**54,400**	**56,590**	**57,870**	100	100	100	100	100
Married couple	41,029	44,751	45,643	46,981	47,443	89	86	84	83	82
Male householder [3]	1,038	1,441	1,816	2,303	2,297	2	3	3	4	4
Female householder [3]	4,099	6,052	6,941	7,306	8,130	9	12	13	13	14
Black, total	**4,856**	**6,184**	**6,778**	**7,470**	**7,989**	100	100	100	100	100
Married couple	3,317	3,433	3,469	3,750	3,714	68	56	51	50	46
Male householder [3]	181	256	344	446	450	4	4	5	6	6
Female householder [3]	1,358	2,495	2,964	3,275	3,825	28	40	44	44	48
Asian or Pacific Islander, total [4]	**(NA)**	**818**	**(NA)**	**1,531**	**1,737**	(NA)	100	(NA)	100	100
Married couple	(NA)	691	(NA)	1,256	1,426	(NA)	84	(NA)	82	82
Male householder [3]	(NA)	39	(NA)	86	79	(NA)	5	(NA)	6	5
Female householder [3]	(NA)	88	(NA)	188	232	(NA)	11	(NA)	12	13
Hispanic, total [2]	**2,004**	**3,029**	**3,939**	**4,840**	**5,940**	100	100	100	100	100
Married couple	1,615	2,282	2,824	3,395	4,033	81	75	72	70	68
Male householder [3]	82	138	210	329	410	4	5	5	7	7
Female householder [3]	307	610	905	1,116	1,498	15	20	23	23	25
NONFAMILY HOUSEHOLDS										
White, total	**10,436**	**18,522**	**20,928**	**23,573**	**24,518**	100	100	100	100	100
Male householder	3,406	7,499	8,608	9,951	10,602	33	40	41	42	43
Female householder	7,030	11,023	12,320	13,622	13,916	67	60	59	58	57
Black, total	**1,367**	**2,402**	**2,703**	**3,015**	**3,292**	100	100	100	100	100
Male householder	564	1,146	1,244	1,313	1,452	41	48	46	44	44
Female householder	803	1,256	1,459	1,702	1,840	59	52	54	56	56
Hispanic, total [2]	**299**	**654**	**944**	**1,093**	**1,423**	100	100	100	100	100
Male householder	150	365	509	587	747	50	56	54	54	52
Female householder	148	289	435	506	676	49	44	46	46	48

NA Not available. [1] Includes other races not shown separately. [2] Hispanic persons may be of any race. 1970 data as of April. [3] No spouse present. [4] 1980 data as of April and are from 1980 Census of Population.

Source: U.S. Bureau of the Census, *Census of Population: 1970, Persons of Spanish Origin*, PC(2)-1C; and *Current Population Reports*, P20-447, and earlier reports; and unpublished data.

No. 71. Family Groups with Children Under 18 Years Old, by Race and Hispanic Origin: 1970 to 1994

[As of **March**. Family groups comprise family households, related subfamilies, and unrelated subfamilies. Excludes members of Armed Forces except those living off post or with their families on post. Based on Current Population Survey; see text, section 1, and Appendix III]

RACE AND HISPANIC ORIGIN OF HOUSEHOLDER OR REFERENCE PERSON	NUMBER (1,000)				PERCENT DISTRIBUTION			
	1970	1980	1990	1994	1970	1980	1990	1994
All races, total [1]	**29,631**	**32,150**	**34,670**	**37,008**	100	100	100	100
Two-parent family groups	25,823	25,231	24,921	25,598	87	79	72	69
One-parent family groups	3,808	6,920	9,749	11,410	13	22	28	31
Maintained by mother	3,415	6,230	8,398	9,854	12	19	24	27
Maintained by father	393	690	1,351	1,556	1	2	4	4
White, total	**26,115**	**27,294**	**28,294**	**29,645**	100	100	100	100
Two-parent family groups	23,477	22,628	21,905	22,310	90	83	77	75
One-parent family groups	2,638	4,664	6,389	7,335	10	17	23	25
Maintained by mother	2,330	4,122	5,310	6,144	9	15	19	21
Maintained by father	307	542	1,079	1,191	1	2	4	4
Black, total	**3,219**	**4,074**	**5,087**	**5,614**	100	100	100	100
Two-parent family groups	2,071	1,961	2,006	1,978	64	48	39	35
One-parent family groups	1,148	2,114	3,081	3,636	36	52	61	65
Maintained by mother	1,063	1,984	2,860	3,350	33	49	56	60
Maintained by father	85	129	221	287	3	3	4	5
Hispanic, total [2]	**(NA)**	**2,194**	**3,429**	**4,369**	(NA)	100	100	100
Two-parent family groups	(NA)	1,626	2,289	2,786	(NA)	74	67	64
One-parent family groups	(NA)	568	1,140	1,583	(NA)	26	33	36
Maintained by mother	(NA)	526	1,003	1,364	(NA)	24	29	31
Maintained by father	(NA)	42	138	219	(NA)	2	4	5

NA Not available. [1] Includes other races, not shown separately. [2] Hispanic persons may be of any race.
Source: U.S. Bureau of the Census, *Current Population Reports*, P20-447, and earlier reports; and unpublished data.

No. 72. Family Groups With Children Under 18 Years Old, by Type, Race and Hispanic Origin: 1994

[As of **March**. Excludes members of Armed Forces except those living off post or with their families on post. Based on Current Population Survey; see text, section 1, and Appendix III]

RACE OR HISPANIC ORIGIN OF HOUSEHOLDER OR REFERENCE PERSON	NUMBER (1,000)					PERCENT DISTRIBUTION				
	Total	Family house-holds	Subfamilies			Total	Family house-holds	Subfamilies		
			Total	Related	Unre-lated			Total	Related	Unre-lated
All races, total [1]	**37,008**	**34,018**	**2,989**	**2,305**	**684**	**100**	**100**	**100**	**100**	**100**
Two-parent family groups	25,598	25,058	540	505	34	69	74	18	22	5
One-parent family groups	11,410	8,961	2,449	1,800	650	31	26	82	78	95
Maintained by mother.	9,854	7,647	2,207	1,636	571	27	22	74	71	83
Maintained by father.	1,556	1,314	242	164	78	4	4	8	7	11
White, total.	**29,645**	**27,642**	**2,004**	**1,443**	**561**	**100**	**100**	**100**	**100**	**100**
Two-parent family groups	22,310	21,884	426	402	24	75	79	21	28	4
One-parent family groups	7,335	5,758	1,578	1,041	536	25	21	79	72	96
Maintained by mother.	6,144	4,748	1,396	925	470	21	17	70	64	84
Maintained by father.	1,191	1,010	182	116	66	4	4	9	8	12
Black, total.	**5,614**	**4,793**	**822**	**735**	**87**	**100**	**100**	**100**	**100**	**100**
Two-parent family groups	1,978	1,924	54	52	2	35	40	7	7	2
One-parent family groups	3,636	2,869	767	683	84	65	60	93	93	97
Maintained by mother.	3,350	2,630	719	644	76	60	55	87	88	87
Maintained by father.	287	238	48	40	9	5	5	6	5	10
Hispanic, total [2]	**4,369**	**3,790**	**579**	**444**	**135**	**100**	**100**	**100**	**100**	**100**
Two-parent family groups	2,786	2,609	177	154	23	64	69	31	35	17
One-parent family groups	1,583	1,181	402	290	112	36	31	69	65	83
Maintained by mother.	1,364	1,006	358	258	100	31	27	62	58	74
Maintained by father.	219	175	44	32	12	5	5	8	7	9

[1] Includes other races, not shown separately. [2] Hispanic persons may be of any race.

Source: U.S. Bureau of the Census, unpublished data.

No. 73. Families, by Size and Presence of Children: 1980 to 1994

[**In thousands, except as indicated.** As of **March**. Excludes members of Armed Forces except those living off post or with their families on post. Based on Current Population Survey; see text, section 1, and Appendix III. For definition of families, see text, section 1]

CHARACTERISTIC	NUMBER				PERCENT DISTRIBUTION			
	1980	1985	1990	1994	1980	1985	1990	1994
Total.	**59,550**	**62,706**	**66,090**	**68,490**	**100**	**100**	**100**	**100**
Size of family:								
Two persons	23,461	25,349	27,606	28,445	39	40	42	42
Three persons	13,603	14,804	15,353	15,979	23	24	23	23
Four persons.	12,372	13,259	14,026	14,479	21	21	21	21
Five persons	5,930	5,894	5,938	6,341	10	9	9	9
Six persons.	2,461	2,175	1,997	2,047	4	4	3	3
Seven or more persons . .	1,723	1,225	1,170	1,198	3	2	2	2
Average per family	3.29	3.23	3.17	3.20	(X)	(X)	(X)	(X)
Own children under age 18:								
None	28,528	31,594	33,801	34,471	48	50	51	50
One	12,443	13,108	13,530	13,824	21	21	20	20
Two	11,470	11,645	12,263	13,086	19	19	19	19
Three	4,674	4,486	4,650	5,193	8	7	7	8
Four or more	2,435	1,873	1,846	1,915	4	3	3	3
Own children under age 6:								
None	46,063	48,505	50,905	52,581	77	77	77	77
One	9,441	9,677	10,304	10,711	16	15	16	16
Two or more	4,047	4,525	4,882	5,199	7	7	7	8

X Not applicable.

Source: U.S. Bureau of the Census, *Current Population Reports*, P20-447, and earlier reports; and unpublished data.

No. 74. Families, by Number of Own Children Under 18 Years Old: 1970 to 1994

[Except as noted, as of **March** and based on Current Population Survey; see headnote, table 73. See also *Historical Statistics, Colonial Times to 1970*, series A 353-358]

RACE, HISPANIC ORIGIN, AND YEAR	NUMBER OF FAMILIES (1,000)					PERCENT DISTRIBUTION				
	Total	No children	One child	Two children	Three or more children	Total	No children	One child	Two children	Three or more children
ALL FAMILIES [1]										
1970	51,586	22,774	9,398	8,969	10,445	100	44	18	17	20
1980	59,550	28,528	12,443	11,470	7,109	100	48	21	19	12
1985	62,706	31,594	13,108	11,645	6,359	100	50	21	19	10
1990	66,090	33,801	13,530	12,263	6,496	100	51	20	19	10
1994	68,490	34,471	13,824	13,086	7,108	100	50	20	19	10
Married couple	53,171	28,113	9,452	10,188	5,418	100	53	18	19	10
Male householder [2]	2,913	1,599	805	368	141	100	55	28	13	5
Female householder [2]	12,406	4,759	3,566	2,531	1,550	100	38	29	20	12
WHITE FAMILIES										
1970	46,261	20,719	8,437	8,174	8,931	100	45	18	18	19
1980	52,243	25,769	10,727	9,977	5,769	100	49	21	19	11
1985	54,400	28,169	11,174	9,937	5,120	100	52	21	18	9
1990	56,590	29,872	11,186	10,342	5,191	100	53	20	18	9
1994	57,870	30,228	11,229	10,846	5,568	100	52	19	19	10
BLACK FAMILIES										
1970	4,887	1,903	858	726	1,401	100	39	18	15	29
1980	6,184	2,364	1,449	1,235	1,136	100	38	23	20	18
1985	6,778	2,887	1,579	1,330	982	100	43	23	20	15
1990	7,470	3,093	1,894	1,433	1,049	100	41	25	19	14
1994	7,989	3,196	1,983	1,630	1,179	100	40	25	20	15
HISPANIC FAMILIES [3]										
1970	2,004	597	390	388	629	100	30	20	19	31
1980	3,029	946	680	698	706	100	31	22	23	23
1985	3,939	1,337	904	865	833	100	34	23	22	21
1990	4,840	1,790	1,095	1,036	919	100	37	23	21	19
1994	5,940	2,150	1,299	1,357	1,135	100	36	22	23	19

[1] Includes other races, not shown separately.   [2] No spouse present.   [3] Hispanic persons may be of any race. 1970 Hispanic data as of April and based on Census of Population.

Source: U.S. Bureau of the Census, *U.S. Census of Population, 1970* (PC-2-4A), and *Current Population Reports*, P20-447, and earlier reports; and unpublished data.

No. 75. Female Family Householders With No Spouse Present—Characteristics, by Race and Hispanic Origin: 1980 to 1994

[As of **March**. Covers persons 15 years old and over. Based on Current Population Survey; see headnote, table 73]

CHARACTERISTIC	Unit	WHITE			BLACK			HISPANIC ORIGIN [1]		
		1980	1990	1994	1980	1990	1994	1980	1990	1994
Female family householder	1,000	6,052	7,306	8,130	2,495	3,275	3,825	610	1,116	1,498
Marital status:										
Never married (single)	Percent	11	15	18	27	39	43	23	27	32
Married, spouse absent	Percent	17	16	17	29	21	20	32	29	27
Widowed	Percent	33	26	22	22	17	13	15	16	15
Divorced	Percent	40	43	43	22	23	23	30	29	26
Presence of children under age 18:										
No own children	Percent	41	43	42	28	32	31	25	33	33
With own children	Percent	59	58	58	72	68	69	75	67	67
One child	Percent	28	30	29	26	30	28	28	25	26
Two children	Percent	20	19	20	23	22	23	23	22	23
Three children	Percent	7	7	7	11	9	11	15	13	12
Four or more children	Percent	3	2	2	11	7	7	9	6	6
Children per family	Number	1.03	0.95	0.99	1.51	1.26	1.28	1.56	1.37	1.40

[1] Persons of Hispanic origin may be of any race.

Source: U.S. Bureau of the Census, *Current Population Reports*, P20-447, and earlier reports; and unpublished data.

No. 76. Family Households With Own Children Under Age 18, by Type of Family, 1980 to 1994, and by Age of Householder, 1994

[As of **March**. Excludes members of Armed Forces except those living off post or with their families on post. Based on Current Population Survey; see text, section 1, and Appendix III]

FAMILY TYPE	1980	1990	1994						
			Total	15 to 24 years old	25 to 34 years old	35 to 44 years old	45 to 54 years old	55 to 64 years old	65 years old and over
NUMBER (1,000)									
Family households with children...	**31,022**	**32,289**	**34,018**	**1,974**	**11,117**	**14,458**	**5,589**	**732**	**148**
Married couple	24,961	24,537	25,058	885	7,722	11,098	4,613	612	128
Male householder [1]	616	1,153	1,314	114	444	503	197	49	7
Female householder [1]	5,445	6,599	7,647	976	2,951	2,857	779	71	13
PERCENT DISTRIBUTION									
Family households with children...	**100**	**100**	**100**	**100**	**100**	**100**	**100**	**100**	**100**
Married couple	81	76	74	45	69	77	83	84	86
Male householder [1]	2	4	4	6	4	3	4	7	5
Female householder [1]	18	20	22	49	27	20	14	10	9
HOUSEHOLDS WITH CHILDREN, AS A PERCENT OF ALL FAMILY HOUSEHOLDS, BY TYPE									
Family households with children, total	**52**	**49**	**50**	**66**	**78**	**81**	**42**	**8**	**1**
Married couple	51	47	47	56	74	81	43	8	1
Male householder [1]	36	40	45	38	58	68	43	19	2
Female householder [1]	63	61	62	87	95	85	37	6	1

[1] No spouse present.

Source: U.S. Bureau of the Census, *Current Population Reports*, P20-447, and earlier reports; and unpublished data.

No. 77. Children Living With Biological, Step, and Adoptive Married-Couple Parents, by Race and Hispanic Origin of Mother: 1980 to 1990

[As of **June**. Covers only those married-couple families with at least one "own child" under age 18 living in their household. "Own children" are children of the householder and/or the householder's spouse. Each child who was the biological child of one of the parents but not of the other parent was classified as a stepchild. If one spouse adopted the biological child of the other spouse, the child was still considered to be a stepchild. Children who were the biological children of both parents were classified as biological children, while all "own" children who were not biological children of either of their parents were classified as adoptive children. Based on Current Population Survey; see text, section 1, and Appendix III]

TYPE OF PARENT	ALL RACES [1]			WHITE			BLACK			Hispanic origin, [2] 1990
	1980	1985	1990	1980	1985	1990	1980	1985	1990	
NUMBER (1,000)										
Own children under 18 years, total	**47,248**	**45,347**	**45,448**	**42,329**	**39,942**	**39,732**	**3,775**	**3,816**	**3,671**	**4,568**
Biological mother and father	39,523	37,213	37,026	35,852	33,202	32,975	2,698	2,661	2,336	3,703
Biological mother-stepfather	5,355	6,049	6,643	4,362	4,918	5,258	877	952	1,149	699
Stepmother-biological father	727	740	608	664	676	549	46	50	38	38
Adoptive mother and father.	1,350	866	974	1,209	754	815	119	76	97	101
Unknown mother or father	293	479	197	242	391	135	35	77	51	27
PERCENT DISTRIBUTION										
Own children under 18 years, total	**100.0**	**100.0**	**100.0**	**100.0**	**100.0**	**100.0**	**100.0**	**100.0**	**100.0**	**100.0**
Biological mother and father	83.7	82.1	81.5	84.7	83.1	83.0	71.5	69.7	63.6	81.1
Biological mother-stepfather	11.3	13.3	14.6	10.3	12.3	13.2	23.2	24.9	31.3	15.3
Stepmother-biological father	1.5	1.6	1.3	1.6	1.7	1.4	1.2	1.3	1.0	0.8
Adoptive mother and father	2.9	1.9	2.1	2.9	1.9	2.1	3.1	2.0	2.6	2.2
Unknown mother or father	0.6	1.1	0.4	0.6	1.0	0.3	0.9	2.0	1.4	0.6

[1] Includes other races not shown separately.   [2] Persons of Hispanic origin may be of any race.

Source: U.S. Bureau of the Census, *Current Population Reports*, P23-180.

No. 78. Living Arrangements of Children Under 18 Years Old, by Selected Characteristic of Parent: 1994

[In thousands. As of March. Covers only those persons under 18 years old who are living with one or both parents. Characteristics are shown for the householder or reference person in married-couple situations. See also headnote, table 73]

CHARACTERISTIC OF PARENT	ALL RACES [1]				WHITE				BLACK				HISPANIC [2]			
	Total	Living with—			Total	Living with—			Total	Living with—			Total	Living with—		
		Both parents	Mother only	Father only		Both parents	Mother only	Father only		Both parents	Mother only	Father only		Both parents	Mother only	Father only
Children under 18 years old	**66,674**	**48,084**	**16,334**	**2,257**	**53,200**	**41,766**	**9,724**	**1,710**	**10,106**	**3,722**	**5,967**	**417**	**9,041**	**6,022**	**2,646**	**373**
Age:																
15 to 24 years old	4,011	1,475	2,362	174	2,706	1,295	1,276	135	1,133	118	994	22	777	337	376	64
25 to 29 years old	8,350	4,905	3,113	333	6,202	4,171	1,794	237	1,779	497	1,207	76	1,560	932	568	60
30 to 34 years old	14,654	10,120	4,039	495	11,431	8,875	2,223	333	2,580	780	1,663	137	2,183	1,415	682	87
35 to 39 years old	16,925	12,854	3,542	529	14,019	11,326	2,268	424	2,018	817	1,123	78	1,899	1,287	536	76
40 to 44 years old	12,514	10,130	2,020	363	10,441	8,817	1,320	304	1,404	749	611	43	1,474	1,155	281	38
45 to 54 years old	8,947	7,502	1,155	291	7,449	6,431	797	221	952	587	310	54	973	748	184	41
55 to 64 years old	1,077	923	90	64	799	710	41	49	208	153	49	8	164	140	18	5
65 years old and over	196	175	14	8	153	142	5	7	31	21	9	1	10	6	-	3
Educational attainment:																
Less than 9th grade	4,117	2,932	1,015	170	3,481	2,546	810	126	268	116	126	26	2,716	1,967	653	96
9th to 12th grade, no diploma	7,948	4,010	3,563	375	5,464	3,373	1,791	299	2,085	405	1,618	62	1,951	1,083	789	79
High school graduate [3]	21,659	14,789	5,993	877	16,740	12,685	3,416	640	4,140	1,534	2,404	202	2,252	1,427	716	108
Some college, no degree or associate degree	17,757	12,754	4,438	565	14,296	11,146	2,725	424	2,689	1,049	1,543	96	1,513	1,032	405	76
Bachelor's degree	9,832	8,714	954	164	8,500	7,701	673	126	692	441	225	26	398	336	57	5
Graduate or professional degree	5,362	4,886	371	105	4,719	4,315	309	95	232	177	51	5	211	176	26	9
Employment status: [4]																
In the civilian labor force	54,878	42,848	10,113	1,917	45,451	37,678	6,291	1,482	6,826	3,012	3,469	345	6,699	5,129	1,252	318
Employed	51,127	40,806	8,616	1,705	42,977	36,035	5,615	1,328	5,736	2,739	2,692	304	6,042	4,710	1,057	275
Both parents employed	27,284	27,284	(X)	(X)	23,933	23,933	(X)	(X)	2,021	2,021	(X)	(X)	2,322	2,322	(X)	(X)
Unemployed	3,751	2,042	1,498	212	2,473	1,643	676	154	1,090	273	777	40	657	419	195	44
Not in the labor force	10,796	4,269	6,202	325	7,008	3,364	3,422	222	3,102	543	2,490	69	2,251	802	1,394	55
Family income:																
Under $5,000	3,651	664	2,775	212	2,049	492	1,414	143	1,428	106	1,261	60	666	164	461	42
$5,000 to $9,999	5,607	1,415	3,980	212	3,375	1,102	2,127	146	1,980	195	1,737	48	1,207	398	781	28
$10,000 to $14,999	4,870	2,261	2,355	253	3,371	1,885	1,304	180	1,170	199	916	55	1,242	741	438	63
$15,000 to $24,999	9,579	5,971	3,022	586	7,320	4,988	1,884	448	1,767	626	1,038	103	2,094	1,482	500	112
$25,000 to $29,999	4,603	3,490	896	217	3,762	3,010	585	166	629	316	270	42	791	665	99	28
$30,000 to $39,999	8,790	6,949	1,542	300	7,282	5,943	1,085	254	1,092	659	408	25	1,143	906	191	45
$40,000 to $49,999	7,655	6,788	646	220	6,694	6,059	468	167	682	480	156	46	678	575	76	27
$50,000 and over	21,921	20,546	1,118	257	19,349	18,288	857	204	1,357	1,140	181	36	1,221	1,090	103	27
Tenure: [5]																
Owned	41,506	35,035	5,366	1,105	36,136	31,348	3,863	925	3,569	2,156	1,289	125	3,523	2,897	510	116
Rented	25,168	13,049	10,968	1,152	17,064	10,418	5,861	785	6,537	1,566	4,678	293	5,518	3,125	2,137	257

- Represents or rounds to zero. X Not applicable. [1] Includes other races, not shown separately. [2] Persons of Hispanic origin may be of any race. [3] Includes equivalency. [4] Excludes children whose parent is in the Armed Forces. [5] Refers to the tenure of the householder (who may or may not be the child's parent).

Source: U.S. Bureau of the Census, unpublished data.

No. 79. Children Under 18 Years Old, by Presence of Parents: 1970 to 1994

[As of **March**. Excludes persons under 18 years old who maintained households or family groups. Based on Current Population Survey; see headnote, table 73]

RACE, HISPANIC ORIGIN, AND YEAR	Number (1,000)	Both parents	PERCENT LIVING WITH—					Father only	Neither parent
			Mother only						
			Total	Divorced	Married, spouse absent	Never married	Wid-owed		
ALL RACES [1]									
1970	69,162	85	11	3	5	1	2	1	3
1980	63,427	77	18	8	6	3	2	2	4
1985	62,475	74	21	9	5	6	2	3	3
1990	64,137	73	22	8	5	7	2	3	3
1994	69,508	69	23	8	6	9	1	3	4
WHITE									
1970	58,790	90	8	3	3	(Z)	2	1	2
1980	52,242	83	14	7	4	1	2	2	2
1985	50,836	80	16	8	4	2	1	2	2
1990	51,390	79	16	8	4	3	1	3	2
1994	54,795	76	18	8	4	4	1	3	3
BLACK									
1970	9,422	59	30	5	16	4	4	2	10
1980	9,375	42	44	11	16	13	4	2	12
1985	9,479	40	51	11	12	25	3	3	7
1990	10,018	38	51	10	12	27	2	4	8
1994	11,177	33	53	10	12	30	1	4	10
HISPANIC [2]									
1970	[3]4,006	78	(NA)	(NA)	(NA)	(NA)	(NA)	(NA)	(NA)
1980	5,459	75	20	6	8	4	2	2	4
1985	6,057	68	27	7	11	7	2	2	3
1990	7,174	67	27	7	10	8	2	3	3
1994	9,496	63	28	6	9	11	2	4	5

NA Not available.   Z Less than 0.5 percent.   [1] Includes other races not shown separately.   [2] Hispanic persons may be of any race.   [3] All persons under 18 years old.

Source: U.S. Bureau of the Census, *Current Population Reports*, P20-450, and earlier reports; and unpublished data.

No. 80. Nonfamily Households, by Sex and Age of Householder: 1980 to 1994

[**In thousands**. As of **March**. See headnote, table 73]

ITEM	MALE HOUSEHOLDER					FEMALE HOUSEHOLDER				
	Total	15 to 24 yr. old	25 to 44 yr. old	45 to 64 yr. old	65 yr. old and over	Total	15 to 24 yr. old	25 to 44 yr. old	45 to 64 yr. old	65 yr. old and over
1980, total	8,807	1,567	3,854	1,822	1,565	12,419	1,189	2,198	3,048	5,983
One person (living alone) .	6,966	947	2,920	1,613	1,486	11,330	779	1,809	2,901	5,842
Nonrelatives present	1,841	620	934	209	79	1,089	410	389	147	141
1990, total	11,606	1,236	5,780	2,536	2,053	15,651	1,032	3,697	3,545	7,377
One person (living alone) .	9,049	674	4,231	2,203	1,943	13,950	536	2,881	3,300	7,233
Nonrelatives present	2,557	560	1,551	334	112	1,701	497	817	245	143
Never married	5,844	1,175	3,689	696	285	4,382	976	2,406	510	491
Married [1]	1,117	28	513	391	187	794	15	261	320	198
Widowed	1,417	-	29	221	1,166	7,428	4	52	1,333	6,038
Divorced	3,228	33	1,550	1,229	416	3,046	37	977	1,382	649
1994, total	12,462	1,210	6,118	2,949	2,183	16,155	1,057	3,844	3,846	7,409
One person (living alone) .	9,440	570	4,359	2,473	2,037	14,171	557	2,872	3,493	7,248
Nonrelatives present	3,022	641	1,759	477	146	1,984	500	972	352	161
Never married	6,283	1,157	3,958	800	367	4,626	998	2,540	638	450
Married [1]	1,204	21	601	402	179	793	22	284	280	206
Widowed	1,411	-	15	211	1,185	7,097	1	75	1,064	5,958
Divorced	3,564	31	1,545	1,537	452	3,639	34	945	1,865	795

- Represents or rounds to zero.   [1] No spouse present.

Source: U.S. Bureau of the Census, *Current Population Reports*, P20-450, and earlier reports; and unpublished data.

No. 81. Persons Living Alone, by Sex and Age: 1970 to 1994

[As of **March**. Based on Current Population Survey; see headnote, table 73]

SEX AND AGE	NUMBER OF PERSONS (1,000)					PERCENT DISTRIBUTION				
	1970	1980	1985	1990	1994	1970	1980	1985	1990	1994
Both sexes	**10,851**	**18,296**	**20,602**	**22,999**	**23,611**	**100**	**100**	**100**	**100**	**100**
15 to 24 years old [1]	556	1,726	1,324	1,210	1,126	5	9	6	5	5
25 to 34 years old	[2]1,604	[2]4,729	3,905	3,972	3,717	[2]15	[2]26	19	17	16
35 to 44 years old	([2])	([2])	2,322	3,138	3,518	([2])	([2])	11	14	15
45 to 64 years old	3,622	4,514	4,939	5,502	5,967	33	25	24	24	25
65 to 74 years old	2,815	3,851	4,130	4,350	4,199	26	21	20	19	18
75 years old and over	2,256	3,477	3,982	4,825	5,086	21	19	19	21	22
Male	**3,532**	**6,966**	**7,922**	**9,049**	**9,440**	**33**	**38**	**39**	**39**	**40**
15 to 24 years old [1]	274	947	750	674	570	3	5	4	3	2
25 to 34 years old	[2]933	[2]2,920	2,307	2,395	2,244	[2]9	[2]16	11	10	10
35 to 44 years old	([2])	([2])	1,406	1,836	2,115	([2])	([2])	7	8	9
45 to 64 years old	1,152	1,613	1,845	2,203	2,473	11	9	9	10	10
65 to 74 years old	611	775	868	1,042	1,031	6	4	4	5	4
75 years old and over	563	711	746	901	1,006	5	4	4	4	4
Female	**7,319**	**11,330**	**12,680**	**13,950**	**14,171**	**68**	**62**	**62**	**61**	**60**
15 to 24 years old [1]	282	779	573	536	557	3	4	3	2	2
25 to 34 years old	[2]671	[2]1,809	1,598	1,578	1,471	[2]6	[2]10	8	7	6
35 to 44 years old	([2])	([2])	916	1,303	1,401	([2])	([2])	4	6	6
45 to 64 years old	2,470	2,901	3,095	3,300	3,493	23	16	15	14	15
65 to 74 years old	2,204	3,076	3,262	3,309	3,168	20	17	16	14	13
75 years old and over	1,693	2,766	3,236	3,924	4,080	16	15	16	17	17

[1] 1970, persons 14 to 24 years old.   [2] Data for persons 35 to 44 years old included with persons 25 to 34 years old.

Source: U.S. Bureau of the Census, *Current Population Reports*, P20-450, and earlier reports; and unpublished data.

No. 82. Population in Institutions and Other Group Quarters, by Type of Group Quarters and State: 1990

[As of **April 1**. See text, section 1, and Appendix III. See *Historical Statistics, Colonial Times to 1970*, series A 359-371, for inmates of institutions]

REGION, DIVISION, AND STATE	Group quarters popula-tion, total [1]	INSTITUTIONALIZED PERSONS		College dormito-ries	REGION, DIVISION, AND STATE	Group quarters popula-tion, total [1]	INSTITUTIONALIZED PERSONS		College dormito-ries
		Total [2]	Nursing homes				Total [2]	Nursing homes	
U.S. . . .	**6,697,744**	**3,334,018**	**1,772,032**	**1,953,558**	DC . . .	41,717	14,070	7,008	16,126
					VA . . .	209,300	84,292	37,762	61,943
Northeast. .	**1,510,088**	**713,335**	**399,329**	**540,689**	WV . . .	36,911	19,469	12,591	15,083
N.E	**445,031**	**179,333**	**119,646**	**198,866**	NC . . .	224,470	83,400	47,014	71,266
ME . . .	37,169	14,136	9,855	14,118	SC . . .	116,543	44,134	18,228	35,488
NH . . .	32,151	11,466	8,202	17,025	GA . . .	173,633	87,266	36,549	39,723
VT . . .	21,642	6,161	4,809	13,435	FL . . .	307,461	173,637	80,298	42,972
MA . . .	214,307	84,345	55,662	100,487	**E.S.C** . . .	**392,424**	**194,314**	**102,900**	**131,846**
RI	38,595	14,801	10,156	18,898	KY . . .	101,176	47,609	27,874	30,600
CT	101,167	48,424	30,962	34,903	TN . . .	129,129	65,389	35,192	43,683
M.A	**1,065,057**	**534,002**	**279,683**	**341,823**	AL . . .	92,402	51,583	24,031	28,859
NY . . .	545,265	267,122	126,175	165,925	MS . . .	69,717	29,733	15,803	28,704
NJ . . .	171,368	92,670	47,054	43,711	**W.S.C** . . .	**658,034**	**373,982**	**184,552**	**161,646**
PA . . .	348,424	174,210	106,454	132,187	AR . . .	58,332	34,223	21,809	16,775
					LA . . .	112,578	67,276	32,072	27,990
Midwest. . .	**1,598,620**	**852,419**	**544,650**	**557,270**	OK . . .	93,677	51,211	29,666	24,924
E.N.C . . .	**1,055,689**	**568,050**	**346,243**	**369,009**	TX . . .	393,447	221,272	101,005	91,957
OH . . .	261,451	152,331	93,769	88,785					
IN	161,992	81,686	50,845	70,873	**West**	**1,294,616**	**622,278**	**269,671**	**239,808**
IL	286,956	149,842	93,662	86,777	**Mountain**	**297,687**	**144,834**	**65,842**	**77,782**
MI	211,692	112,903	57,622	73,093	MT . . .	23,747	11,125	7,764	6,195
WI . . .	133,598	71,288	50,345	49,481	ID . . .	21,490	10,478	6,318	6,676
W.N.C . . .	**542,931**	**284,369**	**198,407**	**188,261**	WY . . .	10,240	5,434	2,679	3,414
MN . . .	117,621	63,279	47,051	39,280	CO . . .	79,472	35,976	18,506	22,749
IA	99,520	47,841	36,455	43,093	NM . . .	28,807	14,024	6,276	8,333
MO . . .	145,397	80,854	52,060	44,033	AZ . . .	80,683	41,508	14,472	18,459
ND . . .	24,234	10,574	8,159	10,377	UT . . .	29,048	12,739	6,222	10,156
SD . . .	25,841	13,305	9,356	9,306	NV . . .	24,200	13,550	3,605	1,800
NE . . .	47,553	25,620	19,171	16,692	**Pacific** . . .	**996,929**	**477,444**	**203,829**	**162,026**
KS . . .	82,765	42,896	26,155	25,480	WA . . .	120,531	55,313	32,840	27,908
					OR . . .	66,205	33,378	18,200	18,970
South	**2,294,420**	**1,145,986**	**558,382**	**615,791**	CA . . .	751,860	376,374	148,362	108,880
S.A	**1,243,962**	**577,690**	**270,930**	**322,299**	AK . . .	20,701	4,574	1,202	1,310
DE . . .	20,071	8,662	4,596	8,806	HI	37,632	7,805	3,225	4,958
MD . . .	113,856	62,760	26,884	30,892					

[1] Includes persons in other types of group quarters not shown separately.   [2] Includes other institutionalized persons not shown separately.

Source: U.S. Bureau of the Census, *1990 Census of Population, General Population Characteristics* (CP-1).

No. 83. Religious Preference, Church Membership, and Attendance: 1967 to 1993

[**In percent**. Covers civilian noninstitutional population, 18 years old and over. Data represent averages of the combined results of several surveys during year or period indicated. Data are subject to sampling variability, see source]

YEAR	RELIGIOUS PREFERENCE					Church/ synagogue members	Persons attending church/ synagogue [1]	AGE AND REGION	Church/ synagogue members, 1992-93
	Protestant	Catholic	Jewish	Other	None				
1967	67	25	3	3	2	[2]73	43	18-29 years old. . . .	59
1975	62	27	2	4	6	71	41	30-49 years old. . . .	68
1980	61	28	2	2	7	69	40	50 years and over . .	76
1985	57	28	2	4	9	71	42	East [3]	69
1990	56	25	2	6	11	65	40	Midwest [4]	72
1991	56	25	2	6	11	68	42	South [5]	76
1992-93	56	26	2	7	9	69	40	West [6]	55

[1] Persons who attended a church or synagogue in the last seven days. [2] 1965 data. [3] ME, NH, RI, NY, CT, VT, MA, NJ, PA, WV, DE, MD, and DC. [4] OH, IN, IL, MI, MN, WI, IA, ND, SD, KS, NE, and MO. [5] KY, TN, VA, NC, SC, GA, FL, AL, MS, TX, AR, OK, and LA. [6] AZ, NM, CO, NV, MT, ID, WY, UT, CA, WA, OR, AK, and HI.

Source: Princeton Religion Research Center, Princeton, NJ, "Emerging Trends," periodical. Based on surveys conducted by The Gallup Organization, Inc.

No. 84. Religious Bodies—Selected Data

[Represents latest information available from religious bodies with memberships of 200,000 or more; excludes a few groups giving no data. Not all groups follow same calendar year nor count membership in same way; some groups give only approximate figures. Data which appear in italics are "noncurrent," i.e., they are reported for 1990 or earlier. All other data are "current" and were reported in 1991 or 1992]

RELIGIOUS BODY	Year reported	Churches reported	Membership (1,000)	Pastors serving parishes [1]
African Methodist Episcopal Church [2]	1991	8,000	3,500	(NA)
African Methodist Episcopal Zion Church	1991	3,000	1,200	2,500
American Baptist Association	*1986*	*1,705*	*250*	*1,740*
American Baptist Churches in the U.S.A.	1992	5,845	1,534	4,506
Antiochian Orthodox Christian Archdiocese of North America, The. . . .	1992	160	250	200
Assemblies of God	1992	11,689	2,258	17,280
Baptist Missionary Association of America.	1992	1,362	237	1,260
Christian and Missionary Alliance, The	1992	1,923	289	1,609
Christian Church (Disciples of Christ)	1992	3,996	1,012	3,883
Christian Churches and Churches of Christ.	*1988*	*5,579*	*1,071*	*5,525*
Christian Methodist Episcopal Church	*1983*	*2,340*	*719*	*2,340*
Christian Reformed Church in North America.	1992	736	224	668
Church of God (Anderson, IN)	1992	2,330	215	2,153
Church of God (Cleveland, TN).	1992	5,776	672	2,301
Church of God in Christ, The	1991	15,300	5,500	28,988
Church of God in Christ, International, The	*1982*	*300*	*200*	*700*
Church of Jesus Christ of Latter-day Saints, The	1992	9,654	4,430	28,962
Church of the Nazarene	1991	5,172	574	4,416
Churches of Christ	1992	13,174	1,685	(NA)
Community Churches, International Council of.	1992	410	500	583
Conservative Baptist Association of America	1992	1,084	200	(NA)
Episcopal Church, The	1991	7,367	2,472	8,040
Evangelical Free Church of America	1992	1,173	214	1,434
Evangelical Lutheran Church in America.	1992	11,055	5,235	9,893
Free Will Baptists, National Association of.	1991	2,495	209	2,800
International Church of the Foursquare Gospel	1992	1,558	207	(NA)
Jehovah's Witnesses	1992	9,890	914	(NA)
Jews [3]	*1990*	*3,416*	*5,981*	*(NA)*
Lutheran Church - Missouri Synod, The	1992	5,369	2,610	5,674
National Baptist Convention of America	*1987*	*2,500*	*3,500*	*8,000*
National Baptist Convention, U.S.A., Inc.	1992	33,000	8,200	32,832
National Missionary Baptist Convention of America.	1992	(NA)	2,500	(NA)
Orthodox Church in America.	1992	700	600	700
Pentecostal Assemblies of the World [2]	*1989*	*1,005*	*500*	*(NA)*
Presbyterian Church in America	1992	1,212	240	1,364
Presbyterian Church (U.S.A.)	1992	11,456	3,758	10,008
Progressive National Baptist Convention, Inc.	1991	1,400	2,500	1,400
Reformed Church in America	1992	927	275	940
Roman Catholic Church, The	1992	19,863	59,221	(NA)
Salvation Army, The	1991	1,151	446	2,710
Seventh-day Adventist Church	1992	4,261	749	2,370
Southern Baptist Convention	1992	38,401	15,359	38,417
United Church of Christ	1992	6,264	1,555	4,512
United Methodist Church, The	1991	37,100	8,789	20,369
United Pentecostal Church International	1992	3,728	550	(NA)
Wisconsin Evangelical Lutheran Synod	*1990*	*1,211*	*420*	*1,167*

NA Not available. [1] Includes other pastors performing pastoral duties. [2] Figures obtained from the *Directory of African American Religious Bodies, 1991.* [3] Estimate of size of Jewish community provided by American Jewish Yearbook. Estimates of the number of Jews holding membership in synagogues or temples of the four branches of Judaism amount to 4,750,000.

Source: Ecumenical Programs in Information and Communications, Inc., Dayton, OH, *Yearbook of American and Canadian Churches,* annual (copyright).

No. 85. Religious Congregations—Summary: 1991

[Excludes Alaska and Hawaii. A religious congregation is a community of people who meet together for worship, for fellowship, and for service to their members and the larger communities in which they live. Excludes informal congregational groups that did not have an official meeting place, denominational organizations, religious charities, and religiously-owned or -affiliated institutions. Based on a sample survey of 1,003 congregations with telephones conducted by the source; for details, see source]

SIZE OF CONGREGATION	Number of congregations	AREAS OF ACTIVITY	Percent of all congregations providing support or service [4]	SOURCE OF REVENUE OR TYPE OF EXPENDITURE	Amount (mil. dol.)
Total	[1]**257,648**	Human services.	91.7	**Revenues, total** [9] **. . . . .**	**48,412**
Fewer than 100 members . .	[2]52,065	Recreation [5]	72.6	Individual giving.	39,223
100-199 members	[3]70,464	Marriage counseling. . . .	70.5	Fees, charges for services.	1,851
200-299 members	39,553	Family counseling	61.8	School tuition	1,352
300-399 members	23,521	Meal services [6]	50.1		
400-499 members	16,051	Single adults programs. .	46.5	**Expenditures, total**	**47,648**
500-999 members	31,826	Health	89.5	Current operating [9]	34,183
1,000-1,999 members	15,451	Visitation and support [7] .	87.4	Wages, salaries	16,532
2,000 or more members . . .	8,717	Alcohol/drug prevention .	47.3	Fringe benefits.	3,696
		International	73.9	Supplies, services.	10,400
Fewer than 100 nonmembers .	136,513	Relief abroad	61.5	Donations [9]	6,626
100-199 nonmembers	63,956	Education &/or health. . .	39.0	Within denomination	4,655
200-299 nonmembers	20,883	Public benefit	62.2	To other organizations	1,317
300-499 nonmembers	12,150	Abortion activities [8]	41.8	Construction, capital improvements [10]	5,051
500 or more nonmembers . .	19,804	Education	53.3	Savings	1,788

[1] Includes those which don't know or did not answer.   [2] Includes churches with fewer than 100 nonmembers.   [3] Includes churches with fewer than 100 members but with 100 or more nonmembers.   [4] Congregations could give multiple responses.   [5] Includes camp programs and other youth programs.   [6] Includes food kitchens.   [7] Programs for sick and shut-ins.   [8] Pro-life or pro-choice.   [9] Includes other items, not shown separately.   [10] Includes acquisition of real property.
Source: INDEPENDENT SECTOR, Washington, DC, *From Belief to Commitment: The Community Service Activities and Finances of Religious Congregations in the United States, 1993 Edition* (copyright).

No. 86. Christian Church Adherents, 1990, and Jewish Population, 1993—States

[Christian church adherents were defined as "all members, including full members, their children and the estimated number of other regular participants who are not considered as communicant, confirmed or full members." Data on Christian church adherents are based on reports of 133 church groupings and exclude 34 church bodies that reported more than 100,000 members to the *Yearbook of American and Canadian Churches*. The Jewish population includes Jews who define themselves as Jewish by religion as well as those who define themselves as Jewish in cultural terms. Data on Jewish population are based primarily on a compilation of individual estimates made by local Jewish federations. Additionally, most large communities have completed Jewish demographic surveys from which the Jewish population can be determined]

REGION, DIVISION, AND STATE	CHRISTIAN ADHERENTS, 1990		JEWISH POPULATION, 1993		REGION, DIVISION, AND STATE	CHRISTIAN ADHERENTS, 1990		JEWISH POPULATION, 1993	
	Number (1,000)	Percent of population [1]	Number (1,000)	Percent of population [1]		Number (1,000)	Percent of population [1]	Number (1,000)	Percent of population [1]
U.S. . .	**131,084**	**52.7**	**5,840**	**2.3**	DC . .	349	57.5	25	4.3
					VA. . .	2,898	46.8	69	1.1
Northeast .	**28,692**	**56.5**	**2,813**	**5.5**	WV . .	740	41.3	2	0.1
N.E.	**7,456**	**56.5**	**405**	**3.1**	NC . .	3,962	59.8	20	0.3
ME . .	439	35.8	8	0.6	SC . .	2,149	61.6	9	0.3
NH . .	431	38.9	8	0.7	GA . .	3,659	56.5	75	1.1
VT. . .	232	41.2	6	0.9	FL. . .	5,106	39.5	622	4.6
MA . .	3,666	60.9	270	4.5	**E.S.C** . .	**9,844**	**64.9**	**39**	**0.3**
RI . .	754	75.1	16	1.6	KY . .	2,216	60.1	12	0.3
CT . .	1,935	58.9	98	3.0	TN . .	2,966	60.8	18	0.4
M.A	**21,235**	**56.5**	**2,408**	**6.4**	AL. . .	2,858	70.7	9	0.2
NY . .	9,970	55.4	1,640	9.1	MS . .	1,804	70.1	1	0.1
NJ. . .	4,305	55.7	437	5.6	**W.S.C.** . .	**17,267**	**64.7**	**133**	**0.5**
PA. . .	6,961	58.6	330	2.8	AR . .	1,423	60.5	2	0.1
Midwest . .	**32,882**	**55.1**	**678**	**1.1**	LA. . .	2,959	70.1	16	0.4
E.N.C . .	**22,220**	**52.9**	**556**	**1.3**	OK . .	2,097	66.7	5	0.2
OH . .	5,307	48.9	129	1.2	TX. . .	10,787	63.5	109	0.6
IN . .	2,617	47.2	18	0.3	**West** . . .	**21,141**	**40.1**	**1,134**	**2.1**
IL . .	6,591	57.7	268	2.3	**Mt**	**6,434**	**47.1**	**155**	**1.1**
MI . .	4,580	49.3	107	1.1	MT . .	341	42.7	(Z)	0.1
WI. . .	3,125	63.9	35	0.7	ID . .	507	50.4	(Z)	0.1
W.N.C. . .	**10,662**	**60.4**	**122**	**0.7**	WY . .	216	47.6	(Z)	0.1
MN . .	2,807	64.2	33	0.7	CO . .	1,244	37.8	51	1.5
IA . .	1,675	60.3	6	0.2	NM . .	883	58.3	7	0.4
MO . .	2,883	56.3	62	1.2	AZ. . .	1,505	41.1	72	1.8
ND . .	484	75.8	1	0.1	UT . .	1,371	79.6	3	0.2
SD . .	474	68.1	(Z)	0.1	NV . .	366	30.5	21	1.6
NE . .	1,000	63.4	7	0.4	**Pac** . . .	**14,707**	**37.6**	**979**	**2.4**
KS . .	1,341	54.1	14	0.6	WA . .	1,580	32.5	33	0.6
South . .	**48,370**	**56.6**	**1,215**	**1.4**	OR . .	903	31.8	18	0.6
S.A.	**21,258**	**48.8**	**1,043**	**2.3**	CA . .	11,665	39.2	919	3.0
DE . .	297	44.6	9	1.4	AK . .	175	31.8	2	0.4
MD . .	2,101	43.9	212	4.3	HI . . .	384	34.6	7	0.6

Z Fewer than 500.   [1] Based on U.S. Bureau of the Census data for resident population enumerated as of April 1, 1990, and estimated as of July 1, 1993.
Source: Christian church adherents—M. Bradley; N. Green, Jr.; D. Jones; M. Lynn; and L. McNeil; *Churches and Church Membership in the United States 1990*, Glenmary Research Center, Atlanta, GA, 1992 (copyright); Jewish population—American Jewish Committee, New York, NY, *American Jewish Year Book, 1993* (copyright).

Figure 2.1
Births and Birth Rates, by Race: 1992

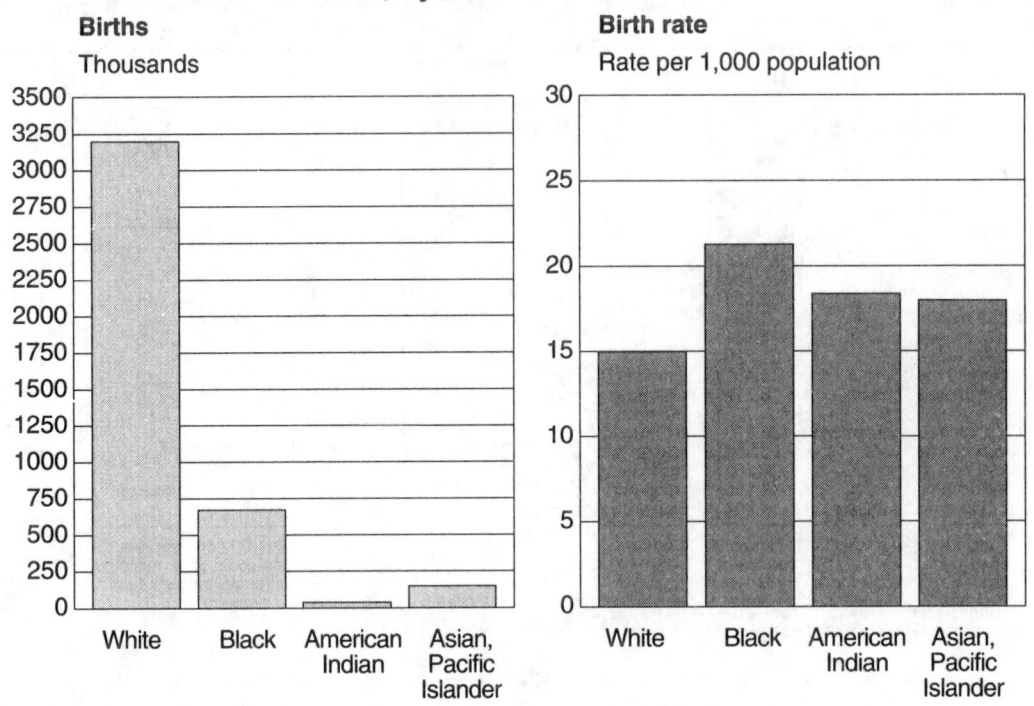

Source: Chart prepared by U.S. Bureau of the Census. For data, see table 89.

Figure 2.2
Live Births by Drinking Status of Mother: 1992

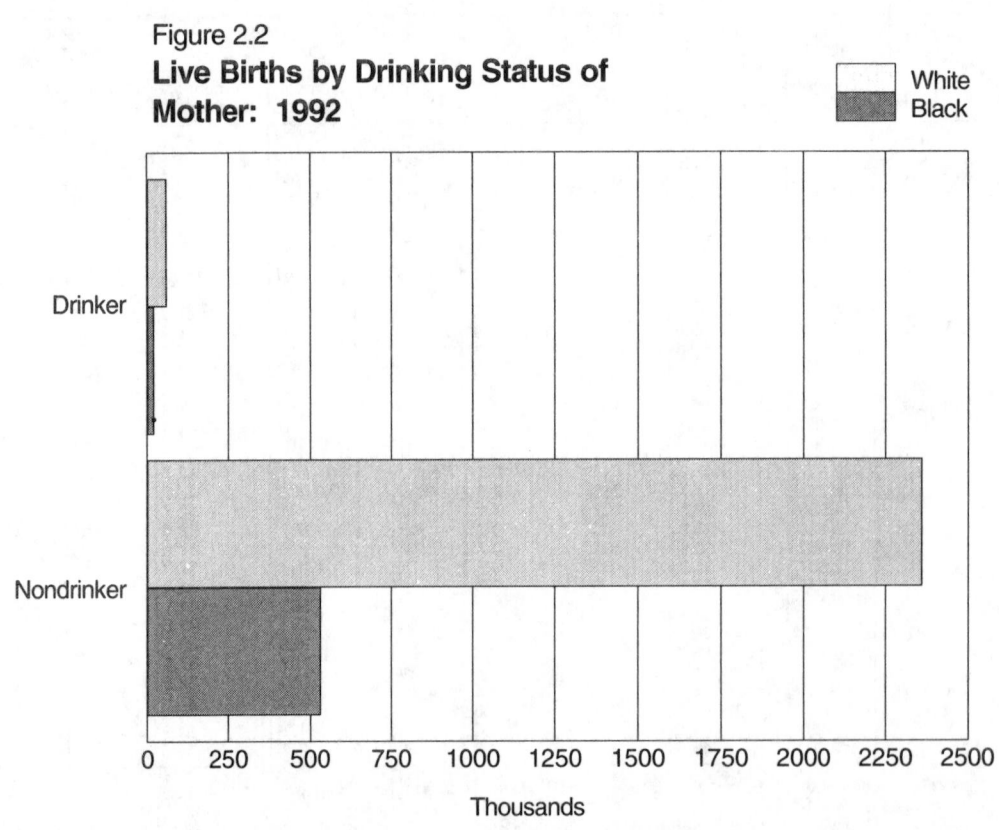

Source: Chart prepared by U.S. Bureau of the Census. For data, see table 110.

Vital Statistics

This section presents vital statistics data on births, deaths, abortions, fetal deaths, fertility, life expectancy, marriages, and divorces. Vital statistics are compiled for the country as a whole by the National Center for Health Statistics (NCHS) and published in its annual report, *Vital Statistics of the United States,* in certain reports of the *Vital and Health Statistics* series, and in the *Monthly Vital Statistics Report.* Reports in this field are also issued by the various State bureaus of vital statistics. Data on fertility, on age of persons at first marriage, and on marital status and marital history are compiled by the Bureau of the Census from its Current Population Survey (CPS; see text, section 1) and published in *Current Population Reports,* P20 series. Data on abortions are published by the Alan Guttmacher Institute, New York, NY in selected issues of *Family Planning Perspectives.*

Registration of vital events.—The registration of births, deaths, fetal deaths, and other vital events in the United States is primarily a State and local function. The civil laws of every State provide for a continuous and permanent birth- and death-registration system. Many States also provide for marriage- and divorce-registration systems. Vital events occurring to U.S. residents outside the United States are not included in the data.

Births and deaths.—The live-birth, death, and fetal-death statistics prepared by NCHS are based on vital records filed in the registration offices of all States, of New York City, and of the District of Columbia. The annual collection of death statistics on a national basis began in 1900 with a national death-registration area of 10 States and the District of Columbia; a similar annual collection of birth statistics for a national birth-registration area began in 1915, also with 10 reporting States and the District of Columbia. Since 1933, the birth- and death-registration areas have comprised the entire United States, including Alaska (beginning 1959) and Hawaii (beginning 1960). National statistics on fetal deaths were

In Brief	
	1994
Births	3,979,000
Deaths	2,286,000
Marriages	2,362,000
Divorces	1,191,000
Acquired Immunodeficiency Syndrome deaths; 1982–94:	
All ages	258,658
13 to 29 years old	45,620
30 to 39 years old	117,759
40 to 49 years old	64,639
50 to 59 years old	21,415
60 years old and over	9,225

first compiled for 1918 and annually since 1922.

Prior to 1951, birth statistics came from a complete count of records received in the Public Health Service (now received in NCHS). From 1951 through 1971, they were based on a 50-percent sample of all registered births (except for a complete count in 1955 and a 20- to 50-percent sample in 1967). Beginning in 1972, they have been based on a complete count for States participating in the Vital Statistics Cooperative Program (VSCP) (for details, see the technical appendix in *Vital Statistics of the United States*) and on a 50-percent sample of all other areas. Beginning 1986 all reporting areas participated in the VSCP. Mortality data have been based on a complete count of records for each area (except for a 50-percent sample in 1972). Beginning in 1970, births to, and deaths of nonresident aliens of the United States and U.S. citizens outside the United States have been excluded from the data. Fetal deaths and deaths among Armed Forces abroad are excluded. Data based on samples are subject to sampling error; for details, see annual issues of *Vital Statistics of the United States.*

Mortality statistics by cause of death are compiled in accordance with World Health Organization regulations according to the *International Classification of Diseases* (ICD). The ICD is revised approximately every 10 years. The ninth revision of the ICD was employed beginning in 1979. Deaths for prior years were classified according to the revision of the ICD in use at the time. Each revision of the ICD introduces a number of discontinuities in mortality statistics; for a discussion of those between the eighth and ninth revisions of the ICD, see *Monthly Vital Statistics Report,* vol. 28, No. 11, supplement.

Some of the tables present age-adjusted death rates in addition to crude death rates. Age-adjusted death rates shown in this section were prepared using the direct method, in which age-specific death rates for a population of interest are applied to a standard population distributed by age. Age adjustment eliminates the differences in observed rates between points in time or among compared population groups that result from age differences in population composition.

Abortions.—The U.S. Centers for Disease Control (CDC) collects data on abortions annually from States which have a central health agency with a statewide reporting system. The Alan Guttmacher Institute, New York, NY also issues data on the number of abortions based on its own surveys of hospitals and physicians. The Guttmacher Institute also publishes data on the characteristics of abortions after adjusting CDC data for changes in the number of States reporting each year.

Fertility and life expectancy.—The total fertility rate, defined as the number of births that 1,000 women would have in their lifetime if, at each year of age, they experienced the birth rates occurring in the specified year, is compiled and published by NCHS. Other data relating to social and medical factors which affect fertility rates, such as contraceptive use and birth expectations, are collected and made available by both NCHS and the Bureau of the Census. NCHS figures are based on information in birth and fetal death certificates and on the periodic National Surveys of Family Growth; Bureau of the Census data are based on decennial censuses and the CPS.

Data on life expectancy, the average remaining lifetime in years for persons who attain a given age, are computed and published by NCHS. For details, see the technical appendix in *Vital Statistics of the United States.*

Marriage and divorce.—The compilation of nationwide statistics on marriages and divorces in the United States began in 1887-88 when the National Office of Vital Statistics prepared estimates for the years 1867-86. Although periodic updates took place after 1888, marriage and divorce statistics were not collected and published annually until 1944 by that Office. In 1957 and 1958, respectively, the same Office established marriage- and divorce-registration areas. Beginning in 1957, the marriage-registration area comprised 30 States, plus Alaska, Hawaii, Puerto Rico, and the Virgin Islands; it currently includes 42 States and the District of Columbia. The divorce-registration area, starting in 1958 with 14 States, Alaska, Hawaii, and the Virgin Islands, currently includes a total of 31 States and the Virgin Islands. Procedures for estimating the number of marriages and divorces in the registration States are discussed in *Vital Statistics of the United States,* vol. III—*Marriage and Divorce.* Total counts of events for registration and nonregistration States are gathered by collecting already summarized data on marriages and divorces reported by State offices of vital statistics and by county offices of registration.

Another important source of data on marriage and divorce trends in the United States is the March supplement to the Current Population Survey conducted by the Bureau of the Census. For information on marital status, see section 1.

Vital statistics rates.—Except as noted, vital statistics rates computed by NCHS are based on decennial census population figures as of April 1 for 1940, 1950, 1960, 1970, 1980, and 1990; and on midyear population figures for other years, as estimated by the Bureau of the Census (see text, section 1).

Race.—Data by race for births, deaths, marriages, and divorces from NCHS are based on information contained in the certificates of registration. The Census Bureau's Current Population Survey obtains information on race by asking respondents to classify their race as: (1) White, (2) Black, (3) American Indian, Eskimo, or Aleut, or (4) Asian or Pacific Islander.

No. 87. Live Births, Deaths, Marriages, and Divorces: 1950 to 1993

[Prior to 1960, excludes Alaska and Hawaii. Beginning 1970, excludes births to and deaths of nonresidents of the United States. See Appendix III. See also *Historical Statistics, Colonial Times to 1970*, series B 1-5, B 142, B 167, and B 216]

YEAR	NUMBER (1,000)					RATE PER 1,000 POPULATION				
	Births [1]	Deaths		Mar-riages [3]	Divor-ces [4]	Births [1]	Deaths		Mar-riages [3]	Divor-ces [4]
		Total	Infant [2]				Total	Infant [2]		
1950	3,632	1,452	104	1,667	385	24.1	9.6	29.2	11.1	2.6
1955	4,097	1,529	107	1,531	377	25.0	9.3	26.4	9.3	2.3
1957	4,300	1,633	112	1,518	381	25.3	9.6	26.3	8.9	2.2
1960	4,258	1,712	111	1,523	393	23.7	9.5	26.0	8.5	2.2
1965	3,760	1,828	93	1,800	479	19.4	9.4	24.7	9.3	2.5
1970	3,731	1,921	75	2,159	708	18.4	9.5	20.0	10.6	3.5
1971	3,556	1,928	68	2,190	773	17.2	9.3	19.1	10.6	3.7
1972	3,258	1,964	60	2,282	845	15.6	9.4	18.5	10.9	4.0
1973	3,137	1,973	56	2,284	915	14.8	9.3	17.7	10.8	4.3
1974	3,160	1,934	53	2,230	977	14.8	9.1	16.7	10.5	4.6
1975	3,144	1,893	51	2,153	1,036	14.6	8.8	16.1	10.0	4.8
1976	3,168	1,909	48	2,155	1,083	14.6	8.8	15.2	9.9	5.0
1977	3,327	1,900	47	2,178	1,091	15.1	8.6	14.1	9.9	5.0
1978	3,333	1,928	46	2,282	1,130	15.0	8.7	13.8	10.3	5.1
1979	3,494	1,914	46	2,331	1,181	15.6	8.5	13.1	10.4	5.3
1980	3,612	1,990	46	2,390	1,189	15.9	8.8	12.6	10.6	5.2
1981	3,629	1,978	43	2,422	1,213	15.8	8.6	11.9	10.6	5.3
1982	3,681	1,975	42	2,456	1,170	15.9	8.5	11.5	10.6	5.1
1983	3,639	2,019	41	2,446	1,158	15.6	8.6	11.2	10.5	5.0
1984	3,669	2,039	40	2,477	1,169	15.6	8.6	10.8	10.5	5.0
1985	3,761	2,086	40	2,413	1,190	15.8	8.8	10.6	10.1	5.0
1986	3,757	2,105	39	2,407	1,178	15.6	8.8	10.4	10.0	4.9
1987	3,809	2,123	38	2,403	1,166	15.7	8.8	10.1	9.9	4.8
1988	3,910	2,168	39	2,396	1,167	16.0	8.9	10.0	9.8	4.8
1989	4,041	2,150	40	[5]2,404	[5]1,163	16.4	8.7	9.8	[5]9.7	[5]4.7
1990	4,158	2,148	38	[5]2,448	[5]1,175	16.7	8.6	9.2	[5]9.8	[5]4.7
1991	4,111	2,170	37	[5]2,371	[5]1,187	16.3	8.6	8.9	[5]9.4	[5]4.7
1992	4,065	2,176	35	2,362	1,215	15.9	8.5	8.5	9.3	4.8
1993	4,039	2,268	33	2,334	1,187	15.7	8.8	8.3	9.0	4.6

[1] Prior to 1960, data adjusted for underregistration.   [2] Infants under 1 year, excluding fetal deaths; rates per 1,000 registered live births.   [3] Includes estimates for some States through 1965 and also for 1976 and 1977 and marriage licenses for some States for all years except 1973 and 1975. Beginning 1978, includes nonlicensed marriages in California.   [4] Includes reported annulments and some estimated State figures for all years.   [5] Preliminary.

Source: U.S. National Center for Health Statistics, *Vital Statistics of the United States*, annual, *Monthly Vital Statistics Report*; and unpublished data.

No. 88. Live Births, by Race and Type of Hispanic Origin—Selected Characteristics: 1990 and 1992

[Represents registered births. Excludes births to nonresidents of the United States. Hispanic origin data are available from only 23 States and the District of Columbia in 1985 and 48 States and DC in 1990]

RACE AND HISPANIC ORIGIN	NUMBER OF BIRTHS (1,000)		BIRTHS TO TEENAGE MOTHERS, PERCENT OF TOTAL		BIRTHS TO UNMARRIED MOTHERS, PERCENT OF TOTAL		PERCENT OF MOTHERS BEGINNING PRENATAL CARE DURING—				PERCENT OF BIRTHS WITH LOW BIRTH WEIGHT [1]	
							First trimester		Third trimester or no care			
	1990	1992	1990	1992	1990	1992	1990	1992	1990	1992	1990	1992
Total	4,158	4,065	12.8	12.7	26.6	30.1	74.2	77.7	6.0	5.2	7.0	7.1
White	3,290	3,202	10.9	10.9	16.9	22.6	77.7	80.8	4.9	4.2	5.7	5.8
Black	684	674	23.1	22.7	66.7	68.1	60.7	63.9	10.9	9.9	13.3	13.3
American Indian, Eskimo, Aleut	39	39	19.5	20.0	53.6	55.3	57.9	62.1	12.9	11.0	6.1	6.2
Asian and Pacific Islander [2]	142	150	5.7	5.6	(NA)	14.7	(NA)	76.6	(NA)	4.9	(NA)	6.6
Filipino	26	29	6.1	5.6	15.9	16.8	77.1	78.7	4.5	4.3	7.3	7.4
Chinese	23	25	1.2	1.0	5.0	6.1	81.3	83.8	3.4	2.9	4.7	5.0
Japanese	9	9	2.9	2.6	9.6	9.8	87.0	88.2	2.9	2.4	6.2	7.0
Hawaiian	6	6	18.4	18.4	45.0	45.7	65.8	69.9	8.7	7.0	7.2	6.9
Hispanic origin [3]	595	643	16.8	17.1	36.7	39.1	60.2	64.2	12.0	9.5	6.1	6.1
Mexican	386	432	17.7	18.0	33.3	36.3	57.8	62.1	13.2	10.5	5.5	5.6
Puerto Rican	59	60	21.7	21.4	55.9	57.5	63.5	67.8	10.6	8.0	9.0	9.2
Cuban	11	11	7.7	7.1	18.2	20.2	84.8	86.8	2.8	2.1	5.7	6.1
Central and South American	83	89	9.0	9.6	41.2	43.9	61.5	66.8	10.9	7.9	5.8	5.8

NA Not available.   [1] Births less than 2,500 grams (5 lb.-8 oz.).   [2] Includes other races not shown separately.   [3] Hispanic persons may be of any race. Includes other types, not shown separately.

Source: U.S. National Center for Health Statistics, *Vital Statistics of the United States*, annual, *Monthly Vital Statistics Report*; and unpublished data.

Vital Statistics

No. 89. Births and Birth Rates: 1970 to 1992

[**Births in thousands and beginning 1980, by race of child.** Excludes births to nonresidents of the United States. For population bases used to derive these data, see text, section 2, and Appendix III. See also *Historical Statistics, Colonial Times to 1970,* series B 1, B 5-10, and B 12-20]

ITEM	1970	1980	1984	1985	1986	1987	1988	1989	1990	1991	1992
Live births [1]	3,731	3,612	3,669	3,761	3,757	3,809	3,910	4,041	4,158	4,111	4,065
White	3,091	2,936	2,967	3,038	3,019	3,044	3,102	3,192	3,290	3,241	3,202
Black	572	568	568	582	593	611	639	673	684	683	674
American Indian	26	29	33	34	34	35	37	39	39	39	39
Asian or Pacific Islander	(NA)	74	99	105	108	117	129	133	142	145	150
Male	1,915	1,853	1,879	1,928	1,925	1,951	2,002	2,069	2,129	2,102	2,082
Female	1,816	1,760	1,790	1,833	1,832	1,858	1,907	1,971	2,029	2,009	1,983
Males per 100 females	106	105	105	105	105	105	105	105	105	105	105
Age of mother:											
Under 20 years old	656	562	480	478	472	473	489	518	533	532	518
20 to 24 years old	1,419	1,226	1,142	1,141	1,102	1,076	1,067	1,078	1,094	1,090	1,070
25 to 29 years old	995	1,108	1,166	1,201	1,200	1,216	1,239	1,263	1,277	1,220	1,179
30 to 34 years old	428	550	658	696	721	761	804	842	886	885	895
35 to 39 years old	180	141	196	214	230	248	270	294	318	331	345
40 years old or more	53	24	28	29	31	36	41	46	50	54	58
Age of father:											
Under 20 years old	189	137	109	108	105	105	111	120	129	130	129
20 to 24 years old	1,015	803	696	685	651	627	617	613	628	625	621
25 to 29 years old	1,085	1,082	1,067	1,081	1,059	1,053	1,055	1,056	1,060	1,007	969
30 to 34 years old	599	739	806	837	845	872	904	922	955	940	940
35 to 39 years old	298	275	356	381	398	413	431	451	474	478	488
40 years old or more	214	139	160	167	174	191	205	221	231	236	242
Age not stated	330	437	475	502	524	549	585	659	681	696	677
Birth rate per 1,000 population	18.4	15.9	15.6	15.8	15.6	15.7	16.0	16.4	16.7	16.3	15.9
White	17.4	15.1	14.8	15.0	14.8	14.9	15.0	15.4	15.8	15.4	15.0
Black	25.3	21.3	20.1	20.4	20.5	20.8	21.5	22.3	22.4	21.9	21.3
American Indian	(NA)	20.7	20.1	19.8	19.2	19.1	19.3	19.7	18.9	18.3	18.4
Asian or Pacific Islander	(NA)	19.9	18.8	18.7	18.0	18.4	19.2	18.7	19.0	18.2	18.0
Male	19.4	16.8	16.4	16.7	16.5	16.5	16.8	17.2	17.6	17.1	16.7
Female	17.4	15.1	14.8	15.0	14.9	14.9	15.2	15.6	15.9	15.6	15.2
Plural birth ratio [2]	(NA)	19.3	20.3	21.0	21.6	22.0	22.4	23.0	23.3	23.9	24.4
White	(NA)	18.5	19.8	20.4	21.2	21.6	22.0	22.5	22.9	23.4	24.0
Black	(NA)	24.1	24.2	25.3	24.9	25.4	25.8	26.9	27.0	27.8	28.2
Birth rate per 1,000 women [3]	87.9	68.4	65.4	66.2	65.4	65.7	67.2	69.2	70.9	69.6	68.9
White [3]	84.1	64.8	63.2	64.1	63.1	63.3	64.5	66.4	68.3	67.0	66.5
Black [3]	115.4	84.7	78.2	78.8	78.9	80.1	82.6	86.2	86.8	85.2	83.2
American Indian [3]	(NA)	82.7	79.8	78.6	75.9	75.6	76.8	79	76.2	75.1	75.4
Asian or Pacific Islander [3]	(NA)	73.2	69.2	68.4	66	67.1	70.2	68.2	69.6	67.6	67.2
Age of mother:											
10 to 14 years old	1.2	1.1	1.2	1.2	1.3	1.3	1.3	1.4	1.4	1.4	1.4
15 to 19 years old	68.3	53.0	50.6	51.0	50.2	50.6	53.0	57.3	59.9	62.1	60.7
20 to 24 years old	167.8	115.1	106.8	108.3	107.4	107.9	110.2	113.8	116.5	115.7	114.6
25 to 29 years old	145.1	112.9	108.7	111.0	109.8	111.6	114.4	117.6	120.2	118.2	117.4
30 to 34 years old	73.3	61.9	67.0	69.1	70.1	72.1	74.8	77.4	80.8	79.5	80.2
35 to 39 years old	31.7	19.8	22.9	24.0	24.4	26.3	28.1	29.9	31.7	32.0	32.5
40 to 44 years old	8.1	3.9	3.9	4.0	4.1	4.4	4.8	5.2	5.5	5.5	5.9
45 to 49 years old	0.5	0.2	0.2	0.2	0.2	0.2	0.2	0.2	0.2	0.2	0.3

NA Not available. [1] Includes other races not shown separately. [2] Number of multiple births per 1,000 live births. [3] Per 1,000 women, 15 to 44 years old in specified group. The rate for *age of mother 45 to 49 years old* computed by relating births to mothers 45 years old and over to women 45 to 49 years old.

Source: U.S. National Center for Health Statistics, *Vital Statistics of the United States,* annual; *Monthly Vital Statistics Report;* and unpublished data.

No. 90. Live Births, by State: 1992

[Registered births. Excludes births to nonresidents of the United States. By race of mother. See Appendix III]

DIVISION AND STATE	All races [1]	WHITE		BLACK		His-panic [2]	Birth rate [3]	Fertility rate [4]
		Total	Non-Hispanic	Total	Non-Hispanic			
United States	**4,065,014**	**3,201,678**	**2,527,207**	**673,633**	**657,450**	**643,271**	**15.9**	**68.9**
Northeast	**761,509**	**606,595**	**491,957**	**126,004**	**116,253**	**92,287**	**14.9**	**(NA)**
New England	**189,088**	**167,197**	**132,905**	**16,203**	**13,614**	**15,682**	**14.3**	**(NA)**
Maine	16,057	15,762	15,033	82	75	101	13.0	56.3
New Hampshire	15,990	15,714	(NA)	109	(NA)	(NA)	14.3	59.5
Vermont	7,737	7,629	6,672	34	32	30	13.5	56.6
Massachusetts	87,231	75,141	67,564	8,647	7,141	8,522	14.6	60.8
Rhode Island	14,500	12,673	10,408	1,186	1,017	1,553	14.5	62.5
Connecticut	47,573	40,278	33,228	6,145	5,349	5,476	14.5	63.2
Middle Atlantic	**572,421**	**439,398**	**359,052**	**109,801**	**102,639**	**76,605**	**15.1**	**(NA)**
New York	287,887	212,579	154,439	60,990	55,549	53,047	15.9	68.1
New Jersey	119,909	90,823	74,348	23,406	22,103	17,609	15.3	66.8
Pennsylvania	164,625	135,996	130,265	25,405	24,987	5,949	13.7	61.6
Midwest	**914,172**	**753,638**	**698,065**	**137,587**	**135,667**	**45,183**	**15.1**	**(NA)**
East North Central	**652,542**	**523,958**	**480,964**	**115,392**	**114,346**	**38,291**	**15.3**	**(NA)**
Ohio	162,247	134,344	131,703	25,994	25,880	2,583	14.7	63.9
Indiana	84,140	73,914	71,956	9,426	9,392	1,941	14.9	64.0
Illinois	191,396	142,842	115,760	42,923	42,346	27,333	16.5	71.4
Michigan	144,089	112,169	102,987	29,742	29,463	4,302	15.3	65.2
Wisconsin	70,670	60,689	58,558	7,307	7,265	2,132	14.2	62.4
West North Central	**261,630**	**229,680**	**217,101**	**22,195**	**21,321**	**6,892**	**14.6**	**(NA)**
Minnesota	65,607	59,187	52,515	2,916	2,132	1,377	14.7	63.7
Iowa	38,469	36,567	35,724	1,184	1,167	853	13.7	63.2
Missouri	76,301	61,908	60,901	13,315	13,282	1,018	14.7	65.5
North Dakota	8,811	7,831	7,657	75	73	119	13.9	63.6
South Dakota	11,018	9,110	9,008	79	74	109	15.6	73.0
Nebraska	23,397	21,403	20,013	1,312	1,306	1,105	14.6	66.0
Kansas	38,027	33,674	31,283	3,314	3,287	2,311	15.1	68.2
South	**1,388,111**	**1,006,482**	**833,487**	**349,657**	**346,605**	**174,970**	**15.7**	**(NA)**
South Atlantic	**681,787**	**467,543**	**425,656**	**198,740**	**196,151**	**43,567**	**15.1**	**(NA)**
Delaware	10,656	7,901	7,504	2,553	2,502	426	15.4	65.2
Maryland	77,815	49,619	46,492	25,426	24,549	2,980	15.8	65.3
District of Columbia	10,960	1,607	1,319	8,803	8,521	893	18.7	71.2
Virginia	97,198	70,137	66,370	23,854	23,737	3,890	15.2	62.6
West Virginia	22,170	21,248	21,185	815	812	75	12.3	54.6
North Carolina	103,967	70,772	68,482	30,333	30,262	2,379	15.2	64.7
South Carolina	56,192	33,977	33,379	21,604	21,535	625	15.6	65.5
Georgia	111,116	68,819	65,794	40,382	40,279	2,932	16.4	66.9
Florida	191,713	143,463	115,131	44,970	43,954	29,367	14.2	68.0
East South Central	**232,395**	**165,390**	**163,868**	**64,744**	**64,660**	**1,552**	**15.0**	**(NA)**
Kentucky	53,840	48,227	47,840	5,188	5,167	372	14.3	61.5
Tennessee	73,614	55,279	54,700	17,510	17,490	595	14.6	62.5
Alabama	62,260	40,180	39,774	21,522	21,488	444	15.0	64.8
Mississippi	42,681	21,704	21,554	20,524	20,515	141	16.3	70.2
West South Central	**473,929**	**373,549**	**243,963**	**86,173**	**85,794**	**129,851**	**17.2**	**(NA)**
Arkansas	34,820	26,289	25,828	8,152	8,133	472	14.5	66.2
Louisiana	70,707	39,757	38,900	29,841	29,751	977	16.5	69.8
Oklahoma	47,557	37,305	35,320	5,164	5,124	2,045	14.8	66.5
Texas	320,845	270,198	143,915	43,016	42,786	126,357	18.1	76.1
West	**1,001,222**	**834,963**	**503,698**	**60,385**	**58,925**	**330,831**	**18.2**	**(NA)**
Mountain	**246,417**	**219,655**	**165,971**	**8,549**	**8,294**	**53,949**	**17.1**	**(NA)**
Montana	11,472	9,981	9,458	49	36	189	14.0	63.6
Idaho	17,362	16,834	15,065	58	55	1,758	16.3	73.5
Wyoming	6,723	6,326	5,852	65	61	482	14.5	62.9
Colorado	54,535	49,644	39,512	3,008	2,919	10,303	15.7	65.0
New Mexico	27,922	23,159	10,331	513	489	12,957	17.7	77.0
Arizona	68,829	59,432	37,790	2,448	2,399	21,862	18.0	80.4
Utah	37,200	35,317	33,062	245	208	2,282	20.5	88.5
Nevada	22,374	18,962	14,901	2,163	2,127	4,116	16.7	73.6
Pacific	**754,805**	**615,308**	**337,727**	**51,836**	**50,631**	**276,882**	**18.5**	**(NA)**
Washington	79,450	70,081	61,224	3,145	2,993	7,182	15.4	66.1
Oregon	42,035	39,068	35,577	955	943	3,561	14.1	62.7
California	601,730	492,487	228,252	46,509	45,510	263,525	19.5	83.1
Alaska	11,726	7,934	7,590	542	531	373	20.0	82.0
Hawaii	19,864	5,738	5,084	685	654	2,241	17.2	75.2

NA Not available. [1] Includes other races not shown separately. [2] Persons of Hispanic origin may be of any race. Births by Hispanic origin of mother. [3] Per 1,000 estimated population. [4] Per 1,000 women aged 15-44 years estimated.

Source: U.S. National Center for Health Statistics, *Vital Statistics of the United States,* annual, and *Monthly Vital Statistics Report.*

No. 91. Total Fertility Rate and Intrinsic Rate of Natural Increase: 1960 to 1992

[Based on race of child and registered births only, thru 1979. Beginning 1980, based on race of mother. Beginning 1970, excludes births to nonresidents of United States. The *total fertility rate* is the number of births that 1,000 women would have in their lifetime if, at each year of age, they experienced the birth rates occurring in the specified year. A total fertility rate of 2,110 represents "replacement level" fertility for the total population under current mortality conditions (assuming no net immigration). The *intrinsic rate of natural increase* is the rate that would eventually prevail if a population were to experience, at each year of age, the birth rates and death rates occurring in the specified year and if those rates remained unchanged over a long period of time. Minus sign (-) indicates decrease. See also Appendix III and *Historical Statistics, Colonial Times to 1970,* series B 11]

ANNUAL AVERAGE AND YEAR	TOTAL FERTILITY RATE			INTRINSIC RATE OF NATURAL INCREASE			ANNUAL AVERAGE AND YEAR	TOTAL FERTILITY RATE			INTRINSIC RATE OF NATURAL INCREASE		
	Total	White	Black and other	Total	White	Black and other		Total	White	Black and other	Total	White	Black and other
1960-64 . . .	3,449	3,326	4,326	18.6	17.1	27.7	1978	1,760	1,668	2,265	-6.8	-8.8	2.9
1965-69 . . .	2,622	2,512	3,362	8.2	6.4	18.6	1979	1,808	1,716	2,310	-5.7	-7.7	3.8
1970-74 . . .	2,094	1,997	2,680	-0.7	-2.5	9.1	1980	1,840	1,773	2,177	-5.1	-7.0	4.0
1975-79 . . .	1,774	1,685	2,270	-6.6	-8.5	3.0	1981	1,812	1,748	2,118	-5.6	-7.4	3.0
1980-84 . . .	1,819	1,731	2,262	-5.4	-7.3	3.0	1982	1,828	1,767	2,107	-5.2	-7.0	3.0
1985-88 . . .	1,870	1,769	2,339	-4.2	-6.3	4.3	1983	1,799	1,741	2,066	-5.8	-7.5	2.2
							1984	1,807	1,749	2,071	-5.6	-7.3	2.1
1970	2,480	2,385	3,067	6.0	4.5	14.4	1985	1,844	1,787	2,109	-4.8	-6.5	2.7
1971	2,267	2,161	2,920	2.6	0.8	12.6	1986	1,838	1,776	2,136	-4.9	-6.7	2.8
1972	2,010	1,907	2,628	-2.0	-3.9	8.6	1987	1,872	1,805	2,198	-4.1	-6.1	4.0
1973	1,879	1,783	2,443	-4.5	-6.5	5.7	1988	1,934	1,857	2,298	-2.9	-5.1	5.7
1974	1,835	1,749	2,339	-5.4	-7.2	4.0	1989	2,014	1,931	2,433	-1.4	-3.6	7.4
1975	1,774	1,686	2,276	-6.7	-8.6	3.0	1990	2,081	2,003	2,480	-0.1	-2.3	8.3
1976	1,738	1,652	2,223	-7.4	-9.3	2.1	1991	2,073	1,996	2,480	-0.2	-2.4	8.2
1977	1,790	1,703	2,279	-6.2	-8.1	3.2	1992	2,065	1,994	2,442	-0.4	-2.5	7.5

Source: U.S. National Center for Health Statistics, *Vital Statistics of the United States,* annual; and unpublished data.

No. 92. Projected Fertility Rates, by Race and Age Group: 1994 and 2010

[For definition of total fertility rate, see headnote, table 91. Birth rates represent live births per 1,000 women in age group indicated. Projections are based on middle fertility assumptions. For explanations of methodology, see text, section 1]

AGE GROUP	ALL RACES [1]		WHITE		BLACK		AMERICAN INDIAN, ESKIMO, ALEUT		ASIAN AND PACIFIC ISLANDERS		HISPANIC [2]	
	1994	2010	1994	2010	1994	2010	1994	2010	1994	2010	1994	2010
Total fertility rate . .	2,079	2,119	1,976	2,009	2,470	2,469	2,779	2,759	2,513	2,406	2,900	2,777
Birth rates:												
10 to 14 years old. . . .	1.4	1.6	0.7	0.9	4.9	5.0	2.0	2.1	0.8	0.8	2.3	2.3
15 to 19 years old. . . .	60.0	62.4	50.0	52.9	113.3	113.8	102.9	105.2	33.4	31.6	99.5	95.8
20 to 24 years old. . . .	118.0	120.0	110.0	112.4	160.9	161.1	188.6	187.0	100.1	95.6	180.5	172.6
25 to 29 years old. . . .	118.8	120.2	118.0	118.8	112.8	113.5	141.4	141.6	160.7	153.4	149.7	143.7
30 to 34 years old. . . .	80.1	82.0	80.2	80.9	67.8	68.4	78.1	78.4	134.2	128.4	95.7	91.5
35 to 39 years old. . . .	31.6	31.8	31.0	30.6	28.0	27.5	34.0	33.5	61.2	57.9	43.0	40.5
40 to 44 years old. . . .	5.4	5.5	5.2	5.1	5.3	5.1	7.2	7.0	12.7	12.0	9.2	8.5
45 to 49 years old. . . .	0.3	0.3	0.2	0.2	0.3	0.3	0.4	0.4	1.3	1.2	0.6	0.5

[1] Includes races not shown separately.   [2] Persons of Hispanic origin may be of any race.

Source: U.S. Bureau of the Census, *Current Population Reports,* P25-1104.

No. 93. Birth Rates, by Live-Birth Order and Race: 1970 to 1992

[**Births per 1,000 women 15 to 44 years old in specified racial group.** Live-birth order refers to number of children born alive. Figures for births of order not stated are distributed. See also headnote, table 89, and *Historical Statistics, Colonial Times to 1970,* series B 20-27]

LIVE-BIRTH ORDER	ALL RACES [1]					WHITE					BLACK				
	1970	1980	1990	1991	1992	1970	1980	1990	1991	1992	1970	1980	1990	1991	1992
Total	87.9	68.4	70.9	69.6	68.9	84.1	65.6	68.3	67.0	66.5	115.4	84.9	86.8	85.2	83.2
First birth	34.2	29.5	29.0	28.3	27.8	32.9	28.8	28.4	27.8	27.3	43.3	33.7	32.4	31.5	30.6
Second birth	24.2	21.8	22.8	22.4	22.3	23.7	21.3	22.4	22.0	22.0	27.1	24.7	25.6	25.0	24.3
Third birth.	13.6	10.3	11.7	11.4	11.3	13.3	9.6	11.1	10.8	10.8	16.1	14.0	15.6	15.4	15.0
Fourth birth	7.2	3.9	4.5	4.5	4.4	6.8	3.4	4.0	4.0	4.0	10.0	6.5	7.4	7.4	7.2
Fifth birth	3.8	1.5	1.7	1.7	1.7	3.4	1.3	1.4	1.4	1.4	6.4	2.9	3.2	3.3	3.3
Sixth and seventh	3.2	1.0	1.0	1.0	1.0	2.7	0.8	0.8	0.8	0.8	7.0	2.1	2.0	2.1	2.2
Eighth and over	1.8	0.4	0.3	0.3	0.3	1.2	0.3	0.2	0.2	0.2	5.6	0.9	0.5	0.6	0.6

[1] Includes other races not shown separately.

Source: U.S. National Center for Health Statistics, *Vital Statistics of the United States,* annual; and *Monthly Vital Statistics Reports.*

No. 94. Births to Unmarried Women, by Race of Child and Age of Mother: 1970 to 1992

[Excludes births to nonresidents of United States. Data for **1970** include estimates for States in which marital status data were not reported. Beginning in **1980**, marital status is inferred from a comparison of the child's and parents' surnames on the birth certificate for those States that do not report on marital status. No estimates included for misstatements on birth records or failures to register births. See also Appendix III and *Historical Statistics, Colonial Times to 1970*, series B 28-35]

RACE OF CHILD AND AGE OF MOTHER	1970	1980	1985	1990	1992	RACE OF CHILD AND AGE OF MOTHER	1970	1980	1985	1990	1992
NUMBER (1,000)						20 to 24 years	31.8	35.6	36.3	34.7	35.6
Total live births [1] .	**399**	**666**	**828**	**1,165**	**1225**	25 to 29 years	10.2	15.0	18.4	19.7	19.1
White	175	320	433	647	722	30 to 34 years	4.8	6.2	8.1	10.1	10.4
Black	215	326	366	473	459	35 years and over	3.1	2.4	3.4	4.5	5.1
Under 15 years old	10	9	9	11	11	AS PERCENT OF ALL BIRTHS IN RACIAL GROUPS					
15 to 19 years old	190	263	271	350	354						
20 to 24 years old	127	237	300	404	436	**Total** [1]	**1J.7**	**18.4**	**22.0**	**28.0**	**30.1**
25 to 29 years old	41	100	152	230	233	White	5.7	11.0	14.5	20.1	22.6
30 to 34 years old	19	41	67	118	128	Black	37.6	55.2	60.1	65.2	68.1
35 years old and over . .	12	16	28	53	63	BIRTH RATE [2]					
PERCENT DISTRIBUTION						**Total** [1][3]	**26.4**	**29.4**	**32.8**	**43.8**	**45.2**
						White [3]	13.9	17.6	21.8	31.8	35.2
Total [1]	**100.0**	**100.0**	**100.0**	**100.0**	**100.0**	Black [3]	95.5	82.9	79.0	93.9	86.5
White	43.9	48.1	52.3	55.6	58.9	15 to 19 years	22.4	27.6	31.4	42.5	44.6
Black	54.0	48.9	44.1	40.6	37.5	20 to 24 years	38.4	40.9	46.5	65.1	68.5
Under 15 years	2.4	1.4	1.1	0.9	0.9	25 to 29 years	37.0	34.0	39.9	56.0	56.5
15 to 19 years	47.8	39.5	32.7	30.0	28.9	30 to 34 years	27.1	21.1	25.2	37.6	37.9

[1] Includes other races not shown separately.   [2] Rate per 1,000 unmarried women (never-married, widowed, and divorced) estimated as of July 1.   [3] Covers women aged 15 to 44 years.

Source: U.S. National Center for Health Statistics, *Vital Statistics of the United States,* annual; *Monthly Vital Statistics Report;* and unpublished data.

No. 95. Low Birth Weight and Births to Teenage Mothers and to Unmarried Women—States: 1980 and 1992

[Represents registered births. Excludes births to nonresidents of the United States. Based on 100 percent of births in all States and the District of Columbia. See Appendix III]

DIVISION AND STATE	PERCENT OF BIRTHS WITH LOW BIRTH WEIGHT[1]		BIRTHS TO TEENAGE MOTHERS, PERCENT OF TOTAL		BIRTHS TO UNMAR-RIED WOMEN, PERCENT OF TOTAL		DIVISION AND STATE	PERCENT OF BIRTHS WITH LOW BIRTH WEIGHT[1]		BIRTHS TO TEENAGE MOTHERS, PERCENT OF TOTAL		BIRTHS TO UNMAR-RIED WOMEN, PERCENT OF TOTAL	
	1980	1992	1980	1992	1980	1992		1980	1992	1980	1992	1980	1992
U.S.	**6.8**	**7.1**	**15.6**	**12.7**	**18.4**	**30.1**	VA	7.5	7.4	15.5	11.0	19.2	28.3
							WV	6.7	7.2	20.1	17.2	13.1	27.7
N.E.	**6.2**	**6.0**	**11.6**	**8.1**	**15.5**	**26.2**	NC	7.9	8.4	19.2	15.4	19.0	31.3
ME	6.5	5.0	15.3	10.2	13.9	25.3	SC	8.6	9.0	19.8	16.6	23.0	35.5
NH	5.4	5.3	10.7	6.7	11.0	19.2	GA	8.6	8.5	20.7	16.2	23.2	35.0
VT	5.9	5.6	13.0	8.5	13.7	23.4	FL	7.6	7.4	18.2	13.5	23.0	34.2
MA	6.1	6.0	10.7	7.7	15.7	25.9	**E.S.C. . . . .**	**7.8**	**8.4**	**21.0**	**18.0**	**20.9**	**33.1**
RI	6.3	6.3	12.3	9.8	[2]15.7	29.6	KY	6.8	6.8	21.1	16.5	15.1	26.3
CT	6.7	6.9	11.4	8.0	[2]17.9	28.7	TN	8.0	8.5	19.9	16.9	19.9	32.7
M.A.	**7.1**	**7.4**	**12.6**	**9.2**	**21.3**	**32.1**	AL	7.9	8.5	20.6	18.2	22.2	32.6
NY	7.4	7.6	11.8	9.0	[2]23.8	34.8	MS	8.7	9.9	23.2	21.4	28.0	42.9
NJ	7.2	7.2	12.3	8.0	21.1	26.4	**W.S.C. . . . .**	**7.3**	**7.4**	**19.1**	**16.6**	**15.8**	**22.9**
PA	6.5	7.2	13.9	10.5	17.7	31.6	AR	7.6	8.2	21.6	19.4	20.5	31.0
E.N.C.	**6.7**	**7.2**	**15.2**	**12.9**	**18.0**	**30.2**	LA	8.6	9.4	20.1	18.1	23.4	40.2
OH	6.8	7.4	15.7	13.6	[2]17.8	31.6	OK	6.8	6.7	19.6	16.8	14.0	28.4
IN	6.3	6.7	17.3	14.1	15.5	29.5	TX	6.9	7.0	18.3	15.9	[2]13.3	17.5
IL	7.2	7.7	15.7	12.9	22.5	33.4	**Mountain . . . .**	**6.6**	**6.9**	**14.3**	**13.3**	**12.7**	**28.3**
MI	6.9	7.5	14.0	13.0	[2]16.2	26.8	MT	5.6	6.0	12.4	11.9	[2]12.5	26.4
WI	5.4	5.9	12.3	10.2	13.9	26.1	ID	5.3	5.5	13.1	13.0	7.9	18.3
W.N.C.	**5.7**	**6.1**	**13.5**	**11.2**	**13.1**	**25.8**	WY	7.3	7.3	15.5	13.2	8.2	24.0
MN	5.1	5.2	10.4	8.1	11.4	23.0	CO	8.2	8.5	13.3	12.0	13.0	23.8
IA	5.0	5.7	12.5	10.2	10.3	23.5	NM	7.6	7.2	18.2	17.0	16.1	39.5
MO	6.6	7.3	16.9	14.5	17.6	31.5	AZ	6.2	6.4	16.5	15.0	18.7	36.2
ND	4.9	5.1	10.9	9.3	9.2	22.6	UT	5.2	5.6	11.0	10.5	6.2	15.1
SD	5.1	5.2	13.5	11.4	13.4	26.6	NV	6.6	7.1	15.4	12.4	[2]13.5	33.3
NE	5.6	5.6	12.1	9.9	11.6	22.6	**Pacific . . . . . .**	**5.8**	**5.8**	**13.6**	**11.6**	**19.6**	**32.6**
KS	5.8	6.4	15.0	12.4	12.3	24.3	WA	5.1	5.3	12.5	10.6	13.6	25.3
S.A.	**8.0**	**8.1**	**18.3**	**13.9**	**22.2**	**33.0**	OR	4.9	5.2	13.3	12.4	14.8	27.0
DE	7.7	7.6	16.7	12.4	24.2	32.6	CA	5.9	5.9	13.9	11.8	[2]21.4	34.3
MD	8.2	8.3	14.8	9.8	25.2	30.5	AK	5.4	4.9	11.8	10.9	15.1	27.4
DC	12.8	14.3	20.7	16.3	56.5	66.9	HI	7.1	7.2	11.5	10.0	17.6	26.2

NA Not available.   [1] Less than 2,500 grams (5 pounds-8 ounces).   [2] Marital status of mother is inferred.

Source: U.S. National Center for Health Statistics, *Vital Statistics of the United States,* annual; and *Monthly Vital Statistics Report.*

No. 96. Live Births, by Place of Delivery, Median and Low Birth Weight, and Prenatal Care: 1970 to 1992

[Represents registered births. Excludes births to nonresidents of the United States. For total number of births, see table 89. See Appendix III]

YEAR	BIRTHS ATTENDED (1,000)			MEDIAN BIRTH WEIGHT [3]			PERCENT OF BIRTHS WITH LOW BIRTH WEIGHT [5]			PERCENT OF BIRTHS BY PERIOD IN WHICH PRENATAL CARE BEGAN	
	In hos-pital [1]	Not in hospital		Total [4]	White	Black	Total [3]	White	Black	1st tri-mester	3d tri-mester or no prenatal care
		Physi-cian	Mid-wife and other [2]								
1970	3,708	5	18	7 lb.-4 oz. . .	7 lb.-5 oz. . .	6 lb.-14 oz. . .	7.9	6.8	13.9	68.0	7.9
1975	3,105	11	28	7 lb.-5 oz. . .	7 lb.-7 oz. . .	6 lb.-15 oz. . .	7.4	6.3	13.1	72.4	6.0
1980	3,576	12	24	7 lb.-7 oz. . .	7 lb.-8 oz. . .	7 lb.-0 oz. . .	6.8	5.7	12.5	76.3	5.1
1985	3,722	10	29	7 lb.-7 oz. . .	7 lb.-9 oz. . .	7 lb.-0 oz. . .	6.8	5.6	12.4	76.2	5.7
1986	3,720	9	27	7 lb.-7 oz. . .	7 lb.-9 oz. . .	7 lb.-0 oz. . .	6.8	5.6	12.5	75.9	6.0
1987	3,774	8	27	7 lb.-7 oz. . .	7 lb.-9 oz. . .	7 lb.-0 oz. . .	6.9	5.7	12.7	76.0	6.1
1988	3,872	9	28	7 lb.-7 oz. . .	7 lb.-9 oz. . .	7 lb.-0 oz. . .	6.9	5.6	13.0	75.9	6.1
1989	3,991	13	22	7 lb.-7 oz. . .	7 lb.-8 oz. . .	6 lb.-15 oz. . .	7.0	5.7	13.2	73.9	6.3
1990	4,110	14	21	7 lb.-7 oz. . .	7 lb.-8 oz. . .	7 lb.-0 oz. . .	7.0	5.7	13.3	74.2	6.0
1991	4,064	12	22	7 lb.-7 oz. . .	7 lb.-8 oz. . .	6 lb.-15 oz. . .	7.1	5.8	13.6	76.2	5.8
1992	4,022	10	21	7 lb.-3 oz. . .	7 lb.-4 oz. . .	6 lb.-9 oz. . .	7.1	5.8	13.3	77.7	5.2

[1] Includes all births in hospitals or institutions and in clinics. [2] Includes births with attendant not specified. [3] Beginning 1989, median birth weight based on race of mother; prior to 1989, based on race of child. [4] Includes other races not shown separately. [5] Through 1975, births of 2,500 grams (5 lb.-8 oz.) or less at birth; thereafter, less than 2,500 grams.
Source: U.S. National Center for Health Statistics, *Vital Statistics of the United States,* annual; *Monthly Vital Statistics Report;* and unpublished data.

No. 97. Cesarean Section Deliveries, by Age of Mother: 1990 to 1993

AGE OF MOTHER	1990	1991	1992	1993
Number of cesarean deliveries, total (1,000)	**945**	**905**	**921**	**917**
Rate: Mothers, all ages [1]	23.5	22.6	22.3	22.8
Under 20 years old	16.6	16.4	17.5	15.6
20 to 24 years old	21.0	19.9	21.4	19.9
25 to 29 years old	23.3	23.3	23.2	23.0
30 to 34 years old	27.8	25.7	27.1	26.3
35 years and over	31.4	29.4	30.1	30.3

[1] Cesarean rates are the number of cesarean deliveries per 100 total deliveries for specified category.
Source: U.S. National Center for Health Statistics, *Vital Statistics of the United States*, annual.

No. 98. Live Births and Deaths—20 Largest Metropolitan Areas: 1988

[Excludes births to and deaths of nonresidents of the United States. Data are by place of residence. Metropolitan statistical areas (MSA's), consolidated metropolitan statistical areas (CMSA's), and New England County Metropolitan Areas (NECMA's) are defined by the U.S. Office of Management and Budget as of December 31, 1992; see Appendix II for definitions and components]

METROPOLITAN AREA	NUMBER (1,000)			RATE PER 1,000 POPULATION		
	Births	Deaths		Births	Deaths	
		Total	Infant [1]		Total	Infant [1]
New York-Northern New Jersey-Long Island, NY-NJ-CT-PA CMSA/NECMA [2]	307,126	189,362	3,354	15.8	9.7	10.9
Los Angeles-Riverside-Orange County, CA CMSA	276,991	101,850	2,458	19.9	7.3	8.9
Chicago-Gary-Kenosha, IL-IN-WI CMSA.	141,570	71,500	1,678	17.3	8.7	11.9
Washington-Baltimore, DC-MD-VA-WV CMSA	107,954	50,890	1,243	16.4	7.7	11.5
San Francisco-Oakland-San Jose, CA CMSA	99,474	47,356	774	16.3	7.8	7.8
Philadelphia-Wilmington-Atlantic City, PA-NJ-DE-MD CMSA . .	94,245	58,748	1,100	16.1	10.0	11.7
Boston-Brockton-Nashua, MA-NH NECMA	85,666	50,656	659	15.2	9.0	7.7
Detroit-Ann Arbor-Flint, MI CMSA	78,425	45,227	967	15.2	8.8	12.3
Dallas-Fort Worth, TX CMSA	74,017	25,596	654	18.9	6.5	8.8
Houston-Galveston-Brazoria, TX CMSA	67,130	22,579	644	18.7	6.3	9.6
Miami-Fort Lauderdale, FL CMSA	48,638	32,785	542	15.8	10.7	11.1
Seattle-Tacoma-Bremerton, WA CMSA	44,475	20,447	395	15.8	7.3	8.9
Atlanta, GA MSA	49,123	19,235	554	17.3	6.8	11.3
Cleveland-Akron, OH CMSA.	42,012	27,524	463	14.7	9.6	11.0
Minneapolis-St. Paul, MN-WI MSA	41,436	16,896	322	16.8	6.8	7.8
San Diego, CA MSA	44,096	16,658	315	18.7	7.0	7.1
St. Louis, MO-IL MSA	40,097	23,302	390	16.1	9.4	9.7
Pittsburgh, PA MSA	30,134	27,206	260	12.5	11.3	8.6
Phoenix-Mesa, AZ MSA.	40,216	16,315	398	18.6	7.5	9.9
Tampa-St. Petersburg-Clearwater, FL MSA	27,201	24,903	290	13.6	12.4	10.7

[1] Infants under 1 year, excluding fetal deaths; rates per 1,000 registered live births. [2] Includes parts of New Haven County, CT, not in the CMSA; excludes parts of Litchfield and Middlesex Counties, CT, in the CMSA.
Source: U.S. National Center for Health Statistics, *Vital Statistics of the United States,* annual; and unpublished data.

No. 99. Women Who Have Had a Child in the Last Year, by Age: 1980 to 1992

[See headnote, table 100]

AGE OF MOTHER	WOMEN WHO HAD A CHILD IN LAST YEAR (1,000)			TOTAL BIRTHS PER 1,000 WOMEN			FIRST BIRTHS PER 1,000 WOMEN		
	1980	1990	1992	1980	1990	1992	1980	1990	1992
Total	**3,247**	**3,913**	**3,688**	**71.1**	**67.0**	**62.9**	**28.5**	**26.4**	**24.8**
15 to 29 years old [1] . . .	2,476	2,568	2,346	103.7	90.8	85.9	48.6	43.2	40.9
15 to 19 years old [2] . .	(NA)	338	311	(NA)	39.8	38.0	(NA)	30.1	27.9
20 to 24 years old [2] . .	1,396	1,038	940	96.6	113.4	103.4	(NA)	51.8	49.4
25 to 29 years old . .	1,081	1,192	1,094	114.8	112.1	109.0	(NA)	46.2	43.7
30 to 44 years old	770	1,346	1,342	35.4	44.7	42.9	6.3	10.6	10.7
30 to 34 years old . .	519	892	856	60.0	80.4	76.1	(NA)	21.9	21.8
35 to 39 years old . .	192	377	404	26.9	37.3	38.0	(NA)	6.5	6.4
40 to 44 years old . .	59	77	82	9.9	8.6	8.7	(NA)	1.2	2.3

NA Not available. [1] For 1980-88, 18 to 29 years old. [2] For 1980-88, 18 to 24 years old.

Source: U.S. Bureau of the Census, *Current Population Reports*, P20-375, P20-454, and P20-470.

No. 100. Characteristics of Women Who Have Had a Child in the Last Year: 1992

[As of **June.** Covers civilian noninstitutional population. Since the number of women who had a birth during the 12-month period was tabulated and not the actual numbers of births, some small underestimation of fertility for this period may exist due to the omission of: (1) Multiple births, (2) Two or more live births spaced within the 12-month period (the woman is counted only once), (3) Women who had births in the period and who did not survive to the survey date, (4) Women who were in institutions and therefore not in the survey universe. These losses may be somewhat offset by the inclusion in the CPS of births to immigrants who did not have their children born in the United States and births to nonresident women. These births would not have been recorded in the vital registration system. Based on Current Population Survey (CPS); see text, section 1, and Appendix III]

CHARACTERISTIC	TOTAL, 15 TO 44 YEARS OLD			15 TO 29 YEARS OLD			30 TO 44 YEARS OLD		
	Number of women (1,000)	Women who have had a child in the last year		Number of women (1,000)	Women who have had a child in the last year		Number of women (1,000)	Women who have had a child in the last year	
		Total births per 1,000 women	First births per 1,000 women		Total births per 1,000 women	First births per 1,000 women		Total births per 1,000 women	First births per 1,000 women
Total [1]	**58,614**	**63**	**25**	**27,312**	**86**	**41**	**31,302**	**43**	**11**
White.	48,157	62	25	22,102	82	41	26,056	44	11
Black.	8,017	69	22	4,070	106	39	3,947	31	5
Asian or Pacific Islander	1,827	64	26	832	69	30	996	59	16
Hispanic [2]	5,555	95	35	2,915	125	60	2,640	62	8
Currently married.	31,878	88	32	9,209	176	80	22,668	52	13
Married, spouse present.	29,531	90	33	8,338	180	84	21,193	54	14
Married, spouse absent [3]	2,347	65	19	871	132	45	1,475	26	3
Widowed or divorced	5,383	27	10	973	75	31	4,409	16	5
Never married.	21,354	35	17	17,129	38	20	4,225	22	5
Educational attainment:									
Less than high school	12,159	67	24	8,422	79	33	3,737	40	4
High school, 4 years	19,063	65	25	7,762	113	50	11,301	33	7
College: 1 or more years	27,392	60	25	11,128	73	40	16,264	51	15
No degree	12,422	59	24	6,362	72	36	6,060	45	10
Associate degree	3,982	56	23	1,420	87	46	2,562	38	11
Bachelor's degree	8,173	65	27	2,864	70	44	5,310	63	18
Grad. or prof. degree . . .	2,814	55	30	482	65	48	2,332	53	27
Labor force status:									
Employed	38,139	45	19	15,906	61	32	22,233	34	11
Unemployed	3,849	69	31	2,418	88	45	1,432	37	9
Not in labor force	16,626	102	35	8,988	129	56	7,637	71	12
Occupation of employed women:									
Managerial-professional.	9,923	47	22	2,918	68	43	7,005	38	13
Tech., sales, admin. support. . . .	16,818	47	21	7,602	58	32	9,216	37	12
Service workers	7,102	46	16	3,763	61	26	3,339	28	4
Farming, forestry, and fishing . . .	512	44	10	207	78	25	306	21	-
Precision prod., craft, repair	738	44	19	238	54	29	500	39	14
Operators, fabricators, laborers . .	3,047	31	12	1,179	61	25	1,868	12	4
Family income: Under $10,000	7,500	95	29	4,426	133	47	3,074	41	3
$10,000 to $19,999.	9,201	70	29	4,946	103	50	4,255	32	5
$20,000 to $24,999.	4,964	66	27	2,480	100	47	2,484	33	7
$25,000 to $29,999.	4,492	57	21	2,086	86	40	2,406	32	5
$30,000 to $34,999.	4,631	61	22	2,078	89	41	2,553	37	6
$35,000 to $49,999.	10,677	58	22	4,444	69	37	6,233	50	11
$50,000 to $74,999.	8,821	53	24	3,407	54	34	5,414	52	18
$75,000 and over	5,259	43	21	2,053	29	20	3,205	52	21

- Represents or rounds to zero. [1] Includes women of other races and women with family income not reported, not shown separately. [2] Persons of Hispanic origin may be of any race. [3] Includes separated women.

Source: U.S. Bureau of the Census, *Current Population Reports*, P20-375, P20-454, and P20-470.

Vital Statistics

No. 101. Women Who Have Had a Child in the Last Year, by Age and Labor Force Status: 1980 to 1992

[See headnote, table 100]

YEAR	TOTAL, 18 TO 44 YEARS OLD			18 TO 29 YEARS OLD			30 TO 44 YEARS OLD		
	Number (1,000)	In the labor force		Number (1,000)	In the labor force		Number (1,000)	In the labor force	
		Number (1,000)	Percent		Number (1,000)	Percent		Number (1,000)	Percent
1980	3,247	1,233	38	2,476	947	38	770	287	37
1981	3,381	1,411	42	2,499	1,004	40	881	407	46
1982	3,433	1,508	44	2,445	1,040	43	988	469	48
1983	3,625	1,563	43	2,682	1,138	42	942	425	45
1984	3,311	1,547	47	2,375	1,058	45	936	489	52
1985	3,497	1,691	48	2,512	1,204	48	984	488	50
1986	3,625	1,805	50	2,452	1,185	48	1,174	620	53
1987	3,701	1,881	51	2,521	1,258	50	1,180	623	53
1988 [1]	3,667	1,866	51	2,384	1,177	49	1,283	688	54
1990 [1]	3,913	2,068	53	2,568	1,275	50	1,346	793	59
1992 [1]	3,688	1,985	54	2,346	1,182	50	1,342	802	60

[1] Lower age limit is 15 years old.
Source: U.S. Bureau of the Census, *Current Population Reports*, P20-470; and unpublished data.

No. 102. Childless Women and Children Ever Born, by Race, Age, and Marital Status: 1992

[See headnote, table 100]

CHARACTERISTIC	Total number of women (1,000)	WOMEN BY NUMBER OF CHILDREN EVER BORN (percent)				CHILDREN EVER BORN	
		Total	None	One	Two or more	Total number (1,000)	Per 1,000 women
ALL RACES [1]							
Women ever married	37,260	100	18	23	59	65,874	1,768
15 to 19 years old.	339	100	44	46	10	228	673
20 to 24 years old.	3,064	100	38	34	28	3,046	994
25 to 29 years old.	6,780	100	28	30	43	9,237	1,362
30 to 34 years old.	9,050	100	17	23	60	15,988	1,767
35 to 39 years old.	9,337	100	12	19	69	18,866	2,020
40 to 44 years old.	8,690	100	11	18	71	18,509	2,130
Women never married.	21,354	100	81	10	9	7,440	348
15 to 19 years old.	7,847	100	95	4	1	511	65
20 to 24 years old.	6,023	100	80	13	7	1,827	303
25 to 29 years old.	3,259	100	70	13	17	1,926	591
30 to 34 years old.	2,199	100	64	15	22	1,728	786
35 to 39 years old.	1,300	100	65	13	22	1,016	782
40 to 44 years old.	726	100	75	11	15	433	596
WHITE							
Women ever married	32,165	100	19	23	58	55,482	1,725
15 to 19 years old.	313	100	45	47	8	200	638
20 to 24 years old.	2,708	100	40	35	26	2,546	940
25 to 29 years old.	5,929	100	28	30	41	7,827	1,320
30 to 34 years old.	7,799	100	17	23	60	13,650	1,750
35 to 39 years old.	7,993	100	13	19	68	15,753	1,971
40 to 44 years old.	7,422	100	12	17	72	15,507	2,089
Women never married.	15,993	100	88	7	5	3,006	188
15 to 19 years old.	6,191	100	96	3	1	272	44
20 to 24 years old.	4,674	100	87	9	4	814	174
25 to 29 years old.	2,287	100	80	10	10	832	364
30 to 34 years old.	1,476	100	77	13	10	641	434
35 to 39 years old.	837	100	82	8	10	307	367
40 to 44 years old.	529	100	88	6	6	140	265
BLACK							
Women ever married	3,585	100	11	23	66	7,686	2,144
15 to 19 years old.	16	100	(B)	(B)	(B)	16	(B)
20 to 24 years old.	238	100	22	28	50	384	1,609
25 to 29 years old.	608	100	19	27	54	1,072	1,763
30 to 34 years old.	858	100	12	22	66	1,707	1,988
35 to 39 years old.	934	100	7	22	71	2,255	2,416
40 to 44 years old.	930	100	7	22	72	2,251	2,421
Women never married.	4,432	100	53	20	27	4,215	951
15 to 19 years old.	1,297	100	88	9	4	226	174
20 to 24 years old.	1,097	100	47	29	23	966	881
25 to 29 years old.	813	100	41	23	37	1,028	1,264
30 to 34 years old.	634	100	31	21	49	1,039	1,639
35 to 39 years old.	412	100	30	24	47	677	1,645
40 to 44 years old.	179	100	34	26	41	278	1,555

B Base figure too small to meet statistical standards for reliability. [1] Includes other races, not shown separately.
Source: U.S. Bureau of the Census, *Current Population Reports*, series P20-470.

No. 103. Lifetime Births Expected per 1,000 Wives: 1971 to 1992

[See headnote, table 100]

YEAR	LIFETIME BIRTHS TO ALL WIVES [1] AGED—			LIFETIME BIRTHS TO WHITE WIVES AGED—			LIFETIME BIRTHS TO BLACK WIVES AGED—			LIFETIME BIRTHS TO HISPANIC [2] WIVES AGED—		
	18 to 24 yrs. old	25 to 29 yrs. old	30 to 34 yrs. old	18 to 24 yrs. old	25 to 29 yrs. old	30 to 34 yrs. old	18 to 24 yrs. old	25 to 29 yrs. old	30 to 34 yrs. old	18 to 24 yrs. old	25 to 29 yrs. old	30 to 34 yrs. old
1971....	2,375	2,619	2,989	2,353	2,577	2,936	2,623	3,112	3,714	(NA)	(NA)	(NA)
1975....	2,173	2,260	2,610	2,147	2,233	2,564	2,489	2,587	3,212	2,223	2,607	3,238
1980....	2,134	2,166	2,248	2,130	2,146	2,223	2,155	2,426	2,522	2,428	2,495	2,909
1985....	2,183	2,236	2,167	2,177	2,227	2,139	2,242	2,259	2,521	2,367	2,628	2,712
1990....	2,244	2,285	2,277	2,218	2,272	2,257	2,509	2,443	2,579	2,404	2,482	2,824
1992....	2,279	2,271	2,218	2,274	2,259	2,208	2,353	2,389	2,362	2,511	2,437	2,600

NA Not available.   [1] Includes other races not shown separately.   [2] Persons of Hispanic origin may be of any race.

No. 104. Lifetime Births Expected by Women, 18 to 34 Years Old, by Selected Characteristics: 1992

[As of June. Covers women in the civilian noninstitutional population. Based on Current Population Survey; see text, section 1, and Appendix III]

CHARACTERISTIC	Women reporting on birth expectations (1,000)	RATE PER 1,000 WOMEN			PERCENTAGE EXPECTING—	
		Births to date	Future births expected	Lifetime births expected	No lifetime births	No future births
Total [1]	**24,223**	**1,135**	**963**	**2,098**	**9.3**	**48.3**
White................	20,141	1,077	1,014	2,091	9.3	46.1
Black................	3,217	1,508	628	2,136	9.3	63.4
Hispanic [2]............	2,357	1,493	838	2,331	5.7	51.4
Not a high school graduate	3,599	1,776	616	2,393	7.6	63.8
High school, 4 years............	8,760	1,325	718	2,043	9.0	57.9
College: 1 or more years	11,864	800	1,249	2,049	10.0	36.5
Some college, no degree	5,871	848	1,216	2,064	10.0	39.2
Associate degree	1,731	1,020	1,018	2,038	8.9	43.4
Bachelor's degree............	3,466	663	1,380	2,043	10.3	31.0
Graduate or professional degree ...	795	563	1,427	1,990	12.0	26.0
In labor force................	17,834	929	1,069	1,998	10.5	44.1
Employed	16,130	903	1,077	1,980	10.7	43.6
Unemployed	1,705	1,176	991	2,167	8.4	49.3
Not in labor force	6,389	1,710	667	2,377	6.0	60.1
Managerial and professional.......	3,760	725	1,232	1,957	11.3	36.8
Technical, sales, and admin. support ..	7,511	835	1,126	1,962	10.2	41.0
Service workers.............	3,127	1,097	974	2,071	9.5	48.2
Farming, forestry, and fishing	198	1,426	972	2,398	14.1	55.5
Precision production, craft, and repair .	299	1,135	714	1,849	12.7	59.5
Operators, fabricators, and laborers...	1,235	1,223	675	1,897	13.5	62.4

[1] Includes other races not shown separately.   [2] Persons of Hispanic origin may be of any race.
Source of tables 103 and 104: U.S. Bureau of the Census, *Current Population Reports*, series P20-470.

No. 105. Pregnancies, Number and Outcome: 1976 to 1992

[**Live births:** source of data is statistics of registered births published annually by National Center for Health Statistics (NCHS). **Induced abortions:** derived from published reports by the Alan Guttmacher Institute. **Fetal losses:** based on the National Survey of Family Growth conducted by NCHS]

YEAR	NUMBER (1,000)				RATE PER 1,000 WOMEN, 15 TO 44 YEARS OLD			
	Total	Live births	Induced abortions	Fetal losses	Total	Live births	Induced abortions	Fetal losses
1976.................	5,002	3,168	1,179	655	102.7	65.0	24.2	13.4
1977.................	5,331	3,327	1,317	687	107.0	66.8	26.4	13.8
1978.................	5,433	3,333	1,410	690	106.7	65.5	27.7	13.5
1979.................	5,714	3,494	1,498	722	109.9	67.2	28.8	13.9
1980.................	5,912	3,612	1,554	746	111.9	68.4	29.4	14.1
1981.................	5,958	3,629	1,577	751	110.5	67.3	29.3	13.9
1982.................	6,024	3,681	1,574	769	110.1	67.3	28.8	14.1
1983.................	5,977	3,639	1,575	763	108.0	65.7	28.5	13.8
1984.................	6,019	3,669	1,577	773	107.4	65.5	28.1	13.8
1985.................	6,144	3,761	1,589	795	108.3	66.3	28.0	14.0
1986.................	6,129	3,757	1,574	798	106.7	65.4	27.4	13.9
1987.................	6,183	3,809	1,559	815	106.8	65.8	26.9	14.1
1988.................	6,341	3,910	1,591	840	109.1	67.3	27.4	14.5
1989.................	6,480	4,041	1,567	873	111.0	69.2	26.8	15.0
1990.................	6,668	4,158	1,609	902	113.8	70.9	27.4	15.4
1991.................	6,563	4,111	1,557	896	111.1	69.6	26.3	15.2
1992.................	6,484	4,065	1,529	890	109.9	68.9	25.9	15.1

Source: U.S. National Center for Health Statistics, *Monthly Vital Statistics Report,* vol. 41, No. 6, Supplement.

No. 106. Pregnancies, by Outcome, Age of Woman, and Race: 1991

[See headnote, table 105]

ITEM	Total	Under 15 years old	15 to 19 years old	20 to 24 years old	25 to 29 years old	30 to 34 years old	35 to 39 years old	40 years old and over
PREGNANCIES								
Non-Hispanic:								
White, pregnancies	3,964	8	489	1,007	1,145	884	368	63
Live births	2,635	3	250	637	834	640	235	36
Induced abortions	774	4	164	264	163	106	58	16
Fetal losses	556	1	75	107	148	138	76	11
Black, pregnancies	1,344	14	272	439	320	202	81	15
Live births	673	6	149	216	160	98	37	6
Induced abortions	507	7	101	178	119	67	29	7
Fetal losses	164	1	22	45	41	37	15	3
Hispanic:								
Pregnancies	965	5	177	306	250	149	64	14
Live births	623	2	105	199	170	100	39	8
Induced abortions	208	1	40	73	50	28	13	4
Fetal losses	134	1	32	33	30	22	12	2
RATE PER 1,000 WOMEN								
Non-Hispanic:								
White, pregnancies	91.8	1.3	84.7	151.4	154.7	107.6	47.3	8.6
Live births	61.0	0.5	43.4	95.7	112.7	77.9	30.2	4.8
Induced abortions	17.9	0.7	28.4	39.6	22.0	12.9	7.4	2.2
Fetal losses	12.9	0.2	13.0	16.0	20.0	16.8	9.7	1.6
Black, pregnancies	174.8	11.0	216.7	337.2	232.3	142.7	63.9	14.4
Live births	87.6	4.9	118.9	166.1	116.3	69.3	28.9	5.7
Induced abortions	65.9	5.1	80.5	136.4	86.3	47.1	23.0	6.2
Fetal losses	21.3	0.9	17.2	34.7	29.7	26.3	12.1	2.4
Hispanic:								
Pregnancies	167.4	4.8	180.2	285.6	224.3	143.9	74.8	19.8
Live births	108.1	2.4	106.7	186.3	152.8	96.1	44.9	11.1
Induced abortions	36.2	1.4	40.4	68.1	44.4	27.1	15.5	5.2
Fetal losses	23.2	1.0	33.1	31.2	27.1	20.7	14.4	3.6

Source: U.S. National Center for Health Statistics, *Monthly Vital Statistics Report,* vol. 43, No. 12.

No. 107. Contraceptive Use by Women, 15 to 44 Years Old: 1990

[Based on samples of the female population of of the United States; see source for details. See Appendix III]

CONTRACEPTIVE STATUS AND METHOD	All women [1]	AGE			RACE			MARITAL STATUS		
		15-24 years	25-34 years	35-44 years	Non-Hispanic White	Non-Hispanic Black	His-panic	Never married	Cur-rently married	For-merly married
All women (1,000)	**58,381**	**17,637**	**21,728**	**19,016**	**42,968**	**7,510**	**5,500**	**20,788**	**30,561**	**7,033**
PERCENT DISTRIBUTION										
Sterile	32.1	3.8	26.4	64.6	32.9	34.0	27.5	7.1	46.0	45.2
Surgically sterile	30.2	3.1	24.8	61.1	31.2	31.4	23.9	5.7	43.9	42.3
Noncontraceptively sterile [2]	5.2	0.3	2.7	12.5	5.4	6.5	3.2	1.1	6.6	10.9
Contraceptively sterile [3]	25.0	2.8	22.1	48.6	25.8	24.9	20.7	4.6	37.3	31.4
Nonsurgically sterile [4]	1.9	0.7	1.6	3.5	1.7	2.6	3.6	1.4	2.1	2.9
Pregnant, postpartum	5.4	7.0	7.9	1.2	5.2	5.5	7.7	3.4	7.3	3.1
Seeking pregnancy	4.0	1.8	7.6	2.0	3.7	4.7	5.1	1.1	6.6	1.5
Other nonusers	24.2	46.4	17.1	12.0	23.6	22.1	28.3	50.0	6.6	24.4
Never had intercourse	9.4	26.4	2.8	1.3	8.7	7.0	16.4	26.4	-	-
No intercourse in last month	7.0	7.7	7.1	6.4	7.2	7.5	5.1	12.5	0.6	18.9
Had intercourse in last month	7.8	12.3	7.2	4.3	7.7	7.6	6.8	11.1	6.0	5.5
Nonsurgical contraceptors	34.3	41.2	41.3	20.1	34.6	33.8	31.7	38.5	33.3	25.8
Pill	16.9	23.9	22.0	4.7	17.3	16.7	16.4	21.7	14.5	12.8
IUD	0.8	0.2	0.4	1.8	0.8	0.8	1.0	0.4	1.0	1.4
Diaphragm	1.7	0.2	2.3	2.4	1.8	1.0	0.8	0.3	2.9	0.5
Condom	10.5	13.9	11.0	6.7	10.3	11.4	8.9	13.0	9.9	5.6
Periodic abstinence	1.6	1.0	2.0	1.6	1.6	0.7	1.9	0.8	2.4	0.4
Natural family planning	0.2	0.1	0.4	0.2	0.2	-	-	-	0.4	-
Withdrawal	0.6	0.6	0.6	0.5	0.6	0.4	0.4	0.7	0.5	0.1
Other methods [5]	2.3	1.4	3.0	2.4	2.2	2.8	2.3	1.6	2.1	5.0

- Represents or rounds to zero.   [1] Includes other races, not shown separately.   [2] Persons who had sterilizing operation and who gave as one reason that they had medical problems with their female organs.   [3] Includes all other sterilization operations, and sterilization of the husband or current partner.   [4] Persons sterile from illness, accident, or congenital conditions.   [5] Douche, suppository, and less frequently used methods.

Source: U.S. National Center for Health Statistics, *Advance Data from Vital and Health Statistics,* No. 182.

No. 108. Live Births—Mothers Who Smoked During Pregnancy, According to Educational Attainment and Race of Mother: 1992

[In thousands, except percents. Excludes California, Indiana, New York, and South Dakota, which did not require reporting of tobacco use during pregnancy]

SMOKING MEASURE AND RACE OF MOTHER	Total	YEARS OF SCHOOL COMPLETED BY MOTHER					
		0-8 years	9-11 years	12 years	13-15 years	16 years or more	Not stated
All races [1]	3,080	144	516	1,144	646	581	49
White	2,414	116	350	878	521	514	34
Black	557	20	149	231	106	41	11
Percent: Smoker [1]	16.9	16.8	30.6	20.1	12.0	3.9	17.2
White	17.9	18.3	35.9	22.1	12.6	4.0	17.5
Black	13.8	11.4	19.3	13.5	10.1	4.7	20.3
PERCENT DISTRIBUTION							
All races [1]: Smoker	100.0	100.0	100.0	100.0	100.0	100.0	100.0
10 cigarettes or less	61.9	55.9	60.5	61.2	64.8	73.9	63.7
11-20 cigarettes	32.8	35.6	33.5	33.8	30.7	22.5	30.8
21 cigarettes or more	5.4	8.5	6.0	5.1	4.4	3.6	5.6
White: Smoker	100.0	100.0	100.0	100.0	100.0	100.0	100.0
10 cigarettes or less	58.6	53.5	56.3	58.0	62.3	73.0	59.9
11-20 cigarettes	35.5	37.3	37.0	36.5	32.8	23.1	33.7
21 cigarettes or more	5.9	9.2	6.8	5.5	4.9	3.8	6.5
Black: Smoker	100.0	100.0	100.0	100.0	100.0	100.0	100.0
10 cigarettes or less	78.3	72.3	77.6	79.2	79.1	81.0	74.1
11-20 cigarettes	19.0	23.9	19.3	18.4	18.9	17.7	23.0
21 cigarettes or more	2.6	3.9	3.1	2.3	2.0	1.2	2.9

[1] Includes races other than White and Black.
Source: U.S. National Center for Health Statistics, *Monthly Vital Statistics Reports.*

No. 109. Percent Low Birthweight, by Smoking Status, Age, and Race of Mother: 1992

[Low birthweight is defined as weight of less than 2,500 grams (5 lb. 8 oz.). Excludes California, Indiana, New York, and South Dakota, which did not require reporting of tobacco use during pregnancy]

SMOKING STATUS AND RACE OF MOTHER	All ages	Under 15 years	15-19 years			20-24 years	25-29 years	30-34 years	35-39 years	40-49 years
			Total	15-17 years	18-19 years					
All races [1], total	**7.3**	**13.4**	**9.6**	**10.5**	**9.1**	**7.4**	**6.3**	**6.6**	**7.7**	**8.7**
Smoker	11.5	13.2	11.0	11.4	10.8	10.1	11.2	12.9	15.6	16.9
Nonsmoker	6.3	13.4	9.2	10.2	8.6	6.6	5.3	5.5	6.4	7.6
Not stated	9.1	14.2	11.8	13.1	11.1	9.4	8.2	8.0	9.7	9.2
White, total	**5.9**	**9.9**	**7.9**	**8.5**	**7.5**	**6.0**	**5.2**	**5.5**	**6.5**	**7.4**
Smoker	9.7	12.6	10.4	11.0	10.1	8.8	9.1	10.3	12.6	14.2
Nonsmoker	5.0	9.3	6.9	7.8	6.5	5.1	4.4	4.7	5.5	6.6
Not stated	7.2	(B)	9.8	10.3	9.6	7.3	6.5	6.4	8.3	7.9
Black, total	**13.4**	**15.9**	**13.5**	**13.9**	**13.2**	**12.3**	**13.1**	**14.8**	**16.2**	**16.7**
Smoker	22.1	(B)	16.7	16.1	17.0	18.8	22.4	25.7	28.6	29.1
Nonsmoker	11.9	16.0	13.2	13.6	12.8	11.3	10.9	11.6	12.8	14.3
Not stated	16.8	14.3	16.2	17.8	15.0	15.6	17.0	18.5	19.4	16.7

B Base figure too small to meet statistical standards for reliability of a derived figure.   [1] Includes races other than White and Black.
Source: U.S. National Center for Health Statistics, *Monthly Vital Statistics Reports.*

No. 110. Live Births—Drinking Status of Mother Who Drank During Pregnancy, According to Age and Race of Mother: 1992

[In thousands, except percents. Excludes California, New York, and South Dakota, which did not require reporting of alcohol abuse during pregnancy]

DRINKING STATUS, DRINKING MEASURE, AND RACE OF MOTHER	All ages	Under 15 years	15-19 years			20-24 years	25-29 years	30-34 years	35-39 years	40-49 years
			Total	15-17 years	18-19 years					
All races [1], total	**3,164.4**	**10.0**	**409.4**	**151.5**	**257.9**	**850.6**	**916.9**	**683.8**	**253.6**	**40.1**
Drinker	78.7	0.1	5.4	1.7	3.7	16.6	22.9	22.7	9.6	1.4
Nondrinker	2,993.1	9.6	392.5	145.4	247.1	810.1	867.8	640.0	235.7	37.4
Not stated	92.6	0.3	11.5	4.4	7.1	23.8	26.2	21.1	8.2	1.4
White, total	**2,487.5**	**3.9**	**268.4**	**91.6**	**176.8**	**637.8**	**755.0**	**578.1**	**211.5**	**32.8**
Drinker	57.5	(Z)	3.7	1.2	2.6	11.1	16.2	17.7	7.7	1.1
Nondrinker	2,359.3	3.7	257.2	87.8	169.4	609.5	718.0	543.1	197.1	30.6
Not stated	70.7	0.1	7.4	2.6	4.8	17.2	20.8	17.3	6.7	1.1
Black, total	**566.1**	**5.8**	**129.7**	**55.7**	**74.0**	**186.5**	**129.1**	**79.4**	**30.5**	**5.0**
Drinker	18.3	(Z)	1.3	0.4	0.9	4.8	5.9	4.4	1.7	0.2
Nondrinker	529.6	5.6	124.8	53.8	71.0	176.0	118.8	72.1	27.7	4.6
Not stated	18.2	0.2	3.7	1.6	2.1	5.8	4.4	2.9	1.1	0.2
Percent: Drinker [1]	2.6	8.0	1.4	1.2	1.5	2.0	2.6	3.4	3.9	3.5
White	2.4	1.2	1.4	1.3	1.5	1.8	2.2	3.2	3.7	3.5
Black	3.3	0.5	1.0	0.7	1.2	2.6	4.7	5.8	5.8	4.1

Z Less than 50.   [1] Includes races other than White or Black.
Source: U.S. National Center for Health Statistics, *Monthly Vital Statistics Reports.*

No. 111. Abortions—Number, Rate, and Ratio, by Race: 1975 to 1992

YEAR	ALL RACES				WHITE				BLACK AND OTHER			
	Women 15-44 years old (1,000)	Abortions			Women 15-44 years old (1,000)	Abortions			Women 15-44 years old (1,000)	Abortions		
		Num-ber (1,000)	Rate per 1,000 women	Ratio per 1,000 live births [1]		Num-ber (1,000)	Rate per 1,000 women	Ratio per 1,000 live births [1]		Num-ber (1,000)	Rate per 1,000 women	Ratio per 1,000 live births [1]
1975 ..	47,606	1,034	21.7	331	40,857	701	17.2	276	6,749	333	49.3	565
1979 ..	52,016	1,498	28.8	420	44,266	1,062	24.0	373	7,750	435	56.2	625
1980 ..	53,048	1,554	29.3	428	44,942	1,094	24.3	376	8,106	460	56.5	642
1981 ..	53,901	1,577	29.3	430	45,494	1,108	24.3	377	8,407	470	55.9	645
1982 ..	54,679	1,574	28.8	428	46,049	1,095	23.8	373	8,630	479	55.5	646
1983 [2] .	55,340	1,575	28.5	436	46,506	1,084	23.3	376	8,834	491	55.5	670
1984 ..	56,061	1,577	28.1	423	47,023	1,087	23.1	366	9,038	491	54.3	646
1985 [2] .	56,754	1,589	28.0	422	47,512	1,076	22.6	360	9,242	513	55.5	659
1986 [2] .	57,483	1,574	27.4	416	48,010	1,045	21.8	350	9,473	529	55.9	661
1987 ..	57,964	1,559	27.1	405	48,288	1,017	21.1	338	9,676	542	56.0	648
1988 [2] .	58,192	1,591	27.3	401	48,325	1,026	21.2	333	9,867	565	57.3	638
1989 [2] .	58,365	1,557	26.8	380	48,104	1,006	20.9	309	10,261	561	54.7	650
1990 [2] .	58,700	1,609	27.4	389	48,224	1,039	21.5	318	10,476	570	54.4	655
1991 ..	59,080	1,557	26.3	379	48,406	982	20.3	303	10,674	574	53.8	661
1992 ..	59,020	1,529	25.9	379	(NA)	(NA)	(NA)	(NA)	(NA)	(NA)	(NA)	(NA)

NA Not available. [1] Live births are those which occurred from July 1 of year shown through June 30 of the following year (to match time of conception with abortions). Births are classified by race of child 1972-1988, and by race of mother after 1988. [2] Total numbers of abortions in 1983 and 1986 have been estimated by interpolation; 1989 and 1990 have been estimated using trends in CDC data.

No. 112. Abortions, by Selected Characteristics: 1985 to 1991

[Number of abortions from surveys conducted by source; characteristics from the U.S. Centers for Disease Control's (CDC) annual abortion surveillance summaries, with adjustments for changes in States reporting data to the CDC each year]

CHARACTERISTIC	NUMBER (1,000)			PERCENT DISTRIBUTION			ABORTION RATIO [1]		
	1985	1990 [1]	1991	1985	1990 [1]	1991	1985	1990 [1]	1991
Total abortions	1,589	1,609	1,557	100	100	100	297	280	275
Age of woman:									
Less than 15 years old	17	13	12	1	1	1	624	515	502
15 to 19 years old	399	351	314	25	22	20	462	403	379
20 to 24 years old	548	532	533	35	33	34	328	328	330
25 to 29 years old	336	360	348	21	22	22	219	224	224
30 to 34 years old	181	216	213	11	13	14	203	196	192
35 to 39 years old	87	108	107	5	7	7	280	249	241
40 years old and over.	21	29	29	1	2	2	409	354	339
Race of woman:									
White.	1,076	1,039	982	68	65	63	265	241	233
Black and other	513	570	574	32	35	37	397	396	398
Marital status of woman:									
Married	281	284	271	18	18	17	88	88	86
Unmarried	1,307	1,325	1,285	82	82	83	605	527	512
Number of prior live births:									
None.	872	780	724	55	49	46	358	316	303
One.	349	396	398	22	25	26	219	230	231
Two.	240	280	281	15	17	18	288	292	294
Three	85	102	105	5	6	7	281	279	285
Four or more.	43	50	50	3	3	3	230	223	218
Number of prior induced abortions:									
None.	944	891	840	60	55	54	(NA)	(NA)	(NA)
One.	416	443	437	26	28	28	(NA)	(NA)	(NA)
Two or more . . . . [2]	228	275	279	14	17	18	(NA)	(NA)	(NA)
Weeks of gestation: [2]									
Less than 9 weeks	779	817	805	49	51	52	(NA)	(NA)	(NA)
9 to 10 weeks	425	418	399	27	26	26	(NA)	(NA)	(NA)
11 to 12 weeks	211	199	188	13	12	12	(NA)	(NA)	(NA)
13 weeks or more	173	175	164	11	11	11	(NA)	(NA)	(NA)

NA Not available. [1] Number of abortions per 1,000 abortions and live births. Live births are those which occurred from July 1 of year shown through June 30 of the following year (to match time of conception with abortions). [2] Beginning 1985, data not exactly comparable with prior years because of a change in the method of calculation.

Source of tables 111 and 112: S.K. Henshaw and J. Van Vort, eds., Abortion Factbook, 1992 Edition: Readings, Trends, and State and Local Data to 1988 (copyright); S.K. Henshaw and J. Van Vort, Abortion Services in the United States, 1991 and 1992: Family Perspectives, 26:100, 1994 (copyright); and unpublished data. Reproduced with the permission of the Alan Guttmacher Institute, from Stanley K. Henshaw and Jennifer Van Vort.

No. 113. Abortions—Number, Rate, and Abortion/Live Birth Ratio, by State: 1980 to 1992

[Number of abortions from surveys of hospitals, clinics, and physicians identified as providers of abortion services conducted by The Alan Guttmacher Institute. Abortion rates are computed per 1,000 women 15 to 44 years of age on **July 1** of specified year; abortion ratios are computed as the number of abortions per 1,000 live births from **July 1** of year shown to **June 30** of following year, by State of occurrence]

DIVISION, REGION, AND STATE	NUMBER OF ABORTIONS (1,000)			RATE PER 1,000 WOMEN, 15 TO 44 YEARS OLD			RATIO: ABORTIONS PER 1,000 LIVE BIRTHS		
	1980	1985	1992	1980	1985	1992	1980	1985	1992
United States......	1,554	1,589	1,529	29.3	28.0	25.9	428	422	379
Northeast............	**396**	**407**	**379**	**34.9**	**(NA)**	**32.1**	**604**	**(NA)**	**506**
New England	84	85	78	28.9	28.6	25.2	530	504	429
Maine	5	5	4	18.6	18.6	14.7	289	308	282
New Hampshire.......	5	7	4	21.1	29.0	14.6	347	419	269
Vermont............	4	3	3	30.4	26.2	21.2	466	448	393
Massachusetts	46	40	41	33.5	29.3	28.4	609	533	472
Rhode Island	7	8	7	30.7	35.5	30.0	529	572	461
Connecticut	19	22	20	25.6	29.3	26 2	561	550	444
Middle Atlantic	312	322	300	37.0	37.6	34.6	627	607	530
New York	188	195	195	45.8	47.4	46.2	780	746	694
New Jersey	56	69	55	32.8	39.6	31.0	591	672	460
Pennsylvania	69	57	50	26.1	21.3	18.6	423	348	302
Midwest............	**318**	**289**	**262**	**23.3**	**(NA)**	**18.9**	**336**	**(NA)**	**287**
East North Central.....	243	221	205	24.9	22.1	20.7	369	356	313
Ohio	67	57	50	26.8	22.4	19.5	397	357	294
Indiana	20	16	16	15.3	12.2	12.0	227	202	185
Illinois	69	65	68	25.9	23.8	25.4	374	372	361
Michigan	65	64	56	29.7	28.7	25.2	457	486	393
Wisconsin	22	18	15	20.1	15.7	13.6	292	246	223
West North Central	75	68	57	19.2	16.7	14.3	260	252	221
Minnesota	20	17	16	20.7	16.6	15.6	288	257	251
Iowa	9	10	7	14.3	15.0	11.4	195	248	185
Missouri...........	22	20	14	19.4	17.3	11.6	273	261	175
North Dakota	3	3	1	21.5	18.5	10.7	235	230	149
South Dakota	1	2	1	9.0	10.6	6.8	103	140	92
Nebraska..........	6	7	6	17.9	18.2	15.7	227	268	246
Kansas	14	10	13	25.6	18.2	22.4	343	264	353
South	**457**	**453**	**450**	**25.9**	**(NA)**	**22.0**	**369**	**(NA)**	**323**
South Atlantic........	255	257	269	29.4	27.1	25.9	462	429	397
Delaware	4	5	6	25.9	30.9	35.2	395	451	502
Maryland	31	30	31	29.2	26.9	26.4	571	480	454
District of Columbia	29	24	21	168.3	145.9	138.4	1,569	1,186	1,104
Virginia	32	34	35	24.2	24.0	22.7	417	412	373
West Virginia	3	5	3	6.9	10.1	7.7	104	185	134
North Carolina.......	32	34	36	22.8	22.6	22.4	377	379	357
South Carolina	14	11	12	18.2	13.7	14.2	274	228	229
Georgia...........	38	38	40	28.4	26.1	24.0	395	397	350
Florida............	74	77	85	35.5	31.8	30.0	547	465	438
East South Central	65	57	54	19.2	15.8	14.9	271	258	228
Kentucky	13	10	10	15.1	11.0	11.4	215	189	191
Tennessee	26	22	19	23.6	19.1	16.2	352	315	243
Alabama	21	19	17	23.1	20.2	18.2	331	333	277
Mississippi.........	6	6	8	10.6	9.7	12.4	132	142	176
West South Central	137	139	127	24.5	21.8	19.6	308	290	266
Arkansas	6	5	7	12.3	10.1	13.5	173	159	213
Louisiana..........	18	19	14	17.6	17.4	13.4	218	240	195
Oklahoma	11	13	9	16.4	17.1	12.5	221	269	193
Texas	102	101	97	30.0	25.5	23.1	367	320	297
West	**383**	**440**	**438**	**36.8**	**(NA)**	**34.1**	**486**	**(NA)**	**446**
Mountain	68	75	70	25.0	23.6	21.0	302	316	280
Montana	4	4	3	20.1	19.0	18.2	265	288	298
Idaho	3	3	2	12.7	11.1	7.2	141	155	97
Wyoming	1	1	(Z)	9.5	7.9	4.3	107	125	74
Colorado	23	24	20	31.4	28.8	23.6	447	438	362
New Mexico	8	6	6	27.0	17.4	17.7	358	219	228
Arizona	16	22	21	25.0	29.9	24.1	310	373	295
Utah	4	4	4	12.3	11.1	9.3	97	116	104
Nevada	9	10	13	46.6	40.5	44.2	697	641	591
Pacific	315	365	368	41.0	42.8	38.7	561	594	501
Washington	37	31	33	37.5	28.0	27.7	522	458	447
Oregon	18	15	16	28.3	22.3	23.9	396	374	372
California..........	250	304	304	43.7	47.9	42.1	598	640	519
Alaska............	2	4	2	17.9	27.7	16.5	196	283	222
Hawaii............	8	11	12	34.4	43.7	46.0	441	611	617

NA Not available.   Z Less than 500.

Source: S.K. Henshaw and J. Van Vort, eds., *Abortion Factbook, 1992 Edition: Readings, Trends, and State and Local Data to 1988* (copyright). S.K. Henshaw and J. Van Vort, *Abortion Services in the United States, 1991 and 1992: Family Perspectives, 26:100, 1994* (copyright); and unpublished data. Reproduced with the permission of the Alan Guttmacher Institute, from Stanley K. Henshaw and Jennifer Van Vort.

No. 114. Expectation of Life at Birth, 1970 to 1993, and Projections, 1995 to 2010

[In years. Excludes deaths of nonresidents of the United States. See also *Historical Statistics, Colonial Times to 1970,* series B 107-115]

YEAR	TOTAL			WHITE			BLACK AND OTHER			BLACK		
	Total	Male	Female	Total	Male	Female	Total	Male	Female	Total	Male	Female
1970............	70.8	67.1	74.7	71.7	68.0	75.6	65.3	61.3	69.4	64.1	60.0	68.3
1975............	72.6	68.8	76.6	73.4	69.5	77.3	68.0	63.7	72.4	66.8	62.4	71.3
1980............	73.7	70.0	77.4	74.4	70.7	78.1	69.5	65.3	73.6	68.1	63.8	72.5
1981............	74.1	70.4	77.8	74.8	71.1	78.4	70.3	66.2	74.4	68.9	64.5	73.2
1982............	74.5	70.8	78.1	75.1	71.5	78.7	70.9	66.8	74.9	69.4	65.1	73.6
1983............	74.6	71.0	78.1	75.2	71.6	78.7	70.9	67.0	74.7	69.4	65.2	73.5
1984............	74.7	71.1	78.2	75.3	71.8	78.7	71.1	67.2	74.9	69.5	65.3	73.6
1985............	74.7	71.1	78.2	75.3	71.8	78.7	71.0	67.0	74.8	69.3	65.0	73.4
1986............	74.7	71.2	78.2	75.4	71.9	78.8	70.9	66.8	74.9	69.1	64.8	73.4
1987............	74.9	71.4	78.3	75.6	72.1	78.9	71.0	66.9	75.0	69.1	64.7	73.4
1988............	74.9	71.4	78.3	75.6	72.2	78.9	70.8	66.7	74.8	68.9	64.4	73.2
1989............	75.1	71.7	78.5	75.9	72.5	79.2	70.9	66.7	74.9	68.8	64.3	73.3
1990............	75.4	71.8	78.8	76.1	72.7	79.4	71.2	67.0	75.2	69.1	64.5	73.6
1991............	75.5	72.0	78.9	76.3	72.9	79.6	71.5	67.3	75.5	69.3	64.6	73.8
1992............	75.8	72.3	79.1	76.5	73.2	79.8	71.8	67.7	75.7	69.6	65.0	73.9
1993............	75.5	72.1	78.9	76.3	73.0	79.5	71.5	67.4	75.5	69.3	64.7	73.7
Projections: [1] 1995 ...	76.3	72.8	79.7	77.0	73.7	80.3	72.5	68.2	76.8	70.3	65.8	74.8
2000 ...	76.7	73.2	80.2	77.6	74.3	80.9	72.9	68.3	77.5	70.2	65.3	75.1
2005 ...	77.3	73.8	80.7	78.2	74.9	81.4	73.6	69.1	78.1	70.7	65.9	75.5
2010 ...	77.9	74.5	81.3	78.8	75.6	82.0	74.3	69.9	78.7	71.3	66.5	76.0

[1] Based on middle mortality assumptions; for details, see source. Source: U.S. Bureau of the Census, *Current Population Reports,* P25-1104.

Source: Except as noted, U.S. National Center for Health Statistics, *Vital Statistics of the United States,* annual, and *Monthly Vital Statistics Reports.*

No. 115. Selected Life Table Values: 1979 to 1992

[See also *Historical Statistics, Colonial Times to 1970,* series B 116-125]

AGE AND SEX	TOTAL [1]			WHITE			BLACK		
	1979-1981	1990	1992	1979-1981	1990	1992	1979-1981	1990	1992
AVERAGE EXPECTATION OF LIFE IN YEARS									
At birth: Male...........	70.1	71.8	72.3	70.8	72.7	73.2	64.1	64.5	65.0
Female..........	77.6	78.8	79.1	78.2	79.4	79.8	72.9	73.6	73.9
Age 20: Male..........	51.9	53.3	53.7	52.5	54.0	54.3	46.4	46.7	47.2
Female..........	59.0	59.8	60.1	59.4	60.3	60.6	54.9	55.3	55.6
Age 40: Male..........	33.6	35.1	35.5	34.0	35.6	36.0	29.5	30.1	30.5
Female..........	39.8	40.6	40.9	40.2	41.0	41.2	36.3	36.8	37.1
Age 50: Male..........	25.0	26.4	26.8	25.3	26.7	27.1	22.0	22.5	23.0
Female..........	30.7	31.3	31.6	31.0	31.6	31.9	27.8	28.2	28.5
Age 65: Male..........	14.2	15.1	15.4	14.3	15.2	15.5	13.3	13.2	13.5
Female..........	18.4	18.9	19.2	18.6	19.1	19.3	17.1	17.2	17.4
EXPECTED DEATHS PER 1,000 ALIVE AT SPECIFIED AGE [2]									
At birth: Male...........	13.9	10.3	9.4	12.3	8.6	7.7	23.0	19.7	18.4
Female..........	11.2	8.2	7.6	9.7	6.6	6.1	19.3	16.3	15.2
Age 20: Male..........	1.8	1.6	1.5	1.8	1.4	1.3	2.2	2.7	2.9
Female..........	0.6	0.5	0.5	0.6	0.5	0.5	0.7	0.7	0.7
Age 40: Male..........	3.0	3.1	3.3	2.6	2.7	2.8	6.9	7.1	7.2
Female..........	1.6	1.4	1.4	1.4	1.2	1.2	3.2	3.1	3.3
Age 50: Male..........	7.8	6.2	6.0	7.1	5.6	5.5	14.9	12.8	12.3
Female..........	4.2	3.5	3.4	3.8	3.2	3.1	7.7	6.6	6.3
Age 65: Male..........	28.2	12.9	23.3	27.4	23.0	22.4	38.5	36.8	34.7
Female..........	14.3	13.5	13.2	13.6	12.8	12.6	21.6	21.4	20.4
NUMBER SURVIVING TO SPECIFIED AGE PER 1,000 BORN ALIVE									
Age 20: Male...........	973	979	980	975	981	983	961	963	964
Female........	982	986	987	984	988	989	972	976	977
Age 40: Male..........	933	938	939	940	946	948	885	880	883
Female........	965	971	972	969	975	976	941	944	945
Age 50: Male..........	890	899	901	901	912	913	801	801	804
Female........	941	950	951	947	957	958	896	904	904
Age 65: Male..........	706	741	748	724	760	767	551	571	582
Female..........	835	851	855	848	864	868	733	751	755

[1] Includes other races not shown separately.   [2] See footnote 1, table 116.

Source: U.S. National Center for Health Statistics, *U.S. Life Tables and Actuarial Tables, 1959-61, 1969-71, and 1979-81; Vital Statistics of the United States,* annual; and unpublished data.

No. 116. Expectation of Life and Expected Deaths, by Race, Sex, and Age: 1992

AGE IN 1990 (years)	EXPECTATION OF LIFE IN YEARS					EXPECTED DEATHS PER 1,000 ALIVE AT SPECIFIED AGE [1]				
	Total	White		Black		Total	White		Black	
		Male	Female	Male	Female		Male	Female	Male	Female
At birth.......	75.8	73.2	79.8	65.0	73.9	8.51	7.68	6.10	18.36	15.23
1...........	75.4	72.8	79.3	65.2	74.1	0.62	0.63	0.46	1.11	0.88
2...........	74.5	71.8	78.3	64.3	73.1	0.46	0.45	0.36	0.79	0.71
3...........	73.5	70.9	77.3	63.4	72.2	0.35	0.34	0.28	0.60	0.58
4...........	72.5	69.9	76.3	62.4	71.2	0.29	0.28	0.22	0.50	0.46
5...........	71.6	68.9	75.4	61.4	70.3	0.25	0.25	0.19	0.45	0.37
6...........	70.6	67.9	74.4	60.5	69.3	0.23	0.23	0.16	0.43	0.30
7...........	69.6	66.9	73.4	59.5	68.3	0.21	0.22	0.15	0.40	0.25
8...........	68.6	65.9	72.4	58.5	67.3	0.18	0.20	0.13	0.34	0.22
9...........	67.6	65.0	71.4	57.5	66.3	0.16	0.17	0.12	0.26	0.20
10...........	66.6	64.0	70.4	56.5	65.4	0.14	0.14	0.12	0.18	0.20
11...........	65.6	63.0	69.4	55.5	64.4	0.14	0.15	0.12	0.17	0.22
12...........	64.6	62.0	68.4	54.6	63.4	0.19	0.21	0.15	0.29	0.24
13...........	63.7	61.0	67.4	53.6	62.4	0.30	0.35	0.20	0.58	0.28
14...........	62.7	60.0	66.5	52.6	61.4	0.44	0.54	0.26	1.00	0.32
15...........	61.7	59.1	65.5	51.7	60.4	0.61	0.76	0.34	1.46	0.38
16...........	60.7	58.1	64.5	50.7	59.5	0.76	0.96	0.41	1.90	0.44
17...........	59.8	57.2	63.5	49.8	58.5	0.88	1.11	0.46	2.28	0.51
18...........	58.8	56.2	62.5	48.9	57.5	0.95	1.20	0.48	2.55	0.57
19...........	57.9	55.3	61.6	48.1	56.6	0.98	1.25	0.47	2.75	0.63
20...........	56.9	54.3	60.6	47.2	55.6	1.00	1.28	0.45	2.93	0.69
21...........	56.0	53.4	59.6	46.3	54.6	1.03	1.32	0.44	3.13	0.76
22...........	55.1	52.5	58.7	45.5	53.7	1.06	1.36	0.44	3.28	0.84
23...........	54.1	51.6	57.7	44.6	52.7	1.08	1.39	0.44	3.37	0.92
24...........	53.2	50.6	56.7	43.8	51.8	1.11	1.42	0.46	3.42	1.02
25...........	52.2	49.7	55.7	42.9	50.8	1.13	1.44	0.48	3.44	1.12
26...........	51.3	48.8	54.8	42.1	49.9	1.16	1.46	0.50	3.48	1.22
27...........	50.4	47.8	53.8	41.2	48.9	1.19	1.51	0.52	3.56	1.32
28...........	49.4	46.9	52.8	40.4	48.0	1.24	1.58	0.54	3.72	1.42
29...........	48.5	46.0	51.8	39.5	47.1	1.31	1.67	0.57	3.93	1.51
30...........	47.5	45.1	50.9	38.7	46.1	1.38	1.77	0.60	4.16	1.61
31...........	46.6	44.1	49.9	37.8	45.2	1.45	1.87	0.64	4.40	1.72
32...........	45.7	43.2	48.9	37.0	44.3	1.53	1.97	0.68	4.65	1.85
33...........	44.7	42.3	48.0	36.2	43.4	1.61	2.06	0.73	4.90	1.99
34...........	43.8	41.4	47.0	35.3	42.4	1.70	2.15	0.78	5.17	2.15
35...........	42.9	40.5	46.0	34.5	41.5	1.80	2.25	0.84	5.46	2.32
36...........	42.0	39.6	45.1	33.7	40.6	1.91	2.36	0.90	5.77	2.50
37...........	41.0	38.7	44.1	32.9	39.7	2.01	2.47	0.97	6.10	2.68
38...........	40.1	37.8	43.2	32.1	38.8	2.11	2.58	1.04	6.44	2.87
39...........	39.2	36.9	42.2	31.3	37.9	2.22	2.69	1.11	6.80	3.06
40...........	38.3	36.0	41.2	30.5	37.1	2.33	2.81	1.19	7.17	3.27
41...........	37.4	35.1	40.3	29.7	36.2	2.47	2.96	1.28	7.58	3.49
42...........	36.5	34.2	39.3	28.9	35.3	2.61	3.12	1.39	8.00	3.72
43...........	35.6	33.3	38.4	28.2	34.4	2.77	3.29	1.52	8.46	3.94
44...........	34.7	32.4	37.5	27.4	33.6	2.94	3.48	1.67	8.95	4.16
45...........	33.8	31.5	36.5	26.7	32.7	3.14	3.71	1.83	9.48	4.41
46...........	32.9	30.6	35.6	25.9	31.9	3.36	3.97	2.01	10.06	4.69
47...........	32.0	29.7	34.7	25.2	31.0	3.63	4.27	2.23	10.63	5.02
48...........	31.1	28.8	33.7	24.4	30.2	3.94	4.61	2.47	11.18	5.41
49...........	30.2	28.0	32.8	23.7	29.3	4.29	5.01	2.75	11.75	5.85
50...........	29.3	27.1	31.9	23.0	28.5	4.68	5.45	3.05	12.33	6.33
51...........	28.5	26.3	31.0	22.3	27.7	5.11	5.96	3.39	13.00	6.85
52...........	27.6	25.4	30.1	21.5	26.8	5.60	6.53	3.75	13.86	7.45
53...........	26.8	24.6	29.2	20.8	26.0	6.15	7.18	4.14	15.00	8.17
54...........	25.9	23.7	28.3	20.1	25.3	6.76	7.91	4.56	16.36	8.96
55...........	25.1	22.9	27.5	19.5	24.5	7.43	8.71	5.01	17.85	9.84
56...........	24.3	22.1	26.6	18.8	23.7	8.15	9.59	5.51	19.38	10.74
57...........	23.5	21.3	25.7	18.2	23.0	8.93	10.57	6.06	20.92	11.64
58...........	22.7	20.6	24.9	17.6	22.2	9.79	11.67	6.68	22.40	12.52
59...........	21.9	19.8	24.1	16.9	21.5	10.71	12.89	7.36	23.87	13.40
60...........	21.1	19.1	23.2	16.3	20.8	11.71	14.20	8.10	25.41	14.30
61...........	20.4	18.3	22.4	15.8	20.1	12.77	15.60	8.90	27.08	15.28
62...........	19.7	17.6	21.6	15.2	19.4	13.91	17.11	9.74	28.83	16.37
63...........	18.9	16.9	20.8	14.6	18.7	15.12	18.76	10.63	30.69	17.61
64...........	18.2	16.2	20.0	14.1	18.0	16.42	20.53	11.57	32.66	18.98
65...........	17.5	15.5	19.3	13.5	17.4	17.81	22.43	12.57	34.68	20.43
70...........	14.2	12.4	15.6	11.0	14.3	26.54	33.64	19.55	49.07	28.93
75...........	11.2	9.6	12.2	8.9	11.4	39.26	50.60	30.19	65.43	38.70
80...........	8.5	7.2	9.2	6.8	8.6	59.53	77.27	48.24	89.10	55.92
85 and over ...	6.2	5.3	6.6	5.1	6.3	1,000.00	1,000.00	1,000.00	1,000.00	1,000.00

[1] Based on the proportion of the cohort who are alive at the beginning of an indicated age interval who will die before reaching the end of that interval. For example, out of every 1,000 people alive and exactly 50 years old at the beginning of the period, between 4 and 5 (4.86) will die before reaching their 51st birthdays.

Source: U.S. National Center for Health Statistics, *Vital Statistics of the United States,* annual; and unpublished data.

Vital Statistics

No. 117. Deaths and Death Rates, by Sex and Race: 1970 to 1993

[**Rates are per 1,000 population for specified groups.** Excludes deaths of nonresidents of the United States and fetal deaths. For explanation of age-adjustment, see text, section 2. The standard population for this table is the total population of the United States enumerated in 1940. See Appendix III. See also *Historical Statistics, Colonial Times to 1970*, series B 167-173 and B 181-192]

SEX AND RACE	1970	1980	1984	1985	1986	1987	1988	1989	1990	1991	1992	1993
Deaths [1] (1,000)	**1,921**	**1,990**	**2,039**	**2,086**	**2,105**	**2,123**	**2,168**	**2,150**	**2,148**	**2,170**	**2,176**	**2,268**
Male [1] (1,000)	1,078	1,075	1,077	1,098	1,104	1,108	1,126	1,114	1,113	1,122	1,122	1,167
Female [1] (1,000)	843	915	963	989	1,001	1,015	1,042	1,036	1,035	1,048	1,053	1,101
White (1,000)	1,682	1,739	1,782	1,819	1,831	1,843	1,877	1,854	1,853	1,869	1,874	1,951
Male (1,000)	942	934	935	950	953	953	965	951	951	956	957	994
Female (1,000)	740	805	847	869	879	890	911	903	902	912	917	957
Black (1,000)	226	233	236	244	250	255	264	268	266	270	269	281
Male (1,000)	128	130	129	134	137	140	144	146	145	147	147	153
Female (1,000)	98	103	107	111	113	115	120	121	120	122	123	128
Death rates [1]	**9.5**	**8.8**	**8.6**	**8.8**	**8.8**	**8.8**	**8.8**	**8.7**	**8.6**	**8.6**	**8.5**	**8.8**
Male [1]	10.9	9.8	9.4	9.5	9.4	9.4	9.5	9.3	9.2	9.1	9.0	9.3
Female [1]	8.1	7.9	7.9	8.1	8.1	8.2	8.3	8.2	8.1	8.1	8.1	8.3
White	9.5	8.9	8.9	9.0	9.0	9.0	9.1	8.9	8.9	8.9	8.8	9.1
Male	10.9	9.8	9.5	9.6	9.6	9.5	9.6	9.4	9.3	9.3	9.2	9.4
Female	8.1	8.1	8.2	8.4	8.4	8.5	8.7	8.5	8.5	8.5	8.4	8.7
Black	10.0	8.8	8.4	8.5	8.6	8.7	8.9	8.9	8.8	8.6	8.5	8.7
Male	11.9	10.3	9.7	9.9	10.0	10.1	10.3	10.3	10.1	10.0	9.8	10.0
Female	8.3	7.3	7.2	7.3	7.4	7.5	7.6	7.6	7.5	7.4	7.4	7.6
Age-adjusted death rates [1]	**7.1**	**5.9**	**5.5**	**5.5**	**5.4**	**5.4**	**5.4**	**5.3**	**5.2**	**5.1**	**5.0**	**5.1**
Male [1]	9.3	7.8	7.2	7.2	7.2	7.1	7.1	6.9	6.8	6.7	6.6	6.7
Female [1]	5.3	4.3	4.1	4.1	4.1	4.0	4.1	4.0	3.9	3.9	3.8	3.9
White	6.8	5.6	5.3	5.2	5.2	5.1	5.1	5.0	4.9	4.9	4.8	4.9
Male	8.9	7.5	6.9	6.9	6.8	6.7	6.7	6.5	6.4	6.3	6.2	6.3
Female	5.0	4.1	3.9	3.9	3.9	3.8	3.9	3.8	3.7	3.7	3.6	3.7
Black	10.4	8.4	7.8	7.9	8.0	8.0	8.1	8.1	7.9	7.8	7.7	7.9
Male	13.2	11.1	10.4	10.5	10.6	10.6	10.8	10.8	10.6	10.5	10.3	10.5
Female	8.1	6.3	5.9	5.9	5.9	5.9	6.0	5.9	5.8	5.8	5.7	5.8

[1] Includes other races, not shown separately.

Source: U.S. National Center for Health Statistics, *Vital Statistics of the United States*, annual; and *Monthly Vital Statistics Report*.

No. 118. Death Rates, by Age, Sex, and Race: 1970 to 1993

[**Number of deaths per 100,000 population in specified group.** See headnote, table 117]

SEX, YEAR, AND RACE	All ages [1]	Under 1 yr. old	1-4 yr. old	5-14 yr. old	15-24 yr. old	25-34 yr. old	35-44 yr. old	45-54 yr. old	55-64 yr. old	65-74 yr. old	75-84 yr. old	85 yr. old and over
MALE [2]												
1970	1,090	2,410	93	51	189	215	403	959	2,283	4,874	10,010	17,822
1980	977	1,429	73	37	172	196	299	767	1,815	4,105	8,817	18,801
1990	918	1,083	52	29	147	204	310	610	1,553	3,492	7,889	18,057
1992	902	957	48	27	142	202	319	592	1,482	3,374	7,483	17,740
1993 [3]	927	965	49	27	144	211	328	603	1,480	3,415	7,720	18,099
White: 1970	1,087	2,113	84	48	171	177	344	883	2,203	4,810	10,099	18,552
1980	983	1,230	66	35	167	171	257	699	1,729	4,036	8,830	19,097
1990	931	896	46	26	131	176	268	549	1,467	3,398	7,845	18,268
1992	917	781	43	25	122	176	277	533	1,399	3,287	7,441	17,956
1993 [3]	944	795	44	26	122	186	282	541	1,391	3,335	7,672	18,229
Black: 1970	1,187	4,299	151	67	321	560	957	1,778	3,257	5,803	9,455	12,222
1980	1,034	2,587	111	47	209	407	690	1,480	2,873	5,131	9,232	16,099
1990	1,008	2,112	86	41	252	431	700	1,261	2,618	4,946	9,130	16,955
1992	978	1,958	78	41	269	413	697	1,223	2,494	4,747	8,745	16,717
1993 [3]	1,005	1,962	77	35	283	410	732	1,277	2,538	4,761	8,969	18,169
FEMALE [2]												
1970	808	1,864	75	32	68	102	231	517	1,099	2,580	6,678	15,518
1980	785	1,142	55	24	58	76	159	413	934	2,145	5,440	14,747
1990	812	856	41	19	49	74	138	343	879	1,991	4,883	14,274
1992	807	771	39	18	47	74	141	326	855	1,971	4,731	13,901
1993 [3]	834	727	40	20	49	74	144	333	864	2,009	4,826	14,512
White: 1970	813	1,615	66	30	62	84	193	463	1,015	2,471	6,699	15,980
1980	806	963	49	23	56	65	138	373	876	2,067	5,402	14,980
1990	847	690	36	18	46	62	117	309	823	1,924	4,839	14,401
1992	844	619	33	16	44	61	117	294	799	1,909	4,696	14,016
1993 [3]	874	611	35	18	45	63	117	296	810	1,929	4,788	14,669
Black: 1970	829	3,369	129	44	112	231	533	1,044	1,986	3,861	6,692	10,707
1980	733	2,124	84	31	71	150	324	768	1,561	3,057	6,212	12,367
1990	748	1,736	68	28	69	160	299	639	1,453	2,866	5,688	13,310
1992	736	1,610	69	26	68	159	314	621	1,405	2,797	5,483	13,264
1993 [3]	758	1,418	64	31	72	147	332	659	1,393	2,968	5,650	13,634

[1] Includes unknown age. [2] Includes other races not shown separately. [3] Includes deaths of nonresidents. Based on a 10-percent sample of deaths.

Source: U.S. National Center for Health Statistics, *Vital Statistics of the United States*, annual; *Monthly Vital Statistics Report*; and unpublished data.

No. 119. Deaths and Death Rates, by State: 1980 to 1993

[By State of residence. Excludes deaths of nonresidents of the United States, except as noted. Caution should be used in comparing death rates by State; rates are affected by the population composition of the area. See also Appendix III]

DIVISION AND STATE	NUMBER OF DEATHS (1,000)							RATE PER 1,000 POPULATION [2]						
	1980	1985	1989	1990	1991	1992	1993 prel. [1]	1980	1985	1989	1990	1991	1992	1993 prel. [1]
United States . .	1,990	2,086	2,150	2,148	2,165	2,176	2,268	8.8	8.8	8.7	8.6	8.6	8.5	8.8
New England	115	118	116	115	112	116	120	9.3	9.3	8.8	8.7	8.5	8.8	9.1
Maine	11	11	11	11	11	11	11	9.6	9.8	9.2	9.0	8.9	9.0	9.3
New Hampshire . .	8	8	8	8	9	9	9	8.3	8.5	7.7	7.7	7.7	7.7	7.9
Vermont	5	5	5	5	5	5	5	9.0	8.8	8.2	8.2	8.0	8.4	8.5
Massachusetts . . .	55	56	54	53	51	54	56	9.6	9.5	9.0	8.8	8.6	9.0	9.4
Rhode Island . . .	9	10	10	10	9	9	10	9.8	10.0	9.6	9.5	9.2	9.5	9.7
Connecticut	27	28	28	28	28	28	29	8.8	8.8	8.6	8.4	8.4	8.6	8.9
Middle Atlantic	365	367	367	361	360	361	370	9.9	9.9	9.8	9.6	9.5	9.5	9.7
New York	173	172	172	169	167	166	170	9.8	9.7	9.5	9.4	9.2	9.2	9.4
New Jersey	69	71	71	70	70	71	73	9.4	9.4	9.2	9.1	9.0	9.1	9.2
Pennsylvania	124	124	124	122	124	124	127	10.4	10.5	10.4	10.3	10.3	10.3	10.5
East North Central .	365	370	372	373	379	373	387	8.8	8.9	8.9	8.9	8.9	8.7	9.0
Ohio	98	99	98	99	99	99	101	9.1	9.2	9.1	9.1	9.1	9.0	9.1
Indiana	47	48	49	50	52	50	52	8.6	8.8	8.9	8.9	9.2	8.8	9.1
Illinois	103	102	103	103	105	102	108	9.0	9.0	9.1	9.0	9.1	8.8	9.2
Michigan	75	79	79	79	80	79	83	8.1	8.7	8.5	8.5	8.5	8.4	8.7
Wisconsin	41	41	42	43	44	42	44	8.7	8.7	8.7	8.7	8.8	8.5	8.7
West North Central .	159	162	161	161	164	162	172	9.2	9.3	9.2	9.1	9.2	9.0	9.5
Minnesota	33	35	34	35	35	35	36	8.2	8.3	7.9	7.9	8.0	7.8	8.0
Iowa	27	28	27	27	26	27	28	9.3	9.8	9.8	9.7	9.3	9.5	9.9
Missouri	50	50	50	50	53	51	56	10.1	10.1	9.9	9.8	10.4	9.8	10.8
North Dakota	6	6	6	6	6	6	6	8.6	8.3	8.5	8.9	8.9	9.0	9.3
South Dakota	7	7	7	6	7	7	7	9.5	9.5	9.4	9.1	9.4	9.5	9.6
Nebraska	14	15	15	15	15	15	15	9.2	9.4	9.4	9.4	9.2	9.2	9.6
Kansas	22	22	22	22	23	22	23	9.3	9.1	9.0	9.0	9.0	8.8	9.2
South Atlantic	330	364	391	392	397	404	424	8.9	9.1	9.1	9.0	8.9	9.0	9.3
Delaware	5	5	6	6	6	6	6	8.5	8.9	8.9	8.7	8.6	8.6	8.7
Maryland	34	37	38	38	38	39	43	8.1	8.3	8.1	8.0	7.8	7.9	8.7
Dist. of Columbia . .	7	7	8	7	7	7	7	11.1	11.0	12.3	12.0	11.7	12.1	11.6
Virginia	43	45	47	48	49	49	52	8.0	7.9	7.7	7.8	7.8	7.7	8.0
West Virginia	19	19	20	19	20	20	20	9.9	10.2	10.8	10.8	11.0	10.9	11.0
North Carolina . . .	48	53	57	57	59	60	63	8.2	8.5	8.8	8.6	8.7	8.7	9.0
South Carolina . . .	25	27	30	30	30	31	31	8.1	8.2	8.6	8.5	8.4	8.5	8.6
Georgia	44	49	52	52	53	53	56	8.1	8.2	8.2	8.0	8.0	7.8	8.1
Florida	105	121	133	134	135	140	146	10.7	10.7	10.5	10.4	10.2	10.4	10.7
East South Central .	134	140	145	146	144	146	155	9.1	9.4	9.6	9.6	9.4	9.4	9.8
Kentucky	34	35	35	35	35	35	37	9.2	9.4	9.6	9.5	9.5	9.3	9.7
Tennessee	41	43	45	46	45	47	50	8.9	9.2	9.4	9.5	9.2	9.3	9.7
Alabama	36	38	39	39	38	39	42	9.1	9.5	9.7	9.7	9.3	9.5	9.9
Mississippi	24	25	25	25	26	25	27	9.4	9.5	9.9	9.8	9.9	9.7	10.1
West South Central .	195	209	217	218	222	222	235	8.2	8.0	8.2	8.2	8.2	8.1	8.4
Arkansas	23	24	25	25	24	25	26	9.9	10.4	10.5	10.5	10.2	10.4	10.9
Louisiana	36	37	38	38	38	38	40	8.5	8.4	8.9	8.9	9.0	8.8	9.3
Oklahoma	28	30	30	30	30	31	33	9.3	9.1	9.5	9.7	9.6	9.5	10.1
Texas	108	118	125	125	129	129	136	7.6	7.3	7.4	7.4	7.4	7.3	7.5
Mountain	80	88	95	97	99	103	108	7.0	6.9	7.1	7.1	7.1	7.2	7.3
Montana	7	7	7	7	7	7	8	8.5	8.2	8.4	8.6	8.7	8.6	8.9
Idaho	7	7	7	7	8	8	8	7.2	7.2	7.5	7.4	7.5	7.4	7.6
Wyoming	3	3	3	3	3	3	4	6.9	6.6	7.1	7.1	6.9	7.1	7.5
Colorado	19	20	21	22	22	22	24	6.6	6.3	6.5	6.6	6.6	6.5	6.7
New Mexico	9	10	11	11	11	11	12	7.0	6.8	7.0	7.0	7.2	7.1	7.3
Arizona	21	25	28	29	29	31	32	7.9	7.7	7.8	7.9	7.8	8.1	8.2
Utah	8	9	9	9	9	10	10	5.6	5.5	5.4	5.3	5.2	5.4	5.5
Nevada	6	7	9	9	9	10	11	7.4	7.6	7.6	7.8	7.2	7.7	7.8
Pacific	247	268	286	286	290	289	296	7.8	7.6	7.5	7.3	7.3	7.1	7.2
Washington	32	35	36	37	38	38	42	7.7	7.8	7.6	7.6	7.5	7.4	8.0
Oregon	22	24	25	25	25	26	27	8.3	8.9	8.9	8.8	8.6	8.7	9.0
California	187	202	217	214	219	216	218	7.9	7.6	7.4	7.2	7.2	7.0	7.0
Alaska	2	2	2	2	2	2	2	4.3	3.9	3.8	4.0	3.8	3.9	3.8
Hawaii	5	6	7	7	7	7	7	5.2	5.6	5.9	6.1	5.9	6.0	6.2

[1] Includes deaths of nonresidents. [2] Rates based on enumerated resident population as of April 1 for 1980; and 1990; estimated resident population as of July 1 for all other years.

Source: U.S. National Center for Health Statistics, *Vital Statistics of the United States,* annual; and *Monthly Vital Statistics Report.*

No. 120. Infant, Maternal, and Neonatal Mortality Rates and Fetal Mortality Ratios, by Race: 1970 to 1992

[Deaths per 1,000 live births, except as noted. Excludes deaths of nonresidents of U.S. Beginning 1980, race for live births tabulated according to race of mother, for infant and neonatal mortality rates. Beginning 1989, race for live births tabulated according to race of mother, for maternal mortality rates and mortality rates. See also Appendix III and *Historical Statistics, Colonial Times to 1970,* series B 136-147]

ITEM	1970	1980	1982	1983	1984	1985	1986	1987	1988	1989	1990	1991	1992
Infant deaths [1]	20.0	12.6	11.5	11.2	10.8	10.6	10.4	10.1	10.0	9.8	9.2	8.9	8.5
White	17.8	10.9	9.9	9.6	9.3	9.2	8.8	8.5	8.4	8.1	7.6	7.3	6.9
Black and other	30.9	20.2	18.3	17.8	17.1	16.8	16.7	16.5	16.1	16.3	15.5	15.1	14.4
Black	32.6	22.2	20.5	20.0	19.2	19.0	18.9	18.8	18.5	18.6	18.0	17.6	16.8
Maternal deaths [2]	21.5	9.2	7.9	8.0	7.8	7.8	7.2	6.6	8.4	7.9	8.2	7.9	7.8
White	14.4	6.7	5.8	5.9	5.4	5.2	4.9	5.1	5.9	5.6	5.4	5.8	5.0
Black and other	55.9	19.8	16.4	16.3	16.9	18.1	16.0	12.0	17.4	16.5	19.1	15.6	18.2
Black	59.8	21.5	18.2	18.3	19.7	20.4	18.8	14.2	19.5	18.4	22.4	18.3	20.8
Fetal deaths [3]	14.2	9.2	8.9	8.5	8.2	7.9	7.7	7.7	7.5	7.5	7.5	7.3	(NA)
White	12.4	8.2	7.9	7.5	7.4	7.0	6.8	6.7	6.4	6.4	6.4	6.2	(NA)
Black and other	22.6	13.4	12.7	12.4	11.5	11.3	11.2	11.5	11.4	11.7	11.9	11.4	(NA)
Neonatal deaths [4]	15.1	8.5	7.7	7.3	7.0	7.0	6.7	6.5	6.3	6.2	5.8	5.6	5.4
White	13.8	7.4	6.7	6.3	6.1	6.0	5.7	5.4	5.3	5.1	4.8	4.5	4.3
Black and other	21.4	13.2	12.0	11.4	10.9	11.0	10.8	10.7	10.3	10.3	9.9	9.5	9.2
Black	22.8	14.6	13.6	12.9	12.3	12.6	12.3	12.3	12.1	11.9	11.6	11.2	10.8

NA Not available.   [1] Represents deaths of infants under 1 year old, exclusive of fetal deaths.   [2] Per 100,000 live births from deliveries and complications of pregnancy, childbirth, and the puerperium. Beginning 1979, deaths are classified according to the ninth revision of the *International Classification of Diseases;* earlier years classified according to the revision in use at the time; see text, section 2.   [3] Includes only those deaths with stated or presumed period of gestation of 20 weeks or more. [4] Represents deaths of infants under 28 days old, exclusive of fetal deaths.

No. 121. Fetal and Infant Deaths—Number and Percent Distribution: 1970 to 1991

[State requirements for reporting of fetal deaths vary. Most States require reporting of fetal deaths of gestations of 20 weeks or more. There is substantial evidence that not all fetal deaths for which reporting is required are reported. For details of methodology, see Appendix III and source]

YEAR	NUMBER						PERCENT DISTRIBUTION					
		Fetal deaths		Infant deaths				Fetal deaths		Infant deaths		
	Total	Early [1]	Late [2]	Neonatal		Post-neo-natal [5]	Total	Early [1]	Late [2]	Neonatal		Post-neo-natal [5]
				Early [3]	Late [4]					Early [3]	Late [4]	
1970	127,628	17,170	35,791	50,821	5,458	18,388	100.0	13.5	28.0	39.8	4.3	14.4
1980	78,879	10754	22,599	25,492	5,126	14,908	100.0	13.6	28.7	32.3	6.5	18.9
1981	75,901	11126	21,470	24,384	4,737	14,184	100.0	14.7	28.3	32.1	6.2	18.7
1982	75,095	11,028	21,666	23,706	4,629	14,066	100.0	14.7	28.9	31.6	6.2	18.7
1983	71,379	10,933	19,819	22,315	4,192	14,120	100.0	15.3	27.8	31.3	5.9	19.8
1984	69,679	10,963	19,136	21,566	4,125	13,889	100.0	15.7	27.5	31.0	5.9	19.9
1985	69,691	10,958	18,703	21,865	4,314	13,851	100.0	15.7	26.8	31.4	6.2	19.9
1986	67,863	11,100	17,872	21,053	4,159	13,679	100.0	16.4	26.3	31.0	6.1	20.2
1987	67,757	11,656	17,693	20,471	4,156	13,781	100.0	17.2	26.1	30.2	6.1	20.3
1988	68,352	11,833	17,609	20,471	4,219	14,220	100.0	17.3	25.8	29.9	6.2	20.8
1989	70,124	12,397	18,072	20,796	4,372	14,487	100.0	17.7	25.8	29.7	6.2	20.7
1990	67,696	12,554	16,791	20,020	4,289	14,042	100.0	18.5	24.8	29.6	6.3	20.7
1991	65,000	12,310	15,924	18,916	4,062	13,788	100.0	18.9	24.5	29.1	6.2	21.2

[1] 20-27 weeks gestation.   [2] 28 weeks or more gestation.   [3] Less than 7 days.   [4] 7-27 days.   [5] 28 days-11 months.

No. 122. Infant Deaths and Infant Mortality Rates, by Cause of Death: 1980 to 1992

[Excludes deaths of nonresidents of the United States. Deaths classified according to ninth revision of *International Classification of Diseases.* See also Appendix III]

CAUSE OF DEATH	NUMBER			PERCENT DISTRIBUTION			INFANT MORTALITY RATE [1]		
	1980	1990	1992	1980	1990	1992	1980	1990	1992
Total	45,526	38,351	34,628	100	100	100	12.6	9.2	8.5
Congenital anomalies	9,220	8,239	7,449	20	21	22	2.6	2.0	1.8
Sudden infant death syndrome	5,510	5,417	4,891	12	14	14	1.5	1.3	1.2
Respiratory distress syndrome	4,989	2,850	2,063	11	7	6	1.4	0.7	0.5
Disorders relating to short gestation and unspecified low birth weight	3,648	4,013	4,035	8	10	12	1.0	1.0	1.0
Newborn affected by maternal complications of pregnancy	1,572	1,655	1,461	4	4	4	0.4	0.4	0.4
Intrauterine hypoxia and birth asphyxia	1,497	762	613	3	2	2	0.4	0.2	0.2
Infections specific to the perinatal period	971	875	901	2	2	3	0.3	0.2	0.2
Accidents and adverse effects	1,166	930	819	3	2	2	0.3	0.2	0.2
Newborn affected by complications of placenta, cord, and membranes	985	975	993	2	3	3	0.3	0.2	0.2
Pneumonia and influenza	1,012	634	600	2	2	2	0.3	0.2	0.1
All other causes	14,956	12,001	10,803	33	31	31	4.1	2.9	2.7

[1] Deaths of infants under 1 year old per 1,000 live births.
Sources of tables 120-122: U.S. National Center for Health Statistics, *Vital Statistics of the United States,* annual, and *Monthly Vital Statistics Report;* and unpublished data.

No. 123. Infant Mortality Rates, by Race—States: 1980 to 1992

[**Deaths per 1,000 live births, by place of residence.** Represents deaths of infants under 1 year old, exclusive of fetal deaths. Excludes deaths of nonresidents of the United States. See Appendix III and *Historical Statistics, Colonial Times to 1970,* series B 143-147, for U.S. totals]

DIVISION AND STATE	TOTAL [1]			WHITE		BLACK		DIVISION AND STATE	TOTAL [1]			WHITE		BLACK	
	1980	1990	1992	1990	1992	1990	1992		1980	1990	1992	1990	1992	1990	1992
U.S .	**12.6**	**9.2**	**8.5**	**7.7**	**6.9**	**18.0**	**16.8**	VA. . . .	13.6	10.2	9.5	7.5	6.9	19.5	17.7
								WV . . .	11.8	9.9	9.2	9.6	8.9	(NA)	(NA)
N.E.	**10.5**	**7.2**	**6.8**	**6.8**	**6.0**	**14.0**	**14.9**	NC . . .	14.5	10.6	10.0	8.3	7.3	16.5	16.5
ME . . .	9.2	6.2	5.6	6.2	5.5	(NA)	(NA)	SC . . .	15.6	11.7	10.4	8.3	7.1	17.3	16.0
NH . . .	9.9	7.1	5.9	7.2	5.8	(NA)	(NA)	GA . . .	14.5	12.4	10.3	9.1	7.1	18.3	15.9
VT . . .	10.7	6.4	7.2	6.5	7.3	(NA)	(NA)	FL . . .	14.6	9.6	8.8	7.6	7.0	16.8	15.1
MA . . .	10.5	7.0	6.5	6.7	5.8	11.9	13.4	**E.S.C . . .**	**14.5**	**10.4**	**9.9**	**8.1**	**7.5**	**16.4**	**16.2**
RI	11.0	8.1	7.4	8.3	6.9	(NA)	(NA)	KY . . .	12.9	8.5	8.3	8.0	7.9	14.3	12.7
CT	11.2	7.9	7.6	6.6	6.2	17.6	17.2	TN . . .	13.5	10.3	9.4	8.0	7.0	17.9	17.4
M.A. . .	**12.8**	**9.5**	**8.8**	**7.5**	**6.8**	**18.7**	**17.5**	AL . . .	15.1	10.8	10.5	8.3	7.6	16.0	16.2
NY . . .	12.5	9.6	8.8	7.7	7.1	18.1	15.8	MS . . .	17.0	12.1	11.9	8.5	8.0	16.2	16.1
NJ . . .	12.5	9.0	8.4	6.8	5.9	18.4	18.7	**W.S.C . . .**	**12.7**	**8.7**	**8.3**	**7.4**	**7.1**	**15.3**	**14.2**
PA . . .	13.2	9.6	9.0	7.8	6.9	20.5	20.4	AR . . .	12.7	9.2	10.3	8.0	8.6	13.9	16.2
E.N.C . . .	**13.0**	**10.1**	**9.5**	**8.0**	**7.4**	**21.0**	**19.6**	LA. . . .	14.3	11.1	9.4	7.3	6.9	16.7	13.0
OH . . .	12.8	9.8	9.4	8.2	7.9	19.5	18.0	OK . . .	12.7	9.2	8.8	9.4	7.9	14.3	16.8
IN . . .	11.9	9.6	9.4	8.9	8.0	17.4	20.3	TX . . .	12.2	8.1	7.8	7.1	6.8	14.7	14.2
IL	14.8	10.7	10.1	7.7	7.4	22.4	19.8	**Mountain**	**11.0**	**8.6**	**7.6**	**8.3**	**7.2**	**18.5**	**16.7**
MI . . .	12.8	10.7	10.2	7.9	7.0	21.6	22.1	MT . . .	12.4	9.0	7.5	8.6	6.7	(NA)	(NA)
WI . . .	10.3	8.2	7.2	7.2	6.4	19.0	13.5	ID	10.7	8.7	8.8	8.7	8.8	(NA)	(NA)
W.N.C . . .	**11.3**	**8.4**	**8.0**	**7.5**	**7.0**	**18.9**	**17.3**	WY	9.8	8.6	8.9	8.8	9.0	(NA)	(NA)
MN . . .	10.0	7.3	7.1	6.7	6.2	23.7	17.5	CO . . .	10.1	8.8	7.6	8.4	7.2	19.4	14.6
IA . . .	11.8	8.1	8.0	7.8	7.7	21.9	19.4	NM . . .	11.5	9.0	7.6	9.3	6.8	(NA)	(NA)
MO . . .	12.4	9.4	8.5	7.8	6.9	18.2	15.9	AZ . . .	12.4	8.8	8.4	8.2	7.8	20.6	16.7
ND . . .	12.1	8.0	7.8	7.9	7.4	(NA)	(NA)	UT . . .	10.4	7.5	5.9	7.4	6.0	(NA)	(NA)
SD . . .	10.9	10.1	9.3	8.6	7.7	(NA)	(NA)	NV . . .	10.7	8.4	6.7	8.1	5.9	14.2	16.6
NE . . .	11.5	8.3	7.4	7.2	6.7	18.9	19.8	**Pacific . .**	**11.2**	**7.9**	**7.0**	**7.6**	**6.4**	**17.1**	**16.7**
KS . . .	10.4	8.4	8.7	7.7	7.5	17.7	21.7	WA . . .	11.8	7.8	6.8	7.6	6.4	20.6	15.9
S.A.	**14.5**	**10.7**	**9.8**	**8.0**	**7.1**	**17.9**	**16.4**	OR . . .	12.2	8.3	7.1	8.1	6.8	(NA)	23.0
DE . . .	13.9	10.1	8.6	7.3	5.8	20.1	18.0	CA . . .	11.1	7.9	7.0	7.6	6.3	16.8	16.8
MD . . .	14.0	9.5	9.8	6.5	6.7	17.1	16.5	AK . . .	12.3	10.5	8.6	8.5	7.3	(NA)	(NA)
DC . . .	25.0	20.7	19.6	12.1	13.1	24.6	22.0	HI	10.3	6.7	6.3	5.1	(NA)	(NA)	(NA)

NA Not available. [1] Includes other races, not shown separately.
Source: U.S. National Center for Health Statistics, *Vital Statistics of the United States,* annual; and unpublished data.

No. 124. Age-Adjusted Death Rates, by Selected Causes: 1980 to 1992

[**Rates per 100,000 population.** For explanation of age-adjustment, see text, section 2. The standard population for this table is the total population of the United States enumerated in 1940. See also headnote, table 125]

CAUSE OF DEATH	1980	1990	1992	CAUSE OF DEATH	1980	1990	1992
All causes.	585.8	520.2	504.5	Pneumonia and influenza	12.9	14.0	12.7
				Pneumonia	12.4	13.7	12.5
Major cardiovascular diseases	256.0	189.8	180.4	Influenza.	0.5	0.3	0.2
Diseases of heart	202.0	152.0	144.3				
Rheumatic fever and rheumatic				Diabetes mellitus.	10.1	11.7	11.9
heart disease	2.6	1.5	1.3	Suicide	11.4	11.5	11.1
Hypertensive heart disease [1].	6.8	5.3	4.8	Chronic liver disease and cirrhosis	12.2	8.6	8.0
Ischemic heart disease	149.8	102.6	95.7	Nephritis, nephrotic syndrome, and			
Other diseases of endocardium . . .	2.0	2.5	2.6	nephrosis	4.5	4.3	4.3
All other forms of heart disease . . .	40.8	40.1	39.4	Homicide and legal intervention	10.8	10.2	10.5
Hypertension [1]	2.0	1.9	2.0				
Cerebrovascular diseases	40.8	27.7	26.2	Septicemia	2.6	4.1	4.0
Atherosclerosis	5.7	2.7	2.4	Other infectious and parasitic diseases . .	1.8	12.0	14.7
Other	5.5	5.4	5.4	Benign neoplasms [3]	2.0	1.7	1.7
Malignancies [2]	132.8	135.0	133.1	Ulcer of stomach and duodenum	1.7	1.3	1.2
Of respiratory and intrathoracic							
organs	36.4	41.4	40.8	Hernia of abdominal cavity and			
Of digestive organs and peritoneum. .	33.0	30.2	29.6	intestinal obstruction [4].	1.4	1.1	1.1
Of genital organs	13.6	13.6	13.5	Anemias.	0.9	0.9	0.9
Of breast	12.5	12.7	12.0	Cholelithiasis and other disorders of			
Of urinary organs	5.2	5.1	5.1	gallbladder	0.8	0.6	0.5
Leukemia	5.4	5.0	4.9	Nutritional deficiencies	0.5	0.5	0.5
				Infections of kidney	0.7	0.2	0.2
Accidents and adverse effects	42.3	32.5	29.4	Tuberculosis	0.6	0.5	0.4
Motor vehicle.	22.9	18.5	15.8	Meningitis.	0.6	0.3	0.2
All other	19.5	14.0	13.7	Viral hepatitis	0.3	0.5	0.6
Chronic obstructive pulmonary diseases				Acute bronchitis and bronchiolitis	0.2	0.1	0.1
and allied conditions.	15.9	19.7	19.9	Hyperplasia of prostate.	0.2	0.1	0.1
Bronchitis, chronic and unspecified . .	1.0	0.8	0.8				
Emphysema	4.0	3.7	3.7	Symptoms, signs, and ill-defined			
Asthma.	1.0	1.4	1.4	conditions	9.8	7.3	6.7
Other	9.9	13.7	14.0	All other causes.	36.8	38.4	38.1

[1] With or without renal disease. [2] Includes other types of malignancies not shown separately. [3] Includes neoplasms of unspecified nature; and carcinoma in situ. [4] Without mention of hernia.
Source: U.S. National Center for Health Statistics, *Vital Statistics of the United States,* annual; *Monthly Vital Statistics Reports;* and unpublished data.

No. 125. Deaths and Death Rates, by Selected Causes: 1970 to 1993

[Excludes deaths of nonresidents of the United States, except as noted. Beginning 1979, deaths classified according to ninth revision of *International Classification of Diseases:* for earlier years, classified according to revision in use at that time. See also Appendix III and *Historical Statistics, Colonial Times to 1970,* series B 149-166]

CAUSE OF DEATH	DEATHS (1,000)					CRUDE DEATH RATE PER 100,000 POPULATION [2]				
	1970	1980	1990	1992 [1]	1993 [1]	1970	1980	1990	1992 [1]	1993 [1]
All causes	1,921.0	1,989.8	2,148.5	2,177.0	2,268.0	945.3	878.3	863.8	853.3	879.3
Major cardiovascular diseases	1,008.0	988.5	916.0	915.4	944.6	496.0	436.4	368.3	358.8	366.3
Diseases of heart	735.5	761.1	720.1	720.5	739.9	362.0	336.0	289.5	282.5	286.9
Percent of total	38.3	38.3	33.5	33.1	32.6	38.3	38.3	33.5	33.1	32.6
Rheumatic fever and rheumatic heart disease	14.9	7.8	6.0	6.0	5.6	7.3	3.5	2.4	2.3	2.2
Hypertensive heart disease [3]	15.0	24.8	23.4	25.3	26.0	7.4	10.9	9.5	8.8	9.0
Ischemic heart disease	666.7	565.8	489.2	480.2	490.0	328.1	249.7	196.7	188.2	190.0
Other diseases of endocardium	6.7	7.2	13.0	15.8	15.1	3.3	3.2	5.2	6.2	5.8
All other forms of heart disease	32.3	155.5	188.4	193.3	203.2	15.9	68.7	75.8	75.8	78.8
Hypertension [3]	8.3	7.8	9.2	10.5	11.5	4.1	3.5	3.7	4.1	4.5
Cerebrovascular diseases	207.2	170.2	144.1	143.6	149.7	101.9	75.1	57.9	56.3	58.1
Atherosclerosis	31.7	29.4	18.0	16.1	17.1	15.6	13.0	7.3	6.3	6.6
Other	25.3	20.0	24.6	24.6	26.4	12.5	8.8	9.9	9.7	10.2
Malignancies [4]	330.7	416.5	505.3	521.1	530.9	162.8	183.9	203.2	204.3	205.8
Percent of total	17.2	20.9	23.5	23.9	23.4	17.2	20.9	23.5	23.9	23.4
Of respiratory and intrathoracic organs	69.5	108.5	146.4	155.0	156.6	34.2	47.9	58.9	60.7	60.7
Of digestive organs and peritoneum	94.7	110.6	120.8	121.4	123.6	46.6	48.8	48.6	47.6	47.9
Of genital organs	41.2	46.4	57.5	58.6	60.9	20.3	20.5	23.1	23.0	23.6
Of breast	29.9	35.9	43.7	44.2	44.1	14.7	15.8	17.6	17.3	17.1
Of urinary organs	15.5	17.8	20.7	22.2	22.2	7.6	7.9	8.3	8.7	8.6
Leukemia	14.5	16.5	18.6	19.2	19.0	7.1	7.3	7.5	7.5	7.3
Accidents and adverse effects	114.6	105.7	92.0	86.3	88.6	56.4	46.7	37.0	33.8	34.4
Motor vehicle	54.6	53.2	46.8	41.7	40.9	26.9	23.5	18.8	16.4	15.9
All other	60.0	52.5	45.2	44.6	47.8	29.5	23.3	18.2	17.5	18.5
Chronic obstructive pulmonary diseases and allied conditions [5]	30.9	56.1	86.7	91.4	101.1	15.2	24.7	34.9	35.8	39.2
Bronchitis, chronic and unspecified	5.8	3.7	3.6	4.2	3.6	2.9	1.6	1.4	1.6	1.4
Emphysema	22.7	13.9	15.7	16.6	18.0	11.2	6.1	6.3	6.5	7.0
Asthma	2.3	2.9	4.8	4.7	5.2	1.1	1.3	1.9	1.8	2.0
Other	([6])	35.6	62.6	66.0	74.3	([6])	15.7	25.2	25.9	28.8
Pneumonia and influenza	62.7	54.6	79.5	76.1	81.7	30.9	24.1	32.0	29.8	31.7
Pneumonia	59.0	51.9	77.4	74.9	80.7	29.0	22.9	31.1	29.3	31.3
Influenza	3.7	2.7	2.1	1.3	1.1	1.8	1.2	0.8	0.5	0.4
Diabetes mellitus	38.3	34.9	47.7	50.2	55.1	18.9	15.4	19.2	19.8	21.4
Suicide	23.5	26.9	30.9	29.8	31.2	11.6	11.9	12.4	11.7	12.1
Chronic liver disease and cirrhosis	31.4	30.6	25.8	24.8	24.7	15.5	13.5	10.4	9.7	9.6
Other infectious and parasitic diseases	6.9	5.1	32.2	40.4	45.9	3.4	2.2	13.0	15.8	17.8
Homicide and legal intervention	16.8	24.3	24.9	26.6	25.5	8.3	10.7	10.0	10.4	9.9
Nephritis, nephrotic syndrome, and nephrosis	8.9	16.8	20.8	22.4	23.5	4.4	7.4	8.3	8.8	9.1
Septicemia	3.5	9.4	19.2	19.9	20.4	1.7	4.2	7.7	7.8	7.9
Certain conditions originating in the perinatal period	43.2	22.9	17.7	15.8	15.8	21.3	10.1	7.1	6.2	6.1
Congenital anomalies	16.8	13.9	13.1	12.4	12.1	8.3	6.2	5.3	4.9	4.7
Benign neoplasms [7]	4.8	6.2	6.8	6.5	7.1	2.4	2.7	2.7	2.5	2.8
Ulcer of stomach and duodenum	8.6	6.1	6.2	5.8	5.6	4.2	0.0	2.5	2.3	2.2
Hernia of abdominal cavity and intestinal obstruction [8]	7.2	5.4	5.8	6.2	5.8	3.6	2.4	2.3	2.4	2.2
Anemias	3.4	3.2	4.1	4.0	4.5	1.7	1.4	1.6	1.6	1.8
Cholelithiasis and other disorders of gall bladder	4.0	3.3	3.0	3.0	2.7	2.0	1.5	1.2	1.2	1.0
Nutritional deficiencies	2.5	2.4	3.0	3.1	3.3	1.2	1.0	1.2	1.2	1.3
Tuberculosis	5.2	2.0	1.8	1.4	1.7	2.6	0.9	0.7	0.5	0.6
Infections of kidney	8.2	2.7	1.3	1.2	1.0	4.0	1.2	0.5	0.5	0.4
Viral hepatitis	1.0	0.8	1.6	1.9	2.5	0.5	0.4	0.6	0.8	1.0
Meningitis	1.7	1.4	1.0	0.7	0.8	0.8	0.6	0.4	0.3	0.3
Acute bronchitis and bronchiolitis	1.3	0.6	0.6	0.5	0.6	0.6	0.3	0.3	0.2	0.2
Hyperplasia of prostate	2.2	0.8	0.5	0.4	0.6	1.1	0.3	0.2	0.1	0.2
Symptoms, signs, and ill-defined conditions	25.8	28.8	24.1	24.2	26.3	12.7	12.7	9.7	9.5	10.2
All other causes	108.8	120.0	172.9	181.0	199.3	53.5	53.0	69.5	70.9	77.3

[1] Based on a 10-percent sample of deaths. Includes deaths of nonresidents. [2] 1970, 1980, and 1990 based on resident population enumerated as of April 1. Other years based on resident population estimated as of July 1. [3] With or without renal disease. [4] Includes other types of malignancies not shown separately. [5] Prior to 1980, data are shown for bronchitis, emphysema, and asthma. [6] Included in "all other causes." Comparable data not available separately. [7] Includes neoplasms of unspecified nature; beginning 1980 also includes carcinoma in situ. [8] Without mention of hernia.

Source: U.S. National Center for Health Statistics, *Vital Statistics of the United States,* annual; *Monthly Vital Statistics Report;* and unpublished data.

No. 126. Deaths, by Selected Causes and Selected Characteristics: 1992

[In thousands. Excludes deaths of nonresidents of the U.S. Deaths classified according to ninth revision of *International Classification of Diseases*. See also Appendix III]

AGE, SEX, AND RACE	Total [1]	Heart disease	Cancer	Accidents and adverse effects	Cerebrovascular diseases	Chronic obstructive pulmonary diseases [2]	Pneumonia, flu	Suicide	Chronic liver disease, cirrhosis	Diabetes mellitus	Homicide and legal intervention
ALL RACES [3]											
Both sexes, total [4] .	853	717.7	520.6	86.8	143.8	91.9	75.7	30.5	25.3	50.1	25.5
Under 1 year old	866	0.7	1.0	0.8	0.2	(Z)	0.6	(Z)	(Z)	(Z)	0.3
1 to 4 years old	44	0.3	0.5	2.5	0.1	0.1	0.2	(Z)	(Z)	(Z)	0.4
5 to 14 years old	23	0.3	1.1	3.4	0.1	0.1	0.1	0.3	(Z)	(Z)	0.6
15 to 24 years old	96	1.0	1.8	13.7	0.2	0.2	0.2	4.7	(Z)	0.1	8.0
25 to 34 years old	138	3.4	5.3	13.8	0.8	0.3	0.7	6.2	0.8	0.7	7.3
35 to 44 years old	229	12.7	16.9	12.0	2.6	0.7	1.4	6.0	3.6	1.6	4.5
45 to 54 years old	456	31.4	41.2	7.5	4.8	2.3	1.6	4.0	4.6	3.2	2.0
55 to 64 years old	1,152	72.5	91.6	6.4	9.7	10.1	3.5	3.1	5.8	7.1	1.0
65 to 74 years old	2,589	156.5	161.2	8.2	25.0	28.7	10.2	3.0	6.3	14.0	0.7
75 to 84 years old	5,776	226.7	142.6	10.2	49.4	34.5	24.0	2.4	3.4	15.0	0.4
85 years old and over . . .	14,973	212.0	58.2	8.3	51.0	15.0	33.3	0.7	0.8	8.3	0.1
Male, total [4]	902	357.5	274.8	57.9	56.6	50.5	35.5	24.5	16.5	21.7	20.1
Under 1 year old	957	0.4	0.1	0.5	0.1	(Z)	0.4	(Z)	(Z)	(Z)	0.2
1 to 4 years old	48	0.2	0.3	1.5	(Z)	(Z)	0.1	(Z)	(Z)	(Z)	0.2
5 to 14 years old	27	0.2	0.6	2.3	(Z)	0.1	0.1	0.2	(Z)	(Z)	0.4
15 to 24 years old	142	0.6	1.1	10.3	0.1	0.1	0.1	4.0	(Z)	0.1	6.9
25 to 34 years old	202	2.3	2.6	10.7	0.4	0.2	0.4	5.1	0.5	0.4	5.8
35 to 44 years old	319	9.5	7.5	9.2	1.4	0.4	0.9	4.7	2.7	1.0	3.5
45 to 54 years old	592	23.3	20.6	5.5	2.6	1.2	1.1	3.0	3.3	1.8	1.6
55 to 64 years old	1,482	50.0	50.9	4.4	5.3	5.6	2.1	2.4	4.0	3.6	0.8
65 to 74 years old	3,374	95.8	90.3	5.0	12.7	16.2	6.0	2.4	3.8	6.4	0.4
75 to 84 years old	7,483	110.4	75.5	5.2	20.4	19.2	12.4	2.0	1.8	6.0	0.2
85 years old and over . . .	17,740	65.1	25.5	3.1	13.6	7.6	11.9	0.6	0.3	2.4	0.1
Female, total [4]	807	360.2	245.7	28.9	87.1	41.5	40.3	6.0	8.8	28.4	5.4
Under 1 year old	771	0.3	(Z)	0.4	0.1	(Z)	0.2	(Z)	(Z)	(Z)	0.1
1 to 4 years old	39	0.1	0.2	1.0	(Z)	(Z)	0.1	(Z)	(Z)	(Z)	0.2
5 to 14 years old	18	0.1	0.5	1.1	(Z)	(Z)	0.1	0.1	(Z)	(Z)	0.2
15 to 24 years old	47	0.3	0.7	3.4	0.1	0.1	0.1	0.6	(Z)	0.1	1.1
25 to 34 years old	74	1.1	2.7	3.1	0.4	0.1	0.2	1.1	0.3	0.3	1.5
35 to 44 years old	141	3.2	9.4	2.8	1.2	0.3	0.5	1.3	0.9	0.6	1.0
45 to 54 years old	326	8.1	20.6	2.0	2.2	1.1	0.6	1.0	1.2	1.4	0.4
55 to 64 years old	855	22.6	40.7	2.0	4.4	4.5	1.3	0.7	1.8	3.6	0.2
65 to 74 years old	1,971	60.7	71.0	3.2	12.3	12.5	4.2	0.6	2.4	7.6	0.2
75 to 84 years old	4,731	116.4	67.2	4.9	29.0	15.3	11.5	0.4	1.6	9.0	0.2
85 years old and over . . .	13,901	147.0	32.7	5.2	37.3	7.5	21.4	0.1	0.5	5.8	0.1
WHITE											
Both sexes, total [4] .	880	633.5	454.5	72.4	124.4	85.2	67.5	27.6	21.3	40.4	12.5
Under 1 year old	702	0.5	0.1	0.5	0.1	(Z)	0.4	(Z)	(Z)	(Z)	0.2
1 to 4 years old	38	0.2	0.4	1.8	(Z)	(Z)	0.1	(Z)	(Z)	(Z)	0.2
5 to 14 years old	21	0.2	0.9	2.5	0.1	0.1	0.1	0.3	(Z)	(Z)	0.3
15 to 24 years old	84	0.6	1.5	11.5	0.1	0.1	0.2	3.9	(Z)	0.1	3.2
25 to 34 years old	119	2.3	4.2	11.3	0.5	0.2	0.4	5.4	0.5	0.5	3.4
35 to 44 years old	197	9.1	13.3	9.6	1.6	0.5	0.8	5.4	2.7	1.2	2.4
45 to 54 years old	412	24.4	33.6	6.0	3.3	1.9	1.2	3.7	3.6	2.3	1.2
55 to 64 years old	1,086	59.4	77.4	5.2	7.1	9.0	2.7	3.0	4.9	5.2	0.7
65 to 74 years old	2,519	135.8	141.8	7.1	20.5	26.6	8.7	2.9	5.6	11.2	0.4
75 to 84 years old	5,740	204.8	128.6	9.2	44.0	32.6	21.8	2.3	3.2	12.8	0.3
85 years old and over . . .	15,104	196.2	52.8	7.7	47.1	14.2	31.0	0.7	0.7	7.2	0.1
BLACK											
Both sexes, total [4] .	851	75.6	58.4	11.8	17.0	5.9	7.1	2.1	3.3	8.7	12.3
Under 1 year old	1,786	0.2	(Z)	0.3	0.1	(Z)	0.2	(Z)	(Z)	(Z)	0.1
1 to 4 years old	73	0.1	0.1	0.6	(Z)	(Z)	0.1	(Z)	(Z)	(Z)	0.2
5 to 14 years old	34	0.1	0.2	0.7	(Z)	(Z)	(Z)	(Z)	(Z)	(Z)	0.3
15 to 24 years old	168	0.3	0.3	1.7	(Z)	0.1	0.1	0.5	(Z)	(Z)	4.6
25 to 34 years old	279	1.1	0.9	2.0	0.2	0.1	0.2	0.6	0.2	0.2	3.8
35 to 44 years old	492	3.3	3.1	2.1	0.9	0.2	0.5	0.5	0.8	0.4	1.9
45 to 54 years old	894	6.4	6.7	1.2	1.4	0.4	0.4	0.2	0.8	0.8	0.7
55 to 64 years old	1,880	12.0	12.6	1.0	2.3	0.9	0.7	0.1	0.8	1.7	0.3
65 to 74 years old	3,601	18.7	17.3	0.9	3.9	1.8	1.3	0.1	0.6	2.5	0.2
75 to 84 years old	6,652	19.4	12.5	0.9	4.8	1.6	1.8	0.1	0.2	2.1	0.1
85 years old and over . . .	14,279	14.0	4.8	0.5	3.4	0.7	1.8	(Z)	(Z)	1.0	(Z)

Z Fewer than 50. [1] Includes other causes not shown separately. [2] Includes allied conditions. [3] Includes other races not shown separately. [4] Includes those deaths with age not stated.

Source: U.S. National Center for Health Statistics, *Vital Statistics of the United States,* annual.

Vital Statistics

No. 127. Deaths, by Age and Leading Cause: 1992

[Excludes deaths of nonresidents of the United States. Deaths classified according to ninth revision of *International Classification of Diseases*. See also Appendix III and *Historical Statistics, Colonial Times to 1970*, series B 149-166]

AGE AND LEADING CAUSE OF DEATH	NUMBER OF DEATHS			DEATH RATE PER 100,000 POPULATION		
	Total	Male	Female	Total	Male	Female
ALL AGES [1]						
All races [2]	2,175,613	1,122,336	1,053,277	852.9	901.6	806.5
White	1,873,781	956,957	916,824	880.0	917.2	844.3
Black	269,219	146,630	122,589	850.5	977.5	736.2
Leading causes of death:						
Heart disease	717,706	357,545	360,161	281.4	287.2	275.8
Malignant neoplasms (cancer)	520,578	274,838	245,740	204.1	220.8	188.2
Cerebrovascular disease (stroke)	143,769	56,645	87,124	56.4	45.5	66.7
Chronic obstructive pulmonary disease	91,938	50,465	41,473	36.0	40.5	31.8
Accidents	86,777	57,862	28,915	34.0	46.5	22.1
Motor vehicle	40,982	27,982	13,000	16.1	22.5	10.0
Pneumonia	75,719	35,465	40,254	29.7	28.5	30.8
Diabetes	50,067	21,672	28,395	19.6	17.4	21.7
Suicide	30,484	24,457	(NA)	12.0	19.6	(NA)
HIV infection [3]	33,566	29,325	(NA)	13.2	23.6	(NA)
Homicide and legal intervention	25,488	20,115	(NA)	10.0	16.2	(NA)
1 TO 4 YEARS OLD						
All causes	6,764	3,809	2,955	43.6	48.0	39.0
Leading causes of death:						
Accidents	2,467	1,513	954	15.9	19.1	12.6
Motor vehicle	860	487	373	5.5	6.1	4.9
Congenital anomalies	856	460	396	5.5	5.8	5.2
Malignant neoplasms (cancer)	479	248	231	3.1	3.1	3.0
Homicide and legal intervention	430	242	188	2.8	3.0	2.5
Heart disease	286	151	135	1.8	1.9	1.8
Pneumonia and influenza	188	95	93	1.2	1.2	1.2
5 TO 14 YEARS OLD						
All causes	8,193	5,080	3,113	22.5	27.2	17.5
Leading causes of death:						
Accidents	3,388	2,280	1,108	9.3	12.2	6.2
Malignant neoplasms (cancer)	1,105	637	468	3.0	3.4	2.6
Congenital anomalies	448	238	210	1.2	1.3	1.2
Homicide and legal intervention	587	375	212	1.6	2.0	1.2
Heart disease	284	160	124	0.8	0.9	0.7
Pneumonia and influenza	104	54	50	0.3	0.3	0.3
15 TO 24 YEARS OLD						
All causes	34,548	26,207	8,341	95.6	141.8	47.2
Leading causes of death:						
Accidents	13,662	10,253	3,409	37.8	55.5	19.3
Motor vehicle	10,305	7,438	2,867	28.5	40.3	16.2
Homicide and legal intervention	8,019	6,891	1,128	22.2	37.3	6.4
Suicide	4,693	4,044	649	13.0	21.9	3.7
Malignant neoplasms (cancer)	1,809	1,084	725	5.0	5.9	4.1
Heart disease	968	626	342	2.7	3.4	1.9
HIV infection [3]	578	419	159	1.6	2.3	0.9
25 TO 44 YEARS OLD						
All causes	149,771	105,890	43,881	181.9	258.3	106.1
Leading causes of death:						
Accidents	25,808	19,981	5,827	31.3	48.7	14.1
Motor vehicle	14,071	10,327	3,744	17.1	25.2	9.1
Malignant neoplasms (cancer)	22,185	10,095	12,090	26.9	24.6	29.2
HIV infection [3]	24,629	21,509	3,120	29.9	52.5	7.5
Heart disease	16,121	11,729	4,392	19.6	28.6	10.6
Homicide and legal intervention	11,803	9,311	2,492	14.3	22.7	6.0
Suicide	12,181	9,782	2,399	14.8	23.9	5.8
45 TO 64 YEARS OLD						
All causes	366,021	226,151	139,870	757.2	970.1	558.8
Leading causes of death:						
Malignant neoplasms (cancer)	132,815	71,501	61,314	274.7	306.7	245.0
Heart disease	103,929	73,229	30,700	215.0	314.1	122.7
Cerebrovascular (stroke)	14,500	7,859	6,641	30.0	33.7	26.5
Accidents	13,882	9,926	3,956	28.7	42.6	15.8
Motor vehicle	6,597	4,409	2,188	13.6	18.9	8.7
Chronic obstructive pulmonary disease	12,372	6,751	5,621	25.6	29.0	22.5
Chronic liver disease and cirrhosis	10,349	7,303	3,046	21.4	31.3	12.2
Diabetes	10,312	5,363	4,949	21.3	23.0	19.8
65 YEARS OLD AND OVER						
All causes	1,575,214	735,298	839,916	4,880.6	5,638.1	4,366.9
Leading causes of death:						
Heart disease	595,314	271,214	324,100	1,844.5	2,079.6	1,685.1
Malignant neoplasms (cancer)	362,060	191,204	170,856	1,121.8	1,466.1	888.3
Cerebrovascular (stroke)	125,392	46,722	78,670	388.5	358.3	409.0
Chronic obstructive pulmonary disease	78,182	42,961	35,221	242.2	329.4	183.1
Pneumonia and influenza	67,489	30,374	37,115	209.1	232.9	193.0
Diabetes	37,328	14,865	22,463	115.7	114.0	116.8
Accidents	26,633	13,335	13,298	82.5	102.3	69.1
Motor vehicle	7,053	3,970	3,083	21.9	30.4	16.0

NA Not available.   [1] Includes those deaths with age not stated.   [2] Includes other races not shown separately.   [3] Human immunodeficiency virus.

Source: U.S. National Center for Health Statistics, *Vital Statistics of the United States,* annual; and unpublished data.

No. 128. Death Rates, by Selected Causes and Age: 1980 to 1992

[Deaths per 100,000 population in specified group. Except as noted, excludes deaths of nonresidents of the United States. See headnote, table 124]

YEAR, RACE, AND AGE	Total [1]	Heart disease	Malignant neoplasms	Accidents and adverse effects	Cerebrovascular diseases	Chronic obstructive pulmonary diseases [2]	Pneumonia, flu	Suicide	Chronic liver disease, cirrhosis	Diabetes mellitus	Homicide and legal intervention
ALL RACES [3]											
Both sexes:											
1980, age-adjusted...	585.8	336.0	183.9	46.7	75.1	24.7	24.1	11.9	13.5	15.4	10.7
1990, age-adjusted...	520.2	289.5	203.2	37.0	57.9	34.9	32.0	12.4	10.4	19.2	10.0
1991, age-adjusted...	513.7	285.9	204.1	35.4	56.9	35.9	30.9	12.2	10.1	19.4	10.5
1992, age-adjusted...	504.5	281.4	204.1	34.0	56.4	36.0	29.7	12.0	9.9	19.6	10.0
15 to 24 years old..	(NA)	2.7	5.0	37.8	0.5	0.5	0.6	13.0	0.1	0.4	22.2
25 to 34 years old..	(NA)	8.1	12.5	32.5	1.9	0.7	1.5	14.5	1.8	1.6	17.3
35 to 44 years old..	(NA)	31.8	42.3	30.1	6.5	1.8	3.4	15.1	9.0	4.0	11.2
45 to 54 years old..	(NA)	114.6	150.3	27.3	17.5	8.3	6.0	14.7	16.7	11.7	7.5
55 to 64 years old..	(NA)	346.5	437.8	30.6	46.4	48.3	16.5	14.8	27.6	34.0	4.7
65 to 74 years old..	(NA)	847.9	873.4	44.2	135.3	155.5	55.3	16.5	33.9	75.7	3.7
75 to 84 years old..	(NA)	2,147.3	1,350.9	96.3	468.2	326.5	227.1	22.8	32.3	142.9	3.8
85 years old and over	(NA)	6,513.5	1,787.3	254.8	1,566.0	460.9	1,022.8	21.9	24.2	253.8	4.1
Male:											
1980, age-adjusted	777.2	368.6	205.3	67.4	63.6	35.1	25.1	18.6	18.0	13.0	17.3
1990, age-adjusted	680.2	297.6	221.3	51.1	46.8	40.8	30.4	20.4	13.7	16.7	16.2
1991, age-adjusted	669.9	292.6	221.5	48.6	46.1	41.1	29.4	20.1	13.2	17.2	16.9
1992, age-adjusted	656.0	287.2	220.8	46.5	45.5	40.5	28.5	19.6	13.2	17.4	16.2
15 to 24 years old ...	(NA)	3.4	5.9	55.5	0.6	0.6	0.7	21.9	(NA)	0.4	37.3
25 to 34 years old ...	(NA)	10.7	12.1	50.6	1.9	0.7	1.9	24.0	2.4	1.8	27.5
35 to 44 years old ...	(NA)	47.8	38.1	46.7	6.9	1.8	4.5	23.7	13.7	4.9	17.6
45 to 54 years old ...	(NA)	173.7	153.8	41.0	19.3	8.7	7.9	22.4	24.8	13.5	11.8
55 to 64 years old ...	(NA)	503.9	513.4	44.8	53.2	56.3	21.2	24.1	40.2	35.9	7.7
65 to 74 years old ...	(NA)	1,178.9	1,111.1	61.1	155.8	199.7	74.1	29.9	46.9	78.5	5.5
75 to 84 years old ...	(NA)	2,754.1	1,882.8	130.8	509.7	478.6	310.4	50.0	44.7	150.9	5.3
85 years old and over.	(NA)	7,157.6	2,802.7	344.3	1,500.8	830.9	1,310.4	62.8	36.5	268.7	7.3
Female:											
1980, age-adjusted	432.6	305.1	163.6	27.1	86.1	15.0	23.2	5.5	9.3	17.6	4.5
1990, age-adjusted	390.6	281.8	186.0	23.6	68.6	29.2	33.4	4.8	7.2	21.5	4.2
1991, age-adjusted	386.5	279.5	187.5	22.9	67.2	31.1	32.2	4.7	7.1	21.6	4.4
1992, age-adjusted	380.3	275.8	188.2	22.1	66.7	31.8	30.8	4.6	6.7	21.7	4.1
15 to 24 years old ...	(NA)	1.9	4.1	19.3	0.4	0.5	0.6	3.7	(NA)	0.3	6.4
25 to 34 years old ...	(NA)	5.4	12.9	14.4	1.9	0.6	1.1	5.0	1.2	1.3	7.1
35 to 44 years old ...	(NA)	16.1	46.5	13.8	6.1	1.7	2.3	6.6	4.5	3.2	4.9
45 to 54 years old ...	(NA)	58.1	147.0	14.2	15.7	7.9	4.2	7.3	8.9	10.0	3.3
55 to 64 years old ...	(NA)	204.9	369.7	17.8	40.3	41.0	12.2	6.5	16.3	32.3	2.0
65 to 74 years old ...	(NA)	587.8	686.5	31.0	119.2	120.7	40.5	5.9	23.7	73.5	2.4
75 to 84 years old ...	(NA)	1,776.1	1,025.6	75.3	442.8	233.4	176.1	6.2	24.8	138.0	2.9
85 years old and over.	(NA)	6,264.0	1,394.1	220.2	1,591.3	317.6	911.3	6.1	19.5	248.0	2.9
WHITE											
Both sexes:											
1980, age-adjusted...	559.4	350.8	189.0	46.3	76.3	26.9	24.8	12.7	13.0	14.8	7.0
1990, age-adjusted...	492.8	305.4	211.6	36.9	59.7	38.4	33.9	13.5	10.3	18.5	5.8
1991, age-adjusted...	486.8	301.9	213.1	35.3	58.7	39.8	32.8	13.3	10.1	18.8	6.1
1992, age-adjusted...	477.5	297.5	213.5	34.0	58.4	40.0	31.7	13.0	10.0	19.0	5.9
Male:											
1980, age-adjusted	745.3	384.0	208.7	66.3	63.3	37.9	25.1	19.9	17.3	12.8	10.9
1990, age-adjusted	644.3	312.7	227.7	50.3	47.0	44.3	31.4	22.0	13.6	16.5	9.0
1991, age-adjusted	634.4	307.6	228.9	47.7	46.3	44.9	30.6	21.7	13.4	16.9	9.3
1992, age-adjusted	620.9	302.4	228.6	45.9	46.1	44.4	29.7	21.2	13.3	17.2	9.1
Female:											
1980, age-adjusted	411.1	319.2	170.3	27.2	88.8	16.4	24.6	5.9	8.8	16.8	3.2
1990, age-adjusted	369.9	298.4	196.1	24.0	71.8	32.8	36.3	5.3	7.1	20.5	2.8
1991, age-adjusted	366.3	296.5	198.0	23.4	70.5	35.0	35.0	5.2	7.1	20.6	3.0
1992, age-adjusted	359.9	292.9	199.0	22.6	70.3	35.8	33.6	5.1	6.8	20.7	2.8
BLACK											
Both sexes:											
1980, age-adjusted...	842.5	274.0	169.1	50.6	75.6	12.7	21.2	6.0	18.0	20.8	38.6
1990, age-adjusted...	789.2	246.4	187.2	40.7	57.1	18.6	24.8	6.9	12.3	26.6	39.8
1991, age-adjusted...	780.7	243.9	185.9	40.0	55.7	18.7	23.7	6.7	11.1	27.3	41.6
1992, age-adjusted...	767.5	238.8	184.5	37.3	53.8	18.5	22.3	6.8	10.5	27.3	38.9
Male:											
1980, age-adjusted	1,112.8	301.0	205.5	77.1	73.1	19.3	26.9	10.3	24.0	16.0	66.6
1990, age-adjusted	1,061.3	256.8	221.9	60.7	53.1	25.2	28.9	12.0	16.6	21.1	69.2
1991, age-adjusted	1,048.8	253.9	217.5	59.8	52.1	24.5	26.7	12.1	14.5	22.1	72.0
1992, age-adjusted	1,026.9	246.9	214.4	54.9	49.5	23.8	25.5	12.0	14.5	21.8	67.5
Female:											
1980, age-adjusted	631.1	249.7	136.5	26.9	77.9	6.8	16.1	2.2	12.6	25.2	13.5
1990, age-adjusted	581.6	237.0	156.1	22.8	60.7	12.6	21.2	2.3	8.5	31.5	13.5
1991, age-adjusted	575.1	235.0	157.4	22.2	59.0	13.4	20.9	1.9	8.1	32.0	14.2
1992, age-adjusted	568.4	231.6	157.6	21.5	57.8	13.7	19.5	2.0	6.8	32.3	13.1

NA Not available. [1] Includes other causes not shown separately. [2] Includes allied conditions. [3] Includes other races not shown separately.

Source: U.S. National Center for Health Statistics, *Vital Statistics of the United States,* annual; and *Monthly Vital Statistics Report.*

No. 129. Death Rates, by Cause—States: 1991 and 1992

[**Deaths per 100,000 resident population enumerated as of April 1.** By place of residence. Excludes nonresidents of the United States. Causes of death classified according to ninth revisions of *International Classification of Diseases*]

DIVISION AND STATE	Total [1] 1992	Heart disease, 1992	Cancer, 1992	Cerebro-vascular dis-eases, 1992	Acci-dents and adverse effects, 1992	Chronic obstruc-tive pulmo-nary dis-eases, 1992[2]	Pneu-monia, influ-enza, 1991	Dia-betes mellitus, 1992	Suicide, 1992	Chronic liver disease and cir-rhosis, 1991	Athero-sclerosis, 1991
U.S. ...	**852.9**	**281.4**	**204.1**	**56.4**	**34.0**	**36.0**	**30.9**	**19.6**	**12.0**	**10.1**	**6.9**
Northeast ..	**932.7**	**330.2**	**228.9**	**53.1**	**27.8**	**35.2**	**(NA)**	**21.2**	**9.2**	**(NA)**	**(NA)**
N.E.	**879.8**	**285.6**	**229.0**	**55.0**	**24.6**	**37.6**	**35.1**	**20.1**	**9.7**	**10.0**	**6.9**
ME	902.5	280.0	237.8	60.3	32.8	50.8	30.4	25.9	12.7	11.0	8.9
NH	766.3	240.7	204.7	50.0	22.8	36.5	24.8	21.5	12.3	8.5	7.3
VT	839.4	277.4	204.1	50.4	29.8	42.4	28.0	21.9	14.0	8.1	5.3
MA	899.1	284.8	236.7	55.6	21.6	35.9	39.8	19.9	8.9	10.1	6.5
RI.....	945.6	323.0	251.4	58.5	22.7	37.6	35.0	22.8	7.3	11.9	8.5
CT	861.6	294.6	217.5	53.5	27.3	35.4	32.9	16.4	9.1	9.8	6.4
M.A.	**951.1**	**345.7**	**228.9**	**52.5**	**29.0**	**34.4**	**34.4**	**21.7**	**9.1**	**10.7**	**5.6**
NY	918.5	354.0	213.3	46.0	26.8	32.3	37.8	16.4	8.5	10.7	5.1
NJ	906.2	304.5	228.5	49.6	25.8	31.0	29.1	26.9	6.6	11.4	5.7
PA	1,029.7	360.2	252.7	64.1	34.3	39.8	32.8	26.2	11.6	10.2	6.3
Midwest ...	**881.2**	**297.2**	**212.1**	**60.7**	**32.8**	**36.7**	**(NA)**	**21.7**	**11.1**	**(NA)**	**(NA)**
E.N.C. ...	**872.0**	**295.3**	**212.1**	**58.2**	**31.1**	**35.7**	**31.6**	**22.7**	**11.0**	**9.7**	**7.5**
OH	899.3	308.7	220.7	55.4	30.5	39.7	28.9	26.3	10.8	8.5	7.2
IN.....	883.0	295.2	212.6	63.1	34.1	40.1	30.9	22.2	12.3	7.6	9.1
IL.....	879.3	296.8	212.0	58.4	30.2	33.3	34.3	20.6	9.8	11.4	5.9
MI	838.3	285.1	204.6	54.1	30.6	32.7	29.7	22.5	11.3	11.3	8.8
WI	846.1	281.5	206.8	66.5	31.8	32.8	35.3	20.9	11.7	7.2	7.2
W.N.C. ...	**903.1**	**301.7**	**212.0**	**66.5**	**36.9**	**39.3**	**38.0**	**19.3**	**11.5**	**7.1**	**9.7**
MN	784.1	229.4	191.3	63.1	33.3	33.5	35.1	17.4	11.5	6.6	7.8
IA.....	948.8	327.5	229.5	72.5	36.4	41.8	44.0	18.1	10.2	6.2	13.8
MO....	982.3	341.9	227.5	66.5	41.1	42.8	36.6	20.8	12.1	8.5	7.6
ND	898.5	300.0	215.0	75.9	36.6	36.9	36.2	22.6	10.3	8.8	15.3
SD	945.4	323.8	222.0	67.9	42.9	42.5	44.4	23.2	11.2	8.3	9.7
NE	915.0	329.6	202.4	64.3	34.9	41.7	41.6	16.6	11.7	6.6	12.1
KS	882.0	295.1	200.1	64.6	34.6	37.8	35.6	20.5	12.4	6.1	10.2
South	**875.9**	**284.6**	**207.6**	**59.6**	**38.6**	**36.4**	**(NA)**	**20.9**	**12.9**	**(NA)**	**(NA)**
S.A.....	**895.9**	**289.3**	**216.3**	**59.3**	**36.1**	**38.2**	**26.9**	**20.5**	**12.9**	**10.6**	**6.0**
DE	859.9	266.9	223.5	46.9	35.8	35.9	26.6	30.0	12.7	9.9	3.8
MD....	790.9	241.6	202.4	42.8	26.2	29.4	24.5	22.5	9.4	9.0	4.2
DC	1,214.9	314.1	260.9	57.4	31.6	28.2	31.3	29.6	5.8	25.8	6.9
VA	772.0	242.4	187.8	53.0	30.3	32.2	27.2	15.1	12.7	7.8	5.3
WV....	1,090.2	382.9	255.1	60.3	46.7	54.3	38.2	30.1	13.3	9.3	8.4
NC	872.0	277.8	204.0	66.9	39.7	35.1	28.5	20.9	12.6	9.8	5.2
SC	850.4	268.0	194.1	69.2	43.0	34.9	23.0	21.7	12.9	11.0	4.1
GA	782.4	243.4	174.2	54.4	38.9	31.2	28.6	14.5	12.0	8.7	6.0
FL	1,036.3	351.0	260.9	64.9	36.1	48.6	25.2	22.8	15.0	13.4	7.8
E.S.C.....	**941.4**	**314.3**	**218.4**	**67.6**	**48.1**	**38.3**	**34.2**	**20.3**	**12.9**	**9.1**	**6.6**
KY	933.3	313.8	227.7	61.6	44.2	45.2	38.4	21.8	13.1	9.5	6.2
TN	926.8	298.8	214.4	73.6	43.9	38.2	34.2	19.9	12.9	9.6	7.5
AL	951.1	311.7	218.6	66.6	49.9	35.2	32.8	20.6	12.6	9.1	6.4
MS	965.9	349.1	212.6	66.1	58.7	33.6	30.6	18.2	12.7	7.5	5.8
W.S.C. ...	**806.3**	**260.4**	**187.1**	**55.5**	**37.3**	**32.5**	**25.4**	**22.0**	**12.9**	**9.7**	**7.4**
AR	1,042.3	344.0	244.2	84.5	47.7	39.3	38.2	21.5	12.2	8.6	7.0
LA	879.7	284.1	207.0	56.5	41.5	29.6	24.5	27.9	12.4	8.3	8.3
OK....	951.9	339.1	211.3	67.2	39.5	43.0	37.3	17.9	14.7	9.4	11.2
TX	730.1	229.0	170.2	49.2	34.5	30.4	21.6	21.3	12.8	10.2	6.6
West......	**711.0**	**213.4**	**166.7**	**49.5**	**33.8**	**35.4**	**(NA)**	**13.7**	**13.9**	**(NA)**	**(NA)**
Mountain .	**716.0**	**204.7**	**165.4**	**44.7**	**39.5**	**40.4**	**26.8**	**16.8**	**17.7**	**10.4**	**7.0**
MT	859.5	231.9	207.6	60.4	49.5	55.5	30.3	19.5	18.6	9.0	13.1
ID.....	739.0	218.1	169.1	59.1	44.7	40.2	28.5	17.8	15.8	6.7	6.5
WY....	709.7	194.1	160.7	52.3	51.0	49.5	22.8	14.6	18.1	8.9	5.9
CO....	647.7	178.1	143.0	41.3	33.1	40.8	28.0	12.6	17.3	9.5	9.3
NM	706.5	187.5	157.4	38.1	52.0	33.8	23.6	23.4	19.2	14.2	6.5
AZ	810.3	243.1	194.2	47.6	42.3	44.3	31.0	17.2	17.0	12.7	6.6
UT	539.5	151.8	108.3	38.7	30.6	23.2	22.5	19.8	14.1	4.8	3.9
NV	769.0	232.1	200.4	37.3	30.8	47.6	18.9	12.9	24.6	13.4	3.7
Pacific ...	**709.2**	**216.5**	**167.2**	**51.2**	**31.8**	**33.6**	**30.6**	**12.7**	**12.6**	**11.3**	**7.0**
WA....	742.1	217.5	184.0	56.7	33.4	40.6	26.9	15.8	13.5	8.1	8.7
OR	866.9	245.3	212.5	70.7	36.6	42.2	27.5	18.9	16.4	9.0	10.4
CA	698.6	217.2	162.1	49.1	30.7	32.6	32.0	11.6	12.1	12.3	6.6
AK	391.8	88.1	88.1	18.4	60.9	15.1	9.1	8.0	15.3	8.8	(NA)
HI.....	602.9	184.8	151.9	48.2	25.4	16.4	26.4	14.8	11.2	6.0	2.6

NA Not available.   [1] Includes other causes not shown separately.   [2] Includes allied conditions.

Source: U.S. National Center for Health Statistics, *Monthly Vital Statistics Report;* and unpublished data.

No. 130. Acquired Immunodeficiency Syndrome (AIDS) Deaths, by Selected Characteristics: 1982 to 1994

[Data are shown by year of death and are subject to substantial retrospective changes. For data on AIDS cases reported, see table 213. Based on reporting by State health departments]

CHARACTERISTIC	NUMBER									PERCENT DISTRIBUTION	
	Total, 1982-1994 [1]	1985	1988	1989	1990	1991	1992	1993	1994	1994	1982-1994
Total [2]	258,658	6,689	19,979	26,266	29,781	34,491	37,619	40,015	31,212	100.0	100.0
Age:											
13 to 19 years old	850	28	54	78	90	115	110	135	112	0.4	0.3
20 to 29 years old	44,770	1,311	3,812	4,795	5,246	5,846	6,073	6,409	4,868	15.6	17.3
30 to 39 years old	117,759	3,071	9,044	12,045	13,659	15,561	16,966	18,149	14,334	45.9	45.5
40 to 49 years old	64,639	1,426	4,499	6,188	7,312	8,916	10,059	10,718	8,396	26.9	25.0
50 to 59 years old	21,415	603	1,704	2,214	2,429	2,811	3,080	3,318	2,550	8.2	8.3
60 years old and over. . .	9,225	250	866	946	1,045	1,242	1,331	1,286	952	3.1	3.6
Sex:											
Male	229,450	6,230	17,947	23,682	26,653	30,624	33,082	34,714	26,660	85.4	88.7
Female	29,619	468	2,050	2,616	3,177	3,920	4,599	5,392	4,620	14.8	11.5
Race/ethnicity:											
White...........	137,602	4,015	10,956	14,439	16,450	18,619	19,392	19,877	14,929	47.8	53.2
Black...........	82,556	1,754	6,061	7,941	8,989	10,706	12,493	14,084	11,453	36.7	31.9
Hispanic.........	36,244	889	2,798	3,647	4,105	4,828	5,404	5,691	4,488	14.4	14.0
Indian	537	6	25	40	49	87	73	117	97	0.3	0.2
Asian...........	1,750	29	129	180	195	240	246	281	280	0.9	0.7

[1] Includes deaths prior to 1982.   [2] Includes other race/ethnicity groups not shown separately.

Source: U.S. Centers for Disease Control, *Surveillance Report,* annual.

No. 131. Death Rates From Heart Disease, by Sex and Age: 1970 to 1992

[**Deaths per 100,000 population in specified age groups.** Excludes deaths of nonresidents of the United States. Beginning 1980, deaths classified according to the ninth revision of the *International Classification of Diseases.* For earlier years, classified according to the revision in use at the time; see text, section 2. See Appendix III]

AGE AT DEATH AND SELECTED TYPE OF HEART DISEASE	MALE					FEMALE				
	1970	1980	1990	1991	1992	1970	1980	1990	1991	1992
Total U.S. rate [1]	422.5	368.6	297.6	292.6	287.2	304.5	305.1	281.8	279.5	275.8
25 to 34 years old	15.2	11.4	10.3	10.7	10.7	7.7	5.3	5.0	5.3	5.4
35 to 44 years old	103.2	68.7	48.1	47.4	47.8	32.2	21.4	15.1	16.0	16.1
45 to 54 years old	376.4	282.6	183.0	179.3	173.7	109.9	84.5	61.0	59.5	58.1
55 to 64 years old	987.2	746.8	537.3	520.8	503.9	351.6	272.1	215.7	210.0	204.9
65 to 74 years old	2,170.3	1,728.0	1,250.0	1,219.1	1,178.8	1,082.7	828.6	616.8	600.6	587.8
75 to 84 years old	4,534.8	3,834.3	2,968.2	2,850.9	2,754.0	3,120.8	2,497.0	1,893.8	1,836.9	1,776.2
85 years old and over	8,426.2	8,752.7	7,418.4	7,262.4	7,156.5	7,591.8	7,350.5	6,478.1	6,362.5	6,263.1
Persons 45 to 54 years old:										
Ischemic heart	338.0	217.3	123.8	119.6	114.9	84.0	52.2	33.6	33.4	31.6
Rheumatic heart..	11.4	3.1	1.1	1.0	1.2	10.6	4.3	1.9	1.8	1.6
Hypertensive heart [2]	4.6	8.3	7.6	8.0	7.6	4.0	5.5	4.3	4.0	4.1
Persons 55 to 64 years old:										
Ischemic heart	904.6	581.1	375.4	360.3	345.1	299.1	189.0	135.4	133.1	126.7
Rheumatic heart..	21.5	6.2	3.4	3.0	2.6	20.8	9.2	4.7	4.6	4.3
Hypertensive heart [2]	11.7	21.8	18.1	18.4	18.9	9.1	13.3	10.9	10.4	11.4
Persons 65 to 74 years old:										
Ischemic heart	2,010.0	1,355.5	898.5	870.2	837.5	978.0	605.3	415.2	398.9	387.9
Rheumatic heart..	31.9	11.8	7.1	6.3	5.7	30.2	18.6	10.5	10.4	9.9
Hypertensive heart [2]	30.6	44.3	33.2	31.5	32.5	24.8	36.2	25.9	24.6	24.5
Persons 75 to 84 years old:										
Ischemic heart	4,222.7	2,953.7	2,129.6	2,032.3	1,961.2	2,866.3	1,842.7	1,287.6	1,236.9	1,186.1
Rheumatic heart..	34.8	16.7	12.3	12.8	12.1	34.3	25.4	22.5	22.2	20.7
Hypertensive heart [2]	80.8	90.7	67.9	68.4	64.8	83.9	101.1	69.7	68.7	66.9
Persons 85 years old and over:										
Ischemic heart	7,781.5	6,501.6	5,120.7	4,964.5	4,878.3	6,951.5	5,280.6	4,257.8	4,145.9	4,056.4
Rheumatic heart..	34.7	19.5	18.7	22.7	19.9	39.2	25.8	33.3	31.8	30.0
Hypertensive heart [2]	182.0	180.3	154.3	155.2	157.8	223.5	250.8	212.1	214.7	216.4

[1] Includes persons under 25 years old not shown separately.   [2] With or without renal disease.

Source: U.S. National Center for Health Statistics, *Vital Statistics of the United States,* annual; and unpublished data.

No. 132. Death Rates From Cancer, by Sex and Age: 1970 to 1992

[**Deaths per 100,000 population in the specified age groups.** See headnote, table 131]

AGE AT DEATH AND SELECTED TYPE OF CANCER	MALE					FEMALE				
	1970	1980	1990	1991	1992	1970	1980	1990	1991	1992
Total [1]	182.1	205.3	221.3	221.5	220.8	144.4	163.6	186.0	187.5	188.2
25 to 34 years	16.3	13.4	12.6	12.2	12.1	16.7	14.0	12.6	12.6	12.9
35 to 44 years	53.0	44.0	38.5	38.8	38.1	65.6	53.1	48.1	47.2	46.5
45 to 54 years	183.5	188.7	162.5	159.0	153.8	181.5	171.8	155.5	151.3	147.0
55 to 64 years	511.8	520.8	532.9	525.7	513.4	343.2	361.7	375.2	379.1	369.7
65 to 74 years	1,006.8	1,093.2	1,122.2	1,120.4	1,111.1	557.9	607.1	677.4	676.9	686.5
75 to 84 years	1,588.3	1,790.5	1,914.4	1,898.4	1,882.7	891.9	903.1	1,010.3	1,020.7	1,025.6
85 years old and over	1,720.8	2,369.5	2,739.9	2,753.3	2,803.3	1,096.7	1,255.7	1,372.1	1,395.2	1,393.9
Persons, 35 to 44 years old:										
Respiratory, intrathoracic	17.0	12.6	9.1	8.6	8.6	6.5	6.8	5.4	5.5	5.6
Digestive organs, peritoneum . .	11.4	9.5	8.9	9.2	9.1	8.6	6.5	5.5	5.7	5.7
Breast	0.1	-	(B)	(B)	0.0	20.4	17.9	17.8	16.9	16.1
Genital organs	1.4	0.7	0.6	0.7	0.6	13.6	8.3	7.3	7.1	7.3
Lymphatic and hematopoietic tissues, excl. leukemia	5.6	4.3	4.5	5.1	4.9	3.2	2.4	2.1	2.2	2.2
Urinary organs	1.9	1.4	1.5	1.5	1.4	1.0	0.6	0.6	0.7	0.7
Lip, oral cavity, and pharynx . . .	1.7	1.8	1.3	1.3	1.2	0.7	0.5	0.3	0.3	0.4
Leukemia	3.4	3.2	2.5	2.3	2.5	2.8	2.6	2.2	2.0	1.8
Persons, 45 to 54 years old:										
Respiratory, intrathoracic	72.1	79.8	63.0	60.6	57.7	22.2	34.8	35.3	33.8	32.5
Digestive organs, peritoneum . .	45.9	44.3	40.4	38.2	37.6	32.5	27.8	23.3	22.3	21.6
Breast	0.4	0.2	0.3	(B)	0.2	52.6	48.1	45.4	44.3	42.8
Genital organs	3.4	3.4	2.9	3.0	2.7	34.4	24.1	19.4	18.4	18.2
Lymphatic and hematopoietic tissues, excl. leukemia	12.8	10.2	10.9	11.0	10.8	8.3	6.6	6.0	6.4	6.1
Urinary organs	8.0	7.4	7.2	7.1	7.4	3.5	3.3	2.9	3.0	2.8
Lip, oral cavity, and pharynx . . .	7.9	8.2	5.9	6.1	5.5	2.8	2.6	1.6	1.6	1.6
Leukemia	6.6	6.2	5.6	5.5	5.2	4.9	4.4	4.1	4.0	4.0
Persons, 55 to 64 years old:										
Respiratory, intrathoracic	202.3	223.8	232.6	226.0	217.0	38.9	74.5	107.6	107.0	108.4
Digestive organs, peritoneum . .	139.0	129.3	124.0	125.4	123.6	86.0	79.1	69.3	70.0	67.8
Breast	0.6	0.7	0.6	0.5	0.5	77.6	80.5	78.6	79.1	73.6
Genital organs	22.8	23.5	27.9	26.8	26.6	58.2	46.8	40.1	40.3	39.2
Lymphatic and hematopoietic tissues, excl. leukemia	27.1	24.4	27.2	26.7	26.5	17.7	16.8	16.7	18.1	17.3
Urinary organs	26.4	22.9	23.5	23.2	23.1	9.4	8.9	8.8	9.6	9.1
Lip, oral cavity, and pharynx . . .	20.1	17.9	16.2	14.7	14.8	6.2	6.0	4.7	5.3	4.4
Leukemia	15.4	14.7	14.7	14.6	14.9	9.0	9.3	8.8	9.1	9.0
Persons, 65 to 74 years old:										
Respiratory, intrathoracic	340.7	422.0	447.3	446.0	439.8	45.6	106.1	181.7	185.8	195.3
Digestive organs, peritoneum . .	293.3	284.1	267.4	262.6	263.5	185.8	173.6	153.0	149.7	148.4
Breast	1.4	1.1	1.1	1.1	1.1	93.8	101.1	111.7	108.6	109.3
Genital organs	103.7	107.6	123.5	122.1	122.0	85.6	73.6	71.0	70.2	70.5
Lymphatic and hematopoietic tissues, excl. leukemia	50.3	48.1	56.8	57.9	58.7	34.6	34.4	39.5	41.1	41.0
Urinary organs	60.3	56.9	50.7	52.8	51.2	20.1	19.7	19.8	19.7	19.8
Lip, oral cavity, and pharynx . . .	26.8	25.4	21.5	20.6	20.3	6.7	8.8	8.3	7.8	7.8
Leukemia	35.3	35.3	36.0	36.1	36.0	19.3	18.7	18.8	19.3	19.0
Persons, 75 to 84 years old:										
Respiratory, intrathoracic	354.2	511.5	594.4	593.9	587.5	56.5	98.0	194.5	207.1	216.0
Digestive organs, peritoneum . .	507.5	496.6	468.0	454.1	444.0	353.3	326.3	293.3	290.0	288.7
Breast	2.7	2.1	1.6	1.7	2.0	127.4	126.4	146.3	145.1	140.8
Genital organs	299.4	315.4	358.5	363.5	355.7	104.9	95.7	95.3	94.8	97.2
Lymphatic and hematopoietic tissues, excl. leukemia	74.0	80.0	104.5	104.1	106.5	49.4	57.8	71.2	75.4	74.6
Urinary organs	112.2	112.4	107.5	103.5	104.5	44.0	37.4	38.5	38.5	40.0
Lip, oral cavity, and pharynx . . .	36.6	31.4	26.1	25.7	23.3	10.8	10.9	11.6	11.3	10.9
Leukemia	68.3	71.5	71.9	69.7	72.3	39.6	38.5	38.8	39.8	38.0
Persons, 85 years old and over:										
Respiratory, intrathoracic	215.3	386.3	538.0	552.1	545.4	56.5	96.3	142.8	154.4	160.8
Digestive organs, peritoneum . .	583.7	705.8	699.5	688.2	683.7	465.0	504.3	497.6	495.6	495.1
Breast	2.9	2.6	2.4	4.1	4.4	157.1	169.3	196.8	197.9	195.5
Genital organs	434.2	612.3	750.0	781.0	808.1	107.3	115.9	115.6	117.8	115.8
Lymphatic and hematopoietic tissues, excl. leukemia	58.1	93.2	140.5	140.7	138.8	41.7	63.0	90.0	92.8	92.5
Urinary organs	140.5	177.0	186.3	186.2	192.8	59.9	63.8	68.5	67.7	69.6
Lip, oral cavity, and pharynx . . .	47.0	40.2	37.4	31.9	32.8	19.2	16.0	17.5	17.1	16.9
Leukemia	83.3	117.1	116.0	111.7	116.8	50.9	61.1	65.0	70.0	67.7

- Represents zero. B Base figure too small to meet statistical standards for reliability of a derived figure. [1] Includes persons under 25 years of age and malignant neoplasms of other and unspecified sites, not shown separately.

Source: U.S. National Center for Health Statistics, *Vital Statistics of the United States,* annual; and unpublished data.

No. 133. Death Rates From Accidents and Violence: 1990 to 1992

[**Rates are per 100,000 population.** Excludes deaths of nonresidents of the United States. Beginning 1980, deaths classified according to the ninth revision of the *International Classification of Diseases*. For earlier years, classified according to the revisions in use at the time; see text, section 2. See Appendix III]

CAUSE OF DEATH AND AGE	WHITE						BLACK					
	Male			Female			Male			Female		
	1990	1991	1992	1990	1991	1992	1990	1991	1992	1990	1991	1992
Total [1]	**81.2**	**78.7**	**76.2**	**32.1**	**31.5**	**30.4**	**142.0**	**143.9**	**134.5**	**38.6**	**38.4**	**36.7**
Motor vehicle accidents	26.1	24.4	22.4	11.4	10.8	10.2	28.1	25.6	24.0	9.4	8.7	8.8
All other accidents	23.6	23.3	23.4	12.4	12.6	12.4	32.7	34.2	30.9	13.4	13.5	12.7
Suicide	22.0	21.7	21.2	5.3	5.2	5.1	12.0	12.1	12.0	2.3	1.9	2.0
Homicide	9.0	9.3	9.1	2.8	3.0	2.8	69.2	72.0	67.5	13.5	14.2	13.1
15 to 24 years old	107.3	104.2	97.4	30.5	31.2	28.4	208.0	231.9	222.2	34.9	37.0	34.9
25 to 34 years old	97.4	94.2	90.4	26.2	24.7	23.6	218.1	213.8	193.6	48.1	47.7	46.1
35 to 44 years old	82.3	78.5	80.3	24.4	23.5	23.5	176.6	171.8	159.8	38.5	40.0	38.9
45 to 54 years old	73.5	72.9	69.8	25.3	25.2	24.2	138.5	132.4	132.9	30.7	33.1	29.5
55 to 64 years old	79.5	75.6	73.0	29.4	26.6	25.7	129.9	124.7	118.7	36.1	32.5	31.8
65 years old and over	150.7	147.4	145.4	80.1	79.6	78.6	175.5	182.2	165.7	81.6	78.6	72.6
65 to 74 years old	99.7	94.8	94.0	40.5	39.0	38.7	141.8	142.6	130.8	50.4	48.1	43.9
75 to 84 years old	195.7	190.5	186.2	89.4	87.1	83.9	206.1	213.5	201.4	95.8	89.7	89.5
85 years old and over	428.3	433.3	421.4	232.4	234.8	234.2	359.1	373.9	340.0	213.0	209.8	178.4

[1] Includes persons under 15 years old, not shown separately.

No. 134. Deaths and Death Rates From Accidents, by Type: 1970 to 1992

[See headnote, table 133 and Appendix III. See also *Historical Statistics, Colonial Times to 1970*, series B 163-165]

TYPE OF ACCIDENT	DEATHS (number)					RATE PER 100,000 POPULATION				
	1970	1980	1990	1991	1992	1970	1980	1990	1991	1992
Total	**114,638**	**105,718**	**91,983**	**89,347**	**86,777**	**56.4**	**46.7**	**37.0**	**35.4**	**34.0**
Motor vehicle accidents	54,633	53,172	46,814	43,536	40,982	26.9	23.5	18.8	17.3	16.1
Traffic	53,493	51,930	45,827	42,621	39,985	26.3	22.9	18.4	16.9	15.7
Nontraffic	1,140	1,242	987	915	997	0.6	0.5	0.4	0.4	0.4
Water-transport accidents	1,651	1,429	923	851	837	0.8	0.6	0.4	0.3	0.3
Air and space transport accidents . .	1,612	1,494	941	1,000	1,094	0.8	0.7	0.4	0.4	0.4
Railway accidents	852	632	663	651	642	0.4	0.3	0.3	0.3	0.3
Accidental falls	16,926	13,294	12,313	12,662	12,646	8.3	5.9	5.0	5.0	5.0
Fall from one level to another. . . .	4,798	3,743	3,194	3,291	3,091	2.4	1.7	1.3	1.3	1.2
Fall on the same level.	828	415	499	474	483	0.4	0.2	0.2	0.2	0.2
Fracture, cause unspecified, and other unspecified falls	11,300	9,136	8,620	8,897	9,072	5.6	4.0	3.5	3.5	3.6
Accidental drowning.	6,391	6,043	3,979	3,967	3,524	3.1	2.7	1.6	1.6	1.4
Accidents caused by—										
Fires and flames	6,718	5,822	4,175	4,120	3,958	3.3	2.6	1.7	1.6	1.6
Firearms.	2,406	1,955	1,416	1,441	1,409	1.2	0.9	0.6	0.6	0.6
Electric current	1,140	1,095	670	626	525	0.6	0.5	0.3	0.2	0.2
Accidental poisoning by—										
Drugs and medicines	2,505	2,492	4,506	5,215	5,951	1.2	1.1	1.8	2.1	2.3
Other solid and liquid substances .	1,174	597	549	483	498	0.6	0.3	0.2	0.2	0.2
Gases and vapors	1,620	1,242	748	736	633	0.8	0.5	0.3	0.3	0.2
Complications due to medical procedures.	3,581	2437	2,669	2,473	2,669	1.8	1.1	1.1	1.0	1.0
Inhalation and ingestion of objects . .	2,753	3,249	3,303	3,240	3,128	1.4	1.5	1.3	1.3	1.2

No. 135. Suicides, by Sex and Method Used: 1970 to 1992

[Excludes deaths of nonresidents of the United States. Beginning 1979, deaths classified according to the ninth revision of the *International Classification of Diseases*. For earlier years, classified according to the revision in use at the time; see text, section 2. See also *Historical Statistics, Colonial Times to 1970*, series H 979-986]

METHOD	MALE						FEMALE					
	1970	1980	1985	1990	1991	1992	1970	1980	1985	1990	1991	1992
Total.	**16,629**	**20,505**	**23,145**	**24,724**	**24,769**	**24,457**	**6,851**	**6,364**	**6,308**	**6,182**	**6,041**	**6,027**
Firearms [1]	9,704	12,937	14,809	16,285	16,120	15,802	2,068	2,459	2,554	2,600	2,406	2,367
Percent of total	58	63	64	66	65	65	30	39	41	42	40	39
Poisoning [2]	3,299	2,997	3,319	3,221	3,316	3,262	3,285	2,456	2,385	2,203	2,228	2,233
Hanging and strangulation [3] .	2,422	2,997	3,532	3,688	3,751	3,822	831	694	732	756	810	856
Other [4]	1,204	1,574	1,485	1,530	1,582	1,571	667	755	637	623	597	571

[1] Includes explosives in 1970. [2] Includes solids, liquids, and gases. [3] Includes suffocation. [4] Beginning 1980, includes explosives.

Source of tables 133-135: U.S. National Center for Health Statistics, *Vital Statistics of the United States,* annual; and unpublished data.

Vital Statistics

No. 136. Suicide Rates, by Sex, Race, and Age Group: 1980 to 1992

[See headnote, tables 128 and 133]

AGE	TOTAL [1]			MALE						FEMALE					
				White			Black			White			Black		
	1980	1990	1992	1980	1990	1992	1980	1990	1992	1980	1990	1992	1980	1990	1992
All ages [2]	11.9	12.4	12.0	19.9	22.0	21.2	10.3	12.0	12.0	5.9	5.3	5.1	2.2	2.3	2.0
10 to 14 years old	0.8	1.5	1.7	1.4	2.3	2.6	0.5	1.6	2.0	0.3	0.9	1.1	0.1	(B)	(B)
15 to 19 years old	8.5	11.1	10.8	15.0	19.3	18.4	5.6	11.5	14.8	3.3	4.0	3.7	1.6	1.9	1.9
20 to 24 years old	16.1	15.1	14.9	27.8	26.8	26.6	20.0	19.0	21.2	5.9	4.4	4.0	3.1	2.6	2.4
25 to 34 years old	16.0	15.2	14.5	25.6	25.6	25.1	21.8	21.9	20.7	7.5	6.0	5.4	4.1	3.7	3.3
35 to 44 years old	15.4	15.3	15.1	23.5	25.3	25.2	15.6	16.9	16.9	9.1	7.4	7.2	4.6	4.0	3.3
45 to 54 years old	15.9	14.8	14.7	24.2	24.8	24.0	12.0	14.8	12.4	10.2	7.5	7.9	2.8	3.2	3.0
55 to 64 years old	15.9	16.0	14.8	25.8	27.5	26.0	11.7	10.8	10.1	9.1	8.0	7.2	2.3	2.6	2.0
65 to 74 years over . . .	16.9	17.9	16.5	32.5	34.2	32.0	11.1	14.7	11.8	7.0	7.2	6.3	1.7	2.6	(B)
75 to 84 years over . . .	19.1	24.9	22.8	45.5	60.2	53.0	10.5	14.4	18.5	5.7	6.7	6.6	1.4	(B)	(B)
85 years and over	19.2	22.2	21.9	52.8	70.3	67.6	18.9	(B)	(B)	5.8	5.4	6.3	0.1	(B)	(B)

B Base figure too small to meet statistical standards for reliability of a derived figure.   [1] Includes other races not shown separately.   [2] Includes other age groups not shown separately.

Source: U.S. National Center for Health Statistics, *Monthly Vital Statistics Report;* and unpublished data.

No. 137. Firearm Mortality Among Children, Youth, and Young Adults, 1 to 34 Years Old: 1992

[**Death rate per 100,000 population.** Deaths classified according to the ninth revision of the *International Classification of Diseases*]

ITEM	Under 5 years old	5 to 9 years old	10 to 14 years old	15 to 19 years old	20 to 24 years old	25 to 29 years old	30 to 34 years old
MALE							
Total: White	0.5	0.5	4.6	29.1	34.6	29.0	26.0
Black	1.4	1.5	11.5	140.5	184.3	129.4	94.8
Accidents: White	0.1	0.3	1.6	2.9	1.6	1.0	0.8
Black	0.2	0.6	2.0	6.3	4.7	2.2	1.2
Suicide: White	(X)	(X)	1.5	13.6	17.7	15.3	14.9
Black	(X)	(X)	1.1	9.0	14.4	13.4	10.5
Homicide: White	0.3	0.3	1.4	11.8	14.9	12.3	10.1
Black	1.1	0.9	8.2	123.6	164.4	113.4	82.9
FEMALE							
Total: White	0.4	0.3	1.0	4.6	5.1	4.9	5.5
Black	1.5	0.5	3.0	12.7	17.7	16.5	13.9
Accidents: White	0.1	0.1	0.1	0.2	0.2	0.1	0.1
Black	0.4	0.1	0.2	0.2	(X)	0.1	0.1
Suicide: White	(X)	(X)	0.4	2.1	2.0	2.4	2.8
Black	(X)	(X)	0.1	0.8	0.7	1.9	0.7
Homicide: White	0.3	0.2	0.5	2.2	2.7	2.3	2.4
Black	1.1	0.4	2.7	11.2	16.8	14.4	13.1

X Not applicable.

Source: U.S. National Center for Health Statistics, *Advance Data from Vital and Health Statistics*, No. 231.

No. 138. Deaths and Death Rates for Injury by Firearms, by Race and Sex: 1980 to 1992

[Age-adjusted rates per 100,000]

YEAR	ALL RACES			WHITE			ALL OTHER					
							Total			Black		
	Both sexes	Male	Female	Both sexes	Male	Female	Both sexes	Male	Female	Both sexes	Male	Female
NUMBER												
1980	33,780	28,322	5,458	24,849	20,714	4,135	8,931	7,608	1,323	8,505	7,265	1,240
1985	31,566	26,382	5,184	24,507	20,389	4,118	7,059	5,993	1,066	6,565	5,584	981
1990	37,155	31,736	5,419	26,299	22,249	4,050	10,856	9,487	1,369	10,175	8,922	1,253
1991	38,317	32,882	5,435	26,455	22,448	4,007	11,862	10,434	1,428	11,025	9,733	1,292
1992	37,776	32,425	5,351	26,120	22,208	3,912	11,656	10,217	1,439	10,906	9,581	1,325
RATE [1]												
1980	14.8	25.3	4.8	12.4	21.1	4.2	29.1	53.0	8.1	33.5	61.8	9.1
1985	12.7	21.8	4.2	11.4	19.4	3.9	19.7	35.4	5.7	23.2	42.2	6.5
1990	14.6	25.4	4.2	11.9	20.5	3.7	26.9	48.9	6.5	33.4	61.5	7.8
1991	15.2	26.4	4.2	12.0	20.7	3.7	29.0	52.9	6.6	35.9	66.4	8.0
1992	14.9	25.9	4.1	11.8	20.4	3.6	28.0	50.9	6.6	35.1	64.5	8.0

[1] Age-adjusted death rate. For method of computation see source.

No. 139. Deaths and Death Rates for Drug-Induced Causes, by Race and Sex: 1980 to 1992

[Age-adjusted rates per 100,000]

YEAR	ALL RACES			WHITE			ALL OTHER					
							Total			Black		
	Both sexes	Male	Female	Both sexes	Male	Female	Both sexes	Male	Female	Both sexes	Male	Female
NUMBER												
1980	6,900	3,771	3,129	5,814	3,088	2,726	1,086	683	403	1,006	648	358
1985	8,663	5,342	3,321	6,946	4,172	2,774	1,717	1,170	547	1,600	1,107	493
1990	9,463	5,897	3,566	7,603	4,646	2,957	1,860	1,251	609	1,703	1,155	548
1991	10,388	6,593	3,795	8,204	5,129	3,075	2,184	1,464	720	2,037	1,385	652
1992	11,703	7,766	3,937	9,360	6,124	3,236	2,343	1,642	701	2,148	1,533	615
RATE [1]												
1980	3.0	3.4	2.6	2.9	3.2	2.6	3.7	4.9	2.5	4.1	5.8	2.7
1985	3.5	4.5	2.6	3.3	4.0	2.5	4.9	7.2	2.9	5.9	8.9	3.3
1990	3.6	4.6	2.6	3.3	4.2	2.5	4.6	6.7	2.8	5.7	8.4	3.4
1991	3.8	5.0	2.7	3.6	4.6	2.6	5.2	7.5	3.2	6.6	9.7	3.9
1992	4.3	5.9	2.8	4.1	5.5	2.7	5.5	8.3	3.1	6.8	10.6	3.6

[1] Age-adjusted death rate. For method of computation see source.

No. 140. Deaths and Death Rates for Alcohol-Induced Causes, by Race and Sex: 1980 to 1992

[Age-adjusted rates per 100,000]

YEAR	ALL RACES			WHITE			ALL OTHER					
							Total			Black		
	Both sexes	Male	Female	Both sexes	Male	Female	Both sexes	Male	Female	Both sexes	Male	Female
NUMBER												
1980	19,765	14,447	5,318	14,815	10,936	3,879	4,950	3,511	1,439	4,451	3,170	1,281
1985	17,741	13,216	4,525	13,216	9,922	3,294	4,525	3,294	1,231	4,114	3,030	1,084
1990	19,757	14,842	4,915	14,904	11,334	3,570	4,853	3,508	1,345	4,337	3,172	1,165
1991	19,233	14,467	4,766	14,825	11,286	3,539	4,408	3,181	1,227	3,883	2,816	1,067
1992	19,568	14,926	4,642	15,143	11,701	3,442	4,425	3,225	1,200	3,809	2,800	1,009
RATE [1]												
1980	8.4	13.0	4.3	6.9	10.8	3.5	18.8	29.5	10.0	20.4	32.4	10.6
1985	7.0	11.0	3.4	5.8	9.2	2.8	14.6	23.5	7.2	16.8	27.7	8.0
1990	7.2	11.4	3.4	6.2	9.9	2.8	13.6	22.0	6.8	16.1	26.6	7.7
1991	6.8	10.9	3.2	6.0	9.7	2.7	11.8	19.2	5.9	13.9	22.9	6.8
1992	6.8	11.0	3.1	6.1	9.9	2.6	11.6	18.9	5.6	13.4	22.3	6.3

[1] Age-adjusted death rate. For method of computation see source.
Source of tables 138-140: U.S. National Center for Health Statistics, *Monthly Vital Statistics Reports.*

No. 141. Deaths—Life Years Lost and Mortality Costs, by Age, Sex, and Cause: 1992

[**Life years lost:** Number of years person would have lived in absence of death. **Mortality cost:** Value of lifetime earnings lost by persons who die prematurely, discounted at 6 percent]

CHARACTER-ISTIC	Number of deaths (1,000)	LIFE YEARS LOST [1] Total (1,000)	LIFE YEARS LOST [1] Per death	MORTALITY COST [2] Total (mil.)	MORTALITY COST [2] Per death	CHARACTER-ISTIC	Number of deaths (1,000)	LIFE YEARS LOST [1] Total (1,000)	LIFE YEARS LOST [1] Per death	MORTALITY COST [2] Total (mil.)	MORTALITY COST [2] Per death
Total.....	**2,176**	**36,707**	**17**	**312,198**	**143,530**	Heart disease .	358	4,722	13	38,714	108,278
Under 5 yrs. . .	41	3,096	75	20,796	502,421	Cancer......	275	4,097	15	36,174	131,618
5-14 yrs.....	8	554	68	5,505	671,889	Cerebrovas-					
15-24 yrs.....	35	1,963	57	30,164	873,096	cular diseases	57	672	12	4,941	87,233
25-44 yrs.....	150	6,338	42	117,657	785,580	Injuries......	58	2,077	36	34,028	588,094
45-64 yrs.....	366	9,011	25	101,882	278,350	Other.......	375	8,399	22	105,947	282,190
65 yrs. and over	1,575	15,745	10	36,194	22,977						
Heart disease .	718	8,959	12	54,081	75,352	**Female . . .**	**1,053**	**16,741**	**16**	**92,394**	**87,730**
Cancer......	521	8,544	16	63,901	122,749	Under 5 yrs. . .	18	1,420	79	8,011	444,126
Cerebrovas-						5-14 yrs......	3	224	72	1,819	584,186
cular diseases	144	1,680	12	8,768	60,984	15-24 yrs.....	8	517	62	6,033	723,352
Injuries......	87	3,007	35	42,823	493,485	25-44 yrs.....	44	2,019	46	26,678	607,969
Other.......	707	14,517	21	142,626	201,797	45-64 yrs.....	140	3,823	27	32,490	232,285
Male.....	**1,122**	**19,966**	**18**	**219,804**	**195,907**	65 yrs. and over	840	8,738	10	17,363	20,672
Under 5 yrs. . .	23	1,676	72	12,785	547,446	Heart disease .	360	4,237	12	15,366	42,665
5-14 yrs.....	5	330	65	3,686	725,633	Cancer......	246	4,448	18	27,727	112,830
15-24 yrs.....	26	1,446	55	24,130	920,756	Cerebrovas-					
25-44 yrs.....	106	4,319	41	90,979	859,182	cular diseases	87	1,009	12	3,826	43,917
45-64 yrs.....	226	5,188	23	69,392	306,841	Injuries......	29	930	32	8,795	304,162
65 yrs. and over	735	7,007	10	18,832	25,611	Other.......	331	6,118	18	36,679	110,701

[1] Based on life expectancy at year of death.   [2] Cost estimates based on the person's age, sex, life expectancy at the time of death, labor force participation rates, annual earnings, value of homemaking services, and a 6-percent discount rate by which to convert to present worth the potential aggregate earnings lost over the years.

Source: Institute for Health and Aging, University of California, San Francisco, CA, unpublished data.

No. 142. Marriages and Divorces: 1970 to 1990

[See also *Historical Statistics, Colonial Times to 1970,* series B 214-217]

YEAR	MARRIAGES [1] Number (1,000)	MARRIAGES [1] Rate per 1,000 population Total	MARRIAGES [1] Rate per 1,000 population Men, 15 yrs. old and over	MARRIAGES [1] Rate per 1,000 population Women, 15 yrs. old and over	MARRIAGES [1] Rate per 1,000 population Unmarried women 15 yrs. old and over	MARRIAGES [1] Rate per 1,000 population Unmarried women 15 to 44 yrs. old	DIVORCES AND ANNULMENTS Number (1,000)	DIVORCES AND ANNULMENTS Rate per 1,000 population Total	DIVORCES AND ANNULMENTS Rate per 1,000 population Married women, 15 yrs. old and over
1970	2,159	10.6	31.1	28.4	76.5	140.2	708	3.5	14.9
1975	2,153	10.0	27.9	25.6	66.9	118.5	1,036	4.8	20.3
1980	2,390	10.6	28.5	26.1	61.4	102.6	1,189	5.2	22.6
1983	2,446	10.5	28.0	25.7	59.9	99.3	1,158	5.0	21.3
1984	2,477	10.5	28.1	25.8	59.5	99.0	1,169	5.0	21.5
1985	2,413	10.1	26.9	24.8	57.0	94.9	1,190	5.0	21.7
1986	2,407	10.0	26.5	24.5	56.2	93.9	1,178	4.9	21.2
1987	2,403	9.9	26.2	24.2	55.7	92.4	1,166	4.8	20.8
1988	2,396	9.7	25.9	23.9	54.6	91.0	1,167	4.8	20.7
1989	(NA)	(NA)	(NA)	(NA)	(NA)	(NA)	1,157	4.7	20.4
1990	(NA)	(NA)	(NA)	(NA)	(NA)	(NA)	1,182	4.7	20.9

NA Not available.   [1] Beginning 1980, includes nonlicensed marriages registered in California.

No. 143. Percent Distribution of Marriages, by Marriage Order: 1970 to 1988

[Excludes marriages with marriage order not stated. See headnote, table 145]

MARRIAGE ORDER	1970	1980	1981	1982	1983	1984	1985	1986	1987	1988
Total.........................	100.0	100.0	100.0	100.0	100.0	100.0	100.0	100.0	100.0	100.0
First marriage of bride and groom	68.6	56.2	54.7	54.8	54.4	54.4	54.3	53.9	53.9	54.1
First marriage of bride, remarriage of groom ...	7.6	11.3	11.8	11.6	11.6	11.5	11.5	11.3	11.3	11.1
Remarriage of bride, first marriage of groom ...	7.3	9.8	10.1	10.3	10.5	10.7	10.9	11.2	11.3	11.4
Remarriage of bride and groom	16.5	22.7	23.4	23.3	23.5	23.4	23.4	23.6	23.5	23.4

Source of tables 142 and 143: U.S. National Center for Health Statistics, *Vital Statistics of the United States,* annual; *Monthly Vital Statistics Report;* and unpublished data.

No. 144. Percent Distribution of Marriages, by Age, Sex, and Previous Marital Status: 1980 and 1988

[Data cover marriage registration area; see text, section 2. Based on a sample and subject to sampling variability; for details, see source]

SEX AND PREVIOUS MARITAL STATUS	Total	Under 20 years old	20-24 years old	25-29 years old	30-34 years old	35-44 years old	45-64 years old	65 years old and over
WOMEN								
All marriages:[1]								
1980	100.0	21.1	37.1	18.7	9.3	7.8	5.0	1.0
1988	100.0	11.8	31.5	24.1	13.2	12.6	5.8	1.0
First marriages:[2]								
1980	100.0	30.4	47.3	16.0	4.0	1.6	0.6	0.1
1988	100.0	17.7	43.3	26.1	8.5	3.7	0.7	0.1
Remarriages.[2][3]								
1980	100.0	1.7	15.3	24.4	20.6	20.8	14.3	2.9
1988	100.0	0.7	9.1	20.5	21.9	29.5	15.4	2.8
Previously divorced:[4] 1980	100.0	1.7	16.7	26.7	22.5	21.6	10.0	0.6
1988	100.0	0.8	9.8	22.2	23.3	30.7	12.5	0.6
MEN								
All marriages:[1]								
1980	100.0	8.5	35.7	23.8	12.3	10.5	7.4	1.8
1988	100.0	4.5	26.9	27.2	15.8	15.1	8.6	1.9
First marriages:[2]								
1980	100.0	12.7	50.0	25.7	7.5	2.9	1.1	0.1
1988	100.0	6.9	38.7	33.9	13.6	5.8	1.1	0.1
Remarriages:[2][3]								
1980	100.0	0.2	7.2	20.1	21.9	25.6	20.0	5.1
1988	100.0	0.1	4.0	14.4	20.1	33.1	23.1	5.2
Previously divorced:[4] 1980	100.0	0.2	7.7	21.7	24.1	27.7	17.3	1.4
1988	100.0	0.1	4.3	15.6	21.8	35.3	21.3	1.6

[1] Includes marriage order not stated. [2] Excludes data for Iowa. [3] Includes remarriages of previously widowed.
[4] Excludes remarriages in Michigan, Ohio, and South Carolina.

No. 145. Marriage Rates and Median Age of Bride and Groom, by Previous Marital Status: 1970 to 1988

[Data cover marriage registration area; see text, section 2. Figures for previously divorced and previously widowed exclude data for Michigan and Ohio for all years, for South Carolina beginning 1975, and for the District of Columbia for 1970. Based on a sample and subject to sampling variability; for details, see source. For definition of median, see Guide to Tabular Presentation. See also *Historical Statistics, Colonial Times to 1970,* series A 158-159]

YEAR	MARRIAGE RATES[1]						MEDIAN AGE AT MARRIAGE (years)					
	Women			Men			Women			Men		
	Single	Divorced	Wid-owed	Single	Divorced	Wid-owed	First mar-riage	Remarriage		First mar-riage	Remarriage	
								Divorced	Widowed		Divorced	Widowed
1970	93.4	123.3	10.2	80.4	204.5	40.6	20.6	30.1	51.2	22.5	34.5	58.7
1975	75.9	117.2	8.3	61.5	189.8	40.4	20.8	30.2	52.4	22.7	33.6	59.4
1980	66.0	91.3	6.7	54.7	142.1	32.2	21.8	31.0	53.6	23.6	34.0	61.2
1985	61.5	81.8	5.7	50.1	121.6	27.7	23.0	32.8	54.6	24.8	36.1	62.7
1986	59.7	79.5	5.5	49.1	117.8	26.8	23.3	33.1	54.3	25.1	36.6	62.9
1987	58.9	80.7	5.4	48.8	115.7	26.1	23.6	33.3	53.9	25.3	36.7	62.8
1988	58.4	78.6	5.3	48.3	109.7	25.1	23.7	33.6	53.9	25.5	37.0	63.0

[1] Rate per 1,000 population 15 years old and over in specified group.

No. 146. Divorces and Annulments—Duration of Marriage, Age at Divorce, and Children Involved: 1970 to 1990

[Data cover divorce-registration area; see text, section 2. Based on a sample and subject to sampling variability; for details, see source. Median age computed on data by single years of age. See also *Historical Statistics, Colonial Times to 1970,* series B 218]

DURATION OF MARRIAGE, AGE AT DIVORCE, AND CHILDREN INVOLVED	1970	1975	1980	1983	1984	1985	1986	1987	1988	1989	1990
Median duration of marriage (years)	6.7	6.5	6.8	7.0	6.9	6.8	6.9	7.0	7.1	7.2	7.2
Median age at divorce:											
Men (years)	32.9	32.2	32.7	34.0	34.3	34.4	34.6	34.9	35.1	35.4	35.6
Women (years)	29.8	29.5	30.3	31.5	31.7	31.9	32.1	32.5	32.6	32.9	33.2
Estimated number of children involved in divorce (1,000)	870	1,123	1,174	1,091	1,081	1,091	1,064	1,038	1,044	1,063	1,075
Avg. number of children per decree	1.22	1.08	0.98	0.94	0.92	0.92	0.90	0.89	0.89	0.91	0.90
Rate per 1,000 children under 18 years of age.	12.5	16.7	17.3	17.4	17.2	17.3	16.8	16.3	16.4	16.8	16.8

Source of tables 144-146: U.S. National Center for Health Statistics of the United States, *Vital Statistics of the United States,* annual, *Monthly Vital Statistics Report;* and unpublished data.

No. 147. First Marriage Dissolution and Years Until Remarriage for Women, by Race and Hispanic Origin: 1988

[For women 15 to 44 years old. Based on 1988 National Survey of Family Growth; see Appendix III. Marriage dissolution includes death of spouse, separation because of marital discord, and divorce]

ITEM	Number (1,000)	YEARS UNTIL REMARRIAGE (cumulative percent)					
		All	1	2	3	4	5
ALL RACES [1]							
Year of dissolution of first marriage:							
All years	11,577	56.8	20.6	32.8	40.7	46.2	49.7
1980-84	3,504	47.5	16.3	28.1	36.4	[2]41.1	[2]45.4
1975-79	3,235	65.3	21.9	36.0	44.7	52.7	55.4
1970-74	1,887	83.2	24.9	38.6	47.9	56.4	61.2
1965-69	1,013	89.9	32.6	48.7	60.2	65.0	72.8
WHITE							
Year of dissolution of first marriage:							
All years	10,103	59.9	21.9	35.2	43.5	49.4	53.0
1980-84	3,030	51.4	18.2	31.1	40.3	[2]45.2	[2]49.8
1975-79	2,839	69.5	23.2	38.5	46.9	55.6	58.4
1970-74	1,622	87.5	24.9	39.8	49.8	59.3	64.3
1965-69	893	91.0	34.7	52.3	64.9	69.3	76.9
BLACK							
Year of dissolution of first marriage:							
All years	1,166	34.0	10.9	16.5	19.6	22.7	25.0
1980-84	380	19.7	[3]4.7	[3]10.6	[3]12.9	[2]14.8	[2]14.8
1975-79	301	32.3	[3]11.4	[3]15.6	18.5	22.2	24.9
1970-74	227	59.0	22.3	29.4	35.3	38.7	42.3
1965-69	98	81.2	[3]20.9	[3]27.3	[3]31.3	40.8	52.1
Hispanic, [4] all years	942	44.7	12.5	16.6	22.7	27.8	29.9

[1] Includes other races.   [2] The percent having remarried is biased downward because the women had not completed the indicated number of years since dissolution of first marriage at the time of the survey.   [3] Figure does not meet standard of reliability or precision.   [4] Hispanic persons may be of any race.

Source: National Center for Health Statistics, *Advance Data from Vital and Health Statistics,* No. 194.

No. 148. Marriage Experience for Women, by Age and Race: 1980 and 1990

[**In percent.** As of **June.** Based on Current Population Survey; see text, section 1]

MARITAL STATUS AND AGE	ALL RACES		WHITE		BLACK		HISPANIC [1]	
	1980	1990	1980	1990	1980	1990	1980	1990
EVER MARRIED								
20 to 24 years old	49.5	38.5	52.2	41.3	33.3	23.5	55.4	45.8
25 to 29 years old	78.6	69.0	81.0	73.2	62.3	45.0	80.2	69.6
30 to 34 years old	89.9	82.2	91.6	85.6	77.9	61.1	88.3	83.0
35 to 39 years old	94.3	89.4	95.3	91.4	87.4	74.9	91.2	88.9
40 to 44 years old	95.1	92.0	95.8	93.4	89.7	82.1	94.2	92.8
45 to 49 years old	95.9	94.4	96.4	95.1	92.5	89.7	94.4	91.7
50 to 54 years old	95.3	95.5	95.8	96.1	92.1	91.9	95.0	91.8
DIVORCED AFTER FIRST MARRIAGE								
20 to 24 years old	14.2	12.5	14.7	12.8	10.5	9.6	9.4	6.8
25 to 29 years old	20.7	19.2	21.0	19.8	20.2	17.8	13.9	13.5
30 to 34 years old	26.2	28.1	25.8	28.6	31.4	26.6	21.1	19.9
35 to 39 years old	27.2	34.1	26.7	34.6	32.9	35.8	21.9	29.7
40 to 44 years old	26.1	35.8	25.5	35.2	33.7	45.1	19.7	26.6
45 to 49 years old	23.1	35.2	22.7	35.5	29.0	39.8	23.9	24.6
50 to 54 years old	21.8	29.5	21.0	28.5	29.0	39.2	22.5	22.9
REMARRIED AFTER DIVORCE								
20 to 24 years old	45.5	38.1	47.0	39.3	(B)	(B)	(B)	(B)
25 to 29 years old	53.4	51.8	56.4	52.8	27.9	44.4	(B)	49.5
30 to 34 years old	60.9	59.6	63.3	61.4	42.0	42.0	58.3	45.9
35 to 39 years old	64.9	65.0	66.9	66.5	50.6	54.0	45.2	51.2
40 to 44 years old	67.4	67.1	68.6	69.5	58.4	50.3	(B)	53.9
45 to 49 years old	69.2	65.9	70.4	67.2	62.7	55.0	(B)	51.0
50 to 54 years old	72.0	63.0	72.6	65.4	72.7	50.2	(B)	62.2
REDIVORCED AFTER REMARRIAGE								
20 to 24 years old	8.5	13.1	(NA)	(NA)	(NA)	(NA)	(NA)	(NA)
25 to 29 years old	15.6	17.8	(NA)	(NA)	(NA)	(NA)	(NA)	(NA)
30 to 34 years old	19.1	22.7	(NA)	(NA)	(NA)	(NA)	(NA)	(NA)
35 to 39 years old	24.7	28.5	(NA)	(NA)	(NA)	(NA)	(NA)	(NA)
40 to 44 years old	28.4	30.6	(NA)	(NA)	(NA)	(NA)	(NA)	(NA)
45 to 49 years old	25.1	36.4	(NA)	(NA)	(NA)	(NA)	(NA)	(NA)
50 to 54 years old	29.0	34.5	(NA)	(NA)	(NA)	(NA)	(NA)	(NA)

B Base is less than 75,000.   NA Not available.   [1] Persons of Hispanic origin may be of any race.

Source: U.S. Bureau of the Census, *Current Population Reports,* P23-180.

No. 149. Marriages and Divorces—Number and Rate, by State: 1980 to 1993

[By place of occurrence]

DIVISION AND STATE	MARRIAGES [1]						DIVORCES [3]					
	Number (1,000)			Rate per 1,000 population [2]			Number (1,000)			Rate per 1,000 population [2]		
	1980	1985	1993, prel.	1980	1985	1993, prel.	1980	1985	1993, prel.	1980	1985	1993, prel.
U.S.	2,390.3	2,412.6	[4]2,334.0	10.6	10.1	9.0	1,189.0	[5]1,190.0	1,187.0	5.2	[5]5.0	4.6
New England.	106.3	114.3	93.9	8.6	9.0	7.1	49.0	49.9	42.6	4.0	3.9	3.2
Maine	12.0	12.2	10.9	10.7	10.5	8.8	6.2	6.1	5.3	5.5	5.2	4.3
New Hampshire. . . .	9.3	11.4	9.6	10.0	11.4	8.5	5.3	4.9	5.0	5.7	4.9	4.5
Vermont	5.2	5.5	6.0	10.2	10.4	10.5	2.6	2.4	2.8	5.1	4.4	4.8
Massachusetts	46.3	49.8	37.5	8.1	8.6	6.2	17.9	21.6	16.0	3.1	3.7	2.7
Rhode Island	7.5	8.0	7.1	7.9	8.3	7.1	3.6	3.7	3.4	3.8	3.8	3.4
Connecticut	26.0	27.3	22.8	8.4	8.6	7.0	13.5	11.2	10.2	4.3	3.5	3.1
Middle Atlantic	294.0	314.3	281.5	8.0	8.5	7.4	124.7	137.1	121.4	3.4	3.7	3.2
New York	144.5	164.0	151.5	8.2	9.2	8.3	62.0	67.6	56.7	3.5	3.8	3.1
New Jersey.	55.8	61.2	53.4	7.6	8.1	6.8	27.8	29.3	24.8	3.8	3.9	3.1
Pennsylvania	93.7	89.1	76.7	7.9	7.5	6.4	34.9	40.2	39.8	2.9	3.4	3.3
East North Central. . .	395.5	[6]362.2	337.9	9.5	[6]8.7	7.9	212.4	[6]192.6	151.5	5.1	[6]4.6	[7]4.1
Ohio	99.8	[6]94.4	88.9	9.2	[6]8.8	8.0	58.8	[6]53.0	51.2	5.4	[6]4.9	4.6
Indiana	57.9	51.1	49.8	10.5	9.3	8.7	40.0	[8]35.3	(NA)	7.3	[8]6.4	(NA)
Illinois	109.8	97.7	91.6	9.6	8.5	7.8	51.0	48.9	43.2	4.5	4.2	3.7
Michigan	86.9	79.0	71.2	9.4	8.7	7.5	45.0	38.8	39.2	4.9	4.3	4.1
Wisconsin.	41.1	40.0	36.5	8.7	8.4	7.2	17.5	16.6	17.9	3.7	3.5	3.5
West North Central . .	173.7	158.3	146.4	10.1	9.0	8.1	79.6	74.3	77.8	4.6	4.2	4.3
Minnesota	37.6	35.1	31.4	9.2	8.4	7.0	15.4	14.8	16.8	3.8	3.5	3.7
Iowa	27.5	24.6	25.0	9.4	8.5	8.9	11.9	10.5	10.9	4.1	3.7	3.9
Missouri	54.6	49.5	44.1	11.1	9.8	8.4	27.6	25.0	26.6	5.6	5.0	5.1
North Dakota	6.1	5.4	4.9	9.3	7.9	7.7	2.1	2.3	2.2	3.3	3.4	3.5
South Dakota	8.8	7.8	7.4	12.7	11.0	10.4	2.8	2.6	2.9	4.1	3.6	4.0
Nebraska	14.2	12.7	12.4	9.1	7.9	7.7	6.4	6.4	6.3	4.1	4.0	3.9
Kansas	24.8	23.3	21.1	10.5	9.5	8.3	13.4	12.8	12.0	5.7	5.2	4.8
South Atlantic	413.1	438.8	436.0	11.2	10.9	9.5	206.3	210.5	233.1	5.6	5.2	5.1
Delaware	4.4	5.4	5.0	7.5	8.6	7.2	2.3	3.0	3.1	3.9	4.8	4.5
Maryland	46.3	46.1	42.3	11.0	10.5	8.5	17.5	16.2	17.0	4.1	3.7	3.4
Dist. of Columbia . . .	5.2	5.0	3.0	8.1	8.1	5.2	4.7	2.7	1.9	7.3	4.3	3.4
Virginia	60.2	66.5	68.4	11.3	11.7	10.5	23.6	24.1	29.5	4.4	4.2	4.5
West Virginia.	17.4	14.6	13.1	8.9	7.5	7.2	10.3	9.9	9.7	5.3	5.1	5.3
North Carolina.	46.7	50.5	47.1	7.9	8.1	6.8	28.1	30.2	34.9	4.8	4.8	5.0
South Carolina	53.9	52.8	52.5	17.3	15.8	14.4	13.6	13.5	15.1	4.4	4.0	4.1
Georgia	70.6	72.3	61.6	12.9	12.1	8.9	34.7	33.4	38.3	6.4	5.6	5.5
Florida	108.3	125.5	142.9	11.1	11.0	10.4	71.6	77.5	83.6	7.3	6.8	6.1
East South Central. . .	[6]168.8	171.8	181.7	11.5	11.4	11.6	87.5	[6]86.2	95.3	6.0	[6]5.7	6.1
Kentucky	[6]32.7	46.0	45.5	8.9	12.3	12.0	16.7	18.3	21.8	4.6	4.9	5.8
Tennessee	59.2	55.0	73.1	12.9	11.5	14.3	30.2	29.9	33.2	6.6	6.3	6.5
Alabama	49.0	46.1	39.5	12.6	11.5	9.4	26.7	25.0	27.0	6.9	6.2	6.5
Mississippi	27.9	24.8	23.7	11.1	9.5	8.9	13.8	[6]13.0	13.3	5.5	[6]5.0	5.0
West South Central . .	298.2	308.6	288.8	12.6	11.6	10.3	155.0	[7]160.9	138.2	6.5	(NA)	[7]5.8
Arkansas	26.5	31.7	36.4	11.6	13.4	15.0	15.9	[6]16.5	16.7	6.9	[6]7.0	6.9
Louisiana	43.5	39.4	36.2	10.3	8.8	8.4	18.1	17.6		4.3	(NA)	(NA)
Oklahoma.	46.5	35.9	30.5	15.4	10.9	9.4	24.2	26.4	22.8	8.0	8.0	7.1
Texas	181.8	201.6	185.6	12.8	12.3	10.3	96.8	100.4	98.7	6.8	6.1	5.5
Mountain	241.7	233.7	254.8	21.3	18.3	17.2	86.1	89.9	76.8	7.6	7.0	[7]5.7
Montana	8.3	7.2	7.0	10.6	8.7	8.4	4.9	4.3	4.3	6.3	5.2	5.1
Idaho.	13.4	12.3	14.0	14.2	12.2	12.7	6.6	6.2	6.9	7.0	6.2	6.3
Wyoming	6.9	5.4	4.6	14.6	10.6	9.8	4.0	3.8	3.1	8.5	7.5	6.5
Colorado	34.9	33.6	34.0	12.1	10.4	9.5	18.6	19.2	19.1	6.4	5.9	5.4
New Mexico	16.6	[9]15.5	12.6	12.8	[9]10.7	7.8	10.4	[10]13.2	9.9	8.0	[10]9.1	6.2
Arizona	30.2	35.7	38.8	11.1	11.2	9.9	19.9	21.2	24.5	7.3	6.6	6.2
Utah	17.0	17.5	20.6	11.6	10.6	11.1	7.8	8.8	8.9	5.3	5.3	4.8
Nevada	114.3	106.5	123.2	142.8	113.7	88.7	13.8	13.3	-	17.3	14.2	(NA)
Pacific	298.8	310.6	294.6	9.4	8.9	7.1	187.9	188.5	51.5	5.9	5.4	[7]5.1
Washington.	47.7	43.8	43.4	11.6	9.9	8.3	28.6	26.3	27.4	6.9	6.0	5.2
Oregon	23.0	22.4	24.3	8.7	8.3	8.0	17.8	15.7	16.0	6.7	5.9	5.3
California [11]	210.9	222.8	203.9	8.9	8.5	6.5	133.5	[12]137.5	-	5.6	[12]5.2	(NA)
Alaska	5.4	6.2	5.5	13.3	11.8	9.2	3.5	4.0	3.2	8.8	7.7	5.3
Hawaii	11.9	15.4	17.5	12.3	14.7	14.9	4.4	4.9	4.9	4.6	4.6	4.2

- Represents or rounds to zero.   NA Not available.   [1] Data are counts of marriages performed, except as noted.   [2] Based on total population residing in area; population enumerated as of April 1 for 1980; estimated as of July 1 for all other years.   [3] Includes annulments.   [4] Estimate for U.S. is based on monthly reports adjusted for observed differences from final monthly figures. State figures are not adjusted in this manner.   [5] Estimated.   [6] Data are incomplete.   [7] Excludes figures for States shown below as not available.   [8] Includes divorce petitions filed for some counties.   [9] Premarital health forms issued.   [10] Divorce petitions filed.   [11] Marriage data include nonlicensed marriages registered.   [12] Data include legal separations.

Source: U.S. National Center for Health Statistics, *Vital Statistics of the United States,* annual; and *Monthly Vital Statistics Reports.*

Figure 3.1
**Personal Health Care Expenditures per Capita:
1970 to 1993**

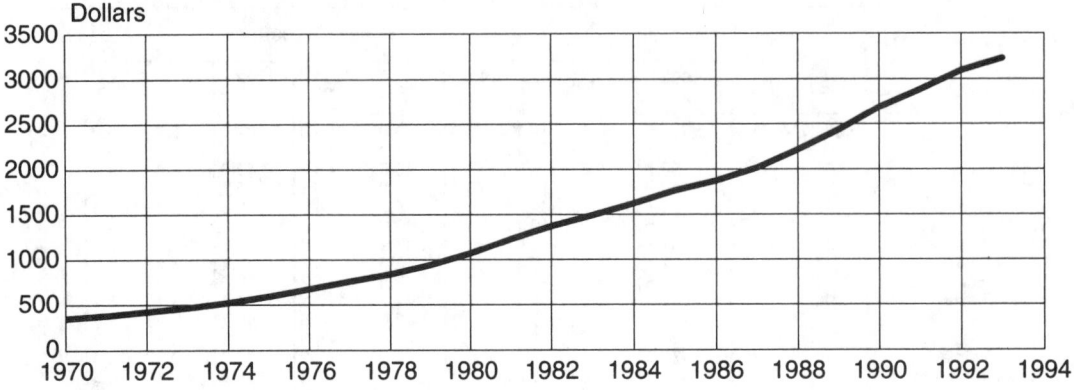

Source: Charts prepared by U.S. Bureau of the Census.
For data, see table 150.

Figure 3.2
**Consumer Price Indexes—
Medical Services: 1970 to 1994**

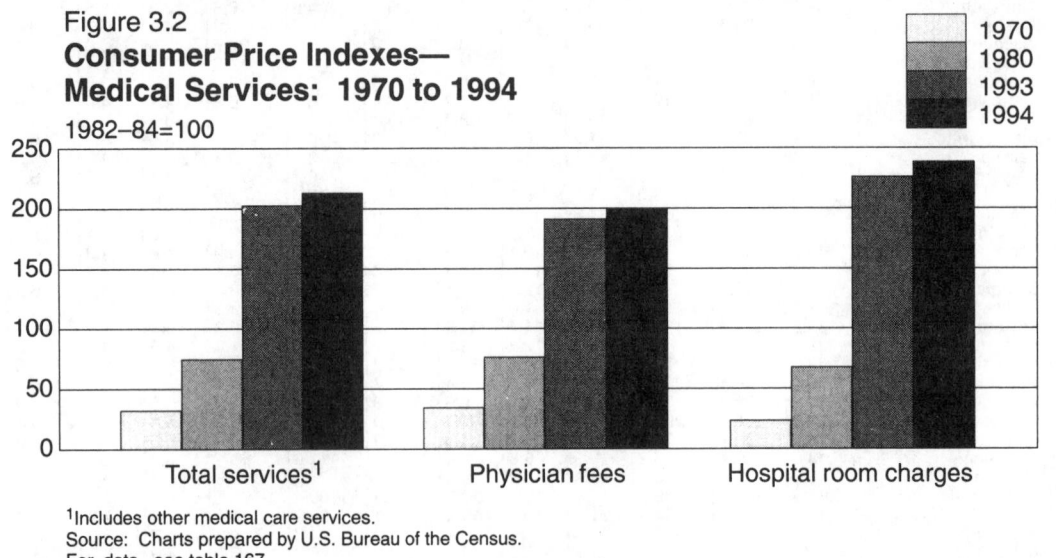

[1]Includes other medical care services.
Source: Charts prepared by U.S. Bureau of the Census.
For data, see table 167.

Figure 3.3
**Per Capita Food Consumption,
by Selected Products: 1970 to 1993**

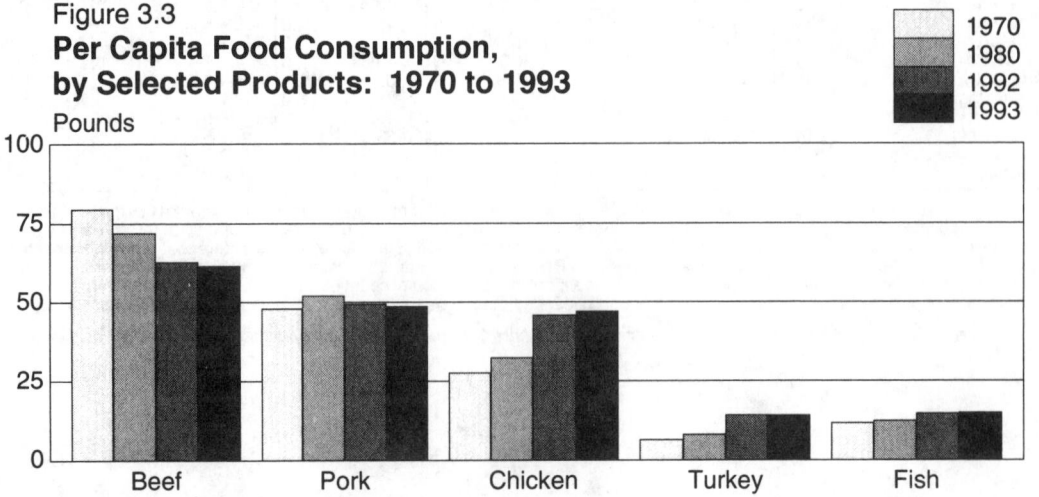

Source: Charts prepared by U.S. Bureau of the Census.
For data, see table 225.

Health and Nutrition

This section presents statistics on health expenditures and insurance coverage, including Medicare and Medicaid; medical personnel; hospitals; nursing homes and other care facilities; incidence of acute and prevalence of chronic conditions; nutritional intake of the population; and food consumption. Summary statistics showing recent trends on health care and discussions of selected health issues are published annually by the U.S. National Center for Health Statistics (NCHS) in *Health, United States.* Data on national health expenditures, medical costs, and insurance coverage are compiled by the U.S. Health Care Financing Administration (HCFA) and appear in the quarterly *Health Care Financing Review* and in the *Annual Medicare Program Statistics* series. Statistics on health insurance are also collected by NCHS and are published in series 10 of *Vital and Health Statistics.* The Census Bureau also publishes data on insurance coverage in *Current Population Reports,* series P70. Statistics on health facilities are collected by NCHS and are published in series 14 of *Vital and Health Statistics.* Statistics on hospitals are published annually by the American Hospital Association, Chicago, IL, in *Hospital Statistics.* Primary sources for data on nutrition are the quarterly *National Food Review* and the annual *Food Consumption, Prices, and Expenditures,* both issued by the U.S. Department of Agriculture. NCHS also conducts periodic surveys of nutrient levels in the population, including estimates of food and nutrient intake, overweight and obesity, hypercholesterolemia, hypertension, and clinical signs of malnutrition.

National health expenditures.—HCFA compiles estimates of national health expenditures (NHE) to measure spending for health care in the United States. With the publication of the 1988 estimates, major revisions to the NHE back to 1960 have been incorporated into the accounts. The NHE accounts are structured to show spending by type of expenditure (i.e., hospital care, physician care, dental care, and other professional care; home health; drugs and other medical nondurables; vision products and other medical durables; nursing home care and other

In Brief	
In 1993:	
40 million with no health insurance.	
Hospital surgeries— percent outpatient:	
1980	*16*
1993	*55*
Per capita consumption of chicken:	
1980	*33 pounds*
1993	*47 pounds*

personal health expenditures; plus nonpersonal health expenditures for such items as public health, research, construction of medical facilities, and administration) and by source of funding (e.g., private health insurance, out-of-pocket payments, and a range of public programs including Medicare, Medicaid, and those operated by the Department of Veterans Affairs (VA)).

In all cases except private insurance (HCFA conducts its own survey of part of the health insurance industry), data used to estimate health expenditures come from existing sources which are tabulated for other purposes. The type of expenditure estimates rely upon statistics produced by such groups as the American Hospital Association, the Internal Revenue Service, the Department of Commerce, and the Department of Health and Human Services (HHS). Source of funding estimates are constructed using administrative and statistical records from the Medicare and Medicaid programs, the Department of Defense and VA medical programs, the Social Security Administration, Census Bureau's *Governmental Finances,* State and local governments, other HHS agencies, and other nongovernment sources. Detailed descriptions of sources and methods, along with the most recent analysis of health care expenditure estimates, are published in the *Health Care Financing Review's* annual article on national health expenditures.

Medicare and Medicaid.—Since July 1966, the Federal Medicare program has provided two coordinated plans for nearly all people age 65 and over: (1) A hospital insurance plan which covers hospital and related services and (2) a voluntary supplementary medical insurance plan, financed partially by monthly premiums paid by participants, which partly covers physicians' and related medical services. Such insurance also applies, since July 1973, to disabled beneficiaries of any age after 24 months of entitlement to cash benefits under the social security or railroad retirement programs and to persons with end stage renal disease.

Under Medicaid, all States offer basic health services to certain very poor people: Individuals who are pregnant, aged, disabled or blind, and families with dependent children. Medicaid eligibility is automatic for almost all cash welfare recipients in these States. Thirty-nine States also extend Medicaid to certain other persons who qualify, except for incomes above regular eligibility levels; those persons include those who have medical expenses which, when subtracted from their income, spend down to a State "medically needy" level or those who meet the higher "medically needy" income restrictions. Within Federal guidelines, each State determines its own Medicaid eligibility criteria and the health services to be provided under Medicaid. The cost of providing Medicaid services is jointly shared by the Federal Government and the States.

Health resources.—Hospital statistics based on data from the American Hospital Association's yearly survey are published annually in *Hospital Statistics,* and cover all hospitals accepted for registration by the Association. To be accepted for registration, a hospital must meet certain requirements relating to number of beds, construction, equipment, medical and nursing staff, patient care, clinical records, surgical and obstetrical facilities, diagnostic and treatment facilities, laboratory services, etc. Data obtained from NCHS cover all U.S. hospitals which meet certain criteria for inclusion. The criteria are published in *Vital and Health Statistics* reports, series 13. NCHS defines a hospital as a non-Federal short-term general or special facility with six or more inpatient beds with an average stay of less than 60 days.

Statistics on the demographic characteristics of persons employed in the health occupations are compiled by the U.S. Bureau of Labor Statistics and reported in *Employment and Earnings* (monthly) (see table 649, section 13). Data based on surveys of health personnel and utilization of health facilities providing long-term care, ambulatory care, and hospital care are presented in NCHS series 13 and series 14, *Data on Health Resources Utilization* and *Data on Health Resources: Manpower and Facilities.* Statistics on patient visits to health care providers, as reported in health interviews, appear in NCHS series 10, *National Health Interview Survey Data.*

The HCFA's *Health Care Financing Review* and *Health Care Financing Program Statistics* present data for hospitals and nursing homes as well as extended care facilities and home health agencies. These data are based on records of the Medicare program and differ from those of other sources because they are limited to facilities meeting Federal eligibility standards for participation in Medicare.

Data on patients in hospitals for the mentally ill and on mental health facilities are collected by the National Institute of Mental Health (NIMH) and appear in *Mental Health, U.S.,* the *Mental Health Statistics* reports, (series CN), and the Mental Health Statistical Note series.

Disability and illness.—General health statistics, including morbidity, disability, injuries, preventive care, and findings from physiological testing are collected by NCHS in its National Health Interview Survey and its National Health and Nutrition Examination Surveys and appear in *Vital and Health Statistics,* series 10 and 11, respectively. The Department of Labor compiles statistics on industrial injuries (see section 13). Annual incidence data on notifiable diseases are compiled by the Public Health Service (PHS) at its Centers for Disease Control and Prevention in Atlanta, Georgia, and are published as a supplement to its *Morbidity and Mortality Weekly Report.* The list of diseases is revised annually and includes those which, by mutual agreement of the States and PHS, are communicable diseases of national importance.

Nutrition.—Statistics on annual per capita consumption of food and its nutrient value are estimated by the U.S. Department of Agriculture and published quarterly in *National Food Review.* Historical data can be found in *Food Consumption, Prices, and Expenditures,* issued annually.

Statistics on food insufficiency and food and nutrient intake are collected by NCHS to estimate the nation's population diet. NCHS also collects physical examination data to assess the population's nutritional status, including growth, overweight/obesity, nutritional deficiencies, and prevalence of nutrition-related conditions, such as hypertension, hypercholesterolemia, and diabetes.

Statistical reliability.—For discussion of statistical collection, estimation, and sampling procedures and measures of reliability applicable to data from NCHS and HCFA, see Appendix III.

Historical statistics.—Tabular headnotes provide cross-references, where applicable, to *Historical Statistics of the United States, Colonial Times to 1970.* See Appendix IV.

No. 150. National Health Expenditures: 1960 to 1993

[Includes Puerto Rico and outlying areas]

YEAR	TOTAL[1]			HEALTH SERVICES AND SUPPLIES						
				Private				Public		
					Out-of-pocket payments				Medical payments	
	Total (bil.dol.)	Per capita (dol.)	Percent of GDP[2]	Total[3] (bil.dol.)	Total (bil.dol.)	Percent of total private	Insurance premiums[4] (bil.dol.)	Total (bil.dol.)	Medicare (bil. dol.)	Public assistance (bil. dol.)
1960	27.1	143	5.3	19.8	13.4	67.5	5.9	5.7	–	0.5
1965	41.6	204	5.9	29.9	19.0	63.6	10.0	8.3	–	1.7
1970	74.3	346	7.4	44.0	25.4	57.7	16.9	25.0	7.7	6.3
1971	82.2	379	7.5	48.1	26.9	55.9	19.2	28.2	8.5	7.7
1972	92.3	421	7.7	53.9	29.6	55.0	22.0	31.8	9.4	8.9
1973	102.4	464	7.6	59.7	32.6	54.5	24.8	35.9	10.8	10.2
1974	115.9	521	7.9	65.9	35.8	54.3	27.5	42.8	13.5	11.9
1975	132.6	591	8.4	74.1	39.1	52.8	32.0	50.2	16.4	14.5
1976	151.9	671	8.6	85.7	43.2	50.4	38.5	56.9	19.8	16.4
1977	172.6	755	8.7	98.6	47.5	48.2	46.7	64.7	23.0	18.8
1978	193.2	838	8.7	109.7	51.0	46.5	53.6	73.6	26.8	20.9
1979	218.3	937	8.8	124.0	55.9	45.1	62.2	84.0	31.0	23.9
1980	251.1	1,068	9.3	141.3	61.3	43.4	72.1	98.1	37.5	28.0
1981	291.4	1,227	9.6	164.3	69.6	42.4	85.1	113.9	44.9	32.6
1982	328.2	1,369	10.4	186.5	76.5	41.0	99.1	126.9	52.5	34.6
1983	360.8	1,490	10.6	205.3	83.0	40.4	110.6	139.5	59.8	38.0
1984	396.0	1,620	10.5	228.0	90.4	39.6	125.1	151.6	66.5	41.1
1985	434.5	1,761	10.8	252.9	98.8	39.1	139.8	165.2	72.2	44.5
1986	466.0	1,871	10.9	268.7	105.0	39.1	147.8	180.4	76.9	49.0
1987	506.2	2,013	11.1	291.3	111.6	38.3	162.3	196.6	82.3	54.0
1988	562.3	2,214	11.5	327.5	123.0	37.6	184.8	213.7	89.4	58.8
1989	623.9	2,433	11.9	361.7	127.8	35.3	211.7	240.1	102.6	66.4
1990	696.6	2,686	12.6	399.8	138.3	34.6	236.9	272.5	112.1	80.5
1991	755.6	2,882	13.2	422.8	143.3	33.9	252.8	308.0	123.3	99.1
1992	820.3	3,094	13.6	451.7	150.6	33.3	272.7	341.2	138.3	113.5
1993	884.2	3,299	13.9	484.3	157.5	32.5	296.1	370.9	154.2	122.9

– Represents zero. [1] Includes medical research and medical facilities construction. [2] GDP=Gross domestic product; see table 701. [3] Includes other sources of funds not shown separately. [4] See footnote 2, table 151.
Source: U. S. Health Care Financing Administration, *Health Care Financing Review,* winter 1994.

No. 151. National Health Expenditures, by Type: 1980 to 1993

[In millions of dollars, except percent. Includes Puerto Rico and outlying areas. See also *Historical Statistics, Colonial Times to 1970*, series B 248-261]

TYPE OF EXPENDITURE	1980	1985	1988	1989	1990	1991	1992	1993
Total	**251,058**	**434,498**	**562,326**	**623,914**	**696,553**	**755,551**	**820,347**	**884,205**
Annual percent change [1]	15.0	9.7	11.1	11.0	11.6	8.5	8.6	7.8
Private expenditures	**145,791**	**259,436**	**336,144**	**370,731**	**410,033**	**432,913**	**462,854**	**496,387**
Health services and supplies	141,338	252,936	327,486	361,682	399,790	422,791	451,694	484,278
Out-of-pocket payments	61,280	98,798	122,974	127,837	138,266	143,296	150,589	157,466
Insurance premiums [2]	72,111	139,796	184,819	211,725	236,950	252,826	272,731	296,142
Other	7,947	14,342	19,694	22,119	24,574	26,669	28,374	30,670
Medical research	292	538	838	881	959	1,091	1,221	1,248
Medical facilities construction	4,161	5,963	7,819	8,168	9,285	9,031	9,939	10,861
Public expenditures	**105,267**	**175,062**	**226,182**	**253,184**	**286,520**	**322,638**	**357,493**	**387,818**
Percent Federal of public	68.4	70.4	68.8	69.1	68.3	69.6	71.1	72.3
Health services and supplies	98,083	165,166	213,678	240,124	272,453	308,004	341,221	370,916
Medicare [3]	37,521	72,190	89,361	102,606	112,064	123,291	138,281	154,202
Public assistance medical payments [4]	28,023	44,465	58,847	66,412	80,473	99,093	113,531	122,917
Temporary disability insurance [5]	52	51	62	64	62	66	70	73
Workers' compensation (medical) [5]	5,141	7,971	12,208	14,298	16,067	17,163	18,975	21,128
Defense Dept. hospital, medical	4,350	7,498	9,755	10,321	11,578	12,849	12,884	13,436
Maternal, child health programs	892	1,262	1,694	1,795	1,892	2,017	2,135	2,209
Public health activities	7,225	12,323	16,425	19,019	21,550	22,938	23,719	24,708
Veterans' hospital, medical care	5,934	8,713	10,016	10,641	11,424	12,377	13,201	14,287
Medical vocational rehabilitation	298	401	498	523	555	594	646	681
State and local hospitals [6]	5,589	7,030	10,729	10,583	11,777	11,858	11,257	10,255
Other [7]	3,059	3,263	4,082	3,860	5,009	5,757	6,521	7,020
Medical research	5,169	7,302	9,665	10,379	11,256	11,804	13,003	13,130
Medical facilities construction	2,014	2,594	2,840	2,681	2,811	2,830	3,270	3,772

[1] Change from immediate prior year. For explanation of average annual percent change, see Guide to Tabular Presentation. [2] Covers insurance benefits and amount retained by insurance companies for expenses, additions to reserves, and profits (net cost of insurance). [3] Represents expenditures for benefits and administrative cost from Federal hospital and medical insurance trust funds under old-age, survivors, disability, and health insurance programs; see text, section 12. [4] Payments made directly to suppliers of medical care (primarily Medicaid). [5] Includes medical benefits paid under public law by private insurance carriers and self-insurers. [6] Expenditures not offset by other revenues. [7] Covers expenditures for Alcohol, Drug Abuse, and Mental Health Administration; Indian Health Service; school health and other programs.

Source: U.S. Health Care Financing Administration, *Health Care Financing Review,* fall 1994.

No. 152. National Health Expenditures, by Object: 1980 to 1993

[In billions of dollars. Includes Puerto Rico and outlying areas. See also *Historical Statistics, Colonial Times to 1970*, series B 221-235]

OBJECT OF EXPENDITURE	1980	1985	1988	1989	1990	1991	1992	1993
Total	**251.1**	**434.5**	**562.3**	**623.9**	**696.6**	**755.6**	**820.3**	**884.2**
Spent by—								
Consumers	133.4	238.6	307.8	339.6	375.2	396.1	423.3	453.6
Government	105.3	175.1	226.2	253.2	286.5	322.6	357.5	387.8
Other [1]	12.4	20.8	28.4	31.2	34.8	36.8	39.5	42.8
Spent for—								
Health services and supplies	239.4	418.1	541.2	601.8	672.2	730.8	792.9	855.2
Personal health care expenses	220.1	380.5	500.2	550.5	612.4	670.8	729.7	782.5
Hospital care	102.7	168.2	211.7	231.8	256.5	282.3	306.0	326.6
Physicians' services	45.2	83.6	116.9	127.3	140.5	150.3	161.8	171.2
Dentists' services	13.3	21.7	27.1	28.6	30.4	31.7	34.7	37.4
Other professional services [2]	6.4	16.6	27.8	32.2	36.0	40.4	46.4	51.2
Home health care	1.9	4.9	6.4	8.1	11.1	13.2	16.8	20.8
Drugs/other medical nondurables	21.6	37.4	49.0	54.4	61.2	67.1	70.8	75.0
Vision products/other med. durables [3]	4.5	7.1	8.9	9.6	10.5	11.3	12.0	12.6
Nursing home care	20.5	34.9	43.9	48.9	54.8	60.8	65.5	69.6
Other health services	4.0	6.1	8.6	9.5	11.4	13.8	15.8	18.2
Net cost of insurance and admin. [4]	12.1	25.3	24.5	32.3	38.3	37.0	39.5	48.0
Government public health activities	7.2	12.3	16.4	19.0	21.6	22.9	23.7	24.7
Medical research	5.5	7.8	10.5	11.3	12.2	12.9	14.2	14.4
Medical facilities construction	6.2	8.6	10.7	10.8	12.1	11.9	13.2	14.6

[1] Includes nonpatient revenues, privately funded construction, and industrial inplant. [2] Includes services of registered and practical nurses in private duty, visiting nurses, podiatrists, optometrists, physical therapists, clinical psychologists, chiropractors, naturopaths, and Christian Science practitioners. [3] Includes expenditures for eyeglasses, hearing aids, orthopedic appliances, artificial limbs, crutches, wheelchairs, etc. [4] Includes administrative expenses of federally financed health programs.

Source: U.S. Health Care Financing Administration, *Health Care Financing Review,* fall 1994.

No. 153. Personal Health Care Expenditures, by State: 1993

[**In millions of dollars.** Data represent spending for services produced by each State's health care providers, as opposed to those consumed by State residents or supplied by State employers]

| STATE | PERSONAL HEALTH CARE (PHC) EXPENDITURES | | | | | | | | | | Medi-care PHC expendi-tures | Medi-caid PHC expendi-tures |
	Total	Hos-pital care	Physi-cian serv-ices	Dental serv-ices	Other profes-sional serv-ices	Home health care	Drugs [1]	Vision prod-ucts [2]	Nursing home care	Other per-sonal health care		
U.S.	778,510	323,919	171,226	37,383	51,220	22,982	74,956	12,636	66,201	17,988	150,374	112,776
AL.	12,060	5,301	2,631	456	641	602	1,247	155	703	323	2,625	1,276
AK.	1,573	701	301	124	127	5	165	26	56	68	101	273
AZ.	10,635	3,999	2,799	551	821	317	1,124	227	567	230	2,276	1,270
AR.	6,111	2,723	1,244	242	332	145	684	56	558	127	1,422	1,007
CA.	94,178	34,827	28,981	5,664	6,859	1,640	9,017	1,522	4,103	1,565	17,347	11,330
CO	10,066	3,932	2,452	605	751	195	919	226	661	327	1,556	967
CT.	12,216	4,380	2,587	685	769	391	996	192	1,749	467	2,134	1,998
DE.	2,260	937	466	104	156	51	214	35	217	79	377	249
DC	4,285	2,612	672	119	267	45	175	34	231	130	603	678
FL.	44,811	17,131	10,498	2,029	3,505	2,323	4,450	872	3,089	912	12,484	4,697
GA	20,104	8,704	4,543	898	1,226	729	2,117	331	1,038	516	3,549	2,753
HI	3,485	1,460	771	235	222	32	416	64	181	104	496	354
ID	2,277	900	486	163	126	49	265	35	197	55	384	290
IL	34,747	15,621	6,970	1,588	2,063	853	3,263	604	3,148	636	6,404	4,609
IN	16,401	6,998	3,263	692	993	308	1,594	270	2,018	264	3,126	2,777
IA	7,341	3,111	1,376	341	431	137	743	148	927	127	1,447	960
KS.	6,903	2,868	1,425	325	470	152	695	107	721	140	1,326	769
KY.	10,384	4,515	2,038	369	691	357	1,196	141	850	228	2,143	1,683
LA	13,014	5,956	2,537	432	736	410	1,269	160	1,186	328	2,730	2,664
ME	3,433	1,376	601	157	210	104	333	46	453	153	605	722
MD	15,154	5,926	3,704	749	942	314	1,749	272	1,185	312	2,692	1,924
MA	23,421	10,034	4,442	1,022	1,524	835	1,961	269	2,737	597	4,712	3,689
MI	27,136	11,711	5,562	1,531	1,844	714	2,937	457	1,849	532	5,405	3,865
MN	14,194	4,796	3,617	741	933	414	1,146	277	1,884	386	2,164	2,229
MS	6,187	2,897	1,107	214	288	300	720	60	460	141	1,367	1,043
MO	15,949	7,652	2,958	602	1,013	347	1,420	244	1,368	346	3,439	1,648
MT	2,103	894	392	103	166	50	209	36	178	74	391	322
NE.	4,400	2,003	825	191	225	74	421	80	482	99	746	561
NV.	3,747	1,362	1,029	215	307	120	408	76	164	67	732	344
NH	3,452	1,388	780	177	269	71	319	43	268	136	473	446
NJ.	25,741	10,312	5,776	1,460	1,870	718	2,452	457	2,128	570	4,838	3,857
NM	3,878	1,848	716	175	254	62	409	69	215	131	565	577
NY.	67,033	28,001	12,003	2,837	3,717	3,562	5,081	1,090	9,106	1,635	11,872	18,041
NC	18,241	7,801	3,717	810	1,102	541	2,027	268	1,562	413	3,553	2,564
ND	2,021	903	445	78	93	16	160	28	246	52	374	269
OH	33,456	14,305	7,118	1,398	1,969	649	3,218	531	3,758	511	6,177	4,665
OK	8,041	3,329	1,640	356	504	273	874	121	748	196	1,665	1,013
OR	7,999	2,966	1,904	578	530	122	762	91	656	391	1,521	955
PA	41,521	19,540	7,460	1,634	3,005	796	3,519	617	4,153	798	10,056	5,116
RI	3,428	1,314	575	150	239	103	310	33	485	219	664	793
SC.	9,029	4,221	1,685	387	472	216	978	115	638	317	1,541	1,324
SD.	1,953	920	342	87	117	16	163	30	216	63	364	264
TN.	16,203	7,208	3,137	609	1,166	899	1,635	228	1,085	235	3,549	2,183
TX.	49,816	21,592	10,526	2,081	3,591	1,583	5,131	883	3,104	1,325	8,765	5,914
UT.	4,118	1,743	864	276	220	100	439	117	260	99	624	477
VT.	1,499	562	265	84	122	52	161	24	148	82	241	232
VA.	16,682	7,031	3,769	863	970	368	2,015	295	976	395	2,736	1,621
WA	15,129	5,305	3,720	1,189	1,102	380	1,474	242	1,291	425	2,360	2,161
WV	5,197	2,346	988	182	326	150	574	74	365	192	1,106	1,075
WI	14,502	5,537	3,362	765	875	265	1,290	240	1,752	415	2,397	2,138
WY	998	417	160	57	68	29	113	17	83	55	150	137

[1] Includes other medical nondurables.   [2] Includes other medical durables.

Source: U.S. Health Care Financing Administration, Office of the Actuary. Estimates prepared by the Office of National Health Statistics.

No. 154. Health Services and Supplies—Per Capita Consumer Expenditures, by Object: 1980 to 1993

[In dollars, except percent. Based on Social Security Administration estimates of total U.S. population as of July 1, including Armed Forces and Federal employees abroad and civilian population of outlying areas for 1960 through 1980. Years 1991 to 1993 are estimated by HCFA. Excludes research and construction. See also *Historical Statistics, Colonial Times to 1970,* series B 222-232]

OBJECT OF EXPENDITURE	1980	1985	1987	1988	1989	1990	1991	1992	1993
Total, national	**1,018**	**1,694**	**1,940**	**2,131**	**2,347**	**2,592**	**2,787**	**2,991**	**3,191**
Annual percent change [1]	14.0	9.1	7.6	9.9	10.1	10.4	7.5	7.3	6.7
Hospital care	437	682	772	834	904	989	1,077	1,154	1,218
Physicians' services	192	339	414	461	497	542	572	609	638
Dentists' services	57	88	101	107	112	117	121	131	139
Other professional services [2]	27	67	90	109	126	139	154	175	191
Home health care	8	20	24	25	31	43	50	63	78
Drugs and other medical nondurables	92	151	180	193	212	236	256	267	280
Vision products and other medical durables [2]	19	29	32	35	37	41	43	45	47
Nursing home care	87	141	161	173	191	211	232	247	260
Other health services	17	25	31	34	37	44	53	60	68
Net cost of insurance and administration [2]	51	102	77	97	126	148	141	149	179
Government public health activities	31	50	58	65	74	83	87	89	92
Total, private consumer [3]	**567**	**967**	**1,089**	**1,212**	**1,324**	**1,447**	**1,511**	**1,597**	**1,693**
Hospital care	187	283	321	354	381	407	429	445	473
Physicians' services	135	234	278	310	329	356	373	398	411
Dentists' services	54	85	98	103	108	113	116	125	132
Other professional services [2]	19	50	67	83	96	104	114	130	138
Home health care	3	6	9	10	12	17	18	22	26
Drugs and other medical nondurables	85	139	164	174	191	211	227	236	245
Vision products and other medical durables [2]	17	23	25	27	28	30	30	31	32
Nursing home care	34	66	74	80	81	93	94	93	92
Net cost of insurance	34	81	53	70	97	117	110	115	142

[1] Change from immediate prior year. [2] See footnotes for corresponding objects in table 152. [3] Represents out-of-pocket payments and private health insurance.

Source: U.S. Health Care Financing Administration, *Health Care Financing Review,* fall 1994.

No. 155. Government Expenditures for Health Services and Supplies: 1993

[In millions of dollars. Includes Puerto Rico and outlying areas. Excludes medical research and construction]

TYPE OF SERVICE	Total [1]	Federal	State and local	Medi-care [2] (OASDHI)	Public assis-tance [3]	OTHER HEALTH SERVICES Veterans	Defense Dept. [4]	Workers' compensa-tion [5]
Total [1]	370,916	268,559	102,357	154,202	122,917	14,287	13,436	21,128
Hospital care	182,864	149,200	33,664	92,700	45,473	11,849	10,449	10,014
Physicians' services	58,143	45,033	13,110	34,817	12,952	126	1,755	7,663
Nursing home care	43,612	28,334	15,278	6,124	36,070	1,418	-	-
Drugs and other medical nondurables	9,177	4,732	4,446	-	8,569	10	142	413
Administration	9,175	6,326	2,849	3,101	5,082	72	170	495
Public health activities	24,708	3,273	21,436	-	-	-	-	-

- Represents zero. [1] Includes other items not shown separately. [2] Covers hospital and medical insurance payments and administrative costs under old-age, survivors, disability, and health insurance program. [3] Covers Medicaid and other medical public assistance. Excludes funds paid into Medicare trust fund by States to cover premiums for public assistance recipients and medically indigent persons. [4] Includes care for retirees and military dependents. [5] Medical benefits.

Source: U.S. Health Care Financing Administration, *Health Care Financing Review,* fall 1994.

No. 156. Expenditures for Health Services and Supplies, by Type of Payer: 1970 to 1991

[In billions of dollars]

TYPE OF PAYER	1970	1975	1980	1985	1986	1987	1988	1989	1990	1991
Total expenditures	**69.1**	**124.7**	**238.9**	**407.2**	**438.9**	**476.9**	**526.2**	**583.6**	**652.4**	**728.6**
Private	50.1	86.2	162.0	279.0	301.8	327.5	362.5	398.3	436.6	474.1
Business	13.7	27.8	64.3	113.5	125.9	131.8	151.0	167.0	187.9	205.4
Share of private health insurance premiums	9.8	19.9	47.9	83.9	92.2	95.0	110.9	122.8	140.2	152.7
Households [1]	35.0	55.9	90.8	153.6	163.1	181.9	196.1	213.8	228.9	247.0
Share of private health insurance premiums	6.0	9.9	16.6	30.0	30.9	37.5	37.7	42.7	46.6	52.2
Out-of-pocket spending	18.9	38.5	59.5	94.4	100.9	108.8	118.5	126.2	136.5	144.3
Nonpatient revenues [2]	1.5	2.5	7.0	12.0	12.9	13.8	15.4	17.5	19.8	21.7
Public	18.9	38.5	76.8	128.2	137.1	149.4	163.7	185.4	215.8	254.5
Federal government	10.4	21.3	42.6	68.9	71.6	77.0	84.3	96.5	113.7	133.8
State/local government	8.5	17.2	34.2	59.3	65.5	72.4	79.4	88.8	102.1	120.7

[1] Includes other items not shown separately. [2] Includes philanthropy.

Source: U.S. Health Care Financing Administration, *Health Care Financing Review,* spring 1993.

No. 157. Personal Health Care—Third Party Payments and Private Consumer Expenditures: 1980 to 1993

[**In billions of dollars, except percent.** See headnote, table 158]

ITEM	1980	1985	1987	1988	1989	1990	1991	1992	1993
Personal health care expenditures.	220.1	380.5	453.8	500.2	550.5	612.4	670.8	729.7	782.5
Third party payments, total	**158.8**	**281.7**	**342.2**	**377.2**	**422.7**	**474.1**	**527.5**	**579.1**	**625.0**
Percent of personal health care	72.2	74.0	75.4	75.4	76.8	77.4	78.6	79.4	79.9
Private insurance payments	64.1	119.8	148.9	167.0	186.8	206.7	223.9	242.1	258.0
Government expenditures.	87.0	148.0	176.4	191.1	214.3	243.5	277.6	309.3	337.0
Other [1]	7.7	13.9	16.9	19.2	21.6	24.0	26.1	27.7	30.0
Private consumer expenditures [2]	**133.1**	**232.5**	**277.4**	**309.1**	**336.3**	**368.9**	**393.2**	**420.4**	**445.5**
Percent met by private insurance	48.2	51.5	53.7	54.0	55.6	56.0	56.9	57.6	57.9
Hospital care	49.0	78.1	90.6	101.1	110.1	119.2	127.5	134.0	143.7
Percent met by private insurance	78.9	78.1	79.6	78.7	80.0	80.3	80.7	81.4	81.9
Physicians' services	32.2	59.1	72.0	81.0	87.0	95.0	100.5	108.4	113.1
Percent met by private insurance	53.3	62.6	65.5	66.0	69.0	70.6	72.1	73.4	74.4

[1] Includes nonpatient revenues and industrial inplant health services.   [2] Includes expenditures not shown separately. Represents out-of-pocket payments and private health insurance benefits. Excludes net cost of insurance.

Source: U.S. Health Care Financing Administration, *Health Care Financing Review,* fall 1994.

No. 158. Personal Health Care Expenditures, by Object and Source of Payment: 1993

[**In millions of dollars, except as indicated.** Includes Puerto Rico and outlying areas. Covers all expenditures for health services and supplies, except net cost of insurance and administration, government public health activities, and expenditures of philanthropic agencies for fund raising activities]

OBJECT OF PAYMENT	Total	Out of pocket payments	THIRD PARTY PAYMENTS				Private payments [2]
			Total	Private health insurance	Government	Other [1]	
Total	**782,513**	**157,466**	**625,047**	**258,050**	**337,033**	**29,965**	**445,480**
Hospital care.	326,559	9,123	317,436	117,752	182,864	16,820	143,695
Physicians' services	171,196	26,235	144,961	84,079	58,143	2,739	113,053
Dentists' services	37,383	18,691	18,692	16,794	1,743	154	35,640
Other professional services [3]	51,220	21,174	30,046	15,843	10,594	3,608	40,626
Home health care.	20,781	4,332	16,449	2,540	11,381	2,528	9,400
Drugs/other medical nondurables	74,956	47,361	27,595	18,417	9,177	-	65,778
Vision products/other med. durables [3]	12,636	7,580	5,056	886	4,170		8,466
Nursing home care	69,621	22,969	46,652	1,739	43,612	1,301	26,009
Other health services	18,162	-	18,162	-	15,348	2,814	2,814

- Represents or rounds to zero.   [1] Includes nonpatient revenues and industrial plant.   [2] Covers out-of-pocket payments, private health insurance, and other.   [3] See footnotes for corresponding items on table 152.

Source: U.S. Health Care Financing Administration, *Health Care Financing Review,* fall 1994.

No. 159. Medicare Enrollees and Expenditures: 1970 to 1993

[**In millions**. Enrollment as of July 1. Includes Puerto Rico and outlying areas and enrollees in foreign countries and unknown place of residence]

ITEM	1970	1975	1980	1985	1990	1991	1992	1993, prel.
ENROLLEES								
Total	20.5	25.0	28.5	31.1	34.2	34.9	35.6	36.3
Hospital insurance	20.4	24.6	28.1	30.6	33.7	34.4	35.2	35.9
Supplementary medical insurance	19.6	23.9	27.4	30.0	32.6	33.2	33.9	34.6
EXPENDITURES								
Total	7,493	16,316	36,802	72,294	110,984	121,447	135,845	150,370
Hospital insurance [1]	5,281	11,581	25,557	48,414	66,997	72,570	85,015	94,391
Inpatient hospital	4,827	10,877	24,116	44,940	59,501	62,839	71,444	76,325
Skilled nursing facility	246	278	395	548	2,528	2,575	3,935	5,473
Home health agency	51	160	540	1,913	3,663	5,342	7,466	10,415
Hospice	-	-	-	43	358	561	846	1,077
Supplementary medical insurance [1]	2,212	4,735	11,245	23,880	43,987	48,877	50,830	55,979
Physician	1,790	3,416	8,187	17,312	29,609	32,313	32,546	35,780
Outpatient hospital	114	643	1,897	4,319	8,482	9,783	10,776	11,543
Home health agency	34	95	234	38	74	65	79	107
Group practice prepayment.	26	80	203	720	2,827	3,531	3,983	5,002
Independent laboratory	11	39	114	558	1,476	1,644	1,876	1,547

- Represents or rounds to zero.   [1] Includes administrative expenses and, for hospital insurance, peer review activity, not shown separately.

Source: U.S. Health Care Financing Administration, Office of the Actuary.

No. 160. Medicare—Persons Served and Reimbursements: 1980 to 1992

[Persons served are enrollees who use covered services, incurred expenses greater than the applicable deductible amounts and for whom Medicare paid benefits. Reimbursements are amounts paid to providers for covered services. Excluded are retroactive adjustments resulting from end of fiscal year cost settlements and certain lump-sum interim payments. Also excluded are beneficiary (or third party payor) liabilities for applicable deductibles, coinsurance amounts, and charges for noncovered services. Includes data for enrollees living in outlying territories and foreign countries]

TYPE OF COVERAGE AND SERVICE	Unit	PERSONS 65 YEARS OLD AND OVER			DISABLED PERSONS [1]		
		1980	1990	1992	1980	1990	1992
Persons served, total [2]	1,000	16,271	24,809	25,491	1,760	2,390	2,627
Hospital insurance [2]	1,000	6,024	6,367	6,746	728	680	753
Inpatient hospital	1,000	5,951	5,906	6,117	721	644	703
Skilled-nursing services [3]	1,000	248	615	759	9	23	27
Home health services [3]	1,000	675	1,818	2,357	51	122	166
Supplementary medical insurance [2]	1,000	16,099	24,687	25,350	1,723	2,365	2,598
Physicians' and other medical services	1,000	15,627	24,193	24,745	1,631	2,249	2,453
Outpatient services	1,000	6,629	14,055	15,658	909	1,496	1,748
Home health services [3]	1,000	302	38	35	25	-	-
Persons served per 1,000 enrollees, total [2]	Rate	638	802	796	594	734	736
Hospital insurance [2]	Rate	240	209	214	246	209	211
Inpatient hospital	Rate	237	194	194	243	198	197
Skilled-nursing services [3]	Rate	10	20	24	3	7	8
Home health services [3]	Rate	27	60	75	17	38	47
Supplementary medical insurance [2]	Rate	652	832	825	634	804	807
Physicians' and other medical services	Rate	633	815	806	600	764	762
Outpatient services	Rate	269	474	510	334	508	543
Home health services [3]	Rate	12	1	1	9	-	-
Reimbursements, total	Mil. dol	29,134	88,778	107,590	4,478	11,239	14,253
Per person served	Dollars	1,791	3,578	4,221	2,544	4,703	5,426
Hospital insurance	Mil. dol	20,353	54,244	68,598	2,765	6,694	8,567
Inpatient hospital	Mil. dol	19,583	48,952	58,596	2,714	6,346	7,876
Skilled-nursing services [3]	Mil. dol	331	1,886	3,146	13	85	126
Home health services [3]	Mil. dol	440	3,406	6,856	38	264	564
Supplementary medical insurance	Mil. dol	8,781	34,533	38,990	1,713	4,545	5,686
Physicians' and other medical services	Mil. dol	7,361	27,379	29,744	997	2,831	3,285
Outpatient services	Mil. dol	1,261	7,077	9,145	701	1,714	2,402
Home health services [3]	Mil. dol	159	78	102	16	-	-

- Represents or rounds to zero.   [1] Age under 65; includes persons enrolled because of end-stage renal disease (ESRD) only.   [2] Persons are counted once for each type of covered service used, but are not double counted in totals.   [3] Beginning 1982, a change in legislation resulted in virtually all home health services being paid under hospital insurance.

Source: U.S. Health Care Financing Administration, *Medicare Program Statistics,* annual; and unpublished data.

No. 161. Medicare—Utilization and Charges: 1970 to 1993

[Data reflect date expense was incurred based on bills submitted for payment and recorded in Health Care Financing Administration central records through May 1993. Includes Puerto Rico, Virgin Islands, Guam, other outlying areas, and enrollees in foreign countries]

ITEM	Unit	PERSONS 65 YEARS OLD AND OVER				DISABLED PERSONS [1]			
		1970	1980	1990	1993	1975	1980	1990	1993
Hospital inpatient care:									
Admissions [2]	1,000	6,141	9,258	9,216	10,038	822	1,271	1,257	1,369
Per 1,000 enrollees [3]	Rate	302	369	309	309	379	429	396	356
Covered days of care	Millions	79	98	82	81	9	13	11	11
Per 1,000 enrollees [3]	Rate	3,902	3,885	2,702	2,493	4,198	4,549	3,464	2,871
Per admission	Days	12.9	10.5	8.9	8.1	11.1	10.6	8.8	8.1
Hospital covered charges	Mil. dol.	5,968	28,615	90,846	125,444	1,371	4,087	11,910	17,016
Per covered day	Dollars	75	293	1,104	1,550	151	303	1,057	1,550
Percent of covered charges reimbursed [4]	Percent	78.0	70.0	47.5	49.6	73.6	68.6	46.5	49.6
Physician allowed charges [5]	Mil. dol.	2,310	9,011	30,447	35,255	367	1,112	2,907	3,917
Percent reimbursed	Percent	71.9	78.0	77.0	76.2	76.1	78.7	75.7	76.2

[1] Disabled persons under age 65 and persons enrolled solely because of end-stage renal disease.   [2] Beginning 1990, represents number of discharges and includes pass-through amounts, except for kidney acquisition.   [3] Based on Hospital Insurance (HI) enrollment as of July 1.   [4] Prior to 1990, billing reimbursements exclude: (1) PPS pass-through amounts for capital, direct medical education, kidney acquisitions, and bad debts by Medicare patients; (2) certain lump-sum interim payments. All years exclude retroactive adjustments resulting from end-of-fiscal year cost reports.   [5] Calendar year data.

Source: U.S. Health Care Financing Administration, unpublished data.

No. 162. Medicare—Summary, by State and Other Areas: 1992 and 1993

STATE AND AREA	1992 Enrollment [1] (1,000)	1992 Payments [2] (mil. dol.)	1993 Enrollment [1] (1,000)	1993 Payments [2] (mil. dol.)	STATE AND AREA	1992 Enrollment [1] (1,000)	1992 Payments [2] (mil. dol.)	1993 Enrollment [1] (1,000)	1993 Payments [2] (mil. dol.)
All areas ..	35,649	129,179	36,271	142,934	MO	805	2,674	814	3,122
U.S.....	34,901	128,618	35,497	142,211	MT........	123	307	125	370
					NE........	243	631	245	689
AL.........	607	2,100	618	2,461	NV........	159	598	170	664
AK.........	28	82	30	97	NH........	145	428	148	462
AZ.........	534	2,077	554	2,178	NJ........	1,130	4,188	1,144	4,749
AR.........	405	1,309	410	1,306	NM........	192	489	198	557
CA.........	3,435	15,653	3,504	16,488	NY........	2,573	10,269	2,594	11,448
CO.........	384	1,242	396	1,430	NC........	945	3,006	971	3,242
CT.........	485	1,953	491	2,053	ND........	101	352	102	347
DE.........	93	267	96	368	OH........	1,603	5,721	1,626	6,086
DC.........	78	1,112	78	1,112	OK........	467	1,471	473	1,547
FL.........	2,448	10,361	2,494	11,722	OR........	444	1,357	452	1,444
GA.........	771	2,864	791	3,302	PA........	2,019	8,365	2,039	9,271
HI.........	137	404	141	473	RI........	164	588	165	628
ID.........	139	300	142	342	SC........	468	1,244	481	1,440
IL.........	1,579	5,565	1,593	6,136	SD........	113	276	115	331
IN.........	791	2,455	803	2,877	TN........	723	2,895	738	3,252
IA.........	467	1,242	469	1,305	TX........	1,926	6,978	1,973	8,007
KS.........	373	1,161	376	1,350	UT........	171	427	177	591
KY.........	555	1,788	565	1,959	VT........	78	200	79	228
LA.........	553	2,318	563	2,607	VA........	761	2,226	779	2,420
ME.........	191	514	194	561	WA........	645	2,145	658	2,167
MD.........	568	2,262	578	2,470	WV........	318	931	322	1,017
MA.........	898	3,780	911	4,487	WI........	736	2,126	745	2,305
MI.........	1,288	4,642	1,309	5,171	WY........	55	98	57	139
MN.........	608	1,943	615	2,106	PR........	446	556	457	709
MS.........	378	1,235	384	1,328	Other areas .	302	5	317	13

[1] Hospital and/or medical insurance enrollment as of September. [2] Benefit payments for all areas represent 100% fee for service experience and actual HMO expenditures through the fiscal year and relate to the State of the provider.

Source: U.S. Health Care Financing Administration, unpublished data.

No. 163. Medicaid—Summary, by State and Other Areas: 1992 and 1993

[Data are for fiscal years]

STATE AND AREA	1992 Recipients [1] (1,000)	1992 Payments [2] (mil. dol.)	1993 Recipients [1] (1,000)	1993 Payments [2] (mil. dol.)	STATE AND AREA	1992 Recipients [1] (1,000)	1992 Payments [2] (mil. dol.)	1993 Recipients [1] (1,000)	1993 Payments [2] (mil. dol.)
All areas ..	30,926	90,814	33,432	101,709	MO	554	1,350	609	1,548
U.S.....	30,028	90,651	32,664	101,547	MT........	60	217	89	287
					NE........	151	468	165	553
AL.........	467	1,056	522	1,192	NV........	78	282	88	301
AK.........	58	187	65	217	NH........	71	340	79	380
AZ.........	402	209	404	212	NJ........	697	2,802	794	3,485
AR.........	321	885	339	998	NM........	212	478	241	543
CA.........	4,486	8,692	4,834	9,650	NY........	2,558	15,281	2,742	17,557
CO.........	259	814	281	911	NC........	785	2,083	898	2,452
CT.........	316	1,663	334	1,825	ND........	57	253	62	273
DE.........	61	219	69	252	OH........	1,442	4,308	1,491	4,667
DC.........	109	499	120	555	OK........	360	1,004	387	1,043
FL.........	1,538	3,518	1,745	4,131	OR........	295	748	325	831
GA.........	864	2,149	955	2,441	PA........	1,175	3,547	1,223	3,886
HI.........	100	270	110	293	RI........	213	774	191	710
ID.........	87	275	100	301	SC........	431	1,151	470	1,249
IL.........	1,313	4,070	1,396	4,625	SD........	64	231	70	264
IN.........	507	2,225	565	2,354	TN........	785	1,735	909	1,977
IA.........	279	855	289	896	TX........	2,025	4,407	2,308	5,575
KS.........	227	620	243	702	UT........	137	365	148	408
KY.........	583	1,543	618	1,707	VT........	78	222	81	235
LA.........	702	2,479	751	2,873	VA........	515	1,511	576	1,623
ME.........	162	642	169	713	WA........	569	1,347	633	1,537
MD.........	377	1,612	445	1,721	WV........	308	795	347	1,056
MA.........	686	3,248	765	2,726	WI........	440	1,677	471	1,786
MI.........	1,129	2,802	1,172	3,077	WY........	42	114	46	125
MN.........	406	1,750	425	1,930	PR........	885	158	757	158
MS.........	487	881	504	896	Virgin Islands	13	5	11	4

[1] Persons who had payments made on their behalf at any time during the fiscal year. [2] Payments are for fiscal year and reflect Federal and State contribution payments. Data exclude disproportionate hospital share payments.

Source: U.S. Health Care Financing Administration, unpublished data.

No. 164. Medicaid—Selected Utilization Measures: 1975 to 1993

[**In thousands.** For fiscal years ending in year shown. Includes Virgin Islands. See text, section 3]

MEASURE	1975	1980	1985	1989	1990	1991	1992	1993
General hospitals:								
Recipients discharged	2,336	2,255	2,390	2,701	3,261	3,638	3,866	4,050
Total days of care	22,941	24,089	29,562	22,754	27,471	28,998	29,921	31,216
Nursing facilities: [1]								
Total recipients	1,212	1,395	1,375	1,438	1,461	1,500	1,573	1,610
Total days of care	199,715	273,497	277,996	367,228	360,044	387,621	408,191	416,200
Intermediate care facilities: [2]								
Total recipients	69	121	147	147	146	146	151	149
Total days of care	9,060	250,124	47,324	50,276	49,730	50,223	53,538	51,716

[1] Includes skilled nursing facilities and intermediate care facilities for all other than the mentally retarded.　[2] Mentally retarded.

Source: U.S. Health Care Financing Administration, Bureau of Data Management and Strategy, Division of Program Systems, *Statistical Report on Medical Care: Eligibles, Recipients, Payments, and Services.*

No. 165. Medicaid—Selected Characteristics of Persons Covered: 1988 to 1993

[**In thousands, except percent.** Represents number of persons as of March of following year who were enrolled at any time in year shown. Person did not have to receive medical care paid for by Medicaid in order to be counted. See headnote, table 590]

POVERTY STATUS	1988	1990	1993							
			Total [1]	White	Black	His-panic [2]	Under 18 years old	18-44 years old	45-64 years old	65 years and over
Persons covered, total	**20,674**	**24,160**	**31,537**	**20,513**	**9,213**	**6,272**	**16,482**	**9,597**	**2,750**	**2,709**
Below poverty level	13,185	15,175	18,801	11,070	6,692	3,872	10,531	5,747	1,493	1,031
Above poverty level	7,489	8,985	12,736	9,443	2,521	2,400	5,951	3,850	1,257	1,678
Percent of population										
covered	**8.5**	**9.7**	**12.2**	**9.5**	**28.0**	**23.6**	**23.8**	**8.8**	**5.5**	**8.8**
Below poverty level	41.5	45.2	47.9	42.2	61.5	47.6	67.0	38.1	31.7	27.5
Above poverty level	3.5	4.2	5.8	5.0	11.4	13.0	11.1	4.1	2.8	6.2

[1] Includes other races not shown separately.　[2] Persons of Hispanic origin may be of any race.

Source: U.S. Bureau of the Census, *Current Population Reports*, P60-188, earlier reports; and unpublished data.

No. 166. Medicaid—Recipients and Payments: 1980 to 1993

[**For fiscal year ending in year shown;** see text, section 10. Includes Puerto Rico and outlying areas. Medical vendor payments are those made directly to suppliers of medical care]

BASIS OF ELIGIBILITY AND TYPE OF SERVICE	RECIPIENTS (1,000)					PAYMENTS (mil. dol.)				
	1980	1985	1990	1992	1993	1980	1985	1990	1992	1993
Total [1] **. . . . .**	**21,605**	**21,814**	**25,255**	**30,926**	**33,432**	**23,311**	**37,508**	**64,859**	**90,814**	**101,709**
Age 65 and over	3,440	3,061	3,202	3,742	3,863	8,739	14,096	21,508	29,078	31,554
Blindness	92	80	83	84	84	124	249	434	530	589
Disabled [2]	2,819	2,937	3,635	4,378	4,932	7,497	13,203	23,969	33,326	38,065
AFDC [3] program	14,210	15,275	17,230	22,058	23,790	6,354	9,160	17,690	26,676	30,109
Other and unknown	1,499	1,214	1,105	664	763	596	798	1,257	1,204	1,391
Inpatient services in—										
General hospital	3,680	3,434	4,593	5,768	5,894	6,412	9,453	16,674	23,503	25,734
Mental hospital	66	60	92	77	75	775	1,192	1,714	2,196	2,161
Intermediate care facilities:										
Mentally retarded	121	147	147	151	149	1,989	4,731	7,354	8,550	8,831
Nursing facility services [4] . . .	1,398	1,375	1,461	1,573	1,610	7,887	11,587	17,693	23,544	25,431
Physicians	13,765	14,387	17,078	21,627	23,746	1,875	2,346	4,018	6,102	6,952
Dental	4,652	4,672	4,552	5,700	6,174	462	458	593	851	961
Other practitioner	3,234	3,357	3,873	4,711	5,229	198	251	372	538	937
Outpatient hospital	9,705	10,072	12,370	15,120	16,436	1,101	1,789	3,324	5,279	6,215
Clinic	1,531	2,121	2,804	4,115	4,839	320	714	1,688	2,818	3,457
Laboratory [5]	3,212	6,354	8,959	11,804	12,970	121	337	721	1,035	1,137
Home health	392	535	719	925	1,067	332	1,120	3,404	4,886	5,601
Prescribed drugs	13,707	13,921	17,294	22,030	23,901	1,318	2,315	4,420	6,765	7,970
Family planning	1,129	1,636	1,752	2,550	2,538	81	195	265	500	538

[1] Recipient data do not add due to small number of recipients that are reported in more than one category. Includes recipients of, and payments for, other care not shown separately.　[2] Permanently and totally.　[3] Aid to families with dependent children. [4] Nursing facility services includes skilled nursing facility services and intermediate care facility services for all other than the mentally retarded.　[5] Includes radiological services.

Source: U.S. Health Care Financing Administration, *Health Care Financing Review,* quarterly.

No. 167. Consumer Price Indexes of Medical Care Prices: 1970 to 1994

[1982-1984=100. Indexes are annual averages of monthly data based on components of consumer price index for all urban consumers; for explanation, see text, section 15. See *Historical Statistics, Colonial Times to 1970,* series B 262-272 for similar data]

| YEAR | Medical care | MEDICAL CARE SERVICES | | | | | Medical care commodities [2] | ANNUAL PERCENT CHANGE [3] | | | | | |
| | | Total [1] | Professional services | | | Hospital room | | Medical care [1] | Medical care services | | | | Medical care commodities [2] |
			Total [1]	Physicians	Dental				Total [1]	Physicians	Dental	Hospital room	
1970	34.0	32.3	37.0	34.5	39.2	23.6	46.5	6.6	7.0	7.5	5.7	12.9	2.4
1975	47.5	46.6	50.8	48.1	53.2	38.3	53.3	12.0	12.6	12.1	10.4	17.1	8.3
1980	74.9	74.8	77.9	76.5	78.9	68.0	75.4	11.0	11.3	10.5	11.9	13.1	9.3
1985	113.5	113.2	113.5	113.3	114.2	115.4	115.2	6.3	6.1	5.9	6.2	5.9	7.2
1987	130.1	130.0	128.8	130.4	128.8	131.1	131.0	6.6	6.6	7.3	6.8	7.2	6.7
1988	138.6	138.3	137.5	139.8	137.5	143.3	139.9	6.5	6.4	7.2	6.8	9.3	6.8
1989	149.3	148.9	146.4	150.1	146.1	158.1	150.8	7.7	7.7	7.4	6.3	10.3	7.8
1990	162.8	162.7	156.1	160.8	155.8	175.4	163.4	9.0	9.3	7.1	6.6	10.9	8.4
1991	177.0	177.1	165.7	170.5	167.4	191.9	176.8	8.7	8.9	6.0	7.4	9.4	8.2
1992	190.1	190.5	175.8	181.2	178.7	208.7	188.1	7.4	7.6	6.3	6.8	8.8	6.4
1993	201.4	202.9	184.7	191.3	188.1	226.4	195.0	5.9	6.5	5.6	5.3	8.5	3.7
1994	211.0	213.4	192.5	199.8	197.1	239.2	200.7	4.8	5.2	4.4	4.8	5.7	2.9

[1] Includes other services not shown separately. 　[2] Prior to 1980, covers drugs and prescriptions only. 　[3] Percent change from the immediate prior year.

Source: U.S. Bureau of Labor Statistics, *CPI Detailed Report,* January 1995; and unpublished data.

No. 168. Average Annual Expenditures per Consumer Unit for Health Care: 1985 to 1993

[In dollars, except percent. See text, section 14, and headnote, table 718. For composition of regions, see table 27]

| ITEM | HEALTH CARE, TOTAL | | Health insurance | Medical services | Drugs and medical supplies [1] | PERCENT DISTRIBUTION | | |
	Amount	Percent of total expenditures				Health insurance	Medical services	Drugs and medical supplies [1]
1985....................	1,108	4.7	375	496	238	33.8	44.8	21.5
1986....................	1,135	4.8	371	502	261	32.7	44.2	23.0
1987....................	1,135	4.6	392	467	276	34.5	41.1	24.3
1988....................	1,298	5.0	474	529	294	36.5	40.8	22.7
1989....................	1,407	5.1	537	542	327	38.2	38.5	23.2
1990....................	1,480	5.2	581	562	337	39.3	38.0	22.8
1991....................	1,554	5.2	656	555	344	42.2	35.7	22.1
1992....................	1,634	5.5	725	533	375	44.4	32.6	22.9
1993....................	**1,776**	**5.8**	**800**	**574**	**402**	**45.0**	**32.3**	**22.6**
Age of reference person:								
Under 25 years old.............	349	2.0	141	140	68	40.4	40.1	19.5
25 to 34 years old.............	1,128	3.9	487	424	217	43.2	37.6	19.2
35 to 44 years old.............	1,673	4.5	671	697	305	40.1	41.7	18.2
45 to 54 years old.............	1,817	4.4	736	631	450	40.5	34.7	24.8
55 to 64 years old.............	2,176	6.6	1,007	655	514	46.3	30.1	23.6
65 to 74 years old.............	2,610	11.0	1,390	555	665	53.3	21.3	25.5
75 years old and over...........	2,883	15.7	1,382	783	718	47.9	27.2	24.9
Race:								
White and other.............	1,890	5.9	842	621	427	44.6	32.9	22.6
Black....................	894	4.3	480	211	202	53.7	23.6	22.6
Region of residence:								
Northeast..................	1,732	5.5	757	602	373	43.7	34.8	21.5
Midwest...................	1,642	5.7	783	481	377	47.7	29.3	23.0
South....................	1,928	6.6	857	613	457	44.5	31.8	23.7
West....................	1,732	5.0	769	595	368	44.4	34.4	21.2
Size of consumer unit:								
One person.................	1,204	6.7	511	403	290	42.4	33.5	24.1
Two or more persons............	2,006	5.6	916	643	448	45.7	32.1	22.3
Two persons..............	2,192	6.9	1,063	580	549	48.5	26.5	25.0
Three persons.............	1,804	5.1	816	596	393	45.2	33.0	21.8
Four persons.............	1,932	4.6	817	749	366	42.3	38.8	18.9
Five persons or more.........	1,863	4.7	767	761	335	41.2	40.8	18.0
Income before taxes:								
Complete income reporters [2]......	1,772	5.6	799	563	409	45.1	31.8	23.1
Quintiles of income:								
Lowest 20 percent..........	1,080	7.7	493	284	302	45.6	26.3	28.0
Second 20 percent..........	1,658	8.4	797	417	444	48.1	25.2	26.8
Third 20 percent..........	1,733	6.5	830	537	367	47.9	31.0	21.2
Fourth 20 percent..........	1,989	5.3	874	696	418	43.9	35.0	21.0
Highest 20 percent..........	2,396	4.0	1,000	880	516	41.7	36.7	21.5
Incomplete reporters of income.....	1,831	6.8	805	645	381	44.0	35.2	20.8

[1] Includes prescription and nonprescription drugs. 　[2] A complete reporter is a consumer unit providing values for at least one of the major sources of income.

Source: Bureau of Labor Statistics, *Consumer Expenditure Survey,* annual.

No. 169. Health Insurance Coverage Status, by Selected Characteristics: 1987 to 1993

[Persons as of following year for coverage in the year shown. Government health insurance includes Medicare, Medicaid, and military plans. Based on Current Population Survey; see text, section 1, and Appendix III]

		NUMBER (mil.)						PERCENT			
		Covered by private or Government health insurance					Not covered by health insur- ance	Covered by private or Government health insurance			Not covered by health insur- ance
CHARACTERISTIC	Total persons	Total [1]	Private		Government			Total [1]	Private	Medi- caid	
			Total	Group health [2]	Medi- care	Medi- caid					
1987	241.2	210.2	182.2	149.7	30.5	20.2	31.0	87.1	75.5	8.4	12.9
1988	243.7	211.0	182.0	150.9	30.9	20.7	32.7	86.6	74.7	8.5	13.4
1989	246.2	212.8	183.6	151.6	31.5	21.2	33.4	86.4	74.6	8.6	13.6
1990	248.9	214.2	182.1	150.2	32.3	24.3	34.7	86.1	73.2	9.7	13.9
1991	251.4	216.0	181.4	150.1	32.9	26.9	35.4	85.9	72.1	10.7	14.1
1992 [3]	254.2	216.8	180.8	148.2	33.7	28.6	37.4	85.3	71.1	11.2	14.7
1993, total [3][4] . .	**220.0**	**182.4**	**148.3**	**33.1**	**31.7**	**39.7**	**84.7**	**70.2**	**12.2**	**15.3**	
Sex:											
Male	126.9	105.3	89.4	74.2	14.1	13.0	21.7	82.9	70.4	10.3	17.1
Female	132.8	114.8	93.0	74.1	19.0	18.7	18.1	86.4	70.0	14.1	13.6
Race:											
White	215.2	184.7	158.6	128.9	29.3	20.6	30.5	85.8	73.7	9.6	14.2
Black	33.0	26.3	16.6	13.7	3.1	9.3	6.8	79.5	50.2	28.1	20.5
Hispanic origin [5]	26.6	18.2	12.0	10.0	1.6	6.3	8.4	68.4	45.1	23.7	31.6
Age:											
Under 18 years . .	69.8	60.2	47.0	39.7	-	16.7	9.6	86.3	67.4	23.9	13.7
18 to 24 years . . .	25.5	18.6	15.7	11.1	0.1	3.0	6.8	73.2	61.5	11.7	26.8
25 to 34 years . . .	41.9	32.9	28.6	25.4	0.5	4.0	9.1	78.4	68.3	9.5	21.6
35 to 44 years . . .	41.5	34.5	31.4	28.1	0.6	2.6	7.0	83.2	75.7	6.3	16.8
45 to 54 years . . .	29.5	25.4	23.3	20.7	0.8	1.5	4.1	86.1	79.0	5.2	13.9
55 to 64 years . . .	20.7	18.0	15.9	13.3	1.5	1.2	2.8	86.6	76.9	5.8	13.4
65 years and over .	30.8	30.4	20.3	9.9	29.4	2.7	0.4	98.8	66.0	8.8	1.2

- Represents zero.   [1] Includes other Government insurance, not shown separately. Persons with coverage counted only once in total, even though they may have been covered by more than one type of policy.   [2] Related to employment of self or other family members.   [3] Beginning 1992, data based on 1990 census adjusted population controls.   [4] Includes other races not shown separately.   [5] Persons of Hispanic origin may be of any race.

Source: U.S. Bureau of the Census, March Supplement to the Current Population Survey, unpublished data.

No. 170. Persons Without Health Insurance, by State: 1991 to 1993

[In percent. Based on the Current Population Survey and subject to sampling error; see text, section 1, and Appendix III]

STATE	1993	2-year average [1], 1992-93	3-year average [1], 1991-93	STATE	1993	2-year average [1], 1992-93	3-year average [1], 1991-93
United States . .	**15.3**	**15.2**	**14.9**	Missouri	12.2	13.3	13.0
Alabama	17.2	17.0	17.4	Montana	15.3	12.4	12.5
Alaska	13.3	15.1	14.6	Nebraska	11.9	10.7	9.9
Arizona	20.2	17.9	17.8	Nevada	18.1	20.6	20.0
Arkansas	19.7	19.8	18.5	New Hampshire	12.5	12.6	11.7
California	19.7	19.9	19.7	New Jersey	13.7	13.5	12.7
Colorado	12.6	12.7	11.9	New Mexico	22.0	20.9	21.3
Connecticut	10.0	9.1	8.6	New York	13.9	13.9	13.5
Delaware	13.4	12.3	12.7	North Carolina	14.0	14.0	14.3
District of Columbia . .	20.7	21.2	22.9	North Dakota	13.4	10.8	9.7
Florida	19.6	19.7	19.4	Ohio	11.1	11.1	10.8
Georgia	18.4	18.8	17.2	Oklahoma	23.6	22.8	21.4
Hawaii [2]	11.1	8.6	8.1	Oregon	14.7	14.2	14.3
Idaho	14.8	15.7	16.4	Pennsylvania	10.8	9.8	9.2
Illinois	12.6	12.9	12.5	Rhode Island	10.3	9.9	10.0
Indiana	11.9	11.5	12.0	South Carolina	16.9	17.1	15.8
Iowa	9.2	9.8	9.5	South Dakota	13.0	14.1	12.7
Kansas	12.7	11.8	11.7	Tennessee	13.2	13.4	13.4
Kentucky	12.5	13.6	13.4	Texas	21.8	22.5	22.6
Louisiana	23.9	23.1	22.4	Utah	11.3	11.6	12.4
Maine	11.1	11.1	11.1	Vermont	11.9	10.7	11.4
Maryland	13.5	12.4	12.7	Virginia	13.0	13.8	14.7
Massachusetts	11.7	11.2	11.1	Washington	12.6	11.5	11.2
Michigan	11.2	10.6	10.1	West Virginia	18.3	16.9	16.5
Minnesota	10.1	9.1	9.2	Wisconsin	8.7	8.9	8.6
Mississippi	17.8	18.6	18.8	Wyoming	15.0	13.4	12.6

[1] Three-year average is recommended when comparing rates between States and 2-year average is recommended when comparing change in State rates to reduce somewhat the chances of misinterpreting differences and lessen the effect of sampling variability.   [2] CPS does not adequately reflect health insurance coverage through State-specific plans, such as those that exist in Hawaii, because the same questions are used for every State.

Source: U.S. Bureau of the Census, Statistical Brief, SB/94-28.

No. 171. Health Insurance Coverage, by Selected Characteristic: 1990-92

[Data represent persons covered by Government or private health insurance coverage during a 32-month period, beginning October 1989. Based on Survey of Income and Program Participation. See text, section 14]

CHARACTERISTIC	All per-sons (mil.)	COVERED BY INSURANCE (mil.)				PERCENT COVERED BY INSURANCE			
		Government or private			Private for entire period	Government or private			Private for entire period
		For entire period	For part of the period	No coverage		For entire period	For part of the period	No coverage	
Total	**235.8**	**176.2**	**50.6**	**8.9**	**152.3**	**74.7**	**21.5**	**3.8**	**64.6**
Under 18 years old	64.0	45.4	16.1	2.5	39.0	71.0	25.2	3.8	61.0
Under 6 years old	23.0	16.0	6.5	0.6	12.9	69.3	28.0	2.6	56.1
18 to 21 years old	13.2	6.9	5.6	0.7	6.2	52.5	42.3	5.2	46.8
22 to 24 years old	10.4	5.5	4.3	0.6	4.7	52.9	41.0	6.2	45.4
25 to 34 years old	41.9	28.6	11.4	1.9	26.4	68.3	27.2	4.4	63.0
35 to 44 years old	36.1	28.2	6.4	1.5	27.0	78.1	17.8	4.1	74.8
45 to 64 years old	45.0	36.5	6.7	1.8	33.1	81.0	15.0	4.0	73.5
65 years old and over	25.3	25.1	0.1	-	15.9	99.4	0.6	-	63.1
Male	113.7	83.5	25.3	4.9	74.1	73.4	22.3	4.3	65.2
Female	122.1	92.8	25.3	4.1	78.3	76.0	20.7	3.3	64.1
White	198.6	151.9	39.6	7.0	135.8	76.5	19.9	3.5	68.4
Black	29.0	18.5	9.0	1.5	12.0	64.0	31.0	5.1	41.5
Hispanic [1]	18.6	9.7	7.0	1.9	6.7	52.0	37.8	10.1	36.1
Residence:									
Northeast	48.0	39.2	7.9	1.0	34.3	81.6	16.4	2.0	71.4
Midwest	62.1	49.1	11.1	1.8	43.8	79.2	18.0	2.8	70.5
South	79.0	53.9	20.8	4.3	45.2	68.2	26.3	5.5	57.2
West	46.8	34.1	10.8	1.9	29.1	72.8	23.1	4.1	62.1
Educational attainment: [2]									
High school	35.8	24.8	8.5	2.5	15.6	69.4	23.7	7.0	43.6
High school, no college	66.3	49.1	14.3	2.8	43.6	74.1	21.6	4.2	65.8
College, 1+ years	69.7	56.8	11.7	1.2	54.1	81.5	16.8	1.7	77.6
Work-status: [3] Worked entire 28 months—									
Full time	53.4	46.7	5.8	0.9	46.4	87.5	10.8	1.7	86.9
Part time	4.8	3.7	0.8	0.2	3.6	77.9	17.5	4.6	74.3
Had at least one work interruption	75.6	46.9	24.5	4.3	39.7	62.0	32.3	5.6	52.4

- Represents zero.   [1] Persons of Hispanic origin may be of any race.   [2] For persons 18 years old and over.   [3] For wage and salary workers.

Source: U.S. Bureau of the Census, *Current Population Reports*, series P70-37; and unpublished data.

No. 172. Health Maintenance Organizations (HMO's): 1980 to 1993

[As of **June 30,** except as noted. Under the Health Maintenance Organization Act, an HMO must have four characteristics: (1) an organized system for providing health care in a geographic area, for which the HMO is responsible for providing or otherwise assuring its delivery; (2) an agreed upon set of basic and supplemental health maintenance and treatment services; (3) a voluntarily enrolled group of people; and (4) community rating. A staff HMO delivers services through a physician group controlled by the HMO unit. A group HMO contracts with one or more medical groups to provide services to members and generally provides all services except hospital care under one roof. A network HMO provides comprehensive health services to members in two or more distinct geographic areas. Individual practice association (IPA) HMO contracts with a physician organization that in turn contracts with individual physicians. IPA physicians provide care to HMO members from their private offices and continue to see their fee-for-service patients. An open-ended product line allows enrollees to receive services from health care providers outside the HMO network for additional out-of-pocket fee (typically a deductible and coinsurance are imposed)]

TYPE OF PRACTICE AND SIZE	1980	1985	1987	1988	1989 (July 1)	1990 (July 1)	1991 (July 1)	1992 (Dec. 1)	1993 (Dec. 31)
NUMBER OF PLANS									
Total	**236**	**393**	**662**	**[1]643**	**[1]590**	**[1]556**	**[1]559**	**[1]546**	**[1]545**
Staff	63	55	64	69	60	50	46	61	57
Group	76	71	74	69	66	62	55	55	55
Network	(NA)	86	107	93	93	82	68	88	94
I.P.A	97	181	417	412	371	350	349	342	339
Mixed	(NA)	(NA)	(NA)	(NA)	(NA)	12	41	(NA)	(X)
ENROLLMENT (1,000)									
Total	**9,100**	**18,894**	**28,587**	**[2]31,366**	**[2]32,493**	**[2]33,622**	**[2]35,052**	**[2]41,386**	**[2]45,205**
Staff	1,673	2,686	3,079	4,276	3,997	3,577	3,425	5,602	5,134
Group	5,732	6,488	7,286	7,985	9,177	9,535	9,471	10,087	10,892
Network	(NA)	5,073	6,895	5,622	5,719	5,874	4,077	6,634	7,912
I.P.A	1,694	4,646	11,327	13,483	13,598	13,879	13,984	19,063	21,267
Mixed	(NA)	(NA)	(NA)	(NA)	(NA)	755	4,096	(X)	(X)
HMO's WITH OPEN-ENDED PRODUCT LINE									
Number of plans	(X)	(X)	(X)	48	78	96	157	271	306
Enrollment (1,000)	(X)	(X)	(X)	482	703	1,041	1,430	2,381	2,634

NA Not available.   X Not applicable.   [1] Includes HMO's containing only open-ended members, not distributed by enrollment size.   [2] Excludes enrollees participating in open-ended plans.

Source: InterStudy, Excelsior, MN, *The InterStudy Competitive Edge*, 1993, vol. 2, No. 2, and earlier publications (copyright); and Group Health Association of America, Inc., Washington, DC, *1994 National Directory of HMO's*.

No. 173. Employment in the Health Service Industries: 1980 to 1994

[**In thousands.** See headnote table 668]

INDUSTRY	1987 SIC code [1]	1980	1985	1990	1992	1993	1994
Health services [2]	80	5,278	6,293	7,814	8,490	8,767	9,032
Offices and clinics of MD's	801	802	1,028	1,338	1,463	1,512	1,562
Offices and clinics of dentist's	802	(NA)	439	513	541	560	590
Offices and clinics of other practitioners	804	96	165	277	327	356	389
Nursing and personal care facilities	805	997	1,198	1,415	1,533	1,580	1,633
Skilled nursing care facilities	8051	(NA)	791	989	1,094	1,130	1,170
Intermediate care facilities	8052	(NA)	(NA)	200	217	222	229
Other, n.e.c. [3]	8059	(NA)	(NA)	227	222	228	233
Hospitals	806	2,750	2,997	3,549	3,750	3,787	3,790
General medical and surgical hospitals	8062	(NA)	2,811	3,268	3,449	3,485	3,492
Psychiatric hospitals	8063	(NA)	59	104	102	97	94
Specialty hospitals, exc. psychiatric	8069	(NA)	126	176	199	205	204
Medical and dental laboratories	807	105	119	166	180	190	202
Home health care services	808	(NA)	152	291	398	462	533

NA Not available. [1] Based on the 1987 Standard Industrial Classification code; see text, section 13. [2] Includes other industries not shown separately. [3] N.e.c. means not elsewhere classified.

Source: U.S. Bureau of Labor Statistics, Bulletin 2445, and *Employment and Earnings,* monthly, March and June issues.

No. 174. Annual Receipts for the Health Service Industries: 1988 to 1993

[**In millions of dollars.** For employer establishments]

INDUSTRY	1987 SIC code [1]	1988	1989	1990	1991	1992	1993
TAXABLE FIRMS							
Health services [2]	80	203,827	220,088	247,305	266,353	289,560	304,135
Offices and clinics of MD's	801	101,034	107,902	117,682	125,490	136,386	139,376
Offices and clinics of dentist's	802	25,726	27,306	29,070	30,394	33,422	35,429
Offices and clinics of doctors of osteopathy	803	2,336	2,323	2,517	2,604	2,743	2,783
Offices and clinics of other practitioners [2]	804	12,167	12,795	15,112	16,015	17,812	19,344
Offices and clinics of chiropractors	8041	4,007	4,476	4,923	5,124	5,984	6,538
Offices and clinics of optometrists	8042	3,773	3,893	4,322	4,497	4,737	5,053
Offices and clinics of podiatrists	8043	(NA)	(NA)	1,710	1,848	1,985	2,100
Nursing and personal care facilities	805	21,507	23,661	26,962	29,408	31,311	33,831
Hospitals	806	22,700	24,846	28,758	31,229	33,578	35,335
General medical and surgical hospitals	8062	(NA)	(NA)	22,047	23,964	26,059	28,117
Psychiatric hospitals	8063	(NA)	(NA)	5,237	5,584	5,576	4,995
Specialty hospitals, exc. psychiatric	8069	(NA)	(NA)	1,474	1,681	1,943	2,223
Medical and dental laboratories	807	8,119	8,933	9,981	10,685	11,328	12,184
Medical laboratories	8071	6,641	7,425	8,296	8,978	9,511	10,318
Dental laboratories	8072	1,506	7,573	1,685	1,707	1,817	1,866
Home health care services	808	(NA)	(NA)	6,374	7,673	9,385	10,864
Miscellaneous allied services, n.e.c. [2][3]	809	(NA)	(NA)	10,849	12,855	13,595	14,989
Kidney dialysis centers	8092	(NA)	(NA)	1,276	1,510	1,883	2,168
Specialty outpatient facilities, n.e.c. [3]	8093	(NA)	(NA)	5,459	6,671	6,639	7,014
TAX EXEMPT FIRMS							
Selected health services [2]	805, 6, 8, 9	(NA)	(NA)	281,248	313,068	340,496	360,963
Offices and clinics of doctors of medicine	801	(NA)	(NA)	12,015	13,745	15,427	17,830
Nursing and personal care facilities	805	8,660	8,901	9,393	10,572	11,849	12,957
Hospitals	806	(NA)	(NA)	251,900	279,628	302,149	317,409
General medical and surgical hospitals	8062	(NA)	(NA)	230,031	255,769	277,991	292,362
Psychiatric hospitals	8063	(NA)	(NA)	9,525	9,917	9,460	9,638
Specialty hospitals, exc. psychiatric	8069	(NA)	(NA)	12,344	13,942	14,698	15,409
Home health care services	808	(NA)	(NA)	3,237	3,864	4,775	5,705
Miscellaneous allied services, n.e.c. [2][3]	809	(NA)	(NA)	4,579	5,125	6,153	6,908
Kidney dialysis centers	8092	(NA)	(NA)	347	406	455	518
Specialty outpatient facilities, n.e.c. [3]	8093	(NA)	(NA)	3,042	3,315	3,836	4,081

NA Not available. [1] Based on the 1987 Standard Industrial Classification code; see text, section 13. [2] Includes other industries not shown separately. [3] N.e.c. means not elsewhere classified.

Source: U.S. Bureau of the Census, Current Business Reports, *Service Annual Survey,* BS/93.

No. 175. Physicians, by Selected Activity: 1970 to 1993

[In thousands. Through 1985, as of Dec. 31; thereafter, as of Jan. 1, except as noted. Includes Puerto Rico and outlying areas. See also *Historical Statistics, Colonial Times to 1970*, series B 275-280]

ACTIVITY	1970	1980	1985	1989	1990	1992	1993
Doctors of medicine, total	**334.0**	**467.7**	**552.7**	**600.8**	**615.4**	**653.1**	**670.3**
Professionally active	311.2	435.5	511.1	549.2	560.0	594.7	605.7
Place of medical education:							
U.S. medical graduates	256.8	343.6	398.4	428.3	437.2	460.4	466.6
Foreign medical graduates [1]	54.4	91.8	112.7	120.8	122.8	134.3	139.1
Sex: Male	289.8	386.7	436.3	458.4	463.9	484.6	488.5
Female	21.4	48.7	74.8	90.7	96.1	110.1	117.2
Active Non-Federal	281.7	417.7	489.5	528.8	539.5	575.5	584.0
Patient care	255.0	361.9	431.5	477.2	487.8	520.2	531.7
Office-based practice	188.9	271.3	329.0	350.1	359.9	387.9	398.8
General and family practice	50.8	47.8	53.9	56.3	57.6	58.6	58.1
Cardiovascular diseases	3.9	6.7	9.1	10.2	10.7	11.4	12.1
Dermatology	2.9	4.4	5.3	5.7	6.0	6.3	6.5
Gastroenterology	1.1	2.7	4.1	4.9	5.2	5.7	6.3
Internal medicine	23.0	40.5	52.7	56.9	57.8	65.1	67.3
Pediatrics	10.3	17.4	22.4	24.7	26.5	29.0	30.8
Pulmonary diseases	0.8	2.0	3.0	3.6	3.7	4.0	4.4
General surgery	18.1	22.4	24.7	24.7	24.5	24.9	24.3
Obstetrics and gynecology	13.8	19.5	23.5	25.2	25.5	27.1	27.6
Ophthalmology	7.6	10.6	12.2	12.8	13.1	13.7	13.9
Orthopedic surgery	6.5	10.7	13.0	14.1	14.2	15.8	16.3
Otolaryngology	3.9	5.3	5.8	6.2	6.4	6.6	6.7
Plastic surgery	1.2	2.4	3.3	3.6	3.8	4.0	4.1
Urological surgery	4.3	6.2	7.1	7.3	7.4	7.7	7.8
Anesthesiology	7.4	11.3	15.3	16.7	17.8	20.0	20.6
Diagnostic radiology	0.9	4.2	7.7	9.0	9.8	10.9	11.9
Emergency medicine	(NA)	(NA)	(NA)	8.0	8.4	9.4	9.8
Neurology	1.2	3.2	4.7	5.4	5.6	6.3	6.8
Pathology, anatomical/clinical	3.0	6.0	6.9	7.0	7.3	7.9	8.5
Psychiatry	10.1	15.9	18.5	19.6	20.0	21.8	22.3
Other specialty	18.2	31.9	35.8	27.8	28.8	31.7	32.4
Hospital-based practice	66.1	90.6	102.5	127.2	127.9	132.3	132.9
Clinical fellows	(NA)	(NA)	(NA)	8.3	8.2	6.8	5.9
Residents and interns	45.8	59.6	72.2	80.0	81.7	85.4	83.1
Full-time hospital staff	20.3	31.0	30.3	38.8	38.0	40.1	43.9
Other professional activity [2]	26.3	35.2	44.0	39.2	39.0	38.7	37.7
Not classified [3]	0.4	20.6	14.0	12.4	12.7	16.6	14.7
Federal	29.5	17.8	21.6	20.4	20.5	19.2	21.7
Patient care	23.5	14.6	17.3	15.9	16.1	15.0	18.8
Office-based practice	3.5	0.7	1.2	1.1	1.1	1.5	0.1
Hospital-based practice	20.0	13.9	16.1	14.8	15.0	13.5	18.7
Other professional activity [2]	6.0	3.2	4.3	4.4	4.4	4.2	2.9
Inactive/unknown address	22.8	32.1	41.6	51.6	55.4	58.4	64.7
Doctors of osteopathy [4]	**14.3**	**18.8**	**24.0**	**29.6**	**30.9**	**33.5**	**33.4**
Medical and osteopathic schools [5]	110	141	142	142	141	141	142
Students [5]	42.6	70.1	73.2	71.6	72.0	73.5	74.5
Graduates [5]	8.8	16.2	17.8	17.2	16.9	17.1	17.1

NA Not available.   [1] Foreign medical graduates received their medical education in schools outside the United States and Canada.   [2] Includes medical teaching, administration, research, and other.   [3] Not classified established in 1970; however, complete data not available until 1972.   [4] As of July. Total DO's. Source: American Osteopathic Association, Chicago, IL.   [5] Number of schools and students as of fall; graduates for academic year ending in year shown. Based on data from annual surveys conducted by the Association of American Medical Colleges and the American Association of Colleges of Osteopathic Medicine.

Source: Except as noted, American Medical Association, Chicago, IL, *Physician Characteristics and Distribution in the U.S.*, annual (copyright).

No. 176. Dentists and Nurses: 1970 to 1993

[As of **end of year,** except as noted. Excludes Puerto Rico and outlying areas. See also *Historical Statistics, Colonial Times to 1970*, series B 281-290]

ITEM	Unit	1970	1975	1980	1985	1989	1990	1991	1992	1993
Dentists, number [1]	1,000	116	127	141	156	168	[2]173	179	183	187
Active (exc. in Federal service) [3]	1,000	96	107	121	136	144	147	149	152	154
Rate per 100,000 population [4]	Rate	47	50	53	57	58	59	59	60	60
Dental schools [5]	Number	53	59	60	60	58	56	55	55	54
Students [5]	1,000	16.6	20.8	22.8	19.6	16.2	16.0	15.9	16.0	16.3
Graduates [5]	1,000	3.7	5.0	5.3	5.4	4.3	4.2	4.0	3.9	3.8
Nurses, number (active registered)	1,000	750	961	1,273	1,538	1,679	1,715	1,758	1,853	(NA)
Rate per 100,000 population [4]	Rate	368	446	560	644	676	690	697	726	(NA)
Nursing programs [6]	Number	1,343	1,360	1,385	1,473	1,457	1,470	1,484	1,484	1,493
Students [6]	1,000	165	250	231	218	201	221	238	258	270
Graduates [6]	1,000	44	75	76	82	62	66	72	81	88

NA Not available.   [1] Includes current year's graduates.   [2] Revised since originally published.   [3] Source: American Dental Association, Bureau of Economic and Behavioral Research, Master Membership file and periodic censuses.   [4] Based on Bureau of Census estimated resident population as of July 1. Estimates reflect revisions based on the 1990 Census of Population.   [5] Number of schools and students as of fall; graduates for academic year ending in year shown. Based on data from the American Dental Association, Council on Dental Education, Annual Report on Dental Education.   [6] Number of programs and students are as of October 15 and number of graduates are for academic year ending in year shown; from National League for Nursing, NLN Data Book, annual issues and State-Approved Schools of Nursing, RN, annual issues.

Source: Except as noted, U.S. Dept. of Health and Human Services, Health Resources and Services Administration, unpublished data. Prior to 1980, data were published by U.S. National Center for Health Statistics in *Health Resources Statistics*, annual.

No. 177. Active Non-Federal Physicians 1993, and Nurses 1992, by State

[Nurses as of March; Physicians as of Jan. 1. Excludes doctors of osteopathy, Federally employed persons and physicians with addresses unknown. Includes all physicians not classified according to activity status]

STATE	PHYSICIANS, 1993		NURSES, 1992		STATE	PHYSICIANS, 1993		NURSES, 1992	
	Total	Rate [1]	Total	Rate [1]		Total	Rate [1]	Total	Rate [1]
United States..	576,771	225	1,853,024	731	Missouri	10,830	207	42,035	812
Alabama.	7,068	170	27,717	673	Montana.	1,407	169	5,848	715
Alaska	818	142	3,583	637	Nebraska	3,025	189	13,257	834
Arizona.	7,606	194	27,093	711	Nevada	2,045	148	7,135	538
Arkansas	3,908	162	14,001	587	New Hampshire	2,373	211	10,743	964
California	74,165	240	173,973	568	New Jersey.	20,657	263	64,519	827
Colorado.	7,830	222	26,697	780	New Mexico	3,049	190	9,393	600
Connecticut.	10,482	321	30,918	946	New York	60,759	334	159,297	881
Delaware	1,453	209	6,137	894	North Carolina	13,574	198	47,602	708
District of Columbia .	3,814	667	11,352	1,966	North Dakota.	1,178	188	6,300	1,007
Florida	29,209	215	94,591	707	Ohio	22,928	207	89,799	816
Georgia	12,456	182	43,386	647	Oklahoma.	4,897	153	16,972	534
Hawaii	2,728	244	7,674	697	Oregon.	6,354	210	23,992	808
Idaho	1,428	131	5,702	537	Pennsylvania	30,640	254	108,663	907
Illinois	26,804	230	93,069	804	Rhode Island.	2,695	271	9,665	971
Indiana.	9,611	168	39,602	700	South Carolina.	6,205	173	20,684	584
Iowa	4,470	159	25,838	922	South Dakota	1,108	156	6,828	973
Kansas.	4,643	185	19,773	794	Tennessee	10,685	210	35,318	706
Kentucky	6,740	179	24,552	659	Texas.	31,699	177	92,810	528
Louisiana	8,591	201	24,233	570	Utah	3,463	187	9,831	545
Maine.	2,365	192	10,584	861	Vermont	1,492	259	5,199	910
Maryland	16,496	335	38,170	783	Virginia.	13,567	215	42,519	684
Massachusetts.	21,676	361	63,751	1,066	Washington.	11,457	220	38,698	761
Michigan.	18,513	195	65,441	694	West Virginia.	3,311	182	11,875	657
Minnesota	10,476	232	39,876	893	Wisconsin	9,982	198	39,883	799
Mississippi	3,401	130	13,415	516	Wyoming	640	137	3,032	658

[1] Per 100,000 civilian population. Based on U.S. Bureau of the Census estimates as of July 1, 1992, for nurses, and July 1, 1993, for physicians.

Source: Physicians: American Medical Association, Chicago, IL, *Physician Characteristics and Distribution in the U.S.,* annual (copyright); Nurses: U.S. Dept. of Health and Human Services, Health Resources and Services Administration, unpublished data.

No. 178. Physician and Dental Contacts, by Patient Characteristics: 1970 to 1993

[See headnote, table 204. Based on National Health Interview Survey; see Appendix III]

| TYPE OF VISIT AND YEAR | TOTAL VISITS (mil.) | | | | VISITS PER PERSON PER YEAR | | | | | | | | | |
| | Sex | | Race [1] | | Sex | | Race [1] | | Age (years) | | | | | |
	Male	Fe-male	White	Black	Male	Fe-male	White	Black	Under 5	5 to 17	18 to 24	25 to 44	45 to 64	65 and over
PHYSICIANS														
1970	396	531	832	87	4.1	5.1	4.8	3.9	[2]5.9	[3]2.9	[4]4.6	4.6	5.2	6.3
1980	426	610	903	115	4.0	5.4	4.8	4.5	[2]6.7	[3]3.2	[4]4.0	4.6	5.1	6.4
1983	470	694	1,018	126	4.3	5.8	5.2	4.6	[2]6.5	[3]3.2	[4]4.0	4.7	5.8	7.6
1985	498	733	1,074	132	4.4	6.1	5.4	4.7	[2]6.3	[3]3.1	[4]4.2	4.9	6.1	8.3
1986	515	756	1,110	131	4.5	6.2	5.5	4.6	6.3	3.3	4.2	4.7	6.6	9.1
1987	523	765	1,118	140	4.5	6.2	5.5	4.9	6.7	3.3	4.4	4.8	6.4	8.9
1988	530	774	1,139	136	4.5	6.2	5.6	4.6	7.0	3.4	3.8	5.1	6.1	8.7
1989	552	771	1,148	140	4.7	6.1	5.6	4.7	6.7	3.5	3.9	5.1	6.1	8.9
1990	558	806	1,178	148	4.7	6.4	5.7	4.9	6.9	3.2	4.3	5.1	6.4	9.2
1991	589	842	1,243	152	4.9	6.6	6.0	4.9	7.1	3.4	3.9	5.1	6.6	10.4
1992	624	889	1,286	181	5.1	6.9	6.1	5.8	6.9	3.5	4.1	5.4	7.2	10.6
1993	634	917	1,314	183	5.1	7.0	6.2	5.7	7.2	3.6	4.0	5.4	7.1	10.9
DENTISTS														
1970	133	171	283	17	1.4	1.7	1.6	0.8	[2]0.5	[3]1.9	[4]1.8	1.7	1.5	1.1
1980	158	207	333	26	1.5	1.8	1.8	1.0	[2]0.5	[3]2.3	[4]1.6	1.7	1.8	1.4
1983	183	239	382	31	1.6	2.0	1.9	1.1	[2]0.5	[3]2.6	[4]1.6	1.9	2.0	1.5
1986	210	256	416	37	1.9	2.2	2.1	1.4	0.7	2.4	1.7	2.0	2.2	2.1
1989	221	271	441	34	1.9	2.2	2.2	1.2	0.5	2.4	1.6	2.0	2.4	2.0

[1] See footnote 2, table 204.　[2] Under 6 years.　[3] 6 to 17 years.　[4] 17 to 24 years.

Source: U.S. National Center for Health Statistics, *Vital and Health Statistics,* series 10, No. 190, and earlier reports; and unpublished data.

No. 179. Visits to Office Based Physicians: 1992

[Based on the National Ambulatory Care Survey and subject to sampling error; see source for details]

CHARACTERISTIC	Number of visits (1,000)	Per-cent distri-bution	Visits per person per year	CHARACTERISTIC	Number of visits (1,000)	Per-cent distri-bution	Visits per person per year
All visits	762,045	100.0	3.0	New problem.	175,370	23.0	(X)
Age:				New patient	112,381	14.7	(X)
Under 15 years old	155,168	20.4	2.7				
15 to 24 years old	72,016	9.5	2.1	Expected source of payment: [1]			
25 to 44 years old	211,897	27.8	2.6	Private/commercial insurance .	250,870	32.9	(X)
45 to 64 years old	154,997	20.3	3.2	Medicaid	84,098	11.0	(X)
65 to 74 years old	90,625	11.9	4.9	HMO/other prepaid	146,338	19.2	(X)
75 years old and over	77,341	10.1	6.3	Patient paid	145,459	19.1	(X)
				Medicare	151,656	19.9	(X)
Sex:				Other government	15,622	2.1	(X)
Male	304,676	40.0	2.5	No charge	12,454	1.6	(X)
Female	457,369	60.0	3.5	Other/unknown	48,100	6.3	(X)
Race:				Disposition: [1]			
White	653,851	85.8	3.1	Return to at specified time . . .	469,155	61.6	(X)
Black	82,599	10.8	2.6	Return if needed	184,144	24.2	(X)
Asian/Pacific Islander.	23,205	3.0	(NA)	No followup	72,881	9.6	(X)
American Indian/Eskimo/Aleut .	2,389	0.3	(NA)	Telephone followup	21,202	2.8	(X)
				Return to other clinic/physician.	22,445	2.9	(X)
Visit status:				Admit to hospital	5,385	0.7	(X)
Old patient	649,664	85.3	(X)	Return to referring physician . .	8,097	1.1	(X)
Old problem	474,294	62.2	(X)	Other	6,408	0.8	(X)

NA Not available.　X Not applicable.　[1] More than one reported source of payment or disposition may be reported.
Source: U.S. National Center for Health Statistics, *Advance Data*, No. 253, August 18, 1994.

No. 180. Medical Practice Characteristics, by Selected Specialty: 1985 to 1992

[**Dollar figures in thousands.** Based on a sample telephone survey of 4,000 non-Federal office and hospital based patient care physicians, excluding residents, with a response rate of 69.1% in 1990, 66.7% in 1991, and 64.4% in 1992. For details, see source. For definition of mean, see Guide to Tabular Presentation]

SPECIALTY	1985	1987	1988	1989	1990	1991	1992
MEAN PATIENT VISITS PER WEEK							
All physicians [1]	117.1	119.3	121.1	121.6	120.9	118.4	114.8
General/Family practice	138.1	138.3	145.6	143.0	146.0	144.4	138.4
Internal medicine	105.2	114.5	113.0	117.9	112.0	110.7	109.4
Surgery.	108.2	107.8	105.0	107.7	107.6	106.9	101.6
Pediatrics	130.8	127.4	135.1	138.1	134.0	133.5	126.9
Obstetrics/Gynecology	112.0	112.7	118.9	115.6	120.0	112.2	110.5
MEAN HOURS IN PATIENT CARE PER WEEK							
All physicians [1]	51.3	52.9	53.1	53.3	53.3	53.3	52.9
General/Family practice	53.6	53.7	54.4	54.4	55.0	54.7	53.1
Internal medicine	52.4	56.0	56.2	56.8	55.7	56.3	55.5
Surgery.	51.2	53.0	53.8	53.3	53.1	53.4	53.0
Pediatrics	50.6	53.6	52.5	53.4	52.4	52.4	52.6
Obstetrics/Gynecology	56.9	57.0	59.4	59.0	60.4	59.5	58.8
MEAN NET INCOME							
All physicians [1]	112.2	132.3	144.7	155.8	164.3	170.6	177.4
General/Family practice	77.9	91.5	94.6	95.9	102.7	111.5	111.8
Internal medicine	102.0	121.8	130.9	146.5	152.5	149.6	159.3
Surgery.	155.0	187.9	207.5	220.5	236.4	233.8	244.6
Pediatrics	76.2	85.3	94.9	104.7	106.5	119.3	121.7
Obstetrics/Gynecology	124.3	163.2	180.7	194.3	207.3	221.8	215.1
MEAN PROFESSIONAL EXPENSES							
All physicians [1]	102.7	123.7	140.8	148.4	150.0	168.4	179.0
General/Family practice	96.5	121.2	122.3	128.5	134.5	146.4	156.3
Internal medicine	90.0	117.8	136.3	139.1	139.2	159.0	172.9
Surgery.	135.7	164.7	188.2	203.2	201.0	215.6	238.6
Pediatrics	87.3	100.2	115.3	132.5	138.0	145.4	168.8
Obstetrics/Gynecology	131.9	173.2	189.6	197.4	212.6	236.2	234.8
MEAN LIABILITY PREMIUM							
All physicians [1]	10.5	15.0	15.9	15.5	14.5	14.9	13.5
General/Family practice	6.8	8.9	9.4	9.0	7.8	8.1	8.1
Internal medicine	5.8	8.4	9.0	8.2	9.2	8.0	8.5
Surgery.	16.6	24.5	26.5	25.8	22.8	22.5	20.6
Pediatrics	4.7	7.1	9.3	7.8	7.8	8.4	7.8
Obstetrics/Gynecology	23.5	35.3	35.3	37.0	34.3	34.9	33.5

[1] Includes other specialties not shown separately.
Source: American Medical Association, Chicago IL, *Socioeconomic Characteristics of Medical Practice*, annual (copyright).

No. 181. Hospital Registered Nursing Personnel—Summary: 1992

[**In percent, except as indicated.** Based on a sample of 5,417 U.S. short term acute care hospitals registered and unregistered by the American Hospital Association, with a response rate of 50.2 percent. For details see source. For an explanation of mean, see Guide to Tabular Presentation]

CHARACTERISTIC	1992	CHARACTERISTIC	1992
Full-time registered nurses per hospital (mean) [1] . . .	112.7	Registered nurse, full-time:	
		Lowest mean hourly wage paid	13.96
LENGTH OF EMPLOYMENT AT HOSPITAL [2]		Highest mean hourly wage paid	19.71
		Mean hourly wage paid.	16.92
Full-time: Less than 1 year	15.5		
1 year to less than 2 years	14.3	**HOSPITAL STAFFING MECHANISMS** [4]	
2 years to less than 5 years.	25.0		
5 years or more	45.2	Per-diem	41.2
		Float-pool [5]	27.3
Part-time: Less than 1 year	13.1	On-call	11.1
1 year to less than 2 years	13.1	Temporary nursing service	16.7
2 years to less than 5 years.	25.2	Other	3.7
5 years or more.	48.7		
		HOSPITAL POSITION SCHEDULES [6]	
EDUCATIONAL ATTAINMENT [3]			
		Days only	32.6
Associate degree in nursing	39.4	Evenings only.	17.1
Nursing diploma	27.7	Nights only.	18.6
Baccalaureate degree in nursing	31.0	Shifts: Day/evening	11.1
Master's degree in nursing or higher.	2.0	Day/night	6.1
		Evening/night	4.2
SALARY/WAGES (dol. per hr.) [2]		Rotate all	10.3
Full-time head nurse:		**HOSPITAL BARGAINING STATUS**	
Lowest mean annual salary paid	17.57		
Highest mean annual salary paid	22.59	Organized for the purpose of collective bargaining. . .	15.8

[1] Source: American Hospital Association, Chicago, IL, 1991 Human Resource Survey.   [2] Full-time: at least 35 hours worked per week. Part-time: less than 35 hours worked per week.   [3] Full-time only.   [4] Percent of positions with each mechanism. [5] In-house nursing staff personnel routinely assigned schedules who work different units in the institution according to the demands of variable patient volume and acuity levels.   [6] Percent of positions.

Source: Except as indicated, American Hospital Association, Chicago, IL, *Report of the Hospital Nursing Personnel Survey, 1992,* copyright 1992 by the American Hospital Association (copyright).

No. 182. Hospitals and Nursing Homes—Summary Characteristics: 1971 to 1993

[Except as indicated, based on National Master Facility Inventory]

YEAR AND TYPE OF FACILITY	Total	FACILITIES UNDER—			FACILITIES WITH—			Resi-dents [2] (1,000)	Full-time employ-ees (1,000)
		Gov't. control	Propri-etary control	Non-profit control	Fewer than 25 beds [1]	25-74 beds	75 or more beds		
1971: All facilities.	29,682	4,178	18,091	7,413	8,902	10,959	9,821	2,262	3,007
Nursing homes [3].	22,004	1,368	17,049	3,587	8,266	8,259	5,479	1,076	568
Hospitals.	7,678	2,810	1,042	3,826	636	2,700	4,342	1,186	2,439
1980: All facilities.	30,116	3,498	19,611	7,007	8,852	8,573	12,691	2,427	3,919
Nursing homes [3][4].	23,065	936	18,669	3,460	8,498	6,362	8,205	1,396	[5]798
Hospitals.	7,051	2,562	942	3,547	354	2,211	4,486	1,031	3,121
1986: All facilities.	32,600	3,275	21,399	7,926	9,903	8,755	13,942	2,427	(NA)
All hospitals [6].	6,954	2,230	1,176	3,548	290	2,150	4,514	874	3,241
General	5,956	1,871	829	3,256	259	1,849	3,848	690	2,871
Psychiatric	584	267	218	99	12	140	432	139	248
Chronic	44	30	4	10	-	6	38	13	21
Tuberculosis	4	3	-	1	-	1	3	-	1
Nursing homes [3].	25,646	1,045	20,223	4,378	9,613	6,605	9,428	1,553	(NA)
1990: All hospitals [6]	6,779	2,145	1,203	3,431	326	2,077	4,376	840	3,562
General	5,611	1,788	711	3,112	290	1,690	3,631	673	3,168
Psychiatric	734	272	350	112	17	211	506	128	262
Chronic	34	27	2	5	-	6	28	10	18
Tuberculosis	4	3	-	1	-	1	3	-	1
1993: All hospitals [6].	6,580	2,046	1,167	3,367	310	2,010	4,260	781	3,783
General	5,403	1,697	660	3,046	260	1,586	3,557	634	3,401
Psychiatric	737	266	358	113	24	242	471	107	231
Chronic	26	21	1	4	1	3	22	9	16
Tuberculosis	4	3	-	1	-	2	2	-	1

- Represents or rounds to zero.   NA Not available.   [1] For hospitals, minimum of six beds; for nursing homes, minimum of three beds.   [2] Number of residents as of date of interview.   [3] See footnotes 1, 3, and 4, table 200.   [4] Includes 1978 data for Alaska and South Dakota.   [5] Estimated.   [6] Includes types not shown separately. Based on data from the American Hospital Association.

Source: U.S. National Center for Health Statistics, *Health Resources Statistics, 1971;* and unpublished data.

No. 183. Hospitals—Summary Characteristics: 1972 to 1993

[Covers hospitals accepted for registration by the American Hospital Association; see text, section 3. Short-term hospitals have an average patient stay of less than 30 days; long-term, an average stay of longer duration. Special hospitals include obstetrics and gynecology; eye, ear, nose, and throat; rehabilitation; orthopedic; and chronic and other special hospitals except psychiatric, tuberculosis, alcoholism, and chemical dependency. See also *Historical Statistics, Colonial Times to 1970*, series B 305-318, B 331-344, and B 413-422]

ITEM	1972	1980	1985	1988	1989	1990	1991	1992	1993
NUMBER									
All hospitals	7,061	6,965	6,872	6,780	6,720	6,649	6,634	6,539	6,467
With 100 beds or more	2,710	3,755	3,805	3,681	3,650	3,620	3,611	3,572	3,558
Non-Federal [1]	6,660	6,606	6,529	6,438	6,380	6,312	6,300	6,214	6,151
Community hospitals [2]	5,746	5,830	5,732	5,533	5,455	5,384	5,342	5,292	5,261
Nongovernmental nonprofit	3,301	3,322	3,349	3,242	3,220	3,191	3,175	3,173	3,154
For profit	738	730	805	790	769	749	738	723	717
State and local government	1,707	1,778	1,578	1,501	1,466	1,444	1,429	1,396	1,390
Long-term general and special	216	157	128	129	138	131	126	115	117
Psychiatric	529	534	610	726	741	757	800	774	741
Tuberculosis	72	11	7	4	4	4	4	4	4
Federal	401	359	343	342	340	337	334	325	316
BEDS (1,000)									
All hospitals [3]	1,550	1,365	1,309	1,241	1,224	1,211	1,197	1,174	1,158
Rate per 1,000 population [4]	7.4	6.0	5.5	5.1	5.0	4.9	4.7	4.6	4.6
Beds per hospital	220	196	190	183	182	182	180	180	179
Non-Federal [1]	1,407	1,248	1,197	1,138	1,124	1,113	1,101	1,085	1,071
Community hospitals [2]	879	988	1,001	944	933	928	924	921	916
Rate per 1,000 population [4]	4.2	4.3	4.2	3.9	3.8	3.7	3.7	3.6	3.6
Nongovernmental nonprofit	617	692	707	666	660	657	656	656	649
For profit	57	87	104	103	103	102	100	99	99
State and local government	205	209	189	175	170	169	168	167	169
Long-term general and special	54	39	31	27	27	25	25	23	21
Psychiatric	457	215	169	163	160	158	150	139	131
Tuberculosis	13	2	1	(Z)	(Z)	(Z)	(Z)	(Z)	(Z)
Federal	143	117	112	104	100	98	95	89	87
OCCUPANCY RATE [5]									
All hospitals	78.0	77.7	69.5	69.6	69.7	69.7	69.1	68.7	67.6
Non-Federal [1]	78.0	77.4	68.9	69.1	69.3	69.4	68.8	68.0	66.9
Community hospitals [2]	75.4	75.6	64.8	65.7	66.2	66.7	66.1	65.6	64.6
Nongovernmental nonprofit	77.5	78.2	67.2	68.4	68.8	69.3	68.6	67.9	66.7
For profit	68.7	65.2	52.2	51.0	51.6	52.6	52.5	52.0	51.1
State and local government	71.0	71.1	62.9	63.9	64.9	65.3	64.4	64.7	64.5
Long-term general and special	83.0	85.9	88.5	87.5	86.6	85.9	84.9	84.5	83.8
Psychiatric	82.8	85.2	87.0	86.3	84.6	82.5	82.4	81.4	80.1
Tuberculosis	61.2	67.0	64.1	67.2	69.3	66.4	76.6	82.9	84.8
Federal	80.0	80.1	76.3	74.4	73.7	73.3	72.8	77.3	76.8
EXPENSES (bil. dol.) [6]									
All hospitals	32.7	91.9	153.3	196.7	214.9	234.9	258.5	282.5	301.5
Non-Federal [1]	30.0	84.0	141.0	182.1	199.8	219.6	241.7	264.3	281.9
Community hospitals [2]	25.5	76.9	130.5	168.7	184.9	203.7	225.0	248.1	266.1
Nongovernmental nonprofit	18.4	55.8	96.1	124.7	136.9	150.7	166.8	183.8	197.2
For profit	1.4	5.8	11.5	15.5	17.2	18.8	20.5	22.5	23.1
State and local government	5.7	15.2	22.9	28.5	30.8	34.2	37.7	41.8	45.8
Long-term general and special	0.7	1.2	1.9	2.3	2.5	2.7	2.9	2.7	2.7
Psychiatric	3.1	5.8	8.3	10.9	12.0	12.9	13.5	13.2	12.7
Tuberculosis	0.1	0.1	0.1	(Z)	(Z)	0.1	(Z)	(Z)	0.1
Federal	3.1	7.9	12.3	14.6	15.1	15.2	16.8	18.2	19.6
PERSONNEL (1,000) [7]									
All hospitals	2,671	3,492	3,625	3,840	3,937	4,063	4,165	4,236	4,289
Non-Federal [1]	2,439	3,213	3,326	3,545	3,648	3,760	3,864	3,929	3,970
Community hospitals [2]	2,051	2,873	2,997	3,205	3,303	3,420	3,535	3,620	3,677
Nongovernmental nonprofit	1,473	2,086	2,216	2,373	2,454	2,533	2,624	2,692	2,711
For profit	105	189	221	249	261	273	281	285	289
State and local government	473	598	561	583	589	614	630	643	676
Long-term general and special	63	56	58	54	56	55	55	49	45
Psychiatric	307	275	263	281	284	280	269	256	242
Tuberculosis	12	3	2	1	1	1	1	1	1
Federal	232	279	299	295	288	303	301	306	320
Personnel per 100 patients [7]	221	329	398	445	462	482	504	525	548
Outpatient visits (mil.)	219.2	263.0	282.1	336.2	352.2	368.2	387.7	417.9	435.6
Emergency	60.1	82.0	80.1	86.6	89.9	92.8	93.5	95.8	97.4
Closures	(NA)	73	59	106	80	63	67	60	83

NA Not available.   Z Less than 500 beds, $50 million, or 0.5 percent.   [1] Short term (average length of stay less than 30 days) general and special (e.g., obstetrics and gynecology; eye, ear, nose and throat; rehabilitation etc. except psychiatric, tuberculosis, alcoholism and chemical dependency). Includes hospital units of institutions.   [2] Excludes hospital units of institutions.   [3] Beginning 1988, number of beds at end of reporting period; prior years, average number in 12 month period.   [4] Based on Bureau of the Census estimated resident population as of July 1. Estimates reflect revisions based on the 1990 Census of Population.   [5] Ratio of average daily census to every 100 beds.   [6] Excludes new construction.   [7] Includes full-time equivalents of part-time personnel.

Source: American Hospital Association, Chicago, IL, *Hospital Statistics,* annual (copyright).

No. 184. Community Hospitals—States and Puerto Rico: 1993

[For definition of community hospitals see footnotes 1 and 2, table 183. See also *Historical Statistics, Colonial Times to 1970,* series B 305-308 and B 359-362 for data on all hospitals]

REGION, DIVISION, AND STATE OR OTHER AREA	Number of hospitals	Beds (1,000)	Patients admitted (1,000)	Average daily census [1] (1,000)	Occupancy rate [2] (percent)	Personnel [3] (1,000)	Outpatient visits (mil.)
United States	**5,261**	**916.2**	**30,748.1**	**591.7**	**64.6**	**3,676.6**	**366.9**
Northeast	**788**	**204.8**	**6,896.6**	**157.3**	**76.8**	**886.5**	**92.9**
New England	**227**	**43.1**	**1,602.7**	**30.6**	**71.0**	**206.5**	**23.4**
Maine	39	4.4	145.1	3.0	68.0	18.5	2.2
New Hampshire	28	3.4	109.7	2.1	63.7	13.8	1.8
Vermont	15	1.9	57.5	1.2	64.2	7.0	0.9
Massachusetts	99	21.1	817.3	15.1	71.5	107.8	12.4
Rhode Island	11	3.0	126.8	2.2	73.3	14.7	1.4
Connecticut	35	9.2	346.3	6.9	74.4	44.8	4.8
Middle Atlantic	**561**	**161.8**	**5,293.9**	**126.7**	**78.3**	**680.0**	**69.5**
New York	231	77.4	2,359.9	64.1	82.8	328.7	33.7
New Jersey	97	31.1	1,103.2	23.9	77.0	121.0	11.2
Pennsylvania	233	53.4	1,830.7	38.7	72.6	230.3	24.6
Midwest	**1,523**	**238.8**	**7,421.8**	**146.5**	**61.4**	**933.8**	**99.9**
East North Central	**809**	**155.1**	**5,221.6**	**96.6**	**62.3**	**653.3**	**73.8**
Ohio	192	41.1	1,413.7	24.9	60.5	176.2	19.4
Indiana	115	21.3	712.3	12.5	58.7	90.6	10.8
Illinois	208	44.1	1,467.8	28.0	63.5	180.0	19.6
Michigan	167	30.9	1,059.4	20.0	64.7	140.9	16.4
Wisconsin	127	17.7	568.4	11.2	63.4	65.5	7.5
West North Central	**714**	**83.7**	**2,200.3**	**49.9**	**59.6**	**280.5**	**26.1**
Minnesota	145	18.4	496.1	12.1	66.0	55.0	5.3
Iowa	119	13.4	348.4	7.7	57.9	44.1	5.1
Missouri	130	23.6	705.1	13.9	58.9	95.9	8.2
North Dakota	45	4.4	90.8	2.8	64.2	12.2	0.8
South Dakota	51	4.3	94.9	2.6	60.6	11.4	0.9
Nebraska	90	8.4	175.1	4.6	55.2	25.7	2.1
Kansas	134	11.3	289.8	6.1	54.2	36.3	3.6
South	**1,982**	**329.1**	**11,025.3**	**201.9**	**61.3**	**1,265.1**	**104.9**
South Atlantic	**790**	**159.1**	**5,502.6**	**103.3**	**64.9**	**632.8**	**52.7**
Delaware	8	2.2	79.3	1.5	70.9	10.9	1.2
Maryland	50	13.0	559.3	9.8	75.3	60.9	4.5
District of Columbia . . .	11	4.2	156.4	3.1	73.2	20.1	1.3
Virginia	96	19.5	690.7	12.5	64.2	76.4	6.6
West Virginia	58	8.3	278.3	5.2	61.9	30.4	3.5
North Carolina	117	22.7	785.5	15.8	69.6	97.0	7.7
South Carolina	68	11.4	394.2	7.7	67.3	45.9	3.9
Georgia	159	26.5	853.1	16.8	63.4	97.7	8.8
Florida	223	51.3	1,705.6	31.0	60.4	193.6	15.2
East South Central	**449**	**69.8**	**2,255.5**	**42.4**	**60.8**	**248.9**	**21.4**
Kentucky	106	15.9	532.6	9.9	62.2	58.5	6.0
Tennessee	130	22.8	747.3	13.9	60.8	86.1	7.4
Alabama	116	18.5	604.9	11.3	60.7	66.0	5.2
Mississippi	97	12.5	370.8	7.4	59.3	38.3	2.8
West South Central . . .	**743**	**100.3**	**3,267.1**	**56.1**	**56.0**	**383.4**	**30.8**
Arkansas	87	11.0	342.1	6.4	58.3	37.5	3.0
Louisiana	132	19.1	598.0	10.9	57.0	73.0	7.1
Oklahoma	110	11.7	363.2	6.4	54.5	44.4	2.9
Texas	414	58.5	1,963.9	32.5	55.5	228.5	17.8
West	**968**	**143.5**	**5,404.4**	**86.0**	**60.0**	**591.2**	**69.2**
Mountain	**350**	**42.1**	**1,430.7**	**24.4**	**57.9**	**166.1**	**18.3**
Montana	52	4.2	97.5	2.7	64.2	11.9	1.2
Idaho	41	3.4	99.0	1.9	55.4	11.4	1.6
Wyoming	25	2.2	42.8	1.1	48.4	8.7	0.7
Colorado	72	10.3	340.0	6.0	58.6	42.2	4.7
New Mexico	37	4.1	151.1	2.2	54.0	18.5	2.5
Arizona	60	9.9	403.6	5.6	57.1	39.8	3.4
Utah	42	4.4	173.5	2.3	53.4	20.7	3.0
Nevada	21	3.7	123.0	2.5	67.8	12.8	1.2
Pacific	**618**	**101.4**	**3,973.7**	**61.7**	**60.8**	**425.1**	**50.9**
Washington	90	12.0	494.2	6.9	57.6	53.2	7.1
Oregon	63	7.4	293.2	4.1	54.7	33.1	4.6
California	429	77.7	3,052.2	47.6	61.2	320.5	36.7
Alaska	16	1.3	37.3	0.7	52.9	4.5	0.6
Hawaii	20	2.9	96.9	2.4	83.1	13.9	2.0
Puerto Rico	50	8.1	400.0	5.9	72.6	27.2	3.1

[1] Inpatients receiving treatment each day; excludes newborn.   [2] Ratio of average daily census to every 100 beds.
[3] Includes full-time equivalents of part-time personnel.

Source: American Hospital Association, Chicago, IL, *Hospital Statistics, 1994-95* (copyright).

No. 185. Hospital Use Rates, by Type of Hospital: 1972 to 1993

[See also *Historical Statistics, Colonial Times to 1970*, series B 384-387]

TYPE OF HOSPITAL	1972	1980	1985	1989	1990	1991	1992	1993
Community hospitals: [1]								
Admissions per 1,000 population [2]	147	159	141	126	125	123	122	119
Admissions per bed	35	37	33	33	34	34	34	33
Average length of stay [3] (days)	7.9	7.6	7.1	7.2	7.2	7.2	7.1	7.0
Outpatient visits per admission	1.8	5.6	6.5	9.2	9.7	10.4	11.2	11.9
Outpatient visits per 1,000 population [2]	777	890	919	1,158	1,208	1,277	1,367	1,423
Surgical operations (million)	14.8	18.8	20.1	21.3	21.9	22.4	22.9	22.8
Number per admission	0.5	0.5	0.6	0.7	0.7	0.7	0.7	0.7
Non-Federal psychiatric:								
Admissions per 1,000 population [2]	2.8	2.5	2.5	2.9	2.9	2.9	2.9	2.9
Days in hospital per 1,000 population [2]	661	295	224	201	190	179	162	149

[1] For definition of community hospitals, see footnotes 1 and 2, table 183.   [2] Based on Bureau of the Census estimated resident population as of July 1. Estimates reflect revisions based on the 1990 Census of Population.   [3] Number of inpatient days divided by number of admissions.

Source: American Hospital Association, Chicago, IL, *Hospital Statistics*, annual (copyright); and unpublished data.

No. 186. Average Cost to Community Hospitals per Patient: 1970 to 1993

[**In dollars, except percent.** Covers non-Federal short-term general or special hospitals (excluding psychiatric or tuberculosis hospitals and, beginning 1975, hospital units of institutions). Total cost per patient based on total hospital expenses (payroll, employee benefits, professional fees, supplies, etc.). Data have been adjusted for outpatient visits]

TYPE OF EXPENSE AND HOSPITAL	1970	1975	1980	1985	1988	1989	1990	1991	1992	1993
Average cost per day, total	**74**	**134**	**245**	**460**	**586**	**637**	**687**	**752**	**820**	**881**
Annual percent change [1]	12.7	17.5	12.9	11.9	8.7	8.7	7.8	9.5	9.0	7.4
Nongovernmental nonprofit	75	133	246	463	591	642	692	758	828	898
For profit	71	133	257	500	649	708	752	820	889	914
State and local government	71	136	239	433	539	582	634	696	754	800
Average cost per stay, total	**605**	**1,030**	**1,851**	**3,245**	**4,207**	**4,588**	**4,947**	**5,360**	**5,794**	**6,132**
Nongovernmental nonprofit	615	1,040	1,902	3,307	4,273	4,649	5,001	5,393	5,809	6,178
For profit	486	876	1,676	3,033	4,023	4,406	4,727	5,134	5,548	5,643
State and local government	614	1,031	1,750	3,106	4,034	4,430	4,838	5,340	5,871	6,206

[1] Change from immediate prior year, except 1970, average annual change from 1965. For explanation of average annual change, see Guide to Tabular Presentation.

Source: American Hospital Association, Chicago, IL, *Hospital Statistics*, annual (copyright); and unpublished data.

No. 187. Average Cost to Community Hospitals per Patient, by State: 1990 to 1993

[**In dollars.** See headnote, table 186]

STATE	AVERAGE COST PER DAY			AVERAGE COST PER STAY			STATE	AVERAGE COST PER DAY			AVERAGE COST PER STAY		
	1990	1992	1993	1990	1992	1993		1990	1992	1993	1990	1992	1993
U.S.	687	820	881	4,947	5,794	6,132	MO	679	792	863	5,022	5,789	6,161
AL	588	729	775	4,175	5,080	5,229	MT	405	474	481	3,973	4,704	4,953
AK	1,070	1,116	1,136	6,249	7,456	7,594	NE	490	600	626	4,675	5,714	6,024
AZ	867	1,051	1,091	4,877	5,502	5,528	NV	854	952	900	5,511	5,778	6,796
AR	534	633	678	3,730	4,376	4,585	NH	671	776	976	4,544	5,480	6,964
CA	939	1,134	1,221	5,709	6,626	6,918	NJ	613	737	829	4,573	5,909	6,540
CO	725	904	961	5,209	5,933	6,212	NM	734	950	1,046	5,094	5,600	5,600
CT	825	1,012	1,058	6,238	7,241	7,478	NY	641	744	784	6,397	7,316	7,716
DE	771	920	1,028	5,112	6,123	7,307	NC	595	711	763	4,408	5,217	5,571
DC	995	1,124	1,201	7,876	8,218	8,594	ND	427	484	507	4,468	5,302	5,403
FL	769	886	940	5,312	6,092	6,169	OH	720	875	940	4,801	5,649	5,923
GA	630	721	775	4,303	5,238	5,554	OK	632	740	797	4,302	4,847	5,093
HI	638	761	823	6,048	6,876	7,633	OR	800	1,011	1,053	4,432	5,112	5,309
ID	547	618	659	3,701	4,346	4,635	PA	662	793	861	5,120	5,955	6,564
IL	717	849	912	5,253	6,048	6,318	RI	663	801	885	4,839	5,355	5,672
IN	667	822	898	4,390	5,305	5,677	SC	590	782	838	4,168	5,617	5,955
IA	495	588	612	4,135	4,920	4,980	SD	391	457	506	3,905	4,653	5,052
KS	532	661	666	4,161	5,115	5,108	TN	633	796	859	4,340	5,392	5,798
KY	563	674	703	3,762	4,652	4,749	TX	752	933	1,010	4,663	5,666	6,021
LA	701	836	875	4,575	5,457	5,781	UT	832	1,036	1,081	4,409	5,104	5,314
ME	574	674	738	4,604	5,142	5,543	VT	598	726	676	4,343	5,046	5,241
MD	678	806	889	4,640	5,139	5,632	VA	635	774	830	4,408	5,226	5,504
MA	788	937	1,036	5,709	6,381	6,843	WA	817	974	1,143	4,519	5,238	5,792
MI	716	847	902	5,358	5,899	6,147	WV	565	655	701	3,918	4,496	4,712
MN	536	618	652	4,782	5,456	5,867	WI	554	674	744	4,083	4,909	5,348
MS	439	516	555	3,116	3,807	4,053	WY	462	515	537	3,990	4,370	4,706

Source: American Hospital Association, Chicago, IL, *Hospital Statistics*, annual (copyright); and unpublished data.

No. 188. Facilities and Services Provided by Community Hospitals: 1993

[Community hospitals are non-Federal short-stay (average length stay fewer than 30 days) excluding hospital units of institutions. Data are for hospitals responding to that portion of the questionnaire 4,845 of a total of 5,261 community hospitals in 1993]

SERVICE	Hospitals with service	Percent of total	SERVICE	Hospitals with service	Percent of total
Adult day care program.	362	7.5	Outpatient surgery services	4,541	93.7
Alzheimer's diagnostic/assessment	475	9.8	Patient representative services.	2,739	56.5
Angioplasty.	1,055	21.8	Psychiatric services:		
Alcoholism/chemical dependency			Emergency	1,694	35.0
outpatient services	1,025	21.2	Outpatient.	1,130	23.3
Birthing rooms.	3,228	66.6	Radiation therapy:		
Blood bank	3,382	69.8	X-ray	967	20.0
Cardiac catheterization	1,610	33.2	Megavoltage (mil. volts).	1,006	20.8
Cardiac rehabilitation	2,374	49.0	Radio-active implants	1,231	25.4
Computed tomographic (CT) scanner . .	3,750	77.4	Radio isotope facilities:		
Emergency department.	4,460	92.1	Diagnostic.	2,988	61.7
Extracorporeal shock wave			Therapeutic.	1,288	26.6
lithotripter	516	10.7	Rehabilitation outpatient		
Genetic counseling services.	501	10.3	department	2,802	57.8
Geriatric services.	3,147	65.0	Reproductive health services	2,130	44.0
Hemodialysis	1,358	28.0	Therapy services:		
Histopathology laboratory	3,105	64.1	Occupational therapy services	2,688	55.5
Home health services.	2,047	42.2	Physical therapy services.	4,143	85.5
Hospice	964	19.9	Recreational therapy services.	1,751	36.1
Hospital auxiliary	3,861	79.7	Respiratory therapy services.	4,420	91.2
AIDS inpatient care	3,564	73.6	Trauma center.	810	16.7
AIDS outpatient care	326	6.7	Ultrasound	4,115	84.9
Magnetic resonance imaging (MRI)	1,507	31.1	Volunteer services department	3,356	69.3
Open-heart surgery facilities	908	18.7	Women's center	1,364	28.2

Source: American Hospital Association, Chicago, IL, *Hospital Statistics, 1994-95* and *1993 Annual Survey of Hospitals* (copyright).

No. 189. Hospital Utilization Rates: 1970 to 1993

[Represents estimates of inpatients discharged from noninstitutional, short-stay hospitals, exclusive of Federal hospitals. Excludes newborn infants. Based on sample data collected from the National Hospital Discharge Survey, a sample survey of hospital records of patients discharged in year shown; subject to sampling variability. For composition of regions, see table 27]

SELECTED CHARACTERISTIC	Patients discharged (1,000)	PATIENTS DISCHARGED PER 1,000 PERSONS [1]			DAYS OF CARE PER 1,000 PERSONS [1]			AVERAGE STAY (days)		
		Total	Male	Female	Total	Male	Female	Total	Male	Female
1970.	29,127	144	118	169	1,122	982	1,251	8.0	8.7	7.6
1980.	37,832	168	139	194	1,217	1,068	1,356	7.3	7.7	7.0
1985.	35,056	148	124	171	954	849	1,053	6.5	6.9	6.2
1986.	34,256	143	121	164	913	817	1,003	6.4	6.8	6.1
1987.	33,387	138	116	159	889	806	968	6.4	6.9	6.1
1988 [2]	31,146	128	107	147	834	757	907	6.5	7.1	6.2
1989 [2]	30,947	126	105	145	815	741	884	6.5	7.0	6.1
1990 [2]	30,788	124	102	144	792	704	875	6.4	6.9	6.1
1991 [2]	31,098	124	103	144	795	715	869	6.4	7.0	6.0
1992 [2]	30,951	122	101	142	751	680	818	6.2	6.7	5.8
1993, [2] total	**30,825**	**120**	**98**	**141**	**720**	**644**	**792**	**6.0**	**6.5**	**5.6**
Age:										
Under 1 year old	710	181	206	156	1,155	1,265	1,041	6.4	6.1	6.7
1 to 4 years old	654	41	46	37	163	169	157	3.9	3.7	4.3
5 to 14 years old	777	21	22	20	108	110	105	5.1	5.1	5.2
15 to 24 years old	3,088	87	37	138	309	204	416	3.5	5.5	3.0
25 to 34 years old	4,655	113	53	171	446	313	575	4.0	5.9	3.4
35 to 44 years old	3,457	85	72	99	431	424	438	5.1	5.9	4.4
45 to 64 years old	6,283	127	132	123	785	831	742	6.2	6.3	6.1
65 to 74 years old	4,890	262	284	245	1,927	2,033	1,844	7.4	7.2	7.5
75 years old and over. . .	6,310	446	476	430	3,665	3,764	3,609	8.2	7.9	8.4
Region:										
Northeast	6,965	136	119	152	952	876	1,023	7.0	7.4	6.7
Midwest	7,097	116	98	134	706	638	771	6.1	6.5	5.8
South	11,580	131	104	156	749	658	834	5.7	6.3	5.4
West	5,183	93	72	114	473	419	527	5.1	5.8	4.6

[1] Based on Bureau of the Census estimated civilian population as of July 1. Estimates for 1980-90 do not reflect revisions based on the 1990 Census of Population. [2] Comparisons beginning 1988 with data for earlier years should be made with caution as estimates of change may reflect improvements in the design rather than true changes in hospital use.

Source: U.S. National Center for Health Statistics, *Vital and Health Statistics,* series 13; and unpublished data.

No. 190. Hospital Outpatient Department Visits: 1992

[An outpatient department is a hospital facility where nonurgent ambulatory care is provided under the supervision of a physician. Data exclude clinics where only ancillary services, such as radiology, are provided. Based on the National Ambulatory Care Survey and subject to sampling error; see source for details]

CHARACTERISTIC	Number of visits (1,000)	Percent distribu-tion	Visits per 100 persons	CHARACTERISTIC	Number of visits (1,000)	Percent distribu-tion	Visits per 100 persons
All visits	**56,605**	**100.0**	**22.5**	Expected source of payment: [1]			
Age:				Medicaid	17,647	31.2	(X)
Under 15 years old	12,713	22.5	22.5	Private/commercial			
15 to 24 years old	7,242	12.8	21.1	insurance	13,478	23.8	(X)
25 to 44 years old	16,484	29.1	20.3	Medicare	9,240	16.3	(X)
45 to 64 years old	11,295	20.0	23.3	Patient paid	7,747	13.7	(X)
65 to 74 years old	5,031	8.9	27.2	HMO/other prepaid	4,364	7.7	(X)
75 years old and over	3,840	6.8	31.2	Other government	3,684	6.5	(X)
Sex:				No charge	1,640	2.9	(X)
Male	21,864	38.6	17.9	Other and unknown	4,828	8.5	(X)
Female	34,741	61.4	26.9				
Race:				Disposition: [1]			
White	42,034	74.3	20.1	Return to clinic:			
Black	12,549	22.2	39.9	By appointment	36,776	65.0	(X)
Asian/Pacific Islander	1,609	2.8	(NA)	As needed	9,720	17.2	(X)
American Indian/Eskimo/				Return to other clinic/			
Aleut	414	0.7	(NA)	physician	3,899	6.9	(X)
Visit status:				Return to referring physician	3,417	6.0	(X)
Old patient	44,180	78.0	(X)	No followup	2,287	4.0	(X)
Old problem	35,635	63.0	(X)	Telephone followup	1,408	2.5	(X)
New problem	8,545	15.1	(X)	Admit to hospital	705	1.2	(X)
New patient	12,425	22.0	(X)	Other	2,736	4.8	(X)

NA Not available.   X Not applicable.   [1] More than one reported source of payment or disposition may be reported.

Source: U.S. National Center for Health Statistics, *Advance Data,* No. 248, March 9, 1994.

No. 191. Hospital Emergency Room Visits: 1993

[An emergency room is a hospital facility staffed by physicians for the provision of providing outpatient services to patients whose conditions require immediate attention and is staffed 24 hours a day. Data are for non-Federal short stay or general hospitals. Based on the National Hospital Ambulatory Care Survey and subject to sampling error]

CHARACTERISTIC	NUMBER OF VISITS (1,000)				VISITS PER 100 PERSONS			
	Total	Urgent [1]	Non-urgent	Injury-related	Total	Urgent [1]	Non-urgent	Injury-related
All visits [2]	**92,814**	**42,048**	**50,766**	**37,712**	**36.5**	**16.5**	**20.0**	**14.8**
Age:								
Under 15 years old	23,285	9,176	14,108	9,114	40.7	16.0	24.6	15.9
15 to 24 years old	15,583	6,291	9,292	7,644	45.4	18.3	27.1	22.3
25 to 44 years old	28,064	11,526	16,537	12,563	34.4	14.1	20.3	15.4
45 to 64 years old	12,822	6,488	6,334	4,625	25.8	13.0	12.7	9.3
65 to 74 years old	5,496	3,523	1,973	1,511	29.5	18.9	10.6	8.1
75 years old and over	7,565	5,044	2,521	2,257	59.8	39.9	19.9	17.8
Sex:								
Male	44,426	20,848	23,578	20,783	35.9	16.9	19.1	16.8
Female	48,388	21,200	27,188	16,930	37.1	16.2	20.8	13.0
Race:								
White	72,354	33,531	38,823	30,859	34.2	15.9	18.4	14.6
Black	18,464	7,849	10,615	6,096	57.6	24.5	33.1	19.0

[1] Patient requires immediate attention.   [2] Includes other races, not shown separately.

Source: U.S. National Center for Health Statistics, unpublished data.

No. 192. Hospital Discharges and Days of Care: 1993

[See headnote, table 189]

AGE AND FIRST-LISTED DIAGNOSIS	DISCHARGES		Days of care per 1,000 persons [1]	Average stay (days)	AGE AND FIRST-LISTED DIAGNOSIS	DISCHARGES		Days of care per 1,000 persons [1]	Average stay (days)
	Number (1,000)	Per 1,000 persons [1]				Number (1,000)	Per 1,000 persons [1]		
MALE					FEMALE				
All ages [2]	12,262	98.4	643.5	6.5	All ages [2]	18,563	140.8	792.1	5.6
					Delivery	4,015	30.5	74.1	2.4
Diseases of heart	2,078	16.7	100.7	6.0	Diseases of heart	1,873	14.2	93.4	6.6
Malignant neoplasms	690	5.5	47.2	8.5	Malignant neoplasms	792	6.0	46.3	7.7
Pneumonia, all forms	598	4.8	36.3	7.6	Pneumonia, all forms	586	4.4	35.7	8.0
Psychoses	500	4.0	46.5	11.6	Psychoses	554	4.2	51.8	12.3
Fractures, all sites	440	3.5	23.7	6.7					
					Under 15 years [2]	948	34.2	184.2	5.4
Under 15 years [2]	1,193	41.1	206.2	5.0	Acute respiratory infection	86	3.1	10.3	3.3
Acute respiratory infection	136	4.7	15.0	3.2	Pneumonia, all forms	83	3.0	16.3	5.4
Pneumonia, all forms	126	4.3	18.7	4.3	Bronchitis, emphysema [3]	63	2.3	8.6	3.8
Bronchitis, emphysema [3]	105	3.6	11.3	3.1	Noninfectious enteritis [4]	43	1.5	3.7	2.4
Congenital anomalies	64	2.2	14.2	6.5	Congenital anomalies	42	1.5	12.5	8.4
Fractures, all sites	45	1.5	6.4	4.2					
					15 to 44 years [2]	8,021	136.0	479.9	3.5
15 to 44 years [2]	3,179	54.5	317.8	5.8	Delivery	4,001	67.8	164.9	2.4
Psychoses	296	5.1	56.1	11.1	Psycoses	268	4.5	49.0	10.8
Fractures, all sites	216	3.7	20.5	5.5	Benign neoplasms	152	2.6	8.9	3.4
Diseases of heart	161	2.8	12.7	4.6	Cholelithiasis	136	2.3	7.1	3.1
Alcohol dependence syndrome	130	2.2	17.9	8.0	Pregnancy w/abortive				
Intervertebral disk disorders	130	2.2	7.4	3.3	outcome	132	2.2	4.4	2.0
45 to 64 years [2]	3,143	131.5	831.0	6.3	45 to 64 years [2]	3,141	122.5	742.2	6.1
Diseases of heart	743	31.1	169.6	5.5	Diseases of heart	423	16.5	91.4	5.5
Malignant neoplasms	201	8.4	74.2	8.8	Malignant neoplasms	258	10.1	75.0	7.4
Psychoses	115	4.8	57.1	11.8	Psychoses	122	4.7	61.2	12.9
Pneumonia, all forms	97	4.0	29.2	7.2	Bronchitis, emphysema [3]	111	4.3	26.9	6.2
Cerebrovascular disease	96	4.0	33.1	8.3	Benign neoplasms	105	4.1	16.8	4.1
65 years old and older [2]	4,748	357.2	2,691.2	7.5	65 years old and older [2]	6,453	330.9	2,666.0	8.1
Diseases of heart	1,167	87.8	580.1	6.6	Diseases of heart	1,362	69.9	489.1	7.0
Malignant neoplasms	409	30.8	265.8	8.6	Malignant neoplasms	402	20.6	176.2	8.6
Pneumonia, all forms	307	23.1	208.9	9.0	Fractures, all sites	381	19.5	182.0	9.3
Cerebrovascular disease	268	20.2	162.3	8.0	Cerebrovascular disease	362	18.5	161.2	8.7
Hyperplasia of prostate	140	10.5	41.5	3.9	Pneumonia, all forms	335	17.2	159.6	9.3

[1] See footnote 1, table 189.   [2] Includes other first-listed diagnoses not shown separately.   [3] Includes asthma.   [4] Includes colitis.

Source: U.S. National Center for Health Statistics, *Health, United States*, 1994; and unpublished data.

No. 193. Outpatient Surgery Performed in Hospitals: 1980 to 1993

TYPE OF HOSPITAL	1980	1985	1987	1988	1989	1990	1991	1992	1993
OUTPATIENT SURGERIES (1,000)									
All hospitals	3,198	7,309	9,758	10,586	10,953	11,678	12,209	12,849	13,098
Ownership:									
Non-Federal hospitals	3,063	6,984	9,145	10,038	10,362	11,085	11,724	12,316	12,641
Community hospitals [1]	3,054	6,951	9,126	10,028	10,351	11,070	11,712	12,308	12,624
Nongovernmental nonprofit	2,416	5,392	6,903	7,577	7,834	8,389	8,989	9,500	9,685
Federal hospitals	135	325	612	548	591	593	486	533	457
Size of hospital: 6 to 99 beds	354	752	1,146	1,229	1,241	1,303	1,366	1,464	1,473
100 to 199 beds	571	1,502	2,030	2,252	2,360	2,498	2,636	2,824	2,927
200 to 299 beds	630	1,521	2,023	2,297	2,383	2,543	2,695	2,790	2,906
300 to 499 beds	977	2,069	2,617	2,845	2,920	3,172	3,293	3,340	3,424
500 beds or more	666	1,465	1,942	1,963	2,049	2,162	2,220	2,431	2,368
OUTPATIENT SURGERIES AS PERCENT OF TOTAL									
All hospitals	16.4	34.5	44.2	47.0	48.7	50.6	52.1	53.6	54.9
Ownership:									
Non-Federal hospitals	16.3	34.5	43.9	46.8	48.5	50.5	52.3	53.8	55.4
Community hospitals [1]	16.3	34.6	43.8	46.8	48.5	50.5	52.3	53.8	55.4
Nongovernmental nonprofit	17.1	35.5	44.2	47.0	48.6	50.7	52.5	54.0	55.7
Federal hospitals	18.6	33.9	49.9	49.7	51.5	51.8	47.8	49.3	45.4
Size of hospital: 6 to 99 beds	17.9	36.5	49.4	52.8	54.1	56.2	58.7	61.1	62.5
100 to 199 beds	15.4	36.3	47.2	50.3	52.3	55.0	56.3	58.3	59.4
200 to 299 beds	16.7	36.4	45.7	49.2	50.7	52.9	54.6	55.3	57.2
300 to 499 beds	17.2	34.4	43.1	46.5	48.0	48.8	50.6	51.9	53.2
500 beds or more	15.1	30.4	39.2	39.6	41.6	43.9	44.4	46.5	46.9

[1] For definition of community hospital, see footnotes 1 and 2, table 183.

Source: American Hospital Association, Chicago, IL, *Hospital Statistics*, annual (copyright); and unpublished data from the Annual Survey of Hospitals.

No. 194. Procedures for Inpatients Discharged From Short-Stay Hospitals: 1980 to 1993

[Excludes newborn infants and discharges from Federal hospitals. See headnote, table 189]

SEX AND TYPE OF PROCEDURE	NUMBER OF PROCEDURES (1,000)				RATE PER 1,000 POPULATION [2]			
	1980	1985	1990 [1]	1993 [1]	1980	1985	1990 [1]	1993 [1]
Surgical procedures, total [3][4]	**24,494**	**24,799**	**23,051**	**22,767**	**108.6**	**104.6**	**92.4**	**88.8**
MALE								
Total [3][4]	**8,505**	**8,805**	**8,538**	**8,355**	**78.1**	**76.8**	**70.6**	**67.1**
Cardiac catheterization	228	439	620	613	2.1	3.8	5.1	4.9
Prostatectomy	335	367	364	317	3.1	3.2	3.0	2.5
Reduction of fracture [5]	325	339	300	294	3.0	3.0	2.5	2.4
Repair of inguinal hernia	483	370	181	96	4.4	3.2	1.5	0.8
FEMALE								
Total [3][4]	**15,989**	**15,994**	**14,513**	**14,411**	**137.1**	**130.6**	**113.0**	**109.3**
Procedures to assist delivery [4]	2,391	2,494	2,491	2,428	20.5	20.4	19.4	18.4
Cesarean section	619	877	945	917	5.3	7.2	7.4	7.0
Repair of current obstetric laceration	355	548	795	860	3.0	4.5	6.2	6.5
Hysterectomy	649	670	591	562	5.6	5.5	4.6	4.3
Diagnostic and other nonsurgical procedures [4][6]	**6,918**	**11,961**	**17,455**	**18,842**	**30.7**	**50.5**	**70.0**	**73.5**
MALE								
Total [4][6]	**3,386**	**5,889**	**7,378**	**7,787**	**31.1**	**51.4**	**61.0**	**62.5**
Angiocardiography and arteriography [7]	355	693	1,051	1,024	3.3	6.0	8.7	8.2
CAT scan [8]	152	671	736	565	1.4	5.9	6.1	4.5
FEMALE								
Total [4][6]	**3,532**	**6,072**	**10,077**	**11,055**	**30.3**	**49.6**	**78.5**	**83.8**
Diagnostic ultrasound	204	756	941	848	1.7	6.2	7.3	6.4
CAT scan [8]	154	707	770	594	1.3	5.8	6.0	4.5

[1] Comparisons beginning 1990 with data for earlier years should be made with caution as estimates of change may reflect improvements in the design rather than true changes in hospital use.   [2] Based on Bureau of the Census estimated civilian population as of July 1. Population estimates for the 1980's do not reflect revised estimates based on the 1990 Census of Population.   [3] Includes other types of surgical procedures not shown separately.   [4] Beginning in 1990, the definition of some surgical and diagnostic and other nonsurgical procedures was revised, causing a discontinuity in the trends for some totals.   [5] Excluding skull, nose, and jaw.   [6] Includes other nonsurgical procedures not shown separately.   [7] Using contrast material.   [8] Computerized axial tomography.

Source: U.S. National Center for Health Statistics, *Vital and Health Statistics,* series 13; and unpublished data.

No. 195. Hospital Discharges—Principal Source of Expected Payment: 1993

[See headnote, table 189]

CHARACTERISTIC	Total discharges [1] (1,000)	PRINCIPAL SOURCE OF EXPECTED PAYMENT—PERCENT DISTRIBUTION							
		Private insurance	Government				Self-pay	No charge	Other [2]
			Medicare	Medicaid	Worker's compensation	Other			
AGE									
All ages	**30,825**	**33.9**	**37.8**	**14.7**	**1.3**	**1.8**	**4.9**	**0.4**	**3.0**
Under 15 years old	2,141	42.2	1.4	40.0	(X)	3.0	5.6	1.4	4.0
15 to 44 years old	11,200	49.4	4.6	25.2	2.1	2.7	8.3	0.6	4.4
45 to 64 years old	6,283	55.4	15.9	11.2	2.0	2.3	6.3	0.5	4.1
65 years old and over	11,201	4.8	90.3	1.3	0.2	0.3	0.5	([3])	0.8
SEX									
Male, all ages	**12,262**	**31.4**	**41.9**	**10.9**	**2.0**	**1.9**	**5.8**	**0.5**	**3.1**
Under 15 years old	1,193	42.2	0.9	41.1	(X)	2.8	5.4	1.4	4.1
15 to 44 years old	3,179	43.5	9.4	15.8	4.8	3.5	12.9	1.0	5.1
45 to 64 years old	3,143	53.9	18.4	9.4	2.4	2.3	6.4	0.5	4.2
65 years old and over	4,748	5.7	89.4	1.1	0.3	0.4	0.6	([3])	0.8
Female, all ages	**18,563**	**35.5**	**35.1**	**17.2**	**0.8**	**1.7**	**4.3**	**0.3**	**2.9**
Under 15 years old	948	42.2	2.0	38.5	(X)	3.2	5.7	1.4	3.9
15 to 44 years old	8,021	51.7	2.7	28.9	1.0	2.4	6.5	0.4	4.1
45 to 64 years old	3,141	56.9	13.3	12.9	1.6	2.3	6.2	0.5	4.0
65 years old and over	6,453	4.0	90.9	1.5	0.2	0.2	0.5	([3])	0.8
RACE									
White	20,101	36.5	41.5	9.6	1.2	1.4	4.2	0.3	3.1
All other	4,912	25.4	25.7	31.6	0.8	2.9	6.8	1.1	3.4
Not stated	5,812	32.0	35.4	17.9	1.8	2.2	5.7	([3])	2.5
REGION									
Northeast	6,965	33.5	38.6	14.7	1.0	0.8	4.7	0.4	3.6
Midwest	7,097	34.9	42.0	12.2	0.7	1.9	4.1	0.3	2.5
South	11,580	33.7	38.0	13.7	1.8	2.3	6.0	0.6	1.4
West	5,183	33.6	30.7	20.4	1.2	1.8	3.8	([3])	6.6

X Not applicable.   [1] Includes discharges for whom expected source of payment was unknown.   [2] Includes all other nonprofit source of payment such as church, welfare, or United Way.   [3] Figure does not meet standards of reliability or precision.

Source: U.S. National Center for Health Statistics, unpublished data.

No. 196. Organ Transplants and Grafts: 1981 to 1994

[**As of end of year.** Based on reports of procurement programs and transplant centers in the United States, except as noted]

PROCEDURE	NUMBER OF PROCEDURES							NUMBER OF CENTERS		Number of people waiting, 1994	1-year sur-vival rates, 1992 (percent)
	1981	1985	1990	1991	1992	1993	1994	1987	1994		
Transplant:											
Heart.........	62	719	1,998	2,125	2,172	2,298	2,342	104	165	2,933	82
Liver........	26	602	2,534	2,954	3,059	3,440	3,646	45	117	4,059	77
Kidney.......	4,883	7,695	9,433	9,949	10,210	10,361	10,463	200	248	27,498	97
Heart-lung	5	30	52	51	48	61	69	23	92	205	59
Lung........	-	2	187	401	535	669	713	(NA)	85	1,625	69
Pancreas/Islet cell	(NA)	130	529	532	557	[1]113	[1]98	31	116	222	89
Cornea grafts [2]...	15,500	26,300	40,631	41,393	42,337	40,215	(NA)	[3]103	(NA)	(NA)	[4]95
Bone grafts	(NA)	(NA)	350,000	350,000	350,000	(NA)	(NA)	(NA)	(NA)	(NA)	(NA)
Skin grafts	(NA)	(NA)	5,500	5,500	5,500	(NA)	(NA)	(NA)	(NA)	(NA)	(NA)

- Represents zero.　NA Not available.　[1] Pancreas only.　[2] 1981 through 1992, number of procedures and eye banks include Canada.　[3] Eye banks.　[4] Success rate.

Source: Transplants: through 1992, U.S. Department of Health and Human Services, Public Health Service, Division of Organ Transplantation; beginning 1993, United Network for Organ Sharing, Richmond, VA; American Association of Tissue Banks, McLean, VA; and Eye Bank Association of America, Washington, DC; and unpublished data.

No. 197. Home Health and Hospice Care Patients, by Selected Characteristics: 1993

[See headnote, table 199]

ITEM	CURRENT PATIENTS [1]			DISCHARGES [2]		
	Total	Home health agency	Hospice	Total	Home health agency	Hospice
Total (1,000).....................	1,501.3	1,451.2	50.1	3,945.1	3,688.0	257.2
PERCENT DISTRIBUTION						
Age:						
Under 45 years old	13.6	13.7	9.9	15.2	15.6	9.9
45-54 years old.....................	3.7	3.7	6.3	4.3	4.2	5.2
55-64 years old.....................	8.3	8.2	12.3	9.4	9.1	13.8
65 years old and over	74.4	74.5	71.5	71.0	71.1	71.2
65-69 years old	9.7	9.6	10.7	10.2	9.8	16.3
70-74 years old	14.5	14.4	18.2	15.0	14.8	18.7
75-79 years old	15.6	15.7	13.0	15.4	15.6	13.2
80-84 years old	16.0	16.1	15.0	14.5	14.8	10.3
85 years old and over...............	18.6	18.7	14.6	15.9	16.1	12.7
Sex:						
Male............................	34.3	34.0	41.1	37.3	36.5	48.6
Female	65.7	66.0	58.9	62.7	63.5	51.4
Race:						
White	68.5	68.0	80.4	68.2	67.5	79.3
Black	13.6	13.7	9.1	9.7	9.8	9.1
Other or unknown	18.0	18.3	10.6	22.1	22.8	11.6
Marital status: [3]						
Married	30.0	29.4	47.6	38.7	37.5	56.0
Widowed.........................	37.4	37.6	31.3	31.4	32.0	22.9
Divorced or separated	5.1	5.1	5.4	4.6	4.5	7.0
Never married.....................	17.1	17.3	10.3	14.6	14.9	11.5
Unknown.........................	10.4	10.6	5.3	10.6	11.2	2.7

[1] Patients on the rolls of the agency as of midnight the day prior to the survey.　[2] Patients removed from the rolls of the agency during the 12 months prior to the day of the survey. A patient could be included more than once if the individual had more than one episode of care during the year.　[3] For current patients, marital status at admission; for discharged patients, status at time of discharge.

Source: U.S. National Center for Health Statistics, unpublished data.

No. 198. Elderly Home Health Care Patients: 1993

[Covers the civilian noninstitutionalized population 65 years old and over who are home health care patients. Home health care is provided to individuals and families in their place of residence. Based on the 1993 National Home and Hospice Care Survey]

ITEM	CURRENT PATIENTS [1]		DISCHARGES [2]		ITEM	CURRENT PATIENTS [1]		DISCHARGES [2]	
	Number (1,000)	Percent distribution	Number (1,000)	Percent distribution		Number (1,000)	Percent distribution	Number (1,000)	Percent distribution
Total 65 years old and over	**1,080.2**	**100.0**	**2,622.7**	**100.0**	Medicare	816.9	75.6	2,235.9	85.3
					Medicaid	97.7	9.0	74.0	2.8
Received help with—					Services rendered last billing period:				
Bathing or showering.	589.0	54.5	1,059.8	40.4	Skilled nursing.	894.2	82.8	2,203.4	84.0
Dressing.	508.6	47.1	873.2	33.3	Personal care	475.9	44.1	842.6	32.1
Eating	132.2	12.2	227.8	8.7	Social services	124.1	11.5	299.3	11.4
Transferring in/out of					Counseling	44.2	4.1	117.7	4.5
a bed or chair	378.0	35.2	782.9	29.9	Medications	63.5	5.9	176.3	6.7
Using the toilet	286.6	26.5	533.2	20.3	Physical therapy . . .	188.8	17.5	822.9	31.4
Doing light house									
work	412.1	38.2	631.1	24.1	Homemaker/				
Managing money . . .	22.4	2.1	21.4	0.8	companion services	201.1	18.6	274.4	10.5
Shopping for					Referral services . . .	19.9	1.8	52.4	2.0
groceries or clothes.	146.9	13.6	196.7	7.5	Dietary and nutrition				
Using the telephone .	36.7	3.4	35.2	1.3	services	27.4	2.5	71.2	2.7
Preparing meals . . .	274.8	25.4	429.1	16.4	Physician services . .	17.0	1.6	39.8	1.5
Taking medications. .	278.7	25.8	650.7	24.8	High tech care.	12.8	1.2	50.5	1.9
Primary source of pay-					Occupational/				
ment of last billing:					vocational therapy .	39.5	3.7	132.5	5.1
Private insurance . . .	32.7	3.0	128.1	4.9	Speech therapy/				
Own income	25.1	2.3	39.5	1.5	audiology	14.5	1.3	41.3	1.6

[1] Patients on the rolls of the agency as of midnight the day prior to the survey.   [2] Patients removed from the rolls of the agency during the 12 months prior to the day of the survey. A patient could be included more than once if the individual had more than one episode of care during the year.

Source: U.S. National Center for Health Statistics, unpublished data.

No. 199. Home Health and Hospice Care Agencies, by Selected Characteristics: 1993

[**In percent, except total in thousands.** Based on the 1993 National Home and Hospice Care Survey. Home health care is provided to individuals and families in their place of residence. Hospice care is available in both the home and inpatient settings. Agencies which provide both types of care are classified according to how the majority of their patients are cared for. See source for details. For composition of regions, see table 27]

ITEM	AGENCIES			CURRENT PATIENTS [1]			DISCHARGES [2]		
	Total	Home health agency	Hospice	Total	Home health agency	Hospice	Total	Home health agency	Hospice
Total (1,000)	**8.4**	**7.4**	**1.0**	**1,501.3**	**1,451.2**	**50.1**	**3,945.1**	**3,688.0**	**257.2**
PERCENT DISTRIBUTION									
Ownership:									
Proprietary	33.1	37.1	3.6	26.5	27.1	8.3	23.5	24.7	7.6
Voluntary nonprofit.	48.5	42.5	93.9	60.1	59.1	90.8	67.4	65.7	91.1
Government and other	18.4	20.5	2.4	13.4	13.8	0.9	9.1	9.6	1.3
Certification:									
Medicare	81.5	82.7	67.6	89.9	89.6	86.5	95.9	96.1	89.4
Medicaid	80.4	82.5	60.0	90.6	90.5	80.1	93.2	93.5	82.5
Region:									
Northeast.	21.8	22.4	17.0	34.5	34.8	23.7	33.4	34.0	25.2
Midwest.	28.3	28.1	29.8	18.7	18.5	25.7	20.0	19.5	26.9
South	35.7	36.0	33.3	33.3	33.3	33.9	26.6	26.3	31.1
West.	14.3	13.5	19.9	13.5	13.4	16.6	20.0	20.3	16.8

[1] Patients on the rolls of the agency as of midnight the day prior to the survey.   [2] Patients removed from the rolls of the agency during the 12 months prior to the day of the survey. A patient could be included more than once if the individual had more than one episode of care during the year.

Source: U.S. National Center for Health Statistics, unpublished data.

No. 200. Nursing and Related Care Facilities: 1971 to 1993

ITEM	Unit	1971	1976	1978	1980	1982	1986	1991	1993
Nursing and related care: [1]									
Facilities	Number .	22,004	20,468	[2]18,722	[3]23,065	[4]25,849	[4]25,646	[4]33,006	(NA)
Beds.	1,000. . .	1,202	1,415	[2]1,349	[3]1,537	[4]1,642	[4]1,707	[4]1,921	(NA)
Resident patients	1,000. . .	1,076	1,293	[2]1,240	[3]1,396	[4]1,493	[4]1,553	[4]1,729	(NA)
Employees, full-time. . . .	1,000. . .	568	653	[2]664	[3]798	(NA)	(NA)	(NA)	(NA)
Per 1,000 patients . . .	Rate . . .	528	505	[2]535	[3]571	(NA)	(NA)	(NA)	(NA)
Skilled nursing facilities [5] . .	Number .	4,277	3,922	4,745	5,052	5,408	6,897	9,674	11,309
Beds.	1,000. . .	307	309	408	436	488	(NA)	567	617
Per 1,000 Medicare enrollees [6]	Rate . . .	15.1	13.7	17.3	17.7	19.1	(NA)	15.3	16.3

NA Not available. [1] Covers nursing homes with three beds or more and all other places providing some form of nursing, personal, or domiciliary care; standards vary widely among States. Includes skilled nursing facilities. 1971-1984 based on National Master Facility Inventory. Some changes in data beginning 1976 may be due to dependence on State collection. 1986 data based on the 1986 Inventory of Long Term Care Places. Data may not be strictly comparable with previous years. 1991 based on National Health Provider Inventory; excludes board and care homes for the mentally retarded. [2] Includes 1976 data for California, District of Columbia, New York, and North Carolina. [3] Excludes hospital-based nursing homes and includes 1978 data for Alaska and South Dakota. [4] Excludes hospital-based nursing homes. [5] Source: Through 1976, U.S. Social Security Administration, *Health Insurance Statistics* and unpublished data. Beginning 1978, U.S. Health Care Financing Administration, *Medicare Participating Providers and Suppliers of Health Services, 1980;* and unpublished data. Covers facilities and beds certified for participation under Medicare as of midyear. Includes facilities which have transfer agreements with one or more participating hospitals, and are engaged primarily in providing skilled nursing care and related services for the rehabilitation of injured, disabled, or sick persons. [6] Based on number of aged persons residing in United States who were enrolled in the Medicare hospital insurance program as of July 1 of year stated.

Source: Except as noted, U.S. National Center for Health Statistics, *Health Resources Statistics,* annual through 1976 and 1978; 1982, 1986, and 1991 *Advance Data from Vital and Health Statistics,* No. 111, No. 147, and No. 244; and unpublished data.

No. 201. Nursing and Related Care Facilities, by Selected Characteristics: 1991

[Excludes hospital-based nursing homes which numbered 767 with 51,897 residents in 1991. Based on the National Health Provider Inventor. For composition of regions, see table 27]

CHARACTERISTIC	TOTAL FACILITIES				NURSING HOMES [1]				BOARD AND CARE HOMES [2]			
	Homes	Beds (1,000)	Average number of beds	Occu-pancy rate	Homes	Beds (1,000)	Average number of beds	Occu-pancy rate	Homes	Beds (1,000)	Average number of beds	Occu-pancy rate
Total	33,006	1,920	58	90.0	14,744	1,558	106	91.5	18,262	362	20	83.6
REGION												
Northeast	5,834	414	71	93.5	2,654	328	124	95.3	3,180	86	27	86.6
Midwest	9,142	583	64	89.7	5,137	519	101	90.3	4,005	64	16	84.7
South	9,499	608	64	89.7	4,708	502	107	91.2	4,791	106	22	83.0
West	8,531	315	37	86.8	2,245	209	93	89.6	6,286	106	17	81.3
OWNERSHIP												
Government.	1,570	113	72	92.3	725	100	138	93.5	845	13	16	83.8
Proprietary.	24,256	1,347	56	89.1	10,522	1,086	103	90.7	13,734	262	19	82.6
Nonprofit.	7,180	459	64	92.2	3,497	372	106	93.5	3,683	87	24	86.8
SIZE												
Fewer than 10 beds . .	10,025	53	5	83.9	165	1	5	81.6	9,860	52	5	83.9
10 to 24 beds	5,281	82	15	85.5	398	7	18	88.5	4,883	74	15	85.2
25 to 49 beds	3,381	124	37	87.9	1,590	61	39	91.1	1,791	62	35	84.9
50 to 74 beds	3,792	229	60	90.9	3,050	184	60	92.1	742	44	60	85.8
75 to 99 beds	2,795	245	88	90.2	2,401	211	88	91.2	394	34	86	83.6
100 to 199 beds.	6,497	854	132	90.8	6,028	792	131	91.5	469	62	132	81.9
200 to 299 beds	942	218	231	90.1	847	196	231	91.3	95	22	228	79.0
300 to 499 beds	248	89	358	89.5	224	80	359	91.0	24	8	347	75.5
500 beds or more	45	28	618	94.7	41	25	608	96.6	4	3	721	78.8

[1] These facilities have three or more beds. [2] These facilities offer no nursing services and provide only personal care or supervisory care. Excludes board and care homes for the mentally retarded.

Source: U.S. National Center for Health Statistics, *Advance Data From Vital and Health Statistics,* No. 244; and unpublished data.

No. 202. Residential Facilities for Persons with Mental Retardation: 1970 to 1993

[For years ending **June 30.** Persons with mental retardation refers to those who have been so designated by State governments in the process of placing them into residential facilities]

ITEM	STATE OPERATED FACILITIES [1]					PRIVATE FACILITIES [3]			
	1970	1980 [2]	1985 [2]	1990 [2]	1993 [2]	1977	1982	1990	1993
Number of facilities [4]	190	394	881	1,321	1,765	10,219	14,605	41,588	58,790
Residents beginning of year	189,956	148,734	117,101	94,625	73,856	(NA)	(NA)	(NA)	(NA)
Admissions [5]	14,985	14,064	7,713	5,548	4,700	22,363	22,431	(NA)	(NA)
Deaths in institutions	3,496	2,142	1,537	1,100	1,167	891	920	(NA)	(NA)
Live releases [6]	14,702	16,225	10,310	7,620	7,258	12,384	12,999	(NA)	(NA)
Residents end of year [7]	186,743	140,230	112,183	91,640	69,760	89,120	115,032	188,902	229,279
Rate per 100,000 population [7]	92.5	62.2	47.5	34.7	31.9	40.9	50.0	76.0	89.6
Average daily residents	187,897	136,304	111,791	92,729	71,477	(NA)	(NA)	(NA)	(NA)
Maintenance expenditures per day per average daily resident (dollars) [8]	13	68	122	196	225	[9]19	[9]37	(NA)	(NA)

NA Not available.   [1] Data as submitted by many State agencies; figures reflect some estimates. Resident patients at the end of a year do not equal the number at the beginning of a succeeding year. Includes estimates for underreporting.   [2] Includes data for 142 facilities in 1980, 121 facilities in 1985, 108 in 1990, and 110 in 1993 operated as mental hospitals or other facilities and which have residents with mental retardation. The average daily number of residents with mental retardation in these facilities was 8,240 in 1980, 5,602 in 1985, 1,487 in 1990, and 1,515 in 1993.   [3] A privately-operated living quarter which provides 24-hour, 7-days-a-week responsibility for room, board, and supervision of mentally retarded persons. Excludes single-family homes providing services to a relative; and nursing homes, boarding homes, and foster homes not formally licensed or contracted as mental retardation service providers.   [4] Beginning 1985, reflects the development of a large number of community based State-operated facilities which were developed in the early 1980's.   [5] Includes readmissions and excludes transfers. Excludes people entering newly opened facilities.   [6] 1970, represents excess of residents released alive from facility over those returning to facility. Beginning 1980, total live releases.   [7] Based on Bureau of the Census estimated civilian population as of July 1. Estimates reflect revisions based on 1990 Census of Population.   [8] Reporting facilities only; includes salaries and wages, purchased provisions, fuel, light, water, etc.   [9] Represents average daily reimbursement rate per resident.

Source: 1970 State-operated facilities: U.S. Office of Human Development Services, *Residents in Public Institutions for the Mentally Retarded,* annual, and unpublished data; later State-operated facilities and private facilities: Center for Residential Services and Community Living (CRSCL), Institute on Community Integration, UAP, University of Minnesota, Minneapolis, MN, Magan, Blake, Prouty, and Larkin, Report No. 40, and earlier reports and unpublished data.

No. 203. Mental Health Facilities—Summary, by Type of Facility: 1990

[Revised 1990 data. Facilities, beds and inpatients as of year-end 1990; other data are for calendar year or fiscal year ending in a month other than December since facilities are permitted to report on either a calendar or fiscal year basis. Excludes private psychiatric office practice and psychiatric service modes of all types in hospitals or outpatient clinics of Federal agencies other than U.S. Dept. of Veterans Affairs. Excludes data from Puerto Rico, Virgin Islands, Guam, and other territories]

TYPE OF FACILITY	Number of facilities	INPATIENT BEDS		INPATIENTS		Average daily inpatients (1,000)	Inpatient care episodes [2] (1,000)	EXPENDITURES		Patient care staff [4] (1,000)
		Total (1,000)	Rate [1]	Total (1,000)	Rate [1]			Total (mil. dol.)	Per capita [3] (dol.)	
Total	5,284	272.2	111.5	229.7	93.0	224.4	2,260.9	28,357	116.3	471.8
Mental hospitals:										
State and county	270	98.4	40.3	90.3	37.0	89.7	365.7	7,705	31.6	112.8
Private [5]	967	75.0	30.7	60.3	24.7	58.4	509.0	8,093	33.2	99.6
General hospitals [6]	1,674	53.5	21.9	38.3	15.7	38.6	997.6	4,662	19.1	80.7
Veterans Administration [7]	141	21.7	8.9	17.2	7.1	17.3	215.6	1,480	6.1	29.7
Free-standing psychiatric outpatient clinics [8]	743	(X)	(X)	(X)	(X)	(X)	(X)	671	2.8	14.3
Other [9]	1,489	23.6	9.7	23.6	8.5	20.4	173.0	5,746	23.5	134.7

X Not applicable.   [1] Rate per 100,000 population. Based on Bureau of the Census estimated civilian population as of July 1.   [2] "Inpatient care episodes" is defined as the number of residents in inpatient facilities at the beginning of the year plus the total additions to inpatient facilities during the year.   [3] Based on Bureau of the Census estimated civilian population as of July 1.   [4] Full-time equivalent.   [5] Includes residential treatment centers for emotionally disturbed children.   [6] Non-Federal hospitals with separate psychiatric services.   [7] Includes U.S. Department of Veterans Affairs (VA) neuropsychiatric hospitals, VA general hospitals with separate psychiatric settings and VA freestanding psychiatric outpatient clinics.   [8] Includes mental health facilities which provide only psychiatric outpatient services.   [9] Includes other multiservice mental health facilities with two or more settings, which are not elsewhere classified, as well as freestanding partial care facilities which only provide psychiatric partial care services. Number of facilities, expenditures, and staff data also include freestanding psychiatric partial care facilities.

Source: U.S. Substance Abuse and Mental Health Services Administration, Center for Mental Health Services, unpublished data.

No. 204. Days of Disability, by Type and Selected Characteristics: 1970 to 1993

[Covers civilian noninstitutional population. Beginning 1985, the levels of estimates may not be comparable to estimates for 1970-1980 because the later data are based on a revised questionnaire and field procedures; for further information, see source. Based on National Health Interview Survey; see Appendix III. For composition of regions, see table 27]

ITEM	TOTAL DAYS OF DISABILITY (millions)						DAYS PER PERSON					
	1970	1980	1985	1990	1992	1993	1970	1980	1985	1990	1992	1993
Restricted-activity days [1] . .	2,913	4,165	3,453	3,669	4,096	4,346	14.6	19.1	14.8	14.9	16.3	17.1
Male	1,273	1,802	1,442	1,558	1,739	1,844	13.2	17.1	12.8	13.1	14.2	14.9
Female	1,640	2,363	2,011	2,111	2,357	2,502	15.8	21.0	16.6	16.7	18.2	19.2
White [2]	2,526	3,518	2,899	3,057	3,384	3,598	14.4	18.7	14.5	14.8	16.2	17.0
Black [2]	365	580	489	536	586	616	16.2	22.7	17.4	17.7	18.6	19.2
Hispanic [3]	(NA)	(NA)	228	(NA)	(NA)	(NA)	(NA)	(NA)	13.2	(NA)	(NA)	(NA)
Under 65 years	2,331	3,228	2,557	2,734	3,005	3,289	12.9	16.6	12.4	12.6	13.6	14.7
65 years and over	582	937	895	936	1,091	1,057	30.7	39.2	33.1	31.4	35.4	33.8
Northeast	709	862	689	656	684	798	14.5	17.9	13.8	13.2	13.7	15.9
Midwest	691	989	744	836	946	978	12.4	17.2	12.7	14.0	15.4	15.8
South	996	1,415	1,308	1,404	1,518	1,564	15.9	19.8	16.3	16.7	18.0	18.3
West	518	899	712	773	948	1,006	15.6	22.0	15.7	14.8	17.1	17.7
Family income:												
Under $10,000	(NA)	(NA)	893	662	712	741	(NA)	(NA)	25.8	27.3	29.0	30.2
$10,000 to $19,999 . . .	(NA)	(NA)	781	758	847	857	(NA)	(NA)	16.7	19.1	22.1	22.3
$20,000 to $34,999 . . .	(NA)	(NA)	791	715	750	849	(NA)	(NA)	12.1	13.5	14.6	15.7
$35,000 or more	(NA)	(NA)	568	912	940	1,086	(NA)	(NA)	9.9	10.3	10.3	11.2
Bed-disability days [4]	1,222	1,520	1,436	1,521	1,585	1,708	6.1	7.0	6.1	6.2	6.3	6.7
Male	503	616	583	625	648	688	5.2	5.9	5.2	5.2	5.3	5.6
Female	720	904	852	896	938	1,020	6.9	8.0	7.1	7.1	7.3	7.8
Under 65 years	959	1,190	1,064	1,115	1,130	1,286	5.3	6.1	5.1	5.2	5.1	5.8
65 years and over	263	330	371	406	455	422	13.8	13.8	13.7	13.6	14.8	13.5
Work-loss days [5]	417	485	575	621	597	666	5.4	5.0	5.3	5.3	5.1	5.6
Male	243	271	287	303	280	315	5.0	4.9	4.8	4.7	4.4	4.8
Female	175	215	288	319	317	351	5.9	5.1	6.0	5.9	5.9	6.4
School-loss days [6]	222	204	217	212	215	250	4.9	5.3	4.8	4.6	4.6	5.3
Male	108	95	100	100	101	121	4.7	4.8	4.4	4.3	4.2	5.0
Female	114	109	117	112	114	129	5.1	5.7	5.3	5.0	5.0	5.5

NA Not available. [1] A day when a person cuts down on his activities for more than half a day because of illness or injury. Includes bed-disability, work-loss, and school-loss days. Total includes other races and unknown income, not shown separately. [2] Beginning 1980, race was determined by asking the household respondent to report his race. In earlier years the racial classification of respondents was determined by interviewer observation. [3] Persons of Hispanic origin may be of any race. [4] A day when a person stayed in bed more than half a day because of illness or injury. Includes those work-loss and school-loss days actually spent in bed. [5] A day when a person lost more than half a workday because of illness or injury. Computed for persons 17 years of age and over (beginning 1985, 18 years of age and over) in the currently employed population, defined as those who were working or had a job or business from which they were not on layoff during the 2-week period preceding the week of interview. [6] Child's loss of more than half a school day because of illness or injury. Computed for children 6-16 years of age. Beginning 1985, children 5-17 years old.

Source: U.S. National Center for Health Statistics, *Vital and Health Statistics,* series 10, No. 190; and earlier reports and unpublished data.

No. 205. Costs of Unintentional Injuries: 1993

[Covers costs for accidents in which deaths or disabling injuries beyond the day of the accident occurred, together with vehicle accidents and fires]

COST	AMOUNT (bil. dol.)					PERCENT DISTRIBUTION				
	Total [1]	Motor vehicle	Work	Home	Other	Total [1]	Motor vehicle	Work	Home	Other
Total	407.5	167.3	111.9	86.5	58.9	100.0	100.0	100.0	100.0	100.0
Wage and productivity losses [2]	216.1	63.4	59.9	55.3	42.3	53.0	37.9	53.5	63.9	71.8
Medical expense	74.7	22.7	20.7	21.5	11.3	18.3	13.6	18.5	24.9	19.2
Administrative expenses [3]	50.0	38.3	14.4	2.0	1.3	12.3	22.9	12.9	2.3	2.2
Motor vehicle damage	40.7	40.7	4.1	(NA)	(NA)	10.0	24.3	3.7	(NA)	(NA)
Employer cost [4]	17.3	2.2	9.7	3.4	2.7	4.2	1.3	8.7	3.9	4.6
Fire loss	8.7	(NA)	3.1	4.3	1.3	2.1	(NA)	2.8	5.0	2.2

NA Not available. [1] Excludes duplication between work and motor vehicle ($17.1 billion) in 1993. [2] Actual loss of wages and household production and the present value of future earnings lost. [3] Includes the administrative cost of public and private insurance and police and legal costs. [4] Estimate of the uninsured costs incurred by employers, representing the money value of time lost by noninjured workers.

Source: National Safety Council, Itasca, IL, *Accident Facts, 1994* (copyright).

No. 206. Injuries Associated With Consumer Products: 1991 and 1992

[For products associated with more than 16,600 injuries in 1992. Estimates calculated from a representative sample of hospitals with emergency treatment departments in the United States. Data are estimates of the number of emergency room treated cases nationwide associated with various products. Product involvement does not necessarily mean the product caused the accident. Products were selected from the U.S. Consumer Product Safety Commission's National Electronic Injury Surveillance System]

PRODUCT	1991	1992	PRODUCT	1991	1992
Home maintenance:			General household appliances:		
Noncaustic cleaning equip. [1]	21,890	26,654	Cooking ranges, ovens, etc.	54,659	53,401
Cleaning agents (except soap)	38,397	43,758	Irons, clothes steamers	18,120	17,266
Paints, solvents, lubricants	21,430	23,383	Refrigerators, freezers	31,741	35,895
Misc. household chemicals	20,369	24,679	Washers, dryers	19,205	22,590
			Misc. household appliances	30,532	34,941
Home workshop equipment:					
Power home tools, except saws	29,014	31,742	Heating, cooling equipment: [4]		
Power home workshop saws	94,076	97,606	Chimneys, fireplaces	24,120	26,664
Welding, soldering, cutting tools	19,368	20,686	Fans (except stove)	21,126	17,050
Workshop manual tools	118,799	125,780	Heating stoves, space heaters	31,439	37,805
Misc. workshop equipment	40,147	46,407	Pipes, heating and plumbing	21,238	23,216
Household packaging and containers:			Home entertainment equipment:		
Cans, other containers	209,407	239,521	Pet supplies, equipment	23,177	26,703
Glass bottles, jars	69,837	63,170	Sound recording equip [5]	42,678	46,022
Paper, cardboard, plastic products	36,931	47,495	Television sets, stands	36,995	42,000
Housewares:					
Cookware, pots, pans	34,868	36,700	Personal use items:		
Cutlery, knives, unpowered	448,525	468,587	Cigarettes, lighters, fuels	20,355	23,547
Drinking glasses	134,790	130,200	Clothing	126,173	142,457
Scissors	30,973	34,602	Grooming devices	32,937	31,991
Small kitchen appliances	40,952	43,453	Jewelry	49,891	55,142
Tableware and accessories	116,796	120,940	Paper money, coins	31,796	30,274
Misc. housewares	55,635	61,201	Pencils, pens, other desk supplies	45,833	49,226
			Razors, shavers, razor blades	43,916	43,365
Home furnishing: [2]			Sewing equipment	32,044	29,814
Bathtub, shower structures	152,770	166,327			
Beds, mattresses, pillows	362,790	400,732	Yard and garden equipment:		
Carpets, rugs	97,784	112,763	Chains and saws	44,019	38,692
Chairs, sofas, sofa beds	381,024	413,759	Hand garden tools	38,796	36,374
Desks, cabinets, shelves, racks	210,188	228,676	Hatchets, axes	18,270	16,760
Electric fixtures, lamps, equipment	55,191	54,097	Lawn garden care equipment	54,507	51,324
Ladders, stools	179,422	189,210	Lawn mowers	76,133	85,202
Mirrors, mirror glass	23,325	24,928	Other power lawn equipment	19,424	21,598
Sinks, toilets	54,847	61,281			
Tables	332,775	345,271	Sports and recreation equipment:		
Other misc. accessories	53,181	57,555	Bicycles, accessories	600,649	649,536
			Exercise equipment	86,210	95,127
Home structures, construction: [3]			Mopeds, minibikes, ATV's [6]	127,371	132,271
Cabinets or door hardware	22,946	24,876	Nonpowder guns, BB's, pellets	32,562	34,552
Ceilings, walls, inside panels	227,618	262,572	Playground equipment	266,869	290,382
Counters, counter tops	33,748	36,888	Skateboards	56,435	44,068
Fences	122,111	123,014	Toboggans, sleds, snow disks, etc	38,282	43,273
Glass doors, windows, panels	217,916	216,193	Trampolines	38,823	43,665
Handrails, railings, banisters	40,765	42,965			
Nails, carpet tacks, etc	241,859	239,711	Miscellaneous products:		
Nonglass doors, panels	336,790	357,149	Dollies, carts	41,363	45,257
Porches, open side floors, etc	118,166	129,152	Gasoline and diesel fuels	18,882	19,205
Stairs, ramps, landings, floors	1,693,175	1,879,029	Nursery equipment	112,753	117,732
Window, door sills, frames	53,523	60,147	Toys	163,624	177,061
Misc. construction materials	85,492	95,147			

[1] Includes detergent.   [2] Includes accessories.   [3] Includes materials.   [4] Includes ventilating equipment.   [5] Includes reproducing equipment.   [6] All-terrain vehicles.

Source: National Safety Council, Itasca, IL, *Accident Facts*, annual (copyright).

No. 207. Injuries, by Sex: 1970 to 1993

[Covers civilian noninstitutional population and comprises incidents leading to restricted activity and/or medical attention. Beginning 1982, data not strictly comparable with other years. See headnote, table 204. Based on National Health Interview Survey; see Appendix III]

YEAR	INJURIES (mil.)		RATE PER 100 POPULATION			YEAR	INJURIES (mil.)		RATE PER 100 POPULATION		
	Male	Female	Total	Male	Female		Male	Female	Total	Male	Female
1970	31.8	24.2	28.0	33.0	23.3	1987	33.6	28.4	26.0	29.1	23.1
1975	39.4	32.5	34.4	39.1	30.0	1988	32.4	26.8	24.6	27.7	21.6
1980	39.0	29.1	31.2	37.1	25.8	1989	31.7	26.3	23.8	26.9	20.9
1983	33.0	28.1	26.6	29.8	23.7	1990	33.6	26.6	24.4	28.1	21.0
1984	33.7	27.4	26.4	30.1	22.9	1991	32.2	27.5	24.0	26.7	21.5
1985	34.6	28.0	26.8	30.6	23.1	1992	32.8	26.8	23.7	26.8	20.7
1986	34.0	28.4	26.4	29.8	23.3	1993	33.4	28.7	24.4	27.0	22.0

Source: U.S. National Center for Health Statistics, *Vital and Health Statistics*, series 10, No. 190, and earlier reports; and unpublished data.

No. 208. Injuries, by Age and Condition: 1993

[See headnote, table 207]

AGE AND TYPE	INJURIES (mil.)			RATE PER 100 POPULATION		
	Total	Male	Female	Total	Male	Female
Total [1]	**62.1**	**33.4**	**28.7**	**24.4**	**27.0**	**22.0**
Under 5 years	5.0	2.7	2.2	24.9	26.6	23.1
5 to 17 years	12.5	7.6	4.9	26.2	31.0	21.2
18 to 44 years	29.1	16.7	12.4	27.5	32.0	23.2
45 years and over	15.6	6.5	9.1	19.2	17.4	20.7
Fractures [2]	7.9	4.3	3.6	3.1	3.5	2.8
Sprains and strains	14.2	7.4	6.8	5.6	6.0	5.2
Open wounds and lacerations	12.5	8.6	3.9	4.9	7.0	3.0
Contusions [3]	12.1	6.2	5.9	4.8	5.0	4.5
Other	15.4	6.8	8.5	6.1	5.5	6.5

[1] Includes unknown place of accident not shown separately. [2] Includes dislocations. [3] Includes superficial injuries.

Source: U.S. National Center for Health Statistics, *Vital and Health Statistics,* series 10, No. 190, and earlier reports; and unpublished data.

No. 209. Persons With Disabilities: 1991-92

[Covers the civilian noninstitutional resident population 15 years old and over and members of the Armed Forces living off post or with their families on post. The criteria for presence of disability varied by age. In general, a disability is considered a reduced ability to perform tasks one would normally do at a given stage in life. Based on the Survey of Income and Program Participation; for details, see source]

CHARACTERISTIC	PERSONS (1,000)			PERCENT DISTRIBUTION		
	Total	Male	Female	Total	Male	Female
Total 15 years old and over	**195,729**	**93,985**	**101,744**	**100.0**	**100.0**	**100.0**
With a disability	46,023	21,040	24,982	23.5	22.4	24.6
Severe	23,588	9,593	13,995	12.1	10.2	13.8
Not severe	22,435	11,447	10,987	11.5	12.2	10.8
With functional limitations	34,163	14,774	19,389	17.5	15.7	19.1
Has difficulty—						
Seeing words and letters	9,685	4,006	5,679	5.0	4.3	5.6
Hearing normal conversation	10,928	6,421	4,506	5.6	6.8	4.4
Having speech understcod	2,284	1,316	968	1.2	1.4	1.0
Lifting or carrying 10 lbs.	16,205	5,218	10,987	8.3	5.6	10.8
Climbing stairs without resting	17,469	6,465	11,003	8.9	6.9	10.8
Walking three city blocks	17,319	6,653	10,665	8.9	7.1	10.5
Is unable to—						
See words and letters	1,590	661	929	0.8	0.7	0.9
Hear normal conversation	924	529	396	0.5	0.6	0.4
Have speech understood	237	141	95	0.1	0.2	0.1
Lift or carry 10 lbs.	7,734	2,375	5,359	4.0	2.5	5.3
Climb stairs without resting	9,116	3,277	5,839	4.7	3.5	5.7
Walk three city blocks	8,972	3,236	5,736	4.6	3.4	5.6
With limitations of activities of daily living	7,919	3,013	4,907	4.1	3.2	4.8
Has difficulty—						
Getting around inside the house	3,664	1,376	2,288	1.9	1.5	2.3
Getting in/out of bed or a chair	5,280	2,006	3,274	2.7	2.1	3.2
Taking a bath or shower	4,501	1,550	2,951	2.3	1.7	2.9
Dressing	3,234	1,262	1,971	1.7	1.3	1.9
Eating	1,077	437	640	0.6	0.5	0.6
Getting to or using the toilet	2,084	767	1,317	1.1	0.8	1.3
Needs personal assistance with—						
Getting around inside the house	1,706	698	1,008	0.9	0.7	1.0
Getting in/out of bed or a chair	2,022	796	1,227	1.0	0.9	1.2
Taking a bath or shower	2,718	1,028	1,691	1.4	1.1	1.7
Dressing	2,060	866	1,193	1.1	0.9	1.2
Eating	487	226	261	0.3	0.2	0.3
Getting to or using the toilet	1,157	477	680	0.6	0.5	0.7
With limitations of instrumental activities of daily living	11,694	4,601	7,093	6.0	4.9	7.0
Has difficulty—						
Going outside the home	7,809	2,759	5,050	4.0	2.9	5.0
Keeping track of money and bills	3,901	1,621	2,280	2.0	1.7	2.2
Preparing meals	4,530	1,699	2,831	2.3	1.8	2.8
Doing light housework	6,313	2,191	4,122	3.2	2.3	4.1
Using the telephone	3,130	1,749	1,381	1.6	1.9	1.4
Needs personal assistance with—						
Going outside the home	6,011	2,017	3,994	3.1	2.2	3.9
Keeping track of money and bills	3,425	1,460	1,965	1.8	1.6	1.9
Preparing meals	3,685	1,447	2,238	1.9	1.5	2.2
Doing light housework	4,745	1,626	3,119	2.4	1.7	3.1
Using the telephone	933	509	424	0.5	0.5	0.4

Source: U.S. Bureau of the Census, *Current Population Reports,* P70-33.

No. 210. Children Immunized Against Specified Diseases: 1991 to 1993

[**In percent.** Covers civilian noninstitutionalized population ages 19 months to 35 months. Based on estimates from the National Health Interview Survey. Excludes respondents with unknown or missing information. See Appendix III]

VACCINATION	1991, total	1992, total	1993 Total	1993 White	1993 Black	1993 Other
Diphtheria-tetanus-pertussis (DPT)/ diphtheria-tetanus:						
3+ doses	68.8	83.0	88.2	89.4	82.6	84.5
4+ doses	43.3	59.0	72.1	73.0	69.2	64.7
Polio: 3+ doses	53.2	72.4	78.9	79.8	73.4	80.8
Hib [1]: 3+ doses	1.7	28.2	55.0	57.0	44.8	56.9
Hepatitis B: 3+ doses	(NA)	(NA)	16.3	16.3	16.0	16.7
Measles containing	82.0	82.5	84.1	86.0	76.9	72.5
3 DPT/3 polio/1 MMR [2]	50.0	68.7	74.5	75.7	69.2	68.0
4 DPT/3 polio/1 MMR [2][3]	37.0	55.3	67.1	68.4	61.8	58.4

NA Not available. [1] Haemophilus B. [2] Measles, measles/rubella, measles/mumps, and measles/mumps/rubella. [3] Up-to-date for age.

Source: U.S. Centers for Disease Control and Prevention, Atlanta, GA, the National Health Interview Survey.

No. 211. Specified Reportable Diseases—Cases Reported: 1970 to 1993

[Figures should be interpreted with caution. Although reporting of some of these diseases is incomplete, the figures are of value in indicating trends of disease incidence. Includes cases imported from outside the United States. See *Historical Statistics, Colonial Times to 1970*, series B 291-303, for related data]

DISEASE	1970	1980	1985	1988	1989	1990	1991	1992	1993
AIDS [1]	(NA)	(NA)	8,249	31,001	33,722	41,595	43,672	45,472	103,691
Amebiasis	2,888	5,271	4,433	2,860	3,217	3,328	2,989	2,942	2,970
Aseptic meningitis	6,480	8,028	10,619	7,234	10,274	11,852	14,526	12,223	12,848
Botulism [2]	12	89	122	84	89	92	114	91	97
Brucellosis (undulant fever)	213	183	153	96	95	85	104	105	120
Chickenpox (1,000)	(3)	190.9	178.2	192.9	185.4	173.1	147.1	158.4	134.7
Diphtheria	435	3	3	2	3	4	5	4	-
Encephalitis:									
Primary infectious [4]	1,580	1,362	1,376	882	981	1,341	1,021	774	919
Post infectious [4]	370	40	161	121	88	105	82	129	170
Haemophilius influenza	(3)	(3)	(3)	(3)	(3)	(3)	2,764	1,412	1,419
Hepatitis: B (serum) (1,000)	8.3	19.0	26.6	23.2	23.4	21.1	18.0	16.1	13.4
A (infectious) (1,000)	56.8	29.1	23.2	28.5	35.8	31.4	24.4	23.1	24.2
Unspecified (1,000)	(3)	11.9	5.5	2.5	2.3	1.7	1.3	0.9	0.6
Non-A, non-B (1,000) [5]	(3)	(3)	4.2	2.6	2.5	2.6	3.6	6.0	4.8
Legionellosis	(3)	(3)	830	1,085	1,190	1,370	1,317	1,339	1,280
Leprosy (Hansen disease)	129	223	361	184	163	198	154	172	187
Leptospirosis	47	85	57	54	93	77	58	54	51
Lyme disease	(3)	(3)	(3)	(3)	(3)	(3)	9,465	9,895	8,257
Malaria	3,051	2,062	1,049	1,099	1,277	1,292	1,278	1,087	1,411
Measles (1,000)	47.4	13.5	2.8	3.4	18.2	27.8	9.6	2.2	0.3
Meningococcal infections	2,505	2,840	2,479	2,964	2,727	2,451	2,130	2,134	2,637
Mumps (1,000)	105.0	8.6	3.0	4.9	5.7	5.3	4.3	2.6	1.7
Pertussis [6] (1,000)	4.2	1.7	3.6	3.5	4.2	4.6	2.7	4.1	6.6
Plague	13	18	17	15	4	2	11	13	10
Poliomyelitis, acute [7]	33	9	7	9	9	6	9	6	3
Psittacosis	35	124	119	114	116	113	94	92	60
Rabies, animal	3,224	6,421	5,565	4,651	4,724	4,826	6,910	8,589	9,377
Rabies, human	3	-	1	-	1	1	3	1	3
Rheumatic fever, acute [8]	3,227	432	90	158	144	108	127	75	112
Rubella [9] (1,000)	56.6	3.9	0.6	0.2	0.4	1.1	1.4	0.2	0.2
Salmonellosis [10] (1,000)	22.1	33.7	65.3	48.9	47.8	48.6	48.2	40.9	41.6
Shigellosis [11] (1,000)	13.8	19.0	17.1	30.6	25.0	27.1	23.5	23.9	32.2
Tetanus	148	95	83	53	53	64	57	45	48
Toxic-shock syndrome	(3)	(3)	384	390	400	322	280	244	212
Trichinosis	109	131	61	45	30	129	62	41	16
Tuberculosis [12] (1,000)	37.1	27.7	22.2	22.4	23.5	25.7	26.3	26.7	25.3
Tularemia	172	234	177	201	152	152	193	159	132
Typhoid fever	346	510	402	436	460	552	501	414	440
Typhus fever:									
Flea-borne (endemic-murine)	27	81	37	54	41	50	43	28	25
Tick-borne (Rocky Mt. spotted fever)	380	1,163	714	609	623	651	628	502	456
Sexually transmitted diseases:									
Gonorrhea (1,000)	600	1,004	911	720	733	690	620	501	439
Syphilis (1,000)	91	69	68	103	111	134	129	113	101
Other (1,000)	2.2	1.0	2.3	5.2	4.9	4.6	4.0	2.2	1.7

- Represents zero. NA Not available. [1] Acquired immunodeficiency syndrome was not a notifiable disease until 1984. Figures are shown for years in which cases were reported to the CDC. Beginning 1993, based on revised classification system and expanded surveillance case definition. [2] Beginning in 1980, includes foodborne, infant, wound, and unspecified cases. [3] Disease was not notifiable. [4] Beginning 1980, reported data reflect new diagnostic categories. [5] Includes some persons positive for antibody to hepatitis C virus who do not have hepatitis. [6] Whooping cough. [7] Revised. Data subject to annual revisions. [8] Based on reports from States: 38 in 1970, 37 in 1980, 31 in 1985, 29 in 1988, 28 in 1989, 30 in 1990, 23 in 1991, and 26 in 1992 and 1993. [9] German measles. [10] Excludes typhoid fever. [11] Bacillary dysentery. [12] Newly reported active cases. New diagnostic standards introduced in 1980.

Source: U.S. Centers for Disease Control and Prevention, Atlanta, GA, *Summary of Notifiable Diseases, United States, Morbidity and Mortality Weekly Report,* vol. 43, No. 32, August 19, 1994.

No. 212. Selected Measures of Hospital Utilization for Patients Discharged With the Diagnosis of Human Immunodeficiency Virus (HIV): 1985 to 1993

[See headnote, table 189]

MEASURE OF UTILIZATION	Unit	1985	1989	1990	1991	1992	1993
Number of patients discharged [1]	1,000....	23	140	146	165	194	225
Rate of patient discharges [2]	Rate	1.0	5.7	5.9	6.6	7.6	8.8
Number of days of care	1,000....	387	1,731	2,188	2,108	2,136	2,561
Rate of days of care [2]	Rate	16.3	70.2	87.7	84.1	84.3	99.9
Average length of stay [3]	Days	17.1	12.4	14.9	12.8	11.0	11.4

[1] Comparisons beginning 1989 with data for earlier years should be made with caution as estimates of change may reflect improvements in the 1988 design rather than true changes in hospital use. [2] Per 10,000 population. Based on Bureau of the Census estimated civilian population as of July 1. Population estimates for the 1980's do not reflect revised estimates based on the 1990 Census of Population. [3] For similar data on all patients, see table 189.

Source: National Center for Health Statistics, *Vital and Health Statistics,* series 13.

No. 213. AIDS Cases Reported, by Patient Characteristic: 1981 to 1994

[**Provisional.** For cases reported in the year shown. For data on AIDS deaths, see table 130. Data are subject to retrospective changes and may differ from those data in table 211]

CHARACTERISTIC	Total	1981-1985	1986	1987	1988	1989	1990	1991	1992	1993	1994
Total [1]	427,392	15,331	13,083	21,503	30,703	33,631	41,762	43,776	45,964	103,360	78,279
Age:											
Under 5 years old	4,711	201	155	271	443	494	583	530	615	680	739
5 to 12 years old	1,184	23	27	56	127	103	144	149	142	202	211
13 to 29 years old	78,838	3,224	2,794	4,382	6,261	6,703	8,087	7,827	7,918	18,671	12,971
30 to 39 years old	195,304	7,214	6,078	9,826	14,176	15,555	18,994	20,026	20,760	47,148	35,527
40 to 49 years old	103,894	3,215	2,685	4,661	6,539	7,351	9,764	10,655	11,632	26,609	20,783
50 to 59 years old	31,319	1,143	966	1,594	2,142	2,418	2,940	3,248	3,442	7,455	5,971
Over 60 years old	12,142	311	378	713	1,015	1,007	1,250	1,341	1,455	2,595	2,077
Sex:											
Male	368,920	14,247	12,028	19,666	27,417	29,973	36,871	38,087	39,608	86,802	64,221
Female	58,472	1,084	1,055	1,837	3,286	3,658	4,891	5,689	6,356	16,558	14,058
Race/ethnic group:											
White [2]	214,061	9,125	7,769	13,253	17,050	18,597	22,378	22,163	22,507	48,039	33,180
Black [2]	146,159	3,981	3,392	5,435	9,141	10,292	13,250	14,684	16,103	38,424	31,457
Hispanic	62,419	2,133	1,810	2,608	4,236	4,371	5,685	6,446	6,789	15,642	12,699
Other/unknown	4,753	92	112	207	276	371	449	483	565	1,255	943
Leading States: [3]											
New York	83,197	5,295	3,804	4,010	6,945	5,991	8,368	8,135	8,322	17,383	14,944
California	78,084	3,498	2,524	5,188	5,692	6,449	7,373	7,713	8,821	18,690	12,136
Florida	43,978	1,066	1,031	1,633	2,650	3,448	4,018	5,471	5,086	10,958	8,617
Texas	30,712	830	949	1,666	2,214	2,382	3,317	3,053	2,930	7,492	5,879
New Jersey	25,089	952	781	1,516	2,461	2,235	2,457	2,296	2,024	5,374	4,993
Illinois	14,255	344	347	628	984	1,120	1,269	1,612	1,887	2,960	3,104
Pennsylvania	12,754	337	305	665	852	1,072	1,223	1,233	1,347	3,192	2,528
Georgia	12,228	285	303	518	841	1,098	1,229	1,468	1,399	2,842	2,245
Maryland	10,534	229	190	457	549	711	983	972	1,201	2,520	2,722
Massachusetts	9,254	296	286	454	708	750	839	959	863	2,698	1,401
District of Columbia	7,129	285	237	466	504	496	733	711	710	1,588	1,399
Louisiana	6,611	177	165	334	402	507	701	822	825	1,439	1,239
Ohio	6,509	95	214	342	504	492	692	631	778	1,577	1,184
Virginia	6,318	174	158	244	350	397	748	682	780	1,623	1,162
Michigan	6,240	104	151	212	455	505	580	636	741	1,821	1,035
Washington	5,922	173	170	324	341	525	752	583	564	1,558	932
Connecticut	5,754	167	180	255	413	432	427	565	649	1,754	912
Missouri	5,635	82	73	241	410	443	580	658	713	1,722	713
North Carolina	5,419	90	81	209	277	446	571	602	585	1,371	1,187
Colorado	4,571	126	166	226	325	388	365	431	406	1,322	816
South Carolina	4,441	55	58	84	174	326	376	342	397	1,471	1,158
Tennessee	3,833	25	72	73	329	266	340	353	408	1,203	764
Arizona	3,774	78	77	214	275	322	315	280	382	1,219	612
Indiana	3,314	55	71	133	78	397	294	313	400	948	622
Alabama	3,023	39	32	154	212	216	239	376	440	733	582
Oregon	2,942	52	61	165	176	227	336	257	288	774	606
Minnesota	2,346	57	98	130	167	176	203	215	217	661	422
Wisconsin	2,180	35	41	96	115	130	212	213	230	729	379
Oklahoma	2,170	33	51	109	152	168	206	188	270	724	269
Nevada	2,162	18	36	89	119	178	189	261	248	637	387
Percent of total	96.0	98.2	97.2	96.9	96.6	96.0	95.6	96.0	95.5	95.8	95.7

[1] Includes other States not shown separately, and persons whose residence is unknown. [2] Non-Hispanic. [3] States with at least 2,000 total cases reported through 1994.

Source: U.S. Centers for Disease Control and Prevention, Atlanta, GA, unpublished data.

No. 214. Acute Conditions, by Type: 1970 to 1993

[Covers civilian noninstitutional population. Estimates include only acute conditions which were medically attended or caused at least 1 day of restricted activity. Based on National Health Interview Survey; see Appendix III. See headnote, table 204. For composition of regions, see table 27]

YEAR AND CHARACTERISTIC	NUMBER OF CONDITIONS (mil.)					RATE PER 100 POPULATION				
	Infective and parasitic	Respiratory Common cold	Influenza	Digestive system	Injuries	Infective and parasitic	Respiratory Common cold	Influenza	Digestive system	Injuries
1970	48.2	(NA)	(NA)	23.0	59.2	24.1	(NA)	(NA)	11.5	29.6
1975	47.6	(NA)	(NA)	21.6	76.2	22.8	(NA)	(NA)	10.3	36.4
1980	53.6	(NA)	(NA)	24.9	72.7	24.6	(NA)	(NA)	11.4	33.4
1985	47.8	(NA)	(NA)	16.3	64.0	20.5	(NA)	(NA)	7.0	27.4
1990	51.7	61.5	106.8	13.0	60.1	21.0	25.0	43.4	5.3	24.4
1991	46.1	71.2	129.6	16.5	59.7	18.5	28.6	52.1	6.6	24.0
1992	56.2	64.6	107.3	17.6	59.6	22.4	25.7	42.7	7.0	23.7
1993, total [1]	**54.3**	**68.2**	**132.6**	**16.1**	**62.1**	**21.3**	**26.8**	**52.2**	**6.3**	**24.4**
Under 5 years old	10.8	13.2	13.0	2.0	5.0	54.4	66.3	65.4	9.9	24.9
5 to 17 years old	20.0	18.9	35.1	4.0	12.5	42.2	39.8	73.7	8.4	26.2
18 to 24 years old	4.2	6.4	13.3	1.7	7.4	17.5	26.4	55.0	7.2	30.5
25 to 44 years old	11.0	17.8	46.6	5.0	21.8	13.5	21.8	57.1	6.1	26.6
45 to 64 years old	5.7	8.0	17.2	2.3	9.3	11.4	16.1	34.6	4.6	18.8
65 years old and over	2.4	3.9	7.5	1.1	6.2	7.8	12.6	23.9	3.6	19.9
Male	23.9	31.5	59.9	6.8	33.4	19.3	25.5	48.4	5.5	27.0
Female	30.3	36.7	72.8	9.3	28.7	23.2	28.1	55.7	7.1	22.0
White	47.1	56.1	117.9	13.1	52.9	22.3	26.6	55.8	6.2	25.0
Black	5.9	9.5	9.6	2.7	7.5	18.3	29.6	29.9	8.5	23.4
Northeast	11.7	13.4	18.5	2.1	11.3	23.3	26.7	37.1	4.2	22.7
Midwest	10.7	17.6	37.0	3.4	18.5	17.3	28.4	59.6	5.4	29.8
South	23.1	20.7	34.0	6.1	19.8	27.1	24.3	39.8	7.1	23.2
West	8.7	16.5	43.1	4.6	12.4	15.3	29.0	75.9	8.0	21.9
Family income:										
Under $10,000	5.7	9.3	14.2	2.5	7.0	23.2	38.0	57.8	10.0	28.6
$10,000 to $19,999	7.4	9.8	21.2	2.7	10.5	19.4	25.5	55.1	7.1	27.4
$20,000 to $34,999	11.9	12.7	31.6	3.6	13.6	22.0	23.5	58.7	6.7	25.2
$35,000 or more	21.7	26.2	49.1	4.9	22.7	22.4	27.1	50.7	5.0	23.5

NA Not available. [1] Includes other races and unknown income not shown separately.
Source: U.S. National Center for Health Statistics, *Vital and Health Statistics,* series 10, No. 190, and earlier reports; and unpublished data.

No. 215. Prevalence of Selected Chronic Conditions, by Age and Sex: 1993

[Covers civilian noninstitutional population. Conditions classified according to ninth revision of International Classification of Diseases. Based on National Health Interview Survey; see Appendix III. See headnote, table 204]

CHRONIC CONDITION	Conditions (1,000)	RATE [1]							
		Male				Female			
		Under 45 years old	45 to 64 years old	65 to 74 years old	75 years old and over	Under 45 years old	45 to 64 years old	65 to 74 years old	75 years old and over
Arthritis	32,642	28.0	182.7	373.8	467.2	36.6	280.6	533.3	583.2
Dermatitis, including eczema	9,896	30.1	34.0	21.4	[2]18.9	49.0	44.3	48.3	40.5
Trouble with—									
Dry (itching) skin	5,170	11.7	20.0	49.9	27.2	20.2	27.4	42.9	29.0
Ingrown nails	6,237	18.0	27.4	23.3	52.8	17.4	37.6	48.1	77.0
Corns and calluses	5,117	9.2	16.3	25.0	35.8	14.0	50.2	54.6	60.9
Visual impairments	9,302	31.4	67.3	89.6	154.1	13.1	32.9	44.6	133.3
Cataracts	6,067	2.5	13.7	87.1	139.4	[2]1.3	25.9	135.9	247.6
Hearing impairments	24,160	48.7	189.3	320.5	458.8	34.3	101.1	206.0	360.4
Tinnitus	8,845	17.3	68.2	110.5	79.4	15.1	52.1	93.5	101.3
Deformities or orthopedic impairments	31,182	101.1	183.1	146.4	183.0	95.5	162.4	178.0	210.2
Ulcer	4,569	11.2	18.9	29.3	38.1	14.2	30.5	41.5	35.0
Hernia of abdominal cavity	4,900	7.2	38.1	69.0	87.6	4.8	27.8	63.0	75.5
Frequent indigestion	6,253	19.1	31.1	21.3	49.9	17.1	39.8	52.7	49.0
Frequent constipation	4,460	4.7	8.6	29.4	60.8	12.2	38.9	43.4	102.6
Diabetes	7,813	8.8	64.8	99.6	102.1	8.5	59.1	103.7	108.3
Migraine	11,023	22.1	23.4	[2]8.7	[2]2.7	63.9	93.2	29.3	27.4
Heart conditions	21,255	27.9	131.3	346.8	375.6	38.1	107.6	223.8	332.8
High blood pressure (Hypertension)	27,549	35.1	210.6	323.3	304.5	32.4	223.1	359.4	387.7
Varicose veins of lower extremities	7,641	4.6	19.2	39.0	33.1	26.5	87.0	93.9	100.7
Hemorrhoids	10,111	21.3	66.3	79.7	42.1	30.2	67.1	72.2	90.7
Chronic bronchitis	13,820	43.8	49.0	58.6	45.9	58.3	72.6	78.2	53.1
Asthma	13,074	53.9	30.1	51.9	[2]26.4	53.8	58.9	53.8	50.0
Hay fever, allergic rhinitis without asthma	23,743	87.4	98.9	75.6	41.9	99.1	113.4	87.4	71.7
Chronic sinusitis	37,293	119.3	174.7	174.5	126.4	150.6	195.2	167.9	115.0

[1] Conditions per 1,000 persons. [2] Figure does not meet standards of reliability or precision.
Source: U.S. National Center for Health Statistics, *Vital and Health Statistics,* series 10, No. 190, and earlier reports; and unpublished data.

No. 216. Substance Abuse Treatment Services: 1992

[As of **September 30.** Based on the National Drug and Alcoholism Treatment Unit Survey (NDATUS), a census of all known drug abuse and alcoholism treatment facilities in the United States. Data collected in cooperation with State agencies which defined what constitutes a facility for reporting purposes]

TYPE OF CARE AND LOCATION	Service locations reporting [1]	All clients	Drug abuse clients only	Alcoholism clients only	Clients with both problems	Clients with a drug problem [2]	Clients with an alcohol problem [3]
Total	**11,315**	**944,880**	**237,004**	**348,677**	**359,198**	**596,202**	**707,876**
TYPE OF CARE							
Detoxification: [4] Hospital inpatient	1,026	8,256	1,444	2,377	4,435	5,879	6,812
Free-standing residential	566	6,656	1,142	2,730	2,785	3,926	5,514
Rehab/residential: [5]							
Hospital inpatient	928	16,582	1,675	4,266	10,641	12,316	14,907
Short-term—30 days or less	963	19,077	2,671	5,580	10,825	13,496	16,406
Long-term—over 30 days	2,481	71,368	16,644	11,708	43,017	59,661	54,725
Ambulatory: [6]							
Outpatient	7,528	752,605	196,239	303,998	252,368	448,607	556,366
Intensive outpatient [7]	2,496	62,234	10,932	17,319	33,983	44,915	51,302
Detoxification [8]	332	8,102	6,258	700	1,144	7,402	1,844
UNIT LOCATION							
Community mental health care	1,440	146,941	30,987	62,094	53,860	84,847	115,954
Free-standing nonresidential facility	4,923	506,774	140,795	208,259	157,721	298,515	365,980
Hospital [9]	1,727	118,599	29,941	33,784	54,873	84,815	88,657
Correctional facility	312	30,658	5,708	3,999	20,951	26,659	24,950
Halfway house	994	23,125	3,447	5,854	13,824	17,272	19,678
Other residential facility	1,480	64,369	15,322	16,153	32,895	48,217	49,048
Other site	139	9,775	2,526	3,316	3,933	6,459	7,249
Multiple sites	255	42,963	7,505	15,046	20,412	27,917	35,458
Unknown	45	1,675	773	173	729	1,502	902

[1] Some units provide more than one type of treatment but are counted only once in the total. [2] The sum of clients with a drug problem and clients with both diagnoses. [3] The sum of clients with an alcohol problem and clients with both diagnoses. [4] 24 hour care for the withdrawal and transition to ongoing treatment. [5] Other than detoxification. Provides treatment services for dependency. [6] Ambulatory care provides care in a nonresidential setting. [7] "Intensive" outpatient involves at least 2 hours of treatment a day for 3 or more days a week. [8] Less than 24 hour care. [9] Includes general hospitals, alcoholism hospitals, mental/psychiatric hospitals, and other specialized hospitals.

Source: U.S. Substance Abuse and Mental Health Services Administration and U.S. Institute on Alcohol Abuse and Alcoholism, *1992 National Drug and Alcoholism Treatment Unit Survey: Final Report.*

No. 217. Drug Use, by Type of Drug and Age Group: 1974 to 1993

[**In percent.** Current users are those who used drugs at least once within month prior to this study. Based on national samples of respondents residing in households. Subject to sampling variability; see source]

AGE AND TYPE OF DRUG	EVER USED					CURRENT USER				
	1974	1979	1985	1988	1993	1974	1979	1985	1988	1993
12 TO 17 YEARS OLD										
Marijuana	23.0	30.9	23.2	17.4	11.7	12.0	16.7	11.9	6.4	4.9
Cocaine	3.6	5.4	4.8	3.4	1.1	1.0	1.4	1.4	1.1	0.4
Inhalants	8.5	9.8	9.6	8.8	5.9	0.7	2.0	3.7	2.0	1.4
Hallucinogens	6.0	7.1	3.2	3.5	2.9	1.3	2.2	1.2	0.8	0.5
Heroin	1.0	0.5	0.4	0.6	0.2	(B)	(B)	0.1	(B)	0.2
Stimulants [1]	5.0	3.4	5.5	4.2	2.1	1.0	1.2	1.6	1.2	0.5
Sedatives [1]	5.0	3.2	4.1	2.3	1.4	1.0	1.1	1.0	0.6	0.2
Tranquilizers [1]	3.0	4.1	4.9	2.0	1.2	1.0	0.6	0.6	0.2	0.2
Analgesics [1]	(NA)	3.2	6.0	4.1	3.7	(NA)	0.6	1.7	0.9	0.7
Alcohol	54.0	70.3	55.4	50.2	41.3	34.0	37.2	31.0	25.2	18.0
Cigarettes	52.0	54.1	45.3	42.3	34.5	25.0	12.1	15.3	11.8	9.6
18 TO 25 YEARS OLD										
Marijuana	52.7	68.2	59.4	56.4	47.4	25.2	35.4	21.9	15.5	11.1
Cocaine	12.7	27.5	24.4	19.7	12.5	3.1	9.3	7.5	4.5	1.5
Inhalants	9.2	16.5	13.0	12.5	9.9	(B)	1.2	0.8	1.7	1.1
Hallucinogens	16.6	25.1	11.6	13.8	12.5	2.5	4.4	1.8	1.9	1.3
Heroin	4.5	3.5	1.3	0.3	0.7	(B)	(B)	0.3	(B)	0.4
Stimulants [1]	17.0	18.2	17.5	11.3	6.4	3.7	3.5	3.8	2.4	0.9
Sedatives [1]	15.0	17.0	11.8	5.5	2.7	1.6	2.8	1.6	0.9	0.6
Tranquilizers [1]	10.0	15.8	12.6	7.8	5.4	1.2	2.1	1.6	1.0	0.6
Analgesics [1]	(NA)	11.8	11.5	9.4	8.7	(NA)	1.0	2.0	1.5	1.4
Alcohol	81.6	95.3	92.0	90.3	87.1	69.3	75.9	70.7	65.3	59.3
Cigarettes	68.8	82.8	75.2	75.0	66.7	48.8	42.6	36.6	35.2	29.0
26 YEARS OLD AND OVER										
Marijuana	9.9	19.6	26.6	30.7	34.3	2.0	6.0	6.0	3.9	3.0
Cocaine	0.9	4.3	9.2	9.9	12.5	(B)	0.9	1.9	0.9	0.5
Inhalants	1.2	3.9	5.3	3.9	4.3	(B)	0.5	0.5	0.2	0.2
Hallucinogens	1.3	4.5	6.0	6.6	8.8	(B)	(B)	(B)	(B)	(B)
Heroin	0.5	1.0	1.1	1.1	1.3	(B)	(B)	(B)	(B)	(B)
Stimulants [1]	3.0	5.8	7.9	6.6	6.5	(B)	0.5	0.7	0.5	0.2
Sedatives [1]	2.0	3.5	5.6	3.3	3.8	(B)	(B)	0.6	0.3	0.2
Tranquilizers [1]	2.0	3.1	7.8	4.5	4.9	(B)	(B)	1.0	0.6	0.2
Analgesics [1]	(NA)	2.7	5.9	4.5	5.5	(NA)	(B)	0.9	0.4	0.5
Alcohol	73.2	91.5	89.2	88.6	88.7	54.5	61.3	59.8	54.8	52.1
Cigarettes	65.4	83.0	80.6	79.6	76.9	39.1	36.9	32.7	29.8	25.3

B Base too small to meet statistical standards for reliability of a derived figure. NA Not available. [1] Nonmedical use; does not include over-the-counter drugs.

Source: U.S. Substance Abuse and Mental Health Services Administration, *National Household Survey on Drug Abuse,* annual.

No. 218. Use of Selected Drugs, by Age of User: 1993

[In percent. See headnote, table 217. For composition of regions, see table 27]

SUBSTANCE AND AGE GROUP	Total [1]	SEX		RACE/ETHNICITY			REGION			
		Male	Female	White [2]	Black [2]	His-panic	North-east	Mid-west	South	West
CURRENT USERS										
Cigarettes: Total	24.2	26.2	22.3	24.7	23.4	21.2	25.4	24.3	24.3	22.7
12 to 17 years old	9.6	9.3	10.0	11.0	4.0	8.4	10.5	11.1	8.4	9.0
18 to 25 years old	29.0	30.9	27.2	32.7	16.3	25.5	32.9	26.9	29.7	26.7
26 to 34 years old	30.1	31.4	28.8	31.1	30.5	24.8	30.6	30.7	31.8	26.2
35 years old and over	23.8	26.7	21.3	23.4	28.0	21.5	24.7	24.5	23.2	22.9
Alcohol: Total	49.6	57.4	42.5	52.7	37.6	45.6	54.1	48.6	44.9	54.2
12 to 17 years old	18.0	18.3	17.7	19.2	13.1	17.5	20.4	19.5	15.4	18.1
18 to 25 years old	59.3	64.5	54.3	65.3	45.0	49.9	61.0	61.2	55.6	62.4
26 to 34 years old	62.8	70.1	55.7	66.3	54.5	56.0	65.0	64.7	58.9	64.6
35 years old and over	48.8	59.1	39.9	51.5	35.5	47.1	54.7	47.0	42.8	55.1
Marijuana: Total	4.3	6.0	2.8	4.2	5.6	4.7	4.2	3.5	4.3	5.5
12 to 17 years old	4.9	5.5	4.3	4.5	5.8	6.7	5.0	3.5	3.7	6.7
18 to 25 years old	11.1	16.5	5.7	12.5	9.2	7.8	12.2	10.2	11.2	10.9
26 to 34 years old	6.7	9.0	4.5	6.8	9.9	4.1	7.3	5.2	6.1	8.7
35 years old and over	1.9	2.5	1.4	1.7	2.7	2.9	1.4	1.5	2.1	2.7
Cocaine: Total	0.6	0.9	0.4	0.5	1.3	1.1	0.7	0.5	0.6	0.8
12 to 17 years old	0.4	0.4	0.4	0.3	0.3	1.0	0.2	0.3	0.4	0.6
18 to 25 years old	1.5	1.7	1.4	1.6	1.3	2.1	1.9	0.5	1.5	2.3
26 to 34 years old	1.0	1.6	0.4	0.9	1.8	1.1	1.3	0.8	0.9	1.0
35 years old and over	0.4	0.6	0.2	0.2	1.4	0.7	0.3	0.5	0.3	0.4
Smokeless tobacco: Total	2.9	5.9	0.2	3.5	1.5	1.1	2.2	3.0	3.9	2.0
12 to 17 years old	2.0	3.9	(3)	2.7	0.2	0.9	0.9	2.2	2.9	1.1
18 to 25 years old	6.4	12.7	0.2	8.5	1.1	1.9	4.2	6.9	7.7	5.5
26 to 34 years old	4.4	8.9	0.1	5.9	0.2	1.0	1.6	4.2	6.6	3.8
35 years old and over	1.9	3.7	0.3	1.9	2.5	0.8	2.3	2.0	2.2	0.6
EVER USED										
Crack: Total	1.8	2.6	1.1	1.6	3.4	2.0	1.7	1.2	1.7	3.0
12 to 17 years old	0.4	0.2	0.5	0.2	0.3	1.2	0.2	0.1	0.4	0.7
18 to 25 years old	3.5	4.6	2.5	4.0	2.1	3.5	3.3	2.4	3.5	4.9
26 to 34 years old	4.2	5.9	2.5	3.8	7.2	3.2	3.5	3.0	4.4	5.7
35 years old and over	0.9	1.5	0.4	0.7	3.3	0.9	1.1	0.6	0.5	1.9
Inhalants: Total	5.3	7.4	3.3	5.8	2.9	4.9	4.3	5.1	4.7	7.3
12 to 17 years old	5.9	5.5	6.3	6.5	1.7	7.7	5.7	4.7	4.6	9.7
18 to 25 years old	9.9	12.4	7.4	12.4	2.0	7.2	10.4	11.5	8.3	10.4
26 to 34 years old	9.4	12.9	6.1	11.5	4.0	5.0	7.7	8.9	10.1	10.5
35 years old and over	2.8	4.7	1.1	2.8	3.1	3.0	1.9	2.9	2.1	4.8
Hallucinogens: Total	8.7	11.8	5.9	10.1	3.0	5.9	7.6	7.5	7.6	13.2
12 to 17 years old	2.9	3.4	2.4	3.1	0.2	4.1	2.0	2.0	2.6	5.5
18 to 25 years old	12.5	15.2	9.9	15.8	1.9	7.8	10.6	12.5	11.2	16.4
26 to 34 years old	15.9	19.7	12.2	19.6	5.3	6.7	13.7	14.1	15.1	20.8
35 years old and over	6.6	10.0	3.7	7.3	3.1	5.1	6.1	5.8	5.1	11.0
Stimulants: [4] Total	6.0	7.4	4.8	6.9	3.0	3.9	6.2	4.4	5.2	9.3
12 to 17 years old	2.1	2.0	2.2	2.5	0.2	2.2	0.9	2.1	2.0	3.1
18 to 25 years old	6.4	7.2	5.7	8.0	1.3	4.4	4.9	5.3	4.6	11.8
26 to 34 years old	10.5	12.1	8.9	12.7	3.2	5.8	7.8	9.7	9.0	16.1
35 years old and over	5.3	7.0	3.8	5.7	4.2	3.3	6.8	3.1	4.8	7.4
Sedatives: [4] Total	3.4	4.1	2.8	3.6	2.2	2.2	2.8	2.0	3.3	6.1
12 to 17 years old	1.4	1.2	1.6	1.4	0.9	2.2	1.2	0.6	1.5	2.4
18 to 25 years old	2.7	3.4	2.0	3.1	1.5	2.4	2.2	1.4	2.8	4.3
26 to 34 years old	4.8	5.5	4.0	5.9	1.8	2.2	3.7	4.2	5.0	5.9
35 years old and over	3.6	4.4	2.8	3.5	2.9	2.1	3.0	1.8	3.1	7.2
Tranquilizers: [4] Total	4.6	5.0	4.1	5.2	2.3	2.8	3.7	4.3	4.2	6.3
12 to 17 years old	1.2	1.0	1.4	1.4	0.4	1.1	1.0	0.4	1.6	1.9
18 to 25 years old	5.4	5.8	4.9	7.0	1.2	2.4	4.0	4.3	6.2	6.2
26 to 34 years old	7.1	8.0	6.2	8.4	3.0	3.6	5.3	6.9	7.1	8.9
35 years old and over	4.2	4.6	3.8	4.5	2.9	3.0	3.6	4.4	3.2	6.3
Analgesics: [4] Total	5.8	6.7	4.9	6.3	3.5	3.9	5.3	4.3	5.3	8.8
12 to 17 years old	3.7	2.8	4.5	4.1	2.7	3.2	3.7	3.0	3.3	5.1
18 to 25 years old	8.7	9.3	8.1	10.6	4.6	4.4	7.6	7.8	7.4	12.5
26 to 34 years old	9.0	11.1	7.0	10.3	3.4	5.9	7.0	7.4	8.0	14.0
35 years old and over	4.4	5.4	3.6	4.6	3.5	2.8	4.5	3.0	4.2	6.7

[1] Includes other races, not shown separately.   [2] Non-Hispanic.   [3] Low precision; no estimate reported.   [4] Nonmedical use; does not include over-the-counter drugs.

Source: U.S. Substance Abuse and Mental Health Services Administration, *National Household Survey on Drug Abuse: 1993*.

No. 219. Current Cigarette Smoking: 1965 to 1992

[In percent. Prior to 1992, a current smoker is a person who has smoked at least 100 cigarettes and who now smokes. Beginning 1992, definition includes persons who smoke only "some days." Excludes unknown smoking status. Based on the National Health Interview Survey; for details, see Appendix III]

SEX, AGE, AND RACE	1965	1974	1979	1983	1985	1987	1990	1991	1992
Total smokers, 18 years old and over	**42.4**	**37.1**	**33.5**	**32.1**	**30.1**	**28.8**	**25.5**	**25.6**	**26.5**
Male, total	51.9	43.1	37.5	35.1	32.6	31.2	28.4	28.1	28.6
18 to 24 years	54.1	42.1	35.0	32.9	28.0	28.2	26.6	23.5	28.0
25 to 34 years	60.7	50.5	43.9	38.8	38.2	34.8	31.6	32.8	32.8
35 to 44 years	58.2	51.0	41.8	41.0	37.6	36.6	34.5	33.1	32.9
45 to 64 years	51.9	42.6	39.3	35.9	33.4	33.5	29.3	29.3	28.6
65 years and over	28.5	24.8	20.9	22.0	19.6	17.2	14.6	15.1	16.1
White, total	51.1	41.9	36.8	34.5	31.7	30.5	28.0	27.4	28.2
18 to 24 years	53.0	40.8	34.3	32.5	28.4	29.2	27.4	25.1	30.0
25 to 34 years	60.1	49.5	43.6	38.6	37.3	33.8	31.6	32.1	33.5
35 to 44 years	57.3	50.1	41.3	40.8	36.6	36.2	33.5	32.1	30.9
45 to 64 years	51.3	41.2	38.3	35.0	32.1	32.4	28.7	28.0	28.1
65 years and over	27.7	24.3	20.5	20.6	18.9	16.0	13.7	13.7	14.9
Black, total	60.4	54.3	44.1	40.6	39.9	39.0	32.5	35.0	32.2
18 to 24 years	62.8	54.9	40.2	34.2	27.2	24.9	21.3	15.0	16.2
25 to 34 years	68.4	58.5	47.5	39.9	45.6	44.9	33.8	39.4	29.5
35 to 44 years	67.3	61.5	48.6	45.5	45.0	44.0	42.0	44.4	47.5
45 to 64 years	57.9	57.8	50.0	44.8	46.1	44.3	36.7	42.0	35.4
65 years and over	36.4	29.7	26.2	38.9	27.7	30.3	21.5	24.3	28.3
Female, total	33.9	32.1	29.9	29.5	27.9	26.5	22.8	23.5	24.6
18 to 24 years	38.1	34.1	33.8	35.5	30.4	26.1	22.5	22.4	24.9
25 to 34 years	43.7	38.8	33.7	32.6	32.0	31.8	28.2	28.4	30.1
35 to 44 years	43.7	39.8	37.0	33.8	31.5	29.6	24.8	27.6	27.3
45 to 64 years	32.0	33.4	30.7	31.0	29.9	28.6	24.8	24.6	26.1
65 years and over	9.6	12.0	13.2	13.1	13.5	13.7	11.5	12.0	12.4
White, total	34.0	31.7	30.1	29.4	27.7	26.7	23.4	23.7	25.1
18 to 24 years	38.4	34.0	34.5	36.5	31.8	27.8	25.4	25.1	28.5
25 to 34 years	43.4	38.6	34.1	32.2	32.0	31.9	28.5	28.4	31.5
35 to 44 years	43.9	39.3	37.2	34.8	31.0	29.2	25.0	27.0	27.6
45 to 64 years	32.7	33.0	30.6	30.6	29.7	29.0	25.4	25.3	25.8
65 years and over	9.8	12.3	13.8	13.2	13.3	13.9	11.5	12.1	12.6
Black, total	33.7	36.4	31.1	32.2	31.0	28.0	21.2	24.4	24.2
18 to 24 years	37.1	35.6	31.8	32.0	23.7	20.4	10.0	11.8	10.3
25 to 34 years	47.8	42.2	35.2	38.0	36.2	35.8	29.1	32.4	26.9
35 to 44 years	42.8	46.4	37.7	32.7	40.2	35.3	25.5	35.3	32.4
45 to 64 years	25.7	38.9	34.2	36.3	33.4	28.4	22.6	23.4	30.9
65 years and over	7.1	8.9	8.5	13.1	14.5	11.7	11.1	9.6	11.1

Source: U.S. National Center for Health Statistics, *Health, United States, 1993*.

No. 220. Cancer—Estimated New Cases, 1994, and Survival Rates, 1974-76 to 1983-90

[The 5-year relative survival rate, which is derived by adjusting the observed survival rate for expected mortality, represents the liklihood that a person will not die from causes directly related to their cancer within 5 years. Survival data shown are based on those patients diagnosed while residents of an area listed below during the time periods shown. Data are based on information collected as part of the National Cancer Institute's Surveillance, Epidemiology and End Results (SEER) program, a collection of population-based registries in Connecticut, New Mexico, Utah, Iowa, Hawaii, Atlanta, Detroit, Seattle-Puget Sound, and San Francisco-Oakland]

SITE	ESTIMATED NEW CASES,[1] 1994 (1,000)			5-YEAR RELATIVE SURVIVAL RATES (percent)							
				White				Black			
	Total	Male	Female	1974–76	1977–79	1980–82	1983–89	1974–76	1977–79	1980–82	1983–90
All sites [2]	**1,208**	**632**	**576**	**50.3**	**50.8**	**51.8**	**55.5**	**38.8**	**38.9**	**39.4**	**40.4**
Lung	172	100	72	12.4	13.6	13.5	13.7	11.4	10.9	12.1	11.1
Breast [3]	183	1	182	74.9	75.2	76.9	81.6	62.9	62.8	65.7	65.9
Colon and rectum	149	75	74	49.8	52.1	54.7	60.1	44.5	45.4	46.2	49.5
Prostate	200	200	(X)	67.7	71.9	74.3	81.3	58.0	62.1	64.4	66.4
Bladder	51	38	13	73.6	75.7	78.8	80.7	47.8	54.9	58.3	60.0
Corpus uteri	31	(X)	31	88.6	86.2	82.7	84.9	60.4	57.5	53.7	55.2
Non-Hodgkin's lymphoma [4]	45	25	20	47.5	48.3	51.6	52.6	47.9	50.4	50.1	45.4
Oral cavity and pharynx	30	20	10	54.9	54.2	55.1	54.6	36.3	36.3	30.5	33.6
Leukemia [4]	29	16	12	34.8	37.5	38.3	39.5	31.5	29.6	32.7	30.8
Melanoma of skin	32	17	15	80.0	81.8	82.3	85.3	66.4	50.8	56.9	70.3
Pancreas	27	13	14	2.6	2.3	2.8	3.0	2.3	3.8	4.8	4.9
Kidney	28	17	11	51.4	50.7	50.9	56.9	48.9	51.4	55.0	52.0
Stomach	24	15	9	14.4	16.0	16.2	17.5	16.3	15.3	19.3	18.8
Ovary	24	(X)	24	36.3	37.5	38.7	41.6	40.1	39.8	37.6	38.4
Cervix uteri [5]	15	(X)	15	69.2	68.8	67.7	69.9	63.5	61.9	60.4	56.4

X Not applicable. [1] Estimates provided by American Cancer Society are based on rates from the National Cancer Institute's SEER program. [2] Includes other sites not shown separately. [3] Survival rates for female only. [4] All types combined. [5] Invasive cancer only.

Source: U.S. National Institutes of Health, National Cancer Institute, *Cancer Statistics Review*, annual.

No. 221. Personal Health Practices, by Selected Characteristic: 1990

[**In percent, except total persons.** For persons 18 years of age and over. Based on the National Health Interview Survey and subject to sampling error; for details see source and Appendix III]

CHARACTERISTIC	Total persons (1,000)	Eats break-fast [1]	Rarely snacks	Exercised regularly [2]	Had two or more drinks on any day [3]	Current smoker	20 percent or more above weight [4]
All persons [5]	**181,447**	**56.4**	**25.5**	**40.7**	**5.5**	**25.5**	**27.5**
Sex: Male	86,278	54.6	25.6	44.0	9.7	28.4	29.6
Female	95,169	58.0	25.4	37.7	1.7	22.8	25.6
Race: White	155,301	57.8	25.8	41.5	5.8	25.6	26.7
Black	20,248	46.9	22.7	34.3	4.3	26.2	38.0
Hispanic origin: Hispanic	14,314	52.5	29.3	34.9	4.6	23.0	27.6
Non-Hispanic	166,599	56.7	25.2	41.2	5.6	25.7	27.5
Marital status:							
Currently married	117,413	57.8	25.3	39.4	5.3	24.6	29.2
Formerly married	30,439	61.5	31.2	34.3	5.3	30.3	29.1
Never married	33,413	46.9	20.9	51.3	6.6	24.3	19.8
Education level:							
Less than 12 years	38,367	58.6	27.8	25.9	5.1	31.8	32.7
12 years	69,405	52.6	24.3	37.0	5.9	29.6	28.6
More than 12 years	73,244	58.8	25.5	52.1	5.4	18.3	23.8
Income: Less than $10,000	18,469	54.1	27.6	32.9	4.8	31.6	29.3
$10,000 to $19,999	30,452	56.6	25.9	32.3	4.9	29.8	28.5
$20,000 to $34,999	40,216	55.2	25.1	40.5	5.8	26.9	28.2
$35,000 to $49,999	29,795	53.7	23.8	46.1	5.6	23.4	27.8
$50,000 or more	36,199	57.2	25.8	51.7	6.7	19.3	24.9

[1] Almost every day.   [2] Or played sports regularly.   [3] On average per day in the past 2 weeks.   [4] Above desirable weight. Based on 1983 Metropolitan Life Insurance Company standards. Height and weight data are self-reported.   [5] Includes persons whose characteristics are unknown.

Source: U.S. National Center for Health Statistics, *Health Promotion and Disease Prevention: United States, 1990, Vital and Health Statistics,* series 10, No. 185.

No. 222. Persons Using Devices or Features to Assist With Impairments, by Age: 1990

[**In percent, except as indicated.** For the civilian noninstitutionalized population. Based on the Current Population Survey; see text, section 1, and Appendix III]

DEVICE OR FEATURE	Total	Under 25 years old	25 to 44 years old	45 to 64 years old	65 to 74 years old	75 years old and over
Persons using assistive technology devices [1] (1,000)	13,128	1,048	2,228	3,022	2,756	4,073
Anatomical devices	28.4	61.7	61.4	34.8	14.1	6.8
Leg brace	6.6	19.9	12.9	6.9	3.5	1.5
Foot brace	1.4	6.8	2.0	1.0	1.1	[2]0.3
Arm brace	1.6	2.7	3.9	2.0	0.7	[2]0.3
Hand brace	1.6	2.7	4.2	2.1	0.8	[2]0.1
Neck brace	2.3	2.6	5.3	3.6	1.0	[2]0.4
Back brace	8.9	6.5	18.8	15.2	4.6	2.4
Other brace	6.5	23.0	16.6	4.8	1.7	1.2
Artificial leg or foot	1.4	[2]0.8	1.3	2.1	1.7	0.9
Artificial arm or hand	0.3	1.1	[2]0.2	[2]0.3	[2]0.3	[2]-
Mobility devices	48.8	22.9	27.3	45.8	52.1	67.2
Crutch	5.1	8.3	7.8	6.9	5.0	1.6
Cane or walking stick	33.5	3.0	14.3	33.5	37.4	49.3
Walker	12.9	3.2	3.2	9.1	12.7	23.5
Wheelchair	10.8	13.3	7.6	10.0	11.8	11.7
Scooter	0.5	[2]0.6	[2]0.5	[2]0.6	[2]0.7	[2]0.3
Other mobility devices	1.9	[2]1.7	1.3	2.2	2.1	2.1
Hearing devices	30.4	14.5	11.5	27.1	41.4	39.7
Hearing aid	28.8	14.1	10.2	24.6	40.0	38.3
TDD/TTY [3]	1.3	2.1	1.0	1.8	0.9	1.2
Special Alarm	0.6	[2]0.7	[2]0.8	0.8	[2]0.2	0.6
Other hearing devices	4.3	2.3	2.5	4.5	5.1	5.0
Persons using home accessibility features (1,000)	7,102	1,395	1,272	1,484	1,284	1,667
Ramps	29.7	41.4	36.0	32.8	25.0	16.0
Extra-wide doors	23.2	28.5	26.2	27.6	19.4	15.8
Elevator or stair lift	5.8	4.7	2.2	3.0	7.6	10.4
Hand rails	47.8	30.5	33.0	46.2	60.6	65.2
Raised toilet	18.6	9.0	10.5	19.2	21.5	30.3
Adaptive door locks	5.8	4.1	2.3	6.1	6.7	8.9
Lowered counters	3.4	3.7	3.7	4.0	1.7	3.7
Slip-resistant floors	3.0	2.9	3.2	5.3	1.9	1.6
Other features	22.5	22.4	24.6	23.3	22.8	19.8

- Represents or rounds to zero.   [1] Includes other devices, not shown separately. Excludes any implanted devices, such as pacemakers.   [2] Figure does not meet standards of reliability or precision.   [3] TDD/TTY is a typewriter-like device for the deaf that communicates over telephone lines using text.

Source: U.S. National Center for Health Statistics, *Advance Data from Vital and Health Statistics,* No. 217, September 16, 1992.

No. 223. Cumulative Percent Distribution of Population, by Height and Sex: 1976-80

[**For persons 18 to 74 years old**. Height was measured without shoes. Based on sample and subject to sampling variability; see source]

HEIGHT	MALES						FEMALES					
	18-24 years	25-34 years	35-44 years	45-54 years	55-64 years	65-74 years	18-24 years	25-34 years	35-44 years	45-54 years	55-64 years	65-74 years
Percent under—												
4'8"	-	-	-	-	-	-	0.05	-	0.10	0.28	0.46	1.04
4'9"	-	-	-	-	-	-	0.43	0.23	0.34	0.35	1.07	2.27
4'10"	-	-	-	-	-	-	0.94	0.64	0.95	1.22	3.02	4.23
4'11"	-	-	-	-	-	-	2.22	1.65	1.94	4.20	6.43	9.33
5'	0.18	0.05	0.27	-	0.27	0.24	4.22	3.65	4.56	8.88	11.40	17.20
5'1"	0.18	0.31	0.34	0.19	0.72	1.22	9.13	8.60	7.75	16.16	19.70	29.00
5'2"	0.34	0.42	0.87	0.70	0.92	2.66	17.75	19.11	18.24	27.68	31.71	44.34
5'3"	0.61	0.54	2.07	1.50	2.78	5.97	29.06	32.96	33.11	39.83	45.87	59.15
5'4"	2.37	1.55	3.68	2.55	5.28	10.53	41.81	47.43	49.90	57.21	63.89	76.44
5'5"	3.85	4.36	6.36	5.72	9.29	18.31	58.09	61.36	63.88	70.47	77.44	86.97
5'6"	8.24	9.51	12.39	11.39	17.54	29.42	74.76	74.92	78.07	84.64	88.91	94.63
5'7"	16.18	15.25	17.63	21.24	29.10	41.63	85.37	85.65	87.95	91.21	94.56	97.86
5'8"	26.68	26.69	26.40	33.56	43.53	57.75	92.30	93.28	93.43	96.28	97.70	99.20
5'9"	38.89	39.68	42.52	50.39	58.21	69.96	96.23	97.19	97.18	98.17	99.36	99.81
5'10"	53.66	55.35	57.01	63.38	81.95	81.95	98.34	99.49	99.19	99.58	99.78	99.92
5'11"	68.25	69.67	70.70	76.94	83.09	89.59	99.38	99.68	99.39	99.84	99.81	100.00
6'	80.14	81.58	81.15	85.83	90.99	94.52	100.00	100.00	100.00	100.00	100.00	100.00
6'1"	88.54	89.95	90.04	93.43	96.28	97.82	100.00	100.00	100.00	100.00	100.00	100.00
6'2"	92.74	95.57	95.05	98.01	97.66	99.17	100.00	100.00	100.00	100.00	100.00	100.00
6'3"	96.17	97.98	97.82	99.35	98.90	99.86	100.00	100.00	100.00	100.00	100.00	100.00
6'4"	98.40	99.23	99.19	99.70	99.79	100.00	100.00	100.00	100.00	100.00	100.00	100.00

- Represents or rounds to zero.

Source: U.S. National Center for Health Statistics, *Vital and Health Statistics,* series 11, No. 238.

No. 224. Nutrition—Nutrients in Foods Available for Civilian Consumption per Capita per Day: 1950 to 1990

[Computed by the Center for Nutrition Policy and Promotion (CNPP). Based on Economic Research Service (ERS) estimates of per capita quantities of food available for consumption from "Food Consumption, Prices, and Expenditures," or imputed consumption data for foods no longer reported by ERS, and on CNPP estimates of quantities of produce from home gardens. Food supply estimates do not reflect loss of food or nutrients from further marketing or home processing. Enrichment and fortofication levels of iron, thiamin, riboflavin, niacin, vitamin A, vitamin B_6, vitamin B_{12}, and ascorbic acid are included. See *Historical Statistics, Colonial Times to 1970,* series G 851-856 for related details]

NUTRIENT	Unit	1950-59	1960-69	1970-79	1980-89	1990
Food energy	Calories	3,100	3,200	3,300	3,500	3,700
Carbohydrate	Grams	382	374	388	416	452
Protein	Grams	93	96	99	101	105
Total fat [1]	Grams	141	150	158	165	165
Saturated	Grams	60	62	59	60	59
Monounsaturated	Grams	57	61	64	66	67
Polyunsaturated	Grams	18	22	28	32	32
Cholesterol	Milligrams	510	490	460	440	410
Vitamin A	Micrograms RE [2]	1,310	1,320	1,520	1,460	1,420
Carotenes	Micrograms RE [2]	420	410	570	580	620
Vitamin E	Milligrams α-TE [3] . . .	11.7	12.4	13.6	14.7	15.7
Vitamin C	Milligrams	101	96	110	113	110
Thiamin	Milligrams	1.9	1.9	2.2	2.4	2.5
Riboflavin	Milligrams	2.4	2.3	2.4	2.5	2.6
Niacin	Milligrams	19.9	21.3	24.4	26.7	27.9
Vitamin B_6	Milligrams	1.9	1.9	2.1	2.1	2.2
Folacin	Micrograms	292	275	287	294	296
Vitamin B_{12}	Micrograms	9.2	9.8	10.1	9.2	8.7
Calcium	Milligrams	940	890	870	880	920
Phosphorus	Milligrams	1,460	1,460	1,480	1,530	1,600
Magnesium	Milligrams	330	320	320	330	350
Iron	Milligrams	14.1	14.5	18.7	17.8	19.3
Zinc	Milligrams	11.8	12.2	12.6	12.6	12.7
Copper	Milligrams	1.6	1.6	1.6	1.7	1.7
Potassium	Milligrams	3,630	3,500	3,480	3,480	3,540

[1] Includes other types of fat not shown separately.   [2] Retinol equivalents.   [3] Alpha-Tocopherol equivalents.

Source: U.S. Dept. of Agriculture, Center for Nutrition Policy and Promotion. Data published by Economic Research Service in *Food Consumption, Prices, and Expenditures,* annual; and *National Food Review,* quarterly.

No. 225. Per Capita Consumption of Major Food Commodities: 1970 to 1993

[In pounds, retail weight except as indicated. Consumption represents the residual after exports, nonfood use and ending stocks are subtracted from the sum of beginning stocks, domestic production, and imports. Based on Bureau of the Census estimated population. Estimates reflect revisions based on the 1990 Census of Population. For similar but unrevised data, see *Historical Statistics, Colonial Times to 1970*, series G 881-915]

COMMODITY	1970	1975	1980	1985	1990	1991	1992	1993
Red meat, total (boneless, trimmed weight) [1][2]	131.7	125.8	126.4	124.9	112.3	111.9	114.1	111.9
Beef	79.6	83.0	72.1	74.6	64.0	63.1	62.8	61.5
Veal	2.0	2.8	1.3	1.5	0.9	0.8	0.8	0.8
Lamb and mutton	2.1	1.3	1.0	1.1	1.0	1.0	1.0	1.0
Pork (excluding lard)	48.0	38.7	52.1	47.7	46.4	46.9	49.5	48.7
Fish and shellfish (edible weight) [3]	11.7	12.1	12.4	15.0	15.0	14.8	14.7	14.9
Fresh and frozen	6.9	7.5	7.8	9.7	9.6	9.6	9.8	10.1
Canned	4.4	4.2	4.3	5.0	5.1	4.9	4.6	4.5
Tuna	2.5	2.8	3.0	3.3	3.7	3.6	3.5	3.5
Cured	0.4	0.4	0.3	0.3	0.3	0.3	0.3	0.3
Poultry products: (boneless weight) [2][4]	33.8	32.9	40.6	45.2	56.0	58.0	60.0	61.1
Chicken	27.4	26.4	32.5	36.1	42.2	43.9	45.9	47.1
Turkey	6.4	6.5	8.1	9.1	13.8	14.1	14.2	14.1
Eggs (farm weight) (number)	308.9	276.0	271.1	255.4	233.3	232.7	234.0	233.4
Dairy products:								
Total (milk equivalent, milkfat basis) [5]	563.8	539.1	543.2	593.7	570.7	565.3	564.9	572.2
Fluid milk and cream [6]	275.1	261.4	245.6	241.0	233.4	233.1	230.9	226.6
Beverage milks	269.1	254.0	237.4	229.7	221.7	221.2	218.7	214.2
Plain whole milk	213.5	174.9	141.7	119.7	87.6	84.7	81.5	77.8
Plain lowfat milk	29.8	53.2	70.1	83.3	98.3	99.7	99.4	97.1
Plain skim milk	11.6	11.5	11.6	12.6	22.9	23.9	25.0	26.7
Flavored whole milk	5.6	6.3	4.7	3.7	2.8	2.7	2.7	2.7
Flavored lowfat and skim milks	3.0	3.3	5.3	6.0	6.6	6.8	6.9	6.9
Buttermilk	5.5	4.7	4.1	4.4	3.5	3.4	3.2	3.0
Yogurt (excl. frozen)	0.8	2.1	2.6	4.1	4.1	4.2	4.3	4.3
Cream [7]	3.8	3.3	3.4	4.4	4.6	4.6	4.8	4.9
Sour cream and dip	1.1	1.6	1.8	2.3	2.5	2.6	2.7	2.7
Condensed and evaporated milk:								
Whole milk	7.0	5.1	3.8	3.6	3.2	3.2	3.3	3.0
Skim milk	5.0	3.5	3.3	3.8	4.8	5.0	5.2	5.2
Cheese [8]	11.4	14.3	17.5	22.5	24.6	25.0	26.0	26.3
American	7.0	8.2	9.6	12.2	11.1	11.1	11.3	11.4
Cheddar	5.8	6.0	6.9	9.8	9.0	9.0	9.2	9.1
Italian	2.1	3.2	4.4	6.5	9.0	9.4	10.0	9.8
Mozzarella	1.2	2.1	3.0	4.6	6.9	7.2	7.7	7.5
Other [9]	2.3	2.9	3.4	3.9	4.5	4.6	4.7	5.0
Swiss	0.9	1.1	1.3	1.3	1.4	1.2	1.2	1.2
Cream and Neufchatel	0.6	0.7	1.0	1.2	1.7	1.8	2.0	2.1
Cottage cheese	5.2	4.6	4.5	4.1	3.4	3.3	3.1	2.9
Ice cream	17.8	18.6	17.5	18.1	15.8	16.3	16.3	16.1
Ice milk	7.7	7.6	7.1	6.9	7.7	7.4	7.1	6.9
Fats and oils:								
Total, fat content only [10]	52.6	52.6	57.2	64.3	62.2	63.8	65.6	65.0
Butter (product weight)	5.4	4.7	4.5	4.9	4.4	4.2	4.2	4.5
Margarine (product weight)	10.8	11.0	11.3	10.8	10.9	10.6	11.0	10.8
Lard (direct use)	4.6	3.2	2.6	1.8	1.9	1.7	1.7	1.8
Edible tallow (direct use)	(NA)	(NA)	1.1	1.9	0.6	1.4	2.4	2.0
Shortening	17.3	17.0	18.2	22.9	22.2	22.4	22.4	22.9
Salad and cooking oils	15.4	17.9	21.2	23.5	24.2	25.2	25.6	24.3
Other edible fats and oils	2.3	2.0	1.5	1.6	1.2	1.3	1.4	1.7
Flour and cereal products	135.3	138.8	144.6	156.1	183.3	185.6	187.0	189.2
Wheat flour [11]	110.9	114.5	116.9	124.6	135.6	136.6	138.1	139.4
Rye flour	1.2	1.0	0.7	0.7	0.6	0.6	0.6	0.6
Rice, milled [12]	6.7	7.6	9.4	9.0	16.2	16.8	16.9	17.5
Corn products	11.1	10.8	12.9	17.1	21.7	21.9	21.9	22.1
Oat products	4.4	4.1	3.7	3.7	8.2	8.6	8.5	8.6
Barley products	1.0	0.9	1.1	1.0	1.0	1.0	0.9	0.9
Caloric sweeteners, total [13]	122.9	119.0	124.4	131.5	139.6	140.6	143.8	147.1
Sugar, refined cane and beet	101.8	89.2	83.6	62.7	64.4	63.8	64.5	64.2
Corn sweeteners (dry weight)	19.6	28.4	39.5	67.5	73.8	75.4	77.9	81.5
Low-calorie sweeteners (sugar sweetness equivalent) [14]	5.8	6.1	7.7	18.1	22.2	24.3	(NA)	(NA)
Saccharin	5.8	6.1	7.7	6.0	6.7	7.3	(NA)	(NA)
Aspartame	-	-	-	12.1	15.5	17.0	(NA)	(NA)
Other:								
Cocoa beans	3.9	3.2	3.4	4.6	5.4	5.7	5.7	5.8
Coffee (green beans)	13.6	12.2	10.3	10.5	10.3	10.4	10.3	10.0
Peanuts (shelled)	5.5	6.0	4.8	6.3	6.0	6.5	6.2	6.0
Tree nuts (shelled)	1.7	1.9	1.8	2.5	2.6	2.3	2.4	2.3

- Represents or rounds to zero. NA Not available. [1] Excludes edible offals. [2] Excludes shipments to Puerto Rico and the other U.S. possessions. [3] Excludes consumption from recreational fishing, approximately 3 to 4 pounds per capita. [4] Includes backs, necks, skin, and giblets. [5] Includes other products, not shown separately. [6] Fluid milk figures are aggregates of commercial sales and milk produced and consumed on farms. [7] Heavy cream, light cream, and half and half. [8] Excludes cottage, pot, and baker's cheese. [9] Includes other cheeses not shown separately. [10] The fat content of butter and margarine is 80 percent of product weight. [11] White, whole wheat, semolina, and durum flour. [12] For crop year beginning in previous year. [13] Dry weight. Includes edible syrups (maple, molasses, etc.) and honey not shown separately. [14] Assumes saccharin is 300 times as sweet as sugar and aspartame 200 times as sweet as sugar.

Source: U.S. Department of Agriculture, Economic Research Service, *Food Consumption, Prices, and Expenditures*, annual.

No. 226. Per Capita Utilization of Selected Commercially Produced Fresh Fruits and Vegetables: 1970 to 1993

[In pounds, farm weight. Domestic food use of fresh fruits and vegetables reflects the fresh-market share of commodity production plus imports and minus exports. All data are on a calendar year basis except for citrus fruits, October or November; apples, August; grapes and pears, July. See headnote, table 225]

COMMODITY	1970	1975	1980	1985	1989	1990	1991	1992	1993
Fresh fruits, total	79.6	83.5	87.3	86.9	96.7	92.5	89.7	98.2	99.9
Noncitrus	50.8	54.5	61.2	65.4	73.1	71.1	70.6	73.9	74.0
Bananas	17.4	17.6	20.8	23.5	24.7	24.4	25.1	27.3	26.8
Apples	17.0	19.5	19.2	17.3	21.4	19.7	18.3	19.3	19.4
Grapes	2.9	3.6	4.0	6.8	7.9	7.9	7.3	7.2	7.0
Nectarines and peaches	5.8	5.0	7.1	5.5	5.7	5.5	6.4	6.0	5.9
Pears	1.9	2.7	2.6	2.8	3.2	3.2	3.2	3.2	3.4
Strawberries	1.7	1.8	2.0	3.0	3.3	3.2	3.6	3.5	3.6
Pineapples	0.7	1.0	1.5	1.5	2.0	2.1	1.9	2.0	2.1
Plums and prunes	1.5	1.3	1.5	1.4	1.4	1.5	1.4	1.8	1.3
Other [1]	1.9	2.0	2.5	3.6	3.5	3.6	3.4	3.6	4.5
Citrus	28.9	29.0	26.1	21.5	23.5	21.4	19.1	24.4	26.0
Oranges	16.2	15.9	14.3	11.6	12.2	12.4	8.5	12.9	14.2
Grapefruit	8.2	8.3	7.3	5.5	6.6	4.4	5.8	5.9	6.2
Other [2]	4.5	4.8	4.5	4.4	4.7	4.6	4.8	5.6	5.6
Selected melons	21.6	17.7	17.9	24.1	26.5	24.6	23.3	24.5	24.4
Watermelons	13.5	11.4	10.7	13.5	13.6	13.3	12.8	14.2	14.2
Cantaloups	7.2	5.2	5.8	8.5	10.4	9.2	8.7	8.3	8.5
Honeydews	0.9	1.1	1.4	2.1	2.5	2.1	1.9	2.0	1.6
Selected fresh vegetables	85.6	88.6	92.5	102.1	114.9	112.3	109.6	114.0	113.0
Asparagus	0.4	0.4	0.3	0.5	0.6	0.6	0.6	0.6	0.6
Broccoli	0.5	1.0	1.4	2.6	3.8	3.4	3.1	3.4	2.8
Cabbage	8.8	9.1	8.1	8.2	7.9	7.8	7.5	7.7	8.4
Carrots	6.0	6.4	6.2	6.5	7.9	8.0	7.5	8.6	8.4
Cauliflower	0.7	0.9	1.1	1.8	2.3	2.2	2.0	1.9	1.7
Celery	7.3	6.9	7.5	7.0	7.5	7.2	6.8	6.7	6.2
Corn	7.8	7.8	6.5	6.4	6.4	6.5	5.7	6.7	6.3
Cucumbers	2.8	2.8	3.9	4.4	4.8	4.7	4.6	5.2	5.5
Iceberg lettuce	22.4	23.5	25.6	23.7	28.8	27.8	26.1	25.9	24.6
Onions	10.1	10.5	11.4	13.6	14.8	15.1	15.7	16.1	15.7
Snap beans	1.5	1.4	1.3	1.3	1.2	1.1	1.1	1.4	1.6
Green peppers	2.2	2.5	2.9	3.8	4.7	4.5	5.1	5.5	5.9
Tomatoes	12.1	12.0	12.8	14.9	16.8	15.5	15.4	15.2	15.9
Other fresh vegetables [3]	3.0	3.4	3.5	7.4	7.4	7.9	8.4	9.1	9.4
Potatoes	121.7	121.9	114.7	122.4	127.1	127.7	130.4	132.4	135.7
Fresh	61.8	52.6	51.1	46.3	50.0	45.8	46.4	48.9	51.9
For freezing	28.5	37.1	35.4	46.4	46.8	50.2	51.3	51.0	51.3
For chips/shoestrings	17.4	15.5	16.5	17.6	17.5	17.0	17.3	17.5	17.5
For dehydrating	12.0	14.7	9.8	11.2	10.8	12.8	13.7	13.2	13.1
For canning	2.0	2.0	1.9	1.9	2.0	1.9	1.7	1.8	1.9
Sweet potatoes [4]	5.4	5.4	4.4	5.4	4.1	4.6	4.0	4.3	3.9
Mushrooms	1.3	1.9	2.7	3.6	3.5	3.7	3.6	3.5	3.9
For fresh	0.3	0.7	1.2	1.8	2.0	2.0	1.9	1.9	1.9
For processing	1.0	1.2	1.5	1.8	1.5	1.7	1.7	1.6	2.0

[1] Includes apricots, avocados, cherries, cranberries, kiwifruit, mangos, and papayas.   [2] Includes tangerines, tangelos, lemons, and limes.   [3] Includes artichokes, Brussels sprouts, eggplant, escarole/endive, garlic, romaine and leaf lettuce (after 1984), radishes, and spinach.   [4] Fresh and processed.

Source: U.S. Dept. of Agriculture, Economic Research Service, *Food Consumption, Prices and Expenditures*, annual; and unpublished data.

No. 227. Per Capita Consumption of Selected Beverages, by Type: 1970 to 1993

[In gallons. See headnote, table 225]

COMMODITY	1970	1975	1980	1985	1989	1990	1991	1992	1993
Nonalcoholic [1]	95.8	103.2	106.3	109.1	116.5	118.1	120.5	120.3	122.1
Milk (plain and flavored)	31.3	29.5	27.6	26.7	26.0	25.7	25.7	25.4	24.8
Whole	25.5	21.1	17.0	14.3	11.3	10.5	10.2	9.8	9.4
Lowfat	4.4	7.1	9.2	10.9	12.3	12.6	12.7	12.7	12.4
Skim	1.3	1.3	1.3	1.5	2.3	2.6	2.8	2.9	3.1
Tea	6.8	7.5	7.3	7.1	6.9	6.8	6.9	7.1	7.1
Coffee	33.4	31.4	26.7	27.4	26.3	27.0	27.1	26.9	26.0
Bottled water	(NA)	(NA)	2.4	4.5	7.4	8.0	8.0	8.2	9.2
Soft drinks	24.3	28.2	35.1	35.7	42.2	43.7	44.9	45.4	46.6
Selected juices	(NA)	6.6	7.2	7.7	7.7	6.9	7.9	7.3	8.4
Alcoholic (adult population)	35.7	39.7	42.8	40.7	39.1	40.0	37.8	37.3	36.8
Beer	30.6	33.9	36.6	34.6	33.9	34.9	33.2	32.6	32.4
Wine	2.2	2.7	3.2	3.5	3.1	2.9	2.7	2.7	2.5
Distilled spirits	3.0	3.1	3.0	2.6	2.2	2.2	2.0	2.0	1.9

NA Not available.   [1] Excludes vegetable juices.

Source: U.S. Dept. of Agriculture, Economic Research Service, *Food Consumption, Prices, and Expenditures*, annual; and unpublished data.

Education

This section presents data primarily concerning formal education as a whole, at various levels, and for public and private schools. Data shown relate to the school-age population and school enrollment, educational attainment, education personnel, and financial aspects of education. In addition, data are shown for libraries, computer usage in schools, and adult education. The chief sources are the decennial census of population and the Current Population Survey (CPS), both conducted by the Bureau of the Census (see text, section 1); annual, biennial, and other periodic surveys conducted by the National Center for Education Statistics, a part of the U.S. Department of Education; and surveys conducted by the National Education Association.

The censuses of population have included data on school enrollment since 1840 and on educational attainment since 1940. The CPS has reported on school enrollment annually since 1945 and on educational attainment periodically since 1947.

The National Center for Education Statistics is continuing the pattern of statistical studies and surveys conducted by the U.S. Office of Education since 1870. The annual *Digest of Education Statistics* provides summary data on pupils, staff, finances, including government expenditures, and organization at the elementary, secondary, and higher education levels. It is also a primary source for detailed information on Federal funds for education, projections of enrollment, graduates, and teachers. *The Condition of Education,* issued annually, presents a summary of information on education of particular interest to policymakers.

Other sources of data include special studies by the National Center for Education Statistics and annual or biennial reports of education agencies in individual States. The census of governments, conducted by the Bureau of the Census every 5 years (for the years ending in "2" and "7"), provides data on school district finances and State and local government

In Brief	
The enrollment rate of 3 to 5 year olds in preprimary school:	
1970	*37 percent*
1993	*55 percent*
Persons 25 years old and over completing college:	
1970	*11 percent*
1994	*22 percent*
Elementary and secondary schools with microcomputers:	
1985	*78 percent*
1994	*97 percent*

expenditures for education. Reports published by the Bureau of Labor Statistics contain data relating civilian labor force experience to educational attainment (see also tables 629, 630, 652, 662, and 663 in section 13).

Types and sources of data.—The statistics in this section are of two general types. One type, exemplified by data from the Bureau of the Census, is based on direct interviews with individuals to obtain information about their own and their family members' education. Data of this type relate to school enrollment and level of education attained, classified by age, sex, and other characteristics of the population. The school enrollment statistics reflect attendance or enrollment in any regular school within a given period; educational attainment statistics reflect the highest grade completed by an individual or, beginning in 1992, the highest diploma or degree received.

For enrollment data starting in October 1981, the CPS used 1980 census population controls; for years 1971 through 1980, 1970 census population controls had been used. This change had little impact on summary measures (e.g., medians) and proportional measures (e.g., enrollment rates); however, use of the controls may have significant impact on absolute numbers.

Beginning with data for 1986, a new edit and tabulation package for school enrollment has been introduced. The data produced increased the estimates of high school enrollment for 1986 by 200,000 and college enrollment by 300,000. See table 237 which presents both earlier and revised estimates. In other enrollment tables, revised estimates are shown. In 1988, a new edit and tabulation package was introduced for educational attainment data.

The second type, generally exemplified by data from the National Center for Education Statistics and the National Education Association, is based on reports from administrators of educational institutions and of State and local agencies having jurisdiction over education. Data of this type relate to enrollment, attendance, staff, and finances for the Nation, individual States, and local areas.

Unlike the National Center for Education Statistics, the Census Bureau does not regularly include specialized vocational, trade, business, or correspondence schools in its surveys. The National Center for Education Statistics includes nursery schools and kindergartens that are part of regular grade schools in their enrollment figures. The Census Bureau includes all nursery schools and kindergartens. At the higher education level, the statistics of both agencies are concerned with institutions granting degrees or offering work acceptable for degree-credit, such as junior colleges.

School attendance.—All States require that children attend school. While State laws vary as to the ages and circumstances of compulsory attendance, generally they require that formal schooling begin by age 6 and continue to age 16.

Schools.—The National Center for Education Statistics defines a *school* as "a division of the school system consisting of students composing one or more grade groups or other identifiable groups, organized as one unit with one or more teachers to give instruction of a defined type, and housed in a school plant of one or more buildings. More than one school may be housed in one school plant, as is the case when the elementary and secondary programs are housed in the same school plant."

Regular schools are those which advance a person toward a diploma or degree. They include public and private nursery schools, kindergartens, graded schools, colleges, universities, and professional schools.

Public schools are schools controlled and supported by local, State, or Federal governmental agencies; *private* schools are those controlled and supported mainly by religious organizations or by private persons or organizations.

The Bureau of the Census defines *elementary* schools as including grades 1 through 8; *high* schools as including grades 9 through 12; and *colleges* as including junior or community colleges, regular 4-year colleges, and universities and graduate or professional schools. Statistics reported by the National Center for Education Statistics and the National Education Association by type of organization, such as elementary level and secondary level, may not be strictly comparable with those from the Bureau of the Census because the grades included at the two levels vary, depending on the level assigned to the middle or junior high school by the local school systems.

School year.—Except as otherwise indicated in the tables, data refer to the school year which, for elementary and secondary schools, generally begins in September of the preceding year and ends in June of the year stated. For the most part, statistics concerning school finances are for a 12-month period, usually July 1 to June 30. Enrollment data generally refer to a specific point in time, such as fall, as indicated in the tables.

Statistical reliability.—For a discussion of statistical collection, estimation, and sampling procedures and measures of statistical reliability applicable to Census Bureau and the National Center for Education Statistics data, see Appendix III.

Historical statistics.—Tabular headnotes provide cross-references, where applicable, to *Historical Statistics of the United States, Colonial Times to 1970.* See Appendix IV.

No. 228. School Enrollment: 1965 to 2004

[In thousands. As of fall. See also *Historical Statistics, Colonial Times to 1970,* series H 421-429]

ITEM AND YEAR	TOTAL		K THROUGH GRADE 8		GRADES 9 THROUGH 12		COLLEGE	
	Public	Private	Public	Private	Public	Private	Public	Private
1965	46,143	8,251	30,563	4,900	11,610	1,400	3,970	1,951
1970	52,322	7,516	32,558	4,052	13,336	1,311	6,428	2,153
1975	53,654	7,350	30,515	3,700	14,304	1,300	8,835	2,350
1980	50,335	7,971	27,647	3,992	13,231	1,339	9,457	2,640
1981	49,691	8,225	27,280	4,100	12,764	1,400	9,647	2,725
1982	49,262	8,330	27,161	4,200	12,405	1,400	9,696	2,730
1983	48,935	8,497	26,981	4,315	12,271	1,400	9,683	2,782
1984	48,686	8,465	26,905	4,300	12,304	1,400	9,477	2,765
1985	48,901	8,325	27,034	4,195	12,388	1,362	9,479	2,768
1986	49,467	8,242	27,420	4,116	12,333	1,336	9,714	2,790
1987	49,982	8,272	27,933	4,232	12,076	1,247	9,973	2,793
1988	50,349	8,136	28,501	4,036	11,687	1,206	10,161	2,894
1989	51,120	8,316	29,152	4,162	11,390	1,193	10,578	2,961
1990	52,061	•8,206	29,878	4,095	11,338	1,137	10,845	2,974
1991	53,357	8,248	30,506	4,074	11,541	1,125	11,310	3,049
1992 prel. . . .	54,123	8,479	30,997	4,212	11,738	1,163	11,388	3,104
1993, est. [1] . . .	54,803	8,621	31,374	4,280	11,979	1,191	11,450	3,150
1994, est.	55,754	8,765	31,837	4,333	12,417	1,232	11,500	3,200
1995, proj.	56,744	8,911	32,275	4,393	12,774	1,267	11,695	3,251
1996, proj.	57,684	9,016	32,841	4,470	13,147	1,304	11,696	3,242
1997, proj.	58,581	9,131	33,395	4,545	13,440	1,333	11,746	3,253
1998, proj.	59,266	9,227	33,798	4,600	13,632	1,352	11,836	3,275
1999, proj.	59,913	9,333	34,145	4,648	13,782	1,367	11,986	3,318
2000, proj.	60,453	9,421	34,441	4,688	13,904	1,379	12,108	3,354
2001, proj.	60,925	9,498	34,670	4,719	14,035	1,392	12,220	3,387
2002, proj.	61,332	9,568	34,846	4,743	14,168	1,405	12,318	3,420
2003, proj.	61,645	9,616	34,955	4,758	14,325	1,421	12,365	3,437
2004, proj.	61,937	9,660	34,923	4,753	14,583	1,446	12,431	3,461

[1] Higher education figures are preliminary.

Source: U.S. National Center for Education Statistics, *Digest of Education Statistics,* annual, and *Projections of Education Statistics,* annual.

No. 229. School Expenditures, by Type of Control and Level of Instruction in Constant (1990-91) Dollars: 1960 to 1993

[In millions of dollars. For school years ending in year shown. Total expenditures for public elementary and secondary schools include current expenditures, interest on school debt and capital outlay. Data deflated by the Consumer Price Index, wage earners, and clerical workers through 1975; thereafter, all urban consumers, on a school year basis (supplied by the National Center for Education Statistics). See also Appendix III. See *Historical Statistics, Colonial Times to 1970,* series H 494, 499, and 500 for related but not comparable data, and H 513-519 for private schools]

YEAR	Total	ELEMENTARY AND SECONDARY SCHOOLS			COLLEGES AND UNIVERSITIES		
		Total	Public	Private [1]	Total	Public	Private [1]
1960	108,747	76,173	71,160	5,013	32,574	17,791	14,783
1970	242,696	153,091	144,228	8,863	89,605	57,552	32,053
1975	280,969	178,013	167,670	10,343	102,956	69,726	33,230
1980	285,706	177,954	165,534	12,420	107,752	71,474	36,279
1983	289,366	175,634	161,580	14,053	113,732	74,139	39,593
1984	300,768	182,884	167,753	15,131	117,884	76,475	41,410
1985	313,572	189,163	173,463	15,700	124,409	80,660	43,749
1986	331,645	199,121	182,876	16,245	132,524	86,231	46,293
1987	351,517	210,929	193,713	17,216	140,588	89,756	50,832
1988	362,270	217,333	199,645	17,687	144,937	92,320	52,618
1989.	383,305	231,362	213,240	18,122	151,943	96,253	55,690
1990	402,950	242,891	223,696	19,195	160,059	102,403	57,657
1991	414,093	248,333	228,933	19,400	165,760	105,631	60,128
1992	427,263	256,146	235,894	20,251	171,117	108,232	62,885
1993 [1]	437,943	262,525	241,948	20,577	175,418	110,685	64,733

[1] Estimated.

Source: U.S. National Center for Education Statistics, *Digest Education Statistics,* annual.

Education

No. 230. School Enrollment, Faculty, Graduates, and Finances, With Projections: 1985 to 2003

[As of **fall, except as indicated**]

ITEM	Unit	1985	1990	1992, prel.	1995, proj.	2002, proj.	2003, proj.
ELEMENTARY AND SECONDARY SCHOOLS							
School-age population [1]	1,000	44,781	45,166	46,661	48,853	53,026	53,384
School enrollment: Total	1,000	44,979	46,448	48,109	50,709	55,162	55,459
Kindergarten through grade 8	1,000	31,229	33,973	35,209	36,668	39,589	39,713
Grades 9 through 12	1,000	13,750	12,475	12,901	14,041	15,573	15,746
Public, total	1,000	39,422	41,217	42,735	45,049	49,014	49,280
Kindergarten through grade 8	1,000	27,034	29,878	30,997	32,275	34,846	34,955
Grades 9 through 12	1,000	12,388	11,338	11,738	12,774	14,168	14,325
Private, total	1,000	5,557	5,232	5,375	5,660	6,148	6,179
Kindergarten through grade 8	1,000	4,195	4,095	4,212	4,393	4,743	4,758
Grades 9 through 12	1,000	1,362	1,137	1,163	1,267	1,405	1,421
Classroom teachers: Total	1,000	2,549	2,753	2,821	(NA)	(NA)	(NA)
Public, total	1,000	2,206	2,398	2,458	(NA)	(NA)	(NA)
Private, total	1,000	343	356	363	(NA)	(NA)	(NA)
High school graduates, total [2]	1,000	2,643	2,503	2,512	(NA)	(NA)	(NA)
Public	1,000	2,383	2,235	2,255	(NA)	(NA)	(NA)
Public schools: [2]							
Average daily attendance (ADA)	1,000	36,523	38,427	38,961	41,791	45,462	45,677
Constant (**1992-93**) dollars:							
Teachers' average salary	Dol.	32,999	35,203	35,027	36,096	38,829	39,030
Current school expenditures	Bil. dol.	179.6	214.9	220.8	242.1	291.8	296.8
HIGHER EDUCATION							
Enrollment, total	1,000	12,247	13,820	14,491	14,946	15,738	15,802
Male	1,000	5,818	6,285	6,526	6,781	7,116	7,161
Full time	1,000	3,608	3,808	3,928	4,031	4,354	4,396
Part time	1,000	2,211	2,477	2,598	2,750	2,762	2,765
Female	1,000	6,429	7,535	7,965	8,165	8,622	8,641
Full time	1,000	3,468	4,013	4,237	4,211	4,569	4,596
Part time	1,000	2,961	3,522	3,728	3,954	4,053	4,045
Public	1,000	9,479	10,844	11,388	11,695	12,318	12,365
Four-year institutions	1,000	5,210	5,848	5,902	6,270	6,628	6,666
Two-year institutions	1,000	4,270	4,996	5,486	5,425	5,690	5,699
Private	1,000	2,768	2,975	3,104	3,251	3,420	3,437
Four-year institutions	1,000	2,506	2,731	2,866	2,985	3,133	3,150
Two-year institutions	1,000	261	244	238	266	287	287
Undergraduate	1,000	10,597	11,959	12,540	12,761	13,596	13,659
Graduate	1,000	1,376	1,586	1,670	1,859	1,829	1,830
First-time professional	1,000	274	274	281	326	313	313
Full-time equivalent	1,000	8,943	9,984	10,440	10,661	11,382	11,449
Public	1,000	6,668	7,558	7,915	8,036	8,592	8,641
Private	1,000	2,276	2,426	2,525	2,625	2,790	2,808
Faculty, total	1,000	715	817	835	889	(NA)	(NA)
Public	1,000	503	574	585	621	(NA)	(NA)
Private	1,000	212	244	250	268	(NA)	(NA)
Degrees conferred, total [2]	1,000	1,830	2,025	2,121	2,231	2,286	2,316
Associate's	1,000	446	482	497	518	554	560
Bachelor's	1,000	988	1,095	1,145	1,214	1,254	1,278
Master's	1,000	289	337	364	383	363	363
Doctorate's	1,000	34	39	41	41	41	41
First-professional	1,000	74	72	74	75	74	74

NA Not available.   [1] Population 5-17 years old. Estimated as of July, except 1990 enumerated as of April 1 (with modifications, see text, section 1).   [2] For school year ending June the following year.

Source: U.S. National Center for Education Statistics, *Digest of Education Statistics,* annual, and *Projections of Educational Statistics,* annual.

No. 231. Federal Funds for Education and Related Programs: 1992 to 1994

[In millions of dollars, except percent. For fiscal years ending in June. Figures represent on-budget funds]

LEVEL, AGENCY, AND PROGRAM	1992	1993	1994 [1]
Total, all programs	**60,479.8**	**67,740.6**	**68,364.2**
Percent of Federal budget outlays	4.5	4.8	4.7
Elementary/secondary education programs	**27,926.9**	**30,834.3**	**34,318.8**
Department of Education [2]	12,057.7	13,059.0	14,825.8
Grants for the disadvantaged	6,158.8	6,615.0	6,900.1
School improvement programs	1,514.9	2,032.6	1,663.4
Indian education	68.5	99.9	82.2
Education for the handicapped	2,243.3	2,564.1	3,603.8
Vocational and adult education	1,079.1	190.4	1,317.2
Department of Agriculture [2]	6,714.1	7,154.5	7,800.9
Child nutrition programs	6,127.0	6,596.6	7,236.7
Agricultural Marketing Service—commodities [3]	400.0	389.9	400.0
Department of Defense [2]	1,197.3	1,259.4	1,206.1
Overseas dependents schools	912.9	895.7	841.8
Section VI schools [4]	229.7	279.6	255.5
Department of Energy	15.2	6.3	6.3
Department of Health and Human Services	3,310.2	4,114.5	4,771.3
Head Start	2,201.8	2,776.3	3,326.3
Social security student benefits	514.2	601.7	585.1
Department of the Interior [2]	517.7	536.5	587.8
Mineral Leasing Act and other funds	167.9	143.8	163.5
Indian Education	349.2	391.8	423.6
Department of Justice	94.7	107.9	125.2
Inmate programs	92.8	106.1	121.8
Department of Labor	3,708.4	4,241.0	4,535.9
Job Corps	925.8	949.3	1,027.0
Department of Veterans Affairs	190.6	222.6	320.2
Vocational rehab for disabled veterans	184.5	216.3	253.0
Other agencies and programs	120.9	132.8	139.2
Higher education programs	**14,384.1**	**17,844.0**	**14,129.0**
Department of Education [2]	11,323.6	14,660.7	10,698.9
Student financial assistance	7,071.4	7,678.3	7,420.6
Guaranteed student loans	3,253.6	5,554.9	1,911.5
Department of Defense	34.2	32.7	33.4
Tuition assistance for military personnel	680.2	696.8	684.5
Service academies [5]	102.4	123.4	132.6
Senior ROTC	125.1	128.0	143.7
Professional development education	193.3	184.1	190.1
Department of Energy [2]	259.3	261.3	218.1
	34.4	17.7	17.7

LEVEL, AGENCY, AND PROGRAM	1992	1993	1994 [1]
Department of Health and Human Services [2]	743.5	720.9	759.5
Health professions training programs	305.8	299.8	305.6
National Health Service Corps scholarships	58.7	33.3	42.3
National Institutes of Health training grants [6]	348.0	350.8	373.4
Department of the Interior	140.3	132.9	147.0
Shared revenues, Mineral Leasing Act and other receipts—estimated education share.	69.0	61.6	70.1
Indian programs	71.3	71.4	76.9
Department of Transportation	54.0	57.6	61.0
Department of Veterans Affairs [2]	854.5	920.0	1,070.4
Post-Vietnam veterans	88.5	65.9	52.0
All-volunteer-force educational assistance	650.5	745.8	912.3
Other agencies and programs [2]	519.5	604.7	656.6
National Endowment for the Humanities	58.5	57.8	56.8
National Science Foundation	210.4	246.6	283.0
United States Information Agency	207.7	256.1	266.3
Other education programs [2]	**3,992.0**	**4,107.2**	**4,805.0**
Department of Education [2]	2,579.9	2,526.4	3,038.6
Administration	368.4	353.5	469.2
Libraries	214.9	181.2	166.1
Rehabilitative services and handicapped research	1,991.9	1,983.8	2,396.9
Department of Agriculture	400.4	443.7	452.7
Department of Health and Human Services	97.6	96.9	110.1
Department of Justice	34.5	37.0	27.2
Department of State	44.1	58.8	38.5
Department of the Treasury [2]	51.7	56.8	58.3
Other agencies and programs [2]	784.5	887.7	1,079.5
Agency for International Development	212.2	215.2	231.2
Library of Congress	296.0	311.5	320.3
National Endowment for the Arts	3.3	2.8	2.3
National Endowment for the Humanities	99.8	100.8	99.1
Research programs at universities and related institutions [2]	**14,176.9**	**14,955.1**	**15,111.4**
Department of Agriculture	438.0	436.2	441.5
Department of Defense	2,071.0	2,002.6	1,857.3
Department of Energy	2,867.5	2,763.5	2,623.3
Department of Health and Human Services	5,210.7	5,953.0	6,065.9
National Aeronautics and Space Administration	1,377.3	1,367.5	1,451.2
National Science Foundation	1,664.7	1,833.6	1,958.3

[1] Estimated. [2] Includes other programs and agencies, not shown separately. [3] Purchased under Section 32 of the Act of August 1935 for use in child-nutrition programs. Program provides for the education of dependents of Federal employees residing on Federal property where free public education is unavailable in the nearby community. [4] Includes stateside schools. [5] Instructional costs only including academics, audiovisual, academic computer center, faculty training, military training, physical education, and libraries. [6] Includes alcohol, drug abuse, and mental health training programs.

Source: U.S. National Center for Education Statistics, *Digest of Education Statistics*, 1994.

No. 232. School Expenditures, by Source of Funds in Constant (1990-91) Dollars: 1970 to 1991

[In billions of dollars. For school years ending in year shown. Includes nursery, kindergarten, and special programs when provided by school system. All nonpublic school data and all data beginning 1980 are estimated. Data are deflated by the Consumer Price Index. For 1970, for wage earners and clerical workers; beginning 1980, for all urban consumers, on a school year basis (supplied by the U.S. National Center for Education Statistics). Due to revised methodology, data for 1970 are not comparable to later years or to table 229]

SOURCE OF FUNDS AND CONTROL OF SCHOOL	1970	1980	1984	1985	1986	1987	1988	1989	1990	1991
Total	249.5	285.7	300.8	313.6	331.6	351.5	362.3	383.3	403.0	414.1
Federal	26.6	32.6	25.9	27.0	29.0	30.4	30.9	32.1	33.4	34.4
State	78.7	111.0	114.4	121.7	129.6	136.3	139.9	143.9	149.9	153.3
Local	80.2	74.6	79.1	80.2	83.6	88.4	91.6	101.8	103.0	105.3
All other	64.1	67.5	81.3	84.7	89.5	96.4	99.9	105.6	116.6	121.0
Public	201.3	237.0	244.3	254.1	269.1	283.5	292.0	309.5	326.1	334.6
Federal	20.6	25.6	19.4	20.0	21.3	21.7	22.1	23.1	24.2	24.9
State	78.4	110.2	113.7	120.9	128.7	135.2	138.6	142.4	148.5	151.8
Local	79.7	74.4	78.8	79.8	83.3	88.1	91.3	101.4	102.6	104.9
All other	22.7	26.9	32.3	33.3	35.8	38.5	40.0	42.5	50.8	53.0
Private	48.2	48.7	56.5	59.5	62.5	68.0	70.3	73.8	76.9	79.5
Federal	6.0	7.1	6.5	7.0	7.6	8.7	8.7	8.9	9.2	9.5
State and local	0.7	1.1	1.1	1.2	1.3	1.4	1.6	1.8	1.9	2.1
All other	41.4	40.6	49.0	51.4	53.7	57.9	59.9	63.1	65.8	68.0
Elementary and secondary	162.0	177.9	182.9	189.2	199.1	210.9	217.3	231.4	242.9	248.3
Federal	12.0	16.2	11.4	11.5	12.2	12.4	12.6	13.2	13.9	14.2
State	56.0	77.1	79.8	84.5	89.9	95.9	98.5	101.5	105.8	108.2
Local	76.9	71.7	76.0	76.9	80.2	84.8	87.9	97.9	98.8	100.9
All other	17.0	12.9	15.6	16.2	16.8	17.8	18.3	18.8	24.6	25.0
Public	145.3	165.6	167.8	173.5	182.9	193.7	199.6	213.2	223.7	228.9
Federal	12.0	16.2	11.4	11.5	12.2	12.4	12.6	13.2	13.7	14.2
State	56.0	77.1	79.8	84.5	89.9	95.9	98.5	101.5	105.8	108.2
Local	76.9	71.7	76.0	76.9	80.2	84.8	87.9	97.9	98.8	100.9
All other [1]	0.3	0.5	0.5	0.5	0.5	0.6	0.6	0.6	5.4	5.6
Private	16.7	12.4	15.1	15.7	16.2	17.2	17.7	18.1	19.2	19.4
Higher education	87.5	107.8	117.9	124.5	132.5	140.6	144.9	151.9	160.1	165.8
Federal	14.6	16.5	14.6	15.5	16.7	18.0	18.3	18.8	19.8	20.3
State	22.7	33.9	34.6	37.2	39.7	40.4	41.4	42.4	44.1	45.1
Local	3.2	3.0	3.1	3.3	3.4	3.6	3.7	4.0	4.2	4.4
All other	47.1	54.5	65.7	68.6	72.8	78.6	81.6	86.8	92.0	95.9
Public	56.0	71.5	76.5	80.7	86.2	89.8	92.3	96.3	102.4	105.6
Federal	8.5	9.4	8.0	8.5	9.1	9.3	9.5	9.9	10.6	10.8
State	22.4	33.1	33.9	36.4	38.8	39.2	40.1	40.9	42.7	43.5
Local	2.8	2.6	2.7	3.0	3.1	3.3	3.4	3.6	3.8	4.0
All other	22.4	26.4	31.9	32.8	35.3	37.9	39.4	41.9	45.4	47.4
Private	31.5	36.3	41.4	43.8	46.3	50.8	52.6	55.7	57.7	60.1
Federal	6.0	7.1	6.5	7.0	7.6	8.7	8.7	8.9	9.2	9.5
State and local	0.7	1.1	1.1	1.2	1.2	1.4	1.6	1.8	1.9	2.1
All other	24.8	28.2	33.9	35.6	37.5	40.7	42.2	44.9	46.6	48.6

[1] Beginning in 1989-90, includes all fees for transportation, books, and food services.

Source: U.S. National Center for Education Statistics, *Digest of Education Statistics*, annual.

No. 233. Enrollment in Public and Private Schools, by Control and Level, With Projections: 1970 to 2004

[In thousands. As of fall. Data are for regular day schools and exclude independent nursery schools and kindergartens, residential schools for exceptional children, subcollegiate departments of colleges, Federal schools for Indians, and federally operated schools on Federal installations. College data include degree-credit and nondegree-credit enrollment]

CONTROL OF SCHOOL AND LEVEL	1970	1980	1985	1990	1992, prel.	1993, est.	1994, est.	1995, proj.	2000, proj.	2003, proj.	2004, proj.
Total	59,838	58,305	57,226	60,267	62,601	63,424	64,519	65,655	69,874	71,261	71,598
Public	52,322	50,335	48,901	52,061	54,122	54,803	55,754	56,744	60,453	61,645	61,937
Private	7,516	7,971	8,325	8,206	8,478	8,621	8,765	8,911	9,421	9,616	9,661
Kindergarten through 8	36,610	31,639	31,229	33,973	35,209	35,654	36,170	36,668	39,129	39,713	39,676
Public	32,558	27,647	27,034	29,878	30,997	31,374	31,837	32,275	34,441	34,955	34,923
Private	4,052	3,992	4,195	4,095	4,212	4,280	4,333	4,393	4,688	4,758	4,753
Grades 9 through 12	14,647	14,570	13,750	12,475	12,901	13,170	13,649	14,041	15,283	15,746	16,029
Public	13,336	13,231	12,388	11,338	11,738	11,979	12,417	12,774	13,904	14,325	14,583
Private	1,311	1,339	1,362	1,137	1,163	1,191	1,232	1,267	1,379	1,421	1,446
College	8,581	12,097	12,247	13,820	14,491	[1]14,600	14,700	14,946	15,462	15,802	15,892
Public	6,428	9,457	9,479	10,845	11,388	11,450	11,500	11,695	12,108	12,365	12,431
Private	2,153	2,640	2,768	2,975	3,104	3,150	3,200	3,251	3,354	3,437	3,461

[1] Higher education figures are preliminary.

Source: U.S. National Center for Education Statistics, *Digest of Education Statistics*, annual; *Projections of Education Statistics*, annual; and unpublished data.

No. 234. School Enrollment: 1970 to 1993

[As of **October.** Covers civilian noninstitutional population enrolled in nursery school and above. Based on Current Population Survey, see text, section 1. See *Historical Statistics, Colonial Times to 1970,* series H 442-476 for enrollment 5-34 years old]

AGE	1970	1980	1985	1987	1988	1989	1990	1991	1992	1993
ENROLLMENT										
Total 3 to 34 years old	**60,357**	**57,348**	**58,013**	**58,692**	**58,846**	**59,235**	**60,588**	**61,276**	**62,084**	**62,730**
3 and 4 years old	1,461	2,280	2,801	2,744	2,797	2,898	3,292	3,068	3,063	3,275
5 and 6 years old	7,000	5,853	6,697	6,956	7,044	6,990	7,207	7,178	7,252	7,298
7 to 13 years old	28,943	23,751	22,849	23,525	24,044	24,431	25,016	25,445	25,768	26,110
14 and 15 years old	7,869	7,282	7,362	6,651	6,481	6,493	6,555	6,634	6,861	7,011
16 and 17 years old	6,927	7,129	6,654	6,881	6,561	6,254	6,098	6,155	6,272	6,339
18 and 19 years old	3,322	3,788	3,716	3,982	4,059	4,125	4,044	3,969	4,012	4,063
20 and 21 years old	1,949	2,515	2,708	2,740	2,724	2,630	2,852	3,041	3,027	2,810
22 to 24 years old	1,410	1,931	2,068	2,052	2,092	2,207	2,231	2,365	2,577	2,579
25 to 29 years old	1,011	1,714	1,942	1,931	1,773	1,960	2,013	2,045	1,907	1,942
30 to 34 years old	466	1,105	1,218	1,229	,1,271	1,248	1,281	1,377	1,344	1,303
35 years old and over	(NA)	1,290	1,766	1,931	2,270	2,230	2,439	2,620	2,473	2,634
ENROLLMENT RATE										
Total 3 to 34 years old	**56.4**	**49.7**	**48.3**	**48.6**	**48.7**	**49.1**	**50.2**	**50.7**	**51.4**	**51.8**
3 and 4 years old	20.5	36.7	38.9	38.3	38.2	39.1	44.4	40.5	39.7	40.4
5 and 6 years old	89.5	95.7	96.1	95.1	96.0	95.2	96.5	95.4	95.5	95.4
7 to 13 years old	99.2	99.3	99.2	99.5	99.7	99.3	99.6	99.7	99.4	99.5
14 and 15 years old	98.1	98.2	98.1	98.6	98.9	98.8	99.0	98.8	99.1	98.9
16 and 17 years old	90.0	89.0	91.7	91.7	91.6	92.7	92.5	93.3	94.1	94.0
18 and 19 years old	47.7	46.4	51.6	55.6	55.7	56.0	57.3	59.6	61.4	61.6
20 and 21 years old	31.9	31.0	35.3	38.7	39.1	38.5	39.7	42.0	44.0	42.7
22 to 24 years old	14.9	16.3	16.9	17.5	18.3	19.9	21.0	22.2	23.7	23.6
25 to 29 years old	7.5	9.3	9.2	9.0	8.3	9.3	9.7	10.2	9.8	10.2
30 to 34 years old	4.2	6.4	6.1	5.9	3.9	5.7	5.8	6.2	6.1	5.9
35 years old and over	(NA)	1.4	1.6	1.8	2.1	2.0	2.1	2.2	2.1	2.2

NA Not available.

Source: U.S. Bureau of the Census, *Current Population Reports*, P20-479; and earlier reports.

No. 235. School Enrollment, by Race, Hispanic Origin, and Age: 1980 to 1993

[See headnote, table 234]

AGE	WHITE			BLACK			HISPANIC ORIGIN [1]		
	1980	1990	1993	1980	1990	1993	1980	1990	1993
ENROLLMENT									
Total 3 to 34 years old	**47,673**	**48,899**	**49,985**	**8,251**	**8,854**	**9,470**	**4,263**	**6,073**	**6,689**
3 and 4 years old	1,844	2,700	2,581	371	452	526	172	249	275
5 and 6 years old	4,781	5,750	5,784	904	1,129	1,139	491	835	844
7 to 13 years old	19,585	20,076	20,739	3,598	3,832	4,081	2,009	2,794	2,991
14 and 15 years old	6,038	5,265	5,572	1,088	1,023	1,111	568	739	793
16 and 17 years old	5,937	4,858	5,060	1,047	962	1,024	454	592	727
18 and 19 years old	3,199	3,271	3,242	494	596	600	226	329	355
20 and 21 years old	2,206	2,402	2,295	242	305	308	111	213	260
22 to 24 years old	1,669	1,781	2,091	196	274	262	93	121	170
25 to 29 years old	1,473	1,706	1,537	187	162	269	84	130	159
30 to 34 years old	942	1,090	1,083	124	119	149	54	72	116
35 years old and over	1,104	2,096	2,167	186	238	321	(NA)	145	149
ENROLLMENT RATE									
Total 3 to 34 years old	**48.9**	**49.5**	**51.1**	**53.9**	**51.9**	**53.6**	**49.8**	**47.4**	**48.9**
3 and 4 years old	36.3	44.9	40.8	38.2	41.6	39.8	28.5	29.8	26.8
5 and 6 years old	95.8	96.5	95.5	95.4	96.3	94.6	94.5	94.8	93.8
7 to 13 years old	99.2	99.6	99.5	99.4	99.8	99.5	99.2	99.4	99.4
14 and 15 years old	98.3	99.1	98.9	97.9	99.2	98.5	94.3	99.0	97.6
16 and 17 years old	88.6	92.5	94.1	90.6	91.7	94.7	81.8	85.4	88.3
18 and 19 years old	46.3	57.1	61.7	45.7	55.2	57.7	37.8	44.1	50.0
20 and 21 years old	31.9	41.0	44.0	23.4	28.4	30.0	19.5	27.2	31.8
22 to 24 years old	16.4	20.2	23.3	13.6	20.0	18.1	11.7	9.9	13.7
25 to 29 years old	9.2	9.9	9.8	8.8	6.1	10.4	6.9	6.3	7.7
30 to 34 years old	6.3	5.9	5.9	6.8	4.4	5.5	5.1	3.6	5.1
35 years old and over	1.3	2.1	2.1	1.8	2.1	2.6	(NA)	2.1	1.9

NA Not available.   [1] Persons of Hispanic origin may be of any race.

Source: U.S. Bureau of the Census, *Current Population Reports*, P20-479; and earlier reports.

No. 236. Enrollment in Public and Private Schools: 1960 to 1993

[In millions, except percent. As of **October.** For civilian noninstitutional population. For **1960,** 5 to 34 years old; for **1970 to 1985,** 3 to 34 years old; **beginning 1986,** for 3 years old and over]

YEAR	PUBLIC						PRIVATE					
	Total	Nur-sery	Kinder-garten	Ele-mentary	High School	College	Total	Nur-sery	Kinder-garten	Ele-mentary	High School	College
1960	39.0	(NA)	([1])	27.5	9.2	2.3	7.2	(NA)	([1])	4.9	1.0	1.3
1970	52.2	0.3	2.6	30.0	13.5	5.7	8.1	0.8	0.5	3.9	1.2	1.7
1975	52.8	0.6	2.9	27.2	14.5	7.7	8.2	1.2	0.5	3.3	1.2	2.0
1976	52.4	0.5	3.0	26.7	14.5	7.7	8.1	1.1	0.5	3.1	1.2	2.2
1977	51.6	0.6	2.7	26.0	14.5	7.9	8.4	1.1	0.5	3.3	1.2	2.3
1978	50.0	0.6	2.5	25.3	14.2	7.4	8.6	1.2	0.5	3.2	1.2	2.4
1979	50.0	0.6	2.6	24.8	14.0	7.7	8.2	1.2	0.4	3.1	1.1	2.3
1980	(NA)	0.6	2.7	24.4	(NA)	(NA)	(NA)	1.4	0.5	3.1	(NA)	(NA)
1981	49.7	0.7	2.6	24.8	13.5	8.2	8.7	1.4	0.5	3.0	1.1	2.6
1982	49.2	0.7	2.7	24.4	13.0	8.4	8.2	1.4	0.6	3.0	1.1	2.6
1983	48.7	0.8	2.7	24.2	12.8	8.2	9.0	1.5	0.7	3.0	1.2	2.6
1984	49.0	0.8	3.0	24.1	12.7	8.5	8.3	1.6	0.5	2.7	1.1	2.4
1985 [2]	49.0	0.9	3.2	23.8	12.8	8.4	9.0	1.6	0.6	3.1	1.2	2.5
1986 [2]	51.2	0.8	3.4	24.2	13.0	9.8	9.4	1.7	0.6	3.0	1.2	2.9
1987 [2]	51.7	0.8	3.4	24.8	12.7	10.0	8.9	1.7	0.6	2.8	1.1	2.8
1988 [2]	52.2	0.9	3.4	25.5	12.2	10.3	8.9	1.8	0.5	2.8	1.0	2.8
1989 [2]	52.5	0.9	3.3	25.9	12.1	10.3	8.9	1.9	0.6	2.7	0.8	2.9
1990 [2]	53.8	1.2	3.3	26.6	11.9	10.7	9.2	2.2	0.6	2.7	0.9	2.9
1991 [2]	54.5	1.1	3.5	26.6	12.2	11.1	9.4	1.8	0.6	3.0	1.0	3.0
1992 [2]	55.0	1.1	3.5	27.1	12.3	11.1	9.4	1.8	0.6	3.1	1.0	3.0
1993 [2]	56.0	1.2	3.5	27.7	12.6	10.9	9.4	1.8	0.7	2.9	1.0	3.0
Percent White:												
1960.	85.7	(NA)	([1])	84.3	88.2	92.2	95.7	(NA)	([1])	95.3	96.7	96.3
1970.	84.5	59.5	84.4	83.1	85.6	90.7	93.4	91.1	88.2	94.1	96.1	92.8
1980.	(NA)	68.2	80.7	80.9	(NA)	(NA)	(NA)	89.0	87.0	90.7	(NA)	(NA)
1990.	79.8	71.7	78.3	78.9	79.2	84.1	87.4	89.6	83.2	88.2	89.4	85.0
1991.	79.3	74.0	78.3	78.6	78.4	82.8	86.7	89.0	81.8	87.9	88.8	84.3
1992.	79.2	71.5	77.8	78.4	78.6	83.1	86.7	89.0	84.9	87.6	87.5	84.5
1993.	78.9	68.5	76.6	78.4	78.3	82.5	85.3	89.7	86.9	87.0	83.1	81.4

NA Not available.   [1] Included in elementary school.   [2] See table 279 for college enrollment 35 years old and over. Also data beginning 1986 based on a revised edit and tabulation package.

Source: U.S. Bureau of the Census, *Current Population Reports,* P20-479; and earlier reports.

No. 237. School Enrollment, by Sex and Level: 1960 to 1993

[In millions. As of **Oct.** For the civilian noninstitutional population. For **1960,** persons 5 to 34 years old; **1970-1979** 3 to 34 years old; **beginning 1980,** 3 years old and over. Elementary includes kindergarten and grades 1-8; high school, grades 9-12; and college, 2-year and 4-year colleges, universities, and graduate and professional schools. Data for college represent degree-credit enrollment]

YEAR	ALL LEVELS [1]			ELEMENTARY			HIGH SCHOOL			COLLEGE		
	Total	Male	Female	Total	Male	Female	Total	Male	Female	Total	Male	Female
1960	46.3	24.2	22.0	32.4	16.7	15.7	10.2	5.2	5.1	3.6	2.3	1.2
1970	60.4	31.4	28.9	37.1	19.0	18.1	14.7	7.4	7.3	7.4	4.4	3.0
1975	61.0	31.6	29.4	33.8	17.3	16.5	15.7	8.0	7.7	9.7	5.3	4.4
1976	60.5	31.2	29.3	33.3	17.0	16.2	15.7	8.1	7.7	10.0	5.3	4.7
1977	60.0	30.8	29.2	32.4	16.6	15.8	15.8	8.0	7.7	10.2	5.4	4.8
1978	58.6	30.1	28.6	31.5	16.1	15.3	15.5	7.8	7.6	9.8	5.1	4.7
1979	57.9	29.5	28.3	30.9	15.9	15.0	15.1	7.7	7.4	10.0	5.0	5.0
1980 [2]	58.6	29.6	29.1	30.6	15.8	14.9	14.6	7.3	7.3	11.4	5.4	6.0
1981 [2]	58.4	29.5	28.9	30.1	15.5	14.7	14.4	7.3	7.1	11.8	5.6	6.2
1981 [3]	59.9	30.3	29.6	31.0	15.9	15.0	14.7	7.5	7.3	12.1	5.8	6.3
1982	59.4	30.0	29.4	30.7	15.8	14.9	14.2	7.2	7.0	12.3	5.9	6.4
1983	59.3	30.1	29.2	30.6	15.7	14.8	14.1	7.1	7.0	12.4	6.0	6.3
1984	58.9	29.9	29.0	30.3	15.6	14.7	13.9	7.1	6.8	12.3	6.0	6.3
1985	59.8	30.0	29.7	30.7	15.7	15.0	14.1	7.2	6.9	12.5	5.9	6.6
1986	60.1	30.4	29.7	31.1	16.1	15.0	14.0	7.1	6.9	12.4	5.8	6.6
1986 [4]	60.5	30.6	30.0	31.1	16.1	15.0	14.2	7.2	7.0	12.7	6.0	6.7
1987	60.6	30.7	29.9	31.6	16.3	15.3	13.8	7.0	6.8	12.7	6.0	6.7
1988	61.1	30.7	30.5	32.2	16.6	15.6	13.2	6.7	6.4	13.1	5.9	7.2
1989	61.5	30.8	30.7	32.5	16.7	15.8	12.9	6.6	6.3	13.2	6.0	7.2
1990	63.0	31.5	31.5	33.2	17.1	16.0	12.8	6.5	6.4	13.6	6.2	7.4
1991	63.9	32.1	31.8	33.8	17.3	16.4	13.1	6.8	6.4	14.1	6.4	7.6
1992	64.6	32.2	32.3	34.3	17.7	16.6	13.3	6.8	6.5	14.0	6.2	7.8
1993	65.4	32.9	32.5	34.8	17.9	16.9	13.6	7.0	6.6	13.9	6.3	7.6

[1] Beginning 1970, includes nursery schools, not shown separately.   [2] Based on 1970 population controls.   [3] Based on 1980 population controls.   [4] Revised. Data beginning 1986, based on a revised edit and tabulation package.

Source: U.S. Bureau of the Census, *Current Population Reports,* P20-479; and earlier reports.

No. 238. Educational Attainment, by Race and Ethnicity: 1960 to 1994

[In percent. For persons 25 years old and over. 1960, 1970, and 1980 as of April 1 and based on sample data from the censuses of population. **Other years as of March** and based on the Current Population Survey; see text, section 1, and Appendix III. See table 239 for data by sex]

YEAR	Total [1]	White	Black	Asian and Pacific Islander	HISPANIC [2] Total [3]	HISPANIC [2] Mexican	HISPANIC [2] Puerto Rican	HISPANIC [2] Cuban
COMPLETED 4 YEARS OF HIGH SCHOOL OR MORE								
1960	41.1	43.2	20.1	(NA)	(NA)	(NA)	(NA)	(NA)
1965	49.0	51.3	27.2	(NA)	(NA)	(NA)	(NA)	(NA)
1970	52.3	54.5	31.4	(NA)	32.1	24.2	23.4	43.9
1975	62.5	64.5	42.5	(NA)	37.9	31.0	28.7	51.7
1980	66.5	68.8	51.2	(NA)	44.0	37.6	40.1	55.3
1985	73.9	75.5	59.8	(NA)	47.9	41.9	46.3	51.1
1990	77.6	79.1	66.2	80.4	50.8	44.1	55.5	63.5
1992 [4]	79.4	80.9	67.7	(NA)	52.6	45.2	60.5	62.0
1993 [4]	80.2	81.5	70.4	(NA)	53.1	46.2	59.8	62.1
1994 [4]	80.9	82.0	72.9	(NA)	53.3	46.7	59.4	64.1
COMPLETED 4 YEARS OF COLLEGE OR MORE								
1960	7.7	8.1	3.1	(NA)	(NA)	(NA)	(NA)	(NA)
1965	9.4	9.9	4.7	(NA)	(NA)	(NA)	(NA)	(NA)
1970	10.7	11.3	4.4	(NA)	4.5	2.5	2.2	11.1
1975	13.9	14.5	6.4	(NA)	(NA)	(NA)	(NA)	(NA)
1980	16.2	17.1	8.4	(NA)	7.6	4.9	5.6	16.2
1985	19.4	20.0	11.1	(NA)	8.5	5.5	7.0	13.7
1990	21.3	22.0	11.3	39.9	9.2	5.4	9.7	20.2
1992 [4]	21.4	22.1	11.9	(NA)	9.3	6.1	8.4	18.4
1993 [4]	21.9	22.6	12.2	(NA)	9.0	5.9	8.0	16.5
1994 [4]	22.2	22.9	12.9	(NA)	9.1	6.3	9.7	16.2

NA Not available.   [1] Includes other races, not shown separately.   [2] Persons of Hispanic origin may be of any race.   [3] Includes persons of other Hispanic origin, not shown separately.   [4] Beginning 1992, persons high school graduates and those with a BA degree or higher.

Source: U.S. Bureau of the Census, *U.S. Census of Population, U.S. Summary,* PC80-1-C1 and *Current Population Reports* P20-455, P20-459, P20-462, P20-465RV, P20-475; and unpublished data.

No. 239. Educational Attainment, by Race, Ethnicity, and Sex: 1960 to 1994

[In percent. **For persons 25 years old and over. 1960, 1970 and 1980 as of April 1** and based on sample data from the censuses of population. **Other years as of March** and based on the Current Population Survey; see text, section 1, and Appendix III. See table 238 for totals for both sexes]

YEAR	ALL RACES [1] Male	ALL RACES [1] Female	WHITE Male	WHITE Female	BLACK Male	BLACK Female	ASIAN AND PACIFIC ISLANDER Male	ASIAN AND PACIFIC ISLANDER Female	HISPANIC [2] Male	HISPANIC [2] Female
COMPLETED 4 YEARS OF HIGH SCHOOL OR MORE										
1960	39.5	42.5	41.6	44.7	18.2	21.8	(NA)	(NA)	(NA)	(NA)
1965	48.0	49.9	50.2	52.2	25.8	28.4	(NA)	(NA)	(NA)	(NA)
1970	51.9	52.8	54.0	55.0	30.1	32.5	(NA)	(NA)	37.9	34.2
1975	63.1	62.1	65.0	64.1	41.6	43.3	(NA)	(NA)	39.5	36.7
1980	67.3	65.8	69.6	68.1	50.8	51.5	(NA)	(NA)	67.3	65.8
1985	74.4	73.5	76.0	75.1	58.4	60.8	(NA)	(NA)	48.5	47.4
1990	77.7	77.5	79.1	79.0	65.8	66.5	84.0	77.2	50.3	51.3
1991	78.5	78.3	79.8	79.9	66.7	66.7	83.8	80.0	51.4	51.2
1992 [3]	79.7	79.2	81.1	80.7	67.0	68.2	(NA)	(NA)	53.7	51.5
1993 [3]	80.5	80.0	81.8	81.3	69.6	71.1	(NA)	(NA)	52.9	53.2
1994 [3]	81.0	80.7	82.1	81.9	71.7	73.8	(NA)	(NA)	53.4	53.2
COMPLETED 4 YEARS OF COLLEGE OR MORE										
1960	9.7	5.8	10.3	6.0	2.8	3.3	(NA)	(NA)	(NA)	(NA)
1965	12.0	7.1	12.7	7.3	4.9	4.5	(NA)	(NA)	(NA)	(NA)
1970	13.5	8.1	14.4	8.4	4.2	4.6	(NA)	(NA)	7.8	4.3
1975	17.6	10.6	18.4	11.0	6.7	6.2	(NA)	(NA)	8.3	4.6
1980	20.1	12.8	21.3	13.3	8.4	8.3	(NA)	(NA)	9.4	6.0
1985	23.1	16.0	24.0	16.3	11.2	11.0	(NA)	(NA)	9.7	7.3
1990	24.4	18.4	25.3	19.0	11.9	10.8	44.9	35.4	9.8	8.7
1991	24.3	18.8	25.4	19.3	11.4	11.6	43.2	35.5	10.0	9.4
1992 [3]	24.3	18.6	25.2	19.1	11.9	12.0	(NA)	(NA)	10.2	8.5
1993 [3]	24.8	19.2	25.7	19.7	11.9	12.4	(NA)	(NA)	9.5	8.5
1994 [3]	25.1	19.6	26.1	20.0	12.8	13.0	(NA)	(NA)	9.6	8.6

NA Not available.   [1] Includes other races, not shown separately.   [2] Persons of Hispanic origin may be of any race.   [3] Beginning 1992, persons high school graduates and those with a BA degree or higher.

Source: U.S. Bureau of the Census, *U.S. Census of Population, 1960, 1970, and 1980, vol.1;* and *Current Population Reports* P20-459, P20-462, P20-475; and unpublished data.

No. 240. Years of School Completed, by Selected Characteristic: 1994

[**For persons 25 years old and over.** As of **March.** Based on Current Population Survey; see text, section 1, and Appendix III. For composition of regions, see table 27]

CHARACTERISTIC	Population (1,000)	PERCENT OF POPULATION—					
		Not a high school graduate	High school graduate	With some college, but no degree	With an associate's degree [1]	With a bachelor's degree	With an advanced degree
Total persons	**164,512**	**19.1**	**34.4**	**17.4**	**7.0**	**14.7**	**7.5**
Age:							
25 to 34 years old	41,946	13.6	34.5	19.9	8.5	18.2	5.2
35 to 44 years old	41,527	11.3	33.2	19.4	9.1	17.9	9.2
45 to 54 years old	29,522	14.9	34.0	17.9	7.1	15.2	11.0
55 to 64 years old	20,737	24.4	37.2	14.8	4.7	11.1	7.7
65 to 74 years old	18,087	32.2	36.6	13.5	4.0	8.5	5.1
75 years old or over	12,692	45.2	30.6	10.8	2.5	7.0	3.9
Sex: Male	78,539	19.0	32.3	17.3	6.3	15.9	9.2
Female	85,973	19.3	36.2	17.4	7.5	13.7	5.9
Race: White	139,760	18.0	34.5	17.5	7.1	15.1	7.9
Black	18,103	27.1	36.2	17.5	6.3	9.5	3.4
Other	6,648	21.0	26.0	14.3	6.3	22.0	10.4
Hispanic origin: Hispanic	13,714	46.7	26.2	13.3	4.7	6.2	2.9
Non-Hispanic	150,798	16.6	35.1	17.7	7.2	15.5	7.9
Region: Northeast	33,797	17.3	37.8	13.4	6.6	15.6	9.3
Midwest	38,427	17.3	37.8	17.0	7.2	14.1	6.7
South	57,025	22.4	33.4	17.4	6.5	13.7	6.6
West	35,262	17.4	28.9	21.5	7.9	16.3	8.0
Marital status:							
Never married	24,026	17.8	31.3	17.2	7.0	19.1	7.6
Married spouse present	103,987	16.2	34.8	17.4	7.3	15.8	8.5
Married spouse absent	6,208	29.0	35.4	17.3	5.8	8.5	3.9
Separated	4,404	28.1	37.4	18.6	5.5	7.0	3.3
Widowed	13,273	42.0	34.0	11.6	3.2	6.4	2.8
Divorced	17,017	17.0	35.7	21.9	8.5	10.9	6.1
Civilian labor force status:							
Employed	102,325	10.7	33.7	19.2	8.5	18.3	9.6
Unemployed	6,268	24.1	38.7	17.4	6.3	9.8	3.7
Not in the labor force	55,151	34.5	35.1	13.8	4.2	8 [7]	3.8

[1] Includes vocational degrees.

Source: U.S. Bureau of the Census, unpublished data.

No. 241. Mean Monthly Income, by Highest Degree Earned: 1993

[**For persons 18 years old and over.** Based on the Survey of Income and Program Participation; see source for details]

CHARACTERISTIC	Total persons	LEVEL OF DEGREE								
		Not a high school graduate	High school graduate only	Some college, no degree	Vocational	Associate's	Bachelor's	Master's	Professional	Doctorate
MEAN MONTHLY INCOME [1] (dol.)										
All persons [2]	**1,687**	**906**	**1,380**	**1,579**	**1,736**	**1,985**	**2,625**	**3,411**	**5,534**	**4,328**
Age: 18 to 24 years old	709	459	783	610	1,017	912	1,128	1,351	1,295	(B)
25 to 34 years old	1,622	936	1,310	1,610	1,643	1,760	2,341	2,648	3,515	3,465
35 to 44 years old	2,082	1,032	1,603	1,936	2,030	2,145	2,891	3,180	6,537	4,032
45 to 54 years old	2,302	1,096	1,711	2,484	1,990	2,534	3,345	3,983	6,606	5,267
55 to 64 years old	1,922	1,045	1,535	1,974	1,731	2,969	3,397	4,462	6,921	4,246
65 years old and over	1,329	878	1,217	1,648	1,516	1,697	2,324	3,163	3,820	3,639
Sex: Male	2,230	1,211	1,812	2,045	2,318	2,561	3,430	4,298	6,312	4,421
Female	1,186	621	1,008	1,139	1,373	1,544	1,809	2,505	3,530	4,020
Race: White	1,756	951	1,422	1,649	1,768	2,021	2,682	3,478	5,590	4,449
Black	1,192	713	1,071	1,222	1,428	1,746	2,333	2,834	3,445	3,778
Hispanic [3]	1,126	786	1,106	1,239	1,329	2,069	2,186	2,605	2,317	2,677

B Base figure too small to meet statistical standards for reliability of a derived figure.   [1] For definition of mean, see Guide to Tabular Presentation.   [2] Includes other races, not shown separately.   [3] Persons of Hispanic origin may be of any race.

Source: U.S. Bureau of the Census, unpublished data.

No. 242. Educational Attainment—States: 1990

[As of **April 1. For persons 25 years old and over, except as indicated.** Based on the 1990 Census of Population; see text, section 1, and Appendix III]

STATE	Population (1,000)	PERCENT OF POPULATION—						
		Not a high school graduate	High school graduate	With some college, but no degree	With an associate's degree	With a bachelor's degree	With an advanced degree	Drop-outs [1]
United States	**158,868**	**24.8**	**30.0**	**18.7**	**6.2**	**13.1**	**7.2**	**11.2**
Alabama............	2,546	33.1	29.4	16.8	5.0	10.1	5.5	12.6
Alaska.............	323	13.4	28.7	27.6	7.2	15.0	8.0	10.9
Arizona............	2,301	21.3	26.1	25.4	6.8	13.3	7.0	14.4
Arkansas	1,496	33.7	32.7	16.6	3.7	8.9	4.5	11.4
California	18,695	23.8	22.3	22.6	7.9	15.3	8.1	14.2
Colorado...........	2,107	15.6	26.5	24.0	6.9	18.0	9.0	9.8
Connecticut.........	2,199	20.8	29.5	15.9	6.6	16.2	11.0	9.0
Delaware	428	22.5	32.7	16.9	6.5	13.7	7.7	10.4
District of Columbia	409	26.9	21.2	15.6	3.1	16.1	17.2	13.9
Florida	8,887	25.6	30.1	19.4	6.6	12.0	6.3	14.3
Georgia	4,023	29.1	29.6	17.0	5.0	12.9	6.4	14.1
Hawaii.............	710	19.9	28.7	20.1	8.3	15.8	7.1	7.5
Idaho.............	601	20.3	30.4	24.2	7.5	12.4	5.3	10.4
Illinois	7,294	23.8	30.0	19.4	5.8	13.6	7.5	10.6
Indiana............	3,489	24.4	38.2	16.6	5.3	9.2	6.4	11.4
Iowa	1,777	19.9	38.5	17.0	7.7	11.7	5.2	6.6
Kansas............	1,566	18.7	32.8	21.9	5.4	14.1	7.0	8.7
Kentucky	2,334	35.4	31.8	15.2	4.1	8.1	5.5	13.3
Louisiana	2,537	31.7	31.7	17.2	3.3	10.5	5.6	12.5
Maine.............	796	21.2	37.1	16.1	6.9	12.7	6.1	8.3
Maryland	3,123	21.6	28.1	18.6	5.2	15.6	10.9	10.9
Massachusetts.......	3,962	20.0	29.7	15.8	7.2	16.6	10.6	8.5
Michigan...........	5,843	23.2	32.3	20.4	6.7	10.9	6.4	10.0
Minnesota..........	2,771	17.6	33.0	19.0	8.6	15.6	6.3	6.4
Mississippi	1,539	35.7	27.5	16.9	5.2	9.7	5.1	11.8
Missouri...........	3,292	26.1	33.1	18.4	4.5	11.7	6.1	11.4
Montana...........	508	19.0	33.5	22.1	5.6	14.1	5.7	8.1
Nebraska..........	996	18.2	34.7	21.1	7.1	13.1	5.9	7.0
Nevada	790	21.2	31.5	25.8	6.2	10.1	5.2	15.2
New Hampshire.......	714	17.8	31.7	18.0	8.1	16.4	7.9	9.4
New Jersey.........	5,166	23.3	31.1	15.5	5.2	16.0	8.8	9.6
New Mexico	923	24.9	28.7	20.9	5.0	12.1	8.3	11.7
New York	11,819	25.2	29.5	15.7	6.5	13.2	9.9	9.9
North Carolina.......	4,253	30.0	29.0	16.8	6.8	12.0	5.4	12.5
North Dakota........	397	23.3	28.0	20.5	10.0	13.5	4.5	4.6
Ohio	6,925	24.3	36.3	17.0	5.3	11.1	5.9	8.9
Oklahoma..........	1,995	25.4	30.5	21.3	5.0	11.8	6.0	10.4
Oregon............	1,855	18.5	28.9	25.0	6.9	13.6	7.0	11.8
Pennsylvania........	7,873	25.3	38.6	12.9	5.2	11.3	6.6	9.1
Rhode Island........	659	28.0	29.5	15.0	6.3	13.5	7.8	11.1
South Carolina.......	2,168	31.7	29.5	15.8	6.3	11.2	5.4	11.7
South Dakota	431	22.9	33.7	18.8	7.4	12.3	4.9	7.7
Tennessee	3,139	32.9	30.0	16.9	4.2	10.5	5.4	13.4
Texas.............	10,311	27.9	25.6	21.1	5.2	13.9	6.5	12.9
Utah	897	14.9	27.2	27.9	7.8	15.4	6.8	8.7
Vermont	357	19.2	34.6	14.7	7.2	15.4	8.9	8.0
Virginia............	3,975	24.8	26.6	18.5	5.5	15.4	9.1	10.0
Washington.........	3,126	16.2	27.9	25.0	7.9	15.9	7.0	10.6
West Virginia........	1,172	34.0	36.6	13.2	3.8	7.5	4.8	10.9
Wisconsin..........	3,094	21.4	37.1	16.7	7.1	12.1	5.6	7.1
Wyoming	278	17.0	33.2	24.2	6.9	13.1	5.7	6.9

[1] For persons 16 to 19 years old. A dropout is a person who is not in regular school and who has not completed the 12th grade or received a general equivalency degree.

Source: U.S. Bureau of the Census, *1990 Census of Population*, CPH-L-96.

No. 243. Preprimary School Enrollment—Summary: 1970 to 1993

[As of **October**. Civilian noninstitutional population. Includes public and nonpublic nursery school and kindergarten programs. Excludes 5 year olds enrolled in elementary school. Based on Current Population Survey; see text, section 1]

ITEM	1970	1975	1980	1985	1989	1990	1991	1992	1993
NUMBER OF CHILDREN (1,000)									
Population, 3 to 5 years old	10,949	10,183	9,284	10,733	11,038	11,207	11,370	11,544	11,954
Total enrolled.[1]	4,104	4,954	4,878	5,865	6,026	6,659	6,334	6,403	6,581
Nursery	1,094	1,745	1,981	2,477	2,825	3,378	2,824	2,857	2,984
Public	332	570	628	846	930	1,202	996	1,074	1,204
Private	762	1,174	1,353	1,631	1,894	2,177	1,827	1,784	1,779
Kindergarten	3,010	3,211	2,897	3,388	3,201	3,281	3,510	3,546	3,597
Public	2,498	2,682	2,438	2,847	2,704	2,767	2,968	2,996	3,020
Private	511	528	459	541	496	513	543	550	577
White	3,443	4,105	3,994	4,757	4,911	5,389	5,104	5,137	5,224
Black	586	731	725	919	872	964	928	966	1,011
Hispanic [2]	(NA)	(NA)	370	496	520	642	675	728	657
3 years old	454	683	857	1,035	1,005	1,205	1,075	1,081	1,097
4 years old	1,007	1,418	1,423	1,765	1,882	2,086	1,993	1,982	2,179
5 years old	2,643	2,852	2,598	3,065	3,139	3,367	3,266	3,340	3,306
ENROLLMENT RATE									
Total enrolled [1]	37.5	48.6	52.5	54.6	54.6	59.4	55.7	55.5	55.1
White	37.8	48.6	52.7	54.7	55.0	59.7	56.2	55.8	55.7
Black	34.9	48.1	51.8	55.8	54.2	57.8	53.1	55.1	52.7
Hispanic [2]	(NA)	(NA)	43.3	43.3	41.6	49.0	46.4	48.4	43.9
3 years old	12.9	21.5	27.3	28.8	27.1	32.6	28.2	27.7	27.1
4 years old	27.8	40.5	46.3	49.1	51.0	56.0	53.0	52.1	53.9
5 years old	69.3	81.3	84.7	86.5	86.4	88.8	86.0	87.2	85.7

NA Not available.   [1] Includes races not shown separately.   [2] Persons of Hispanic origin may be of any race. The method of identifying Hispanic children was changed in 1980 from allocation based on status of mother to status reported for each child. The number of Hispanic children using the new method is larger.

Source: U.S. Bureau of the Census, *Current Population Reports*, P20-479.

No. 244. School Enrollment of 3 to 5 Year Olds, by Education and Labor Force Status of Mother and Family Income: 1993

[**In thousands**. As of **October**. Civilian noninstitutional population. Based on Current Population Survey; see text, section 1]

CHARACTERISTIC	Total population[1]	ENROLLED IN NURSERY SCHOOL			ENROLLED IN KINDERGARTEN			Enrolled in elementary school
		Total	Public	Private	Total	Public	Private	
NUMBER								
Total children 3 to 5 years old	11,954	2,984	1,204	1,779	3,597	3,020	577	236
3 and 4 year olds	8,097	2,732	1,088	1,643	543	369	174	-
5 year olds	3,857	252	116	136	3,054	2,651	403	236
Education of mother:								
Children living with mother	11,058	2,803	1,095	1,708	3,310	2,770	540	206
Elementary: 0 to 8 years	556	53	51	3	166	162	3	14
High school: 1-3 years	1,278	178	152	26	388	369	19	21
High school graduate	3,987	875	437	438	1,215	1,072	143	78
College: Less than a BA degree	3,068	904	300	604	858	715	143	53
BA degree or higher	2,169	793	155	638	683	452	232	40
Labor force status of mother:								
Children living with mother	11,058	2,803	1,095	1,708	3,310	2,770	540	206
Mother in the labor force	6,518	1,761	653	1,109	2,004	1,616	388	129
Employed	5,958	1,651	587	1,064	1,845	1,470	375	116
Full-time	4,158	1,117	402	714	1,295	1,043	252	73
Part-time	1,800	534	185	350	550	427	123	43
Unemployed	559	110	65	45	159	146	13	13
Mother not in the labor force	4,541	1,041	442	599	1,306	1,154	152	76
Children not living with mother	896	181	110	71	287	250	37	30
Family income:								
Less than $10,000	2,048	379	325	54	611	594	16	33
$10,000 to 14,999	1,207	224	151	73	360	333	26	13
$15,000 to 19,999	849	139	90	48	262	243	20	35
$20,000 to 24,999	985	195	109	86	285	260	25	15
$25,000 to 29,999	848	183	82	101	244	207	38	18
$30,000 to 34,999	907	200	52	148	259	214	45	19
$35,000 to 39,999	819	190	64	126	278	209	69	7
$40,000 to 49,999	1,095	325	102	223	348	275	76	20
$50,000 to 74,999	1,595	571	113	458	468	353	115	35
$75,000 and over	956	422	57	365	310	210	100	21
Not reported	645	156	60	96	173	122	51	21

- Represents or rounds to zero.   [1] Includes those not enrolled, not shown separately.

Source: U.S. Bureau of the Census, *Current Population Reports*, P20-479.

No. 245. Public Elementary and Secondary Schools—Summary: 1980 to 1994

[For school year ending in year shown, except as indicated. Data are estimates]

ITEM	Unit	1980	1985	1990	1991	1992	1993	1994
School districts, total.	Number .	16,044	15,812	15,552	15,439	15,360	15,212	15,052
ENROLLMENT								
Population 5-17 years old [1]	1,000. . .	48,041	44,787	44,949	45,166	45,915	46,661	47,419
Percent of resident population	Percent .	21.4	19.0	18.2	18.2	18.2	18.3	18.4
Fall enrollment [2].	1,000. . .	41,778	39,354	40,527	41,198	41,956	42,660	43,303
Percent of population 5-17								
years old [3]	Percent .	87.0	87.9	90.2	91.2	91.4	91.4	91.3
Elementary [3]	1,000. . .	24,397	23,830	26,253	26,927	27,432	27,858	28,212
Secondary [4]	1,000. . .	17,381	15,524	14,274	14,271	14,524	14,802	15,091
Average daily:								
Attendance (ADA)	1,000. . .	38,411	36,530	37,573	38,181	38,927	39,605	40,079
High school graduates	1,000. . .	2,762	2,424	2,327	2,232	2,237	2,248	2,241
INSTRUCTIONAL STAFF								
Total [5]	1,000. . .	2,521	2,473	2,685	2,746	2,763	2,811	2,860
Classroom teachers.	1,000. . .	2,211	2,175	2,362	2,409	2,428	2,466	2,507
Average salaries:								
Instructional staff.	Dollar . .	16,715	24,666	32,638	34,401	35,552	36,454	37,383
Classroom teachers.	Dollar . .	15,970	23,600	31,367	33,085	34,063	35,029	35,819
REVENUES								
Revenue receipts	Mil. dol. .	97,635	141,013	208,656	223,896	234,924	247,706	255,769
Federal	Mil. dol. .	9,020	9,533	13,184	14,178	15,704	17,521	18,423
State	Mil. dol. .	47,929	69,107	100,787	108,021	111,348	115,855	117,646
Local	Mil. dol. .	40,686	62,373	94,685	101,697	107,871	114,330	119,700
Percent of total:								
Federal	Percent .	9.2	6.8	6.3	6.3	6.7	7.1	7.2
State	Percent .	49.1	49.0	48.3	48.2	47.4	46.8	46.0
Local	Percent .	41.7	44.2	45.4	45.4	45.9	46.2	46.8
EXPENDITURES								
Total	Mil. dol. .	96,105	139,382	209,698	227,459	236,750	248,564	260,179
Current expenditures								
(day schools)	Mil. dol. .	85,661	127,230	186,583	200,911	208,352	218,944	229,129
Other current expenditures [6]	Mil. dol. .	1,859	2,109	3,341	3,772	4,611	5,142	5,664
Capital outlay	Mil. dol. .	6,504	7,529	16,012	18,289	18,870	18,770	19,610
Interest on school debt	Mil. dol. .	2,081	2,514	3,762	4,487	4,918	5,707	5,775
Percent of total:								
Current expenditures								
(day schools)	Percent .	89.1	91.3	89.0	88.3	88.0	88.1	88.1
Other current expenditures [6]	Percent .	1.9	1.5	1.6	1.7	2.0	2.1	2.2
Capital outlay	Percent .	6.8	5.4	7.6	8.0	8.0	7.6	7.5
Interest on school debt	Percent .	2.2	1.8	1.8	2.0	2.1	2.3	2.2
In current dollars:								
Revenue receipts per pupil								
enrolled	Dollar . .	2,337	3,583	5,149	5,435	5,599	5,807	5,907
Current expenditures per pupil								
enrolled	Dollar . .	2,050	3,233	4,604	4,877	4,966	5,132	5,291
In constant **(1994)** dollars: [7]								
Revenue receipts per pupil								
enrolled	Dollar . .	4,403	4,951	5,927	6,976	5,923	5,957	5,907
Current expenditures per pupil								
enrolled	Dollar . .	3,863	4,467	5,300	6,260	5,253	5,266	5,291

[1] Estimated resident population as of July 1 of the previous year. Estimates reflect revisions based on the 1990 Census of Population.   [2] Fall enrollment of the previous year.   [3] Kindergarten through grade 6.   [4] Grades 7 through 12.   [5] Full-time equivalent.   [6] Current expenses for summer schools, adult education, post-high school vocational education, personnel retraining, etc., when operated by local school districts and not part of regular public elementary and secondary day-school program.   [7] Compiled by U.S. Bureau of the Census. Deflated by the Consumer Price Index, all urban consumers (for school year) supplied by U.S. National Center for Education Statistics.

Source: Except as noted, National Education Association, Washington, DC, *Estimates of School Statistics,* annual (copyright); *Rankings of the States,* annual (copyright); and unpublished data.

No. 246. Elementary and Secondary Schools--Teachers and Pupil-Teacher Ratios With Projections: 1960 to 1994

[**In thousands, except ratios.** As of **fall.** Data are for full-time equivalents. Schools are classified by type of organization, rather than by grade group; elementary includes kindergarten and secondary includes junior high]

ITEM	TOTAL			PUBLIC			PRIVATE		
	Total	Elemen-tary	Second-ary	Total	Elemen-tary	Second-ary	Total	Elemen-tary	Second-ary
Number of teachers:									
1960.	1,600	991	609	1,408	858	550	192	133	59
1965.	1,933	1,112	822	1,710	965	746	223	147	76
1970.	2,292	1,283	1,009	2,059	1,130	929	233	153	80
1975.	2,453	1,353	1,100	2,198	1,181	1,017	255	172	83
1980.	2,485	1,401	1,084	2,184	1,189	995	301	212	89
1985.	2,549	1,483	1,066	2,206	1,237	969	343	246	97
1986.	2,592	1,521	1,071	2,244	1,271	973	348	250	98
1987.	2,632	1,564	1,068	2,279	1,307	973	353	257	95
1988.	2,668	1,604	1,064	2,323	1,353	970	345	251	94
1989.	2,679	1,622	1,057	2,357	1,387	970	322	235	87
1990.	2,753	1,680	1,073	2,398	1,426	972	356	254	101
1991.	2,787	1,713	1,074	2,432	1,459	973	355	254	101
1992, prel.	2,821	1,742	1,079	2,458	1,482	976	363	260	103
1993, prel.	2,871	1,771	1,100	2,507	1,510	997	364	261	103
1994, proj.	2,890	1,769	1,122	2,520	1,506	1,014	370	263	108
Pupil-teacher ratio:									
1960.	26.4	29.4	21.4	25.8	28.4	21.7	30.7	36.1	18.6
1965.	25.1	28.4	20.6	24.7	27.6	20.8	28.3	33.3	18.4
1970.	22.4	24.6	19.5	22.3	24.3	19.8	23.0	26.5	16.4
1975.	20.3	21.7	18.6	20.4	21.7	18.8	19.6	21.5	15.7
1980.	18.6	20.1	16.6	18.7	20.4	16.8	17.7	18.8	15.0
1985.	17.6	19.1	15.6	17.9	19.5	15.8	16.2	17.1	14.0
1986.	17.4	18.8	15.5	17.7	19.3	15.7	15.7	16.5	13.6
1987.	17.3	18.8	15.0	17.6	19.3	15.2	15.5	l6.4	13.1
1988.	17.0	18.6	14.7	17.3	19.0	14.9	15.2	16.1	12.8
1989.	17.1	18.8	14.5	17.2	19.0	14.6	16.6	17.7	13.7
1990.	16.9	18.5	14.3	17.2	19.0	14.6	14.7	16.1	11.3
1991.	16.9	18.5	14.5	17.3	19.0	14.7	14.6	16.0	11.1
1992, prel.	17.1	18.5	14.8	17.4	18.9	15.2	14.8	16.2	11.3
1993, prel..	17.0	18.4	14.8	17.3	18.7	15.2	15.0	16.4	11.6
1994, proj.	17.2	18.6	15.0	17.6	19.0	15.4	15.0	16.5	11.4

Source: U.S. National Center for Education Statistics, *Digest of Education Statistics,* annual.

No. 247. Public Elementary and Secondary Schools, by Type and Size of School: 1992-93

[Data reported by schools, rather than school districts]

ENROLLMENT SIZE OF SCHOOL	NUMBER OF SCHOOLS					ENROLLMENT (1,000)				
	Total	Elemen-tary [1]	Second-ary [2]	Com-bined [3]	Other [4]	Total	Elemen-tary [1]	Second-ary [2]	Com-bined [3]	Other [4]
Total.	**84,501**	**59,680**	**19,995**	**2,549**	**2,277**	**42,645**	**27,671**	**13,774**	**1,078**	**121**
PERCENT DISTRIBUTION [5]										
Total.	100.0	100.0	100.0	100.0	100.0	100.0	100.0	100.0	100.0	100.0
Under 100 students	8.6	5.9	12.2	27.1	57.4	0.8	0.6	0.9	2.8	17.1
100 to 199 students	10.0	9.5	10.7	14.2	19.5	2.9	3.1	2.3	4.9	18.6
200 to 299 students	11.6	12.6	8.9	11.0	9.4	5.7	6.9	3.2	6.4	15.8
300 to 399 students	13.9	16.2	8.0	8.2	6.3	9.4	12.2	4.1	6.8	14.8
400 to 499 students	13.5	15.9	7.4	7.9	3.1	11.8	15.4	4.8	8.4	9.7
500 to 599 students	11.9	13.9	7.1	6.4	1.3	12.7	16.4	5.6	8.3	5.0
600 to 699 students	8.7	9.6	6.6	5.9	0.7	10.9	13.4	6.2	9.0	3.2
700 to 799 students	6.2	6.5	5.8	3.5	0.4	9.0	10.4	6.3	6.3	1.9
800 to 999 students	7.0	6.3	9.3	6.5	1.0	12.1	12.0	12.1	13.7	6.0
1,000 to 1,499 students . . .	6.0	3.3	13.9	6.5	0.5	13.9	8.3	24.7	18.4	3.8
1,500 to 1,999 students . . .	1.8	0.3	6.2	1.8	0.2	5.9	1.1	15.5	7.1	2.5
2,000 to 2,999 students . . .	0.9	(Z)	3.4	0.9	0.1	4.0	0.2	11.6	5.1	1.8
3,000 or more students. . . .	0.1	(Z)	0.6	0.2	(Z)	1.0	(Z)	2.8	2.9	(Z)
Average enrollment	(X)	(X)	(X)	(X)	(X)	513	464	689	423	146

X Not applicable.   **Z** Less than .05 percent.   [1] Includes schools beginning with grade 6 or below and with no grade higher than 8.   [2] Includes schools with no grade lower than 7.   [3] Includes schools with both elementary and secondary grades.   [4] Includes special education, alternative, and other schools not classified by grade span.   [5] Data for those schools reporting enrollment.

Source: U.S. National Center for Education Statistics, *Digest of Education Statistics,* annual.

No. 248. Public Elementary and Secondary School Enrollment, by State: 1980 to 1993

[**In thousands, except rate**. As of **fall**. Includes unclassified students]

| STATE | ENROLLMENT | | | | | | | | ENROLLMENT RATE [2] | | | |
| | K through Grade 8 [1] | | | | Grades 9 through 12 | | | | | | | |
	1980	1985	1990	1993, est.	1980	1985	1990	1993, est.	1980	1985	1990	1993, est.
United States ...	**27,647**	**27,034**	**29,878**	**31,372**	**13,231**	**12,388**	**11,338**	**11,981**	**86.5**	**87.7**	**91.3**	**91.4**
Alabama.........	528	517	527	524	231	213	195	198	87.6	89.6	93.3	93.6
Alaska..........	60	77	85	93	26	30	29	32	94.0	99.4	97.4	94.7
Arizona.........	357	386	479	512	157	162	161	183	88.9	90.8	93.3	91.2
Arkansas	310	304	314	317	138	130	123	126	90.3	91.8	95.9	95.5
California	2,730	2,927	3,615	3,909	1,347	1,329	1,336	1,430	88.0	89.5	92.8	93.1
Colorado.........	374	379	420	459	172	172	154	167	92.2	92.7	94.6	92.5
Connecticut.......	364	321	347	371	168	141	122	129	83.3	83.4	90.2	91.7
Delaware.........	62	63	73	77	37	30	27	29	79.5	80.1	87.4	86.9
District of Columbia .	71	62	61	59	29	25	19	20	91.8	96.8	100.9	105.3
Florida..........	1,042	1,086	1,370	1,518	468	476	492	524	84.4	86.7	92.6	91.6
Georgia	742	757	849	907	327	323	303	325	86.9	88.2	93.6	94.2
Hawaii..........	110	113	123	130	55	51	49	50	83.4	84.2	87.6	87.8
Idaho..........	144	149	160	164	59	59	61	70	95.4	93.6	96.9	95.5
Illinois.........	1,335	1,246	1,310	1,347	649	580	512	540	82.6	83.3	86.9	88.0
Indiana.........	708	654	676	677	347	312	279	288	88.0	88.4	90.4	91.4
Iowa	351	324	345	349	183	161	139	150	88.4	89.1	92.1	93.1
Kansas..........	283	286	320	330	133	125	117	127	88.7	91.0	92.6	92.0
Kentucky	464	449	459	464	206	195	177	188	83.7	85.8	90.5	92.5
Louisiana	544	573	586	576	234	215	199	209	80.3	83.9	88.2	87.9
Maine..........	153	142	155	158	70	64	60	60	91.5	93.3	96.5	96.5
Maryland	493	446	527	567	258	225	188	202	83.9	84.9	89.1	89.0
Massachusetts.....	676	559	604	642	346	285	230	232	88.6	86.3	88.8	89.4
Michigan.........	1,227	1,086	1,145	1,176	570	517	440	442	90.1	87.8	90.3	90.0
Minnesota.......	482	468	546	577	272	237	211	232	87.2	89.4	91.2	90.6
Mississippi	330	330	372	363	147	141	131	137	79.6	81.0	91.3	91.7
Missouri	567	544	588	617	277	251	228	243	83.8	84.9	86.5	87.4
Montana.........	106	108	111	116	50	46	42	46	92.9	93.8	93.8	93.1
Nebraska	189	184	198	202	91	82	76	81	86.6	87.7	88.7	88.2
Nevada	101	107	150	174	49	48	51	61	93.4	93.3	98.7	95.5
New Hampshire....	112	107	126	137	55	54	46	49	85.3	87.5	89.1	90.3
New Jersey.......	820	740	784	831	426	376	306	316	81.5	82.9	86.1	86.5
New Mexico	186	187	208	219	85	90	94	100	89.5	91.6	94.3	91.9
New York	1,838	1,703	1,828	1,915	1,033	918	770	808	80.8	82.3	86.6	88.0
North Carolina.....	786	749	783	820	343	337	304	306	90.0	91.2	94.8	92.8
North Dakota......	77	84	85	84	40	35	33	35	85.9	89.2	92.8	93.0
Ohio	1,312	1,206	1,258	1,278	645	588	514	517	84.8	85.6	88.0	87.6
Oklahoma........	399	414	425	439	179	178	154	163	92.9	94.3	95.1	95.1
Oregon..........	319	305	340	371	145	142	132	150	88.5	89.7	90.7	92.4
Pennsylvania......	1,231	1,093	1,172	1,240	678	591	496	517	80.4	80.3	83.6	85.0
Rhode Island......	98	90	102	108	51	44	37	39	79.7	81.2	87.3	89.1
South Carolina.....	426	424	452	462	193	183	170	176	88.1	89.6	94.0	94.9
South Dakota.....	86	88	95	98	42	37	34	38	87.4	90.7	89.7	89.5
Tennessee	602	575	598	616	252	239	226	236	87.8	88.3	93.5	93.4
Texas..........	2,049	2,261	2,511	2,649	851	871	872	931	92.4	93.2	98.4	97.8
Utah..........	250	299	325	328	93	105	122	141	98.2	96.3	97.7	97.3
Vermont	66	63	71	74	29	27	25	25	87.9	89.3	93.9	93.4
Virginia.........	703	665	728	774	307	303	270	278	90.7	94.0	94.2	94.3
Washington.......	515	507	613	667	242	243	227	256	91.0	92.2	94.0	93.2
West Virginia.....	270	249	224	215	113	109	98	98	92.6	92.2	95.7	96.9
Wisconsin........	528	501	566	599	303	267	232	250	82.1	83.8	86.0	86.5
Wyoming	70	74	71	71	28	29	27	29	97.3	97.0	97.3	97.1

[1] Data include a small number of pre-kindergarten students.   [2] Percent of persons 5-17 years old. Based on enumerated resident population as of April 1, 1980, and 1990, and estimated resident population as of July 1 for other years. Data not adjusted for revisions based of the 1990 Census of Population.

Source: U.S. National Center for Education Statistics, *Digest of Education Statistics*, annual.

No. 249. Public Elementary and Secondary School Enrollment, by Grade: 1960 to 1992

[**In thousands. 1960,** for school year; thereafter, as of **fall** of year. Beginning 19¯0, kindergarten includes nursery schools. For 1960, enrollment figures are prorated and 12th grade includes postgraduates. See also *Historical Statistics, Colonial Times to 1970,* series H 420-424]

GRADE	1960	1970	1975	1980	1985	1986	1987	1988	1989	1990	1991	1992, prel.
Pupils enrolled	**36,087**	**45,894**	**44,819**	**40,877**	**39,422**	**39,753**	**40,008**	**40,189**	**40,543**	**41,217**	**42,047**	**42,735**
Kindergarten and grades 1-8	27,602	32,558	30,515	27,647	27,034	27,420	27,933	28,501	29,152	29,878	30,506	30,997
Kindergarten	1,923	2,564	2,971	2,689	3,192	3,310	3,388	3,433	3,486	3,610	3,686	3,732
First	3,733	3,817	3,238	2,894	3,239	3,358	3,407	3,460	3,485	3,499	3,556	3,542
Second	3,436	3,654	3,027	2,800	2,941	3,054	3,173	3,223	3,289	3,327	3,360	3,431
Third	3,302	3,663	3,038	2,893	2,895	2,933	3,046	3,167	3,235	3,297	3,334	3,362
Fourth	3,146	3,675	3,112	3,107	2,771	2,896	2,938	3,051	3,182	3,248	3,315	3,342
Fifth	3,118	3,635	3,281	3,130	2,776	2,775	2,901	2,945	3,067	3,197	3,268	3,326
Sixth	3,070	3,598	3,476	3,038	2,789	2,806	2,811	2,937	2,987	3,110	3,239	3,303
Seventh	3,173	3,662	3,619	3,085	2,938	2,899	2,910	2,905	3,027	3,067	3,181	3,299
Eighth	2,701	3,601	3,636	3,086	2,982	2,870	2,839	2,853	2,853	2,979	3,020	3,128
Unclassified [1]	(X)	690	1,116	924	511	520	520	527	540	543	545	533
Grades 9-12	8,485	13,336	14,304	13,231	12,388	12,333	12,076	11,687	11,390	11,338	11,541	11,738
Ninth	2,412	3,654	3,879	3,377	3,439	3,256	3,143	3,106	3,141	3,169	3,313	3,352
Tenth	2,258	3,458	3,723	3,368	3,230	3,215	3,020	2,895	2,868	2,896	2,915	3,028
Eleventh	2,063	3,128	3,354	3,195	2,866	2,954	2,936	2,749	2,629	2,612	2,645	2,656
Twelfth	1,752	2,775	2,986	2,925	2,550	2,601	2,681	2,650	2,473	2,381	2,392	2,432
Unclassified [1]	(X)	321	362	366	303	308	296	288	279	282	275	270

X Not applicable. [1] Includes ungraded and special education.

Source: U.S. National Center for Education Statistics, *Digest of Education Statistics,* annual.

No. 250. Public Elementary and Secondary School Teachers—Selected Characteristics: 1990-91

[**For school year.** Based on survey and subject to sampling error; for details, see source. Excludes prekindergarten teachers. See table 265 for similar data on private school teachers]

CHARACTERISTIC	Unit	AGE				SEX		RACE/ETHNICITY		
		Under 30 years old	30 to 39 years old	40 to 49 years old	Over 50 years old	Male	Fe-male	White [1]	Black [1]	His-panic
Total teachers [2]	**1,000**	**312**	**731**	**1,002**	**514**	**719**	**1,840**	**2,214**	**212**	**87**
Highest degree held:										
Bachelor's	Percent	84.1	56.4	43.8	41.6	44.7	54.7	51.5	50.8	61.0
Master's	Percent	14.4	39.1	48.8	49.9	47.0	40.1	42.7	42.1	32.9
Education specialist	Percent	1.2	3.4	5.9	5.9	5.3	4.3	4.5	5.0	4.3
Doctorate	Percent	-	0.4	1.0	1.4	1.3	0.6	0.7	1.3	0.9
Full-time teaching experience:										
Less than 3 years	Percent	41.8	10.2	3.5	1.5	7.8	10.4	9.7	6.5	14.0
3 to 9 years	Percent	58.1	38.7	16.3	7.3	19.9	28.4	26.3	20.0	33.4
10 to 20 years	Percent	0.1	51.0	49.1	26.0	37.0	39.8	39.0	40.9	39.6
20 years or more	Percent	(X)	0.1	31.1	65.2	35.3	21.4	25.1	32.8	13.1
Full-time teachers	1,000	283	650	925	481	668	1,680	2,021	202	82
Earned income	Dol.	24,918	30,108	36,083	38,614	37,874	31,870	33,611	33,539	32,907
Salary	Dol.	22,779	27,918	33,690	36,333	33,360	30,476	31,293	31,579	30,743
Supplemental contract during school year:										
Teachers receiving	1,000	122	231	313	122	354	435	703	49	25
Salary	Dol.	1,675	2,045	1,914	2,088	2,663	1,357	1,977	1,664	1,709
Supplemental contract during summer:										
Teachers receiving	1,000	54	113	162	64	156	237	321	45	18
Salary	Dol.	1,615	1,969	2,018	2,294	2,328	1,773	1,935	2,251	2,375
Teachers with nonschool employment:										
Teaching/tutoring	1,000	13	30	47	20	39	71	95	8	5
Education related	1,000	9	18	28	12	31	36	59	5	2
Not education related	1,000	33	63	91	42	130	99	204	16	5

- Represents or rounds to zero. X Not applicable. [1] Non-Hispanic. [2] Includes teachers with no degrees and associates degrees, not shown separately.

Source: U.S. National Center for Education Statistics, *Digest of Education Statistics,* 1994.

No. 251. Public Elementary and Secondary Schools—Number and Average Salary of Classroom Teachers, 1960 to 1994, and by State, 1994

[Estimates for school year ending in **June** of year shown. Schools classified by type of organization rather than by grade-group; elementary includes kindergarten]

YEAR AND STATE	TEACHERS [1] (1,000)			AVG. SALARY ($1,000)			YEAR AND STATE	TEACHERS [1] (1,000)			AVG. SALARY ($1,000)		
	Total	Elementary	Secondary	All teachers	Elementary	Secondary		Total	Elementary	Secondary	All teachers	Elementary	Secondary
1960	1,355	834	521	5.0	4.8	5.3	LA	46.8	32.8	14.0	26.3	26.3	26.3
1970	2,008	1,109	899	8.6	8.4	8.9	ME	15.1	9.4	5.7	31.0	30.5	32.1
1975	2,171	1,169	1,001	11.7	11.3	12.0	MD	44.2	25.0	19.2	39.5	38.4	40.6
1980	2,211	1,206	1,005	16.0	15.6	16.5	MA	58.9	25.3	33.6	40.9	40.9	40.9
1985	2,175	1,212	963	23.6	23.2	24.2	MI	84.0	58.9	25.1	45.2	45.2	45.2
1986	2,215	1,242	973	25.2	24.7	25.8	MN	46.6	23.9	22.7	36.1	35.6	37.8
1987	2,249	1,274	975	26.6	26.1	27.2	MS	28.6	15.8	12.7	25.2	24.7	25.7
1988	2,282	1,308	974	28.0	27.5	28.8	MO	54.1	28.3	25.8	30.3	29.5	31.1
1989	2,324	1,354	970	29.6	29.0	30.2	MT	10.0	6.9	3.0	28.2	28.0	28.7
1990	2,362	1,390	972	31.4	30.8	32.0	NE	19.3	11.1	8.3	29.6	29.6	29.6
1991	2,409	1,435	974	33.1	32.5	33.9	NV	12.4	7.2	5.2	34.0	33.4	34.8
1992	2,428	1,466	963	34.1	33.5	34.8	NH	12.0	8.1	3.9	34.1	34.1	34.1
1993	2,466	1,496	970	35.0	34.3	35.9	NJ	84.6	54.0	30.6	44.7	43.7	46.4
							NM	17.8	12.5	5.3	27.9	27.4	28.2
1994, U.S.	**2,507**	**1,517**	**990**	**35.8**	**35.3**	**36.7**	NY	188.5	94.0	94.5	45.8	44.0	47.6
AL	42.6	23.0	19.6	28.7	28.7	28.7	NC	68.6	41.8	26.7	29.7	29.7	29.8
AK	8.2	5.4	2.9	47.5	47.5	47.5	ND	7.8	5.0	2.8	25.5	25.5	25.5
AZ	36.5	28.1	8.4	31.8	31.8	31.8	OH	103.1	68.7	34.4	35.7	35.2	36.6
AR	26.3	12.9	13.4	28.1	27.3	28.0	OK	39.1	20.9	18.2	27.0	26.3	27.8
CA	218.5	161.4	57.1	40.3	39.8	42.3	OR	27.2	17.2	10.0	37.6	37.0	38.5
CO	33.7	17.2	16.5	33.8	33.3	34.4	PA	101.3	52.0	49.3	42.4	41.7	43.1
CT	34.7	24.7	10.0	49.8	49.1	51.7	RI	9.9	5.3	4.6	39.3	39.2	39.3
DE	6.4	3.3	3.1	37.5	36.9	38.1	SC	37.5	25.7	11.8	29.6	29.2	30.3
DC	6.5	4.0	2.5	42.5	41.9	43.5	SD	8.9	6.3	2.6	25.3	24.9	25.3
FL	113.7	62.1	51.6	31.9	31.9	31.9	TN	47.4	33.8	13.6	30.5	30.0	31.7
GA	75.1	54.9	20.2	30.7	30.7	30.7	TX	223.1	120.2	102.9	30.5	29.9	31.1
HI	10.4	5.9	4.5	36.6	36.6	36.6	UT	20.0	11.2	8.8	27.7	27.8	27.8
ID	12.0	6.3	5.7	27.8	27.6	27.9	VT	7.4	4.2	3.1	34.5	33.9	35.4
IL	110.6	77.3	33.3	39.4	37.5	43.7	VA	68.9	41.3	27.6	33.0	32.0	34.5
IN	55.0	29.5	25.5	35.7	35.6	35.7	WA	45.5	27.0	18.5	35.9	35.5	36.4
IA	31.7	14.9	16.8	30.8	29.7	31.7	WV	20.9	12.1	8.8	30.5	30.2	31.0
KS	30.3	16.4	13.9	33.9	33.9	33.9	WI	51.0	34.0	17.0	36.0	35.6	36.9
KY	38.0	26.4	11.6	31.6	31.2	33.3	WY	6.7	3.4	3.3	31.0	30.8	31.1

[1] Full-time equivalent.

Source: National Education Association, Washington, DC, *Estimates of School Statistics, 1993-94,* and earlier issues. (Copyright by the National Education Association. All rights reserved.)

No. 252. Average Starting Salaries of Public School Teachers Compared With Salaries in Private Industry, by Selected Position: 1975 to 1993

[Except as noted, salaries represent what corporations plan to offer graduates graduating in the year shown with bachelors' degrees. Based on a survey of approximately 200 companies]

ITEM AND POSITION	1975	1980	1985	1988	1989	1990	1991	1992	1993
SALARIES (dollars)									
Teachers [1]	8,233	10,764	15,460	19,400	(NA)	20,486	21,481	22,171	22,505
College graduates:									
Engineering	12,744	20,136	26,880	29,856	30,852	32,304	34,236	34,620	35,004
Accounting	11,880	15,720	20,628	25,140	25,908	27,408	27,924	28,404	28,020
Sales—marketing	10,344	15,936	20,616	23,484	27,768	27,828	26,580	26,532	28,536
Business administration	9,768	14,100	19,896	23,880	25,344	26,496	26,256	27,156	27,564
Liberal arts [2]	9,312	13,296	18,828	23,508	25,608	26,364	25,560	27,324	27,216
Chemistry	11,904	17,124	24,216	27,108	27,552	29,088	29,700	30,360	30,456
Mathematics—statistics	10,980	17,604	22,704	25,548	28,416	28,944	29,244	29,472	30,756
Economics—finance	10,212	14,472	20,964	23,928	25,812	26,712	26,424	27,708	28,584
Computer science	(NA)	17,712	24,156	26,904	28,608	29,100	30,924	30,888	31,164
INDEX (1975=100)									
Teachers [1]	100	131	187	236	(NA)	249	261	269	273
College graduates:									
Engineering	100	158	211	234	242	253	268	271	275
Accounting	100	132	174	212	218	230	235	239	236
Sales—marketing	100	154	199	227	268	269	257	256	276
Business administration	100	144	204	244	259	271	268	278	282
Liberal arts [2]	100	143	202	252	275	283	274	293	292
Chemistry	100	144	203	228	231	244	249	255	256
Mathematics—statistics	100	160	207	233	258	263	266	268	280
Economics—finance	100	142	205	234	252	261	258	271	280
Computer science [3]	(NA)	125	171	190	202	205	218	217	218

NA Not available. [1] Estimate. Minimum mean salary. Source: National Education Association, Washington, DC, unpublished data. [2] Excludes Chemistry, Mathematics, Economics, and Computer Science. [3] Computer science index (1978=100).

Source: Except as noted, Northwestern University Placement Center, Evanston, IL, *The Northwestern University Lindquist-Endicott Report* (copyright).

No. 253. Average Salary and Wages Paid in Public School Systems: 1975 to 1994

[**In dollars.** For school year ending in year shown. Data reported by a stratified sample of school systems enrolling 300 or more pupils. Data represent unweighted means of average salaries paid school personnel reported by each school system]

POSITION	1975	1980	1985	1989	1990	1991	1992	1993	1994
ANNUAL SALARY									
Central office administrators:									
Superintendent (contract salary) . . .	30,338	39,344	56,954	71,190	75,425	79,874	83,342	85,120	87,717
Deputy/assoc. superintendent	30,074	37,440	52,877	66,214	69,623	72,428	76,796	77,057	78,672
Assistant superintendent	26,460	33,452	48,003	59,655	62,698	66,553	69,315	70,525	72,701
Administrators for—									
Finance and business	21,850	27,147	40,344	49,933	52,354	55,097	57,036	57,864	59,997
Instructional services	22,608	29,790	43,452	53,716	56,359	59,162	62,102	62,508	64,676
Public relations/information	21,470	24,021	35,287	43,402	44,926	47,938	50,625	50,622	52,366
Staff personnel services	21,470	29,623	44,182	53,972	56,344	59,271	62,269	62,162	63,690
Subject area supervisors	18,601	23,974	34,422	43,555	45,929	48,366	50,580	51,407	52,837
School building administrators:									
Principals:									
Elementary	19,061	25,165	36,452	45,909	48,431	51,453	53,856	54,905	56,906
Junior high/middle	21,136	27,625	39,650	49,427	52,163	55,083	57,504	58,620	60,651
Senior high.	22,894	29,207	42,094	52,987	55,722	59,106	61,768	63,054	64,993
Assistant principals:									
Elementary	15,968	20,708	30,496	38,360	40,916	43,548	45,558	45,377	47,057
Junior high/middle	17,868	23,507	33,793	42,292	44,570	46,981	48,956	49,925	51,518
Senior high.	18,939	24,816	35,491	44,002	46,486	49,009	51,318	52,348	54,170
Classroom teachers.	11,507	15,913	23,587	29,608	31,278	32,915	34,565	35,291	36,531
Auxiliary professional personnel:									
Counselors	14,479	18,847	27,593	34,244	35,979	38,024	39,563	40,413	41,355
Librarians	12,546	16,764	24,981	31,645	33,469	35,417	37,227	37,945	39,319
School nurses	10,673	13,788	19,944	24,804	26,090	27,713	28,721	29,555	30,630
Secretarial/clerical personnel:									
Central office:									
Secretaries/stenographers.	7,318	10,331	15,343	19,045	20,238	21,303	22,309	22,770	23,495
Accounting/payroll clerks.	7,588	10,479	15,421	19,143	20,088	21,202	22,215	22,605	23,275
Clerk-typists	6,089	8,359	12,481	15,192	16,125	16,859	17,646	17,772	18,296
School building level:									
Secretaries/stenographers.	6,046	8,348	12,504	15,364	16,184	16,953	17,784	18,104	18,692
Library clerks	5,052	6,778	9,911	11,751	12,151	12,696	13,347	13,311	13,809
HOURLY WAGE RATE									
Other support personnel:									
Teacher aides:									
Instructional	2.91	4.06	5.89	7.05	7.43	7.77	8.15	8.31	8.50
Noninstructional	2.81	3.89	5.60	6.69	7.08	7.43	7.70	7.82	8.14
Custodians	3.54	4.88	6.90	8.19	8.54	9.05	9.35	9.51	9.76
Cafeteria workers	2.61	3.78	5.42	6.56	6.77	7.19	7.39	7.56	7.72
Bus drivers	3.75	5.21	7.27	8.78	9.21	9.52	10.04	10.15	10.35

Source: Educational Research Service, Arlington, VA, *National Survey of Salaries and Wages in Public Schools,* annual, vols. 2 and 3. (All rights reserved. Copyright.)

No. 254. Public School Employment: 1982 and 1992

[**In thousands.** Covers full-time employment. Excludes Hawaii. 1982 also excludes District of Columbia and New Jersey. 1982 based on sample survey of school districts with 250 or more students. 1992 based on sample survey of school districts with 100 or more employees; see source for sampling variability]

OCCUPATION	1982					1992				
	Total	Male	Female	White [1]	Black [1]	Total	Male	Female	White [1]	Black [1]
All occupations	**3,082**	**1,063**	**2,019**	**2,498**	**432**	**3,376**	**948**	**2,428**	**2,643**	**494**
Officials, administrators	41	31	10	36	3	44	27	17	37	5
Principals and assistant										
principals. . . . .[2]	90	72	19	76	11	93	56	37	74	14
Classroom teachers [2]	1,680	534	1,146	1,435	186	1,862	487	1,375	1,565	202
Elementary schools	798	129	669	667	98	930	123	807	770	108
Secondary schools	706	363	343	619	67	693	312	381	598	67
Other professional staff	235	91	144	193	35	242	59	184	199	31
Teachers aides [3]	215	14	200	146	45	351	58	293	223	76
Clerical, secretarial staff.	210	4	206	177	19	236	6	231	187	27
Service workers [4]	611	316	295	434	132	547	255	292	360	138

[1] Excludes individuals of Hispanic origin.　　[2] Includes other classroom teachers, not shown separately.　　[3] Includes technicians.　　[4] Includes craftworkers and laborers.

Source: U.S. Equal Employment Opportunity Commission, *Elementary-Secondary Staff Information (EEO-5),* biennial.

No. 255. Public Elementary and Secondary School Price Indexes: 1975 to 1993

[1983=100. For years ending **June 30**. Reflects prices paid by public elementary-secondary schools. For explanation of average annual percent change, see Guide to Tabular Presentation]

YEAR	Index, total	PERSONNEL COMPENSATION				CONTRACTED SERVICES, SUPPLIES AND EQUIPMENT						
		Total	Professional salaries	Nonprofessional salaries	Fringe benefits	Total	Services	Supplies and materials	Equipment replacement	Library materials and textbooks	Utilities	Fixed costs
1975	52.7	53.3	56.0	55.6	40.2	50.6	55.7	58.0	53.7	53.8	35.9	45.0
1980	76.5	75.7	76.7	77.8	69.8	79.6	77.4	85.9	79.6	82.1	73.2	77.6
1982	93.7	92.6	92.8	94.4	90.3	97.8	94.6	101.1	95.5	91.6	102.2	94.1
1983	100.0	100.0	100.0	100.0	100.0	100.0	100.0	100.0	100.0	100.0	100.0	100.0
1984	105.6	106.2	105.7	104.5	109.4	103.5	106.2	102.2	103.0	107.3	98.2	106.9
1985	112.6	114.2	113.4	111.3	120.3	106.4	112.3	103.5	105.6	113.0	96.5	111.8
1986	119.6	122.7	121.4	117.6	132.6	107.6	118.8	102.5	108.7	119.0	88.3	117.8
1987	125.7	129.9	128.4	121.9	143.5	109.8	122.8	103.9	111.3	126.8	83.2	124.6
1988	132.7	137.6	135.5	127.5	155.4	113.8	125.3	110.3	111.3	145.2	79.1	131.2
1989	139.6	144.9	142.2	133.3	166.6	119.3	132.2	118.8	116.3	151.4	77.9	137.0
1990	147.6	153.4	150.1	139.4	179.5	125.5	136.7	122.5	120.8	175.9	85.8	142.5
1991	156.0	162.3	158.1	146.5	193.4	132.2	142.5	126.1	124.7	196.1	96.2	147.8
1992	162.9	170.6	165.9	152.4	206.4	133.3	147.1	123.5	127.5	209.9	90.4	153.4
1993	166.8	175.0	169.3	155.1	216.3	135.7	149.0	124.4	130.7	212.7	92.7	158.7

Source: Research Associates of Washington, Washington, DC, *Inflation Measures for Schools, Colleges, and Libraries*, annual (copyright).

No. 256. Finances of Public Elementary and Secondary School Systems, by Enrollment-Size Group: 1990-91

[**In millions of dollars, except as indicated.** Data are estimates subject to sampling variability. For details, see source. See also Appendix III]

ITEM	All school systems	ENROLLMENT SIZE						
		50,000 or more	25,000 to 49,999	15,000 to 24,999	7,500 to 14,999	5,000 to 7,499	3,000 to 4,999	Under 3,000
Enrollment, fall (1,000)	41,255	7,548	4,301	3,746	6,235	3,773	4,764	10,888
General revenue [1]	224,226	42,858	21,680	18,243	31,591	19,421	25,419	65,014
Intergovernmental	122,415	23,839	12,630	10,847	17,038	9,713	12,112	36,236
From Federal government	1,352	284	100	75	150	107	116	520
From States	118,050	23,356	12,193	10,532	16,523	9,367	11,633	34,445
Federal aid distributed by State governments.	11,983	3,071	1,273	979	1,541	913	1,108	3,099
From local governments.	3,013	199	337	239	364	239	363	1,271
From own sources	101,811	19,019	9,050	7,396	14,553	9,708	13,306	28,778
Taxes	69,147	9,283	6,152	5,072	10,017	7,149	9,713	21,759
Property	67,383	8,900	5,962	4,997	9,765	6,963	9,451	21,344
Contribution from parent government	19,135	7,548	1,541	1,046	2,464	1,355	1,995	3,186
Charges and miscellaneous	13,529	2,189	1,356	1,277	2,072	1,203	1,598	3,833
Current charges	6,353	1,168	646	579	959	560	731	1,711
School lunch sales.	3,639	485	357	322	584	370	478	1,042
Interest earnings.	3,584	527	352	324	529	335	428	1,089
Other	3,592	493	359	375	584	309	439	1,033
Employee-retirement revenue	1,007	793	203	11	-	(Z)	-	-
General expenditure [1]	226,803	43,962	22,310	18,601	32,088	19,568	25,730	64,544
Intergovernmental	604	24	31	53	107	64	99	226
Direct.	226,199	43,938	22,279	18,548	31,981	19,503	25,632	64,318
Current operation	203,735	40,010	19,715	16,418	28,559	17,679	22,989	58,364
Salaries and wages	131,966	26,590	13,417	11,203	19,155	11,751	15,147	34,703
Capital outlay.	18,607	3,322	2,131	1,769	2,811	1,489	2,149	4,936
Construction.	11,153	1,944	1,184	1,079	1,783	874	1,383	2,906
Interest on debt	3,857	606	433	360	611	336	493	1,018
Employee-retirement expenditure	324	198	120	5	-	(Z)	-	-
Debt outstanding [2].	63,669	11,110	6,660	5,769	9,820	5,404	8,190	16,716
Long-term.	60,521	11,043	6,519	5,664	9,279	5,105	7,559	15,351
Short-term	3,148	67	141	104	541	298	632	1,365
Long-term debt issued	12,806	2,251	1,460	1,245	2,076	1,008	1,510	3,257
Long-term debt retired	5,777	854	647	479	869	574	765	1,590
Cash and security holdings	50,909	10,177	6,016	3,649	5,854	3,734	5,060	16,419
Employee-retirement holdings	6,278	4,385	1,792	101	-	(Z)		(Z)

- Represents zero.   Z Less than $500,000.   [1] Excludes interschool system transactions.   [2] As of end of fiscal year.

Source: U.S. Bureau of the Census, *Public Education Finances: 1990-91*, GF/91-10.

No. 257. Public Elementary and Secondary Estimated Finances, 1970 to 1993, and by State, 1993

[In millions of dollars, except as noted. For school years ending in June of year shown]

YEAR AND STATE	RECEIPTS						EXPENDITURES				
	Total	Revenue receipts				Non-revenue re-ceipts [1]	Total [2]	Per capita [3] (dol.)	Current expenditures	Average per pupil in ADA [4]	
		Total	Source						Elementary and sec-ondary day schools	Amount (dol.)	Rank
			Federal	State	Local						
1970	41,621	38,192	2,767	15,628	19,797	3,429	39,091	194	32,683	773	(X)
1975	66,319	63,047	5,089	27,472	30,486	3,273	62,340	292	53,333	1,286	(X)
1980	101,724	97,635	9,020	47,929	40,686	4,089	96,105	428	85,661	2,230	(X)
1985	146,976	141,013	9,533	69,107	62,373	5,963	139,382	591	127,230	3,483	(X)
1990	218,126	208,656	13,184	100,787	94,685	9,469	209,698	850	186,583	4,966	(X)
1992	254,510	234,924	15,704	111,348	107,871	19,586	236,750	939	208,352	5,352	(X)
1993, total	268,823	247,706	17,521	115,855	114,330	21,118	248,564	975	218,944	5,528	(X)
Alabama	2,867	2,739	371	1,753	614	128	2,894	700	2,615	3,830	49
Alaska	1,082	972	122	618	231	110	1,058	1,803	962	9,290	2
Arizona	3,784	3,325	285	1,421	1,619	459	3,508	915	2,641	4,140	44
Arkansas	2,046	1,879	186	1,175	518	168	1,825	762	1,578	3,838	48
California	30,126	28,561	2,317	17,903	8,342	1,566	27,315	884	23,743	4,620	39
Colorado	4,004	3,337	165	1,403	1,770	667	3,408	984	2,869	5,050	30
Connecticut	4,099	4,097	200	1,573	2,323	2	4,099	1,250	3,820	8,170	4
Delaware	698	653	57	434	163	45	673	975	614	6,420	12
District of Columbia	622	590	75	-	515	32	621	1,061	572	8,036	5
Florida	11,956	11,370	947	5,511	4,911	586	11,579	857	9,661	5,314	27
Georgia	6,300	6,121	475	3,132	2,514	179	6,015	889	5,317	4,730	36
Hawaii	1,084	1,084	81	982	21	-	1,077	934	963	5,806	17
Idaho	997	894	72	551	271	102	957	898	877	4,025	47
Illinois	17,245	10,551	854	2,926	6,771	6,695	10,687	921	9,101	5,399	25
Indiana	5,809	5,626	294	2,933	2,398	184	5,595	990	4,798	5,439	24
Iowa	2,717	2,653	152	1,284	1,217	64	2,785	992	2,404	5,184	29
Kansas	2,680	2,374	130	1,179	1,065	307	2,538	1,008	2,244	5,490	22
Kentucky	3,340	3,092	309	2,101	682	248	3,158	842	2,861	4,942	31
Louisiana	3,789	3,449	410	1,877	1,162	340	3,426	802	3,129	4,330	43
Maine	1,357	1,277	93	652	531	80	1,357	1,097	1,224	6,162	14
Maryland	4,997	4,841	270	1,988	2,582	156	4,932	1,004	4,494	6,447	11
Massachusetts	5,770	5,759	353	1,943	3,463	10	5,576	929	5,219	6,592	9
Michigan	11,409	10,733	616	3,446	6,671	677	10,896	1,156	9,438	6,402	13
Minnesota	5,477	4,834	225	2,262	2,347	643	5,054	1,130	4,135	5,626	20
Mississippi	1,915	1,811	313	957	541	104	1,769	677	1,604	3,390	50
Missouri	4,642	4,193	271	1,568	2,355	449	3,956	762	3,400	4,489	40
Montana	854	845	78	455	313	8	880	1,070	789	5,459	23
Nebraska	1,351	1,340	64	524	753	10	1,399	872	1,292	4,893	35
Nevada	1,473	1,176	55	402	719	297	1,264	949	1,007	4,929	32
New Hampshire	1,096	1,094	31	90	973	2	1,021	917	936	5,635	19
New Jersey	11,073	10,972	462	4,554	5,957	101	10,429	1,335	9,995	9,491	1
New Mexico	1,396	1,343	170	1,022	151	53	1,453	919	1,231	4,643	38
New York	23,983	22,574	1,352	8,849	12,373	1,409	23,295	1,287	20,898	8,794	3
North Carolina	5,649	5,467	460	3,507	1,500	182	5,589	817	5,067	4,894	34
North Dakota	579	548	62	245	241	31	547	862	503	4,404	41
Ohio	10,419	9,529	575	4,135	4,820	890	10,126	920	8,717	5,260	28
Oklahoma	2,813	2,592	197	1,622	773	221	2,726	850	2,290	4,085	45
Oregon	3,389	3,068	197	1,184	1,687	322	3,146	1,058	2,859	6,088	15
Pennsylvania	12,670	12,609	737	5,375	6,497	61	11,600	967	10,944	6,914	6
Rhode Island	904	904	46	324	534	-	904	903	875	6,649	8
South Carolina	3,313	3,089	292	1,461	1,336	224	3,079	856	2,716	4,669	37
South Dakota	654	603	70	164	369	51	615	868	553	4,367	42
Tennessee	3,489	3,311	351	1,572	1,387	178	3,333	664	3,170	4,033	46
Texas	20,317	18,743	1,534	8,202	9,007	1,573	18,360	1,039	15,868	4,900	33
Utah	1,835	1,657	118	961	578	178	1,557	859	1,393	3,218	51
Vermont	686	662	35	222	405	24	671	1,174	630	6,731	7
Virginia	5,641	5,564	268	1,912	3,385	76	5,757	901	5,137	5,326	26
Washington	5,861	5,422	307	3,933	1,181	439	5,945	1,155	4,634	5,528	21
West Virginia	1,892	1,820	145	1,213	461	73	1,893	1,048	1,673	5,698	18
Wisconsin	6,041	5,347	238	2,048	3,062	694	5,607	1,122	4,934	6,509	10
Wyoming	633	614	35	309	270	20	610	1,314	548	5,822	16

- Represents or rounds to zero.   X Not applicable.   [1] Amount received by local education agencies from the sales of bonds and real property and equipment, loans, and proceeds from insurance adjustments.   [2] Includes interest on school debt and other current expenditures not shown separately.   [3] Based on Bureau of the Census estimated resident population, as of July 1, the previous year. Estimates reflect revisions based on the 1990 Census of Population.   [4] Average daily attendance.

Source: National Education Association, Washington, DC, *Estimates of School Statistics,* annual (copyright); and unpublished data.

No. 258. Microcomputers for Student Instruction in Elementary and Secondary Schools: 1985 and 1994

[As of **fall for public schools; as of midwinter for private schools.** Public school data based on surveys of every school district and all public schools. Private school data based on surveys of all Catholic and private schools. For details, see source]

LEVEL	1984-85				1993-94			
	Total schools	Percent with micros	Number of micros [1]	Students per micro	Total schools	Percent with micros	Number of micros [1]	Students per micro
U.S. total	**105,509**	**77.7**	**631,983**	**62.7**	**105,763**	**97.5**	**4,470,573**	**11.0**
Public schools, total	81,100	85.1	569,825	63.5	83,435	98.6	4,079,260	10.8
Elementary	50,967	82.2	215,393	79.3	50,033	98.7	1,863,499	12.1
Middle/junior high	9,791	93.1	100,331	61.2	12,181	99.6	717,298	11.1
Senior high	15,152	94.6	228,726	51.5	14,322	99.5	1,237,086	9.0
K-12/other	5,190	70.3	25,375	45.8	6,899	86.8	261,377	9.6
Catholic schools, total	9,463	63.4	28,427	73.5	8,345	97.9	197,944	13.0
Elementary	7,831	56.4	15,863	85.1	6,940	97.9	137,275	14.0
Secondary	1,481	87.0	12,147	57.8	1,255	97.9	56,443	10.7
K-12/other	151	46.4	417	(NA)	150	96.2	4,226	10.4
Other private schools, total. . . .	14,946	46.4	33,731	40.5	13,983	85.7	193,369	11.9
Elementary	8,226	45.1	13,400	42.7	7,118	85.9	77,363	13.2
Secondary	950	82.7	6,266	40.1	1,039	86.3	26,339	8.1
K-12/other	5,770	42.4	14,065	(NA)	5,826	85.1	89,666	11.8

NA Not available. [1] Includes estimates for schools not reporting number of micros.

Source: Market Data Retrieval, Shelton, CT, unpublished data.

No. 259. Instructional Use of Computers in Elementary and Secondary Schools: 1985 to 1992

[Includes microcomputers and terminals used by students or teachers. Based on stratified, probability sample of 1,416 public, private, and parochial schools surveyed in spring 1989, and 571 surveyed in spring 1992. Represents all elementary and secondary schools in the United States, except preschools and those that have no grade 5 or higher]

ITEM	Unit	Total, 1985	Total, 1989	1992, BY GRADE LEVEL			
				Total	Grade 5	Grade 8	Grade 11
ALL SCHOOLS							
Computers used for instruction	1,000 . .	1,034	2,355	3,536	1,485	874	1,177
Schools using computers	Percent .	86	96	100	100	100	100
Schools with 15 or more computers	Percent .	24	57	80	77	75	96
SCHOOLS USING COMPUTERS FOR INSTRUCTION							
Mean [1] number of computers	Number.	10	26	37	28	31	65
Median [1]	Number.	8	19	25	23	24	47
Students per computer, median [1]	Number.	42	20	14	15	14	10
Percent of all instructional computers in—							
Classrooms.	Percent.	37	36	37	41	28	33
Computer labs.	Percent.	49	50	50	47	58	52
Other locations	Percent.	14	14	13	12	14	15
Percent of all instructional computers used—							
Usually every day	Percent.	(NA)	71	(NA)	(NA)	(NA)	(NA)
Less than every week or not used at all	Percent.	(NA)	10	(NA)	(NA)	(NA)	(NA)
Median hours of use per week (in rooms with greatest number of computers) [1]	Number.	17	20	20	20	18	22
Percent of all student computer use: [2]							
Learning math	Percent.	(NA)	14	15	18	12	7
Word processing (how to use)	Percent.	(NA)	14	14	12	16	17
Keyboarding (how to)	Percent.	(NA)	13	14	13	15	14
Learning English	Percent.	(NA)	13	13	17	10	7
Programming	Percent.	(NA)	8	5	3	7	8
Recreational use	Percent.	(NA)	8	9	10	10	6
Tools, e.g., spreadsheets.	Percent.	(NA)	7	6	4	8	12
Learning science	Percent.	(NA)	6	7	8	7	6
Learning social studies	Percent.	(NA)	5	7	9	6	3
Business education [3]	Percent.	(NA)	5	4	3	3	10
Industrial arts	Percent.	(NA)	3	2	1	3	6
Fine arts.	Percent.	(NA)	2	2	2	2	2
Learning foreign languages	Percent.	(NA)	1	1	-	1	2
Other.	Percent.	(NA)	1	1	1	1	-

- Represents zero. NA Not available. [1] For definition of mean and median, see Guide to Tabular Presentation.
[2] Estimates supplied by each school's technology coordinator. [3] Other than keyboarding or word processing instruction.

Source: University of Minnesota, Minneapolis, MN, Department of Sociology, IEA Computers in Education Study.

No. 260. Student Use of Computers: 1984 and 1993

[In percent. As of October. Based on the Current Population Survey and subject to sampling error; see Appendix III and source]

CHARACTERISTIC	1984, total	1993					
		Total	Prekinder-garten and kinder-garden	Grades 1-8	Grades 9-12	1st to 4th year of college	5th or later year of college
USING COMPUTERS AT SCHOOL							
Total	27.3	59.0	26.2	68.9	58.2	55.2	52.1
Sex:							
Male	29.0	59.4	25.9	69.5	56.5	57.5	56.7
Female	25.5	58.7	26.5	68.4	60.0	53.3	47.8
Race/ethnicity:							
White [1]	30.0	61.6	29.4	73.7	59.9	54.9	49.8
Black [1]	16.8	51.5	16.5	56.5	54.5	56.9	57.9
Hispanic	18.6	52.3	19.2	58.4	54.1	51.9	53.7
Other	28.6	59.0	23.5	65.7	57.3	60.9	69.4
Household income:							
Less than $5,000	18.7	51.2	19.6	55.0	50.6	61.7	66.7
$5,000 to $9,999	21.0	53.3	24.4	60.3	51.9	53.9	56.2
$10,000 to $14,999	22.4	56.4	20.1	64.7	56.7	50.7	76.1
$15,000 to $19,999	25.9	58.1	23.8	67.5	57.4	51.2	58.5
$20,000 to $24,999	26.7	56.4	23.7	64.3	53.0	57.4	52.4
$25,000 to $29,999	30.5	60.0	28.0	70.1	60.3	51.5	58.0
$30,000 to $34,999	30.5	59.1	23.7	69.6	59.7	51.7	45.3
$35,000 to $39,999	32.3	60.7	27.1	72.1	61.7	49.2	47.9
$40,000 to $49,999	32.8	59.3	28.5	70.3	57.2	53.9	48.6
$50,000 to $74,999	35.5	62.6	28.6	75.6	61.5	57.4	44.2
$75,000 or more	36.0	64.6	33.5	78.7	62.5	60.9	47.7
Control of school:							
Public	27.4	60.2	30.1	68.6	58.1	53.9	54.1
Private	26.5	52.1	18.7	72.5	60.7	60.7	48.0
USING COMPUTERS AT HOME							
Total	11.5	27.0	15.6	24.7	28.7	32.8	52.6
Sex:							
Male	14.0	27.4	15.1	24.8	28.2	36.6	56.1
Female	9.0	26.6	16.1	24.6	29.2	29.7	49.5
Race/ethnicity:							
White [1]	13.7	32.8	19.4	31.4	35.9	36.0	53.6
Black [1]	4.9	10.9	4.2	9.0	10.4	19.4	48.1
Hispanic	3.6	10.4	5.7	7.5	9.8	22.0	52.2
Other	9.0	28.7	17.0	23.2	37.0	33.0	47.1
Household income:							
Less than $5,000	2.9	9.7	1.1	4.1	6.8	25.6	45.2
$5,000 to $9,999	3.2	8.0	0.9	4.5	5.3	21.3	45.6
$10,000 to $14,999	5.0	11.4	4.6	6.4	8.7	29.8	50.0
$15,000 to $19,999	7.5	15.1	6.9	10.9	14.1	28.9	43.0
$20,000 to $24,999	9.9	16.8	7.4	13.1	17.9	27.7	49.6
$25,000 to $29,999	12.8	21.1	12.3	19.3	22.0	26.1	47.0
$30,000 to $34,999	15.8	24.1	18.7	20.5	29.1	26.4	44.4
$35,000 to $39,999	19.4	27.1	13.0	26.3	28.1	32.7	52.7
$40,000 to $49,999	20.4	32.2	21.6	32.9	33.9	32.5	45.9
$50,000 to $74,999	24.2	43.0	25.5	45.3	46.4	40.1	58.2
$75,000 or more	22.1	56.1	38.2	62.3	61.0	47.0	64.7
Control of school:							
Public	11.2	25.3	12.1	23.0	27.2	31.9	50.0
Private	13.8	37.4	22.4	41.5	47.2	36.9	57.7
USING COMPUTERS AT HOME FOR SCHOOL WORK							
Total	4.6	14.9	0.6	10.8	20.9	23.1	36.6
Sex:							
Male	5.9	14.8	0.9	10.1	20.5	26.3	40.3
Female	3.3	15.0	0.4	11.5	21.4	20.5	33.2
Race/ethnicity:							
White [1]	5.4	18.2	0.8	13.8	26.5	25.7	37.8
Black [1]	2.3	5.7	(NA)	4.0	6.9	11.5	30.1
Hispanic	1.4	5.6	(NA)	2.9	6.7	15.9	36.8
Other	3.8	16.0	1.1	9.3	27.0	23.7	29.2
Household income:							
Less than $5,000	1.0	6.7	(NA)	2.5	4.0	18.7	36.0
$5,000 to $9,999	1.5	4.8	(NA)	1.1	3.6	16.1	35.5
$10,000 to $14,999	1.9	7.3	(NA)	2.6	5.6	25.9	34.6
$15,000 to $19,999	3.0	8.6	0.4	4.7	10.8	18.7	31.0
$20,000 to $24,999	3.1	9.8	0.7	5.1	12.6	22.9	35.0
$25,000 to $29,999	5.1	10.4	1.1	6.3	13.4	19.5	34.9
$30,000 to $34,999	4.9	13.0	0.8	8.1	21.9	18.0	35.1
$35,000 to $39,999	7.1	15.4	0.8	12.4	21.0	22.6	37.2
$40,000 to $49,999	9.2	17.1	1.1	14.7	24.2	22.2	32.1
$50,000 to $74,999	11.5	23.2	1.0	19.7	35.0	27.0	38.2
$75,000 or more	9.8	30.4	0.8	29.4	45.2	30.6	41.5
Control of school:							
Public	4.5	14.2	0.5	10.1	19.8	22.7	34.7
Private	5.4	18.8	1.0	17.8	35.4	24.8	40.1

NA Not available. [1] Non-Hispanic.
Source: U.S. National Center for Education Statistics, *Digest of Education Statistics*, 1994.

No. 261. Technology in Public Schools: 1992 to 1995

[For school year ending in year shown. Based on surveys of school districts conducted in the spring and summer of the school year. For details, see source]

TECHNOLOGY	NUMBER				PERCENT OF TOTAL	
	1992	1993	1994	1995	1992	1995
Schools with interactive videodisk players [1]	6,502	11,729	19,189	23,112	8	27
Elementary [2]	2,921	5,986	10,043	12,326	6	24
Junior high [3]	1,258	2,386	3,844	4,672	10	34
Senior high [4]	2,106	3,129	5,026	5,805	14	34
Students represented (1,000)	5,781	9,064	13,434	16,060	14	36
Schools with modems [1]	13,597	18,471	24,277	28,275	16	34
Elementary [2]	5,831	8,492	11,679	14,782	11	29
Junior high [3]	2,608	3,431	4,531	5,393	20	39
Senior high [4]	5,001	6,371	7,853	8,620	30	51
Students represented (1,000)	10,717	13,382	16,476	19,326	25	43
Schools with networks [1]	4,184	11,657	19,272	23,402	5	28
Elementary [2]	1,583	4,683	8,477	11,155	3	22
Junior high [3]	776	2,030	3,611	4,425	6	32
Senior high [4]	1,736	4,895	7,104	8,042	10	48
Students represented (1,000)	3,754	8,043	12,713	15,160	9	34
Schools with CD-ROM's [1]	5,706	11,021	24,526	31,501	7	37
Elementary [2]	1,897	4,457	11,794	16,816	4	33
Junior high [3]	1,231	2,326	4,874	6,170	9	45
Senior high [4]	2,543	4,168	7,724	9,063	15	54
Students represented (1,000)	5,298	8,534	15,576	19,501	12	44
Schools with satellite dishes [1]	1,129	8,812	12,580	14,290	1	17
Elementary [2]	351	2,988	4,269	5,154	1	10
Junior high [3]	166	1,503	2,497	3,004	1	22
Senior high [4]	606	4,292	5,770	6,263	4	37
Students represented (1,000)	1,906	4,668	6,740	7,946	4	18
Schools with cable [1]	(NA)	47,745	58,652	62,593	(NA)	74
Elementary [2]	(NA)	27,923	35,325	37,730	(NA)	73
Junior high [3]	(NA)	9,266	10,696	11,416	(NA)	83
Senior high [4]	(NA)	10,296	12,198	13,089	(NA)	78
Students represented (1,000)	(NA)	27,324	33,510	35,770	(NA)	80

NA Not available. [1] Includes schools for special education and adult education, not shown separately. [2] Includes K-12, preschool, preschool through 3, K-6, and K-8. [3] Includes schools with grade spans of 4-8, 7-8, and 7-9. [4] Includes 7-12, 9-12, 10-12, vocational technical, and alternative high schools.

Source: Quality Education Data, Inc., Denver, CO, Technology in Public Schools, annual.

No. 262. Children and Youth With Disabilities in Educational Programs for the Disabled, by Type of Disability: 1980 to 1993

[For school year ending in year shown. For persons under 22 years old, except as noted. Represents children under 20 served under Chapter 1 of the Elementary and Secondary Education Act (ESEA), State Operated Programs (SOP), and children 3 to 21 served under Individuals with Disabilities Education Act, Part B (IDEA). Excludes outlying areas]

ITEM	1980	1985	1987	1988 [1]	1989 [1]	1990 [1]	1991 [1]	1992 [1]	1993 [1]
All conditions (1,000)	4,005	4,315	4,374	4,128	4,173	4,219	4,320	4,459	4,586
PERCENT DISTRIBUTION									
Learning disabled	31.9	42.4	43.6	47.0	47.8	48.6	49.3	50.1	51.3
Speech impaired	29.6	26.1	25.8	23.2	23.1	23.1	22.8	22.3	21.7
Mentally retarded	21.7	16.1	15.0	14.6	13.8	13.0	12.4	12.0	11.3
Emotionally disturbed	8.2	8.6	8.7	9.1	8.9	9.0	9.0	8.9	8.7
Hard of hearing and deaf	2.0	1.6	1.5	1.4	1.4	1.3	1.3	1.3	1.3
Orthopedically handicapped	1.6	1.3	1.3	1.1	1.1	1.1	1.1	1.1	1.1
Other health impaired	2.6	1.6	1.2	1.1	1.2	1.2	1.3	1.1	1.1
Visually handicapped	0.8	0.7	0.6	0.6	C.5	0.5	0.5	1.3	1.4
Multihandicapped	1.5	1.6	2.2	1.9	2.0	2.0	2.2	0.5	0.5
Deaf-blind	0.1	0.1	(Z)	(Z)	(Z)	(Z)	(Z)	2.2	2.2
Autism	(NA)	(NA)	(NA)	(NA)	(NA)	(NA)	(NA)	(Z)	(Z)
Traumatic brain injury	(NA)	(NA)	(NA)	(NA)	(NA)	(NA)	(NA)	0.1	0.3
								(Z)	0.1

NA Not available. Z Less than .05 percent. [1] For children 6 to 21 years old; total number of children served under 22 years old was 4,494,280 in school year 1987-88, 4,568,118 in school year 1988-89, 4,640,969 in 1989-90, 4,761,742 in 1990-91, 4,940,475 in 1991-92, and 5,110,653 in 1992-93.

Source: U.S. Dept. of Education, Office of Special Education Programs, Annual Report to Congress.

No. 263. Children and Youth With Disabilities, by Age and Educational Environment: 1991

[For school year ending in year shown. Covers children 3 to 21 served under Chapter 1 of ESEA (SOP) and IDEA-B; see headnote, table 262]

ENVIRONMENT	NUMBER (1,000)					PERCENT DISTRIBUTION			
	Total	3-5 years old	6-11 years old	12-17 years old	18-21 years old	3-5 years old	6-11 years old	12-17 years old	18-21 years old
Total	**4,691.2**	**367.5**	**2,284.0**	**1,812.9**	**226.8**	**100.0**	**100.0**	**100.0**	**100.0**
Regular class [1]	1,592.8	163.1	991.2	399.3	39.1	44.4	43.4	22.0	17.2
Resource room [2]	1,618.6	47.8	718.1	773.5	79.3	13.0	31.4	42.7	35.0
Separate class [3]	1,181.6	99.1	492.8	520.1	69.5	27.0	21.6	28.7	30.7
Separate school facility:									
Public	154.0	30.0	42.6	58.2	23.3	8.2	1.9	3.2	10.3
Private	76.4	18.9	24.5	26.7	6.3	5.1	1.1	1.5	2.8
Separate residential facility:									
Public	25.5	1.0	5.4	14.5	4.6	0.3	0.2	0.8	2.0
Private	12.2	0.3	2.5	7.2	2.2	0.1	0.1	0.4	1.0
Correctional facility [4]	9.1	(NA)	(NA)	(NA)	(NA)	(NA)	(NA)	(NA)	(NA)
Home/hospital	30.0	7.2	6.9	13.4	2.5	2.0	0.3	0.7	1.1

NA Not available. [1] Receives special education and related services less than 21 percent of the school day. [2] Receives services between 21 and 60 percent of the school day. [3] Receives services for more than 60 percent of the school day. [4] Students in correctional institutions are also distributed by type of environment, but not duplicated in the total.
Source: U.S. Dept. of Education, Office of Special Education Programs, Data Analysis Systems (DANS), unpublished data.

No. 264. Catholic Elementary and Secondary Schools: 1960 to 1993

[As of **October 1**. Regular sessions only. See also *Historical Statistics, Colonial Times to 1970*, series H 535-544]

ITEM	Unit	1960	1970	1975	1980	1985	1989	1990	1991	1992	1993
Elementary schools	Number	10,501	9,362	8,340	8,043	7,806	7,395	7,291	7,239	7,174	7,114
Pupils enrolled	1,000	4,373	3,359	2,525	2,269	2,057	1,893	1,884	1,964	1,984	1,992
Teachers, total [1]	1,000	108	112	99	97	97	94	91	109	110	112
Religious	1,000	79	52	35	25	18	12	11	12	11	12
Lay	1,000	29	60	64	72	79	82	80	96	98	100
Secondary schools	Number	2,392	1,981	1,653	1,516	1,430	1,324	1,296	1,269	1,249	1,231
Pupils enrolled	1,000	880	1,008	890	837	762	606	592	587	584	585
Teachers, total [1]	1,000	44	54	50	49	50	43	40	44	45	45
Religious	1,000	33	28	20	14	11	8	6	6	6	7
Lay	1,000	11	26	30	35	39	35	34	37	38	38

[1] Beginning 1991, includes part-time teachers.
Source: National Catholic Educational Association, (NCEA) Washington, DC; from the NCEA Data Bank—*U.S. Catholic Schools l967-1968*, (copyright) and *U.S. Catholic Elementary and Secondary Schools 1992-1993 Annual Statistical Report on Schools, Enrollment & Staffing*, NCEA, annual (copyright); and NCEA/Ganley's *Catholic Schools in America*, 1993 edition, annual (copyright).

No. 265. Private Elementary and Secondary School Teachers—Selected Characteristics: 1990-91

[For school year. Based on survey and subject to sampling error; for details, see source. See table 250 for similar data on public school teachers]

CHARACTERISTIC	Unit	AGE				SEX		RACE/ETHNICITY		
		Under 30 years old	30 to 39 years old	40 to 49 years old	Over 50 years old	Male	Female	White [1]	Black [1]	Hispanic
Total teachers [2]	1,000	**68**	**105**	**115**	**67**	**82**	**275**	**329**	**9**	**12**
Highest degree held:										
Bachelor's	Percent	81.4	65.9	55.4	47.0	51.5	65.0	61.8	72.8	60.6
Master's	Percent	9.8	23.5	33.4	38.7	35.3	24.5	27.3	21.7	22.1
Education specialist	Percent	0.8	2.3	3.7	4.8	4.0	2.6	3.0	1.0	1.7
Doctorate	Percent	0.3	1.1	1.9	4.0	4.2	1.0	1.8	0.9	2.7
Full-time teaching experience:										
Less than 3 years	Percent	55.5	27.2	19.3	13.4	25.3	28.1	27.2	28.9	32.4
3 to 9 years	Percent	44.4	43.3	37.6	16.6	33.2	37.6	36.6	43.0	33.0
10 to 20 years	Percent	-	29.5	33.4	28.9	26.4	24.6	25.1	22.5	22.8
20 years or more	Percent	-	-	9.7	41.1	15.1	9.6	11.1	5.6	11.9
Full-time teachers	1,000	61	86	98	55	70	231	278	9	9
Earned income	Dol.	18,658	21,322	22,447	24,197	27,196	19,999	21,569	23,094	22,912
Salary	Dol.	16,403	19,177	20,879	22,534	23,003	18,806	19,709	20,333	20,740

- Represents zero. [1] Non-Hispanic. [2] Includes teachers with no degrees and associates degrees, not shown separately.
Source: U.S. National Center for Education Statistics, *Digest of Education Statistics*, 1994.

No. 266. Private Elementary and Secondary Schools—Enrollment and Tuition, by Orientation: 1991

[For school year ending in year shown. Based on survey and subject to sampling error; for details see source. Revised since originally published]

CHARACTERISTIC	ENROLLMENT (1,000)				SCHOOLS			
	Total	Catholic	Other religious	Non-sectarian	Total	Catholic	Other religious	Non-sectarian
Total	**4,673.9**	**2,555.9**	**1,468.5**	**649.4**	**24,690**	**8,731**	**11,476**	**4,483**
School enrollment:								
Less than 150 students	824.4	176.0	461.9	186.6	13,072	1,703	8,217	3,152
150 to 299 students	1,499.5	904.6	430.0	164.9	7,027	4,148	2,082	797
300 to 499 students	1,112.7	692.8	291.3	128.6	2,923	1,824	775	324
500 to 749 students	682.3	420.3	184.9	77.1	1,122	700	301	121
750 or more students	555.0	362.3	100.5	92.2	458	357	101	(B)
Percent minority students:								
Less than 5 percent	36.0	34.1	44.9	23.0	40.0	38.3	49.0	20.6
5 percent, less than 20 percent . . .	31.9	29.6	31.5	41.9	28.8	28.3	25.8	37.5
20 percent, less than 50 percent	17.6	17.9	14.1	24.6	16.9	15.5	14.9	24.8
50 percent or more	14.5	18.4	9.5	10.4	14.2	17.9	10.3	17.2
Average annual tuition (dol.):								
Total	(X)	(X)	(X)	(X)	2,595	1,776	2,633	5,727
Elementary	(X)	(X)	(X)	(X)	1,705	1,260	2,270	3,846
Secondary	(X)	(X)	(X)	(X)	3,649	3,007	4,070	8,061
Combined	(X)	(X)	(X)	(X)	3,853	(B)	2,711	6,257

B Base too small to meet statistical standards for reliability of a derived figure.   X Not applicable.

Source: U.S. National Center for Education Statistics, *Digest of Education Statistics*, 1994.

No. 267. High School Dropouts, by Race and Hispanic Origin: 1973 to 1993

[In percent. As of **October**]

ITEM	1973	1975	1980	1985	1986	1987 [1]	1988	1989	1990	1991	1992	1993
EVENT DROPOUTS [2]												
Total [3]	**6.3**	**5.8**	**6.0**	**5.2**	**4.3**	**4.1**	**4.8**	**4.5**	**4.0**	**4.0**	**4.3**	**4.2**
White	5.7	5.4	5.6	4.8	4.2	3.7	4.7	3.9	3.8	3.7	4.1	4.1
Male	6.1	5.0	6.4	4.9	4.2	4.1	5.1	4.1	4.1	3.6	3.8	4.1
Female	5.3	5.8	4.9	4.7	4.1	3.4	4.3	3.8	3.5	3.8	4.4	4.1
Black	10.1	8.7	8.3	7.7	4.7	6.4	6.3	7.7	5.1	6.2	4.9	5.4
Male	12.0	8.3	8.0	8.3	4.8	6.2	6.7	6.9	4.1	5.5	3.3	5.7
Female	8.4	9.0	8.5	7.2	4.6	6.4	6.0	8.6	6.0	7.0	6.7	5.0
Hispanic [4]	10.0	10.9	11.5	9.7	11.9	5.6	10.5	7.7	8.0	7.3	7.9	5.4
Male	7.9	10.1	16.9	9.3	11.7	5.0	12.3	7.6	8.7	10.4	5.8	5.7
Female	12.0	11.6	6.9	9.8	12.4	6.2	8.4	7.7	7.2	4.8	8.6	5.0
STATUS DROPOUTS [5]												
Total [3]	**15.7**	**15.6**	**15.6**	**13.9**	**13.8**	**14.5**	**14.6**	**14.4**	**13.6**	**14.2**	**12.7**	**12.7**
White	14.2	13.9	14.4	13.5	13.5	14.2	14.2	14.1	13.5	14.2	12.2	12.2
Male	13.8	13.5	15.7	14.7	14.6	15.1	15.4	15.4	14.2	15.4	13.3	13.0
Female	14.5	14.2	13.2	12.3	12.4	13.2	13.0	12.8	12.8	13.1	11.1	11.5
Black	26.5	27.3	23.5	17.6	16.6	17.0	17.7	16.4	15.1	15.6	16.3	16.4
Male	25.9	27.8	26.0	18.8	18.1	18.7	18.9	18.6	13.6	15.4	15.5	15.6
Female	27.1	26.9	21.5	16.6	15.8	15.4	16.6	14.5	16.2	15.8	17.1	17.2
Hispanic [4]	38.9	34.9	40.3	31.5	27.9	32.8	39.6	37.7	37.3	39.6	33.9	32.7
Male	36.5	32.6	42.6	35.8	37.4	34.5	40.2	40.3	39.8	44.4	38.4	34.7
Female	41.3	36.8	38.1	27.0	31.1	30.8	38.8	35.0	34.5	34.5	29.6	31.0

[1] Beginning 1987 reflects new editing procedures for cases with missing data on school enrollment.   [2] Percent of students who drop out in a single year without completing high school. For grades 10 to 12.   [3] Includes other races, not shown separately.   [4] Persons of Hispanic origin may be of any race.   [5] Percent of the population who have not completed high school and are not enrolled, regardless of when they dropped out. For persons 18 to 24 years old.

Source: U.S. Bureau of the Census, *Current Population Reports*, P20-479.

No. 268. High School Dropouts by Age, Race, and Hispanic Origin: 1970 to 1993

[As of **October. For persons 14 to 24 years old.** See table 270 for definition of dropouts]

AGE AND RACE	NUMBER OF DROPOUTS (1,000)					PERCENT OF POPULATION				
	1970	1980	1985	1990	1993	1970	1980	1985	1990	1993
Total dropouts [1][2]	**4,670**	**5,212**	**4,456**	**3,854**	**3,472**	**12.2**	**12.0**	**10.6**	**10.1**	**9.2**
16 to 17 years	617	709	505	418	326	8.0	8.8	7.0	6.3	4.8
18 to 21 years	2,138	2,578	2,095	1,921	1,658	16.4	15.8	14.1	13.4	12.6
22 to 24 years	1,770	1,798	1,724	1,458	1,412	18.7	15.2	14.1	13.8	12.9
White [2]	3,577	4,169	3,583	3,127	2,683	10.8	11.3	10.3	10.1	8.8
16 to 17 years	485	619	424	334	253	7.3	9.2	7.1	6.4	4.7
18 to 21 years	1,618	2,032	1,678	1,516	1,283	14.3	14.7	13.6	13.1	12.3
22 to 24 years	1,356	1,416	1,372	1,235	1,086	16.3	14.0	13.3	14.0	12.1
Black [2]	1,047	934	748	611	641	22.2	16.0	12.6	10.9	11.2
16 to 17 years	125	80	70	73	50	12.8	6.9	6.5	6.9	4.6
18 to 21 years	500	486	376	345	328	30.5	23.0	17.5	16.0	15.9
22 to 24 years	397	346	279	185	250	37.8	24.0	17.8	13.5	17.2
Hispanic [2][3]	(NA)	919	820	1,122	1,009	(NA)	29.5	23.3	26.8	22.9
16 to 17 years	(NA)	92	97	89	82	(NA)	16.6	14.6	12.9	9.9
18 to 21 years	(NA)	470	335	502	437	(NA)	40.3	29.3	32.9	28.6
22 to 24 years	(NA)	323	365	523	470	(NA)	40.6	33.9	42.8	37.8

NA Not available.　[1] Includes other groups not shown separately.　[2] Includes persons 14 to 15 years, not shown separately.
[3] Persons of Hispanic origin may be of any race.
Source: U.S. Bureau of the Census, *Current Population Reports*, P20-479; and earlier reports.

No. 269. Enrollment Status, by Race, Hispanic Origin, and Sex: 1975 and 1993

[As of **October. For persons 18 to 21 years old.** For the civilian noninstitutional population. Based on the Current Population Survey; see text, section 1 and Appendix III]

CHARACTERISTIC	TOTAL PERSONS 18 TO 21 YEARS OLD (1,000)		PERCENT DISTRIBUTION							
			Enrolled in high school		High school graduates				Not high school graduates	
					Total		In college			
	1975	1993	1975	1993	1975	1993	1975	1993	1975	1993
Total [1]	**15,693**	**13,169**	**5.7**	**7.6**	**78.0**	**78.2**	**33.5**	**42.9**	**16.3**	**12.6**
White	13,448	10,466	4.7	8.0	80.6	79.7	34.6	44.9	14.7	12.3
Black	1,997	2,067	12.5	14.4	60.4	69.6	24.9	29.4	27.0	15.9
Hispanic [2]	899	1,526	12.0	11.3	57.2	59.7	24.4	28.6	30.8	28.6
Male [1]	7,584	6,521	7.4	11.6	76.6	75.4	35.4	40.6	15.9	13.0
White	6,545	5,212	6.2	10.1	79.7	77.1	36.9	42.6	14.1	12.7
Black	911	986	15.9	18.8	55.0	65.1	23.9	25.9	29.0	16.0
Hispanic [2]	416	736	17.3	13.3	54.6	56.2	25.2	25.4	27.9	30.4
Female [1]	8,109	6,648	4.2	6.8	79.2	81.0	31.8	45.3	16.6	12.2
White	6,903	5,255	3.2	5.8	81.4	82.3	32.4	47.1	15.3	11.8
Black	1,085	1,081	9.7	10.4	65.0	73.8	25.8	32.7	25.4	15.7
Hispanic [2]	484	790	7.6	9.7	59.3	62.8	23.6	31.5	33.1	27.1

[1] Includes other races not shown separately.　[2] Persons of Hispanic origin may be of any race.
Source: U.S. Bureau of the Census, *Current Population Reports*, P20-479; and earlier reports.

No. 270. Employment Status of High School Graduates and School Dropouts: 1980 to 1993

[**In thousands, except percent.** As of **October.** For civilian noninstitutional population 16 to 24 years old. Based on Current Population Survey; see text, section 1, and Appendix III]

EMPLOYMENT STATUS, SEX, AND RACE	GRADUATES [1]				DROPOUTS [2]			
	1980	1985	1990	1993	1980	1985	1990	1993
Civilian population	**11,622**	**10,381**	**8,370**	**6,819**	**5,254**	**4,323**	**3,800**	**3,390**
In labor force	9,795	8,825	7,107	5,652	3,549	2,920	2,506	2,084
Percent of population	84.3	85.0	84.9	82.9	67.5	67.5	66.0	61.5
Employed	8,567	7,707	6,279	4,969	2,651	2,165	1,993	1,658
Percent of labor force	87.5	87.3	88.3	87.9	74.7	74.1	79.5	79.6
Unemployed	1,228	1,118	828	683	898	755	513	426
Unemployment rate, total [3]	12.5	12.7	11.7	12.1	25.3	25.9	20.5	20.4
Male	13.5	12.5	11.1	12.2	23.5	23.9	18.8	17.5
Female	11.5	12.9	12.3	11.9	28.7	29.8	23.5	26.8
White	10.8	9.8	9.0	10.6	21.6	23.6	17.0	18.3
Black	26.1	29.4	26.0	21.1	43.9	41.5	43.3	34.4
Not in labor force	1,827	1,556	1,262	1,167	1,705	1,403	1,294	1,305
Percent of population	15.7	15.0	15.1	17.1	32.5	32.5	34.1	38.5

[1] For persons not enrolled in college who have completed 4 years of high school only.　[2] For persons not in regular school and who have not completed the 12th grade nor received a general equivalency degree.　[3] Includes other races not shown separately.
Source: U.S. Bureau of Labor Statistics, Bulletin 2307, *News*, USDL 94-252, May 20, 1994; and unpublished data.

No. 271. Scholastic Assessment Test (SAT) Scores and Characteristics of College-Bound Seniors: 1967 to 1994

[**For school year ending in year shown**. Data are for the SAT I: Reasoning Tests. Prior to 1994, named Scholastic Aptitude Test]

TYPE OF TEST AND CHARACTERISTIC	Unit	1967	1970	1975	1980	1985	1990	1991	1992	1993	1994
TEST SCORES [1]											
Verbal, total [2]	Point . . .	466	460	434	424	431	424	422	423	424	423
Male	Point . . .	463	459	437	428	437	429	426	428	428	425
Female	Point . . .	468	461	431	420	425	419	418	419	420	421
Math, total [2]	Point . . .	492	488	472	466	475	476	474	476	478	479
Male	Point . . .	514	509	495	491	499	499	497	499	502	501
Female	Point . . .	467	465	449	443	452	455	453	456	457	460
PARTICIPANTS											
Total	1,000 . . .	(NA)	(NA)	996	992	977	1,026	1,033	1,034	1,044	1,050
Male	Percent .	(NA)	(NA)	49.9	48.2	48.3	47.8	47.7	47.6	47.4	46.9
White	Percent .	(NA)	(NA)	86.0	82.1	81.0	73.0	72.0	71.5	70.4	69.4
Black	Percent .	(NA)	(NA)	7.9	9.1	7.5	10.0	10.0	10.4	10.8	10.8
Obtaining scores [1] of—											
600 or above:											
Verbal	Percent .	(NA)	(NA)	7.9	7.2	7.9	7.4	7.2	7.3	7.8	7.6
Math	Percent .	(NA)	(NA)	15.6	15.1	17.1	18.4	17.8	18.1	18.8	18.9
Below 400:											
Verbal	Percent .	(NA)	(NA)	37.8	41.8	39.4	41.2	42.4	41.3	41.3	42.3
Math	Percent .	(NA)	(NA)	28.5	30.2	28.2	28.4	29.1	28.2	27.7	27.0
Selected intended area of study:											
Business and commerce	Percent .	(NA)	(NA)	11.5	18.6	21.0	21.0	19.0	16.8	15.0	13.8
Engineering	Percent .	(NA)	(NA)	6.7	11.1	11.7	10.0	10.0	10.5	10.2	9.4
Social science	Percent .	(NA)	(NA)	7.7	7.8	7.5	13.0	12.0	12.1	12.2	12.1
Education	Percent .	(NA)	(NA)	9.1	6.1	4.7	7.0	8.0	8.1	8.0	8.0
SAT average [1] by high school rank:											
Top tenth	Point . . .	(NA)	(NA)	(NA)	539	547	549	548	549	550	549
Second tenth	Point . . .	(NA)	(NA)	(NA)	470	482	481	480	480	481	481
Second fifth	Point . . .	(NA)	(NA)	(NA)	431	442	438	437	438	439	439
Third fifth	Point . . .	(NA)	(NA)	(NA)	386	396	392	391	392	393	394

NA Not available. [1] Minimum score 200; maximum score, 800. [2] 1967 and 1970 are estimates based on total number of persons taking SAT.

Source: College Entrance Examination Board, New York, NY, *National College-Bound Senior,* annual (copyright).

No. 272. American College Testing (ACT) Program Scores and Characteristics of College-Bound Students: 1967 to 1994

[**For academic year ending in year shown**. Except as indicated, test scores and characteristics of college-bound students. Through 1985, data based on 10 percent sample; thereafter, based on all ACT tested seniors]

TYPE OF TEST AND CHARACTERISTIC	Unit	1967	1970	1975	1980	1985	1990 [1]	1991 [1]	1992 [1]	1993 [1]	1994 [1]
TEST SCORES [2]											
Composite	Point . . .	19.9	18.6	18.5	18.5	18.6	20.6	20.6	20.6	20.7	20.8
Male	Point . . .	20.3	19.5	19.3	19.3	19.4	21.0	20.9	20.9	21.0	20.9
Female	Point . . .	19.4	17.8	17.9	17.8	17.9	20.3	20.4	20.5	20.5	20.7
English	Point . . .	18.5	17.7	17.9	17.8	18.1	20.5	20.3	20.2	20.3	20.3
Male	Point . . .	17.6	17.1	17.3	17.3	17.6	20.1	19.8	19.8	19.8	19.8
Female	Point . . .	19.4	18.3	18.3	18.2	18.6	20.9	20.7	20.6	20.6	20.7
Math	Point . . .	20.0	17.6	17.4	17.3	17.2	19.9	20.0	20.0	20.1	20.2
Male	Point . . .	21.1	19.3	18.9	18.9	18.6	20.7	20.6	20.7	20.8	20.8
Female	Point . . .	18.8	16.2	16.2	16.0	16.0	19.3	19.4	19.5	19.6	19.6
Reading [3]	Point . . .	19.7	17.4	17.2	17.2	17.4	(NA)	21.2	21.1	21.2	21.2
Male	Point . . .	20.3	18.7	18.2	18.3	18.3	(NA)	21.3	21.1	21.2	21.1
Female	Point . . .	19.0	16.4	16.4	16.4	16.6	(NA)	21.1	21.1	21.2	21.4
Science reasoning [4]	Point . . .	20.8	21.1	21.1	21.0	21.2	(NA)	20.7	20.7	20.8	20.9
Male	Point . . .	21.6	22.4	22.4	22.3	22.6	(NA)	21.3	21.4	21.5	21.6
Female	Point . . .	20.0	20.0	20.0	20.0	20.0	(NA)	20.1	20.1	20.3	20.4
PARTICIPANTS [5]											
Total	1,000 . . .	788	714	822	836	739	817	796	832	876	892
Male	Percent .	52	46	45	45	46	46	45	45	45	45
White	Percent .	(NA)	77	83	83	82	79	79	80	80	79
Black	Percent .	4	7	8	8	8	9	9	9	9	9
Obtaining composite scores [6] of—											
27 or above	Percent .	14	14	13	13	14	12	11	12	12	13
18 or below	Percent .	21	33	33	33	32	35	35	35	35	34
Planned educational major:											
Business [7]	Percent .	18	21	20	19	21	20	18	17	15	14
Engineering	Percent .	8	6	8	10	9	9	10	11	10	9
Social science [8]	Percent .	10	9	6	6	7	10	10	10	10	9
Education	Percent .	16	12	9	7	6	8	10	9	9	10

NA Not available. [1] Beginning 1990, not comparable with previous years because a new version of the ACT was introduced. Estimated average composite scores for prior years: 1989, 20.6; 1988, 1987, and 1986, 20.8. [2] Minimum score, 1; maximum score, 36. [3] Prior to 1990, social studies; data not comparable with previous years. [4] Prior to 1990, natural sciences; data not comparable with previous years. [5] Beginning 1985, data are for seniors who graduated in year shown and had taken the ACT in their junior or senior years. [6] Prior to 1990, 26 or above and 15 or below. [7] Includes political and persuasive (e.g. sales) fields through 1975; thereafter, business and commerce. [8] Includes religion through 1975.

Source: The American College Testing Program, Iowa City, IA, *High School Profile Report,* annual.

Education

No. 273. Proficiency Test Scores for Selected Subjects, by Characteristic: 1977 to 1992

[Based on The National Assessment of Educational Progress Tests which are administered to a representative sample of students in public and private schools. Test scores can range from 0 to 500. For details, see source]

TEST AND YEAR	Total	SEX		RACE		His-panic origin	PARENTAL EDUCATION				
		Male	Fe-male	White [1]	Black [1]		Less than high school	High school	More than high school		
									Total	Some college	College graduate
READING											
9 year olds:											
1979-80	215	210	220	221	189	190	194	213	226	(NA)	(NA)
1983-84	211	208	214	218	186	187	195	209	223	(NA)	(NA)
1987-88	212	208	216	218	189	194	193	211	220	(NA)	(NA)
1989-90	209	204	215	217	182	189	193	209	218	(NA)	(NA)
1991-92	211	206	215	218	185	192	195	207	220	(NA)	(NA)
13 year olds:											
1979-80	259	254	263	264	233	237	239	254	271	(NA)	(NA)
1983-84	257	253	262	263	236	240	240	253	268	(NA)	(NA)
1987-88	258	252	263	261	243	240	247	253	265	(NA)	(NA)
1989-90	257	251	263	262	242	238	241	251	267	(NA)	(NA)
1991-92	260	254	265	266	238	239	239	252	270	(NA)	(NA)
17 year olds:											
1979-80	286	282	289	293	243	264	262	278	290	(NA)	(NA)
1983-84	289	284	294	295	264	268	269	281	301	(NA)	(NA)
1987-88	290	286	294	295	274	271	267	282	300	(NA)	(NA)
1989-90	290	284	297	297	267	275	270	283	300	(NA)	(NA)
1991-92	290	284	296	297	261	271	271	281	299	(NA)	(NA)
WRITING [2]											
4th graders:											
1983-84	204	201	208	211	182	189	179	192	217	208	218
1987-88	206	199	213	215	173	190	194	199	212	211	212
1989-90	202	195	209	211	171	184	186	197	210	214	209
1991-92	207	198	216	217	175	189	191	202	212	201	214
8th graders:											
1983-84	267	258	276	272	247	247	258	261	276	271	278
1987-88	264	254	274	269	246	250	254	258	271	275	271
1989-90	257	246	268	262	239	246	246	253	265	267	265
1991-92	274	264	285	279	258	265	258	268	283	280	284
11th graders:											
1983-84	290	281	299	297	270	259	274	284	299	298	300
1987-88	291	282	299	296	275	274	276	285	298	296	299
1989-90	287	276	298	293	268	277	268	278	296	292	298
1991-92	287	279	296	294	263	274	271	278	295	292	296
MATHEMATICS											
9 year olds:											
1977-78	219	217	220	224	192	203	200	219	231	230	231
1981-82	219	217	221	224	195	204	199	218	228	225	229
1985-86	222	222	222	227	202	205	201	218	231	229	231
1989-90	230	229	230	235	208	214	210	226	237	236	238
13 year olds:											
1977-78	264	264	265	272	230	238	245	263	280	273	284
1981-82	269	269	268	274	240	252	251	263	280	275	282
1985-86	269	270	268	274	249	254	252	263	278	274	280
1989-90	270	271	270	276	249	255	253	263	279	277	280
17 year olds:											
1977-78	300	304	297	306	268	276	280	294	313	305	317
1981-82	299	302	296	304	272	277	279	293	309	304	312
1985-86	302	305	299	308	279	283	279	293	310	305	314
1989-90	305	306	303	310	289	284	285	294	313	308	316
1991-92	307	309	305	312	286	292	286	298	313	308	316
SCIENCE											
9 year olds:											
1976-77	220	222	218	230	175	192	199	223	233	237	232
1981-82	221	221	221	229	187	189	198	218	230	229	231
1985-86	224	227	221	232	196	199	204	220	235	236	235
1989-90	229	230	227	238	196	206	210	226	236	238	236
13 year olds:											
1976-77	247	251	244	256	208	213	224	245	264	260	266
1981-82	250	256	245	257	217	226	225	243	262	259	264
1985-86	251	256	247	259	222	226	229	245	262	258	264
1989-90	255	259	252	264	226	232	233	247	266	263	268
1991-92	258	260	256	267	224	238	234	246	268	266	269
17 year olds:											
1976-77	290	297	282	298	240	262	265	284	304	296	309
1981-82	283	292	275	293	235	249	259	275	296	290	300
1985-86	289	295	282	298	253	259	258	277	300	295	304
1989-90	290	296	285	301	253	262	261	276	302	297	306
1991-92	294	299	289	304	256	270	262	280	304	296	308

NA Not available. [1] Non-Hispanic. [2] Writing scores revised from previous years; previous writing scores were recorded on a 0 to 400 rather than 0 to 500 scale.

Source: U.S. National Center for Education Statistics, *NAEP Trends in Academic Progress*, Report No. 23-TR01, July 1994.

No. 274. Public High School Graduates, by State: 1980 to 1994

[In thousands. For school year ending in year shown]

STATE	1980	1985	1987	1988	1989	1990	1991	1992	1993, est.	1994, est.
U.S....	2,747.7	2,414.0	2,428.8	2,500.2	2,458.8	2,320.3	2,234.9	2,211.9	2,254.7	2,255.1
AL.......	45.2	40.0	42.5	43.8	43.4	40.5	39.0	38.7	36.0	36.1
AK.......	5.2	5.2	5.7	5.9	5.6	5.4	5.5	5.5	5.6	5.9
AZ.......	28.6	27.9	29.5	29.8	31.9	32.1	31.3	31.3	30.7	29.1
AR.......	29.1	26.3	27.1	27.8	27.9	26.5	25.7	25.8	25.4	25.3
CA.......	249.2	225.4	237.4	249.6	244.6	236.3	234.2	244.6	260.0	261.6
CO.......	36.8	32.3	34.2	36.0	35.5	33.0	31.3	31.1	31.8	32.4
CT.......	37.7	32.1	31.1	32.4	30.9	27.9	27.3	27.1	27.1	27.0
DE.......	7.6	5.9	5.9	6.0	6.1	5.6	5.2	5.3	5.5	5.3
DC.......	5.0	3.9	3.8	3.9	3.6	3.6	3.4	3.4	3.1	3.0
FL.......	87.3	81.1	82.2	89.2	90.8	88.9	87.4	93.7	88.5	92.0
GA.......	61.6	58.7	60.0	61.8	61.9	56.6	60.1	57.7	60.4	59.5
HI.......	11.5	10.1	10.4	10.6	10.4	10.3	9.0	9.2	8.9	9.3
ID.......	13.2	12.1	12.2	12.4	12.5	12.0	12.0	12.7	13.0	13.3
IL.......	135.6	117.0	116.1	119.1	116.7	108.1	103.3	102.7	103.6	105.3
IN.......	73.1	63.3	60.4	64.0	63.6	60.0	57.9	56.6	57.3	56.6
IA.......	43.4	36.1	34.6	35.2	34.3	31.8	28.6	29.2	30.5	30.0
KS.......	30.9	26.0	26.9	27.0	26.8	25.4	24.4	24.1	24.9	25.2
KY.......	41.2	38.0	36.9	39.5	38.9	38.0	35.8	33.9	36.9	37.1
LA.......	46.3	39.7	39.1	39.1	37.2	36.1	33.5	32.2	32.5	33.3
ME.......	15.4	13.9	13.7	13.8	13.9	13.8	13.2	13.2	13.1	13.1
MD.......	54.3	48.3	46.1	47.2	45.8	41.6	39.0	39.2	39.5	39.8
MA.......	73.8	63.4	61.0	59.5	57.3	55.9	50.2	50.8	49.3	45.7
MI.......	124.3	105.9	102.7	106.2	101.8	93.8	88.2	87.8	86.8	88.8
MN.......	64.9	53.4	53.5	54.6	53.1	49.1	46.5	46.2	48.0	48.6
MS.......	27.6	25.3	26.2	27.9	24.2	25.2	23.7	23.0	23.4	23.3
MO.......	62.3	51.3	50.8	51.3	52.0	49.0	46.9	46.6	46.9	46.9
MT.......	12.1	10.0	10.1	10.3	10.5	9.4	9.0	9.0	9.4	9.7
NE.......	22.4	18.0	18.1	18.3	18.7	17.7	16.5	17.1	18.1	17.3
NV.......	8.5	8.6	9.5	9.4	9.5	9.5	9.4	8.8	9.0	9.4
NH.......	11.7	11.1	10.8	11.7	11.3	10.8	10.1	10.3	9.7	9.5
NJ.......	94.6	81.5	79.4	80.9	76.3	69.8	67.0	66.7	67.3	66.5
NM.......	18.4	15.6	15.7	15.9	15.5	14.9	15.2	14.8	15.0	15.3
NY.......	204.1	166.8	163.8	165.4	154.6	143.3	133.6	134.6	135.8	137.5
NC.......	70.9	67.2	65.4	67.8	70.0	64.8	62.8	61.2	60.2	58.3
ND.......	9.9	8.1	7.8	8.4	8.1	7.7	7.6	7.4	7.3	7.7
OH.......	144.2	122.3	121.1	124.5	125.0	114.5	107.5	104.5	105.0	100.0
OK.......	39.3	34.6	35.5	36.1	36.8	35.6	33.0	32.7	30.5	30.0
OR.......	29.9	26.9	27.2	28.1	26.9	25.5	24.6	25.3	26.4	27.2
PA.......	146.5	127.2	121.2	124.4	118.9	110.5	104.8	103.9	103.2	101.8
RI.......	10.9	9.2	8.8	8.9	8.6	7.8	7.7	7.9	7.7	7.5
SC.......	38.7	34.5	36.0	36.1	37.0	32.5	33.0	30.7	32.4	32.3
SD.......	10.7	8.2	8.1	8.4	8.2	7.7	7.1	7.3	8.6	8.2
TN.......	49.8	43.3	44.7	47.9	48.6	46.1	44.8	45.1	45.8	44.1
TX.......	171.4	159.2	168.4	171.4	177.0	172.5	174.3	148.1	158.6	160.1
UT.......	20.0	19.9	20.9	22.2	22.9	21.2	22.2	23.5	25.6	28.2
VT.......	6.7	5.8	6.0	6.2	6.0	6.1	5.2	5.2	5.4	5.4
VA.......	66.6	61.0	65.0	65.7	65.0	60.6	58.4	57.3	58.3	58.4
WA.......	50.4	45.4	49.9	51.8	48.9	45.9	42.5	44.4	47.2	48.4
WV.......	23.4	22.3	22.4	22.4	22.9	21.9	21.1	20.1	20.8	20.5
WI.......	69.3	58.9	56.9	58.4	55.0	52.0	49.3	48.6	52.8	52.5
WY.......	6.1	5.7	5.9	6.1	6.1	5.8	5.7	5.8	6.0	6.0

Source: U.S. National Center for Education Statistics, *Digest of Education Statistics,* annual.

No. 275. General Educational Development (GED) Credentials Issued: 1974 to 1993

YEAR	GED's issued (1,000)	PERCENT DISTRIBUTION BY AGE OF TEST TAKER				
		Under 19 years old	20 to 24 years old	25 to 29 years old	30 to 34 years old	35 years old or over
1974	294	35	27	13	9	17
1975	340	33	26	14	9	18
1980	479	37	27	13	8	15
1983	465	34	29	14	8	15
1984	427	32	28	15	9	16
1985	413	32	26	15	10	16
1986	428	32	26	15	10	17
1987	444	33	24	15	10	18
1988	410	35	22	14	10	18
1989	357	36	22	14	10	17
1990	410	35	25	14	10	17
1991	462	33	27	14	10	17
1992	457	32	28	13	11	16
1993	469	33	27	13	11	16

Source: U.S. National Center for Education Statistics, *Digest of Education Statistics,* 1994.

Education

No. 276. College Enrollment of Recent High School Graduates: 1960 to 1992

[For persons 16 to 24 who graduated from high school in the preceeding 12 months. Includes persons receiving GED's. Based on surveys and subject to sampling error]

YEAR	NUMBER OF HIGH SCHOOL GRADUATES (1,000)					PERCENT ENROLLED IN COLLEGE [2]				
	Total[1]	Male	Female	White	Black	Total	Male	Female	White	Black
1960	1,679	756	923	1,565	(NA)	45.1	54.0	37.9	45.8	(NA)
1961	1,763	790	973	1,612	(NA)	48.0	56.3	41.3	49.5	(NA)
1962	1,838	872	966	1,660	(NA)	49.0	55.0	43.5	50.6	(NA)
1963	1,741	794	947	1,615	(NA)	45.0	52.3	39.0	45.6	(NA)
1964	2,145	997	1,148	1,964	(NA)	48.3	57.2	40.7	49.2	(NA)
1965	2,659	1,254	1,405	2,417	(NA)	50.9	57.3	45.3	51.7	(NA)
1966	2,612	1,207	1,405	2,403	(NA)	50.1	58.7	42.7	51.7	(NA)
1967	2,525	1,142	1,383	2,267	(NA)	51.9	57.6	47.2	53.0	(NA)
1968	2,606	1,184	1,422	2,303	(NA)	55.4	63.2	48.9	56.6	(NA)
1969	2,842	1,352	1,490	2,538	(NA)	53.3	60.1	47.2	55.2	(NA)
1970	2,757	1,343	1,414	2,461	(NA)	51.8	55.2	48.5	52.0	(NA)
1971	2,872	1,369	1,503	2,596	(NA)	53.4	57.6	49.7	54.0	(NA)
1972	2,961	1,420	1,541	2,614	(NA)	49.2	52.7	45.9	49.4	(NA)
1973	3,059	1,458	1,601	2,707	(NA)	46.6	50.1	43.4	48.1	(NA)
1974	3,101	1,491	1,610	2,736	(NA)	47.5	49.4	45.8	47.1	(NA)
1975	3,186	1,513	1,673	2,825	(NA)	50.7	52.6	49.0	51.2	(NA)
1976	2,987	1,450	1,537	2,640	320	48.8	47.2	50.3	48.9	41.9
1977	3,140	1,482	1,658	2,768	335	50.6	52.2	49.3	50.7	49.6
1978	3,161	1,485	1,676	2,750	352	50.1	51.0	49.3	50.1	45.7
1979	3,160	1,474	1,686	2,776	324	49.3	50.4	48.4	49.6	45.4
1980	3,089	1,500	1,589	2,682	361	49.3	46.7	51.8	49.9	41.8
1981	3,053	1,490	1,563	2,626	359	53.9	54.8	53.1	54.6	42.9
1982	3,100	1,508	1,592	2,644	384	50.6	49.0	52.1	52.0	36.5
1983	2,964	1,390	1,574	2,496	392	52.7	51.9	53.4	55.0	38.5
1984	3,012	1,429	1,583	2,514	438	55.2	56.0	54.5	57.9	40.2
1985	2,666	1,286	1,380	2,241	333	57.7	58.6	56.9	59.4	42.3
1986	2,786	1,331	1,455	2,307	386	53.8	55.9	51.9	56.0	36.5
1987	2,647	1,278	1,369	2,207	337	56.8	58.4	55.3	56.6	51.9
1988	2,673	1,334	1,339	2,187	382	58.9	57.0	60.8	60.7	45.0
1989	2,454	1,208	1,245	2,051	337	59.6	57.6	61.6	60.4	52.8
1990	2,355	1,169	1,185	1,921	341	59.9	57.8	62.0	61.5	46.3
1991	2,276	1,139	1,137	1,867	320	62.4	57.6	67.1	64.6	45.6
1992	2,398	1,216	1,182	1,900	353	61.7	59.6	63.8	63.4	47.9

NA Not available. [1] Includes other races, not shown separately. [2] As of October.

Source: U.S. Department of Education Statistics, *Digest of Education Statistics*, 1994.

No. 277. College Enrollment, by Sex and Attendance Status: 1983 to 1993

[As of **fall. In thousands**]

SEX AND AGE	1983		1988		1989		1991		1993, est.	
	Total	Part-time	Total	Part-time	Total	Part-time	Total	Part-time	Total	Part-time
Total	**12,465**	**5,204**	**13,055**	**5,619**	**13,539**	**5,878**	**14,359**	**6,244**	**14,762**	**6,542**
Male	6,024	2,264	6,002	2,340	6,190	2,450	6,502	2,573	6,643	2,664
14 to 17 years old	102	16	55	5	71	12	46	6	84	11
18 to 19 years old	1,256	158	1,290	132	1,342	113	1,217	121	1,256	145
20 to 21 years old	1,241	205	1,243	216	1,189	198	1,306	230	1,329	220
22 to 24 years old	1,158	382	1,106	378	1,090	367	1,214	378	1,300	412
25 to 29 years old	1,115	624	875	485	1,038	639	1,082	587	988	593
30 to 34 years old	570	384	617	456	603	439	664	475	690	509
35 years old and over	583	494	816	668	857	682	972	775	997	777
Female	6,441	2,940	7,053	3,278	7,349	3,428	7,857	3,672	8,119	3,878
14 to 17 years old	142	16	115	17	101	12	76	1	93	6
18 to 19 years old	1,496	179	1,536	195	1,515	184	1,496	185	1,428	183
20 to 21 years old	1,125	204	1,278	218	1,253	213	1,462	239	1,433	297
22 to 24 years old	884	378	932	403	1,104	470	1,072	412	1,296	525
25 to 29 years old	947	658	932	633	1,052	732	1,053	679	1,103	734
30 to 34 years old	721	553	698	499	750	563	804	593	848	612
35 years old and over	1,126	953	1,563	1,313	1,574	1,253	1,895	1,564	1,917	1,520

Source: U.S. National Center for Education Statistics, *Digest of Education Statistics*, annual.

No. 278. College Enrollment, by Selected Characteristics: 1978 to 1992

[**In thousands**. As of **fall**. Totals may differ from other tables because of adjustments to underreported and nonreported racial/ethnic data. Nonresident alien students are not distributed among racial/ethnic groups]

CHARACTERISTIC	1978	1980	1984	1988	1990	1991, est.	1992, prel.
Total	**11,231.2**	**12,086.8**	**12,233.0**	**13,043.1**	**13,819.5**	**14,359.0**	**14,491.2**
Male	5,621.5	5,868.1	5,858.3	5,998.2	6,284.4	6,501.8	6,526.1
Female	5,609.6	6,218.7	6,374.7	7,044.9	7,535.1	7,857.1	7,965.1
Public	8,769.8	9,456.4	9,456.4	10,156.4	10,844.7	11,309.6	11,387.8
Private	2,461.4	2,630.4	2,776.6	2,886.7	2,974.8	3,049.4	3,103.5
2-year	4,028.8	4,521.4	4,526.9	4,868.1	5,240.1	5,651.9	5,723.2
4-year	7,202.4	7,565.4	7,706.1	8,175.0	8,579.4	8,707.1	8,768.0
Undergraduate	9,665.8	10,469.1	10,610.8	11,304.2	11,959.2	12,439.3	12,539.8
Graduate	1,310.4	1,340.9	1,343.7	1,471.9	1,586.2	1,639.1	1,670.0
First professional	255.0	276.8	278.5	267.1	274.1	280.5	281.4
White [1]	9,194.0	9,833.0	9,814.7	10,283.2	10,723.0	10,989.8	10,870.0
Male	4,613.1	4,772.9	4,689.9	4,711.6	4,861.3	4,962.2	4,882.5
Female	4,580.9	5,060.1	5,124.7	5,571.6	5,861.7	6,027.6	5,987.6
Public	7,136.1	7,656.1	7,542.4	7,963.8	8,385.4	8,622.2	8,486.9
Private	2,057.9	2,176.9	2,272.3	2,319.4	2,337.6	2,367.5	2,383.1
2-year	3,166.9	3,558.5	3,514.3	3,701.5	3,954.3	4,198.8	4,123.1
4-year	6,027.1	6,274.5	6,300.4	6,581.6	6,768.7	6,791.0	6,746.9
Undergraduate	7,870.6	8,480.7	8,484.0	8,906.7	9,272.6	9,507.7	9,380.6
Graduate	1,094.1	1,104.7	1,087.3	1,153.2	1,228.4	1,258.0	1,268.4
First professional	229.3	247.7	243.4	223.2	222.0	224.0	220.9
Black [1]	1,054.4	1,106.8	1,075.8	1,129.6	1,247.1	1,335.4	1,393.5
Male	453.3	463.7	436.8	442.7	484.7	517.0	537.1
Female	601.1	643.0	639.0	686.9	762.4	818.4	856.4
Public	839.5	876.1	844.0	881.1	976.5	1,053.4	1,101.1
Private	214.9	230.7	231.8	248.5	270.6	281.9	292.4
2-year	442.6	472.5	458.7	473.3	524.3	577.6	602.0
4-year	611.8	634.3	617.0	656.3	722.8	757.8	791.5
Undergraduate	966.5	1,018.8	994.9	1,038.8	1,147.2	1,229.3	1,281.2
Graduate	76.4	75.1	67.4	76.5	83.9	88.9	94.1
First professional	11.4	12.8	13.4	14.3	16.0	17.2	18.2
Hispanic	417.3	471.7	534.9	680.0	782.6	866.6	954.4
Male	212.5	231.6	253.8	310.3	354.0	390.5	427.4
Female	204.7	240.1	281.2	369.6	428.6	476.0	527.1
Public	362.5	406.2	456.1	586.9	671.4	742.1	821.7
Private	54.7	65.5	78.9	93.1	111.1	124.5	132.7
2-year	226.9	255.1	288.8	383.9	424.2	483.7	544.5
4-year	190.4	216.6	246.1	296.0	358.3	382.9	409.9
Undergraduate	384.0	433.1	495.2	631.2	724.6	804.2	887.2
Graduate	28.0	32.1	31.7	39.5	47.2	50.9	55.2
First professional	5.4	6.5	8.0	9.3	10.9	11.4	12.0
American Indian [1]	77.9	83.9	83.6	92.5	102.8	113.7	118.8
Male	36.8	37.8	37.4	39.1	43.1	47.6	50.1
Female	41.0	46.1	46.1	53.4	59.7	66.1	68.8
Public	68.5	74.2	72.1	81.1	90.4	100.2	103.0
Private	9.5	9.7	11.4	11.5	12.4	13.6	15.9
2-year	43.1	47.0	45.5	50.4	54.9	62.6	64.0
4-year	34.8	36.9	38.1	42.1	47.9	51.1	54.9
Undergraduate	71.9	77.9	77.8	85.9	95.5	105.8	110.4
Graduate	4.9	5.2	4.8	5.6	6.2	6.6	7.0
First professional	1.1	0.8	1.0	1.1	1.1	1.3	1.5
Asian [1]	235.1	286.4	389.5	496.7	572.5	637.2	696.8
Male	126.3	151.3	210.0	259.2	294.9	325.1	351.3
Female	108.7	135.2	179.5	237.5	277.6	312.0	345.5
Public	195.4	239.7	322.7	405.7	461.0	516.3	565.6
Private	39.6	46.7	66.8	91.0	111.6	120.9	131.1
2-year	97.2	124.3	167.1	199.3	215.2	255.7	289.2
4-year	137.8	162.1	222.4	297.4	357.3	381.5	407.6
Undergraduate	202.8	248.7	343.0	436.6	500.5	558.7	612.7
Graduate	27.5	31.6	37.1	45.7	53.2	57.6	61.6
First professional	4.8	6.1	9.3	14.4	18.8	20.8	22.5
Nonresident alien	252.6	305.0	334.6	361.2	391.5	416.4	457.6
Male	179.5	210.8	230.4	235.3	246.3	259.4	277.8
Female	73.1	94.2	104.1	125.9	145.2	157.0	179.8
Public	167.7	204.1	219.0	237.8	260.0	275.3	309.4
Private	84.8	100.8	115.5	123.3	131.5	141.0	148.2
2-year	52.0	64.1	52.5	59.6	67.1	73.5	100.4
4-year	200.5	240.9	282.1	301.5	324.4	342.8	357.2
Undergraduate	170.1	209.9	215.8	205.0	218.7	233.6	267.7
Graduate	79.5	92.2	115.3	151.4	167.3	177.0	183.7
First professional	3.0	2.9	3.4	4.7	5.4	5.8	6.3

[1] Non-Hispanic.

Source: U.S. National Center for Education Statistics, *Digest of Education Statistics*, annual.

No. 279. College Enrollment, by Sex, Age, Race, and Hispanic Origin: 1975 to 1993

[In thousands. As of October for the civilian noninstitutional population, 14 years old and over. Based on the Current Population Survey; see text, section 1, and Appendix III]

CHARACTERISTIC	1975	1980	1985	1986 [1]	1987	1988	1989	1990	1991	1992	1993
Total [2]	10,880	11,387	12,524	12,651	12,719	13,116	13,180	13,621	14,057	14,035	13,898
Male [3]	5,911	5,430	5,906	5,957	6,030	5,950	5,950	6,192	6,439	6,192	6,324
18 to 24 years	3,693	3,604	3,749	3,702	3,867	3,770	3,717	3,922	3,954	3,912	3,994
25 to 34 years	1,521	1,325	1,464	1,545	1,421	1,395	1,443	1,412	1,605	1,392	1,406
35 years old and over . . .	569	405	561	628	625	727	716	772	832	789	873
Female [3]	4,969	5,957	6,618	6,694	6,689	7,166	7,231	7,429	7,618	7,844	7,574
18 to 24 years	3,243	3,625	3,788	3,775	3,826	4,021	4,085	4,042	4,218	4,429	4,199
25 to 34 years	947	1,378	1,599	1,559	1,564	1,568	1,639	1,749	1,680	1,732	1,688
35 years old and over . . .	614	802	1,100	1,240	1,176	1,452	1,396	1,546	1,636	1,575	1,616
White [3]	9,546	9,925	10,781	10,707	10,731	11,140	11,243	11,488	11,686	11,710	11,434
18 to 24 years	6,116	6,334	6,500	6,307	6,483	6,659	6,631	6,635	6,813	6,916	6,763
25 to 34 years	2,147	2,328	2,604	2,617	2,468	2,448	2,597	2,698	2,661	2,582	2,505
35 years old and over . . .	1,031	1,051	1,448	1,609	1,584	1,896	1,868	2,023	2,107	2,053	2,068
Male	5,263	4,804	5,103	5,074	5,104	5,078	5,136	5,235	5,304	5,210	5,222
Female	4,284	5,121	5,679	5,632	5,627	6,063	6,107	6,253	6,382	6,499	6,212
Black [3]	1,099	1,163	1,263	1,359	1,351	1,321	1,287	1,393	1,477	1,424	1,545
18 to 24 years	665	688	734	812	823	752	835	894	828	886	861
25 to 34 years	248	289	295	330	341	330	275	258	373	302	386
35 years old and over . . .	152	156	213	198	155	206	146	207	257	208	284
Male	523	476	552	580	587	494	480	587	629	527	636
Female	577	686	712	779	764	827	807	807	848	897	909
Hispanic origin [3][4]	411	443	580	794	739	747	754	748	830	918	995
18 to 24 years	295	315	375	458	455	450	453	435	516	586	602
25 to 34 years	103	118	189	231	204	191	170	168	196	214	249
35 years old and over . . .	(NA)	(NA)	(NA)	89	73	93	114	130	109	102	129
Male	218	222	279	377	390	391	353	353	364	347	388	442
Female	193	221	299	417	349	391	401	384	483	530	553

NA Not available. [1] Revised. Beginning 1986, based on a revised edit and tabulation package. [2] Includes other races not shown separately. [3] Includes persons 14 to 17 years old, not shown separately. [4] Persons of Hispanic origin may be of any race.

Source: U.S. Bureau of the Census, *Current Population Reports*, P20-479; and earlier reports.

No. 280. College Population, by Selected Characteristics: 1987 and 1993

[In thousands, except percent. As of October. Based on the Current Population Survey. See text, section 1, and Appendix III]

CHARACTERISTIC	Total popula-tion	ENROLLED IN COLLEGE					PERCENT EMPLOYED		
		Total	Type of school			Percent enrolled full-time	Total	Full-time	Part-time
			2-year	4-year	Graduate school				
Total, 1987 [1]	190,058	12,719	3,648	6,656	2,415	62.6	60.4	31.7	28.7
Male	90,610	6,030	1,522	3,356	1,152	67.2	60.6	31.7	28.9
Female.	99,449	6,689	2,127	3,299	1,264	58.4	60.1	31.6	28.5
White.	162,757	10,731	3,039	5,617	2,075	61.6	62.2	32.6	29.6
Black.	21,520	1,351	422	748	181	66.3	50.5	28.6	21.9
Hispanic origin [2].	13,687	739	307	342	90	57.3	65.5	37.0	28.6
14 to 19 years old	21,410	3,284	1,111	2,172	1	88.1	44.0	7.6	36.4
20 and 21 years old . . .	7,078	2,642	624	1,961	58	84.4	53.3	14.5	38.8
22 to 24 years old	11,712	2,006	457	1,055	494	67.2	62.5	29.8	32.7
25 to 34 years old	42,374	2,985	851	996	1,137	36.4	74.0	55.8	18.2
35 years and older	107,484	1,802	605	471	725	22.3	83.1	62.8	20.3
Total, 1993 [1]	197,652	13,898	4,196	7,311	2,391	64.9	59.7	30.8	28.9
Male	94,746	6,324	1,748	3,446	1,130	69.4	59.7	31.1	28.6
Female.	102,905	7,574	2,448	3,865	1,261	61.1	59.7	30.6	29.1
White.	167,086	11,434	3,431	5,990	2,013	63.6	62.4	31.5	30.9
Black.	23,003	1,545	530	833	182	65.7	49.2	33.2	16.0
Hispanic origin [2].	16,329	995	446	451	98	61.0	60.5	30.7	29.8
15 to 19 years old	16,841	3,049	1,077	1,968	3	89.7	43.9	7.1	36.8
20 and 21 years old . . .	6,575	2,734	696	2,025	13	87.4	49.1	9.3	39.8
22 to 24 years old	10,931	2,533	614	1,406	514	70.5	63.3	27.1	36.2
25 to 34 years old	41,099	3,094	965	1,123	1,006	45.1	70.1	50.7	19.4
35 years and older	122,206	2,488	844	789	856	28.6	69.9	58.4	11.5

[1] Includes other races, not shown separately. [2] Persons of Hispanic origin may be of any race.

Source: U.S. Bureau of the Census, *Current Population Reports*, P20-443 and P20-479.

No. 281. Higher Education—Summary: 1970 to 1992

[Institutions, staff, and enrollment as of fall. Finances for fiscal year ending in the following year. Covers universities, colleges, professional schools, junior and teachers colleges, both publicly and privately controlled, regular session. Includes estimates for institutions not reporting. See also Appendix III, and *Historical Statistics, Colonial Times to 1970,* series H 680, H 690-692, H 699-705, and H 710]

ITEM	Unit	1970	1980	1985	1987	1988	1989	1990	1991, est.	1992, prel.
ALL INSTITUTIONS										
Number of institutions [1]	Number.	2,556	3,231	3,340	3,587	3,565	3,535	3,559	3,601	3,638
4-year	Number.	1,665	1,957	2,029	2,135	2,129	2,127	2,141	2,157	2,169
2-year	Number.	891	1,274	1,311	1,452	1,436	1,408	1,418	1,444	1,469
Instructional staff—										
(Lecturer or above) [2]	1,000...	474	686	715	793	804	824	817	826	835
Percent full-time	Percent.	78	66	64	66	(NA)	64	61	65	(NA)
Total enrollment [3]	1,000...	8,581	12,097	12,247	12,767	13,055	13,539	13,818	14,359	14,491
Male	1,000...	5,044	5,874	5,818	5,932	6,002	6,190	6,284	6,502	6,526
Female	1,000...	3,537	6,223	6,429	6,835	7,053	7,349	7,535	7,857	7,965
4-year institutions	1,000...	6,262	7,571	7,716	7,990	8,180	8,388	8,579	8,707	8,768
2-year institutions	1,000...	2,319	4,526	4,531	4,776	4,875	5,151	5,240	5,652	5,724
Full-time	1,000...	5,816	7,098	7,075	7,231	7,437	7,661	7,821	8,115	8,165
Part-time	1,000...	2,765	4,999	5,172	5,536	5,619	5,878	5,998	6,244	6,326
Public	1,000...	6,428	9,457	9,479	9,973	10,161	10,578	10,844	11,310	11,388
Private	1,000...	2,153	2,640	2,768	2,793	2,894	2,961	2,975	3,049	3,104
Undergraduate [4]	1,000...	7,376	10,475	10,597	11,046	11,317	11,743	11,959	12,439	12,540
Men	1,000...	4,254	5,000	4,962	5,068	5,138	5,311	5,380	5,571	5,584
Women	1,000...	3,122	5,475	5,635	5,978	6,179	6,432	6,579	6,868	6,956
First-time freshmen	1,000...	2,063	2,588	2,292	2,246	2,379	2,341	2,257	2,278	2,186
First professional	1,000...	173	278	274	268	267	274	274	281	281
Men	1,000...	159	199	180	170	167	168	167	170	169
Women	1,000...	15	78	94	98	100	105	107	111	112
Graduate [4]	1,000...	1,031	1,343	1,376	1,452	1,472	1,522	1,586	1,639	1,670
Men	1,000...	630	675	677	693	697	710	737	761	773
Women	1,000...	400	670	700	759	774	811	849	878	897
Current funds revenues [5]	Mil. dol.	23,879	65,585	100,438	117,340	128,502	139,635	149,766	161,421	(NA)
Tuition and fees	Mil. dol.	5,021	13,773	23,117	27,837	30,807	33,926	37,434	41,559	(NA)
Federal government	Mil. dol.	4,190	9,748	12,705	14,772	15,894	17,255	18,236	19,833	(NA)
State government	Mil. dol.	6,503	20,106	29,912	33,517	36,031	38,349	39,481	40,587	(NA)
Auxiliary enterprises	Mil. dol.	3,125	7,287	10,674	11,948	12,856	13,938	14,903	15,784	(NA)
Plant funds [6]	Mil. dol.	(NA)	4,774	7,713	(NA)	(NA)	(NA)	(NA)	(NA)	(NA)
Increase in fund balance [7]	Mil. dol.	498	2,793	7,239	(NA)	(NA)	(NA)	(NA)	(NA)	(NA)
Current funds expenditures [5]	Mil. dol.	23,375	64,053	97,536	113,786	123,867	134,656	146,088	156,212	(NA)
Educational and general [8]	Mil. dol.	17,616	50,074	76,128	89,157	96,803	105,585	114,140	121,567	(NA)
Auxiliary enterprises [9]	Mil. dol.	2,988	7,288	10,528	11,400	12,280	13,204	14,272	14,989	(NA)
Gross addition to plant value	Mil. dol.	4,165	6,471	10,149	11,589	13,638	17,107	19,672	(NA)	(NA)
Value of plant	Mil. dol.	46,054	88,761	122,261	139,456	158,693	182,609	190,355	(NA)	(NA)
Endowment (market value)	Mil. dol.	13,714	23,465	50,281	57,392	64,155	67,979	72,049	(NA)	(NA)
TWO-YEAR INSTITUTIONS										
Number of institutions [1][10]	Number.	891	1,274	1,311	1,452	1,436	1,408	1,418	1,444	1,469
Public	Number.	654	945	932	992	984	968	972	999	1,024
Private	Number.	237	329	379	460	452	440	446	445	445
Instructional staff—										
(Lecturer or above) [2]	1,000...	92	192	211	246	(NA)	241	(NA)	(NA)	(NA)
Enrollment [3][4]	1,000...	2,319	4,526	4,531	4,776	4,875	5,151	5,240	5,652	5,723
Public	1,000...	2,195	4,329	4,270	4,541	4,615	4,884	4,996	5,405	5,486
Private	1,000...	124	198	261	235	260	267	244	247	238
Male	1,000...	1,375	2,047	2,002	2,073	2,090	2,217	2,232	2,401	2,414
Female	1,000...	945	2,479	2,529	2,704	2,785	2,934	3,008	3,250	3,309
Current funds revenue [5]	Mil. dol.	2,504	8,505	12,293	14,060	15,387	16,777	18,021	19,695	(NA)
Tuition and fees	Mil. dol.	413	1,618	2,618	3,057	3,376	3,623	4,029	4,649	(NA)
State government	Mil. dol.	926	3,961	5,659	6,350	6,898	7,558	8,001	8,537	(NA)
Local government	Mil. dol.	701	1,623	2,027	2,352	2,662	2,831	3,044	3,259	(NA)
Current funds expenditures	Mil. dol.	2,327	8,212	11,976	13,644	14,726	16,077	17,494	18,814	(NA)
Education and general [8]	Mil. dol.	2,073	7,608	11,118	12,701	13,676	14,936	16,270	17,462	(NA)
Instruction	Mil. dol.	1,205	3,764	5,398	6,082	6,617	7,236	7,903	8,167	(NA)

NA Not available.   [1] Beginning 1974, number of institutions includes count of branch campuses. Due to revised survey procedures, data beginning 1987 are not comparable with previous years.   [2] Due to revised survey methods, data beginning 1987 not comparable with previous years.   [3] Beginning 1974, branch campuses counted according to actual status, e.g., 2-year branch in 2-year category; previously a 2-year branch included in university category.   [4] Includes unclassified students. (Students taking courses for credit, but are not candidates for degrees.)   [5] Includes items not shown separately.   [6] Annual net increase in plant funds.   [7] Includes endowment, and, beginning 1980, annuity and student loans.   [8] Data for 1970 are not strictly comparable with later years.   [9] Includes activities.   [10] Beginning 1980, includes schools accredited by the National Association of Trade and Technical Schools.

Source: U.S. National Center for Education Statistics, *Digest of Education Statistics,* annual; *Projections of Education Statistics,* annual; and unpublished data.

Education

No. 282. Colleges—Number and Enrollment, by State, 1992

[Number of institutions beginning in academic year. Opening fall enrollment of resident and extension students attending full-time or part-time. Excludes students taking courses for credit by mail, radio, or TV and students in branches of U.S. institutions operated in foreign countries. See Appendix III]

STATE	Number of institutions [1]	ENROLLMENT, PREL. (1,000)										
		Total	Male	Female	Public	Private	Full-time	White [2]	Minority enrollment			Non-resident alien
									Total [3]	Black [2]	His-panic	
United States..	**3,638**	**14,491**	**6,526**	**7,965**	**11,388**	**3,104**	**8,165**	**10,870**	**3,164**	**1,393**	**954**	**458**
Alabama.........	86	231	104	127	206	24	155	172	54	49	1	5
Alaska	8	31	13	18	29	2	12	25	6	1	1	1
Arizona.........	40	276	127	149	256	20	124	209	59	9	34	8
Arkansas	34	97	42	56	86	12	69	80	16	14	1	2
California	322	1,977	902	1,076	1,748	229	862	1,115	764	140	315	98
Colorado........	59	240	112	128	211	29	126	198	37	8	20	5
Connecticut......	47	166	73	93	108	58	83	138	23	11	6	5
Delaware	10	43	18	24	35	7	26	35	7	5	1	1
District of Columbia .	18	82	38	44	12	70	50	41	32	25	3	9
Florida..........	105	618	275	343	511	107	299	436	166	73	75	17
Georgia	115	293	130	163	233	61	194	211	76	65	4	6
Hawaii	17	61	28	33	50	12	34	17	39	1	1	5
Idaho	11	58	26	32	47	11	39	53	3	(Z)	1	2
Illinois	169	748	336	412	566	182	375	543	187	94	55	18
Indiana.........	78	297	138	159	235	62	194	260	28	17	5	8
Iowa ......,....	61	178	82	96	128	50	125	158	11	5	3	8
Kansas.........	49	169	76	93	153	16	97	146	17	8	4	6
Kentucky	62	188	78	110	158	30	121	170	15	12	1	3
Louisiana	33	204	88	116	177	27	144	140	59	50	4	5
Maine..........	31	58	24	34	41	17	32	55	3	1	(Z)	1
Maryland	56	268	115	153	228	40	124	189	71	52	5	9
Massachusetts.....	117	423	189	234	183	240	266	343	58	20	15	23
Michigan........	102	560	249	311	473	86	288	461	83	57	10	15
Minnesota.......	99	273	123	150	212	61	160	249	18	6	3	6
Mississippi	46	124	54	69	110	14	94	85	36	34	(Z)	2
Missouri	96	297	134	162	199	98	169	253	36	25	4	8
Montana.........	19	40	19	21	34	6	30	34	5	(Z)	(Z)	1
Nebraska	37	123	56	67	103	19	69	111	9	4	2	3
Nevada	9	64	28	35	63	1	21	51	12	3	4	1
New Hampshire....	29	64	28	36	35	29	40	60	3	1	1	1
New Jersey......	62	342	152	191	278	65	173	247	82	38	26	13
New Mexico	31	99	44	56	95	4	49	59	39	3	29	2
New York	320	1,070	468	602	611	459	674	754	277	129	88	39
North Carolina.....	122	383	168	216	316	68	237	292	85	72	4	6
North Dakota......	20	40	20	20	37	4	32	36	3	(Z)	(Z)	2
Ohio	165	573	263	310	437	136	353	490	67	50	7	16
Oklahoma........	46	182	83	99	159	23	116	144	31	13	3	7
Oregon.........	45	167	79	88	145	23	94	144	17	3	4	6
Pennsylvania.....	220	630	288	342	363	267	395	537	77	46	11	17
Rhode Island......	12	79	36	44	43	36	49	69	8	3	2	3
South Carolina.....	60	171	74	98	146	26	110	128	40	36	1	3
South Dakota	19	38	17	21	30	7	26	34	3	(Z)	(Z)	1
Tennessee	78	243	109	134	192	51	157	198	41	35	2	4
Texas..........	176	939	434	504	832	106	511	617	295	89	169	27
Utah	16	133	68	66	97	36	91	120	7	1	3	6
Vermont	22	37	16	21	21	16	25	35	1	(Z)	(Z)	1
Virginia.........	86	354	157	198	298	57	199	274	74	53	6	6
Washington.......	62	276	123	153	239	38	159	230	40	9	8	6
West Virginia......	28	90	40	50	79	11	61	84	5	3	-	2
Wisconsin........	64	308	138	170	257	51	186	275	26	12	6	7
Wyoming	9	32	14	18	31	1	17	29	2	(Z)	1	1
U.S. military [4] ..	10	53	30	22	53	-	31	40	11	5	4	1

- Represents zero.   Z Fewer than 500.   [1] Branch campuses counted as separate institutions.   [2] Non-Hispanic.
[3] Includes other races not shown separately.   [4] Service schools.

Source: U.S. National Center for Education Statistics, *Digest of Education Statistics*, annual.

No. 283. Higher Education Price Indexes: 1965 to 1993

[1983=100. For years ending **June 30.** Reflects prices paid by colleges and universities]

YEAR	Index, total	PERSONNEL COMPENSATION				CONTRACTED SERVICES, SUPPLIES, AND EQUIPMENT					
		Total	Profes-sional salaries	Nonpro-fessional salaries	Fringe benefits	Total	Serv-ices	Supplies and materials	Equip-ment	Library acquisi-tions	Utilities
1965	29.8	30.5	34.9	31.0	13.0	27.6	35.8	33.8	36.0	19.3	15.7
1970	39.5	42.1	47.7	38.8	24.7	31.9	42.8	37.6	41.9	25.7	16.3
1975	54.3	56.3	60.3	54.6	42.9	48.5	56.8	58.0	58.3	46.7	31.8
1977	61.7	63.5	66.4	63.1	52.8	56.1	63.5	63.8	64.8	58.6	40.5
1978	65.8	67.6	69.9	68.1	58.4	60.4	67.0	66.6	69.3	64.3	45.9
1979	70.6	72.4	74.1	73.4	64.5	65.2	71.0	71.7	74.7	71.4	50.3
1980	77.5	78.4	79.4	80.2	72.6	75.0	76.5	84.6	81.6	79.5	64.1
1981	85.9	85.8	86.3	87.7	81.8	86.2	85.3	95.6	89.6	89.3	79.7
1982	94.0	93.5	93.7	94.6	91.5	95.3	94.8	100.4	96.4	95.5	92.4
1983	100.0	100.0	100.0	100.0	100.0	100.0	100.0	100.0	100.0	100.0	100.0
1984	104.7	105.4	104.7	105.2	108.3	102.8	104.7	103.1	102.2	103.8	100.8
1985	110.5	112.0	111.4	109.1	117.7	106.1	109.2	105.4	104.8	108.5	103.0
1986	115.6	118.8	118.2	113.0	127.7	106.2	114.3	104.2	106.9	117.2	95.5
1987	120.4	125.4	125.0	116.4	137.5	105.2	117.8	103.5	108.8	129.9	84.4
1988	125.8	131.6	130.9	120.4	147.1	108.4	122.1	107.9	110.9	138.7	84.4
1989	133.1	139.5	138.8	125.2	158.8	114.0	129.0	116.9	115.8	149.9	85.2
1990	140.8	148.2	147.6	130.2	171.4	118.8	134.2	118.7	120.8	163.6	88.4
1991	148.3	156.6	155.6	135.5	184.5	123.8	140.2	121.4	123.4	179.0	91.2
1992	153.1	162.4	160.8	140.4	193.9	125.4	144.6	118.1	125.9	189.8	89.4
1993	158.2	167.6	165.1	143.9	204.3	130.4	148.1	118.3	128.0	206.5	95.7

Source: Research Associates of Washington, Washington, DC, *Inflation Measures for Schools, Colleges, and Libraries,* annual (copyright).

No. 284. Institutions of Higher Education—Finances: 1980 to 1992

[**In millions of dollars. For fiscal years ending in year shown.** For coverage, see headnote, table 281. See also Appendix III and *Historical Statistics, Colonial Times to 1970* , series H 729-738 and H 747-749]

ITEM	1980	1985	1988	1989	1990	1991	1992		
							Total	Public	Private
Current funds revenues	**58,520**	**92,473**	**117,340**	**128,502**	**139,635**	**149,766**	**161,421**	**102,198**	**59,224**
Tuition and fees	11,930	21,283	27,837	30,807	33,926	37,434	41,559	17,455	24,104
Federal government.	8,902	11,509	14,772	15,894	17,255	18,236	19,833	10,782	9,051
State government	18,378	27,583	33,517	36,031	38,349	39,481	40,587	39,098	1,489
Local government	1,588	2,387	3,006	3,364	3,640	3,931	4,160	3,768	392
Private gifts, grants, and con-tracts [1]	2,808	4,896	6,359	7,061	7,781	8,361	8,977	4,039	4,938
Endowment earnings	1,177	2,096	2,586	2,914	3,144	3,269	3,442	594	2,848
Educational activities [2]	1,239	2,127	2,918	3,316	3,632	4,055	4,521	2,960	1,561
Auxiliary enterprises.	6,481	10,100	11,948	12,856	13,938	14,903	15,784	9,678	6,106
Hospitals	([3])	7,475	10,627	11,991	13,217	15,150	17,240	11,122	6,118
Other funds revenues [4]	6,015	3,015	3,770	4,269	4,753	4,946	5,318	2,700	2,617
Current funds expenditures [5]	**56,914**	**89,951**	**113,786**	**123,867**	**134,656**	**146,088**	**156,212**	**98,841**	**57,372**
Educational and general	44,543	70,061	89,157	96,803	105,585	114,140	121,567	78,529	43,038
Instruction.	18,497	28,777	35,834	38,813	42,146	45,496	47,997	32,812	15,185
Institutional support	5,054	8,587	10,774	11,529	12,674	13,726	14,475	8,420	6,055
Research	5,099	7,552	10,351	11,432	12,506	13,444	14,262	9,949	4,313
Plant operation [6]	4,700	7,345	8,231	8,740	9,458	10,063	10,347	6,788	3,559
Academic support	3,876	6,074	8,142	8,904	9,438	10,051	10,577	7,272	3,305
Libraries	1,624	2,362	2,836	3,010	3,254	3,344	3,596	2,284	1,312
Student services	2,567	4,178	5,397	5,781	6,388	7,025	7,509	4,690	2,819
Scholarships and fellowships . . .	2,200	3,670	5,325	5,919	6,656	7,551	9,060	3,255	5,805
Unrestricted funds.	905	1,962	2,941	3,283	3,854	4,445	5,206	1,523	3,682
Restricted funds.	1,296	1,709	2,384	2,636	2,802	3,106	3,854	1,732	2,122
Public service	1,817	2,861	3,786	4,227	4,690	5,076	5,489	4,286	1,204
Mandatory transfers	732	1,016	1,318	1,458	1,630	1,707	1,851	1,058	794
Auxiliary enterprises [5].	6,486	10,012	11,400	12,280	13,204	14,272	14,989	9,653	5,336
Hospitals [5].	4,757	8,010	10,406	11,825	12,679	14,326	16,104	10,433	5,672
Independent operations [5]	1,128	1,868	2,823	2,959	3,187	3,350	3,552	226	3,326

[1] Private grants represent nongovernmental revenue for sponsored research and other sponsored programs; includes private contracts.   [2] Sales and service of educational departments only.   [3] Included in other.   [4] Includes sales and services of federally funded research and development centers, and others sources.   [5] Includes mandatory transfers which are primarily current expenditures for plant.   [6] Includes maintenance.

Source: U.S. National Center for Education Statistics, *Digest of Education Statistics,* annual.

No. 285. Major Federal Student Financial Assistance Programs: 1970 to 1993

[For award years July 1 of year shown to the following June 30, except as indicated. Funds utilized exclude operating costs, etc., and represent funds given to students]

PROGRAM	Unit	1970	1980	1985	1988	1989	1990	1991	1992	1993, est.
Pell Grants:										
Number of recipients. . .	1,000. . .	(X)	2,708	2,813	3,198	3,322	3,405	3,786	4,002	3,539
Funds utilized	Mil. dol. .	(X)	2,387	3,597	4,476	4,778	4,935	5,793	6,176	5,683
Average grant	Dollars. .	(X)	882	1,279	1,399	1,438	1,449	1,530	1,543	1,606
Supplemental Educational Opportunity Grants: [1]										
Number of recipients. . .	1,000. . .	253.4	716.5	686.0	678.8	727.6	761.2	881.3	976.3	908.0
Funds utilized	Mil. dol. .	134	368	410	423	466	503	586	651	663
Average grant	Dollars. .	527	513	598	621	641	661	665	667	730
College Work-Study:										
Number of recipients. . .	1,000. . .	425.0	819.1	728.4	672.7	676.7	687.4	697.3	714.4	813.0
Funds utilized [2]	Mil. dol. .	200	660	656	625	664	727	760	780	813
Average annual earnings	Dollars. .	470	806	901	930	980	1,059	1,090	1,097	1,000
Perkins Loans: [3]										
Number of recipients. . .	1,000. . .	452.0	813.4	700.9	692.1	695.9	660.2	654.2	669.0	571.0
Loan funds utilized [2] . . .	Mil. dol. .	241	694	703	874	903	870	868	868	720
Average loan	Dollars. .	532	853	1,003	1,262	1,297	1,318	1,326	1,333	1,261
Loans in default [4]	Mil. dol. .	(NA)	612.0	690.0	749.8	741.1	727.5	744.7	569.3	(NA)
Default rate	Percent .	(NA)	11.6	8.3	7.3	6.8	6.2	6.0	12.2	(NA)
Federal Family Education Loans [5]										
Number of loans.	1,000. . .	1,017	2,905	3,833	4,513	4,713	4,493	4,818	5,130	5,647
Loan funds utilized [6] . . .	Mil. dol. .	1,015	6,200	8,913	11,816	12,466	12,291	13,500	14,749	17,863
Average loan	Dollars. .	998	2,135	2,374	2,618	2,645	2,734	2,804	2,875	3,163
Loans in default [7]	Mil. dol. .	(NA)	1,454	4,272	8,434	10,471	13,151	16,374	19,029	21,534
Default rate [8]	Percent .	(NA)	10.1	9.0	9.2	9.7	10.4	11.6	11.6	11.1

NA Not available.   X Not applicable.   [1] For 1970, data represents Educational Opportunity Grants Program.   [2] Includes institutional matching funds.   [3] Formerly National Direct Student Loans.   [4] Loans in default represents all loans in institutions' portfolio.   [5] Formerly Guaranteed Student Loans. Beginning with 1985, data include activity under the Stafford program, the PLUS (Parent Loans for Undergraduate Students), FISL (Federally Insured Student Loans), and SLS (Supplemental Loans Students) programs.   [6] Represents dollar amount of commitments.   [7] As of September 30 of year shown. Data are cumulative.   [8] Cumulative dollar amount of default claims to lenders, minus cumulative collections as a percent of all loans that have ever gone into repayment.

Source: U.S. Dept. of Education, Office of Postsecondary Education, unpublished data.

No. 286. Finances of Public Colleges, 1990 to 1992, and by State, 1993

[For academic years ending in year shown. Data provided by the State higher education finance officers]

STATE	FTE [1] enroll-ment (1,000)	Appropria-tions for current operations [2] (mil. dol.)	Net tuition reven-ues [3] (mil. dol.)	STATE	FTE [1] enroll-ment (1,000)	Appropria-tions for current operations [2] (mil. dol.)	Net tuition reven-ues [3] (mil. dol.)
Total, 1990	7,887.8	33,791.7	11,318.4	Minnesota	173.8	796.3	350.5
Total, 1991	8,074.2	35,142.0	12,464.8	Mississippi.	99.1	301.8	196.9
Total, 1992	8,309.1	35,304.0	14,207.5	Missouri	138.8	561.3	363.7
				Montana	29.3	108.9	46.0
Total, 1993	**8,380.9**	**35,002.0**	**15,746.3**	Nebraska	69.8	275.1	101.8
Alabama	180.4	569.0	358.5	Nevada	35.4	183.6	36.2
Alaska	16.4	155.7	30.5	New Hampshire	28.4	70.3	122.5
Arizona.	159.0	621.0	275.7	New Jersey	187.9	1,001.5	429.5
Arkansas.	74.3	296.1	135.2	New Mexico.	68.7	349.6	79.8
California.	1,284.9	5,218.0	1,137.7	New York	441.2	2,242.1	906.4
Colorado.	136.7	413.0	372.3	North Carolina	240.0	1,224.3	301.8
Connecticut	62.7	348.9	183.5	North Dakota	31.5	120.1	58.1
Delaware.	26.6	111.6	133.9	Ohio.	355.9	1,181.8	1,001.4
District of Columbia. . . .	8.5	67.8	8.4	Oklahoma	114.1	508.2	138.4
Florida	353.1	1,591.5	484.3	Oregon	102.7	454.3	190.4
Georgia	198.6	850.7	304.4	Pennsylvania	299.1	1,268.6	1,073.5
Hawaii	31.9	275.7	31.0	Rhode Island	28.3	108.7	102.3
Idaho	38.1	184.5	36.9	South Carolina	118.8	452.0	273.0
Illinois.	384.4	1,596.6	440.5	South Dakota	21.9	74.6	49.3
Indiana.	181.1	746.1	466.4	Tennessee.	155.6	606.2	258.8
Iowa.	102.9	504.3	247.5	Texas	625.7	2,336.8	868.2
Kansas.	108.5	440.2	179.2	Utah	75.6	314.2	115.7
Kentucky.	121.4	411.8	197.4	Vermont	16.0	36.1	121.6
Louisiana	136.6	418.6	269.4	Virginia	220.8	733.7	550.8
Maine	29.7	154.9	81.4	Washington	175.3	866.6	239.4
Maryland	158.0	649.0	416.2	West Virginia	63.8	166.0	118.4
Massachusetts.	120.7	460.5	309.6	Wisconsin	186.6	940.3	420.9
Michigan	340.4	1,495.7	1,101.3	Wyoming.	22.0	137.8	29.8

[1] Full-time equivalent (FTE). Credit and noncredit program enrollment including summer session. Excludes medical enrollments.   [2] State and local appropriations. Includes aid to students attending in-State public institutions. Excludes sums for research, agriculture stations and cooperative extension, and hospitals and medical schools.   [3] Excludes appropriated aid to students attending in-State public institutions.

Source: Research Associates of Washington, Washington, DC, *State Profiles: Financing Public Higher Education,* annual (copyright).

No. 287. Institutions of Higher Education—Charges: 1985 to 1994

[In dollars. Estimated. **For the entire academic year ending in year shown.** Figures are average charges per full-time equivalent student. Room and board are based on full-time students]

ACADEMIC CONTROL AND YEAR	TUITION AND REQUIRED FEES [1]				BOARD RATES [2]				DORMITORY CHARGES			
	All institutions	2-yr. colleges	4-yr. colleges	Other 4-yr. schools	All institutions	2-yr. colleges	4-yr. colleges	Other 4-yr. schools	All institutions	2-yr. colleges	4-yr. colleges	Other 4-yr. schools
Public:												
1985.....	971	584	1,386	1,117	1,241	1,302	1,276	1,201	1,196	921	1,237	1,200
1990.....	1,356	756	2,035	1,608	1,635	1,581	1,728	1,561	1,513	962	1,561	1,554
1991.....	1,454	824	2,159	1,707	1,691	1,594	1,767	1,641	1,612	1,050	1,658	1,655
1992.....	1,624	937	2,410	1,933	1,780	1,612	1,852	1,745	1,731	1,074	1,789	1,782
1993.....	1,782	1,025	2,604	2,192	1,841	1,668	1,982	1,761	1,756	1,106	1,856	1,787
1994[3]....	1,939	1,114	2,822	2,368	1,880	1,688	1,989	1,829	1,877	1,204	1,898	1,962
Private:												
1985.....	5,315	3,485	6,843	5,135	1,462	1,294	1,647	1,405	1,426	1,424	1,753	1,309
1990.....	8,174	5,196	10,348	7,778	1,948	1,811	2,339	1,823	1,923	1,663	2,411	1,774
1991.....	8,772	5,570	11,379	8,389	2,074	1,989	2,470	1,943	2,063	1,744	2,654	1,889
1992.....	9,434	5,752	12,192	9,053	2,252	2,090	2,727	2,098	2,221	1,789	2,860	2,038
1993.....	9,942	6,059	13,055	9,533	2,344	1,875	2,825	2,197	2,348	1,970	3,018	2,151
1994[3]....	10,594	6,343	13,812	10,151	2,440	1,981	2,941	2,285	2,498	2,113	3,274	2,266

[1] For in-State students. [2] Beginning 1990, rates reflect 20 meals per week, rather than meals served 7 days a week. [3] Preliminary.

Source: U.S. National Center for Education Statistics, *Digest of Education Statistics,* annual.

No. 288. Average College Costs for Undergraduates: 1993 and 1994

[In dollars. Based on survey responses of colleges, representing 80 percent of all colleges. See source for details. Data are weighted by enrollment to reflect the charges incurred by the average undergraduate enrolled at each type of institution]

TYPE OF INSTITUTION AND ITEM	1992-93				1993-94			
	Public colleges [1]		Private colleges		Public colleges [1]		Private colleges	
	Resident	Commuter	Resident	Commuter	Resident	Commuter	Resident	Commuter
4-year colleges, total	**8,071**	**6,473**	**17,027**	**14,621**	**8,562**	**6,809**	**17,846**	**15,200**
Tuition and fees................	2,315	2,315	10,498	10,498	2,527	2,527	11,025	11,025
Books and supplies..............	528	528	531	531	552	552	556	556
Room and board................	3,526	1,549	4,575	1,762	3,680	1,601	4,793	1,722
Transportation	497	843	487	794	557	870	498	824
Other	1,205	1,238	936	1,036	1,246	1,259	974	1,073
2-year colleges, total	**(B)**	**5,282**	**11,266**	**9,444**	**(B)**	**5,372**	**12,142**	**10,190**
Tuition and fees................	1,292	1,292	5,621	5,621	1,229	1,229	6,175	6,175
Books and supplies..............	502	502	512	512	533	533	566	566
Room and board................	(B)	1,592	3,750	1,558	(B)	1,643	3,980	1,589
Transportation	(B)	926	517	812	(B)	923	487	890
Other	(B)	970	866	941	(B)	1,044	934	970

B Base too small to meet statistical standards for reliability of a derived figure. [1] For in-State students.

Source: The College Board, New York, NY, Annual Survey of Colleges 1992 and 1993.

No. 289. Range of Undergraduate Tuitions at 4-Year Colleges: 1993 and 1994

[See headnote, table 288. Data presented here are unweighted by enrollment and reflect the average amounts charged by each type of institution]

TYPE OF CONTROL AND RANGE OF TUITION	1992-93		1993-94	
	Number of colleges	Percent of enrollment	Number of colleges	Percent of enrollment
Total, public [1] ..	**554**	**100.0**	**526**	**100.0**
$6,000 to $6,499 ..	(NA)	(NA)	1	0.2
$5,500 to $5,599 ..	(NA)	(NA)	1	0.1
$5,000 to $5,400 ..	(NA)	(NA)	6	1.3
$4,500 to $4,999 ..	(NA)	(NA)	11	1.9
$4,000 to $4,499 ..	(NA)	(NA)	20	2.9
$3,500 to $3,999 ..	(NA)	(NA)	38	7.6
$3,000 to $3,499 ..	[2]96	[2]17.8	49	11.3
$2,500 to $2,999 ..	107	20.9	93	18.1
$2,000 to $2,499 ..	84	15.6	88	16.0
$1,500 to $1,999 ..	150	25.5	155	30.1
$1,000 to $1,499 ..	100	18.8	52	9.2
Less than $1,000 ..	17	1.4	12	1.3
Total, private ...	**1,169**	**100.0**	**1,112**	**100.0**
$19,000 or more...	(NA)	(NA)	7	1.0
$18,000 to $18,999 .	(NA)	(NA)	31	4.3
$17,000 to $17,999 .	(NA)	(NA)	29	6.4

TYPE OF CONTROL AND RANGE OF TUITION	1992-93		1993-94	
	Number of colleges	Percent of enrollment	Number of colleges	Percent of enrollment
$16,000 to $16,999 .	(NA)	(NA)	28	3.5
$15,000 to $15,999 .	[3]100	[3]15.6	32	3.5
$14,000 to $14,999 .	29	3.1	23	2.7
$13,000 to $13,999 .	34	3.3	59	5.5
$12,000 to $12,999 .	61	6.0	70	7.6
$11,000 to $11,999 .	82	8.0	90	7.9
$10,000 to $10,999 .	104	10.6	106	12.2
$9,000 to $9,999 ..	110	10.5	118	8.8
$8,000 to $8,999 ..	138	10.0	112	8.0
$7,000 to $7,999 ..	118	7.7	96	7.5
$6,000 to $6,999 ..	97	6.7	81	5.6
$5,000 to $5,999 ..	84	4.7	65	3.6
$4,000 to $4,999 ..	84	5.2	76	2.8
$3,000 to $3,999 ..	66	2.0	48	2.7
$2,000 to $2,999 ..	45	5.5	28	5.2
$1,000 to $1,999 ..	7	0.1	5	0.1
Less than $1,000 ..	10	1.0	8	1.1

NA Not available. [1] For in-State students. [2] $3,000 or more. [3] $15,000 or more.

Source: The College Board, New York, NY, Annual Survey of Colleges 1992 and 1993.

No. 290. Voluntary Financial Support of Higher Education: 1970 to 1993

[For school years ending in years shown; enrollment as of fall of preceding year. Voluntary support, as defined in Gift Reporting Standards, excludes income from endowment and other invested funds as well as all support received from Federal, State, and local governments and their agencies and contract research]

ITEM	Unit	1970	1980	1985	1989	1990	1991	1992	1993
Estimated support, total [1]	Mil. dol.	1,780	3,800	6,320	8,925	9,800	10,200	10,700	11,200
Individuals	Mil. dol.	822	1,757	2,876	4,369	4,770	4,990	5,340	5,510
Alumni	Mil. dol.	381	910	1,460	2,292	2,540	2,680	2,840	2,980
Business corporations	Mil. dol.	269	696	1,574	1,947	2,170	2,230	2,260	2,400
Foundations	Mil. dol.	434	903	1,175	1,742	1,920	2,030	2,090	2,200
Religious organizations	Mil. dol.	102	155	208	237	240	240	240	250
Current operations	Mil. dol.	960	2,250	3,800	5,045	5,440	5,830	6,100	6,300
Capital purposes	Mil. dol.	820	1,550	2,520	3,880	4,360	4,370	4,600	4,900
Enrollment, higher education	1,000	8,094	11,570	12,242	13,055	13,539	13,820	14,359	14,558
Support per student	Dollars	220	328	516	684	724	738	745	769
In 1992-93 dollars	Dollars	829	603	696	804	812	786	768	769
Expenditures, higher education	Bil. dol.	24.7	62.5	98.3	137.5	151.8	165.8	176.5	186.7
Expenditures per student	Dollars	3,052	5,402	8,030	10,532	11,212	11,997	12,292	12,825
In 1992-93 dollars	Dollars	11,509	9,911	10,821	12,383	12,581	12,771	12,676	12,825
Institutions reporting support	Number	1,045	1,019	1,114	1,132	1,056	1,046	1,060	1,106
Total support reported	Mil. dol.	1,472	3,055	5,295	7,546	8,214	8,559	9,033	9,491
Private 4-year institutions	Mil. dol.	1,154	2,178	3,522	4,847	5,072	5,262	5,360	5,767
Public 4-year institutions	Mil. dol.	292	856	1,728	2,625	3,056	3,222	3,583	3,610
2-year colleges	Mil. dol.	26	20	45	74	85	75	89	115

[1] Includes other contributions, not shown separately.

Source: Council for Aid to Education, New York, NY, *Voluntary Support of Education,* annual.

No. 291. Average Salaries for College Faculty Members: 1992 to 1994

[In thousands of dollars. For academic year ending in year shown. Figures are for 9 months teaching for full-time faculty members in 4-year institutions. Fringe benefits in 1993 averaged $11,500 in public institutions and $13,100 in private institutions, and in 1994, $12,000 in public institutions and $13,900 in private ones]

TYPE OF CONTROL AND ACADEMIC RANK	1992	1993	1994	TYPE OF CONTROL AND ACADEMIC RANK	1992	1993	1994
Public: All ranks	45.3	46.0	47.3	Private: [1] All ranks	50.0	51.6	53.8
Professor	57.4	58.4	59.8	Professor	66.1	68.7	71.2
Associate professor	43.4	44.1	45.3	Associate professor	45.6	46.9	48.5
Assistant professor	36.3	37.0	38.0	Assistant professor	37.8	38.6	40.1
Instructor	27.2	27.8	28.8	Instructor	28.5	28.3	30.2

[1] Excludes church-related colleges and universities.

Source: American Association of University Professors, Washington, DC, *AAUP Annual Report on the Economic Status of the Profession.*

No. 292. Tenure Status of Full-Time College Faculty Members: 1993

[In percent. For academic year ending in year shown. Data are for those institutions of higher education reporting tenure status and are preliminary. Excludes schools with no tenure]

TYPE OF INSTITUTION AND CONTROL	Total faculty	ACADEMIC RANK						SEX	
		Professor	Associate professor	Assistant professor	Instructor	Lecturer	No academic rank	Male	Female
All institutions	63.4	95.8	81.3	17.3	9.0	6.4	71.4	70.1	48.9
4-year	61.7	95.9	80.8	14.1	4.2	5.3	21.3	68.9	44.1
University	65.4	97.3	85.7	7.4	3.1	1.7	1.5	72.3	44.2
Other 4-year	59.2	94.8	77.6	17.9	4.6	8.4	28.9	66.5	44.0
2-year	71.2	94.6	86.3	51.1	20.4	21.0	75.9	76.8	63.9
Public institutions	66.3	96.7	84.8	20.7	11.2	7.8	74.1	72.8	52.4
4-year	64.4	97.0	84.6	16.2	5.4	6.5	12.9	71.6	46.3
University	67.2	97.7	89.1	8.0	3.8	1.8	2.0	74.0	45.7
Other 4-year	62.4	96.3	81.0	21.5	6.0	9.8	19.3	69.6	46.7
2-year	72.0	94.7	86.5	52.5	20.8	21.2	77.0	77.5	64.9
Private institutions	56.1	93.6	73.6	10.7	2.2	1.2	37.7	63.5	40.0
4-year	56.4	93.6	73.6	10.6	2.1	1.2	30.3	63.6	40.1
University	61.0	96.1	76.8	5.9	1.0	1.6	0.4	67.8	40.8
Other 4-year	54.0	92.0	72.1	12.6	2.3	0.6	36.7	61.2	39.8
2-year	44.8	89.1	75.5	17.6	6.7	(NA)	46.6	52.0	37.4

NA Not available.

Source: U.S. National Center for Education Statistics, *Digest of Education Statistics,* 1994.

No. 293. Higher Education Registrations in Foreign Languages: 1960 to 1990

[As of **fall**]

ITEM	1960	1968	1970	1974	1977	1980	1983	1986	1990
Registrations [1] (1,000)	[2]647.1	1,127.4	1,111.5	946.6	933.5	924.8	966.0	1,003.2	1,184.1
Index (1960=100)	100.0	174.2	171.8	146.3	144.3	142.9	149.3	155.0	183.0
By selected language (1,000):									
Spanish	178.7	364.9	389.2	362.2	376.7	379.4	386.2	411.3	533.9
French	228.8	388.1	359.3	253.1	246.1	248.4	270.1	275.3	272.5
German	146.1	216.3	202.6	152.1	135.4	126.9	128.2	121.0	133.3
Italian	11.1	30.4	34.2	33.0	33.3	34.8	38.7	40.9	49.7
Japanese	1.7	4.3	6.6	9.6	10.7	11.5	16.1	23.5	45.7
Russian	30.6	40.7	36.1	32.5	27.8	24.0	30.4	34.0	44.6
Latin	[2]25.7	35.0	27.6	25.2	24.4	25.0	24.2	25.0	28.2
Chinese	1.8	5.1	6.2	10.6	9.8	11.4	13.2	16.9	19.5
Ancient Greek	[2]12.7	19.3	16.7	24.4	25.8	22.1	19.4	17.6	16.4
Hebrew	3.8	10.2	16.6	22.4	19.4	19.4	18.2	15.6	13.0
Portuguese	1.0	4.0	5.1	5.1	5.0	4.9	4.4	5.1	6.2
Arabic	0.5	1.1	1.3	2.0	3.1	3.5	3.4	3.4	3.5
12 languages as percent of total	99.3	99.3	99.1	98.5	98.3	98.5	98.6	98.6	98.5

[1] Includes other foreign languages, not shown separately.   [2] Estimated.

Source: Association of Departments of Foreign Languages, New York, NY, *ADFL Bulletin*, vol. 23, No. 3, and earlier issues (copyright).

No. 294. College Freshmen—Summary Characteristics: 1970 to 1994

[**In percent**. As of **fall** for first-time full-time freshmen. Based on sample survey and subject to sampling error; see source]

CHARACTERISTIC	1970	1980	1985	1989	1990	1991	1992	1993	1994
Sex: Male	55	49	48	46	46	47	46	45	46
Female	45	51	52	54	54	53	54	55	54
Applied to three or more colleges	[1]15	26	29	37	36	34	33	37	36
Average grade in high school:									
A- to A+	16	21	21	23	23	24	26	27	28
B- to B+	58	60	59	59	58	57	57	57	56
C to C+	27	19	20	17	19	19	17	16	15
D	1	1	1	-	-	-	-	-	-
Political orientation:									
Liberal	34	20	21	22	23	24	24	25	23
Middle of the road	45	60	57	54	55	54	53	50	53
Conservative	17	17	19	21	20	19	19	21	21
Probable field of study:									
Arts and humanities	16	9	8	9	9	8	8	8	8
Biological sciences	4	4	4	4	4	4	5	6	7
Business	16	24	27	25	21	18	16	16	16
Education	11	7	7	9	10	9	10	10	10
Engineering	9	12	11	10	8	10	9	9	8
Physical science	2	3	2	2	2	2	2	3	2
Social science	14	7	8	10	10	8	9	9	10
Professional	(NA)	15	13	13	15	18	20	20	19
Technical	4	6	5	3	4	4	3	3	3
Data processing/computer programming	(NA)	2	2	1	1	1	1	1	1
Other [2]	(NA)	(NA)	16	15	16	17	17	17	17
Communications	(NA)	2	2	3	2	2	2	2	2
Computer science	(NA)	1	2	2	2	2	1	2	2
Recipient of financial aid:									
Pell grant	(NA)	33	19	22	23	23	23	24	23
Supplemental educational opportunity grant	(NA)	8	5	6	7	7	6	6	6
State scholarship or grant	(NA)	16	14	15	16	13	14	14	16
College grant	(NA)	13	19	20	22	22	24	24	26
Federal guaranteed student loan	(NA)	21	23	23	23	22	23	28	29
Perkins loan [3]	(NA)	9	6	2	8	7	8	8	9
College loan	(NA)	4	4	8	6	5	6	6	8
College work-study grant	(NA)	15	10	10	10	11	12	12	13
Attitudes—agree or strongly agree:									
Activities of married women are best confined to home and family	48	27	22	26	25	26	26	24	25
Capital punishment should be abolished	56	34	27	21	22	21	21	22	20
Legalize marijuana	38	39	22	17	19	21	23	28	32
There is too much concern for the rights of criminals	52	66	(NA)	69	(NA)	65	67	68	73
Abortion should be legalized	(NA)	54	55	65	65	63	64	62	60
Aspires to an advanced degree	49	49	51	60	61	60	55	65	66

- Represents or rounds to zero.   NA Not available.   [1] 1969 data.   [2] Includes other fields, not shown separately.
[3] National Direct Student Loan prior to 1990.

Source: The Higher Education Research Institute, University of California, Los Angeles, CA, *The American Freshman: National Norms,* annual.

No. 295. Foreign (Nonimmigrant) Student Enrollment in College: 1976 to 1994

[For **fall** of the previous year]

REGION OF ORIGIN	ENROLLMENT (1,000)									PERCENT ENROLLED IN—					
										Engineering		Science[1]		Business	
	1976	1980	1985	1989	1990	1991	1992	1993	1994	1980	1992	1980	1992	1980	1992
All regions . . .	179	286	342	366	387	408	420	439	449	25	18	8	10	16	20
Africa	25	36	40	26	25	24	22	21	21	20	15	9	9	19	19
Nigeria	11	16	18	6	4	4	3	2	2	19	12	9	7	22	17
Asia[2]	97	165	200	232	245	263	277	291	294	32	22	8	10	16	20
Taiwan	11	18	23	29	31	34	36	37	37	17	22	15	9	17	21
Hong Kong	12	10	10	11	11	13	13	14	14	22	18	9	6	26	33
India	10	9	15	23	26	29	23	36	35	31	39	16	10	21	14
Indonesia	1	2	7	9	9	10	10	11	11	27	20	7	4	21	41
Iran	20	51	17	9	7	6	5	4	4	45	29	7	15	11	7
Japan	7	12	13	24	30	37	42	43	44	7	4	5	3	19	24
Korea, South	3	5	16	21	22	23	26	29	31	17	16	11	11	15	15
Malaysia	2	4	22	16	14	14	13	13	14	13	29	14	4	22	30
Saudi Arabia	3	10	8	5	4	4	4	4	4	30	24	4	5	14	15
Thailand	7	7	7	7	7	7	8	9	9	17	12	6	3	26	40
Europe	14	23	33	43	46	50	54	58	62	15	10	9	9	14	22
Latin America[3]	30	42	49	45	48	48	43	43	45	20	15	8	7	14	21
Mexico	5	6	6	6	7	7	7	8	8	16	15	7	8	11	18
Venezuela	5	10	10	3	3	3	3	3	4	30	19	8	7	11	20
North America	10	16	16	17	19	19	20	22	23	8	7	6	7	13	14
Canada	10	15	15	16	18	18	19	21	22	8	7	6	7	12	14
Oceania	3	4	4	4	4	4	4	4	4	5	5	7	5	16	19

[1] Physical and life sciences.   [2] Includes countries not shown separately.   [3] Includes Central America, Caribbean, and South America.

Source: Institute of International Education, New York, NY, *Open Doors*, annual (copyright).

No. 296. Salary Offers to Candidates for Degrees: 1990 to 1993

[**In dollars**. Data are average beginning salaries based on offers made by business, industrial, government, and nonprofit and educational employers to graduating students. Data from representative colleges throughout the United States]

FIELD OF STUDY	BACHELOR'S			MASTER'S[1]			DOCTOR'S		
	1990	1992	1993	1990	1992	1993	1990	1992	1993
Accounting	26,391	27,179	27,493	29,647	31,259	30,284	(NA)	(NA)	(NA)
Business, general[2]	23,529	24,305	24,555	36,175	35,734	36,513	(NA)	(NA)	(NA)
Marketing	23,543	23,914	24,361	35,440	39,508	40,104	(NA)	(NA)	(NA)
Engineering:									
Civil	28,136	29,376	29,211	32,336	34,303	34,606	44,481	46,501	48,268
Chemical	35,122	39,203	39,482	37,862	40,611	40,874	50,524	54,451	55,078
Computer	31,490	32,848	33,963	35,748	40,207	39,161	50,526	55,325	53,912
Electrical	31,778	33,754	34,313	37,526	41,024	41,291	53,147	56,826	57,076
Mechanical	32,064	34,462	34,460	36,506	39,298	40,457	49,887	51,880	54,217
Nuclear[3]	31,750	34,447	34,755	36,728	38,607	(NA)	(NA)	(NA)	(NA)
Petroleum	35,202	40,679	38,387	38,412	43,600	(NA)	(NA)	(NA)	(NA)
Engineering technology	29,318	31,051	29,236	(NA)	(NA)	(NA)	(NA)	(NA)	(NA)
Chemistry	27,494	27,557	28,002	32,320	35,104	35,690	45,356	50,719	50,933
Mathematics	27,032	28,434	26,524	30,069	33,636	33,183	42,775	40,954	39,500
Physics	28,002	29,019	26,835	31,480	31,626	31,800	41,486	40,940	50,600
Humanities	23,213	22,941	24,373	(NA)	(NA)	(NA)	(NA)	(NA)	(NA)
Social sciences[4]	21,627	21,623	22,684	(NA)	(NA)	(NA)	(NA)	(NA)	(NA)
Computer science	29,804	30,523	31,329	36,849	39,120	40,115	54,788	61,555	56,513

NA Not available.   [1] Candidates with 1 year or less of full-time nonmilitary employment.   [2] For master's degree, offers are after nontechnical undergraduate degree.   [3] Includes engineering physics.   [4] Excludes economics.

Source: College Placement Council, Inc., Bethlehem, PA, Salary Survey, *A Study of Beginning Offers*, annual (copyright).

No. 297. Time Spent Earning Bachelor's Degree, by Selected Characteristic: 1993

[As of **spring**. Based on Survey of Income and Program Participation; for details, see source]

CHARACTERISTIC	Total with bachelor's degrees (1,000)	YEARS TO BA DEGREE FROM END OF HIGH SCHOOL						Mean duration[1]
		Number (1,000)			Percent			
		4 years or less	5 years or less	6 years or less	4 years or less	5 years or less	6 years or less	
All persons	36,787	15,624	23,810	27,334	42.5	64.7	74.3	6.29
Male	19,351	7,321	11,695	13,827	37.8	60.4	71.5	6.28
Female	17,436	8,302	12,115	13,508	47.6	69.5	77.5	6.30
White	32,279	14,161	21,201	24,235	43.9	65.7	75.1	6.24
Male	17,258	6,717	10,537	12,411	38.9	61.1	71.9	6.22
Female	15,021	7,444	10,664	11,824	49.6	71.0	78.7	6.26
Black	2,314	713	1,258	1,473	30.8	54.4	63.7	7.19
Male	926	264	493	570	28.5	53.2	61.6	6.98
Female	1,388	448	764	904	32.3	55.0	65.1	7.33
Hispanic origin[2]	1,367	363	689	852	26.6	50.4	62.3	6.79
Male	693	187	308	407	27.0	44.4	58.7	7.06
Female	674	176	381	445	26.1	56.5	66.0	6.50
Field of Bachelor's degree:[3]								
Agriculture/Forestry	395	103	209	293	26.1	52.9	74.2	5.78
Biology	624	241	416	471	38.6	66.7	75.5	6.34
Business/Management	5,282	1,952	3,117	3,628	37.0	59.0	68.7	6.72
Economics	660	321	433	479	48.6	65.6	72.6	6.35
Education	3,613	1,522	2,338	2,658	42.1	64.7	73.6	7.03
Engineering	2,577	729	1,392	1,733	28.3	54.0	67.2	6.66
English/Journalism	1,137	553	743	854	48.6	65.3	75.1	6.28
Home Economics	337	177	262	284	52.5	77.7	84.3	4.71
Law	145	73	98	104	(B)	(B)	(B)	6.33
Liberal Arts/Humanities	2,188	894	1,413	1,592	40.9	64.6	72.8	6.44
Mathematics/Statistics	567	283	412	457	49.9	72.7	80.6	5.28
Medicine/Dentistry	142	39	74	104	(B)	(B)	*(B)	6.32
Nursing/Pharmacy/Technical Health	1,626	498	914	1,092	30.6	56.2	67.2	7.10
Physical/Earth Sciences	614	194	362	470	31.6	59.0	76.5	6.25
Police Science/Law Enforcement	326	95	182	240	29.1	55.8	73.6	6.11
Psychology	815	328	555	619	40.2	68.1	76.0	6.02
Religion/Theology	138	52	66	71	(B)	(B)	(B)	7.64
Social Sciences	1,760	683	1,113	1,333	38.8	63.2	75.7	6.44
Vo-tech Studies	181	64	121	135	(B)	(B)	(B)	7.39
Other	1,816	735	1,082	1,302	40.5	59.6	71.7	6.63
Advanced degree	11,843	6,089	8,507	9,417	51.4	71.8	79.5	5.67

B Base is less than 200,000 persons. [1] For definition of mean, see Guide to Tabular Presentation. [2] Persons of Hispanic origin may be of any race. [3] For persons whose highest degree is the BA.

Source: U.S. Bureau of the Census, unpublished data.

No. 298. Earned Degrees Conferred, by Level and Sex, With Projections: 1950 to 2004

[**In thousands, except percent**. Beginning 1960, includes Alaska and Hawaii. See *Historical Statistics, Colonial Times to 1970*, series H-751-763 for similar data. See also Appendix III]

YEAR ENDING	ALL DEGREES		ASSOCIATE'S		BACHELOR'S		MASTER'S		FIRST PROFESSIONAL		DOCTOR'S	
	Total	Percent male	Male	Female	Male	Female	Male	Female	Male	Female	Male	Female
1950 [1]	497	75.7	(NA)	(NA)	329	103	41	17	(NA)	(NA)	6	1
1960 [1]	477	65.8	(NA)	(NA)	254	138	51	24	(NA)	(NA)	9	1
1965	664	61.6	(NA)	(NA)	289	213	78	40	27	1	15	2
1970	1,271	59.2	117	89	451	341	126	83	33	2	26	4
1975	1,666	56.1	191	169	505	418	162	131	49	7	27	7
1980	1,731	51.1	184	217	474	456	151	147	53	17	23	10
1981	1,752	50.3	189	228	470	465	147	149	53	19	23	10
1982	1,788	49.8	197	238	473	480	146	150	52	20	22	10
1983	1,822	49.6	207	249	479	490	145	145	51	22	22	11
1984	1,819	49.6	203	250	482	492	144	141	51	23	22	11
1985	1,828	49.3	203	252	483	497	143	143	50	25	22	11
1986	1,830	49.0	196	250	486	502	144	145	49	25	22	12
1987	1,825	48.4	192	246	481	510	141	148	47	25	22	12
1988	1,835	48.0	190	245	477	518	145	154	45	25	23	12
1989	1,873	47.3	186	250	483	535	149	161	45	26	23	13
1990	1,940	46.6	191	264	492	560	154	171	44	27	24	14
1991	2,025	45.8	199	283	504	590	156	181	44	28	25	15
1992	2,108	45.6	207	297	521	616	162	191	45	29	26	15
1993	2,121	46.0	207	290	529	616	170	194	44	30	26	16
1995, proj.	2,189	46.4	216	302	548	630	182	195	44	31	25	17
2004, proj.	2,284	46.0	218	334	572	676	153	207	47	34	23	20

NA Not available. [1] First-professional degrees are included with bachelor's degrees.

Source: U.S. National Center for Education Statistics, *Digest of Education Statistics*, annual and *Projections of Education Statistics to 2004*, annual.

Education

No. 299. Degrees and Awards Earned Below Bachelor's, by Field: 1992

[Covers associate degrees and other awards based on postsecondary curriculums of less than 4 years in institutions of higher education]

FIELD OF STUDY	LESS THAN 1-YEAR AWARDS		1- TO LESS THAN 4-YEAR AWARDS		ASSOCIATE DEGREES	
	Total	Women	Total	Women	Total	Women
Total	**64,647**	**34,155**	**133,792**	**79,256**	**504,231**	**296,750**
Agriculture and natural resources	1,432	326	3,057	1,652	5,251	1,675
Architecture and related programs	2	2	93	62	443	337
Area, ethnic, and cultural studies	116	77	160	145	29	20
Biological/life sciences	72	17	119	36	1,361	797
Business management and administrative services	13,337	9,980	27,417	22,242	102,227	71,953
Communications and communications technologies	514	161	749	402	3,680	1,645
Computer and information sciences	1,563	809	3,445	2,038	9,290	4,725
Construction trades	944	34	3,735	175	1,560	69
Consumer and personal services	664	444	5,220	4,131	4,420	1,519
Education	420	270	671	598	10,267	6,559
Engineering	2,361	296	7,714	821	38,546	4,101
English language and literature/letters	109	78	62	45	1,019	671
Foreign languages and literatures	328	204	36	30	433	305
Health professions and related sciences	21,234	15,507	33,789	28,636	79,453	68,648
Home economics and vocational home economics	2,880	1,845	8,079	7,075	6,436	5,749
Law and legal studies	936	789	2,252	1,870	7,053	6,146
Liberal/general studies and humanities	71	37	1,048	628	154,594	91,777
Library science	77	64	50	50	103	85
Mathematics	-	-	33	10	744	280
Mechanics and repairers	3,083	123	16,202	1,237	10,264	671
Multi/interdisciplinary studies	59	49	105	61	7,841	4,059
Parks, recreation, leisure, and fitness	38	20	100	54	620	251
Physical sciences	58	26	306	27	2,066	861
Precision production trades	2,385	374	7,114	1,072	9,005	1,872
Protective services	4,345	811	2,260	571	15,117	3,876
Psychology	33	25	16	12	1,209	871
Public administration and services	94	61	333	224	3,162	2,523
Social sciences and history	12	7	94	56	3,160	1,760
Theological studies, religion and philosophy	119	96	1,549	911	556	233
Transportation and material moving	4,900	527	451	90	2,418	440
Visual and performing arts	223	147	4,079	2,662	11,888	7,085
Undistributed	2,238	949	3,454	1,633	10,016	5,187

- Represents zero.
Source: U.S. National Center for Education Statistics, *Digest of Education Statistics*, 1994.

No. 300. Bachelor's Degrees Earned, by Field: 1971 to 1992

FIELD OF STUDY	1971	1980	1985	1990	1992	PERCENT FEMALE	
						1971	1992
Total	**839,730**	**929,417**	**979,477**	**1,051,344**	**1,136,553**	**43.4**	**54.2**
Agriculture and natural resources	12,672	22,802	18,107	12,900	15,124	4.2	34.7
Architecture and environmental design	5,570	9,132	9,325	9,364	8,753	11.9	33.7
Area, ethnic and cultural studies	2,582	2,840	2,985	4,613	5,342	52.4	64.3
Biological sciences/life sciences	35,743	46,370	38,445	37,204	42,941	29.1	51.6
Business and management	114,729	184,867	232,636	248,698	256,603	9.1	47.2
Communications [1]	10,802	28,616	42,002	51,308	54,977	35.3	60.9
Computer and information sciences	2,388	11,154	38,878	27,257	24,557	13.6	28.7
Education	176,307	118,038	88,072	105,112	108,006	74.5	79.0
Engineering [1]	50,046	68,893	95,828	81,322	77,541	0.8	14.0
English language and literature/letters	64,342	32,541	33,218	47,519	54,951	65.6	66.3
Foreign languages	20,536	12,089	10,827	12,386	13,903	74.0	71.3
Health sciences	25,226	63,920	64,422	58,302	61,720	77.1	83.5
Home economics	11,167	18,411	15,157	14,491	14,898	97.3	88.7
Law	545	683	1,157	1,592	2,144	5.0	67.3
Liberal/general studies	7,481	23,196	21,818	27,985	32,174	33.6	60.3
Library and archival sciences	1,013	398	197	77	97	92.0	91.8
Mathematics	24,937	11,872	15,861	15,176	14,783	37.9	46.6
Military technologies	357	38	299	196	184	0.3	14.1
Multi/interdisciplinary studies	6,286	11,277	12,978	16,267	20,647	22.8	58.2
Parks and recreation	1,621	5,753	4,725	4,582	8,446	34.7	50.9
Philosophy, religion, and theology	11,890	13,276	12,447	12,068	12,255	25.5	32.2
Physical sciences [1]	21,412	23,410	23,704	16,066	16,960	13.8	32.6
Protective services	2,045	15,015	12,510	15,354	18,855	9.2	38.2
Psychology	38,187	42,093	39,900	53,952	63,513	44.4	73.2
Public affairs	5,466	16,644	11,754	13,908	15,987	68.4	78.2
Social sciences [2]	155,324	103,662	91,570	118,083	133,974	36.8	45.5
Visual and performing arts	30,394	40,892	38,140	39,934	46,522	59.7	62.1
Unclassified	662	1,535	2,515	5,628	10,696	0.9	31.2

[1] Includes technologies.   [2] Includes history.
Source: U.S. National Center for Education Statistics, *Digest of Education Statistics*, annual.

No. 301. Master's and Doctorate's Degrees Earned, by Field: 1971 to 1992

LEVEL AND FIELD OF STUDY	1971	1980	1985	1990	1992	PERCENT FEMALE	
						1971	1992
MASTER'S DEGREES							
Total...............	**230,509**	**298,081**	**286,251**	**324,301**	**352,838**	**40.1**	**54.1**
Agriculture and natural resources	2,457	3,976	3,928	3,382	3,735	5.9	35.4
Architecture and related programs.......	1,705	3,139	3,275	3,499	3,640	13.8	37.6
Area, ethnic and cultural studies	1,032	852	904	1,212	1,385	38.3	50.3
Biological sciences/life sciences	5,728	6,510	5,059	4,869	4,785	33.6	51.9
Business management and administrative services	25,977	54,484	66,996	76,676	84,642	3.9	35.4
Communications and technologies	1,856	3,082	3,669	4,362	4,464	34.6	62.1
Computer and information sciences	1,588	3,647	7,101	9,677	9,530	10.3	27.8
Education......................	87,666	101,819	74,654	84,881	92,668	56.2	77.1
Engineering and engineering technologies .	16,443	16,243	21,555	24,772	25,977	1.1	14.8
English language and literature/letters	10,686	6,189	5,187	6,567	7,450	60.6	66.3
Foreign languages	5,217	2,854	2,471	2,760	2,926	64.2	66.8
Health sciences..................	5,749	15,704	17,385	20,321	23,065	55.3	79.7
Home economics..................	1,452	2,690	2,375	2,100	2,412	93.9	83.0
Law and legal studies	955	1,817	1,796	1,888	2,369	4.8	32.6
Liberal arts and sciences, general studies and humanities	885	2,646	1,696	1,999	2,394	44.6	63.7
Library science	7,001	5,374	3,870	4,341	4,893	81.3	79.7
Mathematics	5,695	3,382	3,413	4,146	4,011	27.1	38.9
Military technologies	2	46	119	-	-	(Z)	-
Multi/interdisciplinary studies	821	2,306	2,583	2,834	2,126	25.0	53.2
Parks and recreation...............	218	647	596	529	1,358	29.8	52.1
Philosophy, religion, and theology	4,036	5,126	5,602	6,265	6,331	27.1	37.9
Physical sciences and science technologies	6,367	5,219	5,796	5,449	5,374	13.3	27.3
Protective services	194	1,805	1,235	1,151	1,249	10.3	36.2
Psychology....................	5,717	9,938	9,891	10,730	10,215	40.6	70.7
Public administration and services.......	7,785	17,560	15,575	17,399	19,243	50.0	70.0
Social sciences [1]	16,539	12,176	10,503	11,634	12,702	28.5	43.0
Visual and performing arts...........	6,675	8,708	8,718	8,481	9,353	47.4	56.4
Unclassified.....................	63	142	299	2,377	4,541	(Z)	41.6
DOCTORATE'S DEGREES							
Total...............	**32,107**	**32,615**	**32,943**	**38,371**	**40,659**	**14.3**	**37.1**
Agriculture and natural resources	1,086	991	1,213	1,295	1,214	2.9	20.7
Architecture and related programs.......	36	79	89	103	132	8.3	29.5
Area, ethnic and cultural studies	144	151	140	131	155	16.7	41.9
Biological sciences/life sciences	3,645	3,636	3,432	3,844	4,243	16.3	38.3
Business management and administrative services	757	753	831	1,093	1,242	2.8	23.3
Communications and technologies	145	193	234	273	255	13.1	48.2
Computer and information sciences......	128	240	248	627	772	2.3	13.3
Education......................	6,041	7,314	6,612	6,502	6,864	21.0	59.5
Engineering and engineering technology ..	3,638	2,507	3,230	4,981	5,499	0.6	9.6
English language and literature/letters	1,650	1,294	1,041	1,078	1,273	28.8	57.8
Foreign languages	988	755	635	724	850	34.6	55.5
Health sciences..................	466	786	1,199	1,536	1,661	16.5	58.0
Home economics..................	123	192	273	301	293	61.0	75.8
Law and legal studies	20	40	105	111	68	(Z)	26.5
Liberal arts and sciences, general studies and humanities	32	192	112	63	67	31.3	55.2
Library science	39	73	87	42	50	28.2	68.0
Mathematics	1,249	763	734	966	1,082	7.6	21.3
Multi/interdisciplinary studies	59	209	219	272	231	6.8	37.7
Parks and recreation...............	2	21	36	35	61	50.0	32.8
Philosophy, religion, and theology	866	1,693	1,612	1,756	1,734	5.8	16.8
Physical sciences and science technologies	4,390	3,089	3,403	4,164	4,391	5.6	21.9
Protective services	1	18	33	38	24	-	45.8
Psychology....................	2,144	3,395	3,447	3,811	3,373	24.0	59.7
Public administration and services.......	174	342	431	508	432	24.1	52.8
Social sciences [1]	3,660	3,230	2,851	3,010	3,218	13.9	33.9
Visual and performing arts...........	621	655	696	849	906	22.2	44.4
Unclassified.....................	3	4	-	258	569	(Z)	31.6

- Represents zero.   Z Less than .05 percent.   [1] Includes history.

Source: U.S. National Center for Education Statistics, *Digest of Education Statistics,* annual.

No. 302. First Professional Degrees Earned in Selected Professions: 1960 to 1992

[First professional degrees include degrees which require at least 6 years of college work for completion (including at least 2 years of preprofessional training). See Appendix III]

TYPE OF DEGREE AND SEX OF RECIPIENT	1960	1970	1975	1980	1985	1988	1989	1990	1991	1992
Medicine (M.D.):										
Institutions conferring degrees.....	79	86	104	112	120	122	124	124	121	120
Degrees conferred, total.........	7,032	8,314	12,447	14,902	16,041	15,358	15,460	15,075	15,043	15,243
Percent to women	5.5	8.4	13.1	23.4	30.4	33.1	33.3	34.2	36.0	35.7
Dentistry (D.D.S. or D.M.D.):										
Institutions conferring degrees.....	45	48	52	58	59	57	58	57	55	52
Degrees conferred, total.........	3,247	3,718	4,773	5,258	5,339	4,477	4,265	4,100	3,699	3,593
Percent to women	0.8	0.9	3.1	13.3	20.7	26.3	26.8	30.9	32.1	32.3
Law (LL.B. or J.D.):										
Institutions conferring degrees.....	134	145	154	179	181	180	182	182	179	177
Degrees conferred, total.........	9,240	14,916	29,296	35,647	37,491	35,397	35,634	36,485	37,945	38,848
Percent to women	2.5	5.4	15.1	30.2	38.5	40.5	40.9	42.2	43.0	42.7
Theological (B.D., M.Div., M.H.L.):										
Institutions conferring degrees.....	(NA)	(NA)	(NA)	(NA)	(NA)	(NA)	(NA)	(NA)	(NA)	(NA)
Degrees conferred, total.........	(NA)	5,298	5,095	7,115	7,221	6,466	6,012	5,851	5,695	5,251
Percent to women	(NA)	2.3	6.8	13.8	18.5	21.4	22.8	24.8	23.4	23.3

NA Not available.

Source: U.S. National Center for Education Statistics, *Digest of Education Statistics*, annual.

No. 303. Degrees Earned, by Level and Race/Ethnicity: 1981 to 1992

[For **school year ending in year shown.** Data exclude some institutions not reporting field of study and are slight undercounts of degrees awarded]

LEVEL OF DEGREE AND RACE/ETHNICITY	TOTAL					PERCENT DISTRIBUTION		
	1981	1985	1990	1991	1992	1981	1985	1992
Associate's degrees, total	410,174	429,815	450,263	462,030	494,387	100.0	100.0	100.0
White, non-Hispanic	339,167	355,343	369,580	376,081	400,530	82.7	82.7	81.0
Black, non-Hispanic.........	35,330	35,791	35,327	37,657	39,411	8.6	8.3	8.0
Hispanic	17,800	19,407	22,195	24,251	26,905	4.3	4.5	5.4
Asian or Pacific Islander......	8,650	9,914	13,482	13,725	15,596	2.1	2.3	3.2
American Indian/Alaskan Native...............	2,584	2,953	3,530	3,672	4,008	0.6	0.7	0.8
Nonresident alien	6,643	6,407	6,149	6,644	7,937	1.6	1.5	1.6
Bachelor's degrees, total	934,800	968,311	1,048,631	1,081,280	1,129,833	100.0	100.0	100.0
White, non-Hispanic	807,319	826,106	884,376	904,062	936,771	86.4	85.3	82.9
Black, non-Hispanic.........	60,673	57,473	61,063	65,341	72,326	6.5	5.9	6.4
Hispanic	21,832	25,874	32,844	36,612	40,761	2.3	2.7	3.6
Asian or Pacific Islander......	18,794	25,395	39,248	41,618	46,720	2.0	2.6	4.1
American Indian/Alaskan Native...............	3,593	4,246	4,392	4,513	5,176	0.4	0.4	0.5
Nonresident alien	22,589	29,217	26,708	29,134	28,079	2.4	3.0	2.5
Master's degrees, total	294,183	280,421	322,465	328,645	348,682	100.0	100.0	100.0
White, non-Hispanic	241,216	223,628	251,690	255,281	268,371	82.0	79.7	77.0
Black, non-Hispanic.........	17,133	13,939	15,446	16,139	18,116	5.8	5.0	5.2
Hispanic	6,461	6,864	7,950	8,386	9,358	2.2	2.4	2.7
Asian or Pacific Islander......	6,282	7,782	10,577	11,180	12,658	2.1	2.8	3.6
American Indian/Alaskan Native...............	1,034	1,256	1,101	1,136	1,273	0.4	0.4	0.4
Nonresident alien	22,057	26,952	35,701	36,523	38,906	7.5	9.6	11.2
Doctor's degrees, total	32,839	32,307	38,113	38,547	40,090	100.0	100.0	100.0
White, non-Hispanic	25,908	23,934	25,880	25,328	25,813	78.9	74.1	64.4
Black, non-Hispanic.........	1,265	1,154	1,153	1,211	1,223	3.9	3.6	3.1
Hispanic	456	677	788	732	811	1.4	2.1	2.0
Asian or Pacific Islander......	877	1,106	1,235	1,459	1,559	2.7	3.4	3.9
American Indian/Alaskan Native...............	130	119	99	102	118	0.4	0.4	0.3
Nonresident alien	4,203	5,317	8,958	9,715	10,566	12.8	16.5	26.4
First-professional degrees, total ..	71,340	71,057	70,744	71,515	72,129	100.0	100.0	100.0
White, non-Hispanic	64,551	63,219	60,240	60,327	59,800	90.5	89.0	82.9
Black, non-Hispanic.........	2,931	3,029	3,410	3,575	3,560	4.1	4.3	4.9
Hispanic	1,541	1,884	2,427	2,527	2,766	2.2	2.7	3.8
Asian or Pacific Islander......	1,456	1,816	3,362	3,755	4,455	2.0	2.6	6.2
American Indian/Alaskan Native...............	192	248	257	261	296	0.3	0.3	0.4
Nonresident alien	669	861	1,048	1,070	1,252	0.9	1.2	1.7

Source: U.S. National Center for Education Statistics, *Digest of Education Statistics,* annual.

No. 304. Libraries—Number, by Type: 1980 to 1993

TYPE	1980	1985	1990	1993	TYPE	1980	1985	1990	1993
Total [1]	**31,564**	**32,323**	**34,613**	**36,445**	Junior college . . .	1,191	1,188	1,233	1,255
					Colleges,				
United States . . .	28,638	29,843	30,761	32,414	universities	3,400	3,846	3,360	3,364
Public	8,717	8,849	9,060	9,097	Departmental .	1,489	1,824	1,454	1,455
Public branches . . .	5,936	6,330	5,833	6,215	Law,				
Special [2]	7,649	7,530	9,051	10,149	medicine,				
Medicine	1,674	1,667	1,861	1,925	religious	269	531	501	495
Religious	913	839	946	1,011	Government	1,260	1,574	1,735	1,871
Law [3]	417	435	647	1,140	Armed Forces	485	526	489	463
Academic	4,591	5,034	4,593	4,619	Outlying areas . .	113	114	110	(NA)

NA Not available. [1] Includes Canadian libraries, and libraries in regions administered by the United States, not shown separately. Data are exclusive of elementary and secondary school libraries. Law libraries with fewer than 10,000 volumes are included only if they specialize in a particular field. [2] Includes other types of special libraries, not shown separately. Increase between 1985 and 1990 is due mainly to revised criteria for identifying special libraries and improved methods of counting. [3] Increase beginning 1993 due to increased effort in identifying special libraries.

Source: R.R. Bowker Co., New York, NY, *The Bowker Annual: Library and Book Trade Almanac* and *American Library Directory,* annual. (Copyright by Reed Publishing (USA) Inc.)

No. 305. Public Libraries, Selected Characteristics: 1992

[Based on survey of public libraries. Data are for public libraries in the 50 States and the District of Columbia. The response rates for these items are between 97 and 100 percent, except for library visits (82 percent). See source for details]

POPULATION OF SERVICE AREA	NUMBER OF—		OPERATING INCOME			PAID STAFF [3]		Books and serial volumes (per capita)
	Public libraries	Stationary outlets [1]	Total (mil. dol.) [2]	Source (percent)		Total	Librarians with ALA-MLS [4]	
				State government	Local government			
Total	**8,946**	**15,870**	**4,997**	**12.0**	**78.6**	**109,926**	**24,461**	**2.7**
1,000,000 or more	22	866	848	10.1	79.1	13,669	3,855	2.3
500,000 to 999,000	49	1,034	765	18.3	74.4	15,072	3,917	2.5
250,000 to 499,999	98	1,058	605	11.7	81.5	12,711	3,156	2.3
100,000 to 249,999	293	1,820	735	9.9	81.9	16,870	3,786	2.2
50,000 to 99,999	505	1,631	633	12.6	78.8	14,756	3,284	2.4
25,000 to 49,999	861	1,652	575	11.6	79.4	14,028	3,010	2.8
10,000 to 24,999	1,654	2,130	513	10.1	78.8	12,801	2,488	3.3
5,000 to 9,999	1,481	1,647	192	11.1	74.5	5,360	679	4.1
2,500 to 4,999	1,327	1,371	77	7.0	73.4	2,467	199	5.2
1,000 to 2,499	1,661	1,672	44	5.3	67.0	1,628	72	7.4
Fewer than 1,000	995	989	11	9.0	63.9	565	14	13.0

[1] The sum of central and branches libraries. The total number of central libraries was 8,835; the total of branch libraries was 7,035. [2] Includes income from the Federal Government (1.0%) and other sources (8.4%), not shown separately. [3] Full-time equivalents. [4] Librarians with master's degrees from a graduate library education program accredited by the American Library Association (ALA). Total librarians, including those without ALA-MLS, were 35,999.

Source: U.S. National Center for Education Statistics, *Public Libraries in the United States: 1992.*

No. 306. College and University Libraries—Summary: 1975 to 1990

[For school year ending in year shown, except enrollment as of fall of the prior year. Prior to 1982, includes outlying areas]

ITEM	1975	1977	1979	1982	1985	1988	1990
Number of libraries	2,972	3,058	3,122	3,104	3,322	3,438	3,274
Total enrollment (1,000)	10,322	11,121	11,392	12,372	12,242	12,767	13,539
COLLECTIONS (1,000)							
Number of volumes	447,059	481,442	519,895	567,826	631,727	706,504	717,042
Volumes added during year	23,242	22,367	21,608	19,507	20,658	21,907	19,003
Number of serial subscriptions	4,434	4,670	4,775	4,890	6,317	6,416	5,748
STAFF							
Total	56,836	57,087	58,416	58,476	58,476	67,251	69,359
Librarians and professional	23,530	23,308	23,676	23,816	21,822	25,115	26,101
OPERATING EXPENDITURES ($1,000)							
Total [1]	1,091,784	1,259,637	1,502,158	1,943,769	2,404,524	2,770,075	3,257,813
Salaries	592,568	698,090	824,438	1,081,894	1,156,138	1,451,551	1,693,813
Collection	327,904	373,699	450,180	561,199	750,282	891,281	1,040,928

[1] Includes other expenditures, not shown separately.

Source: U.S. National Center for Education Statistics, *Digest of Education Statistics,* 1991; and *Academic Libraries: 1990,* 1992.

No. 307. Participation in Adult Education: 1990-91

[For the civilian noninstitutional population 17 years old and over not enrolled full-time in elementary or secondary school at the time of the survey. Adult education is considered any part-time enrollment in any educational activity at any time in the prior 12 months. Based on a telephone survey and subject to sampling error; source for details]

CHARACTERISTIC	Adult popu-lation (1,000)	PARTICIPANTS IN ADULT EDUCATION					
		Number taking adult ed. courses (1,000)	Per-cent of total	Reason for taking course (percent) [1]			
				Per-sonal/ social	Advance on the job	Train for a new job	Complete degree or diploma
Total..................	181,800	57,391	32	30	60	9	13
Age: 17 to 24 years old...........	21,688	7,125	33	30	38	18	29
25 to 34 years old...........	47,244	17,530	37	25	63	12	14
35 to 44 years old...........	38,565	17,083	44	27	66	8	12
45 to 54 years old...........	25,375	8,107	32	29	70	6	7
55 to 64 years old...........	19,967	4,516	23	35	61	5	5
65 years old and over........	28,960	3,031	10	73	22	4	3
Sex: Male..................	82,154	25,923	32	24	67	8	11
Female................	99,646	31,469	32	35	54	10	14
Race/ethnicity:							
White [2]...................	143,144	47,401	33	30	62	8	13
Black [2]...................	20,141	4,586	23	30	53	14	13
Hispanic..............	13,804	4,032	29	31	48	16	12
Other races [2]...............	4,711	1,371	29	32	51	8	17
Marital status:							
Never married.............	36,652	11,539	31	30	48	14	24
Currently married.............	118,397	39,323	33	30	63	8	10
Other..................	26,752	6,529	24	34	59	11	11
Children under 16 in household:							
Yes...................	68,868	25,349	37	26	65	10	12
No....................	112,932	32,042	28	33	56	9	14
Educational attainment:							
Up to 8th grade.............	10,163	735	7	56	16	5	14
9th to 11th grade...........	17,581	2,520	14	30	43	13	16
Twelfth grade..............	67,129	15,077	22	31	55	13	9
Vocational school after high school	6,994	2,219	32	28	68	6	10
Some college..............	36,823	14,488	39	33	53	10	19
Associate's degree...........	5,034	2,461	49	22	71	7	15
Bachelor's or higher..........	38,076	19,891	52	28	70	6	11
Labor force status:							
Employed.................	115,620	47,143	41	24	68	9	13
Unemployed..............	9,820	2,099	21	27	29	27	25
Not in the labor force..........	56,361	8,149	14	64	17	10	11
Occupation: [3]							
Professional.................	19,898	12,693	64	22	79	5	15
Executive, administrative, and managerial..............	10,574	6,255	59	22	78	6	13
Technical, sales, and related support.............	3,082	1,947	63	18	75	12	13
Sales workers.............	12,234	5,154	42	34	56	12	11
Administrative support [4]........	18,971	7,044	37	28	66	10	15
Service..................	15,904	4,426	28	27	61	11	15
Agriculture, forestry, and fishing....	2,783	303	11	31	62	6	10
Precision production, craft and repair.............	11,393	3,918	34	27	61	13	10
Machine operators, assemblers [5]...	7,768	2,201	28	20	73	10	10
Transportation and materials moving..............	3,962	1,030	26	23	68	7	9
Handlers, equipment cleaners, helpers and laborers..........	3,297	767	23	17	60	18	10
Nonclassifiable, undetermined.....	5,753	1,403	24	8	19	8	6
Income: Under $10,000...........	27,504	3,843	14	37	34	16	14
$10,001 to $15,000.............	15,465	3,178	21	31	48	16	15
$15,001 to $20,000.............	16,117	3,308	21	32	50	13	16
$20,001 to $25,000.............	16,092	4,063	25	32	56	11	14
$25,001 to $30,000.............	17,973	5,445	30	33	53	14	15
$30,001 to $40,000.............	26,110	9,043	35	30	64	10	13
$40,001 to $50,000.............	21,303	9,313	44	29	64	6	12
$50,001 to $75,000.............	24,540	11,235	46	28	67	6	12
More than $75,000.............	16,695	7,963	48	27	66	6	10

[1] Reason for taking at least one course. Includes duplication. Excludes "to improve basic skills," cited by no more than 4 percent of participants.　[2] Non-Hispanic.　[3] For the currently employed.　[4] Includes clerical.　[5] Includes inspectors.

Source: U.S. National Center for Education Statistics, *Adult Education Profile for 1990-91;* and unpublished data.

Law Enforcement, Courts, and Prisons

This section presents data on crimes committed, victims of crimes, arrests, and data related to criminal violations, and the criminal justice system. The major sources of these data are the Bureau of Justice Statistics (BJS) and the Federal Bureau of Investigation (FBI). BJS issues several reports, including *Sourcebook of Criminal Justice Statistics, Criminal Victimization in the United States, Prisoners in State and Federal Institutions, Children in Custody, National Survey of Courts, Census of State Correctional Facilities* and *Survey of Prison Inmates, Census of Jails* and *Survey of Jail Inmates, Parole in the United States, Capital Punishment,* and the annual *Expenditure and Employment Data for the Criminal Justice System.* The Federal Bureau of Investigation's major annual report is *Crime in the United States,* which presents data on reported crimes as gathered from State and local law enforcement agencies.

Other major sources of these data include: *Annual Report of the Director, Federal Court Management Statistics, Federal Offenders,* and *Sentences Imposed Chart* issued by the Administrative Office of the U.S. Courts; *Governmental Finances and Public Employment,* issued annually by the Bureau of the Census; and the *Statistical Report,* issued annually by the Federal Bureau of Prisons.

Legal jurisdiction and law enforcement.—Law enforcement is, for the most part, a function of State and local officers and agencies. The U.S. Constitution reserves general police powers to the States. By act of Congress, Federal offenses include only offenses against the U.S. Government and against or by its employees while engaged in their official duties, and offenses which involve the crossing of State lines or an interference with interstate commerce. Excluding the military, there are 52 separate criminal law jurisdictions in the United States: 1 in each of the 50 States, 1 in the District of Columbia, and the Federal jurisdiction. Each of these has its own criminal law and procedure and its own

In Brief

Crime rate, as reported by the FBI, fell again from 5,660 per 100,000 population in 1992 to 5,438 in 1993

Among the Nation's 23,271 murder victims in 1993, there were 2,697 victims under 18 years old.

Over 1 million child victims in cases of substantiated abuse and neglect in 1993

law enforcement agencies. While the systems of law enforcement are quite similar among the States, there are often substantial differences in the penalties for like offenses.

Law enforcement can be divided into three parts: Investigation of crimes and arrests of persons suspected of committing them; prosecution of those charged with crime; and the punishment or treatment of persons convicted of crime.

Crime.—There are two major approaches taken in determining the extent of crime. One perspective is provided by the FBI through its Uniform Crime Reporting Program (UCR). The FBI receives monthly and annual reports from law enforcement agencies throughout the country, currently representing 98 percent of the national population. Each month, city police, sheriffs, and State police file reports on the number of index offenses that become known to them. The FBI Crime Index offenses are as follows: *Murder and nonnegligent manslaughter,* is based on police investigations, as opposed to the determination of a medical examiner or judicial body, includes willful felonious homicides, and excludes attempts and assaults to kill, suicides, accidental deaths, justifiable homicides, and deaths caused by negligence; *forcible rape* includes forcible rapes and attempts; *robbery* includes stealing or taking anything of value by force or violence or threat of force or violence and includes attempted robbery; *aggravated assault* includes assault with intent to kill; *burglary* includes any unlawful entry to commit a felony or a theft and includes attempted burglary and burglary followed by larceny; *larceny* includes theft of property or articles of value without use of force and violence or fraud and excludes embezzlement, "con games," forgery, etc.; *motor vehicle theft* includes all cases where vehicles are driven away and abandoned, but excludes vehicles taken for temporary use and returned by the taker. Arson was added as the eighth Index offense in April 1979 following a Congressional mandate. *Arson* includes any willful or malicious burning or attempt to burn with or without intent to defraud, a dwelling house, public building, motor vehicle or aircraft, personal property of another, etc. The monthly Uniform Crime Reports also contain data on crimes cleared by arrest and on characteristics of persons arrested for all criminal offenses. In summarizing and publishing crime data, the FBI depends primarily on the adherence to the established standards of reporting for statistical accuracy, presenting the data as information useful to persons concerned with the problem of crime and criminal-law enforcement.

National Crime Victimization Survey (NCVS).—A second perspective on crime is provided by this survey (formerly the National Crime Survey until August 1991) of the Bureau of Justice Statistics. Details about the crimes come directly from the victims. No attempt is made to validate the information against police records or any other source. The NCVS measures rape, robbery, assault, household and personal larceny, burglary, and motor vehicle theft. The NCVS includes offenses reported to the police, as well as those not reported. Police reporting rates (percent of victimizations) varied by type of crime. In 1991, for instance, 59 percent of the rapes were reported; 55 percent of the robberies; 47 percent of assaults; 28 percent of personal larcenies without contact; 50 percent of the household burglaries; and 74 percent of motor vehicle thefts.

Murder and kidnaping are not covered. Commercial burglary and robbery were dropped from the program during 1977. The so-called victimless crimes, such as drunkenness, drug abuse, and prostitution, also are excluded, as are crimes for which

it is difficult to identify knowledgeable respondents or to locate data records.

Crimes of which the victim may not be aware also cannot be measured effectively. Buying stolen property may fall into this category, as may some instances of embezzlement. Attempted crimes of many types probably are under recorded for this reason. Events in which the victim has shown a willingness to participate in illegal activity also are excluded.

In any encounter involving a personal crime, more than one criminal act can be committed against an individual. For example; a rape may be associated with a robbery; or a household offense, such as a burglary, can escalate into something more serious in the event of a personal confrontation. In classifying the survey-measured crimes, each criminal incident has been counted only once—by the most serious act that took place during the incident and ranked in accordance with the seriousness classification system used by the Federal Bureau of Investigation. The order of seriousness for crimes against persons is as follows: Rape, robbery, assault, and larceny. Consequently, if a person were both robbed and assaulted, the event would be classified as robbery; if the victim suffered physical harm, the crime would be categorized as robbery with injury. Personal crimes take precedence over household offenses.

A *victimization,* basic measure of the occurrence of a crime, is a specific criminal act as it affects a single victim. The number of victimizations is determined by the number of victims of such acts. Victimization counts serve as key elements in computing rates of victimization. For crimes against persons, the rates are based on the total number of individuals age 12 and over or on a portion of that population sharing a particular characteristic or set of traits. As general indicators of the danger of having been victimized during the reference period, the rates are not sufficiently refined to represent true measures of risk for specific individuals or households.

An *incident* is a specific criminal act involving one or more victims; therefore, the number of incidents of personal crimes lower than that of victimizations.

Courts.—Statistics on criminal offenses and the outcome of prosecutions are incomplete for the country as a whole, although data are available for many States individually. The only national compilations of such statistics were made by the Bureau of the Census for 1932 to 1945 covering a maximum of 32 States, and by the Bureau of Justice Statistics for 1986, 1988, 1990, and 1992 based on a nationally representative sample survey.

The bulk of civil and criminal litigation in the country is commenced and determined in the various State courts. Only when the U.S. Constitution and acts of Congress specifically confer jurisdiction upon the Federal courts may civil litigation be heard and decided by them. Generally, the Federal courts have jurisdiction over the following types of cases: Suits or proceedings by or against the United States; civil actions between private parties arising under the Constitution, laws, or treaties of the United States; civil actions between private litigants who are citizens of different States; civil cases involving admiralty, maritime, or prize jurisdiction; and all matters in bankruptcy.

There are several types of courts with varying degrees of legal jurisdiction. These jurisdictions include original, appellate, general, and limited or special. A *court of original jurisdiction* is one having the authority initially to try a case and pass judgment on the law and the facts; a *court of appellate jurisdiction* is one with the legal authority to review cases and hear appeals; a *court of general jurisdiction* is a trial court of unlimited original jurisdiction in civil and/or criminal cases, also called a "major trial court"; a *court of limited or special jurisdiction* is a trial court with legal authority over only a particular class of cases, such as probate, juvenile, or traffic cases.

The 94 Federal courts of original jurisdiction are known as the U.S. district courts. One or more of these courts is established in every State and one each in the District of Columbia, Puerto Rico, the Virgin Islands, the Northern Mariana Islands, and Guam. Appeals from the district courts are taken to intermediate appellate courts of which there are 13, known as U.S. courts of appeals and the United States Court of Appeals for the Federal Circuit. The Supreme Court of the United States is the final and highest appellate court in the Federal system of courts.

Juvenile offenders.—For statistical purposes, the FBI and most States classify as juvenile offenders persons under the age of 18 years who have committed a crime or crimes.

Delinquency cases are all cases of youths referred to a juvenile court for violation of a law or ordinance or for seriously "antisocial" conduct. Several types of facilities are available for those adjudicated delinquent, ranging from the short-term physically unrestricted environment to the long-term very restrictive atmosphere.

Prisoners.—Data on prisoners in Federal and State prisons and reformatories were collected annually by the Bureau of the Census until 1950, by the Federal Bureau of Prisons until 1971, transferred then to the Law Enforcement Assistance Administration, and, in 1979, to the Bureau of Justice Statistics. Adults convicted of criminal activity may be given a prison or jail sentence. A *prison* is a confinement facility having custodial authority over adults sentenced to confinement of more than one year. A *jail* is a facility, usually operated by a local law enforcement agency, holding persons detained pending adjudication and/or persons committed after adjudication to one year or less. Nearly every State publishes annual data either for its whole prison system or for each separate State institution.

Statistical reliability.—For discussion of statistical collection, estimation, and sampling procedures and measures of statistical reliability pertaining to the National Crime Victimization Survey and Uniform Crime Reporting Program, see Appendix III.

Historical statistics.—Tabular headnotes provide cross-references, where applicable, to *Historical Statistics of the United States, Colonial Times to 1970*. See Appendix IV.

Figure 5.1
Violent and Property Crime Rates: 1980 to 1993

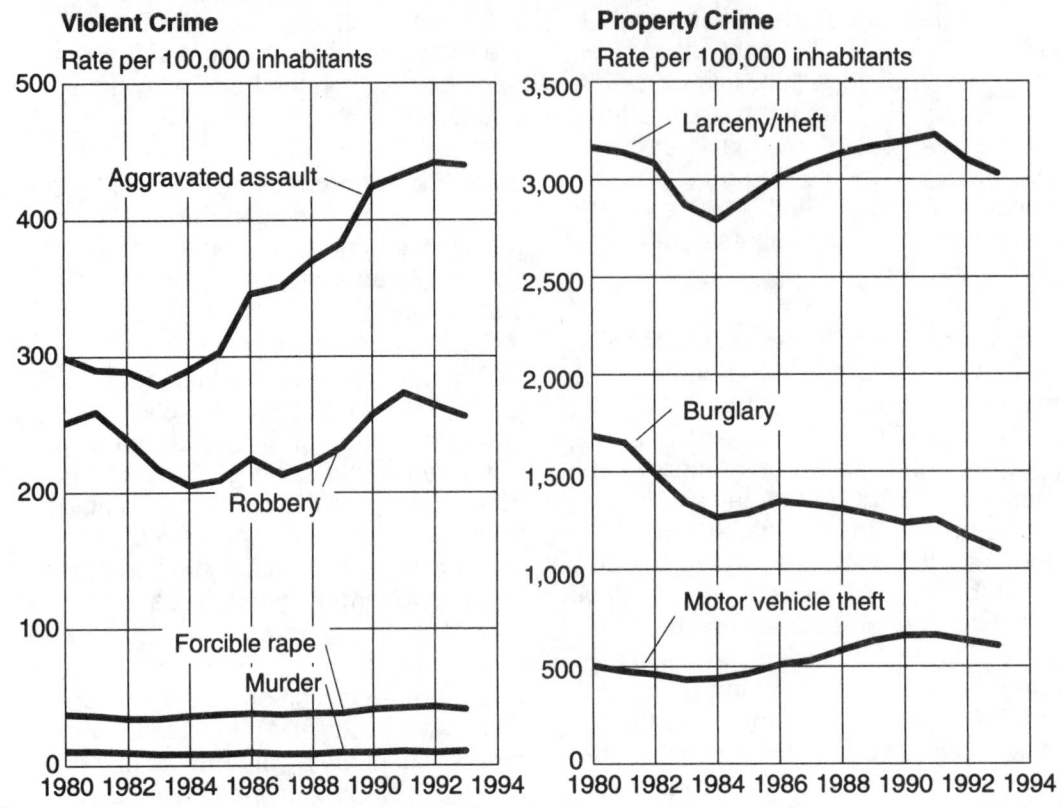

Violent Crime

Rate per 100,000 inhabitants

Aggravated assault

Robbery

Forcible rape

Murder

Property Crime

Rate per 100,000 inhabitants

Larceny/theft

Burglary

Motor vehicle theft

Source: Chart prepared by U.S. Bureau of the Census. For data, see table 308.

Figure 5.2
Child Abuse and Neglect Cases: 1993

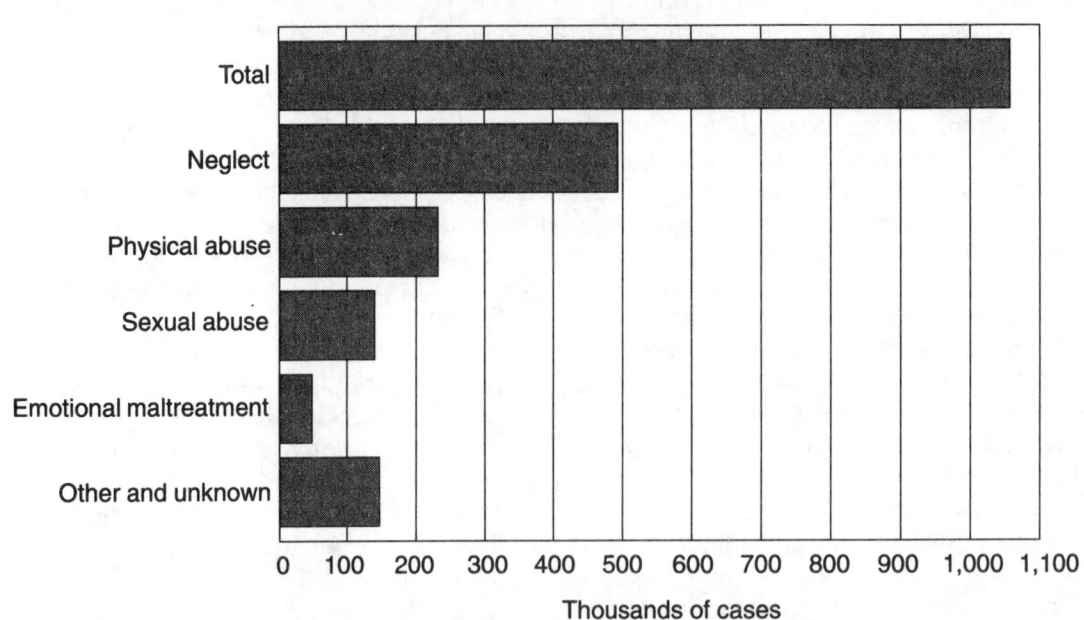

Total

Neglect

Physical abuse

Sexual abuse

Emotional maltreatment

Other and unknown

Thousands of cases

Note: More than one type of maltreatment may be substantiated per child. Therefore, items add up to more than the total shown.
Source: Chart prepared by U.S. Bureau of the Census. For data, see table 346.

No. 308. Crimes and Crime Rates, by Type: 1983 to 1993

[Data refer to offenses known to the police. Rates are based on Bureau of the Census estimated resident population as of **July 1, 1980 and 1990, enumerated as of April 1.** See source for details. Minus sign (-) indicates decrease. For definitions of crimes, see text, section 5. See *Historical Statistics, Colonial Times to 1970,* series H 952-961 for related data]

ITEM AND YEAR	Total	VIOLENT CRIME					PROPERTY CRIME			
		Total	Mur-der[1]	Forcible rape	Rob-bery	Aggra-vated assault	Total	Bur-glary	Larce-ny—theft	Motor vehicle theft
Number of offenses (1,000):										
1983............	12,109	1,258	19.3	78.9	507	653	10,851	3,130	6,713	1,008
1984............	11,882	1,273	18.7	84.2	485	685	10,609	2,984	6,592	1,032
1985............	12,431	1,329	19.0	88.7	498	723	11,103	3,073	6,926	1,103
1986............	13,212	1,489	20.6	91.5	543	834	11,723	3,241	7,257	1,224
1987............	13,509	1,484	20.1	91.1	518	855	12,025	3,236	7,500	1,289
1988............	13,923	1,566	20.7	92.5	543	910	12,357	3,218	7,706	1,433
1989............	14,251	1,646	21.5	94.5	578	952	12,605	3,168	7,872	1,565
1990............	14,476	1,820	23.4	102.6	639	1,055	12,656	3,074	7,946	1,636
1991............	14,873	1,912	24.7	106.6	688	1,093	12,961	3,157	8,142	1,662
1992............	14,438	1,932	23.8	109.1	672	1,127	12,506	2,980	7,915	1,611
1993............	14,141	1,924	24.5	105.0	660	1,135	12,217	2,835	7,821	1,561
Percent change, number of offenses:										
1983 to 1993	16.8	52.9	26.9	33.1	30.2	73.8	12.6	-9.4	16.5	54.9
1991 to 1992	-3.0	1.0	-3.8	2.3	-2.4	3.0	-3.6	-5.9	-2.9	-3.2
1992 to 1993	-2.1	-0.4	2.9	-3.9	-1.8	0.7	-2.4	-5.1	-1.2	-3.2
Rate per 100,000 population:										
1983............	5,175	538	8.3	33.7	217	279	4,637	1,338	2,869	431
1984............	5,031	539	7.9	35.7	205	290	4,492	1,264	2,791	437
1985............	5,207	557	7.9	37.1	209	303	4,651	1,287	2,901	462
1986............	5,480	618	8.6	37.9	225	346	4,863	1,345	3,010	508
1987............	5,550	610	8.3	37.4	213	351	4,940	1,330	3,081	529
1988............	5,664	637	8.4	37.6	221	370	5,027	1,309	3,135	583
1989............	5,741	663	8.7	38.1	233	383	5,078	1,276	3,171	630
1990............	5,820	732	9.4	41.2	257	424	5,089	1,236	3,195	658
1991............	5,898	758	9.8	42.3	273	433	5,140	1,252	3,229	659
1992............	5,660	758	9.3	42.8	264	442	4,903	1,168	3,103	631
1993............	5,483	746	9.5	40.6	256	440	4,737	1,099	3,032	605
Percent change, rate per 100,000 population:										
1983 to 1993	6.0	38.7	14.5	20.5	18.0	57.7	2.2	-17.9	5.7	40.4
1991 to 1992	-4.2	-	-5.4	1.2	-3.3	2.0	-4.8	-7.2	-4.1	-4.4
1992 to 1993	-3.2	-1.6	2.1	-5.4	-3.1	-0.5	-3.5	-6.3	-2.3	-4.3

- Represents or rounds to zero.   [1] Includes nonnegligent manslaughter.

Source: U.S. Federal Bureau of Investigation, *Crime in the United States,* annual.

No. 309. Crimes and Crime Rates, by Type and Area: 1993

[**In thousands, except rate.** Rate per 100,000 population; see headnote, table 308. Estimated totals based on reports from city and rural law enforcement agencies representing 96 percent of the national population. For definitions of crimes, see text, section 5]

TYPE OF CRIME	UNITED STATES		METROPOLITAN AREAS[1]		OTHER CITIES		RURAL AREAS	
	Total	Rate	Total	Rate	Total	Rate	Total	Rate
Total.....................	**14,141**	**5,483**	**12,390**	**6,045**	**1,126**	**5,303**	**625**	**1,971**
Violent crime..................	1,924	746	1,747	852	107	504	71	222
Murder and nonnegligent manslaughter..................	25	10	22	11	1	5	2	5
Forcible rape...................	105	41	89	43	8	39	8	25
Robbery	660	256	639	312	15	71	5	16
Aggravated assault..............	1,135	440	997	486	83	389	56	176
Property crime..................	12,217	4,737	10,643	5,193	1,019	4,799	555	1,749
Burglary	2,835	1,099	2,423	1,182	211	993	201	633
Larceny—theft	7,821	3,032	6,741	3,289	761	3,582	319	1,006
Motor vehicle theft	1,561	605	1,479	721	48	224	35	110

[1] For definition, see Appendix II.

Source: U.S. Federal Bureau of Investigation, *Crime in the United States,* annual.

No. 310. Crime Rates, by State, 1991 to 1993, and by Type, 1993

[**Offenses known to the police per 100,000 population.** Based on Bureau of the Census estimated resident population as of **July 1.** For definitions of crimes, see text, section 5]

REGION, DIVISION, AND STATE	1991, total	1992, total	1993									
			Total	Violent crime					Property crime			
				Total	Mur-der [1]	Forci-ble rape	Rob-bery	Aggra-vated assault	Total	Bur-glary	Larce-ny—theft	Motor vehi-cle theft
United States	**5,898**	**5,660**	**5,483**	**746**	**9.5**	**40.6**	**256**	**440**	**4,737**	**1,099**	**3,032**	**605**
Northeast	**5,155**	**4,837**	**4,613**	**713**	**8.2**	**28.4**	**323**	**354**	**3,900**	**878**	**2,358**	**664**
New England	**4,950**	**4,614**	**4,431**	**538**	**4.1**	**31.4**	**141**	**361**	**3,894**	**925**	**2,366**	**602**
Maine	3,768	3,524	3,154	126	1.6	26.6	21	76	3,028	719	2,175	134
New Hampshire	3,448	3,081	2,905	138	2.0	44.4	27	64	2,767	515	2,058	194
Vermont	3,955	3,410	3,972	114	3.6	39.8	9	62	3,858	874	2,851	133
Massachusetts	5,322	5,003	4,894	805	3.9	33.4	176	592	4,089	1,002	2,271	816
Rhode Island	5,039	4,578	4,499	402	3.9	28.6	101	268	4,097	1,041	2,410	646
Connecticut	5,364	5,053	4,560	456	6.3	24.4	197	229	4,194	978	2,621	596
Middle Atlantic	**5,227**	**4,914**	**4,676**	**774**	**9.6**	**27.3**	**386**	**351**	**3,902**	**862**	**2,355**	**685**
New York	6,245	5,858	5,551	1,074	13.3	27.5	561	472	4,478	999	2,644	835
New Jersey	5,431	5,064	4,801	627	5.3	28.1	296	298	4,174	974	2,486	714
Pennsylvania	3,559	3,393	3,271	418	6.8	26.5	179	205	2,854	582	1,832	440
Midwest	**5,257**	**4,975**	**4,806**	**602**	**7.6**	**42.3**	**204**	**348**	**4,204**	**900**	**2,850**	**454**
East North Central	**5,482**	**5,136**	**4,953**	**661**	**8.3**	**45.9**	**235**	**372**	**4,292**	**910**	**2,883**	**499**
Ohio	5,033	4,666	4,485	504	6.0	49.1	193	256	3,981	878	2,668	435
Indiana	4,818	4,687	4,465	489	7.5	39.1	120	323	3,976	852	2,696	428
Illinois [2]	6,132	5,765	5,618	960	11.4	34.6	381	533	4,658	1,016	3,084	559
Michigan	6,138	5,611	5,453	792	9.8	71.1	239	472	4,661	983	3,063	615
Wisconsin	4,466	4,319	4,054	264	4.4	25.2	113	121	3,790	663	2,762	365
West North Central . . .	**4,722**	**4,594**	**4,454**	**459**	**5.9**	**33.8**	**130**	**290**	**3,995**	**875**	**2,773**	**347**
Minnesota	4,496	4,591	4,386	327	3.4	35.2	113	176	4,059	845	2,872	343
Iowa [3]	4,134	3,957	3,846	326	2.3	24.4	54	245	3,521	731	2,599	191
Missouri	5,416	5,097	5,095	744	11.3	36.2	242	455	4,351	1,026	2,778	548
North Dakota	2,794	2,903	2,820	82	1.7	23.5	8	49	2,738	373	2,216	149
South Dakota	3,079	2,999	2,958	208	3.4	44.5	15	1.46	2,750	549	2,086	115
Nebraska	4,354	4,324	4,117	339	3.9	27.8	55	252	3,778	664	2,913	202
Kansas	5,534	5,320	4,975	496	6.4	40.1	124	326	4,479	1,132	3,024	323
South	**6,417**	**6,155**	**5,983**	**802**	**11.3**	**45.2**	**236**	**510**	**5,181**	**1,286**	**3,339**	**557**
South Atlantic	**6,585**	**6,428**	**6,334**	**872**	**10.8**	**42.8**	**276**	**542**	**5,462**	**1,362**	**3,528**	**573**
Delaware	5,869	4,848	4,872	686	5.0	77.0	187	417	4,186	892	2,979	315
Maryland	6,209	6,225	6,107	998	12.7	44.0	435	506	5,109	1,133	3,293	683
District of Columbia [4] .	10,768	11,407	11,761	2,922	78.5	56.1	1,230	1,558	8,839	1,996	5,449	1,395
Virginia	4,607	4,299	4,116	372	8.3	32.1	142	190	3,743	668	2,790	286
West Virginia	2,663	2,610	2,533	208	6.9	20.1	43	139	2,324	599	1,564	162
North Carolina	5,889	5,802	5,652	679	11.3	34.3	192	441	4,973	1,516	3,169	289
South Carolina	6,179	5,893	5,903	1,023	10.3	52.3	187	773	4,880	1,309	3,227	344
Georgia	6,493	6,405	6,193	723	11.4	35.4	248	428	5,470	1,307	3,569	594
Florida	8,547	8,358	8,351	1,206	8.9	53.8	358	786	7,145	1,835	4,414	896
East South Central	**4,687**	**4,589**	**4,528**	**641**	**10.3**	**41.0**	**159**	**431**	**3,888**	**1,068**	**2,429**	**390**
Kentucky	3,358	3,324	3,260	463	6.6	34.3	90	331	2,797	740	1,841	216
Tennessee	5,367	5,136	5,240	766	10.2	49.9	220	486	4,474	1,183	2,700	591
Alabama	5,366	5,268	4,879	780	11.6	35.1	160	574	4,098	1,089	2,672	338
Mississippi	4,221	4,282	4,418	434	13.5	42.6	139	238	3,984	1,286	2,364	335
West South Central . . .	**7,118**	**6,589**	**6,228**	**779**	**12.7**	**51.3**	**213**	**502**	**5,449**	**1,284**	**3,542**	**624**
Arkansas	5,175	4,762	4,811	593	10.2	42.4	125	416	4,218	1,099	2,796	323
Louisiana	6,425	6,546	6,847	1,062	20.3	42.3	284	715	5,785	1,368	3,803	614
Oklahoma	5,669	5,432	5,294	635	8.4	49.3	122	455	4,659	1,235	2,944	481
Texas	7,819	7,058	6,439	762	11.9	55.0	224	471	5,677	1,297	3,687	692
West	**6,478**	**6,388**	**6,220**	**845**	**9.9**	**42.9**	**283**	**509**	**5,375**	**1,222**	**3,360**	**794**
Mountain	**6,125**	**6,012**	**5,929**	**589**	**6.4**	**43.5**	**130**	**410**	**5,340**	**1,117**	**3,708**	**516**
Montana	3,648	4,596	4,790	178	3.0	27.9	32	114	4,613	714	3,652	246
Idaho	4,196	3,996	3,845	282	2.9	35.3	17	227	3,563	669	2,711	183
Wyoming	4,389	4,575	4,163	286	3.4	34.3	17	231	3,877	643	3,079	155
Colorado	6,074	5,959	5,527	567	5.8	45.8	117	399	4,960	1,010	3,499	450
New Mexico	6,679	6,434	6,266	930	8.0	52.1	138	731	5,336	1,421	3,510	405
Arizona	7,406	7,029	7,432	715	8.6	37.8	163	506	6,717	1,466	4,387	864
Utah	5,608	5,659	5,237	301	3.1	44.6	59	195	4,936	791	3,903	242
Nevada	6,299	6,204	6,180	875	10.4	60.9	340	464	5,305	1,245	3,322	738
Pacific	**6,602**	**6,521**	**6,324**	**936**	**11.2**	**42.6**	**338**	**544**	**5,388**	**1,259**	**3,235**	**894**
Washington	6,304	6,173	5,952	515	5.2	64.4	137	308	5,438	1,067	3,914	456
Oregon	5,755	5,821	5,766	503	4.6	51.3	130	318	5,263	1,025	3,657	581
California	6,773	6,679	6,457	1,078	13.1	37.7	405	622	5,379	1,327	3,029	1,023
Alaska	5,702	5,570	5,568	761	9.0	83.8	122	546	4,807	817	3,539	451
Hawaii	5,970	6,112	6,277	261	3.8	33.6	104	120	6,016	1,136	4,429	451

[1] Includes nonnegligent manslaughter.　　[2] Forcible rape figures for 1991 to 1993 were estimated using the national rate of forcible rapes when grouped by like agencies as figures submitted were not in accordance with national Uniform Crime Reporting program guidelines.　　[3] Data for 1991 were not available; therefore, data presented are estimates.　　[4] Includes offenses reported by the police at the National Zoo.

Source: U.S. Federal Bureau of Investigation, *Crime in the United States,* annual.

No. 311. Crime Rates, by Type—Selected Large Cities: 1993

[**Offenses known to the police per 100,000 population.** Based on Bureau of the Census estimated resident population as of **July 1.** For definitions of crimes, see text, section 5]

CITY RANKED BY POPULATION SIZE, 1992 [1]	Crime index, total	VIOLENT CRIME					PROPERTY CRIME			
		Total	Murder	Forcible rape	Robbery	Aggravated assault	Total	Burglary	Larceny—theft	Motor vehicle theft
New York, NY	8,171	2,090	26.5	38.4	1,171	854	6,081	1,350	3,200	1,531
Los Angeles, CA	8,873	2,374	30.5	50.3	1,090	1,204	6,498	1,425	3,378	1,695
Chicago, IL	(2)	(2)	30.3	(2)	1,262	1,425	7,437	1,637	4,350	1,450
Houston, TX	8,188	1,454	25.9	64.3	625	739	6,734	1,567	3,571	1,596
Philadelphia, PA	6,262	1,255	28.1	50.3	739	437	5,007	969	2,512	1,525
San Diego, CA	7,343	1,160	11.5	34.1	401	714	6,183	1,257	3,262	1,665
Dallas, TX	10,627	1,743	30.4	95.9	712	905	8,884	2,012	5,197	1,675
Phoenix, AZ	9,282	1,146	15.2	42.7	331	757	8,136	1,984	4,655	1,498
Detroit, MI	(2)	(2)	56.8	(2)	1,332	1,274	9,212	2,264	4,198	2,751
San Antonio, TX	9,911	682	22.3	56.1	302	302	9,229	1,813	6,219	1,197
San Jose, CA	4,539	657	5.1	48.3	147	457	3,882	743	2,643	496
Indianapolis, IN	8,877	1,666	18.0	136.9	543	968	7,211	2,020	3,808	1,384
San Francisco, CA	9,524	1,815	17.5	49.0	1,148	600	7,709	1,515	4,693	1,501
Baltimore, MD	12,541	2,994	48.2	91.1	1,689	1,166	9,547	2,442	5,655	1,449
Jacksonville, FL	10,042	1,698	18.6	104.0	536	1,040	8,344	2,250	4,750	1,344
Columbus, OH	8,706	1,105	16.2	101.7	601	386	7,601	2,018	4,491	1,093
Milwaukee, WI	8,094	965	25.2	68.0	646	226	7,128	1,324	4,101	1,704
Memphis, TN	10,041	1,634	32.0	117.1	867	618	8,407	2,474	3,786	2,147
Washington, DC	11,755	2,922	78.5	56.1	1,230	1,558	8,834	1,995	5,444	1,395
Boston, MA	10,030	1,958	17.7	86.7	737	1,117	8,073	1,441	4,477	2,154
El Paso, TX	8,429	1,102	8.5	50.7	282	761	7,327	1,018	5,309	1,000
Seattle, WA	11,798	1,400	12.6	67.0	503	818	10,398	1,741	7,374	1,284
Cleveland, OH	7,910	1,643	33.0	164.9	850	596	6,267	1,588	2,668	2,011
Nashville-Davidson, TN	10,805	1,784	16.9	112.3	527	1,127	9,021	1,781	6,319	921
Austin, TX	10,252	600	7.4	54.0	310	229	9,652	1,684	7,101	868
New Orleans, LA	10,735	2,039	80.3	60.6	1,054	845	8,696	2,275	4,479	1,942
Denver, CO	7,985	1,054	14.8	78.9	374	586	6,931	1,832	3,583	1,516
Fort Worth, TX	10,748	1,506	28.7	109.4	594	775	9,241	2,267	5,678	1,296
Oklahoma City, OK	11,222	1,417	17.5	112.6	377	910	9,806	2,186	6,409	1,211
Portland, OR	11,380	1,857	12.8	105.3	507	1,232	9,523	1,725	5,939	1,860
Long Beach, CA	8,038	1,605	28.4	45.1	839	693	6,433	1,530	3,183	1,720
Kansas City, MO	12,669	2,517	35.1	118.3	894	1,470	10,152	2,780	5,423	1,949
Virginia Beach, VA	4,846	295	5.2	42.8	149	98	4,551	770	3,499	282
Charlotte, NC	11,767	2,300	28.9	84.2	763	1,424	9,467	2,528	6,236	703
Tucson, AZ	11,480	1,023	10.3	73.6	210	730	10,457	1,727	7,524	1,206
Albuquerque, NM	9,582	1,644	12.3	63.6	381	1,187	7,938	2,013	5,046	879
Atlanta, GA	17,354	4,041	50.4	122.1	1,501	2,368	13,313	3,269	7,757	2,288
St. Louis, MO	16,648	3,875	69.0	82.4	1,608	2,116	12,773	3,204	6,969	2,600
Sacramento, CA	10,210	1,254	22.0	43.2	597	592	8,956	2,089	4,828	2,039
Fresno, CA	10,944	1,450	22.9	56.8	758	613	9,494	2,230	3,821	3,443
Tulsa, OK	7,758	1,301	14.3	89.6	302	895	6,458	1,902	3,381	1,175
Oakland, CA	11,916	2,602	40.8	93.6	1,209	1,258	9,314	2,216	5,037	2,061
Honolulu, HI	6,443	286	3.5	32.7	124	126	6,157	1,062	4,586	509
Miami, FL	18,745	3,893	34.1	54.8	1,901	1,903	14,852	3,296	8,556	3,001
Pittsburgh, PA	7,765	1,216	21.7	61.3	756	377	6,550	1,251	3,533	1,766
Cincinnati, OH	8,442	1,536	10.6	123.6	636	765	6,906	1,680	4,663	564
Minneapolis, MN	(2)	(2)	15.8	(2)	867	744	9,268	2,552	5,442	1,274
Toledo, OH	8,588	963	13.6	107.7	481	361	7,625	1,660	4,602	1,363
Buffalo, NY	9,811	1,860	23.4	90.8	892	853	7,951	2,339	3,914	1,699
Wichita, KS	8,845	875	15.3	84.5	423	352	7,970	1,865	5,186	919
Mesa, AZ	7,925	766	2.0	36.4	135	593	7,158	1,531	4,736	892
Colorado Springs, CO	6,441	511	6.2	87.0	128	290	5,930	1,197	4,399	334
Las Vegas, NV	6,741	1,015	12.7	60.6	498	444	5,727	1,364	3,325	1,038
Santa Ana, CA	6,554	1,096	26.8	26.5	648	395	5,458	1,014	3,084	1,360
Tampa, FL	15,707	3,247	14.9	85.5	1,026	2,120	12,460	3,111	6,416	2,933
Arlington, TX	7,181	803	2.5	51.9	252	496	6,378	1,414	4,093	872
Anaheim, CA	6,732	704	11.9	25.3	328	339	6,028	1,423	3,302	1,302
Louisville, KY	6,335	996	13.5	49.3	509	424	5,339	1,537	2,952	850
St. Paul, MN	(2)	(2)	8.1	(2)	352	548	6,518	1,483	4,177	858
Newark, NJ	14,270	3,787	35.6	95.2	2,183	1,474	10,483	2,549	3,861	4,073
Corpus Christi, TX	10,092	819	12.5	71.4	187	548	9,273	1,693	6,964	616
Birmingham, AL	11,823	2,485	45.0	110.5	635	1,694	9,338	2,466	5,554	1,319
Norfolk, VA	8,621	1,075	24.1	79.2	554	417	7,546	1,449	5,254	844
Anchorage, AK	6,438	883	9.2	84.6	227	562	5,555	750	4,252	553
Aurora, CO	8,259	1,807	7.7	67.3	300	1,432	6,452	1,180	4,668	604
Riverside, CA	9,188	1,649	13.7	54.3	534	1,047	7,539	2,064	3,997	1,478
St. Petersburg, FL	9,644	2,167	8.0	73.7	670	1,415	7,477	2,022	4,913	541
Rochester, NY	10,846	1,149	27.2	67.6	696	358	9,697	2,694	5,747	1,255
Lexington-Fayette, KY	6,653	919	3.4	59.1	237	619	5,734	1,356	4,119	260
Jersey City, NJ	8,146	1,991	8.7	43.4	1,086	853	6,156	1,819	2,749	1,587
Baton Rouge, LA	16,195	3,025	32.8	78.5	827	2,086	13,170	3,344	8,050	1,776
Akron, OH	7,205	946	8.4	90.7	373	474	6,259	1,496	3,855	908
Raleigh, NC	6,809	906	12.1	42.0	355	497	5,903	1,315	4,193	394
Stockton, CA	11,200	1,578	20.3	70.8	700	786	9,622	2,417	5,540	1,666

[1] Crime data are not available for Omaha, NE in 1993.   [2] The rates for forcible rape, violent crime, and crime index are not shown because the forcible rape figures were not in accordance with national Uniform Crime Reporting guidelines.

Source: U.S. Federal Bureau of Investigation, *Crime in the United States,* annual.

No. 312. Murder—Circumstances and Weapons Used or Cause of Death: 1980 to 1993

[In percents, except as indicated. Based solely on police investigation. For definition of murder, see text, section 5]

CHARACTERISTIC	1980	1990	1992	1993	CHARACTERISTIC	1980	1990	1992	1993
Murders, total	**21,860**	**20,273**	**22,716**	**23,271**	Other motives	20.6	19.4	19.2	21.7
Percent distribution	100.0	100.0	100.0	100.0	Unknown	15.1	24.8	27.6	27.7
CIRCUMSTANCES					TYPE OF WEAPON OR CAUSE OF DEATH				
Felonies, total	17.7	20.8	21.6	19.1					
Robbery	10.8	9.2	10.0	9.9	Guns	62.4	64.3	68.2	69.6
Narcotics	1.7	6.7	5.7	5.5	Handguns	45.8	49.8	55.4	56.9
Sex offenses	1.5	1.1	0.9	0.7	Cutting or stabbing	19.3	17.4	14.5	12.7
Other felonies	3.7	3.7	5.0	3.0	Blunt objects [1]	5.0	5.4	4.6	4.4
Suspected felonies	6.7	0.7	1.2	0.6	Personal weapons [2]	5.9	5.5	5.0	5.0
Argument, total	39.9	34.4	30.3	30.8	Strangulations,				
Property or money	2.6	2.5	2.1	1.9	asphyxiations	2.3	2.0	1.9	1.9
Romantic triangle	2.3	2.0	1.5	1.9	Fire	1.3	1.4	0.9	0.9
Other arguments	35.0	29.8	26.7	27.0	All other [3]	3.8	4.0	5.0	5.5

[1] Refers to club, hammer, etc. [2] Hands, fists, feet, etc. [3] Includes poison, drowning, explosives, narcotics, and unknown.
Source: U.S. Federal Bureau of Investigation, *Crime in the United States,* annual.

No. 313. Murder Victims, by Age, Sex, and Race: 1993

AGE	Total	Sex			Race			
		Male	Female	Unknown	White	Black	Other	Unknown
Total	**23,271**	**17,949**	**5,278**	**44**	**10,709**	**11,795**	**563**	**204**
Percent distribution	100.0	77.1	22.7	0.2	46.0	50.7	2.4	0.9
Under 18 yrs. old	2,697	1,933	761	3	1,187	1,411	81	18
18 yrs. old and over	20,250	15,800	4,441	9	9,387	10,266	473	124
Infant (under 1 yr. old)	272	150	120	2	135	118	10	9
1 to 4 yrs. old	459	258	200	1	217	225	16	1
5 to 9 yrs. old	173	84	89	-	101	61	10	1
10 to 14 yrs. old	387	258	129	-	185	194	8	-
15 to 19 yrs. old	3,084	2,652	432	-	1,125	1,857	81	21
20 to 24 yrs. old	4,355	3,667	684	4	1,597	2,656	78	24
25 to 29 yrs. old	3,466	2,729	736	1	1,451	1,921	74	20
30 to 34 yrs. old	3,083	2,338	745	-	1,444	1,541	86	12
35 to 39 yrs. old	2,318	1,767	550	1	1,143	1,108	56	11
40 to 44 yrs. old	1,620	1,226	394	-	800	753	52	15
45 to 49 yrs. old	1,077	825	252	-	649	389	28	11
50 to 54 yrs. old	717	549	166	2	443	244	21	9
55 to 59 yrs. old	465	352	112	1	299	149	13	4
60 to 64 yrs. old	393	285	108	-	253	130	9	1
65 to 69 yrs. old	319	210	109	-	209	102	7	1
70 to 74 yrs. old	292	171	121	-	194	93	4	1
75 yrs. old and over	467	212	255	-	329	136	1	1
Age unknown	324	216	76	32	135	118	9	62

- Represents zero.
Source: U.S. Federal Bureau of Investigation, *Crime in the United States,* annual.

No. 314. Homicide Victims, by Race and Sex: 1970 to 1992

[Rates per 100,000 resident population in specified group. Excludes deaths to nonresidents of United States. Beginning 1980, deaths classified according to the ninth revision of the *International Classification of Diseases;* for earlier years, classified according to revision in use at the time; see text, section 2. See also *Historical Statistics, Colonial Times to 1970,* series H 971-978]

YEAR	HOMICIDE VICTIMS					HOMICIDE RATE [2]				
	Total [1]	White		Black		Total [1]	White		Black	
		Male	Female	Male	Female		Male	Female	Male	Female
1970	16,848	5,865	1,938	7,265	1,569	8.3	6.8	2.1	67.6	13.3
1980	24,278	10,381	3,177	8,385	1,898	10.7	10.9	3.2	66.6	13.5
1981	23,646	9,941	3,125	8,312	1,825	10.3	10.4	3.1	64.8	12.7
1982	22,358	9,260	3,179	7,730	1,743	9.6	9.6	3.1	59.1	12.0
1983	20,191	8,355	2,880	6,822	1,672	8.6	8.6	2.8	51.4	11.3
1984	19,796	8,171	2,956	6,563	1,677	8.4	8.3	2.9	48.7	11.2
1985	19,893	8,122	3,041	6,616	1,666	8.3	8.2	2.9	48.4	11.0
1986	21,731	8,567	3,123	7,634	1,861	9.0	8.6	3.0	55.0	12.1
1987	21,103	7,979	3,149	7,518	1,969	8.7	7.9	3.0	53.3	12.6
1988	22,032	7,994	3,072	8,314	2,089	9.0	7.9	2.9	58.0	13.2
1989	22,909	8,337	2,971	8,888	2,074	9.2	8.2	2.8	61.1	12.9
1990	24,932	9,147	3,006	9,981	2,163	10.0	9.0	2.8	69.2	13.5
1991	26,513	9,581	3,201	10,628	2,330	10.5	9.3	3.0	72.0	14.2
1992	25,488	9,456	3,012	10,131	2,187	10.0	9.1	2.8	67.5	13.1

[1] Includes races not shown separately. [2] Rate based on enumerated population figures as of April 1 for 1970, 1980, and 1990; July 1 estimates for other years.
Source: U.S. National Center for Health Statistics, *Vital Statistics of the United States,* annual, and unpublished data.

No. 315. Forcible Rape—Number and Rate: 1970 to 1993

[For definition of rape, see text, section 5]

ITEM	1970	1980	1985	1987	1988	1989	1990	1991	1992	1993
NUMBER										
Total	**37,990**	**82,990**	**88,670**	**91,110**	**92,490**	**94,500**	**102,560**	**106,590**	**109,060**	**104,810**
By force	26,888	63,599	71,060	73,456	75,441	78,411	86,541	91,522	93,825	91,315
Attempt	11,102	19,391	17,610	17,654	17,049	16,089	16,019	15,068	15,235	13,495
RATE										
Per 100,000 population	18.7	36.8	37.1	37.4	37.6	38.1	41.2	42.3	42.8	40.6
Per 100,000 females	30.4	71.6	72.3	73.0	73.4	74.3	80.5	82.5	83.5	79.4
Per 100,000 females 12 years old and over	46.3	86.3	86.6	87.5	88.1	89.3	96.6	100.9	100.5	95 6
AVERAGE ANNUAL PERCENT CHANGE IN RATE [1]										
Per 100,000 population	(NA)	6.1	3.9	−1.3	0.5	1.3	8.1	2.7	1.2	−5.1
Per 100,000 females 12 years old and over	(NA)	6.0	4.3	−1.2	0.7	1.4	8.2	4.5	−0.4	−4.9

NA Not available. [1] Represents annual average from prior year shown except for 1980, from 1979; for 1985, from 1984; and for 1987, from 1986.

No. 316. Robbery and Property Crimes, by Type and Selected Characteristic: 1980 to 1993

[For definition of crime, see text, section 5]

ITEM	NUMBER OF OFFENSES (1,000)				RATE PER 100,000 INHABITANTS				AVERAGE VALUE LOST (dol.)	
	1980	1990	1992	1993	1980	1990	1992	1993	1992	1993
Robbery, total [1]	**566**	**639**	**672**	**660**	**251.1**	**257.0**	**263.6**	**255.8**	**$840**	**$815**
Type of crime:										
Street or highway	293	359	374	361	130.1	144.2	146.7	139.9	672	628
Commercial house	78	73	80	82	34.6	29.5	31.3	31.9	1,380	1,304
Gas station	23	18	17	15	10.4	7.1	6.6	6.0	513	515
Convenience store	38	39	35	35	17.0	15.6	13.8	13.5	402	449
Residence	60	62	68	68	26.8	25.1	26.5	26.3	1,123	1,104
Bank	8	9	11	12	3.8	3.8	4.4	4.6	3,325	3,308
Weapon used:										
Firearm	228	234	271	280	101.3	94.1	106.2	108.4	(NA)	(NA)
Knife or cutting instrument	73	76	71	66	32.3	30.7	27.8	25.5	(NA)	(NA)
Other dangerous weapon	51	61	64	62	22.8	24.5	25.2	24.2	(NA)	(NA)
Strongarm	214	268	267	252	94.8	107.7	104.5	97.7	(NA)	(NA)
Burglary, total	**3,795**	**3,074**	**2,980**	**2,835**	**1,684.1**	**1,235.9**	**1,168.2**	**1,099.2**	**1,278**	**1,185**
Forcible entry	2,789	2,150	2,049	1,932	1,237.5	864.5	803.3	749.3	(NA)	(NA)
Unlawful entry	711	678	692	676	315.6	272.8	271.2	262.2	(NA)	(NA)
Attempted forcible entry	295	245	239	226	131.0	98.7	93.7	87.7	(NA)	(NA)
Residence	2,525	2,033	1,973	1,884	1,120.6	817.4	773.4	730.5	1,215	1,189
Nonresidence	1,270	1,041	1,007	951	563.5	418.5	394.8	368.7	1,400	1,179
Occurred during the night	1,508	1,135	1,099	1,032	669.0	456.4	431.0	400.2	(NA)	(NA)
Occurred during the day	1,263	1,151	1,123	1,070	560.3	462.8	440.1	414.9	(NA)	(NA)
Larceny-theft, total	**7,137**	**7,946**	**7,915**	**7,821**	**3,167.0**	**3,194.8**	**3,103.0**	**3,032.4**	**483**	**504**
Pocket picking	85	81	78	73	37.9	32.4	30.7	28.2	430	411
Purse snatching	107	82	75	68	47.5	32.8	29.3	26.5	292	341
Shoplifting	773	1,291	1,254	1,201	343.0	519.1	491.5	465.6	106	109
From motor vehicles	1,231	1,744	1,792	1,828	546.4	701.3	702.7	708.6	555	531
Motor vehicle accessories	1,366	1,185	1,107	1,091	606.2	476.3	434.0	423.0	297	303
Bicycles	715	443	469	478	317.5	178.2	183.7	185.5	231	241
From buildings	1,187	1,118	1,107	1,029	526.9	449.4	433.9	399.0	802	831
From coin-operated machines	58	63	72	62	25.8	25.4	28.3	23.9	141	208
Other	1,613	1,940	1,961	1,991	715.7	780.0	768.9	772.0	665	740
Motor vehicles, total [2]	**1,132**	**1,636**	**1,611**	**1,561**	**502.2**	**657.8**	**631.5**	**605.3**	**4,713**	**4,808**
Automobiles	845	1,304	1,282	1,236	374.8	524.3	502.5	479.2	(NA)	(NA)
Trucks and buses	149	238	243	240	66.1	95.5	95.1	93.0	(NA)	(NA)

NA Not available. [1] Includes other crimes not shown separately. [2] Includes other types of motor vehicles not shown separately.

Source of tables 315 and 316: U.S. Federal Bureau of Investigation, *Population-at-Risk Rates and Selected Crime Indicators,* annual.

No. 317. Number and Rate of Victimizations for Crimes Against Persons and Households, by Type: 1973 to 1992

[Data based on National Crime Victimization Survey; see text, section 5, and Appendix III]

YEAR	PERSONAL SECTOR								HOUSEHOLD SECTOR			
	Total	Violent crimes						Larce-ny—theft	Total	Bur-glary	Lar-ceny	Motor vehi-cle theft
		Total	Rape	Rob-bery	Assault							
					Total	Aggra-vated	Simple					
NUMBER (1,000)												
1973	20,322	5,351	156	1,108	4,087	1,655	2,432	14,971	15,340	6,459	7,537	1,344
1975	21,867	5,573	154	1,147	4,272	1,631	2,641	16,294	17,400	6,744	9,223	1,433
1980	21,430	6,130	174	1,209	4,747	1,707	3,041	15,300	18,821	6,973	10,468	1,381
1981	22,445	6,582	178	1,381	5,024	1,796	3,228	15,863	19,009	7,394	10,176	1,439
1982	22,012	6,459	153	1,334	4,973	1,754	3,219	15,553	17,744	6,663	9,705	1,377
1983	20,561	5,903	154	1,149	4,600	1,517	3,083	14,657	16,440	6,063	9,114	1,264
1984	19,743	5,954	180	1,117	4,657	1,673	2,984	13,789	15,733	5,643	8,750	1,340
1985	19,296	5,823	138	985	4,699	1,605	3,094	13,474	15,568	5,594	8,703	1,270
1986	18,751	5,515	130	1,009	4,376	1,543	2,833	13,235	15,368	5,557	8,455	1,356
1987	19,371	5,796	148	1,046	4,602	1,587	3,014	13,575	15,966	5,705	8,788	1,473
1988	19,966	5,910	127	1,048	4,734	1,741	2,993	14,056	15,830	5,777	8,419	1,634
1989	19,691	5,861	135	1,092	4,634	1,665	2,969	13,829	16,128	5,352	8,955	1,820
1990	18,984	6,009	130	1,150	4,729	1,601	3,128	12,975	15,419	5,148	8,304	1,968
1991	19,472	6,587	174	1,203	5,210	1,634	3,575	12,885	16,025	5,187	8,702	2,136
1992	18,832	6,621	141	1,226	5,255	1,849	3,406	12,211	14,817	4,757	8,101	1,959
RATE [1]												
1973	123.6	32.6	1.0	6.7	24.9	10.1	14.8	91.1	217.8	91.7	107.0	19.1
1975	128.9	32.8	0.9	6.8	25.2	9.6	15.6	96.0	236.5	91.7	125.4	19.5
1980	116.3	33.3	0.9	6.6	25.8	9.3	16.5	83.0	227.4	84.3	126.5	16.7
1981	120.4	35.3	1.0	7.4	27.0	9.6	17.3	85.1	226.0	87.9	121.0	17.1
1982	116.8	34.3	0.8	7.1	26.4	9.3	17.1	82.5	208.2	78.2	113.9	16.2
1983	107.9	31.0	0.8	6.0	24.1	8.0	16.2	76.9	189.8	70.0	105.2	14.6
1984	102.8	31.0	0.9	5.8	24.3	8.7	15.5	71.8	178.7	64.1	99.4	15.2
1985	99.4	30.0	0.7	5.1	24.2	8.3	15.9	69.4	174.4	62.7	97.5	14.2
1986	95.6	28.1	0.7	5.1	22.3	7.9	14.4	67.5	170.0	61.5	93.5	15.0
1987	98.0	29.3	0.8	5.3	23.3	8.0	15.2	68.7	173.9	62.1	95.7	16.0
1988	100.1	29.6	0.6	5.3	23.7	8.7	15.0	70.5	169.6	61.9	90.2	17.5
1989	97.8	29.1	0.7	5.4	23.0	8.3	14.7	68.7	169.9	56.4	94.4	19.2
1990	93.4	29.6	0.6	5.7	23.3	7.9	15.4	63.8	161.0	53.8	86.7	20.5
1991	95.3	32.2	0.9	5.9	25.5	8.0	17.5	63.1	166.4	53.9	90.4	22.2
1992	91.2	32.1	0.7	5.9	25.5	9.0	16.5	59.2	152.2	48.9	83.2	20.1

[1] Rate per 1,000 persons, 12 years old and over, and per 1,000 households.

Source: U.S. Bureau of Justice Statistics, *Criminal Victimization in the United States,* annual.

No. 318. Personal Crimes—Victimization Rate, by Type of Crime and Characteristic: 1992

[Rate per 1,000 persons age 12 years or older. Based on the National Crime Victimization Survey; see text, section 5, and Appendix III]

ITEM	Total	Rape	Robbery	Assault			Larceny—theft
				Total	Aggra-vated	Simple	
Total	**91.2**	**0.7**	**5.9**	**25.5**	**9.0**	**16.5**	**59.2**
Male	101.4	0.6	8.1	30.1	12.0	18.1	62.6
Female	81.8	0.8	3.9	21.1	6.1	15.0	55.9
12 to 15 yrs. old	171.0	1.1	9.8	64.8	20.1	44.7	95.3
16 to 19 yrs. old	172.7	1.6	15.4	60.9	26.3	34.5	94.8
20 to 24 yrs. old	177.0	2.6	11.4	56.0	18.1	38.0	106.9
25 to 34 yrs. old	111.1	0.5	7.7	29.4	9.3	20.1	73.4
35 to 49 yrs. old	75.1	0.4	3.8	17.1	6.8	10.2	53.9
50 to 64 yrs. old	43.3	0.1	2.8	7.1	2.3	4.8	33.3
65 yrs. old and over	21.1	0.2	1.5	3.1	1.3	1.8	16.3
White	88.7	0.6	4.7	24.6	7.8	16.8	58.8
Black	110.8	1.3	15.6	33.5	18.3	15.2	60.4
Other	88.3	-	5.1	18.6	5.3	13.3	64.6
Hispanic	100.1	0.6	10.6	26.9	10.0	16.8	61.9
Non-Hispanic	90.3	0.7	5.4	25.3	8.9	16.4	58.9

- Represents or rounds to zero.

Source: U.S. Bureau of Justice Statistics, *Criminal Victimization in the United States*, annual.

No. 319. Crime Incidents, by Place and Time of Occurrence and Injury: 1992

INCIDENT CHARACTERISTICS	Rape	ROBBERY			ASSAULT			Personal larceny with contact
		Total	Completed	Attempted	Total	Aggravated	Simple assault	
Incidents, total	131,530	1,113,300	741,590	371,710	4,719,250	1,594,210	3,125,030	478,170
PERCENT DISTRIBUTION								
Place of occurrence	100.0	100.0	100.0	100.0	100.0	100.0	100.0	100.0
Inside own home	[1]16.3	10.1	9.4	11.6	12.4	9.8	13.7	[1]1.4
Near own home, on the street near home	[1]12.4	11.0	10.9	11.3	11.7	14.0	10.5	[1]5.2
Friend's, relative's, or neighbor's home . .	[1]14.1	[1]3.1	[1]3.1	[1]3.0	8.3	9.2	7.9	[1]4.3
Inside commercial property	[1]1.5	4.2	[1]3.8	[1]5.0	12.2	9.1	13.7	23.2
In parking lot or garage	[1]6.5	13.6	12.2	16.3	7.3	8.0	7.0	[1]3.0
Inside school, on school property	[1]7.9	3.9	[1]3.6	[1]4.4	14.1	8.1	17.1	8.6
In park, field, or playground	[1]8.5	6.4	6.6	[1]5.8	4.4	5.1	4.1	[1]1.5
On street not near own or friend's home .	[1]25.9	39.7	44.8	29.5	20.6	27.6	17.1	31.9
Other	[1]6.9	8.0	5.5	13.0	9.0	9.1	9.0	20.9
Time of occurrence:								
Daytime (6 a.m. to 6 p.m.)	40.3	39.5	41.3	35.8	50.2	42.6	54.0	62.9
Nighttime	59.7	58.9	56.7	63.5	49.5	57.4	45.4	35.3
Percent of incidents:								
Involving the presence of a weapon	27.6	54.0	55.4	51.2	31.8	94.1	(X)	(X)
Resulting in victim injury	(NA)	35.7	41.4	24.7	29.7	35.6	26.6	(X)

NA Not available.   X Not applicable.   [1] Estimate based on about 10 or fewer sample cases.

Source: U.S. Bureau of Justice Statistics, *Criminal Victimization in the United States,* annual.

No. 320. Handgun Crime Victimization Rate, by Sex, Race, and Age: 1987-92 Period

[Number of victimizations rates per 1,000 population. Rates do not include murder or nonnegligent manslaughter committed with handguns. Based on National Crime Victimization Survey; see text, section 5, and Appendix III]

AGE OF VICTIM	MALE VICTIMS			FEMALE VICTIMS		
	Total[1]	White	Black	Total[1]	White	Black
All ages	**4.9**	**3.7**	**14.2**	**2.1**	**1.6**	**5.8**
12 to 15 yrs. old	5.0	3.1	14.1	2.5	2.1	4.7
16 to 19 yrs. old	14.2	9.5	39.7	5.1	3.6	13.4
20 to 24 yrs. old	11.8	9.2	29.4	4.3	3.5	9.1
25 to 34 yrs. old	5.7	4.9	12.3	3.1	2.1	9.0
35 to 49 yrs. old	3.3	2.7	8.7	1.7	1.4	3.3
50 to 64 yrs. old	1.5	1.2	3.5	0.8	0.7	1.6
65 yrs. old and older	0.8	0.6	3.7	0.3	0.2	2.3

[1] Includes persons of other races not shown separately.

Source: U.S. Bureau of Justice Statistics, *Guns and Crime,* Crime Data Brief, NCJ-147003.

No. 321. Households Touched by Crime, 1990 and 1992, and by Characteristic, 1992

[A household is considered "touched by crime" if during the year it experienced a burglary, auto theft or household theft, or if a household member was raped, robbed, or assaulted, or a victim of personal theft, no matter where the crime occurred. Data based on the National Crime Victimization Survey; see text, section 5, and Appendix III]

TYPE OF CRIME	1990		1992						
	Number (1,000)	Percent touched	Number (1,000)	Percent touched					
				Total[1]	White	Black	Urban	Suburban	Rural
Total [2]	22,652	23.7	22,093	22.6	21.9	27.2	28.1	21.4	16.9
Violent crime	4,478	4.7	4,888	5.0	4.8	7.1	6.4	4.6	3.8
Rape	104	0.1	149	0.2	0.2	0.1	0.2	0.1	0.1
Robbery	967	1.0	998	1.0	0.9	2.2	1.8	0.7	0.4
Assault	3,591	3.8	3,975	4.1	4.0	5.1	4.7	3.9	3.5
Theft	15,905	16.7	15,343	15.7	15.5	17.1	19.5	15.0	11.4
Burglary	4,557	4.8	4,116	4.2	4.0	5.8	5.0	3.8	3.7
Motor vehicle theft	1,825	1.9	1,947	2.0	1.8	3.3	3.2	1.8	0.6

[1] Includes other races not shown separately.   [2] Types of crime will not add to "total" since each household may report as many crime categories as experienced.

Source: U.S. Bureau of Justice Statistics, *Crime and the Nation's Households, 1992.*

No. 322. Persons Arrested, by Charge and Race: 1993

[Represents arrests (not charges) reported by 10,509 agencies with a total 1993 population 213,093,000 as estimated by FBI]

OFFENSE CHARGED	TOTAL ARRESTS (1,000)					PERCENT DISTRIBUTION				
	Total	White	Black	American Indian or Alaskan Native	Asian or Pacific Islander	Total	White	Black	American Indian or Alaskan Native	Asian or Pacific Islander
Total	11,742	7,855	3,647	126	113	100.0	66.9	31.1	1.1	1.0
Serious crimes [1]	2,419	1,482	884	23	31	100.0	61.3	36.5	0.9	1.3
Murder and nonnegligent manslaughter	20	8	12	(Z)	(Z)	100.0	40.7	57.6	0.6	1.1
Forcible rape	32	18	13	(Z)	(Z)	100.0	56.9	41.3	1.0	0.8
Robbery.	153	56	95	1	2	100.0	36.5	62.1	0.4	1.0
Aggravated assault	441	258	176	4	4	100.0	58.4	39.8	0.9	1.0
Burglary.	338	227	104	3	4	100.0	67.2	30.9	0.9	1.0
Larceny/theft.	1,249	807	412	13	18	100.0	64.6	33.0	1.0	1.4
Motor vehicle theft.	169	96	68	2	3	100.0	57.1	40.3	0.9	1.7
Arson	16	12	4	(Z)	(Z)	100.0	74.6	23.5	0.9	0.9
All other nonserious crimes:										
Other assaults	963	606	336	12	9	100.0	62.9	34.9	1.2	1.0
Forgery and counterfeiting. . . .	89	56	32	1	1	100.0	63.0	35.4	0.6	1.0
Fraud	335	209	123	2	2	100.0	62.3	36.6	0.5	0.7
Embezzlement	11	7	3	(Z)	(Z)	100.0	67.4	31.0	0.4	1.2
Stolen property—buying, receiving, possessing	135	75	57	1	1	100.0	56.1	42.3	0.6	1.1
Vandalism	261	195	60	3	3	100.0	74.8	22.9	1.1	1.2
Weapons; carrying, possessing, etc.	224	124	96	1	2	100.0	55.4	43.0	0.5	1.1
Prostitution and commer- cialized vice	89	55	32	1	1	100.0	62.0	35.9	0.6	1.5
Sex offenses (except forcible rape and prostitution)	88	67	18	1	1	100.0	77.0	20.9	1.0	1.1
Drug abuse violations.	968	578	380	4	5	100.0	59.8	39.3	0.4	0.5
Gambling.	15	7	7	(Z)	1	100.0	48.2	46.9	0.4	4.6
Offenses against family and children	89	58	28	1	2	100.0	65.6	31.2	1.3	2.0
Driving under the influence . . .	1,227	1,070	130	16	11	100.0	87.2	10.6	1.3	0.9
Liquor laws.	417	353	53	10	3	100.0	84.5	12.6	2.3	0.6
Drunkenness	604	482	108	13	2	100.0	79.7	17.8	2.1	0.3
Disorderly conduct.	607	392	204	8	3	100.0	64.6	33.6	1.3	0.5
Vagrancy.	25	14	10	(Z)	(Z)	100.0	56.6	41.2	1.9	0.4
All other offenses (except traffic)	2,928	1,833	1,039	28	27	100.0	62.6	35.5	1.0	0.9
Suspicion.	12	6	6	(Z)	(Z)	100.0	46.9	52.0	0.6	0.5
Curfew and loitering law violations	85	67	15	1	2	100.0	78.8	18.1	1.1	2.0
Runaways	151	118	26	2	5	100.0	78.1	17.2	1.3	3.4

Z Less than 500.   [1] Includes arson.
Source: U.S. Federal Bureau of Investigation, *Crime in the United States*, annual.

No. 323. Juvenile Arrests for Selected Offenses: 1970 to 1993

[Juveniles are persons between the ages 10-17]

OFFENSE	1970	1975	1980	1985	1988	1989	1990	1991	1992	1993
Number of contributing agencies . .	5,073	7,528	8,178	11,263	10,077	10,502	10,765	10,148	11,058	10,277
Population covered (1,000)	145,014	156,854	169,439	206,269	192,275	199,098	204,543	189,962	217,754	213,705
NUMBER										
Violent crime, total.	54,860	76,131	77,220	75,077	71,251	84,551	97,103	95,677	118,358	122,434
Murder.	1,350	1,373	1,475	1,384	1,827	2,204	2,661	2,626	3,025	3,473
Forcible rape.	3,233	3,457	3,668	5,073	4,278	4,691	4,971	4,766	5,451	5,490
Robbery.	29,363	39,388	38,529	31,833	25,459	30,728	34,944	35,632	42,639	44,598
Aggravated assault	20,914	31,913	33,548	36,787	39,687	46,928	54,527	52,653	67,243	68,873
Weapon law violations	17,111	19,341	21,203	27,035	27,473	31,480	33,123	37,575	49,903	54,414
Drug abuse, total	71,517	136,996	86,685	78,660	72,303	86,757	66,300	58,603	73,232	90,618
Sale and manufacturing	([1])	([1])	13,004	14,846	23,174	33,652	24,575	22,929	25,331	27,635
Heroin/cocaine.	10,041	4,902	1,318	2,851	14,914	19,760	17,511	16,915	17,881	18,716
Marijuana	35,818	95,027	8,876	8,646	4,811	6,781	4,372	3,579	4,853	6,144
Synthetic narcotics	8,971	3,010	465	414	846	701	346	570	663	455
Dangerous nonnarcotic drugs .	16,687	34,057	2,345	2,935	2,603	6,410	2,346	1,865	1,934	2,320
Possession.	([1])	([1])	73,681	63,814	49,129	53,105	41,725	35,674	47,901	62,983
Heroin/cocaine.	([1])	([1])	2,614	7,809	15,754	19,745	19,194	13,747	16,855	17,726
Marijuana	([1])	([1])	64,465	50,582	28,885	27,253	20,940	16,490	25,004	37,915
Synthetic narcotics	([1])	([1])	1,524	1,085	1,096	1,115	1,155	885	897	1,008
Dangerous nonnarcotic drugs .	([1])	([1])	5,078	4,338	3,394	4,992	4,436	4,552	5,145	6,334

[1] Prior to 1976, drug abuse arrests were collected with no distinctions between the present day classifications of sales/manufacturing and possession.
Source: U.S. Federal Bureau of Investigation, *Crime in the United States*, annual.

No. 324. Persons Arrested, by Charge, Sex, and Age: 1993

[Represents arrests (not charges) reported by 10,512 agencies (reporting 12 months) with a total 1993 population of 214 million as estimated by FBI]

CHARGE	Total (1,000)	PERCENT DISTRIBUTION							
		Male	Under 15 years	Under 18 years	18-24 years	25-44 years	45-54 years	55-64 years	65 yr. and over
Total arrests	11,766	80.5	6.0	17.1	27.5	47.6	5.4	1.7	0.7
Serious crimes [1]	2,423	77.3	11.9	29.3	25.9	38.9	3.9	1.2	0.7
Murder and nonnegligent manslaughter	20	90.6	1.9	16.2	41.2	35.6	4.5	1.6	0.9
Forcible rape	33	98.7	6.4	16.3	26.7	48.8	5.4	2.0	0.8
Robbery	154	91.3	8.1	28.2	33.7	36.2	1.6	0.2	0.1
Aggravated assault	442	84.3	4.9	15.3	26.8	49.9	5.5	1.7	0.8
Burglary [2]	338	90.1	13.9	34.3	28.5	34.7	2.0	0.4	0.1
Larceny—theft	1,251	67.3	14.1	31.3	23.4	38.2	4.4	1.5	1.1
Motor vehicle theft	169	88.2	13.2	44.6	28.7	25.0	1.4	0.3	0.1
Arson	16	85.3	32.3	49.3	17.0	28.0	3.7	1.3	0.6
All other nonserious crimes	9,343	81.4	4.4	14.0	27.9	49.8	5.8	1.8	0.7
Other assaults	965	82.1	6.7	16.2	24.8	51.8	5.2	1.5	0.6
Forgery and counterfeiting	89	65.3	1.2	7.3	32.8	54.6	4.2	0.9	0.3
Fraud	336	59.4	1.2	4.8	27.4	58.8	6.7	1.7	0.6
Embezzlement	11	59.5	0.7	5.6	34.1	51.7	6.3	1.8	0.4
Stolen property [3]	135	87.1	7.7	27.0	34.0	35.3	2.8	0.7	0.2
Vandalism	261	87.8	21.9	45.6	24.2	27.1	2.2	0.6	0.3
Weapons (carrying, etc.)	224	92.2	7.1	23.3	35.9	34.7	4.1	1.4	0.6
Prostitution and commercialized vice	89	35.7	0.2	1.1	24.0	68.6	4.4	1.3	0.6
Sex offenses [4]	88	91.4	9.7	18.7	19.2	47.8	8.4	3.7	2.2
Drug abuse violations	969	83.8	1.5	9.6	31.9	53.8	3.8	0.7	0.2
Gambling	15	86.0	1.4	7.6	20.7	43.2	15.2	8.9	4.3
Offenses against family and children	89	80.7	1.4	4.4	21.7	65.2	6.7	1.5	0.5
Driving under the influence	1,230	85.9	(Z)	0.9	22.2	62.3	9.8	3.5	1.3
Liquor laws	419	80.7	2.3	21.9	52.0	21.1	3.3	1.3	0.5
Drunkenness	605	88.9	0.3	2.3	20.8	60.5	10.8	4.0	1.5
Disorderly conduct	607	79.3	6.7	20.0	30.3	42.9	4.7	1.4	0.7
Vagrancy	25	87.7	3.7	13.0	21.3	52.3	9.9	2.6	0.9
Suspicion	12	84.6	3.7	11.4	27.8	54.3	5.0	1.2	0.4
Curfew, loitering (juveniles)	85	71.9	30.3	100.0	(X)	(X)	(X)	(X)	(X)
Runaways (juveniles)	152	42.8	44.5	100.0	(X)	(X)	(X)	(X)	(X)
All other offenses, except traffic	2,935	82.1	3.0	10.9	29.7	51.7	5.4	1.6	0.7

X Not applicable. Z Less than .05 percent. [1] Includes arson arrests, a newly established index offense in 1979. [2] Breaking or entering. [3] Buying, receiving, possessing. [4] Excludes forcible rape and prostitution, shown separately.

Source: U.S. Federal Bureau of Investigation, *Crime in the United States,* annual.

No. 325. Drug Use by Arrestees in 24 U.S. Cities, by Type of Drug and Sex: 1992

[Percent testing positive]

CITY	MALE				FEMALE			
	Any drug [1]	Mari- juana	Cocaine	Heroin	Any drug [1]	Mari- juana	Cocaine	Heroin
Atlanta, GA	69	22	58	4	65	13	58	5
Birmingham, AL	64	22	49	3	59	13	46	4
Chicago, IL	69	26	56	19	(NA)	(NA)	(NA)	(NA)
Cleveland, OH	64	17	53	3	74	11	66	5
Dallas, TX	59	28	41	4	66	24	48	8
Denver, CO	60	34	38	2	61	19	50	5
Detroit, MI	58	27	37	8	72	11	62	15
Fort Lauderdale, FL	64	32	46	1	62	21	47	3
Houston, TX	59	24	41	3	54	12	44	4
Indianapolis, IN	52	35	23	4	50	26	25	7
Kansas City, MO	60	28	41	2	73	18	62	3
Los Angeles, CA	67	23	52	10	72	13	58	13
Manhattan, NY	77	22	62	18	85	12	72	24
Miami, FL	68	30	56	2	(NA)	(NA)	(NA)	(NA)
New Orleans, LA	60	19	49	4	52	8	44	6
Omaha, NE	48	38	16	2	(NA)	(NA)	(NA)	(NA)
Philadelphia, PA	78	26	63	12	78	15	67	11
Phoenix, AZ	47	22	26	5	63	15	49	15
Portland, OR	60	28	35	11	73	17	54	22
St. Louis, MO	64	21	50	7	70	11	62	7
San Antonio, TX	54	28	32	15	44	16	25	14
San Diego, CA	77	35	45	16	72	25	37	17
San Jose, CA	50	24	28	4	56	18	32	9
Washington, DC	60	20	44	11	72	8	64	19

NA Not available. [1] Includes other drugs not shown separately.

Source: U.S. National Institute of Justice, *Drug Use Forecasting,* annual.

No. 326. Drug Arrest Rates for Drug Abuse Violations, 1980 to 1993, and by Region, 1993

[Rate per 100,000 inhabitants. Based on Bureau of the Census estimated resident population as of **July 1**, except **1980** and **1990**, enumerated as of **April 1.** For composition of regions, see table 27]

OFFENSE	1980	1990	1991	1992	1993					
					Total	Region				
						North-east	Mid-west	South	West
Drug arrest rate, total	**256.0**	**435.3**	**400.6**	**418.1**	**437.2**	**523.5**	**244.9**	**395.9**	**580.8**
Sale and/or manufacture	57.9	139.0	133.8	131.6	129.8	213.7	72.1	105.2	143.6
Heroin or cocaine [1]	10.8	93.7	90.1	85.9	84.1	173.0	25.3	71.1	77.3
Marijuana	28.4	26.4	24.6	27.1	27.1	31.3	20.2	23.6	34.3
Synthetic or manufactured drugs	2.8	2.7	3.1	2.9	2.5	3.4	1.2	2.9	2.1
Other dangerous nonnarcotic drugs ..	15.9	16.2	16.0	15.7	16.1	6.0	25.5	7.5	29.9
Possession	198.1	296.3	266.8	286.4	307.4	309.8	172.8	290.7	437.2
Heroin or cocaine [1]	22.2	144.4	131.3	136.8	136.1	165.6	49.0	128.2	192.5
Marijuana	146.2	104.9	89.6	106.5	120.6	127.7	93.2	138.4	109.4
Synthetic or manufactured drugs	6.7	6.6	5.6	5.0	5.2	4.9	2.4	7.0	5.1
Other dangerous nonnarcotic drugs ..	23.0	40.4	40.3	38.1	45.6	11.6	28.2	17.1	130.3

[1] Includes other derivatives such as morphine, heroin, and codeine.

Source: U.S. Federal Bureau of Investigation, *Crime in the United States,* annual.

No. 327. Federal Drug Seizures, by Type of Drug: 1990 to 1994

[For fiscal years ending in year shown. Reflects the combined drug seizure effort of the Drug Enforcement Administration, the Federal Bureau of Investigation, the U.S. Customs Services within the jurisdiction of the United States as well as maritime seizures by the U.S. Coast Guard. Based on reports to the Federal-wide Drug Seizure System, which eliminates duplicate reporting of a seizure involving more than one Federal agency]

DRUG	1990	1991	1992	1993	1994, prel.
AMOUNTS (lbs.)					
Heroin	1,794	3,030	2,551	3,514	2,824
Cocaine	235,214	246,324	303,254	244,302	282,086
Marijuana	483,248	499,070	783,343	772,307	778,715
Hashish	17,062	178,211	4,048	26,060	1,616
PERCENT CHANGE					
Heroin	(NA)	68.9	−15.8	37.7	−19.6
Cocaine	(NA)	4.7	23.1	−19.4	15.5
Marijuana	(NA)	3.3	57.0	−1.4	0.8
Hashish	(NA)	944.5	−97.7	543.8	−93.8

NA Not available.

Source: U.S. Bureau of Justice Statistics, *Fact Sheet: Drug Data Summary,* July 1994, series NCJ-148213; and unpublished data.

No. 328. Drug Removals, Laboratory Seizures, and Persons Indicted, by DEA: 1985 to 1993

[Represents domestic drug removals. 1 kg=.454 lbs; du=dosage unit]

ITEM	Unit	1985	1988	1989	1990	1991	1992	1993
Domestic drug removals:								
Heroin...................	kg	447	829	629	637	1,124	696	722
Cocaine	kg	18,129	57,113	82,438	73,635	57,080	78,211	60,666
Cannabis (Marijuana)........	1,000 kg .	745	602	336	149	108	202	143
Dangerous drugs	mil. du ..	26	114	109	148	532	49	84
Clandestine laboratory seizures ..	Number .	338	810	852	549	408	335	286
Narcotic Title III intercepts	Number .	136	129	192	235	256	291	308
Asset removals:								
Total seizures.............	$1,000 ..	246,344	671,290	975,884	1,106,827	956,960	879,058	679,550
DEA seizures	$1,000 ..	171,888	483,355	659,802	886,184	705,003	669,581	553,133
Seizures through inter-agency cooperation	$1,000 ..	74,456	187,936	316,082	220,643	251,957	209,478	126,416
Arrests..................	Number .	15,727	23,994	25,718	23,082	23,025	24,386	21,442
Convictions	Number .	10,519	13,091	15,917	15,662	15,962	17,476	18,371

Source: Drug Enforcement Administration (DEA), *Annual Report.*

No. 329. Authorized Intercepts of Communication—Summary: 1980 to 1993

[Data for jurisdictions with statutes authorizing or approving interception of wire or oral communication]

ITEM	1980	1983	1984	1985	1986	1987	1988	1989	1990	1991	1992	1993
Jurisdictions: [1]												
With wiretap statutes	28	31	31	32	32	33	34	37	40	41	41	41
Reporting interceptions	22	20	24	22	24	22	23	25	25	23	23	23
Intercept applications authorized	564	648	801	784	754	673	738	763	872	856	919	976
Intercept installations	524	602	773	722	676	634	678	720	812	802	846	938
Federal	79	205	277	235	247	233	286	305	321	349	332	444
State	445	397	496	487	429	401	392	415	491	453	514	494
Intercepted communications, average [2] . . . . : . . .	1,058	1,107	1,209	1,320	1,328	1,299	1,251	1,656	1,487	1,584	1,861	1,801
Incriminating	315	229	298	275	253	230	316	337	321	290	347	364
Persons arrested [3]	1,871	1,716	2,393	2,469	2,410	2,226	2,486	2,804	2,057	2,364	2,685	2,428
Convictions [3]	259	521	649	660	761	506	543	706	420	605	607	413
Major offense specified:												
Gambling	199	157	186	206	189	135	126	111	116	98	66	96
Drugs	282	360	483	434	348	379	435	471	520	536	634	679
Homicide and assault	13	31	30	25	34	18	14	20	21	21	35	28
Other	70	100	102	1*9	183	141	163	161	204	201	184	173

[1] Jurisdictions include Federal Government, States, and District of Columbia.   [2] Average per authorized installation.
[3] Based on information received from intercepts installed in year shown; additional arrests/convictions will occur in subsequent years but are not shown here.

Source: Administrative Office of the U.S. Courts, *Report on Applications for Orders Authorizing or Approving the Interception of Wire, Oral or Electronic Communications,* (Wiretap Report), annual.

No. 330. Aliens Expelled and Immigration Violations: 1980 to 1993

[**For fiscal years ending in year shown.** See text, section 9. See also *Historical Statistics, Colonial Times to 1970,* series C 144, C 149, and C 158-160]

ITEM	Unit	1980	1985	1987	1988	1989	1990	1991	1992	1993
Aliens expelled	1,000	737	1,062	1,113	934	860	1,045	1,091	1,143	1,279
Deported	1,000	17	21	22	23	30	26	28	38	37
Required to depart	1,000	719	1,041	1,091	911	830	1,019	1,063	1,105	1,242
Prosecutions disposed of.	**Number** . .	**14,863**	**17,688**	**18,894**	**18,360**	**18,580**	**20,079**	**18,882**	**14,655**	**19,650**
Immigration violations	Number . . .	14,498	16,976	18,200	17,590	17,992	19,351	18,297	14,138	18,958
Nationality violations	Number . . .	365	712	694	770	588	728	585	517	692
Convictions.	**Number** . .	**12,935**	**9,833**	**11,996**	**12,208**	**12,561**	**12,719**	**11,509**	**9,865**	**12,538**
Immigration violations	Number . . .	12,678	9,635	11,786	11,929	12,379	12,515	11,392	9,766	12,252
Nationality violations	Number . . .	257	198	210	279	182	204	117	99	286

No. 331. Immigration Border Patrol and Investigation Activities: 1980 to 1993

[**In thousands, except where indicated. For fiscal years ending in year shown.** See text, section 9]

ITEM	Unit	1980	1985	1987	1988	1989	1990	1991	1992	1993
BORDER PATROL										
Border patrol agents:										
Authorized number	Number . . .	2,484	3,228	4,812	4,812	4,804	4,852	4,968	4,948	4,143
On duty	Number . . .	2,329	3,023	3,180	4,074	3,857	4,360	4,312	4,759	3,991
Border patrol obligations	Mil. dol. . . .	82.5	141.9	194.6	205.3	246.4	261.1	295.5	325.8	354.5
Persons apprehended [1]	1,000	766.6	1,272.4	1,168.9	980.5	906.5	1,123.2	1,152.7	1,221.9	1,281.7
Deportable aliens located [2] . .	1,000	759.4	1,262.4	1,159.0	971.1	893.0	1,103.4	1,132.9	1,199.6	1,263.5
Mexican	1,000	734.2	1,218.7	1,124.6	929.8	832.2	1,054.8	1,095.1	1,168.9	1,230.1
Canadian	1,000	5.3	5.9	4.8	4.3	5.3	5.7	6.7	6.2	5.2
Other	1,000	19.9	37.8	29.6	37.0	55.5	42.8	31.1	24.4	28.1
Number of seizures	Number . . .	1,920	7,827	7,512	6,643	10,789	17,275	14,261	11,391	10,995
Value of seizures	Mil. dol. . .	116.1	122.0	590.6	721.2	1,212.7	843.6	950.2	1,247.9	1,382.9
Narcotics	Mil. dol. . . .	110.3	119.8	582.4	700.5	1,191.5	797.8	910.1	1,216.8	1,337.8
INVESTIGATIONS										
Deportable aliens located. . . .	1,000	150.9	83.9	31.5	37.0	61.1	64.1	63.6	57.4	60.4
Mexican	1,000	83.3	48.3	15.0	19.9	33.1	35.8	35.5	36.2	38.8
Canadian	1,000	1.5	1.1	0.4	0.4	0.5	0.4	0.5	0.4	0.4
Other	1,000	66.1	34.5	16.1	16.7	28.5	30.0	29.7	20.8	21.1

[1] Covers deportable aliens located and U.S. citizens engaged in smuggling or other immigration violations.   [2] Beginning 1988, includes apprehension by the antismuggling unit.

Source of tables 330 and 331: U.S. Immigration and Naturalization Service, *Statistical Yearbook,* annual; and unpublished data.

No. 332. Criminal Justice System—Public Expenditures and Employment, by Activity and Level of Government: 1990

[Based on a sample survey of local governments. Data for State governments were compiled from State financial records and for the Federal Government from the *Budget of the United States Government*]

TYPE OF GOVERNMENT	Total	ACTIVITY					
		Police protection	Judicial	Legal services	Public defense	Corrections	Other justice
TOTAL EXPENDITURES [1] (mil. dol.)							
All governments [2]	74,249	31,805	9,307	5,500	1,742	24,961	934
Federal Government	10,059	4,020	1,553	1,518	406	1,597	964
State and local government [2]	64,918	27,784	7,754	3,982	1,336	23,504	557
State government	28,005	5,197	3,478	1,451	604	16,693	582
Local government	39,667	23,081	4,635	2,686	788	8,244	233
FULL-TIME EQUIVALENT EMPLOYMENT (1,000)							
All governments	1,722	800	225	118	16	556	7
Federal Government	136	65	22	24	(Z)	22	(Z)
State and local government	1,586	735	203	93	15	534	7
State government	576	121	70	30	7	345	5
Local government	1,007	614	133	63	8	188	2

Z Fewer than 500.   [1] Covers direct and intergovernmental expenditures.   [2] Totals are adjusted to exclude duplication from intergovernmental expenditures.

Source: U.S. Bureau of Justice Statistics, *Justice Expenditure and Employment in the U.S., 1990*.

No. 333. State and Local Government Police Protection and Correction—Employment and Expenditures: 1992

[Employment as of **October**. Expenditures for fiscal years. Local government data are estimates subject to sampling variation; see Appendix III and source]

REGION, DIVISION, AND STATE	FULL-TIME EQUIVALENT EMPLOYMENT			EXPENDITURES		REGION, DIVISION, AND STATE	FULL-TIME EQUIVALENT EMPLOYMENT			EXPENDITURES	
	Total	Per 10,000 population [1]		Total [2] (mil. dol.)	Per capita [1] (dol.)		Total	Per 10,000 population [1]		Total [2] (mil. dol.)	Per capita [1] (dol.)
		Police protection	Correction					Police protection	Correction		
U.S.	1,248,277	28.0	20.9	79,502	312	DC	10,144	86.9	86.5	719	1,229
						VA.	29,383	24.1	21.9	1,698	266
Northeast	280,837	32.1	22.8	18,640	365	WV	4,434	16.7	7.8	212	117
N.E.	57,377	27.7	15.8	3,809	289	NC	32,761	25.8	22.1	1,609	235
ME	4,804	23.7	15.1	248	201	SC	17,651	25.0	24.0	869	241
NH	4,407	27.2	12.3	269	241	GA	37,476	27.6	27.7	1,806	267
VT	1,939	21.7	12.2	118	207	FL	87,102	33.6	31.0	5,153	382
MA	26,735	28.5	16.1	1,781	297	**E.S.C**	63,558	23.7	17.2	3,039	196
RI	4,825	30.0	18.2	303	302	KY	14,460	20.4	18.1	722	192
CT	14,667	28.2	16.5	1,091	333	TN	23,142	25.0	21.1	1,135	226
M.A.	223,460	33.7	25.3	14,831	391	AL	16,448	25.6	14.2	825	199
NY	126,843	37.5	32.6	9,000	497	MS	9,508	22.9	13.5	356	136
NJ	49,061	39.5	23.2	2,887	369	**W.S.C**	140,811	27.3	23.8	6,680	242
PA	47,556	24.1	15.6	2,944	245	AR	9,179	22.4	15.9	366	153
Midwest	258,207	26.4	16.2	15,298	252	LA	22,053	28.6	22.9	1,096	256
E.N.C	188,347	27.1	17.0	11,615	272	OK	14,445	27.5	17.6	623	194
OH	44,353	25.1	15.2	2,883	262	TX	95,134	27.5	26.3	4,596	260
IN	22,628	23.4	16.6	1,026	181						
IL	60,289	35.0	16.9	3,255	280	**West**	256,751	26.8	19.7	21,811	396
MI	40,693	22.6	20.6	2,985	316	**Mountain**	69,716	27.5	21.0	4,476	311
WI	20,384	26.1	14.7	1,467	294	MT	3,270	24.4	15.4	173	210
W.N.C	69,860	24.6	14.4	3,683	206	ID	4,390	25.7	15.5	234	220
MN	14,899	21.0	12.4	1,078	241	WY	2,346	33.7	16.8	148	319
IA	8,855	21.7	9.9	452	161	CO	15,640	27.3	17.8	1,051	303
MO	23,490	28.7	16.6	1,020	197	NM	8,279	28.7	23.6	463	293
ND	2,011	21.1	10.6	98	155	AZ	21,303	29.2	26.4	1,404	366
SD	2,342	21.5	11.6	121	170	UT	6,548	20.6	15.5	396	219
NE	6,486	24.6	15.9	310	194	NV	7,940	32.7	26.7	607	454
KS	11,777	27.4	19.4	604	240	**Pacific**	187,035	26.6	19.3	17,335	425
						WA	20,388	21.9	17.7	1,679	327
South	452,482	27.5	23.8	23,753	269	OR	11,994	22.3	18.1	851	286
S.A.	248,113	29.0	26.0	14,034	311	CA	146,321	27.7	19.7	14,032	454
DE	3,621	28.2	24.2	259	375	AK	2,870	27.2	21.7	366	623
MD	25,541	29.7	22.2	1,709	348	HI	5,462	29.7	17.5	407	352

[1] Based on resident population as of July 1.   [2] Covers police protection, corrections, judicial, and legal functions.

Source: U.S. Bureau of the Census, *Public Employment*, series GE, No. 1, annual, and *Government Finances*, series GF, No. 5, annual.

No. 334. General Purpose Law Enforcement Agencies—Number, Employment, and Expenditures: 1987 and 1990

[Includes both full-time and part-time employees. State police data are based on the 49 main State police agencies; Hawaii does not have a State police agency. Expenditure data cover fiscal years ending in year stated]

TYPE OF AGENCY	1987			1990				
	Number of agencies[1]	Number of employees	Expenditures (mil. dol.)	Number of agencies[1]	Number of employees			Expenditures (mil. dol.)
					Total	Sworn	Civilian	
NUMBER								
Total	**15,118**	**757,508**	**28,071.1**	**15,430**	**812,110**	**590,626**	**221,484**	**33,412.7**
Local police	11,989	493,930	18,011.3	12,288	513,596	387,534	126,062	20,586.0
Sheriff	3,080	189,234	6,857.8	3,093	220,380	150,610	69,770	9,137.2
State police	49	74,344	3,202.0	49	78,134	52,482	25,652	3,689.5
PERCENT								
Total	100.0	100.0	100.0	100.0	100.0	100.0	100.0	100.0
Local police	79.3	65.2	64.2	79.6	63.2	65.6	56.9	61.6
Sheriff	20.4	25.0	24.4	20.0	27.1	25.5	31.5	27.3
State police	0.3	9.8	11.4	0.3	9.6	8.9	11.6	11.0

[1] The number of agencies reported here is the result of a weighted sample and not an exact enumeration.
Source: U.S. Bureau of Justice Statistics, *Profile of State and Local Law Enforcement Agencies, 1987*, March 1989, and *State and Local Police Departments, 1990*, February 1992.

No. 335. Federal Agencies Employing 500 or More Full-Time Officers With Authority to Carry Firearms and Make Arrests, by Function: 1993

[As of December]

AGENCY	Total	Police response and patrol	Criminal investigation and enforcement	Other
All agencies [1]	**68,825**	**7,127**	**40,002**	**21,696**
U.S. Customs Service	10,120	43	10,077	-
Federal Bureau of Investigation	10,075	-	10,000	75
Federal Bureau of Prisons	9,984	-	-	9,984
Immigration and Naturalization Service	9,466	3,920	4,457	1,089
Administrative Office of the U.S. Courts	3,763	-	-	3,763
Internal Revenue Service	3,621	-	3,621	-
U.S. Postal Inspection Service	3,587	-	2,129	1,458
Drug Enforcement Administration	2,813	-	2,813	-
U.S. Secret Service	2,186	-	1,594	592
National Park Service	2,160	439	1,563	158
Ranger Activities Division	1,500	-	1,500	-
U.S. Park Police	660	439	63	158
U.S. Marshals Service	2,153	-	-	2153
Bureau of Alcohol, Tobacco and Firearms	1,959	-	1,832	127
U.S. Capitol Police	1,080	122	41	917
Tennessee Valley Authority	740	357	-	383
U.S. Forest Service	732	527	205	-
GSA - Federal Protective Services	732	505	66	161
U.S. Fish and Wildlife Service	620	397	223	-

- Represents or rounds to zero.   [1] Includes agencies not shown separately.
Source: U.S. Bureau of Justice Statistics, *Federal Law Enforcement Officers, 1993*.

No. 336. Law Enforcement Officers Killed and Assaulted: 1980 to 1993

[Covers officers killed feloniously and accidentally in line of duty; includes Federal officers. 1988 excludes Florida and Kentucky. For composition of regions, see table 27. See also *Historical Statistics, Colonial Times to 1970*, series H 987-998]

ITEM	1980	1985	1987	1988	1989	1990	1991	1992	1993
OFFICERS KILLED									
Total killed	**165**	**148**	**148**	**155**	**145**	**132**	**123**	**129**	**129**
Northeast	31	19	24	17	23	13	16	16	12
Midwest	23	23	31	18	22	20	26	15	27
South	72	64	51	77	68	68	55	68	57
West	32	29	40	39	23	23	17	23	22
Puerto Rico	6	10	2	-	8	8	8	7	11
Outlying areas, foreign countries	1	3	-	4	1	-	1	-	-
ASSAULTS									
Population (1,000) [1]	182,288	198,935	190,025	186,418	189,641	199,065	191,397	217,997	210,658
Number of—									
Agencies represented	9,235	9,906	8,957	8,866	9,213	9,483	9,263	10,682	9,809
Police officers	345,554	389,808	378,977	369,743	380,232	412,314	405,069	460,430	454,105
Total assaulted	**57,847**	**61,724**	**63,842**	**58,752**	**62,172**	**71,794**	**62,852**	**81,252**	**66,975**
Firearm	3,295	2,793	2,789	2,759	3,154	3,662	3,532	4,455	4,002
Knife or cutting instrument	1,653	1,715	1,561	1,367	1,379	1,641	1,493	2,095	1,574
Other dangerous weapon	5,415	5,263	5,685	5,573	5,778	7,390	7,014	8,604	7,551
Hands, fists, feet, etc	47,484	51,953	53,807	49,053	51,861	59,101	50,813	66,098	53,848

- Represents zero.   [1] Represents the number of persons covered by agencies shown.
Source: U.S. Federal Bureau of Investigation, *Law Enforcement Officers Killed and Assaulted*, annual.

No. 337. Lawyers—Selected Characteristics: 1960 to 1991

[Data based on editions of Martindale-Hubbell Law Directory. Represents all persons who are members of the bar, including those in industries, educational institutions, etc., and those inactive or retired. See also *Historical Statistics, Colonial Times to 1970*, series H 1028-1062]

CHARACTERISTIC	1960	1970	1980	1985	1988	1991
All lawyers [1]	**285,933**	**355,242**	**542,205**	**655,191**	**723,189**	**805,872**
Lawyers reporting [2]	252,385	324,818	(X)	(X)	(X)	(X)
Male	245,897	315,715	498,019	569,649	606,768	646,495
Female	6,488	9,103	44,185	85,542	116,421	159,377
Status in practice: [3]						
Government	25,621	35,803	50,490	53,035	57,742	66,227
Federal	13,045	18,710	20,132	19,989	23,042	27,985
State	4,316	9,293	30,358	33,046	34,700	38,242
City or county	8,260	7,800	([4])	([4])	([4])	([4])
Judicial [5]	8,180	10,349	19,160	21,677	19,547	21,536
Federal	599	878	2,611	3,003	2,846	3,119
State and county	5,301	7,548	16,549	18,674	16,701	18,417
City	2,280	1,923	([4])	([4])	([4])	([4])
Private practice	192,353	236,085	370,111	460,206	519,941	587,289
Individual	116,911	118,963	179,923	216,336	240,141	262,622
Partner	60,709	92,442	144,279	177,392	194,976	213,016
Associate [5]	14,733	24,680	45,908	66,478	84,824	111,651
Salaried	25,198	40,486	73,862	83,843	85,671	93,849
Private industry	22,533	33,593	54,626	63,622	66,627	71,022
Educational institutions	1,798	3,732	6,606	7,254	7,575	8,177
Other private employment	867	3,161	12,630	12,967	11,469	14,650
Inactive or retired	10,887	16,812	28,582	36,430	40,288	36,971

X Not applicable.   [1] 1960 to 1970 includes lawyers not reporting and an adjustment (subtraction) for duplications; 1980 to 1991, weighted to account for nonreporters and duplicate listings.   [2] 1960 and 1970 includes duplications; 1980-91 figures are weighted to adjust for duplication of entries.   [3] 1960 and 1970, in cases where more than one subentry was applicable, the individual was tabulated in each. In 1980-91 lawyers who were in both private practice and government service are coded in private practice.   [4] Data no longer available separately; included with category above.   [5] Associates are lawyers designated as such by their employers.

Source: American Bar Foundation, Chicago, IL, 1960 to 1970, *The 1971 Lawyer Statistical Report*, 1971 (copyright); 1980, *The Lawyer Statistical Report: A Statistical Profile of the U.S. Legal Profession in the 1980's*, 1985 (copyright); 1985 and 1988, *Supplement to The Lawyer Statistical Report: The U.S. Legal Profession in 1988*, 1991 and similar report for 1985; 1991 Lawyer Statistical Report: The U.S. Legal Profession in the 1990's, 1994 (copyright).

No. 338. U.S. Supreme Court—Cases Filed and Disposition: 1980 to 1993

[Statutory term of court begins first Monday in **October.** See *Historical Statistics, Colonial Times to 1970*, series H 1063-1078, for related but not comparable data]

ACTION	1980	1985	1987	1988	1989	1990	1991	1992	1993
Total cases on docket	**5,144**	**5,158**	**5,268**	**5,657**	**5,746**	**6,316**	**6,770**	**7,245**	**7,786**
Appellate cases on docket	2,749	2,571	2,577	2,587	2,416	2,351	2,451	2,441	2,442
From prior term	527	400	440	446	384	365	365	379	342
Docketed during present term	2,222	2,171	2,137	2,141	2,032	1,986	2,086	2,062	2,100
Cases acted upon [1]	2,324	2,185	2,224	2,271	2,096	2,042	2,125	2,140	2,099
Granted review	167	166	157	130	103	114	103	83	78
Denied, dismissed, or withdrawn	1,999	1,863	1,919	1,973	1,881	1,802	1,914	1,920	1,947
Summarily decided	90	78	66	75	44	81	52	84	34
Cases not acted upon	425	386	353	316	320	309	326	301	343
Pauper cases on docket	2,371	2,577	2,675	3,056	3,316	3,951	4,307	4,792	5,332
Cases acted upon	2,027	2,189	2,263	2,638	2,891	3,436	3,768	4,261	4,621
Granted review	17	20	23	17	19	27	17	14	21
Denied, dismissed, or withdrawn	1,968	2,136	2,210	2,577	2,824	3,369	3,716	4,209	4,566
Summarily decided	32	24	21	32	35	28	22	25	30
Cases not acted upon	344	388	412	418	425	515	539	531	711
Original cases on docket	24	10	16	14	14	14	12	12	12
Cases disposed of during term	7	2	5	2	2	3	1	1	1
Total cases available for argument	**264**	**276**	**280**	**254**	**204**	**201**	**196**	**166**	**145**
Cases disposed of	162	175	175	173	147	131	130	120	105
Cases argued	154	171	167	170	146	125	127	116	99
Cases dismissed or remanded without argument	8	4	8	3	1	6	3	4	6
Cases remaining	102	101	105	81	57	70	66	46	40
Cases decided by signed opinion	144	161	151	156	143	121	120	111	93
Cases decided by per curiam opinion	8	10	9	12	3	4	3	4	6
Number of signed opinions	123	146	139	133	129	112	107	107	84

[1] Includes cases granted review and carried over to next term, not shown separately.

Source: Office of the Clerk, Supreme Court of the United States, unpublished data.

No. 339. U.S. Courts of Appeals—Cases Commenced and Disposition: 1980 to 1994

[For years ending **June 30.** See also *Historical Statistics, Colonial Times to 1970*, series H 1079-1096]

ITEM	1980	1985	1988	1989	1990	1991	1992	1993	1994
Cases commenced [1]	23,200	33,360	37,524	39,734	40,898	42,033	46,032	49,770	48,815
Criminal	4,405	4,989	6,012	8,020	9,493	9,949	10,956	11,885	11,052
U.S. civil	4,654	6,744	6,210	6,349	6,626	6,663	7,113	7,758	7,518
Private civil	10,200	16,827	20,464	20,626	20,490	20,798	22,862	24,030	24,781
Administrative appeals	2,950	3,179	3,043	2,965	2,578	2,764	3,052	3,824	3,560
Cases terminated [1]	20,887	31,387	35,888	37,372	38,520	41,414	42,933	47,466	48,546
Criminal	3,993	4,892	5,284	6,297	7,509	9,198	9,830	11,043	11,519
U.S. civil	4,346	6,363	6,386	6,127	6,379	6,579	6,797	7,462	7,637
Private civil	8,942	15,743	19,798	20,313	20,369	20,698	21,628	23,437	23,943
Administrative appeals	2,643	2,760	2,625	2,914	2,582	3,148	2,801	3,464	3,480
Cases disposed of [2]	10,607	16,369	19,178	19,322	21,006	22,707	23,162	25,567	26,475
Affirmed or granted	8,017	12,286	14,953	15,240	16,629	17,988	18,463	20,604	21,371
Reversed or denied	1,845	2,770	2,664	2,617	2,565	2,503	2,681	2,514	2,636
Other	745	1,313	1,561	1,465	1,812	2,216	2,018	2,449	2,468
Median months [3]	8.9	10.3	10.1	10.3	10.1	10.2	10.5	10.4	10.5

[1] Includes original proceedings and bankruptcy appeals not shown separately. [2] Terminated on the merits after hearing or submission. [3] Prior to 1985, the figure is from filing of complete record to final disposition; beginning 1985, figure is from filing notice of appeal to final disposition. For definition of median, see Guide to Tabular Presentation.

No. 340. U.S. District Courts—Civil and Criminal Cases: 1980 to 1994

[**In thousands, except percent.** For years ending **June 30.** See also *Historical Statistics, Colonial Times to 1970*, series H 1097-1111]

ITEM	1980	1985	1988	1989	1990	1991	1992	1993	1994
Civil cases: Commenced	168.8	273.7	239.6	233.5	217.9	207.7	226.9	228.6	236.0
Cases terminated [1]	155.0	268.6	238.1	234.6	213.4	211.7	239.6	225.2	229.3
No court action	68.7	129.4	79.6	64.3	51.6	44.6	51.4	44.0	40.5
Court action, total	86.2	139.2	158.6	170.4	161.8	166.5	187.6	181.2	188.8
Before pretrial	53.8	95.5	114.7	129.7	127.0	136.9	153.4	152.3	160.0
Pretrial	22.4	31.1	32.2	29.5	25.5	21.1	26.2	21.1	21.0
Trials	10.1	12.6	11.6	11.2	9.2	8.4	8.0	7.9	7.9
Percent reaching trial	6.5	4.7	4.9	4.8	4.3	4.0	3.4	3.5	3.4
Criminal cases: Commenced [2]	28.0	38.5	43.5	44.9	46.5	45.1	47.5	45.7	44.9
Defendants disposed of [3]	36.6	47.4	52.8	54.6	56.5	56.7	58.4	59.5	61.2
Not convicted	8.0	8.8	9.9	10.1	9.8	10.0	10.0	9.2	10.0
Convicted	28.6	38.5	42.9	44.5	46.7	46.8	48.4	50.4	51.1
Imprisonment	13.2	18.7	22.5	24.9	27.8	29.2	31.1	34.2	34.5
Probation	11.1	14.4	16.1	15.0	14.2	13.8	13.1	12.6	12.8
Fine and other	4.4	5.4	4.4	4.7	4.7	3.8	4.3	3.7	3.9

[1] Excludes land condemnation cases. [2] Excludes transfers. [3] Includes Guam, Virgin Islands, and Northern Mariana Islands; 1980 includes Canal Zone.

No. 341. U.S. District Courts—Civil Cases Commenced and Pending: 1991 to 1994

[For years ending **June 30**]

TYPE OF CASE	CASES COMMENCED				CASES PENDING			
	1991	1992	1993	1994	1991	1992	1993	1994
Cases total	**207,690**	**226,895**	**228,562**	**235,996**	**244,570**	**237,040**	**215,574**	**218,396**
Contract actions [1]	42,396	51,246	38,240	31,988	42,497	41,588	40,525	34,036
Recovery of overpayments [2]	7,932	17,475	7,255	2,591	4,686	4,663	5,995	2,585
Real property actions	9,795	10,143	8,436	7,468	8,743	7,657	7,743	6,810
Tort actions	37,287	36,469	40,939	48,067	77,998	69,734	45,148	46,785
Personal injury	34,007	33,147	37,409	44,734	74,141	65,792	41,324	43,105
Personal injury product liability [1]	12,399	10,769	16,545	23,977	47,288	39,264	15,208	14,721
Asbestos	7,142	4,673	4,900	7,111	38,849	31,218	7,154	7,053
Other personal injury	21,608	22,378	20,864	20,757	26,853	26,528	26,116	24,635
Personal property damage	3,280	3,322	3,530	3,333	3,857	3,942	3,824	3,680
Actions under statutes [1]	118,085	128,921	140,811	148,344	114,853	117,538	121,964	130,504
Civil rights [1]	19,337	23,419	26,483	31,521	23,791	24,009	26,477	29,179
Employment	8,144	10,275	12,221	15,256	11,490	11,156	12,530	14,386
Bankruptcy suits	5,013	5,243	6,192	5,675	3,941	4,083	4,203	4,922
Commerce (ICC rates, etc.)	1,556	2,475	1,475	1,228	1,441	1,189	1,238	1,149
Environmental matters	1,075	1,252	1,077	1,059	1,538	1,719	1,943	1,949
Prisoner petitions	42,476	46,452	52,454	56,283	35,793	37,259	39,512	42,956
Forfeiture and penalty	5,581	5,492	4,832	3,548	4,886	4,967	4,850	4,323
Labor laws	14,684	15,800	16,174	15,800	12,112	12,778	13,026	12,859
Protected property rights [3]	5,231	5,670	6,202	7,051	5,448	5,296	5,281	5,559
Securities commodities and exchanges	2,245	1,998	1,875	1,742	4,636	4,555	3,983	3,642
Social Security laws	7,695	8,415	11,602	11,142	8,068	8,154	8,304	11,473
Tax suits	2,639	2,305	2,267	2,275	2,850	2,713	2,255	2,087
Freedom of information	363	439	425	566	451	465	498	478

[1] Includes other types not shown separately. [2] Includes enforcement of judgments in student loan cases, and overpayments of veterans benefits. [3] Includes copyright, patent, and trademark rights.

Source of tables 339-341: Administrative Office of the U.S. Courts, *Annual Report of the Director.*

No. 342. U.S. District Courts—Offenders Convicted and Sentenced to Prison, and Length of Sentence: 1992

MOST SERIOUS OFFENSE OF CONVICTION	Offenders convicted	Convicted offenders sentenced to prison	Length of sentence (mo.)	MOST SERIOUS OFFENSE OF CONVICTION	Offenders convicted	Convicted offenders sentenced to prison	Length of sentence (mo.)
Total [1]	**51,936**	**33,622**	**62.2**	Drug offenses [2]	18,698	16,401	82.2
				Possession	1,120	414	21.8
Violent offenses	2,919	2,618	88.5	Trafficking and			
Property offenses	14,217	6,557	19.9	manufacturing	17,578	15,987	83.8
Fraudulent offenses [2] .	10,253	5,039	19.4	Public-order offenses . . .	16,101	8,045	47.6
Embezzlement. . . .	1,743	718	15.2	Regulatory offenses . .	2,179	856	35.5
Fraud [3]	7,215	3,669	20.3	Other offenses	13,922	7,189	49.1
Forgery	726	336	18.2	Weapons	3,985	3,426	76.9
Other offenses [2]	3,964	1,518	21.8	Immigration.	2,364	1,741	15.1
Larceny	3,086	901	17.0	Tax law violations [4] .	1,062	436	19.0

[1] Total may include offenders for whom offense category could not be determined.   [2] Includes offenses not shown separately.   [3] Excludes tax fraud.   [4] Includes tax fraud.

Source: U.S. Bureau of Justice Statistics, *Federal Criminal Case Processing,* annual.

No. 343. U.S. District Courts—Defendants Charged With Violations of Drug Abuse Prevention and Control Act: 1990 to 1994

[For years ending **June 30**]

ITEM	MARIJUANA				DRUGS				CONTROLLED SUBSTANCES (prescribed drugs)			
	1990	1992	1993	1994	1990	1992	1993	1994	1990	1992	1993	1994
Defendants disposed of.	**5,139**	**5,438**	**5,615**	**5,884**	**12,649**	**12,776**	**12,713**	**11,461**	**1,483**	**2,011**	**3,215**	**3,952**
Not convicted.	1,011	946	870	810	1,850	1,807	1,675	1,613	222	272	422	537
Dismissed [1]	915	850	780	740	1,506	1,474	1,415	1,381	189	233	339	453
Convicted.	4,128	4,492	4,745	5,074	10,799	10,969	11,038	9,848	1,261	1,739	2,793	3,415
By guilty plea and nolo contendere.	3,624	4,056	4,310	4,764	8,423	8,806	9,278	8,439	1,020	1,512	2,430	2,981
Imprisonment, total [2]	**3,004**	**3,585**	**3,906**	**4,091**	**9,804**	**10,050**	**10,230**	**9,289**	**1,030**	**1,397**	**2,412**	**2,974**
Regular sentence	2,931	3,538	3,886	4,040	9,551	9,936	10,005	8,920	980	1,355	2,356	2,883
Avg. sentence (mo.). . .	48.9	51.4	45.7	46.8	86.2	98.1	96.8	96.2	79.3	105.0	93.3	88.0
Other sentences to prison [2]	73	47	20	51	253	114	225	369	50	42	56	91
Probation, total.	**1,054**	**838**	**754**	**913**	**874**	**831**	**724**	**644**	**207**	**285**	**345**	**424**
Avg. sentence (mo.). . .	25.1	32.7	31.1	30.4	40.0	42.4	41.0	40.4	32.3	48.5	36.0	35.5
Fine only.	39	69	84	70	17	88	85	35	8	57	36	17
Other [3]	31	1	4	-	104	3	2	6	16	-	5	4

- Represents zero.   [1] Includes defendants committed under 28 USC 2902, Narcotic Addict Rehabilitation Act of 1966.   [2] Split or mixed sentences of prison and probation in the same case as well as indeterminate and Youth Corrections Act sentences are included under total imprisonment and other sentences to prison.   [3] Includes deportation, suspended sentences, imprisonment for four days or less or for time already served, remitted and suspended fines and life sentences.

Source: Administrative Office of the U.S. Courts, *Annual Report of the Director.*

No. 344. Federal Prosecutions of Public Corruption: 1980 to 1992

[As of **Dec. 31.** Prosecution of persons who have corrupted public office in violation of Federal Criminal Statutes]

PROSECUTION STATUS	1980	1982	1983	1984	1985	1986	1987	1988	1989	1990	1991	1992
Total: [1] Indicted	727	813	1,076	931	1,157	1,208	1,276	1,274	1,348	1,176	1,452	1,189
Convicted	602	671	972	934	997	1,026	1,081	1,067	1,149	1,084	1,194	1,081
Awaiting trial.	213	186	222	269	256	246	368	288	375	300	346	380
Federal officials: Indicted	123	158	[2]460	408	563	596	651	629	695	615	803	624
Convicted	131	147	[2]424	429	470	523	545	529	610	583	665	532
Awaiting trial.	16	38	58	77	90	83	118	86	126	103	149	139
State officials: Indicted	72	49	81	58	79	88	102	66	71	96	115	84
Convicted	51	43	65	52	66	71	76	69	54	79	77	92
Awaiting trial.	28	18	26	21	20	24	26	14	18	28	42	24
Local officials: Indicted.	247	257	270	203	248	232	246	276	269	257	242	232
Convicted	168	232	226	196	221	207	204	229	201	225	180	211
Awaiting trial.	82	58	61	74	49	55	89 79	122	98	88	91	277

[1] Includes individuals who are neither public officials nor employees but who were involved with public officials or employees in violating the law, not shown separately.   [2] Increases in the number indicted and convicted between 1982 and 1983 resulted from a greater focus on federal corruption nationwide and more consistent reporting of cases involving lower-level employees.

Source: U.S. Department of Justice, *Federal Prosecutions of Corrupt Public Officials, 1970-1980* and *Report to Congress on the Activities and Operations of the Public Integrity Section,* annual.

No. 345. Delinquency Cases Disposed by Juvenile Courts, by Reason for Referral: 1982 to 1992

[In thousands. A delinquency offense is an act committed by a juvenile for which an adult could be prosecuted in a criminal court. Disposition of a case involves taking a definite action such as transferring the case to criminal court, dismissing the case, placing the youth on probation, placing the youth in a facility for delinquents, or such actions as fines, restitution, and community service]

REASON FOR REFERRAL	1982	1984	1985	1986	1987	1988	1989	1990	1991	1992
All delinquency offense....	**1,073**	**1,034**	**1,112**	**1,150**	**1,145**	**1,170**	**1,212**	**1,300**	**1,374**	**1,471**
Case rate [1]	39.1	38.7	42.2	43.9	45.7	45.7	47.8	51.0	52.7	55.1
Violent offenses	57	61	67	73	67	71	78	95	105	119
Criminal homicide	2	1	1	2	1	2	2	3	3	3
Forcible rape.	3	3	4	5	4	4	4	4	5	5
Robbery.	26	22	26	26	22	22	23	28	30	33
Aggravated assault	27	35	36	40	39	43	49	60	67	78
Property offenses	475	442	489	496	498	501	525	546	590	599
Burglary.	158	129	139	140	131	129	131	142	151	156
Larceny.	278	276	307	308	314	311	319	327	360	362
Motor vehicle theft	34	31	36	42	47	55	68	71	72	73
Arson	5	6	7	6	6	7	7	7	8	8
Delinquency offenses.	541	530	555	583	590	599	610	658	679	753
Simple assault.	86	73	92	95	100	104	111	125	134	153
Vandalism	64	69	84	84	83	81	83	97	109	122
Drug law violations.	62	65	76	73	73	82	78	71	63	72
Obstruction of justice	47	63	68	76	79	79	82	86	81	87
Other [2]	282	260	235	255	256	253	257	279	293	320

[1] Number of cases disposed per 1,000 youth (ages 10 to 17) at risk.   [2] Includes such offenses as stolen property offenses, trespassing, weapons offenses, other sex offenses, liquor law violations, disorderly conduct, and miscellaneous offenses.

Source: National Center for Juvenile Justice, Pittsburgh, PA, *Juvenile Court Statistics,* annual.

No. 346. Child Abuse and Neglect Cases Substantiated and Indicated— Victim Characteristics: 1990 to 1993

[Based on reports alleging child abuse and neglect that were referred for investigation by the respective child protective services agency in each State. The reporting period may be either calendar or fiscal year. The majority of States provided duplicated counts. Also, varying number of States reported the various characteristics presented below. A substantiated case represents a type of investigation disposition that determines that there is sufficient evidence under State law to conclude that maltreatment occurred or that the child is at risk of maltreatment. An indicated case represents a type of disposition that concludes that there was a reason to suspect maltreatment had occurred]

ITEM	1990		1991		1992		1993	
	Number	Percent	Number	Percent	Number	Percent	Number	Percent
TYPES OF SUBSTANTIATED MALTREATMENT								
Victims, total [1]	801,143	(X)	819,922	(X)	1,044,480	(X)	1,057,255	(X)
Neglect.	358,846	44.8	366,462	44.7	474,871	51.7	492,211	48.8
Physical abuse	205,057	25.6	206,235	25.2	212,300	23.1	232,061	23.0
Sexual abuse	127,853	16.0	129,425	15.8	130,248	14.2	139,326	13.8
Emotional maltreatment	47,673	6.0	46,334	5.7	48,898	5.3	47,659	4.7
Other and unknown	61,714	7.7	71,466	8.7	178,163	19.4	145,998	14.5
SEX OF VICTIM								
Victims, total	775,596	100.0	816,223	100.0	956,076	100.0	915,579	100.0
Male.	360,531	46.5	376,617	46.1	430,280	45.0	413,210	45.0
Female	409,286	52.8	434,729	53.3	488,267	51.1	470,541	51.1
Unknown	5,779	0.7	4,877	0.6	37,529	3.9	31,828	3.9
AGE OF VICTIM								
Victims, total	788,338	100.0	813,057	100.0	953,487	100.0	915,909	100.0
1 year and younger	107,217	13.6	112,227	13.8	122,631	12.9	121,689	13.3
2 to 5 years old.	194,485	24.7	208,183	25.6	244,184	25.6	236,925	25.9
6 to 9 years old.	177,396	22.5	189,124	23.3	216,414	22.7	209,227	22.8
10 to 13 years old.	151,971	19.3	162,049	19.9	183,297	19.2	177,537	19.4
14 to 17 years old.	117,312	14.9	122,603	15.1	138,667	14.5	133,852	14.6
18 and over	7,184	0.9	6,327	0.8	7,377	0.8	6,799	0.7
Unknown	32,773	4.2	12,544	1.5	40,917	4.3	29,880	3.3
RACE/ETHNIC GROUP OF VICTIM [2]								
Victims, total	775,409	100.0	818,527	99.9	956,248	100.0	916,185	100.0
White	424,470	54.7	454,059	55.5	509,111	53.2	497,913	54.3
Black	197,400	25.5	218,044	26.6	242,357	25.3	229,596	25.1
Asian and Pacific Islander.	6,408	0.8	6,585	0.8	7,139	0.7	7,775	0.8
American Indian, Eskimo, and Aleut	10,283	1.3	10,873	1.3	12,782	1.3	13,657	1.5
Other races	11,749	1.5	12,982	1.6	15,094	1.6	13,659	1.5
Hispanic origin	73,132	9.4	77,985	9.5	89,426	9.4	85,026	9.3
Unknown.	51,967	6.7	37,999	4.6	80,339	8.4	68,559	7.5

X Not applicable.   [1] More than one type of maltreatment may be substantiated per child.   [2] Some States were unable to report on the number of Hispanic victims, thus it is probable that nationwide the percentage of Hispanic victims is higher.

Source: U.S. Department of Health and Human Services, National Center on Child Abuse and Neglect, National Child Abuse and Neglect Data System, *Working Paper 2, 1991 Summary Data Component,* May 1993; *Child Maltreatment - 1992,* May 1994; and *Child Maltreatment - 1993,* April 1995.

Law Enforcement, Courts, and Prisons

No. 347. Child Abuse and Neglect Cases Reported and Investigated, by State: 1992 and 1993

[Based on reports alleging child abuse and neglect that were referred for investigation by the respective child protective services agency in each State. The reporting period may be either calendar or fiscal year. The majority of States were unable to provide unduplicated counts. Only nine jurisdictions (Alaska, Hawaii, Michigan, Montana, Ohio, Oregon, South Carolina, Vermont, and Washington) provided unduplicated counts of children subject of report. Excludes the Armed Forces]

STATE	1992				1993			
		Reports		Investi-gation disposition, number of children substan-tiated [2]		Reports		Investi-gation disposition, number of children substan-tiated [2]
	Population under 18 years old	Number of reports [1]	Number of children subject of a report		Population under 18 years old	Number of reports [1]	Number of children subject of a report	
United States . . .	66,166,000	1,898,098	2,876,184	991,549	67,135,000	1,936,242	2,825,594	1,007,953
Alabama	1,076,000	28,311	43,246	23,265	1,077,000	26,758	40,388	19,130
Alaska.	185,000	[3]9,079	9,079	8,335	189,000	[3]9,920	9,920	6,917
Arizona	1,047,000	29,339	51,216	30,556	1,070,000	29,747	51,068	30,729
Arkansas	629,000	17,250	36,089	7,538	635,000	17,489	25,624	10,336
California	8,423,000	326,120	463,090	73,675	8,594,000	342,537	455,526	161,612
Colorado	909,000	34,409	56,305	9,237	938,000	33,287	33,287	7,892
Connecticut	771,000	14,369	22,080	15,957	775,000	17,871	27,710	23,069
Delaware.	172,000	4,586	8,292	2,157	175,000	5,386	9,635	2,271
District of Columbia . . .	117,000	5,596	12,093	3,718	115,000	5,669	12,773	3,327
Florida.	3,106,000	116,403	180,285	88,563	3,169,000	105,468	161,686	81,982
Georgia	1,800,000	51,225	65,908	46,192	1,841,000	52,519	85,118	55,516
Hawaii.	293,000	[3]5,310	5,310	2,277	299,000	[3]5,412	5,412	2,297
Idaho	324,000	12,230	24,020	6,395	333,000	12,494	24,759	6,892
Illinois	3,029,000	74,220	131,592	43,433	3,068,000	72,101	126,960	43,519
Indiana	1,461,000	39,233	58,970	30,283	1,469,000	40,263	59,481	29,136
Iowa	735,000	19,432	28,094	7,834	734,000	20,866	30,776	8,834
Kansas	678,000	[3]22,079	22,079	11,585	684,000	[3]24,797	24,797	12,327
Kentucky	964,000	35,997	56,438	24,437	971,000	36,901	57,706	25,282
Louisiana.	1,238,000	26,087	47,893	16,050	1,243,000	27,218	46,170	15,253
Maine	306,000	4,826	10,177	4,927	307,000	4,286	9,567	4,955
Maryland	1,226,000	30,062	49,191	(NA)	1,241,000	29,412	29,412	(NA)
Massachusetts	1,384,000	32,286	52,581	24,601	1,393,000	31,833	51,941	24,186
Michigan	2,509,000	51,601	117,316	25,931	2,506,000	53,302	126,601	19,522
Minnesota	1,206,000	17,988	27,462	11,217	1,228,000	17,427	26,778	10,535
Mississippi	748,000	17,528	32,076	10,712	758,000	17,606	27,568	8,812
Missouri.	1,350,000	49,286	79,493	24,339	1,363,000	52,268	85,323	20,472
Montana	226,000	9,691	14,760	5,328	232,000	9,005	13,713	4,827
Nebraska.	439,000	7,961	17,029	5,262	439,000	8,439	17,481	5,726
Nevada	338,000	13,914	22,768	7,699	352,000	12,568	12,568	7,085
New Hampshire	280,000	6,755	11,053	917	283,000	6,225	7,234	928
New Jersey	1,863,000	[3]50,443	50,443	17,499	1,896,000	[3]65,102	65,102	10,510
New Mexico	469,000	[3]26,969	26,969	6,716	481,000	[3]24,984	24,984	6,880
New York.	4,422,000	137,779	228,457	92,238	4,468,000	139,468	230,916	59,311
North Carolina	1,662,000	55,411	88,472	29,546	1,704,000	58,376	92,739	29,809
North Dakota	172,000	4,515	7,565	3,669	172,000	4,884	8,252	4,010
Ohio	2,820,000	95,376	148,101	61,327	2,859,000	93,144	147,106	51,850
Oklahoma	858,000	[3]24,092	24,092	8,063	869,000	[3]26,349	26,349	8,359
Oregon	766,000	25,622	41,916	8,705	782,000	25,227	25,227	(NA)
Pennsylvania	2,844,000	[3]25,891	25,891	8,419	2,872,000	[3]24,909	24,909	7,814
Rhode Island	233,000	8,395	12,886	4,931	235,000	8,278	13,065	3,130
South Carolina	945,000	19,712	33,854	11,348	952,000	21,227	40,147	11,263
South Dakota	204,000	[3]10,486	10,486	2,903	208,000	[3]10,284	10,284	2,368
Tennessee	1,246,000	[3]31,231	31,231	11,469	1,269,000	[3]32,739	32,739	12,136
Texas	5,072,000	110,937	174,255	62,342	5,183,000	110,973	177,328	58,304
Utah	654,000	15,910	27,047	10,875	665,000	16,168	27,485	10,976
Vermont	144,000	2,750	2,778	1,498	144,000	2,732	3,190	1,305
Virginia	1,562,000	35,880	55,680	14,472	1,588,000	36,257	55,937	14,066
Washington	1,355,000	39,704	55,836	41,879	1,393,000	40,075	55,689	41,602
West Virginia	438,000	12,932	21,161	(NA)	434,000	12,932	12,932	(NA)
Wisconsin	1,330,000	[3]47,622	47,622	19,213	1,342,000	[3]49,152	49,152	19,189
Wyoming	138,000	3,268	5,457	2,017	138,000	3,908	5,080	1,702

NA Not available.   [1] Except as noted, reports are on incident/family based basis or based on number of reported incidents regardless of the number of children involved in the incidents.   [2] Type of investigation disposition that determines that there is sufficient evidence under State law to conclude that maltreatment occurred or that the child is at risk of maltreatment.   [3] Child-based report that enumerates each child who is a subject of a report.

Source: U.S. Department of Health and Human Services, National Center on Child Abuse and Neglect, *Child Maltreatment - 1992*, May 1994; and *Child Maltreatment -1993*, April 1995.

No. 348. Jail Inmates, by Race and Detention Status: 1978 to 1994

[Excludes Federal and State prisons or other correctional institutions; institutions exclusively for juveniles; State-operated jails in Alaska, Connecticut, Delaware, Hawaii, Rhode Island, and Vermont; and other facilities which retain persons for less than 48 hours. As of **June 30.** For 1978 and 1988, data based on National Jail Census; for other years, based on sample survey and subject to sampling variability]

CHARACTERISTIC	1978	1985	1988	1989	1990	1991	1992	1993	1994
Total inmates [1]	**158,394**	**256,615**	**343,569**	**395,553**	**405,320**	**426,479**	**444,584**	**459,804**	**490,442**
Percent of rated capacity	65	94	101	108	104	101	99	97	97
Male	148,839	235,909	313,158	356,050	368,002	386,865	403,768	415,700	441,219
Female	9,555	19,077	30,411	37,253	37,318	39,614	40,816	44,100	49,223
White [2]	89,418	151,403	166,302	201,732	186,989	190,333	191,362	239,500	255,800
Black [2]	65,104	102,646	141,979	185,910	174,335	187,618	195,156	214,100	227,000
Other races [2]	3,872	2,566	3,932	7,911	5,321	5,391	5,831	6,200	7,600
Hispanic [3]	16,349	35,926	51,455	55,377	57,449	60,129	62,961	69,200	75,500
Non-Hispanic	142,045	220,689	292,114	340,176	347,871	366,350	381,623	390,600	414,942
Adult [4]	156,783	254,986	341,893	393,303	403,019	424,129	441,781	455,500	(NA)
Awaiting arraignment or trial	77,453	127,059	175,669	204,291	207,358	217,671	223,840	228,900	(NA)
Convicted	75,438	123,409	166,224	189,012	195,661	206,458	217,940	226,600	(NA)
Juvenile [5]	1,611	1,629	1,676	2,250	2,301	2,350	2,804	4,300	(NA)

NA Not available. [1] For 1985, 1989-1994, includes juveniles not shown separately by sex, and for 1988 and 1990-1994 includes 31,356, 38,675, 43,138, 52,235, 66,249, and 93,058 persons, respectively, of unknown race not shown separately. [2] For 1993 and 1994, data are estimated and rounded to nearest 100. [3] Hispanic persons may be of any race. Data for 1993 and 1994 are estimated and rounded to nearest 100. [4] Includes inmates not classified by conviction status. [5] Juveniles are persons whose age makes them initially subject to juvenile court authority although they are sometimes tried as adults in criminal court. In 1993, includes juveniles who were tried as adults. In 1994, includes all persons under age 18.
Source: U.S. Bureau of Justice Statistics, *Profile of Jail Inmates, 1978 and 1989; Jail Inmates,* annual; and *1988 Census of Local Jails.*

No. 349. Federal and State Prisoners: 1970 to 1993

[Based on Bureau of the Census estimated resident population, as of **July 1.** Prior to 1970, excludes State institutions in Alaska. Beginning 1980, includes all persons under jurisdiction of Federal and State authorities rather than those in the custody of such authorities. Represents inmates sentenced to maximum term of more than a year. See also *Historical Statistics, Colonial Times to 1970,* series H 1135-1140]

YEAR	PRESENT AT END OF YEAR						RECEIVED FROM COURTS					
	All institutions		Federal		State		All institutions		Federal		State	
	Number	Rate [1]	Number	Rate [1]	Number	Rate [1]	Number	Rate [1]	Number	Rate [1]	Number	Rate [1]
1970 . . .	196,429	96.7	20,038	9.8	176,391	86.8	79,351	39.1	12,047	5.9	67,304	33.1
1975 . . .	240,593	113.3	24,131	11.4	216,462	102.0	129,573	61.0	16,770	7.9	112,803	53.1
1980 . . .	315,974	139.2	20,611	9.1	295,363	130.1	142,122	62.7	10,907	4.8	131,215	57.9
1985 . . .	480,568	216.5	32,695	13.6	447,873	187.6	198,499	82.7	15,368	6.4	183,131	76.3
1986 . . .	522,084	230.4	36,531	15.0	485,553	201.4	219,382	91.0	16,067	7.0	203,315	84.0
1987 . . .	560,812	229.0	39,523	16.0	521,289	214.2	241,887	99.0	16,260	7.0	225,627	92.0
1988 . . .	603,732	244.0	42,738	17.0	560,994	227.0	261,242	106.0	15,932	6.4	245,310	99.3
1989 . . .	680,907	274.3	47,168	19.0	633,739	255.3	316,215	127.4	18,388	7.4	297,827	120.0
1990 . . .	739,980	295.0	50,403	20.1	689,577	274.9	(NA)	(NA)	(NA)	(NA)	323,069	128.8
1991 . . .	789,610	309.6	56,696	22.2	732,914	287.3	(NA)	(NA)	(NA)	(NA)	317,237	124.4
1992 . . .	846,277	331.8	65,706	25.8	780,571	306.0	(NA)	(NA)	(NA)	(NA)	334,301	130.3
1993 . . .	910,080	352.9	74,399	28.8	835,681	324.0	341,722	132.5	23,653	9.2	318,069	123.3

NA Not available. [1] Rate per 100,000 estimated population.
Source: U.S. Bureau of Justice Statistics, *Prisoners in State and Federal Institutions on December 31,* annual, and *Correctional Populations in the United States,* annual.

No. 350. State Prison Inmates—Selected Characteristics: 1986 and 1991

[Based on a sample survey of about 13,986 inmates in 1991 and 13,711 inmates in 1986; subject to sampling variability]

CHARACTERISTIC	NUMBER		PERCENT OF PRISON INMATES		CHARACTERISTIC	NUMBER		PERCENT OF PRISON INMATES	
	1986	1991	1986	1991		1986	1991	1986	1991
Total [1]	**450,416**	**711,643**	**100.0**	**100.0**	Never married	241,707	389,302	53.7	55.3
					Married	91,492	127,389	20.3	18.1
Under 18 years old	2,057	4,552	0.5	0.6	Widowed	8,343	13,036	1.9	1.9
18 to 24 years old	120,384	151,328	26.7	21.3	Divorced	81,264	129,913	18.1	18.5
25 to 34 years old	205,817	325,429	45.7	45.7	Separated	26,985	44,095	6.0	6.3
35 to 44 years old	87,502	161,651	19.4	22.7	Years of school:				
45 to 54 years old	23,524	46,475	5.2	6.5	Less than 12 years . . .	276,309	[2]290,722	61.6	[2]41.2
55 to 64 years old	8,267	16,997	1.8	2.4	12 years or more	172,386	415,451	38.4	58.8
65 years old and over . . .	2,808	5,210	0.6	0.7	Pre-arrest employment status:				
Male	430,604	672,847	95.6	94.5	Employed	309,364	476,068	69.0	67.3
Female	19,812	38,796	4.4	5.5	Not employed	139,097	230,876	31.0	32.7
White	223,648	349,628	49.7	49.1	Looking for work . . .	80,750	115,590	18.0	16.4
Black	211,021	336,920	46.9	47.3	Not looking for work .	58,347	115,286	13.0	16.3
Other races	15,412	25,094	3.4	3.5					

[1] For 1986, includes data not reported for all characteristics except sex. For 1991, includes data not reported for marital status, re-arrest, employment status, and years of school. [2] In 1991, the survey question was revised; therefore, the response may not be entirely comparable with 1986 and before.
Source: U.S. Bureau of Justice Statistics, *Profile of State Prison Inmates, 1986;* and *Survey of State Prison Inmates, 1991.*

No. 351. State Prison Inmates, by Criminal History and Selected Characteristics of the Inmate: 1991

[Violent/nonviolent refers to the current or past criminal offense for which the inmate is or was incarcerated; see table 308 for types of violent crimes. Data based on a sample survey of 13,986 inmates; subject to sampling variability]

CHARACTERISTIC	Total	CRIMINAL HISTORY OF PRISON INMATES							
		First-timers			Recidivists [1]				
		Total	Non-violent	Violent	Total	Non-violent	Prior violent	Current violent only	Current and prior violent
Prison inmates, total	**697,853**	**134,131**	**45,559**	**88,572**	**563,722**	**223,117**	**88,689**	**131,289**	**120,626**
Percent of total	100.0	19.2	6.5	12.7	80.8	32.0	12.7	18.8	17.3
Percent distribution	100.0	100.0	100.0	100.0	100.0	100.0	100.0	100.0	100.0
Male	94.5	92.0	89.7	93.2	95.1	92.1	96.5	96.9	97.8
Female	5.5	8.0	10.3	6.8	4.9	7.9	3.5	3.1	2.2
White	49.0	52.6	50.9	53.4	48.2	52.9	40.1	50.4	42.9
Black	47.5	43.6	45.7	42.6	48.4	43.7	56.5	45.6	54.0
Other races	3.5	3.8	3.4	4.0	3.5	3.4	3.4	4.0	3.1
Median age (years)	30	31	30	31	30	29	30	30	32
Median age at first arrest (years)	18	24	25	23	17	18	16	17	16

[1] An individual who has been previously sentenced to probation or incarceration as a juvenile or adult.

Source: U.S. Bureau of Justice Statistics, *Survey of State Prison Inmates, 1991.*

No. 352. Prisoners Under Jurisdiction of State and Federal Correctional Authorities— Summary, by State: 1980 to 1993

[For years ending **December 31**]

SEX, REGION, DIVISION, AND STATE	1980	1990	1992	1993 Total	1993 Percent change, 1992-1993	SEX, REGION, DIVISION, AND STATE	1980	1990	1992	1993 Total	1993 Percent change, 1992-1993
U.S.	**329,821**	**773,919**	**882,500**	**946,946**	**7.3**	DE [1]	1,474	3,471	4,062	4,210	3.6
Male	316,401	729,840	832,093	891,885	7.2	MD	7,731	17,848	19,977	20,264	1.4
Female	13,420	44,079	50,407	55,061	9.2	DC [1]	3,145	9,947	10,875	10,845	-0.3
Federal	24,363	65,526	80,259	89,587	11.6	VA.	8,920	17,593	21,199	22,850	7.8
State	305,458	708,393	802,241	857,359	6.9	WV [3]	1,257	1,565	1,674	1,805	7.8
						NC	15,513	18,411	20,454	21,892	7.0
Northeast	**45,796**	**123,464**	**138,144**	**145,425**	**5.3**	SC	7,862	17,319	18,643	18,704	0.3
N.E.	**9,926**	**25,151**	**28,781**	**30,975**	**7.6**	GA [2]	12,178	22,411	25,290	27,783	9.9
ME	814	1,523	1,519	1,469	-3.3	FL [2]	20,735	44,387	48,302	53,048	9.8
NH	326	1,342	1,777	1,775	-0.1	**E.S.C.**	**21,055**	**43,451**	**48,571**	**51,795**	**6.6**
VT [1]	480	1,049	1,254	1,223	-2.5	KY	3,588	9,023	10,364	10,440	0.7
MA [2]	3,185	8,345	10,053	10,034	-0.2	TN	7,022	10,388	11,849	12,824	8.2
RI [1]	813	2,392	2,775	2,783	0.3	AL	6,543	15,665	17,453	18,624	6.7
CT [1]	4,308	10,500	11,403	13,691	20.1	MS	3,902	8,375	8,905	9,907	11.3
M.A.	**35,870**	**98,313**	**109,363**	**114,450**	**4.7**	**W.S.C.**	**46,488**	**88,248**	**104,553**	**117,629**	**12.5**
NY	21,815	54,895	61,736	64,569	4.6	AR	2,911	7,322	8,285	8,625	4.1
NJ	5,884	21,128	22,653	23,831	5.2	LA	8,889	18,599	20,980	22,468	7.1
PA	8,171	22,290	24,974	26,050	4.3	OK	4,796	12,285	14,821	16,409	10.7
Midwest	**66,211**	**145,894**	**166,308**	**173,277**	**4.2**	TX [2][3]	29,892	50,042	60,467	70,127	16.0
E.N.C.	**51,175**	**113,806**	**131,267**	**137,705**	**4.9**	**West**	**47,093**	**154,384**	**174,189**	**187,832**	**7.8**
OH	13,489	31,822	38,378	40,641	5.9	**Mt**	**13,141**	**37,433**	**42,360**	**45,073**	**6.4**
IN [2]	6,683	12,736	13,945	14,470	3.8	MT	739	1,425	1,548	1,541	-0.5
IL [2]	11,899	27,516	31,640	34,495	9.0	ID	817	1,961	2,256	2,606	15.5
MI [2]	15,124	34,267	39,113	39,318	0.5	WY	534	1,110	1,063	1,129	6.2
WI	3,980	7,465	8,191	8,781	7.2	CO	2,629	7,671	8,997	9,462	5.2
W.N.C.	**15,036**	**32,088**	**35,041**	**35,572**	**1.5**	NM	1,279	3,187	3,271	3,498	6.9
MN	2,001	3,176	3,822	4,200	9.9	AZ [2]	4,372	14,261	16,477	17,811	8.1
IA [2]	2,481	3,967	4,518	4,898	8.4	UT	932	2,496	2,699	2,888	7.0
MO [2]	5,726	14,943	16,195	16,178	-0.1	NV	1,839	5,322	6,049	6,138	1.5
ND	253	483	477	498	4.4	**Pac**	**33,952**	**116,951**	**131,829**	**142,759**	**8.3**
SD	635	1,341	1,487	1,553	4.4	WA	4,399	7,995	9,959	10,419	4.6
NE	1,446	2,403	2,514	2,518	0.2	OR	3,177	6,492	6,583	6,557	-0.4
KS	2,494	5,775	6,028	5,727	-5.0	CA [2]	24,569	97,309	109,496	119,951	9.5
South	**146,358**	**284,651**	**323,600**	**350,825**	**8.4**	AK [1][2]	822	2,622	2,865	2,703	-5.7
S.A.	**78,815**	**152,952**	**170,476**	**181,401**	**6.4**	HI [1]	985	2,533	2,926	3,129	6.9

[1] Includes both jail and prison inmates (State has combined jail and prison system).　[2] Numbers are custodial, not jurisdictional counts.　[3] Jurisdiction counts exclude prisoners held in jail because of crowding.

Source: U.S. Bureau of Justice Statistics, *Prisoners in 1993,* and earlier reports.

No. 353. Adults on Probation, in Jail or Prison, or on Parole: 1980 to 1992

[As of December 31, except jail counts as of June 30]

ITEM	Total [1]	Probation	Jail	Prison	Parole
1980	1,840,400	1,118,097	[2]182,288	319,598	220,438
1981	2,006,600	1,225,934	[2]195,085	360,029	225,539
1982	2,192,600	1,357,264	207,853	402,914	224,604
1983	2,475,100	1,582,947	221,815	423,898	246,440
1984	2,689,200	1,740,948	233,018	448,264	266,992
1985	3,011,400	1,968,712	254,986	487,593	300,203
1986	3,239,400	2,114,621	272,735	526,436	325,638
1987	3,459,600	2,247,158	294,092	562,814	355,505
1988	3,714,100	2,356,483	341,893	607,766	407,977
1989	4,055,600	2,522,125	393,303	683,367	456,803
1990	4,348,100	2,670,234	403,019	743,382	531,407
1991	4,536,200	2,729,322	424,129	792,535	590,198
1992	**4,763,200**	**2,811,611**	**441,781**	**851,205**	**658,601**
Sex:					
Male	4,050,900	2,257,900	401,100	804,200	587,700
Female	712,300	553,700	40,700	47,100	70,800
Race:					
White	2,682,200	1,689,500	233,000	411,800	347,800
Black	1,781,700	857,100	195,200	427,700	301,600

[1] Totals may not add due to individuals having multiple correctional statuses.   [2] Estimated.

Source: U.S. Bureau of Justice Statistics, *Correctional Populations in the United States, 1992.*

No. 354. Prisoners Under Sentence of Death: 1980 to 1993

[As of December 31. Excludes prisoners under sentence of death who remained within local correction systems pending exhaustion of appellate process or who had not been committed to prison]

CHARACTERISTIC	1980	1990	1991	1992	1993	CHARACTERISTIC	1980	1990	1991	1992	1993
Total [1]	**688**	**2,346**	**2,466**	**2,575**	**2,716**	Unknown	163	279	313	315	332
						Marital status:					
White	418	1,368	1,450	1,508	1,566	Never married	268	998	1,071	1,132	1,222
Black and other	270	978	1,016	1,067	1,150	Married	229	632	663	663	671
						Divorced [2]	217	726	746	780	823
Under 20 years	11	8	14	12	13						
20 to 24 years	173	168	179	188	211	Time elapsed since					
25 to 34 years	334	1,110	1,087	1,078	1,066	sentencing:					
35 to 54 years	186	1,006	1,129	1,212	1,330	Less than 12 months	185	231	252	265	262
55 years and over	10	64	73	85	96	12 to 47 months	389	753	718	720	716
						48 to 71 months	102	438	441	444	422
Years of school						72 months and over	38	934	1,071	1,146	1,316
completed:											
7 years or less	68	178	173	181	185	Legal status at arrest:					
8 years	74	186	181	180	183	Not under sentence	384	1,345	1,415	1,476	1,562
9 to 11 years	204	775	810	836	885	Parole or probation [3]	115	578	615	702	754
12 years	162	729	783	831	887	Prison or escaped	45	128	102	101	102
More than 12 years	43	209	222	232	244	Unknown	170	305	321	296	298

[1] For 1980 to 1991, revisions to the total number of prisoners were not carried to the characteristics except for race.   [2] Includes persons married but separated, widows, widowers, and unknown.   [3] Includes prisoners on mandatory conditional release, work release, leave, AWOL, or bail. Covers 24 prisoners in 1989, 28 in 1990, and 29 in 1991 and 1992.

Source: U.S. Bureau of Justice Statistics, *Capital Punishment,* annual.

No. 355. Movement of Prisoners Under Sentence of Death: 1980 to 1993

[Prisoners reported under sentence of death by civil authorities. The term "under sentence of death" begins when the court pronounces the first sentence of death for a capital offense]

STATUS	1980	1984	1985	1986	1987	1988	1989	1990	1991	1992	1993
Under sentence of death, Jan. 1 . . .	595	1,209	1,420	1,575	1,800	1,967	2,117	2,243	2,346	2,465	2,580
Received death sentence [1][2]	203	296	281	297	299	296	251	244	266	265	282
White	125	173	165	164	190	196	133	147	163	147	146
Black . . . . [2]	77	119	114	123	106	91	114	94	101	114	130
Dispositions other than executions [2]	101	69	108	73	90	128	102	108	116	124	108
Executions	-	21	18	18	25	11	16	23	14	31	38
Under sentence of death, Dec. 31 [1]	688	1,420	1,575	1,800	1,967	2,117	2,243	2,346	2,466	2,575	2,716
White	425	809	896	1,006	1,128	1,238	1,308	1,368	1,450	1,508	1,566
Black	268	595	664	750	813	853	898	940	1,016	1,029	1,109

- Represents zero.   [1] Includes races other than White or Black.   [2] Revisions to total number of prisoners under death sentence not carried to this category.
Source: U.S. Bureau of Justice Statistics, *Capital Punishment,* annual.

No. 356. Prisoners Executed Under Civil Authority: 1930 to 1993

[Excludes executions by military authorities. The Army (including the Air Force) carried out 160 (148 between 1942 and 1950; 3 each in 1954, 1955, and 1957; and 1 each in 1958, 1959, and 1961). Of the total, 106 were executed for murder (including 21 involving rape), 53 for rape, and 1 for desertion. The Navy carried out no executions during the period. See also *Historical Statistics, Colonial Times to 1970,* series H 1155-1167]

YEAR OR PERIOD	Total [1]	White	Black	EXECUTED FOR MURDER			EXECUTED FOR RAPE			EXECUTED, OTHER OFFENSES [2]		
				Total [1]	White	Black	Total [1]	White	Black	Total [1]	White	Black
All years	**4,089**	**1,864**	**2,154**	**3,564**	**1,777**	**1,718**	**455**	**48**	**405**	**70**	**39**	**31**
1930 to 1939	1,667	827	816	1,514	803	687	125	10	115	28	14	14
1940 to 1949	1,284	490	781	1,064	458	595	200	19	179	20	13	7
1950 to 1959	717	336	376	601	316	280	102	13	89	14	7	7
1960 to 1967	191	98	93	155	87	68	28	6	22	8	5	3
1968 to 1976	-	-	-	-	-	-	-	-	-	-	-	-
1977 to 1981	4	4	-	4	4	-	-	-	-	-	-	-
1982	2	1	1	2	1	1	-	-	-	-	-	-
1983	5	4	1	5	4	1	-	-	-	-	-	-
1984	21	13	8	21	13	8	-	-	-	-	-	-
1985	18	11	7	18	11	7	-	-	-	-	-	-
1986	18	11	7	18	11	7	-	-	-	-	-	-
1987	25	13	12	25	13	12	-	-	-	-	-	-
1988	11	6	5	11	6	5	-	-	-	-	-	-
1989	16	8	8	16	8	8	-	-	-	-	-	-
1990	23	16	7	23	16	7	-	-	-	-	-	-
1991	14	7	7	14	7	7	-	-	-	-	-	-
1992	31	19	11	31	19	11	-	-	-	-	-	-
1993	38	23	14	38	23	14	-	-	-	-	-	-

- Represents zero.   [1] Includes races other than White or Black.   [2] Includes 25 armed robbery, 20 kidnapping, 11 burglary, 8 espionage (6 in 1942 and 2 in 1953), and 6 aggravated assault.
Source: Through 1978, U.S. Law Enforcement Assistance Administration; thereafter, U.S. Bureau of Justice Statistics, *Correctional Populations in the United States,* annual.

No. 357. Prisoners Under Sentence of Death and Executed Under Civil Authority, by States: 1977 to 1993

[No executions took place in Delaware, Maine, Massachusetts, Michigan, Minnesota, Montana, New Hampshire, North Dakota, Rhode Island, South Dakota, and Wisconsin from 1977 to 1993. Maine, Minnesota, and Wisconsin never authorized the death penalty during the period. New Hampshire and Rhode Island authorized it for most of the 4 decades but did not apply it. Michigan abolished the penalty and North Dakota allowed the punishment statute to lapse in 1975. Alaska and Hawaii could enter these data after receiving statehood in 1959, but neither has authorized the death penalty]

STATE	1977 to 1989	1990	1991	1992	1993	STATE	1977 to 1989	1990	1991	1992	1993	STATE	1977 to 1989	1990	1991	1992	1993
U.S..	**120**	**23**	**14**	**31**	**38**	IA . . .	-	-	-	-	-	OH . . .	-	-	-	-	-
AL . . .	7	1	-	2	-	KS . . .	-	-	-	-	-	OK . . .	-	-	1	-	2	-
AZ . . .	-	-	-	1	2	KY . . .	-	-	-	-	-	OR . . .	-	-	-	-	-
AR . . .	-	2	-	2	-	LA . . .	18	1	1	-	1	PA . . .	-	-	-	-	-
CA . . .	-	-	-	-	1	MD . . .	-	-	-	-	-	SC . . .	2	1	1	-	-
CO . . .	-	-	-	-	-	MS . . .	4	-	-	-	-	TN . . .	-	-	-	-	-
CT . . .	-	-	-	-	-	MO . . .	1	4	1	1	4	TX . . .	33	4	5	12	17
DC . . .	-	-	-	-	-	NE . . .	-	-	-	-	-	UT . . .	3	-	-	1	-
FL. . . .	21	4	2	2	3	NV . . .	4	1	-	-	-	VT . . .	-	-	-	-	-
GA . . .	14	-	1	-	2	NJ . . .	-	-	-	-	-	VA . . .	-	3	2	4	5
ID . . .	-	-	-	-	-	NM . . .	-	-	-	-	-	WA . . .	-	-	-	-	1
IL	-	1	-	-	-	NY . . .	-	-	-	-	-	WV . . .	-	-	-	-	-
IN	2	-	-	-	-	NC . . .	3	-	1	1	-	WY . . .	-	-	-	1	-

- Represents zero.
Source: Through 1978, U.S. Law Enforcement Assistance Administration; thereafter, U.S. Bureau of Justice Statistics, *Capital Punishment,* annual.

No. 358. Fire Losses—Total and Per Capita: 1970 to 1993

[Includes allowance for uninsured and unreported losses but excludes losses to government property and forests. Represents incurred losses]

YEAR	Total (mil. dol.)	Per capita [1]	YEAR	Total (mil. dol.)	Per capita [1]	YEAR	Total (mil. dol.)	Per capita [1]
1970	2,328	11.41	1978	4,008	18.05	1986	8,488	35.21
1971	2,316	11.20	1979	4,851	21.60	1987	8,504	34.96
1972	2,304	11.01	1980	5,579	24.56	1988	9,626	39.11
1973	2,639	12.49	1981	5,625	24.53	1989	9,514	38.33
1974	3,190	14.95	1982	5,894	25.61	1990	9,495	38.26
1975	3,190	14.81	1983	6,320	27.20	1991	11,302	44.83
1976	3,558	16.35	1984	7,602	32.35	1992	13,588	48.24
1977	3,764	17.13	1985	7,753	32.70	1993	9,990	38.73

[1] Based on Bureau of the Census estimated resident population as of July 1.

Source: Insurance Information Institute, New York, NY, *Insurance Facts,* annual.

No. 359. Fires—Number and Loss, by Type and Property Use: 1990 to 1993

[Based on annual sample survey of fire departments. No adjustments were made for unreported fires and losses. Property loss includes direct property loss only]

TYPE AND PROPERTY USE	NUMBER (1,000)				PROPERTY LOSS (mil. dol.)			
	1990	1991	1992	1993	1990	1991	1992	1993
Fires, total.	**2,019**	**2,041**	**1,965**	**1,953**	**7,818**	**9,467**	**8,295**	**8,546**
Structure	624	640	638	621	6,713	8,320	6,957	7,406
Outside of structure [1]	52	54	50	52	90	55	318	63
Brush and rubbish	787	806	743	732	-	-	-	-
Vehicle	436	428	405	421	967	1,049	965	1,030
Other	120	113	129	127	48	43	55	47
Structure by property use:								
Public assembly	17	16	17	16	317	362	361	298
Educational	9	9	10	9	136	58	68	64
Institutional	11	12	12	10	33	28	35	30
Stores and offices	31	33	33	29	603	[2]931	[3]1,105	741
Residential.	467	478	472	470	4,253	[4]5,552	3,880	4,843
1-2 family units [5]	359	363	358	358	3,534	3,354	3,178	4,111
Apartments.	95	102	101	100	623	609	597	653
Hotels and motels	6	6	6	6	66	52	56	34
Other residential	7	7	7	6	30	37	49	45
Storage [6]	40	44	42	39	534	594	734	651
Industry, utility, defense [6] . .	22	19	19	19	623	605	597	623
Special structures	27	29	33	29	214	190	177	156

- Represents zero. [1] Includes outside storage, crops, timber, etc. [2] Includes one large store and office fire totaling $325 million. [3] Includes estimated loss of $567 million involving 862 structures from the April 1992 civil disturbance in Los Angeles, CA. [4] Includes the Oakland, CA fire which resulted in $1.5 billion in residential property damage. [5] Includes mobile homes. [6] Data underreported as some incidents were handled by private fire brigades or fixed suppression systems which do not report.

Source: National Fire Protection Association, Quincy, MA, "NFPA Reports on U.S. Fire Loss — 1993," *NFPA Journal,* September 1994, and prior issues (copyright 1994).

No. 360. Fires and Property Loss for Incendiary and Suspicious Fires and Civilian Fire Deaths and Injuries, by Selected Property Type: 1990 to 1993

[Based on sample survey of fire departments]

ITEM	1990	1991	1992	1993	ITEM	1990	1991	1992	1993
NUMBER (1,000)					CIVILIAN FIRE DEATHS				
Structure fires, total. . .	624	640	638	621	Deaths, total [2]	5,195	4,465	4,730	4,635
Structure fires of incendiary					Residential property.	4,115	3,575	3,765	3,825
or suspicious origin	97	98	94	85					
					One- and two-family				
Fires of incendiary origin .	58	62	58	54	dwellings	3,370	2,905	3,160	3,035
Fires of suspicious origin .	39	36	36	31	Apartments.	680	595	545	685
					Vehicles	695	605	730	595
PROPERTY LOSS [1] (mil. dol.)									
Structure fires, total. . .	6,713	8,320	6,957	7,406	CIVILIAN FIRE INJURIES				
Structure fires of incendiary					Injuries, total [2]	28,600	29,375	28,700	30,475
or suspicious origin	1,394	1,531	1,999	2,351	Residential property.	20,650	21,850	21,600	22,600
					One- and two-family				
					dwellings	15,250	15,600	15,275	15,700
Fires of incendiary origin .	875	1,072	[3]1,493	[4]1,901	Apartments.	4,975	5,675	5,825	6,300
Fires of suspicious origin .	519	459	506	450	Vehicles	3,350	3,050	3,000	2,675

[1] Direct property loss only. [2] Includes other not shown separately. [3] Includes estimated loss of $567 million from the April 1992 civil disturbance in Los Angeles, CA. [4] Includes fire losses that occurred during the wildfires in California and the World Trade Center bombing in New York City, which resulted in combined estimated losses of $1.039 billion.

Source: National Fire Protection Association, Quincy, MA, September 1994, and prior issues (copyright 1994).

Figure 6.1
National Air Pollutant Emissions: 1983 to 1993

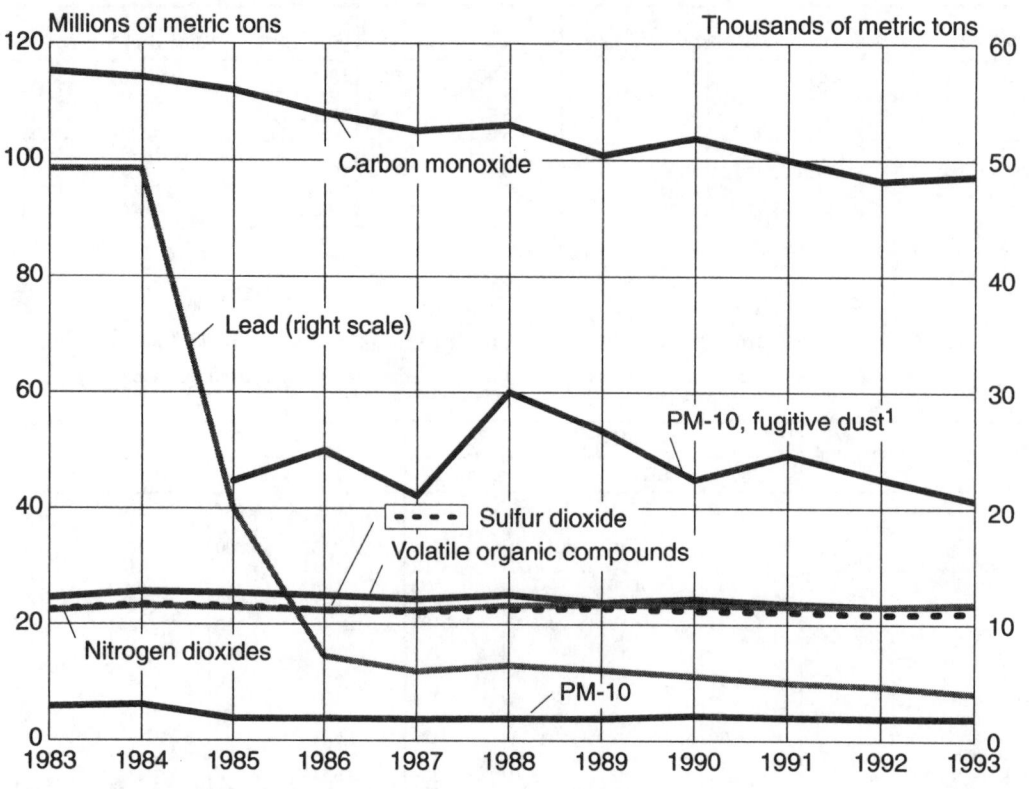

[1] PM-10=Particulate matter of less than ten microns. From sources such as agricultural tilling, construction, mining and quarrying, paved and unpaved roads, and wind erosion.
Source: Chart prepared by U.S. Bureau of the Census. For data, see table 374.

Figure 6.2
Toxic Releases—Top 10 Industries: 1993

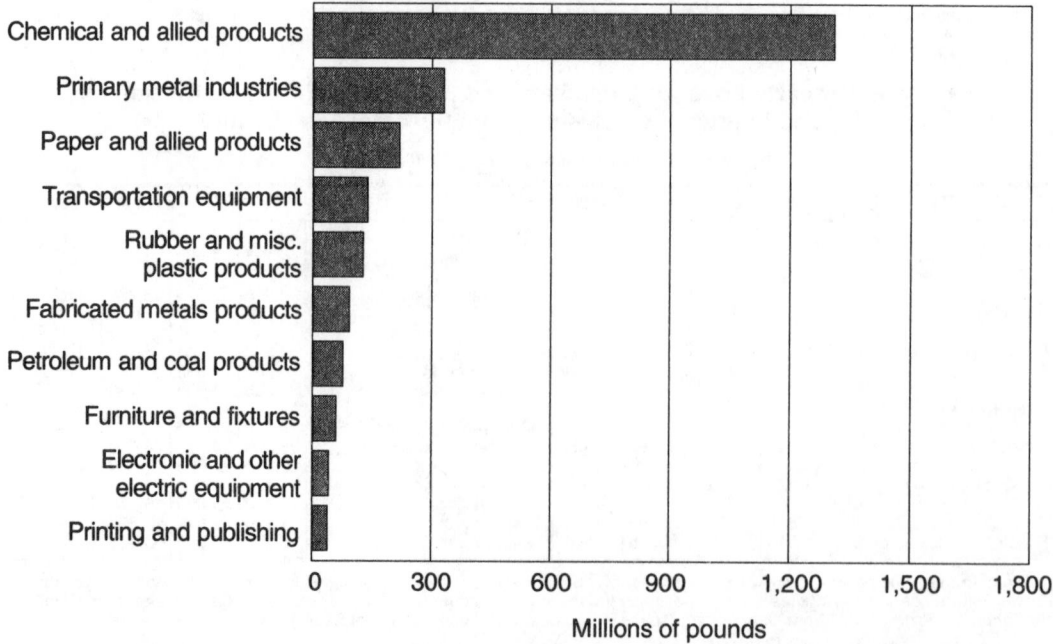

Source: Chart prepared by U.S. Bureau of the Census. For data, see table 379.

Geography and Environment

This section presents a variety of information on the physical environment of the United States, starting with basic area measurement data and ending with climatic data for selected weather stations around the country. The subjects covered between those points are mostly concerned with environmental trends, but include such related subjects as land use, water consumption, air pollutant emissions, toxic releases, oil spills, hazardous waste sites, threatened and endangered wildlife, and expenditures for pollution abatement and control.

The information in this section is selected from a wide range of Federal agencies that compile the data for various administrative or regulatory purposes, such as the Environmental Protection Agency, U.S. Geological Survey, National Oceanic and Atmospheric Administration, Soil Conservation Service, and General Services Administration. Other agencies include the Bureau of the Census, which presents nationwide area measurement information and the Bureau of Economic Analysis, which compiles data on pollution abatement and control expenditures.

Area.—For the 1990 census, area measurements were calculated by computer based on the information contained in a single, consistent geographic data base, the TIGER File (described below), rather than relying on historical, local, and manually calculated information. This especially affects water area figures reported in 1990; these had only included those bodies of water of least 40 acres and those streams with a width of at least one- eighth of a statute mile from 1940 to 1980. Water area figures for 1990 increased because the data reflected all water recorded in the Census Bureau's geographic data base including coastal, Great Lakes and territorial waters.

Geography.—The U.S. Geological Survey conducts investigations, surveys, and research in the fields of geography, geology, topography, geographic information systems, mineralogy, hydrology, and geothermal energy resources as

In Brief

Almost 22 percent of municipal solid waste was recovered or recycled in 1993.

Release of toxic chemicals by manufacturing facilities amounted to 2.8 billion pounds in 1993, down 25 percent from 1990

Emissions of CFC gases in the air down 35% between 1987 and 1992

well as natural hazards. In cooperation with State and local agencies, the U.S. Geological Survey prepares and publishes topographic, land use/land cover, geologic, and hydrologic maps and digital data compilations. The U.S. Geological Survey provides United States cartographic data through the Earth Sciences Information Center, water resources data through the National Water Data Exchange (NAWDEX) and a variety of research and Open-File reports which are announced monthly in New Publications of the U.S. Geological Survey. In a joint project with the Census Bureau, the U.S. Geological Survey provided the basic information on geographic features for input into a national geographic and cartographic data base prepared by the Census Bureau, called the TIGER (Topologically Integrated Geographic Encoding and Referencing) System.

Maps prepared by the Bureau of the Census show the names and boundaries of various types of legal and statistical entities, such as places, county subdivisions, and larger areas, and are available as of the specific decennial census. An inventory is available for the 1990 census, both on computer tape and CD-ROM as the 1990 TIGER/GICS (Geographic Identification Code Scheme) and for the 1992 economic censuses in the Geographic Reference Manual (EC92-R-1). The Census Bureau maintains a current inventory of governmental units and their legal boundaries through its Boundary and Annexation Survey. The TIGER System contains information on the legal and statistical entities used by the Census Bureau, as well as on both manmade and natural features, such as streets, roads, railroads, rivers, and lakes; information is available to the public in the form of machine-readable TIGER extract files.

An inventory of the Nation's land resources by type of use/cover was conducted by the Soil Conservation Service in 1982, 1987, and 1992. The results, published in the 1992 National Inventory of Land Resources, cover all non-Federal land in Puerto Rico, the Virgin Islands, and the U.S. except Alaska.

Environment.— The principal Federal agency responsible for pollution abatement and control activities is the Environmental Protection Agency (EPA). It is responsible for establishing and monitoring national air quality standards, water quality activities, solid and hazardous waste disposal, and control of toxic substances.

National Ambient Air Quality Standards (NAAQS) for suspended particulate matter, sulfur dioxide, photochemical oxidants, carbon monoxide, and nitrogen dioxide were originally set by the EPA in April 1971. Every 5 years each of the NAAQS is reviewed and revised if new health or welfare data indicates that a change is necessary. The standard for photochemical oxidants, now called ozone, was revised in February 1979. Also, a new NAAQS for lead was promulgated in October 1978 and for suspended particulate matter in 1987. Table 363 gives some of the health-related standards for the six air pollutants having NAAQS. Responsibility for demonstrating compliance with or progress toward achieving these standards lies with the State agencies. In 1993, there were 1,508 non-Federal sampling stations for particulates, 692 for sulfur dioxide, 537 for carbon monoxide, 925 for ozone, 377 for nitrogen dioxide, and 430 for lead. Data from these State networks are periodically submitted to EPA's National Aerometric Information Retrieval System (AIRS) for summarization in annual reports on the nationwide status and trends in air quality; for details, see National Air Quality and Emissions Trends Report, 1993.

Pollution abatement and control expenditures.—Data on expenditures for pollution abatement and control are compiled and published by the Bureau of Economic Analysis (BEA) and the U.S. Bureau of the Census. The BEA conducts surveys on national expenditures for pollution abatement and control and presents the data in its Survey of Current Business. The Bureau of the Census collects data on expenditures for pollution control activities for State and local governments and industry. Data on government expenditures are reported in an annual series of publications, Government Finances, which covers expenditures on sewage and sanitation outlays. Industry data are reported annually in Current Industrial Reports. The Council on Environmental Quality published some expenditure data in Environmental Quality along with other environmental indicator.

Climate.—NOAA, through the National Weather Service and the National Environmental Satellite, Data and Information Service, is responsible for data on climate. NOAA maintains about 11,600 weather stations, of which over 3,000 produce autographic precipitation records, about 600 take hourly readings of a series of weather elements, and the remainder record data once a day. These data are reported monthly in the Climatological Data (published by State), and monthly and annually in the Local Climatological Data (published by location for major cities).

The normal climatological temperatures, precipitation, and degree days listed in this publication are derived for comparative purposes and are averages for the 30-year period, 1961-90. For stations that did not have continuous records for the entire 30 years from the same instrument site, the normals have been adjusted to provide representative values for the current location. The information in all other tables is based on data from the beginning of the record at that location through 1993, except as noted.

Historical statistics.—Tabular headnotes provide cross-references, where applicable, to Historical Statistics of the United States, Colonial Times to 1970. See Appendix IV.

No. 361. Land and Water Area of States and Other Entities: 1990

[One square mile=2.59 square kilometers. Excludes territorial water, which was included in the 1993 edition of the *Statistical Abstract*. See *Historical Statistics of the United States, Colonial Times to 1970*, series A 210-263, for land area]

REGION, DIVISION, STATE, AND OTHER AREA	TOTAL AREA		LAND AREA		WATER AREA					
					Total		Inland	Coastal	Great Lakes	
	Sq. mi.	Sq. km.	Sq. mi.	Sq. km.	Sq. mi.	Sq. km.	Sq. mi.	Sq. mi.	Sq. mi.	
United States	3,717,522	9,628,382	3,536,338	9,159,115	181,184	469,267	78,641	42,491	60,052	
Northeast	176,618	457,441	162,274	420,290	14,344	37,151	6,145	3,549	4,650	
New England	68,655	177,816	62,811	162,680	5,844	15,136	3,696	2,148	-	
Maine	33,741	87,389	30,865	79,940	2,876	7,449	2,263	613	-	
New Hampshire	9,283	24,043	8,969	23,230	314	813	314	-	-	
Vermont	9,615	24,903	9,249	23,955	366	948	366	-	-	
Massachusetts	9,241	23,934	7,838	20,300	1,403	3,634	424	979	-	
Rhode Island	1,231	3,188	1,045	2,707	186	482	168	18	-	
Connecticut	5,544	14,359	4,845	12,549	699	1,810	161	538	-	
Middle Atlantic	107,963	279,624	99,463	257,609	8,500	22,015	2,449	1,401	4,650	
New York	53,989	139,832	47,224	122,310	6,765	17,521	1,888	976	3,901	
New Jersey	8,215	21,277	7,419	19,215	796	2,062	371	425	-	
Pennsylvania	45,759	118,516	44,820	116,084	939	2,432	190	-	749	
Midwest	821,765	2,128,371	751,520	1,946,437	70,245	181,935	14,843	-	55,402	
East North Central	301,371	780,551	243,539	630,766	57,832	149,785	4,976	-	52,856	
Ohio	44,828	116,105	40,953	106,068	3,875	10,036	376	-	3,499	
Indiana	36,420	94,328	35,870	92,903	550	1,425	315	-	235	
Illinois	57,918	150,008	55,593	143,986	2,325	6,022	750	-	1,575	
Michigan	96,705	250,466	56,809	147,135	39,896	103,331	1,704	-	38,192	
Wisconsin	65,500	169,645	54,314	140,673	11,186	28,972	1,831	-	9,355	
West North Central	520,394	1,347,820	507,981	1,315,671	12,413	32,150	9,867	-	2,546	
Minnesota	86,943	225,182	79,617	206,208	7,326	18,974	4,780	-	2,546	
Iowa	56,276	145,755	55,875	144,716	401	1,039	401	-	-	
Missouri	69,709	180,546	68,898	178,446	811	2,100	811	-	-	
North Dakota	70,704	183,123	68,994	178,694	1,710	4,429	1,710	-	-	
South Dakota	77,121	199,743	75,896	196,571	1,225	3,173	1,225	-	-	
Nebraska	77,359	200,360	76,878	199,114	481	1,246	481	-	-	
Kansas	82,282	213,110	81,823	211,922	459	1,189	459	-	-	
South	907,237	2,349,744	871,070	2,256,071	36,167	93,673	27,354	8,813	-	
South Atlantic	284,146	735,938	266,221	689,512	17,925	46,426	12,557	5,368	-	
Delaware	2,397	6,208	1,955	5,063	442	1,145	71	371	-	
Maryland	12,297	31,849	9,775	25,317	2,522	6,532	680	1,842	-	
District of Columbia	68	176	61	158	7	18	7	-	-	
Virginia	42,326	109,624	39,598	102,559	2,728	7,066	1,000	1,728	-	
West Virginia	24,232	62,761	24,087	62,385	145	376	145	-	-	
North Carolina	52,672	136,420	48,718	126,180	3,954	10,241	3,954	-	-	
South Carolina	31,189	80,780	30,111	77,987	1,078	2,792	1,006	72	-	
Georgia	58,977	152,750	57,919	150,010	1,058	2,740	1,011	47	-	
Florida	59,988	155,369	53,997	139,852	5,991	15,517	4,683	1,308	-	
East South Central	183,079	474,175	178,615	462,613	4,464	11,562	3,354	1,110	-	
Kentucky	40,411	104,664	39,732	102,906	679	1,759	679	-	-	
Tennessee	42,145	109,156	41,219	106,757	926	2,398	926	-	-	
Alabama	52,237	135,294	50,750	131,443	1,487	3,851	968	519	-	
Mississippi	48,286	125,061	46,914	121,507	1,372	3,553	781	591	-	
West South Central	440,012	1,139,631	426,234	1,103,946	13,778	35,685	11,443	2,335	-	
Arkansas	53,182	137,741	52,075	134,874	1,107	2,867	1,107	-	-	
Louisiana	49,650	128,594	43,566	112,836	6,084	15,758	4,153	1,931	-	
Oklahoma	69,903	181,049	68,679	177,879	1,224	3,170	1,224	-	-	
Texas	267,277	692,247	261,914	678,357	5,363	13,890	4,959	404	-	
West	1,811,902	4,692,826	1,751,474	4,536,318	60,428	156,509	30,299	30,129	-	
Mountain	863,614	2,236,760	856,121	2,217,353	7,493	19,407	7,493	-	-	
Montana	147,046	380,849	145,556	376,990	1,490	3,859	1,490	-	-	
Idaho	83,574	216,457	82,751	214,325	823	2,132	823	-	-	
Wyoming	97,819	253,351	97,105	251,502	714	1,849	714	-	-	
Colorado	104,100	269,619	103,729	268,658	371	961	371	-	-	
New Mexico	121,598	314,939	121,364	314,333	234	606	234	-	-	
Arizona	114,006	295,276	113,642	294,333	364	943	364	-	-	
Utah	84,904	219,901	82,168	212,815	2,736	7,086	2,736	-	-	
Nevada	110,567	286,369	109,806	284,398	761	1,971	761	-	-	
Pacific	948,288	2,456,066	895,353	2,318,964	52,935	137,102	22,806	30,129	-	
Washington	70,637	182,950	66,581	172,445	4,056	10,505	1,545	2,511	-	
Oregon	97,093	251,471	96,002	248,645	1,091	2,826	1,050	41	-	
California	158,869	411,471	155,973	403,970	2,896	7,501	2,674	222	-	
Alaska	615,230	1,593,446	570,374	1,477,269	44,856	116,177	17,501	27,355	-	
Hawaii	6,459	16,729	6,423	16,636	36	93	36	-	-	
Other areas:										
Puerto Rico	3,508	9,085	3,427	8,875	81	210	65	16	-	
American Samoa	90	233	77	200	13	34	7	6	-	
Guam	217	561	210	543	7	18	7	-	-	
No. Mariana Islands	189	490	179	464	10	26	2	8	-	
Palau	241	624	177	458	64	166	40	24	-	
Virgin Islands of the U.S	171	443	134	346	37	96	17	20	-	

- Represents or rounds to zero.

Source: U.S. Bureau of the Census, *1990 Census of Population and Housing*, series CPH-1; and unpublished data. Some corrections have been made subsequent to the 1990 Census reports.

No. 362. Territorial Expansion of the United States and Acquisitions of Other Areas

[One square mile=2.59 square kilometers. Boundaries of all acquisitions listed under "United States" were indefinite, at least in part at time of acquisition. Because different sources are used for land area, the sums of the acquisitions will not equal the United States or the total. See also Historical Statistics, Colonial Times to 1970, series J 1–2]

ACCESSION	Acquisition date	LAND AREA		ACCESSION	Acquisition date	LAND AREA	
		Sq. ml.	Sq. km.			Sq. ml.	Sq. km.
Total[1]	(X)	3,540,558	9,170,043	Alaska[1]	1867	570,374	1,477,267
				Hawaii[1]	1898	6,423	16,636
United States[1]	(X)	3,536,288	9,158,960	Other areas:[1]			
Territory in 1790[2]	(X)	895,415	2,319,125	Puerto Rico	[4]1898	3,427	8,875
Louisiana Purchase	1803	909,380	2,355,294	Guam	[5]1898	210	543
Purchase of Florida[3]	1819	58,666	151,945	American Samoa	[6]1899	77	200
Texas	1845	388,687	1,006,699	Virgin Islands of the U.S. .	1917	134	346
Oregon Territory	1846	286,541	742,141	Palau[7]	1947	179	464
Mexican Cession	1848	529,189	1,370,600	No. Mariana Islands	[8]1947	177	458
Gadsden Purchase	1853	29,670	76,845	All other	(X)	16	41

X Not applicable. [1]Source: U.S. Bureau of the Census, 1990 Census of Population and Housing, series CPH–2. Reflects correction made after publication of results. [2]Includes that part of drainage basin of Red River of the North, south of 49th parallel, sometimes considered part of Louisiana Purchase. [3]Also acquired areas west of the Mississippi River amounting to 22,834 square miles, but relinquished to Spain 97,150 square miles, or a net loss of 15,650 square miles. [4]Ceded by Spain in 1898, ratified in 1899, and became Commonwealth of Puerto Rico by Act of Congress on July 25, 1952. [5]Acquired 1898; ratified 1899. [6]Acquired 1899; ratified 1900. [7]Remaining portion of the Trust Territory of the Pacific Islands, under U.N. trusteeship since 1947. The Federated States of Micronesia and the Marshall Islands, also formerly part of the TTPI, became freely associated States in 1986 and are not included in this table. [8]Attained Commonwealth status in 1986, separate from the TTPI, of which it had been a part since 1947.

Source: Except as noted, U.S. Geological Survey, *Boundaries of the United States and the Several States*, Paper 909, 1976.

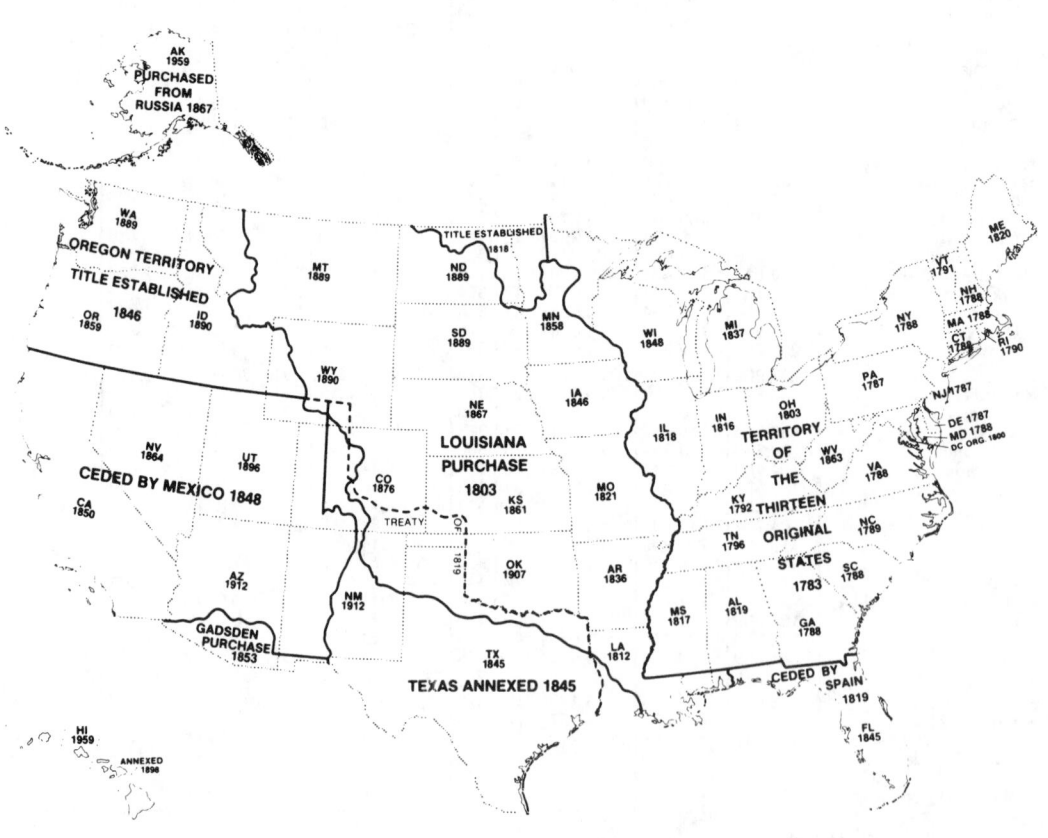

No. 363. Area and Acquisition of the Federal Public Domain: 1781 to 1991

[**In millions of acres.** Areas of acquisitions are as computed in 1912, and do not agree with figures in square miles shown in table 351 which include later adjustments and reflect subsequent remeasurement. Excludes outlying areas of the United States amounting to 645,949 acres in 1978. See also *Historical Statistics, Colonial Times to 1970,* series J 3-6]

YEAR	Land area, total [1]	YEAR	LAND AREA [1]			YEAR AND ACQUISITION	ACREAGE		
			Total	Public domain	Acquired		Total	Land	Inland water
1802 . . .	200.0	1978 . . .	775.2	712.0	63.3	**Aggregate**	**1,837.8**	**1,804.7**	**33.1**
1850 . . .	1,200.0	1979 . . .	744.1	684.3	59.8				
1880 . . .	900.0	1980 . . .	719.5	648.0	71.5	1781-1802 (State Cessions) . . .	236.8	233.4	3.4
1912 . . .	600.0	1981 . . .	730.8	668.7	62.2	1803, Louisiana Purchase [2]	529.9	523.4	6.5
1946 . . .	413.0	1982 . . .	729.8	670.0	59.8	1819, Cession from Spain	46.1	43.3	2.8
1950 . . .	412.0	1983 . . .	732.0	672.4	59.6	Red River Basin [3]	29.6	29.1	0.5
1955 . . .	407.9	1984 . . .	726.6	658.9	67.7				
1959 . . .	768.6	1985 . . .	726.7	656.2	70.5	1846, Oregon Compromise	183.4	180.6	2.7
1960 . . .	771.5	1986 . . .	727.1	662.7	64.4	1848, Mexican Cession [2]	338.7	334.5	4.2
1965 . . .	765.8	1987 . . .	724.3	661.0	63.3	1850, Purchase from Texas	78.9	78.8	0.1
1970 . . .	761.3	1988 . . .	688.2	623.2	65.0	1853, Gadsden Purchase	19.0	19.0	(Z)
1975 . . .	760.4	1989 . . .	662.2	597.9	64.3	1867, Alaska Purchase	375.3	362.5	12.8
1976 . . .	762.2	1990 . . .	649.8	587.4	62.4				
1977 . . .	741.5	1991 . . .	649.3	587.6	61.8				

Z Less than 50,000.   [1] Owned by Federal Government. Comprises original public domain plus acquired lands. Estimated from imperfect data available for indicated years. Prior to 1959, excludes Alaska, and 1960, Hawaii. Source: Beginning 1955, U.S. General Services Administration, *Inventory Report on Real Property Owned by the United States Throughout the World,* annual.
[2] Data for Louisiana Purchase exclude areas eliminated by Treaty of 1819 with Spain. Such areas are included in figures for Mexican Cession.   [3] Represents drainage basin of Red River of the North, south of 49th parallel. Authorities differ as to method and date of its acquisition. Some hold it as part of the Louisiana Purchase; others, as acquired from Great Britain.

Source: Except as noted, U.S. Dept. of the Interior. Estimated area, Bureau of Land Management; all other data, Office of the Secretary, *Areas of Acquisitions to the Territory of the U.S.,* 1922.

No. 364. Total and Federally Owned Land, 1960 to 1991, and by State, 1991

[As of **end of fiscal year;** see text, section 9. Total land area figures are not comparable with those in table 361]

REGION, DIVISION, AND STATE	Total (1,000 acres)	Not owned by Federal Government (1,000 acres)	OWNED BY FEDERAL GOVERNMENT [1]		REGION, DIVISION, AND STATE	Total (1,000 acres)	Not owned by Federal Government (1,000 acres)	OWNED BY FEDERAL GOVERNMENT [1]	
			Acres (1,000)	Percent				Acres (1,000)	Percent
1960	2,273,407	1,501,894	771,512	33.9	**South . . . .**	**561,238**	**540,183**	**21,055**	**3.8**
1965	2,271,343	1,505,546	765,797	33.7	**S.A. . . . .**	**171,325**	**161,181**	**10,144**	**5.9**
1970	2,271,343	1,510,042	761,301	33.5	DE	1,266	1,239	27	2.2
1975	2,271,343	1,510,929	760,414	33.5	MD	6,319	6,133	187	3.0
1980	2,271,343	1,551,822	719,522	31.7	DC	39	29	10	26.1
1985	2,271,343	1,544,658	726,686	32.0	VA	25,496	23,900	1,597	6.3
1988	2,271,343	1,583,090	688,253	30.3	WV	15,411	14,382	1,028	6.7
1989	2,271,343	1,609,185	662,158	29.2	NC	31,403	29,432	1,970	6.3
1990	2,271,343	1,621,541	649,802	28.6	SC	19,374	18,652	722	3.7
1991	2,271,343	1,621,998	649,346	28.6	GA	37,295	35,807	1,488	4.0
1991, total	**2,271,343**	**1,621,998**	**649,346**	**28.6**	FL	34,721	31,607	3,114	9.0
Northeast	**104,700**	**102,411**	**2,288**	**2.2**	**E.S.C . . . . .**	**115,141**	**110,686**	**4,455**	**3.9**
N.E.	**40,401**	**39,079**	**1,322**	**3.3**	KY	25,512	24,433	1,080	4.2
ME	19,848	19,692	155	0.8	TN	26,728	25,734	994	3.7
NH	5,769	5,035	734	12.7	AL	32,678	31,603	1,075	3.3
VT	5,937	5,579	358	6.0	MS	30,223	28,916	1,306	4.3
MA	5,035	4,969	66	1.3	**W.S.C . . . . .**	**274,772**	**268,316**	**6,456**	**2.3**
RI	677	675	2	0.3	AR	33,599	30,837	2,762	8.2
CT	3,135	3,129	6	0.2	LA	28,868	28,123	745	2.6
M.A	**64,299**	**63,332**	**966**	**1.5**	OK	44,088	43,383	705	1.6
NY	30,681	30,472	209	0.7	TX	168,218	165,973	2,245	1.3
NJ	4,813	4,664	149	3.1	**West . . . .**	**1,122,535**	**519,978**	**602,557**	**53.7**
PA	28,804	28,196	608	2.1	**Mountain . . .**	**548,449**	**283,625**	**264,823**	**48.3**
Midwest	**482,870**	**459,425**	**23,446**	**4.9**	MT	93,271	67,129	26,142	28.0
E.N.C	**156,679**	**146,849**	**9,830**	**6.3**	ID	52,933	20,319	32,614	61.6
OH	26,222	25,880	342	1.3	WY	62,343	31,866	30,477	48.9
IN	23,158	22,757	401	1.7	CO	66,486	42,332	24,154	36.3
IL	35,795	34,834	961	2.7	NM	77,766	52,564	25,203	32.4
MI	36,492	31,903	4,589	12.6	AZ	72,688	38,380	34,308	47.2
WI	35,011	31,474	3,537	10.1	UT	52,697	19,036	33,661	63.9
W.N.C	**326,191**	**312,576**	**13,616**	**4.2**	NV	70,264	12,000	58,265	82.9
MN	51,206	45,839	5,367	10.5	**Pacific . . . . .**	**574,086**	**236,353**	**337,733**	**58.8**
IA	35,860	35,524	336	0.9	WA	42,694	30,614	12,080	28.3
MO	44,248	42,152	2,096	4.7	OR	61,599	29,308	32,291	52.4
ND	44,452	42,574	1,879	4.2	CA	100,207	55,500	44,707	44.6
SD	48,882	46,076	2,806	5.7	AK	365,482	117,461	248,021	67.9
NE	49,032	48,322	710	1.4	HI	4,106	3,471	634	15.5
KS	52,511	52,089	422	0.8					

[1] Excludes trust properties.

Source: U.S. General Services Administration, *Inventory Report on Real Property Owned by the United States Throughout the World,* annual.

No. 365. Land Cover/Use, by State: 1992

[In thousands of acres. Excludes Alaska and District of Columbia]

STATE	Total surface area [1]	Federal land	NONFEDERAL LAND							
			Total	Developed [2]	Rural					
					Total	Crop-land	Pasture land	Range-land	Forest land	Minor cover/ use
Total	1,940,011	407,989	1,483,126	92,352	1,390,774	382,317	125,927	398,949	394,958	88,624
United States	1,937,678	407,899	1,480,916	91,946	1,388,970	381,950	125,215	398,803	394,437	88,565
Alabama	33,091	921	31,192	2,046	29,147	3,147	3,760	67	20,968	1,205
Arizona	72,960	30,280	42,408	1,404	41,004	1,198	76	32,227	4,718	2,785
Arkansas	34,040	3,207	29,803	1,322	28,480	7,730	5,727	159	14,267	598
California	101,572	46,792	52,892	5,001	47,892	10,052	1,161	17,140	14,794	4,746
Colorado	66,618	23,923	42,240	1,694	40,547	8,940	1,256	23,537	3,755	3,059
Connecticut	3,212	15	3,054	816	2,238	229	110	-	1,760	140
Delaware	1,309	33	1,213	205	1,008	499	26	-	353	130
Florida	37,545	3,791	30,406	4,645	25,761	2,997	4,373	3,467	12,378	2,545
Georgia	37,702	2,087	34,599	3,077	31,523	5,173	3,075	-	21,714	1,560
Hawaii	4,093	432	3,621	170	3,451	274	88	925	1,483	680
Idaho	53,481	33,298	19,521	587	18,934	5,600	1,243	6,668	4,024	1,399
Illinois	36,061	521	34,766	3,094	31,672	24,100	2,764	-	3,419	1,390
Indiana	23,159	487	22,287	2,095	20,193	13,513	1,866	-	3,626	1,188
Iowa	36,016	184	35,363	1,779	33,584	24,988	3,712		1,931	2,953
Kansas	52,658	606	51,488	1,997	49,491	26,565	2,306	15,723	1,331	3,565
Kentucky	25,862	1,201	23,985	1,653	22,332	5,092	5,859	-	10,312	1,069
Louisiana	30,561	1,264	26,373	1,764	24,609	5,972	2,269	227	12,961	3,181
Maine	21,290	164	19,517	697	18,820	448	111	-	17,557	705
Maryland	6,695	167	6,034	1,095	4,939	1,673	545	-	2,364	356
Massachusetts	5,302	89	4,839	1,309	3,530	272	170	-	2,778	310
Michigan	37,457	3,166	33,040	3,686	29,354	8,985	2,353	-	15,608	2,408
Minnesota	54,017	3,383	47,092	2,418	44,674	21,356	3,282	-	13,815	6,222
Mississippi	30,521	1,726	27,992	1,337	26,655	5,726	4,047	-	15,765	1,117
Missouri	44,606	2,017	41,710	2,336	39,374	13,347	11,911	126	11,656	2,332
Montana	94,109	27,122	65,656	1,096	64,561	15,035	3,370	36,835	5,156	4,165
Nebraska	49,507	739	48,137	1,252	46,885	19,239	2,066	22,669	777	2,135
Nevada	70,759	60,290	10,025	394	9,631	762	297	7,854	353	364
New Hampshire	5,938	747	4,952	563	4,389	142	98	-	3,932	217
New Jersey	4,984	159	4,549	1,588	2,961	650	159	-	1,766	386
New Mexico	77,819	27,394	50,196	866	49,330	1,892	212	39,792	4,600	2,835
New York	31,429	231	29,788	3,005	26,783	5,616	3,001	-	17,178	987
North Carolina	33,708	2,448	28,476	3,542	24,933	5,960	2,019	-	15,979	975
North Dakota	45,250	1,951	42,187	1,344	40,843	24,743	1,168	10,325	426	4,181
Ohio	26,451	375	25,654	3,558	22,096	11,929	2,269	-	6,624	1,275
Oklahoma	44,772	1,202	42,395	1,875	40,520	10,081	7,720	14,061	6,988	1,672
Oregon	62,127	32,291	29,155	1,125	28,030	3,776	1,900	9,375	11,839	1,142
Pennsylvania	28,997	682	27,813	3,432	24,381	5,596	2,326	-	15,316	1,143
Rhode Island	776	4	661	190	472	25	24	-	393	30
South Carolina	19,912	1,156	17,961	1,856	16,105	2,983	1,190	-	10,922	1,010
South Dakota	49,354	2,907	45,459	1,135	44,324	16,436	2,158	21,933	540	3,257
Tennessee	26,972	1,379	24,740	2,161	22,579	4,857	5,165	-	11,580	977
Texas	170,756	3,203	163,687	8,231	155,456	28,261	16,710	94,155	9,960	6,369
Utah	54,336	35,582	16,866	561	16,305	1,815	665	10,050	1,626	2,148
Vermont	6,153	368	5,521	324	5,197	635	349	-	4,138	75
Virginia	26,091	2,389	22,774	2,183	20,591	2,901	3,444	-	13,539	707
Washington	43,608	12,479	29,931	1,851	28,081	6,745	1,352	5,476	12,547	1,960
West Virginia	15,508	1,201	14,138	689	13,449	915	1,609	-	10,534	391
Wisconsin	35,938	1,829	32,747	2,357	30,390	10,813	2,954	-	13,410	3,212
Wyoming	62,598	30,020	32,012	541	31,471	2,272	901	26,015	975	1,309
Caribbean	2,334	90	2,211	407	1,804	367	712	145	521	59

- Represents zero.   [1] Includes water area not shown separately.   [2] Includes urban and built-up areas in units of 10 acres or greater, and rural transportation.

Source: U.S. Dept. of Agriculture, Soil Conservation Service, and Iowa State University, Statistical Laboratory; *Summary Report, 1992 National Resources Inventory.*

No. 366. Extreme and Mean Elevations States and Other Areas

[One foot=.305 meter]

STATE OR OTHER AREA	HIGHEST POINT			LOWEST POINT			APPROXIMATE MEAN ELEVATION	
	Name	Elevation		Name	Elevation			
		Feet	Meters		Feet	Meters	Feet	Meters
U.S.....	**Mt. McKinley (AK)**	**20,320**	**6,198**	**Death Valley (CA)** ...	**−282**	**−86**	**2,500**	**763**
AL	Cheaha Mountain	2,405	733	Gulf of Mexico......	([1])	([1])	500	153
AK	Mount McKinley.	20,320	6,198	Pacific Ocean......	([1])	([1])	1,900	580
AZ	Humphreys Peak..........	12,633	3,853	Colorado River......	70	21	4,100	1,251
AR	Magazine Mountain	2,753	840	Ouachita River......	55	17	650	198
CA	Mount Whitney	14,494	4,419	Death Valley	−282	−86	2,900	885
CO	Mt. Elbert	14,433	4,402	Arkansas River......	3,350	1,022	6,800	2,074
CT	Mt. Frissell on South slope ...	2,380	726	Long Island Sound ...	([1])	([1])	500	153
DE	Ebright Road, [2] New Castle County ...	448	137	Atlantic Ocean......	([1])	([1])	60	18
DC	Tenleytown at Reno Reservoir .	410	125	Potomac River......	1	(Z)	150	46
FL	Sec. 30, T6N, R20W, Walton County.	345	105	Atlantic Ocean......	([1])	([1])	100	31
GA	Brasstown Bald.........	4,784	1,459	Atlantic Ocean......	([1])	([1])	600	183
HI	Puu Wekiu	13,796	4,208	Pacific Ocean......	([1])	([1])	3,030	924
ID	Borah Peak	12,662	3,862	Snake River......	710	217	5,000	1,525
IL	Charles Mound	1,235	377	Mississippi River......	279	85	600	183
IN	Franklin Twp., Wayne Co	1,257	383	Ohio River	320	98	700	214
IA	Sec. 29, T100N, R41W, Osceola County [3]	1,670	509	Mississippi River......	480	146	1,100	336
KS	Mount Sunflower	4,039	1,232	Verdigris River......	679	207	2,000	610
KY	Black Mountain	4,139	2,162	Mississippi River......	257	78	750	229
LA	Driskill Mountain	535	163	New Orleans......	−8	−2	100	31
ME.	Mount Katahdin	5,267	1,606	Atlantic Ocean......	([1])	([1])	600	183
MD.	Backbone Mountain	3,360	1,025	Atlantic Ocean......	([1])	([1])	350	107
MA.	Mount Greylock.........	3,487	1,064	Atlantic Ocean......	([1])	([1])	500	153
MI	Mount Arvon	1,979	604	Lake Erie	571	174	900	275
MN.	Eagle Mountain, Cook Co	2,301	702	Lake Superior	600	183	1,200	366
MS.	Woodall Mountain	806	246	Gulf of Mexico......	([1])	([1])	300	92
MO.	Taum Sauk Mountain	1,772	540	St. Francis River ...	230	70	800	244
MT.	Granite Peak	12,799	3,904	Kootenai River......	1,800	549	3,400	1,037
NE.	Johnson Twp., Kimball Co....	5,424	1,654	Missouri River	840	256	2,600	793
NV.	Boundary Peak	13,140	4,007	Colorado River......	479	146	5,500	1,678
NH.	Mount Washington........	6,288	1,918	Atlantic Ocean......	([1])	([1])	1,000	305
NJ	High Point	1,803	550	Atlantic Ocean......	([1])	([1])	250	76
NM.	Wheeler Peak.........	13,161	4,014	Red Bluff Reservoir ..	2,842	867	5,700	1,739
NY.	Mount Marcy.	5,344	1,630	Atlantic Ocean......	([1])	([1])	1,000	305
NC.	Mount Mitchell.	6,684	2,039	Atlantic Ocean......	([1])	([1])	700	214
ND.	White Butte, Slope Co	3,506	1,069	Red River......	750	229	1,900	580
OH.	Campbell Hill	1,549	472	Ohio River	455	139	850	259
OK.	Black Mesa.	4,973	1,517	Little River......	289	88	1,300	397
OR.	Mount Hood	11,239	3,428	Pacific Ocean......	([1])	([1])	3,300	1,007
PA	Mount Davis	3,213	980	Delaware River......	([1])	([1])	1,100	336
RI	Jerimoth Hill	812	248	Atlantic Ocean......	([1])	([1])	200	61
SC.	Sassafras Mountain	3,560	1,086	Atlantic Ocean......	([1])	([1])	350	107
SD.	Harney Peak.	7,242	2,209	Big Stone Lake......	966	295	2,200	671
TN.	Clingmans Dome.	6,643	2,026	Mississippi River	178	54	900	275
TX.	Guadalupe Peak	8,749	2,668	Gulf of Mexico......	([1])	([1])	1,700	519
UT.	Kings Peak	13,528	4,126	Beaverdam Wash....	2,000	610	6,100	1,861
VT.	Mount Mansfield	4,393	1,340	Lake Champlain......	95	29	1,000	305
VA.	Mount Rogers.	5,729	1,747	Atlantic Ocean......	([1])	([1])	950	290
WA	Mount Rainier.	14,410	4,395	Pacific Ocean......	([1])	([1])	1,700	519
WV	Spruce Knob.	4,861	1,483	Potomac River......	240	73	1,500	458
WI	Timms Hill	1,951	595	Lake Michigan......	579	177	1,050	320
WY	Gannett Peak	13,804	4,210	Belle Fourche River ..	3,099	945	6,700	2,044
'Other areas: Puerto Rico	Cerro de Punta	4,390	1,339	Atlantic Ocean......	([1])	([1])	1,800	549
American Samoa...	Lata Mountain.	3,160	964	Pacific Ocean......	([1])	([1])	1,300	397
Guam	Mount Lamlam	1,332	406	Pacific Ocean......	([1])	([1])	330	101
Virgin Is. ...	Crown Mountain	1,556	475	Atlantic Ocean......	([1])	([1])	750	229

Z Less than 0.5 meter.   [1] Sea level.   [2] At DE-PA State line.   [3] "Sec." denotes section; "T," township; "R," range; "N," north; and "W," west.

Source: U.S. Geological Survey, for highest and lowest points, *Elevations and Distances in the United States, 1990*; for mean elevations, 1983 edition.

No. 367. Water Areas for Selected Major Bodies of Water: 1990

[Includes only that portion of body of water under the jurisdiction of the United States, excluding Hawaii. One square mile=2.59 square kilometers]

BODY OF WATER AND STATE	AREA Sq. mi.	AREA Sq. km.
Atlantic Coast water bodies:		
Chesapeake Bay (MD-VA)	2,747	7,115
Pamlico Sound (NC)	1,622	4,200
Long Island Sound (CT-NY)	914	2,368
Delaware Bay (DE-NJ)	614	1,591
Cape Cod Bay (MA)	598	1,548
Albemarle Sound (NC)	492	1,274
Biscayne Bay (FL)	218	565
Buzzards Bay (MA)	215	558
Tangier Sound (MD-VA)	172	445
Currituck Sound (NC)	116	301
Pocomoke Sound (MD-VA)	111	286
Chincoteague Bay (MD-VA)	105	272
Great South Bay (NY)	94	243
Core Sound (NC)	88	229
Gulf Coast water bodies:		
Mississippi Sound (AL-LA-MS)	813	2,105
Laguna Madre (TX)	733	1,897
Lake Pontchartrain (LA)	631	1,635
Florida Bay (FL)	616	1,596
Breton Sound (LA)	511	1,323
Mobile Bay (AL)	310	802
Lake Borgne (LA-MS)	271	702
Matagorda Bay (TX)	253	656
Atchafalaya Bay (LA)	245	635
Galveston Bay (TX)	236	611
Tampa Bay (FL)	212	549
Vermilion Bay (LA)	189	489
Corpus Christi Bay (TX)	151	392
West Cote Blanche Bay (LA)	146	378
Trinity Bay (TX)	129	335
Choctawhatchee Bay (FL)	122	315
San Antonio Bay (TX)	118	306
Timbalier Bay (LA)	112	291
Charlotte Harbor (FL)	112	291
Aransas Bay (TX)	104	268
Apalachicola Bay (FL)	101	262
Terrebonne Bay (LA)	99	256
East Cote Blanche Bay (LA)	94	243
St George Sound (FL)	93	240
Sabine Lake (LA-TX)	89	229
White Lake (LA)	85	221
Old Tampa Bay (FL)	83	214
Bon Secour Bay (AL)	79	204
Pine Island Sound (FL)	75	194
Pacific Coast water bodies:		
Puget Sound (WA)	808	2,092
San Francisco Bay (CA)	264	684
Willapa Bay (WA)	125	325
Hood Canal (WA)	117	303
Interior water bodies:		
Lake Michigan (IL-IN-MI-WI)	22,342	57,866
Lake Superior (MI-MN-WI)[1]	20,557	53,243
Lake Huron (MI)[1]	8,800	22,792
Lake Erie (MI-NY-OH-PA)[1]	5,033	13,036
Lake Ontario (NY)[1]	3,446	8,926
Great Salt Lake (UT)	1,836	4,756
Green Bay (MI-WI)	1,396	3,617
Lake Okeechobee (FL)	663	1,717
Lake Sakakawea (ND)	563	1,459
Lake Oahe (ND-SD)	538	1,394
Lake of the Woods (MN)[1]	462	1,196
Lake Champlain (NY-VT)[1]	414	1,072
Fort Peck Lake (MT)	379	981
Salton Sea (CA)	364	944
Toledo Bend Reservoir (LA-TX)	268	694
Lower Red Lake (MN)	257	666
Lake Powell (AZ-UT)	250	649
Kentucky Lake (KY-TN)	234	605
Lake Mead (AZ-NV)	233	603
Lake Winnebago (WI)	206	535
Mille Lacs Lake (MN)	200	518
Flathead Lake (MT)	191	495
Lake Tahoe (CA-NV)	187	486
Upper Red Lake (MN)	186	483
Pyramid Lake (NV)	170	440

BODY OF WATER AND STATE	AREA Sq. mi.	AREA Sq. km.
Leech Lake (MN)	162	419
Lake St Clair (MI)[1]	161	416
Eufaula Lake (OK)	157	407
Sam Rayburn Resevoir (TX)	150	389
Goose Lake (CA-OR)	147	381
Utah Lake (UT)	139	361
Lake Marion (SC)	139	360
Lake Francis Case (SD)	134	346
Lake Pend Oreille (ID)	133	343
Lake Texoma (OK-TX)	132	342
Yellowstone Lake (WY)	131	339
Livingston Reservoir (TX)	127	330
Franklin D Roosevelt Lake (WA)	124	322
Moosehead Lake (ME)	116	301
Clark Hill Lake (GA-SC)	105	272
Lake Maurepas (LA)	91	235
Lake Moultrie (SC)	89	230
Lake Winnibigoshish (MN)	87	225
Hartwell Lake (GA-SC)	86	224
Upper Klamath Lake (OR)	85	221
Harry S. Truman Reservoir (MO)	84	217
Oneida Lake (NY)	80	207
Malheur Lake (OR)	75	195
Alaska water bodies:		
Chatham Strait	1,559	4,039
Prince William Sound	1,382	3,579
Clarence Strait	1,199	3,107
Iliamna Lake	1,022	2,646
Frederick Sound	792	2,051
Sumner Strait	791	2,048
Stephens Passage	702	1,819
Kvichak Bay	640	1,659
Montague Strait	463	1,198
Becharof Lake	447	1,158
Icy Strait	436	1,130
Hotham Inlet	433	1,120
Selawik Lake	403	1,044
Nushagak Bay	393	1,018
Baird Inlet	348	902
Yakutat Bay	345	894
Teshekpuk Lake	324	839
Behm Canal	324	839
Turnagain Arm	322	834
Kachemak Bay	310	803
Glacier Bay	310	803
Stefansson Sound	301	780
Revillagigedo Channel	295	764
Kasegaluk Lagoon	293	759
Cordova Bay	241	623
Sitka Sound	229	593
Naknek Lake	225	582
Eschscholtz Bay	210	543
Stepovak Bay	206	534
Keku Strait	206	534
Port Clarence	187	486
Orca Bay	184	476
Knik Arm	169	437
Dall Lake	167	433
Knight Island Passage	167	432
Scammon Bay	163	423
Port Moller	159	412
Ernest Sound	158	410
Spafarief Bay	157	405
Pavlov Bay	153	396
Shishmaref Inlet	153	395
Smith Bay	140	363
Seymour Canal	140	361
Sitkalidak Strait	135	349
Tlevak Strait	135	349
Lake Clark	130	336
Lynn Canal	130	336
Chignik Bay	119	309
Elson Lagoon	119	309
Bucareli Bay	119	307
Hinchinbrook Entrance	118	306

[1] Area measurements for Lake Champlain, Lake Erie, Lake Huron, Lake Ontario, Lake St. Clair, Lake Superior, and Lake of the Woods include only those portions under the jurisdiction of the United States.

Source: U. S. Bureau of the Census, unpublished data from the Census TIGER [TM] data base.

No. 368. Flows of Largest U.S. Rivers—Length, Discharge, and Drainage Area

RIVER	Location of mouth	Source stream (name and location)	Length (miles) [1]	Average discharge at mouth (1,000 cubic ft. per second)	Drainage area (1,000 sq. mi.)
Missouri.	Missouri	Red Rock Creek, MT	2,540	76.2	[5]529
Mississippi	Louisiana	Mississippi River, MN	[2]2,340	[3]593	[4][5]1,150
Yukon	Alaska	McNeil River, Canada	1,980	225	[5]328
St. Lawrence	Canada	North River, MN	1,900	348	[5]396
Rio Grande	Mexico-Texas	Rio Grande, CO	1,900	-	336
Arkansas	Arkansas	East Fork Arkansas River, CO	1,460	41	161
Colorado.	Mexico	Colorado River, CO	1,450	-	246
Atchafalaya [6]	Louisiana	Tierra Blanca Creek, NM	1,420	58	95.1
Ohio	Illinois-Kentucky	Allegheny River, PA	1,310	281	203
Red	Louisiana	Tierra Blanca Creek, NM	1,290	56	93.2
Brazos	Texas	Blackwater Draw, NM	1,280	-	45.6
Columbia.	Oregon-Washington	Columbia River, Canada	1,240	265	[5]258
Snake	Washington	Snake River, WY	1,040	56.9	108
Platte	Nebraska	Grizzly Creek, CO	990	-	84.9
Pecos	Texas	Pecos River, NM	926	-	44.3
Canadian.	Oklahoma	Canadian River, CO	906	-	46.9
Tennessee	Kentucky	Courthouse Creek, NC	886	68	40.9
Colorado (of Texas)	Texas	Colorado River, TX	862	-	42.3
North Canadian.	Oklahoma	Corrumpa Creek, NM	800	-	17.6
Mobile.	Alabama	Tickanetley Creek, GA	774	67.2	44.6
Kansas	Kansas	Arikaree River, CO	743	-	59.5
Kuskokwim.	Alaska	South Fork Kuskokwim River, AK	724	67	48
Yellowstone	North Dakota	North Folk Yellowstone River, WY	692	-	70
Tanana	Alaska	Nabesna River, AK	659	41	44.5
Gila	Arizona	Middle Fork Gila River, NM	649	-	58.2

- Represents zero.   [1] From source to mouth.   [2] The length from the source of the Missouri River to the Mississippi River and thence to the Gulf of Mexico is about 3,710 miles.   [3] Includes about 167,000 cubic ft. per second diverted from the Mississippi into the Atchafalaya River but excludes the flow of the Red River.   [4] Excludes the drainage areas of the Red and Atchafalaya Rivers.   [5] Drainage area includes both the United States and Canada.   [6] In east-central Louisiana, the Red River flows into the Atchafalaya River, a distributary of the Mississippi River. Data on average discharge, length, and drainage area include the Red River, but exclude all water diverted into the Atchafalaya from the Mississippi River.
Source: U.S. Geological Survey, *Largest Rivers in the United States,* Open File Report 87-242, May 1990.

No. 369. Water Withdrawals and Consumptive Use—States and Other Areas: 1990

[**In millions of gallons per day, except as noted.** Figures may not add due to rounding. Withdrawal signifies water physically withdrawn from a source. Includes fresh and saline water]

STATE OR OTHER AREA	WATER WITHDRAWN				Consumptive use, [1] fresh water	STATE OR OTHER AREA	WATER WITHDRAWN				Consumptive use, [1] fresh water
	Total	Per capita (gal. per day) fresh	Source				Total	Per capita (gal. per day) fresh	Source		
			Ground water	Surface water					Ground water	Surface water	
U.S. [2]	407,900	1,340	80,640	327,260	93,980	Montana	9,320	11,600	218	9,100	2,090
						Nebraska	8,940	5,660	4,800	4,150	4,230
Alabama	8,090	2,000	403	7,680	454	Nevada	3,350	2,780	1,070	2,280	1,690
Alaska	641	517	112	529	26	New Hampshire	1,310	378	64	1,250	26
Arizona	6,570	1,790	2,740	3,830	4,350						
Arkansas	7,840	3,330	4,710	3,130	4,140	New Jersey	12,800	287	566	12,200	211
California	46,800	1,180	14,900	31,900	20,900	New Mexico	3,480	2,300	1,760	1,720	2,060
						New York	19,000	583	840	18,100	562
Colorado	12,700	3,850	2,800	9,910	5,250	North Carolina	8,940	1,350	435	8,510	390
Connecticut	4,840	325	165	4,680	103	North Dakota	2,680	4,190	141	2,540	228
Delaware	1,370	1,540	89	1,280	59						
District of Columbia	9	15	1	8	16	Ohio	11,700	1,080	904	10,800	901
						Oklahoma	1,670	452	905	760	659
Florida	17,900	582	4,660	13,200	3,130	Oregon	8,430	2,970	767	7,660	3,160
Georgia	5,350	816	996	4,360	822	Pennsylvania	9,830	827	1,020	8,810	581
Hawaii	2,740	1,070	590	2,150	627	Rhode Island	526	132	25	501	18
Idaho	19,700	19,600	7,590	12,100	6,090						
Illinois	18,000	1,570	945	17,100	750	South Carolina	6,000	1,720	282	5,720	293
Indiana	9,430	1,700	621	8,810	451	South Dakota	592	851	251	341	345
						Tennessee	9,190	1,880	503	8,690	252
Iowa	2,860	1,030	495	2,370	271	Texas	25,200	1,180	7,880	17,300	9,020
Kansas	6,080	2,460	4,360	1,720	4,410	Utah	4,480	2,540	971	3,510	2,230
Kentucky	4,320	1,170	247	4,070	309						
Louisiana	9,350	2,200	1,340	8,010	1,590	Vermont	632	1,120	45	587	29
Maine	1,140	433	85	1,060	51	Virginia	6,860	762	443	6,420	224
						Washington	7,940	1,630	1,450	6,490	2,830
Maryland	6,420	307	239	6,180	126	West Virginia	4,580	2,560	728	3,860	509
Massachusetts	5,520	338	338	5,180	195	Wisconsin	6,510	1,330	681	5,830	461
Michigan	11,600	1,250	707	10,900	738	Wyoming	7,600	16,700	403	7,200	2,730
Minnesota	3,270	748	797	2,480	872						
Mississippi	3,640	1,290	2,670	963	1,800	Puerto Rico	3,040	163	157	2,880	199
Missouri	6,930	1,150	728	6,200	529	Virgin Islands	164	91	3	160	2

[1] Water that has been evaporated, transpired, or incorporated into products, plant, or animal tissue; and therefore, is not available for immediate reuse.   [2] Includes Puerto Rico and Virgin Islands.
Source: U.S. Geological Survey, *Estimated Use of Water in the United States in 1990,* circular 1081.

No. 370. U.S. Water Withdrawals and Consumptive Use Per Day, by End Use: 1940 to 1990

[Includes Puerto Rico. Withdrawal signifies water physically withdrawn from a source. Includes fresh and saline water; excludes water used for hydroelectric power. See also *Historical Statistics, Colonial Times to 1970,* series J 92-103]

YEAR	Total (bil. gal.)	Per capita [1] (gal.)	Irrigation (bil. gal.)	PUBLIC SUPPLY [2] Total (bil. gal.)	PUBLIC SUPPLY [2] Per capita[3] (gal.)	Rural [4] (bil. gal.)	Industrial and misc. [5] (bil. gal.)	Steam electric utilities (bil. gal.)
WITHDRAWALS								
1940	140	1,027	71	10	75	3.1	29	23
1950	180	1,185	89	14	145	3.6	37	40
1955	240	1,454	110	17	148	3.6	39	72
1960	270	1,500	110	21	151	3.6	38	100
1965	310	1,602	120	24	155	4.0	46	130
1970	370	1,815	130	27	166	4.5	47	170
1975	420	1,972	140	29	168	4.9	45	200
1980	440	1,953	150	34	183	5.6	45	210
1985	399	1,650	137	38	189	7.8	31	187
1990	408	1,620	137	41	195	7.9	30	195
CONSUMPTIVE USE								
1960	61	339	52	3.5	25	2.8	3.0	0.2
1965	77	403	66	5.2	34	3.2	3.4	0.4
1970	87	427	73	5.9	36	3.4	4.1	0.8
1975	96	451	80	6.7	38	3.4	4.2	1.9
1980	100	440	83	7.1	38	3.9	5.0	3.2
1985	92	380	74	(6)	(6)	9.2	6.1	6.2
1990	94	370	76	(6)	(6)	8.9	6.7	4.0

[1] Based on Bureau of the Census resident population as of July 1.   [2] Includes commercial water withdrawals.
[3] Based on population served.   [4] Rural farm and nonfarm household and garden use, and water for farm stock and dairies.
[5] For 1940 to 1960, includes manufacturing and mineral industries, rural commercial industries, air-conditioning, resorts, hotels, motels, military and other State and Federal agencies, and miscellaneous; thereafter, includes manufacturing, mining and mineral processing, ordnance, construction, and miscellaneous.   [6] Public supply consumptive use included in end-use categories.

Source: 1940-1960, U.S. Bureau of Domestic Business Development, based principally on committee prints, *Water Resources Activities in the United States,* for the Senate Committee on National Water Resources, U.S. Senate, thereafter, U.S. Geological Survey, *Estimated Use of Water in the United States in 1990,* circular 1081, and previous quinquennial issues.

No. 371. National Ambient Water Quality in Rivers and Streams—Violation Rate: 1980 to 1994

[**In percent.** Violation level based on U.S. Environmental Protection Agency water quality criteria. Violation rate represents the proportion of all measurements of a specific water quality pollutant which exceeds the "violation level" for that pollutant. "Violation" does not necessarily imply a legal violation. Data based on U.S. Geological Survey's National Stream Quality Accounting Network (NASQAN) data system; for details, see source. Years refer to water years. A water year begins in Oct. and ends in Sept. µg=micrograms; mg=milligrams. For metric conversion, see page ix]

POLLUTANT	VIOLATION LEVEL	1980	1985	1988	1989	1990	1991	1992	1993	1994
Fecal coliform bacteria. . . .	Above 200 cells per 100 ml. .	31	28	22	30	26	15	28	31	29
Dissolved oxygen	Below 5 mg per liter.	5	3	2	3	2	2	2	(Z)	(Z)
Phosphorus, total, as phosporous	Above 1.0 mg per liter	4	3	4	2	3	2	2	2	4
Lead, dissolved	Above 50 µg per liter	(Z)	(Z)	(Z)	(Z)	(Z)	(Z)	(Z)	(NA)	(NA)
Cadmium, dissolved	Above 10 µg per liter	1	(Z)	(Z)	(Z)	(Z)	(Z)	(Z)	(NA)	(NA)

Z Less than 1.   NA Not available.

Source: U.S. Geological Survey, national-level data, unpublished; State-level data, *Water-Data Report,* annual series prepared in cooperation with the State governments.

No. 372. Oil Polluting Incidents Reported in and Around U.S. Waters: 1973 to 1993

YEAR	Incidents	Gallons	YEAR	Incidents	Gallons
1973.	11,054	15,289,188	1986.	5,818	4,427,544
1974.	12,083	15,739,792	1987.	5,693	3,759,983
1975.	10,998	21,528,444	1988.	6,733	10,650,138
1976.	11,066	18,517,384	1989.	8,562	25,531,292
1977.	10,979	8,188,398	1990.	10,186	13,907,783
1978.	12,174	11,035,890	1991.	10,405	2,156,063
1979.	11,556	10,051,271	1992.	9,131	1,572,341
1980.	9,886	12,638,848			
1981.	9,589	8,919,789	**1993**.	**9,672**	**1,543,578**
1982.	9,416	10,404,646	Tankships.	185	14,138
1983.	10,530	8,378,719	Tank barges	338	295,243
1984.	10,089	19,007,332	Other vessels	5,220	412,430
1985.	7,740	8,465,055	Nonvessels.	3,929	821,767

Source: U.S. Coast Guard. Based on unpublished data from the *Marine Safety Information System.*

No. 373. National Ambient Air Pollutant Concentrations: 1985 to 1993

[Data represent annual composite averages of pollutant based on daily 24-hour averages of monitoring stations, except carbon monoxide is based on the second-highest, non-overlapping, 8-hour average; ozone, average of the second-highest daily maximum one hour value; and lead, quarterly average of ambient lead levels. Based on data from the Aerometric Information Retrieval System. μg/m³=micrograms of pollutant per cubic meter of air; ppm=parts per million]

POLLUTANT	Unit	Monitoring stations, number	Air quality standard [1]	1985	1987	1988	1989	1990	1991	1992	1993
Carbon monoxide...	ppm....	314	[2]9	6.97	6.69	6.38	6.34	5.87	5.55	5.18	4.88
Ozone.........	ppm....	532	[3].12	0.124	0.126	0.136	0.117	0.114	0.116	0.107	0.110
Sulfur dioxide	ppm....	474	.03	0.009	0.009	0.009	0.009	0.008	0.008	0.007	0.007
Particulates (PM-10) [4]	μg/m³...	799	50	(X)	(X)	33.2	33.0	29.8	29.6	27.2	26.4
Nitrogen dioxide....	ppm....	201	.053	0.022	0.022	0.023	0.022	0.021	0.021	0.020	0.019
Lead..........	μg/m³...	204	[5]1.5	0.291	0.156	0.103	0.080	0.079	0.058	0.050	0.045

X Not applicable.   [1] Refers to the primary National Ambient Air Quality Standard that protects the public health.   [2] Based on 8-hour standard of 9 ppm.   [3] Based on 1-hour standard of .12 ppm.   [4] The particulates (PM-10) standard replaced the previous standard for total suspended particulates in 1987.   [5] Based on 3-month standard of 1.5 μg/m³

Source: U.S. Environmental Protection Agency, *National Air Quality and Emissions Trends Report,* annual.

No. 374. National Air Pollutant Emissions: 1940 to 1993

[**In thousands of tons.** PM-10=Particulate matter of less than ten microns. Methodologies to estimate data for 1900 to 1984 period and 1985 to present emissions differ. Beginning with 1985, the estimates are based on a modified National Acid Precipitation Assessment Program inventory]

Year	PM-10	PM-10, fugitive dust[1]	Sulfur dioxide	Nitrogen dioxide	Volatile organic compounds	Carbon monoxide	Lead
1940	15,956	(NA)	19,954	7,568	17,118	90,865	(NA)
1950	17,133	(NA)	22,384	10,403	20,856	98,785	(NA)
1960	15,558	(NA)	22,245	14,581	24,322	103,777	(NA)
1970	12,838	(NA)	31,096	20,625	30,646	128,079	219,471
1980	6,928	(NA)	25,813	23,281	25,893	115,625	74,956
1983	5,849	(NA)	22,471	22,364	24,607	115,334	49,232
1984	6,126	(NA)	23,396	23,172	25,572	114,262	42,217
1985	3,676	44,701	23,148	22,853	25,417	112,072	20,124
1986	3,679	49,940	22,361	22,409	24,826	108,070	7,296
1987	3,630	42,131	22,085	22,386	24,338	105,117	6,840
1988	3,697	59,975	22,535	23,221	24,961	106,100	6,464
1989	3,661	53,323	22,653	23,250	23,731	100,806	6,099
1990, prel.	4,229	44,929	22,261	23,192	24,276	103,753	5,635
1991, prel.	3,902	49,127	22,149	22,977	23,508	99,898	5,020
1992, prel.	3,676	44,953	21,592	22,991	23,020	96,368	4,741
1993, prel.	3,688	41,801	21,888	23,402	23,312	97,208	4,885

NA Not available.   [1] Sources such as agricultural tilling, construction, mining and quarrying, paved roads, unpaved roads, and wind erosion.

No. 375. Air Pollutant Emissions, by Pollutant and Source: 1993

[**In thousands of tons.** See headnote, table 374]

Source	Particulates[1]	Sulfur dioxide	Nitrogen oxide	Volatile organic compounds	Carbon monoxide	Lead
Total	**45,489**	**21,888**	**23,402**	**23,312**	**97,208**	**4,885**
Fuel combustion, stationary sources.	1,212	19,266	11,690	648	5,433	497
Electric utilities	270	15,836	7,782	36	322	62
Industrial :	219	2,830	3,176	271	667	18
Other fuel combustion	723	600	732	341	4,444	417
Residential	674	178	(NA)	310	4,310	9
Industrial processes	553	1,852	905	3,091	5,219	2,281
Chemical and allied product manufacturing ...	75	450	414	1,811	1,998	109
Metals processing	141	580	82	74	2,091	2,118
Petroleum and related industries	26	409	95	720	398	(NA)
Other	311	413	314	486	732	54
Solvent utilization	2	1	3	6,249	2	(NA)
Storage and transport	55	5	3	1,861	56	(NA)
Waste disposal and recycling	248	37	84	2,271	1,732	518
Highway vehicles	197	438	7,437	6,094	59,989	1,383
Light-duty gas vehicles and motorcycle	(NA)	(NA)	3,685	3,854	39,452	1,033
Light-duty trucks	(NA)	(NA)	1,387	1,612	14,879	(NA)
Heavy-duty gas vehicles................	(NA)	(NA)	304	314	4,292	(NA)
Diesels	(NA)	(NA)	2,061	315	1,366	(NA)
Off highway [2]	395	278	2,986	2,207	15,272	206
Miscellaneous [3]	42,828	11	296	893	9,506	(NA)

NA Not available.   [1] Represents both PM-10 and PM-10 fugitive dust; see table 374.   [2] Includes emissions from farm tractors and other farm machinery, construction equipment, industrial machinery, recreational marine vessels, and small general utility engines such as lawn mowers.   [3] Includes emissions such as from forest fires and various agricultural activities, fugitive dust from paved and unpaved roads, and other construction and mining activities, and natural sources.

Source of tables 374 and 375: U.S. Environmental Protection Agency, *National Air Pollutant Emission Trends, 1900-1993.*

No. 376. Metropolitan Areas Failing to Meet National Ambient Air Quality Standards for Carbon Monoxide—Number of Days Exceeding Standards: 1992 and 1993

[Areas generally represent the officially defined metropolitan area, but may, in some cases, not have all the counties identified as part of the area; see *Federal Register*, 40 CFR, part 81, *Air Quality Designations: Revised*, July 1994. Nonattainment status was as of October 1994]

METROPOLITAN AREA	1992	1993	METROPOLITAN AREA	1992	1993	METROPOLITAN AREA	1992	1993
Albuquerque, NM	-	-	Hartford, CT CMSA	1	-	Phoenix, AZ	5	-
Anchorage, AK	2	2	Klamath County, OR [1]	-	-	Portland, OR-WA CMSA	-	-
Baltimore, MD.	-	-	Lake Tahoe S. Shore, CA [1]	1	-	Provo-Orem, UT	3	2
Boston, MA-NH CMSA	-	-	Las Vegas, NV	2	3	Raleigh-Durham, NC	-	-
Chico, CA	-	-	Longmont, CO[1]	-	-	Reno, NV.	-	-
Cleveland, OH CMSA	-	-	Los Angeles, CA CMSA	35	20	Sacramento, CA	-	-
Colorado Springs, CO	-	-	Medford, OR	-	-	San Diego, CA	-	-
Denver-Boulder, CO CMSA.	7	2	Minneapolis-St. Paul, MN-WI.	-	-	San Francisco, CA CMSA	-	-
Duluth, MN.	-	-	Missoula County, MT [1]	-	-	Seattle-Tacoma, WA CMSA	1	-
El Paso, TX	3	2	Modesto, CA	-	-	Spokane, WA	6	4
Fairbanks, AK [1]	2	5	New York, NY-NJ-CT CMSA	2	-	Stockton, CA	-	-
Fort Collins, CO	-	-	Ogden, UT.	-	-	Washington, DC-MD-VA	-	-
Fresno, CA	-	-	Philadelphia, PA-NJ-DE-MD CMSA	-	-			
Grant Pass, OR [1]	-	-						
Greensboro-Winston-Salem, NC	-	-						

- Represents zero.   [1] Not a metropolitan area.

No. 377. Metropolitan Areas Failing to Meet National Ambient Air Quality Standards for Ozone—Average Number of Days Exceeding Standards: 1991 to 1993

[See headnote, table 376. Nonattainment status was as of October 1994]

METROPOLITAN AREA	1991-93, avg.	1993[1]	METROPOLITAN AREA	1991-93, avg.	1993[1]
Albany-Schenectady-Troy, NY	-	-	Los Angeles South Coast Air, CA [6]	104.3	97.6
Allentown-Bethlehem-Easton, PA-NJ	-	-	Manchester, NH	-	-
Altoona, PA.	-	-	Manitowoc Co, WI	2.0	-
Atlanta, GA	4.2	4.3	Memphis, TN-AR-MS	0.3	1.0
Atlantic City, NJ	1.0	0.0	Miami-Fort Lauderdale, FL CMSA	-	1.0
Baltimore, MD	4.8	6.2	Milwaukee-Racine, WI CMSA	3.9	2.4
Baton Rouge, LA	1.8	3.0	Monterey Bay, CA [7]	0.4	-
Beaumont-Port Arthur, TX	2.7	0.0	Muskegon, MI	2.3	1.0
Birmingham, AL	0.7	2.0	Nashville, TN.	1.1	2.1
Boston-Lawrence-Salem, MA-NH CMSA [2]	3.1	4.0	New York, NY-NJ-CT CMSA [8]	6.1	6.0
Buffalo-Niagara Falls, NY CMSA	-	-	Norfolk-Virginia Beach-Newport News, VA	1.7	3.0
Canton, OH.	0.3	-	Owensboro, KY [4]	-	-
Charleston, WV	0.3	-	Paducah, KY [4]	-	-
Charlotte-Gastonia-Rock Hill, NC-SC [3]	0.7	2.1	Parkersburg-Marietta, WV-OH.	-	-
Chicago-Gary-Lake County, IL-IN-WI CMSA	4.7	2.4	Philadelphia, PA-NJ-DE-MD CMSA	10.3	5.2
Cincinnati-Hamilton, OH-KY-IN CMSA	1.3	1.0	Phoenix, AZ	4.0	2.0
Cleveland-Akron-Lorain, OH CMSA	1.7	-	Pittsburgh-Beaver Valley, PA CMSA	0.7	-
Columbus, OH.	0.3	-	Portland-Vancouver, OR-WA CMSA	0.7	-
Dallas-Fort Worth, TX CMSA	2.0	2.3	Portland, ME.	11.8	3.8
Dayton-Springfield, OH	0.0	1.0	Portsmouth-Dover-Rochester, NH-ME	2.2	1.1
Detroit-Ann Arbor, MI CMSA.	1.0	1.0	Poughkeepsie, NY	1.4	2.0
Door County, WI [4]	1.6	-	Providence, RI [9]	4.0	1.4
Edmonson County, KY [4]	-	-	Reading, PA	0.3	-
El Paso, TX.	3.7	4.1	Reno, NV	-	-
Erie, PA	-	-	Richmond-Petersburg, VA	1.4	3.1
Essex County, NY [4]	-	-	Sacramento, CA.	9.7	3.6
Evansville, IN-KY	-	-	St. Louis, MO-IL.	1.7	2.1
Grand Rapids, MI.	3.4	1.0	Salt Lake City-Ogden, UT	-	-
Greater Connecticut, CT [5]	7.5	6.0	San Diego, CA.	11.8	4.0
Greenbrier County, WV [4]	0.4	-	San Joaquin Valley, CA	18.9	27.5
Hancock and Waldo counties, ME [4]	1.3	-	San Francisco-Bay area, CA	0.7	2.0
Harrisburg-Lebanon-Carlisle, PA	0.0	-	Santa Barbara-Santa Maria-Lompoc, CA	1.0	-
Houston-Galveston-Brazoria, TX CMSA	6.3	10.4	Scranton-Wilkes-Barre, PA.	0.4	-
Huntington-Ashland, WV-KY-OH	1.0	1.0	Seattle-Tacoma, WA	-	-
Indianapolis, IN	-	-	Sheboygan, WI	2.6	-
Jefferson County, NY [4]	-	-	Smyth County, VA [4]	(NA)	(NA)
Jersey Co., IL [4]	0.7	2.0	South Bend-Mishawaka, IN	-	-
Johnstown, PA.	-	-	Southeast Desert Modified AQMD, CA [10]	59.3	72.6
Kent County and Queen Anne's Co., MD [4]	2.8	2.0	Springfield, MA	4.6	6.2
Kewaunee County, WI [4]	0.8	0.0	Sussex County, DE [4]	1.0	-
Knox and Lincoln counties, ME [4]	2.3	1.2	Tampa-St. Petersburg-Clearwater, FL.	-	-
Lake Charles, LA	1.3	-	Toledo, OH.	0.3	1.0
Lancaster, PA	0.3	1.0	Ventura County, CA	15.9	9.0
Lewiston-Auburn, ME	0.3	-	Walworth County, WI.	0.3	-
Lexington-Fayette, KY.	-	-	Washington, DC-MD-VA	1.4	3.1
Louisville, KY-IN.	2.2	2.0	York, PA.	-	-
			Youngstown-Warren, OH [11]	0.3	1.0

- Represents zero.   NA Not available.   [1] May represent a different monitoring location than one used to calculate average.
[2] Includes also both the Worcester, MA, and New Bedford, MA MSA's.   [3] Excludes York Co., SC.   [4] Not a metropolitan area.
[5] Primarily represents Hartford-New Haven area.   [6] Primarily represents Los Angeles and Orange counties.   [7] Primarily represents Monterey, Santa Cruz, and San Benito counties.   [8] Excludes the Connecticut portion.   [9] Covers entire State of Rhode Island.   [10] Represents primarily San Joaquin, Turlock, Merced, Madera, Fresno, Kings, Tulare, and Kern counties.
[11] Includes Sharon, PA.

Source of tables 376 and 377: U.S. Environmental Protection Agency, Published in *1993 Air Quality Update*, October 1994.

No. 378. Emissions of Greenhouse Gases, by Type and Source: 1987 to 1993

[Emission estimates were mandated by Congress through Section 1605(a) of the Energy Policy Act of 1992 (title XVI). Gases that contain carbon can be measured either in terms of the full molecular weight of the gas or just in terms of their carbon content]

TYPE AND SOURCE	Unit	1987	1988	1989	1990	1991	1992	1993
Carbon dioxide:								
Carbon content, total	Mil. metric tons	1,316.6	1,377.9	1,386.9	1,374.8	1,361.8	1,382.5	1,409.2
Energy sources	Mil. metric tons	1,283.4	1,345.4	1,356.9	1,345.5	1,325.9	1,347.8	1,375.5
Cement production	Mil. metric tons	8.6	8.7	8.7	8.8	8.5	8.6	9.0
Gas flaring	Mil. metric tons	1.6	1.9	1.9	2.0	2.2	2.2	2.5
Other industrial	Mil. metric tons	7.7	8.2	8.3	8.3	8.3	8.4	8.3
Other, adjustments	Mil. metric tons	15.2	13.7	11.2	10.2	16.9	15.5	13.8
Methane:								
Gas, total	1,000 metric tons	26.39	26.67	26.81	27.19	27.24	27.23	(NA)
Energy sources	1,000 metric tons	8.15	8.16	8.32	8.37	8.30	8.26	(NA)
Landfills	1,000 metric tons	10.16	10.26	10.27	10.42	10.33	10.18	(NA)
Agricultural sources	1,000 metric tons	8.08	8.25	8.21	8.41	8.61	8.81	(NA)
Industrial sources	1,000 metric tons	0.11	0.12	0.12	0.12	0.11	0.12	(NA)
Nitrous oxide, total	1,000 metric tons	392	417	420	430	437	433	(NA)
Fertilizer	1,000 metric tons	145	150	151	158	161	162	162
Transportation	1,000 metric tons	106	121	127	132	136	136	(NA)
Stationary combustion	1,000 metric tons	48	49	46	46	44	43	44
Industrial sources	1,000 metric tons	92	97	96	95	97	91	93
Nitrogen oxide	Mil. metric tons	20.68	21.43	21.28	21.36	21.23	20.99	(NA)
Energy related	Mil. metric tons	19.69	20.41	20.28	20.35	20.23	19.99	(NA)
Industrial processes	Mil. metric tons	0.79	0.82	0.81	0.81	0.80	0.80	(NA)
Solid waste disposal	Mil. metric tons	0.08	0.08	0.08	0.07	0.07	0.07	(NA)
Transportation	Mil. metric tons	9.61	9.80	9.58	9.67	9.51	9.37	(NA)
Other	Mil. metric tons	0.12	0.12	0.12	0.12	0.12	0.12	(NA)
Nonmethane volatile organic compounds								
(VOC's), total	Mil. metric tons	22.42	22.69	21.68	21.47	21.22	20.61	(NA)
Energy related	Mil. metric tons	10.21	10.07	9.16	8.93	8.72	8.10	(NA)
Industrial processes	Mil. metric tons	9.65	9.99	9.92	9.96	9.98	9.89	(NA)
Solid waste disposal	Mil. metric tons	2.05	2.10	2.08	2.05	2.01	2.10	(NA)
Other	Mil. metric tons	0.51	0.53	0.53	0.52	0.52	0.52	(NA)
Chloroflurocarbons (CFC's) gases [1]	1,000 metric tons	278	278	272	232	193	180	(NA)
Hydrochloroflurocarbons (HCFC's) gases [2]	1,000 metric tons	68	74	76	82	82	86	(NA)

NA Not available.   [1] Covers principally CFC-11, CFC-12, and CFC-113.   [2] Covers principally HCFC-22.

Source: U.S. Energy Information Administration, *Emissions of Greenhouse Gases in the United States, 1985-1992.*

No. 379. Toxic Release Inventory, by Industry and Source: 1989 to 1993

[**In millions of pounds**. Based on reports from almost 23,000 manufacturing facilities which have 10 or more full-time employees and meet established thresholds for manufacturing, processing, or otherwise using the list of more than 300 chemicals covered. Only chemicals that were reportable in all years shown are compared so that data do not reflect any chemicals added or deleted from the list covered. The inventory was established under the Emergency Planning and Community Right-to-Know Act of 1986 (EPCRA)]

INDUSTRY	1987 SIC [1] code	1989	1990	1991	1992	1993 Total [2]	1993 Air [3], point	1993 Air [4], non-point	1993 Water
Total	(X)	4,405.2	3,719.7	3,393.5	3,190.4	2,791.4	1,175.1	480.2	271.1
Food and kindred products	20	37.2	39.2	39.8	38.7	38.0	15.7	11.5	1.4
Tobacco products	21	1.8	2.5	2.3	2.0	2.4	2.1	0.2	-
Textile mill products	22	32.2	27.2	25.2	21.9	20.4	15.3	4.8	0.3
Apparel and other textile prod.	23	1.4	1.3	1.4	1.6	1.1	1.0	0.2	-
Lumber and wood products	24	38.0	35.8	32.6	31.0	29.5	24.6	4.7	0.1
Furniture and fixtures	25	65.5	62.6	56.6	56.7	58.1	50.8	7.0	-
Paper and allied products	26	262.8	254.5	246.4	234.1	216.1	171.9	21.1	18.1
Printing and publishing	27	58.7	56.0	47.2	41.1	36.5	17.2	19.3	0.0
Chemical and allied products	28	2,093.3	1,629.5	1,546.9	1,543.0	1,308.4	320.9	148.1	234.1
Petroleum and coal products	29	99.2	86.9	79.9	84.2	74.5	21.8	35.3	3.3
Rubber and misc. plastic prod.	30	184.6	178.7	151.5	135.6	125.1	86.9	37.5	0.4
Leather and leather products	31	13.5	12.8	10.2	10.7	8.4	4.5	3.0	0.1
Stone, clay, glass products	32	37.2	31.2	29.8	26.1	26.7	15.4	2.6	0.2
Primary metal industries	33	522.9	476.7	424.7	348.6	328.6	106.0	30.6	6.8
Fabricated metals products	34	137.5	128.9	111.6	103.0	91.1	57.8	32.6	0.1
Industrial machinery and equip.	35	58.4	49.4	39.3	34.1	27.5	17.0	10.1	0.2
Electronic, electric equipment	36	100.6	82.5	67.7	53.2	39.6	28.8	9.9	0.3
Transportation equipment	37	206.0	176.6	150.8	137.2	135.5	94.9	38.9	0.1
Instruments and related prod.	38	52.5	44.3	39.7	33.3	26.6	19.9	5.8	0.8
Misc. manufacturing industries.	39	29.3	26.2	20.8	18.9	17.2	11.4	5.8	-
Multiple codes	20-39	362.0	303.0	242.1	220.3	159.6	84.1	46.2	4.5
No codes	20-39	10.8	13.8	27.1	15.1	20.4	7.0	4.7	0.3

- Represents zero.   X Not applicable.   [1] Standard Industrial Classification, see text, section 13.   [2] Includes other releases not shown separately.   [3] Stack.   [4] Fugitive.

Source: U.S. Environmental Protection Agency, *1993 Toxics Release Inventory,* March 1995.

No. 380. Municipal Solid Waste Generation, Recovery, and Disposal: 1960 to 1993

[**In millions of tons, except as indicated.** Covers post-consumer residential and commercial solid wastes which comprise the major portion of typical municipal collections. Excludes mining, agricultural and industrial processing, demolition and construction wastes, sewage sludge, and junked autos and obsolete equipment wastes. Based on material-flows estimating procedure and wet weight as generated]

ITEM AND MATERIAL	1960	1970	1980	1985	1989	1990	1991	1992	1993
Waste generated	87.8	121.9	151.5	164.4	191.4	198.0	196.8	203.0	206.9
Per person per day (lb.)	2.7	3.3	3.7	3.8	4.2	4.3	4.3	4.4	4.4
Materials recovered.	5.9	8.6	14.5	16.4	29.9	32.9	37.3	41.5	45.0
Per person per day (lb.)	0.18	0.23	0.35	0.38	0.7	0.7	0.8	0.9	1.0
Combustion for energy recovery	(NA)	0.4	2.7	7.6	27.1	29.7	31.1	30.5	31.3
Per person per day (lb.)	(NA)	0.02	0.06	0.17	0.6	0.7	0.7	0.7	0.7
Combustion without energy recovery .	27.0	24.7	11.0	4.1	2.0	2.2	2.2	2.2	1.6
Per person per day (lb.)	0.82	0.66	0.27	0.10	0.4	0.05	0.05	0.05	0.03
Landfill, other disposal	54.9	88.2	123.3	136.4	132.4	133.2	126.2	128.8	129.0
Per person per day (lb.)	1.67	2.37	2.97	3.13	2.9	2.9	2.7	2.8	2.7
Percent distribution of generation:									
Paper and paperboard	34.1	36.3	36.1	37.4	37.6	36.7	36.1	36.6	37.6
Glass	7.6	10.4	9.9	8.0	6.7	6.7	6.5	6.5	6.6
Metals	12.0	11.6	9.6	8.6	8.2	8.3	8.5	8.3	8.3
Plastics	0.5	2.5	5.2	7.1	8.0	8.5	8.8	9.1	9.3
Rubber and leather	2.3	2.6	2.8	2.3	2.4	3.0	2.9	3.0	3.0
Textiles	1.9	1.6	1.7	1.7	2.9	3.3	3.1	3.2	3.0
Wood	3.4	3.3	4.4	5.0	6.1	6.2	6.4	6.3	6.6
Food wastes.	13.9	10.5	8.7	8.0	6.9	6.7	6.8	6.6	6.7
Yard wastes	22.8	19.0	18.2	18.2	18.1	17.7	17.8	17.2	15.9
Other wastes	1.6	2.2	3.4	3.6	3.1	3.1	3.2	3.1	3.1

NA Not available.

No. 381. Generation and Recovery of Selected Materials in Municipal Solid Waste: 1960 to 1993

[**In millions of tons, except as indicated.** Covers post-consumer residential and commercial solid wastes which comprise the major portion of typical municipal collections. Excludes mining, agricultural and industrial processing, demolition and construction wastes, sewage sludge, and junked autos and obsolete equipment wastes. Based on material-flows estimating procedure and wet weight as generated]

ITEM AND MATERIAL	1960	1970	1980	1985	1989	1990	1991	1992	1993
Waste generated, total	**87.8**	**121.9**	**151.5**	**164.4**	**191.4**	**198.0**	**196.8**	**203.0**	**206.9**
Paper and paperboard	29.9	44.2	54.7	61.5	71.9	72.7	71.1	74.3	77.8
Ferrous metals	9.9	12.6	11.6	10.9	12.0	12.4	12.6	12.9	12.9
Aluminum	0.4	0.8	1.8	2.3	2.5	2.9	3.0	2.9	3.0
Other nonferrous metals	0.2	0.7	1.1	1.0	1.2	1.1	1.2	1.2	1.2
Glass.	6.7	12.7	15.0	13.2	12.9	13.2	12.7	13.1	13.7
Plastics	0.4	3.1	7.9	11.6	15.4	16.8	17.2	18.5	19.3
Yard waste	20.0	23.2	27.5	30.0	34.7	35.0	35.0	35.0	32.8
Other wastes	20.3	24.6	31.9	33.9	40.8	43.9	44.0	45.1	46.2
Materials recovered, total	**5.9**	**8.6**	**14.5**	**16.4**	**29.9**	**32.9**	**37.3**	**41.5**	**45.0**
Paper and paperboard	5.4	7.4	11.9	13.1	19.1	20.3	22.5	24.5	26.5
Ferrous metals	0.1	0.1	0.4	0.4	1.5	1.7	2.3	2.8	3.4
Aluminum.	-	-	0.3	0.6	0.9	1.0	1.0	1.1	1.1
Other nonferrous metals	-	0.3	0.5	0.5	0.8	0.7	0.7	0.7	0.8
Glass.	0.1	0.2	0.8	1.0	2.5	2.6	2.6	2.9	3.0
Plastics	-	-	-	0.1	0.3	0.4	0.5	0.6	0.7
Yard waste	-	-	-	-	3.5	4.2	5.0	6.0	6.5
Other wastes	0.3	0.6	0.6	0.7	1.3	2.0	2.7	2.9	3.0
Percent of generation recovered, total .	**6.7**	**7.1**	**9.6**	**10.0**	**15.6**	**16.6**	**19.0**	**20.4**	**21.7**
Paper and paperboard	18.1	16.7	21.8	21.3	26.6	27.9	31.7	32.9	34.0
Ferrous metals	1.0	0.8	3.4	3.7	12.6	13.7	18.5	21.6	26.1
Aluminum.	-	-	16.7	26.1	35.5	35.3	34.9	38.1	35.4
Other nonferrous metals	-	42.9	45.5	50.0	68.3	66.4	64.3	62.1	62.9
Glass.	1.5	1.6	5.3	7.6	19.5	20.0	20.1	22.0	22.0
Plastics	-	-	-	0.9	1.7	2.2	2.6	3.2	3.5
Yard waste	-	-	-	-	10.0	12.0	14.3	17.1	19.8
Other wastes	1.5	2.4	1.9	2.1	3.2	4.5	6.1	6.4	6.4

- Represents zero.

Source of tables 380 and 381: Franklin Associates, Ltd., Prairie Village, KS, *Characterization of Municipal Solid Waste in the United States: 1994.* Prepared for the U.S. Environmental Protection Agency.

No. 382. Hazardous Waste Sites on the National Priority List, by State: 1994

[Includes both proposed and final sites listed on the National Priorities List for the Superfund program as authorized by the Comprehensive Environmental Response, Compensation, and Liability Act of 1980 and the Superfund Amendments and Reauthorization Act of 1986]

STATE	Total sites	Rank	Per- cent distri- bution	Fed- eral	Non- Fed- eral	STATE	Total sites	Rank	Per- cent distri- bution	Fed- eral	Non- Fed- eral
Total	1,296	(X)	(X)	160	1,136	Montana	9	41	0.7	-	9
						Nebraska	10	37	0.8	1	9
United States. .	**1,283**	**(X)**	**100.0**	**158**	**1,125**	Nevada	1	50	0.1	-	1
						New Hampshire	17	24	1.3	1	16
Alabama.	13	28	1.0	3	10	New Jersey	108	1	8.4	6	102
Alaska	8	42	0.6	6	2	New Mexico	11	34	0.9	2	9
Arizona.	10	36	0.8	3	7	New York	85	4	6.6	4	81
Arkansas	12	32	0.9	-	12	North Carolina	23	17	1.8	2	21
California	96	3	7.5	23	73	North Dakota	2	49	0.2	-	2
Colorado.	18	22	1.4	3	15	Ohio	38	10	3.0	5	33
Connecticut.	16	25	1.2	1	15	Oklahoma	11	35	0.9	1	10
Delaware	19	20	1.5	1	18	Oregon.	13	28	1.0	2	11
District of Columbia . .	-	(X)	-	-	-	Pennsylvania	102	2	8.0	6	96
Florida	58	6	4.5	5	53	Rhode Island	12	32	0.9	2	10
Georgia	13	28	1.0	2	11	South Carolina.	26	15	2.0	2	24
Hawaii	4	46	0.3	3	1	South Dakota	4	46	0.3	1	3
Idaho	10	37	0.8	2	8	Tennessee	18	22	1.4	4	14
Illinois	37	11	2.9	4	33	Texas.	30	13	2.3	4	26
Indiana.	33	12	2.6	-	33	Utah	16	25	1.2	4	12
Iowa	19	20	1.5	1	18	Vermont	8	42	0.6	-	8
Kansas.	10	37	0.8	1	9	Virginia.	25	16	1.9	6	19
Kentucky	20	19	1.6	1	19	Washington.	56	7	4.4	20	36
Louisiana	14	27	1.1	1	13	West Virginia.	6	44	0.5	2	4
Maine.	10	37	0.8	3	7	Wisconsin	40	9	3.1	-	40
Maryland	13	28	1.0	4	9	Wyoming	3	48	0.2	1	2
Massachusetts.	30	13	2.3	8	22						
Michigan.	77	5	6.0	1	76	Guam	2	(X)	(X)	1	1
Minnesota	41	8	3.2	3	38	Puerto Rico.	9	(X)	(X)	1	8
Mississippi	5	45	0.4	-	5	Virgin Islands.	2	(X)	(X)	-	2
Missouri	23	17	1.8	3	20						

- Represents zero.   X Not applicable.

Source: U.S. Environmental Protection Agency, *Supplementary Materials: National Priorities List, Proposed Rule,* August 1994.

No. 383. Environmental Industry—Revenues and Employment, by Industry Segment: 1980 to 1994

[Covers approximately 59,000 private and public companies engaged in environmental activities]

INDUSTRY SEGMENT	REVENUE (bil. dol.)					EMPLOYMENT (1,000)				
	1980	1990	1992	1993	1994	1980	1990	1992	1993	1994
Industry total	**52.0**	**137.7**	**147.0**	**152.8**	**161.5**	**463**	**1,174**	**1,204**	**1,223**	**1,262**
Analytical services [1]	0.4	1.5	1.6	1.6	1.6	6	20	20	20	20
Water treatment works	9.2	19.8	21.7	23.4	25.7	54	95	100	106	114
Solid waste management [2]	8.5	26.1	28.2	29.4	31.0	83	210	218	222	230
Hazardous waste management	0.6	6.3	6.6	6.5	6.4	7	57	58	55	53
Remediation/Industrial services	0.4	8.5	8.2	8.4	8.6	7	107	99	100	100
Consulting & engineering	1.5	12.5	14.3	14.6	15.3	21	144	158	158	163
Water equipment and chemicals . . .	6.3	12.1	13.0	13.2	13.5	62	98	101	101	101
Instrument manufacturing	0.2	1.6	1.8	1.8	1.9	3	19	23	24	25
Air pollution control equipment.	3.0	3.7	3.8	3.8	3.7	28	83	83	84	83
Waste management equipment	4.0	10.4	11.1	10.9	11.2	42	89	91	88	88
Process and prevention technology . .	0.1	0.4	0.6	0.7	0.8	2	9	13	14	15
Water utilities	11.9	19.8	21.9	23.1	24.2	77	105	111	115	118
Resource recovery	4.4	13.1	12.2	13.3	15.4	49	118	106	113	128
Environmental energy sources.	1.5	1.8	2.0	2.1	2.2	22	21	23	23	24

[1] Covers environmental laboratory testing and services.   [2] Covers such activities as collection, transportation, transfer stations, disposal, landfill ownership, and management for solid waste.

Source: Environmental Business International, Inc., San Diego, CA, *Environmental Business Journal,* monthly, (copyright).

No. 384. Pollution Abatement and Control Expenditures, in Current and Constant (1987) Dollars, 1972 to 1992, and by Media, 1992

[In millions of dollars]

| YEAR | Total expendi-tures | POLLUTION ABATEMENT | | | | | | | Regu-lation and monitor-ing | Research and develop-ment |
| | | Total | Per-sonal con-sump-tion | Busi-ness | Government | | | | | |
					Total	Federal	State and local	Govt. enter-prise[1]		
CURRENT DOLLARS										
1972	16,586	15,397	1,350	10,639	3,409	139	1,311	1,959	367	823
1975	28,442	26,685	3,235	16,554	6,896	432	1,752	4,713	653	1,104
1980	50,399	47,352	6,558	29,706	11,088	494	2,768	7,825	1,296	1,751
1981	54,241	51,153	8,122	32,370	10,660	506	3,144	7,011	1,378	1,711
1982	55,359	52,321	8,287	33,092	10,942	550	3,484	6,908	1,397	1,641
1983	58,873	55,893	9,742	34,804	11,346	795	3,842	6,709	1,385	1,595
1984	65,423	62,561	10,839	39,032	12,690	944	4,280	7,466	1,362	1,501
1985	71,169	68,268	11,991	42,058	14,220	1,225	4,858	8,137	1,279	1,621
1986	75,389	72,111	12,385	43,954	15,772	1,346	5,515	8,912	1,532	1,746
1987	77,649	74,349	11,075	45,432	17,842	1,237	6,266	10,339	1,519	1,781
1988	83,809	80,242	12,284	49,107	18,852	1,402	7,283	10,167	1,695	1,872
1989	87,390	83,543	10,944	52,217	20,382	1,379	8,705	10,299	1,803	2,044
1990 [2]	92,873	89,317	9,238	57,492	22,587	1,391	10,161	11,035	1,784	1,772
1991 [2]	94,799	90,918	7,394	59,618	23,906	1,417	11,547	10,942	1,868	2,013
1992 [2]	101,954	98,136	7,896	64,825	25,414	1,215	13,086	11,113	1,848	1,971
Air	28,560	26,889	7,896	18,667	327	75	22	230	526	1,144
Water	38,222	37,162	-	25,067	12,095	656	556	10,883	741	320
Solid Waste	36,046	35,496	-	22,804	12,692	281	12,411	-	401	149
CONSTANT (1987) DOLLARS										
1972	46,032	42,814	3,450	30,243	9,122	402	3,693	5,027	959	2,259
1975	57,246	53,587	6,172	32,987	14,427	937	3,782	9,708	1,346	2,313
1980	65,590	61,305	7,297	38,673	15,335	679	4,015	10,641	1,873	2,413
1981	63,613	59,681	8,472	37,731	13,477	627	4,070	8,780	1,810	2,123
1982	61,714	58,115	8,494	36,462	13,159	649	4,287	8,224	1,709	1,890
1983	63,836	60,465	9,990	37,454	13,021	911	4,527	7,583	1,608	1,763
1984	68,913	65,812	11,040	40,708	14,063	1,048	4,803	8,212	1,506	1,596
1985	72,813	69,773	11,935	42,833	15,005	1,300	5,200	8,505	1,361	1,678
1986	77,487	74,110	12,831	45,002	16,277	1,402	5,726	9,149	1,589	1,788
1987	77,649	74,349	11,075	45,432	17,842	1,237	6,266	10,339	1,519	1,781
1988	81,465	78,030	12,067	47,805	18,158	1,340	6,953	9,866	1,643	1,792
1989	81,664	78,128	10,438	48,782	18,908	1,271	7,982	9,655	1,657	1,879
1990 [2]	83,901	80,706	8,657	51,881	20,169	1,228	8,864	10,077	1,636	1,560
1991 [2]	83,348	80,002	6,755	52,658	20,589	1,220	9,770	9,599	1,654	1,692
1992 [2]	87,594	84,328	7,019	55,994	21,315	1,041	10,734	9,540	1,619	1,648
Air	25,329	23,900	7,019	16,596	285	64	18	203	467	961
Water	33,919	32,993	-	22,427	10,514	565	613	9,337	660	266
Solid Waste	29,176	28,713	-	18,448	10,265	242	10,023	-	339	124

- Represents or rounds to zero. [1] Fixed capital. [2] Includes "other and unallocated" expenditures (such as for noise, radiation, and pesticide pollution and business expenditures not assigned to media) which may be either positive or negative; therefore, data may not add.

No. 385. Air and Water Pollution Abatement Expenditures in Constant (1987) Dollars: 1972 to 1992

[In millions of dollars. Excludes agricultural production of crops and livestock except feedlots]

YEAR	AIR							WATER				
	Total	Mobile sources [1]			Stationary sources			Total [5]	Industrial		Public sewer systems	
		Total	Cars [2]	Trucks [2]	Total [3]	Industrial			Facil-ities	Oper-ations[4]	Facil-ities	Oper-ations[4]
						Facil-ities	Oper-ations[4]					
1972	16,421	5,096	4,262	834	11,326	6,047	4,819	18,739	3,986	2,482	4,801	3,197
1975	21,291	9,703	7,805	1,898	11,588	6,781	4,318	23,923	4,093	3,066	9,426	3,722
1980	24,486	11,973	9,103	2,870	12,513	6,044	5,782	26,622	4,131	3,586	10,148	5,100
1981	25,688	13,818	11,092	2,726	11,870	5,851	5,360	23,892	3,306	4,011	8,270	5,297
1982	24,976	13,728	10,914	2,813	11,248	5,301	5,263	23,227	3,145	4,062	7,679	5,616
1983	25,906	15,943	12,756	3,186	9,963	3,879	5,353	23,328	2,564	4,231	7,063	5,959
1984	28,164	18,228	14,119	4,109	9,936	3,900	5,418	24,900	2,807	4,389	7,791	6,149
1985	29,050	19,373	14,896	4,477	9,677	3,409	5,730	26,017	2,771	4,590	8,124	6,550
1986	30,464	20,162	15,484	4,678	10,301	3,654	6,142	27,717	2,587	4,959	8,807	7,285
1987	27,421	17,614	13,166	4,448	9,807	3,482	5,843	29,420	2,566	5,257	10,035	7,792
1988	28,955	19,295	14,727	4,568	9,660	3,138	6,089	29,226	2,539	5,467	9,629	8,269
1989	25,982	16,402	12,511	3,892	9,580	3,184	5,965	30,164	3,046	5,613	9,412	8,803
1990	24,687	14,150	10,765	3,385	10,537	3,879	6,247	32,509	3,983	6,080	9,822	9,430
1991	22,903	12,024	8,909	2,809	10,880	4,814	5,644	32,050	3,940	5,623	9,340	10,251
1992	23,900	12,264	9,186	3,077	11,637	5,538	5,664	32,993	3,702	6,146	9,305	10,934

[1] Excludes expenditures to reduce emissions from sources other than cars and trucks. [2] Includes expenditures for devices such as catalytic convertors, and expenditures for devices. [3] Includes other expenditures not shown separately for fixed capital of government enterprises such as Tennessee Valley Authority. [4] Operation of facilities. [5] Includes expenditures for private connectors to sewer systems, by owners of animal feedlots, and by government enterprises.

Source of tables 384 and 385: U.S. Bureau of Economic Analysis, *Survey of Current Business*, May 1994.

No. 386. Pollution Abatement Capital Expenditures and Operating Costs of Manufacturing Establishments, by Selected Industry Group, 1993

[In millions of dollars. Based on probability sample of about 20,000 manufacturing establishments. Excludes apparel and other textile establishments and establishments with less than 20 employees]

YEAR AND INDUSTRY GROUP	POLLUTION ABATEMENT CAPITAL EXPENDITURES					POLLUTION ABATEMENT GROSS OPERATING COSTS [1]				
	Total	Air	Water	Solid waste		Total	Air	Water	Solid waste	
				Hazard-ous	Non-hazard-ous				Hazard-ous	Non-hazard-ous
All industries [2]	**7,177.9**	**4,122.0**	**2,294.9**	**278.8**	**482.1**	**17,555.0**	**5,574.6**	**6,631.8**	**1,874.6**	**3,474.0**
Food and kindred products .	219.9	73.9	113.6	0.8	31.6	1,339.3	156.1	857.8	24.1	301.3
Paper and allied products . .	715.6	307.3	289.2	10.5	108.7	1,901.5	511.2	852.7	46.1	491.4
Chemical and allied products	1,957.9	767.5	937.9	105.2	147.3	4,348.2	1,013.6	1,957.0	688.1	689.5
Petroleum and coal products	2,648.5	1,974.7	567.2	80.8	25.8	2,647.9	1,585.3	685.2	187.2	190.1
Stone, clay, glass products .	118.1	83.2	16.1	5.8	12.9	521.1	269.0	102.4	24.7	125.0
Primary metal industries . . .	442.2	280.7	92.0	15.2	54.3	2,017.2	944.5	598.2	175.4	299.1
Fabricated metals products .	102.9	44.8	39.3	8.0	10.9	679.4	126.6	267.3	116.9	168.5
Machinery, exc. electrical . .	105.0	65.7	20.2	7.3	11.8	445.1	71.9	157.2	63.9	152.1
Electrical, electronic equipment	176.7	92.7	67.9	10.6	5.6	662.4	121.8	297.5	101.9	141.2
Transportation equipment . .	277.6	178.7	67.1	14.1	17.7	1,194.4	302.4	350.9	243.2	298.0
Instruments, related products	105.0	65.1	19.2	13.6	7.1	336.6	59.3	94.1	74.7	108.5

[1] Includes payments to governmental units.   [2] Includes industries not shown separately; excludes Major Group 23, Apparel and Other Textile Products.

Source: U.S. Bureau of the Census, *Current Industrial Reports*, series MA-200, annual.

No. 387. Threatened and Endangered Wildlife and Plant Species—Number: 1994

[As of **October 19.** Endangered species: One in danger of becoming extinct throughout all or a significant part of its natural range. Threatened species: One likely to become endangered in the foreseeable future]

ITEM	Mam-mals	Birds	Rep-tiles	Amphib-ians	Fishes	Snails	Clams	Crusta-ceans	Insects	Arach-nids	Plants
Endangered species, total	**307**	**228**	**79**	**14**	**78**	**15**	**53**	**14**	**23**	**4**	**416**
U.S. only	36	58	8	6	62	14	50	14	16	4	404
U.S. and foreign	19	17	6	-	5	-	1	-	3	-	11
Foreign only [1]	252	153	65	8	11	1	2	-	4	-	1
Threatened species, total	**31**	**16**	**33**	**5**	**36**	**7**	**6**	**3**	**9**	**-**	**90**
U.S. only	6	8	15	4	30	7	6	3	9	-	76
U.S. and foreign	3	8	4	1	6	-	-	-	-	-	12
Foreign only [1]	22	-	14	-	-	-	-	-	-	-	2

- Represents zero.   [1] Species outside United States and outlying areas as determined by Fish and Wildlife Service.

Source: U.S. Fish and Wildlife Service, *Endangered Species Technical Bulletin*, quarterly.

No. 388. Tornadoes, Floods, and Tropical Storms: 1984 to 1994

[See also *Historical Statistics, Colonial Times to 1970*, series J 268-278]

ITEM	1984	1985	1986	1987	1988	1989	1990	1991	1992	1993	1994, prel.
Tornadoes, number [1]	907	684	764	656	702	856	1,133	1,132	1,303	1,173	(NA)
Lives lost, total	122	94	15	59	32	50	53	39	39	33	(NA)
Most in a single tornado	16	18	3	30	5	21	29	13	10	7	(NA)
Property loss of $500,000 and over	125	69	75	38	48	60	91	64	108	72	(NA)
Floods: Lives lost	126	304	80	82	29	81	147	63	87	101	(NA)
Property loss (mil. dol.)	4,000	3,000	4,000	1,490	114	415	2,058	1,416	800	16,400	(NA)
North Atlantic tropical storms and hurricanes: [2]											
Number reaching U.S. coast . . .	12	11	6	7	12	11	14	8	7	8	7
Hurricanes only	1	6	2	1	1	3	-	1	1	1	-
Lives lost in U.S	4	30	9	-	6	56	10	17	26	9	38
Property loss (mil. (1990) dol.)[3]	77	4,457	18	8	9	7,840	57	1,500	25,000	57	973

- Represents zero.   NA Not available.   [1] A violent, rotating column of air descending from a cumulonimbus cloud in the form of a tubular- or funnel-shaped cloud, usually characterized by movements along a narrow path and wind speeds from 100 to over 300 miles per hour. Also known as a "twister" or "waterspout."   [2] Source: National Hurricane Center, Coral Gables, FL, unpublished data. Tropical storms have maximum winds of 39 to 73 miles per hour; hurricanes have maximum winds of 74 miles per hour or higher.   [3] Source: Hebert, Jarrell, & Mayfield, "The Deadliest, Costliest, and Most Intense U.S. Hurricanes of this Century," NOAA Technical Memo, NHC-31, February 1993.

Source: Except as noted, U.S. National Oceanic and Atmospheric Administration, *Storm Data*, monthly.

No. 389. Normal Daily Mean Temperature—Selected Cities

[**In Fahrenheit degrees.** Airport data except as noted. Based on standard 30-year period, 1961 through 1990. See *Historical Statistics, Colonial Times to 1970,* series J 110-136 and J 164-267, for related data]

STATE	STATION	Jan.	Feb.	Mar.	Apr.	May	June	July	Aug.	Sept.	Oct.	Nov.	Dec.	Annual avg.
AL	Mobile	49.9	53.2	60.5	67.8	74.5	80.4	82.3	81.8	77.9	68.4	59.8	53.0	67.5
AK	Juneau	24.2	28.4	32.7	39.7	47.0	53.0	56.0	55.0	49.4	42.2	32.0	27.1	40.6
AZ	Phoenix	53.6	57.7	62.2	69.9	78.8	88.2	93.5	91.5	85.6	74.5	61.9	54.1	72.6
AR	Little Rock	39.1	43.6	53.1	62.1	70.2	78.4	81.9	80.6	74.1	63.0	52.1	42.8	61.8
CA	Los Angeles	56.8	57.6	58.0	60.1	62.7	65.7	69.1	70.5	69.9	66.8	61.6	56.9	63.0
	Sacramento	45.2	50.7	53.6	58.3	65.3	71.6	75.7	75.1	71.5	64.2	53.3	45.3	60.8
	San Diego	57.4	58.6	59.6	62.0	64.1	66.8	71.0	72.6	71.4	67.7	62.0	57.4	64.2
	San Francisco	48.7	52.2	53.3	55.6	58.1	61.5	62.7	63.7	64.5	61.0	54.8	49.4	57.1
CO	Denver	29.7	33.4	39.0	48.2	57.2	66.9	73.5	71.4	62.3	51.4	39.0	31.0	50.3
CT	Hartford	24.6	27.5	37.5	48.7	59.6	68.5	73.7	71.6	63.3	52.2	41.9	29.5	49.9
DE	Wilmington	30.6	33.4	42.7	52.2	62.5	71.5	76.4	75.0	68.0	56.2	46.3	35.8	54.2
DC	Washington	34.6	37.5	47.2	56.5	66.4	75.6	80.0	78.5	71.3	59.7	49.8	39.4	58.0
FL	Jacksonville	52.4	55.2	61.1	67.0	73.4	79.1	81.6	81.2	78.1	69.8	61.9	55.1	68.0
	Miami	67.2	68.5	71.7	75.2	78.7	81.4	82.6	82.8	81.9	78.3	73.6	69.1	75.9
GA	Atlanta	41.0	44.8	53.5	61.5	69.2	76.0	78.8	78.1	72.7	62.3	53.1	44.5	61.3
HI	Honolulu	72.9	73.0	74.4	75.8	77.5	79.4	80.5	81.4	81.0	79.6	77.2	74.1	77.2
ID	Boise	29.0	35.9	42.4	49.1	57.5	66.5	74.0	72.5	62.6	51.8	39.9	30.1	50.9
IL	Chicago	21.0	25.4	37.2	48.6	58.9	68.6	73.2	71.7	64.4	52.8	40.0	26.6	49.0
	Peoria	21.6	26.3	39.0	51.4	61.9	71.5	75.5	73.1	66.1	54.0	41.2	27.0	50.7
IN	Indianapolis	25.5	29.6	41.4	52.4	62.8	71.9	75.4	73.2	66.6	54.7	43.0	30.9	52.3
IA	Des Moines	19.4	24.7	36.3	50.9	62.3	71.8	76.6	73.9	65.1	53.5	39.0	24.4	49.9
KS	Wichita	29.5	34.8	45.4	56.4	65.6	75.7	81.4	79.3	70.3	58.6	44.7	33.0	56.2
KY	Louisville	31.7	35.7	46.3	56.3	65.3	73.2	77.2	75.8	69.5	57.6	47.1	36.9	56.1
LA	New Orleans	51.3	54.3	61.6	68.5	74.8	80.0	81.9	81.5	78.1	69.1	61.1	54.5	68.1
ME	Portland	20.8	23.3	33.0	43.3	53.3	62.4	68.6	67.3	59.1	48.5	38.7	26.5	45.4
MD	Baltimore	31.8	34.8	44.1	53.4	63.4	72.5	77.0	75.6	68.5	56.6	46.8	36.7	55.1
MA	Boston	28.6	30.3	38.6	48.1	58.2	67.7	73.5	71.9	64.8	54.8	45.3	33.6	51.3
MI	Detroit	22.9	25.4	35.7	47.3	58.4	67.6	72.3	70.5	63.2	51.2	40.2	28.3	48.6
	Sault Ste. Marie	12.9	14.0	24.0	38.2	50.5	58.0	63.8	62.6	55.1	45.3	33.0	19.0	39.7
MN	Duluth	7.0	12.3	24.4	38.6	50.8	59.8	66.1	63.7	54.2	43.7	28.4	12.8	38.5
	Minneapolis-St. Paul	11.8	17.9	31.0	46.4	58.5	68.2	73.6	70.5	60.5	48.8	33.2	17.9	44.9
MS	Jackson	44.1	47.9	56.7	64.6	72.0	78.8	81.5	80.9	75.9	64.7	55.8	47.8	64.2
MO	Kansas City	25.7	31.2	42.7	54.5	64.1	73.2	78.5	76.1	67.5	56.6	43.1	30.4	53.6
	St. Louis	29.3	33.9	45.1	56.7	66.1	75.4	79.8	77.6	70.2	58.4	46.2	33.9	56.1
MT	Great Falls	21.2	27.4	33.3	43.6	53.1	61.6	68.2	66.9	56.6	47.5	33.9	23.9	44.8
NE	Omaha	21.1	26.9	38.6	51.9	62.4	72.1	76.9	74.1	65.1	53.4	39.0	25.1	50.6
NV	Reno	32.9	38.0	42.8	48.6	56.5	65.1	71.6	69.6	60.4	50.8	40.3	32.7	50.8
NH	Concord	18.6	21.8	32.4	43.9	55.2	64.2	69.5	67.3	58.8	47.8	37.1	24.3	45.1
NJ	Atlantic City	30.9	33.0	41.5	50.0	60.4	69.4	74.7	73.4	66.1	54.9	45.8	35.8	53.0
NM	Albuquerque	34.2	40.0	46.9	55.2	64.2	74.2	78.5	75.9	68.6	57.0	44.3	35.3	56.2
NY	Albany	20.6	23.5	34.3	46.4	57.6	66.9	71.8	69.6	61.3	50.2	39.7	26.5	47.4
	Buffalo	23.6	24.5	33.8	45.2	56.6	65.9	71.1	69.0	61.9	51.1	40.5	29.1	47.7
	New York [1]	31.5	33.6	42.4	52.5	62.7	71.6	76.8	75.5	68.2	57.5	47.6	36.6	54.7
NC	Charlotte	39.3	42.5	50.9	59.4	67.4	75.7	79.3	78.3	72.4	61.3	52.1	42.6	60.1
	Raleigh	38.9	42.0	50.4	59.0	67.0	74.3	78.1	77.1	71.1	60.1	51.2	42.6	59.3
ND	Bismarck	9.2	15.7	28.2	43.0	55.0	64.4	70.4	68.3	57.0	45.7	28.6	14.0	41.6
OH	Cincinnati	28.1	31.8	43.0	53.2	62.9	71.0	75.1	73.5	67.3	55.1	44.3	33.5	53.2
	Cleveland	24.8	27.2	37.3	47.6	58.0	67.2	71.9	70.4	63.9	52.8	42.6	30.9	49.6
	Columbus	26.4	29.6	40.9	51.0	61.2	69.2	73.2	71.5	65.5	53.7	42.9	31.9	51.4
OK	Oklahoma City	35.9	40.9	50.3	60.4	68.4	76.7	82.0	81.1	73.0	62.0	49.6	39.3	60.0
OR	Portland	39.6	43.6	47.3	51.0	57.1	63.5	68.2	68.6	63.3	54.5	46.1	40.2	53.6
PA	Philadelphia	30.4	33.0	42.4	52.4	62.9	71.8	76.7	75.5	68.2	56.4	46.4	35.8	54.3
	Pittsburgh	26.1	28.7	39.4	49.6	59.5	67.9	72.1	70.5	63.9	52.4	42.3	31.5	50.3
RI	Providence	27.9	29.7	37.4	47.4	57.3	66.2	72.7	71.3	64.1	53.6	44.0	32.8	50.4
SC	Columbia	43.8	46.8	55.2	63.0	70.9	77.4	80.8	79.7	74.2	63.3	54.6	46.9	63.1
SD	Sioux Falls	13.8	19.7	32.5	46.9	58.4	68.3	74.3	71.4	60.9	48.6	33.0	18.3	45.5
TN	Memphis	39.7	44.2	53.1	62.9	71.2	79.1	82.6	81.0	74.2	63.1	52.5	43.7	62.3
	Nashville	36.2	40.4	50.2	59.2	67.7	75.6	79.3	78.1	71.8	60.4	50.0	40.5	59.1
TX	Dallas-Fort Worth	43.4	47.9	56.7	65.5	72.8	81.0	85.3	84.9	77.4	67.2	56.2	46.9	65.4
	El Paso	42.8	48.1	55.1	63.4	71.8	80.4	82.3	80.1	74.4	64.0	52.4	44.1	63.2
	Houston	50.4	53.9	60.6	68.3	74.5	80.4	82.6	82.3	78.2	69.6	61.0	53.5	67.9
UT	Salt Lake City	27.9	34.1	41.8	49.7	58.8	69.1	77.9	75.6	65.2	53.2	40.8	29.7	52.0
VT	Burlington	16.3	18.2	30.7	43.9	56.3	65.2	70.5	67.9	58.9	47.8	36.8	23.0	44.6
VA	Norfolk	39.1	41.0	48.6	57.0	66.1	74.1	78.2	77.2	71.9	61.2	52.5	43.8	59.2
	Richmond	35.7	38.7	48.0	57.3	66.0	73.9	78.0	76.8	70.0	58.6	49.6	40.1	57.7
WA	Seattle-Tacoma	40.1	43.5	45.6	49.2	55.1	60.9	65.2	65.5	60.6	52.8	45.3	40.5	52.0
	Spokane	27.1	33.3	38.7	45.9	53.9	62.0	68.8	68.4	58.9	47.3	35.1	27.8	47.3
WV	Charleston	32.1	35.5	45.9	54.8	63.5	71.4	75.1	73.9	67.7	56.2	46.8	37.0	55.0
WI	Milwaukee	18.9	23.0	33.3	44.4	54.6	65.0	70.9	69.3	61.7	50.3	37.7	24.4	46.1
WY	Cheyenne	26.5	29.3	33.6	42.5	52.0	61.3	68.4	66.4	57.4	47.0	35.2	27.8	45.6
PR	San Juan	77.0	77.1	78.0	79.4	80.9	82.3	82.6	82.7	82.5	81.9	80.0	78.1	80.2

[1] City office data.

Source: U.S. National Oceanic and Atmospheric Administration, *Climatography of the United States,* No. 81.

No. 390. Normal Daily Maximum Temperature—Selected Cities

[**In Fahrenheit degrees.** Airport data except as noted. Based on standard 30-year period, 1961 through 1990]

STATE	STATION	Jan.	Feb.	Mar.	Apr.	May	June	July	Aug.	Sept.	Oct.	Nov.	Dec.	Annual avg.
AL	Mobile	59.7	63.6	70.9	78.5	84.6	90.0	91.3	90.5	86.9	79.5	70.3	62.9	77.4
AK	Juneau	29.4	34.1	38.7	47.2	55.1	60.9	63.9	62.7	55.9	47.1	36.7	31.6	46.9
AZ	Phoenix	65.9	70.7	75.5	84.5	93.6	103.5	105.9	103.7	98.3	88.1	74.9	66.2	85.9
AR	Little Rock	49.0	53.9	64.0	73.4	81.3	89.3	92.4	91.4	84.6	75.1	62.7	52.5	72.5
CA	Los Angeles	65.7	65.9	65.5	67.4	69.0	71.9	75.3	76.6	76.6	74.4	70.3	65.9	70.4
	Sacramento	52.7	60.0	64.0	71.1	80.3	87.8	93.2	92.1	87.3	77.9	63.1	52.7	73.5
	San Diego	65.9	66.5	66.3	68.4	69.1	71.6	76.2	77.8	77.1	74.6	69.9	66.1	70.8
	San Francisco	55.6	59.4	60.8	63.9	66.5	70.3	71.6	72.3	73.6	70.1	62.4	56.1	65.2
CO	Denver	43.2	46.6	52.2	61.8	70.8	81.4	88.2	85.8	76.9	66.3	52.5	44.5	64.2
CT	Hartford	33.2	36.4	46.8	59.9	71.6	80.0	85.0	82.7	74.8	63.7	51.0	37.5	60.2
DE	Wilmington	38.7	41.9	52.1	62.6	72.9	81.4	85.6	84.1	77.7	66.6	55.5	43.9	63.6
DC	Washington	42.3	45.9	56.5	66.7	76.2	84.7	88.5	86.9	80.1	69.1	58.3	47.0	66.9
FL	Jacksonville	64.2	67.0	73.0	79.1	84.7	89.3	91.4	90.7	87.2	80.2	73.6	66.8	78.9
	Miami	75.2	76.5	79.1	82.4	85.3	87.6	89.0	89.0	87.8	84.5	80.4	76.7	82.8
GA	Atlanta	50.4	55.0	64.3	72.7	79.6	85.8	88.0	87.1	81.8	72.7	63.4	54.0	71.2
HI	Honolulu	80.1	80.5	81.6	82.8	84.7	86.5	87.5	88.7	88.5	86.9	84.1	81.2	84.4
ID	Boise	36.4	44.2	52.9	61.4	71.0	80.9	90.2	88.1	77.0	64.6	48.7	37.7	62.8
IL	Chicago	29.0	33.5	45.8	58.6	70.1	79.6	83.7	81.8	74.8	63.3	48.4	34.0	58.6
	Peoria	29.9	34.9	48.1	62.0	72.8	82.2	85.7	83.1	76.9	64.8	49.8	34.6	60.4
IN	Indianapolis	33.7	38.3	50.9	63.3	73.8	82.7	85.5	83.6	77.6	65.8	51.9	38.5	62.1
IA	Des Moines	28.1	33.7	46.9	61.8	73.0	82.2	86.7	84.2	75.6	64.3	48.0	32.6	59.8
KS	Wichita	39.8	45.9	57.2	68.3	76.9	86.8	92.8	90.7	81.4	70.6	55.3	43.0	67.4
KY	Louisville	40.3	44.8	56.3	67.3	76.0	83.5	87.0	85.7	80.3	69.2	56.8	45.1	66.0
LA	New Orleans	60.8	64.1	71.6	78.5	84.4	89.2	90.6	90.2	86.6	79.4	71.1	64.3	77.6
ME	Portland	30.3	33.1	41.4	52.3	63.2	72.7	78.8	77.4	69.3	58.7	47.0	35.1	54.9
MD	Baltimore	40.2	43.7	54.0	64.3	74.2	83.2	87.2	85.4	78.5	67.3	56.5	45.2	65.0
MA	Boston	35.7	37.5	45.8	55.9	66.6	76.3	81.8	79.8	72.8	62.7	52.2	40.4	59.0
MI	Detroit	30.3	33.3	44.4	57.7	69.6	78.9	83.3	81.3	73.9	61.5	48.1	35.2	58.1
	Sault Ste. Marie	21.1	23.2	32.8	48.0	62.6	70.5	76.3	73.8	65.9	54.3	40.0	26.2	49.6
MN	Duluth	16.2	21.7	32.9	48.2	61.9	71.0	77.1	73.9	63.8	52.3	35.2	20.7	47.9
	Minneapolis-St. Paul	20.7	26.6	39.2	56.5	69.4	78.8	84.0	80.7	70.7	58.8	41.0	25.5	54.3
MS	Jackson	55.6	60.1	69.3	77.4	84.0	90.6	92.4	92.0	88.0	79.1	69.2	59.5	76.4
MO	Kansas City	34.7	40.6	52.8	65.1	74.3	83.3	88.7	86.4	78.1	67.5	52.6	38.8	63.6
	St. Louis	37.7	42.6	54.6	66.9	76.1	85.2	89.3	87.3	79.9	68.5	54.7	41.7	65.4
MT	Great Falls	30.6	37.5	43.7	55.3	65.2	74.6	83.3	81.6	69.6	59.3	43.5	33.1	56.4
NE	Omaha	31.3	37.1	49.4	63.8	74.0	83.7	87.9	85.2	76.5	65.6	49.3	34.6	61.5
NV	Reno	45.1	51.7	56.3	63.7	72.9	83.1	91.9	89.6	79.5	68.6	53.8	45.5	66.8
NH	Concord	29.8	33.0	42.8	56.3	68.9	77.3	82.4	79.8	71.6	60.7	47.1	34.2	57.0
NJ	Atlantic City	40.4	42.5	51.6	60.7	71.2	80.0	84.5	83.3	76.6	66.0	55.7	45.3	63.2
NM	Albuquerque	46.8	53.5	61.4	70.8	79.7	90.0	92.5	89.0	81.9	71.0	57.3	47.5	70.1
NY	Albany	30.2	33.2	44.0	57.5	69.7	79.0	84.0	81.4	73.2	61.8	48.7	34.9	58.1
	Buffalo	30.2	31.6	41.7	54.2	66.1	75.3	80.2	77.9	70.8	59.4	47.1	35.3	55.8
	New York [1]	37.6	40.3	50.0	61.2	71.7	80.1	85.2	83.7	76.2	65.3	54.0	42.5	62.3
NC	Charlotte	49.0	53.0	62.3	71.2	78.3	85.8	88.9	87.7	81.9	72.0	62.6	52.3	70.4
	Raleigh	48.9	52.6	62.1	71.7	78.6	85.0	88.0	86.8	81.1	71.6	62.6	52.7	70.1
ND	Bismarck	20.2	26.4	38.5	54.9	67.8	77.1	84.4	82.7	70.8	58.7	39.3	24.5	53.8
OH	Cincinnati	36.6	40.8	53.0	64.2	74.0	82.0	85.5	84.1	77.9	66.0	53.3	41.5	63.2
	Cleveland	31.9	35.0	46.3	57.9	68.6	78.3	82.4	80.5	73.6	62.1	50.0	37.4	58.7
	Columbus	34.1	38.0	50.5	62.0	72.3	80.4	83.7	82.1	76.2	64.5	51.4	39.2	61.2
OK	Oklahoma City	46.7	52.1	62.0	71.9	79.1	87.3	93.4	92.5	83.8	73.6	60.4	49.9	71.1
OR	Portland	45.4	51.0	56.0	60.6	67.1	74.0	79.9	80.3	74.6	64.0	52.6	45.6	62.6
PA	Philadelphia	37.9	41.0	51.6	62.6	73.1	81.7	86.1	84.6	77.6	66.3	55.1	43.4	63.4
	Pittsburgh	33.7	36.9	49.0	60.3	70.6	78.9	82.6	80.8	74.3	62.5	50.4	38.6	59.9
RI	Providence	36.6	38.3	46.1	57.0	67.3	76.9	82.1	80.7	74.3	64.1	53.0	41.2	59.8
SC	Columbia	55.3	59.3	68.2	76.5	83.5	88.8	91.6	90.1	85.1	76.3	67.8	58.8	75.1
SD	Sioux Falls	24.3	29.6	42.3	59.0	70.7	80.5	86.3	83.3	73.1	61.2	43.4	28.0	56.8
TN	Memphis	48.5	53.5	63.2	73.3	81.0	89.3	92.3	90.8	83.9	74.3	62.3	52.5	72.1
	Nashville	45.9	50.8	61.2	70.8	78.8	86.5	89.5	88.4	82.5	72.5	60.4	50.2	69.8
TX	Dallas-Fort Worth	54.1	58.9	67.8	76.3	82.9	91.9	96.5	96.2	87.8	78.5	66.8	57.5	76.3
	El Paso	56.1	62.2	69.9	78.7	87.1	96.5	96.1	93.5	87.1	78.4	66.4	57.5	77.5
	Houston	61.0	65.3	71.1	78.4	84.6	90.1	92.7	92.5	88.4	81.6	72.4	64.7	78.6
UT	Salt Lake City	36.4	43.6	52.2	61.3	71.9	82.8	92.2	89.4	79.2	66.1	50.8	37.8	63.6
VT	Burlington	25.1	27.5	39.3	53.6	67.2	75.8	81.2	77.9	69.0	57.0	44.0	30.4	54.0
VA	Norfolk	47.3	49.7	57.9	66.9	75.3	82.9	86.4	85.1	79.6	69.5	61.2	52.2	67.8
	Richmond	45.7	49.2	59.5	70.0	77.8	85.1	88.4	87.1	80.9	70.7	61.3	50.2	68.8
WA	Seattle-Tacoma	45.0	49.5	52.7	57.2	63.9	69.9	75.2	75.2	69.3	59.7	50.5	45.1	59.4
	Spokane	33.2	40.6	47.7	57.0	65.8	74.7	83.1	82.5	72.0	58.6	41.4	33.8	57.5
WV	Charleston	41.2	45.3	56.7	66.8	75.5	83.1	85.7	84.4	78.8	68.2	57.3	46.0	65.8
WI	Milwaukee	26.1	30.1	40.4	52.9	64.3	74.9	79.9	77.8	70.6	58.7	44.7	31.2	54.3
WY	Cheyenne	37.7	40.5	44.9	54.7	64.6	74.4	82.2	80.0	71.1	60.0	46.8	38.8	58.0
PR	San Juan	83.2	83.6	84.4	85.8	87.2	88.6	88.5	88.7	88.8	88.3	85.9	83.8	86.4

[1] City office data.

Source: U.S. National Oceanic and Atmospheric Administration, *Climatography of the United States*, No. 81.

No. 391. Normal Daily Minimum Temperature—Selected Cities

[**In Fahrenheit degrees.** Airport data except as noted. Based on standard 30-year period, 1961 through 1990]

STATE	STATION	Jan.	Feb.	Mar.	Apr.	May	June	July	Aug.	Sept.	Oct.	Nov.	Dec.	Annual avg.
AL	Mobile	40.0	42.7	50.1	57.1	64.4	70.7	73.2	72.9	68.7	57.3	49.1	43.1	57.4
AK	Juneau	19.0	22.7	26.7	32.1	38.9	45.0	48.1	47.3	42.9	37.2	27.2	22.6	34.1
AZ	Phoenix	41.2	44.7	48.8	55.3	63.9	72.9	81.0	79.2	72.8	60.8	48.9	41.8	59.3
AR	Little Rock	29.1	33.2	42.2	50.7	59.0	67.4	71.5	69.8	63.5	50.9	41.5	33.1	51.0
CA	Los Angeles	47.8	49.3	50.5	52.8	56.3	59.5	62.8	64.2	63.2	59.2	52.8	47.9	55.5
	Sacramento	37.7	41.4	43.2	45.5	50.3	55.3	58.1	58.0	55.7	50.4	43.4	37.8	48.1
	San Diego	48.9	50.7	52.8	55.6	59.1	61.9	65.7	67.3	65.6	60.9	53.9	48.8	57.6
	San Francisco	41.8	45.0	45.8	47.2	49.7	52.6	53.9	55.0	55.2	51.8	47.1	42.7	49.0
CO	Denver	16.1	20.2	25.8	34.5	43.6	52.4	58.6	56.9	47.6	36.4	25.4	17.4	36.2
CT	Hartford	15.8	18.6	28.1	37.5	47.6	56.9	62.2	60.4	51.8	40.7	32.8	21.3	39.5
DE	Wilmington	22.4	24.8	33.1	41.8	52.2	61.6	67.1	65.9	58.2	45.7	37.0	27.6	44.8
DC	Washington	26.8	29.1	37.7	46.4	56.6	65.5	71.4	70.0	62.5	50.3	41.1	31.7	49.2
FL	Jacksonville	40.5	43.3	49.2	54.9	62.1	69.1	71.9	71.8	69.0	59.3	50.2	43.4	57.1
	Miami	59.2	60.4	64.2	67.8	72.1	75.1	76.2	76.7	75.9	72.1	66.7	61.5	69.0
GA	Atlanta	31.5	34.5	42.5	50.2	58.7	66.2	69.5	69.0	63.5	51.9	42.8	35.0	51.3
HI	Honolulu	65.6	65.4	67.2	68.7	70.3	72.2	73.5	74.2	73.5	72.3	70.3	67.0	70.0
ID	Boise	21.6	27.5	31.9	36.7	43.9	52.1	57.7	56.8	48.2	39.0	31.1	22.5	39.1
IL	Chicago	12.9	17.2	28.5	38.6	47.7	57.5	62.6	61.6	53.9	42.2	31.6	19.1	39.5
	Peoria	13.2	17.7	29.8	40.8	50.9	60.7	65.4	63.1	55.2	43.1	32.5	19.3	41.0
IN	Indianapolis	17.2	20.9	31.9	41.5	51.7	61.0	65.2	62.8	55.6	43.5	34.1	23.2	42.4
IA	Des Moines	10.7	15.6	27.6	40.0	51.5	61.2	66.5	63.6	54.5	42.7	29.9	16.1	40.0
KS	Wichita	19.2	23.7	33.6	44.5	54.3	64.6	69.9	67.9	59.2	46.6	33.9	23.0	45.0
KY	Louisville	23.2	26.5	36.2	45.4	54.7	62.9	67.3	65.8	58.7	45.8	37.3	28.6	46.0
LA	New Orleans	41.8	44.4	51.6	58.4	65.2	70.8	73.1	72.8	69.5	58.7	51.0	44.8	58.5
ME	Portland	11.4	13.5	24.5	34.1	43.4	52.1	58.3	57.1	48.9	38.3	30.4	17.8	35.8
MD	Baltimore	23.4	25.9	34.1	42.5	52.6	61.8	66.8	65.7	58.4	45.9	37.1	28.2	45.2
MA	Boston	21.6	23.0	31.3	40.2	49.8	59.1	65.1	64.0	56.8	46.9	38.3	26.7	43.6
MI	Detroit	15.6	17.6	27.0	36.8	47.1	56.3	61.3	59.6	52.5	40.9	32.2	21.4	39.0
	Sault Ste. Marie	4.6	4.8	15.3	28.4	38.4	45.5	51.3	51.3	44.3	36.2	25.9	11.8	29.8
MN	Duluth	-2.2	2.8	15.7	28.9	39.6	48.5	55.1	53.3	44.5	35.1	21.5	4.9	29.0
	Minneapolis-St. Paul	2.8	9.2	22.7	36.2	47.6	57.6	63.1	60.3	50.3	38.8	25.2	10.2	35.3
MS	Jackson	32.7	35.7	44.1	51.9	60.0	67.1	70.5	69.7	63.7	50.3	42.3	36.1	52.0
MO	Kansas City	16.7	21.8	32.6	43.8	53.9	63.1	68.2	65.7	56.9	45.7	33.6	21.9	43.7
	St. Louis	20.8	25.1	35.5	46.4	56.0	65.7	70.4	67.9	60.5	48.3	37.7	26.0	46.7
MT	Great Falls	11.6	17.2	22.8	31.9	40.9	48.6	53.2	52.2	43.5	35.8	24.3	14.6	33.1
NE	Omaha	10.9	16.7	27.7	39.9	50.9	60.4	65.9	62.9	53.6	41.2	28.7	15.6	39.5
NV	Reno	20.7	24.2	29.2	33.3	40.1	46.9	51.3	49.6	41.3	32.9	26.7	19.9	34.7
NH	Concord	7.4	10.4	22.1	31.5	41.4	51.2	56.5	54.7	46.0	34.9	27.0	14.4	33.1
NJ	Atlantic City	21.4	23.5	31.3	39.3	49.6	58.7	64.8	63.5	55.5	43.7	35.8	26.3	42.8
NM	Albuquerque	21.7	26.4	32.2	39.6	48.6	58.3	64.4	62.6	55.2	43.0	31.2	23.1	42.2
NY	Albany	11.0	13.8	24.5	35.1	45.4	54.6	59.6	57.8	49.4	38.6	30.7	18.2	36.6
	Buffalo	17.0	17.4	25.9	36.2	47.0	56.5	61.9	60.1	53.0	42.7	33.9	22.9	39.5
	New York [1]	25.3	26.9	34.8	43.8	53.7	63.0	68.4	67.3	60.1	49.7	41.1	30.7	47.1
NC	Charlotte	29.6	31.9	39.4	47.5	56.4	65.6	69.6	68.9	62.9	50.6	41.5	32.8	49.7
	Raleigh	28.8	31.3	38.7	46.2	55.3	63.6	68.1	67.5	61.1	48.4	39.7	32.4	48.4
ND	Bismarck	-1.7	5.1	17.8	31.0	42.2	51.6	56.4	53.9	43.1	32.5	17.8	3.3	29.4
OH	Cincinnati	19.5	22.7	33.1	42.2	51.8	60.0	64.8	62.9	56.6	44.2	35.3	25.3	43.2
	Cleveland	17.6	19.3	28.2	37.3	47.3	56.8	61.4	60.3	54.2	43.5	35.0	24.5	40.5
	Columbus	18.5	21.2	31.2	40.0	50.1	58.0	62.7	60.8	54.8	42.9	34.3	24.6	41.6
OK	Oklahoma City	25.2	29.6	38.5	48.8	57.7	66.1	70.6	69.6	62.2	50.4	38.6	28.6	48.8
OR	Portland	33.7	36.1	38.6	41.3	47.0	52.9	56.5	56.9	52.0	44.9	39.5	34.8	44.5
PA	Philadelphia	22.8	24.8	33.2	42.1	52.7	61.8	67.2	66.3	58.7	46.4	37.6	28.1	45.1
	Pittsburgh	18.5	20.3	29.8	38.8	48.4	56.9	61.6	60.2	53.5	42.3	34.1	24.4	40.7
RI	Providence	19.1	20.9	28.8	37.7	47.3	56.8	63.2	61.9	53.8	43.0	34.9	24.4	41.0
SC	Columbia	32.1	34.2	42.2	49.4	58.2	66.0	70.0	69.2	63.2	50.1	41.5	34.9	50.9
SD	Sioux Falls	3.3	9.7	22.6	34.8	45.9	56.1	62.3	59.4	48.7	36.0	22.6	8.6	34.2
TN	Memphis	30.9	34.8	43.0	52.4	61.2	68.9	72.9	71.1	64.5	51.9	42.7	34.8	52.4
	Nashville	26.5	29.9	39.1	47.5	56.6	64.7	68.9	67.7	61.1	48.3	39.6	30.9	48.4
TX	Dallas-Fort Worth	32.7	36.9	45.6	54.7	62.6	70.0	74.1	73.6	66.9	55.8	45.4	36.3	54.6
	El Paso	29.4	33.9	40.2	48.0	56.5	64.3	68.4	66.6	61.6	49.6	38.4	30.7	49.0
	Houston	39.7	42.6	50.0	58.1	64.4	70.6	72.4	72.0	67.9	57.6	49.6	42.2	57.3
UT	Salt Lake City	19.3	24.6	31.4	37.9	45.6	55.4	63.7	61.8	51.0	40.2	30.9	21.6	40.3
VT	Burlington	7.5	8.9	22.0	34.2	45.4	54.6	59.7	57.9	48.8	38.6	29.6	15.5	35.2
VA	Norfolk	30.9	32.3	39.3	47.1	56.8	65.2	70.0	69.4	64.2	52.9	43.8	35.4	50.6
	Richmond	25.7	28.1	36.3	44.6	54.2	62.7	67.5	66.4	59.0	46.5	37.9	29.9	46.6
WA	Seattle-Tacoma	35.2	37.4	38.5	41.2	46.3	51.9	55.2	55.7	51.9	45.8	40.1	35.8	44.6
	Spokane	20.8	25.9	29.6	34.7	41.9	49.2	54.4	54.3	45.8	36.0	28.8	21.7	36.9
WV	Charleston	23.0	25.7	35.0	42.8	51.5	59.8	64.4	63.4	56.5	44.2	36.3	28.0	44.2
WI	Milwaukee	11.6	15.9	26.2	35.8	44.8	55.0	62.0	60.8	52.8	41.8	30.7	17.5	37.9
WY	Cheyenne	15.2	18.1	22.1	30.1	39.4	48.3	54.6	52.8	43.7	33.9	23.7	16.7	33.2
PR	San Juan	70.8	70.6	71.6	72.9	74.5	76.1	76.8	76.7	76.2	75.5	74.0	72.4	74.0

[1] City office data.

Source: U.S. National Oceanic and Atmospheric Administration, *Climatography of the United States*, No. 81.

No. 392. Highest Temperature of Record—Selected Cities

[**In Fahrenheit degrees.** Airport data, except as noted. For period of record through 1993]

STATE	STATION	Length of record (yr.)	Jan.	Feb.	Mar.	Apr.	May	June	July	Aug.	Sept.	Oct.	Nov.	Dec.	Annual
AL	Mobile	52	84	82	90	94	100	102	104	102	99	93	87	81	104
AK	Juneau	49	57	57	59	71	82	86	90	83	72	61	56	54	90
AZ	Phoenix	56	88	92	100	105	113	122	118	116	118	107	93	88	122
AR	Little Rock	52	83	85	91	95	98	105	112	108	106	97	86	80	112
CA	Los Angeles	58	88	92	95	102	97	104	97	98	110	106	101	94	110
	Sacramento	43	70	76	88	93	105	115	114	109	108	101	87	72	115
	San Diego	53	88	88	93	98	96	101	95	98	111	107	97	88	111
	San Francisco	66	72	78	85	92	97	106	105	100	103	99	85	75	106
CO	Denver	59	73	76	84	90	96	104	104	101	97	89	79	75	104
CT	Hartford	39	65	73	87	96	97	100	102	101	99	91	81	74	102
DE	Wilmington	46	75	78	86	94	95	99	102	101	100	91	85	74	102
DC	Washington	52	79	82	89	95	99	101	104	103	101	94	86	75	104
FL	Jacksonville	52	85	88	91	95	100	103	105	102	100	96	88	84	105
	Miami	51	88	89	92	96	95	98	98	98	97	95	89	87	98
GA	Atlanta	45	79	80	85	93	95	101	105	102	98	95	84	79	105
HI	Honolulu	24	87	88	88	89	93	92	92	93	94	94	93	89	94
ID	Boise	54	63	71	81	92	98	109	111	110	102	94	74	65	111
IL	Chicago	35	65	71	88	91	93	104	102	101	99	91	78	71	104
	Peoria	54	70	72	86	92	93	105	103	103	100	90	81	71	105
IN	Indianapolis	54	71	74	85	89	93	102	104	102	100	90	81	74	104
IA	Des Moines	54	65	73	91	93	98	103	105	108	101	95	76	69	108
KS	Wichita	41	75	84	89	96	100	110	113	110	107	95	85	83	113
KY	Louisville	46	77	77	86	91	95	102	105	101	104	92	84	76	105
LA	New Orleans	47	83	85	89	92	96	100	101	102	101	92	87	84	102
ME	Portland	53	64	64	86	85	94	98	99	103	95	88	74	69	103
MD	Baltimore	43	75	79	87	94	98	100	104	105	100	92	83	77	105
MA	Boston	42	63	70	81	94	95	100	102	102	100	90	78	73	102
MI	Detroit	35	62	65	81	89	92	104	102	100	98	91	77	68	104
	Sault Ste. Marie	53	45	47	75	85	89	93	97	98	95	80	67	60	98
MN	Duluth	52	52	55	78	88	90	93	97	97	95	86	70	55	97
	Minneapolis-St. Paul	55	58	60	83	95	96	102	105	102	98	89	75	63	105
MS	Jackson	30	82	85	89	94	99	105	106	102	104	95	88	84	106
MO	Kansas City	21	69	76	86	93	92	105	107	109	102	92	82	70	109
	St. Louis	36	76	85	89	93	93	102	107	107	104	94	85	76	107
MT	Great Falls	56	67	70	78	89	93	101	105	106	98	91	76	69	106
NE	Omaha	57	69	78	89	97	99	105	114	110	104	96	80	72	114
NV	Reno	52	70	75	83	89	96	103	104	105	101	91	77	70	105
NH	Concord	52	68	66	85	95	97	98	102	101	98	90	80	68	102
NJ	Atlantic City	50	78	75	87	94	99	106	104	102	99	90	84	75	106
NM	Albuquerque	54	69	76	85	89	98	105	105	101	100	91	77	72	105
NY	Albany	47	62	67	86	92	94	99	100	99	100	89	82	71	100
	Buffalo	50	72	65	81	94	90	96	97	99	98	87	80	74	99
	New York [1]	125	72	75	86	96	99	101	106	104	102	94	84	72	106
NC	Charlotte	54	78	81	90	93	100	103	103	103	104	98	85	77	104
	Raleigh	49	79	84	92	95	97	104	105	105	104	98	88	79	105
ND	Bismarck	54	62	69	81	93	98	107	109	109	105	95	75	65	109
OH	Cincinnati	32	69	73	84	89	93	102	103	102	98	88	81	75	103
	Cleveland	52	73	69	83	88	92	104	103	102	101	90	82	77	104
	Columbus	54	74	73	85	89	94	102	100	101	100	90	80	76	102
OK	Oklahoma City	40	80	84	93	100	104	105	109	110	102	96	87	86	110
OR	Portland	53	63	71	80	87	100	100	107	107	105	92	73	65	107
PA	Philadelphia	52	74	74	87	94	97	100	104	101	100	96	81	72	104
	Pittsburgh	41	69	69	82	89	91	98	103	100	97	87	82	74	103
RI	Providence	40	66	72	80	98	94	97	102	104	100	86	78	70	104
SC	Columbia	46	84	84	91	94	101	107	107	107	101	101	90	83	107
SD	Sioux Falls	48	66	70	87	94	100	110	108	108	104	94	76	61	110
TN	Memphis	52	78	81	85	94	99	104	108	105	103	95	85	81	108
	Nashville	54	78	84	86	91	97	106	107	104	105	94	84	79	107
TX	Dallas-Fort Worth	40	88	88	96	95	103	113	110	108	106	102	89	88	113
	El Paso	54	80	83	89	98	104	111	112	108	104	96	87	80	112
	Houston	24	84	91	91	95	97	103	104	107	102	96	89	83	107
UT	Salt Lake City	65	62	69	78	86	93	104	107	104	100	89	75	67	107
VT	Burlington	50	63	62	84	91	93	97	99	101	94	85	75	65	101
VA	Norfolk	45	78	81	88	97	100	101	103	104	99	95	86	80	104
	Richmond	64	80	83	93	96	100	104	105	102	103	99	86	80	105
WA	Seattle-Tacoma	49	64	70	75	85	93	96	99	99	98	89	74	64	99
	Spokane	46	59	61	71	90	96	101	103	108	98	86	67	56	108
WV	Charleston	46	79	78	89	94	93	98	104	101	102	92	85	80	104
WI	Milwaukee	53	62	65	82	91	93	101	101	103	98	89	77	63	103
WY	Cheyenne	58	66	71	74	83	90	100	100	96	93	83	73	69	100
PR	San Juan	39	92	96	96	97	96	97	95	97	97	98	96	94	98

[1] City office data.

Source: U.S. National Oceanic and Atmospheric Administration, *Comparative Climatic Data,* annual.

No. 393. Lowest Temperature of Record—Selected Cities

[**In Fahrenheit degrees.** Airport data, except as noted. For period of record through 1993]

STATE	STATION	Length of record (yr.)	Jan.	Feb.	Mar.	Apr.	May	June	July	Aug.	Sept.	Oct.	Nov.	Dec.	Annual
AL	Mobile.........	52	3	11	21	32	43	49	60	59	42	30	22	8	3
AK	Juneau.........	49	−22	−22	−15	6	25	31	36	27	23	11	−5	−21	−22
AZ	Phoenix.........	56	17	22	25	32	40	50	61	60	47	34	25	22	17
AR	Little Rock......	52	−4	−5	11	28	40	46	54	52	37	29	17	−1	−5
CA	Los Angeles.....	58	23	32	34	39	43	48	49	51	47	41	34	32	23
	Sacramento......	43	23	23	26	32	36	41	48	49	43	36	26	18	18
	San Diego.......	53	29	36	39	41	48	51	55	57	51	43	38	34	29
	San Francisco....	66	24	25	30	31	36	41	43	42	38	34	25	20	20
CO	Denver.........	59	−25	−30	−11	−2	22	30	43	41	17	3	−8	−25	−30
CT	Hartford.........	39	−26	−21	−6	9	28	37	44	36	30	17	1	−14	−26
DE	Wilmington......	46	−14	−6	2	18	30	41	48	43	36	24	14	−7	−14
DC	Washington.....	52	−5	4	11	24	34	47	54	49	39	29	16	1	−5
FL	Jacksonville......	52	7	19	23	34	45	47	61	63	48	36	21	11	7
	Miami.........	51	30	32	32	46	53	60	69	68	68	51	39	30	30
GA	Atlanta.........	45	−8	5	10	26	37	46	53	55	36	28	3	-	−8
HI	Honolulu........	24	53	53	55	57	60	65	66	67	66	61	57	54	53
ID	Boise.........	54	−17	−15	6	19	22	31	35	34	23	11	−3	−25	−25
IL	Chicago.........	35	−27	−17	−8	7	24	36	40	41	28	17	1	−25	−27
	Peoria.........	54	−25	−18	−10	14	25	39	47	41	26	19	−2	−23	−25
IN	Indianapolis.....	54	−22	−21	−7	16	28	37	44	41	28	17	−2	−23	−23
IA	Des Moines......	54	−24	−20	−22	9	30	38	47	40	26	14	−4	−22	−24
KS	Wichita.........	41	−12	−21	−2	15	31	43	51	48	31	18	1	−16	−21
KY	Louisville........	46	−20	−19	−1	22	31	42	50	46	33	23	−1	−15	−20
LA	New Orleans.....	47	14	19	25	32	41	50	60	60	42	35	24	11	11
ME	Portland	53	−26	−39	−21	8	23	33	40	33	23	15	3	−21	−39
MD	Baltimore........	43	−7	−3	6	20	32	40	50	45	35	25	13	-	−7
MA	Boston	42	−12	−4	6	16	34	45	50	47	38	28	15	−7	−12
MI	Detroit.........	35	−21	−15	−4	10	25	36	41	38	29	17	9	−10	−21
	Sault Ste. Marie ...	53	−36	−35	−24	−2	18	26	36	29	25	16	−10	−31	−36
MN	Duluth.........	52	−39	−33	−29	−5	17	27	35	32	22	8	−23	−34	−39
	Minneapolis-St. Paul	55	−34	−28	−32	2	18	34	43	39	26	15	−17	−29	−34
MS	Jackson.........	30	2	11	15	27	38	47	51	55	35	26	17	4	2
MO	Kansas City......	21	−17	−19	−10	12	30	42	52	43	33	17	1	−23	−23
	St. Louis........	36	−18	−10	−5	22	31	43	51	47	36	23	1	−16	−18
MT	Great Falls.......	56	−37	−35	−29	−6	15	31	40	30	21	−11	−25	−43	−43
NE	Omaha	57	−23	−21	−16	5	27	38	44	43	25	13	−9	−23	−23
NV	Reno	52	−16	−16	−2	13	18	25	33	24	20	8	1	−16	−16
NH	Concord	52	−33	−37	−16	8	21	30	35	29	21	10	−5	−22	−37
NJ	Atlantic City	50	−10	−11	5	12	25	37	42	40	32	20	10	−7	−11
NM	Albuquerque......	54	−17	−5	8	19	28	40	52	50	37	21	−7	−7	−17
NY	Albany	47	−28	−21	−21	10	26	36	40	34	24	16	5	−22	−28
	Buffalo	50	−16	−20	−7	12	26	35	43	38	32	20	9	−10	−20
	New York [1]......	25	−6	−15	3	12	32	44	52	50	39	28	5	−13	−15
NC	Charlotte........	54	−5	5	4	24	32	45	53	53	39	24	11	2	−5
	Raleigh	49	−9	5	11	23	31	38	48	46	37	19	11	4	−9
ND	Bismarck........	54	−44	−39	−31	−12	15	30	35	33	11	−10	−30	−43	−44
OH	Cincinnati........	32	−25	−11	−11	17	27	39	47	43	31	16	1	−20	−25
	Cleveland	52	−19	−15	−5	10	25	31	41	38	32	19	3	−15	−19
	Columbus	54	−19	−13	−6	14	25	35	43	39	31	20	5	−17	−19
OK	Oklahoma City	40	−4	−3	3	20	37	47	53	51	36	16	11	−8	−8
OR	Portland	53	−2	−3	19	29	29	39	43	44	34	26	13	6	−3
PA	Philadelphia......	52	−7	−4	7	19	28	44	51	44	35	25	15	1	−7
	Pittsburgh	41	−18	−12	−1	14	26	34	42	39	31	16	−1	−12	−18
RI	Providence.......	40	−13	−7	1	14	29	41	48	40	33	20	6	−10	−13
SC	Columbia........	46	−1	5	4	26	34	44	54	53	40	23	12	4	−1
SD	Sioux Falls.......	48	−36	−31	−23	5	17	33	38	34	22	9	−17	−28	−36
TN	Memphis........	52	−4	−11	12	29	38	48	52	48	36	25	9	−13	−13
	Nashville........	54	−17	−13	2	23	34	42	51	47	36	26	−1	−10	−17
TX	Dallas-Fort Worth ..	40	4	7	15	29	41	51	59	56	43	29	20	−1	−1
	El Paso.........	54	−8	8	14	23	31	46	57	56	41	25	1	5	−8
	Houston	24	12	20	22	31	44	52	62	60	48	29	19	7	7
UT	Salt Lake City.....	65	−22	−30	2	14	25	35	40	37	27	16	−14	−21	−30
VT	Burlington	50	−30	−30	−20	2	24	33	39	35	25	15	−2	−26	−30
VA	Norfolk	45	−3	8	18	28	36	45	54	49	45	27	20	7	−3
	Richmond	64	−12	−10	11	23	31	40	51	46	35	21	10	−1	−12
WA	Seattle-Tacoma....	49	-	1	11	29	28	38	43	44	35	28	6	6	-
	Spokane	46	−22	−17	−7	17	24	33	37	35	24	10	−21	−25	−25
WV	Charleston.......	46	−15	−6	-	19	26	33	46	41	34	17	6	−12	−15
WI	Milwaukee.......	53	−26	−19	−10	12	21	33	40	44	28	18	−5	−20	−26
WY	Cheyenne	58	−29	−34	−21	−8	16	25	38	36	8	−1	−16	−28	−34
PR	San Juan........	39	61	62	60	64	66	69	69	70	69	67	66	63	60

- Represents zero.   [1] City office data.

Source: U.S. National Oceanic and Atmospheric Administration, *Comparative Climatic Data*, annual.

No. 394. Normal Monthly and Annual Precipitation—Selected Cities

[**In inches.** Airport data, except as noted. Based on standard 30-year period, 1961 through 1990. See *Historical Statistics, Colonial Times to 1970*, series J 164-267, for related data]

STATE	STATION	Jan.	Feb.	Mar.	Apr.	May	June	July	Aug.	Sept.	Oct.	Nov.	Dec.	Annual
AL	Mobile	4.76	5.46	6.41	4.48	5.74	5.04	6.85	6.96	5.91	2.94	4.10	5.31	63.96
AK	Juneau	4.54	3.75	3.28	2.77	3.42	3.15	4.16	5.32	6.73	7.84	4.91	4.44	54.31
AZ	Phoenix	0.67	0.68	0.88	0.22	0.12	0.13	0.83	0.96	0.86	0.65	0.66	1.00	7.66
AR	Little Rock	3.42	3.61	4.91	5.49	5.17	3.57	3.60	3.26	4.05	3.75	5.20	4.83	50.86
CA	Los Angeles	2.40	2.51	1.98	0.72	0.14	0.03	0.01	0.15	0.31	0.34	1.76	1.66	12.01
	Sacramento	3.73	2.87	2.57	1.16	0.27	0.12	0.05	0.07	0.37	1.08	2.72	2.51	17.52
	San Diego	1.80	1.53	1.77	0.79	0.19	0.07	0.02	0.10	0.24	0.37	1.45	1.57	9.90
	San Francisco	4.35	3.17	3.06	1.37	0.19	0.11	0.03	0.05	0.20	1.22	2.86	3.09	19.70
CO	Denver	0.50	0.57	1.28	1.71	2.40	1.79	1.91	1.51	1.24	0.98	0.87	0.64	15.40
CT	Hartford	3.41	3.23	3.63	3.85	4.12	3.75	3.19	3.65	3.79	3.57	4.04	3.91	44.14
DE	Wilmington	3.03	2.91	3.43	3.39	3.84	3.55	4.23	3.40	3.43	2.88	3.27	3.48	40.84
DC	Washington	2.72	2.71	3.17	2.71	3.66	3.38	3.80	3.91	3.31	3.02	3.12	3.12	38.63
FL	Jacksonville	3.31	3.93	3.68	2.77	3.55	5.69	5.60	7.93	7.05	2.90	2.19	2.72	51.32
	Miami	2.01	2.08	2.39	2.85	6.21	9.33	5.70	7.58	7.63	5.64	2.66	1.83	55.91
GA	Atlanta	4.75	4.81	5.77	4.26	4.29	3.56	5.01	3.66	3.42	3.05	3.86	4.33	50.77
HI	Honolulu	3.55	2.21	2.20	1.54	1.13	0.50	0.59	0.44	0.78	2.28	3.00	3.80	22.02
ID	Boise	1.45	1.07	1.29	1.24	1.08	0.81	0.35	0.43	0.80	0.75	1.48	1.36	12.11
IL	Chicago	1.53	1.36	2.69	3.64	3.32	3.78	3.66	4.22	3.82	2.41	2.92	2.47	35.82
	Peoria	1.51	1.42	2.91	3.77	3.70	3.99	4.20	3.10	3.87	2.65	2.69	2.44	36.25
IN	Indianapolis	2.32	2.46	3.79	3.70	4.00	3.49	4.47	3.64	2.87	2.63	3.23	3.34	39.94
IA	Des Moines	0.96	1.11	2.33	3.36	3.66	4.46	3.78	4.20	3.53	2.62	1.79	1.32	33.12
KS	Wichita	0.79	0.96	2.43	2.38	3.81	4.31	3.13	3.02	3.49	2.22	1.59	1.20	29.33
KY	Louisville	2.86	3.30	4.66	4.23	4.62	3.46	4.51	3.54	3.16	2.71	3.70	3.64	44.39
LA	New Orleans	5.05	6.01	4.90	4.50	4.56	5.84	6.12	6.17	5.51	3.05	4.42	5.75	61.88
ME	Portland	3.53	3.33	3.67	4.08	3.62	3.44	3.09	2.87	3.09	3.90	5.17	4.55	44.34
MD	Baltimore	3.05	3.12	3.38	3.09	3.72	3.67	3.69	3.92	3.41	2.98	3.32	3.41	40.76
MA	Boston	3.59	3.62	3.69	3.60	3.25	3.09	2.84	3.24	3.06	3.30	4.22	4.01	41.51
MI	Detroit	1.76	1.74	2.55	2.95	2.92	3.61	3.18	3.43	2.89	2.10	2.67	2.82	32.62
	Sault Ste. Marie	2.42	1.74	2.30	2.35	2.71	3.14	2.71	3.61	3.69	3.23	3.45	2.88	34.23
MN	Duluth	1.22	0.80	1.91	2.25	3.03	3.82	3.61	3.99	3.84	2.49	1.80	1.24	30.00
	Minneapolis-St. Paul	0.95	0.88	1.94	2.42	3.39	4.05	3.53	3.62	2.72	2.19	1.55	1.08	28.32
MS	Jackson	5.24	4.70	5.82	5.57	5.05	3.18	4.51	3.77	3.55	3.26	4.81	5.91	55.37
MO	Kansas City	1.09	1.10	2.51	3.12	5.04	4.72	4.38	4.01	4.86	3.29	1.92	1.58	37.62
	St. Louis	1.81	2.12	3.58	3.50	3.97	3.72	3.85	2.85	3.12	2.68	3.28	3.03	37.51
MT	Great Falls	0.91	0.57	1.10	1.41	2.52	2.39	1.24	1.54	1.24	0.78	0.66	0.85	15.21
NE	Omaha	0.74	0.77	2.04	2.66	4.52	3.87	3.51	3.24	3.72	2.28	1.49	1.02	29.86
NV	Reno	1.07	0.99	0.71	0.38	0.69	0.46	0.28	0.32	0.39	0.38	0.87	0.99	7.53
NH	Concord	2.51	2.53	2.72	2.91	3.14	3.15	3.23	3.32	2.81	3.23	3.66	3.16	36.37
NJ	Atlantic City	3.46	3.06	3.62	3.56	3.33	2.64	3.83	4.14	2.93	2.82	3.58	3.32	40.29
NM	Albuquerque	0.44	0.46	0.54	0.52	0.50	0.59	1.37	1.64	1.00	0.89	0.43	0.50	8.88
NY	Albany	2.36	2.27	2.93	2.99	3.41	3.62	3.18	3.47	2.95	2.83	3.23	2.93	36.17
	Buffalo	2.70	2.31	2.68	2.87	3.14	3.55	3.08	4.17	3.49	3.09	3.83	3.67	38.58
	New York [1]	3.42	3.27	4.08	4.20	4.42	3.67	4.35	4.01	3.89	3.56	4.47	3.91	47.25
NC	Charlotte	3.71	3.84	4.43	2.68	3.82	3.39	3.92	3.73	3.50	3.36	3.23	3.48	43.09
	Raleigh	3.48	3.69	3.77	2.59	3.92	3.68	4.01	4.02	3.19	2.86	2.98	3.24	41.43
ND	Bismarck	0.45	0.43	0.77	1.67	2.18	2.72	2.14	1.72	1.49	0.90	0.49	0.51	15.47
OH	Cincinnati	2.59	2.69	4.24	3.75	4.28	3.84	4.24	3.35	2.88	2.86	3.46	3.15	41.33
	Cleveland	2.04	2.19	2.91	3.14	3.49	3.70	3.52	3.40	3.44	2.54	3.17	3.09	36.63
	Columbus	2.18	2.24	3.27	3.21	3.93	4.04	4.31	3.72	2.96	2.15	3.22	2.86	38.09
OK	Oklahoma City	1.13	1.56	2.71	2.77	5.22	4.31	2.61	2.60	3.84	3.23	1.98	1.40	33.36
OR	Portland	5.35	3.85	3.56	2.39	2.06	1.48	0.63	1.09	1.75	2.67	5.34	6.13	36.30
PA	Philadelphia	3.21	2.79	3.46	3.62	3.75	3.74	4.28	3.80	3.42	2.62	3.34	3.38	41.41
	Pittsburgh	2.54	2.39	3.41	3.15	3.59	3.71	3.75	3.21	2.97	2.36	2.85	2.92	36.85
RI	Providence	3.88	3.61	4.05	4.11	3.76	3.33	3.18	3.63	3.48	3.69	4.43	4.38	45.53
SC	Columbia	4.42	4.12	4.82	3.28	3.68	4.80	5.50	6.09	3.67	3.04	2.90	3.59	49.91
SD	Sioux Falls	0.51	0.64	1.64	2.52	3.03	3.40	2.68	2.85	3.02	1.78	1.09	0.70	23.86
TN	Memphis	3.73	4.35	5.41	5.46	4.98	3.57	3.79	3.43	3.53	3.01	5.10	5.74	52.10
	Nashville	3.58	3.81	4.85	4.37	4.88	3.57	3.97	3.46	3.46	2.62	4.12	4.61	47.30
TX	Dallas-Fort Worth	1.83	2.18	2.77	3.50	4.88	2.98	2.31	2.21	3.39	3.52	2.29	1.84	33.70
	El Paso	0.40	0.41	0.29	0.20	0.25	0.67	1.54	1.58	1.70	0.76	0.44	0.57	8.81
	Houston	3.29	2.96	2.92	3.21	5.24	4.96	3.60	3.49	4.89	4.27	3.79	3.45	46.07
UT	Salt Lake City	1.11	1.23	1.91	2.12	1.80	0.93	0.81	0.86	1.28	1.44	1.29	1.40	16.18
VT	Burlington	1.82	1.63	2.23	2.76	3.12	3.47	3.65	4.06	3.30	2.88	3.13	2.42	34.47
VA	Norfolk	3.78	3.47	3.70	3.06	3.81	3.82	5.06	4.81	3.90	3.15	2.85	3.23	44.64
	Richmond	3.24	3.16	3.61	2.96	3.84	3.62	5.03	4.40	3.34	3.53	3.17	3.26	43.16
WA	Seattle-Tacoma	5.38	3.99	3.54	2.33	1.70	1.50	0.76	1.14	1.88	3.23	5.83	5.91	37.19
	Spokane	1.98	1.49	1.49	1.18	1.41	1.26	0.67	0.72	0.73	0.99	2.15	2.42	16.49
WV	Charleston	2.91	3.04	3.63	3.31	3.94	3.59	4.99	4.01	3.24	2.89	3.59	3.39	42.53
WI	Milwaukee	1.60	1.45	2.67	3.50	2.84	3.24	3.47	3.53	3.38	2.41	2.51	2.33	32.93
WY	Cheyenne	0.40	0.39	1.03	1.37	2.39	2.08	2.09	1.69	1.27	0.74	0.53	0.42	14.40
PR	San Juan	2.81	2.15	2.35	3.76	5.93	4.00	4.37	5.32	5.28	5.71	5.94	4.72	52.34

[1] City office data.

Source: U.S. National Oceanic and Atmospheric Administration, *Climatography of the United States,* No. 81.

No. 395. Average Number of Days With Precipitation of .01 Inch or More— Selected Cities

[Airport data, except as noted. For period of record through 1993, except as noted]

STATE	STATION	Length of record (yr.)	Jan.	Feb.	Mar.	Apr.	May	June	July	Aug.	Sept.	Oct.	Nov.	Dec.	Annual
AL	Mobile.	52	11	10	10	7	9	11	16	14	10	6	8	10	122
AK	Juneau [1]	49	18	17	18	17	17	15	17	18	20	24	20	21	221
AZ	Phoenix.	54	4	4	4	2	1	1	4	5	3	3	3	4	36
AR	Little Rock	51	10	9	10	10	10	8	8	7	7	7	8	9	105
CA	Los Angeles	58	6	6	6	3	1	(Z)	1	(Z)	1	2	3	5	35
	Sacramento	54	10	9	9	5	3	1	(Z)	(Z)	1	3	7	9	58
	San Diego	53	7	6	7	4	2	1	(Z)	1	1	2	5	6	42
	San Francisco	66	11	10	10	6	3	1	(Z)	(Z)	1	4	7	10	62
CO	Denver	59	6	6	9	9	11	9	9	9	6	5	6	5	89
CT	Hartford.	39	11	10	11	11	12	11	10	10	9	9	11	12	127
DE	Wilmington.	46	11	9	11	11	11	10	9	9	8	8	9	10	116
DC	Washington	52	10	9	11	10	11	9	10	9	8	7	9	9	112
FL	Jacksonville	52	8	8	8	6	8	12	14	15	13	8	6	8	116
	Miami	51	7	6	6	6	10	15	16	17	17	14	9	6	129
GA	Atlanta	59	11	10	11	9	9	10	12	10	8	6	8	10	115
HI	Honolulu	44	10	9	9	9	7	6	7	6	7	9	9	10	98
ID	Boise	54	12	10	10	8	8	6	2	3	4	6	10	11	90
IL	Chicago.	35	11	9	13	13	11	10	10	9	10	9	11	11	126
	Peoria.	54	9	8	11	12	11	10	9	8	9	8	9	10	114
IN	Indianapolis	54	12	10	13	12	12	10	10	9	8	8	11	12	126
IA	Des Moines	54	8	7	10	11	11	11	9	9	9	8	7	8	108
KS	Wichita	40	6	5	8	8	11	9	7	7	8	6	5	6	86
KY	Louisville	46	11	11	13	12	12	10	11	8	8	8	10	11	125
LA	New Orleans	45	10	9	9	7	8	11	14	13	10	6	7	10	114
ME	Portland	53	11	10	11	12	12	11	10	9	9	9	12	12	129
MD	Baltimore.	43	10	9	11	11	11	9	9	9	8	7	9	9	113
MA	Boston	42	11	11	12	11	11	11	9	10	9	9	11	12	126
MI	Detroit.	35	13	11	13	13	11	10	10	10	10	10	12	14	136
	Sault Ste. Marie . . .	52	19	15	13	11	11	11	10	11	13	14	17	19	166
MN	Duluth.	52	12	10	11	11	12	13	11	11	12	9	11	12	134
	Minneapolis-St. Paul	55	9	7	10	10	11	12	10	10	10	8	9	9	115
MS	Jackson.	30	11	9	10	9	10	8	10	10	8	6	8	10	110
MO	Kansas City	21	7	7	10	11	11	10	9	9	9	8	8	8	106
	St. Louis	36	8	8	11	11	11	9	9	8	8	8	10	9	111
MT	Great Falls.	56	9	8	9	9	12	12	8	8	7	6	7	8	101
NE	Omaha	57	6	7	9	10	12	11	9	9	8	6	6	6	99
NV	Reno	51	6	6	6	4	4	3	2	2	2	3	5	6	50
NH	Concord	52	11	10	11	12	12	11	10	10	9	9	11	11	126
NJ	Atlantic City	50	11	10	11	11	10	9	9	9	8	7	9	10	112
NM	Albuquerque.	54	4	4	5	3	5	4	9	10	6	5	4	4	61
NY	Albany	47	12	11	12	12	13	11	10	10	10	9	12	12	135
	Buffalo . . . . [2]	50	20	17	16	14	12	10	10	11	11	12	16	20	169
	New York [2]	124	11	10	11	11	11	10	11	10	8	8	9	10	121
NC	Charlotte	54	10	10	11	9	10	9	11	10	7	7	8	10	111
	Raleigh	49	10	10	10	9	10	9	11	10	8	7	8	9	112
ND	Bismarck.	54	8	7	8	8	10	11	9	8	7	5	6	8	96
OH	Cincinnati.	46	12	11	13	13	12	10	10	9	8	8	11	12	130
	Cleveland	52	16	14	15	14	13	11	10	10	10	11	15	16	156
	Columbus	54	13	11	14	13	13	11	11	9	8	9	12	13	137
OK	Oklahoma City	54	6	6	7	8	10	9	6	7	7	6	5	6	83
OR	Portland	53	18	16	17	14	12	9	4	5	7	12	18	19	151
PA	Philadelphia	53	11	9	11	11	11	10	9	9	8	8	9	10	117
	Pittsburgh	41	16	14	16	14	13	11	11	10	10	10	13	16	153
RI	Providence.	40	11	10	12	11	11	11	9	9	8	9	11	12	124
SC	Columbia	46	10	10	11	8	9	9	12	11	8	6	7	9	109
SD	Sioux Falls	48	6	7	9	9	11	11	10	9	8	6	6	6	98
TN	Memphis	43	10	9	11	10	9	9	9	8	7	6	9	10	107
	Nashville	52	11	11	12	11	11	9	10	9	8	7	9	11	119
TX	Dallas-Fort Worth . .	40	7	7	7	8	9	7	5	5	7	6	6	7	79
	El Paso.	54	4	3	2	2	2	3	8	8	5	4	3	4	49
	Houston	24	11	8	9	7	9	9	9	9	9	7	8	9	106
UT	Salt Lake City.	65	10	9	10	9	8	5	5	6	5	6	8	9	91
VT	Burlington	50	14	12	13	12	14	12	12	13	12	12	14	15	154
VA	Norfolk	45	11	10	11	10	10	9	11	10	8	8	8	9	115
	Richmond	56	10	9	11	9	11	9	11	10	8	7	8	9	113
WA	Seattle-Tacoma. . . .	49	18	16	17	14	10	9	5	6	9	13	18	19	154
	Spokane	46	14	11	11	9	9	8	5	5	6	7	13	15	113
WV	Charleston	46	15	14	15	14	13	11	13	11	10	10	12	14	151
WI	Milwaukee	53	11	9	12	12	12	11	10	9	9	9	11	11	125
WY	Cheyenne	58	6	6	9	10	12	11	11	10	7	6	6	6	100
PR	San Juan.	38	17	13	12	13	17	15	19	18	17	17	18	19	196

Z Less than 1/2 day.   [1] For period of record through 1989.   [2] City office data.

Source: U.S. National Oceanic and Atmospheric Administration, *Comparative Climatic Data,* annual.

No. 396. Snow and Ice Pellets—Selected Cities

[**In inches.** Airport data, except as noted. For period of record through 1993. T denotes trace]

STATE	STATION	Length of record (yr.)	Jan.	Feb.	Mar.	Apr.	May	June	July	Aug.	Sept.	Oct.	Nov.	Dec.	Annual
AL	Mobile	52	0.1	0.2	0.1	T	T	-	T	-	-	-	T	0.1	0.5
AK	Juneau	49	26.0	19.0	14.9	3.5	-	T	-	-	T	1.1	11.9	22.6	99.0
AZ	Phoenix	56	T	-	T	T	T	-	-	-	-	T	0.0	0.0	T
AR	Little Rock	51	2.3	1.4	0.5	T	-	-	-	-	-	T	0.2	0.7	5.1
CA	Los Angeles	58	T	T	T	-	-	-	-	-	-	-	-	T	T
	Sacramento	45	T	-	T	-	-	-	-	-	-	-	-	T	T
	San Diego	53	T	-	T	-	-	-	-	-	-	-	T	T	T
	San Francisco	66	0.0	T	T	-	-	-	-	-	-	-	-	-	T
CO	Denver	59	8.2	7.4	12.6	8.9	1.6	-	T	T	1.6	3.8	8.9	7.4	60.4
CT	Hartford	39	12.0	11.4	9.9	1.6	-	T	-	-	-	0.1	2.0	10.3	47.3
DE	Wilmington	46	6.6	6.0	3.3	0.2	T	T	T	-	-	-	0.9	3.3	20.4
DC	Washington	50	5.3	5.3	2.1	-	T	-	T	T	-	-	0.8	3.1	16.6
FL	Jacksonville	52	T	-	-	-	-	-	T	-	-	-	-	-	T
	Miami	51	-	-	-	-	-	-	-	-	-	-	-	-	0.0
GA	Atlanta	59	0.9	0.5	0.4	T	-	-	-	-	-	T	-	0.2	2.0
HI	Honolulu	47	-	-	-	-	-	-	-	-	-	-	-	-	-
ID	Boise	54	6.8	3.6	1.7	0.6	0.1	T	T	T	-	0.1	2.2	5.8	20.9
IL	Chicago	35	10.7	8.1	7.0	1.7	0.1	T	T	T	T	0.4	1.9	8.3	38.2
	Peoria	50	6.6	5.4	4.1	0.9	-	-	T	-	T	0.1	2.1	5.9	25.1
IN	Indianapolis	62	6.1	5.8	3.4	0.5	-	T	-	T	-	0.2	1.8	4.9	22.7
IA	Des Moines	54	8.1	7.2	6.2	1.9	-	T	T	-	T	0.2	3.0	6.6	33.2
KS	Wichita	40	4.6	4.2	2.4	0.3	T	T	T	-	T	0.0	1.3	3.3	16.1
KY	Louisville	46	5.1	4.5	3.2	0.1	T	T	-	-	-	0.1	1.0	2.2	16.2
LA	New Orleans	47	0.0	0.1	T	T	T	-	-	-	-	-	T	0.1	0.2
ME	Portland	53	19.0	17.4	13.0	3.1	0.2	-	-	-	T	0.2	3.0	14.6	70.5
MD	Baltimore	43	5.9	6.5	3.8	0.1	T	-	-	-	-	-	1.0	3.5	20.8
MA	Boston	58	12.0	11.3	7.9	0.9	-	-	-	-	-	-	1.3	7.5	40.9
MI	Detroit	35	10.2	9.1	7.0	1.7	T	-	-	-	T	0.2	3.0	10.2	41.4
	Sault Ste. Marie	52	28.7	18.7	14.8	5.6	0.5	T	-	T	0.1	2.5	15.3	29.9	116.1
MN	Duluth	50	16.8	11.2	13.3	6.5	0.8	-	T	T	0.1	1.4	12.5	15.4	78.0
	Minneapolis-St. Paul	55	9.8	8.4	10.7	2.8	0.1	T	T	T	-	0.5	7.9	9.3	49.5
MS	Jackson	30	0.5	0.2	0.2	-	-	-	-	-	-	-	-	-	0.9
MO	Kansas City	59	5.8	4.5	3.6	0.8	T	T	T	-	T	-	1.1	4.4	20.2
	St. Louis	57	5.3	4.7	4.2	0.4	-	T	-	-	-	T	1.4	3.8	19.8
MT	Great Falls	56	9.9	8.3	10.4	7.2	1.8	0.3	T	0.1	1.5	3.4	7.5	8.7	59.1
NE	Omaha	58	7.4	6.6	6.4	1.0	0.1	T	-	-	T	0.3	2.6	5.5	29.9
NV	Reno	51	6.0	5.2	4.4	1.2	0.9	-	-	-	0.0	0.3	2.2	4.4	24.6
NH	Concord	52	17.7	14.6	10.9	2.4	0.1	T	-	-	T	0.1	3.8	13.6	63.2
NJ	Atlantic City	49	5.2	5.4	2.6	0.3	T	-	T	-	0.0	T	0.4	2.2	16.1
NM	Albuquerque	54	2.5	2.2	1.8	0.6	-	T	T	T	T	0.1	1.3	2.6	11.1
NY	Albany	47	16.0	14.2	11.1	2.7	0.1	T	T	T	T	0.2	4.1	14.9	63.3
	Buffalo	50	23.3	18.2	11.7	3.1	0.3	T	T	T	T	0.3	11.5	22.7	91.1
	New York [1]	125	7.5	8.4	5.0	0.9	T	-	T	-	-	-	0.9	5.4	28.1
NC	Charlotte	54	2.0	1.7	1.2	-	T	-	-	-	-	-	0.1	0.5	5.5
	Raleigh	49	2.2	2.6	1.3	-	-	-	-	T	-	-	0.1	0.8	7.0
ND	Bismarck	54	7.2	6.7	8.1	3.8	0.9	T	T	T	0.3	1.7	6.3	6.9	41.9
OH	Cincinnati	46	6.7	5.5	4.2	0.5	-	T	T	-	-	0.3	2.1	3.9	23.2
	Cleveland	52	12.6	12.3	10.6	2.3	0.1	T	T	-	T	0.6	5.0	11.9	55.4
	Columbus	46	8.1	6.2	4.5	0.9	-	T	-	-	T	0.1	2.3	5.5	27.6
OK	Oklahoma City	54	3.0	2.4	1.4	-	T	T	-	-	T	T	0.5	1.8	9.1
OR	Portland	53	3.3	1.0	0.4	T	-	-	-	T	T	-	0.4	1.4	6.5
PA	Philadelphia	51	6.4	6.4	3.7	0.3	T	T	T	-	-	-	0.6	3.4	20.8
	Pittsburgh	41	11.3	9.3	8.7	1.7	0.1	T	T	-	T	0.4	3.3	8.3	43.1
RI	Providence	40	9.4	9.6	7.6	0.7	0.2	-	-	-	-	0.1	1.0	7.0	35.6
SC	Columbia	46	0.5	0.8	0.3	T	-	-	T	-	-	-	T	0.3	1.9
SD	Sioux Falls	48	6.4	8.1	9.6	2.2	-	T	-	T	-	0.7	5.4	7.2	39.6
TN	Memphis	43	2.3	1.3	0.8	T	T	-	-	-	-	T	0.1	0.6	5.1
	Nashville	52	3.8	3.1	1.4	-	-	T	-	T	-	-	0.4	1.5	10.2
TX	Dallas-Fort Worth	40	1.2	1.0	0.2	T	T	-	-	-	-	T	0.1	0.2	2.7
	El Paso	54	1.4	0.8	0.4	0.3	T	T	T	-	-	T	0.9	1.7	5.5
	Houston	59	0.2	0.2	0.0	T	T	T	-	-	-	-	T	0.0	0.4
UT	Salt Lake City	65	13.5	9.4	9.4	5.0	0.6	T	T	T	0.1	1.3	6.6	12.0	57.9
VT	Burlington	50	18.8	16.8	12.4	3.8	0.2	-	T	T	-	0.2	6.6	18.1	76.9
VA	Norfolk	45	2.6	2.9	1.0	-	-	T	-	T	-	-	-	0.9	7.4
	Richmond	56	4.9	4.1	2.4	0.1	T	-	-	-	-	T	0.4	2.0	13.9
WA	Seattle-Tacoma	49	4.0	1.6	1.4	0.1	T	-	T	-	T	-	1.2	2.5	11.8
	Spokane	46	16.2	7.7	4.1	0.6	0.1	T	-	T	T	0.4	6.2	15.1	50.4
WV	Charleston	46	10.1	8.7	5.1	0.9	0.0	T	T	T	T	0.2	2.2	5.1	32.3
WI	Milwaukee	53	12.8	9.6	8.7	1.7	0.1	T	T	T	T	0.2	3.0	10.4	46.5
WY	Cheyenne	58	6.4	5.9	12.1	9.0	3.4	0.3	T	-	0.8	3.7	7.4	6.2	55.2
PR	San Juan	38	-	-	-	-	-	-	-	-	-	-	-	-	-

- Represents zero or rounds to zero.   [1] City office data.

Source: U.S. National Oceanic and Atmospheric Administration, *Comparative Climatic Data,* annual.

No. 397. Sunshine, Average Wind Speed, Heating and Cooling Degree Days, and Average Relative Humidity—Selected Cities

[Airport data, except as noted. For period of record through 1993, except as noted. M=morning. A=afternoon]

STATE	STATION	AVERAGE PERCENTAGE OF POSSIBLE SUNSHINE [1]		AVERAGE WIND SPEED (m.p.h.)				Heating degree days	Cooling degree days	AVERAGE RELATIVE HUMIDITY (percent)						
											Annual		Jan.		July	
		Length of record (yr.)	Annual	Length of record (yr.)	Annual	Jan.	July			Length of record (yr.)	M	A	M	A	M	A
AL	Mobile	45	60	45	9.0	10.3	7.0	1,702	2,627	31	87	57	82	61	55	90
AK	Juneau	43	23	48	8.3	8.3	7.5	8,897	-	27	84	73	81	78	65	83
AZ	Phoenix	56	81	48	6.2	5.3	7.1	1,350	4,162	33	51	23	67	33	12	44
AR	Little Rock	35	60	51	7.8	8.5	6.7	3,155	2,005	33	84	57	80	61	55	88
CA	Los Angeles	58	72	45	7.5	6.7	7.9	1,458	727	34	79	64	70	59	67	86
	Sacramento	45	72	44	7.9	7.2	9.0	2,749	1,237	33	83	46	90	70	31	77
	San Diego	53	72	53	7.0	5.9	7.4	1,256	984	33	77	62	71	56	67	82
	San Francisco	66	72	66	10.6	7.2	13.6	3,016	145	34	84	62	86	66	58	86
CO	Denver	59	67	45	8.7	8.6	8.3	6,020	679	33	68	40	64	49	35	69
CT	Hartford	39	52	39	8.5	9.0	7.4	6,151	677	34	77	52	71	56	51	78
DE	Wilmington	46	55	45	9.1	9.8	7.8	4,937	1,046	46	78	55	75	60	53	79
DC	Washington	45	55	45	9.4	10.0	8.3	4,047	1,549	33	74	53	70	55	52	76
FL	Jacksonville	45	61	44	8.0	8.2	7.1	1,434	2,551	57	88	56	87	58	57	88
	Miami	44	68	44	9.3	9.5	8.0	200	4,198	29	84	61	84	59	65	84
GA	Atlanta	59	59	55	9.1	10.4	7.6	2,991	1,667	33	82	56	78	59	56	88
HI	Honolulu	44	74	44	11.3	9.5	13.2	-	4,474	24	72	55	81	61	52	67
ID	Boise	54	58	54	8.7	8.0	8.4	5,861	754	54	69	43	81	70	30	54
IL	Chicago	35	52	35	10.4	11.7	8.3	6,536	752	35	80	60	77	67	55	82
	Peoria	50	53	50	10.0	11.1	7.8	6,148	982	34	83	62	79	69	56	87
IN	Indianapolis	62	51	45	9.6	10.9	7.5	5,615	1,014	34	84	62	81	70	56	87
IA	Des Moines	44	55	44	10.8	11.5	8.9	6,497	1,036	32	80	60	76	67	56	82
KS	Wichita	39	62	40	12.3	12.1	11.4	4,791	1,628	40	80	56	79	63	53	79
KY	Louisville	46	53	46	8.3	9.6	6.8	4,514	1,288	33	81	58	76	64	56	85
LA	New Orleans	45	60	45	8.2	9.3	6.1	1,513	2,655	45	88	63	85	66	63	91
ME	Portland	53	55	53	8.8	9.2	7.6	7,378	268	53	79	59	76	60	60	80
MD	Baltimore	43	59	43	9.2	9.7	8.0	4,707	1,137	40	77	54	72	57	52	80
MA	Boston	58	55	36	12.5	13.8	11.0	5,641	678	29	72	58	67	57	58	73
MI	Detroit	35	49	35	10.4	11.9	8.5	6,569	626	35	81	60	80	69	54	82
	Sault Ste. Marie	52	43	52	9.2	9.7	7.8	9,316	131	52	85	67	81	74	61	89
MN	Duluth	45	49	44	11.0	11.6	9.4	9,818	180	32	81	63	77	70	60	85
	Minneapolis-St. Paul . .	55	54	55	10.5	10.5	9.4	7,981	682	34	79	60	74	60	54	81
MS	Jackson	30	59	30	7.4	8.4	5.9	2,467	2,215	30	91	58	87	65	56	94
MO	Kansas City	21	59	21	10.8	11.4	9.5	5,393	1,288	21	81	60	77	64	59	84
	St. Louis	45	55	48	10.6	11.5	8.5	4,758	1,534	33	83	59	81	66	55	84
MT	Great Falls	56	51	52	12.7	15.2	10.0	7,741	388	32	67	45	66	40	40	67
NE	Omaha	48	59	57	10.5	10.9	8.9	6,300	1,072	29	81	59	78	65	55	85
NV	Reno	51	69	51	6.6	5.6	7.1	5,674	508	30	70	31	79	51	22	63
NH	Concord	52	55	51	6.7	7.2	5.7	7,554	328	28	82	54	75	58	52	84
NJ	Atlantic City	35	56	35	10.0	10.9	8.4	5,169	826	29	82	56	78	58	56	83
NM	Albuquerque	54	76	54	9.0	8.0	9.0	4,425	1,244	33	60	29	71	41	18	60
NY	Albany	55	49	55	8.9	9.8	7.5	6,894	507	28	80	57	77	63	56	81
	Buffalo	50	43	54	11.9	14.2	10.3	6,747	477	33	80	63	79	72	56	78
	New York [2]	42	64	58	9.4	10.7	7.6	4,805	1,096	61	72	56	68	60	55	75
NC	Charlotte	45	59	44	7.4	7.8	6.6	3,341	1,582	33	82	54	78	56	55	86
	Raleigh	45	59	44	7.8	8.5	6.7	3,457	1,417	29	85	54	79	55	56	89
ND	Bismarck	54	55	54	10.2	10.0	9.2	8,968	488	34	80	57	75	68	52	84
OH	Cincinnati	42	49	46	9.1	10.7	7.2	5,248	996	31	82	60	79	68	56	85
	Cleveland	52	45	52	10.6	12.2	8.6	6,201	621	33	79	62	78	69	57	81
	Columbus	44	48	44	8.4	9.9	6.6	5,708	797	34	80	59	77	67	55	84
OK	Oklahoma City	44	64	45	12.3	12.6	10.9	3,659	1,859	28	80	55	78	60	56	80
OR	Portland	45	39	45	7.9	10.0	7.6	4,522	371	53	86	59	86	75	49	82
PA	Philadelphia	53	56	53	9.6	10.3	8.2	4,954	1,101	34	76	55	73	59	53	79
	Pittsburgh	41	44	41	9.1	10.6	7.3	5,968	654	33	79	57	76	65	52	82
RI	Providence	40	55	40	10.5	11.1	9.4	5,884	606	30	75	55	71	56	56	77
SC	Columbia	46	60	45	6.9	7.2	6.3	2,649	1,966	27	87	51	83	54	51	89
SD	Sioux Falls	48	57	45	11.1	11.0	9.8	7,809	744	30	82	60	77	68	55	83
TN	Memphis	41	59	45	8.8	10.0	7.5	3,082	2,118	54	81	57	79	63	56	84
	Nashville	52	57	52	8.0	9.1	6.6	3,729	1,616	28	84	57	80	63	55	89
TX	Dallas-Fort Worth	40	64	40	10.7	10.9	9.7	2,407	2,603	30	82	56	80	60	55	81
	El Paso	51	80	51	8.8	8.3	8.3	2,708	2,094	33	57	28	66	35	18	63
	Houston	24	56	24	7.9	8.2	7.0	1,599	2,700	24	90	60	86	64	60	93
UT	Salt Lake City	65	62	64	8.8	7.5	9.5	5,765	1,047	34	68	43	79	70	26	52
VT	Burlington	50	44	50	9.0	9.7	8.0	7,771	388	28	77	59	72	64	55	79
VA	Norfolk	45	58	45	10.6	11.5	9.0	3,495	1,422	45	78	57	74	59	56	81
	Richmond	48	56	45	7.7	8.1	6.9	3,963	1,348	59	83	53	80	57	53	85
WA	Seattle-Tacoma	49	38	45	9.0	9.7	8.3	4,908	190	34	83	62	81	74	53	82
	Spokane	46	47	46	8.9	8.8	8.6	6,842	398	34	78	52	85	79	36	65
WV	Charleston	46	48	46	6.2	7.4	5.0	4,646	1,031	46	83	56	77	63	54	90
WI	Milwaukee	53	52	53	11.5	12.6	9.7	7,324	479	33	80	64	76	68	60	82
WY	Cheyenne	58	64	36	12.9	15.3	10.4	7,326	285	34	65	44	57	50	41	70
PR	San Juan	38	75	38	8.4	8.5	9.6	-	5,558	38	79	65	82	64	66	79

- Represents zero.   [1] Percent of days that are either clear or partly cloudy.   [2]City office data.

Source: U.S. National Oceanic and Atmospheric Administration, *Comparative Climatic Data*, annual.

Parks, Recreation, and Travel

This section presents data on national parks and forests, State parks, recreational activities, the arts and humanities, and domestic and foreign travel.

Parks and recreation.—The Department of the Interior has responsibility for administering the national parks. As part of this function, it issues reports relating to the usage of public parks for recreation purposes. The National Park Service publishes information on visits to national park areas in its annual report, *National Park Statistical Abstract. The National Parks: Index (year)* is a biannual report which has appeared under a variety of *Index* titles prior to 1985. Beginning with the 1985 edition, the report has appeared under the current title. The *Index* contains brief descriptions, with acreages, of each area administered by the Service, plus certain "related" areas. A statistical summary of Service-administered areas is also presented. The annual *Federal Recreation Fee Report* summarizes the prior year's recreation fee receipts and recreation visitation statistics for seven Federal land managing agencies.

Statistics for State parks are compiled by the National Association of State Park Directors which issues its annual *Information Exchange.* The Bureau of Land Management, in its *Public Land Statistics,* also issues data on recreational use of its lands. The Department of Agriculture's Forest Service, in its *Report of the Forest Service,* issues data on recreational uses of the national forests.

Visitation.—Data on visitation to reporting areas are collected by several different agencies and groups. The methodology used to collect these results may vary accordingly, from visual counts and estimates to the use of electromagnetic traffic counters. In using and comparing these data, one should also be aware of several different definitions that follow: Recreation visit, which is the entry of any person into an area for recreation purposes; nonrecreation visits, which include visits going to and from inholdings, through traffic, tradespeople and personnel with business in the area; and visitor hour, which constitutes the presence of a person in a recreation

In Brief

Percent of households with guns:

1974	46%
1993	42%

Attendance at Major League baseball:

1985	47,742,000
1993	71,237,000

area or site for recreational purposes for periods of time aggregating 60 minutes.

Recreation and leisure activities.—Statistics on the participation in various recreation and leisure time activities are based on several sample surveys. Data on participation in fishing, hunting, and other forms of wildlife-associated recreation are published periodically by the U.S. Department of Interior, Fish and Wildlife Service. The most recent data are from the 1991 survey. Data on participation in various sports recreation activities are published by the National Sporting Goods Association.

Travel.—Information on foreign travel and personal expenditures abroad, as well as expenditures by foreign citizens traveling in the United States, is compiled annually by the U.S. Bureau of Economic Analysis and published in selected issues of the monthly *Survey of Current Business.* Statistics on arrivals to the United States are reported by the U.S. Travel and Tourism Administration (USTTA), in cooperation with the U.S. Immigration and Naturalization Service, and are published in *Summary and Analysis of International Travel to the United States.* Sources of statistics on departures from the United States include USTTA's in-flight survey, the Department of Transportation's *International Air Travel Statistics,* and other sources. Data on domestic travel, business receipts and employment of the travel industry, and travel expenditures are published by the U.S. Travel Data Center, the national nonprofit center for travel and tourism research which is located in Washington, DC. Other data on household transportation characteristics may be found in section 21.

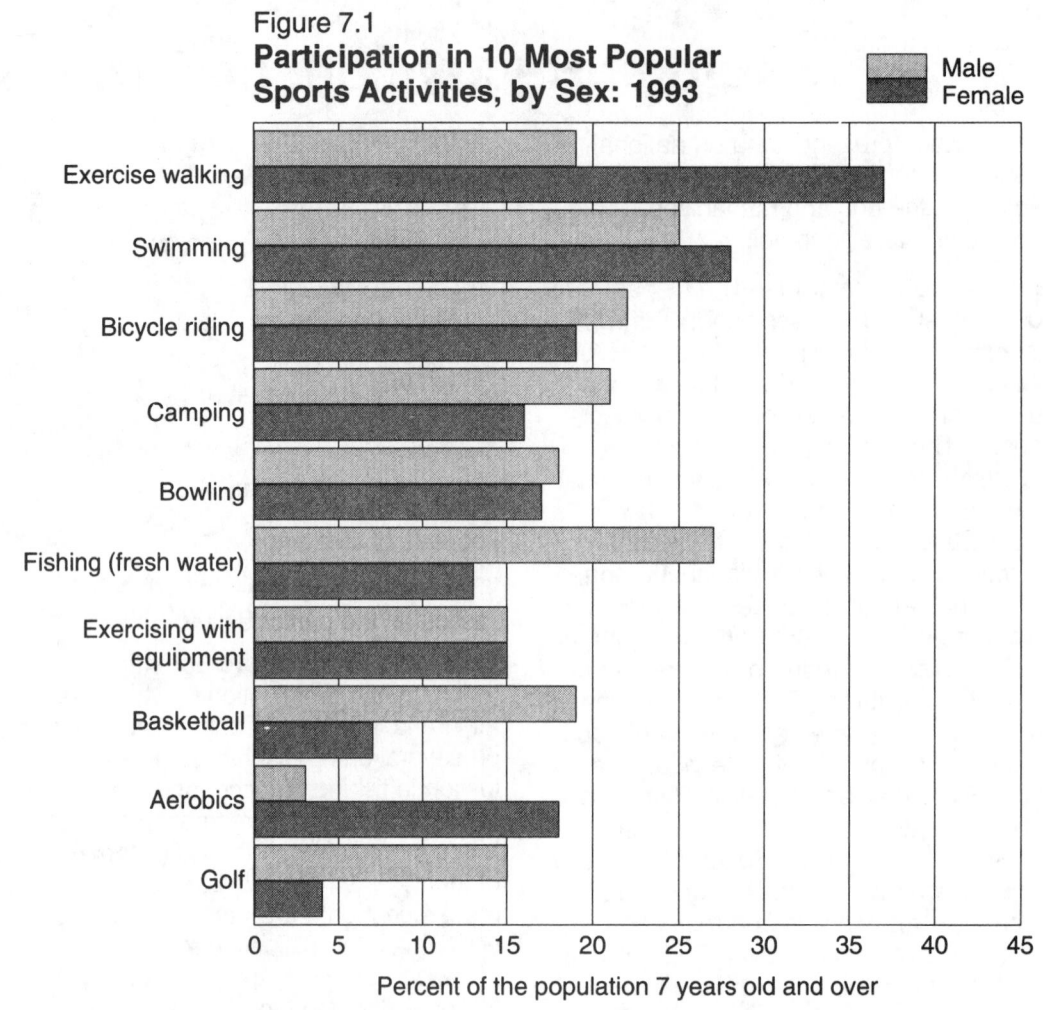

Figure 7.1
Participation in 10 Most Popular Sports Activities, by Sex: 1993

Male
Female

Percent of the population 7 years old and over

Source: Chart prepared by U.S. Bureau of the Census. For data, see table 416.

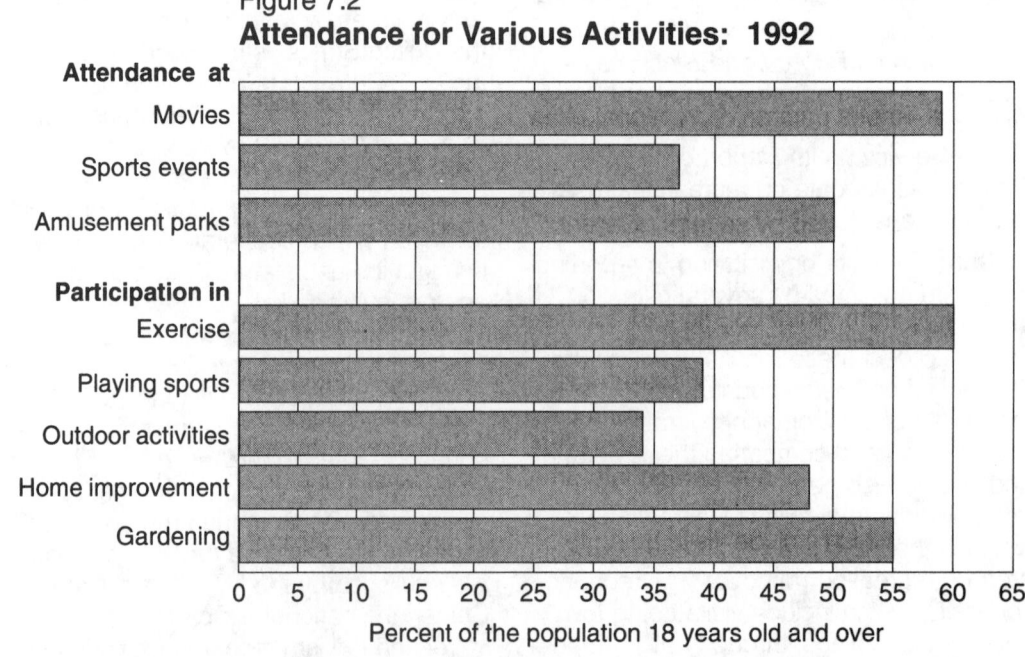

Figure 7.2
Attendance for Various Activities: 1992

Percent of the population 18 years old and over

Source: Chart prepared by U.S. Bureau of the Census. For data, see table 413.

No. 398. Visitation to Federal Recreation Areas: 1980 to 1994

[In **millions of visitor hours.** For years ending **September 30.** Covers persons entering and using a recreation area over a specified period of time. For definition of visitor hour, see text, section 7]

ADMINISTERING FEDERAL AGENCY	1980	1985	1987	1988	1989	1990	1991	1992	1994
All areas	**6,367**	**6,403**	**7,332**	**7,419**	**7,475**	**7,567**	**7,829**	**7,995**	**(NA)**
Fish and Wildlife Service	17	65	72	81	45	(NA)	(NA)	(NA)	(NA)
Forest Service	2,819	2,705	2,861	2,908	3,030	3,157	3,346	3,452	(NA)
U.S. Army Corps of Engineers [1]	1,926	1,721	2,176	2,290	2,296	2,280	2,306	2,306	(NA)
National Park Service	1,042	1,298	1,394	1,376	1,315	1,322	1,344	1,390	1,338
Bureau of Land Management [2]	68	246	515	461	493	518	540	563	(NA)
Bureau of Reclamation	407	289	306	294	286	280	280	269	(NA)
Tennessee Valley Authority [3]	87	79	8	9	10	10	13	14	(NA)

NA Not available. [1] Beginning 1987, not comparable with previous years. [2] Data not comparable for all years. [3] Beginning in 1989, the TVA discontinued reporting visitation to nonfee charging areas. Data for 1987 and 1988 have been adjusted to reflect this policy.

Source: 1980, U.S. Heritage Conservation and Recreation Service, *Federal Recreation Fee Report,* annual; thereafter, U.S. National Park Service.

No. 399. National Park System—Summary: 1985 to 1994

[**For fiscal years ending in year shown, except as noted;** see text, section 10. Includes data for five areas in Puerto Rico and Virgin Islands, one area in American Samoa, and one area in Guam. See also *Historical Statistics, Colonial Times to 1970,* séries H 806-828]

ITEM	1985	1988	1989	1990	1991	1992	1993	1994
Finances (mil. dol.): [1]								
Expenditures reported	848.1	922.9	1,036.8	986.1	1,104.4	1,268.7	1,429.4	1,404.0
Salaries and wages	369.4	423.9	441.4	459.1	495.3	518.1	596.1	627.2
Improvements, maintenance	127.4	154.7	197.5	160.0	179.6	212.1	224.8	222.9
Construction	84.7	86.3	85.2	108.5	134.1	193.3	226.8	205.6
Other	266.6	258.0	312.7	258.5	295.4	345.2	379.7	348.3
Funds available	1,248.2	1,338.4	1,440.0	1,505.5	1,988.4	2,274.8	2,346.5	2,307.7
Appropriations	821.6	874.6	996.7	1,052.5	1,284.7	1,392.8	1,334.0	1,388.8
Other [2]	426.6	463.8	443.3	453.0	703.7	882.0	1,012.5	918.9
Revenue from operations	50.6	77.2	86.3	78.6	78.1	88.3	89.5	97.0
Recreation visits (millions): [3]								
All areas	263.4	282.5	269.4	258.7	267.8	274.7	273.1	267.6
National parks [4]	50.0	56.4	57.4	57.7	57.4	58.7	59.8	60.1
National monuments	15.9	23.2	23.7	23.9	25.8	26.6	26.5	26.5
National historical, commemorative, archaeological [5]	61.9	61.2	63.9	57.5	61.0	63.3	61.9	59.5
National parkways	40.0	42.0	31.2	29.1	28.8	30.7	30.4	29.3
National recreation areas [4]	49.4	54.5	49.6	47.2	49.8	50.3	50.8	52.3
National seashores and lakeshores	25.3	23.2	21.9	23.3	24.4	23.9	24.1	24.0
National Capital Parks	8.3	9.0	8.9	7.5	7.5	8.1	9.1	5.4
Miscellaneous other areas	12.6	12.9	12.8	12.5	13.1	13.1	10.5	10.5
Recreation overnight stays (millions) [3]	15.8	17.0	17.4	17.6	17.7	18.3	17.7	18.3
In commercial lodgings	3.5	3.8	3.9	3.9	4.0	4.1	4.0	3.9
In Park Service campgrounds	7.3	7.9	7.8	7.9	7.8	8.1	7.5	7.6
In tents	3.6	3.9	3.9	4.1	4.2	4.4	4.1	4.2
In recreation vehicles	3.8	3.9	3.9	3.8	3.6	3.7	3.4	3.4
In backcountry	1.7	1.6	1.6	1.7	2.0	2.2	2.4	2.4
Other	3.2	3.7	4.1	4.2	3.9	3.9	3.8	4.4
Land (1,000 acres): [6]								
Total	75,749	76,176	76,331	76,362	76,607	76,492	75,515	74,905
Parks	45,739	45,955	46,081	46,089	46,135	46,208	45,521	48,111
Recreation areas	3,335	3,339	3,342	3,344	3,346	3,347	3,349	3,351
Other	26,675	26,882	26,907	26,929	27,126	26,937	26,645	23,443
Acquisition, gross	34	38	73	21	66	23	39	26
By purchase	29	37	14	18	15	21	29	25
By gift	2	(Z)	58	2	43	1	10	(Z)
By transfer or exchange	3	1	1	3	8	1	1	(Z)
Exclusion	(Z)	(Z)	1	1	(Z)	(Z)	(Z)	(Z)
Acquisition, net	34	38	71	21	66	23	39	26

Z Less than 500 acres. [1] Financial data are those associated with the National Park System. Certain other functions of the National Park Service (principally the activities absorbed from the former Heritage Conservation and Recreation Service in 1981) are excluded. [2] Includes funds carried over from prior years. [3] For calendar year. [4] Combined data for North Cascades National Park and two adjacent National Recreation Areas are included in National Parks total. [5] Includes military areas. [6] Federal land only, as of Dec. 31. Federal land acreages, in addition to National Park Service administered lands, also include lands within national park system area boundaries but under the administration of other agencies. Year-to-year changes in the federal lands figures include changes in the acreages of these other lands and hence often differ from "net acquisition."

Source: U.S. National Park Service, Visits, *National Park Statistical Abstract,* annual; and unpublished data. Other data are unpublished.

No. 400. National Forest Recreation Use, Summary: 1980 to 1993

[For year ending September 30. Estimated. Represents recreational use of National Forest land and water in States which have a Forest Service recreation program. See also *Historical Statistics, Colonial Times to 1970*, series H 829-835]

YEAR AND ACTIVITY	Recreation visitor-days[1] (1,000)	Percent	STATE	Recreation visitor-days[1], 1993 (1,000)	STATE OR OTHER AREA	Recreation visitor-days[1], 1993 (1,000)
1980	233,549	100.0	U.S.	295,473	NV	3,677
1981	235,709	100.0			NH	3,243
1982	233,438	100.0	AL	833	NM	8,775
1983	227,708	100.0	AK	5,515	NY	35
1984	227,554	100.0	AZ	30,973	NC	6,158
1985	225,407	100.0	AR	2,106	ND	135
1986	226,533	100.0	CA	69,981	OH	680
1987	238,458	100.0	CO	30,106	OK	358
1988	242,316	100.0	FL	3,124	OR	19,285
1989	252,495	100.0	GA	3,033	PA	2,950
1990	263,051	100.0	ID	13,455	SC	944
1991	278,849	100.0	IL	1,029	SD	3,352
1992	287,691	100.0	IN	501	TN	2,957
1993, total	295,473	100.0	KS	83	TX	2,303
Mechanized travel and viewing scenery	99,573	33.7	KY	2,106	UT	15,157
Camping, picnicking, and swimming	79,319	26.8	LA	533	VT	1,728
Hiking, horseback riding, and water travel	26,632	9.0	MA	114	VA	4,477
Winter sports	19,230	6.5	MI	5,011	WA	18,735
Hunting	17,279	5.8	MN	5,676	WV	1,354
Resorts, cabins, and organization camps	17,086	5.8	MS	1,318	WI	2,733
Fishing	16,299	5.5	MO	1,931	WY	7,454
Nature studies	2,711	0.9	MT	11,001		
Other[2]	17,343	6.0	NE	260	PR	296

[1] One recreation visitor-day is the recreation use of National Forest land or water that aggregates 12 visitor-hours. This may entail 1 person for 12 hours, 12 persons for 1 hour, or any equivalent combination of individual or group use, either continuous or intermittent. [2] Includes team sports, gathering forest products, attending talks and programs, and other uses.

Source: U.S. Forest Service, unpublished data.

No. 401. Recreational Use of Public Lands Administered by Bureau of Land Management: 1982 to 1993

[In thousands. For year ending Sept. 30. Beginning 1987, increase due to an estimated longer length of stay per visit, especially in California. See text, section 7]

YEAR AND STATE	Number of visits	TYPE OF RECREATION USE (visitor hours)										
		Total	Off-highway vehicle travel	Other motorized travel	Non-motorized travel	Camping	Hunting	Misc. site based	Fishing	Boating	Misc. water based	Snow- and ice-based recreational activity, winter sports
1982	58,135	316,959	19,471	32,646	11,237	63,928	108,996	44,587	19,287	10,101	1,043	5,663
1983	56,270	334,010	24,397	35,534	12,237	84,066	92,974	39,734	20,290	16,869	4,992	2,917
1984	59,228	271,373	21,348	25,433	9,579	73,032	73,898	37,650	14,263	11,184	2,092	2,894
1985	51,739	244,612	36,995	24,053	10,047	65,397	51,842	23,098	14,254	11,710	2,193	5,023
1986	54,253	284,142	49,688	25,866	14,397	95,196	35,570	19,331	18,227	15,891	3,951	6,025
1987	56,427	514,716	123,325	34,325	19,172	195,315	57,624	38,412	22,932	15,140	5,212	3,259
1988	57,460	492,756	122,014	35,748	19,761	178,703	55,285	38,340	21,617	13,294	4,979	3,015
1989	60,957	493,214	65,808	74,075	36,676	173,597	46,760	45,871	23,392	18,491	5,425	3,119
1990	71,820	523,753	63,016	83,445	41,316	165,366	47,053	57,958	28,664	20,806	8,313	7,816
1991	72,541	539,779	50,849	85,835	44,398	196,310	49,593	59,928	20,939	19,676	8,353	3,898
1992	69,418	519,429	46,411	93,477	43,845	181,536	44,557	59,857	19,768	18,735	7,586	3,657
1993, total	(NA)	428,825	40,197	61,113	27,780	162,663	47,246	42,500	19,466	17,127	7,009	3,724
AK	(NA)	5,924	152	466	87	3,719	567	201	432	173	5	122
AZ[1]	(NA)	59,022	749	619	2,473	36,351	2,334	8,748	756	4,927	2,061	4
CA	(NA)	132,143	24,989	10,159	7,177	66,608	7,727	9,213	2,745	1,584	1,688	253
CO	(NA)	27,795	1,418	6,122	946	5,692	9,204	1,535	791	1,710	54	323
Eastern States	(NA)	52	-	-	-	-	1	1	6	2	42	-
ID	(NA)	18,199	1,032	1,326	692	5,168	2,568	1,588	2,288	1,433	570	1,534
MT[2]	(NA)	13,004	2,523	967	503	3,187	2,822	418	1,734	476	57	317
NV	(NA)	26,897	1,668	11,309	2,798	4,191	2,192	2,708	1,434	262	172	163
NM	(NA)	20,098	926	5,137	1,721	3,001	5,329	2,917	600	392	71	4
OR[3]	(NA)	60,564	1,828	8,291	5,625	15,759	6,627	9,718	7,232	3,026	1,902	556
UT	(NA)	56,008	4,618	15,988	5,481	17,341	4,868	3,985	465	2,812	336	114
WY	(NA)	9,119	294	729	277	1,646	3,007	1,468	983	330	51	334

- Represents zero.   NA Not available.   [1] Includes concession visitation data. These data relate to Bureau of Land Management concession leases along the Colorado River. The leases consist of boat docks and storage areas, trailer parks, restaurants, etc. The visitation by the recreating public to these areas and facilities is monitored and recorded. [2] Includes North Dakota and South Dakota. [3] Includes Washington.

Source: U.S. Bureau of Land Management, *Public Land Statistics*, annual.

No. 402. State Parks and Recreation Areas—States: 1992

[**For year ending June 30.** Data are shown as reported by State park directors. In some States, park agency has under its control forests, fish and wildlife areas, and/or other areas. In other States, agency is responsible for State parks only]

STATE	Acreage (1,000)	Visitors (1,000)[1]	REVENUE Total ($1,000)	REVENUE Percent of operating expenditures	STATE	Acreage (1,000)	Visitors (1,000)[1]	REVENUE Total ($1,000)	REVENUE Percent of operating expenditures
United States ...	**11,831**	**724,805**	**488,984**	**45.0**	Missouri	122	16,103	4,300	22.4
					Montana	41	4,491	1,330	48.6
Alabama	50	6,268	23,427	81.4	Nebraska	142	9,227	8,600	71.1
Alaska	3,169	6,321	1,063	19.9	Nevada.........	142	2,679	751	14.5
Arizona.........	33	1,750	3,734	35.9	New Hampshire ...	75	1,737	4,341	51.5
Arkansas........	47	6,725	12,046	56.0	New Jersey	305	10,607	6,123	22.8
California........	1,323	67,301	73,563	49.3	New Mexico......	122	4,089	2,932	29.0
Colorado........	340	9,522	13,373	109.0	New York	260	63,520	36,657	33.5
Connecticut......	173	7,053	3,498	47.9	North Carolina ...	135	9,713	2,108	18.3
Delaware........	13	3,619	4,176	43.0	North Dakota	19	990	809	49.1
Florida	444	12,232	18,061	38.9	Ohio...........	208	49,861	13,178	30.8
Georgia	57	16,284	15,029	42.5	Oklahoma	77	16,183	17,127	76.7
Hawaii	25	19,255	1,161	14.7	Oregon.........	91	42,334	9,171	38.5
Idaho..........	42	2,697	1,958	79.8	Pennsylvania	277	35,542	8,053	15.4
Illinois..........	403	38,555	3,528	11.6	Rhode Island	9	3,423	2,584	44.8
Indiana.........	57	10,570	9,111	73.7	South Carolina....	80	7,876	10,955	60.7
Iowa..........	391	12,230	1,804	24.0	South Dakota	92	5,166	3,946	64.5
Kansas.........	324	4,425	2,523	45.5	Tennessee.......	133	27,360	20,270	59.0
Kentucky........	43	27,831	36,529	63.3	Texas..........	501	24,423	16,366	49.8
Louisiana	39	1,226	2,142	25.0	Utah...........	97	5,577	3,923	31.9
Maine..........	75	2,005	1,478	34.9	Vermont	64	839	4,222	96.2
Maryland........	241	8,891	6,176	26.0	Virginia	66	3,975	2,635	27.6
Massachusetts....	274	11,549	9,256	64.9	Washington	241	47,289	7,360	36.1
Michigan	264	21,172	21,108	77.4	West Virginia	202	8,753	14,806	64.6
Minnesota	231	7,932	7,472	41.6	Wisconsin	125	11,646	8,338	70.0
Mississippi.	23	4,033	5,607	48.0	Wyoming.	120	1,949	275	10.2

[1] Includes overnight visitors.

Source: National Association of State Park Directors, Tallahassee, FL, *1993 Annual Information Exchange.*

No. 403. Personal Consumption Expenditures for Recreation in Constant (1987) Dollars: 1970 to 1993

[**In billions of dollars, except percent.** Represents market value of purchases of goods and services by individuals and nonprofit institutions]

TYPE OF PRODUCT OR SERVICE	1970	1980	1985	1989	1990	1991	1992	1993
Total recreation expenditures	**91.3**	**149.1**	**195.5**	**250.9**	**261.9**	**268.0**	**283.5**	**304.1**
Percent of total personal consumption [1]	5.0	6.1	6.8	7.8	8.0	8.2	8.5	8.8
Books and maps	10.5	10.2	11.4	14.7	15.3	15.4	16.3	16.6
Magazines, newspapers, and sheet music	13.2	18.4	17.9	20.3	20.9	20.3	20.3	20.4
Nondurable toys and sport supplies.	9.5	17.4	22.3	27.5	28.7	29.5	30.6	32.2
Wheel goods, sports and photographic equipment [2]	10.3	20.2	24.4	29.0	28.3	27.5	27.7	28.1
Video and audio products, computer equipment, and musical instruments	8.8	17.6	29.7	49.2	54.1	62.2	70.4	83.7
Radio and television repair.	2.7	3.5	3.3	3.4	3.4	3.2	3.1	3.1
Flowers, seeds, and potted plants................	4.0	5.9	7.0	9.7	9.7	9.1	9.5	10.5
Admissions to specified spectator amusements	8.2	9.9	10.2	10.6	11.5	11.5	11.6	12.5
Motion picture theaters	4.2	3.8	3.6	3.4	3.8	3.9	3.7	4.2
Legitimate theaters and opera, and entertainments of nonprofit institutions [3]	1.3	2.7	2.9	3.5	3.7	3.7	3.9	4.1
Spectator sports [4].	2.8	3.4	3.7	3.7	4.0	3.9	4.0	4.2
Clubs and fraternal organizations except insurance [5] ...	3.8	4.0	6.3	7.4	7.5	7.4	7.5	7.9
Commercial participant amusements [6]	6.3	12.5	16.1	19.0	20.3	20.0	21.6	22.0
Pari-mutuel net receipts.	2.8	3.6	3.2	3.1	3.2	3.0	3.0	2.9
Other [7]	11.3	25.8	43.5	57.1	58.9	59.0	62.0	64.2

[1] See table 709.   [2] Includes boats and pleasure aircraft.   [3] Except athletic.   [4] Consists of admissions to professional and amateur athletic events and to racetracks, including horse, dog, and auto.   [5] Consists of dues and fees excluding insurance premiums.   [6] Consists of billiard parlors; bowling alleys; dancing, riding, shooting, skating, and swimming places; amusement devices and parks; golf courses; sightseeing buses and guides; private flying operations; casino gambling; and other commercial participant amusements.   [7] Consists of net receipts of lotteries and expenditures for purchases of pets and pet care services, cable TV, film processing, photographic studios, sporting and recreation camps, video cassette rentals, and recreational services, not elsewhere classified.

Source: U.S. Bureau of Economic Analysis, *The National Income and Product Accounts of the United States: Volume 2, 1959-88,* and *Survey of Current Business,* August, 1994.

No. 404. Expenditures per Consumer Unit for Entertainment and Reading: 1985 to 1993

[Data are **annual averages. In dollars, except as indicated.** Based on Consumer Expenditure Survey; see text, section 14, for description of survey. See also headnote, table 718. For composition of regions, see table 27]

YEAR AND CHARACTERISTIC	ENTERTAINMENT AND READING		ENTERTAINMENT				Reading
	Total	Percent of total expenditures	Total	Fees and admissions	Television, radios, and sound equipment	Other equipment and services [1]	
1985................	1,311	5.6	1,170	320	371	479	141
1986................	1,289	5.4	1,149	308	371	470	140
1987................	1,335	5.5	1,193	323	379	491	142
1988................	1,479	5.7	1,329	353	416	560	150
1989................	1,581	5.7	1,424	377	429	618	157
1990................	1,575	5.6	1,422	371	454	597	153
1991................	1,635	5.5	1,472	378	468	627	163
1992................	1,662	5.6	1,500	379	492	629	162
1993, total	**1,792**	**5.8**	**1,626**	**414**	**590**	**621**	**166**
Age of reference person:							
Under 25 years old........	982	5.6	910	224	427	258	72
25 to 34 years old......	1,648	5.8	1,511	354	541	616	137
35 to 44 years old.........	2,285	6.1	2,094	555	700	839	191
45 to 54 years old.........	2,702	6.6	2,490	596	1,030	863	212
55 to 64 years old.........	1,724	5.2	1,527	454	504	570	197
65 to 74 years old........	1,363	5.7	1,198	296	356	546	165
75 years old and over........	710	3.9	578	162	243	173	132
Race:							
White and other.............	1,911	6.0	1,734	448	610	676	177
Black....................	855	4.1	772	155	427	190	83
Region of residence:							
Northeast................	1,762	5.6	1,569	439	542	588	193
Midwest...............	1,572	5.4	1,408	365	484	559	164
South	1,798	6.1	1,655	372	700	583	143
West	2,078	6.0	1,897	519	585	793	181
Size of consumer unit:							
One person	977	5.4	854	246	327	281	123
Two or more persons	2,121	5.9	1,937	482	696	759	184
Two persons	1,840	5.8	1,645	428	501	716	195
Three persons............	1,789	5.1	1,620	417	598	605	169
Four persons	3,009	7.1	2,818	613	1,219	985	191
Five persons or more	2,223	5.6	2,062	563	694	805	161

[1] Other equipment and services includes pets, toys, and playground equipment, and sports, exercise, and photographic equipment.

Source: U.S. Bureau of Labor Statistics, *Consumer Expenditure Survey*, annual.

No. 405. Motion Pictures and Amusement and Recreation Services—Annual Receipts: 1988 to 1993

[**In billions of dollars.** For taxable employer and nonemployer firms]

KIND OF BUSINESS	1987 SIC code [1]	1988	1989	1990	1991	1992	1993
Motion pictures.......................	78	31,107	35,035	38,296	41,039	43,645	48,130
Production, distribution, and allied services	781, 782	22,740	24,962	26,640	28,957	31,095	34,720
Theaters	783	4,635	5,518	6,277	6,488	6,234	6,489
Video tape rental........................	784	(NA)	(NA)	5,379	5,594	6,316	6,921
Amusement and recreation services.............	79	40,632	42,161	47,951	48,689	53,685	59,382
Dance studios, schools, and halls.............	791	794	693	614	646	758	839
Theatrical producers (except motion picture), bands, orchestras, and entertainers	792	8,358	8,012	10,003	10,636	11,609	13,987
Bowling centers........................	793	2,726	2,817	2,844	2,807	2,986	2,952
Commercial sports [2]	794	6,961	7,944	9,331	9,670	10,594	10,890
Professional sports clubs and promoters	7941	2,681	3,438	4,429	4,836	5,469	6,312
Racing, including track operation	7948	4,280	4,506	4,902	4,834	5,125	4,578
Miscellaneous amusement and recreation services [3]	799	(NA)	(NA)	25,159	24,930	27,738	30,714
Physical fitness facilities	7991	(NA)	(NA)	3,305	3,022	3,535	3,471
Public golf courses.....................	7992	(NA)	(NA)	2,246	2,375	2,562	2,863
Coin-operated amusement devices	7993	1,804	1,712	1,797	1,815	1,963	2,101
Amusement parks	7996	3,956	4,424	4,692	4,500	4,930	5,202
Membership sports and recreation clubs	7997	4,091	4,147	4,339	4,472	4,565	5,062

NA Not available.   [1] 1987 Standard Industrial Classification code; see text, section 13.   [2] Data for 1988 and 1989 revised from published source.   [3] Includes kinds of businesses, not shown separately.

Source: U.S. Bureau of the Census, *Current Business Reports, Service Annual Survey*, BS/93.

No. 406. Quantity of Books Sold and Value of U.S. Domestic Consumer Expenditures: 1982 to 1993

[Includes all titles released by publishers in the United States and imports which appear under the imprints of American publishers. Multi-volume sets, such as encyclopedias, are counted as one unit]

TYPE OF PUBLICATION AND MARKET AREA	UNITS SOLD (mil.)					CONSUMER EXPENDITURES (mil. dol.)				
	1982	1985	1990	1992	1993	1982	1985	1990	1992	1993
Total [1]	**1,723**	**1,788**	**2,005**	**2,051**	**2,072**	**9,889**	**12,611**	**19,043**	**21,224**	**22,635**
Hardbound, total	646	694	824	826	822	6,190	7,969	11,789	13,046	13,840
Softbound, total	1,077	1,094	1,181	1,225	1,250	3,699	4,642	7,254	8,178	8,795
Trade	459	553	705	760	763	2,484	3,660	6,498	7,793	8,353
Adult	315	360	403	442	460	2,028	2,871	4,777	5,805	6,393
Juvenile	144	193	301	319	303	456	789	1,721	1,988	1,960
Religious	144	134	130	140	141	706	926	1,362	1,567	1,651
Professional	106	110	131	135	141	1,630	2,043	2,957	3,326	3,646
Bookclubs	133	130	108	106	108	510	582	705	722	766
Elhi text	233	234	209	208	223	1,067	1,415	1,948	2,000	2,220
College text	115	110	137	137	136	1,388	1,575	2,319	2,427	2,498
Mail order publications	134	121	138	110	98	581	650	752	650	601
Mass market paperbacks-rack sized	382	382	433	439	446	1,102	1,244	1,775	1,954	2,078
General retailers	756	829	1,010	1,066	1,074	3,743	5,103	8,465	9,900	10,597
College stores	224	225	255	261	264	1,910	2,309	3,403	3,710	3,916
Libraries and institutions [2]	80	80	88	91	94	888	1,090	1,592	1,788	1,911
Schools [2]	262	260	244	244	258	1,313	1,685	2,365	2,462	2,692
Direct to consumers	319	300	304	282	277	1,889	2,214	2,901	3,002	3,144
Other	82	94	104	107	106	146	210	316	361	375

[1] Types of publications include university press publications and subscription reference works, not shown separately. [2] Elhi libraries included in schools.

Source: Book Industry Study Group, Inc., New York, NY, *Book Industry Trends, 1994,* annual, (copyright).

No. 407. Book Purchasing by Adults: 1991 and 1993

[**In percent.** Excludes books purchased for or by children under 13. Based on a survey of 16,000 households conducted over 12 months ending in December of year shown. For details, see source]

CHARACTERISTIC	TOTAL		MASS MARKET [1]		TRADE [2]		HARDCOVER	
	1991	1993	1991	1993	1991	1993	1991	1993
Total	**100.0**	**100.0**	**100.0**	**100.0**	**100.0**	**100.0**	**100.0**	**100.0**
Age of purchaser:								
Under 25 years old	4.3	3.9	3.7	3.4	5.2	4.7	4.4	3.7
25 to 34 years old	18.8	16.8	13.9	13.8	25.4	19.8	19.6	17.2
35 to 44 years old	23.7	28.6	22.8	26.6	25.2	31.7	23.7	27.7
45 to 54 years old	22.4	20.8	26.0	20.9	18.5	20.4	20.5	21.1
55 to 64 years old	15.6	14.2	15.8	15.6	13.9	12.1	17.2	14.7
65 years old and over	15.2	15.7	17.8	19.7	11.8	11.3	14.6	15.6
Household income:								
Under $30,000	37.1	31.2	41.7	36.3	32.6	27.2	34.1	28.9
$30,000 to 49,999	27.2	29.4	27.3	32.8	27.7	27.9	26.5	26.4
$50,000 to 59,999	11.0	8.6	9.8	7.2	12.3	9.4	11.5	9.5
$60,000 to 69,999	6.9	8.8	7.0	7.0	7.2	10.1	6.3	9.6
$70,000 and over	17.8	22.0	14.2	16.7	20.2	25.4	21.6	25.6
Household size:								
Singles	20.8	21.1	17.7	21.0	24.1	21.3	22.8	20.9
Families with no children	40.4	37.9	42.3	40.4	38.0	34.2	39.7	38.9
Families with children	38.8	41.0	40.0	38.6	37.9	44.5	37.5	40.2
Age of reader:								
Under 25 years old	7.3	8.5	5.2	5.9	10.1	11.4	7.7	8.5
25 to 34 years old	18.7	17.1	14.1	13.5	24.7	20.6	20.2	17.8
35 to 44 years old	22.9	26.3	22.3	25.3	24.0	28.0	22.7	25.7
45 to 54 years old	20.8	19.0	24.9	19.9	16.5	18.2	18.4	18.9
55 to 64 years old	14.9	13.5	15.9	15.6	12.7	10.9	15.6	13.8
65 years old and over	15.4	15.6	17.6	19.8	12.0	10.9	15.6	15.3
Category of book:								
Popular fiction	54.9	52.4	93.0	92.4	14.9	15.4	31.8	40.7
General nonfiction	10.3	10.5	3.6	3.6	15.6	15.3	16.5	14.4
Cooking/crafts	10.2	9.6	0.4	0.4	20.6	17.4	18.2	13.1
Other	24.6	27.5	3.0	3.6	48.9	51.9	33.5	31.8
Sales outlet:								
Independent	32.5	24.2	26.5	15.6	44.9	35.9	29.0	22.4
Chain book store	22.0	23.5	17.2	19.6	27.4	28.5	25.2	22.6
Book clubs	16.6	16.0	17.8	15.2	9.5	8.7	22.6	25.6
Other [3]	28.9	36.3	38.5	49.8	18.2	26.9	23.2	29.4

[1] "Pocket size" books sold primarily through magazine and news outlets, supermarkets, variety stores, etc. [2] All paperbound books, except mass market. [3] Includes mail order, price clubs, discount stores, food/drug stores, used book stores, and other outlets.

Source: Book Industry Study Group, Inc., New York, NY, *1993 Consumer Research Study on Book Purchasing,* (copyright).

No. 408. Profile of Consumer Expenditures for Sound Recordings: 1990 to 1993

[In percent, except total value. Based on monthly telephone surveys of the population 10 years old and over]

ITEM	1990	1992	1993	ITEM	1990	1992	1993
Total value (mil. dol.)	7,541.1	9,023.9	10,046.6	Other store	16.2	22.8	24.2
PERCENT DISTRIBUTION [1]				Music club	8.8	10.6	11.3
				Mail order	3.5	4.0	4.4
Age: 10 to 14 years	6.3	7.0	7.2	Music type: [2]			
15 to 19 years	17.1	17.9	16.0	Rock	37.4	33.2	32.6
20 to 24 years	17.1	16.2	15.1	Country	8.8	16.5	17.5
25 to 29 years	15.0	14.3	13.6	Pop	13.6	11.4	11.7
30 to 34 years	13.5	12.8	12.4	Urban Contemporary	(NA)	8.8	9.9
35 to 39 years	10.1	11.2	11.6	Rap	(NA)	7.9	7.8
40 to 44 years	8.3	7.3	8.7	Classical	4.1	4.4	4.0
45 years and over	11.8	12.3	14.6	Jazz	5.2	4.0	3.3
Sex: Male	57.2	54.6	52.8	Gospel	2.4	2.7	3.1
Female	42.8	45.4	47.2	Soundtracks	1.0	0.9	0.8
Sales outlet:				Children's	0.4	0.5	0.3
Record store	71.5	62.1	59.1	Other	7.9	7.8	7.2

NA Not available.   [1] Percent distributions exclude nonresponses and responses of don't know.   [2] As classified by respondent.

Source: Recording Industry Association of America, Inc., Washington, DC, *Inside the Recording Industry: A Statistical Overview: 1993*, and earlier issues.

No. 409. Profile of Adults Living in Cable and Non-Cable TV Households: 1993-94

[Based on survey and subject to sampling error]

CHARACTERIATIC	ALL ADULTS	CABLE TV STATUS			
		No cable	Any cable		
			Total	Basic cable only	Pay cable
Total (mil.)	187.7	69.1	118.6	66.7	51.9
PERCENT DISTRIBUTION					
Age: 18 to 34 years old	36	37	36	33	40
35 to 54 years old	36	33	37	32	42
55 years old and over	28	30	27	35	18
Household income:					
Under $20,000	27	36	20	24	15
$20,000 to $39,999	30	32	29	30	27
$40,000 to $59,999	21	17	24	22	27
$60,000 to $74,999	9	7	11	10	12
$75,000 and over	13	8	16	14	19

Source: Media Dynamics, Inc. New York, NY, *TV Dimensions '95*. Based on data from Mediamark Research, Inc., (copyright).

No. 410. Household Participation in Lawn and Garden Activities: 1989 to 1993

[Based on national household sample survey conducted by the Gallup Organization. Subject to sampling variability; see source]

ACTIVITY	PERCENT HOUSEHOLDS ENGAGED IN					RETAIL SALES (mil. dol.)				
	1989	1990	1991	1992	1993	1989	1990	1991	1992	1993
Total	75	80	78	75	71	16,285	20,802	22,134	22,824	22,410
Lawn care	57	66	62	54	54	5,660	6,412	6,890	7,460	6,446
Indoor houseplants	37	43	42	34	31	822	928	852	926	689
Flower gardening	41	48	41	39	39	1,857	2,275	2,302	2,167	2,396
Insect control	29	39	35	27	24	1,052	1,370	1,260	1,593	1,080
Shrub care	29	38	32	27	28	844	1,099	1,030	1,437	1,274
Vegetable gardening	32	37	31	31	26	1,026	1,384	1,652	1,440	1,063
Tree care	23	31	27	20	21	886	1,445	1,443	1,664	2,011
Landscaping	22	31	26	22	24	2,605	3,837	4,828	4,444	5,006
Flower bulbs	23	31	26	23	22	478	579	520	503	453
Fruit trees	14	19	15	13	13	287	502	371	350	759
Container gardening	11	15	13	9	11	240	359	330	239	441
Raising transplants [1]	11	15	12	8	10	139	181	141	169	201
Herb gardening	7	9	9	7	8	58	84	161	135	175
Growing berries	7	9	7	6	6	73	79	90	62	126
Ornamental gardening	5	7	7	5	6	266	268	264	235	290

[1] Starting plants in advance of planting in ground.

Source: The National Gardening Association, Burlington, VT, *National Gardening Survey*, annual, (copyright).

No. 411. Sport Fishing and Hunting Licenses—Number and Cost: 1970 to 1993

[In millions, except as indicated. For fiscal years ending in year shown; see text, section 9. See also *Historical Statistics, Colonial Times to 1970,* series H 875-876]

ITEM	1970	1975	1980	1985	1988	1989	1990	1991	1992	1993
Fishing licenses: Sales	31.1	34.7	35.2	35.7	36.8	36.6	37.0	37.0	37.4	37.9
Resident.	26.8	30.0	30.1	30.5	31.3	31.0	31.0	31.1	31.4	31.8
Nonresident	4.3	4.7	5.1	5.2	5.5	5.6	6.0	5.9	6.0	6.1
Paid license holders [1]	24.4	27.5	28.0	29.7	31.4	30.3	30.7	30.7	30.6	30.2
Cost to anglers (mil. dol.) . . .	91	142	196	282	330	341	363	375	398	412
Hunting licenses: Sales	22.2	25.9	27.0	27.7	30.0	29.3	30.0	30.7	31.3	31.6
Resident.	21.0	24.7	25.6	26.1	27.7	27.3	27.4	28.5	29.1	29.5
Nonresident	1.2	1.3	1.4	1.6	2.0	2.0	2.3	2.2	2.2	2.0
Paid license holders [1]	15.4	16.6	16.3	15.9	15.9	15.9	15.8	15.7	15.7	15.6
Cost to hunters (mil. dol.) . . .	102	155	222	301	381	400	422	439	481	492
Federal duck stamps sold (1,000)	2,072	2,222	2,090	1,914	1,663	1,395	1,401	1,420	1,330	1,314

[1] Resident and nonresident. Includes multiple counting of license holders who bought nonresident licenses as well as a home State license. "Licenses" includes licenses, tags, permits, and stamps.

Source: U.S. Fish and Wildlife Service, *Federal Aid in Fish and Wildlife Restoration,* annual.

No. 412. Anglers and Hunters: 1991

[**For persons 16 years old and over.** An angler or hunter is anyone who has fished or hunted in 1991. Based on the 1991 National Survey of Fishing, Hunting, and Wildlife-Associated Recreation conducted for the U.S. Fish and Wildlife Service by the U.S. Bureau of the Census]

TYPE OF FISHING	ANGLERS Number (1,000)	ANGLERS Percent of population	Days of fishing [1] (mil.)	Expenditures [2] (mil. dol.)	TYPE OF HUNTING	HUNTERS Number (1,000)	HUNTERS Percent of population	Days of hunting [1] (mil.)	Expenditures [2] (mil. dol.)
All fishing.	[3]35,578	19	[3]511	23,990	**All hunting . . .**	[3]14,063	7	[3]236	12,336
All freshwater fishing .	[3]31,041	16	[3]440	15,149	Big game	10,745	6	128	5,090
Freshwater, except .					Small game	7,642	4	77	1,550
Great Lakes.	30,186	16	431	13,812	Migratory birds . .	3,009	2	22	686
Great Lakes	2,552	1	25	1,337	Other animals . . .	1,411	1	19	255
Saltwater	8,885	5	75	4,992					

[1] Any part of a day constitutes a day.   [2] Totals include expenditures for equipment, trips, magazines, membership dues, contributions, land leasing and ownership, licenses, stamps, tags, and other expenditures. Figures by type of fishing and hunting include only expenditures for trips and equipment.   [3] Includes duplication for persons who participate in more than one category.

Source: U.S. Fish and Wildlife Service, *1991 National Survey of Fishing, Hunting, and Wildlife-Associated Recreation.*

No. 413. Participation in Various Leisure Activities: 1992

[**In percent, except as indicated.** Covers activities engaged in at least once in the prior 12 months. See headnote, table 421. See also table 422]

ITEM	Adult population (mil.)	ATTENDANCE AT— Movies	ATTENDANCE AT— Sports events	ATTENDANCE AT— Amusement park	PARTICIPATION IN— Exercise program	PARTICIPATION IN— Playing sports	PARTICIPATION IN— Outdoor activities [1]	PARTICIPATION IN— Home improvement/repair	PARTICIPATION IN— Gardening
Total.	**185.8**	**59**	**37**	**50**	**60**	**39**	**34**	**48**	**55**
Sex: Male	89.0	60	44	51	61	50	39	53	46
Female	96.8	59	30	50	59	29	29	42	62
Race: White	158.8	60	38	51	61	40	37	50	57
Black	21.1	54	32	45	51	32	10	32	39
Other	5.9	62	20	46	51	38	28	31	42
Age: 18 to 24 years old	24.1	82	51	68	67	59	43	33	31
25 to 34 years old	42.4	70	47	68	67	52	41	47	51
35 to 44 years old	39.8	68	43	58	62	44	42	58	57
45 to 54 years old	27.7	58	35	44	62	34	36	57	64
55 to 64 years old	21.2	40	23	30	56	21	21	53	63
65 to 74 years old	18.3	34	20	29	50	18	21	42	63
75 to 96 years old	12.3	19	7	14	34	7	5	20	55
Education: Grade school	14.3	16	9	24	24	10	11	24	44
Some high school	18.6	35	19	35	39	18	21	34	50
High school graduate.	69.4	54	33	51	55	34	31	47	53
Some college	39.2	21	45	59	71	49	42	53	55
College graduate	26.2	77	51	58	75	55	42	52	61
Graduate school	18.1	81	51	54	79	57	51	65	65

[1] Camping, hiking, and canoeing.

Source: U.S. National Endowment for the Arts, *Arts Participation in America: 1982 to 1992.*

No. 414. Selected Spectator Sports: 1985 to 1993

[See also *Historical Statistics, Colonial Times to 1970*, series H 865-870 and H 872]

SPORT	Unit	1985	1987	1988	1989	1990	1991	1992	1993
Baseball, major leagues: [1]									
Attendance	1,000 . .	47,742	53,182	53,800	55,910	55,512	57,820	56,852	71,237
Regular season	1,000 . .	46,824	52,011	52,999	55,173	54,824	56,814	55,873	70,257
National League	1,000 . .	22,292	24,734	24,499	25,324	24,492	24,696	24,113	36,924
American League	1,000 . .	24,532	27,277	28,500	29,849	30,332	32,118	31,760	33,333
Playoffs	1,000 . .	591	784	541	514	479	633	668	636
World Series	1,000 . .	327	387	260	223	209	373	311	344
Players' salaries: [2]									
Average	$1,000 .	371	412	439	497	598	851	1,029	1,076
Basketball: [3] [4]									
NCAA—Men's college:									
Teams	Number.	753	760	761	772	767	796	813	831
Attendance	1,000 . .	26,584	26,798	27,453	28,270	28,741	29,250	29,378	28,527
NCAA—Women's college:									
Teams	Number.	746	756	754	765	782	806	815	826
Attendance	1,000 . .	2,072	2,156	2,325	2,502	2,777	3,013	3,397	4,193
Pro: [5]									
Teams	Number.	23	23	23	25	27	27	27	27
Attendance, total [6]	1,000 . .	11,534	13,190	14,070	16,586	18,586	18,009	18,609	19,120
Regular season	1,000 . .	10,506	12,065	12,654	15,465	17,369	16,876	17,367	17,778
Average per game	Number.	11,141	12,795	13,419	15,088	15,690	15,245	15,689	16,060
Playoffs	1,000 . .	985	1,091	1,397	1,077	1,203	1,109	1,228	1,322
Players' salaries:									
Average	$1,000 .	325	440	510	603	817	989	1,202	1,348
Football:									
NCAA college: [4]									
Teams	Number.	509	507	524	524	533	548	552	560
Attendance	1,000 . .	34,952	35,008	34,324	35,116	35,330	35,528	35,225	34,871
National Football League: [7]									
Teams	Number.	28	28	28	28	28	28	28	28
Attendance, total [8]	1,000 . .	14,058	[9]15,180	17,024	17,400	17,666	17,752	17,784	14,772
Regular season	1,000 . .	13,345	[9]11,406	13,539	13,626	13,960	13,841	13,829	13,967
Average per game	Number.	59,567	[9]54,315	60,446	60,829	62,321	61,792	61,736	62,352
Postseason games [10]	1,000 . .	711	656	658	686	848	813	815	805
Players' salaries: [11]									
Average	$1,000 .	194	203	239	295	352	415	645	636
Median base salary	$1,000 .	140	175	180	200	236	250	325	330
National Hockey League: [12]									
Regular season attendance . . .	1,000 . .	11,621	12,118	12,418	12,580	12,344	12,770	14,158	16,106
Playoffs attendance	1,000 . .	1,153	1,337	1,327	1,356	1,442	1,328	1,346	1,440
Horseracing: [13] [14]									
Racing days	Number.	13,745	14,208	14,285	14,240	13,841	(NA)	13,644	(NA)
Attendance	1,000 . .	73,346	70,105	69,949	69,551	63,803	(NA)	49,275	(NA)
Pari-mutuel turnover	Mil. dol .	12,222	13,122	13,616	13,867	7,162	14,094	14,078	(NA)
Revenue to government	Mil. dol .	625	608	596	585	611	624	491.3	(NA)
Greyhound: [13]									
Total performances	Number.	9,590	11,156	12,904	13,393	14,915	(NA)	17,528	(NA)
Attendance	1,000 . .	23,853	26,215	26,477	33,818	28,660	(NA)	28,003	(NA)
Pari-mutuel turnover	Mil. dol .	2,702	3,193	3,291	3,278	3,422	3,422	3,306	(NA)
Revenue to government	Mil. dol .	201	221	230	239	235	(NA)	204.2	(NA)
Jai alai: [13]									
Total performances	Number.	2,736	2,906	3,615	3,835	3,620	3,619	3,288	(NA)
Games played	Number.	32,260	38,476	47,716	(NA)	(NA)	(NA)	45,067	(NA)
Attendance	1,000 . .	4,722	6,816	6,414	5,227	5,329	(NA)	4,634	(NA)
Pari-mutuel turnover	Mil. dol .	664.0	707.5	663.6	553.0	545.5	(NA)	425.9	(NA)
Revenue to government	Mil. dol .	50	51	44	39	39	39	30.1	(NA)
Professional rodeo: [15]									
Rodeos	Number.	617	637	707	741	754	798	791	782
Performances	Number.	1,887	1,832	2,037	2,128	2,159	2,241	2,269	2,245
Members	Number.	5,239	5,342	5,479	5,560	5,693	5,748	5,760	6,415
Permit-holders (rookies)	Number.	2,534	2,746	3,310	3,584	3,290	3,006	2,888	3,346

NA Not available. [1] Source: The National League of Professional Baseball Clubs, New York, NY, *National League Green Book;* and The American League of Professional Baseball Clubs, New York, NY, *American League Red Book.* [2] Source: Major League Baseball Players Association, New York, NY. [3] Season ending in year shown. [4] Source: National Collegiate Athletic Assn., Overland Park, KS. For women's attendance total, excludes double-headers with men's teams. [5] Source: National Basketball Assn., New York, NY. [6] Includes All-Star game, not shown separately. [7] Source: National Football League, New York, NY. [8] 1987 through 1992 includes preseason attendance, not shown separately. [9] Season was interrupted by a strike. [10] Includes Pro Bowl, a nonchampionship game and Super Bowl. [11] Source: National Football League Players Association, Washington, DC. [12] For season beginning in year shown. Source: National Hockey League, Montreal, Quebec. [13] Source: Association of Racing Commissioners International, Inc., Lexington, KY. [14] Includes thoroughbred, harness, quarter horse, and fairs. [15] Source: Professional Rodeo Cowboys Association, Colorado Springs, CO., *Official Professional Rodeo Media Guide,* annual, (copyright).

Source: Compiled from sources listed in footnotes.

No. 415. Selected Recreational Activities: 1975 to 1993

[See also *Historical Statistics, Colonial Times to 1970,* series H 862-864, H 871, H 874, and H 877]

ACTIVITY	Unit	1975	1980	1985	1989	1990	1991	1992	1993
Softball, amateur: [1]									
Total participants [2]	Million. .	26	30	41	41	41	41	41	42
Youth participants	1,000 . .	450	650	712	900	1,100	1,205	1,207	1,208
Adult teams [3]	1,000 . .	66	110	152	188	188	200	202	202
Youth teams [3]	1,000 . .	9	18	31	46	46	51	57	62
Golfers (one round or more) [4][5]	1,000 . .	13,036	15,112	17,520	24,200	27,800	24,800	24,800	24,600
Golf rounds played [5]	1,000 . .	308,562	357,701	414,777	469,000	502,000	479,000	505,400	498,600
Golf facilities	Number.	11,370	12,005	12,346	12,658	12,846	13,004	13,210	13,439
Classification:									
Private	Number.	4,770	4,839	4,861	4,862	4,810	4,686	4,568	4,492
Daily fee	Number.	5,014	5,372	5,573	5,833	6,024	6,272	6,552	6,803
Municipal	Number.	1,586	1,794	1,912	1,963	2,012	2,046	2,090	2,144
Tennis: [6]									
Players	1,000 . .	[7]34,000	(NA)	13,000	(NA)	21,000	(NA)	22,630	22,000
Courts	1,000 . .	130	(NA)	220	220	220	230	230	230
Indoor	1,000 . .	8	(NA)	14	14	14	14	14	14
Tenpin bowling:									
Participants, total [8]	Million. .	62.5	72.0	67.0	71.0	71.0	82.0	82.0	79.0
Male	Million. .	29.9	34.0	32.0	35.4	35.4	40.2	40.2	36.3
Female	Million. .	32.6	38.0	35.0	35.6	35.6	41.8	41.8	42.6
Establishments [9]	Number.	8,577	8,591	8,275	7,671	7,544	7,395	7,250	7,183
Lanes [9]	1,000 . .	141	154	155	147	146	144	143	142
Membership, total [9][10]	1,000 . .	8,751	9,595	8,064	6,570	6,357	5,881	5,601	5,202
American Bowling Congress	1,000 . .	4,300	4,688	3,657	3,036	2,922	2,712	2,577	2,455
Women's Bowling Congress	1,000 . .	3,692	4,118	3,714	2,859	2,742	2,523	2,403	2,191
Young American Bowling Alliance [11]	1,000 . .	759	789	693	675	693	646	621	556
Motion picture theaters [12][13]	1,000 . .	15	18	21	23	24	25	26	26
Four-wall	1,000 . .	11	14	18	22	23	24	25	25
Drive-in	1,000 . .	4	4	3	1	1	1	1	1
Receipts, box office	Mil. dol..	2,115	2,749	3,749	5,033	5,022	4,803	4,871	5,154
Admission, average price	Dollars	2.05	2.69	3.55	3.99	4.23	4.21	4.15	4.14
Attendance	Million. .	1,033	1,022	1,056	1,263	1,187	1,141	1,173	1,244
Bicycles: [14]									
Domestic shipments	Million. .	5.6	6.9	5.8	5.3	6.0	7.3	7.4	8.0
Imports	Million. .	1.7	2.0	5.6	5.4	4.8	4.4	4.3	5.0
Boating: [15]									
Recreational boats owned	Million. .	9.7	11.8	13.8	15.6	16.0	16.3	16.2	16.5
Outboard boats	Million. .	5.7	6.8	7.4	7.9	7.9	7.9	7.7	7.8
Inboard boats	Million. .	0.8	1.2	1.4	2.0	2.2	2.4	2.5	2.6
Sailboats	Million. .	0.8	1.0	1.2	1.3	1.3	1.3	1.3	1.3
Canoes	Million. .	2.4	1.3	1.8	2.2	2.3	2.4	2.4	2.4
Rowboats and other	Million. .	([16])	1.5	1.8	2.1	2.3	2.3	2.3	2.4
Expenditures, total [17]	Bil. dol.	4.8	7.4	13.3	17.1	13.7	10.6	10.3	11.3
Outboard motors in use	1,000 . .	7,649	8,241	9,733	11,225	11,524	11,769	12,000	12,240
Motors sold	1,000 . .	435	315	392	430	352	289	272	283
Value, retail	Mil. dol.	411	554	1,319	1,764	1,546	1,311	1,268	1,364
Outboard boats sold	1,000 . .	328	290	305	291	227	195	192	205
Value, retail	Mil. dol.	263	408	759	1,134	978	871	839	914
Inboard/outdrive boats sold	1,000 . .	70	56	115	133	97	73	75	75
Value, retail	Mil. dol.	420	616	1,663	2,354	1,794	1,293	1,239	1,244
Inboard cruisers sold	1,000 . .	6.5	5.3	12.2	12.3	7.5	3.6	3.5	3.4
Value, retail	Mil. dol.	256	457	1,341	1,909	1,383	668	621	655

NA Not available.   [1] Source: Amateur Softball Association, Oklahoma City, OK.   [2] Amateur Softball Association teams and other amateur softball teams.   [3] Amateur Softball Association teams only.   [4] Source: National Golf Foundation, Jupiter, FL. [5] Prior to 1986, for persons 5 years of age and over; thereafter for persons 12 years of age and over.   [6] Source: U.S. Tennis Association, White Plains, NY. Players for persons 12 years old and over who played at least once.   [7] 1974 data.   [8] For season ending in year shown. Persons 5 years old and over. Source: National Bowling Council, Arlington, VA.   [9] Source: American Bowling Congress, Greendale, WI. Season ending in year shown.   [10] Membership totals are for U.S., Canada and for U.S. military personnel worldwide.   [11] Prior to 1985, represents American Jr. Bowling Congress and ABC/WIBC Collegiate Division. [12] Source: Motion Picture Association of America, Inc., Encino, CA.   [13] Prior to 1975, figures represent theaters; thereafter, screens.   [14] Source: Bicycle Manufacturers Association of America, Inc., Washington, DC.   [15] Source: National Marine Manufacturers Association, Chicago, IL.   [16] Included in canoes.   [17] Represents estimated expenditures for new and used boats, motors, accessories, safety equipment, fuel, insurance, docking, maintenance, storage, repairs, and other expenses.

Source: Compiled from sources listed in footnotes.

Parks, Recreation, and Travel

No. 416. Participation in Selected Sports Activities: 1993

[In thousands, except rank. For persons 7 years of age or older. Except as indicated, a participant plays a sport more than once in the year. Based on a sampling of 10,000 households]

ACTIVITY	ALL PERSONS		SEX		AGE								HOUSEHOLD INCOME (dol.)					
	Number	Rank	Male	Female	7-11 years	12-17 years	18-24 years	25-34 years	35-44 years	45-54 years	55-64 years	65 years and over	Under 15,000	15,000-24,999	25,000-34,999	35,000-49,999	50,000-74,999	75,000 and over
Total	**230,406**	(X)	**111,851**	**118,555**	**18,561**	**21,304**	**25,650**	**41,808**	**40,761**	**28,644**	**20,922**	**32,758**	**45,150**	**36,221**	**33,971**	**43,701**	**46,189**	**25,175**
Number participated in:																		
Aerobic exercising [1]	24,386	9	3,527	21,359	647	1,837	4,852	7,514	4,996	2,610	1,181	1,250	3,172	3,092	3,692	5,012	6,299	3,618
Backpacking [2]	9,229	24	6,196	3,033	779	1,280	1,501	2,477	2,067	850	170	104	1,424	1,291	1,207	1,817	2,174	1,316
Baseball	16,682	16	13,451	3,232	5,422	5,283	1,834	1,724	1,658	511	87	164	2,499	2,001	2,440	3,832	4,070	1,840
Basketball	29,631	8	21,332	8,299	5,751	9,361	5,305	4,766	3,257	857	146	189	4,163	3,750	4,935	6,254	6,963	3,566
Bicycle riding [1]	47,918	3	24,562	23,357	11,204	8,794	4,551	8,808	6,980	3,441	2,030	2,111	6,897	6,449	6,685	10,606	10,393	6,888
Bowling	41,305	6	20,714	20,591	3,890	5,039	7,222	9,484	7,625	3,919	1,716	2,410	6,684	6,207	6,487	8,498	9,084	4,346
Calisthenics [1]	10,800	21	4,571	6,230	1,132	2,024	1,508	1,824	1,712	1,099	657	844	1,698	1,202	1,422	2,319	2,540	1,619
Camping [3]	42,698	5	23,165	19,533	5,302	5,336	4,767	10,000	8,580	4,135	2,355	2,224	7,182	7,275	6,277	9,338	8,452	4,175
Exercise walking [1]	64,427	1	21,054	43,373	1,848	2,816	5,690	12,525	14,045	10,185	7,782	9,536	10,491	9,802	9,807	12,325	13,593	8,409
Exercising with equipment [1]	34,900	7	16,901	17,999	425	3,025	6,595	9,105	7,065	4,257	2,217	2,210	3,915	3,948	4,639	7,305	9,412	5,681
Fishing—fresh water	45,333	4	30,449	14,885	4,623	4,945	4,946	9,913	9,561	5,044	3,156	3,146	8,891	7,190	7,158	9,470	9,251	3,373
Fishing—salt water	12,079	20	8,337	3,743	938	882	1,358	2,276	2,593	1,603	1,251	1,178	2,182	2,002	1,344	2,286	2,833	1,432
Football	14,723	17	12,879	1,843	2,495	5,227	3,410	2,203	1,032	202	94	60	2,457	2,295	2,263	2,813	3,105	1,790
Golf	22,633	10	17,212	5,421	840	1,692	3,074	5,192	4,620	3,180	1,956	2,080	1,439	1,925	2,668	4,159	7,342	5,100
Hiking	19,462	13	10,741	8,721	1,851	2,439	2,224	4,604	4,358	1,873	1,035	1,078	2,717	2,964	2,884	3,530	4,314	3,052
Hunting with firearms	18,455	14	16,303	2,152	540	1,695	2,575	4,658	4,282	2,380	1,311	1,014	3,234	2,814	3,555	3,939	3,473	1,440
Racquetball	5,407	25	4,161	1,246	162	550	1,704	1,590	936	380	71	15	705	597	595	1,197	1,592	722
Running/jogging [1]	20,283	12	11,429	8,854	1,727	4,008	4,088	4,393	3,489	1,566	680	331	2,795	2,364	2,506	4,047	5,104	3,468
Skiing—alpine/downhill	10,495	22	6,462	4,033	453	1,549	2,766	2,807	1,698	921	230	70	552	734	930	1,763	3,365	3,150
Skiing—cross country	3,727	26	1,738	1,989	298	469	273	530	1,084	580	314	179	291	317	463	718	1,064	874
Soccer	10,273	23	6,509	3,764	4,543	3,063	889	839	626	254	51	9	1,247	925	1,126	2,387	2,927	1,661
Softball [1]	17,943	15	10,426	7,517	2,886	3,817	3,101	4,446	2,813	532	191	157	2,173	2,335	2,758	3,789	4,530	2,358
Swimming [1]	61,353	2	27,713	33,640	10,507	10,874	7,860	11,293	10,075	4,941	2,756	3,047	8,545	7,936	8,817	13,054	14,284	8,717
Target shooting	12,804	19	10,195	2,609	746	1,640	2,057	3,288	2,723	1,345	546	459	2,086	1,916	2,175	2,877	2,283	1,468
Tennis	14,197	18	8,302	5,896	1,003	2,464	3,375	3,076	2,357	1,091	558	274	1,669	1,390	1,752	2,586	3,758	3,043
Volleyball	20,477	11	9,777	10,700	1,333	5,443	4,402	4,961	3,150	823	252	112	2,890	2,500	3,226	4,289	5,036	2,536

X Not applicable. [1] Participant engaged in activity at least six times in the year. [2] Includes wilderness camping. [3] Vacation/overnight.

Source: National Sporting Goods Association, Mt. Prospect, IL, Sports Participation in 1993: Series I (copyright).

No. 417. Sporting Goods Sales, by Product Category: 1980 to 1994

[In millions of dollars, except percent. Based on a sample survey of consumer purchases of 80,000 households, except recreational transport, which was provided by industry associations. Excludes Alaska and Hawaii]

SELECTED PRODUCT CATEGORY	1980	1985	1987	1988	1989	1990	1991	1992	1993	1994, proj.
Sales, all products	16,691	27,446	33,942	42,093	45,184	44,111	42,943	42,434	44,107	46,150
Annual percent change [1]	−1.4	4.0	10.9	24.0	7.3	−2.4	−2.6	−1.2	3.9	4.6
Percent of retail sales	1.7	2.0	2.2	2.5	2.6	2.4	2.3	2.2	2.1	2.1
Athletic and sport clothing [2]	3,127	3,376	4,645	10,736	11,557	11,382	12,057	10,101	9,643	9,952
Athletic and sport footwear [3]	1,731	2,610	3,524	3,772	5,763	6,263	6,300	6,242	5,919	6,019
Walking shoes	(NA)	263	512	752	1,237	1,509	1,375	1,375	1,367	1,408
Gym shoes, sneakers	465	656	693	783	1,125	1,177	1,181	1,113	936	936
Jogging and running shoes	397	572	475	460	515	519	555	574	574	551
Tennis shoes	359	470	367	353	508	582	597	589	471	462
Aerobic shoes	(NA)	178	401	327	425	389	381	376	318	305
Basketball shoes	86	185	169	226	293	428	449	456	407	407
Golf shoes	68	109	130	128	129	157	173	182	192	202
Athletic and sport equipment [3]	6,487	8,922	9,900	10,705	11,503	11,965	12,063	12,816	13,460	14,449
Firearms and hunting	1,351	1,699	1,804	1,894	2,139	2,202	2,091	2,533	2,565	3,027
Exercise equipment	(NA)	1,216	1,191	1,452	1,748	1,824	2,106	2,050	2,498	2,697
Golf	386	730	946	1,111	1,167	1,219	1,149	1,338	1,255	1,330
Camping	646	724	858	945	996	1,072	1,006	903	908	927
Bicycles (10-12-15-18+ speed)	(NA)	975	930	819	906	1,092	(NA)	(NA)	(NA)	(NA)
Fishing tackle	539	681	830	766	769	776	711	678	708	715
Snow skiing	379	593	661	710	606	606	577	627	629	677
Tennis	237	273	238	264	315	287	295	296	189	191
Archery	149	212	224	235	261	265	270	334	285	294
Baseball and softball	158	176	173	174	206	217	214	245	303	309
Water skis	123	125	148	160	96	88	63	55	51	51
Bowling accessories	107	106	129	129	143	155	155	164	159	156
Recreational transport	5,345	12,539	15,873	16,880	16,360	14,502	12,524	13,275	15,085	15,730
Pleasure boats	2,718	6,753	8,906	9,637	9,319	7,644	5,862	5,765	6,282	6,722
Recreational vehicles	1,178	3,515	4,507	4,839	4,481	4,113	3,615	4,412	4,775	4,838
Bicycles and supplies	1,233	2,109	2,272	2,131	2,259	2,423	2,686	2,723	3,534	3,640
Snowmobiles	216	162	188	273	301	322	362	376	495	530

NA Not available. [1] Represents change from immediate prior year. [2] Category expanded in 1988; not comparable with earlier years. [3] Includes other products not shown separately.

Source: National Sporting Goods Association, Mt. Prospect, IL, *The Sporting Goods Market in 1994*; and prior issues (copyright).

No. 418. Consumer Purchases of Sporting Goods, by Consumer Characteristics: 1993

[In percent. Based on sample survey of consumer purchases of 80,000 households. Excludes Alaska and Hawaii]

CHARACTERISTIC	Total households	FOOTWEAR				EQUIPMENT					
		Aerobic shoes	Gym shoes/ sneakers	Jogging/ running shoes	Walking shoes	Fishing tackle	Camping equipment	Exercise equipment	Hunting equipment	Team sports equipment guns	Golf equipment
Total	100.0	100.0	100.0	100.0	100.0	100.0	100.0	100.0	100.0	100.0	100.0
Age of user:											
Under 14 years old	21	6	40	11	13	6	15	-	5	60	2
14 to 17 years old	5	7	13	11	4	1	8	3	2	17	1
18 to 24 years old	10	9	5	10	4	5	10	6	11	5	5
25 to 34 years old	16	28	12	19	9	21	25	25	35	10	27
35 to 44 years old	16	20	9	24	13	28	20	26	19	6	20
45 to 64 years old	19	21	16	19	35	30	14	31	27	2	31
65 years old and over	13	9	5	5	22	5	2	7	2	-	14
Multiple ages	-	-	-	-	-	5	7	2	1	-	-
Sex of user:											
Male	49	14	48	60	37	81	67	44	91	87	80
Female	51	86	52	40	63	13	26	53	8	12	20
Both sexes	-	-	-	-	-	5	7	3	1	-	-
Education of household head:											
Less than high school	10	2	10	8	7	7	5	6	8	5	3
High school	27	15	21	18	25	29	22	19	28	29	15
Some college	27	37	39	28	35	40	36	33	44	29	31
College graduate	36	47	30	46	33	24	37	41	20	36	51
Annual household income:											
Under $15,000	22	11	16	13	20	9	10	7	8	13	2
$15,000 to $24,999	17	14	16	17	18	12	13	10	11	15	8
$25,000 to $34,999	15	11	14	10	12	15	15	12	18	18	8
$35,000 to $49,999	18	25	17	16	20	23	21	20	24	13	20
$50,000 to $74,999	17	24	22	22	17	21	26	27	29	24	26
$75,000 and over	11	16	16	21	13	20	15	24	10	16	36

- Represents or rounds to zero.

Source: National Sporting Goods Association, Mt. Prospect, IL, *The Sporting Goods Market in 1994* (copyright).

No. 419. Gun Ownership: 1974 to 1993

[**In percent.** For the 50 States and DC, except prior to 1984 excludes Alaska and Hawaii. Represents respondents indicating there is a gun in the home or garage. Based on samples of noninstitutionalized English speaking persons 18 years old and older. For details, see source]

CHARACTERISTIC	1974	1976	1980	1984	1987	1990	1991	TYPE OF FIREARM, 1993			
								Total [1]	Pistol	Shotgun	Rifle
Total	46	47	48	45	46	43	40	42	24	27	23
Age:											
18 to 20 years old	34	38	48	44	43	40	22	48	21	34	21
21 to 29 years old	48	45	48	37	35	34	36	38	21	23	17
30 to 49 years old	49	52	50	48	51	46	40	44	27	27	24
50 years old and older . .	44	44	46	49	47	42	42	42	22	28	25
Sex:											
Male	51	52	56	53	51	53	50	53	28	38	31
Female	42	43	41	40	43	34	32	34	20	19	17
Race:											
White.	48	58	50	48	49	45	42	45	25	29	26
Black/other	32	37	29	30	33	29	29	26	17	14	9
Education:											
Grade school	49	42	51	43	44	47	39	47	18	30	27
High school.	48	50	51	48	50	47	46	46	25	32	27
College	42	44	41	42	43	37	34	38	24	22	20
Religion:											
Protestant.	52	53	56	52	·52	48	46	47	27	31	26
Catholic	37	36	36	34	36	36	30	36	17	23	20
Jewish	7	26	6	22	25	6	10	9	-	4	4
None	40	43	39	36	39	34	31	37	24	17	20
Politics:											
Republican	49	50	53	56	51	48	42	51	29	34	28
Democrat	45	45	46	42	44	40	41	35	18	21	17
Independent	47	48	47	40	44	42	37	42	26	28	25

- Represents or rounds to zero.   [1] Includes other types of firearms, not shown separately.

Source: U.S. Bureau of Justice Statistics, *Sourcebook of Criminal Justice Statistics*, annual.

No. 420. Arts and Humanities—Selected Federal Aid Programs: 1980 to 1993

[**In millions of dollars, except as indicated. For fiscal years ending in year shown,** see text, section 9]

TYPE OF FUND AND PROGRAM	1980	1985	1987	1988	1989	1990	1991	1992	1993
National Endowment for the Arts:									
Funds available [1]	188.1	171.7	170.9	171.1	166.7	170.8	166.5	163.0	159.7
Program appropriation	97.0	118.7	120.8	122.2	123.5	124.3	124.6	123.0	120.0
Matching funds [2]	42.9	29.5	29.3	32.9	23.6	32.4	32.4	30.3	27.4
Grants awarded (number).	5,505	4,801	4,542	4,628	4,604	4,475	4,239	4,229	4,096
Funds obligated	166.4	149.4	151.4	156.3	148.3	157.6	158.0	154.6	148.4
Music.	13.6	15.3	15.1	15.3	15.3	16.5	14.1	14.9	12.4
State programs	22.1	24.4	24.6	24.9	25.5	26.1	37.7	37.0	42.0
Museums	11.2	11.9	11.5	12.6	12.7	12.1	11.3	11.1	9.9
Theater	8.4	10.6	10.8	10.7	10.7	10.6	9.4	9.4	8.3
Dance	8.0	9.0	9.1	9.2	9.5	9.6	8.5	8.2	7.9
Media arts	8.4	9.9	12.9	12.4	12.7	13.9	11.8	12.0	10.2
Challenge [3]	50.8	20.7	20.8	24.8	15.4	19.7	19.7	13.8	11.7
Visual arts.	7.3	6.2	6.2	6.0	6.1	5.9	5.3	5.6	5.1
Other.	36.6	41.3	40.4	40.4	40.2	43.1	40.2	42.7	40.9
National Endowment for the Humanities:									
Funds available [1]	186.2	125.6	128.4	125.2	137.1	140.6	152.1	156.5	158.5
Program appropriation	100.3	95.2	[4]95.8	96.7	108.3	114.2	125.1	131.2	131.9
Matching funds [2]	38.4	30.4	28.5	28.5	28.7	26.3	27.0	25.2	26.5
Grants awarded (number).	2,917	2,241	2,888	2,113	2,285	2,195	2,171	2,199	2,197
Funds obligated	185.5	125.7	128.4	125.2	137.1	141.0	149.8	159.1	160.3
Education programs	18.3	17.9	16.4	16.6	16.5	16.3	18.5	20.0	20.8
State programs	26.0	24.4	25.0	25.3	29.0	29.6	30.8	31.8	32.4
Research grants	32.0	24.4	21.7	21.9	22.1	22.5	24.0	25.3	23.7
Fellowship program	18.0	15.3	15.3	15.3	15.3	15.3	16.2	17.4	18.9
Challenge [3]	53.5	19.6	16.5	16.5	16.7	14.6	15.1	12.4	14.2
Public programs.	25.1	24.1	25.4	24.9	25.1	25.4	25.3	27.0	26.7
Preservation and access [5]	(X)	(X)	4.1	4.7	12.3	17.5	19.9	25.1	23.5
National Capital Arts and Cultural									
Affairs Program	(X)	(X)	4.0	(X)	(X)	(X)	(X)	(X)	(X)
Other.	12.6	(X)	(X)	(X)	(X)	(X)	(X)	(X)	(X)

X Not applicable.   [1] Includes other funds, shown separately. Excludes administrative funds. Gifts are included through 1980; excluded thereafter.   [2] Represents Federal funds appropriated only upon receipt or certification by Endowment of matching non-Federal gifts.   [3] Program designed to stimulate new sources and higher levels of giving to institutions for the purpose of guaranteeing long-term stability and financial independence. Program requires a match of at least 3 private dollars to each Federal dollar. Funds for challenge grants are not allocated by program area because they are awarded on a grant-by-grant basis.   [4] Excludes National Capital Arts and Cultural Affairs Program.   [5] Program designed to support projects which preserve and guarantee access to print and nonprint media in danger of disintegration or deterioration.

Source: U.S. National Endowment for the Arts, *Annual Report;* and U.S. National Endowment for the Humanities, *Annual Report.*

No. 421. Attendance Rates for Various Arts Activities: 1992

[In percent. For persons 18 years old and over. Excludes elementary and high school performances. Based on 1992 household survey Public Participation in the Arts conducted January through December 1992. Data are subject to sampling error; see source. See also tables 413 and 422]

ITEM	ATTENDANCE AT LEAST ONCE IN THE PRIOR 12 MONTHS AT—								Reading litera-ture[1]
	Jazz perfor-mance	Classical music perfor-mance	Opera	Musical play	Non-musical play	Ballet	Art museum	Historic park	
Total	11	13	3	17	14	5	27	35	54
Sex: Male	12	12	3	15	12	4	27	35	47
Female	9	13	4	20	15	6	27	34	60
Race: White	10	13	3	18	14	5	28	37	56
Black	16	7	2	14	12	3	19	18	45
Other	6	12	5	11	10	6	29	23	42
Age: 18 to 24 years old	11	10	3	16	13	5	29	33	53
25 to 34 years old	14	10	3	16	12	5	29	36	54
35 to 44 years old	13	12	3	19	14	5	30	40	59
45 to 54 years old	11	17	4	22	17	5	29	41	57
55 to 64 years old	8	15	4	19	15	5	25	33	53
65 to 74 years old	7	14	4	17	13	4	20	29	50
75 to 96 years old	2	8	2	9	7	2	10	12	40
Education: Grade school	1	2	1	3	2	1	4	8	17
Some high school	2	3	1	5	4	1	7	15	32
High school graduate	6	7	1	12	8	2	16	26	49
Some college	14	14	3	21	16	6	35	43	65
College graduate	20	23	6	30	23	9	46	52	71
Graduate school	25	36	12	37	35	12	59	64	79
Income: Under $5,000	6	5	2	8	8	2	12	17	37
$5,000 to $9,999	5	6	1	7	6	3	14	16	40
$10,000 to $14,999	5	6	2	8	7	2	13	20	43
$15,000 to $24,999	9	11	2	14	11	3	23	31	50
$25,000 to $49,999	11	13	3	18	14	5	29	40	58
$50,000 and over	18	23	8	33	24	10	44	51	71
Not reported	11	13	4	18	15	5	28	33	50

[1] Includes novels, short stories, poetry, or plays.

Source: U.S. National Endowment for the Arts, *Arts Participation in America: 1982 to 1992.*

No. 422. Participation in Various Arts Activities: 1992

[In percent, except as indicated. Covers activities engaged in at least once in the prior 12 months. See headnote, table 421. See also table 413]

ITEM	Adult popu-lation (mil.)	IN THE PAST 12 MONTHS PERCENT ENGAGED AT LEAST ONCE IN—							
		Playing classical music	Modern danc-ing[1]	Pottery work[2]	Needle-work[3]	Photo-graphy[4]	Paint-ing[5]	Creative writing	Buying art work
Total	185.8	4	8	8	25	12	10	7	22
Sex: Male	89.0	3	8	8	5	13	9	7	22
Female	96.8	5	8	9	43	10	10	8	22
Race: White	158.8	4	8	9	26	12	10	7	24
Black	21.1	3	8	8	15	11	5	6	12
Other	5.9	5	9	5	24	9	10	11	8
Age: 18 to 24 years old	24.1	6	11	9	18	11	19	14	13
25 to 34 years old	42.4	3	10	10	24	15	10	7	19
35 to 44 years old	39.8	4	7	10	25	13	10	8	27
45 to 54 years old	27.7	5	6	9	26	13	8	7	29
55 to 64 years old	21.2	5	6	6	27	10	6	5	26
65 to 74 years old	18.3	4	9	6	29	7	6	5	20
75 to 96 years old	12.3	3	5	3	26	2	4	2	17
Education: Grade school	14.3	1	4	2	22	3	1	(Z)	4
Some high school	18.6	1	4	7	25	5	5	3	11
High school graduate	69.4	2	8	8	25	9	9	4	15
Some college	39.2	6	10	12	26	15	13	11	27
College graduate	26.2	8	8	9	26	16	12	12	32
Graduate school	18.1	9	10	8	21	22	13	16	49
Income: Under $5,000	8.6	2	7	7	22	6	8	7	10
$5,000 to $9,999	15.2	2	7	4	27	7	8	7	10
$10,000 to $14,999	19.2	3	7	8	26	8	8	6	14
$15,000 to $24,999	32.9	4	9	8	26	9	10	7	17
$25,000 to $49,999	62.2	5	8	10	25	13	10	7	22
$50,000 and over	32.1	6	8	8	23	17	11	9	40
Not reported	15.6	4	8	8	24	12	11	9	24

Z Less than .05 percent.   [1] Dancing other than ballet (e.g. folk and tap).   [2] Includes ceramics, jewelry, leatherwork, and metalwork.   [3] Includes weaving, crocheting, quilting, and sewing.   [4] Includes making movies or video as an artistic activity.   [5] Includes drawing, sculpture, and printmaking.

Source: U.S. National Endowment for the Arts, *Arts Participation in America: 1982 to 1992.*

No. 423. Performing Arts—Selected Data: 1980 to 1993

[**Receipts and expenditures in millions of dollars.** For season ending in year shown, except as indicated]

ITEM	1980	1985	1986	1987	1988	1989	1990	1991	1992	1993
Legitimate theater: [1]										
Broadway shows:										
New productions	67	31	33	40	31	29	35	28	36	(NA)
Playing weeks [2][3]	1,541	1,062	1,049	1,031	1,114	1,097	1,062	970	901	(NA)
Number of tickets sold (1,000) .	9,380	7,156	6,527	6,968	8,142	7,968	8,039	7,314	7,365	(NA)
Gross box office receipts	143.4	208.0	190.6	207.2	253.4	262.0	283.3	267.2	292.4	(NA)
Road shows:										
Playing weeks [3]	1,351	993	983	901	893	869	944	1,152	1,171	(NA)
Gross box office receipts	181.2	225.9	235.6	224.2	222.9	255.5	367.1	450.2	502.7	(NA)
Nonprofit professional theatres: [4]										
Companies reporting	147	217	201	188	189	192	185	184	182	177
Gross income	113.6	234.7	263.8	271.2	276.4	349.0	307.6	333.9	359.1	342.5
Earned income	67.3	146.1	160.8	165.2	167.0	224.6	188.4	202.6	222.5	209.7
Contributed income.	46.3	88.6	103.0	106.0	109.4	124.4	119.2	131.3	136.6	132.8
Gross expenses	113.6	239.3	263.3	272.8	277.9	349.2	306.3	336.7	365.6	349.3
Productions	1,852	2,710	2,944	2,427	2,369	2,469	2,265	2,277	2,310	2,319
Performances	42,109	52,341	57,727	46,768	46,149	53,263	46,131	48,695	46,184	44,933
Total attendance (mil.).	14.2	14.2	14.8	14.6	13.9	18.7	15.2	16.9	16.0	16.5
OPERA America professional member companies: [5]										
Number of companies [6]	79	97	100	100	99	101	98	98	100	(NA)
Expenses [6]	122.4	216.4	252.6	260.1	294.4	311.7	321.2	346.7	371.8	(NA)
Performances [7]	1,372	1,909	2,054	2,254	2,378	2,429	2,336	2,283	2,424	(NA)
Total attendance (mil.) [7][8]	5.5	6.7	6.2	6.6	6.8	7.4	7.5	7.6	7.3	(NA)
Main season attendance (mil.) [7][9].	(NA)	3.3	3.4	3.8	3.9	4.0	4.1	4.3	4.3	(NA)
Symphony orchestras: [10]										
Concerts	(NA)	19,573	20,051	19,319	21,306	20,630	18,931	18,074	19,778	18,599
Attendance (mil.)	(NA)	24.0	25.4	24.5	27.4	25.8	24.7	26.7	26.3	24.3
Gross revenue	(NA)	252.4	281.2	306.9	325.3	353.2	377.5	394.5	414.0	429.8
Concert income	(NA)	168.6	184.5	200.4	218.0	231.0	253.3	273.8	284.1	293.4
Endowment income	(NA)	(NA)	(NA)	(NA)	42.6	46.8	52.1	52.5	55.3	59.8
Other earned income	(NA)	83.8	96.7	106.5	64.7	75.4	72.1	68.2	74.6	76.6
Operating expenses	(NA)	426.1	469.7	503.5	541.2	583.5	621.7	662.2	683.0	690.5
Artistic personnel	(NA)	231.9	253.4	270.0	288.0	310.2	327.3	355.8	398.9	378.9
Concert production	(NA)	69.2	71.4	79.5	85.8	89.0	104.3	110.3	117.2	114.3
Advertising and promotion	(NA)	32.5	36.6	40.4	42.0	47.5	51.3	57.3	58.3	63.3
General and administrative. . . .	(NA)	51.3	56.2	59.4	61.5	68.4	73.3	75.6	76.2	73.7
Other	(NA)	41.3	52.2	54.3	63.9	68.4	65.6	63.2	32.4	60.3
Support	(NA)	188.1	202.7	219.5	229.2	249.0	257.8	281.2	279.6	293.9
Tax supported grants.	(NA)	42.2	49.0	49.3	52.1	54.5	55.6	58.3	49.1	48.2
Private sector support	(NA)	145.9	153.8	170.1	177.1	194.5	202.1	222.9	230.5	245.8

NA Not Available. [1]Source: *Variety*, New York, NY, various June issues. Reprinted with permission from *Variety* (copyright). [2]All shows (new productions and holdovers from previous seasons). [3]Eight performances constitute one playing week. Source: Theatre Communications Group, New York, NY. For years ending on or prior to Aug. 31. [5]Source: OPERA America, Washington, DC. [6] United States companies. [7]United States and Canadian companies. [8]Includes educational performances, outreach, etc. [9]For paid performances. [10]Source: American Symphony Orchestra League, Inc., Washington DC. For years ending Aug. 31. Data represent all United States orchestras, excluding college/university and youth orchestras.

Source: Compiled from sources in footnotes.

No. 424. Boy Scouts and Girl Scouts—Membership and Units: 1970 to 1993

[**In thousands.** Boy Scouts as of **Dec. 31**; Girl Scouts as of **Sept. 30.** Includes Puerto Rico and outlying areas]

ITEM	1970	1975	1980	1985	1987	1988	1989	1990	1991	1992	1993
BOY SCOUTS OF AMERICA											
Membership	6,287	5,318	4,318	4,845	5,347	5,364	5,356	5,448	5,319	5,338	5,355
Boys	4,683	3,933	3,207	3,755	4,180	4,228	4,247	4,293	4,150	4,150	4,165
Adults	1,604	1,385	1,110	1,090	1,168	1,136	1,109	1,155	1,168	1,188	1,190
Total units (packs, troops, posts, groups).	157	150	129	134	131	131	130	130	128	128	129
GIRL SCOUTS OF THE U.S.A.											
Membership	3,922	3,234	2,784	2,802	2,947	3,052	3,166	3,269	3,383	3,510	3,440
Girls.	3,248	2,723	2,250	2,172	2,274	2,345	2,415	2,480	2,561	2,647	2,613
Adults	674	511	534	630	673	707	751	788	822	863	827
Total units (troops, groups)	164	159	154	166	180	189	196	202	210	219	221

Source: Boy Scouts of America, National Council. Irving, TX, *Annual Report;* and Girl Scouts of the United States of America, New York, NY, *Annual Report.*

No. 425. Travel by U.S. Residents, by Selected Trip Characteristics: 1985 to 1993

[In millions. See headnote, table 426]

CHARACTERISTIC	TRIPS				PERSON TRIPS [1]			
	1985	1990	1992	1993	1985	1990	1992	1993
Total.................	558.4	661.1	650.7	648.2	1,077.6	1,274.5	1,063.0	1,057.5
Purpose:								
Visit friends and relatives........	206.8	246.0	195.2	194.5	430.8	523.3	350.8	338.4
Other pleasure...............	177.6	214.5	221.3	226.9	376.0	447.5	393.3	401.9
Business or convention..........	133.3	155.6	208.2	207.4	185.2	209.5	276.4	275.0
Other....................	40.7	45.0	26.0	19.4	85.6	94.2	42.5	31.7
Mode of transport:								
Auto, truck, recreation vehicle.....	376.1	483.9	462.0	453.7	797.7	1,011.3	807.9	793.1
Airplane...................	140.5	144.9	169.2	168.5	217.3	214.5	223.2	222.1
Other.....................	41.8	32.3	19.5	25.9	62.6	48.7	31.9	42.3
Vacation trip [2]................	339.8	422.3	351.4	350.0	728.7	883.9	637.8	634.5
Weekend trip [2]...............	224.0	280.0	338.4	330.6	470.1	580.2	584.7	571.1

[1] A count of times each person (child or adult) goes on a trip.   [2] A trip can be counted as both a weekend and a vacation trip.

Source: U.S. Travel Data Center, Washington, DC, *National Travel Survey*, annual, (copyright).

No. 426. Characteristics of Business Trips and Pleasure Trips: 1985 to 1993

[Represents trips to places 100 miles or more from home by one or more from home by one or more household members traveling together. Based on a monthly telephone survey of 1,500 U.S. adults. For details, see source]

CHARACTERISTIC	Unit	BUSINESS TRIPS				PLEASURE TRIPS			
		1985	1990	1992	1993	1985	1990	1992	1993
Total trips...............	Million..	133.3	155.6	210.8	210.4	384.4	460.9	411.7	413.4
Average household members on trip..	Number.	1.4	1.4	1.3	1.3	2.1	2.1	1.8	1.8
Average nights per trip.[1]..........	Nights...	3.6	3.7	3.5	3.5	5.6	4.4	4.3	4.0
Average miles per trip.[2]..........	Miles....	1,180	1,020	1,121	1,192	1,010	867	872	858
Traveled primarily by auto/truck/RV [3]									
rental car.................	Percent.	51	58	56	55	73	77	77	79
Traveled primarily by air.........	Percent.	44	37	40	43	21	18	19	18
Used a rental car while on trip......	Percent.	20	14	25	26	6	7	8	9
Stayed in a hotel while on trip.......	Percent.	62	71	70	73	39	37	40	40
Used a travel agent.............	Percent.	28	21	22	25	13	12	8	8
Also a vacation trip...........	Percent.	13	17	14	14	80	82	76	76
Male travelers...............	Percent.	67	71	74	72	48	49	53	55
Female travelers..............	Percent.	33	29	26	28	52	51	47	45
Household income:									
Less than $40,000...........	Percent.	58	42	31	30	73	63	53	47
$40,000 or more.............	Percent.	42	56	69	70	27	38	47	53

[1] Includes no overnight stays.   [2] United States only.   [3] Recreational vehicle.
Source: U.S. Travel Data Center, Washington, DC, *National Travel Survey*, annual, (copyright).

No. 427. Arrangement of Passenger Transportation—Receipts and Expenses, by Source: 1988 to 1993

[In millions of dollars. For taxable employer firms. Data are for SIC 472. Based on the 1987 Standard Industrial Classification code; see text, section 13]

ITEM	1988	1989	1990	1991	1992	1993
RECEIPTS						
Total.........................	8,052	8,878	9,344	8,839	9,274	9,696
Air carriers......................	4,575	5,043	5,247	5,045	5,377	5,571
Water carriers....................	305	333	374	397	409	430
Hotels and motels..................	539	622	649	597	614	637
Motor coaches....................	272	276	294	304	298	311
Railroads.......................	69	81	81	86	81	87
Rental cars......................	134	144	154	155	171	171
Packaged tours...................	1,655	1,804	1,957	1,696	1,800	1,940
Other..........................	503	575	588	559	524	549
EXPENSES						
Total.........................	7,283	7,982	8,538	8,307	8,559	8,921
Annual payroll....................	3,044	3,423	3,814	3,695	3,868	3,973
Employer contributions to Social Security						
and other supplemental benefits....	378	454	502	505	516	546
Lease and rental payments............	671	690	698	687	694	722
Advertising and promotion............	446	486	540	489	510	561
Taxes and licenses.................	119	130	129	110	110	118
Utilities........................	234	257	277	276	299	309
Depreciation.....................	317	301	303	293	272	276
Purchased office supplies.............	247	271	261	242	240	237
Purchased repair services............	98	93	102	96	92	98
Other..........................	1,729	1,877	1,912	1,914	1,958	2,081

Source: U.S. Bureau of the Census, *Current Business Reports, Service Annual Survey*, BS/93.

No. 428. Domestic Travel Expenditures, by State: 1993

[Represents U.S. spending on domestic overnight trips and day trips of 100 miles or more away from home. Excludes spending by foreign visitors and by U.S. residents in U.S. territories and abroad]

STATE	Total (mil. dol.)	Share of total (per-cent)	Rank	STATE	Total (mil. dol.)	Share of total (per-cent)	Rank	STATE	Total (mil. dol.)	Share of total (per-cent)	Rank
U.S., total .	323,272	100	(X)	KS	2,457	0.8	37	ND	828	0.3	50
				KY	3,567	1.1	29	OH	8,546	2.6	11
AL	3,682	1.1	28	LA	4,848	1.5	22	OK	2,698	0.8	35
AK	1,085	0.3	46	ME	1,483	0.5	40	OR	3,795	1.2	27
AZ	5,525	1.7	19	MD	4,922	1.5	21	PA	10,060	3.2	8
AR	2,745	0.8	33	MA	7,452	2.3	14	RI	708	0.2	51
CA	42,480	13.1	1	MI	7,498	2.3	13	SC	4,831	1.5	23
CO	6,122	1.9	17	MN	4,492	1.4	24	SD	834	0.3	49
CT	3,458	1.1	30	MS	2,236	0.7	38	TN	6,779	2.1	15
DE	836	0.3	48	MO	6,215	1.9	16	TX	20,215	6.3	3
DC	3,169	1	31	MT	1,434	0.4	42	UT	2,712	0.8	34
FL	28,629	8.9	2	NE	1,751	0.5	39	VT	1,030	0.3	47
GA	9,186	2.8	9	NV	12,539	3.9	6	VA	9,076	2.8	10
HI	5,866	1.8	18	NH	1,408	0.4	43	WA	5,318	1.6	20
ID	1,462	0.5	41	NJ	11,134	3.4	7	WV	1,371	0.4	44
IL	13,804	4.3	5	NM	2,695	0.8	36	WI	4,453	1.4	25
IN	4,220	1.3	26	NY	19,950	6.2	4	WY	1,142	0.4	45
IA	2,746	0.8	32	NC	7,884	2.4	12				

X Not applicable.
Source: U.S. Travel Data Center, Washington, DC, *Impact of Travel on State Economies, 1993*, (copyright).

No. 429. International Travelers and Expenditures, With Projections: 1970 to 1995

[For coverage, see tables 430 and 431. Beginning 1985, receipts, payments, and fares not comparable with previous years. See source for details. Minus sign (-) indicates deficit. See also *Historical Statistics, Colonial Times to 1970,* series H 921, 928, 941, and 945]

YEAR	TRAVEL AND PASSENGER FARE (mil. dol.)				U.S. net travel and passen-ger payments (mil. dol.)	U.S. travelers to foreign countries (1,000)	Foreign visitors to the U.S. (1,000)
	Payments by U.S. travelers		Receipts from foreign visitors				
	Total [1]	Expenditures abroad	Total [1]	Travel receipts			
1970	5,195	3,980	2,708	2,331	−2,487	(NA)	12,362
1980	14,004	10,397	12,650	10,588	−1,354	[2]22,365	22,326
1985	31,042	24,558	22,173	17,762	−8,869	34,715	25,399
1987	36,593	29,310	30,566	23,563	−6,027	39,410	29,500
1988	39,843	32,114	38,409	29,434	−1,434	40,669	34,095
1989	41,666	33,418	46,863	36,250	5,197	41,138	36,564
1990	47,879	37,349	58,305	43,007	10,426	44,623	39,539
1991	45,334	35,322	64,237	48,384	18,904	41,566	42,986
1992	49,614	39,007	71,257	54,284	21,642	43,897	47,261
1993	51,980	40,564	74,171	57,621	22,191	44,385	45,779
1994, est. . .	55,618	43,059	77,653	60,001	22,035	46,426	45,504
1995, proj. .	57,900	44,825	76,485	58,370	18,585	47,419	42,983

NA Not available.   [1] Includes passenger fares not shown separately.   [2] Mexico visitation data are under-reported.
Source: Travelers and visitors: U.S. Travel and Tourism Administration (USTTA), and unpublished data. Fares and Payments: Through 1980, U.S. Bureau of Economic Analysis, (BEA) *Survey of Current Business;* beginning 1985, USTTA, based on data from BEA.

No. 430. U.S. Travel to Foreign Countries, With Projections: 1985 to 1995

[**Travelers in thousands; expenditures in millions of dollars.** Covers residents of the United States, its territories and possessions. See source for details. See also *Historical Statistics, Colonial Times to 1970,* series H 921-940]

ITEM AND AREA	1985	1989	1990	1991	1992	1993	1994, est.	1995, proj.
Total travelers	**34,715**	**41,138**	**44,623**	**41,566**	**43,897**	**44,385**	**46,426**	**47,419**
Canada	11,558	12,184	12,252	12,003	11,818	11,998	12,543	12,920
Mexico	10,461	14,163	16,381	15,042	16,114	15,285	15,759	15,759
Total overseas	12,696	14,791	15,990	14,521	15,965	17,102	18,124	18,740
Europe	6,780	7,233	8,043	6,316	7,136	7,491	(NA)	(NA)
Latin America [1]	3,592	4,392	4,749	5,155	5,285	5,729	(NA)	(NA)
Other	2,324	3,166	3,198	3,050	3,544	3,882	(NA)	(NA)
Expenditures abroad	**24,558**	**33,418**	**37,349**	**35,322**	**39,007**	**40,564**	**43,059**	**44,825**
Canada	2,506	3,396	3,541	3,705	3,554	3,692	3,826	(NA)
Mexico	2,548	4,276	4,879	5,111	5,159	5,158	5,062	(NA)
Total overseas	19,504	25,746	28,929	26,506	30,293	31,714	34,172	(NA)
Europe	9,403	11,967	13,996	11,524	13,951	14,437	15,512	(NA)
Latin America [1]	3,995	5,123	5,395	3,072	6,351	6,987	7,570	(NA)
Other	6,106	8,656	9,538	11,910	9,991	10,290	11,090	(NA)
Fares to foreign carriers	6,444	8,248	10,530	10,012	10,608	11,416	12,558	(NA)

NA Not available.   [1] Includes Central and South America and the Caribbean.
Source: Travelers: U.S. Travel and Tourism Administration (USTTA), unpublished data. Expenditures: USTTA, based on data from the Bureau of Economic Analysis.

No. 431. Foreign Travel to the United States, With Projections: 1985 to 1995

[Travelers in thousands; receipts in millions of dollars. Includes travelers for business and pleasure, foreigners in transit through the United States, and students; excludes travel by foreign government personnel and foreign businessmen employed in the United States. See source for details. See also *Historical Statistics, Colonial Times to 1970,* series H 946-951]

AREA OF ORIGIN	1985	1989	1990	1991	1992	1993	1994, est.	1995, proj.
International travelers	**25,399**	**36,564**	**39,539**	**42,986**	**47,261**	**45,779**	**45,504**	**42,983**
Canada	10,721	15,325	17,263	19,113	18,598	17,293	14,970	13,668
Mexico	7,141	7,240	7,217	7,718	10,872	9,824	11,325	9,610
Total overseas	7,537	13,999	15,059	16,155	17,791	18,662	19,209	19,705
Europe	2,905	6,251	6,659	7,360	8,262	8,630	8,509	8,803
Latin America [1]	1,795	2,627	2,877	3,080	3,255	3,678	3,672	3,751
Other	2,837	5,121	5,523	5,715	6,274	6,354	7,028	7,151
Total travel receipts	**17,762**	**36,250**	**43,007**	**48,384**	**54,284**	**57,621**	**60,001**	**58,370**
Canada	2,580	5,385	7,093	8,499	8,182	7,458	6,321	(NA)
Mexico	2,101	3,926	5,108	5,367	5,696	5,119	4,930	(NA)
Total overseas	13,081	26,939	30,806	34,518	40,407	45,044	48,749	(NA)
Europe	4,774	11,004	12,602	14,332	17,706	19,204	20,033	(NA)
Latin America [1]	3,122	4,418	5,126	5,927	6,883	8,300	8,816	(NA)
Other	5,185	11,517	13,078	14,259	15,818	17,540	19,900	(NA)
Fares to U.S. carriers	4,411	10,613	15,298	15,854	16,972	16,550	17,651	(NA)

NA Not available.   [1] Includes Central and South America and the Caribbean.

Source: Travelers: U.S. Travel and Tourism Administration (USTTA), unpublished data. Receipts: USTTA, based on data from the Bureau of Economic Analysis.

No. 432. Foreign Visitors for Pleasure Admitted, by Country of Last Residence: 1985 to 1993

[In thousands. For years ending September 30. See headnote, table 7, section 1]

COUNTRY	1985	1990	1992	1993	COUNTRY	1985	1990	1992	1993
Total [1]	**6,609**	**13,418**	**16,450**	**16,900**	Africa [2]	101	105	112	127
					Egypt	16	16	16	16
Europe [2]	2,048	5,383	6,979	7,341	Nigeria	25	11	11	11
Austria	34	87	131	145	Oceania [2]	282	562	581	534
Belgium	39	95	131	147	Australia	195	380	416	381
Denmark	36	75	80	80	New Zealand	74	153	127	117
Finland	24	83	75	56	North America	1,664	2,463	2,605	2,701
France	226	566	697	697	Canada	79	119	166	160
Greece	34	43	44	44	Mexico	773	1,061	1,238	1,256
Ireland	55	81	99	111	Caribbean [2]	584	963	844	881
Italy	155	308	508	491	Bahamas, The	211	332	286	282
Netherlands	82	214	272	301	Barbados	17	34	32	41
Norway	41	80	80	79	Cayman Islands	18	31	30	31
Poland	40	55	38	32	Dominican Republic	57	137	135	145
Soviet Union	2	53	45	47	Haiti	56	57	34	31
Spain	64	183	295	272	Jamaica	74	132	101	117
Sweden	71	230	222	177	Netherlands Antilles	27	31	38	39
Switzerland	110	236	276	282	Trinidad and Tobago	71	81	65	69
United Kingdom	598	1,899	2,395	2,564	Central America [2]	228	320	357	404
Germany [3]	373	969	1,487	1,664	Costa Rica	41	62	75	88
					El Salvador	38	46	52	64
Asia [2]	1,866	3,830	4,699	4,502	Guatemala	53	91	93	103
China [4]	83	187	249	289	Panama	38	43	51	55
Hong Kong	64	111	142	141	South America [2]	606	1,016	1,423	1,593
India	52	75	68	63	Argentina	66	136	302	312
Israel	80	128	124	142	Brazil	148	300	380	446
Japan	1,277	2,846	3,486	3,178	Chile	28	54	79	91
Korea	26	120	230	270	Colombia	123	122	140	162
Philippines	59	76	94	95	Ecuador	42	57	72	70
Saudi Arabia	31	33	40	45	Peru	44	97	92	102
Singapore	23	32	42	42	Venezuela	122	199	291	343

[1] Includes countries unknown or not reported.   [2] Includes countries not shown separately.   [3] Data prior to 1991 for former West Germany.   [4] Includes Taiwan.

Source: U.S. Immigration and Naturalization Service, *Statistical Yearbook*, annual.

Figure 8.1
**Political Party Identification of the
Adult Population: 1960 to 1994**
(Democrat and Republican parties include individuals identifying
themselves as strong, weak, or independent.)

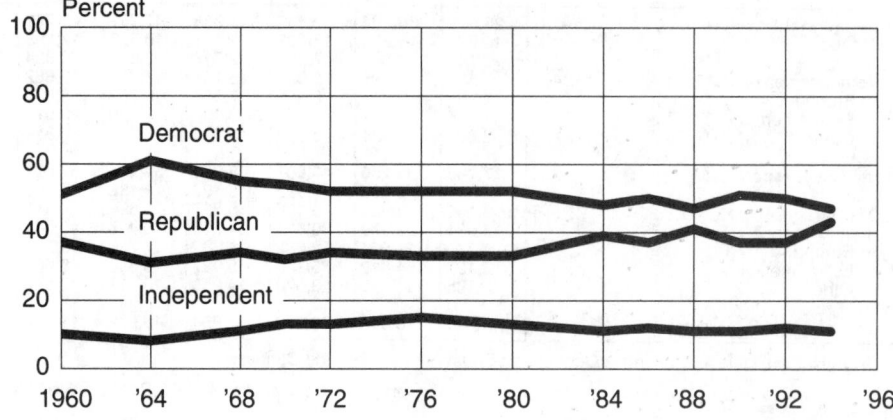

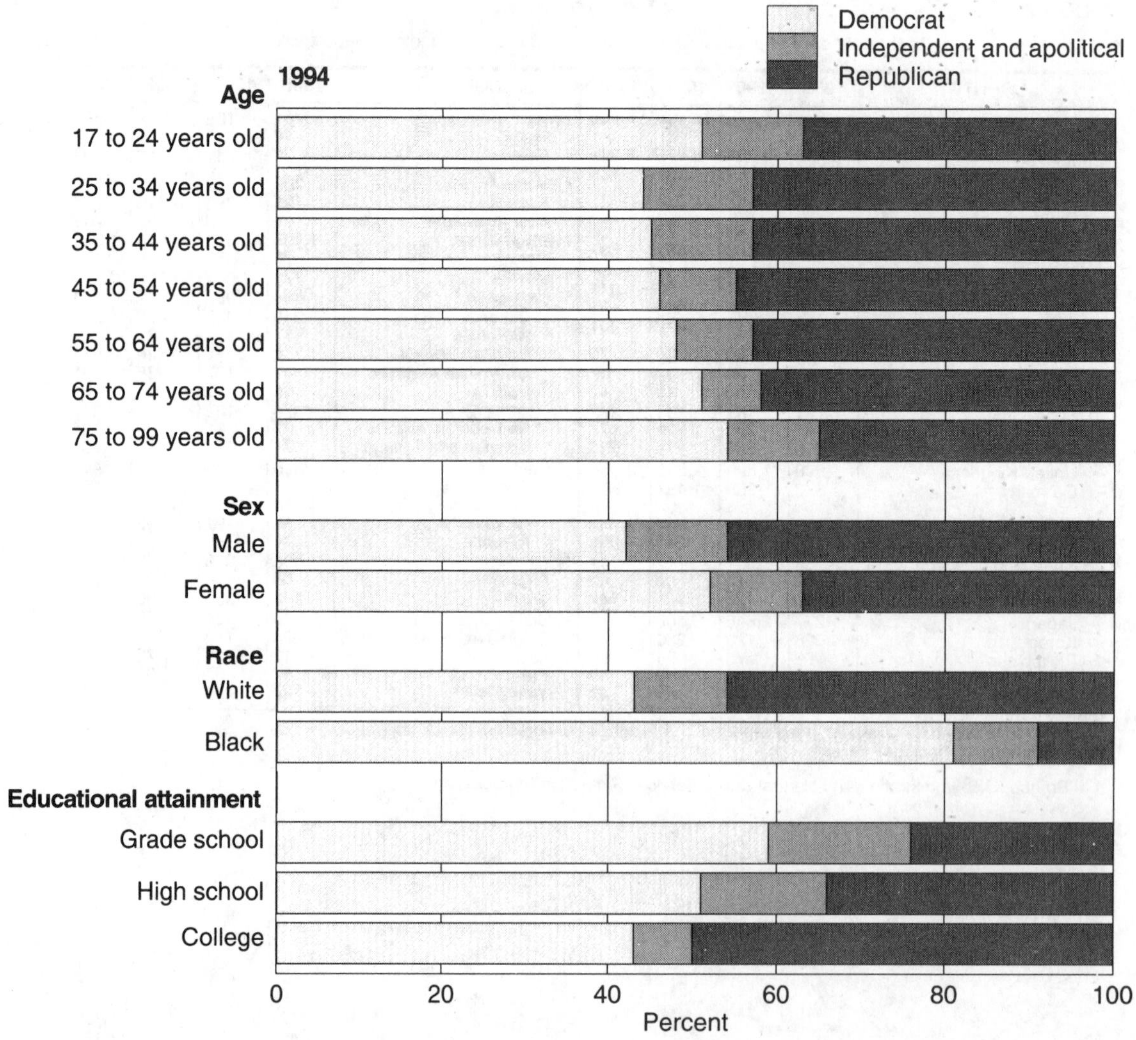

Source: Chart prepared by U.S. Bureau of the Census. For data, see table 458.

Elections

This section relates primarily to Presidential, congressional, and gubernatorial elections. Also presented are summary tables on congressional legislation; State legislatures; Black, Hispanic, and female officeholders; population of voting age; voter participation; and campaign finances.

Official statistics on Federal elections, collected by the Clerk of the House, are published biennially in *Statistics of the Presidential and Congressional Election* and *Statistics of the Congressional Election*. Federal and State elections data appear also in *America Votes*, a biennial volume of the Elections Research Center, Chevy Chase, MD. Federal elections data also appear in the U.S. Congress, *Congressional Directory*, and in official State documents. Data on reported registration and voting for social and economic groups are obtained by the U.S. Bureau of the Census as part of the Current Population Survey (CPS) and are published in *Current Population Reports*, P20 (see text, section 1).

Almost all Federal, State, and local governmental units in the United States conduct elections for political offices and other purposes. The conduct of elections is regulated by State laws or, in some cities and counties, by local charter. An exception is that the U.S. Constitution prescribes the basis of representation in Congress and the manner of electing the President, and grants to Congress the right to regulate the times, places, and manner of electing Federal officers. Amendments to the Constitution have prescribed national criteria for voting eligibility. The 15th Amendment, adopted in 1870, gave all citizens the right to vote regardless of race, color, or previous condition of servitude. The 19th Amendment, adopted in 1919, further extended the right to vote to all citizens regardless of sex. The payment of poll taxes as a prerequisite to voting in Federal elections was banned by the 24th Amendment in 1964. In 1971, as a result of the 26th Amendment, eligibility to vote in national elections was extended to all citizens, 18 years old and over.

In Brief

Percent of voting-age population voting for Representatives:

1990	*33.1%*
1994	*36.0%*

Members of Congress:

	1981	1995
Black	*17*	*41*
Asian, Pacific Islander	*6*	*6*
Hispanic	*6*	*17*
Female	*21*	*55*

Presidential election.—The Constitution specifies how the President and Vice President are selected. Each State elects, by popular vote, a group of electors equal in number to its total of members of Congress. The 23d Amendment, adopted in 1961, grants the District of Columbia three presidential electors, a number equal to that of the least populous State. Subsequent to the election, the electors meet in their respective States to vote for President and Vice President. Usually, each elector votes for the candidate receiving the most popular votes in his or her State. A majority vote of all electors is necessary to elect the President and Vice President. If no candidate receives a majority, the House of Representatives, with each State having one vote, is empowered to elect the President and Vice President, again, with a majority of votes required.

The 22d Amendment to the Constitution, adopted in 1951, limits presidential tenure to two elective terms of 4 years each, or to one elective term for any person who, upon succession to the Presidency, has held the office or acted as President for more than 2 years.

Congressional election.—The Constitution provides that Representatives be apportioned among the States according to their population; that a census of population be taken every 10 years as a basis for apportionment; and that each State have at least one Representative. At the time of each apportionment, Congress decides what the total number of

Representatives will be. Since 1912, the total has been 435, except during 1960 to 1962 when it increased to 437, adding one Representative each for Alaska and Hawaii. The total reverted to 435 after reapportionment following the 1960 census. Members are elected for 2-year terms, all terms covering the same period. The District of Columbia, American Samoa, Guam, and the Virgin Islands each elect one nonvoting Delegate and Puerto Rico elects a nonvoting Resident Commissioner.

The Senate is composed of 100 members, two from each State, who are elected to serve for a term of 6 years. One-third of the Senate is elected every 2 years. Senators were originally chosen by the State legislatures. The 17th Amendment to the Constitution, adopted in 1913, prescribed that Senators be elected by popular vote.

Voter eligibility and participation.—The Census Bureau publishes estimates of the population of voting age and the percent casting votes in each State for Presidential and congressional election years. These voting-age estimates include a number of persons who meet the age requirement but are not eligible to vote, (e.g. aliens and some institutionalized persons). In addition, since 1964, voter participation and voter characteristics data have been collected during November of election years as part of the CPS. These survey data include noncitizens in the voting age population estimates, but exclude members of the Armed Forces and the institutional population.

Statistical reliability.—For a discussion of statistical collection and estimation, sampling procedures, and measures of statistical reliability applicable to Census Bureau data, see Appendix III.

Historical statistics.—Tabular headnotes provide cross-references, where applicable, to *Historical Statistics of the United States, Colonial Times to 1970.* See Appendix IV.

Figure 8.2
Popular Vote Cast for President, by Major Political Party: 1972 to 1992

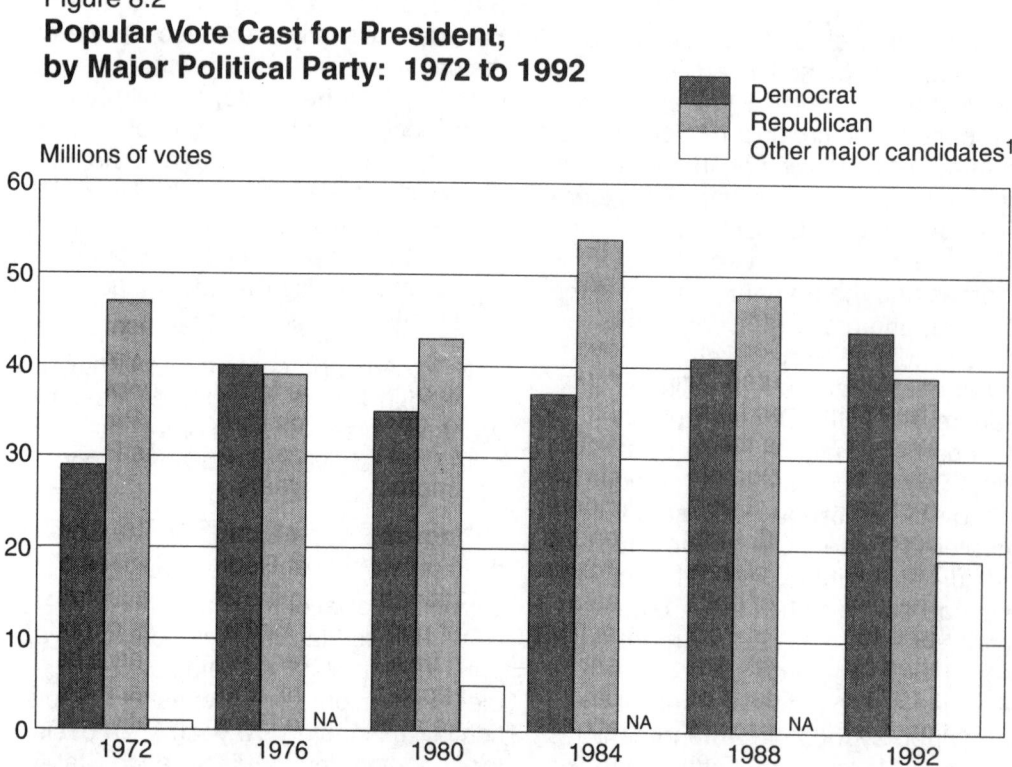

1 1972—American, John Schmitz; 1980—Independent, John Anderson; 1992—Independent, Ross Perot.
Source: Chart prepared by U.S. Bureau of the Census. For data, see table 433 and 434.

No. 433. Vote Cast for President, by Major Political Party: 1936 to 1992

[Prior to 1960, excludes Alaska and Hawaii; prior to 1964, excludes DC. Vote cast for major party candidates include the votes of minor parties cast for those candidates. See also *Historical Statistics, Colonial Times to 1970*, series Y 79-83 and Y 135]

YEAR	CANDIDATES FOR PRESIDENT		VOTE CAST FOR PRESIDENT						
			Total popular vote [1] (1,000)	Democratic			Republican		
	Democratic	Republican		Popular vote		Electoral vote	Popular vote		Electoral vote
				Number (1,000)	Percent		Number (1,000)	Percent	
1936	F. D. Roosevelt	Landon	45,655	27,757	60.8	523	16,684	36.5	8
1940	F. D. Roosevelt	Willkie	49,900	27,313	54.7	449	22,348	44.8	82
1944	F. D. Roosevelt	Dewey	47,977	25,613	53.4	432	22,018	45.9	99
1948	Truman	Dewey	48,794	24,179	49.6	303	21,991	45.1	189
1952	Stevenson	Eisenhower	61,551	27,315	44.4	89	33,936	55.1	442
1956	Stevenson	Eisenhower	62,027	26,023	42.0	73	35,590	57.4	457
1960	Kennedy	Nixon	68,838	34,227	49.7	303	34,108	49.5	219
1964	Johnson	Goldwater	70,645	43,130	61.1	486	27,178	38.5	52
1968	Humphrey	Nixon	73,212	31,275	42.7	191	31,785	43.4	301
1972	McGovern	Nixon	77,719	29,170	37.5	17	47,170	60.7	520
1976	Carter	Ford	81,556	40,831	50.1	297	39,148	48.0	240
1980	Carter	Reagan	86,515	35,484	41.0	49	43,904	50.7	489
1984	Mondale	Reagan	92,653	37,577	40.6	13	54,455	58.8	525
1988	Dukakis	Bush	91,595	41,809	45.6	111	48,886	53.4	426
1992	Clinton	Bush	104,425	44,909	43.0	370	39,104	37.4	168

[1] Include votes for minor party candidates, independents, unpledged electors, and scattered write-in votes.

No. 434. Vote Cast for Leading Minority Party Candidates for President: 1936 to 1992

[See headnote, table 433]

YEAR	Candidate	Party	Popular vote (1,000)	Candidate	Party	Popular vote (1,000)
1936	William Lemke	Union	892	Norman Thomas	Socialist	188
1940	Norman Thomas	Socialist	116	Roger Babson	Prohibition	59
1944	Norman Thomas	Socialist	79	Claude Watson	Prohibition	75
1948	Strom Thurmond	States' Rights	1,176	Henry Wallace	Progressive	1,157
1952	Vincent Hallinan	Progressive	140	Stuart Hamblen	Prohibition	73
1956	T. Coleman Andrews	States' Rights	111	Eric Hass	Socialist Labor	44
1960	Eric Hass	Socialist Labor	48	Rutherford Decker	Prohibition	46
1964	Eric Hass	Socialist Labor	45	Clifton DeBerry	Socialist Workers	33
1968	George Wallace	American Independent	9,906	Henning Blomen	Socialist Labor	53
1972	John Schmitz	American	1,099	Benjamin Spock	People's	79
1976	Eugene McCarthy	Independent	757	Roger McBride	Libertarian	173
1980	John Anderson	Independent	5,720	Ed Clark	Libertarian	921
1984	David Bergland	Libertarian	228	Lyndon H. LaRouche	Independent	79
1988	Ron Paul	Libertarian	432	Lenora B. Fulani	New Alliance	217
1992	H. Ross Perot	Independent	19,742	Andre Marrou	Libertarian	292

Source of tables 433 and 434: Elections Research Center, Chevy Chase, MD, *America at the Polls 2*, 1965, and *America Votes*, biennial (copyright).

No. 435. Democratic and Republican Percentages of Two-Party Presidential Vote, by Selected Characteristics of Voters: 1988 and 1992

[**In percent**. Covers citizens of voting age living in private housing units in the contiguous United States. Percentages for Democratic Presidential vote are computed by subtracting the percentage Republican vote from 100 percent; third-party or independent votes are not included as valid data. Data are from the National Election Studies and are based on a sample and subject to sampling variability; for details, see source]

CHARACTERISTIC	1988		1992		CHARACTERISTIC	1988		1992	
	Democratic	Republican	Democratic	Republican		Democratic	Republican	Democratic	Republican
Total [1]	47	53	58	42	Race:				
Year of birth:					White	41	59	53	47
1959 or later	48	52	58	42	Black	92	8	94	6
1943 to 1958	47	53	58	42					
1927 to 1942	49	51	57	43	Education:				
1911 to 1926	44	56	62	38	Grade school	61	39	70	30
1895 to 1910	47	53	55	45	High school	51	49	63	37
					College	42	58	55	45
Sex:									
Male	44	56	55	45	Union household	59	41	68	32
Female	50	50	61	39	Non-union household	44	56	56	44

[1] Includes other characteristics, not shown separately.

Source: Center for Political Studies, University of Michigan, Ann Arbor, MI, unpublished data, (copyright).

No. 436. Electoral Vote Cast for President, by Major Political Party—States: 1952 to 1992

[D=Democratic, R=Republican. For composition of regions, see table 27. See also *Historical Statistics, Colonial Times to 1970*, series Y 84-134]

REGION, DIVISION, AND STATE	1952	1956[1]	1960[2]	1964	1968[3]	1972[4]	1976[5]	1980	1984	1988[6]	1992
Democratic	89	73	303	486	191	17	297	49	13	111	370
Republican	442	457	219	52	301	520	240	489	525	426	168
Northeast: Democratic .	-	-	121	126	102	14	86	4	-	53	106
Republican .	133	133	12	-	24	108	36	118	113	60	-
Midwest: Democratic . .	-	13	71	149	31	-	58	10	10	29	100
Republican . .	153	140	82	-	118	145	87	135	127	108	29
South: Democratic	89	60	101	121	45	3	149	31	3	8	68
Republican	77	105	50	47	77	165	20	138	174	168	116
West: Democratic	-	-	10	90	13	-	4	4	-	21	96
Republican	79	79	75	5	82	102	97	98	111	90	23
New England: ME	R-5	R-5	R-5	D-4	D-4	R-4	R-4	R-4	R-4	R-4	D-4
NH	R-4	R-4	R-4	D-4	R-4	R-4	R-4	R-4	R-4	R-4	D-4
VT	R-3	R-3	R-3	D-3	R-3	R-3	R-3	R-3	R-3	R-3	D-3
MA	R-16	R-16	D-16	D-14	D-14	D-14	D-14	R-14	R-13	D-13	D-12
RI	R-4	R-4	D-4	D-4	D-4	R-4	D-4	D-4	R-4	D-4	D-4
CT	R-8	R-8	D-8	D-8	D-8	R-8	R-8	R-8	R-8	R-8	D-8
Middle Atlantic: NY . . .	R-45	R-45	D-45	D-43	D-43	R-41	D-41	R-41	R-36	D-36	D-33
NJ	R-16	R-16	D-16	D-17	D-17	R-17	R-17	R-17	R-16	R-16	D-15
PA	R-32	R-32	D-32	D-29	D-29	R-27	D-27	R-27	R-25	R-25	D-23
East North Central: OH	R-25	R-25	R-25	D-26	R-26	R-25	D-25	R-25	R-23	R-23	D-21
IN	R-13	R-13	R-13	D-13	R-13	R-13	R-13	R-13	R-12	R-12	R-12
IL	R-27	R-27	D-27	D-26	R-26	R-26	R-26	R-26	R-24	R-24	D-22
MI	R-20	R-20	R-20	D-21	D-21	R-21	R-21	R-21	R-20	R-20	D-18
WI	R-12	R-12	R-12	D-12	R-12	R-11	D-11	R-11	R-11	D-11	D-11
West North Central: MN	R-11	R-11	D-11	D-10	D-10	R-10	D-10	D-10	D-10	D-10	D-10
IA	R-10	R-10	R-10	D-9	R-9	R-8	R-8	R-8	R-8	D-8	D-7
MO	R-13	D-13	D-13	D-12	R-12	R-12	D-12	R-12	R-11	R-11	D-11
ND	R-4	R-4	R-4	D-4	R-4	R-3	R-3	R-3	R-3	R-3	R-3
SD	R-4	R-4	R-4	D-4	R-4	R-4	R-4	R-4	R-3	R-3	R-3
NE	R-6	R-6	R-6	D-5	R-5	R-5	R-5	R-5	R-5	R-5	R-5
KS	R-8	R-8	R-8	D-7	R-7	R-7	R-7	R-7	R-7	R-7	R-6
South Atlantic: DE	R-3	R-3	D-3	D-3	R-3	R-3	D-3	R-3	R-3	R-3	D-3
MD	R-9	R-9	D-9	D-10	D-10	R-10	D-10	D-10	R-10	R-10	D-10
DC	(X)	(X)	(X)	D-3	D-3	D-3	D-3	D-3	D-3	D-3	D-3
VA	R-12	R-12	R-12	D-12	R-12	[4]R-11	R-12	R-12	R-12	R-12	R-13
WV	D-8	R-8	D-8	D-7	D-7	R-6	D-6	D-6	R-6	[6]D-5	D-5
NC	D-14	D-14	D-14	D-13	[3]R-12	R-13	D-13	R-13	R-13	R-13	R-14
SC	D-8	D-8	D-8	R-8	R-8	R-8	D-8	R-8	R-8	R-8	R-8
GA	D-12	D-12	D-12	R-12	([3])	R-12	D-12	D-12	R-12	R-12	D-13
FL	R-10	R-10	R-10	D-14	R-14	R-17	D-17	R-17	R-21	R-21	R-25
East South Central: KY	D-10	R-10	R-10	D-9	R-9	R-9	D-9	R-9	R-9	R-9	D-8
TN	R-11	R-11	R-11	D-11	R-11	R-10	D-10	R-10	R-11	R-11	D-11
AL	D-11	[1]D-10	[2]D-5	R-10	([3])	R-9	D-9	R-9	R-9	R-9	R-9
MS	D-8	D-8	([2])	R-7	([3])	R-7	D-7	R-7	R-7	R-7	R-7
West South Central: AR	D-8	D-8	D-8	D-6	([3])	R-6	D-6	R-6	R-6	R-6	D-6
LA	D-10	R-10	D-10	R-10	([3])	R-10	D-10	R-10	R-10	R-10	D-9
OK	R-8	R-8	[2]R-7	D-8	R-8	R-8	R-8	R-8	R-8	R-8	R-8
TX	R-24	R-24	D-24	D-25	D-25	R-26	D-26	R-26	R-29	R-29	R-32
Mountain: MT	R-4	R-4	R-4	D-4	R-4	R-4	R-4	R-4	R-4	R-4	D-3
ID	R-4	R-4	R-4	D-4	R-4	R-4	R-4	R-4	R-4	R-4	R-4
WY	R-3	R-3	R-3	D-3	R-3	R-3	R-3	R-3	R-3	R-3	R-3
CO	R-6	R-6	R-6	D-6	R-6	R-7	R-7	R-7	R-8	R-8	D-8
NM	R-4	R-4	D-4	D-4	R-4	R-4	R-4	R-4	R-5	R-5	D-5
AZ	R-4	R-4	R-4	R-5	R-5	R-6	R-6	R-6	R-7	R-7	R-8
UT	R-4	R-4	R-4	D-4	R-4	R-4	R-4	R-4	R-5	R-5	R-5
NV	R-3	R-3	D-3	D-3	R-3	R-3	R-3	R-3	R-4	R-4	D-4
Pacific: WA	R-9	R-9	R-9	D-9	D-9	R-9	[5]R-8	R-9	R-10	D-10	D-11
OR	R-6	R-6	R-6	D-6	R-6	R-6	R-6	R-6	R-7	D-7	D-7
CA	R-32	R-32	R-32	D-40	R-40	R-45	R-45	R-45	R-47	R-47	D-54
AK	(X)	(X)	R-3	D-3	R-3	R-3	R-3	R-3	R-3	R-3	R-3
HI	(X)	(X)	D-3	D-4	D-4	R-4	D-4	D-4	R-4	D-4	D-4

- Represents zero. X Not applicable. [1] Excludes one electoral vote cast for Walter B. Jones in Alabama. [2] Excludes 15 electoral votes cast for Harry F. Byrd as follows: AL 6, MS 8, and OK 1. [3] Excludes 46 electoral votes cast for American Independent George C. Wallace as follows: AL 10, AR 6, GA 12, LA 10, MS 7, and NC 1. [4] Excludes one electoral vote cast for Libertarian John Hospers in Virginia. [5] Excludes one electoral vote cast for Ronald Reagan in Washington. [6] Excludes one electoral vote cast for Lloyd Bentsen for President in West Virginia.

Source: 1952-72, U.S. Congress, Clerk of the House, *Statistics of the Presidential and Congressional Election*, quadrennial; 1976-92, Elections Research Center, Chevy Chase, MD, *America Votes*, biennial (copyright).

No. 437. Popular Vote Cast for President, by Political Party—States: 1988 and 1992

[In thousands, except percent. See also *Historical Statistics, Colonial Times to 1970*, series Y 135-186]

REGION, DIVISION, AND STATE	1988				1992				Percent of total vote		
	Total [1]	Demo-cratic Party	Repub-lican Party	Percent for leading party [2]	Total [1]	Demo-cratic Party	Repub-lican Party	Perot (Inde-pen-dent)	Demo-cratic Party	Repub-lican Party	Perot (Inde-pen-dent)
United States..	**91,595**	**41,809**	**48,886**	**R-53.4**	**104,425**	**44,909**	**39,104**	**19,742**	**43.0**	**37.4**	**18.9**
Northeast........	**19,852**	**9,689**	**9,961**	**R-50.2**	**21,581**	**9,940**	**7,507**	**3,994**	**46.1**	**34.8**	**18.5**
N.E	**5,730**	**2,826**	**2,836**	**R-49.5**	**6,351**	**2,820**	**2,012**	**1,479**	**44.4**	**31.7**	**23.3**
ME	555	244	307	R-55.3	679	263	207	207	38.8	30.4	30.4
NH	451	164	282	R-62.4	538	209	202	121	38.9	37.6	22.6
VT	243	116	124	R-51.1	290	134	88	66	46.1	30.4	22.8
MA	2,633	1,401	1,195	D-53.2	2,774	1,319	805	631	47.5	29.0	22.7
RI	405	225	178	D-55.6	453	213	132	105	47.0	29.0	23.2
CT	1,443	677	750	R-52.0	1,616	682	578	349	42.2	35.8	21.6
M.A	**14,121**	**6,863**	**7,125**	**R-50.5**	**15,230**	**7,120**	**5,495**	**2,515**	**46.7**	**36.1**	**16.5**
NY	6,486	3,348	3,082	D-51.6	6,927	3,444	2,347	1,091	49.7	33.9	15.7
NJ	3,100	1,320	1,743	R-56.2	3,344	1,436	1,357	522	43.0	40.6	15.6
PA	4,536	2,195	2,300	R-50.7	4,960	2,239	1,792	903	45.1	36.1	18.2
Midwest........	**24,663**	**11,556**	**12,915**	**R-52.4**	**27,735**	**11,692**	**10,234**	**5,668**	**42.2**	**36.9**	**20.4**
E.N.C.........	**16,982**	**7,819**	**9,038**	**R-53.2**	**19,102**	**8,199**	**7,104**	**3,702**	**42.9**	**37.2**	**19.4**
OH	4,394	1,940	2,417	R-55.0	4,940	1,985	1,894	1,036	40.2	38.3	21.0
IN	2,169	861	1,298	R-59.8	2,306	848	989	456	36.8	42.9	19.8
IL	4,559	2,216	2,311	R-50.7	5,050	2,453	1,734	841	48.6	34.3	16.6
MI	3,669	1,676	1,965	R-53.6	4,275	1,871	1,555	825	43.8	36.4	19.3
WI	2,192	1,127	1,047	D-51.4	2,531	1,041	931	544	41.1	36.8	21.5
W.N.C.........	**7,681**	**3,737**	**3,877**	**R-50.5**	**8,633**	**3,493**	**3,130**	**1,966**	**40.5**	**36.3**	**22.8**
MN	2,097	1,109	962	D-52.9	2,348	1,021	748	563	43.5	31.9	24.0
IA	1,226	671	545	D-54.7	1,355	586	505	253	43.3	37.3	18.7
MO	2,094	1,002	1,085	R-51.8	2,392	1,054	811	519	44.1	33.9	21.7
ND	297	128	167	R-56.0	308	99	136	71	32.2	44.2	23.1
SD	313	146	165	R-52.8	336	125	137	73	37.1	40.7	21.8
NE	661	259	398	R-60.2	738	217	344	174	29.4	46.6	23.6
KS	993	423	554	R-55.8	1,157	390	450	312	33.7	38.9	27.0
South	**28,558**	**12,004**	**16,327**	**R-57.2**	**33,625**	**14,118**	**14,014**	**5,325**	**42.0**	**41.7**	**15.8**
S.A	**14,234**	**5,927**	**8,207**	**R-57.7**	**17,195**	**7,352**	**7,103**	**2,667**	**42.8**	**41.3**	**15.5**
DE	250	109	140	R-55.9	290	126	102	59	43.5	35.3	20.4
MD	1,714	826	876	R-51.1	1,985	989	707	281	49.8	35.6	14.2
DC	193	159	28	D-82.6	228	193	21	10	84.6	9.1	4.3
VA	2,192	860	1,309	R-59.7	2,559	1,039	1,151	349	40.6	45.0	13.6
WV	653	341	310	D-52.2	684	331	242	109	48.4	35.4	15.9
NC	2,134	890	1,237	R-58.0	2,612	1,114	1,135	358	42.7	43.4	13.7
SC	986	371	606	R-61.5	1,203	480	578	139	39.9	48.0	11.5
GA	1,810	715	1,081	R-59.8	2,321	1,009	995	310	43.5	42.9	13.3
FL	4,302	1,657	2,619	R-60.9	5,314	2,073	2,173	1,053	39.0	40.9	19.8
E.S.C.........	**5,269**	**2,174**	**3,055**	**R-58.0**	**6,145**	**2,689**	**2,751**	**673**	**43.8**	**44.8**	**10.9**
KY	1,323	580	734	R-55.5	1,493	665	617	204	44.6	41.3	13.7
TN	1,636	680	947	R-57.9	1,983	934	841	200	47.1	42.4	10.1
AL	1,378	550	816	R-59.2	1,688	690	804	183	40.9	47.6	10.8
MS	932	364	558	R-59.9	982	400	488	86	40.8	49.7	8.7
W.S.C.........	**9,054**	**3,903**	**5,065**	**R-55.9**	**10,285**	**4,077**	**4,160**	**1,985**	**39.6**	**40.4**	**19.3**
AR	828	349	467	R-56.4	951	506	337	99	53.2	35.5	10.4
LA	1,628	717	884	R-54.3	1,790	816	733	211	45.6	41.0	11.8
OK	1,171	483	678	R-57.9	1,390	473	593	320	34.0	42.6	23.0
TX	5,427	2,353	3,037	R-56.0	6,154	2,282	2,496	1,355	37.1	40.6	22.0
West	**18,522**	**8,560**	**9,683**	**R-52.3**	**21,484**	**9,160**	**7,349**	**4,755**	**42.6**	**34.2**	**22.1**
Mountain	**5,014**	**2,043**	**2,887**	**R-57.6**	**5,970**	**2,167**	**2,272**	**1,437**	**36.3**	**38.1**	**24.1**
MT	366	169	190	R-52.1	411	155	144	107	37.6	35.1	26.1
ID	409	147	254	R-62.1	482	137	203	130	28.4	42.0	27.0
WY	177	67	107	R-60.5	201	68	79	51	34.0	39.6	25.6
CO	1,372	621	728	R-53.1	1,569	630	563	366	40.1	35.9	23.3
NM	521	244	270	R-51.9	570	262	213	92	45.9	37.3	16.1
AZ	1,172	454	703	R-60.0	1,487	543	572	354	36.5	38.5	23.8
UT	647	207	428	R-66.2	744	183	323	203	24.7	43.4	27.3
NV	350	133	206	R-58.9	506	189	176	133	37.4	34.7	26.2
Pacific	**13,509**	**6,517**	**6,797**	**R-50.3**	**15,514**	**6,993**	**5,076**	**3,318**	**45.1**	**32.7**	**21.4**
WA	1,865	934	904	D-50.0	2,288	993	731	542	43.4	32.0	23.7
OR	1,202	616	560	D-51.3	1,463	621	476	354	42.5	32.5	24.2
CA	9,887	4,702	5,055	R-51.1	11,132	5,121	3,631	2,296	46.0	32.6	20.6
AK	200	73	119	R-59.6	259	78	102	73	30.3	39.5	28.4
HI	354	192	159	D-54.3	373	179	137	53	48.1	36.7	14.2

[1] Includes other parties.   [2] D=Democratic, R=Republican. Leading party vote refers to the party vote representing either a majority or a plurality for the victorious party in the area shown.

Source: Elections Research Center, Chevy Chase, MD, *America Votes*, biennial, (copyright).

No. 438. Vote Cast for United States Senators, 1992 and 1994, and Incumbent Senators, 1995—States

[D=Democrat; R=Republican]

DIVISION AND STATE	1992 Total (1,000)	1992 Percent for leading party	1994 Total (1,000)	1994 Percent for leading party	INCUMBENT SENATORS AND YEAR TERM EXPIRES — Name, party, and year	INCUMBENT SENATORS AND YEAR TERM EXPIRES — Name, party, and year
N.E.:						
ME	(X)	(X)	511	R-60.3	William S. Cohen (R) 1997	Olympia Snowe (R) 2001
NH	518	R-48.1	(X)	(X)	Judd Gregg (R) 1999	Robert C. Smith (R) 1997
VT	286	D-54.2	212	R-50.3	Patrick J. Leahy (D) 1999	James M. Jeffords (R) 2001
MA	(X)	(X)	2,179	D-58.1	Edward M. Kennedy (D) 2001	John F. Kerry (D) 1997
RI	(X)	(X)	345	R-64.5	Claiborne Pell (D) 1997	John H. Chafee (R) 2001
CT	1,501	D-58.8	1,080	D-67.0	Christopher J. Dodd (D) 1999	Joseph I. Lieberman (D) 2001
M.A.:						
NY	6,459	R-49.0	4,790	D-55.2	Daniel P. Moynihan (D) 2001	Alfonse M. D'Amato (R) 1999
NJ	(X)	(X)	2,055	D-50.3	Bill Bradley (D) 1997	Frank R. Lautenberg (D) 2001
PA	4,802	R-49.1	3,513	R-49.4	Rick Santorum (R) 2001	Arlen Specter (R) 1999
E.N.C.:						
OH	4,794	D-51.0	3,437	R-53.4	John Glenn (D) 1999	Mike DeWine (R) 2001
IN	2,211	R-57.3	1,544	R-67.4	Dan Coats (R) 1999	Richard G. Lugar (R) 2001
IL	4,940	D-53.3	(X)	(X)	Carol Moseley Braun (D) 1999	Paul Simon (D) 1997
MI	(X)	(X)	3,043	R-51.9	Carl Levin (D) 1997	Spencer Abraham (R) 2001
WI	2,455	D-52.6	1,565	D-58.3	Herb Kohl (D) 2001	Russell Feingold (D) 1999
W.N.C.:						
MN	(X)	(X)	1,773	R-49.1	Paul David Wellstone (D) 1997	Rod Grams (R) 2001
IA	1,292	R-69.6	(X)	(X)	Tom Harkin (D) 1997	Charles E. Grassley (R) 1999
MO	2,355	R-51.9	1,775	R-59.7	Christopher S. Bond (R) 1999	John Ashcroft (R) 2001
ND	304	D-59.0	237	D-58.0	Byron L. Dorgan (D) 1999	Kent Conrad (D) 2001
SD	334	D-64.9	(X)	(X)	Thomas A. Daschle (D) 1999	Larry Pressler (R) 1997
NE	(X)	(X)	579	D-54.8	J. James Exon (D) 1997	J. Robert Kerrey (D) 2001
KS	1,126	R-62.7	(X)	(X)	Bob Dole (R) 1999	Nancy Kassebaum (R) 1997
S.A.:						
DE	(X)	(X)	199	R-55.8	Joseph R. Biden Jr. (D) 1997	William V. Roth, Jr. (R) 2001
MD	1,842	D-71.0	1,369	D-59.1	Barbara A. Mikulski (D) 1999	Paul S. Sarbanes (D) 2001
VA	(X)	(X)	2,057	D-45.6	Charles S. Robb (D) 2001	John W. Warner (R) 1997
WV	(X)	(X)	421	D-69.0	Robert C. Byrd (D) 2001	John D. Rockefeller IV (D) 1997
NC	2,578	R-50.3	(X)	(X)	Lauch Faircloth (R) 1999	Jesse Helms (R) 1997
SC	1,180	D-50.1	(X)	(X)	Ernest F. Hollings (D) 1999	Strom Thurmond (R) 1997
GA	[1]1,254	[1]R-50.6	(X)	(X)	Paul Coverdell (R) 1999	Sam Nunn (D) 1997
FL	4,962	D-65.4	4,105	R-70.5	Bob Graham (D) 1999	Connie Mack (R) 2001
E.S.C.:						
KY	1,331	D-62.9	(X)	(X)	Wendell H. Ford (D) 1999	Mitch McConnell (R) 1997
TN	(X)	(X)	1,480	R-56.4	[2]Fred Thompson (R) 1997	Bill Frist (R) 2001
AL	1,578	D-64.8	(X)	(X)	Howell Heflin (D) 1997	Richard C. Shelby (D) 1999
MS	(X)	(X)	608	R-68.8	Thad Cochran (R) 1997	Trent Lott (R) 2001
W.S.C.:						
AR	920	D-60.2	(X)	(X)	Dale Bumpers (D) 1999	David Pryor (D) 1997
LA	[3]843	[3]D-78.5	(X)	(X)	John B. Breaux (D) 1999	J. Bennett Johnston (D) 1997
OK	1,294	R-58.5	982	R-55.2	James Inhofe (R) 2001	Don Nickles (R) 1999
TX	[4]1,765	[4]R-67.3	4,280	R-60.8	Kay Bailey Hutchison (R) 2001	Phil Gramm (R) 1997
Mountain:						
MT	(X)	(X)	350	R-62.4	Max Baucus (D) 1997	Conrad Burns (R) 2001
ID	479	R-56.5	(X)	(X)	Larry E. Craig (R) 1997	Dirk Kempthorne (R) 1999
WY	(X)	(X)	202	R-58.9	Alan K. Simpson (R) 1997	Craig Thomas (R) 2001
CO	1,552	D-51.8	(X)	(X)	Ben N. Campbell (D) 1999	Hank Brown (R) 1997
NM	(X)	(X)	463	D-54.0	Jeff Bingaman (D) 2001	Pete V. Domenici (R) 1997
AZ	1,382	R-55.8	1,119	R-53.7	John McCain (R) 1999	Jon Kyl (R) 2001
UT	758	R-55.4	519	R-68.8	Robert F. Bennett (R) 1999	Orrin G. Hatch (R) 2001
NV	496	D-51.0	368	D-52.7	Harry Reid (D) 1999	Richard H. Bryan (D) 2001
Pacific:						
WA	2,219	D-54.0	1,700	R-55.7	Patty Murray (D) 1999	Slade Gorton (R) 2001
OR	1,376	R-52.1	(X)	(X)	Mark O. Hatfield (R) 1997	Bob Packwood (R) 1999
CA	10,800	D-47.9	8,503	D-46.8	Barbara Boxer (D) 1999	Dianne Feinstein (D) 2001
AK	240	R-53.0	(X)	(X)	Frank H. Murkowski (R) 1999	Ted Stevens (R) 1997
HI	364	D-57.3	357	D-71.8	Daniel K. Akaka (D) 2001	Daniel K. Inouye (D) 1999

X Not applicable.　　[1] Results of run-off election. In the first election no candidate received more than 50 percent of the vote. First election: Total votes cast, 2,251,587; Democratic candidate, 1,108,416; Republican candidate, 1,073,282.　　[2] In a special election in 1994 to fill an unexpired term, the Republican candidate received 60.4 percent of 1,465,835 total votes cast. [3] Louisiana holds an open-primary election with candidates from all parties running on the same ballot. Any candidate who receives a majority is elected. In 1992 the indicated Senator received more than 50 percent of the vote in the October open-primary. [4] Special election in June 1993 to fill the unexpired term of Senator Bentsen.

Source: Elections Research Center, Chevy Chase, MD, *America Votes*, biennial, (copyright) and Congressional Quarterly, Inc., Washington, DC, *Congressional Quarterly Weekly Report*, vol. 53, No. 15, April 15, 1995, (copyright).

No. 439. Vote Cast for United States Representatives, by Major Political Party—States: 1990 to 1994

[In thousands, except percent. In each State, totals represent the sum of votes cast in each Congressional District or votes cast for Representative at Large in States where only one member is elected. In all years there are numerous districts within the State where either the Republican or Democratic party had no candidate. In some States the Republican and Democratic vote includes votes cast for the party candidate by endorsing parties. See also *Historical Statistics, Colonial Times to 1970*, series Y 211-214]

REGION, DIVISION, AND STATE	1990				1992				1994			
	Total[1]	Demo-cratic	Repub-lican	Percent for leading party	Total[1]	Demo-cratic	Repub-lican	Percent for leading party	Total[1]	Demo-cratic	Repub-lican	Percent for leading party
U.S. [2] . . .	61,513	32,565	27,648	D-52.9	96,239	48,964	43,833	D-50.9	69,770	31,698	36,590	R-52.4
Northeast . . .	12,792	6,483	5,868	D-50.7	19,417	9,567	8,871	D-49.3	14,398	7,016	6,927	D-48.7
N.E.	4,453	2,523	1,742	D-56.7	5,910	3,007	2,334	D-50.9	4,410	2,431	1,754	D-55.1
ME	517	284	233	D-55.0	670	364	278	D-54.3	503	236	234	D-47.0
NH. . . .	291	141	149	R-51.2	511	266	227	D-52.0	309	117	180	R-58.2
VT. . . .	210	6	83	[3]I-56.0	282	22	87	[3]I-57.8	211	-	99	[3]I-49.9
MA	2,051	1,420	567	D-69.2	2,614	1,518	857	D-58.1	1,976	1,363	593	D-69.0
RI	347	182	165	D-52.5	399	193	186	D-48.3	342	209	132	D-61.3
CT. . . .	1,037	489	546	R-52.6	1,435	644	699	R-48.7	1,069	506	516	R-48.3
M.A.	8,339	3,959	4,126	R-47.1	13,507	6,560	6,537	D-48.6	9,987	4,585	5,173	R-51.8
NY [4] . . .	3,662	1,830	1,662	D-50.0	5,925	3,051	2,687	D-51.5	4,611	2,213	2,251	R-48.8
NJ	1,827	837	911	R-49.9	2,992	1,355	1,503	R-50.2	2,005	880	1,091	R-54.4
PA	2,851	1,293	1,552	R-54.5	4,591	2,154	2,347	R-51.1	3,371	1,492	1,831	R-54.3
Midwest . . .	17,484	9,370	7,970	D-53.6	26,232	13,260	12,238	D-50.5	18,769	8,414	10,147	R-54.1
E.N.C	11,699	6,202	5,363	D-53.0	17,899	9,149	8,315	D-51.1	12,348	5,421	6,803	R-55.1
OH	3,418	1,807	1,590	D-52.9	4,577	2,198	2,154	D-48.0	3,298	1,328	1,925	R-58.4
IN	1,514	831	683	D-54.9	2,219	1,206	998	D-54.3	1,546	667	875	R-56.6
IL	3,077	1,646	1,349	D-53.5	4,831	2,678	2,097	D-55.4	3,044	1,460	1,577	R-51.8
MI	2,434	1,321	1,089	D-54.3	3,884	1,913	1,855	D-49.3	3,001	1,418	1,532	R-51.0
WI	1,256	597	652	R-51.9	2,388	1,154	1,211	R-50.7	1,459	548	893	R-61.2
W.N.C	5,785	3,168	2,607	D-54.8	8,333	4,111	3,923	D-49.3	6,420	2,992	3,344	R-52.1
MN	1,781	1,042	736	D-58.5	2,275	1,178	931	D-51.8	1,748	884	847	D-50.6
IA	792	401	385	D-50.6	1,242	493	729	R-58.7	977	407	560	R-57.3
MO	1,353	728	625	D-53.8	2,349	1,269	1,036	D-54.1	1,766	894	834	D-50.6
ND. . . .	234	153	81	D-65.2	298	169	117	D-56.8	235	123	106	D-52.3
SD. . . .	257	174	83	D-67.6	333	230	89	D-69.1	306	183	112	D-59.8
NE. . . .	587	277	309	R-52.7	711	283	427	R-60.1	571	203	365	R-64.0
KS. . . .	781	394	387	D-50.4	1,125	488	592	R-52.6	817	298	519	R-63.5
South [2] . . .	17,180	9,691	7,265	D-56.4	30,107	15,638	13,815	D-51.9	20,394	8,844	11,280	R-55.3
S.A. [2] . . .	9,409	5,222	4,063	D-55.5	15,982	8,088	7,577	D-50.6	10,660	4,566	6,017	R-56.4
DE. . . .	177	116	58	D-65.5	276	117	153	R-55.4	195	52	138	R-70.7
MD	1,091	566	517	D-51.9	1,808	956	843	D-52.9	1,345	662	683	R-50.7
DC. . . .	160	98	42	D-61.7	197	167	20	D-84.8	(NA)	(NA)	(NA)	(NA)
VA	1,153	663	411	D-57.5	2,368	1,149	1,143	D-48.5	1,908	753	1,089	R-57.1
WV	375	251	123	D-67.1	562	439	123	D-78.1	407	269	138	D-66.1
NC. . . .	2,011	1,076	935	D-53.5	2,527	1,282	1,204	D-50.7	1,588	681	907	R-57.1
SC. . . .	670	383	275	D-57.2	1,115	506	581	R-52.1	867	313	552	R-63.6
GA. . . .	1,394	855	539	D-61.3	2,214	1,215	999	D-54.9	1,498	681	816	R-54.5
FL [5] . . .	2,378	1,213	1,163	D-51.0	4,915	2,257	2,511	R-51.1	2,852	1,156	1,694	R-59.4
E.S.C	2,866	1,712	1,070	D-59.7	5,655	3,170	2,292	D-56.1	3,936	1,839	2,041	R-51.9
KY. . . .	764	353	397	R-52.0	1,361	722	638	D-53.0	784	316	451	R-57.5
TN. . . .	717	369	289	D-51.5	1,726	883	738	D-51.2	1,416	615	776	R-54.8
AL	1,017	690	315	D-67.9	1,603	896	643	D-55.9	1,115	554	558	R-50.1
MS	369	299	69	D-81.2	965	670	273	D-69.4	620	354	256	D-57.1
W.S.C	4,906	2,758	2,132	D-56.2	8,470	4,380	3,946	D-51.7	5,798	2,438	3,222	R-55.6
AR [6] . . .	665	369	296	D-55.5	889	525	357	D-59.1	709	336	373	R-52.6
LA [6] . . .	106	106	-	D-100.0	684	285	399	R-58.3	(X)	(X)	(X)	(X)
OK. . . .	857	519	338	D-60.6	1,276	764	504	D-59.9	969	368	555	R-57.3
TX	3,278	1,763	1,498	D-53.8	5,622	2,806	2,686	D-49.9	4,120	1,734	2,294	R-55.7
West	14,057	7,022	6,545	D-50.0	20,483	10,499	8,910	D-51.3	16,209	7,424	8,237	R-50.8
Mountain . .	3,872	1,783	2,043	R-52.8	5,736	2,627	2,886	R-50.3	4,438	1,706	2,580	R-58.1
MT. . . .	317	157	160	R-50.5	404	204	190	D-50.5	352	171	149	D-48.7
ID	315	183	131	D-58.2	473	222	231	R-48.8	393	138	255	R-65.0
WY	158	71	87	R-55.1	197	77	114	R-57.8	196	81	104	R-53.2
CO	1,001	504	487	D-50.3	1,479	691	758	R-51.2	1,056	364	687	R-65.1
NM	359	146	214	R-59.5	556	273	278	R-50.0	462	188	263	R-57.1
AZ. . . .	966	345	621	R-64.3	1,409	582	740	R-52.5	1,099	410	653	R-59.4
UT. . . .	442	234	191	D-52.9	727	331	362	R-49.8	504	216	252	R-50.0
NV. . . .	313	144	151	R-48.2	492	245	214	D-49.9	376	138	216	R-57.4
Pacific. . . .	10,185	5,239	4,502	D-51.4	14,747	7,872	6,024	D-53.4	11,771	5,719	5,657	D-48.6
WA	1,313	696	596	D-53.0	2,223	1,237	912	D-55.6	1,687	827	854	R-50.6
OR	1,053	667	342	D-63.4	1,391	825	553	D-59.3	1,193	647	499	D-54.2
CA. . . .	7,287	3,568	3,347	D-49.0	10,535	5,447	4,365	D-51.7	8,328	3,958	4,066	R-48.8
AK. . . .	192	92	99	R-51.7	239	102	112	R-46.8	208	68	119	R-56.9
HI	341	216	118	D-63.3	358	261	82	D-72.8	354	219	120	D-61.9

- Represents zero.   NA Not available.   X Not applicable.   [1] Includes vote cast for minor parties.   [2] Includes vote cast for nonvoting Delegate at Large in District of Columbia, except for 1994.   [3] Leading party candidate was Independent.   [4] Includes votes cast by other endorsing parties for Democratic and Republican candidates.   [5] State law does not require tabulation of votes for unopposed candidates. In 1990 Districts 8, 10, 12, 13, and 16 were unopposed; in 1992 District 21 was unopposed; in 1994 Districts 4, 10, 13, 14, 18, and 23 were unopposed.   [6] 1990 data are for a general election runoff in one district. 1990 open primary totals-total, 1,186,253; Democratic, 706,004; Republican, 450,867. 1992 data are for general election runoffs in three districts. In 1994 all Representatives won their seats in the open primary.

Source: 1990 and 1992, Elections Research Center, Chevy Chase, MD, *America Votes*, biennial, (copyright); 1994, Congressional Quarterly Inc., *Congressional Quarterly Weekly Report*, vol. 53, No. 15, April 15, 1995, (copyright).

No. 440. Vote Cast for United States Representatives, by Major Political Party—Congressional Districts: 1994

[In some States the Democratic and Republican vote includes votes cast for the party candidate by endorsing parties]

STATE AND DISTRICT	Total vote cast (1,000)	DEMOCRATIC CANDIDATE Name	Percent of total	REPUBLICAN CANDIDATE Name	Percent of total
AL	1,115	(X)	49.7	(X)	50.1
1st...	154	Womack	32.7	Callahan	67.3
2d...	169	Dowling	26.4	Everett	73.6
3d...	148	Browder	63.6	Hand	36.4
4th...	121	Bevill	98.5	(1)	(1)
5th...	176	Cramer	50.5	Parker	49.5
6th...	196	Fortenberry	20.9	Bachus	79.0
7th...	151	Hilliard	76.9	Middleton	23.0
AK	208	Smith	32.7	Young	56.9
AZ	1,099	(X)	37.3	(X)	59.4
1st...	181	Blanchard	39.0	Salmon	56.0
2d...	100	Pastor	62.3	MacDonald	32.7
3d...	207	Sprague	29.9	Stump	70.1
4th...	194	Cure	36.0	Shadegg	60.2
5th...	221	Auerbach	28.7	Kolbe	67.7
6th...	196	English	41.5	Hayworth	54.6
AR	709	(X)	47.4	(X)	52.6
1st...	178	Lambert	53.4	Dupwe	46.6
2d...	170	Thornton	57.4	Powell	42.6
3d...	192	Seitz	32.3	Hutchinson	67.7
4th...	169	Bradford	48.2	Dickey	51.8
CA	8,328	(X)	47.5	(X)	48.8
1st...	201	Hamburg	46.7	Riggs	53.3
2d...	215	Jacobs	26.1	Herger	64.2
3d...	195	Fazio	49.8	Lefever	46.1
4th...	236	Hirning	34.9	Doolittle	61.3
5th...	183	Matsui	68.5	Dinsmore	29.0
6th...	237	Woolsey	58.1	Nugent	37.6
7th...	167	Miller	69.7	Hughes	27.4
8th...	168	Pelosi	81.8	Cheung	18.2
9th...	179	Dellums	72.2	Wright	22.6
10th..	234	Schwartz	38.6	Baker	59.3
11th..	160	Perry	34.9	Pombo	62.1
12th..	176	Lantos	67.4	Wilder	32.6
13th..	151	Stark	64.6	Molton	30.2
14th..	199	Eshoo	60.6	Brink	39.4
15th..	200	Mineta	59.9	Wick	40.1
16th..	115	Lofgren	65.0	Smith	35.0
17th..	167	Farr	52.2	McCampbell	44.5
18th..	139	Condit	65.5	Carter	31.7
19th..	184	Lehman	39.6	Radanovich	56.8
20th..	101	Dooley	56.7	Young	43.3
21st..	172	Evans	27.7	Thomas	68.1
22d...	209	Capps	48.5	Seastrand	49.3
23d...	172	Ready	27.5	Gallegly	66.2
24th..	193	Beilenson	49.4	Sybert	47.5
25th..	170	Gilmartin	31.4	McKeon	64.9
26th..	88	Berman	62.6	Forsch	32.2
27th..	167	Kahn	42.1	Moorhead	53.0
28th..	164	Randle	30.5	Dreier	67.1
29th..	190	Waxman	68.0	Stepanek	28.3
30th..	66	Becerra	66.2	Ramirez	28.2
31st..	85	Martinez	59.1	Flores	40.9
32d...	126	Dixon	77.6	Farhat	17.6
33d...	42	Roybal-Allard	81.5	(1)	(1)
34th..	117	Torres	61.7	Nunez	34.1
35th..	84	Waters	78.1	Truman	21.9
36th..	196	Harman	48.0	Brooks	47.6
37th..	83	Tucker III	77.4	(1)	(1)
38th..	146	Mathews	36.8	Horn	58.5
39th..	170	Davis	29.0	Royce	66.4
40th..	164	Rusk	29.3	Lewis	70.7
41st..	132	Tessier	37.9	Kim	62.1
42d...	115	Brown	51.1	Guzman	48.8
43d...	154	Takano	38.4	Calvert	54.7
44th..	172	Clute	38.1	Bono	55.6
45th..	179	Williamson	30.9	Rohrabacher	69.1
46th..	88	Farber	37.1	Dornan	57.1
47th..	213	Kingsbury	24.9	Cox	71.7
48th..	195	Leschick	22.3	Packard	73.4
49th..	186	Schenk	46.0	Bilbray	48.5
50th..	104	Filner	56.7	Acevedo	35.4
51st..	207	Tamerius	27.7	Cunningham	66.9
52d...	171	Gastil	31.1	Hunter	64.0
CO	1,056	(X)	34.5	(X)	65.1
1st...	155	Schroeder	60.0	Eggert	39.9
2d...	187	Skaggs	56.8	Miller	43.2
3d...	209	Powers	30.4	McInnis	69.6
4th...	188	Kipp	27.7	Allard	72.3
5th...	139	(1)	(1)	Hefley	100.0
6th...	178	Hallen	28.0	Schaefer	69.8
CT	1,069	(X)	47.4	(X)	48.3
1st...	189	Kennelly	73.4	Putman	24.8
2d...	186	Gejdenson	42.6	Munster	42.5
3d...	175	DeLauro	63.4	Johnson	36.6
4th...	147	Kantrowitz	23.8	Shays	74.4
5th...	179	Maloney	45.5	Franks	52.2
6th...	193	Koskoff	31.5	Johnson	63.9
DE	195	DeSantis	26.6	Castle	70.7
FL	2,852	(X)	40.5	(X)	59.4
1st...	183	Whibbs	38.4	Scarborough	61.6
2d...	191	Peterson	61.3	Griffin	38.7
3d...	111	Brown	57.7	Little	42.3
4th...	(NA)	(1)	(1)	Fowler	(NA)
5th...	220	Thurman	57.2	Garlits	42.8
6th...	150	(1)	(1)	Stearns	99.1
7th...	179	Goddard	26.6	Mica	73.4
8th...	132	(1)	(1)	McCollum	99.7
9th...	177	(1)	(1)	Bilirakis	99.9
10th..	(NA)	(1)	(1)	Young	(NA)
11th..	149	Gibbons	51.6	Sharpe	48.4
12th..	163	Connors	35.0	Canady	65.0
13th..	(NA)	(1)	(1)	Miller	(NA)
14th..	(NA)	(1)	(1)	Goss	(NA)
15th..	218	Munsey	46.2	Weldon	53.7
16th..	211	Comerford	41.9	Foley	58.1
17th..	76	Meek	100.0	(1)	(1)
18th..	(NA)	(1)	(1)	Ros-Lehtinen	(NA)
19th..	223	Johnston	66.1	Tsakanikas	33.9
20th..	187	Deutsch	61.2	Kennedy	38.8
21st..	91	(1)	(1)	Diaz-Balart	100.0
22d...	189	Wiener	36.6	Shaw	63.4
23d...	(NA)	Hastings	(NA)	(1)	(1)
GA	1,498	(X)	45.5	(X)	54.5
1st...	116	Beckworth	23.4	Kingston	76.6
2d...	99	Bishop	66.2	Clayton	33.8
3d...	145	Overby	34.5	Collins	65.5
4th...	156	Yates	42.1	Linder	57.9
5th...	123	Lewis	69.1	Dixon	30.9
6th...	186	Jones	35.8	Gingrich	64.2
7th...	137	Darden	48.1	Barr	51.9
8th...	143	Mathis	37.3	Chambliss	62.7
9th...	137	Deal	57.9	Castello	42.1
10th..	147	Johnson	34.8	Norwood	65.2
11th..	109	McKinney	65.6	Lovett	34.4
HI	354	(X)	61.9	(X)	33.8
1st...	177	Abercrombie	53.6	Swindle	43.4
2d...	177	Mink	70.1	Garner	24.2
ID	393	(X)	35.0	(X)	65.0
1st...	202	LaRocco	44.6	Chenoweth	55.4
2d...	192	Fletcher	25.0	Crapo	75.0

See footnotes at end of table.

No. 440. Vote Cast for United States Representatives, by Major Political Party— Congressional Districts: 1994—Continued

[See headnote, p. 276]

STATE AND DISTRICT	Total vote cast (1,000)	DEMOCRATIC CANDIDATE Name	Percent of total	REPUBLICAN CANDIDATE Name	Percent of total
IL.....	3,044	(X)	48.0	(X)	51.8
1st...	149	Rush	75.7	Kelly	24.3
2d...	96	Reynolds	98.1	(1)	(1)
3d...	171	Lipinski	54.2	Nalepa	45.8
4th...	62	Gutierrez	75.2	Valtierra	24.8
5th...	138	Rosten-kowski	45.6	Flanagan	54.4
6th...	157	Berry	23.6	Hyde	73.5
7th...	117	Collins	79.6	Mobley	20.4
8th...	136	Walberg	35.1	Crane	64.9
9th...	143	Yates	66.1	Larney	33.9
10th...	153	Krupp	24.9	Porter	75.1
11th...	160	Giglio	39.4	Weller	60.6
12th...	154	Costello	65.9	Morris	34.1
13th...	170	Riley	26.9	Fawell	73.1
14th...	144	Denari	23.5	Hastert	76.5
15th...	160	Alexander	31.8	Ewing	68.2
16th...	166	Sullivan	29.4	Manzullo	70.6
17th...	175	Evans	54.5	Anderson	45.5
18th...	199	Stephens	39.3	LaHood	60.2
19th...	197	Poshard	58.4	Winters	41.6
20th...	197	Durbin	54.8	Owens	45.2
IN.....	1,546	(X)	43.2	(X)	56.6
1st...	122	Visclosky	56.5	Larson	43.5
2d...	172	Hogsett	45.5	McIntosh	54.5
3d...	131	Roemer	55.2	Burkett	44.8
4th...	160	Long	44.6	Souder	55.4
5th...	160	Beaty	28.3	Buyer	69.5
6th...	178	Bruner	23.0	Burton	77.0
7th...	160	Harmless	34.9	Myers	65.1
8th...	178	McCloskey	47.6	Hostettler	52.4
9th...	176	Hamilton	52.0	Leising	48.0
10th...	110	Jacobs	53.5	Scott	46.5
IA.....	977	(X)	41.7	(X)	57.3
1st...	183	Winkauf	37.9	Leach	60.2
2d...	198	Nagle	43.4	Nussle	56.0
3d...	193	Baxter	41.0	Lightfoot	57.8
4th...	213	Smith	46.4	Ganske	52.5
5th...	189	McGuire	39.0	Latham	60.8
KS.....	817	(X)	36.5	(X)	63.5
1st...	219	Nichols	22.6	Roberts	77.4
2d...	207	Carlin	34.4	Brownback	65.6
3d...	181	Hancock	43.4	Meyers	56.6
4th...	211	Glickman	47.1	Tiahrt	52.9
KY.....	784	(X)	40.3	(X)	57.5
1st...	127	Barlow	49.0	Whitfield	51.0
2d...	151	Adkisson	40.2	Lewis	59.8
3d...	152	Ward	44.4	Stokes	44.1
4th...	130	Skaggs	25.9	Bunning	74.1
5th...	104	Blevins	20.6	Rogers	79.4
6th...	119	Baesler	58.8	Wills	41.2
LA[2].....	(X)	(X)	(X)	(X)	(X)
1st...	(X)	(X)	(X)	Livingston[3]	(X)
2d...	(X)	Jefferson[3]	(X)	(X)	(X)
3d...	(X)	Tauzin[3]	(X)	(X)	(X)
4th...	(X)	Fields[3]	(X)	(X)	(X)
5th...	(X)	(X)	(X)	McCrery[3]	(X)
6th...	(X)	(X)	(X)	Baker[3]	(X)
7th...	(X)	Hayes[3]	(X)	(X)	(X)
ME.....	503	(X)	47.0	(X)	46.6
1st...	263	Dutremble	48.1	Longley	51.9
2d...	240	Baldacci	45.7	Bennett	40.8
MD.....	1,345	(X)	49.2	(X)	50.7
1st...	179	Gies	32.3	Gilchrest	67.7
2d...	199	Brewster	37.2	Ehrlich	62.8
3d...	165	Cardin	71.0	Tousey	29.0
4th...	124	Wynn	75.0	Dyson	25.0
5th...	168	Hoyer	58.8	Devine	41.2
6th...	186	Muldowney	34.1	Bartlett	65.9
7th...	119	Mfume	81.5	Kondner	18.5
8th...	204	Van Grack	29.7	Morella	70.3
MA.....	1,976	(X)	69.0	(X)	30.0
1st...	151	Olver	99.4	(1)	(1)
2d...	200	Neal	58.6	Briare	36.4
3d...	212	O'Sullivan	44.2	Blute	54.6
4th...	170	Frank	99.5	(1)	(1)
5th...	201	Meehan	69.9	Coleman	30.1
6th...	239	Tierney	47.4	Torkildsen	50.5
7th...	227	Markey	64.4	Bailey	35.6
8th...	114	Kennedy	99.0	(1)	(1)
9th...	210	Moakley	69.8	Murphy	30.2
10th...	251	Studds	68.8	Hemeon	31.2
MI.....	3,001	(X)	47.3	(X)	51.0
1st...	213	Stupak	56.9	Ziegler	42.0
2d...	194	Hoover	23.7	Hoekstra	75.3
3d...	185	Flory	23.5	Ehlers	73.9
4th...	199	Frasier	25.5	Camp	73.1
5th...	193	Barcia	65.5	Anderson	31.8
6th...	166	Taylor	25.5	Upton	73.5
7th...	177	McCaughtry	32.3	Smith	65.1
8th...	212	Mitchell	44.9	Chrysler	51.6
9th...	189	Kildee	51.2	O'Neill	47.0
10th...	196	Bonior	62.3	Lobsinger	37.7
11th...	227	Breshgold	30.5	Knollenberg	68.2
12th...	198	Levin	52.4	Pappa-george	46.9
13th...	173	Rivers	51.9	Schall	45.1
14th...	158	Conyers	81.5	Fornier	16.6
15th...	142	Collins	84.1	Savage	14.1
16th...	179	Dingell	59.1	Larkin	39.8
MN.....	1,748	(X)	50.6	(X)	48.4
1st...	213	Hottinger	44.7	Gutknecht	55.2
2d...	220	Minge	52.0	Revier	45.0
3d...	237	Olson	26.3	Ramstad	73.2
4th...	211	Vento	54.9	Newinski	41.9
5th...	196	Sabo	61.9	LeGrand	37.3
6th...	228	Luther	49.9	Jude	49.7
7th...	211	Peterson	51.2	Omann	48.6
8th...	233	Oberstar	65.7	Herwig	34.2
MS.....	620	(X)	57.1	(X)	41.3
1st...	128	Wheeler	36.9	Wicker	63.1
2d...	127	Thompson	53.7	Jordan	38.9
3d...	123	Montgomery	67.6	Dabbs	32.4
4th...	121	Parker	68.5	Wood	31.5
5th...	122	Taylor	60.1	Barlos	39.9
MO.....	1,766	(X)	50.6	(X)	47.3
1st...	153	Clay	63.4	Counts	32.9
2d...	230	Kelly	30.6	Talent	67.3
3d...	204	Gephardt	57.7	Gill	39.7
4th...	203	Skelton	67.8	Noland	32.2
5th...	178	McCarthy	56.6	Freeman	43.4
6th...	212	Danner	66.1	Tucker	33.9
7th...	196	Fossard	39.7	Hancock	57.3
8th...	185	Thompson	26.5	Emerson	70.1
9th...	205	Volkmer	50.5	Hulshof	45.0
MT.....	352	Williams	48.7	Jamison	42.2
NE.....	571	(X)	35.6	(X)	64.0
1st...	189	Combs	37.3	Bereuter	62.6
2d...	185	Hoagland	49.0	Christensen	49.9
3d...	197	Chapin	21.3	Barrett	78.7
NV.....	376	(X)	36.6	(X)	57.4
1st...	152	Bilbray	47.5	Ensign	48.5
2d...	224	Greeson	29.2	Vucanovich	63.5
NH.....	309	(X)	37.7	(X)	58.2
1st...	148	Verge	28.7	Zeliff	65.6
2d...	162	Swett	46.0	Bass	51.4
NJ.....	2,005	(X)	43.9	(X)	54.4
1st...	150	Andrews	72.3	Hogan	27.7
2d...	159	Magazzu	35.4	LoBiondo	64.6
3d...	174	Smith	31.2	Saxton	66.4
4th...	162	Walsh	30.6	Smith	67.9
5th...	189	Auer	21.9	Roukema	74.2
6th...	147	Pallone	60.4	Herson	37.5
7th...	166	Carroll	38.7	Franks	59.6
8th...	141	Klein	48.6	Martini	49.9
9th...	160	Torricelli	62.5	Russo	36.1
10th...	98	Payne	75.9	Ford	21.9
11th...	180	Herbert	28.0	Freling-huysen	71.2
12th...	184	Youssouf	30.4	Zimmer	68.3
13th...	95	Menendez	70.9	Alonso	25.2

See footnotes at end of table.

No. 440. Vote Cast for United States Representatives, by Major Political Party— Congressional Districts: 1994—Continued

[See headnote, p. 276]

STATE AND DISTRICT	Total vote cast (1,000)	DEMOCRATIC CANDIDATE Name	Percent of total	REPUBLICAN CANDIDATE Name	Percent of total	STATE AND DISTRICT	Total vote cast (1,000)	DEMOCRATIC CANDIDATE Name	Percent of total	REPUBLICAN CANDIDATE Name	Percent of total
NM....	462	(X)	40.6	(X)	57.1	12th..	172	Ruccia	33.3	Kasich	66.5
1st...	162	Zollinger	26.1	Schiff	73.9	13th..	190	Brown	49.1	White	45.5
2d...	142	Chavez	31.9	Skeen	63.3	14th..	185	Sawyer	51.9	Slaby	48.1
3d...	157	Richardson	63.6	Bemis	34.1	15th..	160	Buckel	29.1	Pryce	70.7
NY....	4,611	(X)	48.0	(X)	48.8	16th..	183	Finn	25.0	Regula	75.0
1st...	172	Hochbrueckner	46.5	Forbes	52.5	17th..	192	Traficant	77.4	Meister	22.6
2d...	147	Manfre	28.0	Lazio	68.2	18th..	191	DiDonato	46.0	Ney	54.0
3d...	195	Grill	40.0	King	59.2	19th..	206	Fingerhut	43.5	LaTourette	48.5
4th...	175	Schiliro	37.3	Frisa	50.2	OK....	969	(X)	38.0	(X)	57.3
5th...	171	Ackerman	55.0	Lally	43.3	1st...	171	Price	37.3	Largent	62.7
6th...	85	Flake	80.4	Bhagwandin	19.6	2d...	158	Cooper	47.9	Coburn	52.1
7th...	68	Manton	87.1	(1)	(1)	3d...	157	Brewster	73.8	Tallant	26.2
8th...	134	Nadler	82.0	Askren	15.8	4th...	155	Perryman	43.3	Watts	51.6
9th...	131	Schumer	72.6	McCall	27.4	5th...	175	(1)	(1)	Istook	78.1
10th...	87	Towns	89.0	Parker	9.2	6th...	152	Tollett	29.8	Lucas	70.2
11th...	70	Owens	88.9	Popkin	9.5	OR....	1,193	(X)	54.2	(X)	41.8
12th...	43	Velazquez	92.3	(1)	(1)	1st...	254	Furse	47.7	Witt	47.6
13th...	135	Butler	25.1	Molinari	71.4	2d...	234	Kupillas	38.7	Cooley	57.3
14th...	153	Maloney	64.2	Millard	35.4	3d...	223	Wyden	72.5	Hall	19.4
15th...	81	Rangel	96.5	(1)	(1)	4th...	238	DeFazio	66.8	Newkirk	33.2
16th...	61	Serrano	96.3	(1)	(1)	5th...	244	Webber	46.8	Bunn	49.8
17th...	94	Engel	77.6	Marshall	17.9	PA....	3,371	(X)	44.3	(X)	54.3
18th...	160	Lowey	57.3	Hartzell	40.9	1st...	122	Foglietta	81.5	Gordon	18.5
19th...	192	Fish	36.8	Kelly	52.1	2d...	140	Fattah	85.9	Watson	14.1
20th...	178	Julian	29.4	Gilman	67.5	3d...	148	Borski	62.7	Hasher	37.3
21st...	221	McNulty	67.0	Gomez	31.2	4th...	186	Klink	64.2	Peglow	35.8
22d...	215	Lawrence	26.6	Solomon	73.4	5th...	145	(1)	(1)	Clinger	99.9
23d...	176	Skeele	23.1	Boehlert	70.5	6th...	159	Holden	56.7	Levering	43.3
24th...	159	Francis	21.4	McHugh	78.6	7th...	197	Nichols	30.3	Weldon	69.7
25th...	198	Jezer	42.4	Walsh	57.6	8th...	167	Murray	26.7	Greenwood	66.1
26th...	195	Hinchey	49.1	Moppert	48.5	9th...	147	(1)	(1)	Shuster	99.7
27th...	205	Long	25.5	Paxon	74.5	10th...	163	Schreffler	31.1	McDade	65.7
28th...	196	Slaughter	56.6	Davison	40.1	11th...	153	Kanjorski	66.5	Podolak	33.5
29th...	187	LaFalce	55.2	Miller	43.0	12th...	171	Murtha	68.9	Choby	31.1
30th...	186	Franczyk	33.0	Quinn	67.0	13th...	195	Mezvinsky	45.2	Fox	49.4
31st...	143	(1)	(1)	Houghton	84.8	14th...	164	Coyne	64.1	Clark	32.4
NC....	1,588	(X)	42.9	(X)	57.1	15th...	151	McHale	47.8	Yeager	47.4
1st...	109	Clayton	61.1	Tyler	38.9	16th...	157	Chertok	30.3	Walker	69.7
2d...	141	Mocre	44.0	Funderburk	56.0	17th...	134	(1)	(1)	Gekas	99.9
3d...	137	Lancaster	47.3	Jones	52.7	18th...	186	Doyle	54.8	McCarty	45.2
4th...	154	Price	49.6	Heineman	50.4	19th...	125	(1)	(1)	Goodling	99.5
5th...	148	Sands	42.7	Burr	57.3	20th...	179	Mascara	53.1	McCormick	46.9
6th...	98	(1)	(1)	Coble	100.0	21st...	181	Leavens	46.9	English	49.5
7th...	122	Rose	51.6	Anderson	48.4	RI....	342	(X)	61.3	(X)	38.7
8th...	120	Hefner	52.4	Morgan	47.6	1st...	166	Kennedy	54.1	Vigilante	45.9
9th...	127	Blake	35.0	Myrick	65.0	2d...	176	Reed	68.0	Elliot	32.0
10th...	151	Avery	28.5	Ballenger	71.5	SC....	867	(X)	36.1	(X)	63.6
11th...	193	Lauterer	39.9	Taylor	60.1	1st...	147	Barber	32.4	Sanford	66.3
12th...	88	Watt	65.8	Martino	34.2	2d...	134	(1)	(1)	Spence	99.8
ND....	235	Pomeroy	52.3	Porter	45.0	3d...	150	Bryan	39.9	Graham	60.1
OH....	3,298	(X)	40.3	(X)	58.4	4th...	149	Fowler	26.4	Inglis	73.5
1st...	166	Mann	43.9	Chabot	56.1	5th...	148	Spratt	52.1	Bigham	47.8
2d...	194	Mann	22.6	Portman	77.4	6th...	139	Clyburn	63.8	McLeod	36.2
3d...	178	Hall	59.3	Westbrock	40.7	SD....	306	Johnson	59.8	Berkhout	36.6
4th...	140	(1)	(1)	Oxley	100.0	TN....	1,416	(X)	43.4	(X)	54.8
5th...	185	Tudor	26.6	Gillmor	73.4	1st...	141	Christian	24.6	Quillen	72.9
6th...	179	Strickland	49.1	Cremeans	50.9	2d...	142	(1)	(1)	Duncan	90.5
7th...	140	(1)	(1)	Hobson	100.0	3d...	162	Button	45.6	Wamp	52.3
8th...	148	(1)	(1)	Boehner	99.9	4th...	144	Whorley	42.0	Hilleary	56.6
9th...	157	Kaptur	75.3	Whitman	24.7	5th...	159	Clement	60.2	Osborne	38.7
10th...	184	Gaul	38.6	Hoke	51.9	6th...	180	Gordon	50.6	Gill	49.4
11th...	148	Stokes	77.2	Sykora	22.8	7th...	170	Byrd	38.6	Bryant	60.2
						8th...	154	Tanner	63.8	Morris	36.2
						9th...	164	Ford	57.8	DeBerry	42.2

See footnotes at end of table.

No. 440. Vote Cast for United States Representatives, by Major Political Party—Congressional Districts: 1994—Continued

[See headnote, p. 276]

STATE AND DISTRICT	Total vote cast (1,000)	DEMOCRATIC CANDIDATE Name	Percent of total	REPUBLICAN CANDIDATE Name	Percent of total	STATE AND DISTRICT	Total vote cast (1,000)	DEMOCRATIC CANDIDATE Name	Percent of total	REPUBLICAN CANDIDATE Name	Percent of total
TX	4,120	(X)	42.1	(X)	55.7	1st...	192	Sinclair	23.5	Bateman	74.3
1st...	156	Chapman ..	55.3	Blankenship	40.9	2d ...	138	Pickett	59.1	Chapman..	40.9
2d...	154	Wilson	57.0	Peterson ..	43.0	3d ...	137	Scott	79.4	Ward.....	20.6
3d...	173	(¹)	(¹)	Johnson ..	91.0	4th ...	187	Sisisky	61.6	Sweet	38.4
4th...	169	Hall	58.8	Bridges ...	39.8	5th ...	179	Payne	53.3	Landrith..	46.7
5th...	124	Bryant ...	50.1	Sessions ..	47.3	6th ...	127	(¹)	(¹)	Goodlatte..	99.9
6th...	201	Jesmore ..	22.0	Barton....	75.6	7th ...	211	(¹)	(¹)	Bliley....	84.0
7th...	117	(¹)	(¹)	Archer....	100.0	8th ...	203	Moran....	59.4	McSlarrow..	39.3
8th...	161	(¹)	(¹)	Fields....	92.0	9th ...	175	Boucher ...	58.8	Fast	41.2
9th...	157	Brooks	45.7	Stockman..	51.9	10th ...	176	(¹)	(¹)	Wolf.....	87.3
10th..	202	Doggett....	56.3	Baylor....	39.8	11th ...	186	Byrne....	45.3	Davis....	52.9
11th..	130	Edwards....	59.2	Broyles..	40.8	WA	1,687	(X)	49.0	(X)	50.6
12th..	140	Geren.....	68.7	Anderson..	31.3	1st...	195	Cantwell..	48.3	White....	51.7
13th..	143	Sarpalius..	44.6	Thornberry.	55.4	2d ...	197	Spanel....	45.3	Metcalf..	54.7
14th..	155	Laughlin..	55.6	Deats....	44.4	3d ...	193	Unsoeld ..	44.6	Smith	52.0
15th..	104	De La Garza.	59.0	Haughey..	39.4	4th ...	174	Inslee....	46.7	Hastings..	53.3
16th..	87	Coleman...	57.1	Ortiz.....	42.9	5th ...	216	Foley....	49.1	Nethercutt..	50.9
17th..	156	Stenholm..	53.7	Boone....	46.3	6th ...	181	Dicks....	58.3	Gregg....	41.7
18th..	115	Lee....	73.5	Burley	24.4	7th ...	197	McDermott..	75.1	Harris....	24.9
19th..	121	(¹)	(¹)	Combest..	100.0	8th ...	185	Wyrick....	23.9	Dunn....	76.1
20th..	96	Gonzalez ..	62.5	Colyer....	37.5	9th ...	150	Kreidler....	48.2	Tate	51.8
21st..	184	(¹)	(¹)	Smith....	90.0	WV	407	(X)	66.1	(X)	33.9
22d ..	163	Cunningham	23.8	DeLay....	73.7	1st...	147	Mollohan..	70.3	Riley....	29.7
23d ..	118	Rios......	37.4	Bonilla..	62.6	2d ...	142	Wise....	63.7	Cravotta..	36.3
24th..	123	Frost....	52.8	Harrison..	47.2	3d ...	117	Rahall....	63.9	Waldman..	36.1
25th..	119	Bentsen ...	52.3	Fontenot ..	45.0	WI	1,459	(X)	37.6	(X)	61.2
26th..	177	Bryant	22.4	Armey....	76.4	1st...	170	Barca....	48.8	Neumann..	49.4
27th..	110	Ortiz....	59.4	Stone....	40.6	2d ...	193	Hecht....	28.7	Klug....	69.2
28th..	104	Tejeda	70.9	Slatter..	27.6	3d ...	160	Stower....	41.0	Gunderson.	55.7
29th..	60	Green....	73.4	Eide....	26.6	4th ...	175	Kleczka..	53.7	Reynolds..	44.8
30th..	101	Johnson....	72.6	Cain....	25.7	5th ...	141	Barrett....	62.4	Hollingshead..	36.4
UT	504	(X)	42.8	(X)	50.0	6th ...	120	(¹)	(¹)	Petri.....	99.5
1st...	163	Coray....	35.5	Hansen....	64.5	7th ...	179	Obey....	54.3	West....	45.7
2d...	187	Shepherd ..	35.9	Waldholtz..	45.8	8th ...	179	Gruszynski.	36.3	Roth....	63.7
3d...	155	Orton	59.0	Thompson .	39.9	9th ...	142	(¹)	(¹)	Sensenbrenner ...	99.8
VT⁴	211	(¹)	(¹)	Carroll....	46.6	WY	196	Schuster ..	41.3	Cubin....	53.2
VA	1,908	(X)	39.4	(X)	57.1						

NA Not available.   X Not applicable.   ¹ No candidate.   ² Louisiana holds an open-primary election with candidates from all parties running on the same ballot. Any candidate who receives a majority is elected; if no candidate receives 50 percent, there is a run-off election in November between the top two finishers.   ³ Candidate listed won seat in open-primary.   ⁴ The winning candidate was Sanders, an Independent, who received 49.9 percent of the vote.

Source: Congressional Quarterly Inc., *Congressional Quarterly Weekly Report*, vol. 53, No. 15, April 15, 1995, (copyright).

No. 441. Composition of Congress, by Political Party: 1971 to 1995

[D=Democratic, R=Republican. Data for beginning of first session of each Congress (as of January 3). Excludes vacancies at beginning of session. See also *Historical Statistics, Colonial Times to 1970*, series Y 204-210]

YEAR	Party and President	Congress	HOUSE Majority party	HOUSE Minority party	HOUSE Other	SENATE Majority party	SENATE Minority party	SENATE Other
1971 [1]	R (Nixon)	92d	D-254	R-180	-	D-54	R-44	2
1973 [1][2]	R (Nixon)	93d	D-239	R-192	1	D-56	R-42	2
1975 [3]	R (Ford)	94th	D-291	R-144	-	D-60	R-37	2
1977 [4]	D (Carter)	95th	D-292	R-143	-	D-61	R-38	1
1979 [4]	D (Carter)	96th	D-276	R-157	-	D-58	R-41	1
1981 [4]	R (Reagan)	97th	D-243	R-192	-	R-53	D-46	1
1983	R (Reagan)	98th	D-269	R-165	-	R-54	D-46	-
1985	R (Reagan)	99th	D-252	R-182	-	R-53	D-47	-
1987	R (Reagan)	100th	D-258	R-177	-	D-55	R-45	-
1989	R (Bush)	101st	D-259	R-174	-	D-55	R-45	-
1991 [5]	R (Bush)	102d	D-267	R-167	1	D-56	R-44	-
1993 [5]	D (Clinton)	103d	D-258	R-176	1	D-57	R-43	-
1995 [5]	D (Clinton)	104th	R-230	D-204	1	R-52	D-48	-

- Represents zero.   ¹ Senate had one Independent and one Conservative-Republican.   ² House had one Independent-Democrat.   ³ Senate had one Independent, one Conservative-Republican, and one undecided (New Hampshire).   ⁴ Senate had one Independent.   ⁵ House had one Independent-Socialist.

Source: U.S. Congress, Joint Committee on Printing, *Congressional Directory*, annual; beginning 1977, biennial.

No. 442. Composition of Congress, by Political Party Affiliation—States: 1989 to 1995

[Figures are for the beginning of the first session (as of January 3). Dem.=Democratic; Rep.=Republican]

REGION, DIVISION, AND STATE	REPRESENTATIVES 101st Cong.,[1] 1989 Dem.	Rep.	102d Cong.,[2] 1991 Dem.	Rep.	103rd Cong.,[2] 1993 Dem.	Rep.	104th Cong.,[2] 1995 Dem.	Rep.	SENATORS 101st Cong., 1989 Dem.	Rep.	102d Cong., 1991 Dem.	Rep.	103rd Cong., 1993 Dem.	Rep.	104th Cong., 1995 Dem.	Rep.
U.S.	259	174	267	167	258	176	204	230	55	45	56	44	57	43	48	52
Northeast	55	40	56	38	50	37	47	40	10	8	10	8	11	7	9	9
N.E	14	10	16	7	14	8	14	8	7	5	7	5	7	5	6	6
ME	1	1	1	1	1	1	1	1	1	1	1	1	1	1	-	2
NH	-	2	1	1	1	1	-	2	-	2	-	2	-	2	-	2
VT	-	1	-	-	-	-	-	-	1	1	1	1	1	1	1	1
MA	10	1	10	1	8	2	8	2	2	-	2	-	2	-	2	-
RI	-	2	1	1	1	1	2	-	1	1	1	1	1	1	1	1
CT	3	3	3	3	3	3	3	3	2	-	2	-	2	-	2	-
M.A	41	30	40	31	36	29	33	32	3	3	3	3	4	2	3	3
NY	21	13	21	13	18	13	17	14	1	1	1	1	1	1	1	1
NJ	8	6	8	6	7	6	5	8	2	-	2	-	2	-	2	-
PA	12	11	11	12	11	10	11	10	-	2	-	2	1	1	-	2
Midwest	64	48	68	45	61	44	46	59	13	11	14	10	15	9	13	11
E.N.C	47	32	49	31	43	31	32	42	7	3	7	3	8	2	6	4
OH	11	10	11	10	10	9	6	13	2	-	2	-	2	-	1	1
IN	6	3	8	2	7	3	4	6	-	2	-	2	-	2	-	2
IL	14	8	15	7	12	8	10	10	2	-	2	-	2	-	2	-
MI	11	7	11	7	10	6	9	7	2	-	2	-	2	-	1	1
WI	5	4	4	5	4	5	3	6	1	1	1	1	2	-	2	-
W.N.C	17	16	19	14	18	13	14	17	6	8	7	7	7	7	7	7
MN	5	3	6	2	6	2	6	2	-	2	1	1	1	1	1	1
IA	2	4	2	4	1	4	-	5	1	1	1	1	1	1	1	1
MO	5	4	6	3	6	3	6	3	-	2	-	2	-	2	-	2
ND	1	-	1	-	1	-	1	-	2	-	2	-	2	-	2	-
SD	1	-	1	-	1	-	1	-	1	1	1	1	1	1	1	1
NE	1	2	1	2	1	2	-	3	2	-	2	-	2	-	2	-
KS	2	3	2	3	2	3	-	4	-	2	-	2	-	2	-	2
South	95	46	95	47	92	57	71	78	22	10	22	10	20	12	16	16
S.A	47	22	45	24	42	33	31	44	11	5	11	5	9	7	9	7
DE	1	-	1	-	-	1	-	1	1	1	1	1	1	1	1	1
MD	6	2	5	3	4	4	4	4	2	-	2	-	2	-	2	-
VA	5	5	6	4	7	4	6	5	1	1	1	1	1	1	1	1
WV	4	-	4	-	3	-	3	-	2	-	2	-	2	-	2	-
NC	8	3	7	4	8	4	4	8	1	1	1	1	-	2	-	2
SC	4	2	4	2	3	3	2	4	1	1	1	1	1	1	1	1
GA	9	1	9	1	7	4	4	7	2	-	2	-	1	1	1	1
FL	10	9	9	10	10	13	8	15	1	1	1	1	1	1	1	1
E.S.C	18	9	20	8	19	8	14	13	5	3	5	3	5	3	3	5
KY	4	3	4	3	4	2	2	4	1	1	1	1	1	1	1	1
TN	6	3	6	3	6	3	4	5	2	-	2	-	2	-	-	2
AL	4	2	5	2	4	3	4	3	2	-	2	-	2	-	2	-
MS	4	1	5	-	5	-	4	1	-	2	-	2	-	2	-	2
W.S.C	30	15	30	15	31	16	26	21	6	2	6	2	6	2	4	4
AR	3	1	3	1	2	2	2	2	2	-	2	-	2	-	2	-
LA	4	4	4	4	4	3	4	3	2	-	2	-	2	-	2	-
OK	4	2	4	2	4	2	1	5	1	1	1	1	1	1	-	2
TX	19	8	19	8	21	9	19	11	1	1	1	1	1	1	-	2
West	45	40	48	37	55	38	40	53	10	16	10	16	11	15	10	16
Mountain	9	15	11	13	11	13	6	18	6	10	6	10	6	10	5	11
MT	1	1	1	1	1	-	1	-	1	1	1	1	1	1	1	1
ID	1	1	2	-	1	1	-	2	-	2	-	2	-	2	-	2
WY	-	1	-	1	-	1	-	1	-	2	-	2	-	2	-	2
CO	3	3	3	3	2	4	2	4	1	1	1	1	1	1	1	1
NM	1	2	1	2	1	2	1	2	1	1	1	1	1	1	1	1
AZ	1	4	1	4	3	3	1	5	1	1	1	1	1	1	-	2
UT	1	2	2	1	2	1	1	2	-	2	-	2	-	2	-	2
NV	1	1	1	1	1	1	-	2	2	-	2	-	2	-	2	-
Pacific	36	25	37	24	44	25	34	35	4	6	4	6	5	5	5	5
WA	5	3	5	3	8	1	2	7	1	1	1	1	1	1	1	1
OR	3	2	4	1	4	1	3	2	-	2	-	2	-	2	-	2
CA	27	18	26	19	30	22	27	25	1	1	1	1	2	-	2	-
AK	-	1	-	1	-	1	-	1	-	2	-	2	-	2	-	2
HI	1	1	2	-	2	-	2	-	2	-	2	-	2	-	2	-

- Represents zero.   [1] Alabama and Indiana had one vacancy each.   [2] Vermont had one Independent-Socialist Representative.

Source: U.S. Congress, Joint Committee on Printing, *Congressional Directory,* biennial; and unpublished data.

No. 443. Members of Congress—Incumbents Re-elected: 1964 to 1994

YEAR	REPRESENTATIVES						SENATORS					
	Retire-ments[1]	Incumbent candidates					Retire-ments[1]	Incumbent candidates				
		Total	Re-elected		Defeated in—			Total	Re-elected		Defeated in—	
			Num-ber	Per-cent of candi-dates	Pri-mary	Gen-eral elec-tion			Num-ber	Per-cent of candi-dates	Pri-mary	Gen-eral election
PRESIDENTIAL-YEAR ELECTIONS												
1964	33	397	344	86.6	8	45	2	33	28	84.8	1	4
1968	23	409	396	96.8	4	9	6	28	20	71.4	4	4
1972	40	390	365	93.6	12	13	6	27	20	74.1	2	5
1976	47	384	368	95.8	3	13	8	25	16	64.0	-	9
1980	34	398	361	90.7	6	31	5	29	16	55.2	4	9
1984	22	411	392	95.4	3	16	4	29	26	89.7	-	3
1988	23	409	402	98.3	1	6	6	27	23	85.2	-	4
1992	65	368	325	88.3	[2]19	[3]24	7	28	23	82.1	1	4
MIDTERM ELECTIONS												
1966	22	411	362	88.1	8	41	3	32	28	87.5	3	1
1970	29	401	379	94.5	10	12	4	31	24	77.4	1	6
1974	43	391	343	87.7	8	40	7	27	23	85.2	2	2
1978	49	382	358	93.7	5	19	10	25	15	60.0	3	7
1982	40	393	354	90.1	[2]10	29	3	30	28	93.3	-	2
1986	40	394	385	97.7	3	6	6	28	21	75.0	-	7
1990	27	406	390	96.1	1	15	3	32	31	96.9	-	1
1994	[4]27	383	347	90.6	4	35	[4]8	26	24	92.3	-	2

- Represents zero.   [1] Does not include persons who died or resigned before the election.   [2] Number of incumbents defeated in primaries by other incumbents due to redistricting: six in 1982 and four in 1992.   [3] Five incumbents defeated in general election by other incumbents due to redistricting.   [4] As of September 9, 1994.

Source: Ornstein, Norman J., Thomas E. Mann, and Michael J. Malbin, *Vital Statistics on Congress, 1993-1994,* Congressional Quarterly, Inc., Washington, DC, 1994; Congressional Quarterly, Inc., Washington, DC, *Congressional Quarterly Weekly Report,* vol. 52, No. 44, Nov. 12, 1994, and selected prior issues; and *Congressional Monitor,* vol. 30, No. 161, Nov. 10, 1994 (copyright).

No. 444. Members of Congress—Selected Characteristics: 1981 to 1995

[As of beginning of first session of each Congress, (January 3). Figures for Representatives exclude vacancies]

MEMBERS OF CONGRESS AND YEAR	Male	Fe-male	Black[1]	Asian, Pacific Islan-der[2]	His-panic[3]	AGE[4] (in years)					SENIORITY[5]				
						Under 40	40 to 49	50 to 59	60 to 69	70 and over	Less than 2 yrs.	2 to 9 yrs.	10 to 19 yrs.	20 to 29 yrs.	30 yrs. or more
REPRESENTATIVES															
97th Cong., 1981 . . .	416	19	17	3	6	94	142	132	54	13	77	231	96	23	8
98th Cong., 1983 . . .	413	21	21	3	8	86	145	132	57	14	83	224	88	28	11
99th Cong., 1985 . . .	412	22	20	3	10	71	154	131	59	19	49	237	104	34	10
100th Cong., 1987 . .	412	23	23	4	11	63	153	137	56	26	51	221	114	37	12
101st Cong., 1989 . .	408	25	24	5	10	41	163	133	74	22	39	207	139	35	13
102d Cong., 1991 . .	407	28	25	3	11	39	152	134	86	24	55	178	147	44	11
103d Cong., 1993[6] .	388	47	38	4	17	47	151	128	89	15	118	141	132	32	12
104th Cong., 1995 . .	388	47	40	4	17	53	155	135	79	13	92	188	110	36	9
SENATORS															
97th Cong., 1981 . . .	98	2	-	3	-	9	35	36	14	6	19	51	17	11	2
98th Cong., 1983 . . .	98	2	-	2	-	7	28	39	20	6	5	61	21	10	3
99th Cong., 1985 . . .	98	2	-	2	-	4	27	38	25	6	8	56	27	7	2
100th Cong., 1987 . .	98	2	-	2	-	5	30	36	22	7	14	41	36	7	2
101st Cong., 1989 . .	98	2	-	2	-	-	30	40	22	8	23	22	43	10	2
102d Cong., 1991 . .	98	2	-	2	-	-	23	46	24	7	5	34	47	10	4
103d Cong., 1993[6] .	93	7	1	2	-	1	16	48	22	12	15	30	39	11	5
104th Cong., 1995 . .	92	8	1	2	-	1	14	41	27	17	12	38	30	15	5

- Represents zero.   [1] Source: Joint Center for Political and Economic Studies, Washington, DC, *Black Elected Officials: A National Roster,* annual (copyright).   [2] Source: Library of Congress, Congressional Research Service, "Asian Pacific Americans in the United States Congress", Report 94-767 GOV.   [3] Source: National Association of Latino Elected and Appointed Officials, Washington, DC, *National Roster of Hispanic Elected Officials,* annual.   [4] Some members do not provide date of birth.   [5] Represents consecutive years of service.   [6] Includes members elected to fill vacant seats through June 14, 1993.

Source: Except as noted, compiled by U.S. Bureau of the Census from data published in *Congressional Directory,* biennial.

No. 445. U.S. Congress—Measures Introduced and Enacted and Time in Session: 1977 to 1994

[Excludes simple and concurrent resolutions. See also *Historical Statistics, Colonial Times to 1970*, series Y 189-198]

ITEM	95th Cong., 1977-78	96th Cong., 1979-80	97th Cong., 1981-82	98th Cong., 1983-84	99th Cong., 1985-86	100th Cong., 1987-88	101st Cong., 1989-90	102d Cong., 1991-92	103d Cong., 1993-94
Measures introduced.............	19,387	12,583	11,490	11,156	9,885	9,588	6,664	6,775	8,544
Bills......................	18,045	11,722	10,582	10,134	8,697	8,515	5,977	6,212	7,883
Joint resolutions.............	1,342	861	908	1,022	1,188	1,073	687	563	661
Measures enacted.............	803	736	529	677	483	761	666	609	473
Public....................	633	613	473	623	466	713	650	589	465
Private....................	170	123	56	54	17	48	16	20	8
HOUSE OF REPRESENTATIVES									
Number of days..............	323	326	303	266	281	298	281	280	265
Number of hours.............	1,898	1,876	1,420	1,705	1,794	1,659	1,688	1,796	1,887
Number of hours per day.........	5.9	5.8	4.7	6.4	6.4	5.6	6.0	6.4	7.1
SENATE									
Number of days..............	337	333	312	281	313	307	274	287	291
Number of hours.............	2,510	2,324	2,158	1,951	2,531	2,341	2,254	2,292	2,514
Number of hours per day.........	7.4	7.0	6.9	6.9	8.1	7.6	8.2	8.0	8.6

Source: U.S. Congress, *Congressional Record* and *Daily Calendar*, selected issues.

No. 446. Congressional Bills Vetoed: 1961 to 1994

[See also *Historical Statistics, Colonial Times to 1970*, series Y 199-203]

PERIOD	President	Total vetoes	Regular vetoes	Pocket vetoes	Vetoes sustained	Bills passed over veto
1961-63..............	Kennedy..................	21	12	9	21	-
1963-69..............	Johnson..................	30	16	14	30	-
1969-74..............	Nixon...................	43	26	17	36	7
1974-77..............	Ford....................	66	48	18	54	12
1977-81..............	Carter..................	31	13	18	29	2
1981-89..............	Reagan..................	78	39	39	69	9
1989-93..............	Bush...................	44	29	15	43	1
1993-94..............	Clinton..................	-	-	-	-	-

- Represents zero.

Source: U.S. Congress, Senate Library, *Presidential Vetoes ... 1789-1968*; U.S. Congress, *Calendars of the U.S. House of Representatives and History of Legislation*, annual.

No. 447. Congressional Staff, by Location of Employment: 1970 to 1991

[Excludes those persons employed in Congressional support agencies such as the U.S. General Accounting Office, the Library of Congress, and the Congressional Budget Office]

YEAR	PERSONAL STAFF House	PERSONAL STAFF Senate	YEAR	STANDING COMMITTEE STAFF House	STANDING COMMITTEE STAFF Senate	LOCATION OF EMPLOYMENT	1981	1985	1989	1990	1991
1972 ..	5,280	2,426	1970..	702	635	Total	17,422	18,136	17,306	17,625	17,821
1978 ..	6,944	3,268	1978..	1,844	1,151						
1979 ..	7,067	3,593	1979..	1,909	1,269	House of Representatives...	11,217	11,636	11,184	11,064	11,041
1980 ..	7,371	3,746	1980..	1,917	1,191	Committee staff [2].......	1,917	2,146	2,267	2,173	2,321
1981 ..	7,487	3,945	1981..	1,843	1,022	Personal staff	7,487	7,528	7,569	7,496	7,278
1982 ..	7,511	4,041	1982..	1,839	1,047	Leadership staff........	127	144	133	156	149
1983 ..	7,606	4,059	1983..	1,970	1,075	Officers of House, staff ...	1,686	1,818	1,215	1,239	1,293
1984 ..	7,385	3,949	1984..	1,944	1,095						
1985 ..	7,528	4,097	1985..	2,009	1,080	Senate	6,079	6,369	5,984	6,425	6,635
1986 ..	[1]7,920	[1]3,774	1986..	1,954	1,075	Committee staff [2].......	1,150	1,178	1,116	1,207	1,154
1987 ..	7,584	4,075	1987..	2,024	1,074	Personal staff	3,945	4,097	3,837	4,162	4,294
			1988..	1,976	970	Leadership staff........	106	118	105	94	95
1989 ..	7,569	3,837	1989..	1,986	1,013	Officers of Senate, staff...	878	976	926	962	1,092
1990 ..	7,496	4,162	1990..	1,993	1,090						
1991 ..	7,278	4,294	1991..	2,201	1,030	Joint committee staff	126	131	138	136	145

[1] House figure is average for year, and Senate figure only covers period following implementation of Gramm-Rudman budget reductions. [2] Covers standing, select, and special committees.

Source: Ornstein, Norman J., Thomas E. Mann, and Michael J. Malbin, *Vital Statistics on Congress, 1993-1994*, Congressional Quarterly, Inc., Washington, DC, 1994, (copyright).

No. 448. Number of Governors, by Political Party Affiliation: 1970 to 1995

[Reflects results of elections in previous year and holdover incumbents]

YEAR	Demo-cratic	Repub-lican	Inde-pendent	YEAR	Demo-cratic	Repub-lican	Inde-pendent	YEAR	Demo-cratic	Repub-lican	Inde-pendent
1970	18	32	-	1986	34	16	-	1991 [1] ...	28	20	2
1975	36	13	1	1987	26	24	-	1992	27	21	2
1980	31	19	-	1988	27	23	-	1993	30	18	2
1984	35	15	-	1989	28	22	-	1994	28	20	2
1985	34	16	-	1990	29	21	-	1995	19	30	1

- Represents zero.   [1] Reflects result of runoff election in Arizona in February 1991.
Source: National Governors' Association, Washington, DC, *Directory of Governors of the American States, Commonwealths & Territories,* annual, (copyright).

No. 449. Vote Cast for and Governor Elected, by State: 1988 to 1994

[**In thousands, except percent**. D=Democratic, R=Republican, I=Independent]

DIVISION AND STATE	1988 Total vote [1]	1988 Percent leading party	1990 Total vote [1]	1990 Percent leading party	1992 Total vote [1]	1992 Percent leading party	1994 Total vote [1]	1994 Percent leading party	Candidate elected at most recent election
N.E.:									
ME	(X)	(X)	522	R-46.7	(X)	(X)	511	I-35.4	Angus King
NH	442	R-60.4	295	R-60.3	516	R-56.0	312	R-69.9	Steve Merrill
VT	243	D-55.4	211	R-51.8	286	D-74.7	212	D-68.7	Howard Dean
MA	(X)	(X)	2,343	R-50.2	(X)	(X)	2,164	R-70.9	William Weld
RI	401	R-50.8	357	D-74.1	425	D-61.5	361	R-47.4	Lincoln Almond
CT	(X)	(X)	1,141	I-40.4	(X)	(X)	1,147	R-36.2	John Rowland
M.A.:									
NY[2]	(X)	(X)	4,057	D-53.2	(X)	(X)	5,204	R-48.8	George Pataki
NJ[2]	(X)	(X)	2,254	D-61.2	2,506	R-49.3	(X)	(X)	Christine T. Whitman
PA	(X)	(X)	3,053	D-67.7	(X)	(X)	3,585	R-45.4	Thomas Ridge
E.N.C.:									
OH	(X)	(X)	3,478	R-55.7	(X)	(X)	3,346	R-71.8	George Voinovich
IN	2,141	D-53.2	(X)	(X)	2,229	D-62.0	(X)	(X)	Evan Bayh
IL	(X)	(X)	3,257	R-50.7	(X)	(X)	3,107	R-63.9	Jim Edgar
MI	(X)	(X)	2,565	R-49.8	(X)	(X)	3,088	R-61.5	John Engler
WI	(X)	(X)	1,380	R-58.2	(X)	(X)	1,563	R-67.3	Tommy Thompson
W.N.C.:									
MN	(X)	(X)	1,807	R-49.6	(X)	(X)	1,766	R-62.0	Arne Carlson
IA	(X)	(X)	976	R-60.6	(X)	(X)	997	R-56.8	Terry Branstad
MO	2,086	R-64.2	(X)	(X)	2,344	D-58.7	(X)	(X)	Mel Carnahan
ND	299	D-59.9	(X)	(X)	305	R-57.9	(X)	(X)	Edward T. Schafer
SD	(X)	(X)	257	D-58.9	(X)	(X)	312	R-55.4	William Janklow
NE	(X)	(X)	587	D-49.9	(X)	(X)	580	D-73.0	Ben Nelson
KS	(X)	(X)	783	D-48.6	(X)	(X)	821	R-64.1	Bill Graves
S.A.:									
DE	240	R-70.7	(X)	(X)	277	D-64.7	(X)	(X)	Thomas R. Carper
MD[2]	(X)	(X)	1,111	D-59.8	(X)	(X)	1,410	D-50.2	Parris Glendening
VA[2]	(X)	(X)	1,789	D-50.1	1,794	R-58.3	(X)	(X)	George F. Allen
WV	650	D-58.9	(X)	(X)	657	D-56.0	(X)	(X)	Gaston Caperton
NC	2,180	R-56.1	(X)	(X)	2,595	D-52.7	(X)	(X)	James B. Hunt
SC	(X)	(X)	761	R-69.5	(X)	(X)	934	R-50.4	David Beasley
GA	(X)	(X)	1,450	D-52.9	(X)	(X)	1,545	D-51.1	Zell Miller
FL	(X)	(X)	3,531	D-56.5	(X)	(X)	4,206	D-50.8	Lawton Chiles
E.S.C.:									
KY[3]	781	D-64.6	835	D-64.7	(X)	(X)	(X)	(X)	Brereton C. Jones
TN	(X)	(X)	790	D-60.8	(X)	(X)	1,487	R-54.3	Don Sundquist
AL	(X)	(X)	1,216	R-52.1	(X)	(X)	1,202	R-50.3	Fob James, Jr.
MS[3]	722	D-53.4	711	R-50.8	(X)	(X)	(X)	(X)	Kirk Fordice
W.S.C.:									
AR	(X)	(X)	696	D-57.5	(X)	(X)	717	D-59.8	Jim Guy Tucker
LA	[4]1,559	[4]33.1	[5]1,728	[5]D-61.2	(X)	(X)	(X)	(X)	Edwin W. Edwards
OK	(X)	(X)	911	D-57.4	(X)	(X)	995	R-46.9	Frank Keating
TX	(X)	(X)	3,893	D-49.5	(X)	(X)	4,396	R-53.5	George W. Bush
Mountain:									
MT	367	R-51.9	(X)	(X)	408	R-51.3	(X)	(X)	Marc Racicot
ID	(X)	(X)	321	D-68.2	(X)	(X)	413	R-52.3	Phil Batt
WY	(X)	(X)	160	D-65.4	(X)	(X)	201	R-58.7	Jim Geringer
CO	(X)	(X)	1,011	D-61.9	(X)	(X)	1,116	D-55.5	Roy Romer
NM	(X)	(X)	411	D-54.6	(X)	(X)	468	R-49.8	Gary Johnson
AZ	(X)	(X)	[6]941	[6]R-52.4	(X)	(X)	1,129	R-52.5	Fife Symington
UT	649	R-40.1	(X)	(X)	763	R-42.2	(X)	(X)	Mike Leavitt
NV	(X)	(X)	321	D-64.8	(X)	(X)	371	D-53.9	Bob Miller
Pacific:									
WA	1,875	D-62.2	(X)	(X)	2,271	D-52.2	(X)	(X)	Mike Lowry
OR	(X)	(X)	1,113	D-45.7	(X)	(X)	1,221	D-50.9	John Kitzhaber
CA	(X)	(X)	7,699	R-49.2	(X)	(X)	8,659	R-55.2	Pete Wilson
AK	(X)	(X)	195	I-38.9	(X)	(X)	213	D-41.1	James Campbell
HI	(X)	(X)	340	D-59.8	(X)	(X)	369	D-36.6	Ben Cayetano

X Not applicable.   [1] Includes minor party and scattered votes.   [2] Voting years 1989 and 1993.   [3] Voting years 1987 and 1991.   [4] Primary election in Oct. 1987, held on a nonparty basis. Winner was Democratic. Runner-up withdrew from runoff.   [5] Result of runoff election in 1991.   [6] Result of runoff election in February 1991.
Source: Elections Research Center, Chevy Chase, MD, *America Votes,* biennial; and unpublished data, (copyright) and Congressional Quarterly, Inc., Washington, DC, *Congressional Quarterly Weekly Report,* vol. 53, No. 15, April 15, 1995, (copyright).

No. 450. Composition of State Legislatures, by Political Party Affiliation: 1988 to 1994

[Data reflect election results in year shown for most States; and except as noted, results in previous year for other States. Figures reflect immediate results of elections, including holdover members in State houses which do not have all of their members running for re-election. Dem.=Democrat, Rep.=Republican. In general, Lower House refers to body consisting of State Representatives; Upper House, of State Senators]

STATE	LOWER HOUSE								UPPER HOUSE							
	1988 [1,2]		1990 [3,4]		1992 [5,6]		1994 [7,8]		1988 [1,9]		1990 [3,10]		1992 [5,11]		1994 [7,12]	
	Dem.	Rep.	Dem.	Rep.	Dem.	Rep.	Dem.	Rep.	Dem.	Rep.	Dem.	Rep.	Dem.	Rep.	Dem.	Rep.
U.S. . . .	3,277	2,176	3,242	2,202	3,186	2,223	2,817	2,603	1,192	751	1,186	757	1,132	799	1,021	905
AL [13] . . .	85	17	82	23	82	23	74	31	28	6	28	7	27	8	23	12
AK [14] . . .	23	17	23	17	20	18	17	22	8	12	10	10	10	10	8	12
AZ [15] . . .	26	34	27	33	25	35	22	38	13	17	17	13	12	18	11	19
AR [14] . . .	88	11	90	9	88	11	88	12	31	4	31	4	30	5	28	7
CA [14] . . .	46	33	47	33	47	33	39	40	24	15	25	13	21	16	21	17
CO [14] . . .	26	39	27	38	31	34	24	41	11	24	12	23	16	19	16	19
CT [15] . . .	88	63	87	64	85	64	90	61	23	13	20	16	19	17	17	19
DE [14] . . .	18	23	17	24	18	23	14	27	13	8	15	6	15	6	12	9
FL [14] . . .	73	47	74	46	71	49	63	57	23	17	22	18	20	20	19	21
GA [15] . . .	144	36	145	35	128	51	114	65	45	11	45	11	41	15	35	20
HI [14] . . .	45	6	45	6	47	4	44	7	22	3	22	3	22	3	23	2
ID [15] . . .	20	64	28	56	20	50	13	57	19	23	21	21	12	23	8	27
IL [14] . . .	67	51	72	46	67	51	54	64	31	28	31	28	27	32	26	33
IN [14] . . .	50	50	52	48	55	45	44	56	24	26	24	26	22	28	20	30
IA [14] . . .	61	39	55	45	49	51	36	64	30	20	29	21	27	23	27	23
KS [14] . . .	58	67	63	62	59	66	45	80	18	22	18	22	13	27	13	27
KY [14] . . .	72	28	68	32	71	29	64	36	30	8	27	11	25	13	21	17
LA [13] . . .	86	17	89	16	88	16	86	17	34	5	34	5	33	6	33	6
ME [15] . . .	97	54	97	54	93	58	77	74	20	15	21	14	20	15	16	18
MD [13] . . .	125	16	116	25	116	25	100	41	40	7	38	9	38	9	32	15
MA [15] . . .	128	32	118	37	123	34	125	34	32	8	25	15	31	9	30	10
MI [14] . . .	61	49	61	49	55	55	53	56	18	20	18	20	16	22	16	22
MN [14] . . .	80	53	78	56	85	49	71	63	44	23	46	21	45	22	43	21
MS [13] . . .	112	9	98	23	91	29	89	31	44	8	43	9	37	15	36	14
MO [14] . . .	104	58	99	64	98	65	87	76	22	12	23	11	20	14	19	15
MT [14] . . .	52	48	61	39	47	53	33	67	23	27	29	21	30	20	19	31
NE . . .	(16)	(16)	(16)	(16)	(16)	(16)	(16)	(16)	(16)	(16)	(16)	(16)	(16)	(16)	(16)	(16)
NV [14] . . .	30	12	22	19	27	12	21	21	8	13	10	10	10	11	8	13
NH [15] . . .	119	281	125	268	136	258	112	286	8	16	11	13	11	13	6	18
NJ [14] . . .	44	36	22	58	27	53	28	52	22	17	13	27	16	24	16	24
NM [14] . . .	45	25	49	21	53	17	46	24	26	16	26	16	27	15	27	15
NY [15] . . .	92	58	95	55	100	50	94	56	27	34	26	35	26	35	25	36
NC [15] . . .	74	46	81	39	78	42	52	68	37	13	36	14	39	11	26	24
ND [14] . . .	45	61	48	58	33	65	23	75	32	21	27	26	25	24	20	29
OH [14] . . .	59	40	61	38	53	46	43	56	14	19	12	21	13	20	13	20
OK [14] . . .	68	32	68	33	70	31	65	36	33	15	37	11	37	11	35	13
OR [14] . . .	32	28	28	32	28	32	26	34	19	11	20	10	16	14	11	19
PA [14] . . .	104	99	107	94	105	98	101	102	23	27	24	26	24	25	21	29
RI [15] . . .	83	17	89	11	85	15	84	16	41	9	45	5	39	11	40	10
SC [14] . . .	87	37	79	43	71	52	58	62	35	11	33	13	30	16	29	17
SD [15] . . .	24	46	25	45	28	42	24	46	15	20	17	18	20	15	16	19
TN [14] . . .	59	40	57	42	63	36	59	40	22	11	20	13	19	14	18	15
TX [14] . . .	93	57	93	57	91	58	89	61	23	8	22	9	18	13	17	14
UT [14] . . .	28	47	31	44	26	49	20	55	7	22	10	19	11	18	10	19
VT [15] . . .	74	76	73	75	87	57	86	61	16	14	15	15	14	16	12	18
VA [14] . . .	59	39	58	41	52	47	52	47	30	10	22	18	22	18	22	18
WA [14] . . .	63	35	58	40	65	33	38	60	24	25	24	25	28	21	25	24
WV [14] . . .	81	19	74	26	79	21	69	30	29	5	33	1	32	2	26	8
WI [14] . . .	56	43	58	41	51	47	48	51	20	13	19	14	16	17	16	17
WY [14] . . .	23	41	22	42	19	41	13	47	11	19	10	20	10	20	10	20

[1] Status as of Jan. 1989, except for NJ and VA which are as of Jan. 1990. [2] Excludes one Independent for AR; two Independents for VA; one Independent Democrat for MS; one vacancy each for CA, MN, MO, and OK; two vacancies for LA; and three vacancies for AL. [3] Status as of May 1992; reflects results of elections held in LA, KY, MS, and NJ in 1991. [4] Excludes one Independent each for MA, MS, NH, SC, and VA; one Independent Democrat for NH; two Independents for VT; one vacancy each for AR, NV, and SC; two vacancies for PA; four vacancies for MA; and five vacancies for NH. [5] Status as of November 11, 1993. [6] Excludes one Independent each for AR, LA, NH, SC, and VA; two Independents each for AK and MS; four Independents for VT; members of political parties other than Democratic, Republican, or Independent (one in MA, two in VT, and four in NH); one vacancy each for GA, NH, TX, and WI; two vacancies each for CT and MA; and three vacancies for NV. [7] Status as of December 7, 1994. [8] Excludes one Independent each for AK, CA, LA, and VA; two Independents each for MS and VT; four Independents for SC; members of political parties other than Democratic, Republican, or Independent (one each in MA and VT and two in NH); one undecided in GA; and one vacancy each in LA, MI, and WV. [9] Excludes one Independent for CA and one vacancy each for AL and NJ. [10] Excludes two Independents for CA; and one vacancy for NV. [11] Excludes two Independents for CA; and one vacancy each for CA and PA. [12] Excludes one Independent in ME, two independents in CA, one vacancy in GA, two vacancies in MS, and three vacancies in MN. [13] Members of both houses serve 4-year terms. [14] Upper House members serve 4-year terms and Lower House members serve 2-year terms. [15] Members of both houses serve 2-year terms. [16] Single chamber (unicameral body) of 49 members, elected without party designation.

Source: 1988 and 1990, The Council of State Governments, Lexington, KY, *State Elective Officials and the Legislatures*, biennial (copyright); ©1993 The Council of State Governments. Reprinted with permission from *The Book of States* (copyright). 1992 and 1994. National Conference of State Legislatures, Denver, CO, unpublished data, (copyright).

No. 451. Political Party Control of State Legislatures, by Party: 1971 to 1995

[As of beginning of year. Until 1972 there were two nonpartisan legislatures in Minnesota and Nebraska. Since then only Nebraska has had a nonpartisan legislature]

YEAR	LEGISLATURES UNDER—			YEAR	LEGISLATURES UNDER—			YEAR	LEGISLATURES UNDER—		
	Democratic control	Split control or tie	Republican control		Democratic control	Split control or tie	Republican control		Democratic control	Split control or tie	Republican control
1971...	23	9	16	1981...	28	6	15	1990...	29	11	9
1973...	27	6	16	1983 [1].	34	4	11	1992...	29	14	6
1975...	37	7	5	1985...	27	11	11	1993...	25	16	8
1977...	36	8	5	1987...	28	12	9	1994...	24	17	8
1979...	30	7	12	1989 [2].	28	13	8	1995...	18	12	19

[1] Two 1984 midterm recall elections resulted in a change in control of the Michigan State Senate. At the time of the 1984 election, therefore, Democrats controlled 33 legislatures.   [2] A party change during the year by a Democratic representative broke the tie in the Indiana House of Representatives, giving the Republicans control of both chambers.

Source: National Conference of State Legislatures, Denver, CO, *State Legislatures*, periodic.

No. 452. Local Elected Officials, by Sex, Race, Hispanic Origin, and Type of Government: 1992

SEX, RACE, AND HISPANIC ORIGIN	Total	GENERAL PURPOSE			SPECIAL PURPOSE	
		County	Municipal	Town, township	School district	Special district
Total.....................	**491,669**	**56,390**	**135,580**	**127,009**	**88,610**	**84,080**
Male	324,487	43,582	94,828	76,258	54,582	55,237
Female....................	100,597	12,528	26,831	27,713	24,772	8,753
Sex not reported	66,585	280	13,921	23,038	9,256	20,090
White......................	406,199	52,726	114,898	102,733	74,064	61,778
Black	11,560	1,716	4,566	371	4,233	674
American Indian, Eskimo, Aleut.........	1,811	147	783	90	564	227
Asian, Pacific Islander.................	514	80	97	16	184	137
Hispanic....................	5,871	906	1,701	217	2,471	576
Non-Hispanic.................	414,213	53,763	118,643	102,993	76,574	62,240
Race, Hispanic origin not reported.......	71,585	1,721	15,236	23,799	9,565	21,264

Source: U.S. Bureau of the Census, *Census of Governments, Popularly Elected Officials in 1992, Preliminary Report* (GC92-2(P).

No. 453. Women Holding State Public Offices, by Office and State: 1995

[As of **January**. For data on women in U.S. Congress, see table 444]

STATE	State-wide elective executive office[1]	State legislature	STATE	State-wide elective executive office[1]	State legislature	STATE	State-wide elective executive office[1]	State legislature
United States .	**84**	**1,535**	Kentucky	1	11	North Dakota ...	5	22
Alabama	3	5	Louisiana	2	14	Ohio	2	32
Alaska........	1	14	Maine	-	50	Oklahoma	3	16
Arizona	3	27	Maryland	1	54	Oregon	1	24
Arkansas	2	17	Massachusetts ..	-	48	Pennsylvania ...	2	30
California	2	25	Michigan	2	33	Rhode Island ...	1	36
Colorado	3	31	Minnesota	3	50	South Carolina ..	1	21
Connecticut	2	50	Mississippi	-	20	South Dakota ...	3	19
Delaware	4	13	Missouri........	[2]2	39	Tennessee	1	18
Florida........	1	31	Montana	1	36	Texas	2	33
Georgia	1	43	Nebraska......	1	12	Utah	2	15
Hawaii........	1	16	Nevada	1	22	Vermont........	1	53
Idaho........	2	30	New Hampshire..	-	128	Virginia	-	16
Illinois........	2	42	New Jersey	1	16	Washington	4	58
Indiana	4	33	New Mexico	2	23	West Virginia ...	-	20
Iowa	1	27	New York	1	38	Wisconsin......	-	32
Kansas	4	46	North Carolina...	-	27	Wyoming	2	19

- Represents zero.   [1] Excludes women elected to the judiciary, women appointed to State cabinet-level positions, women elected to executive posts by the legislature, and elected members of university Board of Trustees or Board of Education.   [2] Includes one official who was appointed to an elective position.

Source: Center for the American Woman and Politics, Eagleton Institute of Politics, Rutgers University, New Brunswick, NJ, information releases, (copyright).

Elections

No. 454. Local Elected Officials, by Level of Government and State: 1992

[Preliminary]

STATE	Total	State govern- ment officials	LOCAL GOVERNMENT OFFICIALS					
			Total	General purpose			Special purpose	
				County	Municipal	Township	School district	Special district
U.S.	510,497	18,828	491,669	56,390	135,580	127,009	88,610	84,080
Northeast.	120,408	3,810	116,598	5,367	18,805	63,426	17,726	11,274
N.E	54,903	1,539	53,364	379	2,771	40,831	4,040	5,343
ME	6,569	210	6,359	110	292	4,463	872	622
NH	7,347	430	6,917	72	288	5,032	1,084	441
VT	8,534	186	8,348	73	563	5,914	1,367	431
MA	22,168	225	21,943	124	794	18,935	539	1,551
RI	1,138	155	983	-	127	516	26	314
CT	9,147	333	8,814	-	707	5,971	152	1,984
M.A	65,505	2,271	63,234	4,988	16,034	22,595	13,686	5,931
NY	25,937	950	24,987	1,317	4,156	9,721	4,753	5,040
NJ	9,087	121	8,966	204	2,184	1,285	4,407	886
PA	30,481	1,200	29,281	3,467	9,694	11,589	4,526	5
Midwest.	218,161	5,302	212,859	21,576	60,024	63,583	39,416	28,260
E.N.C	109,888	2,462	107,426	9,315	32,817	34,606	22,412	8,276
OH	19,377	231	19,146	1,429	8,829	5,266	3,087	535
IN	11,629	506	11,123	1,776	3,174	4,078	1,503	592
IL	42,338	623	41,715	2,398	11,456	10,809	10,997	6,055
MI	18,704	652	18,052	1,399	4,747	7,348	3,990	568
WI	17,840	450	17,390	2,313	4,611	7,105	2,835	526
W.N.C.	108,273	2,840	105,433	12,261	27,207	28,977	17,004	19,984
MN	18,933	623	18,310	1,024	4,645	9,010	2,913	718
IA	16,486	319	16,167	6,133	6,357	-	2,418	1,259
MO	17,291	994	16,297	1,752	5,773	1,547	3,311	3,914
ND	15,486	205	15,281	631	2,122	7,824	1,420	3,284
SD	9,701	155	9,546	669	1,596	5,175	1,023	1,083
NE	13,899	201	13,698	1,064	2,809	1,355	3,670	4,800
KS	16,477	343	16,134	988	3,905	4,066	2,249	4,926
South	104,663	6,744	97,919	23,084	41,847	-	17,114	15,874
S.A	31,407	2,971	28,436	6,627	15,206	-	2,338	4,265
DE	1,171	80	1,091	36	406	-	98	551
MD	2,122	356	1,766	323	868	-	-	575
DC	348	-	348	-	348	-	-	-
VA	3,104	143	2,961	989	1,737	-	-	235
WV	2,772	205	2,567	461	1,712	-	275	119
NC	5,831	593	5,238	1,665	3,028	-	-	545
SC	3,948	195	3,753	765	1,638	-	585	765
GA	6,528	465	6,063	1,551	3,231	-	984	297
FL	5,583	934	4,649	837	2,238	-	396	1,178
E.S.C	23,168	1,618	21,550	7,907	9,619	-	1,999	2,025
KY	7,058	565	6,493	1,728	2,774	-	877	1,114
TN	6,950	321	6,629	3,835	2,184	-	77	533
AL	4,391	436	3,955	768	2,700	-	422	65
MS	4,769	296	4,473	1,576	1,961	-	623	313
W.S.C.	50,088	2,155	47,933	8,550	17,022	-	12,777	9,584
AR	8,407	349	8,058	1,796	4,027	-	1,810	425
LA	5,051	629	4,422	1,622	2,122	-	660	18
OK	9,002	362	8,640	641	3,502	-	2,807	1,690
TX	27,628	815	26,813	4,491	7,371	-	7,500	7,451
West	67,265	2,972	64,293	6,363	14,904	-	14,354	28,672
Mountain	30,662	1,573	29,089	3,257	7,117	-	5,595	13,120
MT	5,116	201	4,915	657	825	-	1,838	1,595
ID	4,775	171	4,604	482	1,055	-	576	2,491
WY	2,747	121	2,626	264	531	-	379	1,452
CO	8,608	280	8,328	528	1,973	-	1,004	4,823
NM	2,201	220	1,981	310	699	-	482	490
AZ	3,286	239	3,047	433	589	-	1,004	1,021
UT	2,711	200	2,511	299	1,328	-	204	680
NV	1,218	141	1,077	284	117	-	108	568
Pacific	36,603	1,399	35,204	3,106	7,787	-	8,759	15,552
WA	7,724	537	7,187	445	1,905	-	1,477	3,360
OR	7,842	290	7,552	307	1,592	-	1,886	3,767
CA	18,918	226	18,692	2,013	2,910	-	5,396	8,373
AK	1,936	255	1,681	312	1,369	-	-	-
HI	183	91	92	29	11	-	-	52

- Represents zero.

Source: U.S. Bureau of the Census, *1992 Census of Governments, Popularly Elected Officials in 1992, Preliminary Report*, GC92-2(P).

No. 455. Black Elected Officials, by Office, 1970 to 1993, and by Region and State, 1993

[As of **January 1993**, no Black elected officials had been identified in Hawaii, Idaho, Montana, North Dakota, or Utah]

REGION, DIVISION, AND STATE	Total	U.S. and State legisla-tures[1]	City and county offices[2]	Law enforce-ment[3]	Educa-tion[4]	REGION, DIVISION, AND STATE	Total	U.S. and State legisla-tures[1]	City and county offices[2]	Law enforce-ment[3]	Educa-tion[4]
1970 (Feb.)	1,469	179	715	213	362	South	5,492	328	3,675	518	971
1980 (July)	4,890	326	2,832	526	1,206	S.A.	2,200	173	1,522	147	358
1985 (Jan.)	6,016	407	3,517	661	1,431	DE	23	3	14	-	6
1990 (Jan.)	7,335	436	4,485	769	1,645	MD	140	32	79	23	6
1991 (Jan.)	7,445	473	4,496	847	1,629	DC	198	[5]4	185	-	9
1992 (Jan.)	7,517	499	4,557	847	1,614	VA	155	14	126	15	-
1993 (Jan.)	7,984	561	4,819	922	1,682	WV	21	1	17	3	-
Northeast	777	96	291	126	264	NC	468	28	328	31	81
N.E.	109	35	60	4	10	SC	450	26	269	15	140
ME	1	-	1	-	-	GA	545	43	371	32	99
NH	2	2	-	-	-	FL	200	22	133	28	17
VT	2	2	-	-	-	E.S.C.	1,681	85	1,175	175	246
MA	30	8	18	2	2	KY	63	4	47	5	7
RI	12	9	3	-	-	TN	168	16	104	24	24
CT	62	14	38	2	8	AL	699	23	529	58	89
M.A.	668	61	231	122	254	MS	751	42	495	88	126
NY	299	30	63	70	136	W.S.C	1,611	70	978	196	367
NJ	211	13	113	-	85	AR	380	13	214	51	102
PA	158	18	55	52	33	LA	636	33	346	104	153
Midwest	1,361	106	757	171	327	OK	123	6	95	1	21
E.N.C.	1,119	78	604	143	294	TX	472	18	323	40	91
OH	219	16	124	30	49	West	354	31	96	107	120
IN	72	12	50	4	6	Mountain	49	11	11	16	11
IL	465	25	282	37	121	WY	1	-	-	-	1
MI	333	17	133	68	115	CO	20	4	4	10	2
WI	30	8	15	4	3	NM	3	-	-	2	1
W.N.C	242	28	153	28	33	AZ	15	4	3	3	5
MN	16	1	2	10	3	NV	10	3	4	1	2
IA	11	1	6	1	3	Pacific	305	20	85	91	109
MO	185	18	134	14	19	WA	19	2	9	5	3
SD	3	1	2	-	-	OR	10	4	2	4	-
NE	6	1	2	-	3	CA	273	13	72	82	106
KS	21	6	7	3	5	AK	3	1	2	-	-

- Represents zero.   [1] Includes elected State administrators.   [2] County commissioners and councilmen, mayors, vice mayors, aldermen, regional officials, and other.   [3] Judges, magistrates, constables, marshals, sheriffs, justices of the peace, and other.   [4] Members of State education agencies, college boards, school boards, and other.   [5] Includes two shadow senators and one shadow representative.

Source: Joint Center for Political and Economic Studies, Washington, DC, *Black Elected Officials: A National Roster*, annual, (copyright).

No. 456. Hispanic Public Officials, by Office, 1985 to 1994, and by State, 1994

[As of **September**. For States not shown, no Hispanic public officials had been identified]

REGION, DIVISION, AND STATE	Total	State executives and legisla-tors[1]	County and munici-pal officials	Judicial and law enforce-ment	Educa-tion and school boards	REGION, DIVISION, AND STATE	Total	State executives and legisla-tors[1]	County and munici-pal officials	Judicial and law enforce-ment	Educa-tion and school boards
1985	3,147	129	1,316	517	1,185	South	2,298	61	1,059	410	768
1990	4,004	144	1,819	583	1,458	S.A.	68	16	35	13	4
1991	4,202	151	1,867	596	1,588	DE	1	-	1	-	-
1992	4,994	150	1,908	628	2,308	MD	2	-	1	-	1
1993	5,170	182	2,023	633	2,332	DC	1	-	-	1	-
1994	5,459	199	2,197	651	2,412	FL	64	16	33	12	3
Northeast	156	28	42	13	73	W.S.C	2,230	45	1,024	397	764
N.E.	28	13	9	-	6	AR	2	1	-	-	1
MA	1	-	-	-	1	LA	12	3	1	8	-
RI	1	1	-	-	-	OK	1	-	1	-	-
CT	26	12	9	-	5	TX	2,215	41	1,022	389	763
M.A.	128	15	33	13	67	West	2,088	95	1,053	220	720
NY	83	12	13	11	47	Mountain	1,270	74	697	167	332
NJ	37	2	17	1	17	MT	2	-	-	1	-
PA	8	1	3	1	3	ID	2	1	1	-	-
Midwest	917	15	43	8	851	WY	3	1	2	-	-
E.N.C	903	8	39	7	849	CO	201	9	140	10	42
OH	4	-	1	2	1	NM	716	50	410	105	151
IN	8	1	5	1	1	AZ	341	11	144	50	136
IL	881	7	26	3	[2]845	UT	1	1	-	-	-
MI	8	-	5	1	2	NV	4	1	-	1	2
WI	2	-	2	-	-	Pacific	818	21	356	53	388
W.N.C.	14	7	4	1	2	WA	14	2	4	2	6
MN	3	2	-	1	-	OR	5	-	3	1	1
MO	1	-	1	-	-	CA	796	16	349	50	381
NE	3	-	2	-	1	AK	1	1	-	-	-
KS	7	5	1	-	1	HI	2	2	-	-	-

- Represents zero.   [1] Includes U.S. Representatives.   [2] Includes local school council members in the Chicago area.

Source: National Association of Latino Elected and Appointed Officials, Washington, DC, *National Roster of Hispanic Elected Officials*, annual.

No. 457. Public Confidence Levels in Selected Public and Private Institutions: 1994

[Based on a sample survey of 1,509 persons 18 years old and over conducted during the spring and subject to sampling variability; see source]

INSTITUTION	LEVEL OF CONFIDENCE				
	A great deal	Quite a lot	Some	Very little	Can't say/ no answer
Religious organizations	21.3	28.3	30.9	16.7	2.8
Private higher colleges or universities	14.4	33.9	30.9	12.4	8.4
Private elementary or secondary education	13.4	31.9	34.7	13.9	6.2
Federated charitable appeals	11.3	26.1	36.1	21.2	5.3
Health organizations	11.2	24.4	43.0	16.6	4.7
Environmental organizations.	10.7	22.9	40.3	20.5	5.6
Human service organizations	10.3	22.9	45.0	15.4	6.5
Arts, culture, & humanities organizations	8.1	21.2	40.5	18.7	11.6
Private and community foundations	8.0	22.5	43.9	16.7	8.9
Public /society benefit organizations [1]	6.0	17.9	45.5	24.4	6.1
International/foreign organizations [2]	3.7	14.9	38.3	30.7	12.5
Small businesses	16.2	36.7	36.8	7.2	3.2
Military	15.8	32.8	34.0	14.1	3.2
Public higher colleges or universities	11.4	33.9	39.2	10.7	4.8
Public elementary or secondary education	11.3	30.7	40.6	14.7	2.7
Organized labor	6.7	15.9	43.9	29.1	4.4
Media (e.g. newspapers, TV, radio)	6.1	19.8	40.5	32.0	1.6
Major corporations	5.1	17.2	50.6	22.7	4.4
State government.	4.4	16.4	46.0	31.2	1.9
Political organizations, parties.	3.9	12.7	40.3	39.7	3.4
Local government.	3.8	19.4	45.6	29.0	2.1
Federal government	3.5	15.5	44.2	34.8	1.9
Congress	3.2	12.0	40.9	41.3	2.6

[1] Civil rights, social justice, or community improvement organizations.　　[2] Culture exchange or relief organizations.

Source: Hodgkinson, Virginia, Murray Weitzman, and the Gallup Organization, Inc., *Giving & Volunteering in the United States: 1994 Edition.* (Copyright and published by INDEPENDENT SECTOR, Washington, DC, 1994.)

No. 458. Political Party Identification of the Adult Population, by Degree of Attachment, 1972 to 1994, and by Selected Characteristics, 1994

[**In percent.** Covers citizens of voting-age living in private housing units in the contiguous United States. Data are from the National Election Studies and are based on a sample and subject to sampling variability; for details, see source]

YEAR AND SELECTED CHARACTERISTIC	Total	Strong Democrat	Weak Democrat	Independent Democrat	Independent	Independent Republican	Weak Republican	Strong Republican	Apolitical
1972	100	15	26	11	13	11	13	10	1
1980	100	18	23	11	13	10	14	9	2
1984	100	17	20	11	11	12	15	12	2
1986	100	18	22	10	12	11	15	11	2
1988	100	18	18	12	11	13	14	14	2
1990	100	20	19	12	11	12	15	10	2
1992	100	18	18	14	12	12	14	11	1
1994, total [1]	**100**	**15**	**19**	**13**	**10**	**12**	**15**	**16**	**1**
Age:									
17 to 24 years old. . . .	100	9	20	22	10	8	19	10	1
25 to 34 years old. . . .	100	11	19	14	12	11	16	16	1
35 to 44 years old. . . .	100	13	18	14	12	11	14	18	-
45 to 54 years old. . . .	100	15	16	15	7	16	12	17	1
55 to 64 years old. . . .	100	18	22	8	8	16	12	15	-
65 to 74 years old. . . .	100	28	17	6	8	13	14	15	-
75 to 99 years old. . . .	100	19	26	9	9	5	17	13	2
Sex:									
Male.	100	13	17	12	11	14	14	18	1
Female	100	18	21	13	10	9	15	13	1
Race:									
White	100	12	19	12	10	13	16	17	1
Black	100	38	23	20	8	4	2	3	1
Education:									
Grade school	100	26	26	7	13	7	11	6	4
High school	100	15	22	14	13	10	13	11	1
College	100	14	16	13	7	13	16	21	-

- Represents zero.　　[1] Includes other characteristics, not shown separately.

Source: Center for Political Studies, University of Michigan, Ann Arbor, MI, unpublished data. Data prior to 1988 published in Warren E. Miller and Santa A. Traugott *American National Election Studies Data Sourcebook, 1952-1986.* Reprinted with permission from Harvard University Press, Cambridge, MA, 1989, (copyright).

No. 459. Voting-Age Population, Percent Reporting Registered, and Voted: 1980 to 1994

[As of **November**. Covers civilian noninstitutional population 18 years old and over. Includes aliens. Figures are based on Current Population Survey (see text, section 1, and Appendix III) and differ from those in table 461 based on population estimates and official vote counts]

CHARACTERISTIC	VOTING-AGE POPULATION (mil.)								PERCENT REPORTING THEY REGISTERED								PERCENT REPORTING THEY VOTED							
									Presidential election years				Congressional election years				Presidential election years				Congressional election years			
	1980	1982	1984	1986	1988	1990	1992	1994	1980	1984	1988	1992	1982	1986	1990	1994	1980	1984	1988	1992	1982	1986	1990	1994
Total [1]	157.1	165.5	170.0	173.9	178.1	182.1	185.7	190.3	66.9	68.3	66.6	68.2	64.1	64.3	62.2	62.0	59.2	59.9	57.4	61.3	48.5	46.0	45.0	44.6
18 to 20 years old	12.3	12.1	11.2	10.7	10.7	10.8	9.7	10.3	44.7	47.0	44.9	48.3	35.0	35.4	35.4	37.2	35.7	36.7	33.2	38.5	19.8	18.6	18.4	16.5
21 to 24 years old	15.9	16.7	16.7	15.7	14.8	14.0	14.6	14.9	52.7	54.3	50.6	55.3	47.8	46.6	43.3	45.5	43.1	43.5	38.3	45.7	28.4	24.2	22.0	22.3
25 to 34 years old	35.7	38.8	40.3	41.9	42.7	42.7	41.6	41.1	62.0	63.3	57.8	60.6	57.1	55.8	52.0	51.5	54.6	54.5	48.0	53.2	40.4	35.1	33.8	32.2
35 to 44 years old	25.6	28.1	30.7	33.0	35.2	37.9	39.7	41.9	70.6	70.9	69.3	69.2	67.5	67.9	65.5	63.3	64.4	63.5	61.3	63.6	52.2	49.3	48.4	46.0
45 to 64 years old	43.6	44.2	44.3	44.8	45.9	46.9	49.1	50.9	75.8	76.6	75.5	75.3	75.6	74.8	71.4	71.0	69.3	69.8	67.9	70.0	62.2	58.7	55.8	56.0
65 years old and over	24.1	25.6	26.7	27.7	28.8	29.9	30.8	31.1	74.6	76.9	78.4	78.0	75.2	76.9	76.5	75.6	65.1	67.7	68.8	70.1	59.9	60.9	60.3	60.7
Male	74.1	78.0	80.3	82.4	84.5	86.6	88.6	91.0	66.6	67.3	65.2	66.9	63.7	63.4	61.2	60.8	59.1	59.0	56.4	60.2	48.7	45.8	44.6	44.4
Female	83.0	87.4	89.6	91.5	93.6	95.5	97.1	99.3	67.1	69.3	67.8	69.3	64.4	65.0	63.1	63.2	59.4	60.8	58.3	62.3	48.4	46.1	45.4	44.9
White	137.7	143.6	146.8	149.9	152.9	155.6	157.8	160.3	68.4	69.6	67.9	70.1	65.6	65.3	63.8	64.2	60.9	61.4	59.1	63.6	49.9	47.0	46.7	46.9
Black	16.4	17.6	18.4	19.0	19.7	20.4	21.0	21.8	60.0	66.3	64.5	63.9	59.1	64.0	58.8	58.3	50.5	55.8	51.5	54.0	43.0	43.2	39.2	37.0
Hispanic [2]	8.2	8.8	9.5	11.8	12.9	13.8	14.7	17.5	36.3	40.1	35.5	35.0	35.3	35.9	32.3	30.0	29.9	32.6	28.8	28.9	25.3	24.2	21.0	19.1
Region: [3]																								
Northeast	35.5	36.4	36.9	37.3	37.9	38.1	38.3	38.4	64.8	66.6	64.8	67.0	62.5	62.0	61.0	60.9	58.5	59.7	57.4	61.2	49.8	44.4	45.2	45.2
Midwest	41.5	41.9	42.1	42.8	43.3	43.9	44.4	44.5	73.8	74.6	72.5	74.6	71.1	70.7	68.2	68.7	65.8	65.7	62.9	67.2	54.7	49.5	48.6	48.8
South	50.6	55.4	57.6	59.2	60.7	62.4	63.7	66.4	64.8	66.9	65.6	67.2	61.7	63.0	61.3	60.7	55.6	56.8	54.5	59.0	41.8	43.0	42.4	40.5
West	29.5	31.9	33.4	34.6	36.2	37.7	39.3	41.0	63.3	64.7	63.0	63.6	60.6	60.8	57.7	58.1	57.2	58.5	55.6	58.5	50.7	48.4	45.0	46.4
School years completed:																								
8 years or less	22.7	22.4	20.6	19.6	19.1	17.7	15.4	14.7	53.0	53.4	47.5	43.9	52.3	50.5	44.0	40.1	42.6	42.9	36.7	35.1	35.7	32.7	27.7	23.2
High school:																								
1 to 3 years	22.5	22.3	22.1	21.4	21.1	21.0	[4]21.0	[4]20.7	54.6	54.9	52.8	[4]50.4	53.3	52.4	47.9	[4]44.7	45.6	44.4	41.3	[4]41.2	37.7	33.8	30.9	[4]27.0
4 years	61.2	65.2	67.8	68.6	70.0	71.5	[5]65.5	[5]64.9	66.4	67.3	64.6	[5]64.9	62.9	62.9	60.0	[5]58.9	58.9	58.7	54.7	[5]57.5	47.1	44.1	42.2	[5]40.5
College:																								
1 to 3 years	26.7	28.8	30.9	33.0	34.3	36.3	[6]46.7	[6]50.4	74.4	75.7	73.5	[6]75.4	70.0	70.0	68.7	[6]68.4	67.2	67.5	64.5	[6]68.7	53.3	49.9	50.0	[6]49.1
4 years or more	24.0	26.9	28.6	31.3	33.6	35.6	[7]37.4	[7]39.4	84.3	83.8	83.1	[7]84.8	79.4	77.8	77.3	[7]76.3	79.9	79.1	77.6	[7]81.0	66.5	62.5	62.5	[7]63.1
Employed	95.0	97.2	104.2	108.5	113.8	115.5	116.3	122.6	68.7	69.4	67.1	69.9	65.5	64.4	62.6	62.9	61.8	61.6	58.4	63.8	50.0	45.7	45.1	45.2
Unemployed	6.9	10.8	7.4	6.6	5.8	6.7	8.3	6.5	50.3	54.3	50.4	53.7	49.8	50.6	44.6	46.4	41.2	44.0	38.6	46.2	34.1	31.2	27.9	28.3
Not in labor force	55.2	57.5	58.4	58.8	58.5	59.9	61.1	61.2	65.8	68.1	67.2	66.8	65.8	65.4	63.4	61.9	57.0	58.9	57.3	58.7	48.7	48.2	46.7	45.3

[1] Includes other races not shown separately. [2] Hispanic persons may be of any race. [3] For composition of regions, see table 27. [4] Represents those who completed 9th to 12th grade, but have no high school diploma. [5] High school graduate. [6] Some college or associate degree. [7] Bachelor's or advanced degree.

Source: U.S. Bureau of the Census, *Current Population Reports*, P20-453 and P20-466; and unpublished data.

No. 460. Persons Reported Registered and Voted, by State: 1994

[See headnote, table 459]

STATE	Voting-age population (1,000)	PERCENT OF VOTING-AGE POPULATION		STATE	Voting-age population (1,000)	PERCENT OF VOTING-AGE POPULATION	
		Registered	Voted			Registered	Voted
U.S.....	190,267	62.0	44.6	DC	440	66.9	55.6
				VA.....	4,760	60.0	45.7
Northeast....	38,386	60.9	45.2	WV.....	1,396	60.8	33.9
N.E......	9,865	67.8	51.0	NC.....	5,211	60.8	35.7
ME	909	81.6	58.2	SC.....	2,681	60.8	45.2
NH	832	64.3	41.2	GA.....	5,105	54.9	35.4
VT.....	432	70.7	48.8	FL.....	10,582	55.5	42.3
MA	4,532	65.6	51.6	E.S.C	11,662	66.7	41.9
RI	729	64.2	50.6	KY	2,807	62.5	34.5
CT	2,431	68.4	51.3	TN	3,856	63.7	43.0
M.A	28,521	58.5	43.1	AL.....	3,136	70.6	45.8
NY	13,599	56.8	44.6	MS	1,863	72.6	44.3
NJ.....	5,918	61.6	40.3	W.S.C	20,273	61.0	38.5
PA.....	9,004	58.9	42.7	AR	1,801	60.0	41.6
Midwest.....	44,505	68.7	48.7	LA	3,013	70.6	34.2
E.N.C	31,463	66.4	46.1	OK	2,325	65.8	46.8
OH	8,152	64.6	46.6	TX.....	13,134	58.2	37.6
IN	4,191	55.6	38.7	West	41,009	58.1	46.4
IL	8,561	63.0	42.8	Mountain...	10,911	60.0	45.9
MI	6,921	73.7	52.2	MT	619	73.2	60.7
WI.....	3,638	77.2	49.6	ID	798	63.0	50.7
W.N.C	13,042	74.3	55.2	WY	333	69.0	63.5
MN	3,296	80.9	58.4	CO	2,703	64.3	46.4
IA	2,059	71.7	52.5	NM	1,175	58.8	46.8
MO	3,797	72.3	54.5	AZ.....	2,971	56.0	41.6
ND	441	93.3	61.1	UT	1,231	59.4	44.1
SD	495	75.4	63.9	NV	1,081	49.5	40.1
NE	1,156	72.6	54.3	Pacific	30,098	57.4	46.6
KS	1,798	65.3	50.5	WA	3,924	66.8	46.3
South......	66,364	60.7	40.5	OR	2,309	72.7	60.9
S.A......	34,429	58.4	41.2	CA	22,639	54.2	45.0
DE	528	58.7	41.2	AK	393	71.7	59.1
MD	3,726	62.6	46.2	HI	833	51.5	46.0

Source: U.S. Bureau of the Census, unpublished data.

No. 461. Participation in Elections for President and U.S. Representatives: 1932 to 1994

[As of **November**. Estimated resident population 21 years old and over, 1932-70, except as noted, and 18 years old and over thereafter; includes Armed Forces. Prior to 1960, excludes Alaska and Hawaii. District of Columbia is included in votes cast for President beginning 1964 and in votes cast for Representative from 1972 to 1992]

YEAR	Resident population (incl. aliens) of voting age [1] (1,000)	VOTES CAST				YEAR	Resident population (incl. aliens) of voting age [1] (1,000)	VOTES CAST			
		For President [2] (1,000)	Per-cent of voting-age population	For U.S. Representa-tives (1,000)	Per-cent of voting-age population			For President [2] (1,000)	Per-cent of voting-age population	For U.S. Representa-tives (1,000)	Per-cent of voting-age population
1932 ...	75,768	39,758	52.5	37,657	49.7	1964 ...	114,090	70,645	61.9	65,895	57.8
1934 ...	77,997	(X)	(X)	32,256	41.4	1966 ...	116,638	(X)	(X)	52,908	45.4
1936 ...	80,174	45,654	56.9	42,886	53.5	1968 ...	120,285	73,212	60.9	66,288	55.1
1938 ...	82,354	(X)	(X)	36,236	44.0	1970 ...	124,498	(X)	(X)	54,173	43.5
1940 ...	84,728	49,900	58.9	46,951	55.4	1972 ...	140,777	77,719	55.2	71,430	50.7
1942 ...	86,465	(X)	(X)	28,074	32.5	1974 ...	146,338	(X)	(X)	52,495	35.9
1944 ...	85,654	47,977	56.0	45,103	52.7	1976 ...	152,308	81,556	53.5	74,422	48.9
1946 ...	92,659	(X)	(X)	34,398	37.1	1978 ...	158,369	(X)	(X)	55,332	34.9
1948 ...	95,573	48,794	51.1	45,933	48.1	1980 ...	163,945	86,515	52.8	77,995	47.6
1950 ...	98,134	(X)	(X)	40,342	41.1	1982 ...	169,643	(X)	(X)	64,514	38.0
1952 ...	99,929	61,551	61.6	57,571	57.6	1984 ...	173,995	92,653	53.3	83,231	47.8
1954 ...	102,075	(X)	(X)	42,580	41.7	1986 ...	177,922	(X)	(X)	59,619	33.5
1956 ...	104,515	62,027	59.3	58,426	55.9	1988 ...	181,956	91,595	50.3	81,786	44.9
1958 ...	106,447	(X)	(X)	45,818	43.0	1990 ...	185,812	(X)	(X)	61,513	33.1
1960 ...	109,672	68,838	62.8	64,133	58.5	1992 ...	189,524	104,425	55.1	96,239	50.8
1962 ...	112,952	(X)	(X)	51,267	45.4	1994 ...	193,650	(X)	(X)	69,770	36.0

X Not applicable.   [1] Population 18 and over in Georgia, 1944-70, and in Kentucky, 1956-70; 19 and over in Alaska and 20 and over in Hawaii, 1960-70.   [2] Source: 1932-58, U.S. Congress, Clerk of the House, *Statistics of the Presidential and Congressional Election*, biennial.

Source: Except as noted, U.S. Bureau of the Census, *Current Population Reports*, P25-1085; Elections Research Center, Chevy Chase, MD, *America Votes*, biennial, (copyright); and 1994, Congressional Quarterly Inc., *Congressional Quarterly Weekly Report*, vol. 53, No. 15, April 15, 1995, (copyright).

No. 462. Resident Population of Voting Age and Percent Casting Votes— States: 1988 to 1994

[As of **November. Estimated population, 18 years old and over**. Includes Armed Forces stationed in each State, aliens, and institutional population]

REGION, DIVISION, AND STATE	VOTING-AGE POPULATION						PERCENT CASTING VOTES FOR—				
	1988 (1,000)	1990 (1,000)	1992 (1,000)	1994, proj. (1,000)			Presidential electors		U.S. Representatives		
				Total	Black	His-panic [1]	1988	1992	1990	1992	1994
U.S.	181,956	185,812	189,524	193,650	22,172	17,103	50.3	55.1	33.1	50.8	36.0
Northeast	38,670	38,838	38,920	38,849	4,303	2,826	51.3	55.4	32.9	49.9	37.1
N.E	10,069	10,137	10,091	10,017	456	420	56.9	62.9	43.9	58.6	44.0
ME	902	924	932	931	2	5	61.5	72.9	56.0	71.8	54.0
NH	817	835	838	843	3	8	55.2	64.2	34.8	61.0	36.7
VT	411	422	429	429	-	2	59.1	67.5	49.7	65.6	49.3
MA	4,642	4,646	4,616	4,564	226	208	56.7	60.1	44.1	56.6	43.3
RI	772	776	768	764	29	37	52.5	59.0	44.7	51.9	44.8
CT	2,525	2,534	2,508	2,486	196	160	57.1	64.4	40.9	57.2	43.0
M.A.	28,601	28,701	28,829	28,832	3,847	2,406	49.4	52.8	29.1	46.9	34.6
NY	13,659	13,683	13,705	13,646	2,248	1,618	47.5	50.5	26.8	43.2	33.8
NJ	5,905	5,927	5,964	5,974	795	608	52.5	56.1	30.8	50.2	33.6
PA	9,037	9,091	9,161	9,212	804	180	50.2	54.1	31.4	50.1	36.6
Midwest	43,684	44,160	44,803	45,529	4,131	1,276	56.5	61.9	39.6	58.5	41.2
E.N.C.	30,775	31,133	31,636	32,083	3,497	1,064	55.2	60.4	37.6	56.6	38.5
OH	7,986	8,066	8,207	8,313	845	104	55.0	60.2	42.4	55.8	39.7
IN	4,046	4,105	4,209	4,298	319	76	53.6	54.8	36.9	52.7	36.0
IL	8,411	8,495	8,598	8,712	1,219	674	54.2	58.7	36.2	56.2	34.9
MI	6,774	6,851	6,947	6,983	942	145	54.2	61.5	35.5	55.9	43.0
WI	3,559	3,616	3,675	3,777	172	65	61.6	68.9	34.7	65.0	38.6
W.N.C	12,910	13,027	13,167	13,446	634	212	59.5	65.6	44.4	63.3	47.7
MN	3,167	3,222	3,272	3,362	63	39	66.2	71.8	55.3	69.5	52.0
IA	2,053	2,061	2,073	2,112	37	25	59.7	65.3	38.4	59.9	46.3
MO	3,770	3,813	3,851	3,902	385	46	55.5	62.1	35.5	61.0	45.2
ND	470	462	462	467	2	2	63.2	66.7	50.6	64.5	50.4
SD	498	498	505	522	2	2	62.9	66.6	51.7	65.9	58.6
NE	1,145	1,152	1,164	1,192	40	29	57.7	63.4	50.9	61.1	47.9
KS	1,809	1,819	1,840	1,889	105	69	54.9	62.9	42.9	61.1	43.3
South	62,134	63,821	65,609	67,501	11,569	5,407	46.0	51.3	26.9	45.9	30.2
S.A	32,148	33,312	34,210	35,211	6,689	1,895	44.3	50.3	28.2	46.7	30.3
DE	490	507	521	534	88	11	51.0	55.6	35.0	53.0	36.5
MD	3,536	3,640	3,705	3,750	940	106	48.5	53.6	30.0	48.8	35.9
DC	503	481	467	452	281	26	38.4	48.7	33.2	42.1	(NA)
VA	4,572	4,716	4,855	4,967	891	132	47.9	52.7	24.4	48.8	38.4
WV	1,358	1,349	1,376	1,389	38	9	48.1	49.7	27.8	40.9	29.3
NC	4,903	5,061	5,190	5,364	1,088	66	43.5	50.3	39.7	48.7	29.6
SC	2,505	2,587	2,669	2,740	753	26	39.4	45.1	25.9	41.8	31.7
GA	4,631	4,791	5,006	5,159	1,292	94	39.1	46.4	29.1	44.2	29.0
FL	9,651	10,180	10,422	10,856	1,318	1,425	44.6	51.0	[2]23.4	[2]47.2	[2]26.3
E.S.C.	11,085	11,252	11,547	11,813	2,091	76	47.5	53.2	25.5	49.0	33.3
KY	2,710	2,740	2,798	2,857	194	16	48.8	53.4	27.9	48.6	27.5
TN	3,609	3,685	3,796	3,913	567	28	45.3	52.2	19.5	45.5	36.2
AL	2,950	2,995	3,080	3,138	721	19	46.7	54.8	34.0	52.0	35.5
MS	1,816	1,832	1,873	1,905	609	13	51.3	52.4	20.1	51.5	32.6
W.S.C	18,901	19,257	19,852	20,477	2,789	3,436	47.9	51.8	25.5	42.7	28.3
AR	1,717	1,737	1,774	1,817	247	18	48.2	53.6	38.3	50.1	39.0
LA	3,006	2,988	3,045	3,100	882	77	54.2	58.8	[3]3.5	[3]22.4	[3](X)
OK	2,300	2,310	2,352	2,394	161	62	50.9	59.1	37.1	54.2	40.5
TX	11,878	12,222	12,681	13,166	1,499	3,279	45.7	48.5	26.8	44.3	31.3
West	37,468	38,993	40,194	41,771	2,169	7,594	49.4	53.5	36.0	51.0	38.8
Mountain	9,524	9,856	10,370	10,906	287	1,519	52.6	57.6	39.3	55.3	40.7
MT	574	579	600	623	1	8	63.8	68.4	54.8	67.3	56.5
ID	683	707	750	803	2	41	59.9	64.3	44.5	63.0	49.0
WY	321	319	329	343	2	20	55.1	61.0	49.5	59.9	57.2
CO	2,397	2,447	2,579	2,713	106	321	57.2	60.8	40.9	57.4	38.9
NM	1,047	1,075	1,121	1,167	21	434	49.8	50.8	33.4	49.6	39.6
AZ	2,610	2,696	2,812	2,923	80	513	44.9	52.9	35.8	50.1	37.6
UT	1,070	1,104	1,169	1,246	9	60	60.5	63.6	40.1	62.2	40.5
NV	824	929	1,011	1,088	66	122	42.5	50.1	33.7	48.7	34.6
Pacific	27,943	29,137	29,824	30,865	1,882	6,075	48.3	52.0	35.0	49.4	38.1
WA	3,465	3,650	3,812	4,000	108	170	53.8	60.0	36.0	58.3	42.2
OR	2,055	2,140	2,220	2,311	35	88	58.5	65.9	49.2	62.6	51.6
CA	21,250	22,124	22,521	23,225	1,701	5,740	46.5	49.4	32.9	46.8	35.9
AK	369	382	405	429	16	13	54.2	63.8	50.2	59.0	48.5
HI	804	841	866	900	22	64	44.0	43.1	40.5	41.4	39.3

- Represents or rounds to zero.   NA Not available.   X Not applicable.   [1] Persons of Hispanic origin may be of any race.
[2] State law does not require tabulation of votes for unopposed candidates.   [3] See footnote 6, table 139.

Source: Compiled by U.S. Bureau of the Census. Population data from U.S. Bureau of the Census, *Current Population Reports*, P25-1117; votes cast from Elections Research Center, Chevy Chase, MD, *America Votes*, biennial, (copyright); and 1994, Congressional Quarterly Inc., *Congressional Quarterly Weekly Report*, vol. 53, No. 15, April 15, 1995, (copyright).

No. 463. Political Party Financial Activity, by Major Political Party: 1981 to 1992

[**In millions of dollars**. Covers financial activity during 2-year calendar period indicated. Some political party financial activities, such as building funds and State and local election spending, are not reported to the source. Also excludes contributions earmarked to Federal candidates through the party organizations, since some of those funds never passed through the committees' accounts]

YEAR AND TYPE OF COMMITTEE	DEMOCRATIC				REPUBLICAN			
	Receipts, net [1]	Disburse-ments, net [1]	Contribu-tions to candi-dates	Monies spent on behalf of party's nomi-nees [2]	Receipts, net [1]	Disburse-ments, net [1]	Contribu-tions to candi-dates	Monies spent on behalf of party's nomi-nees [2]
1981-82	39.3	40.1	1.7	3.3	215.0	214.0	5.6	14.3
1983-84	98.5	97.4	2.6	9.0	297.9	300.8	4.9	20.1
1985-86	64.8	65.9	1.7	9.0	255.2	258.9	3.4	14.3
1987-88, total	**135.2**	**129.1**	**1.8**	**17.9**	**267.1**	**261.0**	**3.4**	**22.7**
National committee	52.3	47.0	0.1	8.1	91.0	89.9	0.3	8.3
Senatorial committee	16.3	16.3	0.4	6.2	65.9	63.3	0.8	10.2
Congressional committee	12.5	12.5	0.7	2.4	34.7	33.7	1.6	4.1
Conventions, other national	19.2	19.2	-	-	9.6	9.6	-	-
State and local	35.0	34.1	0.6	1.2	65.9	64.5	0.7	0.1
1989-90, total	**85.8**	**90.9**	**1.5**	**8.7**	**206.3**	**213.5**	**2.9**	**10.7**
National committee	14.5	18.5	0.1	0.1	68.7	70.4	0.3	0.1
Senatorial committee	17.5	17.6	0.4	4.5	65.1	67.6	0.7	7.7
Congressional committee	9.1	9.1	0.4	2.9	33.2	34.4	0.9	2.8
Conventions, other national	8.8	9.2	-	-	-	-	-	-
State and local	35.8	36.4	0.5	1.2	39.3	41.1	1.0	0.2
1991-92, total	**189.2**	**184.0**	**1.9**	**28.0**	**278.9**	**267.4**	**3.0**	**33.8**
National committee	65.8	65.0	-	11.3	85.4	81.9	0.8	11.3
Senatorial committee	25.4	25.5	0.6	11.2	73.8	71.3	0.7	16.5
Congressional committee	12.8	12.6	0.8	4.1	35.3	34.3	0.7	5.2
Conventions, other national	21.3	20.7	-	-	11.6	11.3	-	-
State and local	63.9	60.2	0.5	1.4	72.8	68.6	0.8	0.9

- Represents zero.   [1] Excludes monies transferred between affiliated committees.   [2] Monies spent in the general election.

Source: U.S. Federal Election Commission, *FEC Reports on Financial Activity, Final Report, Party and Non-Party Political Committees*, biennial.

No. 464. Independent Expenditures for Presidential and Congressional Campaigns: 1985 to 1994

[**In thousands of dollars**. Covers campaign finance activity during 2-year calendar period indicated. An "independent expenditure" is money spent to support or defeat a clearly identified candidate. According to Federal election law, such an expenditure must be made without cooperation or consultation with the candidate or his/her campaign. Independent expenditures are not limited, as are contributions]

TYPE OF OFFICE AND YEAR	ALL PARTIES			DEMOCRATS		REPUBLICANS		OTHERS	
	Total	For	Against	For	Against	For	Against	For	Against
TOTAL									
1985-86	10,205	8,832	1,373	3,450	888	5,376	485	6	-
1987-88	21,341	16,654	4,687	2,865	4,248	13,784	439	6	-
1989-90	5,774	4,177	1,597	1,530	735	2,645	862	2	-
1991-92	11,052	8,710	2,342	3,044	1,483	5,548	847	118	12
1993-94	4,980	3,256	1,724	672	1,119	2,571	590	13	15
PRESIDENTIAL									
1985-86	841	795	45	76	28	719	17	-	-
1987-88	14,127	10,628	3,499	568	3,352	10,054	146	6	-
1989-90	497	322	174	5	169	318	5	-	-
1991-92	4,431	3,695	736	583	561	3,052	163	60	12
1993-94	112	27	85	12	84	15	(Z)	-	1
SENATE									
1985-86	5,312	4,331	980	988	632	3,343	348	-	-
1987-88	4,401	3,641	761	831	617	2,810	143	(Z)	-
1989-90	3,506	2,362	1,144	756	428	1,604	716	2	-
1991-92	2,604	1,912	692	1,025	462	886	230	1	-
1993-94	2,627	1,612	1,015	261	476	1,351	539	(Z)	-
HOUSE OF REPRESENTATIVES									
1985-86	4,053	3,706	347	2,386	227	1,314	120	6	-
1987-88	2,813	2,385	427	1,466	279	920	149	(Z)	-
1989-90	1,772	1,493	279	770	138	723	141	-	-
1991-92	4,017	3,103	914	1,436	460	1,610	454	57	-
1993-94	2,241	1,617	624	399	559	1,205	51	13	14

- Represents zero.   Z Less than $500.

Source: U.S. Federal Election Commission, *FEC Index of Independent Expenditures, 1987-88,* May 1989; press release of May 19, 1989; and unpublished data.

No. 465. Political Action Committees—Number, by Committee Type: 1980 to 1994

[As of **December 31**]

COMMITTEE TYPE	1980	1985	1989	1990	1991	1992	1993	1994
Total	**2,551**	**3,992**	**4,178**	**4,172**	**4,094**	**4,195**	**4,210**	**3,954**
Corporate	1,206	1,710	1,796	1,795	1,738	1,735	1,789	1,660
Labor	297	388	349	346	338	347	337	333
Trade/membership/health	576	695	777	774	742	770	761	792
Nonconnected	374	1,003	1,060	1,062	1,083	1,145	1,121	980
Cooperative	42	54	59	59	57	56	56	53
Corporation without stock	56	142	137	136	136	142	146	136

Source: U.S. Federal Election Commission, press release of January 9, 1995.

No. 466. Political Action Committees—Financial Activity Summary, by Committee Type: 1987 to 1992

[**In millions of dollars.** Covers financial activity during 2-year calendar period indicated. Data have not been adjusted for transfers between affiliated committees]

COMMITTEE TYPE	RECEIPTS			DISBURSEMENTS [1]			CONTRIBUTIONS TO CANDIDATES		
	1987-88	1989-90	1991-92	1987-88	1989-90	1991-92	1987-88	1989-90	1991-92
Total	**384.6**	**372.1**	**392.8**	**364.2**	**357.6**	**402.3**	**159.2**	**159.1**	**188.9**
Corporate	96.9	106.5	112.5	89.8	101.1	112.4	56.2	58.1	68.4
Labor	78.5	88.9	89.9	74.1	84.6	94.6	35.5	34.7	41.4
Trade/membership/health	89.5	92.5	95.7	83.7	88.1	97.5	41.2	44.8	53.9
Nonconnected	106.3	71.6	73.8	104.9	71.4	76.2	20.3	15.1	18.3
Cooperative	4.9	5.0	4.8	4.5	4.8	4.9	2.7	2.9	3.0
Corporation without stock	8.5	7.6	8.7	7.2	7.7	9.2	3.3	3.4	4.0

[1] Comprises contributions to candidates, independent expenditures, and other disbursements.

Source: U.S. Federal Election Commission, *FEC Reports on Financial Activity, Final Report, Party and Non-Party Political Committees,* biennial.

No. 467. Presidential Campaign Finances—Federal Funds for General Election: 1980 to 1992

[**In millions of dollars.** Based on FEC certifications, audit reports, and Dept. of Treasury reports]

1980		1984		1988		1992	
Candidate	Amount	Candidate	Amount	Candidate	Amount	Candidate	Amount
Total	**62.7**	**Total**	**80.3**	**Total**	**92.2**	**Total**	**110.4**
Anderson [1]	4.2	Mondale	40.2	Bush	46.1	Bush	55.2
Carter	29.4	Reagan	40.1	Dukakis	46.1	Clinton	55.2
Reagan	29.2					Perot	-

- Represents zero.   [1] John Anderson, as the candidate of a new party, was permitted to raise funds privately. Total receipts for the Anderson campaign, including Federal funds, were $17.6 million, and total expenditures were $15.6 million.

Source: U.S. Federal Election Commission, periodic press releases.

No. 468. Presidential Campaign Finances—Primary Campaign Receipts and Disbursements: 1983 to 1992

[**In millions of dollars.** Covers campaign finance activity during 2-year calendar period indicated. Covers candidates who received Federal matching funds or who had significant financial activity]

ITEM	TOTAL			DEMOCRATIC			REPUBLICAN		
	1983-84 [1]	1987-88 [2]	1991-92 [3]	1983-84	1987-88	1991-92	1983-84	1987-88	1991-92
Receipts, total [4]	**105.0**	**213.8**	**126.9**	**77.5**	**91.9**	**70.8**	**27.1**	**116.0**	**50.5**
Individual contributions	62.8	141.1	82.5	46.2	59.4	44.7	16.4	76.8	34.5
Federal matching funds	34.9	65.7	43.2	24.6	30.1	25.2	10.1	34.7	15.7
Disbursements	**103.6**	**210.7**	**121.8**	**77.4**	**90.2**	**66.0**	**25.9**	**114.6**	**50.1**

[1] Includes Citizens Party candidate, not shown separately.   [2] Includes a minor party candidate who sought several party nominations and a Democratic candidate who did not receive Federal matching funds, but who had significant financial activity.   [3] Includes other parties, not shown separately.   [4] Includes other types of receipts, not shown separately.

Source: U.S. Federal Election Commission, *FEC Reports on Financial Activity, Final Report, Presidential Pre-Nomination Campaigns,* quadrennial.

No. 469. Congressional Campaign Finances—Receipts and Disbursements: 1987 to 1992

[Covers all campaign finance activity during 2-year calendar period indicated for primary, general, run-off, and special elections. For 1987-88 relates to 1,582 House of Representatives candidates and 210 Senate candidates; for 1989-90 to 1,580 House of Representatives candidates and 179 Senate candidates; for 1991-92 to 2,580 House of Representatives candidates and 365 Senate candidates. Data have been adjusted to eliminate transfers between all committees within a campaign. For further information on legal limits of contributions, see Federal Election Campaign Act of 1971, as amended]

ITEM	HOUSE OF REPRESENTATIVES						SENATE					
	Amount (mil. dol.)			Percent distribution			Amount (mil. dol.)			Percent distribution		
	1987-88	1989-90	1991-92	1987-88	1989-90	1991-92	1987-88	1989-90	1991-92	1987-88	1989-90	1991-92
Total receipts [1]	**278.3**	**285.4**	**395.9**	**100**	**100**	**100**	**199.3**	**186.3**	**263.4**	**100**	**100**	**100**
Individual contributions	129.9	129.9	192.4	47	46	49	128.1	119.6	162.8	64	64	62
Other committees	102.2	108.5	127.4	37	38	32	45.7	41.2	51.2	23	22	19
Candidate loans	23.2	20.9	43.0	8	7	11	8.2	10.0	28.7	4	5	11
Candidate contributions	4.9	4.8	11.4	2	2	3	6.8	2.4	6.5	3	1	2
Democrats	160.3	163.4	217.7	58	57	55	107.7	89.5	143.8	54	48	55
Republicans	117.0	120.9	174.3	42	42	44	91.3	96.8	118.4	46	52	45
Others	1.0	1.1	3.9	(Z)	(Z)	1	0.3	(Z)	1.2	(Z)	(Z)	(Z)
Incumbents	175.6	181.9	203.5	63	64	51	98.3	118.7	99.7	49	64	38
Challengers [2]	52.5	47.7	91.3	19	17	23	56.3	54.8	95.6	28	29	36
Open seats [2]	50.2	55.9	101.1	18	20	26	44.7	12.8	68.2	22	7	26
Total disbursements	**257.6**	**265.8**	**408.2**	**100**	**100**	**100**	**201.4**	**180.4**	**272.1**	**100**	**100**	**100**
Democrats	145.6	151.0	228.3	57	57	56	107.9	87.6	147.6	54	49	54
Republicans	111.0	113.7	176.0	43	43	43	93.1	92.9	123.2	46	52	45
Others	1.0	1.1	3.9	(Z)	(Z)	1	0.3	(Z)	1.2	(Z)	(Z)	(Z)
Incumbents	156.6	163.4	218.5	61	62	53	101.2	113.5	107.2	50	63	39
Challengers [2]	51.7	47.0	90.0	20	18	22	56.1	54.9	95.3	28	30	35
Open seats [2]	49.3	55.4	99.6	19	21	24	44.1	12.1	69.6	22	7	26

Z Less than $50,000 or 0.5 percent.   [1] Includes other types of receipts, not shown separately.   [2] Elections in which an incumbent did not seek re-election.

Source: U.S. Federal Election Commission, *FEC Reports on Financial Activity, Final Report, U.S. Senate and House Campaigns*, biennial.

No. 470. Contributions to Congressional Campaigns by Political Action Committees (PAC), by Type of Committee: 1981 to 1992

[**In millions of dollars**. Covers amounts given to candidates in primary, general, run-off, and special elections during the 2-year calendar period indicated. For number of political action committees, see table 465]

TYPE OF COMMITTEE	Total	Democrats	Republicans	Incumbents	Challengers	Open seats [1]
HOUSE OF REPRESENTATIVES						
1981-82	61.1	34.2	26.8	40.8	10.9	9.4
1983-84	75.7	46.3	29.3	57.2	11.3	7.2
1985-86	87.4	54.7	32.6	65.9	9.1	12.4
1987-88	102.2	67.4	34.7	82.2	10.0	10.0
1989-90	108.5	72.2	36.2	87.5	7.3	13.6
1991-92, total [2]	**127.4**	**85.4**	**41.7**	**94.4**	**12.2**	**20.8**
Corporate	42.9	23.4	19.5	35.1	2.8	5.0
Trade association [3]	38.8	23.2	15.5	29.2	2.9	6.6
Labor	30.7	29.0	1.5	20.0	4.5	6.2
Nonconnected [4]	10.4	6.7	3.7	6.3	1.7	2.4
SENATE						
1981-82	22.6	11.2	11.4	14.3	5.2	3.0
1983-84	29.7	14.0	15.6	17.9	6.3	5.4
1985-86	45.3	20.2	25.1	23.7	10.2	11.4
1987-88	45.7	24.2	21.5	28.7	8.0	9.0
1989-90	41.2	20.2	21.0	29.5	8.2	3.5
1991-92, total [2]	**51.2**	**29.0**	**22.2**	**31.9**	**9.4**	**10.0**
Corporate	21.2	8.7	12.5	14.6	2.9	3.8
Trade association [3]	12.5	6.6	5.9	8.2	1.8	2.4
Labor	8.6	8.3	0.4	3.8	2.9	1.9
Nonconnected [4]	7.0	4.2	2.8	4.0	1.5	1.5

[1] Elections in which an incumbent did not seek re-election.   [2] Includes other types of political action committees not shown separately.   [3] Includes membership organizations and health organizations.   [4] Represents "ideological" groups as well as other issue groups not necessarily ideological in nature.

Source: U.S. Federal Election Commission, *FEC Reports on Financial Activity, Final Report, U.S. Senate and House Campaigns*, biennial.

State and Local Government Finances and Employment

This section presents data on revenues, expenditures, debt, and employment of State and local governments. Nationwide statistics relating to State and local governments, their numbers, finances, and employment, are compiled primarily by the Bureau of the Census through a program of censuses and surveys. Every fifth year (for years ending in "2" and "7") the Bureau conducts a Census of Governments involving collection of data for all governmental units in the United States. In addition, the Bureau conducts annual surveys which cover all the State governments and a sample of local governments.

Publications issued annually by the Bureau of the Census include a report on finances which presents figures for the Federal Government, nationwide totals for State and local governments by type, and State-local data by States. Also issued annually is a series of publications on State, city, county, and school finances, and on city, county, and other public employment. Financial data are published in the GF publication series, employment data in the GE series. There is also a series of quarterly reports covering tax revenue and finances of major public employee retirement systems.

Basic information for Census Bureau statistics on governments is obtained by mail canvass from State and local officials; however, financial data for each of the State governments and for many of the large local governments are compiled from their official records and reports by Census Bureau personnel. In over two thirds of the States, all or part of local government financial data are obtained through central collection arrangements with State governments. Financial data on the Federal Government is primarily based on the *Budget* published by the Office of Management and Budget (see text, Section 10).

Governmental units.—The governmental structure of the United States includes, in addition to the Federal Government and the States, thousands of

In Brief

State government revenue (from own sources) in 1992: $574,330 million

Taxes	*57%*
Insurance trust funds	*23%*
Charges	*9%*
Interest earnings	*5%*
Utility and liquor stores	*1%*

State government direct expenditures in 1992: $498,640 million

Public welfare	*25%*
Education	*17%*
Insurance trust funds	*16%*
Health and hospitals	*8%*

local governments—counties, municipalities, townships, school districts, and numerous kinds of "special districts." In 1992, 86,743 local governments were identified by the Census of Governments. As defined by the census, governmental units include all agencies or bodies having an organized existence, governmental character, and substantial autonomy. While most of these governments can impose taxes, many of the special districts—such as independent public housing authorities, and numerous local irrigation, power, and other types of districts—are financed from rentals, charges for services, benefit assessments, grants from other governments, and other nontax sources. The count of governments excludes semi-autonomous agencies through which States, cities, and counties sometimes provide for certain functions—for example, "dependent" school systems, State institutions of higher education, and certain other "authorities" and special agencies which are under the administrative or fiscal control of an established governmental unit.

Finances.—The financial statistics relate to government fiscal years ending June 30, or at some date within the 12 previous months. The following governments are exceptions and are included as though they were part of the June 30 group; ending September 30, the State governments of Alabama and Michigan, The District of Columbia, and Alabama school districts; and ending August 31, the State government of Texas and Texas school districts. New York State ends its fiscal year on March 31. The Federal Government ended the fiscal year June 30 until 1976 when its fiscal year, by an act of Congress, was revised to extend from Oct. 1 to Sept. 30. A 3-month quarter (July 1 to Sept. 30, 1976) bridged the transition.

Nationwide government finance statistics have been classified and presented in terms of uniform concepts and categories, rather than according to the highly diverse terminology, organization, and fund structure utilized by individual governments. Accordingly, financial statistics which appear here for the Federal Government and for individual States or local governments have been standardized and may not agree directly with figures appearing in the original sources.

Statistics on governmental finances distinguish among general government, utilities, liquor stores, and insurance trusts. *General government* comprises all activities except utilities, liquor stores, and insurance trusts. Utilities include government water supply, electric light and power, gas supply, and transit systems. Liquor stores are operated by 17 States and by local governments in 6 States. Insurance trusts relate to employee retirement, unemployment compensation, and other social insurance systems administered by the Federal, State, and local governments.

Data for cities relate only to municipal corporations and their dependent agencies and do not include amounts for other local governments overlying city areas. Therefore, expenditure figures for "education" do not include spending by the separate school districts which administer public schools within most municipal areas. Variations in the assignment of governmental responsibility for public assistance, health, hospitals, public housing, and other functions to a lesser degree also have an important effect upon reported amounts of city expenditure, revenue, and debt. Therefore, any intercity comparisons based upon these figures should be made with caution and with due recognition of variations that exist among urban areas in the relative role of the municipal corporation.

Employment and payrolls.—These data are based mainly on mail canvassing of State and local governments. Payroll includes all salaries, wages, and individual fee payments for the month specified, and employment relates to all persons on governmental payrolls during a pay period of the month covered—including paid officials, temporary help, and (unless otherwise specified) part-time as well as full-time personnel. Beginning 1986, statistics for full-time equivalent employment have been computed with a formula using hours worked by part-time employees. A payroll based formula was used prior to 1985. Full-time equivalent employment statistics were not computed for 1985. Figures shown for individual governments cover major dependent agencies such as institutions of higher education, as well as the basic central departments and agencies of the government.

Statistical reliability.—For a discussion of statistical collection and estimation, sampling procedures, and measures of statistical reliability applicable to Census Bureau data, see Appendix III.

Historical statistics.—Tabular headnotes provide cross-references, where applicable, to *Historical Statistics of the United States, Colonial Times to 1970.* See Appendix IV.

No. 471. Number of Governmental Units, by Type: 1942 to 1992

TYPE OF GOVERNMENT	1942	1952 [1]	1957 [1]	1962	1967	1972	1977	1982	1987	1992
Total	155,116	116,807	102,392	91,237	81,299	78,269	79,913	81,831	83,237	86,743
U.S. Government	1	1	1	1	1	1	1	1	1	1
State government	48	50	50	50	50	50	50	50	50	50
Local governments	155,067	116,756	102,341	91,186	81,248	78,218	79,862	81,780	83,186	86,692
County	3,050	3,052	3,050	3,043	3,049	3,044	3,042	3,041	3,042	3,043
Municipal	16,220	16,807	17,215	18,000	18,048	18,517	18,862	19,076	19,200	19,296
Township and town	18,919	17,202	17,198	17,142	17,105	16,991	16,822	16,734	16,691	16,666
School district	108,579	67,355	50,454	34,678	21,782	15,781	15,174	14,851	14,721	14,556
Special district	8,299	12,340	14,424	18,323	21,264	23,885	25,962	28,078	29,532	33,131

[1] Adjusted to include units in Alaska and Hawaii which adopted statehood in 1959.

No. 472. Number of Local Governments, by Type—States: 1992

[Governments in existence in January. Limited to governments actually in existence. Excludes, therefore, a few counties and numerous townships and "incorporated places" existing as areas for which statistics can be presented as to population and other subjects, but lacking any separate organized county, township, or municipal government]

STATE	All govern-mental units [1]	County [2]	Muni-cipal [2]	Town-ship [2]	School district	SPECIAL DISTRICT			
						Total [3]	Natural resources	Fire protection	Housing and com-munity develop-ment
United States	86,743	3,043	19,296	16,666	14,556	33,131	6,564	5,354	3,663
Alabama	1,134	67	440	-	129	497	68	4	153
Alaska	176	12	149	-	-	14	-	-	13
Arizona	598	15	86	-	228	268	71	130	-
Arkansas	1,473	75	489	-	324	584	230	48	130
California	4,495	57	460	-	1,080	2,897	489	395	92
Colorado	1,826	62	266	-	180	1,317	170	247	96
Connecticut	575	-	30	149	17	378	1	59	95
Delaware	281	3	57	-	19	201	192	-	4
Dist. of Columbia	2	-	1	-	-	1	-	-	-
Florida	1,041	66	390	-	95	489	136	60	107
Georgia	1,321	157	536	-	185	442	38	6	207
Hawaii	21	3	1	-	-	16	16	-	-
Idaho	1,105	44	199	-	116	745	170	130	13
Illinois	6,810	102	1,282	1,433	997	2,995	928	813	117
Indiana	2,976	91	566	1,008	310	1,000	132	1	62
Iowa	1,904	99	953	-	445	406	242	72	19
Kansas	3,918	105	627	1,355	324	1,506	261	-	207
Kentucky	1,345	119	438	-	177	610	128	93	24
Louisiana	461	61	301	-	66	32	2	-	1
Maine	799	16	22	468	88	204	13	-	27
Maryland	416	23	155	-	-	237	165	-	21
Massachusetts	851	12	39	312	86	401	14	15	255
Michigan	2,727	83	534	1,242	587	280	82	2	-
Minnesota	3,616	87	854	1,804	477	393	111	-	172
Mississippi	898	82	294	-	176	345	256	-	57
Missouri	3,368	114	933	324	553	1,443	175	208	159
Montana	1,305	54	128	-	544	578	129	150	18
Nebraska	2,997	93	534	452	842	1,075	96	422	137
Nevada	212	16	18	-	17	160	33	14	17
New Hampshire	531	10	13	221	168	118	10	16	23
New Jersey	1,625	21	320	247	550	486	17	171	83
New Mexico	494	33	99	-	94	267	220	-	5
New York	3,319	57	620	929	714	998	2	909	-
North Carolina	954	100	518	-	-	335	150	-	104
North Dakota	2,795	53	366	1,351	284	740	79	277	38
Ohio	3,534	88	942	1,317	665	521	98	41	59
Oklahoma	1,822	77	589	-	614	541	102	18	124
Oregon	1,487	36	240	-	340	870	202	268	22
Pennsylvania	5,397	66	1,022	1,548	516	2,244	10	1	88
Rhode Island	128	-	8	31	4	84	3	38	26
South Carolina	705	46	270	-	91	297	48	85	46
South Dakota	1,803	64	310	971	184	273	109	51	42
Tennessee	960	93	339	-	14	513	117	-	96
Texas	4,919	254	1,171	-	1,101	2,392	432	96	402
Utah	635	29	228	-	40	337	77	20	18
Vermont	690	14	50	237	278	110	14	22	9
Virginia	461	95	230	-		135	44	-	-
Washington	1,796	39	268	-	296	1,192	160	410	51
West Virginia	708	55	231	-	55	366	15	-	36
Wisconsin	2,752	72	583	1,267	430	399	179	-	188
Wyoming	576	23	97	-	56	399	128	62	-

- Represents zero. [1] Includes the Federal Government and the 50 State governments not shown separately. [2] Includes "town" governments in the six New England States and in Minnesota, New York, and Wisconsin. [3] Includes other special districts not shown separately.

Source of tables 471 and 472: U.S. Bureau of the Census, 1992 Census of Governments, *Government Organization*.

No. 473. County, Municipal, and Township Governments: 1992

[Number of governments as of **January 1992**. Population enumerated as of **April 1, 1990**. Consolidated city-county governments are classified as municipal rather than county governments. Township governments include "towns" in the six New England States, Minnesota, New York, and Wisconsin]

POPULATION-SIZE GROUP	COUNTY GOVERNMENTS			MUNICIPAL GOVERNMENTS			TOWNSHIP GOVERNMENTS		
	Number, 1992	Population, 1990		Number, 1992	Population, 1990		Number, 1992	Population, 1990	
		Number (1,000)	Percent		Number (1,000)	Percent		Number (1,000)	Percent
Total	3,043	224,924	100	19,279	153,819	100	16,656	53,051	100
200,000 or more	[1]174	[1]120,551	[1]54	76	47,809	31	6	2,140	4
100,000 to 199,999	[2]244	[2]37,336	[2]17	119	16,390	11	27	3,554	7
50,000 to 99,999	377	26,555	12	310	21,282	14	77	5,214	10
25,000 to 49,999	612	21,510	10	566	19,877	13	249	8,461	16
10,000 to 24,999	908	14,851	7	1,290	20,324	13	728	11,225	21
5,000 to 9,999	[3]728	[3]4,121	[3]2	1,566	11,135	7	1,019	7,112	13
2,500 to 4,999	(NA)	(NA)	(NA)	2,036	7,238	5	1,800	6,301	12
1,000 to 2,499	(NA)	(NA)	(NA)	3,670	5,894	4	3,626	5,796	11
Less than 1,000	(NA)	(NA)	(NA)	9,646	3,874	3	9,124	3,251	6

NA Not available.   [1] For population-size group of 250,000 or more.   [2] 100,000 to 249,999.   [3] Less than 10,000.

Source: U.S. Bureau of the Census, *Census of Governments: 1992,* vol. 1, No. 1, *Government Organization.*

Figure 9.1
State Lottery Proceeds: 1980 to 1994

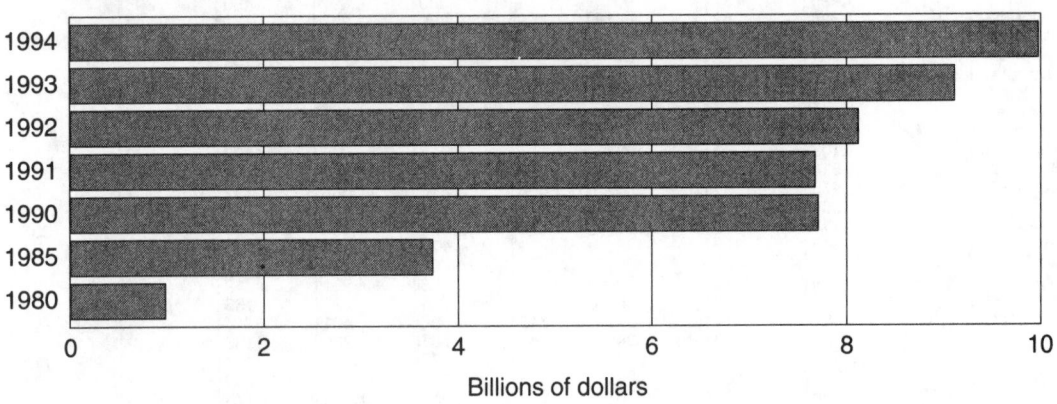

Billions of dollars

Percent distribution of
1993
State lottery proceeds
($9 billion)

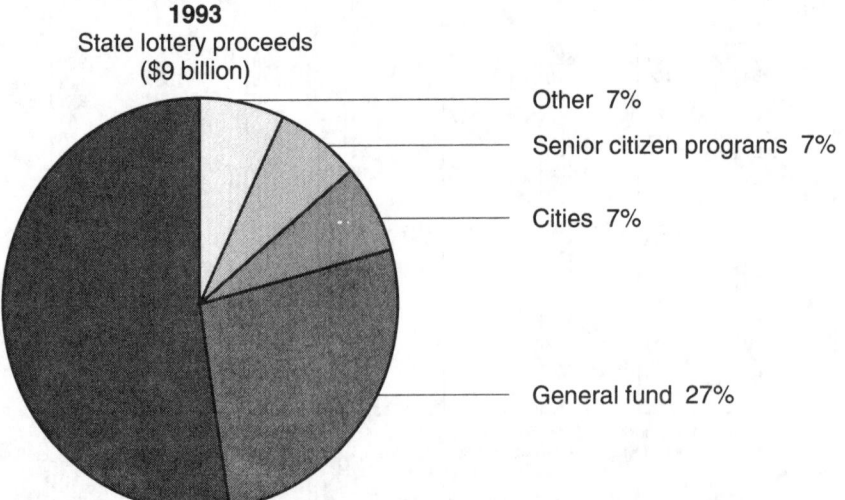

Other 7%

Senior citizen programs 7%

Cities 7%

General fund 27%

Education 53%

Source: Chart prepared by U.S. Bureau of the Census. For data, see table 496.

No. 474. All Governments—Revenue, Expenditure, and Debt: 1980 to 1992

[For fiscal year ending in year shown; see text, section 9. Local government amounts are estimates subject to sampling variation; see Appendix III and source. See also *Historical Statistics, Colonial Times to 1970*, series Y 505-637 and Y 652-848]

ITEM	All govern-ments (bil. dol.)	FEDERAL [1]		STATE AND LOCAL (bil. dol.)			PER CAPITA [2] (dollars)		
		Total (bil. dol.)	Percent of total	Total	State	Local	Total	Federal	State and local
Revenue: [3] 1980	[4]932	565	60.7	[4]452	277	258	[4]4,115	2,496	1,993
1990	[4]2,047	1,155	56.4	[4]1,032	632	580	[4]8,230	4,642	4,150
1991	[4]2,124	1,201	56.5	[4]1,081	660	612	[4]8,425	4,762	4,287
1992	[4]2,262	1,259	47.2	[4]1,185	744	648	[4]8,869	4,938	4,647
Intergovernmental: 1980	(X)	2	(X)	[4]83	64	102	(X)	8	366
1990	(X)	3	(X)	[4]137	126	191	(X)	12	550
1991	(X)	3	(X)	[4]154	170	216	(X)	14	611
1992	(X)	3	(X)	[4]179	170	216	(X)	13	703
General, own sources:									
1980	717	417	58.2	299	169	130	3,163	1,842	1,321
1990	1,493	780	52.2	713	391	322	6,004	3,138	2,866
1991	1,557	809	52.0	748	408	340	6,176	3,209	2,967
1992	1,645	851	51.8	793	436	357	6,449	3,338	3,111
Taxes: [3] 1980	574	351	61.1	223	137	86	2,535	1,548	986
1990	1,134	632	55.7	502	300	201	4,559	2,542	2,017
1991	1,167	642	55.0	525	311	215	4,630	2,546	2,084
1992	1,215	659	54.3	556	328	227	4,763	2,584	2,179
Property: 1980	68	(X)	(X)	68	3	66	302	(X)	302
1990	156	(X)	(X)	156	6	150	626	(X)	626
1991	168	(X)	(X)	168	6	162	666	(X)	666
1992	179	(X)	(X)	179	7	172	700	(X)	700
Individual income:									
1980	286	244	85.3	42	37	5	1,263	1,077	186
1990	573	467	81.6	106	96	10	2,302	1,877	425
1991	577	468	81.1	109	99	10	2,289	1,855	434
1992	592	476	80.5	115	105	11	2,320	1,868	452
Corporate income:									
1980	78	65	82.9	13	13	-	344	285	59
1990	117	94	80.3	24	22	2	471	376	95
1991	120	98	81.5	22	20	2	477	389	88
1992	124	100	81.0	24	22	2	486	393	93
Sales or gross receipts:									
1980	112	[5]32	28.6	80	68	12	494	[5]141	353
1990	232	[5]54	23.3	178	147	31	932	[5]217	715
1991	244	[5]58	24.0	186	154	32	968	[5]232	736
1992	260	[5]64	24.7	196	163	33	1,021	[5]252	769
Current charges and miscellaneous: 1980	142	67	46.7	76	32	44	629	294	335
1990	359	148	41.3	211	91	120	1,445	596	849
1991	390	167	42.9	223	98	125	1,547	663	883
1992	430	192	44.7	238	108	130	1,687	754	932
Expenditures: [3] 1980	[4]959	617	64.4	[4]434	258	261	[4]4,232	2,724	1,916
1990	[4]2,219	1,393	62.8	[4]976	572	581	[4]8,921	5,601	3,924
1991	[4]2,577	1,480	62.2	[4]1,261	629	632	[4]10,222	5,868	5,002
1992	[4]2,488	1,527	61.4	[4]1,355	700	655	[4]9,755	5,989	5,313
Intergovernmental: 1980	(X)	91	(X)	[4]2	85	2	(X)	401	8
1990	(X)	147	(X)	[4]3	175	6	(X)	591	13
1991	(X)	160	(X)	[4]3	187	5	(X)	635	14
1992	(X)	186	(X)	[4]4	201	7	(X)	729	14
Direct: [3] 1980	959	526	54.9	432	173	259	4,232	2,323	1,908
1990	2,219	1,246	56.2	973	397	575	8,921	5,010	3,911
1991	2,379	1,319	55.5	1,060	442	618	9,436	5,233	4,203
1992	2,488	1,341	53.9	1,147	499	648	9,755	5,259	4,496
Current operation: 1980	2,577	209	40.5	308	108	200	11,376	923	1,359
1990	1,190	490	41.2	700	258	442	4,785	1,970	2,815
1991	1,283	522	40.6	762	287	475	5,087	2,069	3,022
1992	1,324	500	37.7	823	322	501	5,191	1,962	3,229
Capital outlay: 1980	99	36	36.7	63	23	40	439	161	278
1990	221	98	44.3	123	46	78	888	394	495
1991	227	96	42.1	132	48	84	901	379	522
1992	228	93	40.9	135	50	84	893	365	527
Debt outstanding: [6] 1980	1,250	914	73.2	337	122	214	5,517	4,036	1,486
1990	4,127	3,266	79.2	861	318	542	16,592	13,132	3,460
1991	4,599	3,683	80.1	916	346	570	18,240	14,608	3,632
1992	5,054	4,083	80.8	970	372	599	19,817	16,010	3,804

- Represents or rounds to zero.   X Not applicable.   [1] Data adjusted to system for reporting State and local data and therefore differ from figures in section 10 tables.   [2] 1980 and 1990 based on enumerated resident population as of April 1; all other years based on estimated resident population as of July 1.   [3] Includes amounts not shown separately.   [4] Excludes duplicative transactions between levels of government; see source.   [5] Includes customs.   [6] End of fiscal year.

Source: U.S. Bureau of the Census, *Government Finances*, series GF, No. 5, annual.

No. 475. All Governments—Detailed Finances: 1992

[**For fiscal year ending in year shown,** see text, section 9. Local government amounts are estimates subject to sampling variation; see Appendix III and source. See also *Historical Statistics, Colonial Times to 1970,* series Y 505-637 and Y 652-848]

ITEM	All governments (mil. dol.)	Federal (mil. dol.)	State (mil. dol.)	Local (mil. dol.)	PER CAPITA [1] (dol.) Federal	State and local
Revenue	2,261,849	1,259,383	744,232	647,872	4,938	5,459
Intergovernmental revenue	(2)	3,431	169,902	216,305	13	1,514
Revenue from own sources	2,261,849	1,255,952	574,330	431,567	4,925	3,944
General revenue from own sources	1,644,789	851,390	435,980	357,419	3,338	3,111
Taxes [3]	1,214,651	659,041	328,370	227,240	2,584	2,179
Property	178,536	(X)	6,673	171,863	(X)	700
Individual income	591,636	476,465	104,609	10,562	1,868	452
Corporation income	123,865	100,270	21,566	2,029	393	93
Sales and gross receipts	260,394	64,282	162,721	33,391	252	769
Customs duties	17,480	17,480	(X)	(X)	69	(X)
General	130,830	(X)	107,757	23,073	(X)	513
Selective [3]	112,084	46,802	54,964	10,318	184	256
Motor fuel	42,809	19,865	22,250	694	78	90
Alcoholic beverages	11,787	7,907	3,599	281	31	15
Tobacco products	11,500	5,190	6,119	191	20	25
Public utilities	21,338	7,851	7,762	5,725	31	53
Motor vehicle and operators' licenses	12,601	(X)	11,771	830	(X)	49
Death and gift	15,629	11,143	4,456	30	44	18
Charges and miscellaneous [3]	430,138	192,349	107,610	130,179	754	932
Current charges [3]	226,382	89,482	52,941	83,959	351	537
National defense and international relations	8,677	8,677	(X)	(X)	34	-
Postal service	45,158	45,158	(X)	(X)	177	-
Education [3]	39,102	-	28,901	10,201	-	153
School lunch sales	3,737	-	-	3,737	-	15
Higher education	32,027	-	28,434	3,593	-	126
Natural resources	16,970	15,148	1,396	426	59	7
Hospitals	37,876	124	12,729	25,023	(Z)	148
Sewerage and sanitation	3,115	(X)	287	2,828	(X)	12
Parks and recreation	3,899	110	788	3,001	(Z)	15
Housing and community development	5,749	2,708	213	2,828	11	12
Airports	5,888	21	650	5,217	(Z)	23
Water transport and terminals	2,889	1,265	393	1,231	5	6
Special assessments	368	(X)	127	241	(X)	1
Sale of property	4,445	3,723	183	539	15	3
Interest earnings	65,746	10,397	26,603	28,746	41	217
Utility and liquor store revenue	62,431	(X)	6,579	55,852	(X)	245
Insurance trust revenue	554,629	404,562	131,771	18,296	1,586	588
Expenditure	2,487,885	1,527,311	699,954	655,325	5,989	5,314
Intergovernmental expenditure	(2)	186,036	201,314	7,355	729	818
Direct expenditure	2,487,885	1,341,275	498,640	647,970	5,259	4,496
General expenditure [3]	1,858,519	886,545	409,132	562,842	3,476	3,811
Education [3]	353,591	26,821	86,650	240,120	105	1,281
Elementary and secondary education	228,917	-	2,221	226,696	-	898
Higher education	84,328	-	70,904	13,424	-	331
Public welfare	201,956	47,722	125,500	28,734	187	605
Health and hospitals	118,791	30,679	41,643	46,469	120	345
Highways	67,290	813	40,266	26,211	3	261
Police protection	41,248	6,703	4,863	29,682	26	135
Fire protection	14,358	(X)	(X)	14,358	(X)	56
Corrections	31,017	2,411	18,306	10,300	9	112
Natural resources	63,650	51,501	9,022	3,127	202	48
Sewerage and sanitation	32,398	(X)	2,235	30,163	(X)	127
Housing and community development	32,549	15,482	1,606	15,461	61	67
Governmental administration	67,180	16,845	19,847	30,488	66	197
Parks and recreation	17,712	1,984	2,688	13,040	8	62
Interest on general debt	254,968	199,713	24,622	30,633	783	217
Utility and liquor store expenditure	84,361	(X)	9,613	74,748	(X)	331
Insurance trust expenditure	545,006	454,730	79,895	10,381	1,783	354
By character and object:						
Current operation	1,323,835	500,341	322,353	501,141	1,962	3,229
Capital outlay	227,807	93,095	50,126	84,586	365	528
Construction	99,797	10,920	39,001	49,876	43	348
Equip., land, and existing structures	112,433	82,175	11,125	19,133	322	119
Assistance and subsidies	129,852	96,622	20,784	12,446	379	130
Interest on debt (general and utility)	264,611	199,713	25,482	39,416	783	254
Insurance benefits and repayments	545,006	454,730	79,895	10,381	1,783	354
Expenditure for salaries and wages [4]	*540,355*	*161,551*	*112,685*	*266,119*	*633*	*1,485*

- Represents or rounds to zero.   X Not applicable.   Z Less than 50 cents.   [1] Based on estimated resident population as of July 1. See table 2.   [2] Aggregates exclude duplicative transactions between levels of government; see source.   [3] Includes amounts not shown separately.   [4] Included in items shown above.

Source: U.S. Bureau of the Census, *Government Finances,* series GF, No. 5, annual.

No. 476. All Governments—Capital Outlays: 1970 to 1992

[In millions of dollars, except percent. For fiscal year ending in year shown; see text, section 9. Except for 1987, local government amounts are subject to sampling variation; see Appendix III and source. See also *Historical Statistics, Colonial Times to 1970*, series Y 523-524, Y 673-674, Y 740-741, and Y 787-788]

LEVEL AND FUNCTION	1970	1980	1985	1986	1987	1988	1989	1990	1991	1992
Total	47,519	99,386	156,912	176,096	195,713	197,844	211,734	220,960	227,225	227,616
Federal Government:										
Total	17,869	36,492	77,014	85,647	96,871	93,531	99,790	97,891	95,575	93,095
Annual percent change [1]	-6	11	6	11	13	-3	7	-2	-2	-3
Percent of direct expenditure	10	7	8	9	9	8	9	8	6	7
By function:										
National defense [2]	14,027	28,161	64,154	71,995	78,222	74,790	78,891	75,624	72,775	69,061
Education	9	97	39	5	13	7	9	41	97	90
Highways	9	132	121	204	173	173	165	181	143	310
Health and hospitals	166	673	916	1,160	1,327	1,228	1,403	1,096	1,387	1,594
Natural resources	1,691	4,046	4,092	3,651	4,058	3,581	3,786	4,698	4,721	5,466
Housing [3]	853	317	1,935	2,515	3,642	5,180	5,032	4,343	4,147	4,017
Air transportation	234	151	785	391	494	407	658	664	778	879
Water transportation [4]	285	1,003	583	245	315	370	306	385	459	506
Other	595	1,912	4,389	5,481	8,627	7,792	9,540	10,859	10,068	11,172
State and local governments:										
Total	29,650	62,894	79,898	90,449	98,842	104,313	111,944	123,069	131,650	134,712
Annual percent change [1]	5	7	13	13	9	6	7	10	7	2
Percent of direct expenditure	20	15	12	13	13	13	13	13	12	9
By function:										
Education [5]	7,621	10,737	13,477	15,490	17,803	18,529	21,854	25,997	27,251	30,854
Higher education	2,705	2,972	4,629	5,217	6,141	6,397	6,851	7,441	7,064	9,180
Elementary and secondary	4,658	7,362	8,358	10,009	11,355	11,789	11,789	18,057	19,852	21,328
Highways	10,762	19,133	23,900	26,807	28,352	31,635	32,754	33,867	36,409	37,031
Health and hospitals	790	2,443	2,709	2,810	3,029	3,436	3,445	3,848	4,142	4,331
Natural resources	789	1,052	1,736	1,803	2,157	1,894	2,019	2,545	2,474	2,266
Housing [3]	1,319	2,248	3,217	3,516	3,394	3,619	3,765	3,997	4,389	4,182
Air transportation	691	1,391	1,875	2,183	2,632	2,896	2,965	3,434	3,941	4,605
Water transportation [4]	258	623	717	911	869	911	943	924	984	778
Sewerage	1,385	6,272	5,926	6,461	7,483	8,300	8,343	8,356	9,104	8,926
Parks and recreation	684	2,023	2,196	2,554	2,838	3,142	3,350	3,877	4,702	3,934
Utilities	2,437	9,933	13,435	15,340	15,638	14,782	15,371	16,601	17,028	17,785
Water	1,201	3,335	4,160	5,134	6,135	6,052	6,372	6,873	7,499	7,567
Electric	820	4,572	5,247	6,127	5,086	4,473	4,291	3,976	3,579	3,950
Transit	366	1,921	3,830	3,830	4,165	3,998	4,430	5,443	5,636	5,836
Gas	50	105	198	250	253	259	279	310	314	432
Other	2,915	7,039	10,711	12,573	14,645	15,172	17,135	19,623	21,226	20,020

[1] Change from prior year shown except 1970, change from 1969, and 1980, change from 1975. [2] Includes international relations and U.S. service schools. [3] Includes community development. [4] Includes terminals. [5] Includes other education.

Source: U.S. Bureau of the Census, *Historical Statistics on Governmental Finances and Employment*; and *Government Finances*, series GF, No. 5, annual.

No. 477. All Governments—Expenditure for Public Works: 1980 to 1992

[In millions of dollars. Public works include expenditures on highways, airports, water transport and terminals, sewerage, solid waste management, water supply, and mass transit systems. Represents direct expenditures excluding intergovernmental grants]

ITEM	Total	High-ways	Airport transpor-tation	Water transport and ter-minals	Sew-erage	Solid waste manage-ment	Water supply	Mass transit
1980: Total	72,177	33,745	5,071	3,278	9,892	3,322	9,228	7,641
Federal	5,114	434	2,570	2,110	-	-	-	-
State	22,832	20,661	360	360	334	-	91	1,026
Local	44,231	12,650	2,141	808	9,558	3,322	9,137	6,615
Capital expenditures (percent)	48	57	30	50	63	11	36	25
1990: Total	146,762	61,913	10,983	4,524	18,309	10,144	22,101	18,788
Federal	7,911	856	4,499	2,556	-	-	-	-
State	43,787	36,464	635	504	636	891	136	4,521
Local	95,064	24,593	5,848	1,464	17,673	9,253	21,966	14,267
Capital expenditures (percent)	42	55	37	29	46	18	31	29
1992: Total	162,872	67,196	12,791	4,582	20,138	12,022	24,264	21,879
Federal	8,213	813	4,679	2,721	-	-	-	-
State	48,469	40,266	963	504	908	1,327	209	4,292
Local	106,190	26,117	7,149	1,357	19,230	10,695	24,055	17,587
Capital expenditures (percent)	42	56	43	28	44	13	31	27

- Represents or rounds to zero.

Source: U.S. Bureau of the Census, *Government Finances*, series GF, No. 5, annual.

No. 478. Federal Grants-in-Aid Summary: 1970 to 1995

[For fiscal year ending in year shown; see text, section 9. Minus sign (-) indicates decrease]

YEAR	CURRENT DOLLARS							CONSTANT (1987) DOLLARS	
	Total grants (bil. dol.)	Average annual percent change [1]	Grants to individuals		Grants as percent of—			Total grants (bil. dol.)	Average annual percent change [1]
			Total (bil. dol.)	Percent of total grants	State-local govt. outlays [2]	Federal outlays	Gross domestic product		
1970	24.1	17.8	8.7	36.3	19.0	12.3	2.4	73.6	11.3
1975	49.8	2.8	16.8	33.7	22.6	15.0	3.3	105.4	0.6
1980	91.5	1.8	32.7	35.7	25.8	15.5	3.5	127.6	-0.2
1985	105.9	1.6	49.4	46.6	20.9	11.2	2.7	113.0	0.8
1988	115.4	2.1	62.4	54.1	17.7	10.8	2.4	110.8	0.7
1989	122.0	5.6	67.4	55.2	17.3	10.7	2.4	112.2	1.3
1990	135.4	10.5	77.1	57.0	19.4	10.8	2.5	119.5	6.3
1991	154.6	13.3	90.7	58.7	20.5	11.7	2.7	130.9	9.1
1992	178.1	14.3	110.0	61.8	21.5	12.9	3.0	146.8	11.5
1993	193.7	8.4	121.5	62.7	21.9	13.7	3.1	155.5	5.8
1994	210.6	8.4	131.1	63.3	23.0	14.4	3.2	165.9	6.5
1995, est.	228.0	8.0	140.4	63.9	(NA)	14.8	3.2	174.7	5.2

NA Not available. [1] Average annual percent change from prior year shown. For explanation, see Guide to Tabular Presentation. 1970, change from 1969. [2] Outlays as defined in the national income and product accounts.

Source: Advisory Commission on Intergovernmental Relations, Washington, DC, *Significant Features of Fiscal Federalism*, 1994 Edition, vol. II, based on *Budget of the United States Government*, FY 96.

No. 479. Federal Aid to State and Local Governments: 1970 to 1995

[In millions of dollars. For fiscal year ending in year shown; see text, section 9. Includes trust funds. See *Historical Statistics, Colonial Times to 1970*, series Y 638-651, for related data]

PROGRAM	1970	1980	1990	1991	1992	1993	1994	1995
Grant-in-aid shared revenue [1]	[2]24,065	91,451	135,377	154,570	178,117	193,664	210,596	228,015
National defense	37	93	241	185	318	152	169	109
Natural resources and environment	411	5,363	3,745	4,040	3,929	3,796	3,765	4,052
Environmental Protection Agency	194	4,603	2,874	3,071	3,038	2,852	2,700	2,837
Energy	25	499	461	457	448	460	466	521
Agriculture	604	569	1,285	1,220	1,142	1,117	937	871
Transportation [1]	4,599	13,087	19,225	19,878	20,608	22,343	23,633	24,823
Airports	83	590	1,220	1,541	1,672	1,931	1,620	1,785
Highways	4,395	9,208	14,171	14,417	15,250	16,409	18,667	19,179
Urban mass transit	104	3,129	3,730	3,821	3,585	3,885	3,267	3,777
Community and regional development [1]	1,780	6,486	4,965	4,273	4,539	5,666	7,789	9,331
Appalachian development	184	335	124	157	125	138	181	158
Community development block grants	(X)	3,902	2,818	2,976	3,090	3,198	3,651	4,330
Education, employment, training, social services [1]	6,417	21,862	23,359	26,566	28,795	30,160	32,744	36,138
Compensatory education for the disadvantaged [3]	1,470	3,370	4,437	5,193	6,129	6,582	6,819	7,009
School improvement programs [3]	86	523	1,080	1,243	1,361	1,903	1,358	1,451
Bilingual and immigrant education [3]	-	166	152	148	160	101	176	209
Federally affected areas impact aid	622	622	799	747	785	468	797	1,084
Vocational and adult education	285	854	1,287	1,038	1,020	1,133	1,292	1,486
Libraries	105	158	127	132	190	159	125	134
Payments to States for Family Support Activities	81	383	265	546	594	736	839	937
Social services-block grants to States	574	2,763	2,749	2,822	2,708	2,785	2,728	2,996
Human development services	390	1,548	2,267	2,920	3,621	3,614	3,998	4,435
Training and employment assistance	954	6,191	3,042	2,985	3,388	3,245	3,310	3,549
Health [1]	3,849	15,758	43,890	55,783	71,416	79,665	86,265	93,244
Alcohol, drug abuse, and mental health [4]	146	679	1,241	1,744	1,778	1,994	2,132	2,462
Medicaid [4]	2,727	13,957	41,103	52,533	67,827	75,774	82,034	88,438
Income security [1]	5,795	18,495	35,189	38,864	43,486	46,991	51,532	55,098
Family support payments to States [4]	4,142	6,888	12,246	13,520	15,103	15,628	16,508	17,260
Food stamps-administration	559	412	1,199	1,406	1,611	2,611	2,688	2,879
Child nutrition and special milk programs [4]	380	3,388	4,871	5,418	5,993	6,589	6,938	7,530
Housing assistance [4]	436	3,435	9,516	10,444	12,262	14,100	15,791	17,774
Veterans benefits and services	18	90	134	141	164	189	199	242
Administration of justice	42	529	574	940	987	987	992	1,300
General government [5]	479	8,616	2,309	2,224	2,274	2,131	2,098	2,279

- Represents or rounds to zero. X Not applicable. [1] Includes items not shown separately. [2] Includes $5 million for international affairs subsequently provided to a private institution. [3] The 1983 Budget proposed dismantlement of the Dept. of Education (DED). Budget data for elementary and secondary education previously performed by DED are included in the Foundation for Education Assistance under compensatory education for the disadvantaged, school improvement (formerly titled "Special programs and populations") programs and bilingual and immigrant education. [4] Includes grants for payments to individuals. [5] Includes general purpose fiscal assistance.

Source: U.S. Office of Management and Budget, *Historical Tables, Budget of the United States Government*, annual.

No. 480. Federal Aid to State and Local Governments—Selected Programs, by State: 1994

[In millions of dollars, except per capita. For fiscal year ending September 30]

STATE	FEDERAL AID [1] Total	Per capita [2] (dol.)	OE [3] compensatory education [4]	EPA [5] waste treatment facilities construction	HHS [6] Administration for Children and Families [7]	Medicaid	HUD [8] Lower income housing assistance [9]	Community development	ETA [10] employment/ training	DOT [11] highway trust fund
United States [12]	214,239	811	6,819	1,971	32,968	82,034	13,266	3,653	6,733	18,623
Alabama	3,209	761	125	24	297	1,287	169	63	97	272
Alaska	1,063	1,755	24	9	129	176	88	6	40	225
Arizona	2,996	735	99	9	496	1,103	152	46	99	271
Arkansas	1,966	802	76	15	213	834	98	30	63	185
California	26,219	834	777	144	6,825	7,861	1,574	389	997	2,015
Colorado	2,102	575	65	7	284	649	146	32	77	257
Connecticut	3,028	924	60	24	500	1,175	260	38	111	393
Delaware	472	669	16	9	69	153	23	7	18	53
District of Columbia	2,222	3,898	26	17	310	395	74	35	28	72
Florida	8,018	575	297	81	1,107	2,945	474	141	301	795
Georgia	5,028	713	172	19	785	2,080	281	74	123	384
Hawaii	1,088	923	18	7	176	243	88	19	36	222
Idaho	778	686	25	10	95	235	37	10	33	115
Illinois	8,506	724	290	106	1,325	2,780	750	205	316	728
Indiana	3,553	618	102	31	423	1,591	200	73	102	353
Iowa	2,015	712	49	24	284	693	92	63	64	247
Kansas	1,666	652	52	16	230	602	65	36	42	215
Kentucky	3,096	809	116	14	395	1,330	180	48	83	215
Louisiana	5,233	1,213	178	13	292	3,256	190	75	118	239
Maine	1,269	1,023	32	11	185	604	82	16	37	262
Maryland	3,637	727	93	52	519	1,191	243	54	104	88
Massachusetts	6,261	1,036	134	195	1,072	2,104	597	112	184	298
Michigan	7,117	749	280	108	1,436	2,914	330	158	273	963
Minnesota	3,515	770	81	10	597	1,390	230	60	273	417
Mississippi	2,507	939	121	14	289	1,068	116	31	101	293
Missouri	3,971	752	112	41	520	1,577	210	82	68	173
Montana	906	1,059	25	9	110	247	56	11	133	439
Nebraska	1,114	686	31	6	119	389	61	18	28	165
Nevada	797	547	17	10	97	192	63	10	27	150
New Hampshire	956	840	15	11	117	496	55	9	40	125
New Jersey	6,163	780	179	82	821	2,431	567	110	208	69
New Mexico	1,714	1,036	57	15	238	531	73	17	42	510
New York	22,445	1,235	628	110	3,571	11,323	1,456	403	468	148
North Carolina	4,862	688	141	41	653	2,098	251	60	138	780
North Dakota	702	1,100	17	7	87	201	37	7	23	473
Ohio	8,366	754	261	124	1,350	3,504	594	167	219	705
Oklahoma	2,359	724	78	14	376	782	163	34	75	249
Oregon	2,355	763	68	22	374	755	127	32	83	203
Pennsylvania	9,705	805	308	67	1,462	3,998	712	207	319	757
Rhode Island	1,100	1,103	22	7	130	445	128	18	36	136
South Carolina	2,726	744	90	23	243	1,329	130	31	77	232
South Dakota	724	1,004	20	10	78	206	56	11	22	134
Tennessee	3,940	761	122	35	342	1,803	209	54	98	284
Texas	12,669	689	578	137	1,482	5,386	575	206	387	1,071
Utah	1,209	634	31	15	174	406	42	20	46	110
Vermont	546	942	16	4	118	187	34	9	18	48
Virginia	3,180	485	110	48	422	1,006	237	53	120	307
Washington	3,924	734	98	40	677	1,441	223	53	146	462
West Virginia	2,166	1,189	61	26	216	989	101	21	57	172
Wisconsin	3,450	678	110	61	494	1,427	190	55	106	339
Wyoming	714	1,501	11	5	54	98	18	7	18	114
Outlying areas	3,852	6,600	252	17	304	129	360	113	131	94

[1] Includes programs not shown separately. [2] Based on estimated resident population as of July 1, 1994. [3] Department of Education, Office of Elementary and Secondary Education. [4] For the disadvantaged. [5] Environmental Protection Agency. [6] Department of Health and Human Services. [7] Includes family support payments (Aid to Families with Dependent Children), social services block grants, children and family services, foster care and adoption assistance, community services block grants, refugee assistance, and assistance for legalized aliens. [8] Department of Housing and Urban Development. [9] Includes public housing, housing payments (section 8) to public agencies, and college housing. [10] Department of Labor, Employment and Training Administration, Insurance and Employment Service Operations: and Community Service. [11] Department of Transportation, Highway Trust Fund. [12] Includes undistributed amounts not shown separately.

Source: U.S. Bureau of the Census, Federal Expenditures by State for Fiscal Year 1994.

No. 481. State and Local Governments—Summary of Finances: 1980 to 1992

[**For fiscal year ending in year shown;** see text, section 9. Local government amounts are estimates subject to sampling variation; see Appendix III and source. See also *Historical Statistics, Colonial Times to 1970*, series Y 652-709]

ITEM	TOTAL (mil. dol.)				PER CAPITA [1] (dol.)			
	1980	1990	1991	1992	1980	1990	1991	1992
Revenue [2]	451,537	1,032,115	1,080,862	1,185,191	1,993	4,150	4,287	4,647
From Federal Government	83,029	136,802	154,099	179,184	366	550	611	703
Public welfare	24,921	59,961	72,661	91,788	110	241	288	360
Highways	8,980	14,368	14,561	14,800	40	58	58	58
Education	14,435	23,233	25,197	27,821	64	93	100	109
Health and hospitals	2,513	5,904	6,504	7,293	11	24	26	29
Housing and community development	3,905	9,655	10,233	10,876	17	39	41	43
Other and unallocable	28,275	23,683	24,943	26,606	125	95	99	104
From State and local sources	368,509	895,313	926,763	1,006,007	1,627	3,600	3,676	3,945
General, net intergovernmental	299,293	712,700	748,108	793,399	1,321	2,866	2,967	3,111
Taxes	223,463	501,619	525,355	555,610	986	2,017	2,084	2,179
Property	68,499	155,613	167,999	178,536	302	626	666	700
Sales and gross receipts	79,927	177,885	185,570	196,112	353	715	736	769
Individual income	42,080	105,640	109,341	115,170	186	425	434	452
Corporation income	13,321	23,566	22,242	23,595	59	95	88	93
Other	19,636	38,915	40,202	42,197	87	156	159	165
Charges and miscellaneous	75,830	211,081	222,753	237,789	335	849	883	932
Utility and liquor stores	25,560	58,642	60,736	62,540	113	236	241	245
Water supply system	6,766	17,674	18,034	19,147	30	71	72	75
Electric power system	11,387	29,268	30,489	30,999	50	118	121	122
Transit system	2,397	5,216	5,629	5,742	11	21	22	23
Gas supply system	1,809	3,043	3,013	3,034	8	12	12	12
Liquor stores	3,201	3,441	3,571	3,618	14	14	14	14
Insurance trust revenue [3]	43,656	123,970	117,919	150,067	193	498	468	588
Employee retirement	25,441	94,268	87,206	108,310	112	379	346	425
Unemployment compensation	13,529	18,441	18,025	27,019	60	74	71	106
Direct expenditure	432,328	972,662	1,059,805	1,146,610	1,908	3,911	4,203	4,496
By function:								
Direct general expenditure [3]	367,340	834,786	908,108	971,973	1,621	3,356	3,602	3,811
Education [3]	133,211	288,148	309,302	326,769	588	1,159	1,227	1,281
Elementary and secondary	92,930	202,009	217,643	228,917	410	812	863	898
Higher education	33,919	73,418	78,749	84,329	150	295	312	331
Highways	33,311	61,057	64,937	66,477	147	245	258	261
Public welfare	45,552	110,518	130,402	154,235	201	444	517	605
Health	8,387	24,223	26,706	29,344	37	97	106	115
Hospitals	23,787	50,412	54,404	58,768	105	203	216	230
Police protection	13,494	30,577	32,772	34,545	60	123	130	135
Fire protection	5,718	13,186	13,796	14,358	25	53	55	56
Natural resources	5,509	12,330	12,575	13,049	24	50	50	51
Sanitation and sewerage	13,214	28,453	31,014	32,398	58	114	123	127
Housing and community development	6,062	15,479	16,648	17,067	27	62	66	67
Parks and recreation	6,520	14,326	15,930	15,728	29	58	63	62
Financial administration	6,719	16,217	16,995	18,090	30	65	67	71
Interest on general debt [4]	14,747	49,739	52,234	55,255	65	200	207	217
Utility and liquor stores [4]	36,191	77,801	81,004	84,361	160	313	321	331
Water supply system	9,228	22,101	23,561	24,378	41	89	93	96
Electric power system	15,016	30,997	31,090	31,983	66	125	123	125
Transit system	7,641	18,788	20,379	21,879	34	76	81	86
Gas supply system	1,715	2,989	2,970	3,058	8	12	12	12
Liquor stores	2,591	2,926	3,005	3,063	11	12	12	12
Insurance trust expenditure [3]	28,797	63,321	74,159	90,276	127	255	294	354
Employee retirement	14,008	38,355	42,121	46,419	62	154	167	182
Unemployment compensation	12,070	16,499	22,135	32,887	53	66	88	129
By character and object:								
Current operation	307,811	700,131	762,007	823,494	1,359	2,815	3,022	3,229
Capital outlay	62,894	123,069	131,650	134,521	278	495	522	527
Construction	51,492	89,114	96,654	100,533	227	358	383	394
Equipment, land, and existing structures	11,402	33,955	34,996	33,988	50	137	139	133
Assistance and subsidies	15,222	27,227	30,456	33,230	67	109	121	130
Interest on debt (general and utility)	17,604	58,914	61,533	64,789	78	237	244	254
Insurance benefits and repayments	28,797	63,321	74,159	90,276	127	255	294	354
Expenditure for salaries and wages	*163,896*	*341,158*	*366,406*	*378,804*	*723*	*1,372*	*1,453*	*1,485*
Debt outstanding, year end	335,603	860,584	915,711	970,043	1,481	3,460	3,632	3,804
Long-term	322,456	841,278	894,019	948,710	1,423	3,383	3,546	3,720
Short-term	13,147	19,306	21,692	21,333	58	78	86	84
Long-term debt:								
Issued	42,364	108,468	118,054	155,060	187	436	468	608
Retired	17,404	64,831	65,666	99,233	77	261	260	389

[1] 1980 and 1990 based on enumerated resident population as of April 1. Other years based on estimated resident population as of July 1; see table 2. [2] Aggregates exclude duplicative transactions between State and local governments; see source. [3] Includes amounts not shown separately. [4] Interest on utility debt included in "utility expenditure." For total interest on debt, see "Interest on debt (general and utility)."

Source: U.S. Bureau of the Census, *Historical Statistics on Governmental Finances and Employment* and *Government Finances*, series GF, No. 5, annual.

No. 482. State and Local Government Receipts and Expenditures in the National Income and Product Accounts: 1980 to 1993

[**In billions of dollars.** For explanation of national income, see text, section 14]

ITEM	1980	1985	1986	1987	1988	1989	1990	1991	1992	1993
Receipts	**361.4**	**528.7**	**571.2**	**594.3**	**631.3**	**681.5**	**730.0**	**783.6**	**842.9**	**891.0**
Personal tax and nontax receipts [1]	56.2	94.0	101.6	111.8	117.6	131.4	138.9	147.9	159.1	166.1
Income taxes	42.6	72.1	77.4	86.0	89.9	101.4	106.3	110.4	118.1	123.3
Nontaxes	5.0	9.9	11.4	11.9	12.7	14.1	15.3	19.2	21.8	22.7
Corporate profits tax accruals	14.5	20.2	22.7	23.9	26.0	24.2	22.3	23.0	24.2	30.3
Indirect business tax and nontax accruals [1]	172.3	271.4	292.0	306.5	324.5	352.8	378.2	398.4	423.1	440.7
Sales taxes	82.9	131.1	140.4	149.8	161.4	172.3	183.3	189.9	202.1	212.4
Property taxes	68.8	107.0	114.5	121.1	127.6	143.5	155.5	167.6	177.5	184.0
Contributions for social insurance	29.7	42.8	47.3	49.2	51.9	54.8	58.3	61.0	64.5	67.8
Federal grants-in-aid	88.7	100.3	107.6	102.8	111.3	118.2	132.3	153.3	172.2	186.1
Expenditures	**336.6**	**472.6**	**517.0**	**554.2**	**593.0**	**636.7**	**704.9**	**766.6**	**818.1**	**864.7**
Purchases	298.0	428.1	465.3	496.6	531.7	573.6	620.9	651.6	676.3	704.7
Compensation of employees	193.5	283.2	305.9	327.3	351.9	379.8	412.7	437.9	461.7	483.0
Transfer payments to persons	65.7	101.2	110.9	119.6	130.0	143.6	165.4	199.2	229.0	250.4
Net interest paid [2]	−19.3	−38.7	−40.4	−41.2	−44.2	−52.3	−51.3	−52.3	−53.1	−53.4
Less: Dividends received	1.9	4.5	5.1	5.9	6.9	8.1	9.0	9.5	10.1	10.4
Subsidies [3]	−5.8	−13.5	−13.7	−14.9	−17.5	−20.1	−21.1	−22.5	−24.0	−26.7
Surplus	**24.8**	**56.1**	**54.3**	**40.1**	**38.4**	**44.8**	**25.1**	**17.0**	**24.8**	**26.3**
Social insurance funds	26.9	46.9	52.7	54.8	56.8	62.3	60.7	63.4	66.4	66.3

[1] Includes other items not shown separately.   [2] Interest paid less interest received.   [3] Less current surplus of government.

Source: U.S. Bureau of Economic Analysis, *National Income and Product Accounts of the United States: volume 2, 1959-88,* and *Survey of Current Business,* July 1994.

No. 483. State and Local Government Detailed Expenditures in the National Income and Product Accounts: 1980 to 1993

[**In billions of dollars.** For explanation of national income, see text, section 14]

EXPENDITURE	1980	1985	1986	1987	1988	1989	1990	1991	1992	1993
Purchases	298.0	428.1	465.3	496.6	531.7	573.6	620.9	651.6	676.3	704.7
Durable goods	12.8	22.3	24.6	26.0	28.1	31.9	34.9	35.0	35.7	36.9
Nondurable goods	28.8	38.7	39.1	42.3	45.5	50.7	56.2	58.0	59.9	62.6
Services	207.4	307.5	335.1	357.3	382.2	410.1	442.8	466.2	486.2	505.7
Compensation of employees	193.5	283.2	305.9	327.3	351.9	379.8	412.7	437.9	461.7	483.0
Other services	13.9	24.3	29.2	29.9	30.3	30.4	30.1	28.4	24.5	22.6
Structures	49.0	59.5	66.4	71.0	75.9	80.9	87.1	92.4	94.5	99.6
Transfers	65.7	101.2	110.9	119.6	130.0	143.6	165.4	199.2	229.0	250.4
Benefits from social insurance funds	17.8	30.4	33.9	37.4	40.9	44.6	49.6	55.2	61.8	68.4
State and local employee retirement	15.1	25.5	28.4	31.2	34.1	36.9	40.6	44.8	50.5	56.6
Temporary disability insurance	0.8	1.4	1.5	1.6	1.8	1.9	2.2	2.8	3.0	2.5
Workers' compensation	2.0	3.5	3.9	4.6	5.1	5.8	6.9	7.6	8.3	9.3
Public assistance	42.8	65.1	70.7	75.6	82.0	91.3	107.0	134.4	156.7	170.7
Medical care	24.6	41.2	45.4	49.8	55.0	62.9	75.6	100.1	120.5	133.2
Aid to Families with Dependent Children	12.4	15.4	16.4	16.7	17.3	18.0	19.8	22.0	23.3	23.9
Supplemental Security Income	2.0	2.3	2.6	2.9	3.1	3.4	3.8	3.8	4.1	3.9
General assistance	1.4	2.4	2.5	2.6	2.7	2.8	3.0	2.9	3.3	3.3
Other	2.3	3.7	3.7	3.6	4.0	4.1	4.8	5.4	5.6	6.3
Other	4.9	5.6	6.3	6.5	7.0	7.7	8.7	9.6	10.5	11.3

Source: U.S. Bureau of Economic Analysis, *National Income and Product Accounts of the United States: volume 2, 1959-88,* and *Survey of Current Business,* July 1994.

No. 484. New Issues of Long-Term State and Local Government Securities: 1980 to 1994

[In billions of dollars. Beginning 1985, includes outlying areas]

ITEM	1980	1985	1987	1988	1989	1990	1991	1992	1993	1994
All issues, new capital and refunding [1]	38.7	194.3	100.4	114.1	119.4	123.1	166.3	226.7	287.8	160.0
General obligations	11.2	37.1	30.0	30.5	36.8	39.7	55.9	78.8	90.9	55.3
Revenue	27.4	157.3	70.4	83.6	82.6	83.3	110.4	147.9	197.0	104.7
Type of issuer:	38.7	194.3	100.4	114.1	119.4	123.1	166.3	[2]226.7	[2]287.8	[2]160.0
City, town	6.4	34.6	17.3	20.6	23.2	22.5	30.7	44.1	51.0	26.5
College or university	0.1	2.7	1.1	1.9	2.0	1.6	3.7	4.0	5.1	2.8
County/parish	3.8	15.5	9.6	10.7	9.8	9.7	14.3	19.2	24.0	16.9
District	2.4	15.2	10.0	13.0	13.1	14.7	22.6	30.4	36.8	20.8
Local authority	7.9	49.8	22.1	21.7	23.1	20.8	27.7	41.0	57.4	26.3
State/Province	5.1	10.9	10.1	9.4	11.6	14.8	19.4	25.2	28.2	19.7
State authority	13.0	65.7	30.2	36.8	36.5	38.9	47.8	62.8	85.4	47.0
Issues for new capital	37.1	123.9	55.2	77.5	84.0	97.9	112.7	104.5	93.7	110.6
Use of proceeds:										
Airports	0.4	2.5	1.2	3.2	1.2	4.7	3.4	4.9	1.7	3.0
Economic development	0.1	1.8	2.2	1.3	1.6	1.5	2.2	1.9	2.2	3.0
Education	2.6	10.3	8.3	11.1	13.8	16.3	17.6	16.9	14.4	20.0
Electric & public power	3.6	8.4	1.6	1.2	2.1	1.3	3.3	2.8	3.2	2.4
General purpose/public improvement	9.6	21.4	17.4	24.7	28.2	32.2	40.8	34.2	31.3	39.1
Health care	1.7	15.9	3.7	5.6	8.0	8.2	11.1	8.1	8.5	7.5
Multi family housing	2.2	20.1	1.9	1.6	1.8	1.0	1.5	2.2	2.0	3.4
Pollution control	2.1	7.8	1.6	0.7	0.8	1.2	1.6	1.4	1.8	1.3
Single family housing	10.6	14.6	4.4	9.9	6.4	10.2	6.7	5.4	3.3	7.6
Solid waste/Resource Rec.	0.4	3.3	1.0	2.0	1.9	2.3	2.5	1.9	3.0	2.8
Student loans	0.2	2.7	1.3	2.9	1.3	0.9	1.4	2.6	3.0	2.3
Transportation	0.9	5.7	2.5	3.4	5.0	6.9	6.3	9.3	7.3	7.6
Water, sewer, and gas facilities	1.6	4.9	5.5	6.8	6.9	7.5	10.9	9.1	8.6	7.3

[1] Excludes short term issues, private placements, not-for-profit issuers.   [2] Includes amounts not shown separately.

Source: Securities Data Company, Newark, NJ, Municipal New Issues Database.(copyright)

No. 485. State and Local Governments—Indebtedness: 1980 to 1992

[In billions of dollars, except per capita. For fiscal year ending in year shown; see text, section 9. Local government amounts are estimates subject to sampling variation; see Appendix III and source. See *Historical Statistics, Colonial Times to 1970*, series Y 680, Y 747, and Y 794, for debt outstanding]

ITEM	DEBT OUTSTANDING						LONG-TERM		
	Total	Per capita [1] (dol.)	Long-term			Short-term	Net long-term	Debt issued	Debt retired
			Local schools [2]	Utilities	All other				
1980: Total	335.6	1,477	32.3	55.2	235.0	13.1	262.9	42.4	17.4
State	122.0	537	3.8	4.6	111.5	2.1	79.8	16.4	5.7
Local	213.6	940	28.5	50.6	123.5	11.0	183.1	25.9	11.7
1985: Total	568.6	2,390	43.8	90.8	414.5	19.6	430.5	101.2	43.5
State	211.9	891	6.7	8.6	193.8	2.8	110.4	41.7	16.4
Local	356.7	1,499	37.1	82.2	220.6	16.8	320.1	59.5	27.2
1986: Total	658.9	2,744	43.0	104.8	492.8	18.3	458.9	162.0	74.4
State	247.7	1,032	4.1	10.0	232.0	1.6	129.1	64.0	26.4
Local	411.2	1,712	38.9	94.9	260.6	16.7	329.8	98.1	48.0
1987: Total	727.1	3,001	49.2	120.5	541.5	15.9	518.3	134.4	83.0
State	265.7	1,097	7.9	11.9	244.1	1.6	143.4	50.2	33.3
Local	461.5	1,905	41.3	108.6	297.3	14.3	375.0	84.1	49.8
1988: Total	755.0	3,088	47.5	124.9	566.9	15.7	425.4	89.7	63.8
State	276.8	1,132	3.3	12.2	260.0	1.3	108.8	36.4	26.1
Local	478.2	1,956	44.2	112.7	306.9	14.4	316.5	53.3	37.6
1989: Total	798.4	3,235	52.7	127.5	600.2	18.0	445.5	102.2	63.8
State	295.5	1,197	3.7	12.2	277.4	2.3	118.2	42.0	26.9
Local	502.9	2,037	49.0	115.3	322.8	15.7	327.2	60.2	36.8
1990: Total	860.6	3,451	60.4	134.8	646.1	19.3	477.0	108.5	64.8
State	318.3	1,276	4.4	12.3	298.8	2.8	125.5	43.5	22.9
Local	542.3	2,175	56.0	122.4	347.4	16.5	351.5	65.0	42.0
1991: Total	915.8	3,632	71.0	141.2	703.5	21.7	509.9	118.1	65.7
State	345.6	1,371	5.9	12.5	327.1	3.4	139.9	50.5	25.4
Local	570.2	2,261	65.1	128.7	376.4	18.3	369.9	67.6	40.3
1992: Total	971.0	3,807	78.4	150.4	742.2	21.4	561.6	155.1	99.2
State	371.9	1,458	7.6	13.7	350.7	2.9	125.4	70.2	45.0
Local	599.1	2,349	70.9	136.7	391.5	18.4	409.1	85.0	54.3

[1] 1980 and 1990 based on enumerated resident population as of April 1; other years based on estimated resident population as of July 1; see table 2.   [2] Includes debt for education activities other than higher education.

Source: U.S. Bureau of the Census, *Government Finances*, series GF, No. 5, annual; and unpublished data.

No. 486. Bond Ratings, for State Government, by State: 1994

[**As of fourth quarter.** Key to investment grade ratings are: **S&P:** AAA, AA1, AA, AA-, A+, A, A-, BBB+, BBB; **Moody's:** AAA, AA1, AA, A1, A, BBA1, BBB; **Fitch:** AAA, AA+, AA, AA-, A+, BBB+, BBB]

STATE	Standard & Poor's	Moody's	Fitch	STATE	Standard & Poor's	Moody's	Fitch
Alabama	AA	AA	AA	Montana	AA-	AA	(1)
Alaska	AA	AA	AA	Nebraska	(1)	(1)	(1)
Arizona	(1)	(1)	(1)	Nevada	AA	AA	(1)
Arkansas	AA	AA	(1)	New Hampshire	AA	AA	AA
California	A	A1	A	New Jersey	AA+	AA1	AA+
Colorado	(1)	(1)	(1)	New Mexico	AA+	AA1	(1)
Connecticut	AA-	AA	AA+	New York	A-	A	A+
Delaware	AA+	AA1	(1)	North Carolina	AAA	AAA	AAA
Florida	AA	AA	AA	North Dakota	AA-	AA	(1)
Georgia	AA+	AAA	AAA	Ohio	AA	AA	(1)
Hawaii	AA	AA	(1)	Oklahoma	AA-	AA	AA
Idaho	(1)	(1)	(1)	Oregon	AA-	AA	AA
Illinois	AA-	A1	(2)	Pennsylvania	AA-	A1	AA-
Indiana	(1)	(1)	(1)	Rhode Island	AA-	A1	AA-
Iowa	(1)	(1)	(1)	South Carolina	AA+	AAA	AAA
Kansas	(1)	(1)	(1)	South Dakota	(1)	(1)	(1)
Kentucky	AA	AA	(1)	Tennessee	AA+	AAA	AAA
Louisiana	A	BAA1	(1)	Texas	AA	AA	AA+
Maine	AA+	AA	(1)	Utah	AAA	AAA	AAA
Maryland	AAA	AAA	AAA	Vermont	AA-	AA	AA
Massachusetts	A+	A1	A+	Virginia	AAA	AAA	AAA
Michigan	AA	A1	AA	Washington	AA	AA	AA
Minnesota	AA+	AA1	AAA	West Virginia	A+	A1	A+
Mississippi	AA-	AA	(1)	Wisconsin	AA	AA	(2)
Missouri	AAA	AAA	AAA	Wyoming	(1)	(1)	(1)

[1] Not reviewed.   [2] Under general review.

Sources: Standard & Poor's, New York, NY; Moody's Investors Service, New York, NY; Fitch Investor Services, New York, NY. (All data copyrighted).

No. 487. Bond Ratings for City Government, by Largest Cities: 1994

[**As of fourth quarter.** For key to investment grade ratings, see headnote in table above]

CITIES RANKED BY 1992 POPULATION	Standard & Poors	Moody's	Fitch	CITIES RANKED BY 1992 POPULATION	Standard & Poors	Moody's	Fitch
New York, NY	A-	BAA1	A-	Sacramento, CA	AA	AA1	(1)
Los Angeles, CA	AA	AA1	(1)	Fresno, CA	(1)	(1)	(1)
Chicago, IL	A	A	(1)	Tulsa, OK	AA	AA	(1)
Houston, TX	AA-	AA	AA	Oakland, CA	AA-	A1	(1)
Philadelphia, PA	BBB-	BA	BB	Honolulu, HI	AA	AA	(1)
San Diego, CA	AA+	AAA	(1)	Miami, FL	(1)	A	(1)
Dallas, TX	AAA	AA1	(1)	Pittsburgh, PA	(1)	BAA1	A-
Phoenix, AZ	AA+	AA	(1)	Cincinnati, OH	AA+	AA	(1)
Detroit, MI	BBB	BA1	(1)	Minneapolis, MN	AAA	AAA	(1)
San Antonio, TX	AA	AA	AA	Omaha, NE	AAA	AAA	(1)
San Jose, CA	(1)	AA	(1)	Toledo, OH	(1)	BAA1	(1)
Indianapolis, IN	(1)	AAA	AAA	Buffalo, NY	BBB	BAA	(1)
San Francisco, CA	AA-	A1	AA	Wichita, KS	AA	AA	(1)
Baltimore, MD	A	A1	AAA	Mesa, AZ	A+	A1	(1)
Jacksonville, FL	AA	A1	AA	Colorado Springs, CO	AA-	AA-	(1)
Columbus, OH	AA+	AA1	(1)	Santa Ana, CA	(1)	(1)	(1)
Milwaukee, WI	AA+	AA	AA+	Tampa, FL	(1)	(1)	(1)
Memphis, TN	AA	AA	(1)	Arlington, TX	AA	AA	(1)
Washington, DC	BBB-	BAA	(1)	Anaheim, CA	AA	AA1	(1)
Boston, MA	A	A	(1)	Louisville, KY	AA-	A1	(1)
El Paso, TX	AA	AA	(1)	St. Paul, MN	AA+	AA	(1)
Seattle, WA	AA+	AA1	(1)	Newark, NJ	BBB+	BAA1	(1)
Cleveland, OH	A	A	A-	Corpus Christi, TX	AA-	A	(1)
Nashville-Davidson, TN	(1)	AA	(1)	Birmingham, AL	AA	A1	(1)
Austin, TX	AA	AA	AA	Norfolk, VA	AA	AA	(1)
New Orleans, LA	A-	BAA	(1)	Anchorage, AK	(1)	A1	(1)
Denver, CO	AA	AA	AA	Aurora, CO	AA-	A1	(1)
Fort Worth, TX	AA	AA	AA	Riverside, CA	(1)	(1)	(1)
Oklahoma City, OK	AA	AA	(1)	St. Petersburg, FL	(1)	A1	(1)
Portland, OR	AA+	AAA	(1)	Rochester, NY	AA	A1	(1)
Long Beach, CA	(1)	(1)	(1)	Lexington-Fayette, KY	AAA	(1)	(1)
Kansas City, MO	AA	AA	(1)	Jersey City, NJ	BBB	BAA	(1)
Virginia Beach, VA	AA	AA	(1)	Baton Rouge, LA	(1)	(1)	(1)
Charlotte, NC	AAA	AAA	(1)	Akron, OH	AA-	A	(1)
Tucson, AZ	AA-	A1	(1)	Raleigh, NC	AAA	AAA	(1)
Albuquerque, NM	AA	AA	(1)	Stockton CA	(1)	(1)	(1)
Atlanta, GA	AA	AA	(1)	Richmond, VA	AA	A1	(1)
St. Louis, MO	BBB	BAA	BBB	Mobile, AL	(1)	A	(1)

[1] Not rated.

Sources: Standard & Poor's, New York, NY; Moody's Investors Service, New York, NY; Fitch Investors Service, New York, NY (All data copyrighted).

No. 488. State Governments—Revenue, by State: 1993

[In millions of dollars, except as noted. Data will not match other tables due to later revisions. For fiscal year ending in year shown; see text, section 9]

STATE	Total revenue [1]	GENERAL REVENUE							
		Total		Per capita [2]		Intergovernmental revenue		Taxes	Charges and miscella-neous
		Amount	Rank	Total (dol.)	Rank	From Federal Govern-ment	From local govern-ments		
United States.....	804,495	653,135	(X)	2,534	(X)	177,560	11,070	353,328	111,177
Alabama	11,389	9,688	23	2,317	32	2,926	39	4,640	2,083
Alaska.	7,358	6,160	31	10,303	1	892	13	2,227	3,028
Arizona	10,843	8,808	25	2,233	40	2,141	285	5,282	1,100
Arkansas	6,446	5,627	34	2,319	31	1,826	6	2,943	852
California	108,222	84,409	1	2,704	19	23,599	1,879	48,738	10,192
Colorado	10,028	7,840	27	2,200	43	2,101	36	3,789	1,915
Connecticut	12,744	11,011	20	3,359	6	2,380	5	6,675	1,951
Delaware	2,876	2,532	45	3,625	4	437	8	1,340	747
Florida.	33,216	27,654	5	2,015	47	6,996	237	16,407	4,013
Georgia.	16,565	14,077	13	2,039	46	4,358	35	8,150	1,534
Hawaii.	5,543	4,838	37	4,151	2	1,006	6	2,748	1,078
Idaho	3,408	2,746	43	2,495	25	676	11	1,560	498
Illinois	30,351	24,971	6	2,137	45	6,188	272	14,500	4,011
Indiana	14,653	13,465	16	2,360	30	3,707	116	6,915	2,727
Iowa	8,224	7,123	30	2,525	24	1,806	83	3,902	1,333
Kansas	6,730	5,836	33	2,302	35	1,631	18	3,276	911
Kentucky	11,011	9,632	24	2,539	23	2,814	14	5,277	1,527
Louisiana	13,348	11,636	19	2,712	18	4,306	24	4,366	2,940
Maine	3,926	3,428	40	2,765	16	1,042	4	1,764	619
Maryland	14,842	12,071	18	2,435	27	2,707	87	7,175	2,101
Massachusetts	21,493	19,252	10	3,199	8	4,645	513	10,383	3,711
Michigan	28,760	24,638	7	2,605	21	6,404	217	13,177	4,840
Minnesota	16,245	13,397	17	2,961	13	2,977	270	8,137	2,012
Mississippi	7,205	6,031	32	2,285	37	2,209	88	2,983	751
Missouri.	12,559	10,335	21	1,974	50	3,198	22	5,480	1,634
Montana	3,023	2,408	46	2,863	14	752	17	1,130	508
Nebraska	3,890	3,712	39	2,301	34	946	22	1,981	763
Nevada	4,500	3,185	41	2,305	36	596	41	2,207	341
New Hampshire	3,011	2,550	44	2,269	38	780	70	993	707
New Jersey	29,614	23,816	9	3,031	11	5,682	236	13,026	4,873
New Mexico	6,303	5,376	35	3,327	7	1,208	49	2,777	1,343
New York.	78,209	62,986	2	3,470	5	18,841	4,764	31,291	8,090
North Carolina	19,377	16,370	11	2,355	29	4,290	395	9,757	1,927
North Dakota	2,288	2,010	47	3,156	9	620	27	877	487
Ohio	38,341	24,483	8	2,213	42	6,932	210	12,788	4,553
Oklahoma	8,679	7,275	29	2,250	39	1,817	45	4,166	1,246
Oregon	10,826	7,772	28	2,561	22	2,299	40	3,658	1,774
Pennsylvania	37,779	29,912	4	2,486	26	7,879	197	16,601	5,235
Rhode Island	3,765	3,018	42	3,019	12	921	52	1,433	611
South Carolina	10,637	8,429	26	2,322	33	2,458	105	4,289	1,577
South Dakota	1,942	1,591	50	2,221	41	576	9	589	416
Tennessee	11,864	10,135	22	1,989	48	3,585	42	5,117	1,391
Texas	42,019	35,688	3	1,980	49	10,747	78	18,241	6,622
Utah	5,348	4,437	38	2,386	28	1,218	37	2,212	970
Vermont	1,953	1,742	49	3,026	10	561	2	793	386
Virginia	16,307	13,973	14	2,159	44	2,729	154	7,572	3,518
Washington	19,930	14,587	12	2,774	15	3,437	69	8,904	2,178
West Virginia	6,047	5,016	36	2,759	17	1,774	13	2,475	755
Wisconsin	18,677	13,610	15	2,698	20	3,261	88	7,956	2,305
Wyoming	2,181	1,851	48	3,940	3	678	19	662	492

X Not applicable.   [1] Includes items not shown separately.   [2] Based on estimated resident population as of July 1.

Source: U.S. Bureau of the Census, *State Government Finances*, series GF, No. 3, annual; and unpublished data.

No. 489. State Governments—Expenditures and Debt, by State: 1993

[In millions of dollars, except as indicated. Data will not match other tables due to later revisions. For fiscal year ending in year shown; see text, section 9]

STATE	Total expenditure [1]	GENERAL EXPENDITURE							DEBT OUTSTANDING	
		Total		Selected functions					Total	Per capita [2] (dol.)
		Amount	Per capita [2] (dol.)	Education	Public welfare	Highways	Health and hospitals	Corrections		
United States.....	742,936	646,088	2,506	221,342	168,421	51,268	53,202	20,690	387,680	1,504
Alabama	10,242	9,340	2,234	3,663	2,017	856	1,300	182	4,163	996
Alaska............	5,423	4,934	8,253	1,267	564	586	209	135	4,427	7,405
Arizona	9,783	8,782	2,226	3,017	2,159	921	531	345	3,053	774
Arkansas.........	5,915	5,455	2,249	2,248	1,312	608	406	119	1,884	777
California........	104,567	89,037	2,852	31,282	25,118	4,593	7,209	3,050	41,295	1,323
Colorado	8,673	7,472	2,097	3,132	1,837	719	400	266	3,117	875
Connecticut	12,507	10,582	3,228	2,524	2,776	753	1,130	444	12,848	3,920
Delaware.........	2,557	2,320	3,321	811	319	265	166	90	3,490	4,997
Florida..........	30,103	27,689	2,017	9,362	6,135	2,369	2,426	1,073	13,635	993
Georgia..........	15,308	14,061	2,037	5,746	3,684	1,031	1,087	605	4,519	655
Hawaii...........	5,606	5,088	4,365	1,447	651	361	479	113	5,023	4,310
Idaho	2,776	2,442	2,219	1,023	428	292	96	65	1,290	1,172
Illinois	28,133	24,682	2,112	7,540	6,862	2,489	1,690	655	19,893	1,702
Indiana	14,136	13,480	2,363	5,139	3,390	1,370	842	321	5,458	957
Iowa............	7,766	7,198	2,551	2,816	1,514	916	660	158	1,837	651
Kansas..........	5,742	5,275	2,081	2,270	982	654	461	179	935	369
Kentucky	10,543	9,550	2,517	3,716	2,565	933	515	210	6,820	1,798
Louisiana........	12,893	11,726	2,733	3,836	3,095	829	1,370	300	9,585	2,234
Maine	3,889	3,405	2,747	1,039	1,107	311	185	53	2,999	2,419
Maryland	13,537	11,406	2,301	3,712	2,682	985	939	592	8,731	1,761
Massachusetts	21,557	18,684	3,105	3,544	5,425	1,256	1,734	681	25,415	4,223
Michigan	27,051	23,358	2,469	7,952	6,192	1,635	2,569	910	8,849	935
Minnesota	14,295	13,003	2,874	4,642	3,259	1,204	981	205	4,145	916
Mississippi.......	6,235	5,585	2,116	2,042	1,349	571	421	91	1,659	628
Missouri.........	10,809	9,817	1,875	3,701	2,498	853	790	208	6,516	1,245
Montana	2,663	2,283	2,715	849	406	285	132	40	1,749	2,080
Nebraska.........	3,823	3,717	2,304	1,300	807	481	401	84	1,587	984
Nevada	4,051	3,151	2,280	1,165	513	302	110	154	1,653	1,196
New Hampshire	2,970	2,584	2,298	518	919	223	140	50	5,242	4,663
New Jersey	28,923	23,630	3,007	7,117	5,741	1,615	1,456	679	21,779	2,771
New Mexico.......	5,599	5,190	3,212	1,977	758	823	465	137	1,597	989
New York........	74,280	61,558	3,391	16,661	21,975	2,297	5,419	2,076	59,219	3,262
North Carolina	16,916	15,495	2,229	6,440	3,198	1,555	1,307	606	4,002	576
North Dakota	2,129	1,919	3,015	686	411	215	106	16	830	1,303
Ohio............	31,665	25,038	2,264	8,760	7,021	2,141	1,999	755	12,486	1,129
Oklahoma	8,272	7,058	2,183	3,052	1,575	697	608	202	3,919	1,212
Oregon	9,013	7,685	2,532	2,493	1,472	800	805	200	5,821	1,918
Pennsylvania	34,359	28,705	2,386	8,689	8,959	2,303	2,592	627	12,989	1,080
Rhode Island	4,176	3,539	3,541	845	886	209	252	107	5,147	5,150
South Carolina	10,388	8,793	2,422	3,138	2,064	616	1,076	331	4,901	1,350
South Dakota	1,686	1,604	2,239	481	319	229	94	34	1,818	2,539
Tennessee........	11,028	10,288	2,020	3,525	3,073	1,067	823	366	2,632	517
Texas	39,091	35,111	1,948	14,777	8,984	2,991	2,675	1,562	8,684	482
Utah	4,834	4,370	2,350	2,076	742	360	389	106	2,193	1,179
Vermont	1,849	1,696	2,947	572	405	185	57	42	1,419	2,465
Virginia	14,721	13,398	2,070	5,265	2,449	1,381	1,472	642	7,438	1,149
Washington	18,003	15,141	2,879	6,622	3,216	1,231	1,067	368	7,848	1,492
West Virginia	5,943	4,833	2,658	1,870	1,394	584	196	37	2,684	1,476
Wisconsin	14,621	13,272	2,631	4,396	3,002	1,065	867	390	7,674	1,521
Wyoming..........	1,887	1,657	3,528	597	211	253	99	27	781	1,662

[1] Includes items not shown separately. [2] Based on estimated resident population as of July 1.

Source: U.S. Bureau of the Census, *State Government Finances*, series GF, No. 3, annual.

No. 490. State Governments—Summary of Finances: 1980 to 1993

[For fiscal year ending in year shown; see text section 9. See also *Colonial Times to 1970*, series Y 710-782]

ITEM	TOTAL (mil. dol.)				PER CAPITA [1] (dollars)			
	1980	1990	1992	1993	1980	1990	1992	1993
Borrowing and revenue	**293,356**	**672,994**	**802,030**	**882,014**	**1,295**	**2,706**	**3,145**	**3,422**
Borrowing	16,394	40,532	60,177	77,519	72	163	236	301
Revenue	276,962	632,462	741,853	804,495	1,223	2,543	2,909	3,121
General revenue	233,592	517,720	605,334	653,135	1,031	2,082	2,374	2,534
Taxes	137,075	300,779	327,822	353,328	605	1,209	1,285	1,371
Sales and gross receipts	67,855	147,404	162,308	174,218	300	593	636	676
General	43,168	99,929	107,579	114,909	191	402	422	446
Motor fuels	9,722	19,379	22,198	23,568	43	78	87	91
Alcoholic beverages	2,478	3,191	3,509	3,584	11	13	14	14
Tobacco products	3,738	5,541	6,103	6,229	16	22	24	24
Other	8,750	19,365	22,919	25,928	39	78	90	101
Licenses	8,690	18,849	21,691	23,319	38	76	85	90
Motor vehicles	4,936	9,850	10,766	11,502	22	40	42	45
Corporations in general	1,388	3,096	4,104	4,317	6	12	16	17
Other	2,366	5,903	6,821	7,500	10	24	27	29
Individual income	37,089	96,076	104,401	112,555	164	386	409	437
Corporation net income	13,321	21,751	21,566	24,208	59	87	85	94
Property	2,892	5,775	6,594	7,053	13	23	26	27
Other	7,227	10,922	11,262	11,975	32	44	44	46
Charges and miscellaneous	32,190	90,612	107,610	111,177	142	364	422	431
Intergovernmental revenue	64,326	126,329	169,902	188,630	284	508	666	732
From Federal Government	61,892	118,353	159,041	177,560	273	476	624	689
Public welfare	24,680	59,397	91,091	101,765	109	239	357	395
Education	12,765	21,271	25,867	28,164	56	86	101	109
Highways	8,860	13,931	14,367	16,475	39	56	56	64
Other	15,587	23,754	27,716	31,156	69	96	109	121
From local governments	2,434	7,976	10,861	11,070	11	32	43	43
Utility revenue	1,304	3,305	3,512	3,675	6	13	14	14
Liquor store revenue	2,765	2,907	3,067	3,070	12	12	12	12
Insurance trust revenue [2]	39,301	108,530	129,940	144,614	173	436	510	561
Employee retirement	21,146	78,898	88,281	94,347	93	317	346	366
Unemployment compensation	13,468	18,370	26,921	34,442	59	74	106	134
Expenditure and debt redemption	**263,494**	**592,213**	**736,095**	**805,076**	**1,163**	**2,381**	**2,886**	**3,123**
Expenditure	257,812	572,318	700,894	742,936	1,138	2,301	2,748	2,882
General expenditure	228,223	508,284	611,922	646,088	1,007	2,044	2,399	2,506
Education	87,939	184,935	211,570	221,342	388	744	830	859
Public welfare	44,219	104,971	156,364	168,421	195	422	613	653
Highways	25,044	44,249	48,747	51,268	111	178	191	199
Health and hospitals	17,855	42,666	48,123	53,202	79	172	189	206
Corrections	4,449	17,266	20,120	20,690	20	69	79	80
Natural resources	4,346	9,909	10,521	11,212	19	40	41	43
General control	3,232	8,384	10,020	10,452	14	34	39	41
Financial administration	3,031	8,616	9,751	10,546	13	35	38	41
Police protection	2,263	5,166	5,489	5,600	10	21	22	22
Employment security	2,001	3,003	3,702	3,930	9	12	15	15
Housing and community development	601	2,856	2,668	2,830	3	11	10	11
Other and unallocable	33,243	76,263	84,847	86,594	147	307	333	336
Utility expenditure	2,401	7,131	7,036	7,240	11	29	28	28
Liquor store expenditure	2,206	2,452	2,577	2,558	10	10	10	10
Insurance trust expenditure [2]	24,981	54,452	79,359	87,050	110	219	311	338
Employee retirement	10,256	29,562	35,628	40,117	45	119	140	156
Unemployment compensation	12,006	16,423	32,761	35,197	53	66	128	137
By character and object:								
Intergovernmental expend	84,504	175,028	201,313	213,937	373	704	789	830
Direct expenditure	173,307	397,291	499,580	528,999	765	1,597	1,959	2,052
Current operation	108,131	258,046	323,830	345,397	477	1,038	1,270	1,340
Capital outlay	23,325	45,524	50,126	49,776	103	183	197	193
Construction	19,736	34,803	39,001	39,220	87	140	153	152
Land and existing structure	1,345	3,471	3,822	3,129	6	14	15	12
Equipment	2,243	7,250	7,303	7,427	10	29	29	29
Assistance and subsidies	9,818	16,902	20,784	21,976	43	68	81	85
Interest on debt	7,052	22,367	25,482	24,800	31	90	100	96
Insurance benefits [3]	24,981	54,452	79,359	87,050	110	219	311	338
Debt outstanding, year end	**121,958**	**318,254**	**371,901**	**387,680**	**538**	**1,280**	**1,458**	**1,504**
Long-term	119,821	315,490	368,951	383,810	529	1,269	1,447	1,489
Full-faith and credit	49,364	74,972	96,598	103,667	218	301	379	402
Nonguaranteed	70,457	240,518	272,353	280,143	311	967	1,068	1,087
Short-term	2,137	2,764	2,949	3,870	9	11	12	15
Net long-term	79,810	125,524	152,423	180,944	352	505	598	702
Full-faith and credit only	39,357	63,481	85,258	93,077	174	255	334	361
Debt redemption	5,682	19,895	35,201	62,140	25	80	138	241

[1] 1980 and 1990 based on enumerated resident population as of April 1; other years based on estimated resident population as of July 1.   [2] Includes other items not shown separately.   [3] Includes repayments.

Source: U.S. Bureau of the Census, *State Government Finances*, series GF, No. 3, annual; and unpublished data.

No. 491. State Resources, Expenditures, and Balances: 1993 and 1994

[**For fiscal year ending in year shown;** see text; section 9. **General funds** exclude special funds earmarked for particular purposes, such as highway trust funds and federal funds; they support most on-going broad-based State services and are available for appropriation to support any governmental activity. Minus sign (-) indicates deficit]

STATE	Total, 1993 (mil. dol.)	EXPENDITURES BY FUND SOURCE 1994[1]				STATE GENERAL FUND					
		Total[2] (mil. dol.)	General fund (percent)	Federal funds (percent)	Other State funds (percent)	Resources[3][4] 1993 (mil. dol.)	1994[1] (mil. dol.)	Expenditures[4] 1993 (mil. dol.)	1994[1] (mil. dol.)	Balance[5] 1993 (mil. dol.)	1994[1] (mil. dol.)
United States..	626,423	675,218	47	27	24	321,838	338,491	311,997	327,599	9,649	10,322
Alabama.........	9,993	10,831	36	33	31	3,685	3,964	3,555	3,845	130	119
Alaska..........	4,327	4,980	61	19	20	2,738	3,208	2,738	3,208	-	-
Arizona.........	8,132	8,752	45	34	19	3,793	4,138	3,707	3,951	86	187
Arkansas	6,369	6,748	33	28	38	2,077	2,270	2,077	2,270	-	-
California	86,061	86,729	45	37	15	41,459	38,880	40,948	39,299	[6]511	[6]-419
Colorado........	6,641	7,861	46	21	33	3,577	3,897	3,250	3,560	[6]327	[6]338
Connecticut......	12,077	13,677	63	14	15	7,569	7,889	7,456	7,748	114	141
Delaware	2,828	3,021	45	15	35	1,470	1,659	1,260	1,345	[6]210	[6]313
Florida	34,378	36,741	36	19	43	12,371	13,283	11,990	13,280	381	3
Georgia	14,715	16,403	54	28	12	8,311	9,003	8,089	8,792	99	90
Hawaii	6,238	6,256	49	13	24	3,327	3,350	3,063	3,059	264	291
Idaho..........	2,349	2,561	44	33	23	1,043	1,185	1,032	1,147	11	38
Illinois.........	23,101	25,676	44	23	30	12,235	13,068	12,063	12,838	172	230
Indiana.........	11,417	12,512	53	30	16	6,319	6,730	6,309	6,640	10	90
Iowa..........	8,085	8,651	41	23	36	3,455	3,578	3,403	3,487	52	90
Kansas.........	5,934	7,035	45	24	30	3,075	3,516	2,690	3,155	385	361
Kentucky	10,152	10,946	43	29	27	4,560	4,744	4,521	4,646	39	98
Louisiana	12,516	14,573	30	35	33	4,301	4,438	4,200	4,438	101	-
Maine..........	3,545	3,598	44	29	25	1,611	1,602	1,607	1,599	4	3
Maryland	12,086	12,541	53	20	23	6,393	6,634	6,382	6,574	11	60
Massachusetts.....	16,184	17,385	69	23	3	11,848	12,259	11,646	12,077	133	123
Michigan........	20,824	22,524	35	30	35	7,834	8,307	7,808	7,958	26	-
Minnesota......	11,900	13,267	63	20	15	8,202	9,009	7,326	8,260	[6]876	[6]749
Mississippi	5,414	6,428	33	41	26	2,160	2,481	1,985	2,149	175	332
Missouri	9,543	10,587	44	27	28	4,525	4,934	4,299	4,758	226	176
Montana........	2,248	2,273	22	29	49	564	531	523	498	41	33
Nebraska	3,676	4,035	40	24	36	1,737	1,764	1,614	1,612	123	152
Nevada	(NA)	(NA)	(NA)	(NA)	(NA)	1,006	1,123	1,008	1,023	-2	100
New Hampshire....	2,179	2,415	34	36	29	818	829	787	817	31	12
New Jersey......	21,593	21,966	67	20	11	15,413	16,081	14,301	15,130	[6]1,112	[6]951
New Mexico	(NA)	(NA)	(NA)	(NA)	(NA)	2,387	2,754	2,172	2,630	[6]215	[6]124
New York	54,796	57,907	52	28	17	30,896	32,229	30,896	32,229	-	-
North Carolina.....	15,272	17,515	51	25	19	8,458	9,891	7,879	9,004	[6]579	[6]888
North Dakota.....	1,674	1,651	35	33	31	673	639	653	611	20	28
Ohio	25,854	28,618	39	26	32	13,764	15,019	13,674	14,719	90	300
Oklahoma.......	7,268	7,419	44	26	30	3,423	3,420	3,318	3,302	105	118
Oregon.........	9,041	10,136	31	16	53	3,182	3,512	2,820	3,081	362	432
Pennsylvania	27,113	29,966	50	29	20	14,178	15,270	13,960	14,968	218	302
Rhode Island.....	3,383	3,326	44	25	29	1,639	1,543	1,631	1,538	9	5
South Carolina.....	8,957	10,093	37	31	30	3,680	4,184	3,521	3,776	[6]159	[6]407
South Dakota.....	1,470	1,603	37	40	23	585	626	585	626	-	-
Tennessee	10,044	11,740	39	34	24	4,870	5,080	4,604	4,884	[6]266	[6]196
Texas..........	33,556	35,768	55	29	14	19,731	21,300	18,401	19,492	1,330	1,808
Utah	4,039	4,360	48	23	26	1,986	2,140	1,975	2,114	11	26
Vermont	1,493	1,551	41	34	21	597	657	643	657	-46	-
Virginia.........	14,102	15,382	43	17	38	6,605	7,076	6,436	6,814	[6]169	[6]262
Washington......	13,683	15,229	54	23	20	8,052	8,419	7,818	8,029	234	390
West Virginia	5,073	5,365	39	35	25	2,100	2,189	2,029	2,079	71	69
Wisconsin	13,323	14,824	50	25	26	7,094	7,616	6,926	7,383	168	[6]234
Wyoming	1,777	1,793	28	23	49	464	572	421	500	43	73

- Represents zero.   NA Not available.   [1] Estimated.   [2] Includes bonds not shown separately.   [3] Includes funds budgeted, adjustments, and balances from previous year.   [4] May or may not include budget stabilization fund transfers, depending on State accounting practices.   [5] Resources less expenditures.   [6] Ending balance is held in a budget stabilization fund.

Source: National Association of State Budget Officers, Washington, DC, *1994 State Expenditure Report,* and National Governors' Association and NASBO, *Fiscal Survey of the States,* semi-annual (copyright).

No. 492. State Government Tax Collections, by State: 1993

[In millions of dollars. For fiscal year ending in year shown; see text; section 9. Includes local shares of State-imposed taxes]

STATE	Total [1]	Sales and gross receipts						Indi-vidual income	Corpo-ration net income	Death and gift	Sever-ance
		Total [1]	Gen-eral sales and gross receipts	Motor fuels	Alco-holic bever-ages and tobacco prod-ucts	Public util-ities	Motor vehicle and opera-tors' licenses				
United States . . .	**353,328**	**174,218**	**114,909**	**23,568**	**9,812**	**8,268**	**12,517**	**112,555**	**24,208**	**4,659**	**4,908**
Alabama	4,640	2,515	1,190	436	178	357	162	1,333	190	32	73
Alaska	2,227	99	(X)	41	29	2	24	(X)	872	1	1,125
Arizona	5,282	2,992	2,256	387	94	115	216	1,381	245	40	(X)
Arkansas	2,943	1,649	1,119	305	105	(X)	100	905	154	14	15
California	48,738	21,575	16,672	2,556	974	43	1,519	17,200	4,728	459	35
Colorado	3,789	1,582	998	380	85	5	123	1,765	138	20	23
Connecticut	6,675	3,097	2,056	398	158	146	213	2,254	713	248	(X)
Delaware	1,340	198	(X)	76	32	23	21	513	114	40	(X)
Florida	16,407	12,720	9,295	1,186	987	448	827	(X)	756	297	64
Georgia	8,150	3,855	2,980	468	198	(X)	181	3,390	471	39	(X)
Hawaii	2,748	1,684	1,303	74	72	86	58	923	53	12	(X)
Idaho	1,560	703	486	141	35	1	57	609	84	9	2
Illinois	14,500	7,326	4,370	1,064	378	749	690	4,815	1,097	164	(X)
Indiana	6,915	3,148	2,300	572	142	4	133	2,807	656	102	1
Iowa	3,902	1,807	1,252	338	107	(X)	252	1,467	167	77	(X)
Kansas	3,276	1,641	1,172	264	104	(Z)	121	1,040	219	57	103
Kentucky	5,277	2,342	1,466	375	70	(X)	174	1,733	255	71	200
Louisiana	4,366	2,222	1,332	471	134	20	103	930	245	51	447
Maine	1,764	911	642	146	83	(X)	58	615	75	9	(X)
Maryland	7,175	3,055	1,718	559	164	129	261	3,080	260	93	(X)
Massachusetts	10,383	3,297	2,124	557	252	(X)	344	5,375	959	267	(X)
Michigan	13,177	4,838	3,467	783	367	(X)	571	5,204	1,843	163	40
Minnesota	8,137	3,570	2,374	469	223	(Z)	450	3,322	510	21	3
Mississippi	2,983	1,967	1,414	308	87	(X)	84	588	171	10	40
Missouri	5,480	2,767	2,017	444	103	2	229	2,006	193	59	(Z)
Montana	1,130	200	(X)	116	29	12	47	357	85	13	97
Nebraska	1,981	1,041	695	222	54	2	63	685	103	15	2
Nevada	2,207	1,811	1,034	156	61	5	89	(X)	(X)	20	20
New Hampshire	993	673	(X)	97	52	32	60	36	126	22	(Z)
New Jersey	13,026	6,778	3,651	419	333	1,693	346	4,350	947	284	(X)
New Mexico	2,777	1,665	1,319	200	37	10	114	527	90	14	310
New York	31,291	11,310	6,284	525	781	1,696	634	15,300	2,638	673	(X)
North Carolina	9,757	4,212	2,354	869	199	257	343	3,992	711	103	2
North Dakota	877	490	289	78	18	13	47	126	54	2	131
Ohio	12,788	6,404	3,971	1,122	318	669	463	4,722	677	75	9
Oklahoma	4,166	1,647	1,014	355	127	14	441	1,300	142	51	394
Oregon	3,658	478	(X)	312	96	6	268	2,383	205	41	70
Pennsylvania	16,601	7,790	4,829	742	479	638	508	4,658	1,470	563	(X)
Rhode Island	1,433	763	413	99	44	62	48	497	70	13	(X)
South Carolina	4,289	2,201	1,557	295	142	38	93	1,495	176	15	(X)
South Dakota	589	471	306	83	23	1	28	(X)	28	22	6
Tennessee	5,117	3,991	2,853	643	144	5	200	95	365	56	1
Texas	18,241	14,504	9,142	2,086	1,010	226	780	(X)	(X)	142	1,178
Utah	2,212	1,179	894	186	43	(X)	56	842	84	8	20
Vermont	793	375	161	56	28	10	42	286	33	7	(X)
Virginia	7,572	3,013	1,666	651	112	96	290	3,585	365	48	2
Washington	8,904	6,638	5,305	608	264	194	227	(X)	(X)	36	65
West Virginia	2,475	1,335	714	221	40	191	84	621	179	27	170
Wisconsin	7,956	3,436	2,261	590	213	268	238	3,446	492	54	1
Wyoming	662	251	195	37	7	(X)	37	(X)	(X)	4	257

X Not applicable.   Z less than $500,000.   [1] Includes amounts not shown separately.

Source: U.S. Bureau of the Census, *State Government Tax Collections*, series GF, No. 1, annual.

No. 493. Estimated State and Local Taxes Paid by a Family of Four in Selected Cities: 1992

[Preliminary. Data based on average family of four (two wage earners and two school age children) owning their own home and living in a city where taxes apply. Comprises State and local sales, income, auto, and real estate taxes. For definition of median see Guide to Tabular Presentation]

CITY	TOTAL TAXES PAID, BY GROSS FAMILY INCOME LEVEL (dollars)				TOTAL TAXES PAID AS PERCENT OF INCOME			
	$25,000	$50,000	$75,000	$100,000	$25,000	$50,000	$75,000	$100,000
Albuquerque, NM	1,478	3,434	5,943	8,461	5.9	6.9	7.9	8.5
Atlanta, GA	2,838	5,593	9,107	12,019	11.4	11.2	12.1	12.0
Baltimore, MD	4,068	8,246	12,791	16,659	16.3	16.5	17.1	16.7
Bridgeport, CT	4,519	9,416	16,270	21,185	18.1	18.8	21.7	21.2
Burlington, VT	1,909	4,132	7,197	10,134	7.6	8.3	9.6	10.1
Charleston, WV	1,691	3,542	6,373	8,836	6.8	7.1	8.5	8.8
Charlotte, NC	2,085	4,412	7,253	9,734	8.3	8.8	9.7	9.7
Chicago, IL	2,954	5,938	9,326	12,084	11.8	11.9	12.4	12.1
Columbus, OH	2,151	4,713	7,712	10,650	8.6	9.4	10.3	10.7
Columbia, SC	1,971	4,799	8,151	10,905	7.9	9.6	10.9	10.9
Des Moines, IA	1,844	4,120	6,770	9,109	7.4	8.2	9.0	9.1
Detroit, MI	4,723	9,680	14,773	19,290	18.9	19.4	19.7	19.3
Honolulu, HI	1,853	4,306	7,272	9,921	7.4	8.6	9.7	9.9
Indianapolis, IN	2,017	3,703	6,268	8,061	8.1	7.4	8.4	8.1
Jackson, MS	1,451	3,421	6,080	8,237	5.8	6.8	8.1	8.2
Kansas City, MO	1,965	4,358	7,024	9,224	7.9	8.7	9.4	9.2
Louisville, KY	2,439	5,100	8,099	10,777	9.8	10.2	10.8	10.8
Memphis, TN	1,718	2,896	4,506	5,702	6.9	5.8	6.0	5.7
Milwaukee, WI	3,274	7,288	11,425	15,071	13.1	14.6	15.2	15.1
Newark, NJ	5,853	11,445	17,696	23,420	23.4	22.9	23.6	23.4
New York City, NY	2,603	6,579	11,199	15,247	10.4	13.2	14.9	15.2
Omaha, NE	2,159	4,529	7,872	10,668	8.6	9.1	10.5	10.7
Philadelphia, PA	3,956	7,610	11,361	14,755	15.8	15.2	15.1	14.8
Portland, ME	2,132	5,144	9,361	12,759	8.5	10.3	12.5	12.8
Portland, OR	2,428	5,369	8,623	11,542	9.7	10.7	11.5	11.5
Providence, RI	4,271	8,393	13,542	17,945	17.1	16.8	18.1	17.9
Salt Lake City, UT	2,038	4,682	7,564	10,020	8.2	9.4	10.1	10.0
Sioux Falls, SD	1,837	3,180	5,312	6,701	7.3	6.4	7.1	6.7
Virginia Beach, VA	2,089	4,423	7,521	9,930	8.4	8.8	10.0	9.9
Washington, DC	2,278	5,041	8,416	11,556	9.1	10.1	11.2	11.6
Median [1]	1,970	4,306	7,253	9,921	7.9	8.6	9.7	9.9

[1] Median of all 51 cities. For complete list of cities, see table 481.

Source: Government of the District of Columbia, Department of Finance and Revenue, *Tax Rates and Tax Burdens in the District of Columbia: A Nationwide Comparison*, annual.

No. 494. Residential Property Tax Rates in Selected Cities: 1992

CITY	EFFECTIVE TAX RATE PER $100		Assessment level (percent)	Nominal rate per $100	CITY	EFFECTIVE TAX RATE PER $100		Assessment level (percent)	Nominal rate per $100
	Rank	Rate				Rank	Rate		
Detroit, MI	1	4.53	49.4	9.17	Billings, MT	27	1.47	3.9	38.21
Milwaukee, WI	2	3.83	99.9	3.84	Jackson, MS	28	1.47	10.0	14.73
Newark, NJ	3	3.14	15.8	19.96	Salt Lake City, UT	29	1.43	95.0	1.50
Manchester, NH	4	2.75	99.0	2.78	Minneapolis, MN	30	1.39	12.1	11.50
Des Moines, IA	5	2.66	65.8	4.04	Columbia, SC	31	1.25	4.0	31.36
Philadelphia, PA	6	2.64	32.0	8.26	Charlotte, NC	32	1.17	98.2	1.20
Providence, RI	7	2.55	100.0	2.55	Kansas City, MO	33	1.15	19.0	6.03
Bridgeport, CT	8	2.49	39.4	6.33	Boston, MA	34	1.12	100.0	1.12
Baltimore, MD	9	2.44	40.0	6.11	Virginia Beach, VA	35	1.09	100.0	1.09
Sioux Falls, IA	10	2.36	84.9	2.78	Seattle, WA	36	1.05	95.5	1.10
Portland, OR	11	2.32	100.0	2.32	Oklahoma City, OK	37	1.04	11.0	9.45
Omaha, NE	12	2.29	88.3	2.60	Albuquerque, NM	38	1.04	33.3	3.11
Jacksonville, FL	13	2.15	100.0	2.15	Las Vegas, NV	39	1.02	35.0	2.92
Houston, TX	14	2.00	100.0	2.00	Denver, CO	40	0.97	14.3	6.73
Boise City, ID	15	1.98	95.0	2.08	Little Rock, AR	41	0.95	18.7	5.08
Columbus, OH	16	1.80	35.0	5.14	Louisville, KY	42	0.95	92.0	1.03
Fargo, ND	17	1.78	4.3	41.49	Wilmington, DE	43	0.94	57.7	1.63
Wichita, KS	18	1.76	12.0	14.66	Washington, DC	44	0.91	94.7	0.96
Indianapolis, IN	19	1.75	15.0	11.65	New York City, NY	45	0.87	8.0	10.89
Atlanta, GA	20	1.74	30.0	5.81	Cheyenne, WY	46	0.74	9.5	7.83
Portland, ME	21	1.74	46.4	3.75	Birmingham, AL	47	0.70	10.0	6.95
Anchorage, AK	22	1.71	95.0	1.80	Charleston, WV	48	0.68	39.8	1.70
New Orleans, LA	23	1.61	10.0	16.06	Memphis, TN	49	0.67	25.0	2.68
Phoenix, AZ	24	1.53	10.0	15.28	Los Angeles, CA	50	0.63	61.2	1.03
Burlington, VT	25	1.51	59.8	2.52	Honolulu, HI	51	0.30	84.3	0.35
Chicago, IL	26	1.49	16.0	9.31					

Source: Government of the District of Columbia, Department of Finance and Revenue, *Tax Rates and Tax Burdens in the District of Columbia: A Nationwide Comparison*, annual.

No. 495. Gross Revenue From Parimutuel and Amusement Taxes and Lotteries, by State: 1993

[For **fiscal years**; see text, section 9]

STATE	Gross revenue (mil. dol.)	Parimutuel taxes (mil. dol.)	Amuse- ment taxes[1] (mil. dol.)	LOTTERY REVENUE			
				Total[2] (mil. dol.)	Apportionment of funds (percent)		
					Prizes	Administra- tion	Proceeds available from ticket sales
United States[3] ...	**24,984**	**539**	**992**	**23,453**	**53**	**6**	**41**
Alabama	6	6	(Z)	-	(X)	(X)	(X)
Alaska	1	-	1	-	(X)	(X)	(X)
Arizona	252	8	1	243	50	10	40
Arkansas	17	17	-	-	(X)	(X)	(X)
California	1,761	106	-	1,655	50	9	41
Colorado	257	8	1	248	58	11	31
Connecticut	614	40	50	524	51	3	45
Delaware	85	(Z)	-	85	57	8	35
Florida	2,124	106	2	2,016	50	6	45
Idaho	58	1	-	57	54	20	25
Illinois	1,544	45	93	1,406	51	3	46
Indiana	467	-	-	467	63	6	31
Iowa	199	4	9	186	59	11	31
Kansas	110	1	-	109	54	14	33
Kentucky	460	6	(Z)	454	69	8	23
Louisiana	467	7	2	458	53	5	42
Maine	119	1	-	118	54	9	37
Maryland	844	3	5	836	55	4	40
Massachusetts	1,915	16	9	1,891	68	4	28
Michigan	1,162	19	-	1,143	57	5	39
Minnesota	369	1	57	311	53	15	31
Missouri	241	-	-	241	57	10	32
Montana	35	(Z)	-	35	51	23	26
Nebraska	11	1	10	-	(X)	(X)	(X)
Nevada	391	-	391	-	(X)	(X)	(X)
New Hampshire	108	6	2	99	53	5	42
New Jersey	1,557	7	260	1,290	43	3	54
New York	2,234	71	1	2,161	49	3	48
North Dakota	7	-	7	-	(X)	(X)	(X)
Ohio	1,871	14	-	1,857	58	5	37
Oklahoma	10	4	6	-	(X)	(X)	(X)
Oregon	537	4	-	532	61	24	15
Pennsylvania	1,346	11	(Z)	1,335	52	3	45
Rhode Island	127	9	(Z)	117	56	3	41
South Carolina	24	-	24	-	(X)	(X)	(X)
South Dakota	78	(Z)	-	77	20	6	74
Texas	1,701	-	15	1,686	58	3	39
Vermont	47	(Z)	-	47	57	8	34
Virginia	823	-	(Z)	823	54	10	36
Washington	370	5	(Z)	365	49	14	37
West Virginia	110	-	(Z)	110	56	12	32
Wisconsin	480	10	(Z)	470	59	7	35

- Represents or rounds to zero.   X Not applicable.   Z Less than $500,000.   [1] Represents nonlicense taxes.   [2] Excludes commissions.   [3] Includes States whose gross revenues were less than $1 million not shown separately.

Source: U.S. Bureau of the Census, *State Government Finances*, series GF, No. 3, annual.

No. 496. Lottery Sales—Type of Game and Use of Proceeds: 1980 to 1994

[In millions of dollars. For fiscal years]

GAME	1980	1985	1990	1992	1993	1994	USE OF PROFITS	Cumu- lative[1]
Total ticket sales	2,393	9,035	20,017	22,069	25,170	28,514	Total	81,865
Passive[2]	206	88	(NA)	(NA)	(NA)	(NA)	Education	47,116
Instant[3]	527	1,296	5,204	6,104	7,948	9,681	General fund	17,532
Three digit[4]	1,554	3,376	4,572	4,767	4,861	5,294	Cities	7,582
Four digit[4]	55	693	1,302	1,637	1,739	1,872	Senior citizen programs ..	8,077
Lotto[5]	52	3,583	8,563	8,506	9,516	10,024	Taxes	(NA)
Other[6]	(NA)	(NA)	409	1,055	1,106	1,642	Economic development...	1,066
							Infrastructure	(NA)
State proceeds (net income)[7] ..	978	3,735	7,703	8,118	9,106	9,977	Environment	356
							Other	134

NA Not available.   [1] Cumulative profits tracks lottery revenue to government from March 12, 1964 - June 30, 1994.   [2] Also known as draw game or ticket. Player must match his ticket to winning numbers drawn by lottery. Players cannot choose their numbers.   [3] Player scratches a latex section on ticket which reveals instantly whether ticket is a winner.   [4] Players choose and bet on three or four digits, depending on game, with various payoffs for different straight order or mixed combination bets. [5] Players typically select six digits out of a large field of numbers. Varying prizes are offered for matching three through six numbers drawn by lottery.   [6] Includes breakopen tickets, spiel, keno, video lottery, etc.   [7] Net income equals total sales, net a lottery's direct and direct costs or expenses.

Source: TLF Publications, Inc., Boyds, MD, *1995 World Lottery Almanac* annual; *LaFleur's Fiscal 1994 Lottery Special Report;* and *LaFleur's Lottery World Government Profits Report* (copyright).

No. 497. State Government Intergovernmental Expenditures, by State: 1993

[For fiscal year ending in year shown; see text, section 9]

STATE	Total (mil. dol.)	Per capita [1] (dol.)	Rank	Percent of general expenditure	STATE	Total (mil. dol.)	Per capita [1] (dol.)	Rank	Percent of general expenditure
United States .	**213,937**	**830**	**(X)**	**33**	Missouri	2,824	539	44	29
					Montana	660	785	14	29
Alabama	2,212	529	46	24	Nebraska	1,030	638	33	28
Alaska	1,086	1,816	1	22	Nevada	1,166	844	10	37
Arizona	3,220	816	11	37	New Hampshire . .	301	268	49	12
Arkansas	1,506	621	35	28	New Jersey	8,099	1,031	7	34
California	44,177	1,415	2	50	New Mexico	1,666	1,031	6	32
Colorado	2,378	667	26	32	New York	23,848	1,314	4	39
Connecticut	2,112	644	32	20	North Carolina . . .	5,419	779	15	35
Delaware	410	587	38	18	North Dakota . . .	411	645	31	21
Florida	9,303	678	24	34	Ohio	8,315	752	17	33
Georgia	4,121	597	37	29	Oklahoma	2,255	698	22	32
Hawaii	133	114	50	3	Oregon	2,258	744	18	29
Idaho	806	732	20	33	Pennsylvania . . .	8,378	696	23	29
Illinois	7,139	611	36	29	Rhode Island . . .	484	484	47	14
Indiana	4,386	769	16	33	South Carolina . .	2,099	578	40	24
Iowa	2,287	811	12	32	South Dakota . . .	299	418	48	19
Kansas	1,670	659	28	32	Tennessee	2,774	545	43	27
Kentucky	2,521	664	27	26	Texas	10,373	576	41	30
Louisiana	2,806	654	30	24	Utah	1,214	653	29	28
Maine	773	623	34	23	Vermont	303	526	46	18
Maryland	2,707	546	42	24	Virginia	3,749	579	39	28
Massachusetts . .	4,287	712	21	23	Washington	4,658	886	9	31
Michigan	7,694	813	13	33	West Virginia	1,226	674	25	25
Minnesota	4,804	1,062	5	37	Wisconsin	5,006	992	8	38
Mississippi	1,946	737	19	35	Wyoming	639	1,360	3	39

X Not applicable.   [1] Based on estimated resident population as of July 1.

Source: U.S. Bureau of the Census, *State Government Finances*, series GF, No. 3, annual.

No. 498. Local Government General Revenue, by State: 1992

[In millions of dollars. For fiscal year ending in year shown; see text, section 9. Data are estimates subject to sampling variation; see Appendix III and source]

STATE	Total [1]	INTERGOVERN-MENTAL FROM— Federal	INTERGOVERN-MENTAL FROM— State	FROM OWN SOURCES Total	FROM OWN SOURCES Taxes	STATE	Total [1]	INTERGOVERN-MENTAL FROM— Federal	INTERGOVERN-MENTAL FROM— State	FROM OWN SOURCES Total	FROM OWN SOURCES Taxes
U.S. . . .	**572,274**	**20,047**	**195,539**	**356,687**	**226,696**	MO	8,133	261	2,543	5,329	3,515
AL	6,078	222	2,122	3,734	1,720	MT	1,487	102	460	925	561
AK	2,201	87	799	1,315	665	NE	3,106	110	829	2,167	1,345
AZ	8,116	309	2,997	4,810	2,921	NV	3,298	191	1,252	1,855	889
AR	3,061	90	1,355	1,617	887	NH	2,049	51	256	1,742	1,510
CA	90,382	2,650	39,996	47,736	25,946	NJ	20,615	244	7,382	12,989	10,080
CO	8,061	242	2,226	5,593	3,493	NM	2,806	122	1,451	1,233	586
CT	6,924	201	2,018	4,704	3,976	NY	70,750	1,804	23,169	45,778	33,880
DE	1,054	41	479	534	277	NC	11,857	417	4,866	6,575	3,387
DC	4,712	1,776	(X)	2,936	2,407	ND	1,056	46	393	617	363
FL	31,384	948	8,887	21,549	11,377	OH	21,808	815	7,278	13,714	9,222
GA	13,823	517	3,776	9,530	5,102	OK	4,985	155	1,869	2,960	1,475
HI	1,239	94	137	1,008	683	OR	6,449	380	1,706	4,363	2,916
ID	1,716	51	710	954	496	PA	23,993	1,074	7,920	14,999	9,998
IL	24,779	1,176	6,884	16,719	12,146	RI	1,550	70	400	1,080	938
IN	9,887	228	3,606	6,052	3,631	SC	5,520	183	1,896	3,441	1,771
IA	5,599	156	1,902	3,541	2,093	SD	1,019	54	236	729	543
KS	4,852	77	1,318	3,457	2,138	TN	7,744	305	2,149	5,290	2,868
KY	5,271	199	2,246	2,826	1,508	TX	35,085	864	9,635	24,586	15,808
LA	7,719	342	2,490	4,887	2,826	UT	3,037	82	1,102	1,853	1,093
ME	2,052	70	669	1,313	995	VT	927	13	276	638	540
MD	9,710	421	2,506	6,783	4,965	VA	11,902	392	3,563	7,947	5,659
MA	11,775	622	3,934	7,218	5,406	WA	11,361	402	4,545	6,414	3,467
MI	19,334	395	6,154	12,785	8,718	WV	2,601	63	1,198	1,341	651
MN	12,279	439	4,801	7,039	3,631	WI	11,584	291	4,951	6,342	4,220
MS	4,163	170	1,653	2,340	964	WY	1,379	31	548	800	440

X Not applicable.   [1] Excludes duplicative intergovernmental transactions.

Source: U.S. Bureau of the Census, *Government Finances*, series GF, No. 5, annual.

No. 499. County Governments—Summary of Finances, by Population-Size Group: 1980 to 1991

[For fiscal year ending in year shown; see text, section 9. Represents all counties and their dependent agencies (including dependent school systems where applicable). Size classifications based on 1986 populations; counties distributed according to their 1990 enumerated population]

ITEM	ALL COUNTIES [1] (mil. dol.)			PER CAPITA (dollars), 1991								
				All counties		Counties with 1990 population (1,000) of—						
	1980	1990	1991	Total (3,043) [2]	Per-cent distri-bution	Less than 100 [1] (2,631)	100 to 149.9 (133)	150 to 199.9 (66)	200 to 299.9 (74)	300 to 499.9 (62)	500 to 999.9 (52)	1,000 or more (24)
General revenue	54,573	135,775	137,223	610	100	539	527	544	551	551	733	704
Intergovernmental revenue[3]	24,746	53,953	49,863	222	36	194	195	184	179	184	228	305
From State governments	18,969	49,225	44,535	198	32	174	175	162	157	167	200	274
From Federal government	4,948	2,780	3,058	14	2	12	14	14	14	9	15	16
Tax revenue [3]	18,813	48,750	52,154	232	38	189	184	234	212	227	333	239
Property	14,300	35,723	38,610	172	28	136	135	163	156	169	232	195
Charges and miscella-neous	11,014	33,072	35,207	157	26	157	148	126	160	140	173	160
General expenditure	54,291	127,626	139,267	619	100	535	542	568	559	562	764	710
Capital outlay.	6,505	13,467	15,332	68	11	53	60	62	63	61	104	71
Current expenditure . . .	47,786	114,159	123,934	551	89	482	482	506	496	501	660	638
Education	8,412	18,395	19,821	88	14	111	103	120	86	80	126	22
Public welfare	8,591	18,114	20,171	90	14	50	74	71	70	97	97	151
Hospitals.	5,975	13,018	14,164	63	10	65	47	22	56	32	60	95
Health	2,806	8,791	9,362	42	7	32	40	40	42	39	47	53
Highways	5,227	9,415	10,246	46	7	68	42	45	37	38	39	28
Police protection	2,661	6,693	7,382	33	5	27	28	36	29	28	35	44
Correction.	1,759	6,590	7,447	33	5	17	21	25	31	31	46	53
Natural resources	687	1,314	1,371	6	1	5	4	4	3	5	4	11
Parks and recreation. . .	1,094	2,487	2,830	13	2	5	6	10	10	13	27	15
Financial administration .	1,521	3,363	3,613	16	3	17	14	17	17	15	16	16
General control [4]	3,374	9,149	9,948	42	7	51	23	22	24	28	35	58
General public buildings.	1,072	2,182	2,317	10	2	10	10	11	12	10	14	7
Interest on general debt.	1,542	7,976	8,223	37	6	27	30	29	32	30	52	47
Other and unallocable. .	9,570	20,139	22,372	102	16	49	101	116	109	117	167	111
Debt outstanding, year end.	32,993	118,608	121,755	541	100	401	433	468	459	480	732	697
Long-term	31,543	115,392	117,041	520	96	395	426	459	449	458	715	643
Short-term.	1,450	3,216	4,714	21	4	6	8	9	10	22	18	54

[1] Data for counties under 100,000 population are estimates subject to sampling variation; see Appendix III and source. [2] Figures in parentheses represent number of counties in each size group. [3] Includes other revenues not shown separately. [4] Includes judicial and legal as well as other administrative expenditures.
Source: U.S. Bureau of the Census, *County Government Finances*, series GF, No. 8, annual.

No. 500. Gross Assessed Value of Property and Government Revenue From Property Taxes: 1975 to 1992

[In billions of dollars, except percent. Data are estimates subject to sampling variation; see Appendix III and source]

ITEM	1975	1979	1981	1984	1986	1988	1989	1990	1991	1992
Gross assessed value of property [1] . .	1,096	1,679	2,958	4,053	4,818	(NA)	6,013	(NA)	6,924	(NA)
State assessed	75	114	159	200	243	(NA)	257	(NA)	286	(NA)
Locally assessed.	1,022	1,565	2,799	3,853	4,575	(NA)	5,756	(NA)	6,638	(NA)
Real property	882	1,359	2,515	3,447	4,105	(NA)	5,220	(NA)	6,044	(NA)
Percent of locally assessed . .	86	87	90	89	90	(NA)	91	(NA)	91	(NA)
Net assessed value of locally taxable property [2]	1,063	1,607	2,838	3,869	4,620	(NA)	5,791	(NA)	6,682	(NA)
Percent of gross assessed	97	96	96	96	96	(NA)	96	(NA)	97	(NA)
REVENUE FROM PROPERTY TAXES										
State and local governments.	52	65	75	97	112	132	143	156	168	178
Percent of general revenue	23	19	18	18	17	18	18	18	19	18
Percent of tax revenue	36	32	31	30	30	30	30	31	32	32
State governments	2	3	3	4	4	5	5	6	6	7
Percent of general revenue	1	1	1	1	1	1	1	1	1	1
Percent of tax revenue	2	2	2	2	2	2	2	2	2	2
Local governments	50	63	72	93	107	127	137	150	162	172
Annual percent change from prior year	[3]7	6	7	8	8	9	8	9	9	6
Percent of general revenue	32	27	25	25	25	29	29	29	30	30
Percent of tax revenue	82	78	76	75	74	74	74	75	75	74

NA Not available. [1] Gross assessed value amounts may include prior year components for those States unable to report data for indicated year at time of publication. See sources for definitions of terms and limitations of data. [2] Value subject to local general property taxation, including State-assessed property, after deduction of partial exemptions. [3] Change from 1971.
Source: U.S. Bureau of the Census, *1982* and *1987 Census of Governments*, vol. 2; *Property Values Subject to Local General Property Taxation in the United States: 1975* and *1979*, and *Government Finances*, series GF, No. 5, annual.

No. 501. City Governments—Summary of Finances: 1980 to 1992

[For fiscal year ending in year shown; see text, section 9. Represents all municipalities and their dependent agencies (including dependent school systems where applicable); excludes other local governments overlying city areas. Includes sample-based estimates for cities of less 50,000; thus subject to sampling variation. See Appendix III and source]

ITEM	TOTAL (mil. dol.)				PER CAPITA [1] (dol.)			
	1980	1990	1991	1992	1980	1990	1991	1992
Revenue	94,862	202,393	210,498	220,048	672	1,316	1,368	1,430
General revenue	76,056	158,301	164,319	171,618	539	1,029	1,068	1,116
Intergovernmental revenue	28,270	45,306	46,260	48,152	200	295	301	313
From State governments only	15,939	34,243	34,901	36,222	113	223	227	235
Taxes	31,256	68,788	72,213	75,486	222	447	469	491
Property	16,859	35,024	37,654	39,706	119	228	245	258
Percent of total taxes	54	51	52	53	(X)	(X)	(X)	(X)
Sales and gross receipts	8,208	19,190	19,604	20,190	58	125	127	131
General	5,096	11,645	11,738	11,976	36	76	76	78
Selective	3,112	7,545	7,866	8,214	22	49	51	53
Income, licenses, and other	6,189	14,574	14,954	15,590	44	95	97	101
Charges and miscellaneous	16,530	44,207	45,846	47,980	117	287	298	312
Current charges only	9,875	25,265	27,221	29,449	70	164	177	191
Utility and liquor store revenue	15,719	33,266	34,486	35,460	111	216	224	231
Water system	4,989	11,578	12,067	12,724	35	75	78	83
Electric power system	8,007	17,312	17,926	18,232	57	113	117	119
Gas supply system	1,444	2,335	2,299	2,321	10	15	15	15
Transit system	1,032	1,766	1,924	1,892	7	11	13	13
Liquor stores	247	275	270	292	2	2	2	2
Insurance trust revenue	3,088	10,827	11,693	12,969	22	70	76	84
Expenditure	93,699	198,822	211,506	219,293	664	1,293	1,375	1,426
General expenditure	72,433	153,717	164,226	170,680	513	999	1,068	1,110
Police protection	8,200	18,183	19,388	20,420	58	118	126	133
Fire protection	4,535	9,487	10,045	10,412	32	62	65	68
Highways	5,977	12,106	12,627	12,961	42	79	82	84
Sewerage and sanitation	7,907	16,476	17,603	18,260	56	107	114	119
Public welfare	3,801	7,890	8,941	9,528	27	51	58	62
Education	9,284	17,368	18,793	19,382	66	113	122	126
Libraries	883	1,939	2,119	2,106	6	13	14	14
Health and hospitals	4,457	9,141	9,818	10,338	32	59	64	67
Parks and recreation	3,433	7,584	8,450	8,232	24	49	55	54
Housing and community develop.	3,459	7,661	8,286	8,576	25	50	54	56
Airports	1,100	2,878	2,970	3,552	8	19	19	23
Financial administration	1,843	3,895	3,907	4,172	13	25	25	27
General control [2]	2,015	5,274	6,195	6,055	14	34	40	39
General public buildings	1,090	1,767	1,947	1,884	8	11	13	12
Interest on general debt	3,054	11,317	11,370	12,429	22	74	74	81
Other and unallocable	11,395	20,751	21,767	22,373	81	135	142	145
Utility and liquor store expenditure	18,274	38,436	39,728	40,740	130	250	257	265
Water system	5,933	13,579	14,229	14,661	42	88	93	95
Electric power system	8,596	17,490	17,656	18,023	61	114	115	117
Gas supply system	1,334	2,263	2,218	2,177	9	15	14	14
Transit system	2,189	4,855	5,375	5,613	16	32	35	36
Liquor stores	222	250	250	266	2	2	2	2
Insurance trust expenditure	2,993	6,669	7,552	7,873	21	43	49	51
By character and object:								
Direct expenditure	91,692	193,933	206,637	213,379	650	1,261	1,343	1,387
Current operation	66,687	138,818	147,644	153,501	473	902	960	998
Capital outlay	16,285	31,779	34,106	33,274	115	207	222	216
Construction	13,341	22,842	23,977	23,929	95	148	156	156
Land and existing structures [3]	2,944	8,937	10,129	9,345	21	58	66	61
Assistance payments	1,546	2,212	2,549	2,788	11	14	17	18
Interest on debt	4,182	14,455	14,786	15,944	30	94	96	104
Insurance benefits, repayments	2,992	6,669	7,552	7,873	21	43	49	52
Intergovernmental expenditure	2,007	4,890	4,869	5,913	14	32	32	34
Expenditure for salaries and wages [4]	*34,709*	*66,973*	*72,108*	*74,192*	*246*	*435*	*469*	*482*
Debt outstanding, year end	86,019	212,919	226,554	241,551	610	1,384	1,473	1,570
Long-term	82,346	207,487	220,591	236,144	584	1,349	1,434	1,535
Full faith and credit	39,570	68,510	75,147	81,748	280	445	489	531
Nonguaranteed	42,776	138,977	145,444	154,396	303	903	946	1,004
Short-term	3,673	5,432	5,963	5,407	26	35	39	34
Net long-term debt outstanding	72,528	139,109	152,880	167,329	514	904	994	1,088
Long-term debt issued	12,582	27,991	30,166	35,795	89	182	196	233
Long-term debt retired	5,541	17,980	16,245	22,227	39	117	106	144

X Not applicable.   [1] 1980 data based on April 1 enumerated urban population; all other years based on April 1, 1990 enumerated urban population.   [2] Includes judicial and legal as well as other governmental administration.   [3] Includes equipment.   [4] Included in items shown above.

Source: U.S. Bureau of the Census, *City Government Finances,* series GF, No. 4, annual.

No. 502. City Governments—Total and Per Capita Finances for Largest Cities: 1992

[For fiscal year ending in year show; see text, section 9. Cities ranked by size except Honolulu and Baton Rouge ranked by county population. Data reflect inclusion of fiscal activity of dependent systems where applicable. Intercity comparisons should be made with caution due to variations in responsibilities am areas; for details see text, section 9, and source]

CITIES RANKED BY 1990 POPULATION	GENERAL REVENUE		INTERGOV. REVENUE		TAXES		GENERAL EXPENDITURE		DEBT OUTSTANDING	
	Total (mil. dol.)	Per capita [1] (dol.)	Total (mil. dol.)	Per capita [1] (dol.)	Total (mil. dol.)	Per capita [1] (dol.)	Total (mil. dol.)	Per capita [1] (dol.)	Total (mil. dol.)	Per capita [1] (dol.)
New York City, NY [2]	36,782	5,023	14,480	1,977	17,141	2,341	34,331	4,688	34,984	4,778
Los Angeles, CA	3,889	1,116	522	150	1,933	554	3,534	1,014	8,003	2,296
Chicago, IL	3,298	1,185	822	295	1,592	572	3,281	1,179	6,012	2,160
Houston, TX	1,417	869	64	39	779	478	1,452	890	3,962	2,430
Philadelphia, PA [2]	2,818	1,777	874	551	1,483	935	2,823	1,780	3,835	2,418
San Diego, CA	1,174	1,057	233	210	383	345	1,084	976	1,646	1,482
Detroit, MI	1,567	1,524	706	686	551	536	1,577	1,534	1,685	1,640
Dallas, TX	1,083	1,076	58	58	505	502	1,373	1,363	3,586	3,562
Phoenix, AZ	988	1,005	312	317	334	339	924	940	2,310	2,349
San Antonio, TX	555	593	118	126	224	239	657	702	4,239	4,529
San Jose, CA	642	821	95	122	328	419	710	908	1,249	1,597
Baltimore, MD [2]	1,760	2,391	882	1,198	664	903	1,550	2,106	1,308	1,777
Indianapolis, IN [2]	933	1,276	284	388	419	574	895	1,223	1,232	1,685
San Francisco, CA [2]	2,640	3,647	900	1,243	977	1,349	2,302	3,180	3,174	4,382
Jacksonville, FL [2]	731	1,151	145	229	248	391	779	1,227	4,654	7,326
Columbus, OH	558	881	105	166	287	453	600	947	1,247	1,070
Milwaukee, WI	601	957	307	490	166	265	584	930	600	956
Memphis, TN	882	1,445	573	939	159	260	879	1,439	811	1,328
Washington, DC [2]	4,419	7,282	1,508	2,485	2,407	3,965	4,586	7,556	3,942	6,495
Boston, MA [2]	1,595	2,778	657	1,144	641	1,117	1,560	2,716	1,071	1,864
Seattle, WA	713	1,381	98	189	370	718	737	1,428	1,032	1,999
El Paso, TX	271	526	31	59	129	250	268	520	448	870
Cleveland, OH	535	1,058	132	262	273	539	552	1,091	761	1,506
New Orleans, LA [2]	658	1,323	123	247	301	605	684	1,376	1,126	1,265
Nashville-Davidson, TN [2]	989	2,026	258	529	479	980	857	1,754	2,216	4,537
Denver, CO [2]	1,046	2,236	249	532	391	836	1,513	3,236	3,344	7,151
Austin, TX	560	1,203	34	74	176	378	611	1,313	3,190	6,850
Fort Worth, TX	381	851	42	94	196	437	436	974	935	2,067
Oklahoma City, OK	355	798	19	42	194	436	362	813	571	1,294
Portland, OR	402	920	66	150	203	464	495	1,131	759	1,735
Kansas City, MO	541	1,244	57	130	330	758	570	1,310	905	2,080
Long Beach, CA	604	1,407	115	267	183	425	598	1,393	791	1,841
Tucson, AZ	361	891	120	295	132	326	343	845	825	2,034
St. Louis, MO [2]	494	1,247	74	186	277	698	517	1,303	767	1,933
Charlotte, NC	428	1,080	111	279	165	416	500	1,263	999	2,523
Atlanta, GA	695	1,763	138	350	223	566	624	1,583	1,433	3,637
Virginia Beach, VA [2]	736	1,872	271	689	374	950	682	1,734	566	1,439
Albuquerque, NM	470	1,222	151	392	132	344	395	1,238	754	3,300
Oakland, CA	540	1,451	102	274	222	596	508	1,364	1,144	3,073
Pittsburgh, PA	373	1,009	91	245	237	640	379	1,024	661	1,787
Sacramento, CA	331	895	31	83	154	417	352	954	452	1,224
Minneapolis, MN	620	1,682	170	461	192	522	736	1,998	2,290	6,215
Tulsa, OK	416	1,133	29	79	167	454	444	1,210	1,585	4,315
Honolulu, HI [2]	871	1,042	123	147	482	577	892	1,066	1,051	1,256
Cincinnati, OH	523	1,437	96	263	238	653	525	1,443	260	713
Miami, FL	306	854	48	135	171	476	324	903	565	1,575
Fresno, CA	242	682	47	132	109	306	236	666	248	701
Omaha, NE	228	678	36	107	144	429	209	621	195	580
Toledo, OH	235	705	45	134	128	384	234	703	194	582
Buffalo, NY	690	2,101	467	1,425	143	436	757	2,308	500	1,524
Wichita, KS	247	812	76	250	80	262	260	857	539	1,772
Santa Ana, CA	180	613	39	134	103	349	204	694	304	1,035
Mesa, AZ	183	636	59	204	45	158	197	685	484	1,681
Colorado Springs, CO	286	1,016	27	96	85	302	306	1,087	730	2,597
Tampa, FL	306	1,094	50	178	126	449	327	1,169	683	2,438
Newark, NJ	453	1,646	265	963	97	353	450	1,634	207	750
St. Paul, MN	414	1,522	142	521	93	343	409	1,504	865	3,177
Louisville, KY	255	946	57	211	147	547	255	947	442	1,642
Anaheim, CA	267	1,003	39	145	112	421	333	1,252	766	2,874
Birmingham, AL	277	1,042	30	111	158	595	309	1,162	807	3,035
Arlington, TX	180	686	11	42	96	367	154	589	378	1,446
Norfolk, VA [2]	566	2,167	211	807	216	827	586	2,244	1,023	3,914
Las Vegas, NV	235	912	101	393	64	250	246	951	134	518
Corpus Christi, TX	164	637	15	59	71	276	154	596	429	1,668
St. Petersburg, FL	237	993	33	138	91	381	212	889	574	2,405
Rochester, NY	615	2,656	362	1,563	140	602	628	2,712	284	1,228
Riverside, CA	216	955	32	140	74	325	219	966	727	3,208
Anchorage, AK [2]	696	3,074	270	1,191	179	792	699	3,088	1,055	4,662
Lexington-Fayette, KY [2]	197	873	16	73	101	450	190	842	414	1,837
Akron, OH	200	898	41	182	95	426	200	895	152	683
Aurora, CO	173	777	16	74	100	452	157	706	429	1,932
Baton Rouge, LA [2]	414	1,089	56	147	203	533	476	1,040	1,269	1,984
Stockton, CA	146	693	21	102	68	322	145	687	283	1,342

[1] Based on enumerated population as of April 1, 1990.   [2] Represents, in effect, city-county consolidated government.

Source: U.S. Bureau of the Census, *City Government Finances*, series GF, No. 4, annual.

No. 503. City Governments—Finances, by Population-Size Groups: 1992

[**For fiscal year ending in year shown;** see text, section 9. Represents all municipalities and their dependent agencies, including dependent school systems where applicable]

ITEM	All cities [1]	CITIES HAVING A **1990** POPULATION OF—						
		Less than 75,000 [1]	75,000 to 99,999	100,000 to 199,999	200,000 to 299,999	300,000 to 499,999	500,000 to 999,999	1,000,000 or more
Number of cities, 1992	19,296	19,003	98	119	24	28	16	8
Population, 1990 (1,000)	153,827	81,012	8,455	16,390	5,975	11,088	10,954	19,953
FINANCES, 1992 (mil. dol.)								
General revenue [2]	**171,618**	**55,827**	**7,963**	**15,995**	**7,228**	**13,884**	**18,694**	**52,027**
Taxes [2]	75,486	23,630	3,704	7,047	2,691	5,940	8,108	24,366
Property	39,706	13,983	2,404	4,351	1,396	2,593	4,313	10,666
Sales and gross receipts	20,190	6,355	991	2,038	787	2,313	1,791	5,915
Intergovernmental [2]	48,152	12,655	1,824	4,338	2,189	3,118	6,269	17,759
From State governments	36,222	9,201	1,414	3,128	1,518	1,970	3,580	15,411
From Federal Government	8,033	1,638	316	775	420	732	2,147	2,005
Current charges	29,449	11,900	1,479	2,632	1,370	2,875	2,611	6,582
Utility and liquor store revenue	35,460	17,321	1,703	3,597	1,445	2,095	3,698	5,601
General expenditure [2]	**170,680**	**56,198**	**8,128**	**16,373**	**7,423**	**14,629**	**18,475**	**49,454**
Police and fire protection	30,832	12,451	1,710	3,444	1,438	2,698	2,992	6,099
Education	19,382	3,328	1,229	2,414	1,058	1,018	2,261	8,074
Sewerage and sanitation	18,260	8,040	756	1,770	714	1,646	1,791	3,543
Highways	12,961	6,478	748	1,367	581	1,070	940	1,777
Health and hospitals	10,338	2,872	335	284	267	622	1,693	4,265
Public welfare	9,528	367	68	282	146	183	1,320	7,162
Housing and community development	8,576	1,934	466	828	597	701	956	3,094
Interest on general debt	12,429	3,838	557	1,207	681	1,735	1,326	3,085
Utility and liquor store expenditure	40,740	17,791	1,978	3,804	1,596	2,340	4,456	8,775
Debt outstanding	**241,551**	**73,666**	**10,772**	**22,488**	**12,701**	**29,081**	**29,129**	**63,714**
Long-term	236,144	71,806	10,581	22,110	12,476	28,753	28,865	61,553
Short-term	5,407	1,857	192	379	226	328	264	2,161
PERCENT DISTRIBUTION								
General revenue [2]	**100.0**	**100.0**	**100.0**	**100.0**	**100.0**	**100.0**	**100.0**	**100.0**
Taxes [2]	44.0	42.3	46.5	44.1	37.2	42.8	43.4	46.8
Property	23.1	25.0	30.2	27.2	19.3	18.7	23.1	20.5
Sales and gross receipts	11.8	11.4	12.4	12.7	10.9	16.7	9.6	11.4
Intergovernmental	28.1	22.7	22.9	27.1	30.3	22.5	33.5	34.1
Current charges	21.1	16.5	17.8	19.6	21.0	14.2	19.2	29.6
General expenditure [2]	**100.0**	**100.0**	**100.0**	**100.0**	**100.0**	**100.0**	**100.0**	**100.0**
Police and fire protection	18.1	22.2	21.0	21.0	19.4	18.4	16.2	12.3
Education	11.4	5.9	15.1	14.7	14.3	7.0	12.2	16.3
Sewerage and sanitation	10.7	14.3	9.3	10.8	9.6	11.3	9.7	7.2
Highways	7.6	11.5	9.2	8.3	7.8	7.3	5.1	3.6
Health and hospitals	6.1	5.1	4.1	1.7	3.6	4.3	9.2	8.6
Public welfare	5.6	0.7	0.8	1.7	2.0	1.3	7.1	14.5
Housing and community development	5.0	3.4	5.7	5.1	8.0	4.8	5.2	6.3
Interest on general debt	7.3	6.8	6.9	7.4	9.2	11.9	7.2	6.2
PER CAPITA [3] **(dollars)**								
General revenue [2]	**1,116**	**689**	**942**	**976**	**1,210**	**1,252**	**1,707**	**2,607**
Taxes [2]	491	292	438	430	450	536	740	1,221
Property	258	173	284	265	234	234	394	535
Sales and gross receipts	131	78	117	124	132	209	163	296
Intergovernmental [2]	313	156	216	265	366	281	572	890
From State governments	235	114	167	191	254	178	327	772
From Federal Government	52	20	37	47	70	66	196	100
Current charges	191	147	175	161	229	259	238	330
Utility and liquor store revenue	231	214	201	219	242	189	338	281
General expenditure [2]	**1,110**	**694**	**961**	**999**	**1,242**	**1,319**	**1,687**	**2,479**
Police and fire protection	200	154	202	210	241	243	273	306
Education	126	41	145	147	177	92	206	405
Sewerage and sanitation	119	99	89	108	120	148	164	178
Highways	84	80	88	83	97	96	86	89
Health and hospitals	67	35	40	17	45	56	155	214
Public welfare	62	5	8	17	24	17	121	359
Housing and community development	56	24	55	50	100	63	87	155
Interest on general debt	81	47	66	74	114	156	121	155
Utility and liquor store expenditure	265	220	234	232	267	211	407	440
Debt outstanding	**1,570**	**909**	**1,274**	**1,372**	**2,126**	**2,623**	**2,659**	**3,193**
Long-term	1,535	886	1,251	1,349	2,088	2,593	2,635	3,085
Short-term	35	23	23	23	38	30	24	108

[1] Data are estimates subject to sampling variation, see Appendix III and source.   [2] Includes items not shown separately.
[3] Based on 1990 enumerated resident population as of April 1.

Source: U.S. Bureau of the Census, *City Government Finances*, series GF, No. 4, annual.

No. 504. City Governments—Revenue and Debt for Largest Cities: 1992

[**In millions of dollars.** For fiscal year ending in year shown; see text, section 9. See headnote, table 502]

CITIES RANKED BY 1990 POPULATION	REVENUE								Debt out-stand-ing
	Total [1]	General revenue						Utility and liquor store	
		Total [1]	Intergovernmental		Taxes				
			From State and local govts.	From Federal Government	Total [1]	Property	Sales and gross receipts		
New York City, NY [2]	44,888	36,782	13,330	1,150	17,141	7,899	3,432	1,993	34,984
Los Angeles, CA	6,993	3,889	385	137	1,933	774	758	2,141	8,003
Chicago, IL	4,514	3,298	565	256	1,592	596	855	228	6,012
Houston, TX	1,802	1,417	23	41	779	400	359	235	3,962
Philadelphia, PA [2]	3,471	2,818	717	157	1,483	330	73	587	3,835
San Diego, CA	1,427	1,174	142	92	383	156	194	125	1,646
Detroit, MI	2,043	1,567	576	130	551	215	44	169	1,685
Dallas, TX	1,371	1,083	16	42	505	295	201	122	3,586
Phoenix, AZ	1,152	988	230	82	334	117	197	103	2,310
San Antonio, TX	1,427	555	96	22	224	124	94	839	4,239
San Jose, CA	768	642	86	9	328	129	146	8	1,249
Baltimore, MD [2]	1,997	1,760	828	53	664	458	48	52	1,308
Indianapolis, IN [2]	965	933	248	35	419	322	20	7	1,232
San Francisco, CA [2]	3,417	2,640	778	122	977	536	233	225	3,174
Jacksonville, FL [2]	1,556	731	88	57	248	198	41	729	4,654
Columbus, OH	647	558	58	47	287	23	6	89	1,247
Milwaukee, WI	833	601	257	50	166	155	5	48	600
Memphis, TN	1,891	882	546	27	159	118	30	844	811
Washington, DC [2]	4,754	4,419	58	1,451	2,407	903	672	54	3,942
Boston, MA [2]	1,830	1,595	634	23	641	599	25	69	1,071
Seattle, WA	1,104	713	76	21	370	128	154	332	1,032
El Paso, TX	359	271	8	22	129	66	59	42	448
Cleveland, OH	703	535	69	63	273	49	4	167	761
New Orleans, LA [2]	747	658	45	78	301	138	137	56	1,126
Nashville-Davidson, TN [2]	1,636	989	246	13	479	263	173	605	2,216
Denver, CO [2]	1,171	1,046	221	27	391	99	246	85	3,344
Austin, TX	1,130	560	26	8	176	98	74	500	3,190
Fort Worth, TX	501	381	23	19	196	130	61	65	935
Oklahoma City, OK	407	355	8	10	194	27	161	38	571
Portland, OR	455	402	54	12	203	138	31	52	759
Kansas City, MO	671	541	29	28	330	62	147	47	905
Long Beach, CA	725	604	73	42	183	72	91	120	791
Tucson, AZ	455	361	98	22	132	24	104	76	825
St. Louis, MO [2]	604	494	41	32	277	37	109	30	767
Charlotte, NC	473	428	89	22	165	140	12	34	999
Atlanta, GA	811	695	82	55	223	123	68	61	1,433
Virginia Beach, VA [2]	775	736	179	91	374	233	113	39	566
Albuquerque, NM	514	470	122	29	132	47	80	43	1,269
Oakland, CA	566	540	73	29	222	113	68	-	1,144
Pittsburgh, PA	407	373	70	21	237	122	29	-	661
Sacramento, CA	386	331	30	1	154	52	90	20	452
Minneapolis, MN	750	620	144	26	192	142	38	23	2,290
Tulsa, OK	473	416	14	15	167	19	144	44	1,585
Honolulu, HI [2]	962	871	62	61	482	389	59	91	1,051
Cincinnati, OH	675	523	69	27	238	43	4	64	260
Miami, FL	381	306	35	14	171	127	35	-	565
Fresno, CA	320	242	34	13	109	39	50	23	248
Omaha, NE	259	228	32	4	144	66	70	-	195
Toledo, OH	255	235	31	13	128	10	-	21	194
Buffalo, NY	709	690	422	45	143	122	15	20	500
Wichita, KS	313	247	66	10	80	52	25	25	539
Santa Ana, CA	197	180	22	17	103	48	47	17	304
Mesa, AZ	255	183	52	6	45	5	37	71	484
Colorado Springs, CO	546	286	15	12	85	18	66	260	730
Tampa, FL	383	306	38	12	126	58	59	30	683
Newark, NJ	491	453	203	62	97	62	8	37	207
St. Paul, MN	448	414	102	40	93	72	17	22	865
Louisville, KY	317	255	36	21	147	38	1	62	442
Anaheim, CA	510	267	17	21	112	38	65	243	766
Birmingham, AL	326	277	16	13	158	28	56	-	807
Arlington, TX	212	180	2	9	96	57	37	33	378
Norfolk, VA [2]	633	566	163	48	216	127	69	33	1,023
Las Vegas, NV	235	235	98	3	64	30	14	-	134
Corpus Christi, TX	214	164	5	10	71	36	34	50	429
St. Petersburg, FL	296	237	30	3	91	58	29	49	574
Rochester, NY	641	615	308	54	140	126	11	26	284
Riverside, CA	414	216	28	4	74	25	42	197	727
Anchorage, AK [2]	815	696	264	6	179	165	7	94	1,055
Lexington-Fayette, KY [2]	221	197	6	11	101	24	6	1	414
Akron, OH	226	200	18	22	95	18	-	25	152
Aurora, CO	205	173	14	2	100	16	80	25	429
Baton Rouge, LA [2]	455	414	32	24	203	54	137	3	754
Stockton, CA	152	146	17	5	68	18	40	6	283

- Represents or rounds to zero.   [1] Includes items not shown separately.   [2] Represents, in effect, city-county consolidated government.

Source: U.S. Bureau of the Census, *City Government Finances*, series GF, No. 4, annual.

No. 505. City Governments—Expenditures for Largest Cities: 1992

[In millions of dollars. For fiscal year ending in year shown; see text, section 9. See headnote, table 502]

CITIES RANKED BY 1990 POPULATION	Total expenditure [1]	General expenditure								Utility and liquor store
		Total [1]	Education	Housing and community development	Public welfare	Health and hospitals	Police protection	Fire protection	Highways	
New York City, NY [2]	42,499	34,331	8,008	2,445	6,840	3,646	1,872	699	795	4,690
Los Angeles, CA	6,577	3,534	9	256	-	11	650	265	153	2,411
Chicago, IL	3,887	3,281	35	128	110	97	627	231	365	198
Houston, TX	1,758	1,452	-	21	-	59	269	147	128	238
Philadelphia, PA [2]	3,723	2,823	17	89	213	335	345	123	95	607
San Diego, CA	1,311	1,084	-	90	(Z)	2	168	75	76	181
Detroit, MI	2,131	1,577	6	51	-	98	290	93	100	305
Dallas, TX	1,620	1,373	-	14	-	19	168	75	63	146
Phoenix, AZ	1,091	924	1	57	-	1	155	83	68	143
San Antonio, TX	1,501	657	9	13	12	18	99	66	53	829
San Jose, CA	760	710	-	110	-	-	110	55	64	17
Baltimore, MD [2]	1,687	1,550	537	63	2	58	154	84	144	46
Indianapolis, IN [2]	954	895	-	30	77	176	88	38	49	24
San Francisco, CA [2]	3,024	2,302	58	75	313	549	164	101	42	490
Jacksonville, FL [2]	1,686	779	-	50	17	21	78	56	45	867
Columbus, OH	729	600	-	4	-	23	127	67	53	129
Milwaukee, WI	684	584	-	46	-	12	118	54	46	37
Memphis, TN	1,762	879	435	20	-	16	74	59	37	819
Washington, DC [2]	5,036	4,586	743	219	872	535	273	97	122	78
Boston, MA [2]	1,781	1,560	479	45	26	237	137	86	51	57
Seattle, WA	1,173	737	-	49	-	14	95	62	51	384
El Paso, TX	359	268	-	5	1	15	43	23	24	74
Cleveland, OH	803	552	-	68	(Z)	10	123	67	48	252
New Orleans, LA [2]	773	684	-	82	6	14	77	37	39	54
Nashville-Davidson, TN [2]	1,525	857	271	5	11	80	64	39	35	629
Denver, CO [2]	1,649	1,513	-	11	133	134	92	53	65	113
Austin, TX	1,113	611	-	5	1	142	52	35	22	478
Fort Worth, TX	523	436	-	6	-	11	53	32	52	65
Oklahoma City, OK	417	362	-	6	-	1	68	48	41	49
Portland, OR	581	495	-	20	-	-	71	48	64	50
Kansas City, MO	662	570	24	8	(Z)	41	78	41	51	62
Long Beach, CA	737	598	-	70	-	25	95	56	26	137
Tucson, AZ	463	343	-	33	2	1	51	24	47	110
St. Louis, MO [2]	603	517	3	27	4	31	88	26	21	28
Charlotte, NC	566	500	-	12	1	3	43	33	53	61
Atlanta, GA	767	624	19	15	(Z)	-	74	39	25	82
Virginia Beach, VA [2]	716	682	334	5	15	17	41	19	56	34
Albuquerque, NM	546	476	-	17	5	7	55	29	38	70
Oakland, CA	554	508	4	46	1	-	75	40	17	-
Pittsburgh, PA	429	379	-	9	(Z)	7	58	43	22	16
Sacramento, CA	399	352	(Z)	-	-	2	73	40	49	28
Minneapolis, MN	795	736	-	131	-	10	56	29	49	29
Tulsa, OK	491	444	-	5	-	19	46	34	28	42
Honolulu, HI [2]	1,101	892	-	102	-	9	114	44	44	209
Cincinnati, OH	659	525	-	54	-	32	65	50	44	81
Miami, FL	359	324	-	17	1	(Z)	88	46	9	-
Fresno, CA	303	236	-	9	-	-	41	21	30	43
Omaha, NE	222	209	(Z)	10	-	1	33	25	30	-
Toledo, OH	258	234	-	10	-	5	46	31	28	24
Buffalo, NY	774	757	362	68	-	2	55	41	21	17
Wichita, KS	309	260	-	10	2	7	27	17	69	32
Santa Ana, CA	221	204	-	47	-	3	52	22	18	17
Mesa, AZ	265	197	-	4	(Z)	-	40	19	22	68
Colorado Springs, CO	590	306	-	4	-	109	34	19	54	284
Tampa, FL	408	327	-	5	-	4	54	22	26	54
Newark, NJ	491	450	(Z)	66	45	13	66	44	6	34
St. Paul, MN	451	409	-	59	-	8	34	25	55	27
Louisville, KY	291	255	-	23	11	7	33	22	18	37
Anaheim, CA	600	333	-	97	-	1	47	25	22	266
Birmingham, AL	329	309	3	1	-	3	36	28	25	-
Arlington, TX	189	154	-	13	-	1	24	16	21	34
Norfolk, VA [2]	646	586	196	66	32	30	34	21	20	44
Las Vegas, NV	246	246	-	4	(Z)	2	39	26	54	(Z)
Corpus Christi, TX	195	154	-	1	-	5	25	13	14	42
St. Petersburg, FL	285	212	-	3	-	5	40	16	33	58
Rochester, NY	645	628	320	54	-	-	38	27	18	17
Riverside, CA	398	219	-	18	-	1	37	17	28	180
Anchorage, AK [2]	868	699	284	2	6	27	40	22	43	162
Lexington-Fayette, KY [2]	203	190	-	21	5	13	22	19	8	5
Akron, OH	232	200	-	10	-	7	27	20	22	32
Aurora, CO	188	157	-	2	-	(Z)	30	17	22	29
Baton Rouge, LA [2]	423	395	-	11	1	31	39	20	41	6
Stockton, CA	152	145	-	4	-	1	35	21	9	7

- Represents or rounds to zero.   Z Less than $500,000.   [1] Includes items not shown separately.   [2] Represents, in effect, city-county consolidated government.

Source: U.S. Bureau of the Census, *City Government Finances*, series GF, No. 4, annual.

No. 506. Governmental Employment and Payrolls: 1980 to 1992

[For **October.** Covers both full-time and part-time employees. Except for 1987, local government data are estimates subject to sampling variation; see Appendix III and source. See also *Historical Statistics, Colonial Times to 1970*, series Y 272-307]

TYPE OF GOVERNMENT	1980	1983	1984	1985	1986	1987	1988	1989	1990	1991	1992
EMPLOYEES (1,000)											
Total	**16,213**	**16,034**	**16,436**	**16,690**	**16,933**	**17,212**	**17,588**	**17,879**	**18,369**	**18,554**	**18,745**
Federal (civilian) [1]	2,898	2,875	2,942	3,021	3,019	3,091	3,112	3,114	3,105	3,103	3,047
State and local	13,315	13,159	13,494	13,669	13,913	14,121	14,476	14,765	15,263	15,452	15,698
Percent of total	82	82	82	82	82	82	82	83	83	83	84
State	3,753	3,816	3,898	3,984	4,068	4,116	4,236	4,365	4,503	4,521	4,595
Local	9,562	9,344	9,595	9,685	9,846	10,005	10,240	10,400	10,760	10,930	11,103
Counties	1,853	1,811	1,872	1,891	1,926	1,963	2,024	2,085	2,167	2,196	2,253
Municipalities	2,561	2,424	2,434	2,467	2,494	2,493	2,570	2,569	2,642	2,662	2,665
School districts	4,270	4,211	4,387	4,416	4,502	4,627	4,679	4,774	4,950	5,045	5,134
Townships	394	379	386	392	400	393	415	405	418	415	424
Special districts	484	519	516	519	524	529	552	568	585	612	627
OCTOBER PAYROLLS (mil. dol.)											
Total	**19,935**	**24,525**	**26,904**	**28,945**	**30,670**	**32,669**	**34,203**	**36,763**	**39,228**	**41,237**	**43,120**
Federal (civilian) [1]	5,205	6,301	7,137	7,580	7,561	7,924	7,976	8,636	8,999	9,687	9,937
State and local	14,730	18,224	19,767	21,365	23,109	24,745	26,227	28,127	30,229	31,551	33,183
Percent of total	74	74	74	74	75	76	77	77	77	77	77
State	4,285	5,346	5,815	6,329	6,810	7,263	7,842	8,443	9,083	9,437	9,828
Local	10,445	12,878	13,952	15,036	16,298	17,482	18,385	19,684	21,146	22,113	23,355
Counties	1,936	2,387	2,596	2,819	3,009	3,270	3,532	3,855	4,192	4,404	4,698
Municipalities	2,951	3,640	3,872	4,191	4,407	4,770	4,979	5,274	5,564	5,784	6,207
School districts	4,683	5,729	6,283	6,746	7,517	7,961	8,298	8,852	9,551	9,975	10,394
Townships	330	398	421	446	474	522	556	599	642	664	685
Special districts	546	724	780	834	892	959	1,020	1,104	1,197	1,287	1,370

[1] Includes employees outside the United States.

Source: U.S. Bureau of the Census, *Historical Statistics on Governmental Finances and Employment*, and *Public Employment*, series GE, No. 1, annual.

No. 507. All Governments—Employment and Payroll, by Function: 1992

[For **October.** Covers both full-time and part-time employees. Local government amounts are estimates subject to sampling variation; see Appendix III and source]

FUNCTION	EMPLOYEES (1,000)					OCTOBER PAYROLLS (mil. dol.)				
	Total	Federal (civil-ian) [1]	State and local			Total	Federal (civil-ian) [1]	State and local		
			Total	State	Local			Total	State	Local
Total	**18,745**	**3,047**	**15,698**	**4,595**	**11,103**	**43,120**	**9,937**	**33,183**	**9,828**	**23,355**
National defense [2]	984	984	(X)	(X)	(X)	2,913	2,913	(X)	(X)	(X)
Postal Service	774	774	(X)	(X)	(X)	2,654	2,654	(X)	(X)	(X)
Space research and technology	25	25	(X)	(X)	(X)	112	112	(X)	(X)	(X)
Education	8,239	14	8,225	2,050	6,174	16,565	45	16,521	3,774	12,747
Highways.	565	4	561	261	300	1,271	19	1,252	626	626
Health and hospitals	1,854	310	1,544	721	823	4,292	952	3,340	1,613	1,727
Public welfare.	506	10	496	215	281	1,051	36	1,015	471	544
Police protection	858	88	770	87	683	2,396	335	2,061	247	1,814
Fire protection	344	(X)	344	(X)	344	825	(X)	825	(X)	825
Sanitation and sewerage . .	244	(X)	244	3	241	554	(X)	554	8	547
Parks and recreation	345	27	318	42	276	514	72	441	70	371
Natural resources	436	232	204	164	40	1,249	818	431	355	76
Financial administration . . .	493	138	355	151	205	1,176	425	751	351	400
Other government administration	399	29	370	52	318	668	100	568	125	443
Judicial and legal	374	51	323	114	209	1,013	181	832	350	482
Other	2,303	360	1,943	734	1,209	5,865	1,273	4,592	1,839	2,753

X Not applicable.   [1] Includes employees outside the United States.   [2] Includes international relations.

Source: U.S. Bureau of the Census, *Public Employment*, series GE, No. 1.

No. 508. State and Local Government—Full-Time Employment and Salary, by Sex and Race/Ethnic Group: 1973 to 1993

[As of June 30. Excludes school systems and educational institutions. Based on reports from State governments (44 in 1973, 48 in 1975, 1976, and 1979, 47 in 1977 and 1983, 45 in 1978, 42 in 1980, 49 in 1981 and 1984 through 1987, and 50 in 1989 through 1993) and a sample of county, municipal, township, and special district jurisdictions employing 15 or more nonelected, nonappointed full-time employees. Data for 1974, 1982, 1988 and 1992 not available. For definition of median, see Guide to Tabular Presentation]

YEAR AND OCCUPATION	EMPLOYMENT (1,000)							MEDIAN ANNUAL SALARY ($1,000)					
	Total	Male	Female	White [1]	Minority			Male	Female	White [1]	Minority		
					Total [2]	Black [1]	Hispanic [3]				Total [2]	Black [1]	Hispanic [3]
1973	3,809	2,486	1,322	3,115	693	523	125	9.6	7.0	8.8	7.5	7.4	7.4
1975	3,899	2,436	1,464	3,102	797	602	147	11.3	8.2	10.2	8.8	8.6	8.9
1976	4,369	2,724	1,645	3,490	880	664	165	11.8	8.6	10.7	9.2	9.1	9.4
1977	4,415	2,737	1,678	3,480	935	705	175	12.4	9.1	11.3	9.7	9.5	9.9
1978	4,447	2,711	1,736	3,481	966	723	181	13.3	9.7	12.0	10.4	10.1	10.7
1979	4,576	2,761	1,816	3,568	1,008	751	192	14.1	10.4	12.8	10.9	10.6	11.4
1980	3,987	2,350	1,637	3,146	842	619	163	15.2	11.4	13.8	11.8	11.5	12.3
1981	4,665	2,740	1,925	3,591	1,074	780	205	17.7	13.1	16.1	13.5	13.3	14.7
1983	4,492	2,674	1,818	3,423	1,069	768	219	20.1	15.3	18.5	15.9	15.6	17.3
1984	4,580	2,700	1,880	3,458	1,121	799	233	21.4	16.2	19.6	17.4	16.5	18.4
1985	4,742	2,789	1,952	3,563	1,179	835	248	22.3	17.3	20.6	18.4	17.5	19.2
1986	4,779	2,797	1,982	3,549	1,230	865	259	23.4	18.1	21.5	19.6	18.7	20.2
1987	4,849	2,818	2,031	3,600	1,249	872	268	24.2	18.9	22.4	20.9	19.3	21.1
1989	5,257	3,030	2,227	3,863	1,394	961	308	26.1	20.6	24.1	22.1	20.7	22.7
1990	5,374	3,071	2,302	3,918	1,456	994	327	27.3	21.8	25.2	23.3	22.0	23.8
1991	5,459	3,110	2,349	3,965	1,494	1,011	340	28.4	22.7	26.4	23.8	22.7	24.5
1993, total . .	**5,024**	**2,820**	**2,204**	**3,588**	**1,436**	**948**	**341**	**30.6**	**24.3**	**28.5**	**25.9**	**24.2**	**26.8**
Officials/admin- istrators	273	188	86	231	42	27	10	(NA)	40.9	(NA)	(NA)	(NA)	(NA)
Professionals. . .	1,206	587	619	923	283	168	59	37.8	32.5	35.3	32.8	31.8	34.1
Technicians. . . .	465	270	195	348	117	69	31	30.4	24.5	28.3	25.6	24.6	27.6
Protective serv ice.	846	725	120	632	214	145	58	31.4	27.2	30.9	30.3	28.8	34.3
Paraprofes- sionals	360	100	260	218	142	111	23	22.6	20.4	21.5	21.7	19.8	21.4
Admin. support .	897	116	781	610	287	183	75	22.7	21.1	21.0	21.9	21.2	21.8
Skilled craft. . . .	395	378	17	299	96	59	28	28.5	22.9	28.2	27.7	27.0	29.7
Service/mainte- nance.	582	455	127	327	255	186	57	23.1	17.8	22.2	22.6	21.0	23.0

NA Not available. [1] Non-Hispanic. [2] Includes other minority groups not shown separately. [3] Persons of Hispanic origin may be of any race.

Source: U.S. Equal Employment Opportunity Commission, *State and Local Government Information Report,* biennially.

No. 509. State and Local Government—Employer Costs per Hour Worked: 1994

[As of March. Based on a sample; see source for details. For additional data, see table 683]

ITEM	Total compensation	Wages and salaries	BENEFITS						
			Total	Paid leave	Supplemental pay	Insurance	Retirement and savings	Legally required benefits	Other [1]
All State & local government workers .	$25.27	$17.57	$7.71	$1.94	$0.20	$2.15	$1.90	$1.49	$0.03
Occupational group:									
White-collar occupations	28.60	20.38	8.22	2.05	0.12	2.31	2.11	1.60	0.03
Professional specialty and technical	34.04	24.90	9.15	2.03	0.13	2.52	2.60	1.83	0.04
Teachers	37.22	27.77	9.45	1.78	0.04	2.72	2.97	1.90	0.04
Executive, admin., & managerial .	31.81	22.04	9.77	3.19	0.15	2.20	2.37	1.85	0.02
Admin. support including clerical .	16.10	10.53	5.58	1.50	0.09	1.94	1.01	1.02	(Z)
Blue-collar occupations	19.42	12.49	6.93	1.78	0.36	1.94	1.34	1.49	0.02
Service occupations	17.71	11.25	6.45	1.66	0.39	1.73	1.53	1.12	0.02
Industry group:									
Services	26.94	19.25	7.69	1.80	0.14	2.24	1.97	1.50	0.03
Health services	20.03	13.37	6.65	2.05	0.52	1.60	1.08	1.39	0.02
Hospitals	20.28	13.64	6.64	2.08	0.50	1.56	1.07	1.41	0.02
Educational services	28.60	20.67	7.93	1.75	0.07	2.37	2.17	1.54	0.03
Elementary and secondary education.	28.78	20.82	7.96	1.65	0.05	2.48	2.23	1.51	0.05
Higher education	28.94	20.91	8.03	2.03	0.13	2.15	2.07	1.65	(Z)
Public administration	22.11	14.47	7.64	2.19	0.29	1.90	1.86	1.37	0.02

Z Cost per hour is less than one cent. [1] Includes severance pay and supplemental unemployment benefits.

Source: U.S. Bureau of Labor Statistics, News, *Employer Costs for Employee Compensation,* USDL 94-220.

No. 510. State and Local Government—Employee Benefits: 1992

[In percent. For January through July. Covers full-time employees in State and local governments. Covers only benefits for which the employer pays part or all of the premium or expenses involved, except unpaid maternity and paternity leave, and long-term care insurance. Based on sample. For data on employee benefits in businesses, see table 685]

BENEFIT	All employees	White collar employees [1]	Teachers [2]	Blue collar employees [3]	BENEFIT	All employees	White collar employees [1]	Teachers [2]	Blue collar employees [3]
Paid: Vacations	67	87	10	91	Life	89	89	87	89
Holidays	75	88	38	91	Noncontributory	75	76	73	77
Jury duty leave	97	97	98	97	Accident/sickness	22	25	15	23
Funeral leave	65	64	61	70	Noncontributory	16	18	13	17
Rest time	53	68	20	64	Long-term disability	28	30	33	22
Military leave	83	87	76	85	Noncontributory	22	23	27	18
Sick leave	95	94	97	94	Retirement and savings plans:				
Personal leave	38	31	55	33	Defined benefit pension	87	86	89	87
Lunch time	10	6	14	13	Noncontributory	24	25	22	24
Unpaid: Maternity leave	59	59	63	54	Defined contribution	9	10	8	9
Paternity leave	44	46	44	40	Money purchase pension [4]	7	7	7	8
Insurance plans:					Additional benefits:				
Medical	90	91	90	89	Child care	8	10	6	7
Dental	65	65	65	64	Educational assistance:				
Extended care facility	76	76	75	75	Job related	66	73	57	64
Home health care	78	79	77	77	Not job related	18	20	14	18
Hospital/room & board	90	91	90	89	Eldercare	13	14	15	11
In HMO's	27	25	25	30	Employee assistance				
Inpatient surgery	90	91	90	89	program	63	70	47	68
Mental health care:					Flexible benefits plans	5	5	7	4
Inpatient	89	90	88	88	In-house infirmary	17	18	16	14
Outpatient	83	85	83	84	Long-term care insurance	5	6	5	3
Vision	35	34	33	38	Nonproduction bonuses,				
Alcohol abuse treatment:					cash	38	43	26	44
Inpatient detox	89	90	89	89	Prepaid legal services	7	8	7	7
Inpatient rehab	65	66	64	65	Recreation facilities	15	15	19	12
Outpatient	67	67	65	67	Reimbursement accounts [5]	50	55	44	48
Drug abuse treatment:					Severance pay	32	30	31	35
Inpatient detox	89	90	88	88	Travel accident insurance	15	17	13	13
Inpatient rehab	64	65	62	64	Wellness programs	30	34	23	30
Outpatient	66	66	63	66					

[1] Includes all professional, administrative, technical, and clerical employees except teachers. [2] Includes all personnel in primary and secondary schools, junior colleges, and universities whose primary duty is teaching or closely related activities. [3] Includes police, firefighters, and all production and service employees. [4] Fixed contributions are periodically placed in an employee's account and benefits are based on how much money has accumulated at retirement. [5] Account which is used throughout the year to pay for plan premiums or to reimburse the employee for benefit related expenses. Account may be financed by employer, employee, or both.

Source: U.S. Bureau of Labor Statistics, *Employee Benefits in State and Local Governments, 1992.*

No. 511. State and Local Government Major Collective Bargaining Agreements— Average Percent Changes in Wage and Compensation Rates Negotiated: 1987 to 1994

[In percent, except as indicated. Averages presented are means; for definition, see Guide to Tabular Presentation]

ITEM	1987	1988	1989	1990	1991	1992	1993	1994
Compensation rate changes, [1] all settlements:								
First year	4.9	5.4	5.1	5.1	1.8	0.6	0.9	2.8
Over life of contract [2]	4.8	5.3	4.9	5.1	2.9	1.9	1.8	3.1
State government: First year	4.3	5.3	4.9	4.4	1.9	0.2	1.2	2.8
Over life of contract [2]	4.3	4.9	4.6	3.9	2.8	2.0	2.1	2.9
Local government: First year	5.4	5.5	5.6	5.4	1.6	1.2	0.7	2.8
Over life of contract [2]	5.1	5.8	5.5	5.8	2.9	1.5	1.6	3.3
Wage rate changes, [3] all settlements:								
First year	4.9	5.1	5.1	4.9	2.3	1.1	1.1	2.7
Over life of contract [2]	5.1	5.3	5.1	5.0	2.8	2.1	2.1	3.0
State government: First year	4.1	5.3	5.0	4.7	2.0	0.5	1.3	3.0
Over life of contract [2]	4.2	5.0	4.7	4.2	3.0	2.0	2.4	3.2
Local government: First year	5.3	5.0	5.2	5.0	2.5	1.7	1.0	2.5
Over life of contract [2]	5.5	5.5	5.4	5.2	2.7	2.1	1.9	3.0
Number of workers affected (mil.) [4]	1.3	1.1	1.1	0.9	0.8	1.2	1.7	1.2
State government	0.5	0.4	0.5	0.2	0.4	0.6	0.6	0.4
Local government	0.8	0.7	0.6	0.7	0.4	0.6	1.1	0.8
Wage rate changes, all agreements [5]	4.9	4.7	5.1	4.6	2.6	1.9	2.8	3.3
Source: Current settlements	2.7	2.3	2.5	2.0	0.6	0.8	1.6	1.4
Prior settlements	2.2	2.4	2.6	2.6	1.8	1.1	1.1	1.9
Cost-of-living adjustments	(Z)	(Z)	(Z)	(Z)	0.1	(Z)	(Z)	(Z)
State government	4.3	4.1	4.0	4.7	2.5	1.6	3.4	1.1
Local government	5.3	5.1	5.9	4.6	2.6	2.1	2.2	1.7

Z Less than .05 percent. [1] Data relate to settlements of 5,000 workers or more in each calendar year, whether wages and benefits were changed or not. [2] Average annual rate of change. [3] Data relate to settlements covering 1,000 workers or more in each calendar year but exclude possible changes in wages under cost-of-living adjustment (COLA) clauses, except increases guaranteed by the contract. Includes all settlements, whether wages were changed or not. [4] Number of workers covered by settlements reached in each calendar year. [5] Data relate to all wage changes implemented in the year stemming from settlements reached in the year, deferred from prior-year agreements, and cost-of-living clauses.

Source: U.S. Bureau of Labor Statistics, *Current Wage Developments*, monthly.

No. 512. State and Local Government Full-Time Equivalent Employment, by Selected Function and State: 1992

[**In thousands,** for **October.** Local government amounts are estimates subject to sampling variation; see Appendix III and source]

STATE	EDUCATION				HEALTH AND HOSPITALS		HIGHWAYS		POLICE AND FIRE PROTECTION		PUBLIC WELFARE	
	Total		Higher education									
	State	Local	State	Local	State	Local	State	Local	State [1]	Local	State	Local
United States..	**1,412.4**	**5,243.1**	**1,285.7**	**261.3**	**685.8**	**736.3**	**257.3**	**286.5**	**86.2**	**887.7**	**211.7**	**261.0**
Alabama.........	34.1	81.7	30.1	-	18.9	21.8	4.3	7.1	1.1	13.8	4.5	1.3
Alaska.........	9.3	11.8	5.9	-	0.8	0.1	3.0	0.6	0.4	1.7	1.7	0.2
Arizona.........	21.5	81.0	18.8	7.4	3.4	7.3	3.2	3.7	1.7	13.0	5.0	3.4
Arkansas........	17.5	53.7	14.9	-	8.8	4.4	4.0	3.3	0.9	6.4	3.6	0.4
California........	111.1	528.8	106.6	63.5	44.7	107.1	19.3	21.1	11.1	108.2	3.1	47.0
Colorado........	28.8	68.9	27.3	1.2	6.0	9.5	3.1	4.7	1.0	11.8	1.3	4.1
Connecticut......	15.1	61.4	12.4	-	12.7	1.8	3.7	3.6	1.5	11.8	4.2	2.0
Delaware........	6.7	12.1	6.4	-	3.6	0.2	1.4	0.6	0.7	1.5	1.6	0.1
District of Columbia .	(X)	12.8	(X)	1.5	(X)	7.6	(X)	0.9	(X)	7.0	(X)	1.9
Florida.........	39.3	252.0	36.7	20.3	28.7	42.2	10.9	13.9	3.8	57.7	9.7	5.3
Georgia........	37.5	152.9	32.8	0.6	29.4	44.8	6.2	7.0	2.1	24.7	7.5	0.8
Hawaii.........	28.9	-	7.1	-	6.2	0.1	0.9	1.1	-	5.1	1.2	0.1
Idaho.........	7.8	23.9	7.1	0.9	2.0	4.4	1.8	1.5	0.4	3.0	1.6	0.1
Illinois........	49.4	228.8	46.5	19.4	23.8	22.6	8.9	11.0	3.8	51.6	12.6	7.4
Indiana.........	50.1	113.8	45.2	0.0	13.4	23.5	4.8	5.8	1.8	17.0	5.4	2.9
Iowa.........	19.7	66.7	18.5	5.7	8.8	10.2	2.8	5.7	0.8	7.0	3.3	1.7
Kansas.........	20.6	67.6	19.9	5.7	8.4	8.3	3.7	5.1	1.0	8.3	1.7	0.7
Kentucky........	32.3	80.7	28.1	-	7.7	8.5	5.8	3.0	1.7	8.7	4.9	0.6
Louisiana........	31.0	96.1	27.4	0.2	23.9	12.1	5.6	5.0	1.1	15.0	5.9	0.6
Maine.........	7.1	30.0	5.7	-	2.9	1.2	2.8	1.7	0.6	3.6	1.9	0.2
Maryland........	22.1	92.9	20.2	7.3	13.0	3.1	5.1	5.2	2.3	18.4	7.1	1.8
Massachusetts.....	21.5	105.6	20.7	0.1	20.5	8.9	4.7	5.6	2.0	27.5	7.3	1.8
Michigan........	67.2	202.9	65.2	12.4	14.9	21.3	3.9	8.9	3.1	25.0	12.8	2.8
Minnesota.......	34.8	90.6	33.2	2.6	9.4	17.8	5.1	7.4	0.8	10.7	1.7	10.2
Mississippi.......	15.9	67.0	14.5	5.0	10.9	15.2	3.5	4.4	0.9	7.3	3.2	0.3
Missouri.........	22.5	103.0	20.5	4.6	15.3	11.4	6.3	6.0	1.9	17.8	6.8	2.4
Montana.........	6.3	26.0	5.6	0.2	1.8	0.8	1.9	1.3	0.4	2.1	1.2	0.9
Nebraska........	10.7	38.4	9.9	2.5	4.9	4.6	2.4	3.1	0.7	4.4	2.6	1.3
Nevada.........	6.3	23.6	6.0	-	1.5	3.9	1.4	1.0	0.5	5.6	1.0	0.3
New Hampshire....	5.5	22.3	5.2	-	1.8	0.2	1.9	1.4	0.4	3.9	1.1	2.3
New Jersey......	33.9	170.6	27.3	8.6	22.4	10.6	8.3	10.4	3.7	34.4	5.9	11.1
New Mexico......	17.6	38.2	16.7	1.8	7.5	2.6	2.7	1.5	0.6	5.3	2.0	0.4
New York........	48.3	409.0	42.7	18.9	71.8	85.1	14.9	35.6	5.5	83.2	7.4	57.0
North Carolina.....	41.8	151.6	38.8	13.4	17.8	28.6	12.1	3.1	3.1	19.8	1.2	11.8
North Dakota.....	7.1	13.3	6.8	-	3.2	0.2	1.1	1.1	0.2	1.4	0.2	0.9
Ohio.........	68.3	205.7	66.0	4.3	22.2	30.8	8.9	13.0	2.3	37.3	2.1	23.0
Oklahoma........	25.6	75.6	23.6	-	11.6	8.1	3.5	5.4	1.7	10.8	7.9	0.3
Oregon.........	15.3	64.1	14.1	6.8	7.6	5.1	3.9	3.8	1.1	8.5	4.4	0.7
Pennsylvania.....	50.8	213.8	48.1	8.1	25.6	5.1	12.7	10.5	5.3	29.3	9.8	21.9
Rhode Island.....	6.7	17.4	5.8	-	2.8	0.1	1.0	0.9	0.3	4.8	1.6	0.1
South Carolina....	29.0	74.6	26.1	-	16.7	14.5	5.2	2.0	1.8	10.0	5.0	0.1
South Dakota.....	4.7	17.0	4.3	-	2.1	0.7	1.3	1.5	0.3	1.6	1.1	0.3
Tennessee.......	30.6	87.9	28.6	-	14.2	20.9	4.8	6.7	1.5	16.8	4.7	3.6
Texas.........	86.7	459.7	81.9	27.2	51.1	58.9	14.3	17.2	3.0	63.1	15.5	2.6
Utah.........	20.0	33.6	19.2	-	5.5	2.0	1.8	1.4	0.6	4.4	2.6	0.5
Vermont........	4.8	13.5	4.5	-	1.0	-	1.1	1.0	0.5	1.0	1.1	0.0
Virginia.........	45.7	137.3	42.5	-	25.0	8.5	11.3	3.9	2.4	19.7	2.4	8.1
Washington.......	41.0	89.5	39.3	-	14.2	11.6	6.2	6.4	1.9	15.3	7.5	1.0
West Virginia......	13.0	50.8	11.5	-	3.2	4.4	5.8	0.9	0.8	3.1	2.3	-
Wisconsin.......	37.6	107.4	36.3	9.4	10.1	10.3	2.1	8.7	0.9	16.6	1.2	13.1
Wyoming........	3.3	15.5	3.2	1.7	2.1	3.3	1.9	0.8	0.2	1.7	0.3	0.1

- Represents or rounds to zero.   X Not applicable.   [1] For State government, represents police protection only.

Source: U.S. Bureau of the Census, *Public Employment,* series GE, No. 1, annual.

No. 513. State and Local Government Employment and Average Earnings, by State: 1986 and 1992

[For October]

STATE	FULL-TIME EQUIVALENT EMPLOYMENT (1,000)				FULL-TIME EQUIVALENT EMPLOYMENT PER 10,000 POPULATION [2]				AVERAGE OCTOBER EARNINGS [3] (dol.)			
	State		Local [1]		State		Local [1]		State		Local [1]	
	1986	1992	1986	1992	1986	1992	1986	1992	1986	1992	1986	1992
United States.....	3,437	3,856	8,415	9,513	143	151	349	373	2,052	2,621	1,992	2,539
Alabama............	70	81	131	154	174	196	324	373	1,884	2,243	1,532	1,830
Alaska.............	21	24	20	22	393	413	377	371	3,228	3,258	3,324	3,590
Arizona............	43	54	119	145	128	141	358	379	2,126	2,361	2,185	2,557
Arkansas...........	39	47	71	82	163	194	299	342	1,724	2,195	1,388	1,724
California..........	279	323	965	1,108	104	104	358	359	2,751	3,420	2,535	3,281
Colorado...........	50	53	122	132	155	153	375	381	2,368	3,016	2,017	2,450
Connecticut........	56	54	95	97	175	165	297	296	2,336	3,286	2,089	3,160
Delaware...........	17	20	16	18	272	293	252	254	1,795	2,463	1,991	2,669
District of Columbia	(X)	(X)	51	55	(X)	(X)	817	928	(X)	(X)	2,594	3,175
Florida............	124	164	407	500	106	122	348	370	1,748	2,202	1,872	2,294
Georgia............	91	114	239	283	149	170	391	419	1,811	2,075	1,589	1,968
Hawaii	41	51	12	14	389	437	113	120	1,844	2,554	2,010	3,031
Idaho.............	18	20	33	40	175	190	332	373	1,766	2,265	1,535	1,943
Illinois............	130	137	385	431	113	117	333	370	2,165	2,642	2,166	2,672
Indiana............	75	95	182	202	136	168	330	358	2,056	2,506	1,686	2,199
Iowa	57	47	101	108	199	168	355	386	2,049	2,895	1,735	2,179
Kansas............	43	48	96	109	174	190	390	433	1,687	2,191	1,700	2,133
Kentucky	63	76	102	121	170	203	275	322	1,651	2,349	1,596	1,980
Louisiana..........	86	89	151	161	191	207	337	375	1,673	2,227	1,494	1,800
Maine.............	20	22	36	43	168	178	307	349	1,714	2,437	1,590	2,101
Maryland	80	82	143	158	178	167	321	321	2,046	2,720	2,233	2,892
Massachusetts......	88	85	192	192	151	142	329	321	2,034	2,645	2,082	2,775
Michigan...........	128	138	315	323	140	146	344	342	2,541	3,134	2,329	2,906
Minnesota..........	61	67	137	173	145	150	326	385	2,428	3,101	2,318	2,673
Mississippi.........	42	47	95	108	161	181	364	412	1,430	2,000	1,324	1,608
Missouri...........	66	74	157	174	130	143	310	334	1,621	2,075	1,826	2,133
Montana...........	16	17	29	37	192	207	349	451	1,864	2,300	1,727	1,995
Nebraska	29	29	65	71	184	179	407	441	1,509	2,185	1,785	2,198
Nevada	15	19	33	47	154	144	343	353	1,990	2,738	2,140	2,772
New Hampshire	18	16	29	36	172	147	285	320	1,759	2,416	1,701	2,456
New Jersey.........	96	116	283	302	126	149	372	387	2,278	3,100	2,146	3,062
New Mexico	34	42	49	60	231	267	332	381	1,792	2,253	1,680	1,858
New York	272	267	810	884	153	148	456	488	2,355	3,143	2,266	3,147
North Carolina	93	109	216	260	147	159	341	380	1,935	2,413	1,662	2,092
North Dakota........	15	16	22	21	222	259	318	331	1,805	2,231	2,017	2,269
Ohio..............	122	140	365	399	113	127	340	363	1,984	2,691	1,911	2,417
Oklahoma..........	64	67	109	121	195	209	329	376	1,733	2,044	1,595	1,903
Oregon............	44	50	91	106	163	167	338	354	1,975	2,607	2,018	2,599
Pennsylvania........	124	143	340	367	104	119	286	305	1,915	2,696	1,976	2,622
Rhode Island........	19	20	24	28	195	198	245	276	2,041	2,817	2,215	2,832
South Carolina	69	78	109	124	204	216	322	344	1,705	2,098	1,558	1,970
South Dakota	13	14	23	26	177	190	330	361	1,684	2,166	1,441	1,833
Tennessee	71	76	157	178	147	151	327	354	1,746	2,153	1,554	2,004
Texas.............	193	240	633	748	115	136	379	424	1,927	2,351	1,748	2,107
Utah	33	40	47	53	197	219	283	294	1,842	2,100	1,900	2,204
Vermont	11	13	15	18	211	227	270	309	1,842	2,514	1,653	2,240
Virginia............	102	116	195	229	177	182	336	359	1,895	2,270	1,787	2,322
Washington.........	79	98	143	177	177	191	320	345	2,231	2,760	2,134	2,738
West Virginia	34	34	61	59	180	185	317	324	1,574	1,969	1,625	2,002
Wisconsin..........	74	73	168	189	154	145	351	377	2,128	3,216	2,035	2,594
Wyoming	11	12	25	25	213	242	494	543	1,924	2,055	1,967	2,202

X Not applicable.   [1] Estimates subject to sampling variation; see Appendix III and source.   [2] Based on estimated resident population as of July 1.   [3] For full-time employees.

Source: U.S. Bureau of the Census, *Public Employment*, series GE, No. 1, annual.

No. 514. City Government Employment and Payroll: 1980 to 1992

[For **October**. Includes only those school systems operated as part of the city government. 1982 and 1987 based on complete census of all cities; other years based on sample and subject to sampling variation]

YEAR	ALL EMPLOYEES, FULL-TIME AND PART-TIME (1,000)		OCTOBER PAYROLLS (mil. dol.)		ANNUAL		FULL-TIME EQUIVALENT EMPLOYMENT [1] (1,000)			AVERAGE EARNINGS IN OCTOBER, FULL-TIME EMPLOYEES (dol.)	
	Total	Excl. education	Total	Excl. education	All employees	October payroll	Total	Education	Other	Education	Other
1980	2,561	2,130	2,942	2,403	[2]0.3	[2]7.8	2,166	360	1,806	1,501	1,338
1981	2,469	2,056	3,222	2,640	-3.6	9.5	2,111	346	1,765	1,686	1,500
1982	2,396	2,015	3,428	2,861	-2.9	6.4	2,088	317	1,770	1,791	1,625
1983	2,423	2,051	3,640	3,059	1.1	6.2	2,060	300	1,760	1,962	1,739
1984	2,434	2,070	3,872	3,268	0.4	6.4	2,090	300	1,790	2,033	1,831
1985	2,467	2,102	4,191	3,536	1.4	8.2	(NA)	(NA)	(NA)	2,117	1,953
1986	2,494	2,126	4,407	3,724	1.1	5.1	2,181	320	1,860	2,186	2,044
1987	2,493	2,110	4,770	3,977	(Z)	8.2	2,223	337	1,885	2,406	2,163
1988	2,570	2,188	4,979	4,136	3.1	4.4	2,251	342	1,910	2,566	2,220
1989	2,569	2,190	5,274	4,405	(Z)	5.9	2,268	341	1,927	2,669	2,343
1990	2,642	2,237	5,564	4,675	2.8	5.5	2,295	338	1,957	2,683	2,449
1391	2,662	2,324	5,784	4,878	0.7	4.0	2,303	338	1,965	2,739	2,547
1992	2,665	2,312	6,207	5,146	0.1	7.3	2,340	371	1,969	2,931	2,683

NA Not available.   Z Less than .05 percent.   [1] Beginning 1986, data not comparable to previous years due to a change in how full-time equivalent is calculated; see text, section 9.   [2]Percent change from 1979.

Source: U.S. Bureau of the Census, *Compendium of Public Employment*, and *City Employment*, series GE, No. 2, annual.

No. 515. City Government Employment and Payroll, by Function: 1980 to 1992

[For **October**]

ITEM	EMPLOYEES (1,000)					OCTOBER PAYROLLS (mil. dol.)				
	All cities [1]				Cities with 75,000 population or more, [2] 1992	All cities [1]				Cities with 75,000 population or more, [2] 1992
	1980	1990	1991	1992		1980	1990	1991	1992	
Total	2,561	2,642	2,662	2,665	1,568	2,942	5,564	5,784	6,207	4,281
Full-time	2,071	2,149	2,153	2,197	1,418	2,826	5,334	5,543	5,980	4,178
Part-time	489	493	509	468	150	116	229	241	227	103
Full-time equivalent [3]	2,166	2,295	2,303	2,340	1,480	(X)	(X)	(X)	(X)	(X)
Education [4]	360	338	338	371	301	539	889	906	1,061	880
Percent of total	17	15	15	16	20	18	16	16	17	21
Instructional staff	266	264	262	261	209	436	754	765	848	698
Others	94	74	76	110	92	102	134	141	212	182
Libraries	34	45	45	45	27	38	80	84	86	57
Public welfare	41	57	58	55	49	47	118	116	132	121
Hospitals	131	124	124	125	82	143	282	297	301	217
Health	35	42	41	43	35	47	93	94	104	89
Highways	121	133	132	130	56	141	274	283	301	152
Police protection	365	412	418	423	234	550	1,093	1,162	1,249	783
Fire protection	190	199	201	200	117	300	579	603	642	416
Correction	18	35	36	36	34	27	90	94	108	103
Parks and recreation	103	121	123	123	71	116	211	222	232	141
Housing and community development	44	46	46	45	38	57	104	108	115	97
Sewerage	60	74	75	76	38	74	155	164	172	95
Solid waste management	104	86	85	83	49	118	174	177	193	135
Financial administration	69	74	75	74	35	85	164	169	179	96
Judicial, legal, other governmental administration	112	129	129	132	73	147	314	326	345	209
Local utilities [5]	209	226	226	226	144	306	594	619	615	439
Water supply	93	101	103	103	53	116	219	230	240	137
Electric power	44	51	51	51	28	67	142	149	159	101
Transit	66	66	65	64	60	115	217	224	198	191
Other	171	154	152	152	97	208	350	360	372	252

X Not applicable.   [1] Data are estimates subject to sampling variation; see Appendix III and source.   [2] Based on enumerated resident population as of April 1, 1990.   [3] 1980 data not directly comparable to later years due to a change in 1986 in how full-time equivalent was calculated; see text, section 9.   [4] City-operated schools and colleges only.   [5] Includes gas supply not shown separately.

Source: U.S. Bureau of the Census, *City Employment*, series GE, No. 2, annual.

No. 516. City Government Employment and Payroll—Largest Cities: 1980 and 1992

[**For October.** See footnote 2, table 504, for those areas representing city-county consolidated governments]

CITIES RANKED BY 1990 POPULATION	TOTAL EMPLOYMENT (1,000)		FULL-TIME EQUIVALENT EMPLOYMENT [1]				OCTOBER PAYROLL (mil. dol.)		AVERAGE EARNINGS IN OCTOBER, FULL-TIME EMPLOYEES (dol.)	
			Total (1,000)		Per 10,000 population [2]					
	1980	1992	1980	1992	1980	1992	1980	1992	1980	1992
New York, NY [3][4]	364	442	319	415	451	557	504	1,307	1,587	3,154
Los Angeles, CA	42	50	41	50	138	140	73	188	1,806	3,815
Chicago, IL	47	41	45	41	150	148	71	135	1,569	3,269
Houston, TX	18	21	18	21	111	129	26	51	1,499	2,404
Philadelphia, PA	33	31	32	30	189	189	51	92	1,611	3,092
San Diego, CA	8	11	7	9	81	93	12	29	1,773	2,894
Detroit, MI	22	19	22	19	179	180	40	49	1,852	2,700
Dallas, TX	14	14	14	14	153	137	20	36	1,465	2,642
Phoenix, AZ	9	11	9	11	114	110	14	32	1,517	3,104
San Antonio, TX	10	14	10	13	128	140	13	32	1,282	2,472
San Jose, CA [3][6]	[5]4	7	[5]4	6	[5]60	76	[5]7	24	[5]1,714	4,206
Baltimore, MD [3][6]	44	28	40	27	514	372	47	70	1,172	2,613
Indianapolis, IN	13	13	12	13	174	172	13	26	1,098	2,164
San Francisco, CA	21	26	21	26	310	354	37	99	1,761	3,881
Jacksonville, FL	[7]11	11	[7]11	10	[7]202	156	[7]11	27	[7]1,031	2,888
Columbus, OH	8	8	7	8	122	125	10	20	1,498	2,607
Milwaukee, WI	10	9	9	8	145	133	15	23	1,631	2,782
Memphis, TN [3]	25	24	22	22	342	366	29	53	1,335	2,361
Washington, DC [3][4]	45	48	42	46	651	763	73	138	1,761	3,022
Boston, MA [3]	[5]28	21	[5]25	21	[5]444	361	[5]35	61	[5]1,398	2,949
Seattle, WA	10	11	9	10	188	197	17	35	1,830	3,494
El Paso, TX	5	5	4	5	104	99	3	11	942	2,220
Cleveland, OH	10	9	9	8	160	167	13	20	1,460	2,742
New Orleans, LA	[8]13	10	[8]13	10	[8]225	149	[8]11	12	[8]919	1,623
Nashville-Davidson, TN [3]	[9]18	18	[9]17	17	[9]374	340	[9]22	40	[9]1,295	2,430
Denver, CO	13	14	12	12	244	266	18	35	1,540	2,859
Austin, TX	8	12	7	11	199	246	10	27	1,515	2,496
Fort Worth, TX	[7]5	5	[7]5	5	[7]120	114	[7]5	11	[7]1,198	2,277
Oklahoma City, OK	5	5	4	5	104	104	6	12	1,323	2,567
Portland, OR	5	[10]5	4	[10]5	115	[10]104	8	[10]15	1,916	[10]3,363
Kansas City, MO	7	[10]6	7	[10]6	145	[10]146	9	[10]16	1,368	[10]2,485
Long Beach, CA	[5]5	6	[5]4	5	[5]122	123	[5]7	18	[5]1,678	3,627
Tucson, AZ	4	5	4	5	124	118	6	12	1,474	2,645
St. Louis, MO	13	8	13	7	280	188	15	18	1,279	2,405
Charlotte, NC	4	5	4	5	125	115	5	11	1,290	2,436
Atlanta, GA	8	8	8	8	187	197	10	18	1,230	2,373
Virginia Beach, VA [3]	10	15	9	14	346	356	11	30	1,204	2,275
Albuquerque, NM	[7]4	7	[7]4	6	[7]119	147	[7]4	12	[7]1,135	2,100
Oakland, CA	4	6	4	5	109	130	7	17	2,011	3,985
Pittsburgh, PA	[8]6	7	[8]6	5	[8]135	145	[8]6	14	[8]1,116	3,092
Sacramento, CA	3	4	3	4	119	107	6	13	1,762	3,384
Minneapolis, MN	6	7	5	6	136	161	9	18	1,821	3,097
Tulsa, OK	[5]4	4	[5]4	4	[5]115	120	[5]5	11	[5]1,184	2,463
Honolulu, HI	9	11	9	9	117	111	12	29	1,401	3,139
Cincinnati, OH	7	8	7	7	174	191	10	20	1,527	3,092
Miami, FL	4	4	4	4	118	101	6	14	1,408	3,994
Fresno, CA	3	3	3	3	115	73	4	8	1,607	3,043
Omaha, NE	3	3	3	3	92	81	5	8	1,684	3,138
Toledo, OH	4	3	3	3	96	86	6	9	1,758	2,955
Buffalo, NY [3]	14	14	13	13	348	390	18	36	1,475	2,986
Wichita, KS	3	3	3	3	111	97	4	7	1,327	2,429
Santa Ana, CA	2	2	1	2	68	64	2	9	1,819	5,162
Mesa, AZ	1	2	1	2	89	82	2	7	1,592	2,908
Colorado Springs, CO	4	5	3	5	158	181	5	13	1,445	2,594
Tampa, FL	5	4	5	4	165	140	5	11	1,178	2,861
Newark, NJ [11]	12	3	12	4	374	139	17	12	1,387	3,220
St. Paul, MN	4	3	3	3	125	119	6	11	1,734	3,429
Louisville, KY	6	4	6	4	186	160	7	8	1,358	1,965
Anaheim, CA	2	1	2	3	91	98	3	10	1,616	4,235
Birmingham, AL	4	4	4	4	128	145	5	9	1,333	2,293
Arlington, TX	[7]1	2	[7]1	2	[7]63	73	[7]1	5	[7]1,180	2,721
Norfolk, VA [3]	11	11	10	10	380	394	12	24	1,222	2,349

[1] 1992 data not comparable with 1980 due to a change in 1986 in how full-time equivalent was calculated; see text, section 9.   [2] 1980 based on enumerated resident population as of April 1, 1980. 1992 based on enumerated resident population as of April 1, 1990.   [3] Includes city-operated elementary and secondary schools.   [4] Includes city-operated university or college.   [5] 1979 data.   [6] Prior to 1990, includes data for city operated colleges.   [7] 1978 data.   [8] 1977 data.   [9] Noneducation data are for 1979.   [10] 1991 data.   [11] Prior to 1983, city-operated elementary and secondary schools.

Source: U.S. Bureau of the Census, *City Employment,* series GE, No. 2, annual; and unpublished data.

Federal Government Finances and Employment

This section presents statistics relating to the financial structure and the civilian employment of the Federal Government. The fiscal data cover taxes, other receipts, outlays, and debt. The principal sources of fiscal data are *The Budget of the United States Government* and related documents, published annually by the Office of Management and Budget (OMB), and the Department of the Treasury's *United States Government Annual Report* and its *Appendix.* Detailed data on tax returns and collections are published annually by the Internal Revenue Service. Personnel data relating to staffing and payrolls for the various public functions and agencies, to employee characteristics, and to civil service status; are published by the Office of Personnel Management and the Bureau of Labor Statistics. The primary source for data on public lands is *Public Land Statistics,* published annually by the Bureau of Land Management, Department of the Interior. Data on federally owned land and real property are collected by the General Services Administration and presented in its annual *Inventory Report on Real Property Owned by the United States Throughout the World.*

Budget concept.—Under the unified budget concept, all Federal monies are included in one comprehensive budget. These monies comprise both Federal funds and trust funds. Federal funds are derived mainly from taxes and borrowing and are not restricted by law to any specific government purpose. Trust funds, such as the Unemployment Trust Fund, collect certain taxes and other receipts for use in carrying out specific purposes or programs in accordance with the terms of the trust agreement or statute. Fund balances include both cash balances with Treasury and investments in U.S. securities. Part of the balance is obligated, part unobligated. Prior to 1985, the budget totals, under provisions of law, excluded some Federal activities— including the Federal Financing Bank, the Postal Service, the Synthetic Fuels Corporation, and the lending activities of

In Brief	
	1995
Gross Federal debt	$4,962 bil.
Net interest on the public debt	$334 bil.

the Rural Electrification Administration. The Balanced Budget and Emergency Deficit Control Act of 1985 (P.L.99-177) repealed the off-budget status of these entities and placed social security (Federal old-age and survivors insurance and the Federal disability insurance trust funds) off-budget. Though social security is now off-budget and, by law, excluded from coverage of the congressional budget resolutions, it continues to be a Federal program.

Receipts arising from the Government's sovereign powers are reported as governmental receipts; all other receipts, i.e., from business-type or market-oriented activities, are offset against outlays. Outlays are reported on a checks-issued (net) basis (i.e., outlays are recorded at the time the checks to pay bills are issued).

Debt concept.—For most of U.S. history, the total debt consisted of debt borrowed by the Treasury (i.e., public debt). The present debt series includes both public debt and agency debt. The *gross Federal debt* includes money borrowed by the Treasury and by various Federal agencies; it is the broadest generally used measure of the Federal debt. *Total public debt* is covered by a statutory debt limitation and includes only borrowing by the Treasury.

Treasury receipts and outlays.—All receipts of the Government, with a few exceptions, are deposited to the credit of the U.S. Treasury regardless of ultimate disposition. Under the Constitution, no money may be withdrawn from the Treasury unless appropriated by the Congress.

The day-to-day cash operations of the Federal Government clearing through the accounts of the U.S. Treasury are reported in the *Daily Treasury Statement.* Extensive detail on the public debt is published in the *Monthly Statement of the Public Debt of the United States.*

Budget receipts such as taxes, customs duties, and outlays represented by checks issued and cash payments made by disbursing officers as well as government agencies are reported in the *Daily Treasury Statement of Receipts and Outlays of the United States Government* and in the Treasury's *United States Government Annual Report* and its *Appendix.* These deposits in and payments from accounts maintained by Government agencies are on the same basis as the unified budget.

The quarterly *Treasury Bulletin* contains data on fiscal operations and related Treasury activities, including financial statements of Government corporations and other business-type activities.

Income tax returns and tax collections.—Tax data are compiled by the Internal Revenue Service of the Treasury Department. The *Annual Report of the Commissioner and Chief Counsel of the Internal Revenue Service* gives a detailed account of tax collections by kind of tax and by regions, districts, and States. The agency's annual *Statistics of Income* reports present detailed data from individual income tax returns and corporation income tax returns. The quarterly *Statistics of Income Bulletin* has, in general, replaced the supplemental *Statistics of Income* publications which presented data on such diverse subjects as tax-exempt organizations, unincorporated businesses, fiduciary income tax and estate tax returns, sales of capital assets by individuals, international income and taxes reported by corporations and individuals, and estate tax wealth.

Employment and payrolls.—The Office of Personnel Management collects employment and payroll data from all departments and agencies of the Federal Government, except the Central Intelligence Agency, the National Security Agency, and the Defense Intelligence Agency. Employment figures represent the number of persons who occupied civilian positions at the end of the report month shown and who are paid for personal services rendered for the Federal Government, regardless of the nature of appointment or method of payment.

Federal payrolls include all payments for personal services rendered during the report month and payments for accumulated annual leave of employees who separate from the service. Since most Federal employees are paid on a biweekly basis, the calendar month earnings are partially estimated on the basis of the number of work days in each month where payroll periods overlap.

Federal employment and payroll figures are published by the Office of Personnel Management in its *Federal Civilian Workforce Statistics—Employment and Trends.* It also publishes biennial employment data for minority groups, data on occupations of white- and blue-collar workers, and data on employment by geographic area; reports on salary and wage distribution of Federal employees are published annually. General schedule is primarily white-collar; wage system primarily blue-collar. Data on Federal employment are also issued by the Bureau of Labor Statistics in its *Monthly Labor Review* and in *Employment and Earnings* and by the Bureau of the Census in its annual *Public Employment.*

Public lands.—These data refer to transactions which involve the disposal, under public land laws, of Federal public lands to non-Federal owners. In general, original entries and selections are applications to secure title to public lands which have been accepted as properly filed (i.e., allowed). Some types of applications, however, are not reported until issuance of the final certificate, which passes equitable title to the land to the applicant. Applications are approved when full compliance with the requirements of the laws is shown and become final entries (perfected entries) upon issuance of a final certificate. Patents are Government deeds which pass legal title to the land to the applicant. Certifications are issued in lieu of patents in connection with certain State selections.

Historical statistics.—Tabular headnotes provide cross-references, where applicable, to *Historical Statistics of the United States, Colonial Times to 1970.* See Appendix IV.

Figure 10.1
The Government of the United States
(As of July 1, 1993)

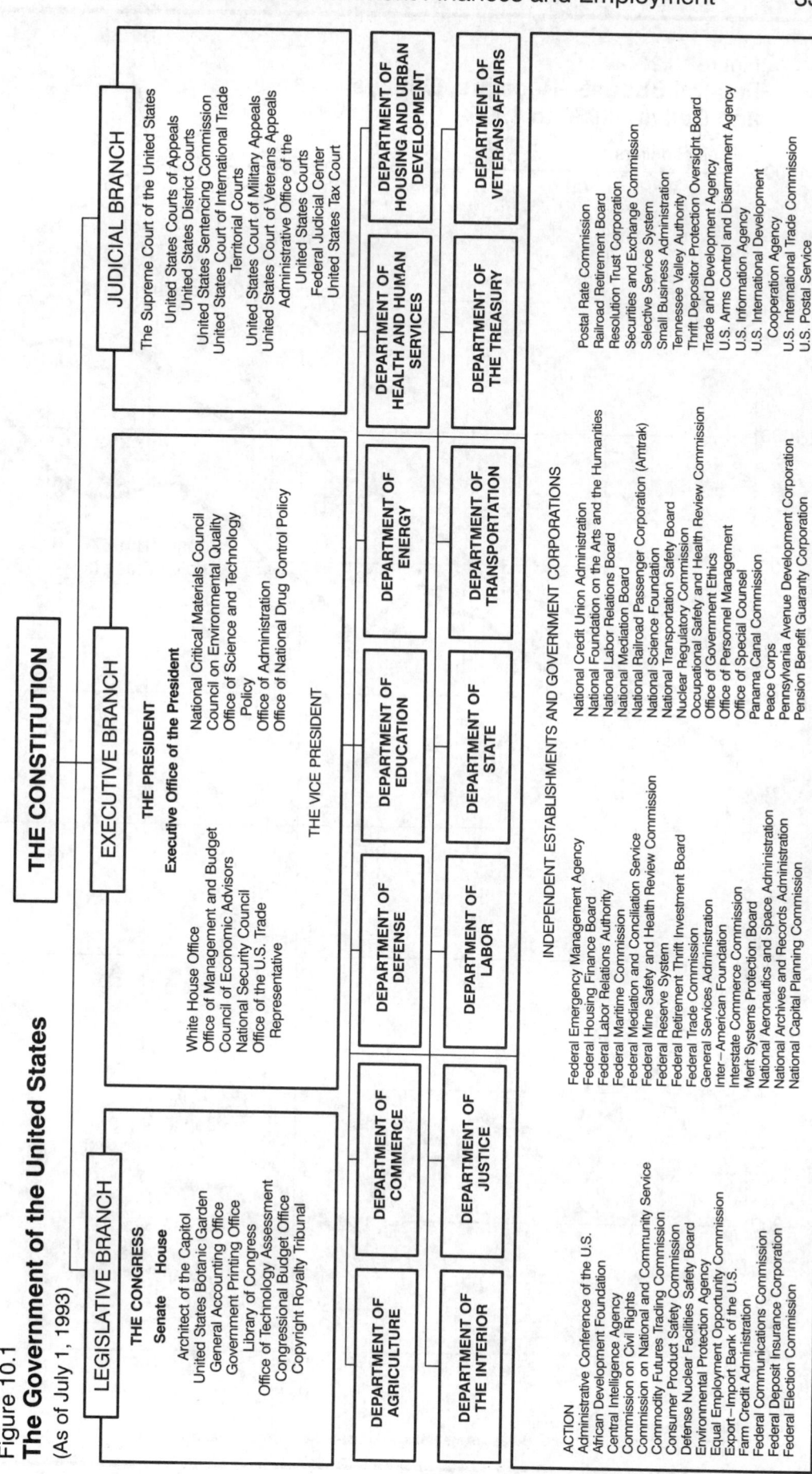

Source: Chart prepared by U.S. Bureau of the Census.

Figure 10.2
Federal Budget—Receipts, Outlays, and Deficit: 1970 to 1995

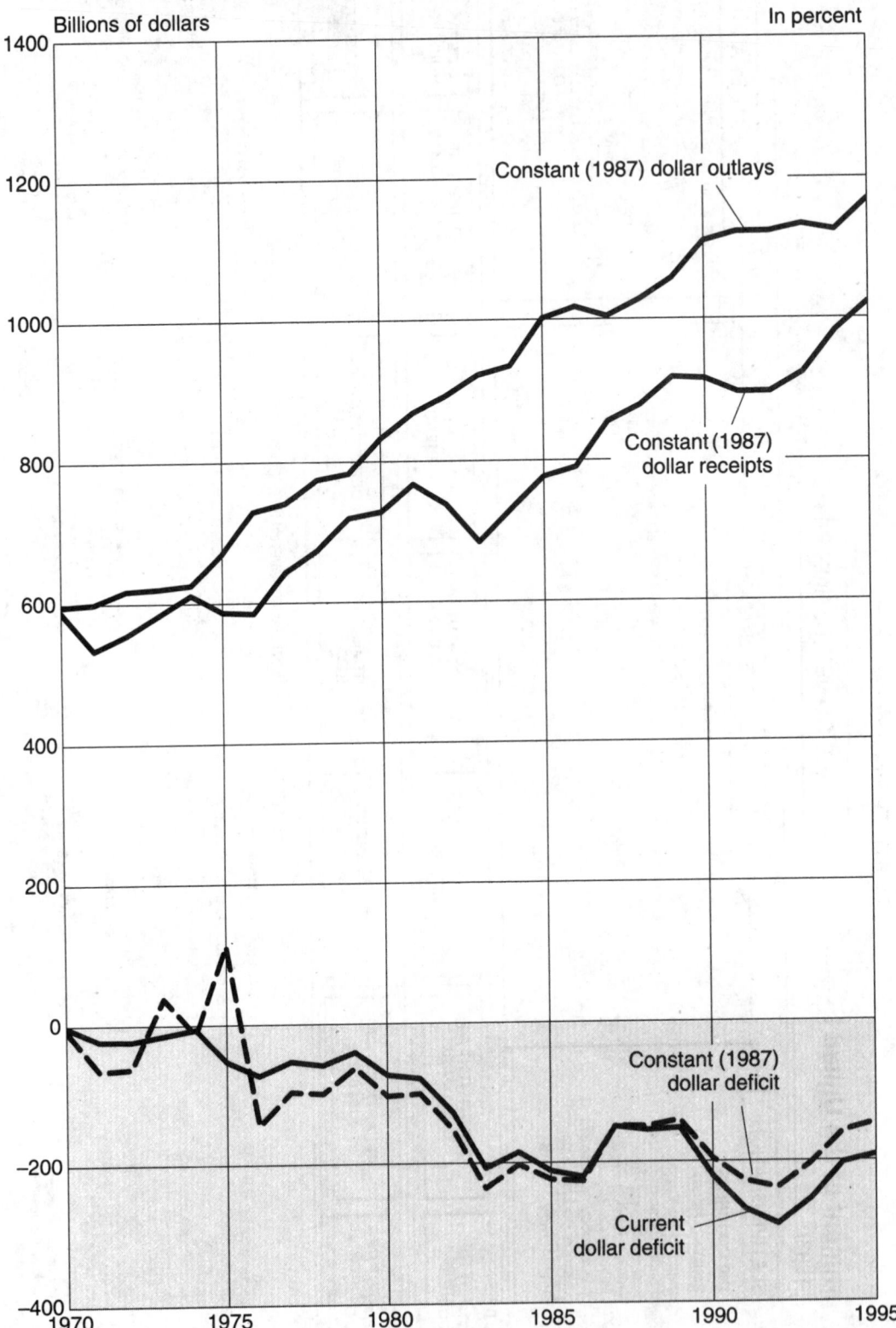

Billions of dollars

In percent

Constant (1987) dollar outlays

Constant (1987) dollar receipts

Constant (1987) dollar deficit

Current dollar deficit

Note: Data for 1995 is estimated.
Source: Chart prepared by U.S. Bureau of the Census. For data, see tables 517 and 521.

No. 517. Federal Budget—Summary: 1945 to 1995

[In millions of dollars, except percent. For fiscal years ending in year shown; see text, section 9. The Balanced Budget and Emergency Deficit Control Act of 1985 put all the previously off-budget Federal entities into the budget and moved Social Security off-budget. Minus sign (-) indicates deficit or decrease]

YEAR	Receipts[1]	Outlays[1] Total	Outlays Human resources	Outlays National defense	Outlays Percent of GDP[2]	Surplus or deficit (-)	Gross federal debt[3] Total	Held by Federal Gov't Account	Held by The public	Held by Federal Reserve System	As percent of GDP[2]	Annual % change Receipts	Annual % change Outlays	Annual % change Gross Federal debt[3]	Outlays, off-budget
1945	45,159	92,712	1,859	82,965	43.7	-47,553	260,123	24,941	235,182	21,792	122.7	3.2	1.5	27.5	143
1950	39,443	42,562	14,221	13,724	16.0	-3,119	256,853	37,830	219,023	18,331	96.6	0.1	9.6	1.7	524
1955	65,451	68,444	14,908	42,729	17.8	-2,993	274,366	47,751	226,616	23,607	71.3	-6.0	-3.4	1.3	3,983
1960	92,492	92,191	26,184	48,130	18.3	301	290,525	53,686	236,840	26,523	57.6	16.7	0.1	1.1	10,850
1965	116,817	118,228	36,576	50,620	17.6	-1,411	322,318	61,540	260,778	39,100	48.0	3.7	-0.3	2.0	16,529
1970	192,807	195,649	75,349	81,692	19.9	-2,842	380,921	97,723	283,198	57,714	38.7	3.2	6.5	4.1	27,607
1972	207,309	230,681	107,211	79,174	20.1	-23,373	435,936	113,559	322,377	71,426	38.0	10.8	9.8	6.8	36,857
1973	230,799	245,707	119,522	76,681	19.3	-14,908	466,291	125,381	340,910	75,181	36.6	11.3	6.5	7.0	45,589
1974	263,224	269,359	135,783	79,347	19.2	-6,135	483,893	140,194	343,699	80,648	34.5	14.0	9.6	3.8	52,089
1975	279,090	332,332	173,245	86,509	22.0	-53,242	541,925	147,225	394,700	84,993	35.9	6.0	23.4	12.0	60,440
1976	298,060	371,792	189,524	89,619	22.1	-73,732	628,970	151,566	477,404	94,714	37.3	6.8	11.9	16.1	69,609
1976[5]	81,232	95,975	52,065	22,269	21.6	-14,744	643,561	148,052	495,505	96,702	36.2	(X)	(X)	(X)	19,421
1977	355,559	409,218	221,895	97,241	21.3	-53,659	706,398	157,295	549,103	105,004	36.8	19.3	10.1	12.3	80,716
1978	399,561	458,746	242,329	104,495	21.3	-59,186	776,602	169,477	607,125	115,480	36.0	12.4	12.1	9.9	89,657
1979	463,302	504,032	267,574	116,342	20.7	-40,729	829,470	189,162	640,308	115,594	34.1	16.0	9.8	6.7	99,978
1980	517,112	590,947	313,374	133,995	22.3	-73,835	909,050	199,212	709,838	120,846	34.4	11.6	17.4	9.6	114,329
1981	599,272	678,249	362,022	157,513	22.9	-78,976	994,845	209,507	785,338	124,466	33.6	15.9	14.8	9.4	135,196
1982	617,766	745,755	388,681	185,309	23.9	-127,989	1,137,345	217,560	919,785	134,497	36.4	3.1	10.0	14.3	131,151
1983	600,562	808,380	426,003	209,903	24.4	-207,818	1,371,710	240,114	1,131,596	155,527	41.4	-2.8	8.4	20.6	147,108
1984	666,457	851,846	432,042	227,413	23.1	-185,388	1,564,657	264,159	1,300,498	155,122	42.3	11.0	5.4	14.1	165,813
1985	734,057	946,391	471,822	252,748	23.9	-212,334	1,817,521	317,612	1,499,908	169,806	45.8	10.1	11.1	16.2	176,807
1986	769,091	990,336	481,594	273,375	23.5	-221,245	2,120,629	383,919	1,736,709	190,855	50.3	4.8	4.6	16.7	183,498
1987	854,143	1,003,911	502,196	281,999	22.5	-149,769	2,346,125	457,444	1,888,680	212,040	52.7	11.1	1.4	10.6	193,832
1988	908,954	1,064,140	533,404	290,361	22.1	-155,187	2,601,307	550,507	2,050,799	229,218	54.1	6.4	6.0	10.9	202,691
1989	990,691	1,143,172	568,668	303,559	22.1	-152,481	2,868,039	678,157	2,189,882	220,088	55.4	9.0	7.4	10.3	210,911
1990	1,031,321	1,252,705	619,329	299,331	22.9	-221,384	3,206,564	795,841	2,410,722	234,410	58.5	4.1	9.6	11.8	225,065
1991	1,054,272	1,323,441	689,666	273,292	23.3	-269,169	3,598,498	910,362	2,688,137	258,591	63.4	2.2	5.7	12.2	241,687
1992	1,090,453	1,380,856	772,440	298,350	23.3	-290,403	4,002,136	1,003,302	2,998,834	296,397	67.6	3.4	4.3	11.2	252,339
1993	1,153,535	1,408,675	827,535	291,086	22.5	-255,140	4,351,416	1,103,945	3,247,471	325,653	69.5	5.8	2.0	8.7	266,587
1994	1,257,745	1,460,914	869,418	281,563	22.0	-203,169	4,643,711	1,211,498	3,432,213	355,150	70.0	9.0	3.7	6.7	279,372
1995, est.	1,346,414	1,538,920	926,000	271,600	21.9	-192,506	4,961,529	1,321,380	3,640,149	(NA)	70.6	7.0	5.3	6.8	291,984

NA Not available. X Not applicable. [1] Includes off-budget receipts and outlays. [2] Gross domestic product as of fiscal year; for calendar year GDP, see section 14. [3] See text, section 10, for discussion of debt concept. [4] Change from previous year. [5] Represents transition quarter, July-Sept.

Source: U.S. Office of Management and Budget, Historical Tables, annual.

No. 518. Federal Receipts, by Source: 1980 to 1995

[In millions of dollars. For fiscal years ending in year shown; see text, section 9. Receipts reflect collections. Covers both Federal funds and trust funds; see text, section 10. Excludes government-sponsored but privately-owned corporations, Federal Reserve System, District of Columbia government, and money held in suspense as deposit funds. See *Historical Statistics, Colonial Times to 1970,* series Y 343-351, and Y 472-487 for related data]

SOURCE	1980	1990	1991	1992	1993	1994	1995, est.
Total receipts [1]	517,112	1,031,321	1,054,272	1,090,453	1,153,535	1,257,745	1,346,414
Individual income taxes	244,069	466,884	467,827	475,964	509,680	543,055	588,460
Corporation income taxes	64,600	93,507	98,086	100,270	117,520	140,385	150,864
Social insurance	157,803	380,047	396,016	413,689	428,300	461,475	484,409
Employment taxes and contributions	138,748	353,891	370,526	385,491	396,939	428,810	451,794
Old-age and survivors insurance	96,581	255,031	265,503	273,137	281,735	302,607	284,189
Disability insurance	16,628	26,625	28,382	29,289	30,199	32,419	67,067
Hospital insurance	23,217	68,556	72,842	79,108	81,224	90,062	96,657
Railroad retirement/ pension fund	2,323	2,292	2,371	2,449	2,367	2,323	2,386
Railroad social security equivalent account	-	1,387	1,428	1,508	1,414	1,399	1,495
Unemployment insurance	15,336	21,635	20,922	23,410	26,556	28,004	28,057
Other retirement contributions	3,719	4,522	4,568	4,788	4,805	4,661	4,558
Excise taxes [1]	24,329	35,345	42,402	45,569	48,057	55,225	57,600
Federal funds	15,563	15,591	18,275	21,836	24,522	31,226	28,992
Alcohol	5,601	5,695	7,364	8,011	7,583	7,539	7,551
Tobacco	2,443	4,081	4,706	5,049	5,875	5,691	5,657
Ozone depletion	-	360	562	637	854	761	717
Trust funds [1]	8,766	19,754	24,127	23,733	23,535	23,999	28,608
Highways	6,620	13,867	16,979	16,733	18,039	16,668	20,665
Airport and airway	1,874	3,700	4,910	4,645	3,262	5,189	5,562
Black lung disability	272	665	652	626	634	567	636
Hazardous substance response	-	818	810	818	826	807	842
Aquatic resources	-	218	260	271	276	301	301
Leaking underground storage	-	122	123	157	153	152	155
Vaccine injury compensations	-	159	81	118	38	179	140
Oil spill liability	-	143	254	295	229	48	204
Estate and gift taxes	6,389	11,500	11,138	11,143	12,577	15,225	15,587
Customs duties	7,174	16,707	15,949	17,359	18,802	20,099	20,913
Federal Reserve deposits	11,767	24,319	19,158	22,920	14,908	18,023	24,559

- Represents or rounds to zero.   [1] Totals reflect interfund and intragovernmental transactions and/or other functions, not shown separately.

Source: U.S. Office of Management and Budget, *Historical Tables,* annual.

No. 519. Federal Trust Fund Receipts, Outlays, and Balances: 1993 to 1995

[In billions of dollars. For fiscal years ending in year shown; see text, section 9. Receipts deposited. Outlays on a checks-issued basis less refunds collected. Balances: That which have not been spent. See text, section 10, for discussion of the budget concept and trust funds]

DESCRIPTION	INCOME			OUTLAYS			BALANCES [1]		
	1993	1994	1995, est.	1993	1994	1995, est.	1993	1994	1995, est.
Total [2]	702	749	783	602	653	684	1,080	1,181	1,281
Airport and airway trust fund	4	6	7	7	7	7	13	12	12
Federal employees retirement funds	63	65	67	35	37	38	319	346	375
Federal old-age, survivors and disability insurance trust funds	351	378	399	305	321	339	374	423	483
Foreign military sales trust fund	13	13	13	13	13	14	7	6	6
Health insurance trust funds	156	164	173	146	163	177	149	151	146
Medicare: Hospital insurance	(NA)	106	115	(NA)	103	112	(NA)	130	133
Supplemental medical insurance	(NA)	57	58	(NA)	60	66	(NA)	21	13
Transportation	(NA)	24	28	(NA)	29	29	(NA)	30	30
Surface transportation	(NA)	18	22	(NA)	22	22	(NA)	18	18
Federal employees health benefits	(NA)	16	16	(NA)	16	16	(NA)	8	8
Military retirement trust funds	35	35	34	26	27	27	98	120	127
Railroad retirement trust funds	11	11	12	11	11	11	12	12	13
Unemployment trust funds	41	34	32	40	31	26	37	40	47
Veterans life insurance trust funds	2	2	2	1	2	2	13	14	14
Other trust funds [3]	8	10	11	4	8	9	36	32	34

NA Not available.   [1] Balances available on a cash basis (rather than an authorization basis) at the end of the year. Balances are primarily invested in Federal debt securities.   [2] Includes funds not shown separately.   [3] Effective August 9, 1989, the permanent insurance fund of the FDIC was classified under law as a Federal fund.

Source: U.S. Office of Management and Budget, *Analytical Perspectives,* annual.

No. 520. Federal Budget Outlays—Defense, Human and Physical Resources, and Net Interest Payments: 1940 to 1995

[In millions of dollars. For fiscal year ending in year shown. Minus sign (-) indicates offsets]

YEAR	Outlays, total	National defense	HUMAN RESOURCES							PHYSICAL RESOURCES			Net interest	Other	Undistributed offsets
			Total	Social Security	Income security	Medicare	Health	Education[1]	Veterans benefits	Total[2]	Transportation	Commerce and housing			
1940	9,468	1,660	4,139	28	1,514	(NA)	55	1,972	570	2,312	392	550	899	775	-317
1945	92,712	82,965	1,859	267	1,137	(NA)	211	134	110	1,747	3,654	-2630	3,112	4,418	-1,389
1950	42,562	13,724	14,221	781	4,097	(NA)	268	241	8,834	3,667	967	1,035	4,812	7,955	-1,817
1955	68,444	42,729	14,908	4,427	5,071	(NA)	291	445	4,675	2,732	1,246	92	4,850	6,718	-3,493
1960	92,191	48,130	26,184	11,602	7,378	(NA)	795	968	5,441	7,991	4,126	1,618	6,947	7,760	-4,820
1965	118,228	50,620	36,576	17,460	9,462	(NA)	1,791	2,140	5,723	11,264	5,730	1,157	8,591	17,086	-5,908
1966	134,532	58,111	43,257	20,694	9,671	64	2,543	4,363	5,923	13,410	5,936	3,245	9,386	16,911	-6,542
1967	157,464	71,417	51,272	21,725	10,253	2,748	3,351	6,453	6,743	14,674	6,316	3,979	10,268	17,126	-7,294
1968	178,134	81,926	59,375	23,854	11,806	4,649	4,390	7,548	7,042	16,002	6,526	4,280	11,090	17,786	-8,045
1969	183,640	82,497	66,410	27,298	13,066	5,695	5,162	7,634	7,642	11,869	7,008	-119	12,699	18,151	-7,986
1970	195,649	81,692	75,349	30,270	15,645	6,622	5,907	8,634	8,679	15,574	8,052	2,112	14,380	17,286	-8,632
1971	210,172	78,872	91,901	35,872	22,936	7,479	6,843	9,849	9,778	18,286	8,392	2,366	14,841	16,379	-10,107
1972	230,681	79,174	107,211	40,157	27,638	8,052	8,674	12,529	10,732	19,574	9,066	2,222	15,478	18,828	-9,583
1973	245,707	76,681	119,522	49,090	28,264	9,639	9,356	12,745	12,015	20,614	9,172	931	17,349	24,950	-13,409
1974	269,359	79,347	135,783	55,867	33,699	12,875	10,733	16,022	13,388	25,106	10,918	4,705	21,449	24,423	-16,749
1975	332,332	86,509	173,245	64,658	50,160	15,834	12,930	18,910	16,599	35,449	13,739	9,947	23,244	27,487	-13,602
1976	371,792	89,619	203,594	73,899	60,784	15,834	15,734	18,910	18,433	39,188	13,739	7,619	26,727	27,050	-14,386
1976 [3]	95,975	22,269	52,065	19,763	14,981	4,264	3,924	5,169	3,963	9,512	3,358	931	6,949	9,388	-4,206
1977	409,218	97,241	221,895	85,061	61,044	19,345	17,302	21,104	18,038	40,746	14,829	3,093	29,901	34,315	-14,879
1978	458,746	104,495	242,329	93,861	61,488	22,768	18,524	26,710	18,978	52,591	15,521	6,254	35,458	39,594	-15,720
1979	504,032	116,342	267,574	104,073	66,359	26,495	20,494	30,223	19,931	54,559	17,532	4,686	42,636	40,396	-17,476
1980	590,947	133,995	313,374	118,547	86,540	32,090	23,169	31,843	21,185	65,985	21,329	9,390	52,538	44,996	-19,942
1981	678,249	157,513	362,022	139,584	99,723	39,149	26,866	33,709	22,991	70,886	23,379	8,206	68,774	47,095	-28,041
1982	745,755	185,309	388,681	155,964	107,717	46,567	27,445	27,029	23,958	61,752	20,625	6,256	85,044	51,069	-26,099
1983	808,380	209,903	426,003	170,724	122,598	52,588	28,641	26,606	24,846	57,600	21,334	6,681	89,828	59,023	-33,976
1984	851,846	227,413	432,042	178,223	112,668	57,540	30,417	27,579	25,614	57,938	23,669	6,917	111,123	55,287	-31,957
1985	946,391	252,748	471,822	188,623	128,200	65,822	33,542	29,342	26,292	56,789	25,838	4,229	129,504	68,227	-32,698
1986	990,336	273,375	481,594	198,757	119,796	70,164	35,936	30,585	26,356	58,614	28,117	4,890	136,047	73,713	-33,007
1987	1,003,911	281,999	502,196	207,353	123,250	75,120	39,967	29,724	26,782	54,932	26,222	6,182	138,652	62,588	-36,455
1988	1,064,140	290,361	533,404	219,341	129,332	78,878	44,487	31,938	29,428	68,283	27,272	18,815	151,838	57,222	-36,967
1989	1,143,172	303,559	568,668	232,542	136,031	84,964	48,390	36,674	30,066	81,069	27,608	29,211	169,266	57,822	-37,212
1990	1,252,705	299,331	619,329	248,623	147,022	98,102	57,716	38,755	29,112	125,546	29,485	67,142	184,221	60,893	-36,615
1991	1,323,441	273,292	689,666	269,015	170,276	104,489	71,183	43,354	31,349	134,217	31,099	75,312	194,541	71,081	-39,356
1992	1,380,856	298,350	772,440	287,585	196,948	119,024	89,497	45,248	34,138	74,789	33,333	10,093	199,421	75,136	-39,280
1993	1,408,675	291,086	827,535	304,585	207,250	130,552	99,415	50,012	35,720	45,896	35,004	-22,719	198,811	82,733	-37,386
1994	1,460,914	281,563	869,418	319,565	214,036	144,747	107,122	46,307	37,642	69,749	38,134	-5,122	202,957	74,998	-37,772
1995, est.	1,538,920	271,600	926,000	336,149	223,006	157,288	115,098	56,065	38,392	66,274	39,154	-11,958	234,224	82,215	-41,392

NA Not available. [1] Also includes training, employment, and social services. [2] Includes outlays not shown separately. [3] Transition quarter, July to September.

Source: U.S. Office of Management and Budget, *Historical Tables*, annual.

No. 521. Federal Budget Outlays in Constant (1987) Dollars: 1980 to 1995

[Dollar amounts in billions of dollars. For fiscal years ending in year shown; see text, section 9. Given the inherent imprecision in deflating outlays, the data shown in constant dollars present a reasonable perspective—not precision. The deflators and the categories that are deflated are as comparable over time as feasible. See headnote, table 517. Minus sign (-) indicates offset]

OUTLAYS	1980	1984	1985	1986	1987	1988	1989	1990	1991	1992	1993	1994	1995, est.
Outlays, total	**832.1**	**933.5**	**1001.3**	**1017.3**	**1003.9**	**1027.1**	**1057.2**	**1110.4**	**1123.2**	**1133.4**	**1,125.8**	**1140.3**	**1168.1**
National defense	187.1	241.7	261.2	276.4	282.0	283.3	285.9	272.6	240.5	249.7	237.2	220.6	206.7
Nondefense outlays	645.0	691.7	740.1	740.8	721.9	743.8	771.3	837.7	882.7	883.7	888.6	919.7	961.5
Payments for individuals	394.9	446.5	458.6	467.5	471.3	480.0	490.4	509.6	541.3	587.3	614.8	634.9	655.8
Direct payments	348.6	396.0	405.6	411.4	413.5	420.2	428.8	442.3	464.2	496.6	517.0	530.2	546.6
Grants to State and local gov'ts	46.3	50.5	53.0	56.2	57.8	59.9	61.6	67.3	77.1	90.7	97.8	104.7	109.2
Other grants	81.2	57.8	59.8	59.6	50.5	50.8	50.3	51.9	53.6	55.7	57.4	61.0	65.3
Net interest	74.4	122.3	137.3	140.1	138.7	146.5	156.3	163.1	165.4	164.6	160.3	160.5	180.4
All other	122.9	100.0	118.7	107.6	97.9	102.4	108.6	145.5	155.6	108.0	85.2	91.5	90.0
Undistributed offsetting receipts	-28.5	-34.8	-34.3	-34.0	-36.5	-35.8	-34.4	-32.4	-33.1	-32.0	-29.2	-28.2	-30.1
PERCENT OF GDP													
Outlays, total	22.3	23.1	23.9	23.5	22.5	22.1	22.1	22.9	23.3	23.3	22.5	22.0	21.9
National defense	5.1	6.2	6.4	6.5	6.3	6.0	5.9	5.5	4.8	5.0	4.7	4.2	3.9
Nondefense outlays	17.3	16.9	17.5	17.0	16.2	16.1	16.2	17.4	18.5	18.3	17.9	17.8	18.0
Payments for individuals	10.5	10.9	10.8	10.7	10.6	10.4	10.4	10.7	11.5	12.3	12.5	12.4	12.4
Direct payments	9.3	9.6	9.5	9.4	9.3	9.1	9.1	9.2	9.8	10.4	10.5	10.4	10.4
Grants to State and local gov'ts	1.2	1.2	1.4	1.3	1.3	1.3	1.3	1.4	1.6	1.9	2.0	2.0	2.1
Other grants	2.2	1.4	1.4	1.4	1.1	1.1	1.1	1.1	1.1	1.1	1.1	1.1	1.2
Net interest	2.0	3.0	3.3	3.2	3.1	3.2	3.3	3.4	3.4	3.4	3.2	3.1	3.3
All other	3.3	2.5	2.9	2.5	2.2	2.2	2.3	3.0	3.2	2.2	1.7	1.8	1.7
Undistributed offsetting receipts	-0.8	-0.9	-0.8	-0.8	-0.8	-0.8	-0.7	-0.7	-0.7	-0.7	-0.6	-0.6	-0.6
PERCENT OF OUTLAYS													
Outlays, total	100.0	100.0	100.0	100.0	100.0	100.0	100.0	100.0	100.0	100.0	100.0	100.0	100.0
National defense	22.7	26.7	26.7	27.6	28.1	27.3	26.6	23.9	20.7	21.6	20.7	19.3	17.6
Nondefense outlays	77.3	73.3	73.3	72.4	71.9	72.7	73.4	76.1	79.3	78.4	79.3	80.7	82.4
Payments for individuals	47.1	47.1	45.2	45.6	46.9	47.0	46.9	46.6	49.1	52.7	55.6	56.3	56.8
Direct payments	41.6	41.8	39.9	40.1	41.2	41.2	41.0	40.5	42.1	44.6	46.7	47.0	47.4
Grants to State and local gov'ts	5.5	5.3	5.2	5.5	5.8	5.9	5.9	6.2	7.0	8.1	8.9	9.3	9.4
Other grants	9.9	6.1	6.0	5.9	5.0	5.0	4.8	4.7	4.7	4.8	4.9	5.1	5.4
Net interest	8.9	13.0	13.7	13.7	13.8	14.3	14.8	14.7	14.7	14.4	14.1	13.9	15.2
All other	14.7	10.8	12.0	10.6	9.8	9.9	10.2	13.1	13.8	9.3	7.4	8.0	7.6
Undistributed offsetting receipts	-3.4	-3.8	-3.5	-3.3	-3.6	-3.5	-3.3	-2.9	-3.0	-2.8	-2.7	-2.6	-2.7

Source: U.S. Office of Management and Budget, *Historical Tables*, annual.

No. 522. Federal Outlays, by Detailed Function: 1980 to 1995

[In millions of dollars. **For fiscal years ending in year shown;** outlays stated in terms of checks issued or cash payments. See headnote, table 518]

FUNCTION	1980	1990	1991	1992	1993	1994	1995, est.
Total outlays	590,947	1,252,705	1,323,441	1,380,856	1,408,675	1,460,914	1,538,920
Legislative branch.	1,224	2,241	2,296	2,677	2,406	2,561	2,793
The Judiciary	567	1,646	1,997	2,308	2,628	2,677	3,101
Funds appropriated to President [1] . .	8,542	10,087	11,724	11,113	11,534	10,511	10,860
Departments:							
Agriculture	34,785	46,012	54,119	56,437	63,144	60,753	62,313
Commerce	3,129	3,734	2,585	2,567	2,798	2,915	3,601
Defense-Military	130,912	289,755	261,925	286,632	278,574	268,635	260,269
Defense-Civil	15,161	24,975	26,543	28,270	29,266	30,407	31,207
Education	14,770	23,109	25,339	26,047	30,290	24,699	32,888
Energy	6,467	12,084	12,479	15,523	16,942	17,839	16,135
Health and Human Services	68,255	175,531	198,110	231,560	253,835	278,901	301,439
Housing and Urban Development .	12,735	20,167	22,751	24,470	25,181	25,845	26,854
Interior	4,472	5,790	6,088	6,539	6,784	6,900	7,329
Justice	2,641	6,507	8,244	9,802	10,170	10,005	11,821
Labor [2]	29,510	25,215	33,954	47,078	44,651	37,047	31,942
State.	1,940	3,979	4,252	5,007	5,377	5,718	6,272
Transportation.	19,802	28,650	30,511	32,491	34,457	37,228	37,992
Treasury	76,568	255,172	276,339	292,987	298,804	307,577	351,816
Veterans Affairs.	21,137	28,998	31,214	33,897	35,487	37,401	38,231
Independent agencies:							
Environmental Protection Agency .	5,603	5,108	5,769	5,950	5,930	5,855	6,274
General Services Administration. .	249	−123	487	469	743	334	1,131
NASA [3]	4,959	12,429	13,878	13,961	14,305	13,695	14,241
Office of Personnel Management .	15,056	31,949	34,808	35,596	36,794	38,596	40,308
Small Business Administration . . .	2,026	692	613	546	785	779	703
Other independent agencies	16,338	72,998	79,659	18,007	−11,428	10,356	7,934
Undistributed offsetting receipts. . . .	−31,988	−98,930	−110,005	−117,111	−119,711	−123,469	−132,857
Outlays, by function	590,947	1,252,705	1,323,441	1,380,856	1,408,675	1,460,914	1,538,920
National defense	133,995	299,331	273,292	298,350	291,086	281,563	271,600
Dept. of Defense—Military.	130,912	289,755	262,389	286,892	278,561	268,611	260,155
Military personnel	40,897	75,622	83,439	81,171	75,904	73,137	70,750
Operation and maintenance . . .	44,788	88,340	101,769	91,984	94,094	87,880	90,129
Procurement	29,021	80,972	82,028	74,881	69,936	61,758	54,671
R and D, test, and evaluation. .	13,127	37,458	34,589	34,632	36,968	34,762	34,981
Military construction	2,450	5,080	3,497	4,262	4,831	4,979	5,621
Family housing	1,680	3,501	3,296	3,271	3,255	3,316	3,457
Other.	−1,050	−1,218	−46,229	−3,308	−6,428	2,779	547
Atomic energy defense activities .	2,878	8,988	10,004	10,619	11,017	11,892	10,471
Defense related activities	206	587	899	839	1,508	1,060	973
International affairs	12,714	13,764	15,851	16,107	17,248	17,083	18,713
International development and							
humanitarian assistance	3,626	5,498	5,141	6,133	5,835	7,061	7,311
Conduct of foreign affairs	1,366	3,050	3,282	3,894	4,325	4,557	5,050
Other	7,722	5,216	7,428	6,080	7,088	5,465	6,352
Income security	86,540	147,022	170,276	196,948	207,250	214,036	223,006
General retirement and disability							
insurance	5,083	5,148	4,945	5,483	4,347	5,720	5,026
Federal employee retirement and							
disability.	26,594	51,983	56,106	57,572	60,047	62,487	64,788
Housing assistance	5,632	15,891	17,175	18,904	21,542	23,888	26,694
Food and nutrition assistance . . .	14,016	23,964	28,481	32,622	35,148	36,773	38,892
Other income security	17,163	31,146	36,485	42,901	48,366	56,439	63,768
Unemployment compensation . . .	18,051	18,889	27,084	39,466	37,802	28,729	23,839
Health.	23,169	57,716	71,183	89,497	99,415	107,122	115,098
Health care services	18,003	47,642	60,723	77,719	86,860	94,259	101,423
Health research	4,161	8,611	8,899	10,021	10,794	11,000	11,660
Consumer and occupational							
health and safety	1,006	1,462	1,560	1,757	1,762	1,863	2,015
Medicare.	32,090	98,102	104,489	119,024	130,552	144,747	157,288
Social Security	118,547	248,623	269,015	287,585	304,585	319,565	336,149
Veterans benefits and services	21,185	29,112	31,349	34,138	35,720	37,642	38,392
Income security for veterans . . .	11,688	15,241	16,961	17,296	17,758	19,613	18,768
Educ., training, and rehab.	2,342	278	427	783	826	1,115	1,292
Hospital and medical care.	6,515	12,134	12,889	14,091	14,812	15,678	16,527
Housing for veterans	−23	517	85	901	1,299	197	708
Other	665	943	987	1,067	1,025	1,039	1,097

See footnotes at end of table.

No. 522. Federal Outlays, by Detailed Function: 1980 to 1995—Continued

[In millions of dollars. See headnote, table 518]

FUNCTION	1980	1990	1991	1992	1993	1994	1995, est.
Education, training, employment, and social services.	31,843	38,755	43,354	45,248	50,012	46,307	56,065
Elementary, secondary, and vocational education.	6,893	9,918	11,372	12,402	13,481	14,258	15,844
Higher education.	6,723	11,107	11,961	11,268	14,483	7,876	14,024
Research and general educ. aids	1,212	1,577	1,773	1,996	2,040	2,086	2,291
Training and employment	10,345	5,619	5,934	6,479	6,700	7,097	7,423
Other labor services.	551	810	788	884	948	958	985
Social services	6,119	9,723	11,526	12,219	12,360	14,031	15,497
Commerce and housing credit.	9,390	67,142	75,312	10,093	−22,719	−5,122	−11,958
Mortgage credit.	5,887	3,845	5,362	4,320	1,554	−501	−2,603
Postal Service.	1,246	2,116	1,828	1,169	1,602	1,233	842
Deposit insurance	−285	58,081	66,042	2,518	−27,957	−7,570	−12,278
Other commerce	2,542	3,100	2,079	2,085	2,083	1,715	2,082
Transportation	21,329	29,485	31,099	33,333	35,004	38,134	39,154
Ground transportation	15,274	18,954	19,545	20,347	21,251	23,940	24,832
Air transportation.	3,723	7,234	8,184	9,313	10,049	10,146	10,132
Water transportation.	2,229	3,151	3,148	3,430	3,423	3,716	3,867
Other transportation	104	146	223	244	281	333	324
Natural resources and environment	13,858	17,080	18,559	20,025	20,239	21,064	21,891
Water resources	4,223	4,401	4,366	4,559	4,258	4,528	5,064
Conservation and land management. .	1,043	3,553	4,047	4,581	4,777	5,161	4,907
Recreational resources.	1,677	1,876	2,137	2,378	2,620	2,619	2,802
Pollution control and abatement	5,510	5,170	5,861	6,075	6,061	6,050	6,438
Other natural resources	1,405	2,080	2,148	2,432	2,522	2,706	2,680
Energy	10,156	3,341	2,436	4,500	4,319	5,219	4,589
Supply.	8,367	1,976	1,945	3,226	3,286	3,899	3,235
Conservation	569	365	386	468	521	582	681
Emergency preparedness	342	442	−235	319	336	275	241
Information, policy, and regs	878	559	340	486	176	462	431
Community/regional develop.	11,252	8,498	6,811	6,838	9,052	10,454	12,598
Community development	4,907	3,530	3,543	3,643	3,681	4,133	4,996
Area and regional development	4,303	2,868	2,743	2,315	2,443	2,166	2,757
Disaster relief and insurance	2,043	2,100	525	881	2,928	4,156	4,845
Agriculture.	8,839	11,958	15,183	15,205	20,490	15,121	14,401
Farm income stabilization	7,441	9,761	12,924	12,666	17,847	12,426	11,662
Research and services.	1,398	2,197	2,259	2,539	2,643	2,695	2,739
Net interest	52,538	184,221	194,541	199,421	198,811	202,957	234,224
On-budget	*54,877*	*200,212*	*214,763*	*223,059*	*225,599*	*232,160*	*267,800*
Off-budget	*−2,339*	*−15,991*	*−20,222*	*−23,637*	*−26,788*	*−29,203*	*−33,576*
Interest on the public debt.	74,808	264,724	285,455	292,323	292,502	296,278	333,704
Interest received by on-budget trust funds	−9,707	−46,321	−50,426	−54,193	−55,537	−56,494	−57,889
Interest received by off-budget trust funds	−2,339	−15,991	−20,222	−23,637	−26,788	−29,203	−33,576
Other interest	−10,224	−18,191	−20,266	−15,071	−11,367	−7,623	−8,015
General science, space, and technology .	5,832	14,444	16,111	16,409	17,030	16,227	16,977
Gen. science and basic research	1,381	2,835	3,154	3,571	3,938	3,863	4,173
General government	13,028	10,734	11,661	12,990	13,009	11,312	14,493
Legislative functions.	1,038	1,763	1,916	2,124	2,124	2,051	2,246
Exec. direction and management	97	160	190	188	197	244	294
Central fiscal operations	2,612	6,004	6,097	6,612	6,976	7,417	7,792
General property and records management.	327	31	657	692	1,005	590	1,322
General purpose fiscal assistance . . .	8,582	2,161	2,100	1,865	1,935	1,899	2,129
Other general government	569	800	1,280	1,782	1,329	995	1,234
Deductions, offsetting receipts	−351	−361	−718	−480	−739	−2,087	−700
Administration of justice	4,584	9,993	12,276	14,426	14,955	15,256	17,631
Federal law enforcement.	2,239	4,648	5,661	6,462	6,674	6,624	7,060
Federal litigative and judicial	1,347	3,577	4,352	5,054	5,336	5,470	6,417
Federal correctional activities.	342	1,291	1,600	2,114	2,124	2,315	2,824
Criminal justice assistance	656	477	663	795	822	847	1,330
Undistributed offsetting receipts.	*−19,942*	*−36,615*	*−39,356*	*−39,280*	*−37,386*	*−37,772*	*−41,392*

[1] Represents international affairs funds mainly.   [2] Includes Pension Benefit Guaranty Corporation.   [3] National Aeronautics and Space Administration.

Source: U.S. Office of Management and Budget, *Budget of the United States Government,* annual.

No. 523. Tax Expenditures, by Function: 1994 to 1997

[In millions of dollars. For years ending, Sept. 30, except as noted. Tax expenditures are defined as *revenue losses* attributable to provisions of the Federal tax laws which allow a special exclusion, exemption, or deduction from gross income or which provide a special credit, a preferential rate of tax, or a deferral of liability. Represents tax expenditures of **$1 billion or more in 1997**]

DESCRIPTION	1994	1995	1996	1997
National defense:				
Excl. benefits/allowances to Armed Forces personnel	2,000	2,005	2,020	2,030
International affairs: [1]				
Exclusion of income of foreign sales corporations	1,300	1,400	1,500	1,600
Deferral of income from controlled foreign corps. [2]	1,600	1,700	1,800	2,000
Inventory property sales source rules exception	1,200	1,300	1,400	1,500
General science, space, and technology: [1]				
Expensing of research and experimentation [2]	2,235	2,390	2,560	2,735
Energy:				
Excess of percent over cost depletion: Oil and gas	785	920	955	1,005
Commerce and housing credit: [1]				
Exclusion of interest on—				
Life insurance savings	9,410	10,365	11,160	12,000
Owner-occupied mortgage subsidy bonds	1,760	1,785	1,775	1,715
Capital gains (excl. agri., timber, iron ore and coal) [2]	5,745	6,135	6,205	6,335
Deferral of capital gains on home sales	16,640	17,140	17,850	18,180
Exclusion of capital gains on home sales for persons age 55 and over	4,690	4,820	4,920	5,010
Deductibility of—				
Mortgage interest on owner-occupied homes	48,430	51,270	54,165	57,240
Property tax on owner-occupied homes	14,020	14,845	15,680	16,570
Accelerated depreciation on rental housing [2]	1,145	1,290	1,425	1,580
Accelerated deprec. of bldgs. excl. rental housing [2]	5,145	4,920	4,385	3,580
Step-up basis of capital gains at death	26,850	28,305	29,480	30,285
Accelerated depreciation of machinery and equipment [3]	17,620	19,400	20,850	21,885
Graduated corporation income tax rate [2]	3,775	3,960	4,120	4,240
Exception from passive loss rules for $25,000 rental loss	4,765	4,255	4,170	4,120
Transportation:				
Exclusion of reimbursed employee parking expenses	1,845	1,930	2,015	2,100
Community and regional development: [1]				
Credit for low income housing investments	1,925	2,260	2,600	2,945
Education, training, employment, and social services: [1]				
Deductibility of—				
Charitable contributions (education)	1,610	1,705	1,810	1,915
Charitable contributions other than education	2,085	2,210	2,340	2,490
Charitable contributions other than education and health	17,805	18,910	19,995	21,135
Credit for child and dependent care expenses	2,820	2,900	2,995	3,060
Health: [1]				
Excl. of employer contrib. for medical insurance premiums and medical care	56,000	60,670	66,620	72,300
Deductibility of medical expenses	3,380	3,660	3,965	4,295
Excl. of interest on State and local debt for private nonprofit health facilities	1,455	1,495	1,535	1,585
Deductibility of charitable contributions (health)	2,085	2,210	2,340	2,490
Social Security: [1]				
Exclusion of Social Security benefits:				
Disability insurance benefits	1,815	1,895	2,100	2,300
OASI benefits for retired workers	18,295	16,875	17,395	18,110
Benefits for dependents and survivors	3,620	3,610	3,730	3,940
Income security: [1]				
Exclusion of workmen's compensation benefits	4,240	4,475	4,860	5,120
Net exclusion of pension contributions and earnings:				
Employer plans	48,750	55,540	59,010	59,490
Individual Retirement Accounts	5,185	6,245	6,375	6,120
Keoghs	3,915	4,435	4,825	5,195
Exclusion of other employee benefits:				
Premiums on group term life insurance	2,750	2,880	3,020	3,170
Special ESOP rules (other than investment credit)	2,155	1,830	1,680	1,575
Additional deduction for the elderly [4]	1,470	1,490	1,510	1,520
Earned income credit	4,020	5,110	5,740	6,440
Veterans benefits and services: [1]				
Exclusion of veterans disability compensation	1,910	1,985	1,930	1,975
Deferral of interest on savings bonds	1,250	1,360	1,470	1,600
General purpose fiscal assistance: [1]				
Excl. of interest on public State & local debt	11,970	12,350	12,690	13,085
Deductibility of nonbusiness State & local taxes other than on owner-occupied homes	25,745	27,250	28,795	30,425
Tax credit for corporations receiving income from doing business in United States possessions	2,890	2,630	2,680	2,735

[1] Total (after interactions). [2] Normal tax method. [3] Pre-1983 budget method. [4] Data on calendar year basis.

Source: U.S. Office of Management and Budget, *Budget of the United States Government,* annual.

No. 524. Government—Human and Capital Investment—Summary: 1993 to 1995

[Discretionary budget authority, **in millions of dollars, except as indicated**]

INVESTMENT	1993, actual	1994, enacted	1995, proposed	PERCENT CHANGE 1993-94	PERCENT CHANGE 1994-95
HUMAN INVESTMENTS					
Young children	5,977	7,064	8,054	18.2	14.0
Immunization funds [1]	341	528	888	54.8	68.2
Head Start funds	2,776	3,326	4,026	19.8	21.0
WIC (women, infants, and children) funds	2,860	3,210	3,564	12.2	11.0
Family preservation and support funds	-	60	150	(X)	150.0
Children receiving immunization (1,000) [2]	(NA)	(NA)	13,186	(NA)	(NA)
Head Start slots (1,000)	714	750	840	5.0	12.0
Percent of targeted population reached [3]	51.0	54.0	60.0	5.9	11.1
WIC Recipients (1,000)	5,920	6,510	7,220	10.0	10.9
Percent of target population reached [4]	79.0	85.0	95.0	7.6	11.8
Education	7,278	7,539	9,089	3.6	20.6
Workforce Investments	5,010	5,474	6,480	9.3	18.4
Grants for training the disadvantaged	1,692	1,647	1,729	-2.7	5.0
Dislocated worker assistance	651	1,118	1,465	71.7	31.0
Job Corps	966	1,040	1,157	7.7	11.3
Summer youth employment	1,025	888	1,056	-13.4	18.9
School-to-work	-	50	150	(X)	200.0
One-stop career shopping	-	50	250	(X)	400.0
Other employment and training	676	681	673	0.7	-1.2
National Service	279	575	850	106.1	47.8
INFRASTRUCTURE INVESTMENT (bil. dol.)					
Transportation (DOT):					
Highways:					
Core categorical highway grants	16.5	19.1	19.8	15.8	3.7
Emergency repair [5]	0.5	0.7	0.1	40.0	-85.7
Highway demonstrations and other projects	1.0	0.5	0.4	-50.0	-20.0
Mass transit:					
Formula capital grants	0.9	1.6	2.3	77.8	43.7
Discretionary grants	1.7	1.7	1.5	-	-11.8
Railroads:					
Northeast corridor	0.2	0.2	0.2	-	-
Penn Station redevelopment	-	-	0.1	(X)	(X)
Amtrak capital	0.2	0.2	0.3	-	50.0
Air transportation:					
Air traffic control facilities and equip	2.3	2.1	2.3	-8.7	9.5
Grants for airports	1.8	1.7	1.7	-5.6	-
Water treatment and supply (EPA):					
Clean water State revolving funds	1.9	1.2	1.6	-36.8	33.3
Drinking water State revolving funds	-	0.6	0.7	(X)	16.7
Targeted whitewater assistance	0.6	0.6	0.3	-	-50.0
Rural water and wastewater programs (Dept. of Agri.):					
Grants and loans	0.5	0.6	0.7	20.0	16.7
Loan level	-0.8	-0.8	-1.0	-	25.0
Water resources development:					
Army Corps of engineers	1.7	1.6	1.2	-5.9	-25.0
Bureau of Reclamation (Dept. of Interior)	0.5	0.4	0.4	-20.0	-
Community development block grants	0.8	0.9	0.9	12.5	-

- Represents or rounds to zero.   NA Not available.   X Not applicable.   [1] 1995 funding shows a combined $464 million (current discretionary immunization program) and $424 million (new entitlement program).   [2] Represents children through age 18.   [3] Target population is 1.4 million Head Start eligible children.   [4] Based on a 1993 CBO study estimating that 84 percent of all WIC eligibles will apply for WIC.   [5] Does not include estimates associated with the recent San Fernando earthquake.

Source: U.S. Office of Management and Budget, *Budget of the United States Government*, annual.

No. 525. Federal Debt Held by the Public: 1980 to 1994

[In billions of dollars, except percents. Based on end of fiscal year]

ITEM	1980	1985	1990	1991	1992	1993	1994, est.
Current dollars	709	1,499	2,410	2,688	2,999	3,247	3,472
Constant (1987) dollars [1]	1,005	1,590	2,134	2,284	2,472	2,607	2,743
Percent of GDP	26.8	37.8	44.0	47.4	50.5	51.6	52.3
Percent of credit market debt [2]	18.6	22.7	22.9	24.4	25.9	26.8	(NA)
Interest as percent of total outlays [3]	10.6	16.2	16.2	16.2	15.5	14.9	14.3

NA Not available. [1] Debt in current dollars deflated by the gross domestic product (GDP) deflator with FY 1987=100.
[2] Unpublished and preliminary estimates from the Federal Reserve Board flow of funds accounts. Total credit market debt owed by domestic nonfinancial sectors, modified to be consistent with budget concepts for the measurement of Federal debt.
[3] Represents *interest on the public debt* less *interest received by trust funds* subfunction 901 less subfunction 902 and 903. Excludes the comparatively small amount of interest on agency debt or the offsets for other interest received by Government accounts.

Source: U.S. Office of Management and Budget, *Budget of the United States Government*, annual.

No. 526. Summary of Federal Debt: 1985 to 1994

[In millions of dollars. Based on end of fiscal year]

ITEM	1985	1990	1992	1993	1994
Debt outstanding, total	**1,827,470**	**3,266,073**	**4,082,871**	**4,436,171**	**4,721,293**
Public debt securities	1,823,103	3,233,313	4,064,621	4,411,489	4,692,750
Agency securities	4,366	32,758	18,250	24,682	28,543
Securities held by—					
Government accounts, total	317,612	795,907	1,016,453	1,116,713	1,213,115
Public debt securities	316,545	795,762	1,016,330	1,116,693	1,213,098
Agency securities	1,067	145	123	21	17
The public, total	1,509,857	2,470,166	3,066,418	3,319,458	3,508,178
Public debt securities	1,506,558	2,437,551	3,048,291	3,924,796	3,479,652
Agency securities	3,299	32,613	18,127	24,661	28,526
Interest-bearing public debt, total	**1,821,010**	**3,210,943**	**4,061,801**	**4,408,567**	**4,689,524**
Marketable, total	1,360,179	2,092,759	2,677,476	2,904,910	3,091,602
Treasury bills	384,220	482,454	634,287	658,381	697,295
Treasury notes	776,449	1,218,081	1,566,349	1,734,161	1,867,507
Treasury bonds	199,510	377,224	461,840	497,367	511,800
Nonmarketable, total	460,831	1,118,184	1,384,325	1,503,657	1,597,922
U.S. savings bonds	77,011	122,152	148,266	167,024	176,413
Foreign series: Government	6,638	36,041	37,039	42,459	41,996
Government account series, total	313,928	779,412	1,011,020	1,114,289	1,211,689
Airport and airway trust fund	7,410	14,312	15,090	12,672	12,206
Bank insurance fund	16,130	8,438	4,664	4,325	13,972
Employees life insurance fund	6,312	9,561	12,411	13,575	14,929
Exchange stabilization fund	2,073	1,863	3,314	5,637	7,326
Federal disability insurance trust fund	5,443	11,254	12,774	10,162	6,025
Federal employees retirement funds	127,253	223,229	273,732	301,711	329,602
Federal hospital insurance trust fund	20,721	96,249	120,647	126,078	128,716
Federal Housing Administration	3,485	6,678	6,077	5,380	5,933
Fed. old-age & survivors insurance trust fund	30,968	203,717	306,524	355,510	413,425
Fed. S&L Corp., resolution fund	4,953	929	1,346	828	1,649
Fed. supplementary medical insur. trust fund	10,736	14,286	18,534	23,269	21,489
Government life insurance fund	269	184	134	125	114
Highway trust fund	9,422	9,530	11,167	11,475	7,751
National service life insurance fund	9,296	10,917	11,310	11,666	11,852
Postal Service fund	2,362	3,063	4,679	3,826	1,270
Railroad retirement account	4,232	8,356	10,081	10,457	10,596
Treasury deposit funds	681	304	212	147	130
Unemployment trust fund	16,454	50,186	34,898	36,563	39,745
Other	35,728	106,376	163,426	180,883	184,959
State and local government series	62,778	161,248	157,570	149,449	137,386
Domestic series	(X)	18,886	29,995	29,995	29,995
Other	477	447	435	442	445
MATURITY DISTRIBUTION					
Amount outstanding, privately held	**1,185,675**	**1,841,903**	**2,363,802**	**2,562,336**	**2,719,861**
Maturity class:					
Within 1 year	472,661	626,297	808,705	858,135	877,932
1-5 years	402,766	630,144	866,329	978,714	1,128,322
5-10 years	159,383	267,573	295,921	306,663	289,998
10-20 years	62,853	82,713	84,706	94,345	88,208
20 years and over	88,012	235,176	308,141	324,479	335,401

X Not applicable.

Source: U.S. Department of the Treasury, *Treasury Bulletin*, quarterly.

No. 527. Federal Participation in Domestic Credit Markets: 1970 to 1994

[**In billions of dollars, except percent.** Federal credit programs are primarily in three forms: direct loans from the Federal Government, Federal guarantees of private lending, and lending by privately-owned government-sponsored enterprises]

TYPE OF PARTICIPATION	1970	1975	1980	1985	1990	1991	1992	1993	1994
Total net borrowing in credit market [1]	**88**	**170**	**325**	**806**	**689**	**494**	**534**	**572**	**620**
Federal borrowing from the public	4	51	70	199	221	277	311	247	185
Guaranteed borrowing.	8	9	32	22	41	22	20	-2	39
Government-sponsored enterprise borrowing [2]	5	5	21	58	115	125	151	170	166
Total, Federal and federally assisted borrowing. . .	16	65	123	279	377	424	481	416	390
Federal borrowing participation rate (percent)	18.4	38.3	37.7	34.6	54.7	85.9	90.1	72.7	62.9
Total net lending in credit market [1]	**88**	**170**	**325**	**806**	**689**	**494**	**534**	**572**	**620**
Direct loans.	3	13	24	28	3	-8	7	-2	-1
Guaranteed loans.	8	9	32	22	41	22	20	-2	39
Government-sponsored enterprise loans.	5	6	24	61	90	91	145	163	145
Total, Federal and federally assisted lending	16	27	80	110	134	105	172	160	182
Federal lending participation rate (percent)	18.1	15.9	24.6	13.7	19.4	21.3	32.2	27.8	29.4

[1] Total net borrowing (or lending) in credit market by domestic nonfinancial sectors, excluding equities. Financial sectors are omitted to avoid double counting.   [2] Most Government-sponsored enterprises (GSE's) are financial intermediaries. In order to avoid double counting, GSE borrowing and lending are calculated net of transactions with Federal agencies, transactions between GSE's, and transactions in guaranteed loans.

Source: U.S. Office of Management and Budget, *Analytical Perspectives,* annual.

No. 528. U.S. Savings Bonds: 1970 to 1994

[**In billions of dollars, except percent. As of end of fiscal year,** see text, section 9. See *Historical Statistics, Colonial Times to 1970,* series Y 500, for similar but not exactly comparable data]

ITEM	1970	1980	1985	1987	1988	1989	1990	1991	1992	1993	1994
Amounts outstanding, total [1]	52	73	77	97	107	114	123	134	149	167	177
Funds from sales	5	5	5	10	7	8	8	9	14	17	9
Accrued discounts	1	4	5	6	8	8	8	10	9	9	9
Redemptions [2]	6	17	6	5	6	7	8	8	7	8	9
Percent of total outstanding. . .	12.2	23.0	7.4	5.1	5.6	6.3	6.1	5.6	5.0	4.7	5.1

[1] Interest-bearing debt only for amounts end of year.   [2] Matured and unmatured bonds.

Source: U.S. Dept. of the Treasury, *Treasury Bulletin,* quarterly.

No. 529. Government-Sponsored Enterprise Securities and Guarantees Outstanding: 1970 to 1991

[As of December 31. In billions of dollars]

ENTERPRISE	1970	1980	1990	1991	ENTERPRISE	1970	1980	1990	1991
Total	**39**	**177**	**981**	**1,082**	Mortgage-backed securities . .	(X)	(X)	300	372
Farm credit system:					Freddie Mac: [2]				
Farm credit banks	11	52	42	40	Debt	(X)	5	28	28
Banks for cooperatives	2	9	13	13	Mortgage-backed securities . .	(X)	17	316	359
Fannie Mae: [1]					Fed. home loan bank system . .	11	37	118	108
Debt	15	55	123	134	Sallie Mae [3]	(X)	3	39	43

X Not applicable.   [1] Federal National Mortgage Association.   [2] Federal Home Loan Mortgage Corporation.   [3] Student Loan Mortgage Association.

Source: Congressional Budget Office, *Controlling the Risks of Government-Sponsored Enterprises,* April 1991.

No. 530. Federal Funds—Summary Distribution, by State: 1994

[In millions of dollars. For year ending Sept. 30. Data for grants, salaries and wages and direct payments to individuals are on an expenditures basis; procurement is on obligation basis]

REGION, DIVISION, AND STATE	FEDERAL FUNDS		Defense	Non-defense	Direct payments to individuals	Procure-ment	Grants to State and local govern-ments	Salaries and wages
	Total [1]	Per capita [2] (dol.)						
U.S. [3]	1,320,132	4,996	227,525	1,092,607	691,666	197,959	214,239	168,951
Northeast.	**259,892**	**5,057**	**28,002**	**231,889**	**151,071**	**26,363**	**51,473**	**23,600**
New England	**71,193**	**5,365**	**12,402**	**58,790**	**37,284**	**11,478**	**13,160**	**6,631**
Maine	6,708	5,409	1,502	5,206	3,518	1,023	1,269	773
New Hampshire.	4,636	4,078	607	4,029	2,648	487	956	432
Vermont.	2,411	4,157	155	2,256	1,435	109	546	268
Massachusetts	35,374	5,856	6,251	29,123	17,672	6,609	6,261	3,112
Rhode Island	5,473	5,489	845	4,628	3,109	499	1,100	641
Connecticut	16,591	5,066	3,042	13,548	8,902	2,751	3,028	1,405
Middle Atlantic	**188,699**	**4,949**	**15,600**	**173,099**	**113,787**	**14,885**	**38,313**	**16,969**
New York	90,346	4,973	5,533	84,813	51,909	6,142	22,445	7,428
New Jersey	37,328	4,723	4,719	32,609	22,685	4,218	6,163	3,739
Pennsylvania	61,025	5,064	5,348	55,677	39,193	4,525	9,705	5,802
Midwest.	**269,918**	**4,396**	**28,404**	**241,516**	**160,046**	**25,441**	**44,699**	**26,126**
East North Central.	**178,708**	**4,138**	**14,645**	**164,064**	**112,810**	**13,432**	**30,992**	**16,253**
Ohio	48,023	4,326	5,198	42,825	29,488	4,775	8,366	4,467
Indiana	22,104	3,843	2,470	19,634	13,804	1,674	3,553	2,101
Illinois	49,936	4,249	3,149	46,788	31,367	3,222	8,506	5,402
Michigan	38,975	4,104	2,601	36,374	25,535	2,479	7,117	2,887
Wisconsin	19,670	3,870	1,227	18,443	12,616	1,282	3,450	1,396
West North Central	**91,210**	**5,009**	**13,759**	**77,452**	**47,236**	**12,009**	**13,707**	**9,873**
Minnesota	18,797	4,116	1,585	17,212	10,113	1,798	3,515	1,617
Iowa	12,979	4,588	564	12,416	7,590	637	2,015	954
Missouri.	31,766	6,019	7,797	23,968	14,889	7,455	3,971	3,332
North Dakota	3,909	6,127	473	3,436	1,704	210	702	566
South Dakota	3,814	5,289	331	3,483	1,848	197	724	541
Nebraska	7,439	4,584	936	6,504	4,178	561	1,114	971
Kansas	12,506	4,897	2,073	10,433	6,914	1,151	1,666	1,892
South	**472,832**	**5,214**	**94,127**	**378,707**	**239,074**	**71,431**	**67,290**	**78,486**
South Atlantic.	**265,846**	**5,730**	**59,141**	**206,706**	**128,265**	**42,355**	**32,311**	**52,763**
Delaware	2,950	4,179	398	2,552	1,784	167	472	455
Maryland	36,576	7,306	7,588	28,988	13,600	8,228	3,637	7,414
District of Columbia . . .	21,766	38,186	2,308	19,458	2,523	4,103	2,222	11,415
Virginia	45,890	7,004	19,023	26,867	17,168	11,689	3,180	12,147
West Virginia	9,550	5,242	416	9,134	6,003	445	2,166	788
North Carolina.	28,858	4,082	5,313	23,546	16,481	1,897	4,862	4,833
South Carolina	17,097	4,666	3,494	13,603	8,839	2,721	2,726	2,503
Georgia	32,067	4,545	8,463	23,604	15,486	4,799	5,028	5,945
Florida.	71,092	5,095	12,138	58,954	46,381	8,306	8,018	7,263
East South Central	**78,912**	**4,966**	**12,039**	**66,873**	**42,833**	**11,459**	**12,752**	**9,941**
Kentucky	17,504	4,574	2,618	14,886	10,068	1,322	3,096	2,608
Tennessee	25,056	4,842	2,272	22,784	13,461	4,478	3,940	2,669
Alabama	22,280	5,281	4,058	18,222	11,996	3,364	3,209	3,125
Mississippi	14,072	5,272	3,091	10,981	7,308	2,295	2,507	1,539
West South Central	**128,074**	**4,509**	**22,947**	**105,128**	**67,976**	**17,617**	**22,227**	**15,782**
Arkansas	11,376	4,638	1,072	10,305	7,298	596	1,966	1,020
Louisiana	21,672	5,022	3,541	18,131	10,656	3,037	5,233	2,136
Oklahoma	15,718	4,824	2,796	12,922	8,943	1,142	2,359	2,627
Texas	79,308	4,315	15,538	63,770	41,079	12,842	12,669	9,999
West	**282,254**	**4,964**	**60,266**	**221,985**	**136,223**	**51,058**	**45,865**	**39,523**
Mountain	**74,919**	**4,924**	**13,634**	**61,284**	**35,279**	**14,151**	**11,216**	**11,222**
Montana	4,638	5,418	330	4,307	2,250	204	906	611
Idaho	4,965	4,382	401	4,564	2,520	844	778	612
Wyoming	2,344	4,924	249	2,095	1,070	121	714	358
Colorado	18,989	5,194	4,897	14,092	7,987	4,472	2,102	3,540
New Mexico	11,274	6,816	1,764	9,510	4,041	3,596	1,714	1,590
Arizona	19,011	4,665	3,624	15,388	10,558	2,679	2,996	2,269
Utah	7,594	3,980	1,452	6,141	3,444	1,190	1,209	1,479
Nevada	6,104	4,189	917	5,187	3,409	1,045	797	763
Pacific	**207,335**	**4,979**	**46,632**	**160,701**	**100,944**	**36,907**	**34,649**	**28,301**
Washington	26,644	4,987	5,028	21,615	13,381	4,086	3,924	4,187
Oregon	13,057	4,231	643	12,415	8,275	493	2,355	1,419
California	155,391	4,944	36,198	119,192	75,466	30,416	26,219	18,830
Alaska	4,640	7,656	1,567	3,072	924	1,007	1,063	1,367
Hawaii.	7,603	6,449	3,196	4,407	2,898	905	1,088	2,498
Undistributed	24,318	(X)	15,423	8,896	193	23,043	1,059	23

X Not applicable.   [1] Includes other programs not shown separately.   [2] Based on 1993 population estimates.   [3]Includes outlying areas not shown separately.

Source: U.S. Bureau of the Census, *Federal Expenditures by State for Fiscal Year,* annual.

No. 531. Tax Returns Filed—Examination Coverage: 1970 to 1992

[In thousands, except as indicated. Identification of returns with either schedule C (nonfarm sole proprietorships) or schedule F (farm proprietorships) for audit examination purposes was based on the largest source of income on the return and certain other characteristics. Therefore, the number with schedule C is not comparable to the number of nonfarm sole proprietorships returns in table 849]

YEAR AND ITEM	Returns filed [1]	RETURNS EXAMINED					AVERAGE TAX AND PENALTY—DOLLARS PER RETURN		
		Total	Percent of returns filed	By—			Revenue agents	Tax auditors	Service centers
				Revenue agents	Tax auditors	Service centers			
INDIVIDUAL RETURNS									
1970	76,431	1,672	2.2	(NA)	(NA)	-	(NA)	(NA)	-
1975	81,272	1,839	2.3	355.2	1,483.4	-	2,609	219	-
1980	90,727	1,834	2.0	292.5	1,346.3	195.1	1,335	602	39
1981	93,052	1,644	1.8	289.5	1,193.1	161.5	6,374	579	223
1982	94,013	1,455	1.6	285.5	1,066.6	103.2	7,505	751	364
1983	95,419	1,428	1.5	277.9	1,001.9	147.9	10,248	990	316
1984	95,541	1,216	1.3	276.2	859.4	80.4	11,584	1,314	692
1985	96,497	1,266	1.3	332.6	810.9	122.1	10,854	1,539	496
1986	99,529	1,091	1.1	298.9	732.5	59.6	14,052	1,945	862
1987	101,751	1,109	1.1	317.5	610.4	181.3	12,235	2,107	4,084
1988	103,251	1,061	1.0	352.8	532.3	175.7	9,750	2,190	4,195
1989	107,029	985	0.9	243.0	542.7	199.0	11,347	1,827	2,393
1990	109,868	883	0.8	202.8	517.2	163.2	16,248	1,965	3,817
1991	112,305	1,124	1.0	200.7	499.9	422.9	19,981	2,403	3,436
1992, total	**113,829**	**1,039**	**0.9**	**210.2**	**536.6**	**292.6**	**18,648**	**2,280**	**3,072**
1040A, income under $25,000	43,431	300	0.7	12.4	154.4	133.7	15,839	1,489	2,647
Non 1040A, income: [2]									
Under $25,000	18,656	120	0.6	16.0	83.4	20.3	8,276	1,502	3,129
$25,000 - $49,999, simple	27,492	162	0.6	25.5	106.9	29.2	7,685	1,948	2,307
$50,000 - $99,999, complex	13,657	138	1.0	27.5	81.2	29.3	8,386	2,323	2,073
$100,000 and over	3,173	156	4.9	47.1	45.8	63.2	40,785	3,920	4,761
Schedule C-TGR: [3]									
Under $25,000	2,185	33	1.5	9.8	21.3	1.5	6,703	2,721	1,110
$25,000 - $99,999	2,805	56	2.0	24.3	26.5	5.1	9,749	5,080	1,528
$100,000 and over	1,582	63	4.0	41.7	11.5	9.3	19,881	7,881	4,182
Schedule F-TGR: [3]									
Under $100,000	572	7	1.1	1.8	4.0	0.4	6,015	1,214	829
$100,000 and over	278	6	2.2	4.0	1.7	0.6	25,234	2,496	6,031
1992—OTHER RETURNS									
Fiduciary	2,779	3	0.1	1.9	-	1.5	15,064	-	807
Partnerships	1,631	12	0.7	8.2	-	3.7	-	-	-
Corporations, total	2,622	78	3.0	75.8	-	2.6	238,289	-	8,536
Estate, total	65	12	18.6	11.9	-	0.1	101,791	-	4,571
Gift	157	2	1.3	2.1	-	-	93,737	-	-
Excise	821	46	5.6	42.8	2.8	0.2	8,400	1,226	332
Employment	28,465	73	0.3	65.1	7.7	-	8,528	2,169	4,549
Windfall profit	-	2	-	0.3	-	1.6	540,380	-	365
Miscellaneous	-	1	-	0.6	-	0.1	41,382	-	9,348
Service center corrections	-	169	-	-	-	168.7	-	-	1,608

- Represents zero. NA Not available. [1] Returns filed in previous calendar year. [2] Income from positive sources only. [3] Total gross receipts.

Source: U.S. Internal Revenue Service, *Annual Report of the Commissioner and Chief Counsel of the Internal Revenue Service.*

No. 532. Internal Revenue Gross Collections, by Source: 1980 to 1993

[For fiscal year ending in year shown; see text, section 9. See also *Historical Statistics, Colonial Times to 1970,* series Y 358-373]

SOURCE OF REVENUE	COLLECTIONS (bil. dol.)					PERCENT OF TOTAL				
	1980	1985	1990	1992	1993	1980	1985	1990	1992	1993
All taxes	**519**	**743**	**1,056**	**1,121**	**1,177**	**100.0**	**100.0**	**100.0**	**100.0**	**100.0**
Individual income taxes	288	397	540	558	586	54.9	53.4	51.1	50.0	49.8
Withheld by employers	224	299	388	408	431	43.1	40.2	36.8	36.4	36.6
Employment taxes [1]	128	225	367	400	412	24.7	30.2	34.8	35.7	35.0
Old-age and disability insurance	123	216	358	390	402	23.6	29.0	33.8	34.8	34.2
Unemployment insurance	3	6	6	6	6	0.6	0.8	0.5	0.5	0.5
Corporation income taxes	72	77	110	118	132	13.9	10.4	10.4	10.5	11.2
Estate and gift taxes	7	7	12	12	13	1.3	0.9	1.1	1.0	1.1
Excise taxes	25	37	27	34	35	4.7	5.0	2.6	3.0	3.0
Alcohol and tobacco	8	10	10	13	14	1.6	1.3	1.0	1.2	1.1
Manufactures	7	10	11	17	17	1.3	1.3	1.0	1.5	1.4
Windfall profits tax	3	5	(Z)	(Z)	(Z)	0.6	0.7	(Z)	(Z)	(Z)
Other	10	17	6	4	5	1.9	2.3	0.6	0.3	0.4

Z Less than $50 million or .05 percent. [1] Includes railroad retirement, not shown separately.

Source: U.S. Internal Revenue Service, *Annual Report,* and Bureau of Alcohol, Tobacco, and Firearms, *Alcohol and Tobacco Tax Collections.*

No. 533. Federal Individual Income Tax Returns With Adjusted Gross Income (AGI)—Summary: 1980 to 1992

[Includes Puerto Rico and Virgin Islands. Includes returns of resident aliens, based on a sample of unaudited returns as filed. Data are not comparable for all years because of tax changes and other changes, as indicated. See Statistics of Income, Individual Income Tax Returns publications for a detailed explanation. See Appendix III. See Historical Statistics, Colonial Times to 1970, series Y 393-411, for related data]

ITEM	NUMBER OF RETURNS (1,000)				AMOUNT (mil. dol.)				AVERAGE AMOUNT (dollars)			
	1980	1985	1990	1992	1980	1985	1990	1992	1980	1985	1990	1992
Total returns	93,902	101,660	113,717	113,605	1,613,731	2,305,951	3,405,427	3,629,130	17,185	22,683	29,947	31,945
Form 1040	57,123	67,006	69,270	65,871	1,310,088	1,938,263	2,772,625	2,888,436	22,935	28,927	40,026	43,850
Salaries and wages	83,802	87,198	96,730	96,264	1,349,843	1,928,201	2,599,401	2,805,703	16,108	22,113	26,873	29,146
Interest received	49,020	64,526	70,370	67,281	102,009	182,109	227,084	162,343	2,081	2,822	3,227	2,413
Dividends in AGI	10,739	15,528	22,904	23,715	38,761	55,046	80,169	77,926	3,609	3,545	3,500	3,286
Business or profession profit less loss	8,881	11,900	11,222	11,727	55,129	78,773	141,430	154,002	6,207	6,620	12,603	13,132
Sales of capital assets, net gain less loss, in AGI	9,971	11,126	14,288	16,491	30,029	67,694	114,231	118,230	3,012	6,084	7,995	7,169
Pensions and annuities in AGI	7,374	13,133	17,041	17,676	43,340	95,096	159,294	186,492	5,878	7,241	9,348	10,551
Rents and royalties, net income less loss	8,208	9,964	10,317	10,155	4,105	-10,946	-3,156	4,559	500	-1,099	-306	449
Partnerships and S Corporations [1] profit less loss	3,910	5,488	5,977	5,358	10,099	-2,527	67,022	87,652	2,583	-460	11,213	16,359
Farm profit less loss	2,608	2,621	2,321	2,288	-1,792	-12,005	-434	-2,536	-687	-4,580	-187	-1,108
Statutory adjustments, total	13,149	37,763	16,648	17,171	28,614	95,082	33,974	35,464	2,176	2,518	2,041	2,065
Individual Retirement Arrangements	2,564	16,206	5,224	4,478	3,431	38,212	9,858	8,696	1,338	2,358	1,887	1,942
Self-employed retirement (Keogh) plan	569	676	824	(NA)	2,008	5,182	6,778	7,592	3,529	7,666	8,226	8,261
Married couples who both work	(NA)	24,835	(NA)	(NA)	919	24,615	(NA)	(NA)	(NA)	991	(NA)	(NA)
Exemptions, total [2]	227,925	244,180	227,549	230,547	227,569	253,720	485,985	523,042	998	1,039	2,135	2,269
Age 65 or older	11,847	16,749	(NA)	(NA)	(NA)	(NA)	(NA)	(NA)	(NA)	(NA)	(NA)	(NA)
Blind	185	327	(NA)	(NA)	(NA)	(NA)	(NA)	(NA)	(NA)	(NA)	(NA)	(NA)
Standard and itemized deductions, total [3]	88,105	96,849	112,796	112,613	362,776	554,734	789,942	848,479	4,118	5,728	7,003	7,534
Itemized deductions, total [3]	28,950	39,848	32,175	32,541	218,028	405,024	458,485	481,946	7,531	10,164	14,250	14,810
Medical and dental expenses	19,458	10,777	5,091	5,508	14,972	22,926	21,457	25,747	769	2,127	4,215	4,674
Taxes paid	28,749	39,548	31,594	31,959	69,404	128,085	140,011	160,453	2,414	3,239	4,432	5,021
Interest paid	26,677	36,287	29,395	27,347	91,187	180,095	208,354	208,656	3,418	4,963	7,088	7,630
Contributions	26,601	36,162	29,230	29,603	25,810	47,963	57,243	63,843	970	1,326	1,958	2,157
Taxable income [4]	88,105	96,124	93,148	90,717	1,279,985	1,820,741	2,263,661	2,395,690	14,528	18,942	24,302	26,408
Income tax before credits	76,136	85,994	93,089	90,633	256,294	332,165	453,128	482,631	3,366	3,863	4,868	5,325
Tax credits, total [2] [5]	19,674	20,995	12,484	12,733	7,216	10,248	6,831	7,749	367	488	547	609
Child care	4,231	8,418	6,144	5,980	956	3,128	2,549	2,527	226	372	415	423
Elderly and disabled	562	463	339	240	135	109	61	51	240	235	180	213
Residential energy	4,670	2,979	(NA)	(NA)	562	812	(NA)	(NA)	120	273	(NA)	(NA)
Foreign tax	393	454	772	1,069	1,342	783	1,682	2,047	3,415	1,725	2,179	1,915
General business credit [6]	(NA)	4,614	263	252	(NA)	4,791	616	575	(NA)	1,038	2,342	2,282
Income tax, total [7]	73,906	82,846	89,862	86,732	250,341	325,710	447,127	476,239	3,387	3,932	4,976	5,491

NA Not available. [1] S Corporations are certain small corporations with up to 35 shareholders (25 for 1982; 15 for 1980-81; 10 for 1970-75), mostly individuals, electing to be taxed at the shareholder level. [2] Includes items not shown separately. Beginning 1991, total exemptions amount is after limitation. [3] For 1985, includes charitable deduction for nonitemizers. Starting 1989, includes additional standard deductions for age 65 or older or for blindness. Beginning 1991, total itemized deductions are after limitation. [4] For 1980 and 1985, includes amounts "taxed" at zero percent. [5] For 1981, includes tax reduction credit. [6] Investment credit was included in the more-inclusive general business tax credit starting with 1984. With exceptions, investment credit was repealed effective 1986. [7] Includes minimum tax or alternative minimum tax.

Source: U.S. Internal Revenue Service, Statistics of Income Bulletin, and Statistics of Income, Individual Income Tax Returns, annual.

No. 534. Individual Income Tax Returns—Number, Income Tax, and Average Tax, by Size of Adjusted Gross Income: 1991 and 1992

[Number in thousands; money amounts in billions of dollars, except as indicated]

SIZE OF ADJUSTED GROSS INCOME	NUMBER OF RETURNS		ADJUSTED GROSS INCOME (AGI)		TAXABLE INCOME		INCOME TAX TOTAL [1]		TAX AS PERCENT OF AGI [2]		AVERAGE TAX ($1,000) [2]	
	1991	1992, prel.	1991	1992, prel.	1991	1992, prel.	1991	1992, prel.	1991	1992, prel.	1991	1992, prel.
Total.........	114,730	113,605	3,464.2	3,629.1	2,284.1	2,395.7	448.4	476.2	13.4	13.7	5.0	5.5
Less than $1,000 [3] .	3,775	3,515	−49.9	−49.9	0.1	0.1	0.2	0.1	3.4	3.2	0.1	0.1
$1,000-$2,999	7,084	6,568	13.9	13.1	1.0	0.9	0.2	0.1	4.7	4.7	0.1	0.1
$3,000-$4,999	6,136	5,890	24.5	23.5	1.7	1.3	0.3	0.2	3.6	3.2	0.1	0.1
$5,000-$6,999	6,103	5,962	36.7	35.8	4.1	3.6	0.6	0.6	3.3	3.5	0.2	0.2
$7,000-$8,999	6,100	5,909	48.8	47.2	9.7	7.8	1.5	1.2	4.9	4.2	0.4	0.3
$9,000-$10,999 ...	5,871	5,694	58.6	56.8	15.0	12.9	2.2	1.9	6.1	5.9	0.6	0.6
$11,000-$12,999...	5,573	5,583	66.8	66.9	20.5	19.1	2.8	2.7	6.4	6.4	0.8	0.8
$13,000-$14,999 ..	5,364	4,968	75.2	69.5	29.2	24.7	3.8	3.3	7.1	6.9	1.0	1.0
$15,000-$16,999 ..	5,104	4,871	81.6	77.9	36.3	32.2	4.7	4.2	7.3	7.4	1.2	1.2
$17,000-$18,999 ..	4,478	4,506	80.6	81.0	39.1	36.8	5.3	4.9	7.4	7.1	1.3	1.3
$19,000-$21,999 ..	6,106	6,215	125.1	127.3	66.6	64.5	9.6	9.1	7.9	7.6	1.6	1.6
$22,000-$24,999 ..	5,592	5,451	131.2	128.0	75.0	70.9	11.1	10.5	8.7	8.3	2.0	2.0
$25,000-$29,999 ..	7,874	7,590	216.1	208.2	131.5	123.6	20.0	18.5	9.4	9.0	2.6	2.5
$30,000-$39,999 ..	12,347	12,325	429.1	428.5	279.5	274.0	45.1	43.7	10.6	10.3	3.7	3.6
$40,000-$49,999 ..	8,817	9,009	393.5	403.1	266.3	269.2	43.5	43.6	11.1	10.9	4.9	4.9
$50,000-$74,999 ..	11,390	11,796	685.6	712.3	481.2	495.9	87.8	88.5	12.8	12.4	7.7	7.5
$75,000-$99,999 ..	3,572	3,988	305.0	340.6	222.0	247.4	47.0	51.6	15.4	15.1	13.2	12.9
$100,000-$199,999 .	2,598	2,811	339.1	368.4	258.3	280.7	62.8	67.4	18.6	18.3	24.2	24.0
$200,000-$499,999 .	676	746	196.3	218.6	165.2	186.1	46.3	52.0	23.6	23.8	68.5	69.8
$500,000-$999,999 .	118	141	79.6	95.4	69.7	84.3	20.5	24.8	25.8	26.0	173.4	175.7
$1,000,000 or more .	52	67	127.1	176.9	112.1	159.7	33.3	47.5	26.3	26.9	641.3	706.7

[1] Consists of income after credits, and alternative minimum tax.   [2] Computed using taxable returns only.   [3] In addition to low income taxpayers, this size class (and others) includes taxpayers with "tax preferences," not reflected in adjusted gross income or taxable income which are subject to the "alternative minimum tax" (included in total income tax).

Source: U.S. Internal Revenue Service, *Statistics of Income Bulletin,* quarterly and *Statistics of Income, Individual Income Tax Returns,* annual.

No. 535. Individual Income Tax Returns—Itemized Deductions and Statutory Adjustments, by Size of Adjusted Gross Income: 1992

[Preliminary]

ITEM	Unit	ADJUSTED GROSS INCOME CLASS							
		Total	Under $10,000	$10,000 to $19,999	$20,000 to $29,999	$30,000 to $39,999	$40,000 to $49,999	$50,000 to $99,999	$100,000 and over
Returns with itemized deductions:									
Number [1]	1,000 ..	32,541	796	2,409	3,705	4,608	5,057	12,408	3,557
Amount.................	Mil. dol .	481,946	7,429	23,423	35,810	46,875	56,368	183,780	128,262
Medical and dental expenses:									
Returns	1,000 ..	5,508	486	1,242	1,250	890	668	876	96
Amount	Mil. dol .	25,746	2,669	7,002	5,237	3,284	2,349	3,901	1,304
Taxes paid: Returns, total....	1,000 ..	31,960	690	2,216	3,616	4,542	5,015	12,336	3,546
State, local income taxes..	1,000 ..	27,222	366	1,534	3,037	3,888	4,395	10,869	3,133
Real estate taxes	1,000 ..	28,744	583	1,843	3,110	3,984	4,423	11,455	3,346
Amount, total	Mil. dol .	154,366	1,063	3,676	7,477	11,284	15,380	57,530	57,956
State, local income taxes..	Mil. dol .	96,946	162	983	3,000	5,790	8,405	34,723	43,883
Real estate taxes	Mil. dol .	57,243	902	2,693	4,478	5,494	6,795	22,808	14,073
Interest paid: Returns	1,000 ..	27,347	517	1,563	2,889	3,891	4,385	11,042	3,060
Amount	Mil. dol .	208,656	2,799	8,406	15,536	21,592	26,443	83,845	50,035
Home mortgages interest:									
Returns	1,000 ..	26,985	507	1,542	2,853	3,856	4,345	10,942	2,940
Amount	Mil. dol .	196,946	2,740	8,138	15,161	21,155	25,980	81,487	42,285
Contributions: Returns	1,000 ..	29,603	542	1,923	3,164	4,137	4,648	11,749	3,439
Amount	Mil. dol .	63,844	477	2,381	3,953	5,902	6,741	22,637	21,753
Employee business expense:									
Returns...............	1,000 ..	8,703	51	401	878	1,306	1,634	3,592	841
Amount	Mil. dol .	25,240	125	1,080	2,176	3,019	4,154	9,740	4,946
Returns with statutory adjus'mts: [2]									
Returns...............	1,000 ..	17,173	2,917	3,045	2,757	2,299	1,770	3,006	1,379
Amount of adjustments	Mil. dol .	35,466	1,728	3,340	4,095	3,706	3,023	8,427	11,147
Payments to IRA's: [3] Returns ..	1,000 ..	5,875	281	777	1,316	1,154	906	957	484
Amount	Mil. dol .	8,697	409	1,195	1,953	1,616	1,040	1,617	867
Payments to Keogh plans:									
Returns..............	1,000 ..	920	6	46	47	62	83	321	355
Amount	Mil. dol .	7,593	18	84	127	200	275	1,622	5,267
Alimony paid: Returns........	1,000 ..	682	54	85	72	94	70	192	115
Amount.................	Mil. dol .	5,512	253	414	318	493	394	1,582	2,058

[1] After limitations.   [2] Includes disability income exclusion, employee business expenses, moving expenses, forfeited interest penalty, alimony paid, deduction for expense of living abroad, and other data not shown separately.   [3] Individual Retirement Account.

Source: U.S. Internal Revenue Service, *Statistics of Income, Individual Income Tax Returns,* annual.

No. 536. Federal Individual Income Tax Returns—Adjusted Gross Income (AGI), by Source of Income and Income Class for Taxable Returns: 1992

[**In millions of dollars, except as indicated.** Minus sign (-) indicates net loss was greater than net income. See headnote, table 533]

ITEM	Total [1]	Under $10,000	$10,000 to $19,999	$20,000 to $29,999	$30,000 to $39,999	$40,000 to $49,999	$50,000 to $99,999	$100,000 and over
Number of returns(1,000)	86,732	11,586	17,697	16,705	12,239	8,982	15,753	3,761
Adjusted gross income (AGI) by source	3,483,882	70,244	268,721	412,066	425,474	401,920	1,050,981	858,513
Salaries and wages.	2,650,365	52,673	194,999	333,218	356,280	338,227	868,341	506,627
Percent of AGI for taxable returns . . .	76.3	75.0	72.6	80.9	83.7	84.2	82.6	59.0
Interest received.	188,730	6,402	21,187	19,773	16,240	14,828	43,630	66,670
Dividends in AGI.	73,747	1,533	5,126	5,323	5,414	4,485	17,775	33,971
Business; profession, net profit less loss.	143,786	2,644	7,870	13,568	12,731	11,511	36,823	58,639
Pensions and annuities in AGI	173,960	4,110	30,924	29,840	23,263	20,553	48,572	16,698
Sales of property, net [2]	111,098	660	1,997	2,205	3,343	3,986	16,250	82,657
Rents, royalties, net [3]	10,139	55	213	125	-809	-122	-1,100	11,777
Other sources, net	175,220	2,795	8,095	10,477	10,164	10,998	29,473	103,193
Percent of all returns: [4]								
Number of returns.	76.3	10.2	15.6	14.7	10.8	7.9	13.9	3.3
Adjusted gross income.	96.0	1.9	7.4	11.4	11.7	11.1	28.9	23.7
Salaries and wages.	94.5	1.9	7.0	11.9	12.7	12.1	30.9	18.1
Interest received.	87.6	9.0	13.3	14.2	12.6	10.5	22.7	34.6
Dividends in AGI.	94.3	2.0	6.6	6.8	6.9	5.7	22.8	43.5
Business; profession, net profit less loss.	93.4	1.7	5.1	8.8	8.3	7.5	23.9	38.1
Pensions and annuities in AGI	93.3	2.2	16.6	16.0	12.5	11.0	26.0	9.0
Sales of property [2]	96.1	0.6	1.7	1.9	2.9	3.4	14.1	71.5

[1] Includes a small number of taxable returns with no adjusted gross income.   [2] Includes sales of capital assets and other property; net gain less loss.   [3] Excludes rental passive losses disallowed in the computation of AGI; net income less loss. [4] Without regard to taxability.

Source: U.S. Internal Revenue Service, *Statistics of Income, Individual Income Tax Returns,* 1992.

No. 537. Federal Individual Income Tax Returns, by State, 1992

YEAR, DIVISION, STATE	Number of returns [1] (1,000)	Adjusted gross income (AGI) [2]	INCOME TAX Total [3] (mil. dol.)	INCOME TAX Per capita [4] (dol.)	YEAR, DIVISION, STATE	Number of returns [1] (1,000)	Adjusted gross income (AGI) [2]	INCOME TAX Total [3] (mil. dol.)	INCOME TAX Per capita [4] (dol.)
U.S.	**115,621**	**3,831,409**	**493,920**	**1,936**	DC. . . .	305	10,226	1,559	2,665
					VA	2,926	96,314	13,334	2,085
Northeast . .	**23,321**	**829,767**	**121,362**	**2,374**	WV . . .	693	18,243	2,263	1,251
N.E.	**6,160**	**220,673**	**32,584**	**2,469**	NC. . . .	3,097	88,167	11,137	1,629
ME . . .	550	14,947	1,835	1,485	SC. . . .	1,565	41,733	5,014	1,392
NH. . . .	532	17,825	2,525	2,265	GA. . . .	2,987	89,568	11,878	1,754
VT. . . .	263	7,417	947	1,658	FL. . . .	6,239	187,754	27,732	2,057
MA . . .	2,793	99,257	14,551	2,428	**E.S.C** . . .	**6,529**	**176,515**	**23,017**	**1,482**
RI	450	14,139	1,880	1,878	KY. . . .	1,531	41,645	5,297	1,411
CT. . . .	1,572	67,088	10,846	3,308	TN. . . .	2,213	62,725	8,729	1,737
M.A.	**17,161**	**609,094**	**88,778**	**2,341**	AL. . . .	1,745	47,859	6,126	1,480
NY. . . .	7,950	291,690	43,144	2,382	MS . . .	1,040	24,286	2,865	1,096
NJ. . . .	3,782	148,626	22,328	2,886	**W.S.C** . . .	**11,695**	**329,604**	**46,495**	**1,687**
PA	5,429	168,778	23,306	1,943	AR. . . .	990	24,763	3,092	1,292
Midwest . . .	**27,463**	**844,543**	**115,522**	**1,905**	LA	1,696	45,044	5,992	1,400
E.N.C . . .	**19,380**	**606,534**	**83,487**	**1,954**	OK. . . .	1,337	35,342	4,556	1,452
OH . . .	5,083	148,230	19,741	1,791	TX. . . .	7,672	224,455	32,855	1,858
IN	2,526	75,257	10,066	1,779	**West.**	**25,070**	**790,488**	**108,753**	**1,973**
IL	5,364	181,322	26,720	2,301	**Mountain** .	**6,667**	**187,585**	**25,212**	**1,753**
MI	4,122	131,884	17,823	1,889	MT. . . .	374	9,168	1,165	1,417
WI	2,285	69,841	9,137	1,830	ID	461	12,478	1,580	1,482
W.N.C . . .	**8,083**	**238,009**	**32,035**	**1,788**	WY . . .	212	6,198	895	1,925
MN . . .	2,065	67,253	9,149	2,048	CO . . .	1,662	52,167	7,366	2,126
IA	1,268	34,818	4,496	1,604	NM . . .	887	17,171	2,119	1,339
MO . . .	2,294	66,759	9,037	1,741	AZ. . . .	1,669	47,305	6,107	1,594
ND. . . .	284	7,228	963	1,519	UT. . . .	730	21,057	2,524	1,394
SD. . . .	318	8,071	1,129	1,594	NV. . . .	672	22,041	3,456	2,587
NE. . . .	741	20,431	2,691	1,681	**Pacific.** . . .	**18,403**	**602,903**	**83,541**	**2,050**
KS. . . .	1,113	33,449	4,570	1,817	WA . . .	2,411	81,105	11,940	2,322
South	**38,696**	**1,133,247**	**145,334**	**1,761**	OR . . .	1,348	39,711	5,145	1,731
S.A.	**20,472**	**627,128**	**85,822**	**1,903**	CA. . . .	13,722	453,941	62,480	2,022
DE. . . .	330	11,114	1,504	2,177	AK. . . .	353	9,747	1,504	2,558
MD . . .	2,330	84,009	11,401	2,319	HI	569	18,399	2,472	2,138

[1] Includes returns filled by nonresident aliens and certain self-employment tax returns.   [2] Less deficit.   [3] Includes additional tax for tax preferences, self-employment tax, tax from investment credit recapture, and other income-related taxes.   Total is before earned income credit.   [4] Based on resident population as of July 1.

Source: U.S. Internal Revenue Service, *Statistics of Income Bulletin,* quarterly.

No. 538. Federal Individual Income Tax—Tax Liability, Effective and Marginal Tax Rates, for Selected Income Groups: 1985 to 1994

[Refers to income after exclusions. Effective rate represents tax liability divided by stated income. The marginal tax rate is the percentage of the first additional dollar of income which would be paid in income tax. Computations assume the low income allowance, standard deduction, zero bracket amount, or itemized deductions equal to 10 percent of adjusted gross income, whichever is greatest. Excludes self employment tax. See *Historical Statistics, Colonial Times to 1970*, series Y 412-439, for similar data on net income]

ADJUSTED GROSS INCOME	1985	1988	1990	1991	1992	1993	1994
TAX LIABILITY							
Single person, no dependents:							
$5,000 [1]	177	8	-	-	-	-	-306
$10,000	888	758	705	668	615	593	563
$20,000	2,854	2,258	2,205	2,168	2,115	2,093	2,063
$25,000	4,125	3,294	2,988	2,918	2,865	2,843	2,813
$35,000	6,916	5,954	5,718	5,573	5,360	5,233	5,093
$50,000	12,067	9,734	9,498	9,353	9,168	9,069	8,957
$75,000	22,195	17,154	16,718	16,134	15,867	15,719	15,555
Married couple, two dependents: [2]							
$5,000 [3]	-550	-800	-700	-865	-920	-975	-1,500
$10,000 [3]	132	-858	-953	-1,235	-1,384	-1,511	2,528
$20,000 [4]	1,682	1,080	926	701	409	235	-359
$25,000	2,566	1,830	1,703	1,605	1,470	1,410	1,275
$35,000	4,916	3,330	3,203	3,105	2,970	2,910	2,828
$50,000	9,086	6,549	5,960	5,576	5,220	5,160	5,078
$75,000	17,649	12,849	12,386	12,072	11,670	11,471	11,216
EFFECTIVE RATE							
Single person, no dependents:							
$5,000 [1]	3.5	0.2	-	-	-	-	-6.1
$10,000	8.9	7.6	7.1	6.7	6.2	5.9	5.6
$20,000	14.3	11.3	11.0	10.8	10.6	10.5	10.3
$25,000	16.5	13.2	12.0	11.7	11.5	11.4	11.3
$35,000	19.8	17.0	16.3	15.9	15.3	15.0	14.6
$50,000	24.1	19.5	19.0	18.7	18.3	18.1	17.9
$75,000	29.6	22.9	22.3	21.5	21.2	21.0	20.7
Married couple, two dependents: [2]							
$5,000 [3]	-11.0	-14.0	-14.0	-17.3	-18.4	-19.5	-30.0
$10,000 [3]	1.3	-8.6	-9.5	-12.4	-13.8	-15.1	-25.3
$20,000 [4]	8.4	5.4	4.6	3.5	2.0	1.2	-1.8
$25,000	10.3	7.3	6.8	6.4	5.9	5.6	5.1
$35,000	14.0	9.5	9.2	8.9	8.5	8.3	8.1
$50,000	18.2	13.1	11.9	11.2	10.4	10.3	10.2
$75,000	23.5	17.1	16.5	16.1	15.6	15.3	15.0
MARGINAL TAX RATE							
Single person, no dependents:							
$5,000 [1]	12	15	-	-	-	-	7.7
$10,000	16	15	15	15	15	15	15
$20,000	26	15	15	15	15	15	15
$25,000	26	28	28	28	15	15	15
$35,000	34	28	28	28	28	28	28
$50,000	42	28	28	28	28	28	28
$75,000	48	33	33	31	31	31	31
Married couple, two dependents: [2]							
$5,000 [3]	-11.0	-14	-14	-17.3	-18.4	-19.5	-30
$10,000 [3]	24.2	10	-	-	-	-	-
$20,000 [4]	16	15	25	27.4	28.1	28.9	32.7
$25,000	18	15	15	15	15	15	32.7
$35,000	25	15	15	15	15	15	15
$50,000	33	28	28	28	15	15	15
$75,000	42	28	28	28	28	28	28

- Represents zero.   [1] 1994, refundable earned income credit.   [2] Only one spouse is assumed to work.   [3] Refundable earned income credit.   [4] Beginning 1990, refundable earned income credit.

Source: U.S. Dept. of the Treasury, Office of Tax Analysis, unpublished data.

No. 539. Federal Individual Income Tax—Current Income Equivalent to 1990 Constant Income for Selected Income Groups: 1985 to 1994

[Constant 1990 dollar incomes calculated by using the NIPA Personal Consumption Expenditure (PCE) deflator: 1970, 35.6; 1985, 93.1; 1988, 104.2; 1990, 114.9; 1991, 119.7; 1992, 123.5; 1993, 126.6; and 1994, 129.4 (estimated). See *Historical Statistics, Colonial Times to 1970*, series 412-439, for similar data on net income]

ADJUSTED GROSS INCOME	1985	1988	1990	1991	1992	1993	1994
REAL INCOME EQUIVALENT							
Single person, no dependents:							
$5,000	4,050	4,530	5,000	5,210	5,370	5,510	5,630
$10,000	8,100	9,070	10,000	10,420	10,750	11,020	11,260
$20,000	16,210	18,140	20,000	20,840	21,500	22,040	22,520
$25,000	20,260	22,670	25,000	26,040	26,870	27,550	28,150
$35,000	28,360	31,740	35,000	36,460	37,620	38,560	39,420
$50,000	40,510	45,340	50,000	52,090	53,740	55,090	56,310
$75,000	60,770	68,020	75,000	78,130	80,610	82,640	84,460
Married couple, two dependents: [1]							
$5,000	4,050	4,530	5,000	5,210	5,370	5,510	5,630
$10,000	8,100	9,070	10,000	10,420	10,750	11,020	11,260
$20,000	16,210	18,140	20,000	20,840	21,500	22,040	22,520
$25,000	20,260	22,670	25,000	26,040	26,870	27,550	28,150
$35,000	28,360	31,740	35,000	36,460	37,620	38,560	39,420
$50,000	40,510	45,340	50,000	52,090	53,740	55,090	56,310
$75,000	60,770	68,020	75,000	78,130	80,610	82,640	84,460
EFFECTIVE RATE (percent)							
Single person, no dependents:							
$5,000 [2]	1.7	-	-	-	-	-	-4.6
$10,000	7.4	6.8	7.1	7.0	6.8	6.8	6.7
$20,000	12.3	10.9	11.0	11.0	10.9	10.9	10.8
$25,000	14.4	11.7	12.0	11.9	11.7	11.7	11.7
$35,000	17.7	16.2	16.3	16.3	16.1	16.0	16.0
$50,000	21.5	18.9	19.0	19.0	18.8	18.8	18.7
$75,000	26.6	22.2	22.3	21.8	21.6	21.6	21.5
Married couple, two dependents: [1]							
$5,000 [3]	−11.0	−14.0	−14.0	−17.3	−18.4	−19.5	−30.0
$10,000 [3]	−3.8	−9.6	−9.5	−11.9	−12.9	−13.7	−22.0
$20,000 [4]	6.7	4.2	4.6	4.5	3.9	3.7	2.1
$25,000	8.5	6.5	6.8	6.8	6.5	6.5	6.4
$35,000	11.6	9.0	9.2	9.1	8.9	8.9	8.9
$50,000	15.6	11.6	11.9	11.8	11.4	11.4	11.2
$75,000	20.7	16.3	16.5	16.5	16.2	16.2	16.1
MARGINAL TAX RATE (percent)							
Single person, no dependents:							
$5,000 [2]	11	-	-	-	-	-	7.7
$10,000	15	15	15	15	15	15	15
$20,000	20	15	15	15	15	15	15
$25,000	26	15	28	28	15	15	15
$35,000	30	28	28	28	28	28	28
$50,000	38	28	28	28	28	28	28
$75,000	42	33	33	31	31	31	31
Married couple, two dependents: [1]							
$5,000 [3]	−11	−14	−14	−17.3	−18.4	−19.5	−30
$10,000 [3]	23.2	-	-	-	-	-	17.7
$20,000 [4]	14	25	25	27.4	28.1	28.9	32.7
$25,000	16	15	15	15	15	15	15
$35,000	22	15	15	15	15	15	15
$50,000	28	28	28	28	28	28	28
$75,000	38	28	28	28	28	28	28

- Represents zero.   [1] Only one spouse is assumed to work.   [2] 1994, refundable earned income credit.   [3] Refundable earned income credit.   [4] Beginning 1988, refundable earned income credit.

Source: U.S. Dept. of the Treasury, Office of Tax Analysis, unpublished data.

No. 540. Federal Civilian Employment, by Branch and Agency: 1985 to 1994

[As of September 30]

AGENCY	1985	1990	1991	1992	1993	1994, prel.
Total, all agencies	3,020,531	3,128,267	3,111,912	3,085,323	3,013,508	2,971,357
Legislative Branch, total [1]	38,764	37,495	38,504	38,509	38,258	35,357
Congress [1]	19,656	19,474	20,178	20,084	20,336	18,903
U.S. Senate	7,294	7,369	7,571	7,620	7,550	7,370
House of Representatives	12,351	12,089	12,587	12,446	12,769	11,518
Architect of the Capitol.	2,145	2,235	2,316	2,346	2,355	2,182
Judicial Branch	18,225	23,605	25,805	27,987	28,120	28,035
Supreme Court	337	332	343	353	354	347
U.S. Courts	17,888	23,221	25,392	27,551	27,677	27,688
Executive Branch, total	2,963,542	3,067,167	3,047,603	3,018,827	2,947,130	2,907,965
Executive Office of the President [1]	1,526	1,731	1,758	1,866	1,631	1,568
White House Office	367	396	347	392	404	378
Office of the Vice-President	20	21	16	20	21	20
Office of Management and Budget . . .	566	574	609	586	527	519
Office of Administration	194	205	228	247	209	188
Council of Economic Advisors	30	34	34	34	28	32
Executive Departments	1,789,270	2,065,542	2,054,094	2,038,675	1,972,569	1,907,668
State	25,254	25,288	25,699	25,734	26,077	25,596
Treasury	130,084	158,655	166,433	161,951	156,073	156,373
Defense	1,084,549	1,034,152	1,012,716	982,774	921,179	879,651
Justice	64,433	83,932	90,821	96,927	97,898	97,910
Interior	77,485	77,679	81,683	85,260	84,864	80,704
Agriculture	117,750	122,594	125,640	128,324	124,199	119,558
Commerce	35,150	69,920	38,087	38,086	38,680	37,642
Labor	18,260	17,727	17,938	17,889	17,407	16,732
Health & Human Services	140,151	123,959	129,483	131,191	130,216	128,244
Housing & Urban Development	12,289	13,596	14,998	13,701	13,459	13,218
Transportation	62,227	67,364	69,831	70,558	69,144	64,896
Energy	16,749	17,731	19,539	20,962	20,336	19,899
Education	4,889	4,771	5,081	5,113	5,002	4,813
Veterans Affairs [2]	247,156	248,174	256,145	260,205	268,035	262,432
Independent agencies [1]	1,172,746	999,894	991,751	978,286	972,930	998,729
Environmental Protection Agency	13,788	17,123	18,218	18,196	18,415	18,092
Equal Employment Opportunity Comm	3,222	2,880	2,889	2,899	2,868	2,914
Federal Deposit Insurance Corporation	6,723	17,641	22,007	22,467	21,701	18,775
Fed. Emergency Management Agency	3,133	3,137	3,130	5,632	5,099	5,221
General Services Administration	25,782	20,277	21,122	20,770	20,502	19,257
National Aeronautics & Space Admin .	22,562	24,872	25,737	25,425	24,826	23,338
Nuclear Regulatory Commission	3,605	3,353	3,534	3,528	3,476	3,336
Office of Personnel Management	6,353	6,636	6,757	6,941	6,776	6,240
Small Business Administration	4,960	5,128	4,867	5,897	5,526	5,340
Smithsonian Institution, Summary	4,757	5,092	5,360	5,514	5,497	5,527
Tennessee Valley Authority	32,035	28,392	24,870	19,493	18,986	18,846
U.S. Information Agency	8,851	8,555	8,213	8,342	8,283	7,888
U.S. International Development Cooperation Agency	5,054	4,698	4,575	4,542	4,273	4,059
U.S. Postal Service	750,021	816,886	804,338	791,992	790,286	822,699

[1] Includes branches, or agencies, not shown separately.   [2] Formerly Veterans Administration.

Source: U.S. Office of Personnel Management, *Federal Civilian Workforce Statistics— Employment and Trends,* bimonthly.

No. 541. Paid Full-Time Federal Civilian Employment, all Areas: 1990 to 1994

[As of March 31. Excludes employees of Congress and Federal courts, maritime seamen of Dept. of Commerce, and small number for whom rates were not reported. See text, section 10, for explanation of general schedule and wage system. See also *Historical Statistics, Colonial Times to 1970,* series Y 318-331]

COMPENSATION AUTHORITY	EMPLOYEES (1,000)				AVERAGE PAY			
	1990	1992	1993	1994	1990	1992	1993	1994
Total	2,697	2,776	2,709	2,681	31,174	35,357	37,327	39,129
General Schedule	1,506	1,537	1,520	1,479	31,239	35,254	37,332	39,070
Wage System	369	328	315	290	26,565	28,852	30,136	31,299
Postal pay system [1]	661	725	692	729	29,264	31,839	32,458	33,592
Other	161	186	182	183	41,149	42,689	49,743	51,996

[1] Source: Employees—U.S. Postal Service, *Annual Report of the Postmaster General.* Average pay—U.S. Postal Service, *Comprehensive Statement of Postal Operations,* annual.

Source: Except as noted, U.S. Office of Personnel Management, *Pay Structure of the Federal Civil Service,* annual.

No. 542. Federal Civilian Employment and Annual Payroll, by Branch: 1970 to 1993

[Average annual employment: **For fiscal year ending in year shown**; see text, section 9. Includes employees in U.S. territories and foreign countries. Data represent employees in active-duty status, including intermittent employees. Annual employment figures are averages of monthly figures. Excludes Central Intelligence Agency, National Security Agency, and, as of November 1984, the Defense Intelligence Agency. See also *Historical Statistics, Colonial Times to 1970*, series Y 308-317]

YEAR	EMPLOYMENT Total (1,000)	Percent of U.S. employed[1]	Executive Total (1,000)	Executive Defense	Legislative (1,000)	Judicial (1,000)	PAYROLL (mil. dol.) Total	Executive Total	Executive Defense	Legislative	Judicial
1970	[2]2,997	3.8	2,961	1,263	29	7	27,322	26,894	11,264	338	89
1971	2,899	3.7	2,861	1,162	31	7	29,475	29,007	11,579	369	98
1972	2,882	3.5	2,842	1,128	32	8	31,626	31,102	12,181	411	112
1973	2,822	3.3	2,780	1,076	33	9	33,240	32,671	12,414	447	121
1974	2,825	3.3	2,781	1,041	35	9	35,661	35,035	12,789	494	132
1975	2,877	3.4	2,830	1,044	37	10	39,126	38,423	13,418	549	154
1976	2,879	3.2	2,831	1,025	38	11	42,259	41,450	14,699	631	179
1977	2,855	3.1	2,803	997	39	12	45,895	44,975	15,696	700	219
1978	2,875	3.0	2,822	987	40	13	49,921	48,899	16,995	771	251
1979	2,897	2.9	2,844	974	40	13	53,590	52,513	18,065	817	260
1980	[3]2,987	3.0	2,933	971	40	14	58,012	56,841	18,795	883	288
1981	2,909	2.9	2,855	986	40	15	63,793	62,510	21,227	922	360
1982	2,871	2.9	2,816	1,019	39	16	65,503	64,125	22,226	980	398
1983	2,878	2.9	2,823	1,033	39	16	69,878	68,420	23,406	1,013	445
1984	2,935	2.8	2,879	1,052	40	17	74,616	73,084	25,253	1,081	451
1985	3,001	2.8	2,944	1,080	39	18	80,599	78,992	28,330	1,098	509
1986	3,047	2.8	2,991	1,089	38	19	82,598	80,941	29,272	1,112	545
1987	3,075	2.7	3,018	1,084	38	19	85,543	83,797	29,786	1,153	593
1988	3,113	2.7	3,054	1,073	38	21	88,841	86,960	29,609	1,226	656
1989	3,133	2.7	3,074	1,067	38	22	92,847	90,870	30,301	1,266	711
1990	[4]3,233	2.7	3,173	1,060	38	23	99,138	97,022	31,990	1,329	787
1991	3,101	2.7	3,038	1,015	38	25	104,273	101,965	32,956	1,434	874
1992	3,106	2.6	3,040	1,004	39	27	108,054	105,402	31,486	1,569	1,083
1993	3,043	2.6	2,976	952	39	28	114,323	111,523	32,755	1,609	1,191

[1] Civilian only. See table 628.　[2] Includes 33,000 temporary census workers.　[3] Includes 81,116 temporary census workers.　[4] Includes 111,020 temporary census workers.

Source: U.S. Office of Personnel Management, *Federal Civilian Workforce Statistics—Employment and Trends*, bimonthly; and unpublished data.

No. 543. Federal Executive Branch (non-Postal) Employment, by Race and National Origin: 1985 to 1993

[As of **Sept. 30**. Covers total employment for only Executive branch agencies participating in OPM's Central Personnel Data File (CPDF)]

PAY SYSTEM	1985	1990	1991	1992	1993
All personnel	**2,087,722**	**2,150,359**	**2,183,403**	**2,175,715**	**2,110,510**
White, non-Hispanic	1,553,218	1,562,846	1,581,388	1,570,812	1,515,700
General schedule and equivalent	1,196,576	1,218,188	1,239,964	1,228,634	1,190,705
Grades 1-4 ($11,903 - $21,307)	187,779	132,028	127,344	112,948	99,006
Grades 5-8 ($18,340 - $32,710)	344,312	337,453	344,483	338,182	320,410
Grades 9-12 ($27,789 - $52,385)	467,803	510,261	517,004	509,978	500,616
Grades 13-15 ($47,920 - $86,589)	196,682	238,446	251,133	267,526	270,673
Total Executives/Senior Pay Levels [1]	7,179	9,337	12,998	13,661	13,162
Wage pay system	283,107	244,220	238,136	232,753	215,122
Other pay systems	66,356	91,101	90,290	95,764	96,711
Black	338,435	356,867	363,864	360,725	351,879
General schedule and equivalent	248,732	272,657	281,559	277,264	272,393
Grades 1-4 ($11,903 - $21,307)	78,413	65,077	64,396	56,650	51,142
Grades 5-8 ($18,340 - $32,710)	98,928	114,993	119,566	120,259	118,438
Grades 9-12 ($27,789 - $52,385)	59,332	74,985	78,109	78,970	80,130
Grades 13-15 ($47,920 - $86,589)	12,059	17,602	19,488	21,385	22,683
Total Executives/Senior Pay Levels [1]	343	479	630	662	716
Wage pay system	84,492	72,755	71,615	69,976	65,422
Other pay systems	4,868	10,976	10,060	12,823	13,348
Hispanic	102,421	115,170	118,769	120,296	117,935
General schedule and equivalent	69,241	83,218	88,051	87,947	87,200
Grades 1-4 ($11,903 - $21,307)	18,002	15,738	16,308	14,240	13,027
Grades 5-8 ($18,340 - $32,710)	23,876	28,727	30,852	31,708	30,985
Grades 9-12 ($27,789 - $52,385)	22,737	31,615	32,965	33,121	33,758
Grades 13-15 ($47,920 - $86,589)	4,626	7,138	7,926	8,878	9,430
Total Executives/Senior Pay Levels [1]	92	154	250	281	274
Wage pay system	30,177	26,947	26,294	26,151	24,515
Other pay systems	2,911	4,851	4,174	5,917	5,946
American Indian, Alaska Natives, Asians, and Pacific	93,648	115,476	119,382	123,882	124,996

[1] General schedule pay rates as of January 1993. Senior Pay Levels effective as of October 1, 1991.

Source: Office of Personnel Management, Central Personnel Data File.

No. 544. Paid Civilian Employment in the Federal Government: 1992

[As of **December 31**. Excludes Central Intelligence Agency, Defense Intelligence Agency, seasonal and on-call employees, and National Security Agency]

DIVISION AND STATE	Total (1,000)	Percent Defense	DIVISION AND STATE	Total (1,000)	Percent Defense
United States	2,988	30.0	District of Columbia	223	7.7
			Virginia.	168	64.1
Northeast	483	25.1	West Virginia.	17	10.2
New England.	127	24.5	North Carolina	51	32.6
Maine	16	53.6	South Carolina	33	53.1
New Hampshire.	8	17.2	Georgia	93	39.5
Vermont.	6	10.8	Florida	114	28.2
Massachusetts	62	18.3	**East South Central**.	176	33.1
Rhode Island.	10	40.9	Kentucky	38	37.4
Connecticut.	24	19.6	Tennessee	54	13.4
Middle Atlantic	355	25.3	Alabama.	58	45.3
New York	149	11.9	Mississippi	26	40.6
New Jersey.	74	33.1	**West South Central**	280	33.5
Pennsylvania.	132	36.1	Arkansas	21	23.7
Midwest	512	23.6	Louisiana	35	25.0
East North Central	331	25.5	Oklahoma	46	47.4
Ohio	94	37.4	Texas.	179	32.7
Indiana.	43	36.0	**West**	655	35.4
Illinois	106	18.1	Mountain.	202	29.0
Michigan	59	19.6	Montana.	12	10.4
Wisconsin.	30	10.9	Idaho.	11	13.3
West North Central	180	20.1	Wyoming	7	16.3
Minnesota.	34	8.6	Colorado	57	24.7
Iowa	20	7.7	New Mexico	28	33.7
Missouri	66	27.5	Arizona	40	23.9
North Dakota.	8	23.5	Utah	35	55.4
South Dakota	10	13.4	Nevada	12	17.9
Nebraska	16	23.5	**Pacific**	453	38.3
Kansas	26	24.9	Washington.	69	42.5
South.	1,297	32.7	Oregon	31	10.0
South Atlantic	840	32.3	California	312	37.7
Delaware	5	31.4	Alaska	16	31.4
Maryland	136	30.0	Hawaii	25	73.4

Source: U.S. Office of Personnel Management, *Biennial Report of Employment by Geographic Area.*

No. 545. Federal General Schedule Employee Pay Increases: 1965 to 1994

[Percent change from prior year shown, except 1965, change from 1964. Represents legislated pay increases. For some years data based on range; for details see source]

DATE	AVERAGE INCREASE		DATE	AVERAGE INCREASE		DATE	AVERAGE INCREASE	
	Civilian	Military		Civilian	Military		Civilian	Military
1965	3.6	10.4	1974	5.5	5.5	1985	3.5	4.0
1966	2.9	3.2	1975	5.0	5.0	1986	-	3.0
1967	4.5	5.6	1976	5.2	3.6	1987	3.0	3.0
1968	4.9	6.9	1977	7.0	6.2	1988	2.0	2.0
1969	9.1	12.6	1978	5.5	5.5	1989	4.1	4.1
1970	6.0	8.1	1979	7.0	7.0	1990	3.6	3.6
1971	6.0	7.9	1980	9.1	11.7	1991	4.1	4.1
1972	5.5	7.2	1981	4.8	14.3	1992	4.2	(NA)
1972	5.1	6.7	1982	4.0	4.0	1993	3.7	(NA)
1973	4.8	6.2	1984	4.0	4.0	1994	(^{1})	(NA)

- Represents zero.   NA Not available.   [1] Locality pay, 3.09 percent to 8.00 percent.

Source of tables: U.S. Office of Personnel Management, *Pay Structure of the Federal Civil Service,* annual.

No. 546. Accessions to and Separations From Employment in the Federal Government: 1993 and 1994

[As of September 30]

| AGENCY | ACCESSIONS | | | | SEPARATIONS | | | |
| | Number | | Rate | | Number | | Rate | |
	1993	1994	1993	1994	1993	1994	1993	1994
Total, all agencies	599,530	529,026	20.0	18.0	659,487	565,035	22.0	19.2
Legislative Branch, total [1]	1,147	840	6.3	5.0	2,037	2,800	11.2	16.7
General Accounting Office	181	160	3.5	3.5	483	794	9.4	17.1
Government Printing Office	92	84	1.9	1.9	245	593	5.1	13.4
Library of Congress	511	360	10.3	7.8	663	860	13.3	18.6
Judicial Branch	14	3	16.3	(Z)	9	9	10.5	(Z)
Executive Branch, total	598,369	528,183	20.1	18.0	657,441	562,226	22.1	19.2
Executive Office of the President	860	311	45.3	19.6	934	367	49.2	23.1
Executive Departments	358,106	293,901	17.9	15.2	397,609	370,148	19.8	19.2
State	4,166	3,502	16.0	13.5	4,060	3,893	15.6	15.1
Treasury	53,484	45,954	32.5	28.8	59,243	52,550	36.1	32.9
Defense	152,473	124,483	16.0	13.8	197,838	172,624	20.8	19.2
Justice	9,149	9,268	9.3	9.5	4,481	6,749	4.6	6.9
Interior	20,898	12,463	25.6	15.7	17,393	14,958	21.3	18.8
Agriculture	34,258	31,255	28.3	27.0	39,365	39,209	32.6	33.9
Commerce	8.013	5,228	20.9	13.9	6,312	6,434	16.5	17.1
Labor	1,083	889	6.1	5.2	1,593	1,593	9.0	9.3
Health & Human Services	15,702	13,042	11.9	10.1	13,441	14,362	10.2	11.1
Housing & Urban Development	971	675	7.3	5.1	1,235	1,124	9.3	8.6
Transportation	3,208	1,647	4.6	2.5	5,469	6,692	7.8	10.0
Energy	1,570	1,596	7.6	7.9	2,083	1,888	10.1	9.4
Education	583	628	11.6	12.8	353	613	7.0	12.5
Veterans Affairs [2]	52,548	43,271	19.9	16.4	44,743	47,459	17.0	18.0
Independent agencies [1]	239,403	233,971	24.7	23.5	258,898	191,711	26.7	19.3
Board of Governors, Fed RSRV System	249	182	15.2	10.9	167	189	10.2	11.3
Environmental Protection Agency	2,196	1,451	11.9	8.0	1,961	1,732	10.6	9.5
Equal Employment Opportunity Comm	179	242	6.1	8.4	168	136	5.7	4.7
Federal Deposit Insurance Corporation	3,280	1,246	14.9	6.2	4,168	4,527	18.9	22.6
Fed. Emergency Management Agency	2,759	5,310	60.3	93.9	2,621	3,438	57.3	60.8
General Services Administration	1,926	430	9.3	2.2	1,705	1,210	8.2	6.1
National Aeronautics & Space Admin	2,130	2,341	8.5	9.7	2,669	3,695	10.6	15.3
National Archives & Records Admin	644	585	20.4	18.8	316	200	10.0	6.4
Nuclear Regulatory Commission	150	127	4.2	3.7	195	240	5.5	7.0
Office of Personnel Management	707	340	10.3	5.5	864	1,448	12.6	23.5
Panama Canal Comm	1,388	1,125	16.2	13.1	1,289	1,131	15.1	13.2
Railroad Retirement Board	92	50	5.1	2.9	131	151	7.2	8.8
Securities and Exchange Commission	349	367	12.9	13.7	278	335	10.3	12.5
Small Business Administration	2,057	4,575	36.4	70.7	2,452	3,464	43.4	53.5
Smithsonian Institution	849	793	15.4	14.5	892	853	16.2	15.6
Tennessee Valley Authority	951	674	5.0	3.6	1,402	716	7.3	3.8
U.S. Information Agency	529	338	6.4	4.2	556	830	6.7	10.2
U.S. International Dev. Coop. Agency	463	397	10.5	9.5	733	621	16.6	14.8
U.S. Postal Service	215,964	210,663	27.5	25.9	233,602	164,082	29.7	20.2

Z Less than .05.   [1] Includes other branches, or other agencies, not shown separately.   [2] Formerly Veterans Administration.

Source: U.S. Office of Personnel Management, *Federal Civilian Workforce Statistics, Employment and Trends,* bimonthly.

No. 547. Federal Land and Buildings Owned and Leased, and Predominant Land Usage: 1980 to 1991

[**For fiscal years ending in years shown;** see text, section 9. Covers Federal real property throughout the world, except as noted. Cost of land figures represent total cost of property owned in year shown. For further details see source. For data on Federal land by State, see table 354]

ITEM AND AGENCY	Unit	1980	1985	1986	1987	1988	1989	1990	1991
Federally owned: Land	Mil. acres	720	727	727	724	688	662	650	650
Buildings, number [1]	1,000	403	454	429	412	442	451	446	441
Cost of land, buildings, etc.[2]	Bil. dol.	107	148	158	165	164	164	180	181
Federally leased: Land	Mil. acres	1.4	1.3	1.3	1.6	1.6	1.5	0.9	(NA)
Buildings, floor area [1]	Mil. sq/ft	214	237	246	246	248	254	234	242
Rental property, cost	Mil. dol	1,054	1,681	1,774	1,893	2,001	2,127	2,125	(NA)
Predominant usage (U.S. only)	Mil. acres	720	727	727	724	688	662	650	650
Forest and wildlife	Mil. acres	422	431	431	431	400	375	368	(NA)
Grazing	Mil. acres	162	155	155	154	151	151	154	(NA)
Parks and historic sites	Mil. acres	93	94	96	96	99	98	96	(NA)
Other	Mil. acres	43	48	46	43	38	39	33	(NA)

NA Not available.   [1] Excludes data for Dept. of Defense military functions outside United States.   [2] Includes other uses not shown separately.

Source: U.S. General Services Administration, *Inventory Report on Real Property Owned by the United States Throughout the World,* annual.

Figure 11.1
Military and Civilian Personnel: 1985 to 1994

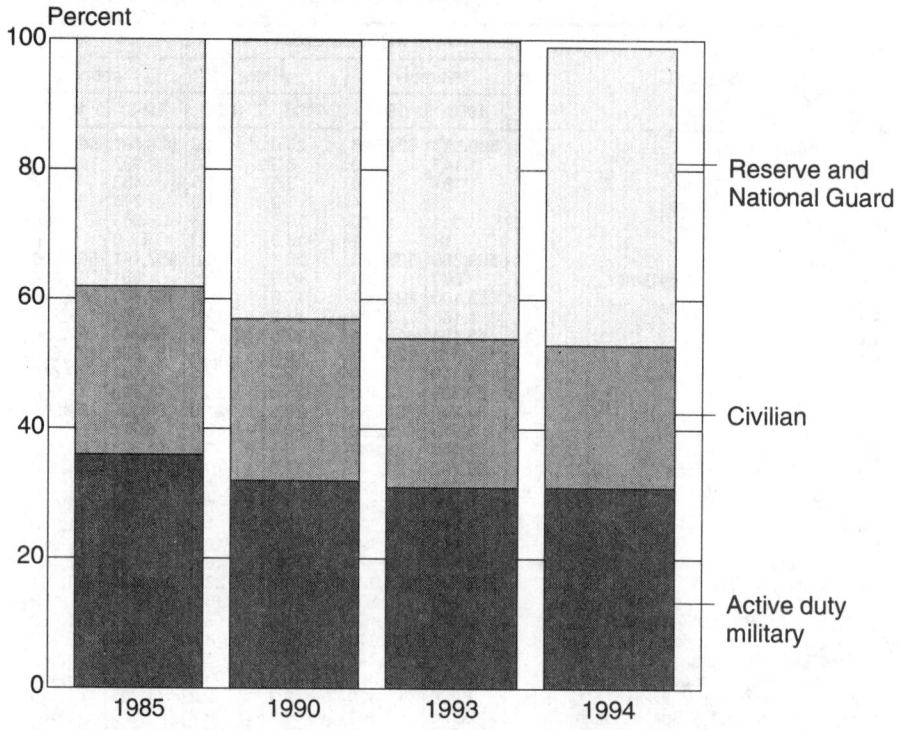

Source: Chart prepared by U.S. Bureau of the Census. For data, see table 552.

Figure 11.2
**Military and Civilian Expenditures,
by Major Location: 1994**

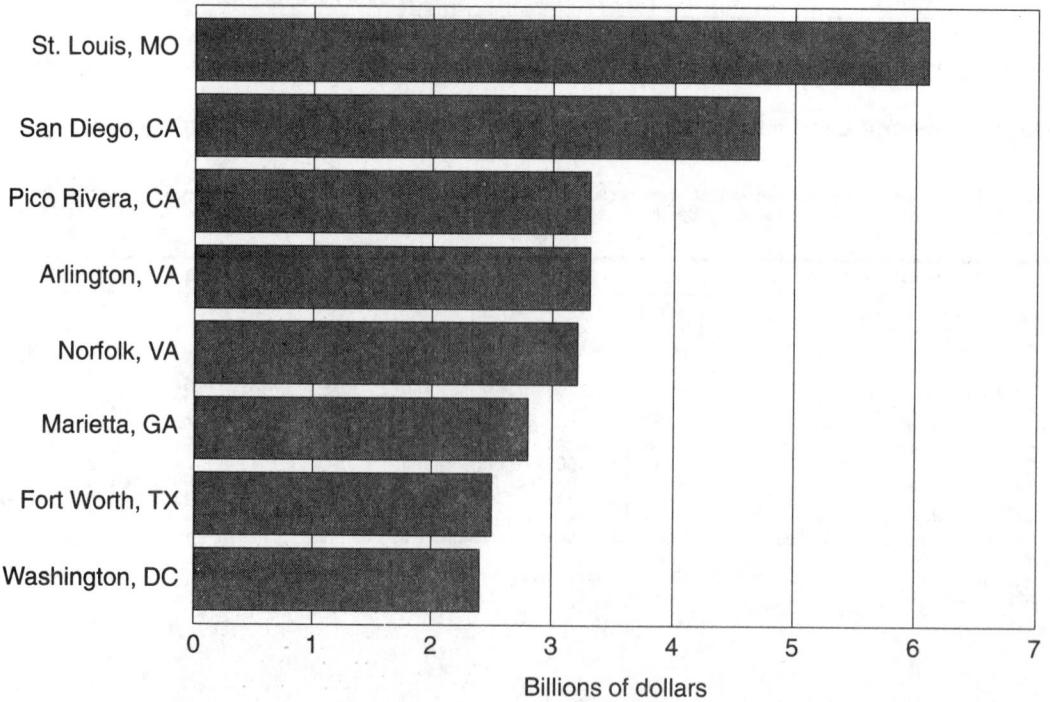

Billions of dollars

Source: Chart prepared by U.S. Bureau of the Census. For data, see table 552.

National Defense and Veterans Affairs

This section presents data on national defense and its human and financial costs; active and reserve military personnel; ships, equipment and aircraft; and federally sponsored programs and benefits for veterans. The principal sources of these data are the annual *Selected Manpower Statistics* and the *Atlas/Data Abstract for the United States and Selected Areas* issued by the Office of the Secretary of Defense; *Annual Report of Secretary of Veterans Affairs, Department of Veterans Affairs,* and *The Budget of the United States Government,* Office of Management and Budget. For more data on expenditures, personnel, and ships, see section 31.

Department of Defense (DOD).—DOD is responsible for providing military forces of the United States. The President serves as Commander in Chief of the Armed Forces; from him, the authority flows to the Secretary of Defense and through the Joint Chiefs of Staff to the commanders of unified and specified commands (e.g., United States European Command).

Reserve components.—Reserve personnel of the Armed Forces consist of the Army National Guard, Army Reserve, Naval Reserve, Marine Corps Reserve, Air National Guard, Air Force Reserve, and Coast Guard Reserve. They provide trained personnel available for active duty in the Armed Forces in time of war or national emergency and at such other times as authorized by law. The National Guard has dual Federal-State responsibilities and uses jointly provided equipment, facilities, and budget support. The President is empowered to mobilize the National Guard and to use such of the Armed Forces as he considers necessary to enforce Federal authority in any State.

The ready reserve includes selected reservists who are intended to assist active forces in a war and the individual ready reserve who, in a major war, would be used to fill out active and reserve units and later would be a source of combat replacements; a portion of the ready reserve serves in an active status. The

In Brief	
	1993
Worldwide military expenditures	$869 bil.
U.S. miliary expenditures	$298 bil.

standby reserve cannot be called to active duty unless the Congress gives explicit approval. The retired reserve represents a low potential for mobilization.

Department of Veterans Affairs.—The Department of Veterans Affairs administers laws authorizing benefits for eligible former and present members of the Armed Forces and for the beneficiaries of deceased members. Veterans benefits available under various acts of Congress include compensation for service-connected disability or death; pensions for nonservice-connected disability or death; vocational rehabilitation, education, and training; home loan insurance; life insurance; health care; special housing and automobiles or other conveyances for certain disabled veterans; burial and plot allowances; and educational assistance to families of deceased or totally disabled veterans, servicemen missing in action, or prisoners of war. Since these benefits are legislated by Congress, the dates they were enacted and the dates they apply to veterans may be different from the actual dates the conflicts occurred.

VA estimates of veterans cover all persons with active duty service during periods of war or armed conflict and until 1982 include those living outside the United States. Veteran population estimates for September 1982 are for the 50 States, the District of Columbia and Puerto Rico. Veterans whose active duty service was entirely during periods of peacetime are eligible for some veterans benefits and, where appropriate, are included in VA estimates.

Historical statistics.—Tabular headnotes provide cross-references, where applicable, to *Historical Statistics of the United States, Colonial Times to 1970.* See Appendix IV.

No. 548. National Defense Outlays and Veterans Benefits: 1960 to 1995

[For fiscal year ending in year shown; see text, section 9. Includes outlays of Department of Defense, Department of Veterans Affairs, and other agencies for activities primarily related to national defense and veterans programs. For explanation of average annual percent change, see Guide to Tabular Presentation. Minus sign (-) indicates decline. See Historical Statistics, Colonial Times to 1970, series Y 472, 473, and Y 476, for related data]

| YEAR | NATIONAL DEFENSE AND VETERANS OUTLAYS | | | | ANNUAL PERCENT CHANGE [1] | | | DEFENSE OUTLAYS, PERCENT OF— | |
| | Total outlays (bil. dol.) | Defense outlays | | Veterans outlays (bil. dol.) | Total outlays | Defense outlays | Veterans outlays | Federal outlays | Gross domestic product [2] |
		Current dollars (bil. dol.)	Constant (1987) dollars (bil. dol.)						
1960	53.5	48.1	220.1	5.4	2.5	2.4	3.1	52.2	9.5
1965	56.3	50.6	203.9	5.7	-6.8	-7.6	0.7	42.8	7.5
1966	64.0	58.1	225.9	5.9	13.7	14.8	3.5	43.2	7.9
1967	78.1	71.4	269.1	6.7	22.1	22.9	13.8	45.4	9.0
1968	88.9	81.9	295.5	7.0	13.8	14.7	4.4	46.0	9.7
1969	90.1	82.5	282.5	7.6	1.3	0.7	8.5	44.9	8.9
1970	90.4	81.7	262.9	8.7	0.3	-1.0	13.6	41.8	8.3
1971	88.7	78.9	236.9	9.8	-1.9	-3.5	12.7	37.5	7.5
1972	89.9	79.2	219.7	10.7	1.4	0.4	9.8	34.3	6.9
1973	88.7	76.7	197.2	12.0	1.3	-3.1	12.0	31.2	6.0
1974	92.7	79.3	185.3	13.4	4.6	3.5	11.4	29.5	5.7
1975	103.1	86.5	183.9	16.6	11.2	9.0	24.0	26.0	5.7
1976	108.1	89.6	177.8	18.4	4.8	3.6	11.0	24.1	5.3
1976, TQ [3]	26.2	22.3	42.4	4.0	(X)	(X)	(X)	23.2	5.0
1977	115.2	97.2	176.8	18.0	6.7	8.5	-2.1	23.8	5.1
1978	123.5	104.5	177.2	19.0	7.1	7.5	5.2	22.8	4.8
1979	136.2	116.3	180.4	19.9	10.4	11.3	5.0	23.1	4.8
1980	155.2	134.0	187.1	21.2	13.9	15.2	6.3	22.7	5.1
1981	180.5	157.5	198.2	23.0	16.3	17.6	8.5	23.2	5.3
1982	209.3	185.3	214.3	24.0	15.9	17.6	4.2	24.8	5.9
1983	234.7	209.9	230.4	24.8	12.1	13.3	3.3	26.0	6.3
1984	253.0	227.4	241.7	25.6	7.8	8.3	3.2	26.7	6.2
1985	279.0	252.7	261.2	26.3	10.3	11.1	2.7	26.7	6.4
1986	299.8	273.4	276.4	26.4	7.4	8.2	0.4	27.6	6.5
1987	308.8	282.0	282.0	26.8	3.0	3.1	1.5	28.1	6.3
1988	319.8	290.4	283.3	29.4	3.6	3.0	9.7	27.3	6.0
1989	333.7	303.6	285.9	30.1	4.3	4.5	2.4	26.6	5.9
1990	328.4	299.3	272.6	29.1	-1.6	-1.4	-3.3	23.9	5.5
1991	304.6	273.3	240.5	31.3	-7.2	-8.7	7.6	20.7	4.8
1992	332.5	298.4	249.7	34.1	12.0	12.4	8.0	21.6	5.0
1993	326.1	291.1	237.2	35.7	-1.9	-2.4	4.6	20.7	4.7
1994	319.2	281.6	220.6	37.6	-2.3	-3.3	5.3	19.3	4.2
1995	310.0	271.6	206.7	38.4	-2.9	-3.6	2.1	17.6	3.9

X Not applicable.   [1] Change from prior year shown; for 1960, change from 1955.   [2] Represents fiscal year GDP; for definition, see text, section 14.   [3] Transition quarter, July-Sept.

Source: U.S. Office of Management and Budget, Historical Tables, annual.

No. 549. Federal Budget Outlays for National Defense Functions: 1970 to 1995

[In billions of dollars, except percent. For fiscal year ending in year shown; see text, section 9. Minus sign (-) indicates decline. See Historical Statistics, Colonial Times to 1970, series Y 473, for total]

DEFENSE FUNCTION	1970	1980	1985	1987	1988	1989	1990	1991	1992	1993	1994	1995, est.
Total	81.7	134.0	252.7	282.0	290.4	303.6	299.3	273.3	298.4	291.1	281.6	271.6
Percent change [1]	10.1	15.2	11.1	3.1	3.0	4.5	-1.4	-8.7	9.2	-2.4	0.6	-3.6
Defense Dept., military	80.1	130.9	245.2	274.0	281.9	294.9	289.8	262.4	286.9	278.6	268.6	260.2
Military personnel	29.0	40.9	67.8	72.0	76.3	80.7	75.6	83.4	81.2	75.9	73.1	70.8
Percent of military	36.2	31.2	27.7	26.3	27.1	27.0	26.1	31.8	28.3	27.2	27.2	27.2
Operation, maintenance	21.6	44.8	72.4	76.2	84.5	87.0	88.3	101.8	92.0	94.1	87.9	90.1
Procurement	21.6	29.0	70.4	80.7	77.2	81.6	81.0	82.0	74.9	69.9	61.8	54.7
Research and development	7.2	13.1	27.1	33.6	34.8	37.0	37.5	34.6	34.6	37.0	34.8	35.0
Military construction	1.2	2.5	4.3	5.9	5.9	5.3	5.1	3.5	4.3	4.8	5.0	5.6
Family housing	0.6	1.7	2.6	2.9	3.1	3.3	3.5	3.3	3.3	3.3	3.3	3.5
Other [2]	-1.1	-1.1	0.6	2.6	0.2	0.1	-1.2	-46.2	-3.3	-6.4	2.8	0.5
Atomic energy activities [3]	1.4	2.9	7.1	7.5	7.9	8.1	9.0	10.0	10.6	11.0	11.9	10.5
Defense-related activities [4]	0.2	0.2	0.5	0.6	0.5	0.6	0.6	0.9	0.8	1.5	1.1	1.0

[1] Change from prior year; for 1970, change from 1965.   [2] Revolving and management funds, trust funds, special foreign currency program, allowances, and offsetting receipts.   [3] Defense activities only.   [4] Includes civil defense activities.

Source: U.S. Office of Management and Budget, Historical Tables, annual.

No. 550. National Defense—Budget Authority and Outlays: 1980 to 1995

[**In billions of dollars, except percent. For fiscal year ending in year shown,** except as noted; see text, section 9. See *Historical Statistics, Colonial Times to 1970,* series Y 458-460 for outlays]

ITEM	1980	1985	1987	1988	1989	1990	1991	1992	1993	1994	1995, est.
Budget authority [1]	143.9	294.7	287.4	292.0	299.6	303.3	288.9	295.1	281.1	263.3	263.5
Department of Defense-Military [2]	140.6	286.8	279.5	283.8	290.8	293.0	276.2	282.1	267.2	251.4	252.6
Atomic energy [1][3]	3.2	7.3	7.5	7.7	8.1	9.7	11.6	12.0	12.1	10.9	10.3
Outlays (Defense) [1]	134.0	252.7	282.0	290.4	303.6	299.3	273.3	298.4	291.1	281.6	271.6
Department of Defense-Military	130.9	245.2	274.0	281.9	294.9	289.8	262.4	286.9	278.6	268.6	260.2
Atomic energy [1][3]	3.1	7.6	8.0	8.4	8.7	9.6	10.0	10.6	11.0	11.9	10.5

[1] Includes defense budget authority, balances, and outlays by other departments. [2] Excluding accruals. [3] Includes other defense related activities.

Source: U.S. Office of Management and Budget, *Historical Tables,* annual.

No. 551. Defense-Related Agencies: 1980 to 1993

[**In thousands, except percent.** Annual averages]

EMPLOYMENT	1980	1985	1987	1988	1989	1990	1991	1992	1993
Total U.S. employment [1]	100,907	108,856	114,177	116,677	119,030	119,550	118,440	119,164	120,791
Federal	4,386	4,608	4,709	4,690	4,662	4,577	4,541	4,549	4,403
Resident Armed Forces	1,604	1,706	1,737	1,709	1,688	1,637	1,564	1,566	1,485
Civilian personnel [2]	2,987	3,001	3,075	3,113	3,133	3,233	3,101	2,983	2,918
DOD-Civilian employment [3]	948	1,073	1,079	1,041	1,067	1,024	1,083	1,044	973
Percent of Federal civilian personnel.	31.7	35.8	35.1	33.4	34.1	31.7	34.9	35.0	33.3
DOD-Military and civilian employment	2,552	2,779	2,816	2,750	2,755	2,661	2,647	2,610	2,458
Percent of total Federal	58.2	60.3	59.8	58.6	59.1	58.1	58.3	57.4	55.8
Percent of total U.S.	2.5	2.6	2.5	2.4	2.3	2.2	2.2	2.2	2.0

[1] Includes resident Armed Forces. [2] See table 542. [3] Source: U.S. Dept. of Defense, *Civilian Manpower Statistics,* annual (Sept. issues).

Source: Except as noted, U.S. Bureau of Labor Statistics, *Employment and Earnings,* monthly.

No. 552. Military and Civilian Personnel and Expenditures: 1985 to 1994

ITEM	1985	1990	1991	1992	1993	1994
Personnel, total [1] (1,000)	3,808	3,693	3,872	3,889	3,762	3,623
Active duty military	1,354	1,185	1,263	1,214	1,171	1,131
Civilian	976	931	911	899	847	810
Reserve and National Guard.	1,478	1,577	1,697	1,777	1,744	1,682
Expenditures, total (mil. dol.)	216,045	209,904	221,089	211,534	214,655	210,138
Payroll outlays	75,949	88,650	96,970	99,250	100,510	99,822
Active duty military pay	29,818	33,705	39,118	39,447	38,782	37,694
Civilian pay	24,815	28,230	29,901	31,205	31,619	30,587
Retired military pay	17,029	21,159	22,584	23,936	25,658	26,386
Reserve and National Guard pay.	4,287	5,556	5,366	4,661	4,451	5,154
Prime contract awards [2] (mil. dol.)	140,096	121,254	124,119	112,285	114,145	110,316
Supply contracts	92,375	66,895	66,981	54,880	54,856	48,642
Service contracts	24,224	28,540	31,222	30,503	32,163	33,040
R and D contracts	18,752	21,955	20,469	21,508	22,076	21,513
Construction contracts	3,245	2,088	3,469	2,894	2,829	4,786
Civil function contracts	1,500	1,775	1,979	2,500	2,222	2,335
Major area of work (mil. dol.):						
Aircraft, fixed wing	11,683	6,329	6,543	8,197	6,926	6,277
Research, devel'mt, testing and evaluation (RDTE)	(NA)	(NA)	(NA)	1,266	1,422	3,256
RDTE/Aircraft-Engineering development	(NA)	(NA)	(NA)	1,266	1,422	1,769
RDTE/Missile and space systems-op systems	(NA)	(NA)	(NA)	(NA)	(NA)	1,487
Gas turbines and jet engines	2,848	1,856	1,236	974	(NA)	(NA)
Guided missiles	(NA)	928	921	(NA)	793	494
Guided missile handling and servicing equip.	(NA)	446	921	(NA)	757	(NA)
Major location of expenditures (mil. dol.):						
San Diego, CA	4,027	4,820	4,628	5,289	6,405	4,748
Pico Rivera, CA.	(NA)	(NA)	2,600	4,284	2,428	3,272
St. Louis, MO	7,412	5,616	5,869	3,462	5,442	6,087
Norfolk, VA.	2,200	2,741	2,928	3,257	3,265	3,228
Arlington, VA.	(NA)	2,527	2,836	2,974	3,246	3,284
Fort Worth, TX	3,912	3,594	3,973	2,948	3,136	2,492
Washington, DC	(NA)	2,771	2,706	2,828	3,045	2,347
Marietta, GA.	(NA)	(NA)	(NA)	2,573	2,734	2,828
Los Angeles, CA	7,125	2,459	(NA)	2,319	(NA)	(NA)
San Antonio, TX	(NA)	(NA)	(NA)	2,117	(NA)	(NA)

NA Not available. [1] Includes those based ashore and excludes those temporarily shore-based, in a transient status, or afloat. [2] Represents contract awards over $25,000.

Source: U.S. Dept. of Defense, *Atlas/Data Abstract for the United States and Selected Areas,* annual.

No. 553. Military Prime Contract Awards to All Businesses, by Program: 1980 to 1993

[In billions of dollars. Net values for fiscal year ending in year shown; see text, section 9. Includes all new prime contracts; debit or credit changes in contracts are also included. Actions cover official awards, amendments, or other changes in prime contracts to obtain military supplies, services, or construction. Excludes term contracts and contracts which do not obligate a firm total dollar amount or fixed quantity, but includes job orders, task orders, and delivery orders against such contracts]

DOD PROCUREMENT PROGRAM	1980	1985	1987	1988	1989	1990	1991	1992	1993
Total	83.7	163.7	156.5	151.4	139.3	144.7	150.9	136.3	138.3
Intragovernmental [1]	10.2	12.4	8.8	8.9	9.6	10.0	11.9	9.6	12.9
For work outside the U.S.	5.4	8.6	8.9	8.2	6.4	7.1	9.2	5.9	5.8
Educ. and nonprofit institutions	1.5	3.1	3.5	3.5	3.3	3.5	3.6	3.4	3.4
With business firms for work in the U.S. [2]	66.7	139.6	135.3	130.8	120.0	123.8	125.9	117.2	116.0
Major hard goods	41.0	98.1	93.0	85.9	79.9	79.1	74.1	67.1	64.5
Aircraft	12.5	34.6	27.7	25.0	24.2	24.0	23.6	24.1	23.0
Electronics and communication equip..	9.6	22.0	22.6	17.8	18.1	18.5	15.2	14.2	14.2
Missiles and space systems	7.9	18.7	19.8	19.7	18.7	17.1	16.4	13.1	12.1
Ships	6.0	10.4	11.5	13.7	9.6	10.3	9.3	8.3	9.0
Tanks, ammo. and weapons	5.1	12.5	11.6	9.7	9.2	9.2	9.6	7.4	6.2
Services	5.9	9.1	11.0	12.0	11.7	14.6	16.9	17.3	17.5

[1] Covers only purchases from other Federal agencies and reimbursable purchases on behalf of foreign governments.
[2] Includes Department of Defense. Includes other business not shown separately. Contracts awarded for work in U.S. possessions, and other areas subject to complete sovereignty of United States; contracts in a classified location; and any intragovernmental contracts entered into overseas.

Source: U.S. Dept. of Defense, *Prime Contract Awards,* semiannual.

No. 554. Department of Defense Contract Awards, Payroll, and Civilian and Military Personnel—States: 1994

[For years ending Sept. 30. Contracts refer to awards made in year specified; expenditures relating to awards may extend over several years. Civilian employees include United States citizen and foreign national direct hire civilians subject to Office of Management and Budget (OMB) ceiling controls and civilian personnel involved in civil functions in the United States. Excludes indirect hire civilians and those direct hire civilian not subject to OMB ceiling controls. Military personnel include active duty personnel based ashore. Excludes personnel temporarily shore-based in a transient status, or afloat. Payroll outlays include the gross earnings of civilian and active duty military personnel for services rendered to the government and for cash allowances for benefits. Excludes employer's share of employee benefits, accrued military retirement benefits and most permanent change of station costs]

REGION, DIVISION, AND STATE	Contract awards [1] (mil. dol.)	Payroll (mil. dol.)	PERSONNEL (1,000)		REGION, DIVISION, AND STATE	Contract awards [1] (mil. dol.)	Payroll (mil. dol.)	PERSONNEL (1,000)	
			Civilian	Military				Civilian	Military
U.S.	110,316	99,822	810.2	1,130.7	DC	1,096	1,251	15.8	13.8
					VA	8,017	11,483	98.8	90.0
Northeast	18,752	9,116	103.8	56.1	WV	176	224	1.5	0.6
N.E.	9,329	3,053	26.1	18.0	NC	1,163	4,186	17.4	96.2
ME	925	584	6.0	2.2	SC	998	2,529	14.5	39.0
NH	369	236	1.4	0.3	GA	4,121	4,273	35.0	61.8
VT	57	94	0.6	0.2	FL	5,910	6,164	30.3	60.8
MA	5,106	1,081	9.9	6.1	E.S.C.	5,470	6,537	53.7	70.2
RI	422	436	4.0	3.6	KY	769	1,902	12.2	33.6
CT	2,450	621	4.2	5.6	TN	1,173	1,068	6.3	7.3
M.A.	9,424	6,064	77.6	38.1	AL	1,673	2,320	24.3	16.7
NY	3,629	1,894	15.5	23.7	MS	1,855	1,246	10.9	12.6
NJ	3,034	1,524	22.0	9.1	W.S.C.	11,426	11,272	86.7	157.0
PA	2,760	2,646	40.1	5.3	AR	374	701	4.2	5.9
Midwest	16,593	11,168	109.7	108.2	LA	2,148	1,355	8.6	20.3
E.N.C.	7,916	6,494	76.2	45.3	OK	759	2,015	19.6	28.3
OH	2,966	2,215	31.9	9.6	TX	8,145	7,201	54.3	102.5
IN	1,319	1,170	14.3	3.8	West	32,229	28,026	204.0	340.7
IL	1,256	1,810	16.8	27.3	Mountain	6,234	7,307	52.4	99.5
MI	1,602	878	9.8	3.8	MT	63	258	1.1	4.6
WI	774	420	3.3	0.8	ID	66	315	1.5	4.3
W.N.C.	8,677	4,674	33.5	63.0	WY	56	189	1.0	3.9
MN	1,137	403	2.7	0.9	CO	2,620	2,298	13.3	34.2
IA	309	236	1.4	0.4	NM	658	1,056	8.6	16.2
MO	6,147	1,566	16.6	15.3	AZ	1,975	1,642	9.3	21.9
ND	120	340	1.7	9.8	UT	521	906	15.5	5.7
SD	75	251	1.3	5.0	NV	274	643	2.2	8.6
NE	310	612	3.6	9.7	Pacific	25,995	20,720	151.6	241.2
KS	580	1,266	6.2	21.9	WA	1,861	3,416	27.0	35.8
South	42,741	51,511	392.8	625.8	OR	131	496	3.0	1.0
S.A.	25,844	33,702	252.4	398.6	CA	22,573	13,467	99.9	143.2
DE	108	285	1.6	4.6	AK	627	923	4.7	19.0
MD	4,256	3,308	37.5	31.8	HI	803	2,417	17.0	42.2

[1] Military awards for supplies, services, and construction. Net value of contracts of over $25,000 for work in each State and DC. Figures reflect impact of prime contracting on State distribution of defense work. Often the State in which a prime contractor is located in is not the State where the subcontracted work is done. See also headnote, table 553. Undistributed civilians and military personnel, their payrolls, and prime contract awards for performance in classified locations are excluded.

Source: U.S. Dept. of Defense, *Atlas/Data Abstract for the United States and Selected Areas,* annual.

No. 555. Worldwide Military Expenditures: 1985 to 1993

[In billions of dollars. For military expenditures and Armed Forces by country, see section 31. GNP=Gross national product]

COUNTRY GROUP	1985	1986	1987	1988	1989	1990	1991	1992	1993
Current dollars, total [1]	**943**	**988**	**1,020**	**1,047**	**1,059**	**1,073**	**1,021**	**932**	**869**
United States	258	281	288	293	304	306	280	305	298
Percent of total	27.4	28.4	28.2	28.0	28.7	28.5	27.5	32.7	34.2
Developed countries [2]	756	797	833	860	867	849	787	689	648
Developing countries [2]	188	191	188	187	192	224	234	244	221
NATO countries [3]	405	432	448	456	475	486	467	489	480
Constant (1993) dollars, total [1]	**1,234**	**1,259**	**1,260**	**1,245**	**1,204**	**1,171**	**1,073**	**953**	**868**
United States	338	358	356	349	346	334	294	312	298
Percent of total	27.4	28.4	28.2	28.0	28.7	28.5	27.4	32.7	34.3
Developed countries [2]	989	1,016	1,028	1,023	986	926	827	704	648
Developing countries [2]	245	243	232	222	218	245	245	249	221
NATO countries [3]	530	550	553	542	541	530	490	500	480
Percent of GNP	**5.4**	**5.4**	**5.2**	**4.9**	**4.6**	**4.4**	**4.1**	**3.7**	**3.3**
United States	6.4	6.6	6.3	6.0	5.8	5.5	4.9	5.1	4.7
Developed countries [2]	5.4	5.4	5.4	5.1	4.8	4.5	4.0	3.7	3.4
Developing countries [2]	5.4	5.2	4.7	4.3	4.0	4.4	4.2	3.7	3.1
NATO countries [3]	4.8	4.9	4.8	4.5	4.3	4.2	3.8	3.8	3.6

[1] Includes countries not shown separately. [2] Twenty-eight developed countries; see table 556 for selected countries; for complete list, see source. [3] North Atlantic Treaty Organization.

No. 556. Arms Trade in Constant (1992) Dollars—Selected Countries: 1991 to 1993

[In millions of dollars, except percent. Because some countries exclude arms imports or exports from their trade statistics and their "total" imports and exports are therefore understated, and because arms transfers may be estimated independently of trade data, the ratio of arms to total imports or exports may be overstated and may even exceed 100 percent]

COUNTRY	1991	1992	1993 Total	1993 Arms imports as percent of total imports	COUNTRY	1991	1992	1993 Total	1993 Arms imports as percent of total imports
World total [1]	**31,790**	**24,710**	**21,960**	**0.6**	India	896	615	10	-
					Iran	2,215	369	1,000	6.2
Exporters: [1]					Iraq	-	-	-	-
Canada	517	1,025	200	0.1	Israel	554	795	850	3.8
China	1,582	897	950	1.0	Italy	200	82	50	(NA)
Czechoslovakia	243	144	(NA)	1.2	Japan	1,266	666	340	0.1
France	1,687	1,435	675	0.3	Jordan	53	21	20	0.6
Poland	116	21	10	0.1	Korea, North	95	10	-	-
United Kingdom	4,957	4,511	4,300	2.4	Korea, South	633	349	875	1.0
United States	11,390	10,360	10,300	2.2	Kuwait	380	769	650	9.9
Germany	2,531	1,128	1,100	0.3	Libya	432	82	-	-
					Morocco	32	51	20	0.3
Importers: [1]					Nicaragua	84	5	5	(NA)
Afghanistan	2,004	5	-	-	Oman	42	10	60	3.8
Algeria	137	-	10	0.1	Pakistan	211	379	430	4.5
Angola	53	10	100	(NA)	Peru	53	62	10	0.2
Argentina	11	10	10	0.1	Poland	-	-	-	-
Australia	253	185	300	0.7	Romania	179	10	-	-
Canada	253	431	210	0.2	Saudi Arabia	6,538	7,382	5,100	(NA)
Cuba	554	103	100	5.9	Spain	190	215	190	0.2
Czechoslovakia	53	-	(NA)	-	Syria	685	538	120	2.9
Egypt	712	897	1,100	13.4	Turkey	1,055	846	975	3.3
El Salvador	63	31	30	1.6	*United States*	*2,004*	*1,538*	*1,400*	*0.2*
Ethiopia	84	-	-	-	Venezuela	200	72	60	0.5
Germany	659	718	250	0.1	Vietnam	211	21	10	0.3
Greece	232	590	725	(NA)	Yemen (Sanaa)	32	5	20	1.3
Hungary	-	-	875	0.1					

- Represents or rounds to zero. NA Not available. [1] Includes countries not shown separately.

Source of tables 555 and 556: U.S. Arms Control and Disarmament Agency, *World Military Expenditures and Arms Transfers,* annual.

No. 557. Arms Transfers—Cumulative Value for Period 1991-93, by Major Supplier and Recipient Country

[In millions of dollars]

RECIPIENT	Total [1]	SUPPLIER				
		United States	France	United Kingdom	China	Germany
World, total	**76,550**	**31,175**	**3,635**	**13,380**	**3,285**	**4,555**
Africa [1]	**2,015**	**195**	**95**	**230**	**295**	**15**
Algeria	145	-	-	-	5	-
Angola	160	-	-	-	-	-
Ethiopia	80	-	-	-	-	-
Libya	480	-	-	-	50	10
Morocco	105	80	10	5	-	-
Mozambique	55	-	-	-	-10	-
Nigeria	295	5	50	190	-	-
Sudan	160	-	-	-	100	-
Zaire	30	-	-	-	10	-
Zimbabwe	155	-	-	30	80	-
Asia [1]	**10,635**	**5,745**	**335**	**520**	**875**	**615**
Afghanistan	1,905	-	-	-	-	-
Bahrain	190	190	-	-	-	-
Bangladesh	105	5	-	-	10	-
Burma	660	-	-	-	525	5
China	1,780	10	50	-	-	-
Taiwan	1,690	1,600	-	-	-	60
Cyprus	190	-	170	-	-	-
Egypt	2,695	2,400	20	10	-	5
Indonesia	210	70	100	-	-	40
India	1,430	70	-	-	-	150
Iran	3,575	-	-	-	875	40
Israel	2,200	2,000	-	-	-	200
Japan	2,230	2,200	-	-	-	30
Jordan	85	50	-	30	-	-
Korea, North	105	-	-	-	-	-
Korea, South	1,810	975	60	460	-	300
Kuwait	1,720	1,500	190	-	-	-
Laos	40	-	-	-	30	-
Malaysia	110	30	-	50	-	-
Oman	125	60	5	60	-	-
Pakistan	1,000	30	120	20	750	-
Philippines	240	180	-	-	-	-
Qatar	50	-	10	-	-	-
Saudi Arabia	18,570	5,200	1,000	10,200	280	525
Singapore	560	230	120	10	-	150
Sri Lanka	75	-	-	-	40	-
Syria	1,310	-	30	-	20	-
Thailand	925	450	-	-	320	30
United Arab Emir.	905	360	100	-	-	50
Vietnam	230	-	-	-	-	-
Europe [1]	**14,240**	**7,485**	**1,030**	**475**	**-**	**2,255**
Austria	90	20	10	-	-	-
Belgium	620	360	-	-	-	-
Czechoslovakia	50	-	-	-	-	-
Denmark	140	140	-	-	-	-
Finland	750	20	310	110	-	250
France	435	320	(NA)	10	-	-
Germany	1,560	1,100	50	100	-	(NA)
Greece	1,510	410	360	20	-	480
Hungary	865	-	-	-	-	40
Italy	330	270	-	50	-	-
Netherlands	770	675	20	5	-	-
Norway	670	130	-	50	-	280
Portugal	780	200	50	20	-	500
Romania	180	-	-	-	-	-
Slovakia	150	-	-	-	-	-
Spain	580	500	-	10	-	20
Sweden	275	140	100	-	-	5
Switzerland	660	80	80	100	-	400
Turkey	2,890	2,300	50	-	-	280
United Kingdom	840	800	-	(NA)	-	-
America:						
Canada	875	400	40	20	-	5
Chile	165	20	50	5	-	10
Colombia	320	60	-	-	-	160
El Salvador	120	120	-	-	-	-
Honduras	40	40	-	-	-	-
Nicaragua	80	-	-	-	-	-
Peru	120	10	-	-	20	-
United States	*4,825*	*(X)*	*210*	*1,700*	*100*	*460*
Venezuela	325	50	50	70	-	40
Oceania	980	640	-	20	-	-

- Nil or negligible ($2.5 million or less).   X Not applicable.   NA Not available.   [1] Includes countries not shown separately.

Source: U.S. Arms Control and Disarmament Agency, *World Military Expenditures and Arms Transfers,* annual.

No. 558. Arms Delivered, by Selected Supplier and Major Weapon Type: 1988-93

[The suppliers included are the five largest single exporters of major weapons in terms of magnitude of deliveries as well as other countries of the two major alliances; excluded are Albania, Bulgaria, Greece, Malta, Spain, Turkey, and Yugoslavia]

TYPE OF WEAPON	Total [1]	United States [2]	France	United Kingdom	China
Land armaments: Tanks	6,868	728	90	70	510
Artillery, field and anti-air [3][4]	10,153	533	420	10	3,110
Armored personnel carriers	9,824	1,164	190	110	390
Naval craft: Major surface combatants [5]	41	-	4	6	5
Other surface combatants [6]	353	21	35	20	37
Submarines	19	-	-	-	-
Missile attack boats	9	-	-	-	6
Aircraft: Combat aircraft (supersonic)	1,581	431	80	50	250
Combat aircraft (subsonic)	278	78	-	70	10
Other aircraft [7]	928	118	20	50	100
Helicopters	1,195	195	150	30	-
Missiles (surface-to-air)	15,374	2,424	1,830	620	450

- Represents $2.5 million or less. [1] Includes other countries not shown separately. [2] United States data are by fiscal years, while other suppliers' data are by calendar years. [3] Includes weapons over 23 millimeters. [4] Includes mobile rocket launchers mortars, and recoilless rifles over 100 millimeters. [5] Includes aircraft carriers, cruisers, destroyers, destroyer and frigates. [6] Includes motor torpedo boats, subchasers, and minesweepers. [7] Includes reconnaissance aircraft, trainers, transports, and utility aircraft.

Source: U.S. Arms Control and Disarmament Agency, *World Military Expenditures and Arms Transfers*, annual.

No. 559. Estimates of Total Dollar Costs of American Wars

[**In millions of dollars, except percent.** Service-connected veterans' benefits estimated at 40 percent of total veterans benefits, except as noted]

ITEM	World War II	Vietnam Conflict	Korean Conflict	World War I	Civil War: Union	Civil War: Confederacy	Spanish American War	American Revolution	War of 1812	Mexican War
Original incremental, direct costs: [1]										
Current dollars	360,000	140,600	50,000	32,700	2,300	1,000	270	100-140	89	82
Constant (1967) dollars	816,300	148,800	69,300	100,000	8,500	3,700	1,100	400-680	170	300
Percent 1 year's GNP	188	14	15	43	74	123	2	104	14	4
Veterans benefits to 1993 [2]	301,000	136,000	72,000	81,000	8,574	-	5,964	80	49	64
Interest, pmts. on war loans [3]	[4]	[4]	[4]	11,000	1,200	[4]	60	20	14	10
Current cost to 1993 [5]	[4]	[4]	[4]	124,700	12,074	[4]	6,294	220	152	156

- Represents zero. [1] Figures are rounded and taken from Claudia D. Goldin, *Encyclopedia of American Economic History*, p. 938. [2] Total cost to Oct. 1, 1993. Veterans benefits are total benefits related to each war and are therefore not comparable to earlier estimates which included only service-connected benefits. [3] Total cost to 1992. Interest payments are a very rough approximation based on the percentage of the original costs of each war financed by money creation and debt, the difference between the level of public debt at the beginning of the war and at its end, and the approximate time required to pay off the war debts. [4] Unknown. [5] Figures are rounded estimates.

Source: Originally presented in U.S. Congress, Joint Economic Committee, *The Military Budget and National Economic Priorities*, part 1, 91st Congress, 1st session (statement of James L. Clayton); subsequently revised and updated by James L. Clayton, University of Utah, Salt Lake City, Utah.

No. 560. U.S. Military Sales and Assistance to Foreign Governments: 1950 to 1993

[**In millions of dollars,** except as indicated. **For fiscal year ending in year shown;** see text, section 9. Department of Defense (DOD) sales deliveries cover deliveries against DOD sales orders authorized under Arms Export Control Act, as well as earlier and applicable legislation. For details regarding individual programs, see source]

ITEM	1950-85 [1]	1986	1987	1988	1989	1990	1991	1992	1993
Military sales agreements	143,136	6,207	6,147	11,344	10,201	12,118	20,889	14,746	32,398
Weapons and ammunition	61,670	2,102	1,759	4,988	4,213	4,631	6,141	7,443	17,382
Support equipment [2]	19,310	611	741	974	860	1,296	4,205	1,043	2,492
Spare parts and mods	30,653	1,466	1,556	2,943	2,315	2,601	4,746	2,689	6,452
Support services	31,503	2,028	2,091	2,439	2,813	3,590	5,797	3,571	6,072
Military constr. sales agrmts	16,103	70	128	209	76	178	677	682	818
Military sales deliveries [3]	105,979	7,806	11,114	9,195	7,385	7,801	9,040	10,574	11,583
Military sales financing	44,456	4,916	4,053	4,049	4,273	4,758	4,693	4,274	4,124
Military assistance programs [4]	56,742	834	958	697	535	137	177	116	508
Military assist. program delivery [5]	54,844	76	83	56	53	27	150	87	54
IMET program/deliveries [5]	1,949	51	53	45	46	43	46	42	43
Students trained (1,000)	533	6	6	6	5	5	5	4	4

[1] Includes transition quarter, July-September 1976. [2] Includes aircraft, ships, support vehicles, communications equipment, and other supplies. [3] Includes military construction sales deliveries. [4] Also includes Military Assistance Service Funded (MASF) program data, section 506(a) drawdown authority, and MAP Merger Funds. [5] Includes Military Assistance Service Funded (MASF) program data and section 506(a) drawdown authority.

Source: U.S. Defense Security Assistance Agency, *Foreign Military Sales, Foreign Military Construction Sales, and Military Assistance Facts*, annual; and unpublished data.

No. 561. U.S. Military Sales Deliveries to Foreign Governments, by Country: 1950 to 1993

[In millions of dollars. For fiscal years ending in year shown; see text, section 9. Represents Department of Defense military sales]

COUNTRY	1950-1985 [1]	1986	1987	1988	1989	1990	1991	1992	1993 Total	1993 Percent distribution
Total [2]	105,979	7,806	11,114	9,195	7,385	7,801	9,040	10,574	11,583	100.0
Australia	3,318	399	593	850	384	267	206	162	245	2.1
Belgium	1,777	28	27	222	153	178	184	40	51	0.4
Canada	1,909	113	127	212	144	103	164	109	130	1.1
Denmark	1,041	24	62	149	93	38	50	44	56	0.5
Egypt	3,504	615	962	498	322	441	573	1,096	1,340	11.6
El Salvador	240	108	77	93	92	87	58	65	43	0.4
France	508	142	99	37	36	109	32	35	41	0.4
Germany	8,021	206	315	382	633	359	480	503	347	3.0
Greece	1,938	73	79	129	138	113	124	172	206	1.8
Indonesia	281	13	23	32	32	189	18	20	42	0.4
Israel	8,975	164	1,294	751	230	151	239	686	780	6.7
Italy	937	66	71	62	64	61	69	54	54	0.5
Japan	2,281	151	235	212	166	220	324	551	327	2.8
Jordan	1,412	63	50	55	59	42	23	20	25	0.2
Kuwait	824	69	58	41	46	52	112	828	913	7.9
Korea, South	2,827	343	344	327	315	293	217	295	315	2.7
Morocco	684	37	43	74	33	41	20	39	20	0.2
Netherlands	2,719	256	417	327	391	381	371	306	123	1.1
Norway	1,488	43	83	117	96	117	82	38	42	0.4
Pakistan	1,528	127	134	139	175	548	-	-	-	-
Philippines	217	37	32	69	72	62	97	96	44	0.4
Portugal	163	27	26	15	32	72	40	89	86	0.7
Saudi Arabia	29,500	2,773	3,382	1,330	976	1,154	3,109	2,681	3,701	32.0
Singapore	356	135	143	191	38	47	64	25	61	0.5
Spain	1,114	262	822	637	686	423	156	139	205	1.8
Sudan	217	27	26	24	30	-	-	-	-	-
Taiwan	2,995	244	368	484	353	460	556	828	731	6.3
Thailand	1,298	115	95	291	212	176	180	104	108	0.9
Tunisia	359	26	44	20	25	33	27	20	17	0.2
Turkey	1,827	282	277	700	619	720	707	703	751	6.5
United Kingdom	4,411	363	205	180	131	205	245	154	230	2.0
Venezuela	620	65	50	27	13	20	23	16	22	0.2

- Represents or rounds to zero.   [1] Includes transactions for the transition quarter, July-September 1976.   [2] Includes countries not shown.

Source: U.S. Defense Security Assistance Agency, *Foreign Military Sales, Foreign Military Construction Sales,* and *Military Assistance Facts,* annual.

No. 562. Summary of Active and Reserve Military Personnel and Forces: 1989 to 1995

ITEM	1989	1994	1995, est.	ITEM	1989	1994	1995, est.
Military personnel (1,000):				Navy air wings	2	1	1
Active	2,130	1,611	1,523	Navy aircraft carrier	-	-	1
Guard and Reserve	1,171	1,025	965	Other navy ships	26	16	19
				Marine divisions and air wings	1	1	1
Active Forces:				Air Force tactical wings	12	9	8
Army divisions	18	12	12	Nuclear Deterrent:			
Navy aircraft carriers	16	12	11	Intercontinental Ballistic Missiles	1,000	642	585
Navy air wings	13	11	10	Ballistic missile submarines	34	15	16
Navy combatants & attack subs	287	196	197	Missiles	608	352	384
Marine divisions and air wings	3	3	3	Bombers	268	152	140
Air Force tactical wings	25	13	13	Mobility Forces:			
Reserve Forces:				Strategic airlift aircraft	367	356	354
Army combat brigades	56	48	48	Sealift ships [1]	163	174	149

- Represents or rounds to zero.   [1] Includes ships in the Ready Reserve Force funded.

Source: U.S. Office of Management and Budget, *Budget,* annual.

No. 563. Military Installations in the United States: 1994

[Represents bases with active-duty populations of 300 or more. Excludes the Coast Guard]

STATE AND BRANCH	Active duty personnel	Family members	Civilians	STATE AND BRANCH	Active duty personnel	Family members	Civilians
United States	1,048,249	1,244,283	552,011	Michigan	3,909	6,336	2,593
Alabama	24,679	29,615	29,495	Air Force	3,909	6,336	2,593
Army	13,703	14,615	19,973	Minnesota	-	-	-
Navy	5,488	7,500	4,761	Mississippi	13,763	22,438	8,760
Air Force	5,488	7,500	4,761	Navy	7,400	6,900	2,994
Alaska	19,152	24,184	5,204	Air Force	6,363	15,538	5,766
Army	7,700	9,635	2,640	Missouri	8,716	12,297	5,120
Navy	1,405	-	86	Army	5,125	6,297	4,482
Air Force	10,047	14,549	2,478	Air Force	3,591	6,000	638
Arizona	22,444	38,249	9,909	Montana	4,611	7,158	527
Army	5,682	4,760	5,597	Air Force	4,611	7,158	527
Marine Corps	6,553	6,789	1,113	Nebraska	9,677	15,380	2,828
Air Force	10,209	26,700	3,199	Air Force	9,677	15,380	2,828
Arkansas	4,763	7,673	1,429	Nevada	8,120	18,686	2,100
Army	350	247	622	Navy	1,100	2,000	1,000
Air Force	4,413	7,426	807	Air Force	7,020	16,686	1,100
California	230,566	158,903	108,667	New Hampshire	597	1,077	4,100
Army	9,842	7,302	4,465	Navy	597	1,077	4,100
Navy	133,630	44,293	46,022	New Jersey	10,264	13,809	13,800
Marine Corps	55,604	48,633	23,609	Army	2,910	5,489	8,867
Air Force	31,490	58,675	34,571	Navy	3,014	1,200	3,283
Colorado	36,503	48,252	12,734	Air Force	4,340	7,120	1,650
Army	17,918	37,572	4,703	New Mexico	16,975	24,153	22,942
Air Force	18,585	10,680	8,031	Army	1,061	1,626	7,505
Connecticut	10,000	22,500	1,800	Air Force	15,914	22,527	15,437
Navy	10,000	22,500	1,800	New York	25,695	35,383	9,584
Delaware	4,388	6,446	1,616	Army	17,092	20,240	6,519
Air Force	4,388	6,446	1,616	Navy	2,500	3,000	-
District of Columbia . .	9,617	90	10,945	Air Force	6,103	12,143	3,065
Army	5,200	50	5,200	North Carolina	104,793	101,619	18,061
Navy	2,000	-	4,550	Army	40,000	11,500	6,000
Marine Corps	1,168	40	-	Marine Corps	55,076	77,737	10,576
Air Force	1,249	-	1,195	Air Force	9,717	12,382	1,485
Florida	86,161	156,885	32,054	North Dakota	9,300	12,840	1,450
Navy	57,119	99,674	21,547	Air Force	9,300	12,840	1,450
Air Force	29,042	57,211	10,507	Ohio	8,754	18,308	15,400
Georgia	73,470	93,666	41,920	Air Force	8,754	18,308	15,400
Army	56,544	62,789	20,986	Oklahoma	28,241	44,511	20,616
Navy	7,400	18,350	4,250	Army	16,806	38,911	5,930
Marine Corps	1,000	2,000	3,000	Air Force	11,435	5,600	14,686
Air Force	8,526	10,527	13,684	Oregon	-	-	-
Hawaii	56,720	50,952	21,947	Pennsylvania	6,001	7,045	7,396
Army	18,277	17,600	4,653	Army	1,233	1,745	1,482
Navy	23,631	15,141	11,162	Navy	4,768	5,300	5,914
Marine Corps	10,007	10,604	2,118	Rhode Island	3,652	3,000	3,976
Air Force	4,805	7,607	4,014	Navy	3,652	3,000	3,976
Idaho	4,004	3,700	467	South Carolina	36,718	75,586	13,478
Navy	500	300	-	Army	5,388	11,691	2,226
Air Force	3,504	3,400	467	Navy	13,726	35,000	6,700
Illinois	22,753	28,166	14,137	Marine Corps	7,151	9,286	1,646
Army	2,120	3,560	8,390	Air Force	10,453	19,609	2,906
Navy	14,000	15,000	2,200	South Dakota	5,022	7,754	850
Air Force	6,633	9,606	3,547	Air Force	5,022	7,754	850
Indiana	2,500	3,000	5,500	Tennessee	9,839	4,050	3,269
Army	2,500	3,000	5,500	Navy	9,839	4,050	3,269
Iowa	-	-	-	Texas	133,847	183,152	61,899
Kansas	21,008	28,341	4,986	Army	81,471	134,052	22,449
Army	18,000	21,300	4,590	Navy	6,469	12,800	7,908
Air Force	3,008	7,041	396	Air Force	45,907	36,300	31,542
Kentucky	34,600	41,194	8,304	Utah	5,000	-	11,000
Army	34,600	41,194	8,304	Air Force	5,000	-	11,000
Louisiana	19,865	27,930	8,271	Vermont	-	-	-
Army	10,396	18,438	4,952	Virginia	173,032	170,023	69,253
Navy	3,669	1,295	2,119	Army	22,989	23,511	19,993
Air Force	5,800	8,197	1,200	Navy	139,493	141,512	46,469
Maine	2,903	3,550	930	Marine Corps	10,550	5,000	2,791
Navy	2,903	3,550	930	Air Force	8,811	10,573	2,613
Air Force	-	-	-	Washington	48,550	72,872	35,895
Maryland	41,343	33,414	70,261	Army	15,500	24,600	5,500
Army	21,538	15,026	52,903	Navy	23,689	35,018	27,258
Navy	9,796	8,400	14,158	Air Force	9,361	13,254	3,137
Air Force	10,009	9,988	3,200	West Virginia	-	-	-
Massachusetts	6,163	6,143	4,585	Wisconsin	300	725	2,200
Army	3,328	4,388	2,271	Army	300	725	2,200
Navy	600	-	250	Wyoming	3,500	5,000	650
Air Force	2,235	1,755	2,064	Air Force	3,500	5,000	650

- Represents or rounds to zero.
Source: Army Times Publishing Co. Springfield, VA 22159, *Guide to Military Installations in the U. S.,* annual.

No. 564. Department of Defense Manpower: 1950 to 1993

[**In thousands.** As of **end of fiscal year;** see text, section 9. Includes National Guard, Reserve, and retired regular personnel on extended or continuous active duty. Excludes Coast Guard. Other officer candidates are included under enlisted personnel. See also *Historical Statistics, Colonial Times to 1970,* series Y 904-916]

YEAR	Total [1][2]	ARMY			NAVY [3]			MARINE CORPS			AIR FORCE		
		Total [2]	Offi-cers	Enlist-ed	Total [2]	Offi-cers	Enlist-ed	Total [2]	Offi-cers	Enlist-ed	Total [2]	Offi-cers	Enlist-ed
1950	1,459	593	73	519	381	45	333	74	7	67	411	57	354
1955	2,935	1,109	122	986	661	75	583	205	18	187	960	137	823
1960	2,475	873	101	770	617	70	545	171	16	154	815	130	683
1961	2,483	859	100	757	626	70	552	177	16	161	821	129	690
1962	2,806	1,066	116	949	664	75	585	191	17	174	884	135	746
1963	2,699	976	108	866	664	76	584	190	17	173	869	134	733
1964	2,686	973	111	861	666	76	585	190	17	173	857	133	721
1965	2,654	969	112	855	670	78	588	190	17	173	825	132	690
1966	3,092	1,200	118	1,080	743	80	659	262	21	241	887	131	753
1967	3,375	1,442	144	1,297	750	82	664	285	24	262	897	135	759
1968	3,546	1,570	166	1,402	764	85	674	307	25	283	905	140	762
1969	3,458	1,512	173	1,337	774	85	684	310	26	284	862	135	723
1970	3,065	1,323	167	1,153	691	81	606	260	25	235	791	130	657
1971	2,713	1,124	149	972	622	75	542	212	22	191	755	126	625
1972	2,322	811	121	687	587	73	511	198	20	178	726	122	600
1973	2,252	801	116	682	564	71	490	196	19	177	691	115	572
1974	2,162	783	106	674	546	67	475	189	19	170	644	110	529
1975	2,128	784	103	678	535	66	466	196	19	177	613	105	503
1976	2,082	779	99	678	525	64	458	192	19	174	585	100	481
1977	2,075	782	98	680	530	63	462	192	19	173	571	96	470
1978	2,062	772	98	670	530	63	463	191	18	172	570	95	470
1979	2,027	759	97	657	523	62	457	185	18	167	559	96	459
1980	2,051	777	99	674	527	63	460	188	18	170	558	98	456
1981	2,083	781	102	675	540	65	470	191	18	172	570	99	467
1982	2,109	780	103	673	553	67	481	192	19	173	583	102	476
1983	2,123	780	106	669	558	68	485	194	20	174	592	105	483
1984	2,138	780	108	668	565	69	491	196	20	176	597	106	486
1985	2,151	781	110	667	571	71	495	198	20	178	602	108	489
1986	2,169	781	110	667	581	72	504	199	20	179	608	109	495
1987	2,174	781	108	668	587	72	510	200	20	179	607	107	495
1988	2,138	772	107	660	593	72	516	197	20	177	576	105	467
1989	2,130	770	107	658	593	72	516	197	20	177	571	104	463
1990	2,044	732	104	624	579	72	503	197	20	177	535	100	431
1991	1,986	711	104	603	570	71	495	194	20	174	510	97	409
1992	1,807	610	95	511	542	69	468	185	19	165	470	90	376
1993	1,705	572	88	480	510	66	439	178	18	160	444	84	356

[1] Beginning 1980, excludes Navy Reserve personnel on active duty for Training and Administration of Reserves (TARS). From 1969, the full-time Guard and Reserve. [2] Includes Cadets. [3] Prior to 1980, includes Navy Reserve personnel on active duty for Training and Administration of Reserves (TARS).

Source: U.S. Dept. of Defense, *Selected Manpower Statistics,* annual.

No. 565. Military Personnel on Active Duty, by Location: 1970 to 1993

[**In thousands. 1970 as of Dec. 31;** thereafter, **as of end of fiscal year;** see text, section 9]

ITEM	1970	1980	1985	1986	1987	1988	1989	1990	1991	1992	1993, prel.
Total	3,065	2,051	2,151	2,169	2,174	2,138	2,130	2,044	1,986	1,807	1,705
Shore-based [1]	2,798	1,840	1,920	1,929	1,928	1,891	1,884	1,794	1,743	1,589	1,505
Afloat [2]	268	211	231	240	246	248	246	252	243	218	200
United States [3]	2,033	1,562	1,636	1,644	1,650	1,598	1,620	1,437	1,539	1,463	1,397
Foreign countries	1,033	488	516	526	524	541	510	609	448	344	308

[1] Includes Navy personnel temporarily on shore. [2] Includes Marine Corps. [3] Includes outlying areas.

Source: U.S. Dept. of Defense, *Selected Manpower Statistics,* annual.

No. 566. Military Personnel on Active Duty in Foreign Countries: 1993

[As of **end of fiscal year**]

COUNTRY	1993	COUNTRY	1993	COUNTRY	1993
In foreign countries	308,020	Ecuador.	20	Nigeria.	16
		Egypt	605	Norway	196
Ashore	263,194	El Salvador.	42	Oman	26
Afloat	44,826	Ethopia	17	Pakistan.	33
Antarctica.	58	Finland	18	Panama.	10,542
Antigua	71	France.	74	Paraguay	11
Argentina	23	Germany	105,254	Peru	20
Australia	339	Greece	807	Philippines	53
Austria.	34	Greenland	131	Poland.	18
Bahamas, The.	25	Guatemala	22	Portugal	1,320
Bahrain	379	Haiti	12	Romania	12
Bangladesh	10	Honduras	696	Russia	70
Barbados	12	Hong Kong	34	Saudi Arabia.	950
Belgium	1,808	Hungary	18	Senegal	11
Bermuda	527	Iceland	2,878	Singapore	162
Bolivia	21	India	32	Somalia	6,345
Brazil.	54	Indonesia	49	South Africa	24
Bulgaria	12	Israel.	42	Spain	3,820
Burma	10	Italy.	10,333	Sri Lanka	11
Cameroon	10	Jamaica	16	Sudan	11
Canada	547	Japan	46,131	Sweden	13
Chile	23	Jordan	21	Switzerland.	30
China	38	Kenya	33	Syria	10
Colombia	41	Korea, South	34,830	Thailand.	106
Costa Rica	12	Kuwait	233	Tonga	23
Cote D'Ivoire.	18	Liberia	10	Tunisia.	19
Croatia	10	Malaysia	20	Turkey	4,049
Cuba (Guantanamo). . . .	2,189	Mexico.	30	United Arab Emirates . . .	25
Cyprus.	18	Morocco.	22	United Kingdom.	16,100
Czech Republic.	17	Nepal	10	Uruguay	12
Denmark	45	Netherlands	2,226	Venezuela	38
Diego Garcia.	1,233	New Zealand	67	Zimbabwe	10
Dominican Republic	14	Nicaragua	15		

[1] Includes areas not shown separately.

Source: U.S. Department of Defense, *Selected Manpower Statistics,* annual.

No. 567. Coast Guard Personnel on Active Duty: 1970 to 1994

[As of **end of fiscal year;** see text, section 9]

YEAR	Total	Officers	Cadets	Enlisted	YEAR	Total	Officers	Cadets	Enlisted
1970.	37,689	5,512	653	31,524	1991.	38,377	7,192	900	30,285
1975.	36,788	5,630	1,177	29,981	1992.	39,388	7,507	919	30,962
1980.	39,381	6,463	877	32,041	1993.	39,234	7,628	907	30,699
1985.	38,595	6,775	733	31,087	1994.	37,802	7,656	881	29,265
1990.	36,939	6,876	927	29,136					

Source: U.S. Dept. of Transportation, *Annual Report of the Secretary of Transportation.*

No. 568. Vietnam Conflict—U.S. Military Forces in Vietnam and Combat Area Casualties: 1957 to 1992

[Military forces as of **Dec. 31.** All U.S. forces withdrawn by Jan. 27, 1973]

ITEM	Unit	1957-1992 total [1]	1957-1964	1965	1966	1967	1968	1969	1970	1971	1972	1973-1989
Military forces [2].	1,000. . .	(X)	[3]23.3	184.3	385.3	485.6	536.1	475.2	234.6	156.8	24.2	-
Battle deaths [4]	Number .	47,366	279	1,432	5,047	9,463	14,623	9,426	4,230	1,376	361	1,118
Killed.	Number .	38,506	197	1,124	4,142	7,525	12,624	8,117	3,486	1,082	205	-
Died of wounds	Number .	5,224	10	111	579	1,598	979	1,168	555	160	28	22
Died while missing [5].	Number .	3,636	72	197	326	401	959	141	189	134	128	1,068

- Represents zero.   X Not applicable.   [1] Number in this column indicates 11 more deaths than a tally of the number by time period, due to revisions. The Cambodia area includes North and South Vietnam, Cambodia, Thailand, Laos, and China. [2] Source: U.S. Dept. of Defense, *Selected Manpower Statistics,* annual.   [3] For 1964 only.   [4] Casualties from enemy action. Deaths exclude 10,799 servicemen who died in accidents, from disease, or other causes.   [5] Includes servicemen who died while captured.

Source: Except as indicated, National Archives and Records Administration, unpublished data from Combat Area Casualties database, as of November 1992.

No. 569. Armed Forces Personnel—Summary of Major Conflicts

[For Revolutionary War, number of personnel serving not known, but estimates range from 184,000 to 250,000; for War of 1812, 286,730 served; for Mexican War, 78,718 served. Dates of the major conflicts may differ from those specified in various laws providing benefits for veterans. See table 557 for data on Vietnam conflict. See also *Historical Statistics, Colonial Times to 1970,* series Y 856-903]

ITEM	Unit	Civil War [1]	Spanish-American War	World War I	World War II	Korean conflict	Vietnam conflict
Personnel serving [2]	1,000	2,213	307	4,735	[3]16,113	[4]5,720	[5]8,744
Average duration of service	Months	20	8	12	33	.19	23
Service abroad: Personnel serving	Percent	(NA)	[6]29	53	73	[7]56	(NA)
Average duration [8]	Months	(NA)	1.5	6	16	13	(NA)
Casualties: [9] Battle deaths [2]	1,000	140	(Z)	53	292	34	[10]47
Wounds not mortal [2]	1,000	282	2	204	671	103	[10]153
Draftees: Classified	1,000	777	(X)	24,234	36,677	9,123	[5]75,717
Examined	1,000	522	(X)	3,764	17,955	3,685	[5]8,611
Rejected	1,000	160	(X)	803	6,420	1,189	[5]3,880
Inducted	1,000	46	(X)	2,820	10,022	1,560	[5]1,759

NA Not available.　X Not applicable.　Z Fewer than 500.　[1] Union forces only. Estimates of the number serving in Confederate forces range from 600,000 to 1.5 million.　[2] Source: U.S. Department of Defense, *Selected Manpower Statistics,* annual.　[3] Covers Dec. 1, 1941, to Dec. 31, 1946.　[4] Covers June 25, 1950, to July 27, 1953.　[5] Covers Aug. 4, 1964, to Jan. 27, 1973.　[6] Army and Marines only.　[7] Excludes Navy. Covers July 1950 through Jan. 1955. Far East area only.　[8] During hostilities only.　[9] For periods covered, see footnotes 3, 4, and 5.　[10] Covers Jan. 1, 1961, to Jan. 27, 1973. Includes known military service personnel who have died from combat related wounds.

Source: Except as noted, the President's Commission on Veterans' Pensions, Veterans' *Benefits in the United States,* vol. I, 1956; and U.S. Dept. of Defense, unpublished data.

No. 570. Enlisted Military Personnel Accessions: 1990 to 1993

[In thousands. For years ending Sept. 30]

BRANCH OF SERVICE	1990	1991	1992	1993	BRANCH OF SERVICE	1990	1991	1992	1993
Total	461.0	433.1	427.5	406.0	First enlistments	62.0	49.8	42.7	51.1
First enlistments	216.0	184.9	186.0	187.4	Reenlistments	58.6	60.7	56.9	51.6
Reenlistments	237.0	218.9	221.5	200.7	Marine Corps	48.0	45.0	47.7	46.4
Reserves to active duty	15.6	29.3	19.9	17.9	First enlistments	33.0	29.7	32.1	34.0
Army	182.0	159.7	155.4	151.8	Reenlistments	14.4	14.1	14.9	11.9
First enlistments	85.0	75.1	75.8	70.5	Air Force	104.0	94.6	105.9	87.9
Reenlistments	96.5	79.9	79.4	81.2	First enlistments	37.0	30.3	35.4	31.9
Navy	135.0	133.8	118.8	119.9	Reenlistments	67.5	64.0	70.1	55.9

Source: U.S. Dept. of Defense, *Selected Manpower Statistics,* annual.

No. 571. Military Personnel on Active Duty and Monthly Basic Pay: 1990 to 1993

[Personnel as of Sept. 30; basic pay as of January, except as noted]

RANK/GRADE	PERSONNEL (1,000)				MONTHLY BASIC PAY (dollars)			
	1990	1991	1992	1993	1990	1991	1992	1993
Total [1]	2,043.7	1,985.6	1,807.2	1,705.1	(X)	(X)	(X)	(X)
Recruit—E-1	97.6	74.6	83.2	75.4	684	710	752	769
Private—E-2	140.3	125.8	110.9	114.1	803	838	873	909
Pvt. 1st class—E-3	280.1	275.6	233.5	214.6	871	900	937	976
Corporal—E-4	427.8	426.1	383.5	352.2	1,014	1,066	1,107	1,154
Sergeant—E-5	361.5	355.5	305.1	295.6	1,245	1,297	1,356	1,409
Staff Sgt.—E-6	239.1	238.9	227.4	214.6	1,480	1,563	1,634	1,711
Sgt. 1st class—E-7	134.1	134.2	130.5	124.7	1,784	1,866	1,946	2,028
Master Sgt.—E-8	38.0	36.1	33.2	31.6	2,117	2,210	2,302	2,406
Sgt. Major—E-9	15.3	14.8	13.5	12.8	2,583	2,682	2,794	2,933
Warrant Officer—W-1	3.2	2.8	2.2	2.4	1,686	1,747	1,809	1,849
Chief Warrant—W-4	3.0	3.0	2.7	2.4	2,943	3,085	3,214	3,383
2d Lt.—O-1	31.9	27.3	25.8	25.0	1,485	1,562	1,627	1,697
1st Lt.—O-2	37.9	37.6	33.5	29.7	2,056	2,135	2,220	2,311
Captain—O-3	106.6	106.1	100.2	93.0	2,618	2,727	2,829	2,924
Major—O-4	53.2	53.1	50.4	48.0	3,196	3,321	3,453	3,588
Lt. Colonel—O-5	32.3	32.2	30.9	29.5	3,894	4,041	4,197	4,359
Colonel—O-6	14.0	13.7	13.2	12.5	4,758	4,942	5,137	5,371
Brig. General—O-7	0.5	0.5	0.5	0.4	5,751	5,987	6,238	6,469
Major General—O-8	0.4	0.3	0.3	0.3	6,516	6,783	7,068	7,330
Lt. General—O-9	0.1	0.1	0.1	0.1	6,516	7,482	7,788	8,075
General—O-10	(Z)	(Z)	(Z)	(Z)	6,516	8,441	8,733	9,017

X Not applicable.　Z Fewer than 50.　[1] Includes cadets and midshipmen and warrant officers, W-2 and W-3.

Source: U.S. Dept. of Defense, *Selected Manpower Statistics,* annual, and Office of the Comptroller, unpublished data.

No. 572. Military Reserve Personnel: 1970 to 1994

[In thousands. As of end of fiscal year; see text, section 9. Excludes U.S. Coast Guard Reserve. The ready reserve includes selected reservists who are intended to assist active forces in a war and the individual ready reserve who, in a major war, would be used to fill out active and reserve units and later would be a source of combat replacements; a portion of the ready reserve serves in an active status. The standby reserve cannot be called to active duty unless the Congress gives its explicit approval. The retired reserve represents a low potential for mobilization]

RESERVE STATUS AND BRANCH OF SERVICE	1970	1975	1980	1985	1986	1987	1988	1989	1990	1991	1992	1993	1994
Total reserves	**3,639**	**1,836**	**1,349**	**1,610**	**1,653**	**1,657**	**1,677**	**1,661**	**1,671**	**1,786**	**1,883**	**1,867**	**1,805**
Ready reserve	2,574	1,471	1,263	1,566	1,612	1,620	1,642	1,631	1,641	1,758	1,858	1,841	1,779
Standby reserve	492	365	86	44	41	38	34	29	29	28	25	26	26
Retired reserve	573	(NA)	338	372	390	412	469	477	462	474	442	461	482
Army	2,221	1,168	804	1,045	1,067	1,064	1,070	1,062	1,050	1,124	1,156	1,132	1,077
Navy	808	273	207	214	228	238	244	248	252	271	297	302	317
Marine Corp	(NA)	124	94	92	93	88	87	82	83	96	107	112	109
Air Force	610	271	243	259	266	268	275	270	286	295	323	321	302

NA Not available.

Source: U.S. Dept. of Defense, *Official Guard and Reserve Manpower Strengths and Statistics,* quarterly.

No. 573. Ready Reserve Personnel Profile—Race, and Sex: 1990 to 1994

ITEM	RACE					PERCENT DISTRIBUTION			
	Total	White	Black	Asian	American Indian	White	Black	Asian	American Indian
1990	1,558,867	1,269,278	271,470	14,608	3,511	81.4	17.4	0.9	0.2
1991	1,154,515	906,748	190,214	12,711	5,652	78.5	16.5	1.1	0.5
1992	1,114,905	725,963	172,770	11,479	4,842	65.1	15.5	1.0	0.4
1993	1,057,676	829,797	173,444	13,350	4,785	78.5	16.4	1.3	0.5
1994, total [1]	1,137,048	771,068	163,427	13,686	4,584	67.8	14.4	1.2	0.4
Male	998,330	681,062	124,683	11,897	3,800	68.2	12.5	1.2	0.4
Officers	153,809	117,107	7,630	1,620	292	76.1	5.0	1.1	0.2
Enlisted	844,521	563,955	117,053	10,277	3,508	66.8	13.9	1.2	0.4
Female	138,718	90,006	38,744	1,789	784	64.9	27.9	1.3	0.6
Officers	24,197	19,200	3,731	287	59	79.3	15.4	1.2	0.2
Enlisted	114,521	70,806	35,013	1,502	725	61.8	30.6	1.3	0.6

[1] Includes unknown sex.

Source: U.S. Dept. of Defense, *Official Guard and Reserve Manpower Strengths and Statistics,* annual.

No. 574. Military Reserve Costs: 1980 to 1993

[In millions of dollars. As of end of fiscal year; see text, section 9. Army and Air Force data include National Guard]

TYPE OF COST	1980	1985	1987	1988	1989	1990	1991	1992	1993
Total	**7,969**	**19,414**	**18,947**	**19,234**	**19,797**	**21,526**	**21,811**	**21,867**	**22,825**
Operations and maintenance	3,526	5,734	6,168	6,670	6,694	6,687	7,398	7,714	8,095
Personnel	2,456	7,703	8,382	8,837	8,637	8,621	8,543	9,272	9,062
Procurement	1,459	5,009	3,316	2,533	3,520	4,914	4,480	3,533	4,398
Active-duty support	408	566	601	610	611	638	700	731	682
Construction	120	402	480	584	605	666	690	617	588

Source: U.S. Dept. of Defense, unpublished data.

No. 575. National Guard—Summary: 1980 to 1993

[As of end of fiscal year; see text, section 9. Includes Puerto Rico]

ITEM	Unit	1980	1985	1987	1988	1989	1990	1991	1992	1993
Army National Guard: Units .	**Number** . .	**3,379**	**4,353**	**6,125**	**5,982**	**5,715**	**4,055**	**6,470**	**6,727**	**6,339**
Personnel [1]	1,000	368	438	452	455	457	444	446	427	410
Funds obligated [2]	Bil. dol. . . .	1.8	4.4	5.0	5.3	5.4	5.2	5.4	6.3	6.3
Value of equipment	Bil. dol. . . .	7.6	18.8	22.3	27.4	30.1	29.0	29.0	29.0	31.0
Air National Guard: Units . . .	**Number** . .	**1,054**	**1,184**	**1,281**	**1,272**	**1,339**	**1,339**	**1,450**	**1,425**	**1,330**
Personnel [1]	1,000	96	109	115	115	116	118	115	119	117
Funds obligated [2]	Bil. dol. . . .	1.7	2.8	2.9	3.1	3.2	3.2	1.2	1.9	2.6
Value of equipment (est.) [3] .	Bil. dol. . . .	5.2	21.4	23.7	25.7	27.5	26.4	27.1	38.3	41.7

[1] Officers and enlisted personnel.   [2] Federal funds; includes personnel, operations, maintenance, and military construction.   [3] Beginning 1985, increase due to repricing of aircraft to current year dollars to reflect true replacement value. Beginning 1993 includes value of aircraft and support equipment.

Source: National Guard Bureau, *Annual Review of the Chief, National Guard Bureau;* and unpublished data.

No. 576. Wartime Veterans—States: 1994

[In thousands. As of end of fiscal year; see text, section 9. Data were estimated starting with veteran's place of residence as of April 1, 1980, based on 1980 Census of Population data, extended to later years on the basis of estimates of veteran interstate migration, separations from the Armed Forces, and mortality; not directly comparable with earlier estimates previously published by the VA. Excludes 423,000 veterans whose only active-duty military service occurred since September 8, 1980, and who failed to satisfy the minimum service requirement. Also excludes a small indeterminate number of National Guard personnel or reservists who incurred service-connected disabilities while on an initial tour of active duty for training only]

STATE	Total veterans [1]	War veterans [1]	World War I	World War II	Korean conflict	Vietnam era [2]	Persian Gulf War
United States	**26,365**	**20,327**	**18**	**7,770**	**4,563**	**8,246**	**1,230**
Northeast	5,126	3,980	4	1,672	887	1,405	195
New England	1,418	1,088	1	441	246	412	48
Maine	155	118	(Z)	42	26	50	8
New Hampshire	137	102	(Z)	35	23	46	5
Vermont	63	47	(Z)	16	10	20	3
Massachusetts	606	469	1	201	107	166	18
Rhode Island	111	87	(Z)	38	20	31	4
Connecticut	346	265	(Z)	109	60	99	10
Middle Atlantic	3,708	2,892	3	1,231	641	993	147
New York	1,569	1,215	1	507	269	416	67
New Jersey	756	590	1	255	137	201	23
Pennsylvania	1,383	1,087	1	469	235	376	57
North Central	6,297	4,892	3	1,837	1,061	1,904	304
East North Central	4,370	3,382	3	1,281	720	1,304	210
Ohio	1,204	936	1	362	197	357	59
Indiana	599	458	(Z)	168	100	181	29
Illinois	1,092	854	1	332	186	321	49
Michigan	961	739	1	272	152	293	48
Wisconsin	514	395	(Z)	147	85	152	25
West North Central	1,927	1,510	(Z)	556	341	600	94
Minnesota	468	360	(Z)	125	78	151	19
Iowa	296	237	(Z)	90	53	87	16
Missouri	592	462	(Z)	175	106	183	29
North Dakota	60	48	(Z)	16	11	19	4
South Dakota	75	59	(Z)	21	15	22	5
Nebraska	170	134	(Z)	49	32	52	9
Kansas	266	210	(Z)	80	46	86	12
South	9,293	7,156	3	2,705	1,627	3,013	504
South Atlantic	5,076	3,874	2	1,510	889	1,622	247
Delaware	79	60	(Z)	23	13	24	4
Maryland	536	394	(Z)	139	89	174	23
District of Columbia	52	40	(Z)	16	11	15	3
Virginia	710	526	(Z)	175	125	261	33
West Virginia	202	163	(Z)	66	37	59	11
North Carolina	714	542	(Z)	195	121	232	38
South Carolina	381	289	(Z)	101	65	130	25
Georgia	687	509	(Z)	157	111	247	41
Florida	1,715	1,351	2	638	317	480	69
East South Central	1,556	1,213	(Z)	447	277	490	100
Kentucky	371	291	(Z)	108	63	117	21
Tennessee	520	401	(Z)	144	89	170	28
Alabama	430	336	(Z)	123	81	135	31
Mississippi	235	185	(Z)	72	44	68	20
West South Central	2,661	2,069	1	748	461	901	157
Arkansas	260	206	(Z)	82	46	79	18
Louisiana	384	304	(Z)	114	65	119	30
Oklahoma	355	282	(Z)	107	66	119	18
Texas	1,662	1,277	1	445	284	584	91
West	5,651	4,297	2	1,556	989	1,919	227
Mountain	1,608	1,242	(Z)	452	286	546	76
Montana	97	77	(Z)	28	17	31	6
Idaho	113	88	(Z)	33	19	36	7
Wyoming	49	39	(Z)	13	8	17	3
Colorado	390	299	(Z)	94	67	148	19
New Mexico	173	133	(Z)	48	30	60	9
Arizona	460	355	(Z)	144	83	146	19
Utah	140	112	(Z)	42	25	45	8
Nevada	186	139	(Z)	50	37	63	5
Pacific	4,043	3,055	2	1,104	703	1,373	151
Washington	636	480	(Z)	161	107	232	27
Oregon	374	291	(Z)	111	60	124	16
California	2,852	2,152	2	796	507	945	101
Alaska	65	46	(Z)	8	8	30	2
Hawaii	116	86	(Z)	28	21	42	5

Z Less than 500.　[1] Veterans who served in more than one wartime period are counted only once. "All Veterans" includes Vietnam era (no prior wartime service), Korean conflict (no prior wartime service), World War II, post Vietnam era, Persian Gulf War era, and other.　[2] Excludes reservists.

Source: U.S. Dept. of Veterans Affairs, Management Sciences Service (008B2), *Annual Report of the Secretary of Veterans Affairs.*

No. 577. Veterans Living in the United States and Puerto Rico, by Age and by Service: 1994

[In thousands, except as indicated. As of July 1. Estimated. Excludes 500,000 veterans whose only active duty military service of less than 2 years occurred since Sept. 30, 1980. See headnote, table 576. See *Historical Statistics, Colonial Times to 1970*, series Y 943-956, for all veterans]

AGE	Total veterans	WARTIME VETERANS						Peace-time veterans
		Total [1]	Persian Gulf	Vietnam era	Korean con-flict	World War II	World War I	
1994	**26,497**	**20,425**	**1,236**	**8,281**	**4,597**	**7,795**	**19**	**6,072**
All ages	26,497	20,425	1,236	8,281	4,597	7,795	19	6,072
Under 30 years old . . .	1,236	675	675	(Z)	-	-	-	561
30-34 years old	1,328	215	203	12	-	-	-	1,113
35-39 years old	1,610	588	112	498	-	-	-	1,022
40-44 years old	2,194	1,951	126	1,920	-	-	-	244
45-49 years old	3,530	3,390	81	3,371	-	-	-	141
50-54 years old	2,545	1,548	28	1,538	-	-	-	997
55-59 years old	2,435	960	9	409	625	-	-	1,475
60-64 years old	3,037	2,653	2	260	2,524	110	-	384
65 years old and over .	8,581	8,446	(Z)	272	1,448	7,685	19	135

- Represents zero.   Z Less than 500.   [1] Veterans who served in more than one wartime period are counted only once.

Source: U.S. Dept. of Veterans Affairs, Office of Information Management and Statistics, *Veteran Population*, annual.

No. 578. Disabled Veterans Receiving Compensation: 1970 to 1994

[In thousands, except as indicated. As of end of fiscal year; see text, section 9. Represents veterans receiving compensation for service-connected disabilities. Totally disabled refers to veterans with any disability, mental or physical, deemed to be total and permanent which prevents the individual from maintaining a livelihood and are rated for disability at 100 percent]

MILITARY SERVICE	1970	1980	1985	1988	1989	1990	1991	1992	1993	1994
Disabled, all periods [1]	**2,092**	**2,274**	**2,240**	**2,199**	**2,192**	**2,184**	**2,179**	**2,181**	**2,198**	**2,218**
Peace-time	185	262	352	398	421	444	468	500	471	492
World War I [1]	85	30	12	6	5	3	3	2	1	1
World War II	1,416	1,193	1,049	947	912	876	841	805	769	731
Korea	239	236	223	215	212	209	205	202	198	195
Vietnam	167	553	604	633	643	652	662	671	682	694
Persian Gulf	(X)	(X)	(X)	(X)	(X)	(X)	(X)	(X)	76	106
Totally disabled, all periods [1].	**124**	**121**	**136**	**131**	**131**	**131**	**131**	**132**	**135**	**138**
Peace-time	16	20	26	26	26	27	27	28	28	29
World War I [1]	11	3	1	1	(Z)	(Z)	(Z)	(Z)	(Z)	(Z)
World War II	63	51	54	47	45	43	41	39	37	36
Korea	16	16	17	16	16	16	16	15	15	15
Vietnam	18	31	38	41	43	44	46	49	52	56
Persian Gulf	(X)	(X)	(X)	(X)	(X)	(X)	(X)	(X)	2	2
Compensation (mil. dol.) . . .	**2,393**	**6,104**	**8,270**	**8,722**	**8,937**	**9,284**	**9,612**	**10,031**	**10,545**	**10,977**

X Not applicable.   Z Less than 500.   [1] Includes Spanish-American War and Mexican Border service, not shown separately.

Source: U.S. Dept. of Veterans Affairs, *Annual Report of the Secretary of Veterans Affairs;* and unpublished data.

No. 579. Veterans Benefits—Expenditures, by Program: 1970 to 1992

[In millions of dollars. For fiscal years ending in year shown; see text, section 9. Beginning with fiscal year 1988, data are for outlays]

PROGRAM	1970	1980	1985	1987	1988	1989	1990	1991	1992
Total	**10,201**	**23,187**	**29,359**	**31,812**	**29,271**	**30,041**	**28,998**	**31,214**	**33,894**
Medical programs	1,765	6,042	9,227	9,876	10,283	10,745	11,582	12,472	13,815
Construction	75	300	557	589	649	703	661	608	639
General operating expenses	243	605	765	765	781	766	811	884	914
Compensation and pension	5,252	11,044	14,037	14,241	14,710	15,009	14,674	16,080	16,282
Vocational rehabilitation and education	1,032	2,350	1,164	847	717	589	452	541	695
All other [1]	1,835	2,846	3,609	5,494	2,130	2,228	818	629	1,549

[1] Includes insurance and indemnities, and miscellaneous funds and expenditures. (Excludes expenditures from personal funds of patients.)

Source: U.S. Dept. of Veterans Affairs, *Trend Data, Fiscal Years 1968-1992*.

No. 580. Veterans Compensation and Pension Benefits—Number on Rolls and Average Payment, by Period of Service and Status: 1980 to 1993

[As of **Sept. 30.** Living refers to veterans receiving compensation for disability incurred or aggravated while on active duty and war veterans receiving pension and benefits for nonservice connected disabilities. Deceased refers to deceased veterans whose dependents were receiving pensions and compensation benefits. See also *Historical Statistics, Colonial Times to 1970,* series Y 998-999]

PERIOD OF SERVICE AND VETERAN STATUS	VETERANS ON ROLLS (1,000)					AVERAGE PAYMENT (annual basis) [1] (dol.)				
	1980	1990	1991	1992	1993	1980	1985	1990	1991	1992
Total	**4,646**	**3,584**	**3,509**	**3,428**	**3,374**	**2,370**	**3,505**	**4,335**	**4,552**	**4,712**
Living veterans	3,195	2,746	2,709	2,674	2,660	2,600	3,666	4,320	4,491	4,611
Service connected	2,273	2,184	2,179	2,181	2,198	2,669	3,692	4,250	4,406	4,593
Nonservice connected	922	562	530	493	462	2,428	3,581	4,591	4,837	4,689
Deceased veterans	1,451	838	800	754	714	1,863	3,066	4,382	4,761	5,071
Service connected	358	320	318	314	310	3,801	5,836	7,349	7,815	8,244
Nonservice connected	1,093	518	482	440	404	1,228	1,809	2,548	2,748	2,810
Prior to World War I	14	4	4	3	3	1,432	1,855	2,616	2,921	3,073
Living	(Z)	(Z)	(Z)	(Z)	(Z)	2,634	4,436	10,502	10,441	8,176
World War I	692	198	172	146	124	1,683	2,461	3,435	3,674	3,754
Living	198	18	13	9	6	2,669	4,439	6,922	7,239	6,476
World War II	2,520	1,723	1,638	1,543	1,453	2,307	3,317	4,052	4,238	4,334
Living	1,849	1,294	1,226	1,153	1,083	2,462	3,460	4,123	4,278	4,333
Korean conflict [2]	446	390	388	387	377	2,691	4,114	5,105	5,330	5,462
Living	317	305	304	300	296	2,977	4,260	5,103	5,288	5,390
Peacetime	312	495	518	550	518	3,080	3,973	4,132	4,216	4,292
Living	262	444	468	500	471	2,828	3,589	3,709	3,789	3,866
Vietnam era [3]	662	774	789	804	821	2,795	4,021	4,945	5,242	5,551
Living	569	685	698	711	727	2,709	3,849	4,671	4,936	5,234
Persian Gulf War [4]	(X)	(X)	(X)	(Z)	78	(X)	(X)	(X)	(X)	1,673
Living	(X)	(X)	(X)	(Z)	76	(X)	(X)	(X)	(X)	1,386

X Not applicable.　Z Fewer than 500.　[1] Averages calculated by multiplying average monthly payment by 12.　[2] Service during period June 27, 1950, to Jan. 31, 1955.　[3] Service from Aug. 5, 1964, to May 7, 1975.　[4] Service from August 2, 1990, to the present.

Source: U.S. Dept. of Veterans Affairs, *Annual Report of the Secretary of Veterans Affairs;* and unpublished data.

No. 581. Veterans Administration Health Care Summary: 1980 to 1993

[For years ending **Sept. 30**]

ITEM	Unit	1980	1990	1993	ITEM	Unit	1980	1990	1993
Facilities operating:					Obligations [2]	Mil. dol.	6,215	11,827	15,079
Hospitals	Number	172	172	171	Prescriptions dispensed .	Millions	36.7	58.6	59.1
Domiciliaries	Number	16	32	37	Laboratory	Millions	215	188	(NA)
Outpatient clinics	Number	226	339	353	Inpatients treated [3]	1,000. .	1,359	1,113	1,043
Nursing home units . .	Number	92	126	128	Average daily	1,000. .	105	88	84
Employment [1]	1,000. .	194	199	210	Outpatient visits	Millions	18.0	22.6	24.2

NA Not available.　[1] Net full-time equivalent.　[2] 1980, cost basis; thereafter, obligation basis.　[3] Based on the number of discharges and deaths during the fiscal year, plus the number on the rolls (bed occupants and patients on authorized leave of absence) at the end of the fiscal year. Excludes interhospital transfers.

Source: U.S. Dept. of Veterans Affairs, *Annual Report of the Secretary of Veterans Affairs; Directory of VA Facilities,* biennial; and unpublished data.

No. 582. Veterans Assistance—Education and Training: 1980 to 1994

[**In thousands, except where indicated. For fiscal years ending in year shown;** see text, section 9. Represents persons in training during year]

PROGRAM	1980	1985	1989	1990	1991	1992	1993	1994
Veteran Education Assistance [1]	1,107	402	164	102	143	195	246	284
Institutions of higher education	842	326	144	94	132	177	223	258
Resident schools other than college	149	54	13	6	9	14	18	19
Correspondence schools	42	7	3	1	1	3	3	4
On-the-job training	74	15	3	1	1	2	2	3
Children's Educational Assistance	82.6	55.3	38.7	37.5	37.3	37.2	36.4	35.7
Institutions of higher education	75.5	50.0	36.2	35.3	35.2	35.1	34.3	33.7
Schools other than college	6.5	5.2	2.4	2.1	2.1	2.1	2.0	1.9
Special restorative training	0.1	(Z)	(Z)	(Z)	(Z)	(Z)	(Z)	(Z)
On-the-job training	0.5	0.2	0.1	0.1	(Z)	(Z)	(Z)	(Z)
Spouses, Widows/Widowers Educational								
Assistance Program	13.0	6.6	4.6	4.5	4.4	4.5	4.4	4.6
Institutions of higher education	10.8	5.7	4.1	4.1	4.0	4.0	4.0	4.1
Schools other than college	2.2	1.0	0.5	0.4	0.4	0.4	0.4	0.4
Disabled Veterans Vocational Rehab	25.5	26.9	27.0	27.8	35.9	36.8	40.7	44.2
Guaranteed and insured loans, (1,000) . . .	297.4	178.9	189.7	196.6	181.2	266.0	383.3	(NA)
Guaranteed and insured loans, (mil. dol.) . .	14,815	11,452	14,416	15,779	15,454	22,960	34,635	(NA)
Guaranty and insurance (mil. dol.)	6,370	4,363	5,211	5,561	5,299	7,819	11,601	(NA)

NA Not available.　Z Fewer than 50.　[1] Data for 1980-89 are for Post-Korean Conflict GI Bill (Title 38 USC Chapter 34). Data for 1990-94 are for the Active Duty Montgomery GI Bill (Title 38 USC Chapter 30).

Source: U.S. Dept. of Veterans Affairs, *Annual Report of the Secretary of Veterans Affairs;* and unpublished data.

Social Insurance and Human Services

This section presents data related to governmental expenditures for social welfare; governmental programs for old-age, survivors, disability, and health insurance (OASDHI); governmental employee retirement; private pension plans; government unemployment and temporary disability insurance; Federal supplemental security income payments and aid to the needy; child and other welfare services; and Federal food programs. Also included here are selected data on workers' compensation, vocational rehabilitation; child support; child care; charity contributions; and philanthropic trusts and foundations.

The principal sources for these data are the Social Security Administration's quarterly *Social Security Bulletin* and the *Annual Statistical Supplement to the Social Security Bulletin* which present current data on many of the programs. Current data on employment security are published annually in the Department of Labor's *Unemployment Insurance, Financial Data.* Statistics on aid to families with dependent children (AFDC) are presented in the U.S. Administration for Children and Families' annual publication, *Quarterly Public Assistance Statistics.*

Social insurance under the Social Security Act.—Programs established by the Social Security Act provide protection against wage loss resulting from retirement, prolonged disability, death, or unemployment, and protection against the cost of medical care during old age and disability. The Federal OASDHI program provides monthly benefits to retired or disabled insured workers and their dependents and to survivors of insured workers. To be eligible, a worker must have had a specified period of employment in which OASDHI taxes were paid. A worker becomes eligible for full benefits at age 65, although reduced benefits may be obtained up to 3 years earlier; the worker's spouse is under the same limitations. Survivor benefits are payable to dependents of deceased insured

In Brief

In 1993, households below poverty level receiving:

Medicaid	*49%*
Food stamps	*35%*

Social Security beneficiaries, 1993:

Total	*42 million*
Retired workers	*26 million*

workers. Disability benefits are payable to an insured worker under age 65 with a prolonged disability and to the disabled worker's dependents on the same basis as dependents of retired workers. Disability benefits are provided at age 50 to the disabled widow or widower of a deceased worker who was fully insured at the time of death. Disabled children, aged 18 or older, of retired, disabled, or deceased workers are also eligible for benefits. A lump-sum benefit is generally payable on the death of an insured worker to a spouse or minor children. For information on the Medicare program, see section 3.

Retirement, survivors, disability, and hospital insurance benefits are funded by a payroll tax on annual earnings (up to a maximum of earnings set by law) of workers, employers, and the self-employed. The maximum taxable earnings are adjusted annually to reflect increasing wage levels (see table 592). Effective January 1994, there is no dollar limit on wages and self-employment income subject to hospital insurance tax. Tax receipts and benefit payments are administered through Federal trust funds. Special benefits for uninsured persons; hospital benefits for persons 65 and over with specified amounts of Social Security coverage less than that required for cash benefit eligibility; and that part of the cost of supplementary medical insurance not financed by contributions from participants are financed from Federal general revenues.

Unemployment insurance is presently administered by the U.S. Employment and Training Administration and each State's employment security agency. By agreement with the U.S. Secretary of Labor, State agencies also administer unemployment compensation for eligible ex-service members and Federal employees, unemployment assistance under the Disaster Relief Act of 1970, and workers assistance and relocation allowances under the Trade Act. Under State unemployment insurance laws, benefits related to the individual's past earnings are paid to unemployed eligible workers. State laws vary concerning the length of time benefits are paid and their amount. In most States, benefits are payable for 26 weeks and, during periods of high unemployment, extended benefits are payable under a Federal-State program to those who have exhausted their regular State benefits. The basic benefit can vary among States by over 100 percent. Some States also supplement the basic benefit with allowances for dependents.

Unemployment insurance is funded by a Federal unemployment tax levied on the taxable payrolls of most employers. Taxable payroll under the Federal Act and 12 State laws is the first $7,000 in wages paid each worker during a year. Forty-one States have taxable payrolls above $7,000. Employers are allowed a percentage credit of taxable payroll for contributions paid to States under State unemployment insurance laws. The remaining percent of the Federal tax finances administrative costs, the Federal share of extended benefits, and advances to States. About 97 percent of wage and salary workers are covered by unemployment insurance.

Retirement Programs for Government Employees.—The Civil Service Retirement System (CSRS) and the Federal Employees' Retirement System (FERS) are the two major programs providing age and service, disability, and survivor annuities for Federal civilian employees. In general, employees hired after December 31, 1983, are covered under FERS and the social security program (OASDHI), and employees on staff prior to that date are members of CSRS and are covered under Medicare. CSRS employees were offered the option of

transferring to FERS during 1987. There are separate retirement systems for the uniformed services (supplementing OASDHI) and for certain special groups of Federal employees. State and local government employees are covered for the most part by State and local retirement systems similar to the Federal civil service retirement system. In many jurisdictions these benefits supplement OASDHI coverage.

Workers' compensation.—All States provide protection against work-connected injuries and deaths, although some States exclude certain workers (e.g., domestic help). Federal laws cover Federal employees, private employees in the District of Columbia, and longshoremen and harbor workers. In addition, the Social Security Administration and the Department of Labor administer "black lung" benefits programs for coal miners disabled by pneumoconiosis and for specified dependents and survivors. Specified occupational diseases are compensable to some extent. In most States, benefits are related to the worker's salary. The benefits may or may not be augmented by dependents' allowances or automatically adjusted to prevailing wage levels.

Public aid.—State-administered public assistance programs (Aid to Families with Dependent Children (AFDC), emergency assistance and general assistance) and the Federal Supplemental Security Income (SSI) program administered by the Social Security Administration provide benefits to persons who qualify. AFDC and emergency assistance are in part federally funded while the costs of general assistance are met entirely with State and local funds. The SSI program replaced Federal grants for aid to the aged, blind, and disabled in the 50 States and the District of Columbia in 1974. Residents of the Northern Mariana Islands became eligible in 1978. Federal grants continue for aid to the aged, blind, and disabled in Guam, Puerto Rico, and the Virgin Islands. The SSI program provides a minimum income for the aged, blind, and disabled and establishes uniform national basic eligibility requirements and payment standards. Most States supplement the basic SSI payment.

Federal Food Stamp program.—Under the Food Stamp program, single persons and those living in households meeting nationwide standards for income and assets may receive coupons redeemable for food at most retail food stores. The monthly amount of coupons a unit receives is determined by household size and income. Households without income receive the determined monthly cost of a nutritionally adequate diet for their household size. This amount is updated to account for food price increases. Households with income receive the difference between the amount of a nutritionally adequate diet and 30 percent of their income, after certain allowable deductions.

To qualify for the program, a household must have less than $2,000 in disposable assets ($3,000 if one member is aged 60 or older), gross income below 130 percent of the official poverty guidelines, and net income below 100 percent of the poverty guidelines. Households with a person aged 60 or older or a disabled person receiving SSI, Social Security, or veterans' disability benefits may have gross income exceeding 130 percent of the poverty guidelines. All households must meet these requirements, even those receiving other Federal assistance payments. Households are certified for varying lengths of time, depending on their income sources and individual circumstances.

Health and welfare services.—Programs providing health and welfare services are aided through Federal grants to States for child welfare services, vocational rehabilitation, activities for the aged, maternal and child health services, maternity and infant care projects, comprehensive health services, and a variety of public health activities. For information about the Medicaid program, see section 3.

Noncash benefits.—The Bureau of the Census annually collects data on the characteristics of recipients of noncash (in-kind) benefits to supplement the collection of annual money income data in the Current Population Survey (see text, section 1 and section 15). Noncash benefits are those benefits received in a form other than money which serve to enhance or improve the economic well-being of the recipient. As for money income, the data for noncash benefits are for the calendar year prior to the date of the interview. The major categories of noncash benefits covered are public transfers (e.g. food stamps, school lunch, public housing, and Medicaid) and employer or union-provided benefits to employees.

Statistical reliability.—For discussion of statistical collection, estimation, and sampling procedures and measures of statistical reliability applicable to HHS and Census Bureau data, see Appendix III.

Historical statistics.—Tabular headnotes provide cross-references, where applicable, to *Historical Statistics of the United States, Colonial Times to 1970*. See Appendix IV.

Social Insurance and Human Services

No. 583. Social Welfare Expenditures Under Public Programs: 1970 to 1992

[In billions of dollars, except percent. See headnote, table 585]

YEAR	Total	Social insur-ance	Public aid	Health and medical programs [1]	Veterans pro-grams	Educa-tion	Housing	Other social welfare	All health and medical care [2]
Total:									
1970.	146	55	16	10	9	51	1	4	25
1980.	493	230	73	27	21	121	7	14	100
1985.	732	370	98	39	27	172	13	14	171
1989.	957	468	129	57	30	239	18	17	240
1990.	1,050	514	147	62	31	258	19	18	276
1991.	1,161	561	181	67	33	277	22	20	317
1992.	1,264	617	208	70	35	292	21	22	354
Federal:									
1970.	77	45	10	5	9	6	1	2	16
1980.	303	191	49	13	21	13	6	9	69
1985.	451	310	63	18	27	14	11	8	122
1989.	565	387	82	24	30	19	15	8	165
1990.	617	422	93	27	30	18	17	9	190
1991.	676	454	113	30	32	19	19	10	213
1992.	749	496	139	32	34	20	18	11	250
State and local:									
1970.	68	9	7	5	(Z)	45	(Z)	2	9
1980.	190	39	23	14	(Z)	108	1	5	31
1985.	281	59	35	21	(Z)	158	2	6	49
1989.	392	81	47	33	(Z)	220	3	8	75
1990.	433	92	54	35	(Z)	240	3	9	85
1991.	484	108	68	37	1	258	3	10	103
1992.	514	121	69	38	1	272	3	11	105
Percent Federal:									
1970.	53	83	59	48	99	12	83	55	65
1980.	62	83	68	47	99	11	91	65	69
1985.	62	84	64	46	99	8	88	56	71
1990.	59	82	64	44	98	7	85	50	69
1991.	58	81	62	44	98	7	87	50	68
1992.	59	80	67	46	98	7	87	50	71
Per capita (current dollars): [3]									
1970.	698	262	79	46	43	244	3	20	120
1980.	2,126	990	314	118	92	523	30	59	434
1985.	3,009	1,516	405	161	111	708	52	56	705
1990.	4,131	2,017	579	250	120	1,018	77	71	1,084
1991.	4,530	2,184	708	266	126	1,083	84	77	1,237
1992.	4,863	2,369	801	274	130	1,126	79	83	1,364
Per capita (constant (1992) dollars): [3][4]									
1970.	2,421	908	275	160	150	847	12	69	418
1980.	3,678	1,712	544	204	159	905	51	102	750
1985.	3,993	2,011	537	215	147	940	69	74	940
1990.	4,440	2,168	622	269	129	1,094	83	76	1,171
1991.	4,531	2,185	705	271	126	1,083	87	77	1,234
1992.	4,863	2,369	801	274	130	1,126	79	83	1,364

Z Less than $500 million.   [1] Excludes program parts of social insurance, public aid, veterans, and other social welfare.
[2] Combines "Health and medical programs" with medical services included in social insurance, public aid, veterans, vocational rehabilitation, and antipoverty programs.   [3] Excludes payments within foreign countries for education, veterans, OASDHI, and civil service retirement.   [4] Constant dollar figures are based on implicit price deflators for personal consumption expenditures published by U.S. Bureau of Economic Analysis in *Survey of Current Business*, July 1994.

No. 584. Social Welfare Expenditures Under Public Programs as Percent of GDP and Total Government Outlays: 1970 to 1992

[See headnote, table 585]

YEAR	TOTAL EXPENDITURES				FEDERAL				STATE AND LOCAL GOVERNMENT			
	Total (bil. dol.)	Percent change [1]	Percent of—		Total (bil. dol.)	Percent change [1]	Percent of—		Total (bil. dol.)	Percent change [1]	Percent of—	
			Total GDP [2]	Total govt. outlays			Total GDP [2]	Total Federal outlays			Total GDP [2]	Total State and local outlays
1970. . . .	146	14.6	14.8	46.5	77	13.2	7.8	40.0	68	16.3	6.9	57.9
1980. . . .	493	14.7	18.6	57.2	303	15.2	11.4	54.4	190	13.8	7.2	62.9
1985. . . .	732	8.0	18.4	52.2	451	7.1	11.3	48.7	281	9.3	7.1	59.9
1989. . . .	957	7.9	18.5	55.2	565	7.2	10.9	49.5	392	8.8	7.6	68.0
1990. . . .	1,050	9.7	18.9	56.7	617	9.0	11.1	51.4	433	10.7	7.8	68.0
1991. . . .	1,161	10.6	20.3	58.6	676	9.7	11.8	52.8	484	12.0	8.5	70.4
1992. . . .	1,264	8.9	21.0	61.6	749	10.8	12.4	57.1	514	6.2	8.5	70.6

[1] Percent change from immediate prior year.   [2] Gross domestic product.
Source of tables 583 and 584: U.S. Social Security Administration, *Social Security Bulletin,* summer 1993; and unpublished data.

No. 585. Social Welfare Expenditures, by Source of Funds and Public Program: 1980 to 1992

[In millions of dollars. For fiscal years ending in year shown; see text, section 9. Represents outlays from trust funds (mostly social insurance funds built up by earmarked contributions from insured persons, their employers, or both) and budgetary outlays from general revenues. Includes administrative expenditures, capital outlay, and some expenditures and payments outside the United States. See *Historical Statistics, Colonial Times to 1970*, series H 1-47, for related but not comparable data]

PROGRAM	FEDERAL				STATE AND LOCAL			
	1980	1990	1991	1992	1980	1990	1991	1992
Total	303,167	616,639	676,411	749,406	189,547	433,036	484,409	514,457
Social insurance	191,162	422,257	453,534	495,710	38,592	91,565	107,641	121,266
Old-age, survivors, disability, health	152,110	355,264	382,290	416,564	(X)	(X)	(X)	(X)
Health insurance (Medicare).........	34,992	109,709	116,651	132,246	(X)	(X)	(X)	(X)
Public employee retirement [1]	26,983	53,541	56,880	58,229	12,507	36,851	40,391	45,099
Railroad employee retirement	4,769	7,230	7,532	7,737	(X)	(X)	(X)	(X)
Unemployment insurance and employment services [2]	4,408	3,096	3,613	9,928	13,919	16,878	24,793	31,238
Other railroad employee insurance [3]	224	105	94	95	(X)	(X)	(X)	(X)
State temporary disability insurance [4] ...	(X)	(X)	(X)	(X)	1,377	3,224	3,879	4,009
Workers' compensation [5]	2,668	3,021	3,125	3,157	10,789	34,613	38,578	40,919
Hospital and medical benefits.......	130	457	506	571	3,596	13,849	15,503	17,344
Public aid.............	49,394	92,858	113,235	138,704	23,309	53,953	68,104	69,241
Public assistance [6]	23,542	54,747	69,315	86,747	21,522	50,347	64,354	65,264
Medical assistance payments [7].....	14,550	40,690	53,393	69,766	13,020	35,485	48,521	47,848
Social services	1,757	2,065	2,117	2,031	586	688	706	677
Supplemental Security Income........	6,440	13,625	15,896	19,446	1,787	3,605	3,751	3,978
Food stamps	9,083	16,254	19,471	23,233	(X)	(X)	(X)	(X)
Other [8]	10,329	8,232	8,553	9,279	(X)	(X)	(X)	(X)
Health and medical programs.........	12,840	27,204	29,700	31,965	14,423	35,151	37,300	37,861
Hospital and medical care..........	6,636	14,816	17,128	17,781	5,667	11,479	11,836	11,407
Civilian programs	2,438	3,654	4,388	5,012	5,667	11,479	11,836	11,407
Defense Department [9]	4,198	11,162	12,740	12,769	(X)	(X)	(X)	(X)
Maternal and child health programs	351	492	522	580	519	1,374	1,461	1,532
Medical research.............	4,428	9,172	9,445	10,641	496	1,679	1,854	1,931
Medical facilities construction.........	210	413	-	-	1,450	1,922	2,056	2,388
Other	1,215	2,311	2,605	2,963	6,291	18,697	20,093	20,603
Veterans programs	21,255	30,428	32,331	34,212	212	488	526	555
Pensions and compensation	11,306	15,793	16,284	16,539	(X)	(X)	(X)	(X)
Health and medical programs	6,204	12,004	13,222	14,567	(X)	(X)	(X)	(X)
Hospital and medical care	5,750	11,321	12,190	13,452	(X)	(X)	(X)	(X)
Hospital construction	323	445	776	845	(X)	(X)	(X)	(X)
Medical and prosthetic research	131	238	256	270	(X)	(X)	(X)	(X)
Education	2,401	523	570	772	(X)	(X)	(X)	(X)
Life insurance [10]	665	1,038	1,039	1,114	(X)	(X)	(X)	(X)
Welfare and other	679	1,070	1,217	1,220	212	488	526	555
Education [11]	13,452	18,374	19,084	20,188	107,597	240,011	258,063	272,011
Elementary and secondary [12]	7,430	9,944	11,979	12,891	79,720	189,333	203,819	214,015
Construction [13]	41	23	39	43	6,483	10,613	12,324	14,638
Higher..............	4,468	6,747	5,339	5,392	21,708	50,678	54,243	57,996
Construction	42	-	31	30	1,486	3,953	3,950	4,839
Vocational and adult [13]	1,207	1,293	1,314	1,452	6,169	([12])	([12])	([12])
Housing....................	6,278	16,612	18,696	17,950	601	2,856	2,826	2,668
Other social welfare	8,786	8,905	9,831	10,677	4,813	9,012	9,949	10,855
Vocational rehabilitation	1,006	1,661	1,751	1,912	245	466	485	534
Medical services and research	237	415	438	478	56	116	121	134
Institutional care [14]	74	143	142	144	408	486	523	541
Child nutrition [15]	4,209	5,470	6,098	6,722	643	1,696	1,869	2,054
Child welfare [16]	57	253	274	274	743	(NA)	(NA)	(NA)
Special CSA and ACTION programs [17] ..	2,303	169	192	194	(X)	(X)	(X)	(X)
Welfare, not elsewhere classified [18]	1,137	1,209	1,375	1,431	2,774	6,365	7,072	7,726

- Represents zero. NA Not available. X Not applicable. [1] Excludes refunds to those leaving service. Federal data include military retirement. [2] Includes compensation for Federal employees and ex-servicemen, trade adjustment and cash training allowance, and payments under extended, emergency, disaster, and special unemployment insurance programs. [3] Unemployment and temporary disability insurance. [4] Cash and medical benefits in five areas. Includes private plans where applicable. [5] Benefits paid by private insurance carriers, State funds, and self-insurers. Federal includes black lung benefit programs. [6] Includes payments under State general assistance programs and work incentive activities, not shown separately. [7] Medicaid payments and State and local general assistance medical payments. [8] Refugee assistance, surplus food for the needy, and work-experience training programs under the Comprehensive Employment and Training Act. Beginning 1990, includes low-income energy assistance program. [9] Includes medical care for military dependent families. [10] Excludes servicemen's group life insurance. [11] Federal expenditures include administrative costs (Department of Education) and research, not shown separately. [12] Beginning 1990, all State and local vocational education costs included with elementary-secondary. [13] Construction costs of vocational and adult education programs included under elementary-secondary expenditures. [14] Federal expenditures represent primarily surplus foods for nonprofit institutions. [15] Surplus food for schools and programs under National School Lunch and Child Nutrition Acts. [16] Represents primarily child welfare services under Title V of the Social Security Act. [17] Includes domestic volunteer programs under ACTION and community action and migrant workers programs under Community Services Administration. Beginning 1990, represents ACTION funds only. [18] Federal expenditures include administrative expenses of the Secretary of Health and Human Services; Indian welfare and guidance; and aging and juvenile delinquency activities. State and local include antipoverty and manpower programs, child care and adoption services, legal assistance, and other unspecified welfare services.

Source: U.S. Social Security Administration, *Social Security Bulletin*, summer 1993; and unpublished data.

No. 586. Private Expenditures for Social Welfare, by Type: 1980 to 1992

[In millions of dollars, except percent]

TYPE	1980	1985	1987	1988	1989	1990	1991	1992
Total expenditures	**255,859**	**471,794**	**555,643**	**610,812**	**678,275**	**728,034**	**768,165**	**824,719**
Percent of gross domestic product	9.4	11.7	12.2	12.5	12.9	13.1	13.4	13.7
Health.	145,800	259,400	298,600	336,100	370,700	410,000	432,900	462,900
Income maintenance	54,103	119,442	144,116	149,357	167,726	165,283	172,553	185,572
Private pension plan payments [1] [2] . .	37,560	98,450	120,442	124,546	140,911	137,739	144,237	156,888
Short-term sickness and disability [2] . .	9,214	11,261	12,579	13,613	14,457	14,566	14,720	15,526
Long-term disability [2]	1,282	1,937	2,293	2,295	2,892	2,926	3,172	3,143
Life insurance and death [3]	5,075	7,489	8,166	8,418	9,063	9,278	9,472	9,442
Supplemental unemployment [2]	972	305	636	485	403	774	952	573
Education	33,180	54,038	65,498	72,137	80,383	87,864	93,813	100,491
Welfare and other services	22,776	38,914	47,429	53,218	59,466	64,887	68,899	75,756

[1] Covers benefits paid for solely by employers and all benefits of employment-related pension plans to which employee contributions are made. Excludes individual savings plans such as IRA's and Keogh plans. Pension plan benefits include monthly benefits and lump-sum distributions to retired and disabled employees and their dependents and to survivors of deceased employees. Also includes preretirement lump-sum distributions. [2] Covers wage and salary workers in private industry. [3] Covers all wage and salary workers.

Source: U.S. Social Security Administration, *Annual Statistical Supplement* to the *Social Security Bulletin*, annual.

No. 587. Public Income-Maintenance Programs—Cash Benefit Payments: 1980 to 1993

[Includes payments outside the United States and benefits to dependents, where applicable]

PROGRAM	PAYMENTS (bil. dol.)									PERCENT		
	1980	1985	1987	1988	1989	1990	1991	1992	1993	1980	1990	1992
Total [1]	**228.1**	**335.2**	**372.0**	**393.8**	**421.9**	**455.8**	**504.4**	**539.2**	**(NA)**	**100**	**100**	**100**
Percent of personal income [2]	10.1	9.9	9.8	9.7	9.6	9.8	10.4	10.5	(NA)	(X)	(X)	(X)
OASDI [3]	120.3	186.1	204.7	216.4	229.6	245.6	265.6	281.7	296.2	53	54	52
Public employee retirement [4]	40.6	63.0	72.1	78.0	83.8	90.4	97.3	103.7	(NA)	18	20	19
Railroad retirement	4.9	6.3	6.5	6.7	6.9	7.2	7.5	7.3	7.9	2	2	2
Veterans' pensions, compensation.	11.4	14.1	14.3	14.7	15.3	15.8	16.3	16.5	16.9	5	3	3
Unemployment benefits [5]	18.9	14.4	14.4	13.2	16.4	20.0	31.3	37.3	21.5	8	4	7
Temporary disability benefits.	1.4	1.8	2.5	2.8	2.9	3.2	3.9	4.0	(NA)	1	1	1
Workers' compensation [6]	9.7	22.3	27.1	30.3	33.8	37.6	41.7	44.1	43.4	4	8	8
Public assistance	12.1	15.3	16.5	17.0	17.4	19.3	21.2	22.3	22.9	5	4	4
Supplemental Security Income . . .	7.9	11.1	13.6	14.7	14.9	15.2	18.5	22.3	24.7	3	4	4

NA Not available. X Not applicable. [1] Includes lump sum death benefits, not shown separately. Lump sum death benefits for State and local government employee retirement systems are not available beginning 1987. [2] For base data, see table 710. [3] Old-age, survivors, and disability insurance under Federal Social Security Act; see text, section 12. [4] Excludes refunds of contributions to employees who leave service. [5] Beginning 1985, covers State unemployment insurance, Ex-Servicemen's Compensation Act and railroad unemployment insurance only. [6] Includes black lung benefits.

Source: U.S. Social Security Administration, *Social Security Bulletin*, quarterly; and unpublished data.

No. 588. Selected Social Insurance Programs—Estimated Payrolls of Covered Employment in Relation to Wages and Salaries: 1980 to 1992

[**In billions of dollars, except percent.** Data for Federal civilian and military personnel cover all areas. Gross amount before deduction of social insurance contributions. OASDHI: Old-age, survivors, disability, and health insurance programs under Social Security Act; see text, section 12. See also *Historical Statistics, Colonial Times to 1970*, series H 57-69]

PROGRAM	1980	1984	1985	1986	1987	1988	1989	1990	1991	1992
Total earnings [1]	1,553	2,073	2,232	2,377	2,573	2,767	2,934	3,108	3,192	3,369
All wages and salaries [1]	1,372	1,839	1,975	2,094	2,250	2,443	2,586	2,745	2,816	2,955
Civilian.	1,342	1,794	1,928	2,044	2,198	2,390	2,531	2,688	2,754	2,894
Payrolls covered by—										
Retirement programs [2]	1,318	1,775	1,896	2,011	2,158	2,343	2,493	2,634	2,714	(NA)
OASDHI [3]	1,229	1,665	1,782	1,896	2,042	2,225	2,368	2,511	2,565	2,719
Railroad retirement [3]	13	13	13	12	12	12	12	12	12	13
Federal civil service	52	65	70	72	74	80	83	88	92	(NA)
State and local government	123	162	175	190	203	219	235	253	255	(NA)
Unemployment insurance [3]	1,303	1,739	1,870	1,983	2,046	2,205	2,336	2,492	2,549	2,697
Workers' compensation program [4] . .	1,136	1,516	1,618	1,725	1,845	1,997	2,115	2,250	2,300	(NA)
Net earnings in self-employment covered by OASDHI.	98	117	130	139	156	208	221	200	200	214
Percent of civilian payrolls covered by—										
Retirement programs [2]	96.0	96.5	96.0	96.0	95.9	95.9	96.4	96.0	96.5	(NA)
Unemployment insurance [3]	97.1	97.0	97.0	97.0	93.1	92.3	92.3	92.7	92.7	93.2
Workers' compensation programs [4] . .	84.6	84.5	83.9	84.3	84.0	84.0	83.9	83.9	83.6	(NA)

NA Not available. [1] Data from U.S. Bureau of Economic Analysis. Earnings include self-employed; wages and salaries represent civilian and military pay in cash and in kind. [2] Adjusted for duplication in coverage by both OASDHI and State and local government retirement systems; beginning 1984 adjusted for duplication in coverage by both OASDHI and Federal civil service retirement. [3] Taxable plus estimated nontaxable wages and salaries. [4] Excludes railroad employees.

Source: U.S. Social Security Administration, *Annual Statistical Supplement to the Social Security Bulletin*; and unpublished data.

No. 589. Cash and Noncash Benefits for Persons With Limited Income: 1990 and 1992

[For years ending September 30, except as noted. Programs covered provide cash, goods, or services to persons who make no payment and render no service in return. In case of job and training programs and some educational benefits, recipients must work or study for wages, training allowances, stipends, grants, or loans. Most of the programs base eligibility on individual, household, or family income, but some use group or area income tests; and a few offer help on the basis of presumed need]

PROGRAM	AVERAGE MONTHLY RECIPIENTS (1,000)		EXPENDITURES (mil. dol.)					
			Total		Federal		State and local	
	1990	1992	1990	1992	1990	1992	1990	1992
Total [1]	(X)	(X)	210,176	289,880	151,478	207,566	58,698	82,314
Medical care [2]	(X)	(X)	86,144	134,032	50,190	78,529	35,954	55,503
Medicaid [3] [4]	25,253	30,776	72,492	118,067	41,103	67,827	31,389	50,240
Veterans [5] [6] [7]	585	580	6,624	7,838	6,624	7,838	-	-
General assistance [7]	(NA)	(NA)	4,212	4,850	-	-	4,212	4,850
Indian Health Services [8]	1,100	1,160	1,176	1,431	1,176	1,431	-	-
Maternal and child health services	(NA)	(NA)	907	1,059	554	646	353	413
Cash aid [2]	(X)	(X)	54,255	69,350	36,445	48,374	17,810	20,976
A.F.D.C. [4] [9]	11,465	13,754	21,200	24,923	11,507	13,569	9,693	11,354
Supplemental Security Income [4] ...	4,938	5,559	17,233	22,774	[10]13,607	[10]18,744	3,626	4,030
Earned income tax credit (refunded portion) [11]	37,836	39,909	5,303	9,553	5,303	9,553	-	-
Foster care	168	222	2,741	4,170	1,473	2,233	1,268	1,937
Pensions for needy veterans [12] [13] ...	1,106	969	3,954	3,667	3,954	3,667	-	-
General assistance [11]	1,205	1,205	2,924	3,340	-	-	2,924	3,340
Food benefits [2]	(X)	(X)	25,106	34,107	23,871	32,661	1,235	1,446
Food stamps [4] [14]	21,500	26,900	17,686	24,918	16,512	23,540	1,174	1,378
School lunch program [15] [16]	11,600	13,000	3,154	3,895	3,154	3,895	(NA)	(NA)
Women, infants and children [17] ...	4,500	5,400	2,126	2,600	2,126	2,600	-	-
School breakfast [15]	3,600	4,500	548	782	548	782	-	-
Nutrition program for elderly [8] [18] ..	3,540	3,349	575	659	514	591	61	68
Child and adult care food program [19]	842	1,019	447	624	447	624	-	-
Housing benefits [2]	(X)	(X)	17,548	20,535	17,548	20,535	-	-
Low-income housing asst. (Sec. 8) [20]	2,500	2,797	10,577	12,307	10,577	12,307	-	-
Low-rent public housing [20]	1,405	1,409	3,918	5,008	3,918	5,008	(NA)	(NA)
Rural housing loans [21] [22]	26	26	1,311	1,468	1,311	1,468	-	-
Interest reduction payments [21]	531	510	630	652	630	652	-	-
Education aid [2]	(X)	(X)	14,390	16,037	13,761	15,423	629	614
Stafford loans [23]	4,496	5,135	5,648	5,683	5,648	5,683	-	-
Pell grants [23] [24]	3,214	4,259	4,484	5,374	4,484	5,374	-	-
Head Start	541	621	1,940	2,753	1,552	2,202	388	551
Services [2]	(X)	(X)	6,460	8,551	3,781	5,346	2,679	3,205
Social services (Title 20) [25]	(NA)	(NA)	5,346	5,419	2,762	2,800	2,584	2,619
Child care and development block grant [26]	(X)	570	(X)	825	(X)	825	(X)	-
Child care for AFDC recipients and ex-recipients [26]	(NA)	265	211	755	116	438	95	317
"At risk" child care (to avert AFDC eligibility) ..	(X)	(NA)	(X)	604	(X)	335	(X)	269
Jobs and training [2]	(X)	(X)	4,242	5,500	3,975	5,024	267	476
Training for disadvantaged adults and youth [27] [28] [29]	630	602	1,745	1,774	1,745	1,774	-	-
Summer youth employment program [28] [29] [30]	585	783	709	1,183	709	1,183	-	-
JOBS and WIN (for AFDC recipients) [31]	444	510	452	1,010	265	623	187	387
Job Corps [28] [29]	61	65	803	955	803	955	-	-
Energy assistance [2]	(X)	(X)	1,728	1,768	1,604	1,674	124	94
Low-income energy assistance [4] [32] [33]	5,800	6,200	1,567	1,594	1,443	1,500	124	94

- Represents zero. NA Not available. X Not applicable. [1] Includes State Legalization Impact Assistance Grants to offset State and local costs of welfare, health care, and education provided to legalized aliens. [2] Includes other programs not shown separately. [3] Recipient data represent unduplicated annual number. [4] Expenditures include administrative expenses. [5] Medical care for veterans with a nonservice-connected disability. [6] Recipients are estimated number of inpatients. [7] Estimated expenditures. [8] Recipients data represent annual numbers. [9] Aid to Families with Dependent Children program. Excludes data for foster care program and child support operations (cost and collections). [10] Excludes Federal sums spent for SSI (State supplements) to Indochinese refugees. [11] Estimated recipients. [12] Estimated recipients as of September. [13] Includes dependents and survivors. [14] Includes Puerto Rico's nutritional assistance program. [15] Free and reduced-price segments. [16] Includes estimate of commodity assistance. [17] Special supplemental food program for women, infants and children. [18] No income test required but preference given to those with greatest need. [19] Recipient data are numbers of children receiving free or reduced price meals and snacks in child care centers and estimates of children in family day care homes with incomes below 185 percent of poverty. Adult participants and funding are not included. [20] Recipient data represent units eligible for payment at end of year. [21] Recipient data represent total families or dwelling units during year. [22] Expenditure data represent amount of loans obligated. [23] Recipient data are total numbers for the school year ending in year shown. [24] Expenditure data are appropriations available for school year ending the fiscal year named. [25] Non-Federal expenditure data are rough estimates. [26] Recipient data are estimated number of children served. [27] Recipient data are average monthly enrollment for program year. [28] Programs represent specific titles under the Job Training and Partnership Act (JTPA). [29] Federal funds are appropriations. [30] Total participants (June-August). [31] Job opportunities and basic skills training program (JOBS) and work incentive (WIN) program. [32] Households served during the year with heating and winter crisis aid. [33] Federal funds include amounts transferred to other programs serving the needy. State spending includes funds received as "oil overcharge" settlements.

Source: Library of Congress, Congressional Research Service, "Cash and Noncash Benefits for Persons With Limited Income: Eligibility Rules, Recipient and Expenditure Data, FY 1990-92," Report 93-832 EPW, and earlier reports.

No. 590. Households Receiving Means-Tested Noncash Benefits: 1980 to 1993

[**In thousands, except percent**. Households as of **March** of following year. Covers civilian noninstitutional population, including persons in the Armed Forces living off post or with their families on post. A means-tested benefit program requires that the household's income and/or assets fall below specified guidelines in order to qualify for benefits. The means-tested noncash benefits covered are food stamps, free or reduced-price school lunches, public or subsidized housing, and Medicaid. There are general trends toward underestimation of noncash beneficiaries. Households are classified according to poverty status of family or nonfamily householder; for explanation of poverty level, see text, section 14. Data for 1980-90 based on 1980 census population controls; beginning 1992, based on 1990 census population controls. Based on Current Population Survey; see text, section 1, and Appendix III]

TYPE OF BENEFIT RECEIVED	1980	1985	1990	1992	1993			
					Total	Below poverty level		Above poverty level
						Number	Percent distribution	
Total households	82,368	88,458	94,312	96,426	97,107	13,777	100	83,330
Receiving at least one noncash benefit . .	14,266	14,466	16,098	18,639	19,937	8,817	64	11,120
Not receiving cash public assistance . .	7,860	7,860	8,819	10,431	11,573	3,824	28	7,749
Receiving cash public assistance [1] . . .	6,407	6,607	7,279	8,208	8,365	4,993	36	3,372
Total households receiving—								
Food stamps.	6,769	6,779	7,163	8,669	9,167	4,827	35	4,340
School lunch.	5,532	5,752	6,252	7,264	8,109	3,929	29	4,180
Public housing.	2,777	3,799	4,339	4,550	5,183	2,909	21	2,274
Medicaid	8,287	8,178	10,321	12,476	13,134	6,746	49	6,388

[1] Households receiving money from Aid to Families with Dependent Children program, Supplemental Security Income program or other public assistance programs.

Source: U.S. Bureau of the Census, *Current Population Reports*, P60-155, and earlier reports; and unpublished data.

No. 591. Persons Participating in Selected Means-Tested Government Assistance Programs, by Selected Characteristics: 1987 to 1991

[**Average monthly participation**. Covers noninstitutionalized population. Persons are considered participants in Aid to Families with Dependent Children (AFDC), General Assistance, and the Food Stamp Program if they are the primary recipient or if they are covered under another persons's allotment. Persons receiving Supplemental Security Income (SSI) payments are considered to be participants in an assistance program as are persons covered by Medicaid or living in public or subsidized rental housing. Based on the Survey of Income and Program Participation; for details on sample survey, see source]

YEAR AND SELECTED CHARACTERISTIC	NUMBER OF PARTICIPANTS (1,000)					PERCENT OF POPULATION PARTICIPATING				
	Major means-tested assistance programs [1]	AFDC or General Assistance	Food stamps	Medi-caid	Housing assistance	Major means-tested assistance programs [1]	AFDC or General Assistance	Food stamps	Medi-caid	Housing assistance
1987	27,412	10,385	17,365	17,474	9,222	11.4	4.3	7.2	7.3	3.8
1990	28,461	10,573	17,136	19,110	10,694	11.5	4.3	6.9	7.7	4.3
1991, total	**30,859**	**11,556**	**18,870**	**21,379**	**10,951**	**12.4**	**4.6**	**7.6**	**8.6**	**4.4**
Under 18 years old.	13,639	7,020	9,686	10,461	4,488	20.8	10.7	14.7	15.9	6.8
18 to 64 years old	13,702	4,451	8,089	8,698	4,937	8.9	2.9	5.3	5.7	3.2
65 years old and over . . .	3,517	85	1,095	2,220	1,526	11.7	0.3	3.6	7.4	5.1
White.	19,104	5,950	10,902	12,930	6,145	9.1	2.8	5.2	6.1	2.9
Black	10,302	4,836	7,029	7,282	4,332	33.4	15.7	22.8	23.6	14.1
Hispanic origin [2].	5,740	2,166	3,672	3,966	1,995	26.3	9.9	16.9	18.2	9.2
Poverty status: [3] Below the poverty level	18,463	9,239	14,550	13,971	6,526	54.5	27.3	43.0	41.3	19.3
At or above the poverty level	12,396	2,316	4,320	7,408	4,425	5.7	1.1	2.0	3.4	2.0
Family status: In married-couple families	11,493	2,750	6,380	6,975	2,972	6.7	1.6	3.7	4.1	1.7
With related children under 18 years old.	9,497	2,667	5,683	5,658	2,465	8.9	2.5	5.3	5.3	2.3
In families with female householder, no spouse present	13,846	8,216	10,324	11,049	5,476	39.1	23.2	29.2	31.2	15.5
With related children under 18 years old.	12,700	8,127	9,923	10,262	5,120	47.7	30.5	37.3	38.5	19.2
Unrelated individuals . .	4,538	258	1,626	2,612	2,243	12.6	0.6	4.5	7.2	6.2

[1] Covers AFDC, General Assistance, SSI, food stamps, Medicaid, and housing assistance. [2] Persons of Hispanic origin may be of any race. [3] For explanation of poverty level, see text, section 14.

Source: U.S. Bureau of the Census, *Current Population Reports*, P70-41.

No. 592. Social Security—Covered Employment, Earnings, and Contribution Rates: 1970 to 1993

[Includes Puerto Rico, Virgin Islands, American Samoa, and Guam. Represents all reported employment. Data are estimated. OASDHI=Old-age, survivors, disability, and health insurance; SMI=Supplementary medical insurance. See also *Historical Statistics, Colonial Times to 1970*, series H 172-185]

ITEM	Unit	1970	1980	1985	1987	1988	1989	1990	1991	1992	1993
Workers with insured status [1]	Million	105.7	137.4	148.7	152.7	155.4	158.2	161.2	163.6	165.8	167.9
Male	Million	61.9	75.4	79.7	81.5	82.6	83.7	85.1	86.1	87.2	88.1
Female	Million	43.8	62.0	69.0	71.2	72.8	74.5	76.1	77.5	78.6	79.9
Under 25 years old	Million	17.7	25.5	22.3	21.3	21.3	21.3	21.3	21.2	20.7	20.5
25 to 34 years old	Million	22.3	34.9	39.9	40.6	41.0	41.4	41.5	41.5	41.2	40.8
35 to 44 years old	Million	19.0	22.4	28.5	31.2	32.3	33.5	34.9	36.2	37.3	38.1
45 to 54 years old	Million	19.0	18.6	19.0	19.8	20.5	21.4	22.1	22.8	24.1	25.5
55 to 59 years old	Million	7.8	9.2	9.1	8.9	8.8	8.7	8.7	8.7	8.8	9.0
60 to 64 years old	Million	6.3	7.9	8.7	8.7	8.7	8.6	8.7	8.7	8.7	8.5
65 to 69 years old	Million	5.1	6.7	7.3	7.6	7.7	7.8	8.1	8.2	8.2	8.2
70 years old and over	Million	8.5	12.1	13.9	14.7	15.0	15.5	15.8	16.3	16.8	17.3
Workers reported with—											
Taxable earnings [2]	Million	93	113	120	126	130	132	133	132	133	135
Maximum earnings [2]	Million	24	10	8	8	8	8	8	8	8	8
Earnings in covered employment [2]	Bil. dol	532	1,329	1,937	2,237	2,433	2,583	2,703	2,780	2,929	3,021
Reported taxable [2]	Bil. dol	416	1,181	1,723	1,960	2,089	2,239	2,363	2,423	2,534	2,637
Percent of total	Percent	78.2	88.9	88.9	87.6	85.9	86.7	87.4	87.2	86.5	87.2
Annual maximum taxable earnings [3]	Dollars	7,800	25,900	39,600	43,800	45,000	48,000	51,300	53,400	55,500	57,600
Maximum tax	Dollars	374	1,588	2,792	3,132	3,380	3,605	3,924	5,123	5,329	5,529
Contribution rates for OASDHI: [4]											
Each employer and employee	Percent	4.80	6.13	7.05	7.15	7.51	7.51	7.65	7.65	7.65	7.65
Self-employed [5]	Percent	6.90	8.10	14.10	14.30	15.02	15.02	15.30	15.30	15.30	15.30
SMI, monthly premium [6]	Dollars	5.30	9.60	15.50	17.90	24.80	31.90	28.60	29.90	31.80	36.60

[1] Fully insured for retirement and/or survivor benefits as of beginning of year. [2] Includes self-employment. [3] The maximum taxable earnings for HI was $125,000 in 1991; $130,200 in 1992, and $135,000 in 1993. [4] As of January 1, 1994 and 1995, each employee and employer pays 7.65 percent and the self-employed pay 15.3 percent. [5] Self-employed pays 11.8 percent in 1985, 12.3 percent in 1987, and 13.02 percent in 1988 and 1989. The additional amount is supplied from general revenues. Beginning 1990, self-employed pays 15.3 percent, and half of the tax is deductible for income tax purposes and for computing self-employment income subject to social security tax. [6] 1970 and 1980, as of July 1; beginning 1985, as of January 1. As of January 1, 1994, the monthly premium is $41.10 and as of January 1, 1995, the monthly premium is $46.10.

Source: U.S. Social Security Administration, *Annual Statistical Supplement* to the *Social Security Bulletin;* and unpublished data.

No. 593. Social Security Trust Funds: 1980 to 1993

[**In billions of dollars.** See also *Historical Statistics, Colonial Times to 1970*, series H 238-242]

TYPE OF TRUST FUND	1980	1985	1987	1988	1989	1990	1991	1992	1993
Old-age and survivors insurance (OASI):									
Net contribution income [1]	103.5	180.2	206.0	233.2	252.6	272.4	278.4	286.8	296.2
Interest received [2]	1.8	1.9	4.7	7.6	12.0	16.4	20.8	24.3	27.0
Benefit payments [3]	105.1	167.2	[4]183.6	[4]195.5	208.0	223.0	240.5	[4]254.9	[4]267.8
Assets, end of year	22.8	[5]35.8	62.1	102.9	155.1	214.2	267.8	319.2	369.3
Disability insurance (DI):									
Net contribution income [1]	13.3	17.4	19.7	22.1	24.1	28.7	29.3	30.4	31.5
Interest received [2]	0.5	0.9	0.6	0.6	0.7	0.9	1.1	1.1	0.8
Benefit payments [3]	15.5	18.8	[4]20.5	[4]21.7	22.9	24.8	27.7	[4]31.1	[4]34.6
Assets, end of year	3.6	[6]6.3	6.7	6.9	7.9	11.1	12.9	12.3	9.0
Hospital insurance (HI):									
Net contribution income [1][7]	23.9	47.7	58.8	62.6	68.5	71.1	78.4	82.4	84.9
Interest received [2]	1.1	3.4	4.5	5.8	7.3	8.5	9.5	10.5	12.5
Benefit payments	25.1	47.5	49.5	52.5	60.0	66.2	71.5	83.9	93.5
Assets, end of year	13.7	[8]20.5	53.7	69.6	85.6	98.9	115.2	124.0	127.8
Supplementary medical insurance (SMI):									
Net premium income	3.0	5.6	7.4	8.8	10.8	11.3	11.9	14.1	14.2
Transfers from general revenue	7.5	18.3	23.6	26.2	30.9	33.0	37.6	41.4	41.5
Interest received	0.4	1.2	0.9	0.9	1.1	1.6	1.7	1.8	2.6
Benefit payments	10.6	22.9	30.8	34.0	38.4	42.5	47.3	49.3	55.8
Assets, end of year	4.5	10.9	8.4	9.0	12.2	15.5	17.8	24.2	24.1

[1] Includes deposits by States and deductions for refund of estimated employee-tax overpayment. Beginning in 1985, includes government contributions on deemed wage credits for military service in 1957 and later. Beginning 1985, includes tax credits on net earnings from self-employment in 1985-89; and taxation of benefits (OASI and DI, only). [2] Beginning in 1985, includes interest on advance tax transfers and interest on reimbursement for unnegotiated checks. Data for 1985 reflect interest on interfund borrowing. [3] Includes payments for vocational rehabilitation services furnished to disabled persons receiving benefits because of their disabilities. Beginning in 1985, amounts reflect deductions for unnegotiated benefit checks. [4] Data adjusted to reflect 12 months of benefit payments. [5] Includes $13.2 billion borrowed from the DI and HI Trust Funds. [6] Excludes $2.5 billion lent to the OASI Trust Fund. [7] Includes premiums from aged ineligibles enrolled in HI. [8] Excludes $10.6 billion lent to the OASI Trust Fund.

Source: U.S. Social Security Administration, *Annual Report of Board of Trustees, OASI, DI, HI, and SMI Trust Funds*. Also published in *Social Security Bulletin,* quarterly.

No. 594. Social Security (OASDI)—Benefits, by Type of Beneficiary: 1970 to 1993

[A person eligible to receive more than one type of benefit is generally classified or counted only once as a retired-worker beneficiary. OASDI=Old-age, survivors, and disability insurance. See also headnote, table 592; Appendix III; and *Historical Statistics, Colonial Times to 1970*, series H 197-229]

TYPE OF BENEFICIARY	1970	1980	1985	1987	1988	1989	1990	1991	1992	1993
	BENEFITS IN CURRENT-PAYMENT STATUS[1] (end of year)									
Number of benefits (1,000) ...	**26,229**	**35,585**	**37,058**	**38,190**	**38,627**	**39,151**	**39,832**	**40,592**	**41,507**	**42,246**
Retired workers [2] (1,000)	13,349	19,562	22,432	23,440	23,858	24,327	24,838	25,289	25,758	26,104
Disabled workers [3] (1,000)	1,493	2,859	2,657	2,786	2,830	2,895	3,011	3,195	3,468	3,726
Wives and husbands [2][4] (1,000)	2,952	3,477	3,375	3,381	3,367	3,365	3,367	3,370	3,382	3,367
Children (1,000)	4,122	4,607	3,319	3,244	3,204	3,165	3,187	3,268	3,391	3,527
Under age 18	3,315	3,423	2,699	2,604	2,534	2,488	2,497	2,558	2,664	2,777
Disabled children [5]	271	450	526	561	574	586	600	616	637	656
Students [6]	537	733	94	79	96	91	89	95	90	94
Of retired workers	546	639	457	439	432	423	422	426	432	436
Of deceased workers	2,688	2,610	1,917	1,837	1,809	1,780	1,776	1,791	1,808	1,836
Of disabled workers	889	1,358	945	968	963	962	989	1,052	1,151	1,255
Widowed mothers [7] (1,000)	523	562	372	329	318	312	304	301	294	289
Widows and widowers [2][8] (1,000)	3,227	4,411	4,863	4,984	5,029	5,071	5,111	5,158	5,205	5,224
Parents [2] (1,000)	29	15	10	8	7	6	6	5	5	5
Special benefits [9] (1,000)	534	93	32	19	14	10	7	5	4	2
Average monthly benefit, current dollars										
Retired workers [2]	118	341	479	513	537	567	603	629	653	674
Retired worker and wife [2]	199	567	814	873	914	966	1,027	1,072	1,111	1,145
Disabled workers [3]	131	371	484	508	530	556	587	609	626	642
Wives and husbands [2][4]	59	164	236	253	265	281	298	311	322	332
Children of retired workers	45	140	198	216	228	242	259	273	285	297
Children of deceased workers	82	240	330	352	368	385	406	420	432	443
Children of disabled workers	39	110	142	146	151	157	164	168	170	173
Widowed mothers [7]	87	246	332	353	368	388	409	424	438	448
Widows and widowers, nondisabled [2]	102	311	433	468	493	522	557	584	608	630
Parents [2]	103	276	378	407	428	454	482	506	526	547
Special benefits [9]	45	105	138	145	151	158	167	173	178	183
Average monthly benefit, constant (1993) dollars [10]										
Retired workers [2]	432	576	639	648	650	656	657	665	671	674
Retired worker and wife [2]	729	958	1,086	1,103	1,106	1,117	1,119	1,133	1,142	1,145
Disabled workers [3]	480	627	646	642	641	643	640	644	643	642
Wives and husbands [2][4]	216	277	315	320	321	325	325	329	331	332
Children of deceased workers	300	405	442	445	445	445	442	444	444	443
Widowed mothers [7]	319	416	443	446	445	449	446	448	450	448
Widows and widowers, nondisabled [2]	374	525	578	591	597	604	606	616	625	630
	BENEFITS AWARDED DURING YEAR (1,000)									
Number of benefits	**3,722**	**4,215**	**3,796**	**3,734**	**3,681**	**3,646**	**3,717**	**3,865**	**4,051**	**4,001**
Retired workers [2]	1,338	1,620	1,690	1,682	1,654	1,657	1,665	1,695	1,708	1,661
Disabled workers [3]	350	389	377	416	409	426	468	536	637	635
Wives and husbands [2][4]	436	469	440	411	391	380	379	380	383	365
Children	1,091	1,174	714	685	706	675	695	727	795	816
Widowed mothers [7]	112	108	72	65	63	60	58	58	56	56
Widows and widowers [2][8]	363	452	502	475	458	449	452	469	472	466
Parents [2]	2	1	(Z)	(Z)	(Z)	(Z)	(Z)	(Z)	(Z)	(Z)
Special benefits [9]	30	1	1	(Z)	(Z)	(Z)	(Z)	(Z)	(Z)	(Z)
	BENEFIT PAYMENTS DURING YEAR (bil. dol.)									
Total amount [11]	**31.9**	**120.5**	**186.2**	**204.2**	**217.2**	**230.9**	**247.8**	**268.1**	**286.0**	**302.4**
Monthly benefits [12]	31.6	120.1	186.0	204.0	217.0	230.6	247.6	267.9	285.8	302.2
Retired workers [2]	18.4	70.4	116.8	128.5	137.0	146.0	156.8	169.1	179.4	188.4
Disabled workers [3]	2.4	12.8	16.5	18.1	19.2	20.3	22.1	24.7	27.9	30.9
Wives and husbands [2][4]	2.2	7.0	11.1	12.1	12.8	13.6	14.5	15.5	16.4	16.9
Children	3.5	10.5	10.7	11.0	11.3	11.5	12.0	12.8	13.6	14.6
Under age 18	2.7	7.4	8.5	8.5	8.7	8.7	9.0	9.5	10.1	10.8
Disabled children [5]	0.3	1.0	1.8	2.0	2.2	2.3	2.5	2.8	3.0	3.3
Students [6]	0.6	2.1	0.4	0.4	0.5	0.5	0.5	0.5	0.5	0.5
Of retired workers	0.3	1.1	1.1	1.2	1.2	1.2	1.3	1.4	1.5	1.6
Of deceased workers	2.8	7.4	7.8	7.8	8.1	8.3	8.6	9.0	9.4	9.9
Of disabled workers	0.5	2.0	1.8	1.9	2.0	2.0	2.2	2.4	2.7	3.1
Widowed mothers [7]	0.6	1.6	1.5	1.4	1.4	1.4	1.4	1.5	1.5	1.5
Widows and widowers [2][8]	4.1	17.6	29.3	32.8	35.2	37.7	40.7	44.1	47.1	49.7
Parents [2]	(Z)	0.1	0.1	(Z)	(Z)	(Z)	(Z)	(Z)	(Z)	(Z)
Special benefits [9]	0.3	0.1	0.1	(Z)	(Z)	(Z)	(Z)	(Z)	(Z)	(Z)
Lump sum	0.3	0.4	0.2	0.2	0.2	0.2	0.2	0.2	0.2	0.2

Z Fewer than 500 or less than $50 million.   [1] Benefit payment actually being made at a specified time with no deductions or with deductions amounting to less than a month's benefits; i.e., the benefits actually being received.   [2] 62 years and over.   [3] Disabled workers under age 65.   [4] Includes wife beneficiaries with entitled children in their care and entitled divorced wives.   [5] 18 years old and over. Disability began before age 18 and, beginning 1973, before age 22.   [6] Full-time students aged 18-21 through 1984 and aged 18 and 19 beginning 1985.   [7] Includes surviving divorced mothers with entitled children in their care and, beginning 1980, widowed fathers with entitled children in their care.   [8] Includes widows aged 60-61, surviving divorced wives aged 60 and over, disabled widows and widowers aged 50 and over; and beginning 1980, widowers aged 60-61.   [9] Benefits for persons aged 72 and over not insured under regular or transitional provisions of Social Security Act.   [10] Constant dollar figures are based on the consumer price index for December as published by the U.S. Bureau of Labor Statistics.   [11] Represents total disbursements of benefit checks by the U.S. Dept. of the Treasury during the years specified.   [12] Distribution by type estimated.

Source: U.S. Social Security Administration, *Annual Statistical Supplement* to the *Social Security Bulletin;* and unpublished data.

No. 595. Social Security—Beneficiaries, Annual Payments, and Average Monthly Benefit, 1980 to 1993, and by State and Other Areas, 1993

[Number of beneficiaries in current-payment status and average monthly benefit as of **December**. Data for number of beneficiaries based on 10-percent sample of administrative records. See also headnote, table 594, and Appendix III]

YEAR, DIVISION, STATE, AND OTHER AREA	NUMBER OF BENEFICIARIES (1,000)				ANNUAL PAYMENTS (mil. dol.)				AVERAGE MONTHLY BENEFIT (dol.)		
	Total	Retired workers and dependents [1]	Survivors	Disabled workers and dependents	Total	Retired workers and dependents [1]	Survivors [2]	Disabled workers and dependents	Retired workers [3]	Disabled workers	Widows and widowers [4]
1980	35,585	23,309	7,598	4,678	120,472	78,025	27,010	15,437	341	371	311
1990	39,832	28,369	7,197	4,266	247,796	172,042	50,951	24,803	603	587	557
1991	40,592	28,824	7,255	4,513	268,098	185,545	54,891	27,662	629	609	584
1992	41,497	29,296	7,297	4,903	285,980	196,688	58,203	31,089	653	626	608
1993, total [5]	42,238	29,633	7,341	5,264	302,402	206,365	61,440	34,598	674	642	630
United States	41,230	29,033	7,117	5,085	297,824	203,837	60,225	33,763	(NA)	(NA)	(NA)
New England	2,266	1,665	336	263	16,770	12,045	2,990	1,735	(NA)	(NA)	(NA)
Maine	228	161	36	31	1,521	1,040	295	185	621	581	598
New Hampshire	176	131	25	20	1,291	934	226	131	676	647	659
Vermont	95	66	15	14	664	454	126	84	663	618	629
Massachusetts	1,027	744	155	127	7,528	5,307	1,380	841	677	630	661
Rhode Island	187	139	27	21	1,370	1,002	230	137	672	611	656
Connecticut	553	424	78	51	4,396	3,308	733	355	739	648	702
Middle Atlantic	6,537	4,758	1,086	694	50,329	35,600	9,784	4,944	(NA)	(NA)	(NA)
New York	2,937	2,113	474	351	22,670	15,962	4,202	2,506	720	674	676
New Jersey	1,286	955	202	129	10,239	7,439	1,866	934	739	672	695
Pennsylvania	2,314	1,690	410	214	17,420	12,199	3,716	1,504	693	664	664
East North Central	7,087	4,985	1,260	841	53,612	36,427	11,357	5,827	(NA)	(NA)	(NA)
Ohio	1,882	1,300	357	225	13,951	9,213	3,191	1,546	690	667	660
Indiana	951	667	165	120	7,161	4,877	1,476	808	702	657	669
Illinois	1,815	1,298	318	200	13,940	9,668	2,879	1,393	713	667	680
Michigan	1,569	1,086	281	201	12,096	8,106	2,557	1,434	720	698	678
Wisconsin	870	634	139	96	6,464	4,563	1,254	646	691	648	664
West North Central	3,137	2,264	541	336	22,342	15,536	4,629	2,177	(NA)	(NA)	(NA)
Minnesota	698	514	117	67	4,956	3,502	1,010	443	659	621	632
Iowa	535	393	91	52	3,871	2,727	805	339	674	629	644
Missouri	952	664	165	124	6,739	4,549	1,382	808	660	631	623
North Dakota	114	82	22	11	769	523	181	66	634	605	599
South Dakota	134	95	25	14	883	605	194	84	624	583	593
Nebraska	278	204	48	27	1,982	1,396	416	170	664	616	647
Kansas	426	312	73	42	3,142	2,234	641	267	693	614	658
South Atlantic	7,723	5,427	1,307	989	53,987	36,939	10,532	6,517	(NA)	(NA)	(NA)
Delaware	115	85	18	13	864	616	160	88	702	666	667
Maryland	653	469	119	65	4,775	3,301	1,016	458	674	663	642
District of Columbia	79	55	15	9	495	333	105	57	573	573	523
Virginia	901	618	163	121	6,192	4,105	1,302	786	642	629	587
West Virginia	380	231	82	66	2,669	1,551	678	440	666	687	601
North Carolina	1,174	791	204	180	7,909	5,237	1,530	1,142	635	607	558
South Carolina	591	387	107	97	3,949	2,552	775	623	633	621	550
Georgia	964	613	186	165	6,449	4,021	1,391	1,037	632	619	566
Florida	2,866	2,178	413	274	20,685	15,223	3,575	1,886	672	653	651
East South Central	2,808	1,748	564	498	18,347	11,129	4,207	3,012	(NA)	(NA)	(NA)
Kentucky	687	415	140	133	4,509	2,622	1,068	820	623	642	564
Tennessee	891	575	169	147	5,957	3,752	1,301	904	633	607	572
Alabama	752	472	157	124	4,949	3,020	1,175	755	625	614	557
Mississippi	478	286	98	94	2,932	1,735	663	533	590	591	512
West South Central	4,117	2,716	838	563	27,789	17,731	6,597	3,461	(NA)	(NA)	(NA)
Arkansas	489	315	90	84	3,153	1,973	668	513	611	611	544
Louisiana	689	408	160	121	4,500	2,564	1,215	720	627	646	576
Oklahoma	562	389	104	69	3,849	2,571	844	434	643	626	603
Texas	2,377	1,604	484	289	16,287	10,623	3,870	1,794	654	631	611
Mountain	2,175	1,549	344	282	15,293	10,577	2,870	1,846	(NA)	(NA)	(NA)
Montana	148	103	25	21	1,028	688	204	136	653	651	632
Idaho	170	123	27	20	1,183	828	230	125	654	648	640
Wyoming	68	49	11	8	485	338	95	53	674	636	645
Colorado	469	326	77	66	3,279	2,191	652	436	655	639	635
New Mexico	244	162	45	36	1,579	1,029	338	211	632	623	593
Arizona	658	481	97	80	4,755	3,377	823	555	682	669	656
Utah	213	153	34	26	1,495	1,056	285	154	679	628	661
Nevada	205	152	28	25	1,489	1,070	243	176	680	670	658
Pacific	5,380	3,921	841	619	39,356	27,851	7,259	4,246	(NA)	(NA)	(NA)
Washington	762	562	115	85	5,696	4,068	1,032	595	700	653	672
Oregon	530	395	79	56	3,878	2,804	695	379	684	645	664
California	3,891	2,814	618	460	28,405	19,953	5,302	3,151	688	645	658
Alaska	39	25	8	6	271	174	59	38	673	649	597
Hawaii	158	125	21	12	1,106	852	171	83	664	640	608
Puerto Rico	593	327	118	149	2,678	1,355	599	724	433	534	390
Guam	6	4	2	1	28	15	10	3	482	553	447
American Samoa	5	2	2	1	17	6	7	4	390	504	370
Virgin Islands	11	7	2	2	64	40	15	9	569	612	501
Abroad	357	250	90	16	1,791	1,112	584	95	458	558	469

NA Not available. [1] Includes special benefits; see footnote 9, table 594. [2] Includes lump-sum payments to survivors of deceased workers. [3] Excludes persons with special benefits. [4] Nondisabled only. [5] Number of beneficiaries includes those with State or area unknown.

Source: U.S. Social Security Administration, *Social Security Bulletin*, quarterly.

No. 596. Public Employee Retirement Systems—Participants and Finances: 1980 to 1992

[For fiscal year of retirement system, except data for the Thrift Savings Plan are for calendar year]

RETIREMENT PLAN	Unit	1980	1985	1986	1987	1988	1989	1990	1991	1992
TOTAL PARTICIPANTS [1]										
Federal retirement systems:										
Defined benefit:										
Civil Service Retirement System	1,000	4,629	4,919	4,970	4,295	4,261	4,332	4,167	4,086	4,014
Federal Employees Retirement System [2]	1,000	(X)	(X)	(X)	800	924	1,068	1,180	1,325	1,367
Military Service Retirement System [3]	1,000	3,380	3,672	3,725	3,765	3,762	3,790	3,763	3,732	3,579
Thrift Savings Plan [4]	1,000	(X)	(X)	(X)	1,022	1,317	1,446	1,625	1,700	1,900
State and local retirement systems [5][6]	1,000	(NA)	15,234	15,426	15,093	15,777	16,684	16,858	17,502	(NA)
ACTIVE PARTICIPANTS										
Federal retirement systems:										
Defined benefit:										
Civil Service Retirement System	1,000	2,700	2,800	2,800	2,080	2,011	1,918	1,826	1,726	1,654
Federal Employees Retirement System [2]	1,000	(X)	(X)	(X)	800	919	1,052	1,136	1,260	1,276
Military Service Retirement System [3]	1,000	2,050	2,192	2,219	2,229	2,196	2,188	2,130	2,064	1,868
Thrift Savings Plan [4]	1,000	(X)	(X)	(X)	960	1,099	1,269	1,419	1,200	1,300
State and local retirement systems [5][6]	1,000	(NA)	10,364	10,529	10,744	10,732	11,357	11,345	11,696	(NA)
ASSETS										
Total	Bil. dol.	258	529	622	732	825	922	1,047	1,150	(NA)
Federal retirement systems	Bil. dol.	73	154	186	219	262	289	326	367	411
Defined benefit	Bil. dol.	73	154	186	218	260	284	318	355	394
Civil Service Retirement System	Bil. dol.	73	142	161	175	198	204	220	237	256
Federal Employees Retirement System [2]	Bil. dol.	(X)	(X)	(X)	4	8	12	18	24	32
Military Service Retirement System [3]	Bil. dol.	([7])	12	25	39	53	68	80	94	106
Thrift Savings Plan [4]	Bil. dol.	(X)	(X)	(X)	1	3	5	8	12	16
State and local retirement systems [5]	Bil. dol.	185	374	437	513	563	633	721	783	(NA)
CONTRIBUTIONS										
Total	Bil. dol.	43	90	95	97	100	104	108	115	(NA)
Federal retirement systems	Bil. dol.	19	54	56	56	58	60	61	65	68
Defined benefit	Bil. dol.	19	54	56	55	56	58	59	62	64
Civil Service Retirement System	Bil. dol.	19	27	28	24	25	26	28	29	30
Federal Employees Retirement System [2]	Bil. dol.	(X)	(X)	(X)	2	3	4	4	5	6
Military Service Retirement System [3]	Bil. dol.	([7])	27	28	29	29	28	27	28	28
Thrift Savings Plan [4]	Bil. dol.	(X)	(X)	(X)	1	2	2	2	3	4
State and local retirement systems [5]	Bil. dol.	24	37	39	42	43	44	46	49	(NA)
BENEFITS										
Total	Bil. dol.	39	62	67	71	77	83	89	96	(NA)
Federal retirement systems	Bil. dol.	27	40	42	44	47	50	53	57	58
Defined benefit	Bil. dol.	27	40	42	44	47	50	53	56	58
Civil Service Retirement System	Bil. dol.	15	23	25	26	28	30	31	33	33
Federal Employees Retirement System [2]	Bil. dol.	(X)	(X)	(X)	(Z)	(Z)	(Z)	(Z)	(Z)	(Z)
Military Service Retirement System [3]	Bil. dol.	12	17	18	18	19	20	22	23	25
Thrift Savings Plan [4]	Bil. dol.	(X)	(X)	(X)	(Z)	(Z)	(Z)	(Z)	(Z)	(Z)
State and local retirement systems [5]	Bil. dol.	12	22	24	27	30	33	36	39	(NA)

NA Not available.   X Not applicable.   Z Less than $500 million.   [1] Includes active, separated vested, retired employees, and survivors.   [2] The Federal Employees Retirement system was established June 6, 1986.   [3] Includes nondisability and disability retirees, surviving families, and all active personnel with the exception of active reserves.   [4] The Thrift Savings Plan (a defined contribution plan) was established April 1, 1987.   [5] Excludes state and local plans that are fully supported by employee contributions.   [6] Not adjusted for double counting of individuals participating in more than one plan.   [7] The Military Retirement System was unfunded until October 1, 1984.

Source: Employee Benefit Research Institute, Washington, DC, *EBRI Databook on Employee Benefits, Third Edition* (copyright).

No. 597. Federal Civil Service Retirement: 1980 to 1993

[As of **Sept. 30** or for **year ending Sept. 30**. Covers both Civil Service Retirement System and Federal Employees Retirement System. See also *Historical Statistics, Colonial Times to 1970*, series H 262-270]

ITEM	Unit	1980	1985	1987	1988	1989	1990	1991	1992	1993
Employees covered [1]	1,000	2,720	2,750	2,810	2,800	2,880	2,945	2,885	2,933	2,843
Annuitants, total	1,000	1,675	1,955	2,032	2,089	2,120	2,143	2,184	2,185	2,242
Age and service	1,000	905	1,122	1,186	1,237	1,267	1,288	1,325	1,322	1,378
Disability	1,000	343	332	318	311	305	297	289	282	274
Survivors	1,000	427	501	528	541	548	558	570	581	589
Receipts, total [2]	Mil. dol.	24,389	40,790	43,640	46,696	49,249	52,689	56,815	59,737	62,878
Employee contributions	Mil. dol.	3,686	4,679	4,641	4,544	4,491	4,501	4,563	4,713	4,703
Federal government contributions	Mil. dol.	15,562	22,301	23,144	24,258	25,367	27,368	29,509	30,785	32,668
Disbursements, total [3]	Mil. dol.	14,977	23,203	25,772	28,306	29,713	31,416	33,209	33,187	35,123
Age and service annuitants [4]	Mil. dol.	12,639	19,414	21,678	23,889	25,095	26,495	27,997	27,684	29,288
Survivors	Mil. dol.	1,912	3,158	3,485	3,749	4,033	4,366	4,716	5,093	5,377
Average monthly benefit:										
Age and service	Dollars	992	1,189	1,267	1,263	1,310	1,369	1,439	1,493	1,537
Disability	Dollars	723	881	893	930	966	1,008	1,059	1,094	1,120
Survivors	Dollars	392	528	552	583	616	653	698	731	760
Cash and security holdings	Bil. dol.	73.7	142.3	178.7	197.1	216.7	238.0	261.6	289.6	317.4

[1] Excludes employees in Leave Without Pay status.   [2] Includes interest on investments.   [3] Includes refunds, death claims, and administration.   [4] Includes disability annuitants.

Source: U.S. Office of Personnel Management, *Compensation Report*, annual.

No. 598. State and Local Government Retirement Systems—
Beneficiaries and Finances: 1980 to 1991

[In millions of dollars, except as indicated. For fiscal years closed during the 12 months ending June 30]

YEAR AND LEVEL OF GOVERNMENT	Number of benefi- ciaries (1,000)	RECEIPTS					BENEFITS AND WITHDRAWALS			Cash and security holdings
		Total	Em- ployee contri- butions	Government contributions		Earn- ings on invest- ments	Total	Ben- efits	With- drawals	
				State	Local					
1980: All systems	(NA)	37,313	6,466	7,581	9,951	13,315	14,008	12,207	1,801	185,226
State-administered . . .	(NA)	28,603	5,285	7,399	5,611	10,308	10,257	8,809	1,448	144,682
Locally administered . .	(NA)	8,710	1,180	181	4,340	3,008	3,752	3,399	353	40,544
1985: All systems	3,378	71,411	9,468	12,227	15,170	34,546	24,413	21,999	2,414	374,433
State-administered . . .	2,661	55,960	7,901	11,976	8,944	27,139	18,230	16,183	2,047	296,951
Locally administered . .	716	15,451	1,567	251	6,226	7,407	6,183	5,816	367	77,481
1990: All systems	4,026	111,339	13,853	13,994	18,583	64,907	38,396	35,966	2,430	703,772
State-administered . . .	3,232	89,162	11,648	13,964	11,538	52,012	29,603	27,562	2,041	565,641
Locally administered . .	794	22,177	2,205	32	7,045	12,895	8,793	8,404	389	138,131
1991: All systems	4,179	108,240	16,268	14,473	18,691	58,808	42,028	39,421	2,607	783,405
State-administered . . .	3,357	85,576	12,563	14,455	11,553	47,006	32,323	30,167	2,156	630,551
Locally administered . .	822	22,664	3,705	18	7,138	11,803	9,706	9,255	451	152,854

NA Not available.

Source: U.S. Bureau of the Census, *Finances of Employee-Retirement Systems of State and Local Governments*, series GF, No. 2, annual.

No. 599. Private Pension Plans—Summary, by Type of Plan: 1980 to 1991

["Pension plan" is defined by the Employee Retirement Income Security Act (ERISA) as "any plan, fund, or program which was heretofore or is hereafter established or maintained by an employer or an employee organization, or by both, to the extent that such plan (a) provides retirement income to employees, or (b) results in a deferral of income by employees for periods extending to the termination of covered employment or beyond, regardless of the method of calculating the contributions made to the plan, the method of calculating the benefits under the plan, or the method of distributing benefits from the plan." A defined benefit plan provides a definite benefit formula for calculating benefit amounts - such as a flat amount per year of service or a percentage of salary times years of service. A defined contribution plan is a pension plan in which the contributions are made to an individual account for each employee. The retirement benefit is dependent upon the account balance at retirement. The balance depends upon amounts contributed, investment experience, and, in the case of profit sharing plans, amounts which may be allocated to the account due to forfeitures by terminating employees. Employee Stock Ownership Plans (ESOP) (see table 866) and 401(k) plans (see table 601) are included among defined contribution plans. Data are based on Form 5500 series reports filed with the Internal Revenue Service]

ITEM	Unit	TOTAL				DEFINED CONTRIBUTION PLAN				DEFINED BENEFIT PLAN			
		1980	1985	1990	1991	1980	1985	1990	1991	1980	1985	1990	1991
Number of plans [1]	1,000 . .	488.9	632.1	712.3	699.3	340.8	462.0	599.2	597.5	148.1	170.2	113.1	101.8
Total participants [2][3] . .	Million . .	57.9	74.7	76.9	77.7	19.9	35.0	38.1	38.6	38.0	39.7	38.8	39.0
Active participants [2][4] . .	Million . .	49.0	62.3	61.8	61.5	18.9	33.2	35.5	35.8	30.1	29.0	26.3	25.7
Contributions [5]	Bil. dol. .	66.2	95.1	98.8	111.1	23.5	53.1	75.8	80.9	42.6	42.0	23.0	30.1
Benefits [6]	Bil. dol. .	35.3	101.9	129.4	135.6	13.1	47.4	63.0	64.0	22.1	54.5	66.4	71.5

[1] Excludes all plans covering only one participant.   [2] Includes double counting of workers in more than one plan.   [3] Total participants include active participants, vested separated workers, and retirees.   [4] Any workers currently in employment covered by a plan and who are earning or retaining credited service under a plan. Includes any nonvested former employees who have not yet incurred breaks in service.   [5] Includes both employer and employee contributions.   [6] Benefits paid directly from trust and premium payments made from plan to insurance carriers. Excludes benefits paid directly by insurance carriers.

Source: U.S. Dept. of Labor, Pension and Welfare Benefits Administration, *Private Pension Plan Bulletin*, summer 1993; and unpublished data.

No. 600. Pension Plan Coverage of Workers, by Selected Characteristics: 1993

[Covers workers as of **March 1994** who had earnings in year 1993. Based on Current Population Survey; see text, section 1, and Appendix III]

SEX AND AGE	NUMBER WITH COVERAGE (1,000)				PERCENT OF TOTAL WORKERS			
	Total [1]	White	Black	Hispanic [2]	Total [1]	White	Black	Hispanic [2]
Total	**53,742**	**46,571**	**5,364**	**2,964**	**39.2**	**39.9**	**36.6**	**24.8**
Male.	29,923	26,440	2,506	1,739	40.8	41.8	35.6	24.4
Under 65 years old	29,331	25,913	2,451	1,713	41.6	42.7	35.6	24.5
15 to 24 years old	1,437	1,242	156	128	11.5	11.6	11.6	8.2
25 to 44 years old	17,190	15,100	1,466	1,133	45.0	46.5	36.9	27.5
45 to 64 years old	10,704	9,571	829	452	54.0	54.6	53.0	34.2
65 years old and over	592	528	55	25	21.5	21.0	34.5	20.4
Female.	23,819	20,131	2,858	1,225	37.3	37.5	37.5	25.4
Under 65 years old	23,331	19,707	2,799	1,215	37.8	38.1	37.6	25.6
15 to 24 years old	1,193	1,030	137	104	10.5	10.8	10.4	9.6
25 to 44 years old	13,833	11,573	1,717	783	42.1	42.7	40.0	29.5
45 to 64 years old	8,305	7,103	945	328	47.6	47.4	51.4	32.7
65 years old and over	488	424	59	11	22.6	21.8	32.4	14.4

[1] Includes other races, not shown separately.   [2] Hispanic persons may be of any race.

Source: U.S. Bureau of the Census, unpublished data.

Social Insurance and Human Services

No. 601. 401(k) Plans—Summary: 1985 to 1991

[A 401(k) plan is a qualified retirement plan that allows participants to have a portion of their compensation (otherwise payable in cash) contributed pretax to a retirement account on their behalf]

ITEM	1985	1986	1987	1988	1989	1990	1991
Number of plans [1]	29,869	37,420	45,054	68,121	83,301	97,614	114,667
Active participants [2] (1,000)	10,339	11,559	13,131	15,451	17,337	19,548	20,958
Assets (mil. dol.)	143,939	182,784	215,477	276,995	357,015	384,859	447,689
Contributions (mil. dol.)	24,322	29,226	33,185	39,412	46,081	48,998	52,546
Benefits (mil. dol.)	16,399	22,898	22,215	25,235	30,875	32,028	33,325
Percentage of all private defined contribution plans:							
Assets	34	37	41	46	52	54	53
Contributions	46	50	53	60	57	64	64
Benefits	35	37	40	42	43	51	51

[1] Excludes single-participant plans.   [2] May include some employees who are eligible to participate in the plan but have not elected to join. 401(k) participants may participate in one or more additional plans.

Source: Employee Benefit Research Institute, Washington, DC, *EBRI Databook on Employee Benefits, Third Edition* (copyright).

No. 602. State Unemployment Insurance—Summary: 1980 to 1993

[Includes unemployment compensation for State and local government employees where covered by State law. See also *Historical Statistics, Colonial Times to 1970*, series H 305-317]

ITEM	Unit	1980	1985	1986	1987	1988	1989	1990	1991	1992	1993
Insured unemployment, avg. weekly	1,000	3,350	2,611	2,641	2,330	2,081	2,158	2,522	3,342	3,245	2,751
Percent of covered employment [1]	Percent	3.9	2.9	2.8	2.3	2.0	2.1	2.4	3.3	3.1	2.6
Percent of civilian unemployed	Percent	43.9	31.4	32.1	31.4	31.0	33.0	36.0	40.0	34.0	32.0
Unemployment benefits, avg. weekly	Dollars	99	127	135	140	145	152	162	170	174	180
Percent of weekly wage	Percent	37.5	35.3	35.8	35.3	34.9	35.4	36.2	36.4	35.4	36.0
Weeks compensated	Million	149.0	119.3	121.4	105.2	94.2	97.6	116.0	155.1	150.2	125.6
Beneficiaries, first payments	1,000	10,001	8,350	8,361	7,205	6,861	7,369	8,629	10,075	9,243	7,884
Average duration of benefits [2]	Weeks	14.9	14.3	14.5	14.6	13.7	13.2	13.4	15.4	16.2	15.9
Claimants exhausting benefits	1,000	3,072	2,575	2,688	2,409	1,979	1,940	2,323	3,472	3,838	3,204
Percent of first payment [3]	Percent	33.2	31.3	32.1	30.6	28.5	28.0	29.4	34.8	39.9	39.2
Contributions collected [4]	Bil. dol.	11.4	19.3	18.1	17.6	17.7	16.5	15.2	14.5	17.0	19.8
Benefits paid	Bil. dol.	13.8	14.0	15.4	14.2	13.2	14.3	18.1	25.4	25.2	21.8
Funds available for benefits [5]	Bil. dol.	11.4	16.0	19.6	23.2	31.1	37.5	38.4	31.9	27.9	28.9
Average employer contribution rate [6]	Percent	2.5	3.1	2.7	2.6	2.5	2.2	2.0	2.1	2.4	2.3

[1] Insured unemployment as percent of average covered employment in preceding year.   [2] Weeks compensated divided by first payment.   [3] Based on first payments for 12-month period ending June 30.   [4] Contributions from employers; also employees in States which tax workers.   [5] End of year. Sum of balances in State clearing accounts, benefit-payment accounts, and State accounts in Federal unemployment trust funds.   [6] As percent of taxable wages.

No. 603. State Unemployment Insurance, by State and Other Areas: 1993

[See headnote, table 602. For State data on insured unemployment, see table 664]

STATE OR OTHER AREA	Beneficiaries, first payments (1,000)	Benefits paid (mil. dol.)	Avg. weekly unemployment benefits (dol.)	STATE OR OTHER AREA	Beneficiaries, first payments (1,000)	Benefits paid (mil. dol.)	Avg. weekly unemployment benefits (dol.)	STATE OR OTHER AREA	Beneficiaries, first payments (1,000)	Benefits paid (mil. dol.)	Avg. weekly unemployment benefits (dol.)
Total	7,884	21,763	180	KY	117	209	156	OH	265	740	183
AL	159	189	129	LA	82	161	119	OK	53	123	164
AK	41	103	171	ME	46	102	163	OR	128	355	180
AZ	79	177	149	MD	122	361	180	PA	435	1,524	210
AR	81	164	158	MA	211	811	234	RI	49	158	211
CA	1,258	3,425	156	MI	395	1,050	215	SC	106	176	147
CO	72	168	186	MN	119	378	210	SD	8	12	131
CT	151	539	224	MS	56	99	127	TN	154	238	131
DE	25	61	183	MO	153	320	149	TX	387	1,105	184
DC	25	112	223	MT	26	50	151	UT	32	73	181
FL	276	693	167	NE	30	47	138	VT	22	57	163
GA	202	298	150	NV	54	134	175	VA	99	215	169
HI	36	156	252	NH	27	41	142	WA	221	728	192
ID	41	79	162	NJ	287	1,220	234	WV	53	122	167
IL	349	1,250	195	NM	26	65	144	WI	197	421	183
IN	112	196	142	NY	556	2,164	200	WY	10	24	164
IA	83	179	177	NC	155	275	168	PR	133	207	89
KS	63	176	189	ND	14	26	150	VI	3	8	177

Source of tables 602 and 603: U.S. Employment and Training Administration, *Unemployment Insurance Data Summary*, annual.

No. 604. Workers' Compensation Payments: 1980 to 1993

[**In billions of dollars**, except as indicated. See headnote, table 605. See also *Historical Statistics, Colonial Times to 1970*, series H 332-345]

ITEM	1980	1984	1985	1986	1987	1988	1989	1990	1991	1992	1993
Workers covered [1] (mil.)	79	82	84	86	88	91	94	95	94	95	96
Premium amounts paid . . .	**22.3**	**25.1**	**29.2**	**34.0**	**38.1**	**43.3**	**48.0**	**53.1**	**55.2**	**55.5**	**57.3**
Private carriers.	15.7	16.6	19.5	22.8	25.4	28.5	31.9	35.1	35.7	32.8	33.6
State funds	3.0	3.0	3.5	4.5	5.3	6.7	7.2	8.0	8.7	9.6	10.9
Federal programs [2]	1.1	1.6	1.7	1.8	1.8	1.9	2.0	2.2	2.1	2.2	2.3
Self-insurers	2.4	3.9	4.5	4.9	5.5	6.2	6.9	7.9	8.7	10.4	10.6
Annual benefits paid	**13.6**	**19.7**	**22.2**	**24.6**	**27.3**	**30.7**	**34.3**	**38.2**	**42.2**	**44.7**	**42.9**
By private carriers [3]	7.0	10.6	12.3	13.8	15.5	17.5	19.9	22.2	24.5	24.0	21.8
From State funds [4]	4.3	5.4	5.7	6.2	6.8	7.5	8.0	8.7	9.7	11.0	11.3
Employers' self-insurance [5]	2.3	3.7	4.1	4.5	5.1	5.7	6.4	7.4	7.9	9.6	9.7
Type of benefit:											
Medical/hospitalization	3.9	6.4	7.5	8.6	9.9	11.5	13.4	15.2	16.8	18.3	17.5
Compensation payments	9.7	13.3	14.7	16.0	17.4	19.2	20.9	23.1	25.3	26.4	25.4
Disability.	8.4	11.7	13.1	14.3	15.8	17.6	19.2	21.2	23.3	24.4	23.5
Survivor	1.3	1.6	1.7	1.6	1.6	1.6	1.7	1.8	2.0	2.0	2.0
Percent of covered payroll:											
Workers' compensation costs [6][7]	1.96	1.66	1.82	1.99	2.07	2.16	2.27	2.36	2.40	2.31	2.30
Benefits [7]	1.07	1.21	1.30	1.37	1.43	1.49	1.58	1.66	1.79	1.82	1.68

[1] Estimated per month.   [2] Includes Federal employer compensation program and that portion of Federal black lung benefits program financed from employer contributions.   [3] Net cash and medical benefits paid under standard workers' compensation policies.   [4] Net cash and medical benefits paid by competitive and exclusive State funds and by Federal workers' compensation programs, including black lung benefit program.   [5] Cash and medical benefits paid by self-insurers, plus value of medical benefits paid by employers carrying workers' compensation policies that exclude standard medical coverage.   [6] Premiums written by private carriers and State funds, and benefits paid by self-insurers increased by 5-10 percent to allow for administrative costs. Also includes benefits paid and administrative costs of Federal system for government employees.   [7] Excludes programs financed from general revenue—black lung benefits and supplemental pensions in some States.

Source: U.S. Social Security Administration, *Annual Statistical Supplement* to the *Social Security Bulletin*.

No. 605. Workers' Compensation Payments, by State: 1980 to 1993

[**In millions of dollars.** Calendar-year data, except fiscal-year data for Federal civilian and other programs and for a few States with State funds. Payments represent cash and medical benefits and include insurance losses paid by private insurance carriers (compiled from the *Spectator (Insurance by States . . . of Casualty Lines)*, from reports of State insurance commissions, and from A. M. Best Co.); net disbursements of State funds (from the *Spectator*, from *Argus Casualty and Surety Chart*, and from State reports), estimated for some States; and self-insurance payments, estimated from available State data. Includes benefit payments under Longshoremen's and Harbor Workers' Compensation Act and Defense Bases Compensation Act for States in which such payments are made]

STATE	1980	1990	1991	1992	1993	STATE	1980	1990	1991	1992	1993
Total	13,618	38,238	42,169	44,660	42,925	Nevada	69	339	392	529	553
						New Hampshire	48	169	203	206	194
Alabama.	112	444	472	481	461	New Jersey	316	844	916	956	968
Alaska	60	113	124	127	122	New Mexico	54	228	232	216	182
Arizona.	120	371	368	399	402	New York	637	1,752	2,014	2,317	2,370
Arkansas	83	229	251	244	224	North Carolina	131	480	545	705	671
California	1,628	6,065	7,248	7,907	7,625	North Dakota.	17	60	73	71	60
Colorado.	114	595	657	722	683	Ohio	776	1,960	2,195	2,364	2,353
Connecticut.	147	694	773	783	798	Oklahoma.	127	369	434	476	493
Delaware	21	75	80	89	84						
District of Columbia .	69	86	91	126	122	Oregon.	275	573	587	476	468
Florida	362	1,976	1,961	1,861	1,705	Pennsylvania.	572	2,019	2,329	2,531	2,551
Georgia	185	735	791	1,004	911	Rhode Island.	55	219	214	266	185
Hawaii	60	216	250	288	324	South Carolina. . . .	79	277	292	350	344
Idaho	37	105	115	123	125	South Dakota	13	56	64	69	72
Illinois	699	1,607	1,745	1,750	1,668	Tennessee	129	463	515	522	487
Indiana	110	350	380	375	364	Texas.	701	2,896	3,264	2,682	2,119
Iowa	99	231	241	259	240	Utah	39	187	183	219	248
Kansas.	84	266	295	297	307	Vermont	15	61	67	73	73
Kentucky	161	383	432	475	457	Virginia.	182	507	545	542	539
						Washington.	324	883	949	1,253	1,346
Louisiana	301	575	560	517	403	West Virginia.	176	389	417	456	476
Maine.	81	380	419	429	341	Wisconsin.	170	561	627	598	608
Maryland	187	505	523	565	548	Wyoming	22	49	59	66	76
Massachusetts.	296	1,235	1,276	1,205	976						
Michigan.	626	1,205	1,286	1,428	1,437	Federal programs:					
Minnesota	260	582	646	743	734	Civilian employ-					
Mississippi	60	198	203	247	214	ees.	776	1,448	1,595	1,751	1,822
Missouri	124	496	557	698	656	Black lung					
Montana.	41	150	168	260	210	benefits [1]	1,739	1,435	1,391	1,396	1,356
Nebraska	42	137	146	157	160	Other [2]	8	11	11	11	11

[1] Includes payments by Social Security Administration and by Department of Labor.   [2] Primarily payments made to dependents of reservists who died while on active duty in the Armed Forces.

Source: U.S. Social Security Administration, *Social Security Bulletin,* fall 1993, and selected prior issues; and unpublished data.

No. 606. Persons With Work Disability, by Selected Characteristics: 1993

[In thousands, except percent. As of March. Covers civilian noninstitutional population and members of Armed Forces living off post or with their families on post. Persons are classified as having a work disability if they (1) have a health problem or disability which prevents them from working or which limits the kind or amount of work they can do; (2) have a service-connected disability or ever retired or left a job for health reasons; (3) did not work in survey reference week or previous year because of long-term illness or disability; or (4) are under age 65, and are covered by Medicare or receive Supplemental Security Income. Based on Current Population Survey; see text, section 1, and Appendix III]

AGE AND PARTICIPATION STATUS IN ASSISTANCE PROGRAMS	Total [1]	Male	Female	White	Black	Hispanic [2]
Persons with work disability	**16,777**	**8,548**	**8,229**	**12,912**	**3,223**	**1,578**
16 to 24 years old	1,467	759	708	1,009	382	148
25 to 34 years old	2,843	1,460	1,383	2,106	600	307
35 to 44 years old	3,802	1,956	1,846	2,903	737	376
45 to 54 years old	3,902	2,034	1,867	3,047	715	361
55 to 64 years old	4,763	2,338	2,425	3,848	789	387
Percent work disabled of total population	10.1	10.4	9.8	9.3	15.8	9.5
16 to 24 years old	4.5	4.6	4.3	3.9	7.9	3.4
25 to 34 years old	6.8	7.0	6.6	6.1	11.0	6.1
35 to 44 years old	9.2	9.5	8.8	8.4	14.6	10.2
45 to 54 years old	13.2	14.1	12.4	12.1	23.5	16.3
55 to 64 years old	23.0	23.5	22.4	21.3	38.8	28.3
Percent of work disabled—						
Receiving Social Security income	28.3	29.1	27.5	29.3	25.9	23.4
Receiving food stamps	25.7	19.8	31.8	20.9	43.5	37.2
Covered by Medicaid	32.8	26.3	39.6	28.3	48.9	46.5
Residing in public housing	6.2	4.1	8.3	4.3	13.2	7.6
Residing in subsidized housing	3.5	2.2	4.8	2.8	6.5	4.9

[1] Includes other races not shown separately.　[2] Hispanic persons may be of any race.
Source: U.S. Bureau of the Census, unpublished data.

No. 607. Vocational Rehabilitation—Summary: 1980 to 1993

[For fiscal years ending in year shown; see text, section 9. Includes Puerto Rico, Guam, Virgin Islands, American Samoa, Northern Mariana Islands, and Trust Territory of the Pacific Islands. Vocational rehabilitation of the disabled defined as restoration, preservation, or development of the ability to function in productive activity. Rehabilitation services provided by State vocational rehabilitation agencies with matching State and Federal funds include medical restoration, training, counseling, guidance, and placement services. See also Historical Statistics, Colonial Times to 1970, series H 392-397]

ITEM	Unit	1980	1985	1987	1988	1989	1990	1991	1992	1993
Federal and State expenditures [1]	Mil. dol.	[2]1,076	1,452	1,649	1,776	1,867	1,910	2,092	2,240	2,383
Federal expenditures	Mil. dol.	[2]817	1,100	1,275	1,373	1,446	1,525	1,622	1,731	1,804
Applicants processed for program eligibility	1,000	717	594	597	606	623	625	619	713	615
Percent accepted into program	Percent	58	60	58	58	58	57	57	57	60
Total persons rehabilitated [3]	1,000	277	228	220	218	220	216	203	192	194
Rehabilitation rate [4]	Percent	64	64	63	63	63	62	60	58	56
Severely disabled persons rehabilitated [3][5]	1,000	143	135	136	141	147	146	140	134	139
Rehabilitation rate [4]	Percent	61	62	62	62	62	62	59	57	55
Percent of total persons rehabilitated	Percent	51	59	62	65	67	68	69	70	72
Persons served, total [6]	1,000	1,095	932	917	919	929	938	942	949	1,049
Persons served, severely disabled [5][6]	1,000	606	581	584	604	625	640	654	668	767
Percent of total persons served	Percent	55	62	64	66	67	68	69	70	73

[1] Includes expenditures only under the basic support provisions of the Rehabilitation Act.　[2] Estimates based on amounts appropriated.　[3] Persons successfully placed into gainful employment.　[4] Persons rehabilitated as a percent of all active case closures (whether rehabilitated or not).　[5] Severely disabled individuals fall into any of the following three categories: (a) clients with specified major disabling conditions such as blindness and deafness; (b) clients who at any time in the vocational rehabilitation process had been Social Security disability beneficiaries or recipients of Supplemental Security Income; and (c) other individuals with substantial loss in conducting certain specified activities.　[6] Includes active cases accepted for rehabilitation services during year plus active cases on hand at beginning of year.

Source: U.S. Dept. of Education, Rehabilitation Services Administration, Caseload Statistics of State Vocational Rehabilitation Agencies in Fiscal Years, and State Vocational Rehabilitation Agency Program Data in Fiscal Years, both annual.

No. 608. Protection Against Short-Term Sickness Income Loss: 1980 to 1992

[In millions of dollars, except percent. "Short-term sickness" refers to short-term or temporary nonwork-connected disability (lasting not more than 6 months) and the first 6 months of long-term disability. See also Historical Statistics, Colonial Times to 1970, series H 115-124]

ITEM	1980	1985	1986	1987	1988	1989	1990	1991	1992
Short-term sickness: Income loss	33,933	48,745	51,867	55,839	60,115	63,788	67,661	69,522	73,565
Total protection provided [1]	**16,777**	**22,131**	**22,980**	**25,384**	**27,922**	**30,006**	**31,203**	**32,346**	**34,788**
Protection as percent of loss	49.4	45.4	44.3	45.5	46.4	47.0	46.1	46.5	47.3
Benefits provided by protection:									
Individual insurance	1,280	1,796	1,774	2,062	2,057	2,451	2,701	2,588	3,497
Group benefits to workers in private employment	9,984	12,440	12,713	14,275	15,392	16,364	16,835	17,537	18,147
Private cash insurance [2]	3,271	2,601	2,275	2,692	2,903	2,732	2,711	2,645	2,475
Publicly operated cash sickness funds [3]	770	1,179	1,255	1,696	1,779	1,907	2,269	2,817	2,975
Sick leave	5,943	8,660	9,183	9,887	10,710	11,725	11,855	12,075	12,697
Sick leave for government employees	5,338	7,700	8,299	8,827	10,266	10,967	11,393	11,910	12,748

[1] Provided by individual insurance, group benefits to workers in private employment, and sick leave for government employees. Includes benefits for the sixth month of disability payable under old-age, survivors, disability, and health insurance program, not shown separately.　[2] Group accident and sickness insurance and self-insurance privately written either on a voluntary basis or in compliance with State temporary disability insurance laws in CA, HI, NJ, and NY. Includes a small but undetermined amount of group disability insurance benefits paid to government workers and to self-employed persons through farm, trade, or professional associations.　[3] Includes State-operated plans in RI, CA, and NJ; State Insurance Fund and special fund for disabled unemployed in New York; and provisions of Railroad Unemployment Insurance Act.

Source: U.S. Social Security Administration, Social Security Bulletin, fall 1994 and unpublished data.

No. 609. Public Aid—Recipients and Average Monthly Cash Payments Under Supplemental Security Income (SSI) and Public Assistance: 1980 to 1993

[As of **December**, except as noted. Public assistance data for all years include Puerto Rico, Guam, and Virgin Islands; SSI data are for federally administered payments only. See text, section 12. Excludes payments made directly to suppliers of medical care. See also Appendix III and *Historical Statistics, Colonial Times to 1970*, series H 355-367]

PROGRAM	RECIPIENTS (1,000)					AVG. MONTHLY PAYMENTS (dol.)				
	1980	1990	1991	1992	1993	1980	1990	1991	1992	1993
SSI, total.................	4,142	4,817	5,118	5,566	5,984	168	299	321	358	345
Aged..................	1,808	1,454	1,465	1,471	1,475	128	213	221	227	237
Blind..................	78	84	85	85	85	213	342	351	362	359
Disabled	2,256	3,279	3,569	4,010	4,424	198	337	361	407	381
Old-age assistance [1]...........	19	17	17	17	16	39	45	55	41	45
Aid to the blind [1].............	(Z)	(Z)	(Z)	(Z)	(Z)	36	42	56	37	40
Aid to permanently, totally disabled [1] .	21	26	27	28	28	35	40	58	40	41
AFDC: [2] Families	3,843	4,218	4,708	4,936	5,050	288	392	388	382	377
Recipients [3]	11,101	12,159	13,489	14,035	14,257	100	136	135	134	133
Children.................	7,599	8,208	9,104	9,471	9,598	(NA)	(NA)	(NA)	(NA)	(NA)
General assistance cases	796	1,060	1,078	979	971	161	(NA)	(NA)	(NA)	(NA)

NA Not available.   Z Fewer than 500.   [1] Average monthly recipients and payments for the year.   [2] Aid to Families with Dependent Children program.   [3] Includes the children and one or both parents, or one caretaker relative other than a parent, in families where the needs of such adults were considered in determining the amount of assistance.

No. 610. Public Aid Payments: 1980 to 1993

[**In millions of dollars**. See headnote, table 609. Supplemental Security Income data cover federally- and State-administered payments. See also Appendix III and *Historical Statistics, Colonial Times to 1970*, series H 346-354]

PROGRAM	1980	1985	1986	1987	1988	1989	1990	1991	1992	1993
Payments, total	[1]21,994	26,431	28,311	29,556	30,910	32,762	36,047	39,788	44,661	47,659
Supplemental Security Income [2] . .	7,941	11,060	12,081	12,951	13,786	14,980	16,599	18,524	22,233	24,557
Aged..................	2,734	3,035	3,096	3,194	3,299	3,476	3,736	3,890	4,140	4,248
Blind..................	190	264	277	291	302	316	334	347	371	375
Disabled	5,014	7,755	8,700	9,458	10,177	11,180	12,521	14,268	17,711	19,928
Public assistance	[1]14,048	15,371	16,230	16,605	17,124	17,782	19,448	21,264	22,428	23,102
Old-age assistance	9	8	8	7	7	7	7	11	8	9
Blind...............	(Z)	(Z)	(Z)	(Z)	(Z)	(Z)	(Z)	(Z)	(Z)	(Z)
Permanently, totally disabled ...	9	10	11	11	11	12	12	19	14	14
Families with dependent children.	12,475	15,196	16,033	16,373	16,827	17,466	19,078	20,931	22,106	22,688
Emergency assistance	113	157	178	214	279	297	349	303	301	391

Z Less than $500,000.   [1] Includes general assistance payments.   [2] Includes data not available by reason for eligibility.

Source of tables 609 and 610: U.S. Social Security Administration, *Social Security Bulletin*, quarterly and *Annual Statistical Supplement* to the *Social Security Bulletin*, and U.S. Administration for Children and Families, *Quarterly Public Assistance Statistics*, annual.

No. 611. Public Aid Recipients as Percent of Population, by State: 1990 and 1993

[Total recipients as of **June** of Aid to Families with Dependent Children and of Federal Supplemental Security Income as percent of resident population. Based on resident population as of April 1 for 1990 and as of July 1 for 1993]

DIVISION AND STATE	1990	1993	DIVISION AND STATE	1990	1993	DIVISION AND STATE	1990	1993	DIVISION AND STATE	1990	1993
U.S ...	**6.5**	**7.7**	IL	7.1	7.9	WV	8.9	9.6	**Mountain . .**	**4.2**	**5.3**
			MI	8.6	9.3	NC	5.6	7.3	MT	4.9	5.6
N.E	**5.6**	**6.9**	WI	6.6	6.7	SC	5.8	6.8	ID	2.7	3.2
ME	6.6	7.6	**W.N.C. ....**	**4.8**	**5.5**	GA	7.1	8.4	WY	3.8	5.0
NH	2.2	3.4	MN	4.9	5.5	FL	4.6	7.0	CO	4.3	4.8
VT	5.7	7.0	IA	4.7	4.9	**E.S.C. .....**	**7.9**	**9.1**	NM	5.8	8.3
MA	6.4	7.7	MO	5.8	6.9	KY	7.9	9.5	AZ	4.7	6.5
RI	6.4	8.3	ND	3.6	4.2	TN	7.2	9.4	UT	3.3	3.7
CT	4.7	6.2	SD	4.2	4.5	AL	6.5	7.0	NV	2.9	3.7
M.A	**6.7**	**8.0**	NE	3.7	4.2	MS	11.4	11.3	**Pacific ....**	**8.4**	**10.0**
NY	7.7	9.6	KS	4.1	4.7				WA	6.0	7.1
NJ	5.3	6.1	**S.A .....**	**5.4**	**7.0**	**W.S.C. ....**	**6.2**	**6.9**	OR	4.3	5.3
PA	6.0	7.0	DE	4.4	5.3	AR	6.3	6.6	CA	9.4	11.2
E.N.C.	**7.0**	**7.8**	MD	5.1	5.9	LA	9.8	9.9	AK	4.6	7.2
OH	7.3	8.3	DC	10.9	15.0	OK	5.6	6.2	HI	5.2	6.3
IN	3.9	5.1	VA	3.9	4.8	TX	5.4	6.3			

Source: Compiled by U.S. Bureau of the Census. Data from U.S. Social Security Administration, *Social Security Bulletin*, quarterly, and U.S. Administration for Children and Families, *Quarterly Public Assistance Statistics*, annual.

No. 612. Aid to Families With Dependent Children (AFDC) and Supplemental Security Income (SSI)—Recipients and Payments, by State and Other Areas: 1990 to 1993

[Recipients as of **December**. Data for SSI cover Federal SSI payments and/or federally-administered State supplementation except as noted. For explanation of methodology, see Appendix III]

DIVISION AND STATE OR OTHER AREA	AFDC Recipients [1] (1,000)			AFDC Payments for year (mil. dol.)			AFDC Average monthly payment per family		SSI Recipients (1,000)		SSI Payments for year (mil. dol.)	
	1990	1992	1993	1990	1992	1993	1990	1993	1990	1993	1990	1993
Total	12,159	14,035	14,257	19,078	22,106	22,688	$392	$377	[2]4,817	[2]5,984	16,133	[2]23,991
U.S.	11,958	13,834	14,061	18,995	22,017	22,598	396	381	4,817	5,984	16,133	23,988
New England	577	680	661	1,250	1,502	1,516	535	527	209	259	652	981
ME.	62	67	65	104	118	115	422	404	24	28	56	80
NH.	21	29	30	35	55	58	431	433	[3]7	[3]9	[3]19	[3]30
VT.	25	29	28	51	70	65	527	543	10	12	31	45
MA.	282	335	313	647	750	755	556	549	119	149	397	597
RI.	52	61	63	104	130	136	499	506	17	21	53	79
CT.	135	159	163	309	379	388	571	560	[3]32	[3]40	[3]96	[3]149
Middle Atlantic	1,903	2,120	2,194	3,623	4,073	4,337	472	469	711	907	2,533	3,947
NY.	1,031	1,171	1,240	2,337	2,633	2,887	556	546	415	536	1,557	2,421
NJ.	323	347	340	459	518	531	352	356	105	134	340	533
PA.	549	601	614	827	922	919	382	371	191	236	635	993
East North Central .	2,397	2,519	2,528	3,611	3,708	3,739	379	357	622	840	2,021	3,475
OH.	657	721	694	896	979	976	328	317	156	214	483	869
IN	164	199	220	174	221	209	263	235	[3]60	[3]82	[3]174	[3]308
IL.	656	682	709	868	891	908	342	324	[3]177	[3]245	[3]593	[3]1,032
MI	684	684	676	1,232	1,167	1,208	464	438	143	192	483	795
WI	236	233	228	441	450	439	464	460	86	106	288	470
West North Central .	647	719	731	955	1,077	1,079	366	356	216	273	584	951
MN.	177	186	189	355	388	386	512	501	[3]40	[3]55	[3]110	[3]190
IA	96	101	109	154	164	165	371	370	33	39	86	133
MO	218	260	264	237	286	284	274	261	[3]85	[3]105	[3]237	[3]374
ND.	16	19	17	24	28	28	359	365	[3]7	[3]9	[3]18	[4]26
SD.	19	20	19	22	25	25	272	291	10	13	26	42
NE.	44	48	46	60	66	65	336	325	[3]16	[3]20	[3]42	[3]67
KS.	77	86	87	103	121	126	332	346	25	33	65	118
South Atlantic	1,654	2,212	2,189	1,844	2,499	2,566	272	263	847	1,038	2,370	3,586
DE.	22	28	28	30	38	40	292	291	8	10	22	34
MD.	198	222	215	304	335	306	370	319	60	74	185	281
DC.	54	63	74	87	101	118	380	383	16	19	54	73
VA.	158	194	195	181	228	233	265	262	[3]95	[3]118	[3]257	[3]395
WV.	109	119	116	112	121	122	249	246	[4]47	[4]60	[4]146	[4]238
NC.	255	335	334	257	343	358	237	227	[3]149	[3]175	[3]403	[3]558
SC.	118	147	142	97	119	118	203	184	[3]90	[3]104	[3]234	[3]342
GA.	320	400	394	333	427	434	265	255	159	187	415	615
FL.	420	704	692	443	787	837	263	275	222	293	653	1,049
East South Central .	742	858	808	510	600	610	168	168	501	603	1,371	2,115
KY.	204	229	211	185	214	208	224	211	[3]115	[3]146	[3]337	[3]544
TN.	230	316	301	176	210	221	186	168	140	168	384	566
AL.	132	141	135	63	88	95	115	154	[3]133	[3]156	[3]351	[3]535
MS.	176	172	161	86	89	86	120	120	114	134	300	470
West South Central .	1,154	1,268	1,258	811	941	942	180	177	564	702	1,478	2,444
AR.	73	73	70	57	60	59	190	186	76	91	187	299
LA.	279	269	256	188	184	176	167	164	133	170	378	685
OK.	129	142	132	135	173	171	279	297	[3]60	[3]70	[3]158	[3]233
TX.	673	784	799	431	524	536	165	159	[4]295	[4]371	[4]755	[4]1,226
Mountain	454	575	592	523	739	783	297	321	162	221	476	800
MT.	29	34	35	40	46	47	344	331	10	12	29	43
ID.	17	21	23	20	24	30	266	307	[3]10	[3]14	[3]29	[3]52
WY.	16	18	17	20	27	25	313	332	[3]3	[3]5	[3]9	[3]17
CO.	109	125	126	138	163	163	320	319	[3]38	[3]51	[3]110	[3]186
NM.	67	94	101	66	109	124	273	324	[3]32	[3]40	[3]90	[3]139
AZ.	144	194	203	146	252	271	268	318	[3]45	[3]63	[3]139	[3]233
UT.	47	53	50	65	76	78	347	354	13	18	38	69
NV.	25	35	37	28	41	45	278	282	11	17	33	60
Pacific.	2,427	2,883	3,100	5,866	6,878	7,025	606	558	984	1,141	4,646	5,691
WA.	237	283	290	447	572	610	452	498	62	82	208	333
OR.	99	116	115	150	200	203	374	395	[3]32	[3]43	[3]95	[3]155
CA.	2,023	2,395	2,597	5,107	5,875	5,953	637	568	873	994	4,278	5,112
AK.	24	35	37	62	100	111	651	748	[3]5	[3]6	[3]14	[3]21
HI	44	54	60	100	130	148	581	654	14	17	51	71
PR	193	191	186	74	77	77	103	106	(X)	(X)	(X)	(X)
GU	4	6	6	6	8	10	418	534	(X)	(X)	(X)	(X)
VI	3	4	4	3	3	3	279	229	(X)	(X)	(X)	(X)
N. Mariana	(X)	(X)	(X)	(X)	(X)	(X)	(X)	(X)	[4]1	[4]1	[4]2	[4]2

X Not applicable.   [1] See footnote 3, table 609.   [2] Includes data for those recipients whose residence was "unknown". [3] Data for persons with Federal SSI payments only; State has State-administered supplementation.   [4] Data for persons with Federal SSI payments only; State supplementary payments not made.

Source: U.S. Social Security Administration, *Social Security Bulletin*, quarterly, and *Annual Statistical Supplement* to the *Social Security Bulletin*; and U.S. Administration for Children and Families, *Quarterly Public Assistance Statistics*, annual.

No. 613. Federal Food Stamp and National School Lunch Programs, by State: 1990 to 1994

[Cost data for years ending Sept. 30. Data on food stamp households and persons are average monthly number participating in year ending Sept. 30. Data on pupils participating in National School Lunch Program are for month in which the highest number of children participated nationwide. For National School Lunch Program, covers public and private elementary and secondary schools and residential child care institutions. Food Stamp costs are for benefits only and exclude administrative expenditures. National School Lunch Program costs include Federal cash reimbursements at rates set by law for each meal served but do not include the value of USDA donated commodities utilized in this program]

REGION, DIVISION, AND STATE	Households participating, 1994 Number (1,000)	Households participating, 1994 Percent of all households	Persons (1,000) 1990	Persons (1,000) 1993	Persons (1,000) 1994	Cost (mil. dol.) 1990	Cost (mil. dol.) 1993	Cost (mil. dol.) 1994	Persons (1,000) 1990	Persons (1,000) 1993	Persons (1,000) 1994	Cost (mil. dol.) 1990	Cost (mil. dol.) 1993	Cost (mil. dol.) 1994
Total [1]	11,094	(NA)	20,067	26,982	27,476	14,187	22,006	22,752	24,589	25,356	25,730	3,214	4,081	4,283
U.S.	11,083	11.6	20,036	26,952	27,440	14,153	21,969	22,707	24,019	24,793	25,215	3,098	3,966	4,158
Northeast	2,203	11.6	3,589	4,769	4,927	2,462	3,959	4,191	4,033	4,091	4,143	489	628	676
N.E.	443	8.9	707	1,007	1,020	426	738	759	991	964	993	95	129	137
ME	61	12.8	94	138	136	63	112	111	108	106	107	11	15	15
NH	26	6.2	31	60	62	20	46	46	91	87	92	6	9	10
VT	29	13.0	38	58	65	22	38	44	47	49	50	4	6	6
MA	191	8.4	347	443	442	207	326	330	454	440	455	44	58	63
RI	40	10.8	64	92	93	42	73	76	60	56	60	7	10	11
CT	97	7.9	133	215	223	72	143	152	231	226	229	23	30	33
M.A.	1,760	12.5	2,882	3,762	3,907	2,036	3,221	3,432	3,042	3,128	3,149	393	500	538
NY	1,004	15.0	1,548	2,045	2,154	1,086	1,796	1,945	1,546	1,625	1,666	232	289	317
NJ	227	8.0	382	531	545	289	464	486	507	518	494	60	81	85
PA	530	11.6	952	1,186	1,208	661	961	1,001	990	985	990	102	130	137
Midwest	2,392	10.4	4,806	5,814	5,821	3,566	4,779	4,775	5,806	5,913	6,005	619	766	789
E.N.C.	1,783	11.1	3,616	4,305	4,316	2,765	3,626	3,616	3,687	3,738	3,840	421	520	532
OH	531	12.7	1,089	1,269	1,245	861	1,100	1,077	919	943	1,026	109	130	130
IN	196	9.1	311	497	521	226	406	415	635	602	602	54	68	69
IL	499	11.6	1,013	[2]1,179	1,189	835	[2]1,060	1,070	932	959	965	131	161	168
MI	434	12.4	917	1,022	1,031	663	837	834	733	746	758	82	106	107
WI	122	6.4	286	337	330	180	223	221	468	487	490	45	56	58
W.N.C.	609	8.8	1,190	1,510	1,506	801	1,152	1,159	2,119	2,176	2,164	197	246	256
MN	133	7.7	263	317	316	165	228	230	489	512	523	42	54	56
IA	79	7.3	170	[2]196	196	109	[2]147	145	392	383	380	31	38	39
MO	240	11.9	431	[2]591	593	312	[2]477	483	547	562	543	58	72	76
ND	18	7.5	39	48	45	25	36	34	94	92	89	8	10	10
SD	19	7.3	50	56	53	35	43	41	102	108	107	12	14	14
NE	45	7.3	95	113	111	59	81	79	191	203	211	18	22	23
KS	76	7.9	142	188	192	96	141	146	302	316	312	29	37	39
South	4,379	13.0	8,040	11,197	11,188	5,928	9,235	9,355	9,890	10,174	10,344	1,334	1,696	1,769
S.A.	1,927	11.0	2,993	4,705	4,726	2,223	3,934	4,009	4,454	4,577	4,672	558	737	776
DE	22	8.3	33	58	59	25	46	48	59	61	65	6	8	9
MD	165	9.0	255	375	387	203	336	351	347	352	367	40	52	56
DC	41	17.5	62	87	91	43	81	87	47	47	47	10	12	13
VA	232	9.5	346	535	547	247	433	448	586	586	601	60	78	80
WV	126	17.9	262	322	321	192	261	261	198	199	204	29	31	31
NC	259	9.7	419	627	630	282	480	490	749	751	767	91	113	117
SC	146	10.9	299	394	385	240	306	303	451	459	461	60	76	80
GA	329	12.8	536	807	832	382	658	696	908	948	975	106	140	151
FL	607	11.1	781	1,500	1,474	609	1,334	1,324	1,110	1,172	1,186	158	227	241
E.S.C.	912	15.4	1,938	2,401	2,318	1,386	1,906	1,868	2,085	2,109	2,111	281	334	340
KY	196	13.6	458	530	522	334	422	416	498	521	518	61	75	76
TN	307	15.6	527	774	735	372	610	601	590	601	608	68	85	87
AL	215	13.6	454	560	551	328	457	453	570	564	567	77	89	92
MS	194	20.4	499	537	511	352	416	397	428	423	418	76	86	85
W.S.C.	1,540	15.0	3,109	4,091	4,145	2,319	3,395	3,479	3,351	3,489	3,561	495	625	653
AR	108	11.6	235	285	283	155	209	212	292	310	318	41	51	51
LA	278	18.0	727	779	756	549	653	642	694	691	687	104	121	125
OK	150	12.2	267	370	376	186	294	305	362	370	375	46	59	62
TX	1,003	15.3	1,880	2,657	2,730	1,429	2,239	2,320	2,003	2,119	2,182	304	394	414
West	2,109	10.4	3,601	5,172	5,504	2,197	3,996	4,386	4,289	4,614	4,723	657	876	925
Mountain	542	9.7	988	1,415	1,435	726	1,134	1,157	1,362	1,466	1,506	170	224	239
MT	28	8.6	57	70	71	41	54	56	84	87	91	10	12	12
ID	30	7.4	59	79	82	40	57	57	131	139	142	14	18	19
WY	13	7.3	28	34	34	21	26	27	57	58	59	5	7	7
CO	107	7.5	221	273	268	156	226	223	282	296	304	31	40	41
NM	86	14.7	157	244	244	117	194	194	179	183	187	30	37	39
AZ	187	12.4	317	489	512	239	394	418	331	365	381	47	67	73
UT	46	7.7	99	133	128	71	97	94	233	249	255	24	31	32
NV	44	7.9	50	93	97	41	86	88	67	89	87	8	13	15
Pacific	1,567	10.7	2,613	3,757	4,069	1,471	2,863	3,228	2,927	3,148	3,217	487	651	686
WA	196	9.6	340	462	468	229	368	390	361	406	411	43	60	65
OR	127	10.6	216	283	286	168	235	241	234	250	251	26	35	37
CA	1,179	10.9	1,955	2,866	3,155	968	2,083	2,391	2,147	2,296	2,350	396	527	554
AK	15	7.2	25	43	46	25	45	53	39	45	46	8	12	12
HI	50	13.1	77	103	115	81	132	153	145	150	160	14	17	18

NA Not available.   [1] Includes Puerto Rico (for NSLP), other outlying areas and Dept. of Defense overseas.   [2] Includes disaster relief.

Source: U.S. Dept. of Agriculture, Food and Nutrition Service. In "Annual Historical Review of FNS Programs" and unpublished data.

No. 614. Federal Food Programs: 1980 to 1994

[For fiscal years ending in year shown; see text, section 9. Program data include Puerto Rico, Virgin Islands, Guam, American Samoa, Northern Marianas, and the former Trust Territory when a Federal food program was operated in these areas. Participation data are average monthly figures except as noted. Participants are not reported for the nutrition program for the elderly and the commodity distribution programs. Cost data are direct Federal benefits to recipients; they exclude Federal administrative payments and applicable State and local contributions. Federal costs for commodities and cash-in-lieu of commodities are shown separately from direct cash benefits for those programs receiving both]

PROGRAM	Unit	1980	1985	1989	1990	1991	1992	1993	1994, prel.
Food Stamp:									
Participants	Million . .	21.1	19.9	18.8	20.1	22.6	25.4	27.0	27.5
Federal cost	Mil. dol . .	8,721	10,744	11,676	14,187	17,339	20,906	22,006	22,752
Monthly average coupon value per recipient .	Dollars . .	34.47	44.99	51.85	58.92	63.86	68.57	67.96	69.00
Nutrition assistance program for Puerto Rico: [1]									
Federal cost	Mil. dol . .	(X)	825	908	937	963	1,002	1,040	1,079
National school lunch program (NSLP): [2]									
Free lunches served	Million . .	1,671	1,657	1,627	1,662	1,748	1,891	1,981	2,046
Reduced-price lunches served	Million . .	308	255	263	273	293	285	287	298
Children participating [3]	Million . .	26.6	23.6	24.3	24.1	24.2	24.6	24.9	25.2
Federal cost	Mil. dol . .	2,279	2,578	3,005	3,214	3,525	3,856	4,081	4,283
School breakfast (SB): [3]									
Children participating [3]	Million . .	3.6	3.4	3.8	4.1	4.4	4.9	5.4	5.8
Federal cost	Mil. dol . .	288	379	513	596	685	787	869	955
Special supplemental food program (WIC): [4]									
Participants	Million . .	1.9	3.1	4.1	4.5	4.9	5.4	5.9	6.5
Federal cost	Mil. dol . .	584	1,193	1,489	1,637	1,752	1,959	2,115	2,340
Commodity supplemental food program: [5]									
Participants	Million . .	0.1	0.2	0.2	0.3	0.3	0.3	0.4	0.4
Federal cost	Mil. dol . .	19	42	62	71	76	87	94	87
Child and adult care (CC): [6]									
Participants [7]	Million . .	0.7	1.0	1.4	1.5	1.6	1.8	2.0	2.1
Federal cost	Mil. dol . .	207	390	612	720	834	966	1,082	1,193
Summer feeding (SF): [8]									
Children participating [9]	Million . .	1.9	1.5	1.7	1.7	1.8	1.9	2.1	2.1
Federal cost	Mil. dol . .	104	103	132	145	160	182	195	210
Nutrition program for the elderly:									
Meals served	Million . .	166	225	243	246	245	245	244	247
Federal cost	Mil. dol . .	75	134	146	142	140	151	153	151
Federal cost of commodities donated to— [10]									
Child nutrition (NSLP, CC, SF and SB)	Mil. dol . .	930	840	793	646	729	740	704	705
Charitable institutions, summer camps	Mil. dol . .	71	170	136	104	93	116	92	98
Emergency feeding [11]	Mil. dol . .	(X)	973	266	286	253	230	231	198

X Not applicable.   [1] Puerto Rico was included in the food stamp program until June 30, 1982.   [2] See headnote, table 613. [3] Nine month (September through May) average daily meals (lunches or breakfasts) served divided by the ratio of average daily attendance to enrollment.   [4] WIC serves women, infants, and children.   [5] Program provides commodities to women, infants, children, and the elderly.   [6] Program provides year-round subsidies to feed preschool children in child care centers and family day care homes. Certain care centers serving disabled or elderly adults also receive meal subsidies.   [7] Quarterly average daily attendance at participating institutions.   [8] Program provides free meals to children in poor areas during summer months. [9] Peak month (July) average daily attendance at participating institutions.   [10] Includes the Federal cost of commodity entitlements, cash-in-lieu of commodities, and bonus foods.   [11] Provides free commodities to needy persons for home consumption through food banks, hunger centers, soup kitchens, and similar nonprofit agencies. Includes the Emergency Food Assistance Program, the commodity purchases for soup kitchens/food banks program, and commodity disaster relief.

Source: U.S. Dept. of Agriculture, Food and Nutrition Service. In "Annual Historical Review of FNS Programs" and unpublished data.

No. 615. Primary Child Care Arrangements Used by Employed Mothers for Children Under 5 Years Old: 1991

[As of fall. Data were obtained for the three youngest children in the household. Based on the Survey of Income and Program Participation; see text, section 14]

TYPE OF ARRANGEMENT	Total	AGE			MONTHLY FAMILY INCOME			
		Under 1 year	1 to 2 years	3 to 4 years	Less than $1,500	$1,500 to $2,999	$3,000 to $4,499	$4,500 or more
Children under 5 years old, total (1,000) . .	9,854	1,650	4,021	4,183	1,618	3,173	2,594	2,403
PERCENT DISTRIBUTION								
Care in child's home	35.7	40.5	38.7	31.1	37.4	39.6	36.2	29.5
By father	20.0	21.6	21.2	18.3	21.2	25.3	20.3	12.2
By grandparent	7.2	8.7	8.0	5.8	5.6	7.6	8.2	6.6
By other relative	3.2	2.7	3.9	2.7	7.0	3.2	2.2	1.7
By nonrelative	5.4	7.5	5.5	4.3	3.6	3.5	5.5	9.0
Care in another home	31.0	40.5	33.8	24.5	32.8	31.2	32.6	27.2
By grandparent	8.6	14.3	8.6	6.3	10.8	9.5	9.9	3.9
By other relative	4.5	5.6	4.7	3.8	5.7	6.0	3.8	2.5
By nonrelative	17.9	20.5	20.4	14.4	16.3	15.7	18.9	20.8
Organized child care facilities	23.0	11.5	17.5	32.9	20.4	17.5	21.9	33.7
Day/group care center	15.8	9.8	15.2	18.6	14.8	10.9	17.0	21.9
Nursery school/preschool	7.3	1.7	2.3	14.2	5.6	6.6	4.9	11.8
School-based activity	0.5	-	0.1	1.1	0.4	1.1	-	0.5
Mother cares for child at work [1]	8.7	7.6	9.9	7.9	7.2	10.3	7.8	7.9
Other arrangements [2]	1.1	-	-	2.5	1.8	0.4	1.3	1.2

- Represents or rounds to zero.   [1] Includes mothers working at home or away from home.   [2] Includes children in kindergarten/grade school.

Source: U.S. Bureau of the Census, Current Population Reports, P70-36.

No. 616. Child Support—Award and Recipiency Status of Custodial Parent: 1991

[In thousands except as noted. Custodial parents 15 years and older with own children under 21 years of age present from absent parents as of spring 1992. Covers civilian noninstitutional population. Based on Current Population Survey; see text, section 1, and Appendix III. For definition of mean, see Guide to Tabular Presentation]

AWARD AND RECIPIENCY STATUS	ALL CUSTODIAL PARENTS				CUSTODIAL PARENTS BELOW THE POVERTY LEVEL			
	Total		Mothers	Fathers	Total		Mothers	Fathers
	Number	Percent distribution			Number	Percent distribution		
Total....................	11,502	100	9,918	1,584	3,720	100	3,513	207
Payments awarded...............	6,190	54	5,542	648	1,438	39	1,368	71
Supposed to receive payments in 1991..	5,326	46	4,883	443	1,257	34	1,200	57
Not supposed to receive payments	864	8	659	205	181	5	168	14
Payments not awarded.............	5,312	46	4,376	936	2,282	61	2,145	136
Supposed to receive payments.......	5,326	100	4,883	443	1,257	100	1,200	57
Actually received payments in 1991......	4,006	75	3,728	278	859	68	845	14
Received full amount.............	2,742	51	2,552	189	499	40	497	2
Received partial amount............	1,265	24	1,176	89	360	29	348	12
Did not receive payments	1,320	25	1,156	164	398	32	355	43
MEAN INCOME AND CHILD SUPPORT								
Received child support payments in 1991:								
Mean total money income (dol.).......	19,217	(X)	18,144	33,579	5,734	(X)	5,687	(B)
Mean child support received (dol.).....	2,961	(X)	3,011	2,292	1,910	(X)	1,922	(B)
Received no payments in 1991:								
Mean total money income (dol.).......	15,919	(X)	14,602	25,184	5,399	(X)	5,525	(B)
Without child support agreement or award:								
Mean total money income (dol.).......	13,283	(X)	10,226	27,578	4,979	(X)	4,942	5,560

B Base too small to meet statistical standards for reliability.   X Not applicable.
Source: U.S. Bureau of the Census, *Current Population Reports*, P60-187.

No. 617. Child Support—Selected Characteristics of Custodial Parents: 1991

[See headnote, table 616. For definition of mean, see Guide to Tabular Presentation]

RECIPIENCY STATUS OF PARENT	Unit	Total [1]	AGE			RACE		His-pan-ic [2]	CURRENT MARITAL STATUS			
			18 to 29 years	30 to 39 years	40 years and over	White	Black		Divorced	Married [3]	Never married	Separated
ALL CUSTODIAL PARENTS												
All parents, total........	1,000 ..	11,502	3,197	5,058	3,154	8,319	2,886	1,160	3,599	3,428	2,685	1,705
Payments agreed to or awarded .	1,000 ..	6,190	1,321	2,997	1,862	5,035	1,009	410	2,477	2,208	712	755
Percent of total	Percent.	54	41	59	59	61	35	35	69	64	27	44
Supposed to receive child support in 1991 .	1,000 ..	5,326	1,175	2,647	1,499	4,357	834	356	2,190	1,909	600	597
Percent received payment ..	Percent.	75	70	75	79	77	69	65	76	75	74	74
Mean child support........	Dollars .	2,961	1,790	3,052	3,625	3,131	2,079	2,165	3,544	2,799	1,537	2,707
Percent of total income .	Percent.	15	16	16	14	16	15	15	15	15	14	19
Parents with incomes below the poverty level in 1991..	1,000 ..	3,720	1,529	1,555	575	2,134	1,478	591	935	410	1,487	874
Payments agreed to or awarded .	1,000 ..	1,438	545	664	224	962	438	152	514	221	362	333
Percent of total	Percent.	39	36	43	39	45	30	26	55	54	24	38
Supposed to receive child support in 1991.....	1,000 ..	1,257	486	577	191	858	364	138	472	194	313	274
Percent received payment ..	Percent.	68	69	69	65	66	74	61	67	68	73	67
Mean child support........	Dollars .	1,910	1,390	2,042	2,919	1,839	2,106	2,580	2,453	1,492	1,500	1,786
Percent of total income ..	Percent.	33	26	32	62	33	34	51	36	37	26	36
ALL CUSTODIAL MOTHERS												
All mothers, total	1,000 ..	9,918	3,022	4,379	2,429	6,966	2,698	1,043	3,052	2,707	2,565	1,514
Payments agreed to or awarded .	1,000 ..	5,542	1,269	2,691	1,571	4,459	958	368	2,221	1,888	693	702
Percent of total	Percent.	56	42	61	65	64	36	35	73	70	27	46
Supposed to receive child support in 1991 .	1,000 ..	4,883	1,132	2,446	1,299	3,976	791	324	2,027	1,679	583	563
Percent received payment ..	Percent.	76	71	76	82	78	70	68	77	76	74	74
Mean child support........	Dollars .	3,011	1,816	3,127	3,719	3,193	2,102	2,200	3,623	2,831	1,534	2,753
Percent of total income ..	Percent.	17	17	17	16	17	15	16	16	18	14	20
Mothers with incomes below the poverty level in 1991..........	1,000 ..	3,513	1,472	1,455	528	1,979	1,433	563	877	338	1,449	836
Payments agreed to or awarded .	1,000 ..	1,368	534	621	207	896	433	140	486	187	359	328
Percent of total	Percent.	39	36	43	39	45	30	25	55	55	25	39
Supposed to receive child support in 1991	1,000 ..	1,200	474	539	184	804	361	126	448	169	311	268
Percent received payment ..	Percent.	70	70	72	67	68	74	67	69	73	72	68
Mean child support........	Dollars .	1,922	1,399	2,058	2,939	1,869	2,083	2,580	2,474	1,477	1,515	1,786
Percent of total income ..	Percent.	34	26	33	62	34	33	51	36	40	26	36

[1] Includes other items, not shown separately.   [2] Hispanic persons may be of any race.   [3] Remarried parents whose previous marriage ended in divorce and persons in first marriage.
Source: U.S. Bureau of the Census, *Current Population Reports*, P60-187.

No. 618. Child Support Enforcement Program—Caseload and Collections: 1980 to 1993

[For years ending Sept. 30. Includes Puerto Rico, Guam, and the Virgin Islands. The Child Support Enforcement program locates absent parents, establishes paternity of children born out-of-wedlock, and establishes and enforces support orders. By law, these services are available to all families that need them. The program is operated at the State and local government level but 68 percent of administrative costs are paid by the Federal government. Child support collected for families not receiving Aid to Families with Dependent Children (AFDC) goes to the family to help it remain self-sufficient. Most of the child support collected on behalf of AFDC families goes to Federal and State governments to offset AFDC payments. Based on data reported by State agencies. Minus sign (-) indicates net outlay]

ITEM	Unit	1980	1985	1988	1989	1990	1991	1992	1993
Total cases	1,000 . . .	5,432	8,401	11,078	11,876	12,796	13,423	15,159	17,110
AFDC and AFDC arrears only caseload .	1,000 . . .	(NA)	(NA)	7,501	7,610	7,953	8,034	8,705	9,619
AFDC cases	1,000 . . .	4,583	6,242	5,703	5,709	5,872	6,166	6,753	7,472
AFDC arrears only cases [1]	1,000 . . .	(NA)	(NA)	1,798	1,901	2,082	1,868	1,952	2,147
Non-AFDC cases	1,000 . . .	849	2,159	3,577	4,266	4,843	5,389	6,454	7,491
Cases for which a collection was made:									
AFDC cases	1,000 . . .	503	684	621	658	701	755	831	874
AFDC arrears only cases [1]	1,000 . . .	(NA)	(NA)	181	202	224	278	255	290
Non-AFDC cases	1,000 . . .	243	654	1,083	1,247	1,363	1,555	1,749	1,956
Percentage of cases with collections:									
AFDC cases	Percent .	11.0	11.0	10.9	11.5	11.9	12.2	12.3	11.7
AFDC arrears only cases [1]	Percent .	(NA)	(NA)	10.1	10.6	10.8	14.9	13.1	13.5
Non-AFDC cases	Percent .	28.7	30.3	30.3	29.2	28.1	28.9	27.1	26.1
Absent parents located, total	1,000 . . .	643	878	1,388	1,628	2,062	2,577	3,706	4,484
Paternities established, total	1,000 . . .	144	232	307	339	393	472	516	554
Support obligations established, total [2]	1,000 . . .	374	669	870	938	1,022	821	893	1,045
FINANCES									
Collections, total	Mil. dol .	1,478	2,694	4,605	5,241	6,010	6,886	7,965	8,908
AFDC collections	Mil. dol . .	603	1,090	1,486	1,593	1,750	1,984	2,259	2,416
State share	Mil. dol . .	274	415	525	563	620	700	787	847
Incentive payments to States	Mil. dol . .	72	145	222	266	264	278	299	339
Federal share	Mil. dol . .	246	341	449	458	533	626	738	777
Payments to AFDC families [3]	Mil. dol . .	10	189	289	307	334	381	435	453
Non-AFDC collections	Mil. dol . .	874	1,604	3,119	3,648	4,260	4,902	5,706	6,492
Administrative expenditures, total	Mil. dol . .	466	814	1,171	1,363	1,606	1,804	1,995	2,241
State share	Mil. dol . .	117	243	366	426	545	593	652	724
Federal share	Mil. dol . .	349	571	804	938	1,061	1,212	1,343	1,517
Program savings, total	Mil. dol . .	127	86	26	−77	−190	−201	−171	−278
State share	Mil. dol . .	230	317	381	403	338	385	434	462
Federal share	Mil. dol . .	−103	−231	−355	−480	−528	−586	−605	−740
Total fees and costs recovered for									
non-AFDC cases	Mil. dol . .	5	3	7	7	22	34	29	31
Percentage of AFDC payments recovered .	Percent .	5.2	7.3	9.8	10.0	10.3	10.7	11.4	12.0

NA Not available.   [1] Reflects cases that are no longer receiving AFDC but still have outstanding child support due.   [2] Through 1990 covers new support orders and modifications. Beginning 1991 covers only new support orders.   [3] Beginning 1985, States were required to pass along to the family the first $50 of any current child support collected each month.
Source: U.S. Department of Health and Human Services, Office of Child Support Enforcement, *Annual Report to Congress.*

No. 619. Percent of Adult Population Doing Volunteer Work: 1993

[Covers persons 18 years and over. Volunteers are persons who worked in some way to help others for no monetary pay during the previous year. See headnote, table 620]

AGE, SEX, RACE AND HISPANIC ORIGIN	Percent of population volunteering	Average hours volunteered per week	EDUCATIONAL ATTAINMENT AND HOUSEHOLD INCOME	Percent of population volunteering	Average hours volunteered per week	TYPE OF ACTIVITY	Percent of volunteers involved in activity
Total	47.7	4.2	Elementary school . . .	31.8	(B)	Arts, culture, humanities . .	4.4
			Some high school	29.9	(B)	Education	15.7
18-24 years old	45.3	4.0	High school graduate .	40.4	3.6	Environment	6.2
25-34 years old	46.1	3.1	Technical, trade, or			Health	10.8
35-44 years old	54.5	4.8	business school	49.2	5.0	Human services	9.8
45-54 years old	53.8	5.2	Some college	56.9	4.3		
55-64 years old	46.6	4.1	College graduate	67.2	5.0	Informal	17.2
65-74 years old	42.9	4.8				International, foreign	1.3
75 years old and over .	36.4	(B)	Under $10,000	34.0	(B)	Political organizations . . .	3.7
			$10,000-$19,999	37.0	3.7	Private, community	
Male	43.9	4.3	$20,000-$29,999	52.5	4.2	foundations	2.2
Female	51.2	4.2	$30,000-$39,999	56.3	4.9		
			$40,000-$49,999	55.1	3.6	Public and societal benefit .	5.4
White	51.1	4.2	$50,000-$59,999	56.9	4.1	Recreation - adults	5.4
Black	29.1	3.7	$60,000-$74,999	66.6	6.1	Religion	24.1
			$75,000-$99,999	58.1	(B)	Work-related organizations	6.9
Hispanic [1]	32.4	(B)	$100,000 or more	67.5	(B)	Youth development	11.7

B Base figure too small to meet statistical standards for reliability.   [1] Hispanic persons may be of any race.

Source: Hodgkinson, Virginia, Murray Weitzman, and the Gallup Organization, Inc., *Giving and Volunteering in the United States: 1994 Edition.* (Copyright and published by INDEPENDENT SECTOR, Washington, DC, fall 1994.)

No. 620. Charity Contributions—Average Dollar Amount and Percent of Household Income, 1987 to 1993, and by Age of Respondent and Household Income, 1993

[Estimates cover households' contribution activity for the year and are based on respondents' replies as to contribution and volunteer activity of household. Based on a sample survey conducted during the spring of the following year and subject to sampling variability; see source]

YEAR AND AGE	ALL CONTRIBUTING HOUSEHOLDS		CONTRIBUTORS AND VOLUNTEERS		HOUSEHOLD INCOME	ALL CONTRIBUTING HOUSEHOLDS		CONTRIBUTORS AND VOLUNTEERS	
	Average amount (dol.)	Percent of household income	Average amount (dol.)	Percent of household income		Average amount (dol.)	Percent of household income	Average amount (dol.)	Percent of household income
1987	790	1.9	1,021	2.4	**1993—**				
1991	899	2.2	1,155	2.6	Under $10,000	207	2.7	(B)	(B)
1993, total	**880**	**2.1**	**1,193**	**2.6**	$10,000-$19,999. . .	332	2.3	460	3.1
18-24 years.	514	1.2	(B)	(B)	$20,000-$29,999. . .	668	2.7	862	3.4
25-34 years.	520	1.4	666	1.6	$30,000-$39,999. . .	715	2.0	824	2.3
35-44 years.	978	1.8	1,376	2.5	$40,000-$49,999. . .	572	1.3	713	1.6
45-54 years. . . : . .	1,241	2.5	1,766	3.3	$50,000-$59,999. . .	632	1.1	758	1.4
55-64 years.	1,037	2.4	1,222	2.6	$60,000-$74,999 . . .	1,572	2.3	2,006	3.0
65-74 years.	1,135	3.9	1,832	4.8	$75,000-$99,999. . .	1,720	2.0	(B)	(B)
75 years and over . .	666	3.2	(B)	(B)	$100,000 and over .	3,213	3.2	(B)	(B)

B Base too small to meet statistical standards for reliability.

No. 621. Charity Contributions—Percent of Households Contributing, by Dollar Amount, 1987 to 1993, and Type of Charity, 1993

[**In percent, except as noted**. See headnote, table 620]

ANNUAL AMOUNT OF HOUSEHOLD CONTRIBUTIONS	ALL HOUSEHOLDS			GIVERS			TYPE OF CHARITY	1993	
	1987	1991	1993	1987	1991	1993		Percentage of households	Average contribution [1] (dol.)
None	28.9	27.8	26.6	(X)	(X)	(X)	Arts, culture, humanities . . .	8.1	139
Givers.	71.0	72.2	73.4	100.0	100.0	100.0	Education.	17.5	424
$1 to $100	20.8	14.9	20.9	32.7	24.9	32.3	Environment	11.6	89
$101 to $200	7.4	8.1	9.8	11.6	13.5	15.2	Health	25.7	139
$201 to $300	6.6	7.3	5.6	10.5	12.2	8.6	Human services.	26.7	208
$301 to $400	3.5	3.3	3.7	5.6	5.6	5.8	International	2.8	(B)
$401 to $500	3.2	3.2	4.0	5.0	5.4	6.2	Private, community		
$501 to $600	2.3	2.6	3.0	3.7	4.4	4.6	foundations.	5.3	144
$601 to $700	2.0	2.5	2.0	3.2	4.2	3.1	Public, societal benefit	11.2	160
$701 to $999	3.7	3.4	2.9	5.8	5.7	4.6	Recreation - adults.	4.6	193
$1,000 or more	13.9	14.5	12.8	21.9	24.2	19.7	Religion	49.2	817
Not reported	7.6	12.4	8.6	(X)	(X)	(X)	Youth development	17.9	106

B Base too small to meet statistical standards for reliability.   X Not applicable.   [1] Average contribution per contributing household.

Source of tables 620 and 621: Hodgkinson, Virginia, Murray Weitzman, and the Gallup Organization, Inc., *Giving and Volunteering in the United States: 1994 Edition*. (Copyright and published by INDEPENDENT SECTOR, Washington, DC, fall 1994.)

No. 622. Private Philanthropy Funds, by Source and Allocation: 1980 to 1993

[**In billions of dollars.** Estimates for sources of funds based on U.S. Internal Revenue Service reports of individual charitable deductions, household surveys of giving by Independent Sector, and, for years prior to 1986, an econometric model. For corporate giving, data are those prepared by the Council for Aid to Education. Data about foundation donations are based upon surveys of foundations and data provided by the Foundation Center. Estimates of the allocation of funds were derived from surveys of nonprofits conducted by source and other groups. See *Historical Statistics, Colonial Times to 1970*, series H 398-411, for similar but not comparable data]

SOURCE AND ALLOCATION	1980	1982	1983	1984	1985	1986	1987	1988	1989	1990	1991	1992	1993
Total funds	**48.6**	**59.2**	**63.2**	**68.8**	**73.2**	**83.9**	**90.3**	**98.4**	**107.0**	**111.9**	**117.1**	**121.9**	**126.2**
Individuals.	40.7	47.6	52.1	56.5	58.7	67.6	72.3	80.1	87.8	91.5	95.6	99.2	102.6
Foundations.	2.8	3.2	3.6	4.0	4.9	5.4	5.9	6.2	6.6	7.2	7.7	8.6	9.2
Corporations	2.2	3.2	3.7	4.3	4.8	5.1	5.5	5.6	5.8	5.9	6.0	5.9	5.9
Charitable bequests	2.9	5.2	3.9	4.0	4.8	5.7	6.6	6.6	7.0	7.6	7.8	8.2	8.5
Allocation:													
Religion.	22.2	28.1	31.8	35.6	38.2	41.7	43.5	45.2	47.8	49.8	53.9	54.9	57.2
Health.	5.3	6.2	6.7	6.8	7.7	8.4	9.2	9.6	9.9	9.9	9.7	10.2	10.8
Education	5.0	6.0	6.7	7.3	8.2	9.4	9.8	10.2	11.0	12.4	13.5	14.3	15.1
Human service	4.9	6.3	7.2	7.9	8.5	9.1	9.8	10.5	11.4	11.8	11.1	11.6	12.5
Arts, culture and humanities . .	3.2	5.0	4.2	4.5	5.1	5.8	6.3	6.8	7.5	7.9	8.8	9.3	9.6
Public/societal benefit.	1.5	1.7	1.9	1.9	2.2	2.5	2.9	3.2	3.8	4.9	4.9	5.1	5.4
Environment/wildlife	(1)	(1)	(1)	(1)	(1)	(1)	2.1	2.4	2.0	2.6	2.9	3.1	3.2
International	(1)	(1)	(1)	(1)	(1)	(1)	0.9	1.0	1.2	1.5	1.8	1.7	1.9
Unclassified	6.5	6.0	4.8	4.8	3.3	7.0	5.7	10.0	12.5	11.0	10.5	11.7	10.7

[1] Included in "Unclassified."
Source: AAFRC Trust for Philanthropy, New York, NY, *Giving USA*, annual, (copyright).

No. 623. Foundations—Number and Finances, by Asset Size

[Figures are for latest year reported by foundations, usually **1991** or **1992**. Covers nongovernmental nonprofit organizations with funds and programs managed by their own trustees or directors, whose goals were to maintain or aid social, educational, religious, or other activities deemed to serve the common good. Excludes organizations that make general appeals to the public for funds, act as trade associations for industrial or other special groups, or do not currently award grants]

ASSET SIZE	Number	Assets (mil. dol.)	Gifts received (mil. dol.)	Expenditures (mil. dol.)	Grants (mil. dol.)	PERCENT DISTRIBUTION				
						Number	Assets	Gifts received	Expenditures	Grants
Total	35,765	176,825	6,180	12,403	10,209	100.0	100.0	100.0	100.0	100.0
Under $50,000.	8,283	148	246	312	287	23.1	0.1	3.9	2.5	2.9
$50,000-$99,999	3,498	255	76	101	88	9.8	0.1	1.2	0.8	0.9
$100,000-$249,999.	5,866	962	182	249	218	16.4	0.5	2.9	2.0	2.1
$250,000-$499,999.	4,457	1,594	214	304	266	12.5	0.9	3.5	2.4	2.6
$500,000-$999,999.	4,057	2,898	259	394	338	11.3	1.6	4.2	3.2	3.3
$1,000,000-$4,999,999	6,292	13,977	1,203	1,539	1,307	17.6	7.9	19.5	12.4	12.8
$5,000,000-$9,999,999	1,384	9,686	664	877	722	3.9	5.5	10.7	7.1	7.1
$10,000,000-$49,999,999 . . .	1,471	30,237	1,359	2,481	2,048	4.1	17.1	22.0	20.0	20.1
$50,000,000-$99,999,999 . . .	229	15,848	622	971	794	0.6	9.0	10.1	7.8	7.8
$100,000,000-$249,999,999. . .	137	20,474	899	1,368	1,043	0.4	11.6	14.6	11.0	10.2
$250,000,000 or more.	91	80,746	454	3,807	3,097	0.3	45.7	7.3	30.7	30.3

Source: The Foundation Center, New York, NY, *Guide to U.S. Foundations, Their Trustees, Officers, and Donors*, vol. 1, 1994.

No. 624. Foundations—Grants Reported, by Subject Field and Recipient Organization: 1993

[Covers grants of $10,000 or more in size. Based on reports of 1,020 foundations. Grant sample totaling $5.62 billion represented over half of all grant dollars awarded by private, corporate, and community foundations. For definition of foundations, see headnote, table 623]

SUBJECT FIELD	NUMBER OF GRANTS		DOLLAR VALUE OF GRANTS		RECIPIENT ORGANIZATION [1]	NUMBER OF GRANTS		DOLLAR VALUE OF GRANTS	
	Number	Percent distribution	Amount (mil. dol.)	Percent distribution		Number	Percent distribution	Amount (mil. dol.)	Percent distribution
Total	68,495	100.0	5,621	100.0	Community improvement				
Arts and culture	10,041	14.7	835	14.8	organizations	3,044	4.4	210	3.7
Education	15,036	22.0	1,337	23.8	Educational institutions.	19,805	28.9	2,036	36.2
Environment & animals . .	3,768	5.5	290	5.2	Colleges & universities . . .	11,518	16.8	1,356	24.1
					Educational support				
Health	9,326	13.6	1,025	18.2	agencies.	2,940	4.3	267	4.7
Human services.	15,205	22.2	822	14.6	Schools	3,481	5.1	231	4.1
International affairs,					Federated funds	2,310	3.4	228	4.1
development & peace . .	2,167	3.2	205	3.6	Hospitals/medical care				
					facilities	3,818	5.6	372	6.6
Public/societal benefit . . .	7,913	11.6	632	11.2	Human service agencies. . . .	12,287	17.9	626	11.1
Science and technology .	2,029	3.0	222	3.9	Museums/historical societies .	2,943	4.3	352	6.3
					Performing arts groups.	3,631	5.3	231	4.1
Social sciences	1,255	1.8	153	2.7	Professional societies &				
Religion	1,668	2.4	95	1.7	associations	2,053	3.0	182	3.2
Other.	87	0.1	7	0.1	Public administration				
					agencies	2,161	3.2	222	3.9

[1] Grants may be awarded to multiple types of recipient organizations and would thereby be double-counted.

Source: The Foundation Center, New York, NY, *The Foundation Grants Index, 1995*, 23rd Edition, 1994.

No. 625. Corporate Philanthropy—Donations, by Type of Beneficiary: 1980 to 1992

[**In millions of dollars.** Based on a sample of corporations that gave at least $100,000; see source]

BENEFICIARY	1980	1984	1985	1986	1987	1988	1989	1990	1991	1992
Total [1]	994.6	1,444.3	1,694.7	1,673.7	1,658.4	1,645.7	1,820.1	2,051.5	2,245.5	2,061.4
Health and human services [1]	337.9	399.9	494.1	468.6	450.5	480.2	481.0	580.2	608.9	570.8
Federated drives	170.7	193.9	(NA)	225.9	203.6	235.0	218.3	262.6	285.0	271.4
Education [1]	375.8	561.7	650.0	718.0	610.1	614.1	699.8	789.2	783.6	764.7
Employee matching gifts [2]	45.4	72.2	(NA)	98.7	108.3	108.2	115.0	105.0	142.0	143.7
Culture and art	108.7	154.7	187.5	198.7	178.6	183.6	201.2	243.6	265.4	243.6
Civic, community activities [1]	116.8	271.6	279.5	220.5	236.1	212.1	253.5	254.5	253.5	214.3
Community improvement.	47.0	30.5	(NA)	12.6	53.4	57.3	87.0	43.0	(NA)	(NA)
Environment; ecology	10.8	97.1	(NA)	35.9	44.0	17.3	11.7	18.7	22.0	(NA)

NA Not available.   [1] Includes other beneficiaries not shown separately.   [2] Higher education institutions.

Source: The Conference Board, New York, NY, *Annual Survey of Corporate Contributions* (copyright).

Labor Force, Employment, and Earnings

This section presents statistics on the labor force; its distribution by occupation and industry affiliation; and the supply of, demand for, and conditions of labor. The chief source of these data is the Current Population Survey conducted by the U.S. Bureau of the Census. Comprehensive historical data are published by the Bureau of Labor Statistics (BLS) in *Labor Force Statistics Derived From the Current Population Survey, 1948-87, BLS Bulletin 2307.* These data are supplemented on a current basis by the BLS monthly publications *Employment and Earnings* and the *Monthly Labor Review.* Detailed data on the labor force are also available from the Census Bureau's decennial census of population.

Types of data.—Most statistics in this section are obtained by two methods: household interviews or questionnaires, and reports of establishment payroll records. Each method provides data which the other cannot suitably supply. Population characteristics, for example, are readily obtainable only from the household survey, while detailed industrial classifications can be readily derived only from establishment records.

Household data are obtained from a monthly sample survey of the population. The Current Population Survey (CPS) is used to gather data for the calendar week including the 12th of the month and provides current comprehensive data on the labor force (see text, section 1). The CPS provides information on the work status of the population without duplication since each person is classified as employed, unemployed, or not in the labor force. Employed persons holding more than one job are counted only once, according to the job at which they worked the most hours during the survey week.

Monthly data from the CPS are published by the Bureau of Labor Statistics in *Employment and Earnings* and the related reports mentioned above. Data presented include national totals of the number of persons in the civilian labor force by sex, race, Hispanic origin, and age; the number employed; hours of work; industry and

---

In Brief

Labor force participation rate of married women with children under 6 years old:

1960	*18.6%*
1970	*30.3%*
1980	*45.1%*
1994	*61.7%*

Fastest growing occupations, 1992–2005:

Home health aids	*+138%*
Human services workers	*+136%*
Personal and home care aides	*+130%*
Computer engineers and scientists	*+112%*

---

occupational groups; and the number unemployed, reasons for, and duration of unemployment. Monthly data from the CPS are also presented for regions and 11 large States. Annual data shown in this section are averages of monthly figures for each calendar year, unless otherwise specified.

In addition to monthly data, the CPS also produces annual estimates of employment and unemployment for each State, 50 large metropolitan statistical areas, and selected cities. These estimates are published by BLS in its annual *Geographic Profile of Employment and Unemployment.* More detailed geographic data (e.g., for counties and cities) are provided by the decennial population censuses.

Data based on establishment records are compiled by BLS and cooperating State agencies as part of an ongoing Current Employment Statistics Program. Data, gathered from a sample of employers who voluntarily complete mail questionnaires monthly, are supplemented by data from other government agencies and adjusted at intervals to data from government social insurance program reports. The estimates exclude proprietors of unincorporated firms, self-employed persons, private household workers, unpaid family workers, agricultural workers, and the Armed Forces. In March 1993, reporting establishments employed 9 million manufacturing workers (51 percent of the total manufacturing employment at the time), 20 million workers in nonmanufacturing industries (27 percent of the total in nonmanufacturing), and 15 million Federal, State, and local government employees (77 percent of total government).

The establishment survey counts workers each time they appear on a payroll during the reference week (as with the CPS, the week including the 12th of the month). Thus, unlike the CPS, a person with two jobs is counted twice. The establishment survey is designed to provide detailed industry information for the Nation, States, and metropolitan areas on nonfarm wage and salary employment, average weekly hours, and average hourly and weekly earnings. Establishment survey data are published in *Employment and Earnings* and the *Monthly Labor Review,* cited above. Historical national and geographic data are published in *BLS Bulletin 2445, Employment, Hours, and Earnings, United States, 1909-94;* and *Bulletin 2411, Employment, Hours, and Earnings, States and Areas, 1987-92.*

Labor force.—According to the CPS definitions, the civilian labor force comprises all civilians in the noninstitutional population 16 years and over classified as "employed" or "unemployed" according to the following criteria: Employed civilians comprise (a) all civilians, who, during the reference week, did any work for pay or profit (minimum of an hour's work) or worked 15 hours or more as unpaid workers in a family enterprise, and (b) all civilians who were not working but who had jobs or businesses from which they were temporarily absent for noneconomic reasons (illness, weather conditions, vacation, labor-management dispute, etc.) whether they were paid for the time off or were seeking other jobs. Unemployed persons comprise all civilians who had no employment during the reference week, who made specific efforts to find a job within the previous 4 weeks (such as applying directly to an employer, or to a public employment service, or checking with friends), and who were available for work during that week, except for temporary illness. Persons on layoff from a job and expecting recall are also classified as unemployed. All other civilian persons,

16 years old and over, are "not in the labor force."

Beginning in 1982, changes in the estimation procedures and the introduction of 1980 census data caused substantial increases in the population and estimates of persons in all labor force categories. Rates on labor force characteristics, however, were essentially unchanged. In order to avoid major breaks in series, some 30,000 labor force series were adjusted back to 1970. The effect of the 1982 revisions on various data series and an explanation of the adjustment procedure used are described in "Revisions in the Current Population Survey in January 1982," in the February 1982 issue of *Employment and Earnings.* The revisions did not, however, smooth out the breaks in series occurring between 1972 and 1979, and data users should make allowances for them in making certain data comparisons.

Beginning in January 1985, and again in January 1986, the CPS estimation procedures were revised due to the implementation of a new sample design (for the 1985 revision) and to reflect an explicit estimate of the number of undocumented immigrants (for the 1986 revision). The greatest impact of these revisions was on estimates of persons of Hispanic origin. Where possible, these estimates were revised back to January 1980. A description of the changes and an indication of their effect on the national estimates of labor force characteristics appear in the February 1985 and February 1986 issues of *Employment and Earnings* respectively.

Beginning in January 1994, several of changes were introduced into the CPS that effect all data comparisons with prior years. These changes include the results of a major redesign of the survey questionnaire and collection methodology, revisions to some of the labor force concepts and definitions, and the introduction of 1990 census population controls, adjusted for the estimated undercount. An explanation of the changes and their effects on the labor force data appears in "Revisions in the Current Population Survey Effective January 1994" in the February 1994 issue of *Employment and Earnings.*

Hours and earnings.—Average hourly earnings, based on establishment data, are gross earnings (i.e., earnings before payroll deductions) and include overtime premiums; they exclude irregular bonuses and value of payments in kind. Hours are those for which pay was received. Wages and salaries from the CPS consist of total monies received for work performed by an employee during the income year. It includes wages, salaries, commissions, tips, piece-rate payments, and cash bonuses earned before deductions were made for taxes, bonds, union dues, etc. Persons who worked 35 hours or more are classified as working full time (see table 632).

Industrial and occupational groups.— Establishments responding to the establishment survey are classified into industries on the basis of their principal product or activity (determined by annual sales volume) in accordance with the *Standard Industrial Classification (SIC) Manual,* Office of Management and Budget. The SIC is a classification structure for the entire national economy. The structure provides data on a division and industry code basis, according to the level of industrial detail. For example, manufacturing is a major industrial division; food and kindred products (code 20) is one of its major groups. One of the ways this group is further divided is into meat products (code 201) and meat packing plants (code 2011). Periodically, the SIC is revised to reflect changes in the industrial composition of the economy. The *1987 SIC Manual* has been issued; the previous was the *1972 SIC Manual.* Tables shown in this *Abstract* indicate which *SIC Manual* the data shown are based on.

Industry data derived from the CPS for 1983-91 utilize the 1980 census industrial classification developed from the 1972 SIC. CPS data from 1971 to 1982 were based on the 1970 census classification system which was developed from the 1967 SIC. Most of the industry categories were not affected by the change in classification.

The occupational classification system used in the 1980 census and in the CPS for 1983-91 evolved from the 1980 Standard Occupational Classification (SOC) system, first introduced in 1977. Occupational categories used in the 1980 census classification system are so radically different from the 1970 census system used in the CPS through 1982, that their implementation represented a break in historical data series. In cases where data have not yet been converted to the 1980 classifications and still reflect the 1970 classifications (e.g., table 668), comparisons between the two systems should not be made. To help users bridge the data gap, a limited set of estimates was developed for the 1972-82 period based on the new classifications. The estimates were developed by means of applying conversion factors created by double coding a 20-percent sample of CPS occupational records for 6 months during 1981-82. For further details, contact BLS.

Beginning in January 1992, the occupational and industrial classification system used in the 1990 census were introduced into the CPS. (These systems were largely based on the 1980 Standard Occupational Classification and the 1987 Standard Industrial Classification.) There were a few breaks in comparability between the 1980 and 1990 census– based systems, particularly within the "technical, sales, and administrative support" categories. The most notable changes in industry classification were the shift of several industries from "business services" to "professional services" and the splitting of some industries into smaller, more detailed categories. A number of industry titles were changed as well, with no change in content.

Productivity.—The Bureau of Labor Statistics (BLS) publishes data on productivity as measured by output per hour (labor productivity), output per combined unit of labor and capital input (multifactor productivity), and, for manufacturing industries, output per combined unit of capital, labor, energy, materials, and purchased service inputs. Labor productivity and related indexes are published for the business sector as a whole and its major subsectors: nonfarm business, manufacturing, nonfinancial corporations, 177 specific industries, and various functional areas of the Federal and State and local governments. Multifactor productivity and related measures are published for the private business sector and its major subsectors. Productivity indexes which take into account capital, labor, energy, materials, and service inputs are published for the 20 major two-digit industry groups which comprise the manufacturing sector and for the tire and inner tubes, footwear, steel, farm and garden machinery, motor vehicles, and railroad transportation industries. The major sector data are published in the BLS quarterly news release, *Productivity and Costs* and in the annual *Multifactor Productivity Measures* release. The specific industry productivity measures are published annually in the BLS Bulletin, *Productivity Measures for Selected Industries and Government Services,* and the *Handbook of Labor Statistics.* Detailed information on methods, limitations, and data sources appears in the *BLS Handbook of Methods,* BLS Bulletin 2414 (1992), chapters 10 and 11.

Unions.—As defined here, unions include traditional labor unions and employee associations similar to labor unions. Data on union membership status provided by BLS are for employed wage and salary workers and relate to their principal job. Earnings by union membership status are usual weekly earnings of full-time wage and salary workers. The information is collected through the Current Population Survey. For a full description of the method of collection and comparability with earlier data, see "New Data on Union Members and Their Earnings" in the January 1985 issue of *Employment and Earnings,* and "Changing Employment Patterns of Organized Workers" in the February 1985 issue of the *Monthly Labor Review.* Collective bargaining settlements data are available for bargaining situations involving 1,000 or more workers in private industry and State and local government.

Work stoppages.—Work stoppages include all strikes and lockouts known to BLS which last for at least one full day or shift and involve 1,000 or more workers. All stoppages, whether or not authorized by a union, legal or illegal, are counted. Excluded are work slowdowns and instances where employees report to work late, or leave early, to attend mass meetings or mass rallies.

Seasonal adjustment.—Many economic statistics reflect a regularly recurring seasonal movement which can be estimated on the basis of past experience. By eliminating that part of the change which can be ascribed to usual seasonal variation (e.g., climate or school openings and closings), it is possible to observe the cyclical and other nonseasonal movements in the series. However, in evaluating deviations from the seasonal pattern—that is, changes in a seasonally adjusted series— it is important to note that seasonal adjustment is merely an approximation based on past experience. Seasonally adjusted estimates have a broader margin of possible error than the original data on which they are based, since they are subject not only to sampling and other errors, but also are affected by the uncertainties of the adjustment process itself.

Statistical reliability.—For discussion of statistical collection, estimation, sampling procedures, and measures of statistical reliability applicable to Census Bureau and BLS data, see Appendix III.

Historical statistics.—Tabular headnotes provide cross-references, where applicable, to *Historical Statistics of the United States, Colonial Times to 1970.* See Appendix IV.

Figure 13.1
Fastest Growing Occupations: 1992 to 2005

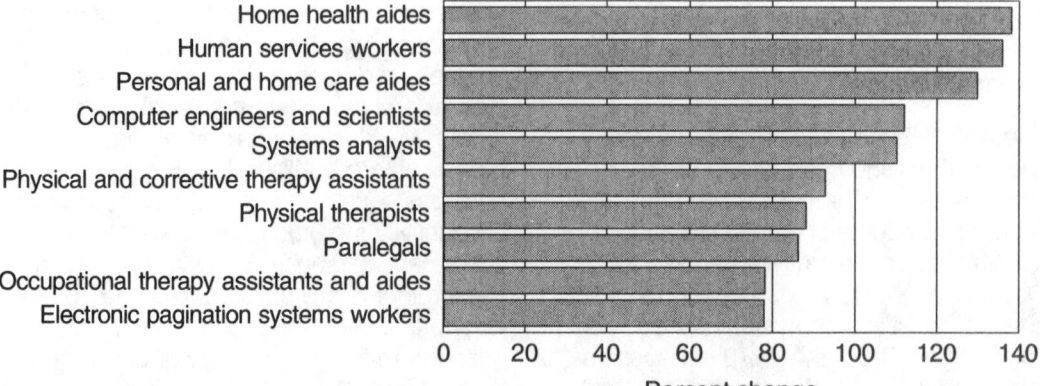

Source: Chart prepared by U.S. Bureau of the Census. For data, see table 639.

No. 626. Employment Status of the Civilian Population: 1950 to 1994

[In thousands, except as indicated. Annual averages of monthly figures. For the civilian noninstitutional population 16 years old and over. Based on Current Population Survey; see text, section 1, and Appendix III. See also *Historical Statistics, Colonial Times to 1970*, series D 11-19 and D 85-86]

YEAR	Civilian noninstitutional population	CIVILIAN LABOR FORCE							NOT IN LABOR FORCE	
		Total	Percent of population	Employed	Employment/population ratio [1]	Unemployed			Number	Percent of population
						Number	Percent of labor force			
1950	104,995	62,208	59.2	58,918	56.1	3,288	5.3		42,787	40.8
1960	117,245	69,628	59.4	65,778	56.1	3,852	5.5		47,617	40.6
1970	137,085	82,771	60.4	78,678	57.4	4,093	4.9		54,315	39.6
1980	167,745	106,940	63.8	99,303	59.2	7,637	7.1		60,806	36.2
1983	174,215	111,550	64.0	100,834	57.9	10,717	9.6		62,665	36.0
1984	176,383	113,544	64.4	105,005	59.5	8,539	7.5		62,839	35.6
1985	178,206	115,461	64.8	107,150	60.1	8,312	7.2		62,744	35.2
1986	180,587	117,834	65.3	109,597	60.7	8,237	7.0		62,752	34.7
1987	182,753	119,865	65.6	112,440	61.5	7,425	6.2		62,888	34.4
1988	184,613	121,669	65.9	114,968	62.3	6,701	5.5		62,944	34.1
1989	186,393	123,869	66.5	117,342	63.0	6,528	5.3		62,523	33.5
1990	188,049	124,787	66.4	117,914	62.7	6,874	5.5		63,262	33.6
1991	189,765	125,303	66.0	116,877	61.6	8,426	6.7		64,462	34.0
1992	191,576	126,982	66.3	117,598	61.4	9,384	7.4		64,593	33.7
1993 [2]	193,550	128,040	66.2	119,306	61.6	8,734	6.8		65,509	33.8
1994 [2]	196,814	131,056	66.6	123,060	62.5	7,996	6.1		65,758	33.4

[1] Civilian employed as a percent of the civilian noninstitutional population.   [2] Data beginning 1994, not directly comparable with earlier years. See text, section 13, and February 1994 issue of *Employment and Earnings*.

Source: U.S. Bureau of Labor Statistics, Bulletin 2307; and *Employment and Earnings*, monthly, January issues.

No. 627. Civilian Labor Force and Participation Rates, With Projections: 1970 to 2005

[For civilian noninstitutional population 16 years old and over. Annual averages of monthly figures. Rates are based on annual average civilian noninstitutional population of each specified group and represent proportion of each specified group in the civilian labor force. Based on Current Population Survey; see text, section 1, and Appendix III. See also *Historical Statistics, Colonial Times to 1970*, series D 42-48]

RACE, SEX, AND AGE	CIVILIAN LABOR FORCE (millions)						PARTICIPATION RATE (percent)					
	1970	1980	1990	1994 [1]	2000, proj.	2005, proj.	1970	1980	1990	1994 [1]	2000, proj.	2005, proj.
Total [2]	82.8	106.9	124.8	131.0	141.8	150.5	60.4	63.8	66.4	66.6	68.2	68.8
White	73.6	93.6	107.2	111.1	118.8	124.8	60.2	64.1	66.8	67.1	68.7	69.3
Male	46.0	54.5	59.3	60.7	63.8	66.0	80.0	78.2	76.9	75.9	76.0	75.3
Female	27.5	39.1	47.9	50.3	55.1	58.8	42.6	51.2	57.5	58.9	61.8	63.6
Black [3]	9.2	10.9	13.5	14.5	16.0	17.4	61.8	61.0	63.3	63.4	65.5	66.2
Male	5.2	5.6	6.7	7.1	7.8	8.3	76.5	70.3	70.1	69.1	70.8	70.5
Female	4.0	5.3	6.8	7.4	8.2	9.0	49.5	53.1	57.8	58.7	61.2	62.6
Hispanic [4]	(NA)	6.1	9.6	12.0	14.3	16.6	(NA)	64.0	67.0	66.1	68.0	68.4
Male	(NA)	3.8	5.8	7.2	8.7	9.6	(NA)	81.4	81.2	79.2	80.2	79.5
Female	(NA)	2.3	3.8	4.8	5.8	7.0	(NA)	47.4	53.0	52.9	55.8	57.3
Male	51.2	61.5	68.2	70.8	75.3	78.7	79.7	77.4	76.1	75.1	75.3	74.7
16 to 19 years	4.0	5.0	3.9	3.9	4.4	4.6	56.1	60.5	55.7	54.1	55.4	55.5
20 to 24 years	5.7	8.6	7.3	7.5	7.2	8.1	83.3	85.9	84.3	83.1	84.0	84.4
25 to 34 years	11.3	17.0	19.8	18.9	17.2	16.5	96.4	95.2	94.2	92.6	73.1	93.5
35 to 44 years	10.5	11.8	17.3	19.0	20.7	19.6	96.9	95.5	94.4	92.8	93.7	93.5
45 to 54 years	10.4	9.9	11.2	13.0	15.8	18.1	94.3	91.2	90.7	89.1	90.4	90.2
55 to 64 years	7.1	7.2	6.8	6.4	7.7	9.6	83.0	72.1	67.7	65.5	69.1	69.7
65 years and over	2.2	1.9	2.0	2.2	2.1	2.2	26.8	19.0	16.4	16.8	15.0	14.7
Female	31.5	45.5	56.6	60.2	66.6	71.8	43.3	51.5	57.5	58.8	61.6	63.2
16 to 19 years	3.2	4.4	3.5	3.6	4.0	4.2	44.0	52.9	51.8	51.3	52.0	52.4
20 to 24 years	4.9	7.3	6.6	6.6	6.4	7.2	57.7	68.9	71.6	71.0	72.5	73.6
25 to 34 years	5.7	12.3	16.0	15.5	14.9	14.8	45.0	65.5	73.6	74.0	78.1	80.7
35 to 44 years	6.0	8.6	14.6	16.3	18.8	18.6	51.1	65.5	76.5	77.1	83.0	86.2
45 to 54 years	6.5	7.0	9.3	11.4	14.7	17.4	54.4	59.9	71.2	74.6	79.7	82.8
55 to 64 years	4.2	4.7	5.1	5.3	6.2	7.8	43.0	41.3	45.3	48.9	50.3	52.4
65 years and over	1.1	1.2	1.5	1.7	1.6	1.7	9.7	8.1	8.7	9.2	8.5	8.8

NA Not available.   [1] See footnote 2, table 626.   [2] Beginning 1980, includes other races not shown separately.   [3] For 1970, Black and other.   [4] Persons of Hispanic origin may be of any race.

Source: U.S. Bureau of Labor Statistics, Bulletin 2307; *Employment and Earnings*, monthly, January issues; *Monthly Labor Review*, November 1993; and unpublished data.

No. 628. Employment Status of the Civilian Population: 1960 to 1994

[In thousands, except as indicated. Annual averages of monthly figures. For the civilian noninstitutional population 16 years old and over. Based on Current Population Survey; see text, section 1, and Appendix III. See also *Historical Statistics, Colonial Times to 1970*, series D 11-19 and D 85-86]

YEAR, SEX, RACE, AND HISPANIC ORIGIN	Civilian noninsti- tutional popula- tion	CIVILIAN LABOR FORCE						NOT IN LABOR FORCE	
		Total	Percent of popula- tion	Employed	Employ- ment/ popula- tion ratio [1]	Unemployed			
						Number	Percent of labor force	Number	Percent of population
Total: [2]									
1960.	117,245	69,628	59.4	65,778	56.1	3,852	5.5	47,617	40.6
1970.	137,085	82,771	60.4	78,678	57.4	4,093	4.9	54,315	39.6
1980.	167,745	106,940	63.8	99,303	59.2	7,637	7.1	60,806	36.2
1985.	178,206	115,461	64.8	107,150	60.1	8,312	7.2	62,744	35.2
1990.	188,049	124,787	66.4	117,914	62.7	6,874	5.5	63,262	33.6
1991.	189,765	125,303	66.0	116,877	61.6	8,426	6.7	64,462	34.0
1992.	191,576	126,982	66.3	117,598	61.4	9,384	7.4	64,593	33.7
1993.	193,550	128,040	66.2	119,306	61.6	8,734	6.8	65,509	33.8
1994 [3] . . .	196,814	131,056	66.6	123,060	62.5	7,996	6.1	65,758	33.4
Male:									
1960.	55,662	46,388	83.3	43,904	78.9	2,486	5.4	9,274	16.7
1970.	64,304	51,228	79.7	48,990	76.2	2,238	4.4	13,076	20.3
1980.	79,398	61,453	77.4	57,186	72.0	4,267	6.9	17,945	22.6
1985.	84,469	64,411	76.3	59,891	70.9	4,521	7.0	20,058	23.7
1990.	89,650	68,234	76.1	64,435	71.9	3,799	5.6	21,417	23.9
1991.	90,552	68,411	75.5	63,593	70.2	4,817	7.0	22,141	24.5
1992.	91,541	69,184	75.6	63,805	69.7	5,380	7.8	22,356	24.4
1993.	92,620	69,633	75.2	64,700	69.9	4,932	7.1	22,987	24.8
1994 [3] . . .	94,355	70,817	75.1	66,450	70.4	4,367	6.2	23,538	24.9
Female:									
1960.	61,582	23,240	37.7	21,874	35.5	1,366	5.9	38,343	62.3
1970.	72,782	31,543	43.3	29,688	40.8	1,855	5.9	41,239	56.7
1980.	88,348	45,487	51.5	42,117	47.7	3,370	7.4	42,861	48.5
1985.	93,736	51,050	54.5	47,259	50.4	3,791	7.4	42,686	45.5
1990.	98,399	56,554	57.5	53,479	54.3	3,075	5.4	41,845	42.5
1991.	99,214	56,893	57.3	53,284	53.7	3,609	6.3	42,321	42.7
1992.	100,035	57,798	57.8	53,793	53.8	4,005	6.9	42,237	42.2
1993.	100,930	58,407	57.9	54,606	54.1	3,801	6.5	42,522	42.1
1994 [3] . . .	102,460	60,239	58.8	56,610	55.3	3,629	6.0	42,221	41.2
White:									
1960.	105,282	61,915	58.8	58,850	55.9	3,065	5.0	43,367	41.2
1970.	122,174	73,556	60.2	70,217	57.5	3,339	4.5	48,618	39.8
1980.	146,122	93,600	64.1	87,715	60.0	5,884	6.3	52,523	35.9
1985.	153,679	99,926	65.0	93,736	61.0	6,191	6.2	53,753	35.0
1990.	160,415	107,177	66.8	102,087	63.6	5,091	4.7	53,237	33.2
1991.	161,511	107,486	66.6	101,039	62.6	6,447	6.0	54,025	33.4
1992.	162,658	108,526	66.7	101,479	62.4	7,047	6.5	54,132	33.3
1993.	163,921	109,359	66.7	102,812	62.7	6,547	6.0	54,562	33.3
1994 [3] . . .	165,555	111,082	67.1	105,190	63.5	5,892	5.3	54,473	32.9
Black:									
1973.	14,917	8,976	60.2	8,128	54.5	846	9.4	5,941	39.8
1980.	17,824	10,865	61.0	9,313	52.2	1,553	14.3	6,959	39.0
1985.	19,664	12,364	62.9	10,501	53.4	1,864	15.1	7,299	37.1
1990.	21,300	13,493	63.3	11,966	56.2	1,527	11.3	7,808	36.7
1991.	21,615	13,542	62.6	11,863	54.9	1,679	12.4	8,074	37.4
1992.	21,958	13,891	63.3	11,933	54.3	1,958	14.1	8,067	36.7
1993.	22,329	13,943	62.4	12,146	54.4	1,796	12.9	8,386	37.6
1994 [3] . . .	22,879	14,502	63.4	12,835	56.1	1,666	11.5	8,377	36.6
Hispanic: [4]									
1980.	9,598	6,146	64.0	5,527	57.6	620	10.1	3,451	36.0
1985.	11,915	7,698	64.6	6,888	57.8	811	10.5	4,217	35.4
1990.	14,297	9,576	67.0	8,808	61.6	769	8.0	4,721	33.0
1991.	14,770	9,762	66.1	8,799	59.6	963	9.9	5,008	33.9
1992.	15,244	10,131	66.5	8,971	58.9	1,160	11.4	5,113	33.5
1993.	15,753	10,377	65.9	9,272	58.9	1,104	10.6	5,377	34.1
1994 [3] . . .	18,117	11,975	66.1	10,788	59.5	1,187	9.9	6,142	33.9
Mexican:									
1986.	7,377	4,941	67.0	4,387	59.5	555	11.2	2,436	33.0
1990.	8,742	5,970	68.3	5,478	62.7	492	8.2	2,773	31.7
1992.	9,368	6,319	67.5	5,581	59.6	739	11.7	3,049	32.5
1993.	9,693	6,499	67.0	5,805	59.9	693	10.7	3,194	33.0
1994 [3] . . .	11,174	7,567	67.7	6,800	60.9	766	10.1	3,608	32.3
Puerto Rican:									
1986.	1,494	804	53.8	691	46.3	113	14.0	690	46.2
1990.	1,546	859	55.6	780	50.5	79	9.1	687	44.4
1992.	1,628	934	57.4	802	49.2	132	14.1	694	42.6
1993.	1,676	950	56.7	828	49.4	122	12.8	725	43.3
1994 [3] . . .	1,854	1,026	55.4	907	48.9	119	11.6	828	44.6
Cuban:									
1986.	842	570	67.7	533	63.3	36	6.4	272	32.3
1990.	847	552	65.1	512	60.4	40	7.2	295	34.8
1992.	867	529	61.1	488	56.3	42	7.9	337	38.9
1993.	927	554	59.8	511	55.1	43	7.8	373	40.2
1994 [3] . . .	1,002	604	60.3	555	55.4	49	8.1	398	39.7

[1] Civilian employed as a percent of the civilian noninstitutional population. [2] Includes other races, not shown separately. [3] See footnote 2, table 626. [4] Persons of Hispanic origin may be of any race. Includes persons of other Hispanic origin, not shown separately.

Source: U.S. Bureau of Labor Statistics, Bulletin 2307; and *Employment and Earnings*, monthly, January issues.

No. 629. Civilian Labor Force and Participation Rates, by Educational Attainment, Sex, and Race: 1970 to 1991

[As of **March,**. For civilian noninstitutional population 25 to 64 years of age. Beginning 1992, the method of computing educational attainment data was changed. See table 630 for later data. Based on Current Population Survey; see text, section 1, and Appendix III]

ITEM	CIVILIAN LABOR FORCE					PARTICIPATION RATE [1]				
	Total (1,000)	Percent distribution				Total	Less than high school	High school graduate	College	
		Less than high school	High school graduate	College					1-3 years	4 years or more
				1-3 years	4 years or more					
Total: [2] 1970	61,765	36.1	38.1	11.8	14.1	70.3	65.5	70.2	73.8	82.3
1980	78,010	20.6	39.8	17.6	22.0	73.9	60.7	74.2	79.5	86.1
1990	99,175	13.4	39.5	20.7	26.4	78.6	60.7	78.2	83.3	88.4
1991	100,480	13.0	39.4	21.1	26.5	78.6	60.7	78.1	83.2	88.4
Male: 1970	39,303	37.5	34.5	12.2	15.7	93.5	89.3	96.3	95.8	96.1
1980	45,417	22.2	35.7	17.7	24.3	89.4	78.8	91.9	92.4	95.3
1990	54,476	15.1	37.2	19.7	28.0	88.8	75.1	89.9	91.5	94.5
1991	55,165	14.7	37.5	20.2	27.6	88.6	75.1	89.3	92.0	94.2
Female: 1970	22,462	33.5	44.3	10.9	11.2	49.0	43.0	51.3	50.9	60.9
1980	32,593	18.4	45.4	17.4	18.7	59.5	43.7	61.2	66.4	73.4
1990	44,699	11.3	42.4	21.9	24.5	68.9	46.2	68.7	75.9	81.1
1991	45,315	10.9	41.6	22.2	25.2	69.1	46.2	68.6	75.2	81.8
White: 1970	55,044	33.7	39.3	12.2	14.8	70.1	65.2	69.7	73.3	81.9
1980	68,509	19.1	40.2	17.7	22.9	74.2	61.4	73.7	79.2	86.0
1990	85,238	12.6	39.6	20.6	27.1	79.2	62.5	78.4	83.3	88.3
1991	86,344	12.2	39.3	21.1	27.4	79.4	62.5	78.3	83.1	88.6
Black: 1970	6,721	55.5	28.2	8.0	8.3	72.0	67.1	76.8	81.0	87.4
1980	7,731	34.7	38.1	16.3	11.0	71.5	58.1	79.2	82.0	90.1
1990	10,537	19.9	42.5	22.1	15.5	74.6	54.5	78.2	84.2	92.0
1991	10,650	19.5	42.9	22.1	15.4	73.9	53.9	77.1	84.1	90.2

[1] Percent of the civilian population in each group in the civilian labor force.   [2] Includes other races, not shown separately. For 1970, White and Black races only.

Source: U.S. Bureau of Labor Statistics, Bulletin 2307; and unpublished data.

No. 630. Civilian Labor Force and Participation Rates, by Educational Attainment, Sex, Race, and Hispanic Origin: 1992 to 1994

[**As of March**. For the civilian noninstitutional population 25 to 64 years of age. See table 663 for unemployment data. Based on Current Population Survey; see text, section 1, and Appendix III]

YEAR, SEX, AND RACE	CIVILIAN LABOR FORCE (1,000)					PARTICIPATION RATE [1]				
	Total	Less than high school diploma	High school graduate, no degree	Less than a bachelor's degree	College graduate	Total	Less than high school diploma	High school gradu-ates, no degree	Less than a bachelor's degree	College graduate
Total: [2]										
1992	102,387	12.2	36.2	25.2	26.4	79.0	60.3	78.3	83.5	88.4
1993	103,504	11.5	35.2	26.3	27.0	78.9	59.6	77.7	82.9	88.3
1994 [3]	104,868	11.0	34.0	27.6	27.3	78.9	58.3	77.8	83.2	88.2
Male:										
1992	55,917	13.9	34.7	23.8	27.5	88.6	75.1	89.0	91.8	93.7
1993	56,544	13.2	33.9	24.7	28.1	88.1	74.9	88.1	90.6	93.7
1994 [3]	56,633	12.7	32.9	25.8	28.6	87.0	71.5	86.8	90.3	93.2
Female:										
1992	46,469	10.2	37.9	26.9	25.0	70.0	45.6	69.1	76.2	82.2
1993	46,961	9.3	36.7	28.2	25.8	70.0	44.2	68.8	76.1	82.2
1994 [3]	48,235	9.1	35.3	29.8	25.8	71.1	44.7	70.0	77.0	82.5
White:										
1992	87,656	11.3	36.1	25.5	27.1	79.8	61.5	78.7	83.8	88.7
1993	88,457	10.7	35.0	26.4	27.9	79.7	61.1	78.2	83.1	88.8
1994 [3]	89,009	10.5	33.7	27.7	28.1	79.8	60.3	78.3	83.5	88.5
Black:										
1992	10,936	19.2	40.3	24.9	15.6	74.4	55.4	76.9	83.4	89.1
1993	11,051	16.8	39.5	27.6	16.1	73.8	53.4	74.7	83.0	89.6
1994 [3]	11,368	14.5	39.3	29.2	17.0	73.5	49.4	75.2	82.5	89.5
Hispanic: [4]										
1992	7,702	39.1	30.2	19.3	11.4	73.8	64.6	77.5	84.2	87.1
1993	8,010	38.7	29.4	21.0	10.9	73.9	64.9	76.8	84.0	87.3
1994 [3]	8,984	38.6	28.7	21.5	11.1	73.2	63.9	77.5	81.9	86.3

[1] See footnote 1, table 629.   [2] Includes other races, not shown separately.   [3] See footnote 2, table 626.   [4] Persons of Hispanic origin may be of any race.

Source: U.S. Bureau of Labor Statistics, unpublished data.

No. 631. Civilian Labor Force—Percent Distribution, by Sex and Age: 1960 to 1994

[For civilian noninstitutional population 16 years old and over. Annual averages of monthly figures. Based on Current Population Survey; see text, section 1, and Appendix III. See *Historical Statistics, Colonial Times to 1970,* series D 29-41, for similar but not exactly comparable data]

YEAR AND SEX	Civilian labor force (1,000)	PERCENT DISTRIBUTION						
		16 to 19 years	20 to 24 years	25 to 34 years	35 to 44 years	45 to 54 years	55 to 64 years	65 yrs. and over
Total: 1960	69,628	7.0	9.6	20.7	23.4	21.3	13.5	4.6
1970	82,771	8.8	12.8	20.6	19.9	20.5	13.6	3.9
1980	106,940	8.8	14.9	27.3	19.1	15.8	11.2	2.9
1985	115,461	6.8	13.6	29.1	22.6	15.0	10.4	2.5
1990	124,787	5.9	11.1	28.7	25.5	16.4	9.5	2.8
1991	125,303	5.5	10.9	28.2	26.3	16.9	9.4	2.8
1992	126,982	5.3	10.8	27.6	26.5	17.6	9.3	2.8
1993	128,040	5.3	10.6	26.9	26.8	18.4	9.3	2.7
1994 [1]	131,056	5.7	10.8	26.2	26.9	18.6	8.9	2.9
Male: 1960	46,388	6.0	8.9	22.1	23.6	20.6	13.8	4.9
1970	51,228	7.8	11.2	22.1	20.4	20.3	13.9	4.2
1980	61,453	8.1	14.0	27.6	19.3	16.1	11.8	3.1
1985	64,411	6.4	12.9	29.2	22.5	15.3	11.0	2.7
1990	68,234	5.7	10.7	29.0	25.3	16.4	9.9	3.0
1991	68,411	5.2	10.6	28.6	26.1	16.8	9.8	2.9
1992	69,184	5.1	10.5	28.0	26.3	17.5	9.7	3.0
1993	69,633	5.1	10.3	27.4	26.6	18.1	9.5	2.9
1994 [1]	70,817	5.5	10.6	26.6	26.8	18.3	9.1	3.1
Female: 1960	23,240	8.8	11.1	17.8	22.8	22.7	12.8	3.9
1970	31,543	10.3	15.5	18.1	18.9	20.7	13.2	3.3
1980	45,487	9.6	16.1	26.9	19.0	15.4	10.4	2.6
1985	51,050	7.4	14.6	28.9	22.7	14.6	9.7	2.3
1990	56,554	6.3	11.6	28.3	25.8	16.5	9.0	2.7
1991	56,893	5.9	11.3	27.7	26.6	17.0	8.9	2.7
1992	57,798	5.5	11.2	27.2	26.7	17.8	8.9	2.6
1993	58,407	5.6	10.9	26.4	26.9	18.7	9.0	2.5
1994 [1]	60,239	6.0	10.9	25.7	27.0	18.9	8.8	2.8

[1] See footnote 2, table 626.

Source: U.S. Bureau of Labor Statistics, Bulletin 2307, and *Employment Earnings,* monthly, January issues.

No. 632. Civilian Labor Force, by Selected Metropolitan Area: 1994

[For the civilian noninstitutional population 16 years old and over. Annual averages of monthly figures. Except as noted, data are derived from the Local Area Unemployment Statistics Program. For composition of metropolitan areas, see Appendix II]

METROPOLITAN AREAS RANKED BY LABOR FORCE SIZE, 1994	Civilian labor force (1,000)	Unemployment rate [1]	METROPOLITAN AREAS RANKED BY LABOR FORCE SIZE, 1994	Civilian labor force (1,000)	Unemployment rate [1]
U.S. total	**131,056**	6.1	San Jose, CA	857.2	6.3
Los Angeles-Long Beach, CA [2]	4,396.0	9.4	Fort Worth-Arlington, TX	805.1	5.6
Chicago, IL.	3,964.6	5.5	Indianapolis, IN	803.8	4.1
New York, NY	3,830.2	8.1	Cincinnati, OH-KY-IN	801.6	4.8
Washington, DC-MD-VA-WV	2,585.3	4.1	Milwaukee-Waukesha, WI	776.0	4.5
Philadelphia, PA-NJ	2,434.8	5.9	Columbus, OH	767.8	4.1
Detroit, MI	2,131.0	5.7	Orlando, FL	751.5	5.8
Houston, TX	1,958.8	6.4	Fort Lauderdale, FL	713.5	6.5
Atlanta, GA.	1,846.6	4.7	Norfolk-Virginia Beach-Newport News,		
Boston, MA-NH	1,753.9	5.2	VA-NC	713.1	5.5
Dallas, TX	1,672.6	5.3	Sacramento, CA	711.8	7.3
Minneapolis-St. Paul, MI-WI.	1,580.4	3.3	San Antonio, TX	700.4	4.9
Nassau-Suffolk, NY	1,359.1	5.7	Charlotte-Gastonia-Rock Hill, NC-SC. . . .	696.4	3.8
Orange County, CA	1,342.1	5.8	Bergen-Passaic-NJ	650.0	7.1
St. Louis, MO-IL [3]	1,279.3	4.8	Salt Lake City-Ogden, UT	627.1	3.5
Riverside-San Bernardino, CA	1,273.7	9.4	Greensboro-Winston-Salem-High Point,		
Phoenix-Mesa, AZ	1,267.0	5.0	NC	614.6	3.6
San Diego, CA	1,234.5	7.2	Hartford, CT	604.8	5.9
Baltimore, MD.	1,218.2	6.0	New Orleans, LA	600.9	7.4
Seattle-Bellevue-Everett, WA	1,193.8	5.7	Nashville, TN	595.4	3.3
Pittsburgh, PA	1,137.0	6.2	Austin-San Marcos, TX	582.9	3.6
Oakland, CA.	1,135.7	6.3	Middlesex-Somerset-Hunterdon, NJ . . .	582.3	5.2
Cleveland-Lorain-Elyria, OH.	1,085.6	5.8	Providence-Fall River-Warwick, RI-MA. .	580.6	7.5
Tampa-St. Petersburg-Clearwater, FL . . .	1,083.4	5.5	Buffalo-Niagara Falls, NY	576.1	6.2
Miami, FL.	1,039.2	8.0	Las Vegas, NV-AZ	573.3	6.3
Denver, CO	1,014.7	3.9	Rochester, NY	569.1	5.2
Newark, NJ.	981.9	7.0	Raleigh-Durham-Chapel Hill, NC.	552.8	3.0
Portland-Vancouver, OR-WA	937.0	4.4	Grand Rapids-Muskegon-Holland, MI . . .	528.7	4.7
San Francisco, CA.	910.4	5.7	Louisville, KY-IN	523.0	4.6
Kansas City, MO-KS.	894.2	4.6			

[1] Percent unemployed of the civilian labor force.   [2] Derived from the Current Population Survey.   [3] Excludes the part of Sullivan City in Crawford County, Missouri.

Source: U.S. Bureau of Labor Statistics, *Employment and Earnings,* May 1995.

No. 633. Characteristics of the Civilian Labor Force, by State: 1994

[**In thousands, except ratio and rate.** For civilian noninstitutional population, 16 years old and over. Annual averages of monthly figures. Because of separate processing and weighting procedures, the totals for the United States may differ from results obtained by aggregating totals for States]

STATE	TOTAL		EMPLOYED		Em-ployed/popula-tion ratio [1]	UNEMPLOYED					PARTICIPATION RATE [3]	
	Num-ber	Fe-male	Total	Fe-male		Total		Rate [2]			Male	Female
						Num-ber	Fe-male	Total	Male	Fe-male		
United States .	**131,056**	**60,239**	**123,060**	**56,610**	**62.5**	**7,996**	**3,629**	**6.1**	**6.2**	**6.0**	**75.1**	**58.8**
Alabama	2,031	938	1,909	868	59.1	122	70	6.0	4.7	7.5	72.1	54.8
Alaska	305	140	282	132	68.5	24	9	7.8	9.1	6.2	81.2	67.5
Arizona	1,988	900	1,862	836	61.3	126	64	6.4	5.7	7.1	74.1	57.4
Arkansas	1,207	554	1,142	520	61.3	65	34	5.3	4.7	6.1	72.7	57.3
California	15,471	6,819	14,141	6,243	60.3	1,330	576	8.6	8.7	8.4	75.4	56.9
Colorado	1,996	915	1,912	878	69.4	84	37	4.2	4.4	4.0	79.4	65.7
Connecticut	1,726	818	1,630	769	64.9	96	48	5.6	5.3	5.9	76.9	61.5
Delaware	384	173	365	164	67.3	19	9	4.9	4.5	5.3	78.3	63.4
District of Columbia .	314	153	289	140	61.5	26	12	8.2	8.3	8.0	74.0	60.9
Florida	6,824	3,164	6,376	2,945	58.5	448	219	6.6	6.3	6.9	70.7	55.4
Georgia	3,566	1,676	3,381	1,586	64.1	185	90	5.2	5.0	5.4	76.0	60.1
Hawaii	583	284	547	270	64.0	35	14	6.1	7.1	5.0	74.1	62.8
Idaho	591	265	558	250	67.2	33	15	5.6	5.6	5.6	79.2	63.3
Illinois	6,000	2,775	5,660	2,623	63.9	340	153	5.7	5.8	5.5	76.5	59.7
Indiana	3,056	1,455	2,905	1,377	66.4	151	78	4.9	4.5	5.4	78.3	62.5
Iowa	1,565	721	1,508	697	70.4	58	25	3.7	3.9	3.4	80.9	65.6
Kansas	1,331	624	1,261	593	67.0	70	31	5.3	5.6	5.0	78.4	63.8
Kentucky	1,825	853	1,727	811	59.0	98	42	5.4	5.8	4.9	70.3	55.3
Louisiana	1,939	897	1,783	817	56.3	156	80	8.0	7.3	9.0	70.1	53.3
Maine	613	290	567	272	59.5	45	18	7.4	8.3	6.3	70.3	58.6
Maryland	2,691	1,292	2,554	1,235	67.0	137	58	5.1	5.7	4.5	77.8	64.2
Massachusetts	3,179	1,482	2,988	1,402	63.8	191	80	6.0	6.6	5.4	75.7	60.7
Michigan	4,753	2,181	4,473	2,052	62.7	280	129	5.9	5.9	5.9	75.2	58.7
Minnesota	2,565	1,212	2,462	1,171	72.6	103	41	4.0	4.6	3.4	81.6	69.8
Mississippi	1,254	578	1,171	537	59.3	83	40	6.6	6.3	6.9	72.7	55.2
Missouri	2,695	1,244	2,564	1,184	64.7	131	60	4.9	4.9	4.8	75.9	60.6
Montana	437	205	414	195	64.8	22	10	5.1	5.3	4.8	75.2	61.8
Nebraska	876	416	851	403	71.0	25	14	2.9	2.5	3.3	79.8	66.9
Nevada	779	345	731	323	65.8	48	22	6.2	5.9	6.5	77.8	62.4
New Hampshire	628	287	599	273	68.9	29	14	4.6	4.4	4.8	78.8	65.7
New Jersey	3,991	1,811	3,719	1,688	61.4	272	123	6.8	6.8	6.8	75.1	57.4
New Mexico	770	342	722	324	59.8	48	18	6.3	7.1	5.3	72.8	55.3
New York	8,571	3,965	7,978	3,720	57.0	593	245	6.9	7.5	6.2	70.5	53.2
North Carolina	3,609	1,722	3,451	1,639	64.1	158	83	4.4	4.0	4.8	74.6	60.4
North Dakota	338	158	324	153	68.8	13	5	3.9	4.4	3.3	77.9	65.6
Ohio	5,537	2,562	5,231	2,434	62.1	307	139	5.5	5.6	5.4	75.0	57.6
Oklahoma	1,540	693	1,451	655	59.9	90	37	5.8	6.2	5.4	73.4	54.7
Oregon	1,643	739	1,553	702	65.1	89	37	5.4	5.8	5.0	75.4	62.2
Pennsylvania	5,829	2,639	5,468	2,486	58.9	361	153	6.2	6.5	5.8	71.7	54.6
Rhode Island	505	244	470	228	61.2	36	16	7.1	7.6	6.5	73.5	59.3
South Carolina	1,828	873	1,713	812	62.0	115	61	6.3	5.6	7.0	74.2	59.1
South Dakota	374	175	362	169	69.4	12	6	3.3	3.1	3.6	78.2	65.7
Tennessee	2,664	1,267	2,537	1,201	63.7	127	66	4.8	4.4	5.2	74.4	60.2
Texas	9,385	4,166	8,780	3,891	64.8	604	275	6.4	6.3	6.6	78.9	60.1
Utah	975	435	938	417	71.5	36	18	3.7	3.4	4.2	83.3	65.5
Vermont	321	155	306	148	67.7	15	7	4.7	5.0	4.4	77.5	65.3
Virginia	3,422	1,622	3,255	1,539	66.0	167	82	4.9	4.7	5.1	76.4	63.0
Washington	2,708	1,229	2,534	1,151	63.0	174	78	6.4	6.5	6.3	75.0	59.9
West Virginia	788	353	717	326	49.7	70	26	8.9	10.1	7.5	63.5	46.6
Wisconsin	2,795	1,299	2,663	1,244	69.7	132	55	4.7	5.2	4.2	79.2	67.3
Wyoming	249	114	236	108	67.5	13	6	5.3	5.4	5.2	78.8	64.1

[1] Civilian employment as a percent of civilian noninstitutional population.   [2] Percent unemployed of the civilian labor force.
[3] Percent of civilian noninstitutional population of each specified group in the civilian labor force.

Source: U.S. Bureau of Labor Statistics, *Geographic Profile of Employment and Unemployment, 1994.*

No. 634. Hispanic Persons—Civilian Labor Force Participation: 1993 and 1994

[For civilian noninstitutional population, 16 years old and over. Annual averages of monthly figures. Based on Current Population Survey; see text, section 1, and Appendix III]

ITEM	1993					1994 [1]				
	Total	Mexi-can	Puerto Rican	Cuban	Other His-panic origin [2]	Total	Mexi-can	Puerto Rican	Cuban	Other His-panic origin [2]
Total (1,000).............	15,753	9,693	1,676	927	3,457	18,117	11,174	1,854	1,002	4,087
Percent in labor force:										
Male.....................	80.0	81.5	70.6	73.3	81.2	79.2	81.5	67.6	70.3	79.7
Female..................	52.0	51.9	45.3	47.9	56.7	52.9	52.9	44.9	50.9	57.1
Employed (1,000)............	9,272	5,805	828	511	2,128	10,788	6,800	907	555	2,526
Percent by occupation..........	100.0	100.0	100.0	100.0	100.0	100.0	100.0	100.0	100.0	100.0
Managerial and professional	14.1	11.5	19.1	25.0	16.6	14.1	11.6	19.5	25.5	16.3
Tech., sales, and admin. support .	24.9	23.3	32.1	32.9	24.3	24.5	22.4	31.0	36.5	24.9
Services	19.9	19.1	19.9	12.9	23.8	19.8	19.1	18.0	11.7	23.9
Precision production, craft, and repair...............	13.2	14.4	9.8	10.2	12.0	13.0	13.9	10.1	10.6	12.3
Operators, fabricators and laborers	22.2	23.7	17.9	17.0	20.9	22.9	25.0	20.2	14.4	20.3
Farming, forestry, and fishing....	5.8	8.0	1.2	2.2	2.3	5.7	8.0	1.3	1.3	2.3
Percent of labor force unemployed:										
Male.....................	10.4	10.2	14.4	7.8	10.1	9.4	9.5	11.0	7.9	8.9
Female..................	10.9	11.4	10.8	7.7	10.8	10.7	11.1	12.4	8.4	9.4

[1] See footnote 2, table 626.   [2] Includes Central or South American and other Hispanic origin.

Source: U.S. Bureau of Labor Statistics, *Employment and Earnings*, monthly, January issues.

No. 635. School Enrollment and Labor Force Status: 1980 and 1993

[**In thousands, except percent.** As of **October.** For the civilian noninstitutional population 16 to 24 years old. Based on Current Population Survey; see text, section 1, and Appendix III]

CHARACTERISTIC	POPULATION		CIVILIAN LABOR FORCE			EMPLOYED		UNEMPLOYED		
	1980	1993	1980, total	1993		1980	1993	1980, total	1993	
				Total	Per-cent [1]				Total	Rate [2]
Total, 16 to 24 years [3].....	37,103	30,844	24,918	19,899	64.5	21,454	17,464	2,464	2,435	12.2
Enrolled in school [3]	15,713	15,790	7,454	7,692	48.7	6,433	6,677	1,021	1,015	13.2
16 to 19 years	11,126	10,396	4,836	4,363	42.0	4,029	3,581	807	781	17.9
20 to 24 years	4,587	5,394	2,618	3,330	61.7	2,404	3,096	214	233	7.0
Sex:										
Male..................	7,997	8,063	3,825	3,836	47.6	3,259	3,280	566	556	14.5
Female................	7,716	7,727	3,629	3,856	49.9	3,174	3,398	455	459	11.9
College level	7,664	8,311	3,996	4,816	58.0	3,632	4,396	364	420	8.7
Full-time................	6,396	6,906	2,854	3,559	51.5	2,554	3,205	300	355	10.0
Race:										
White	13,242	12,689	6,687	6,696	52.8	5,889	5,941	798	755	11.3
Below college	6,566	5,830	3,095	2,511	43.1	2,579	2,053	516	458	18.3
College level	6,678	6,859	3,592	4,185	61.0	3,310	3,888	282	296	7.1
Black..................	2,028	2,195	595	686	31.3	406	469	189	217	31.7
Below college	1,282	1,323	294	288	21.8	174	167	120	121	41.9
College level	747	872	300	398	45.6	230	301	70	97	24.3
Not enrolled [3]	21,390	15,054	17,464	12,207	81.1	15,021	10,787	2,443	1,420	11.6
White	18,103	12,122	15,121	10,153	83.8	13,318	9,117	1,803	1,037	10.2
Black	2,864	2,401	2,055	1,675	69.7	1,451	1,331	604	344	20.5

[1] Percent of civilian noninstitutional population.   [2] Percent of civilian labor force in each category.   [3] Includes other races, not shown separately.

Source: U.S. Bureau of Labor Statistics, Bulletin 2307; *News*, USDL 94-252, May 20, 1994; and unpublished data.

No. 636. Labor Force Participation Rates, by Marital Status, Sex, and Age: 1960 to 1994

[Annual averages of monthly figures. See table 633 for definition of participation rate. Based on Current Population Survey; see text, section 1, and Appendix III]

MARITAL STATUS AND YEAR	MALE PARTICIPATION RATE							FEMALE PARTICIPATION RATE						
	Total	16-19 years	20-24 years	25-34 years	35-44 years	45-64 years	65 and over	Total	16-19 years	20-24 years	25-34 years	35-44 years	45-64 years	65 and over
Single:														
1960 ..	69.8	42.6	80.3	91.5	88.6	80.1	31.2	58.6	30.2	77.2	83.4	82.9	79.8	24.3
1970 ..	65.5	54.6	73.8	87.9	86.2	75.7	25.2	56.8	44.7	73.0	81.4	78.6	73.0	19.7
1975 ..	68.7	57.9	77.9	86.7	83.2	69.9	21.0	59.8	49.6	72.5	80.8	78.6	68.3	15.8
1980 ..	72.6	59.9	81.3	89.2	82.2	66.9	16.8	64.4	53.6	75.2	83.3	76.9	65.6	13.9
1985 ..	73.8	56.3	81.5	89.4	84.6	65.5	15.6	66.6	52.3	76.3	82.4	80.8	67.9	9.8
1990 ..	74.9	55.1	81.5	89.9	84.6	67.1	15.7	66.9	51.8	74.7	81.2	81.0	66.1	12.2
1991 ..	74.2	52.6	80.6	89.6	84.8	66.8	14.0	66.5	50.3	73.5	80.3	81.2	68.4	12.7
1992 ..	74.6	52.9	80.7	89.8	84.9	67.6	16.3	66.4	49.2	73.7	80.5	80.6	68.2	11.3
1993 ..	74.2	52.5	80.5	89.2	84.5	68.2	15.0	66.4	49.8	74.2	79.1	79.1	68.8	12.5
1994 [1] .	73.9	53.6	80.5	88.4	83.1	67.8	17.8	66.7	51.4	73.6	78.9	78.7	68.8	12.7
Married: [2]														
1960 ..	89.2	91.5	97.1	98.8	98.6	93.7	36.6	31.9	27.2	31.7	28.8	37.2	36.0	6.7
1970 ..	86.1	92.3	94.7	98.0	98.1	91.2	29.9	37.8	47.9	38.8	46.8	44.0	7.3	
1975 ..	83.0	92.9	95.3	97.4	97.1	86.8	23.3	44.3	46.2	57.0	48.4	52.0	43.8	7.0
1980 ..	80.9	91.3	96.9	97.5	97.2	84.3	20.5	49.8	49.3	61.4	58.8	61.8	46.9	7.3
1985 ..	78.7	91.0	95.6	97.4	96.8	81.7	16.8	53.8	49.6	65.7	65.8	68.1	49.4	6.6
1990 ..	78.2	92.3	95.6	96.9	96.8	82.5	17.6	58.4	50.0	66.5	69.8	74.0	56.5	8.5
1991 ..	77.8	93.2	95.4	96.6	96.6	82.3	16.8	58.5	48.7	65.0	70.1	74.3	57.1	8.3
1992 ..	77.6	90.2	94.8	96.6	96.2	82.7	17.2	59.2	49.0	66.3	70.9	74.8	58.6	7.9
1993 ..	77.3	91.2	95.0	96.6	96.1	82.5	16.6	59.4	50.1	65.6	70.8	74.7	60.0	7.6
1994 [1] .	77.4	88.7	94.2	95.9	95.6	81.9	18.1	60.7	48.9	65.8	71.6	75.8	61.9	9.4
Other: [3]														
1960 ..	63.1	(B)	96.9	95.2	94.4	83.2	22.7	41.6	43.5	58.0	63.1	70.0	60.0	11.4
1970 ..	60.7	(B)	90.4	93.7	91.1	78.5	19.3	40.3	48.6	60.3	64.6	68.8	61.9	10.0
1975 ..	63.4	(B)	88.8	92.4	89.4	73.4	15.4	40.1	47.6	65.3	68.6	69.2	59.0	8.3
1980 ..	67.5	(B)	92.6	94.1	91.9	73.0	13.7	43.6	50.0	68.4	76.5	77.1	60.2	8.2
1985 ..	68.7	(B)	95.1	93.7	91.8	72.8	11.4	45.1	51.9	66.2	76.9	81.6	61.0	7.5
1990 ..	68.3	(B)	93.1	93.0	90.8	74.6	12.0	47.2	54.4	65.6	77.3	82.3	65.0	8.5
1991 ..	67.7	(B)	93.9	92.1	90.5	73.5	12.3	46.8	45.8	63.3	74.8	82.1	65.2	8.4
1992 ..	68.0	(B)	91.8	93.5	90.3	74.7	12.2	47.0	47.8	66.9	75.7	81.6	66.4	8.4
1993 ..	67.4	(B)	91.7	91.9	89.6	74.2	12.0	47.1	53.3	65.2	75.2	81.6	66.9	8.2
1994 [1] .	66.8	65.1	91.0	90.3	88.6	72.6	11.9	47.5	46.2	66.6	74.3	80.4	67.6	8.7

B For 1960, percentage not shown where base is less than 50,000; beginning 1970, 35,000.   [1] See footnote 2, table 626.   [2] Spouse present.   [3] Widowed, divorced, and married (spouse absent).

Source: U.S. Bureau of Labor Statistics, Bulletins 2217 and 2340; and unpublished data.

No. 637. Marital Status of Women in the Civilian Labor Force: 1960 to 1994

[Annual averages of monthly figures. For civilian noninstitutional population 16 years old and over. Based on Current Population Survey; see text, section 1, and Appendix III. See also *Historical Statistics, Colonial Times to 1970,* series D 49-62]

YEAR	FEMALE LABOR FORCE (1,000)				FEMALE PARTICIPATION RATE [3]			
	Total	Single	Married [1]	Other [2]	Total	Single	Married [1]	Other [2]
1960	23,240	5,410	12,893	4,937	37.7	58.6	31.9	41.6
1965	26,200	5,976	14,829	5,396	39.3	54.5	34.9	40.7
1970	31,543	7,265	18,475	5,804	43.3	56.8	40.5	40.3
1975	37,475	9,125	21,484	6,866	46.3	59.8	44.3	40.1
1979	44,235	11,597	24,378	8,260	50.9	64.6	49.0	43.1
1980	45,487	11,865	24,980	8,643	51.5	64.4	49.9	43.6
1981	46,696	12,124	25,428	9,144	52.1	64.5	50.5	44.6
1982	47,755	12,460	25,971	9,324	52.6	65.1	51.1	44.8
1983	48,503	12,659	26,468	9,376	52.9	65.0	51.8	44.4
1984	49,709	12,867	27,199	9,644	53.6	65.6	52.8	44.7
1985	51,050	13,163	27,894	9,993	54.5	66.6	53.8	45.1
1986	52,413	13,512	28,623	10,277	55.3	67.2	54.9	45.6
1987	53,658	13,885	29,381	10,393	56.0	67.4	55.9	45.7
1988	54,742	14,194	29,921	10,627	56.6	67.7	56.7	46.2
1989	56,030	14,377	30,548	11,104	57.4	68.0	57.8	47.0
1990	56,554	14,229	30,970	11,354	57.5	66.9	58.4	47.2
1991	56,893	14,295	31,175	11,423	57.3	66.5	58.5	46.8
1992	57,798	14,477	31,720	11,601	57.8	66.4	59.2	47.0
1993	58,407	14,624	31,978	11,805	57.9	66.4	59.4	47.1
1994 [4]	60,239	15,333	32,888	12,018	58.8	66.7	60.7	47.5

[1] Husband present.   [2] Widowed, divorced, or separated.   [3] See table 633 for definition of participation rate.   [4] See footnote 2, table 626.

Source: U.S. Bureau of Labor Statistics, Bulletin 2307; and unpublished data.

No. 638. Employment Status of Women, by Marital Status and Presence and Age of Children: 1960 to 1994

[As of **March.** For 1960, civilian noninstitutional persons 14 years and over, thereafter 16 years old and over. Based on Current Population Survey; see text, section 1, and Appendix III]

ITEM	TOTAL			WITH ANY CHILDREN								
				Total			Children 6 to 17 only			Children under 6		
	Single	Mar-ried [1]	Other [2]	Single	Mar-ried [1]	Other [2]	Single	Mar-ried [1]	Other [2]	Single	Mar-ried [1]	Other [2]
IN LABOR FORCE (mil.)												
1960	5.4	12.3	4.9	(NA)	6.6	1.5	(NA)	4.1	1.0	(NA)	2.5	0.4
1970	7.0	18.4	5.9	(NA)	10.2	1.9	(NA)	6.3	1.3	(NA)	3.9	0.6
1980	11.2	24.9	8.8	0.6	13.7	3.6	0.2	8.4	2.6	0.3	5.2	1.0
1985	12.9	27.7	10.3	1.1	14.9	4.0	0.4	8.5	2.9	0.7	6.4	1.1
1990	14.0	31.0	11.2	1.5	16.5	4.2	0.6	9.3	3.0	0.9	7.2	1.2
1991	14.1	31.1	11.1	1.7	16.6	4.1	0.6	9.1	3.0	1.1	7.4	1.2
1992	14.1	31.7	11.5	1.7	16.8	4.2	0.7	9.5	3.0	1.0	7.3	1.2
1993 [3]	14.1	32.2	11.3	1.9	16.9	4.2	0.7	9.7	3.0	1.1	7.3	1.2
1994 [3]	14.9	32.9	11.9	2.2	17.6	4.4	0.8	9.9	3.2	1.4	7.7	1.2
PARTICIPATION RATE [4]												
1960	44.1	30.5	40.0	(NA)	27.6	56.0	(NA)	39.0	65.9	(NA)	18.6	40.5
1970	53.0	40.8	39.1	(NA)	39.7	60.7	(NA)	49.2	66.9	(NA)	30.3	52.2
1980	61.5	50.1	44.0	52.0	54.1	69.4	67.6	61.7	74.6	44.1	45.1	60.3
1985	65.2	54.2	45.6	51.6	60.8	71.9	64.1	67.8	77.8	46.5	53.4	59.7
1990	66.4	58.2	46.8	55.2	66.3	74.2	69.7	73.6	79.7	48.7	58.9	63.6
1991	65.1	58.5	46.2	53.6	66.8	72.7	64.8	73.6	79.5	48.8	59.9	59.8
1992	64.7	59.3	46.7	52.5	67.8	73.2	67.2	75.4	80.0	45.8	59.9	60.5
1993 [3]	64.5	59.4	45.9	54.4	67.5	72.1	70.2	74.9	78.3	47.4	59.6	60.0
1994 [3]	65.1	60.6	47.3	56.9	69.0	73.1	67.5	76.0	78.4	52.2	61.7	62.2
EMPLOYMENT (mil.)												
1960	5.1	11.6	4.6	(NA)	6.2	1.3	(NA)	3.9	0.9	(NA)	2.3	0.4
1970	6.5	17.5	5.6	(NA)	9.6	1.8	(NA)	6.0	1.2	(NA)	3.6	0.6
1980	10.1	23.6	8.2	0.4	12.8	3.3	0.2	8.1	2.4	0.2	4.8	0.9
1985	11.6	26.1	9.4	0.9	13.9	3.5	0.3	8.1	2.6	0.5	5.9	0.9
1990	12.9	29.9	10.5	1.2	15.8	3.8	0.5	8.9	2.7	0.7	6.9	1.1
1991	12.9	29.7	10.4	1.4	15.7	3.7	0.5	8.8	2.7	0.8	6.9	1.0
1992	12.8	30.1	10.6	1.4	15.9	3.7	0.6	9.1	2.7	0.8	6.8	1.0
1993 [3]	12.7	30.8	10.5	1.5	16.1	3.9	0.6	9.3	2.8	0.9	. 6.8	1.1
1994 [3]	13.4	31.4	11.0	1.7	16.8	4.0	0.7	9.5	2.9	1.1	7.3	1.0
UNEMPLOY-MENT RATE [5]												
1960	6.0	5.4	6.2	(NA)	6.0	8.4	(NA)	4.9	6.8	(NA)	7.8	12.5
1970	7.1	4.8	4.8	(NA)	6.0	7.2	(NA)	4.8	5.9	(NA)	7.9	9.8
1980	10.3	5.3	6.4	23.2	5.9	9.2	15.6	4.4	7.9	29.2	8.3	12.8
1985	10.2	5.7	8.5	23.8	6.6	12.1	15.4	5.5	10.6	28.5	8.0	16.1
1990	8.2	3.5	5.7	18.4	4.2	8.5	14.5	3.8	7.7	20.8	4.8	10.2
1991	8.8	4.6	6.8	17.9	5.3	9.1	10.7	4.2	7.7	22.0	6.7	12.7
1992	9.1	4.9	7.6	17.3	5.7	10.8	14.1	4.6	8.6	19.4	7.0	16.3
1993 [3]	9.8	4.4	6.9	19.2	4.8	8.5	13.7	3.8	7.0	22.8	6.2	12.5
1994 [3]	10.0	4.5	7.4	19.5	5.0	9.8	13.2	4.5	7.7	23.0	5.6	15.1

NA Not available. 　[1] Husband present. 　[2] Widowed, divorced, or separated. 　[3] See footnote 2, table 626. 　[4] Percent of women in each specific category in the labor force. 　[5] Unemployed as a percent of civilian labor force in specified group.
Source: U.S. Bureau of Labor Statistics, Bulletin 2307; and unpublished data.

No. 639. Labor Force Participation Rates for Wives, Husband Present, by Age of Own Youngest Child: 1975 to 1994

[As of **March.** For civilian noninstitutional population, 16 years old and over. For definition of participation rate, see table 638. Based on Current Population Survey; see text, section 1, and Appendix III]

PRESENCE AND AGE OF CHILD	TOTAL			WHITE			BLACK		
	1975	1985	1994 [1]	1975	1985	1994 [1]	1975	1985	1994 [1]
Wives, total	**44.4**	**54.2**	**60.6**	**43.6**	**53.3**	**60.3**	**54.1**	**63.8**	**65.6**
No children under 18	43.8	48.2	53.2	43.6	47.5	53.0	47.6	55.2	55.6
With children under 18	44.9	60.8	69.0	43.6	59.9	68.7	58.4	71.7	75.2
Under 6, total	36.7	53.4	61.7	34.7	52.1	61.2	54.9	69.6	70.6
Under 3	32.7	50.5	59.7	30.7	49.4	59.3	50.1	66.2	68.3
1 year or under	30.8	49.4	58.8	29.2	48.6	58.8	50.0	63.7	64.2
2 years	37.1	54.0	64.5	35.1	52.7	63.2	56.4	69.9	80.5
3 to 5 years	42.2	58.4	64.6	40.1	56.6	63.9	61.2	73.8	74.0
3 years	41.2	55.1	62.9	39.0	52.7	61.7	62.7	72.3	74.8
4 years	41.2	59.7	63.9	38.7	58.4	62.4	64.9	70.6	77.7
5 years	44.4	62.1	67.1	43.8	59.9	67.5	56.3	79.1	70.5
6 to 13 years	51.8	68.2	75.5	50.7	67.7	75.3	65.7	73.3	81.2
14 to 17 years	53.5	67.0	77.2	53.4	66.6	77.8	52.3	74.4	73.7

[1] See footnote 2, table 626.
Source: U.S. Bureau of Labor Statistics, Bulletin 2340; and unpublished data.

No. 640. Civilian Labor Force—Employment Status, by Sex, Race, and Age: 1994

[For civilian noninstitutional population 16 years old and over. Annual averages of monthly figures. Based on Current Population Survey; see text, section 1, and Appendix III]

AGE AND RACE	TOTAL (1,000)	MALE (1,000)			FEMALE (1,000)			PERCENT OF LABOR FORCE			
		Total	Em-ployed	Unem-ployed	Total	Em-ployed	Unem-ployed	Employed		Unemployed	
								Male	Fe-male	Male	Fe-male
All workers [1] ..	131,056	70,817	66,450	4,367	60,239	56,610	3,629	93.8	94.0	6.2	6.0
16 to 19 years.....	7,481	3,896	3,156	740	3,585	3,005	580	81.0	83.8	19.0	16.2
20 to 24 years.....	14,131	7,540	6,771	768	6,592	5,987	605	89.8	90.8	10.2	9.2
25 to 34 years.....	34,353	18,854	17,741	1,113	15,499	14,545	954	94.1	93.8	5.9	6.2
35 to 44 years.....	35,226	18,966	18,111	855	16,259	15,488	772	95.5	95.3	4.5	4.7
45 to 54 years.....	24,318	12,962	12,439	522	11,357	10,908	449	96.0	96.0	4.0	4.0
55 to 64 years.....	11,713	6,423	6,142	281	5,289	5,085	204	95.6	96.1	4.4	3.9
65 years and over ..	3,834	2,176	2,089	88	1,658	1,592	66	96.0	96.0	4.0	4.0
White	111,082	60,727	57,452	3,275	50,356	47,738	2,617	94.6	94.8	5.4	5.2
16 to 19 years.....	6,357	3,315	2,776	540	3,042	2,622	420	83.7	86.2	16.3	13.8
20 to 24 years.....	11,688	6,294	5,738	555	5,394	4,997	397	91.2	92.6	8.8	7.4
25 to 34 years.....	28,580	15,879	15,052	827	12,702	12,049	652	94.8	94.9	5.2	5.1
35 to 44 years.....	29,626	16,188	15,562	626	13,439	12,880	558	96.1	95.8	3.9	4.2
45 to 54 years.....	21,026	11,327	10,910	417	9,699	9,338	361	96.3	96.3	3.7	3.7
55 to 64 years.....	10,319	5,726	5,490	236	4,593	4,423	170	95.9	96.3	4.1	3.7
65 years and over ..	3,486	1,998	1,925	74	1,487	1,429	58	96.3	96.1	3.7	3.9
Black	14,502	7,089	6,241	848	7,413	6,595	818	88.0	89.0	12.0	11.0
16 to 19 years.....	852	443	276	167	409	275	133	62.3	67.4	37.6	32.6
20 to 24 years.....	1,800	891	718	173	909	731	178	80.6	80.4	19.4	19.6
25 to 34 years.....	4,199	2,068	1,850	218	2,131	1,882	249	89.5	88.3	10.6	11.7
35 to 44 years.....	4,068	1,975	1,795	180	2,093	1,926	166	90.9	92.0	9.1	8.0
45 to 54 years.....	2,308	1,102	1,030	72	1,206	1,147	59	93.5	95.1	6.5	4.9
55 to 64 years.....	1,007	484	455	29	523	497	26	94.0	95.1	6.0	4.9
65 years and over ..	267	125	115	10	142	136	6	91.8	95.6	8.2	4.4
Hispanic [2]	11,975	7,210	6,530	680	4,765	4,258	508	90.6	89.3	9.4	10.7
16 to 19 years.....	807	463	341	121	345	268	77	73.7	77.8	26.3	22.2
20 to 24 years.....	1,863	1,184	1,056	128	679	587	92	89.2	86.5	10.8	13.5
25 to 34 years.....	3,865	2,430	2,227	203	1,435	1,290	145	91.6	89.9	8.4	10.1
35 to 44 years.....	2,965	1,713	1,600	113	1,252	1,137	115	93.4	89.8	6.6	9.2
45 to 54 years.....	1,626	922	847	75	704	648	57	91.9	92.0	8.1	8.0
55 to 64 years.....	698	410	379	30	288	268	21	92.6	92.9	7.4	7.1
65 years and over ..	151	89	79	9	62	59	2	89.5	96.4	10.5	3.6

[1] Includes other races not shown separately. [2] Persons of Hispanic origin may be of any race.

Source: U.S. Bureau of Labor Statistics, *Employment and Earnings*, monthly, January 1995.

No. 641. Employed Civilians and Weekly Hours: 1970 to 1994

[**In thousands, except as indicated. For civilian noninstitutional population 16 years old and over**. Annual averages of monthly figures. Based on Current Population Survey; see text, section 1, and Appendix III]

ITEM	1970	1980	1985	1990	1991	1992	1993	1994 [1]
Total employed	78,678	99,303	107,150	117,914	116,877	117,598	119,306	123,060
Age:								
16 to 19 years old	6,144	7,710	6,434	6,261	5,628	5,398	5,530	6,161
20 to 24 years old	9,731	14,087	13,980	12,622	12,233	12,157	12,137	12,758
25 to 34 years old	16,318	27,204	31,208	33,831	32,914	32,441	32,107	32,286
35 to 44 years old	15,922	19,523	24,732	30,543	31,286	31,662	32,402	33,599
45 to 54 years old	16,473	16,234	16,509	19,765	20,164	21,246	22,412	23,348
55 to 64 years old	10,974	11,586	11,474	11,464	11,268	11,267	11,311	11,228
65 years old and over...........	3,118	2,960	2,813	3,428	3,384	3,427	3,409	3,681
Class of worker:								
Nonagriculture................	75,215	95,938	103,971	114,728	113,644	114,391	116,232	119,651
Wage and salary worker	69,491	88,525	95,871	105,715	104,520	105,540	107,011	110,517
Self-employed	5,221	7,000	7,811	8,760	8,899	8,619	9,003	9,003
Unpaid family workers...........	502	413	289	252	225	232	218	131
Agriculture................	3,463	3,364	3,179	3,186	3,233	3,207	3,074	3,409
Wage and salary worker	1,154	1,425	1,535	1,679	1,673	1,696	1,637	1,715
Self-employed	1,810	1,642	1,458	1,400	1,442	1,398	1,332	1,645
Unpaid family workers...........	499	297	185	107	118	113	105	49
Weekly hours:								
Nonagriculture:								
Wage and salary workers........	38.3	38.1	38.7	39.2	39.0	38.8	39.3	39.1
Self-employed	45.0	41.2	41.1	40.8	40.4	40.1	40.5	39.5
Unpaid family workers...........	37.9	34.7	35.1	33.9	35.4	34.5	34.2	33.7
Agriculture:								
Wage and salary workers........	40.0	41.6	40.8	41.3	41.0	40.6	40.8	41.0
Self-employed	51.0	49.3	48.2	46.9	46.8	47.1	46.5	43.0
Unpaid family workers...........	40.0	38.6	38.5	38.5	40.3	40.5	36.9	39.0

[1] See footnote 2, table 626.

Source: U.S. Bureau of Labor Statistics, *Employment and Earnings*, monthly, January issues; and unpublished data.

No. 642. Persons At Work, by Hours Worked: 1994

[For civilian noninstitutional population 16 years old and over. Annual averages of monthly figures. Based on Current Population Survey; see text, section 1, and Appendix III]

HOURS OF WORK	PERSONS AT WORK (1,000)			PERCENT DISTRIBUTION		
	Total	Agriculture industries	Non-agriculture industries	Total	Agriculture industries	Non-agriculture industries
Total	**117,441**	**3,208**	**114,233**	**100.0**	**100.0**	**100.0**
1 to 34 hours	30,851	1,063	29,788	26.3	33.1	26.1
1 to 4 hours	1,271	84	1,187	1.1	2.6	1.0
5 to 14 hours	4,992	262	4,730	4.3	8.2	4.1
15 to 29 hours	15,115	493	14,623	12.9	15.4	12.8
30 to 34 hours	9,473	225	9,248	8.1	7.0	8.1
35 hours and over	86,590	2,144	84,445	73.7	66.9	73.9
35 to 39 hours	8,684	168	8,516	7.4	5.2	7.5
40 hours	40,587	624	39,963	34.6	19.4	35.0
41 hours and over	37,319	1,352	35,966	31.8	42.2	31.5
41 to 48 hours	14,075	242	13,832	12.0	7.6	12.1
49 to 58 hours	13,366	381	12,985	11.4	11.9	11.4
60 hours and over	9,878	729	9,149	8.4	22.7	8.0
Average weekly hours:						
Total at work	39.2	41.9	39.1	(X)	(X)	(X)
Persons usually working full time	43.4	49.9	43.3	(X)	(X)	(X)

X Not applicable.

Source: U.S. Bureau of Labor Statistics, *Employment and Earnings,* monthly, January 1995.

No. 643. Self-Employed Workers, by Industry and Occupation: 1970 to 1994

[**In thousands.** For civilian noninstitutional population 16 years old and over. Annual averages of monthly figures. Data from 1992 forward are not fully comparable with data for prior years because of the introduction of the occupational and industrial classification used in the 1990 census. Based on the Current Population Survey; see text, section 1, and Appendix III]

ITEM	1970	1975	1980	1985	1990	1992	1993	1994 [1]
Total self-employed	**7,031**	**7,427**	**8,642**	**9,269**	**10,160**	**10,017**	**10,335**	**10,648**
Industry: Agriculture	1,810	1,722	1,642	1,458	1,400	1,398	1,332	1,645
Nonagriculture	5,221	5,705	7,000	7,811	8,760	8,619	9,003	9,003
Mining	14	16	28	20	24	23	17	13
Construction	687	839	1,173	1,301	1,463	1,466	1,555	1,506
Manufacturing	264	273	358	347	429	392	442	426
Transportation and public utilities	196	223	282	315	302	337	372	385
Trade	1,667	1,709	1,899	1,792	1,859	1,776	1,890	1,906
Finance, insurance, and real estate	254	335	458	558	635	630	664	625
Services	2,140	2,310	2,804	3,477	4,048	3,995	4,062	4,142
Occupation:								
Managerial and professional specialty	(NA)	(NA)	(NA)	2,585	3,067	2,919	3,102	3,106
Technical, sales, and administrative support	(NA)	(NA)	(NA)	2,059	2,252	2,192	2,336	2,380
Service occupations	(NA)	(NA)	(NA)	980	1,213	1,079	1,043	1,178
Precision production, craft, and repair	(NA)	(NA)	(NA)	1,611	1,680	1,803	1,891	1,740
Operators, fabricators, and laborers	(NA)	(NA)	(NA)	568	568	626	632	639
Farming, forestry, and fishing	(NA)	(NA)	(NA)	1,465	1,380	1,390	1,331	1,605

NA Not available. [1] See footnote 2, table 626.

Source: U.S. Bureau of Labor Statistics, Bulletin 2307; *Employment and Earnings,* monthly, January issues; and unpublished data.

No. 644. Persons With a Job But Not at Work: 1970 to 1994

[**In thousands, except percent.** For civilian noninstitutional population 16 years old and over. Annual averages of monthly figures. Based on Current Population Survey; see text, section 1, and Appendix III. See *Historical Statistics, Colonial Times to 1970,* series D 116-126, for related but not comparable data]

REASON FOR NOT WORKING	1970	1975	1980	1985	1988	1989	1990	1991	1992	1993	1994 [1]
All industries, number	**4,645**	**5,221**	**5,881**	**5,789**	**5,831**	**6,170**	**6,157**	**5,909**	**6,082**	**6,028**	**5,619**
Percent of employed	**5.9**	**6.1**	**5.9**	**5.4**	**5.1**	**5.3**	**5.2**	**5.1**	**5.2**	**5.1**	**4.6**
Reason for not working:											
Vacation	2,341	2,815	3,320	3,338	3,236	3,437	3,531	3,297	3,414	3,330	2,877
Illness	1,324	1,343	1,426	1,308	1,364	1,405	1,341	1,302	1,258	1,290	1,184
Bad weather	128	139	155	141	122	133	89	118	126	151	165
Industrial dispute	156	95	105	42	30	63	24	17	19	24	15
All other	696	829	876	960	1,080	1,132	1,172	1,175	1,265	1,233	1,378

[1] See footnote 2, table 626.

Source: U.S. Bureau of Labor Statistics, *Employment and Earnings,* monthly, January issues; and unpublished data.

No. 645. Part-time Workers, by Reason: 1994

[**In thousands, except hours.** For persons working 1 to 34 hours per week. For civilian noninstitutional population 16 years old and over. Annual average of monthly figures. Based on the Current Population Survey and subject to sampling error; see text, section 1, and Appendix III]

REASON	ALL INDUSTRIES			NONAGRICULTURAL INDUSTRIES		
	Total	Usually Work—		Total	Usually Work—	
		Full-time	Part-time		Full-time	Part-time
Total working fewer than 35 hours	**30,851**	**9,980**	**20,871**	**29,788**	**9,680**	**20,107**
Economic reasons	4,625	1,392	3,232	4,414	1,314	3,100
Slack work or business conditions	2,432	1,128	1,304	2,311	1,077	1,235
Could find only part-time work	1,871	-	1,871	1,824	-	1,824
Seasonal work	135	77	58	95	54	41
Job started or ended during the week	188	188	-	183	183	-
Noneconomic reasons	26,226	8,588	17,638	25,374	8,367	17,007
Child-care problems	819	68	751	805	67	738
Other family or personal obligations	5,531	721	4,810	5,349	697	4,652
Health or medical limitations	673	-	673	639	-	639
In school or training	6,022	75	5,947	5,875	72	5,803
Retired or Social Security limit on earnings	1,822	-	1,822	1,665	-	1,665
Vacation or personal day	2,971	2,971	-	2,919	2,919	-
Holiday, legal, or religious	1,087	1,087	-	1,077	1,077	-
Weather related curtailment	1,005	1,005	-	938	938	-
Other	6,295	2,660	3,635	6,106	2,596	3,511
Average hours per week:						
Economic reasons	22.6	23.8	22.0	22.6	23.9	22.1
Noneconomic reasons	21.5	26.0	19.3	21.6	26.1	19.4

- Represents or rounds to zero.

Source: U.S. Bureau of Labor Statistics, *Employment and Earnings,* monthly, January 1995.

No. 646. Multiple Jobholders: 1994

[**Annual average of monthly figures.** For the civilian noninstitutional population 16 years old and over. Multiple jobholders are employed persons who, either 1) had jobs as wage or salary workers with two employers or more; 2) were self-employed and also held a wage and salary job; or 3) were unpaid family workers on their primary jobs but also held wage and salary job. Based on the Current Population Survey; see text, section 1, and Appendix III]

CHARACTERISTIC	TOTAL		MALE		FEMALE	
	Number (1,000)	Percent of employed	Number (1,000)	Percent of employed	Number (1,000)	Percent of employed
Total [1]	**7,260**	**5.9**	**3,924**	**5.9**	**3,336**	**5.9**
Age:						
16 to 19 years old	307	5.0	129	4.1	178	5.9
20 to 24 years old	880	6.9	428	6.3	452	7.6
25 to 54 years old	5,478	6.1	3,016	6.2	2,462	6.0
55 to 64 years old	509	4.5	295	4.8	215	4.2
65 years old and over	85	2.3	57	2.7	29	1.8
Race and Hispanic origin:						
White	6,392	6.1	3,462	6.0	2,930	6.1
Black	630	4.9	337	5.4	293	4.4
Hispanic origin [2]	394	3.7	243	3.7	151	3.6
Marital status:						
Married, spouse present	4,096	5.6	2,516	6.1	1,580	5.0
Widowed, divorced, or separated	1,159	6.2	407	5.5	752	6.7
Single, never married	2,005	6.4	1,001	5.7	1,003	7.2
Full- or part-time status:						
Primary job full-time, secondary job part-time	4,182	(X)	2,509	(X)	1,673	(X)
Both jobs part-time	1,602	(X)	513	(X)	1,089	(X)
Both jobs full-time	242	(X)	179	(X)	63	(X)
Hours vary on primary or secondary job	1,193	(X)	705	(X)	488	(X)

X Not applicable.   [1] Includes a small number of persons who work part time on their primary job and full time on their secondary job(s), not shown separately. Includes other races, not shown separately.   [2] Persons of Hispanic origin may be of any race.

Source: U.S. Bureau of Labor Statistics, *Employment and Earnings,* monthly, January 1995.

No. 647. Workers on Flexible and Shift Schedules: 1985 and 1991

[**In thousands, except percent**. As of **May.** For employed persons 16 years old and over who usually work full-time and who were at work during the survey reference week. Based on Current Population Survey; see text, section 1, and Appendix III]

| CHARACTERISTIC | Total employ-ed [1] | WORK SCHEDULES—PERCENT DISTRIBUTION | | | | | | |
| | | Regular daytime schedules | | Shift workers | | | | |
		Total	Workers on flexible sched-ules [2]	Total	Evening	Night	Rotating	Other [3]
Total, 1985 [4]	73,395	84.1	12.3	15.9	6.3	2.7	4.3	2.6
Total, 1991 [4]	**80,452**	**81.8**	**15.1**	**17.8**	**5.1**	**3.7**	**3.4**	**5.7**
Age: 16 to 19 years old	1,413	70.6	10.6	28.6	12.0	5.5	3.2	7.9
20 to 24 years old	8,332	74.8	12.0	25.0	8.5	4.7	4.6	7.2
25 to 34 years old	25,523	81.3	15.7	18.3	5.0	3.9	3.8	5.6
35 to 44 years old	22,749	83.7	16.5	16.0	4.1	3.5	3.2	5.2
45 to 54 years old	14,306	83.6	15.3	16.2	4.6	2.9	2.9	5.7
55 to 64 years old	7,197	84.1	12.2	15.3	4.2	3.4	2.4	5.3
65 years old and over.	933	88.1	16.4	11.7	2.3	2.7	1.1	5.7
Sex:								
Male	46,308	79.5	15.5	20.2	5.4	4.2	4.0	6.5
Female	34,145	85.0	14.5	14.6	4.6	2.9	2.6	4.6
Race and Hispanic origin:								
White.	68,795	82.6	15.5	17.1	4.6	3.4	3.3	5.9
Black.	8,943	76.0	12.1	23.3	8.4	5.6	4.7	4.7
Hispanic [5].	6,598	80.3	10.6	19.1	6.4	4.6	2.7	5.5
Marital status: Single	18,420	77.6	15.7	22.0	7.0	4.0	4.0	6.9
Married, spouse present	49,101	83.9	14.7	15.8	4.2	3.3	3.2	5.2
Other.	12,932	80.1	15.7	19.4	5.8	4.4	3.4	5.9
Occupation:								
Managerial and professional	22,630	89.6	22.1	10.0	1.6	1.4	1.8	5.1
Technical, sales, administrative.	24,116	85.9	17.7	13.8	3.5	2.4	2.7	5.3
Service occupations	8,389	57.1	10.5	42.5	14.7	8.7	7.9	11.2
Precision production, craft, and repair .	10,270	85.3	8.1	14.4	4.3	3.7	3.4	3.0
Operators, fabricators, and laborers . .	13,514	73.4	7.3	26.2	8.6	6.8	4.8	5.9
Farming, forestry, and fisheries.	1,533	89.2	11.3	10.4	1.1	1.2	0.7	7.4

[1] Includes a small number of workers who did not report data on shift worked.   [2] A flexible schedule allows workers to vary the time they begin and end their work day.   [3] Includes employer arranged irregular schedules.   [4] Data for 1985 are not strictly comparable to those for 1991 because of the addition of the "irregular" category in the May 1991 survey. Includes other races, not shown separately.   [5] Persons of Hispanic origin may be of any race.

Source: U.S. Bureau of Labor Statistics, *News,* USDL 92-491, August 14, 1992; and unpublished data.

No. 648. Persons Not in the Labor Force: 1994

[**In thousands. Annual average of monthly figures.** For the civilian noninstitutional population 16 years old and over. Based on the Current Population Survey; see text, section 1, and Appendix III]

| STATUS AND REASON | Total | AGE | | | SEX | |
		16 to 24 years old	25 to 54 years old	55 years old and over	Male	Female
Total, not in the labor force	**65,758**	**10,937**	**18,720**	**36,101**	**23,538**	**42,221**
Do not want a job now.	59,540	8,635	15,790	35,116	21,089	38,452
Want a job now	6,218	2,302	2,930	985	2,449	3,769
In the previous year—						
Did not search for a job.	3,588	1,263	1,611	714	1,311	2,277
Did search for a job	2,630	1,040	1,319	272	1,138	1,492
Not available for work now	823	400	379	44	308	515
Available for work now, not looking for work.	1,807	639	939	228	830	977
Reason for not currently looking:						
Discouraged over job prospects [1] . . .	500	143	278	79	296	204
Family responsibilities.	213	44	153	17	31	183
In school or training	267	213	52	1	137	129
Ill health or disability.	150	21	92	36	69	81
Other [2].	677	219	364	94	298	379

[1] Includes believes no work available, could not find work, lack necessary schooling or training, employer thinks too young or old, and other types of discrimination.   [2] Includes such things as child care and transportation problems.

Source: U.S. Bureau of Labor Statistics, *Employment and Earnings,* monthly, January 1995.

No. 649. Employed Civilians, by Occupation, Sex, Race, and Hispanic Origin: 1983 and 1994

[**For civilian noninstitutional population 16 years old and over.** Annual average of monthly figures. Based on Current Population Survey; see text, section 1, and Appendix III. Persons of Hispanic origin may be of any race. See headnote, table 643]

OCCUPATION	1983				1994 [1]			
	Total employed (1,000)	Percent of total			Total employed (1,000)	Percent of total		
		Female	Black	His-panic		Female	Black	His-panic
Total	100,834	43.7	9.3	5.3	123,060	46.0	10.4	8.8
Managerial and professional specialty	23,592	40.9	5.6	2.6	33,847	48.1	7.1	4.5
Executive, administrative, and managerial [2]	10,772	32.4	4.7	2.8	16,312	43.0	6.8	4.9
Officials and administrators, public	417	38.5	8.3	3.8	598	46.1	12.7	4.2
Financial managers	357	38.6	3.5	3.1	608	49.1	7.0	5.7
Personnel and labor relations managers	106	43.9	4.9	2.6	111	61.6	8.9	6.1
Purchasing managers	82	23.6	5.1	1.4	130	37.0	1.7	4.3
Managers, marketing, advertising and public relations	396	21.8	2.7	1.7	564	34.3	2.6	4.3
Administrators, education and related fields	415	41.4	11.3	2.4	701	62.0	12.2	4.7
Managers, medicine and health	91	57.0	5.0	2.0	614	79.7	5.4	4.0
Managers, properties and real estate	305	42.8	5.5	5.2	479	50.6	6.3	8.7
Management-related occupations [2]	2,966	40.3	5.8	3.5	4,269	53.7	8.8	5.0
Accountants and auditors	1,105	38.7	5.5	3.3	1,483	51.8	9.0	4.4
Professional specialty [2]	12,820	48.1	6.4	2.5	17,536	52.8	7.4	4.0
Architects	103	12.7	1.6	1.5	141	16.8	1.4	3.7
Engineers [2]	1,572	5.8	2.7	2.2	1,866	8.3	3.7	3.3
Aerospace engineers	80	6.9	1.5	2.1	75	14.5	0.9	4.5
Chemical engineers	67	6.1	3.0	1.4	56	7.3	1.8	1.3
Civil engineers	211	4.0	1.9	3.2	240	8.2	2.8	2.9
Electrical and electronic	450	6.1	3.4	3.1	556	6.7	4.2	2.2
Industrial engineers	210	11.0	3.3	2.4	245	14.7	5.9	3.9
Mechanical	259	2.8	3.2	1.1	341	5.1	3.1	4.9
Mathematical and computer scientists [2]	463	29.6	5.4	2.6	1,186	33.6	6.5	3.7
Computer systems analysts, scientists	276	27.8	6.2	2.7	916	31.4	7.2	3.5
Operations and systems researchers and analysts	142	31.3	4.9	2.2	222	41.4	3.9	4.9
Natural scientists [2]	357	20.5	2.6	2.1	535	31.0	3.8	1.6
Chemists, except biochemists	98	23.3	4.3	1.2	144	36.8	4.5	1.4
Geologists and geodesists	65	18.0	1.1	2.6	57	13.2	0.9	0.2
Biological and life scientists	55	40.8	2.4	1.8	120	36.5	4.5	0.6
Health diagnosing occupations [2]	735	13.3	2.7	3.3	932	21.5	3.7	4.4
Physicians	519	15.8	3.2	4.5	628	22.3	4.2	5.2
Dentists	126	6.7	2.4	1.0	148	13.3	3.7	4.5
Health assessment and treating occupations	1,900	85.8	7.1	2.2	2,708	86.2	8.8	3.4
Registered nurses	1,372	95.8	6.7	1.8	1,956	93.8	9.3	2.9
Pharmacists	158	26.7	3.8	2.6	182	38.3	2.6	4.1
Dietitians	71	90.8	21.0	3.7	86	92.0	14.3	2.1
Therapists [2]	247	76.3	7.6	2.7	430	74.3	8.3	4.5
Inhalation therapists	69	69.4	6.5	3.7	98	57.8	11.1	8.2
Physical therapists	55	77.0	9.7	1.5	106	66.2	3.7	3.7
Speech therapists	51	90.5	1.5	-	92	94.6	3.3	1.6
Physicians' assistants	51	36.3	7.7	4.4	53	54.3	5.5	7.8
Teachers, college and university	606	36.3	4.4	1.8	838	42.5	5.0	2.9
Teachers, except college and university [2]	3,365	70.9	9.1	2.7	4,330	74.9	8.9	4.3
Prekindergarten and kindergarten	299	98.2	11.8	3.4	496	98.1	11.0	5.4
Elementary school	1,350	83.3	11.1	3.1	1,634	85.6	10.2	4.2
Secondary school	1,209	51.8	7.2	2.3	1,197	55.6	7.6	4.0
Special education	81	82.2	10.2	2.3	308	83.7	6.9	3.8
Counselors, educational and vocational	184	53.1	13.9	3.2	237	68.1	13.7	8.1
Librarians, archivists, and curators	213	84.4	7.8	1.6	219	81.6	9.5	3.7
Librarians	193	87.3	7.9	1.8	196	84.1	10.5	3.7
Social scientists and urban planners [2]	261	46.8	7.1	2.1	440	53.6	7.0	4.1
Economists	98	37.9	6.3	2.7	106	47.4	3.8	3.3
Psychologists	135	57.1	8.6	1.1	280	58.6	8.3	4.9
Social, recreation, and religious workers [2]	831	43.1	12.1	3.8	1,209	51.4	17.3	5.7
Social workers	407	64.3	18.2	6.3	667	69.3	24.0	7.0
Recreation workers	65	71.9	15.7	2.0	105	70.5	14.4	3.8
Clergy	293	5.6	4.9	1.4	371	11.1	8.7	3.2
Lawyers and judges	651	15.8	2.7	1.0	861	24.8	3.3	3.0
Lawyers	612	15.3	2.6	0.9	821	24.6	3.3	3.1
Writers, artists, entertainers, and athletes [2]	1,544	42.7	4.8	2.9	2,011	47.8	5.3	5.3
Authors	62	46.7	2.1	0.9	112	53.3	2.8	2.9
Technical writers	([3])	([3])	([3])	([3])	72	57.8	4.0	0.2
Designers	393	52.7	3.1	2.7	548	55.3	3.4	5.8
Musicians and composers	155	28.0	7.9	4.4	164	31.8	10.2	6.1
Actors and directors	60	30.8	6.6	3.4	86	41.2	3.8	3.2
Painters, sculptors, craft-artists, and artist printmakers	186	47.4	2.1	2.3	225	50.5	4.6	5.2
Photographers	113	20.7	4.0	3.4	148	28.4	4.6	5.1
Editors and reporters	204	48.4	2.9	2.1	267	48.8	5.4	3.6
Public relations specialists	157	50.1	6.2	1.9	142	63.1	5.0	3.9
Athletes	58	17.6	9.4	1.7	81	21.8	10.5	2.8

See footnotes at end of table.

No. 649. Employed Civilians, by Occupation, Sex, Race, and Hispanic Origin: 1983 and 1994—Continued

[See headnote, page 411]

OCCUPATION	1983				1994 [1]			
	Total employed (1,000)	Percent of total			Total employed (1,000)	Percent of total		
		Female	Black	Hispanic		Female	Black	Hispanic
Technical, sales, and administrative support	**31,265**	**64.6**	**7.6**	**4.3**	**37,306**	**64.3**	**9.7**	**7.1**
Technicians and related support	3,053	48.2	8.2	3.1	3,869	52.0	9.7	5.3
Health technologists and technicians [2]	1,111	84.3	12.7	3.1	1,590	81.6	13.9	5.3
Clinical laboratory technologists and technicians	255	76.2	10.5	2.9	341	77.2	13.9	4.4
Dental hygienists	66	98.6	1.6	-	97	100.0	0.2	2.9
Health record technologists and technicians	(3)	(3)	(3)	(3)	(3)	(3)	(3)	(3)
Radiologic technicians	101	71.7	8.6	4.5	154	74.1	8.1	7.6
Licensed practical nurses	443	97.0	17.7	3.1	397	95.1	18.7	4.3
Engineering and related technologists and technicians [2]	822	18.4	6.1	3.5	916	19.5	7.4	6.2
Electrical and electronic technicians	260	12.5	8.2	4.6	316	15.1	9.9	5.9
Drafting occupations	273	17.5	5.5	2.3	239	19.8	4.1	4.5
Surveying and mapping technicians	(3)	(3)	(3)	(3)	68	7.8	1.5	3.8
Science technicians [2]	202	29.1	6.6	2.8	266	36.7	9.5	4.3
Biological technicians	52	37.7	2.9	2.0	89	52.9	10.4	1.2
Chemical technicians	82	26.9	9.5	3.5	77	25.5	8.8	6.6
Technicians, except health, engineering, and science [2]	917	35.3	5.0	2.7	1,098	40.0	5.7	4.8
Airplane pilots and navigators	69	2.1	-	1.6	104	2.6	1.5	0.4
Computer programmers	443	32.5	4.4	2.1	549	29.3	6.0	3.5
Legal assistants	128	74.0	4.3	3.6	262	79.9	5.4	9.4
Sales occupations	11,818	47.5	4.7	3.7	14,817	49.1	7.1	6.8
Supervisors and proprietors	2,958	28.4	3.6	3.4	4,443	37.5	5.3	5.8
Sales representatives, finance and business services [2]	1,853	37.2	2.7	2.2	2,361	40.0	4.8	4.1
Insurance sales	551	25.1	3.8	2.5	601	35.1	5.9	4.1
Real estate sales	570	48.9	1.3	1.5	708	48.4	2.6	3.9
Securities and financial services sales	212	23.6	3.1	1.1	391	29.9	4.2	2.9
Advertising and related sales	124	47.9	4.5	3.3	147	51.6	4.5	2.6
Sales representatives, commodities, except retail	1,442	15.1	2.1	2.2	1,476	23.3	2.8	4.2
Sales workers, retail and personal services	5,511	69.7	6.7	4.8	6,440	66.1	10.3	9.1
Cashiers	2,009	84.4	10.1	5.4	2,745	79.8	14.2	10.1
Sales-related occupations	54	58.7	2.8	1.3	96	67.3	3.6	6.4
Administrative support, including clerical	16,395	79.9	9.6	5.0	18,620	78.9	11.8	7.6
Supervisors	676	53.4	9.3	5.0	753	59.7	13.6	6.9
Computer equipment operators	605	63.9	12.5	6.0	550	60.7	14.1	6.9
Computer operators	597	63.7	12.1	6.0	546	60.6	14.2	6.9
Secretaries, stenographers, and typists [2]	4,861	98.2	7.3	4.5	4,163	98.0	9.2	6.7
Secretaries	3,891	99.0	5.8	4.0	3,397	98.9	8.4	6.2
Typists	906	95.6	13.8	6.4	661	94.1	14.6	9.6
Information clerks	1,174	88.9	8.5	5.5	1,755	88.4	10.6	9.2
Receptionists	602	96.8	7.5	6.6	931	96.4	10.1	10.2
Records processing occupations, except financial [2]	866	82.4	13.9	4.8	890	78.5	15.6	9.2
Order clerks	188	78.1	10.6	4.4	202	75.1	18.5	8.5
Personnel clerks, except payroll and time keeping	64	91.1	14.9	4.6	66	86.6	17.3	11.9
Library clerks	147	81.9	15.4	2.5	147	77.7	10.8	5.0
File clerks	287	83.5	16.7	6.1	280	78.9	16.8	12.7
Records clerks	157	82.8	11.6	5.6	181	78.0	13.4	6.4
Financial records processing [2]	2,457	89.4	4.6	3.7	2,278	91.4	6.0	5.5
Bookkeepers, accounting, and auditing clerks	1,970	91.0	4.3	3.3	1,829	91.9	4.9	5.0
Payroll and time keeping clerks	192	82.2	5.9	5.0	155	91.7	9.5	4.7
Billing clerks	146	88.4	6.2	3.9	177	90.0	11.9	8.3
Cost and rate clerks	96	75.6	5.9	5.3	(3)	(3)	(3)	(3)
Billing, posting, and calculating machine operators	(3)	(3)	(3)	(3)	70	90.7	8.4	8.8
Duplicating, mail and other office machine operators	68	62.6	16.0	6.1	58	41.5	17.2	9.5
Communications equipment operators	256	89.1	17.0	4.4	179	86.6	20.8	8.2
Telephone operators	244	90.4	17.0	4.3	165	88.8	21.7	8.3
Mail and message distributing occupations	799	31.6	18.1	4.5	982	38.9	18.5	7.9
Postal clerks, except mail carriers	248	36.7	26.2	5.2	311	44.4	28.2	7.8
Mail carrier, postal service	259	17.1	12.5	2.7	354	34.0	11.6	8.5
Mail clerks, except postal service	170	50.0	15.8	5.9	170	50.5	24.2	5.9
Messengers	122	26.2	16.7	5.2	147	25.7	8.1	8.9
Material recording, scheduling, and distributing [2][4]	1,562	37.5	10.9	6.6	1,798	43.6	12.6	9.8
Dispatchers	157	45.7	11.4	4.3	226	51.4	7.6	6.6
Production coordinators	182	44.0	6.1	2.2	200	56.0	8.0	8.2
Traffic, shipping, and receiving clerks	421	22.6	9.1	11.1	571	28.7	14.7	12.9
Stock and inventory clerks	532	38.7	13.3	5.5	459	44.1	13.5	9.9
Weighers, measurers, and checkers	79	47.2	16.9	5.8	71	50.9	15.8	5.2
Expediters	112	57.5	8.4	4.3	196	65.9	11.4	7.5
Adjusters and investigators	675	69.9	11.1	5.1	1,414	74.5	13.9	6.8
Insurance adjusters, examiners, and investigators	199	65.0	11.5	3.3	364	74.6	13.3	4.1
Investigators and adjusters, except insurance	301	70.1	11.3	4.8	788	74.5	12.3	6.0
Eligibility clerks, social welfare	69	88.7	12.9	9.4	109	80.6	18.7	16.8
Bill and account collectors	106	66.4	8.5	6.5	153	69.7	20.6	9.9
Miscellaneous administrative support [2]	2,397	85.2	12.5	5.9	3,799	81.6	13.9	8.4
General office clerks	648	80.6	12.7	5.2	696	80.2	13.0	8.1
Bank tellers	480	91.0	7.5	4.3	441	90.4	10.4	9.2
Data entry keyers	311	93.6	18.6	5.6	627	83.8	18.3	7.2
Statistical clerks	96	75.7	7.5	3.4	75	81.6	23.4	7.9
Teachers' aides	348	93.7	17.8	12.6	582	90.3	14.3	14.6

See footnotes at end of table.

No. 649. Employed Civilians, by Occupation, Sex, Race, and Hispanic Origin: 1983 and 1994—Continued

[See headnote, page 411]

OCCUPATION	1983 Total em-ployed (1,000)	1983 Percent of total Fe-male	1983 Black	1983 His-panic	1994 [1] Total em-ployed (1,000)	1994 Percent of total Fe-male	1994 Black	1994 His-panic
Service occupations [2]	**13,857**	**60.1**	**16.6**	**6.8**	**16,912**	**59.6**	**17.1**	**12.6**
Private household [2]	980	96.1	27.8	8.5	817	96.3	16.7	27.2
Child care workers	408	96.9	7.9	3.6	286	97.3	8.4	20.5
Cleaners and servants	512	95.8	42.4	11.8	500	95.8	20.0	31.0
Protective service	1,672	12.8	13.6	4.6	2,249	16.7	18.1	7.4
Supervisors, protective service	127	4.7	7.7	3.1	219	12.0	12.4	4.5
Supervisors, police and detectives	58	4.2	9.3	1.2	109	12.2	12.3	4.7
Firefighting and fire prevention	189	1.0	6.7	4.1	210	2.1	9.7	5.5
Firefighting occupations	170	1.0	7.3	3.8	195	2.1	9.1	5.4
Police and detectives	645	9.4	13.1	4.0	968	15.6	17.8	5.6
Police and detectives, public service	412	5.7	9.5	4.4	532	13.2	13.8	6.2
Sheriffs, bailiffs, and other law enforcement officers	87	13.2	11.5	4.0	130	16.4	12.2	5.6
Correctional institution officers	146	17.8	24.0	2.8	305	19.3	27.1	4.5
Guards	711	20.6	17.0	5.6	851	22.9	22.0	10.8
Guards and police, except public service	602	13.0	18.9	6.2	717	15.8	24.1	11.4
Service except private household and protective	11,205	64.0	16.0	6.9	13,847	64.3	16.9	12.6
Food preparation and service occupations [2]	4,860	63.3	10.5	6.8	5,960	57.9	12.4	13.4
Bartenders	338	48.4	2.7	4.4	322	55.1	2.9	4.4
Waiters and waitresses	1,357	87.8	4.1	3.6	1,446	78.6	5.5	7.6
Cooks	1,452	50.0	15.8	6.5	2,071	43.3	17.9	16.8
Food counter, fountain, and related occupations	326	76.0	9.1	6.7	351	70.2	11.2	8.9
Kitchen workers, food preparation	138	77.0	13.7	8.1	265	73.7	9.7	9.8
Waiters' and waitresses' assistants	364	38.8	12.6	14.2	433	47.6	12.8	21.8
Health service occupations	1,739	89.2	23.5	4.8	2,157	87.9	26.4	8.9
Dental assistants	154	98.1	6.1	5.7	188	96.6	2.7	10.2
Health aides, except nursing	316	86.8	16.5	4.8	333	78.1	25.6	7.8
Nursing aides, orderlies, and attendants	1,269	88.7	27.3	4.7	1,636	88.8	29.3	8.9
Cleaning and building service occupations [2]	2,736	38.8	24.4	9.2	2,948	45.2	22.4	17.7
Maids and housemen	531	81.2	32.3	10.1	680	83.3	27.9	20.2
Janitors and cleaners	2,031	28.6	22.6	8.9	2,048	34.0	20.8	17.1
Personal service occupations [2]	1,870	79.2	11.1	6.0	2,782	80.1	13.6	8.3
Barbers	92	12.9	8.4	12.1	98	21.8	27.6	10.3
Hairdressers and cosmetologists	622	88.7	7.0	5.7	753	90.6	10.3	8.0
Attendants, amusement and recreation facilities	131	40.2	7.1	4.3	201	39.0	10.2	6.7
Public transportation attendants	63	74.3	11.3	5.9	104	81.1	13.9	5.7
Welfare service aides	77	92.5	24.2	10.5	81	84.8	29.6	15.2
Family child care providers	(NA)	(NA)	(NA)	(NA)	428	98.7	10.8	9.0
Early childhood teachers' assistants	(NA)	(NA)	(NA)	(NA)	416	96.4	14.4	7.5
Precision production, craft, and repair	**12,328**	**8.1**	**6.8**	**6.2**	**13,489**	**9.3**	**7.7**	**10.4**
Mechanics and repairers	4,158	3.0	6.8	5.3	4,419	4.5	7.9	8.2
Mechanics and repairers, except supervisors [2]	3,906	2.8	7.0	5.5	4,183	4.2	8.1	8.3
Vehicle and mobile equipment mechanics/repairers [2]	1,683	0.8	6.9	6.0	1,734	1.2	6.6	9.7
Automobile mechanics	800	0.5	7.8	6.0	864	1.0	6.8	11.4
Aircraft engine mechanics	95	2.5	4.0	7.6	129	4.6	6.3	7.0
Electrical and electronic equipment repairers [2]	674	7.4	7.3	4.5	666	12.4	9.8	7.0
Data processing equipment repairers	98	9.3	6.1	4.5	163	18.0	7.6	3.6
Telephone installers and repairers	247	9.9	7.8	3.7	191	16.8	9.9	7.5
Construction trades	4,289	1.8	6.6	6.0	5,008	2.2	6.5	11.4
Construction trades, except supervisors	3,784	1.9	7.1	6.1	4,304	2.3	6.9	12.5
Carpenters	1,160	1.4	5.0	5.0	1,265	1.0	4.6	9.9
Extractive occupations	196	2.3	3.3	6.0	142	1.0	5.9	8.5
Precision production occupations	3,685	21.5	7.3	7.4	3,921	23.9	9.0	11.8
Operators, fabricators, and laborers [2]	**16,091**	**26.6**	**14.0**	**8.3**	**17,876**	**24.3**	**15.0**	**13.8**
Machine operators, assemblers, and inspectors [2]	7,744	42.1	14.0	9.4	7,754	38.1	15.1	14.8
Textile, apparel, and furnishings machine operators [2]	1,414	82.1	18.7	12.5	1,139	74.4	21.8	20.0
Textile sewing machine operators	806	94.0	15.5	14.5	619	86.0	19.4	24.1
Pressing machine operators	141	66.4	27.1	14.2	127	62.8	18.7	21.6
Fabricators, assemblers, and hand working occupations	1,715	33.7	11.3	8.7	1,994	31.5	12.4	13.0
Production inspectors, testers, samplers, and weighers	794	53.8	13.0	7.7	749	52.9	16.0	13.1
Transportation and material moving occupations	4,201	7.8	13.0	5.9	5,136	9.4	14.6	10.0
Motor vehicle operators	2,978	9.2	13.5	6.0	3,882	11.0	14.7	10.4
Trucks, heavy and light	2,195	3.1	12.3	5.7	2,815	4.5	12.4	10.7
Transportation occupations, except motor vehicles	212	2.4	6.7	3.0	176	2.1	12.0	2.3
Material moving equipment operators	1,011	4.8	12.9	6.3	1,078	4.7	14.6	9.5
Industrial truck and tractor operators	369	5.6	19.6	8.2	483	6.9	23.3	12.2
Handlers, equipment cleaners, helpers, and laborers [2]	4,147	16.8	15.1	8.6	4,986	18.1	15.3	16.3
Freight, stock, and material handlers	1,488	15.4	15.3	7.1	2,024	20.1	16.4	12.9
Laborers, except construction	1,024	19.4	16.0	8.6	1,240	18.2	15.1	15.4
Farming, forestry, and fishing	**3,700**	**16.0**	**7.5**	**8.2**	**3,629**	**19.3**	**5.1**	**17.1**
Farm operators and managers	1,450	12.1	1.3	0.7	1,453	25.4	0.2	2.0
Other agricultural and related occupations	2,072	19.9	11.7	14.0	1,992	15.3	8.3	27.1
Farm workers	1,149	24.8	11.6	15.9	748	16.6	6.7	37.9
Forestry and logging occupations	126	1.4	12.8	2.1	132	7.0	9.9	11.9
Fishers, hunters, and trappers	53	4.5	1.8	2.5	52	6.2	1.9	7.4

- Represents or rounds to zero.   NA Not available.   [1] See footnote 2, table 626.   [2] Includes other occupations, not shown separately.   [3] Level of total employment below 50,000.   [4] Includes clerks.

Source: U.S. Bureau of Labor Statistics, *Employment and Earnings,* monthly, January issues.

No. 650. Civilian Employment in Occupations With the Largest Job Growth: 1992 to 2005

[Occupations are in descending order of absolute employment change 1992-2005 (moderate growth). Includes wage and salary jobs, self-employed, and unpaid family members. Estimates based on the Current Employment Statistics estimates and the Occupational Employment Statistics estimates. See source for methodological assumptions. Minus sign (-) indicates decrease]

OCCUPATION	EMPLOYMENT (1,000)				PERCENT CHANGE 1992-2005		
	1992	2005 [1]			Low	Moderate	High
		Low	Moderate	High			
Total, all occupations [2]	121,099	139,007	147,482	154,430	14.8	21.8	27.5
Salespersons, retail	3,660	4,137	4,446	4,611	13.1	21.5	26.0
Registered nurses	1,835	2,479	2,601	2,637	35.1	41.7	43.7
Cashiers	2,747	3,201	3,417	3,520	16.5	24.4	28.1
General office clerks	2,688	3,143	3,342	3,489	16.9	24.3	29.8
Truck drivers light and heavy	2,391	2,836	3,039	3,235	18.6	27.1	35.3
Waiters and waitresses	1,756	2,280	2,394	2,415	29.8	36.3	37.5
Nursing aides, orderlies, and attendants	1,308	1,824	1,903	1,937	39.4	45.4	48.0
Janitors and cleaners [3]	2,862	3,246	3,410	3,519	13.4	19.1	23.0
Food preparation workers	1,223	1,661	1,748	1,775	35.8	42.9	45.1
Systems analysts	455	891	956	1,001	95.7	110.1	120.0
Home health aides	347	794	827	835	128.7	138.1	140.6
Teachers, secondary school	1,263	1,640	1,724	1,789	29.9	36.6	41.7
Child care workers	684	1,100	1,135	1,183	60.6	65.8	72.8
Guards	803	1,138	1,211	1,255	41.7	50.8	56.2
Marketing and sales worker supervisors	2,036	2,303	2,443	2,565	13.1	20.0	26.0
Teacher aides and educational assistants	885	1,209	1,266	1,308	36.6	43.1	47.8
General managers and top executives	2,871	3,050	3,251	3,418	6.2	13.2	19.0
Maintenance repairers, general utility	1,145	1,388	1,464	1,542	21.2	27.8	34.7
Gardeners and groundskeepers, except farm	884	1,152	1,195	1,261	30.3	35.2	42.7
Teachers, elementary	1,456	1,683	1,767	1,830	15.6	21.3	25.6
Food counter, fountain, and related workers	1,564	1,776	1,872	1,895	13.6	19.7	21.2
Receptionists and information clerks	904	1,149	1,210	1,245	27.1	33.8	37.7
Accountants and auditors	939	1,167	1,243	1,301	24.3	32.3	38.6
Clerical supervisors and managers	1,267	1,473	1,568	1,622	16.3	23.8	28.0
Cooks, restaurant	602	837	879	889	39.0	45.8	47.5
Teachers, special education	358	594	625	648	65.9	74.4	81.0
Licensed practical nurses	659	879	920	933	33.4	39.7	41.6
Cooks, short order and fast food	714	921	971	978	29.0	36.0	37.0
Human services workers	189	429	445	451	127.6	135.9	139.2
Computer engineers and scientists	211	409	447	484	93.9	111.9	129.2
Teachers, preschool and kindergarten	434	646	669	682	48.9	54.3	57.2
Food service and lodging managers	532	732	764	787	37.6	43.5	48.0
Hairdressers, hairstylists, and cosmetologists	628	824	846	876	31.2	34.7	39.4
Blue collar worker supervisors	1,757	1,844	1,974	2,131	5.0	12.4	21.3
College and university faculty	812	976	1,026	1,064	20.2	26.4	31.1
Carpenters	978	1,131	1,176	1,317	15.7	20.2	34.6
Correction officers	282	452	479	503	60.0	69.9	78.1
Physicians	556	720	751	769	29.5	35.0	38.3
Lawyers	626	781	821	850	24.7	31.1	35.8
Social workers	484	645	676	693	33.3	39.5	43.0
Financial managers	701	828	875	917	18.1	24.8	30.7
Computer programmers	555	673	723	759	21.3	30.4	36.8
Automotive mechanics	739	857	907	960	15.9	22.7	29.8
Personal and home care aides	127	283	293	296	122.0	129.8	132.0
Legal secretaries	280	415	439	447	48.3	57.1	59.9
Stock clerks	1,782	1,801	1,940	2,024	1.0	8.8	13.6
Marketing, advertising, and public relations managers	432	548	588	616	26.8	36.1	42.6
Traffic, shipping, and receiving clerks	824	889	971	1,034	7.9	17.8	25.4
Dining room and cafeteria attendants and bar helpers	441	546	572	580	23.8	29.8	31.5
Painters and paperhangers, construction and maintenance	440	547	569	624	24.3	29.2	41.8
Medical assistants	181	296	308	313	63.5	70.5	73.0
Secretaries, except legal and medical	2,810	2,766	2,930	3,067	-1.5	4.3	9.2
Teachers and instructors, vocational ed. and training	305	396	416	430	29.7	36.5	41.1
Freight, stock, and material movers, hand	845	885	955	1,011	4.8	13.1	19.7
Bus drivers, school	395	471	504	519	19.3	27.6	31.5
Engineering, mathematical, and natural science managers	337	410	444	476	21.5	31.5	41.1
Medical secretaries	235	326	341	345	39.0	45.2	47.0
Radiologic technologists and technicians	162	252	264	267	55.4	62.7	64.6
Personnel, training, and labor relations specialists	281	360	383	398	28.1	36.1	41.7
Electricians	518	588	618	698	13.6	19.3	34.7
Amusement and recreation attendants	207	294	303	309	41.9	46.1	49.2
Instructors and coaches, sports and physical training	260	343	355	363	31.6	36.2	39.3
Bill and account collectors	235	309	328	339	31.9	40.0	44.5
Adjustment clerks	352	412	445	462	17.2	26.5	31.2
Electrical and electronics engineers	370	422	459	501	14.0	24.2	35.4
Management analysts	208	283	297	313	35.8	42.7	50.2
Counter and rental clerks	242	314	331	341	29.5	36.3	40.6

[1] Based on low, moderate, or high trend assumptions. [2] Includes other occupations, not shown separately. [3] Includes maids and housekeepers.

Source: U.S. Bureau of Labor Statistics, *Monthly Labor Review*, November 1993.

No. 651. Civilian Employment in the Fastest Growing and Fastest Declining Occupations: 1992 to 2005

[Occupations are in order of employment percent change 1992-2005 (moderate growth). Includes wage and salary jobs, self-employed, and unpaid family members. Estimates based on the Current Employment Statistics estimates and the Occupational Employment Statistics estimates. See source for methodological assumptions. Minus sign (-) indicates decrease]

OCCUPATION	EMPLOYMENT (1,000)				PERCENT CHANGE 1992-2005		
	1992	2005 [1]			Low	Moderate	High
		Low	Moderate	High			
Total, all occupations [2]	121,099	139,007	147,482	154,430	14.8	21.8	27.5
FASTEST GROWING							
Home health aides	347	794	827	835	128.7	138.1	140.6
Human services workers	189	429	445	451	127.6	135.9	139.2
Personal and home care aides	127	283	293	296	122.0	129.8	132.0
Computer engineers and scientists	211	409	447	484	93.9	111.9	129.2
Systems analysts	455	891	956	1,001	95.7	110.1	120.0
Physical and corrective therapy assistants and aides	61	113	118	119	84.6	92.7	95.1
Physical therapists	90	163	170	173	80.2	88.0	91.4
Paralegals	95	166	176	180	75.8	86.1	89.8
Occupational therapy assistants and aides	12	20	21	21	70.5	78.1	80.1
Electronic pagination systems workers	18	29	32	33	65.1	77.9	84.0
Teachers, special education	358	594	625	648	65.9	74.4	81.0
Medical assistants	181	296	308	313	63.5	70.5	73.0
Detectives, except public	59	94	100	104	60.1	70.2	76.8
Correction officers	282	452	479	503	60.0	69.9	78.1
Child care workers	684	1,100	1,135	1,183	60.6	65.8	72.8
Travel agents	115	167	191	196	45.2	65.7	69.9
Radiologic technologists and technicians	162	252	264	267	55.4	62.7	64.6
Nursery (farm) workers	72	110	116	123	53.1	62.0	71.3
Medical records technicians	76	118	123	125	54.4	61.5	63.6
Operations research analysts	45	67	72	75	50.1	61.4	68.0
Occupational therapists	40	61	64	65	52.9	59.6	62.5
Subway and streetcar operators	22	33	35	37	48.1	57.2	64.9
Legal secretaries	280	415	439	447	48.3	57.1	59.9
Teachers, preschool and kindergarten	434	646	669	682	48.9	54.3	57.2
Manicurists	35	54	55	56	51.2	54.1	58.3
EEG technologists	6	9	10	10	46.6	53.8	55.4
Producers, directors, actors, and entertainers	129	190	198	205	47.0	53.5	58.7
Speech-language pathologists and audiologists	73	105	110	113	44.6	51.3	55.7
Flight attendants	93	121	140	144	30.3	51.0	55.5
Guards	803	1,138	1,211	1,255	41.7	50.8	56.2
Nuclear medicine technologists	12	17	18	18	43.1	50.1	51.6
Insurance adjusters, examiners, and investigators	147	205	220	220	39.3	49.1	49.5
Respiratory therapists	74	104	109	110	41.4	48.3	49.9
Psychologists	143	204	212	222	42.1	48.0	54.7
FASTEST DECLINING							
Frame wirers, central office	11	2	3	3	-77.4	-75.3	-74.7
Signal or track switch maintainers	3	1	1	1	-76.6	-74.6	-72.9
Peripheral EDP equipment operators	30	11	12	12	-62.6	-60.2	-59.0
Directory assistance operators	27	12	13	14	-54.9	-50.6	-49.4
Central office operators	48	22	24	24	-54.7	-50.3	-49.1
Station installers and repairers, telephone	40	18	20	20	-54.7	-50.3	-49.1
Portable machine cutters	11	5	6	6	-48.3	-40.1	-39.4
Computer operators, except peripheral equipment	266	151	161	168	-43.2	-39.3	-36.6
Shoe sewing machine operators and tenders	16	9	10	10	-46.3	-38.4	-35.8
Central office and PBX installers and repairers	70	41	45	46	-41.3	-35.6	-34.1
Child care workers, private household	350	220	227	242	-37.1	-35.1	-31.0
Job printers	15	9	10	10	-39.4	-35.0	-33.2
Roustabouts	33	20	22	32	-38.4	-33.2	-2.0
Separating and still machine operators and tenders	21	13	14	15	-37.0	-32.8	-29.8
Cleaners and servants, private household	483	316	326	347	-34.6	-32.5	-28.2
Coil winders, tapers, and finishers	20	12	14	16	-41.2	-32.4	-22.1
Billing, posting, and calculating machine operators	93	62	66	68	-33.6	-29.5	-27.0
Sewing machine operators, garment	556	338	393	396	-39.1	-29.2	-28.7
Compositors and typesetters, precision	11	7	8	8	-30.7	-26.5	-23.3
Data entry keyers, composing	16	11	12	12	-31.7	-26.4	-23.8
Motion picture projectionists	9	7	7	7	-29.3	-25.8	-24.0
Telephone and cable TV line installers and repairers	165	117	125	134	-29.4	-24.4	-18.7
Cutting and slicing machine setters [3]	94	68	73	76	-28.1	-22.6	-19.5
Watchmakers	9	7	7	8	-26.5	-22.6	-18.4
Tire building machine operators	14	10	11	12	-29.4	-22.3	-19.0
Packaging and filling machine operators and tenders	319	232	248	257	-27.1	-22.3	-19.4
Head sawyers and sawing machine operators and tenders [4]	59	44	46	53	-25.7	-22.3	-10.3
Switchboard operators	239	177	188	194	-25.9	-21.3	-18.8
Farmers	1,088	831	857	914	-23.7	-21.2	-16.0
Machine forming operators and tenders, metal and plastic	155	112	123	133	-27.8	-20.8	-14.3
Cement and gluing machine operators and tenders	35	26	28	30	-25.7	-20.2	-12.7

[1] Based on low, moderate, or high trend assumptions. [2] Includes other occupations, not shown separately. [3] Includes operators and tenders. [4] Includes setters and set-up operators.

Source: U.S. Bureau of Labor Statistics, *Monthly Labor Review*, November 1993.

Labor Force, Employment, and Earnings

No. 652. Occupations of the Employed, by Selected Characteristics: 1994

[In thousands. Annual averages of monthly figures. For civilian noninstitutional population 25 to 64 years old. Based on Current Population Survey; see text, section 1, and Appendix III]

SEX, RACE, AND EDUCATIONAL ATTAINMENT	Total employed	Managerial/professional	Tech./sales/administrative	Service [1]	Precision production [2]	Operators/fabricators [3]	Farming, forestry, fishing
Male, total [4]	**54,434**	**16,069**	**10,667**	**4,544**	**10,736**	**10,357**	**2,061**
Less than a high school diploma	6,392	311	456	806	1,727	2,434	659
High school graduates, no college	17,811	1,923	2,864	1,748	5,185	5,288	802
Less than a bachelor's degree	14,183	3,285	3,782	1,433	3,130	2,155	398
College graduates	16,047	10,550	3,565	558	694	480	201
White	47,013	14,458	9,315	3,399	9,618	8,371	1,853
Less than a high school diploma	5,242	270	380	573	1,509	1,953	557
High school graduates, no college	15,267	1,751	2,496	1,265	4,710	4,318	727
Less than a bachelor's degree	12,277	2,957	3,297	1,116	2,807	1,725	374
College graduates	14,227	9,480	3,142	445	592	374	194
Black	5,131	909	892	847	786	1,566	131
Less than a high school diploma	787	26	52	152	139	355	62
High school graduates, no college	1,976	113	274	378	364	796	52
Less than a bachelor's degree	1,417	234	353	246	224	348	14
College graduates	950	536	213	71	60	67	1
Female, total [4]	**46,026**	**14,784**	**18,746**	**7,214**	**1,107**	**3,627**	**548**
Less than a high school diploma	3,858	195	753	1,579	185	1,022	125
High school graduates, no college	16,069	2,145	7,827	3,392	554	1,930	221
Less than a bachelor's degree	13,755	3,839	7,196	1,762	274	551	130
College graduates	12,344	8,605	2,969	481	94	124	71
White	38,690	12,903	16,135	5,513	870	2,755	514
Less than a high school diploma	2,969	162	645	1,130	146	782	104
High school graduates, no college	13,577	1,907	6,952	2,600	433	1,471	213
Less than a bachelor's degree	11,524	3,340	6,029	1,403	219	406	126
College graduates	10,619	7,492	2,509	381	71	96	70
Black	5,453	1,297	1,960	1,353	158	668	17
Less than a high school diploma	641	24	71	357	23	157	10
High school graduates, no college	1,970	170	684	649	88	376	4
Less than a bachelor's degree	1,795	388	952	292	38	122	1
College graduates	1,047	715	254	55	9	14	-

- Represents or rounds to zero.   [1] Includes private household workers.   [2] Includes craft and repair.   [3] Includes laborers.   [4] Includes other races, not shown separately.

Source: U.S. Bureau of Labor Statistics, unpublished data.

No. 653. Employment, by Industry: 1970 to 1994

[In thousands, except percent. See headnote, table 634. Data from 1985 to 1990, and also beginning 1994, not strictly comparable with other years due to changes in industrial classification]

INDUSTRY	1970	1980	1985	1990	1994 [1] Total	Percent Female	Percent Black	Percent Hispanic[2]
Total employed	**78,678**	**99,303**	**107,150**	**117,914**	**123,060**	**46.0**	**10.4**	**8.8**
Agriculture	3,463	3,364	3,179	3,186	3,409	25.1	4.0	16.4
Mining	516	979	939	730	669	15.7	4.5	5.5
Construction	4,818	6,215	6,987	7,696	7,493	9.6	6.4	10.5
Manufacturing	20,746	21,942	20,879	21,184	20,157	32.1	10.1	9.9
Transportation, communication, and other public utilities	5,320	6,525	7,548	8,136	8,692	28.4	13.7	7.8
Wholesale and retail trade	15,008	20,191	22,296	24,269	25,699	47.2	8.5	9.7
Wholesale trade	2,672	3,920	4,341	4,651	4,713	28.9	6.5	9.2
Retail trade	12,336	16,270	17,955	19,618	20,986	51.3	8.9	9.9
Finance, insurance, real estate	3,945	5,993	7,005	8,021	8,141	58.9	9.1	6.7
Services [3]	20,385	28,752	33,322	39,084	42,986	61.8	11.9	7.8
Business and repair services [3]	1,403	3,848	5,969	7,409	7,304	36.3	11.2	10.0
Advertising	147	191	263	277	272	52.6	5.6	4.2
Services to dwellings and buildings	(NA)	370	571	813	849	49.2	16.4	20.3
Personnel supply services	(NA)	235	590	704	804	61.3	20.5	6.7
Computer and data processing	(NA)	221	549	799	1,017	34.5	7.1	3.8
Detective/protective services	(NA)	213	318	373	477	17.6	24.0	10.6
Automobile services	600	952	1,322	1,429	1,546	13.5	8.9	12.9
Personal services [3]	4,276	3,839	4,352	4,667	4,339	69.0	13.6	15.2
Private households	1,782	1,257	1,254	1,023	976	89.3	17.5	25.4
Hotels and lodging places	979	1,149	1,451	1,780	1,328	54.7	16.1	17.8
Entertainment and recreation	717	1,047	1,278	1,503	2,134	42.6	8.4	7.9
Professional and related services [3]	12,904	19,853	21,563	25,335	29,030	68.8	12.0	6.0
Hospitals	2,843	4,036	4,269	4,690	5,009	76.5	16.4	5.5
Health services, except hospitals	1,628	3,345	3,641	4,757	5,579	78.9	13.3	6.8
Elementary, secondary schools	6,126	5,550	5,431	6,028	6,447	74.6	11.8	7.1
Colleges and universities	([4])	2,108	2,281	2,609	2,743	52.3	9.7	4.7
Social services	828	1,590	1,682	2,234	3,046	81.3	17.5	7.8
Legal services	429	776	995	1,217	1,286	55.0	5.2	5.3
Public administration [5]	4,476	5,342	4,995	5,608	5,814	43.0	16.4	5.8

NA Not available.   [1] See footnote 2, table 626.   [2] Persons of Hispanic origin may be of any race.   [3] Includes industries not shown separately.   [4] Included with elementary/secondary schools.   [5] Includes workers involved in uniquely governmental activities, e.g., judicial and legislative.

Source: U.S. Bureau of Labor Statistics, *Employment and Earnings*, monthly, January issues.

No. 654. Employment by Selected Industry, With Projections: 1979 to 2005

[Figures may differ from those in other tables since these data exclude establishments not elsewhere classified (SIC 99); in addition, agriculture services (SIC 074, 5, 8) are included in agriculture, not services. See source for details. Minus sign (-) indicates decrease]

INDUSTRY	1987 SIC [1] code	EMPLOYMENT (1,000)			ANNUAL GROWTH RATE	
		1979	1992	2005 proj. [2]	1979-1992	1992-2005 proj. [2]
Total.........................	(X)	101,363	121,093	147,484	1.4	1.5
Nonfarm wage and salary.............	(X)	89,491	107,888	132,960	1.4	1.6
Goods-producing (excluding agriculture)	(X)	26,461	23,142	23,717	-1.0	0.2
Mining..........................	10-14	958	631	562	-3.2	-0.9
Construction.....................	15,16,17	4,463	4,471	5,632	-	1.8
Manufacturing....................	20-39	21,040	18,040	17,523	-1.2	-0.2
Durable manufacturing.............	24,25,32-39	12,730	10,237	9,673	-1.7	-0.4
Lumber and wood products...........	24	782	674	690	-1.1	0.2
Furniture and fixtures............	25	498	476	523	-0.3	0.7
Stone, clay and glass products	32	674	512	437	-2.1	-1.2
Primary metal industries	33	1,254	693	618	-4.5	-0.9
Blast furnaces/basic steel products ...	331	571	250	224	-6.1	-0.9
Fabricated metal products.............	34	1,713	1,322	1,196	-2.0	-0.8
Industrial machinery and equipment	35	2,508	1,922	1,868	-2.0	-0.2
Computer equipment	3571,2,5,7	318	353	237	0.8	-3.0
Electronic and other electric equipment [3]	36	1,793	1,526	1,354	-1.2	-0.9
Telephone and telegraph apparatus........	3661	171	108	81	-3.4	-2.3
Semiconductors and related devices.....	3674	201	218	224	0.6	0.2
Transportation equipment	37	2,059	1,822	1,765	-0.9	-0.2
Motor vehicles and equipment	371	990	809	759	-1.5	-0.5
Instruments and related products [3]	38	1,006	925	887	-0.6	-0.3
Measuring/controlling devices, watches	382	431	300	255	-2.8	-1.2
Medical instruments and supplies	3841-3	144	216	295	3.2	2.4
Miscellaneous manufacturing industries	39	445	363	334	-1.5	-0.6
Nondurable manufacturing	20-23,26-31	8,310	7,804	7,851	-0.5	-
Food and kindred products	20	1,733	1,655	1,648	-0.4	-
Tobacco manufactures	21	70	49	37	-2.7	-2.1
Textile mill products.............	22	885	671	571	-2.1	-1.2
Apparel and other textile products	23	1,304	1,005	760	-2.0	-2.1
Paper and allied products	26	697	687	729	-0.1	0.4
Printing and publishing.............	27	1,235	1,504	1,751	1.5	1.2
Chemicals and allied products	28	1,109	1,083	1,090	-0.2	0.1
Petroleum and coal products	29	210	159	128	-2.1	-1.6
Rubber/misc. plastics products.........	30	821	872	1,066	0.5	1.6
Leather and leather products	31	246	119	71	-5.4	-3.9
Service producing	(X)	63,030	84,746	109,243	2.3	2.0
Transportation, communications, utilities.........	40-42,44-49	5,136	5,709	6,497	0.8	1.0
Transportation	40-42,44-47	3,019	3,486	4,310	1.1	1.6
Communications	48	1,309	1,268	1,116	-0.2	-1.0
Electric, gas, and sanitary services	49	807	955	1,072	1.3	0.9
Wholesale trade....................	50,51	5,221	6,045	7,191	1.1	1.3
Retail trade.....................	52-59	14,972	19,346	23,777	2.0	1.6
Eating and drinking places	58	4,513	6,602	8,778	3.0	2.2
Finance, insurance, and real estate.............	60-67	4,975	6,571	7,969	2.2	1.5
Services.............	70-87,89	16,779	28,422	41,788	4.1	3.0
Hotels and other lodging places	70	1,060	1,572	2,209	3.1	2.6
Personal services [3]	72	821	1,111	1,382	2.4	1.7
Business services [3]	73	2,410	5,313	8,370	6.3	3.6
Advertising.....................	731	146	226	288	3.4	1.9
Services to buildings	734	487	805	1,000	3.9	1.7
Personnel supply services.............	736	508	1,649	2,581	9.5	3.5
Computer and data processing services	737	271	831	1,626	9.0	5.3
Auto repair, services, and garages.............	75	575	878	1,293	3.3	3.0
Miscellaneous repair shops	76	282	345	449	1.6	2.0
Motion pictures.............	78	228	404	499	4.5	1.6
Video tape rental.............	784	(NA)	125	107	(NA)	-1.2
Amusement and recreation services.............	79	751	1,169	1,626	3.5	2.6
Health services.............	80	4,993	8,523	12,539	4.2	3.0
Offices of health practitioners.............	801,2,3,4	1,200	2,387	3,617	5.4	3.2
Nursing and personal care facilities.............	805	951	1,543	2,306	3.8	3.1
Hospitals, private.............	806	2,608	3,760	5,040	2.9	2.3
Health services, n.e.c. [4]	807,8,9	234	833	1,577	10.3	5.0
Legal services.............	81	460	915	1,355	5.4	3.1
Educational services.............	82	1,090	1,700	2,162	3.5	1.9
Social services.............	83	1,081	1,958	3,691	4.7	5.0
Museums, zoos, and membership organizations.............	84,86,8733	1,652	2,164	2,674	2.1	1.6
Engineering, management, and services, n.e.c. [4][5]	87,89	1,341	2,370	3,538	4.5	3.1
Government.....................	(X)	15,947	18,653	22,021	1.2	1.3
Federal government	(X)	2,773	2,969	2,815	0.5	-0.4
State and local government	(X)	13,174	15,683	19,206	1.4	1.6
Agriculture.....................	01,02,07,08,09	3,398	3,295	3,325	-0.2	0.1
Private households....................	88	1,264	1,116	802	-1.0	-2.5
Nonagriculture self-employed and unpaid family	(X)	7,210	8,794	10,397	1.5	1.3

- Rounds to zero.   NA Not available.   X Not applicable.   [1] 1987 Standard Industrial Classification; see text, section 13.
[2] Based on assumptions of moderate growth; see source.   [3] Includes other industries, not shown separately.   [4] N.e.c. means not elsewhere classified.   [5] Excludes SIC 8733.

Source: U.S. Bureau of Labor Statistics, *Monthly Labor Review*, November 1993.

No. 655. High Technology Industries—Summary: 1993

[For workers on private industry payrolls and excludes the self-employed. Based on surveys of the Occupational Employment Statistics Program and subject to sampling error; for details see source]

INDUSTRY	1987 SIC [1] code	Establish- ments (1,000)	EMPLOYMENT Total (1,000)	EMPLOYMENT Percent distribution	Average annual pay (dol.)
All high technology industries [2]	(X)	**363.2**	**9,600**	**100.0**	**41,595**
Level I industries [3]	(X)	327.2	8,329	86.8	42,842
Crude petroleum and natural gas operations	131	9.4	172	1.8	56,814
Cigarettes	211	(Z)	33	0.3	50,758
Industrial inorganic chemicals	281	1.6	135	1.4	46,530
Plastics materials and synthetics	282	1.0	165	1.7	44,222
Drugs	283	1.8	264	2.8	49,112
Soap, cleaners, and toilet goods	284	2.6	156	1.6	40,569
Paints and allied products	285	1.5	58	0.6	36,653
Industrial organic chemicals	286	1.0	149	1.6	51,152
Agricultural chemicals	287	1.2	56	0.6	42,320
Miscellaneous chemical products	289	2.7	92	1.0	40,763
Petroleum refining	291	0.7	113	1.2	53,863
Miscellaneous petroleum and coal products	299	0.5	13	0.1	36,259
Nonferrous rolling and drawing	335	1.3	161	1.7	36,350
Special industry machinery	355	4.2	148	1.5	36,467
Computer and office equipment	357	2.7	366	3.8	49,780
Electrical industrial apparatus	362	1.9	153	1.6	31,302
Communications equipment	366	2.3	240	2.5	42,547
Electronic components and accessories	367	6.5	528	5.5	36,480
Motor vehicles and equipment	371	5.8	837	8.7	42,215
Aircraft and parts	372	2.8	540	5.6	44,556
Guided missiles, space vehicles, parts	376	0.3	123	1.3	49,633
Search and navigation equipment	381	0.9	206	2.1	47,200
Measuring and controlling devices	382	5.3	283	3.0	37,718
Medical instruments and supplies	384	4.4	269	2.8	35,520
Photographic equipment and supplies	386	0.9	91	1.0	47,373
Computer and data-processing services	737	66.0	894	9.3	45,172
Engineering and architectural services	871	66.1	761	7.9	41,750
Research and testing services	873	24.3	577	6.0	38,996
Management and public relations	874	98.3	707	7.4	42,508
Services, n.e.c. [4]	899	9.0	42	0.4	48,235
Level II industries [5]	(X)	36.0	1,272	13.3	33,428
Miscellaneous textile goods	229	1.0	51	0.5	28,265
Pulp mills	261	0.1	13	0.1	46,827
Miscellaneous converted paper products	267	3.1	243	2.5	32,890
Ordinance and accessories, n.e.c. [4]	348	0.4	60	0.6	35,172
Engines and turbines	351	0.5	88	0.9	43,055
General industry machinery	356	4.6	237	2.5	34,164
Industrial machines, n.e.c. [4]	359	22.2	299	3.1	30,052
Household audio and video equipment	365	1.2	83	0.9	35,968
Miscellaneous electrical equipment and supplies	369	1.8	151	1.6	33,860
Miscellaneous transportation equipment	379	1.1	46	0.5	29,719

Z Less than 50.   X Not applicable.   [1] 1987 Standard Industrial Classification; see text, section 13.   [2] Those industries whose proportion of R&D employment is at least equal to the average proportion of all industries surveyed.   [3] Industries whose proportion of R&D employment is at least 50 percent higher than the average of all industries surveyed.   [4] N.e.c. means not elsewhere classified.   [5] Industries whose proportion of R&D employment is at least equal to the average of all industries surveyed, but less than 50 percent higher than the average.

Source: U.S. Bureau of Labor Statistics, *Employment and Wages, Annual Averages 1993*, BLS Bulletin 2449.

No. 656. Occupational and Employer Tenure, by Occupation: 1991

[As of January. For the 35 occupations with the longest occupational tenure. Covers occupations with 50,000 or more workers. Based on Current Population Survey; see text section 1, and Appendix III]

CURRENT OCCUPATION	Number (1,000)	OCCUPATIONAL TENURE [1]		EMPLOYER TENURE [2]		Median age [3]
		Total (years)	Rank	Total (years)	Rank	
Total employed, 16 years old and over [4]	**114,979**	**6.5**	**(X)**	**4.5**	**(X)**	**37.2**
Airplane pilots and navigators	116	12.2	30	4.5	32	36.2
Automobile body and related repairers	202	12.1	31	3.1	34	34.1
Barbers.	111	27.2	1	11.0	12	51.7
Brickmasons and stonemasons	160	12.6	21	5.1	30	38.2
Chemical engineers	72	12.6	21	6.4	22	38.0
Civil engineers	284	13.2	15	7.4	18	42.0
Crane and tower operators	77	13.7	13	6.1	24	41.9
Dental laboratory & medical appliance technicians . . .	59	12.9	17	5.5	27	39.9
Dentists	136	15.1	7	13.7	7	40.5
Electrical power installers and repairers	128	12.6	21	12.5	9	39.2
Electricians	718	12.3	27	4.9	31	38.3
Farmers, except horticultural.	1,037	21.8	2	20.2	2	48.0
Geologists and geodesists	60	12.3	27	7.3	19	40.8
Health specialties teachers	50	15.1	7	11.4	11	45.7
Heavy equipment mechanics	158	13.7	13	6.7	20	38.1
Locomotive operators	58	19.8	3	19.7	3	46.5
Machinists.	526	12.3	27	6.6	21	39.3
Managers, farms, except horticultural	145	11.6	34	8.9	15	36.9
Millwrights	79	12.5	24	6.2	23	43.1
Musicians and composers	143	15.2	5	5.4	29	36.8
Operating engineers	247	12.0	32	5.7	26	37.8
Pharmacists.	182	12.7	20	5.8	25	39.1
Plumbers, pipefitters, and steamfitters	427	13.1	16	5.5	27	38.4
Public transportation attendants.	60	12.5	24	8.2	17	39.2
Railroad conductors and yardmasters.	56	15.2	5	18.8	4	43.1
Stationary engineers	120	15.4	4	11.8	10	42.2
Structural metal workers.	52	12.4	26	1.1	35	36.5
Supervisors, firefighting & fire prevention.	65	15.0	10	20.3	1	44.5
Supervisors, police and detectives	69	12.9	17	15.1	6	41.5
Teachers, elementary school.	1,592	12.0	32	8.4	16	41.3
Teachers, secondary school	1,392	14.1	11	9.5	14	42.0
Telephone installers and repairers	193	12.9	17	16.5	5	40.3
Timber cutting and logging	68	11.5	35	3.5	33	33.3
Tool and die makers	125	15.1	7	12.6	8	39.5
Veterinarians	66	14.0	12	10.2	13	39.5

X Not applicable.   [1] Cumulative tenure in current occupation.   [2] Continuous tenure with current employer.   [3] For definition of median, see Guide to Tabular Presentation.   [4] Includes other occupations, not shown separately.
Source: U.S. Bureau of Labor Statistics, *News*, USDL 92-386; and unpublished data.

No. 657. Displaced Workers, by Selected Characteristics: 1994

[As of February. In percent, except total. For persons 20 years old and over with tenure of 3 years or more who lost or left a job between January 1991 and December 1993 because of plant closings or moves, slack work, or the abolishment of their positions. Based on Current Population Survey and subject to sampling error; see source and Appendix III]

SEX, AGE, RACE, AND HISPANIC ORIGIN	Total (1,000)	EMPLOYMENT STATUS			REASON FOR JOB LOSS		
		Employed	Unemployed	Not in the labor force	Plant or company closed down or moved	Slack work	Position or shift abolished
Total [1]	**4,473**	**68.0**	**19.1**	**12.9**	**42.3**	**29.9**	**27.7**
Males	2,614	71.6	19.9	8.4	40.9	33.0	26.1
20 to 24 years old	77	58.7	35.6	5.6	43.7	42.2	14.1
25 to 54 years old	2,097	76.2	19.1	4.7	40.7	32.8	26.4
55 to 64 years old	383	57.0	21.5	21.6	42.9	31.0	26.0
65 years old and over	57	(2)	(2)	(2)	(2)	(2)	(2)
Females	1,859	62.9	17.9	19.2	44.3	25.6	30.1
20 to 24 years old	76	68.6	13.1	18.3	47.4	30.3	22.4
25 to 54 years old	1,443	68.4	18.0	13.6	42.3	27.1	30.6
55 to 64 years old	228	47.4	23.0	29.6	54.4	16.2	29.4
65 years old and over	112	19.5	9.1	71.4	45.9	23.4	30.6
White	3,859	69.3	17.9	12.8	41.2	30.2	28.6
Male	2,291	73.4	18.4	8.2	40.2	33.1	26.6
Female.	1,568	63.3	17.2	19.5	42.7	25.9	31.4
Black	427	61.5	26.1	12.4	51.4	25.3	23.3
Male	219	59.3	32.1	8.7	50.7	25.2	24.0
Female.	209	63.7	19.8	16.4	52.1	25.3	22.6
Hispanic origin [3]	361	55.6	30.5	13.9	49.2	35.5	15.4
Male	243	57.8	34.0	8.1	44.9	42.0	13.1
Female.	118	51.0	23.1	25.9	58.0	21.8	20.2

[1] Includes other races, not shown separately.   [2] Data not shown where base is less than 75,000.   [3] Persons of Hispanic origin may be of any race.
Source: U.S. Bureau of Labor Statistics, *News*, USDL 94-434.

No. 658. Unemployed Workers—Summary: 1980 to 1994

[**In thousands, except as indicated**. For civilian noninstitutional population 16 years old and over. Annual averages of monthly figures. For data on unemployment insurance, see table 602. See also *Historical Statistics, Colonial Times to 1970*, series D 87-101]

AGE, SEX, RACE, HISPANIC ORIGIN	1980	1985	1989	1990	1991	1992	1993	1994 [1]
UNEMPLOYED								
Total [2]	7,637	8,312	6,528	6,874	8,426	9,384	8,734	7,996
16 to 19 years old	1,669	1,468	1,194	1,149	1,290	1,352	1,296	1,320
20 to 24 years old	1,835	1,738	1,218	1,221	1,477	1,546	1,421	1,373
25 to 44 years old	2,964	3,681	3,010	3,273	4,106	4,603	4,220	3,694
45 to 64 years old	1,075	1,331	1,016	1,124	1,437	1,748	1,686	1,456
65 years and over	94	93	91	107	116	135	111	153
Male	4,267	4,521	3,525	3,799	4,817	5,380	4,932	4,367
16 to 19 years old	913	806	658	629	709	761	728	740
20 to 24 years old	1,076	944	660	666	849	884	808	768
25 to 44 years old	1,619	1,950	1,572	1,774	2,331	2,603	2,348	1,968
45 to 64 years old	600	766	585	668	862	1,062	983	803
65 years and over	58	55	49	61	66	69	65	88
Female	3,370	3,791	3,003	3,075	3,609	4,005	3,801	3,629
16 to 19 years old	755	661	536	519	581	591	568	580
20 to 24 years old	760	794	558	555	628	662	613	605
25 to 44 years old	1,345	1,732	1,437	1,498	1,775	1,999	1,871	1,726
45 to 64 years old	473	566	430	456	575	686	703	653
65 years and over	36	39	41	46	50	66	46	66
White [3]	5,884	6,191	4,770	5,091	6,447	7,047	6,547	5,892
16 to 19 years old	1,291	1,074	863	856	977	983	943	960
20 to 24 years old	1,364	1,235	856	844	1,063	1,084	991	952
Black [3]	1,553	1,864	1,544	1,527	1,679	1,958	1,796	1,666
16 to 19 years old	343	357	300	258	270	313	302	300
20 to 24 years old	426	455	322	335	362	401	371	351
Hispanic [3][4]	620	811	750	769	963	1,160	1,104	1,187
16 to 19 years old	145	141	132	131	149	185	173	198
20 to 24 years old	138	171	158	135	172	193	191	220
Full-time workers	6,269	6,793	5,211	5,541	6,932	7,746	7,146	6,513
Part-time workers	1,369	1,519	1,317	1,332	1,494	1,638	1,588	1,483
UNEMPLOYMENT RATE (percent) [5]								
Total [2]	7.1	7.2	5.3	5.5	6.7	7.4	6.8	6.1
16 to 19 years old	17.8	18.6	15.0	15.5	18.6	20.0	19.0	17.6
20 to 24 years old	11.5	11.1	8.6	8.8	10.8	11.3	10.5	9.7
25 to 44 years old	6.0	6.2	4.5	4.8	6.0	6.7	6.1	5.3
45 to 64 years old	3.7	4.5	3.2	3.5	4.4	5.1	4.8	4.0
65 years and over	3.1	3.2	2.6	3.0	3.3	3.8	3.2	4.0
Male	6.9	7.0	5.2	5.6	7.0	7.8	7.1	6.2
16 to 19 years old	18.3	19.5	15.9	16.3	19.8	21.5	20.4	19.0
20 to 24 years old	12.5	11.4	8.8	9.1	11.7	12.2	11.3	10.2
25 to 44 years old	5.6	5.9	4.3	4.8	6.2	6.9	6.2	5.2
45 to 64 years old	3.5	4.5	3.3	3.7	4.7	5.6	5.1	4.1
65 years and over	3.1	3.1	2.4	3.0	3.3	3.3	3.2	4.0
Female	7.4	7.4	5.4	5.4	6.3	6.9	6.5	6.0
16 to 19 years old	17.2	17.6	14.0	14.7	17.4	18.5	17.4	16.2
20 to 24 years old	10.4	10.7	8.3	8.5	9.8	10.2	9.6	9.2
25 to 44 years old	6.4	6.6	4.8	4.9	5.7	6.4	6.0	5.4
45 to 64 years old	4.0	4.6	3.1	3.2	3.9	4.4	4.4	3.9
65 years and over	3.1	3.3	2.9	3.1	3.3	4.5	3.1	4.0
White [3]	6.3	6.2	4.5	4.7	6.0	6.5	6.0	5.3
16 to 19 years old	15.5	15.7	12.7	13.4	16.4	17.1	16.2	15.1
20 to 24 years old	9.9	9.2	7.2	7.2	9.2	9.4	8.7	8.1
Black [3]	14.3	15.1	11.4	11.3	12.4	14.1	12.9	11.5
16 to 19 years old	38.5	40.2	32.4	31.1	36.3	39.8	38.9	35.2
20 to 24 years old	23.6	24.5	18.0	19.9	21.6	23.9	22.0	19.5
Hispanic [3][4]	10.1	10.5	8.0	8.0	9.9	11.4	10.6	9.9
16 to 19 years old	22.5	24.3	19.4	19.5	22.9	27.5	26.2	24.5
20 to 24 years old	12.1	12.6	10.7	9.1	11.6	13.2	13.1	11.8
Experienced workers [6]	6.9	6.8	5.0	5.3	6.5	7.1	6.5	5.9
Women maintaining families [2]	9.2	10.5	8.1	8.2	9.1	9.9	9.5	8.9
White	7.3	8.1	6.1	6.3	7.2	7.8	7.7	(NA)
Black	14.0	16.4	13.0	13.1	13.9	14.7	13.7	(NA)
Married men, wife present [2]	4.2	4.3	3.0	3.4	4.4	5.0	4.4	3.7
White	3.9	4.0	2.8	3.1	4.2	4.7	4.1	3.4
Black	7.4	8.0	5.8	6.2	6.5	8.3	7.2	6.0
Percent without work for—								
Fewer than 5 weeks	43.1	42.1	48.6	46.1	40.1	34.8	36.2	34.1
5 to 10 weeks	23.4	22.2	22.2	23.5	22.9	20.9	20.6	20.6
11 to 14 weeks	9.0	8.0	8.1	8.6	9.5	8.5	8.3	9.5
15 to 26 weeks	13.8	12.3	11.2	11.8	14.5	15.2	14.6	15.5
27 weeks and over	10.7	15.4	9.9	10.1	13.0	20.6	20.4	20.3
Unemployment duration, average (weeks)	11.9	15.6	11.9	12.1	13.8	17.9	18.1	18.8

NA Not available. [1] See footnote 2, table 626. [2] Includes other races, not shown separately. [3] Includes other ages, not shown separately. [4] Persons of Hispanic origin may be of any race. [5] Unemployed as percent of civilian labor force in specified group. [6] Wage and salary workers.

Source: U.S. Bureau of Labor Statistics, *Employment and Earnings*, monthly, January issues; and unpublished data.

No. 659. Unemployed Persons, by Sex and Reason: 1970 to 1994

[In thousands. For civilian noninstitutional population 16 years old and over. Annual averages of monthly figures. Based on Current Population Survey; see text, section 1, and Appendix III]

SEX AND REASON	1970	1980	1985	1986	1987	1988	1989	1990	1991	1992	1993	1994 [1]
Male, total	**2,238**	**4,267**	**4,521**	**4,530**	**4,101**	**3,655**	**3,525**	**3,799**	**4,817**	**5,380**	**4,932**	**4,367**
Job losers [2]	1,199	2,649	2,749	2,725	2,432	2,078	1,975	2,208	3,105	3,518	3,091	2,416
Job leavers	282	438	409	520	494	503	495	511	492	479	490	408
Reentrants	533	776	876	805	761	697	726	782	865	950	914	1,265
New entrants	224	405	487	480	413	376	328	298	356	433	437	278
Female, total	**1,855**	**3,370**	**3,791**	**3,707**	**3,324**	**3,046**	**3,003**	**3,075**	**3,609**	**4,005**	**3,801**	**3,629**
Job losers [2]	614	1,297	1,390	1,308	1,134	1,014	1,008	1,114	1,503	1,773	1,677	1,399
Job leavers	267	453	468	494	471	480	529	503	487	496	456	383
Reentrants	696	1,152	1,380	1,355	1,213	1,112	1,117	1,101	1,222	1,278	1,230	1,521
New entrants	279	468	552	549	506	440	349	357	398	457	438	326

[1] See footnote 2, table 626.   [2] Beginning 1994, persons who completed temporary jobs are identified separately and are included as job losers.

Source: U.S. Bureau of Labor Statistics, *Employment and Earnings,* monthly, January issues; Bulletin 2307; and unpublished data.

No. 660. Unemployment Rates, by Industry, 1975 to 1994, and by Sex, 1980 and 1994

[In percent. For civilian noninstitutional population 16 years old and over. Annual averages of monthly figures. Rate represents unemployment as a percent of labor force in each specified group. Data for 1985-90, and also beginning 1993, not strictly comparable with other years due to changes in industrial classification]

INDUSTRY	1975	1980	1985	1990	1993	1994 [1]	MALE		FEMALE	
							1980	1994 [1]	1980	1994 [1]
All unemployed [2]	**8.5**	**7.1**	**7.2**	**5.5**	**6.8**	**6.1**	**6.9**	**6.2**	**7.4**	**6.0**
Industry: [3]										
Agriculture	10.4	11.0	13.2	9.7	11.6	11.3	9.7	11.2	15.1	11.5
Mining	4.1	6.4	9.5	4.8	7.3	5.4	6.7	5.9	4.5	2.7
Construction	18.0	14.1	13.1	11.1	14.3	11.8	14.6	12.2	8.9	7.3
Manufacturing	10.9	8.5	7.7	5.8	7.2	5.6	7.4	5.0	10.8	6.7
Transportation and public utilities	5.6	4.9	5.1	3.8	5.1	4.8	5.1	5.2	4.4	4.0
Wholesale and retail trade	8.7	7.4	7.6	6.4	7.8	7.4	6.6	6.8	8.3	8.1
Finance, insurance, and real estate	4.9	3.4	3.5	3.0	4.1	3.6	3.2	3.1	3.5	3.9
Services	7.1	5.9	6.2	5.0	6.1	5.9	6.3	6.2	5.8	5.7
Government	4.1	4.1	3.9	2.6	3.3	3.4	3.9	3.5	4.3	3.3

[1] See footnote 2, table 626.   [2] Includes the self-employed, unpaid family workers, and persons with no previous work experience, not shown separately.   [3] Covers unemployed wage and salary workers.

Source: U.S. Bureau of Labor Statistics, *Employment and Earnings,* monthly, January issues.

No. 661. Unemployment by Occupation, 1985 to 1994, and by Sex, 1994

[For civilian noninstitutional population 16 years old and over. Annual averages of monthly data. Rate represents unemployment as a percent of the labor force for each specified group. Based on Current Population Survey; see text, section 1, and Appendix III. See also headnote, table 643 concerning 1994 data]

OCCUPATION	NUMBER (1,000)			UNEMPLOYMENT RATE				
	1985	1990	1994 [1]	1985	1990	1994 [1]		
						Total	Male	Female
Total [2]	**8,312**	**6,874**	**7,996**	**7.2**	**5.5**	**6.1**	**6.2**	**6.0**
Managerial and professional specialty	645	662	907	2.4	2.1	2.6	2.4	2.8
Executive, administrative, and managerial	329	348	454	2.6	2.3	2.7	2.4	3.1
Professional specialty	316	314	453	2.3	1.9	2.5	2.5	2.6
Technical sales, and administrative support	1,694	1,605	1,962	4.9	4.2	5.0	4.3	5.4
Technicians and related support	110	115	127	3.3	2.9	3.2	3.2	3.1
Sales occupations	702	702	907	5.3	4.7	5.8	4.3	7.3
Administrative support, including clerical	882	788	928	4.9	4.1	4.7	5.0	4.7
Service occupations	1,386	1,110	1,471	8.8	6.6	8.0	8.4	7.7
Private household	69	45	91	6.4	5.5	10.0	19.2	9.6
Protective service	85	73	96	4.7	3.5	4.1	3.9	4.8
Service except private household and protective	1,233	992	1,285	9.5	7.1	8.5	9.9	7.7
Precision production, craft, and repair	1,038	847	910	7.2	5.8	6.3	6.4	6.0
Mechanics and repairers	225	173	201	4.8	3.7	4.3	4.3	5.2
Construction trades	531	475	518	10.1	8.4	9.4	9.3	11.2
Other precision production, craft, and repair	281	199	191	6.4	4.7	4.5	4.2	5.6
Operators, fabricators, and laborers	2,140	1,673	1,761	11.3	8.6	9.0	8.7	9.9
Machine operators, assemblers, inspectors	980	711	672	11.1	8.1	8.0	6.9	9.6
Transportation and material moving occupations	422	325	364	8.5	6.3	6.6	6.7	6.1
Handlers, equipment cleaners, helpers, laborers	739	637	725	14.3	11.6	12.7	12.7	12.5
Construction laborers	186	172	172	21.3	18.1	18.9	18.9	(B)
Farming, forestry, and fishing	315	226	333	8.3	6.2	8.4	8.3	9.0

B Base is less than 35,000.   [1] See footnote 2, table 626.   [2] Includes persons with no previous work experience and those whose last job was in the Armed Forces.

Source: U.S. Bureau of Labor Statistics, *Employment and Earnings,* monthly, January issues.

No. 662. Unemployment Rates, by Educational Attainment, Sex, and Race: 1970 to 1991

[In percent. As of **March.** For the civilian noninstitutional population 25 to 64 years of age. Due to a change in the method of reporting educational attainment, 1992 are not comparable with data for earlier years. See table 663 for data beginning 1992. Based on the Current Population Survey; see text, section 1, and Appendix III]

ITEM	1970	1975	1980	1984	1985	1986	1987	1988	1989	1990	1991
Total	3.3	6.9	5.0	6.6	6.1	6.1	5.7	4.7	4.4	4.5	6.1
Less than 4 years of high school [1]	4.6	10.7	8.4	12.1	11.4	11.6	11.1	9.4	8.9	9.6	12.3
4 years of high school, only	2.9	6.9	5.1	7.2	6.9	6.9	6.3	5.4	4.8	4.9	6.7
College: 1-3 years	2.9	5.5	4.3	5.3	4.7	4.7	4.5	3.7	3.4	3.7	5.0
4 years or more	1.3	2.5	1.9	2.7	2.4	2.3	2.3	1.7	2.2	1.9	2.9
Male: Total	2.9	6.7	4.9	6.9	6.1	6.2	6.0	5.1	4.7	4.8	6.8
Less than 4 years of high school [1]	4.0	10.5	8.2	12.3	11.2	11.7	11.2	10.0	9.4	9.6	13.4
4 years of high school, only	2.4	6.7	5.3	8.1	7.2	7.4	6.7	6.2	5.4	5.3	7.7
College: 1-3 years	2.7	5.1	4.4	5.2	4.5	4.7	5.0	3.9	3.2	3.9	5.2
4 years or more	1.1	2.2	1.7	2.7	2.4	2.3	2.5	1.6	2.3	2.1	3.2
Female: Total	4.0	7.4	5.0	6.1	6.0	5.8	5.2	4.2	4.0	4.2	5.2
Less than 4 years of high school [1]	5.7	10.5	8.9	11.7	11.7	11.4	10.9	8.5	8.1	9.5	10.7
4 years of high school, only	3.6	7.1	5.0	6.3	6.5	6.3	5.8	4.6	4.2	4.6	5.5
College: 1-3 years	3.1	6.3	4.1	5.3	4.8	4.8	4.0	3.4	3.7	3.5	4.8
4 years or more	1.9	3.4	2.2	2.7	2.5	2.4	2.1	1.9	2.0	1.7	2.5
White: Total	3.1	6.5	4.4	5.7	5.3	5.5	5.0	4.0	3.8	4.0	5.6
Less than 4 years of high school [1]	4.5	10.1	7.8	10.9	10.6	10.9	10.2	8.3	7.7	8.3	11.6
4 years of high school, only	2.7	6.5	4.6	6.4	6.1	6.2	5.5	4.6	4.2	4.4	6.2
College: 1-3 years	2.8	5.1	3.9	4.6	3.9	4.2	4.1	3.2	3.0	3.3	4.6
4 years or more	1.3	2.4	1.8	2.4	2.1	2.2	2.2	1.5	2.0	1.8	2.7
Black: Total [2]	4.7	10.9	9.6	13.3	12.0	10.7	10.6	10.0	9.2	8.6	10.1
Less than 4 years of high school [1]	5.2	13.5	11.7	17.4	15.3	15.3	14.8	14.6	14.6	15.9	15.9
4 years of high school, only	5.2	10.7	9.5	14.5	13.0	11.7	11.7	11.2	9.2	8.6	10.3
College: 1-3 years	3.5	9.8	9.0	9.7	10.6	8.7	7.6	7.4	6.9	6.5	8.0
4 years or more	0.9	3.9	4.0	6.2	5.4	3.2	4.2	3.3	4.7	1.9	5.2

[1] Includes persons reporting no school years completed.   [2] For 1970 and 1975, data refer to Black and other workers.

Source: U.S. Bureau of Labor Statistics, Bulletin 2307; and unpublished data.

No. 663. Unemployed and Unemployment Rates, by Educational Attainment, Sex, Race, and Hispanic Origin: 1992 to 1994

[As of March. For the civilian noninstitutional population 25 to 64 years old. See table 630 for civilian labor force and participation rate data Based on Current Population Survey; see text, section 1, and Appendix III]

YEAR, SEX, AND RACE	UNEMPLOYED (1,000)					UNEMPLOYMENT RATE [1]				
	Total	Less than high school diploma	High school graduates, no degree	Less than a bachelor's degree	College graduate	Total	Less than high school diploma	High school graduate, no degree	Less than a bachelor's degree	College graduate
Total: [2]										
1992	6,846	1,693	2,851	1,521	782	6.7	13.5	7.7	5.9	2.9
1993 [3]	6,596	1,550	2,666	1,492	888	6.4	13.0	7.3	5.5	3.2
1994 [3]	6,126	1,463	2,388	1,453	823	5.8	12.6	6.7	5.0	2.9
Male:										
1992	4,207	1,151	1,709	854	493	7.5	14.8	8.8	6.4	3.2
1993 [3]	4,152	1,059	1,667	882	543	7.3	14.1	8.7	6.3	3.4
1994 [3]	3,498	920	1,333	779	466	6.2	12.8	7.2	5.3	2.9
Female:										
1992	2,639	542	1,142	666	289	5.7	11.4	6.5	5.3	2.5
1993 [3]	2,444	490	999	609	345	5.2	11.2	5.8	4.6	2.9
1994 [3]	2,628	543	1,055	674	357	5.4	12.4	6.2	4.7	2.9
White:										
1992	5,247	1,285	2,146	1,176	641	6.0	12.9	6.8	5.3	2.7
1993 [3]	5,129	1,175	2,025	1,166	763	5.8	12.4	6.5	5.0	3.1
1994 [3]	4,598	1,092	1,738	1,109	659	5.2	11.7	5.8	4.5	2.6
Black:										
1992	1,353	361	619	291	81	12.4	17.2	14.1	10.7	4.8
1993 [3]	1,201	321	542	266	72	10.9	17.3	12.4	8.7	4.1
1994 [3]	1,202	286	546	277	94	10.6	17.4	12.2	8.3	4.9
Hispanic: [4]										
1992	757	408	224	88	36	9.8	13.6	9.6	5.9	4.2
1993 [3]	826	449	215	117	46	10.3	14.5	9.1	7.0	5.2
1994 [3]	871	465	215	139	52	9.7	13.4	8.3	7.2	5.2

[1] Percent unemployed of the civilian labor force.   [2] Includes other races, not shown separately.   [3] See footnote 2, table 626.   [4] Persons of Hispanic origin may be of any race.

Source: U.S. Bureau of Labor Statistics, unpublished data.

No. 664. Total Unemployed and Insured Unemployed—States: 1980 to 1993

[For civilian noninstitutional population 16 years old and over. Annual averages of monthly figures. Total unemployment estimates based on the Current Population Survey (CPS); see text, section 1, and Appendix III. U.S. totals derived by independent population controls; therefore State data may not add to U.S. totals. See table 633 for 1994 unemployment]

STATE	TOTAL UNEMPLOYED								INSURED UNEMPLOYED [2]			
	Number (1,000)				Percent [1]				Number (1,000)		Percent [3]	
	1980	1985	1990	1993	1980	1985	1990	1993	1992	1993	1992	1993
United States	7,637	8,312	6,874	8,734	7.1	7.2	5.5	6.8	[4]3,245	[4]2,751	[4]3.1	[4]2.6
Alabama	147	160	128	149	8.8	8.9	6.8	7.5	38.8	33.4	2.5	2.1
Alaska	18	24	18	23	9.7	9.7	6.9	7.6	13.9	12.2	6.4	5.5
Arizona	83	96	96	113	6.7	6.5	5.3	6.2	34.2	28.0	2.3	1.9
Arkansas	76	91	77	71	7.6	8.7	6.9	6.2	31.5	27.1	3.6	3.0
California	790	934	850	1,410	6.8	7.2	5.6	9.2	552.5	478.6	4.5	3.9
Colorado	88	101	87	99	5.9	5.9	4.9	5.2	26.4	23.9	1.8	1.6
Connecticut	94	83	93	110	5.9	4.9	5.1	6.2	57.3	49.5	3.8	3.3
Delaware	22	17	19	20	7.7	5.3	5.1	5.3	7.9	6.8	2.4	2.1
District of Columbia	24	27	22	27	7.3	8.4	6.6	8.5	11.0	9.8	2.5	2.3
Florida	251	320	383	463	5.9	6.0	5.9	7.0	127.0	122.5	2.4	2.3
Georgia	163	188	179	199	6.4	6.5	5.4	5.8	56.4	45.1	2.0	1.6
Hawaii	21	27	15	24	4.9	5.6	2.8	4.2	11.6	12.7	2.3	2.5
Idaho	34	37	29	34	7.9	7.9	5.8	6.1	14.3	13.4	3.7	3.3
Illinois	459	513	362	444	8.3	9.0	6.2	7.4	156.0	136.9	3.1	2.7
Indiana	252	215	148	157	9.6	7.9	5.3	5.3	42.3	33.6	1.8	1.4
Iowa	82	112	61	62	5.8	8.0	4.2	4.0	24.8	22.4	2.1	1.9
Kansas	53	62	56	66	4.5	5.0	4.4	5.0	22.7	20.1	2.2	1.9
Kentucky	133	161	103	111	8.0	9.5	5.8	6.2	33.9	29.1	2.5	2.1
Louisiana	121	229	114	139	6.7	11.5	6.2	7.4	40.9	32.1	2.7	2.1
Maine	39	30	32	50	7.8	5.4	5.1	7.9	19.3	14.2	4.0	2.9
Maryland	140	104	120	164	6.5	4.6	4.6	6.2	59.9	47.2	3.1	2.5
Massachusetts	162	120	194	218	5.6	3.9	6.0	6.9	100.8	78.7	3.7	2.9
Michigan	534	433	345	327	12.4	9.9	7.1	7.0	133.7	108.4	3.6	2.9
Minnesota	125	133	115	125	5.9	6.0	4.8	5.1	44.2	39.1	2.2	1.9
Mississippi	79	116	88	77	7.5	10.3	7.5	6.3	27.3	20.4	3.1	2.2
Missouri	167	158	149	170	7.2	6.4	5.7	6.4	61.7	51.5	2.8	2.3
Montana	23	31	23	26	6.1	7.7	5.8	6.0	8.8	9.2	3.1	3.2
Nebraska	31	44	18	22	4.1	5.5	2.2	2.6	9.3	8.4	1.3	1.2
Nevada	27	41	32	53	6.2	8.0	4.9	7.2	20.2	17.8	3.3	2.9
New Hampshire	22	21	36	41	4.7	3.9	5.6	6.6	10.7	7.0	2.3	1.5
New Jersey	260	217	201	292	7.2	5.7	5.0	7.4	131.7	109.9	4.0	3.3
New Mexico	42	57	44	56	7.5	8.8	6.3	7.5	13.5	11.8	2.5	2.2
New York	597	544	459	663	7.5	6.5	5.2	7.7	281.2	223.8	3.7	3.0
North Carolina	187	168	142	173	6.6	5.4	4.1	4.9	60.8	41.5	2.0	1.4
North Dakota	15	20	13	14	5.0	5.9	3.9	4.3	4.7	4.1	2.0	1.7
Ohio	426	455	305	356	8.4	8.9	5.7	6.5	127.5	96.3	2.8	2.1
Oklahoma	66	112	84	92	4.8	7.1	5.6	6.0	22.8	18.9	2.0	1.6
Oregon	107	116	82	115	8.3	8.8	5.5	7.2	51.1	46.3	4.3	3.8
Pennsylvania	425	443	311	413	7.8	8.0	5.4	7.0	195.5	164.0	4.1	3.4
Rhode Island	34	25	35	40	7.2	4.9	6.7	7.7	20.5	16.4	5.0	4.0
South Carolina	96	107	82	137	6.9	6.8	4.7	7.5	37.6	30.5	2.6	2.1
South Dakota	16	18	13	13	4.9	5.1	3.7	3.5	2.6	2.4	0.9	0.9
Tennessee	152	180	124	141	7.3	8.0	5.2	5.7	55.4	42.8	2.7	2.0
Texas	352	565	530	641	5.2	7.0	6.2	7.0	152.3	137.5	2.2	2.0
Utah	40	43	35	35	6.3	5.9	4.3	3.9	10.7	9.5	1.6	1.4
Vermont	16	13	15	17	6.4	4.8	5.0	5.4	9.5	7.9	4.0	3.3
Virginia	128	160	138	168	5.0	5.6	4.3	5.0	41.8	30.8	1.6	1.2
Washington	156	170	124	203	7.9	8.1	4.9	7.5	83.9	83.9	4.0	3.9
West Virginia	74	100	63	85	9.4	13.0	8.3	10.8	21.4	18.9	3.7	3.2
Wisconsin	167	171	113	127	7.2	7.2	4.4	4.7	62.0	53.9	2.8	2.4
Wyoming	9	18	13	13	4.0	7.1	5.4	5.4	4.2	3.6	2.3	1.9

[1] Total unemployment as percent of civilian labor force. [2] Source: U.S. Employment and Training Administration, *Unemployment Insurance, Financial Data,* annual updates. [3] Insured unemployment as percent of average covered employment in the previous year. [4] Includes 55,100 in Puerto Rico and the Virgin Islands in 1992 and 57,600 in 1993.
Source: Except as noted, U.S. Bureau of Labor Statistics, *Geographic Profile of Employment and Unemployment,* annual.

No. 665. Job Openings and Placements and Help-Wanted Advertising: 1970 to 1993

[Openings 1970 and 1980, for years ending Sept. 30; beginning 1985, for years ending June 30]

ITEM	1970	1980	1985	1988	1989	1990	1991	1992	1993
Job openings: [1] Received (1,000)	6,130	8,122	7,529	7,240	6,998	5,651	5,635	5,752	6,355
Average per month	511	677	627	603	583	471	470	479	530
Nonagricultural placements [1] (1,000)	4,604	5,610	3,270	4,503	4,284	3,714	3,507	3,396	3,340
Index of help-wanted advertising in newspapers [2] (1967=100)	93	128	138	158	151	129	93	92	101

[1] As reported by State employment agencies. Beginning 1985, all placements. Placements include duplication for individuals placed more than once. [2] Source: U.S. Bureau of Economic Analysis, *Survey of Current Business,* monthly. Based on data from the The Conference Board, New York, NY. Index based on the number of advertisements in classified sections of 51 newspapers, each in a major employment area.
Source: Except as noted, U.S. Employment and Training Administration, unpublished data.

No. 666. Nonfarm Establishments, Employees, Hours, and Earnings, by Industry: 1960 to 1994

[Based on data from establishment reports. Includes all full- and part-time employees who worked during, or received pay for, any part of the pay period reported. Excludes proprietors, the self-employed, farm workers, unpaid family workers, private household workers, and Armed Forces. Establishment data shown here conform to industry definitions in the 1987 Standard Industrial Classification and are adjusted to March 1993 employment benchmarks, and reflect historical corrections to previously published data. Based on the Current Employment Statistics Program; see Appendix III. See also *Historical Statistics, Colonial Times to 1970*, series D 127-141 and D 803, 878, 881, 884, and 890]

| ITEM AND YEAR | Total | GOODS-PRODUCING | | | | SERVICE-PRODUCING | | | | | | |
		Total	Mining	Con-struc-tion	Manu-factur-ing	Total	Trans-portation and public utilities	Whole-sale trade	Retail trade	Finance, insur-ance, and real estate	Serv-ices	Govern-ment
EMPLOYEES (1,000)												
1960	54,189	20,434	712	2,926	16,796	33,755	4,004	3,153	8,238	2,628	7,378	8,353
1965	60,765	21,926	632	3,232	18,062	38,839	4,036	3,477	9,239	2,977	9,036	10,074
1970	70,880	23,578	623	3,588	19,367	47,302	4,515	4,006	11,034	3,645	11,548	12,554
1975	76,945	22,600	752	3,525	18,323	54,345	4,542	4,430	12,630	4,165	13,892	14,686
1980	90,406	25,658	1,027	4,346	20,285	64,748	5,146	5,292	15,018	5,160	17,890	16,241
1985	97,387	24,842	927	4,668	19,248	72,544	5,233	5,727	17,315	5,948	21,927	16,394
1990	109,419	24,905	709	5,120	19,076	84,514	5,793	6,173	19,601	6,709	27,934	18,304
1991	108,256	23,745	689	4,650	18,406	84,511	5,762	6,081	19,284	6,646	28,336	18,402
1992	108,604	23,231	635	4,492	18,104	85,377	5,721	5,997	19,356	6,602	29,052	18,645
1993	110,525	23,256	611	4,642	18,003	87,269	5,787	5,958	19,717	6,712	30,278	18,817
1994	113,429	23,584	605	4,916	18,063	89,844	5,843	6,060	20,310	6,788	31,804	19,040
PERCENT DISTRIBUTION												
1960	100.0	37.7	1.3	5.4	31.0	62.3	7.4	5.8	15.2	4.9	13.6	15.4
1965	100.0	36.1	1.0	5.3	29.7	63.9	6.6	5.7	15.2	4.9	14.9	16.6
1970	100.0	33.3	0.9	5.1	27.3	66.7	6.4	5.7	15.6	5.1	16.3	17.8
1975	100.0	29.4	1.0	4.6	23.8	70.6	5.9	5.8	16.4	5.4	18.1	19.1
1980	100.0	28.4	1.1	4.8	22.4	71.6	5.7	5.9	16.6	5.7	19.8	18.0
1985	100.0	25.5	1.0	4.8	19.8	74.5	5.4	5.9	17.8	6.1	22.5	16.8
1990	100.0	22.8	0.6	4.7	17.4	77.2	5.3	5.6	17.9	6.1	25.5	16.7
1991	100.0	21.0	0.6	4.3	17.0	78.1	5.3	5.6	17.8	6.1	26.2	17.0
1992	100.0	21.4	0.6	4.1	16.7	78.6	5.3	5.5	17.8	6.1	26.8	17.2
1993	100.0	21.0	0.6	4.2	16.3	79.0	5.2	5.4	17.8	6.1	27.4	17.0
1994	100.0	20.8	0.5	4.3	15.9	79.2	5.2	5.3	17.9	6.0	28.0	16.8
WEEKLY HOURS [1]												
1960	38.6	(NA)	40.4	36.7	39.7	(NA)	(NA)	40.5	38.0	37.2	(NA)	(NA)
1965	38.8	(NA)	42.3	37.4	41.2	(NA)	41.3	40.8	36.6	37.2	35.9	(NA)
1970	37.1	(NA)	42.7	37.3	39.8	(NA)	40.5	39.9	33.8	36.7	34.4	(NA)
1975	36.1	(NA)	41.9	36.4	39.5	(NA)	39.7	38.6	32.4	36.5	33.5	(NA)
1980	35.3	(NA)	43.3	37.0	39.7	(NA)	39.6	38.4	30.2	36.2	32.6	(NA)
1985	34.9	(NA)	43.4	37.7	40.5	(NA)	39.5	38.4	29.4	36.4	32.5	(NA)
1990	34.5	(NA)	44.1	38.2	40.8	(NA)	38.9	38.1	28.8	35.8	32.5	(NA)
1991	34.3	(NA)	44.4	38.1	40.7	(NA)	38.7	38.1	28.6	35.7	32.4	(NA)
1992	34.4	(NA)	43.9	38.0	41.0	(NA)	38.9	38.2	28.8	35.8	32.5	(NA)
1993	34.5	(NA)	44.3	38.4	41.4	(NA)	39.6	38.2	28.8	35.8	32.5	(NA)
1994	34.6	(NA)	44.7	38.8	42.0	(NA)	39.9	38.3	28.9	35.8	32.5	(NA)
HOURLY EARNINGS [1]												
1960	$2.09	(NA)	$2.60	$3.07	$2.26	(NA)	(NA)	$2.24	$1.52	$2.02	(NA)	(NA)
1965	2.46	(NA)	2.92	3.70	2.61	(NA)	$3.03	2.60	1.82	2.39	$2.05	(NA)
1970	3.23	(NA)	3.85	5.24	3.35	(NA)	3.85	3.43	2.44	3.07	2.81	(NA)
1975	4.53	(NA)	5.95	7.31	4.83	(NA)	5.88	4.72	3.36	4.06	4.02	(NA)
1980	6.66	(NA)	9.17	9.94	7.27	(NA)	8.87	6.95	4.88	5.79	5.85	(NA)
1985	8.57	(NA)	11.98	12.32	9.54	(NA)	11.40	9.15	5.94	7.94	7.90	(NA)
1990	10.01	(NA)	13.68	13.77	10.83	(NA)	12.97	10.79	6.75	9.97	9.83	(NA)
1991	10.32	(NA)	14.19	14.00	11.18	(NA)	13.22	11.15	6.94	10.39	10.23	(NA)
1992	10.57	(NA)	14.54	14.15	11.46	(NA)	13.45	11.39	7.12	10.82	10.54	(NA)
1993	10.83	(NA)	14.60	14.37	11.74	(NA)	13.63	11.73	7.29	11.35	10.79	(NA)
1994	11.12	(NA)	14.89	14.69	12.06	(NA)	13.88	12.01	7.49	11.83	11.07	(NA)
WEEKLY EARNINGS [1]												
1960	$81	(NA)	$105	$113	$90	(NA)	(NA)	$91	$58	$75	(NA)	(NA)
1965	95	(NA)	124	138	108	(NA)	$125	106	67	89	$74	(NA)
1970	120	(NA)	164	195	133	(NA)	156	137	82	113	97	(NA)
1975	164	(NA)	249	266	191	(NA)	233	182	109	148	135	(NA)
1980	235	(NA)	397	368	289	(NA)	351	267	147	210	191	(NA)
1985	299	(NA)	520	464	386	(NA)	450	351	175	289	257	(NA)
1990	345	(NA)	603	526	442	(NA)	505	411	194	357	319	(NA)
1991	354	(NA)	630	533	455	(NA)	512	425	198	371	331	(NA)
1992	364	(NA)	638	538	470	(NA)	523	435	205	387	343	(NA)
1993	374	(NA)	647	552	486	(NA)	540	448	210	406	351	(NA)
1994	385	(NA)	666	570	507	(NA)	554	460	216	424	360	(NA)

NA Not available.　[1] Average hours and earnings. Private production and related workers in mining, manufacturing, and construction; nonsupervisory employees in other industries.

Source: U.S. Bureau of Labor Statistics, Bulletin 2445, and *Employment and Earnings,* monthly, March and June issues.

No. 667. Employees in Nonfarm Establishments—States: 1980 to 1994

[**In thousands.** For coverage, see headnote, table 666. National totals differ from the sum of the State figures because of differing benchmarks among States and differing industrial and geographic stratification. Based on 1987 *Standard Industrial Classification Manual,* see text, section 13]

STATE	1980	1993	1994							
			Total [1]	Con-struc-tion	Manu-factur-ing	Trans-porta-tion and public utilities	Whole-sale and retail trade	Finance, insur-ance, and real estate	Serv-ices	Govern-ment
United States	**90,406**	**110,525**	**113,429**	**4,916**	**18,063**	**5,843**	**26,370**	**6,788**	**31,804**	**19,040**
Alabama	1,356	1,717	1,753	82	386	86	393	77	373	345
Alaska	169	253	260	13	17	24	53	12	58	74
Arizona	1,014	1,586	1,685	109	193	85	411	111	480	285
Arkansas	742	994	1,035	42	254	59	233	42	229	172
California	9,849	12,045	12,136	466	1,771	614	2,821	790	3,549	2,094
Colorado	1,251	1,671	1,750	97	191	107	426	111	502	300
Connecticut	1,427	1,531	1,542	49	285	70	335	136	450	217
Delaware	259	349	355	17	64	15	78	39	91	51
District of Columbia	616	670	657	9	13	21	53	31	260	270
Florida	3,576	5,571	5,797	298	484	295	1,506	376	1,924	907
Georgia	2,159	3,109	3,264	141	576	210	814	173	779	563
Hawaii	405	539	536	[2]29	18	42	133	39	164	112
Idaho	330	437	463	29	72	22	117	24	103	93
Illinois	4,850	5,331	5,463	213	953	317	1,276	394	1,513	783
Indiana	2,130	2,627	2,712	128	662	137	645	131	610	392
Iowa	1,110	1,279	1,319	53	245	59	331	77	327	226
Kansas	945	1,133	1,166	50	188	68	283	59	277	233
Kentucky	1,210	1,548	1,599	75	304	89	379	64	377	282
Louisiana	1,579	1,659	1,727	105	188	111	401	80	446	350
Maine	418	519	531	21	92	23	135	27	141	94
Maryland	1,712	2,102	2,145	126	179	103	514	134	668	420
Massachusetts	2,652	2,841	2,905	87	449	127	667	209	974	392
Michigan	3,443	4,006	4,142	143	949	163	968	197	1,073	639
Minnesota	1,770	2,243	2,311	81	416	114	559	140	636	358
Mississippi	829	1,002	1,053	44	261	48	218	40	221	217
Missouri	1,970	2,395	2,473	111	416	156	588	147	665	386
Montana	280	326	341	15	23	21	93	16	92	76
Nebraska	628	767	796	33	109	48	199	52	202	151
Nevada	400	671	737	55	34	38	144	34	328	92
New Hampshire	385	502	522	18	101	19	134	30	144	77
New Jersey	3,060	3,491	3,550	122	510	243	835	231	1,039	568
New Mexico	465	626	658	42	45	30	156	30	177	163
New York	7,207	7,752	7,800	248	954	401	1,575	738	2,459	1,420
North Carolina	2,380	3,245	3,361	166	859	161	764	142	724	541
North Dakota	245	285	295	13	21	19	77	14	81	67
Ohio	4,367	4,918	5,076	206	1,071	222	1,225	270	1,328	740
Oklahoma	1,138	1,247	1,279	47	171	73	301	64	317	270
Oregon	1,045	1,308	1,364	62	220	69	343	89	346	234
Pennsylvania	4,753	5,123	5,188	202	942	272	1,166	310	1,560	715
Rhode Island	398	430	434	13	87	15	95	26	137	62
South Carolina	1,189	1,570	1,607	85	376	70	366	68	344	297
South Dakota	238	319	333	14	44	16	85	18	87	68
Tennessee	1,747	2,329	2,421	101	538	133	564	108	601	370
Texas	5,851	7,482	7,740	381	1,007	458	1,874	442	2,000	1,416
Utah	551	810	861	48	116	50	206	46	225	161
Vermont	200	257	264	12	44	11	63	12	77	45
Virginia	2,157	2,919	3,006	164	405	153	676	164	829	603
Washington	1,608	2,253	2,309	124	337	117	565	125	600	438
West Virginia	646	653	675	35	82	40	154	26	174	137
Wisconsin	1,938	2,413	2,483	98	582	115	570	134	615	365
Wyoming	210	210	217	14	10	14	50	8	45	58

[1] Includes mining, not shown separately.   [2] Hawaii includes mining with construction.

Source: U.S. Bureau of Labor Statistics, *Employment and Earnings,* monthly, May issues. Compiled from data supplied by cooperating State agencies.

No. 668. Nonfarm Industries—Employees and Earnings: 1980 to 1994

[Annual averages of monthly figures. Covers all full- and part-time employees who worked during, or received pay for, any part of the pay period including the 12th of the month. For mining and manufacturing, data refer to production and related workers; for construction, to employees engaged in actual construction work; and for other industries, to nonsupervisory employees and working supervisors. See also headnote table 666. See *Historical Statistics, Colonial Times to 1970*, series D 127-151, D 802-810, and D 877-892, for related data]

INDUSTRY	1987 SIC [1] code	ALL EMPLOYEES TOTAL (1,000)			PRODUCTION WORKERS					
					Total (1,000)			Average hourly earnings (dollars)		
		1980	1990	1994	1980	1990	1994	1980	1990	1994
Total	(X)	90,406	109,419	113,429	(NA)	(NA)	(NA)	(NA)	(NA)	(NA)
Private sector [2]	(X)	74,166	91,115	94,389	60,331	73,800	77,042	6.66	10.01	11.12
Mining	(B)	1,027	709	605	762	509	431	9.17	13.68	14.89
Metal mining	10	98	58	51	74	46	41	10.26	14.05	16.13
Coal mining	12	246	147	114	204	119	92	10.86	16.71	17.74
Oil and gas extraction	13	560	395	339	389	261	222	8.59	12.94	14.10
Nonmetallic minerals, except fuels	14	123	110	101	96	83	76	7.52	11.58	13.08
Construction	(C)	4,346	5,120	4,916	3,421	3,974	3,802	9.94	13.77	14.69
General building contractors	15	1,173	1,298	1,166	900	938	827	9.22	13.01	13.95
Heavy construction, except building	16	895	770	722	720	643	603	9.20	13.34	14.42
Special trade contractors	17	2,278	3,051	3,029	1,802	2,393	2,372	10.63	14.20	15.02
Manufacturing	(D)	20,285	19,076	18,063	14,214	12,947	12,445	7.27	10.83	12.06
Durable goods [3]	(X)	12,159	11,109	10,267	8,416	7,363	6,978	7.75	11.35	12.67
Lumber and wood products [3]	24	704	733	731	587	603	604	6.57	9.08	9.83
Logging	241	88	85	77	71	70	63	8.64	11.22	11.46
Sawmills and planing mills	242	215	198	184	190	172	160	6.70	9.22	10.05
Millwork, plywood, and structural members	243	206	262	265	170	210	213	6.44	9.04	9.88
Wood containers	244	43	45	47	37	38	40	4.95	6.64	7.39
Mobile homes	2451	46	41	56	36	33	47	6.08	8.67	9.79
Furniture and fixtures [3]	25	466	506	496	376	400	393	5.49	8.52	9.55
Household furniture	251	301	289	281	253	241	235	5.12	7.87	9.02
Office furniture	252	51	68	63	40	51	46	5.91	9.64	10.35
Partitions and fixtures	254	63	78	78	47	57	58	6.68	9.77	10.77
Stone, clay, and glass products [3]	32	629	556	529	486	432	409	7.50	11.12	12.11
Flat glass	321	18	17	15	14	13	11	9.65	15.15	18.34
Glass and glassware, pressed and blown	322	124	83	75	105	72	63	7.97	12.40	13.65
Products of purchased glass	323	45	60	60	32	46	46	6.50	9.75	10.63
Cement, hydraulic	324	31	18	18	25	14	14	10.55	13.90	15.57
Structural clay products	325	46	36	33	34	28	25	6.14	9.55	10.69
Pottery and related products	326	47	39	41	39	31	32	6.25	9.62	10.53
Concrete, gypsum, and plaster	327	204	206	199	157	157	152	7.45	10.76	11.62
Primary metal industries [3]	33	1,142	756	687	878	574	528	9.77	12.92	14.31
Blast furnaces and basic steel products	331	512	276	234	396	212	178	11.39	14.82	16.86
Iron and steel foundries	332	209	132	125	167	105	101	8.20	11.55	13.24
Primary nonferrous metals	333	71	46	40	53	34	30	10.63	14.36	15.43
Nonferrous rolling and drawing	335	211	172	163	151	124	121	8.81	12.29	13.39
Nonferrous foundries (castings)	336	90	84	83	72	66	67	7.30	10.21	11.35
Fabricated metal products [3]	34	1,609	1,419	1,366	1,194	1,045	1,020	7.45	10.83	11.93
Metal cans and shipping containers	341	75	50	40	63	43	35	9.84	14.27	15.42
Cutlery, handtools, and hardware	342	164	131	128	125	96	96	7.02	10.78	11.91
Plumbing and heating, exc. electric	343	71	60	59	52	43	43	6.59	9.75	10.56
Fabricated structural metal products	344	506	427	403	351	303	290	7.27	10.16	11.01
Screw machine products	345	109	96	95	84	73	74	6.96	10.70	11.78
Metal forgings and stampings	346	260	225	229	205	178	183	8.56	12.70	14.41
Industrial machinery and equipment [3]	35	2,517	2,095	1,945	1,614	1,260	1,208	8.00	11.77	12.98
Engines and turbines	351	135	89	88	87	58	56	9.73	14.55	16.27
Farm and garden machinery	352	169	106	104	116	78	76	8.78	10.99	12.52
Construction and related machinery	353	389	229	210	255	141	132	8.60	11.92	12.91
Metalworking machinery	354	398	330	317	290	236	224	8.13	12.27	13.65
Special industry machinery	355	194	159	152	125	94	88	7.53	11.90	13.47
General industrial machinery	356	300	247	239	196	158	153	7.95	11.32	12.75
Computer and office equipment	357	420	438	338	181	137	117	6.75	11.51	13.06
Refrigeration and service machinery	358	175	177	190	120	125	135	7.23	10.93	11.60
Electronic and other elec. equip. [3]	36	1,771	1,673	1,552	([4])	1,055	1,000	([4])	10.30	11.51
Electric distribution equipment	361	117	97	81	82	67	57	6.96	10.15	11.24
Electrical industrial apparatus	362	232	169	159	163	119	112	([4])	11.00	10.90
Household appliances	363	162	124	124	128	99	101	6.95	10.26	10.89
Electric lighting and wiring equip	364	211	189	178	157	136	128	6.43	10.12	11.25
Household audio and video equip	365	109	85	86	79	59	57	6.42	9.68	11.46
Communications equipment	366	([4])	264	235	([4])	133	120	([4])	11.03	12.28
Electronic components and accessories	367	539	582	536	325	329	316	6.05	10.00	11.32
Transportation equipment [3]	37	1,881	1,989	1,728	1,220	1,224	1,129	9.35	14.08	16.49
Motor vehicles and equipment	371	789	812	885	575	617	684	9.85	14.56	16.97
Aircraft and parts	372	633	712	479	344	345	220	9.28	14.79	17.98
Ship and boat building and repairing	373	221	188	158	176	141	123	8.22	10.94	12.49
Railroad equipment	374	71	33	32	53	25	24	9.93	13.41	15.60
Guided missiles, space vehicles, and parts	376	111	185	108	35	57	31	9.22	14.39	17.48

See footnotes at end of table.

No. 668. Nonfarm Industries—Employees and Earnings: 1980 to 1994—Continued

[See headnote, p. 426]

INDUSTRY	1987 SIC [1] code	ALL EMPLOYEES TOTAL (1,000)			PRODUCTION WORKERS					
					Total (1,000)			Average hourly earnings (dollars)		
		1980	1990	1994	1980	1990	1994	1980	1990	1994
Durable goods—Continued	(X)									
Instruments and related products	38	1,022	1,006	855	(4)	499	419	(4)	11.29	12.47
Search and navigation equipment	381	(4)	284	181	(4)	94	56	(4)	14.62	16.77
Measuring and controlling devices	382	(4)	323	276	(4)	180	141	(4)	10.68	12.25
Medical instruments and supplies	384	(4)	246	266	(4)	144	153	(4)	9.85	11.13
Ophthalmic goods	385	44	43	38	31	30	25	5.30	8.18	9.30
Photographic equipment and supplies	386	135	100	86	67	43	38	8.83	14.08	15.01
Watches, clocks, watchcases, and parts	387	22	11	9	17	8	7	5.24	7.70	8.52
Misc. manufacturing industries [3]	39	418	375	378	313	272	269	5.46	8.61	9.65
Jewelry, silverware, and plated ware	391	56	52	51	40	37	36	5.76	9.23	9.88
Toys and sporting goods	394	117	104	110	88	76	78	5.01	7.94	9.06
Pens, pencils, office and art supplies	395	37	34	32	27	24	21	5.58	8.89	10.67
Costume jewelry and notions	396	(4)	34	29	(4)	25	21	(4)	7.40	8.23
Nondurable goods [3]	(X)	**8,127**	**7,968**	**7,797**	**5,798**	**5,584**	**5,467**	**6.56**	**10.12**	**11.25**
Food and kindred products [3]	20	1,708	1,661	1,667	1,175	1,194	1,222	6.85	9.62	10.67
Meat products	201	358	422	446	298	359	379	6.99	7.94	8.71
Dairy products	202	175	155	152	96	95	96	6.86	10.56	12.01
Preserved fruits and vegetables	203	246	247	246	202	206	205	5.94	8.95	10.20
Grain mill products	204	144	128	126	99	89	90	7.67	11.52	13.09
Bakery products	205	230	213	211	139	133	138	7.14	10.85	11.74
Sugar and confectionery products	206	108	99	102	81	78	80	6.56	10.26	11.54
Fats and oils	207	44	31	31	32	22	21	7.03	10.10	11.28
Beverages	208	234	184	177	105	78	84	8.12	13.51	15.05
Tobacco products	21	69	49	39	54	36	30	7.74	16.23	18.76
Cigarettes	211	46	35	27	35	26	21	9.23	19.57	23.37
Textile mill products [3]	22	848	691	672	737	593	571	5.07	8.02	9.14
Broadwoven fabric mills, cotton	221	150	91	84	135	82	74	5.25	8.31	9.53
Broadwoven fabric mills, synthetics	222	116	77	70	104	68	59	5.30	8.63	10.06
Broadwoven fabric mills, wool	223	19	17	17	16	14	15	5.21	8.61	9.60
Narrow fabric mills	224	23	24	22	20	20	19	4.63	7.39	8.37
Knitting mills	225	224	205	196	194	179	169	4.77	7.37	8.35
Textile finishing, except wool	226	74	62	72	62	50	59	5.39	8.45	9.36
Carpets and rugs	227	54	61	64	44	50	51	5.20	8.25	9.15
Yarn and thread mills	228	125	103	95	113	92	85	4.76	7.68	8.88
Apparel and other textile products [3]	23	1,264	1,036	954	1,079	869	799	4.56	6.57	7.33
Men's and boys' suits and coats	231	77	50	40	67	42	33	5.34	7.34	7.93
Men's and boys' furnishings	232	362	274	264	310	235	227	4.23	6.06	6.97
Women's and misses outerwear	233	417	328	283	360	274	236	4.61	6.26	6.95
Women's and children's undergarments	234	90	62	53	76	51	44	4.15	6.18	6.96
Girls' and children's outerwear	236	64	56	45	55	47	38	4.20	5.95	6.57
Paper and allied products [3]	26	685	697	684	519	522	518	7.84	12.31	13.76
Papermills	262	178	180	167	133	136	128	9.05	15.10	17.06
Paperboard mills	263	65	52	50	51	40	38	9.28	15.26	17.32
Paperboard containers and boxes	265	205	209	213	157	162	167	6.94	10.39	11.71
Misc. converted paper products	267	220	241	241	163	174	175	6.89	10.79	12.01
Printing and publishing [3]	27	1,252	1,569	1,529	699	871	840	7.53	11.24	12.13
Newspapers	271	420	474	453	164	166	156	7.72	11.17	12.02
Periodicals	272	90	129	129	16	47	43	7.16	11.95	13.47
Books	273	101	121	124	52	66	66	6.76	10.10	11.30
Commercial printing	275	410	552	548	304	401	396	7.85	11.52	12.31
Blankbooks and bookbinding	278	62	72	68	51	56	53	5.78	8.83	9.56
Chemicals and allied products [3]	28	1,107	1,086	1,054	626	600	574	8.30	13.54	15.18
Industrial inorganic chemicals	281	161	138	130	88	70	56	9.07	14.66	16.81
Plastics materials and synthetics	282	205	180	159	137	116	106	8.21	13.97	15.61
Drugs	283	196	237	265	97	105	122	7.69	12.90	14.83
Soap, cleaners, and toilet goods	284	141	159	152	86	98	95	7.67	11.71	12.68
Paints and allied products	285	65	61	58	33	31	30	7.39	11.99	12.98
Industrial organic chemicals	286	174	155	144	88	86	79	9.67	15.97	18.19
Agricultural chemicals	287	72	56	56	45	34	32	8.12	13.73	15.27
Petroleum and coal products [3]	29	198	157	148	125	103	96	10.10	16.24	19.11
Petroleum refining	291	155	118	110	93	75	70	10.94	17.58	19.76
Asphalt paving and roofing materials	295	31	27	26	24	21	20	7.69	12.87	14.04
Rubber and misc. plastics products [3]	30	764	888	935	588	687	727	6.58	9.76	10.70
Tires and inner tubes	301	115	84	79	81	62	57	9.74	15.42	17.74
Rubber and plastics footwear	302	22	11	11	20	9	9	4.43	6.66	7.81
Leather and leather products [3]	31	233	133	115	197	109	91	4.58	6.91	7.97
Leather tanning and finishing	311	19	15	15	16	12	12	6.10	9.04	10.59
Footwear, except rubber	314	144	74	60	123	63	50	4.42	6.61	7.49
Luggage	316	16	11	11	12	8	8	4.90	6.91	7.89
Handbags and personal leather goods	317	30	15	12	25	12	8	4.33	6.08	7.25

See footnotes at end of table.

No. 668. Nonfarm Industries—Employees and Earnings: 1980 to 1994—Continued

[See headnote, p. 426]

INDUSTRY	1987 SIC [1] code	ALL EMPLOYEES TOTAL (1,000)			PRODUCTION WORKERS					
					Total (1,000)			Average hourly earnings (dollars)		
		1980	1990	1994	1980	1990	1994	1980	1990	1994
Transp. and public utilities [3]	(E)	**5,146**	**5,793**	**5,843**	**4,293**	**4,807**	**4,890**	**8.87**	**12.97**	**13.88**
Railroad transportation	40	532	279	246	(4)	(4)	(4)	(4)	(4)	(4)
Class I railroads [5]	4011	482	241	214	(4)	(4)	(4)	[6]9.92	[6]16.08	[6]16.76
Local and interurban passenger transit	41	265	338	387	244	308	355	6.34	9.23	10.16
Trucking and warehousing	42	1,280	1,625	1,749	1,121	1,416	1,517	9.13	11.71	12.60
Water transportation	44	211	177	166	(4)	(4)	(4)	(4)	(4)	(4)
Transportation by air	45	453	745	734	(4)	(4)	(4)	(4)	(4)	(4)
Pipelines, except natural gas	46	21	19	18	15	14	14	10.50	17.04	20.04
Transportation services	47	198	345	367	159	278	290	6.94	10.43	11.67
Communication [3]	48	1,357	1,309	1,255	1,014	978	963	8.50	13.51	15.25
Telephone communication	481	1,072	913	858	779	658	638	8.72	14.13	15.94
Radio and television broadcasting	483	192	234	233	154	193	195	7.44	12.71	14.85
Cable and other pay television services	484	(4)	126	140	(4)	105	118	(4)	10.50	11.72
Electric, gas, and sanitary services [3]	49	829	957	921	678	759	726	8.90	15.23	17.33
Electric services	491	391	454	416	316	351	324	9.12	15.80	18.06
Gas production and distribution	492	168	165	159	138	129	124	8.27	14.25	16.81
Combination utility services	493	197	193	182	162	156	140	9.64	17.58	20.77
Sanitary services	495	50	115	133	44	99	115	7.16	11.55	12.29
Wholesale trade	(F)	**5,292**	**6,173**	**6,060**	**4,328**	**4,959**	**4,890**	**6.95**	**10.79**	**12.01**
Retail trade [3]	(G)	**15,018**	**19,601**	**20,310**	**13,484**	**17,358**	**17,858**	**4.88**	**6.75**	**7.49**
General merchandise stores	53	2,245	2,540	2,473	2,090	2,380	2,311	4.77	6.83	7.45
Food stores	54	2,384	3,215	3,244	2,202	2,953	2,951	6.24	7.31	7.93
Automotive dealers and service stations	55	1,689	2,063	2,147	1,430	1,718	1,787	5.66	8.92	10.07
Apparel and accessory stores	56	957	1,183	1,149	820	991	939	4.30	6.25	7.18
Furniture and home furnishings stores	57	606	820	895	502	670	726	5.53	8.53	9.82
Eating and drinking places	58	4,626	6,509	7,056	4,256	5,905	6,363	3.69	4.97	5.47
Finance, insurance, real estate	(H)	**5,160**	**6,709**	**6,788**	**3,907**	**4,860**	**4,943**	**5.79**	**9.97**	**11.83**
Depository institutions	60	(4)	2,251	2,041	(4)	1,632	1,472	(4)	8.43	9.39
Nondepository institutions	61	(4)	373	477	(4)	270	352	(4)	10.40	12.41
Security and commodity brokers	62	227	424	503	(4)	(4)	(4)	(4)	(4)	(4)
Insurance carriers	63	1,224	1,462	1,517	854	982	1,071	6.29	11.18	14.00
Insurance, agents, brokers, service	64	464	663	665	(4)	(4)	(4)	(4)	(4)	(4)
Real estate	65	989	1,315	1,353	(4)	(4)	(4)	(4)	(4)	(4)
Holding and other investment offices	67	115	221	233	(4)	(4)	(4)	(4)	(4)	(4)
Services [3]	(I)	**17,890**	**27,934**	**31,804**	**15,921**	**24,387**	**27,783**	**5.85**	**9.83**	**11.07**
Hotels and other lodging places	70	1,076	1,631	1,607	(4)	(4)	(4)	(4)	(4)	(4)
Hotels and motels	701	1,038	1,578	1,551	954	1,398	1,365	4.45	6.98	7.72
Personal services [3]	72	818	1,104	1,137	(4)	(4)	(4)	(4)	(4)	(4)
Laundry, cleaning, garment services	721	356	426	432	318	379	383	4.47	6.82	7.33
Beauty shops	723	284	372	383	264	333	343	4.26	7.10	8.13
Business services [3]	73	2,564	5,139	6,447	(4)	4,522	5,741	(4)	9.48	10.36
Advertising	731	153	235	240	116	169	176	8.07	13.51	15.53
Personnel supply services	736	543	1,535	2,341	(4)	(4)	(4)	(4)	(4)	(4)
Employment agencies	7361	(4)	246	321	(4)	(4)	(4)	(4)	(4)	(4)
Help supply services	7363	(4)	1,288	2,021	(4)	1,245	1,963	(4)	8.09	8.46
Computer and data processing services	737	304	772	989	254	603	801	7.16	15.11	17.01
Prepackaged software	7372	(4)	113	155	(4)	(4)	(4)	(4)	(4)	(4)
Data processing and preparation	7374	(4)	197	232	(4)	(4)	(4)	(4)	(4)	(4)
Auto repair, services, and parking	75	571	914	1,044	488	756	860	6.10	8.77	9.61
Automotive repair shops	753	350	524	591	297	429	479	6.52	9.67	10.65
Motion pictures	78	(4)	408	483	(4)	344	401	(4)	10.95	13.86
Motion picture theaters	783	124	112	115	(4)	(4)	(4)	(4)	(4)	(4)
Amusement and recreation services	79	(4)	1,076	1,269	(4)	944	1,110	(4)	8.11	8.62
Health services [3]	80	5,278	7,814	9,032	4,712	6,948	7,996	5.68	10.41	12.10
Offices and clinics of medical doctors	801	802	1,338	1,562	(4)	1,105	1,274	(4)	10.58	12.22
Nursing and personal care facilities	805	997	1,415	1,633	898	1,279	1,471	4.17	7.24	8.47
Hospitals	806	2,750	3,549	3,790	2,522	3,248	3,465	6.06	11.79	13.83
Home health care services	808	(4)	291	533	(4)	269	493	(4)	8.72	10.67
Legal services	81	498	908	942	427	748	755	7.35	14.16	15.66
Educational services	82	1,138	1,661	1,745	(4)	(4)	(4)	(4)	(4)	(4)
Social services	83	1,134	1,734	2,249	(4)	1,494	1,948	(4)	7.11	8.11
Membership organizations	86	1,539	1,946	2,054	(4)	(4)	(4)	(4)	(4)	(4)
Engineering and management services	87	(4)	2,478	2,610	(4)	1,886	2,004	(4)	13.56	15.36
Government	(J)	**16,241**	**18,304**	**19,040**	**(NA)**	**(NA)**	**(NA)**	**(NA)**	**(NA)**	**(4)**
Federal government	(X)	2,866	3,085	2,870	(NA)	(NA)	(NA)	(NA)	(NA)	(4)
State government	(X)	3,610	4,305	4,552	(NA)	(NA)	(NA)	(NA)	(NA)	(4)
Local government	(X)	9,765	10,914	11,617	(NA)	(NA)	(NA)	(NA)	(NA)	(4)

NA Not available. X Not applicable. [1] 1987 Standard Industrial Classification, see text, section 13. [2] Excludes government. [3] Includes industries not shown separately. [4] Included in totals; not available separately. [5] For changes in "Class I" classification, see text, section 21. [6] Includes all employees except executives, officials, and staff assistants who received pay during the month.

Source: U.S. Bureau of Labor Statistics, Bulletin 2445, and *Employment and Earnings,* March and June issues.

No. 669. Indexes of Output per Hour—Selected Industries: 1975 to 1993

[See text, section 13. Minus sign (-) indicates decrease. See also *Historical Statistics, Colonial Times to 1970*, series W 14, 17, and 19, W 30-54, and 62-65]

INDUSTRY	1987 SIC code [1]	INDEXES (1987=100)						AVERAGE ANNUAL PERCENT CHANGE [2] 1975-92
		1975	1980	1985	1990	1992	1993, prel.	
Mining:	(B)							
Coal mining	12	57.8	61.9	85.2	118.4	132.5	144.4	5.0
Crude petroleum and natural gas	1311	142.9	97.5	83.4	96.8	102.2	106.5	-2.0
Nonmetallic minerals, except fuels	14	79.4	84.6	93.9	105.0	109.0	111.1	1.9
Manufacturing:	(D)							
Red meat products	2011,13	69.1	87.6	99.7	92.3	103.0	(NA)	2.4
Poultry dressing and processing	2015	64.6	77.8	98.2	106.1	121.5	(NA)	3.8
Dairy products	202	66.3	77.4	93.3	104.5	112.2	111.4	3.1
Preserved fruits and vegetables	203	77.8	83.7	94.6	97.0	99.3	(NA)	1.4
Grain mill products	204	58.4	70.4	93.8	104.1	(NA)	(NA)	(NA)
Bakery products	2051,52	81.2	81.5	95.5	93.8	89.8	(NA)	0.6
Bottled and canned soft drinks	2086	55.7	66.6	85.2	126.7	144.1	144.6	5.8
Cotton and synthetic broadwoven fabrics	2211,21	65.2	79.0	94.1	106.1	116.0	(NA)	3.4
Hosiery	2251,52	81.5	92.9	101.3	105.7	117.0	122.9	2.1
Yarn spinning mills	2281	65.3	64.3	87.5	107.1	114.7	(NA)	3.4
Sawmills and planing mills, general	2421	67.4	70.9	92.3	100.3	111.1	107.3	3.0
Millwork	2431	103.8	97.0	95.5	98.3	94.1	(NA)	-0.6
Wood kitchen cabinets	2434	83.6	95.0	85.2	94.4	116.5	(NA)	2.0
Household furniture	251	82.4	84.5	94.6	100.8	106.6	(NA)	1.5
Office furniture	252	71.8	94.1	98.6	95.6	97.9	(NA)	1.8
Pulp, paper, and paperboard mills	2611,21,31	62.8	76.1	89.1	103.2	109.2	(NA)	3.3
Corrugated and solid fiber boxes	2653	78.1	90.1	99.3	100.3	100.9	104.1	1.5
Industrial inorganic chemicals	281	69.6	75.9	86.1	90.3	94.5	(NA)	1.8
Industrial inorganic chemicals, n.e.c. [3]	2819 (pt.)	74.3	79.9	87.4	86.5	93.2	(NA)	1.3
Synthetic fibers	2823,24	53.7	73.4	86.2	99.1	105.4	(NA)	4.0
Cosmetics and other toiletries	2844	94.7	84.2	88.9	100.3	105.8	(NA)	0.7
Industrial organic chemicals, n.e.c. [3]	2869	64.9	75.4	85.7	98.0	92.2	(NA)	2.1
Petroleum refining	2911	77.0	81.6	84.3	109.9	112.6	120.9	2.3
Tires and inner tubes	3011	53.1	59.2	88.1	108.3	117.6	125.8	4.8
Miscellaneous plastics products, n.e.c. [3]	308	67.0	74.3	88.0	100.1	113.4	(NA)	3.1
Footwear	314	94.6	92.5	100.3	92.6	92.7	95.9	-0.1
Concrete products	3271,72	88.7	87.2	97.3	105.8	105.5	(NA)	1.0
Ready-mixed concrete	3273	93.3	89.0	93.2	99.6	99.4	(NA)	0.4
Steel	331	61.3	67.5	91.4	110.4	116.1	130.5	3.8
Gray and ductile iron foundries	3321	90.3	84.5	96.1	103.7	106.2	(NA)	1.0
Fabricated structural metal	3441	82.4	86.4	99.6	97.2	104.3	(NA)	1.4
Metal doors, sash, and trim	3442	86.2	87.3	102.5	98.3	102.5	(NA)	1.0
Metal stampings	3465,66,69	80.8	86.7	90.6	98.3	106.4	(NA)	1.6
Valves and pipe fittings	3491,92,94	83.0	92.5	94.4	102.1	102.3	(NA)	1.2
Farm and garden machinery	352	90.4	86.3	93.3	117.7	113.9	(NA)	1.4
Construction machinery	3531	85.8	89.1	96.7	114.5	102.8	(NA)	1.1
Pumps and compressors	3561,63,94	75.1	82.4	89.6	105.9	105.0	(NA)	2.0
Refrigeration and heating equipment	3585	85.0	88.7	98.3	105.9	105.5	(NA)	1.3
Motors and generators	3621	82.7	85.7	95.9	102.6	112.4	(NA)	1.8
Major household appliances	3631,32,33,39	70.0	79.0	93.0	102.6	112.1	(NA)	2.8
Lighting fixtures and equipment	3645,46,47,48	79.9	83.5	96.4	94.4	98.8	(NA)	1.3
Motor vehicles and equipment	371	69.6	71.9	95.0	102.0	104.8	108.4	2.4
Aircraft	3721	84.0	101.0	92.4	106.2	137.4	(NA)	2.9
Instruments to measure electricity	3825	72.0	81.6	98.3	108.0	124.1	(NA)	3.3
Photographic equipment and supplies	3861	71.2	84.4	90.3	109.5	118.0	(NA)	3.0
Service producing:	(E,G,H,I)							
Railroad transportation, revenue traffic	4011	43.4	52.0	78.4	122.4	140.3	150.9	7.1
Air transportation [4]	4512,13,22 (pts)	59.9	72.8	93.6	92.4	97.3	100.5	2.9
Telephone communications	481	50.0	68.6	90.5	113.3	127.5	135.9	5.7
Gas and electric utilities	491,2,3	101.6	103.2	97.4	106.3	110.1	116.4	0.5
Hardware stores	5251	84.0	95.9	96.0	110.5	107.4	108.7	1.5
Department stores	5311	64.3	74.5	93.1	95.0	101.3	106.3	2.7
Variety stores	5331	143.3	126.1	129.1	132.0	136.3	135.3	-0.3
Food stores	54	106.0	107.5	102.4	94.8	93.4	92.9	-0.7
New and used car dealers	5511	83.9	87.9	99.8	106.0	106.3	106.7	1.4
Auto and home supply stores	5531	70.8	84.0	95.0	114.2	120.4	120.2	3.2
Gasoline service stations	5541	58.8	72.3	93.7	101.1	106.2	108.9	3.5
Apparel and accessory stores	56	72.6	81.4	102.0	101.4	109.8	109.0	2.5
Home furniture, furnishings, & equipment stores	57	64.6	75.3	92.4	111.3	126.1	132.7	4.0
Eating and drinking places	581	107.5	106.5	96.2	103.2	104.1	103.9	-0.2
Drug stores and proprietary stores	5912	89.5	101.5	101.4	106.6	109.2	112.5	1.2
Liquor stores	5921	89.9	95.2	101.6	107.8	113.0	98.1	1.4
Commercial banks	602	76.3	78.6	94.3	108.5	117.2	129.9	2.6
Hotels and motels	7011	100.2	103.8	101.1	90.6	97.5	97.4	-0.2
Laundry, cleaning, and garment services	721	112.5	105.9	103.2	99.0	97.1	96.4	-0.9
Beauty and barber shops	7231,41	83.2	86.8	94.7	92.2	92.8	90.0	0.6
Automotive repair shops	753	107.0	100.7	99.4	106.4	102.9	102.0	-0.2

NA Not available.   [1] 1987 Standard Industrial Classification; see text, section 13.   [2] Average annual percent change based on compound rate formula.   [3] N.e.c. means not elsewhere classified.   [4] Refers to output per employee.

Source: U.S. Bureau of Labor Statistics, Bulletin 2461, *Productivity Measures for Selected Industries and Government Services*, April 1995.

No. 670. Productivity and Related Measures: 1970 to 1994

[See text, section 13. Minus sign (-) indicates decrease. See also *Historical Statistics, Colonial Times to 1970*, series D 689-704 and W 22-25]

ITEM	1970	1975	1980	1985	1990	1991	1992	1993	1994
INDEXES (1982=100)									
Output per hour, business sector	87.0	95.5	98.6	106.3	110.7	112.1	115.5	117.2	119.9
Nonfarm business	88.5	96.7	99.0	105.6	109.1	110.7	113.7	115.4	117.9
Manufacturing	(NA)	(NA)	92.9	106.7	122.1	124.9	127.5	131.6	138.0
Output,[1] business sector	75.8	85.0	100.5	116.7	133.3	132.0	135.5	140.6	148.1
Nonfarm business	75.7	84.9	100.8	116.8	133.5	132.2	135.5	141.0	148.3
Manufacturing	(NA)	(NA)	102.0	114.0	130.6	128.2	130.1	135.4	143.7
Hours,[2] business sector	87.2	89.0	101.9	109.8	120.5	117.7	117.4	120.0	123.5
Nonfarm business	85.6	87.9	101.8	110.7	122.4	119.5	119.2	122.2	125.7
Manufacturing	(NA)	(NA)	109.8	106.8	107.0	102.6	102.0	102.9	104.2
Compensation per hour,[3] business sector	36.7	54.5	85.0	113.2	140.6	147.4	154.9	160.5	165.6
Nonfarm business	37.0	54.9	84.9	112.8	139.2	146.2	153.7	158.7	163.6
Manufacturing	(NA)	(NA)	83.3	111.3	134.7	141.9	147.9	152.8	157.1
Real hourly compensation,[3] business sector	91.3	97.8	99.5	101.5	103.8	104.4	106.6	107.2	107.8
Nonfarm business	92.0	98.4	99.4	101.1	102.8	103.6	105.7	106.0	106.6
Manufacturing	(NA)	(NA)	97.5	99.8	99.5	100.5	101.7	102.0	102.3
Unit labor costs,[4] business sector	42.2	57.1	86.2	106.5	127.1	131.5	134.2	136.9	138.1
Nonfarm business	41.8	56.8	85.7	106.8	127.6	132.1	135.2	137.5	138.8
Manufacturing	(NA)	(NA)	89.7	104.2	110.4	113.7	116.0	116.1	113.8
ANNUAL PERCENT CHANGE [5]									
Output per hour, business sector	1.4	2.4	-0.8	1.4	0.7	1.3	3.0	1.5	2.3
Nonfarm business	1.0	2.3	-0.9	0.8	0.4	1.5	2.7	1.5	2.2
Manufacturing	(NA)	(NA)	-2.2	3.2	1.8	2.3	2.1	3.2	4.9
Output,[1] business sector	-0.5	-1.9	-1.6	3.6	0.7	-1.0	2.7	3.8	5.3
Nonfarm business	-0.6	-2.0	-1.7	3.4	0.6	-1.0	2.4	4.1	5.2
Manufacturing	(NA)	(NA)	-6.7	2.4	-0.4	-1.9	1.5	4.1	6.1
Hours,[2] business sector	-1.8	-4.2	-0.9	2.1	0.1	-2.3	-0.3	2.2	2.9
Nonfarm business	-1.5	-4.2	-0.8	2.5	0.2	-2.4	-0.3	2.5	2.9
Manufacturing	(NA)	(NA)	-4.6	-0.7	-2.2	-4.1	-0.6	0.8	1.2
Compensation per hour,[3] business sector	7.5	10.0	10.7	4.5	5.7	4.8	5.1	3.6	3.2
Nonfarm business	7.2	10.0	10.7	4.1	5.5	5.0	5.1	3.3	3.1
Manufacturing	(NA)	(NA)	11.9	5.0	5.3	5.3	4.2	3.3	2.8
Real hourly compensation,[3] business sector	1.7	0.8	-2.5	0.9	0.3	0.6	2.0	0.6	0.6
Nonfarm business	1.4	0.8	-2.5	0.6	0.1	0.8	2.0	0.2	0.5
Manufacturing	(NA)	(NA)	-1.4	1.4	-0.1	1.1	1.2	0.3	0.2
Unit labor costs,[4] business sector	6.1	7.5	11.5	3.0	5.0	3.5	2.1	2.0	0.8
Nonfarm business	6.2	7.5	11.7	3.3	5.1	3.5	2.4	1.7	0.9
Manufacturing	(NA)	(NA)	14.3	1.8	3.5	3.0	2.1	0.1	-2.0

NA Not available.　[1] Refers to gross domestic product originating in the sector, in 1987 prices.　[2] Hours at work of all persons engaged in the business and nonfarm business sectors (employees, proprietors, and unpaid family workers); employees' and proprietors' hours in manufacturing.　[3] Wages and salaries of employees plus employers' contributions for social insurance and private benefit plans. Also includes an estimate of same for self-employed. Real compensation deflated by the consumer price index for all urban consumers, see text, section 15.　[4] Hourly compensation divided by output per hour.　[5] All changes are from the immediate prior year.

Source: U.S. Bureau of Labor Statistics, *Employment and Earnings,* monthly; and unpublished data.

No. 671. Workers Using Computers on the Job: 1993

[**In percent.** For workers 18 years old and over. Based on the Current Population Survey and subject to sampling error; see Appendix III and source]

CHARACTERISTIC	Number using computers [1] (1,000)	Percent of total	TYPE OF APPLICATION						
			Book-keeping/inventory	Word processing	Communications [2]	Analysis/spreadsheets	Data-bases	Desktop publishing	Sales and telemarketing
Total	51,106	45.8	36.1	45.0	38.7	34.5	22.3	16.2	44.4
Age:									
18 to 25 years old	4,965	34.4	25.0	45.3	27.1	27.1	15.9	19.9	34.7
25 to 29 years old	8,424	48.3	37.2	45.2	38.7	35.0	22.8	17.0	45.7
30 to 39 years old	14,969	50.7	38.8	45.4	40.4	36.0	25.0	16.4	45.0
40 to 49 years old	13,854	51.3	38.6	45.1	42.0	36.8	23.4	14.5	47.5
50 to 59 years old	6,881	43.9	34.5	44.3	38.8	33.3	20.4	15.0	43.9
60 years old and over	2,014	27.2	28.0	42.7	31.6	27.4	15.0	16.9	40.0
Sex: Male	24,414	40.3	41.1	45.2	39.4	35.2	25.3	18.1	40.7
Female	26,692	52.4	31.6	44.8	38.1	33.8	19.6	14.5	47.8
Race/ethnicity:									
White [3]	43,020	48.7	37.2	45.8	39.3	35.2	23.0	16.7	45.9
Black [3]	4,016	36.2	27.5	38.3	37.3	31.2	16.8	12.9	35.5
Hispanic	2,492	29.3	29.1	45.6	32.1	27.6	18.7	16.0	33.6
Other	1,578	43.9	39.7	39.4	37.2	33.5	22.6	10.2	44.5
Educational attainment:									
Not a high school graduate	1,190	10.0	19.1	54.4	20.4	22.2	9.9	20.6	16.0
High school graduate	13,307	34.2	23.7	52.5	29.4	25.8	13.3	17.6	30.8
Some college	11,548	50.4	33.5	49.5	38.5	33.9	20.6	18.0	40.9
Associate's degree	5,274	58.2	37.5	47.0	39.7	34.7	21.7	14.9	41.6
Bachelor's degree	13,162	68.8	46.9	40.0	45.1	41.5	28.8	17.0	54.8
Master's degree	4,628	71.2	47.9	29.3	48.5	41.9	35.3	10.4	63.8
Doctorate or professional degree	1,999	66.9	42.8	27.9	45.9	39.2	28.3	5.2	66.5

[1] Includes other applications, not shown separately. A person may be counted in more than one application.　[2] Includes bulletin boards and electronic mail.　[3] Non-Hispanic.

Source: U.S. National Center for Education Statistics, *Digest of Education Statistics,* 1994.

No. 672. Annual Total Compensation and Wages and Salaries Per Full-Time Equivalent Employee, by Industry: 1985 to 1993

[**In dollars.** Wage and salary payments include executives' compensation, bonuses, tips, and payments-in-kind; total compensation includes in addition to wages and salaries, employer contributions for social insurance, employer contributions to private and welfare funds, director's fees, jury and witness fees, etc. 1985 based on 1972 Standard Industrial Classification Code (SIC); beginning 1990, based on the 1987 SIC. See text, section 13]

INDUSTRY	ANNUAL TOTAL COMPENSATION				ANNUAL WAGES AND SALARIES			
	1985	1990	1992	1993	1985	1990	1992	1993
Domestic industries	**25,263**	**31,398**	**34,583**	**35,803**	**21,059**	**26,138**	**28,455**	**29,367**
Agriculture, forestry, and fisheries	13,084	17,672	18,449	18,973	11,773	15,299	15,977	16,363
Mining	38,883	46,216	52,114	54,047	32,054	37,903	42,127	43,561
Construction	26,721	32,826	34,920	35,247	22,775	27,679	29,264	29,363
Manufacturing	30,145	36,572	40,472	42,069	24,600	29,746	32,400	33,604
Transportation	30,638	35,430	38,766	39,944	25,240	28,916	31,439	32,339
Communication	39,635	47,926	53,670	57,004	31,342	38,382	42,081	44,389
Electric, gas, and sanitary services	39,179	47,936	53,757	56,413	31,653	38,930	43,030	44,929
Wholesale trade	29,195	37,147	40,451	42,152	25,016	31,772	34,255	35,568
Retail trade	15,694	18,588	20,372	20,848	13,603	16,036	17,411	17,761
Finance, insurance, and real estate	27,873	37,049	42,602	46,485	23,724	31,682	36,171	39,536
Services	21,441	28,381	31,053	31,970	18,698	24,801	26,831	27,517
Government and government enterprises	27,839	35,616	39,748	41,334	21,988	27,772	30,538	31,533

Source: U.S. Bureau of Economic Analysis, *The National Income and Product Accounts of the United States, Volume 2, 1958-88;* and *Survey of Current Business,* July 1994; and unpublished data.

No. 673. Average Hourly and Weekly Earnings, by Private Industry Group: 1980 to 1994

[Average earnings include overtime. Data are for production and related workers in mining, manufacturing, and construction, and nonsupervisory employees in other industries. Excludes agriculture. See headnote, table 666. See also *Historical Statistics, Colonial Times to 1970,* series D 877-892]

PRIVATE INDUSTRY GROUP	CURRENT DOLLARS					CONSTANT (**1982**) DOLLARS [1]				
	1980	1985	1990	1993	1994	1980	1985	1990	1993	1994
Average hourly earnings	**6.66**	**8.57**	**10.01**	**10.83**	**11.12**	**7.78**	**7.77**	**7.52**	**7.39**	**7.40**
Mining	9.17	11.98	13.68	14.60	14.89	10.71	10.86	10.28	9.96	9.91
Construction	9.94	12.32	13.77	14.37	14.69	11.61	11.17	10.35	9.80	9.77
Manufacturing	7.27	9.54	10.83	11.74	12.06	8.49	8.65	8.14	8.01	8.02
Transportation, public utilities	8.87	11.40	12.97	13.63	13.88	10.36	10.34	9.74	9.30	9.23
Wholesale trade	6.95	9.15	10.79	11.73	12.01	8.12	8.30	8.11	8.00	7.99
Retail trade	4.88	5.94	6.75	7.29	7.49	5.70	5.39	5.07	4.97	4.98
Finance, insurance, real estate	5.79	7.94	9.97	11.35	11.83	6.76	7.20	7.49	7.74	7.87
Services	5.85	7.90	9.83	10.79	11.07	6.83	7.16	7.39	7.36	7.37
Average weekly earnings	**235**	**299**	**345**	**374**	**385**	**275**	**271**	**259**	**255**	**256**
Mining	397	520	603	647	666	464	471	453	441	443
Construction	368	464	526	552	570	430	421	395	376	379
Manufacturing	289	386	442	486	507	337	350	332	332	337
Transportation, public utilities	351	450	505	540	554	410	408	379	368	368
Wholesale trade	267	351	411	448	460	312	318	309	306	306
Retail trade	147	175	194	210	216	172	158	146	143	144
Finance, insurance, real estate	210	289	357	406	424	245	262	268	277	282
Services	191	257	319	351	360	223	233	240	239	239

[1] Earnings in current dollars divided by the Consumer Price Index (CPI-W) on a 1982 base; see text, section 15.

Source: U.S. Bureau of Labor Statistics, Bulletin 2445, and *Employment and Earnings,* monthly, March and June issues.

No. 674. Annual Percent Changes in Earnings and Compensation: 1980 to 1994

[Annual percent change from immediate prior year. Minus sign (-) indicates decrease]

ITEM	1980	1985	1988	1989	1990	1991	1992	1993	1994
Current dollars:									
Hourly earnings, total [1]	8.1	3.0	3.3	4.1	3.6	3.1	2.4	2.5	2.7
Hourly earnings, manufacturing	8.5	3.8	2.8	2.8	3.3	3.2	2.5	2.4	2.7
Compensation per employee-hour [1]	10.6	4.1	4.2	3.3	5.5	5.0	5.1	3.2	3.0
Constant (**1982**) dollars:									
Hourly earnings, total [1]	−4.8	−0.4	−0.5	−0.7	−1.6	−0.9	−0.5	−0.3	0.1
Hourly earnings, manufacturing	−4.5	0.3	−1.2	−1.9	−1.7	−0.9	−0.4	−0.4	0.1
Compensation per employee-hour [1]	−2.6	0.5	0.1	−1.4	0.1	0.8	2.0	0.2	0.5
Consumer Price Index [2]	13.5	3.6	4.1	4.8	5.4	4.2	3.0	3.0	2.6

[1] Nonfarm business sector. [2] See text, section 15.

Source: U.S. Bureau of Labor Statistics, *Monthly Labor Review;* and unpublished data.

No. 675. Average Annual Pay, by State: 1992 and 1993

[In dollars, except percent change. For workers covered by State unemployment insurance laws and for Federal civilian workers covered by unemployment compensation for Federal employees, approximately 96 percent of wage and salary civilian employment in 1993. Excludes most agricultural workers on small farms, all Armed Forces, elected officials in most States, railroad employees, most domestic workers, most student workers at school, employees of certain nonprofit organizations, and most self-employed individuals. Pay includes bonuses, cash value of meals and lodging, and tips and other gratuities]

STATE	AVERAGE ANNUAL PAY		Percent change, 1992-93 [1]	STATE	AVERAGE ANNUAL PAY		Percent change, 1992-93 [1]
	1992	1993 [1]			1992	1993 [1]	
United States......	25,897	26,362	1.8	Missouri...........	23,550	23,898	1.5
Alabama............	22,340	22,786	2.0	Montana...........	19,378	19,932	2.9
Alaska.............	31,825	32,336	1.6	Nebraska..........	20,355	20,815	2.3
Arizona............	23,153	23,501	1.5	Nevada............	24,743	25,461	2.9
Arkansas...........	20,108	20,337	1.1	New Hampshire......	24,866	24,962	0.4
California..........	28,902	29,468	2.0	New Jersey.........	32,073	32,716	2.0
Colorado..........	25,040	25,682	2.6	New Mexico........	21,051	21,731	3.2
Connecticut........	32,603	33,169	1.7	New York..........	32,399	32,919	1.6
Delaware..........	26,596	27,143	2.1	North Carolina......	22,249	22,770	2.3
District of Columbia....	37,951	39,199	3.3	North Dakota.......	18,945	19,382	2.3
Florida............	23,145	23,571	1.8	Ohio..............	24,845	25,339	2.0
Georgia...........	24,373	24,867	2.0	Oklahoma.........	21,698	22,003	1.4
Hawaii............	25,538	26,325	3.1	Oregon............	23,514	24,093	2.5
Idaho.............	20,649	21,188	2.6	Pennsylvania.......	25,785	26,274	1.9
Illinois............	27,910	28,420	1.8	Rhode Island.......	24,315	24,889	2.4
Indiana...........	23,570	24,109	2.3	South Carolina......	21,398	21,928	2.5
Iowa.............	20,937	21,441	2.4	South Dakota.......	18,016	18,613	3.3
Kansas...........	21,982	22,430	2.0	Tennessee.........	22,807	23,368	2.5
Kentucky..........	21,858	22,170	1.4	Texas.............	25,088	25,545	1.8
Louisiana..........	22,342	22,632	1.3	Utah..............	21,976	22,250	1.2
Maine.............	21,808	22,026	1.0	Vermont...........	22,360	22,704	1.5
Maryland..........	27,145	27,684	2.0	Virginia...........	24,940	25,496	2.2
Massachusetts.......	29,664	30,229	1.9	Washington.........	25,553	25,760	0.8
Michigan..........	27,463	28,260	2.9	West Virginia.......	22,168	22,373	0.9
Minnesota.........	25,324	25,711	1.5	Wisconsin..........	23,008	23,610	2.6
Mississippi.........	19,237	19,694	2.4	Wyoming..........	21,215	21,745	2.5

[1] Preliminary.

Source: U.S. Bureau of Labor Statistics, *Employment and Wages Annual Averages 1993;* and USDL News Release 94-451, *Average Annual Pay by State and Industry, 1993.*

No. 676. Average Annual Pay, by Selected Metropolitan Areas: 1992 and 1993

[In dollars. Metropolitan areas ranked by average pay 1993. Includes data for Metropolitan Statistical Areas and Primary Metropolitan Statistical Areas defined as of June 30, 1993. In the New England areas, the New England County Metropolitan Area (NECMA) definitions were used. See source for details. See also headnote table 675]

METROPOLITAN AREA	1992	1993 [1]	METROPOLITAN AREA	1992	1993 [1]
Metropolitan areas............	27,051	27,540	Denver, CO...................	27,734	28,607
New York, NY..................	38,802	39,381	Brazoria, TX..................	27,979	28,453
San Jose, CA..................	37,068	38,040	Atlanta, GA...................	27,925	28,359
Middlesex-Somerset-Hunterdon, NJ......	34,796	35,573	Minneapolis-St. Paul, MN-WI.....	27,938	28,345
San Francisco, CA..............	34,364	35,278	Monmouth-Ocean, NJ...........	27,488	28,045
Newark, NJ....................	34,302	35,129	Ann Arbor, MI.................	27,195	27,930
New Haven-Bridgeport-Stamford-Danbury-			Saginaw-Bay City-Midland, MI.....	26,650	27,686
Waterbury, CT.................	34,517	35,058	Rochester, NY.................	27,256	27,645
Trenton, NJ...................	33,960	34,365	Rochester, MN.................	27,416	27,624
Bergen-Passaic, NJ.............	33,555	34,126	Sacramento, CA...............	27,105	27,476
Anchorage, AK.................	33,007	33,782	Honolulu, HI..................	26,534	27,253
Washington, DC-MD-VA-WV.......	32,337	33,170	Baltimore, MD.................	26,795	27,236
Jersey City, NJ................	31,638	32,815	Yolo, CA.....................	26,099	27,187
Hartford, CT..................	31,967	32,555	Springfield, IL................	25,706	26,998
Los Angeles-Long Beach, CA......	31,165	31,760	Cleveland-Lorain-Elyria, OH......	26,501	26,989
Oakland, CA..................	30,623	31,701	Lansing-East Lansing, MI........	26,548	26,848
Detroit, MI...................	30,534	31,622	Fort Worth-Arlington, TX.........	25,745	26,622
Chicago, IL...................	30,210	30,720	Albany-Schenectady-Troy, NY.....	26,099	26,604
Boston-Worcester-Lawrence-Lowell-			Indianapolis, IN...............	25,896	26,587
Brockton, MA-NH..............	30,100	30,642	Ventura, CA..................	26,267	26,567
Flint, MI.....................	29,672	30,512	St Louis, MO-IL...............	26,198	26,544
Nassau-Suffolk, NY.............	29,708	30,226	San Diego, CA................	26,153	26,531
Houston, TX..................	29,794	30,069	Pittsburgh, PA................	25,872	26,478
Orange County, CA.............	29,353	29,916	Cincinnati, OH-KY-IN...........	26,023	26,465
Philadelphia, PA-NJ............	29,392	29,839	Portland-Vancouver, OR-WA......	25,703	26,360
Dutchess County, NY...........	29,262	29,730	West Palm Beach-Boca Raton, FL..	26,055	26,348
Kokomo, IN...................	28,676	29,672	Bloomington-Normal, IL..........	25,581	26,285
Dallas, TX....................	28,813	29,489	Boulder-Longmont, CO..........	25,829	26,215
Seattle-Bellevue-Everett, WA......	29,466	29,399	Milwaukee-Waukesha, WI........	25,541	26,202
Huntsville, AL.................	28,944	29,243	Melbourne-Titusville-Palm Bay, FL..	26,032	26,095
Wilmington-Newark, DE-MD........	28,635	29,232	Raleigh-Durham-Chapel Hill, NC...	25,503	26,063
New London-Norwich, CT.........	27,926	28,630	Decatur, IL...................	25,292	26,040

[1] Preliminary.

Source: U.S. Bureau of Labor Statistics, USDL News Release 94-516, *Average Annual Pay Levels in Metropolitan Areas, 1993.*

No. 677. Full-Time Wage and Salary Workers—Number and Earnings: 1983 to 1994

[**In current dollars of usual weekly earnings**. Data represent annual averages of quarterly data. See text, section 13, and headnote table 643, for a discussion of occupational data. Based on Current Population Survey; see text, section 1, and Appendix III. For definition of median, see Guide to Tabular Presentation]

CHARACTERISTIC	NUMBER OF WORKERS (1,000)				MEDIAN WEEKLY EARNINGS (dol.)			
	1983	1985	1990	1994 [1]	1983	1985	1990	1994 [1]
All workers [2]	70,976	77,002	85,082	87,379	313	343	415	467
Male	42,309	45,589	49,015	49,992	378	406	485	522
16 to 24 years old	6,702	6,956	6,313	6,040	223	240	283	294
25 years old and over	35,607	38,632	42,702	43,952	406	442	514	576
Female	28,667	31,414	36,068	37,386	252	277	348	399
16 to 24 years old	5,345	5,621	5,001	4,403	197	210	254	276
25 years old and over	23,322	25,793	31,066	32,983	267	296	370	421
White	61,739	66,481	72,637	73,500	319	355	427	484
Male	37,378	40,030	42,563	42,816	387	417	497	547
Female	24,361	26,452	30,075	30,685	254	281	355	408
Black	7,373	8,393	9,642	10,199	261	277	329	371
Male	3,883	4,367	4,909	5,099	293	304	360	400
Female	3,490	4,026	4,733	5,100	231	252	308	346
Hispanic origin [3]	(NA)	(NA)	6,993	8,274	(NA)	(NA)	307	324
Male	(NA)	(NA)	4,410	5,295	(NA)	(NA)	322	343
Female	(NA)	(NA)	2,583	2,979	(NA)	(NA)	280	305
Family relationship:								
Husbands	28,720	30,260	31,326	(NA)	410	455	532	(NA)
Wives	14,884	16,270	18,666	(NA)	257	285	363	(NA)
Women who maintain families	3,948	4,333	5,007	(NA)	256	278	339	(NA)
Men who maintain families	1,331	1,313	1,786	(NA)	377	396	444	(NA)
Other persons in families:								
Men	5,518	6,173	6,434	(NA)	219	238	296	(NA)
Women	4,032	4,309	4,475	(NA)	201	213	271	(NA)
All other men [4]	6,740	7,841	9,468	(NA)	350	380	442	(NA)
All other women [4]	5,803	6,503	7,920	(NA)	274	305	376	(NA)
Occupation, male:								
Managerial and professional	10,312	11,078	12,263	13,021	516	583	731	803
Exec., admin., managerial	5,344	5,835	6,401	6,785	530	593	742	797
Professional specialty	4,967	5,243	5,863	6,236	506	571	720	809
Technical, sales, and administrative support	8,125	8,803	9,596	9,764	385	420	496	548
Tech. and related support	1,428	1,563	1,747	1,638	424	472	570	622
Sales	3,853	4,227	4,666	4,836	389	431	505	575
Admin. support, incl. clerical	2,844	3,013	3,183	3,289	362	391	440	482
Service	3,723	3,947	4,476	4,784	255	272	320	350
Private household	11	13	12	14	(B)	(B)	(B)	(B)
Protective	1,314	1,327	1,523	1,674	355	391	477	538
Other service	2,398	2,607	2,942	3,096	217	230	273	293
Precision production [5]	9,180	10,026	10,169	9,824	387	408	488	515
Mechanics and repairers	3,418	3,752	3,669	3,593	377	400	477	519
Construction trades	2,966	3,308	3,603	3,407	375	394	480	492
Other	2,796	2,966	2,897	2,824	408	433	510	553
Operators, fabricators and laborers	9,833	10,585	11,257	11,333	308	325	378	406
Machine operators, assemblers, and inspectors	4,138	4,403	4,510	4,469	319	341	391	415
Transportation and material moving	3,199	3,459	3,721	3,854	335	369	418	469
Handlers, equipment cleaners, helpers, and laborers	2,496	2,724	3,027	3,010	251	261	308	319
Farming, forestry, and fishing	1,137	1,150	1,253	1,266	200	216	263	290
Occupation, female:								
Managerial and professional	7,139	8,302	10,595	12,187	357	399	511	592
Exec., admin., managerial	2,772	3,492	4,764	5,548	339	383	485	541
Professional specialty	4,367	4,810	5,831	6,639	367	408	534	623
Technical, sales, and administrative support	13,517	14,622	16,202	15,954	247	269	332	376
Tech. and related support	1,146	1,200	1,470	1,536	299	331	417	466
Sales	2,460	2,929	3,531	3,633	204	226	292	324
Admin. support, incl. clerical	9,911	10,494	11,202	10,785	248	270	332	374
Service	3,598	3,963	4,531	4,702	173	185	230	257
Private household	267	330	298	311	116	130	171	177
Protective	139	156	216	277	250	278	405	430
Other service	3,193	3,477	4,017	4,115	176	188	231	256
Precision production [5]	784	906	893	970	256	268	316	370
Mechanics and repairers	120	144	139	160	337	392	459	520
Construction trades	45	53	50	52	(B)	265	394	408
Other	619	709	704	758	244	253	300	342
Operators, fabricators, and laborers	3,486	3,482	3,675	3,412	204	216	262	293
Machine operators, assemblers, and inspectors	2,853	2,778	2,840	2,563	202	216	260	292
Transportation and material moving	159	189	227	242	253	252	314	361
Handlers, equipment cleaners, helpers and laborers	474	514	608	608	211	209	250	279
Farming, forestry, and fishing	143	138	171	161	169	185	216	234

B Data not shown where base is less than 50,000.   NA Not available.   [1] See footnote 2, table 626.   [2] Includes other races, not shown separately.   [3] Persons of Hispanic origin may be of any race.   [4] The majority of these persons are living alone or with nonrelatives. Also included are persons in families where the husband, wife or other person maintaining the family is in the Armed Forces, and persons in unrelated subfamilies.   [5] Includes craft and repair.

Source: U.S. Bureau of Labor Statistics, Bulletin 2307, and *Employment and Earnings*, monthly, January issues.

No. 678. Families With Earners—Number and Earnings: 1980 to 1993

[In current dollars of usual weekly earnings. Annual averages of quarterly figures based on Current Population Survey; see text, section 1, and Appendix III. For families with wage and salary earners]

CHARACTERISTIC	NUMBER OF FAMILIES (1,000)				MEDIAN WEEKLY EARNINGS (dollars)			
	1980	1985	1990	1993	1980	1985	1990	1993
TOTAL								
Total families with earners [1]	**41,162**	**41,616**	**43,759**	**44,383**	**400**	**522**	**653**	**707**
Married-couple families	33,825	33,459	34,219	34,257	433	582	732	804
One earner	14,797	13,347	12,166	12,185	303	385	455	481
Husband	12,127	10,346	8,994	8,643	336	440	520	565
Wife	2,059	2,243	2,407	2,773	159	217	267	314
Other family member	611	758	764	769	163	204	280	282
Two or more earners [2]	19,028	20,112	22,053	22,071	535	715	880	973
Husband and wife only	12,990	14,019	15,934	16,349	507	684	844	944
Husband and other family member(s) .	2,369	2,159	1,751	1,509	557	689	825	875
Wife and other family member(s)	426	514	527	574	350	454	557	613
Other family members only	139	176	176	150	356	468	554	605
Families maintained by women	5,690	6,470	7,323	7,792	222	297	363	393
One earner	4,022	4,397	4,983	5,452	184	234	288	307
Householder	3,104	3,432	3,937	4,402	188	243	296	315
Other family member	918	965	1,045	1,050	168	200	254	263
Two or more earners	1,668	2,073	2,340	2,340	370	487	607	655
Families maintained by men	1,647	1,688	2,218	2,334	360	450	514	523
One earner	1,016	1,031	1,352	1,523	283	346	396	429
Two or more earners	631	656	866	811	502	625	778	763
WHITE								
Total families with earners [1]	**35,786**	**35,848**	**37,239**	**37,458**	**411**	**543**	**681**	**739**
Married-couple families	30,316	29,899	30,361	30,288	438	589	745	816
One earner [2]	13,437	12,097	10,856	10,790	311	395	473	492
Husband	11,152	9,496	8,162	7,755	343	452	535	583
Wife	1,740	1,925	2,044	2,383	160	218	270	313
Two or more earners	16,878	17,802	19,505	19,497	542	723	892	984
Husband and wife only	11,448	12,394	14,148	14,546	511	691	855	954
Families maintained by women	4,140	4,616	5,127	5,355	233	311	382	415
Families maintained by men	1,331	1,333	1,751	1,816	374	475	539	547
BLACK								
Total families with earners [1]	**4,503**	**4,668**	**5,082**	**5,268**	**299**	**378**	**459**	**490**
Married-couple families	2,802	2,671	2,724	2,698	366	487	601	674
One earner [2]	1,103	902	893	909	210	257	304	344
Husband	769	580	527	539	244	292	345	381
Wife	279	257	290	287	151	206	243	321
Two or more earners	1,700	1,769	1,831	1,789	472	622	748	846
Husband and wife only	1,238	1,258	1,297	1,285	461	603	713	819
Families maintained by women	1,438	1,703	1,986	2,168	192	259	314	334
Families maintained by men	263	294	372	403	307	360	397	413
HISPANIC ORIGIN [3]								
Total families with earners [1]	**(NA)**	**(NA)**	**3,624**	**3,879**	**(NA)**	**(NA)**	**496**	**505**
Married-couple families	(NA)	(NA)	2,599	2,800	(NA)	(NA)	555	566
One earner [2]	(NA)	(NA)	1,050	1,177	(NA)	(NA)	322	334
Husband	(NA)	(NA)	814	912	(NA)	(NA)	356	365
Wife	(NA)	(NA)	164	183	(NA)	(NA)	236	262
Two or more earners	(NA)	(NA)	1,549	1,622	(NA)	(NA)	716	744
Husband and wife only	(NA)	(NA)	924	1,032	(NA)	(NA)	672	733
Families maintained by women	(NA)	(NA)	691	749	(NA)	(NA)	326	353
Families maintained by men	(NA)	(NA)	334	330	(NA)	(NA)	468	432

NA Not available.   [1] Excludes families in which there is no wage or salary earner or in which the husband, wife, or other person maintaining the family is either self-employed or in the Armed Forces.   [2] Includes other earners, not shown separately. [3] Persons of Hispanic origin may be of any race.

Source: U.S. Bureau of Labor Statistics, Bulletin 2307; and *Employment and Earnings,* monthly, January issues.

No. 679. Workers With Earnings, by Occupation of Longest Job Held and Sex: 1993

[Covers persons 15 years old and over as of **March 1994.** Based on Current Population Survey; see text, section 1, and Appendix III. For definition of median, see Guide to Tabular Presentation]

MAJOR OCCUPATION OF LONGEST JOB HELD	ALL WORKERS				YEAR ROUND FULL-TIME			
	Women		Men		Women		Men	
	Number (1,000)	Median earnings	Number (1,000)	Median earnings	Number (1,000)	Median earnings	Number (1,000)	Median earnings
Total [1]	63,660	13,896	73,198	22,443	33,524	21,747	49,818	30,407
Executive, administrators, and managerial	7,402	25,282	9,294	40,335	5,503	28,876	7,873	42,722
Professional specialty	9,629	25,865	8,577	40,505	5,521	31,906	6,597	45,136
Technical and related support	2,429	21,583	1,982	31,081	1,533	26,324	1,481	35,048
Sales	8,653	8,238	7,967	25,319	3,514	18,743	5,807	32,327
Admin. support, incl. clerical	16,233	15,733	4,341	20,733	9,456	20,683	2,924	26,746
Precision production, craft and repair	1,414	17,340	13,181	23,175	956	21,357	9,234	27,653
Machine operators, assemblers, and inspectors	3,273	12,046	5,093	20,277	1,955	15,379	3,664	23,378
Transportation and material moving	560	12,125	5,005	21,987	218	19,652	3,382	26,532
Handlers, equipment cleaners, helpers, and laborers	1,070	7,465	5,009	9,913	397	14,826	2,005	17,556
Service workers	12,118	6,684	8,393	10,795	4,165	13,126	4,205	20,860
Private household	1,045	2,446	77	2,340	190	8,460	16	(B)
Service, except private household	11,073	7,127	8,316	10,872	3,976	13,419	4,189	20,868
Farming, forestry, and fishing	794	3,106	3,521	8,416	237	10,581	1,702	15,655

B Base less than 75,000.   [1] Includes persons whose longest job was in the Armed Forces.

Source: U.S. Bureau of the Census, *Current Population Reports*, P60-188.

No. 680. Employment Cost Index (ECI), by Industry and Occupation: 1982 to 1994

[As of **December.** The ECI is a measure of the rate of change in employee compensation (wages, salaries, and employer costs for employee benefits). Data are not seasonally adjusted: 1982-1985 based on fixed employment counts from 1970 Census of Population; thereafter, based on fixed employment counts from the 1980 Census of Population]

ITEM	INDEXES (June 1989=100)						PERCENT CHANGE FOR 12 MONTHS ENDING—				
	1982	1985	1990	1992	1993	1994	1985	1990	1992	1993	1994
Civilian workers [1]	74.8	86.8	107.6	116.1	120.2	123.8	4.3	4.9	3.5	3.5	3.0
Workers, by occupational group:											
White-collar occupations	72.9	85.8	108.3	116.6	120.6	124.4	4.9	5.2	3.4	3.4	3.2
Blue-collar occupations	78.2	88.4	106.5	115.2	119.4	122.7	3.3	4.4	3.7	3.6	2.8
Service occupations	74.3	87.2	108.0	116.7	120.5	124.3	3.9	5.1	3.2	3.3	3.2
Workers, by industry division:											
Manufacturing	76.9	87.8	107.2	116.5	121.3	125.1	3.3	5.1	3.8	4.1	3.1
Nonmanufacturing	73.9	86.4	107.8	116.0	119.8	123.4	4.7	4.9	3.3	3.3	3.0
Service industries	70.5	84.1	110.2	119.2	122.9	126.4	4.7	6.3	4.0	3.1	2.8
Public administration [2]	71.9	85.4	108.7	116.3	120.0	124.2	4.9	5.3	3.3	3.2	3.5
Private industry workers [3]	75.8	87.3	107.0	115.6	119.8	123.5	3.9	4.6	3.5	3.6	3.1
Workers, by occupational group:											
White-collar occupations	73.7	86.4	107.4	115.9	120.2	124.1	4.9	4.9	3.3	3.7	3.2
Blue-collar occupations	78.4	88.5	106.4	115.0	119.3	122.6	3.1	4.4	3.6	3.7	2.8
Service occupations	76.3	88.4	107.3	115.9	119.5	122.9	3.0	4.7	3.1	3.1	2.8
Workers, by industry division:											
Manufacturing	76.9	87.8	107.2	116.5	121.3	125.1	3.3	5.1	3.8	4.1	3.1
Nonmanufacturing	75.1	87.0	106.9	115.1	119.0	122.6	4.3	4.5	3.2	3.4	3.0
Service industries	(NA)	84.1	109.3	118.9	123.1	126.6	(NA)	6.2	4.3	3.5	2.8
Business services	(NA)	(NA)	107.4	115.9	118.6	123.0	(NA)	6.0	4.3	2.3	3.7
Health services	(NA)	83.7	110.8	121.8	126.0	128.7	(NA)	6.8	4.5	3.4	2.1
Hospitals	(NA)	(NA)	110.7	121.6	125.6	128.6	(NA)	7.0	4.7	3.3	2.4
Workers by bargaining status:											
Union	79.6	90.1	106.2	115.9	120.9	124.2	2.6	4.3	4.3	4.3	2.7
Nonunion	74.3	86.3	107.3	115.5	119.5	123.2	4.6	4.8	3.2	3.5	3.1
State and local government	70.8	84.6	110.4	118.6	121.9	125.6	5.6	5.8	3.7	2.8	3.0
Workers, by occupational group:											
White-collar occupations	70.4	84.2	110.9	118.9	121.9	125.5	5.8	6.0	3.8	2.5	3.0
Blue-collar workers	73.9	86.7	108.7	117.8	121.4	124.7	5.3	4.8	4.3	3.1	2.7
Workers, by industry division:											
Service industries	70.0	84.0	111.3	119.6	122.6	126.1	5.9	6.3	3.7	2.5	2.9
Schools	69.0	83.6	111.6	119.9	122.9	126.3	6.2	6.0	3.7	2.5	2.8
Elementary and secondary	68.6	83.6	112.1	120.7	123.6	126.5	6.4	6.3	3.9	2.4	2.3
Colleges and universities	(NA)	(NA)	110.2	117.2	120.7	125.5	(NA)	5.3	3.3	3.0	4.0
Services, excluding schools [4]	73.1	85.2	110.2	118.6	121.9	125.6	4.7	6.8	3.7	2.8	3.0
Public administration [2]	71.9	85.4	108.7	116.3	120.0	124.2	4.9	5.3	3.3	3.2	3.5

NA Not available.   [1] Includes private industry and State and local government workers and excludes farm, household, and Federal government workers.   [2] Consists of legislative, judicial, administrative, and regulatory activities.   [3] Excludes farm and household workers.   [4] Includes library, social, and health services. Formerly called hospitals and other services.

Source: U.S. Bureau of Labor Statistics, *News, Employment Cost Index*, quarterly.

No. 681. Effective Federal Minimum Hourly Wage Rates: 1950 to 1994

[The Fair Labor Standards Act of 1938 and subsequent amendments provide for minimum wage coverage applicable to specified nonsupervisory employment categories. Exempt from coverage are executives and administrators or professionals]

IN EFFECT	MINIMUM RATES FOR NONFARM			Minimum rates for farm work-ers [4]	IN EFFECT	MINIMUM RATES FOR NONFARM			Minimum rates for farm work-ers [4]
	Laws prior to 1966 [1]	Percent, average earn-ings [2]	1966 and later [3]			Laws prior to 1966 [1]	Percent, average earn-ings [2]	1966 and later [3]	
Jan. 25, 1950 . . .	$0.75	54	(X)	(X)	Jan. 1, 1976	2.30	46	2.20	2.00
Mar. 1, 1956	1.00	52	(X)	(X)	Jan. 1, 1977	(5)	42	2.30	2.20
Sept. 3, 1961 . . .	1.15	50	(X)	(X)	Jan. 1, 1978	2.65	44	2.65	2.65
Sept. 3, 1963 . . .	1.25	51	(X)	(X)	Jan. 1, 1979	2.90	45	2.90	2.90
Feb. 1, 1967	1.40	50	$1.00	$1.00	Jan. 1, 1980	3.10	44	3.10	3.10
Feb. 1, 1968	1.60	54	1.15	1.15	Jan. 1, 1981	3.35	43	3.35	3.35
Feb. 1, 1969	(5)	51	1.30	1.30	Apr. 1, 1990	3.80	35	3.80	3.80
Feb. 1, 1970	(5)	49	1.45	(5)	Apr. 1, 1991	4.25	38	4.25	4.25
Feb. 1, 1971	(5)	46	1.60	(5)	Apr. 1, 1992	(5)	37	(5)	(5)
May 1, 1974	2.00	46	1.90	1.60	Apr. 1, 1993	(5)	36	(5)	(5)
Jan. 1, 1975	2.10	45	2.00	1.80	Apr. 1, 1994	(5)	35	(5)	(5)

X Not applicable.   [1] Applies to workers covered prior to 1961 amendments and, after Sept. 1965, to workers covered by 1961 amendments. Rates set by 1961 amendments were: Sept. 1961, $1.00; Sept. 1964, $1.15; and Sept. 1965, $1.25.   [2] Percent of gross average hourly earnings of production workers in manufacturing.   [3] Applies to workers newly covered by amendments of 1966, 1974, and 1977, and Title IX of Education amendments of 1972.   [4] Included in coverage as of 1966, 1974, and 1977 amendments.   [5] No change in rate.

Source: U.S. Department of Labor, Employment Standards Administration, *Minimum Wage and Maximum Hours Standards Under the Fair Labor Standards Act,* 1981, annual; and unpublished data.

No. 682. Workers Paid Hourly Rates, by Selected Characteristics: 1994

[Annual average of monthly figures; for employed wage and salary workers. Based on Current Population Survey; see text, section 1, and Appendix III]

CHARACTERISTIC	NUMBER OF WORKERS [1] (1,000)				PERCENT OF ALL WORKERS PAID HOURLY RATES			Median hourly earnings of workers paid hourly rates [2]
	Total paid hourly rates	At or below $4.25			At or below $4.25			
		Total	At $4.25	Below $4.25	Total	At $4.25	Below $4.25	
Total, 16 years and over [3]	**66,549**	**4,127**	**2,132**	**1,995**	**6.2**	**3.2**	**3.0**	**$8.01**
16 to 24 years	15,258	2,217	1,271	946	14.5	8.3	6.2	5.62
16 to 19 years	5,493	1,295	767	528	23.6	14.0	9.6	4.91
25 years and over	51,291	1,911	861	1,050	3.7	1.7	2.0	9.12
Male, 16 years and over	33,528	1,565	891	674	4.7	2.7	2.0	9.00
16 to 24 years	7,939	955	617	338	12.0	7.8	4.3	5.88
16 to 19 years	2,773	583	380	203	21.0	13.7	7.3	4.98
25 years and over	25,589	610	274	336	2.4	1.1	1.3	10.29
Women, 16 years and over	33,021	2,563	1,241	1,322	7.8	3.8	4.0	7.25
16 to 24 years	7,319	1,262	654	608	17.2	8.9	8.3	5.32
16 to 19 years	2,720	712	387	325	26.2	14.2	11.9	4.83
25 years and over	25,702	1,301	587	714	5.1	2.3	2.8	8.05
White	55,151	3,384	1,657	1,727	6.1	3.0	3.1	8.11
Black	8,586	561	356	205	6.5	4.1	2.4	7.29
Hispanic origin [4]	7,130	612	401	211	8.6	5.6	3.0	6.93
Full-time workers [5]	49,682	1,519	734	785	3.1	1.5	1.6	8.98
Part-time workers [5]	16,773	2,602	1,395	1,207	15.5	8.3	7.2	5.65
Private sector	57,927	3,847	1,953	1,894	6.6	3.4	3.3	7.81
Goods-producing industries [6] . .	18,295	435	246	189	2.4	1.3	1.0	9.32
Service-producing industries [7] . .	39,632	3,412	1,707	1,705	8.6	4.3	4.3	7.07
Public sector	8,623	281	180	101	3.3	2.1	1.2	10.16

[1] Excludes the incorporated self-employed.   [2] For definition of median, see Guide to Tabular Presentation.   [3] Includes races not shown separately. Includes a small number of multiple jobholders whose full- part- time status can not be determined for their principal job.   [4] Persons of Hispanic origin may be of any race.   [5] Working fewer than 35 hours per week.   [6] Includes agriculture, mining, construction, and manufacturing.   [7] Includes transportation and public utilities; wholesale trade; finance, insurance, and real estate; private households; and other service industries, not shown separately.

Source: U.S. Bureau of Labor Statistics, unpublished data.

No. 683. Employer Costs for Employee Compensation per Hour Worked: 1994

[**In dollars.** As of **March,** for private industry workers. Based on a sample of establishments; see source for details]

COMPENSATION COMPONENT	Total	Goods producing [1]	Service producing [2]	Manufacturing	Non-manufacturing	Union members	Non-union members	Full-time workers	Part-time workers
Total compensation . . .	**17.08**	**20.85**	**15.82**	**20.72**	**16.19**	**23.26**	**16.04**	**19.28**	**8.80**
Wages and salaries	12.14	13.87	11.56	13.69	11.76	14.76	11.70	13.52	6.97
Total benefits.	4.94	6.98	4.26	7.03	4.43	8.51	4.34	5.77	1.83
Paid leave	1.11	1.38	1.02	1.55	1.00	1.66	1.02	1.33	0.27
Vacation.	0.54	0.72	0.48	0.79	0.48	0.90	0.48	(NA)	(NA)
Holiday	0.38	0.50	0.34	0.57	0.33	0.53	0.36	(NA)	(NA)
Sick	0.14	0.11	0.15	0.13	0.14	0.16	0.14	(NA)	(NA)
Other	0.05	0.05	0.05	0.06	0.05	0.08	0.04	(NA)	(NA)
Supplemental pay	0.44	0.71	0.36	0.72	0.38	0.75	0.39	0.52	0.14
Premium pay	0.19	0.40	0.12	0.40	0.14	0.50	0.14	(NA)	(NA)
Nonproduction bonuses .	0.20	0.23	0.19	0.22	0.19	0.11	0.21	(NA)	(NA)
Shift pay	0.06	0.08	0.05	0.10	0.04	0.14	0.04	(NA)	(NA)
Insurance	1.23	1.85	1.03	1.96	1.06	2.46	1.03	1.48	0.30
Health insurance	1.14	1.70	0.95	1.79	0.98	2.28	0.94	(NA)	(NA)
Retirement and savings . . .	0.52	0.85	0.41	0.81	0.45	1.23	0.40	0.63	0.11
Pensions	0.41	0.68	0.32	0.63	0.35	1.12	0.29	(NA)	(NA)
Savings and thrift	0.11	0.17	0.09	0.17	0.09	0.12	0.11	(NA)	(NA)
Legally required [3]	1.60	2.08	1.44	1.87	1.53	2.30	1.48	1.75	1.02
Social Security	1.02	1.20	0.95	1.20	0.97	1.27	0.97	(NA)	(NA)
Federal unemployment . .	0.03	0.03	0.03	0.03	0.03	0.03	0.03	(NA)	(NA)
State unemployment . . .	0.13	0.17	0.11	0.16	0.12	0.17	0.12	(NA)	(NA)
Workers compensation . .	0.41	0.68	0.32	0.48	0.39	0.75	0.35	(NA)	(NA)
Other benefits [4]	0.04	0.11	0.02	0.12	0.02	0.11	0.03	0.05	(Z)

NA Not available.   Z Represents or rounds to zero.   [1] Mining, construction, and manufacturing.   [2] Transportation, communications, public utilities, wholesale trade, retail trade, finance, insurance, real estate, and services.   [3] Includes railroad retirement, railroad unemployment, railroad supplemental unemployment, and other legally required benefits, not shown separately.   [4] Includes severance pay, and supplemental unemployment benefits.

Source: U.S. Bureau of Labor Statistics, *News, Employer Costs for Employee Compensation, USDL, 94-290.*

No. 684. Employees With Employer- or Union-Provided Pension Plans or Group Health Plans: 1993

[For wage and salary workers 15 years old and over as of **March 1994.** Based on Current Population Survey; see text, section 1, and Appendix III. Data based on 1990 population controls]

OCCUPATION	Total (1,000)	PERCENT WITH—		CHARACTERISTIC	Total (1,000)	PERCENT WITH—	
		Pension plan	Group health plan			Pension plan	Group health plan
Total.	**137,095**	**39.2**	**51.9**	AGE			
Executive, admin., managerial . . .	16,710	51.5	66.7	**Total . . . .**	**137,095**	**39.2**	**51.9**
Professional specialty	18,209	58.2	66.9	15 to 24 years	23,858	11.0	23.4
				25 to 44 years	71,056	43.7	57.2
Technical/related support	4,412	54.4	67.1	45 to 64 years	37,270	51.0	61.9
Sales workers	16,661	26.4	41.6	65 years and over	4,912	22.0	37.5
Admin. support, inc. clerical	20,636	45.8	57.3	WORK EXPERIENCE			
				Worked	**137,095**	**39.2**	**51.9**
Precision prod., craft/repair	14,601	40.1	56.5	Full-time	106,406	47.1	61.6
				50 weeks or more	83,390	53.4	68.6
Mach. operators, assemblers [1] . . .	8,380	41.1	60.5	27 to 49 weeks	13,057	30.4	45.9
Transportation/material moving. . .	5,569	40.5	57.1	26 weeks or fewer	9,960	16.1	23.8
Handlers, equipment cleaners [2] . .	6,096	23.6	36.2	Part-time	30,689	11.7	18.2
				50 weeks or more	12,902	17.6	25.5
Service workers	20,528	20.9	30.5	27 to 49 weeks	6,823	11.9	18.0
Private households	1,122	1.0	5.1	26 weeks or fewer	10,965	4.8	9.8
Other	19,406	22.0	32.0	EMPLOYER SIZE			
				Under 25	44,467	15.5	29.3
Farming, forestry and fishing	4,373	8.6	20.4	25 to 99	18,239	32.8	51.6
				100 to 499	19,250	46.5	62.2
Armed Forces	919	70.3	25.7	500 to 999	8,250	54.1	65.1
				Over 1,000.	46,889	58.6	66.9

[1] Includes inspectors.   [2] Includes helpers and laborers.

Source: U.S. Bureau of the Census, unpublished data.

Labor Force, Employment, and Earnings

No. 685. Employee Benefits in Private Establishments: 1992 and 1993

[Covers full-time employees in private industry. Medium and large establishments exclude establishments with fewer than 100 workers, executive and traveling operating employees, and Alaska and Hawaii. Small establishments include those with fewer than 100 employees. Covers only benefits for which the employer pays part or all of the premium or expenses involved, except unpaid parental leave and long-term care insurance. Based on a sample survey of establishments; for details, see sources. For data on employee benefits in State and local governments, see table 510]

MEDIUM AND LARGE PRIVATE ESTABLISHMENTS, 1993	All employees	Professional, technical and related	Clerical and sales	Production and service	SMALL PRIVATE ESTABLISHMENTS, 1992	All employees	Professional, technical and related	Clerical and sales	Blue collar and service
Percent of employees participating in—					Percent of employees participating in—				
Paid: Vacations	97	97	98	96	Paid: Vacations	88	94	94	81
Holidays	91	89	93	92	Holidays	82	94	90	74
Jury duty leave	90	95	92	85	Jury duty leave	58	76	65	47
Funeral leave.	83	86	85	80	Funeral leave.	50	60	56	43
Rest time	68	54	66	76	Rest time	49	40	43	56
Military leave	53	66	54	44	Military leave	21	33	27	13
Sick leave	65	85	80	45	Sick leave	53	74	70	35
Personal leave	21	27	31	13	Personal leave	12	19	16	7
Lunch time	9	5	5	13	Lunch time	9	12	8	8
Maternity leave	3	4	3	1	Maternity leave	2	3	2	1
Paternity leave	1	2	1	(Z)	Paternity leave	1	1	(Z)	(Z)
Unpaid: Maternity leave. . . .	60	63	60	59	Unpaid: Maternity leave. . .	18	27	20	13
Paternity leave	53	55	51	52	Paternity leave	8	13	9	6
Insurance plans:					Insurance plans:				
Medical care	82	84	79	82	Medical care	71	83	78	61
Noncontributory	37	31	32	44	Noncontributory	37	43	40	34
Hospital/room and board	82	84	79	82	Hospital/room and board	71	83	78	61
Inpatient surgery	82	84	79	82	Inpatient surgery	71	83	78	61
Mental health care:					Mental health care:				
Inpatient care	80	83	77	80	Inpatient	68	80	76	57
Outpatient care	80	82	77	79	Outpatient	67	80	74	57
Dental.	62	68	63	58	Dental.	33	43	37	27
Extended care facility. .	67	71	68	66	Extended care facility. .	60	72	66	49
Home health care	71	74	70	68	Home health care . . .	57	69	66	46
Hospice care	53	56	54	52	Hospice care	40	50	44	34
Vision	26	27	26	27	Vision	10	9	10	10
In HMO's	19	24	21	15	In HMO's	14	14	13	16
Alcohol abuse treatment:					Alcohol abuse treatment:				
Inpatient detoxification	80	82	77	80	Inpatient detoxification	67	79	74	59
					Inpatient.				
Inpatient rehabilitation	66	66	63	58	rehabilitation	50	58	52	43
Outpatient	67	69	65	68	Outpatient	50	61	55	43
Drug abuse treatment: .					Drug abuse treatment:				
Inpatient detoxification	80	82	77	80	Inpatient detoxification	66	78	71	58
					Inpatient				
Inpatient rehabilitation	64	65	60	66	rehabilitation	48	57	50	41
Outpatient	66	68	64	65	Outpatient	49	60	53	41
Life	91	95	92	89	Life	64	77	73	53
Noncontributory	87	84	87	89	Noncontributory	53	66	62	42
Accident/sickness	44	28	37	57	Accident/sickness	26	24	27	27
Noncontributory	75	65	67	81	Noncontributory	17	17	16	18
Long-term disability	41	64	50	23	Long-term disability	23	43	31	10
Noncontributory	73	69	71	80	Noncontributory	18	38	26	6
Retirement and savings plans .	78	83	78	76	Retirement and savings plans:				
Defined benefit pension . . .	56	57	54	56	Defined benefit pension . .	22	21	25	20
Earnings-based formula [1]	40	50	45	32	Earnings-based formula [1]	15	19	20	9
Defined contribution	49	60	54	40	Defined contribution	33	43	38	26
Savings and thrift	29	38	34	21	Savings and thrift	14	20	17	9
Employee stock owner-ship	3	3	4	2	Employee stock owner-ship	1	1	1	1
Deferred profit sharing. . .	13	12	16	12	Deferred profit sharing. .	16	18	19	14
Money purchase pension .	8	13	7	6	Money purchase pension	5	9	5	4
Additional benefits:					Additional benefits:				
Parking [2]	88	86	85	92	Parking [4]	86	84	85	88
Educational assistance	72	85	72	65	Educational assistance . . .	36	51	43	26
Travel accident insurance . .	44	59	52	32	Travel accident insurance .	16	24	19	11
Severance pay	42	56	48	31	Severance pay	15	26	21	8
Relocation allowance [2]	31	50	30	21	Relocation allowance . . .	12	22	15	6
Recreation facilities [2]	26	34	25	23	Recreation facilities	7	13	7	4
Nonproduction bonuses, cash	38	37	38	38	Nonproduction bonuses, cash	47	52	50	43
Child care.	7	12	6	4	Child care.	2	3	3	(Z)
Flexible benefits plans . . [3]	12	21	13	6	Flexible benefits plans . .	2	4	4	(Z)
Reimbursement accounts [3] .	52	68	62	37	Reimbursement accounts [4]	14	24	20	7
Eldercare	31	33	32	29	Eldercare	3	4	5	2
Long-term care insurance . .	6	8	8	3	Long-term care insurance . .	1	2	1	1
Wellness programs.	37	51	38	29	Wellness programs.	17	24	21	12
Employee assistance programs	62	74	64	53	Employee assistance programs	17	24	21	12

Z Represents or rounds to zero.   [1] Earnings-based formulas pay a percent of employee's annual earnings (usually earnings in the final years of employment) per year of service.   [2] 1991 data.   [3] Account which is used throughout the year to pay for plan premiums or to reimburse the employee for benefit related expenses. Account may be financed by employer, employee, or both.   [4] 1990 data.

Source: U.S. Bureau of Labor Statistics, *Employee Benefits in Medium and Large Private Establishments, 1993*, Bulletin 2456; and *Employee Benefits in Small Private Establishments, 1992*, Bulletin 2441.

No. 686. Major Collective Bargaining Agreements—Average Percent Wage Rate Changes Under All Agreements: 1970 to 1994

[In percent, except as indicated. Data represent all wage rate changes implemented under the terms of private nonfarm industry agreements affecting 1,000 workers or more. Series covers production and related workers in manufacturing and nonsupervisory workers in nonmanufacturing industries. Data measure all wage rate changes effective in the year stemming from settlements reached in the year, deferred from prior year settlements, and cost-of-living adjustment (COLA) clauses]

CHANGES	1970	1975	1980	1985	1989	1990	1991	1992	1993	1994
Average wage rate change (prorated over all workers)	8.8	8.7	9.9	3.3	3.2	3.5	3.6	3.1	3.0	2.7
Source:										
Current settlements	5.1	2.8	3.6	0.7	1.2	1.3	1.1	0.8	0.9	0.6
Prior settlements	3.1	3.7	3.5	1.8	1.3	1.5	1.9	1.9	1.9	1.9
COLA provisions	0.6	2.2	2.8	0.7	0.7	0.7	0.5	0.4	0.2	0.2
Industry:										
Manufacturing	7.1	8.5	10.2	2.8	3.5	4.4	3.7	3.1	3.3	2.4
Nonmanufacturing	10.5	8.9	9.7	3.6	3.0	3.0	3.5	3.1	2.8	2.9
Construction	(NA)	8.1	9.9	3.0	3.1	3.4	3.4	3.4	2.7	2.7
Transportation and public utilities	(NA)	9.7	10.8	3.6	2.3	2.2	3.3	2.7	3.0	2.8
Wholesale and retail trade	(NA)	9.2	7.6	3.3	3.2	3.6	3.5	3.5	2.3	2.9
Services	(NA)	6.4	8.1	5.1	5.3	4.3	4.9	3.7	3.4	3.3
Nonmanufacturing, excluding construction	(NA)	9.3	9.6	3.7	3.0	2.9	3.6	3.0	2.8	2.9
Average wage rate increase for workers receiving an increase	9.4	9.0	10.1	4.2	4.0	4.2	4.0	3.7	3.5	3.3
Source:										
Current settlements	11.9	10.2	9.4	4.1	4.2	4.1	4.2	3.6	3.2	3.2
Prior settlements	5.8	5.2	5.6	3.7	3.4	3.3	3.7	3.8	3.4	3.4
COLA provisions	3.7	4.8	7.7	2.2	3.3	2.7	2.0	2.0	1.3	1.7
Total number of workers receiving a wage rate increase (mil.)	10.2	9.7	8.9	5.5	4.8	4.9	5.1	4.7	4.8	4.6
Source (mil.):										
Current settlements	4.7	2.7	3.5	1.4	1.7	1.9	1.5	1.3	1.7	1.1
Prior settlements	5.7	7.3	5.6	3.4	2.3	2.7	3.0	2.8	3.0	3.0
COLA provisions	1.8	4.7	3.4	2.3	1.3	1.4	1.3	1.0	0.9	0.8
Number of workers not receiving a wage rate increase (mil.)	0.6	0.4	0.2	1.5	1.2	1.0	0.5	0.9	0.7	0.8

NA Not available.

Source: U.S. Bureau of Labor Statistics, *Compensation and Working Conditions*, monthly.

No. 687. Major Collective Bargaining Settlements—Average Percent Changes in Wage and Compensation Rates Negotiated: 1970 to 1994

[In percent, except as indicated. Data represent private nonfarm industry settlements affecting production and related workers in manufacturing and nonsupervisory workers in nonmanufacturing industries. Wage data cover units with 1,000 workers or more. Compensation data relate to units of 5,000 or more. Data relate to contracts negotiated in each calendar year but exclude possible changes in wage rates under cost-of-living adjustment (COLA) clauses, except increases guaranteed by the contract. Includes all settlements, whether wage and benefit rates were changed or not. Minus sign (-) indicates decrease]

CHANGES	1970	1975	1980	1985	1988	1989	1990	1991	1992	1993	1994
Compensation rates:											
First year	13.1	11.4	10.4	2.6	3.1	4.5	4.6	4.1	3.0	3.0	2.3
Over life of contract [1]	9.1	8.1	7.1	2.7	2.5	3.4	3.2	3.4	3.1	2.4	2.4
Wage rates:											
All industries:											
First year	11.9	10.2	9.5	2.3	2.5	4.0	4.0	3.6	2.7	2.3	2.0
Contracts with COLA	(NA)	12.2	8.0	1.6	2.4	3.9	3.4	3.4	2.7	2.8	2.7
Contracts without COLA	(NA)	9.1	11.7	2.7	2.7	4.0	4.4	3.7	2.7	2.1	1.8
Over life of contract [1]	8.9	7.8	7.1	2.7	2.4	3.4	3.2	3.2	3.0	2.1	2.3
Contracts with COLA	(NA)	7.1	5.0	2.5	1.8	2.8	1.9	3.0	2.5	1.4	2.5
Contracts without COLA	(NA)	8.3	10.3	2.8	2.8	3.5	4.0	3.3	3.1	2.5	2.3
Manufacturing:											
First year	8.1	9.8	7.4	0.8	2.2	3.9	3.7	3.9	2.6	2.7	2.4
Over life of contract [1]	6.0	8.0	5.4	1.8	2.1	3.2	2.1	3.1	2.6	1.5	2.3
Nonmanufacturing:											
First year	15.2	10.4	10.9	3.3	2.8	4.0	4.3	3.4	2.7	2.1	1.8
Over life of contract [1]	11.5	7.8	8.3	3.3	2.5	3.4	4.0	3.3	3.0	2.5	2.3
Number of workers affected (mil.)	4.7	2.9	3.8	2.2	1.8	1.9	2.0	1.8	1.6	2.1	1.6
Manufacturing (mil.)	2.2	0.8	1.6	0.9	0.7	0.4	0.9	0.6	0.3	0.8	0.4
Nonmanufacturing (mil.)	2.5	2.1	2.2	1.3	1.1	1.5	1.1	1.2	1.3	1.3	1.1

NA Not available.   [1] Average annual rate of change.

Source: U.S. Bureau of Labor Statistics, *Compensation and Working Conditions*, monthly.

No. 688. Workers Killed or Disabled on the Job: 1960 to 1993

[Data for 1993 are preliminary estimates. Estimates based on data from the U.S. National Center for Health Statistics, State Departments of Health, and State industrial commissions. Numbers of workers based on data from the U.S. Bureau of Labor Statistics]

YEAR	DEATHS						Disabling injur-ies [2] (mil.)	YEAR AND INDUSTRY GROUP	DEATHS		Disabling injur-ies [2] (1,000)
	Total		Manufacturing		Nonmanufacturing				Number (1,000)	Rate [1]	
	Number (1,000)	Rate [1]	Number (1,000)	Rate [1]	Number (1,000)	Rate [1]					
1960 ...	13.8	21	1.7	10	12.1	25	2.0	**1993, total**	9,100	8	3,200
1965 ...	14.1	20	1.8	10	12.3	24	2.1	Agriculture [3]	1,100	35	130
1970 ...	13.8	18	1.7	9	12.1	21	2.2	Mining and quarrying [4]..	200	33	20
1975 ...	13.0	15	1.6	9	11.4	17	2.2	Construction.........	1,300	22	280
1980 ...	13.2	13	1.7	8	11.5	15	2.2	Manufacturing........	700	4	560
1985 ...	11.5	11	1.2	6	10.3	12	2.0	Transportation and			
1986 ...	11.1	10	1.0	5	10.1	11	1.8	utilities...........	1,200	20	230
1987 ...	11.3	10	1.0	5	10.3	11	1.8	Trade [5]	1,300	5	710
1988 ...	11.0	10	1.1	6	9.9	10	1.8	Services [6]	1,300	3	780
1989 ...	10.9	9	1.1	6	9.8	10	1.7	Government.........	2,000	11	490
1990 ...	10.1	9	1.0	5	9.1	9	3.9				
1991 ...	9.8	8	0.8	4	9.0	9	3.5				
1992 ...	9.2	8	0.7	4	8.5	9	3.3				
1993 ...	9.1	8	0.7	4	8.4	8	3.2				

[1] Per 100,000 workers.   [2] Disabling injury defined as one which results in death, some degree of physical impairment, or renders the person unable to perform regular activities for a full day beyond the day of the injury. Due to change in methodology, data beginning 1990 not comparable with prior years.   [3] Includes forestry and fishing.   [4] Includes oil and gas extraction. [5] Includes wholesale and retail trade.   [6] Includes finance, insurance, and real estate.

Source: National Safety Council, Itasca, IL, *Accident Facts,* annual (copyright).

No. 689. Worker Deaths and Injuries and Production Time Lost: 1991 to 1993

ITEM	DEATHS (1,000)			DISABLING INJURIES [1] (mil.)			PRODUCTION TIME LOST (mil. days)					
							In the current year			In future years [2]		
	1991	1992	1993	1991	1992	1993	1991	1992	1993	1991	1992	1993
All accidents	42.6	40.9	42.4	8.5	8.6	8.4	170	200	195	435	420	430
On the job	9.3	9.2	9.1	3.6	3.6	3.2	70	80	75	115	120	120
Off the job.............	33.3	31.7	33.3	4.9	5.0	5.2	100	120	120	320	300	310
Motor vehicle..........	21.4	19.3	19.8	1.2	1.1	1.0	(NA)	(NA)	(NA)	(NA)	(NA)	(NA)
Public nonmotor vehicle....	5.9	6.2	7.0	1.9	2.0	2.3	(NA)	(NA)	(NA)	(NA)	(NA)	(NA)
Home	6.0	6.2	6.5	1.8	1.9	1.9	(NA)	(NA)	(NA)	(NA)	(NA)	(NA)

NA Not available.   [1] See footnote 2, table 688, for a definition of disabling injuries. Data revised here beginning 1991. [2] Based on an average of 5,850 days lost in future years per fatality and 565 days lost in future years per permanent injury.

Source: National Safety Council, Itasca, IL, *Accident Facts,*

No. 690. Industries with the Highest Total Case Incidence Rates for Nonfatal Injuries and Illnesses: 1992 and 1993

[**Rates per full-time employees.** Industries shown are those with highest rates in 1993. See headnote, table 691]

INDUSTRY	1987 SIC [1] code	1992	1993	INDUSTRY	1987 SIC [1] code	1992	1993
Private industry............	(X)	8.9	8.5	Truck trailers................	3715	25.0	22.7
				Truck and bus bodies............	3713	22.3	22.7
Meat packing plants.............	2011	44.4	39.0	Malt........................	2083	26.6	22.3
Ship building and repairing.......	3731	37.8	34.3	Metal barrels, drums, and pails......	3412	21.3	22.1
Motor vehicles and car bodies......	3711	32.3	31.2	Secondary nonferrous metals......	3341	-	20.9
Metal sanitary ware	3431	35.0	29.0	Flat glass...................	3211	21.1	20.9
Special product sawmills, n.e.c. [2]....	2429	-	28.0	Structural wood members, n.e.c. [2] ...	2439	22.4	20.8
Household appliances, n.e.c. [2]	3639	27.2	27.5	Iron and steel forgings..........	3462	21.1	20.7
Mobile homes.................	2451	23.0	27.5	Aluminum foundries	3365	20.1	20.3
Gray and ductile iron foundries.....	3321	31.6	27.0	Knit underwear mills...........	2254	18.9	20.3
Automotive stampings..........	3465	29.2	26.7	Motor homes.................	3716	19.5	20.2
Malleable iron foundries	3322	20.3	25.9	Leather tanning and finishing.......	3111	20.5	19.9
Motorcycles, bicycles, and parts.....	3751	22.5	23.8	Lawn and garden equipment	3524	17.0	19.9
Poultry slaughtering processing	2015	23.2	23.2	Sausages and other prepared meats..	2013	21.0	19.7
Steel foundries, n.e.c............	3325	24.4	23.1	Commerical laundry equipment	3582	17.4	19.6
Aluminum die-castings	3363	20.5	22.8	Nonferrous die-casting except aluminum	3364	-	19.6
Prefabricated wood buildings	2452	21.3	22.8	Fresh or frozen prepared fish.......	2092	20.3	19.4

- Represents or rounds to zero.   X Not applicable.   [1] 1987 Standard Industrial Classification; see text, section 13.   [2] N.e.c. means not elsewhere classified.

Source: U.S. Bureau of Labor Statistics, *Occupational Injuries and Illnesses in the United States by Industry,* annual.

No. 691. Nonfatal Occupational Injury and Illness Incidence Rates: 1992 and 1993

[Rates per 100 full-time employees. For nonfarm employment data, see table 668. Rates refer to any occupational injury or illness resulting in (1) lost workday cases, or (2) nonfatal cases without lost workdays. Incidence rates were calculated as: Number of injuries and illnesses divided by total hours worked by all employees during year multiplied by 200,000 as base for 100 full-time equivalent workers (working 40 hours per week, 50 weeks a year)]

INDUSTRY	1987 SIC [1] code	1992	1993	INDUSTRY	1987 SIC [1] code	1992	1993
Private sector [2]	(X)	**8.9**	**8.5**	Local passenger transit	41	11.0	11.5
Agriculture, forestry, fishing [2]	A	**11.6**	**11.2**	Trucking and warehousing	42	13.4	13.8
Mining [3]	B	**7.3**	**6.8**	Water transportation	44	11.5	10.4
Metal mining [3]	10	6.1	5.9	Transportation by air	45	13.8	15.1
Coal mining [3]	12	12.5	10.3	Pipelines, except natural gas	46	3.1	3.8
Oil and gas extraction	13	6.0	6.1	Transportation services	47	3.9	4.0
Nonmetallic minerals, exc. fuels	14	6.5	6.3	Communications	48	3.4	3.9
Construction	C	**13.1**	**12.2**	Electric, gas, sanitary services	49	7.6	7.5
General building contractors	15	12.2	11.5	**Wholesale and retail trade**	F, G	**8.4**	**8.1**
Heavy construction, except building	16	12.1	11.1	Wholesale trade	F	7.6	7.8
				Retail trade	G	8.7	8.2
Special trade contractors	17	13.8	12.8	**Finance, insurance, real estate**	H	**2.9**	**2.9**
Manufacturing	D	**12.5**	**12.1**	Depository institutions	60	2.1	2.5
Durable goods	(X)	13.4	13.1	Nondepository institutions	61	1.0	1.3
Lumber and wood products	24	16.3	15.9	Security and commodity brokers	62	0.7	0.9
Furniture and fixtures	25	14.8	14.6	Insurance carriers	63	(NA)	2.4
Stone, clay, and glass products	32	13.6	13.8	Insurance agents, brokers, and service	64	1.4	1.5
Primary metal industries	33	17.5	17.0	Real estate	65	6.8	6.2
Fabricated metal products	34	16.8	16.2	Holding and other investment offices	67	2.7	2.4
Industrial machinery and equip	35	11.1	11.1	**Services** [4]	I	**7.1**	**6.7**
Electronic/other electric equip	36	8.4	8.3	Hotels and other lodging places	70	11.2	10.7
Transportation equipment	37	18.7	18.5	Personal services	72	5.1	4.3
Instruments/related products	38	5.9	5.6	Business services	73	5.4	5.0
Miscellaneous manufacturing industries	39	10.7	10.0	Auto repair, services, and parking	75	7.8	7.5
Nondurable goods	(X)	11.3	10.7	Miscellaneous repair services	76	8.7	8.2
Food and kindred products	20	18.8	17.6	Motion pictures	78	(NA)	3.3
Tobacco products	21	6.0	5.8	Amusement and recreation services	79	10.1	10.3
Textile mill products	22	9.9	9.7	Health services	80	10.2	9.6
Apparel and other textile products	23	9.5	9.0	Legal services	81	1.2	1.3
Paper and allied products	26	11.0	9.9	Educational services	82	5.6	4.6
Printing and publishing	27	7.3	6.9	Social services	83	8.0	7.3
Chemicals and allied products	28	6.0	5.9	Museums, botanical, zoological gardens	84	7.8	9.1
Petroleum and coal products	29	5.9	5.2	Engineering and management services	87	2.4	2.6
Rubber and misc. plastics products	30	14.5	13.9	Services, n.e.c. [5]	89	2.7	2.4
Leather and leather products [3]	31	12.1	12.1				
Transportation/public utilities [3]	E	**9.1**	**9.5**				
Railroad transportation [3]	40	6.6	5.8				

NA Not available.   X Not applicable.   [1] 1987 Standard Industrial Classification; see text, section 13.   [2] Excludes farms with fewer than 11 employees.   [3] Data conforming to OSHA definitions for employers in the railroad industry and for mining operators in coal, metal, and nonmetal mining. Independent mining contractors are excluded from the coal, metal, and nonmetal mining industries.   [4] Includes categories not shown separately.   [5] N.e.c means not elsewhere classified.

Source: U.S. Bureau of Labor Statistics, *Occupational Injuries and Illnesses in the United States by Industry*, annual.

No. 692. Fatal Work Injuries, by Cause: 1993

[For the 50 States and DC. Based on the 1993 Census of Fatal Occupational Injuries. Due to methodological differences, data differ from those in table 688. For details, see source]

CAUSE	Number of fatalities	Percent distribution	CAUSE	Number of fatalities	Percent distribution
Total	**6,271**	**100**	Contacts with objects and equipment [1]	1,039	17
			Struck by object [1]	563	9
Transportation accidents [1]	2,482	40	Struck by falling objects	345	6
Highway accidents [1]	1,232	20	Struck by flying object	81	1
Collision between vehicles, mobile equipment	652	10	Caught in or compressed by— equipment or objects	308	5
Noncollision accidents	333	5	collapsing materials	138	2
Nonhighway accident (farm, industrial premises)	392	6	Falls	611	10
Aircraft accidents	280	4	Exposure to harmful substances or environments [1]	590	9
Workers struck by a vehicle	361	6	Contact with electric current	324	5
Water vehicle accidents	119	2	Exposure to caustic, noxious or allergenic substances	116	2
Railway accidents	85	1	Oxygen deficiency	111	2
Assaults and violent acts [1]	1,309	21	Drowning, submersion	89	1
Homicides [1]	1,063	17			
Shooting	874	14	Fires and explosions	201	3
Stabbing	95	2	Other events and exposures	38	1
Self-inflicted injury	215	3			

[1] Includes other causes, not shown separately.

Source: U.S. Bureau of Labor Statistics, *Monthly Labor Report*, October, 1994.

No. 693. Fatal Occupational Injuries, by Industry and Event: 1993

[See headnote, table 692]

INDUSTRY	1987 SIC [1] code	Fatal-ities [2]	EVENT OR EXPOSURE—PERCENT DISTRIBUTION					Rate [5]
			Trans-portation incidents	Assaults/ violent acts	Contact with objects [3]	Falls	Expo-sure [4]	
Total.	(X)	6,271	40	21	17	10	9	5
Private industry	(X)	5,590	38	21	18	10	10	6
Agriculture, forestry, fishing	A	855	51	5	26	6	11	26
Mining [6]	B	174	27	3	42	8	14	26
Coal mining.	12	40	12	-	70	-	15	35
Oil and gas extraction	13	94	33	4	32	10	15	25
Construction.	C	924	25	4	20	30	17	14
General building contractors	15	152	23	5	21	38	10	-
Heavy construction, except building.	16	255	37	3	29	11	16	-
Special trade contractors	17	517	20	4	16	36	20	-
Manufacturing [6]	D	762	29	9	36	8	11	4
Food and kindred products	20	82	35	10	24	10	15	5
Lumber and wood products	24	204	28	2	63	3	-	29
Transportation and public utilities [6] . . .	E	890	65	16	8	3	5	13
Local passenger transit	41	130	18	78	-	-	-	28
Trucking and warehousing	42	467	79	5	9	2	2	22
Transportation by air	45	79	87	-	5	4	-	11
Electric, gas, sanitary services	49	72	38	7	19	6	22	5
Wholesale trade	F	250	55	15	13	8	4	5
Retail trade [6]	G	784	18	70	5	2	3	4
Food stores.	54	223	7	89	-	2	-	6
Automotive dealer and service stations	55	138	28	54	8	3	4	7
Eating and drinking places	58	199	15	76	3	2	4	3
Finance, insurance, real estate.	H	116	31	40	3	15	11	2
Services [6]	I	758	35	28	10	9	13	2
Business services.	73	188	32	26	9	15	12	4
Auto repair, services, and parking	75	116	22	32	22	3	11	8
Government.	J	681	52	23	7	7	6	3

- No data reported or data do not meet publication standards.　X Not applicable.　[1] 1987 Standard Industrial Classification code, see text section 13.　[2] Includes 77 fatalities, not available by type of industry. Includes fatalities caused by fires and explosions, not shown separately.　[3] Includes equipment.　[4] Exposure to harmful substances or environments.　[5] Rate per 100,000 employed civilians 16 years old and over.　[6] Includes other industries, not shown separately.

Source: U.S. Bureau of Labor Statistics, *Monthly Labor Report,* October, 1994.

No. 694. Work Stoppages: 1960 to 1994

[Excludes work stoppages involving fewer than 1,000 workers and lasting less than 1 day. Information is based on reports of labor disputes appearing in daily newspapers, trade journals, and other public sources. The parties to the disputes are contacted by telephone, when necessary, to clarify details of the stoppages]

YEAR	Number of work stop-pages [1]	Workers involved [2] (1,000)	DAYS IDLE		YEAR	Number of work stop-pages [1]	Workers involved [2] (1,000)	DAYS IDLE	
			Number [3] (1,000)	Percent esti-mated working time [4]				Number [3] (1,000)	Percent esti-mated working time [4]
1960.	222	896	13,260	0.09	1981.	145	729	16,908	0.07
1965.	268	999	15,140	0.10	1982.	96	656	9,061	0.04
1969.	412	1,576	29,397	0.16	1983.	81	909	17,461	0.08
1970.	381	2,468	52,761	0.29	1984.	62	376	8,499	0.04
1971.	298	2,516	35,538	0.19	1985.	54	324	7,079	0.03
1972.	250	975	16,764	0.09	1986.	69	533	11,861	0.05
1973.	317	1,400	16,260	0.08	1987.	46	174	[5]4,481	0.02
1974.	424	1,796	31,809	0.16	1988.	40	118	[5]4,381	0.02
1975.	235	965	17,563	0.09	1989.	51	452	16,996	0.07
1976.	231	1,519	23,962	0.12	1990.	44	185	5,926	0.02
1977.	298	1,212	21,258	0.10	1991.	40	392	4,584	0.02
1978.	219	1,006	23,774	0.11	1992.	35	364	3,989	0.01
1979.	235	1,021	20,409	0.09	1993.	35	182	3,981	0.01
1980.	187	795	20,844	0.09	1994.	45	322	5,021	0.02

[1] Beginning in year indicated.　[2] Workers counted more than once if involved in more than one stoppage during the year.　[3] Resulting from all stoppages in effect in a year, including those that began in an earlier year.　[4] Agricultural and government employees are included in the total working time; private household and forestry and fishery employees are excluded.　[5] Revised since originally published.

Source: U.S. Bureau of Labor Statistics, *Compensation and Conditions,* monthly.

No. 695. Labor Union Membership, by Sector: 1983 to 1994

[See headnote, table 697]

SECTOR	1983	1985	1988	1989	1990	1991	1992	1993	1994 [1]
TOTAL (1,000)									
Wage and salary workers:									
Union members	17,717.4	16,996.1	17,001.7	16,960.5	16,739.8	16,568.4	16,390.3	16,598.1	16,740.3
Covered by unions	20,532.1	19,358.1	19,241.3	19,197.6	19,057.8	18,733.8	18,540.1	18,646.4	18,842.5
Public sector workers:									
Union members	5,737.2	5,743.1	6,299.2	6,424.2	6,485.0	6,632.0	6,653.1	7,017.8	7,091.0
Covered by unions	7,112.2	6,920.6	7,485.1	7,614.4	7,691.4	7,796.0	7,840.6	8,162.4	8,191.8
Private sector workers:									
Union members	11,980.2	11,253.0	10,702.4	10,536.2	10,254.8	9,936.5	9,737.2	9,580.3	9,649.4
Covered by unions	13,419.9	12,437.5	11,756.3	11,583.1	11,366.4	10,937.8	10,699.5	10,484.0	10,650.6
PERCENT									
Wage and salary workers:									
Union members	20.1	18.0	16.8	16.4	16.1	16.1	15.8	15.8	15.5
Covered by unions	23.3	20.5	19.0	18.6	18.3	18.2	17.9	17.7	17.4
Public sector workers:									
Union members	36.7	35.7	36.6	36.7	36.5	36.9	36.6	37.7	38.7
Covered by unions	45.5	43.1	43.5	43.5	43.3	43.3	43.2	43.8	44.7
Private sector workers:									
Union members	16.5	14.3	12.7	12.3	11.9	11.7	11.4	11.1	10.8
Covered by unions	18.5	15.9	14.0	13.5	13.2	12.9	12.5	12.1	11.9

[1] See footnote 2, table 626.

Source: The Bureau of National Affairs, Inc., Washington, DC, *Union Membership and Earnings Data Book 1994: Compilations from the Current Population Survey,* (copyright by BNA); authored by Barry Hirsch and David Macpherson of Florida State University.

No. 696. U.S. Membership in AFL-CIO Affiliated Unions, by Selected Union: 1979 to 1993

[**In thousands**. Figures represent the labor organizations as constituted in 1993 and reflect past merger activity. Membership figures based on average per capita paid membership to the AFL-CIO for the 2-year period ending in June of the year shown and reflect only actively-employed members. Labor unions shown had a membership of 50,000 or more in 1993]

LABOR ORGANIZATION	1979	1989	1993	LABOR ORGANIZATION	1979	1989	1993
Total [1]	13,621	14,100	13,299	Longshoreman's Association	63	62	58
Actors and Artists	75	97	93	Machinists and Aerospace (IAM) [2]	688	517	474
Automobile, Aerospace and Agriculture (UAW)	(X)	917	771	Marine Engineers Beneficial Assn.	23	48	52
Bakery, Confectionery and Tobacco	131	103	99	Mine Workers	(X)	(X)	75
Boiler Makers, Iron Ship-builders [2] [3]	129	75	58	Office and Professional Employees	83	84	89
Bricklayers [2]	106	84	84	Oil, Chemical, Atomic Workers (OCAW)	146	71	86
Carpenters [2]	626	613	408	Painters	160	128	106
Clothing and Textile Workers (ACTWU) [2]	308	180	143	Paperworkers Int'l	262	210	188
Communication Workers (CWA)	485	492	472	Plumbing and Pipefitting	228	220	220
Electrical Workers (IBEW)	825	744	710	Postal Workers	245	213	249
Electronic, Electrical and Salaried [2] [4]	243	171	143	Retail, Wholesale Department Stores	122	137	80
Operating Engineers	313	330	305	Rubber, Cork, Linoleum, Plastic	158	92	81
Fire Fighters	150	142	151	Seafarers	84	80	80
Food and Commercial Workers (UFCW) [2]	1,123	999	997	Service Employees (SEIU) [2] [5]	537	762	919
Garment Workers (ILGWU)	314	153	133	Sheet Metal Workers	120	108	108
Glass, Molders, Pottery, and Plastics [2]	50	86	73	Stage Employees, Moving Picture Machine Operators	50	50	51
Government, American Federation (AFGE)	236	156	149	State, County, Municipal (AFSCME) [5]	889	1,090	1,167
Graphic Communications [2]	171	124	95	Steelworkers	964	481	421
Hotel Employees and Restaurant Employees	373	278	258	Teachers (AFT)	423	544	574
Ironworkers	146	111	91	Teamsters [6]	(X)	1,161	1,316
Laborers	475	406	408	Transit Union	94	96	94
Letter Carriers (NALC)	151	201	210	Transport Workers	85	85	78
				Transportation Union, United	121	(X)	60

X Not applicable. [1] Includes other AFL-CIO affiliated unions, not shown separately. [2] Figures reflect mergers with one or more unions since 1979. For details see source. [3] Includes Blacksmiths, Forgers, and Helpers. [4] Includes Machine and Furniture Workers. [5] Excludes Hospital and Health Care Employees which merged into both unions on June 1, 1989, (membership of 23,000 in 1985; 60,000 in 1987; and 58,000 in 1989). [6] Includes Chauffeurs, Warehousemen, and Helpers.

Source: American Federation of Labor and Congress of Industrial Organizations, Washington, DC, *Report of the AFL-CIO Executive Council,* biennial.

Labor Force, Employment, and Earnings

No. 697. Labor Union Membership, by State: 1983 and 1994

[Annual averages of monthly figures. For wage and salary workers. Data represent union members by place of residence. Based on the Current Population Survey and subject to sampling error. For methodological details, see source. U.S. totals here for 1994 differ slightly from those published by BLS due to revisions made subsequent to the publication of the official estimates]

| STATE | UNION MEMBERS (1,000) | | WORKERS COVERED BY UNIONS (1,000) | | PERCENT OF WORKERS— | | | | | |
| | | | | | Union members | | Covered by unions | | Private manufacturing sector union members | |
	1983	1994 [1]	1983	1994 [1]	1983	1994 [1]	1983	1994 [1]	1983	1994 [1]
United States..	17,717.4	16,740.3	20,532.1	18,842.5	20.1	15.5	23.3	17.4	27.8	18.2
Alabama.........	228.2	236.1	268.2	270.0	16.9	13.9	19.8	15.9	25.9	19.6
Alaska..........	41.7	47.1	49.2	54.4	24.9	19.3	29.3	22.3	23.3	14.4
Arizona.........	125.0	126.7	156.4	161.3	11.4	7.9	14.3	10.1	7.8	2.9
Arkansas........	82.2	77.1	103.2	98.2	11.0	7.9	13.8	10.1	18.7	12.4
California........	2,118.9	2,185.1	2,505.2	2,470.3	21.9	17.9	25.9	20.3	21.0	11.0
Colorado........	177.9	179.1	209.6	214.2	13.6	10.9	16.0	13.0	13.1	6.8
Connecticut.......	314.0	290.1	345.1	298.1	22.7	20.0	25.0	20.5	28.1	14.0
Delaware	49.2	39.9	54.1	50.6	20.1	15.3	22.1	19.3	27.3	15.6
District of Columbia .	52.4	44.2	69.4	48.6	19.5	13.3	25.9	14.6	17.6	22.0
Florida..........	393.7	452.0	532.9	607.3	10.2	8.2	13.8	11.0	11.3	5.1
Georgia	267.0	244.1	345.1	287.9	11.9	8.0	15.3	9.4	16.9	9.8
Hawaii	112.6	135.2	124.9	144.0	29.2	28.0	32.4	29.9	35.6	24.1
Idaho...........	41.3	38.7	53.7	48.7	12.5	8.5	16.2	10.7	19.0	10.6
Illinois..........	1,063.8	1,006.6	1,205.1	1,086.9	24.2	19.9	27.4	21.4	32.4	22.7
Indiana..........	503.3	494.3	544.5	535.0	24.9	19.3	27.0	20.9	48.7	36.0
Iowa	185.9	161.0	231.3	193.5	17.2	13.2	21.5	15.9	40.3	22.8
Kansas..........	125.2	106.4	170.4	152.2	13.7	10.0	18.7	14.3	25.5	15.7
Kentucky	223.7	171.3	259.8	200.2	17.9	11.5	20.8	13.4	37.4	22.5
Louisiana	204.2	121.4	267.8	148.5	13.8	7.7	18.1	9.4	24.9	14.1
Maine...........	88.0	71.6	100.4	80.3	21.0	15.6	24.0	17.5	24.8	20.0
Maryland	346.5	371.7	423.1	434.4	18.5	16.0	22.6	18.7	29.2	24.0
Massachusetts.....	603.2	419.4	661.4	453.5	23.7	15.9	26.0	17.2	26.7	11.7
Michigan.........	1,005.4	960.6	1,084.6	1,028.2	30.4	23.8	32.8	25.5	46.2	33.2
Minnesota........	393.9	413.5	439.4	442.9	23.2	19.7	25.9	21.1	22.3	16.2
Mississippi	79.4	66.5	99.7	85.3	9.9	6.4	12.5	8.2	18.9	11.5
Missouri	374.4	329.1	416.7	362.3	20.8	14.8	23.2	16.3	36.6	21.2
Montana	49.5	60.4	55.5	66.3	18.3	18.8	20.5	20.6	33.0	28.4
Nebraska	80.6	77.5	94.8	97.1	13.6	10.7	16.0	13.4	19.1	16.3
Nevada	90.0	120.9	106.7	136.0	22.4	18.4	26.6	20.7	10.8	6.8
New Hampshire....	48.5	55.1	60.8	66.8	11.5	10.7	14.4	13.0	10.6	7.4
New Jersey.......	822.1	779.5	918.2	849.2	26.9	23.1	30.0	25.2	31.4	22.7
New Mexico	52.6	56.2	70.6	68.5	11.8	9.3	15.8	11.4	11.9	6.2
New York	2,155.6	2,050.0	2,385.9	2,174.9	32.5	28.9	36.0	30.6	31.0	24.2
North Carolina.....	178.7	158.6	238.1	201.4	7.6	5.2	10.2	6.6	6.9	5.1
North Dakota......	28.4	24.3	35.1	31.1	13.2	9.4	16.3	12.0	27.4	18.2
Ohio	1,011.0	896.6	1,125.0	976.7	25.1	19.1	27.9	20.8	40.9	29.2
Oklahoma........	131.5	110.7	168.2	136.4	11.5	8.8	14.7	10.9	25.2	15.2
Oregon..........	222.9	275.3	261.9	294.9	22.3	21.5	26.2	23.0	28.7	23.4
Pennsylvania......	1,195.7	962.3	1,350.0	1,039.2	27.5	19.6	31.1	21.2	42.3	26.5
Rhode Island......	85.8	66.7	93.7	72.1	21.5	16.3	23.5	17.6	16.9	11.4
South Carolina.....	69.6	59.3	100.6	80.3	5.9	3.8	8.6	5.2	5.5	3.2
South Dakota	26.8	23.4	34.8	29.7	11.5	8.3	14.9	10.5	19.0	11.8
Tennessee	252.4	265.3	300.9	307.4	15.1	11.9	18.0	13.8	21.4	18.0
Texas...........	583.7	543.0	712.8	680.4	9.7	7.0	11.9	8.8	16.1	9.1
Utah	81.6	79.8	100.9	105.0	15.2	9.7	18.9	12.8	14.9	5.2
Vermont	25.9	22.7	31.5	27.0	12.6	9.4	15.3	11.1	13.5	7.8
Virginia..........	268.3	210.7	346.1	280.8	11.7	7.3	15.1	9.8	21.2	11.9
Washington.......	419.9	486.9	499.7	560.5	27.1	22.0	32.3	25.3	35.5	30.9
West Virginia......	142.7	113.1	160.6	120.1	25.3	17.6	28.5	18.7	41.3	35.3
Wisconsin........	465.5	430.6	526.7	455.7	23.8	18.3	26.9	19.4	36.0	23.8
Wyoming	27.1	22.2	31.8	28.0	13.9	11.5	16.2	14.4	14.6	12.8

[1] See footnote 2, table 626.

Source: The Bureau of National Affairs, Inc., Washington, DC, *Union Membership and Earnings Data Book 1994: Compilations from the Current Population Survey,* (copyright by BNA); authored by Barry Hirsch and David Macpherson of Florida State University.

No. 698. Union Members, by Selected Characteristics: 1983 and 1994

[Annual averages of monthly data. Covers employed wage and salary workers 16 years old and over. Excludes self-employed workers whose businesses are incorporated although they technically qualify as wage and salary workers. See headnote table 643 regarding data by occupation and industry. Based on Current Population Survey, see text, section 1, and Appendix III]

CHARACTERISTIC	EMPLOYED WAGE AND SALARY WORKERS						MEDIAN USUAL WEEKLY EARNINGS [4] (dol.)							
	Total (1,000)		Percent union members [2]		Percent represented by unions [3]		Total [1]		Union members [2]		Represented by unions [3]		Not represented by unions [1]	
	1983	1994 [1]	1983	1994 [1]	1983	1994 [1]	1983	1994 [1]	1983	1994 [1]	1983	1994 [1]	1983	1994 [1]
Total [5]	88,290	107,989	20.1	15.5	23.3	17.5	313	467	388	592	383	587	288	432
16 to 24 years old	19,305	18,207	9.1	6.2	11.1	7.2	210	286	281	366	275	364	203	281
25 to 34 years old	25,978	29,617	19.6	12.7	23.1	14.5	321	439	382	532	376	522	304	421
35 to 44 years old	18,722	29,160	24.8	18.5	28.6	20.8	369	537	411	623	407	618	339	508
45 to 54 years old	13,150	19,675	27.0	22.5	30.5	24.8	366	566	404	639	402	636	335	520
55 to 64 years old	9,201	8,924	26.9	20.3	30.3	22.8	346	501	392	588	390	589	316	472
65 years and over	1,934	2,406	10.1	8.9	12.1	10.2	260	384	338	549	330	549	238	361
Men	47,856	56,570	24.7	17.9	27.7	19.6	378	522	416	621	414	620	349	495
Women	40,433	51,419	14.6	12.9	18.0	15.1	252	399	309	522	307	517	237	377
White	77,046	91,290	19.3	14.8	22.3	16.7	319	484	396	609	391	604	295	451
Men	42,168	48,351	24.0	17.2	26.9	18.9	387	547	423	640	421	638	362	513
Women	34,877	42,939	13.5	12.1	16.7	14.1	254	408	314	546	313	538	240	386
Black	8,979	12,229	27.2	20.5	31.7	23.3	261	371	331	493	324	487	222	338
Men	4,477	5,834	31.7	23.3	36.1	25.9	293	400	366	524	360	518	244	359
Women	4,502	6,395	22.7	18.1	27.4	20.8	231	346	292	452	287	446	209	323
Hispanic [6]	(NA)	10,017	(NA)	14.2	(NA)	15.9	(NA)	324	(NA)	470	(NA)	468	(NA)	307
Men	(NA)	6,002	(NA)	15.5	(NA)	17.0	(NA)	343	(NA)	506	(NA)	501	(NA)	316
Women	(NA)	4,015	(NA)	12.1	(NA)	14.2	(NA)	305	(NA)	402	(NA)	413	(NA)	289
Full-time workers	70,976	87,379	22.9	17.3	26.4	19.4	313	467	388	592	383	587	288	432
Part-time workers	17,314	20,431	8.4	7.9	10.3	9.2	(X)	(X)	(X)	(X)	(X)	(X)	(X)	(X)
Managerial and professional specialty	19,657	28,568	17.1	14.4	21.9	17.3	437	683	423	729	421	720	446	672
Technical sales, and admin. support	28,024	33,509	12.1	10.3	15.0	12.1	281	420	350	518	341	511	270	407
Service occupations	12,875	15,597	15.3	14.3	17.9	15.7	205	294	305	483	299	470	182	268
Precision, production, craft, and repair	10,542	11,354	32.9	23.9	35.7	25.6	377	504	456	672	450	663	322	458
Operators, fabricators, and laborers	15,416	17,142	35.4	24.1	37.9	25.6	275	373	366	514	361	510	226	327
Farming, forestry, and fishing	1,775	1,820	5.5	5.7	6.9	6.7	196	282	292	416	287	406	189	273
Agricultural wage and salary workers	1,446	1,487	3.4	2.3	3.8	2.8	198	282	(B)	(B)	(B)	(B)	195	279
Private nonagri. wage and salary workers	71,225	88,163	16.8	10.9	18.8	12.0	307	448	389	562	385	556	286	427
Mining	869	652	20.7	17.0	23.1	17.0	481	639	470	664	470	656	488	634
Construction	4,109	4,866	27.5	18.8	29.4	19.9	348	477	518	696	510	687	296	425
Manufacturing	19,066	19,267	27.8	18.2	30.5	19.7	335	482	370	533	368	533	315	464
Transportation and public utilities	5,142	6,512	42.4	28.4	46.2	30.7	417	584	449	665	445	657	386	531
Wholesale and retail trade, total	18,081	22,319	8.7	6.2	9.8	6.8	252	359	353	453	348	439	242	352
Finance, insurance, and real estate	5,559	6,897	2.9	2.3	4.1	3.1	296	484	284	471	285	467	297	485
Services	18,400	27,649	7.7	6.2	9.6	7.3	272	425	303	485	303	488	268	420
Government	15,618	18,339	36.7	38.7	45.5	44.7	351	564	386	623	381	617	316	493

B Data not shown where base is less than 50,000. NA Not available. X Not applicable. [1] See footnote 2, table 626. [2] Members of a labor union or an employee association similar to a labor union. [3] Members of a labor union or an employee association similar to a union as well as workers who report no union affiliation but whose jobs are covered by a union or an employee association contract. [4] For full-time employed wage and salary workers; 1983 revised since originally published. [5] Includes races not shown separately. For 1994, includes a small number of multiple jobholders whose full- part-time status can not be determined for their principal job. [6] Persons of Hispanic origin may be of any race.

Source: U.S. Bureau of Labor Statistics, Employment and Earnings, January issues.

Figure 14.1
Disposable Personal Income Per Person: 1994
(Percent of national average)

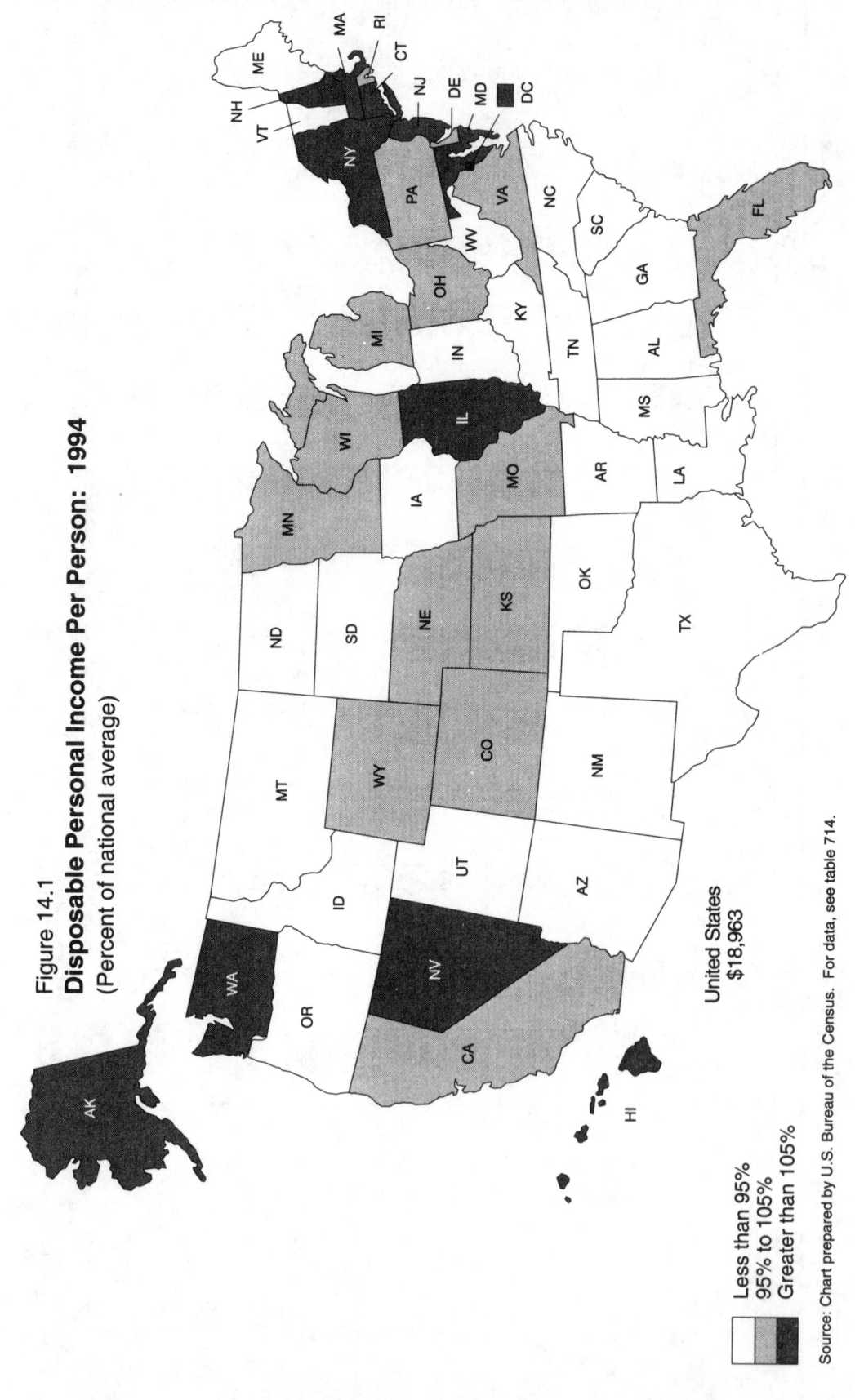

United States
$18,963

Less than 95%
95% to 105%
Greater than 105%

Source: Chart prepared by U.S. Bureau of the Census. For data, see table 714.

Income, Expenditures, and Wealth

This section presents data on gross domestic product (GDP), gross national product (GNP), national and personal income, saving and investment, money income, poverty, and national and personal wealth. The data on income and expenditures measure two aspects of the U.S. economy. One aspect relates to the national income and product accounts (NIPA's), a summation reflecting the entire complex of the Nation's economic income and output and the interaction of its major components; the other relates to the distribution of money income to families and individuals, or consumer income.

The primary source for data on GDP, GNP, national and personal income, gross saving and investment, and fixed reproducible tangible wealth is the *Survey of Current Business,* published monthly by the Bureau of Economic Analysis (BEA). A comprehensive revision to the NIPA's was completed in December 1991. A discussion of the revision appears in the August through October, 1991 and the December 1991 issues of *Survey of Current Business.* Detailed historical data appear in *The National Income and Product Accounts of the United States, volume 1, 1929-58* and *volume 2, 1959-88* and the July 1992; detailed data for the most recent years are normally published each July in the *Survey.*

Sources of income distribution data are the decennial censuses of population and the Current Population Survey (CPS), both products of the Bureau of the Census (see text, section 1). Annual data on income of families, individuals, and households are presented in *Current Population Reports-Consumer Income,* P60 series.

Data on individuals' saving and assets are published by the Board of Governors of the Federal Reserve System in the quarterly *Flow of Funds Accounts;* and detailed information on personal wealth is published periodically by the Internal Revenue Service (IRS) in *SOI Bulletin.*

In Brief

Gross domestic product, in constant (1987) dollars reached a record $5.4 trillion in 1994, 4.1% above 1993

Median household income in 1993: $31,241

Poverty status of persons in 1993:
Number below poverty level: 39.3 million
Percent below poverty level: 15.1

National income and product.—
Gross domestic product is the total output of goods and services produced by labor and property located in the United States, valued at market prices. GDP can be viewed in terms of expenditure categories that comprise purchases of goods and services by consumers and government, gross private domestic investment, and net exports of goods and services. The goods and services included are largely those bought for final use (excluding illegal transactions) in the market economy. A number of inclusions, however, represent imputed values, the most important of which is rental value of owner-occupied housing. GDP, in this broad context, measures the output attributable to the factors of production located in the United States. *Gross State product* (GSP) is the gross market value of the goods and services attributable to labor and property located in a State. It is the State counterpart of the Nation's gross domestic product.

Gross national product measures the output attributable to all labor and property supplied by United States residents. GNP differs from "national income" mainly in that GNP includes allowances for depreciation and for indirect business taxes (sales and property taxes); see table 705.

In December 1991, the Bureau of Economic Analysis began featuring gross domestic product rather than gross national product as the primary measure of U.S. production. GDP is now the standard measure of growth because it is the appropriate measure for much of the short-term monitoring and analysis of the economy. In addition, the use of GDP facilitates comparisons of economic activity in the United States with that in other countries. GDP is the primary measure of production in the United Nation's System of National Accounts, the set of international guidelines for economic accounting that the U.S. economic accounts will be moving toward in the mid-1990's. Virtually all other countries already use GDP as their primary measure of production. The dollar levels of GDP and GNP differ little, but percentage changes often differ. The annual rates of growth of real GNP have been slightly less than the annual rates of growth of real GDP in most years of the 1980's. The quarterly differences are larger and they fluctuate more.

National income is the aggregate of labor and property earnings which arises in the current production of goods and services. It is the sum of employee compensation, proprietors' income, rental income of persons, corporate profits, and net interest. It measures the total factor costs of the goods and services produced by the economy. Income is measured before deduction of taxes.

Capital consumption adjustment for corporations, and for nonfarm sole proprietorships and partnerships is the difference between capital consumption based on income tax returns and capital consumption measured at straight-line depreciation, consistent service lives, and replacement cost. The tax return data are valued at historical costs and reflect changes over time in service lives and depreciation patterns as permitted by tax regulations. *Inventory valuation adjustment* represents the difference between the book value of inventories used up in production and the cost of replacing them.

Personal income is the current income received by persons from all sources minus their personal contributions for social insurance. Classified as "persons" are individuals (including owners of unincorporated firms), nonprofit institutions that primarily serve individuals, private trust funds, and private noninsured welfare

funds. Personal income includes transfers (payments not resulting from current production) from government and business such as Social Security benefits, public assistance, etc., but excludes transfers among persons. Also included are certain nonmonetary types of income—chiefly estimated net rental value to owner-occupants of their homes and the value of services furnished without payment by financial intermediaries.

Disposable personal income is personal income less personal tax and nontax payments. It is the income available to persons for spending or saving. Personal tax and nontax payments are tax payments (net of refunds) by persons (except personal contributions for social insurance) that are not chargeable to business expense, and certain personal payments to general government that are treated like taxes. Personal taxes include income, estate and gift, and personal property taxes and motor vehicle licenses. Nontax payments include passport fees, fines and forfeitures, and donations.

Consumer Expenditure Survey.—The Consumer Expenditure Survey program was begun in late 1979. The principal objective of the survey is to collect current consumer expenditure data which provide a continuous flow of data on the buying habits of American consumers. The data are necessary for future revisions of the Consumer Price Index.

The survey conducted by the Bureau of the Census for the Bureau of Labor Statistics, consists of two components: (1) An interview panel survey in which the expenditures of consumer units are obtained in five interviews conducted every 3 months; and (2) a diary or record-keeping survey completed by participating households for two consecutive 1-week periods.

Each component of the survey queries an independent sample of consumer units representative of the U.S. total population. Over 52 weeks of the year, 5,000 consumer units are sampled for the diary survey. Each consumer unit keeps a diary for two 1-week periods yielding approximately 10,000 diaries a year. The interview sample is selected on a rotating panel basis, targeted at 5,000 consumer units per quarter. Data are collected in 88 urban and 16 rural areas of the country that are representative of the U.S. total population. The survey includes students in student housing. Data from the two surveys are combined; integration is necessary to permit analysis of total family expenditures because neither the diary nor quarterly interview survey was designed to collect a complete account of consumer spending.

The Diary survey is designed to obtain expenditures on small, frequently purchased items which are normally difficult for respondents to recall. Detailed records of expenses are kept for food and beverages, both at home and in eating places, tobacco, housekeeping supplies, nonprescription drugs, and personal care products and services.

The Interview survey is designed to obtain data on the types of expenditures which respondents can be expected to recall for a period of 3 months or longer. In general, these include relatively large expenditures, such as those for property, automobiles, and major appliances, or expenditures which occur on a fairly regular basis, such as rent, utilities, or insurance premiums. Including "global estimates" for food, it is estimated that about 95 percent of expenditures are covered in the interview. Excluded are nonprescription drugs, household supplies, and personal care items. The interview survey also provides data on expenditures incurred while on trips. Both surveys exclude all business related expenditures for which the family is reimbursed.

Distribution of money income to families and individuals.—Money income statistics are based on data collected in various field surveys of income conducted since 1936. Since 1947, the Bureau of the Census has collected the data on an annual basis and published them in *Current Population Reports,* P60 series. In each of the surveys, field representatives interview samples of the population with respect to income received during the previous year. Money income as defined by the Bureau of the Census differs from the BEA concept of "personal income."

Data on consumer income collected in the CPS by the Bureau of the Census cover money income received (exclusive of certain money receipts such as capital gains) before payments for personal income taxes, Social Security, union dues, Medicare deductions, etc. Therefore, money income does not reflect the fact that some families receive part of their income in the form of noncash benefits (see section 12) such as food stamps, health benefits, and subsidized housing; that some farm families receive noncash benefits in the form of rent-free housing and goods produced and consumed on the farm; or that noncash benefits are also received by some nonfarm residents which often take the form of the use of business transportation and facilities, full or partial payments by business for retirement programs, medical and educational expenses, etc. These elements should be considered when comparing income levels. For data on noncash benefits, see section 12. None of the aggregate income concepts (GDP, national income, or personal income) is exactly comparable with money income, although personal income is the closest.

Beginning in the March 1981 Current Population Survey, 1980 census population controls were used; for income years 1971 through 1979, 1970 census population controls had been used. This change had little impact on income summary measures (means and medians) and proportional measures (percent distributions and poverty rates); however, use of the controls may have significant impact on the absolute numbers.

Several changes were made in the collection and processing of the March 1994 CPS data. These changes included (1) a change in the data collection method from paper and pencil to computer-assisted interviewing, (2) revisions allowing for the coding of different income amounts on selected questionnaire items (limits either increased or decreased in the following categories: earnings increased to $999,999, Social Security increased to $49,999, Supplemental Security Income and Public Assistance increased to $24,999, Veterans' Benefits increased to $99,999, Child Support and Alimony decreased to $49,999), and (3) the introduction of 1990 census population controls. A detailed description of these changes and their effects on estimates can be found in *Current Population Reports*, Series P60–188.

In October 1983, the Census Bureau began to collect data under the new Survey of Income and Program Participation (SIPP). The information supplied by this survey is expected to provide better measures of the status and changes in income distribution and poverty of households and persons in the United States. The data collected in SIPP will be used to study Federal and State aid programs (such as food stamps, welfare, Medicaid, and subsidized housing), to estimate program costs and coverage, and to assess the effects of proposed changes in program eligibility rules or benefit levels. The core questions are repeated at each interview and cover labor force activity, the types and amounts of income received, and participation status in various programs. The core also contains questions covering attendance in postsecondary schools and private health insurance coverage. Various supplements or topical modules covering areas such as educational attainment, assets and liabilities, and pension plan coverage are periodically included.

Poverty.—Families and unrelated individuals are classified as being above or below the poverty level using the poverty index originated at the Social Security Administration in 1964 and revised by Federal Interagency Committees in 1969 and 1980. The poverty index is based solely on money income and does not reflect the fact that many low-income persons receive noncash benefits such as food stamps, Medicaid, and public housing. The index is based on the Department of Agriculture's 1961 Economy Food Plan and reflects the different consumption requirements of families based on their size and composition. The poverty thresholds are updated every year to reflect changes in the Consumer Price Index. The following technical changes to the thresholds were made in 1981: (1) distinctions based on sex of householder have been eliminated; (2) separate thresholds for farm families have been dropped; and (3) the matrix has been expanded to families of nine or more persons from the old cutoff of seven or more persons. These changes have been incorporated in the calculation of poverty data beginning with 1981.

In the recent past, the Bureau of the Census has published a number of technical papers that presented experimental poverty estimates based on income definitions that counted the value of selected government noncash benefits. The Census Bureau has also published annual reports on after-tax income. The *Current Population Reports,* series P60-186RD brings together the benefit and tax data that previously appeared in the separate reports. This report shows the distribution of income among households and the prevalence of poverty under the official definition of money income and under definitions that add or subtract income components.

The poverty statistics presented by the Bureau of the Census and Congressional Budget Office reflect alternative adjustments for inflation. The study used a variation of the Consumer Price Index to adjust poverty thresholds for the effects of changing prices since 1967. The alternative measure of inflation uses estimates of the cost of renting equivalent housing to assess homeownership costs; this methodology has been used in the official Consumer Price Index since 1983. See text, section 15, and source for more details.

Personal wealth.—Personal wealth estimates, issued by the IRS, are based on a sample of Federal estate tax returns which must be filed for deceased persons. Estimates are weighted to adjust for age, sex, and "social class" (as determined by the IRS through insurance holdings). Gross estate is the gross value of all assets, including the full face value of life insurance (reduced by policy loans), before reduction by the amount of debts. The level of gross estate or gross assets required for filing estate tax returns was $600,000 in 1989. Net worth is one's level of worth after all debts have been removed.

Statistical reliability.—For a discussion of statistical collection and estimation, sampling procedures, and measures of statistical reliability pertaining to Census Bureau data, see Appendix III.

Historical statistics.—Tabular headnotes provide cross-references, where applicable, to *Historical Statistics of the United States, Colonial Times to 1970.* See Appendix IV.

No. 699. GDP in Current and Constant (1987) Dollars: 1929 to 1994

[**In billions of dollars.** For explanation of gross domestic product, see text, section 14]

ITEM	1929	1940	1950	1960	1970	1980	1983	1984	1985
CURRENT DOLLARS									
Gross domestic product (GDP) .	103.1	100.0	287.0	513.4	1,010.7	2,708.0	3,405.0	3,777.2	4,038.7
Personal consumption expenditures . .	77.5	71.2	192.7	332.4	646.5	1,748.1	2,257.5	2,460.3	2,667.4
Durable goods	9.2	7.8	30.8	43.5	85.3	212.5	275.0	317.9	352.9
Nondurable goods	37.7	37.0	98.2	153.1	270.4	682.9	817.8	873.0	919.4
Services	30.5	26.4	63.7	135.9	290.8	852.7	1,164.7	1,269.4	1,395.1
Gross private domestic investment . . .	16.7	13.6	54.2	78.7	150.3	467.6	546.7	718.9	714.5
Fixed investment	14.9	11.2	48.3	75.5	148.1	477.1	552.2	647.8	689.9
Nonresidential	11.0	7.7	27.8	49.2	106.7	353.8	400.2	468.9	504.0
Residential	4.0	3.5	20.5	26.3	41.4	123.3	152.0	178.9	185.9
Change in business inventories . . .	1.7	2.4	5.9	3.2	2.3	−9.5	−5.5	71.1	24.6
Net exports of goods and services . . .	0.4	1.4	0.7	2.4	1.2	−14.7	−51.4	−102.7	−115.6
Exports	5.9	4.8	12.3	25.3	57.0	279.2	276.7	302.4	302.1
Imports	5.6	3.4	11.6	22.8	55.8	293.9	328.1	405.1	417.6
Government purchases	8.6	13.8	39.5	99.8	212.7	507.1	652.3	700.8	772.3
Federal	1.5	6.0	20.2	55.3	100.1	209.1	292.0	310.9	344.3
National defense	-	2.3	14.3	45.3	76.8	142.7	214.4	233.1	258.6
State and local	7.1	7.8	19.3	44.5	112.6	298.0	360.3	389.9	428.1
CONSTANT (1987) DOLLARS									
Gross domestic product (GDP) .	821.8	906.0	1,418.5	1,970.8	2,873.9	3,776.3	3,906.6	4,148.5	4,279.8
Personal consumption expenditures . .	554.5	595.2	874.3	1,210.8	1,813.5	2,447.1	2,619.4	2,746.1	2,865.8
Durable goods	48.1	48.3	95.0	115.4	183.7	262.7	297.7	338.5	370.1
Nondurable goods	238.5	293.0	400.4	526.9	717.2	860.5	900.3	934.6	958.7
Services	267.9	253.9	378.9	568.5	912.5	1,323.9	1,421.4	1,473.0	1,537.0
Gross private domestic investment . . .	152.8	121.8	256.4	290.8	429.7	594.4	599.5	757.5	745.9
Fixed investment	142.1	107.1	233.9	282.7	423.8	602.7	595.1	689.6	723.8
Nonresidential	100.6	69.0	132.5	173.3	292.0	437.8	420.8	490.2	521.8
Residential	41.6	38.1	101.4	109.4	131.8	164.8	174.2	199.3	202.0
Change in business inventories . . .	10.6	14.7	22.5	8.1	5.9	−8.3	4.4	67.9	22.1
Net exports of goods and services . . .	1.9	8.2	3.2	−7.6	−35.2	30.7	−56.1	−122.0	−145.3
Exports	36.0	37.5	53.0	88.4	161.3	320.5	285.9	305.7	309.2
Imports	34.1	29.2	49.7	96.1	196.4	289.9	342.1	427.7	454.6
Government purchases	112.6	180.7	284.5	476.9	665.8	704.2	743.8	766.9	813.4
Federal	21.9	76.2	145.6	259.0	315.0	284.8	320.8	331.0	355.2
National defense	-	-	-	-	-	194.2	234.2	245.8	265.6
State and local	90.7	104.5	138.9	217.9	350.9	419.4	423.0	436.0	458.2

	1986	1987	1988	1989	1990	1991	1992	1993	1994
CURRENT DOLLARS									
Gross domestic product (GDP) .	4,268.6	4,539.9	4,900.4	5,250.8	5,546.1	5,724.8	6,020.2	6,343.3	6,738.4
Personal consumption expenditures . .	2,850.6	3,052.2	3,296.1	3,523.1	3,761.2	3,902.4	4,136.9	4,378.2	4,628.4
Durable goods	389.6	403.7	437.1	459.4	468.2	456.6	492.7	538.0	591.5
Nondurable goods	952.2	1,011.1	1,073.8	1,149.5	1,229.2	1,257.8	1,295.5	1,339.2	1,394.3
Services	1,508.8	1,637.4	1,785.2	1,914.2	2,063.8	2,188.1	2,348.7	2,501.0	2,642.7
Gross private domestic investment . . .	717.6	749.3	793.6	832.3	808.9	744.8	788.3	882.0	1,032.9
Fixed investment	709.0	723.0	777.4	789.9	802.0	746.6	785.2	866.7	980.7
Nonresidential	492.4	497.8	545.4	568.1	586.7	557.0	561.4	616.1	697.6
Residential	216.6	225.2	232.0	230.9	215.3	189.6	223.8	250.6	283.0
Change in business inventories . . .	8.6	26.3	16.2	33.3	6.9	−1.8	3.0	15.4	52.2
Net exports of goods and services . . .	−132.5	−143.1	−108.0	−79.7	−71.4	−19.9	−30.3	−65.3	−98.2
Exports	319.2	364.0	444.2	508.0	557.1	601.1	638.1	659.1	718.7
Imports	451.7	507.1	552.2	587.7	628.5	620.9	668.4	724.3	816.9
Government purchases	833.0	881.5	918.7	975.2	1,047.4	1,097.4	1,125.3	1,148.4	1,175.3
Federal	367.8	384.9	387.0	401.6	426.5	445.8	449.0	443.6	437.3
National defense	276.7	292.1	295.6	299.9	314.0	322.8	314.2	302.7	292.3
State and local	465.3	496.6	531.7	573.6	620.9	651.6	676.3	704.7	738.0
CONSTANT (1987) DOLLARS									
Gross domestic product (GDP) .	4,404.5	4,540.0	4,718.6	4,838.0	4,897.3	4,867.6	4,979.3	5,134.5	5,344.0
Personal consumption expenditures . .	2,969.1	3,052.2	3,162.4	3,223.3	3,272.6	3,259.4	3,349.5	3,458.7	3,579.6
Durable goods	402.0	403.7	428.7	440.7	443.1	425.3	452.6	489.9	532.1
Nondurable goods	991.0	1,011.1	1,035.1	1,051.6	1,060.7	1,047.8	1,057.7	1,078.5	1,109.5
Services	1,576.1	1,637.4	1,698.5	1,731.0	1,768.8	1,786.3	1,839.1	1,890.3	1,938.1
Gross private domestic investment . . .	735.1	749.3	773.4	784.0	746.8	683.8	725.3	819.9	951.5
Fixed investment	726.5	723.0	753.4	754.2	741.1	684.9	722.9	804.6	903.8
Nonresidential	500.3	497.8	530.8	540.0	546.5	515.4	525.9	591.6	672.4
Residential	226.2	225.2	222.7	214.2	194.5	169.5	196.9	213.0	231.3
Change in business inventories . . .	8.5	26.3	19.9	29.8	5.7	−1.1	2.5	15.3	47.8
Net exports of goods and services . . .	−155.1	−143.0	−104.0	−73.7	−54.7	−19.5	−32.3	−73.9	−110.0
Exports	329.6	364.0	421.6	471.8	510.5	542.6	578.8	602.5	657.0
Imports	484.7	507.1	525.7	545.4	565.1	562.1	611.2	676.3	766.9
Government purchases	855.4	881.5	886.8	904.4	932.6	944.0	936.9	929.8	922.8
Federal	373.0	384.9	377.3	376.1	384.1	386.7	373.5	356.6	337.6
National defense	280.6	292.1	287.0	281.4	283.6	281.4	261.4	243.7	226.7
State and local	482.4	496.6	509.6	528.3	548.5	557.2	563.3	573.1	585.2

- Represents or rounds to zero.

Source: U.S. Bureau of Economic Analysis, *National Income and Product Accounts of the United States: volume 1, 1929-58, and volume 2, 1959-88,* and *Survey of Current Business,* August 1993, July 1994, and March 1995.

No. 700. Gross Domestic Product, by Industry: 1980 to 1992

[**In billions of dollars.** 1980 data are based on the 1972 Standard Industrial Classification (SIC), and 1990-92 are based on the 1987 SIC. Data include nonfactor charges (capital consumption allowances, indirect business taxes, etc.) as well as factor charges against gross product; corporate profits and capital consumption allowances have been shifted from a company to an establishment basis]

INDUSTRY	CURRENT DOLLARS				CONSTANT (1987) DOLLARS			
	1980	1990	1991	1992	1980	1990	1991	1992
Gross domestic product	**2,708**	**5,546**	**5,725**	**6,020**	**3,776**	**4,897**	**4,868**	**4,979**
Private industries	2,370	4,682	5,002	5,256	3,203	4,324	4,313	4,431
Agriculture, forestry, and fishing	67	112	107	116	63	96	98	110
Farms	56	85	79	86	51	72	71	81
Agricultural services	11	27	29	30	12	24	28	30
Mining [1]	113	103	92	85	80	92	92	89
Construction	129	240	223	222	185	210	195	201
Manufacturing	588	1,025	1,033	1,063	725	929	911	925
Durable goods	349	564	554	568	424	537	526	534
Lumber and wood products	19	31	29	31	22	28	26	25
Furniture and fixtures	8	16	16	17	12	14	14	15
Stone, clay, and glass products	18	25	23	25	24	26	23	25
Primary metal industries	44	44	42	40	49	35	38	36
Fabricated metal products	45	67	65	70	55	60	57	60
Machinery, except electrical	77	(X)	(X)	(X)	81	(X)	(X)	(X)
Industrial machinery	(X)	109	101	103	(X)	102	101	108
Electric and electronic equipment	55	(X)	(X)	(X)	70	(X)	(X)	(X)
Electronic & other electric equipment	(X)	86	88	86	(X)	91	94	93
Motor vehicles and equipment	27	46	45	57	40	49	44	51
Other transportation equipment	26	65	66	61	38	64	61	54
Instruments and related products	20	56	59	60	24	50	51	50
Misc. manufacturing industries	10	19	19	20	10	17	17	17
Nondurable goods	239	461	478	495	301	392	385	391
Food and kindred products	52	97	102	104	64	84	83	83
Tobacco manufactures	7	16	17	19	20	9	9	8
Textile mill products	15	22	22	24	17	21	21	23
Apparel and other textile products	17	25	26	27	20	24	24	25
Paper and allied products	23	46	46	46	31	42	42	44
Printing and publishing	33	72	74	77	53	62	59	58
Chemicals and allied products	48	104	107	111	58	88	86	88
Petroleum and coal products	24	40	44	43	15	26	25	25
Rubber and misc. plastic products	17	35	36	39	19	32	33	35
Leather and leather products	4	4	4	5	5	4	4	4
Transportation and public utilities	242	481	507	529	336	463	479	495
Transportation	103	177	184	194	120	169	175	184
Railroad transportation	21	22	23	23	19	24	26	26
Local & interurban passenger transit	5	10	11	11	9	9	9	9
Trucking and warehousing	40	73	75	78	51	69	72	77
Water transportation	7	10	11	10	9	8	8	8
Transportation by air	18	40	41	46	19	40	40	45
Pipelines, except natural gas	5	4	4	5	5	5	5	5
Transportation services	6	17	19	20	9	15	15	15
Communications	69	147	154	162	94	141	148	154
Telephone and telegraph	62	123	128	135	81	121	126	131
Radio and television broadcasting	7	24	27	28	14	20	23	23
Electric, gas, and sanitary services	70	158	169	173	122	153	156	157
Wholesale trade	192	363	373	394	191	320	325	341
Retail trade	245	516	532	558	320	478	473	487
Finance, insurance, and real estate [2]	418	982	1,041	1,106	693	868	869	893
Depository institutions	(X)	159	181	194	(X)	135	129	125
Insurance carriers	37	70	85	85	61	60	68	73
Real estate	289	642	664	699	453	567	565	575
Nonfarm housing	208	459	484	512	325	398	404	409
Services [3]	377	1,040	1,093	1,183	609	869	871	890
Hotels and other lodging places	20	50	52	54	31	45	46	46
Personal services	17	36	37	39	28	31	30	30
Business services	69	198	199	221	104	173	168	174
Amusement and recreation services	14	40	45	51	20	35	37	41
Health services	111	304	335	364	196	241	248	252
Legal services	25	80	82	89	52	66	65	66
Social services & membership organization	26	61	65	70	38	55	58	60
Private households	6	9	9	10	7	9	8	9
Government	324	676	722	756	509	582	587	584
Federal	115	221	240	248	179	193	194	189
General government	96	180	193	200	139	156	157	152
Government enterprise	19	41	47	48	39	37	37	37
State and local	209	455	482	508	330	388	392	395
General government	194	413	438	462	301	353	357	360
Government enterprise	15	42	44	46	29	35	35	35
Statistical discrepancy	14	8	2	9	19	7	1	7
Residual	(X)	(X)	(X)	(X)	46	-15.3	-33.7	-43.0

X Not applicable.   [1] For additional mining industries, see table 1173.   [2] For additional finance, real estate, and insurance industries, see table 782.   [3] For additional service industries, see table 1288.

Source: U.S. Bureau of Economic Analysis, *Survey of Current Business,* May and November 1993.

No. 701. Gross Domestic Product, by Type of Product and Sector: 1980 to 1994

[In billions of dollars]

ITEM	1980	1985	1987	1988	1989	1990	1991	1992	1993	1994
Gross domestic product . . .	**2,708.0**	**4,038.7**	**4,539.9**	**4,900.4**	**5,250.8**	**5,546.1**	**5,724.8**	**6,020.2**	**6,343.3**	**6,738.4**
PRODUCT										
Goods	1,176.2	1,652.6	1,794.5	1,942.0	2,097.0	2,185.2	2,223.9	2,295.0	2,405.8	2,584.7
Services	1,215.4	1,939.0	2,267.2	2,460.9	2,642.1	2,849.4	3,028.9	3,227.2	3,405.5	3,576.2
Structures	316.4	447.1	478.2	497.5	511.7	511.5	472.0	498.0	532.0	577.6
SECTOR										
Business	2,328.9	3,473.5	3,890.8	4,201.0	4,495.9	4,725.9	4,847.6	5,090.4	5,371.4	5,723.2
Households and institutions	89.3	141.7	170.5	187.6	206.1	227.5	246.7	268.6	285.3	302.7
General government	289.8	423.6	478.7	511.7	548.8	592.8	630.5	661.2	686.3	712.6

Source: U.S. Bureau of Economic Analysis, *National Income and Product Accounts of the United States: volume 2, 1959-88*, and *Survey of Current Business*, July 1994 and March 1995.

No. 702. GDP Components—Annual Percent Change: 1980 to 1994

[Change from previous year; for 1980, change from 1979 and for 1986, change from 1985. Minus sign (-) indicates decrease]

ITEM	1980	1986	1987	1988	1989	1990	1991	1992	1993	1994
CURRENT DOLLARS										
Gross domestic product	8.8	5.7	6.4	7.9	7.2	5.6	3.2	5.2	5.4	6.2
Personal consumption expenditures	10.4	6.9	7.1	8.0	6.9	6.8	3.8	6.0	5.8	5.7
Durable goods	-0.8	10.4	3.6	8.3	5.1	1.9	-2.5	7.9	9.2	9.9
Nondurable goods	11.3	3.6	6.2	6.2	7.0	6.9	2.3	3.0	3.4	4.1
Services	12.8	8.1	8.5	9.0	7.2	7.8	6.0	7.3	6.5	5.7
Gross private domestic investment .	-2.6	0.4	4.4	5.9	4.9	-2.8	-7.9	5.8	11.9	17.1
Fixed investment	2.1	2.8	2.0	7.5	2.8	0.4	-6.9	5.2	10.4	13.2
Nonresidential	8.4	-2.3	1.1	9.6	4.2	3.3	-5.1	0.8	9.7	13.2
Residential	-12.6	16.5	4.0	3.0	-0.5	-6.8	-11.9	18.0	12.0	12.9
Exports of goods and services . . .	22.0	5.7	14.0	22.0	14.4	9.7	7.9	6.2	3.3	9.0
Imports of goods and services . . .	16.3	8.2	12.3	8.9	6.4	6.9	-1.2	7.7	8.4	12.8
Government purchases	13.1	7.9	5.8	4.2	6.1	7.4	4.8	2.5	2.1	2.3
Federal	16.6	6.8	4.6	0.5	3.8	6.2	4.5	0.7	-1.2	-1.4
State and local	10.7	8.7	6.7	7.1	7.9	8.2	4.9	3.8	4.2	4.7
CONSTANT (1987) DOLLARS										
Gross domestic product	-0.5	2.9	3.1	3.9	2.5	1.2	-0.6	2.3	3.1	4.1
Personal consumption expenditures	-0.1	3.6	2.8	3.6	1.9	1.5	-0.4	2.8	3.3	3.5
Durable goods	-9.1	8.6	0.4	6.2	2.8	0.5	-4.0	6.4	8.2	8.6
Nondurable goods	-0.3	3.4	2.0	2.4	1.6	0.9	-1.2	1.0	2.0	2.9
Services	2.1	2.5	3.9	3.7	1.9	2.2	1.0	3.0	2.8	2.5
Gross private domestic investment .	-11.2	-1.4	1.9	3.2	1.4	-4.7	-8.4	6.1	13.0	16.1
Fixed investment	-8.1	0.4	-0.5	4.2	0.1	-1.7	-7.6	5.5	11.3	12.3
Nonresidential	-2.5	-4.1	-0.5	6.6	1.7	1.2	-5.7	2.0	12.5	13.7
Residential	-20.5	12.0	-0.4	-1.1	-3.8	-9.2	-12.9	16.2	8.2	8.6
Exports of goods and services . . .	9.2	6.6	10.4	15.8	11.9	8.2	6.3	6.7	4.1	9.0
Imports of goods and services . . .	-4.7	6.6	4.6	3.7	3.7	3.6	-0.5	8.7	10.7	13.4
Government purchases	2.2	5.2	3.1	0.6	2.0	3.1	1.2	-0.8	-0.8	-0.8
Federal	4.8	5.0	3.2	-2.0	-0.3	2.1	0.7	-3.4	-4.5	-5.3
State and local	0.4	5.3	2.9	2.6	3.7	3.8	1.6	1.1	1.7	2.1

Source: U.S. Bureau of Economic Analysis, *National Income and Product Accounts of the United States: volume 2, 1959-88*, and *Survey of Current Business*, July 1994 and March 1995.

Income, Expenditures, and Wealth

No. 703. Gross State Product in Current and Constant (1987) Dollars: 1980 to 1991

[**In billions of dollars.** For definition of gross State product, see text, section 14]

DIVISION AND STATE	CURRENT DOLLARS					CONSTANT (1987) DOLLARS				
	1980	1985	1989	1990	1991	1980	1985	1989	1990	1991
United States	2,685	4,038	5,232	5,518	5,691	3,697	4,271	4,836	4,888	4,883
New England	141	230	320	327	332	200	247	297	290	285
Maine	10	16	22	23	23	14	17	21	20	20
New Hampshire.	9	17	23	24	24	13	18	21	21	21
Vermont	5	7	11	11	11	7	8	10	10	10
Massachusetts	67	110	152	154	156	95	118	141	137	134
Rhode Island	10	15	20	21	21	13	16	18	18	18
Connecticut	41	66	91	94	96	58	71	85	84	83
Middle Atlantic	441	664	880	919	943	626	712	814	813	807
New York	222	341	445	467	476	321	367	414	414	409
New Jersey	89	144	201	207	213	125	154	185	182	181
Pennsylvania	130	179	234	245	255	179	191	215	216	217
East North Central.	483	680	859	891	914	665	723	796	795	789
Ohio	123	170	214	223	228	168	180	198	199	197
Indiana	59	82	108	111	114	80	87	99	99	99
Illinois	145	202	259	271	279	199	215	240	240	240
Michigan	103	152	185	187	189	145	162	173	168	164
Wisconsin.	53	73	94	100	103	73	78	87	89	89
West North Central	195	279	348	368	380	265	295	322	327	328
Minnesota	49	72	95	100	103	66	77	88	89	89
Iowa	34	42	52	55	56	45	44	48	49	48
Missouri.	53	79	99	103	106	73	84	92	92	92
North Dakota	8	11	11	12	12	10	11	10	11	10
South Dakota	7	10	12	13	14	9	10	11	11	12
Nebraska	18	25	31	34	35	24	27	29	30	31
Kansas	28	40	48	52	53	37	42	44	46	46
South Atlantic.	385	627	872	920	958	551	674	804	813	816
Delaware	7	12	18	20	21	10	13	17	17	18
Maryland	45	74	104	109	112	65	80	96	96	95
District of Columbia	18	26	35	37	38	28	28	32	32	32
Virginia	58	95	133	140	145	85	102	123	123	123
West Virginia	19	23	27	28	29	24	24	25	26	26
North Carolina.	59	95	133	141	148	86	103	122	123	125
South Carolina	27	42	59	64	66	38	45	55	57	57
Georgia	56	96	131	137	144	77	103	121	122	124
Florida.	96	164	231	245	255	137	176	213	216	218
East South Central	139	201	260	272	286	190	213	240	243	247
Kentucky	37	50	64	67	70	50	53	59	60	60
Tennessee	45	68	92	95	101	62	73	85	85	87
Alabama	35	52	67	71	74	49	55	62	63	64
Mississippi	22	31	38	39	41	29	32	35	35	36
West South Central	332	481	527	569	590	418	479	486	499	505
Arkansas	20	29	36	38	41	27	30	34	34	35
Louisiana	65	85	84	92	95	77	80	77	79	81
Oklahoma.	38	51	53	57	58	48	51	50	50	50
Texas	210	316	353	382	396	266	317	326	335	339
Mountain.	140	209	258	275	290	188	218	239	245	252
Montana.	9	11	13	13	14	12	11	12	12	13
Idaho.	10	13	17	18	19	13	14	16	16	16
Wyoming	11	13	12	13	13	12	12	11	12	12
Colorado	37	57	68	73	77	51	60	63	64	66
New Mexico	16	23	25	27	30	20	23	23	24	27
Arizona	30	49	65	68	70	41	52	60	61	60
Utah	15	24	29	31	33	21	25	26	28	29
Nevada	12	18	29	32	33	17	20	27	29	29
Pacific.	429	668	908	977	998	596	709	839	864	854
Washington	51	73	102	112	119	71	79	94	99	102
Oregon	30	40	53	56	59	42	42	48	50	51
California	320	511	703	753	764	447	546	650	665	652
Alaska	16	26	23	27	26	17	23	22	24	23
Hawaii	12	18	26	29	31	18	20	24	26	26

Source: U.S. Bureau of Economic Analysis, *Survey of Current Business*, August 1994; and unpublished data.

No. 704. Gross State Product, by Industry: 1991

[**In billions of dollars.** For definition of gross state product, see text, section 14. Industries based on 1987 Standard Industrial Classification]

DIVISION AND STATE	Total [1]	Farms, forestry, fisheries [2]	Construction	Manufacturing	Transportation, public utilities	Wholesale trade	Retail trade	Finance, insurance, real estate	Services	Government [3]
United States . .	**5,691**	**109**	**223**	**1,026**	**506**	**375**	**532**	**1,040**	**1,090**	**698**
New England	332	3	11	65	24	22	30	72	73	32
Maine	23	1	1	4	2	1	3	4	4	3
New Hampshire. . . .	24	(Z)	1	5	2	1	2	5	5	2
Vermont	11	(Z)	1	2	1	1	1	2	2	1
Massachusetts	156	1	5	29	11	11	13	33	38	14
Rhode Island . . .	21	(Z)	1	4	1	1	2	5	4	2
Connecticut	96	1	3	20	7	7	9	23	19	9
Middle Atlantic	943	6	34	156	84	65	77	211	205	102
New York	476	3	16	67	40	32	37	119	107	54
New Jersey.	213	1	8	37	20	18	17	44	45	22
Pennsylvania	255	3	10	52	24	16	23	47	53	26
East North Central. . . .	914	14	35	224	80	64	85	155	159	94
Ohio	228	3	8	60	20	15	22	36	39	23
Indiana	114	2	5	33	11	7	11	17	17	12
Illinois	279	4	11	53	28	23	25	53	54	27
Michigan	189	2	7	49	14	13	18	32	33	21
Wisconsin.	103	3	4	28	8	6	9	18	16	11
West North Central . . .	380	18	13	73	37	28	36	63	63	45
Minnesota	103	3	4	22	9	8	9	18	18	11
Iowa	56	4	2	13	5	4	5	9	8	7
Missouri	106	2	4	22	12	8	11	17	19	12
North Dakota	12	1	(Z)	1	1	1	1	2	2	2
South Dakota	14	2	(Z)	1	1	1	1	3	2	2
Nebraska	35	4	1	4	4	3	3	6	5	5
Kansas	53	2	2	10	6	4	5	8	8	7
South Atlantic	958	18	41	156	88	61	93	164	182	149
Delaware	21	(Z)	1	5	1	1	1	7	3	2
Maryland	112	1	7	11	9	7	11	21	25	19
District of Columbia .	38	(Z)	1	1	2	1	1	5	13	14
Virginia	145	2	6	23	13	8	13	24	27	28
West Virginia.	29	(Z)	1	5	4	2	3	4	4	4
North Carolina. . . .	148	4	5	45	12	9	14	20	19	18
South Carolina . . .	66	1	3	17	6	3	7	9	9	11
Georgia	144	3	5	26	16	13	13	23	24	19
Florida	255	7	12	23	24	17	29	51	58	34
East South Central . . .	286	7	10	67	26	17	29	40	44	40
Kentucky	70	2	3	17	6	4	7	9	10	9
Tennessee	101	2	4	24	8	7	11	15	18	13
Alabama	74	2	3	16	7	4	7	10	11	12
Mississippi	41	1	1	10	5	2	4	6	5	6
West South Central . . .	590	12	21	102	64	38	55	89	97	68
Arkansas	41	2	1	10	5	2	4	6	6	5
Louisiana	95	1	4	18	10	5	8	13	13	10
Oklahoma.	58	2	2	9	6	3	6	9	9	9
Texas	396	7	15	64	43	27	37	61	69	44
Mountain	290	8	13	35	28	16	29	47	60	42
Montana.	14	1	1	1	2	1	1	2	2	2
Idaho.	19	2	1	3	2	1	2	3	3	2
Wyoming	13	(Z)	(Z)	1	2	(Z)	1	2	1	2
Colorado	77	2	3	10	8	5	8	13	16	11
New Mexico	30	1	1	4	3	1	3	4	5	5
Arizona	70	2	3	9	5	4	8	13	14	10
Utah	33	(Z)	1	5	3	2	3	5	6	5
Nevada	33	(Z)	2	1	3	1	3	5	12	3
Pacific.	998	23	44	148	74	64	98	200	208	125
Washington.	119	4	6	20	9	8	12	20	22	17
Oregon	59	2	2	11	5	4	6	10	10	7
California	764	16	33	115	54	49	74	160	167	91
Alaska	26	1	1	1	3	1	1	3	2	4
Hawaii	31	1	2	1	3	1	4	6	7	6

Z Less than $500 million.   [1] Includes mining not shown separately.   [2] Includes agricultural services.   [3] Includes Federal civilian and military and State and local government.

Source: U.S. Bureau of Economic Analysis, *Survey of Current Business,* August 1994.

No. 705. Relation of GDP, GNP, Net National Product, National Income, Personal Income, Disposable Personal Income, and Personal Saving: 1980 to 1994

[**In billions of dollars.** For definitions, see text, section 14]

ITEM	1980	1985	1988	1989	1990	1991	1992	1993	1994
Gross domestic product	2,708.0	4,038.7	4,900.4	5,250.8	5,546.1	5,724.8	6,020.2	6,343.3	6,738.4
Plus: Receipts of factor income from the rest of the world [1]	80.6	97.3	128.7	157.5	168.6	155.7	133.5	136.6	167.1
Less: Payments of factor income to the rest of the world [2]	46.5	82.4	120.8	141.5	146.9	139.7	127.9	132.1	178.6
Equals: Gross national product	2,742.1	4,053.6	4,908.2	5,266.8	5,567.8	5,740.8	6,025.8	6,347.8	6,726.9
Less: Consumption of fixed capital	311.9	454.5	534.0	580.4	602.7	626.5	658.5	669.1	715.3
Equals: Net national product [3]	2,430.2	3,599.1	4,374.2	4,686.4	4,965.1	5,114.3	5,367.3	5,678.7	6,011.5
Less: Indirect business tax and nontax liability	212.0	329.9	385.3	414.7	444.0	478.3	504.4	525.3	554.0
Plus: Subsidies [4]	4.8	6.4	10.9	5.4	4.5	−0.1	3.5	9.0	0.7
Equals: National income [3]	2,198.2	3,268.4	4,002.6	4,249.5	4,491.0	4,608.2	4,829.5	5,131.4	5,458.4
Less: Corporate profits [5]	177.7	280.8	365.0	362.8	380.6	390.3	405.1	485.8	542.7
Net interest	191.2	326.2	387.7	452.7	463.7	447.4	420.0	399.5	409.7
Contributions for social insurance	216.6	353.8	442.3	473.2	503.1	525.9	556.4	585.6	626.0
Plus: Personal interest income	274.0	498.1	583.2	668.2	698.2	695.1	665.2	637.9	664.0
Personal dividend income	57.1	87.9	108.4	126.5	144.4	150.5	161.0	181.3	194.3
Government transfer payments to persons	312.6	468.1	555.9	603.8	666.3	749.2	837.9	892.6	939.9
Business transfer payments to persons	8.8	17.8	20.8	21.1	21.3	20.8	22.3	22.8	23.5
Wage accruals less disbursements	-	−0.2	-	-	0.1	−0.1	−20.0	20.0	-
Equals: Personal income	2,265.4	3,379.8	4,075.9	4,380.3	4,673.8	4,860.3	5,154.3	5,375.1	5,701.7
Less: Personal tax and nontax payments	312.4	436.8	527.7	593.3	623.3	623.7	648.6	686.4	742.1
Equals: Disposable personal income	1,952.9	2,943.0	3,548.2	3,787.0	4,050.5	4,236.6	4,505.8	4,688.7	4,959.6
Less: Personal outlays	1,799.1	2,753.7	3,392.5	3,634.9	3,880.6	4,025.0	4,257.8	4,496.2	4,756.5
Equals: Personal saving	153.8	189.3	155.7	152.1	170.0	211.6	247.9	192.6	203.1

- Represents or rounds to zero. [1] Consists largely of receipts by U.S. residents of interest and dividends and reinvested earnings of foreign affiliates of U.S. corporations. [2] Consists largely of payments to foreign residents of interest and dividends and reinvested earnings of U.S. affiliates of foreign corporations. [3] Includes items not shown separately. [4] Less current surplus of government enterprises. [5] With inventory valuation and capital consumption adjustments.

Source: U.S. Bureau of Economic Analysis, *National Income and Product Accounts of the United States: volume 2, 1959-88*, and *Survey of Current Business,* July 1994 and March 1995.

No. 706. Selected Per Capita Income and Product Items: 1929 to 1994

[Based on Bureau of the Census estimated population including Armed Forces abroad; based on quarterly averages. Prior to 1960, excludes Alaska and Hawaii]

YEAR	CURRENT DOLLARS					CONSTANT (1987) DOLLARS			
	Gross domestic product	Gross national product	Personal income	Disposable personal income	Personal consumption expenditures	Gross domestic product	Gross national product	Disposable personal income	Personal consumption expenditures
1929	846	852	691	672	636	6,743	6,789	4,807	4,550
1940	757	760	586	568	539	6,857	6,878	4,747	4,505
1945	1,523	1,526	1,215	1,068	857	11,453	11,470	6,367	5,107
1950	1,892	1,902	1,502	1,369	1,270	9,352	9,398	6,214	5,764
1955	2,446	2,461	1,903	1,693	1,568	10,699	10,764	6,842	6,335
1960	2,840	2,858	2,264	1,994	1,839	10,903	10,969	7,264	6,698
1965	3,616	3,643	2,845	2,527	2,287	12,712	12,807	8,508	7,703
1970	4,928	4,959	4,052	3,521	3,152	14,013	14,099	9,875	8,842
1971	5,283	5,320	4,302	3,779	3,372	14,232	14,329	10,111	9,022
1972	5,750	5,791	4,671	4,042	3,658	14,801	14,904	10,414	9,425
1973	6,368	6,428	5,184	4,521	4,002	15,422	15,564	11,013	9,752
1974	6,819	6,893	5,637	4,893	4,337	15,185	15,346	10,832	9,602
1975	7,343	7,404	6,053	5,329	4,745	14,917	15,036	10,906	9,711
1976	8,109	8,187	6,632	5,796	5,241	15,502	15,646	11,192	10,121
1977	8,961	9,055	7,269	6,316	5,772	16,039	16,201	11,406	10,425
1978	10,029	10,127	8,121	7,042	6,384	16,635	16,795	11,851	10,744
1979	11,055	11,198	9,032	7,787	7,035	16,867	17,082	12,039	10,876
1980	11,892	12,042	9,948	8,576	7,677	16,584	16,790	12,005	10,746
1981	13,177	13,321	11,021	9,455	8,375	16,710	16,890	12,156	10,770
1982	13,564	13,694	11,589	9,989	8,868	16,194	16,348	12,146	10,782
1983	14,531	14,657	12,216	10,642	9,634	16,672	16,813	12,349	11,179
1984	15,978	16,081	13,345	11,673	10,408	17,549	17,659	13,029	11,617
1985	16,933	16,995	14,170	12,339	11,184	17,944	18,007	13,258	12,015
1986	17,735	17,773	14,917	13,010	11,843	18,299	18,337	13,552	12,336
1987	18,694	18,712	15,655	13,545	12,568	18,694	18,712	13,545	12,568
1988	19,994	20,026	16,630	14,477	13,448	19,252	19,284	13,890	12,903
1989	21,224	21,209	17,706	15,307	14,241	19,556	19,615	14,005	13,029
1990	22,189	22,276	18,699	16,205	15,048	19,593	19,670	14,101	13,093
1991	22,656	22,719	19,234	16,766	15,444	19,263	19,321	14,003	12,899
1992	23,564	23,586	20,175	17,636	16,192	19,490	19,515	14,279	13,110
1993	24,559	24,576	20,810	18,153	16,951	19,879	19,901	14,341	13,391
1994	25,818	25,744	21,846	19,003	17,734	20,476	20,450	14,696	13,716

Source: U.S. Bureau of Economic Analysis, *National Income and Product Accounts of the United States: volume 2, 1959-88*, and *Survey of Current Business,* July 1994 and March 1995.

No. 707. National Income, by Type of Income: 1980 to 1994

[In billions of dollars]

INCOME	1980	1985	1988	1989	1990	1991	1992	1993	1994
National income	**2,198.2**	**3,268.4**	**4,002.6**	**4,249.5**	**4,491.0**	**4,608.2**	**4,829.5**	**5,131.4**	**5,458.4**
Compensation of employees	1,644.4	2,382.8	2,921.3	3,100.2	3,297.6	3,404.8	3,591.2	3,780.4	4,004.6
Wages and salaries	1,376.6	1,986.3	2,443.0	2,586.4	2,745.0	2,816.0	2,954.8	3,100.8	3,279.0
Government	261.4	373.7	449.0	478.5	516.0	545.4	567.3	583.8	602.8
Other	1,115.2	1,612.6	1,994.0	2,107.9	2,229.0	2,270.6	2,387.5	2,517.0	2,676.2
Supplements to wages and salaries	267.8	396.5	478.3	513.8	552.5	588.8	636.4	679.6	725.6
Employer contributions for social insurance	127.9	204.7	247.8	261.9	278.3	289.8	307.7	324.3	344.6
Other labor income	139.8	191.8	230.5	251.9	274.3	299.0	328.7	355.3	381.0
Proprietors' income [1][2]	171.8	259.9	324.3	347.3	363.3	376.2	418.7	441.6	473.7
Farm	11.5	21.5	30.9	40.2	41.9	36.7	44.4	37.3	39.5
Nonfarm	160.3	238.4	293.4	307.0	321.4	339.5	374.4	404.3	434.2
Rental income of persons [1]	13.2	18.7	4.3	−13.5	−14.2	−10.5	−5.5	24.1	27.7
Corporate profits [1][2]	177.7	280.8	365.0	362.8	380.6	390.3	405.1	485.8	542.7
Corporate profits [2]	197.8	225.3	320.3	325.4	354.7	370.9	389.4	456.2	505.0
Profits before tax	240.9	225.0	347.5	342.9	365.7	365.2	395.9	462.4	524.5
Profits tax liability	84.8	96.5	137.0	141.3	138.7	131.1	139.7	173.2	202.5
Profits after tax	156.1	128.5	210.5	201.6	227.1	234.1	256.2	289.2	322.0
Dividends	59.0	92.4	115.3	134.6	153.5	160.0	171.1	191.7	205.2
Undistributed profits	97.1	36.1	95.2	67.1	73.6	74.1	85.1	97.5	116.9
Inventory valuation adjustment	−43.0	0.2	−27.3	−17.5	−11.0	5.8	−6.4	−6.2	−19.5
Capital consumption adjustment	−20.2	55.5	44.7	37.4	25.9	19.4	15.7	29.5	37.7
Net interest	191.2	326.2	387.7	452.7	463.7	447.4	420.0	399.5	409.7
Addenda:									
Corporate profits after tax [1][2]	92.9	184.2	228.0	221.5	241.9	259.2	265.4	312.5	340.2
Net cash flow [1][2]	218.9	369.7	440.3	439.3	456.7	482.6	491.1	528.7	567.3
Undistributed profits [1][2]	33.9	91.9	112.6	86.9	88.5	99.2	94.3	120.9	135.1
Consumption of fixed capital	185.1	277.8	327.6	352.4	368.2	383.3	396.8	407.8	432.2
Less: Inventory valuation adjustment	−43.0	0.2	−27.3	−17.5	−11.0	5.8	−6.4	−6.2	−19.5
Equals: Net cash flow	262.0	369.5	467.5	456.9	467.7	476.8	497.5	534.9	586.8

[1] With capital consumption adjustment.　[2] With inventory valuation adjustment.

Source: U.S. Bureau of Economic Analysis, *National Income and Product Accounts of the United States: volume 2, 1959-88*, and *Survey of Current Business*, July 1994 and March 1995.

No. 708. National Income, by Sector: 1980 to 1993

[In billions of dollars]

SECTOR	1980	1985	1988	1989	1990	1991	1992	1993
National income	**2,198.2**	**3,268.4**	**4,002.6**	**4,249.5**	**4,491.0**	**4,608.2**	**4,829.5**	**5,131.4**
Domestic business	1,785.0	2,688.3	3,295.4	3,478.6	3,649.1	3,715.0	3,894.1	4,155.0
Corporate business	1,318.8	1,957.9	2,399.1	2,524.6	2,643.1	2,680.3	2,804.9	3,010.9
Compensation of employees	1,119.4	1,615.3	1,965.2	2,075.8	2,185.0	2,225.4	2,340.9	2,471.6
Corporate profits [1]	142.7	250.0	315.9	303.4	312.6	321.8	344.5	420.5
Net interest	56.7	92.6	118.0	145.5	145.6	133.1	119.5	118.8
Sole proprietorships and partnerships	310.9	470.6	584.9	631.0	658.5	670.9	715.6	747.9
Compensation of employees	104.9	139.1	177.8	185.9	202.0	207.7	220.1	233.8
Proprietors' income [1]	170.5	258.2	322.5	345.4	361.4	374.1	416.5	439.3
Net interest	35.4	73.3	84.6	99.7	95.1	89.1	78.9	74.9
Other private business [2]	122.1	210.3	251.0	259.3	278.5	291.2	296.5	317.7
Compensation of employees	7.8	13.8	18.7	20.1	21.7	22.1	23.3	24.7
Proprietors' income [1]	1.3	1.7	1.8	1.9	2.0	2.1	2.2	2.3
Rental income of persons [3]	13.2	18.7	4.3	−13.5	−14.2	−10.5	−5.5	24.1
Net interest	99.8	176.0	226.2	250.9	269.1	277.5	276.5	266.5
Government enterprises [4]	33.2	49.6	60.4	63.7	68.9	72.7	77.2	78.6
Households and institutions [5]	89.3	141.7	187.6	206.1	227.5	246.7	268.6	285.3
General government [4]	289.8	423.6	511.7	548.8	592.8	630.5	661.2	686.6
Rest of the world	34.1	14.8	7.9	16.0	21.7	16.0	5.6	4.5

[1] With inventory valuation and capital consumption adjustments.　[2] Consists of all business activities reported on the individual income tax return in Schedule E—Supplemental Income Schedule; tax-exempt cooperatives; and owner-occupied nonfarm housing and buildings and equipment owned and used by nonprofit institutions servicing individuals, which are considered to be business activities selling their current services to their owners.　[3] With capital consumption adjustment.　[4] Compensation of employees.　[5] Compensation of employees in private households; nonprofit social and athletic clubs; labor organizations; nonprofit schools and hospitals; religious, charitable, and welfare organizations; and all other nonprofit organizations serving individuals.

Source: U.S. Bureau of Economic Analysis, *National Income and Product Accounts of the United States, volume 2, 1959-88*, and *Survey of Current Business*, July 1994.

Income, Expenditures, and Wealth

No. 709. Personal Consumption Expenditures, by Type: 1980 to 1993

[In billions of dollars]

EXPENDITURE	CURRENT DOLLARS				CONSTANT (1987) DOLLARS			
	1980	1990	1992	1993	1980	1990	1992	1993
Total [1]	1,748.1	3,761.2	4,136.9	4,378.2	2,447.1	3,272.6	3,349.5	3,458.7
Food and tobacco [1]	362.6	648.2	678.0	700.3	487.5	555.8	545.9	553.6
Food purchased for off-premise consumption	241.7	400.2	410.5	422.2	307.5	345.0	336.8	340.4
Purchased meals and beverages [2]	93.4	193.1	204.2	215.2	132.3	168.8	167.8	173.5
Tobacco products	20.9	43.4	51.2	50.5	38.7	32.0	31.1	29.6
Clothing, accessories, and jewelry [1]	131.8	259.3	281.7	293.9	157.1	229.6	234.7	241.5
Shoes	17.4	31.4	32.7	33.0	19.9	28.1	27.5	27.6
Clothing	89.8	175.7	194.8	202.1	106.0	157.9	165.6	169.9
Jewelry and watches	15.0	81.3	33.5	36.2	16.8	25.4	24.9	26.3
Personal care	26.9	59.2	63.4	65.8	38.0	52.3	52.8	53.7
Housing [1]	255.2	547.5	601.3	629.0	399.4	474.6	485.2	492.6
Owner-occupied nonfarm dwellings-space rent	178.4	379.5	417.6	438.3	278.7	326.6	334.6	340.3
Tenant-occupied nonfarm dwellings-space rent	61.8	141.1	154.6	160.2	98.2	125.5	129.5	131.2
Household operation [1]	233.6	437.3	476.7	508.2	315.3	408.4	430.3	449.1
Furniture [3]	20.7	36.7	38.8	42.5	25.8	34.8	35.3	37.7
Semidurable house furnishings [4]	10.6	21.2	23.8	25.2	14.9	19.8	21.5	22.5
Cleaning and polishing preparations	22.9	51.8	54.1	56.1	31.2	45.5	46.2	47.8
Household utilities	81.1	136.7	148.9	159.3	111.7	124.3	128.0	132.6
Electricity	37.2	70.8	76.4	80.4	54.0	66.2	67.5	69.7
Gas	19.1	26.7	29.3	32.4	27.6	26.1	27.8	28.9
Water and other sanitary services	9.4	26.1	30.2	32.5	16.2	21.5	21.5	21.9
Fuel oil and coal	15.4	13.2	13.0	14.0	14.0	10.5	11.2	12.1
Telephone and telegraph	27.6	53.8	64.3	68.2	41.1	54.9	65.5	68.7
Medical care [1]	207.2	597.8	705.1	760.5	346.5	483.5	510.4	523.0
Drug preparations and sundries [5]	21.8	60.6	66.3	69.0	38.8	49.3	47.5	47.8
Physicians	42.8	133.8	156.4	165.6	72.9	108.5	112.6	113.0
Dentists	13.7	31.6	35.9	38.6	22.4	26.1	25.9	26.4
Hospitals and nursing homes [6]	98.7	268.4	322.8	346.8	164.0	217.1	232.5	238.1
Health insurance	12.8	36.6	39.8	46.2	23.0	25.2	26.2	26.2
Medical care [7]	7.6	30.8	34.2	37.1	17.7	19.9	21.3	21.6
Personal business [1]	101.6	296.0	354.0	373.3	175.5	249.7	262.1	271.1
Expense of handling life insurance [8]	23.4	57.5	69.4	72.6	37.8	49.8	54.8	54.5
Legal services	13.6	49.2	53.8	56.1	26.6	41.5	41.1	41.1
Funeral and burial expenses	4.6	8.5	9.6	10.4	8.8	7.4	7.5	7.8
Transportation	235.7	453.9	466.3	504.2	274.8	403.1	390.3	410.5
User-operated transportation [1]	214.9	414.0	426.9	461.9	247.4	369.1	357.5	377.0
New autos	46.4	96.6	87.4	93.4	60.2	91.5	77.9	81.3
Net purchases of used autos	10.8	33.1	38.6	45.9	20.8	33.0	34.9	38.0
Tires, tubes, accessories, etc.	14.9	22.9	24.4	26.4	15.3	21.8	22.7	24.9
Repair, greasing, washing, parking, storage, rental, and leasing	33.7	82.6	89.5	98.4	48.3	72.6	73.2	77.5
Gasoline and oil	86.7	108.4	105.5	105.6	72.0	86.4	85.6	86.5
Purchased local transportation	4.8	8.9	9.1	9.3	7.8	7.9	7.2	7.2
Mass transit systems	2.9	5.7	5.8	5.9	5.3	5.1	4.7	4.6
Taxicab	1.9	3.2	3.3	3.4	2.5	2.8	2.6	2.6
Purchased intercity transportation [1]	16.1	30.9	30.3	33.0	19.7	26.2	25.6	26.2
Railway (commutation)	0.3	0.7	0.7	0.7	0.5	0.6	0.6	0.5
Bus	1.4	1.4	1.5	1.3	2.4	1.3	1.2	1.1
Airline	13.5	26.4	26.0	28.5	15.2	22.4	22.0	22.7
Recreation [1][9]	117.6	285.7	318.2	339.9	149.1	261.9	283.5	304.1
Magazines, newspapers, and sheet music	12.0	23.8	25.8	26.8	18.4	20.9	20.3	20.4
Nondurable toys and sport supplies	14.6	32.1	35.2	37.4	17.4	28.7	30.6	32.2
Radio and television receivers, records, and musical instruments	19.9	50.4	58.8	65.7	17.6	54.1	70.4	83.7
Education and research	33.6	86.2	98.9	105.5	51.7	73.6	76.7	78.6
Religious and welfare activities	38.6	101.6	116.9	123.0	51.3	90.1	97.6	100.6

[1] Includes other expenditures not shown separately. [2] Consists of purchases (including tips) of meals and beverages from retail, service, and amusement establishments; hotels; dining and buffet cars; schools; school fraternities; institutions; clubs; and industrial lunch rooms. Includes meals and beverages consumed both on and off-premise. [3] Includes mattresses and bedsprings. [4] Consists largely of textile house furnishings including piece goods allocated to house furnishing use. Also includes lamp shades, brooms, and brushes. [5] Excludes drug preparations and related products dispensed by physicians, hospitals, and other medical services. [6] Consists of (1) current expenditures (including consumption of fixed capital) of nonprofit hospitals and nursing homes and (2) payments by patients to proprietary and government hospitals and nursing homes. [7] Consists of (1) premiums, less benefits and dividends, for health, hospitalization and accidental death and dismemberment insurance provided by commercial insurance carriers and (2) administrative expenses (including consumption of fixed capital) of Blue Cross and Blue Shield plans and of other independent prepaid and self-insured health plans. [8] Consists of (1) operating expenses of life insurance carriers and private noninsured pension plans and (2) premiums, less benefits and dividends of fraternal benefit societies. Excludes expenses allocated by commercial carriers to accident and health insurance. [9] For additional details, see table 403.

Source: U.S. Bureau of Economic Analysis, *National Income and Product Accounts, volume 2, 1959-88,* and *Survey of Current Business,* July 1994.

No. 710. Personal Income and Its Disposition: 1980 to 1994

[**In billions of dollars, except percent.** For definition of personal income, see text, section 14]

ITEM	1980	1985	1989	1990	1991	1992	1993	1994
Personal income	**2,265.4**	**3,379.8**	**4,380.3**	**4,673.8**	**4,860.3**	**5,154.3**	**5,375.1**	**5,701.7**
Wage and salary disbursements	1,376.6	1,986.5	2,586.4	2,745.0	2,816.1	2,974.8	3,080.8	3,279.0
Commodity-producing industries [1]	471.9	612.2	724.2	745.7	738.4	757.6	773.8	818.2
Manufacturing	355.7	461.3	542.2	555.6	557.4	578.3	588.4	617.5
Distributive industries [2]	336.4	475.9	607.0	635.1	648.0	682.3	701.9	748.5
Service industries [3]	306.9	524.5	776.8	848.3	884.2	967.6	1,021.4	1,109.5
Government	261.4	373.9	478.5	515.9	545.5	567.3	583.8	602.8
Other labor income	139.8	191.8	251.9	274.3	299.0	328.7	355.3	381.0
Proprietors' income [4]	171.8	259.9	347.3	363.3	376.2	418.7	441.6	473.7
Rental income of persons [5]	13.2	18.7	–13.5	–14.2	–10.5	–5.5	24.1	27.7
Personal dividend income	57.1	87.9	126.5	144.4	150.5	161.0	181.3	194.3
Personal interest income	274.0	498.1	668.2	698.2	695.1	665.2	637.9	664.0
Transfer payments to persons	321.5	485.9	625.0	687.6	770.1	860.2	915.4	963.4
Old-age, survivors, disability, and health insurance benefits	154.2	253.4	325.1	352.0	382.3	414.0	444.4	473.5
Gov't unemployment insurance benefits	16.1	15.7	14.4	19.0	26.7	38.9	33.9	23.3
Veterans benefits	15.0	16.7	17.3	17.8	18.3	19.3	20.1	20.1
Gov't employees retirement benefits	43.0	66.6	87.5	94.5	102.4	109.9	118.7	126.9
Other transfer payments	93.2	133.5	180.6	204.3	240.3	278.1	298.3	319.6
Less: Personal contributions for social insurance	*88.6*	*149.1*	*211.4*	*224.9*	*236.2*	*248.7*	*261.3*	*281.4*
Less: Personal tax and nontax payments	*312.4*	*436.8*	*593.3*	*623.3*	*623.7*	*648.6*	*686.4*	*742.1*
Equals: Disposable personal income	**1,952.9**	**2,943.0**	**3,787.0**	**4,050.5**	**4,236.6**	**4,505.8**	**4,688.7**	**4,959.6**
Less: Personal outlays	*1,799.1*	*2,753.7*	*3,634.9*	*3,880.6*	*4,025.0*	*4,257.8*	*4,496.2*	*4,756.5*
Personal consumption expenditures	1,748.1	2,667.4	3,523.1	3,761.2	3,902.4	4,136.9	4,378.2	4,628.4
Interest paid by persons	49.4	83.6	103.0	109.3	112.2	111.4	108.2	117.6
Personal transfer payments to foreigners (net)	1.6	2.7	8.9	10.1	10.4	9.5	9.9	10.5
Equals: Personal saving	**153.8**	**189.3**	**152.1**	**170.0**	**211.6**	**247.9**	**192.6**	**203.1**
Percent of disposable personal income	7.9	6.4	4.0	4.2	5.0	5.5	4.1	4.1
Disposable personal income, 1987 dollars	2,733.6	3,162.1	3,464.9	3,524.5	3,538.5	3,648.1	3,704.1	3,835.7
PERCENT DISTRIBUTION								
Personal income	**100**	**100**	**100**	**100**	**100**	**100**	**100**	**100**
Wage and salary disbursements	61	59	59	59	58	58	57	58
Other labor income	6	6	6	6	6	6	7	7
Proprietors' income [4]	8	8	8	8	8	8	8	8
Rental income of persons [5]	1	1	(-Z)	(-Z)	(-Z)	(-Z)	(Z)	(Z)
Personal dividend income	3	3	3	3	3	3	3	3
Personal interest income	12	15	15	15	14	13	12	12
Transfer payments	14	14	14	15	16	17	17	17
Less: Personal contributions for social insurance	4	4	5	5	5	5	5	5

Z Less than 0.5 percent. [1] Comprises agriculture, forestry, fishing, mining, construction, and manufacturing. [2] Comprises transportation, communication, public utilities, and trade. [3] Comprises finance, insurance, real estate, services, and rest of world. [4] With capital consumption and inventory valuation adjustments. [5] With capital consumption adjustment.

Source: U.S. Bureau of Economic Analysis, *National Income and Product Accounts of the United States, volume 2, 1959-88,* and *Survey of Current Business,* July 1992, August 1993, July 1994, and March 1995.

No. 711. Gross Saving and Investment: 1980 to 1994

[In billions of dollars]

ITEM	1980	1985	1988	1989	1990	1991	1992	1993	1994
Gross saving	**465.4**	**610.4**	**704.0**	**741.8**	**722.7**	**751.4**	**722.9**	**787.5**	**920.6**
Gross private saving	499.6	735.7	802.3	819.4	861.1	937.3	980.8	1,002.5	1,053.5
Personal saving	153.8	189.3	155.7	152.1	170.0	211.6	247.9	192.6	203.1
Undistributed corporate profits [1]	33.9	91.9	112.6	86.9	88.5	99.2	94.3	120.9	135.1
Undistributed profits	97.1	36.1	95.2	67.1	73.6	74.1	85.1	97.5	116.9
Inventory valuation adjustment	–43.0	0.2	–27.3	–17.5	–11.0	5.8	–6.4	–6.2	–19.5
Capital consumption adjustment	–20.2	55.5	44.7	37.4	25.9	19.4	15.7	29.5	37.7
Corporate consumption of fixed capital	185.1	277.8	327.6	352.4	368.2	383.3	396.8	407.8	432.2
Noncorporate consumption of fixed capital	126.8	176.7	206.4	228.0	234.5	243.1	261.8	261.2	283.1
Wage accruals less disbursements							–20.0	20.0	
Government surplus or deficit (-) [2]	–35.3	–125.3	–98.3	–77.5	–138.4	–185.9	–257.8	–215.0	–132.9
Federal	–60.1	–181.4	–136.6	–122.3	–163.5	–202.9	–282.7	–241.4	–159.1
State and local	24.8	56.1	38.4	44.8	25.1	17.0	24.8	26.3	26.2
Capital grants received by the U.S. (net)	1.2								
Gross investment	**479.1**	**596.5**	**675.6**	**742.9**	**730.4**	**752.9**	**731.7**	**789.8**	**889.7**
Gross private domestic investment	467.6	714.5	793.6	832.3	808.9	744.8	788.3	882.0	1,032.9
Net foreign investment	11.5	–118.1	–118.0	–89.3	–78.5	8.1	–56.6	–92.3	–143.2
Statistical discrepancy	**13.6**	**–13.9**	**–28.4**	**1.1**	**7.8**	**1.5**	**8.8**	**2.3**	**–30.9**

- Represents or rounds to zero. [1] With inventory valuation and capital consumption adjustments. [2] National income and product accounts basis.

Source: U.S. Bureau of Economic Analysis, *National Income and Product Accounts of the United States, volume 2, 1959-88,* and *Survey of Current Business,* July 1992, August 1993, July 1994, and March 1995.

No. 712. Personal Income, by State: 1980 to 1994

[In billions of dollars, except percent. 1994 preliminary. Represents a measure of income received from all sources during the calendar year by residents of each State. Data exclude Federal employees overseas and U.S. residents employed by private U.S. firms on temporary foreign assignment. Totals may differ from those in tables 705, 706, and 710. For definition of average annual percent change, see Guide to Tabular Presentation]

REGION, DIVISION, AND STATE	CURRENT DOLLARS				CONSTANT (1987) DOLLARS				Average annual percent change		Percent distribution	
	1980	1990	1993	1994	1980	1990	1993	1994	1980-1994	1993-1994	1980	1994
United States . . .	2,259.0	4,655.4	5,362.0	5,677.8	3,163.9	4,051.7	4,235.4	4,391.2	2.4	3.7	100.0	100.0
Northeast	526.2	1,103.6	1,237.9	1,299.0	736.9	960.5	977.8	1,004.7	2.2	2.7	23.3	22.9
New England	130.9	290.0	320.0	336.0	183.3	252.4	252.8	259.9	2.5	2.8	5.8	5.9
Maine	9.3	21.0	23.3	24.4	13.0	18.3	18.4	18.9	2.7	2.6	0.4	0.4
New Hampshire	9.1	22.5	25.1	26.6	12.7	19.6	19.9	20.6	3.5	3.8	0.4	0.5
Vermont	4.4	9.8	11.2	11.7	6.1	8.6	8.8	9.1	2.8	2.7	0.2	0.2
Massachusetts	61.2	133.9	146.9	154.8	85.7	116.5	116.0	119.7	2.4	3.2	2.7	2.7
Rhode Island	9.1	19.1	21.2	22.2	12.7	16.6	16.8	17.2	2.2	2.3	0.4	0.4
Connecticut	37.9	83.6	92.3	96.3	53.0	72.8	72.9	74.5	2.5	2.2	1.7	1.7
Middle Atlantic	395.3	813.6	917.9	963.0	553.6	708.1	725.0	744.8	2.1	2.7	17.5	17.0
New York	191.6	401.8	450.6	472.4	268.3	349.7	355.9	365.3	2.2	2.6	8.5	8.3
New Jersey	85.9	187.2	211.2	221.6	120.3	162.9	166.8	171.4	2.6	2.7	3.8	3.9
Pennsylvania	117.8	224.6	256.0	269.1	165.0	195.5	202.2	208.1	1.7	2.9	5.2	4.7
Midwest	581.6	1,079.8	1,240.3	1,329.7	814.6	939.8	979.7	1,028.4	1.7	5.0	25.7	23.4
East North Central . . .	420.3	769.9	885.7	948.0	588.6	670.1	699.6	733.1	1.6	4.8	18.6	16.7
Ohio	105.2	190.6	217.9	232.3	147.3	165.9	172.1	179.7	1.4	4.4	4.7	4.1
Indiana	50.6	93.4	109.6	117.2	70.9	81.3	86.6	90.7	1.8	4.7	2.2	2.1
Illinois	124.4	230.8	263.6	279.5	174.3	200.9	208.2	216.2	1.6	3.8	5.5	4.9
Michigan	94.0	169.8	194.7	212.1	131.6	147.8	153.8	164.0	1.6	6.6	4.2	3.7
Wisconsin	46.1	85.3	99.9	106.8	64.5	74.2	78.9	82.6	1.8	4.7	2.0	1.9
West North Central . .	161.4	309.9	354.6	381.8	226.0	269.7	280.1	295.3	1.9	5.4	7.1	6.7
Minnesota	40.8	82.4	94.9	102.5	57.1	71.7	75.0	79.3	2.4	5.8	1.8	1.8
Iowa	27.3	46.4	51.6	57.3	38.2	40.4	40.7	44.3	1.1	8.9	1.2	1.0
Missouri	45.6	89.2	102.4	109.3	63.8	77.7	80.9	84.6	2.0	4.6	2.0	1.9
North Dakota	5.0	9.8	10.9	11.8	7.0	8.5	8.6	9.2	1.9	6.6	0.2	0.2
South Dakota	5.3	10.9	12.8	14.1	7.5	9.5	10.1	10.9	2.8	8.0	0.2	0.2
Nebraska	14.1	27.5	31.7	33.2	19.8	23.9	25.1	25.7	1.9	2.6	0.6	0.6
Kansas	23.3	43.8	50.3	53.4	32.6	38.1	39.7	41.3	1.7	3.8	1.0	0.9
South	678.4	1,448.4	1,706.4	1,814.9	950.2	1,260.6	1,347.9	1,403.6	2.8	4.1	30.0	32.0
South Atlantic	341.9	797.7	927.8	987.3	478.8	694.2	732.8	763.6	3.4	4.2	15.1	17.4
Delaware	6.2	13.2	15.3	16.1	8.6	11.5	12.1	12.5	2.7	3.4	0.3	0.3
Maryland	45.7	106.0	118.5	124.8	64.1	92.2	93.6	96.5	3.0	3.1	2.0	2.2
District of Columbia .	8.0	14.9	17.1	17.8	11.2	12.9	13.5	13.7	1.5	1.8	0.4	0.3
Virginia	52.9	121.4	140.2	148.0	74.1	105.7	110.7	114.5	3.2	3.4	2.3	2.6
West Virginia	15.6	25.0	29.4	31.4	21.8	21.8	23.2	24.2	0.8	4.4	0.7	0.6
North Carolina	47.2	108.3	129.8	139.1	66.1	94.3	102.5	107.5	3.5	4.9	2.1	2.4
South Carolina . . .	23.7	52.9	61.2	64.8	33.2	46.0	48.3	50.1	3.0	3.7	1.0	1.1
Georgia	45.8	111.4	132.9	142.9	64.2	97.0	104.9	110.5	4.0	5.3	2.0	2.5
Florida	96.8	244.6	283.4	302.4	135.5	212.9	223.9	233.9	4.0	4.5	4.3	5.3
East South Central . . .	113.6	225.0	268.5	287.2	159.1	195.8	212.1	222.1	2.4	4.7	5.0	5.1
Kentucky	29.5	54.5	64.1	68.1	41.3	47.4	50.6	52.7	1.8	4.1	1.3	1.2
Tennessee	36.9	77.8	93.9	100.8	51.6	67.7	74.2	78.0	3.0	5.1	1.6	1.8
Alabama	29.9	60.3	71.6	76.0	41.8	52.5	56.6	58.8	2.5	3.9	1.3	1.3
Mississippi	17.4	32.4	38.9	42.3	24.3	28.2	30.7	32.7	2.1	6.3	0.8	0.7
West South Central . .	223.0	425.8	510.1	540.4	312.3	370.5	403.0	417.9	2.1	3.7	9.9	9.5
Arkansas	16.9	32.5	38.8	41.4	23.6	28.2	30.6	32.1	2.2	4.6	0.7	0.7
Louisiana	36.7	60.2	71.3	76.2	51.3	52.4	56.3	58.9	1.0	4.6	1.6	1.3
Oklahoma	28.3	47.6	55.0	57.8	39.7	41.4	43.5	44.7	0.9	2.8	1.3	1.0
Texas	141.1	285.5	345.0	364.9	197.6	248.5	272.5	282.2	2.6	3.6	6.2	6.4
West	472.8	1,023.6	1,177.3	1,234.1	662.2	890.9	930.0	954.5	2.6	2.6	20.9	21.7
Mountain	108.3	227.5	279.2	300.6	151.6	198.0	220.5	232.4	3.1	5.4	4.8	5.3
Montana	6.9	11.8	14.6	15.3	9.6	10.3	11.5	11.8	1.5	2.5	0.3	0.3
Idaho	8.0	15.5	19.3	20.7	11.2	13.5	15.2	16.0	2.6	5.0	0.4	0.4
Wyoming	5.4	7.7	9.3	9.7	7.5	6.7	7.3	7.5	-	2.8	0.2	0.2
Colorado	30.9	62.2	76.6	81.6	43.3	54.1	60.5	63.1	2.7	4.3	1.4	1.4
New Mexico	10.7	21.6	26.4	28.3	15.0	18.8	20.9	21.9	2.8	4.9	0.5	0.5
Arizona	25.4	59.8	71.3	77.4	35.5	52.1	56.4	59.9	3.8	6.3	1.1	1.4
Utah	11.7	24.3	30.0	32.5	16.4	21.2	23.7	25.1	3.1	6.1	0.5	0.6
Nevada	9.4	24.7	31.6	35.0	13.1	21.5	25.0	27.1	5.3	8.3	0.4	0.6
Pacific	364.5	796.1	898.2	933.6	510.5	692.8	709.5	722.0	2.5	1.8	16.1	16.4
Washington	44.5	94.4	114.5	120.8	62.4	82.2	90.4	93.4	2.9	3.3	2.0	2.1
Oregon	26.1	49.2	59.0	63.0	36.5	42.8	46.6	48.7	2.1	4.6	1.2	1.1
California	278.0	617.7	683.5	707.0	389.3	537.6	539.9	546.8	2.5	1.3	12.3	12.5
Alaska	5.5	11.5	13.8	14.4	7.8	10.1	10.9	11.2	2.6	2.4	0.2	0.3
Hawaii	10.4	23.3	27.4	28.4	14.6	20.2	21.6	21.9	2.9	1.3	0.5	0.5

- Represents zero.

Source: U.S. Bureau of Economic Analysis, *Survey of Current Business,* August issues; and unpublished data.

No. 713. Personal Income Per Capita, by State: 1980 to 1994

[1994 data preliminary. See headnote, table 712]

REGION, DIVISION, AND STATE	CURRENT DOLLARS					CONSTANT (1987) DOLLARS					Income rank	
	1980	1990	1992	1993	1994	1980	1990	1992	1993	1994	1980	1994
United States ...	9,940	18,666	20,137	20,800	21,809	13,922	16,245	16,305	16,430	16,867	(X)	(X)
Northeast..........	10,699	21,699	23,417	24,141	25,275	14,984	18,886	18,961	19,069	19,548	(X)	(X)
New England	10,582	21,934	23,398	24,179	25,319	14,821	19,090	18,946	19,099	19,582	(X)	(X)
Maine	8,218	17,039	18,137	18,780	19,663	11,510	14,829	14,686	14,834	15,207	38	34
New Hampshire....	9,803	20,227	21,840	22,357	23,434	13,730	17,604	17,684	17,660	18,124	23	10
Vermont.........	8,546	17,442	18,809	19,437	20,224	11,969	15,180	15,230	15,353	15,641	35	31
Massachusetts	10,659	22,247	23,588	24,410	25,616	14,929	19,362	19,100	19,281	19,811	12	4
Rhode Island	9,576	19,032	20,206	21,244	22,251	13,412	16,564	16,361	16,780	17,209	26	19
Connecticut	12,170	25,427	27,338	28,151	29,402	17,045	22,130	22,136	22,236	22,739	2	1
Middle Atlantic	10,738	21,617	23,424	24,128	25,260	15,039	18,814	18,967	19,058	19,536	(X)	(X)
New York........	10,906	22,321	24,128	24,824	25,999	15,275	19,426	19,537	19,608	20,108	7	3
New Jersey	11,648	24,182	26,111	26,876	28,038	16,314	21,046	21,143	21,229	21,684	4	2
Pennsylvania	9,923	18,883	20,610	21,281	22,324	13,898	16,434	16,688	16,810	17,265	17	18
Midwest...........	9,872	18,067	19,626	20,320	21,659	13,826	15,724	15,892	16,051	16,751	(X)	(X)
East North Central...	10,077	18,297	19,834	20,619	21,952	14,113	15,924	16,060	16,287	16,978	(X)	(X)
Ohio	9,738	17,548	18,945	19,696	20,928	13,639	15,272	15,340	15,558	16,186	25	22
Indiana	9,215	16,816	18,415	19,213	20,378	12,906	14,635	14,911	15,176	15,760	31	28
Illinois	10,875	20,159	21,784	22,560	23,784	15,231	17,545	17,639	17,820	18,394	8	9
Michigan	10,154	18,237	19,707	20,584	22,333	14,221	15,872	15,957	16,259	17,272	15	16
Wisconsin	9,772	17,398	19,103	19,806	21,019	13,686	15,142	15,468	15,645	16,256	24	21
West North Central ..	9,374	17,520	19,133	19,610	20,965	13,129	15,248	15,492	15,490	16,214	(X)	(X)
Minnesota	9,982	18,779	20,485	20,979	22,453	13,980	16,344	16,587	16,571	17,365	16	15
Iowa	9,346	16,684	18,148	18,275	20,265	13,090	14,520	14,695	14,435	15,673	27	29
Missouri........	9,256	17,409	18,949	19,557	20,717	12,964	15,151	15,343	15,448	16,022	30	24
North Dakota	7,641	15,321	17,098	17,072	18,546	10,702	13,334	13,845	13,485	14,343	47	38
South Dakota	7,701	15,630	17,280	17,879	19,577	10,786	13,603	13,992	14,122	15,141	45	35
Nebraska	8,988	17,379	19,189	19,672	20,488	12,588	15,125	15,538	15,539	15,845	32	25
Kansas	9,829	17,642	19,210	19,849	20,896	13,766	15,354	15,555	15,679	16,161	22	23
South	8,958	16,895	18,343	19,084	20,011	12,546	14,704	14,853	15,074	15,477	(X)	(X)
South Atlantic......	9,204	18,230	19,465	20,284	21,279	12,891	15,866	15,761	16,022	16,457	(X)	(X)
Delaware	10,356	19,719	21,208	21,852	22,828	14,504	17,162	17,172	17,261	17,655	14	11
Maryland	10,824	22,090	23,186	23,908	24,933	15,160	19,225	18,774	18,885	19,283	9	5
District of Columbia .	12,508	24,648	27,953	29,500	31,136	17,518	21,452	22,634	23,302	24,080	(X)	(X)
Virginia	9,857	19,537	20,934	21,653	22,594	13,805	17,003	16,951	17,103	17,474	19	13
West Virginia	7,972	13,967	15,554	16,169	17,208	11,165	12,156	12,594	12,772	13,309	43	46
North Carolina....	8,000	16,275	17,831	18,670	19,669	11,204	14,164	14,438	14,747	15,212	42	33
South Carolina ...	7,558	15,106	16,200	16,861	17,695	10,585	13,147	13,117	13,318	13,685	48	44
Georgia	8,353	17,123	18,495	19,249	20,251	11,699	14,903	14,976	15,205	15,662	37	30
Florida.........	9,835	18,788	19,664	20,650	21,677	13,775	16,352	15,922	16,311	16,765	21	20
East South Central ..	7,730	14,792	16,447	17,095	18,075	10,826	12,874	13,317	13,503	13,979	(X)	(X)
Kentucky	8,051	14,747	16,418	16,889	17,807	11,276	12,835	13,294	13,340	13,772	40	42
Tennessee	8,010	15,905	17,647	18,439	19,482	11,218	13,842	14,289	14,565	15,067	41	36
Alabama	7,656	14,903	16,518	17,129	18,010	10,723	12,970	13,375	13,530	13,929	46	40
Mississippi	6,868	12,571	14,070	14,745	15,838	9,619	10,941	11,393	11,647	12,249	50	50
West South Central ..	9,329	15,908	17,575	18,238	19,024	13,066	13,845	14,231	14,406	14,713	(X)	(X)
Arkansas	7,371	13,784	15,572	15,995	16,898	10,324	11,997	12,609	12,634	13,069	49	49
Louisiana	8,672	14,281	15,876	16,612	17,651	12,146	12,429	12,855	13,122	13,651	34	45
Oklahoma	9,308	15,119	16,460	17,026	17,744	13,036	13,158	13,328	13,449	13,723	28	43
Texas	9,840	16,749	18,460	19,145	19,857	13,782	14,577	14,947	15,122	15,357	20	32
West	10,889	19,296	20,526	21,005	21,705	15,251	16,794	16,620	16,592	16,787	(X)	(X)
Mountain	9,455	16,589	18,100	18,891	19,755	13,242	14,438	14,656	14,922	15,278	(X)	(X)
Montana	8,728	14,741	16,361	17,376	17,865	12,224	12,829	13,248	13,725	13,817	33	41
Idaho	8,433	15,301	16,679	17,512	18,231	11,811	13,317	13,505	13,833	14,100	36	39
Wyoming	11,356	16,902	18,896	19,719	20,436	15,905	14,710	15,300	15,576	15,805	6	26
Colorado	10,616	18,814	20,585	21,498	22,333	14,868	16,374	16,668	16,981	17,272	13	17
New Mexico	8,147	14,213	15,538	16,346	17,106	11,410	12,370	12,581	12,912	13,230	39	47
Arizona	9,272	16,265	17,468	18,085	19,001	12,986	14,156	14,144	14,285	14,695	29	37
Utah	7,942	14,060	15,501	16,136	17,043	11,123	12,237	12,551	12,746	13,181	44	48
Nevada	11,559	20,254	21,972	22,894	24,023	16,189	17,628	17,791	18,084	18,579	5	7
Pacific	11,403	20,240	21,381	21,762	22,418	15,971	17,615	17,313	17,190	17,338	(X)	(X)
Washington	10,716	19,265	21,333	21,774	22,610	15,008	16,767	17,274	17,199	17,486	11	12
Oregon	9,863	17,199	18,667	19,437	20,419	13,814	14,969	15,115	15,353	15,792	18	27
California	11,681	20,654	21,593	21,895	22,493	16,360	17,976	17,484	17,295	17,396	3	14
Alaska.........	13,692	20,881	22,258	23,070	23,788	19,176	18,173	18,023	18,223	18,398	1	8
Hawaii.........	10,774	20,906	22,476	23,504	24,057	15,090	18,195	18,199	18,566	18,606	10	6

X Not applicable.

Source: U.S. Bureau of Economic Analysis, *Survey of Current Business*, August issues; and unpublished data.

Income, Expenditures, and Wealth

No. 714. Disposable Personal Income Per Capita, by State: 1980 to 1994

[1994 data preliminary]

REGION, DIVISION, AND STATE	CURRENT DOLLARS							CONSTANT (1987) DOLLARS			
	1980	1990	1993	1994	Income rank			1980	1990	1993	1994
					1980	1990	1994				
United States....	8,569	16,173	18,142	18,963	(X)	(X)	(X)	12,001	14,076	14,330	14,666
Northeast	9,140	18,538	20,717	21,611	(X)	(X)	(X)	12,801	16,134	16,364	16,714
New England	9,055	18,827	20,710	21,625	(X)	(X)	(X)	12,682	16,386	16,359	16,725
Maine	7,283	15,062	16,780	17,559	38	27	32	10,200	13,109	13,254	13,580
New Hampshire	8,611	18,117	19,907	20,780	15	7	8	12,060	15,768	15,724	16,071
Vermont	7,485	15,223	17,082	17,763	35	24	28	10,483	13,249	13,493	13,738
Massachusetts.....	9,052	18,925	20,733	21,649	13	3	4	12,678	16,471	16,377	16,743
Rhode Island	8,306	16,568	18,697	19,544	26	14	13	11,633	14,419	14,769	15,115
Connecticut	10,321	21,605	23,681	24,732	2	1	1	14,455	18,803	18,705	19,128
Middle Atlantic	9,169	18,436	20,719	21,606	(X)	(X)	(X)	12,842	16,045	16,366	16,710
New York........	9,249	18,733	21,140	22,047	10	4	3	12,954	16,304	16,698	17,051
New Jersey	9,974	20,852	23,062	23,929	5	2	2	13,969	18,148	18,216	18,507
Pennsylvania	8,549	16,416	18,554	19,418	17	17	16	11,973	14,287	14,656	15,018
Midwest	8,494	15,676	17,718	18,816	(X)	(X)	(X)	11,897	13,643	13,995	14,552
East North Central ...	8,672	15,863	17,992	19,079	(X)	(X)	(X)	12,146	13,806	14,212	14,756
Ohio............	8,405	15,248	17,180	18,195	24	24	23	11,772	13,271	13,570	14,072
Indiana	7,988	14,637	16,862	17,801	30	32	27	11,188	12,739	13,319	13,767
Illinois...........	9,276	17,412	19,613	20,587	9	11	10	12,992	15,154	15,492	15,922
Michigan	8,779	15,836	18,060	19,517	14	20	14	12,296	13,782	14,265	15,094
Wisconsin	8,401	15,046	17,166	18,151	25	28	24	11,766	13,095	13,559	14,038
West North Central ...	8,065	15,231	17,066	18,194	(X)	(X)	(X)	11,296	13,256	13,480	14,071
Minnesota	8,505	15,986	17,746	18,919	18	19	20	11,912	13,913	14,017	14,632
Iowa............	7,987	14,517	15,744	17,529	31	33	33	11,186	12,634	12,436	13,557
Missouri	8,030	15,248	17,282	18,226	28	23	22	11,246	13,271	13,651	14,096
North Dakota	6,600	13,837	15,294	16,664	48	38	38	9,244	12,043	12,081	12,888
South Dakota	6,890	14,121	16,205	17,751	45	37	29	9,650	12,290	12,800	13,729
Nebraska........	7,769	15,340	17,463	18,089	32	21	26	10,881	13,351	13,794	13,990
Kansas	8,419	15,261	17,314	18,140	23	22	25	11,791	13,282	13,676	14,029
South	7,768	14,827	16,830	17,593	(X)	(X)	(X)	10,879	12,904	13,294	13,607
South Atlantic	7,956	15,859	17,735	18,543	(X)	(X)	(X)	11,143	13,802	14,009	14,341
Delaware........	8,502	16,544	18,673	19,381	19	15	17	11,908	14,399	14,750	14,989
Maryland.........	9,097	18,701	20,507	21,293	12	5	5	12,741	16,276	16,198	16,468
District of Columbia..	10,542	20,316	24,521	25,832	(X)	(X)	(X)	14,765	17,681	19,369	19,978
Virginia	8,443	16,881	18,796	19,501	21	13	15	11,825	14,692	14,847	15,082
West Virginia	6,944	12,481	14,563	15,445	43	47	46	9,725	10,862	11,503	11,945
North Carolina	6,939	14,236	16,291	17,116	44	36	36	9,718	12,390	12,868	13,237
South Carolina	6,627	13,331	14,986	15,709	47	40	42	9,282	11,602	11,837	12,149
Georgia..........	7,309	14,893	16,855	17,677	37	29	30	10,237	12,962	13,314	13,671
Florida	8,595	16,538	18,220	19,076	16	16	18	12,038	14,393	14,392	14,753
East South Central ...	6,834	13,203	15,230	16,049	(X)	(X)	(X)	9,571	11,491	12,030	12,412
Kentucky	7,066	12,897	14,715	15,446	41	43	45	9,896	11,225	11,623	11,946
Tennessee........	7,117	14,317	16,509	17,387	40	35	35	9,968	12,460	13,040	13,447
Alabama.........	6,741	13,231	15,284	16,022	46	42	40	9,441	11,515	12,073	12,391
Mississippi........	6,122	11,484	13,415	14,362	50	50	50	8,574	9,995	10,596	11,108
West South Central ...	8,050	14,063	16,249	16,906	(X)	(X)	(X)	11,275	12,239	12,835	13,075
Arkansas........	6,502	12,240	14,241	14,995	49	48	48	9,106	10,653	11,249	11,597
Louisiana........	7,523	12,730	14,865	15,754	34	45	41	10,536	11,079	11,742	12,184
Oklahoma	8,017	13,293	14,966	15,575	29	41	44	11,228	11,569	11,821	12,046
Texas	8,459	14,787	17,080	17,668	20	30	31	11,847	12,869	13,491	13,664
West..............	9,422	16,642	18,340	18,913	(X)	(X)	(X)	13,196	14,484	14,487	14,627
Mountain	8,247	14,522	16,566	17,250	(X)	(X)	(X)	11,550	12,639	13,085	13,341
Montana	7,565	12,832	15,196	15,615	33	44	43	10,595	11,168	12,003	12,077
Idaho	7,452	13,834	15,745	16,293	36	39	39	10,437	12,040	12,437	12,601
Wyoming.........	9,705	15,111	17,675	18,271	6	26	21	13,592	13,151	13,961	14,131
Colorado	9,130	16,228	18,430	19,022	11	18	19	12,787	14,124	14,558	14,712
New Mexico.......	7,246	12,658	14,654	15,308	39	46	47	10,148	11,017	11,575	11,839
Arizona.........	8,147	14,340	15,993	16,748	27	34	37	11,410	12,480	12,633	12,953
Utah............	6,987	12,154	14,202	14,938	42	49	49	9,786	10,578	11,218	11,553
Nevada..........	10,058	17,589	19,918	20,815	4	10	7	14,087	15,308	15,733	16,098
Pacific............	9,843	17,381	18,976	19,520	(X)	(X)	(X)	13,786	15,127	14,989	15,097
Washington	9,317	16,888	19,206	19,886	7	12	11	13,049	14,698	15,171	15,380
Oregon	8,425	14,709	16,707	17,419	22	31	34	11,800	12,802	13,197	13,472
California........	10,084	17,688	19,083	19,593	3	9	12	14,123	15,394	15,073	15,153
Alaska..........	11,639	18,348	20,548	21,175	1	6	6	16,301	15,969	16,231	16,377
Hawaii...........	9,286	17,693	20,166	20,587	8	8	9	13,006	15,399	15,929	15,922

X Not applicable.

Source: U.S. Bureau of Economic Analysis, *Survey of Current Business*, August issues; and unpublished data.

No. 715. Personal Income, by Metropolitan Area: 1990 to 1993

[As defined **June 30, 1994.** CMSA=Consolidated Metropolitan Statistical Area; NECMA=New England County Metropolitan Area; MSA=Metropolitan Statistical Area. See Appendix II]

METROPOLITAN AREA RANKED BY 1990 POPULATION	PERSONAL INCOME				PER CAPITA PERSONAL INCOME			
	1990 (mil. dol.)	1992 (mil. dol.)	1993 (mil. dol.)	Annual percent change, 1992-93	1990 (dol.)	1992 (dol.)	1993 (dol.)	Percent of national average, 1993
United States [1]	**4,655,420**	**5,135,452**	**5,361,968**	**4.4**	**18,666**	**20,137**	**20,800**	**100.0**
New York-Northern New Jersey-Long Island, NY-NJ-CT-PA CMSA.	491,234	534,717	552,496	3.3	25,230	27,334	28,122	135.2
Los Angeles-Riverside-Orange County, CA CMSA	301,614	320,326	325,310	1.6	20,659	21,266	21,388	102.8
Chicago-Gary-Kenosha, IL-IN-WI CMSA	178,641	196,557	205,307	4.5	21,635	23,400	24,251	116.6
Washington-Baltimore, DC-MD-VA-WV CMSA	159,226	173,378	181,313	4.6	23,594	25,084	25,956	124.8
San Francisco-Oakland-San Jose, CA CMSA .	155,119	170,661	176,570	3.5	24,767	26,623	27,293	131.2
Philadelphia-Wilmington-Atlantic City, PA-NJ-DE-MD CMSA	126,512	138,266	142,974	3.4	21,444	23,325	24,064	115.7
Boston-Brockton-Nashua, MA-NH NECMA . . .	128,494	136,412	141,698	3.9	22,589	24,043	24,861	119.5
Detroit-Ann Arbor-Flint, MI CMSA	104,758	113,208	118,551	4.7	20,174	21,621	22,600	108.7
Dallas-Fort Worth, TX CMSA.	80,619	91,805	97,146	5.8	19,870	21,824	22,702	109.1
Houston-Galveston-Brazoria, TX CMSA.	73,025	84,801	88,727	4.6	19,456	21,467	22,028	105.9
Miami-Fort Lauderdale, FL CMSA	62,388	63,966	70,793	10.7	19,464	19,284	21,108	101.5
Seattle-Tacoma-Bremerton, WA CMSA	63,334	73,589	76,128	3.4	21,157	23,494	23,873	114.8
Atlanta, GA MSA.	60,882	68,383	73,206	7.1	20,446	21,812	22,675	109.0
Cleveland-Akron, OH CMSA	55,519	59,933	62,495	4.3	19,398	20,760	21,595	103.8
Minneapolis-St. Paul, MN-WI MSA	54,579	61,042	64,093	5.0	21,418	23,327	24,145	116.1
San Diego, CA MSA	49,587	53,672	54,719	2.0	19,729	20,629	20,950	100.7
St. Louis, MO-IL MSA	50,212	54,820	56,936	3.9	20,116	21,788	22,521	108.3
Pittsburgh, PA MSA	45,437	50,675	52,531	3.7	18,970	21,073	21,825	104.9
Phoenix-Mesa, AZ MSA	40,237	44,523	47,490	6.7	17,919	19,087	19,853	95.4
Tampa-St. Petersburg-Clearwater, FL MSA . .	37,291	40,542	42,742	5.4	17,966	19,153	20,004	96.2
Denver-Boulder-Greeley, CO CMSA	40,913	46,992	50,359	7.2	20,595	22,509	23,463	112.8
Cincinnati-Hamilton, OH-KY-IN CMSA.	33,873	37,486	39,025	4.1	18,588	20,133	20,744	99.7
Portland-Salem, OR-WA CMSA	33,612	38,407	40,832	6.3	18,610	20,222	21,001	101.0
Milwaukee-Racine, WI CMSA	31,851	35,331	36,935	4.5	19,784	21,690	22,600	108.7
Kansas City, MO-KS MSA.	30,369	33,729	35,291	4.6	19,135	20,894	21,639	104.0
Sacramento-Yolo, CA CMSA	28,820	32,122	33,052	2.9	19,269	20,578	20,969	100.8
Norfolk-Virginia Beach-Newport News, VA-NC MSA	24,258	27,003	27,984	3.6	16,719	18,053	18,485	88.9
Indianapolis, IN MSA	26,638	30,048	31,775	5.7	19,227	21,095	22,019	105.9
Columbus, OH MSA	24,664	27,750	29,195	5.2	18,264	19,947	20,717	99.6
San Antonio, TX MSA	20,691	23,720	25,172	6.1	15,586	17,226	17,889	86.0
New Orleans, LA MSA	21,038	23,447	24,623	5.0	16,386	18,053	18,882	90.8
Orlando, FL MSA	21,645	24,151	25,641	6.2	17,468	18,530	19,224	92.4
Buffalo-Niagara Falls, NY MSA	21,277	23,143	23,863	3.1	17,877	19,401	20,013	96.2
Charlotte-Gastonia-Rock Hill, NC-SC MSA. . .	21,727	24,102	25,726	6.7	18,593	19,913	20,856	100.3
Hartford, CT NECMA	27,085	28,507	29,275	2.7	24,091	25,417	26,147	125.7
Salt Lake City-Ogden, UT MSA	16,429	18,934	20,181	6.6	15,259	16,797	17,481	84.0
Rochester, NY MSA.	21,245	22,837	23,657	3.6	19,954	21,101	21,719	104.4
Greensboro-Winston-Salem-High Point, NC MSA	19,457	21,446	22,682	5.8	18,467	19,892	20,772	99.9
Memphis, TN-AR-MS MSA	18,001	20,125	21,247	5.6	17,824	19,508	20,386	98.0
Nashville, TN MSA	18,127	21,100	22,597	7.1	18,334	20,649	21,634	104.0
Oklahoma City, OK MSA	15,701	17,477	18,250	4.4	16,357	17,805	18,328	88.1
Dayton-Springfield, OH MSA	16,900	18,523	19,267	4.0	17,751	19,324	20,093	96.6
Louisville, KY-IN MSA	17,294	19,592	20,543	4.9	18,195	20,284	21,092	101.4
Grand Rapids-Muskegon-Holland, MI MSA . .	16,308	18,446	19,545	6.0	17,317	19,126	20,062	96.5
Providence-Warwick, RI NECMA	17,372	18,447	19,369	5.0	18,941	20,156	21,189	101.9
Jacksonville, FL MSA.	16,443	18,210	19,346	6.2	18,015	19,172	20,102	96.6
West Palm Beach-Boca Raton, FL MSA	25,319	28,517	30,031	5.3	29,103	31,372	32,230	155.0
Richmond-Petersburg, VA MSA	18,535	20,084	21,074	4.9	21,313	22,457	23,262	111.8

[1] Includes other areas not listed separately.

Source: U.S. Bureau of Economic Analysis, *Survey of Current Business,* April issues; and unpublished data.

No. 716. Percent Distribution of Shares of National Income: 1980 to 1994

INCOME	1980	1985	1988	1989	1990	1991	1992	1993	1994
National income	100.0	100.0	100.0	100.0	100.0	100.0	100.0	100.0	100.0
Compensation of employees	74.8	72.9	73.0	73.0	73.4	73.9	74.4	73.7	73.4
Wages and salaries	62.6	60.8	61.0	60.9	61.1	63.1	61.2	60.4	60.1
Supplements to wages, salaries . .	12.2	12.1	11.9	12.1	12.3	12.8	13.2	13.2	13.3
Proprietors' income [1]	7.8	8.0	8.1	8.2	8.1	8.2	8.7	8.6	8.7
Farm	0.5	0.7	0.8	0.9	0.9	0.8	0.9	0.7	0.7
Nonfarm	7.3	7.3	7.3	7.2	7.2	7.4	7.8	7.9	8.0
Rental income of persons [2]	0.6	0.6	0.1	−0.3	−0.3	−0.2	−0.1	0.5	0.5
Corporate profits [1]	8.1	8.6	9.1	8.5	8.5	8.5	8.4	9.5	9.9
Profits before tax	11.0	6.9	8.7	8.1	8.1	7.9	8.2	9.0	9.6
Profits after tax	7.1	3.9	5.3	4.7	5.1	5.1	5.3	5.6	5.9
Inventory valuation adjustment . . .	−2.0	-	−0.7	−0.4	−0.2	0.1	−0.1	−0.1	−0.4
Capital consumption adjustment . .	−0.9	1.7	1.1	0.9	0.6	0.4	0.3	0.6	0.7
Net interest	8.7	10.0	9.7	10.7	10.3	9.7	8.7	7.8	7.5

- Represents or rounds to zero.   [1] With inventory valuation and capital consumption adjustments.   [2] With capital consumption adjustment.

Source: U.S. Bureau of Economic Analysis, *National Income and Product Accounts of the United States, volume 2, 1959-88,* and *Survey of Current Business,* July 1994, and March 1995.

No. 717. Flow of Funds Accounts—Composition of Individuals' Savings: 1980 to 1994

[**In billions of dollars.** Combined statement for households, farm business, and nonfarm noncorporate business. Minus sign (-) indicates decrease. See *Historical Statistics, Colonial Times to 1970,* series F 566-594, for similar but not exactly comparable data]

COMPOSITION OF SAVINGS	1980	1985	1988	1989	1990	1991	1992	1993	1994
Increase in financial assets	**329.6**	**631.9**	**508.5**	**594.9**	**502.3**	**442.2**	**532.1**	**524.1**	**582.1**
Checkable deposits and currency	9.3	29.0	27.2	−1.2	5.4	63.0	131.1	81.7	14.3
Time and savings deposits	121.6	117.2	136.2	79.6	38.5	−117.4	−112.1	−91.1	14.6
Money market fund shares	23.5	2.3	15.9	76.8	28.6	8.7	−41.8	−10.7	20.8
Securities	13.6	109.2	103.4	23.2	191.4	56.6	257.4	133.3	357.1
U.S. savings bonds	−7.3	5.3	8.5	8.2	8.5	11.9	19.1	14.7	8.0
Other U.S. Treasury securities	24.7	−3.2	60.9	12.5	106.8	−54.8	33.1	31.8	145.2
U.S. Government agency securities	7.7	13.1	63.4	46.3	12.7	7.9	49.2	−39.8	207.1
Tax-exempt securities	2.4	72.2	39.7	55.6	17.7	34.9	−34.8	−15.8	−29.6
Corporate and foreign bonds	−14.5	−0.8	−21.8	−17.2	38.0	10.3	−4.8	26.2	58.5
Open-market paper	2.9	58.4	31.3	−9.0	−8.3	−34.8	5.2	−37.7	−19.7
Mutual fund shares	2.1	75.5	14.1	36.0	37.7	115.1	146.5	187.0	76.6
Other corporate equities	−4.3	−111.2	−92.6	−109.1	−21.7	−33.8	43.8	−33.1	−89.0
Private life insurance reserves	9.7	10.4	24.9	28.4	25.3	25.6	27.7	35.7	20.4
Private insured pension reserves	22.3	63.4	85.0	77.8	84.4	81.1	75.2	102.0	80.7
Private noninsured pension reserves	59.0	136.2	−28.4	142.4	−10.9	192.5	75.0	96.9	−83.2
Government insurance and pension reserves .	35.8	72.5	76.0	101.3	92.0	86.8	99.0	109.9	116.1
Investment in bank personal trusts	−1.0	10.2	2.2	19.6	29.7	16.1	−7.1	1.6	4.6
Miscellaneous financial assets	35.7	81.5	66.1	46.9	18.0	29.1	27.7	64.9	36.6
Gross investment in tangible assets	**406.4**	**651.9**	**779.1**	**822.0**	**807.4**	**758.4**	**825.9**	**905.2**	**1,023.9**
Owner-occupied homes	101.8	161.5	206.8	206.8	191.5	173.1	205.5	230.2	260.9
Other fixed assets [1]	98.4	130.8	145.2	152.8	144.5	129.4	122.2	140.7	163.0
Consumer durables	212.5	353.0	437.1	459.4	468.2	456.6	492.7	538.0	591.4
Inventories [1]	−6.3	6.7	−10.0	3.1	3.3	−0.7	5.5	−3.7	8.7
Capital consumption allowances	**314.3**	**435.5**	**532.4**	**580.0**	**614.2**	**649.3**	**693.8**	**712.5**	**776.6**
Owner-occupied homes	50.3	67.7	80.0	92.1	93.2	97.4	111.6	107.1	113.3
Other fixed assets [1]	77.8	110.6	127.9	137.5	142.9	147.5	152.2	156.2	172.1
Consumer durables	186.2	257.1	324.5	350.4	378.1	404.4	430.1	449.1	491.2
Net investment in tangible assets	**92.0**	**216.4**	**246.7**	**242.0**	**193.2**	**109.2**	**132.1**	**192.7**	**247.4**
Owner-occupied homes	51.5	93.7	126.7	114.6	98.3	75.7	94.0	123.1	147.6
Other fixed assets [1]	20.6	20.2	17.3	15.3	1.6	−18.0	−30.0	−15.5	−9.0
Consumer durables	26.3	95.8	112.6	109.0	90.0	52.2	62.6	88.9	100.2
Inventories [1]	−6.3	6.7	−10.0	3.1	3.3	−0.7	5.5	−3.7	8.7
Net increase in liabilities	**200.2**	**444.3**	**363.1**	**360.0**	**252.2**	**159.7**	**191.8**	**309.4**	**396.5**
Mortgage debt on nonfarm homes	94.1	171.7	234.3	223.8	185.0	163.3	179.0	183.3	191.3
Other mortgage debt [1]	50.9	98.1	44.1	43.8	18.3	−2.1	−27.6	−12.4	3.6
Consumer credit	4.8	82.3	50.1	45.8	16.0	−15.0	5.5	62.3	117.5
Security credit	7.3	18.9	1.7	−1.0	−3.7	16.3	−1.8	22.7	−2.5
Policy loans	6.7	−0.1	−0.1	3.2	4.1	4.8	5.7	5.7	6.4
Other liabilities [1]	36.4	73.6	33.0	44.4	32.5	−7.5	30.9	47.9	80.2
Personal saving	**221.5**	**404.0**	**392.1**	**476.9**	**443.3**	**391.7**	**472.4**	**407.4**	**433.0**
Less: Government insurance and pension reserve	35.8	72.5	76.0	101.3	92.0	86.8	99.0	109.9	116.1
Net investment in consumer durables	26.3	95.8	112.6	109.0	90.0	52.2	62.6	88.9	100.2
Net saving by farm corporations	0.5	0.9	1.4	1.8	2.2	1.6	0.8	0.4	0.3
Equals: Personal saving, flow of funds basis.	**158.9**	**234.8**	**202.1**	**264.8**	**259.0**	**251.1**	**310.1**	**208.2**	**216.4**
Personal saving, NIPA basis	153.9	189.3	155.7	152.1	170.0	211.5	247.9	192.5	203.7
Difference [2]	5.1	45.6	46.4	112.7	89.0	39.6	62.2	15.7	12.7

[1] Includes corporate farms.   [2] Personal saving on national income account basis measures personal saving as income less taxes and consumption; flow-of-funds basis measures the same concept from acquisition of assets less borrowing.

Source: Board of Governors of the Federal Reserve System, *Flow of Funds Accounts,* quarterly.

No. 718. Average Annual Expenditures of All Consumer Units, by Race and Age of Householder: 1993

[**In dollars.** Based on Consumer Expenditure Survey. Data are averages for the noninstitutional population. Expenditures reported here are out-of-pocket]

ITEM	All consumer units	White and other	Black	AGE Under 25 yrs.	25 to 34 yrs.	35 to 44 yrs.	45 to 54 yrs.	55 to 64 yrs.	65 yrs. and over
Expenditures, total	30,692	31,967	20,684	17,468	28,594	37,429	41,020	32,973	21,322
Food	4,399	4,517	3,399	2,631	4,170	5,360	5,485	4,638	3,245
Food at home	2,735	2,772	2,421	1,339	2,519	3,336	3,212	2,897	2,344
Cereals and bakery products	434	444	348	206	392	544	522	434	375
Cereals and cereal products	160	161	151	86	153	206	200	143	127
Bakery products	274	283	196	119	239	338	322	292	248
Meats, poultry, fish, and eggs	734	720	862	337	636	892	876	844	629
Beef	234	234	238	110	209	287	273	278	190
Pork	154	148	200	66	130	185	178	180	142
Other meats	98	97	101	41	84	116	120	120	81
Poultry	131	127	169	61	114	166	163	135	110
Fish and seafood	87	84	118	42	70	104	109	99	79
Eggs	30	29	35	16	29	34	34	32	28
Dairy products	295	307	193	141	283	368	333	304	251
Fresh milk and cream	128	132	93	65	125	164	139	127	107
Other dairy products	167	175	100	77	158	204	194	177	144
Fruits and vegetables	444	450	387	186	387	509	518	470	451
Fresh fruits	137	140	108	46	110	158	165	151	146
Fresh vegetables	132	135	107	52	113	150	159	143	134
Processed fruits	96	97	86	49	93	109	105	92	96
Processed vegetables	79	78	86	40	71	92	89	84	75
Other food at home	827	850	631	469	821	1,023	962	845	639
Nonalcoholic beverages	225	230	181	126	203	288	281	228	169
Food away from home	1,664	1,746	978	1,293	1,651	2,024	2,273	1,741	901
Alcoholic beverages	268	288	98	304	307	324	293	250	148
Housing	9,636	9,928	7,341	5,297	9,683	12,005	12,027	9,683	6,908
Shelter	5,415	5,585	4,106	3,297	5,794	7,002	6,744	5,017	3,440
Owned dwellings	3,331	3,559	1,585	424	2,719	4,804	4,803	3,583	2,197
Mortgage interest and charges	1,878	2,001	936	300	1,900	3,301	2,818	1,633	417
Property taxes	825	886	359	73	471	912	1,204	1,115	883
Maintenance, repair, insurance, other	628	672	290	50	348	592	782	835	896
Rented dwellings	1,714	1,625	2,395	2,678	2,857	1,817	1,297	929	966
Other lodging	370	402	126	196	219	380	643	505	278
Utilities, fuels, and public services	2,112	2,121	2,048	1,082	1,886	2,351	2,580	2,425	1,920
Natural gas	279	274	318	110	223	295	329	342	302
Electricity	836	845	769	389	727	947	1,046	963	754
Fuel oil and other fuels	99	106	46	13	69	97	118	118	133
Telephone	658	650	719	512	687	734	782	707	484
Water and other public services	241	247	196	58	180	277	304	295	247
Household operations	469	496	256	156	514	671	408	377	433
Personal services	228	238	148	113	402	408	106	85	100
Other household expenses	241	258	109	43	112	263	302	292	333
Housekeeping supplies	410	427	263	161	356	458	537	424	396
Household furnishings and equipment	1,230	1,299	667	600	1,133	1,524	1,758	1,439	718
Household textiles	102	107	66	21	67	126	160	106	94
Furniture	317	325	257	224	368	402	426	302	144
Floor coverings	87	94	34	14	69	91	140	163	40
Major appliances	143	150	88	73	112	171	174	191	118
Small appliances, misc. housewares	87	93	40	43	71	114	103	107	68
Miscellaneous household equipment	493	530	182	225	445	620	755	570	254
Apparel and services	1,676	1,681	1,638	1,198	1,752	2,071	2,200	1,695	937
Men and boys	426	437	334	274	457	574	551	410	203
Women and girls	658	658	662	332	566	828	883	749	456
Children under 2 years old	79	77	103	104	166	78	61	47	20
Footwear	249	244	292	248	257	289	327	236	142
Other apparel products and services	264	266	247	241	307	302	377	253	116
Transportation	5,453	5,759	3,092	3,948	5,099	6,651	7,479	6,340	3,081
Vehicle purchases (net outlay)	2,319	2,493	981	2,139	2,146	2,847	3,104	2,833	1,137
Cars and trucks, new	1,216	1,328	349	1,077	1,023	1,427	1,752	1,665	577
Cars and trucks, used	1,079	1,137	631	1,053	1,069	1,388	1,329	1,151	560
Gasoline and motor oil	977	1,017	666	652	960	1,199	1,299	1,069	589
Other vehicle expenses	1,843	1,932	1,154	1,008	1,711	2,272	2,622	2,032	1,129
Vehicle finance charges	244	254	172	154	282	331	345	256	72
Maintenance and repair	620	649	396	368	560	781	833	685	404
Vehicle insurance	678	711	422	364	598	767	964	773	500
Rent, lease, licenses, other	301	319	164	123	270	393	480	318	153
Public transportation	314	317	291	148	282	333	453	406	225
Health care [1]	1,776	1,890	894	349	1,128	1,673	1,817	2,176	2,733
Entertainment [2]	1,626	1,734	772	910	1,511	2,094	2,490	1,527	918
Personal care products and services	385	393	310	228	358	455	478	384	323
Reading	166	177	83	72	137	191	212	197	150
Education	455	475	305	907	270	438	1,114	209	107
Tobacco products and smoking supplies	268	277	198	202	280	324	345	316	141
Miscellaneous	715	751	434	266	646	898	893	921	503
Cash contributions	961	1,029	436	95	465	811	1,473	1,301	1,292
Personal insurance and pensions	2,908	3,067	1,685	1,061	2,787	4,133	4,716	3,336	837
Life and other personal insurance	399	414	284	56	229	431	717	579	302
Pensions and Social Security	2,509	2,653	1,401	1,006	2,558	3,702	3,999	2,757	535
Personal taxes	2,978	3,173	1,413	873	2,701	4,127	5,138	3,318	1,110

[1] For additional health care expenditures, see table 168. [2] For additional recreation expenditures, see table 404.
Source: U.S. Bureau of Labor Statistics, *Consumer Expenditures in 1993;* and unpublished data.

Income, Expenditures, and Wealth

No. 719. Average Annual Expenditures of All Consumer Units, by Region and Size of Unit: 1993

[See headnote, page 465]

ITEM	REGION				SIZE OF CONSUMER UNIT				
	North-east	Mid-west	South	West	One person	Two per-sons	Three per-sons	Four per-sons	Five or more
Expenditures, total	**31,634**	**28,884**	**29,247**	**34,348**	**17,999**	**31,603**	**35,416**	**42,397**	**39,981**
Food	4,712	4,178	4,200	4,686	2,341	4,361	5,199	6,274	6,533
Food at home	2,984	2,559	2,564	2,985	1,308	2,634	3,247	3,986	4,604
Cereals and bakery products	489	410	398	470	207	412	500	650	754
Cereals and cereal products	168	148	156	175	70	146	183	244	314
Bakery products	321	262	242	295	137	266	317	406	440
Meats, poultry, fish, and eggs	853	675	718	716	311	707	922	1,070	1,274
Beef	253	222	235	228	90	233	296	349	393
Pork	153	156	164	135	61	147	189	217	300
Other meats	118	96	85	100	44	90	124	145	168
Poultry	179	112	118	129	59	123	166	200	216
Fish and seafood	119	63	84	91	42	86	114	120	137
Eggs	31	25	31	34	15	28	35	40	60
Dairy products	331	283	265	325	141	275	341	444	524
Fresh milk and cream	128	129	121	138	58	109	150	194	262
Other dairy products	203	154	144	187	83	166	191	250	262
Fruits and vegetables	502	395	407	506	233	446	509	606	713
Fresh fruits	154	125	120	164	74	140	151	184	224
Fresh vegetables	151	110	122	156	69	143	147	174	201
Processed fruits	113	88	83	109	53	87	120	138	152
Processed vegetables	84	72	82	77	38	77	91	110	137
Other food at home	809	796	776	969	416	793	975	1,216	1,338
Nonalcoholic beverages	223	227	219	233	110	209	274	333	372
Food away from home	1,728	1,619	1,636	1,700	1,033	1,727	1,952	2,287	1,928
Alcoholic beverages	314	250	215	334	244	289	280	291	222
Housing	10,759	8,686	8,762	11,123	6,300	9,554	10,955	13,107	12,359
Shelter	6,367	4,563	4,532	6,967	3,909	5,210	6,045	7,167	6,832
Owned dwellings	3,815	2,936	2,843	4,141	1,614	3,344	3,959	5,195	4,518
Mortgage interest and charges	1,842	1,498	1,648	2,756	691	1,562	2,468	3,430	3,071
Property taxes	1,315	852	570	728	467	984	872	1,069	935
Maintenance, repair, insurance, other	657	585	624	657	456	798	619	696	511
Rented dwellings	2,140	1,270	1,366	2,405	2,081	1,409	1,660	1,549	1,931
Other lodging	413	357	323	422	214	458	425	423	383
Utilities, fuels, and public services	2,207	2,073	2,215	1,896	1,355	2,194	2,389	2,675	2,784
Natural gas	329	437	172	215	191	284	307	333	397
Electricity	774	719	1,041	702	490	893	965	1,085	1,088
Fuel oil and other fuels	236	90	58	41	66	115	102	124	102
Telephone	677	616	673	664	472	656	740	803	854
Water and other public services	191	212	272	274	135	245	276	331	343
Household operations	505	370	485	526	247	362	604	798	743
Personal services	265	200	221	234	53	82	387	536	478
Other household expenses	241	169	263	292	194	280	217	262	266
Housekeeping supplies	398	406	398	447	215	433	484	593	520
Household furnishings and equipment	1,282	1,274	1,132	1,287	573	1,354	1,432	1,873	1,480
Household textiles	103	94	99	117	43	112	119	182	103
Furniture	302	333	326	298	147	339	370	482	415
Floor coverings	88	149	48	79	21	106	137	120	93
Major appliances	134	152	139	147	61	169	178	171	200
Small appliances, misc. housewares	82	73	86	112	47	104	107	116	78
Miscellaneous household equipment	573	473	434	535	254	525	521	802	590
Apparel and services	1,834	1,662	1,558	1,732	901	1,676	1,967	2,432	2,370
Men and boys	486	438	369	445	228	419	495	628	617
Women and girls	712	692	601	658	357	695	747	957	844
Children under 2 years old	79	73	76	93	18	43	125	159	183
Footwear	279	239	240	243	119	215	318	378	435
Other apparel products and services	278	220	272	293	179	304	282	309	292
Transportation	4,991	5,430	5,384	6,057	2,727	5,720	6,696	7,671	7,265
Vehicle purchases (net outlay)	1,832	2,504	2,407	2,435	993	2,432	2,990	3,325	3,258
Cars and trucks, new	1,132	1,261	1,258	1,173	534	1,433	1,477	1,716	1,354
Cars and trucks, used	693	1,206	1,128	1,229	429	987	1,494	1,566	1,875
Gasoline and motor oil	843	950	1,023	1,067	505	1,003	1,173	1,397	1,329
Other vehicle expenses	1,868	1,718	1,733	2,152	993	1,927	2,227	2,587	2,334
Vehicle finance charges	175	271	265	247	109	236	324	382	331
Maintenance and repair	595	560	597	758	338	636	773	849	808
Vehicle insurance	763	594	635	765	389	711	818	919	826
Rent, lease, licenses, other	335	294	236	382	157	343	311	436	370
Public transportation	449	257	221	404	236	358	307	362	345
Health care [1]	1,732	1,642	1,928	1,732	1,204	2,192	1,804	1,932	1,863
Entertainment [2]	1,569	1,408	1,655	1,897	854	1,645	1,620	2,818	2,062
Personal care products and services	379	372	367	435	209	408	455	526	505
Reading	193	164	143	181	123	195	169	191	161
Education	533	446	412	460	292	326	593	739	692
Tobacco products and smoking supplies	267	299	278	217	176	260	337	348	335
Miscellaneous	645	637	718	874	488	752	805	887	861
Cash contributions	861	1,011	906	1,088	763	1,210	985	870	846
Personal insurance and pensions	2,845	2,697	2,723	3,533	1,378	3,016	3,549	4,312	3,909
Life and other personal insurance	356	323	468	420	170	434	444	557	650
Pensions and Social Security	2,489	2,374	2,256	3,113	1,208	2,582	3,105	3,755	3,258
Personal taxes	**3,215**	**2,781**	**2,539**	**3,634**	**1,679**	**3,261**	**3,381**	**4,336**	**3,326**

[1] For additional health care expenditures, see table 168.   [2] For additional recreation expenditures, see table 404.

Source: U.S. Bureau of Labor Statistics, *Consumer Expenditures in 1993;* and unpublished data.

No. 720. Average Annual Expenditures of All Consumer Units, by Type of Household
Unit: 1993

[See headnote, page 465]

ITEM	Husband and wife only	HUSBAND AND WIFE WITH CHILDREN				One parent, at least one child under 18	Single person and other consumer units
		Total	Oldest child under 6	Oldest child 6 to 17	Oldest child 18 and over		
Expenditures, total	**34,566**	**43,644**	**38,569**	**43,691**	**47,418**	**20,937**	**20,573**
Food	4,632	6,258	5,001	6,614	6,593	4,043	2,838
Food at home	2,780	3,896	3,317	4,081	4,021	2,926	1,689
Cereals and bakery products	442	635	500	688	644	464	261
Cereals and cereal products	156	239	190	265	227	195	92
Bakery products	287	396	310	423	417	268	168
Meats, poultry, fish, and eggs	747	1,012	809	1,034	1,145	817	453
Beef	256	326	274	346	330	251	135
Pork	155	205	146	207	252	177	97
Other meats	93	138	104	136	173	115	60
Poultry	129	186	159	187	208	141	84
Fish and seafood	85	117	97	116	135	102	57
Eggs	29	41	30	42	47	31	20
Dairy products	295	438	383	469	423	276	179
Fresh milk and cream	115	193	176	204	186	141	77
Other dairy products	180	245	208	265	237	135	101
Fruits and vegetables	480	607	519	632	633	417	282
Fresh fruits	154	185	150	193	200	120	87
Fresh vegetables	152	172	137	180	186	123	86
Processed fruits	92	141	138	144	137	90	61
Processed vegetables	82	109	93	114	110	84	48
Other food at home	815	1,204	1,105	1,258	1,175	952	515
Nonalcoholic beverages	215	330	253	350	355	226	143
Food away from home	1,852	2,362	1,685	2,533	2,572	1,117	1,149
Alcoholic beverages	288	297	301	266	358	124	265
Housing	10,181	13,292	13,350	13,898	12,099	7,656	6,967
Shelter	5,467	7,346	7,449	7,733	6,545	4,344	4,183
Owned dwellings	3,879	5,466	5,319	5,752	5,044	1,628	1,792
Mortgage interest and charges	1,780	3,615	3,842	3,898	2,916	1,000	819
Property taxes	1,150	1,140	888	1,151	1,312	372	503
Maintenance, repair, insurance, other	949	710	589	704	815	255	470
Rented dwellings	1,028	1,366	1,886	1,468	780	2,622	2,170
Other lodging	560	514	244	513	721	95	221
Utilities, fuels, and public services	2,292	2,678	2,278	2,669	2,998	1,855	1,599
Natural gas	295	343	297	338	388	262	223
Electricity	947	1,094	884	1,115	1,213	751	592
Fuel oil and other fuels	127	119	88	122	136	49	75
Telephone	647	780	728	753	868	639	551
Water and other public services	275	343	281	340	394	154	159
Household operations	357	807	1,374	837	321	543	274
Personal services	27	527	1,190	517	44	422	88
Other household expenses	329	280	185	320	277	122	187
Housekeeping supplies	482	594	533	598	641	267	254
Household furnishings and equipment	1,584	1,867	1,716	2,061	1,593	647	657
Household textiles	129	158	126	191	117	58	51
Furniture	385	482	457	530	411	226	178
Floor coverings	142	150	185	154	110	22	24
Major appliances	194	189	186	187	197	95	82
Small appliances, misc. housewares	117	125	128	116	137	47	53
Miscellaneous household equipment	617	763	635	883	622	198	269
Apparel and services	1,767	2,424	2,134	2,522	2,471	1,434	1,098
Men and boys	451	638	483	705	631	296	282
Women and girls	744	932	650	1,010	1,023	637	409
Children under 2 years old	46	158	455	87	47	102	28
Footwear	212	376	303	403	384	214	170
Other apparel products and services	313	320	243	316	386	185	209
Transportation	6,363	8,169	6,690	7,249	11,013	2,728	3,332
Vehicle purchases (net outlay)	2,831	3,621	3,095	2,988	5,200	863	1,247
Cars and trucks, new	1,723	1,870	1,493	1,562	2,730	184	625
Cars and trucks, used	1,092	1,712	1,574	1,389	2,420	675	598
Gasoline and motor oil	1,049	1,433	1,128	1,380	1,764	681	639
Other vehicle expenses	2,078	2,759	2,151	2,570	3,581	1,008	1,191
Vehicle finance charges	252	399	362	374	474	138	139
Maintenance and repair	686	932	733	894	1,161	388	401
Vehicle insurance	749	977	758	834	1,409	361	468
Rent, lease, licenses, other	391	451	298	468	536	122	182
Public transportation	405	355	316	311	469	176	255
Health care [1]	2,648	2,102	1,710	2,098	2,408	885	1,219
Entertainment [2]	1,805	2,526	2,877	2,595	2,083	1,038	1,009
Personal care products and services	460	533	433	558	568	275	245
Reading	213	202	156	210	223	90	131
Education	321	815	166	769	1,393	259	317
Tobacco products and smoking supplies	236	329	258	300	438	230	236
Miscellaneous	768	916	856	917	967	513	554
Cash contributions	1,542	1,107	759	992	1,585	260	687
Personal insurance and pensions	3,342	4,673	3,877	4,704	5,220	1,404	1,674
Life and other personal insurance	508	650	416	582	953	211	196
Pensions and Social Security	2,834	4,024	3,461	4,122	4,268	1,193	1,478
Personal taxes	**3,671**	**4,500**	**3,272**	**4,556**	**5,393**	**1,086**	**1,887**

[1] For additional health care expenditures, see table 168. [2] For additional recreation expenditures, see table 404.
Source: U.S. Bureau of Labor Statistics, *Consumer Expenditures in 1993;* and unpublished data.

No. 721. Average Annual Expenditures of All Consumer Units, by Type of Expenditure: 1987 to 1993

[In dollars. See headnote, table 718]

ITEM	1987	1988	1989	1990	1991	1992	1993
Number of consumer units (1,000).	94,150	94,862	95,818	96,968	97,918	100,019	100,049
Total expenditures	**24,414**	**25,892**	**27,810**	**28,381**	**29,614**	**29,846**	**30,692**
Food.	3,664	3,748	4,152	4,296	4,271	4,273	4,399
Food at home	2,099	2,136	2,390	2,485	2,651	2,643	2,735
Cereal and bakery products	299	312	359	368	404	411	434
Meats, poultry, fish, and eggs	572	551	611	668	709	687	734
Dairy products	274	274	304	295	294	302	295
Fruits and vegetables	356	373	408	408	429	428	444
Other food at home.	598	625	708	746	815	814	828
Food away from home	1,565	1,612	1,762	1,811	1,620	1,631	1,664
Alcoholic beverages.	289	269	284	293	297	301	268
Housing.	7,569	7,918	8,434	8,703	9,252	9,477	9,636
Shelter.	4,154	4,332	4,660	4,836	5,191	5,411	5,415
Fuels, utilities, public services	1,671	1,747	1,835	1,890	1,990	1,984	2,112
Household operations, furnishings.	1,403	1,477	1,546	1,571	1,648	1,649	1,699
Housekeeping supplies	341	361	394	406	424	433	410
Apparel and services	1,446	1,489	1,582	1,618	1,735	1,710	1,676
Transportation	4,600	5,093	5,187	5,120	5,151	5,228	5,453
Vehicle purchase	2,022	2,361	2,291	2,129	2,111	2,189	2,319
Gasoline and motor oil	888	932	985	1,047	995	973	977
Other transportation	1,690	1,800	1,911	1,944	2,045	2,066	2,157
Health care	1,135	1,298	1,407	1,480	1,554	1,634	1,776
Tobacco products, smoking supplies.	232	242	261	274	276	275	268
Life and other personal insurance	294	314	346	345	356	353	399
Pensions and Social Security	1,881	1,935	2,125	2,248	2,431	2,397	2,509
Other expenditures	3,305	3,586	4,030	4,003	4,291	4,198	4,308

No. 722. Average Annual Expenditures of All Consumer Units, by Metropolitan Area: 1993

[In dollars. Metropolitan areas defined June 30, 1983, CMSA=Consolidated Metropolitan Statistical Area; MSA=Metropolitan Statistical Area; PMSA=Primary Metropolitan Statistical Area. See text, section 1, and Appendix II. See headnote, table 718]

METROPOLITAN AREA	Total expenditures [1]	Food	HOUSING		Apparel and services	TRANSPORTATION			Health care
			Total [1]	Shelter		Total [1]	Vehicle purchases	Gasoline and motor oil	
Anchorage, AK MSA	39,804	5,192	13,104	8,239	1,905	6,536	2,394	957	1,904
Atlanta, GA MSA	36,893	4,210	12,690	7,241	2,103	6,368	2,702	1,066	1,971
Baltimore, MD MSA	30,820	4,574	10,690	6,425	1,753	4,067	1,184	916	1,608
Boston-Lawrence-Salem, MA-NH CMSA	33,631	4,329	12,338	7,784	1,990	5,525	2,343	968	1,640
Buffalo-Niagara Falls, NY CMSA	24,297	4,663	7,865	4,641	1,313	3,960	1,394	713	1,399
Chicago-Gary-Lake County, IL-IN-WI CMSA	35,370	5,060	11,708	6,814	2,285	6,396	2,926	1,001	1,825
Cincinnati-Hamilton, OH-KY-IN CMSA .	32,751	4,801	9,940	5,493	2,003	6,021	2,515	1,077	1,656
Cleveland-Akron-Lorain, OH CMSA . . .	27,677	4,368	8,191	4,443	1,503	5,266	2,447	854	1,681
Dallas-Fort Worth, TX CMSA	37,258	4,898	11,401	6,180	1,837	7,444	3,620	1,201	1,916
Detroit-Ann Arbor, MI CMSA.	32,542	4,307	10,718	6,201	1,936	6,832	3,213	1,019	1,255
Honolulu, HI MSA.	38,997	7,104	12,261	8,352	2,086	5,490	1,809	819	1,661
Houston-Galveston-Brazoria, TX CMSA	34,062	4,705	10,060	5,247	1,819	6,388	2,770	1,106	1,813
Kansas City, MO-Kansas City, KS CMSA	33,089	4,492	9,887	4,989	2,016	6,526	2,822	1,043	1,915
Los Angeles-Long Beach, CA PMSA . .	35,319	4,725	12,750	8,533	1,980	5,911	2,197	1,045	1,519
Miami-Fort Lauderdale, FL CMSA	30,744	4,934	10,018	6,152	1,625	5,596	2,216	931	1,583
Milwaukee, WI PMSA	32,690	4,444	10,162	6,082	1,934	6,154	3,153	1,012	1,602
Minneapolis-St. Paul, MN-WI MSA . . .	38,775	4,898	12,398	6,985	2,014	5,917	2,369	1,082	1,687
New York-Northern New Jersey-Long Island, NY-NJ-CT CMSA	35,760	5,241	13,080	8,487	2,435	4,882	1,337	826	1,689
Philadelphia-Wilmington-Trenton, PA-NJ-DE-MD CMSA	34,591	4,700	12,180	6,737	2,422	4,858	1,423	828	1,803
Pittsburgh-Beaver Valley, PA CMSA. . .	28,976	4,476	8,607	4,295	2,185	4,981	2,108	800	1,903
Portland-Vancouver, OR-WA CMSA. . .	32,027	4,434	10,487	6,519	1,654	5,827	2,715	942	1,573
San Diego, CA MSA	35,320	4,739	12,413	8,433	1,752	5,985	2,263	1,054	1,561
San Francisco-Oakland-San Jose, CA CMSA	40,969	5,337	14,155	9,658	1,849	7,017	2,929	1,087	1,444
Seattle-Tacoma, WA CMSA	36,211	4,722	11,813	7,361	1,923	6,712	2,783	1,082	1,594
St. Louis-East St. Louis-Alton, MO-IL CMSA.	27,656	4,188	8,297	4,358	1,211	4,832	2,208	908	1,609
Washington, DC-MD-VA MSA	40,507	5,031	14,233	8,901	2,027	5,753	1,918	976	1,723

[1] Includes expenditures not shown separately.

Sources of tables 721 and 722: U.S. Bureau of Labor Statistics, *Consumer Expenditures in 1993,* and unpublished data.

No. 723. Money Income of Households—Percent Distribution, by Income Level, Race, and Hispanic Origin, in Constant (1993) Dollars: 1970 to 1993

[Constant dollars based on CPI-U-X1 deflator. Households as of **March** of **following year.** Based on Current Population Survey; see text, sections 1 and 14, and Appendix III. For definition of median, see Guide to Tabular Presentation]

YEAR	Number of house-holds (1,000)	PERCENT DISTRIBUTION							Median income (dollars)
		Under $10,000	$10,000-$14,999	$15,000-$24,999	$25,000-$34,999	$35,000-$49,999	$50,000-$74,999	$75,000 and over	
ALL HOUSEHOLDS [1]									
1970	64,778	15.0	8.5	16.9	18.0	20.4	14.8	6.4	30,558
1975	72,867	14.4	9.6	17.2	16.6	19.7	15.5	6.9	30,340
1980	82,368	14.2	9.0	17.4	15.0	19.4	16.3	8.8	31,095
1985	88,458	14.4	8.7	16.7	15.1	17.9	16.5	10.6	31,717
1990	94,312	13.4	8.6	16.4	14.7	17.7	16.6	12.6	33,105
1991	95,669	14.0	9.0	16.4	15.0	17.4	16.2	12.0	31,962
1992	96,426	14.4	9.3	16.6	14.6	17.1	16.4	11.7	31,553
1993	97,107	14.2	9.2	16.9	14.7	16.3	16.1	12.5	31,241
WHITE									
1970	57,575	13.8	8.0	16.3	18.3	21.2	15.5	6.8	31,828
1975	64,392	12.9	9.2	16.9	16.8	20.4	16.4	7.5	31,728
1980	71,872	12.4	8.5	17.0	15.2	20.1	17.2	9.5	32,805
1985	76,576	12.7	8.2	16.5	15.3	18.5	17.2	11.5	33,450
1990	80,968	11.5	8.3	16.2	15.0	18.2	17.5	13.3	34,529
1991	81,675	11.9	8.7	16.3	15.2	17.9	17.1	12.9	33,493
1992	81,795	12.2	8.9	16.4	14.8	17.6	17.4	12.6	33,173
1993	82,387	12.2	8.9	16.6	14.9	17.0	17.0	13.4	32,960
BLACK									
1970	6,180	27.2	13.0	22.2	15.4	13.1	7.4	1.7	19,373
1975	7,489	27.6	14.0	19.7	15.2	13.9	7.7	1.9	19,047
1980	8,847	28.1	13.4	20.7	12.9	13.2	9.0	2.7	18,899
1985	9,797	28.1	12.6	19.4	13.4	13.3	9.7	3.5	19,901
1990	10,671	28.2	11.3	18.3	13.2	13.8	9.6	5.5	20,648
1991	11,083	29.5	11.1	18.0	13.7	13.9	9.4	4.6	19,953
1992	11,269	29.6	12.2	18.2	13.1	13.3	9.0	4.6	19,316
1993	11,281	28.9	11.8	19.2	13.8	12.0	9.3	5.2	19,533
HISPANIC [2]									
1975	2,948	18.5	13.2	22.9	17.8	16.9	8.2	2.4	22,793
1980	3,906	18.2	12.3	22.2	15.9	16.3	11.2	4.1	23,968
1985	5,213	20.4	12.7	19.8	15.8	15.1	11.2	4.8	23,454
1990	6,220	18.6	12.9	19.1	16.3	16.3	10.8	5.9	24,688
1991	6,379	19.4	11.8	20.6	15.8	15.5	11.1	5.9	24,074
1992	7,153	20.1	12.2	21.1	15.6	14.9	10.8	5.3	23,273
1993	7,362	20.0	12.4	21.5	16.5	13.4	10.8	5.4	22,886

[1] Includes other races not shown separately.   [2] Persons of Hispanic origin may be of any race. Income data for Hispanic origin households are not available prior to 1972.

No. 724. Money Income of Households—Median Income, by Race and Hispanic Origin, in Current and Constant (1993) Dollars: 1970 to 1993

[See headnote, table 723]

YEAR	MEDIAN INCOME IN CURRENT DOLLARS					MEDIAN INCOME IN CONSTANT (1993) DOLLARS				
	All house-holds [1]	White	Black	Asian, Pacific Islander	His-panic [2]	All house-holds [1]	White	Black	Asian, Pacific Islanders	His-panic [2]
1970	8,734	9,097	5,537	(NA)	(NA)	30,558	31,828	19,373	(NA)	(NA)
1975	11,800	12,340	7,408	(NA)	8,865	30,340	31,728	19,047	(NA)	22,793
1980	17,710	18,684	10,764	(NA)	13,651	31,095	32,805	18,899	(NA)	23,968
1981	19,074	20,153	11,309	(NA)	15,300	30,590	32,321	18,137	(NA)	24,538
1982	20,171	21,117	11,968	(NA)	15,178	30,489	31,918	18,090	(NA)	22,942
1983 [3]	20,885	21,902	12,429	(NA)	15,906	30,300	31,775	18,032	(NA)	23,076
1984	22,415	23,647	13,471	(NA)	16,992	31,174	32,887	18,735	(NA)	23,632
1985	23,618	24,908	14,819	(NA)	17,465	31,717	33,450	19,901	(NA)	23,454
1986	24,897	26,175	15,080	(NA)	18,352	32,825	34,510	19,882	(NA)	24,196
1987 [4]	26,061	27,458	15,672	(NA)	19,336	33,150	34,927	19,935	(NA)	24,596
1988	27,225	28,781	16,407	32,267	20,359	33,255	35,155	20,041	39,413	24,868
1989	28,906	30,406	18,083	36,102	21,921	33,685	35,433	21,073	42,070	25,545
1990	29,943	31,231	18,676	38,450	22,330	33,105	34,529	20,648	42,510	24,688
1991	30,126	31,569	18,807	36,449	22,691	31,962	33,493	19,953	38,670	24,074
1992	30,786	32,368	18,660	38,153	22,848	31,708	33,337	19,219	39,295	23,532
1992 [5]	30,636	32,209	18,755	37,801	22,597	31,553	33,173	19,316	38,933	23,273
1993	31,241	32,960	19,533	38,347	22,886	31,241	32,960	19,533	38,347	22,886

NA Not available.   [1] Includes other races not shown separately.   [2] Persons of Hispanic origin may be of any race.
[3] Beginning 1983, data based on revised Hispanic population controls and not directly comparable with prior years.   [4] Beginning 1987, based on revised processing procedures and not directly comparable with prior years.   [5] Based on 1990 population controls.

Source of tables 723 and 724: U.S. Bureau of the Census, *Current Population Reports*, P60-188; and unpublished data.

No. 725. Money Income of Households—Percent Distribution, by Income Level and Selected Characteristics: 1993

[See headnote, table 723. For composition of regions, see table 27]

CHARACTERISTIC	Number of households (1,000)	Under $10,000	$10,000-$14,999	$15,000-$24,999	$25,000-$34,999	$35,000-$49,999	$50,000-$74,999	$75,000 and over	Median income (dollars)
Total [1]	97,107	14.3	9.2	16.9	14.7	16.3	16.1	12.5	31,241
Age of householder:									
15 to 24 years	5,265	26.0	12.6	25.5	16.7	11.8	5.3	2.1	19,333
25 to 34 years	19,717	12.2	7.9	17.9	17.7	19.6	16.9	7.8	31,281
35 to 44 years	22,293	8.9	5.6	12.9	14.4	19.7	21.9	16.7	40,862
45 to 54 years	16,837	8.1	5.4	11.1	12.5	16.9	22.3	23.6	46,207
55 to 64 years	12,188	13.1	8.2	15.7	14.9	16.8	16.7	14.6	33,474
65 years and over	20,806	24.8	17.2	23.6	13.6	9.8	6.5	4.6	17,751
White	82,387	12.2	8.9	16.6	14.9	17.0	17.0	13.4	32,960
Black	11,281	28.9	11.8	19.2	13.8	12.0	9.3	5.1	19,533
Hispanic [2]	7,362	20.1	12.4	21.5	16.5	13.4	10.8	5.4	22,886
Northeast	19,470	14.3	8.3	15.4	13.5	16.3	17.0	15.2	33,747
Midwest	23,385	13.9	8.9	17.1	15.1	17.5	16.5	10.9	31,400
South	33,904	16.0	10.1	18.1	15.3	15.6	14.5	10.5	28,441
West	20,347	11.8	9.0	16.2	14.6	15.9	17.4	15.0	33,739
Size of household:									
One person	23,611	31.2	15.9	21.8	13.6	9.7	5.2	2.6	16,065
Two persons	31,211	9.2	9.1	18.9	16.5	17.4	16.7	12.2	32,434
Three persons	16,898	9.8	6.0	13.6	14.6	18.9	20.8	16.3	39,414
Four persons	15,073	7.3	4.6	11.5	13.4	19.5	23.2	20.5	45,087
Five persons	6,749	8.3	5.7	11.9	13.7	19.6	22.0	18.9	42,241
Six persons	2,186	8.3	6.4	13.6	14.4	17.9	21.8	17.6	41,094
Seven or more persons	1,379	9.5	8.3	18.6	16.3	16.5	16.2	14.6	33,120
Family households	68,490	9.0	7.1	15.3	15.0	18.2	19.6	15.8	37,484
Married-couple	53,171	4.3	5.4	14.0	14.9	19.6	22.7	19.0	43,129
Male householder, wife absent	2,913	11.3	9.7	20.0	18.5	18.9	12.9	8.7	29,849
Female householder, husband absent	12,406	28.6	13.7	19.9	14.5	12.1	7.8	3.4	18,545
Nonfamily households	28,617	26.9	14.3	20.7	14.2	11.6	7.7	4.6	18,880
Male householder	12,462	17.0	12.3	21.2	17.1	14.9	10.4	7.0	24,728
Female householder	16,155	34.5	15.8	20.4	11.9	9.1	5.6	2.8	14,883
Educational attainment of householder: [3]									
Total	91,842	13.6	9.0	16.4	14.6	16.5	16.7	13.1	32,166
Less than 9th grade	8,587	35.1	18.3	22.3	11.7	7.2	3.9	1.5	13,920
9th to 12th grade (no diploma)	9,712	28.2	14.5	20.9	15.8	11.6	6.5	2.5	17,966
High school graduate	29,420	13.6	10.2	19.3	17.3	18.0	14.9	6.7	28,700
Some college, no degree	16,295	9.2	7.5	17.0	15.9	19.5	19.6	11.3	35,220
Associate degree	6,032	7.2	5.9	13.9	16.3	21.3	22.4	13.1	39,583
Bachelor's degree or more	21,795	3.7	3.4	8.5	10.2	16.9	25.0	32.3	56,116
Bachelor's degree	13,808	4.3	3.9	10.2	11.0	18.2	25.6	26.9	51,480
Master's degree	5,153	2.8	2.6	6.3	9.8	17.1	26.4	35.0	60,341
Professional degree	1,630	2.6	2.9	5.1	5.2	9.4	18.5	56.3	87,666
Doctorate degree	1,204	2.2	2.2	3.8	8.9	11.3	21.7	49.8	74,753
Tenure:									
Owner occupied	62,374	8.5	7.4	14.8	14.1	18.0	19.9	17.2	38,903
Renter occupied	32,901	24.3	12.5	20.6	15.9	13.2	9.3	4.1	21,131
Occupier paid no cash rent	1,831	31.6	13.2	21.4	13.6	10.3	7.6	2.3	17,597

[1] Includes other races not shown separately. [2] Persons of Hispanic origin may be of any race. [3] 25 years old and over.

Source: U.S. Bureau of the Census, *Current Population Reports*, P60-188; and unpublished data.

No. 726. Money Income of Households—Aggregate and Average Income, by Race and Hispanic Origin: 1993

[See headnote, table 723]

CHARACTERISTIC	ALL RACES [1]		WHITE		BLACK		HISPANIC [2]	
	Aggregate income (bil. dol.)	Mean income (dollars)	Aggregate income (bil. dol.)	Mean income (dollars)	Aggregate income (bil. dol.)	Mean income (dollars)	Aggregate income (bil. dol.)	Mean income (dollars)
Total.................	4,022.9	41,428	3,566.1	43,285	307.2	27,229	223	30,291
Age of householder:								
15 to 24 years old.............	121.3	23,041	102.7	24,298	12.4	16,009	12.7	21,423
25 to 34 years old.............	739.6	37,510	642.1	40,020	64.4	23,455	60.9	28,666
35 to 44 years old.............	1,102.9	49,473	966.7	52,205	89.5	31,666	64.1	34,520
45 to 54 years old.............	972.9	57,770	861.0	60,106	70.8	38,156	46.4	38,042
55 to 64 years old.............	546.2	44,814	493.2	46,650	38.7	29,450	22.5	29,316
65 years old and over..........	540.2	25,965	500.5	26,761	31.4	17,782	16.3	20,459
Region:								
Northeast.................	882.4	45,319	792.5	46,823	58.4	30,161	36.4	27,311
Midwest.................	922.4	39,442	843.3	40,963	63.3	26,580	15.8	31,364
South	1,296.8	38,249	1,111.2	40,897	156.6	25,853	72.8	30,551
West	921.4	45,284	819.2	46,269	28.8	31,883	98.1	31,185
Size of household:								
One person	524.6	22,217	463.6	22,946	47.1	16,808	19.4	18,233
Two persons.................	1,322.5	42,374	1,214.1	44,195	77.6	26,602	48.9	29,265
Three persons.................	811.6	48,030	710.4	50,805	70.7	31,356	43.1	30,631
Four persons.................	836.8	55,516	735.4	58,306	63.4	36,018	48.0	34,042
Five persons.................	354.1	52,473	305.7	55,456	26.8	30,862	34.1	35,474
Six persons	112.1	51,259	92.0	55,575	12.3	33,978	14.9	35,576
Seven or more persons..........	61.2	44,401	45.1	47,388	9.2	29,373	14.7	33,937

[1] Includes other races not shown separately.   [2] Persons of Hispanic origin may be of any race.

Source: U.S. Bureau of the Census, *Current Population Reports*, P60-188; and unpublished data.

No. 727. Money Income of Households—Median Income and Income Level, byHousehold Type: 1993

[See headnote, table 723]

ITEM	All households	FAMILY HOUSEHOLDS				NONFAMILY HOUSEHOLDS		
		Total	Married couple	Male householder, wife absent	Female householder, husband absent	Total [1]	Single-person household	
							Male householder	Female householder
MEDIAN INCOME (dollars)								
All households.........	31,241	37,484	43,129	29,849	18,545	18,880	21,372	12,995
White.................	32,960	39,841	43,785	31,177	21,583	19,639	22,383	13,468
Black.................	19,533	22,221	35,409	22,000	12,423	13,857	15,893	10,082
Hispanic [2].................	22,886	24,530	28,867	25,013	13,223	15,799	17,324	8,672
NUMBER (1,000)								
All households.........	97,107	68,490	53,171	2,913	12,406	28,617	9,440	14,171
Under $5,000	4,407	2,176	708	102	1,366	2,230	704	1,386
$5,000 to $9,999	9,467	4,002	1,594	228	2,180	5,464	1,257	4,013
$10,000 to $14,999	8,956	4,873	2,895	283	1,695	4,083	1,324	2,439
$15,000 to $19,999	8,319	5,181	3,534	277	1,370	3,138	1,106	1,678
$20,000 to $24,999	8,103	5,310	3,906	306	1,098	2,793	1,080	1,279
$25,000 to $34,999	14,318	10,261	7,920	540	1,801	4,057	1,639	1,578
$35,000 to $49,999	15,791	12,467	10,417	549	1,500	3,325	1,217	1,083
$50,000 to $74,999	15,632	13,429	12,084	376	968	2,204	698	520
$75,000 and over...........	12,114	10,792	10,112	253	428	1,322	414	196

[1] Includes other nonfamily households not shown separately.   [2] Persons of Hispanic origin may be of any race.

Source: U.S. Bureau of the Census, *Current Population Reports*, P60-188; and unpublished data.

Income, Expenditures, and Wealth

No. 728. Money Income of Households—Percent Distribution, by Income Quintile and Top 5 Percent: 1993

[See headnote, table 723. For composition of regions, see table 27]

CHARACTERISTIC	Number (1,000)	PERCENT DISTRIBUTION						
		Total	Lowest fifth	Second fifth	Third fifth	Fourth fifth	Highest fifth	Top 5 percent
Total	97,107	100.0	20.0	20.0	20.0	20.0	20.0	5.0
Age of householder:								
15 to 24 years old	5,265	100.0	33.8	29.9	21.9	10.3	4.1	0.5
25 to 34 years old	19,717	100.0	16.8	20.7	24.0	23.1	15.3	2.8
35 to 44 years old	22,293	100.0	12.1	14.9	20.2	25.8	26.9	6.4
45 to 54 years old	16,837	100.0	11.4	12.9	17.2	23.7	34.8	9.9
55 to 64 years old	12,188	100.0	18.2	18.3	20.5	20.4	22.6	6.4
65 years old and over.	20,806	100.0	35.9	29.1	17.4	9.9	7.6	1.9
White	82,387	100.0	17.7	19.7	20.4	21.0	21.4	5.4
Black . . . . [1]	11,281	100.0	36.8	22.6	18.0	13.3	9.3	1.7
Hispanic origin [1]	7,362	100.0	27.9	25.6	21.4	15.1	10.0	1.8
Northeast.	19,470	100.0	19.6	18.0	18.7	20.5	23.2	6.6
Midwest.	23,385	100.0	19.5	20.1	20.5	21.5	18.5	3.7
South	33,904	100.0	22.2	21.6	20.4	18.5	17.4	4.1
West.	20,347	100.0	17.4	19.2	19.9	20.3	23.1	6.4
Family households.	68,490	100.0	13.1	17.9	20.7	23.2	25.1	6.4
Married-couple families	53,171	100.0	7.3	16.1	20.9	25.8	30.0	7.8
Male householder	2,913	100.0	16.7	24.1	24.7	20.5	14.0	3.1
Female householder.	12,406	100.0	37.4	24.4	19.0	12.6	6.6	0.9
Nonfamily households	28,617	100.0	36.5	25.0	18.3	12.4	7.8	1.8
Male householder	12,462	100.0	24.9	25.1	22.2	16.1	11.8	2.8
Living alone.	9,440	100.0	30.0	27.3	22.0	13.3	7.3	1.8
Female householder.	16,155	100.0	45.4	24.9	15.4	9.6	4.8	1.0
Living alone.	14,171	100.0	50.0	25.9	14.3	7.3	2.5	0.5
Worked	69,282	100.0	10.0	17.5	21.8	24.7	26.0	6.6
Worked at full-time jobs.	60,539	100.0	7.1	16.3	22.1	26.4	28.1	7.1
Worked at part-time jobs	8,744	100.0	30.2	25.9	19.3	13.1	11.4	2.8
Did not work.	27,825	100.0	44.8	26.3	15.6	8.2	5.1	1.1

[1] Persons of Hispanic origin may be of any race.

Source: U.S. Bureau of the Census, Current Population Survey, unpublished data.

No. 729. Money Income of Households—Percent Distribution, by Income Level, Race, and Hispanic Origin: 1993

[See headnote, table 723]

TYPE OF HOUSEHOLD	Number of house-holds (1,000)	PERCENT DISTRIBUTION									Median income (dollars)
		Under $5,000	$5,000-$9,999	$10,000-$14,999	$15,000-$24,999	$25,000-$34,999	$35,000-$49,999	$50,000-$74,999	$75,000-$99,999	$100,000 and over	
HOUSEHOLDS											
Total [1]	97,107	4.5	9.7	9.2	16.9	14.7	16.3	16.1	6.7	5.8	31,241
White.	82,387	3.6	8.6	8.9	16.6	14.9	17.0	17.0	7.1	6.3	32,960
Black	11,281	10.9	18.0	11.8	19.2	13.8	12.0	9.3	3.3	1.9	19,533
Asian, Pacific Islander [2].	2,233	5.5	8.1	7.2	14.4	12.4	12.9	20.0	10.5	9.0	38,347
Hispanic [2].	7,362	5.9	14.1	12.4	21.5	16.5	13.4	10.8	3.1	2.3	22,886
FAMILIES											
Total [1]	68,490	3.2	5.8	7.1	15.3	15.0	18.2	19.6	8.4	7.4	37,484
White.	57,870	2.2	4.6	6.5	14.9	15.2	19.0	20.8	8.8	8.0	39,841
Black	7,989	9.9	14.8	11.2	18.5	14.1	13.3	11.3	4.4	2.4	22,221
Asian, Pacific Islander [2].	1,737	4.0	5.9	6.4	12.3	11.6	13.9	22.7	12.6	10.5	45,251
Hispanic [2].	5,940	5.0	11.6	12.2	22.1	17.0	14.6	11.8	3.2	2.4	24,530
NONFAMILIES											
Total [1]	28,617	7.8	19.1	14.3	20.7	14.2	11.6	7.7	2.6	2.0	18,880
White.	24,518	7.0	18.2	14.5	20.7	14.3	12.1	8.1	2.9	2.2	19,639
Black	3,292	13.2	25.8	13.1	20.8	13.0	8.6	4.4	0.7	0.5	13,857
Asian, Pacific Islander [2].	496	10.5	15.5	10.1	22.0	15.1	9.3	10.3	3.4	4.0	21,407
Hispanic [2].	1,423	9.7	24.7	13.4	19.0	14.3	8.1	6.8	2.6	1.5	15,799

[1] Includes other races not shown separately.   [2] Persons of Hispanic origin may be of any race.

Source: U.S. Bureau of the Census, Current Population Reports, P60-188; and unpublished data.

No. 730. Money Income of Households—Median Income, by State, in Constant (1993) Dollars: 1985 to 1993

[Constant dollars based on the CPI-U-X1 deflator. Data based on the Current Population Survey; see text, sections 1 and 14, and Appendix III. The CPS is designed to collect reliable data on income primarily at the national level and secondarily at the regional level. When the income data are tabulated by State, the estimates are considered less reliable and, therefore, particular caution should be used when trying to interpret the results]

STATE	1985	1986	1987 [1]	1988	1989	1990	1991	1992 [2]	1993 [3]
United States....	$31,717	$32,825	$33,054	$33,255	$33,685	$33,105	$31,962	$31,553	$31,241
Alabama...........	24,620	25,224	25,102	24,366	24,803	25,823	25,830	26,581	25,082
Alaska............	46,710	41,341	42,273	40,434	41,959	43,447	43,087	43,053	42,931
Arizona...........	32,065	33,620	34,025	32,290	33,272	32,310	32,610	30,237	30,510
Arkansas	23,436	24,694	23,948	24,640	24,976	25,192	24,863	24,597	23,039
California	36,234	38,248	38,346	36,995	38,466	36,805	35,715	35,948	34,073
Colorado..........	37,847	35,851	33,678	32,020	31,238	33,978	33,419	33,456	34,488
Connecticut........	41,752	43,140	41,801	44,233	49,318	42,974	44,723	42,064	39,516
Delaware	30,861	33,786	37,199	37,261	37,370	34,056	34,571	36,746	36,064
District of Columbia	28,304	32,067	34,923	32,663	31,175	30,284	31,706	31,152	27,304
Florida	28,662	30,125	31,150	31,033	30,397	29,503	28,913	28,168	28,550
Georgia	28,267	32,130	33,980	32,450	32,095	30,471	28,870	29,659	31,663
Hawaii	38,893	38,238	44,548	40,338	40,827	43,030	39,516	43,374	42,662
Idaho	27,881	27,356	26,401	28,643	28,730	27,977	27,708	28,533	31,010
Illinois	33,399	34,953	34,451	36,063	36,475	35,978	33,827	32,496	32,857
Indiana...........	30,451	29,965	28,644	32,116	30,180	29,771	28,740	29,384	29,475
Iowa	28,104	29,611	28,226	29,688	30,607	30,169	30,293	29,603	28,663
Kansas...........	30,603	31,545	32,542	31,228	31,303	33,076	31,080	31,254	29,770
Kentucky	23,315	26,202	26,296	24,316	27,132	27,396	25,212	24,188	24,376
Louisiana	28,442	27,542	27,156	25,036	26,640	24,771	26,841	26,201	26,312
Maine............	27,556	30,883	30,019	32,249	32,887	30,364	29,566	30,504	27,438
Maryland	40,471	40,349	44,482	44,647	41,970	42,960	39,204	38,317	39,939
Massachusetts.......	37,880	40,000	41,011	40,569	42,052	40,074	37,890	37,447	37,064
Michigan..........	32,555	35,077	35,237	35,999	35,863	33,098	34,074	33,233	32,662
Minnesota.........	32,037	34,863	35,721	35,529	35,175	34,787	31,275	31,908	33,682
Mississippi	22,042	21,771	23,549	22,189	23,210	22,308	20,662	21,186	22,191
Missouri	29,463	28,907	30,172	28,635	30,878	30,218	29,628	28,180	28,682
Montana..........	27,176	26,801	26,043	27,155	27,609	25,843	26,340	27,319	26,470
Nebraska	29,275	28,705	29,597	30,731	30,670	30,384	31,350	30,948	31,008
Nevada	31,256	34,565	34,189	34,180	34,191	35,404	34,944	32,863	35,814
New Hampshire.......	35,458	40,275	41,134	42,293	43,737	45,113	38,228	40,617	37,964
New Jersey........	41,604	41,814	43,555	44,324	45,587	42,824	42,490	40,168	40,500
New Mexico	27,427	26,164	26,404	23,570	26,339	27,683	28,157	26,634	26,758
New York	31,746	32,994	33,561	35,319	36,703	34,927	33,732	31,981	31,697
North Carolina.......	28,807	28,822	28,951	29,822	30,772	29,109	28,489	28,602	28,820
North Dakota........	28,477	28,357	28,717	29,428	29,400	27,931	27,470	27,766	28,118
Ohio	33,807	33,112	32,783	33,884	33,819	33,182	31,605	32,344	31,285
Oklahoma.........	28,477	27,618	27,591	28,909	27,580	26,959	27,014	26,041	26,260
Oregon...........	29,402	32,661	31,849	33,893	33,245	32,373	32,030	32,883	33,138
Pennsylvania.......	30,722	31,388	32,340	32,665	33,433	32,067	32,218	30,777	30,995
Rhode Island........	33,070	34,991	35,988	36,451	35,104	35,343	32,715	31,343	33,509
South Carolina.......	26,907	28,963	31,863	31,188	27,732	31,769	29,137	28,404	26,053
South Dakota	24,364	26,234	26,904	27,231	28,094	27,165	26,141	27,045	27,737
Tennessee	23,875	24,069	26,940	25,475	26,349	24,977	25,943	25,046	25,102
Texas............	31,885	31,856	31,445	30,492	30,166	31,208	29,423	28,790	28,727
Utah	33,893	34,650	33,745	32,141	35,795	33,325	29,723	35,276	35,786
Vermont	34,916	32,432	32,328	35,408	36,469	34,381	30,932	33,736	31,065
Virginia...........	38,178	39,177	38,155	39,879	39,758	38,776	38,339	39,341	36,433
Washington.........	32,230	35,441	34,750	39,486	37,245	35,503	36,040	34,915	35,655
West Virginia........	21,464	21,707	21,887	23,639	25,261	24,474	24,558	20,878	22,421
Wisconsin.........	31,218	34,846	33,542	36,125	33,938	33,954	33,030	34,305	31,766
Wyoming	29,653	31,061	35,095	32,270	34,402	32,571	30,820	31,113	29,442

[1] Beginning 1987, data based on revised processing procedures and not directly comparable with prior years. [2] Implementation of 1990 census population controls. [3] Data collection method changed from paper and pencil to computer assisted interviewing. In addition, the March 1994 income supplement was revised to allow for the coding of different income amounts on selected questionnaire items.

Source: U.S. Bureau of the Census, *Current Population Reports*, P60-188.

No. 731. Money Income of Families—Percent Distribution, by Income Level, Race, and Hispanic Origin, in Constant (1993) Dollars: 1970 to 1993

[Constant dollars based on CPI-U-X1 deflator. Families as of **March** of following year. Beginning with 1980 based on householder concept and restricted to primary families. Based on Current Population Survey; see text, sections 1 and 14, and Appendix III. For definition of median, see Guide to Tabular Presentation. See also *Historical Statistics, Colonial Times to 1970*, series G 1-8, G 16-23, G 190-192, and G 197-199]

YEAR	Number of families (1,000)	Under $10,000	$10,000-$14,999	$15,000-$24,999	$25,000-$34,999	$35,000-$49,999	$50,000-$74,999	$75,000 and over	Median income (dollars)
ALL FAMILIES [1]									
1970	52,227	8.2	7.3	16.6	19.6	23.6	17.3	7.5	34,523
1975	56,245	7.6	7.9	16.6	17.7	23.0	18.7	8.4	35,274
1980	60,309	8.0	7.1	16.1	15.6	22.2	20.0	10.9	36,912
1985	63,558	9.0	7.0	15.5	15.5	19.9	19.9	13.3	37,246
1990	66,322	8.3	6.5	14.8	14.6	19.8	20.0	15.9	39,086
1991	67,173	9.0	6.8	14.8	15.3	19.3	19.7	15.0	38,129
1992	68,216	9.5	7.1	15.2	14.6	19.1	19.9	14.7	37,668
1993	68,506	9.6	7.2	15.5	14.8	17.9	19.4	15.5	36,959
WHITE									
1970	46,535	7.0	6.7	15.8	19.8	24.5	18.2	8.0	35,814
1975	49,873	6.3	7.3	16.1	17.9	23.7	19.7	9.0	36,686
1980	52,710	6.4	6.3	15.6	15.9	23.1	21.1	11.8	38,458
1985	54,991	7.3	6.3	15.0	15.6	20.6	20.8	14.4	39,149
1990	56,803	6.3	5.9	14.4	14.9	20.5	21.1	16.9	40,813
1991	57,224	6.7	6.3	14.4	15.5	20.1	20.8	16.2	40,085
1992	57,669	7.1	6.4	14.8	14.9	19.8	21.2	15.8	39,828
1993	57,881	7.3	6.6	15.1	15.1	18.8	20.6	16.6	39,300
BLACK									
1970	4,928	20.1	13.0	23.9	17.2	15.1	8.8	1.9	21,969
1975	5,586	19.6	14.2	20.9	16.8	16.5	9.6	2.3	22,572
1980	6,317	20.7	13.9	21.2	14.2	15.2	11.4	3.5	22,253
1985	6,921	22.8	11.9	19.9	14.5	15.1	11.5	4.3	22,543
1990	7,471	22.9	11.3	18.6	13.1	15.7	11.5	7.0	23,685
1991	7,716	25.0	10.7	18.1	14.2	15.2	11.3	5.6	22,861
1992	7,982	25.7	11.8	18.4	13.0	14.4	10.8	5.8	21,735
1993	7,993	25.8	11.4	18.6	13.7	12.9	10.9	6.6	21,542
HISPANIC ORIGIN [2]									
1975	2,499	14.9	12.9	23.3	18.9	18.4	9.0	2.7	24,557
1980	3,235	14.5	12.1	22.2	17.0	17.6	12.3	4.3	25,838
1985	4,206	16.7	13.0	19.8	16.7	15.9	12.5	5.4	25,552
1990	4,981	16.1	12.5	20.0	16.0	17.1	11.8	6.5	25,905
1991	5,177	17.5	11.8	20.1	16.8	15.4	12.1	6.4	25,351
1992	5,733	17.5	12.4	21.8	15.6	15.5	11.5	5.7	24,260
1993	5,946	17.9	12.5	22.2	16.6	14.0	11.4	5.5	23,654

[1] Includes other races not shown separately.   [2] Persons of Hispanic origin may be of any race.

No. 732. Money Income of Families—Median Income, by Race and Hispanic Origin, in Current and Constant (1993) Dollars: 1970 to 1993

[See headnote, table 731]

YEAR	MEDIAN INCOME IN CURRENT DOLLARS					MEDIAN INCOME IN CONSTANT (1993) DOLLARS				
	All families [1]	White	Black	Asian, Pacific Islander	His-panic [2]	All families [1]	White	Black	Asian, Pacific Islander	His-panic [2]
1970	9,867	10,236	6,279	(NA)	(NA)	34,523	35,814	21,969	(NA)	(NA)
1975	13,719	14,268	8,779	(NA)	9,551	35,274	36,686	22,572	(NA)	24,557
1980	21,023	21,904	12,674	(NA)	14,716	36,912	38,458	22,253	(NA)	25,838
1981	22,388	23,517	13,266	(NA)	16,401	35,905	37,716	21,276	(NA)	26,303
1982	23,433	24,603	13,598	(NA)	16,227	35,419	37,188	20,553	(NA)	24,527
1983 [3]	24,580	25,757	14,506	(NA)	16,956	35,661	37,368	21,045	(NA)	24,600
1984	26,433	27,686	15,431	(NA)	18,832	36,762	38,505	21,461	(NA)	26,191
1985	27,735	29,152	16,786	(NA)	19,027	37,246	39,149	22,543	(NA)	25,552
1986	29,458	30,809	17,604	(NA)	19,995	38,838	40,620	23,210	(NA)	26,362
1987 [4]	30,970	32,385	18,406	(NA)	20,300	39,394	41,194	23,413	(NA)	25,822
1988	32,191	33,915	19,329	36,560	21,769	39,320	41,426	23,610	44,657	26,590
1989	34,213	35,975	20,209	40,351	23,446	39,869	41,922	23,550	47,022	27,322
1990	35,353	36,915	21,423	42,246	23,431	39,086	40,813	23,685	46,707	25,905
1991	35,939	37,783	21,548	40,974	23,895	38,129	40,085	22,861	43,471	25,351
1992	36,812	38,909	21,161	42,556	23,901	37,914	40,074	21,794	43,830	24,616
1992 [5]	36,573	38,670	21,103	42,255	23,555	37,668	39,828	21,735	43,520	24,260
1993	36,959	39,300	21,542	44,456	23,654	36,959	39,300	21,542	44,456	23,654

NA Not available.   [1] Includes other races not shown separately.   [2] Persons of Hispanic origin may be of any race. [3] Beginning 1983, data based on revised Hispanic population controls and not directly comparable with prior years.   [4] Beginning 1987, data based on revised processing procedures and not directly comparable with prior years.   [5] Based on 1990 census population controls.

Source of tables 731 and 732: U.S. Bureau of the Census, *Current Population Reports*, P60-188; and unpublished data.

No. 733. Money Income of Families—Percent Distribution of Aggregate Income Received by Quintile and Income at Selected Positions, in Constant (1993) Dollars: 1980 and 1993

[See headnote, table 731. For composition of regions, see table 27. See also *Historical Statistics, Colonial Times to 1970*, series G 31-138]

ITEM	All families, 1980	1993						
		All families	RACE		REGION			
			White	Black	North-east	Midwest	South	West
Number (1,000).................	60,309	68,506	57,881	7,993	13,456	16,210	24,438	14,402
INCOME AT SELECTED POSITIONS (dollars)								
Upper limit of each fifth:								
Lowest........	17,535	16,952	19,017	8,000	18,500	18,080	15,000	18,000
Second	29,645	30,000	32,024	16,010	33,010	30,920	26,998	31,413
Third.................	41,988	45,020	47,293	27,742	49,861	45,316	40,820	48,044
Fourth.................	58,871	66,794	69,039	46,502	73,100	64,693	62,600	70,500
Lower limit of top 5 percent..........	92,158	113,182	117,278	83,600	126,000	104,616	106,200	122,349
PERCENT DISTRIBUTION OF AGGREGATE INCOME								
Lowest fifth	5.2	4.2	4.7	3.0	4.0	4.6	4.1	4.3
Second fifth	11.5	10.1	10.5	7.9	10.0	10.9	9.8	10.0
Third fifth	17.5	15.9	16.1	14.5	15.9	16.8	15.6	15.8
Fourth fifth.................	24.3	23.6	23.4	24.1	23.3	24.0	23.6	23.5
Highest fifth.................	41.5	46.2	45.4	50.6	46.8	43.7	47.0	46.6
Top 5 percent	15.3	19.1	18.8	20.3	19.7	17.1	19.5	19.4

Source: U.S. Bureau of the Census, *Current Population Reports*, P60-188; and unpublished data.

No. 734. Money Income of Families—Percent Distribution, by Income Quintile and Top 5 Percent: 1993

[See headnote, table 731]

CHARACTERISTIC	Number (1,000)	PERCENT DISTRIBUTION						
		Total	Lowest fifth	Second fifth	Third fifth	Fourth fifth	Highest fifth	Top 5 percent
All families.................	**68,506**	**100.0**	**20.0**	**20.0**	**20.0**	**20.0**	**20.0**	**5.0**
Age of householder:								
15 to 24 years old	2,999	100.0	49.6	27.3	16.2	4.5	2.5	0.3
25 to 34 years old	14,248	100.0	25.0	22.0	21.1	20.4	11.5	2.2
35 to 44 years old	17,810	100.0	15.3	15.9	21.1	23.9	23.8	5.5
45 to 54 years old	13,281	100.0	11.3	12.7	17.7	24.0	34.2	9.4
55 to 64 years old	8,951	100.0	15.7	18.6	21.0	21.0	23.7	6.7
65 years old and over............	11,217	100.0	26.9	31.7	19.8	12.0	9.6	2.5
White	57,881	100.0	16.9	19.9	20.7	21.2	21.4	5.5
Black	7,993	100.0	41.4	21.6	15.9	12.1	9.0	1.5
Hispanic origin [1]	5,946	100.0	35.3	26.3	18.4	11.9	8.1	1.5
Type of family:								
Married-couple families..........	53,181	100.0	12.7	18.8	21.1	23.1	24.4	6.2
Male householder, wife absent......	2,914	100.0	29.8	26.4	21.2	13.3	9.3	2.1
Female householder, husband absent .	12,411	100.0	49.1	23.4	15.2	8.5	3.9	0.7
Presence of related children under 18 years old:								
No related children..............	32,050	100.0	16.6	21.6	20.4	20.2	21.3	5.4
One or more related children	36,456	100.0	23.0	18.6	19.7	19.8	18.9	4.7
One child	14,827	100.0	22.8	19.5	19.6	19.1	19.0	4.3
Two children or more..........	21,629	100.0	23.2	18.0	19.7	20.4	18.7	4.9
Education attainment of householder: [2]								
Total.................	65,506	100.0	18.6	19.7	20.2	20.7	20.8	5.2
Less than 9th grade..............	5,614	100.0	45.3	29.4	15.8	6.3	3.2	0.2
9th to 12th grade (no diploma)........	6,756	100.0	37.4	28.2	19.1	10.4	4.9	0.9
High school graduate (includes equivalency)	21,340	100.0	19.5	23.9	23.9	20.9	11.8	1.7
Some college, no degree	11,815	100.0	14.6	19.1	22.5	24.6	19.1	3.5
Associate degree	4,408	100.0	11.8	15.8	22.6	28.2	21.7	3.2
Bachelor's degree or more	15,574	100.0	4.7	8.2	14.7	25.0	47.4	15.6
Bachelor's degree	9,673	100.0	5.6	9.3	16.7	27.1	41.3	10.8
Master's degree.................	3,687	100.0	3.3	6.8	13.4	24.5	52.0	16.6
Professional degree	1,297	100.0	2.7	5.2	6.8	17.0	68.3	40.3
Doctorate degree.................	918	100.0	2.6	6.5	10.6	16.0	64.3	27.0

[1] Persons of Hispanic origin may be of any race.   [2] 25 years old and over.

Source: U.S. Bureau of the Census, Current Population Survey, unpublished data.

Income, Expenditures, and Wealth

No. 735. Money Income of Families—Median Income, by Race and Hispanic Origin: 1993

[See headnote, table 731. For composition of regions, see table 27]

CHARACTERISTIC	NUMBER (1,000)				MEDIAN INCOME (dollars)			
	All families [1]	White	Black	His-panic [2]	All families [1]	White	Black	His-panic [2]
All families............	**68,506**	**57,881**	**7,993**	**5,946**	**36,959**	**39,300**	**21,542**	**23,654**
Region:								
Northeast................	13,456	11,690	1,298	1,001	40,987	42,526	25,002	19,580
Midwest.................	16,210	14,258	1,643	405	37,942	40,158	20,794	27,501
South..................	24,438	19,461	4,461	1,915	33,365	36,504	20,372	23,651
West...................	14,402	12,472	591	2,624	38,881	39,614	26,182	24,781
Type of family:								
Married-couple families........	53,181	47,452	3,715	4,038	43,005	43,675	35,218	28,454
Wife in paid labor force......	32,194	28,539	2,417	2,121	51,204	51,630	44,805	35,973
Wife not in paid labor force ...	20,988	18,913	1,298	1,917	30,218	30,878	22,207	20,721
Male householder, wife absent...	2,914	2,298	450	410	26,467	28,269	19,476	21,717
Female householder, husband absent..............	12,411	8,131	3,828	1,498	17,443	20,000	11,909	12,047
With related children, under 18	36,456	29,234	5,525	4,153	36,200	39,837	18,671	22,117
Married couple............	26,121	22,670	2,147	2,747	45,548	46,376	36,659	28,499
Male householder, wife absent...	1,577	1,202	295	239	22,348	24,272	18,857	17,835
Female householder, husband absent..............	8,758	5,361	3,084	1,167	13,472	16,020	10,375	10,497
Number of earners:								
No earners...............	10,546	8,622	1,574	860	15,515	17,656	6,858	8,362
One earner	19,301	15,556	2,999	2,044	26,193	28,574	16,571	17,121
Two earners..............	30,137	26,336	2,620	2,248	47,424	48,332	37,124	32,172
Three earners.............	6,367	5,486	651	538	57,745	58,651	49,489	40,724
Four or more earners.........	2,155	1,882	149	256	72,673	73,269	59,678	49,876

[1] Includes other races not shown separately. [2] Persons of Hispanic origin may be of any race.

No. 736. Money Income of Families—Percent Distribution, by Income Level and Selected Characteristics: 1993

[See headnote, table 731. See *Historical Statistics, Colonial Times to 1970*, series G 1-8 for U.S. data on total, White, Black, and other races. For composition of regions, see table 27]

ITEM	Number of fami-lies (1,000)	PERCENT DISTRIBUTION								Median income (dollars)
		Under $5,000	$5,000 to $9,999	$10,000 to $14,999	$15,000 to $24,999	$25,000 to $34,999	$35,000 to $49,999	$50,000 to $74,999	$75,000 and over	
All families [1]	**68,506**	**3.5**	**6.1**	**7.2**	**15.5**	**14.8**	**17.9**	**19.4**	**15.5**	**36,959**
White, total	57,881	2.5	4.8	6.6	15.1	15.1	18.8	20.6	16.6	39,300
Northeast.............	11,690	2.6	4.6	5.7	13.5	13.5	18.3	21.5	20.3	42,526
Midwest.............	14,258	2.2	4.2	5.8	14.9	15.6	20.7	21.8	14.8	40,158
South..............	19,461	2.7	5.1	7.6	16.4	16.0	18.4	19.0	14.9	36,504
West...............	12,472	2.4	5.1	6.7	14.9	14.5	17.7	20.8	17.8	39,614
Black, total	7,993	10.7	15.1	11.4	18.6	13.7	12.9	10.9	6.6	21,542
Northeast	1,298	11.0	14.1	9.6	15.3	14.1	14.0	13.4	8.5	25,002
Midwest	1,643	12.7	18.0	10.0	17.3	13.1	12.2	9.7	6.8	20,794
South..............	4,461	10.2	15.0	12.6	20.2	13.3	13.2	10.2	5.4	20,372
West..............	591	8.8	10.0	10.0	17.6	17.1	10.8	15.1	11.2	26,182
Hispanic, [2] total	5,946	5.8	12.1	12.5	22.2	16.6	14.0	11.4	5.4	23,654
Northeast.............	1,001	9.1	19.3	11.9	19.5	13.6	12.7	8.5	5.5	19,580
Midwest	405	4.2	10.9	10.6	20.2	17.5	18.0	13.6	5.2	27,501
South..............	1,915	6.1	10.9	13.3	23.1	16.9	12.4	11.1	6.2	23,651
West..............	2,624	4.6	10.4	12.3	22.9	17.3	14.9	12.4	4.9	24,781
Presence of related children under 18 years old:										
All families..........	68,506	3.5	6.1	7.2	15.5	14.8	17.9	19.4	15.5	36,959
No children........	32,050	1.5	4.0	7.4	17.1	15.9	17.7	19.7	16.6	37,849
One or more children..	36,456	5.3	7.9	7.1	14.2	13.9	18.1	19.1	14.5	36,200
Married-couple families ...	53,181	1.4	3.0	5.5	14.1	14.9	19.5	22.7	18.9	43,005
No children........	27,060	1.4	3.3	6.7	16.2	15.6	17.6	20.8	18.5	40,293
One or more children ..	26,121	1.4	2.8	4.2	11.8	14.2	21.6	24.7	19.4	45,548
Female householder, no husband present.......	12,411	12.4	18.4	14.0	20.3	14.0	11.2	7.1	2.7	17,443
No children........	3,653	2.8	8.1	11.8	22.5	18.0	18.0	13.1	5.6	27,184
One or more children ...	8,758	16.4	22.7	15.0	19.4	12.3	8.3	4.5	1.5	13,472

[1] Includes other races not shown separately. [2] Persons of Hispanic origin may be of any race.

Source of tables 735 and 736: U.S. Bureau of the Census, *Current Population Reports*, P60-188; and unpublished data.

No. 737. Money Income of Families—Distribution, by Type of Family and Income Level: 1993

[See headnote, table 731]

TYPE OF FAMILY	Number of families (1,000)	DISTRIBUTION (1,000)								Median income (dollars)
		Under $9,999	$10,000-$14,999	$15,000-$19,999	$20,000-$24,999	$25,000-$34,999	$35,000-$49,999	$50,000-$74,999	$75,000 and over	
All families	**68,506**	**6,570**	**4,966**	**5,261**	**5,379**	**10,162**	**12,287**	**13,280**	**10,600**	**36,959**
Married-couple families. . .	53,181	2,323	2,923	3,556	3,926	7,931	10,391	12,072	10,057	43,005
Wife worked	34,411	678	815	1,338	1,832	4,681	7,425	9,571	8,072	50,798
Wife did not work.	18,770	1,646	2,109	2,219	2,094	3,250	2,965	2,502	1,986	28,779
Male householder [1]	2,914	428	302	318	322	498	508	332	207	26,467
Female householder [1]	12,411	3,819	1,741	1,386	1,131	1,733	1,387	876	337	17,443
With related children [2] . . .	36,456	4,787	2,597	2,556	2,605	5,072	6,611	6,957	5,271	36,200
Married-couple	26,121	1,075	1,100	1,416	1,673	3,722	5,635	6,439	5,060	45,548
Female householder [1] . .	8,758	3,421	1,311	938	757	1,073	730	396	132	13,472

[1] No spouse present. [2] Children under 18 years old. Includes male householders not shown separately.
Source: U.S. Bureau of the Census, *Current Population Reports*, P60-188, and earlier reports; and unpublished data.

No. 738. Median Income of Families, by Type of Family in Current and Constant (1993) Dollars: 1970 to 1993

[See headnote, table 731. See also *Historical Statistics, Colonial Times to 1970*, series G 179-188]

YEAR	CURRENT DOLLARS						CONSTANT (1993) DOLLARS					
	Total	Married-couple families			Male householder, no wife present	Female householder, no husband present	Total	Married-couple families			Male householder, no wife present	Female householder, no husband present
		Total	Wife in paid labor force	Wife not in paid labor force				Total	Wife in paid labor force	Wife not in paid labor force		
1970	9,867	10,516	12,276	9,304	9,012	5,093	34,523	36,793	42,951	32,553	31,531	17,819
1975	13,719	14,867	17,237	12,752	12,995	6,844	35,274	38,226	44,319	32,788	33,412	17,597
1980	21,023	23,141	26,879	18,972	17,519	10,408	36,912	40,630	47,193	33,310	30,759	18,274
1981	22,388	25,065	29,247	20,325	19,889	10,960	40,199	44,906	46,906	32,597	31,897	17,577
1982	23,433	26,019	30,342	21,299	20,140	11,484	35,419	39,328	45,862	32,194	30,442	17,358
1983 [1]	24,580	27,286	32,107	21,890	21,845	11,789	35,661	39,587	46,581	31,758	31,693	17,104
1984 [1]	26,433	29,612	34,668	23,582	23,325	12,803	36,762	41,183	48,215	32,797	32,439	17,806
1985	27,735	31,100	36,431	24,556	22,622	13,660	37,246	41,765	48,925	32,977	30,380	18,345
1986 [2]	29,458	32,805	38,346	25,803	24,962	13,647	38,838	43,251	50,557	34,019	32,911	17,993
1987 [2]	30,970	34,879	40,751	26,640	25,208	14,683	39,394	44,366	51,836	33,886	32,065	18,677
1988	32,191	36,389	42,709	27,220	26,827	15,346	39,320	44,448	52,168	33,248	32,768	18,745
1989	34,213	38,547	45,266	28,747	27,847	16,442	39,869	44,920	52,749	33,500	32,451	19,160
1990	35,353	39,895	46,777	30,265	29,046	16,932	39,086	44,107	51,716	33,461	32,113	18,720
1991	35,939	40,995	48,169	30,075	28,351	16,692	38,129	43,493	51,104	31,908	30,079	17,709
1992 [3]	36,812	42,064	49,984	30,326	27,821	17,221	37,914	43,323	51,480	31,234	28,654	17,737
1992 [3]	36,573	41,890	49,775	30,174	27,576	17,025	37,668	43,144	51,265	31,077	28,402	17,535
1993	36,959	43,005	51,204	30,218	26,467	17,443	36,959	43,005	51,204	30,218	26,467	17,443

[1] Beginning 1984, data based on revised Hispanic population controls and not directly comparable with prior years.
[2] Beginning 1987, data based on revised processing procedures and not comparable with prior years. [3] Based on 1990 census population controls.
Source: U.S. Bureau of the Census, *Income and Poverty: 1993* series CD-INPO-94-03, on compact disc.

No. 739. Median Income of Year-Round Full-Time Workers With Income: 1980 to 1993

[Age as of **March of following year.** Prior to 1990, earnings are for civilian workers only. For definition of median, see Guide to Tabular Presentation]

ITEM	FEMALE					MALE				
	1980	1990	1991	1992	1993	1980	1990	1991	1992	1993
Total with income . . .	**$11,591**	**$20,591**	**$21,245**	**$22,093**	**$22,469**	**$19,173**	**$28,979**	**$30,332**	**$30,832**	**$31,077**
15 to 19 years old	6,779	[1]13,944	[1]14,242	[1]14,662	[1]15,227	7,753	[1]15,462	[1]15,307	[1]15,658	[1]15,948
20 to 24 years old	9,407	(NA)	(NA)	(NA)	(NA)	12,109	(NA)	(NA)	(NA)	(NA)
25 to 34 years old	12,190	20,184	21,022	21,941	21,949	17,724	25,355	26,100	26,410	26,087
35 to 44 years old	12,239	22,505	23,385	24,125	25,282	21,777	32,607	33,588	34,714	35,233
45 to 54 years old	12,116	21,938	22,630	24,489	24,412	22,323	35,732	37,198	37,926	39,685
55 to 64 years old	11,931	20,755	21,325	22,581	22,587	21,053	33,169	35,720	35,537	35,736
65 years old and over. . . .	12,342	22,957	21,780	21,556	24,875	17,307	35,520	34,473	35,341	37,085
White.	11,703	20,839	21,555	22,349	22,979	19,720	30,081	30,953	31,565	31,832
Black.	10,915	18,544	19,134	20,258	20,315	13,875	21,481	22,628	22,991	23,566
Hispanic [2]	9,887	16,181	16,548	17,674	17,112	13,790	19,358	20,027	19,855	20,423

NA Not available. [1] 15 to 24 years old. [2] Persons of Hispanic origin may be of any race.
Source: U.S. Bureau of the Census, *Current Population Reports*, P60-188, and earlier reports; and unpublished data.

Income, Expenditures, and Wealth

No. 740. Money Income of Persons—Percent Distribution, by Income Level, in Constant (1993) Dollars: 1970 to 1993

[Constant dollars based on CPI-U-X1 deflator. As of **March of following year.** For 1970, persons 14 years old and over; thereafter, 15 years old and over. For definition of median, see Guide to Tabular Presentation. See also *Historical Statistics, Colonial Times to 1970*, series G 257-268. For composition of regions, see table 27]

ITEM	All persons (mil.)	PERSONS WITH INCOME									
		Total (mil.)	Percent distribution								Median income (dollars)
			$1 to $2,499 or loss [1]	$2,500 to $4,999	$5,000 to $9,999	$10,000 to $14,999	$15,000 to $24,999	$25,000 to $49,999	$50,000 to $74,999	$75,000 and over	
MALE											
1970	70.6	65.0	8.3	5.9	10.8	9.8	19.5	35.6	7.1	3.1	23,337
1980	82.9	78.7	7.2	5.1	11.9	11.1	20.0	32.9	8.1	3.6	22,000
1981	84.0	79.7	7.6	5.8	12.1	10.9	20.1	32.1	7.8	3.6	21,608
1982	85.0	79.7	8.2	5.6	12.2	10.6	21.1	30.6	7.6	4.0	21,086
1983 [2]	86.0	80.8	8.3	5.6	12.1	11.7	20.1	30.1	8.4	3.8	21,220
1984	87.3	82.2	7.6	5.5	12.6	11.1	19.0	31.3	8.7	4.1	21,696
1985	88.5	83.6	7.3	5.5	12.0	11.6	19.8	30.6	8.9	4.3	21,905
1986 [3]	89.4	84.5	7.0	5.1	11.8	11.1	19.3	31.3	9.6	4.8	22,564
1987 [3]	90.3	85.7	6.7	5.1	11.6	11.1	19.7	31.0	9.8	5.0	22,624
1988	91.0	86.6	6.7	4.9	11.7	11.0	20.1	31.1	9.5	5.0	23,096
1989	92.0	87.5	6.3	4.7	11.6	11.2	20.5	30.7	9.4	5.5	23,182
1990	92.8	88.2	6.4	4.7	12.3	11.5	20.9	30.4	9.0	5.0	22,436
1991	93.8	88.7	6.4	5.1	12.5	12.4	20.3	30.2	8.4	4.8	21,716
1992 [4]	94.9	89.6	6.9	5.1	12.9	12.3	20.6	29.0	8.4	4.8	21,067
1993	**96.8**	**90.2**	**7.0**	**4.9**	**12.1**	**12.4**	**20.8**	**28.8**	**8.7**	**5.2**	**21,102**
15 to 24 years old . .	18.2	13.8	27.7	15.0	21.0	14.9	15.2	5.6	0.5	0.2	6,429
25 to 34 years old . .	20.9	20.2	3.7	3.7	9.5	12.8	27.8	33.8	6.3	2.4	21,927
35 to 44 years old . .	20.5	19.9	3.7	2.2	6.9	8.1	18.9	39.3	13.3	7.6	30,342
45 to 54 years old . .	14.5	14.1	3.6	1.9	7.0	7.1	15.4	37.2	16.5	11.2	33,154
55 to 64 years old . .	9.9	9.6	3.8	3.1	11.0	11.7	20.1	31.6	10.7	7.9	25,139
65 yr. old and over . .	12.7	12.6	1.4	4.6	21.6	22.5	25.2	18.1	4.0	2.6	14,983
White	82.0	77.7	6.5	4.5	11.3	12.2	20.7	29.8	9.3	5.7	21,981
Black . . . [5] . . .	10.6	8.9	11.1	7.5	18.0	14.1	21.8	22.2	4.1	1.2	14,605
Hispanic [5]	9.3	8.2	7.8	7.1	20.1	18.5	23.1	18.4	3.5	1.4	13,689
Northeast	19.3	17.9	6.4	4.8	11.3	11.8	19.9	29.5	10.0	6.3	22,283
Midwest	22.5	21.4	7.0	4.9	10.7	12.4	21.2	31.2	8.7	4.1	21,696
South	33.5	31.0	7.4	5.2	13.7	13.0	21.4	26.6	7.8	4.8	19,714
West	21.4	19.9	7.0	4.3	12.2	12.1	20.1	29.1	9.0	6.1	21,536
FEMALE											
1970	77.6	51.6	20.8	16.3	20.4	15.0	18.0	8.9	0.5	0.2	7,827
1980	91.1	80.8	20.3	12.8	22.3	14.4	18.3	10.8	0.8	0.3	8,638
1981	92.2	82.1	19.9	12.6	22.8	14.1	18.6	11.0	0.8	0.2	8,753
1982	93.1	82.5	19.8	12.2	22.4	13.6	18.9	11.7	1.0	0.4	8,898
1983 [2]	94.3	83.8	18.9	12.1	21.7	14.6	18.4	12.7	1.2	0.4	9,292
1984	95.3	85.6	18.1	11.9	22.0	14.1	18.2	13.9	1.4	0.5	9,552
1985	96.4	86.5	17.7	12.0	21.7	14.0	18.1	14.4	1.5	0.5	9,692
1986 [3]	97.3	87.8	17.1	11.6	21.6	13.7	18.4	15.2	1.7	0.6	10,033
1987 [3]	98.2	89.7	16.0	11.4	21.2	13.8	19.1	15.8	1.9	0.7	10,551
1988	99.0	90.6	15.9	11.1	21.3	14.0	18.9	16.1	2.1	0.7	10,852
1989	99.8	91.4	15.1	11.1	20.6	13.9	19.6	16.6	2.2	0.8	11,215
1990	100.7	92.2	14.9	11.2	20.9	14.4	19.1	16.4	2.3	0.8	11,133
1991	101.5	92.6	14.3	10.8	21.7	14.9	19.0	16.3	2.2	0.8	11,114
1992 [4]	102.4	93.2	14.6	10.9	21.3	14.7	18.7	16.7	2.2	0.8	11,035
1993	**104.0**	**94.4**	**14.1**	**10.9**	**21.4**	**14.4**	**19.1**	**16.5**	**2.6**	**0.9**	**11,046**
15 to 24 years old . .	18.1	13.5	30.5	17.4	23.5	13.2	12.2	3.0	0.1	0.1	5,351
25 to 34 years old . .	21.1	19.6	13.2	8.4	16.3	14.5	24.1	20.6	2.3	0.6	13,988
35 to 44 years old . .	21.0	19.7	13.0	7.1	14.6	13.3	21.5	25.0	4.0	1.7	15,844
45 to 54 years old . .	15.1	14.0	12.7	5.9	14.7	13.2	22.5	24.7	4.9	1.5	16,324
55 to 64 years old . .	10.8	10.0	15.8	11.2	20.3	14.1	18.4	16.1	3.0	1.1	10,829
65 yr. old and over . .	18.0	17.7	4.0	16.7	38.9	17.9	14.2	6.7	1.2	0.5	8,499
White	86.8	79.5	14.2	10.4	21.0	14.5	19.3	16.9	2.7	1.0	11,266
Black	12.9	11.3	11.8	14.7	25.3	14.7	17.7	13.8	1.5	0.5	9,508
Hispanic [5]	9.1	7.1	16.3	14.5	27.1	15.3	15.7	9.8	1.0	0.4	8,100
Northeast	21.3	19.5	13.3	10.6	21.8	13.1	18.4	17.8	3.5	1.4	11,375
Midwest	24.5	22.9	14.0	11.0	21.4	14.8	20.3	16.0	2.0	0.6	11,031
South	36.4	32.4	14.4	11.7	22.0	14.9	19.2	15.1	2.1	0.7	10,557
West	21.9	19.6	14.6	9.8	19.9	14.6	18.3	18.2	3.2	1.3	11,568

[1] Includes persons with income deficit. [2] Beginning 1983, data based on revised Hispanic population controls and not directly comparable with prior years. [3] Beginning 1987, data based on revised processing procedures and not directly comparable with prior years. [4] Based on 1990 populations controls. [5] Persons of Hispanic origin may be of any race.

Source: U.S. Bureau of the Census, *Current Population Reports*, P60-188; and unpublished data.

No. 741. Median Income of Married-Couple Families, by Work Experience of Husbands and Wives: 1993

March 1994. Based on Current Population Survey; see text, sections 1 and 14, and Appendix III]

WORK EXPERIENCE OF HUSBAND	NUMBER (1,000)				MEDIAN INCOME (dollars)			
		Wife worked		Wife did not work		Wife worked		Wife did not work
	Total	Total	Worked year-round, full-time		Total	Total	Worked year-round, full-time	
All families [1]	**53,181**	**34,411**	**18,657**	**18,770**	**43,005**	**50,798**	**56,078**	**28,779**
Husband worked	42,072	31,419	17,170	10,653	49,450	52,494	57,891	37,482
Worked year-round, full-time . . .	33,357	25,423	14,325	7,934	52,869	56,017	60,711	41,776
Husband did not work	11,109	2,992	1,487	8,117	23,128	30,131	34,661	20,987
White.	47,452	30,574	16,231	16,878	43,675	51,205	56,519	29,571
Husband worked	37,634	28,069	14,993	9,565	49,988	52,863	58,269	38,601
Worked year-round, full-time . . .	29,808	22,690	12,470	7,118	53,356	56,341	61,062	42,456
Husband did not work	9,818	2,505	1,238	7,313	23,822	30,777	35,421	21,709
Black.	3,715	2,562	1,617	1,153	35,218	44,446	51,192	20,953
Husband worked	2,763	2,171	1,427	592	43,181	47,815	53,146	29,354
Worked year-round, full-time . . .	2,214	1,759	1,210	455	47,002	51,442	55,517	30,966
Husband did not work	953	392	190	561	17,211	25,712	29,380	13,962
Hispanic [2].	4,038	2,236	1,166	1,802	28,454	35,919	43,856	19,989
Husband worked	3,395	2,047	1,078	1,349	31,198	37,282	45,587	21,681
Worked year-round, full-time . . .	2,483	1,543	885	939	35,357	42,191	48,607	25,254
Husband did not work	643	190	88	453	17,042	21,431	28,779	14,714

[1] Includes other races not shown separately.   [2] Persons of Hispanic origin may be of any race.

No. 742. Average Earnings of Year-Round, Full-Time Workers: 1993

[In dollars. For persons 25 years old and over as of March 1994]

AGE AND SEX	All workers	Less than 9th grade	HIGH SCHOOL		COLLEGE		
			9th to 12th grade (no diploma)	High school graduate (includes equivalency)	Some college, no degree	Associate degree	Bachelor's degree or more
Male, total	**$39,806**	**$18,697**	**$23,797**	**$30,384**	**$34,967**	**$36,002**	**$59,276**
25 to 34 years old	30,224	15,860	19,796	25,532	28,135	31,355	42,296
35 to 44 years old	41,940	18,123	24,755	31,675	36,005	36,679	60,381
45 to 54 years old	49,219	20,085	26,398	35,783	42,060	40,627	73,445
55 to 64 years old	41,195	21,994	28,200	32,216	39,735	39,721	62,219
65 years old and over. . . .	37,533	14,939	22,468	24,011	28,864	(B)	64,705
Female, total	**26,165**	**13,051**	**18,030**	**20,924**	**23,655**	**26,430**	**37,109**
25 to 34 years old	23,865	11,878	14,108	19,151	21,499	23,990	32,154
35 to 44 years old	27,787	13,040	14,940	21,821	24,215	28,542	39,394
45 to 54 years old	27,113	13,377	17,078	21,471	24,987	27,883	39,963
55 to 64 years old	26,518	13,504	28,018	21,548	26,339	25,102	41,010
65 years old and over. . . .	21,308	(B)	(B)	20,757	20,780	(B)	(B)

B Base figure too small to meet statistical standards for reliability of derived figure.

No. 743. Per Capita Money Income in Current and Constant (1993) Dollars, by Race and Hispanic Origin: 1970 to 1993

[In dollars. Constant dollars based on CPI-U-X1 deflator. As of March of following year]

YEAR	CURRENT DOLLARS				CONSTANT (1993) DOLLARS			
	All races [1]	White	Black	Hispanic [2]	All races [1]	White	Black	Hispanic [2]
1970	3,177	3,354	1,869	(NA)	11,116	11,735	6,539	(NA)
1975	4,818	5,072	2,972	2,847	12,388	13,041	7,642	7,320
1980 [3]	7,787	8,233	4,804	4,865	13,672	14,455	8,435	8,542
1985 [3]	11,013	11,671	6,840	6,613	14,790	15,673	9,186	8,881
1986 [4]	11,670	12,352	7,207	7,000	15,386	16,285	9,502	9,229
1987 [4]	12,391	13,143	7,645	7,653	15,761	16,718	9,724	9,735
1988	13,123	13,896	8,271	7,956	16,029	16,974	10,103	9,718
1989	14,056	14,896	8,747	8,390	16,380	17,359	10,193	9,777
1990	14,387	15,265	9,017	8,424	15,906	16,877	9,969	9,313
1991	14,617	15,510	9,170	8,662	15,508	16,455	9,729	9,190
1992 [5]	15,033	15,981	9,296	8,874	15,483	16,459	9,574	9,140
1992 [5]	14,847	15,785	9,239	8,591	15,291	16,258	9,516	8,848
1993	15,777	16,800	9,863	8,830	15,777	16,800	9,863	8,830

NA Not available.   [1] Includes other races not shown separately.   [2] Persons of Hispanic origin may be of any race.   [3] Beginning 1983, data based on revised Hispanic population controls and not directly comparable with prior years.   [4] Beginning 1987, data based on revised processing procedures and not directly comparable with prior years.   [5] Based on 1990 population controls.

Source of tables 741-743: U.S. Bureau of the Census, Current Population Reports, P60-188.

No. 744. Persons Below Poverty Level and Below 125 Percent of Poverty Level: 1960 to 1993

[Persons as of **March of the following year**. Based on Current Population Survey; see text, sections 1 and 14, and Appendix III]

YEAR	NUMBER BELOW POVERTY LEVEL (1,000)				PERCENT BELOW POVERTY LEVEL				BELOW 125 PERCENT OF POVERTY LEVEL		AVERAGE INCOME CUTOFFS FOR NONFARM FAMILY OF FOUR [3]	
	All races [1]	White	Black	His-panic [2]	All races [1]	White	Black	His-panic [2]	Number (mil.)	Per-cent of total popula-tion	At poverty level	At 125 percent of poverty level
1960	39,851	28,309	(NA)	(NA)	22.2	17.8	(NA)	(NA)	54,560	30.4	3,022	3,778
1966	28,510	19,290	8,867	(NA)	14.7	11.3	41.8	(NA)	41,267	21.3	3,317	4,146
1969	24,147	16,659	7,095	(NA)	12.1	9.5	32.2	(NA)	34,665	17.4	3,743	4,679
1970	25,420	17,484	7,548	(NA)	12.6	9.9	33.5	(NA)	35,624	17.6	3,968	4,960
1975	25,877	17,770	7,545	2,991	12.3	9.7	31.3	23.0	37,182	17.6	5,500	6,875
1976	24,975	16,713	7,595	2,783	11.8	9.1	31.1	26.9	35,509	16.7	5,815	7,269
1977	24,720	16,416	7,726	2,700	11.6	8.9	31.3	24.7	35,659	16.7	6,191	7,739
1978	24,497	16,259	7,625	2,607	11.4	8.7	30.6	22.4	34,155	15.8	6,662	8,328
1979 [4]	26,072	17,214	8,050	2,921	11.7	9.0	31.0	21.6	36,616	16.4	7,412	9,265
1980	29,272	19,699	8,579	3,491	13.0	10.2	32.5	21.8	40,658	18.1	8,414	10,518
1981	31,822	21,553	9,173	3,713	14.0	11:1	34.2	25.7	43,748	19.3	9,287	11,609
1982 [5]	34,398	23,517	9,697	4,301	15.0	12.0	35.6	26.5	46,520	20.3	9,862	12,328
1983 [5]	35,303	23,984	9,882	4,633	15.2	12.1	35.7	29.9	47,150	20.3	10,178	12,723
1984	33,700	22,955	9,490	4,806	14.4	11.5	33.8	28.0	45,288	19.4	10,609	13,261
1985	33,064	22,860	8,926	5,236	14.0	11.4	31.3	28.4	44,166	18.7	10,989	13,736
1986	32,370	22,183	8,983	5,117	13.6	11.0	31.1	29.0	43,486	18.2	11,203	14,004
1987 [6]	32,221	21,195	9,520	5,422	13.4	10.4	32.4	27.3	43,032	17.9	11,611	14,514
1988	31,745	20,715	9,356	5,357	13.0	10.1	31.3	28.0	42,551	17.5	12,092	15,115
1989	31,528	20,785	9,302	5,430	12.8	10.0	30.7	26.7	42,653	17.3	12,674	15,843
1990	33,585	22,326	9,837	6,006	13.5	10.7	31.9	26.2	44,837	18.0	13,359	16,699
1991 [7]	35,708	23,747	10,242	6,339	14.2	11.3	32.7	28.1	47,527	18.9	13,924	17,405
1992 [7]	38,014	25,259	10,827	7,592	14.8	11.9	33.4	29.6	50,592	19.7	14,335	17,919
1993	39,265	26,226	10,877	8,126	15.1	12.2	33.1	30.6	51,801	20.0	14,763	(NA)

NA Not available.   [1] Includes other races not shown separately.   [2] Persons of Hispanic origin may be of any race. [3] Beginning 1981, income cutoffs for nonfarm families are applied to all families, both farm and nonfarm.   [4] Population controls based on 1980 census; see text, sections 1 and 14.   [5] Beginning 1983, data based on revised Hispanic population controls and not directly comparable with prior years.   [6] Beginning 1987, data based on revised processing procedures and not directly comparable with prior years.   [7] Beginning 1992, based on 1990 population controls.

Source: U.S. Bureau of the Census, *Current Population Reports*, P60-188.

No. 745. Children Below Poverty Level, by Race and Hispanic Origin: 1970 to 1993

[Persons as of **March of the following year**. Covers only related children in families under 18 years old. Based on Current Population Survey; see text, sections 1 and 14, and Appendix III]

YEAR	NUMBER BELOW POVERTY LEVEL (1,000)				PERCENT BELOW POVERTY LEVEL			
	All races [1]	White	Black	Hispanic [2]	All races [1]	White	Black	Hispanic [2]
1970	10,235	6,138	3,922	(NA)	14.9	10.5	41.5	(NA)
1975	10,882	6,748	3,884	1,619	16.8	12.5	41.4	33.1
1980	11,114	6,817	3,906	1,718	17.9	13.4	42.1	33.0
1981	12,068	7,429	4,170	1,874	19.5	14.7	44.9	35.4
1982	13,139	8,282	4,388	2,117	21.3	16.5	47.3	38.9
1983 [3]	13,427	8,534	4,273	2,251	21.8	17.0	46.2	37.7
1984	12,929	8,086	4,320	2,317	21.0	16.1	46.2	38.7
1985	12,483	7,838	4,057	2,512	20.1	15.6	43.1	39.6
1986	12,257	7,714	4,037	2,413	19.8	15.3	42.7	37.1
1987 [4]	12,275	7,398	4,234	2,606	19.7	14.7	44.4	38.9
1988	11,935	7,095	4,148	2,576	19.0	14.0	42.8	37.3
1989	12,001	7,164	4,257	2,496	19.0	14.1	43.2	35.5
1990	12,715	7,696	4,412	2,750	19.9	15.1	44.2	37.7
1991	13,658	8,316	4,637	2,977	21.1	16.1	45.6	39.8
1992 [5]	14,521	8,752	5,015	3,440	21.6	16.5	46.3	39.0
1993	14,961	9,123	5,030	3,666	22.0	17.0	45.9	39.9

NA Not available.   [1] Includes other races not shown separately.   [2] Persons of Hispanic origin may be of any race. [3] Beginning 1983, data based on revised Hispanic population controls and not directly comparable with prior years.   [4] Beginning 1987, data based on revised processing procedures and not directly comparable with prior years.   [5] Beginning 1992, based on 1990 population controls.

Source: U.S. Bureau of the Census, *Current Population Reports*, P60-188.

No. 746. Weighted Average Poverty Thresholds: 1980 to 1993

[Official poverty thresholds; see text, section 14]

SIZE OF UNIT	1980[1]	1986	1987	1988	1989	1990	1991	1992	1993
One person (unrelated individual) . . .	$4,190	$5,572	$5,778	$6,022	$6,310	$6,652	$6,932	$7,143	$7,363
Under 65 years	4,290	5,701	5,909	6,155	6,451	6,800	7,086	7,299	$7,518
65 years and over	3,949	5,255	5,447	5,674	5,947	6,268	6,532	6,729	6,930
Two persons	5,363	7,138	7,397	7,704	8,076	8,509	8,865	9,137	9,414
Householder under 65 years	5,537	7,372	7,641	7,958	8,343	8,794	9,165	9,443	9,728
Householder 65 years and over . . .	4,983	6,630	6,872	7,157	7,501	7,905	8,241	8,487	8,740
Three persons	6,565	8,737	9,056	9,435	9,885	10,419	10,860	11,186	11,522
Four persons	8,414	11,203	11,611	12,092	12,674	13,359	13,924	14,335	14,763
Five persons	9,966	13,259	13,737	14,304	14,990	15,792	16,456	16,952	17,449
Six persons	11,269	14,986	15,509	16,146	16,921	17,839	18,587	19,137	19,718
Seven persons	12,761	17,049	17,649	18,232	19,162	20,241	21,058	21,594	22,383
Eight persons	14,199	18,791	19,515	20,253	21,328	22,582	23,605	24,053	24,838
Nine or more persons	16,896	22,497	23,105	24,129	25,480	26,848	27,942	28,745	29,529

[1] Poverty levels for nonfarm families.

Source: U.S. Bureau of the Census, Current Population Reports, P60-188; and earlier reports.

No. 747. Persons Below Poverty Level, by Selected Characteristics: 1993

[Persons as of **March 1994.** Based on Current Population Survey; see text, sections 1 and 14, and Appendix III. For composition of regions, see table 27]

AGE AND REGION	NUMBER BELOW POVERTY LEVEL (1,000)				PERCENT BELOW POVERTY LEVEL			
	All races [1]	White	Black	Hispanic [2]	All races [1]	White	Black	Hispanic [2]
Total	**39,265**	**26,226**	**10,877**	**8,126**	**15.1**	**12.2**	**33.1**	**30.6**
Under 18 years old	15,727	9,752	5,125	3,873	22.7	17.8	46.1	40.9
18 to 24 years old	4,854	3,274	1,264	1,047	19.1	16.0	34.4	31.0
25 to 34 years old	5,804	3,885	1,556	1,279	13.8	11.3	28.4	25.4
35 to 44 years old	4,415	3,001	1,156	879	10.6	8.7	23.0	23.8
45 to 54 years old	2,522	1,776	586	446	8.5	7.0	19.2	20.2
55 to 59 years old	1,057	742	254	154	9.9	8.0	23.6	20.6
60 to 64 years old	1,129	857	233	151	11.3	9.7	24.4	24.4
65 years old and over . . .	3,755	2,939	702	297	12.2	10.7	28.0	21.4
Northeast	6,839	4,817	1,744	1,527	13.3	11.0	31.2	37.3
Midwest	8,172	5,454	2,413	476	13.4	10.3	35.9	26.5
South	15,375	8,876	6,063	2,349	17.1	12.8	33.6	28.0
West	8,879	7,080	658	3,774	15.6	14.6	25.9	30.7

[1] Includes other races not shown separately.   [2] Persons of Hispanic origin may be of any race.

Source: U.S. Bureau of the Census, Current Population Reports, P60-188; and unpublished data.

No. 748. Persons 65 Years Old and Over Below Poverty Level: 1970 to 1993

[Persons as of **March of following year**]

CHARACTERISTIC	NUMBER BELOW POVERTY LEVEL (1,000)					PERCENT BELOW POVERTY LEVEL				
	1970	1979 [1]	1990 [2]	1992	1993	1970	1979 [1]	1990 [2]	1992	1993
Total [3]	**4,793**	**3,682**	**3,658**	**3,983**	**3,755**	**24.6**	**15.2**	**12.2**	**12.9**	**12.2**
White	4,011	2,911	2,707	2,992	2,939	22.6	13.3	10.1	10.9	10.7
Black	683	740	860	887	702	48.0	36.2	33.8	33.3	28.0
Hispanic [4]	(NA)	154	245	269	297	(NA)	26.8	22.5	22.0	21.4
In families	2,013	1,380	1,172	1,484	1,343	14.8	8.4	5.8	7.1	6.5
Unrelated individuals	2,779	2,299	2,479	2,498	2,412	47.2	29.4	24.7	24.9	24.1

NA Not available.   [1] Population controls based on 1980 census; see text, section 14.   [2] Beginning 1987, data based on revised processing procedures and not directly comparable with prior years.   [3] Beginning 1979, includes members of unrelated subfamilies not shown separately. For earlier years, unrelated subfamily members are included in the "In families" category.   [4] Persons of Hispanic origin may be of any race.

Source: U.S. Bureau of the Census, Current Population Reports, P60-188; and earlier reports.

Income, Expenditures, and Wealth

No. 749. Persons Below Poverty Level, by State: 1980 to 1993

[Based on the Current Population Survey; see text, sections 1 and 14, and Appendix III. The CPS is designed to collect reliable data on income primarily at the national level and secondarily at the regional level. When the income data are tabulated by State, the estimates are considered less reliable and, therefore, particular caution should be used when trying to interpret the results; for additional detail, see source]

STATE	NUMBER BELOW POVERTY LEVEL (1,000)					PERCENT BELOW POVERTY LEVEL				
	1980	1990 [1]	1991	1992	1993	1980	1990 [1]	1991	1992	1993
United States.	29,272	33,585	35,708	36,880	39,265	13.0	13.5	14.2	14.5	15.1
Alabama	810	779	786	715	725	21.2	19.2	18.8	17.1	17.4
Alaska.	36	57	62	53	52	9.6	11.4	11.8	10.0	9.1
Arizona	354	484	532	554	615	12.8	13.7	14.8	15.1	15.4
Arkansas.	484	472	425	424	484	21.5	19.6	17.3	17.4	20.0
California.	2,619	4,128	4,825	4,925	5,803	11.0	13.9	15.7	15.8	18.2
Colorado	247	461	347	353	354	8.6	13.7	10.4	10.6	9.9
Connecticut	255	196	287	303	277	8.3	6.0	8.6	9.4	8.5
Delaware.	68	48	53	55	73	11.8	6.9	7.5	7.6	10.2
District of Columbia	131	120	98	108	158	20.9	21.1	18.6	20.3	26.4
Florida.	1,692	1,896	2,069	2,097	2,507	16.7	14.4	15.4	15.3	17.8
Georgia.	727	1,001	1,077	1,151	919	13.9	15.8	17.2	17.8	13.5
Hawaii.	81	121	90	129	91	8.5	11.0	7.7	11.0	8.0
Idaho	138	157	144	160	150	14.7	14.9	13.9	15.0	13.1
Illinois	1,386	1,606	1,598	1,836	1,600	12.3	13.7	13.5	15.3	13.6
Indiana	645	714	866	660	704	11.8	13.0	15.7	11.7	12.2
Iowa.	311	289	271	327	290	10.8	10.4	9.6	11.3	10.3
Kansas	215	259	317	277	327	9.4	10.3	12.3	11.0	13.1
Kentucky	701	628	683	723	763	19.3	17.3	18.8	19.7	20.4
Louisiana.	868	952	795	1,020	1,119	20.3	23.6	19.0	24.2	26.4
Maine	158	162	171	170	196	14.6	13.1	14.1	13.4	15.4
Maryland	389	468	432	568	479	9.5	9.9	9.1	11.6	9.7
Massachusetts	542	626	637	580	641	9.5	10.7	11.0	10.0	10.7
Michigan	1,194	1,315	1,308	1,254	1,475	12.9	14.3	14.1	13.5	15.4
Minnesota	342	524	564	554	506	8.7	12.0	12.9	12.8	11.6
Mississippi	591	684	635	660	639	24.3	25.7	23.7	24.5	24.7
Missouri	625	700	740	797	832	13.0	13.4	14.8	15.6	16.1
Montana	102	134	127	113	127	13.2	16.3	15.4	13.7	14.9
Nebraska.	199	167	157	169	169	13.0	10.3	9.5	10.3	10.3
Nevada	70	119	141	188	141	8.3	9.8	11.4	14.4	9.8
New Hampshire	63	68	81	99	112	7.0	6.3	7.3	8.6	9.9
New Jersey	659	711	754	771	866	9.0	9.2	9.7	10.0	10.9
New Mexico.	268	319	349	327	282	20.6	20.9	22.4	21.0	17.4
New York.	2,391	2,571	2,736	2,699	2,981	13.8	14.3	15.3	15.3	16.4
North Carolina	877	829	964	1,047	966	15.0	13.0	14.5	15.7	14.4
North Dakota	99	87	92	73	70	15.5	13.7	14.5	11.9	11.2
Ohio.	1,046	1,256	1,488	1,381	1,461	9.8	11.5	13.4	12.4	13.0
Oklahoma	406	481	541	600	662	13.9	15.6	17.0	18.4	19.9
Oregon	309	267	401	340	363	11.5	9.2	13.5	11.3	11.8
Pennsylvania	1,142	1,328	1,340	1,426	1,598	9.8	11.0	11.0	11.7	13.2
Rhode Island	97	71	99	116	108	10.7	7.5	10.4	12.0	11.2
South Carolina	534	548	582	687	678	16.8	16.2	16.4	18.9	18.7
South Dakota	127	93	96	105	102	18.8	13.3	14.8	14.8	14.2
Tennessee	884	833	744	849	998	19.6	16.9	15.5	17.0	19.6
Texas	2,247	2,684	2,965	3,079	3,177	15.7	15.9	17.5	17.8	17.4
Utah	148	143	222	162	203	10.0	8.2	12.9	9.3	10.7
Vermont	62	61	73	63	59	12.0	10.9	12.6	10.4	10.0
Virginia	647	705	608	584	627	12.4	11.1	9.9	9.4	9.7
Washington	538	434	474	555	634	12.7	8.9	9.5	11.0	12.1
West Virginia	297	328	327	396	400	15.2	18.1	17.9	22.3	22.2
Wisconsin	403	448	492	551	636	8.5	9.3	9.9	10.8	12.6
Wyoming	49	51	47	49	64	10.4	11.0	9.9	10.3	13.3

[1] Beginning 1987, data based on revised processing procedures and not directly comparable with prior years.

Source: U.S. Bureau of the Census, *Current Population Reports*, P60-188.

No. 750. Persons Below Poverty Level, by Race and Family Status: 1979 to 1993

[Persons as of March of following year. Based on Current Population Survey; see text, sections 1 and 14, and Appendix III]

RACE AND FAMILY STATUS	NUMBER BELOW POVERTY LEVEL (mil.)					PERCENT BELOW POVERTY LEVEL				
	1979 [1]	1990 [2]	1991	1992 [3]	1993	1979 [1]	1990 [2]	1991	1992 [3]	1993
All persons [4]	**26.1**	**33.6**	**35.7**	**38.0**	**39.3**	**11.7**	**13.5**	**14.2**	**14.8**	**15.1**
In families	20.0	25.2	27.1	29.0	30.0	10.2	12.0	12.8	13.3	13.6
Householder	5.5	7.1	7.7	8.1	8.4	9.2	10.7	11.5	11.9	12.3
Related children under 18 years	10.0	12.7	13.7	14.5	15.0	16.0	19.9	21.1	21.6	22.0
Unrelated individuals	5.7	7.4	7.8	8.1	8.4	21.9	20.7	21.1	21.9	22.1
Male	2.0	2.9	3.0	3.2	3.3	16.9	16.9	17.3	18.2	18.1
Female	3.8	4.6	4.7	4.9	5.1	26.0	24.0	24.5	25.3	25.7
White [4]	**17.2**	**22.3**	**23.7**	**25.3**	**26.2**	**9.0**	**10.7**	**11.3**	**11.9**	**12.2**
In families	12.5	15.9	17.3	18.3	19.0	7.4	9.0	9.7	10.1	10.5
Householder	3.6	4.6	5.0	5.3	5.5	6.9	8.1	8.8	9.1	9.4
Related children under 18 years	5.9	7.7	8.3	8.8	9.1	11.4	15.1	16.1	16.5	17.0
Unrelated individuals	4.5	5.7	5.9	6.1	6.4	19.7	18.6	18.8	19.7	20.1
Black [4]	**8.1**	**9.8**	**10.2**	**10.8**	**10.9**	**31.0**	**31.9**	**32.7**	**33.4**	**33.1**
In families	6.8	8.2	8.5	9.1	9.2	30.0	31.0	32.0	32.9	32.9
Householder	1.7	2.2	2.3	2.5	2.5	27.8	29.3	30.4	31.1	31.3
Related children under 18 years	3.7	4.4	4.6	5.0	5.0	40.8	44.2	45.6	46.3	45.9
Unrelated individuals	1.2	1.5	1.6	1.6	1.5	37.3	35.1	35.3	35.6	33.4
In families with female householder, no spouse present	9.4	12.6	13.8	14.2	14.6	34.9	37.2	39.7	39.0	38.7
Householder	2.6	3.8	4.2	4.3	4.4	30.4	33.4	35.6	35.4	35.6
Related children under 18 years	5.6	7.4	8.1	8.4	8.5	48.6	53.4	55.5	54.6	53.7

[1] Population controls based on 1980 census; see text, section 14.   [2] Beginning 1987, data based on revised processing procedures and not directly comparable with prior years.   [3] Beginning 1992, based on 1990 population controls.   [4] Includes other races and members of unrelated subfamilies not shown separately.

Source: U.S. Bureau of the Census, Current Population Reports, P60-188; and unpublished data.

No. 751. Monthly Measures of Poverty Status, by Selected Characteristics: 1990-91 Period

[In thousands, except percent. Covers 2-year calendar period. Based on Survey of Income and Program Participation, see text, section 14]

CHARACTERISTIC	PERSONS POOR IN AN AVERAGE MONTH		PERSONS POOR 2 OR MORE MONTHS		PERSONS POOR ALL 24 MONTHS OF 1990-91		Median duration of poverty spells (months)
	Number	Percent	Number	Percent	Number	Percent	
Total [1]	**31,818**	**12.9**	**45,638**	**18.9**	**10,619**	**4.5**	**4.0**
Under 18 years old	13,027	20.1	17,672	27.7	4,820	7.5	(NA)
18 to 64 years old	16,009	10.5	24,454	16.4	4,401	3.0	(NA)
65 years old and over	2,783	9.4	3,512	12.5	1,399	5.3	(NA)
White	21,233	10.2	32,042	15.7	5,969	3.0	3.9
Black	9,152	30.1	11,621	39.2	4,060	13.9	5.8
Hispanic origin [2]	5,465	26.1	7,345	37.5	1,949	10.4	4.9
Region: [3]							
Northeast	5,139	10.2	6,980	14.4	2,007	4.2	3.8
Midwest	7,345	11.9	10,472	16.9	2,689	4.3	3.9
South	13,458	15.9	19,606	23.8	4,570	5.7	4.4
West	5,876	11.6	8,579	17.7	1,354	2.9	4.2
Educational attainment: [4]							
Less than 4 years of high school	8,392	20.8	11,229	29.2	3,366	9.1	5.3
High school graduate, no college	6,350	9.3	9,927	14.6	1,776	2.7	3.9
One or more years of college	4,050	5.5	6,809	9.6	658	0.9	3.7
Disability status: [5]							
With a work disability	5,304	17.8	7,149	25.8	1,899	7.3	4.9
With no work disability	12,944	9.0	20,378	14.4	3,239	2.3	3.9

NA Not available.   [1] Includes other characteristics not shown separately.   [2] Persons of Hispanic origin may be of any race.   [3] For composition of regions, see table 27.   [4] Persons 18 years old and over.   [5] Persons 15 to 69 years old.

Source: U.S. Bureau of the Census, Current Population Reports, P70-42.

No. 752. Families Below Poverty Level and Below 125 Percent of Poverty Level: 1960 to 1993

[Families as of **March of the following year.** Based on Current Population Survey, see text, sections 1 and 14, and Appendix III]

YEAR	NUMBER BELOW POVERTY LEVEL (1,000)				PERCENT BELOW POVERTY LEVEL				BELOW 125 PERCENT OF POVERTY LEVEL	
	All races [1]	White	Black	His-panic [2]	All races [1]	White	Black	His-panic [2]	Number (1,000)	Percent
1960	8,243	6,115	(NA)	(NA)	18.1	14.9	(NA)	(NA)	11,525	25.4
1970	5,260	3,708	1,481	(NA)	10.1	8.0	29.5	(NA)	7,516	14.4
1972	5,075	3,441	1,529	477	9.3	7.1	29.0	20.6	7,347	13.5
1973	4,828	3,219	1,527	468	8.8	6.6	28.1	19.8	7,044	12.8
1974	4,922	3,352	1,479	526	8.8	6.8	26.9	21.2	7,195	12.9
1975	5,450	3,838	1,513	627	9.7	7.7	27.1	25.1	7,974	14.2
1976	5,311	3,560	1,617	598	9.4	7.1	27.9	23.1	7,647	13.5
1977	5,311	3,540	1,637	591	9.3	7.0	28.2	21.4	7,713	13.5
1978 [3]	5,280	3,523	1,622	559	9.1	6.9	27.5	20.4	7,417	12.8
1979 [3]	5,461	3,581	1,722	614	9.2	6.9	27.8	20.3	7,784	13.1
1980	6,217	4,195	1,826	751	10.3	8.0	28.9	23.2	8,764	14.5
1981	6,851	4,670	1,972	792	11.2	8.8	30.8	24.0	9,568	15.7
1982	7,512	5,118	2,158	916	12.2	9.6	33.0	27.2	10,279	16.7
1983 [4]	7,647	5,220	2,161	981	12.3	9.7	32.3	25.9	10,358	16.7
1984	7,277	4,925	2,094	991	11.6	9.1	30.9	25.2	9,901	15.8
1985	7,223	4,983	1,983	1,074	11.4	9.1	28.7	25.5	9,753	15.3
1986	7,023	4,811	1,987	1,085	10.9	8.6	28.0	24.7	9,476	14.7
1987 [5]	7,005	4,567	2,117	1,168	10.7	8.1	29.4	25.5	9,338	14.3
1988	6,874	4,471	2,089	1,141	10.4	7.9	28.2	23.7	9,284	14.1
1989	6,784	4,409	2,077	1,133	10.3	7.8	27.8	23.4	9,267	14.0
1990	7,098	4,622	2,193	1,244	10.7	8.1	29.3	25.0	9,564	14.4
1991	7,712	5,022	2,343	1,372	11.5	8.8	30.4	26.5	10,244	15.3
1992 [6]	8,144	5,255	2,484	1,529	11.9	9.1	31.1	26.7	10,736	15.8
1993	8,393	5,452	2,499	1,625	12.3	9.4	31.3	27.3	10,959	16.1

NA Not available.   [1] Includes other races not shown separately.   [2] Persons of Hispanic origin may be of any race.
[3] Population controls based on 1980 census; see text, section 14.   [4] Beginning 1983, data based on revised Hispanic population controls and not directly comparable with prior years.   [5] Beginning 1987, data based on revised processing procedures and not directly comparable with prior years.   [6] Beginning 1992, based on 1990 population controls.

Source: U.S. Bureau of the Census, *Current Population Reports*, P60-188.

No. 753. Families Below Poverty Level, by Selected Characteristics: 1993

[Families as of **March 1994.** Based on Current Population Survey; see text, sections 1 and 14, and Appendix III. For composition of regions, see table 27]

CHARACTERISTIC	NUMBER BELOW POVERTY LEVEL (1,000)				PERCENT BELOW POVERTY LEVEL			
	All races [1]	White	Black	His-panic [2]	All races [1]	White	Black	His-panic [2]
Total	**8,393**	**5,452**	**2,499**	**1,625**	**12.3**	**9.4**	**31.3**	**27.3**
Size of family:								
Two persons	2,688	1,874	718	343	9.5	7.5	26.6	21.9
Three persons	2,020	1,274	649	357	12.6	9.7	29.7	25.9
Four persons	1,723	1,105	516	370	11.9	9.1	30.6	27.4
Five persons	1,095	689	327	273	17.3	13.2	41.3	30.2
Six persons	451	279	136	138	22.0	18.0	40.2	34.8
Seven persons or more	415	231	153	144	34.6	28.6	52.9	41.1
Average size	3.57	3.50	3.66	4.21	(X)	(X)	(X)	(X)
Avg. number of children per family with children . .	2.22	2.18	2.28	2.56	(X)	(X)	(X)	(X)
Education of householder: [3]								
No high school diploma	3,109	2,033	882	969	25.1	20.6	44.4	37.2
High school diploma, no college	2,492	1,557	840	329	11.7	8.6	31.4	23.5
Some college, less than bachelor's degree	1,295	875	367	116	8.0	6.3	19.7	11.5
Bachelor's degree or more	355	255	47	42	2.3	1.8	5.3	8.4
Work experience of householder:								
Total [4]	7,616	4,925	2,286	1,537	15.4	11.7	42.5	35.2
Worked during year	3,992	2,746	1,074	848	8.1	6.5	20.0	19.4
Year-round, full-time	1,265	924	278	323	3.4	2.8	7.5	10.7
Not year-round, full-time	2,727	1,822	796	524	23.4	19.1	47.8	39.3
Did not work	3,624	2,179	1,212	689	46.0	37.5	72.5	63.0

X Not applicable.   [1] Includes other races not shown separately.   [2] Hispanic persons may be of any race.   [3] Householder 25 years old and over.   [4] Persons 16 years old and over.

Source: U.S. Bureau of the Census, *Current Population Reports*, P60-188; and unpublished data.

No. 754. Persons Below Poverty Level, by Definition of Income: 1993

[Persons as of **March 1994.** For explanation of income definitions, see text, section 14]

Defi-nition num-ber	DEFINITION	NUMBER BELOW POVERTY LEVEL (1,000)				PERCENT BELOW POVERTY LEVEL			
		All races [1]	White	Black	His-panic [2]	All races [1]	White	Black	His-panic [2]
	All persons.	259,278	214,899	32,910	26,559	(X)	(X)	(X)	(X)
	INCOME BEFORE TAXES								
1	Money income excluding capital gains [3].	35,616	23,386	10,203	7,390	13.7	10.9	31.0	27.8
2	Definition 1 less government money transfers .	57,293	41,439	13,190	9,384	22.1	19.3	40.1	35.3
3	Definition 2 plus capital gains.	57,070	41,198	13,210	9,353	22.0	19.2	40.1	35.2
4	Definition 3 plus health insurance supplements to wage or salary income [4] . . .	55,368	39,956	12,828	9,025	21.4	18.6	39.0	34.0
	INCOME AFTER TAXES								
5	Definition 4 less Social Security payroll taxes .	57,678	41,869	13,132	9,523	22.2	19.5	39.9	35.9
6	Definition 5 less Federal income taxes (excluding EITC) [5]	58,049	42,149	13,201	9,601	22.4	19.6	40.1	36.2
7	Definition 6 plus EITC [5]	56,275	40,791	12,880	9,217	21.7	19.0	39.1	34.7
8	Definition 7 less State income taxes	56,581	41,027	12,945	9,235	21.8	19.1	39.3	34.8
9	Definition 8 plus nonmeans-tested government cash transfers [6]	38,406	25,201	10,963	7,951	14.8	11.7	33.3	29.9
10	Definition 9 plus value of Medicare	37,521	24,582	10,715	7,797	14.5	11.4	32.6	29.4
11	Definition 10 plus value of regular-price school lunches.	37,506	24,567	10,715	7,794	14.5	11.4	32.6	29.3
12	Definition 11 plus means-tested government cash transfers [7]	34,026	22,291	9,773	7,048	13.1	10.4	29.7	26.5
13	Definition 12 plus value of Medicaid	31,981	20,897	9,254	6,470	12.3	9.7	28.1	24.4
14	Definition 13 plus means-tested government noncash transfers [8]	27,818	18,444	7,794	5,586	10.7	8.6	23.7	21.0
15	Definition 14 plus net imputed return on equity in own home [9]	25,409	16,535	7,366	5,232	9.8	7.7	22.4	19.7

X Not applicable.   [1] Includes other races not shown separately.   [2] Persons of Hispanic origin may be of any race.   [3] Official definition based on income before taxes and includes government cash transfers.   [4] Employer contributions to the health insurance plans of employees.   [5] Earned Income Tax Credit.   [6] Includes Social Security and Railroad Retirement, veterans payments, unemployment and workers' compensation, Black Lung payments, Pell Grants, and other government educational assistance.   [7] Includes AFDC and other public assistance or welfare payments, Supplemental Security Income, and veterans payments. Households must meet certain eligibility requirements in order to qualify for these benefits.   [8] Includes Medicaid, food stamps, subsidies from free or reduced-price school lunches, and rent subsidies.   [9] Estimated amount of income a household would receive if it chose to shift amount held as home equity into an interest bearing account.

Source: U.S. Bureau of the Census, *Current Population Reports*, P60-188.

No. 755. Top Wealthholders With Gross Assets of $600,000 or More: 1989

[Figures are estimates based on samples of estate tax returns. Net worth equals assets minus debts and mortgages]

SIZE OF NET WORTH	ALL WEALTHHOLDERS			MALE WEALTHHOLDERS			FEMALE WEALTHHOLDERS		
	Number (1,000)	Assets (bil. dol.)	Net worth (bil. dol.)	Number (1,000)	Assets (bil. dol.)	Net worth (bil. dol.)	Number (1,000)	Assets (bil. dol.)	Net worth (bil. dol.)
Total.	3,417	5,390	4,804	1,989	3,150	2,733	1,428	2,241	2,071
Under $600,000 [1]	812	483	299	610	356	212	202	127	87
$600,000 to $999,999. . . .	1,344	1,118	1,024	673	575	514	672	542	510
$1,000,000 to $2,499,999 .	945	1,539	1,404	523	869	778	422	670	626
$2,500,000 to $4,999,999 .	206	770	696	119	456	403	86	314	293
$5,000,000 to $9,999,999 .	73	530	492	43	311	287	31	218	205
$10,000,000 or more	36	951	890	22	582	539	15	369	351

[1] Includes top wealthholders with negative net worth.

Source: U.S. Internal Revenue Service, *Statistics of Income Bulletin,* spring 1993.

No. 756. Nonfinancial Assets Held by Families, by Type of Asset: 1989 and 1992

[Median value in thousands of constant 1992 dollars. Constant dollar figures are based on consumer price index data published by U.S. Bureau of Labor Statistics. Families include one-person units; for definition of family, see text, section 1. Based on Survey of Consumer Finance; see Appendix III. For data on financial assets, see table 789. For definition of median, see Guide to Tabular Presentation]

AGE OF FAMILY HEAD AND FAMILY INCOME	Total	Vehicles	Primary residence	Investment real estate	Business	Other nonfinancial assets
1989, total	89.1	83.6	63.8	20.0	13.2	11.9
1992, total	**91.3**	**86.4**	**63.8**	**20.0**	**14.9**	**8.5**
Under 35 years old	86.7	84.8	37.0	8.4	11.3	8.1
35 to 44 years old	93.0	89.3	64.1	17.1	20.1	9.3
45 to 54 years old	94.5	92.5	75.5	26.6	18.9	10.1
55 to 64 years old	93.1	87.2	77.9	35.8	19.2	6.7
65 to 74 years old	92.0	86.3	78.9	26.7	11.3	7.9
75 years old and over	90.7	72.4	76.7	16.6	4.1	8.4
Less than $10,000.	67.8	55.8	38.8	5.9	3.6	5.0
$10,000 to $24,999	92.2	88.2	54.2	12.3	8.4	5.7
$25,000 to $49,999	97.5	93.9	68.8	20.3	14.1	8.2
$50,000 to $99,999	99.1	96.9	84.2	30.6	23.6	11.3
$100,000 and more	100.0	96.8	87.6	54.2	46.4	21.6
MEDIAN VALUE [1]						
1989, total	74.5	7.7	78.2	48.0	50.3	7.8
1992, total	**69.5**	**6.9**	**81.8**	**50.0**	**50.0**	**7.2**
Under 35 years old	16.6	5.9	69.0	40.0	19.3	3.5
35 to 44 years old	82.3	7.6	90.0	38.5	45.0	8.5
45 to 54 years old	101.5	8.6	95.0	70.0	100.3	11.3
55 to 64 years old	114.2	8.3	85.0	55.0	92.0	10.4
65 to 74 years old	79.0	5.6	70.0	60.0	80.0	11.0
75 years old and over	70.3	4.5	70.0	52.0	80.0	5.0
Less than $10,000.	20.6	2.4	40.0	33.0	29.0	1.5
$10,000 to $24,999	34.3	4.3	50.0	21.0	20.0	5.0
$25,000 to $49,999	71.5	8.1	75.0	45.0	55.5	5.0
$50,000 to $99,999	140.3	11.0	115.0	65.0	25.0	12.0
$100,000 and more	442.3	14.9	225.0	160.0	260.0	20.0

[1] Median value of financial asset for families holding such assets.

Source: Board of Governors of the Federal Reserve System, *Federal Reserve Bulletin*, October 1994.

No. 757. Family Net Worth—Mean and Median Net Worth, by Age and Family Income: 1989 and 1992

[Value in thousands of constant 1992 dollars. Constant dollar figures are based on consumer price index data published by U.S. Bureau of Labor Statistics. Families include one-person units; for definition of family, see text, section 1. Based on Survey of Consumer Finance; see Appendix III. For definition of median, see Guide to Tabular Presentation]

AGE OF FAMILY HEAD FAMILY INCOME AND HOUSING TENURE	1989			1992		
	Percent of families	Net worth		Percent of families	Net worth	
		Mean	Median		Mean	Median
All families	**100.0**	**197.2**	**51.5**	**100.0**	**220.3**	**52.2**
Under 35 years old	27.2	60.4	8.4	25.9	60.2	10.4
35 to 44 years old	23.4	156.0	63.1	22.7	157.0	46.3
45 to 54 years old	14.4	308.1	103.9	16.2	304.5	97.1
55 to 64 years old	13.9	304.5	100.6	13.1	371.0	133.3
65 to 74 years old	12.0	306.4	80.5	12.7	369.8	103.6
75 years old and over	9.0	228.4	75.8	9.4	257.6	87.0
Less than $10,000.	16.9	24.4	1.7	17.6	44.3	3.9
$10,000 to $24,999	26.1	77.5	26.0	28.0	73.0	23.4
$25,000 to $49,999	30.5	118.9	58.7	27.8	144.3	58.3
$50,000 to $99,999	19.6	225.3	127.4	19.3	283.8	139.6
$100,000 and more	6.9	1,344.7	450.3	7.3	1,324.2	569.0
Owner occupied	63.8	283.7	109.0	63.8	317.1	108.5
Renter occupied or other	36.2	45.0	2.2	36.2	49.9	3.7

Source: Board of Governors of the Federal Reserve System, *Federal Reserve Bulletin*, October 1994.

No. 758. Household and Nonprofit Organization Sector Balance Sheet: 1980 to 1993

[In billions of dollars. As of December 31. For details of financial assets and liabilities, see table 787]

ITEM	1980	1985	1986	1987	1988	1989	1990	1991	1992	1993
Assets	11,109	16,271	17,781	19,036	20,448	22,510	22,797	24,820	26,022	27,511
Tangible assets	4,703	6,603	7,100	7,656	8,103	8,709	8,775	9,286	9,557	9,973
Reproducible assets	3,339	4,392	4,758	5,157	5,409	5,774	6,107	6,358	6,662	7,067
Residential structures	2,109	2,693	2,903	3,148	3,223	3,440	3,633	3,777	3,975	4,239
Owner-occupied housing	2,062	2,634	2,841	3,082	3,157	3,370	3,560	3,704	3,902	4,164
Nonprofit institutions	47	58	62	66	67	70	73	73	73	75
Nonprofit plant & equipment	216	308	328	350	377	404	427	443	464	493
Consumer durable goods	1,014	1,391	1,527	1,660	1,808	1,930	2,047	2,139	2,222	2,336
Land	1,364	2,211	2,343	2,499	2,694	2,935	2,668	2,928	2,895	2,906
Owner-occupied [1]	1,227	2,016	2,138	2,287	2,463	2,688	2,456	2,780	2,807	2,836
Nonprofit institutions	137	195	205	211	231	247	212	148	88	70
Financial assets	6,406	9,668	10,680	11,380	12,346	13,802	14,023	15,534	16,465	17,538
Liabilities	1,443	2,333	2,602	2,859	3,174	3,496	3,738	3,920	4,143	4,464
Home mortgages	905	1,379	1,574	1,795	2,023	2,253	2,455	2,614	2,788	2,970
Net worth	9,666	13,938	15,178	16,177	17,274	19,014	19,059	20,900	21,879	23,047
Memo:										
Owner-occupied real estate [2]	3,289	4,650	4,978	5,369	5,620	6,059	6,016	6,484	6,709	7,000
Home mortgages as percent of owner-occupied real estate	28	30	32	33	36	37	41	40	42	42

[1] Includes vacant land. [2] Owner-occupied housing plus owner-occupied land.

Source: Board of Governors of the Federal Reserve System, *Balance Sheets for the U.S. Economy.*

No. 759. Gross and Net Stock of Fixed Reproducible Tangible Wealth: 1970 to 1993

[In billions of dollars. As of December 31]

ITEM	1970	1980	1985	1986	1987	1988	1989	1990	1991	1992	1993
CURRENT DOLLARS											
Gross stock	4,428	14,306	19,330	20,503	21,774	22,966	24,361	25,675	26,645	27,784	29,270
Private	2,689	9,364	12,747	13,536	14,388	15,078	16,022	16,871	17,437	18,137	19,090
Nonresidential equipment	679	2,389	3,374	3,599	3,775	4,010	4,257	4,506	4,636	4,783	4,974
Nonresidential structures	790	2,683	3,783	3,951	4,156	4,478	4,755	4,979	5,109	5,269	5,516
Residential	1,219	4,292	5,590	5,986	6,457	6,590	7,010	7,387	7,692	8,085	8,600
Government	1,060	2,979	3,772	3,916	4,083	4,306	4,516	4,729	4,874	5,067	5,309
Equipment	274	488	695	732	764	814	873	952	1,017	1,085	1,132
Structures	785	2,491	3,077	3,184	3,319	3,492	3,643	3,777	3,857	3,982	4,177
Federal	424	885	1,176	1,227	1,269	1,325	1,394	1,477	1,535	1,606	1,668
Military	276	493	678	715	738	776	818	881	922	977	1,015
State and local	636	2,094	2,596	2,690	2,814	2,981	3,122	3,252	3,339	3,461	3,640
Consumer durable goods	680	1,963	2,811	3,051	3,303	3,582	3,823	4,075	4,334	4,580	4,872
Net stock	2,708	8,619	11,367	12,063	12,803	13,458	14,245	14,947	15,387	15,941	16,718
Private	1,674	5,814	7,752	8,224	8,729	9,108	9,650	10,117	10,385	10,751	11,291
Government	662	1,790	2,224	2,311	2,414	2,542	2,665	2,784	2,864	2,967	3,091
Consumer durable goods	372	1,014	1,391	1,527	1,660	1,808	1,930	2,047	2,139	2,222	2,336
CONSTANT (1987) DOLLARS											
Gross stock	12,476	17,469	20,091	20,753	21,400	22,062	22,717	23,344	23,883	24,437	25,096
Private	8,131	11,585	13,322	13,728	14,112	14,504	14,886	15,245	15,525	15,803	16,162
Nonresidential equipment	1,839	3,009	3,518	3,633	3,737	3,855	3,979	4,091	4,180	4,274	4,424
Nonresidential structures	2,411	3,255	3,870	3,983	4,088	4,191	4,293	4,400	4,480	4,541	4,599
Residential	3,881	5,321	5,934	6,112	6,286	6,458	6,614	6,754	6,865	6,989	7,139
Government	3,001	3,544	3,849	3,934	4,026	4,115	4,204	4,309	4,412	4,514	4,613
Equipment	662	625	698	730	768	802	837	880	920	959	989
Structures	2,339	2,918	3,152	3,204	3,259	3,313	3,367	3,429	3,492	3,556	3,623
Federal	1,141	1,122	1,204	1,233	1,266	1,293	1,319	1,352	1,382	1,411	1,432
Military	723	641	691	716	743	767	786	814	835	855	866
State and local	1,860	2,421	2,645	2,701	2,760	2,822	2,885	2,957	3,029	3,104	3,181
Consumer durable goods	1,344	2,340	2,920	3,091	3,262	3,444	3,627	3,790	3,946	4,119	4,321
Net stock	7,691	10,524	11,823	12,214	12,577	12,942	13,293	13,603	13,810	14,030	14,344
Private	5,074	7,198	8,112	8,346	8,558	8,774	8,980	9,158	9,262	9,374	9,563
Government	1,884	2,123	2,269	2,320	2,380	2,430	2,482	2,539	2,595	2,646	2,690
Consumer durable goods	733	1,203	1,442	1,547	1,639	1,738	1,831	1,907	1,954	2,010	2,092

Source: U.S. Bureau of Economic Analysis, *Survey of Current Business*, January 1992, September 1993, and August 1994 issues.

Figure 15.1
**Annual Percent Change in Producer Price
Indexes by Stage of Processing: 1970 to 1994**

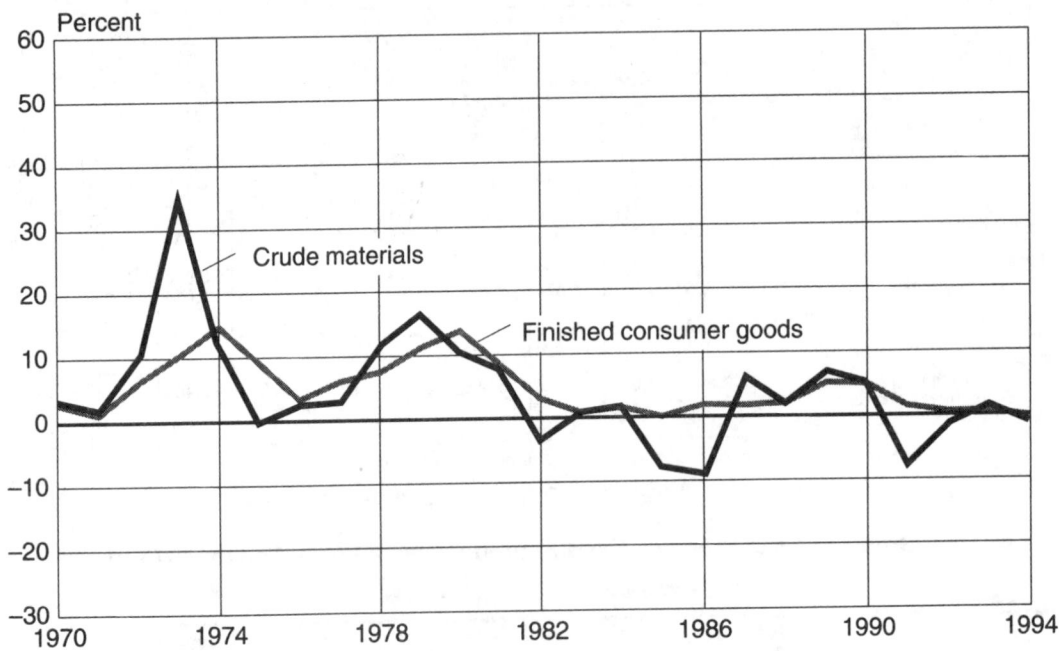

Source: Chart prepared by U.S. Bureau of the Census. For data, see table 767.

Figure 15.2
**Annual Percent Change in Consumer
Price Indexes: 1970 to 1994**

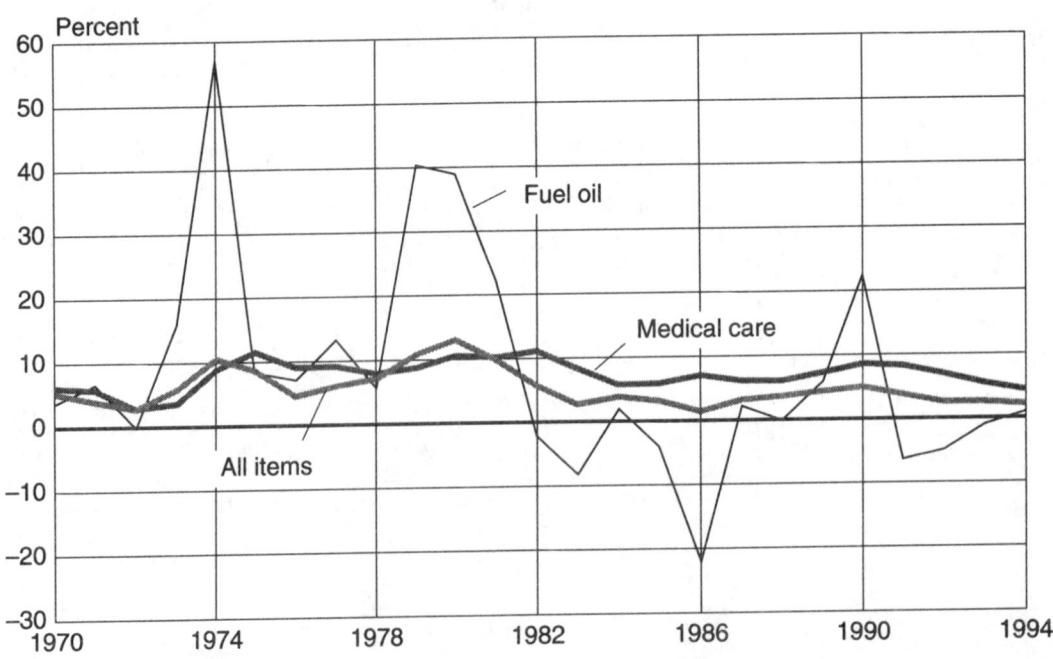

Source: Chart prepared by U.S. Bureau of the Census. For data, see table 761.

This section presents indexes of producer and consumer prices, actual prices for selected commodities, and energy prices. The primary sources of these data are monthly publications of the Department of Labor, Bureau of Labor Statistics (BLS), which include *Monthly Labor Review, Consumer Price Index, Detailed Report; Producer Price Indexes;* and *U.S. Import and Export Price Indexes.* The Department of Commerce, Bureau of Economic Analysis is the source for gross domestic product measures.

Producer price index (PPI).—This index, dating from 1890, is the oldest continuous statistical series published by BLS. It is designed to measure average changes in prices received by producers of all commodities, at all stages of processing, produced in the United States.

The index has undergone several revisions (see *Monthly Labor Review,* February 1962, April 1978, and August 1988). It is now based on approximately 3,200 commodity price series and 80,000 quotations per month. Indexes for the net output of manufacturing and mining industries have been added in recent years. Prices used in constructing the index are collected from sellers, and generally apply to the first significant large volume commercial transaction for each commodity—i.e., the manufacturer's or other producer's selling price or the selling price on an organized exchange or at a central market.

The weights used in the index represent the total net selling value of commodities produced or processed in this country. Values are f.o.b. (free-on-board) production point and are exclusive of excise taxes. Effective with the release of data for January 1988, many important producer price indexes were changed to a new reference base year, 1982=100, from 1967=100. The reference year of the PPI shipment weights has been taken primarily from the 1987 Census of Manufactures. For further detail regarding the PPI, see the *BLS Handbook of Methods, Bulletin 2414,* Chapter 16.

Consumer price indexes (CPI).—The CPI is a measure of the average change in prices over time in a fixed "market

In Brief

Consumer price changes:
1993-94:

All items index up 2.6 percent
Medical care index up 4.8 percent
Fuel oil index down -1.8 percent

basket" of goods and services purchased either by urban wage earners and clerical workers or by all urban consumers.

In 1919, BLS began to publish complete indexes at semiannual intervals, using a weighting structure based on data collected in the expenditure survey of wage-earner and clerical-worker families in 1917-19 (BLS Bulletin 357, 1924). The first major revision of the CPI occurred in 1940, with subsequent revisions in 1953, 1964, 1978, and 1987.

Beginning with the release of data for January 1988 in February 1988, most Consumer Price Indexes shifted to a new reference base year. All indexes previously expressed on a base of 1967=100, or any other base through December 1981, have been rebased to 1982-84=100. Selection of the 1982-84 period was made to coincide with the updated expenditure weights, which are based upon data tabulated from the Consumer Expenditure Surveys for 1982, 1983, and 1984.

BLS publishes CPI's for two population groups: (1) a CPI for All Urban Consumers (CPI-U) which covers approximately 80 percent of the total population; and (2) a CPI for Urban Wage Earners and Clerical Workers (CPI-W) which covers 32 percent of the total population. The CPI-U includes, in addition to wage earners and clerical workers, groups which historically have been excluded from CPI coverage, such as professional, managerial, and technical workers, the self-employed, short-term workers, the unemployed, and retirees and others not in the labor force.

The current CPI is based on prices of food, clothing, shelter, fuels, transportation fares, charges for doctors' and dentists' services, drugs, etc., purchased for day-to-day living. Prices are collected in 85 areas across the country from over

57,000 housing units and 19,000 establishments. Area selection was based on the 1980 census. All taxes directly associated with the purchase and use of items are included in the index. Prices of food, fuels, and a few other items are obtained every month in all 85 locations. Prices of most other commodities and services are collected monthly in the five largest geographic areas and every other month in other areas.

In calculating the index, each item is assigned a weight to account for its relative importance in consumers' budgets. Price changes for the various items in each location are then averaged. Local data are then combined to obtain a U.S. city average. Separate indexes are also published for regions, area size-classes, cross-classifications of regions and size-classes, and for 29 local areas, usually consisting of the Metropolitan Statistical Area (MSA); see Appendix II. Area definitions are those established by the Office of Management and Budget in 1983. Definitions do not include revisions made since 1983. Area indexes do not measure differences in the level of prices among cities; they only measure the average change in prices for each area since the base period. For further detail regarding the CPI, see the BLS *Handbook of Methods,* Bulletin 2414, Chapter 19; the Consumer Price Index, and Report 736, the CPI: 1987 Revision. In January 1983, the method of measuring homeownership costs in the CPI-U was changed to a rental equivalence approach. This treatment calculates homeowner costs of shelter based on the implicit rent owners would pay to rent the homes they own. The rental equivalence approach was introduced into the CPI-W in 1985. The CPI-U was used to prepare the consumer prices tables in this section.

International price indexes—The BLS International Price Program produces export and import price indexes for non-military goods traded between the United States and the rest of the world. The export price index provides a measure of price change for all products sold by U.S. residents to foreign buyers. The import price index provides a measure of price change for goods purchased from other countries by U.S. residents. The reference period for the indexes is 1990=100, unless otherwise indicated.

The product universe for both the import and export indexes includes raw materials, agricultural products, semifinished manufactures, and finished manufactures, including both capital and consumer goods. Price data for these items are collected primarily by mail questionnaire. In nearly all cases, the data are collected directly from the exporter or importer, although in a few cases, prices are obtained from other sources.

To the extent possible, the data gathered refer to prices at the U.S. border for exports and at either the foreign border or the U.S. border for imports. For nearly all products, the prices refer to transactions completed during the first week of the month. Survey respondents are asked to indicate all discounts, allowances, and rebates applicable to the reported prices, so that the price used in the calculation of the indexes is the actual price for which the product was bought or sold.

In addition to general indexes for U.S. exports and imports, indexes are also published for detailed product categories of exports and imports. These categories are defined according to the five-digit level of detail for the Bureau of Economic Analysis End-use Classification, the three-digit level of detail for the Standard International Trade Classification (SITC), and the four-digit level of detail for the Harmonized System. Aggregate import indexes by country or region of origin are also available.

Other price indexes.—The *fixed-weighted price index* is a weighted average of the detailed price indexes used in the deflation of goods and services that make up the gross domestic product (GDP). These price indexes are combined using weights that reflect the composition of GDP in 1987. Because the same weights are used for each period, changes in this index measure changes in prices over any period.

Measures of inflation.—Inflation is defined as a time of generally rising prices for goods and factors of production. The Bureau of Labor Statistics samples prices of items in a representative market basket and publishes the results as the CPI. The media invariably announce the inflation rate as the percent change in the CPI from month to month. A much more meaningful indicator of inflation is the percent change from the same month of the prior year.

The Producer Price Index (PPI) measures prices at the producer/manufacturing level only. The PPI shows the same general pattern of inflation as does the CPI, but is more volatile. The PPI can be roughly viewed as a leading indicator. It often tends to foreshadow trends that later occur in the CPI.

Other measures of inflation include the index of industrial materials prices; the Dow Jones Commodity Spot Price Index; Futures Price Index, the Employment Cost Index, the Hourly Compensation Index, or the Unit Labor Cost Index as a measure of the change in cost of the labor factor of production, and changes in long-term interest rates that are often used to measure changes in the cost of the capital factor of production.

Statistical reliability.—For a discussion of statistical collection and estimation, sampling procedures, and measures of statistical reliability pertaining to the producer price index and the CPI, see Appendix III.

Historical statistics.—Tabular headnotes provide cross-references, where applicable, to *Historical Statistics of the United States, Colonial Times to 1970.* See Appendix IV.

No. 760. Purchasing Power of the Dollar: 1950 to 1994

[**Indexes: PPI, 1982=$1.00; CPI, 1982–84=$1.00.** Producer prices prior to 1961, and consumer prices prior to 1964, exclude Alaska and Hawaii. Producer prices based on finished goods index. Obtained by dividing the average price index for the 1982=100, PPI; 1982–84=100, CPI base periods (100.0) by the price index for a given period and expressing the result in dollars and cents. Annual figures are based on average of monthly data]

YEAR	ANNUAL AVERAGE AS MEASURED BY—		YEAR	ANNUAL AVERAGE AS MEASURED BY—		YEAR	ANNUAL AVERAGE AS MEASURED BY—	
	Producer prices	Consumer prices		Producer prices	Consumer prices		Producer prices	Consumer prices
1950	$3.546	$4.151	1965	2.933	3.166	1980	1.136	1.215
1951	3.247	3.846	1966	2.841	3.080	1981	1.041	1.098
1952	3.268	3.765	1967	2.809	2.993	1982	1.000	1.035
1953	3.300	3.735	1968	2.732	2.873	1983	0.984	1.003
1954	3.289	3.717	1969	2.632	2.726	1984	0.964	0.961
1955	3.279	3.732	1970	2.545	2.574	1985	0.955	0.928
1956	3.195	3.678	1971	2.469	2.466	1986	0.969	0.913
1957	3.077	3.549	1972	2.392	2.391	1987	0.949	0.880
1958	3.012	3.457	1973	2.193	2.251	1988	0.926	0.846
1959	3.021	3.427	1974	1.901	2.029	1989	0.880	0.807
1960	2.994	3.373	1975	1.718	1.859	1990	0.839	0.766
1961	2.994	3.340	1976	1.645	1.757	1991	0.822	0.734
1962	2.985	3.304	1977	1.546	1.649	1992	0.812	0.713
1963	2.994	3.265	1978	1.433	1.532	1993	0.802	0.692
1964	2.985	3.220	1979	1.289	1.380	1994	0.797	0.675

Source: U.S. Bureau of Labor Statistics. Monthly data in U.S. Bureau of Economic Analysis, *Survey of Current Business.*

No. 761. Consumer Price Indexes (CPI-U), by Major Groups: 1960 to 1994

[**1982-84=100.** Represents annual averages of monthly figures. Reflects buying patterns of all urban consumers. Minus sign (-) indicates decrease. See text, section 15. See *Historical Statistics, Colonial Times to 1970*, series E 135-173 for similar data]

YEAR	All items	Energy	Food	Shelter	Apparel and upkeep	Transportation	Medical care	Fuel oil	Electricity	Utility (piped) gas	Telephone services	All commodities
1960	29.6	22.4	30.0	25.2	45.7	29.8	22.3	13.5	29.9	17.6	58.3	33.6
1961	29.9	22.5	30.4	25.4	46.1	30.1	22.9	14.0	29.9	17.9	58.5	33.8
1962	30.2	22.6	30.6	25.8	46.3	30.8	23.5	14.0	29.9	17.9	58.5	34.1
1963	30.6	22.6	31.1	26.1	46.9	30.9	24.1	14.3	29.9	17.9	58.6	34.4
1964	31.0	22.5	31.5	26.5	47.3	31.4	24.6	14.0	29.8	17.9	58.6	34.8
1965	31.5	22.9	32.2	27.0	47.8	31.9	25.2	14.3	29.7	18.0	57.7	35.2
1966	32.4	23.3	33.8	27.8	49.0	32.3	26.3	14.7	29.7	18.1	56.5	36.1
1967	33.4	23.8	34.1	28.8	51.0	33.3	28.2	15.1	29.9	18.1	57.3	36.8
1968	34.8	24.2	35.3	30.1	53.7	34.3	29.9	15.6	30.2	18.2	57.3	38.1
1969	36.7	24.8	37.1	32.6	56.8	35.7	31.9	15.9	30.8	18.6	58.0	39.9
1970	38.8	25.5	39.2	35.5	59.2	37.5	34.0	16.5	31.8	19.6	58.7	41.7
1971	40.5	26.5	40.4	37.0	61.1	39.5	36.1	17.6	33.9	21.0	61.6	43.2
1972	41.8	27.2	42.1	38.7	62.3	39.9	37.3	17.6	35.6	22.1	65.0	44.5
1973	44.4	29.4	48.2	40.5	64.6	41.2	38.8	20.4	37.4	23.1	66.7	47.8
1974	49.3	38.1	55.1	44.4	69.4	45.8	42.4	32.2	44.1	26.0	69.5	53.5
1975	53.8	42.1	59.8	48.8	72.5	50.1	47.5	34.9	50.0	31.1	71.7	58.2
1976	56.9	45.1	61.6	51.5	75.2	55.1	52.0	37.4	53.1	36.3	74.3	60.7
1977	60.6	49.4	65.5	54.9	78.6	59.0	57.0	42.4	56.6	43.2	75.2	64.2
1978	65.2	52.5	72.0	60.5	81.4	61.7	61.8	44.9	60.9	47.5	76.0	68.8
1979	72.6	65.7	79.9	68.9	84.9	70.5	67.5	63.1	65.6	55.1	75.8	76.6
1980	82.4	86.0	86.8	81.0	90.9	83.1	74.9	87.7	75.8	65.7	77.7	86.0
1981	90.9	97.7	93.6	90.5	95.3	93.2	82.9	107.3	87.2	74.9	84.6	93.2
1982	96.5	99.2	97.4	96.9	97.8	97.0	92.5	105.0	95.8	89.8	93.2	97.0
1983	99.6	99.9	99.4	99.1	100.2	99.3	100.6	96.5	98.9	104.7	99.2	99.8
1984	103.9	100.9	103.2	104.0	102.1	103.7	106.8	98.5	105.3	105.5	107.5	103.2
1985	107.6	101.6	105.6	109.8	105.0	106.4	113.5	94.6	108.9	104.8	111.7	105.4
1986	109.6	88.2	109.0	115.8	105.9	102.3	122.0	74.1	110.4	99.7	117.2	104.4
1987	113.6	88.6	113.5	121.3	110.6	105.4	130.1	75.8	110.0	95.1	116.5	107.7
1988	118.3	89.3	118.2	127.1	115.4	108.7	138.6	75.8	111.5	94.5	116.0	111.5
1989	124.0	94.3	125.1	132.8	118.6	114.1	149.3	80.3	114.7	97.1	117.2	116.7
1990	130.7	102.1	132.4	140.0	124.1	120.5	162.8	98.6	117.4	97.3	117.7	122.8
1991	136.2	102.5	136.3	146.3	128.7	123.8	177.0	92.4	121.8	98.5	119.7	126.6
1992	140.3	103.0	137.9	151.2	131.9	126.5	190.1	88.0	124.2	100.3	120.4	129.1
1993	144.5	104.2	140.9	155.7	133.7	130.4	201.4	87.2	126.7	106.5	121.2	131.5
1994	148.2	104.6	144.3	160.5	133.4	134.3	211.0	85.6	126.7	108.5	123.1	133.8
PERCENT CHANGE [1]												
1960	1.7	2.3	1.0	2.0	1.6	-	3.7	-1.5	1.4	6.7	1.6	0.9
1961	1.0	0.4	1.3	0.8	0.9	1.0	2.7	3.7	-	1.7	0.3	0.6
1962	1.0	0.4	0.7	1.6	0.4	2.3	2.6	-	-	-	0.2	0.9
1963	1.3	-	1.6	1.2	1.3	0.3	2.6	2.1	-	-	-	0.9
1964	1.3	-0.4	1.3	1.5	0.9	1.6	2.1	-2.1	-0.3	-	-	1.2
1965	1.6	1.8	2.2	1.9	1.1	1.6	2.4	2.1	-0.3	0.6	-1.5	1.1
1966	2.9	1.7	5.0	3.0	2.5	1.3	4.4	2.8	-	0.6	-2.1	2.6
1967	3.1	2.1	0.9	3.6	4.1	3.1	7.2	2.7	0.7	-	1.4	1.9
1968	4.2	1.7	3.5	4.5	5.3	3.0	6.0	3.3	1.0	0.6	-	3.5
1969	5.5	2.5	5.1	8.3	5.8	4.1	6.7	1.9	2.0	2.2	1.2	4.7
1970	5.7	2.8	5.7	8.9	4.2	5.0	6.6	3.8	3.2	5.4	1.2	4.5
1971	4.4	3.9	3.1	4.2	3.2	5.3	6.2	6.7	6.6	7.1	4.9	3.6
1972	3.2	2.6	4.2	4.6	2.0	1.0	3.3	-	5.0	5.2	5.5	3.0
1973	6.2	8.1	14.5	4.7	3.7	3.3	4.0	15.9	5.1	4.5	2.6	7.4
1974	11.0	29.6	14.3	9.6	7.4	11.2	9.3	57.8	17.9	12.6	4.2	11.9
1975	9.1	10.5	8.5	9.9	4.5	9.4	12.0	8.4	13.4	19.6	3.2	8.8
1976	5.8	7.1	3.0	5.5	3.7	10.0	9.5	7.2	6.2	16.7	3.6	4.3
1977	6.5	9.5	6.3	6.6	4.5	7.1	9.6	13.4	6.6	19.0	1.2	5.8
1978	7.6	6.3	9.9	10.2	3.6	4.6	8.4	5.9	7.6	16.0	1.1	7.2
1979	11.3	25.1	11.0	13.9	4.3	14.3	9.2	40.5	7.7	16.0	-0.3	11.3
1980	13.5	30.9	8.6	17.6	7.1	17.9	11.0	39.0	15.5	19.2	2.5	12.3
1981	10.3	13.6	7.8	11.7	4.8	12.2	10.7	22.3	15.0	14.0	8.9	8.4
1982	6.2	1.5	4.1	7.1	2.6	4.1	11.6	-2.1	9.9	19.9	10.2	4.1
1983	3.2	0.7	2.1	2.3	2.5	2.4	8.8	-8.1	3.2	16.6	6.4	2.9
1984	4.3	1.0	3.8	4.9	1.9	4.4	6.2	2.1	6.5	0.8	8.4	3.4
1985	3.6	0.7	2.3	5.6	2.8	2.6	6.3	-4.0	3.4	-0.7	3.9	2.1
1986	1.9	-13.2	3.2	5.5	0.9	-3.9	7.5	-21.7	1.4	-4.9	-0.6	-0.9
1987	3.6	0.5	4.1	4.7	4.4	3.0	6.6	2.3	-0.4	-4.6	-0.6	3.2
1988	4.1	0.8	4.1	4.8	4.3	3.1	6.5	-	1.4	-0.6	-0.4	3.5
1989	4.8	5.6	5.8	4.5	2.8	5.0	7.7	5.9	2.9	2.8	1.0	4.7
1990	5.4	8.3	5.8	5.4	4.6	5.6	9.0	22.8	2.4	0.2	0.4	5.2
1991	4.2	0.4	2.9	4.5	3.7	2.7	8.7	-6.3	3.7	1.2	1.7	3.1
1992	3.0	0.5	1.2	3.3	2.5	2.2	7.4	-4.8	2.0	1.8	0.6	2.0
1993	3.0	1.2	2.2	3.0	1.4	3.1	5.9	-0.9	2.0	6.2	0.7	1.9
1994	2.6	0.4	2.4	3.1	-0.2	3.0	4.8	-1.8	-	1.9	1.6	1.7

- Represents zero.   [1] Change from immediate prior year.

Source: Bureau of Labor Statistics, *Monthly Labor Review* and *Handbook of Labor Statistics*, periodic.

No. 762. Consumer Price Indexes for All Urban Consumers (CPI-U) for Selected Items and Groups: 1980 to 1994

[1982-84=100. Annual averages of monthly figures. See headnote, table 761]

ITEM	1980	1985	1988	1989	1990	1991	1992	1993	1994
All items	**82.4**	**107.6**	**118.3**	**124.0**	**130.7**	**136.2**	**140.3**	**144.5**	**148.2**
Food and beverages	86.7	105.6	118.2	124.9	132.1	136.8	138.7	141.6	144.9
Food	86.8	105.6	118.2	125.1	132.4	136.3	137.9	140.9	144.3
Food at home	88.4	104.3	116.6	124.2	132.3	135.8	136.8	140.1	144.1
Cereals and bakery products	83.9	107.9	122.1	132.4	140.0	145.8	151.5	156.6	163.0
Cereals and cereal products	84.2	107.2	122.5	133.8	141.1	147.5	153.3	157.9	164.8
Cereals	76.3	111.3	132.9	147.9	158.6	168.1	175.4	183.3	134.8
Rice, pasta, and cornmeal	90.9	102.1	114.4	120.0	122.0	126.5	128.3	129.7	190.6
Bakery products	83.8	108.2	121.8	131.5	139.2	144.7	150.4	155.7	139.7
White bread	85.9	105.8	118.6	129.4	136.4	139.3	146.2	152.2	161.9
Cookies, cakes, and cupcakes	81.5	110.2	125.0	134.5	142.7	151.1	155.6	159.3	159.0
Meats, poultry, fish and eggs	92.0	100.1	114.3	121.3	130.0	132.6	130.9	135.5	137.2
Meats	92.7	98.9	112.2	116.7	128.5	132.5	130.7	134.6	135.4
Beef and veal	98.4	98.2	112.1	119.3	128.8	132.4	132.3	137.1	136.0
Ground beef excl. canned	104.6	95.9	103.4	108.6	118.1	119.9	118.9	121.7	119.7
Chuck roast	99.8	95.6	108.1	116.8	130.3	135.8	137.1	141.9	140.3
Round steak	98.9	97.0	110.6	116.6	125.1	129.5	129.9	134.4	133.0
Sirloin steak	96.2	99.7	120.0	126.0	130.6	133.5	132.4	138.5	137.5
Pork	81.9	99.1	112.5	113.2	129.8	134.1	127.8	131.7	133.9
Bacon	73.5	101.3	100.9	95.8	113.4	119.8	104.6	110.8	118.1
Chops	82.9	98.7	118.8	122.7	140.2	141.7	138.9	144.6	144.2
Ham	85.5	99.8	116.5	117.3	132.4	139.9	135.6	137.9	139.3
Poultry	93.7	106.2	120.7	132.7	132.5	131.5	131.4	136.9	141.5
Fresh whole chicken	94.4	104.5	125.1	137.1	134.9	131.7	131.9	138.0	140.1
Fresh, frozen chicken parts	91.7	104.6	123.3	135.7	135.9	134.7	134.4	140.1	145.6
Fish and seafood	87.5	107.5	137.4	143.6	146.7	148.3	151.7	156.6	163.7
Canned fish and seafood	93.7	97.8	117.0	124.3	119.5	119.0	118.7	121.5	123.8
Fresh and frozen fish and seafood	84.1	112.9	144.2	155.2	161.4	163.8	168.7	174.5	183.6
Eggs	88.6	91.0	93.6	118.5	124.1	121.2	108.3	117.1	114.3
Dairy products	90.9	103.2	108.4	115.6	126.5	125.1	128.5	129.4	131.7
Fruits and vegetables	82.1	108.4	128.1	138.0	149.0	155.8	155.4	159.0	165.0
Fresh fruits	84.8	116.3	143.0	152.4	170.9	193.9	184.2	188.8	201.2
Apples	92.1	113.1	134.2	140.5	147.5	172.8	179.5	169.0	174.0
Bananas	91.5	99.9	119.2	131.3	138.2	145.0	139.9	135.5	143.6
Oranges, tangerines	72.6	119.7	144.6	147.0	160.6	249.4	176.2	190.1	189.9
Fresh vegetables	79.0	103.5	129.3	143.1	151.1	154.4	157.9	168.7	172.3
Potatoes	81.0	101.6	119.1	153.5	162.6	144.6	141.5	154.6	174.3
Lettuce	77.8	106.1	148.6	151.5	150.3	159.8	155.7	178.2	170.3
Tomatoes	81.9	103.6	123.1	136.2	160.8	153.1	171.8	168.0	173.5
Processed fruits	82.1	109.5	122.0	125.9	136.9	131.8	137.7	132.3	133.1
Processed vegetables	83.1	104.4	112.2	124.2	127.5	128.5	128.8	130.8	136.6
Coffee	111.6	105.5	115.0	120.4	117.5	115.3	110.7	109.8	140.4
Lunch away from home	83.8	107.8	121.5	127.6	133.9	138.4	141.3	144.0	146.4
Dinner away from home	84.2	108.8	121.6	126.9	132.3	136.3	138.9	141.3	143.8
Alcoholic beverages	86.4	106.4	118.6	123.5	129.3	142.8	147.3	149.6	151.5
Alcoholic beverages at home	87.3	105.2	114.2	117.9	123.0	137.8	141.6	142.2	142.5
Beer and ale	84.8	106.7	114.4	118.2	123.6	138.4	143.5	143.2	143.4
Distilled spirits	89.8	105.3	116.1	119.9	125.7	139.2	141.5	143.2	144.3
Wine	89.5	100.2	107.8	110.9	114.4	129.9	132.6	134.0	133.3
Alcoholic beverages away from home	82.9	111.1	130.6	137.4	144.4	156.9	162.5	167.4	171.6
Housing	81.1	107.7	118.5	123.0	128.5	133.6	137.5	141.2	144.8
Shelter	81.0	109.8	127.1	132.8	140.0	146.3	151.2	155.7	160.5
Renters' cost	(NA)	115.4	133.6	138.9	146.7	155.6	160.9	165.0	169.4
Rent, residential	80.9	111.8	127.8	132.8	138.4	143.3	146.9	150.3	154.0
Tenants' insurance	78.9	109.4	124.9	128.3	130.6	133.2	136.5	140.8	145.8
Homeowners' costs	(NA)	113.1	131.1	137.3	144.6	150.2	155.3	160.2	165.5
Owners' equivalent rent	(NA)	113.2	131.1	137.4	144.8	150.4	155.5	160.5	165.8
Household insurance	(NA)	111.4	129.0	132.6	135.3	138.4	142.2	146.9	152.3
Maintenance and repair	82.4	106.5	114.7	118.0	122.2	126.3	128.6	130.6	130.8
Fuels and other utilities	75.4	106.5	104.4	107.8	111.6	115.3	117.8	121.3	122.8
Fuels	74.8	104.5	98.0	100.9	104.5	106.7	108.1	111.2	111.7
Fuel oil and other	86.1	95.9	78.1	81.7	99.3	94.6	90.7	90.3	88.8
Fuel oil	87.7	94.6	75.8	80.3	98.6	92.4	88.0	87.2	85.6
Gas (piped) and electricity	71.4	107.1	104.6	107.5	109.3	112.6	114.8	118.5	119.2
Electricity	75.8	108.9	111.5	114.7	117.4	121.8	124.2	126.7	126.7
Utility (piped) gas	65.7	104.8	94.5	97.1	97.3	98.5	100.3	106.5	108.5
Telephone services	77.7	111.7	116.0	117.2	117.7	119.7	120.4	121.2	123.1
Local charges	72.8	120.4	141.3	146.5	149.3	153.9	155.7	156.4	156.9
Interstate toll charges	83.3	94.9	72.3	70.0	68.2	67.6	68.0	69.6	75.2
Intrastate toll charges	85.2	106.8	101.5	97.0	95.1	93.1	91.4	90.7	90.2
Water and sewerage maintenance	74.0	113.4	132.7	140.8	150.2	161.1	172.1	181.4	190.6
Cable television	(NA)	110.6	132.9	144.0	158.4	175.7	186.2	198.9	197.4
Refuse collection	(NA)	109.9	142.5	155.6	171.2	189.2	207.3	220.5	231.4

See footnotes at end of table.

No. 762. Consumer Price Indexes for All Urban Consumers (CPI-U) for Selected Items and Groups: 1980 to 1994—Continued

[1982-84=100. Annual averages of monthly figures. See headnote, table 761]

ITEM	1980	1985	1988	1989	1990	1991	1992	1993	1994
Household furnishings and operations . .	86.3	103.8	109.4	111.2	113.3	116.0	118.0	119.3	121.0
Housefurnishings.	88.5	101.7	105.1	105.5	106.7	107.5	109.0	109.5	111.0
Furniture and bedding	88.0	104.9	113.2	113.9	115.7	116.6	120.6	123.5	128.2
Bedroom furniture	83.5	107.4	117.7	117.6	118.5	120.1	126.8	132.5	135.1
Sofas	(NA)	103.0	114.3	117.0	118.4	118.3	119.4	120.1	125.2
Living room chairs and tables . . .	(NA)	103.2	111.0	112.5	116.7	118.4	121.9	125.0	132.7
Appliances and electronic equip. . . .	93.5	95.2	90.2	89.1	87.8	86.0	84.6	83.4	82.3
Video and audio equipment	100.7	91.9	83.6	82.2	80.8	79.4	78.4	77.1	76.0
Television.	104.6	88.7	77.6	76.1	74.6	72.9	72.4	70.7	69.9
Video products other than TV .	(NA)	(NA)	(NA)	96.8	91.5	84.6	81.0	78.5	73.8
Audio products	97.7	94.4	92.7	92.8	93.2	94.6	94.4	93.9	93.8
Housekeeping supplies.	83.2	106.2	114.7	120.9	125.2	128.9	129.6	130.7	132.3
Housekeeping services.	84.3	106.1	114.3	117.3	120.1	127.5	132.1	135.8	138.5
Postage	76.2	108.8	121.4	125.1	125.1	143.6	145.3	145.3	145.3
Apparel and upkeep	90.9	105.0	115.4	118.6	124.1	128.7	131.9	133.7	133.4
Apparel commodities.	92.9	104.0	113.7	116.7	122.0	126.4	129.4	131.0	130.4
Apparel commodities less footwear. . .	93.0	104.3	114.4	117.1	122.8	127.4	130.2	131.9	131.2
Men's and boy's apparel	89.4	105.0	113.4	117.0	120.4	124.2	126.5	127.5	126.4
Women's and girl's apparel	96.0	104.9	114.9	116.4	122.6	127.6	130.4	132.6	130.9
Infants' and toddlers'.	85.5	107.2	116.4	119.1	125.8	128.9	129.3	127.1	128.1
Footwear.	91.8	102.3	109.9	114.4	117.4	120.9	125.0	125.9	126.0
Transportation	83.1	106.4	108.7	114.1	120.5	123.8	126.5	130.4	134.3
Private transportation.	84.2	106.2	107.6	112.9	118.8	121.9	124.6	127.5	131.4
New vehicles	88.5	106.1	116.5	119.2	121.4	126.0	129.2	132.7	137.6
New cars	88.4	106.1	116.9	119.2	121.0	125.3	128.4	131.5	136.0
New trucks	(NA)	105.5	113.5	117.0	121.6	127.0	130.9	135.7	141.7
Used cars	62.3	113.7	118.0	120.4	117.6	118.1	123.2	133.9	141.7
Motor fuel	97.4	98.7	80.9	88.5	101.2	99.4	99.0	98.0	98.5
Automobile maintenance and repair . .	81.5	106.8	119.7	124.9	130.1	136.0	141.3	145.9	150.2
Automobile insurance	82.0	119.2	156.6	166.6	177.9	191.5	205.5	216.7	224.8
Automobile finance charges.	86.4	94.5	91.3	100.5	99.6	98.0	86.1	78.6	83.8
Vehicle rental, registration, other	78.3	111.7	128.1	135.0	148.1	154.8	162.3	169.8	174.2
Public transportation	69.0	110.5	123.3	129.5	142.6	148.9	151.4	167.0	172.0
Airline fares	68.0	112.5	124.2	131.6	148.4	155.2	155.2	178.7	185.5
Other intercity transportation	73.1	114.7	132.6	138.5	143.3	149.0	152.5	150.9	152.8
Intracity transportation	69.7	107.7	121.7	125.2	133.5	138.9	146.9	150.7	152.7
Medical care	74.9	113.5	138.6	149.3	162.8	177.0	190.1	201.4	211.0
Medical care commodities	75.4	115.2	139.9	150.8	163.4	176.8	188.1	195.0	200.7
Prescription drugs	72.5	120.1	152.0	165.2	181.7	199.7	214.7	223.0	230.6
Nonprescription drugs, medical sup. . .	(NA)	(NA)	108.1	114.6	120.6	126.3	131.2	135.5	138.1
Medical care services	74.8	113.2	138.3	148.9	162.7	177.1	190.5	202.9	213.4
Professional medical services	77.9	113.5	137.5	146.4	156.1	165.7	175.8	184.7	192.5
Physicians' services	76.5	113.3	139.8	150.1	160.8	170.5	181.2	191.3	199.8
Dental services	78.9	114.2	137.5	146.1	155.8	167.4	178.7	188.1	197.1
Eye care.	(NA)	(NA)	108.7	112.4	117.3	121.9	127.0	130.4	133.0
Hospital and related services	69.2	116.1	143.9	160.5	178.0	196.1	214.0	231.9	245.6
Hospital rooms	68.0	115.4	143.3	158.1	175.4	191.9	208.7	226.4	239.2
Entertainment	83.6	107.9	120.3	126.5	132.4	138.4	142.3	145.8	150.1
Entertainment commodities.	84.5	105.8	115.0	119.8	124.0	128.6	131.3	133.4	136.1
Reading materials	77.7	110.7	124.3	129.5	136.2	144.7	150.9	156.2	161.3
Newspapers	79.4	109.3	123.7	129.2	134.6	146.5	154.8	161.1	168.2
Magazines, periodicals, and books .	75.9	112.1	125.0	130.0	137.9	143.3	147.4	151.8	155.1
Sporting goods, equipment	88.5	104.6	108.1	111.1	114.9	118.5	120.2	120.1	122.2
Sport vehicles, including bicycles . .	87.9	106.3	108.9	112.3	115.3	117.5	119.7	120.6	122.3
Toys, hobbies; other entertainment . . .	86.5	103.3	113.2	118.5	121.5	123.9	124.7	126.0	127.4
Pet supplies and expenses	83.3	106.4	114.5	120.7	124.6	129.1	128.1	128.8	130.9
Entertainment services.	82.3	110.9	127.7	135.4	143.2	150.6	155.9	160.8	166.8
Club membership	(NA)	(NA)	107.2	112.6	117.0	122.5	125.2	128.4	130.7
Admissions.	83.8	112.8	131.1	141.4	151.2	159.3	164.5	167.3	175.2
Tobacco and smoking products.	72.0	116.7	145.8	164.4	181.5	202.7	219.8	228.4	220.0
Personal care	81.9	108.3	119.4	125.0	130.4	134.9	138.3	141.5	144.6
Personal care services	83.7	108.9	120.7	126.8	132.8	137.0	140.0	144.0	147.9
Beauty parlor services for women. . . .	83.4	108.8	120.3	126.5	133.0	137.2	139.8	143.6	147.7
Haircuts, etc. for men.	84.4	109.0	121.7	127.3	131.5	135.9	140.3	144.6	147.9
Personal and educational expenses.	70.9	119.1	147.9	158.1	170.2	183.7	197.4	210.7	223.2
School books and supplies	71.4	118.2	148.1	158.0	171.3	180.3	190.3	197.6	205.5
Personal and educational services	70.8	119.2	148.0	158.3	170.4	184.2	198.1	211.9	224.8
Tuition and other school fees	71.2	119.7	151.0	162.7	175.7	191.4	208.5	225.3	239.8
College tuition.	70.8	119.9	150.0	161.9	175.0	192.8	213.5	233.5	249.8
Elementary and high school tuition . . .	72.3	119.0	154.6	168.0	182.8	198.0	213.7	228.9	242.6
Day care and nursery school	(NA)	(NA)	(NA)	(NA)	(NA)	103.2	108.3	113.6	119.6
All commodities	86.0	105.4	111.5	116.7	122.8	126.6	129.1	131.5	133.8
All commodities less food	85.7	105.2	107.7	112.0	117.4	121.3	124.2	126.3	127.9
Energy	86.0	101.6	89.3	94.3	102.1	102.5	103.0	104.2	104.6

NA Not available.
Source: U.S. Bureau of Labor Statistics, *Monthly Labor Review* and *CPI Detailed Report*, January issues.

No. 763. Consumer Price Indexes (CPI-U)—Selected Areas: 1980 to 1994

[1982-84=100, except as indicated. Represents annual averages of monthly figures. Local area CPI indexes are byproducts of the national CPI program. Each local index has a smaller sample size than the national index and is therefore, subject to substantially more sampling and other measurement error. As a result, local area indexes show greater volatility than the national index, although their long- term trends are similar. Area definitions are those established by the Office of Management and Budget in 1983. For further detail see the U.S. Bureau of Labor Statistics Handbook of Methods, Bulletin 2285, Chapter 19, the Consumer Price Index, and Report 736, the CPI: 1987 Revision. See also text, section 15]

AREA	1980	1985	1990	1991	1992	1993	1994								
							All items	Food and beverages	Food	Housing	Apparel and upkeep	Transportation	Medical care	Entertainment	Fuel and other utilities
U.S. city average	82.4	107.6	130.7	136.2	140.3	144.5	148.2	144.9	144.3	141.8	133.4	134.3	211.0	150.1	122.8
Anchorage, AK MSA	85.5	105.8	118.6	124.0	128.2	132.2	135.0	131.9	130.5	122.9	128.9	136.9	197.8	166.6	142.1
Atlanta, GA MSA	80.3	108.9	131.7	135.9	138.5	143.4	146.7	141.1	142.9	140.1	167.3	123.8	227.0	172.3	132.2
Baltimore, MD MSA	83.7	108.2	130.8	136.4	140.1	143.1	146.9	149.7	150.3	138.4	135.3	132.8	218.1	154.7	113.1
Boston-Lawrence-Salem, MA-NH CMSA	82.6	109.4	138.9	145.0	148.6	152.9	154.9	150.0	149.8	147.9	146.8	135.0	251.1	163.9	119.9
Buffalo-Niagara Falls, NY CMSA	83.5	108.6	127.7	133.4	137.9	142.7	146.8	143.1	143.0	155.9	118.7	120.9	174.5	177.7	127.0
Chicago-Gary-Lake County, IL-IN-WI CMSA	82.2	107.7	131.7	137.0	134.1	145.4	148.6	147.0	145.8	144.8	131.0	130.3	213.2	160.0	110.7
Cincinnati-Hamilton, OH-KY-IN CMSA	82.1	106.6	126.5	131.4	136.8	137.8	142.4	135.6	134.5	135.2	140.5	129.4	213.8	147.1	117.5
Cleveland-Akron-Lorain, OH CMSA	78.9	107.8	129.0	134.2	133.9	140.3	144.4	144.4	144.8	142.4	128.8	128.6	195.8	149.4	121.8
Dallas-Fort Worth, TX CMSA	81.5	108.2	125.1	130.8	130.3	137.3	141.2	142.2	140.3	129.0	148.2	134.5	205.6	147.1	126.3
Denver-Boulder, CO CMSA	78.4	107.1	120.9	125.6	128.6	135.8	141.8	134.4	135.5	131.1	96.8	148.4	230.3	145.6	121.3
Detroit-Ann Arbor, MI CMSA	85.3	106.8	128.6	133.1	135.9	139.6	144.0	138.7	137.8	137.6	136.1	138.6	199.7	145.7	116.8
Honolulu, HI MSA	83.0	106.8	138.1	148.0	155.1	160.1	164.5	153.4	153.2	171.6	118.7	156.4	206.0	142.3	121.3
Houston-Galveston-Brazoria, TX CMSA	82.7	104.9	120.6	125.1	127.1	133.4	137.9	137.5	136.8	120.4	146.7	132.9	204.6	157.4	107.6
Kansas City, MO-KS CMSA	83.6	107.7	126.0	131.2	134.3	138.1	141.3	140.2	140.1	133.3	123.3	128.1	202.9	160.5	125.7
Los Angeles-Anaheim-Riverside, CA CMSA	83.7	108.4	135.9	141.4	146.5	150.3	152.3	148.5	146.7	151.0	129.6	140.5	215.2	137.2	143.1
Miami-Fort Lauderdale, FL CMSA	81.1	106.5	128.0	132.3	134.5	139.1	143.6	152.7	152.7	135.2	143.5	135.3	188.1	134.4	111.9
Milwaukee, WI PMSA	81.4	107.0	126.2	132.2	137.1	142.1	147.0	141.5	142.2	148.0	122.5	134.2	201.7	130.2	106.3
Minneapolis-St. Paul, MN-WI MSA	78.9	107.0	127.0	130.4	135.0	139.2	143.6	149.1	147.0	129.6	148.1	134.2	205.4	151.8	112.5
New Orleans, LA MSA	(NA)	(NA)	111.5	116.0	120.2	124.7	129.0	123.6	124.8	115.9	185.5	120.7	169.1	134.8	127.7
New York-Northern New Jersey-Long Island, NY-NJ-CT CMSA	82.1	108.7	138.5	144.8	150.0	154.5	158.2	151.9	151.6	159.9	126.2	141.8	217.6	154.0	112.4
Philadelphia-Wilmington-Trenton, PA-NJ-DE-MD CMSA	83.6	108.8	135.8	142.2	146.6	150.2	154.6	142.7	141.3	155.1	105.8	144.0	223.9	160.3	120.5
Pittsburgh-Beaver Valley, PA CMSA	81.0	106.9	126.2	131.3	136.0	139.9	144.6	140.6	139.2	145.2	133.2	122.3	207.0	153.6	136.1
Portland-Vancouver, OR-WA CMSA	87.2	106.7	127.4	133.9	139.8	144.7	148.9	135.9	135.2	149.5	123.7	138.6	192.8	157.7	124.3
San Diego, CA MSA	79.4	110.4	138.4	143.4	147.4	150.6	154.5	147.6	146.8	153.4	141.7	141.8	217.8	157.8	114.7
San Francisco-Oakland-San Jose, CA CMSA	80.4	108.4	132.1	137.9	142.5	146.3	148.7	148.9	149.0	151.5	115.5	125.7	204.3	164.5	142.8
Seattle-Tacoma, WA CMSA	82.7	105.6	126.8	134.1	139.0	142.9	147.8	146.9	146.7	147.9	120.9	135.0	199.8	146.7	112.7
St. Louis-East St. Louis, MO-IL CMSA	82.5	107.1	128.1	132.1	134.7	137.5	141.3	144.0	143.0	136.7	125.1	129.2	201.7	142.6	119.8
Tampa-St. Petersburg-Clearwater, FL MSA [1]	(NA)	(NA)	111.7	116.4	119.2	124.0	126.5	121.9	121.4	121.4	143.6	118.8	172.8	109.9	115.9
Washington, DC-MD-VA MSA	82.9	109.0	135.6	141.2	144.7	149.3	152.2	144.2	143.7	150.9	141.5	137.0	203.5	155.9	123.5

NA Not available.   [1] 1987=100.

Source: U.S. Bureau of Labor Statistics, *Monthly Labor Review* and *CPI Detailed Report*, January issues.

No. 764. Consumer Price Index for All Urban Consumers (CPI-U), by Region: 1980 to 1994

[1982-84=100. For composition of regions, see table 27]

ITEM	1980	1984	1985	1986	1987	1988	1989	1990	1991	1992	1993	1994
U.S. city average, all items . . .	82.4	103.9	107.6	109.6	113.6	118.3	124.0	130.7	136.2	140.3	144.5	148.2
Food	86.8	103.2	105.6	109.0	113.5	118.2	125.1	132.4	136.3	137.9	140.9	144.3
Housing	81.1	103.6	107.7	110.9	114.2	118.5	123.0	128.5	133.6	137.5	141.2	144.8
Gas (piped) and electricity . .	71.4	105.4	107.1	105.7	103.8	104.6	107.5	109.3	112.6	114.8	118.5	119.2
Northeast:												
All items	82.2	104.5	108.4	111.1	116.0	121.8	128.6	136.3	142.5	147.3	151.4	155.1
Food	86.5	103.3	106.2	110.1	115.8	121.1	128.7	135.9	139.8	141.9	145.1	148.4
Housing	80.7	104.6	109.0	112.7	117.3	124.0	130.8	138.0	144.4	149.0	152.6	156.4
Gas (piped) and electricity . .	73.8	104.7	105.9	104.6	101.2	100.2	105.4	109.6	113.4	117.2	121.4	125.1
North Central:												
All items	82.4	103.6	106.8	108.0	111.9	116.1	121.5	127.4	132.4	136.1	140.0	144.0
Food	88.5	102.7	104.4	107.5	111.8	116.0	122.2	129.6	133.5	135.0	137.8	140.9
Housing	80.0	103.5	107.0	109.4	112.4	115.9	119.9	124.1	128.5	132.1	135.8	139.2
Gas (piped) and electricity . .	70.1	106.1	108.6	107.1	104.6	104.3	105.5	104.0	105.6	107.6	111.6	109.6
South:												
All items	81.9	103.8	107.1	108.9	112.4	116.4	121.5	127.9	132.9	136.5	140.8	144.7
Food	86.6	103.6	105.7	108.8	113.1	117.6	124.2	131.6	135.0	136.1	138.6	142.4
Housing	80.8	103.0	106.3	109.0	111.0	113.9	117.2	121.8	125.6	128.8	132.8	136.4
Gas (piped) and electricity . .	70.2	105.0	106.0	105.1	104.3	106.1	108.2	110.4	112.9	114.9	118.3	118.3
West:												
All items	83.3	103.6	108.0	110.5	114.3	119.0	124.6	131.5	137.3	142.0	146.0	149.6
Food	85.2	103.6	106.1	109.0	112.9	117.6	124.9	132.0	136.4	138.5	141.9	145.3
Housing	83.3	103.3	108.8	113.0	116.5	120.7	124.8	130.9	136.9	141.2	144.6	148.0
Gas (piped) and electricity . .	72.1	105.6	108.1	105.8	105.5	108.8	112.9	115.8	122.9	123.6	126.6	129.1

Source: U.S. Bureau of Labor Statistics, *Monthly Labor Review* and *CPI Detailed Report,* January issues.

No. 765. Annual Percent Changes in Consumer Prices, United States and OECD Countries: 1975 to 1992

[Covers member countries of Organization for Economic Cooperation (OECD). For consumer price indexes for OECD countries, see section 30]

COUNTRY	1975	1980	1981	1982	1983	1984	1985	1986	1987	1988	1989	1990	1991	1992
United States	9.1	13.5	10.3	6.1	3.2	4.3	3.5	1.9	3.7	4.1	4.8	5.4	4.2	3.0
OECD	11.7	13.5	10.8	8.0	5.6	5.6	4.9	3.0	3.6	4.3	5.4	5.8	5.2	4.0
Australia	15.1	9.8	10.1	11.2	10.1	3.9	6.7	9.1	8.5	7.3	7.5	7.3	3.2	1.0
Canada	10.7	10.2	12.4	10.8	5.8	4.3	4.0	4.2	4.4	4.0	5.0	4.8	5.6	1.5
Japan	11.8	7.8	4.9	2.7	1.9	2.2	2.0	0.6	0.1	0.7	2.3	3.1	3.3	1.7
New Zealand	14.7	17.2	15.4	16.2	7.3	6.2	15.4	13.2	15.8	6.4	5.7	6.1	2.6	1.0
Austria	8.4	6.3	6.8	5.4	3.3	5.7	3.2	1.7	1.4	1.9	2.6	3.3	3.3	4.0
Belgium	12.8	6.7	7.1	8.7	7.7	6.3	4.9	1.3	1.6	1.2	3.1	3.4	3.2	2.4
Denmark	9.6	12.3	11.7	10.1	6.9	6.3	4.7	3.6	4.0	4.6	4.8	2.7	2.4	2.1
Finland	17.9	11.6	12.0	9.6	8.3	7.1	5.9	2.9	4.1	5.1	6.6	6.1	4.3	2.9
France	11.8	13.6	13.4	11.8	9.6	7.4	5.8	2.7	3.1	2.7	3.6	3.4	3.2	2.4
Greece	13.6	24.7	24.5	21.0	20.2	18.5	19.3	23.0	16.4	13.5	13.7	20.4	19.5	15.9
Ireland	20.9	18.3	20.4	17.1	10.5	8.6	5.5	3.8	3.1	2.1	4.1	3.3	3.2	3.1
Italy [1]	17.2	21.1	18.7	16.3	15.0	10.6	8.6	6.1	4.6	5.0	6.6	6.1	6.5	5.3
Luxembourg	10.7	6.3	8.1	9.4	8.7	5.6	4.1	0.3	−0.1	1.4	3.4	3.7	3.1	3.2
Netherlands	10.2	6.5	6.7	5.9	2.7	3.3	2.3	0.1	−0.7	0.7	1.1	2.5	3.9	3.7
Norway	11.7	10.9	13.7	11.3	8.4	6.3	5.7	7.2	8.7	6.7	4.6	4.1	3.4	2.3
Portugal [2]	20.4	16.6	20.0	22.4	25.5	28.8	19.6	11.8	9.4	9.7	12.6	13.4	11.4	8.9
Spain	17.0	15.6	14.5	14.4	12.2	11.3	8.8	8.8	5.2	4.8	6.8	6.7	5.9	5.9
Sweden	9.8	13.7	12.1	8.6	8.9	8.0	7.4	4.2	4.2	5.8	6.4	10.5	9.3	2.3
Switzerland	6.7	4.0	6.5	5.6	3.0	2.9	3.4	0.8	1.4	1.9	3.2	5.4	5.8	4.0
Turkey [2]	19.5	110.2	36.6	29.7	31.4	48.4	45.0	34.6	38.9	75.4	63.3	60.3	66.0	70.1
United Kingdom	24.2	18.0	11.9	8.6	4.6	5.0	6.1	3.4	4.1	4.9	7.8	9.5	5.9	3.7
Germany	5.9	5.5	6.3	5.3	3.3	2.4	2.2	−0.1	0.2	1.3	2.8	2.7	3.5	4.0

[1] Households of wage and salary earners.   [2] Excludes rent.

Source: Organization for Economic Cooperation and Development, Paris, France, *Main Economic Indicators,* monthly.

No. 766. Cost of Living Index—Selected Metropolitan Areas: First Quarter 1994

[Measures relative price levels for consumer goods and services in participating areas for a midmanagement standard of living. The national average equals 100, and each index is read as a percent of the national average. The index does not measure inflation, but compares prices at a single point in time. Excludes taxes. Metropolitan areas as defined by the Office of Management and Budget. For definitions and components of MSA's, see source for details. Selection based on 1990 MSA population]

METROPOLITAN AREAS (MA)	Composite index (100%)	Grocery items (13%)	Housing (28%)	Utilities (9%)	Transportation (10%)	Misc. goods and services (35%)
Birmingham, AL MSA	102.0	98.3	101.1	118.6	96.8	101.5
Decatur, AL MSA: Decatur-Hartselle	90.7	93.7	82.4	97.7	97.7	93.2
Dothan, AL MSA: Dothan	89.3	96.1	78.2	95.1	97.3	92.6
Gadsden, AL MSA: Gadsden	90.8	93.0	73.7	116.7	99.0	94.0
Mobile, AL MSA: Mobile	94.6	99.8	76.8	109.9	110.6	99.0
Montgomery, AL MSA: Montgomery	95.7	97.3	79.9	118.1	96.7	101.6
Anchorage, AK MSA: Anchorage	127.4	123.3	142.1	101.0	115.2	123.0
Las Vegas, NV-AZ MSA: Lake Havasu City AZ	101.1	101.4	95.3	108.5	101.8	101.9
Phoenix-Mesa, AZ MSA:						
Phoenix	102.5	101.9	90.3	102.9	120.3	105.2
Scottsdale	106.1	100.0	108.7	102.8	121.6	101.4
Tucson, AZ MSA:						
Tucson	103.0	105.5	96.6	101.1	109.5	104.9
Yuma, AZ	98.9	100.9	82.5	120.8	117.1	100.4
Fayetteville-Springdale-Rogers, AR MSA: Fayetteville	90.5	98.4	75.8	85.5	94.3	100.8
Fort Smith, AR-OK MSA: Fort Smith, AR	89.8	97.5	73.1	101.9	91.5	96.7
Little Rock-North Little Rock, AR MSA:						
Little Rock-North Little Rock	89.8	95.3	79.4	113.9	95.0	89.6
Bakersfield, CA MSA: Bakersfield	110.3	106.4	108.4	122.0	117.0	105.2
Los Angeles-Long Beach, CA PMSA	125.2	106.7	158.2	90.0	108.5	118.5
San Diego, CA MSA: San Diego	127.5	110.4	174.1	72.7	133.4	108.3
Visalia-Tulare-Porterville, CA MSA:						
Visalia	114.9	112.1	118.6	120.6	105.1	113.6
Boulder-Longmont, CO PMSA:						
Boulder	119.4	100.1	170.4	92.6	101.4	101.2
Longmont	109.5	103.9	143.3	66.8	108.7	95.7
Colorado Springs, CO MSA: Colorado Springs	98.9	103.5	98.1	76.9	103.9	101.4
Denver, CO PMSA: Denver	107.8	99.6	123.5	92.3	105.5	100.4
Lakewood, CO	119.4	109.3	144.4	92.3	121.2	108.8
Fort Collins-Loveland, CO MSA: Loveland	94.2	102.4	97.3	77.4	98.9	90.7
Greeley, CO PMSA	93.3	101.1	73.1	97.6	110.3	99.4
Pueblo, CO MSA: Pueblo	90.3	108.2	79.8	76.7	94.5	92.1
Dover, DE MSA: Dover	108.7	110.8	110.6	114.3	98.7	107.6
Wilmington-Newark, DE-MD PMSA: Wilmington, DE	111.8	113.5	116.7	116.9	99.2	108.0
Fort Myers-Cape Coral, FL MSA: Fort Myers	102.7	99.5	105.8	110.8	106.5	98.6
Gainesville, FL MSA: Gainesville	101.3	97.0	96.2	100.6	113.0	103.1
Jacksonville, FL MSA: Jacksonville	96.3	99.4	86.3	100.0	104.9	97.5
Miami, FL PMSA:						
Miami/Dade County FL	109.8	96.6	107.3	125.0	125.6	104.7
Ocala, FL MSA: Ocala	90.9	96.2	75.8	104.9	98.6	96.0
Orlando, FL MSA: Orlando	99.3	99.1	93.2	108.3	95.6	101.5
Pensacola, FL MSA: Pensacola	93.6	100.7	81.5	89.8	88.9	102.7
Sarasota-Bradenton, FL MSA: Sarasota	110.6	98.5	124.5	114.4	105.5	106.2
Tallahassee, FL MSA: Tallahassee	105.8	102.9	109.3	115.6	103.0	102.9
Tampa-St. Petersburg-Clearwater, FL MSA: Tampa	98.2	99.7	95.4	102.8	99.3	97.2
West Palm Beach-Boca Raton, FL MSA:						
Boca Raton	112.7	96.7	126.8	116.6	121.2	105.0
West Palm Beach	112.8	98.4	123.9	117.7	109.7	109.1
Albany, GA MSA: Albany	94.3	96.6	78.9	99.7	93.0	105.2
Atlanta, GA MSA: Atlanta	100.6	103.5	100.8	110.8	101.1	95.2
Augusta-Aiken, GA-SC MSA: Augusta GA MSA	95.7	93.8	87.5	105.8	100.8	98.8
Macon, GA MSA: Macon	100.4	99.3	95.4	107.2	98.9	104.4
Boise City, ID MSA: Boise	105.0	98.6	117.4	76.3	102.9	103.9
Bloomington-Normal, IL MSA: Bloomington-Normal	103.6	100.8	101.4	121.5	99.7	103.9
Champaign-Urbana, IL MSA: Champaign-Urbana	101.8	105.6	95.9	116.7	100.3	100.3
Chicago, IL PMSA: Schaumburg	121.6	110.3	147.0	108.7	107.9	112.2
Davenport-Moline-Rock Island, IA-IL MSA:						
Quad Cities, IL-IA	99.3	97.9	99.0	91.7	102.2	101.1
Decatur, IL MSA: Decatur	93.6	99.4	83.6	114.5	95.3	93.8
Peoria-Pekin, IL MSA: Peoria	104.5	105.2	108.7	96.1	104.7	104.7
Rockford, IL MSA: Rockford	104.7	100.9	101.5	109.8	109.6	106.1
Springfield, IL MSA: Springfield	94.4	102.6	90.3	91.5	94.2	96.2
Bloomington, IN MSA: Bloomington	102.9	101.9	102.5	105.5	92.7	106.3
Evansville-Henderson, IN-KY MSA: Evansville IN	93.7	99.0	90.6	96.6	89.2	95.6
Fort Wayne, IN MSA: Fort Wayne	91.0	100.6	87.6	104.4	92.2	87.0
Indianapolis, IN MSA:						
Anderson	96.5	99.1	96.4	97.4	97.3	95.6
Lafayette, IN MSA: Lafayette	101.2	104.8	100.4	112.0	91.7	100.7
Muncie, IN MSA: Muncie	99.0	100.8	106.6	99.4	100.7	93.2
South Bend, IN MSA: South Bend-Mishawaka	92.7	92.5	89.6	111.2	87.2	92.6
Cedar Rapids, IA MSA: Cedar Rapids	99.3	95.8	103.6	101.7	96.0	99.0
Iowa City, IA MSA:						
Iowa City-Coralville, IA	109.8	96.3	137.9	108.6	101.3	97.5
Waterloo-Cedar Falls, IA MSA: Waterloo-Cedar Falls	96.7	99.9	95.1	86.4	102.7	98.5
Cincinnati, OH-KY-IN PMSA:						
Northern, KY	94.3	92.4	95.9	98.5	90.4	92.6
Lexington, KY MSA	100.2	96.8	101.2	84.9	95.2	105.4
Louisville, KY-IN MSA: Louisville KY	92.5	99.0	85.8	83.8	97.7	96.6

See footnotes at end of table.

No. 766. Cost of Living Index—Selected Metropolitan Areas: First Quarter 1994—Continued

[See headnote, page 497]

METROPOLITAN AREAS (MA)	Composite index (100%)	Grocery items (13%)	Housing (28%)	Utilities (9%)	Transportation (10%)	Misc. goods and services (35%)
Owensboro, KY MSA: Owensboro	93.1	96.2	86.4	86.0	92.1	99.6
Alexandria, LA MSA: Alexandria	95.6	95.4	91.4	87.4	103.7	101.3
Baton Rouge, LA MSA: Baton Rouge	100.9	98.9	98.0	134.1	106.8	95.0
Lafayette, LA MSA: Lafayette	98.4	99.1	90.3	112.7	105.2	100.1
Lake Charles, LA MSA: Lake Charles	100.3	102.8	90.0	107.8	98.2	107.6
Monroe, LA MSA: Monroe	99.7	99.1	80.5	132.0	103.0	106.8
Baltimore, MD PMSA: Baltimore	103.8	100.6	108.6	92.5	110.2	100.3
Cumberland, MD-WV MSA: Cumberland MD	97.9	104.5	99.5	112.6	85.6	94.9
Hagerstown, MD PMSA: Hagerstown	101.9	92.5	116.9	96.3	97.3	97.0
Boston, MA-NH PMSA: Boston PMSA (MA Part)	135.6	118.6	163.4	180.0	125.9	108.4
Benton Harbor, MI MSA: Benton Harbor-St Joseph	105.9	108.0	116.0	93.4	99.2	103.7
Grand Rapids-Muskegon-Holland, MI MSA:						
Holland	99.0	102.5	110.4	75.3	94.9	97.2
Lansing-East Lansing, MI MSA: Lansing	103.5	105.7	120.2	85.4	95.7	94.7
Minneapolis-St Paul, MN-WI MSA:						
Minneapolis, MN	102.2	99.8	95.2	88.9	118.3	105.5
St. Paul, MN	109.4	107.6	103.7	91.0	125.4	111.4
Rochester, MN MSA: Rochester	103.3	104.3	100.6	106.4	112.2	101.6
St. Cloud, MN MSA	97.0	97.8	84.6	97.0	110.3	102.5
Jackson, MS MSA: Jackson	102.1	98.6	101.3	105.7	108.1	104.0
Columbia, MO MSA: Columbia	93.9	99.8	87.5	77.7	96.4	99.0
Joplin, MO MSA: Joplin	87.5	92.4	84.4	86.0	82.2	89.5
Kansas City, MO-KS MSA	97.5	100.1	94.0	108.5	93.3	97.1
Lee's Summit, MO	97.0	102.1	88.0	111.9	91.1	99.0
St Joseph, MO MSA: St Joseph	91.4	95.6	95.6	97.6	87.5	86.0
St Louis, MO-IL MSA:						
St Charles, MO	96.1	107.1	97.9	111.7	83.9	89.6
St Louis, MO-IL	97.0	98.9	98.1	109.7	91.0	93.0
Springfield, MO MSA: Springfield	92.4	89.3	83.8	94.4	98.1	97.9
Billings, MT MSA: Billings	105.8	106.1	114.3	80.8	103.9	106.2
Lincoln, NE MSA: Lincoln	89.9	95.5	78.8	82.8	103.8	94.9
Omaha, NE-IA MSA: Omaha NE	91.9	97.1	84.9	97.9	104.1	90.9
Las Vegas, NV-AZ MSA: Las Vegas NV	109.3	101.1	113.6	87.9	117.6	110.2
Reno, NV MSA: Reno-Sparks	111.1	107.1	123.7	87.6	103.7	107.5
Albuquerque, NM MSA: Albuquerque	104.9	95.2	115.8	93.3	104.7	101.6
Las Cruces, NM MSA: Las Cruces	98.5	95.8	102.1	89.9	104.4	97.6
Santa Fe, NM MSA: Santa Fe, NM	120.1	100.4	158.2	114.2	112.4	102.0
Binghamton, NY MSA: Binghamton/Broome County	101.6	109.5	86.9	118.6	104.4	106.5
Buffalo-Niagara Falls, NY MSA: Buffalo	118.5	117.0	121.5	133.0	120.7	113.8
Rochester, NY MSA	111.8	116.4	117.6	120.7	116.9	102.9
Syracuse, NY MSA: Syracuse	104.2	110.7	92.6	138.3	108.9	100.0
Utica-Rome, NY MSA	107.1	109.6	100.6	132.5	104.5	104.9
Charlotte-Gastonia-Rock Hill, NC-SC MSA:						
Charlotte, NC	100.1	97.6	98.7	99.5	93.2	103.1
Gastonia, NC	90.4	95.2	88.1	99.0	96.3	88.0
Fayetteville, NC MSA: Fayetteville	95.8	96.7	84.5	102.7	96.3	102.5
Goldsboro, NC MSA: Goldsboro	90.7	94.3	77.5	112.3	94.2	93.0
Greensboro-Winston-Salem-High Point, NC MSA:						
Burlington	93.9	95.6	94.7	98.7	85.9	94.4
Greensboro	97.7	96.4	92.9	100.2	96.7	103.4
Winston-Salem	95.2	95.0	95.6	98.8	91.3	96.3
Greenville, NC MSA: Greenville	97.2	96.3	96.7	97.1	87.9	100.7
Hickory-Morganton, NC MSA: Hickory	98.1	95.6	105.6	99.1	84.0	98.2
Raleigh-Durham-Chapel Hill, NC MSA: Raleigh-Durham	98.5	90.9	96.8	105.6	97.4	100.2
Rocky Mount, NC MSA: Rocky Mount	101.5	97.9	91.7	127.8	100.3	105.1
Fargo-Moorhead, ND-MN MSA: Fargo ND	95.9	107.1	91.1	88.3	95.0	96.9
Cincinnati, OH-KY-IN PMSA: Cincinnati	103.8	95.7	105.8	109.3	104.3	104.6
Cleveland-Lorain-Elyria, OH PMSA: Cleveland	105.2	101.5	109.6	123.9	111.8	96.8
Columbus, OH MSA: Columbus	105.6	98.4	110.6	90.7	109.3	107.8
Dayton-Springfield, OH MSA: Dayton-Springfield	100.5	93.4	98.8	106.4	104.6	103.1
Mansfield, OH MSA: Mansfield	97.1	95.5	93.0	124.1	94.4	95.3
Toledo, OH MSA: Toledo	100.7	93.4	98.1	118.2	110.2	99.0
Oklahoma City, OK MSA: Oklahoma City	93.8	100.0	80.3	108.0	91.9	98.6
Tulsa, OK MSA: Tulsa	90.0	93.9	81.0	90.0	85.2	96.0
Eugene-Springfield, OR MSA: Eugene	104.7	96.9	121.8	75.9	104.2	99.6
Portland-Vancouver, OR-WA PMSA: Portland OR	108.5	104.1	124.6	68.5	111.5	104.2
Salem, OR PMSA: Salem	105.0	97.6	106.9	85.2	109.7	108.0
Allentown-Bethlehem-Easton, PA MSA:						
Allentown-Bethlehem-Easton	106.2	106.4	106.3	108.6	98.6	108.4
Erie, PA MSA: Erie	107.3	98.7	121.7	113.9	106.0	98.8
Lancaster, PA MSA: Lancaster	107.0	101.7	108.6	125.8	108.0	105.1
Philadelphia, PA-NJ PMSA: Philadelphia PA	129.7	116.5	148.1	175.6	113.0	115.2
Pittsburgh, PA MSA: Pittsburgh	113.3	101.2	107.3	158.2	114.9	111.9
Scranton-Wilkes Barre-Hazleton, PA MSA:						
Wilkes Barre	99.1	106.5	106.1	93.3	87.5	96.4
Williamsport, PA MSA: Williamsport/Lycoming County	102.1	102.6	107.3	109.9	91.9	99.3
York, PA MSA:						
Hanover	100.1	102.3	105.9	92.2	91.8	100.5
York County	98.9	98.1	99.0	95.9	112.0	96.7
Charleston-North Charleston SC MSA	99.6	93.6	96.9	96.7	96.4	104.8

See footnotes at end of table.

No. 766. Cost of Living Index—Selected Metropolitan Areas: First Quarter 1994—Continued

[See headnote, page 497]

METROPOLITAN AREAS (MA)	Composite index (100%)	Grocery items (13%)	Housing (28%)	Utilities (9%)	Transportation (10%)	Misc. goods and services (35%)
Charlotte-Gastonia-Rock Hill, NC-SC MSA:						
Rock Hill, SC	100.7	96.3	102.4	108.3	97.5	101.4
Columbia, SC MSA: Columbia	95.1	98.4	92.9	96.8	84.9	97.7
Florence, SC MSA: Florence	92.4	97.5	81.6	101.1	87.8	98.5
Greenville-Spartanburg-Anderson, SC MSA:						
Greenville	97.9	97.8	96.6	99.3	92.0	102.1
Spartanburg	97.0	97.3	96.2	97.6	87.4	101.1
Myrtle Beach, SC MSA: Myrtle Beach	96.1	97.0	90.8	97.7	94.3	100.8
Sumter, SC MSA: Sumter	94.3	96.2	79.3	107.5	94.4	103.1
Sioux Falls, SD MSA: Sioux Falls	97.0	98.5	100.2	90.4	100.3	94.6
Chattanooga, TN-GA MSA: Chattanooga	92.2	97.2	83.7	99.5	90.6	95.6
Clarksville-Hopkinsville, TN-KY MSA: Clarksville, TN	90.4	94.9	80.8	92.8	98.2	95.1
Johnson City-Kingsport-Bristol, TN-VA MSA:						
Johnson City, TN	98.2	94.2	105.0	89.9	93.4	98.6
Kingsport, TN	94.7	95.0	89.0	78.1	95.1	104.8
Knoxville, TN MSA: Knoxville	93.3	93.8	85.7	98.3	91.0	98.8
Memphis, TN-AR-MS MSA: Memphis, TN	98.3	105.8	90.6	92.2	109.3	100.0
Nashville, TN MSA: Nashville-Franklin	90.6	95.1	86.3	89.0	92.2	93.7
Abilene, TX MSA: Abilene	92.7	94.5	86.3	93.9	95.1	94.3
Amarillo, TX MSA: Amarillo	90.7	101.6	85.3	73.4	94.0	95.2
Austin-San Marcos, TX MSA:						
Austin, TX	106.1	89.5	116.1	109.8	104.1	104.0
Georgetown, TX	100.3	99.9	97.8	93.4	103.7	102.8
San Marcos, TX	100.7	98.9	101.7	108.8	97.9	101.1
Beaumont-Port Arthur, TX MSA: Beaumont	91.7	104.3	75.8	93.8	113.0	94.1
Brazoria, TX PMSA: Brazoria	94.6	94.0	89.1	97.6	101.6	95.8
Brownsville-Harlingen-San Benito, TX MSA: Harlingen	89.2	95.6	73.7	106.8	95.6	92.0
Corpus Christi, TX MSA	93.8	90.2	90.8	108.2	78.8	99.6
Dallas, TX PMSA	104.9	101.3	99.6	117.1	106.6	105.2
El Paso, TX MSA: El Paso	100.9	98.6	98.2	92.6	119.1	101.6
Fort Worth-Arlington, TX PMSA:						
Arlington	99.2	99.4	88.5	117.8	101.9	100.3
Weatherford	91.1	94.8	77.7	112.1	97.8	94.1
Houston, TX PMSA	98.8	100.9	91.4	100.7	113.0	97.7
Killeen-Temple, TX MSA: Killeen	95.1	98.3	87.1	112.3	88.4	98.6
Longview-Marshall, TX MSA: Longview	90.4	93.9	84.1	90.5	89.1	96.0
Lubbock, TX MSA: Lubbock	92.4	97.5	84.5	73.7	97.5	99.9
McAllen-Edinburg-Mission, TX MSA: McAllen	91.9	93.3	80.6	107.3	94.9	96.7
Odessa-Midland, TX MSA:						
Midland, TX	96.3	93.2	81.5	112.2	101.9	102.8
Odessa, TX	97.2	97.5	79.5	112.1	107.6	103.2
San Antonio, TX MSA: San Antonio	97.4	91.0	97.1	91.6	99.9	100.4
Waco, TX MSA	96.6	94.1	87.4	117.7	102.2	98.8
Wichita Falls, TX MSA: Wichita Falls	96.4	100.1	85.9	125.3	90.5	98.4
Provo-Orem,, UT MSA: Provo-Orem	98.6	93.7	107.0	82.8	108.2	94.9
Salt Lake City-Ogden, UT MSA: Salt Lake City	95.7	91.1	99.3	88.3	89.2	97.1
Johnson City-Kingsport-Bristol, TN-VA MSA:						
Bristol, VA	92.0	95.3	82.0	95.4	87.8	100.4
Lynchburg, VA MSA: Lynchburg	92.5	97.1	89.4	86.9	85.5	97.5
Norfolk-Virginia Beach-Newport News, VA-NC MSA:						
Virginia Peninsula, VA	97.8	95.1	86.9	114.8	105.7	100.7
Richmond-Petersburg, VA MSA: Richmond	106.6	97.7	104.5	114.3	116.2	107.3
Roanoke, VA MSA: Roanoke	95.0	97.4	89.7	88.0	99.5	99.7
Washington, DC-MD-VA-WV PMSA: Prince William, VA	115.4	104.4	137.5	116.2	114.3	103.2
Bellingham, WA MSA: Bellingham	105.6	101.4	112.4	58.8	97.6	112.9
Olympia, WA PMSA: Olympia	107.2	104.9	119.8	69.4	103.1	104.2
Portland-Vancouver, OR-WA PMSA: Vancouver, WA	102.3	95.2	117.1	64.6	99.2	100.0
Richland-Kennewick-Pasco, WA MSA:						
Richland-Kennewick-Pasco	107.4	102.0	116.4	84.0	96.6	107.5
Spokane, WA MSA	108.2	104.3	130.8	56.0	102.3	104.6
Tacoma, WA PMSA: Tacoma	103.0	110.2	101.1	61.6	106.3	105.2
Yakima, WA MSA: Yakima	101.5	104.2	105.4	71.6	99.4	102.9
Charleston, WV MSA: Charleston	96.9	97.2	94.2	100.2	108.3	94.8
Huntington-Ashland, WV-KY-OH MSA:						
Huntington, WV	105.2	93.4	106.5	103.9	100.2	111.4
Washington, DC-MD-VA-WV PMSA:						
Martinsburg/Berkeley County, WV	90.9	92.4	93.5	86.8	90.3	90.2
Wheeling, WV-OH MSA: Wheeling	95.9	99.9	94.6	103.7	86.9	97.0
Appleton-Oshkosh-Neenah, WI MSA:						
Appleton-Neenah-Menasha	98.0	96.8	99.8	93.9	96.7	98.1
Oshkosh	104.0	101.5	118.1	92.4	89.8	99.7
Eau Claire, WI MSA: Eau Claire	100.2	102.5	110.7	95.6	94.0	92.9
Green Bay, WI MSA: Green Bay	97.5	96.8	100.0	94.5	94.4	97.7
Janesville-Beloit, WI MSA: Janesville	101.3	103.4	117.3	84.1	94.1	94.4
La Crosse, WI-MN MSA: La Crosse WI	103.3	99.3	113.6	96.0	95.2	97.6
Milwaukee-Waukesha, WI PMSA	107.0	106.5	124.1	99.5	103.6	97.0
Wausau, WI MSA: Wausau	106.8	100.2	125.9	103.0	90.5	99.8

Source: ACCRA, Louisville KY 40206-6749, *ACCRA Cost of Living Index,* Third Quarter 1992 (copyright).

No. 767. Producer Price Indexes, by Stage of Processing: 1960 to 1994

[**1982=100**. Minus sign (-) indicates decline. See text, section 15. See *Historical Statistics, Colonial Times to 1970*, series E 73-86 for similar data]

YEAR	CRUDE MATERIALS				Inter-mediate materials, supplies, and com-ponents	FINISHED GOODS		CONSUMER FOODS		Finished con-sumer goods excl. food
	Total	Food-stuffs and feed-stuffs	Fuel	Crude nonfood mate-rials except fuel		Con-sumer goods	Capital equip-ment	Crude	Proc-essed	
1960	30.4	38.4	10.5	26.9	30.8	35.5	30.2	35.2	28.4	33.5
1961	30.2	37.9	10.5	27.2	30.6	35.4	30.3	35.3	28.4	33.4
1962	30.5	38.6	10.4	27.1	30.6	35.7	30.5	35.6	28.4	33.4
1963	29.9	37.5	10.5	26.7	30.7	35.3	30.6	35.2	28.5	33.4
1964	29.6	36.6	10.5	27.2	30.8	35.4	31.0	35.2	28.4	33.3
1965	31.1	39.2	10.6	27.7	31.2	36.8	31.5	36.8	28.8	33.6
1966	33.1	42.7	10.9	28.3	32.0	39.2	32.5	39.2	29.3	34.1
1967	31.3	40.3	11.3	26.5	32.2	38.5	33.8	38.8	30.0	34.7
1968	31.8	40.9	11.5	27.1	33.0	40.0	35.0	40.0	30.6	35.5
1969	33.9	44.1	12.0	28.4	34.1	42.4	36.2	42.3	31.5	36.3
1970	35.2	45.2	13.8	29.1	35.4	43.8	38.1	43.9	32.5	37.4
1971	36.0	46.1	15.7	29.4	36.8	44.5	39.6	44.7	33.5	38.7
1972	39.9	51.5	16.8	32.3	38.2	41.5	42.8	48.0	47.2	39.4
1973	54.5	72.6	18.6	42.9	42.4	46.0	44.2	63.6	55.8	41.2
1974	61.4	76.4	24.8	54.5	52.5	53.1	50.5	71.6	63.9	48.2
1975	61.6	77.4	30.6	50.0	58.0	58.2	58.2	71.7	70.3	53.2
1976	63.4	76.8	34.5	54.9	60.9	60.4	62.1	76.7	69.0	56.5
1977	65.5	77.5	42.0	56.3	64.9	64.3	66.1	79.5	72.7	60.6
1978	73.4	87.3	48.2	61.9	69.5	69.4	71.3	85.8	79.4	64.9
1979	85.9	100.0	57.3	75.5	78.4	77.5	77.5	92.3	86.8	73.5
1980	95.3	104.6	69.4	91.8	90.3	88.6	85.8	93.9	92.3	87.1
1981	103.0	103.9	84.8	109.8	98.6	96.6	94.6	104.4	97.2	96.1
1982	100.0	100.0	100.0	100.0	100.0	100.0	100.0	100.0	100.0	100.0
1983	101.3	101.8	105.1	98.8	100.6	101.3	102.8	102.4	100.9	101.2
1984	103.5	104.7	105.1	101.0	103.1	103.3	105.2	111.4	104.9	102.2
1985	95.8	94.8	102.7	94.3	102.7	103.8	107.5	102.9	104.8	103.3
1986	87.7	93.2	92.2	76.0	99.1	101.4	109.7	105.6	107.4	98.5
1987	93.7	96.2	84.1	88.5	101.5	103.6	111.7	107.1	109.6	100.7
1988	96.0	106.1	82.1	85.9	107.1	106.2	114.3	109.8	112.7	103.1
1989	103.1	111.2	85.3	95.8	112.0	112.1	118.0	119.6	118.6	108.9
1990	108.9	113.1	84.8	107.3	114.5	118.2	122.9	123.0	124.4	115.3
1991	101.2	105.5	82.9	97.5	114.4	120.5	126.7	119.3	124.4	118.7
1992	100.4	105.1	84.0	94.2	114.7	121.7	129.1	107.6	124.4	120.8
1993	102.4	108.4	87.1	94.1	116.2	123.0	131.4	114.4	126.5	121.7
1994	101.7	106.5	82.5	96.9	118.5	123.3	134.1	111.2	127.9	121.6
PERCENT CHANGE										
1960	-2.3	-1.0	1.0	-4.3	-	2.0	1.3	1.4	0.7	0.6
1961	-0.7	-1.3	-	1.1	-0.6	-0.3	0.3	0.3	-	-0.3
1962	1.0	1.8	-1.0	-0.4	-	0.8	0.7	0.8	-	-
1963	-2.0	-2.8	1.0	-1.5	0.3	-1.1	0.3	-1.1	0.4	-
1964	-1.0	-2.4	-	1.9	0.3	0.3	1.3	-	-0.4	-0.3
1965	5.1	7.1	1.0	1.8	1.3	4.0	1.6	4.5	1.4	0.9
1966	6.4	8.9	2.8	2.2	2.6	6.5	3.2	6.5	1.7	1.5
1967	-5.4	-5.6	3.7	-6.4	0.6	-1.8	4.0	-1.0	2.4	1.8
1968	1.6	1.5	1.8	2.3	2.5	3.9	3.6	3.1	2.0	2.3
1969	6.6	7.8	4.3	4.8	3.3	6.0	3.4	5.7	2.9	2.3
1970	3.8	2.5	15.0	2.5	3.8	3.3	5.2	3.8	3.2	3.0
1971	2.3	2.0	13.8	1.0	4.0	1.6	3.9	1.8	3.1	3.5
1972	10.8	11.7	7.0	9.9	3.8	-6.7	8.1	7.4	40.9	1.8
1973	36.6	41.0	10.7	32.8	11.0	10.8	3.3	32.5	18.2	4.6
1974	12.7	5.2	33.3	27.0	23.8	15.4	14.3	12.6	14.5	17.0
1975	0.3	1.3	23.4	-8.3	10.5	9.6	15.2	0.1	10.0	10.4
1976	2.9	-0.8	12.7	9.8	5.0	3.8	6.7	7.0	-1.8	6.2
1977	3.3	0.9	21.7	2.6	6.6	6.5	6.4	3.7	5.4	7.3
1978	12.1	12.6	14.8	9.9	7.1	7.9	7.9	7.9	9.2	7.1
1979	17.0	14.5	18.9	22.0	12.8	11.7	8.7	7.6	9.3	13.3
1980	10.9	4.6	21.1	21.6	15.2	14.3	10.7	1.7	6.3	18.5
1981	8.1	-0.7	22.2	19.6	9.2	9.0	10.3	11.2	5.3	10.3
1982	-2.9	-3.8	17.9	-8.9	1.4	3.5	5.7	-4.2	2.9	4.1
1983	1.3	1.8	5.1	-1.2	0.6	1.3	2.8	2.4	0.9	1.2
1984	2.2	2.8	-	2.2	2.5	2.0	2.3	8.8	4.0	1.0
1985	-7.4	-9.5	-2.3	-6.6	-0.4	0.5	2.2	-7.6	-0.1	1.1
1986	-8.5	-1.7	-10.2	-19.4	-3.5	-2.3	2.0	2.6	2.5	-4.6
1987	6.8	3.2	-8.8	16.4	2.4	2.2	1.8	1.4	2.0	2.2
1988	2.5	10.3	-2.4	-2.9	5.5	2.5	2.3	2.5	2.8	2.4
1989	7.4	4.8	3.9	11.5	4.6	5.6	3.2	8.9	5.2	5.6
1990	5.6	1.7	-0.6	12.0	2.2	5.4	4.2	2.8	4.9	5.9
1991	-7.1	-6.7	-2.2	-9.1	-0.1	1.9	3.1	-3.0	-	2.9
1992	-0.9	-0.4	1.3	-3.4	0.3	1.0	1.9	-9.8	-	1.8
1993	2.0	3.1	3.7	-0.1	1.3	1.1	1.8	6.3	1.7	0.7
1994	-0.7	-1.8	-5.3	3.0	2.0	0.2	2.1	-2.8	1.1	-0.1

- Represents or rounds to zero.

Source: U.S. Bureau of Labor Statistics, *Producer Price Indexes,* monthly and annual.

No. 768. Producer Price Indexes for Selected Commodity Groupings, by Stage of Processing: 1970 to 1994

[1982=100, except as indicated]

COMMODITY	1970	1980	1985	1990	1991	1992	1993	1994
Finished goods	**39.3**	**88.0**	**104.7**	**119.2**	**121.7**	**123.2**	**124.7**	**125.5**
Finished consumer goods	39.1	88.6	103.8	118.2	120.5	121.7	123.0	123.3
Finished consumer foods	43.8	92.4	104.6	124.4	124.1	123.3	125.7	126.8
Fresh fruits	42.3	100.3	108.1	118.1	129.9	84.0	84.5	82.4
Fresh and dried vegetables	47.5	88.9	99.5	118.1	103.8	115.0	135.2	129.0
Eggs	71.0	95.7	95.7	117.6	110.7	94.1	105.9	97.8
Bakery products	40.0	90.0	113.9	141.0	146.6	152.5	156.6	160.0
Milled rice	52.4	131.5	105.0	102.5	109.9	108.8	101.3	118.5
Beef and veal	46.7	106.2	90.3	116.0	112.2	109.5	112.9	103.6
Pork	44.6	78.4	89.1	119.8	113.4	98.9	105.7	101.2
Processed young chickens	61.2	106.8	106.5	111.0	105.1	104.9	109.5	113.3
Processed turkeys	69.1	109.2	121.3	107.6	107.3	102.3	101.0	108.4
Fish	29.7	87.8	114.6	147.2	149.5	156.1	156.5	161.5
Dairy products	44.7	92.7	100.2	117.2	114.6	117.9	118.1	119.4
Processed fruits and vegetables	40.3	83.3	108.0	124.7	119.6	120.8	118.2	121.2
Soft drinks	37.8	81.8	107.7	122.3	125.5	125.6	126.2	126.9
Roasted coffee	37.7	110.4	107.2	113.0	107.8	100.5	100.5	128.0
Shortening and cooking oils	47.7	99.5	124.0	123.2	116.5	115.1	122.9	138.9
Finished consumer goods excl. foods	37.4	87.1	103.3	115.3	118.7	120.8	121.7	121.6
Alcoholic beverages	53.3	88.9	107.7	117.2	123.7	126.1	126.0	124.8
Women's apparel	62.8	86.9	105.4	116.1	117.9	119.9	120.2	119.7
Men's and boys' apparel	51.2	91.3	105.0	120.2	122.7	126.0	127.7	128.5
Girls', children's, and infants' apparel	58.8	87.1	103.1	115.3	117.8	119.0	120.1	120.0
Textile housefurnishings	43.4	86.8	100.6	109.5	111.8	113.7	115.8	117.3
Footwear	46.2	95.2	104.8	125.6	128.6	132.0	134.4	135.5
Residential natural gas (December 1990=100)	(NA)	(NA)	(NA)	(NA)	99.2	100.9	107.3	108.6
Gasoline	14.4	93.3	83.3	78.7	69.9	68.1	63.9	61.7
Fuel oil No. 2	(NA)	82.8	81.6	73.3	65.2	61.7	59.1	56.2
Pharmaceutical preps, ethical (Prescription)	52.0	80.6	132.0	200.8	217.5	231.7	242.2	249.9
Pharmaceutical preps, propri.; Over-counter	42.3	81.3	121.6	156.8	165.4	173.6	180.0	183.2
Soaps and synthetic detergents	41.5	85.8	107.9	117.7	117.5	120.6	122.2	121.4
Cosmetics and other toilet preparations	47.8	83.8	109.0	121.6	124.6	126.7	129.1	128.7
Tires, tubes, tread, etc	42.7	92.8	93.0	96.8	98.2	98.9	98.9	98.7
Sanitary papers and health products	32.5	91.9	106.6	135.3	136.2	136.9	134.6	133.0
Household furniture	48.6	89.1	108.5	125.1	128.0	130.0	133.4	138.0
Floor coverings	54.9	90.0	105.6	119.0	120.4	120.3	120.2	121.3
Household appliances	52.9	87.5	106.7	110.8	111.3	111.4	112.9	112.9
Home electronic equipment	106.0	103.8	90.8	82.7	83.2	82.0	80.2	80.2
Household glassware	33.1	84.7	121.8	132.5	136.0	141.6	142.9	146.9
Household flatware	32.7	148.0	98.6	122.1	119.5	125.2	130.7	133.8
Lawn and garden equip., excl. tractors	46.8	87.5	110.3	123.0	124.7	125.3	126.2	128.4
Passenger cars	50.0	88.9	106.9	118.3	124.1	126.9	129.8	133.9
Toys, games, and children's vehicles	48.5	89.2	103.8	118.1	120.2	121.4	121.5	122.4
Sporting and athletic goods	52.7	90.6	99.7	112.6	115.3	118.2	118.6	120.1
Tobacco products	35.2	76.0	132.5	221.4	249.7	275.3	260.3	224.5
Mobile homes	(NA)	(NA)	101.7	117.5	120.4	121.7	127.8	137.2
Capital equipment	**40.1**	**85.8**	**107.5**	**122.9**	**126.7**	**129.1**	**131.4**	**134.1**
Agricultural machinery and equipment	36.4	83.3	108.7	121.7	125.7	129.5	133.6	136.8
Construction machinery and equipment	33.7	84.2	105.4	121.6	125.2	128.7	132.0	133.6
Metal cutting machine tools	30.8	85.1	107.3	129.8	134.6	138.9	141.1	143.1
Metal forming machine tools	28.6	85.7	107.0	128.7	133.5	135.9	138.4	141.9
Tools, dies, jigs, fixtures, and ind. molds	(NA)	(NA)	106.3	117.2	122.7	125.1	128.4	131.4
Pumps, compressors, and equipment	33.0	82.8	102.6	119.2	124.6	129.1	132.8	135.2
Industrial material handling equipment	39.8	88.4	102.7	115.0	117.4	118.4	120.2	122.4
Textile machinery	45.4	87.2	107.6	128.8	135.0	138.9	143.7	144.9
Paper industries machinery (June 1982=100)	(NA)	(NA)	109.8	134.8	140.1	142.7	144.9	147.4
Printing trades machinery	42.5	89.7	109.0	124.9	126.5	126.8	129.5	131.1
Transformers and power regulators	44.7	82.4	105.0	120.9	123.9	123.5	123.0	125.3
Oil field and gas field machinery	27.0	76.3	96.8	102.4	108.6	107.6	108.2	110.8
Mining machinery and equipment	30.9	85.2	105.4	121.0	125.2	127.4	129.5	131.1
Office and store machines and equipment	68.3	93.1	101.6	109.5	109.8	111.0	111.0	111.3
Commercial furniture	41.6	85.7	111.9	133.4	136.2	138.1	140.5	144.7
Light motor trucks	42.0	83.3	112.2	130.0	135.5	142.4	150.3	157.1
Heavy motor trucks	36.3	82.3	108.8	120.3	123.6	128.6	133.9	139.2
Truck trailers	(NA)	(NA)	106.2	110.8	112.1	115.1	118.2	122.2
Railroad equipment	33.2	90.4	104.9	118.6	122.2	123.7	125.2	129.2
Photographic equipment	72.0	94.9	89.5	97.2	99.3	101.1	101.5	98.0
Intermed. materials, supplies, components	**35.4**	**90.3**	**102.7**	**114.5**	**114.4**	**114.7**	**116.2**	**118.5**
Intermediate foods and feeds	45.6	105.5	97.3	113.3	111.1	110.7	112.7	114.8
Flour	55.3	102.3	99.8	103.6	96.8	109.5	108.9	110.6
Crude vegetable oils	75.8	127.1	137.6	115.8	103.0	97.1	110.5	135.4
Prepared animal feeds	49.1	107.3	90.1	107.4	106.8	108.3	111.0	111.4

See footnotes at end of table.

No. 768. Producer Price Indexes for Selected Commodity Groupings by Stage of Processing: 1970 to 1994—Continued

[1982=100, except as indicated]

COMMODITY	1970	1980	1985	1990	1991	1992	1993	1994
Intermediate materials less foods and feeds	**34.8**	**89.4**	**103.0**	**114.5**	**114.6**	**114.9**	**116.4**	**118.7**
Leather	34.6	99.8	113.4	177.5	168.4	163.7	168.6	179.6
Liquefied petroleum gas	(NA)	102.3	86.3	77.4	75.4	65.8	63.7	58.2
Electric power	26.1	79.1	111.6	117.6	124.3	126.3	128.5	128.7
Jet fuels	(NA)	87.5	81.0	76.0	66.4	61.9	59.1	53.9
No. 2 diesel fuel	(NA)	85.8	81.2	74.1	65.6	61.9	60.7	56.0
Residual fuel	10.6	81.3	83.2	57.7	49.1	45.9	49.6	48.2
Industrial chemicals	28.6	91.9	96.0	113.2	111.8	109.3	110.5	114.3
Prepared paint	42.8	89.5	105.3	124.8	129.9	131.6	133.2	135.3
Paint materials	33.3	89.9	109.5	136.3	135.8	131.1	131.5	132.1
Medicinal and botanical chemicals	44.4	91.0	102.3	102.2	109.0	111.3	120.6	125.4
Fats and oils, inedible	49.7	111.6	110.6	88.1	86.8	93.0	95.7	110.6
Mixed fertilizers	35.2	90.0	96.1	103.3	105.2	102.6	98.9	105.7
Nitrogenates	32.7	90.0	96.3	92.3	98.5	95.4	99.5	112.3
Phosphates	27.5	93.0	91.6	96.5	98.1	92.5	83.0	95.5
Other agricultural chemicals	23.2	80.1	98.7	119.9	125.6	129.2	134.5	140.8
Plastic resins and materials	32.0	98.5	107.5	124.1	120.0	116.4	117.2	122.4
Synthetic rubber	34.0	85.3	96.8	111.9	106.1	103.8	105.7	108.9
Plastic construction products	65.5	103.9	108.6	117.2	115.1	112.7	116.8	122.9
Softwood lumber	35.2	107.3	107.4	123.8	125.7	148.6	193.5	198.1
Hardwood lumber	43.7	96.0	117.1	131.0	128.5	140.7	163.3	168.3
Millwork	41.5	93.2	111.7	130.4	135.5	143.3	156.5	162.4
Plywood	46.7	106.2	99.6	114.2	114.3	133.3	152.7	158.6
Woodpulp	28.9	100.3	91.4	151.3	119.2	118.9	104.3	115.9
Paper	38.8	89.7	106.0	128.8	126.9	123.2	123.8	126.0
Paperboard	39.7	92.0	107.7	135.7	130.2	134.3	130.0	140.5
Paper boxes and containers	43.3	89.4	108.8	129.9	128.6	130.6	130.0	136.1
Building paper and board	42.2	86.1	107.4	112.2	111.8	119.6	132.9	144.1
Commercial printing (June 1982=100)	(NA)	(NA)	111.6	128.0	130.0	131.1	134.8	136.5
Foundry and forge shop products	32.4	89.7	105.2	117.2	119.0	120.1	121.3	123.9
Steel mill products	32.7	86.6	104.7	112.1	109.5	106.4	108.2	113.4
Primary nonferrous metals	44.9	132.7	93.6	133.4	114.0	108.1	98.1	115.7
Aluminum mill shapes	36.7	89.3	107.8	127.9	123.2	121.9	120.3	127.7
Copper and brass mill shapes	63.4	112.6	106.9	174.6	160.5	166.0	150.8	167.3
Nonferrous wire and cable	62.6	107.5	100.9	142.6	139.2	136.7	133.2	139.8
Metal containers	34.3	90.9	109.0	114.0	115.5	113.9	109.5	108.1
Hardware	39.8	85.8	109.1	125.9	130.2	132.7	135.2	137.5
Plumbing fixtures and brass fittings	39.9	88.5	111.9	144.3	149.7	153.1	155.8	159.6
Heating equipment	46.6	87.0	109.5	131.6	134.1	137.3	140.3	142.5
Fabricated structural metal products	36.7	88.8	103.2	121.8	122.4	122.1	123.2	127.3
Mechanical power transmission equipment.	36.9	84.5	108.2	125.3	129.1	132.1	136.2	140.5
Ball and roller bearings	33.1	80.0	105.9	130.6	136.7	139.0	141.8	145.7
Wiring devices	35.9	81.9	111.7	132.2	133.9	134.8	138.6	141.5
Motors, generators, motor generator sets	37.7	86.0	113.3	132.9	134.9	136.6	138.6	140.2
Switchgear, switchboard, etc., equipment.	40.5	88.4	106.7	124.4	128.5	131.5	134.6	136.8
Electronic components and accessories	57.4	88.8	112.4	118.4	118.6	117.5	117.8	116.6
Internal combustion engines	34.5	81.7	104.9	120.2	126.0	128.4	130.2	132.9
Machine shop products	31.1	81.0	112.8	124.3	125.9	126.8	128.0	129.7
Flat glass	52.2	88.7	101.7	107.5	105.9	106.5	107.5	110.5
Concrete products	37.7	92.0	107.5	113.5	116.6	117.2	120.1	124.6
Asphalt felts and coatings	25.8	99.6	102.6	97.1	98.2	96.2	96.9	95.3
Gypsum products	38.9	100.1	132.3	105.2	99.3	99.9	108.4	136.1
Glass containers	33.9	82.3	106.8	120.4	125.4	125.1	125.9	127.5
Motor vehicle parts	32.9	72.9	102.5	111.2	112.5	113.1	113.7	114.3
Photographic supplies	41.0	97.2	107.4	127.6	125.8	125.6	124.3	124.7
Crude materials for further processing	**35.2**	**95.3**	**95.8**	**108.9**	**101.2**	**100.4**	**102.4**	**101.8**
Crude foodstuffs and feedstuffs	45.2	104.6	94.8	113.1	105.5	105.1	108.3	106.5
Wheat	39.7	108.3	87.6	87.6	79.4	98.5	98.4	104.8
Corn	54.5	119.2	105.9	100.9	97.0	96.0	92.9	100.1
Cattle	46.9	104.9	91.2	122.5	115.8	115.4	116.7	105.8
Hogs	45.5	74.5	80.7	94.1	82.7	70.7	76.1	65.9
Live chickens (broilers and fryers)	48.5	103.4	110.5	119.5	111.9	114.6	124.9	127.7
Live turkeys	59.9	112.2	144.6	116.9	109.5	106.6	113.1	119.6
Fluid milk	40.8	96.0	93.7	100.8	89.5	96.1	93.8	95.7
Soybeans	45.3	117.0	94.2	100.8	95.1	97.3	104.8	106.0
Cane sugar, raw	39.9	148.3	104.6	119.2	113.7	112.1	113.2	115.2
Crude nonfood materials	**23.8**	**84.6**	**96.9**	**101.5**	**94.6**	**93.5**	**94.7**	**94.8**
Raw cotton	43.6	135.7	97.7	118.2	116.2	89.8	91.9	121.3
Leaf tobacco	40.3	82.1	101.2	95.8	101.1	101.0	99.6	100.2
Cattle hides	30.4	104.6	126.1	217.8	173.4	171.4	180.2	200.9
Coal	28.1	87.4	102.2	97.5	97.2	95.0	96.1	96.7
Natural gas	7.9	63.3	102.9	80.4	79.1	80.6	84.6	78.8
Crude petroleum	14.5	75.9	84.5	71.0	61.9	58.0	51.4	47.1
Logs, timber, etc.	(NA)	(NA)	96.0	142.8	144.1	164.8	211.9	219.1
Wastepaper	103.2	172.2	122.9	138.9	121.4	117.5	118.0	209.5
Iron ore	35.9	87.8	97.5	83.3	83.6	83.7	82.7	82.7
Iron and steel scrap	59.6	140.9	112.6	166.0	147.6	139.2	172.6	192.9
Nonferrous metal ores (Dec. 1983=100)	(NA)	(NA)	73.2	98.3	82.6	75.4	67.3	81.4
Copper base scrap	100.9	138.9	95.4	181.3	170.0	162.9	135.7	155.5
Aluminum base scrap	34.4	183.9	123.4	172.6	143.1	137.6	129.1	172.9
Construction sand, gravel, and crushed stone ..	40.9	85.3	110.7	125.4	128.6	130.6	133.9	137.9

NA Not available.

Source: U.S. Bureau of Labor Statistics, *Producer Price Indexes*, monthly and annual.

No. 769. Producer Price Indexes for the Net Output of Selected Industries: 1985 to 1994

[Indexes are based on selling prices reported by establishments of all sizes by probability sampling. Industries selected by value added. N.e.c.= not elsewhere classified. See text, section 27]

ITEM	SIC code [1]	Index base	1985	1990	1991	1992	1993	1994
Meat packing plants	2011	12/80	90.9	119.8	115.1	108.9	113.6	108.0
Sausages and other prepared meats	2013	12/82	95.7	112.7	113.0	108.7	110.4	108.9
Fluid milk	2026	12/82	102.6	121.4	119.0	121.6	121.3	123.6
Canned fruits and vegetables	2033	06/81	112.7	129.9	129.4	129.8	127.3	130.1
Frozen specialties	2038	12/82	110.8	127.3	130.4	131.0	130.6	132.1
Bread, cake, and related products	2051	06/80	127.1	159.4	165.0	173.3	179.1	182.6
Cookies and crackers	2052	06/83	112.0	141.9	148.5	151.2	152.2	154.5
Malt beverages	2082	06/82	110.0	115.2	121.3	123.6	122.2	119.9
Bottled and canned soft drinks	2086	06/81	112.5	127.2	130.3	131.0	132.5	134.0
Coffee	2095	06/81	111.5	120.0	116.5	110.0	109.8	134.7
Food preparations, n.e.c	2099	12/85	(NA)	114.3	117.3	117.2	118.6	119.8
Cigarettes	2111	12/82	110.7	197.6	225.0	250.5	235.0	198.9
Synthetic fiber and silk broadwoven fabric	2221	06/81	101.2	115.6	115.2	115.9	114.5	109.8
Women's, misses', and juniors' dresses	2335	12/80	108.0	125.6	129.0	129.7	130.1	127.2
Logging camps and logging contractors	2411	12/81	94.8	135.6	135.0	151.3	186.1	192.6
Sawmills and planing mills	2421	12/80	97.3	109.9	111.5	127.9	159.3	162.0
Millwork	2431	06/83	103.2	120.4	125.8	134.5	148.6	152.8
Wood household furniture, except upholstered	2511	12/79	133.3	158.9	163.3	166.9	173.4	180.3
Paper mill products except building paper	2621	06/81	109.5	134.0	131.0	126.6	126.6	128.4
Paperboard mills	2631	12/82	112.0	146.0	140.7	142.6	138.3	152.2
Corrugated and solid fiber boxes	2653	03/80	119.7	139.6	134.5	137.3	135.8	146.2
Newspaper publishing	2711	12/79	164.0	220.4	235.7	248.7	259.3	269.2
Periodical publishing	2721	12/79	157.9	205.7	217.8	227.9	233.1	239.1
Book publishing	2731	12/80	134.1	175.2	183.4	189.7	194.9	202.2
Commercial printing, lithographic	2752	06/82	111.0	127.9	129.7	130.8	135.0	136.5
Commercial printing, n.e.c	2759	06/82	112.9	136.1	140.8	143.6	145.6	147.4
Manifold business forms	2761	12/83	106.2	124.6	123.9	121.0	128.6	133.8
Industrial inorganic chemicals, n.e.c	2819	12/82	100.4	117.9	119.4	118.9	117.2	115.8
Plastic materials and resins	2821	12/80	113.6	139.5	137.9	131.8	132.4	137.4
Noncellulosic manmade fibers	2824	06/81	97.6	102.7	101.9	101.6	101.8	102.9
Pharmaceutical preparations	2834	06/81	141.3	203.5	217.3	231.2	240.8	244.6
Soap and other detergents	2841	06/83	104.2	115.2	116.0	118.5	120.0	119.6
Specialty cleaning, polish. and sanitation preps.	2842	06/83	103.9	118.6	121.5	123.1	124.7	126.3
Toilet preparations	2844	03/80	135.4	153.2	158.0	162.6	166.7	166.6
Paints and allied products	2851	06/83	104.9	125.0	130.3	132.3	133.6	135.9
Cyclic (coal tar) crudes and intermediates	2865	12/82	96.9	114.1	113.3	113.3	116.3	117.5
Industrial organic chemicals, n.e.c	2869	12/82	101.3	125.6	129.1	127.8	123.8	126.1
Chemicals and chemical preparations, n.e.c	2899	06/85	(NA)	112.5	115.7	117.1	120.0	123.7
Petroleum refining	2911	06/85	98.3	90.1	80.9	78.3	75.3	72.2
Tires and inner tubes	3011	06/81	96.8	103.0	105.0	106.0	106.3	106.4
Ready-mixed concrete	3273	06/81	108.6	114.3	116.9	117.4	121.0	125.7
Blast furnaces and steel mills	3312	06/82	104.9	110.8	108.4	105.8	107.5	112.3
Gray iron foundries	3321	12/80	115.6	123.4	125.6	127.0	128.2	131.7
Nonferrous wire drawing and insulating	3357	12/82	100.5	148.7	145.0	141.8	138.2	144.8
Metal cans	3411	06/81	110.4	116.6	118.1	117.0	113.1	110.8
Hardware, n.e.c.	3429	06/85	(NA)	110.6	113.3	114.9	116.9	118.6
Fabricated structural metal	3441	06/82	103.0	118.6	117.3	116.6	118.2	121.6
Fabricated plate work	3443	03/80	120.8	142.3	145.8	147.0	146.5	149.7
Sheet metal work	3444	12/82	107.2	129.4	128.2	126.6	127.1	130.0
Automotive stampings	3465	12/82	110.4	112.6	111.7	111.5	111.3	111.9
Metal stampings, n.e.c	3469	06/84	101.4	121.1	122.5	123.2	123.1	124.2
Fabricated metal products, n.e.c	3499	06/85	(NA)	117.6	119.0	119.2	120.4	122.9
Internal combustion engines, n.e.c	3519	12/82	103.4	115.7	120.7	123.3	125.5	128.0
Farm machinery and equipment	3523	12/82	105.3	116.8	120.5	124.1	126.6	129.6
Construction machinery	3531	12/80	119.5	137.6	142.0	146.9	151.3	153.7
Spec. tools, dies, jigs, fixtures and indus. molds	3544	06/81	113.5	124.5	129.3	131.2	134.3	137.7
Special industry machinery, n.e.c	3559	12/81	116.4	137.5	142.4	146.2	151.0	152.9
Refrigeration and heating equipment	3585	12/82	104.7	119.0	119.7	121.1	122.2	123.0
Machinery, except electrical, n.e.c	3599	06/84	102.0	113.9	114.4	114.3	116.1	118.8
Electric motors and generators	3621	06/83	108.2	127.5	129.7	131.5	133.5	134.3
Telephone and telegraph apparatus	3661	12/85	(NA)	112.0	112.8	112.3	115.0	116.9
Semiconductors and related devices	3674	06/81	106.6	105.0	102.8	98.4	98.2	97.2
Electronic components, n.e.c	3679	06/82	108.6	115.1	115.2	117.8	119.7	119.0
Motor vehicles and passenger car bodies	3711	06/82	107.2	119.9	125.3	129.1	133.2	137.9
Motor vehicle parts and accessories	3714	12/82	100.6	108.9	110.3	111.0	111.6	112.0
Aircraft	3721	12/85	(NA)	116.0	120.4	124.3	128.5	133.0
Aircraft engines and engine parts	3724	12/85	(NA)	112.6	117.9	123.6	125.7	129.0
Aircraft parts and auxiliary equipment, n.e.c	3728	06/85	(NA)	116.3	120.3	124.9	128.0	130.7
Ship building and repairing	3731	12/85	(NA)	114.0	116.2	118.3	123.7	127.2
Photographic equipment and supplies	3861	12/83	101.5	112.2	111.9	112.1	112.7	111.8

NA Not available. [1] Standard Industrial Classification code.
Source: U.S. Bureau of Labor Statistics, *Producer Price Indexes,* monthly.

No. 770. Fixed-Weighted Price Indexes for Personal Consumption Expenditures: 1960 to 1994
[1987=100]

YEAR	Personal consumption expenditures [1]	Motor vehicles and parts	Furniture [2]	Food	Clothing and shoes	Gasoline and oil	Housing	Household operation	Electricity and gas	Transportation	Medical care
1960	30.8	40.6	79.2	27.4	46.1	30.5	28.8	32.0	24.6	25.5	17.8
1961	31.1	40.6	78.2	27.7	46.4	30.2	29.2	32.2	24.7	26.5	18.3
1962	31.3	40.8	76.5	28.0	46.5	30.4	29.5	32.3	24.8	26.8	18.8
1963	31.6	40.8	75.5	28.4	46.9	30.3	29.9	32.5	24.7	26.4	19.2
1964	31.9	41.0	74.9	29.0	47.3	30.1	30.2	32.6	24.7	26.4	19.9
1965	32.2	40.5	73.1	29.5	47.7	31.2	30.5	32.6	24.6	27.1	20.5
1966	32.8	40.1	71.5	30.7	49.0	32.0	30.9	32.5	24.6	27.9	21.5
1967	33.7	40.6	71.8	31.2	51.1	33.0	31.5	33.0	24.8	28.4	22.9
1968	35.0	41.9	73.0	32.3	54.0	33.5	32.3	33.6	25.0	29.2	24.6
1969	36.3	42.6	74.1	33.7	57.1	34.6	33.4	34.5	25.5	30.8	26.1
1970	37.9	43.8	74.9	35.9	59.4	34.9	34.8	35.6	26.4	33.8	27.9
1971	39.5	45.9	75.6	36.9	61.3	35.2	36.4	38.0	28.2	37.3	29.3
1972	40.8	45.9	76.2	38.6	62.7	35.7	37.7	39.9	29.7	38.6	30.7
1973	42.7	46.2	76.9	42.6	64.9	39.1	39.4	41.6	31.3	39.4	32.1
1974	46.7	49.1	80.6	48.7	69.5	52.7	40.9	45.8	36.6	42.1	34.7
1975	50.5	53.9	85.9	52.7	72.2	56.2	43.6	49.8	41.9	44.5	38.3
1976	53.3	57.8	88.3	54.4	74.5	58.6	46.5	53.6	45.6	49.3	41.7
1977	56.7	61.2	89.9	57.9	77.6	62.0	50.4	57.0	50.0	54.7	45.7
1978	60.7	65.3	92.9	63.1	79.5	64.7	54.0	60.2	53.8	57.9	50.0
1979	65.8	70.3	97.2	69.4	81.7	86.8	58.3	63.6	59.1	62.2	54.4
1980	72.6	75.6	98.2	75.9	85.2	120.7	63.8	69.7	69.0	71.9	60.4
1981	78.9	81.3	101.7	82.1	88.2	134.4	70.4	78.1	79.0	79.2	67.6
1982	83.2	85.1	103.6	85.4	90.0	127.5	75.9	86.7	89.1	83.0	74.7
1983	86.7	87.9	102.6	87.6	91.8	123.4	80.5	92.1	95.8	86.9	80.1
1984	89.9	90.5	101.7	91.1	93.1	121.5	84.9	96.3	100.0	89.6	85.0
1985	93.3	93.0	100.8	93.4	95.8	122.5	90.0	98.9	102.2	91.0	90.4
1986	96.1	95.7	99.5	96.5	95.8	96.2	95.4	100.4	101.7	94.0	94.6
1987	100.0	100.0	100.0	100.0	100.0	100.0	100.0	100.0	100.0	100.0	100.0
1988	104.3	101.5	101.0	104.0	104.2	100.9	104.9	101.4	100.8	104.9	107.1
1989	109.5	104.6	101.6	109.8	106.7	110.2	109.6	103.8	103.9	109.6	115.7
1990	115.2	105.3	102.4	115.7	111.4	125.5	115.4	105.8	105.6	114.9	124.3
1991	120.3	109.2	103.0	120.1	115.4	123.9	120.2	109.8	108.9	122.3	131.2
1992	124.6	112.4	103.9	122.0	117.9	123.3	124.1	112.3	111.0	129.3	139.1
1993	128.1	116.1	104.3	124.4	119.2	122.1	127.9	115.4	114.4	134.3	147.3
1994	131.2	120.5	105.7	127.3	118.3	122.8	131.9	117.5	115.0	136.4	153.5
PERCENT CHANGE											
1960	1.3	−1.7	0.3	1.3	1.2	2.9	1.5	2.2	2.4	3.5	3.6
1961	0.8	-	−1.3	0.9	0.5	−0.9	1.3	0.7	0.5	3.7	2.7
1962	0.6	0.5	−2.2	1.2	0.2	0.6	1.2	0.4	-	1.3	2.8
1963	0.9	-	−1.3	1.4	1.0	−0.2	1.1	0.7	−0.1	−1.5	2.6
1964	1.1	0.4	−0.8	2.1	0.7	−0.6	1.0	0.3	−0.3	−0.1	3.2
1965	1.0	−1.2	−2.4	1.8	1.0	3.8	1.0	−0.2	−0.3	2.8	3.3
1966	1.8	−1.0	−2.2	3.9	2.6	2.3	1.4	−0.2	0.1	2.8	4.7
1967	2.6	1.3	0.4	1.7	4.2	3.3	1.9	1.5	0.7	2.0	6.6
1968	3.8	3.1	1.7	3.5	5.7	1.5	2.5	1.8	0.9	2.8	7.5
1969	3.8	1.9	1.5	4.6	5.7	3.3	3.4	2.6	2.0	5.3	5.9
1970	4.4	2.8	1.1	6.3	4.1	0.9	4.2	3.3	3.7	9.7	6.9
1971	4.4	4.8	0.9	2.9	3.2	0.8	4.6	6.6	6.8	10.3	5.1
1972	3.3	-	0.8	4.6	2.2	1.3	3.6	5.1	5.0	3.5	5.0
1973	4.6	0.6	0.9	10.4	3.6	9.5	4.4	4.2	5.6	2.1	4.4
1974	9.3	6.2	4.8	14.3	7.1	34.9	3.9	10.1	17.0	6.8	8.4
1975	8.1	9.9	6.6	8.2	3.8	6.7	6.6	8.6	14.5	5.7	10.1
1976	5.6	7.3	2.8	3.3	3.3	4.2	6.7	7.7	8.8	10.9	9.0
1977	6.4	5.7	1.8	6.5	4.1	5.8	8.5	6.3	9.6	10.9	9.6
1978	7.0	6.8	3.3	9.0	2.4	4.4	7.0	5.6	7.5	5.9	9.2
1979	8.5	7.6	4.6	10.0	2.9	34.2	8.0	5.7	9.9	7.3	9.0
1980	10.3	7.6	1.0	9.3	4.3	39.0	9.4	9.5	16.8	15.7	10.9
1981	8.7	7.5	3.6	8.2	3.5	11.3	10.3	12.1	14.4	10.2	11.8
1982	5.4	4.7	1.9	4.0	2.1	−5.1	7.8	11.1	12.8	4.7	10.6
1983	4.3	3.2	−1.0	2.6	2.0	−3.3	6.1	6.2	7.5	4.8	7.2
1984	3.7	3.0	−0.8	3.9	1.4	−1.5	5.4	4.6	4.5	3.1	6.1
1985	3.8	2.8	−1.0	2.6	3.0	0.8	6.1	2.7	2.2	1.5	6.4
1986	3.0	3.0	−1.2	3.3	-	−21.5	6.0	1.5	−0.5	3.3	4.6
1987	4.1	4.5	0.5	3.6	4.3	4.0	4.8	−0.4	−1.7	6.4	5.7
1988	4.3	1.5	1.0	4.0	4.2	0.9	4.9	1.4	0.8	4.9	7.1
1989	5.0	3.1	0.5	5.6	2.4	9.2	4.6	2.4	3.1	4.5	8.0
1990	5.3	0.7	0.8	5.4	4.4	13.9	5.3	1.9	1.6	4.8	7.4
1991	4.4	3.7	0.6	3.8	3.6	−1.3	4.2	3.8	3.1	6.4	5.6
1992	3.6	2.9	0.9	1.6	2.2	−0.5	3.2	2.3	1.9	5.7	6.0
1993	2.8	3.3	0.4	2.0	1.1	−1.0	3.1	2.8	3.1	3.9	5.9
1994	2.4	3.8	1.3	2.3	−0.8	0.6	3.1	1.8	0.5	5.9	4.2

- Represents or rounds to zero.   [1] Includes items not shown separately.   [2] Includes household equipment.
Source: U.S. Bureau of Economic Analysis, *The National Income and Product Accounts of the United States: Volume 2, 1959-88;* and *Survey of Current Business,* August 1993, July 1994, and March 1995; and unpublished data.

No. 771. Fixed-Weighted Price Indexes: 1980 to 1994

[1987=100]

ITEM	1980	1985	1986	1988	1989	1990	1991	1992	1993	1994
Gross domestic product	(NA)	94.3	97.0	104.0	108.6	113.6	118.1	121.9	125.5	128.9
Personal consumption expenditures. . .	72.6	93.3	96.1	104.3	109.5	115.2	120.3	124.6	128.1	131.2
Durable goods	84.7	96.0	97.1	102.0	104.5	106.3	109.1	111.6	113.9	117.0
Nondurable goods.	79.6	96.2	96.1	103.8	109.5	116.2	120.5	123.0	125.0	126.6
Services	65.3	90.9	95.8	105.1	110.7	116.8	123.0	128.7	133.5	137.6
Gross private domestic investment:										
Fixed investment	(NA)	95.7	97.9	103.3	106.3	109.1	110.8	112.0	114.4	117.5
Nonresidential.	(NA)	97.3	98.8	102.8	105.6	108.4	110.2	111.2	113.0	115.5
Structures	78.5	96.9	98.5	104.6	109.0	112.4	113.9	114.1	117.3	121.2
Producers' durable equipment .	(NA)	97.5	99.0	101.9	103.9	106.2	108.3	109.7	110.7	112.5
Residential.	75.3	92.1	95.8	104.3	107.8	110.7	111.9	113.6	117.4	122.0
Exports of goods and services	(NA)	98.2	97.3	105.7	108.2	110.0	112.6	113.9	115.3	118.1
Imports of goods and services	(NA)	94.6	93.8	105.4	108.5	112.4	113.8	115.4	115.2	117.2
Government purchases	73.3	95.4	97.6	103.7	107.9	112.6	116.8	120.8	124.5	128.6
Federal	75.2	97.9	99.0	102.8	107.0	111.8	116.5	121.5	126.1	131.1
National defense	76.3	98.8	99.5	103.1	107.1	112.1	116.5	122.0	126.6	131.5
Nondefense	71.9	94.9	97.5	102.0	106.7	110.8	116.6	119.8	124.3	130.1
State and local	71.9	93.5	96.5	104.3	108.6	113.2	117.0	120.3	123.4	126.6

NA Not available.

Source: U.S. Bureau of Economic Analysis, *The National Income and Product Accounts of the United States: Volume 2 1959-1988,* and *Survey of Current Business,* July 1994 and March 1995.

No. 772. Fixed-Weighted Price Indexes—Annual Percent Change: 1985 to 1994

[1987=100]

ITEM	1985-86	1986-87	1987-88	1988-89	1989-90	1990-91	1991-92	1992-93	1993-94
Gross domestic product	2.8	3.1	4.0	4.5	4.6	4.0	3.2	3.0	2.7
Personal consumption expend. . . .	3.0	4.1	4.3	5.0	5.3	4.4	3.5	2.8	2.5
Durable goods	1.2	3.0	2.0	2.4	1.7	2.6	2.3	2.1	2.7
Nondurable goods.	-	4.0	3.8	5.5	6.2	3.7	2.1	1.6	1.3
Services	5.4	4.4	5.1	5.3	5.6	5.2	4.7	3.7	3.1
Gross private domestic invest.:									
Fixed investment	2.3	2.2	3.3	3.0	2.6	1.5	1.1	2.1	2.8
Nonresidential.	1.6	1.2	2.8	2.7	2.6	1.7	0.9	1.6	2.2
Structures	1.6	1.5	4.6	4.2	3.1	1.3	0.3	2.8	3.3
Producers' durable equip. .	1.6	1.0	1.9	2.0	2.3	2.0	1.3	0.9	1.6
Residential.	4.0	4.4	4.3	3.4	2.7	1.1	1.5	3.3	4.0
Exports of goods and services . . .	−0.9	2.8	5.7	2.4	1.7	2.3	1.2	1.2	2.5
Imports of goods and services . . .	−0.8	6.6	5.4	3.0	3.5	1.3	1.5	−0.2	1.8
Government purchases	2.2	2.5	3.7	4.1	4.3	3.7	3.5	3.1	3.3
Federal	1.2	1.0	2.8	4.1	4.5	4.2	4.3	3.7	4.0
National defense	0.7	0.5	3.1	3.9	4.7	3.9	4.7	3.7	3.8
Nondefense	2.7	2.6	2.0	4.6	3.8	5.2	2.8	3.7	4.6
State and local	3.1	3.7	4.3	4.1	4.2	3.4	2.8	2.5	2.7

- Represents zero.

Source: U.S. Bureau of Economic Analysis, *The National Income and Product Accounts of the United States: Volume 2, 1959-1988;* and *Survey of Current Business,* September 1993, July 1994, and March 1995.

No. 773. Commodity Research Bureau Futures Price Index: 1975 to 1993

[1967=100. Index computed daily. Represents unweighted geometric average of commodity futures prices (through 9 months forward) of 21 major commodity futures markets. Represents end of year index]

ITEM	1975	1980	1983	1984	1985	1986	1987	1988	1989	1990	1991	1992	1993
All commodities	191.0	308.5	277.6	244.2	229.2	209.1	232.5	251.8	229.9	222.6	208.0	205.9	212.4
Imported	259.4	426.0	326.0	291.7	398.2	321.2	356.1	365.2	271.7	276.0	264.4	232.4	246.9
Industrial	154.8	324.6	249.0	217.0	211.7	210.4	252.5	248.2	249.6	245.5	217.2	224.7	235.0
Grains	195.6	312.1	249.6	224.9	198.5	164.6	186.1	261.9	205.7	171.2	196.1	196.9	193.8
Oilseeds	181.6	314.6	316.6	273.5	245.4	189.8	223.6	309.6	254.2	223.6	195.4	218.8	239.8
Livestock and meats	180.8	217.4	229.7	240.8	206.9	200.2	189.9	199.1	206.5	226.2	174.0	179.8	201.4
Metals (precious) [1]	141.0	531.4	328.5	243.3	256.6	296.6	346.4	318.7	296.9	257.8	226.0	228.5	242.2

[1] Prior to 1980, index for metals only.

Source: Commodity Research Bureau (CRB), New York City, NY, *CRB Commodity Index Report,* weekly (copyright).

No. 774. Indexes of Spot Primary Market Prices: 1980 to 1993

[1967=100. Computed weekly for 1980; daily thereafter. Represents unweighted geometric average of price quotations of 23 commodities; much more sensitive to changes in market conditions than is a monthly producer price index]

ITEMS AND NUMBER OF COMMODITIES	1980 (6-24)	1983 (5-23)	1984 (5-22)	1985 (5-21)	1986 (5-20)	1987 (5-26)	1988 (5-27)	1989 (5-26)	1990 (5-25)	1991 (5-28)	1992 (5-26)	1993 (5-23)
All commodities (23)	265.1	249.8	293.9	251.4	218.0	250.0	270.3	281.3	279.2	235.3	242.3	237.7
Foodstuffs (10)	260.9	246.1	299.9	248.1	205.5	215.2	230.1	222.5	231.5	197.7	201.3	208.3
Raw industrials (13)	268.0	252.3	289.7	253.6	226.9	277.3	302.0	329.0	317.0	265.2	275.5	260.4
Livestock and products (5)	250.5	278.1	364.5	284.5	231.2	303.3	316.1	285.2	306.9	286.6	276.4	291.3
Metals (5)	257.9	225.9	253.4	220.2	191.2	239.5	276.7	347.1	313.9	348.8	262.7	236.2
Textiles and fibers (4)	234.7	208.0	248.1	220.8	216.9	247.1	247.3	253.5	259.4	201.8	218.6	205.3
Fats and oils (4)	229.5	225.9	363.5	273.1	168.5	201.2	230.4	208.1	193.3	185.0	180.7	190.1

Source: Commodity Research Bureau, a Knight-Ridder Business Information Service, New York, NY, *CRB Commodity Index Report,* weekly (copyright).

No. 775. Average Prices of Selected Fuels and Electricity: 1980 to 1993

[In dollars per unit, except electricity, in cents per kWh. Represents price to end-users, except as noted]

ITEM	Unit [1]	1980	1984	1985	1986	1987	1988	1989	1990	1991	1992	1993
Crude oil, composite [2]	Barrel	28.07	28.63	26.75	14.55	17.90	14.67	17.97	22.22	19.06	18.43	16.41
Motor gasoline: [3]												
Unleaded regular	Gallon	1.25	1.21	1.20	0.93	0.95	0.95	1.02	1.16	1.14	1.13	1.11
Unleaded premium	Gallon	(NA)	1.37	1.34	1.09	1.09	1.11	1.20	1.35	1.32	1.32	1.30
No. 2 heating oil	Gallon	0.79	0.92	0.85	0.56	0.58	0.54	0.59	0.73	0.67	0.63	0.60
No. 2 diesel fuel	Gallon	0.82	0.82	0.79	0.48	0.55	0.50	0.59	0.73	0.65	0.62	0.60
Residual fuel oil	Gallon	0.61	0.69	0.61	0.34	0.42	0.33	0.33	0.44	0.34	0.34	0.34
Natural gas, residential	1,000 cu/ft	3.68	6.12	6.12	5.83	5.54	5.47	5.64	5.80	5.82	5.89	6.16
Electricity, residential	kWh	5.4	7.5	7.8	7.4	7.4	7.5	7.6	7.8	8.1	8.2	8.34

NA Not available. [1] See headnote. [2] Refiner acquisition cost. [3] Average, all service.

Source: U.S. Energy Information Administration, *Monthly Energy Review.*

No. 776. Weekly Food Cost: 1990 and 1994

[In dollars. Assumes that food for all meals and snacks is purchased at the store and prepared at home. See source for details on estimation procedures]

FAMILY TYPE	DECEMBER 1990				JANUARY 1994			
	Thrifty plan	Low-cost plan	Moderate-cost plan	Liberal plan	Thrifty plan	Low-cost plan	Moderate-cost plan	Liberal plan
FAMILIES								
Family of two:								
20-50 years	48.10	60.60	74.70	92.70	51.90	65.80	81.00	100.90
51 years and over	45.60	58.30	71.80	85.80	49.10	63.20	77.90	93.30
Family of four:								
Couple, 20-50 years and children—								
1-2 and 3-5 years	70.10	87.30	106.60	131.00	75.60	94.80	115.70	142.40
6-8 and 9-11 years	80.10	102.60	128.30	154.40	86.60	111.30	139.00	167.50
INDIVIDUALS [1]								
Child:								
1-2 years	12.70	15.40	18.00	21.80	13.70	16.80	19.60	23.80
3-5 years	13.70	16.80	20.70	24.90	14.70	18.20	22.50	26.90
6-8 years	16.60	22.20	27.90	32.50	18.00	24.10	30.20	35.10
9-11 years	19.80	25.30	32.50	37.60	21.40	27.40	35.20	40.70
Male:								
12-14 years	20.60	28.60	35.70	42.00	22.30	31.10	38.70	45.40
15-19 years	21.40	29.60	36.80	42.60	23.10	32.00	39.90	46.20
20-50 years	22.90	29.30	36.60	44.30	24.80	31.90	39.60	48.10
51 years and over	20.90	27.90	34.30	41.10	22.40	30.30	37.20	44.70
Female:								
12-19 years	20.80	24.80	30.10	36.30	22.40	26.90	32.60	39.40
20-54 years	20.80	25.80	31.30	40.00	22.40	27.90	34.00	43.60
55 years and over	20.60	25.10	31.00	36.90	22.20	27.20	33.60	40.10

[1] The costs given are for individuals in four-person families. For individuals in other size families, the following adjustments are suggested: one-person, add 20 percent; two-person, add 10 percent; three-person, add 5 percent; five- or six-person, subtract 5 percent; seven- (or more) person, subtract 10 percent.

Source: U.S. Dept. of Agriculture, *Agricultural Research Service,* monthly.

No. 777. Food—Retail Prices of Selected Items: 1988 to 1994

[In dollars per pound, except as indicated. As of **December**]

FOOD	1988	1989	1990	1991	1992	1993	1994
Cereals and bakery products:							
Flour, white, all purpose	0.22	0.24	0.24	0.22	0.23	0.22	0.23
Rice, white, lg. grain, raw	0.48	0.50	0.49	0.51	0.53	0.50	0.53
Spaghetti and macaroni	0.85	0.87	0.85	0.86	0.86	0.84	0.87
Bread, white, pan	0.66	0.69	0.70	0.72	0.74	0.76	0.75
Meats, poultry, fish and eggs:							
Ground chuck, 100% beef	1.79	1.88	2.02	1.93	1.91	1.91	1.84
Rib roast, USDA Choice	4.03	4.21	4.54	4.59	4.69	4.73	4.88
Round steak, USDA Choice	3.01	3.17	3.42	3.38	3.34	3.32	3.24
Sirloin steak, bone-in	3.23	3.46	3.65	3.78	3.75	3.69	(NA)
T-bone steak	4.97	5.04	5.45	5.21	5.39	5.77	5.86
Pork:							
Bacon, sliced	1.79	1.96	2.28	1.99	1.86	2.02	1.89
Chops, center cut, bone-in	2.65	2.85	3.32	3.12	3.15	3.24	3.03
Shoulder picnic, bone-in, smoked	1.10	1.17	1.41	1.30	1.18	1.19	1.13
Sausage	1.92	2.12	2.42	2.24	2.14	1.99	1.85
Poultry:							
Chicken, fresh, whole	0.89	0.88	0.86	0.86	0.88	0.91	0.90
Chicken breast, bone-in	2.06	2.01	2.00	2.02	2.08	2.17	1.91
Chicken legs, bone-in	1.17	1.14	1.17	1.14	1.14	1.13	1.12
Turkey, frozen, whole	0.97	0.95	0.96	0.91	0.93	0.95	0.98
Eggs, Grade A, large, (dozen)	0.83	1.14	1.00	1.01	0.93	0.87	0.87
Dairy products:							
Milk, fresh, whole, fortified (1/2 gal.)	1.21	1.37	1.39	1.40	1.39	1.43	1.44
Butter, salted, grade AA, stick	2.15	2.11	1.92	1.94	1.64	1.61	1.54
Ice cream, prepack., bulk,reg.(1/2 gal.)	2.54	2.67	2.54	2.63	2.49	2.59	2.62
Fruits and vegetables:							
Fresh fruits and vegetables:							
Apples, red Delicious	0.71	0.57	0.77	0.86	0.76	0.78	0.72
Bananas	0.41	0.42	0.43	0.42	0.40	0.41	0.46
Oranges, navel	0.56	0.53	0.56	0.65	0.52	0.56	0.55
Grapefruit	0.45	0.47	0.56	0.53	0.52	0.50	0.47
Lemons	0.91	0.96	0.97	1.21	0.90	1.05	1.04
Pears, Anjou	0.64	0.76	0.79	0.88	0.80	0.89	(NA)
Potatoes, white	0.30	0.31	0.32	0.28	0.31	0.36	0.34
Lettuce, iceberg	0.77	0.52	0.58	0.69	0.66	0.53	0.91
Tomatoes, field grown	0.81	0.90	0.86	0.79	1.23	1.31	1.43
Cabbage	0.33	0.34	0.39	0.46	0.38	0.37	0.45
Carrots, short trimmed and topped	0.39	0.35	0.44	0.51	0.44	0.41	0.48
Celery	0.44	0.46	0.49	0.45	0.48	0.49	0.52
Cucumbers	0.49	0.64	0.56	0.55	0.51	0.93	0.69
Processed fruits and vegetables:							
Orange juice, frozen concentrate,							
12 oz. can, per 16 oz	1.82	1.80	2.02	1.74	1.70	1.67	1.55
Potatoes, frozen, french fried	0.70	0.80	0.85	0.92	0.86	0.87	0.84

No. 778. Average Price of Energy in Selected Metropolitan Areas: 1994

[**In dollars per unit shown.** As of **January**. One therm contains approximately 100 cubic feet of natural gas.
See Appendix II]

CITY/MSA	Utility (piped) gas (100 therms)	Electricity (500 kWh)	Fuel oil No. 2 (gallon)	GASOLINE		
				All types [1]	Unleaded regular	Unleaded premium
U.S. city average	66.47	48.2	0.92	1.11	1.04	1.24
Baltimore, MD MSA	64.44	48.62	1.01	1.16	1.07	1.26
Boston-Lawrence-Salem, MA-NH CMSA	94.34	57.26	0.92	1.14	1.05	1.30
Chicago-Gary-Lake County, IL-IN-WI CMSA	68.07	45.07	0.99	1.11	1.05	1.24
Cleveland-Akron-Lorain, OH CMSA	55.06	54.24	(NA)	1.03	1.00	1.17
Dallas-Fort Worth, TX CMSA	57.21	50.81	(NA)	1.07	1.00	1.17
Detroit-Ann Arbor, MI CMSA	52.91	49.27	0.93	0.98	0.94	1.12
Houston-Galveston-Brazoria, TX CMSA	52.19	43.77	(NA)	1.04	0.96	1.17
Los Angeles-Anaheim-Riverside, CA CMSA	67.12	61.5	(NA)	1.20	1.13	1.34
Miami-Fort Lauderdale, FL CMSA	90.39	43.83	(NA)	1.22	1.15	1.35
New York-N. NJ-Long Island, NY-NJ-CT CMSA	96.89	72.47	1.01	1.21	1.11	1.35
Philadelphia-Wilmington-Trenton, PA-NJ-DE-MD CMSA . .	74.92	59.1	0.91	1.16	1.03	1.27
Pittsburgh-Beaver Valley, PA CMSA	65.15	54.82	(NA)	1.09	1.01	1.24
St. Louis-East St. Louis, MO-IL CMSA	60.99	41.49	(NA)	0.95	0.88	1.09
San Francisco-Oakland-San Jose, CA CMSA	62.05	62.98	(NA)	1.21	1.14	1.37
Washington, DC-MD-VA MSA	77.73	42.52	1.05	1.18	1.09	1.29

NA Not available.   [1] Includes types of gasoline not shown separately.

Source of tables 777 and 778: U.S. Bureau of Labor Statistics, *CPI Detailed Report,* January issues.

No. 779 Import Price Indexes—Selected Commodities: 1985 to 1994

[1990=100. Indexes are weighted by the 1990 Tariff Schedule of the United States Annotated, a scheme for describing and reporting product composition and value of U.S. imports. Import prices are based on U.S. dollar prices paid by importer. F.o.b. = Free on board; c.i.f. = Cost, insurance, and freight; n.e.s.=Not elsewhere specified]

COMMODITY	1985	1988	1989	1990 [1]	1991	1992	1993	1994
All commodities	**80.2**	**93.9**	**96.8**	**96.1**	**98.8**	**100.3**	**100.5**	**101.9**
Food and live animals	87.2	100.5	98.2	98.6	102.4	97.9	101.1	109.0
Meat	68.8	78.4	80.3	100.0	105.6	94.9	99.3	91.0
Meat of bovine animals	77.1	91.2	95.2	98.5	100.8	91.1	100.8	86.5
Fish	75.5	99.1	94.1	96.7	107.6	107.9	107.9	121.2
Crustaceans; fresh, chilled, frozen, salted or dried	85.0	105.2	98.4	97.4	107.3	105.4	106.4	129.8
Cereals and cereal preparations	63.2	91.0	91.2	98.7	96.4	99.3	102.9	102.0
Sugar [2]	87.4	94.0	95.5	99.7	96.7	95.3	95.1	98.2
Coffee, tea and cocoa	145.1	140.0	128.0	99.4	93.2	77.3	81.2	137.1
Beverages and tobacco	77.1	90.3	91.1	99.2	110.8	113.4	112.6	113.2
Beverages	75.9	92.0	92.6	99.3	110.3	112.5	112.9	112.8
Crude materials	77.8	106.6	111.6	101.9	95.9	95.8	95.3	106.7
Crude rubber	98.3	147.1	100.6	101.2	98.4	100.8	102.9	106.3
Cork and wood	93.4	99.1	100.0	102.4	107.7	116.8	130.3	159.9
Pulp and waste paper	56.9	90.1	106.6	102.8	79.2	74.4	63.7	70.1
Crude fertilizers and minerals	102.8	103.1	106.9	99.6	100.9	89.0	82.5	82.3
Metalliferous ores and metal scrap	59.9	105.1	133.1	100.8	93.6	91.1	88.3	89.6
Crude animal and vegetable materials, n.e.s.	83.9	131.2	97.6	103.9	103.7	107.2	106.1	131.2
Mineral fuels and related products	114.5	72.8	84.2	73.1	83.2	86.7	79.9	76.3
Crude petroleum and petroleum products	112.1	71.7	83.8	72.0	82.8	86.7	79.2	75.7
Crude petroleum	123.8	70.9	82.7	66.8	81.4	87.8	76.6	73.6
Natural gas	(NA)	(NA)	88.5	89.4	88.1	83.7	90.3	83.7
Animal and vegetable oils, fats and waxes	115.5	116.8	123.3	100.6	102.2	134.9	117.8	135.1
Chemicals and related products	83.7	97.0	100.4	98.5	100.7	101.7	102.8	102.6
Intermediate manufactured products	73.1	97.4	100.3	99.5	99.2	99.4	99.3	101.0
Rubber manufactures	85.9	93.0	96.9	99.8	100.6	102.0	103.8	102.4
Cork and wood manufactures	69.0	96.1	97.2	100.4	98.6	108.1	120.6	126.5
Paper and paperboard products	82.7	98.0	100.0	100.4	101.0	94.1	96.7	95.6
Textiles	77.6	94.6	95.8	98.7	103.0	106.0	108.1	108.9
Nonmetallic mineral manufactures	60.1	89.0	93.4	99.8	103.3	105.5	108.0	108.5
Iron and steel	79.3	100.7	105.8	99.7	99.3	97.6	98.2	99.1
Nonferrous metals	69.0	109.9	109.2	98.7	89.0	88.6	76.6	85.2
Silver, platinum and other platinum group metals	71.2	102.7	89.6	93.6	90.2	75.5	69.1	74.8
Copper	57.6	85.3	98.5	98.6	88.7	88.5	75.9	89.3
Nickel	62.4	154.9	152.2	95.5	97.6	87.5	72.9	75.3
Aluminum	(NA)	131.6	117.3	98.7	85.8	86.4	79.1	89.6
Zinc	56.7	76.2	108.9	113.4	77.2	89.3	67.7	65.8
Manufactures of metals, n.e.s.	72.9	93.2	97.4	98.9	101.2	103.0	104.5	104.6
Machinery and transport equipment	75.1	96.6	98.1	98.7	101.6	103.5	105.0	106.8
Machinery specialized for particular industries	59.1	91.8	89.3	97.3	101.7	105.4	107.5	109.7
Metalworking machinery	64.8	93.9	92.0	98.7	100.6	103.9	107.7	110.1
General industrial machinery, parts, n.e.s.	62.6	91.8	91.3	97.7	101.5	104.9	107.0	109.0
Computer equipment and office machines	85.0	103.1	103.0	99.8	97.3	95.7	91.9	87.1
Computer equipment	112.8	107.6	105.0	100.3	96.9	92.4	85.5	76.5
Telecommunications [3]	90.1	102.3	104.1	100.2	97.8	97.1	98.0	97.4
Electrical machinery and equipment	77.4	95.9	100.1	98.7	100.6	102.1	103.9	106.1
Electronic valves, diodes, transistors & integr. cir.	98.7	99.9	110.0	98.2	99.5	99.4	104.3	108.0
Road vehicles	75.1	97.0	98.5	98.4	103.5	105.6	108.4	112.7
Miscellaneous manufactured articles	74.3	94.2	94.9	98.9	100.6	103.7	105.2	105.4
Plumbing, heating & lighting fixtures	68.9	88.7	91.9	98.4	100.1	101.5	102.0	99.6
Furniture and parts	74.0	93.0	94.0	99.1	101.2	103.4	104.1	103.9
Articles of apparel and clothing	81.7	94.1	98.1	100.5	98.8	101.8	102.1	102.2
Footwear	70.6	93.3	92.0	99.0	100.9	102.6	101.2	100.2
Prof., scientific & contrlng instr & appratus, n.e.s.	64.4	95.5	91.4	97.5	102.1	104.4	110.5	113.0
Photographic apparatus [4]	73.5	96.1	95.1	98.0	100.1	102.9	106.9	109.1
Miscellaneous manufactured articles, n.e.s.	71.1	94.3	93.8	97.9	101.8	106.0	108.3	108.5

NA Not available. [1] June 1990 may not equal 100 because indexes were reweighted to an "average" trade value in 1990. [2] Includes sugar preparations and honey. [3] Includes sound recording and reproducing equipment. [4] Includes photographic supplies, optical goods, watches, and clocks.

Source: U.S. Bureau of Labor Statistics, *News*, quarterly.

No. 780. Export Price Indexes—Selected Commodities: 1985 to 1994

[1990=100. Indexes are weighted by 1980 export values according to the Schedule B classification system of the U.S. Bureau of the Census. Prices used in these indexes were collected from a sample of U.S. manufacturers of exports and are factory transaction prices, except as noted. F.a.s. = free alongside ship. N.e.s. = not elsewhere specified. F.o.b. = free on board]

COMMODITY	1985	1988	1989	1990 [1]	1991	1992	1993	1994
All commodities	**88.4**	**96.6**	**99.7**	**99.5**	**100.6**	**101.0**	**101.4**	**103.2**
Food and live animals	96.3	99.1	110.6	104.3	100.7	102.8	97.8	103.9
Meat	78.6	104.3	102.0	98.5	101.9	106.1	111.6	107.3
Fish	78.5	112.5	123.2	98.4	94.7	98.1	96.5	98.0
Cereals and cereal preparations	109.3	93.0	113.5	108.6	96.8	104.8	90.9	101.8
Wheat	115.5	101.6	134.4	112.1	91.2	108.4	94.1	91.2
Rice	110.9	115.5	104.5	101.7	112.1	106.7	92.5	113.6
Maize	107.8	86.8	105.2	108.6	97.8	102.2	87.7	105.6
Other cereals	105.0	86.5	103.6	104.7	97.6	104.6	88.7	112.0
Fruits and vegetables	88.6	92.4	100.6	102.0	121.5	100.0	103.0	109.6
Feeding stuff for animals	74.9	130.3	118.8	97.6	100.0	102.2	100.7	106.2
Miscellaneous food products	90.6	93.2	97.9	99.9	100.5	100.2	100.3	97.8
Beverages and tobacco	79.9	88.3	93.8	99.3	105.7	109.8	113.1	113.5
Tobacco and tobacco manufactures	79.6	88.1	93.8	99.4	105.7	109.6	112.8	113.1
Crude materials	74.4	102.4	104.7	100.5	95.4	93.4	99.6	108.1
Raw hides and skins	63.3	108.3	97.4	105.2	81.5	80.8	79.2	94.4
Oil seeds and oleaginous fruits	92.8	125.8	114.3	97.1	99.4	98.4	97.9	112.9
Crude rubber, f.a.s.	85.6	91.0	98.3	99.1	103.2	101.0	99.2	96.1
Cork and wood	56.2	85.2	97.2	102.1	97.9	110.1	161.4	149.4
Pulp and waste paper	57.6	103.2	111.2	100.2	86.6	82.6	70.2	94.6
Textile fibers	85.3	90.6	95.3	102.6	107.0	86.0	83.5	105.0
Cotton textile fibers	87.4	92.0	93.8	103.7	107.9	79.7	77.5	101.3
Crude fertilizers and minerals	100.8	94.6	99.6	100.1	101.1	99.7	95.0	95.6
Metalliferous ores and metal scrap	70.7	102.3	110.1	99.9	89.1	85.1	83.9	91.2
Ferrous waste and scrap	73.0	107.6	112.4	99.8	93.4	82.2	99.0	95.6
Nonferrous base metal waste and scrap	56.5	106.1	112.5	99.4	84.2	86.0	72.2	92.7
Mineral fuels and related materials	104.6	84.4	88.4	91.1	89.9	86.5	88.0	87.4
Coal, coke and briquettes	103.1	94.5	96.8	100.1	98.6	96.9	93.9	93.9
Crude petroleum and petroleum products	(NA)	75.1	81.4	83.9	80.1	77.2	80.7	80.3
Animal and vegetable oils, fats and waxes	123.5	105.9	95.1	103.0	93.8	94.9	98.4	110.0
Chemicals and related products	84.5	102.6	102.9	97.4	99.7	97.4	96.1	99.0
Organic chemicals	80.5	115.7	116.0	94.9	94.6	91.5	90.5	92.7
Hydrocarbons, n.e.s. and derivatives, f.a.s.	73.9	123.2	114.8	93.3	76.2	77.8	80.1	92.4
Alcohols, phenols, phenol-alcohols, & deriv., f.a.s.	78.6	113.2	147.1	96.3	101.8	93.1	93.2	89.3
Chemical materials and products, n.e.s.	86.7	88.3	95.0	98.7	103.4	102.9	105.7	108.7
Intermediate manufactured products	81.3	95.5	99.9	99.8	100.1	100.6	100.7	104.4
Rubber manufactures	86.6	94.0	97.6	98.9	105.0	105.6	108.5	109.2
Paper and paperboard products	76.7	98.6	102.1	99.5	99.5	98.4	93.9	96.2
Textiles	84.3	90.8	97.1	99.6	104.1	105.6	106.8	106.7
Nonmetallic mineral manufactures	(NA)	89.6	96.1	99.6	101.2	103.5	105.4	107.3
Nonferrous metals	77.1	108.4	110.2	100.2	88.1	87.9	81.3	92.5
Manufactures of metals, n.e.s.	84.9	91.7	97.1	99.8	102.7	103.6	105.1	107.3
Machinery and transport equipment [2]	90.7	94.3	97.2	99.8	102.9	104.4	104.5	104.1
Power generating machinery [3]	85.2	92.3	96.0	99.8	104.7	109.6	110.7	112.8
Rotating electric plant and parts thereof, n.e.s.	76.8	89.7	95.0	99.7	101.9	104.7	106.1	107.4
Machinery specialized for particular industries	87.7	90.8	95.4	99.3	103.3	105.5	108.0	109.8
Agricultural machinery and parts [4]	89.4	91.6	94.2	100.0	102.1	104.9	107.3	109.4
Civil engineering and contractors, plant and equip.	90.7	89.0	95.2	98.8	103.9	102.0	105.5	109.6
Metalworking machinery	82.1	91.2	96.5	99.6	106.5	109.1	111.0	110.7
General industrial machines, parts, n.e.s.	84.4	91.2	95.6	99.7	103.7	106.1	108.3	110.1
Computer equipment and office machines	105.9	101.5	100.6	100.3	98.4	94.7	87.7	81.0
Computer equipment	113.0	105.1	101.7	100.3	97.8	94.0	83.5	75.2
Telecommunications [5]	89.6	94.1	96.8	100.1	106.4	108.3	109.4	107.3
Electrical machinery and equipment	93.8	96.1	99.0	99.9	100.6	103.6	103.5	103.2
Electronic valves, diodes, transistors & integr. cir.	106.5	103.5	100.1	100.6	98.5	103.7	102.3	100.0
Road vehicles	89.8	94.1	96.8	99.6	102.4	104.0	105.2	106.3
Other transport equipment	81.7	90.2	94.4	99.8	112.4	113.0	117.4	120.1
Miscellaneous manufactured articles	85.4	92.0	96.1	99.1	104.2	106.2	106.9	107.1

NA Not available.   [1] June 1990 may not equal 100 because indexes were reweighted to an "average" trade value in 1990.   [2] Excludes military and commercial aircraft.   [3] Includes equipment.   [4] Excludes tractors.   [5] Includes sound recording and reproducing equipment.

Source: U.S. Bureau of Labor Statistics, *News,* quarterly.

No. 781. Refiner/Reseller Sales Price of Gasoline, by State: 1991 to 1993

[In cents per gallon. As of **March**. Represents all refinery and gas plant operators' sales through company-operated retail outlets. Gasoline prices exclude excise taxes]

STATE	Gasoline excise taxes 1993 [1]	AVERAGE, ALL GRADES			LEADED REGULAR			UNLEADED REGULAR			PREMIUM		
		1991	1992	1993	1991	1992	1993	1991	1992	1993	1991	1992	1993
United States.	18	76.5	72.2	75.5	71.6	70.7	75.2	73.6	68.3	71.6	87.3	84.3	87.8
Northeast:													
New England:													
Maine.	19	90.0	80.8	80.9	(NA)	(2)	(2)	86.9	77.0	76.4	102.2	93.2	93.6
New Hampshire . . .	18	85.2	79.6	80.3	(D)	(2)	(2)	82.0	75.3	75.2	95.7	92.3	94.6
Vermont	15	91.6	83.6	82.7	(D)	(2)	(2)	88.2	79.8	78.1	102.8	93.7	94.8
Massachusetts. . . .	21	83.1	76.5	79.0	86.4	(D)	(2)	78.8	71.0	73.3	94.4	88.4	92.6
Rhode Island	28	82.9	74.4	77.6	(NA)	(2)	(2)	78.9	69.4	72.2	91.7	83.6	87.3
Connecticut	29	83.0	78.3	81.6	(D)	(2)	(2)	78.5	72.7	75.3	93.7	89.8	96.2
Middle Atlantic:													
New York	8	87.0	74.8	75.8	87.1	74.9	(D)	83.2	70.1	70.5	99.5	88.6	91.1
New Jersey	11	83.4	77.8	85.4	(NA)	(2)	(2)	77.9	70.5	77.1	94.2	89.3	98.9
Pennsylvania	12	82.4	72.5	72.3	(D)	(2)	(2)	78.5	67.7	67.2	94.2	85.2	84.9
Midwest:													
East North Central:													
Ohio	22	73.4	73.3	71.4	78.4	74.0	71.0	70.7	70.0	68.1	84.6	85.2	80.2
Indiana	15	77.3	68.9	71.6	84.8	80.3	79.3	75.0	66.1	69.2	87.6	78.1	76.7
Illinois.	19	76.1	69.6	74.1	88.2	72.7	80.9	73.4	66.3	71.0	86.2	81.3	83.6
Michigan.	15	74.0	67.2	70.8	79.2	76.4	81.6	71.7	64.4	68.2	84.9	79.1	80.0
Wisconsin	23	76.8	69.2	73.5	82.2	74.8	77.5	75.1	67.2	71.4	86.6	78.3	84.1
West North Central:													
Minnesota	20	77.6	73.0	81.1	79.3	73.3	80.2	76.1	71.4	79.3	85.0	80.3	90.2
Iowa	20	80.0	70.9	72.9	83.7	77.5	75.2	79.1	69.9	71.9	86.4	78.3	81.3
Missouri	13	75.6	68.4	69.8	78.7	70.3	73.6	73.1	65.4	66.9	85.5	79.3	78.3
North Dakota	17	82.8	79.1	85.1	85.5	81.6	89.8	82.2	78.4	84.0	85.6	85.1	93.2
South Dakota	18	80.8	75.9	78.2	80.2	77.1	85.1	79.9	75.1	76.9	90.4	86.2	89.1
Nebraska	23	80.9	73.5	76.8	78.6	75.3	79.2	79.0	72.4	75.7	87.9	80.7	85.2
Kansas	18	76.2	72.2	73.1	77.8	74.0	75.5	74.9	70.5	71.3	85.3	82.5	84.8
South:													
South Atlantic:													
Delaware	22	83.8	74.0	74.8	(NA)	(2)	(2)	78.8	68.6	69.7	98.4	87.7	88.3
Maryland	24	78.8	78.1	75.5	(NA)	(2)	(2)	73.0	72.2	70.0	93.3	91.1	87.9
District of Columbia.	20	(D)	(D)	(D)	(D)	(2)	(2)	(D)	(D)	(D)	(D)	(D)	(D)
Virginia.	18	77.2	73.3	75.4	72.4	(D)	(2)	72.7	67.7	69.2	89.1	86.6	89.6
West Virginia	21	81.1	76.8	78.4	(D)	(D)	(2)	76.9	72.3	73.6	95.8	89.4	90.7
North Carolina	22	76.2	69.9	71.2	(D)	(D)	(2)	72.3	64.5	65.9	88.3	83.3	84.5
South Carolina. . . .	16	75.6	69.3	69.8	(D)	(D)	(2)	71.3	64.5	64.7	91.0	84.7	85.5
Georgia	8	75.9	70.8	72.6	75.9	64.8	73.1	71.3	74.9	77.1	89.2	84.9	86.9
Florida	4	78.5	72.2	77.2	-	(D)	(2)	73.9	66.1	70.6	89.1	84.7	91.2
East South Central:													
Kentucky	15	78.6	72.3	72.9	83.8	70.3	(D)	75.5	68.8	68.4	90.2	82.9	84.9
Tennessee	20	74.4	70.3	72.5	(D)	(D)	(D)	70.0	64.9	66.4	87.5	82.9	85.9
Alabama	16	78.4	73.6	74.5	(D)	(D)	(D)	75.1	69.4	69.7	90.1	86.3	87.6
Mississippi	18	78.9	70.6	74.5	(D)	(D)	(D)	75.2	66.7	69.9	90.4	81.5	86.7
West South Central:													
Arkansas	19	77.5	70.1	72.8	79.5	67.3	67.8	74.8	66.9	69.3	90.6	81.9	86.0
Louisiana	20	77.2	73.6	75.3	(D)	(D)	(D)	73.2	68.5	69.8	88.4	85.2	88.3
Oklahoma	16	75.8	69.5	71.5	77.6	69.1	75.7	74.3	67.3	69.1	81.6	78.3	82.3
Texas.	20	76.1	72.4	74.8	79.0	71.4	79.4	73.1	67.7	70.0	85.5	83.9	87.7
West:													
Mountain:													
Montana	24	81.3	73.1	77.1	80.4	73.3	76.5	90.6	71.9	76.4	86.6	78.1	81.9
Idaho	22	67.0	71.7	72.6	66.0	71.1	72.4	66.4	70.8	71.7	77.8	81.1	82.4
Wyoming	9	79.4	77.7	80.2	78.9	77.0	79.7	78.2	76.5	78.9	87.0	85.8	88.4
Colorado.	22	73.4	74.7	80.4	73.3	75.3	83.3	71.3	71.8	77.0	83.0	84.4	93.3
New Mexico	22	77.8	73.7	85.9	75.6	72.3	85.0	76.9	72.2	84.4	88.1	85.7	97.7
Arizona.	18	78.6	73.3	84.6	75.9	69.2	79.7	77.5	71.7	83.2	89.3	87.0	99.3
Utah	19	66.2	69.2	74.8	65.3	71.1	75.7	64.4	66.9	72.0	73.8	76.3	82.3
Nevada	23	79.2	77.8	83.1	74.5	73.4	81.2	77.6	76.1	80.6	90.4	90.1	97.1
Pacific:													
Washington.	23	72.4	69.8	69.6	68.1	64.7	64.0	71.1	68.3	68.0	84.3	84.0	84.9
Oregon.	24	75.8	78.3	79.9	71.5	73.7	74.5	75.1	77.5	78.9	89.8	92.3	96.1
California	17	65.3	73.7	84.4	61.4	(2)	(D)	63.2	69.9	80.6	75.2	85.4	98.6
Alaska	8	108.7	103.9	107.7	(NA)	100.0	104.7	108.6	104.4	(NA)	109.2	103.6	109.1
Hawaii	16	99.1	104.2	108.5	(NA)	(2)	(2)	93.0	97.5	103.0	110.3	115.3	119.2

- Represents zero.   D Withheld to avoid disclosure of individual company data.   NA Not available.   [1] Source: U.S. Advisory Commission on Intergovernmental Relations, *Significant Features of Fiscal Federalism,* annual, vol. I, based on CCH, *State Tax Reporter.*   [2] No data reported.

Source: Except as noted, U.S. Energy Information Administration, *Petroleum Marketing Monthly.*

Banking, Finance, and Insurance

This section presents data on the Nation's finances, various types of financial institutions, money and credit, securities, and insurance. The primary sources of these data are publications of several departments of the Federal Government, especially the Treasury Department, and independent agencies such as the Federal Deposit Insurance Corporation, the Federal Reserve System, and the Securities and Exchange Commission. National data on insurance are available primarily from private organizations, such as the American Council of Life Insurance.

Flow of funds.—The flow of funds accounts of the Federal Reserve System (see tables 784 to 787) bring together statistics on all of the major forms of financial transactions and financial claims to present an economy-wide view of asset and liability relationships. In flow form, the accounts relate borrowing and lending to one another and to the nonfinancial activities that generate income and production. Each claim outstanding is included simultaneously as an asset of the lender and as a liability of the debtor. The accounts also indicate the balance between asset totals and liability totals over the economy as a whole. Several publications of the Board of Governors of the Federal Reserve System contain information on the flow of funds accounts: Summary data on flows and outstandings, in the *Federal Reserve Bulletin, Flow of Funds Accounts* (quarterly), and *Annual Statistical Digest;* and concepts and organization of the accounts, in *Guide to the Flow of Funds Accounts* (1993).

Banking system.—Banks in this country are organized under the laws of both the States and the Federal Government and are regulated by several bank supervisory agencies. National banks are supervised by the Comptroller of the Currency. *Reports of Condition* have been collected from national banks since 1863. Summaries of these reports are published in the Comptroller's *Annual Report,* which also presents data on the structure of the national banking system.

In Brief

Conventional new-home mortgage rates:
1980	13.95%
1990	10.08%
1994	8.58%

Dow-Jones industrial average:
1980	891.4
1990	2,678.9
1994	3,794.2

The Federal Reserve System was established in 1913 to exercise central banking functions, some of which are shared with the U.S. Treasury. It includes national banks and such State banks that voluntarily join the System. Statements of State bank members are consolidated by the Board of Governors of the Federal Reserve System with data for national banks collected by the Comptroller of the Currency into totals for all member banks of the System. Balance sheet data for member banks and other commercial banks are published quarterly in the *Federal Reserve Bulletin*. The Federal Deposit Insurance Corporation (FDIC), established in 1933, insures each depositor up to $100,000. Major item balance sheet and income data for all commercial banks are published in the *FDIC Quarterly Banking Profile*.

The FDIC is the primary federal regulator of State-chartered banks that are not members of the Federal Reserve System and of most savings banks insured by the Bank Insurance Fund (BIF). The agency also has certain back–up supervisory authority, for safety and soundness purposes, over State-chartered banks that are members of the Federal Reserve System, national banks, and savings associations.

Savings institutions.—Savings institutions are primarily involved in credit extension in the form of mortgage loans. Statistics on savings institutions are collected by the U.S. Office of Thrift Supervision and the FDIC. The Financial Institutions Reform, Recovery, and Enforcement Act of 1989 (FIRREA) authorized the establishment of the Resolution Trust Corporation (RTC). The RTC is responsible for the disposal of assets from failed savings institutions. FIRREA gave the FDIC the job of managing the federal deposit insurance fund for savings institutions (SAIF=Savings Association Insurance Fund). Major balance sheet and income data for all insured savings institutions are published in the *FDIC Quarterly Banking Profile*.

Credit Unions.—Federally chartered credit unions are under the supervision of the National Credit Union Administration, established in 1970. State-chartered credit unions are supervised by the respective State supervisory authorities. The Administration publishes comprehensive program and statistical information on all Federal and federally insured State credit unions in the *Annual Report of the National Credit Union Administration*. Deposit insurance (up to $100,000 per account) is provided to members of all Federal and those State credit unions that are federally-insured by the National Credit Union Share Insurance Fund which was established in 1970. Deposit insurance for State chartered credit unions is also available in some States under private or State-administered insurance programs.

Other credit agencies.—Insurance companies, finance companies dealing primarily in installment sales financing, and personal loan companies represent important sources of funds for the credit market. Statistics on loans, investments, cash, etc., of life insurance companies are published principally by the American Council of Life Insurance in its *Life Insurance Fact Book* and in the *Federal Reserve Bulletin*. Consumer credit data are published currently in the *Federal Reserve Bulletin*.

Government corporations and credit agencies make available credit of specified types or to specified groups of private borrowers, either by lending directly or by insuring or guaranteeing loans made by private lending institutions. Data on operations of Government credit agencies, along with other Government corporations, are available in reports of individual agencies; data on their debt outstanding are published in the *Federal Reserve Bulletin*.

Currency.—Currency, including coin and paper money, represents about 31 per-

cent of all media of exchange in the United States, with most payments made by check. All currency is now issued by the Federal Reserve Banks.

Securities.—The Securities and Exchange Commission (SEC) was established in 1934 to protect the interests of the public and investors against malpractices in the securities and financial markets and to provide the fullest possible disclosure of information regarding securities to the investing public. Statistical data are published in the *SEC Annual Report*.

Insurance.—Insuring companies, which are regulated by the various States or the District of Columbia, are classified as either life or property. Companies that underwrite accident and health insurance only and those that underwrite accident and health insurance in addition to one or more property lines are included with property insurance. Insuring companies, other than those classified as life, are permitted to underwrite one or more property lines provided they are so licensed and have the necessary capital or surplus.

There are a number of published sources for statistics on the various classes of insurance—life, health, fire, marine, and casualty. Individual States collect data on all insurers operating within their respective jurisdictions, and many of the States publish an annual insurance report giving individual company data and aggregates of certain items for the companies operating within the State. Organizations representing certain classes of insurers publish reports for these classes. Among them are the annual commercial publishers, such as The National Underwriter Company whose *Argus Health Chart* (annual) contains financial and operating data for individual health and accident insurance companies, including Blue Cross and Blue Shield Plans. The American Council of Life Insurance publishes statistics on life insurance purchases, ownership, benefit payments, and assets in its biennial *Life Insurance Fact Book*.

Historical statistics.—Tabular headnotes provide cross-references, where applicable, to *Historical Statistics of the United States, Colonial Times to 1970*. See Appendix IV.

No. 782. Gross Domestic Product in Finance, Insurance, and Real Estate, in Current and Constant (1987) Dollars: 1987 to 1992

[In billions of dollars, except percent. For definition of gross domestic product, see text, section 14. Based on 1987 Standard Industrial Classification]

INDUSTRY	CURRENT DOLLARS				CONSTANT (1987) DOLLARS			
	1987	1990	1991	1992	1987	1990	1991	1992
Finance, insurance, real estate, total	809.7	982.4	1,041.1	1,106.1	809.7	868.3	868.8	893.4
Percent of gross domestic product	17.8	17.7	18.2	18.4	17.8	17.7	17.9	17.9
Depository institutions	134.7	158.7	181.3	193.9	134.7	135.1	129.4	125.3
Nondepository institutions	17.4	20.7	23.0	25.9	17.4	17.9	18.2	19.5
Security and commodity brokers	37.9	37.9	37.1	49.6	37.9	38.4	38.9	51.0
Insurance carriers	51.2	69.9	84.7	84.8	51.2	60.1	67.5	73.0
Insurance agents, brokers, and services	30.2	37.7	38.5	40.4	30.2	32.1	31.2	31.3
Real estate	521.5	641.7	664.2	698.7	521.5	566.7	565.2	575.0
Nonfarm housing services	375.6	458.7	483.6	512.0	375.6	398.3	403.9	409.4
Other real estate	145.9	183.0	180.6	186.7	145.9	168.5	161.3	165.7
Holding and other investment offices	16.9	15.8	12.1	12.8	16.9	18.1	18.5	18.3

Source: U.S. Bureau of Economic Analysis, *Survey of Current Business*, October 1994.

No. 783. Finance, Insurance, and Real Estate—Establishments, Employees, and Payroll: 1990 and 1992

[Covers establishments with payroll. Excludes government employees, railroad employees, self-employed persons, etc. For statement on methodology, see Appendix III]

KIND OF BUSINESS	1987 SIC code [1]	ESTABLISHMENTS (1,000)		EMPLOYEES (1,000)		PAYROLL (bil. dol.)	
		1990	1992	1990	1992	1990	1992
Finance, insurance, real estate	(H)	544.7	596.9	6,957	6,906	197.4	221.0
Depository institutions [2]	60	81.2	104.5	2,033	2,158	48.4	57.9
Central reserve depositories	601	0.1	0.1	31	29	0.9	1.0
Commercial banks	602	52.3	65.0	1,472	1,576	35.6	42.5
Savings institutions	603	21.7	21.1	417	355	8.8	8.8
Credit unions	606	3.6	13.2	51	123	1.0	2.5
Functions closely related to banking	609	2.8	4.5	44	51	1.4	1.7
Nondepository institutions [2]	61	42.0	40.9	506	457	14.0	16.0
Federal and fed.-sponsored credit	611	0.6	0.8	14	15	0.4	0.5
Personal credit institutions	614	25.0	19.9	236	159	5.5	4.5
Business credit institutions	615	3.7	4.4	88	99	3.1	3.9
Mortgage bankers and brokers	616	10.9	15.1	153	181	4.6	7.1
Security and commodity brokers [2]	62	25.2	32.1	411	426	26.6	34.1
Security brokers and dealers	621	15.9	18.7	308	311	20.8	26.4
Commodity contracts brokers, dealers	622	1.2	1.4	15	13	0.7	0.7
Security and commodity exchanges	623	0.2	0.1	9	9	0.5	0.4
Security and commodity services	628	7.1	11.5	76	92	4.5	6.5
Insurance carriers [2]	63	43.3	52.6	1,407	1,569	41.5	50.8
Life insurance	631	14.1	14.5	572	626	16.3	19.5
Medical service and health insurance [2]	632	2.1	2.9	188	234	5.1	6.8
Accident and health insurance	6321	1.1	1.4	48	61	1.3	1.6
Hospital and medical service plans	6324	1.0	1.5	139	172	3.8	5.3
Fire, marine, and casualty insurance	633	18.3	21.7	533	584	17.0	20.6
Surety insurance	635	0.6	0.8	15	17	0.5	0.7
Title insurance	636	3.2	3.6	57	54	1.6	1.7
Pension, health and welfare funds	637	3.8	8.5	25	47	0.6	1.2
Insurance agents, brokers, and service	64	110.8	114.0	712	642	20.3	19.4
Real estate [2]	65	217.0	224.0	1,374	1,326	28.5	28.4
Real estate operators and lessors	651	95.7	91.6	509	475	8.7	8.3
Real estate agents and managers	653	72.2	92.1	585	637	13.3	15.0
Title abstract offices	654	3.1	4.2	24	29	0.5	0.8
Subdividers and developers [2]	655	19.6	17.8	140	123	3.4	3.0
Subdividers and developers, n.e.c. [3]	6552	10.8	9.2	88	75	2.3	2.0
Cemetery subdividers and developers	6553	4.4	5.9	35	39	0.6	0.8
Holding and other investment offices [2]	67	22.6	27.3	263	266	10.0	11.3
Holding offices	671	6.2	7.5	124	138	5.4	6.6
Investment offices	672	1.0	1.3	16	16	1.0	0.9
Trusts	673	7.8	10.7	65	65	1.4	1.7
Educational, religious, etc. trusts	6732	3.6	4.6	42	37	0.9	0.9
Miscellaneous investing	679	5.0	6.6	44	44	1.5	1.9
Patent owners and lessors	6794	0.9	1.1	15	18	0.4	0.6
Administrative and auxiliary	(X)	2.6	1.4	251	63	8.2	3.0

X Not applicable.   [1] Standard Industrial Classification; see text, section 13.   [2] Includes industries not shown separately.
[3] N.e.c.=Not elsewhere classified.

Source: U.S. Bureau of the Census, *County Business Patterns*, annual.

No. 784. Flow of Funds Accounts—Financial Assets of Financial and Nonfinancial Institutions, by Holder Sector: 1980 to 1994

[In billions of dollars. As of Dec. 31. See also *Historical Statistics, Colonial Times to 1970*, series X 192, X 229, X 821,and X 835]

SECTOR	1980	1985	1987	1988	1989	1990	1991	1992	1993	1994
All sectors	**13,527**	**22,319**	**27,282**	**29,724**	**33,098**	**34,188**	**37,338**	**39,679**	**42,776**	**44,435**
Households [1]	6,406	9,668	11,380	12,346	13,802	14,023	15,534	16,465	17,538	17,997
Nonfinancial business	1,340	2,067	2,473	2,704	2,849	2,981	3,032	3,161	3,233	3,376
Farm	24	33	39	43	45	47	50	53	57	60
Nonfarm noncorporate	140	310	364	404	432	445	440	454	460	474
Nonfinancial corporations	1,176	1,723	2,070	2,257	2,373	2,489	2,542	2,654	2,716	2,842
State and local government	249	521	637	680	712	723	732	716	720	629
U.S. Government	229	372	371	361	369	441	499	474	474	432
U.S. Government-sponsored credit enterprises and mortgage pools	307	692	1,043	1,165	1,321	1,494	1,650	1,821	1,980	2,225
Monetary authorities . .	174	243	286	304	315	344	366	382	424	452
Commercial banking [2]	1,482	2,376	2,774	2,952	3,232	3,339	3,443	3,657	3,896	4,162
Domestic commercial banks	1,266	1,990	2,257	2,385	2,545	2,644	2,677	2,775	2,932	3,123
Foreign banking offices in U.S.	98	144	236	266	360	368	439	511	546	596
Nonbank finance	2,881	5,486	7,055	7,734	8,727	8,966	10,071	10,843	12,043	12,393
Funding corporations	14	46	71	99	117	153	178	235	291	345
Savings institutions	792	1,275	1,505	1,640	1,513	1,358	1,172	1,079	1,029	1,013
Credit unions	68	134	178	192	202	217	240	264	281	295
Life insurance	464	796	1,005	1,133	1,260	1,367	1,505	1,614	1,785	1,888
Other insurance	182	299	405	454	503	533	576	597	641	670
Private pension funds	504	1,093	1,367	1,422	1,706	1,629	2,056	2,214	2,450	2,356
State and local govt. retirement funds	197	399	524	609	767	820	941	1,059	1,151	1,223
Finance companies	205	365	484	535	571	611	634	637	654	742
Mortgage companies	16	25	24	29	49	49	60	60	60	34
Real estate investment trusts	3	8	10	14	15	13	14	14	17	18
Mutual funds	62	240	460	478	566	602	814	1,042	1,429	1,463
Closed-end funds	8	8	21	43	52	52	72	91	107	114
Money market funds	76	244	316	338	428	498	540	544	559	605
Security brokers, dealers	45	156	138	136	237	262	333	372	454	443
Asset-backed securities issuers	-	39	131	169	226	278	329	392	473	528
Bank personal trusts	245	358	414	444	515	522	608	630	661	656
Rest of the world	459	894	1,264	1,478	1,770	1,879	2,011	2,160	2,468	2,770

- Represents zero.   [1] Includes nonprofit organizations.   [2] Includes other sectors not shown separately.
Source: Board of Governors of the Federal Reserve System, *Flow of Funds Accounts*, March 1995 quarterly diskettes. Data are also published in the quarterly Z.1 release.

No. 785. Flow of Funds Accounts—Credit Market Debt Outstanding: 1980 to 1994

[In billions of dollars. As of Dec. 31. N.e.c.=Not elsewhere classified]

ITEM	1980	1985	1987	1988	1989	1990	1991	1992	1993	1994
Credit market debt	**4,700**	**8,462**	**10,697**	**11,704**	**12,725**	**13,597**	**14,232**	**15,036**	**16,018**	**17,051**
U.S. government	735	1,590	1,950	2,105	2,251	2,498	2,776	3,080	3,336	3,492
Private domestic nonfinancial	3,189	5,382	6,612	7,208	7,819	8,215	8,405	8,640	9,027	9,490
Households [1]	1,391	2,243	2,771	3,074	3,380	3,614	3,785	4,002	4,292	4,641
Farm	161	173	144	134	134	135	135	136	138	141
Nonfarm noncorporate business . . .	440	860	1,034	1,097	1,137	1,147	1,116	1,074	1,049	1,069
Corporations	886	1,543	1,970	2,169	2,366	2,469	2,458	2,500	2,554	2,676
State and local government	310	563	693	735	803	849	911	928	993	964
Rest of the world	197	237	245	251	261	285	299	311	358	346
Financial sectors	579	1,254	1,890	2,140	2,393	2,599	2,752	3,005	3,297	3,722
Government-sponsored enterprises [2]	163	264	308	353	378	399	408	448	528	701
Federally-related mortgage pools . . .	114	369	670	745	870	1,020	1,156	1,272	1,353	1,448
Commercial banks	49	79	82	79	77	77	65	74	79	89
Bank holding companies	43	106	131	136	142	115	112	115	123	132
Funding corporations	13	39	80	118	130	146	139	162	170	201
Thrift institutions [3]	55	110	163	184	169	139	95	88	99	112
Life insurance companies	-	-	-	-	-	-	-	-	-	1
Finance companies	127	224	299	323	350	374	393	389	391	441
Mortgage companies	12	17	14	15	25	25	22	30	29	16
Real estate investment trusts	5	5	8	10	12	12	14	14	17	19
Security brokers, dealers	-	1	3	8	14	15	19	22	34	34
Asset-backed securities issuers	-	39	131	169	226	278	329	392	473	528
CORPORATE CREDIT MARKET DEBT OUTSTANDING, BY TYPE OF INSTRUMENT										
Total	886	1,543	1,970	2,169	2,366	2,469	2,458	2,500	2,554	2,676
Tax-exempt debt [4]	46	127	116	116	115	115	114	114	114	112
Corporate bonds	366	578	784	887	961	1,008	1,087	1,154	1,230	1,252
Mortgages	114	96	191	186	204	192	193	166	153	152
Bank loans, n.e.c.	230	424	482	519	554	555	530	518	515	564
Commercial paper	28	72	74	86	107	117	98	107	118	139
Other loans	102	245	322	375	425	481	435	441	424	456
Savings institutions	1	15	20	25	24	17	10	6	5	5
Finance companies	71	127	171	196	216	235	234	237	236	269
U.S. government	8	14	11	10	10	9	8	8	8	9
Acceptance liabilities to banks	17	28	33	33	36	29	23	20	17	15
Rest of the world	5	60	86	111	138	187	153	160	141	140
Asset-backed securities issuers	-	-	-	-	2	5	7	9	17	19

- Represents zero.   [1] Includes nonprofit organizations.   [2] U.S. Government.   [3] Covers savings institutions and credit unions.   [4] Industrial revenue bonds.
Source: Board of Governors of the Federal Reserve System, *Flow of Funds Accounts*, March 1995 quarterly diskettes. Data are also published in the quarterly Z.1 release.

No. 786. Flow of Funds Accounts—Financial Assets and Liabilities of Financial and Nonfinancial Institutions, by Sector and Type of Instrument: 1994

[In billions of dollars. As of **Dec. 31**. Preliminary. A=Assets; L=Liabilities, SDR=Special drawing rights, IMF=International Monetary Fund. RP's=Repurchase Agreements. "N.e.c."=Not elsewhere classified]

TYPE OF INSTRUMENT	All sectors, total A	All sectors, total L	Private total A	Private total L	Households[1] A	Households[1] L	Business A	Business L	State & local govts. A	State & local govts. L	U.S. Govt. A	U.S. Govt. L	Financial total[2] A	Financial total[2] L	Commercial banking A	Commercial banking L	Nonbank finance A	Nonbank finance L	Fed. sponsored credit agencies & mortgage pools A	Fed. sponsored credit agencies & mortgage pools L	Foreign sector A	Foreign sector L
Total	44,435	35,476	22,002	11,435	17,997	4,821	3,376	5,622	629	993	432	3,943	19,231	18,537	4,162	4,028	12,393	11,850	2,225	2,211	2,770	1,561
Gold stock and SDR's	21	-									10		11									
IMF position	12	12									12											12
Official foreign exchange	41	41									19		22									41
Treasury currency, SDR certificates	31	26										26	31									
Checkable deposits, currency	1,200	1,241	1,055		722		303		30		28		92	1,241	3	756	88	112	2		25	
Time and savings accounts	2,596	2,596	2,282		2,031		202		49				276	2,596		1,708	188	887	88		38	
Fed. funds and security RP's	375	537	132				47		85		1		216	537		392	117	145			27	
Money market fund shares	605	605	399		352		48						206	605			206	605				
Foreign deposits	282	282	266				266						16				16					282
Life insurance reserves	488	488	488		488							11		478				478				
Pension fund reserves	5,061	5,061	5,061		5,061							359		4,702				4,702				
Interbank claims[3]	270	264											68	264	66	195	3	3			202	
Mutual fund shares[3]	1,463	1,463	989		969		20						474	1,463	2		472	1,463				
Other corporate equities[4]	6,049	-	2,913		2,913								2,795		7		2,788				341	
Credit market instruments[5]	17,051	17,051	2,663	9,490	1,932	4,641	304	3,885	427	964	197	3,492	12,886	3,722	3,253	221	7,148	1,352	2,117	2,149	1,304	346
U.S. Treasury securities[6]	3,466	3,466	1,091		677		113		301			3,466	1,686		290		967		64		688	
Federal agency securities[7]	2,176	2,176	421		407		10		5			27	1,614	2,149	428		1,054		128	2,149	141	
Tax-exempt securities	1,203	1,203	428	1,203	403	135	13	112	12	956			775		98		678					
Corporate and foreign bonds	2,417	2,417	198	1,252	198		25	1,252	109				1,908	945	104	141	1,803	804			311	220
Mortgages	4,409	4,409	322	4,401	187	3,346	90	1,055			63		4,025	9	1,012		1,292	9	1,720			
Consumer credit	984	984	90	984		984							894		461		433					
Bank loans, n.e.c	832	832		755		36		719					832	51	832			51	14			26
Open-market paper	624	624	113	139	108			139					487	443	6	55	468	388			24	41
Security credit	276	276	108	73	60	73	54						168	203	95		73	203				
Trade credit[8]	1,204	1,102	1,057	1,010		89	1,057	893		29	26	48	70	8	2		70	9			51	34
Taxes payable	61	87	38	79				79	38		23			8				8				
Proprietors' equity	2,485	-	2,485		2,485																	
Investment in bank personal trusts	656	656	656		656									656				656				
Miscellaneous claims	4,207	3,688	1,410	783	281	18	1,128	765			115	7	1,899	2,053	736	753	1,136	1,233	18	61	783	845

- Represents or rounds to zero. [1] Includes nonprofit organizations. [2] Includes monetary authority, not shown separately. [3] Nonbank finance liability is redemption value of shares of open-end investment companies for amounts outstanding. [4] Assets shown at market value. No specific liability attributed to issuers of stocks other than open-end investment companies. [5] Includes "Other loans," not shown separately. [6] Includes savings bonds and other nonmarketable debt held by public. [7] Issues by agencies in the budget and by Government-sponsored enterprises in financial sectors; issues backed by federally-related mortgage pools, and loan participation certificates. [8] Asset is corporate only; noncorporate credit deducted in liability total to conform to quarterly flow tables.

Source: Board of Governors of the Federal Reserve System, *Flow of Funds Accounts*, quarterly.

Banking, Finance, and Insurance

No. 787. Flow of Funds Accounts—Assets and Liabilities of Households: 1980 to 1994

[As of **December 31.** Includes nonprofit organizations. See also *Historical Statistics, Colonial Times to 1970,* series X 114-147]

TYPE OF INSTRUMENT	TOTAL (bil. dol.)							PERCENT DISTRIBUTION		
	1980	1985	1990	1991	1992	1993	1994	1980	1990	1994
Total financial assets	**6,406**	**9,668**	**14,023**	**15,534**	**16,465**	**17,538**	**17,997**	**100.0**	**100.0**	**100.0**
Deposits	1,573	2,454	3,152	3,109	3,080	3,060	3,104	24.6	22.5	17.2
Checkable deposits and currency	264	348	449	511	635	713	722	4.1	3.2	4.0
Small time and savings deposits	1,091	1,690	2,069	2,021	1,957	1,888	1,883	17.0	14.8	10.5
Large time deposits	155	222	260	194	147	128	148	2.4	1.9	0.8
Money market fund shares	62	195	375	383	341	331	352	1.0	2.7	2.0
Credit market instruments	461	862	1,499	1,447	1,523	1,526	1,932	7.2	10.7	10.7
U.S. Government securities	212	350	648	600	699	702	1,084	3.3	4.6	6.0
Treasury issues	181	306	449	406	462	503	677	2.8	3.2	3.8
Savings bonds	73	80	126	138	157	172	180	1.1	0.9	1.0
Other Treasury	108	226	323	268	304	331	497	1.7	2.3	2.8
Agency issues	31	44	199	194	237	199	407	0.5	1.4	2.3
Tax-exempt securities	76	257	448	483	449	433	403	1.2	3.2	2.2
Corporate and foreign bonds	31	31	95	105	107	142	198	0.5	0.7	1.1
Mortgages	111	125	177	162	166	177	187	1.7	1.3	1.0
Open-market paper	31	99	131	96	103	71	60	0.5	0.9	0.3
Mutual fund shares	46	192	452	592	734	972	969	0.7	3.2	5.4
Corporate equities	934	1,210	1,717	2,469	2,810	3,088	2,913	14.6	12.2	16.2
Life insurance reserves	216	257	380	406	433	468	488	3.4	2.7	2.7
Pension fund reserves [1]	949	2,032	3,484	4,138	4,516	4,975	5,061	14.8	24.8	28.1
Investment in bank personal trusts	245	358	522	608	630	661	656	3.8	3.7	3.6
Equity in noncorporate business	1,892	2,134	2,529	2,444	2,412	2,422	2,485	29.5	18.0	13.8
Security credit	16	35	62	87	76	103	108	0.3	0.4	0.6
Miscellaneous assets	74	133	224	234	251	264	281	1.1	1.6	1.6
Total liabilities	**1,443**	**2,333**	**3,738**	**3,920**	**4,143**	**4,464**	**4,821**	**100.0**	**100.0**	**100.0**
Credit market instruments	1,391	2,243	3,614	3,785	4,002	4,292	4,641	96.4	96.7	96.3
Home mortgages	905	1,379	2,455	2,614	2,788	2,970	3,156	62.7	65.7	65.5
Consumer credit	355	602	812	797	803	867	984	24.6	21.7	20.4
Tax-exempt debt	17	81	86	93	108	120	135	1.2	2.3	2.8
Commercial mortgages	31	63	139	152	164	181	190	2.2	3.7	3.9
Bank loans, not elsewhere classified	28	34	12	9	11	20	36	1.9	0.3	0.7
Other loans	55	84	110	120	128	134	141	3.8	2.9	2.9
Security credit	25	51	39	55	53	76	73	1.7	1.0	1.5
Trade credit	14	24	69	64	72	80	89	1.0	1.8	1.8
Unpaid life insurance premiums [2]	13	15	16	16	16	17	18	0.9	0.4	0.4

[1] See also table 834. [2] Includes deferred premiums.

Source: Board of Governors of the Federal Reserve System, *Flow of Funds Accounts,* March 1995 diskettes. Data are also published in the quarterly Z.1 release.

No. 788. Percent Distribution of Amount of Debt Held by Families, by Type and Purpose of Debt and Type of Lending Institution: 1989 and 1992

[Families include one-person units; for definition of family, see text, section 1. Based on Survey of Consumer Finance; see source]

TYPE OF DEBT	1989	1992	PURPOSE OF DEBT	1989	1992	TYPE OF LENDING INSTITUTION	1989	1992
Total	**100.0**	**100.0**	**Total**	**100.0**	**100.0**	**Total**	**100.0**	**100.0**
Home mortgage and home equity lines of credit	56.7	63.3	Home purchase	53.1	58.6	Commercial bank	29.7	31.8
			Home improvement	2.0	1.9	Savings and loan	23.5	18.9
Installment loans	13.9	9.2	Investment, excluding real estate	2.6	1.4	Credit union	3.2	4.0
Credit card balances	2.3	2.8	Vehicles	8.6	5.7	Finance or loan company	9.4	12.9
Other lines of credit	1.0	0.8	Goods and services	4.8	4.9	Brokerage	3.0	3.9
Investment real estate mortgages	24.5	22.0	Investment real estate	25.8	22.4	Real estate lender	13.2	13.4
Other debt	1.7	1.9	Education	1.9	2.1	Individual lender	6.8	4.0
			Unclassifiable loans	1.2	2.9	Other nonfinancial	1.9	2.5
						Government	2.1	1.2
						Credit and store cards	2.3	2.9
						Unclassifiable loans	4.9	4.5

Source: Board of Governors of the Federal Reserve System, *Federal Reserve Bulletin,* October 1994.

No. 789. Financial Assets Held by Families, by Type of Asset: 1989 and 1992

[Median value in thousands of constant 1992 dollars. Constant dollar figures are based on consumer price index data published by U.S. Bureau of Labor Statistics. Families include one-person units; for definition of family, see text, section 1. Based on Survey of Consumer Finance; see source. For definition of median, see Guide to Tabular Presentation]

AGE OF FAMILY HEAD AND FAMILY INCOME	Total [1]	Transaction accounts [2]	Certificates of deposit	Mutual funds [3]	Stocks [4]	Bonds [4]	Retirement accounts [5]	Savings bonds	Other managed [6]
PERCENT OF FAMILIES OWNING ASSET									
1989, total	88.4	85.1	19.4	7.1	16.2	5.3	35.4	23.8	3.5
1992, total	**90.7**	**87.5**	**16.6**	**11.2**	**17.8**	**4.7**	**39.3**	**22.7**	**4.3**
Under 35 years old	86.8	82.5	7.4	5.8	11.1	1.4	29.7	22.8	1.9
35 to 44 years old	90.9	86.9	9.0	10.8	20.7	3.1	47.3	29.4	3.3
45 to 54 years old	93.1	89.2	15.1	10.5	19.2	6.5	52.9	25.4	6.0
55 to 64 years old	92.9	90.7	21.2	16.6	23.0	5.0	53.4	21.4	6.0
65 to 74 years old	91.7	89.8	31.7	16.5	19.0	9.2	36.7	14.1	6.3
75 years old and over	92.6	91.7	36.6	13.4	18.2	8.3	6.3	14.5	5.6
Less than $10,000	70.2	63.7	11.1	3.3	4.2	1.0	7.0	6.6	0.9
$10,000 to $24,999	88.1	83.7	15.1	5.7	8.8	1.9	21.6	13.3	2.4
$25,000 to $49,999	98.2	95.4	17.1	11.8	18.2	3.7	45.2	27.9	4.7
$50,000 to $99,999	99.3	98.7	22.2	18.5	31.0	6.9	70.7	39.5	6.8
$100,000 and more	98.7	98.7	19.5	29.9	48.7	22.4	78.6	32.1	11.6
PERCENT DISTRIBUTION OF AMOUNT OF FINANCIAL ASSETS [7]									
1989	100.0	19.7	10.4	5.0	14.6	11.0	18.8	1.6	6.6
1992	100.0	16.4	7.9	7.2	21.0	7.7	22.7	1.1	6.4
MEDIAN VALUE [8]									
1989, total	12.0	2.3	12.6	11.2	7.3	27.9	11.2	0.6	22.3
1992, total	**13.1**	**2.4**	**13.5**	**18.0**	**10.0**	**25.0**	**15.0**	**0.7**	**25.0**
Under 35 years old	4.2	1.4	5.0	3.8	2.0	10.0	4.7	0.4	20.0
35 to 44 years old	10.8	2.2	5.0	18.0	5.0	19.3	9.8	0.6	20.0
45 to 54 years old	24.7	3.4	10.0	20.0	12.0	25.2	30.0	1.0	25.0
55 to 64 years old	40.1	4.0	20.0	20.4	20.0	40.0	35.7	1.0	30.0
65 to 74 years old	30.2	4.0	25.0	30.0	24.0	25.3	23.0	0.9	40.0
75 years old and over	20.2	4.0	24.0	22.3	28.0	52.0	28.0	1.1	55.0
Less than $10,000	1.5	0.7	7.0	15.0	10.0	15.7	9.0	0.5	12.0
$10,000 to $24,999	3.9	1.1	16.0	7.0	4.0	11.0	5.1	0.5	20.0
$25,000 to $49,999	14.1	2.3	13.0	15.0	5.0	25.0	10.0	0.5	20.0
$50,000 to $99,999	47.0	5.6	12.0	22.0	8.0	20.0	25.0	1.0	32.0
$100,000 and more	184.0	25.5	28.0	30.0	40.0	51.0	66.0	1.2	95.0

[1] Includes other types of financial assets, not shown separately. [2] Checking, savings, and money market accounts. [3] Excludes money market mutual funds, individual retirement accounts (IRA's), Keogh accounts, and any type of pension plan invested in mutual funds. [4] Covers only those stocks and bonds that are directly held by families outside mutual funds, IRA's, Keogh or pension accounts. [5] Covers IRA's, Keogh accounts, and employer-provided pension plans from which withdrawals can be made, such as 401(k) plans. [6] Includes trusts, annuities, managed investment accounts, and other such assets. [7] Of all families. [8] Median value of financial asset for families holding such assets.

No. 790. Percent of Families Holding Financial Debt, by Type of Debt: 1989 and 1992

[See headnote, table 789]

AGE OF FAMILY HEAD AND FAMILY INCOME	Total	Mortgage and home equity	Installment	Credit cards	Other lines of credit	Investment real estate	Other debt [1]
PERCENT OF FAMILIES HOLDING DEBTS							
1989, total	73.0	40.0	50.1	40.4	3.2	7.3	6.7
1992, total	**73.3**	**38.7**	**45.8**	**43.4**	**2.5**	**8.3**	**8.7**
Under 35 years old	82.1	30.6	62.1	52.6	2.9	4.8	6.5
35 to 44 years old	86.5	55.5	58.2	50.3	3.3	9.3	12.6
45 to 54 years old	85.8	61.8	48.6	48.4	2.8	14.5	10.3
55 to 64 years old	69.2	40.0	38.0	36.7	2.3	13.8	10.8
65 to 74 years old	51.9	18.3	22.9	30.2	1.1	5.4	5.4
75 years old and over	30.2	6.7	8.0	19.5	(B)	0.7	4.5
Less than $10,000	47.5	9.6	29.8	23.7	(B)	0.6	5.2
$10,000 to $24,999	69.5	21.8	46.8	43.2	1.5	3.5	6.4
$25,000 to $49,999	82.5	47.4	54.6	54.8	2.9	7.3	10.7
$50,000 to $99,999	84.6	66.1	50.2	49.0	4.3	13.5	10.1
$100,000 and more	85.0	67.6	35.3	32.9	4.2	34.6	14.9
MEDIAN DEBT [2]							
1989, total	17.6	38.0	5.9	1.1	2.2	35.7	2.2
1992, total	**17.6**	**44.0**	**4.5**	**1.0**	**2.2**	**28.0**	**2.5**
Under 35 years old	10.2	52.0	4.6	0.9	1.6	18.0	1.2
35 to 44 years old	33.3	54.0	5.0	1.3	1.8	28.0	3.0
45 to 54 years old	30.9	42.0	5.0	1.7	5.0	49.5	3.0
55 to 64 years old	20.8	28.0	3.9	1.0	4.0	34.7	3.0
65 to 74 years old	5.6	17.0	4.2	0.7	4.0	17.0	2.0
75 years old and over	2.3	15.0	3.1	0.6	(B)	104.0	1.1
Less than $10,000	2.0	16.0	1.6	0.6	(B)	6.5	0.7
$10,000 to $24,999	5.6	17.4	2.7	0.8	3.0	6.1	1.0
$25,000 to $49,999	21.1	40.0	5.6	1.3	1.5	18.0	2.0
$50,000 to $99,999	57.2	58.0	7.8	1.5	2.0	41.0	3.0
$100,000 and more	131.0	103.0	10.8	3.9	18.0	75.0	6.0

B Base figure too small. [1] Includes loans on insurance policies, loans against pension accounts, and other unclassified loans. [2] Median amount of financial debt for families holding such debts.

Source of tables 789 and 790: Board of Governors of the Federal Reserve System, *Federal Reserve Bulletin*, October 1994.

No. 791. Selected Financial Institutions—Number and Assets, by Asset Size: 1993

[As of **December**. FDIC=Federal Deposit Insurance Corporation]

ASSET SIZE	NUMBER OF INSTITUTIONS			ASSETS (bil. dol.)		
	F.D.I.C.-insured		Credit unions [2]	F.D.I.C.-insured		Credit unions [2]
	Commercial banks	Savings institutions [1]		Commercial banks [3]	Savings institutions [1]	
Total................	**10,958**	**2,262**	**12,317**	**3,706.2**	**1,000.9**	**277.2**
Less than $5.0 million.........	([4])	([4])	6,553	([4])	([4])	11.4
$5.0 million to $9.9 million......	([4])	([4])	1,851	([4])	([4])	13.2
$10.0 million to $24.9 million....	[4]2,217	[4]191	1,845	[4]35.9	[4]3.1	29.6
$25.0 million to $49.9 million....	2,789	343	952	101.5	12.9	33.2
$50.0 million to $99.9 million....	2,782	514	560	197.7	37.4	38.6
$100.0 million to $499.9 million...	2,543	900	507	502.6	202.2	99.5
$500.0 million to $999.9 million...	245	140	36	174.4	96.6	24.5
$1.0 billion to $2.9 billion......	187	116	11	305.6	190.9	15.6
$3.0 billion or more..........	195	58	2	2,388.5	457.8	11.6
	PERCENT DISTRIBUTION					
Total................	**100.0**	**100.0**	**100.0**	**100.0**	**100.0**	**100.0**
Less than $5.0 million.........	([4])	([4])	53.3	([4])	([4])	4.1
$5.0 million to $9.9 million......	([4])	([4])	15.0	([4])	([4])	4.8
$10.0 million to $24.9 million....	[4]20.2	[4]8.4	15.0	[4]0.9	[4]0.3	10.7
$25.0 million to $49.9 million....	25.5	15.2	7.7	2.7	1.3	12.0
$50.0 million to $99.9 million....	25.4	22.7	4.5	5.3	3.7	13.9
$100.0 million to $499.9 million...	23.2	39.8	4.1	13.6	20.2	35.9
$500.0 million to $999.9 million...	2.2	6.2	0.3	4.7	9.7	8.8
$1.0 billion to $2.9 billion......	1.7	5.1	0.1	8.3	19.1	5.6
$3.0 billion or more..........	1.8	2.6	(Z)	64.5	45.7	4.2

Z Less than 0.05 percent.   [1] Excludes institutions in Resolution Trust Corporation conservatorship.   [2] Source: National Credit Union Administration, *National Credit Union Administration Year-end Statistics 1993*. Excludes nonfederally insured State chartered credit unions and federally insured corporate credit unions.   [3] Includes foreign branches of U.S. banks.   [4] Data for institutions with assets less than $10 million included with those with assets of $10.0 million to $24.9 million.

Source: Except as noted, U.S. Federal Deposit Insurance Corporation, *Statistics on Banking, 1993*.

No. 792. Banking Offices, by Type of Bank: 1980 to 1994

[As of **December 31**. Includes Puerto Rico and outlying areas. Covers all FDIC-insured commercial banks and all Bank Insurance Fund-insured savings banks as well as those State-chartered Savings Association Insurance Fund-insured savings banks that are regulated by the FDIC. Data for 1980 include automatic teller machines which were reported by many banks as branches. See also *Historical Statistics, Colonial Times to 1970*, series X 716-724]

ITEM	1980	1985	1988	1989	1990	1991	1992	1993	1994
All banking offices	**57,232**	**60,890**	**63,960**	**64,570**	**66,945**	**67,783**	**67,777**	**68,664**	**70,284**
Number of banks	15,330	14,809	13,629	13,201	12,819	12,390	11,997	11,552	11,060
Number of branches	41,902	46,081	50,331	51,369	54,126	55,393	55,780	57,112	59,224
Commercial banks, total.........	53,649	57,764	60,200	60,796	63,160	64,006	63,903	64,078	65,594
Member, Federal Reserve System .	29,985	33,854	35,763	36,755	38,201	39,449	39,271	39,639	40,998
National banks.............	24,217	27,844	29,270	30,019	31,279	31,771	31,064	30,879	31,633
State banks..............	5,768	6,010	6,493	6,736	6,922	7,678	8,207	8,760	9,365
Insured nonmember banks	[1]23,664	23,910	24,437	24,041	24,959	24,557	24,632	24,439	24,596
Savings banks, insured	[1]3,583	3,126	3,760	3,774	3,785	3,777	3,874	4,586	4,690

[1] Includes noninsured banks.

Source: U.S. Federal Deposit Insurance Corporation, 1980, *Annual Report* and, beginning 1985, *Statistics on Banking*, annual.

No. 793. BIF-Insured Commercial and Savings Banks Closed or Assisted Due to Financial Difficulties and Problem Banks: 1980 to 1994

[Banks are closed either permanently or temporarily by order of supervisory authorities or by directors of banks. B.I.F.=Bank Insurance Fund. See also *Historical Statistics, Colonial Times to 1970*, series X 741, 748, 756, and 761]

ITEM	Unit	1980	1985	1988	1989	1990	1991	1992	1993	1994
Total banks closed or assisted....	Number.	11	120	221	207	169	127	122	41	13
Assets, closed and assisted banks .	Bil. dol. .	7.9	8.7	52.6	29.4	15.7	63.2	44.2	3.5	1.4
Deposits, closed and assisted banks	Bil. dol. .	5.2	8.1	37.2	24.1	14.5	53.8	41.2	3.1	1.2
Problem banks [1].............	Number.	217	1,140	1,406	1,109	1,046	1,090	863	474	265
Assets, problem banks..........	Bil. dol. .	(NA)	238	352	236	409	610	465	269	42

NA Not available.   [1] BIF-insured commercial and savings banks considered to be problem banks by the supervisory authorities, end-of-period.

Source: U.S. Federal Deposit Insurance Corporation, *Annual Report, The FDIC Quarterly Banking Profile*, and *Failed Bank Cost Analysis Report*, 1994.

No. 794. Insured Commercial Banks—Assets and Liabilities: 1980 to 1994

[**In billions of dollars, except as indicated**. As of **Dec. 31**. Includes outlying areas. Except as noted, includes foreign branches of U.S. banks. See *Historical Statistics, Colonial Times to 1970*, series X 588-609, for related data]

ITEM	1980	1985	1988	1989	1990	1991	1992	1993	1994 [1]
Number of banks	14,435	14,417	13,137	12,713	12,345	11,926	11,462	10,958	10,450
Assets, total	**1,856**	**2,731**	**3,131**	**3,299**	**3,389**	**3,431**	**3,506**	**3,706**	**4,011**
Net loans and leases	1,006	1,608	1,886	2,004	2,055	1,998	1,977	2,097	2,306
Real estate loans	269	438	675	762	830	851	868	923	998
Home equity lines of credit [2]	(NA)	(NA)	40	51	61	70	73	73	(NA)
Commercial and industrial loans	391	578	600	618	615	559	536	539	589
Loans to individuals	187	309	378	401	404	392	385	419	487
Farm loans	32	36	30	31	33	35	35	37	39
Other loans and leases	158	288	265	261	242	227	216	239	251
Less: Reserve for losses	10	23	47	54	56	55	54	53	52
Less: Unearned income	21	18	16	15	14	11	9	7	6
Investment securities	325	439	536	559	605	691	773	837	823
Other	524	684	709	736	730	742	755	773	882
Domestic office assets	1,533	2,326	2,726	2,897	2,999	3,033	3,110	3,258	(NA)
Foreign office assets	323	406	405	402	390	398	396	448	(NA)
Liabilities and capital, total	1,856	2,731	3,131	3,299	3,389	3,431	3,506	3,706	4,011
Noninterest-bearing deposits [3]	432	471	479	483	489	480	541	572	572
Interest-bearing deposits [4]	1,049	1,646	1,952	2,065	2,162	2,207	2,158	2,182	2,302
Subordinated debt	7	15	17	19	24	25	34	37	41
Other liabilities	260	429	486	526	496	486	510	618	783
Equity capital	108	169	197	205	219	232	263	297	312
Domestic office deposits	1,187	1,796	2,117	2,237	2,357	2,383	2,412	2,424	2,442
Foreign office deposits	294	322	315	312	293	305	287	330	432

NA Not available. [1] Preliminary. [2] For one- to four-family residential properties. [3] Prior to 1985, demand deposits. [4] Prior to 1985, time and savings deposits.

Source: U.S. Federal Deposit Insurance Corporation, *The FDIC Quarterly Banking Profile, Annual Report*, and *Statistics on Banking*, annual.

No. 795. Insured Commercial Banks—Income and Selected Measures of Financial Condition: 1980 to 1994

[**In billions of dollars, except as indicated**. Includes outlying areas. Includes foreign branches of U.S. banks. See *Historical Statistics, Colonial Times to 1970*, series X 588-609, for related data]

ITEM	1980	1985	1988	1989	1990	1991	1992	1993	1994 [1]
Interest income	177.4	248.2	272.3	317.3	320.4	289.2	255.2	245.1	257.8
Interest expense	120.1	157.3	165.0	205.1	204.9	167.3	121.8	105.7	111.3
Net interest income	57.3	90.9	107.2	112.2	115.5	121.9	133.4	139.3	146.6
Provisions for loan losses	4.5	17.8	17.2	31.0	32.1	34.3	26.0	16.8	10.9
Noninterest income	13.3	31.1	45.0	50.9	54.9	59.7	65.6	75.0	76.2
Noninterest expense	46.7	82.4	101.3	108.1	115.7	124.8	130.9	139.7	144.2
Income taxes	5.0	5.6	10.0	9.5	7.7	8.3	14.5	19.8	22.4
Securities gain/loss, net	−0.5	1.6	0.3	0.8	0.5	3.0	4.0	3.1	−0.6
Extraordinary gains, net	-	0.2	0.8	0.3	0.6	0.7	0.4	2.1	-
Net income	14.0	18.0	24.8	15.6	16.0	17.9	32.0	43.1	44.7
RATIOS OF CONDITION									
Return on assets [2] (percent)	0.80	0.70	0.82	0.49	0.48	0.53	0.93	1.20	1.15
Return on equity [3] (percent)	13.66	11.31	13.19	7.71	7.45	7.94	12.98	15.35	14.63
Equity capital to assets (percent)	5.80	6.20	6.28	6.21	6.45	6.75	7.51	8.00	7.78
Nonperforming assets	(NA)	51.0	67.1	75.4	98.1	102.2	91.5	69.2	(NA)
Nonperforming assets to assets (percent)	(NA)	1.87	2.14	2.30	2.94	3.02	2.54	1.61	1.01
Net charge-offs [4]	3.6	13.6	18.6	22.9	29.7	32.9	25.6	17.5	11.2
Net charge-offs to loans and leases (percent)	0.36	0.84	1.00	1.16	1.43	1.59	1.27	0.85	0.50
Net interest margin [5] (percent)	3.66	4.09	4.02	4.02	3.94	4.11	4.41	4.40	4.36
Percentage of banks losing money	3.7	17.1	14.7	12.5	13.4	11.6	6.9	4.9	3.8

- Represents or rounds to zero. NA Not available. [1] Preliminary. [2] Net income (including securities transactions and nonrecurring items) as a percentage of average total assets. [3] Net income as a percentage of average total equity capital. [4] Total loans and leases charged off (removed from balance sheet because of uncollectibility), less amounts recovered on loans and leases previously charged off. [5] Interest income less interest expense as a percentage of average earning assets (i.e. the profit margin a bank earns on its loans and investments).

Source: U.S. Federal Deposit Insurance Corporation, *Annual Report; Statistics on Banking*, annual; and *FDIC Quarterly Banking Profile*.

No. 796. Insured Commercial Banks—Selected Measures of Financial Condition, by Asset Size and Region: 1994

[In percent, except as indicated. Preliminary. See headnote, table 795]

ASSET SIZE AND REGION	Number of banks	Return on assets	Return on equity	Equity capital to assets	Nonper-forming assets to total assets	Net charge-offs to loans and leases	Percentage of banks losing money
Total	10,450	1.15	14.63	7.78	1.01	0.50	3.8
Less than $100 million . .	7,258	1.13	11.36	9.84	0.86	0.24	4.3
$100 million to $1 billion .	2,800	1.20	13.48	8.80	0.92	0.37	2.6
$1 billion to $10 billion. . .	328	1.31	16.04	7.94	0.90	0.54	3.7
$10 billion or more	64	1.06	15.01	7.01	1.13	0.57	1.6
Northeast [1]	834	1.07	14.71	7.33	1.28	0.75	6.2
Southeast [2]	1,740	1.18	14.78	7.84	0.72	0.27	3.6
Central [3]	2,272	1.13	14.08	7.88	0.66	0.29	3.3
Midwest [4]	2,622	1.46	16.76	8.43	0.68	0.46	1.7
Southwest [5]	1,857	1.12	13.49	8.16	0.67	0.16	2.9
West [6]	1,125	1.24	14.48	8.33	1.33	0.58	9.7

[1] CT, DE, DC, ME, MD, MA, NH, NJ, NY, PA, PR, RI, and VT.   [2] AL, FL, GA, MS, NC, SC, TN, VA, and WV.   [3] IL, IN, KY, MI, OH, and WI.   [4] IA, KS, MN, MO, NE, ND, and SD.   [5] AR, LA, NM, OK, and TX.   [6] AK, AZ, CA, CO, HI, ID, MT, NV, OR, Pacific Islands, UT, WA, and WY.

Source: U.S. Federal Deposit Insurance Corporation, *The FDIC Quarterly Banking Profile*, Fourth Quarter 1994.

No. 797. Insured Commercial Banks, 1993, and Banks Closed or Assisted, 1994, by State and Other Area

[In billions of dollars, except as indicated. Includes foreign branches of U.S. banks]

STATE	COMMERCIAL BANKS, 1993 [1]			BANKS CLOSED OR ASSISTED, 1994 [2]		STATE	COMMERCIAL BANKS, 1993 [1]			BANKS CLOSED OR ASSISTED, 1994 [2]	
	Number	Assets	Deposits	Number	Deposits		Number	Assets	Deposits	Number	Deposits
Total .	10,957	3,705.9	2,753.9	13	1.2	WV	148	19.9	16.6	-	-
U.S.	10,941	3,683.7	2,737.5	13	1.2	NC	71	104.0	70.3	-	-
Northeast.	718	1,227.2	839.6	4	0.5	SC	78	27.7	20.6	-	-
N.E	183	166.1	121.2	4	0.5	GA	399	90.1	63.3	-	-
ME	20	8.7	6.8	-	-	FL	375	150.2	123.4	-	-
NH	26	7.4	5.8	-	-	E.S.C	891	173.9	139.6	-	-
VT	20	5.8	4.8	-	-	KY	309	45.5	35.1	-	-
MA	61	97.7	70.0	2	0.2	TN	250	57.0	46.6	-	-
RI	10	13.5	10.0	-	-	AL	214	46.9	37.4	-	-
CT	46	32.9	23.6	2	0.3	MS	118	24.4	20.5	-	-
M.A.	535	1,061.1	718.4	-	-	W.S.C.	1,856	281.1	235.0	-	-
NY	175	770.5	493.9	-	-	AR	257	26.0	22.8	-	-
NJ	99	100.3	84.4	-	-	LA	217	40.1	34.0	-	-
PA	261	190.4	140.1	-	-	OK	371	31.0	27.0	-	-
Midwest.	4,808	817.9	633.3	1	(Z)	TX	1,011	184.0	151.2	-	-
E.N.C.	2,102	566.6	433.2	-	(Z)	West	1,284	566.3	453.0	8	0.7
OH	263	132.9	96.5	-	-	Mountain . . .	702	141.7	112.0	-	-
IN.	237	61.5	49.5	-	-	MT	117	7.9	6.8	-	-
IL.	958	212.0	161.2	-	-	ID.	21	10.9	8.3	-	-
MI.	208	106.0	81.6	-	-	WY	55	5.2	4.5	-	-
WI	436	54.2	44.4	-	-	CO	322	34.4	30.0	-	-
W.N.C.	2,706	251.3	200.0	1	(Z)	NM	81	12.8	11.2	-	-
MN	573	62.3	47.9	-	-	AZ	37	37.1	29.7	-	-
IA.	530	38.7	32.0	-	-	UT	48	15.4	11.2	-	-
MO	490	68.5	55.7	-	-	NV	21	18.0	10.2	-	-
ND	141	8.1	7.1	-	-	Pacific	582	424.6	341.0	8	0.7
SD	121	19.2	11.0	-	-	WA	87	41.4	34.5	-	-
NE	361	24.1	20.9	-	-	OR	45	27.4	21.4	-	-
KS	490	30.3	25.5	1	(Z)	CA	425	328.5	267.0	8	0.7
						AK	8	5.0	3.8	-	-
South	4,131	1,072.3	811.6	-	-	HI.	17	22.3	14.3	-	-
S.A	1,384	617.3	437.1	-	-						
DE	36	85.8	34.9	-	-	AM	1	0.1	(Z)	-	-
MD	94	52.0	40.7	-	-	PR	12	21.5	15.8	-	-
DC	18	13.3	9.8	-	-	GU	2	0.6	0.6	-	-
VA	165	74.4	57.5	-	-	Pac. Is . .	1	0.1	(Z)	-	-

- Represents zero.   Z Less than $50 million.   [1] As of December 31.   [2] Includes Bank Insurance Fund-insured savings banks.

Source: U.S. Federal Deposit Insurance Corporation, *Annual Report; Statistics on Banking*, annual; and *FDIC Quarterly Banking Profile*.

No. 798. U.S. Banking Offices of Foreign Banks—Summary: 1980 to 1994

[In billions of dollars, except as indicated. As of December, except as indicated. Covers agencies, branches, subsidiary commercial banks, and New York State investment companies]

YEAR	Assets	LOANS		Deposits	COUNTRY	NUMBER OF—		Assets	Loans, commercial and industrial	Deposits
		Total	Business			Banks with U.S. offices	U.S. offices			
1980	200.6	121.4	59.6	80.4	**1994** [2]					
1985	440.8	247.4	108.8	236.7	Japan	52	142	392.6	101.1	223.7
1989	735.7	369.8	184.3	376.1	Canada	6	42	61.0	17.6	32.9
1990	791.1	397.9	193.3	383.9	Switzerland . . .	6	15	44.6	14.0	19.7
1991	860.7	412.3	206.4	444.5	France	12	32	88.7	12.9	41.8
1992	869.0	407.5	208.7	464.3	Netherlands . . .	3	22	48.8	12.4	28.9
1993	855.6	383.3	196.5	468.7	United Kingdom	9	32	61.9	10.1	38.2
Share: [1] 1980 . .	11.9	13.4	18.2	6.6	Italy	12	24	35.6	5.1	15.3
1985 . .	16.1	15.4	22.5	12.1	Hong Kong . . .	10	33	22.9	4.5	15.7
1990 . .	21.4	18.0	30.8	14.5	Germany	12	21	36.1	4.0	26.1
1993 . .	21.1	17.0	33.4	16.6	Korea, South . .	8	30	12.1	3.8	2.3

[1] Percent of "domestically owned" commercial banks plus U.S. offices of foreign banks.   [2] As of June 30. Source: American Banker-Bond Buyer, New York, NY, *American Banker Ranking The Banks*, annual, (copyright).

Source: Except as noted, Board of Governors of the Federal Reserve System, unpublished data.

No. 799. Foreign Lending by U.S. Banks, by Type of Borrower and Country: 1994

[In millions of dollars. As of December. Covers 140 U.S. banking organizations which do nearly all of the foreign lending in the country. Data represent claims on foreign residents and institutions held at all domestic and foreign offices of covered banks. Data cover only cross-border and nonlocal currency lending. These result from a U.S. bank's office in one country lending to residents of another country or lending in a currency other than that of the borrower's country. Excludes local currency loans and other claims and local currency liabilities held by banks' foreign offices on residents of the country in which the office was located (e.g. Deutsche mark loans to German residents booked at the German branch of the reporting U.S. bank). Criteria for country selection is $2.7 billion or more]

COUNTRY	Total	Bank	Public	Private non-bank	COUNTRY	Total	Bank	Public	Private non-bank
Total [1]	**232,539**	**85,022**	**58,114**	**89,405**	Hong Kong	7,594	3,802	31	3,762
Argentina	9,970	946	2,585	6,439	Italy.	5,679	1,695	2,913	1,071
Australia.	3,147	1,011	334	1,801	Japan	16,593	7,705	2,803	6,085
Bahamas, The.	4,293	3,981	28	283	Korea, South	5,868	3,503	152	2,213
Belgium-Luxembourg .	5,908	2,724	1,192	1,992	Mexico.	22,825	4,116	12,760	5,949
Brazil.	11,683	2,029	4,631	5,023	Netherlands	4,809	1,731	1,144	1,935
Canada	9,565	2,621	3,377	3,568	Singapore	4,913	2,155	93	2,665
Cayman Islands. . . .	8,195	5,487	25	2,683	Spain	3,336	1,181	1,549	605
Chile	3,848	517	1,580	1,751	Switzerland.	4,543	1,372	154	3,017
Colombia	2,760	400	1,215	1,146	Thailand.	2,898	1,015	55	1,828
France.	8,810	5,731	1,263	1,817	United Kingdom.	31,205	17,255	582	13,368
Germany	5,452	2,093	1,937	1,422	Venezuela	4,586	52	3,021	1,514 .

[1] Includes other countries, not shown separately.

Source: Board of Governors of the Federal Reserve System, Federal Financial Institutions Examination Council, statistical release.

No. 800. Federal and State-Chartered Credit Unions—Summary: 1980 to 1993

[Except as noted, as of December 31. Federal data include District of Columbia, Puerto Rico, Canal Zone, Guam, and Virgin Islands. Excludes State-insured, privately-insured, and noninsured State-chartered credit unions and corporate central credit unions which have mainly other credit unions as members. See also *Historical Statistics, Colonial Times to 1970*, series X 864-878]

YEAR	OPERATING CREDIT UNIONS		Number of failed institutions [1]	MEMBERS (1,000)		ASSETS (mil. dol.)		LOANS OUTSTANDING (mil. dol.)		SAVINGS (mil. dol.)	
	Federal	State		Federal	State	Federal	State	Federal	State	Federal	State
1980 . . .	12,440	4,910	239	24,519	12,338	40,092	20,870	26,350	14,582	36,263	18,469
1985 . . .	10,125	4,920	94	29,579	15,689	78,188	41,525	48,241	26,168	71,616	37,917
1988 . . .	9,118	4,760	85	34,438	18,519	114,565	60,740	73,766	39,977	104,431	55,217
1989 . . .	8,821	4,550	114	35,612	18,858	120,666	63,175	80,272	42,373	109,653	57,658
1990 . . .	8,511	4,349	164	36,241	19,454	130,073	68,133	83,029	44,102	117,892	62,082
1991 . . .	8,229	4,731	130	37,081	21,619	143,940	83,133	84,150	49,268	130,164	75,626
1992 . . .	7,908	4,686	114	38,124	23,238	162,066	96,312	87,350	52,192	145,637	87,371
1993 . . .	7,696	4,621	37	39,756	23,997	172,854	104,316	94,640	57,695	153,506	93,482

[1] For year ending September 30. A failed institution is defined as a credit union which has ceased operation because it was involuntarily liquidated or merged with assistance from the National Credit Union Share Insurance Fund. Assisted mergers were not identified until 1981.

Source: National Credit Union Administration, *Annual Report of the National Credit Union Administration*, and unpublished data.

No. 801. Insured Savings Institutions—Financial Summary: 1990 to 1994

[**In billions of dollars, except number of institutions**. As of **December 31**. Includes Puerto Rico, Guam, and Virgin Islands. Covers SAIF (Savings Association Insurance Fund)- and BIF (Bank Insurance Fund)-insured savings institutions. Minus sign (-) indicates debt or loss]

ITEM	INSURED SAVINGS INSTITUTIONS [1]					RTC CONSERVATORSHIPS [4]			
	1990	1991	1992 [2]	1993 [2]	1994 [2][3]	1991	1992	1993	1994
Number of institutions	2,816	2,560	2,390	2,262	2,152	91	81	63	2
Assets, total.	1,267	1,119	1,030	1,001	1,009	44	37	22	2
Loans and leases, net	816	727	648	626	635	24	17	10	1
Liabilities, total	1,200	1,051	956	923	929	48	42	27	2
Deposits	987	907	828	774	737	37	31	18	1
Equity capital	68	69	74	78	80	-4	-4	-5	(Z)
Interest and fee income	117	98	78	66	63	3	1	1	(Z)
Interest expense.	91	70	46	35	33	3	1	1	(Z)
Net interest income	26	28	32	32	30	(Z)	(Z)	(Z)	(Z)
Net income	-5	1	7	7	6	-2	-3	-2	-2

Z Less than $500 million. [1] Excludes institutions in RTC conservatorship. [2] Excludes one self-liquidating institution. [3] Preliminary. [4] RTC=Resolution Trust Corporation. These savings institutions are members of the Savings Association Insurance Fund.

Source: U.S. Federal Deposit Insurance Corporation, *Statistics on Banking*, annual and *FDIC Quarterly Banking Profile*.

No. 802. Insured Savings Institutions—Finances, by Asset Size: 1993

[**In billions of dollars, except as indicated**. See headnote, table 801. Excludes institutions in Resolution Trust Corporation conservatorship]

ITEM	Total	Less than $100 million	$100 million to $1 billion	$1 billion or more	ITEM	Total	Less than $100 million	$100 million to $1 billion	$1 billion or more
Number of institutions	2,262	1,048	1,040	174	Equity capital	78	5	26	48
Assets, total	1,001	53	299	649					
Investment securities . . .	276	12	83	181	Interest and fee income . . .	66	3	21	42
Loans and leases, net [1]	626	34	186	406	Interest expense	35	2	10	22
Real estate loans	595	33	178	384	Net interest income . . .	32	1	11	20
Commercial and					Provisions for loan losses . .	4	(Z)	1	3
industrial loans	10	(Z)	3	7	Noninterest income	7	(Z)	2	5
Loans to individuals . .	38	2	10	26	Noninterest expense	25	1	8	16
Less: Reserve for					Net operating income,				
losses	8	(Z)	2	6	pretax	10	(Z)	4	6
Liabilities, total	923	48	273	601	Securities gain/loss, net . . .	(Z)	(Z)	(Z)	(Z)
Deposits	774	46	249	478	Income taxes	4	(Z)	2	2
Noninterest-bearing. . .	29	1	8	20	Net income	7	(Z)	3	4
Interest-bearing	745	45	241	459	Net charge-offs [2]	4	(Z)	(Z)	4

Z Less than $500 million. [1] Includes other items, not shown separately. [2] Total loans and leases charged off (removed from balance sheet because of uncollectibility), less amounts recovered on loans and leases previously charged off.

Source: U.S. Federal Deposit Insurance Corporation, *Statistics on Banking, 1993*.

No. 803. Volume of Long-Term Mortgage Loans Originated, by Type of Property, 1980 to 1993, and by Lender, 1993

[**In billions of dollars**. Covers credit extended in primary mortgage markets for financing real estate acquisitions]

TYPE OF PROPERTY	1980	1985	1988	1989	1990	1991	1992	1993, BY LENDER				
								Total [1]	Commercial banks	Mortgage companies	Savings and loan	Life insurance companies
Loans, total	**197.2**	**430.0**	**673.6**	**642.3**	**710.5**	**793.3**	**1,124.0**	**1,238.4**	**435.6**	**529.6**	**189.7**	**27.0**
1-4 unit family home . .	133.8	289.8	446.3	452.9	458.4	562.1	893.7	1010.3	259.5	526.5	179.3	0.8
New units	49.1	59.0	85.2	90.4	110.7	120.0	132.4	117.3	45.5	56.0	13.6	0.2
Existing units	84.6	230.8	361.1	362.5	347.7	442.1	761.3	893.0	214.0	470.5	165.7	0.6
Multifamily residential .	12.5	31.9	38.2	31.1	32.6	25.5	25.7	32.0	19.1	2.0	6.2	1.5
New units	8.6	10.6	9.0	8.3	6.5	6.1	4.9	4.4	2.0	-	0.3	0.5
Existing units	3.9	21.3	29.2	22.8	26.0	19.4	20.9	27.6	17.1	2.0	5.9	1.0
Nonresidential	35.9	99.4	181.6	150.0	209.5	194.6	184.4	178.5	144.7	1.1	4.2	24.1
Farm properties	15.0	9.0	7.6	8.3	10.0	11.1	20.2	17.6	12.3	-	-	0.6

- Represents zero. [1] Includes other lenders not shown separately.

Source: U.S. Dept. of Housing and Urban Development, monthly and quarterly press releases based on the Survey of Mortgage Lending Activity.

No. 804. Mortgage Debt Outstanding, by Type of Property and Holder: 1980 to 1993

[**In billions of dollars**. As of **Dec. 31**. Includes Puerto Rico and Guam. See also *Historical Statistics, Colonial Times to 1970,* series N 273 and N 276]

TYPE OF PROPERTY AND HOLDER	1980	1984	1985	1986	1987	1988	1989	1990	1991	1992	1993
Mortgage debt, total.	1,460	2,051	2,303	2,634	2,990	3,288	3,549	3,764	3,926	4,056	4,215
Residential nonfarm	1,107	1,520	1,716	1,981	2,244	2,505	2,715	2,926	3,088	3,259	3,438
One- to four-family homes.	965	1,334	1,501	1,724	1,964	2,208	2,408	2,617	2,781	2,963	3,147
Savings institutions.	487	529	554	559	602	672	669	600	538	490	470
Mortgage pools or trusts [1]	125	322	407	553	702	790	887	1,044	1,214	1,380	1,494
Government National Mortgage Assoc	92	176	207	257	309	331	358	392	416	411	405
Federal Home Loan Mortgage Corp . .	13	70	100	167	206	220	266	308	352	402	438
Commercial banks	160	196	213	236	276	334	390	456	484	508	557
Individuals and others [2]	113	175	206	235	247	267	319	350	370	383	387
Federal and related agencies	61	98	110	127	124	134	131	153	163	192	230
Federal National Mortgage Assoc . . .	52	82	92	91	90	96	91	94	100	124	151
Life insurance companies	18	14	12	13	13	11	12	13	12	11	9
Five or more units	142	185	214	257	280	297	306	309	307	295	290
Commercial	255	419	482	556	659	698	754	759	759	717	697
Farm	97	112	106	96	88	85	80	78	79	81	81
TYPE OF HOLDER											
Savings institutions	603	710	760	778	860	925	910	802	705	628	598
Commercial banks	263	379	429	503	592	674	767	845	876	895	940
Life insurance companies.	131	157	172	194	212	233	254	268	265	247	229
Individuals and others [2]	203	296	341	393	414	444	502	531	563	575	579
Mortgage pools or trusts [1]	146	351	439	565	718	812	918	1,079	1,251	1,426	1,551
Government National Mortgage Assoc. . . .	94	180	212	263	318	341	368	404	425	420	414
Federal Home Loan Mortgage Corp	17	71	100	171	213	226	273	316	359	408	443
Federal National Mortgage Association . . .	-	36	55	97	140	178	228	300	372	445	496
Farmers Home Administration [3]	32	45	48	(Z)	(Z)	(Z)	(Z)	(Z)	(Z)	(Z)	(Z)
Federal and related agencies	115	159	167	204	193	201	198	239	266	286	317
Federal National Mortgage Association	57	88	98	98	97	103	99	105	112	138	167
Farmers Home Administration [3]	3	1	1	48	43	42	41	41	42	42	41
Federal Land Banks.	38	52	47	40	34	32	30	29	29	29	28
Federal Home Loan Mortgage Corp	5	10	14	12	13	17	22	22	27	34	51
Federal Housing and Veterans Admin	6	5	5	5	6	6	6	9	11	13	12
Government National Mortgage Assoc. . . .	5	2	1	1	(Z)	(Z)	(Z)	(Z)	(Z)	(Z)	(Z)
Resolution Trust Corporation	(X)	(X)	(X)	(X)	(X)	(X)	(Z)	33	46	32	17

- Represents zero.   X Not applicable.   Z Less than $500 million.   [1] Outstanding principal balances of mortgage pools backing securities insured or guaranteed by the agency indicated. Includes other pools not shown separately.   [2] Includes mortgage companies, real estate investment trusts, State and local retirement funds, noninsured pension funds, State and local credit agencies, credit unions, and finance companies.   [3] FmHA-guaranteed securities sold to the Federal Financing Bank were reallocated from FmHA mortgage pools to FmHA mortgage holdings in 1986 because of accounting changes by the Farmers Home Administration.

Source: Board of Governors of the Federal Reserve System, *Federal Reserve Bulletin,* monthly.

No. 805. Characteristics of Conventional First Mortgage Loans for Purchase of Single-Family Homes: 1980 to 1994

[**In percent, except as indicated**. Annual averages. Refers to loans originated directly by Savings Association Insurance Fund-insured savings institutions, mortgage bankers, commercial banks, and Federal Deposit Insurance Corporation-insured savings banks. Excludes interim construction loans, refinancing loans, junior liens, and federally underwritten loans]

LOAN CHARACTERISTICS	NEW HOMES						EXISTING HOMES					
	1980	1990	1991	1992	1993	1994	1980	1990	1991	1992	1993	1994
Contract interest rate, [1]												
all loans	12.3	9.7	9.0	8.0	7.0	7.3	12.5	9.8	9.1	7.8	6.9	7.3
Fixed-rate loans	(NA)	10.1	9.3	8.3	7.3	7.9	(NA)	10.1	9.4	8.2	7.3	8.0
Adjustable-rate loans [2]	(NA)	8.9	8.1	6.6	5.8	6.5	(NA)	8.9	8.0	6.3	5.5	6.2
Initial fees, charges [3]	2.09	1.98	1.72	1.59	1.29	1.29	1.91	1.74	1.54	1.58	1.19	1.07
Effective interest rate, [4]												
all loans	12.7	10.1	9.3	8.2	7.2	7.5	12.9	10.1	9.3	8.1	7.1	7.5
Fixed-rate loans	(NA)	10.4	9.6	8.5	7.5	8.1	(NA)	10.4	9.7	8.5	7.5	8.2
Adjustable-rate loans [2]	(NA)	9.2	8.4	6.9	5.9	6.6	(NA)	9.2	8.2	6.5	5.7	6.4
Term to maturity (years)	28.1	27.3	26.8	25.6	26.1	27.5	26.9	27.0	26.5	25.4	25.4	27.1
Purchase price ($1,000)	83.2	154.1	155.2	158.1	163.7	170.7	68.3	140.3	145.8	144.1	139.6	136.4
Loan to price ratio	73.2	74.9	75.0	76.6	78.0	78.7	73.5	74.9	74.4	76.5	77.1	80.1
Percent of number of loans with adjustable rates	(NA)	31	25	17	18	41	(NA)	27	22	21	20	39

NA Not available.   [1] Initial interest rate paid by the borrower as specified in the loan contract.   [2] Loans with a contractual provision for periodic adjustments in the contract interest rate.   [3] Includes all fees, commissions, discounts and "points" paid by the borrower, or seller, in order to obtain the loan. Excludes those charges for mortgage, credit, life or property insurance; for property transfer; and for title search and insurance.   [4] Contract interest rate plus fees and charges amortized over a 10-year period.

Source: U.S. Federal Housing Finance Board, annual and monthly press releases.

No. 806. Mortgage Delinquency and Foreclosure Rates: 1980 to 1994

[**In percent, except as indicated**. Covers one- to four-family residential nonfarm mortgage loans]

ITEM	1980	1985	1988	1989	1990	1991	1992	1993	1994
Number of mortgage loans outstanding (1,000)	30,033	35,353	41,802	43,571	45,187	45,812	46,887	48,639	(NA)
Delinquency rates: [1]									
Total	5.0	5.8	4.8	4.8	4.7	5.0	4.6	4.2	4.0
Conventional loans	3.1	4.0	2.9	3.1	3.0	3.3	2.9	2.7	2.6
VA loans	5.3	6.6	6.2	6.4	6.4	6.8	6.5	6.3	6.1
FHA loans	6.6	7.5	6.6	6.7	6.7	7.3	7.1	7.1	7.0
Foreclosure rates: [2]									
Total	0.5	1.0	1.2	1.0	0.9	1.0	1.0	1.0	1.0
Conventional loans	0.2	0.7	0.7	0.6	0.7	0.8	0.8	0.8	0.7
VA loans	0.6	1.1	1.6	1.3	1.2	1.3	1.3	1.3	1.4
FHA loans	0.7	1.3	1.8	1.4	1.3	1.4	1.4	1.5	1.5

NA Not available.   [1] Number of loans delinquent 30 days or more as percentage of mortgage loans serviced in survey. Annual average of quarterly figures.   [2] Percentage of loans in the foreclosure process at yearend, not seasonally adjusted.

Source: Mortgage Bankers Association of America, Washington, DC, *National Delinquency Survey*, quarterly.

No. 807. Mortgage Delinquency Rates, by Division: 1990 to 1994

[**In percent. Annual average of quarterly figures**. Covers one- to four-family residential nonfarm mortgage loans. Represents number of loans delinquent 30 days or more as percentage of loans serviced in survey. Excludes loans in foreclosure. For composition of divisions, see table 27]

YEAR	U.S., total	New England	Middle Atlantic	East North Central	West North Central	South Atlantic	East South Central	West South Central	Moun- tain	Pacific
1990	4.67	3.53	4.54	5.06	3.82	4.80	6.32	6.45	5.10	3.21
1991	5.01	4.14	5.05	5.20	3.99	5.53	6.69	6.41	5.01	3.45
1992	4.56	4.02	4.86	4.56	3.34	5.05	5.93	5.50	4.12	3.45
1993	4.22	3.54	4.60	4.05	3.18	4.61	5.37	5.01	3.60	3.43
1994	4.09	3.52	4.48	3.69	3.22	4.43	5.13	4.91	3.33	3.56

Source: Mortgage Bankers Association of America, Washington, DC, *National Delinquency Survey*, quarterly.

No. 808. Home Equity Lending—Percentage of Homeowners with Credit, Sources of Credit, and Uses for Funds Borrowed: 1988 and 1993-94

[**In percent**. A "traditional home equity loan" is a closed-end loan extended for a specific period that generally requires repayment of interest and principal in equal monthly installments. Such a loan typically has a fixed interest rate. A "home equity line of credit" is a revolving account that permits borrowing from time to time, at the homeowner's discretion, up to the amount of the credit line. It usually has a more flexible repayment schedule and a variable interest rate. Based on the Surveys of Consumers, a sample survey (2,527 households in 1993-94) conducted by the Survey Research Center of the University of Michigan]

ITEM	HOME EQUITY LINES OF CREDIT		TRADITIONAL HOME EQUITY LOANS		USES FOR FUNDS BORROWED	1993-94 [1]	
	1988	1993-94	1988	1993-94		Home equity lines of credit	Traditional home equity loans
Percentage of homeowners with home equity credit	5.7	8.3	5.4	4.9	Home improvement	64	38
					Repayment of other debts	45	68
SOURCE OF HOME EQUITY CREDIT					Education	21	4
Total	100	100	100	100	Real estate	12	8
Commercial banks	54	60	33	29	Auto or truck	30	3
Savings institutions [2]	31	21	27	30	Medical expenses	5	1
Credit unions	11	13	8	11	Business expenses	28	1
Other creditors [3]	4	7	32	29	Vacation	6	1
					Other [4]	1	3

[1] Percentages sum to more than 100 because respondents were allowed to cite multiple uses for a single loan or drawdown and more than one draw for one line of credit.   [2] Includes savings banks and savings and loan associations.   [3] Includes finance and loan companies, brokerage firms, mortgage companies, and individuals.   [4] Includes purchase of furniture or appliance, purchase of boat or other recreational vehicle, payment of taxes, and personal financial investments.

Source: Board of Governors of the Federal Reserve System, *Federal Reserve Bulletin*, July 1994.

No. 809. Estimated Home Equity Debt Outstanding, by Type and Source of Credit: 1988 to 1994

[In billions of dollars. See headnote, table 808]

YEAR	Total	HOME EQUITY LINES OF CREDIT			TRADITIONAL HOME EQUITY LOANS		
		All lenders	Commer-cial banks	Other sources	All lenders	Commer-cial banks	Other sources
1988	210-265	75	40	35	135-190	(NA)	(NA)
1989	(NA)	90	51	39	(NA)	(NA)	(NA)
1990	258	105	61	44	153	54	99
1991	262	114	70	44	148	53	95
1992	258	114	73	41	144	50	94
1993	255	110	73	37	145	49	96
1994	(NA)	(NA)	76	(NA)	(NA)	54	(NA)

NA Not available.

Source: Board of Governors of the Federal Reserve System, *Federal Reserve Bulletin*, July 1994.

No. 810. Consumer Installment Credit Outstanding and Finance Rates: 1980 to 1994

[In billions of dollars, except percent. Estimated amounts of seasonally adjusted credit outstanding as of end of year; finance rates, annual averages. See also *Historical Statistics, Colonial Times to 1970*, series X 551-560]

TYPE OF CREDIT	1980	1984	1985	1986	1987	1988	1989	1990	1991	1992	1993	1994
Installment credit outstanding...	**298.2**	**442.6**	**517.7**	**572.0**	**608.7**	**663.0**	**724.4**	**734.9**	**728.4**	**731.1**	**794.3**	**911.3**
Automobile paper	112.0	173.6	210.2	247.8	266.3	285.5	292.5	283.1	259.6	257.7	282.0	324.5
Revolving [1]	55.1	100.3	121.8	135.8	153.1	174.3	198.5	223.5	245.3	257.3	287.9	337.7
Other	131.1	168.8	185.7	188.4	189.3	203.2	233.3	228.3	223.5	216.1	224.4	249.1
FINANCE RATES (percent)												
Commercial banks:												
New automobiles (48 months) [2] ...	14.30	13.71	12.91	11.33	10.46	10.85	12.07	11.78	11.14	9.29	8.09	8.12
Mobile homes (120 months) [2] ...	14.99	15.58	14.96	14.00	13.38	13.54	14.11	14.02	13.70	12.67	11.87	11.69
Other consumer goods (24 months).	15.47	16.47	15.94	14.83	14.23	14.68	15.44	15.46	15.18	14.04	13.47	13.19
Credit-card plans.............	17.31	18.77	18.69	18.26	17.93	17.79	18.02	18.17	18.23	17.78	16.83	16.19
Finance companies:												
New automobiles.............	14.82	14.62	11.98	9.44	10.73	12.60	12.62	12.54	12.41	9.93	9.48	9.79
Used automobiles	19.10	17.85	17.59	15.95	14.61	15.11	16.18	15.99	15.60	13.80	12.79	13.49

[1] Consists mainly of outstanding balances on credit card accounts, but also includes borrowing under check credit and overdraft plans, and unsecured personal lines of credit. [2] For 1980, maturities were 36 months for new car loans and 84 months for mobile home loans.

Source: Board of Governors of the Federal Reserve System, *Federal Reserve Bulletin*, monthly; and *Annual Statistical Digest*.

No. 811. Usage of General Purpose Credit Cards by Families: 1989 and 1992

[General purpose credit cards include Mastercard, Visa, Optima, and Discover cards. Median value in constant 1992 dollars. Constant dollar figures are based on consumer price index data published by U.S. Bureau of Labor Statistics. Families include one-person units; for definition of family, see text, section 1. Based on Survey of Consumer Finance; see Appendix III. For definition of median, see Guide to Tabular Presentation]

AGE OF FAMILY HEAD AND FAMILY INCOME	Percent having a general purpose credit card	Median number of cards	Median new charges on last month's bills	Percent having a balance after last month's bills	Median balance [1]	PERCENT OF CARDHOLDING FAMILIES WHO—		
						Almost always pay off the bal-ance	Some-times pay off the balance	Hardly ever pay off the bal-ance
1989, total	56.4	2	$200	52.8	$1,100	52.0	21.8	26.1
1992, total	**63.3**	**2**	**200**	**51.3**	**1,000**	**54.5**	**19.1**	**26.4**
Under 35 years old	57.6	2	200	67.7	900	39.6	25.0	35.4
35 to 44 years old..........	64.2	2	200	61.6	1,500	45.5	22.0	32.5
45 to 54 years old..........	72.5	2	300	53.3	1,900	52.1	19.7	28.2
55 to 64 years old..........	68.0	2	200	40.0	1,000	64.8	16.3	18.9
65 to 74 years old..........	65.0	1	200	32.3	800	74.9	11.0	14.1
75 years old and over	52.1	1	100	19.1	800	78.9	10.6	10.5
Less than $10,000..........	25.9	1	100	45.5	800	57.4	12.2	30.4
$10,000 to $24,999	52.3	1	100	54.6	900	49.5	21.3	29.1
$25,000 to $49,999	73.1	2	200	61.1	1,200	47.0	21.2	31.7
$50,000 to $99,999	88.5	2	300	46.6	1,500	58.7	18.6	22.8
$100,000 and more	91.2	2	500	30.5	3,000	75.2	14.3	10.5

[1] Among families having a balance.

Source: Board of Governors of the Federal Reserve System, unpublished data.

No. 812. Credit Cards—Holders, Numbers, Spending, and Debt, 1990 and 1994, and Projections, 2000

TYPE OF CREDIT CARD	CARDHOLDERS (mil.)			NUMBER OF CARDS (mil.)			CREDIT CARD SPENDING (bil. dol.)			CREDIT CARD DEBT (bil. dol.)		
	1990	1994	2000, proj.	1990	1994	2000, proj.	1990	1994	2000, proj.	1990	1994	2000, proj.
Total [1]	113	124	141	1,026	1,131	1,344	466	731	1,443	236.4	366.4	660.9
Bank [2]	79	91	106	217	315	469	243	437	974	154.1	251.3	486.0
Oil company	85	84	82	123	114	105	27	26	31	3.3	3.5	4.1
Phone	97	106	132	141	161	203	14	17	24	1.7	2.1	3.0
Retail store	96	100	121	469	463	476	75	96	137	51.0	70.2	98.9
Travel and entertainment [3]	23	22	26	28	27	32	85	109	205	13.8	17.5	35.3
Other [4]	11	9	10	48	51	60	22	46	71	12.5	21.8	33.7

[1] Cardholders may hold more than one type of card.   [2] Visa and MasterCard credit cards. Excludes debit cards.   [3] Includes American Express and Diners Club.   [4] Includes Air Travel Card, automobile rental, Discover (except for cardholders), and miscellaneous cards.

Source: HSN Consultants Inc., Oxnard, CA, *The Nilson Report*, bimonthly. (Copyright used by permission.)

No. 813. Delinquency Rates on Bank Installment Loans, by Type of Loan: 1980 to 1994

[**In percent, except as indicated**. As of **end of year**; seasonally adjusted, except as noted. Number of loans having an installment past due for 30 days or more as a percentage of total installment loans outstanding]

TYPE OF CREDIT	1980	1985	1986	1987	1988	1989	1990	1991	1992	1993	1994
DELINQUENCY RATES											
Closed-end installment loans, total	2.82	2.32	2.26	2.47	2.49	2.64	2.57	2.58	2.43	1.77	1.72
Personal loans [1]	3.53	3.63	3.11	3.66	3.34	3.52	3.37	2.95	3.18	2.30	2.38
Automobile, direct loans [2]	1.81	1.64	1.80	1.59	1.92	2.03	2.22	2.14	2.08	1.58	1.46
Automobile, indirect loans [3]	2.29	2.02	2.09	2.20	2.46	2.61	2.59	2.66	2.33	1.65	1.65
Property improvement [4]	1.93	1.91	1.77	1.88	2.06	2.25	2.30	2.38	2.18	1.61	1.66
Home equity and second mortgage loans [5]	(NA)	2.06	1.85	2.01	1.86	1.85	1.45	2.06	1.89	1.66	1.38
Mobile home loans	3.14	2.39	3.04	2.57	3.12	2.51	3.03	2.86	4.02	3.70	3.68
Recreational vehicle loans	1.94	1.84	1.92	1.99	2.07	2.24	2.63	2.25	2.27	1.26	1.23
Marine financing [5]	(NA)	(NA)	(NA)	(NA)	(NA)	(NA)	(NA)	(NA)	2.52	1.72	1.51
Bank card loans	2.72	2.95	3.15	2.33	2.19	2.24	2.86	3.29	2.93	2.49	2.93
Revolving credit loans	2.70	1.96	1.53	2.33	2.87	2.92	3.00	2.75	2.63	2.90	2.38
Home equity lines of credit loans (open-end) [5]	(NA)	(NA)	(NA)	0.74	0.68	0.78	0.85	0.88	0.85	0.70	0.63
REPOSSESSIONS PER 1,000 LOANS OUTSTANDING											
Mobile home	1.57	1.21	2.50	1.58	1.77	1.63	1.19	1.62	1.30	1.21	1.18
Automobile, direct loans [2]	1.10	1.11	1.15	0.86	1.03	1.03	1.75	1.17	0.92	0.83	0.53
Automobile, indirect loans [3]	2.75	2.08	1.95	2.04	1.86	1.70	1.61	2.07	1.47	0.97	1.17
Marine financing [5]	(NA)	(NA)	(NA)	(NA)	(NA)	(NA)	(NA)	(NA)	1.21	1.03	0.82

NA Not available.   [1] Beginning 1985, includes home appliance loans.   [2] Made directly by bank's lending function.   [3] Made by automobile dealerships; loans in bank's portfolio.   [4] Beginning 1985, own plan and FHA Title I loans.   [5] Not seasonally adjusted.

Source: American Bankers Association, Washington, DC, *Consumer Credit Delinquency Bulletin*, quarterly.

No. 814. Electronic Funds Transfer Volume: 1980 to 1994

[As of **September**, except as noted. Electronic funds transfer cover automated teller machine (ATM) transactions and transactions at point-of-sale (POS) terminals. Point-of-sale terminals are electronic terminals in retail stores that allow a customer to pay for goods through a direct debit to a customer's account at the bank]

ITEM	Unit	1980	1985	1988	1989	1990	1991	1992	1993	1994
Total number of transactions	Million	(NA)	3,579	4,581	5,274	5,942	6,642	7,537	8,135	8,958
ATM transactions	Million	(NA)	3,565	4,480	5,116	5,751	6,418	7,206	7,705	8,334
POS transactions	Million	(NA)	14	92	157	191	223	289	430	624
ATM terminals, total	1,000	18.5	60.0	72.5	75.6	80.2	83.5	87.3	94.8	109.1
Monthly transactions per terminal	Number	5,405	4,951	5,151	5,638	5,980	6,403	6,876	6,772	6,367
Shared terminals	1,000	(NA)	35.5	65.1	70.1	75.3	79.6	84.7	92.6	108.1
Proprietary terminals	1,000	(NA)	24.5	7.4	5.5	4.9	4.0	2.6	2.3	1.0
POS terminals, total	1,000	(NA)	(NA)	(NA)	(NA)	53.1	78.1	95.2	155.0	340.5
Grocery stores	1,000	(NA)	(NA)	(NA)	(NA)	21.5	31.8	45.1	75.3	187.4
Gasoline service stations	1,000	(NA)	(NA)	(NA)	(NA)	18.7	21.5	26.3	50.4	85.9
Specialty stores	1,000	(NA)	(NA)	(NA)	(NA)	10.1	13.4	16.6	22.1	53.2
Convenience stores	1,000	(NA)	(NA)	(NA)	(NA)	2.7	3.1	7.1	7.2	14.0

NA Not available.

Source: Faulkner & Gray, Chicago, IL, *Bank Network News*, vol. 13, No. 13, November 25, 1994, (copyright).

No. 815. Money Stock and Liquid Assets: 1980 to 1994

[In billions of dollars. As of December. Seasonally adjusted averages of daily figures. See Historical Statistics, Colonial Times to 1970, series X 410-417 for similar data]

ITEM	1980	1981	1982	1983	1984	1985	1986	1987	1988	1989	1990	1991	1992	1993	1994
M1, total	408	436	474	521	552	620	724	750	787	794	826	897	1,024	1,129	1,148
Currency [2]	115	123	133	146	156	168	181	197	212	223	247	267	293	322	354
Travelers checks [3]	4	4	4	5	5	6	6	7	7	7	8	8	8	8	8
Demand deposits [4]	261	231	234	238	244	267	302	287	287	279	277	289	339	384	382
Other checkable deposits [4]	28	78	104	132	147	180	236	260	281	285	294	333	385	415	403
M2, total	1,629	1,793	1,953	2,188	2,378	2,576	2,820	2,922	3,084	3,243	3,356	3,458	3,515	3,584	3,613
M1	408	436	474	521	552	620	724	750	787	794	826	897	1,024	1,129	1,148
Nontransaction components in M2 [5]	1,221	1,357	1,479	1,667	1,826	1,956	2,096	2,173	2,297	2,449	2,530	2,561	2,491	2,455	2,465
Overnight repurchase (RP) agreements and Eurodollars [6]	29	38	41	57	63	76	85	87	85	82	78	80	83	97	117
Money market funds, general purpose and broker/dealer	62	151	186	139	168	178	211	224	246	322	358	374	357	360	390
Money market deposit accounts (MMDA) and savings deposits	401	344	400	685	705	815	941	938	927	891	920	1,041	1,184	1,216	1,144
Commercial banks	186	159	190	363	389	457	534	535	542	541	582	666	755	786	752
Thrift institutions [7]	215	185	210	322	316	359	407	403	384	350	338	376	429	430	392
Small time deposits [7]	729	823	851	784	889	886	859	923	1,039	1,154	1,174	1,067	869	785	817
Commercial banks	286	348	380	351	388	386	369	392	452	535	611	602	508	469	502
Thrift institutions	442	475	471	433	501	499	490	530	587	618	563	464	361	316	314
M3, total	1,989	2,236	2,443	2,696	2,995	3,200	3,489	3,676	3,916	4,066	4,123	4,176	4,183	4,243	4,302
M2	1,629	1,793	1,953	2,188	2,378	2,576	2,820	2,922	3,084	3,243	3,356	3,458	3,515	3,584	3,613
Nontransaction components in M3 [5]	359	443	490	509	617	624	668	754	832	823	767	718	668	659	689
Large time deposits [8]	260	303	327	328	417	422	420	467	518	541	481	417	354	333	361
Commercial banks [9]	215	249	264	231	270	271	270	304	344	380	360	333	287	271	297
Thrift institutions	45	54	64	97	147	152	150	163	175	161	121	83	67	62	64
Term RP's and term Eurodollars [6][10]	84	103	115	141	141	139	166	199	229	184	162	133	128	144	159
Money market funds, institution only	15	38	50	41	63	64	85	90	90	107	134	180	200	198	181
L, total	2,326	2,599	2,853	3,158	3,536	3,828	4,129	4,335	4,670	4,896	4,973	4,991	5,061	5,150	5,283
M3	1,989	2,236	2,443	2,696	2,995	3,200	3,489	3,676	3,916	4,066	4,123	4,176	4,183	4,243	4,302
Savings bonds	72	68	68	71	74	79	92	101	109	118	126	138	157	172	180
Short-term Treasury securities [11]	134	150	184	212	261	298	280	253	269	326	333	318	336	334	365
Bankers acceptances	32	40	44	45	45	42	37	45	40	41	36	24	15	15	10
Commercial paper [12]	99	105	114	133	161	207	231	261	335	346	355	335	365	387	426

[1] Currency outside U.S. Treasury, Federal Reserve Banks and the vaults of depository institutions. [2] Outstanding amount of nonbank issuers. [3] At commercial banks and foreign-related institutions. [4] Consists of negotiable order of withdrawal (NOW) and automatic transfer service (ATS) accounts at all depository institutions, credit union share draft balances, and demand deposits at thrift institutions. [5] This sum is seasonally adjusted as a whole. [6] Not seasonally adjusted. [7] Issued in amounts of less than $100,000. Includes retail repurchase agreements. Excludes individual retirement accounts (IRA's) and Keogh accounts. [8] Issued in amounts of $100,000 or more. Excludes those booked at international banking facilities. [9] Excludes those held by money market mutual funds, depository institutions, and foreign banks and official institutions. [10] Excludes those held by depository institutions and money market mutual funds. [11] U.S. Treasury bills and coupons with remaining maturities of less than 12 months held by other than depository institutions, Federal Reserve banks, money market mutual funds, and foreign entities. [12] Excludes commercial paper held by money market mutual funds.

Source: Board of Governors of the Federal Reserve System, Federal Reserve Bulletin, monthly, and Money Stock, Liquid Assets, and Debt Measures, Federal Reserve Statistical Release H.6, weekly.

No. 816. Bank Debits and Deposit Turnover: 1980 to 1993

[Debits in trillions of dollars; turnover as ratio of debits to deposits. Annual averages of monthly data]

ITEM	1980	1983	1984	1985	1986	1987	1988	1989	1990	1991	1992	1993
Debits to—												
Demand deposits, all banks [1]	63.1	112.3	131.6	156.3	188.8	214.9	219.2	256.2	277.6	277.8	313.1	334.2
Major New York City banks	25.3	47.6	57.3	70.7	91.6	110.4	115.5	129.7	131.9	137.3	165.4	171.2
Other banks	37.9	64.7	74.2	85.6	97.1	104.5	103.7	126.5	145.7	140.4	147.7	163.0
Other checkable deposits [2] .	0.2	1.4	1.6	1.8	2.2	2.2	2.5	2.9	3.4	3.6	3.8	3.5
Money market deposit accounts	(NA)	0.6	0.9	1.2	1.6	1.9	2.3	2.7	2.9	[3]3.2	[3]3.3	[3]3.5
Savings deposits	(NA)	0.5	0.4	0.4	0.4	0.5	0.5	0.6	0.6	([3])	([3])	([3])
Deposit turnover:												
Demand deposits, all banks [1]	203	386	441	501	557	608	620	734	799	804	826	785
Major New York City banks	816	1,522	1,840	2,200	2,500	2,670	2,904	3,435	3,831	4,263	4,795	4,198
Other banks	135	249	278	306	322	335	331	406	466	448	429	424

NA Not available.   [1] Represents accounts of individuals, partnerships, and corporations and of States and political subdivisions at insured commercial banks.   [2] Accounts authorized for negotiable orders of withdrawal (NOW) and accounts authorized for automatic transfer to demand deposits (ATS).   [3] Beginning 1991, savings deposits included in money market deposit accounts.

Source: Board of Governors of the Federal Reserve System, *Federal Reserve Bulletin*, monthly, and *Annual Statistical Digest*.

No. 817. Selected Time Deposits and Other Accounts at Insured Commercial Banks— Deposits and Interest Rates: 1985 to 1994

[As of **December**. Estimates based on data collected from a sample of about 500 banks]

TYPE OF DEPOSIT	AMOUNT OUTSTANDING (bil. dol.)						ANNUAL EFFECTIVE YIELD (percent)					
	1985	1990	1991	1992	1993	1994	1985	1990	1991	1992	1993	1994
NOW accounts [1]	45.3	209.9	244.6	286.5	305.2	303.7	6.14	4.89	3.76	2.33	1.86	1.96
Savings deposits	330.0	570.3	652.1	738.3	766.4	734.5	6.91	5.84	4.30	2.88	2.46	2.91
Interest-bearing time deposits: [2]												
7-91 day	25.7	50.2	47.1	38.5	29.5	32.4	7.34	6.94	4.18	2.90	2.65	3.81
92-182 day.	148.5	168.0	158.6	127.8	110.1	95.9	7.48	7.19	4.41	3.16	2.91	4.44
183 day-1 year	67.1	221.0	209.7	163.1	146.6	161.8	7.77	7.33	4.59	3.37	3.13	5.12
1-2½ year	81.0	150.2	171.7	153.0	141.2	162.5	8.23	7.42	4.95	3.88	3.55	5.74
2½ year or more.	117.2	139.4	158.1	169.7	181.5	190.9	8.73	7.53	5.52	4.77	4.29	6.30
All IRA and Keogh Plan deposits .	59.6	131.0	147.3	147.4	144.0	143.4	(NA)	(NA)	(NA)	(NA)	(NA)	(NA)

NA Not available.   [1] Negotiable order of withdrawal account containing an agreement between depositor and depository such that some or all funds deposited are eligible to earn more than 5.25 percent. As of January 1, 1986, interest rate ceilings were removed from all NOW accounts. Beginning with the December 1990 data the NOW accounts category includes all NOW accounts, including those accounts which were subject to a 5.25 percent regulatory interest rate restriction prior to January 1, 1986. Estimates for NOW accounts beginning in December 1990 are based on reports of deposits.   [2] All interest-bearing time deposits and open account time deposits with balances of less than $100,000, including those held in IRA's and Keogh Plan deposits.

Source: Board of Governors of the Federal Reserve System, *Money Stock, Liquid Assets, and Debt Measures, Federal Reserve Statistical Release H.6*, Special Supplementary Table, Monthly Survey of Selected Deposits, monthly.

No. 818. Commercial Paper Outstanding, by Type of Company: 1980 to 1994

[**In billions of dollars**. As of **December 31**. Seasonally adjusted. Commercial paper is an unsecured promissory note having a fixed maturity of no more than 270 days]

TYPE OF COMPANY	1980	1985	1986	1987	1988	1989	1990	1991	1992	1993	1994
All issuers	**124.4**	**298.8**	**330.0**	**359.0**	**458.5**	**525.8**	**562.7**	**528.8**	**545.6**	**555.1**	**601.9**
Financial companies [1]	87.7	213.8	252.9	277.1	354.7	394.6	414.7	395.5	398.1	399.3	436.4
Dealer-placed paper [2]	19.9	78.4	101.1	102.7	159.8	183.6	214.7	213.0	226.5	218.9	225.4
Directly-placed paper [3]	67.8	135.3	151.8	174.3	194.9	210.9	200.0	182.5	171.6	180.4	211.0
Nonfinancial companies [4]	36.7	85.0	77.1	81.9	103.8	131.3	147.9	133.4	147.6	155.7	165.5

[1] Institutions engaged primarily in activities such as, but not limited to, commercial, savings, and mortgage banking; sales, personal, and mortgage financing; factoring, finance leasing, and other business lending; insurance underwriting; and other investment activities.   [2] Includes all financial company paper sold by dealers in the open market.   [3] As reported by financial companies that place their paper directly with investors.   [4] Includes public utilities and firms engaged primarily in such activities as communications, construction, manufacturing, mining, wholesale and retail trade, transportation, and services.

No. 819. Federal Reserve Bank of New York—Discount Rates: 1980 to 1995

[**Percent per year**. Rates for short-term adjustment credit. For rates applicable to other types of discount window credit, see source. See also *Historical Statistics, Colonial Times to 1970*, series X 454-455]

EFFECTIVE DATE	Rate	EFFECTIVE DATE	Rate	EFFECTIVE DATE	Rate	EFFECTIVE DATE	Rate
1980: [1] Sept. 26	11	Aug. 27	10	April 21	6½	Sept. 13	5
Nov. 17	12	Oct. 12	9½	July 11	6	Nov. 6	4½
Dec. 5	13	Nov. 22	9	Aug. 21	5½	Dec. 20	3½
1981: [1] May 5	14	Dec. 15	8½	**1987:** Sept. 4	6	**1992:** July 2	3
Nov. 2	13	**1984:** April 9	9	**1988:** Aug. 9	6½	**1994:** May 17	3½
Dec. 4	12	Nov. 21	8½	**1989:** Feb. 24	7	Aug. 16	4
1982: July 20	11½	Dec. 24	8	**1990:** Dec. 19	6½	Nov. 15	4¾
Aug. 2	11	**1985:** May 20	7½	**1991:** Feb. 1	6	**1995:** Feb. 1	5¼
Aug. 16	10½	**1986:** March 7	7	April 30	5½	In effect, **Apr. 28, '95** .	5¼

[1] The discount rates for 1980 and 1981 do not include the surcharge applied to frequent borrowings by large institutions. The surcharge reached 3 percent in 1980 and 4 percent in 1981. Surcharge was eliminated in Nov. 1981.

Source of tables 818 and 819: Board of Governors of the Federal Reserve System, *Federal Reserve Bulletin*, monthly, and *Annual Statistical Digest*.

No. 820. Money Market Interest Rates and Mortgage Rates: 1970 to 1994

[Percent per year. Annual averages of monthly data, except as indicated. See also *Historical Statistics, Colonial Times to 1970,* series X 444-453]

TYPE	1970	1980	1981	1982	1983	1984	1985	1986	1987	1988	1989	1990	1991	1992	1993	1994
Federal funds, effective rate [1][2]	7.17	13.35	16.39	12.24	9.09	10.23	8.10	6.80	6.66	7.57	9.21	8.10	5.69	3.52	3.02	4.21
Commercial paper, 3-month [1][2]	(NA)	12.61	15.34	11.90	8.88	10.12	7.95	6.49	6.82	7.66	8.99	8.06	5.87	3.75	3.22	4.66
Commercial paper, 6-month [1][2]	7.71	12.24	14.77	11.89	8.90	10.18	8.00	6.39	6.85	7.68	8.80	7.95	5.85	3.80	3.30	4.93
Prime rate charged by banks	7.91	15.26	18.87	14.85	10.79	12.04	9.93	8.33	8.21	9.32	10.87	10.01	8.46	6.25	6.00	7.15
Eurodollar deposits, 3-month	8.52	14.00	16.79	13.12	9.57	10.75	8.27	6.70	7.07	7.85	9.16	8.16	5.86	3.70	3.18	4.63
Finance paper, 3-month [2][3]	7.18	11.45	14.09	11.24	8.71	9.75	7.77	6.38	6.54	7.38	8.72	7.87	5.71	3.65	3.16	4.53
Finance paper, 6-month [2][3]	7.20	11.25	13.74	11.20	8.70	9.67	7.74	6.31	6.37	7.14	8.16	7.53	5.60	3.63	3.15	4.56
Bankers acceptances, 3-month [2][4]	7.23	12.67	15.34	11.89	8.91	10.17	7.91	6.38	6.75	7.56	8.87	7.93	5.70	3.62	3.13	4.56
Bankers acceptances, 6-month [2][4]	(NA)	12.20	14.68	11.83	8.92	10.21	7.95	6.28	6.78	7.60	8.67	7.80	5.67	3.67	3.21	4.83
Large negotiable CD's, 3-month, secondary market [5]	7.56	13.07	15.91	12.27	9.07	10.37	8.05	6.52	6.86	7.73	9.09	8.15	5.83	3.68	3.17	4.63
Taxable money market funds [5]	(NA)	12.68	16.82	12.23	8.58	10.04	7.71	6.26	6.12	7.11	8.87	7.82	5.71	3.37	2.70	3.75
Tax-exempt money market funds [5]	(NA)	(NA)	(NA)	(NA)	(NA)	(NA)	(NA)	(NA)	(NA)	(NA)	(NA)	(NA)	(NA)	2.59	1.97	2.38
Certificates of deposit (CD's): [6]																
6-month	(NA)	(NA)	(NA)	(NA)	(NA)	9.99	7.83	6.51	6.47	7.18	8.34	7.35	5.67	3.46	2.84	3.37
1-year	(NA)	(NA)	(NA)	(NA)	(NA)	10.37	8.29	6.75	6.77	7.47	8.41	7.42	5.88	3.72	3.12	3.94
2½-year	(NA)	(NA)	(NA)	(NA)	10.06	10.82	9.00	7.13	7.16	7.77	8.33	7.52	6.29	4.47	3.73	4.49
5-year	(NA)	(NA)	(NA)	(NA)	(NA)	11.25	9.66	7.60	7.66	8.11	8.30	7.71	6.83	5.62	4.88	5.30
U.S. Government securities:																
Secondary market:																
3-month Treasury bill	6.39	11.39	14.04	10.60	8.62	9.54	7.47	5.97	5.78	6.67	8.11	7.50	5.38	3.43	3.00	4.25
6-month Treasury bill	6.48	11.32	13.81	11.06	8.74	9.78	7.65	6.02	6.03	6.91	8.03	7.46	5.44	3.54	3.12	4.64
1-year Treasury bill	6.48	10.85	13.16	11.07	8.80	9.94	7.81	6.07	6.33	7.13	7.92	7.35	5.52	3.71	3.29	5.02
Auction average: [8]																
3-month Treasury bill	6.46	11.51	14.03	10.69	8.63	9.35	7.47	5.98	5.82	6.68	8.12	7.51	5.42	3.45	3.02	4.29
6-month Treasury bill	6.56	11.37	13.78	11.08	8.75	9.77	7.64	6.03	6.05	6.92	8.04	7.47	5.49	3.57	3.14	4.66
1-year Treasury bill	6.39	10.75	13.16	11.10	8.86	9.91	7.76	6.07	6.33	7.17	7.91	7.36	5.54	3.75	3.33	4.98
Home mortgages: [9]																
HUD series:																
FHA insured, secondary market [10]	9.02	13.44	16.31	15.30	13.11	13.81	12.24	9.91	10.16	10.49	10.24	10.17	9.25	8.46	7.46	8.68
Conventional, new-home [11][12]	8.52	13.95	16.52	15.79	13.43	13.80	12.28	10.07	10.17	10.30	10.21	10.08	9.20	8.43	7.37	8.58
Conventional, existing-home [11]	8.56	13.95	16.55	15.82	13.44	13.81	12.29	10.09	10.17	10.31	10.22	10.08	9.20	8.43	7.36	8.59

NA Not available. [1] Based on daily offering rates of dealers. [2] Yields are quoted on a bank-discount basis, rather than an investment yield basis (which would give a higher figure). [3] Placed directly; averages of daily offering rates quoted by finance companies. [4] Based on representative closing yields. From Jan. 1, 1981, rates of top-rated banks only. [5] 12 month return for period ending December 31. Source: IBC/Donoghue, Inc., Ashland, MA, *IBC's Money Market Insight,* monthly (copyright). [6] Annual averages. Source: Financial Rates, Inc., North Palm Beach, FL, *Bank Rate Monitor,* weekly (copyright). [7] Averages based on daily closing bid yields in secondary market, bank discount basis. [8] Averages computed on an issue-date basis; bank discount basis. [9] HUD=Housing and Urban Development. [10] Averages based on quotations for 1 day each month as compiled by FHA. [11] Primary market. [12] Average contract rates on new commitments.

Source: Except as noted, Board of Governors of the Federal Reserve System, *Federal Reserve Bulletin,* monthly, and *Annual Statistical Digest.*

No. 821. Security Prices: 1980 to 1994

[Annual averages of daily figures, except as noted. See also *Historical Statistics, Colonial Times to 1970*, series X 492-498]

CLASS OR ITEM	1980	1981	1982	1983	1984	1985	1986	1987	1988	1989	1990	1991	1992	1993	1994
BOND PRICES (dollars per $100 bond)															
Dow Jones and Co., Inc.: [1][2]															
Yearly high [3]	76.6	65.8	71.5	77.8	72.9	83.7	93.7	95.5	91.3	94.2	93.0	98.9	103.9	109.8	105.6
Yearly low	61.0	55.0	55.7	69.4	64.8	72.3	83.7	81.3	86.9	87.4	88.4	91.3	98.4	103.5	93.6
STOCK PRICES															
Standard & Poor's common index (500 stocks) (1941-43=10) [3]	118.7	128.0	119.7	160.4	160.5	186.8	236.3	268.8	265.9	323.1	335.0	376.2	415.7	451.6	460.4
Industrial	134.5	144.2	133.6	180.5	181.3	207.8	262.2	330.5	306.5	392.9	391.4	445.8	489.8	517.4	540.6
N.Y. Stock Exchange common stock index (Dec. 31, 1965=50):															
Composite	68.1	74.0	68.9	92.6	92.5	108.1	136.0	161.8	150.0	180.1	183.7	206.4	229.0	249.7	254.2
Yearly high [4]	81.0	79.1	82.4	99.6	98.1	121.9	145.8	188.0	159.4	199.3	201.1	229.4	242.1	260.7	267.7
Yearly low [4]	55.3	65.0	58.8	79.8	85.1	94.6	117.8	125.9	136.7	155.0	162.2	171.0	217.9	236.2	243.1
Industrial	78.6	85.4	78.2	107.5	108.0	123.8	155.9	195.3	180.8	228.0	226.1	258.2	284.3	300.1	315.3
Transportation	60.5	72.6	60.4	89.4	85.6	104.1	119.9	140.5	134.1	174.9	158.8	174.0	201.0	242.7	247.2
Utility	37.3	38.9	39.8	47.0	46.4	56.8	71.4	74.3	72.2	94.3	90.7	92.6	99.5	114.6	105.0
Finance	64.3	73.5	72.0	95.3	89.3	114.2	147.2	146.5	127.4	162.0	133.2	150.8	179.3	216.6	209.8
American Stock Exchange Market Value Index (Aug. 31, 1973=50)	150.6	171.8	141.3	216.5	208.0	229.1	264.4	316.4	295.1	356.7	338.3	360.3	391.3	438.8	449.5
NASDAQ composite index [5]	202.3	195.9	232.4	278.6	247.4	324.9	348.8	330.5	381.4	454.8	373.9	586.3	677.0	776.8	752.0
Industrial	261.4	229.3	273.6	323.7	260.7	330.2	349.3	338.9	379.0	448.0	406.1	669.0	724.9	805.8	753.8
Insurance	166.8	194.3	226.4	257.6	283.1	382.1	404.1	351.1	429.1	546.0	451.8	601.1	803.9	920.6	925.9
Banks	118.4	143.1	156.4	203.8	229.8	349.4	412.5	390.7	435.3	391.0	254.9	350.6	532.9	689.4	697.1
Dow Jones and Co., Inc.: [1]															
Composite [6]	328.2	364.6	345.4	472.2	463.1	541.6	702.5	849.5	772.2	966.9	965.2	1,048.3	1,210.3	1,304.1	1,316.4
Industrial (30 stocks)	891.4	932.9	884.4	1,190.3	1,178.5	1,328.2	1,792.8	2,276.0	2,060.8	2,508.9	2,678.9	2,929.3	3,284.3	3,524.7	3,794.2
Transportation (20 stocks)	307.2	398.6	359.8	544.6	513.8	645.1	785.4	929.2	863.8	1,194.3	1,040.2	1,170.2	1,349.6	1,606.5	1,608.1
Utility (15 stocks)	110.4	108.6	112.0	130.0	131.8	157.6	195.2	202.2	179.7	205.7	211.5	210.3	214.4	239.0	191.4
Wilshire 5000 equity index (Dec. 31, 1980=1404.596) [7]	1,220.7	1,343.7	1,233.7	1,691.5	1,644.6	1,923.8	2,418.8	2,843.7	2,636.9	3,172.6	3,187.3	3,604.6	4,041.1	4,468.0	4,571.3

[1] Source: Dow Jones and Co., Inc., New York, NY.   [2] A 20-bond average consisting of 10 utility bonds and 10 industrial bonds.   [3] The index includes 400 industrial stocks, 20 transportation, 40 public utility, and 40 financial stocks.   [4] Source: New York Stock Exchange, Inc., New York, NY. *Fact Book*, annual.   [5] Source: National Association of Securities Dealers, Washington, DC. *Fact Book*, annual. December monthly closing values.   [6] Based on stocks listed on the New York Stock Exchange and NASDAQ/NMS.   [7] Represents return on the market value of all common equity securities for which daily pricing is available. Source: Wilshire Associates, Santa Monica, CA, releases.

Source: Except as noted, Board of Governors of the Federal Reserve System, *Federal Reserve Bulletin*, monthly; *Annual Statistical Digest*; and unpublished data.

No. 822. Dow-Jones U.S. Equity Market Index, by Industry: 1992 to 1994

INDUSTRY	1992	1993	1994	INDUSTRY	1992	1993	1994
U.S. Equity Market Index, total .	413.29	442.19	433.07	Energy.	264.73	290.55	286.70
				Financial services	410.85	436.98	408.25
Basic materials	401.09	443.38	456.55	Industrial	390.48	432.52	399.78
Consumer, cyclical.	527.62	596.43	532.55	Technology.	320.10	361.45	406.48
Consumer, noncyclical	734.03	684.89	740.25	Utilities	286.74	316.02	272.82

Source: Dow Jones & Company, Inc., New York, NY, *Wall Street Journal*, January 3, 1995, (copyright).

No. 823. Bond and Stock Dividend Yields: 1980 to 1994

[**Percent per year**. Annual averages of daily figures, except as indicated. See also *Historical Statistics, Colonial Times to 1970*, series X 474-491]

TYPE	1980	1985	1986	1987	1988	1989	1990	1991	1992	1993	1994
U.S. Treasury, constant maturities: [1] [2]											
3-year	11.51	9.64	7.06	7.68	8.26	8.55	8.26	6.82	5.30	4.44	6.27
5-year	11.45	10.12	7.30	7.94	8.47	8.50	8.37	7.37	6.19	5.14	6.69
7-year	11.40	10.50	7.54	8.23	8.71	8.52	8.52	7.68	6.63	5.54	6.91
10-year	11.43	10.62	7.67	8.39	8.85	8.49	8.55	7.86	7.01	5.87	7.69
20-year	(NA)	(NA)	(NA)	(NA)	(NA)	(NA)	(NA)	(NA)	(NA)	6.29	7.47
30-year	11.27	10.79	7.78	8.59	8.96	8.45	8.61	8.14	7.67	6.59	7.37
U.S. Govt., long-term bonds [2] [3] . . .	10.81	10.75	8.14	8.64	8.98	8.58	8.74	8.16	7.52	6.45	7.41
State and local govt. bonds, Aaa [4] . . .	7.86	8.60	6.95	7.12	7.36	7.00	6.96	6.56	6.09	5.38	5.77
State and local govt. bonds, Baa [4] . . .	9.02	9.58	7.75	8.17	7.84	7.40	7.29	6.99	6.48	5.82	6.17
Municipal (Bond Buyer, 20 bonds) . . .	8.59	9.11	7.32	7.63	7.68	7.23	7.27	6.92	6.44	5.60	6.18
Corporate Aaa seasoned [4]	11.94	11.37	9.02	9.38	9.71	9.26	9.32	8.77	8.14	7.22	7.97
Corporate Baa seasoned [4]	13.67	12.72	10.39	10.58	10.83	10.18	10.36	9.80	8.98	7.93	8.63
Corporate (Moody's) [4] [5]	12.75	12.05	9.71	9.91	10.18	9.66	9.77	9.23	8.55	7.54	8.26
Industrials (49 bonds) [6]	12.35	11.80	9.96	9.83	9.91	9.66	9.77	9.25	8.52	7.51	8.21
Public utilities (51 bonds) [7]	13.15	12.29	9.46	9.98	10.45	9.66	9.76	9.21	8.57	7.56	8.30
Stocks (Standard & Poor's):											
Common: Composite (500 stocks) .	5.26	4.25	3.48	3.08	3.64	3.45	3.61	3.24	2.99	2.78	2.82

NA Not available.   [1] Yields on the more actively traded issues adjusted to constant maturities by the U.S. Treasury.   [2] Yields are based on closing bid prices quoted by at least five dealers.   [3] Averages (to maturity or call) for all outstanding bonds neither due nor callable in less than 10 years, including several very low yielding "flower" bonds.   [4] Source: Moody's Investors Service, New York, NY.   [5] For 1980-88 includes railroad bonds which were discontinued as part of composite in 1989.   [6] Covers 40 bonds for 1980, 38 bonds for 1985 and 1986, and 37 bonds for 1987 and 1988.   [7] Covers 40 bonds for period 1980-88.

Source: Except as noted, Board of Governors of the Federal Reserve System, *Federal Reserve Bulletin*, monthly.

No. 824. New Security Issues of Corporations, by Type of Offering and Industry Group: 1985 to 1993

[**In billions of dollars**. Represents gross proceeds of issues maturing in more than one year. Figures are the principal amount or the number of units multiplied by the offering price. Excludes secondary offerings, employee stock plans, investment companies other than closed-end, intracorporate transactions, equities sold abroad, and Yankee bonds. Stock data include ownership securities issued by limited partnerships]

TYPE OF OFFERING AND INDUSTRY GROUP	1985	1990	1991	1992	1993	TYPE OF OFFERING AND INDUSTRY GROUP	1985	1990	1991	1992	1993
Total	**239.2**	**339.1**	**465.2**	**559.8**	**755.0**	Stocks, total	35.5	40.2	75.4	88.3	113.5
Bonds, total	203.7	298.9	389.8	471.5	641.5	Preferred	6.5	4.0	17.1	21.3	18.9
Public, domestic. .	119.7	188.8	286.9	378.1	486.9	Common.	29.0	19.4	48.2	57.1	82.7
Private placement,						Private place-					
domestic	46.2	87.0	74.9	65.9	116.2	ment	(NA)	16.7	10.1	9.9	11.9
Sold abroad	37.8	23.1	28.0	27.6	38.4						
Manufacturing . . .	63.6	51.8	86.6	82.1	88.0	Manufacturing . . .	5.7	5.6	24.1	22.7	22.3
Commercial and						Commercial and					
miscellaneous . .	17.2	40.7	36.7	43.1	60.3	miscellaneous . .	9.1	10.2	19.4	20.2	25.8
Transportation . . .	6.0	12.8	13.6	10.0	10.8	Transportation . . .	1.5	0.4	2.4	2.6	2.2
Public utility	13.6	17.6	23.9	48.1	56.3	Public utility	2.0	0.4	3.5	6.5	7.1
Communication . .	10.9	6.7	9.4	15.4	31.9	Communication . .	1.0	3.8	0.5	2.4	3.4
Real estate and						Real estate and					
financial	92.3	169.3	219.6	272.9	394.2	financial	16.2	19.7	25.5	33.9	52.0

NA Not available.

Source: Board of Governors of the Federal Reserve System, *Federal Reserve Bulletin*, monthly, and *Annual Statistical Digest*.

No. 825. Equities, Corporate Bonds, and Tax-Exempt Securities—Holdings and Net Purchases, by Type of Investor: 1980 to 1994

[In billions of dollars. Holdings as of **Dec. 31.** Minus sign (-) indicates net sales]

TYPE OF INVESTOR	HOLDINGS					NET PURCHASES				
	1980	1990	1992	1993	1994	1980	1990	1992	1993	1994
EQUITIES [1]										
Total [2]	**1,535**	**3,530**	**5,463**	**6,186**	**6,049**	**14.5**	**–45.6**	**84.1**	**120.1**	**31.6**
Household sector [3]	934	1,717	2,810	3,088	2,913	–4.3	–21.7	43.8	–33.1	–89.0
Rest of the world [4]	65	222	300	340	341	4.2	–16.0	–5.8	20.5	0.9
Life insurance companies	46	98	122	146	159	0.4	–5.7	2.7	7.8	8.2
Other insurance companies.	32	80	97	103	105	3.1	–7.0	–0.4	0.8	5.3
Private pension funds	223	658	962	1,079	1,047	16.4	–14.4	–2.6	–13.6	–26.7
State and local retirement funds. . .	44	296	449	507	520	5.3	12.3	16.7	48.0	30.9
Mutual funds	42	233	452	669	738	–1.8	14.4	67.2	128.9	122.7
Bank personal trusts	135	190	217	181	156	–7.2	0.5	–37.0	–55.2	–20.4
CORPORATE & FOREIGN BONDS										
Total [2]	**508**	**1,696**	**2,023**	**2,277**	**2,417**	**36.2**	**114.7**	**160.4**	**252.9**	**142.4**
Household sector [3]	31	95	107	142	198	–14.5	38.0	–4.8	26.2	58.5
Rest of the world [4]	37	217	252	273	311	9.2	5.3	18.1	30.0	38.2
Commercial banking	11	89	95	98	104	1.1	4.6	–1.6	3.5	6.0
Life insurance companies	179	567	654	719	766	8.7	55.8	58.9	65.5	46.7
Other insurance companies.	24	89	98	103	105	-	9.9	0.7	5.3	1.6
Private pension funds	78	235	292	309	295	14.0	9.3	16.4	17.4	–14.9
State and local retirement funds. . .	92	169	223	238	258	9.2	2.8	27.8	14.8	19.9
Mutual funds	8	88	120	176	173	1.3	13.6	19.8	56.1	–2.9
TAX-EXEMPT SECURITIES [5]										
Total [2]	**365**	**1,040**	**1,140**	**1,218**	**1,203**	**23.9**	**48.7**	**31.1**	**78.1**	**–15.1**
Household sector [3]	76	448	449	433	403	2.4	17.7	–34.8	–15.8	–29.6
Commercial banking	149	117	98	99	98	13.2	–16.4	–5.7	1.7	–1.5
Other insurance companies.	81	137	134	146	153	7.7	2.2	7.5	11.8	7.3
Mutual funds	4	109	173	218	213	0.4	15.6	36.3	44.6	–5.4
Money market mutual funds	2	84	95	103	111	1.6	14.3	5.0	8.3	7.5
Bank personal trusts	26	81	96	109	120	–1.6	7.7	6.1	12.9	11.3

- Represents or rounds to zero.   [1] Excludes mutual fund shares.   [2] Includes other types not shown separately.   [3] Includes nonprofit organizations.   [4] Holdings of U.S. issues by foreign residents.   [5] Includes small amounts of taxable securities.

Source: Board of Governors of the Federal Reserve System, *Flow of Funds Accounts*, March 1995 quarterly diskettes. Data are also published in the quarterly Z.1 release.

No. 826. United States Purchases and Sales of Foreign Stocks and Bonds, 1980 to 1994, and by Selected Country, 1994

[**In billions of dollars.** See headnote, table 827. Minus sign (-) indicates net sales by U.S. investors or a net inflow of capital into the United States]

YEAR AND COUNTRY	NET PURCHASES			TOTAL TRANSACTIONS [1]			PURCHASES		SALES	
	Total	Bonds	Stocks	Total	Bonds	Stocks	Bonds	Stocks	Bonds	Stocks
1980.	3.1	1.0	2.1	53.1	35.2	17.9	18.1	10.0	17.1	7.9
1985.	7.9	4.0	3.9	212.1	166.4	45.7	85.2	24.8	81.2	20.9
1990.	31.2	21.9	9.2	906.7	652.2	254.5	337.1	131.9	315.1	122.6
1991.	46.8	14.8	32.0	948.6	675.5	273.2	345.1	152.6	330.3	120.6
1992.	47.9	15.6	32.3	1,375.1	1,042.8	332.4	529.2	182.3	513.6	150.1
1993.	128.6	60.8	67.8	2,289.7	1,729.7	559.9	895.2	313.9	834.5	246.1
1994, total [2]	**67.3**	**20.3**	**47.1**	**2,644.6**	**1,829.4**	**815.1**	**924.9**	**431.1**	**904.6**	**384.0**
United Kingdom	–17.1	–23.4	6.3	1,242.1	963.4	278.6	470.0	142.5	493.4	136.2
Canada.	7.3	4.9	2.4	273.4	237.9	35.5	121.4	19.0	116.5	16.5
Japan	17.5	2.7	14.7	184.6	74.9	109.8	38.8	62.3	36.1	47.5
France	4.0	1.9	2.1	106.0	82.6	23.4	42.3	12.8	40.3	10.7
Hong Kong	–0.5	–2.9	2.4	83.9	34.6	49.4	15.8	25.9	18.8	23.5
Mexico	4.1	2.7	1.4	58.8	20.3	38.5	11.5	20.0	8.8	18.5
Germany	3.5	2.1	1.4	58.0	24.3	33.7	13.2	17.6	11.1	16.1

[1] Total purchases plus total sales.   [2] Includes other countries, not shown separately.

Source: U.S. Dept. of Treasury, *Treasury Bulletin*, quarterly.

No. 827. Foreign Purchases and Sales of U.S. Securities, by Type of Security, 1980 to 1994, and by Selected Country, 1994

[In billions of dollars. Covers transactions in all types of long-term domestic securities by foreigners as reported by banks, brokers, and other entities in the United States (except nonmarketable U.S. Treasury notes, foreign series; and nonmarketable U.S. Treasury bonds and notes, foreign currency series). Data cover new issues of securities, transactions in outstanding issues, and redemptions of securities. Includes transactions executed in the United States for the account of foreigners, and transactions executed abroad for the account of reporting institutions and their domestic customers. Data by country show the country of domicile of the foreign buyers and sellers of the securities; in the case of outstanding issues, this may differ from the country of the original issuer. The term "foreigner" covers all institutions and individuals domiciled outside the United States, including U.S. citizens domiciled abroad, and the foreign branches, subsidiaries and other affiliates abroad of U.S. banks and businesses; the central governments, central banks, and other official institutions of foreign countries; and international and regional organizations. "Foreigner" also includes persons in the United States to the extent that they are known by reporting institutions to be acting on behalf of foreigners. Minus sign (-) indicates net sales by foreigners or a net outflow of capital from the United States]

YEAR AND COUNTRY	NET PURCHASES					TOTAL TRANSACTIONS [4]				
	Total	Treasury bonds and notes [1]	U.S. Govt. corporations [2] bonds	Corporate bonds [3]	Corporate stocks	Total	Treasury bonds and notes [1]	U.S. Govt. corporations [2] bonds	Corporate bonds [3]	Corporate stocks
1980	15.8	4.9	2.6	2.9	5.4	198	97	17	9	75
1985	78.3	29.2	4.3	39.8	4.9	1,256	968	46	84	159
1988	74.8	48.8	6.7	21.2	-2.0	3,581	3,072	56	89	364
1989	96.5	54.2	15.1	17.3	9.9	4,767	4,140	88	121	418
1990	18.7	17.9	6.3	9.7	-15.1	4,204	3,620	104	117	362
1991	58.1	19.9	10.2	16.9	11.1	4,706	4,016	124	155	411
1992	73.2	39.3	18.3	20.8	-5.1	5,282	4,444	204	187	448
1993	111.6	24.2	36.1	29.8	21.5	6,317	5,197	263	240	617
1994, total [5]	141.1	77.6	22.3	38.5	2.6	6,542	5,311	300	222	708
United Kingdom	55.5	22.7	6.4	25.8	0.6	2,526	2,140	86	104	197
Japan	36.3	29.6	3.3	2.1	1.3	842	760	31	14	37
British West Indies	-9.8	-12.9	-0.7	2.5	1.3	430	292	60	15	63
Canada	5.1	3.2	2.0	1.1	-1.1	361	264	5	14	78
Netherlands Antilles	8.2	10.5	(Z)	0.8	-3.0	344	267	14	8	55
Bermuda	-1.9	-4.4	1.1	0.8	0.7	230	157	27	11	35

Z Less than $50 million. [1] Marketable bonds and notes. [2] Includes federally-sponsored agencies. [3] Includes transactions in directly placed issues abroad by U.S. corporations and issues of States and municipalities. [4] Total purchases plus total sales. [5] Includes other countries, not shown separately.

Source: U.S. Dept. of Treasury, *Treasury Bulletin*, quarterly.

No. 828. Sales of Stocks and Options on Registered Exchanges: 1980 to 1993

[Excludes over-the-counter trading. See also *Historical Statistics, Colonial Times to 1970*, series X 517-530]

EXCHANGE	Unit	1980	1985	1986	1987	1988	1989	1990	1991	1992	1993
Market value of all sales, all exchanges [1][2]	Bil. dol	522	1,260	1,868	2,492	1,702	2,010	1,752	1,903	2,149	2,734
New York	Bil. dol	398	1,024	1,453	1,987	1,380	1,581	1,394	1,534	1,759	2,278
American	Bil. dol	47	38	63	102	59	80	65	67	69	83
Chicago [3]	Bil. dol	21	79	102	122	87	101	74	77	87	107
CBOE [4]	Bil. dol	28	38	56	124	64	88	81	74	63	65
Pacific	Bil. dol	13	40	55	71	49	64	53	63	65	70
Philadelphia	Bil. dol	11	23	35	48	34	50	41	39	49	55
STOCKS [5]											
Shares sold, all exchanges [2]	Million	15,488	37,046	48,338	63,771	52,533	54,239	53,338	58,025	65,463	82,808
New York	Million	12,390	30,222	39,258	53,038	44,018	44,140	43,829	47,674	53,344	68,732
American	Million	1,659	2,115	2,999	3,496	2,576	3,248	3,125	3,103	3,631	4,470
Chicago [3]	Million	598	2,274	2,784	3,329	2,771	2,960	2,511	2,715	3,035	3,792
Pacific	Million	435	1,352	1,750	2,034	1,576	1,791	1,682	2,068	2,087	2,330
Market value, all exchanges [2]	Bil. dol	476	1,200	1,705	2,284	1,587	1,845	1,612	1,776	2,032	2,610
New York	Bil. dol	398	1,023	1,450	1,983	1,378	1,577	1,390	1,532	1,758	2,276
American	Bil. dol	35	26	43	53	31	43	36	40	42	54
Chicago [3]	Bil. dol	21	79	102	122	87	101	74	77	87	107
Pacific	Bil. dol	11	37	51	57	41	52	45	63	58	62
OPTIONS [6]											
Contracts traded, all exchanges [2]	Million	97	233	289	305	196	227	210	199	202	233
CBOE [4]	Million	53	149	180	182	112	127	130	122	122	141
American	Million	29	49	65	71	45	50	41	39	42	48
Market value of contracts traded, all exchanges [2]	Bil. dol	45.8	59.1	87.9	118.9	62.6	76.8	79.0	76.1	72.2	75.2
CBOE [4]	Bil. dol	27.9	38.4	55.9	76.9	39.7	47.3	55.4	50.7	44.5	45.5
American	Bil. dol	12.5	11.6	19.0	25.7	12.4	15.1	12.8	14.0	14.1	14.9
Options exercised:											
Number of contracts	Million	4.9	10.5	14.5	17.0	11.4	15.6	12.1	10.8	9.9	10.0
Value	Bil. dol	20.4	49.2	72.8	85.9	51.5	85.2	55.8	49.2	43.9	48.4

[1] Includes market value of stocks, rights, warrants, and options trading beginning 1986. [2] Includes other registered exchanges, not shown separately. [3] The Chicago Stock Exchange, Inc. was formerly the Midwest Stock Exchange. [4] Chicago Board Options Exchange, Inc. [5] Includes voting trust certificates, American Depository Receipts, and certificate of deposit for stocks. [6] Data for 1980 exclude nonequity options.

Source: U.S. Securities and Exchange Commission, *SEC Monthly Statistical Review* (discontinued Feb. 1989); and unpublished data.

No. 829. Volume of Trading on New York Stock Exchange: 1980 to 1994

[**Round lot**: A unit of trading or a multiple thereof. On the NYSE the unit of trading is generally 100 shares in stocks. For some inactive stocks, the unit of trading is 10 shares. **Odd lot**: An amount of stock less than the established 100-share unit or 10-share unit of trading]

ITEM	Unit	1980	1985	1987	1988	1989	1990	1991	1992	1993	1994
Shares traded	Million .	**11,562**	**27,774**	**48,143**	**41,118**	**42,022**	**39,947**	**45,599**	**51,826**	**67,461**	**74,003**
Round lots	Million . .	11,352	27,511	47,801	40,850	41,699	39,665	45,266	51,376	66,923	73,420
Average daily shares	Million . .	44.9	109.2	189.0	161.5	165.5	156.8	178.9	202.3	264.5	291.4
High day	Million . .	84.3	181.0	608.1	343.9	416.4	292.4	317.4	389.0	379.5	482.8
Low day	Million . .	16.1	62.1	86.7	72.1	68.9	56.9	69.6	95.1	89.9	113.8
Odd lots	Million . .	209	263	342	268	324	282	[1]333	450	538	583
Value of shares traded . .	**Bil. dol** .	**382**	**981**	**1,889**	**1,366**	**1,556**	**1,336**	**1,533**	**1,765**	**2,305**	**2,477**
Round lots	Bil. dol . .	375	971	1,874	1,356	1,543	1,325	1,520	1,745	2,283	2,454
Odd lots	Bil. dol . .	8	10	15	10	13	11	[1]13	19	22	22
Bond volume [2]	**Mil. dol** .	**5,190**	**9,046**	**9,727**	**7,702**	**8,836**	**10,894**	**12,698**	**11,629**	**9,743**	**7,197**
Daily average	Mil. dol .	20.5	35.9	38.4	30.4	35.1	43.1	50.2	45.8	38.5	28.6

[1] Excludes odd lot statistics for February which were not available.   [2] Par value.

Source: New York Stock Exchange, Inc., New York, NY, *Fact Book,* annual.

No. 830. Securities Listed on New York Stock Exchange: 1980 to 1994

[As of **December 31**, except **cash dividends** are for **calendar year**]

ITEM	Unit	1980	1985	1986	1987	1988	1989	1990	1991	1992	1993	1994
BONDS												
Number of issuers	Number .	1,045	1,010	951	885	846	794	743	705	636	574	583
Number of issues	Number .	3,057	3,856	3,611	3,346	3,106	2,961	2,912	2,727	2,354	2,103	2,141
Face value	Bil. dol . .	602	1,327	1,380	1,651	1,610	1,435	1,689	2,219	2,009	2,342	2,526
Market value	Bil. dol..	508	1,339	1,458	1,621	1,561	1,412	1,610	2,227	2,044	2,528	2,367
Average price.	Percent .	84.41	100.90	105.66	98.20	96.94	98.42	95.31	100.34	101.77	107.96	93.73
STOCKS												
Companies	Number .	1,570	1,541	1,575	1,647	1,681	1,720	1,774	1,885	2,088	2,361	2,570
Number of issues	Number .	2,228	2,298	2,257	2,244	2,234	2,246	2,284	2,426	2,658	2,904	3,060
Shares listed	Billion. . .	33.7	52.4	59.6	72.0	76.1	83.0	90.7	99.6	115.8	131.1	142.3
Market value	Bil. dol . .	1,243	1,950	2,199	2,216	2,457	3,030	2,820	3,713	4,035	4,541	4,448
Average price.	Dollars . .	36.87	37.20	36.89	30.87	32.30	36.51	31.08	37.27	34.83	34.65	31.26
Cash dividends on common stock	Bil. dol . .	53.1	74.2	76.2	84.4	102.2	101.8	103.2	123.4	109.7	120.2	130.0

Source: New York Stock Exchange, Inc., New York, NY, *Fact Book*, annual.

No. 831. NASDAQ—Securities Listed and Volume of Trading: 1980 to 1994

ITEM	Unit	1980	1985	1987	1988	1989	1990	1991	1992	1993	1994
Member firms	Number. . .	2,932	6,307	6,722	6,432	6,141	5,827	5,386	5,254	5,296	5,426
Branch offices.	Number. . .	7,555	15,375	21,479	22,714	29,998	24,457	29,158	33,484	44,181	57,105
Companies listed.	Number. . .	2,894	4,136	4,706	4,451	4,293	4,132	4,094	4,113	4,611	4,902
Issues.	Number. . .	3,050	4,784	5,537	5,144	4,963	4,706	4,684	4,768	5,393	5,761
Shares traded.	Million	6,692	20,699	37,890	31,070	33,530	33,380	41,311	48,455	66,541	74,353
Average daily volume . . .	Million . .	26.5	82.1	149.8	122.8	133.1	131.9	163.3	190.8	263.0	295.1
Value of shares traded	Bil. dol. . . .	69	234	500	347	431	452	694	891	1,350	1,449

Source: National Association of Securities Dealers, Washington, DC, *Fact Book*, annual.

No. 832. Commodity Futures Trading on U.S. Exchanges—Volume of Trading: 1980 to 1994

[In millions. For year ending Sept. 30]

COMMODITY	1980	1985	1986	1987	1988	1989	1990	1991	1992	1993	1994
Number of contracts traded .	**82.7**	**152.6**	**183.1**	**213.5**	**241.8**	**267.7**	**272.2**	**261.4**	**289.5**	**325.5**	**411.1**
Grain.	18.3	10.7	10.3	10.9	15.9	15.9	17.0	16.6	17.6	16.0	20.0
Oilseeds/products	15.7	14.9	13.8	14.2	22.5	21.1	20.4	19.8	18.6	20.7	21.0
Livestock/products	11.8	7.9	8.6	8.8	9.6	8.2	8.0	6.9	6.4	5.8	6.1
Other agriculturals	7.8	5.1	6.7	5.7	9.8	10.7	11.0	9.5	9.4	10.8	12.3
Energy products	1.1	7.0	11.5	20.3	26.3	31.3	35.2	31.8	38.4	42.8	50.5
Metals	14.1	18.4	16.2	19.4	18.9	17.9	17.8	13.9	12.2	15.2	18.2
Financial instruments	10.2	72.1	96.9	114.3	117.6	136.7	135.7	134.1	148.2	185.4	252.6
Currencies	3.7	16.4	19.1	19.9	21.2	25.7	27.2	28.8	38.7	28.8	30.4

Source: U.S. Commodity Futures Trading Commission, *Annual Report.*

No. 833. Securities Industry—Revenues and Expenses: 1980 to 1994

[In millions of dollars]

TYPE	ALL SECURITIES FIRMS								MEMBERS OF NY STOCK EXCHANGE [1]	
	1980	1985	1988	1989	1990	1991	1992	1993	1993	1994, proj.
Revenues, total	**19,829**	**49,844**	**66,100**	**76,864**	**71,356**	**84,890**	**90,584**	**109,416**	**73,182**	**69,809**
Commissions	6,777	10,955	11,932	13,452	12,032	14,210	16,249	19,938	13,707	14,027
Trading/investment gains	5,091	14,549	16,667	16,247	15,746	22,641	21,838	25,526	18,472	12,958
Underwriting profits	1,571	4,987	5,607	4,537	3,728	6,593	8,300	11,251	10,061	6,927
Margin interest	2,151	2,746	3,155	3,860	3,179	2,771	2,690	3,242	3,130	3,991
Mutual fund sales	278	2,754	2,644	3,038	3,242	4,176	5,950	8,116	3,541	3,593
Other	3,960	13,854	26,096	35,731	33,428	34,498	35,557	41,343	24,270	28,313
Expenses, total	**16,668**	**43,342**	**62,623**	**74,041**	**70,566**	**76,234**	**81,467**	**96,358**	**64,582**	**68,444**
Interest expense	3,876	11,470	19,502	29,822	28,093	27,512	24,576	27,061	16,995	20,651
Compensation	7,619	18,112	23,418	23,740	22,931	26,916	32,071	39,167	28,968	28,584
Commissions/clearance paid	1,055	2,314	2,804	3,057	2,959	3,200	3,722	5,364	2,306	2,685
Other	4,119	11,446	16,899	17,422	16,583	18,605	21,098	24,766	16,312	16,523
Net income, pretax	**3,160**	**6,502**	**3,477**	**2,823**	**790**	**8,656**	**9,117**	**13,058**	**8,600**	**1,365**

[1] Covers all members of New York Stock Exchange doing public business. Source: Securities Industry Association, New York, NY, *Securities Industry Association Fact Book*, annual.

Source: Except as noted, U.S. Securities and Exchange Commission, *Annual Report*.

No. 834. Assets of Private and Public Pension Funds, by Type of Fund: 1980 to 1994

[**In billions of dollars**. As of **end of year**. Except for corporate equities, represents book value. Excludes Social Security trust funds and U.S. Government pension funds; see tables 593 and 597]

TYPE OF PENSION FUND	1980	1985	1988	1989	1990	1991	1992	1993	1994
Total, all types	**873**	**1,883**	**2,653**	**3,172**	**3,234**	**3,862**	**4,213**	**4,644**	**4,702**
Private funds	676	1,485	2,044	2,405	2,413	2,921	3,154	3,492	3,480
Insured	172	392	622	700	784	865	940	1,042	1,123
Noninsured [1] [2]	504	1,093	1,422	1,706	1,629	2,056	2,214	2,450	2,356
Small time and savings deposits	28	74	120	144	134	174	183	186	162
Mutual fund shares	7	11	31	42	45	64	86	137	151
Corporate equities	223	464	609	735	658	889	962	1,079	1,047
Credit market instruments [2]	151	378	509	590	607	693	730	771	728
U.S. government securities	51	190	250	311	322	363	384	401	378
Treasury	32	115	164	209	221	254	271	286	276
Agency	18	74	86	102	101	109	112	115	103
Corporate and foreign bonds	78	155	204	226	235	276	292	309	295
State and local pension funds [2]	197	399	609	767	820	941	1,059	1,151	1,223
Corporate equities	44	120	220	300	296	387	449	507	520
Credit market instruments [2]	147	257	353	399	434	480	514	543	586
U.S. government securities	40	124	182	198	225	235	238	251	273
Treasury	21	83	124	125	142	151	155	171	187
Agency	19	41	58	73	82	84	83	79	86
Corporate and foreign bonds	92	107	135	167	169	195	223	238	258

[1] Covers all pension funds of corporations, nonprofit organizations, unions, and multi-employer groups. Also includes deferred profit-sharing plans and Federal Employees Retirement System (FERS) Thrift Savings Fund. Excludes health, welfare, and bonus plans.   [2] Includes other types of assets not shown separately.

Source: Board of Governors of the Federal Reserve System, *Flow of Funds Accounts*, March 1995 quarterly diskettes. Data are also published in the quarterly Z.1 release.

No. 835. Individual Retirement Accounts (IRA) Plans—Value, by Type of Holder: 1985 to 1994

[As of **December 31**. Estimated]

TYPE OF HOLDER	AMOUNT (bil. dol.)									PERCENT DISTRIBUTION		
	1985	1987	1988	1989	1990	1991	1992	1993	1994	1985	1990	1994
Total	200	334	390	455	529	657	746	868	917	100	100	100
Savings institutions	56	77	90	98	95	91	85	76	74	28	18	8
Commercial banks	52	77	88	99	119	134	137	134	133	26	22	15
Mutual funds	32	72	86	112	127	169	211	284	285	16	24	31
Self directed	29	59	68	82	117	181	225	271	318	15	22	35
Life insurance companies	17	26	33	38	42	50	56	70	75	9	8	8
Credit unions	14	23	25	26	29	32	32	32	32	7	6	4

Source: Investment Company Institute, Washington, DC, *Mutual Fund Fact Book*, annual (copyright).

No. 836. 401(k) Plan Assets—Summary, 1984 to 1993, and Projections, 2000

YEAR	Total assets (bil. dol.)	TYPE OF ASSET	Percent of companies offering investment option	ASSETS, 1993		FINANCIAL INSTITUTION MANAGING ASSETS	ASSETS, 1993	
				Amount (bil. dol.)	Percent distribution		Amount (bil. dol.)	Percent distribution
1984	55	Total	(X)	475	100	All defined contribution plans [2]	885	100
1985	105	Guaranteed investment				Insurance companies	320	36
1986	155	account [1]	56	130	27	Banks	275	31
1987	190	Equity	78	75	16	Mutual fund groups	175	20
1988	230	Money market	54	35	7	Other	115	13
1989	270	Balanced account	51	60	13			
1990	300							
1991	350	Bond fund	46	35	7	401(k) plans	475	100
1992	410	Company stock	22	115	24	Insurance companies	160	34
1993	475	Other	20	25	6	Banks	130	27
						Mutual fund groups	125	26
2000, proj.	1,250					Other	60	13

X Not applicable.   [1] Covers bank certificate of deposits, guaranteed investment contracts (GIC's), GIC alternatives, and insurance company participating contracts.   [2] Includes 401(k) plans.

Source: Access Research, Inc., Windsor, CT, *1993 Marketplace Update*, 1993, (copyright).

No. 837. Mutual Funds—Summary: 1980 to 1994

[A mutual fund is an open-end investment company that continuously issues and redeems shares that represent an interest in a pool of financial assets. See also *Historical Statistics, Colonial Times to 1970*, series X 536-539]

TYPE OF FUND	Unit	1980	1985	1988	1989	1990	1991	1992	1993	1994
Number of funds, total	**Number**	564	1,528	2,715	2,917	3,105	3,427	3,850	4,558	5,371
Equity funds	Number	267	579	1,016	1,080	1,127	1,217	1,356	1,615	1,951
Income and bond funds [1]	Number	191	492	1,094	1,173	1,235	1,389	1,629	2,023	2,457
Money market funds, tax-exempt [2]	Number	10	111	174	201	235	267	279	292	319
Money market funds, taxable [3]	Number	96	346	431	463	508	554	586	628	644
Shareholder accounts, total	**Millions**	12.1	34.7	54.7	58.2	62.6	68.6	80.3	95.5	114.9
Equity funds	Millions	5.8	11.5	20.6	21.5	23.0	26.1	33.2	42.1	59.0
Income and bond funds [1]	Millions	1.5	8.3	15.6	15.4	16.6	18.9	23.4	29.7	30.5
Money market funds, tax-exempt [2]	Millions	(NA)	0.5	0.9	1.1	1.4	1.7	1.9	2.0	2.0
Money market funds, taxable [3]	Millions	4.8	14.4	17.6	20.2	21.6	21.9	21.8	21.6	23.3
Assets, total	**Bil. dol**	135	496	810	982	1,067	1,396	1,646	2,075	2,162
Equity funds	Bil. dol	44	117	195	249	246	412	523	749	866
Income and bond funds [1]	Bil. dol	14	135	278	305	323	441	577	761	684
Money market funds, tax-exempt [2]	Bil. dol	2	36	66	69	84	90	95	103	111
Money market funds, taxable [3]	Bil. dol	74	208	272	359	415	453	451	462	500
Sales, total	**Bil. dol**	248	954	1,177	1,445	1,565	2,037	2,751	3,189	3,077
Equity funds	Bil. dol	6	30	31	55	71	99	145	229	271
Income and bond funds [1]	Bil. dol	4	84	64	71	79	138	220	282	203
Money market funds, tax-exempt [2]	Bil. dol	5	109	178	185	197	231	286	342	369
Money market funds, taxable [3]	Bil. dol	232	730	903	1,135	1,219	1,570	2,100	2,336	2,234
Redemptions, total	**Bil. dol**	217	865	1,167	1,327	1,471	1,879	2,548	2,905	2,929
Equity funds	Bil. dol	6	18	35	38	45	54	62	93	142
Income and bond funds [1]	Bil. dol	3	15	58	53	53	62	103	139	188
Money market funds, tax-exempt [2]	Bil. dol	4	99	175	181	190	227	282	337	370
Money market funds, taxable [3]	Bil. dol	204	732	899	1,055	1,183	1,536	2,101	2,337	2,229

NA Not available.   [1] Includes municipal bond funds.   [2] Funds invest in municipal securities with relatively short maturities.   [3] Funds invest in short-term, high-grade securities sold in the money market.

Source: Investment Company Institute, Washington, DC, *Mutual Fund Fact Book*, annual (copyright).

No. 838. Mutual Fund Shares—Holdings and Net Purchases, by Type of Investor: 1980 to 1994

[In billions of dollars. Holdings as of Dec. 31. Minus sign (-) indicates net sales]

TYPE OF INVESTOR	HOLDINGS					NET PURCHASES				
	1980	1990	1992	1993	1994	1980	1990	1992	1993	1994
Total	**61.8**	**602.1**	**1,042.1**	**1,429.3**	**1,463.0**	**3.5**	**65.3**	**211.9**	**317.0**	**128.3**
Households, nonprofit organizations .	45.6	451.9	733.9	972.5	968.5	2.1	37.7	146.5	187.0	76.6
Nonfinancial corporate business. . . .	1.5	8.2	15.6	22.4	20.3	0.3	-1.3	4.7	6.8	-1.3
Commercial banking	-	1.9	3.4	3.9	2.0	-	-0.3	-0.4	0.5	-1.9
Credit unions	-	1.4	4.1	4.2	-	-	0.2	1.5	0.1	-4.2
Life insurance companies	1.1	30.7	70.7	105.6	128.0	0.1	12.6	18.7	34.8	26.1
Private pension funds	7.2	45.4	86.4	137.3	150.5	1.4	6.7	15.2	42.8	17.9
Bank personal trusts	6.4	62.7	128.1	183.5	193.7	-0.3	9.7	25.8	44.9	15.1

- Represents or rounds to zero.

Source: Board of Governors of the Federal Reserve System, *Flow of Funds Accounts*, March 1995 quarterly diskettes. Data are also published in the quarterly Z.1 release.

No. 839. Households Owning Mutual Funds, by Age of Head of Household and Income: 1989 and 1992

[In percent. Income in thousands of constant 1992 dollars. Constant dollar figures are based on consumer price index data published by U.S. Bureau of Labor Statistics. Families include one-person units; for definition of family, see text, section 1. Based on Survey of Consumer Finance; see source]

AGE AND ANNUAL INCOME	PERCENT OF HOUSEHOLDS OWNING LONG-TERM MUTUAL FUNDS [1]		PERCENT OF HOUSEHOLDS' TOTAL FINANCIAL ASSETS HELD IN—			
			Long-term mutual funds [1]		Short-term mutual funds and bank deposits	
	1989	1992	1989	1992	1989	1992
Total	**11.8**	**15.5**	**9.8**	**13.2**	**36.7**	**30.7**
Less than 35 years old	6.1	8.4	3.6	5.2	37.5	41.3
35 to 44 years old	14.3	18.7	9.6	12.4	33.5	33.6
45 to 54 years old	14.6	18.0	10.8	14.0	33.0	23.0
55 to 64 years old	14.9	22.2	10.9	17.2	41.0	22.1
65 years old and over	12.3	14.6	9.7	11.9	36.8	36.0
Less than $30,000	4.9	5.7	4.1	7.7	60.5	51.4
$30,000 to $49,999	12.5	19.9	8.6	17.0	42.9	35.5
$50,000 to $99,999	26.2	28.4	11.0	13.1	36.9	30.2
$100,000 to $199,999	42.6	41.8	12.2	14.2	33.2	23.0
$200,000 or more.	51.7	55.5	11.8	14.4	19.2	18.7

[1] Excludes all money market mutual funds except those in retirement accounts.

Source: Board of Governors of the Federal Reserve System, *Federal Reserve Bulletin*, November 1993.

No. 840. Health Insurance—Premium Income and Benefit Payments of Insurance Companies: 1980 to 1992

[In billions of dollars. Includes Puerto Rico and other U.S. outlying areas. Represents premium income of and benefits paid by insurance companies only. Excludes Blue Cross-Blue Shield plans, medical-society sponsored plans, and all other independent plans]

ITEM	1980	1982	1983	1984	1985	1986	1987	1988	1989	1990	1991	1992
Premiums [1]	**43.7**	**58.3**	**63.2**	**70.4**	**75.2**	**75.5**	**84.1**	**98.2**	**108.0**	**112.9**	**116.4**	**125.0**
Group policies [2]	36.8	50.0	54.9	60.8	64.4	65.9	74.0	87.6	96.1	100.2	103.0	110.4
Individual and family policies. .	6.9	8.3	8.3	9.6	10.8	9.6	10.1	10.6	11.8	12.7	13.3	14.6
Benefit payments	**37.0**	**49.2**	**51.7**	**56.0**	**60.0**	**64.3**	**72.5**	**83.0**	**89.4**	**92.5**	**97.6**	**104.8**
Group policies [2]	33.0	44.2	46.9	50.3	53.7	58.9	66.5	76.4	82.2	84.4	88.8	95.2
Individual and family policies. .	4.0	5.0	4.8	5.7	6.3	5.4	5.9	6.6	7.2	8.2	8.8	9.6
Type of coverage:												
Loss of income	5.3	5.5	4.9	5.2	5.6	5.6	6.4	6.4	7.2	7.4	7.5	8.3
Medical expense	27.9	38.8	41.5	44.1	47.2	50.9	57.4	66.4	72.0	73.8	77.9	82.9
Dental	2.8	4.0	4.4	4.9	5.3	5.3	5.9	6.3	6.5	6.4	6.4	7.1
Medicare supplement	1.0	0.8	1.0	1.8	1.9	2.5	2.8	3.8	3.7	5.0	5.8	6.4

[1] Earned premiums.   [2] Insurance company group premiums and benefit payments include administrative service agreements and minimum premium plans.

Source: Health Insurance Association of America, Washington, DC, *Source Book of Health Insurance Data*, annual.

No. 841. Property and Casualty Insurance—Summary: 1987 to 1993

[**In billions of dollars**. Minus sign (-) indicates loss]

ITEM	1987	1988	1989	1990	1991	1992	1993, est.
Premiums, net written	193.2	202.0	208.4	217.8	223.0	227.5	241.6
Automobile, private [1]	64.3	69.5	73.6	78.4	82.8	88.4	93.4
Automobile, commercial [1]	16.9	16.9	17.3	17.0	16.6	16.1	16.3
Liability other than auto	24.9	23.1	22.7	22.1	20.9	21.1	22.1
Fire and allied lines	7.7	6.9	7.0	7.1	7.2	7.1	7.9
Homeowners' multiple peril	16.7	17.1	17.7	18.6	19.3	20.5	21.5
Commercial multiple peril	17.2	17.7	17.5	17.7	17.0	16.4	17.3
Workers' compensation	23.4	26.1	28.5	31.0	31.3	29.7	30.3
Marine, inland and ocean	5.5	5.5	5.6	5.7	5.5	5.5	6.1
Accident and health	3.8	4.7	4.6	5.0	5.1	5.4	6.8
Other lines	12.8	14.5	14.2	15.2	17.4	17.3	19.8
Losses and expenses	196.4	208.6	223.6	234.7	239.3	259.6	(NA)
Underwriting gain/loss	-9.6	-11.2	-19.2	-20.9	-19.4	-35.5	(NA)
Net investment income	24.0	27.7	31.2	32.9	34.2	33.7	(NA)
Operating earnings after taxes	11.0	12.9	9.0	9.0	10.4	-3.3	(NA)
Assets	426.7	476.9	527.0	556.3	601.4	637.3	661.5
Policyholders' surplus	104.0	118.2	134.0	138.4	158.7	163.1	(NA)

NA Not available.   [1] Includes premiums for automobile liability and physical damage.

Source: Insurance Information Institute, New York, NY, *The Fact Book, Property/Casualty Insurance Facts*, annual (copyright).

No. 842. Automobile Insurance—Average Expenditures Per Insured Vehicle, by State: 1991 to 1993

[**In dollars**. The average expenditures for automobile insurance in a State are affected by a number of factors, including the underlying rate structure, the coverages purchased, the deductibles and limits selected, the types of vehicles insured, and the distribution of driver characteristics]

STATE	1991	1992	1993	STATE	1991	1992	1993	STATE	1991	1992	1993
U.S.	**597**	**616**	**638**	KS	368	392	422	ND	329	319	349
				KY	435	473	506	OH	494	503	493
AL	475	498	513	LA	679	724	752	OK	422	448	470
AK	643	685	712	ME	484	468	477	OR	529	535	564
AZ	647	667	700	MD	689	702	707	PA	610	642	645
AR	398	424	445	MA	814	860	909	RI	823	837	871
CA	783	766	803	MI	606	662	677	SC	502	534	569
CO	588	653	698	MN	530	566	595	SD	309	333	364
CT	841	878	925	MS	482	519	541	TN	466	478	488
DE	718	745	738	MO	469	493	517	TX	612	646	666
DC	863	880	879	MT	370	393	432	UT	436	463	515
FL	669	684	698	NE	346	352	403	VT	474	484	501
GA	546	514	536	NV	640	673	726	VA	506	503	508
HI	874	974	953	NH	646	638	649	WA	549	588	641
ID	386	402	429	NJ	879	957	961	WV	519	557	581
IL	552	534	572	NM	517	543	589	WI	463	492	503
IN	474	497	494	NY	754	799	832	WY	330	366	401
IA	359	379	397	NC	432	448	440				

Source: National Association of Insurance Commissioners, Kansas City, MO, *State Average Expenditures and Premiums for Personal Automobile Insurance,* annual (copyright).

No. 843. Life Insurance in Force in the United States—Summary: 1980 to 1993

[As of **December 31** or **calendar year,** as applicable. Covers life insurance with life insurance companies only. Represents all life insurance in force on lives of U.S. residents whether issued by U.S. or foreign companies. For definition of household, see text, section 1. See also *Historical Statistics, Colonial Times to 1970*, series X 879-889]

YEAR	Number of policies, total (mil.)	LIFE INSURANCE IN FORCE Value (bil. dol.)					AVERAGE SIZE POLICY IN FORCE (dollars)				AVERAGE AMOUNT ($1,000)		Disposable personal income per household ($1,000)
		Total	Ordinary	Group	Industrial	Credit [1]	Ordinary	Group	Industrial	Credit [1]	Per household	Per insured household	
1980	402	3,541	1,761	1,579	36	165	11,920	13,410	620	2,110	41.9	51.1	24.2
1985	386	6,053	3,247	2,562	28	216	22,780	19,720	640	3,100	66.6	82.2	33.9
1987	395	7,452	4,139	3,043	27	243	28,510	22,380	650	3,330	78.7	98.4	36.5
1988	391	8,020	4,512	3,232	25	251	31,390	23,410	660	3,570	84.5	105.6	38.8
1989	394	8,694	4,940	3,470	24	260	34,410	24,510	670	3,600	89.9	112.4	40.8
1990	389	9,393	5,367	3,754	24	248	37,910	26,630	670	3,500	98.4	124.5	44.1
1991	375	9,986	5,678	4,058	22	228	41,450	28,760	680	3,580	102.7	130.0	44.9
1992	366	10,406	5,942	4,241	21	202	42,960	29,930	700	3,610	106.6	136.6	47.0
1993	363	11,105	6,428	4,456	21	200	45,770	31,430	700	3,850	111.6	143.1	48.8

[1] Insures borrower to cover consumer loan in case of death.

Source: American Council of Life Insurance, Washington, DC, *Life Insurance Fact Book*, biennial.

No. 844. Life Insurance Purchases in the United States—Number and Amount: 1980 to 1993

[Excludes revivals, increases, dividend additions, and reinsurance acquired. Includes long-term credit insurance (life insurance on loans of more than 10 years' duration). See also headnote, table 843]

YEAR	NUMBER OF POLICIES PURCHASED (1,000)						AMOUNT PURCHASED (bil. dol.)					
		Ordinary						Ordinary				
	Total	Total	Percent—		Group	Indus-trial	Total	Total	Percent—		Group	Indus-trial
			Whole life [1]	Term [2]					Whole life [1]	Term [2]		
1980	29,007	14,750	78	22	11,379	2,878	573	386	43	57	183	4
1985	33,880	17,104	78	22	16,243	533	1,231	911	57	43	320	1
1987	33,153	16,225	75	25	16,698	230	1,353	987	55	45	366	(Z)
1988	31,589	15,579	81	19	15,793	217	1,407	996	56	44	411	(Z)
1989	29,960	14,694	80	20	15,110	156	1,442	1,021	53	47	421	(Z)
1990	28,791	14,066	79	21	14,592	133	1,529	1,070	52	48	459	(Z)
1991	29,813	13,471	78	22	16,230	112	[3]1,616	1,042	50	50	[3]574	(Z)
1992	28,382	13,350	76	24	14,930	102	1,489	1,048	49	51	441	(Z)
1993	31,238	13,574	75	25	17,574	90	1,678	1,101	56	44	577	(Z)

Z Less than $500 million.   [1] Life insurance payable to a beneficiary at the death of the insured whenever that occurs. Premiums may be payable for a specified number of years or for life. Includes a small number of endowment and retirement income policies.   [2] Life insurance payable to a beneficiary only when an insured dies within a specified period.   [3] Includes Servicemen's Group Life Insurance: $167 billion in 1991.

Source: American Council of Life Insurance, Washington, DC, *Life Insurance Fact Book*, biennial.

No. 845. U.S. Life Insurance Companies—Summary: 1980 to 1993

[As of **December 31** or **calendar year**, as applicable. Covers domestic and foreign business of U.S. companies. See also *Historical Statistics, Colonial Times to 1970*, series X 879 and X 890-917]

ITEM	Unit	1980	1985	1986	1987	1988	1989	1990	1991	1992	1993
U.S. companies	Number .	1,958	2,261	2,254	2,337	2,343	2,270	2,195	2,064	1,944	1,840
Sales	**Bil. dol. .**	**655**	**1,530**	[1]**1,578**	**1,656**	**1,716**	**1,788**	**2,024**	[1]**2,014**	**1,881**	**2,130**
Ordinary	Bil. dol .	461	1,187	1,178	1,267	1,287	1,343	1,368	1,403	1,395	1,520
Group	Bil. dol .	190	342	[1]400	388	428	444	655	[1]611	485	610
Industrial	Bil. dol . .	4	1	(Z)	(Z)	(Z)	(Z)	(Z)	(Z)	1	(Z)
Income	**Bil. dol. .**	**130.9**	**234.0**	**282.3**	**314.3**	**338.1**	**367.3**	**402.2**	**411.0**	**426.9**	**466.4**
Life insurance premiums	Bil. dol . .	40.8	60.1	66.2	76.7	73.5	73.3	76.7	79.3	83.9	94.5
Percent of total	Percent .	31.2	25.7	23.5	24.4	21.7	20.0	19.1	19.3	19.7	20.3
Annuity considerations	Bil. dol .	22.4	53.9	83.7	88.7	103.3	115.0	129.1	123.6	132.6	156.4
Health insurance premiums . . .	Bil. dol .	29.4	41.8	44.2	47.6	52.3	56.1	58.2	60.9	65.5	68.7
Investment and other	Bil. dol .	38.3	78.2	88.2	101.3	109.0	122.9	138.2	147.2	144.9	146.8
Disbursements	**Bil. dol. .**	**88.2**	**151.8**	**186.5**	**202.3**	**221.4**	**246.8**	**277.1**	**299.2**	**305.0**	**318.9**
Payments to policyholders [2] [3] .	Bil. dol .	59.0	95.7	131.4	144.4	156.8	178.3	200.9	218.6	222.1	231.9
Percent of total	Percent .	66.9	63.0	70.5	71.4	70.8	72.2	72.5	73.1	72.8	72.7
Death payments	Bil. dol .	12.9	18.5	19.6	20.7	22.4	23.5	25.5	26.4	28.0	29.8
Matured endowments	Bil. dol .	0.8	0.8	0.8	0.8	0.8	0.8	0.8	0.7	0.7	0.6
Annuity payments	Bil. dol .	7.4	19.7	17.8	20.3	21.9	26.0	28.6	31.8	32.4	36.4
Policy dividends	Bil. dol .	8.1	12.4	12.4	13.0	13.8	14.9	15.7	15.8	15.3	15.8
Surrender values [3]	Bil. dol .	6.4	15.9	49.6	53.7	58.1	73.4	90.2	101.2	100.5	103.1
Disability benefits . . . . . [3] .	Bil. dol .	0.5	0.5	0.5	0.5	0.4	0.5	0.5	0.5	0.6	0.5
Commissions, expenses, etc. [3] .	Bil. dol . .	27.8	53.1	51.4	54.7	61.3	63.5	70.2	75.1	77.8	80.1
Dividends to stockholders	Bil. dol .	1.4	3.0	3.7	3.3	3.4	5.0	6.0	5.5	5.1	6.9
BALANCE SHEET											
Assets	**Bil. dol. .**	**479**	**826**	**938**	**1,045**	**1,167**	**1,300**	**1,408**	**1,551**	**1,665**	**1,839**
Government securities	Bil. dol . .	33	125	145	151	160	178	211	269	320	384
Corporate securities	Bil. dol . .	227	374	433	502	585	664	711	789	863	982
Percent of total assets . . .	Percent .	47.4	45.3	46.2	48.1	50.1	51.1	50.5	50.8	51.8	53.4
Bonds	Bil. dol . .	180	297	342	406	480	538	583	624	670	730
Stocks	Bil. dol . .	47	77	91	97	104	126	128	165	193	252
Mortgages	Bil. dol . .	131	172	194	214	233	254	270	265	247	229
Real estate	Bil. dol . .	15	29	32	34	37	40	43	47	51	54
Policy loans	Bil. dol . .	41	54	54	54	54	57	63	66	72	78
Other	Bil. dol . .	32	72	81	90	98	106	110	115	112	112
Interest earned on assets [4]	Percent .	8.02	9.63	9.35	9.10	9.03	9.10	8.89	8.63	8.08	7.52
Liabilities [2] [5]	Bil. dol . .	445	769	873	977	1,092	1,216	1,317	1,445	1,549	1,711
Policy reserves [2]	**Bil. dol. .**	**390**	**665**	**762**	**862**	**969**	**1,084**	**1,197**	**1,305**	**1,407**	**1,550**
Annuities	Bil. dol . .	181	410	489	562	642	730	815	895	960	1,062
Group	Bil. dol . .	140	303	356	393	434	474	516	548	560	602
Individual [6]	Bil. dol . .	41	107	133	169	208	256	299	347	400	460
Life insurance	Bil. dol . .	198	236	252	276	300	324	349	372	402	436
Health insurance	Bil. dol . .	11	19	21	24	27	30	33	38	45	52
Asset valuation reserve [7]	Bil. dol . .	6	11	15	16	18	19	15	19	21	25
Capital and surplus [2]	Bil. dol . .	34	57	64	67	75	84	91	106	115	128

Z Less than $500 million.   [1] Includes Servicemen's Group Life Insurance: $51 billion in 1986 and $167 billion in 1991; as well as Federal Employees' Group Life Insurance: $11 billion in 1986.   [2] Includes operations of accident and health departments of life insurance companies.   [3] Beginning in 1986, data not comparable to prior years due to change in accounting method.   [4] Net rate.   [5] Includes other obligations not shown separately.   [6] Includes reserves for supplementary contracts with and without life contingencies.   [7] The asset valuation reserve is carried as a liability in financial statements but functions as surplus.

Source: American Council of Life Insurance, Washington, DC, *Life Insurance Fact Book*, biennial; and unpublished data.

Figure 17.1
Mergers and Acquisitions: 1985 to 1993

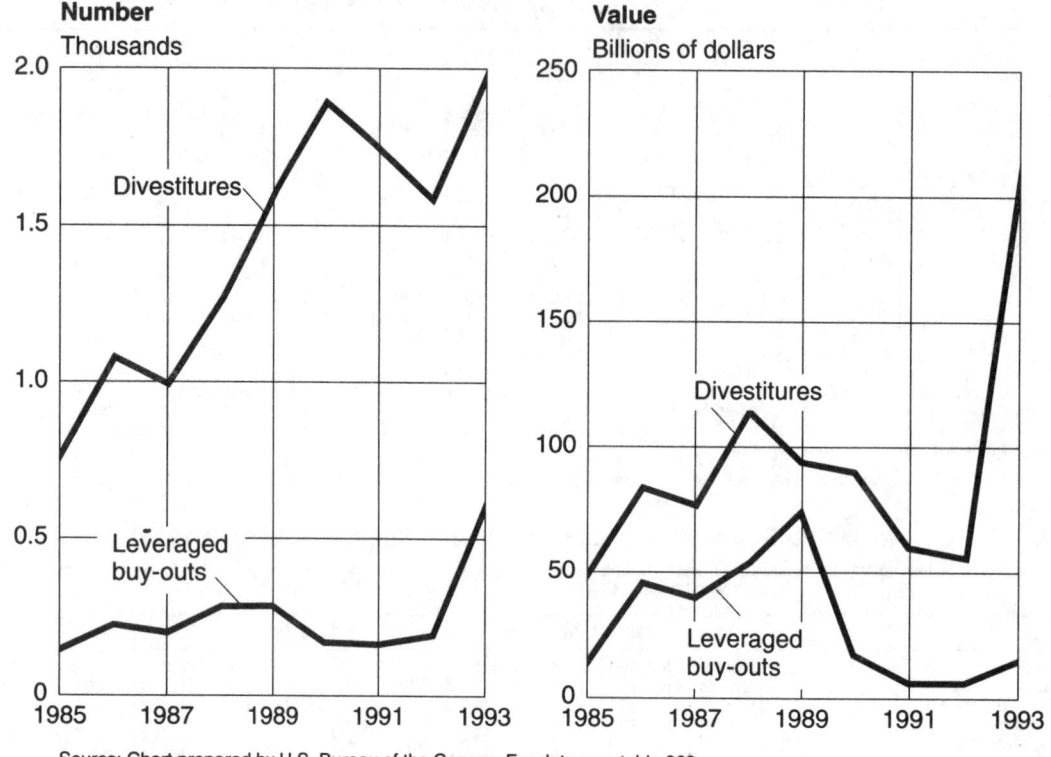

Source: Chart prepared by U.S. Bureau of the Census. For data, see table 869.

Figure 17.2
**Venture Capital Commitments:
1980 to 1994**

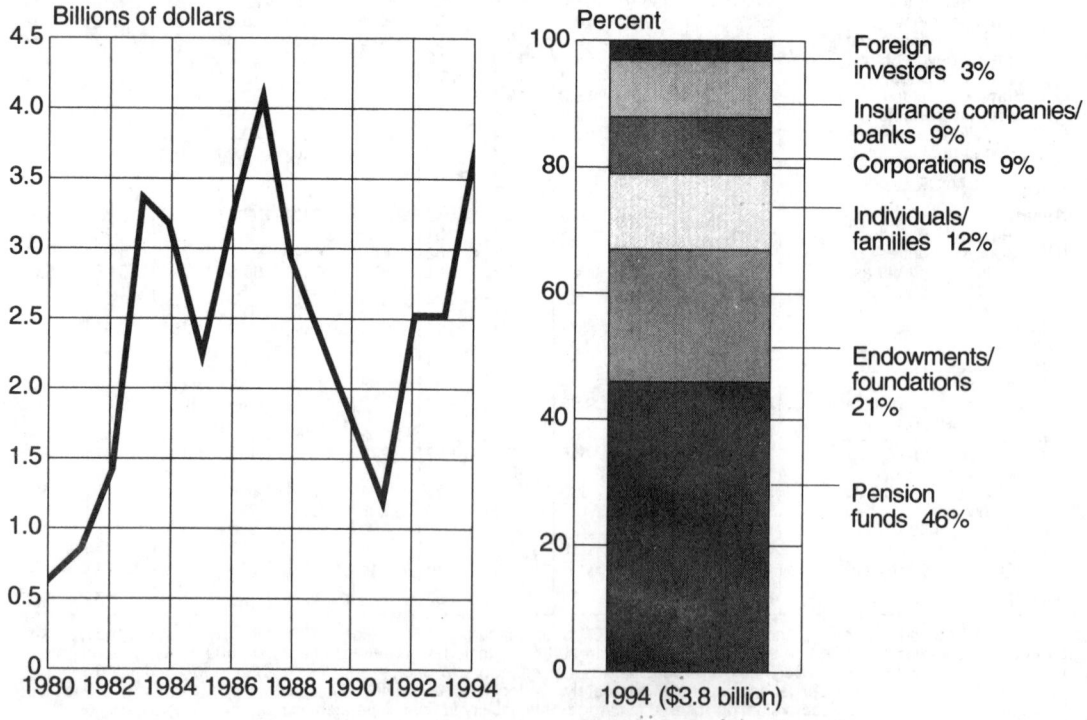

Source: Chart prepared by U.S. Bureau of the Census. For data, see tables 867.

Business Enterprise

This section relates to the place and behavior of the business firm and to business initiative in the American economy. It includes data on the number, type, and size of businesses; financial data of domestic and multinational U.S. corporations; business investment, expenditures, and profits; sales and inventories; and business failures. Additional business data may be found in other sections, particularly 27 and 28.

The principal sources of these data are the *Survey of Current Business,* published by the Bureau of Economic Analysis (BEA), the *Federal Reserve Bulletin,* issued by the Board of Governors of the Federal Reserve System, the annual *Statistics of Income* reports of the Internal Revenue Service (IRS), *The Business Failure Record* issued by The Dun & Bradstreet Corporation, Milton, CT, and *Fortune* and *The Fortune Directory,* issued by Time, Inc., New York.

Business firms.—A **firm** is generally defined as a business organization under a single management and may include one or more establishments (i.e., a single physical location at which business is conducted). The terms **firm, business, company,** and **enterprise** are used interchangeably throughout this section. Examples of series where the industrial distribution is based on data collected from establishments are those on capital stock, those on gross domestic product by industry, and those on employment and earnings (section 13). Examples of company-based series are those on business expenditures for new plant and equipment, those from IRS *Statistics of Income*, and those on corporation profits by industry. A firm doing business in more than one industry is classified by industry according to the major activity of the firm as a whole. The industrial classification is based on the *Standard Industrial Classification (SIC) Manual* (see text, section 13). The IRS concept of a business firm relates primarily to the legal entity used for tax reporting purposes. The IRS *Statistics of Income* reports present data, based on a sample of tax returns before audit, separately for sole proprietorships, partnerships, and corporations. Data presented are for active

In Brief

Patents issued in 1993: 109,700
  Percent issued to foreign country
  residents: *44%*
Bankruptcies filed in 1994: 845,257
  Business: *7%*
  Nonbusiness: *93%*
  Change from 1993   –8%

enterprises only. A *sole proprietorship* is an unincorporated business owned by one person including large enterprises with many employees and hired managers and part-time operations in which the owner is the only person involved. A *partnership* is an unincorporated business owned by two or more persons, each of whom has a financial interest in the business. The "persons" could be individuals, estates, trusts, other partnerships, or corporations. A *corporation* is a business that is legally incorporated under State laws. The IRS recognizes many types of businesses as corporations, including joint-stock companies, insurance companies, and unincorporated associations such as business trusts, etc. While many corporations file consolidated tax returns, most corporate tax returns represent individual corporations, some of which are affiliated through common ownership or control with other corporations filing separate returns.

Assets and liabilities.—In its annual report, *Statistics of Income, Corporation Income Tax Returns,* the IRS presents balance sheet and income estimates for all active U.S. corporations. The Bureau of the Census issues the *Quarterly Financial Report for Manufacturing, Mining, and Trade Corporations* (QFR), which presents quarterly income account and balance sheet data for manufacturing, mining, and trade industries. This report was prepared by the Federal Trade Commission until responsibilities for QFR were transferred to Census beginning with the fourth quarter 1982 report.

One of the most comprehensive measures of the investment position of the business sector (and the only measure adjusted to current replacement cost) is the BEA capital stock series. See

Survey of Current Business, January 1992, September 1993, and August 1994.

Income, profits, dividends, and taxes.— Several agencies, among them IRS and BEA, compile corporate income account data. These data, however, are not comparable because of differing definitions and methods of compilation. A reconciliation of the two can be found in table 8.22 of *Survey of Current Business,* published by BEA. The IRS publishes financial data for all business enterprises. These data appear in *Statistics of Income, Corporation Income Tax Returns* and the *Statistics of Income Bulletin* (partnerships and sole proprietorships). Data on international income and taxes reported by U.S. corporations are also included in the *Statistics of Income Bulletin* and in the periodic *Compendium of Studies of International Income and Taxes.*

Corporate data issued by BEA are a part of its national income and product accounts (see text, section 14). The primary sources for BEA estimates of profits, taxes, dividends, and undistributed profits are the original corporate tax returns submitted to IRS. Various adjustments of IRS data are required by the national income treatment—particularly with respect to profits which would be disclosed if all tax returns were audited: depletion, capital gain or loss, treatment of bad debts, measurement of income received from abroad, and intercorporate dividends—to make the figures comparable with other entries in the national income accounts. For a discussion of two types of adjustments (inventory valuation and capital consumption), see text, section 14. The BEA's corporate profits data also include net earnings of Federal Reserve banks, credit unions, private noninsured pension funds, and several quasi-government credit agencies not included in IRS data.

Sources and uses of corporate funds.— These data show capital requirements of corporations and the manner in which they are financed. Sources of funds should be equal to their uses. Certain discrepancies, however, interfere with this equality due to omission of (1) money accruing to corporations from an excess of sales over purchases of used plant and equipment, (2) transactions in securities held as permanent investments except public offerings, and (3) net purchases of land. Also, the balance sheet data upon which many of the financial flow estimates are based are not fully comparable with the tax-return based estimates of internal sources or the establishment series underlying the figures on inventory change.

Fortune 500.—Sales include service and rental revenues but exclude dividends, interest, and other non-operating revenues. All companies must have derived more than 50 percent of their sales from manufacturing and/or mining. Sales of subsidiaries are included when they are consolidated. **Assets** are those shown at the company's year-end. **Net income** is shown after taxes and after extraordinary credits or charges when any are shown on the income statement. **Stockholder's equity** is the sum of capital stock, surplus, and retained earnings at the company's year-end. Redeemable preferred stock is excluded when its redemption is either mandatory or outside the control of the company, except in the case of cooperatives. **Total returns to investors** include both price appreciation and dividend yield. Returns are adjusted for stock splits, stock dividends, recapitalizations, and corporate reorganizations as they occur. For further discussion, see Time, Inc., New York, NY, *The Fortune Directories.*

Economic censuses.—The economic censuses constitute comprehensive and periodic canvasses of the Nation's industrial and business activities. The first economic census of the United States was conducted as part of the 1810 decennial census, when inquiries on manufacturing were included with the census of population. Minerals data were collected in 1840. The first censuses of construction and business were taken for 1929. An integrated economic census program was begun for 1954. In that year, the censuses covered the retail and wholesale trades, selected service industries, manufactures, and mineral industries. The economic censuses are taken at 5-year intervals covering years ending in "2" and "7." Special surveys are conducted every 5 years as part of the economic censuses to determine the extent of business ownership by specific minority groups and women.

No. 846. Number of Returns and Business Receipts, by Size of Receipts and Type of Business: 1970 to 1992

[Covers active enterprises only. Figures are estimates based on sample of unaudited tax returns; see Appendix III. The industrial distribution is based on data collected from companies; see text, section 17. See also *Historical Statistics, Colonial Times to 1970*, series V 1-12]

SIZE-CLASS OF RECEIPTS	RETURNS (1,000)					BUSINESS RECEIPTS [1] (bil. dol.)				
	1970	1980	1990	1991	1992	1970	1980	1990	1991	1992
Corporations	1,665	2,711	3,717	3,803	(NA)	1,706	6,172	10,914	10,962	(NA)
Under $25,000 [2]	452	557	879	924	(NA)	3	4	5	5	(NA)
$25,000 to $49,999	171	208	252	260	(NA)	6	8	9	10	(NA)
$50,000 to $99,999	220	323	359	376	(NA)	16	22	26	28	(NA)
$100,000 to $499,999	517	926	1,162	1,180	(NA)	123	224	291	295	(NA)
$500,000 to $999,999	141	280	416	416	(NA)	99	197	294	296	(NA)
$1,000,000 or more	165	418	649	647	(NA)	1,459	5,717	10,289	10,329	(NA)
Partnerships	936	1,380	1,554	1,515	1,485	92	286	541	539	571
Under $25,000 [2]	502	638	963	956	921	4	5	4	4	4
$25,000 to $49,999	125	182	126	113	113	5	7	5	4	4
$50,000 to $99,999	120	184	133	120	126	9	13	10	9	9
$100,000 to $499,999	162	290	222	222	220	33	64	51	51	50
$500,000 to $999,999	17	48	49	49	50	12	33	36	36	35
$1,000,000 or more	10	37	55	55	56	30	164	435	436	470
Nonfarm proprietorships [3]	6,494	9,730	14,783	15,181	15,495	199	411	731	713	737
Under $25,000 [2]	4,738	6,916	10,196	10,558	10,392	30	44	69	71	71
$25,000 to $49,999	746	1,079	1,660	1,725	1,817	27	39	58	61	64
$50,000 to $99,999	562	836	1,282	1,327	1,269	40	59	91	93	92
$100,000 to $499,999	420	796	1,444	1,389	1,454	76	159	296	284	297
$500,000 to $999,999	21	74	143	123	133	14	50	97	82	90
$1,000,000 or more	7	29	57	60	58	12	60	119	121	123

NA Not available. [1] Excludes investment income except for partnerships and corporations in finance, insurance, and real estate. Starting 1983, investment income no longer included for S corporations. S corporations are certain small companies with 35 shareholders (15 in 1980 and 10 in 1970), mostly individuals, electing to be taxed through shareholders. [2] Includes firms with no receipts. [3] Number of businesses for 1970 and 1980. Number of nonfarm sole proprietorship returns is not available by size prior to 1981. However, the number of returns and the number of businesses are very closely related. The ratio of number of returns to the number of businesses is approximately 1 to 1.3.

Source: U.S. Internal Revenue Service, *Statistics of Income; Statistics of Income Bulletin;* and unpublished data.

No. 847. Number of Returns, Receipts, and Net Income, by Type of Business and Industry: 1980 to 1991

[See headnote, table 846. Minus sign (-) indicates net loss]

ITEM	NUMBER OF RETURNS (1,000)			BUSINESS RECEIPTS [2] (bil. dol.)			NET INCOME (less loss) [3] (bil. dol.)		
	Nonfarm proprietor- ships [1]	Partner- ships	Corpo- rations	Nonfarm proprietor- ships [1]	Partner- ships	Corpo- rations	Nonfarm proprietor- ships [1]	Partner- ships	Corpora- tions
1980	8,932	1,380	2,711	411	286	6,172	55	8	239
1985	11,929	1,714	3,277	540	349	8,050	79	-9	240
1987	13,091	1,648	3,612	611	428	9,186	106	-5	328
1988	13,679	1,654	3,563	672	516	9,804	126	15	413
1989	14,298	1,635	3,628	693	524	10,440	133	14	389
1990	14,783	1,554	3,717	731	541	10,914	141	17	371
1991 [4]	15,181	1,515	3,803	713	539	10,962	142	21	345
Agriculture, forestry, fishing [5]	432	127	130	17	8	81	3	2	1
Mining	150	39	39	7	18	91	1	1	4
Construction	1,735	57	417	93	27	503	15	1	6
Manufacturing	427	24	300	23	66	3,409	3	1	132
Transportation, public utilities	660	26	165	33	38	897	5	-1	38
Wholesale and retail trade [6]	2,678	171	1,044	246	100	3,291	13	3	30
Wholesale	410	18	329	42	40	1,591	5	1	15
Retail	2,267	152	709	204	60	1,694	8	2	15
Finance, insurance, real estate	1,291	804	618	44	113	1,924	15	-13	125
Services	7,642	260	1,062	247	171	762	87	28	10

[1] In 1980, represents individually owned businesses, including farms; thereafter, represents only nonfarm proprietors, i.e., business owners. [2] Excludes investment income except for partnerships and corporations in finance, insurance, and real estate. Starting 1985, investment income no longer included for S corporations. [3] Net income (less loss) is defined differently by form of organization, basically as follows: (a) Proprietorships: Total taxable receipts less total business deductions, including cost of sales and operations, depletion, and certain capital expensing, excluding charitable contributions and owners' salaries; (b) Partnerships: Total taxable receipts (including investment income except capital gains) less deductions, including cost of sales and operations and certain payments to partners, excluding charitable contributions, oil and gas depletion, and certain capital expensing; (c) Corporations: Total taxable receipts (including investment income, capital gains, and income from foreign subsidiaries deemed received for tax purposes, except for S corporations beginning 1983) less business deductions, including cost of sales and operations, depletion, certain capital expensing, and officers' compensation excluding S corporation charitable contributions and investment expenses starting 1983; net income is before income tax. [4] Includes businesses not allocable to individual industries. [5] Represents agricultural services only. [6] Includes trade business not identified as wholesale or retail.

Source: U.S. Internal Revenue Service, *Statistics of Income,* various publications.

No. 848. Number of Returns and Business Receipts, by Industry, Type of Business, and Size of Business Receipts: 1991

[Number of returns in thousands; receipts and net income in billions of dollars. Covers active enterprises only. Figures are estimates based on a sample of unaudited tax returns; see Appendix III. The industrial distribution is based on data collected from establishments; see text, section 17. See also *Historical Statistics, Colonial Times to 1970*, series V 42-53, for number of active corporations. Minus sign (-) indicates net loss]

INDUSTRY	Non-farm pro-prietor-ships	Partner-ships	CORPORATIONS				
			Under $1 mil. [1]	$1 mil.-$4.9 mil.	$5 mil.-$9.9 mil.	$10 mil.-$49.9 mil.	$50 mil. or more
Total: [2] Number	15,181	1,515	3,156	483	82	66	15
Business receipts [3]	713	539	633	1,029	571	1,330	7,399
Net income (less loss)	142	21	-13	9	9	36	304
Agriculture, forestry, fishing: Number	432	127	117	11	1	1	(Z)
Business receipts [3]	17	8	18	23	8	13	19
Mining: Number	150	39	34	4	1	1	(Z)
Business receipts [3]	7	18	4	8	4	12	62
Construction: Number	1,735	57	335	66	9	6	1
Business receipts [3]	93	27	85	134	66	107	110
Manufacturing: Number	427	24	199	57	15	14	5
Business receipts [3]	23	66	54	150	104	294	2,807
Transportation, public utilities: Number	660	26	132	25	4	3	1
Business receipts [3]	33	38	26	56	30	50	734
Wholesale and retail trade: Number	2,678	171	774	198	36	31	5
Business receipts [3]	246	100	214	427	251	614	1,786
Finance, insurance, real estate: Number	1,291	804	571	31	6	7	3
Business receipts [3]	44	113	61	67	43	137	1,615
Services: Number	7,642	260	965	81	10	5	1
Business receipts [3]	247	171	168	161	66	102	265

Z Less than 500 returns.   [1] Includes businesses without receipts.   [2] Includes businesses not allocable to individual industries.   [3] Excludes investment income except for partnerships and corporations (other than S corporations) in finance, insurance, and real estate.

Source: U.S. Internal Revenue Service, *Statistics of Income*, various publications; and unpublished data.

No. 849. Sole Proprietorships—Selected Income and Deduction Items: 1970 to 1992

[In millions of dollars, except as indicated. Covers nonfarm sole proprietorships. All figures are estimates based on sample. Tax law changes have affected the comparability of the data over time; see *Statistics of Income* reports for a description. See also *Historical Statistics, Colonial Times to 1970*, series V 4-6]

ITEM	1970	1980	1985	1987	1988	1989	1990	1991	1992
Number of returns (1,000)	5,770	8,932	11,929	13,091	13,679	14,298	14,783	15,181	15,495
Businesses with net income (1,000).	(NA)	(NA)	8,641	9,884	10,492	11,018	11,223	11,551	11,720
Inventory, end of year	11,061	21,996	24,970	26,333	27,313	30,060	30,422	29,783	29,898
Business receipts	198,582	411,206	540,045	610,823	671,970	692,811	730,606	712,568	737,082
Income from sales and operations .	(NA)	407,169	528,675	598,315	658,687	678,616	719,008	700,681	725,666
Business deductions [1]	168,045	356,258	461,273	505,362	545,735	560,175	589,250	571,154	583,147
Cost of goods sold/operations [1] . . .	109,149	209,890	232,294	255,045	277,880	283,709	291,011	272,627	274,220
Purchases	88,586	168,302	(NA)	173,400	197,220	204,681	210,225	200,861	204,317
Labor costs	7,704	10,922	14,504	19,631	21,143	22,540	22,680	21,918	18,838
Materials and supplies	6,216	12,909	(NA)	23,842	27,800	29,870	30,195	28,072	28,825
Commissions	1,274	3,333	(NA)	6,262	6,540	6,843	8,816	7,628	10,457
Salaries and wages (net)	15,107	26,561	38,266	42,330	43,007	45,469	46,998	48,890	52,316
Car and truck expenses	(NA)	13,378	17,044	17,470	19,640	20,789	21,766	22,594	23,920
Rent paid. . . .	4,637	9,636	15,259	16,358	19,470	20,952	23,392	23,643	25,148
Repairs	2,445	5,032	(NA)	7,438	8,104	8,149	8,941	9,159	9,706
Taxes paid	3,776	7,672	(NA)	8,449	9,495	9,948	10,342	10,629	12,618
Utilities	(NA)	4,790	(NA)	13,362	14,618	13,601	13,539	13,260	14,547
Insurance	2,310	6,003	(NA)	11,719	12,528	12,879	13,358	13,065	13,260
Interest paid	1,784	7,190	11,914	11,616	12,071	13,280	13,312	12,077	10,406
Depreciation	5,452	13,953	26,291	25,557	26,078	24,479	23,735	23,076	23,274
Pension and profit sharing plans . .	73	141	311	548	450	539	586	519	528
Net income (less loss)	30,537	54,947	78,773	105,461	126,323	132,738	141,430	141,516	153,960
Businesses with net income	33,736	68,010	98,776	123,783	145,518	152,416	161,657	162,427	173,473

NA Not available.   [1] Includes other amounts not shown separately.

Source: U.S. Internal Revenue Service, *Statistics of Income Bulletin*.

No. 850. Partnerships—Selected Items, by Industry: 1980 to 1992

[In millions of dollars, except number of partners and partnerships in thousands. Covers active partnerships only. Includes partnerships not allocable by industry. Figures are estimates based on samples. See Appendix III]

YEAR	NUMBER OF PARTNERSHIPS			Number of part-ners	Total assets[1]	Business re-ceipts[2][3]	Total deduc-tions[3]	Net income less loss[3]	Net in-come[3]	Net loss[3]
	Total	With net income	With net loss							
All industries:										
1980	1,380	774	605	8,420	597,504	285,967	283,749	8,249	45,062	36,813
1985	1,714	876	838	13,245	1,269,434	349,169	376,001	-8,884	77,045	85,928
1989	1,635	898	737	18,432	1,791,027	523,774	475,434	14,099	113,886	99,787
1990	1,554	854	700	17,095	1,735,285	540,647	549,603	16,610	116,318	99,708
1991	1,515	856	660	15,801	1,816,567	539,027	541,230	21,406	113,408	92,002
1992	1,485	856	629	15,735	1,907,345	571,427	553,770	42,916	121,834	78,918
Agriculture, forestry, fishing:										
1980	126	72	54	381	24,595	21,611	22,859	472	2,539	2,067
1985	136	76	60	585	27,027	6,529	10,495	-1,049	2,797	3,846
1989	131	83	48	591	25,219	7,708	10,133	1,380	3,679	2,299
1990	125	77	48	503	27,580	9,497	11,805	1,667	3,905	2,238
1991	127	78	49	552	32,391	8,422	10,892	1,740	3,992	2,252
1992	125	81	44	504	32,884	8,932	10,547	2,227	3,951	1,724
Mining:										
1980	35	15	20	722	24,742	13,201	18,248	-4,208	3,920	8,128
1985	62	33	30	2,207	66,930	19,922	21,920	1,482	7,884	6,402
1989	46	26	20	3,771	62,073	19,701	20,751	1,965	7,027	5,062
1990	41	29	14	2,149	58,246	19,967	20,869	2,183	7,009	4,825
1991	39	26	13	1,415	53,725	18,147	19,966	780	5,285	4,505
1992	36	23	13	1,389	53,697	16,706	18,230	1,009	5,271	4,263
Construction:										
1980	67	51	16	160	9,811	18,407	17,202	1,560	2,119	559
1985	57	41	16	134	15,008	21,476	20,080	2,207	2,743	536
1989	62	46	16	165	21,150	30,052	28,397	2,647	3,313	666
1990	59	45	15	162	17,989	30,716	29,672	1,908	3,020	1,112
1991	57	42	15	152	16,730	26,625	25,766	1,494	2,563	1,069
1992	59	42	17	158	15,663	25,946	24,501	1,906	2,648	743
Transportation, public utilities:										
1980	20	11	10	73	9,291	5,868	5,821	248	1,092	844
1985	25	15	10	186	26,468	11,253	14,814	-3,066	1,360	4,426
1989	22	10	12	435	54,171	26,727	30,319	-1,977	3,695	5,671
1990	25	14	11	503	63,334	32,800	35,989	-117	5,887	6,004
1991	26	14	12	519	72,512	37,611	40,873	-1,431	4,710	6,142
1992	24	12	12	527	81,070	42,081	43,127	1,054	6,585	5,531
Manufacturing:										
1980	30	20	10	92	11,252	15,327	16,142	-472	1,199	1,671
1985	30	12	18	105	24,838	22,588	24,225	-1,085	1,228	2,314
1989	26	14	12	185	56,601	55,336	55,816	1,398	4,154	2,756
1990	28	15	13	246	59,789	65,354	65,833	1,166	4,791	3,626
1991	24	13	11	175	65,140	65,818	66,385	904	4,909	4,005
1992	24	14	11	225	74,240	78,028	78,996	1,870	5,779	3,909
Wholesale and retail trade:										
1980	200	123	77	487	17,727	65,793	63,988	2,475	3,374	900
1985	201	113	88	493	20,568	69,079	68,119	1,977	3,467	1,490
1989	173	98	75	496	27,294	90,306	89,418	2,529	4,550	2,021
1990	176	100	77	481	28,423	98,120	97,131	2,610	4,717	2,107
1991	171	97	74	448	29,786	99,749	98,940	2,628	4,718	2,090
1992	162	86	76	425	32,777	107,870	106,639	2,553	4,758	2,205
Finance, insurance, and real estate:										
1980	637	313	325	5,566	454,531	87,133	91,382	-4,249	15,169	19,418
1985	844	369	475	7,755	979,787	92,309	118,237	-25,929	30,383	56,311
1989	853	419	434	11,327	1,394,319	71,243	91,965	-20,824	47,753	68,576
1990	822	401	422	10,846	1,329,452	64,313	87,011	-19,213	47,577	66,790
1991	804	410	394	10,317	1,386,914	57,398	126,042	-12,786	47,595	60,381
1992	797	427	370	10,328	1,438,303	87,773	72,853	-752	50,044	50,796
Services:										
1980	263	169	94	938	45,510	58,627	48,106	12,424	15,649	3,224
1985	341	207	134	1,713	106,597	104,197	96,202	16,541	26,942	10,400
1989	299	189	110	2,370	148,688	162,325	147,280	26,652	39,296	12,643
1990	267	173	96	2,153	150,063	161,702	145,789	26,453	39,383	12,930
1991	260	170	91	2,207	159,117	169,073	152,011	28,036	39,588	11,552
1992	253	169	84	2,167	178,577	181,603	158,260	33,004	42,748	9,744

[1] Total assets are understated because not all partnerships file complete balance sheets.   [2] Includes investment income for partnerships in finance, insurance, and real estate.   [3] Beginning 1981, only net (not gross) income from farming, rents, and royalties are included.

Source: U.S. Internal Revenue Service, *Statistics of Income Bulletin,* various publications.

No. 851. Partnerships—Selected Income and Balance Sheet Items: 1980 to 1992

[In billions of dollars, except as indicated. Covers active partnerships only. All figures are estimates based on samples. See Appendix III and *Historical Statistics, Colonial Times to 1970*, series V 7-9]

ITEM	1980	1985	1986	1987	1988	1989	1990	1991	1992
Number of returns (1,000)	1,380	1,714	1,703	1,648	1,654	1,635	1,554	1,515	1,485
Number with net income (1,000). . .	774	876	851	865	901	898	854	856	856
Number with balance sheets (1,000)	1,194	1,227	1,203	1,129	1,155	1,149	1,081	1,048	975
Number of partners (1,000).	8,420	13,245	15,229	16,963	17,291	18,432	17,095	15,801	15,735
Assets [1] [2]	598	1,269	1,404	1,381	1,580	1,791	1,735	1,817	1,907
Depreciable assets (net)	239	696	780	567	621	670	681	696	701
Inventories, end of year	33	27	47	45	51	59	57	57	62
Land	70	152	179	178	200	214	215	213	213
Liabilities [1] [2]	489	1,269	1,176	1,386	1,580	1,791	1,415	1,460	1,508
Accounts payable	34	47	44	41	49	52	67	63	79
Short-term debt [3]	48	103	92	82	87	87	88	117	115
Long-term debt [4]	178	382	429	430	474	512	498	491	486
Nonrecourse loans.	119	328	365	388	437	461	470	474	476
Partners' capital accounts [2]	109	200	228	247	267	356	320	357	399
Receipts [1]	292	367	397	443	541	551	565	563	596
Business receipts [5]	271	303	327	428	516	524	541	539	571
Interest received [6]	11	21	22	18	19	21	21	20	16
Deductions [1]	284	376	415	423	465	475	550	541	554
Cost of goods sold/operations	114	146	164	237	253	233	243	237	249
Salaries and wages	22	34	36	41	47	54	56	58	62
Taxes paid	10	8	8	7	8	9	9	10	10
Interest paid	28	29	29	20	23	33	30	28	25
Depreciation	22	23	23	19	20	20	19	19	20
Net income (less loss)	8	−9	−17	−5	14	14	17	21	43
Net income.	45	77	80	88	111	114	116	113	122

[1] Includes items not shown separately. [2] Assets, liabilities, and partners' capital accounts are understated because not all partnerships file complete balance sheets. [3] Mortgages, notes, and bonds payable in less than 1 year. [4] Mortgages, notes, and bonds payable in 1 year or more. [5] Includes investment income for partnerships in finance, insurance, and real estate. [6] For 1985-86, also includes dividends.

Source: U.S. Internal Revenue Service, *Statistics of Income Bulletin,* various publications.

No. 852. Corporate Funds—Sources and Uses: 1980 to 1994

[In billions of dollars, except percent. Covers nonfarm nonfinancial corporate business. See text, section 17]

ITEM	1980	1985	1987	1988	1989	1990	1991	1992	1993	1994
Sources	**336.1**	**493.8**	**564.7**	**634.2**	**567.9**	**535.5**	**471.7**	**560.5**	**557.4**	**661.5**
Internal	199.7	351.9	375.9	404.3	399.6	411.6	426.0	438.4	462.3	501.9
U.S. undistributed profits.	69.2	21.7	41.3	73.6	32.2	20.5	4.7	29.8	17.5	54.8
IVA and CCA [1]	−61.4	54.4	30.6	15.7	19.8	21.8	35.2	22.0	36.5	33.3
Capital consumption allowances. .	173.2	256.0	279.2	295.1	314.8	326.6	338.6	349.3	357.6	378.5
Foreign earnings [2]	18.7	19.8	24.8	19.9	32.8	42.8	47.6	37.3	50.8	35.4
External [3]	136.4	142.0	188.8	229.9	168.2	123.9	45.7	122.2	95.1	159.5
Credit market funds	78.4	84.7	89.3	95.0	68.0	48.3	8.7	67.9	67.1	80.3
Securities and mortgages	35.9	13.2	39.9	−4.7	−37.6	−20.1	96.1	67.0	81.2	−21.4
Equity issues	10.4	−84.5	−75.5	−129.5	−124.2	−63.0	18.3	27.0	21.3	−40.9
Bonds and mortgages [4]	25.5	97.7	115.4	124.8	86.6	42.9	77.8	40.0	59.9	19.5
Loans and short-term paper. . .	42.4	71.5	49.4	99.8	105.6	68.3	−87.4	0.9	−14.1	101.7
Other	21.7	31.8	64.4	100.7	96.2	95.1	−9.3	31.4	−17.5	21.7
Profit taxes payable	2.9	−3.2	5.1	1.7	−3.1	−5.0	−8.2	7.2	2.0	1.7
Trade debt	38.0	34.0	39.9	59.2	30.5	29.3	12.3	30.1	26.0	56.7
Foreign direct investment in U.S.	13.2	17.8	52.3	69.4	61.8	55.9	12.0	9.0	−9.8	22.7
Uses	**334.5**	**467.2**	**492.3**	**575.8**	**509.4**	**488.7**	**435.3**	**527.8**	**523.4**	**648.2**
Capital expenditures	252.4	370.2	361.5	391.0	401.1	402.8	379.8	386.0	440.4	521.5
Increase in financial assets.	82.1	97.0	130.9	184.8	108.3	85.9	55.6	141.8	83.0	126.8
Discrepancy (sources less uses) . . .	*1.6*	*26.7*	*72.4*	*58.4*	*58.4*	*46.7*	*36.4*	*32.8*	*34.0*	*13.2*

[1] Inventory valuation and capital consumption adjustment. [2] Foreign earnings of subsidiaries retained abroad. [3] Net increases in liability. [4] Includes industrial pollution control revenue bonds issued by State and local governments.

Source: Board of Governors of the Federal Reserve System. Data derived from *Flow of Funds Accounts,* annual.

No. 853. Nonfinancial Corporate Business-Sector Balance Sheet: 1980 to 1994

[In billions of dollars. Represents year-end outstandings]

ITEM	1980	1984	1985	1986	1987	1988	1989	1990	1991	1992	1993	1994
Assets	**4,455**	**5,829**	**6,122**	**6,445**	**6,821**	**7,313**	**7,707**	**7,815**	**7,585**	**7,473**	**7,681**	**8,097**
Tangible assets (current cost)	3,278	4,215	4,399	4,546	4,751	5,057	5,334	5,326	5,043	4,819	4,965	5,230
Reproducible	2,771	3,514	3,658	3,771	3,937	4,182	4,394	4,573	4,620	4,709	4,875	5,136
Land	508	702	741	775	814	875	940	753	422	110	90	93
Financial assets	1,176	1,613	1,723	1,899	2,070	2,257	2,373	2,489	2,542	2,654	2,716	2,868
Liquid assets [1]	197	459	508	595	643	674	741	783	801	811	813	857
Checkable deposits and currency	57	105	132	154	172	171	185	193	201	191	194	195
Time deposits	38	74	80	88	92	106	103	99	104	97	101	102
Consumer credit	29	38	43	47	54	61	64	67	63	65	80	90
Mutual fund shares	2	7	11	16	13	11	10	8	11	16	22	20
Trade credit	478	585	624	649	694	766	810	825	822	854	867	942
Miscellaneous assets	471	524	538	593	666	745	749	806	845	908	933	957
Liabilities	**1,416**	**2,084**	**2,313**	**2,606**	**2,910**	**3,246**	**3,537**	**3,705**	**3,724**	**3,825**	**3,914**	**4,152**
Credit market debt	886	1,369	1,543	1,774	1,970	2,169	2,366	2,469	2,458	2,500	2,561	2,681
Profit taxes payable	44	42	39	43	48	50	47	42	33	41	43	45
Trade debt	348	452	486	500	540	599	629	659	671	701	727	800
Miscellaneous liabilities	138	221	245	290	352	428	496	536	562	583	584	627
Net worth	**3,039**	**3,745**	**3,809**	**3,838**	**3,911**	**4,068**	**4,170**	**4,109**	**3,861**	**3,648**	**3,767**	**3,945**

[1] Includes other assets not shown separately.

Source: Board of Governors of the Federal Reserve System, *Balance Sheets for the U.S. Economy.*

No. 854. Corporations—Selected Financial Items: 1980 to 1992

[In billions of dollars, except as noted. Covers active corporations only. All corporations are required to file except those specifically exempt. See source for changes in law affecting comparability of historical data. Based on samples; see Appendix III. See also *Historical Statistics, Colonial Times to 1970*, series Y 381-392]

ITEM	1980	1985	1986	1987	1988	1989	1990	1991	1992
Number of returns (1,000)	2,711	3,277	3,429	3,612	3,563	3,628	3,717	3,803	3,869
Number with net income (1,000)	1,597	1,820	1,908	1,995	1,909	1,922	1,911	1,942	2,064
S Corporation returns [1] (1,000)	545	725	826	1,128	1,257	1,423	1,575	1,698	1,785
Assets [2]	7,617	12,773	14,163	15,311	16,568	17,647	18,190	19,030	20,002
Cash	529	683	763	754	785	824	771	787	806
Notes and accounts receivable	1,985	3,318	3,594	3,763	4,099	4,196	4,198	4,191	4,169
Inventories	535	715	733	829	846	879	894	884	915
Investments in Government obligations	472	917	1,059	1,092	1,095	1,262	1,302	1,069	1,248
Mortgage and real estate	894	1,259	1,377	1,455	1,605	1,610	1,538	1,529	1,567
Other investments	1,214	2,414	2,848	3,227	3,614	3,971	4,137	4,750	4,971
Depreciable assets	2,107	3,174	3,383	3,603	3,821	4,070	4,318	4,549	4,755
Depletable assets	72	112	116	123	124	134	129	142	131
Land	93	141	150	159	177	191	210	215	221
Liabilities [2]	7,617	12,773	14,163	15,311	16,568	17,647	18,190	19,030	20,002
Accounts payable	542	892	909	998	1,023	1,090	1,094	1,681	1,605
Short-term debt [3]	505	1,001	1,084	1,247	1,431	1,602	1,803	1,500	1,560
Long-term debt [4]	987	1,699	1,958	2,141	2,352	2,490	2,665	2,698	2,742
Capital stock	417	920	1,191	1,292	1,429	1,477	1,585	1,741	1,881
Paid-in or capital surplus	532	1,421	1,726	1,988	2,154	2,595	2,814	3,257	3,656
Retained earnings [5]	1,070	1,366	1,394	1,417	1,493	1,522	1,410	1,441	1,431
Net worth	1,944	3,304	3,698	3,947	4,207	4,603	4,739	5,277	5,700
Receipts [3][6]	6,361	8,398	8,669	9,582	10,265	10,935	11,410	11,436	11,742
Business receipts [6][7]	5,732	7,370	7,535	8,415	8,950	9,427	9,860	9,966	10,360
Interest [8]	367	635	662	706	805	967	977	920	829
Rents and royalties	54	105	110	113	116	129	133	137	140
Deductions [3][6]	6,125	8,158	8,395	9,244	9,853	10,545	11,033	11,087	11,330
Cost of sales and operations [7]	4,205	4,894	4,923	5,596	5,945	6,317	6,611	6,654	6,772
Compensation of officers	109	171	185	200	203	198	205	201	221
Rent paid on business property	72	135	145	154	161	173	185	193	196
Taxes paid	163	201	203	211	222	236	251	258	274
Interest paid	345	569	573	590	672	832	825	733	597
Depreciation	157	304	313	317	328	337	333	334	346
Advertising	52	92	99	107	114	124	126	129	134
Net income (less loss) [6][9]	239	240	270	328	413	389	371	345	402
Net income	297	364	409	465	556	556	553	536	570
Deficit	58	124	139	137	143	167	182	191	168
Income subject to tax	247	266	276	312	383	371	366	350	378
Income tax before credits [10]	104	109	109	115	127	123	119	116	126
Tax credits [3]	42	48	37	31	35	32	32	29	30
Foreign tax credit	25	24	21	21	27	24	25	21	22
Income tax after credits [11]	62	61	72	84	92	96	96	93	102

[1] Represents certain small corporations with up to 35 shareholders (15 in 1980), mostly individuals, electing to be taxed at the shareholder level.   [2] Includes items not shown separately.   [3] Payable in less than 1 year.   [4] Payable in 1 year or more.   [5] Appropriated and unappropriated.   [6] Except for 1980, receipts, deductions and net income of S corporations are limited to those from trade or business. Those from investments are excluded.   [7] Beginning 1987, includes gross sales and cost of sales of securities, commodities, and real estate by exchanges, brokers, or dealers selling on their own accounts. Previously, net gain included in total receipts only. Excludes investment income.   [8] Includes tax-exempt interest in State and local government obligations.   [9] Excludes regulated investment companies.   [10] Consists of regular (and alternative tax) only.   [11] Includes minimum tax, alternative minimum tax, adjustments for prior year credits, and other income-related taxes.

Source: U.S. Internal Revenue Service, *Statistics of Income, Corporation Income Tax Returns*, annual.

No. 855. Corporations—Selected Financial Items, by Industry: 1980 to 1992

[**In billions of dollars, except as indicated.** Covers active corporations only. Industrial distribution based on data collected from companies; see text, section 17. Excludes corporations not allocable by industry]

INDUSTRY	1980	1985	1987	1988	1989	1990	1991	1992
Agriculture, forestry, and fishing:								
Returns (1,000)	81	103	117	120	123	126	130	138
Assets	40.7	52.7	55.4	60.5	63.4	68.3	67.8	71.8
Liabilities [1]	29.3	37.2	37.2	40.2	42.3	45.0	45.0	46.7
Receipts [2]	52.1	70.5	77.1	86.3	86.6	88.1	85.9	95.6
Deductions [2]	51.4	70.6	75.4	84.6	85.1	86.9	85.3	94.0
Net income (less loss) [2]	0.7	−0.1	1.6	1.6	1.6	1.2	0.6	1.6
Mining:								
Returns (1,000)	26	41	42	41	42	40	39	37
Assets	126.9	240.8	220.1	225.6	236.3	219.2	213.0	218.2
Liabilities [1]	72.9	136.0	110.6	113.8	109.9	108.9	106.4	112.1
Receipts [2]	176.7	142.0	96.8	100.4	102.4	111.4	103.3	112.8
Deductions [2]	169.1	145.4	96.7	96.8	99.5	106.5	99.5	110.3
Net income (less loss) [2]	7.8	−2.5	0.3	4.1	3.1	5.3	4.0	2.7
Construction:								
Returns (1,000)	272	318	371	381	393	407	417	408
Assets	132.9	215.3	222.1	241.4	249.7	243.8	243.0	231.1
Liabilities [1]	100.1	160.6	168.1	178.9	183.0	180.0	172.4	159.5
Receipts [2]	267.2	387.2	454.8	499.7	517.5	534.7	515.1	499.4
Deductions [2]	262.1	382.8	446.1	488.4	508.8	527.8	509.2	493.9
Net income (less loss) [2]	5.3	4.4	8.7	11.3	8.7	6.8	6.1	5.5
Manufacturing:								
Returns (1,000)	243	277	294	300	301	302	300	300
Assets	1,709.5	2,644.4	3,111.7	3,390.4	3,721.2	3,921.3	4,028.4	4,113.1
Liabilities [1]	960.3	1,544.7	1,920.0	2,137.2	2,347.7	2,529.1	2,547.2	2,701.2
Receipts [2]	2,404.3	2,831.1	3,141.4	3,349.0	3,531.2	3,688.7	3,658.5	3,760.3
Deductions [2]	2,290.6	2,733.1	3,012.1	3,170.0	3,377.1	3,545.1	3,548.7	3,633.8
Net income (less loss) [2]	125.7	113.8	145.5	205.1	180.5	171.4	132.3	143.6
Transportation and public utilities:								
Returns (1,000)	111	138	148	149	156	160	165	178
Assets	758.4	1,246.4	1,352.5	1,411.2	1,474.4	1,522.0	1,573.8	1,642.0
Liabilities [1]	467.7	755.9	842.4	891.8	963.1	1,013.4	1,044.9	1,106.3
Receipts [2]	523.8	772.4	786.2	838.8	906.5	936.3	954.9	997.6
Deductions [2]	504.0	747.8	749.0	792.5	867.6	901.0	917.8	956.5
Net income (less loss) [2]	20.0	25.1	37.5	46.9	39.1	35.4	37.7	41.8
Wholesale and retail trade:								
Returns (1,000)	800	917	972	985	1,013	1,023	1,044	1,053
Assets	646.9	1,010.0	1,177.7	1,295.8	1,390.6	1,447.3	1,483.4	1,581.9
Liabilities [1]	424.6	723.7	861.2	963.9	1,047.8	1,092.5	1,108.6	1,177.7
Receipts [2]	1,955.5	2,473.9	2,766.7	2,978.0	3,184.9	3,309.0	3,380.6	3,503.9
Deductions [2]	1,919.5	2,440.4	2,728.5	2,935.5	3,148.8	3,279.1	3,350.9	3,463.4
Net income (less loss) [2]	35.8	33.1	38.0	42.8	36.2	30.1	30.0	41.3
Finance, insurance, and real estate:								
Returns (1,000)	493	518	521	572	593	609	618	635
Assets	4,022.2	7,029.5	8,732.3	9,411.5	9,957.5	10,193.3	10,780.7	11,480.5
Liabilities [1]	3,491.7	5,867.5	7,097.4	7,632.1	7,929.3	8,051.3	8,267.1	8,531.3
Receipts [2] [3]	697.5	1,182.0	1,589.2	1,714.4	1,868.0	1,954.7	1,924.3	1,900.4
Deductions [2]	652.6	1,104.6	1,476.7	1,596.0	1,730.5	1,809.9	1,771.2	1,724.3
Net income (less loss) [2]	33.1	60.7	87.4	91.9	108.9	109.9	124.5	147.0
Services:								
Returns (1,000)	671	939	1,120	995	990	1,029	1,062	1,100
Assets	178.2	331.0	435.6	530.3	552.1	572.8	636.8	661.6
Liabilities [1]	125.3	241.1	323.1	402.2	419.8	429.7	459.1	465.0
Receipts [2]	279.9	534.6	663.1	695.3	735.5	779.3	809.7	869.5
Deductions [2]	271.8	528.7	654.0	686.3	724.9	769.0	800.2	851.1
Net income (less loss) [2]	8.2	5.9	9.3	9.3	11.0	10.6	9.8	18.5
ANNUAL PERCENT CHANGE RECEIPTS [4]								
Agriculture, forestry, and fishing	−2.4	5.9	−0.5	11.9	0.3	1.7	−2.5	11.3
Mining	33.3	15.0	−1.8	3.7	1.9	8.8	−7.3	9.2
Construction	5.7	14.4	10.2	9.8	3.6	3.3	−3.7	−3.0
Manufacturing	11.7	2.3	11.7	6.6	5.4	4.5	−0.8	2.8
Transportation and public utilities	17.5	6.4	3.1	6.6	8.1	3.3	2.0	4.5
Wholesale and retail trade	11.6	7.2	8.6	7.6	6.9	3.9	2.2	3.6
Finance, insurance, and real estate	24.3	14.4	16.4	7.8	9.0	4.6	−1.6	−1.2
Services	14.2	9.0	12.0	4.8	5.8	6.0	3.9	7.4

[1] Liabilities does not include net worth.   [2] Beginning 1987, receipts, deductions, and net income of S corporations are limited to those from trade or business; those from investments are generally excluded. S corporations are certain small corporations with up to 35 shareholders (15 in 1980), mostly individuals, electing to be taxed at the shareholder level.   [3] Beginning 1987, includes gross sales (previously net sales) of securities, commodities, and real estate by exchanges, brokers, or dealers selling on their own account.   [4] Change from preceding year.

Source: U.S. Internal Revenue Service, *Statistics of Income, Corporation Income Tax Returns*, annual.

No. 856. Corporations, by Asset-Size Class and Industry: 1991

[**In millions of dollars, except number of returns and percent distribution.** Covers active corporations only. Excludes corporations not allocable by industry. The industrial distribution is based on data collected from companies; see text, section 17. Detail may not add to total because of rounding. See also *Historical Statistics, Colonial Times to 1970*, series V 167-183 and V 193-196]

INDUSTRY	Total	ASSET-SIZE CLASS					
		Under $10 mil. [1]	$10-$24.9 mil.	$25-$49.9 mil.	$50-$99.9 mil.	$100-$249.9 mil.	$250 mil. and over
Agriculture, forestry, and fishing:							
Returns	129,886	129,373	316	110	52	24	12
Assets	67,757	46,567	4,861	3,895	3,765	3,925	4,744
Receipts	85,946	60,551	5,260	5,317	4,837	4,952	5,028
Deductions	85,332	60,195	5,263	5,242	4,897	4,885	4,849
Net income (less loss)	626	341	(Z)	74	-62	67	206
Mining:							
Returns	39,199	38,272	450	186	113	80	97
Assets	212,963	16,971	6,919	6,751	8,110	13,687	160,525
Receipts	103,286	20,208	5,862	4,222	4,954	8,148	59,893
Deductions	99,538	19,956	5,859	4,282	4,931	7,963	56,546
Net income (less loss)	4,001	244	-6	-63	22	186	3,618
Construction:							
Returns	416,987	414,894	1,476	348	155	71	43
Assets	243,036	134,116	22,168	12,032	12,506	11,354	50,860
Receipts	515,129	366,281	44,501	21,493	19,089	17,157	46,607
Deductions	509,248	363,033	43,847	21,139	18,910	16,944	45,373
Net income (less loss)	6,104	3,207	635	348	166	227	1,520
Manufacturing:							
Returns	300,122	288,768	5,728	2,292	1,292	952	1,091
Assets	4,028,360	194,210	89,369	79,953	91,337	172,063	3,401,427
Receipts	3,658,501	460,024	160,241	123,824	128,380	205,641	2,580,391
Deductions	3,548,747	456,013	156,315	120,039	124,944	199,369	2,492,066
Net income (less loss)	132,269	3,981	3,908	3,769	3,463	6,802	110,346
Transportation and public utilities:							
Returns	164,980	162,537	1,207	421	247	201	367
Assets	1,573,824	57,739	18,493	15,056	17,364	31,602	1,433,570
Receipts	954,945	148,430	22,889	17,799	16,185	26,925	722,716
Deductions	917,838	148,218	22,902	17,650	16,398	26,389	686,280
Net income (less loss)	37,743	197	-24	148	-217	608	37,031
Wholesale and retail trade:							
Returns	1,043,534	1,034,263	5,902	1,670	765	496	439
Assets	1,483,428	419,387	88,349	57,811	53,106	79,406	785,368
Receipts	3,380,599	1,500,494	252,213	158,692	139,379	192,858	1,136,963
Deductions	3,350,909	1,496,314	250,041	157,188	137,781	191,740	1,117,845
Net income (less loss)	29,951	4,112	2,156	1,512	1,602	1,132	19,437
Finance, insurance, and real estate:							
Returns	617,557	593,275	7,277	5,073	4,446	3,844	3,642
Assets	10,780,681	246,705	118,301	181,633	315,463	601,295	9,317,284
Receipts [2]	1,924,318	196,406	28,096	27,643	45,987	89,921	1,536,266
Deductions	1,771,169	194,879	28,043	25,820	41,605	78,102	1,402,720
Net income (less loss)	124,546	1,043	-209	1,290	3,218	8,918	110,285
Services:							
Returns	1,061,657	1,057,496	2,252	906	446	314	242
Assets	636,752	183,809	34,864	31,714	31,481	49,476	305,408
Receipts	809,724	468,297	44,147	34,727	34,877	45,927	181,750
Deductions	800,164	462,686	43,911	34,609	34,822	45,344	178,792
Net income (less loss)	9,770	5,589	226	98	39	571	3,247
PERCENT DISTRIBUTION RECEIPTS							
Agriculture, forestry, and fishing	100	70	6	6	6	6	6
Mining	100	20	6	4	5	8	58
Construction	100	71	9	4	4	3	9
Manufacturing	100	13	4	3	4	6	71
Transportation and public utilities	100	16	2	2	2	3	76
Wholesale and retail trade	100	44	7	5	4	6	34
Finance, insurance, and real estate [2]	100	10	1	1	2	5	80
Services	100	58	5	4	4	6	22

Z Less than $500,000.   [1] Includes returns with zero assets.   [2] Includes investment income.

Source: U.S. Internal Revenue Service, *Statistics of Income, Corporation Income Tax Returns*, annual.

No. 857. Employees and Payroll, by Employment-Size Class: 1980 to 1992

[Excludes government employees, railroad employees, self-employed persons, etc. See "General Explanation" in source for definitions and statement on reliability of data. An **establishment** is a single physical location where business is conducted or where services or industrial operations are performed]

EMPLOYMENT-SIZE CLASS	Unit	1980	1985	1986	1987	1988	1989	1990	1991	1992
Employees, total [1]	1,000 ..	**74,844**	**81,111**	**83,379**	**85,484**	**87,882**	**91,631**	**93,476**	**92,302**	**92,801**
Under 20 employees	1,000 ..	19,423	21,810	22,296	23,069	23,583	23,992	24,373	24,482	25,000
20 to 99 employees	1,000 ..	21,168	23,539	24,311	25,221	25,930	26,829	27,414	26,906	27,030
100 to 499 employees	1,000 ..	17,840	19,410	20,260	20,615	21,307	22,387	22,926	22,369	22,227
500 to 999 employees	1,000 ..	5,689	5,716	5,780	5,922	6,078	6,442	6,551	6,325	6,270
1,000 or more employees	1,000 ..	10,716	10,645	10,734	10,657	10,984	11,981	12,212	12,220	12,275
Annual payroll, total [1]	Bil. dol.	**1,035**	**1,514**	**1,608**	**1,724**	**1,860**	**1,990**	**2,104**	**2,145**	**2,272**
Under 20 employees	Bil. dol .	231	352	375	414	440	461	485	502	536
20 to 99 employees	Bil. dol .	261	388	414	449	485	514	547	555	586
100 to 499 employees	Bil. dol .	249	362	391	417	452	488	518	523	550
500 to 999 employees	Bil. dol .	91	126	132	140	152	163	174	175	186
1,000 or more employees	Bil. dol .	208	286	298	305	331	364	381	390	413

[1] Prior to 1987, totals for employees and annual payroll have been revised. Detail may not add to totals because revisions for size class are not available.

Source: U.S. Bureau of the Census, *County Business Patterns,* annual.

No. 858. Establishments, Employees, and Payroll, by Industry: 1980 to 1992

[See headnote, table 843. Beginning 1990, data are based on the 1987 Standard Industrial Classification (SIC). Prior to 1990, data are based on the 1972 SIC]

INDUSTRY	ESTABLISHMENTS (1,000)				EMPLOYEES (1,000)				PAYROLL (bil. dol.)			
	1980	1985	1990	1992	1980	1985	1990	1992	1980	1985	1990	1992
All industries [1]	**4,543**	**5,701**	**6,176**	**6,318**	**74,844**	**81,111**	**93,476**	**92,801**	**1,035**	**1,513**	**2,104**	**2,272**
Agricultural services [2]	46	64	85	97	290	380	531	594	3	5	9	10
Mining	30	37	30	29	994	943	723	651	22	28	27	26
Construction	418	476	578	589	4,473	4,480	5,239	4,500	75	98	132	122
Manufacturing	319	358	378	387	21,165	19,429	19,173	18,162	355	458	544	563
Transportation [3]	168	203	235	259	4,623	4,809	5,592	5,517	88	123	166	175
Wholesale trade	385	438	476	492	5,211	5,624	6,328	6,094	89	130	181	191
Retail trade	1,223	1,407	1,530	1,564	15,047	16,851	19,815	19,672	124	178	242	259
Finance and insurance [4]	421	488	545	597	5,295	6,005	6,956	6,906	77	132	197	221
Services	1,278	1,712	2,059	2,218	17,186	21,549	28,800	30,654	197	346	599	704

[1] Includes nonclassifiable establishments not shown separately. [2] Includes forestry and fisheries. [3] Includes public utilities. [4] Includes real estate.

Source: U.S. Bureau of the Census, *County Business Patterns,* annual.

No. 859. Establishments, Employees, and Payroll, by Employment-Size Class and Industry: 1992

[See headnote, table 857. Data are based on the 1987 Standard Industrial Classification]

EMPLOYMENT SIZE-CLASS	Unit	All industries [1]	Agricultural services [2]	Mining	Construction	Manufacturing	Transportation [3]	Wholesale trade	Retail trade	Finance and insurance [4]	Services
Establishments, total	1,000 ..	**6,318**	**97**	**29**	**589**	**387**	**259**	**492**	**1,564**	**597**	**2,218**
Under 20 employees	1,000 ..	5,507	92	23	545	262	212	425	1,330	541	1,989
20 to 99 employees	1,000 ..	678	5	4	40	89	38	60	211	47	185
100 to 499 employees	1,000 ..	118	(Z)	1	4	31	8	7	23	7	38
500 to 999 employees	1,000 ..	9	(Z)	(Z)	(Z)	3	1	(Z)	1	1	3
1,000 or more employees	1,000 ..	6	(Z)	(Z)	(Z)	2	(Z)	(Z)	(Z)	(Z)	3
Employees, total	1,000 ..	**92,801**	**594**	**651**	**4,500**	**18,162**	**5,517**	**6,094**	**19,672**	**6,906**	**30,654**
Under 20 employees	1,000 ..	25,000	339	112	2,075	1,526	989	2,203	7,064	2,221	8,428
20 to 99 employees	1,000 ..	27,030	164	181	1,490	3,909	1,545	2,257	8,276	1,828	7,370
100 to 499 employees	1,000 ..	22,227	64	202	665	6,347	1,440	1,208	3,753	1,433	7,114
500 to 999 employees	1,000 ..	6,270	14	77	99	2,336	437	223	352	528	2,203
1,000 or more employees	1,000 ..	12,275	13	77	171	4,044	1,106	204	228	895	5,538
Annual payroll, total	Bil. dol.	**2,272**	**10.0**	**25.6**	**122.1**	**563.1**	**175.5**	**190.8**	**258.6**	**221.0**	**703.6**
Under 20 employees	Bil. dol .	536	5.8	3.3	48.7	37.3	24.1	63.3	88.6	60.8	202.4
20 to 99 employees	Bil. dol .	586	2.7	6.2	42.8	104.1	44.1	100.9	58.8	157.7
100 to 499 employees	Bil. dol .	550	1.1	8.7	21.7	180.8	48.1	41.1	55.5	48.9	144.4
500 to 999 employees	Bil. dol .	186	0.3	3.6	3.4	75.3	16.7	8.9	7.4	18.3	52.3
1,000 or more employees	Bil. dol .	413	0.2	3.8	5.4	165.6	42.4	8.5	6.2	34.2	146.8

Z Less than 500 establishments. [1] Includes nonclassifiable establishments not shown separately. [2] Includes forestry and fisheries. [3] Includes public utilities. [4] Includes real estate.

Source: U.S. Bureau of the Census, *County Business Patterns,* annual.

No. 860. New Business Incorporations and Business Failures: 1970 to 1994

[1970 excludes Hawaii; 1970 and 1975 exclude Alaska. Total concerns and failure data prior to 1984 exclude agriculture, forestry, and fishing; finance, insurance, and real estate; and services; therefore, are not directly comparable with data for 1984 and later. See also *Historical Statistics, Colonial Times to 1970*, series V 20-30]

YEAR	Total concerns in business [1] (1,000)	Index of net business formations [2] (1967 =100)	New incorporations (1,000)	FAILURES [3] Number	FAILURES [3] Rate per 10,000 concerns	FAILURES [3] Current liabilities [4] (mil. dol.)	YEAR	Total concerns in business [1] (1,000)	Index of net business formations [2] (1967 =100)	New incorporations (1,000)	FAILURES [3] Number	FAILURES [3] Rate per 10,000 concerns	FAILURES [3] Current liabilities [4] (mil. dol.)
1970....	2,442	108.8	264	10,748	44	1,888	1987....	6,004	121.2	686	61,111	102	34,724
1975....	2,679	109.9	326	11,432	43	4,380	1988....	5,804	124.1	685	57,098	98	39,573
1980....	2,780	129.9	534	11,742	42	4,635	1989....	7,694	124.8	677	50,361	65	42,329
1981....	2,745	124.8	581	16,794	61	6,955	1990....	8,038	120.7	647	60,747	74	56,130
1982....	2,806	116.4	567	24,908	88	15,611	1991....	8,218	115.2	629	88,140	107	96,825
1983....	2,851	117.5	600	31,334	110	16,073	1992....	8,805	116.3	667	97,069	110	94,318
1984....	4,885	121.3	635	52,078	107	29,269	1993....	8,966	121.1	70	86,133	96	47,755
1985....	4,990	120.9	664	57,078	115	36,937	1994, prel.	(NA)	126.2	(NA)	71,520	79	29,357
1986....	5,119	120.4	703	61,616	120	44,724							

NA Not available.   [1] Data through 1983 represent number of names listed in July issue of *Dun & Bradstreet Reference Book*. Data for 1984-93 represent the number of establishments listed in the Dun's Census of American Business. The base has been changed due to expanded business failure coverage.   [2] Source: U.S. Bureau of Economic Analysis, *Survey of Current Business*. [3] Includes concerns discontinued following assignment, voluntary or involuntary petition in bankruptcy, attachment, execution, foreclosure, etc.; voluntary withdrawals from business with known loss to creditors; also enterprises involved in court action, such as receivership and reorganization or arrangement which may or may not lead to discontinuance; and businesses making voluntary compromise with creditors out of court.   [4] Liabilities exclude long-term publicly held obligations; offsetting assets are not taken into account.

Source: Except as noted, Dun & Bradstreet Corporation, New York, NY, *New Business Incorporations*, monthly; and *Monthly Failure Report*.

No. 861. New Business Incorporations and Business Failures, by State: 1992 to 1994

[1993 preliminary]

DIVISION AND STATE	NEW BUSINESS INCORPORATIONS 1992	NEW BUSINESS INCORPORATIONS 1993	NUMBER OF FAILURES 1993	NUMBER OF FAILURES 1994	DIVISION AND STATE	NEW BUSINESS INCORPORATIONS 1992	NEW BUSINESS INCORPORATIONS 1993	NUMBER OF FAILURES 1993	NUMBER OF FAILURES 1994
United States ...	666,800	706,537	86,133	71,520	District of Columbia ..	2,256	2,256	197	167
					Virginia	16,936	17,212	1,741	1,455
Northeast..........	143,119	146,557	18,242	14,215	West Virginia	2,236	2,406	316	297
New England	28,686	30,233	5,339	3,757	North Carolina	12,580	13,424	1,194	1,051
Maine	2,431	2,664	383	334	South Carolina	6,189	6,483	397	499
New Hampshire	2,577	2,884	621	410	Georgia	21,046	23,084	2,355	1,958
Vermont..........	1,589	1,617	174	131	Florida...........	86,037	88,048	5,091	3,605
Massachusetts	12,197	12,850	2,712	2,097	East South Central ..	26,514	28,184	3,217	2,585
Rhode Island	2,553	2,696	346	212	Kentucky	7,155	7,758	845	706
Connecticut	7,339	7,522	1,103	573	Tennessee	8,514	8,859	1,210	957
Middle Atlantic	114,433	116,324	12,903	10,458	Alabama	7,087	7,179	839	669
New York..........	67,503	69,835	6,924	5,533	Mississippi	3,758	4,388	323	253
New Jersey	29,983	29,603	2,848	2,182	West South Central ...	58,135	58,805	9,389	8,026
Pennsylvania	16,947	16,886	3,131	2,743	Arkansas	6,078	5,410	186	365
Midwest...........	127,541	138,387	13,540	11,470	Louisiana	10,839	10,656	668	657
East North Central....	92,792	101,052	9,097	7,768	Oklahoma	7,207	7,832	1,443	116
Ohio.............	18,730	20,082	2,131	1,988	Texas	34,011	34,907	7,092	5,838
Indiana	11,119	11,542	1,098	904	West	113,428	125,490	28,767	24,490
Illinois...........	30,928	32,756	2,092	1,749	Mountain	49,841	56,871	5,606	4,293
Michigan	24,726	28,790	2,554	1,956	Montana	1,948	2,261	174	179
Wisconsin	7,289	7,882	1,222	1,171	Idaho	2,127	2,511	351	277
West North Central ...	34,749	37,335	4,443	3,702	Wyoming	1,707	1,747	90	84
Minnesota	10,002	10,845	918	723	Colorado	14,876	15,452	1,548	1,311
Iowa	4,918	4,804	508	473	New Mexico	2,843	3,232	449	328
Missouri..........	10,020	11,544	1,231	1,064	Arizona	9,148	11,170	2,069	1,405
North Dakota	984	932	145	89	Utah	4,582	5,270	356	261
South Dakota	1,218	1,337	174	168	Nevada	12,610	15,228	569	448
Nebraska	3,302	3,458	398	315	Pacific	63,587	68,619	23,161	20,197
Kansas	4,305	4,415	1,069	870	Washington	12,500	13,444	2,032	2,000
South............	282,712	296,103	25,584	21,345	Oregon	8,861	9,874	969	1,025
South Atlantic.......	198,063	209,114	12,978	10,734	California	36,973	40,072	19,746	16,803
Delaware........	33,582	39,111	138	88	Alaska...........	1,461	1,437	108	111
Maryland	17,201	17,090	1,549	1,614	Hawaii...........	3,792	3,792	306	258

Source: Dun & Bradstreet Corporation, New York, NY, *New Business Incorporations*, monthly; and *Business Failure Record*, annual, (copyright).

Business Enterprise

No. 862. Business Failures, by Industry: 1990 to 1994

INDUSTRY	NUMBER					RATE PER 10,000 FIRMS				
	1990	1991	1992	1993	1994	1990	1991	1992	1993	1994
Total	60,747	88,140	97,069	86,133	71,520	74	107	109	90	74
Agriculture, forestry, fishing	1,733	2,256	2,871	2,289	1,872	50	65	80	64	62
Mining	388	411	430	310	241	88	95	99	73	62
Construction	8,162	11,963	12,452	10,552	8,301	91	128	129	109	91
Manufacturing	4,740	6,595	7,120	6,163	4,643	92	127	131	114	90
Food and kindred products	232	305	350	299	204	91	122	133	116	82
Textile mill products	102	143	171	149	99	97	135	158	139	98
Apparel, other textile products	318	505	566	567	410	114	177	191	191	146
Lumber and wood products	420	576	554	440	327	97	129	122	98	86
Furniture and fixtures	258	383	398	305	233	151	223	226	174	139
Paper and allied products	68	86	88	86	70	105	129	128	124	102
Printing and publishing	734	1,062	1,245	1,059	823	74	105	118	100	78
Chemicals and allied products	139	207	219	169	141	86	128	129	101	89
Petroleum refining	21	33	35	17	15	83	137	161	78	73
Rubber and misc. products	158	209	185	197	150	101	134	113	119	92
Leather and leather products	40	40	35	43	42	113	114	95	120	127
Stone, clay, and glass products	161	220	215	168	132	80	111	107	85	74
Primary metal products	115	145	141	95	81	123	157	152	104	91
Fabricated metal products	397	593	662	584	400	90	135	145	128	90
Machinery, exc. electric	656	823	951	860	618	84	105	117	107	79
Electric and electronic equipment	287	380	421	327	271	114	149	157	124	108
Transportation equipment	242	318	263	229	170	147	198	158	140	114
Instruments and related equipment	120	192	175	157	148	68	106	92	83	81
Miscellaneous	272	375	446	412	309	74	98	106	97	73
Transportation, public utilities	2,630	3,891	3,922	3,102	2,448	94	134	126	99	77
Wholesale trade	4,423	6,170	6,744	6,014	4,635	77	109	113	73	55
Retail trade	12,972	17,242	19,084	15,661	12,575	65	90	76	78	66
Finance, insurance, real estate	3,819	5,962	6,260	4,989	3,907	60	90	87	68	52
Services	16,119	22,852	26,871	24,371	20,595	49	87	93	65	50
Public administration	10	20	30	24	20	(NA)	(NA)	(NA)	(NA)	(NA)
Nonclassifiable establishments	5,751	10,778	11,285	12,658	12,283	(NA)	(NA)	(NA)	(NA)	(NA)

NA Not available.

Source: The Dun and Bradstreet Corporation, New York, NY, *Business Failure Record,* annual, (copyright).

No. 863. Bankruptcy Cases, by State: 1991 to 1994

[In thousands. For years ending June 30. Includes outlying areas, not shown separately. Covers only bankruptcy cases filed under the Bankruptcy Reform Act of 1978. Bankruptcy: legal recognition that a company or individual is insolvent and must restructure or liquidate. Petitions "filed" means the commencement of a proceeding through the presentation of a petition to the clerk of the court]

STATE	1991	1992	1993	1994	STATE	1991	1992	1993	1994
United States	880.4	972.5	918.7	845.3	Missouri	17.3	19.2	16.6	14.4
Alabama	27.8	27.8	25.5	23.7	Montana	2.1	2.1	1.9	1.9
Alaska	1.1	1.1	1.0	0.9	Nebraska	4.5	4.4	3.9	3.6
Arizona	19.3	20.4	18.5	17.0	Nevada	6.9	7.7	7.9	7.7
Arkansas	7.7	8.6	7.5	6.7	New Hampshire	3.4	4.0	3.7	3.3
California	124.2	152.8	159.7	150.9	New Jersey	19.4	24.0	24.9	23.8
Colorado	17.0	16.6	14.9	13.2	New Mexico	4.5	4.5	4.3	3.5
Connecticut	6.9	8.9	9.4	8.7	New York	40.3	49.6	51.3	47.8
Delaware	1.3	1.4	1.6	1.3	North Carolina	15.5	16.3	13.8	13.0
District of Columbia	1.2	1.4	1.4	1.3	North Dakota	1.2	1.2	1.1	1.1
Florida	43.4	52.4	46.6	41.9	Ohio	42.8	44.0	37.9	32.5
Georgia	49.0	48.7	42.9	40.5	Oklahoma	16.2	15.3	13.9	13.0
Hawaii	1.0	1.3	1.5	1.5	Oregon	13.5	14.3	13.3	12.7
Idaho	4.2	4.1	3.9	3.4	Pennsylvania	20.8	24.3	23.0	20.2
Illinois	40.5	43.4	41.4	38.4	Rhode Island	3.1	3.6	3.5	3.1
Indiana	26.8	28.2	24.8	22.0	South Carolina	6.9	7.4	6.8	6.4
Iowa	5.8	6.4	5.9	5.3	South Dakota	1.6	1.4	1.4	1.3
Kansas	9.6	9.6	8.3	7.9	Tennessee	40.6	41.6	38.2	35.6
Kentucky	15.6	15.5	12.8	11.6	Texas	46.6	49.5	47.3	41.8
Louisiana	13.3	14.2	13.2	12.3	Utah	8.0	8.3	7.5	6.6
Maine	2.2	2.3	2.0	1.8	Vermont	0.8	1.0	0.9	0.8
Maryland	12.8	16.0	16.2	15.4	Virginia	25.3	29.1	26.8	24.4
Massachusetts	12.9	15.9	16.4	14.8	Washington	17.2	18.7	17.9	17.5
Michigan	23.3	26.7	25.1	22.9	West Virginia	4.0	4.5	4.0	3.6
Minnesota	16.7	17.8	15.5	13.9	Wisconsin	12.1	12.4	11.3	10.2
Mississippi	12.3	12.7	11.1	9.8	Wyoming	1.5	1.4	1.3	1.2

Source: Administrative Office of the U.S. Courts, unpublished data.

No. 864. Bankruptcy Petitions Filed and Pending, by Type and Chapter: 1985 to 1994

[For years ending June 30. Covers only bankruptcy cases filed under the Bankruptcy Reform Act of 1978. Bankruptcy: legal recognition that a company or individual is insolvent and must restructure or liquidate. Petitions "filed" means the commencement of a proceeding through the presentation of a petition to the clerk of the court; "pending" is a proceeding in which the administration has not been completed]

ITEM	1985	1987	1988	1989	1990	1991	1992	1993	1994
Total, filed	364,536	561,278	594,567	642,993	725,484	880,399	972,490	918,734	845,257
Business [1]	66,651	88,278	68,501	62,534	64,688	67,714	72,650	66,428	56,748
Nonbusiness [2]	297,885	473,000	526,066	580,459	660,796	812,685	899,840	852,306	788,509
Voluntary	362,939	559,658	593,158	641,528	723,886	878,626	971,047	917,350	844,087
Involuntary	1,597	1,620	1,409	1,465	1,598	1,773	1,443	1,384	1,170
Chapter 7 [3]	244,650	397,551	423,796	457,240	505,337	612,330	679,662	638,916	578,903
Chapter 9 [4]	3	10	3	7	7	20	15	9	17
Chapter 11 [5]	21,425	22,566	18,891	17,465	19,591	22,495	24,029	20,579	17,098
Chapter 12 [6]	(X)	4,824	3,099	1,717	1,351	1,358	1,634	1,434	976
Chapter 13 [7]	98,452	136,300	148,771	166,539	199,186	244,192	267,121	257,777	248,246
Section 304 [8]	6	27	7	25	12	4	29	19	17
Total, pending . . .	608,945	808,504	814,195	869,340	961,919	1,123,433	1,237,357	1,183,009	1,134,036

X Not applicable.   [1] Business bankruptcies include those filed under chapters 7, 9, 11, or 12.   [2] Bankruptcies include those filed under chapters 7, 11, or 13.   [3] Chapter 7, liquidation of nonexempt assets of businesses or individuals.   [4] Chapter 9, adjustment of debts of a municipality.   [5] Chapter 11, individual or business reorganization.   [6] Chapter 12, adjustment of debts of a family farmer with regular income, effective November 26, 1986.   [7] Chapter 13, adjustment of debts of an individual with regular income.   [8] Chapter 11 U.S.C., Section 304, cases ancillary to foreign proceedings.

Source: Administrative Office of the U.S. Courts, Annual Report of the Director.

No. 865. Small Business Administration Loans to Small Businesses: 1980 to 1994

[For fiscal year ending in year shown; see text, section 9. A small business must be independently owned and operated, must not be dominant in its particular industry, and must meet standards set by the Small Business Administration as to its annual receipts or number of employees. Loans include both direct and guaranteed loans to small business establishments. Does not include Disaster Assistance Loans]

LOANS APPROVED	Unit	1980	1985	1986	1987	1988	1989	1990	1991	1992	1993	1994
Loans, all businesses	1,000. . .	31.7	19.3	16.8	17.1	17.1	17.0	18.8	19.4	25.1	28.0	38.8
Loans, minority-owned businesses . .	1,000. . .	6.0	2.8	2.0	2.1	2.2	2.4	2.4	2.9	3.6	4.3	6.9
Percent of all business loans	Percent .	19	15	12	12	13	14	13	15	14	15	18
Value of total loans [1]	Mil. dol. .	3,858	3,217	3,013	3,232	3,434	3,490	4,354	4,625	6,339	7,412	8,426
Value of loans to minority-operated businesses [2]	Mil. dol. .	470	324	265	299	343	385	473	601	808	928	1,328

[1] Includes both SBA and bank portions of loans.   [2] SBA direct loans and guaranteed portion of bank loans only.

Source: U.S. Small Business Administration, unpublished data.

No. 866. Employee Stock Ownership Plans: 1975 to 1992
[As of end of year]

YEAR	Number of plans	Number of employees (1,000)	YEAR	Number of plans	Number of employees (1,000)	YEAR	Number of plans	Number of employees (1,000)
1975	1,601	248	1983	6,456	5,397	1988	8,862	9,076
1979	4,551	3,039	1984	6,904	6,576	1989	9,385	10,631
1980	5,009	4,048	1985	7,402	7,353	1990	9,870	11,271
1981	5,680	4,537	1986	8,046	7,860	1991	9,888	11,329
1982	6,082	4,745	1987	8,514	8,860	1992	9,764	11,153

Source: National Center for Employee Ownership, Inc., Oakland, CA, unpublished data.

No. 867. Venture Capital Commitments, by Source: 1980 to 1994

[1993 data preliminary. **Venture capital commitment:** investment in venture capital partnerships]

SOURCE	1980	1985	1987	1988	1989	1990	1991	1992	1993	1994
Capital commitments (mil. dol.). .	**661**	**2,327**	**4,184**	**2,947**	**2,399**	**1,847**	**1,271**	**2,548**	**2,545**	**3,764**
PERCENT DISTRIBUTION										
Individuals/families	16	13	12	8	6	11	12	11	7	12
Endowments/foundations	14	8	10	12	12	13	24	18	11	21
Insurance companies/banks	13	11	15	9	13	9	5	15	11	9
Foreign investors	8	23	13	14	13	7	12	11	4	2
Corporations	19	12	11	11	20	7	5	3	8	9
Pension funds	30	33	39	46	36	53	42	42	59	46

Source: Venture Economics Investor Services, Boston, MA, *Venture Capital Journal,* monthly.

No. 868. Venture Capital Disbursements, by Stage and Industry: 1993

[**Preliminary. Venture capital disbursement:** investment by venture capital partnerships in young, high-growth companies that have the potential to contribute to technological development and to become strong competitors in regional, national or international markets]

ITEM	Compa-nies [1]	INVESTMENT			Number of invest-ments [1]
		Total ($1,000)	Percent	Average ($1,000)	
STAGE					
Total	**1,057**	**3,098,395**	**100.0**	**1,081**	**2,867**
Expansion.	504	1,689,536	54.5	1,188	1,422
LBO/acquisition	34	188,172	6.1	2,444	77
Bridge loans, public purchases	224	470,930	15.2	768	613
Other early-stage	93	319,670	10.3	1,269	252
Seed.	104	212,518	6.9	767	277
Start-up	98	217,571	7.0	963	226
INDUSTRY					
Total	**972**	**3,098,395**	**100.0**	**1,014**	**3,055**
Biotechnology	92	284,097	9.2	950	299
Commercial communications	33	136,584	4.4	1,897	72
Computer hardware and systems	55	92,733	3.0	545	170
Consumer-related.	84	325,792	10.5	1,894	172
Energy-related.	4	6,767	0.2	1,353	5
Industrial automation.	7	29,775	1.0	1,985	15
Industry products and machinery.	43	54,590	1.8	501	109
Medical/healthcare-related	159	446,513	14.4	830	538
Other electronics	68	87,821	2.8	374	235
Other products and services.	110	604,731	19.5	1,344	450
Software and services.	203	640,178	20.7	1,010	634
Telephone and data communications	114	308,813	12.5	1,092	356

[1] Figures for total number of companies and financings differ with actual totals reported as a company may receive financings in more than one stage during the year.

Source: Venture Economics Investor Services, Boston, MA, *Venture Capital Journal,* monthly.

No. 869. Mergers and Acquisitions—Summary: 1985 to 1993

[Covers transactions valued at $5 million or more. Values based on transactions for which price data revealed. **All activity** includes mergers, acquisitions, acquisitions of partial interest that involve a 40% stake in the target or an investment of at least $100 million, divestitures, and leveraged transactions that result in a change in ownership. **Divestiture:** sale of a business, division, or subsidiary by corporate owner to another party. **Leveraged buyout:** acquisition of a business in which buyers use mostly borrowed money to finance purchase price and incorporate debt into capital structure of business after change in ownership]

ITEM	Unit	1985	1986	1987	1988	1989	1990	1991	1992	1993
All activity: Number	Number	1,719	2,497	2,479	2,970	3,752	4,239	3,446	3,502	(NA)
Value	Bil. dol.	149.6	223.1	198.8	281.8	316.8	205.6	141.5	125.3	(NA)
Divestitures: Number	Number	780	1,090	1,004	1,274	1,615	1,907	1,759	1,598	1,993
Value	Bil. dol.	51	84.7	77.8	115.8	94.9	90.8	61.4	57.2	213.4
Leveraged buyouts: Number	Number	154	233	208	291	293	177	171	199	621
Value	Bil. dol.	16.3	46.5	40.5	55.2	75.5	17.6	7.3	7.2	16.4
Foreign acquisitions of U.S. companies:										
Number	Number	259	345	365	536	693	773	504	361	(NA)
Value	Bil. dol.	27.9	31.4	55.3	66	69.2	56.4	29.1	17.6	(NA)
U.S. acquisitions overseas:										
Number	Number	91	111	162	223	347	392	402	455	(NA)
Value	Bil. dol.	3.7	3.4	6.9	11.1	27.1	20.5	14.8	13.7	(NA)

NA Not available.

Source: Securities Data Company, Newark, NJ, Merger & Corporate Transactions Database (copyright).

No. 870. Mergers and Acquisitions, by Industry: 1994

[See headnote table 869]

INDUSTRY	TOTAL		U.S. COMPANY ACQUIRING U.S. COMPANY		FOREIGN COMPANY ACQUIRING U.S. COMPANY		U.S. COMPANY ACQUIRING FOREIGN COMPANY	
	Number	Value (mil. dol.)	Number	Value (mil. dol.)	Number	Value (mil. dol.)	Number	Value (mil. dol.)
Total activity [1]	3,129	358,718	1,497	186,181	173	38,169	149	17,612
Construction firms	46	2,926	17	760	3	524	2	248
Food and kindred products	107	19,451	23	8,730	5	3,954	8	632
Textile and apparel products	56	5,387	23	1,775	2	37	1	5
Wood products, furniture, and fixtures	29	1,415	9	223	(NA)	(NA)	1	299
Paper and allied products	44	5,684	7	604	4	2,295	3	178
Chemicals and allied products	71	7,262	21	2,126	3	86	5	328
Drugs	41	26,419	17	14,715	8	8,889	6	214
Soaps, cleaners, & personal-care products	16	4,494	7	1,250	1	1,550	(NA)	(NA)
Rubber & misc. plastic products	41	1,441	16	714	3	40	1	55
Stone, clay, glass and concrete products	53	4,085	10	900	7	206	3	177
Metal and metal products	95	6,610	27	1,071	10	838	9	509
Machinery	83	5,274	36	2,647	6	229	9	452
Computer and office equipment	31	2,030	20	1,720	5	87	1	15
Prepackaged software	51	4,727	34	3,856	5	483	5	208
Electronic and electrical equipment	80	7,210	31	4,223	10	897	8	912
Communications equipment	35	3,005	16	1,576	4	56	3	203
Transportation equipment	39	2,943	13	995	2	59	4	429
Aerospace and aircraft	13	9,166	9	7,995	2	536	(NA)	(NA)
Measuring, medical, photo equip; clocks	71	5,859	38	4,102	9	1,032	3	165
Miscellaneous manufacturing	19	1,089	13	838	(NA)	(NA)	1	78
Air transportation and shipping	19	1,713	3	344	(NA)	(NA)	1	17
Transportation and shipping (except air)	107	4,648	27	1,750	5	276	3	84
Telecommunications	52	14,129	39	5,844	(NA)	(NA)	3	5,623
Radio & television broadcasting stations	85	15,064	62	12,641	2	823	4	301
Printing, publishing, and allied services	59	6,627	24	3,115	1	8	4	820
Electric, gas, water distribution	41	5,315	19	2,809	(NA)	(NA)	2	705
Sanitary services	17	1,227	10	704	2	291	1	46
Services: Hotels and casinos	99	6,478	40	3,338	5	301	4	594
Amusement and recreation services	30	2,240	19	1,965	2	21	(NA)	(NA)
Motion picture production and distribution	20	9,150	12	8,928	1	119	(NA)	(NA)
Business services	183	16,702	114	10,504	10	3,367	10	421
Advertising services	15	1,047	8	604	(NA)	(NA)	(NA)	(NA)
Health services	84	14,760	64	14,139	4	243	1	86
Wholesale trade-durable goods	101	3,716	44	1,629	6	267	8	800
Wholesale trade-nondurable goods	66	7,642	35	4,334	5	1,922	2	76
Retail trade-general merchandise and apparel	26	3,063	11	915	(NA)	(NA)	2	307
Retail trade-food stores	29	2,890	11	1,880	3	483	(NA)	(NA)
Miscellaneous retail trade	54	5,393	21	1,684	3	708	3	181
Commercial banks, bank holding companies	212	23,629	145	10,609	4	822	1	72
Savings and loans, mutual savings banks	78	6,664	77	6,656	1	8	(NA)	(NA)
Credit institutions	14	3,399	8.00	3,120	(NA)	(NA)	(NA)	(NA)
Real estate, mortgage bankers and brokers	210	12,088	110	4,905	1	79	(NA)	(NA)
Investment & commodity firms, dealers, exc.	107	13,996	33	5,686	4	1,715	5	146
Insurance	90	18,175	44	7,234	1	7	5	606
Mining	55	9,689	7	718	5	2,011	2	392
Oil and gas; petroleum refining	140	14,545	77	6,807	9	493	11	1,114

NA Not available.   [1] Includes other items not shown separately.

Source: Securities Data Company, Newark, NJ, Merger & Corporate Transactions Database, (copyright).

No. 871. Patents and Trademarks: 1980 to 1993

[**In thousands.** Calendar year data. Covers patents issued to citizens of the United States and residents of foreign countries. For data on foreign countries, see table 1392. See also *Historical Statistics, Colonial Times to 1970,* series W 96-108]

ITEM	1980	1985	1987	1988	1989	1990	1991	1992	1993
Patent applications filed.	113.0	127.1	139.8	151.9	166.3	176.7	178.4	187.2	189.4
Inventions	104.3	117.0	127.9	139.8	152.8	164.6	164.3	173.1	174.7
Designs	7.8	9.6	11.2	11.3	12.6	11.3	13.1	13.1	13.6
Botanical plants	0.2	0.2	0.4	0.4	0.4	0.4	0.4	0.4	0.4
Reissues.	0.6	0.3	0.4	0.4	0.5	0.5	0.6	0.6	0.6
Patents issued.	66.2	77.3	89.6	84.4	102.7	99.2	106.8	107.4	109.7
Inventions	61.8	71.7	83.0	77.9	95.5	90.4	96.5	97.4	98.3
Individuals	13.8	12.9	15.3	14.3	18.0	17.3	18.1	17.3	16.5
Corporations: United States.	27.7	31.2	33.8	31.5	38.7	36.1	39.2	40.3	41.8
Foreign [1]	19.1	26.4	32.9	31.4	38.0	36.0	38.1	38.7	38.8
U.S. Government.	1.2	1.1	1.0	0.7	0.9	1.0	1.2	1.2	1.2
Designs	3.9	5.1	6.0	5.7	6.1	8.0	9.6	9.3	10.6
Botanical plants	0.1	0.2	0.2	0.4	0.6	0.3	0.4	0.3	0.4
Reissues.	0.3	0.3	0.2	0.2	0.3	0.4	0.3	0.4	0.3
U.S. residents [2]	40.8	43.3	47.7	44.6	54.6	52.8	57.7	58.7	61.1
Foreign country residents [2]	25.4	33.9	41.7	39.7	47.9	46.2	49.0	48.7	48.7
Percent of total	38.4	43.9	46.6	47.1	46.7	46.7	46.0	45.3	44.3
Other published documents [3]	(Z)	(Z)	0.2	0.2	0.2	0.1	0.1	0.1	0.1
Trademarks:									
Applications filed.	46.8	65.1	71.3	78.3	94.4	127.3	123.3	127.8	150.4
Issued	24.7	71.7	51.4	54.3	63.1	60.8	52.4	85.8	86.9
Trademarks	18.9	65.8	47.3	47.4	55.3	53.6	46.6	80.2	80.6
Trademark renewals.	5.9	5.9	4.1	6.9	7.8	7.2	5.8	5.6	6.3

Z Less than 50.   [1] Includes patents to foreign governments.   [2] Includes patents for inventions, designs, botanical plants, and reissues.   [3] Includes Defensive Publications, a practice which began in November 1968 and ended in July 1986; and Statutory Invention Registrations, the current practice, which began May 1985. These documents are patent applications, which are published to provide the defensive properties of a patent, but do not have the enforceable rights of a patent.

Source: U.S. Patent and Trademark Office. Fiscal-year figures are published in the *Commissioner of Patents and Trademarks Annual Report.*

No. 872. Patents, by State: 1993

[Includes only U.S. patents granted to residents of the United States and territories]

STATE	Total	Inventions	Designs	Botanical plants	Reissues	STATE	Total	Inventions	Designs	Botanical plants	Reissues
United States [1]	**61,065**	**53,213**	**7,410**	**235**	**207**	District of Columbia	60	53	6	-	1
						Virginia	983	875	105	-	3
Northeast	**16,801**	**14,862**	**1,868**	**20**	**51**	West Virginia . . .	180	172	8	-	-
New England	**5,225**	**4,581**	**615**	**9**	**20**	North Carolina . . .	1,068	908	154	1	5
Maine	142	114	28	-	-	South Carolina . . .	501	423	77	-	1
New Hampshire .	404	363	38	2	1	Georgia	861	705	154	-	2
Vermont.	154	131	23	-	-	Florida.	2,114	1,777	316	12	9
Massachusetts . .	2,504	2,210	276	7	11	**East South Central**.	**1,424**	**1,204**	**210**	**1**	**9**
Rhode Island . .	275	219	56	-	-	Kentucky	323	277	43	-	3
Connecticut	1,746	1,544	194	-	8	Tennessee	637	554	78	-	5
Middle Atlantic . . .	**11,576**	**10,281**	**1,253**	**11**	**31**	Alabama	324	271	51	1	1
New York	5,355	4,691	647	2	15	Mississippi	140	102	38	-	-
New Jersey	3,228	2,913	302	4	9	**West South Central**.	**5,040**	**4,530**	**484**	**4**	**22**
Pennsylvania . . .	2,993	2,677	304	5	7	Arkansas	154	114	36	4	-
Midwest	**15,408**	**13,406**	**1,919**	**27**	**56**	Louisiana	480	431	47	-	2
East North Central.	**11,843**	**10,361**	**1,416**	**23**	**43**	Oklahoma	681	595	78	-	8
Ohio	2,976	2,529	426	11	10	Texas	3,725	3,390	323	-	12
Indiana	1,107	972	129	4	2	**West**	**15,033**	**12,792**	**2,025**	**169**	**47**
Illinois	3,312	2,846	447	5	14	**Mountain**	**3,401**	**3,004**	**383**	**-**	**14**
Michigan	3,112	2,875	227	3	7	Montana	108	88	20	-	-
Wisconsin	1,336	1,139	187	-	10	Idaho	356	332	23	-	1
West North Central.	**3,565**	**3,045**	**503**	**4**	**13**	Wyoming	43	35	8	-	-
Minnesota	1,767	1,544	214	1	8	Colorado	1,054	910	140	-	4
Iowa	434	366	67	-	1	New Mexico	259	233	26	-	-
Missouri.	747	632	113	-	2	Arizona	928	848	75	-	5
North Dakota . . .	66	60	5	-	1	Utah	471	419	49	-	3
South Dakota . . .	44	32	12	-	-	Nevada	182	139	42	-	1
Nebraska.	191	169	21	1	-	**Pacific**	**11,632**	**9,788**	**1,642**	**169**	**33**
Kansas	316	242	71	2	1	Washington	1,075	900	170	1	4
South.	**13,823**	**12,153**	**1,598**	**19**	**53**	Oregon	819	588	225	5	1
South Atlantic.	**7,359**	**6,419**	**904**	**14**	**22**	California	9,568	8,170	1,211	159	28
Delaware	521	507	13	1	-	Alaska.	64	50	14	-	-
Maryland	1,071	999	71	-	1	Hawaii.	106	80	22	4	-

- Represents zero.   [1] Includes U.S. territories not shown separately.

Source: U.S. Patent and Trademark Office, Technology Assessment and Forecast Data Base.

No. 873. Patents, by Industry: 1980 to 1993

[Based on the 1972 Standard Industrial Classification (SIC). Includes all patents for inventions granted to residents of the United States, its territories, and foreign citizens. Individual industries may not add to total since a patent may be recorded in more than one industry category. Except for total, data for all years have been revised to reflect the U.S. Patent Classification System as of 1993]

INDUSTRY	SIC code	1980	1985	1990	1991	1992	1993
Total	. . . . . .	61,819	71,662	90,365	96,515	97,441	98,344
Durable goods:							
Stone, clay, and glass products	32	1,280	1,369	1,726	1,964	1,904	1,899
Primary metals	33, 3462-3 .	673	751	893	924	919	1,026
Fabricated metal products [1]	34	5,154	5,689	7,030	7,156	6,664	6,336
Machinery, except electrical	35	14,387	16,818	18,994	20,046	20,560	20,995
Electronic and other electric equipment	36, 3825 . .	10,645	13,861	19,101	20,964	21,312	21,670
Transportation equipment	37, 348 . . .	2,942	3,588	4,438	4,795	4,597	4,347
Instruments and related products [2]	38	7,402	8,791	12,254	13,204	13,156	13,554
Nondurable goods:							
Food and kindred products	20	483	547	728	688	668	635
Textile mill products	22	421	503	507	498	558	600
Chemicals and allied products	28	9,825	10,242	12,437	13,424	14,176	14,703
Oil and gas extraction, petroleum products .	13, 29	731	964	842	863	776	784
Rubber and miscellaneous plastics products .	30	2,615	3,077	3,849	4,063	4,274	4,320
Other industries	. . . . . .	5,261	5,462	7,566	7,926	7,877	7,475

[1] Excludes SIC groups 3462, 3463, and 348.   [2] Excludes SIC group 3825.

Source: U.S. Patent and Trademark Office, *Patenting Trends in the United States, State Country Report, 1963-1993.*

No. 874. New Product Introductions of Consumer Packaged Goods: 1980 to 1994

[**Consumer packaged goods:** consumable products packaged by the manufacturer for retail sale primarily through grocery and drug stores. **New product:** a product not previously offered for sale by a particular manufacturer including new varieties, formats, sizes, and packaging for existing products]

ITEM	Food	Beverages	Health and beauty	Household products	Pet products	Miscellaneous products
Domestic and imports:						
1980	1,192	256	834	331	86	197
1981	1,356	262	868	315	74	237
1982	1,762	332	919	390	103	113
1983	3,013	587	1,355	473	138	105
1984	2,678	569	1,094	303	108	227
1985	2,327	585	1,222	463	139	294
1986	2,764	657	1,327	365	107	194
1987	2,895	634	1,526	362	152	292
1988	2,781	597	1,496	310	151	222
1989	2,866	524	1,492	313	204	206
1990	3,453	630	1,531	432	164	154
1991	3,130	589	1,614	422	175	113
1992	2,987	587	1,869	417	213	127
1993	3,107	767	2,068	376	173	161
1994, total	3,883	807	2,655	378	161	97
Percent:						
New brands [1]	21.1	32.6	19.3	17.2	31.7	39.2
Brand extensions [2]	1.4	1.1	1.0	2.9	0.6	4.1
Line extensions [3]	77.5	66.3	79.7	79.9	67.7	56.7
Types of new product innovation (percent): [4]						
Formulation [5]	56.5	50.8	47.8	51.9	50	51.8
New market [6]	0.9	-	3.4	-	11.1	3.4
Packaging [7]	13.3	17.5	8.6	11.1	-	3.4
Positioning [8]	29.3	31.7	39.1	37.0	33.3	34.5
Technology [9]	-	-	1.1	-	5.6	6.9
CUMULATIVE						
Domestic, except imports, 1980-94	36,289	7,127	20,636	5,409	2,078	2,563
Imports, 1980-94 [10]	3,905	1,256	1,234	241	70	176
International, 1985-94 [11]	13,938	4,000	12,194	2,523	567	832

-Represents or rounds to zero.   [1] Product introduced under completely or partly new brand name.   [2] Product introduced in a category with an existing brand name which has not been used in the category before.   [3] Introduction of a new variety, format, size, or package of an existing product/brand name.   [4] Product which offers consumers something significantly different from existing products.   [5] Added or new ingredient which offers a benefit not previously provided by existing products in its category.   [6] Special category for new products which do not compete with any existing category of products.   [7] New product packaged in a way that makes it easier to store, handle, prepare, or dispense than others in its category.   [8] New product presented for new users or uses compared to existing products in its category.   [9] New product with added consumer benefits resulting from use of a new technology.   [10] New products introduced in the United States by foreign companies.   [11] New products introduced by U.S. and foreign companies outside the United States.

Source: Marketing Intelligence Service Ltd., Naples, NY, *Product Alert Weekly.* Publication contains extract from data base, Productscan.

No. 875. Gross Stock of Fixed Private Capital, by Industry: 1990 to 1993

[**In billions of dollars.** Estimates as of **Dec. 31.** Based on the 1987 Standard Industrial Classification]

INDUSTRY	CURRENT DOLLARS				CONSTANT (1987) DOLLARS			
	1990	1991	1992	1993	1990	1991	1992	1993
Fixed private capital	16,871	17,437	18,137	19,090	15,245	15,525	15,803	16,162
Nonresidential	9,485	9,745	10,052	10,490	8,491	8,660	8,814	9,023
Agriculture, forestry, and fishing	416	416	416	423	370	363	356	352
Farms	369	364	360	362	327	318	308	300
Agr. services, forestry, fishing	48	51	56	61	43	45	49	52
Mining	536	527	492	477	449	434	414	396
Metal mining	41	40	40	40	37	36	35	34
Coal mining	49	48	48	49	44	43	42	42
Oil and gas extraction	418	409	374	358	344	330	312	295
Nonmetallic minerals, exc. fuels	28	29	30	30	25	26	25	25
Construction	113	115	117	120	101	101	100	100
Manufacturing	2,114	2,177	2,250	2,347	1,876	1,917	1,952	2,000
Durable goods	1,138	1,161	1,188	1,234	1,017	1,030	1,040	1,062
Lumber and wood products	42	41	41	42	37	36	35	36
Furniture and fixtures	19	20	20	21	17	17	18	18
Stone, clay, glass products	65	64	64	65	58	57	56	57
Primary metal industries	206	207	209	212	180	179	177	176
Fabricated metal products	126	129	130	134	112	112	112	112
Industrial machinery and equipment	198	202	208	216	180	184	188	194
Electronic and electric equipment	168	174	181	190	152	157	161	167
Motor vehicles and equipment	120	123	125	132	106	107	107	111
Other transportation equipment	96	100	104	110	86	89	91	94
Instruments, related products	78	82	86	91	72	75	78	80
Misc. manufacturing industries	19	20	20	21	17	17	17	18
Nondurable goods	977	1,016	1,062	1,113	859	887	912	938
Food and kindred products	192	201	213	225	169	175	182	188
Tobacco products	14	15	15	15	13	13	13	13
Textile mill products	52	52	53	54	46	45	45	45
Apparel, other textile products	18	18	18	19	16	16	16	16
Paper and allied products	145	151	156	161	126	130	132	135
Printing and publishing	82	85	89	94	74	77	80	83
Chemicals, allied products	272	286	305	324	238	250	261	272
Petroleum and coal products	128	132	136	140	113	116	117	118
Rubber, misc. plastic products	68	71	74	78	60	62	64	65
Leather and leather products	4	4	4	4	4	4	4	3
Transportation, communication, and public utilities	2,400	2,442	2,511	2,600	2,141	2,155	2,173	2,193
Transportation	616	613	620	636	553	541	534	528
Railroad transportation	250	246	248	259	226	221	217	213
Local, interurban passenger transit	13	12	12	12	12	11	11	10
Trucking and warehousing	107	104	102	101	96	91	87	83
Water transportation	56	55	55	55	49	48	47	46
Transportation by air	107	110	116	120	95	95	98	100
Pipelines, exc. natural gas	41	42	43	44	36	36	36	36
Transportation services	44	44	45	46	39	40	40	39
Communications	609	622	639	663	563	569	575	580
Telephone and telegraph	527	535	545	561	487	488	488	488
Radio and television	82	88	94	102	76	81	86	92
Electric, gas, and sanitary services	1,175	1,206	1,252	1,300	1,026	1,046	1,065	1,085
Electric services	909	930	958	991	790	802	811	822
Gas services	208	214	224	233	182	185	189	193
Sanitary services	58	63	70	77	54	59	65	70
Wholesale trade	402	415	435	458	374	388	404	422
Retail trade	605	636	673	726	549	574	600	636
Finance, insurance, real estate	2,046	2,136	2,238	2,372	1,855	1,930	1,995	2,075
Depository institutions	415	439	467	497	379	401	423	447
Nondepository institutions	107	114	123	135	97	103	111	121
Security and commodity brokers	13	13	13	14	12	13	13	13
Insurance carriers	125	133	145	159	121	134	148	163
Insurance agents, brokers, and service	6	6	6	6	6	6	6	6
Real estate	1,353	1,404	1,456	1,533	1,212	1,247	1,268	1,297
Holding, other investment offices	28	27	28	29	27	27	27	28
Services	852	882	920	966	777	799	821	851
Hotels, other lodging places	129	131	132	135	116	117	115	114
Personal services	32	33	36	39	30	31	33	36
Business services	225	234	246	259	203	208	215	225
Auto repair, services, parking	151	157	165	172	140	144	150	155
Misc. repair services	15	15	16	17	14	14	14	15
Motion pictures	20	22	23	25	18	20	22	23
Amusement, recreation services	41	42	43	45	38	38	38	39
Other services	239	248	260	274	219	228	236	245
Health services	130	136	144	153	118	122	126	131
Legal services	26	27	28	29	24	26	27	28
Educational services	5	6	6	7	5	5	6	6
Other [1]	79	80	83	86	73	75	77	80
Residential	7,387	7,692	8,085	8,600	6,754	6,865	6,989	7,139
Farms	160	163	166	171	146	145	143	141
Real estate	7,227	7,530	7,919	8,429	6,608	6,720	6,846	6,998

[1] Consists of social services, membership organizations, and miscellaneous professional services.

Source: U.S. Bureau of Economic Analysis, *Survey of Current Business,* January 1992, August 1992, September 1993, and August 1994.

No. 876. Fixed Nonresidential Private Capital: 1980 to 1993

[In billions of dollars. Stocks as of **Dec. 31;** depreciation over entire calendar year. Data refer to privately owned assets and are based on the fixed capital formation components of the gross domestic product. Excludes residential capital and government enterprises; includes nonprofit institutions. Gross stocks allow for retirement; net stocks allow for retirement and depreciation. Net stock and depreciation estimates are based on the straight-line depreciation formula. For manufacturing industry, see table 1254]

ITEM	CURRENT DOLLARS						CONSTANT (1987) DOLLARS					
	1980	1985	1990	1991	1992	1993	1980	1985	1990	1991	1992	1993
Gross stocks . . .	5,072	7,156	9,485	9,745	10,052	10,490	6,264	7,389	8,491	8,660	8,814	9,023
Equipment . . .	2,389	3,374	4,506	4,636	4,783	4,974	3,009	3,518	4,091	4,180	4,274	4,424
Structures . . .	2,683	3,783	4,979	5,109	5,270	5,516	3,255	3,870	4,400	4,480	4,541	4,599
Net stocks.	2,974	4,113	5,321	5,420	5,550	5,770	3,677	4,248	4,773	4,829	4,877	4,980
Equipment . . .	1,360	1,852	2,417	2,463	2,525	2,631	1,709	1,929	2,202	2,231	2,268	2,360
Structures . . .	1,615	2,261	2,904	2,957	3,025	3,139	1,968	2,319	2,571	2,598	2,609	2,620
Depreciation . . .	240	358	471	489	506	519	308	368	436	447	461	472
Equipment . . .	161	240	321	335	347	357	211	250	303	313	324	335
Structures . . .	78	118	150	154	158	162	97	118	132	134	137	137

Source: U.S. Bureau of Economic Analysis, *Survey of Current Business,* August 1992, September 1993, and August 1994 issues, unpublished data.

No. 877. Business Expenditures for New Plant and Equipment: 1980 to 1994

[In billions of dollars. Represents expenditures for new facilities and for expansion or replacement of existing facilities that are chargeable to fixed asset accounts and for which depreciation or amortization accounts are ordinarily maintained. Excludes expenditures for land and mineral rights; maintenance and repair; used plant and equipment, including that purchased or acquired through mergers or acquisitions; assets located in foreign countries; residential structures; etc. They also differ from the nonresidential fixed investment data in type of detail, data sources, coverage, and timing. For further information, see the February 1985 *Survey of Current Business]*

INDUSTRY	1980	1985	1986	1987	1988	1989	1990	1991	1992	1993	1994
All industries [1]	**286.4**	**410.1**	**399.4**	**410.5**	**455.5**	**507.4**	**532.6**	**528.4**	**546.6**	**586.7**	**638.4**
Constant (1987) dollars [2]	**354.6**	**424.5**	**405.9**	**410.6**	**443.2**	**482.3**	**496.2**	**488.9**	**512.1**	**563.4**	**616.3**
Manufacturing	112.6	152.9	138.0	141.1	163.5	183.8	192.6	182.8	174.0	179.5	192.6
Durable goods	54.8	70.9	65.7	68.0	77.0	82.6	82.6	77.6	73.3	81.5	92.8
Primary metals	6.7	7.5	6.7	8.6	11.0	12.0	12.2	10.7	9.8	9.9	12.5
Blast furnaces, steel works	3.7	4.7	3.8	5.3	7.0	7.9	7.8	6.5	5.6	5.6	7.9
Nonferrous metals	2.0	1.8	1.8	2.0	2.5	2.6	2.9	2.8	2.7	2.6	2.4
Fabricated metals	3.3	3.3	3.6	3.6	3.9	4.2	4.4	4.0	3.7	3.9	4.1
Electrical machinery	10.2	17.1	15.6	16.8	20.8	20.5	22.0	21.0	20.4	24.4	27.2
Machinery, except electrical	10.7	13.8	11.4	11.9	13.7	14.6	13.7	12.7	10.6	9.7	9.6
Transportation equipment	16.1	19.6	18.9	16.7	15.8	18.7	17.9	17.2	16.1	19.2	23.1
Motor vehicles	8.5	13.4	12.8	10.9	9.8	11.5	11.3	10.2	8.7	12.3	15.8
Aircraft	3.6	3.5	3.9	3.6	3.5	4.2	4.0	4.1	4.4	3.2	3.0
Stone, clay, and glass.	3.7	3.6	3.1	3.3	3.6	4.0	3.3	2.9	3.4	4.3	5.3
Other durables	4.3	6.1	6.3	7.1	8.2	8.6	9.2	9.1	9.4	10.1	11.1
Nondurable goods	57.8	82.0	72.3	73.0	86.4	101.2	110.0	105.2	100.7	98.0	99.8
Food and beverage	8.5	11.4	11.6	12.1	14.2	15.9	16.4	17.4	19.0	18.8	18.0
Textiles	1.6	1.8	1.7	2.0	2.2	2.3	2.2	2.0	2.1	2.3	2.4
Paper	6.4	8.1	8.3	8.5	10.9	15.6	16.5	11.5	10.5	10.3	10.7
Chemicals.	10.6	14.4	14.5	13.9	16.6	18.5	20.6	21.5	23.2	21.8	23.4
Petroleum.	22.8	34.1	23.1	22.1	26.0	30.1	34.8	35.6	29.6	28.7	27.4
Rubber.	1.7	3.3	3.3	2.9	3.3	3.8	3.5	3.4	3.9	3.3	3.8
Other nondurables	6.2	9.0	9.8	11.5	13.3	15.2	16.1	13.7	12.6	12.8	14.1
Nonmanufacturing.	173.8	257.2	261.4	269.5	292.0	323.6	340.0	345.6	372.6	407.3	445.8
Mining	12.7	12.0	8.2	8.3	9.3	9.2	9.9	10.0	8.9	10.1	11.2
Transportation.	13.6	14.6	15.1	15.1	16.6	18.8	21.5	22.7	22.6	21.8	21.2
Railroad	5.9	5.7	5.3	4.7	5.5	6.3	6.4	6.0	6.7	6.1	6.7
Air.	3.7	4.1	5.2	5.3	5.6	6.7	8.9	10.2	8.9	6.4	4.0
Other.	4.0	4.8	4.6	5.0	5.5	5.9	6.2	6.5	7.0	9.2	10.5
Public utilities	41.3	59.6	56.6	56.3	60.4	66.3	67.2	66.6	72.2	76.0	76.4
Electric.	33.3	44.0	41.0	39.1	40.9	44.8	44.1	43.8	48.2	52.6	52.3
Gas and other	8.0	15.6	15.6	17.2	19.5	21.5	23.1	22.8	24.0	23.4	24.2
Commercial and other	106.2	171.1	181.6	189.8	205.8	229.3	241.4	246.3	268.8	299.4	336.9
Wholesale and retail trade	32.0	60.1	65.4	68.5	76.4	84.5	95.6	105.0	116.2	131.4	(NA)
Finance and insurance	22.6	45.2	49.6	54.1	59.2	70.3	69.0	64.0	72.8	80.5	(NA)
Personal and business services [3] . .	24.9	28.8	28.4	30.1	32.9	34.6	33.7	34.7	38.3	42.6	(NA)
Communication	26.8	37.1	38.2	37.2	37.2	39.8	43.1	42.7	41.5	45.0	(NA)

NA Not available.   [1] Surveyed quarterly.   [2] For preparation of constant-dollar estimates, see source for detail.   [3] Includes construction.

Source: U.S. Bureau of the Census, *Plant and Equipment Expenditures and Plans,* quarterly.

No. 878. Gross Private Domestic Investment: 1980 to 1993

[In billions of dollars]

YEAR	CURRENT DOLLARS						CONSTANT (1987) DOLLARS					
	Gross private domestic investment				Less: Con-sumption of fixed capital	Equals: Net private domestic invest-ment	Gross private domestic investment				Less: Con-sumption of fixed capital	Equals: Net private domestic invest-ment
	Total [1]	Fixed invest-ment	Non-resi-dential	Resi-dential			Total [1]	Fixed invest-ment	Non-resi-dential	Resi-dential		
1980	468	477	354	123	312	156	594	603	438	165	401	194
1981	558	533	410	123	362	196	631	607	455	152	418	213
1982	503	519	414	106	399	104	541	558	434	124	430	111
1983	547	552	400	152	418	128	600	595	421	174	447	152
1984	719	648	469	179	433	286	758	690	490	199	456	302
1985	715	690	504	186	455	260	746	724	522	202	472	274
1986	718	709	492	217	479	239	735	727	500	226	487	248
1987	749	723	498	225	502	247	749	723	498	225	502	247
1988	794	777	545	232	534	260	773	753	531	223	519	255
1989	832	799	568	231	580	252	784	754	540	214	545	239
1990	809	802	587	215	603	206	747	741	547	195	555	192
1991	775	747	557	190	627	118	684	685	515	170	570	114
1992	788	785	561	234	659	130	725	723	526	197	596	130
1993	882	867	616	251	669	213	820	805	592	213	600	220

[1] Includes change in business inventories, not shown separately.

Source: U.S. Bureau of Economic Analysis, *National Income and Product Accounts, volume 2, 1959-88*, and *Survey of Current Business*, July 1994.

No. 879. Composite Indexes of Economic Cyclical Indicators: 1980 to 1993

[See source for discussion of composite indexes. Minus sign (-) indicates decrease. **Leading indicators** are economic time series that tend to reach their cyclical high and low points earlier than the corresponding peaks and troughs in the overall economy. **Coincident indicators** are economic time series that tend to reach their cyclical high and low points about the same time as the corresponding peaks and troughs in the overall economy. **Lagging indicators** are economic time series that tend to reach their cyclical high and low points later than the corresponding peaks and troughs in the overall economy]

ITEM	Unit	1980	1985	1986	1987	1988	1989	1990	1991	1992	1993
LEADING INDICATORS											
Composite index.	1987=100 . . .	88.6	95.3	97.7	100.0	100.1	99.7	98.5	97.2	98.2	98.8
Building permits [1]	1967=100 . . .	96.7	138.1	141.2	122.9	115.8	107.7	89.6	75.4	87.6	96.3
Common stock prices, index [2]	1941-43=10. .	118.8	186.8	236.4	286.8	265.8	322.8	334.6	376.2	415.7	451.4
Initial claims, unemployment insurance . .	1,000	480	383	370	314	305	327	383	444	411	365
Change in sensitive materials prices [3][4] . .	Percent	4.3	-8.2	3.4	12.3	5.0	0.6	-3.0	-7.3	3.2	-3.2
Vendor performance, slower deliveries . .	Percent	40.6	48.0	50.6	57.4	57.7	47.6	47.9	47.3	50.2	51.6
Average workweek, manufacturing [5]	Hours.	39.7	40.5	40.7	41.0	41.1	41.0	40.8	40.7	41.0	41.4
Plant and equipment contracts and orders (1987 dol.)	Bil. dol.	358	350	341	373	422	437	420	381	401	447
Manufacturers new orders for consumer goods and materials (1987 dol.)	Bil. dol.	1,016	1,144	1,167	1,226	1,264	1,250	1,227	1,186	1,231	1,305
Money supply (M2) [6] (1987 dol.)	Bil. dol.	2,163	2,630	2,795	2,874	2,906	2,882	2,880	2,852	2,826	2,775
Change in manufacturers' unfilled orders, durable goods (1987 dol.) [4]	Bil. dol	-13	3	2	20	18	22	13	-15	-37	-34
COINCIDENT INDICATORS											
Composite index.	1987=100 . . .	85.6	95.0	97.2	100.0	103.5	105.8	106.7	105.3	106.7	109.4
Industrial production index	1987=100 . . .	84.1	94.4	95.3	100.0	104.4	106.0	106.0	104.3	107.6	112.0
Employees, nonagricultural payrolls	Million	90.4	97.4	99.3	102.0	105.2	107.9	109.4	108.3	108.6	110.5
Personal income less transfer payments (1987 dol.)	Bil. dol.	2,722	3,110	3,200	3,260	3,357	3,436	3,469	3,416	3,477	3,523
Sales, mfg. and trade (1987 dol.)	Bil. dol.	4,522	5,109	5,307	5,505	5,736	5,825	5,837	5,755	5,929	6,262
LAGGING INDICATORS											
Composite index.	1987=100 . . .	99.0	98.9	100.2	100.0	102.1	104.6	104.7	102.1	97.3	96.3
Change in labor cost per unit of output, manufacturing [4]	Percent	10.1	1.8	-0.2	-2.5	4.6	2.6	3.0	2.8	0.1	-0.2
Ratio, consumer installment credit to personal income	Percent	13.2	14.3	15.3	15.5	15.7	16.0	15.7	15.0	14.1	14.1
Average prime rate charged by banks. . .	Percent	15.3	9.9	8.3	8.2	9.3	10.9	10.0	8.5	6.2	6.0
Average duration of unemployment.	Weeks	11.9	15.6	15.0	14.5	13.5	11.9	12.1	13.8	17.9	18.1
Ratio, mfg. and trade inventories to sales (1987 dol.)	Ratio	1.61	1.59	1.58	1.55	1.54	1.59	1.62	1.64	1.59	1.53
Commercial and industrial loans outstand-ing (1987 dol.) [7]	Bil. dol.	231	338	359	364	375	400	413	398	373	371
Change in CPI for services [4][8]	Percent	15.2	5.0	4.8	4.2	4.7	5.0	5.9	4.5	3.8	3.8

[1] New private housing units authorized.   [2] Standard and Poor's 500 stocks.   [3] Producer prices of selected crude and intermediate materials and spot market prices of selected raw industrial materials.   [4] Smoothed by an autoregressive-moving-average filter developed by Statistics Canada.   [5] Production workers.   [6] See table 802.   [7] Includes commercial paper issued by nonfinancial companies.   [8] Consumer Price Index.

Source: U.S. Bureau of Economic Analysis, *Survey of Current Business*, monthly.

No. 880. Business Cycle Expansions and Contractions—Months of Duration: 1919 to 1994

[A trough is the low point of a business cycle; a peak is the high point. Contraction, or recession, is the period from peak to subsequent trough; expansion is the period from trough to subsequent peak. Business cycle reference dates are determined by the National Bureau of Economic Research, Inc.]

BUSINESS CYCLE REFERENCE DATE		Contraction (trough from previous peak)	Expansion (trough to peak)	LENGTH OF CYCLE	
Trough	Peak			Trough from previous trough	Peak from previous peak
March 1919.	January 1920	[1]7	10	[2]51	[1]17
July 1921.	May 1923	18	22	28	40
July 1924.	October 1926	14	27	36	41
November 1927.	August 1929.	13	21	40	34
March 1933.	May 1937	43	50	64	93
June 1938.	February 1945	13	80	63	93
October 1945.	November 1948	8	37	88	45
October 1949.	July 1953.	11	45	48	56
May 1954.	August 1957.	10	39	55	49
April 1958.	April 1960	8	24	47	32
February 1961.	December 1969	10	106	34	116
November 1970.	November 1973	11	36	117	47
March 1975.	January 1980.	16	58	52	74
July 1980.	July 1981.	6	12	64	18
November 1982.	July 1990.	16	92	28	108
March 1991.	(X)	8	(X)	100	(X)
Average, all cycles:					
1919 to 1945 (six cycles).		18	35	53	53
1945 to 1991 (nine cycles).		11	50	61	61

X Not applicable.   [1] Previous peak: August 1918.   [2] Previous trough: December 1914.

Source: U.S. Bureau of Economic Analysis, *Survey of Current Business*, October 1994.

No. 881. Manufacturing and Trade—Sales and Inventories in Current and Constant (1987) Dollars: 1980 to 1994

[In billions of dollars, except ratios]

ITEM	1980	1985	1987	1988	1989	1990	1991	1992	1993	1994
CURRENT DOLLARS										
Sales, average monthly	**393**	**507**	**549**	**595**	**628**	**651**	**646**	**674**	**712**	**768**
Manufacturing	185	233	248	268	279	287	283	293	310	337
Retail trade	96	138	154	166	176	184	186	195	207	224
Merchant wholesalers	112	136	148	161	173	179	178	185	194	207
Inventories [1]	**(NA)**	**664**	**710**	**765**	**811**	**834**	**830**	**839**	**861**	**917**
Manufacturing	(NA)	335	338	367	387	399	386	379	377	392
Retail trade	(NA)	182	208	219	237	240	243	252	268	290
Merchant wholesalers	(NA)	147	164	179	187	196	200	208	216	235
Inventory-sales ratios [2]	**(NA)**	**1.31**	**1.29**	**1.29**	**1.29**	**1.28**	**1.28**	**1.24**	**1.21**	**1.19**
Manufacturing	(NA)	1.44	1.36	1.37	1.39	1.39	1.36	1.29	1.22	1.16
Retail trade	(NA)	1.32	1.35	1.32	1.35	1.30	1.31	1.29	1.29	1.29
Merchant wholesalers	(NA)	1.08	1.11	1.11	1.08	1.09	1.12	1.12	1.11	1.14
CONSTANT (1987) DOLLARS										
Sales, average monthly [3]	**381**	**431**	**464**	**484**	**490**	**483**	**489**	**510**	**542**	**579**
Manufacturing	179	194	206	216	218	215	219	227	245	263
Retail trade	103	123	134	139	141	141	139	149	157	166
Merchant wholesalers	99	113	124	128	130	127	130	134	140	150
Inventories	**605**	**686**	**724**	**751**	**784**	**791**	**789**	**789**	**802**	**832**
Manufacturing	320	336	340	355	374	377	371	360	360	364
Retail trade	147	194	214	220	231	229	230	234	243	258
Merchant wholesalers	138	156	170	176	179	184	188	195	199	210
Inventory-sales ratios [4]	**1.59**	**1.59**	**1.56**	**1.55**	**1.60**	**1.64**	**1.62**	**1.55**	**1.48**	**1.44**
Manufacturing	1.79	1.73	1.65	1.64	1.71	1.75	1.69	1.58	1.47	1.39
Retail trade	1.42	1.57	1.60	1.58	1.63	1.63	1.65	1.57	1.55	1.56
Merchant wholesalers	1.40	1.38	1.37	1.37	1.37	1.45	1.45	1.45	1.43	1.40

NA Not available.   [1] Seasonally adjusted end-of-year data. See text, section 17.   [2] End-of-year seasonally adjusted inventories to seasonally adjusted sales.   [3] Average monthly sales for fourth quarter.   [4] End of fourth quarter inventories to average monthly sales for fourth quarter.

Source: Current dollars from U.S. Bureau of the Census, Current Business Reports, *"Manufacturing and Trade Inventories and Sales"* February 1994, and unpublished data; constant dollars from U.S. Bureau of Economic Analysis, *Survey of Current Business*.

No. 882. Manufacturing Corporations—Number, Assets, and Profits, by Asset Size: 1980 to 1992

[Corporations and assets as of **end of 4th quarter;** profits for **entire year.** Based on complete canvass. The asset value for complete canvass was $25 million in 1980 and raised in 1988 to $50 million. Asset sizes less than these values are sampled, except as noted. For details regarding methodology, see source for first quarter, 1988]

YEAR	Unit	Total	ASSET-SIZE CLASS						
			Under [1] $10 mil.	$10-$25 mil.	$25-$50 mil.	$50-$100 mil.	$100-$250 mil.	$250 mil.-$1 bil.	$1 bil. and over
Corporations:									
1980.	Number.	(NA)	(NA)	1,777	941	590	491	369	244
1985.	Number.	(NA)	(NA)	(NA)	896	744	608	428	281
1986.	Number.	(NA)	(NA)	(NA)	962	741	628	445	291
1987.	Number.	(NA)	(NA)	(NA)	1,007	811	676	481	318
1988.	Number.	(NA)	(NA)	(NA)	(NA)	783	729	550	334
1989.	Number.	(NA)	(NA)	(NA)	(NA)	781	750	579	347
1990.	Number.	(NA)	(NA)	(NA)	(NA)	834	774	597	367
1991.	Number.	(NA)	(NA)	(NA)	(NA)	868	799	608	373
1992.	Number.	(NA)	(NA)	(NA)	(NA)	956	843	648	407
Assets:									
1980.	Mil. dol .	1,384,474	126,639	43,569	34,930	41,963	75,284	179,959	882,129
1985.	Mil. dol .	1,932,766	153,883	64,324	52,669	58,019	96,748	208,403	1,298,720
1986.	Mil. dol .	1,994,120	140,864	67,663	55,974	58,233	97,908	217,341	1,356,137
1987.	Mil. dol .	2,135,266	147,919	65,623	50,171	60,874	109,458	235,368	1,465,853
1988.	Mil. dol .	2,339,690	149,276	77,068	53,461	62,190	110,411	261,880	1,625,404
1989.	Mil. dol .	2,501,097	144,814	73,487	56,548	68,149	117,014	282,056	1,759,029
1990.	Mil. dol .	2,629,458	142,498	74,477	55,914	72,554	123,967	287,512	1,872,536
1991.	Mil. dol .	2,688,422	140,056	70,567	58,549	72,694	127,748	295,743	1,923,066
1992.	Mil. dol .	2,796,625	141,766	70,446	65,718	75,967	132,742	302,287	2,007,698
Net profit: [2]									
1980.	Mil. dol .	92,443	7,770	2,235	1,904	2,479	4,532	11,485	62,041
1985.	Mil. dol .	87,647	8,601	2,551	2,305	2,819	3,628	7,312	60,431
1986.	Mil. dol .	83,122	6,659	2,988	2,129	2,514	3,884	7,572	57,376
1987.	Mil. dol .	115,600	7,273	3,849	2,753	3,338	5,237	9,636	83,514
1988.	Mil. dol .	154,583	11,364	4,488	3,199	3,978	5,473	13,994	112,086
1989.	Mil. dol .	136,490	10,381	5,173	2,921	3,105	4,434	11,824	98,651
1990.	Mil. dol .	111,561	8,527	5,160	2,769	2,676	3,531	7,245	81,652
1991.	Mil. dol .	67,516	6,820	4,271	2,564	1,714	1,730	5,119	45,299
1992.	Mil. dol .	23,212	9,567	4,748	3,245	3,050	4,585	5,976	-7,956

NA Not available.   [1] Beginning 1986, excludes estimates for corporations with less than $250,000 in assets at time of sample selection. Prior periods include estimates for corporations in this size category.   [2] After taxes.
Source: U.S. Bureau of the Census, *Quarterly Financial Report for Manufacturing, Mining and Trade Corporations.*

No. 883. U.S. Largest Public Companies—Profitability and Growth: 1994

[**In percent, except ranks. For fiscal years ending in the 12 month period ending September 30.** Included in the Forbes Universe of 1,305 companies is every firm with revenue of over $400 million in **1993**, electric and banking firms $800 million. Represents industry medians; calculated by listing companies in rank order and selecting the midpoint. Where there is an even number of companies, an arithmetic average of the two middle companies is substituted. Minus sign (-) indicates decrease]

INDUSTRY	PROFITABILITY					GROWTH					
	Return on equity [1]			Return on capital, [2] latest 12 months	Debt/capital	Sales [3]			Earnings per share		
	5-year rank	5-year average	Latest 12 months			5-year rank	5-year average	Latest 12 months	5-year rank	5-year average	Latest 12 months
All industries, median .	(X)	11.4	12.6	9.4	32.8	(X)	5.5	6.3	(X)	−18.8	11.8
Health.	1	17.3	17.9	13.4	24.2	1	12.7	8.1	1	9.5	16.5
Food, drink and tobacco . . .	3	15.9	14.1	10.6	38.1	7	6.4	4.3	6	−8.7	1.7
Consumer nondurables . . .	2	16.9	16.1	11.5	26.5	4	8.0	5.2	7	−11.5	3.0
Retailing	6	12.8	11.8	9.3	32.6	2	12.1	8.5	8	−13.5	9.4
Chemicals	10	12.1	15.5	11.3	29.3	19	3.4	6.1	13	−29.6	14.8
Insurance	5	14.2	12.1	10.9	19.8	8	6.2	3.9	2	7.7	5.1
Food distribution	9	12.1	8.6	8.1	41.5	12	4.5	3.2	5	−4.1	10.7
Financial services	4	14.5	16.0	12.3	33.1	16	3.8	4.4	3	6.8	12.0
Business services/supplies .	11	11.9	14.0	11.2	30.2	6	6.8	9.9	9	−15.5	15.8
Computers/communications.	15	10.2	13.7	10.7	19.6	3	12.0	15.2	15	(NS)	31.1
Electric utilities	12	11.5	11.7	6.2	37.3	18	3.5	3.3	4	−4.0	−0.8
Entertainment and information	8	12.2	14.8	13.2	28.0	9	5.3	7.0	15	(NS)	15.2
Aerospace and defense . . .	7	12.7	11.3	10.2	37.3	21	−3.0	−0.8	11	−20.8	10.3
Capital goods	13	10.8	13.0	10.2	29.8	11	5.2	8.4	15	(NS)	17.6
Forest prod./packaging. . . .	19	7.1	5.6	4.7	41.6	15	3.8	5.2	15	(NS)	13.2
Transport.	16	10.1	12.8	8.2	36.2	10	5.3	9.4	10	−15.5	27.6
Energy	17	9.1	8.9	6.6	39.6	13	4.5	1.1	12	−23.4	0.9
Consumer durables	18	8.4	15.2	11.6	31.7	14	3.9	11.3	15	(NS)	30.4
Metals.	21	4.6	6.7	7.3	34.0	20	−2.4	7.8	15	(NS)	27.4
Construction.	20	5.9	8.4	6.2	39.1	17	3.7	10.4	14	−31.8	24.1
Travel	14	10.7	8.3	6.5	53.8	5	7.6	7.8	15	(NS)	18.8

NS Not significant.   X Not applicable.   [1] Represents primary earnings per share before extraordinary item divided by common shareholders' equity per share. Common shareholders' equity is total shareholders' equity including the stated value of all preferred stock at the beginning of each year minus the involuntary liquidating value of nonconvertible preferred shares. [2] After-tax profits, the amount remaining if the interest paid on long-term debt was taxed, and minority interest divided by a firm's total capitalization. Total capitalization is long-term debt, common and preferred equity, deferred taxes, investment tax credits, and minority interest in consolidated subsidiaries.   [3] Net sales plus other operating revenue.
Source: Forbes, Inc., New York, NY, *Forbes Annual Report on American Industry,* Reprinted with permission of FORBES Magazine. © Forbes, Inc., 1994.

No. 884. 500 Largest Industrial Corporations—Sales, Assets, and Profits by Sales Group Rank: 1990 to 1993

[In billions of dollars. Excludes large privately owned companies that do not publish sales. Includes service and rental revenues, but companies must derive more than 50 percent of revenues from manufacturing or mining for years ending not later than **Dec. 31 of year stated,** sales exclude excise taxes collected by manufacturer and include discontinued operations. Minus sign (-) indicates decrease]

SALES RANK	SALES				ASSETS [1]				PROFITS [2]			
	1990	1991	1992	1993	1990	1991	1992	1993	1990	1991	1992	1993
Total	2,303	2,264	2,365	2,370	2,443	2,466	2,565	2,676	93.4	[3]55.1	[3](-Z)	62.6
Top 100.	(NA)	1,619	1,681	1,676	(NA)	1,844	1,902	2,015	(NA)	38.5	-7.9	49.0
101-200	(NA)	323	341	343	(NA)	328	351	337	(NA)	9.1	2.9	12.0
201-300	(NA)	160	171	175	(NA)	151	160	163	(NA)	4.2	2.7	2.0
301-400	(NA)	96	104	107	(NA)	77	91	102	(NA)	2.6	1.9	-1.0
401-500	(NA)	65	69	70	(NA)	57	60	59	(NA)	0.8	(Z)	1.0

NA Not available.   Z Less than $500 million.   [1] Total assets employed in business at end of fiscal year, less depreciation and depletion.   [2] After taxes, special charges, and credits.   [3] Total profits of $55 billion in 1991 and $200 million in 1992 include charge-offs for accounting rule change on retiree health benefits. Profits before charge-offs were $60 billion and $71 billion in 1991 and 1992 respectively.

No. 885. 500 Largest Industrial Corporations—Selected Financial Items: 1980 to 1993

ITEM	Unit	1980	1985	1987	1988	1989	1990	1991	1992	1993
Sales per employee	$1,000 . . .	78.1	106.0	124.4	137.9	146.0	153.9	159.2	169.3	174.5
Changes in profits.	Percent . . .	3.6	-19.1	41.3	26.9	-8.1	-11.6	[1]-41.0	[1]-100.4	[1]1.8
Sales per dollar of stockholder's equity . .	Dollar	3.00	2.80	2.77	2.93	2.96	2.97	2.81	2.91	3.02
Return on stockholder's equity	Percent . . .	14.4	11.6	14.4	16.2	15.0	12.7	[2]10.2	[2]9.0	[2]10.3
Return on sales	Percent . . .	4.8	3.9	5.1	5.5	4.7	4.1	3.1	2.4	2.9
Total return to investors [3]	Percent . . .	21.1	26.3	6.6	14.1	17.5	-10.2	29.5	9.1	11.1

[1] Changes in profits of -41% in 1991 and -100.4% in 1992 include charge-offs for accounting rule change on retiree health benefits. Changes before charge-offs were -35.8%, 18.3% and 15.1% in 1991, 1992, and 1993 respectively.   [2] For 1991-92 data, the return is on common stockholders' equity. For prior years and again with 1993 data, the return is on total equity.   [3] Includes both price appreciation and dividend yield, i.e., to an investor in the company's stock.

No. 886. 500 Largest Industrial Corporations—Selected Financial Items, by Industry: 1992 and 1993

[Data are medians and are ranked based on sales per employee for latest year shown. See headnote, table 884. Minus sign (-) indicates decrease. For definition of median, see Guide to Tabular Presentation]

INDUSTRY	SALES PER EMPLOYEE ($1,000)		CHANGES IN PROFITS FROM PREVIOUS YEAR [1] (percent)		SALES PER DOLLAR OF STOCK-HOLDER'S EQUITY (dol.)		RETURN ON COMMON EQUITY (percent)		RETURN ON SALES (percent)		TOTAL RETURN TO INVESTORS [2] (percent)	
	1992	1993	1992	1993	1992	1993	1992	1993	1992	1993	1992	1993
Total.	169.3	174.5	-6.9	1.8	2.91	3.02	9.0	-10.3	2.4	2.9	9.1	11.1
Petroleum refining	609.2	654.8	-76.5	26.1	4.30	3.85	2.0	8.2	0.2	2.3	-1.7	15.7
Mining, crude-oil production	306.2	330.9	-16.5	-6.1	1.61	1.40	7.0	6.3	5.1	3.0	-0.7	9.6
Tobacco	274.7	229.4	17.5	3.4	2.06	4.65	21.9	16.5	2.4	3.2	0.4	-24.2
Soaps, cosmetics	244.3	217.8	6.6	-14.6	2.69	3.38	14.4	12.9	5.7	3.4	8.3	-8.4
Food	229.8	216.2	7.9	-2.7	5.09	5.00	15.6	12.7	3.4	2.4	1.1	-5.8
Beverages	229.6	233.1	-28.7	30.8	3.14	3.00	9.7	15.1	2.1	4.1	4.6	8.8
Chemicals	227.7	242.8	-27.8	-37.2	2.37	2.78	10.5	6.7	2.3	2.0	9.0	6.1
Metals	185.4	188.9	-90.5	-19.0	2.70	3.02	-13.9	3.2	-1.2	0.1	13.3	6.9
Forest and paper products	181.1	186.1	-1.1	35.4	2.22	2.41	5.7	6.3	2.1	2.1	14.6	12.6
Pharmaceuticals	179.8	185.8	8.2	2.3	1.96	1.93	26.7	22.0	11.4	12.5	-10.2	-7.3
Toys, sporting goods	178.2	(NA)	73.5	(NA)	2.65	(NA)	17.0	(NA)	6.5	(NA)	18.7	(NA)
Computers, office equipment	177.4	211.2	-36.6	100.0	2.50	2.87	4.6	9.5	1.0	3.2	25.9	5.8
Publishing, printing.	153.1	149.6	-7.4	21.5	2.18	2.01	11.3	11.9	5.6	6.4	14.7	12.9
Building materials, glass	151.0	141.7	-104.0	-528.6	2.16	6.56	-26.0	0.7	-3.0	0.3	-0.6	23.8
Industrial and farm equipment	144.5	143.3	-97.1	-2.9	3.66	4.23	0.4	10.0	0.2	2.2	6.3	33.8
Aerospace	143.0	154.8	-52.3	-20.7	4.10	3.91	0.3	13.6	-0.2	2.5	16.4	30.8
Motor vehicles and parts	138.7	143.9	-72.5	7.4	4.82	6.91	-11.1	10.5	-1.3	1.7	43.2	31.4
Metal products	136.5	132.7	14.5	-14.3	3.18	3.18	12.1	7.9	4.1	2.5	13.1	11.0
Rubber and plastic products	135.5	129.2	3.0	7.5	3.13	3.61	10.6	14.7	3.0	4.4	23.3	18.6
Scientific, photo, control equip	132.8	132.4	8.0	-71.3	2.68	2.99	15.4	4.9	5.6	2.2	7.1	9.6
Electronics, electrical equip	124.0	139.3	5.1	9.1	2.82	2.45	9.1	11.7	2.9	5.4	16.5	32.1
Transportation equipment [3]	122.4	130.8	-52.7	-122.1	3.38	3.39	3.6	-0.4	-0.3	1.0	20.7	15.8
Furniture	102.7	117.4	17.5	16.7	2.75	3.05	12.0	10.4	4.0	4.0	24.3	47.8
Textiles	98.8	98.7	65.7	13.7	3.19	3.56	7.6	10.6	2.1	2.2	30.3	10.7
Apparel	63.7	69.7	46.9	20.9	3.53	2.55	11.6	10.3	2.5	5.3	-11.0	-10.0

NA Not available.   [1] Changes in profits of -41% in 1991 and -100.4% in 1992 include charge-offs for accounting rule change on retiree health benefits. Changes before charge-offs were -35.8%, 18.3%, and 15.1% in 1991, 1992, and 1993 respectively.   [2] 1991, return on common equity; 1993, return on total equity.   [3] Excludes motor vehicles and aircraft.

Source of tables 884-886: Time Warner, New York, NY, The Fortune Directories (copyright).

No. 887. Corporate Profits, Taxes, and Dividends: 1980 to 1994

[In billions of dollars. Covers corporations organized for profit and other entities treated as corporations. Represents profits to U.S. residents, without deduction of depletion charges and exclusive of capital gains and losses; intercorporate dividends from profits of domestic corporations are eliminated; net receipts of dividends, reinvested earnings of incorporated foreign affiliates, and earnings of unincorporated foreign affiliates are added]

ITEM	1980	1984	1985	1986	1987	1988	1989	1990	1991	1992	1993	1994
Profits before taxes	241	241	225	218	288	348	343	366	365	396	462	525
Less: Income tax liability [1]	85	94	97	107	127	137	141	139	131	140	173	203
Equals: Profits after taxes	156	146	129	111	161	211	202	227	234	256	289	322
Less: Net dividends [2]	59	83	92	110	106	115	135	154	160	171	192	205
Equals: Undistributed profits	97	64	36	2	55	95	67	74	74	85	98	117
Capital consumption allowances [3]	165	294	333	338	354	372	390	394	403	412	437	470
Profits after tax plus capital consumption allowances [3]	321	440	462	450	515	583	591	621	637	669	727	792

[1] Federal, State, and local.   [2] Disbursements to U.S. residents, measured after eliminations of intercorporate dividends. [3] Without capital consumption adjustment. Includes depreciation and accidental damages.

No. 888. Corporate Profits, by Industry: 1990 to 1993

[In billions of dollars. Profits are without inventory valuation and capital consumption adjustments. Minus sign (-) indicates loss. See headnote, table 887]

INDUSTRY	BEFORE TAXES				AFTER TAXES			
	1990	1991	1992	1993	1990	1991	1992	1993
Total	365.7	362.3	395.9	462.4	227.1	234.1	256.2	289.2
Domestic industries	297.8	296.7	335.3	397.2	159.1	165.6	195.6	223.9
Agriculture, forestry, fishing	1.6	1.1	2.0	1.8	1.0	0.6	1.4	1.2
Mining.	2.2	0.8	1.9	2.1	0.6	-0.4	0.8	0.7
Construction.	11.0	8.3	8.2	8.8	8.7	6.4	6.4	6.7
Manufacturing.	112.7	86.3	95.6	113.8	66.2	48.4	57.2	67.7
Transportation	0.9	0.9	1.5	6.2	-2.1	-1.5	-1.3	2.5
Communications	19.3	22.6	27.0	28.0	11.2	14.6	18.2	18.5
Public utilities	24.4	27.0	28.4	31.0	15.4	17.2	18.6	19.4
Wholesale and retail trade	43.7	48.1	58.4	65.6	28.6	33.7	42.3	45.8
Finance, insurance, real estate	62.3	79.4	81.6	104.3	14.8	29.4	27.1	32.9
Services	19.8	22.1	30.7	35.5	14.6	17.0	24.9	28.5
Rest of world [1]	67.9	68.5	60.6	65.3	67.9	68.5	60.6	65.3

[1] Consists of receipts by all U.S. residents, including both corporations and persons, of earnings of unincorporated foreign affiliates, dividends from their incorporated foreign affiliates, and their share of their incorporated foreign affiliates, net of corresponding outflows.

No. 889. Corporate Profits With Inventory Valuation and Capital Consumption Adjustments—Financial and Nonfinancial Industries: 1980 to 1994

[In billions of dollars. Minus sign (-) indicates loss. See headnote, table 887]

ITEM	1980	1985	1986	1987	1988	1989	1990	1991	1992	1993	1994
Corporate profits with IVA [1] and CCA [2]	**177.7**	**280.8**	**271.6**	**319.8**	**365.0**	**362.8**	**380.6**	**390.3**	**405.1**	**485.8**	**542.7**
Domestic industries	142.7	250.0	238.7	280.3	315.9	303.4	312.6	321.8	344.5	420.5	482.3
Financial	22.0	28.6	34.9	36.1	41.5	48.2	56.2	72.6	67.9	89.5	88.3
Nonfinancial	120.7	221.4	203.8	244.2	274.4	255.2	256.4	249.2	276.6	330.9	394.0
Rest of the world.	35.0	30.8	32.9	39.5	49.1	59.4	67.9	68.5	60.6	65.3	60.5
Corporate profits with IVA [1] . .	**197.8**	**225.3**	**227.6**	**273.4**	**320.3**	**325.4**	**354.7**	**370.9**	**389.4**	**456.2**	**505.0**
Domestic industries	162.9	194.5	194.6	233.9	271.2	266.0	286.7	302.4	328.8	391.0	444.6
Financial	24.3	28.7	35.8	36.4	41.8	50.6	65.7	84.3	81.9	103.7	104.0
Federal Reserve banks	11.8	16.3	15.5	15.7	17.6	20.1	21.4	20.3	17.8	16.0	17.3
Other	12.6	12.4	20.3	20.7	24.2	30.5	44.3	64.0	64.2	87.7	86.7
Nonfinancial	138.5	165.8	158.9	197.5	229.4	215.3	221.1	218.1	246.9	287.3	340.6
Manufacturing	75.8	80.1	59.0	87.0	117.5	108.0	109.1	90.1	94.5	114.2	145.8
Durable goods [3]	17.9	29.0	30.0	42.2	52.2	49.3	39.2	30.3	35.5	49.4	72.1
Primary metal industries . . .	2.6	-0.9	0.9	2.6	5.9	6.1	3.3	1.1	-0.4	0.2	0.5
Fabricated metal products . .	4.3	4.7	5.3	5.2	6.4	6.6	6.1	5.3	7.5	6.8	9.3
Machinery, except electrical . .	7.5	5.3	3.2	7.3	10.5	10.3	9.6	4.3	6.1	7.4	9.1
Electric and electronic equipment	5.0	2.4	2.6	6.2	7.6	9.3	7.9	9.2	9.0	11.9	19.8
Motor vehicles and equipment.	-4.3	7.3	4.4	3.7	5.7	2.3	-2.2	-5.6	-1.5	4.1	10.5
Nondurable goods [3]	57.8	51.1	29.0	44.8	65.3	58.8	69.9	59.8	58.9	64.9	73.5
Food and kindred products . .	6.0	8.4	7.5	11.4	11.8	10.7	14.0	17.7	17.5	16.9	20.2
Chemicals and allied products.	5.5	6.0	8.0	15.1	19.3	18.5	16.2	15.5	15.8	17.5	19.2
Petroleum and coal products .	33.6	17.1	-8.5	-3.6	10.4	5.7	17.3	5.0	-1.4	4.7	6.1
Transportation and public utilities .	18.3	34.1	36.5	43.4	47.5	42.1	44.0	53.6	55.6	65.0	72.3
Wholesale and retail trade	22.8	43.1	46.3	39.9	37.1	39.7	37.2	46.7	54.8	61.2	67.6
Other	21.6	8.5	17.1	27.2	27.3	25.5	30.8	27.7	42.0	46.9	55.1

[1] Inventory valuation adjustment.   [2] Capital consumption adjustment.   [3] Includes other industries not shown separately.
Source of tables 887-889: U.S. Bureau of Economic Analysis, *National Income and Product Accounts of the United States, volume 2, 1959-88; Survey of Current Business*, July 1992, August 1993, July 1994, and March 1995.

No. 890. Manufacturing, Mining, and Trade Corporations—Profits and Stockholders' Equity Ratios: 1990 to 1994

[Averages of quarterly figures at annual rates. Beginning 1990, manufacturing data exclude estimates for corporations with less than $250,000 in assets at time of sample selection. Data are not necessarily comparable from year to year due to changes in accounting procedures, industry classifications, sampling procedures, etc.; for detail, see source. Based on sample; see source for discussion of methodology. Minus sign (-) indicates loss]

INDUSTRY	RATIO OF PROFITS TO STOCKHOLDERS' EQUITY (percent)				PROFITS PER DOLLAR OF SALES (cents)				RATIO OF STOCKHOLDERS' EQUITY TO DEBT			
	1990	1992	1993	1994	1990	1992	1993	1994	1990	1992	1993	1994
Manufacturing corporations	**10.7**	**2.2**	**8.1**	**15.7**	**4.0**	**0.8**	**2.8**	**5.4**	**1.3**	**1.3**	**1.3**	**1.4**
Durable goods	8.0	−5.0	5.7	16.3	3.0	−1.7	1.9	5.2	1.6	1.4	1.5	1.7
Lumber and wood products	(NA)	15.1	18.6	21.8	(NA)	3.8	4.7	5.7	(NA)	1.4	1.6	1.8
Furniture and fixtures	(NA)	11.5	13.5	14.7	(NA)	2.7	3.4	3.5	(NA)	1.3	1.7	1.6
Stone, clay, and glass products. . . .	5.4	−2.3	5.8	9.1	1.8	−0.7	2.1	3.4	0.8	0.7	0.8	1.1
Primary metal industries	9.5	−8.3	−2.5.	13.6	2.6	−2.1	−0.7	3.6	1.1	0.9	1.0	1.1
Iron and steel	6.6	−20.9	16.4	16.4	1.0	−2.4	−0.4	3.8	0.6	0.4	0.8	1.1
Nonferrous metals.	10.4	−5.1	−2.8	11.6	4.0	−1.8	−0.9	3.4	1.6	1.2	1.1	1.1
Fabricated metal products	11.7	10.3	7.1	13.4	3.4	3.1	2.1	3.7	1.3	1.3	1.3	1.3
Machinery, exc. electrical	8.1	−7.5	−6.0	12.4	4.4	−3.5	−2.3	4.4	2.2	1.8	1.5	1.7
Electrical and electronic equipment . .	7.5	8.6	21.6	16.0	3.0	3.6	5.0	6.7	1.6	1.7	2.0	2.2
Transportation equipment.	3.8	−40.3	9.8	24.3	1.3	−8.7	1.9	5.1	1.9	1.2	1.3	1.8
Motor vehicles and equipment . . .	−1.0	−72.9	6.9	32.1	−0.5	−13.8	1.1	5.4	2.2	1.1	1.3	2.0
Aircraft, guided missiles and parts .	11.5	−5.3	13.1	14.8	3.4	−1.4	3.6	4.7	1.6	1.4	1.4	1.6
Instruments and related products . . .	12.9	7.4	21.6	17.0	6.6	3.9	5.1	9.2	1.6	1.8	1.9	2.1
Miscellaneous manufacturing	(NA)	12.9	14.6	17.8	(NA)	3.5	4.1	4.9	(NA)	1.4	1.6	1.7
Nondurable goods	13.3	8.4	10.1	15.2	4.9	3.1	3.7	5.5	1.2	1.2	1.1	1.2
Food and kindred products [1]	16.1	15.0	13.5	18.0	4.1	4.3	3.7	5.0	0.8	0.9	0.9	0.9
Tobacco products	([1])	([1])	([1])	([1])	([1])	([1])	([1])	([1])	([1])	([1])	([1])	([1])
Textile mill products	3.4	12.5	7.7	9.7	0.8	3.4	2.3	2.8	0.7	1.1	1.2	1.0
Apparel (includes leather)	(NA)	28.2	16.8	11.7	(NA)	5.1	3.3	2.6	(NA)	1.0	1.1	1.3
Paper and allied products	10.6	2.5	−0.4	11.0	4.2	0.9	−0.2	3.7	1.1	0.9	0.8	0.8
Printing and publishing	8.3	7.2	9.1	12.6	3.6	3.2	3.6	5.1	1.2	1.3	1.0	1.2
Chemicals and allied products	17.3	8.9	10.2	19.1	8.2	4.1	4.7	8.5	1.4	1.3	1.3	1.3
Industrial	13.8	−4.4	6.7	13.5	7.0	−2.1	3.3	6.0	1.4	1.1	1.1	1.1
Drugs	27.1	22.6	22.0	25.4	15.7	12.9	12.4	14.3	2.2	2.2	2.0	1.8
Residual of chemicals	(NA)	13.3	2.6	19.6	(NA)	5.1	0.9	6.9	(NA)	1.3	1.3	1.2
Petroleum and coal products	12.8	2.4	10.3	11.5	5.7	1.2	4.9	5.6	1.7	1.5	1.5	1.6
Rubber and misc. plastics products . .	6.9	7.1	11.9	17.1	1.8	1.7	3.0	4.3	1.0	1.0	1.0	1.2
Mining corporations [2]	**8.1**	**−0.7**	**4.1**	**2.2**	**5.7**	**−0.6**	**3.7**	**1.9**	**1.3**	**1.4**	**1.5**	**1.4**
Retail trade corporations [2]	**8.4**	**5.7**	**9.7**	**13.5**	**1.1**	**0.8**	**1.5**	**2.1**	**0.6**	**0.7**	**0.8**	**0.9**
Wholesale trade corporations [2] . .	**5.0**	**5.4**	**6.6**	**5.2**	**0.6**	**0.7**	**0.9**	**0.7**	**1.0**	**0.8**	**0.8**	**0.8**

NA Not available.   [1] After 1980, tobacco included in food and kindred products.   [2] Asset cut-off raised to $50 million from $25 million in 1985.

No. 891. Manufacturing Corporations—Selected Finances: 1980 to 1994

[**In billions of dollars.** Data are not necessarily comparable from year to year due to changes in accounting procedures, industry classifications, sampling procedures, etc.; for detail, see source. See also *Historical Statistics, Colonial Times to 1970,* series P 93-106]

YEAR	ALL MANUFACTURING CORPS.					DURABLE GOODS INDUSTRIES					NONDURABLE GOODS INDUSTRIES				
	Sales	Profits		Stockholders' equity [1]	Debt [1]	Sales	Profits		Stockholders' equity [1]	Debt [1]	Sales	Profits		Stockholders' equity [1]	Debt [1]
		Before taxes	After taxes				Before taxes	After taxes				Before taxes	After taxes		
1980 . .	1,897	145	92	665	292	883	57	36	316	143	1,014	88	57	349	149
1981 . .	2,145	159	101	743	335	979	67	42	350	159	1,165	91	60	393	176
1982 . .	2,039	108	71	770	371	913	35	22	356	177	1,126	74	49	415	193
1983 . .	2,114	133	86	813	368	973	49	30	372	168	1,141	84	56	440	200
1984 . .	2,335	166	108	864	405	1,108	76	49	396	166	1,228	90	59	469	239
1985 . .	2,331	137	88	866	454	1,143	61	39	421	187	1,189	76	49	445	267
1986 [2]	2,221	129	83	875	501	1,126	52	33	436	203	1,096	77	51	438	298
1987 . .	2,378	173	116	901	553	1,178	78	53	444	229	1,200	95	63	457	324
1988 . .	2,596	216	155	958	622	1,285	92	67	469	265	1,312	124	88	489	357
1989 . .	2,745	189	136	999	733	1,357	75	56	501	308	1,388	114	81	498	425
1990 . .	2,812	160	112	1,044	782	1,357	58	41	515	328	1,454	102	71	529	453
1991 . .	2,761	100	68	1,064	814	1,304	14	7	507	338	1,457	86	60	557	476
1992 . .	2,890	33	23	1,035	819	1,390	−34	−24	474	335	1,500	66	47	561	485
1993 . .	3,014	119	84	1,040	819	1,490	39	28	483	327	1,524	79	56	557	492
1994 . .	3,261	244	175	1,114	815	1,660	121	87	533	316	1,601	123	89	581	500

[1] Annual data are average equity or debt for the year using four end-of-quarter figures.   [2] Beginning 1986, data exclude estimates for corporations with less than $250,000 in assets at time of sample selection.

Source of tables 890 and 891: Through 1981, U.S. Federal Trade Commission; thereafter, U.S. Bureau of Census, *Quarterly Financial Report for Manufacturing, Mining, and Trade Corporations.* In U.S. Council of Economic Advisers, *Economic Report of the President,* annual.

No. 892. Corporate Philanthropy: 1985 to 1992

[Percent of worldwide pretax net income. Data are based on a sample greater than 1,200 corporations. Medians by industry]

INDUSTRY	1985	1986	1987	1988	1989	1990	1991	1992
All firms, median.	**1.0**	**1.0**	**0.9**	**0.8**	**0.9**	**1.0**	**1.3**	**1.0**
Manufacturing firms, median	1.1	1.2	1.0	0.8	0.9	1.0	1.3	1.1
Chemicals	1.1	1.1	0.8	0.7	0.8	0.9	1.0	0.9
Electrical machinery and equipment	1.6	1.3	1.2	0.6	0.7	1.0	1.8	0.7
Food, beverage, tobacco	1.2	1.5	1.3	1.0	1.4	1.1	1.1	0.9
Machinery, nonelectrical	1.1	2.4	1.0	0.9	0.7	0.7	0.8	0.9
Paper and like products	1.2	0.7	0.7	0.6	0.7	1.4	1.9	1.2
Petroleum and gas [1]	0.7	1.2	0.9	0.5	0.8	0.8	2.1	1.3
Pharmaceuticals	1.0	0.9	1.0	1.1	1.0	1.1	1.4	1.1
Primary metal industries	1.1	1.4	(NA)	(NA)	0.5	0.8	1.0	1.4
Printing and publishing	1.3	1.4	0.8	2.3	1.7	1.2	1.5	1.3
Transportation equipment [2]	1.0	1.6	0.9	1.1	1.2	2.0	1.1	1.8
Nonmanufacturing firms, median	0.9	0.9	0.7	0.9	1.0	0.9	1.2	0.9

NA Not available.   [1] Includes mining firms.   [2] Includes rubber and miscellaneous plastic firms.

Source: The Conference Board, New York, NY, *Annual Survey of Corporate Contributions* (copyright).

No. 893. Foreign Corporate Activity in the United States: 1991

[**In millions of dollars, except number of returns.** Includes U.S. corporations controlled or owned by any foreign person (i.e., an individual, partnership, corporation, estate, or trust), directly or indirectly, based on 50 percent or more of a U.S. corporation's voting stock at the end of the tax year]

COUNTRY [1]	Number of returns	Assets	Receipts [2]	Net income (less deficit)	U.S. INCOME TAX Before credits	U.S. INCOME TAX After credits
All corporations in the U.S..	**3,802,788**	**19,029,509**	**11,436,475**	**344,860**	**121,121**	**92,566**
U.S. corporations controlled by a foreign person	**48,247**	**1,827,337**	**1,143,823**	**−4,888**	**7,237**	**6,092**
Canada	8,720	195,129	103,630	−1,009	598	537
Latin America	6,412	44,906	37,500	−554	221	181
Other Western Hemisphere	372	16,591	14,314	−115	58	53
Europe	18,311	939,945	594,215	2,878	4,755	3,873
European Economic Community [3]	15,001	795,244	502,642	3,155	4,135	3,377
Belgium	129	18,162	14,016	658	298	139
France	1,795	97,141	66,096	−606	321	238
West Germany	2,880	124,026	103,504	584	600	498
Netherlands	2,183	209,693	116,175	41	637	531
United Kingdom	5,574	292,877	179,466	3,172	2,108	1,879
Sweden	880	31,009	22,472	−228	102	82
Switzerland	1,248	97,648	56,421	431	470	369
Africa	457	11,047	980	−100	1	1
Asia [3]	11,082	542,903	352,179	−5,610	1,358	1,278
Hong Kong	1,372	21,594	7,184	−625	14	14
Japan	6,830	478,500	314,424	−4,228	1,234	1,163
Korea, South	222	8,512	10,805	−282	13	13
Oceania	541	53,529	19,360	−585	44	37
Puerto Rico and U.S. possessions	89	3,533	1,729	125	87	25
Country not stated	2,263	19,755	19,916	82	116	107

[1] Geographic location of the foreign owners' country of residence, incorporation, organization, creation, or administration.
[2] Includes business and investment receipts.   [3] Includes countries not shown separately.

Source: U.S. Internal Revenue Service, *Statistics of Income Bulletin,* winter 1994.

No. 894. U.S. Multinational Companies—Gross Product: 1982 and 1989

[In millions of dollars. Gross product measures valued added by a firm. Consists of nonbank U.S. parent companies and their nonbank foreign affiliates. A U.S. parent comprises the domestic operations of a multinational and is a U.S. person that owns or controls 10 percent or more of the voting securities, or the equivalent, of a foreign business enterprise. A U.S. person can be an incorporated business enterprise. A majority-owned foreign affiliate is a foreign business enterprise in which a U.S. parent company owns or controls 50% or more of the voting securities]

INDUSTRY	U.S. MULTINATIONALS		U.S. PARENTS		MAJORITY-OWNED FOREIGN AFFILIATES	
	1982	1989	1982	1989	1982	1989
All industries	1,019,734	1,364,878	796,017	1,044,884	223,717	319,994
Petroleum	211,937	165,680	134,096	93,128	77,841	72,552
Manufacturing	542,689	793,771	421,050	586,568	121,639	207,203
Food and kindred products	46,069	79,472	35,804	60,310	10,265	19,162
Chemical and allied products	93,054	141,006	66,234	97,119	26,820	43,887
Primary and fabricated metals	43,592	45,775	37,215	37,556	6,377	8,219
Machinery, except electrical	84,046	116,146	60,597	70,887	23,449	45,259
Electric and electronic equipment	69,259	68,515	59,323	56,139	9,936	12,376
Transportation equipment	91,170	160,292	71,256	121,141	19,914	39,151
Other	115,499	182,567	90,621	143,417	24,878	39,150
Wholesale trade	17,427	28,766	13,604	22,587	3,823	6,179
Finance, insurance, real estate	31,823	62,715	22,801	50,535	9,022	12,180
Finance, except banking	4,991	16,948	4,730	15,103	261	1,845
Insurance	23,539	41,233	17,954	34,948	5,585	6,285
Real estate	135	668	120	558	15	110
Holding companies	3,005	2,808	−2	−75	3,007	2,883
Services	29,362	66,999	25,997	57,090	3,365	9,909
Hotels and other lodging places	2,838	6,676	2,693	5,780	145	896
Business services	10,026	24,067	8,501	18,756	1,525	5,311
Advertising	2,627	3,960	1,947	2,349	680	1,611
Equipment rental (exc. auto, computers)	652	193	646	175	6	18
Computer and data processing	2,313	6,361	2,135	5,353	178	1,008
Other	4,434	13,551	3,773	10,878	661	2,673
Automotive rental and leasing	(1)	4,998	(1)	4,212	(1)	786
Motion pictures, television tape and film	941	3,465	825	2,663	116	802
Health services	5,420	8,965	5,234	8,559	186	406
Engineering, architectural, surveying	3,350	3,498	2,422	2,998	928	500
Management and public relations	(1)	1,702	(1)	1,180	(1)	522
Other	6,787	13,629	6,322	12,943	465	686
Other industries	186,496	246,946	178,469	234,975	8,027	11,971

[1] Included in "other" services.

Source: U.S. Bureau of Economic Analysis, *Survey of Current Business*, February 1994.

No. 895. U.S. Multinational Companies—Selected Characteristics: 1992

[Preliminary. In billions of dollars, except as indicated. Consists of nonbank U.S. parent companies and their nonbank foreign affiliates. U.S. parent is a U.S. person that owns or controls directly or indirectly, 10 percent or more of the voting securities of an incorporated foreign business enterprise, or an equivalent interest in an unincorporated foreign business enterprise. A U.S. person can be an incorporated business enterprise. A foreign affiliate is a foreign business enterprise owned or controlled by a U.S. parent company]

INDUSTRY [1]	U.S. PARENTS				FOREIGN AFFILIATES				U.S. exports shipped to foreign affiliates	U.S. imports shipped from foreign affiliates
	Total assets	Sales	Employ-ment (1,000)	Employee compen-sation	Total assets	Sales	Employ-ment (1,000)	Employee compen-sation		
All industries	5,570.5	3,353.0	17,617.2	722.8	1,746.8	1,578.7	6,727.5	201.4	120.3	109.2
Petroleum	523.2	383.8	553.9	31.9	228.7	306.4	230.2	11.1	2.5	12.5
Manufacturing	2,071.5	1,638.9	9,307.4	417.4	591.6	757.6	4,006.5	121.7	82.2	85.9
Food and kindred products	200.1	223.8	1,167.2	33.3	69.1	89.2	495.1	11.1	2.4	1.4
Chemical and allied products	341.6	267.3	1,194.9	61.5	131.4	143.0	587.1	21.2	9.7	4.9
Primary and fabricated metals	87.1	86.2	557.2	24.5	26.7	27.9	198.9	5.6	2.0	1.8
Machinery (except electrical)	379.3	223.8	1,306.8	67.3	91.9	124.9	507.2	20.7	13.3	15.3
Electric and electronic equipment	103.5	95.4	685.1	28.7	47.8	56.8	557.0	10.7	9.6	12.9
Transportation equipment	476.1	367.2	1,808.8	97.5	102.6	183.9	738.7	25.7	33.5	39.6
Other	483.8	375.1	2,587.4	104.6	122.0	131.9	922.4	26.7	11.7	9.9
Wholesale trade	100.9	184.0	406.7	14.4	142.6	263.2	550.8	24.2	32.7	9.1
Finance (except banking), insurance, real estate	1,936.6	416.2	1,033.4	53.8	594.0	79.0	150.3	7.4	0.0	0.0
Services	154.8	125.3	1,610.7	47.4	73.6	61.1	569.1	17.5	0.8	0.1
Other	783.6	604.9	4,705.1	157.8	116.3	111.4	1,220.8	19.4	2.0	1.7

[1] Represents industry of U.S. parent or industry of foreign affiliate.

Source: U.S. Bureau of Economic Analysis, *Survey of Current Business*, May 1994.

Figure 18.1
Media Usage by Consumers: 1984 to 1998

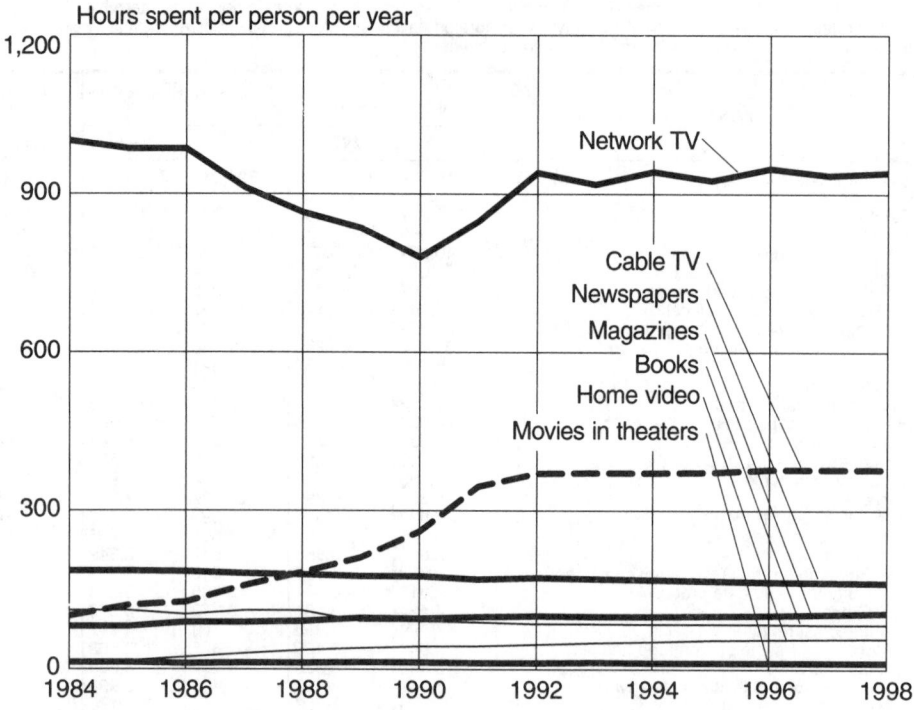

Note: Data for 1993 to 1998 are projected.
Source: Chart prepared by U.S. Bureau of the Census. For data, see table 899.

Figure 18.2
Microcomputer Software Sales: 1994

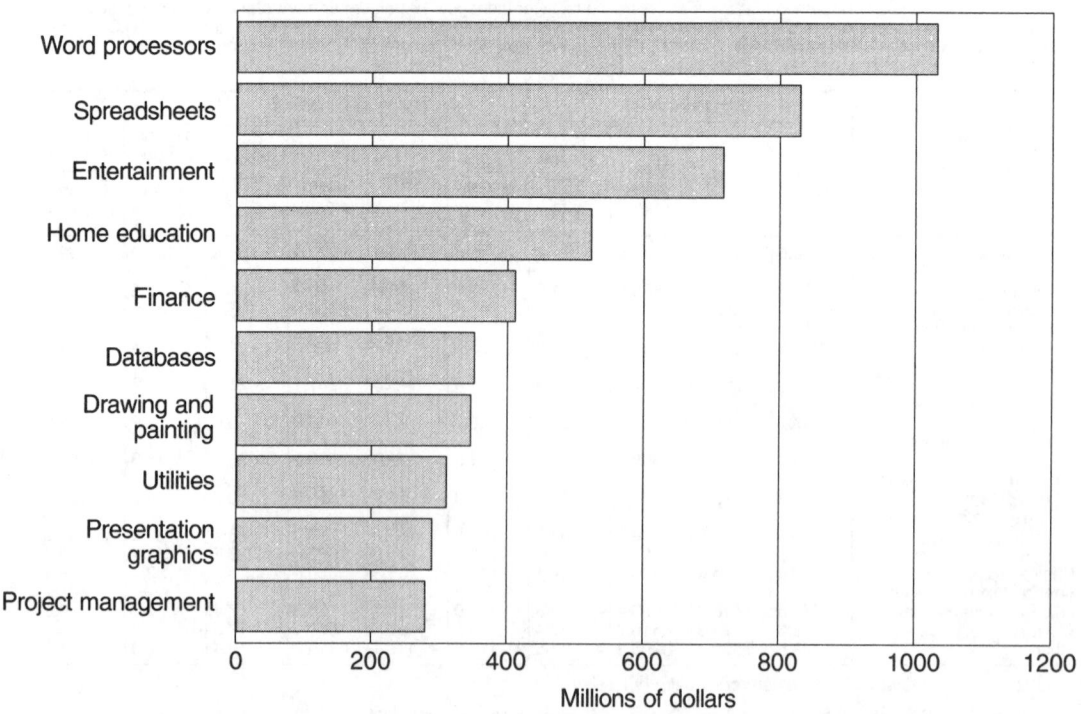

Source: Chart prepared by U.S. Bureau of the Census. For data, see table 914.

Communications and Information Technology

This section presents statistics on the various communications media: telephone, telegraph, radio, television, newspapers and periodicals, and the usage, finances, and operations of the Postal Service. Expenditure data for advertising in the media are also included.

Communication media.—The Bureau of the Census *Annual Survey of Communication Services* (ASCS) covers all employer firms with one or more establishments that are primarily engaged in providing point-to-point communication services, whether by wire or radio, and whether intended to be received aurally or visually. This includes telephone communications, including cellular and other radiotelephone services; telegraph and other message communications, such as electronic mail services, facsimile transmission services, telex services, and so on; radio and television broadcasting stations and networks; cable and other pay television services; and other communication services, such as radar station operations, satellite earth stations, satellite or missile tracking stations, and so on. The report presents statistics that are summarized by kind-of-business classification based on the 1987 edition of the *Standard Industrial Classification Manual.*

The Federal Communications Commission (FCC), established in 1934, regulates wire and radio communications. Only the largest carriers and holding companies file annual or monthly financial reports. The FCC has jurisdiction over interstate and foreign communication services, but not over intrastate or local services. The gross operating revenues of the telephone carriers reporting annually to the FCC, however, are estimated to cover about 90 percent of the revenues of all U.S. telephone companies. Data are not comparable with Bureau of the Census *Annual Survey of Communication Services* because of coverage (*ASCS* includes all domestic long-distance telephone companies, all local exchange carriers, and all cellular telephone companies) and different

In Brief	
Consumer spending in 1993:	
Basic cable	$101
Books	$75
Home video	$69
Daily newspapers	$52
Recorded music	$47
Magazines	$35
Movies in theaters	$24

accounting practices for those telephone companies which report to the FCC.

Reports filed by the broadcasting industry cover substantially all radio and television stations operating in the United States. The private radio services represent the largest and most diverse group of licensees regulated by the FCC. These services provide voice, data communications, point-to-point and point-to-multipoint radio communications for fixed and mobile communicators. Major users of these services are small businesses, the aviation industry, the maritime trades, the land transportation industry, manufacturing industries, State and local public safety and governmental authorities, emergency medical service providers, amateur radio operators, and personal radio operations (CB and the General Mobile Radio Service). The FCC also licenses entities as private and common carriers. Private and common carriers provide fixed and land mobile communications service on a for-profit basis. Principal sources of wire, radio, and television data are the FCC's *Annual Report* and its annual *Statistics of Communications Common Carriers.*

Statistics on the printed media are available from the U.S. Bureau of the Census, as well as from various private agencies. The censuses of manufactures (conducted by the Census Bureau every 5 years, for the years ending in "2" and "7") provide statistics on the number and circulation of newspapers and periodicals and on sales of books and pamphlets. Editor & Publisher Co. New York, NY, presents annual data on the number and circulation of daily and Sunday newspapers in its *International Year Book.* Monthly data on new books and new editions appear in *Publishers Weekly,* issued by R. R. Bowker Company, New York. (See table 921 for annual data.)

Advertising.—Data on advertising expenditures are compiled primarily by McCann-Erickson, Inc., (see table 928). Monthly index figures of advertising in certain media are also published periodically by McCann-Erickson in *Advertising Age.*

The Broadcast Advertisers Reports distinguishes between spot and local advertising primarily on the basis of the type of advertiser to whom the time is sold, rather than how and by whom it is sold. In general, time purchased on behalf of retail or service establishments in the market is considered local, even though the establishments may be part of a national or regional chain. That is, spot advertising promotes a product, while local advertising promotes a given establishment. Network advertising, mutually exclusive of spot and local, is broadcast through the network system.

Postal Service.—The Postal Service provides mail processing and delivery services within the United States. The Postal Reorganization Act of 1970 created the Postal Service, effective July 1971, as an independent establishment of the Federal Executive Branch.

Revenue and cost analysis describes the Postal Service's system of attributing revenues and costs to classes of mail and service. This system draws primarily upon probability sampling techniques to develop estimates of revenues, volumes, and weights, as well as costs by class of mail and special service. The costs attributed to classes of mail and special services are primarily incremental costs which vary in response to changes in volume; they account for roughly 60 percent of the total costs of the Postal Service. The balance represents "institutional costs." Statistics on revenues, volume of mail, and distribution of expenditures are presented in the Postal Service's annual report, *Cost and Revenue Analysis,* and its *Annual Report of the Postmaster General* and its *Annual Comprehensive Report on Postal Operations.*

Statistical reliability.—For a discussion of statistical collection and estimation, sampling procedures, and measures of statistical reliability applicable to Census Bureau data, see Appendix III.

Historical statistics.—Tabular headnotes provide cross-references, where applicable, to *Historical Statistics of the United States, Colonial Times to 1970.* See Appendix IV.

No. 896. Communications Industry—Summary: 1992

[For establishments with payroll]

INDUSTRY	1987 SIC[1] code	Establish- ments	Revenue ($1,000)	Payroll ($1,000)	Paid employees[2]
Communications	48	39,244	230,667,167	47,057,941	1,294,236
Total, except broadcasting and cable ..	**481, 2, 9**	**26,227**	**174,926,125**	**36,522,874**	**943,518**
Telephone	481	24,730	171,580,095	35,900,576	928,245
Radiotelephone	4812	3,063	12,269,735	2,091,368	61,077
Other telephone	4813	21,667	159,310,360	33,809,208	867,168
Telegraph communications	482	489	988,142	217,800	5,536
Communication services, n.e.c.[3]	489	1,008	2,357,888	404,498	9,737
Broadcasting and cable	483, 4	13,017	55,741,042	10,535,067	350,718
Radio and television broadcasting	483	8,549	28,228,942	6,976,376	221,755
Radio	4832	6,956	6,865,419	2,547,700	112,385
Television	4833	1,593	21,363,523	4,428,676	109,370
Cable and other pay television	484	4,468	27,512,100	3,558,691	128,963

[1]1987 Standard Industrial Classification code; see text, section 13.   [2]For the pay period including March 12.
[3] N.e.c. means not elsewhere classified.
   Source: U.S. Bureau of the Census, *Census of Transportation, Communications, and Utilities,* UC92-A-1.

No. 897. Utilization of Selected Media: 1970 to 1994

ITEM	Unit	1970	1980	1985	1988	1989	1990	1991	1992	1993	1994
Households with—											
Telephone service [1]	Percent .	87.0	93.0	91.8	92.9	93.0	93.3	93.6	93.9	94.2	93.9
Radio [2]	Millions .	62.0	78.6	87.1	91.1	92.8	94.4	95.5	96.6	97.3	98.0
Percent of total households . .	Percent .	98.6	99.0	99.0	99.0	99.0	99.0	99.0	99.0	99.0	99.0
Average number of sets	Number .	5.1	5.5	5.5	5.6	5.6	5.6	5.6	5.6	5.6	5.6
Television [3]	Millions .	59	76	85	89	90	92	93	92	93	94
Percent of total households . .	Percent .	95.3	97.9	98.1	98.1	98.2	98.2	98.2	98.3	98.3	98.3
Television sets in homes	Millions .	81	128	155	168	176	193	193	192	201	211
Average number of sets per home	Number	1.4	1.7	1.8	1.9	1.9	2.1	2.1	2.1	2.2	2.2
Color sets . .	Millions .	21	63	78	85	87	90	91	91	92	93
Cable television [4]	Millions .	4	15	36	44	48	52	55	55	57	59
Percent of TV households . . .	Percent .	6.7	19.9	42.8	49.4	52.8	56.4	58.9	60.2	61.4	62.4
VCR's [4]	Millions .	(NA)	1	18	51	58	63	67	69	72	74
Percent of TV households . . .	Percent .	(NA)	1.1	20.8	58.0	64.6	68.6	71.9	75.0	77.1	79.0
Commercial radio stations: [2]											
AM.	Number .	4,323	4,589	[5]4,718	4,932	4,975	4,987	4,985	4,961	4,994	4,913
FM. . . . . [6]	Number .	2,196	3,282	[5]3,875	4,155	4,269	4,392	4,570	4,785	4,971	5,109
Television stations: [6]											
Total.	Number .	862	1,011	1,182	1,362	1,403	1,442	1,459	1,481	1,506	1,512
Commercial [3]	Number .	677	734	883	1,028	1,061	1,092	1,099	1,118	1,137	1,145
VHF	Number .	501	516	520	539	545	547	547	551	552	561
UHF	Number .	176	218	363	489	516	545	552	567	585	584
Cable television:											
Systems [6]	Number .	2,490	4,225	6,844	8,500	9,050	9,575	10,704	11,075	11,217	11,230
Subscribers served [7]	Millions .	4.5	17.7	39.9	48.6	52.6	54.9	55.8	56.4	57.2	60.5
Daily newspaper circulation [8]	Millions .	62	62	63	63	63	62	61	60	60	60

NA Not available. [1] For occupied housing units. 1970 and 1980 as of April 1; all other years as of March. Source: U.S. Bureau of the Census, *1970* and *1980 Census of Housing*, vol. 1; and unpublished data. [2] As of December 31, except as noted. Source: Radio Advertising Bureau, New York, NY, through 1992, *Radio Facts*, annual, (copyright); beginning 1993, *Radio Marketing Guide and Fact Book for Advertisers*, annual, (copyright). Number of stations on the air compiled from Federal Communications Commission reports. [3] 1970, as of September of prior year; all other years as of January of year shown. Excludes Alaska and Hawaii. Source: Television Bureau of Advertising, Inc., *Trends in Television*, annual, (copyright). [4] As of February. Excludes Alaska and Hawaii. Source: See footnote 3. [5] As of February 1986. [6] As of January 1. Source: Warren Publishing, Washington DC, *Television and Cable Factbook*. [7] Source: AC Nielsen Company, *Nielsen Station Index*, November diary estimates. [8] As of September 30. Source: Editor & Publisher, Co., New York, NY, *Editor & Publisher International Year Book*, annual, (copyright).

Source: Compiled from sources mentioned in footnotes.

No. 898. Multimedia Audiences—Summary: 1994

[**In percent, except as indicated.** As of **spring.** For persons **18 years old and over.** Represents the number of people viewing/listening during a specified time period. Based on sample and subject to sampling error; see source for details]

ITEM	Total population (1,000)	Television viewing	Television prime time viewing	Cable viewing	Radio listening	Newspaper reading
Total.	**188,654**	**92.1**	**78.4**	**61.6**	**84.7**	**82.9**
18 to 24 years old	24,247	91.0	73.0	59.6	93.5	80.0
25 to 34 years old	43,548	91.0	76.8	60.2	92.3	81.5
35 to 44 years old	40,581	90.7	77.4	64.4	89.7	85.6
45 to 54 years old	27,501	91.3	78.8	66.1	87.7	85.6
55 to 64 years old	21,394	93.6	81.0	63.4	77.8	84.6
65 years old and over	31,383	95.9	83.8	56.3	63.0	80.0
Male	90,177	91.7	76.9	63.5	86.6	83.0
Female.	98,478	92.4	79.8	59.9	83.0	82.8
White.	160,581	91.7	78.0	64.0	84.8	83.6
Black.	21,415	94.5	81.1	48.1	84.7	82.2
Other.	6,658	92.8	79.7	47.0	82.9	68.5
Spanish speaking.	16,247	93.6	81.1	49.1	88.0	75.2
Not high school graduate.	37,489	93.7	81.1	48.3	72.7	65.0
High school graduate	65,896	92.7	80.0	62.8	84.9	82.8
Attended college	47,506	91.3	76.3	66.4	90.1	88.5
College graduate	37,763	90.3	75.5	66.6	89.4	93.8
Employed:						
Full-time	102,971	90.6	76.1	65.6	91.6	86.4
Part-time	16,348	91.2	74.4	60.2	90.5	88.1
Not employed	69,335	94.6	82.8	56.0	73.2	76.5
Household income:						
Less than $10,000	19,620	92.3	81.1	42.3	70.9	62.9
$10,000 to $19,999	29,530	93.6	80.5	49.4	77.3	75.3
$20,000 to $29,999	29,135	93.5	80.4	57.0	82.7	80.4
$30,000 to $34,999	13,658	94.0	80.3	63.1	85.6	83.5
$35,000 to $39,999	13,087	92.2	78.1	62.6	87.6	84.8
$40,000 to $49,999	22,163	92.1	78.7	67.3	89.2	88.4
$50,000 or more	61,461	90.1	75.0	73.2	91.3	91.6

Source: Mediamark Research Inc., New York, NY, *Multimedia Audiences*, fall 1994 (copyright).

No. 899. Media Usage and Consumer Spending: 1985 to 1998

[Estimates of time spent were derived using data for television and radio, survey research and consumer purchase data for recorded music, newspapers, magazines, books, home video, and admissions for movies. Adults 18 and older except for recorded music and movies in theaters, where estimates include persons 12 and older]

| YEAR | Total [1] | TELEVISION | | | | Recorded music | Daily news-papers | Con-sumer maga-zines | Con-sumer books | Home video [4] | Movies in theaters |
		Net-work sta-tions [2]	Inde-pen-dent sta-tions [2]	Basic cable [3]	Pay cable						
HOURS PER PERSON PER YEAR											
1985	3,307	985	335	120	90	185	185	110	80	15	12
1986	3,313	985	339	126	72	173	184	103	88	22	10
1987	3,258	912	332	157	84	200	180	110	88	29	11
1988	3,310	865	349	182	94	215	178	110	90	35	11
1989	3,288	835	345	210	95	220	175	90	96	39	12
1990	3,276	780	340	260	90	235	175	90	95	42	12
1991	3,283	848	230	345	90	219	169	88	98	43	11
1992	3,378	940	160	370	80	233	172	85	100	46	11
1993	3,304	918	162	371	78	248	170	85	99	49	12
1994 proj.	3,307	942	148	371	78	261	168	84	99	51	11
1995 proj.	3,297	925	149	372	79	274	166	84	100	54	11
1996 proj.	3,348	948	146	377	81	287	164	84	101	55	11
1997 proj.	3,332	935	146	377	82	295	163	83	103	56	11
1998 proj.	3,344	940	144	377	83	305	162	83	105	57	11
CONSUMER SPENDING PER PERSON PER YEAR (dollars)											
1985	218.22	-	-	45.43	(5)	22.39	41.84	25.60	43.39	20.43	19.13
1986	235.77	-	-	49.71	(5)	23.52	43.28	26.89	44.81	28.45	19.11
1987	265.26	-	-	56.66	(5)	27.92	44.76	29.31	49.72	35.58	21.33
1988	315.99	-	-	66.89	(5)	31.01	46.15	29.88	54.29	44.04	22.10
1989	347.20	-	-	75.50	(5)	32.25	47.48	31.49	61.24	50.84	24.67
1990	380.38	-	-	85.31	(5)	36.64	49.35	33.14	63.90	56.48	24.40
1991	398.95	-	-	92.36	(5)	37.73	48.38	33.45	68.18	58.88	23.13
1992	426.21	-	-	96.71	(5)	43.05	50.31	34.26	71.37	63.41	23.24
1993	449.29	-	-	101.06	(5)	47.42	52.02	35.27	74.90	69.42	24.33
1994 proj.	469.99	-	-	98.96	(5)	51.26	54.02	36.60	78.83	76.04	24.02
1995 proj.	497.32	-	-	100.91	(5)	55.47	56.21	38.20	84.02	81.64	24.52
1996 proj.	528.35	-	-	105.65	(5)	59.86	58.88	39.73	89.51	86.02	25.32
1997 proj.	556.53	-	-	110.43	(5)	63.29	61.37	41.20	95.47	89.64	25.82
1998 proj.	584.95	-	-	115.03	(5)	66.78	64.01	42.59	102.08	92.80	26.33

- Represents zero. [1] Includes other media, not shown separately. [2] Affiliates of the Fox network are counted as network affiliates for part of 1991 and all latter years, but as independent stations in earlier years. [3] Includes TBS beginning in 1992. [4] Playback of prerecorded tapes only. [5] Included with basic cable.

Source: Veronis, Suhler & Associates, New York, NY, *Communications Industry Forecast Report*, annual, (copyright).

No. 900. Communications Industry—Finances: 1990 to 1993

[**In millions of dollars.** Covers 349 publicly reporting companies with revenues of over $1 million in 11 communication industry segments]

| INDUSTRY | REVENUE | | | | OPERATING INCOME | | | |
	1990	1991	1992	1993	1990	1991	1992	1993
Total	**119,279**	**125,859**	**135,100**	**141,863**	**15,908**	**14,948**	**17,951**	**19,680**
Television & radio broadcasting [1] . . .	19,210	18,758	19,689	20,555	2,795	2,053	2,490	3,338
Television network companies	11,631	11,448	12,078	12,405	1,608	1,108	1,203	1,796
TV & radio station broadcasters	7,579	7,310	7,611	8,150	1,187	944	1,287	1,543
Cable television	15,083	16,581	18,235	19,583	2,212	2,960	3,640	3,938
Cable system operators	11,313	12,495	13,563	14,511	1,663	2,208	2,777	2,973
Cable network companies	3,770	4,086	4,672	5,072	549	752	863	966
Filmed entertainment	10,501	12,112	14,138	15,016	1,154	915	1,341	1,271
Recorded music	6,085	6,703	7,040	7,363	611	684	763	793
Newspaper publishing	20,126	19,203	19,263	19,639	3,126	2,347	2,662	2,737
Book publishing	7,587	9,126	9,821	10,519	989	1,110	1,267	1,275
Magazine publishing	8,232	8,571	9,189	9,350	909	721	914	991
Consumer magazine	6,327	6,761	7,344	7,537	678	577	742	829
Business & professional	1,905	1,810	1,846	1,813	231	144	172	162
Business information services	18,014	19,078	20,754	21,845	2,674	2,781	3,192	3,534
Advertising agencies [2]	6,807	7,300	7,768	7,655	630	598	677	695
Interactive digital media [3]	2,176	2,666	3,192	3,788	166	106	240	186
Miscellaneous communications	5,459	5,762	6,011	6,551	643	671	767	922

[1] Excludes agency commissions. [2] Net revenue including only commissions, fees, and other income, not gross billings. [3] Software for consumer data and transactions, consumer reference, education, games, home shopping, and infomercials.

Source: Veronis, Suhler & Associates, New York, NY, *Communications Industry Report*, annual, (copyright).

No. 901. Telephone and Telegraph Systems: 1980 to 1993

[Covers principal carriers filing annual reports with Federal Communications Commission. Minus sign (-) indicates loss. See *Historical Statistics, Colonial Times to 1970*, series R 46-70 and R 75-88, for data on telegraph systems]

ITEM	Unit	1980	1985	1987	1988	1989	1990	1991	1992	1993
DOMESTIC TELEPHONE [1]										
Carriers [2]	Number .	59	39	37	54	53	53	54	56	55
Access lines	Million .	(NA)	103	111	122	126	130	137	140	147
Miles of wire	Million . .	1,131	1,313	1,371	1,483	1,502	1,528	(NA)	(NA)	(NA)
Gross book cost of plant	Bil. dol. .	147	195	222	250	260	265	270	279	282
Depreciation reserves [3]	Bil. dol. .	27	50	70	85	94	98	102	108	117
Ratio to book cost	Percent .	18	26	31	34	36	37	38	39	41
Capital stock and premium	Bil. dol. .	31	48	43	45	46	46	47	48	42
Operating revenues	Bil. dol. .	56	89	95	100	102	104	106	122	126
Operating expenses [4]	Bil. dol. .	37	61	66	74	77	78	80	95	98
Net operating income [5]	Bil. dol. .	10	12	15	17	16	16	16	17	17
Net income	Bil. dol. .	7	10	11	13	12	13	12	12	8
Return on investment (domestic and overseas) [6]	Percent .	9	9	10	10	10	10	9	10	10
Employees	1,000. . .	938	(NA)	(NA)	688	663	648	616	608	592
Compensation of employees	Bil. dol. .	20	(NA)	(NA)	25	24	26	25	26	27
OVERSEAS TELEPHONE										
Number of overseas calls	Million . .	200	412	580	706	1,008	1,201	2,279	2,750	3,095
Revenue from overseas calls [7]	Mil. dol. .	1,535	1,799	2,127	2,573	3,513	4,362	5,835	6,974	7,704
Ocean cable systems	Number .	24	26	26	26	23	24	26	(NA)	(NA)
Communications satellites [8]	Number .	5	6	11	14	15	16	16	(NA)	(NA)
TELEGRAPH [9]										
Carriers	Number .	8	7	7	6	6	3	3	2	2
Revenue messages transmitted	Million .	75	42	25	(NA)	(NA)	(NA)	(NA)	(NA)	(NA)
Message revenues [10]	Mil. dol. .	676	708	594	483	521	259	219	(NA)	(NA)
Total operating revenues	Mil. dol. .	1,232	1,367	1,076	882	1,019	408	383	317	367
Operating revenue deductions	Mil. dol. .	1,008	1,292	1,125	942	995	447	421	343	416
Operating income [11]	Mil. dol. .	147	102	-48	-56	24	-28	-28	-77	-76
Return on investment [6]	Percent .	16	7	3	-6	4	1	-12	(NA)	(NA)

NA Not available.   [1] Includes Virgin Islands, and prior to 1991, Puerto Rico. Excludes intercompany duplications. Gross operating revenues of carriers reporting estimated at 90 percent of all carriers. Beginning 1988, based on new accounting rules; prior years not directly comparable.   [2] Beginning 1985, number of carriers changed due to change in dollar requirement of reporting carriers from $1 million to $100 million.   [3] Includes amortization reserves.   [4] Excludes taxes.   [5] After tax deductions.   [6] Ratio of net operating income (after taxes) to average net book cost of communications plant.   [7] Beginning 1991, includes calls to and from Alaska, Hawaii, Puerto Rico, Canada, and Mexico.   [8] Excludes contingency and retired satellites.   [9] Domestic and overseas except for South American and most Caribbean operations of All America Cables and Radio, Inc.   [10] Includes telex service; for domestic telegraph, excludes TWX.   [11] After Federal income taxes.

Source: U.S. Federal Communications Commission, *Statistics of Communications Common Carriers,* annual; and unpublished data.

No. 902. Telephone Communications—Operating Revenue and Expenses: 1989 to 1993

[Based on a sample of employer firms with one or more establishments that are primarily engaged in providing telephone, voice, and data communication services. For SIC 481. Based on the 1987 Standard Industrial Classification Code; see text, section 13]

ITEM	TOTAL (mil. dol.)					PERCENT DISTRIBUTION		
	1989	1990	1991	1992	1993	1990	1992	1993
OPERATING REVENUE								
Total	151,195	157,075	161,241	167,936	177,843	100.0	100.0	100.0
Local service	37,371	39,327	40,476	42,421	44,351	25.0	25.3	24.9
Long-distance service	64,496	66,261	67,542	67,972	70,771	42.2	40.5	39.8
Network access	29,251	29,406	29,311	30,340	31,207	18.7	18.1	17.5
Cellular and other radiotelephone	4,400	5,875	6,724	8,986	11,795	3.7	5.4	6.6
Directory advertising	7,708	8,195	8,496	8,734	8,932	5.2	5.2	5.0
Other	7,969	8,011	8,692	9,483	10,787	5.1	5.6	6.1
OPERATING EXPENSES								
Total	124,789	128,527	134,600	139,999	153,770	100.0	100.0	100.0
Annual payroll	29,209	30,782	31,149	31,661	32,455	23.9	22.6	21.1
Employer contributions to Social Security and other supplemental benefits	6,995	7,162	7,870	8,452	8,225	5.6	6.0	5.3
Access charges	23,576	23,769	24,614	25,126	26,121	18.5	17.9	17.0
Depreciation	23,227	23,474	24,164	24,190	25,203	18.3	17.3	16.4
Lease and rental	3,734	3,628	3,959	4,348	4,200	2.8	3.1	2.7
Purchased repairs	2,838	3,048	3,025	2,985	3,198	2.4	2.1	2.1
Insurance	196	197	223	228	223	0.2	0.2	0.1
Telephone and other purchased communication services	433	517	557	724	858	0.4	0.5	0.6
Purchased utilities	1,125	1,132	1,177	1,207	1,226	0.9	0.9	0.8
Purchased advertising	1,933	2,383	2,607	2,700	3,356	1.9	1.9	2.2
Taxes	5,032	5,208	5,358	5,319	5,494	4.1	3.8	3.6
Other	26,491	27,227	29,897	33,059	43,211	21.2	23.6	28.1

Source: U.S. Bureau of the Census, *Annual Survey of Communication Services,* (BC/93).

No. 903. Telephone Companies—Summary: 1988 to 1993

[**As of Dec. 31** or **calendar year,** as applicable. January 1, 1988, marked the beginning of significant rules changes in the way local exchange carriers account for assets, liabilities, revenue, expenses, and income. Any comparisons with earlier data would not be meaningful. See also Historical Statistics, Colonial Times to 1970, series R 1-12 and 31-45]

ITEM	Unit	INDEPENDENT COMPANIES [1]				ALL TELEPHONE COMPANIES			
		1988	1990	1992	1993	1988	1990	1992	1993
All companies	Number .	1,349	1,310	1,308	1,305	1,371	1,332	1,327	1,324
Access lines	Millions .	29	32	34	35.4	130	138	145	150.2
Total telephone plant.	Bil. dol. .	59	65	71	74.1	238	256	272	281.7
Operating revenues	Bil. dol. .	21	22	26	26.7	90	90	95	98
Avg. daily conversations [2] . .	Millions .	(NA)	(NA)	(NA)	(NA)	1,700	9,515	9,885	10,665
Reporting companies [3]	Number .	585	594	622	573	607	616	641	592
Access lines	Millions .	29	30	32	33.8	130	136	143	148.7
Telephone plant in service . .	Bil. dol. .	57	63	68	70.7	233	251	265	274.8
Depreciation reserves [4]	Bil. dol. .	20	24	27	29	80	95	106	113.8
Operating revenues [5]	Bil. dol. .	21	22	24	24.2	86	89	92	95.5
Operating expenses [5]	Bil. dol. .	14	16	16	17.3	61	65	67	70
Net income	Bil. dol. .	3	3	4	2	12	12	10	7
Stockholders' equity	Bil. dol. .	20	22	24	24.2	76	80	83	79.6
Net income to stockholders equity	Percent .	16	15	15	8.3	16	14	12	8.8
Employees	1,000. . .	170	161	152	140	639	606	560	536

NA Not available. [1] Companies independent of the Bell System, prior to divestiture of January 1984. [2] Average business day conversations in 1988. Average business day minutes of use beginning in 1990. [3] Comprises only companies submitting operating information to source cited below. [4] Total accumulated depreciation and amortization. [5] Excludes Federal income tax.

Source: United States Telephone Association, Washington, DC, *Statistics of the Local Exchange Carriers,* annual, (copyright).

No. 904. Percent of Households with Telephone Service: 1984 and 1994

[**Annual averages of quarterly data.** Based on Current Population Survey; see text, section 1, and Appendix III]

CHARACTERISTIC	1984				1994			
	All races	White	Black	Hispanic [1]	All races	White	Black	Hispanic [1]
Total	92	93	80	81	94	95	86	86
Age of householder:								
15 to 24 years old [2]	77	80	58	61	84	86	74	72
25 to 54 years old	92	93	80	83	93	95	85	86
55 to 59 years old	95	96	87	87	96	96	91	89
60 to 64 years old	95	96	87	87	96	97	90	92
65 to 69 years old	96	97	88	90	97	97	92	93
70 years old and over	95	96	88	84	97	97	92	92
Household size:								
1 person	88	90	75	73	92	93	82	82
2 to 3 persons	93	95	82	82	95	96	88	87
4 to 5 persons.	93	94	82	84	94	96	87	88
6 or more persons	87	90	76	79	89	91	82	83
Household level:								
Under $5,000	71	75	63	55	76	80	69	66
$5,000 to $7,499	83	86	75	70	83	85	77	73
$7,500 to $9,999	87	88	77	75	87	89	81	81
$10,000 to $12,499	90	91	81	80	90	91	82	83
$12,500 to $14,999	92	93	85	87	92	93	86	85
$15,000 to $19,999	(NA)	(NA)	(NA)	(NA)	94	94	87	88
$15,000 to $17,499.	94	94	89	88	(NA)	(NA)	(NA)	(NA)
$17,500 to $19,999.	95	96	92	91	(NA)	(NA)	(NA)	(NA)
$20,000 to $24,999	97	97	93	93	95	96	90	91
$25,000 to $29,999	98	98	95	96	97	97	94	92
$30,000 to $34,999	99	99	97	99	97	98	94	92
$35,000 to $39,999	99	99	98	98	98	98	94	95
$40,000 to $49,999	99	99	97	99	99	99	97	96
$50,000 to $74,999	99	100	98	100	(NA)	(NA)	(NA)	(NA)
$50,000 to $59,999.	(NA)	(NA)	(NA)	(NA)	99	99	96	100
$60,000 to $74,999.	(NA)	(NA)	(NA)	(NA)	99	99	100	98
$75,000 and over.	99	99	97	98	99	99	99	99
Labor force status of persons, 15 years old and over: [3]								
Total civilian noninstitutional population.	93	94	83	83	95	96	88	87
Employed	94	95	86	86	96	96	90	89
Unemployed	82	84	75	74	88	90	81	84
Not in labor force	92	94	81	80	93	95	85	86

NA Not available. [1] Persons of Hispanic origin may be of any race. [2] 16 to 24 years old in 1984. [3] 16 years old and over in 1984.

Source: Federal Communications Commission, *Telephone Subscribership in the U.S.,* April 1995.

No. 905. Cellular Telephone Industry: 1987 to 1994

[Calendar year data, except as noted. Based on a survey mailed to all cellular systems. For 1994 data, the universe was 1,581 systems and the response rate was 85 percent]

ITEM	Unit	1987	1988	1989	1990	1991	1992	1993	1994
Systems	Number .	312	517	584	751	1,252	1,506	1,529	1,581
Subscribers	1,000 . .	1,231	2,069	3,509	5,283	7,557	11,033	16,009	24,134
Cell sites [1]	Number .	2,305	3,209	4,169	5,616	7,847	10,307	12,805	17,920
Employees	Number .	7,147	11,400	15,927	21,382	26,327	34,348	39,775	53,902
Service revenue	Mil. dol. .	1,151	1,959	3,340	4,548	5,708	7,822	10,891	14,229
Roamer revenue [2]	Mil. dol. .	(NA)	89	294	456	704	974	1,360	1,830
Capital investment	Mil. dol. .	2,235	3,274	4,480	6,282	8,672	11,262	13,946	18,939
Average monthly bill [3]	Dollars . .	96.83	98.02	89.30	80.90	72.74	68.68	61.48	56.21
Average length of call [3]	Minutes .	2.33	2.26	2.48	2.20	2.38	2.58	2.41	2.24

NA Not available. [1] The basic geographic unit of a cellular system. A city or county is divided into smaller "cells," each of which is equipped with a low-powered radio transmitter/receiver. The cells can vary in size depending upon terrain, capacity demands, etc. By controlling the transmission power, the radio frequencies assigned to one cell can be limited to the boundaries of that cell. When a cellular phone moves from one cell toward another, a computer at the Switching Office monitors the movement and at the proper time, transfers or hands off the phone call to the new cell and another radio frequency. [2] Service revenue generated by subscribers' calls outside of their system areas. [3] For 6 months ending December 31.

Source: Cellular Telecommunications Industry Association, Washington, DC, *State of the Cellular Industry,* annual, (copyright).

No. 906. Private Radio Stations Authorized, by Class: 1990 to 1993

[In thousands. As of September 30. Includes Puerto Rico and Virgin Islands. See also *Historical Statistics, Colonial Times to 1970,* series R 140-148]

CLASS	1990	1991	1992	1993	CLASS	1990	1991	1992	1993
Private radio services [1] .	2,880	2,935	2,956	3007	Railroad	16	17	18	18
Personal	528	566	611	655	Taxicab	6	6	6	5
General mobile	32	31	28	27	Interurban property	6	6	6	6
Amateur and disaster . .	496	535	583	628	Other	12	12	12	11
Aviation	251	241	210	199	Marine	623	641	634	664
Aircraft	210	200	193	182	Ship	607	626	619	648
Aeronautical and fixed . .	12	12	12	13	Alaskan	2	2	2	2
Civil air patrol	24	24	(Z)	(Z)	Coastal and other	13	13	13	14
Other	5	5	5	5	Public safety	235	240	245	251
Industrial	865	854	840	828	Police	51	52	53	54
Power	46	47	48	49	Fire	44	45	46	47
Business	628	616	27	591	Forestry conservation . .	11	12	12	12
Petroleum	27	27	603	26	Highway maintenance . .	15	16	16	16
Forest products	12	12	12	12	Special emergency	41	41	41	40
Special industrial	114	112	110	108	Other	73	75	78	81
Other	39	40	41	43	Operational fixed				
Land transportation	40	41	41	41	services [2]	33	35	36	37

Z Less than 500. [1] Includes items not shown separately. Each license, construction permit, or combination construction permit and license is counted one as station; therefore, a station might include a transmitter and many mobile units. 1991 data exclude restricted permits. [2] Includes microwave operations.

Source: U.S. Federal Communications Commission, *Annual Report;* and unpublished data.

No. 907. Radio and Television Broadcasting Services—Finances: 1990 to 1993

[In millions of dollars. Based on a sample of taxable employer firms with one of more establishments primarily engaged in broadcasting to the public, except cable and other pay television services. Based on the 1987 Standard Industrial Classification Code; see text, section 13]

ITEM	TOTAL (SIC 483)			RADIO (SIC 4832)			TELEVISION (SIC 4833)		
	1990	1992	1993	1990	1992	1993	1990	1992	1993
Operating revenue	**29,134**	**28,968**	**29,408**	**7,347**	**7,180**	**7,640**	**21,787**	**21,788**	**21,768**
Station time sales	19,815	19,357	20,031	6,759	6,630	7,072	13,056	12,727	12,959
Network compensation	570	476	461	111	100	92	459	376	369
National/regional advertising	7,508	6,993	7,189	1,608	1,387	1,514	5,900	5,606	5,675
Local advertising	11,737	11,888	12,381	5,040	5,143	5,466	6,697	6,745	6,915
Network time sales	8,183	8,510	8,332	322	292	301	7,861	8,218	8,031
Other	1,136	1,101	1,045	266	258	267	870	843	778
Operating expenses	**25,101**	**25,102**	**24,403**	**6,670**	**6,485**	**6,610**	**18,431**	**18,617**	**17,793**
Annual payroll	6,745	7,024	7,073	2,583	2,627	2,697	4,162	4,397	4,376
Employer contributions to Social Security and other supplemental benefits	1,064	1,161	1,192	347	365	379	717	796	813
Broadcast rights	7,823	7,919	7,342	277	220	247	7,546	7,699	7,095
Music license fees	386	383	351	167	157	169	219	226	182
Depreciation	1,388	1,304	1,225	500	471	452	888	833	773
Lease and rental	484	468	485	206	201	217	278	267	268
Purchased repairs	239	233	240	83	81	83	156	152	157
Insurance	148	163	161	67	69	70	81	94	91
Telephone and other purchased communication services	249	245	243	121	122	121	128	123	122
Purchased utilities	254	265	262	104	107	103	150	158	159
Purchased advertising	978	824	835	386	330	326	592	494	509
Taxes	182	193	190	63	68	72	119	125	118
Other	5,161	4,920	4,804	1,766	1,667	1,674	3,395	3,253	3,130

Source: U.S. Bureau of the Census, *Annual Survey of Communication Services,* (BC/93).

No. 908. Copyright Registration, by Subject Matter: 1990 to 1994

[In thousands. For years ending September 30. Comprises claims to copyrights registered for both U.S. and foreign works. See also Historical Statistics, Colonial Times to 1970, series W 82-95]

SUBJECT MATTER	1990	1992	1993	1994	SUBJECT MATTER	1990	1992	1993	1994
Total	643.5	606.2	564.9	530.3	Sound recordings	37.5	33.1	32.4	36.1
Monographs [1]	179.7	190.2	185.8	162.6	Renewals	51.8	49.1	37.7	33.3
Semiconductor chip products	1.0	0.9	1.0	1.1	Musical works [2]	185.3	162.1	152.3	136.1
Serials	111.5	92.9	82.6	75.1	Works of the visual arts [3]	76.7	78.0	73.5	86.1

[1] Includes computer software and machine readable works.   [2] Includes dramatic works, accompanying music, choreography, pantomimes, motion pictures, and filmstrips.   [3] Two-dimensional works of fine and graphic art, including prints and art reproductions; sculptural works; technical drawings and models; photographs; commercial prints and labels; works of applied arts, cartographic works, and multimedia works.

Source: The Library of Congress, Copyright Office, Annual Report.

No. 909. Public Television Programming: 1980 to 1992

[For fiscal years; 1988 to 1992 surveys used October through September seasons. General programming is directed at the general community. Instructional programming is directed at students in the classroom or otherwise in the general context of formal education]

ITEM	1980	1982	1984	1986	1988	1990	1992
Stations broadcasting	281	291	303	305	322	341	349
Number of broadcasters [1]	160	164	169	178	186	193	198
Average annual hours per broadcaster	5,128	5,421	5,542	5,650	6,135	6,392	6,303
BROADCAST HOURS, PERCENT DISTRIBUTION							
Program content [2]	100	100	100	100	100	100	100
General	87	87	88	86	85	86	90
News and public affairs [2]	12	12	14	16	16	18	17
Information and skills	23	25	26	30	32	32	29
Cultural	22	23	20	21	18	19	18
General children's and youth's	9	8	8	7	6	6	15
Sesame Street	16	15	15	11	12	11	11
Other	6	5	6	2	1	1	1
Instructional [3]	15	14	13	15	16	14	12
Children and youth	14	13	12	(NA)	(NA)	(NA)	9
Adult	1	1	1	(NA)	(NA)	(NA)	3
Producer	100	100	100	100	100	100	100
Local	7	7	6	5	5	5	5
Any public TV source	46	46	44	38	27	32	35
Consortium	3	3	3	3	10	10	1
Children's TV Workshop	17	16	16	[4]29	16	15	14
Independent producer	8	11	9	([4])	19	19	25
Foreign producer, international coproduction	13	10	13	15	14	12	11
Commercial producer	3	4	3	6	4	4	5
Other	4	4	5	4	4	3	4
Distributor	100	100	100	100	100	100	100
Local distribution only	7	6	6	5	6	6	5
Public broadcasting service	70	67	65	64	62	59	63
Regional public television network	8	11	13	14	18	24	23
Other	16	16	16	17	14	11	9

NA Not available.   [1] Beginning 1990, only broadcasters in the 50 U.S. States were surveyed.   [2] Beginning 1988, this category includes "Business or Consumer."   [3] Some general audience programs with instructional applications were double counted if aired during school hours when school was in session. "The Electric Company" was one such program. [4] Independent producer included with Children's TV Workshop for 1986.

Source: Corporation for Public Broadcasting, Washington, DC, PTV Programming Survey, biennial.

No. 910. Public Broadcasting Systems—Income, by Source: 1980 to 1993

[In millions of dollars, except number of stations and percents. Stations as of Dec. 31; fiscal year data for income. Includes nonbroadcast income]

NUMBER OF STATIONS AND INCOME SOURCE	1980	1985	1989	1990	1991	1992	1993	PERCENT DISTRIBUTION		
								1980	1990	1993
CPB-qualified public radio stations [1]	217	288	313	318	373	391	400	(X)	(X)	(X)
Public television stations	290	317	340	341	349	349	352	(X)	(X)	(X)
Total income	705	1,096	1,549	1,581	1,721	1,790	1,790	100	100	100
Federal government	193	179	264	267	333	374	370	27	17	21
State and local government [2]	272	358	454	474	503	485	475	39	30	27
Subscribers and auction/marathon	102	248	347	364	384	404	412	15	23	23
Business and industry	72	171	242	262	290	300	301	10	17	17
Foundation	24	43	69	71	70	80	100	3	5	6
Other	43	97	173	143	139	148	132	6	9	7

X Not applicable.   [1] Includes CPB-supported developmental grantees/stations and excludes repeater stations.   [2] Includes income received from State and other public colleges and universities.

Source: Corporation for Public Broadcasting (CPB), Washington, DC, Public Broadcasting Income, Fiscal Year, 1993; and unpublished data.

No. 911. Cable Television—Systems and Subscribers: 1970 to 1995

[Subscribers in thousands, except percent. Estimated]

YEAR (As of Jan. 1)	Systems	Subscribers	YEAR (As of Jan. 1)	Systems	Subscribers	SUBSCRIBER SIZE-GROUP	NUMBER OF [1]—		PERCENT OF [1]—	
							Systems	Subscribers	Systems	Subscribers
1970	2,490	4,500	1985	6,600	32,000	**1994, total** [2]	10,521	56,373	100	100
1975	3,506	9,800	1986	7,600	37,500	50,000 and over	239	23,584	2	42
1976	3,681	10,800	1987	7,900	41,100	20,000 to 49,999	439	13,378	4	24
1977	3,832	11,900	1988	8,500	44,000	10,000 to 19,999	507	7,176	5	13
1978	3,875	13,000	1989	9,050	47,500	5,000 to 9,999	671	4,764	6	9
1979	4,150	14,100	1990	9,575	50,000	3,500 to 4,999	426	1,794	4	3
1980	4,225	16,000	1991	10,704	51,000	1,000 to 3,499	1,928	3,679	18	7
1981	4,375	18,300	1992	11,075	53,000	500 to 999	1,450	1,039	14	2
1982	4,825	21,000	1993	11,100	55,000	250 to 499	1,526	547	15	1
1983	5,600	25,000	1994	11,200	57,000	Less than 250	3,335	411	32	1
1984	6,200	30,000	1995	11,216	58,000					

[1] As of October 1.   [2] Excludes 695 systems not available by subscriber size-group.
Source: Warren Publishing, Inc., Washington, DC, *Television & Cable Factbook,* annual, (copyright).

No. 912. Cable and Pay TV—Summary: 1970 to 1994

[Cable TV for calendar year. Pay TV as of **Dec. 31** of year shown]

YEAR	CABLE TV				PAY TV				Percent of homes passed by cable with pay TV	Percent of homes with cable TV with pay TV
	Avg. basic subscribers (1,000)	Avg. monthly basic rate (dol.)	Revenue [1] (mil. dol.)		Units [2] (1,000)		Monthly rate (dol.)			
			Total	Basic	Total [3]	Pay cable	Total pay [3]	Pay cable		
1970	5,100	5.50	345	337	(X)	(X)	(X)	(X)	(X)	(X)
1980	17,500	7.69	2,549	1,615	10,389	9,144	9.09	8.80	28	51
1985	35,500	9.73	8,938	4,145	31,063	30,596	10.46	10.42	47	84
1988	44,200	13.86	13,595	7,351	39,127	38,819	10.25	10.18	50	85
1989	47,500	15.21	15,678	8,670	41,234	41,095	10.26	10.21	50	83
1990	50,520	16.78	17,855	10,169	41,656	41,505	10.43	10.38	48	80
1991	52,600	18.10	19,463	11,414	43,314	39,900	10.35	10.27	45	75
1992	54,300	19.08	21,045	12,433	44,714	40,700	10.18	10.06	45	74
1993	56,200	[4]19.39	22,782	[4]13,528	46,397	41,500	9.27	9.11	46	73
1994	58,500	21.62	22,786	15,164	51,000	45,000	[5]8.62	8.37	49	75

X Not applicable.   [1] Includes installation revenue, subscriber revenue, and nonsubscriber revenue.   [2] Individual program services sold to subscribers.   [3] Includes multipoint distribution service (MDS) and satellite TV (STV).   [4] Weighted average representing 8 months of unregulated basic rate and 4 months of FCC rolled-back rate.   [5] Direct broadcast satellite average rate not included.
Source: Paul Kagan Associates Inc., Carmel, CA, *The Cable TV Financial Databook,* annual, (copyright); *The Kagan Census of Cable and Pay TV,* 1991, and *The Cable TV Investor,* June 1995.

No. 913. Cable and Pay TV—Revenue and Expenses: 1989 to 1993

[Based on a sample of taxable employer firms with one or more establishments that are primarily engaged in the dissemination of visual and textual television programs on a subscription or fee basis. For SIC 4841. Based on the 1987 Standard Industrial Classification Code; see text, section 13]

ITEM	TOTAL (mil. dol.)					PERCENT DISTRIBUTION		
	1989	1990	1991	1992	1993	1990	1992	1993
Revenue	17,513	20,312	21,897	24,424	26,881	100.0	100.0	100.0
Advertising	1,349	1,725	1,924	2,283	2,633	8.5	9.3	9.8
Program revenue	2,723	3,497	3,768	4,053	4,461	17.2	16.6	16.6
Basic service	8,760	10,019	10,983	12,401	13,609	49.3	50.8	50.6
Pay-per-view and other premium service . .	3,734	3,987	4,092	4,314	4,756	19.6	17.7	17.7
Installation fees	250	277	297	357	400	1.4	1.5	1.5
Other cable and pay TV revenue.	697	807	833	1,016	1,022	4.0	4.1	3.8
Operating expenses	(NA)	17,694	18,433	19,457	20,948	100.0	100.0	100.0
Annual payroll	(NA)	2,748	2,902	3,448	3,768	15.5	17.7	18.0
Employer contributions to Social Security and other supplemental benefits	(NA)	574	651	782	865	3.2	4.0	4.1
Program and production costs	(NA)	5,340	5,693	6,094	6,711	30.2	31.3	32.0
Depreciation	(NA)	3,254	3,274	3,338	3,529	18.4	17.2	16.8
Lease and rental payments	(NA)	462	465	531	570	2.6	2.7	2.7
Purchased repairs	(NA)	309	307	336	366	1.7	1.7	1.7
Insurance	(NA)	99	104	131	150	0.6	0.7	0.7
Telephone, other purchased communications . .	(NA)	120	125	142	162	0.7	0.7	0.8
Purchased utilities	(NA)	169	181	198	217	1.0	1.0	1.0
Purchased advertising	(NA)	421	425	484	530	2.4	2.5	2.5
Taxes	(NA)	279	299	368	394	1.6	1.9	1.9
Other operating expenses	(NA)	3,919	4,007	3,605	3,686	22.1	18.6	17.8

NA Not available.
Source: U.S. Bureau of the Census, *Annual Survey of Communication Services: 1993,* (BC/93).

No. 914. Microcomputer Software Sales: 1992 and 1994

[**In millions of dollars**. Estimated North American retail sales. Figures may not add to totals because individual applications and totals are derived independently]

APPLICATION	1992					1994				
	Total	PC/MS-DOS	Win-dows	Macin-tosh	Other	Total	PC/MS-DOS	Win-dows	Macin-tosh	Other
Total	5,745	2,584	1,935	990	237	7,382	1,280	4,781	1,249	72
Entertainment	342	267	30	31	14	716	404	219	94	(B)
Home education.	146	104	12	23	7	522	120	305	96	2
Finance	296	220	45	31	(B)	411	136	230	45	(B)
Word processors	830	249	418	144	18	1,031	96	827	94	13
Spreadsheets	795	332	344	93	27	830	63	690	69	9
Databases	349	267	31	48	2	351	29	280	41	1
Integrated.	148	66	29	48	5	135	8	79	48	(B)
Utilities.	322	154	99	68	(B)	331	104	157	55	15
Presentation graphic. . . .	289	94	142	49	4	290	9	235	45	1
Drawing and painting . . .	262	3	145	110	4	346	(B)	128	210	8
Desktop publishing	141	10	76	54	(B)	198	(B)	125	(B)	(B)
Other graphics.	264	103	88	70	4	342	36	231	74	1
Project management. . . .	(NA)	(NA)	(NA)	(NA)	(NA)	280	29	227	23	(B)
Personal info. manager . .	(NA)	(NA)	(NA)	(NA)	(NA)	151	4	126	21	(B)
Languages and tools . . .	260	79	87	18	75	176	18	142	13	3
Other productivity	1,302	634	389	203	76	1,272	224	781	249	18

B Base figure too small to meet statistical standards for reliability of a derived figure.   NA Not available.

Source: Software Publishers Association, Washington, DC, *SPA Software Sales Report,* News Release, March 22, 1994 and April 3, 1995.

No. 915. Recording Media—Manufacturers' Shipments and Value: 1975 to 1994

[Domestic shipments based on reports of manufacturers representing more than 85 percent of the market. Domestic value data based on list prices of records and other media]

YEAR	UNIT SHIPMENTS [1] (mil.)					MANUFACTURES' VALUE (mil. dol.)				
	Vinyl singles	Albums-LP's/EP's	CD's	Cassettes	Cassette singles	Vinyl singles	Albums-LP's/EP's	CD's	Cassettes	Cassette singles
1975 . . .	164.0	257.0	(X)	16.2	(X)	211.5	1,485.0	(X)	98.8	(X)
1980 . . .	164.3	322.8	(X)	110.2	(X)	269.3	2,290.3	(X)	776.4	(X)
1984 . . .	131.5	204.6	5.8	332.0	(X)	298.7	1,548.8	103.3	2,383.9	(X)
1985 . . .	120.7	167.0	22.6	339.1	(X)	281.0	1,280.5	389.5	2,411.5	(X)
1986 . . .	93.9	125.2	53.0	344.5	(X)	228.1	983.0	930.1	2,499.5	(X)
1987 . . .	82.0	107.0	102.1	410.0	[2]5.1	203.3	793.1	1,593.6	2,959.7	[2]14.3
1988 . . .	65.6	72.4	149.7	450.1	22.5	180.4	532.2	2,089.9	3,385.1	57.3
1989 . . .	36.6	34.6	207.2	446.2	76.2	116.4	220.3	2,587.7	3,345.8	194.6
1990 . . .	27.6	11.7	286.5	442.2	87.4	94.4	86.5	3,451.6	3,472.4	257.9
1991 . . .	22.0	4.8	333.3	360.1	69.0	63.9	29.4	4,337.7	3,019.6	230.4
1992 . . .	19.8	2.3	407.5	336.4	84.6	66.4	13.5	5,326.5	3,116.3	298.8
1993 . . .	15.1	1.2	495.4	339.5	85.6	51.2	10.6	6,511.4	2,915.8	298.5
1994 . . .	11.7	1.9	662.1	345.4	81.1	47.2	17.8	8,464.5	2,976.4	274.9

X Not applicable.   [1] Net units, after returns.   [2] Represents 6 months of sales.

Source: Recording Industry Association of America, Washington, DC, *Inside the Recording Industry: A Statistical Overview-1994 Update.*

No. 916. Publishing Industry—Summary: 1982 to 1992

[**In millions of dollars,** except as noted. Number in parentheses represents Standard Industrial Classification code; see text, section 13]

ITEM	NEWSPAPERS (SIC 2711)			PERIODICALS (SIC 2721)			BOOKS (SIC 2731)		
	1982	1987	1992	1982	1987	1992	1982	1987	1992
Establishments	8,846	9,091	8,644	3,328	4,020	4,695	2,130	2,298	2,503
With 20 or more employees	2,554	2,617	2,606	690	876	992	419	424	508
Employees [1] (1,000).	402	435	416	94	110	117	67	70	84
Payroll	6,555	9,025	10,506	1,986	2,983	4,076	1,327	1,860	2,869
Value of receipts	21,276	31,849	32,425	11,478	17,329	(NA)	7,740	12,620	(NA)
Cost of materials	6,006	7,533	6,937	4,568	5,873	6,214	2,420	3,663	5,350
Value added [2]	15,275	24,311	27,264	6,911	11,452	15,761	5,292	9,111	11,862
New capital expends.	1,029	1,523	1,667	195	246	269	174	240	342
Fixed assets, gross assets.	8,701	14,028	(NA)	1,370	2,528	(NA)	1,109	1,680	(NA)
Inventories, Dec. 31	755	857	784	724	902	1,084	1,380	2,091	3,008

NA Not available.   [1] Represents the average number of production workers plus the number of other employees in mid-March.   [2] By manufacture, derived by subtracting the cost of materials, supplies, containers, fuel, purchased electricity, and contract work from the value of shipments. This result is then adjusted by the addition of value added by merchandising operations, plus the net change in finished goods and work-in-process inventories between the beginning and the end of the year.

Source: U.S. Bureau of the Census, *1992 Census of Manufactures,* Industry Reports, series MC92-I-27A (P).

No. 917. Newspapers and Periodicals—Number, by Type: 1980 to 1995

[Data refer to year of compilation of the Directory cited as the source, i.e., generally to year preceding year shown. See also *Historical Statistics, Colonial Times to 1970*, series R 232-243]

TYPE	1980	1985	1987	1988	1989	1990	1991	1992	1993	1994	1995
Newspapers [1]	9,620	9,134	9,031	10,088	10,457	11,471	11,689	11,339	12,597	12,513	12,246
Semiweekly	537	517	510	555	567	579	574	562	639	661	705
Weekly	7,159	6,811	6,750	7,438	7,622	8,420	8,546	8,293	9,177	9,067	9,011
Daily	1,744	1,701	1,646	1,745	1,773	1,788	1,781	1,755	1,850	1,831	1,710
Periodicals [1]	10,236	11,090	11,593	11,229	11,556	11,092	11,239	11,143	11,863	12,136	11,179
Weekly	1,716	1,367	1,400	880	828	553	511	466	485	487	513
Semimonthly [2]	645	801	858	619	622	435	412	371	199	209	216
Monthly	3,985	4,088	4,031	4,192	4,445	4,239	4,340	4,326	4,545	4,494	4,067
Bimonthly	1,114	1,361	1,402	1,558	1,880	2,087	2,116	2,143	2,359	2,475	2,568
Quarterly	1,444	1,759	1,984	2,245	2,513	2,758	2,861	3,024	3,199	3,370	3,621

[1] Includes other items not shown separately. [2] Includes fortnightly (every 2 weeks).

Source: Gale Research Inc., *1995 Gale Directory of Publications and Broadcast Media*, 127th edition; and earlier editions, (copyright).

No. 918. Daily and Sunday Newspapers—Number and Circulation: 1970 to 1993

[Number of newspapers as of **February 1** the following year. Circulation figures as of **September 30** of year shown. For English language newspapers only. See also *Historical Statistics, Colonial Times to 1970*, series R 224-231]

TYPE	1970	1975	1980	1984	1985	1986	1987	1988	1989	1990	1991	1992	1993
NUMBER													
Daily: Total [1]	1,748	1,756	1,745	1,688	1,676	1,657	1,645	1,642	1,626	1,611	1,586	1,570	1,556
Morning	334	339	387	458	482	499	511	529	530	559	571	596	623
Evening	1,429	1,436	1,388	1,257	1,220	1,188	1,166	1,141	1,125	1,084	1,042	996	954
Sunday	586	639	736	783	798	802	820	840	847	863	875	891	884
CIRCULATION (mil.)													
Daily: Total [1]	62.1	60.7	62.2	63.1	62.8	62.5	62.8	62.7	62.6	62.3	60.7	60.1	59.8
Morning	25.9	25.5	29.4	35.4	36.4	37.4	39.1	40.5	40.7	41.3	41.5	42.4	43.1
Evening	36.2	35.2	32.8	27.7	26.4	25.1	23.7	22.2	21.9	21.0	19.2	17.8	16.7
Sunday	49.2	51.1	54.7	57.5	58.8	58.9	60.1	61.5	62.0	62.6	62.1	62.2	62.6
PER CAPITA CIRCULATION													
Daily: Total [1]	0.30	0.28	0.27	0.27	0.26	0.26	0.26	0.26	0.25	0.25	0.24	0.24	0.23
Morning	0.13	0.12	0.13	0.15	0.15	0.16	0.16	0.17	0.16	0.17	0.16	0.17	0.17
Evening	0.18	0.16	0.14	0.12	0.11	0.10	0.10	0.09	0.09	0.08	0.08	0.07	0.06
Sunday	0.24	0.24	0.24	0.24	0.25	0.25	0.25	0.25	0.25	0.25	0.25	0.24	0.24

[1] All-day newspapers are counted in both morning and evening columns but only once in total. Circulation is divided equally between morning and evening.

Source: Editor & Publisher Co., New York, NY, *Editor & Publisher International Year Book,* annual, (copyright).

No. 919. Daily Newspapers—Number and Circulation, by Size of City: 1980 to 1993

[Number of newspapers as of **February 1** the following year. Circulation as of **September 30** of year shown. For English language newspapers only. See table 45 for number of cities by population size. All-day newspapers are counted in both morning and evening columns; circulation is divided equally between morning and evening]

TYPE OF DAILY AND POPULATION-SIZE CLASS	NUMBER					NET PAID CIRCULATION (1,000)				
	1980	1985	1990	1992	1993	1980	1985	1990	1992	1993
Morning dailies, total	387	482	559	596	623	29,413	36,361	41,311	42,388	43,093
In cities of—										
1,000,001 or more	20	22	18	20	26	8,795	9,367	6,508	6,340	9,923
500,001 to 1,000,000	27	24	22	20	22	5,705	6,897	4,804	4,865	5,207
100,001 to 500,000	99	121	138	142	150	8,996	12,197	20,051	20,099	17,178
50,001 to 100,000	75	87	100	123	132	2,973	3,653	4,373	5,238	5,565
25,001 to 50,000	64	83	102	104	105	1,701	2,145	3,209	3,369	2,908
Less than 25,000	102	145	179	187	188	1,243	2,099	2,365	2,477	2,310
Evening dailies, total	1,388	1,220	1,084	996	954	32,788	26,407	21,017	17,777	16,717
In cities of—										
1,000,001 or more	11	8	7	7	7	2,984	2,169	1,423	1,289	975
500,001 to 1,000,000	23	14	12	10	10	4,101	1,626	1,350	1,105	1,419
100,001 to 500,000	123	102	71	50	51	8,178	6,987	4,687	3,266	3,182
50,001 to 100,000	156	127	94	88	83	4,896	3,942	2,941	2,676	2,374
25,001 to 50,000	246	229	204	183	174	5,106	4,606	4,278	3,529	3,221
Less than 25,000	829	740	696	658	629	7,523	7,075	6,338	5,912	5,543

Source: Editor & Publisher Co., New York, NY, *Editor & Publisher International Year Book,* annual, (copyright).

No. 920. Daily and Sunday Newspapers—Number and Circulation, by State: 1993

[Number of newspapers as of February 1 the following year. Circulation as of September 30 of the year shown. For English language newspapers only. New York, Massachusetts, and Virginia Sunday newspapers include national circulation]

STATE	DAILY Number	DAILY Circulation[1] Net paid (1,000)	DAILY Circulation[1] Per capita[2]	SUNDAY Number	SUNDAY Net paid circulation[1] (1,000)	STATE	DAILY Number	DAILY Circulation[1] Net paid (1,000)	DAILY Circulation[1] Per capita[2]	SUNDAY Number	SUNDAY Net paid circulation[1] (1,000)
U.S.	1,556	59,812	0.23	884	62,566	MO	45	1,051	0.20	21	1,351
AL	26	759	0.18	19	771	MT	11	193	0.23	7	202
AK	7	113	0.19	4	131	NE	18	468	0.29	7	443
AZ	22	763	0.19	15	873	NV	8	274	0.20	4	307
AR	32	482	0.20	16	529	NH	11	242	0.22	6	203
CA	104	6,260	0.20	68	6,584	NJ	21	1,598	0.20	17	1,916
CO	28	1,045	0.29	11	1,249	NM	18	310	0.19	13	301
CT	19	825	0.25	11	835	NY	71	6,902	0.38	42	5,643
DE	3	155	0.22	2	181	NC	49	1,404	0.20	37	1,510
DC	2	903	1.56	2	1,204	ND	10	186	0.29	7	190
FL	40	3,158	0.23	35	4,009	OH	84	2,694	0.24	36	2,912
GA	34	1,073	0.16	18	1,307	OK	46	699	0.22	41	873
HI	6	241	0.21	5	260	OR	19	684	0.23	10	717
ID	12	219	0.20	8	236	PA	89	3,070	0.26	37	3,321
IL	68	2,566	0.22	28	2,742	RI	6	276	0.28	3	307
IN	73	1,498	0.26	22	1,372	SC	16	667	0.18	14	754
IA	39	704	0.25	10	722	SD	11	170	0.24	4	142
KS	47	510	0.20	16	463	TN	27	915	0.18	16	1,108
KY	23	663	0.17	12	681	TX	92	3,217	0.18	86	4,270
LA	25	746	0.17	20	860	UT	6	305	0.16	6	348
ME	7	264	0.21	2	191	VT	8	129	0.22	3	105
MD	15	639	0.13	7	670	VA	28	2,577	0.40	15	1,001
MA	39	1,890	0.31	14	1,772	WA	24	1,199	0.23	16	1,290
MI	52	2,128	0.23	27	2,424	WV	23	419	0.23	11	408
MN	25	954	0.21	14	1,197	WI	36	1,108	0.22	20	1,220
MS	22	407	0.15	15	389	WY	9	93	0.20	4	70

[1] Circulation figures based on the principal community served by a newspaper which is not necessarily the same location as the publisher's office. [2] Per capita based on estimated resident population as of July 1.

Source: Editor & Publisher Co., New York, NY, *Editor & Publisher International Year Book*, annual, (copyright).

No. 921. New Books and Editions Published and Imports, by Subject: 1980 to 1992

[Covers listings in Bowker's Weekly Record in year shown, plus titles issued in that year which were listed in following 6 months. Comprises new books (published for first time) and new editions (with changes in text or format). Excludes government publications; books sold only by subscription; dissertations; periodicals and quarterlies; and pamphlets under 49 pages. See also *Historical Statistics, Colonial Times to 1970*, series R 191-216]

SUBJECT	NEW BOOKS AND NEW EDITIONS 1980	1985	1989	1990	1991	1992	IMPORTS 1980	1985	1989	1990	1991	1992
Total[1]	42,377	50,070	53,446	46,738	48,146	49,276	5,390	7,304	7,315	6,414	5,867	6,506
Agriculture	461	536	562	514	523	565	104	118	104	86	81	93
Art	1,691	1,545	1,569	1,262	1,283	1,392	157	166	128	94	101	156
Biography	1,891	1,953	2,193	1,957	2,120	2,007	126	216	144	115	124	124
Business	1,185	1,518	1,569	1,191	1,421	1,367	74	196	152	134	140	126
Education	1,011	1,085	1,054	1,039	1,129	1,184	133	211	233	234	176	232
Fiction	2,835	5,105	5,941	5,764	5,424	5,690	71	171	119	166	250	246
General works	1,643	2,905	2,332	1,760	1,886	2,153	132	329	322	266	252	313
History	2,220	2,327	2,563	2,243	2,331	2,322	296	395	376	329	314	348
Home economics	879	1,228	949	758	789	826	40	41	31	19	23	25
Juvenile	2,859	3,801	5,413	5,172	5,111	5,144	58	92	101	103	69	50
Language	529	632	586	649	566	617	134	216	182	202	171	164
Law	1,102	1,349	1,096	896	1,177	1,063	112	170	156	138	171	197
Literature	1,686	1,964	2,298	2,049	2,087	2,227	183	267	275	242	196	274
Medicine	3,292	3,579	3,447	3,014	3,027	3,234	671	598	712	588	447	514
Music	357	364	375	289	300	346	35	70	78	52	71	69
Philosophy, psychology	1,429	1,559	2,058	1,683	1,766	1,806	218	267	348	284	256	291
Poetry and drama	1,179	1,166	1,128	874	890	899	120	220	147	119	115	136
Religion	2,055	2,564	2,586	2,285	2,389	2,540	94	173	173	176	129	165
Science	3,109	3,304	3,288	2,742	2,710	2,729	1,069	1,242	1,187	1,030	795	840
Sociology, economics	7,152	7,441	7,971	7,042	7,241	7,432	1,050	1,559	1,575	1,368	1,278	1,521
Sports, recreation	971	1,154	1,077	973	1,063	1,113	85	107	94	75	93	112
Technology	2,337	2,526	2,690	2,092	2,421	2,152	373	419	638	546	558	458
Travel	504	465	701	495	492	468	55	61	39	48	57	52

[1] Increase in new books and editions after 1980 is due largely to a major improvement in the recording of paperbound books.

Source: R. R. Bowker Co., New York, NY, *Publishers Weekly*. (Copyright by Reed Publishing USA.)

No. 922. Books—Average Retail Prices: 1980 to 1993

[Covers listings in Bowker's Weekly Record in year shown, plus titles issued in that year which were listed in following 6 months. Comprises new books (published for first time) and new editions (with changes in text or format). See also Historical Statistics, Colonial Times to 1970, series R 191-216. For definition of mean see Guide to Tabular Presentation]

SUBJECT	1980	1985	1987	1988	1989	1990	1991	1992	1993, prel.
Hardcover [1]	24.64	31.46	36.29	39.00	40.61	42.12	44.17	45.05	43.26
Agriculture	27.55	36.77	46.25	49.36	51.17	54.24	57.73	53.76	57.15
Art	27.70	35.15	37.72	39.96	50.30	42.18	44.99	44.59	46.29
Biography	19.77	22.20	25.05	25.99	27.34	29.58	27.52	30.41	30.38
Business	22.45	28.84	33.31	37.51	37.94	45.48	43.38	43.91	42.34
Education	17.01	27.28	31.59	33.55	37.62	38.72	41.26	48.77	42.02
Fiction	12.46	15.29	18.20	17.63	18.69	19.83	21.30	20.39	20.35
General works	29.84	37.91	43.82	50.35	49.73	54.77	51.74	56.29	53.58
History	22.78	27.02	31.74	33.44	37.95	36.43	39.87	39.19	40.69
Home economics	13.31	17.50	20.14	21.38	22.17	23.80	24.23	24.88	20.70
Juvenile	8.16	9.95	11.48	11.79	13.01	13.01	16.64	14.46	14.30
Language	22.16	28.68	37.80	40.42	47.35	42.98	51.71	49.68	60.87
Law	33.25	41.70	49.65	50.85	58.62	60.78	64.89	76.21	70.70
Literature	18.70	24.53	28.70	30.85	32.74	35.80	36.76	39.23	38.58
Medicine	34.28	44.36	57.68	66.59	69.87	72.24	71.44	75.22	75.17
Music	21.79	28.79	35.83	36.95	41.73	41.86	41.04	47.37	41.65
Philosophy, psychology	21.70	28.11	33.33	34.75	36.55	40.58	42.74	46.85	44.91
Poetry and drama	17.85	22.14	28.59	28.02	31.12	32.19	33.29	36.76	38.11
Religion	17.61	19.13	24.52	26.73	28.12	31.31	32.33	35.31	32.22
Science	37.45	51.19	62.16	66.91	68.90	74.39	80.14	81.95	79.39
Sociology, economics	31.76	33.33	34.39	37.25	41.26	42.10	48.43	45.53	46.46
Sports, recreation	15.92	23.43	23.96	27.33	29.42	30.52	30.68	34.62	33.42
Technology	33.64	50.37	60.24	65.26	71.04	76.80	76.40	82.18	78.40
Travel	16.80	24.66	28.08	26.22	31.37	30.41	32.43	33.28	28.51
Paperbacks:									
Mass market [2]	(NA)	3.63	4.00	4.54	4.32	4.57	5.08	5.22	5.70
Trade	8.60	13.98	14.56	15.01	17.16	17.45	18.40	18.81	19.24

NA Not available.   [1] Excludes publications of the United States and other governmental units, books sold only by subscription, and dissertations.   [2] "Pocket-sized" books sold primarily through magazine and news outlets, supermarkets, variety stores, etc.

Source: R. R. Bowker Co., New York, NY, *Publishers Weekly*, March 1994 and *Bowker Annual: Library and Book Trade Almanac.* (Copyright by Reed Publishing USA.)

No. 923. Periodicals—Average Retail Prices: 1989 to 1993

[See headnote, table 922]

SUBJECT	1989	1990	1991	1992	1993
Agriculture	185.63	200.26	241.68	254.22	292.75
Anthropology	110.78	121.16	136.60	146.61	148.49
Art and architecture	67.25	73.14	79.05	85.51	91.23
Astronomy	480.66	494.29	606.25	655.25	810.84
Biology	347.81	372.62	443.14	474.94	548.21
Botany	278.86	296.56	345.73	375.98	439.65
Business and economics	119.56	131.08	159.79	175.55	196.86
Chemistry	608.29	641.26	789.09	915.75	1,042.36
Education	82.41	92.03	107.48	113.67	130.57
Engineering and technology	298.67	323.34	415.76	480.38	530.49
Food science	254.80	256.59	339.03	367.88	422.85
General science	180.49	190.34	234.15	300.35	348.18
General works	51.40	55.64	65.05	63.28	68.44
Geography	141.36	155.85	193.25	218.88	236.79
Geology	283.69	297.66	366.22	380.53	443.72
Health sciences	236.70	256.64	307.17	337.36	380.06
History	53.95	57.20	63.49	69.10	74.16
Language and literature	49.32	51.36	59.02	62.08	67.57
Law	55.02	58.92	68.86	73.98	83.86
Library and information science	82.65	91.52	106.11	119.82	127.08
Math and computer science	356.43	385.19	466.66	506.08	567.11
Music	39.01	43.18	47.97	53.53	56.61
Philosophy and religion	61.27	64.92	75.43	78.62	88.53
Physics	631.46	680.06	812.40	927.27	1,090.34
Political science	70.77	76.47	92.58	99.94	112.50
Psychology	99.09	109.06	122.49	136.98	149.29
Recreation	45.60	47.95	56.86	60.75	65.81
Sociology	89.40	98.54	113.13	123.95	138.00
Zoology	265.97	291.92	335.23	362.22	413.42

Source: Library Journal, New York, NY, *Library Journal,* April 15, 1993, and earlier issues. (Copyright by Reed Publishing USA.)

No. 924. U.S. Postal Service—Summary: 1980 to 1994

[**Employees in thousands; revenue and expenditures in millions of dollars,** except as indicated. **For fiscal years;** see text, section 9. Includes Puerto Rico and all outlying areas except Canal Zone. See text, section 18. See also *Historical Statistics, Colonial Times to 1970,* series R 163-171]

ITEM	1980	1985	1988	1989	1990	1991	1992	1993	1994
Number of post offices	30,326	29,557	29,203	29,083	28,959	28,912	28,837	28,728	28,657
Pieces of mail handled (est.) (bil.)	106.3	140.1	161.0	161.6	166.3	165.9	166.4	171.2	177.1
First-class, number (bil.) [1]	60.3	72.4	84.7	85.9	89.3	90.3	90.8	92.2	94.4
Percent	56.7	51.7	52.6	53.2	53.7	54.4	54.5	53.8	53.3
Second class (bil.).	8.4	10.4	10.4	10.5	10.7	10.4	10.3	10.3	10.2
Employees, total	**667**	**744**	**824**	**817**	**819**	**808**	**819**	**818**	**852**
Regular	536	586	764	764	757	746	725	692	729
Postmasters.	29	28	28	27	27	27	26	25	27
Office supervisors and tech. personnel . .	36	46	55	55	53	54	54	42	46
Office clerks and mail handlers [2]	229	249	347	345	333	324	318	308	320
City carriers and vehicle drivers.	160	179	243	243	240	235	232	221	238
Rural carriers.	33	35	39	41	42	43	43	44	45
Other	49	48	52	54	62	64	52	52	53
Substitute (part-time).	130	159	60	53	62	62	84	84	86
Transitional	(X)	(X)	(X)	(X)	(X)	(X)	10	42	38
Compensation and employee benefits (mil. dol.)	16,541	24,349	30,749	32,368	34,214	36,076	37,122	38,447	39,609
Avg. salary per employee (dol.) [3]	24,799	29,621	33,057	35,045	37,570	39,597	41,509	42,711	44,342
Pieces of mail per employee, avg	159	188	195	198	203	205	203	209	208
Total revenue [4]	**19,106**	**28,956**	**35,939**	**38,920**	**40,074**	**44,202**	**47,105**	**47,986**	**49,576**
Operating postal revenue.	17,143	27,736	35,036	37,979	39,201	43,323	46,151	47,418	49,252
Stamps, postal cards, etc	4,287	6,520	7,784	8,381	8,638	9,148	10,071	10,357	10,851
Second-class postage paid in money (pound rates) [5]	881	1,339	1,455	1,519	1,509	1,668	1,751	1,740	1,757
Other postage paid under permit and meter	10,828	17,747	22,676	24,534	25,311	28,019	29,777	30,621	32,079
Box rents	160	230	296	362	394	413	457	481	489
Miscellaneous	892	1,774	2,683	2,959	3,124	3,877	3,941	4,053	4,246
Money-order revenues.	95	126	142	148	154	148	154	166	154
Government appropriations	1,610	970	517	436	453	562	545	164	131
Percent of total revenue	8.4	3.3	1.4	1.1	1.1	1.3	1.2	0.3	0.3
Investment income, net	353	250	386	504	420	317	409	404	193
Mail and service: [1]									
First-class mail [1]	10,146	16,740	21,402	23,234	24,023	26,649	28,296	28,828	29,395
Priority mail [6]	612	960	1,329	1,416	1,555	1,765	2,070	2,300	2,649
Second-class publishers' mail [7]	864	1,093	1,400	1,519	1,509	1,668	1,751	1,740	1,757
Third-class mail [8]	2,412	4,887	7,311	7,924	8,082	8,956	9,490	9,817	10,511
Bulk rate	2,168	4,697	7,096	7,668	7,844	8,699	9,209	9,553	10,240
Single piece rate and fees.	244	190	215	256	238	257	281	264	271
Fourth-class mail [9]	805	763	929	908	920	1,001	1,186	1,183	1,351
Zone rate mail (parcels, catalogs, etc.)	500	524	647	612	655	721	873	882	1,017
Special fourth-class rate	272	199	223	235	215	234	266	257	292
Library rate and fees	33	40	59	61	50	46	48	44	42
Government mail [10]	745	934	(NA)	(NA)	(NA)	(NA)	(NA)	(NA)	(NA)
International mail [11]	596	882	992	1,081	1,163	1,206	1,276	1,407	1,411
Special services	518	918	1,136	1,314	1,310	1,403	1,434	1,509	1,506
Express mail	184	544	524	572	631	668	639	627	671
Mailgrams	15	15	12	10	8	7	8	7	2
Other [12]	2,205	1,220	903	938	873	879	955	568	323
Expenditures [13]	**19,412**	**29,207**	**36,119**	**38,370**	**40,490**	**43,291**	**45,653**	**46,322**	**48,455**

NA Not available.   X Not applicable.   [1] Items mailed at 1st-class rates and weighing 12 ounces or less.   [2] Includes mobile unit employees.   [3] Beginning 1985, for career bargaining unit employees. Includes fringe benefits.   [4] Net revenues after refunds of postage. Includes operating reimbursements, embossed envelope purchases, indemnity claims, and miscellaneous revenue and expenditure offsets. Shown in year which gave rise to the earnings.   [5] Includes controlled circulation publications.   [6] Items otherwise qualified as 1st-class or airmail that exceeds 12 ounces and 8 ounces, respectively.   [7] Includes mail paid at other than bulk rates. Publishers' mail includes printed publications periodically issued and mailed at a known post office to paid subscribers, such as regular rate newspapers and magazines, and classroom and nonprofit rate publications. See source for further detail. [8] Items less than 16 ounces in weight not mailed at either 1st- or 2d-class rates.   [9] Items not mailed at 1st-, 2d-, or 3d-class rates, except government and international mail. May include parcel post, catalogs weighing 16 ounces or more, books, films, and records.   [10] Penalty and franked. Beginning in 1988 penalty and franked mail are included in their appropriate classes of mail. [11] Mail from United States to foreign countries paid at international mail rates.   [12] Consists of unassignable revenues. [13] Shown in year in which obligation was incurred.

Source: U.S. Postal Service, *Annual Report of the Postmaster General* and *Comprehensive Statement on Postal Operations,* annual; and unpublished data.

No. 925. U.S. Postal Service—Volume of Mail, by Class: 1980 to 1994

[**In millions, except per capita. For fiscal years;** see text section 9. Includes Puerto Rico and all outlying areas except Canal Zone. For definition of classes of mail, see footnotes, table 924. See also *Historical Statistics, Colonial Times to 1970*, series R 172-186]

CLASS OF MAIL	PIECES OF MAIL					WEIGHT OF MAIL (lbs.)				
	1980	1990	1992	1993	1994	1980	1990	1992	1993	1994
Total	**106,311**	**166,301**	**166,443**	**171,220**	**177,062**	**12,958**	**18,826**	**18,368**	**19,598**	**20,976**
Domestic	105,348	165,503	165,654	170,313	176,202	12,742	18,577	18,140	19,353	20,736
1st class and express [1]	60,332	89,343	90,842	92,229	94,438	2,213	3,452	3,560	3,733	3,802
Priority mail	248	518	584	664	768	591	1,007	1,109	1,175	1,330
2d class	10,221	10,680	10,319	10,306	10,228	3,478	4,233	3,830	4,041	4,088
3d class	30,381	63,725	62,547	65,773	69,400	3,240	7,648	7,123	8,007	8,797
4th class	633	663	764	744	871	2,661	2,109	2,397	2,284	2,618
Penalty	2,992	(NA)	(NA)	(NA)	(NA)	503	(NA)	(NA)	(NA)	(NA)
Franked and free for blind	540	574	598	596	498	56	127	122	114	100
International	963	798	789	907	860	216	249	228	245	240
Per capita: [2]										
Total, all domestic mail [3]	463	662	648	656	671	56	74	71	74	79
1st class and express	265	354	356	355	360	10	14	14	14	14
2d class	45	43	40	40	39	15	17	15	16	16
3d class	133	255	244	253	264	14	31	28	31	33
4th class	3	3	3	3	3	12	8	9	9	10

NA Not available.   [1] Includes mailgrams.   [2] 1980 and 1990 based on April 1 population, including Armed Forces abroad; other years based on estimated total population as of Jan. 1, including Armed Forces abroad.   [3] Includes types of mail not shown separately.

Source: U.S. Postal Service, *Annual Report of the Postmaster General;* and unpublished data.

No. 926. U.S. Postal Service Rates for Letters and Post Cards: 1958 to 1995

[Domestic airmail letters, as a separate class of service, discontinued in 1973 at 13 cents per ounce. See also *Historical Statistics, Colonial Times to 1970*, series R 188-191]

DATE OF RATE CHANGE	Letters			Postal and post cards	Express mail [1]	DATE OF RATE CHANGE	Letters			Postal and post cards	Express mail [1]
	Each oz.	First oz.	Each added oz.				Each oz.	First oz.	Each added oz.		
1958 (Aug. 1)	$0.04	(X)	(X)	$0.03	(X)	1978 (May 29)	(X)	$0.15	$0.13	$0.10	(X)
1963 (Jan. 7)	$0.05	(X)	(X)	$0.04	(X)	1981 (Mar. 22)	(X)	$0.18	$0.17	$0.12	(X)
1968 (Jan. 7)	$0.06	(X)	(X)	$0.05	(X)	1981 (Nov. 1)	(X)	$0.20	$0.17	$0.13	$9.35
1971 (May 16)	$0.08	(X)	(X)	$0.06	(X)	1985 (Feb. 17)	(X)	$0.22	$0.17	$0.14	$10.75
1974 (Mar. 2)	$0.10	(X)	(X)	$0.08	(X)	1988 (Apr. 3)	(X)	$0.25	$0.20	$0.15	[3]$12.00
1975 (Sept. 14)	(X)	$0.10	$0.09	$0.07	(X)	1991 (Feb. 3)	(X)	$0.29	$0.23	$0.19	[3]$13.95
1975 (Dec. 31) [2]	(X)	$0.13	$0.11	$0.09	(X)	1995 (Jan. 1)	(X)	$0.32	$0.23	$0.20	[3]$15.00

X Not applicable.   [1] Post Office to addressee rates. Rates shown are for weights up to 2 pounds, all zones. Beginning Feb. 17, 1985, for weights between 2 and 5 lbs, $12.85 is charged. Prior to Nov. 1, 1981, rate varied by weight and distances. Over 5 pounds still varies by distance.   [2] As of October 11, 1975, surface mail service upgraded to level of airmail.   [3] Over 8 ounces and up to 2 pounds.

No. 927. International Air Mail Rates From the United States: 1961 to 1991

[Excludes Canada and Mexico. Zones discontinued as of February 1991]

DATE OF RATE CHANGE	ZONE 1 [1]		ZONE 1 [2]		ZONE 1 [3]		Postal and post cards	Aero-grammes
	Each 1/2 oz. up to 2 ozs.	Each added 1/2 oz.	Each 1/2 oz. up to 2 ozs.	Each added 1/2 oz.	Each 1/2 oz. up to 2 ozs.	Each added 1/2 oz.		
1961 (July 1)	$0.13	$0.13	$0.15	$0.15	$0.25	$0.25	$0.11	$0.11
1967 (May 1)	$0.15	$0.15	$0.20	$0.20	$0.25	$0.25	$0.13	$0.13
1971 (July 1)	$0.17	$0.17	$0.21	$0.21	$0.21	$0.21	$0.13	$0.13
1974 (March 2)	$0.21	$0.17	$0.26	$0.21	$0.26	$0.21	$0.18	$0.18
1976 (January 3)	$0.25	$0.21	$0.31	$0.26	$0.31	$0.26	$0.21	$0.22
1981 (January 1)	$0.35	[4]$0.30	$0.40	[5]$0.35	$0.40	[5]$0.35	$0.28	$0.30
1985 (February 17)	$0.39	[6]$0.33	$0.44	[7]$0.39	$0.44	[7]$0.39	$0.33	$0.36
1988 (April 17) [8]	$0.45	$0.42	$0.45	$0.42	$0.45	$0.42	$0.36	$0.39
1991 (February 3) [8][9]	(X)	(X)	(X)	(X)	(X)	(X)	$0.40	$0.45

X Not applicable.   [1] Caribbean, Central and South America. The airmail letter rate to South America, 1961 to 1967, was the same as that to Europe. Beginning January 3, 1976, the airmail letter rate to all South American countries except Colombia and Venezuela is the same as Europe; Columbia and Venezuela are included in the first zone.   [2] Europe and Mediterranean Africa.   [3] Rest of world.   [4] Up to 32 oz.; 30 cents per additional ounce over 32.   [5] Up to 32 oz.; 35 cents per additional ounce over 32.   [6] Up to 32 oz.; 33 cents per additional ounce over 32.   [7] Up to 32 oz.; 39 cents per additional ounce over 32.   [8] Air letters collapsed to a single schedule.   [9] First 1/2 ounce= 50 cents; second 1/2 ounce= 45 cents, 39 cents for each additional 1/2 ounce up to the limit of 64 oz.

Sources of tables 926 and 927: U.S. Postal Service, *"United States Domestic Postage Rate: Recent History;"* and unpublished data.

No. 928. Advertising—Indexes of National Advertising Expenditures, by Medium: 1980 to 1993

[1982-84=100. Based on the average monthly expenditure for those major media which give national coverage. See also *Historical Statistics, Colonial Times to 1970,* series T 472-484]

MEDIUM	1980	1983	1984	1985	1986	1987	1988	1989	1990	1991	1992	1993
General index	71	98	114	118	124	128	136	141	146	138	145	148
Network television	72	97	116	113	117	119	128	128	131	125	134	131
Spot television	67	99	112	123	134	140	146	150	159	145	154	159
Magazines	73	99	115	120	124	131	142	156	159	152	163	171
Newspapers	71	99	112	122	123	127	130	135	140	134	131	131

Source: McCann-Erickson, Inc., New York, NY. Compiled for Crain Communications, Inc. in *Advertising Age,* (copyright).

No. 929. Advertising—Estimated Expenditures, by Medium: 1980 to 1994

[**In millions of dollars.** See text, section 18, for definitions of types of advertising. See also *Historical Statistics, Colonial Times to 1970,* series R 106-109, R 123-126, and T 444-471]

MEDIUM	1980	1985	1987	1988	1989	1990	1991	1992	1993	1994 [1]
Total	**53,550**	**94,750**	**109,650**	**118,050**	**123,930**	**128,640**	**126,400**	**131,290**	**138,080**	**148,960**
National	29,815	53,355	60,625	65,610	68,990	72,780	72,635	76,020	80,010	86,700
Local	23,735	41,395	49,025	52,440	54,940	55,860	53,765	55,270	58,070	62,260
Newspapers	14,794	25,170	29,412	31,197	32,368	32,281	30,409	30,737	32,025	34,360
National	1,963	3,352	3,494	3,586	3,720	3,867	3,685	3,602	3,620	3,910
Local	12,831	21,818	25,918	27,611	28,648	28,414	26,724	27,135	28,405	30,450
Magazines	3,149	5,155	5,607	6,072	6,716	6,803	6,524	7,000	7,357	7,980
Weeklies	1,418	2,297	2,445	2,646	2,813	2,864	2,670	2,739	2,850	3,236
Women's	782	1,294	1,417	1,504	1,710	1,713	1,671	1,853	2,009	2,170
Monthlies	949	1,564	1,745	1,922	2,193	2,226	2,183	2,408	2,498	2,574
Farm publications	130	186	196	196	212	215	215	231	243	255
Television.	11,469	21,022	23,904	25,686	26,891	28,405	27,402	29,409	30,584	33,710
TV networks [2]	5,130	8,060	8,500	9,172	9,110	9,863	9,533	10,249	10,209	11,075
Cable networks . . .	45	594	760	942	1,197	1,393	1,521	1,685	1,970	2,245
Syndication (nat'l) [2] .	50	520	762	901	1,288	1,109	1,253	1,370	1,576	1,735
Spot (national).	3,269	6,004	6,846	7,147	7,354	7,788	7,110	7,551	7,800	8,735
Spot (local).	2,967	5,714	6,833	7,270	7,612	7,856	7,565	8,079	8,435	9,235
Cable (non-network) .	8	130	203	254	330	396	420	475	594	685
Radio	3,702	6,490	7,206	7,798	8,323	8,726	8,476	8,654	9,457	10,295
Network	183	365	413	425	476	482	490	424	458	495
Spot	779	1,335	1,330	1,418	1,547	1,635	1,575	1,505	1,657	1,800
Local	2,740	4,790	5,463	5,955	6,300	6,609	6,411	6,725	7,342	8,000
Yellow Pages	2,900	5,800	7,300	7,781	8,330	8,926	9,182	9,320	9,517	9,830
National	330	695	830	944	1,011	1,132	1,162	1,188	1,230	1,295
Local	2,570	5,105	6,470	6,837	7,319	7,794	8,020	8,132	8,287	8,535
Direct mail	7,596	15,500	19,111	21,115	21,945	23,370	24,460	25,391	27,266	29,310
Business papers	1,674	2,375	2,458	2,610	2,763	2,875	2,882	3,090	3,260	3,425
Outdoor.	578	945	1,025	1,064	1,111	1,084	1,077	1,031	1,090	1,120
Miscellaneous.	7,558	12,107	13,431	14,531	15,271	15,955	15,773	16,427	17,281	18,675

[1] Projected from 9 months of data.   [2] Beginning 1990, Fox included in TV networks, rather than syndication; therefore, data not comparable with previous years.

Source: McCann-Erickson, Inc., New York, NY. Compiled for Crain Communications, Inc. in *Advertising Age* (copyright).

No. 930. Magazine Advertising—Expenditures, by Product: 1980 to 1993

[**In millions of dollars.** Space cost based on one-time rate; special rates used where applicable. Year-to-year data not strictly comparable, as a few minor publications are added or deleted]

PRODUCT	1980	1985	1987	1988	1989	1990	1991	1992	1993
Total	2,846	4,961	5,390	5,943	6,611	6,753	6,608	7,186	7,625
Apparel, footwear, accessories	112	251	323	363	396	428	419	496	511
Automotive, accessories, equipment.	230	549	678	801	881	900	941	1,035	1,054
Beer, wine, and liquor	239	240	208	213	255	277	279	247	203
Computers, office equipment.	79	250	247	252	284	283	291	354	367
Business and consumer services	190	463	491	466	522	516	453	513	621
Drugs and remedies	79	135	142	145	135	163	167	299	367
Food and food products	199	342	377	377	435	444	437	459	468
Household equipment and supplies	65	100	97	102	104	118	115	161	140
Household furnishings	73	87	111	116	126	116	123	117	143
Jewelry, cameras, optical goods	79	101	121	142	156	157	157	158	167
Mail orders/direct response.	(NA)	328	407	467	513	531	574	617	719
Publishing and media	146	188	186	192	191	212	197	202	215
Retail	(NA)	121	138	176	211	255	201	190	221
Smoking materials	290	383	334	352	393	305	265	224	210
Toiletries and toilet goods.	206	385	455	554	651	679	640	734	810
Travel, hotels, and resorts	123	245	273	311	374	380	346	350	376
Other	736	793	802	914	984	989	1,005	1,030	1,033

NA Not available.

Source: Publishers Information Bureau, Inc., New York, NY, as compiled by Leading National Advertisers.

No. 931. Television—Expenditures for Network Advertising: 1992 to 1994

[**In millions of dollars.** See text, section 18, for a definition of network advertising]

PRODUCT	1992	1993 [1]	1994 [1]	PRODUCT	1992	1993 [1]	1994 [1]
Total	**9,973**	**10,893**	**11,893**	Home electronics equipment	121	105	150
Apparel, footwear, accessories	305	332	320	Horticulture	26	32	40
Automotive	1,541	1,589	1,696	Household equipment, supplies,			
Beer and wine	313	330	341	and furnishings	307	286	315
Building material, equipment,				Insurance	142	147	141
fixtures	77	64	65	Jewelry, cameras, optical goods	118	116	121
Computers, office equipment,				Laundry soaps, cleansers,			
and stationery	124	150	187	polishes	285	348	280
Confectionery, soft drinks	531	941	679	Movies	236	373	446
Consumer services	501	783	916	Pet products	67	73	75
Department, discount stores	318	308	383	Proprietary medicines	882	957	988
Financial planning services	95	99	97	Publishing and media	56	51	50
Food and food products	1,375	1,306	1,429	Restaurants and drive-ins	601	743	839
Freight, industrial development	91	77	61	Toiletries and toilet goods	937	1,064	1,095
Gas, lubricants, etc.	67	57	77	Toys and sporting goods	157	271	305
Home centers and hardware				Travel, hotels, and resorts	122	97	181
stores	51	58	68	Other	527	136	548

[1] Includes the Fox network.

Source: Television Bureau of Advertising, Inc., New York, NY. Data compiled by Competitive Media Reporting, New York, NY.

No. 932. Television—Estimated Time Charges for Spot Advertising: 1992 to 1994

[**In millions of dollars.** Data represent activity in the top 75 markets monitored by Competitive Media Reporting, currently covering approximately 382 stations. See text, section 18, for definitions of types of advertising]

PRODUCT	1992	1993	1994	PRODUCT	1992	1993	1994
Total	**5,469**	**5,619**	**6,580**	Home electronics equipment	108	83	129
				Horticulture	40	34	42
Agriculture and farming	12	11	13	Household equipment, supplies,			
Apparel, footwear,				and furnishings	111	139	166
accessories	85	88	84	Insurance	115	135	199
Automotive	1,635	1,820	2,312	Jewelry, cameras, optical goods	25	32	31
Beer and wine	201	196	179	Laundry soaps, cleaners,			
Building material, equipment,				polishes	110	94	84
fixtures	56	58	60	Pet products	28	20	29
Computers, office equip-				Political, unions, religious	76	46	55
ment and stationery	14	16	26	Proprietary medicines	238	177	172
Confectionery, soft drinks	316	308	315	Publishing and media	108	100	95
Consumer services	442	498	666	Toiletries and toilet goods	248	249	276
Food and food products	856	867	963	Toys and sporting goods	245	293	277
Freight, industrial development	48	39	34	Travel, hotels, and resorts	185	140	189
Gasoline, lubricants, etc.	134	136	140	Other	32	40	44

Source: Television Bureau of Advertising, Inc., New York, NY. Data compiled by Competitive Media Reporting, New York, NY, in the top 75 markets.

No. 933. Television—Expenditures for Retail/Local Advertising: 1992 to 1994

[**In millions of dollars.** See headnote, table 932]

PRODUCT	1992	1993	1994	PRODUCT	1992	1993	1994
Total	**5,271**	**5,566**	**6,313**	Hotels, resorts, U.S.	69	84	86
Amusements, entertainment	144	151	160	Insurance agencies	20	26	31
Appliance stores	203	231	269	Jewelry stores	21	26	27
Auto repair, service stations	83	84	93	Legal services	113	126	129
Auto supply, accessory stores	40	41	62	Leisure time stores and services	147	173	201
Auto, truck dealers	283	338	405	Loan, mortgage companies	38	55	75
Banks, S&L associations	183	187	157	Medical, dental services	141	146	158
Builders, home improvement	24	32	35	Movies	242	296	314
Carpet, floor covering stores	52	58	61	Newspapers	30	29	29
Clothing stores	133	143	163	Office equipment/supply stores	16	18	35
Department stores	213	185	198	Optical services, supplies	56	54	57
Discount department stores	119	119	149	Political	170	69	352
Drug stores	118	101	97	Radio, cable TV	186	192	208
Education services	102	99	105	Realtors, real estate developers	21	25	29
Financial planning services	28	28	25	Rental services (nonauto)	30	28	27
Food stores, supermarkets	316	300	289	Restaurants, drive-ins	892	991	1,075
Furniture stores	268	302	359	Shoe stores	31	33	32
Gas, electric, water companies	41	40	42	Shopping centers	24	28	29
Health clubs, reducing salons	128	140	99	Sport, hobby, toy stores	44	58	64
Home centers and hardware	131	138	172	Other	371	392	415

Source: Television Bureau of Advertising, Inc., New York, NY. Data compiled by Competitive Media Reporting, New York, NY, in the top 75 markets.

Figure 19.1
Energy Supply and Disposition: 1970 to 1993

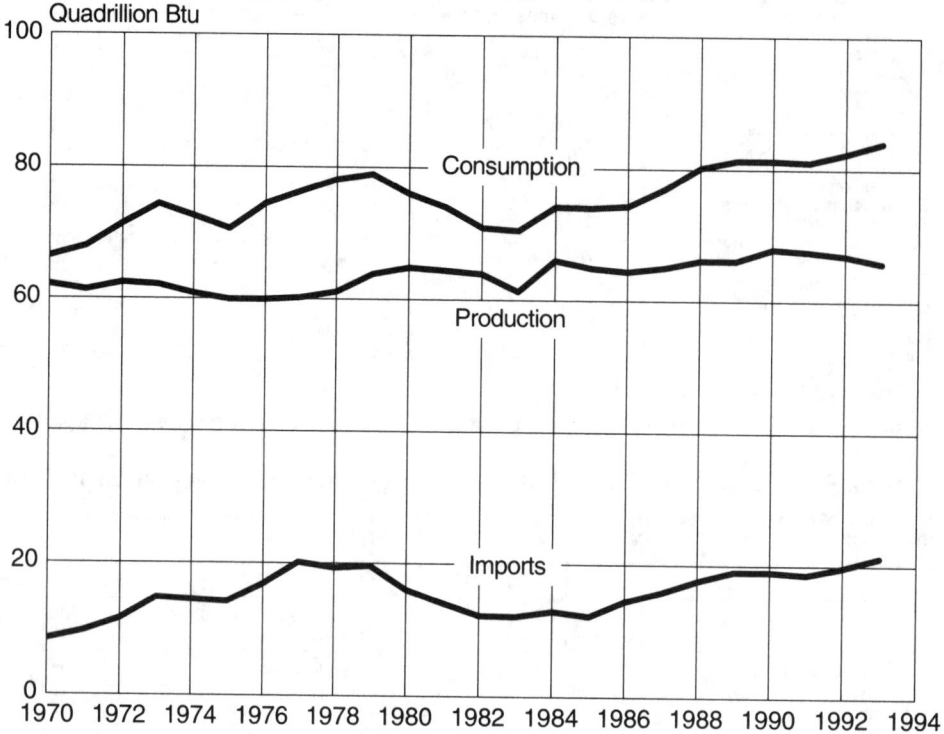

Source: Chart prepared by U.S. Bureau of the Census. For data, see table 936.

Figure 19.2
**Commercial Nuclear Power Generation—
Top 10 Countries: 1993**

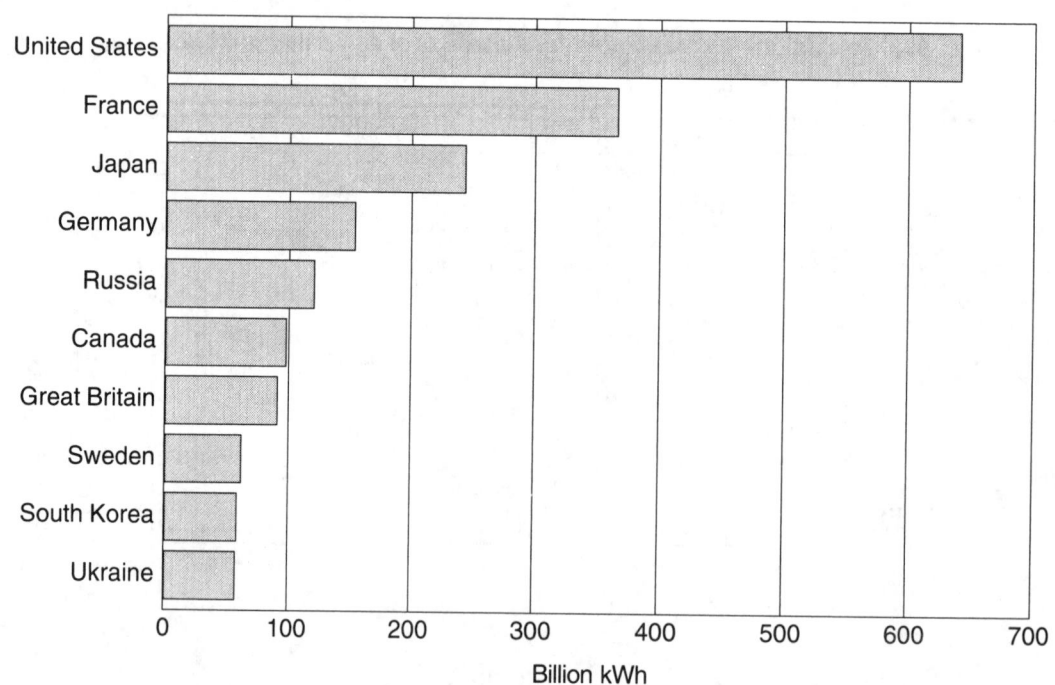

Billion kWh

Source: Chart prepared by U.S. Bureau of the Census. For data, see table 968.

Energy

This section presents statistics on fuel resources, energy production and consumption, electric energy, hydroelectric power, nuclear power, solar energy, wood energy and the electric and gas utility industries. The principal sources are the U.S. Department of Energy's Energy Information Administration (EIA), the Edison Electric Institute, Washington, DC, and the American Gas Association, Arlington, VA. For additional data on transportation, see section 21; on fuels, see section 24; and on energy-related housing characteristics, see section 25.

The EIA, in its *Annual Energy Review,* provides statistics and trend data on energy supply, demand, and prices. Information is included on petroleum and natural gas, coal, electricity, hydroelectric power, nuclear power, solar, wood, and geothermal energy. Among its annual reports are *Annual Energy Review, Electric Power Annual, Natural Gas Annual, Petroleum Supply Annual, State Energy Data Report, State Energy Price and Expenditure Report, Financial Statistics of Selected Electric Utilities, Performance Profiles of Major Energy Producers, Annual Energy Outlook,* and *International Energy Annual.* These various publications contain State, national, and international data on production of electricity, net summer capability of generating plants, fuels used in energy production, energy sales and consumption, and hydroelectric power. The EIA also issues the *Monthly Energy Review,* which presents current supply, disposition, and price data, and monthly publications on petroleum, coal, natural gas, and electric power. Data on residential energy consumption, expenditures, and conservation activities are available from EIA's Residential Energy Consumption Survey and are published triennially in *Residential Energy Consumption Survey: Consumption and Expenditures,* and *Residential Energy Consumption Survey: Housing Characteristics,* and several other reports.

The Edison Electric Institute's monthly bulletin and annual *Statistical Year Book of the Electric Utility Industry for the Year* contain data on the distribution of electric

In Brief

Energy production projected to increase 1.3 percent by the year 2000 while consumption will rise 8.4 percent.

Crude oil imports surpass domestic production in 1994 with 7.0 million barrels per day compared to 6.6 for production.

Net generation of electric energy by utilities reached a record 2.9 trillion kWh in 1993.

energy by public utilities; information on the electric power supply, expansion of electric generating facilities, and the manufacture of heavy electric power equipment is presented in the annual *Year End Summary of the Electric Power Situation in the United States.* The American Gas Association, in its monthly and quarterly bulletins and its yearbook, *Gas Facts,* presents data on gas utilities, including sales, revenues, customers, prices, and other financial and operating statistics.

Btu conversion factors.—Various energy sources are converted from original units (e.g., short tons, cubic feet, barrels, kilowatt-hours) to the thermal equivalent using British thermal units (Btu). A Btu is the amount of energy required to raise the temperature of 1 pound of water 1 degree Fahrenheit (F) at or near 39.2 degrees F. Factors are calculated annually from the latest final annual data available; some are revised as a result. The following list provides conversion factors used in 1992 for production and consumption, in that order, for various fuels: Petroleum, 5.800 and 5.376 mil. Btu per barrel; total coal, 21.675 and 21.164 mil. Btu per short ton; and natural gas (dry), 1,030 Btu per cubic foot for both. The factors for the production of nuclear power and geothermal power were 10,740 and 20,997 Btu per kilowatt-hour, respectively. The fossil fuel steam-electric power plant generation factor of 10,332 Btu per kilowatt-hour was used for hydroelectric power generation and for wood and waste, wind, photovoltaic, and solar thermal energy consumed at electric utilities.

No. 934. Total Horsepower of All Prime Movers: 1960 to 1992

[In millions, except percent. As of **January,** except as noted. Prime movers are mechanical engines and turbines, and work animals, which originally convert fuels or force (as wind or falling water) into work and power. Electric motors, which obtain their power from prime movers, are excluded to avoid duplication. See also *Historical Statistics, Colonial Times to 1970,* series S 1-14]

YEAR	Total horse-power	AUTOMOTIVE [1][2]		NONAUTOMOTIVE							
		Total	Percent of total	Total	Facto-ries[3][4]	Mines[3][4]	Rail-roads[5]	Merchant ships and sailing vessels[4]	Farms	Electric central sta-tions[2]	Air-craft[5][6]
1960......	11,008	10,367	94.2	641	42	35	47	24	240	217	37
1965......	15,096	14,306	94.8	790	48	40	44	24	272	307	55
1970......	20,408	19,325	94.7	1,083	54	45	54	22	290	435	183
1975......	25,100	23,752	94.6	1,348	60	47	62	22	318	654	185
1980......	28,922	27,362	94.6	1,564	64	48	63	28	345	806	210
1981......	29,507	27,909	94.6	1,598	64	48	65	29	345	835	212
1982......	30,495	28,852	94.6	1,643	64	48	64	29	352	854	232
1983......	31,337	29,662	94.7	1,675	64	47	62	29	356	877	240
1984......	31,819	30,117	94.7	1,702	65	47	61	30	359	886	254
1985......	32,529	30,792	94.7	1,737	65	47	58	29	358	912	268
1986......	32,660	30,893	94.6	1,767	65	47	56	29	358	942	270
1987......	33,266	31,488	94.7	1,778	65	47	53	29	357	958	269
1988......	34,200	32,415	94.8	1,785	65	47	53	28	356	969	267
1989......	34,579	32,790	94.8	1,789	65	47	50	28	356	976	267
1990......	34,958	33,158	94.7	1,800	67	48	50	28	356	984	267
1991......	34,962	33,158	94.8	1,804	67	48	50	27	355	991	266
1992......	35,300	33,431	94.7	1,869	68	47	50	29	352	[7]1,057	266

[1] Includes passenger cars, trucks, buses, and motorcycles.　[2] As of July 1, except beginning 1992, as of January 1.
[3] Beginning 1965, data are estimates.　[4] This is an extension of trends, since government agencies suspended compilation of these power capacity statistics. Beginning 1992, includes vessels on the Great Lakes.　[5] Beginning 1965, not strictly comparable with earlier years.　[6] Includes private planes and commercial airlines.　[7] Includes 57 million horsepower in cogenerating and industrial electric power capacity.
Source: John A. Waring, Arlington, VA, unpublished estimates.

No. 935. Energy Supply and Disposition, by Type of Fuel—Projections: 1993 to 2010

[**Quadrillion Btu per year, except percent change**. Projections are "reference" or mid-level forecasts. See report for methodology and assumptions used in generating projections]

TYPE OF FUEL	1993	2000	2005	2010	PERCENT CHANGE		
					1993-2000	2000-2005	2005-2010
Production, total	**69.62**	**70.51**	**72.75**	**75.86**	**1.3**	**3.2**	**4.3**
Crude oil and lease condensate	14.50	11.33	10.92	11.42	−21.9	−3.6	4.6
Natural gas plant liquids	2.41	2.57	2.69	2.81	6.6	4.7	4.5
Natural gas	18.90	19.65	20.53	21.51	4.0	4.5	4.8
Coal............................	20.23	22.08	23.21	24.51	9.1	5.1	5.6
Nuclear power	6.52	6.96	6.97	6.36	6.7	0.1	−8.8
Renewable energy and other	7.06	7.92	8.43	9.25	12.2	6.4	9.7
Imports, total...................	**21.40**	**28.20**	**30.87**	**32.62**	**31.8**	**9.5**	**5.7**
Crude oil.........................	14.79	19.14	19.72	19.53	29.4	3.0	−1.0
Petroleum products..................	3.79	5.18	7.10	8.12	36.7	37.1	14.4
Natural gas	2.32	3.17	3.33	3.97	36.6	5.0	19.2
Other imports......................	0.50	0.71	0.73	1.00	42.0	2.8	37.0
Exports, total...................	**4.21**	**4.40**	**4.49**	**4.83**	**4.5**	**2.0**	**7.6**
Petroleum........................	2.11	1.97	1.68	1.64	−6.6	−14.7	−2.4
Natural gas	0.15	0.21	0.27	0.31	40.0	28.6	14.8
Coal............................	1.96	2.22	2.54	2.89	13.3	14.4	13.8
Consumption, total	**87.27**	**94.61**	**99.37**	**103.88**	**8.4**	**5.0**	**4.5**
Petroleum products.................	33.71	36.89	39.30	40.82	9.4	6.5	3.9
Natural gas	20.81	22.78	23.76	25.30	9.5	4.3	6.5
Coal............................	19.43	20.14	21.01	21.97	3.7	4.3	4.6
Nuclear power	6.52	6.96	6.97	6.36	6.7	0.1	−8.8
Renewable energy/other	6.80	7.83	8.32	9.41	15.1	6.3	13.1

Source: U.S. Energy Information Administration, *Annual Energy Outlook 1995*.

No. 936. Energy Supply and Disposition, by Type of Fuel: 1970 to 1993

[In quadrillion British thermal units (Btu). For Btu conversion factors, see text, section 19]

TYPE OF FUEL	1970	1973	1975	1980	1985	1986	1987	1988	1989	1990	1991	1992	1993
Production	62.1	62.1	59.9	64.8	64.9	64.4	65.0	66.1	66.1	[1]67.9	67.5	66.9	65.81
Crude oil [2]	20.4	19.5	17.7	18.3	19.0	18.4	17.7	17.3	16.1	15.6	15.7	15.2	14.48
Natural gas liquids	2.5	2.6	2.4	2.3	2.2	2.2	2.2	2.3	2.2	2.2	2.3	2.4	2.40
Natural gas [3]	21.7	22.2	19.6	19.9	17.0	16.5	17.1	17.6	17.9	18.4	18.2	18.4	18.98
Coal	14.6	14.0	15.0	18.6	19.3	19.5	20.1	20.7	21.4	22.5	21.6	21.6	20.49
Nuclear electric power	0.2	0.9	1.9	2.7	4.2	4.5	4.9	5.7	5.7	6.2	6.6	6.6	6.52
Hydroelectric power	2.6	2.9	3.2	2.9	3.0	3.1	2.6	2.3	2.8	2.9	2.9	2.5	2.76
Geothermal and other	(Z)	(Z)	0.1	0.1	0.2	0.2	0.2	0.2	0.2	0.2	0.2	0.2	0.18
Net trade [4]	-5.7	-12.7	-11.7	-12.3	-7.9	-10.3	-11.9	-13.2	-14.2	-14.1	-13.4	-14.6	-16.9
Exports	2.7	2.1	2.4	3.7	4.2	4.1	3.9	4.4	4.8	4.9	5.2	5.0	4.31
Coal	1.9	1.4	1.8	2.4	2.4	2.3	2.1	2.5	2.6	2.8	2.9	2.7	1.95
Imports	8.4	14.7	14.1	16.0	12.1	14.4	15.8	17.6	19.0	19.0	18.6	19.7	21.19
Crude oil	2.8	6.9	8.7	11.2	6.8	9.0	10.1	11.0	12.6	12.8	12.6	13.3	14.63
Consumption	66.4	74.3	70.6	76.0	74.0	74.3	76.9	80.2	81.3	81.3	81.1	82.1	[5]83.96
Petroleum products	29.5	34.8	32.7	34.2	30.9	32.2	32.9	34.2	34.2	33.6	32.9	33.5	33.77
Natural gas [3]	21.8	22.5	20.0	20.4	17.8	16.7	17.7	18.6	19.4	19.3	19.6	20.1	20.79
Coal	12.3	13.0	12.7	15.4	17.5	17.3	18.0	18.9	18.9	19.1	18.8	18.9	19.63
Nuclear power	0.2	0.9	1.9	2.7	4.2	4.5	4.9	5.7	5.7	6.2	6.6	6.6	6.52
Hydroelectric power [6]	2.7	3.0	3.2	3.1	3.4	3.5	3.1	2.7	2.9	3.0	3.1	2.8	3.06
Geothermal and other	(Z)	(Z)	0.1	0.1	0.2	0.2	0.3	0.3	0.3	0.2	0.2	0.2	0.20

Z Less than 50 trillion. [1] Represents peak year for U.S. energy production. [2] Includes lease condensate. [3] Dry marketed gas. [4] Exports minus imports. [5] Represents peak year for U.S. energy consumption. [6] Includes industrial generation of hydropower and net electricity imports.

No. 937. Energy Imports and Exports, by Type of Fuel: 1970 to 1993

[In quadrillion of Btu. For definition of Btu, see text, section 19]

TYPE OF FUEL	1970	1973	1975	1980	1985	1987	1988	1989	1990	1991	1992	1993
Net imports:[1]												
Coal	-1.93	-1.42	-1.74	-2.39	-2.39	-2.05	-2.45	-2.57	-2.70	-2.77	-2.59	-1.77
Natural Gas (dry)	0.77	0.98	0.90	0.96	0.90	0.94	1.22	1.28	1.46	1.67	1.94	2.14
Petroleum	6.92	12.98	12.51	13.50	8.95	12.53	14.01	15.33	15.29	14.22	14.96	16.19
Other [2]	-0.04	0.14	0.08	0.18	0.41	0.49	0.37	0.14	0.03	0.24	0.32	0.31
Imports:												
Coal	(Z)	(Z)	0.02	0.03	0.05	0.04	0.05	0.07	0.07	0.08	0.10	0.18
Natural Gas (dry)	0.85	1.06	0.98	1.01	0.95	0.99	1.30	1.39	1.55	1.80	2.16	2.29
Petroleum	7.47	13.47	12.95	14.66	10.61	14.16	15.75	17.16	17.12	16.35	16.97	18.30
Other [2]	0.07	0.20	0.16	0.28	0.49	0.57	0.47	0.33	0.25	0.35	0.43	0.42
Exports:												
Coal	1.94	1.43	1.76	2.42	2.44	2.09	2.50	2.64	2.77	2.85	2.68	1.95
Natural Gas (dry)	0.07	0.08	0.07	0.05	0.06	0.05	0.07	0.11	0.09	0.13	0.22	0.14
Petroleum	0.55	0.49	0.44	1.16	1.66	1.63	1.74	1.84	1.82	2.13	2.01	2.11
Other [2]	0.11	0.06	0.08	0.09	0.08	0.08	0.10	0.10	0.18	0.23	0.11	0.10

Z Less than .005 quadrillion Btu. [1] Net imports equals imports minus exports. Minus sign (-) denotes an excess of exports over imports. [2] Coal coke and small amounts of electricity transmitted across U.S. borders with Canada and Mexico.

No. 938. Selected Energy Indicators—Summary: 1970 to 1993

[Btu=British thermal unit. For Btu conversion factors, see text, section 19. Minus sign (-) indicates decrease]

ITEM	1970	1973	1975	1980	1985	1986	1987	1988	1989	1990	1991	1992	1993
AVERAGE ANNUAL PERCENT CHANGE [1]													
Gross domestic product [2]	3.0	1.7	-0.7	-0.1	0.6	2.9	3.0	3.9	2.5	1.2	-0.6	2.3	3.1
Energy production, total [3]	4.6	-0.2	-1.8	0.3	-0.3	-0.8	0.9	1.8	(Z)	2.6	-0.5	-0.9	-2.1
Crude oil [4]	4.2	-0.9	-4.7	0.2	0.2	-3.3	-3.9	-2.3	-6.9	-3.4	0.8	-3.1	-4.9
Natural gas	6.4	-0.0	-6.1	-0.2	-1.2	-2.6	3.5	2.7	1.4	2.8	-0.7	0.8	2.8
Coal	2.2	-0.2	3.4	1.2	-0.4	1.0	3.2	2.9	2.9	5.1	-3.9	(Z)	-6.5
Energy consumption, total [3]	4.6	1.4	-2.6	-1.8	-0.0	0.4	3.4	4.2	1.4	-0.1	-0.2	1.3	2.1
Petroleum products	4.8	1.9	-3.1	-1.6	-0.1	4.0	2.1	4.1	(Z)	-1.9	-2.1	2.1	0.9
Natural gas (dry)	6.5	-0.3	-6.0	-0.3	-0.7	-6.5	6.0	4.5	4.4	-0.5	1.6	2.6	3.6
Coal	1.1	2.4	-1.2	0.5	0.5	-1.2	4.2	4.6	0.4	0.9	-1.7	0.5	2.9
PER CAPITA [5] (mil. Btu)													
Energy production	304	294	278	285	273	268	268	270	268	272	268	262	254
Energy consumption	327	351	327	334	311	309	317	328	329	326	322	322	325
Energy consumption per dollar of GDP [2] (1,000 Btu)	23.1	22.7	21.9	20.1	17.3	16.9	16.9	17.0	16.8	16.6	16.7	16.5	16.3

Z Less than .05 percent. [1] Represents percent change from immediate prior year; for example, 1970, change from 1965. Percent change derived from Btu values. [2] Gross domestic product in constant (1987) dollars. [3] Includes types of fuel or power, not shown separately. [4] Includes lease condensate. [5] Based on resident population estimated as of July 1.

Source of tables 936 to 938: U.S. Energy Information Administration, *Annual Energy Review*, and *Monthly Energy Review*.

No. 939. Energy Consumption—End-Use Sector and Selected Source, by State: 1992

[In trillions of Btu, except as indicated. For Btu conversion factors, see text, section 19]

REGION, DIVISION, AND STATE	Total[1]	Per capita[2] (mil. Btu)	END-USE SECTOR				SOURCE				
			Resi-dential	Com-mercial	Indus-trial	Trans-porta-tion	Petro-leum	Natural gas (dry)	Coal	Hydro-electric power	Nuclear electric power
United States ..	82,128	322.0	16,193	12,875	[3]30,597	22,464	33,525	20,139	18,846	2,793	6,607
Northeast	12,746	249.3	3,233	2,730	3,366	3,418	5,766	2,784	1,997	455	1,541
New England	3,132	237.4	904	684	673	871	1,712	529	190	138	411
Maine	370	299.5	78	53	135	104	225	5	22	50	57
New Hampshire . . .	244	218.9	71	40	59	74	143	17	35	21	84
Vermont	140	244.9	42	26	27	45	79	8	1	24	40
Massachusetts . . .	1,370	228.5	407	342	236	386	751	306	111	20	51
Rhode Island	247	246.5	66	45	79	57	101	79	-	10	
Connecticut	762	232.3	240	179	137	206	414	114	22	14	179
Middle Atlantic	9,614	253.5	2,328	2,046	2,694	2,546	4,055	2,254	1,807	317	1,131
New York	3,616	199.7	995	1,021	723	878	1,574	987	337	306	258
New Jersey	2,401	307.0	495	484	614	809	1,213	561	63	[4]-1	231
Pennsylvania	3,597	299.9	838	542	1,357	860	1,268	707	1,408	13	642
Midwest	19,663	324.3	4,411	3,115	7,349	4,788	6,815	4,877	6,487	213	1,693
East North Central . .	13,816	323.4	3,148	2,164	5,359	3,145	4,482	3,583	4,509	52	1,267
Ohio	3,733	338.7	822	579	1,551	780	1,137	839	1,419	3	158
Indiana	2,408	425.5	426	271	1,154	556	808	489	1,297	6	-
Illinois	3,487	300.3	852	636	1,238	762	1,143	1,011	693	1	787
Michigan	2,784	295.1	700	442	943	699	914	909	702	8	201
Wisconsin	1,404	281.3	348	236	473	348	481	335	399	35	120
West North Central .	5,846	326.2	1,263	951	1,991	1,643	2,333	1,294	1,978	161	426
Minnesota	1,369	306.4	307	189	498	376	540	312	300	60	119
Iowa	927	330.6	203	139	361	224	320	232	327	10	36
Missouri	1,499	288.8	369	286	353	492	648	241	523	15	86
North Dakota	327	516.1	51	38	169	70	118	38	399	25	-
South Dakota	205	289.2	48	32	53	72	104	27	34	41	-
Nebraska	506	316.0	116	106	131	152	207	105	141	11	93
Kansas	1,014	402.9	170	162	425	257	396	339	254	-	91
South	34,187	387.7	5,835	4,374	15,033	8,945	14,276	8,667	7,937	509	2,614
South Atlantic	12,670	281.0	2,945	2,315	3,620	3,790	5,243	1,655	3,600	181	1,659
Delaware	241	348.2	47	35	93	65	141	41	46	-	-
Maryland	1,204	244.8	321	185	353	344	498	186	248	19	114
Dist. of Columbia . .	174	297.3	34	80	33	27	34	33	1	-	-
Virginia	1,853	289.8	429	392	468	565	732	208	344	4	249
West Virginia	794	439.1	131	88	416	159	295	137	805	12	-
North Carolina	2,019	295.3	468	344	666	541	754	186	600	60	243
South Carolina	1,224	339.8	240	165	513	307	405	142	288	28	486
Georgia	2,095	309.3	454	330	640	671	808	352	616	56	299
Florida	3,066	227.4	821	695	438	1,112	1,577	370	653	2	268
East South Central . .	5,946	382.8	1,106	580	2,650	1,610	2,101	987	2,262	244	462
Kentucky	1,532	408.2	271	180	691	391	539	201	814	39	-
Tennessee	1,793	356.7	382	140	810	461	608	249	591	99	167
Alabama	1,653	399.6	286	159	784	425	538	287	771	106	207
Mississippi	968	370.0	167	102	365	333	415	251	87	-	87
West South Central .	15,571	565.0	1,783	1,478	8,764	3,546	6,932	6,024	2,076	85	493
Arkansas	796	332.5	157	101	307	231	286	227	221	35	121
Louisiana	3,558	831.4	288	211	2,314	745	1,508	1,614	224	-	111
Oklahoma	1,302	406.2	224	173	529	377	473	558	307	33	-
Texas	9,915	560.7	1,114	993	5,614	2,194	4,665	3,626	1,324	17	262
West	15,506	281.2	2,716	2,657	4,820	5,313	6,667	3,812	2,425	1,615	759
Mountain	4,605	320.3	849	859	1,501	1,396	1,731	1,034	2,200	275	273
Montana	341	414.1	56	50	145	90	149	47	190	85	-
Idaho	387	362.7	76	75	145	91	123	50	10	67	-
Wyoming	422	908.7	33	38	268	82	120	131	491	7	-
Colorado	959	276.8	213	233	233	280	349	259	332	16	-
New Mexico	584	369.4	78	96	195	215	241	211	268	3	-
Arizona	945	246.5	206	207	194	338	364	134	369	71	273
Utah	557	307.4	100	87	210	159	208	132	363	6	-
Nevada	412	307.9	87	72	112	141	176	71	179	21	-
Pacific	10,901	267.5	1,866	1,798	3,319	3,917	4,936	2,778	225	1,340	486
Washington	1,991	387.2	363	288	698	642	860	175	106	697	61
Oregon	942	317.1	194	162	284	302	369	127	41	388	49
California	7,092	229.6	1,240	1,256	1,915	2,681	3,243	2,090	65	244	376
Alaska	612	1040.4	46	59	358	149	206	384	13	10	-
Hawaii	263	227.6	23	33	64	143	258	3	1	1	-

- Represents zero.   [1] Sources of energy includes geothermal, wood and waste, and net interstate sales of electricity, including losses, not shown separately.   [2] Based on estimated resident population as of July 1.   [3] Includes 27.2 trillion Btu of net imports of coal coke not allocated by State.   [4] A negative number occurs when more electricity is expended than is created to provide electricity during peak demand periods.

Source: U.S. Energy Information Administration, *State Energy Data Report, 1992.*

No. 940. Energy Consumption, by End-Use Sector: 1970 to 1993

[Btu=British thermal unit. For residential and commercial, industrial, and transportation, represents consumption of fossil fuels only. For Btu conversion factors, see text, section 19]

YEAR	Total consumption (quad. Btu)	Residential and commercial (quad. Btu)	Industrial and miscel-laneous (quad. Btu)	Transporta-tion (quad. Btu)	PERCENT OF TOTAL		
					Residential and commercial	Industrial and miscel-laneous	Transpor-tation
1970	66.4	21.7	28.6	16.1	32.7	43.1	24.2
1973	74.3	24.1	31.5	18.6	32.5	42.4	25.0
1975	70.6	23.9	28.4	18.3	33.9	40.3	25.9
1976	74.4	25.0	30.2	19.1	33.6	40.7	25.7
1977	76.3	25.4	31.1	19.8	33.3	40.7	26.0
1978	78.1	26.1	31.4	20.6	33.4	40.2	26.4
1979	78.9	25.8	32.6	20.5	32.7	41.3	25.9
1980	76.0	25.7	30.6	19.7	33.8	40.3	25.9
1981	74.0	25.2	29.2	19.5	34.1	39.5	26.4
1982	70.9	25.6	26.1	19.1	36.2	36.9	26.9
1983	70.5	25.6	25.8	19.1	36.3	36.5	27.1
1984	74.1	26.5	27.9	19.8	35.7	37.6	26.7
1985	74.0	26.7	27.2	20.1	36.1	36.8	27.1
1986	74.3	26.9	26.6	20.8	36.1	35.8	28.0
1987	76.9	27.6	27.8	21.5	35.9	36.2	27.9
1988	80.2	28.9	29.0	22.3	36.1	36.1	27.8
1989	81.3	29.4	29.4	22.6	36.1	36.1	27.7
1990	81.3	28.8	29.9	22.5	35.4	36.8	27.7
1991	81.1	29.4	29.6	22.1	36.3	36.5	27.3
1992	82.1	29.1	30.6	22.5	35.4	37.2	27.3
1993	84.0	30.3	30.8	22.8	36.1	36.6	27.2

Source: U.S. Energy Information Administration, *Annual Energy Review.*

No. 941. Energy Expenditures and Average Fuel Prices, by Source and Sector: 1970 to 1992

[For definition of Btu, see text, section 19. End-use sector and electric utilities exclude expenditures and prices on energy sources such as hydropower, solar, wind, and geothermal. Also excludes expenditures for reported amounts of energy consumed by the energy industry for production, transportation, and processing operations]

SOURCE AND SECTOR	1970	1973	1975	1980	1985	1987	1988	1989	1990	1991	1992
EXPENDITURES (mil. dol.)											
Total[1][2]	82,579	111,616	171,782	373,900	435,444	393,525	407,597	434,354	469,420	467,029	472,756
Natural gas	10,891	13,933	20,061	51,061	72,938	58,019	61,089	65,383	64,102	64,697	68,401
Petroleum products[2]	48,088	65,305	103,859	238,408	223,196	186,413	189,261	206,277	234,461	221,916	221,764
Motor gasoline	31,596	39,667	59,446	124,408	118,044	99,809	103,211	112,585	126,472	123,051	125,158
Coal	4,594	6,229	13,048	22,648	29,719	27,586	28,371	28,106	28,382	27,869	27,411
Electricity sales	23,351	33,780	50,680	98,098	149,242	154,692	162,070	169,340	176,742	184,822	186,956
Residential sector	20,083	27,078	36,844	68,825	98,307	97,552	102,773	108,423	109,265	114,739	115,150
Commercial sector	10,668	15,104	22,835	46,881	70,263	68,777	71,579	75,467	78,922	81,483	82,398
Industrial sector	16,458	23,531	41,169	94,520	105,723	89,975	91,315	93,827	100,903	99,603	102,035
Transportation sector[2]	35,370	45,904	70,934	163,674	161,150	137,220	141,930	156,637	180,330	171,204	173,173
Motor gasoline	30,525	38,598	57,992	121,809	115,201	97,527	100,988	110,168	123,775	120,557	122,700
Electric utilities	4,316	7,817	16,396	37,435	42,558	36,692	37,435	38,895	38,443	36,501	35,763
AVERAGE FUEL PRICES (dol. per mil. Btu)											
All sectors	1.65	2.02	3.33	6.91	8.42	7.37	7.30	7.69	8.37	8.32	8.27
Residential sector	2.12	2.73	3.83	7.55	11.14	10.95	10.90	11.26	12.14	12.34	12.27
Commercial sector	1.97	2.56	4.09	7.88	11.71	11.06	10.91	11.40	12.03	12.21	12.32
Industrial sector	0.83	1.08	2.20	4.71	6.09	5.19	5.03	5.11	5.40	5.34	5.29
Transportation sector	2.31	2.57	4.02	8.61	8.26	6.57	6.56	7.16	8.26	7.97	7.93
Electric utilities	0.32	0.46	0.96	1.75	1.85	1.51	1.45	1.48	1.46	1.37	1.34

[1] Includes electricity sales; excludes electricity generation.   [2] Includes sources or fuel types not shown separately.

Source: U.S. Energy Information Administration, *State Energy Price and Expenditure Report,* annual.

No. 942. Energy Expenditures—End-Use Sector and Selected Source, by State: 1992

[In millions of dollars, except as indicated. End-use sector and electric utilities exclude expenditures on energy sources such as hydropower, solar, wind, and geothermal. Also excludes expenditures for reported amounts of energy consumed by the energy industry for production, transportation, and processing operations]

REGION, DIVISION, AND STATE	Total[1]	Per capita[2] (dol.)	END-USE SECTOR				SOURCE				
			Residential	Commercial	Industrial	Transportation	Petroleum products		Natural gas	Coal	Electricity sales
							Total	Gasoline			
U.S.	472,756	1,853	115,150	82,398	[3]102,035	173,173	221,764	125,158	68,401	27,411	186,956
Northeast.	92,317	1,806	27,816	20,802	15,284	28,416	40,167	21,922	14,636	3,159	38,434
N.E	24,923	1,889	7,879	5,265	3,725	8,055	12,269	6,719	3,108	357	10,094
ME	2,567	2,077	704	375	552	937	1,475	714	28	57	1,039
NH	2,002	1,796	638	322	362	681	1,027	604	105	60	893
VT	1,145	2,005	363	201	164	417	671	339	38	2	436
MA	10,848	1,810	3,434	2,504	1,410	3,500	5,189	2,864	1,721	193	4,347
RI	1,867	1,865	567	359	408	533	777	452	435	-	657
CT	6,494	1,980	2,173	1,504	829	1,988	3,129	1,745	780	44	2,722
M.A	67,394	1,777	19,937	15,537	11,559	20,361	27,898	15,203	11,528	2,802	28,340
NY	28,751	1,588	9,272	8,150	3,558	7,772	11,162	6,294	5,365	525	13,091
NJ	16,156	2,066	4,161	3,615	2,764	5,616	7,541	3,641	2,758	108	5,975
PA	22,487	1,875	6,504	3,773	5,237	6,973	9,196	5,268	3,405	2,169	9,274
Midwest.	112,265	1,851	28,172	18,171	27,416	38,507	49,002	28,978	20,130	9,126	41,591
E.N.C	78,919	1,847	20,363	13,114	19,981	25,461	32,205	19,438	15,394	6,757	30,140
OH	21,156	1,920	5,365	3,555	5,653	6,584	8,410	5,128	3,706	2,073	8,718
IN	11,606	2,051	2,597	1,428	3,442	4,140	5,079	2,697	1,977	1,845	4,042
IL	21,273	1,832	5,899	4,070	4,926	6,378	8,061	4,908	4,433	1,180	8,599
MI	16,744	1,775	4,313	2,807	4,268	5,356	6,849	4,344	3,784	1,109	6,009
WI	8,140	1,630	2,189	1,256	1,693	3,003	3,804	2,362	1,495	551	2,772
W.N.C	33,346	1,861	7,809	5,057	7,434	13,046	16,797	9,540	4,736	2,369	11,452
MN	7,648	1,712	1,829	939	1,783	3,097	3,862	2,380	1,170	371	2,593
IA	5,295	1,889	1,328	752	1,348	1,867	2,472	1,454	953	373	1,807
MO	9,237	1,779	2,345	1,597	1,507	3,788	4,616	2,781	1,099	699	3,489
ND	1,566	2,471	289	192	510	576	792	402	110	474	412
SD	1,287	1,818	302	172	227	586	766	425	110	41	404
NE	3,024	1,889	646	533	543	1,302	1,618	858	419	110	982
KS	5,288	2,103	1,069	872	1,516	1,831	2,673	1,241	875	300	1,765
South	174,910	1,983	39,823	25,702	43,992	65,393	86,374	45,903	21,453	12,249	70,406
S.A	78,331	1,737	21,243	13,883	13,625	29,580	36,437	22,617	6,672	5,973	35,913
DE	1,379	1,970	368	220	278	514	724	393	154	78	568
MD	8,209	1,670	2,334	1,140	1,644	3,092	3,910	2,509	913	390	3,468
DC	1,143	1,954	234	485	175	249	282	206	213	2	650
VA	11,258	1,761	3,036	2,158	1,548	4,517	5,398	3,400	942	529	4,782
WV	3,761	2,079	773	464	1,218	1,305	1,949	990	478	1,184	1,193
NC	12,886	1,913	3,530	2,063	2,712	4,580	5,787	3,636	769	1,038	6,213
SC	6,733	1,869	1,628	936	1,771	2,399	2,865	1,870	550	451	3,230
GA	12,605	1,861	3,188	2,220	2,526	4,671	5,429	3,377	1,576	1,108	5,530
FL	20,357	1,510	6,154	4,198	1,753	8,253	10,094	6,237	1,078	1,192	10,280
E.S.C	30,073	1,936	6,416	3,232	8,289	12,136	14,401	8,456	3,096	3,223	12,141
KY	7,263	1,935	1,452	838	1,985	2,989	3,657	2,013	696	991	2,781
TN	9,529	1,896	2,062	780	2,922	3,765	4,422	2,747	939	765	4,040
AL	8,357	2,019	1,840	973	2,305	3,239	3,787	2,313	932	1,328	3,362
MS	4,924	1,883	1,062	641	1,077	2,144	2,535	1,383	529	139	1,958
W.S.C	66,506	2,413	12,164	8,587	22,078	23,677	35,536	14,829	11,686	3,054	22,352
AR	4,691	1,959	1,125	609	1,089	1,869	2,184	1,343	676	366	1,864
LA	12,378	2,893	1,947	1,334	4,933	4,164	6,584	2,189	2,440	345	3,824
OK	6,048	1,887	1,382	920	1,130	2,617	3,013	1,754	1,282	382	2,207
TX	43,390	2,454	7,711	5,725	14,927	15,027	23,756	9,544	7,289	1,961	14,457
West	93,164	1,690	19,340	17,723	15,245	40,857	46,221	28,355	12,182	2,876	36,525
Mountain	25,922	1,803	5,495	4,819	4,575	11,034	12,900	7,860	2,965	2,511	10,050
MT	1,719	2,091	298	235	394	792	991	529	180	140	542
ID	1,930	1,811	368	319	449	794	1,006	598	170	18	736
WY	1,550	3,334	176	176	574	624	783	341	231	390	488
CO	5,443	1,571	1,217	1,170	695	2,360	2,706	1,798	823	369	1,902
NM	3,004	1,899	535	570	499	1,399	1,698	953	341	354	1,010
AZ	6,884	1,797	1,800	1,529	900	2,656	2,923	2,015	493	515	3,517
UT	2,861	1,580	579	434	575	1,273	1,451	842	475	463	868
NV	2,530	1,894	520	387	488	1,135	1,344	784	253	262	987
Pacific	67,242	1,650	13,845	12,903	10,670	29,824	33,321	20,496	9,217	366	26,475
WA	8,888	1,728	1,603	1,140	1,363	4,782	5,266	2,748	611	154	3,015
OR	5,101	1,716	953	746	915	2,488	2,814	1,682	460	48	1,850
CA	49,418	1,600	10,651	10,358	7,861	20,548	22,619	15,249	7,897	119	20,378
AK	1,867	3,175	337	338	188	1,004	1,255	307	211	43	430
HI	1,968	1,702	302	322	343	1,002	1,367	510	39	2	803

- Represents zero.   [1] Includes sources not shown separately. Total expenditures are the sum of purchases for each source (including electricity sales) less electric utility purchases of fuel.   [2] Based on estimated resident population as of July 1.   [3] Includes net imports of coal coke not shown separately by State.

Source: U.S. Energy Information Administration, *State Energy Price and Expenditure Report*, annual.

No. 943. Residential Energy Consumption, Expenditures, and Average Price, 1980 to 1990, and by Region, 1990

[**For period April to March for 1980-1985; January to December for 1987 and 1990.** Excludes Alaska and Hawaii in 1980. Covers occupied units only. Excludes household usage of gasoline for transportation and the use of wood or coal. Based on Residential Energy Consumption Survey; see Appendix III. For composition of regions, see table 27. Btu=British thermal unit; see text, section 19]

TYPE OF FUEL	Unit	1980	1982	1983	1985	1987	1990 Total	1990 North-east	1990 Mid-west	1990 South	1990 West
CONSUMPTION											
Total	Quad. Btu . .	9.74	9.51	8.62	9.04	9.13	9.22	2.30	2.81	2.60	1.51
Avg. per household	Mil. Btu . .	126	114	103	105	101	98	120	122	81	78
Natural gas	Quad. Btu . .	5.31	5.39	4.77	4.98	4.83	4.86	1.03	1.88	1.03	0.92
Electricity	Quad. Btu . .	2.42	2.48	2.42	2.48	2.76	3.03	0.47	0.66	1.36	0.54
Fuel oil, kerosene	Quad. Btu . .	1.71	1.33	1.14	1.26	1.22	1.04	0.78	0.13	0.11	0.02
Liquid petroleum gas	Quad. Btu . .	0.31	0.31	0.29	0.31	0.32	0.28	0.02	0.13	0.10	0.03
EXPENDITURES											
Total	Bil. dol.	63.2	85.0	87.8	97.0	97.7	110.2	28.3	26.9	37.2	17.9
Avg. per household	Dollars	815	1,022	1,048	1,123	1,080	1,172	1,471	1,166	1,151	920
Natural gas	Bil. dol.	17.8	24.5	27.1	29.8	26.1	27.3	7.3	9.2	5.9	4.8
Electricity	Bil. dol.	32.6	45.9	48.4	54.5	61.6	71.5	14.6	15.4	29.1	12.5
Fuel oil, kerosene	Bil. dol.	10.7	11.8	9.6	9.6	7.2	8.3	6.1	1.0	1.0	0.2
Liquid petroleum gas	Bil. dol.	2.1	2.7	2.7	3.1	2.8	3.1	0.3	1.3	1.2	0.4
AVERAGE PRICE											
Total	Dol./mil. Btu.	6.49	8.93	10.18	10.73	10.71	12.0	12.3	9.6	14.3	11.8
Natural gas	Dol./mil. Btu .	3.36	4.55	5.67	5.97	5.41	5.6	7.1	4.9	5.7	5.2
Electricity	Dol./mil. Btu .	13.46	18.51	19.98	21.94	22.34	23.6	31.2	23.2	21.4	23.2
Fuel oil, kerosene	Dol./mil. Btu .	6.29	8.89	8.42	7.64	5.89	7.9	7.9	7.8	8.4	7.9
Liquid petroleum gas	Dol./mil. Btu .	6.71	8.74	9.42	9.91	8.91	11.2	14.3	9.7	12.2	12.2

Source: U.S. Energy Information Administration, *Household Energy Consumption and Expenditures, 1990,* and prior reports. Survey not conducted in 1984, 1986, 1988, and 1989.

No. 944. Residential Energy Consumption and Expenditures, by Type of Fuel and Selected Household Characteristic: 1990

[**For period January through December 1990.** Quad.=quadrillion. See headnote, table 943]

CHARACTERISTIC	CONSUMPTION (Btu's) Total [1] (quad.)	CONSUMPTION (Btu's) Avg. per house-hold[1] (mil.)	CONSUMPTION (Btu's) Natural gas (quad.)	CONSUMPTION (Btu's) Elec-tricity (quad.)	CONSUMPTION (Btu's) Fuel oil[2] (quad.)	EXPENDITURES Total[1] (bil. dol.)	EXPENDITURES Avg. per house-hold[1] (dol.)	EXPENDITURES Natural gas (bil. dol.)	EXPENDITURES Elec-tricity (bil. dol.)	EXPENDITURES Fuel oil[2] (bil. dol.)
Total households	9.22	98	4.86	3.03	1.05	110.2	1,172	27.3	71.5	8.3
Single family detached.	6.61	113	3.45	2.20	0.74	78.2	1,340	18.8	51.0	5.9
Single family attached	0.52	87	0.28	0.19	0.06	6.8	1,129	1.7	4.6	0.5
Two-to-four unit building.	0.94	95	0.62	0.20	0.11	10.2	1,015	3.8	5.3	0.9
Five-or-more unit building.	0.73	51	0.36	0.28	0.08	9.8	677	2.2	7.1	0.5
Mobile home	0.41	78	0.15	0.16	0.04	5.3	1,011	0.8	3.5	0.4
Year house built:										
1939 or earlier	2.57	120	1.57	0.51	0.42	26.1	1,216	9.0	13.0	3.3
1940 to 1949	0.74	105	0.45	0.19	0.07	7.9	1,130	2.5	4.5	0.6
1950 to 1959	1.47	110	0.81	0.41	0.22	16.8	1,254	4.6	10.2	1.7
1960 to 1969	1.41	95	0.77	0.48	0.13	17.1	1,155	4.4	11.4	1.0
1970 to 1979	1.82	85	0.78	0.82	0.17	24.5	1,143	4.2	18.3	1.3
1980 to 1984	0.58	72	0.21	0.32	0.01	9.0	1,120	1.2	7.4	0.1
1985 to 1990	0.63	80	0.28	0.30	(B)	8.8	1,117	1.4	6.8	(B)
Heating and cooling degree day zones: [3]										
Less than 2,000 CDD and —										
More than 7,000 HDD.	1.12	111	0.53	0.29	0.21	11.5	1,132	2.7	6.3	1.6
5,500 to 7,000 HDD	3.29	123	2.04	0.75	0.43	33.4	1,251	10.8	18.4	3.5
4,000 to 5,499 HDD	2.12	102	1.06	0.67	0.34	25.6	1,222	6.6	15.6	2.7
Less than 4,000 HDD	1.41	73	0.72	0.59	0.04	19.4	1,008	4.2	14.3	0.3
More than 2,000 CDD and less than 4,000 HDD	1.28	75	0.50	0.74	(B)	20.4	1,197	3.0	16.9	(B)
1990 family income:										
Less than $10,000.	1.27	80	0.70	0.36	0.15	14.1	888	4.0	8.2	1.2
$10,000 to $19,999	1.66	84	0.88	0.53	0.17	19.4	978	5.0	12.3	1.4
$20,000 to $34,999	2.27	93	1.17	0.77	0.25	27.1	1,115	6.4	17.9	2.1
$35,000 to $49,999	1.75	105	0.90	0.62	0.19	21.7	1,296	5.1	14.6	1.5
$50,000 or more	2.27	132	1.21	0.75	0.27	27.9	1,618	6.8	18.6	2.2

B Base figure too small to meet statistical standards for reliability of derived figure. [1] Includes liquid petroleum gas not shown separately. [2] Includes kerosene. [3] CDD=Cooling degree day; HDD=Heating degree day.
Source: U.S. Energy Information Administration, *Household Energy Consumption and Expenditures, 1990.*

No. 945. Manufacturing Primary Energy Consumption for all Purposes, by Type of Fuel and Major Industry Group: 1991

[In trillions of Btu. Estimates represented in this table are for the primary consumption of energy for heat and power and as feedstocks or raw material inputs. Primary consumption is defined as the consumption of the energy that was originally produced offsite or was produced onsite from input materials not classified as energy. Examples of the latter are hydrogen produced from the electrolysis of brine; the output of captive (onsite) mines or wells; woodchips, bark, and woodwaste from wood purchased as a raw material input; and waste materials such as wastepaper and packing materials. Primary consumption excludes quantities of energy that are produced from other energy inputs and, therefore, avoids double counting. Based on the 1991 Manufacturing Energy Consumption Survey and subject to sampling variability]

INDUSTRY	SIC [1] code	Total	Net electricity [2]	Residual fuel oil	Distillate fuel oil [3]	Natural gas [4]	LPG	Coal	Coke and breeze	Other [5]
All industries	(X)	20,257	2,370	454	146	6,095	1,574	2,006	308	7,304
Food and kindred products	20	956	169	27	17	(D)	5	154	(D)	(D)
Tobacco products	21	24	3	1	(Z)	4	(Z)	15	-	(Z)
Textile mill products	22	274	101	12	6	108	2	31	-	13
Apparel and other textile products	23	44	19	(S)	1	19	1	2	-	1
Lumber and wood products	24	451	61	2	16	41	4	2	-	325
Furniture and fixtures	25	68	17	1	1	19	1	4	-	26
Paper and allied products	26	2,506	201	156	9	(D)	5	296	(D)	(D)
Printing and publishing	27	108	53	(Z)	2	48	1	-	-	4
Chemicals and allied products	28	5,051	440	(D)	14	2,227	(D)	(D)	10	526
Petroleum and coal products	29	5,967	105	65	21	838	(D)	(D)	(D)	4,864
Rubber and misc. plastic products	30	238	116	8	3	96	3	7	-	6
Leather and leather products	31	12	3	1	1	5	(Z)	(S)	-	1
Stone, clay, and glass products	32	880	105	9	20	381	(D)	293	(D)	(D)
Primary metal industries	33	2,467	499	(D)	11	708	(D)	853	278	72
Fabricated metal products	34	307	102	3	6	175	4	5	(D)	(D)
Industrial machinery & equipment	35	237	101	3	4	109	2	11	1	5
Electric and electronic equipment	36	212	102	4	2	79	1	(D)	(D)	(D)
Transportation equipment	37	323	118	12	7	133	2	(D)	(D)	17
Instruments and related products	38	98	42	3	(D)	26	(S)	(D)	-	(D)
Misc. manufacturing industries	39	32	12	1	(D)	15	(Z)	1	-	(S)

- Represents or rounds to zero. D Withheld to avoid disclosing data for individual establishments. S Withheld because Relative Standard Error is greater than 50 percent. X Not applicable. Z Less than 0.5 trillion Btu. [1] Standard Industrial Classification Code; see text, section 13. [2] Net electricity is obtained by aggregating purchases, transfers in, and generation from noncombustible renewable resources minus quantities sold and transferred out. Excludes electricity inputs from onsite cogeneration or generation from combustible fuels because that energy has already been included as generating fuel (for example, coal). [3] Includes Nos.1, 2, and 4 fuel oils and Nos. 1, 2, and 4 diesel fuels. [4] Includes natural gas obtained from utilities, transmission pipelines, and any other supplier such as brokers and producers. [5] Includes net steam, and other energy that respondents indicated was used to produce heat and power or as feedstock/raw material inputs.
Source: U.S. Energy Information Administration, *Manufacturing Energy Consumption 1991.*

No. 946. Manufacturing Energy Consumption for Fuel Purposes, by Type of Fuel and End-Use: 1991

[In trillions of Btu. See headnote, table 945]

END-USE CATEGORIES [1]	Total	Net electricity [2]	Residual fuel oil	Distillate fuel oil and diesel fuel [3]	Natural gas [4]	LPG	Coal (excluding coal coke and breeze)	Other [5]
Total inputs	15,027	2,370	414	139	5,506	105	1,184	5,309
Boiler fuel	(X)	(D)	296	40	2,098	18	859	(X)
Direct process uses	(X)	1,864	109	34	2,578	64	314	(X)
Process heating	(X)	235	107	19	2,382	49	314	(X)
Process cooling and refrigeration	(X)	124	(Z)	(Z)	13	(Z)	-	(X)
Machine drive	(X)	1,187	2	14	127	15	-	(X)
Electro-chemical processes	(X)	304	(X)	(X)	(X)	(X)	(X)	(X)
Other process use	(X)	15	(Z)	1	56	(Z)	(Z)	(X)
Direct nonprocess uses	(X)	396	7	53	702	19	(D)	(X)
Facility heating, ventilation, and air conditioning [6]	(X)	192	4	8	283	3	(Z)	(X)
Facility lighting	(X)	161	(X)	(X)	(X)	(X)	(X)	(X)
Facility support	(X)	36	(D)	(Z)	23	(Z)	(Z)	(X)
Onsite transportation	(X)	4	(X)	38	(Z)	16	(X)	(X)
Conventional electricity generation	(X)	(X)	2	4	347	(Z)	(D)	(X)
Other nonprocess use	(X)	4	(D)	2	49	(Z)	(X)	(X)
End-use not reported	5,547	(D)	2	12	128	4	(D)	5,309

- Represents or rounds to zero. D Withheld to avoid disclosing data for individual establishments. X Not applicable. Z Less that .5 trillion. [1] Allocations to specific end-uses are made on the basis of reasonable approximations by respondents. [2] "Net electricity" is obtained by summing purchases, transfers in, and generation from noncombustible renewable resources, minus quantities sold and transferred out. It does not include electricity inputs from onsite cogeneration or generation from combustible fuels because that energy has already been included as generating fuel (for example, coal). [3] Includes Nos. 1, 2, and 4 fuel oils and Nos. 1, 2, and 4 diesel fuels. [4] Includes natural gas obtained from utilities, transmission pipelines, and any other supplier(s) such as brokers and producers. [5] Includes net steam (the sum of purchases, generation from renewables, and net transfers) and other energy that respondents indicated was used to produce heat and power. [6] Excludes steam and hot water.
Source: U.S. Energy Information Administration, *Manufacturing Energy Consumption 1991.*

No. 947. Commercial Buildings—Energy Consumption and Expenditures, by Major Fuel Type Used: 1992

[Covers buildings using one or more major fuel. Excludes industrial buildings predominantly residential buildings, and buildings of less than 1,000 sq. ft. Based on a sample survey of building representatives and energy suppliers; therefore, subject to sampling variability. For characteristics of commercial buildings, see tables in section 25. Tril. = trillion]

TYPE OF FUEL	MAJOR FUEL CONSUMPTION				MAJOR FUEL EXPENDITURES			
	Total (tril. Btu)	Per building (mil. Btu)	Per square feet (1,000 Btu)	Per worker (mil. Btu)	Total (mil. dol.)	Per building (1,000 dol.)	Per square feet (dollars)	Per mil. Btu (dollars)
All buildings	**5,803**	**1,207**	**85.5**	**81.5**	**72,599**	**15.1**	**1.07**	**12.51**
Energy sources (more than one may apply):								
Electricity.	5,802	1,258	87.2	81.5	72,595	15.7	1.09	12.51
Natural gas	4,576	1,722	101.7	89.4	52,563	19.8	1.17	11.49
Fuel oil	1,526	2,727	115.4	84.4	17,972	32.1	1.36	11.78
District heat	839	8,872	160.0	117.5	9,106	96.3	1.74	10.85
District chilled water	292	10,369	152.6	107.8	3,167	112.5	1.65	10.85
Propane	220	653	64.9	76.3	3,561	10.6	1.05	16.18
Other	67	411	43.3	50.9	992	6.1	0.64	14.78

Source: U.S. Energy Information Administration, *Commercial Buildings Energy Consumption and Expenditures, 1992.*

No. 948. Commercial Buildings—Energy Consumption and Expenditures: 1992

[Covers buildings using one or more major fuel. Excludes industrial buildings, predominantly residential buildings, and buildings of less than 1,000 sq. ft. Based on a sample survey of building representatives and energy suppliers; therefore, subject to sampling variability. For characteristics of commercial buildings, see tables in section 25. For composition of regions, see table 27]

BUILDING CHARACTERISTIC	ALL BUILDINGS USING ANY MAJOR FUEL		CONSUMPTION (tril. Btu)			EXPENDITURES (mil. dol.)		
	Number (1,000)	Square feet (mil.)	Major fuel, total [1]	Electricity	Natural gas	Major fuel, total [1]	Electricity	Natural gas
All buildings	**4,615**	**66,538**	**5,803**	**2,609**	**2,487**	**72,599**	**57,619**	**10,679**
Region:								
Northeast	755	13,235	1,090	419	354	16,226	12,250	2,014
Midwest	1,141	16,909	1,688	622	858	17,204	12,745	3,258
South	1,874	23,979	1,888	1,002	760	22,843	19,097	2,998
West.	845	12,415	1,137	566	515	16,326	13,527	2,408
Year constructed:								
1900 or before	169	1,721	118	38	62	1,447	1,029	281
1901 to 1920	244	3,401	213	67	102	2,516	1,711	516
1921 to 1945	681	8,385	878	217	522	8,244	5,263	2,152
1946 to 1960	839	10,135	825	332	380	9,820	7,477	1,688
1961 to 1970	757	12,473	1,200	528	501	14,576	11,617	1,947
1974 to 1979	945	13,781	1,261	629	528	16,459	13,659	2,187
1980 to 1983	855	14,153	1,133	689	345	16,834	14,510	1,668
1984 to 1986	127	2,489	173	109	48	2,702	2,354	239
Principal activity within building:								
Assembly [2]	704	9,123	510	233	202	6,460	4,939	995
Education	301	8,470	637	235	291	7,389	5,526	1,271
Food sales/services.	390	2,248	584	251	320	7,200	5,609	1,483
Health care	63	1,763	403	138	189	3,733	2,640	662
Lodging.	154	2,891	463	189	193	5,459	4,030	929
Mercantile/services	1,270	12,399	892	444	381	12,907	10,583	1,899
Office	749	12,319	1,272	704	413	18,125	15,511	1,641
Public order and safety	24	1,652	52	(B)	9	811	743	43
Warehouse	685	11,179	590	253	259	6,750	5,386	939
Other	65	1,124	270	78	(B)	2,178	1,479	(B)
Vacant	210	3,371	131	47	61	1,585	1,172	290
Square footage:								
1,001 to 5,000	2,539	6,995	715	334	333	10,604	8,536	1,761
5,001 to 10,000	954	7,057	682	251	378	8,481	6,336	1,828
10,001 to 25,000	628	10,097	1,038	335	611	10,373	7,758	2,129
25,001 to 50,000	275	9,856	794	347	324	9,864	7,619	1,559
50,001 to 100,000.	114	7,926	642	308	255	8,483	6,806	1,184
100,001 to 200,000	70	9,658	640	347	206	8,413	6,935	893
200,001 to 500,000	25	7,678	711	361	215	8,457	6,847	742
500,001 and over	9	7,271	581	325	165	7,924	6,783	582

B Base figure too small to meet statistical standards for reliability of a derived figure.   [1] Includes fuel oil, propane, and purchased steam not shown separately.   [2] Includes public assembly, public order and safety, and religious worship.

Source: U.S. Energy Information Administration, *Commercial Buildings Energy Consumption and Expenditures, 1992.*

No. 949. Fossil Fuel Prices in Current and Constant (1987) Dollars: 1970 to 1993

[In cents per million British thermal units (Btu), except as indicated. All fuel prices taken as close to the point of production as possible. See text, section 19, for explanation of Btu conversions from mineral fuels]

FUEL	1970	1973	1975	1980	1985	1986	1987	1988	1989	1990	1991	1992	1993
CURRENT DOLLARS													
Composite [1]	31.7	39.8	82.1	204.2	251.2	165.3	170.0	153.3	167.1	184.3	167.0	165.8	165.1
Crude oil	54.8	67.1	132.2	372.2	415.3	215.7	265.5	216.9	273.4	345.3	285.2	275.7	245.5
Natural gas	15.4	20.1	40.2	144.8	225.7	174.8	150.2	152.4	152.7	154.6	148.0	156.8	177.5
Bituminous coal [2]	26.2	36.5	83.9	109.4	114.8	108.2	104.9	100.8	100.0	99.5	98.9	96.9	95.0
Anthracite coal	48.8	61.7	149.5	185.9	204.2	191.1	188.9	189.8	183.6	174.5	161.0	151.7	167.5
CONSTANT (1987) DOLLARS													
Composite [1]	90.1	96.4	166.9	284.8	266.1	170.6	170.0	147.5	154.0	162.7	141.9	136.9	132.9
Crude oil	155.7	162.5	268.7	519.1	439.9	222.6	265.5	208.8	252.0	304.8	242.3	227.7	197.7
Natural gas	43.8	48.7	81.7	202.0	239.1	180.4	150.2	146.7	140.7	136.5	125.7	129.5	142.9
Bituminous coal [2]	74.4	88.4	170.5	152.6	121.6	111.7	104.9	97.0	92.2	87.8	84.0	80.0	76.5
Anthracite coal	138.6	149.4	303.9	259.3	216.3	197.2	188.9	182.7	169.2	154.0	136.8	125.3	134.9
GDP implicit price deflator[3] (1987=100)	35.2	41.3	49.2	71.7	94.4	96.9	100.0	103.9	108.5	113.2	117.8	121.9	123.5

[1] Weighted by relative importance of individual fuels in total fuels production.   [2] Includes subbituminous and lignite.   [3] GDP=Gross domestic product; see text, section 15.

Source: U.S. Energy Information Administration, *Annual Energy Review*.

No. 950. World Energy Consumption, by Region and Energy Source: 1970 to 1992

[In tons of coal equivalent. Metric ton=1.1023 short tons. Kilogram=2.205 pounds. See text, section 30, for general comments about the data]

REGION AND ENERGY SOURCE	CONSUMPTION (mil. metric tons)				PER CAPITA (kilograms)				PERCENT DISTRIBUTION			
	1970	1980	1990	1992	1970	1980	1990	1992	1970	1980	1990	1992
World, total	**6,412**	**8,783**	**10,826**	**10,948**	**1,208**	**1,626**	**2,004**	**1,993**	**100.0**	**100.0**	**100.0**	**100.0**
North America [1]	2,486	2,825	3,196	3,267	5,949	6,667	7,543	7,495	38.8	32.2	29.5	29.8
United States	2,205	2,391	2,687	2,740	8,910	9,566	10,749	10,737	34.4	27.2	24.8	25.0
South America	142	247	313	330	490	841	1,064	1,083	2.2	2.8	2.9	3.0
Europe	1,709	2,230	2,346	3,797	2,963	3,854	4,056	5,218	26.7	25.4	21.7	34.7
Soviet Union	999	1,592	1,919	(2)	3,476	5,502	6,592	(2)	15.6	18.1	17.7	(2)
Asia	904	1,592	2,624	3,112	292	506	834	939	14.1	18.1	24.2	28.4
Oceania	72	107	149	154	2,753	3,993	5,597	5,601	1.1	1.2	1.4	1.4
Africa	101	191	279	288	(NA)	(NA)	434	423	1.6	2.2	2.6	2.6
Energy source:												
Solid fuels	2,143	2,650	3,238	3,213	586	595	612	586	33.5	30.8	29.9	29.3
Liquid fuels	2,802	3,806	4,000	3,982	770	855	756	727	44.0	44.2	36.9	36.4
Natural gas	1,289	1,838	2,539	2,664	351	413	480	486	20.1	21.5	23.5	24.3
Electricity	178	489	1,049	1,089	48	110	198	199	2.4	3.5	9.7	9.9

NA Not available.   [1] Includes Central America.   [2] Beginning 1992, Soviet Union included with Europe.

Source: Statistical Office of the United Nations, New York, NY, *Energy Statistics Yearbook*, annual (copyright).

No. 951. World Primary Energy Production, by Region and Type: 1973 to 1992

[In quadrillion Btu. Btu=British thermal units. For Btu conversion factors, see source]

REGION AND TYPE	1973	1975	1980	1985	1986	1987	1988	1989	1990	1991	1992
World, total	**244.8**	**245.0**	**286.6**	**302.1**	**312.1**	**319.6**	**332.1**	**339.6**	**344.0**	**340.8**	**343.1**
North America	73.3	71.1	80.5	84.1	82.7	84.1	86.2	86.2	88.2	89.1	88.8
United States	62.0	59.8	64.7	64.6	64.1	64.6	65.8	65.8	67.7	67.4	66.7
Central and South America	12.9	10.6	12.1	13.5	14.3	14.3	15.2	15.7	16.6	17.4	17.6
Western Europe	19.6	21.4	28.7	36.4	37.4	37.9	38.4	37.9	37.8	39.0	39.3
Eastern Europe and Soviet Union	51.4	55.9	69.3	74.5	77.4	79.4	81.8	81.5	79.1	70.8	67.0
Middle East	46.6	43.5	42.2	25.7	30.6	32.1	36.0	39.6	41.0	40.2	43.9
Africa	14.8	13.3	17.3	18.4	18.1	18.5	19.5	20.5	21.5	23.4	23.7
Far East and Oceania	26.2	29.3	36.5	49.5	51.6	53.2	54.9	58.3	59.9	60.9	62.8
Crude oil	117.8	111.6	127.6	115.4	120.2	121.0	125.8	127.8	129.3	128.6	129.2
Natural gas	43.2	43.9	52.8	60.6	61.9	64.9	68.1	70.6	72.0	74.0	74.3
Natural gas liquids	4.2	4.4	5.5	5.7	6.0	6.3	6.6	6.7	7.0	7.3	7.6
Coal	63.8	66.3	75.0	84.2	86.5	88.2	90.3	92.9	92.8	86.7	87.6
Hydroelectric power	13.5	15.0	18.2	20.7	21.1	21.3	22.0	21.8	22.5	22.9	22.9
Nuclear electric power	2.2	3.9	7.6	15.4	16.3	17.8	19.3	19.8	20.3	21.3	21.5

Source: U.S. Energy Information Administration, *International Energy Annual*.

No. 952. U.S. Foreign Trade in Selected Mineral Fuels: 1970 to 1994

[Minus sign (-) indicates an excess of imports over exports. See also *Historical Statistics, Colonial Times to 1970*, series M 100, 101, 127, 128, 140, 141, 178, and 181]

MINERAL FUEL	Unit	1970	1973	1975	1980	1985	1990	1991	1992	1993	1994
NATURAL GAS											
Imports	Bil. cu. ft.	821	1,033	953	985	950	1,532	1,773	2,138	2,350	2,558
Exports	Bil. cu. ft.	70	77	73	49	55	86	129	216	140	144
Net trade	Bil. cu. ft.	−751	−956	−880	−936	−894	−1,446	−1,644	−1,922	−2,210	−2,414
CRUDE OIL											
Imports [1]	Mil. bbl.	483	1,184	1,498	1,926	1,168	2,151	2,110	2,220	2,477	2,565
Exports	Mil. bbl.	5	1	2	105	75	40	42	32	36	36
Net trade	Mil. bbl.	−478	−1,183	−1,496	−1,821	−1,093	−2,112	−2,068	−2,188	−2,441	−2,529
PETROLEUM PRODUCTS											
Imports	Mil. bbl.	765	1,099	712	603	681	775	673	659	669	694
Exports	Mil. bbl.	89	84	74	94	211	273	323	314	330	308
Net trade	Mil. bbl.	−676	−1,015	−638	−509	−470	−502	−350	−345	−339	−387
COAL											
Imports	1,000 sh. tons	36	127	940	1,194	1,952	2,699	3,390	3,803	7,309	7,584
Exports	1,000 sh. tons	71,733	53,587	66,309	91,742	92,680	105,804	108,969	102,516	74,519	71,359
Net trade	1,000 sh. tons	71,697	53,460	65,369	90,548	90,728	103,105	105,579	98,713	67,210	63,775

[1] Beginning 1980, includes strategic petroleum reserve imports.

Source: U.S. Energy Information Administration, *Natural Gas Monthly, Petroleum Supply Monthly,* and *Monthly Energy Review.*

No. 953. Daily International Flow of Crude Oil, by Area: 1991

[In thousands of barrels per day]

EXPORTING AREA	Total [1]	IMPORTING AREA		Central and South America	Western Europe	Eastern Europe	Middle East and Africa	Japan	Other Far East and Oceania
		U.S.	Canada						
World, total	**28,406**	**5,782**	**551**	**1,641**	**10,245**	**834**	**1,143**	**4,180**	**4,030**
United States	116	(X)	5	[2]111	-	-	-	-	-
North America, except U.S.	2,121	1,502	15	58	346	-	32	157	11
Central and South America	1,842	927	35	615	208	-	-	9	48
Western Europe	2,939	183	348	11	2,374	-	23	-	-
Eastern Europe and U.S.S.R.	1,205	1	-	5	637	493	16	2	51
Middle East	12,947	1,770	89	682	3,567	246	731	3,034	2,828
Africa	4,969	1,160	59	147	3,101	95	323	11	73
Far East and Oceania	2,267	239	-	12	12	-	18	967	1,019

- Represents zero.   X Not applicable.   [1] Includes stocks at sea, exchanges, transshipments, and other statistical discrepancies not shown separately.   [2] Includes shipments to Puerto Rico and Virgin Islands.

Source: U.S. Energy Information Administration, *International Energy Annual.*

No. 954. Crude Oil Imports Into United States, by Country of Origin: 1970 to 1994

[In millions of barrels. Barrels contain 42 gallons]

COUNTRY OF ORIGIN	1970	1973	1975	1980	1985	1987	1988	1989	1990	1991	1992	1993	1994
Total	483	1,184	1,498	1,921	1,168	1,706	1,864	2,133	2,151	2,110	2,226	2,477	2,565
Canada	245	365	219	73	171	222	249	230	235	271	292	329	345
Mexico	-	(Z)	26	185	261	220	246	261	251	277	288	315	343
Norway	-	-	4	53	11	26	23	46	35	27	43	50	69
Trinidad-Tobago	(Z)	22	42	42	36	27	26	27	28	26	26	20	23
United Kingdom	-	-	(Z)	63	101	111	93	58	57	39	73	114	145
OPEC [1]	222	765	1,172	1,410	479	876	984	1,232	1,283	1,233	1,247	1,346	1,307
Algeria	2	44	96	166	31	42	21	22	23	16	9	9	9
Ecuador	-	17	21	6	20	8	12	29	14	19	23	28	(2)
Gabon	-	-	10	9	19	13	5	18	23	31	45	55	71
Indonesia	26	73	138	115	107	96	68	58	36	37	26	24	34
Iran	12	79	101	3	10	36	(Z)	-	-	12	-	-	-
Iraq	-	1	1	10	17	30	125	161	188	-	-	-	-
Kuwait	12	15	1	10	1	26	29	57	29	2	14	126	112
Libya	17	49	81	200	-	-	-	-	-	-	-	-	-
Nigeria	17	164	272	307	102	193	222	292	286	249	243	264	228
Qatar	-	3	7	8	-	-	-	1	1	-	-	-	-
Saudi Arabia	15	169	256	456	48	234	333	407	436	622	585	468	473
United Arab Emirates	23	26	43	63	13	20	8	8	3	1	-	4	4
Venezuela	98	126	144	57	112	178	160	181	243	244	302	369	376
Other	16	32	34	95	108	225	244	279	264	237	257	304	333

- Represents zero.   Z Less than 500,000 barrels.   [1] Organization of Petroleum Exporting Countries.   [2] On December 31, 1992, Ecuador withdrew as a member of OPEC. Effective January 1, 1994, imports from Ecuador appear under imports from "Other."

Source: 1970, U.S. Bureau of Mines, *Minerals Yearbooks, vol. I;* thereafter, U.S. Energy Information Administration, *Petroleum Supply Annual,* vol. I.

No. 955. Crude Oil and Refined Products—Summary: 1973 to 1994

[Barrels of 42 gallons. Data are averages]

YEAR	CRUDE OIL (1,000 bbl. per day)					REFINED OIL PRODUCTS (1,000 bbl. per day)			Total oil imports[2] (1,000 bbl. per day)	CRUDE OIL STOCKS [3] (mil. bbl.)	
	Input to refineries	Domestic production	Imports Total [1]	Strategic reserve	Exports	Domestic demand	Imports	Exports		Total	Strategic reserve
1973	12,431	9,208	3,244	(X)	2	17,308	3,012	229	6,256	242	(X)
1974	12,133	8,774	3,477	(X)	3	16,653	2,635	218	6,112	265	(X)
1975	12,442	8,375	4,105	(X)	6	16,322	1,951	204	6,056	271	(X)
1976	13,416	8,132	5,287	(X)	8	17,461	2,026	215	7,313	285	(X)
1977	14,602	8,245	6,615	21	50	18,431	2,193	193	8,807	348	7
1978	14,739	8,707	6,356	161	158	18,847	2,008	204	8,363	376	67
1979	14,648	8,552	6,519	67	235	18,513	1,937	236	8,456	430	91
1980	13,481	8,597	5,263	44	287	17,056	1,646	258	6,909	466	108
1981	12,470	8,572	4,396	256	228	16,058	1,599	367	5,996	594	230
1982	11,774	8,649	3,488	165	236	15,296	1,625	579	5,113	644	294
1983	11,685	8,688	3,329	234	164	15,231	1,722	575	5,051	723	379
1984	12,044	8,879	3,426	197	181	15,726	2,011	541	5,437	796	451
1985	12,002	8,971	3,201	118	204	15,726	1,866	577	5,067	814	493
1986	12,716	8,680	4,178	48	154	16,281	2,045	631	6,224	843	512
1987	12,854	8,349	4,674	73	151	16,665	2,004	613	6,678	890	541
1988	13,246	8,140	5,107	51	155	17,283	2,295	661	7,402	890	560
1989	13,401	7,613	5,843	56	142	17,325	2,217	717	8,061	921	580
1990	13,409	7,355	5,894	27	109	16,988	2,123	748	8,018	908	586
1991	13,301	7,417	5,782	-	116	16,714	1,844	885	7,627	893	569
1992	13,411	7,171	6,083	10	89	17,033	1,805	861	7,888	893	575
1993	13,613	6,847	6,787	15	98	17,237	1,833	904	8,620	922	587
1994	13,872	6,627	7,027	12	99	17,679	1,902	843	8,929	929	592

- Represents zero.   X Not applicable.   [1] Includes Strategic Petroleum Reserve.   [2] Crude oil (including Strategic Petroleum Reserve imports) plus refined products.   [3] End of year.

Source: U.S. Energy Information Administration, *Monthly Energy Review,* February 1995.

No. 956. Strategic Petroleum Reserve: 1977 to 1993

[Million barrels, except as noted. The Strategic Petroleum Reserve is a stock of petroleum maintained by the Federal Government for use during periods of major supply interruption]

YEAR	Crude oil imports	Domestic crude oil deliveries	STOCKS AT YEAR-END			Days of net petroleum imports [3]
			Quantity [1]	Percent of crude oil stocks [2]	Percent of total petroleum stocks	
1977	7.54	[4]0.37	7.46	2.1	0.6	1
1980	16.07	1.30	107.80	23.1	7.7	17
1985	43.12	0.17	493.32	60.6	32.5	115
1987	26.52	2.69	540.65	60.8	33.6	91
1988	18.76	0.01	559.52	62.9	35.0	85
1989	20.35	-	579.86	62.9	36.7	81
1990	9.77	-	585.69	64.5	36.1	82
1991	-	-	568.51	63.7	35.2	86
1992	3.59	2.60	574.72	64.5	36.1	83
1993	5.37	6.96	587.08	63.6	35.7	78

- Represents zero. [1] Stocks do not include imported quantities in transit to Strategic Petroleum Reserve terminals, pipeline fill, and above ground storage. [2] Including lease condensate stocks. [3] Derived by dividing end-of-year strategic petroleum reserve stocks by annual average daily net imports of all petroleum. Calculated prior to rounding. [4] The quantity of domestic fuel oil which was in storage prior to injection of foreign crude oil.

Source: U.S. Energy Information Administration, *Annual Energy Review.*

No. 957. World Petroleum Consumption, by Major Consuming Country: 1983 to 1993
[Million barrels per day]

REGION AND COUNTRY	1983	1985	1986	1987	1988	1989	1990	1991	1992	1993
World, total	**58.74**	**60.10**	**61.76**	**63.01**	**64.83**	**66.03**	**66.16**	**66.71**	**66.57**	**66.72**
North America, total	18.03	18.70	19.28	19.74	20.53	20.73	20.41	20.14	20.51	20.75
Canada	1.45	1.50	1.51	1.55	1.69	1.73	1.69	1.62	1.64	1.66
Mexico	1.35	1.47	1.49	1.52	1.55	1.66	1.73	1.80	1.83	1.84
United States	15.23	15.73	16.28	16.67	17.28	17.33	16.99	16.71	17.03	17.24
Central & South America, total . . .	3.19	3.19	3.41	3.52	3.57	3.58	3.60	3.65	3.74	3.89
Brazil	0.98	1.08	1.24	1.26	1.30	1.32	1.34	1.35	1.37	1.41
Western Europe, total	12.38	12.39	12.79	12.93	13.08	13.16	13.25	13.66	13.81	13.80
France	1.84	1.78	1.77	1.79	1.80	1.86	1.82	1.94	1.93	1.91
Germany	2.66	2.70	2.86	2.77	2.74	2.58	2.66	2.83	2.84	2.90
Italy	1.75	1.72	1.74	1.86	1.84	1.93	1.87	1.86	1.94	1.88
United Kingdom	1.53	1.63	1.65	1.60	1.70	1.74	1.75	1.80	1.80	1.80
Eastern Europe and former U.S.S.R.	10.47	10.46	10.46	10.51	10.38	10.19	9.73	9.43	7.85	6.81
Middle East, total	2.61	2.85	2.98	3.06	3.15	3.36	3.47	3.40	3.40	3.49
Africa, total	1.70	1.83	1.83	1.84	1.91	1.99	2.10	2.15	2.18	2.17
Far East & Oceania, total.	10.36	10.69	11.03	11.42	12.21	13.03	13.61	14.28	15.09	15.82
China	1.73	1.89	2.00	2.12	2.28	2.38	2.30	2.50	2.66	3.11
India	0.77	0.90	0.95	0.99	1.08	1.15	1.17	1.19	1.28	1.29
Japan	4.40	4.38	4.44	4.48	4.75	4.98	5.14	5.28	5.45	5.38

Source: U.S. Energy Information Administration, *Annual Energy Review* and *Monthly Energy Review,* monthly.

No. 958. Energy Producing Companies—Selected Financial and Investment Indicators: 1983 to 1993

[Based on data from major publicly-owned domestic crude oil producing companies which either had at least 1 percent of domestic production or reserves of oil, natural gas, coal, or uranium, or at least 1 percent of refining capacity or petroleum product sales. There were 25 companies in 1983 and 1993; 22 during 1984 through 1987; and 23 in 1988 to 1992]

ITEM	1983	1985	1986	1987	1988	1989	1990	1991	1992	1993
INCOME STATEMENT (bil. dol.)										
Operating revenues	511.0	492.5	378.5	417.4	419.8	433.6	510.4	469.3	472.8	448.1
Operating expenses	462.8	444.2	354.4	383.7	381.6	397.7	470.1	443.3	449.5	423.0
Operating income	48.2	48.3	24.0	33.7	38.2	35.9	40.2	26.0	23.3	25.1
Pretax income	47.4	43.6	20.6	25.0	34.3	32.3	37.5	25.1	22.5	(NA)
Net income	21.9	17.4	9.2	11.3	22.3	19.8	21.6	14.7	1.8	15.5
Funds from operations [1]	60.7	63.5	53.1	51.6	57.8	48.3	54.9	47.8	44.8	(NA)
BALANCE SHEET (bil. dol.)										
Net property, plant, and equipment	278.4	297.7	291.1	297.6	293.6	293.2	302.5	305.5	309.7	307.9
Net investment in place [2]	296.3	315.4	310.0	316.4	309.6	309.9	319.7	325.6	331.6	331.5
Total assets	421.8	438.4	427.0	443.6	437.8	434.5	457.2	447.1	453.6	451.3
RATIOS (percent)										
Net income to operating revenues	4.3	3.5	2.4	2.7	5.3	4.6	4.2	3.1	[3]0.4	3.5
Net income to total assets	5.2	4.0	2.2	2.5	5.1	4.6	4.7	3.3	0.4	3.4
Net income to stockholders' equity	11.4	10.5	5.6	6.8	13.5	12.3	12.9	8.8	1.1	9.6
Long-term debt to stockholders' equity [4] . . .	34.8	54.3	56.0	57.6	56.6	56.4	53.0	54.3	59.4	55.3
Long-term debt to total assets[4]	15.9	20.5	21.6	21.5	21.3	20.9	19.4	20.3	20.6	19.8

NA Not available. [1] The sum of net income, depreciation, depletion and amortization, deferred taxes, dry hole expenses, etc. [2] Composed of net property, plant and equipment plus investment, and advances to unconsolidated subsidiaries. [3] The implementation of the new "Financial Accounting Standard No. 106" greatly reduced the reported profitability of large publicly traded corporations. Net income without these accounting changes would have been $12.5 billion. [4] Long-term debt includes amounts applicable to capitalized leases.

Source: U.S. Energy Information Administration, *Performance Profiles of Major Energy Producers,* annual.

No. 959. Petroleum and Coal Products Corporations—Sales, Net Profit, and Profit Per Dollar of Sales: 1980 to 1993

[Represents SIC group 29. Profit rates are averages of quarterly figures at annual rates. Beginning 1986, excludes estimates for corporations with less than $250,000 in assets]

ITEM	Unit	1980	1983	1984	1985	1986	1987	1988	1989	1990	1991	1992	1993
Sales	Bil. dol. .	333.2	312.7	338.4	320.9	226.5	248.3	252.2	265.3	318.5	282.2	278.0	266.1
Net profit:													
Before income taxes	Bil. dol. .	39.1	27.1	24.5	17.7	9.8	14.2	27.3	23.7	23.3	12.2	2.0	15.0
After income taxes	Bil. dol. .	25.5	19.3	17.2	12.7	8.8	10.9	21.2	19.5	18.0	10.9	3.2	13.1
Depreciation[1]	Bil. dol. .	11.6	17.5	20.7	22.1	21.9	20.3	20.0	18.5	18.7	18.0	18.3	17.4
Profits per dollar of sales:													
Before income taxes	Cents . .	11.7	8.7	7.2	5.5	4.1	5.8	10.8	9.0	7.4	4.3	0.4	5.6
After income taxes	Cents . .	7.7	6.2	5.1	4.0	3.8	4.5	8.5	7.4	5.7	3.9	0.9	4.9
Profits on stockholders' equity:													
Before income taxes	Percent .	30.7	17.8	14.3	11.7	6.8	10.1	19.2	17.8	16.6	8.6	1.5	11.9
After income taxes	Percent .	20.0	12.7	10.0	8.5	6.1	7.7	14.9	14.6	12.8	7.7	2.4	10.3

[1] Includes depletion and accelerated amortization of emergency facilities.
Source: 1980, U.S. Federal Trade Commission; thereafter, U.S. Bureau of the Census, *Quarterly Financial Report for Manufacturing, Mining and Trade Corporations*.

No. 960. Major Petroleum Companies—Financial Data Summary: 1973 to 1993

[Data represent a composite of approximately 42 major worldwide petroleum companies aggregated on a consolidated, total company basis]

ITEM	1973	1975	1980	1985	1987	1988	1989	1990	1991	1992	1993
FINANCIAL DATA (bil. dol.)											
Net income	11.8	11.6	32.9	19.4	15.0	24.6	24.7	26.8	18.7	12.1	18.9
Depreciation, depletion, etc	10.5	11.3	32.5	53.0	45.0	34.3	33.7	38.7	36.5	43.3	36.6
Cash flow[1]	22.3	22.8	65.4	72.4	60.0	58.9	58.4	65.5	55.2	55.4	55.5
Dividends paid	4.0	4.7	9.3	12.0	12.4	14.0	16.0	15.9	16.3	16.5	15.5
Net internal funds available for investment or debt repayment [2]	18.3	18.1	56.1	60.4	47.6	44.9	42.4	49.6	38.9	38.9	40
Capital and exploratory expenditures . . .	16.3	26.9	62.1	58.3	50.1	62.4	55.1	59.6	61.5	53.6	51.8
Long-term capitalization	102.9	121.1	211.4	272.1	282.2	287.8	290.0	300.0	307.4	290.7	291.6
Long-term debt	22.5	28.9	49.8	93.5	88.4	88.5	91.4	90.4	95.9	94.0	91.5
Preferred stock	0.4	0.4	2.0	3.3	4.1	4.5	6.4	5.2	4.1	5.3	5.8
Common stock and retained earnings [3].	80.0	91.9	159.6	175.3	189.7	194.8	192.2	204.4	207.4	191.4	194.3
Excess of expenditures over cash income [4]	−2.0	8.9	6.0	−2.1	−2.5	17.5	12.7	10.0	22.6	14.7	11.8
RATIOS [5] (percent)											
Long-term debt to long-term capitalization	22.0	23.8	23.6	34.4	31.3	30.8	31.5	30.1	31.2	32.3	31.4
Net income to total average capital	12.0	10.0	17.0	7.0	4.6	8.6	8.3	9.1	6.2	4.1	6.5
Net income to average common equity . .	15.6	13.1	22.5	10.8	7.3	12.8	12.4	13.5	9.1	6.1	9.8

[1] Generally represents internally-generated funds from operations. Sum of net income and noncash charges such as depreciation, depletion, and amortization.   [2] Cash flow minus dividends paid.   [3] Includes common stock, capital surplus, and earned surplus accounts after adjustments.   [4] Capital and exploratory expenditures plus dividends paid minus cash flow.
[5] Represents approximate year-to-year comparisons because of changes in the makeup of the group due to mergers and other corporate changes.
Source: Carl H. Pforzheimer & Co., New York, NY, *Comparative Oil Company Statements, 1993-1992*, and earlier reports.

No. 961. Electric Utility Sales and Average Prices, by End-Use Sector: 1970 to 1993

[Prior to 1980, covers Class A and B privately-owned electric utilities; thereafter, Class A utilities whose electric operating revenues were $100 million or more during the previous year]

YEAR	SALES (bil. kWh)				AVERAGE PRICE OF ELECTRICITY SOLD (cents per kWh)							
					Current dollars				Constant (**1987**) dollars [2]			
	Total [1]	Resi-dential	Com-mer-cial	Indus-trial	Total [1]	Resi-dential	Com-mer-cial	Indus-trial	Total [1]	Resi-dential	Com-mer-cial	Indus-trial
1970	1,392	466	307	571	1.7	2.2	2.1	1.0	4.8	6.3	6.0	2.8
1973	1,713	579	388	686	2.0	2.5	2.4	1.3	4.8	6.1	5.8	3.1
1975	1,747	588	403	688	2.9	3.5	3.5	2.1	5.9	7.1	7.1	4.3
1980	2,094	717	488	815	4.7	5.4	5.5	3.7	6.6	7.5	7.7	5.2
1981	2,147	722	514	826	5.5	6.2	6.3	4.3	7.0	7.9	8.0	5.4
1982	2,086	730	526	745	6.1	6.9	6.9	5.0	7.3	8.2	8.2	6.0
1983	2,151	751	544	776	6.3	7.2	7.0	5.0	7.2	8.3	8.0	5.7
1984	2,286	780	583	838	6.3	7.2	7.1	4.8	6.9	7.9	7.8	5.3
1985	2,324	794	606	837	6.4	7.4	7.3	5.0	6.8	7.8	7.7	5.3
1986	2,369	819	631	831	6.4	7.4	7.2	4.9	6.6	7.6	7.4	5.1
1987	2,457	850	660	858	6.4	7.4	7.1	4.8	6.4	7.4	7.1	4.8
1988	2,578	893	699	896	6.4	7.5	7.0	4.7	6.2	7.2	6.7	4.5
1989	2,647	906	726	926	6.5	7.6	7.2	4.7	6.0	7.0	6.6	4.3
1990	2,713	924	751	946	6.6	7.8	7.3	4.7	5.8	6.9	6.4	4.1
1991	2,762	955	766	947	6.7	8.0	7.5	4.8	5.7	6.8	6.4	4.1
1992	2,763	936	761	973	6.8	8.2	7.7	4.8	5.6	6.8	6.4	4.0
1993	2,865	994	790	983	6.9	8.3	7.7	4.9	5.6	6.7	6.2	3.9

[1] Includes other sectors not shown separately.   [2] Based on the GDP implicit price deflator.
Source: U.S. Energy Information Administration, *Annual Energy Review*.

No. 962. Electric Utility Industry—Net Generation, Net Summer Capability, Generating Units, and Consumption of Fuels: 1970 to 1993

[Net Generation for **calendar years;** other data as of **December 31.** See also *Historical Statistics, Colonial Times to 1970,* series S 32-52, S 78-82, and S 86-107]

ITEM	Unit	1970	1975	1980	1985	1988	1989	1990	1991	1992	1993
NET GENERATION											
Total	Bil. kWh	1,532	1,918	2,286	2,470	2,704	2,784	2,808	2,825	2,797	2,883
Average annual change [1]	Percent	7.3	4.5	3.5	1.5	3.0	2.9	0.9	0.6	–1.0	3.0
Net generation, kWh per kW of net summer capability [2]	Rate	4,560	3,904	3,951	3,770	3,990	4,064	4,064	4,076	4,024	4,130
Investor owned	Bil. kWh	1,183	1,487	1,783	1,918	2,146	2,192	2,203	2,213	2,214	2,271
Percent of total utilities	Percent	77.2	77.5	78.0	77.7	79.4	78.7	78.4	78.4	79.2	78.8
Publicly owned	Bil. kWh	349	431	503	552	559	592	606	610	582	611
Municipal	Bil. kWh	71	82	87	74	97	100	98	97	94	103
Federal	Bil. kWh	186	221	235	233	201	224	235	241	225	232
Cooperatives and other	Bil. kWh	91	128	182	245	261	269	273	272	263	276
Source of energy:											
Coal [3]	Percent	46.0	44.6	51.0	57.2	57.4	56.2	55.5	54.9	56.3	56.9
Nuclear	Percent	1.4	9.0	11.0	15.5	19.5	19.0	20.5	21.7	22.1	21.2
Oil	Percent	12.0	15.1	10.8	4.1	5.5	5.7	4.2	3.9	3.2	3.5
Gas	Percent	24.3	15.6	15.1	11.8	9.3	9.6	9.4	9.4	9.4	9.0
Hydro	Percent	16.2	15.6	12.1	11.4	8.2	9.5	10.0	9.8	8.6	9.2
Type of prime mover: [4]											
Hydro [5]	Bil. kWh	248	300	276	281	223	265	280	276	239	265
Steam conventional [5]	Bil. kWh	1,240	1,414	1,726	1,778	1,921	1,950	1,919	1,905	1,906	1,973
Gas turbine and internal combustion	Bil. kWh	22	28	28	16	22	29	22	22	21	25
Steam nuclear	Bil. kWh	22	173	251	384	527	529	577	613	619	610
Other	Bil. kWh	1	3	6	11	12	11	11	10	10	10
NET SUMMER CAPABILITY											
Total [6]	Mil. kW	336	491	579	655	678	685	691	693	695	698
Average annual change [1]	Percent	7.2	7.6	3.3	2.5	1.1	1.1	0.9	0.3	0.3	0.4
Hydro	Mil. kW	64	78	82	89	90	91	91	92	93	94
Steam conventional [7]	Mil. kW	248	333	397	437	442	444	448	447	447	447
Gas turbine	Mil. kW	13	37	43	44	44	45	46	48	50	52
Steam nuclear	Mil. kW	7	37	52	79	95	98	100	100	99	99
Internal combustion	Mil. kW	4	5	5	5	5	5	5	5	5	5
Geothermal and other	Mil. kW	(Z)	1	1	2	2	2	2	2	2	2
NUMBER OF GENERATING UNITS											
Total [8]	Number	9,717	(NA)	11,084	(NA)	10,305	10,325	10,296	10,260	10,221	10,105
Hydro	Number	3,108	(NA)	3,275	(NA)	3,496	3,479	3,479	3,476	3,497	3,388
Steam conventional	Number	2,813	(NA)	2,862	(NA)	2,383	2,383	2,354	2,284	2,307	2,221
Gas turbine	Number	658	(NA)	1,447	(NA)	1,397	1,438	1,460	1,485	1,501	1,411
Steam nuclear	Number	16	(NA)	74	(NA)	108	110	111	111	109	109
Internal combustion	Number	3,118	(NA)	3,410	(NA)	2,872	2,889	2,847	2,803	2,807	2,976
CONSUMPTION OF FUELS											
Net generation by fuel [9]	Bil. kWh	1,284	1,618	2,010	2,189	2,481	2,519	2,525	2,539	2,548	2,608
Average annual change [1]	Percent	(NA)	4.6	4.3	1.7	4.2	1.5	0.2	0.6	0.4	2.3
Coal	Bil. kWh	704	853	1,162	1,402	1,541	1,554	1,560	1,551	1,576	1,639
Percent of total	Percent	54.8	52.7	57.8	64.0	62.1	61.7	61.7	(NA)	(NA)	(NA)
Petroleum	Bil. kWh	184	289	246	100	149	158	117	111	89	100
Gas	Bil. kWh	373	300	346	292	253	267	264	264	264	259
Nuclear	Bil. kWh	22	173	251	384	527	529	577	613	619	610
Fuel consumed:											
Total energy equivalent	Quad. Btu	13.40	15.19	18.57	18.79	20.12	20.54	20.32	20.06	19.99	20.71
Coal	Mil. sh. tons	320	406	569	694	758	767	774	772	780	814
Oil	Mil. bbl.	339	507	421	175	250	270	200	189	152	169
Gas	Bil. cu. ft	3,932	3,158	3,682	3,044	2,636	2,787	2,787	2,789	2,766	2,680

NA Not available.   Z Less than 0.5 million kW.   [1] Change from immediate prior year except for 1970, change from 1960. For explanation of average annual percent change, see Guide to Tabular Presentation.   [2] Net summer capability is the steady hourly output that generating equipment is expected to supply to system load, exclusive of auxiliary power as demonstrated by test at the time of summer peak demand.   [3] Includes small percentage (.5 percent) from wood and waste, geothermal, and petroleum coke.   [4] A prime mover is the engine, turbine, water wheel, or similar machine which drives an electric generator.   [5] Fossil fuels only.   [6] Includes wind, solar thermal, and photovoltaic, not shown separately.   [7] Includes fossil steam, wood, and waste.   [8] Each prime mover type in combination plants counted separately. Includes geothermal, wind, and solar, not shown separately.   [9] Includes small amounts of wood, waste, wind, geothermal, solar thermal, and photovoltaic.

Source: 1970, U.S. Federal Power Commission, *Electric Power Statistics,* and press releases; thereafter, U.S. Energy Information Administration, 1975 and 1980, *Power Production, Fuel Consumption, and Installed Capacity Data-Annual,* and unpublished data; thereafter, *Electric Power Annual, Annual Energy Review,* and unpublished data.

No. 963. Electric Utility Industry—Capability, Peak Load, and Capacity Margin: 1970 to 1993

[Excludes Alaska and Hawaii. Capability represents the maximum kilowatt output with all power sources available and with hydraulic equipment under actual water conditions, allowing for maintenance, emergency outages, and system operating requirements. Capacity margin is the difference between capability and peak load]

YEAR	CAPABILITY AT THE TIME OF— Summer peak load (1,000 kW) Amount	Change from prior year[2]	Winter peak load[1] (1,000 kW) Amount	Change from prior year[2]	NONCOINCIDENT PEAK LOAD Summer	Winter[1]	CAPACITY MARGIN Summer Amount (1,000 kW)	Percent of capability	Winter[1] Amount (1,000 kW)	Percent of capability
1970	326,900	26,600	339,050	27,600	274,650	248,550	52,250	16.0	90,500	26.7
1975	479,300	34,900	492,450	25,050	356,800	331,100	122,500	25.6	161,350	32.8
1978	545,700	29,700	561,550	23,950	408,050	383,100	137,650	25.2	178,450	31.8
1979 [3]	544,506	(X)	554,525	(X)	398,424	368,876	146,082	26.8	185,649	33.5
1980	558,237	13,731	572,195	17,670	427,058	384,567	131,179	23.5	187,628	32.8
1981	572,219	13,982	586,569	14,374	429,349	397,800	142,870	25.0	188,769	32.2
1982	586,142	13,923	598,066	11,497	415,618	373,985	170,524	29.1	224,081	37.5
1983	596,449	10,307	612,453	14,387	447,526	410,779	148,923	25.0	201,674	32.9
1984	604,240	7,791	622,125	9,672	451,150	436,374	153,090	25.3	185,751	29.9
1985	621,597	17,357	636,475	14,350	460,503	423,660	161,094	25.9	212,815	33.4
1986	633,291	11,694	646,721	10,246	476,320	422,857	156,971	24.8	223,864	34.6
1987	648,118	14,827	662,977	16,256	496,185	448,277	151,933	23.4	214,700	32.4
1988	661,580	13,462	676,940	13,963	529,460	466,533	132,120	20.0	210,407	31.1
1989	673,316	11,736	685,249	8,309	523,432	496,378	149,884	22.3	188,871	27.6
1990	685,091	11,775	696,757	11,508	545,537	484,014	139,554	20.4	212,743	30.5
1991	690,915	5,824	703,212	6,455	551,320	485,435	139,595	20.2	217,777	31.0
1992	695,436	4,521	707,752	4,540	548,707	492,983	146,729	21.1	214,769	30.3
1993	694,250	1,186	711,957	4,205	575,356	521,733	118,894	17.1	190,224	26.7

X Not applicable.   [1] 1970 is for the month of December.   [2] For 1970 and 1975, change from 1969 and 1974, respectively.
[3] Beginning 1979, data are not entirely comparable with prior years due to change in data source.

Source: Edison Electric Institute, Washington, DC, *Statistical Yearbook of the Electric Utility Industry,* annual.

No. 964. Electric Energy Sales, by Class of Service, 1970 to 1993, and by State, 1993

[In billions of kilowatt-hours]

REGION, DIVISION, AND STATE	Total[1]	Residential	Commercial	Industrial	REGION, DIVISION, AND STATE	Total[1]	Residential	Commercial	Industrial
1970	1,392.3	466.3	306.7	570.9	**South**	**1,220.3**	**459.5**	**296.7**	**424.2**
1973	1,712.9	579.2	388.3	686.1	**South Atlantic**	**582.4**	**236.5**	**167.5**	**159.9**
1975	1,747.1	588.1	403.0	687.7	Delaware	9.1	3.0	2.6	3.4
1980	2,094.4	717.5	488.2	815.1	Maryland	53.9	21.5	11.3	20.2
1985	2,309.5	791.0	609.0	824.5	Dist. of Columbia	10.4	1.6	5.4	3.0
1988	2,578.1	892.9	699.1	896.5	Virginia	81.4	32.5	22.7	17.4
1989	2,646.8	905.5	725.9	925.7	West Virginia	24.4	8.7	5.5	10.2
1990	2,712.6	924.0	751.0	945.5	North Carolina	99.8	37.7	26.7	33.5
1991	2,762.0	955.4	765.7	946.6	South Carolina	61.5	20.7	13.2	26.9
1992	2,763.3	935.9	761.3	972.7	Georgia	89.2	33.9	25.2	29.1
1993, total [2]	**2,861.5**	**994.8**	**794.6**	**977.2**	Florida	152.7	76.8	54.9	16.3
Northeast	**420.6**	**141.5**	**147.1**	**115.9**	**East South Central**	**247.8**	**85.3**	**32.9**	**124.6**
New England	**104.8**	**38.1**	**38.7**	**26.2**	Kentucky	68.1	19.2	9.8	36.3
Maine	12.0	3.9	2.9	5.0	Tennessee	79.8	30.2	5.2	43.5
New Hampshire	8.8	3.4	2.1	3.1	Alabama	65.1	22.6	11.3	30.5
Vermont	5.0	2.0	1.6	1.4	Mississippi	34.7	13.2	6.7	14.2
Massachusetts	45.3	15.8	18.9	9.6	**West South Central**	**390.0**	**137.8**	**96.3**	**139.7**
Rhode Island	6.5	2.4	2.5	1.4	Arkansas	31.7	11.8	6.7	12.6
Connecticut	27.2	10.6	10.7	5.6	Louisiana	67.8	22.4	14.4	28.4
Middle Atlantic	**315.8**	**103.4**	**108.5**	**89.7**	Oklahoma	40.5	15.9	10.8	11.7
New York	130.2	39.9	47.7	30.2	Texas	250.1	87.7	64.3	86.9
New Jersey	65.6	22.0	28.5	14.6	**West**	**529.8**	**173.1**	**169.0**	**168.7**
Pennsylvania	120.0	41.5	32.3	44.9	**Mountain**	**171.2**	**54.0**	**53.8**	**56.7**
Midwest	**690.9**	**220.7**	**181.7**	**268.4**	Montana	12.9	3.6	3.0	5.8
East North Central	**489.0**	**146.3**	**127.3**	**200.5**	Idaho	18.7	6.2	5.0	7.2
Ohio	148.6	42.0	33.3	68.8	Wyoming	11.9	1.9	2.5	7.4
Indiana	81.9	25.0	17.0	39.4	Colorado	33.0	10.7	14.4	7.0
Illinois	117.8	35.2	34.4	40.2	New Mexico	14.9	3.9	4.8	4.8
Michigan	87.6	26.8	28.9	30.6	Arizona	44.4	16.7	14.8	11.0
Wisconsin	53.2	17.4	13.7	21.4	Utah	16.9	4.7	5.0	6.2
West North Central	**201.8**	**74.4**	**54.4**	**67.9**	Nevada	18.5	6.3	4.3	7.2
Minnesota	49.2	15.6	8.5	24.4	**Pacific**	**358.6**	**119.1**	**115.2**	**112.0**
Iowa	32.1	11.1	7.3	12.5	Washington	90.5	30.9	19.5	36.6
Missouri	58.6	24.2	19.9	13.6	Oregon	44.6	16.7	12.2	15.0
North Dakota	7.4	3.2	1.8	1.9	California	210.5	67.4	79.1	56.2
South Dakota	6.9	3.1	1.6	1.8	Alaska	4.4	1.6	2.1	0.5
Nebraska	18.7	7.2	5.5	5.0	Hawaii	8.7	2.5	2.4	3.8
Kansas	28.8	10.0	9.8	8.7					

[1] Includes other service not shown separately.   [2] Preliminary.

Source: U.S. Energy Information Administration, *Electric Power Annual.*

No. 965. Electric Energy—Net Generation and Net Summer Capability, by State: 1990 to 1993

[Capacity as of **Dec. 31.** Covers utilities for public use]

DIVISION AND STATE	NET GENERATION (bil. kWh)				NET SUMMER CAPABILITY (mil. kW)		DIVISION AND STATE	NET GENERATION (bil. kWh)				NET SUMMER CAPABILITY (mil. kW)	
			1993							1993			
	1990	1992	Total	Per-cent from coal	1990	1993		1990	1992	Total	Per-cent from coal	1990	1993
U.S.	**2,808.2**	**2,797.2**	**2,882.5**	**56.9**	**690.5**	**700.0**	VA	47.2	49.0	52.2	47.4	13.7	14.1
							WV	77.4	72.3	71.1	99.2	14.4	14.4
N.E	**94.1**	**84.6**	**83.9**	**17.9**	**23.4**	**22.4**	NC	79.8	83.0	88.8	66.9	20.2	20.2
ME	9.1	8.3	8.1	-	2.4	2.4	SC	69.3	71.5	75.6	35.1	14.9	16.1
NH	10.8	13.5	14.6	22.4	2.6	2.5	GA	97.6	91.8	95.7	66.1	20.7	21.5
VT	5.0	4.7	4.3	-	1.1	1.1	FL	123.6	134.0	140.1	44.2	32.7	34.8
MA	36.5	32.8	28.2	34.9	9.9	9.5	**E.S.C.**	**246.9**	**264.0**	**274.0**	**79.2**	**59.5**	**58.5**
RI	0.6	0.1	0.1	-	0.3	0.2	KY	73.8	77.4	85.0	96.1	15.5	15.3
CT	32.2	25.2	28.7	6.6	7.1	6.8	TN	73.9	75.4	71.6	83.2	17.0	16.2
M.A.	**330.8**	**309.4**	**306.8**	**41.6**	**78.4**	**80.0**	AL	76.2	90.8	94.1	70.9	20.0	20.0
NY	128.7	112.2	106.3	20.5	31.2	32.7	MS	22.9	20.5	23.2	38.0	7.0	7.0
NJ	36.5	31.2	34.3	15.9	13.7	13.9	**W.S.C.**	**374.3**	**378.5**	**394.4**	**49.4**	**101.2**	**103.3**
PA	165.7	166.0	166.2	60.4	33.4	33.4	AR	37.1	37.4	38.0	47.4	9.6	9.7
E.N.C.	**485.8**	**487.6**	**513.8**	**73.3**	**113.1**	**114.2**	LA	58.2	55.2	59.4	32.6	16.8	16.9
OH	126.5	136.3	133.7	92.0	27.0	27.2	OK	45.1	45.9	48.8	59.4	12.8	12.9
IN	97.7	97.3	100.0	98.8	20.6	20.9	TX	234.0	240.0	248.2	51.7	62.0	63.9
IL	127.0	∆24.8	140.1	42.7	32.6	32.8	**Mountain**	**247.4**	**257.2**	**255.0**	**75.9**	**49.3**	**49.8**
MI	89.1	82.7	92.3	66.7	22.3	22.4	MT	25.7	25.5	23.4	58.7	4.9	4.9
WI	45.6	46.5	47.8	70.3	10.6	10.9	ID	8.6	6.3	9.0	-	2.3	2.3
W.N.C.	**218.4**	**212.8**	**218.4**	**75.9**	**54.2**	**54.8**	WY	39.4	41.9	40.2	97.9	5.8	5.9
MN	41.6	37.8	41.3	65.7	8.8	8.9	CO	31.3	31.9	32.7	93.2	6.6	6.6
IA	29.0	29.4	31.0	86.0	8.0	8.1	NM	28.5	27.7	28.4	89.9	5.0	5.1
MO	59.0	56.6	53.2	76.5	15.2	15.4	AZ	62.3	70.1	68.0	54.4	14.9	15.0
ND	26.8	28.6	28.5	94.9	4.5	4.5	UT	32.3	32.9	33.5	95.4	4.8	4.8
SD	6.4	6.2	5.3	50.3	2.7	2.7	NV	19.3	21.0	19.8	78.8	4.9	5.2
NE	21.6	22.4	22.7	64.9	5.5	5.5	**Pacific**	**276.7**	**255.7**	**261.0**	**4.8**	**82.1**	**82.0**
KS	33.9	31.8	36.4	73.6	9.6	9.7	WA	100.5	84.1	83.8	10.5	24.2	24.3
S.A.	**533.8**	**547.5**	**575.4**	**58.5**	**129.2**	**134.9**	OR	49.2	41.2	40.7	8.6	11.2	10.1
DE	7.1	6.3	8.3	62.4	2.0	2.3	CA	114.5	119.3	125.8	-	43.7	44.3
MD	31.5	39.6	43.5	57.2	9.8	10.7	AK	4.5	4.2	4.6	7.1	1.5	1.7
DC	0.4	0.1	0.2	-	0.8	0.8	HI	8.0	6.9	6.1	-	1.5	1.6

- Represents zero.

Source: U.S. Energy Information Administration, *Electric Power Annual, Electric Power Monthly,* December issues, and *Inventory of Power Plants in the United States,* annual.

No. 966. Nuclear Power Plants—Number of Units, Net Generation, and Net Summer Capability, by State: 1993

REGION, DIVISION, AND STATE	Number of units	NET GENERATION		NET SUMMER CAPABILITY		REGION, DIVISION, AND STATE	Number of units	NET GENERATION		NET SUMMER CAPABILITY	
		Total (mil. kWh)	Percent of total[1]	Total (mil. kW)	Percent of total[1]			Total (mil. kWh)	Percent of total[1]	Total (mil. kW)	Percent of total[1]
U.S.	**109**	**610,291**	**21.2**	**99.04**	**14.1**	**South**	**43**	**227,417**	**18.3**	**40.34**	**13.6**
Northeast	**27**	**155,451**	**39.8**	**23.79**	**23.2**	**S.A.**	**27**	**158,058**	**27.5**	**23.66**	**17.5**
N.E.	**8**	**44,299**	**52.8**	**6.39**	**28.6**	MD	2	12,301	28.3	1.66	15.5
ME	1	5,740	71.1	0.87	36.2	VA	4	22,689	43.5	3.35	23.8
NH	1	9,047	62.0	1.15	45.9	NC	5	23,759	26.8	4.64	23.0
VT	1	3,372	78.4	0.50	45.3	SC	7	46,189	61.1	6.36	39.5
MA	1	4,339	15.4	0.67	7.0	GA	4	27,233	28.4	3.83	17.8
CT	4	21,802	75.9	3.21	47.5	FL	5	25,887	18.5	3.83	11.0
M.A.	**19**	**111,152**	**36.2**	**17.39**	**21.7**	**E.S.C.**	**8**	**29,032**	**10.6**	**8.20**	**14.0**
NY	6	26,889	25.3	4.83	14.8	TN	2	3,305	4.6	2.22	13.7
NJ	4	24,932	72.7	3.85	27.8	AL	5	17,823	18.9	4.84	24.2
PA	9	59,331	35.7	8.71	26.1	MS	1	7,904	34.0	1.14	16.2
Midwest	**31**	**166,681**	**22.8**	**25.70**	**15.2**	**W.S.C**	**8**	**40,327**	**10.2**	**8.48**	**8.2**
E.N.C.	**23**	**128,374**	**25.0**	**20.11**	**17.6**	AR	2	13,522	35.5	1.69	17.5
OH	2	10,011	7.5	2.04	7.5	LA	2	14,398	24.3	2.01	11.9
IL	13	78,373	55.9	12.61	38.5	TX	4	12,407	5.0	4.78	7.5
MI	5	28,525	30.9	3.97	17.7	**West**	**8**	**60,743**	**11.8**	**9.22**	**7.0**
WI	3	11,465	24.0	1.50	13.7	**Mountain**	**3**	**22,049**	**8.6**	**3.81**	**7.6**
W.N.C	**8**	**38,307**	**17.5**	**5.58**	**10.2**	AZ	3	22,049	32.4	3.81	25.3
MN	3	11,986	29.1	1.55	17.5	**Pacfic**	**5**	**38,694**	**14.8**	**5.41**	**6.6**
IA	1	3,235	10.4	0.52	6.4	WA	1	7,135	8.5	1.10	4.5
MO	1	8,381	15.8	1.13	7.3	OR	-	−21	−0.1	-	-
NE	2	6,805	29.9	1.25	22.8	CA	4	31,581	25.1	4.31	9.7
KS	1	7,900	21.7	1.13	11.7						

- Represents zero. [1] For total capability and generation, see table 965.

Source: U.S. Energy Information Administration, *Electric Power Annual* and *Electric Power Monthly,* December issues.

No. 967. Nuclear Power Plants—Number, Capacity, and Generation: 1965 to 1993

ITEM	1965	1970	1975	1980	1985	1987	1988	1989	1990	1991	1992	1993
Operable generating units[1]	6	18	54	70	95	107	108	110	111	111	109	109
Net summer capability[1][2] (mil. kW)	0.8	7.0	37.3	51.8	79.4	93.6	94.7	98.2	99.6	99.6	99.0	99.1
Net generation (bil. kWh)	3.7	21.8	172.5	251.1	383.7	455.3	527.0	529.4	576.9	612.6	618.8	610.3
Percent of total electric utility generation	0.3	1.4	9.0	11.0	15.5	17.7	19.5	19.0	20.5	21.7	22.1	21.2
Capacity factor[3]	(NA)	(NA)	55.9	56.3	58.0	57.4	63.5	62.2	66.0	70.2	70.9	70.5

NA Not available.　[1] As of yearend.　[2] Net summer capability is the peak steady hourly output that generating equipment is expected to supply to system load, exclusive of auxiliary and other powerplant, as demonstrated by test at the time of summer peak demand.　[3] Weighted average of monthly capacity factors. Monthly factors are derived by dividing actual monthly generation by the maximum possible generation for the month (hours in month times net maximum dependable capacity).

Source: U.S. Energy Information Administration, *Annual Energy Review*.

No. 968. Commercial Nuclear Power Generation, by Country: 1970 to 1993

[Generation for **calendar years**; other data as of **December**]

COUNTRY	REACTORS				GROSS ELECTRICITY GENERATED (bil. kWh)				GROSS CAPACITY (1,000 kW)			
	1970	1980	1990	1993	1970	1980	1990	1993	1970	1980	1990	1993
Total	64	208	368	421	73.9	617.8	1,743.9	2,134.6	15,186	128,847	301,745	349,171
United States	15	74	112	110	23.2	265.2	606.4	641.2	5,211	56,529	105,998	105,276
Argentina	-	1	2	2	-	2.3	7.0	7.7	-	357	1,005	1,005
Belgium	1	3	7	7	0.3	12.5	42.7	41.9	11	1,744	5,740	5,843
Brazil	-	-	1	1	-	-	2.0	4.4	-	-	657	657
Bulgaria	(NA)	(NA)	(NA)	6	(NA)	(NA)	(NA)	14.0	(NA)	(NA)	(NA)	3,760
Canada	1	9	19	22	0.9	40.4	74.0	97.5	220	5,588	13,855	16,709
China: Taiwan	-	2	6	6	-	8.2	32.9	34.3	-	1,272	5,146	5,146
Czech Republic	(NA)	(NA)	(NA)	4	(NA)	(NA)	(NA)	3.6	(NA)	(NA)	(NA)	1,782
Finland	-	4	4	4	-	7.0	18.9	19.6	-	2,296	2,400	2,400
France	4	22	58	56	5.7	61.2	314.1	365.8	1,606	15,412	58,862	59,751
Germany	4	11	22	22	5.3	43.7	147.2	153.5	907	8,996	23,973	24,143
Great Britain	27	33	42	37	26.5	37.2	68.8	90.5	4,783	9,012	15,274	14,832
Hungary	-	-	4	4	-	-	13.6	13.8	-	-	1,760	1,840
India	2	4	6	9	2.2	2.9	6.0	6.2	400	860	1,330	2,020
Italy	3	4	2	-	3.3	2.2	-	-	631	1,490	1,132	-
Japan	3	22	40	46	3.3	81.0	191.9	243.5	828	15,117	31,645	37,351
Mexico	-	-	1	1	-	-	2.1	4.9	-	-	675	675
Netherlands	1	2	2	2	0.4	4.2	3.4	3.9	55	529	540	540
Pakistan	-	1	1	1	-	0.1	0.4	0.4	-	137	137	137
Russia	(NA)	(NA)	(NA)	29	(NA)	(NA)	(NA)	120.4	(NA)	(NA)	(NA)	21,316
Slovenia[1]	-	-	1	1	-	-	4.6	4.0	-	-	664	664
South Africa	-	-	2	2	-	-	8.9	7.7	-	-	1,930	1,930
South Korea	-	1	9	9	-	3.5	52.8	58.1	-	587	7,616	7,616
Spain	1	3	10	9	0.9	5.2	54.3	56.0	160	1,117	7,984	7,405
Sweden	1	8	12	12	(Z)	26.7	68.2	61.4	12	5,770	10,344	10,394
Switzerland	1	4	5	5	1.9	14.3	23.6	23.3	364	2,034	3,079	3,099
Ukraine	(NA)	(NA)	(NA)	14	(NA)	(NA)	(NA)	57.0	(NA)	(NA)	(NA)	12,880

- Represents zero.　NA Not available.　Z Less than 50 million kWh.　[1] Formerly Yugoslavia.

Source: McGraw-Hill, Inc., New York, NY, *Nucleonics Week*, March issues (copyright).

No. 969. Uranium Supply, Enrichment, and Discharged Commercial Reactor Fuel: 1980 to 1994

[Years ending **Dec. 31**, except as noted. For additional data on uranium, see section 25 on mining. For explanation of kilogram, see weights and measures]

ITEM	Unit	1980	1985	1988	1989	1990	1991	1992	1993	1994
URANIUM CONCENTRATE										
Production	Mil. lb	43.70	11.31	13.13	13.84	8.89	7.95	5.65	3.07	(NA)
Exports	Mil. lb	5.80	5.30	3.30	2.10	2.00	3.50	2.80	2.80	(NA)
Imports	Mil. lb	3.60	11.70	15.80	13.10	23.70	16.30	23.30	17.70	(NA)
Avg price of domestic purchases	Dol./lb	(NA)	31.43	26.15	19.56	15.70	13.66	13.45	(NA)	(NA)
ENRICHMENT [1]										
Enriched product [2]	Mil. Swu[3]	10.69	10.2	9.9	11.9	10.2	10.3	(NA)	(NA)	(NA)
For domestic customers	Mil. Swu[3]	6.89	6.0	6.3	7.6	6.8	6.7	(NA)	(NA)	(NA)
For foreign customers	Mil. Swu[3]	3.80	4.2	3.6	4.3	3.4	3.6	(NA)	(NA)	(NA)
Sales	Mil. dol	1,379	1,403	1,094	1,320	1,148	1,156	(NA)	(NA)	(NA)
DISCHARGED COMMERCIAL REACTOR FUEL [4]										
Annual discharge	Metric tons	1,193	1,330	1,672	1,914	2,028	1,794	2,255	2,082	1,925
Inventory, year-end [5]	Metric tons	6,434	12,481	17,178	19,092	21,120	22,914	25,169	27,251	29,176

NA Not available.　[1] Beginning 1985, represents fiscal years.　[2] Based on sales.　[3] Separative work units. The standard measure of enrichment services is based on operating tails assay in effect at the time the enriched product was placed in inventory.　[4] Uranium content. Source: Nuclear Assurance Corporation, Atlanta, GA.　[5] Reprocessed fuel not included as inventory.

Source: Except as noted, U.S. Energy Information Administration, *Annual Energy Review, Uranium Industry Annual* and unpublished data.

No. 970. Electric Utilities—Generation, Sales, Revenue, and Customers: 1970 to 1993

[Sales and revenue are to and from ultimate customers]

CLASS	Unit	1970	1975	1980	1985	1988	1989	1990	1991	1992	1993, prel.
Generation [1]	Bil. kWh	1,532	1,918	2,286	2,470	2,704	2,784	2,808	2,825	2,797	2,883
Sales [2]	Bil. kWh	1,391	1,733	2,126	2,306	2,554	2,621	2,684	2,737	2,735	2,836
Residential or domestic	Bil. kWh	448	586	734	793	886	899	916	949	929	990
Percent of total	Percent	32.2	33.8	34.5	34.4	34.7	34.3	34.1	34.7	34.0	34.9
Commercial [3]	Bil. kWh	313	418	524	606	698	716	739	753	756	782
Industrial [4]	Bil. kWh	573	662	794	820	882	913	932	935	949	964
Revenue [2]	Bil. dol	22.1	46.9	95.5	149.2	162.4	169.6	176.5	185.1	187.3	196.4
Residential or domestic	Bil. dol	9.4	18.8	37.6	58.6	66.4	68.8	71.7	76.4	76.4	82.3
Percent of total	Percent	42.7	40.1	39.4	39.3	40.9	40.5	40.7	41.2	40.8	41.9
Commercial [3]	Bil. dol	6.3	13.5	27.4	44.1	49.1	51.6	54.2	56.8	58.0	60.3
Industrial [4]	Bil. dol	5.4	12.7	27.3	41.4	41.6	43.7	44.9	45.9	46.8	47.5
Ultimate customers, Dec. 31 [2]	Million	72.5	81.8	92.7	101.6	106.4	108.5	110.1	111.4	113.1	114.8
Residential or domestic	Million	64.0	72.6	82.2	89.8	93.9	95.6	97.0	98.2	99.6	101.1
Commercial [3]	Million	7.9	8.6	9.7	10.9	11.6	12.0	12.1	12.3	12.5	12.7
Industrial [4]	Million	0.4	0.4	0.5	0.5	0.5	0.5	0.5	0.5	0.5	0.5
Avg. kWh used per customer	1,000	19.4	21.4	23.2	22.9	24.2	24.4	24.6	24.7	24.4	24.9
Residential	1,000	7.1	8.2	9.0	8.9	9.5	9.5	9.5	9.7	9.4	9.9
Commercial [3]	1,000	40.0	49.0	54.5	56.1	60.4	60.6	61.3	61.6	61.0	62.4
Avg. annual bill per customer	Dollar	307	579	1,040	1,482	1,536	1,576	1,614	1,670	1,667	1,726
Residential	Dollar	149	262	462	658	712	725	744	782	772	821
Commercial [3]	Dollar	804	1,580	2,848	4,080	4,256	4,363	4,494	4,646	4,681	4,814
Avg. revenue per kWh sold	Cents	1.59	2.70	4.49	6.47	6.36	6.47	6.57	6.76	6.85	6.93
Residential	Cents	2.10	3.21	5.12	7.39	7.49	7.65	7.83	8.05	8.22	8.32
Commercial [3]	Cents	2.01	3.23	5.22	7.27	7.04	7.20	7.33	7.55	7.67	7.72
Industrial [4]	Cents	0.95	1.92	3.44	5.04	4.71	4.79	4.81	4.91	4.93	4.93

[1] Source: 1970 and 1975, U.S. Federal Power Commission; thereafter, U.S. Energy Information Administration, *Monthly Energy Review*, monthly. [2] Includes other types not shown separately. [3] Small light and power. [4] Large light and power.
Source: Except as noted, Edison Electric Institute, Washington, DC, *Statistical Yearbook of the Electric Utility Industry*, annual.

No. 971. Major Investor-Owned Electric Utilities—Balance Sheet and Income Account of Privately Owned Companies: 1982 to 1993

[In billions of dollars. As of Dec. 31. As of 1990, covers approximately 180 investor-owned electric utilities that during each of the last 3 years met any one or more of the following conditions — 1 mil. megawatthours of total sales; 100 megawatthours of sales for resale, 500 megawatthours of gross interchange out, and 500 megawatthours of wheeling for other. See also *Historical Statistics, Colonial Times to 1970*, series S 133-146 and V 197-212]

ITEM	1982	1985	1986	1987	1988	1989	1990	1991	1992	1993
COMPOSITE BALANCE SHEET										
Total assets and other debits	315.0	404.7	426.1	446.3	454.3	465.7	477.9	487.5	506.4	566.6
Total electric utility plant	321.2	396.9	419.5	434.6	449.4	462.4	480.6	497.9	518.8	537.3
Electric depreciation and amortization	67.6	85.1	93.9	103.2	113.5	125.0	135.7	148.3	160.5	173.4
Net electric utility plant	253.6	311.8	325.6	331.4	335.9	337.5	344.9	349.6	358.3	363.8
Total other utility plant	16.7	19.9	21.2	23.1	24.6	26.3	28.5	31.0	33.4	36.4
Other utility depreciation and amortization	5.3	6.5	7.2	7.8	8.5	9.2	10.0	10.8	11.7	12.4
Net other utility plant	11.4	13.4	14.0	15.2	16.1	17.1	18.6	20.2	21.7	24.0
Total all utility plant	337.9	431.1	455.9	475.7	493.0	507.9	528.7	548.4	571.9	593.6
All utility plant depreciation and amortization	72.9	97.4	107.7	118.7	131.3	144.6	157.4	171.7	185.1	199.8
Net all utility plant	265.0	333.8	348.2	357.0	361.6	363.2	371.3	376.8	386.9	393.8
Other property and investments	9.1	12.1	13.5	15.6	15.2	16.1	17.7	17.4	18.0	20.1
Current and accrued assets	31.7	39.4	38.4	40.9	39.1	41.5	41.5	43.4	43.4	42.4
Deferred debits	9.3	19.4	26.1	32.9	38.3	44.8	47.3	50.0	58.0	110.3
Liabilities and other credits	315.0	404.7	426.1	446.3	454.3	465.7	477.9	487.5	506.4	566.6
Capital stock [1]	70.3	82.8	81.6	79.9	80.7	82.9	83.2	83.6	86.1	87.1
Other paid-in capital [2]	27.7	36.3	38.4	40.3	40.4	39.1	40.5	42.9	44.7	47.2
Retained earnings	27.9	41.1	46.0	48.0	47.1	47.7	48.1	49.0	49.7	49.9
Subsidiary earnings	1.6	2.2	2.3	2.6	2.5	2.8	2.9	3.0	2.7	2.9
Long-term debt	124.0	152.7	157.2	158.4	160.7	162.6	167.9	171.9	174.1	174.9
Current and accrued liabilities	28.6	32.0	34.0	39.3	38.4	42.0	44.3	43.4	45.6	48.9
Deferred credits and operating reserves [3]	15.1	20.9	22.4	25.6	28.1	28.5	28.8	29.2	31.1	40.9
Deferred income taxes as deferred credits	19.4	32.7	39.6	45.9	50.2	53.3	56.5	59.2	65.0	105.0
COMPOSITE INCOME ACCOUNTS										
Electric operating revenues	109.3	135.3	136.3	138.5	143.9	150.9	157.3	166.8	169.5	176.4
Electric operating expenses	91.1	111.1	110.2	111.6	115.3	121.6	127.9	135.9	139.0	146.1
Net electric utility operating income	18.1	24.1	26.1	27.0	28.6	29.4	29.4	30.9	30.5	30.2
Other than electric utility operating income	0.9	1.2	1.1	1.1	1.2	1.2	1.1	1.2	1.3	1.5
Net utility operating income	19.1	25.3	27.2	28.1	29.8	30.6	30.5	32.1	31.8	31.7
Total other income	5.3	7.4	7.2	6.6	5.0	5.2	4.1	3.9	2.9	2.8
Total income [4]	24.4	32.7	34.4	34.6	34.8	35.8	34.6	36.0	34.7	34.6
Income deductions [5]	9.4	14.0	14.0	15.6	18.8	18.5	17.7	19.1	16.3	16.7
Net income	15.0	18.7	20.4	19.0	16.0	17.3	16.9	16.9	18.4	17.9

[1] Composed of Common Stock Issued and Preferred Stock Issued. [2] Composed of Capital Stock Subscribed, Liability and Premium and Other Paid-in Capital. [3] Composed of Total Deferred Credits less Accumulated Deferred Income Taxes as Deferred Credits. [4] Composed of Net Utility Operating Income plus Total Other Income. [5] Composed of the difference between Total Income less Net Income.
Source: U.S. Energy Information Administration, 1982, *Financial Statistics of Selected Electric Utilities,* annual; thereafter, *Financial Statistics of Major U.S. Investor-Owned Electric Utilities,* annual.

No. 972. Nonutility Electric Power Producers—Summary, by Type of Fuel: 1989 to 1993

TYPE OF FUEL	INSTALLED CAPACITY OF 5 MEGAWATT OR MORE					INSTALLED CAPACITY OF 1 MEGAWATT OR MORE	
	1989	1990	1991	1992	1993	1992	1993
Installed capacity (megawatts) ...	**36,645**	**42,869**	**48,171**	**55,163**	**59,055**	**56,814**	**60,778**
Coal [1]	6,229	6,712	7,291	8,443	9,712	8,503	9,772
Petroleum [2]	917	811	1,207	1,579	1,869	1,730	2,043
Natural gas [3]	13,999	16,682	20,259	21,104	23,009	21,542	23,463
Petroleum/natural gas (combined).	4,439	6,167	5,049	8,354	8,377	8,478	8,505
Hydroelectric	1,386	1,477	1,587	2,133	2,173	2,684	2,741
Geothermal	944	1,031	1,048	1,243	1,307	1,254	1,318
Solar	200	360	360	360	360	360	360
Wind	1,339	1,405	1,652	1,786	1,775	1,822	1,813
Wood [4]	5,254	5,786	6,580	6,735	6,983	6,805	7,046
Waste [5]	1,742	2,230	2,627	2,805	2,910	3,006	3,131
Nuclear [6]	20	20	20	20	20	20	20
Other [7]	176	187	491	602	562	611	566
Gross generation (mil. kWh)	**187,356**	**217,241**	**248,448**	**289,856**	**318,843**	**296,001**	**325,226**
Coal [1]	31,511	32,131	40,587	47,160	53,166	47,363	53,367
Petroleum [2]	5,742	7,330	7,814	10,692	13,089	10,963	13,364
Natural gas [3]	98,875	116,706	131,340	156,317	171,765	158,798	174,282
Hydroelectric	5,931	6,235	6,243	7,611	9,583	9,446	11,511
Geothermal	5,046	6,872	7,651	8,533	9,704	8,578	9,749
Solar	489	663	779	746	897	746	897
Wind	1,833	2,251	2,606	2,872	2,999	2,916	3,052
Wood [4]	27,835	30,812	33,785	36,024	37,206	36,255	37,421
Waste [5]	8,296	11,415	13,956	16,330	17,187	17,352	18,325
Nuclear [6]	49	116	80	67	78	67	78
Other [7]	1,750	2,710	3,609	3,504	3,169	3,516	3,181

[1] Includes coal, anthracite, culm and coal waste. [2] Includes petroleum, petroleum coke, diesel, kerosene, and petroleum sludge and tar. [3] Includes natural gas, butane, ethane, propane, waste heat and waste gases. [4] Includes wood, wood waste, peat, wood liquors, railroad ties, pitch and wood sludge. [5] Includes municipal solid waste, agricultural waste, straw, tires, landfill gases and other waste. [6] Nuclear reactor and generator at Argonne National Laboratory used primarily for research and development in testing reactor fuels as well as for training. The generation from the unit is used for internal consumption. [7] Includes hydrogen, sulfur, batteries, chemicals, and spent sulfite liquor. Data previously published for other energy sources in 1989 and 1990 have been reclassified and are included in the category that best reflects its characteristics.
Source: Energy Information Administration, *Electric Power Annual.*

No. 973. Water Power—Developed and Undeveloped Capacity, by Division: 1950 to 1993

[**In millions of kilowatts.** As of **Dec. 31.** Excludes Alaska and Hawaii for 1950 and all capacity of reversible equipment at pumped storage projects. Also excludes capacity precluded from development due to wild and scenic river legislation. For composition of divisions, see table 27. See also *Historical Statistics, Colonial Times to 1970,* series S 160-175]

DIVISION	DEVELOPED INSTALLED CAPACITY							ESTIMATED UNDEVELOPED CAPACITY						
	1950	1960	1970	1980	1990	1992	1993	1950	1960	1970	1980	1990	1992	1993
United States	**18.7**	**33.2**	**52.0**	**64.4**	**73.0**	**74.1**	**73.8**	**87.6**	**114.2**	**128.0**	**129.9**	**73.9**	**73.6**	**73.6**
New England	1.2	1.5	1.5	1.5	1.9	1.9	2.0	3.3	2.9	3.3	4.7	4.4	4.4	4.4
Middle Atlantic	1.7	2.5	4.3	4.3	4.9	4.9	4.9	6.6	7.6	4.5	5.1	5.1	4.9	4.9
East North Central	0.9	0.9	0.9	0.9	1.1	1.2	1.2	2.3	3.0	1.6	2.0	1.7	1.7	1.7
West North Central	0.6	1.6	2.7	2.8	3.1	3.1	3.1	5.8	6.4	4.4	3.4	3.1	3.1	3.1
South Atlantic	2.8	3.8	5.3	5.9	6.7	6.7	6.7	8.2	8.4	9.6	9.6	7.0	7.2	7.2
East South Central	2.7	3.8	5.2	5.6	5.9	5.9	5.9	4.7	4.6	3.8	3.3	2.4	2.4	2.4
West South Central	0.5	0.9	1.9	2.3	2.7	2.7	2.7	3.6	3.9	3.3	4.7	4.6	4.6	4.6
Mountain	2.3	4.6	6.2	7.4	9.2	9.5	9.5	23.4	23.6	26.7	34.2	19.4	19.1	19.1
Pacific	6.0	13.6	23.9	33.7	37.5	38.2	37.8	29.8	53.8	70.9	62.9	26.2	26.2	26.2

Source: U.S. Federal Energy Regulatory Commission (formerly U.S. Federal Power Commission), *Hydroelectric Power Resources of the United States, Developed and Undeveloped,* January 1, 1988; and unpublished data.

No. 974. Solar Collector Shipments, by Type, End Use, and Market Sector: 1980 to 1993

[**In thousands of square feet, except number of manufacturers.** Solar collector is a device for intercepting sunlight, converting the light to heat, and carrying the heat to where it will be either used or stored. 1985 data are not available]

YEAR	Number of manufac-turers	Total ship-ments	COLLECTOR TYPE		END USE			MARKET SECTOR		
			Low temperature	Medium temperature, special, other	Pool heating	Hot water	Space heating	Residential	Commercial	Industrial
1980	233	19,398	12,233	7,165	12,029	4,790	1,688	16,077	2,417	488
1981	203	20,133	8,677	11,456	9,781	7,204	2,017	15,773	2,561	1,518
1982	265	18,621	7,476	11,145	7,035	7,444	2,367	13,729	3,789	560
1983	203	16,828	4,853	11,975	4,839	9,323	2,082	11,780	3,039	1,665
1984 [2]	225	17,191	4,479	11,939	4,427	8,930	2,370	13,980	2,091	289
1986 [2]	98	9,360	3,751	1,111	3,494	1,181	127	4,131	703	13
1987 [2]	59	7,269	3,157	957	3,111	964	23	3,775	305	11
1988 [2]	51	8,174	3,326	732	3,304	726	7	3,796	255	7
1989 [2]	44	11,482	4,283	1,989	4,688	1,374	205	5,804	424	42
1990	51	11,409	3,645	2,527	5,016	1,091	2	5,835	294	22
1991	48	6,574	5,585	989	5,535	989	24	6,322	225	13
1992	45	7,086	6,187	897	6,210	801	35	6,832	204	27
1993	41	6,968	6,025	931	6,040	880	15	6,694	215	31

[1] Includes high temperature collectors, end uses such as process heating, and utility and other market sectors not shown separately. [2] Declines between 1984 and 1989 are primarily due to the expiration of the Federal energy tax credit and industry consolidation.
Source: U.S. Energy Information Administration, *Solar Collector Manufacturing Activity,* annual.

No. 975. Renewable Energy Consumption Estimates, by Type: 1990 to 1992

[Renewable energy is obtained from sources that are essentially inexhaustible unlike fossil fuels of which there is a finite supply]

SOURCE AND SECTOR	QUANTITY (quadrillion Btu)			PERCENT CHANGE	
	1990	1991	1992	1990-91	1991-92
SOURCES					
Total	**6.01**	**6.20**	**6.04**	**3.2**	**-2.6**
Consumption for electricity	3.77	4.01	3.77	6.4	-6.0
Electric utilities	3.13	3.09	2.70	-1.3	-12.6
Hydroelectric power	2.93	2.90	2.51	-1.0	-13.4
Geothermal energy	0.18	0.17	0.17	-5.6	0.0
Biofuels [1]	0.02	0.02	0.02	0.0	0.0
Wind energy [2]	(Z)	(Z)	(Z)	(X)	(X)
Nonutility power generators	0.62	0.69	0.78	11.3	13.0
Hydroelectric power	0.08	0.08	0.10	1.2	19.0
Geothermal, solar, and wind energy	0.10	0.11	0.13	10.0	18.2
Biofuels [1]	0.44	0.49	0.55	13.0	11.3
Net imported electricity	0.02	0.23	0.29	1,050.0	26.1
Consumption for other uses [3]	2.23	2.19	2.27	-1.8	3.7
Biofuels [1]	2.17	2.13	2.21	-1.8	3.8
Solar and photovoltaic energy	0.06	0.06	0.06	0.0	0.0
SECTORS					
Total	**6.01**	**6.20**	**6.04**	**3.2**	**-2.6**
Residential and commercial	0.64	0.67	0.71	4.7	6.0
Industrial	2.13	2.14	2.26	0.5	5.6
Transportation	0.08	0.07	0.08	-12.5	14.3
Electric utilities	3.15	3.32	3.00	5.4	-9.6

Z Less than 0.005 quadrillion Btu.   X Not applicable.   [1] Biofuels are fuelwood, wood byproducts, waste wood, municipal solid waste, manufacturing process waste, and alcohol fuels.   [2] Also includes photovoltaic and solar thermal energy.   [3] Included are nonutility thermal energy uses, such as space heating and industrial process heat production. Excluded are estimates for mechanical energy, such as shaft power from dams, wind machines, and solar-powered motors and activators.
Source: U.S. Energy Information Administration, *Annual Energy Review.*

No. 976. Privately Owned Gas Utility Industry—Balance Sheet and Income Account: 1980 to 1993

[**In millions of dollars.** The gas utility industry consists of pipeline and distribution companies. Excludes operations of companies distributing gas in bottles or tanks. See also *Historical Statistics, Colonial Times to 1970,* series S 205-218]

ITEM	1980	1985	1987	1988	1989	1990	1991	1992	1993
COMPOSITE BALANCE SHEET									
Assets, total [1]	**75,851**	**104,478**	**109,390**	**121,667**	**123,820**	**121,686**	**124,120**	**129,400**	**131,508**
Total utility plant	67,071	88,121	93,540	99,933	106,017	112,863	119,772	129,272	131,377
Depreciation and amortization	*26,162*	*36,377*	*41,162*	*44,423*	*47,054*	*49,483*	*52,400*	*57,005*	*58,738*
Utility plant (net)	40,909	51,744	52,378	55,510	58,963	63,380	67,372	72,267	72,640
Investment and fund accounts [1]	15,530	23,871	25,660	31,552	28,111	23,872	22,883	21,883	23,218
Current and accrued assets	17,243	24,771	21,025	23,402	24,836	23,268	23,023	23,783	20,560
Deferred debits [2]	2,169	4,092	8,633	9,658	10,364	9,576	9,277	9,776	13,142
Liabilities, total [1]	**75,851**	**104,478**	**109,390**	**121,667**	**123,820**	**121,686**	**124,120**	**129,400**	**131,508**
Capitalization, total [1]	51,382	65,799	66,312	69,875	74,753	74,958	75,463	81,183	80,000
Capital stock [1]	29,315	39,517	38,212	39,898	43,889	43,810	43,435	46,318	47,547
Long-term debts	22,067	26,282	28,100	29,977	30,864	31,148	32,028	34,865	32,441
Current and accrued liabilities	18,119	26,125	26,664	33,735	31,005	29,550	28,128	26,438	26,127
Deferred income taxes [3]	4,149	7,769	9,901	10,685	11,292	11,360	10,527	10,952	12,889
Other liabilities and credits	2,201	4,785	6,513	7,372	6,770	5,818	10,002	10,827	12,494
COMPOSITE INCOME ACCOUNT									
Operating revenues, total	**85,918**	**103,945**	**69,566**	**69,754**	**70,363**	**66,027**	**63,922**	**66,405**	**70,420**
Operating expenses [4]	*81,789*	*98,320*	*64,409*	*64,696*	*64,262*	*60,137*	*59,165*	*60,042*	*63,326*
Operation and maintenance	74,508	88,572	56,054	57,032	55,990	51,627	50,867	48,054	50,752
Federal, State, and local taxes	4,847	6,590	5,179	4,241	4,843	4,957	4,446	6,031	6,221
Operating income	4,129	5,625	5,157	5,058	6,101	5,890	4,756	6,363	7,094
Utility operating income	4,471	6,030	5,452	5,202	6,274	6,077	4,962	6,552	7,292
Income before interest charges [1]	6,929	7,636	6,845	7,472	8,764	8,081	5,530	7,223	8,850
Net income [1]	4,194	3,785	2,971	3,352	4,641	4,410	1,894	3,750	5,610
Dividends	2,564	4,060	3,453	3,151	3,113	3,191	4,341	3,889	3,241

[1] Beginning 1980, not comparable with earlier years due to Federal Power Commission ruling requiring adoption of the equity method in reporting earnings of subsidiaries.   [2] Includes capital stock discount and expense and reacquired securities.   [3] Includes reserves for deferred income taxes.   [4] Includes expenses not shown separately.
Source: American Gas Association, Arlington, VA, *Gas Facts,* annual, (copyright).

No. 977. Gas Utility Industry—Summary: 1970 to 1993

[Covers natural, manufactured, mixed, and liquid petroleum gas. Based on questionnaire mailed to all privately and municipally owned gas utilities in United States, except those with annual revenues less than $25,000. See also *Historical Statistics, Colonial Times to 1970*, series S 190-204]

ITEM	Unit	1970	1975	1980	1985	1988	1989	1990	1991	1992	1993
Customers [1]	1,000	41,482	44,555	47,223	49,971	52,422	53,356	54,261	55,174	56,132	57,759
Residential	1,000	38,097	40,950	43,489	45,929	48,133	48,980	49,802	50,634	51,525	52,770
Commercial	1,000	3,131	3,367	3,498	3,816	4,069	4,161	4,246	4,322	4,397	4,777
Industrial and other	1,000	199	184	187	179	168	168	166	168	165	160
Sales [2]	Tril. Btu	16,044	14,863	15,413	12,616	10,705	10,551	9,842	9,605	9,906	10,415
Residential	Tril. Btu	4,923	4,991	4,826	4,513	4,695	4,798	4,468	4,550	4,694	5,097
Percent of total	Percent	30.7	33.6	31.3	35.8	43.9	45.5	45.4	47.4	47.4	48.9
Commercial	Tril. Btu	2,007	2,387	2,453	2,338	2,306	2,322	2,192	2,198	2,209	2,451
Industrial	Tril. Btu	8,439	6,837	7,957	5,635	3,544	3,243	3,010	2,631	2,772	2,677
Other	Tril. Btu	674	648	177	130	160	188	171	226	231	189
Revenues [2]	Mil. dol	10,283	19,101	48,303	63,293	46,162	47,493	45,153	44,647	46,178	51,787
Residential	Mil. dol	5,207	8,445	17,432	26,864	24,828	26,172	25,000	25,729	26,702	29,959
Percent of total	Percent	50.6	44.2	36.1	42.4	53.8	55.1	55.4	57.6	57.8	57.9
Commercial	Mil. dol	1,620	3,303	8,183	12,722	10,681	11,074	10,604	10,669	10,865	12,337
Industrial	Mil. dol	3,181	6,745	22,215	23,086	10,113	9,666	8,996	7,576	7,913	8,039
Other	Mil. dol	274	608	473	621	538	581	553	674	698	1,452
Prices per mil. Btu [3]	Dollars	0.64	1.29	3.13	5.02	4.31	4.50	4.59	4.65	4.66	4.90
Residential	Dollars	1.06	1.69	3.61	5.95	5.29	5.45	5.60	5.66	5.69	5.87
Commercial	Dollars	0.81	1.38	3.34	5.44	4.63	4.77	4.84	4.85	4.92	5.03
Industrial	Dollars	0.38	0.99	2.79	4.10	2.85	2.98	2.99	2.88	2.85	3.07
Gas mains mileage	1,000	913	980	1,052	1,119	1,169	1,185	1,207	1,225	1,254	1,264
Field and gathering	1,000	66	69	84	94	92	91	90	86	86	77
Transmission	1,000	252	263	266	271	276	276	280	282	285	272
Distribution	1,000	595	648	702	754	801	818	837	857	883	914
Construction expenditures [4]	Mil. dol	2,507	2,466	5,350	5,671	6,166	7,341	7,899	9,036	11,068	9,357
Transmission	Mil. dol	1,019	590	1,583	1,562	1,568	2,081	2,886	3,656	5,739	3,336
Distribution	Mil. dol	913	910	1,869	2,577	3,389	3,980	3,714	3,842	3,867	4,366
Production and storage	Mil. dol	203	555	1,150	790	268	276	309	430	349	266

[1] Annual average.　[2] Excludes sales for resale.　[3] For definition, see text, section 19.　[4] Includes general.

Source: American Gas Association, Arlington, VA, *Gas Facts*, annual (copyright).

No. 978. Gas Utility Industry—Customers, Sales, and Revenues, by State: 1993

[See headnote, table 977. For definition of Btu, see text, section 19]

REGION, DIVISION, AND STATE	CUSTOMERS[1] (1,000) Total[2]	Resi-dential	SALES[3] (tril. Btu) Total[2]	Resi-dential	REVENUES[3] (mil. dol.) Total[2]	Resi-dential	REGION, DIVISION, AND STATE	CUSTOMERS[1] (1,000) Total[2]	Resi-dential	SALES[3] (tril. Btu) Total[2]	Resi-dential	REVENUES[3] (mil. dol.) Total[2]	Resi-dential
U.S.	57,759	52,770	10,415	5,097	51,787	29,959	DC	147	133	33	13	234	109
							VA	754	678	135	61	806	452
Northeast	11,237	10,290	1,914	1,055	12,286	7,844	WV	393	359	78	40	384	247
N.E.	2,089	1,887	397	187	2,762	1,573	NC	683	604	162	49	798	325
ME	19	14	5	1	30	7	SC	422	377	111	26	507	180
NH	81	70	17	7	110	50	GA	1,527	1,410	332	167	1,269	761
VT	29	25	8	3	40	18	FL	581	530	87	18	502	153
MA	1,266	1,152	234	113	1,594	928	E.S.C.	2,753	2,465	517	219	2,408	1,197
RI	217	198	35	21	263	170	KY	728	655	140	77	605	357
CT	477	429	98	44	725	401	TN	815	705	169	59	808	330
M.A	9,148	8,403	1,518	867	9,524	6,271	AL	780	718	113	53	633	362
NY	4,297	3,975	593	387	4,330	3,092	MS	430	387	95	29	361	147
NJ	2,278	2,052	469	204	2,499	1,360	W.S.C.	6,179	5,667	1,679	427	7,062	2,300
PA	2,572	2,376	455	276	2,695	1,820	AR	578	514	90	46	419	246
Midwest	18,146	16,318	3,247	2,038	16,013	10,730	LA	1,007	943	387	59	1,178	349
E.N.C	12,925	11,634	2,298	1,517	11,591	8,039	OK	932	841	188	81	699	386
OH	3,095	2,851	547	370	2,896	2,025	TX	3,662	3,369	1,015	240	4,766	1,319
IN	1,573	1,426	306	169	1,567	968	West	13,964	13,043	1,961	905	8,564	5,100
IL	3,665	3,354	632	460	3,216	2,416	Mt	3,649	3,319	531	298	2,379	1,484
MI	3,021	2,795	550	388	2,518	1,816	MT	213	188	40	23	174	103
WI	1,572	1,207	263	131	1,393	814	ID	168	146	23	13	110	65
W.N.C.	5,221	4,685	949	521	4,422	2,691	WY	137	121	29	14	114	62
MN	1,149	1,042	258	126	1,193	668	CO	1,176	1,058	184	108	785	488
IA	958	853	176	97	854	523	NM	435	395	66	35	282	183
MO	1,382	1,252	213	136	1,050	707	AZ	660	612	67	29	351	200
ND	104	91	21	11	98	56	UT	522	484	83	56	368	265
SD	145	128	26	13	117	65	NV	338	314	40	22	195	119
NE	614	539	98	51	436	252	Pac	10,315	9,725	1,430	607	6,185	3,616
KS	870	779	158	86	673	419	WA	4		4		56	10
South	14,413	13,119	3,292	1,100	14,924	6,285	OR	9,170	8,717	1,187	507	5,081	3,092
S.A.	5,481	4,988	1,096	454	5,454	2,788	CA	88	76	29	14	104	54
DE	106	97	23	9	117	56	AK	424	371	74	31	372	191
MD	869	800	136	72	837	506	HI	629	560	137	55	571	268

- Represents zero.　[1] Averages for the year.　[2] Includes other service, not shown separately.　[3] Excludes sales for resale.

Source: American Gas Association, Arlington, VA, *Gas Facts*, annual (copyright).

Science and Technology

This section presents statistics on scientific, engineering, and technological resources, with emphasis on patterns of research and development (R&D) funding and on scientific, engineering, and technical personnel, education, and employment. Also included are statistics on space program outlays and accomplishments. Principal sources of these data are the National Science Foundation (NSF) and the National Aeronautics and Space Administration (NASA).

NSF gathers data chiefly through recurring surveys. Current NSF publications containing data on funds for research and development and on scientific and engineering personnel include the *Science Resources Studies Highlights* summaries series; Detailed Statistical Tables; and annual, biennial, triennial, and special reports. Titles or the areas of coverage of these reports include the following: *Science and Engineering Indicators; National Patterns of R&D Resources; Science and Engineering Personnel-A National Overview; Women and Minorities in Science and Engineering;* science and technology data presented in chart and tabular form in a pocket-size publication; *International Science and Technology Data Update;* profiles on human resources and funding in individual fields of science and engineering; *Federal Funds for Research and Development; Federal R&D Funding by Budget Function; Federal Support to Universities, Colleges, and Selected Nonprofit Institutions; Scientific and Engineering Facilities at Universities and Colleges; Geographic Distribution of Industrial R&D Expenditures; Research and Development in Industry;* R&D funds and graduate enrollment and support in academic science and engineering; characteristics of doctoral scientists and engineers and of recent graduates in the United States; *U.S. Scientists and Engineers;* and scientists, engineers, and technicians in manufacturing, nonmanufacturing, and trade and regulated industries. Statistical surveys in these areas pose problems of concept and definition and the data should, therefore, be regarded as broad estimates

In Brief

R&D expenditures in constant (1987) dollars:

1970	*74.6*	*bil.*
1980	*87.6*	*bil.*
1994	*137.0*	*bil.*

Nondefense R&D spending as percent of GNP: 1992

Japan	*2.8*
Unified Germany	*2.4*
United States	*2.1*
France	*1.9*
Italy	*1.7*
United Kingdom	*1.3*

rather than precise quantitative statements. See sources for details.

The National Science Board's biennial *Science and Engineering Indicators* contains data and analyses of international and domestic science and technology, including measures of inputs and outputs. *The Budget of the United States Government,* published by the U.S. Office of Management and Budget, contains summary financial data on Federal R&D programs.

Research and development outlays.—NSF defines research as a "systematic and intensive study directed toward a fuller knowledge of the subject studied" and development as "the systematic use of scientific knowledge directed toward the production of useful materials, devices, systems, methods, or processes." National coverage of R&D expenditures is developed primarily from periodic surveys in four principal economic sectors: (1) *Government,* made up primarily of Federal executive agencies; (2) *industry,* consisting of manufacturing and nonmanufacturing firms and the federally funded research and development centers (FFRDC's) they administer; (3) *universities and colleges,* composed of universities, colleges, and their affiliated institutions, agricultural experiment stations, and associated schools of agriculture, and FFRDC's administered by educational institutions; and (4) *other nonprofit institutions,* consisting of such organizations as private philanthropic foundations, nonprofit research institutes, voluntary health agencies, and FFRDC's administered by nonprofit organizations. The R&D funds reported consist of current operating costs, including planning and administration costs, except as otherwise noted. They exclude funds for routine testing, mapping and surveying, collection of general-purpose data, dissemination of scientific information, and training of scientific personnel.

Scientists, engineers, and technicians.—Scientists and engineers are defined as persons engaged in scientific and engineering work at a level requiring a knowledge of sciences equivalent at least to that acquired through completion of a 4-year college course. Technicians are defined as persons engaged in technical work at a level requiring knowledge acquired through a technical institute, junior college, or other type of training less extensive than 4-year college training. Craftsmen and skilled workers are excluded.

Historical statistics.—Tabular headnotes provide cross-references, where applicable, to *Historical Statistics of the United States, Colonial Times to 1970.* See Appendix IV.

Figure 20.1
Top 15 Universities—Federal Research and Development Obligations: 1992

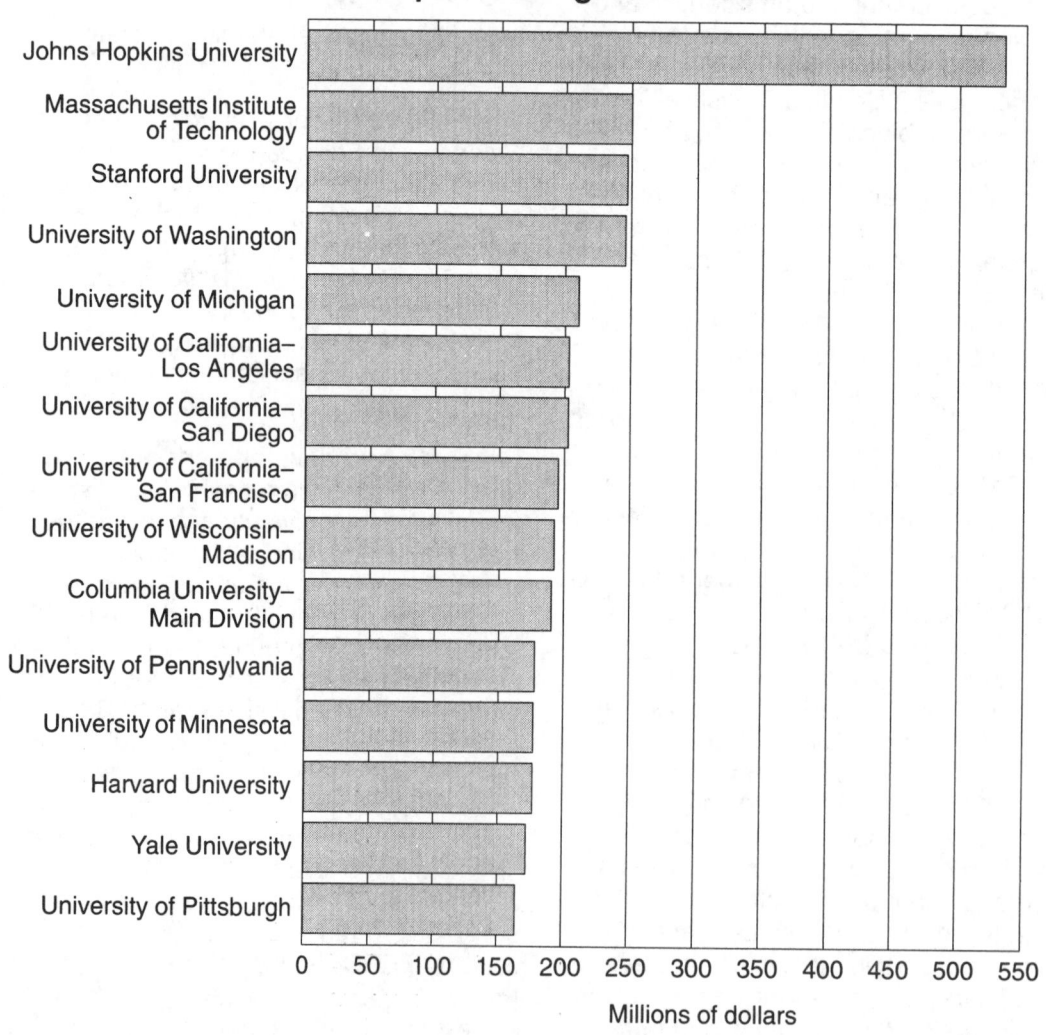

Source: Chart prepared by U.S. Bureau of the Census. For data, see table 988.

No. 979. R&D Expenditures: 1960 to 1994

[Includes basic research, applied research, and development. Defense-related outlays comprise all research and development spending by Dept. of Defense, including space activities, and a portion of Department of Energy funds. Space-related outlays are those of the National Aeronautics and Space Administration; they exclude space activities of other Federal agencies, estimated at less than 5 percent of all space research and development spending. Minus sign (-) indicates decrease]

YEAR	CURRENT DOLLARS (bil. dol.)			CONSTANT (1987) DOLLARS [1]		ANNUAL PERCENT CHANGE [3]		PERCENT OF TOTAL R&D OUTLAYS				
	Total	Defense space related	Other	Total (bil. dol.)	Percent of GDP [2]	Current dollars	Constant dollars	Federally funded defense/space-related			Other outlays	
								Total	Defense	Space	Non-Federal	Federal
1960	13.5	7.5	6.0	52.0	2.6	9.4	7.6	55	52	3	35	9
1965	20.0	10.8	9.3	70.6	2.9	6.3	3.7	54	33	21	35	11
1970	26.1	11.4	14.7	74.6	2.6	2.0	-3.2	44	33	10	43	13
1972	28.5	11.6	16.9	73.7	2.4	6.7	1.9	41	33	8	44	15
1973	30.7	11.9	18.9	74.9	2.3	7.9	1.7	39	32	7	47	15
1974	32.9	11.8	21.1	73.9	2.3	7.0	-1.4	36	29	7	49	15
1975	35.2	12.3	23.0	72.2	2.2	7.2	-2.3	35	27	7	49	17
1976	39.0	13.4	25.6	75.0	2.2	10.8	3.9	34	27	8	49	17
1977	42.8	14.3	28.5	76.7	2.2	9.6	2.2	33	27	7	50	17
1978	48.1	15.3	32.8	80.1	2.2	12.5	4.4	32	26	6	50	18
1979	54.9	16.6	38.4	84.1	2.2	14.2	5.0	30	25	6	51	19
1980	62.6	18.4	44.2	87.6	2.3	13.9	4.3	29	24	5	53	18
1981	71.9	21.2	50.6	91.4	2.4	14.8	4.3	30	24	5	54	17
1982	80.0	24.6	55.4	95.5	2.5	11.3	4.5	31	26	5	54	15
1983	89.1	28.3	60.9	102.3	2.6	11.4	7.1	32	27	4	54	14
1984	101.2	31.8	69.3	111.2	2.7	13.5	8.7	31	28	3	55	14
1985	113.8	37.5	76.3	120.6	2.8	12.5	8.5	33	30	3	54	13
1986	119.6	40.5	79.1	123.3	2.8	5.0	2.3	34	31	3	55	12
1987	125.4	43.2	82.2	125.4	2.8	4.9	1.7	34	31	3	54	12
1988	132.9	43.7	89.2	128.0	2.7	6.0	2.1	33	30	3	55	12
1989	141.0	43.4	97.6	130.0	2.7	6.1	1.6	31	27	4	58	12
1990	151.5	44.4	107.1	134.1	2.7	7.5	3.2	29	25	4	59	11
1991	160.1	42.9	117.2	136.4	2.8	5.6	1.7	27	22	4	62	11
1992	166.7	42.4	124.3	138.1	2.8	4.1	1.3	25	21	4	64	11
1993, prel. .	169.5	42.9	126.6	137.4	2.7	1.7	-0.5	25	21	4	64	11
1994, est...	172.6	42.8	129.8	137.0	2.6	1.8	-0.3	25	20	4	64	11

[1] Based on GDP implicit price deflator. [2] GDP = Gross Domestic Product. [3] Change from immediate prior year.
Source: U.S. National Science Foundation, *National Patterns of R&D Resources,* annual.

No. 980. R&D, Source of Funds and Performance Sector: 1970 to 1994

[In millions of dollars. See headnote, table 981]

YEAR	Total	SOURCE OF FUNDS				PERFORMANCE SECTOR				
		Federal Govt.	Industry	Univ., colleges	Other [1]	Federal Govt.	Industry	Univ., colleges	Associated FFRDC's [2]	Other [1]
Current dollars:										
1970.........	26,134	14,891	10,444	462	337	4,079	18,067	2,335	737	916
1975.........	35,213	18,109	15,820	749	535	5,354	24,187	3,409	987	1,276
1980.........	62,596	29,455	30,912	1,326	903	7,632	44,505	6,063	2,246	2,150
1985.........	113,818	52,127	57,978	2,369	1,344	12,945	84,239	9,686	3,523	3,425
1987.........	125,376	57,913	62,643	3,192	1,628	13,413	92,155	12,152	4,206	3,450
1988.........	132,889	59,546	68,044	3,463	1,836	14,281	97,015	13,462	4,531	3,600
1989.........	140,981	59,893	75,046	3,921	2,121	15,121	102,055	14,975	4,730	4,100
1990.........	151,544	61,493	83,380	4,329	2,342	16,002	109,727	16,283	4,832	4,700
1991.........	160,096	60,219	92,485	4,835	2,557	15,238	116,952	17,577	5,079	5,250
1992.........	166,697	60,239	98,695	5,018	2,745	15,690	121,314	18,794	5,249	5,650
1993.........	169,515	61,411	100,124	5,111	2,869	16,556	122,000	19,911	5,298	5,750
1994.........	172,550	62,200	102,050	5,300	3,000	17,200	123,800	20,500	5,100	5,950
Constant (1987) dollars: [3]										
1970.........	74,597	42,622	29,673	1,335	966	11,789	51,327	6,749	2,130	2,602
1975.........	72,237	37,396	32,162	1,574	1,105	11,248	49,161	7,162	2,074	2,593
1980.........	87,649	41,385	43,118	1,878	1,268	10,810	62,071	8,588	3,181	2,999
1985.........	120,599	55,245	61,418	2,512	1,425	13,727	89,236	10,271	3,736	3,628
1987.........	125,376	57,913	62,643	3,192	1,628	13,413	92,155	12,152	4,206	3,450
1988.........	127,991	57,386	65,492	3,343	1,770	13,785	93,373	12,994	4,374	3,465
1989.........	130,025	55,275	69,169	3,624	1,958	13,975	94,060	13,840	4,372	3,779
1990.........	134,135	54,587	73,604	3,865	2,079	14,288	96,846	14,538	4,314	4,148
1991.........	136,385	51,407	78,652	4,143	2,183	13,057	99,449	15,062	4,352	4,464
1992.........	138,099	50,002	81,641	4,178	2,278	13,064	100,342	15,649	4,371	4,673
1993.........	137,397	49,837	81,077	4,155	2,328	13,460	98,785	16,188	4,307	4,656
1994.........	137,025	49,479	80,934	4,226	2,386	13,716	98,176	16,348	4,067	4,718

[1] Nonprofit institutions. [2] University associated federally-funded R&D centers. [3] Based on gross domestic product implicit price deflator.
Source: U.S. National Science Foundation, *National Patterns of R&D Resources,* annual.

No. 981. R&D Funds, by Performance Sector: 1980 to 1994

[In millions of dollars, except percent. Data primarily on calendar year basis—calendar year data for industry and other nonprofit institutions combined with Federal and university fiscal year data. Data refer, in general, to natural sciences including engineering, and to social sciences in all but industry sector. Excludes capital expenditures data. Expenditures at associated federally funded research and development centers administered by industry and other nonprofit institutions included in totals of respective sectors. See also *Historical Statistics, Colonial Times to 1970,* series W 109-125]

PERFORMANCE SECTOR	1980	1985	1989	1990	1991	1992	1993	1994
Total R&D [1]	**62,596**	**113,818**	**140,981**	**151,544**	**160,096**	**166,697**	**169,515**	**172,550**
In 1987 dollars [2]	87,649	120,599	130,025	134,135	136,385	138,099	137,397	137,025
Percent Federal as source	47.2	45.8	42.5	40.7	37.7	36.2	36.3	36.1
Percent of gross domestic product	2.3	2.8	2.7	2.7	2.8	2.8	2.7	2.6
Federal Government	7,632	12,945	15,121	16,002	15,238	15,690	16,556	17,200
Industry	44,505	84,239	102,055	109,727	116,952	121,314	122,000	123,800
Federal funds	14,029	27,196	28,554	28,125	26,372	24,660	24,000	24,000
Industry funds	30,476	57,043	73,501	81,602	90,580	96,654	98,000	99,800
Universities and colleges	6,063	9,686	14,975	16,283	17,577	18,794	19,911	20,500
Federal funds	4,098	6,063	8,988	9,634	10,230	11,090	11,957	12,200
Industry funds	236	560	995	1,128	1,205	1,291	1,374	1,450
University and college funds [3]	1,326	2,369	3,921	4,329	4,835	5,018	5,111	5,300
Other nonprofit institutions funds [3]	403	694	1,071	1,192	1,307	1,395	1,469	1,550
Universities and colleges, associated federally funded R&D centers	2,246	3,523	4,730	4,832	5,079	5,249	5,298	5,100
Other nonprofit institutions	2,150	3,425	4,100	4,700	5,250	5,650	5,750	5,950
Federal funds	1,450	2,400	2,500	2,900	3,300	3,550	3,600	3,700
Industry funds	200	375	550	650	700	750	750	800
Other [4]	500	650	1,050	1,150	1,250	1,350	1,400	1,450
Total research, basic and applied	**22,045**	**39,537**	**53,525**	**57,144**	**65,342**	**68,422**	**71,060**	**72,190**
In 1987 dollars [2]	27,513	41,046	51,018	53,144	59,813	61,762	63,411	63,744
Percent Federal as source	54.8	50.8	46.5	47.9	45.2	44.4	45.4	45.2
Federal Government	3,666	5,056	5,982	5,953	6,539	6,616	7,360	7,600
Industry	9,775	21,117	27,907	29,913	35,595	36,969	37,600	38,000
Federal funds	2,190	5,836	6,082	7,721	8,141	7,743	7,900	7,900
Industry funds	7,585	15,281	21,825	22,192	27,454	29,226	29,700	30,100
Universities and colleges	5,566	8,973	13,844	14,986	16,079	17,218	18,277	18,860
Federal funds	3,739	5,604	8,276	8,802	9,245	10,053	10,880	11,150
Industry funds	219	521	925	1,049	1,121	1,201	1,278	1,340
University and college funds [3]	1,233	2,203	3,647	4,026	4,497	4,667	4,753	4,930
Other nonprofit institutions funds [3]	375	645	996	1,109	1,216	1,297	1,366	1,440
Universities and colleges, associated federally funded R&D centers	1,553	2,351	2,952	3,052	3,519	3,779	3,903	3,720
Other nonprofit institutions	1,485	2,040	2,840	3,240	3,610	3,840	3,920	4,010
Federal funds	930	1,250	1,600	1,850	2,100	2,200	2,250	2,250
Industry funds	160	300	440	520	560	610	610	660
Other [4]	395	490	800	870	950	1,030	1,060	1,100
Total basic research	**8,435**	**14,210**	**21,248**	**22,322**	**27,985**	**29,579**	**30,676**	**31,150**
In 1987 dollars [2]	11,902	15,064	19,620	19,860	23,906	24,563	24,901	24,788
Percent of total R&D	13.5	12.5	15.1	14.7	17.5	17.7	18.1	18.1
Percent Federal as source	70.1	64.7	61.9	61.9	57.9	57.1	58.3	58.3
Federal Government	1,182	1,923	2,371	2,366	2,446	2,397	2,605	2,700
Industry	1,325	2,862	5,216	5,128	9,423	9,794	9,700	9,700
Federal funds	290	489	1,384	1,368	2,953	2,792	2,700	2,700
Industry funds	1,035	2,373	3,832	3,760	6,470	7,002	7,000	7,000
Universities and colleges	4,036	6,555	9,789	10,640	11,601	12,504	13,270	13,700
Federal funds	2,861	4,342	6,192	6,645	7,123	7,713	8,379	8,650
Industry funds	141	342	598	678	734	803	845	850
University and college funds [3]	793	1,447	2,356	2,601	2,947	3,120	3,143	3,250
Other nonprofit institutions funds [3]	241	424	643	716	797	868	903	950
Universities and colleges, associated federally funded R&D centers	1,132	1,765	2,352	2,428	2,595	2,844	2,941	2,900
Other nonprofit institutions	760	1,105	1,520	1,760	1,920	2,040	2,160	2,150
Federal funds	450	675	850	1,000	1,100	1,150	1,250	1,200
Industry funds	95	170	250	300	320	350	350	370
Other [4]	215	260	420	460	500	540	560	580
Total development	**40,551**	**74,281**	**87,456**	**94,400**	**94,754**	**98,275**	**98,455**	**100,360**
In 1987 dollars [2]	56,669	78,698	80,635	83,453	80,650	81,353	79,761	79,643
Percent of total R&D	64.8	65.3	62.0	62.3	59.2	59.0	58.1	58.2
Percent Federal as source	42.9	43.1	40.0	36.1	32.4	30.4	29.6	29.5

[1] Basic research, applied research, and development.   [2] Based on gross domestic product implicit price deflator.
[3] Includes State and local government funds received by these institutions and used for research and development.   [4] Includes estimates for independent nonprofit hospitals and voluntary health agencies.

Source: U.S. National Science Foundation, *National Patterns of R&D Resources,* annual.

No. 982. Funds for R&D—Performance Sector, by State: 1991

[**In millions of dollars.** See headnote, table 981. Data shown here are unrevised]

STATE	Total	Federal government [1]	Industry	Universities and colleges [2]	Other non-profit [3]	STATE	Total	Federal government [1]	Industry	Universities and colleges [2]	Other non-profit [3]
U.S. ...	145,385	15,238	102,246	22,701	5,200	MO	(NA)	71	([7])	306	22
						MT	(NA)	26	([6])	38	1
AL......	1,503	701	521	245	36	NE......	211	22	59	124	6
AK......	146	59	18	67	2	NV......	261	109	83	67	3
AZ......	1,399	132	944	311	11	NH	(NA)	88	([9])	79	-
AR......	198	35	106	55	2	NJ......	8,768	513	7,810	433	12
CA......	28,337	1,885	21,279	4,700	473	NM	2,582	393	1,064	1,111	15
CO......	(NA)	275	([4])	340	106	NY......	10,363	174	8,268	1,751	170
CT......	1,913	47	1,535	317	15	NC......	1,965	151	1,285	502	27
DE......	(NA)	9	([5])	45	3	ND	(NA)	24	([7])	31	1
DC......	1,737	1,433	40	118	145	OH	5,975	689	4,726	504	57
FL......	3,700	658	2,599	438	5	OK	604	41	392	153	18
GA......	1,479	121	868	484	6	OR	600	47	349	179	24
HI	145	45	11	78	11	PA......	7,621	315	6,262	906	138
ID	(NA)	37	([6])	42	1	RI......	485	226	152	88	18
IL......	6,417	68	5,027	1,275	47	SC......	595	14	419	151	10
IN	2,347	92	1,988	262	4	SD......	32	9	5	16	2
IA	777	27	461	286	3	TN......	1,139	124	737	251	28
KS......	(NA)	12	([7])	124	5	TX......	6,635	405	4,755	1,218	257
KY......	317	62	154	98	2	UT......	665	103	356	202	4
LA......	457	43	172	240	2	VT......	(NA)	5	([8])	47	5
ME	(NA)	14	([8])	27	16	VA......	2,771	1,107	1,115	366	182
MD......	5,864	3,432	1,203	1,078	151	WA	3,890	133	3,215	350	193
MA......	8,561	278	6,335	1,338	610	WV	(NA)	76	([10])	73	5
MI......	8,851	92	8,116	601	42	WI......	1,573	32	1,140	388	13
MN	2,228	41	1,810	332	46	WY	41	9	2	23	7
MS	299	157	41	97	4	Other [11] ...	3,835	577	675	349	2,234

- Represents or rounds to zero.   NA Not available.   [1] Total funds used by Federal government from Federal sources.
[2] Distribution by States includes R&D performed in only doctoral degree granting institutions; U.S. total includes R&D performed in all institutions.   [3] For other sector, funds distributed by State include only Federal obligations to organizations in the nonprofit sector. Nonprofit R&D performance using non-Federal funds are undistributed.   [4] Between $1,751 and $2,593 million.   [5] Between $863 and $995 million.   [6] Under $95 million.   [7] Under $1,963 million.   [8] Under $284 million.   [9] Between $102 and $120 million.   [10] Between $69 and $201 million.   [11] Includes unknown.

Source: U.S. National Science Foundation, *Science and Engineering Indicators*, 1993.

No. 983. Federal Obligations for R&D, by Agency: 1975 to 1994

[**In millions of dollars. For fiscal years ending in year shown;** see text, section 9. Includes those agencies with obligations of $1 billion or more in 1994. See *Historical Statistics, Colonial Times to 1970*, series W 142, for total R&D expenditures]

AGENCY	1975	1980	1985	1989	1990	1991	1992	1993	1994, est.
CURRENT DOLLARS									
Obligations, total [1]	19,039	29,830	48,360	61,407	63,668	61,295	65,593	71,445	71,244
Dept. of Defense	9,013	13,981	29,792	37,577	37,268	32,135	36,130	38,987	37,523
Dept. of Health and Human Services	2,281	3,780	5,451	7,903	8,406	9,756	8,988	10,344	10,723
National Aeronautics and Space Administration................	3,064	3,234	3,327	5,394	6,533	7,280	7,658	8,190	8,637
Dept. of Energy	2,047	4,754	4,966	5,193	5,631	5,983	6,172	6,586	6,582
National Science Foundation.......	595	882	1,346	1,670	1,690	1,785	1,868	2,073	2,217
Dept. of Agriculture	420	688	943	1,038	1,108	1,237	1,327	1,331	1,368
CONSTANT (1987) DOLLARS [2]									
Obligations, total [1]	39,998	42,253	51,283	56,753	56,846	52,479	54,525	57,850	56,275
Dept. of Defense	18,935	19,803	31,592	34,729	33,275	27,513	30,033	31,568	29,639
Dept. of Health and Human Services	4,792	5,354	5,780	7,304	7,505	8,353	7,471	8,376	8,470
National Aeronautics and Space Administration................	6,437	4,581	3,528	4,985	5,833	6,233	6,366	6,632	6,822
Dept. of Energy	4,300	6,733	5,266	4,799	5,028	5,122	5,131	5,333	5,199
National Science Foundation.......	1,250	1,249	1,427	1,543	1,509	1,528	1,553	1,679	1,751
Dept. of Agriculture	882	974	1,000	959	989	1,059	1,103	1,078	1,081

[1] Includes other agencies, not shown separately.   [2] Based on gross domestic product implicit price deflator.

Source: U.S. National Science Foundation, *Federal Funds for Research and Development,* annual.

No. 984. Federal Funding for R&D, by Selected Budget Functions: 1970 to 1995

[In millions of dollars. For fiscal years ending in year shown; see text, section 9. Excludes R&D plant. Represents budget authority. Functions shown are those for which $1 billion or more was authorized for 1993. See *Historical Statistics, Colonial Times to 1970*, series W 126, for total obligations]

FUNCTION	1970	1980	1985	1990	1991	1992	1993	1994, est.	1995, est.
CURRENT DOLLARS									
Total [1]	**15,339**	**29,739**	**49,887**	**63,781**	**65,898**	**68,398**	**69,884**	**68,311**	**71,361**
Eight functions, percent of total	96.6	96.5	98.3	98.0	97.9	98.0	98.1	97.8	97.5
National defense	7,981	14,946	33,698	39,925	39,328	40,083	41,249	38,020	39,496
Health	1,084	3,694	5,418	8,308	9,226	10,055	10,280	10,936	11,417
Space research and technology	3,606	2,738	2,725	5,765	6,511	6,744	6,988	7,212	7,665
Energy	574	3,603	2,389	2,715	2,943	3,099	2,677	2,854	2,943
General science	452	1,233	1,862	2,410	2,635	2,659	2,691	2,717	2,866
Natural resources and environment	340	999	1,059	1,386	1,582	1,688	1,802	1,992	1,998
Transportation	535	887	1,030	1,045	1,231	1,523	1,703	1,892	1,999
Agriculture	238	585	836	950	1,052	1,155	1,152	1,188	1,190
CONSTANT (1987) DOLLARS [2]									
Total [1]	**44,332**	**42,123**	**52,902**	**56,947**	**56,420**	**56,856**	**56,586**	**53,958**	**54,851**
National defense	23,066	21,170	35,735	35,647	33,671	33,319	33,400	30,032	30,358
Health	3,133	5,232	5,745	7,418	7,899	8,358	8,324	8,638	8,776
Space research and technology	10,422	3,878	2,890	5,147	5,574	5,606	5,658	5,697	5,892
Energy	1,659	5,103	2,533	2,424	2,520	2,576	2,168	2,254	2,262
General science	1,306	1,746	1,975	2,152	2,256	2,210	2,179	2,146	2,203
Natural resources and environment	983	1,415	1,123	1,238	1,354	1,403	1,459	1,573	1,536
Transportation	1,546	1,256	1,092	933	1,054	1,266	1,379	1,494	1,537
Agriculture	688	829	887	848	901	960	933	938	915

[1] Includes other functions, not shown separately.   [2] Based on gross domestic product implicit price deflator.

Source: U.S. National Science Foundation, *Federal R&D Funding by Budget Function,* annual.

No. 985. National R&D Expenditures as a Percent of Gross Domestic Product, by Country: 1975 to 1993

YEAR	TOTAL R&D						NONDEFENSE R&D [1]					
	United States	Japan	Unified Germany	France	United Kingdom	Italy	United States	Japan	Unified Germany	France	United Kingdom	Italy
1975	2.22	1.91	2.24	1.79	2.05	0.84	1.61	1.90	2.10	1.44	1.42	0.83
1980	2.31	2.01	2.45	1.82	(NA)	0.75	1.76	2.00	2.33	1.41	(NA)	0.74
1985	2.82	2.58	2.72	2.25	2.27	1.13	1.98	2.56	2.58	1.78	1.68	1.06
1990	2.73	2.89	2.75	2.42	2.19	1.30	2.01	2.87	2.61	1.85	1.81	1.25
1991	2.80	2.87	2.65	2.42	2.13	1.32	2.11	2.84	2.53	1.92	1.73	1.26
1992	2.77	2.80	2.53	2.36	2.12	1.38	2.10	2.77	2.42	1.92	1.71	1.33
1993	2.67	(NA)	(NA)	(NA)	(NA)	1.40	2.02	(NA)	(NA)	(NA)	(NA)	1.35

NA Not available.   [1] Estimated.

Source: National Science Foundation, *National Patterns of R&D Resources,* annual; and Organization for Economic Co-operation and Development.

No. 986. R&D Expenditures in Science and Engineering at Universities and Colleges: 1981 to 1993

[In millions of dollars]

CHARACTERISTIC	1981	1990	1993 [1]	CHARACTERISTIC	1981	1990	1993 [1]
CURRENT DOLLARS				**CONSTANT (1987) DOLLARS** [2]			
Total	**6,846**	**16,334**	**19,911**	**Total**	**8,799**	**14,493**	**16,122**
Basic research	4,593	10,680	13,270	Basic research	5,904	9,476	10,745
Applied R&D	2,253	5,654	6,641	Applied R&D	2,896	5,017	5,377
Source of funds:				Source of funds:			
All governments	5,115	10,976	13,516	All governments	6,575	9,739	10,944
Institutions' own funds	1,004	3,033	3,552	Institutions' own funds	1,290	2,691	2,876
Industry	292	1,130	1,374	Industry	375	1,003	1,113
Other	435	1,195	1,469	Other	559	1,060	1,189
Fields:				Fields:			
Physical sciences	765	1,809	2,124	Physical sciences	983	1,605	1,720
Environmental sciences	550	1,080	1,318	Environmental sciences	707	958	1,067
Mathematical sciences	87	221	272	Mathematical sciences	112	196	220
Computer sciences	144	514	597	Computer sciences	185	456	483
Life sciences	3,695	8,748	10,828	Life sciences	4,749	7,762	8,768
Psychology	127	258	349	Psychology	163	229	283
Social sciences	366	706	896	Social sciences	470	626	726
Other sciences	145	335	375	Other sciences	186	297	304
Engineering	967	2,663	3,151	Engineering	1,243	2,363	2,551

[1] Preliminary.   [2] Based on gross domestic product implicit price deflator.

Source: U.S. National Science Foundation, *Survey of Scientific and Engineering Expenditures at Universities and Colleges,* annual.

No. 987. Federal Obligations to Universities and Colleges: 1970 to 1992

[In millions of dollars, except percent. For fiscal years ending in year shown; see text, section 9. Minus sign (-) indicates decrease]

ITEM	1970	1980	1985	1988	1989	1990	1991	1992
CURRENT DOLLARS								
Federal obligations, total	**3,237**	**8,299**	**10,972**	**14,066**	**15,504**	**15,198**	**17,552**	**19,047**
Annual percent change [1]	-6.5	9.1	9.3	4.7	10.2	-2.0	15.5	8.5
Academic science/engineering obligations	2,188	4,791	7,258	9,136	10,075	10,443	11,829	12,730
Percent of total	67.6	57.7	66.2	65.0	65.0	68.7	67.4	66.8
Research and development	1,447	4,161	6,246	7,719	8,523	9,006	10,027	10,864
Research and development plant	45	38	114	203	237	125	152	195
Other science/engineering activities	696	593	898	1,214	1,315	1,312	1,650	1,671
Nonscience/engineering activities	1,049	3,508	3,714	4,930	5,429	4,755	5,723	6,318
CONSTANT (1987) DOLLARS [2]								
Federal obligations, total	**9,355**	**11,755**	**11,635**	**13,577**	**14,329**	**13,570**	**15,028**	**15,833**
Annual percent change [1]	-11.4	0.0	5.4	1.1	5.5	-5.9	10.7	5.4
Academic science/engineering obligations	6,324	6,786	7,697	8,819	9,311	9,324	10,128	10,582
Percent of total	67.6	57.7	66.2	65.0	65.0	68.7	67.4	66.8
Research and development	4,182	5,894	6,624	7,451	7,877	8,041	8,585	9,031
Research and development plant	130	54	121	196	219	111	130	162
Other science/engineering activities	2,012	840	952	1,172	1,215	1,172	1,413	1,389
Nonscience/engineering activities	3,032	4,969	3,938	4,759	5,018	4,245	4,900	5,252

[1] Percent change from immediate prior year. [2] Based on gross domestic product implicit price deflator.

Source: U.S. National Science Foundation, *Survey of Federal Support to Universities, Colleges, and Nonprofit Institutions,* annual.

No. 988. Federal R&D Obligations to Selected Universities and Colleges: 1981 to 1992

[For fiscal years ending in year shown; see text, section 9. For the top 40 institutions receiving Federal R&D funds in 1992. Awards to the administrative offices of university systems are excluded from totals for individual institutions because that allocation of funds is unknown, but those awards are included in "total all institutions"]

MAJOR INSTITUTION RANKED BY TOTAL 1992 FEDERAL R&D OBLIGATIONS	OBLIGATIONS ($1,000)			RANK		
	1981	1985	1992	1981	1985	1992
Total, all institutions [1]	**4,410,931**	**6,246,181**	**10,863,940**	**(X)**	**(X)**	**(X)**
40 institutions, percent of total	59.0	57.5	56.1	(X)	(X)	(X)
Johns Hopkins University	363,429	297,374	534,128	1	1	1
Massachusetts Institute of Technology	146,035	189,558	249,852	2	2	2
Stanford University	106,073	174,961	246,589	3	3	3
University of Washington	99,965	146,179	245,428	4	4	4
University of Michigan	73,999	108,035	210,000	11	11	5
University of California—Los Angeles	94,945	128,211	202,754	5	5	6
University of California—San Diego	91,403	103,633	202,477	6	13	7
University of California—San Francisco	64,814	98,536	195,156	15	16	8
University of Wisconsin—Madison	86,918	124,604	192,414	8	7	9
Columbia University—Main Division	83,659	127,331	190,310	9	6	10
University of Pennsylvania	76,136	103,119	178,002	10	15	11
University of Minnesota	72,001	103,272	177,182	14	14	12
Harvard University	87,830	109,414	176,967	7	9	13
Yale University	73,526	109,227	172,304	12	10	14
University of Pittsburgh	38,512	58,620	164,183	29	28	15
Cornell University	72,671	119,966	162,177	13	8	16
University of California—Berkeley	64,065	106,710	154,682	16	12	17
Pennsylvania State University	47,099	76,726	148,172	21	19	18
University of Colorado	46,146	71,424	147,935	22	23	19
University of Southern California	49,221	89,706	141,449	20	17	20
Duke University	44,287	69,169	139,864	23	26	21
Washington University	54,170	71,978	134,336	17	22	22
University of North Carolina at Chapel Hill	38,447	63,105	130,144	30	27	23
University of Illinois—Urbana	53,583	83,122	111,061	19	18	24
University of Texas at Austin	43,756	72,379	110,616	24	21	25
University of Arizona	36,308	49,740	106,229	33	37	26
University of Rochester	42,983	70,379	103,020	25	25	27
University of Chicago	53,992	71,194	98,668	18	24	28
California Institute of Technology	32,959	55,083	97,956	40	32	29
New York University	40,636	74,577	96,349	28	20	30
University of Florida	30,845	47,716	92,533	43	41	31
University of Iowa	35,300	55,117	92,133	34	31	32
University of California—Davis	31,757	43,156	90,500	42	47	33
Ohio State University	42,899	56,065	90,377	26	30	34
Case Western Reserve University	33,744	47,994	88,518	38	40	35
Indiana University	29,276	39,118	88,348	45	49	36
Baylor College of Medicine	35,062	45,837	84,947	35	45	37
Vanderbilt University	27,426	39,909	84,390	49	48	38
University of Alabama—Birmingham	29,970	44,093	84,055	44	46	39
Boston University	27,019	46,152	79,255	51	43	40

X Not applicable. [1] Includes other institutions, not shown separately.

Source: U.S. National Science Foundation, *Federal Support to Universities and Colleges and Nonprofit Institutions,* annual.

No. 989. Funds for Performance of Industrial R&D, by Source of Funds and Selected Industries: 1970 to 1992

[In millions of dollars. For calendar years. Covers basic research, applied research, and development. See also *Historical Statistics, Colonial Times to 1970,* series W 144-160]

INDUSTRY	1987 SIC[1] code	1970	1975	1980	1985	1990	1992
CURRENT DOLLARS							
Total funds	(X)	18,067	24,187	44,505	84,239	104,606	121,314
Chemicals and allied products	28	1,773	2,727	4,636	8,540	12,344	16,711
Petroleum refining and extraction	13,29	515	693	1,552	(D)	2,129	2,339
Machinery	35	1,729	3,196	5,901	12,216	14,696	15,135
Electrical equipment	36	4,220	5,105	9,175	14,432	17,723	13,546
Motor vehicles and motor vehicles equipment	371	1,591	2,340	4,955	6,984	(D)	(D)
Aircraft and missiles	372,376	5,219	5,713	9,198	22,231	25,356	16,119
Professional and scientific instruments	38	744	1,173	3,029	5,013	6,194	9,652
All other[2]	(X)	2,276	3,240	6,059	(D)	(D)	(D)
Company funds	(X)	10,288	15,582	30,476	57,043	73,980	96,654
Chemicals and allied products	28	1,593	2,490	4,264	8,310	12,277	16,420
Petroleum refining and extraction	13,29	493	(D)	1,401	2,194	2,113	2,330
Machinery	35	1,469	2687	5,254	10,721	13,780	14,073
Electrical equipment	36	2,008	2,798	5,431	9,271	12,131	9,689
Motor vehicles and motor vehicles equipment	371	1,278	2,022	4,300	6,164	8,548	(D)
Aircraft and missiles	372,376	1,213	1,285	2,570	5,649	6,140	6,248
Professional and scientific instruments	38	550	1,001	2,456	4,622	6,095	7,426
All other[2]	(X)	1,684	(D)	4,800	10,132	12,896	(D)
CONSTANT (1987) DOLLARS[3]							
Total funds	(X)	51,327	49,161	62,071	89,236	92,326	100,176
Chemicals and allied products	28	5,037	5,543	6,466	9,047	10,895	13,799
Petroleum refining and extraction	13,29	1,463	1,409	2,165	(D)	1,879	1,931
Machinery	35	4,912	6,496	8,230	12,941	12,970	12,497
Electrical equipment	36	11,989	10,376	12,796	15,288	15,642	11,185
Motor vehicles and motor vehicles equipment	371	4,520	4,756	6,911	7,398	(D)	(D)
Aircraft and missiles	372,376	14,827	11,612	12,828	23,550	22,379	13,310
Professional and scientific instruments	38	2,114	2,384	4,225	5,310	5,466	7,970
All other[2]	(X)	6,466	6,585	8,450	(D)	(D)	(D)
Company funds	(X)	29,227	31,671	42,505	60,427	65,295	79,813
Chemicals and allied products	28	4,526	5,061	5,947	8,803	10,835	13,559
Petroleum refining and extraction	13,29	1,401	(D)	1,954	2,324	1,865	1,924
Machinery	35	4,173	5,461	7,328	11,357	12,162	11,621
Electrical equipment	36	5,705	5,687	7,575	9,821	10,707	8,000
Motor vehicles and motor vehicles equipment	371	3,631	4,110	5,997	6,530	7,544	(D)
Aircraft and missiles	372,376	3,446	2,612	3,584	5,984	5,419	5,159
Professional and scientific instruments	38	1,563	2,035	3,425	4,896	5,379	6,132
All other[2]	(X)	4,784	(D)	6,695	10,733	11,382	(D)

D Figure withheld to avoid disclosure of information pertaining to a specific organization or individual.　　X Not applicable.
[1] Prior to 1992, 1972 Standard Industrial Classification; beginning 1992, 1987 Standard Industrial Classification; see text, section 13.　　[2] All other manufacturing and nonmanufacturing.　　[3] Based on gross domestic product implicit price deflator.

Source: U.S. National Science Foundation, *Research and Development in Industry,* annual.

No. 990. R&D Funds in R&D-Performing Manufacturing Companies, by Industry: 1970 to 1992

INDUSTRY	1987 SIC[1] code	TOTAL R&D FUNDS AS A PERCENT OF NET SALES					COMPANY R&D FUNDS AS A PERCENT OF NET SALES				
		1970	1980	1985	1990	1992	1970	1980	1985	1990	1992
Total[2]	(X)	3.7	3.0	4.4	4.7	4.2	2.2	2.1	3.0	3.3	3.3
Food and kindred products[3]	20	0.5	0.4	(D)	(D)	0.5	0.5	(D)	0.6	0.5	0.5
Paper and allied products	26	0.9	1.0	(D)	0.8	1.1	(D)	1.0	0.8	0.8	1.0
Chemicals and allied products	28	3.9	3.6	5.0	5.6	6.0	3.5	3.3	4.9	5.6	5.9
Petroleum refining and extraction	13,29	1.0	0.6	(D)	1.0	1.0	0.9	0.5	0.9	1.0	1.0
Rubber products	30	2.3	2.2	(D)	(D)	(D)	1.7	(D)	1.8	1.7	2.5
Stone, clay, and glass products	32	1.8	1.4	(D)	(D)	(D)	1.7	1.3	2.3	2.4	1.7
Primary metals	33	0.8	0.7	(D)	(D)	0.6	0.8	0.5	0.9	1.0	0.6
Fabricated metal products	34	1.2	1.4	1.5	1.2	1.6	1.1	1.2	1.4	1.0	1.1
Machinery	35	4.0	5.0	7.6	8.9	7.8	3.4	4.5	6.7	8.3	7.3
Electrical equipment	36	7.3	6.6	7.6	6.9	5.7	3.4	3.9	4.8	4.7	4.1
Motor vehicles and motor vehicle equipment	371	3.5	4.9	3.8	(D)	(D)	2.8	4.2	3.1	3.9	4.0
Aircraft and missiles	372,376	16.2	13.7	14.9	14.3	11.8	3.8	3.8	3.9	3.5	4.6
Professional and scientific instruments	38	5.7	7.5	8.9	7.8	8.9	4.2	6.1	8.3	7.6	7.2

D Figure withheld to avoid disclosure of information pertaining to a specific organization or individual.　　X Not applicable.
[1] Prior to 1992, 1972 Standard Industrial Classification; beginning 1992, 1987 Standard Industrial Classification; see text, section 13.　　[2] Includes all manufacturing industries.　　[3] Includes tobacco products (SIC 21) beginning 1985.

Source: U.S. National Science Foundation, *Research and Development in Industry,* annual.

No. 991. Federal Obligations for Research, by Field of Science: 1980 to 1994

[In millions of dollars. For fiscal years ending in year shown; see text, section 9. Excludes R&D plant]

FIELD	1980	1985	1988	1989	1990	1991	1992	1993	1994, est.
CURRENT DOLLARS									
Research, total	11,597	16,133	18,650	20,766	21,731	23,968	24,491	27,452	28,124
Basic	4,674	7,819	9,474	10,602	11,286	12,171	12,490	13,897	14,346
Applied	6,923	8,315	9,177	10,164	10,446	11,798	12,001	13,555	13,778
Life sciences	4,192	6,363	7,725	8,495	8,830	9,622	9,910	10,950	11,373
Psychology	199	327	390	422	449	482	298	354	346
Physical sciences	2,001	3,046	3,317	3,705	3,809	4,235	4,439	4,915	4,832
Environmental sciences	1,261	1,404	1,607	1,773	2,174	2,150	2,208	2,412	2,542
Mathematics and computer sciences	241	575	643	735	841	904	1,160	1,363	1,469
Engineering	2,830	3,618	3,956	4,442	4,335	4,945	4,977	5,840	6,005
Social sciences	524	460	486	551	630	727	690	704	709
Other sciences, n.e.c. [1]	350	342	527	642	664	903	808	913	847
CONSTANT (1987) DOLLARS [2]									
Research, total	16,427	17,109	18,002	19,192	19,403	20,521	20,358	22,228	22,215
Basic	6,621	8,291	9,144	9,799	10,077	10,420	10,382	11,253	11,332
Applied	9,806	8,817	8,858	9,394	9,327	10,101	9,976	10,976	10,883
Life sciences	5,938	6,747	7,457	7,851	7,884	8,238	8,238	8,866	8,983
Psychology	282	347	376	390	401	413	248	287	273
Physical sciences	2,834	3,230	3,202	3,424	3,401	3,626	3,690	3,980	3,817
Environmental sciences	1,786	1,489	1,551	1,639	1,941	1,841	1,835	1,953	2,008
Mathematics and computer sciences	341	610	621	679	751	774	964	1,104	1,160
Engineering	4,009	3,836	3,819	4,105	3,871	4,234	4,137	4,729	4,743
Social sciences	742	488	469	509	563	622	574	570	560
Other sciences, n.e.c. [1]	495	362	508	593	593	773	672	739	669

[1] N.e.c. = Not elsewhere classified.   [2] Based on gross domestic product implicit price deflator.

Source: U.S. National Science Foundation, *Federal Funds for Research and Development,* annual.

No. 992. R&D Scientists and Engineers—Employment and Cost, by Industry: 1975 to 1992

[Data are estimates; on average full-time-equivalent (FTE) basis. See *Historical Statistics, Colonial Times to 1970,* series W 167, for total cost per scientist or engineer]

INDUSTRY	1987 SIC [1] code	1975	1980	1985	1987	1988	1989	1990	1991	1992
EMPLOYED SCIENTISTS										
Average FTE of scientists and engineers (1,000) [2][3]	(X)	363.9	469.2	646.8	702.2	714.4	725.6	717.5	741.7	783.2
Chemicals [4]	28	44.8	53.1	73.5	75.5	76.7	78.3	78.9	82.2	87.4
Machinery	35	54.3	65.7	85.7	97.1	99.1	106.1	109.8	103.3	99.4
Electrical equipment [5]	36	81.5	100.7	115.6	131.5	136.6	139.3	137.9	114.8	91.2
Motor vehicles	371	25.7	36.7	31.3	46.9	46.6	47.8	47.6	45.0	44.9
Aircraft and missiles	372,376	67.2	90.6	137.5	136.4	139.4	135.4	123.2	105.4	94.0
CONSTANT (1987) DOLLARS [6]										
Cost per scientist or engineer ($1,000) [3][7]	(X)	135.2	132.3	138.0	131.2	131.9	129.7	128.7	126.3	127.9
Chemicals [4]	28	123.8	121.9	123.2	127.6	135.2	135.2	138.1	142.4	158.0
Machinery	35	119.7	125.4	151.0	(D)	(D)	127.7	118.3	125.6	125.8
Electrical equipment [5]	36	127.5	127.0	132.4	120.6	114.5	112.2	113.4	125.0	122.7
Motor vehicles	371	185.2	188.5	236.4	(D)	(D)	(D)	(D)	(D)	183.6
Aircraft and missiles	372,376	173.0	141.7	171.3	179.4	179.0	174.7	181.7	150.4	141.7

D Withheld to avoid disclosure.   X Not applicable.   [1] Prior to 1992, 1972 Standard Industrial Classification; beginning 1992, 1987 Standard Industrial Classification; see text, section 13.   [2] The mean number of FTE R&D scientists and engineers employed in January of the year shown and the following January.   [3] Includes industries not shown separately.   [4] Includes allied products.   [5] Includes communication.   [6] Based on gross domestic product implicit price deflator.   [7] Represents the arithmetic mean of the numbers of R&D scientists and engineers reported in each industry for January in 2 consecutive years divided into total R&D expenditures in each industry.

Source: U.S. National Science Foundation, *Research and Development in Industry,* annual.

No. 993. Scientists and Engineers Employed in R&D: 1970 to 1991

[**For full-time equivalent employees.** Data are estimates. Yearly averages for industry sector only. Excludes those employed by State and local government agencies]

SECTOR	1970	1980	1982	1983	1984	1985	1987	1989	1991
Total [1] (1,000)	543.8	651.1	711.8	751.6	797.6	801.9	877.8	924.2	960.5
PERCENT DISTRIBUTION									
Industry (excl. social scientists)	69.1	72.1	73.8	74.8	75.6	80.9	80.0	79.3	80.8
Federal Government	12.4	9.0	8.4	8.2	7.8	6.5	6.2	6.4	6.1
Other [2]	18.5	18.9	17.8	17.0	16.6	12.6	13.8	14.3	13.1

[1] Due to change in methodology, data beginning 1985 are not comparable with data for previous years.   [2] Includes professional R&D personnel employed at universities and colleges, other nonprofit institutions, and federally funded R&D centers administered by organizations in these sectors and graduate students engaged in R&D at universities and colleges.

Source: U.S. National Science Foundation, *National Patterns of R&D Resources,* annual.

No. 994. Civilian Employment of Scientists, Engineers, and Technicians, by Occupation and Industry: 1992

[**In thousands.** Based on sample and subject to sampling error. For details, see source]

OCCUPATION	Total [1]	WAGE AND SALARY WORKERS								Self employed
		Mining [2]	Construction	Manufacturing	Transportation [3]	Trade	FIRE [4]	Services	Government	
Scientists and engineers .	**2,673.7**	**41.6**	**27.1**	**913.5**	**108.4**	**86.8**	**99.3**	**761.1**	**461.6**	**163.0**
Scientists	1,319.8	19.5	1.2	272.8	33.1	30.8	88.0	458.9	271.7	134.0
Physical scientists	197.5	14.8	0.1	59.4	3.2	2.5	0.6	65.3	45.2	6.0
Life scientists.	182.1	0.1	-	27.6	0.9	1.7	(NA)	57.7	72.9	12.0
Mathematical scientists	16.3	-	-	1.5	0.7	-	1.6	7.4	5.1	-
Social scientists	257.8	0.3	-	-	1.3	-	7.7	99.0	65.1	84.0
Computer systems analysts, engineers and scientists. . . .	666.2	4.2	1.1	184.4	26.9	26.5	78.1	229.5	83.3	32.0
Engineers [5]	1,353.8	22.2	25.9	640.7	75.4	56.0	11.3	302.2	189.9	29.0
Civil engineers.	172.8	1.1	10.9	8.3	6.2	0.5	0.9	66.2	73.7	5.0
Electrical/electronics	369.9	0.9	5.8	167.6	34.5	35.5	1.1	78.7	39.8	6.0
Mechanical engineers	227.0	1.7	4.0	136.6	5.1	7.1	1.3	52.3	13.8	5.0
Engineering and science technicians.	1,253.1	19.2	25.5	449.5	74.0	84.4	5.1	400.3	160.8	26.0
Electrical/electronics technicians	322.8	1.6	5.1	128.0	26.0	62.1	1.8	67.3	26.7	4.0
Engineering technicians	372.1	5.4	4.5	132.0	26.6	11.4	0.3	94.7	90.4	6.0
Drafters	314.2	2.7	15.9	100.1	17.5	6.6	1.1	144.9	11.3	12.0
Science technicians	244.1	9.5	-	89.3	3.9	4.3	1.9	93.4	32.4	4.0
Surveyors	99.3	2.6	3.3		3.3	-	0.6	55.9	23.0	10.0
Computer programmers.	554.7	3.4	1.3	80.8	24.1	57.0	75.4	246.1	50.1	16.0

- Represents or rounds to zero.   NA Not available.   [1] Includes agriculture, forestry, and fishing not shown separately.   [2] Includes oil and gas extraction.   [3] Includes communications and public utilities.   [4] Finance, insurance, and real estate.   [5] Includes kinds of engineers and technicians not shown separately.

Source: U.S. Bureau of Labor Statistics, *Monthly Labor Review,* November 1993. (Data collected biennially.)

No. 995. Graduate Science/Engineering Students in Doctorate-Granting Colleges: 1985 to 1992

[As of **fall.** Includes outlying areas]

FIELD OF SCIENCE OR ENGINEERING	TOTAL (1,000)			PERCENT—							
				Female			Foreign		Part-time		
	1985	1990	1992	1985	1990	1992	1990	1992	1985	1990	1992
Total, all surveyed fields	**353.8**	**394.8**	**427.8**	**34.5**	**37.5**	**38.6**	**25.6**	**25.1**	**32.2**	**30.7**	**29.9**
Science/engineering	314.8	347.4	374.8	29.4	32.2	33.2	27.9	27.5	30.4	28.5	27.7
Engineering, total	89.7	99.1	108.3	11.5	13.6	14.4	36.7	36.3	39.5	35.6	33.7
Sciences, total	225.1	248.2	266.5	36.6	39.6	40.8	24.3	23.9	26.8	25.6	25.3
Physical sciences	29.4	32.4	33.6	20.5	23.4	24.5	37.1	36.8	11.7	11.2	10.7
Environmental	14.3	13.0	14.0	25.4	29.2	31.0	20.1	21.0	23.9	23.6	24.3
Mathematical sciences . .	15.2	17.2	17.9	29.1	30.4	31.2	36.1	33.9	26.9	23.4	22.4
Computer sciences	23.4	27.4	29.0	24.9	22.8	21.8	33.2	35.0	48.0	46.6	46.4
Agricultural sciences . . .	10.7	10.4	10.9	25.6	29.2	31.5	29.1	27.8	18.2	17.7	18.2
Biological sciences.	42.1	46.2	50.2	42.4	45.5	46.3	24.2	24.9	16.0	14.6	14.8
Psychology.	30.4	34.7	37.7	59.7	65.5	67.3	4.6	4.7	30.1	28.4	27.9
Social sciences	59.6	66.8	73.2	39.7	42.9	44.1	21.9	20.4	34.1	32.4	31.3
Health fields, total.	39.0	47.4	53.0	75.5	76.6	76.4	8.6	8.1	46.2	47.1	45.7

Source: U.S. National Science Foundation, *Survey of Graduate Science Engineering Students and Postdoctorates,* annual.

No. 996. Science and Engineering Degree Recipients in 1991 and 1992: 1993

[Based on survey and subject to sampling error; see source for details]

DEGREE AND FIELD	Graduates 1991 and 1992 (1,000)	1993 [1]—PERCENT DISTRIBUTION				Median salary [4] ($1,000)
		In school [2]	In S&E [3]	In other	Not employed or FT students	
Bachelor's recipients	**639.4**	**22**	**22**	**50**	**6**	**24.0**
All science fields	521.1	24	13	57	6	22.1
Computer and mathematical sciences	77.6	11	32	51	5	28.5
Life and related sciences.	99.7	38	14	43	6	21.0
Physical and related sciences	33.8	39	28	29	4	26.0
Social and related sciences	310.0	21	6	66	6	21.0
All engineering fields	118.4	15	60	20	5	33.8
Aerospace and related engineering	7.3	23	35	37	6	29.0
Chemical engineering	6.7	16	70	10	4	40.0
Civil and architectural engineering.	15.6	12	69	15	4	31.0
Electrical, electronics, computer and communications engineering	41.8	16	59	18	7	35.0
Industrial engineering	7.7	7	59	30	3	33.0
Mechanical engineering.	25.1	13	65	19	3	35.0
Other engineering	14.1	17	53	25	5	33.0
Master's recipients	**115.6**	**23**	**48**	**24**	**5**	**38.1**
All science fields	74.6	26	37	31	5	33.8
Computer and mathematical sciences	24.1	16	48	31	5	40.0
Life and related sciences.	13.2	28	35	31	6	29.0
Physical and related sciences	10.6	38	46	13	4	34.0
Social and related sciences	26.7	31	24	39	6	28.0
All engineering fields	41.0	17	68	11	4	42.9
Aerospace and related engineering	1.9	26	56	16	3	40.0
Chemical engineering	1.7	33	56	7	4	44.0
Civil and architectural engineering.	4.9	15	74	7	5	38.8
Electrical, electronics, computer and communications engineering	15.7	15	71	10	4	44.0
Industrial engineering	2.6	13	63	20	4	42.5
Mechanical engineering.	6.4	17	72	6	4	42.0
Other engineering	7.9	18	61	18	3	43.0

[1] As of April. [2] Full-time graduate students. [3] In science and engineering. [4] Excludes students and the self-employed.
Source: National Science Foundation/SRS, *National Survey of Recent College Graduates: 1993*.

No. 997. Doctorates Conferred, by Recipients' Characteristics: 1980 and 1993

[In percent, except as indicated]

CHARACTERISTIC	1980, total	1993									
		All fields [1]	Engineering	Physical sciences [2]	Earth sciences	Mathematics	Computer sciences	Biological sciences [3]	Agricultural	Social sciences [4]	Psychology
Total conferred (number)	**31,020**	**39,754**	**5,696**	**3,682**	**790**	**1,146**	**878**	**5,090**	**969**	**3,514**	**3,419**
Male	69.7	62.0	90.9	78.8	79.2	77.0	84.4	76.5	59.7	62.9	38.9
Female.	30.3	38.0	9.1	21.2	20.8	23.0	15.6	23.5	40.3	37.1	61.1
Median age [5]	32.2	34.1	31.6	30.0	33.4	31.1	32.3	31.4	34.5	34.8	33.8
CITIZENSHIP [6]											
Total conferred (number)	**30,156**	**38,559**	**5,474**	**3,573**	**756**	**1,107**	**857**	**4,993**	**954**	**3,405**	**3,304**
U.S. citizen	83.6	68.4	40.6	58.3	62.6	44.8	49.5	69.0	47.9	59.9	92.8
Foreign citizen	16.4	31.6	59.4	41.7	37.4	55.2	50.5	31.0	52.1	40.1	7.2
RACE/ETHNICITY [7]											
Total conferred (number)	**26,512**	**28,636**	**2,691**	**1,199**	**516**	**590**	**498**	**3,747**	**506**	**2,215**	**3,606**
White [8]	84.7	83.8	75.1	65.2	89.9	80.7	80.3	83.9	86.4	85.0	77.6
Black [8]	4.2	4.5	1.9	3.3	1.0	1.4	1.2	2.0	3.2	6.0	3.3
Asian/Pacific [8]	4.2	7.0	19.5	21.9	4.5	13.4	15.5	9.8	5.7	3.3	14.6
Indian/Alaskan [8]	0.3	0.4	0.1	0.4	0.8	0.2	0.2	0.2	0.2	0.2	0.4
Hispanic	1.8	3.4	2.4	6.8	2.5	2.7	1.4	3.0	4.0	4.0	3.6
Other/unknown	4.9	0.9	1.0	2.3	1.4	1.7	1.4	1.1	0.6	1.4	0.4

[1] Includes other fields, not shown separately. [2] Astronomy, physics, and chemistry. [3] Biochemistry, botany, microbiology, physiology, zoology, and related fields. [4] Anthropology, sociology, political science, economics, international relations, and related fields. [5] For definition of median, see Guide to Tabular Presentation. [6] For those with known citizenship. Includes those with temporary visas. [7] Excludes those with temporary visas. [8] Non-Hispanic.

Source: U.S. National Science Foundation, Division of Science Resources Studies, Survey of Earned Doctorates, *Selected Data on Science and Engineering Doctorate Awards: 1993*, annual.

No. 998. Space Vehicle Systems—Net Sales and Backlog Orders: 1965 to 1993

[In millions of dollars. Backlog orders as of Dec. 31. Based on data from major companies engaged in manufacture of aerospace products. Includes parts but excludes engines and propulsion units]

YEAR	NET SALES			BACKLOG ORDERS			YEAR	NET SALES			BACKLOG ORDERS		
	Total	Military	Non-military	Total	Military	Non-military		Total	Military	Non-military	Total	Military	Non-military
1965	2,449	602	1,847	2,203	503	1,700	1986	6,304	4,579	[1]1,725	8,063	6,028	[1]2,035
1970	1,956	1,025	931	1,184	786	398	1987	8,051	5,248	[1]2,803	12,393	9,460	[1]2,933
1975	2,119	1,096	1,023	1,304	1,019	285	1988	8,622	6,190	[1]2,432	10,838	7,880	[1]2,958
1980	3,483	1,461	2,022	1,814	951	863	1989	9,758	6,457	[1]3,301	13,356	9,192	[1]4,164
1981	3,856	1,736	2,120	3,174	2,164	1,010	1990	9,691	6,556	[1]3,135	12,462	8,130	[1]4,332
1982	4,749	2,606	2,143	4,337	2,403	1,934	1991	10,515	6,770	[1]3,745	11,664	6,221	[1]5,443
1983	4,940	2,420	2,520	4,865	2,733	2,132	1992	9,266	5,887	[1]3,379	12,809	7,622	[1]5,187
1984	5,225	3,019	2,206	4,624	3,099	1,525	1993	9,341	5,534	[1]3,807	13,282	7,129	[1]6,153
1985	6,300	4,241	2,059	6,707	4,941	1,766							

[1] Includes data for nonmilitary missile systems and parts.

Source: U.S. Bureau of the Census, *Current Industrial Reports*, MA-37D, *Aerospace Industry (Orders, Sales, and Backlog).*

No. 999. Federal Outlays for General Science, Space, and Other Technology: 1970 to 1995

[In billions of dollars. For fiscal years ending in year shown; see text, section 9]

YEAR	CURRENT DOLLARS			CONSTANT (1987) DOLLARS		
	Total	General science/basic research	Space and other technologies	Total	General science/basic research	Space and other technologies
1970	4.5	0.9	3.6	13.9	2.9	11.0
1975	4.0	1.0	3.0	8.2	2.1	6.0
1980	5.8	1.4	4.4	8.2	1.9	6.3
1981	6.5	1.5	5.0	8.1	1.8	6.2
1982	7.2	1.6	5.6	8.5	1.9	6.6
1983	7.9	1.6	6.3	8.9	1.8	7.1
1984	8.3	1.8	6.5	9.0	2.0	7.0
1985	8.6	2.0	6.6	9.1	2.1	6.9
1986	9.0	2.2	6.8	9.2	2.3	6.9
1987	9.2	2.2	7.0	9.2	2.2	7.0
1988	10.8	2.4	8.4	10.5	2.3	8.2
1989	12.8	2.6	10.2	11.9	2.4	9.5
1990	14.4	2.8	11.6	12.8	2.5	10.3
1991	16.1	3.1	13.0	13.7	2.7	11.0
1992	16.4	3.5	12.8	13.7	3.0	10.7
1993	17.0	3.9	13.1	13.9	3.2	10.7
1994	16.2	3.8	12.4	12.7	3.0	9.7
1995	16.9	4.1	12.8	13.0	3.2	9.8

Source: U.S. Office of Management and Budget, *Budget of the United States*, annual.

No. 1000. NASA Financial Summary: 1970 to 1994

[In millions of dollars. For fiscal year ending in year shown; see text, section 9]

YEAR	TOTAL		R&D		COMMUNICA-TIONS [1]		FACILITIES CONSTRUCTION		RESEARCH AND PROGRAM DEVELOPMENT	
	Appro-priations	Outlays	Appro-priations	Outlays	Appro-priations	Outlays	Appro-priations	Outlays	Appro-priations	Outlays
1970	3,749	3,753	3,006	2,992	-	-	53	54	690	707
1975	3,231	3,267	2,331	2,420	-	-	140	85	760	761
1980	5,243	4,852	4,091	3,701	-	-	156	140	996	1,010
1985	7,552	7,318	2,468	2,118	3,602	3,707	150	170	1,332	1,323
1986	7,764	7,404	2,638	2,615	3,689	3,267	133	189	1,303	1,332
1987	10,621	7,592	3,166	2,436	5,561	3,597	469	149	1,425	1,409
1988	9,002	9,092	3,414	2,916	3,908	4,362	178	166	1,501	1,648
1989 [2]	10,898	11,051	4,267	3,922	4,464	5,030	305	190	1,862	1,908
1990 [2]	12,296	12,428	5,221	5,094	4,555	5,117	588	218	1,923	1,991
1991 [2]	15,078	13,877	6,024	5,766	6,334	5,590	498	326	2,212	2,185
1992 [2]	14,302	13,818	6,396	6,261	5,124	5,311	525	448	2,242	1,784
1994, est. [2]	14,551	(NA)	7,529	(NA)	4,854	(NA)	518	(NA)	1,636	(NA)

- Represents zero.   NA Not available.   [1] Space flight, control, and data communications.   [2] Include appropriations and outlays for the Inspector General, not shown separately.

Source: U.S. National Aeronautics and Space Administration, *1995 Budget Summary.*

No. 1001. National Aeronautics and Space Administration—Budget Summary: 1993 to 1995

[**In millions of dollars**. Data represent budget authority for fiscal years]

ITEM	1993	1994	1995
Total	**14,322.5**	**14,551.4**	**14,300.0**
Human space flight.	6,672.0	6,069.7	5,719.9
Space station	2,162.0	1,937.0	1,889.6
Russian cooperation	79.5	170.8	150.1
Space shuttle	3,988.2	3,549.3	3,324.0
Payload and utilization operations	442.3	412.6	356.2
Science, aeronautics and technology	4,908.7	5,847.3	5,901.2
Space science	1,510.4	1,721.9	1,766.0
Life and microgravity sciences and applications	407.5	515.3	470.9
Mission to planet earth.	936.3	1,024.5	1,238.1
Aeronautical research and technology	769.4	1,102.2	898.5
Advanced concepts and technology	464.9	495.3	608.4
Launch services	180.8	313.5	340.9
Mission communication services	546.5	589.1	481.2
Academic programs.	92.9	85.5	97.2
Mission support	2,727.2	2,619.0	2,662.9
Safety, reliability and quality assurance	32.7	34.3	38.7
Space communication services	333.7	214.4	268.9
Research and program management	2,171.4	2,148.2	2,220.3
Construction of facilities	189.4	222.1	135.0
Inspector General.	14.6	15.4	16.0

Source: U.S. National Aeronautics and Space Administration, *1995 Budget Summary*.

No. 1002. U.S. Commercial Space Revenues: 1990 to 1994

[**In millions of dollars**. For calendar years]

INDUSTRY	1990	1991	1992	1993	1994 [1]
Total	**3,385**	**4,370**	**4,860**	**5,295**	**6,490**
Commercial satellites delivered.	1,000	1,300	1,300	1,100	1,400
Satellite services	800	1,200	1,500	1,850	2,300
Fixed	735	1,115	1,275	1,600	1,950
Mobile.	65	85	225	250	350
Satellite ground equipment.	860	1,300	1,400	1,600	1,850
Mobile-equipment	145	280	350	420	480
Commercial launches	570	380	450	465	580
Remote sensing data and services	155	190	210	250	300
Commercial R&D infrastructure.	-	-	-	30	60

- Represents zero.   [1] Forecast.

Source: U.S. Department of Commerce, International Trade Administration, *U.S. Industrial Outlook, 1994*.

No. 1003. NASA Space Shuttle Operations Expenditures: 1993 to 1995

[**In millions of dollars**. Data are funding requirements fiscal years shown]

OPERATION	1993	1994	1995
Total.	**2,857.2**	**2,570.6**	**2,420.1**
Orbiter.	477.0	364.1	292.8
System integration	200.6	211.2	190.5
External tank.	300.2	305.3	379.6
Space shuttle main engine.	239.9	191.8	144.4
Redesigned solid rocket	409.4	368.9	373.1
Solid rocket booster	172.0	156.4	144.9
Launch and landing operations.	697.1	650.1	596.4
Mission and crew operations	361.0	322.8	298.4

Source: U.S. National Aeronautics and Space Administration, *1995 Budget Summary*.

No. 1004. Space Shuttle Flights—Summary: 1981 to November 1994

FLIGHT NUMBER	Date	Mission/ Orbiter name	Days duration	FLIGHT NUMBER	Date	Mission/ Orbiter name	Days duration
1	4/12/81	Columbia	2	36	2/28/90	Atlantis	5
4	6/27/81	Columbia	7	31	4/24/90	Discovery	6
2	11/12/81	Columbia	2	41	10/6/90	Discovery	4
3	3/22/82	Columbia	8	38	11/15/90	Atlantis	4
5	11/11/82	Columbia	5	35	12/2/90	Columbia	9
6	4/4/83	Challenger	5	39	4/28/91	Discovery	8
7	6/18/83	Challenger	6	37	4/5/91	Atlantis	6
8	8/30/83	Challenger	6	40	6/5/91	Columbia	9
9	11/28/83	Columbia	10	43	8/2/91	Atlantis	9
10	2/3/84	Challenger	8	44	11/24/91	Atlantis	7
11	4/6/84	Challenger	7	42	1/22/92	Discovery	8
12	8/30/84	Discovery	6	45	3/24/92	Atlantis	8
13	10/5/84	Challenger	8	49	5/7/92	Endeavour	8
14	11/8/84	Discovery	8	50	6/25/92	Columbia	13
15	1/24/85	Discovery	3	46	7/31/92	Atlantis	7
16	4/12/85	Discovery	7	47	9/12/92	Endeavour	7
17	4/29/85	Challenger	7	52	10/22/92	Columbia	9
18	6/17/85	Discovery	7	53	12/2/92	Discovery	7
19	7/29/85	Challenger	8	54	1/13/93	Endeavour	6
20	8/27/85	Discovery	7	56	4/8/93	Discovery	9
21	10/3/85	Atlantis	4	55	4/26/93	Columbia	10
22	10/30/85	Challenger	7	57	6/21/93	Endeavour	10
23	11/26/85	Atlantis	7	51	9/12/93	Discovery	10
24	1/12/86	Columbia	6	58	10/18/93	Columbia	14
25	1/28/86	Challenger	-	61	12/2/93	Endeavour	11
26	9/29/88	Discovery	4	60	2/3/94	Discovery	8
27	12/2/88	Atlantis	4	62	3/4/94	Columbia	14
29	3/13/89	Discovery	5	59	4/9/94	Endeavour	11
30	5/4/89	Atlantis	4	65	7/8/94	Columbia	14
28	8/8/89	Columbia	5	64	9/9/94	Discovery	10
34	10/18/89	Atlantis	5	68	9/30/94	Endeavour	11
33	11/22/89	Discovery	5	66	11/3/94	Atlantis	10
32	1/9/90	Columbia	10				

- Represents zero.

Source: U.S. National Aeronautics and Space Administration, *Payload Flight Assignments NASA Mixed Fleets,* January 1992, and "Space Shuttle Flights as of November 1994".

No. 1005. World-Wide Successful Space Launches: 1957 to 1993

[Criterion of success is attainment of Earth orbit or Earth escape]

COUNTRY	Total	1957-1964	1965-1969	1970-1974	1975-1979	1980-1984	1985-1989	1989	1990	1991	1992	1993
Total	3,569	289	586	555	607	605	550	101	116	88	94	79
Soviet Union/CIS [1]	2,415	82	302	405	461	483	447	74	75	59	54	47
United States	1,001	207	279	139	126	93	61	18	27	18	28	23
Japan	45	-	-	5	10	12	11	2	3	2	1	1
ESA [2]	57	-	-	-	1	8	21	7	5	8	7	7
China	33	-	-	2	6	6	9	-	5	1	3	1
France	10	-	4	3	3	-	-	-	-	-	-	-
India	4	-	-	-	-	3	-	-	-	-	1	-
Israel	2	-	-	-	-	-	1	-	1	-	-	-
Australia	1	-	1	-	-	-	-	-	-	-	-	-
United Kingdom	1	-	-	1	-	-	-	-	-	-	-	-

- Represents zero.   [1] Commonwealth of Independent States.   [2] European Space Agency.

Source: Library of Congress, Congressional Research Service, Science Policy Research Division, *Space Activities of the United States, CIS, and Other Launching Countries/Organizations 1957-1993,* March 29, 1994.

No. 1006. Nobel Prize Laureates in Chemistry, Physics, and Physiology/Medicine—Selected Countries: 1901 to 1993

[Presented by location of award-winning research and by date of award]

COUNTRY	1901-1993				1901-1930	1931-1945	1946-1960	1961-1975	1976-1990	1991-1993
	Total	Physics	Chemistry	Physiology/ Medicine						
Total	420	144	119	157	93	49	74	92	98	14
United States	170	59	38	73	6	14	38	41	63	8
United Kingdom	69	21	24	24	15	11	14	20	9	-
Germany [1]	59	17	28	14	27	11	4	8	7	2
France	24	10	7	7	13	2	-	5	2	2
Soviet Union	10	7	1	2	2	-	4	3	1	-
Japan	4	3	1	-	-	-	1	2	1	-
Other countries	84	27	20	37	30	11	13	13	15	2

- Represents zero.   [1] Between 1946 and 1991, data are for the former West Germany only.

Source: U.S. National Science Foundation, unpublished data.

Transportation—Land

This section presents statistics on revenues, passenger and freight traffic volume, and employment in various revenue-producing modes of the transportation industry, including motor vehicles, trains, and pipelines. Data are also presented on commuting travel, highway mileage and finances, motor vehicle travel, accidents, sales, and registrations, automobile operating costs, and characteristics of public transit, railroads, and pipelines.

In Brief

Transportation outlays reached $1,064 billion in 1993

State gasoline tax rates for 1994—
Lowest rate, 7.5 cents/gallon in Georgia
Highest rate, 31 cents/gallon in Connecticut

The principal compiler of data on public roads and on operation of motor vehicles is the U.S. Department of Transportation's (DOT) Federal Highway Administration (FHWA). These data appear in FHWA's annual *Highway Statistics* and other publications. The U.S. Interstate Commerce Commission (ICC) presents data on interstate land transport in its publications, the *Annual Report to Congress* and the *Transport Statistics in the United States,* which contain data on railroads and motor carriers subject to ICC regulations.

The U.S. National Highway Traffic Safety Administration issues data on traffic accident deaths and death rates in two annual reports: the *Fact Book* and the *Fatal Accident Reporting System Annual Report*. DOT's Federal Railroad Administration presents data on accidents involving railroads in its annual *Accident/Incident Bulletin,* and the *Rail-Highway Crossing Accident/Incident and Inventory Bulletin.*

Various censuses and surveys conducted by the U.S. Bureau of the Census also provide data. Results of the censuses of transportation are presented in the *Truck Inventory and Use Survey.* The *Annual Survey of Manufactures* and reports of the censuses of manufactures, wholesale and retail trade, and service industries contain statistics on the motor vehicle and equipment industry and on retail, wholesale, and services aspects of this industry. Data on persons commuting to work were collected as part of the 1980 census and are in various census reports.

Data are also presented in many non-government publications. Among them are the weekly and annual *Cars of Revenue Freight Loaded* and the annual *Yearbook of Railroad Facts,* both published by the Association of American Railroads, Washington, DC; and the *Transit Fact Book,* containing electric railway and motorbus statistics, published annually by the American Public Transit Association, Washington, DC. Useful annual handbooks in the field of transportation are *Motor Vehicle Facts and Figures* and *World Motor Vehicle Data,* issued by the American Automobile Manufacturers Association (AAMA), Detroit, MI; *Accident Facts,* issued by the National Safety Council, Chicago, IL; and *Transportation in America,* issued by the ENO Foundation for Transportation, Westport, Connecticut.

Urban and rural highway mileage.—
Beginning in 1980, mileage is classified in urban and rural categories, rather than municipal and rural. Urban denotes the Federal-aid legislation definition of an area. Such areas include, as a minimum, a census place with a population of 5,000 to 49,999 or a designated urbanized area with a population of 50,000 or more. These Federal-aid urban areas may extend beyond corporate and census boundaries, and thus are not necessarily coextensive with municipal boundaries. Rural in 1980 refers to non-Federal-aid urban area mileage. Prior to 1980, municipal referred to roads within incorporated places, densely populated New England towns, and certain of the

more populous unincorporated areas and rural to non-municipal roads.

Federal-aid Highway Systems.—The Intermodal Surface Transportation Efficiency Act (ISTEA of 1991 eliminated the historical Federal-aid Systems and created the National Highway System (NHS) and other Federal-aid highway categories. The final NHS has not been approved by Congress. In the interim, a system consisting of the Interstate, Other Freeways and Expressways, and Other Principal Arterial functional systems, serves as the NHS.

Functional Systems.—Roads and streets are assigned to groups according to the character of service they are intended to provide. The functional systems are: (1) arterial highways that generally handle the long trips, (2) collector facilities that collect and disperse traffiC between the arterials and the lower systems, and (3) local roads and streets that primarily serve direct access to residential areas.

Regulatory bodies.—The ICC, created by the U.S. Congress to regulate transportation in interstate commerce, has jurisdiction over railroads, trucking companies, bus lines, freight forwarders, water carriers, coal slurry pipelines, and transportation brokers. The Federal Energy Regulatory Commission is responsible for setting rates and charges for transportation and sale of natural gas and for establishing rates or charges for transportation.

Motor carriers.—For 1960-73, class I for-hire motor carriers of freight were classified by the ICC as those with $1 million or more of gross annual operating revenue; 1974-79, the class I minimum was $3 million. Effective January 1, 1980, class I carriers are those with $5 million or more in revenue. For 1960-68, class I motor carriers of passengers were classified by the ICC as those with $200,000 or more of gross annual operating revenue; for 1969-76, as those with revenues of $1 million or more; and since 1977, as those with $3 million or more. Effective January 1, 1988, class I motor carriers of passengers are those with $5 million or more in operating revenues; class II less than $5 million in operating revenues.

Railroads.—Railroad companies reporting to the ICC are divided into specific groups as follows: (1) Regular line-haul (interstate) railroads (and their non-operating subsidiaries); (2) switching and terminal railroads; (3) private railroads prior to 1964 (identified by ICC as "circular" because they reported on brief circulars); and (4) unofficial railroads, so designated when their reports are received too late for tabulation. For the most part, the last three groups are not included in the statistics shown here.

For years prior to 1978, class I railroads were those with annual revenues of $1 million or more for 1950-55; $3 million or more for 1956-64; $5 million or more for 1965-75; and $10 million or more for 1976-77. In 1978, the classification became class I, those having more than $50 million gross annual operating revenue; class II, from $10 million to $50 million; and class III, less than $10 million. Effective January 1, 1982, the ICC adopted a procedure to adjust the threshold for inflation by restating current revenues in constant 1978 dollars. In 1990, the criteria for class I and class II railroads were $94.4 million and $18.9 million, respectively. Also effective January 1, 1982, the ICC adopted a *Carrier Classification Index Survey Form* for carriers not filing annual report form R-1 with the commission. Effective January 1, 1992, the ICC adopted new revenue classification levels as follows: Class I–$250 million or more; Class II–less than $250 million but in excess of $20 million; Class III–$20 million or less. The inflation adjustment index still applies. Class II and class III railroads are currently exempted from filing any financial report with the Commission. The form is used for reclassifying carriers.

Statistical reliability.—For a discussion of statistical collection and estimation, sampling procedures, and measures of statistical reliability, see Appendix III.

Historical statistics.—Tabular headnotes provide cross-references, where applicable, to *Historical Statistics of the United States, Colonial Times to 1970.* See Appendix IV.

No. 1007. Passenger and Freight Transportation Outlays, by Type of Transport: 1975 to 1993

[In billions of dollars. Freight data include outlays for mail and express. ICC=Interstate Commerce Commission]

TYPE OF TRANSPORT	1975	1980	1981	1982	1983	1984	1985	1986	1987	1988	1989	1990	1991	1992	1993
Total outlays [1]	**298**	**543**	**593**	**591**	**643**	**716**	**753**	**761**	**808**	**869**	**916**	**965**	**952**	**997**	**1,064**
Passenger, total	187	338	374	379	411	460	492	493	528	572	604	630	613	638	683
Private transportation	161	285	317	321	348	387	418	415	445	481	508	528	509	532	571
Automobiles [2]	157	277	307	313	340	379	410	407	436	472	498	517	499	522	560
New and used cars	46	73	83	86	105	126	139	157	151	164	164	166	153	164	173
Tires, tubes, accessories	12	22	25	25	26	27	30	29	21	23	24	25	26	26	28
Gasoline and oil	54	100	111	105	106	106	107	82	94	97	107	121	114	115	115
Insurance less claims	5	12	11	11	12	12	12	14	17	19	19	20	25	27	29
Interest on debt	7	18	21	22	20	25	27	27	29	34	37	36	32	26	30
Registration and operator's permit fees	2	3	4	4	4	5	5	6	6	6	7	7	7	8	9
Repair, greasing, washing, parking, tolls [3]	22	39	42	45	47	52	60	60	75	84	90	94	94	102	112
Air	5	8	9	8	7	8	8	8	9	10	10	10	10	10	11
For-hire transportation [4]	26	53	57	59	63	72	74	77	84	91	96	103	104	106	112
Local [4]	11	20	22	24	24	27	27	30	31	32	33	34	36	36	37
Bus and transit [5]	5	9	10	11	12	13	14	15	15	16	16	17	18	18	18
School bus	2	4	5	5	5	6	6	6	7	7	7	8	8	8	8
Taxi	3	5	5	5	5	6	6	6	6	7	7	8	8	7	8
Intercity	13	28	30	30	33	39	40	40	44	48	51	53	53	53	58
Air	11	25	27	27	30	34	36	36	40	44	47	50	49	49	54
Rail [6]	1	2	2	2	2	2	2	2	2	2	2	2	2	2	2
Bus	1	2	2	2	2	2	2	2	2	2	2	2	2	2	2
International	3	5	5	5	6	7	7	7	9	11	12	15	16	17	18
Freight, total [4]	116	214	228	222	243	268	274	281	294	313	329	352	356	376	397
Highway	85	155	165	163	182	200	206	213	225	239	254	271	274	293	311
Truck, intercity	47	95	97	100	111	121	123	158	135	143	151	162	165	177	190
Truck, local	37	61	68	63	71	79	82	85	90	96	103	108	110	116	122
Rail	17	28	31	27	27	31	29	28	29	30	30	30	30	31	31
Water	8	16	17	16	16	18	18	19	19	20	20	21	20	20	21
Oil pipeline	2	8	8	9	9	9	9	9	9	8	8	8	8	9	9
Air carrier	2	4	4	4	5	6	7	8	9	10	12	14	14	15	16
Percent change, total	5.4	10.3	9.1	-0.2	8.8	11.3	5.2	1.0	6.1	7.6	5.4	5.4	-1.4	4.7	6.7
Passenger, total	9.4	9.9	10.6	1.4	8.3	11.9	7.1	0.1	7.2	8.3	5.6	4.4	-2.7	4.1	7.0
Private transportation	9.2	7.9	11.2	1.3	8.4	11.4	8.0	-0.7	7.0	8.2	5.6	4.0	-3.5	4.5	7.3
Automobiles [2]	9.3	7.7	11.1	1.7	8.8	11.4	8.3	-0.8	7.1	8.1	5.6	3.9	-3.5	4.5	7.3
Air	6.8	14.1	16.0	-12.8	-9.8	10.8	-3.7	3.8	3.7	11.8	-	9.5	-2.9	1.0	7.8
For-hire transportation	11.0	23.3	7.3	2.1	8.0	14.2	2.4	4.6	8.2	8.7	5.8	6.7	1.3	2.5	5.7
Freight	-0.4	10.8	6.9	-2.8	9.5	10.2	2.1	2.7	4.7	6.4	5.1	6.9	1.0	5.6	5.6

[1] Total outlays less than sum of passenger and freight totals, as estimated freight costs included in costs of new cars, gasoline, oil, tires, and tubes have been excluded to prevent duplication. [2] Includes business-owned vehicles. [3] Includes storage and rental. [4] Includes items not shown separately. [5] Includes Federal, State, and local government operating subsidies and capital grants. [6] Includes Federal operating subsidies and capital grants for Amtrak.

Source: Eno Transportation Foundation, Inc., Lansdowne, VA, *Transportation in America*, annual (copyright).

No. 1008. Employment and Earnings in Transportation, by Industry: 1980 to 1994

[Annual averages of monthly figures. Based on Current Employment Statistics program; see Appendix III. See also *Historical Statistics, Colonial Times to 1970*, series Q36-42]

INDUSTRY	SIC [1] code	1980	1985	1988	1989	1990	1991	1992	1993	1994
NUMBER (1,000)										
Total transportation	(X)	2,960	2,997	3,303	3,415	3,527	3,502	3,498	3,587	3,667
Railroads	40	532	359	298	293	279	262	254	250	246
Class I railroads	4011	482	323	259	252	241	231	222	218	214
Local and interurban passengers	41	265	277	309	326	338	354	361	374	387
Trucking and warehousing	42	1,280	1,361	1,548	1,595	1,625	1,606	1,611	1,685	1,749
Water transportation	44	211	185	171	172	177	184	173	167	166
Air transportation	45	453	522	646	683	745	733	730	737	734
Pipelines, exc. natural gas	46	21	19	19	19	19	19	19	18	18
Transportation services	47	198	275	311	329	345	344	348	356	367
AVERAGE WEEKLY EARNINGS (dol.)										
Class I railroads	4011	427	595	674	693	727	707	736	782	786
Local and interurban passengers	41	217	261	293	305	310	323	334	339	345
Trucking and warehousing	42	358	405	419	437	451	455	468	479	494
Pipelines, exc. natural gas	46	441	629	662	671	711	733	772	817	872

X Not applicable. [1] 1987 Standard Industrial Classification, see text, section 13.

Source: U.S. Bureau of Labor Statistics, Bulletin 2445 and, *Employment and Earnings,* March and June issues.

No. 1009. Volume of Domestic Intercity Freight and Passenger Traffic, by Type of Transport: 1970 to 1993

[Freight traffic in bil. ton-miles; passenger traffic in bil. passenger-miles. A ton-mile is the movement of 1 ton (2,000 pounds) of freight for the distance of 1 mile. A passenger-mile is the movement of 1 passenger for the distance of 1 mile. Comprises public and private traffic, both revenue and nonrevenue. See also *Historical Statistics, Colonial Times to 1970*, series Q1-22]

TYPE OF TRANSPORT	TRAFFIC VOLUME						PERCENT DISTRIBUTION					
	1970	1980	1985	1990	1992	1993	1970	1980	1985	1990	1992	1993
Freight traffic, total	1,936	2,487	2,458	2,895	3,009	3,105	100.0	100.0	100.0	100.0	100.0	100.0
Railroads	771	932	895	1,091	1,138	1,183	39.8	37.5	36.4	37.7	37.8	38.1
Truck:												
ICC truck	167	242	250	311	342	365	8.6	9.7	10.2	10.7	11.4	11.8
Non-ICC truck	245	313	360	424	473	506	12.7	12.6	14.6	14.6	15.7	16.3
Water:												
Rivers/canals	205	311	306	390	397	393	10.6	12.5	12.4	13.5	13.2	12.7
Great Lakes	114	96	76	85	77	74	5.9	3.9	3.1	2.9	2.6	2.4
Oil pipelines	431	588	564	584	571	572	22.3	23.6	23.0	20.2	19.0	18.4
Domestic airways [1]	3	5	7	10	11	12	0.2	0.2	0.3	0.4	0.4	0.4
Passenger traffic, total	1,181	1,467	1,635	1,993	2,079	2,126	100.0	100.0	100.0	100.0	100.0	100.0
Private automobiles	1,026	1,210	1,310	1,598	1,675	1,718	86.9	82.5	80.1	80.2	80.6	80.8
Domestic airways [2]	119	219	290	359	367	370	10.1	14.9	17.7	18.1	17.6	17.4
Bus [3]	25	27	24	23	24	23	2.1	1.8	1.5	1.2	1.1	1.1
Railroads [4]	11	11	11	13	14	14	0.9	0.8	0.7	0.7	0.7	0.7

[1] Revenue service only for scheduled and nonscheduled carriers, with small section 418 all-cargo carriers included from 1980. Includes express mail, and excess baggage. [2] Includes general aviation (mostly private business) flying. [3] Excludes school and urban transit buses. [4] Includes intercity (Amtrak) and rail commuter service.

Source: Eno Transportation Foundation, Inc., Lansdowne VA, *Transportation in America,* annual (copyright).

No. 1010. Passenger Transportation Arrangement: 1990 to 1992

[In millions of dollars, except percent. Represents SIC 4722]

SOURCE OF RECEIPTS	1990	1991	1992	OPERATING EXPENSES	1990	1991	1992
Receipts, total [1]	9,036	8,547	8,968	**Expenses, total**	8,262	8,039	8,278
Air carriers	5,106	4,909	5,234	Payroll, annual	3,696	3,580	3,747
Water carriers	362	384	396	Employer contributions [2]	487	489	500
Hotels and motels	627	577	595	Lease and rental payments	676	666	671
Motor coaches	279	288	282	Advertising and promotion	516	467	487
Railroads	79	83	78	Taxes and licenses	125	107	106
Rental cars	151	152	167	Utilities	268	267	289
Package tours	1,872	1,623	1,720	Depreciation	293	282	262
Other	560	531	496	Office supplies	254	236	234
				Repair services	99	93	89

[1] Receipts for firms primarily engaged in arranging passenger transportation. These estimates exclude receipts of transportation companies (airlines, railroads, etc.). [2] Includes contributions to Social Security and other supplemental benefits.

Source: U.S. Bureau of the Census, *Service Annual Survey.*

No. 1011. Transportation Accidents, Deaths, and Injuries: 1980 to 1993

[For related data, see also tables 1033 and 1055]

| YEAR AND CASUALTY | Total (1,000) | Motor vehi-cle[1] (1,000) | Rail-road[2] | Air carriers | | | | Gen-eral avia-tion[6] | Recre-ational boat-ing[7] | Gas pipe-lines[8] | Liquid pipe-lines[9] | Water-borne[10] | Haz-ardous mate-rials[11] |
				Total	Air-lines[3]	Com-muter air car-riers[4]	On demand air car-riers[5]						
Accidents:													
1980....	17,940	17,900	8,451	228	19	38	171	3,590	5,513	1,996	219	4,624	15,737
1985....	19,322	19,300	3,275	195	22	21	152	2,738	6,237	331	183	3,439	6,019
1990....	11,525	11,500	2,879	147	24	15	108	2,214	6,411	199	177	3,613	8,883
1991....	11,324	11,300	2,814	136	26	22	88	2,170	6,573	233	216	2,222	9,110
1992....	10,022	10,000	2,531	117	18	23	76	2,074	6,408	192	224	3,297	9,351
1993....	11,928	11,900	2,785	110	23	16	71	2,022	6,335	216	328	3,188	12,817
Deaths:													
1980....	54.5	51.1	584	143	1	37	105	1,239	1,360	11	3	206	19
1985....	47.3	43.8	454	639	526	37	76	955	1,116	26	5	131	8
1990....	44.6	44.6	599	94	39	6	49	766	865	5	3	85	8
1991....	41.5	41.5	586	200	50	77	73	781	924	14	-	30	10
1992....	39.2	39.2	591	120	33	21	70	812	816	15	5	105	15
1993....	40.1	40.1	653	67	1	24	42	715	800	14	-	104	15
Injuries:													
1980....	2,063	2,000	58,356	74	17	14	43	675	2,650	45	3	176	626
1985....	1,736	1,700	31,617	89	30	16	43	517	2,757	106	18	172	253
1990....	1,728	1,700	22,736	86	39	11	36	391	3,822	67	7	175	425
1991....	1,627	1,600	21,374	83	26	30	27	420	3,967	89	8	110	439
1992....	2,224	2,200	19,408	37	13	5	19	418	3,683	87	38	172	604
1993....	2,019	2,000	17,284	44	18	2	24	383	3,559	97	10	146	626

- Represents or rounds to zero. [1] Data on deaths are from U.S. National Highway Traffic Safety Administration and are based on 30 day definition; see table 1033. Other data are from National Safety Council. [2] Accidents which result in damages to railroad property. Grade crossing accidents are also included when classified as a train accident. Deaths exclude fatalities in railroad-highway grade crossing accidents. [3] Includes scheduled and nonscheduled (charter) air carriers. Represents serious injuries. [4] All scheduled service. Represents serious injuries. [5] All nonscheduled service. Represents serious injuries. [6] 1975 excludes commuter and on-demand air taxis. [7] Accidents resulting in death; injury or requiring medical treatment beyond first aid; damages exceeding $200; or a person's disappearance. [8] Pipeline accidents/incidents are credited to year of occurrence. Beginning 1985, prior data are credited to the year filed. Fatalities and injuries as reported in annual report. [9] Pipelines carrying hazardous materials, petroleum, and liquid petroleum products. [10] Covers accidents involving commercial vessels which must be reported to U.S. Coast Guard if there is property damage exceeding $1,500; material damage affecting the seaworthiness or efficiency of a vessel; stranding or grounding; loss of life; or injury causing a person's incapacity for more than 3 days. [11] Accidents, deaths, and injuries involving hazardous materials cover all types of transport.

Source: U.S. Dept. of Transportation, Bureau of Transportation Statistics, *National Transportation Statistics Annual,* and Historical Compendium Information Report, 1960-1992.

No. 1012. Highway Mileage—Urban and Rural, by Type and Control, and Federal-Aid Highway System: 1980 to 1993

[In thousands, except percent. As of Dec. 31. Data for urban and rural mileage are not comparable to years prior to 1980 because of classification changes; see text, section 21. See also *Historical Statistics, Colonial Times to 1970,* series Q 50, 51, and 55]

TYPE AND CONTROL	1980	1985	1987	1988	1989	1990	1991	1992	1993
Total mileage [1]	[2]3,955	3,862	3,874	3,871	3,877	3,880	3,889	3,902	3905
Urban mileage..........	624	691	710	739	754	757	750	785	803
Under State control.....	79	111	95	96	97	96	96	104	106
Under local control	543	578	614	642	656	661	653	680	696
Rural mileage	[2]3,331	3,171	3,164	3,132	3,123	3,123	3,139	3,117	3102
Percent surfaced [3].....	77.5	88.1	88.4	88.1	88.4	88.6	89.7	88.9	88.7
Under State control.....	702	773	704	704	706	703	703	697	675
Under local control	2,270	2,173	2,249	2,244	2,238	2,242	2,255	2,239	2247
Under Federal control	262	225	212	183	178	178	182	181	180

[1] Beginning 1985, includes only public road mileage as defined 23 USC 402. [2] Includes 98,000 miles of nonpublic road mileage previously contained in other rural categories. [3] Covers soil-surfaced roads and roads with slag, gravel, stone, bituminous, or concrete surfaces.

Source: U.S. Federal Highway Administration, *Highway Statistics,* annual.

No. 1013. Highway Mileage—Functional Systems and Urban/Rural: 1993

[As of Dec. 31. For definition of urban, rural, see text, section 21]

STATE	FUNCTIONAL SYSTEMS					Urban	Rural
	Total	Interstate	Other arterial	Collector	Local		
U.S	3,904,721	45,530	381,643	800,414	2,677,134	803,078	3,101,643
AL................	92,209	899	8,721	20,317	62,272	19,381	72,828
AK................	13,849	1,087	1,516	2,487	8,759	1,742	12,107
AZ................	55,763	1,189	4,813	8,974	40,787	16,340	39,423
AR................	77,192	543	6,821	20,202	49,626	7,595	69,597
CA................	169,201	2,423	28,157	32,531	106,090	81,061	88,140
CO	78,721	954	8,286	16,286	53,195	12,903	65,818
CT................	20,357	343	2,969	3,145	13,900	11,543	8,814
DE................	5,544	41	620	938	3,945	1,869	3,675
DC................	1,107	14	280	157	656	1,107	-
FL................	112,808	1,443	11,028	14,988	85,349	49,178	63,630
GA	110,879	1,243	13,109	23,084	73,443	26,274	84,605
HI	4,106	44	666	749	2,647	1,799	2,307
ID	58,835	611	3,539	9,695	44,990	3,416	55,419
IL	136,965	2,051	13,967	21,220	99,727	35,181	101,784
IN	92,374	1,138	8,059	22,605	60,572	19,262	73,112
IA	112,708	783	9,396	31,513	71,016	9,218	103,490
KS................	133,256	871	9,282	33,006	90,097	9,580	123,676
KY................	72,632	761	5,412	17,619	48,840	10,139	62,493
LA................	59,599	871	5,331	12,524	40,873	13,766	45,833
ME	22,510	366	2,285	5,987	13,872	2,583	19,927
MD	29,313	482	3,778	4,980	20,073	13,671	15,642
MA	30,563	565	5,821	5,452	18,725	19,636	10,927
MI	117,659	1,240	12,250	26,033	78,136	28,174	89,485
MN	129,959	914	12,408	29,321	87,316	14,886	115,073
MS	72,834	685	7,007	15,519	49,623	7,904	64,930
MO	121,787	1,178	9,514	25,099	85,996	16,150	105,637
MT	69,768	1,190	6,014	16,459	46,105	2,380	67,388
NE................	92,702	481	7,888	20,737	63,596	5,054	87,648
NV................	45,778	545	2,784	4,899	37,550	4,597	41,181
NH	14,938	224	1,596	2,702	10,416	2,869	12,069
NJ................	35,097	413	5,452	4,736	24,496	24,029	11,068
NM	60,812	998	4,524	6,758	48,532	5,851	54,961
NY................	111,882	1,500	14,207	20,820	75,355	39,293	72,589
NC	96,028	970	9,125	17,905	68,028	21,723	74,305
ND	86,727	571	5,872	18,784	61,500	1,818	84,909
OH	113,823	1,573	10,323	23,062	78,865	31,568	82,255
OK	112,467	929	7,995	25,357	78,186	12,794	99,673
OR	96,036	727	6,820	18,385	70,104	10,028	86,008
PA................	117,038	1,588	13,708	19,646	82,096	32,616	84,422
RI	6,057	70	929	864	4,194	4,723	1,334
SC................	64,158	810	6,877	13,393	43,078	10,521	53,637
SD................	83,305	678	6,084	19,482	57,061	1,860	81,445
TN................	85,037	1,062	8,636	17,756	57,583	16,521	68,516
TX................	294,142	3,234	28,883	61,741	200,284	79,132	215,010
UT................	40,508	937	3,337	7,689	28,545	6,106	34,402
VT................	14,166	320	1,320	3,111	9,415	1,324	12,842
VA................	68,429	1,106	7,895	14,008	45,420	15,581	52,848
WA	79,428	763	7,574	16,778	54,313	17,218	62,210
WV	35,045	550	3,173	8,849	22,473	3,137	31,908
WI	110,978	638	11,925	21,458	76,957	15,591	95,387
WY	37,642	914	3,667	10,604	22,457	2,386	35,256

- Represents zero.

Source: U.S. Federal Highway Administration, *Highway Statistics,* annual.

No. 1014. Highway Pavement Condition, by Type of Road System: 1993

CONDITION	URBAN AREAS						RURAL AREAS				
	Total	Inter-state	Other				Total	Inter-state	Other prin-cipal arter-ial	Minor arter-ial	Major collec-tor
			Free-ways and express-ways	Prin-cipal arter-ial	Minor arter-ial	Collec-tor					
Percent of road mileage rated—											
Poor	11	11	10	16	8	11	9	8	10	12	8
Mediocre	19	25	32	28	14	17	18	24	28	23	14
Fair	34	20	22	23	39	39	34	19	23	26	40
Good	19	26	21	19	19	17	22	33	25	24	19
Very good	17	18	15	14	20	16	17	16	14	15	18

No. 1015. Funding for Highways, by Level of Government: 1980 to 1993

[In millions of dollars. Data compiled from reports of State and local authorities. For Federal highway trust fund receipts, disbursements, and balances, see table 519. State data include District of Columbia]

TYPE	1980	1985	1990	1991	1992	1993		
						Total [1]	Federal	State
Total receipts	**39,715**	**61,506**	**75,294**	**82,379**	**86,703**	**87,305**	**18,204**	**45,298**
Current income	37,604	54,957	69,730	75,452	77,404	79,745	18,204	41,281
Imposts on highway users [2]	22,559	35,599	44,264	50,349	50,889	53,236	15,776	35,890
Other taxes and fees	11,808	15,127	19,827	19,077	19,933	20,534	1,611	3,298
Investment income, other receipts . . .	3,237	4,231	5,639	6,026	6,582	5,975	817	2,093
Bond issue proceeds [3]	2,111	6,549	5,564	6,927	9,299	7,560	-	4,017
Intergovernmental payments [4]	(X)	(X)	(X)	(X)	(X)	(X)	-17,059	8,352
Funds from (+) or to (-) reserves [4]	2,080	-4,058	114	-3,768	-3,155	-766	-222	-777
Total funds available	41,795	57,448	75,408	78,611	83,548	86,539	923	52,873
Total disbursements	**41,795**	**57,448**	**75,408**	**78,611**	**83,548**	**86,539**	**923**	**52,873**
Current disbursements	40,084	54,725	72,457	74,895	78,959	81,713	923	50,079
Capital outlay	20,337	27,138	35,151	36,638	38,309	39,725	324	29,874
Maintenance and traffic services	11,445	16,032	20,365	21,222	22,223	23,360	68	9,529
Administration and research	3,022	4,033	6,501	6,856	7,718	7,887	531	4,656
Law enforcement and safety	3,824	5,334	7,235	7,040	7,088	7,138	-	3,865
Interest on debt	1,456	2,188	3,205	3,139	3,621	3,603	-	2,155
Debt retirement [3]	1,711	2,723	2,951	3,716	4,589	4,826	-	2,794

- Represents zero.   X Not applicable.   [1] Includes other levels of government not shown separately.   [2] Excludes amounts later allocated for nonhighway purposes.   [3] Excludes issue and redemption of short-term notes or refunding bonds.   [4] Plus sign (+) indicates net receipt of funds from other levels of government; minus sign (-) indicates net disbursement of funds to other levels.

No. 1016. Disbursements of State Highway Funds, by State: 1990 to 1993

[In millions of dollars. Comprises disbursements from current revenues or loans for construction, maintenance, interest and principal payments on highway bonds, transfers to local units, and miscellaneous. Includes transactions by State toll authorities. Excludes amounts allocated for collection expenses and nonhighway purposes, and bonds redeemed by refunding. See also Historical Statistics, Colonial Times to 1970, series Q 90-94]

STATE	1990	1992	1993	STATE	1990	1992	1993	STATE	1990	1992	1993
U.S.	53,580	59,458	62,192	KS	697	858	780	ND	189	212	230
				KY	1,008	1,411	1,127	OH	2,271	2,424	2,523
AL	866	820	942	LA	923	1,014	980	OK	827	858	738
AK	336	398	436	ME	332	341	339	OR	765	830	825
AZ	1,525	1,172	1,188	MD	1,464	1,212	1,171	PA	2,885	2,988	3,065
AR	456	616	645	MA	1,055	1,832	2,034	RI	214	211	316
CA	4,294	5,002	5,186	MI	1,526	1,718	1,734	SC	585	622	668
CO	714	745	914	MN	1,228	1,367	1,320	SD	232	259	287
CT	1,204	1,202	1,050	MS	529	650	685	TN	1,174	1,177	1,117
DE	315	401	360	MO	937	1,056	1,111	TX	3,001	2,926	3,380
DC	273	268	289	MT	302	312	328	UT	355	368	410
FL	1,677	2,627	2,882	NE	449	544	537	VT	165	194	210
GA	1,278	1,334	1,294	NV	309	321	355	VA	1,874	1,688	1,578
HI	297	426	400	NH	299	328	368	WA	1,251	1,377	1,602
ID	300	292	312	NJ	1,831	2,657	2,457	WV	650	627	765
IL	2,645	2,820	2,802	NM	409	428	519	WI	979	1,228	1,214
IN	1,218	1,318	1,303	NY	2,874	3,268	4,529	WY	297	246	261
IA	869	1,010	1,000	NC	1,428	1,457	1,626				

Source of tables 1014-1016: U.S. Federal Highway Administration, *Highway Statistics*, annual.

No. 1017. Federal Grants to State and Local Governments for Highway Trust Fund and Federal Transit Administration (FTA), by State: 1994

[Year ending **Sept. 30**]

STATE	HIGHWAY TRUST FUND Total (mil. dol.)	Per capita [1]	FTA [2] Total (mil. dol.)	Per capita [1]	STATE	HIGHWAY TRUST FUND Total (mil. dol.)	Per capita [1]	FTA [2] Total (mil. dol.)	Per capita [1]	STATE	HIGHWAY TRUST FUND Total (mil. dol.)	Per capita [1]	FTA [2] Total (mil. dol.)	Per capita [1]
U.S.	**17,826**	**68.5**	**3,909**	**15.0**	KS...	215	84.3	7	2.7	ND...	105	164.9	2	3.8
					KY...	239	62.5	20	5.3	OH...	705	63.5	91	8.2
AL...	272	64.5	17	4.0	LA...	262	60.8	28	6.5	OK...	249	76.4	11	3.3
AK...	225	370.5	3	4.3	ME...	88	71.2	5	4.1	OR...	203	65.7	103	33.3
AZ...	271	66.4	25	6.2	MD...	298	59.5	96	19.1	PA...	757	62.8	251	20.9
AR...	185	75.4	6	2.5	MA...	963	159.4	132	21.9	RI...	136	136.9	13	13.4
CA...	2,015	64.1	566	18.0	MI...	417	43.9	59	6.2	SC...	232	63.3	11	2.9
CO...	257	70.2	51	14.0	MN...	293	64.1	33	7.2	SD...	134	185.8	3	3.5
CT...	393	120.1	73	22.3	MS...	173	65.0	8	3.0	TN...	284	54.9	28	5.3
DE...	53	75.6	2	3.5	MO...	439	83.1	38	7.2	TX...	1,071	58.3	187	10.2
DC...	72	126.7	269	472.1	MT...	165	193.3	3	3.5	UT...	110	57.8	9	4.7
FL...	795	57.0	111	8.0	NE...	150	92.7	6	3.8	VT...	48	83.3	-	0.8
GA...	384	54.4	81	11.5	NV...	125	86.1	5	3.6	VA...	307	46.8	26	4.0
HI...	222	187.9	16	13.4	NH...	69	60.8	3	2.8	WA...	462	86.4	29	5.5
ID...	115	101.6	2	1.9	NJ...	510	64.6	262	33.2	WV...	172	94.5	8	4.6
IL...	728	62.0	337	28.7	NM...	148	89.7	6	3.7	WI...	339	66.7	26	5.2
IN...	353	61.4	26	4.4	NY...	780	42.9	777	42.8	WY...	114	240.2	1	2.8
IA...	247	87.3	12	4.4	NC...	473	66.9	23	3.3					

[1] Based on Bureau of the Census resident population as of July 1, 1994; excluding population of the territories. [2] Federal Transit Administration.

Source: U.S. Bureau of the Census, *Federal Expenditures by State for Fiscal Year,* annual.

No. 1018. State Gasoline Tax Rates, 1993 and 1994, and Motor Fuel Tax Receipts, 1993

[See also *Historical Statistics, Colonial Times to 1970,* series Q 233-234]

STATE	RATE [1] (cents/gal.) 1993	1994	Receipts, [2] 1993 (mil. dol.)	STATE	RATE [1] (cents/gal.) 1993	1994	Receipts, [2] 1993 (mil. dol.)	STATE	RATE [1] (cents/gal.) 1993	1994	Receipts, [2] 1993 (mil. dol.)
Federal .	18.4	18.4	(NA)	IA ...	20	20	332	NC...	22	21.3	850
State...	(NA)	(NA)	(NA)	KS...	18	18	276	ND...	17	18	74
				KY[3]...	15.4	16.4	370	OH...	22	22	1,204
AL...	18	18	500	LA...	20	20	471	OK[4]...	17	17	343
AK...	8	8	29	ME...	19	19	137	OR...	24	24	336
AZ...	18	18	437	MD...	23.5	23.5	570	PA...	22.35	22.35	1,249
AR...	18.7	18.7	299	MA...	21	21	564	RI...	28	28	110
CA...	17	18	2,340	MI...	15	15	712	SC...	16	16	368
CO...	22	22	397	MN...	20	20	459	SD...	18	18	82
CT...	29	31	394	MS...	18.4	18.4	297	TN[5]...	20	20	612
DE...	22	22	80	MO...	13.03	15.05	440	TX...	20	20	2,069
DC...	20	20	35	MT...	24	27	113	UT...	19	19	185
FL...	11.8	12.1	1,127	NE...	24.4	25.4	224	VT...	16	16	59
GA...	7.5	7.5	353	NV...	24	24	188	VA[3]...	17.5	17.5	660
HI...	16	16	65	NH...	18.7	18.7	103	WA...	23	23	601
ID...	21	21	144	NJ...	10.5	10.5	378	WV...	25.35	25.35	251
IL...	19	19	1,054	NM...	23	21	185	WI...	23.2	23.1	602
IN...	15	15	605	NY...	22.89	22.56	1,474	WY...	9	9	44

NA Not available. [1] In effect Dec. 31. [2] Represents net gallonage receipts. [3] Trucks or combinations with more than two axles pay tax of 2 cents per gallon more in Kentucky, and 3.5 cents per gallon more in Virginia. [4] .08 cents per gallon is for inspection fee. [5] Includes 1 cent per gallon inspection fee.

No. 1019. Public Highway Debt—State and Local Governments: 1970 to 1993

[**In millions of dollars.** Long-term obligations. Data are for varying calendar and fiscal years. Excludes duplicated and interunit obligations. See also *Historical Statistics, Colonial Times to 1970,* series Q 136-147]

ITEM	1970	1980	1985	1987	1988	1989	1990	1991	1992	1993 [1]
Total debt issued	1,892	2,357	8,194	6,898	4,594	5,900	5,838	9,516	12,988	20,070
State	1,306	1,135	5,397	4,395	2,702	3,775	3,277	6,252	9,460	10,035
Local	586	1,222	2,797	2,503	1,892	2,125	2,561	3,264	3,528	3,757
Total debt redeemed ..	1,270	1,982	4,606	4,924	2,774	3,729	5,158	6,138	7,665	16,164
State	800	1,109	3,835	3,211	1,547	2,813	2,041	4,352	5,388	8,082
Local	470	873	771	1,713	1,227	916	3,117	1,786	2,277	2,324
Total debt outstanding .	19,124	27,519	33,379	39,843	41,663	43,834	44,514	47,892	53,539	57,445
Local	5,104	7,427	12,100	15,262	15,927	17,136	16,580	18,058	19,353	22,037

[1] Estimated.

Source of tables 1018 and 1019: U.S. Federal Highway Administration, *Highway Statistics,* annual.

No. 1020. Price Trends for Federal-Aid Highway Construction: 1980 to 1994

YEAR	Common exca-vation (cu. yd.)	SURFACING			STRUCTURES				Com-posite index
		Portland cement concrete (sq. yd.)	Bitumi-nous concrete (ton)	Index	Rein forcing steel (lb.)	Struc-tural steel (lb.)	Struc-tural concrete (cu. yd.)	Index	
Average contract price:									
1980	1.83	14.92	25.29	(X)	0.48	0.94	226.68	(X)	(X)
1985	2.24	14.31	28.52	(X)	0.44	0.80	243.60	(X)	(X)
1986	2.28	15.63	26.48	(X)	0.44	0.85	236.37	(X)	(X)
1987	2.42	14.80	24.65	(X)	0.44	0.89	240.81	(X)	(X)
1988	2.72	14.33	24.91	(X)	0.49	0.92	274.12	(X)	(X)
1989	2.40	15.17	24.08	(X)	0.56	1.02	283.40	(X)	(X)
1990	2.38	15.91	24.52	(X)	0.53	1.01	286.18	(X)	(X)
1991	2.32	16.58	25.52	(X)	0.51	1.03	264.98	(X)	(X)
1992	2.20	17.80	24.66	(X)	0.52	0.92	259.61	(X)	(X)
1993	2.50	18.81	26.26	(X)	0.47	0.86	261.89	(X)	(X)
1994 (3d qtr.)	3.12	21.09	30.29	(X)	0.49	0.86	285.08	(X)	(X)
Index:									
1980	75.5	101.3	102.6	102.2	109.6	106.3	94.1	100.0	97.2
1985	92.4	97.1	115.7	109.6	100.7	89.9	101.2	98.1	102.0
1986	94.0	106.1	107.4	107.0	100.3	96.0	98.2	98.0	101.1
1987	100.0	100.0	100.0	100.0	100.0	100.0	100.0	100.0	100.0
1988	112.2	97.3	101.1	99.8	112.1	104.4	113.8	111.0	106.6
1989	99.0	103.0	97.7	99.4	126.2	115.0	117.7	118.4	107.7
1990	98.1	108.0	99.5	102.3	120.0	114.1	118.8	117.8	108.5
1991	95.5	112.5	103.6	106.5	114.6	116.4	110.0	112.5	107.5
1992	90.8	120.8	100.1	106.9	117.9	103.5	107.8	108.4	105.1
1993	103.2	127.7	106.6	113.5	106.0	97.3	108.7	105.3	108.3
1994 (3d qtr.)	128.6	143.2	122.9	129.5	111.1	96.9	118.4	111.5	121.4

X Not applicable.
Source: U.S. Federal Highway Administration, *Price Trends for Federal-Aid Highway Construction, Third Quarter 1994.*

No. 1021. New Plant and Equipment Expenditures and Capacity Utilization: 1980 to 1994

[In percent]

YEAR	NEW PLANT AND EQUIPMENT EXPENDITURES					CAPACITY UTILIZATION			
	Total United States	Total manufac-turing	Motor vehicle and parts mfg.			All manufacturing		Motor vehicle and parts mfg.	
			Total	Percent of—		Total	Percent change	Total	Percent change
				Total mfg.	Total U.S.				
1980	286.40	112.60	8.54	7.6	3.0	80.2	−6.1	57.8	−27.0
1985	410.12	152.88	13.39	8.8	3.3	79.5	−1.1	83.4	6.1
1986	399.36	137.95	12.79	9.3	3.2	79.0	−0.6	79.5	−4.7
1987	410.52	141.06	10.88	7.7	2.7	81.4	3.0	78.1	−1.8
1988	455.49	163.45	9.75	6.0	2.1	83.9	3.1	80.5	3.1
1989	507.40	183.80	11.49	6.3	2.3	83.9	0.0	79.2	−1.6
1990	532.61	192.61	11.28	5.9	2.1	81.1	−3.3	72.6	−8.3
1991	528.39	182.81	10.20	5.6	1.9	77.8	−4.1	67.5	−7.0
1992	546.60	174.02	8.67	5.0	1.6	78.6	1.0	71.9	6.5
1993	585.64	179.18	12.23	6.8	2.1	80.6	2.5	76.6	6.5
1994	634.02	191.60	15.69	8.2	2.5	(NA)	(NA)	(NA)	(NA)

NA Not available.
Source: American Automobile Manufacturers Association, Washington, DC, *Facts and Figures*, annual.

No. 1022. Alternative Fueled Vehicles in Use, by Fuel Type: 1992 to 1995

FUEL	ALTERNATIVE FUELED VEHICLES (1,000)			FUEL CONSUMPTION (1,000 gasoline-equivalent gallons)		
	1992	1993	1995	1992	1993	1995
All fuels	251,470	315,145	418,626	134,230,646	135,912,985	140,250,410
Liquified petroleum gases (LPG)	221,000	269,000	299,000	208,142	264,655	293,773
Compressed natural gas (CNG)	23,191	32,714	93,186	16,823	21,603	66,783
Liquified natural gas (LNG)	90	299	447	585	1,900	2,734
M85 (Mixture: 85% methanol + 15% gasoline)	4,850	10,263	20,040	1,069	1,593	3,411
Neat methanol (M100)	404	414	413	2,547	3,166	3,160
E85 (Mixture: 85% ethanol+15% gasoline) .	172	441	828	21	48	89
E95 (Mixture: 95% ethanol + 5% gasoline) .	38	27	33	85	80	104
Electricity	1,725	1,847	2,250	374	309	525

Source: Energy Information Administration, *Alternatives to Traditional Transportation Fuels 1993.*

No. 1023. Motor Vehicle Registrations, 1990 to 1993, Vehicle Miles of Travel, 1993, and Drivers Licenses, 1993, by State

[**In thousands, except as indicated.** Motor vehicle registrations cover publicly, privately, and commercially owned vehicles. For uniformity, data have been adjusted to a calendar-year basis as registration years in States differ; figures represent net numbers where possible, excluding re-registrations and nonresident registrations]

| STATE | AUTOMOBILES, TRUCKS, AND BUSES [1] | | | | | 1993 | | | | |
| | 1990 | 1991 | 1992 | 1993 | | Motor-cycle [1] regis-tration (incl. official) | Public road and street mileage (1,000 mi.) | Vehicle miles of travel | | Drivers licenses |
				Total	Auto mobiles (incl. taxis)			Total (bil. mi.)	Per mile of road (1,000)	
U.S	188,798	188,136	190,362	194,063	146,314	3,978	3,905	2,297	588	173,149
AL.	3,744	3,484	3,304	3,390	2,136	40	92	47.3	513	3,009
AK.	477	471	486	489	310	12	14	3.9	283	438
AZ.	2,825	2,849	2,801	2,892	2,068	73	56	39.2	702	2,624
AR.	1,448	1,480	1,501	1,528	987	14	77	24.0	311	1,751
CA.	21,926	22,253	22,202	22,824	17,301	587	169	266.4	1,575	20,123
CO	3,155	3,045	2,915	3,032	2,254	88	79	32.7	416	2,591
CT.	2,623	2,589	2,569	2,594	2,456	37	20	27.0	1,326	2,180
DE.	526	534	545	555	429	10	6	6.9	1,244	506
DC	262	246	256	264	250	2	1	3.5	3,148	361
FL.	10,950	9,980	10,232	10,170	8,072	189	113	120.5	1,068	10,762
GA	5,489	5,714	5,899	5,632	3,960	55	111	78.4	707	4,613
HI	771	785	774	763	659	24	4	8.1	1,966	734
ID	1,054	1,055	1,034	1,023	636	32	59	11.5	195	770
IL	7,873	8,193	7,982	8,070	6,650	201	137	89.7	655	7,462
IN	4,366	4,414	4,516	4,670	3,414	96	92	60.5	655	3,791
IA	2,632	2,668	2,706	2,738	1,948	149	113	25.1	223	1,899
KS.	2,012	1,879	1,921	1,922	1,264	53	133	24.1	181	1,774
KY.	2,909	2,942	2,983	2,629	1,713	32	73	39.6	545	2,469
LA.	2,995	3,046	3,094	3,166	2,010	35	60	36.4	610	2,577
ME	977	979	978	1,028	793	31	23	12.2	541	906
MD	3,607	3,630	3,689	3,560	2,957	41	29	43.3	1,478	3,274
MA	3,726	3,664	3,663	3,837	3,327	68	31	46.7	1,527	4,161
MI	7,209	7,245	7,311	7,399	5,731	137	118	85.7	728	6,527
MN	3,508	3,273	3,484	3,716	2,906	126	130	42.2	325	2,637
MS	1,875	1,887	1,954	2,000	1,526	28	73	26.9	369	1,640
MO	3,905	3,950	4,004	4,066	2,858	57	122	54.8	450	3,472
MT	783	766	907	939	555	22	70	8.7	125	531
NE.	1,384	1,404	1,355	1,439	942	19	93	14.8	159	1,141
NV.	853	881	921	937	632	20	46	11.6	254	976
NH	946	906	894	959	743	36	15	10.3	692	869
NJ.	5,652	5,519	5,591	5,641	5,180	89	35	59.7	1,702	5,459
NM	1,301	1,320	1,352	1,421	856	31	61	18.9	312	1,148
NY.	10,196	9,771	9,780	10,163	8,747	195	112	112.2	1,003	10,327
NC	5,162	5,216	5,307	5,365	3,841	64	96	69.5	724	4,725
ND	630	629	655	662	397	18	87	6.2	71	438
OH	8,410	8,685	9,030	9,279	7,483	233	114	97.0	852	7,635
OK	2,649	2,669	2,737	2,771	1,759	56	112	35.5	316	2,336
OR	2,445	2,507	2,583	2,624	2,001	61	96	28.4	295	2,373
PA.	7,971	8,038	8,179	8,282	6,599	172	117	90.7	775	8,055
RI	672	628	622	695	589	20	6	7.2	1,193	675
SC.	2,521	2,471	2,601	2,684	1,997	34	64	36.1	563	2,431
SD.	704	702	720	808	485	26	83	7.4	89	507
TN.	4,444	4,542	4,645	4,964	3,989	84	85	52.1	613	3,543
TX.	12,800	12,697	12,767	13,118	8,881	144	294	167.6	570	11,876
UT.	1,206	1,230	1,252	1,335	840	23	41	17.1	421	1,190
VT.	462	447	465	483	362	17	14	6.0	422	431
VA.	4,938	5,022	5,239	5,408	4,126	62	68	64.2	938	4,580
WA	4,257	4,404	4,466	4,413	3,123	109	79	46.1	581	3,699
WV	1,225	1,273	1,273	1,345	829	19	35	16.8	479	1,302
WI	3,815	3,685	3,735	3,815	2,460	197	111	49.2	443	3,502
WY	528	469	483	558	283	12	38	6.8	180	350

[1] Excludes vehicles owned by military services.

Source: U.S. Federal Highway Administration, *Highway Statistics,* annual; and *Selected Highway Statistics and Charts,* annual.

No. 1024. Motor Vehicle Production and Trade: 1980 to 1993

ITEM	Unit	1980	1985	1988	1989	1990	1991	1992	1993
Production:									
Passenger car production	1,000...	6,376	8,185	7,137	6,825	6,078	5,439	5,664	5,981
Truck and bus production	1,000...	1,634	3,468	4,101	4,051	3,706	3,372	4,065	4,883
Imports:									
Passenger cars (new) [1][2]	1,000...	3,116	4,398	4,450	4,043	3,945	3,736	3,615	3,808
Canada	1,000...	595	1,145	1,191	1,151	1,220	1,196	1,200	1,468
Germany, Federal Republic of	1,000...	339	473	264	217	245	172	206	184
Japan	1,000...	1,992	2,527	2,123	2,052	1,868	1,789	1,678	1,597
Trucks and buses (new) [2]	1,000...	747	1,253	938	953	766	716	777	722
Japan	1,000...	483	800	542	420	302	283	197	154
All-terrain vehicles [3]	1,000...	(NA)	683	210	121	100	(NA)	(NA)	(NA)
Motorcycles, total [3]	1,000...	1,120	733	287	253	169	(NA)	(NA)	(NA)
Import value:									
Passenger cars (new) [1]	Mil. dol.	16,675	36,474	47,005	44,417	45,716	45,564	46,729	52,208
Trucks and buses, (new) [1]	Mil. dol.	1,985	7,734	8,089	8,591	8,155	8,221	10,000	10,104
Motorcycles [3][4]	Mil. dol.	1,142	783	512	542	361	(NA)	(NA)	(NA)
Exports:									
Passenger cars (new) [1]	1,000...	617	704	781	778	794	755	851	864
Trucks and buses (new) exports	1,000...	186	183	230	189	159	208	161	181
Export value [1][5]	Mil. dol.	16,015	22,820	29,519	31,574	38,086	(NA)	(NA)	(NA)
Passenger cars (new) [5]	Mil. dol.	3,932	6,027	8,318	8,895	9,708	9,886	11,893	12,476
Trucks and buses (new) [5]	Mil. dol.	2,977	2,789	3,683	3,471	2,845	3,388	3,073	3,399
Parts and accessories [6]	Mil. dol.	9,106	14,004	17,518	19,208	24,996	(NA)	(NA)	(NA)
Factory sales:									
Passenger cars	1,000...	6,400	8,002	7,105	6,807	6,050	5,407	5,685	5,960
Trucks and buses	1,000...	1,667	3,357	4,121	4,062	3,725	3,387	4,062	4,895
Retail sales:									
Passenger cars (new) [1]	1,000...	8,979	11,042	10,530	9,772	9,300	8,175	8,213	8,518
Domestics [7]	1,000...	6,581	8,205	7,526	7,073	6,897	6,137	6,277	6,734
Imports [8]	1,000...	2,398	2,838	3,004	2,699	2,403	2,038	1,937	1,783
Trucks and buses [9]	1,000...	2,232	3,984	4,608	4,483	4,261	3,842	4,513	5,318
Light duty (up to 14,000 GVW) [10]	1,000...	1,964	3,700	4,273	4,171	3,984	3,621	4,264	5,015
Med. duty (14,001-26,000 GVW) [10]	1,000...	92	53	83	73	71	50	57	64
Heavy duty (over 26,000 GVW) [10]	1,000...	176	231	251	239	207	171	192	239
Under 6,000 pounds	1,000...	985	2,408	2,926	2,854	2,866	2,724	3,217	3,756
Utility	1,000...	51	429	445	447	490	549	666	721
Van	1,000...	79	115	47	43	31	17	21	18
Minivan (cargo)	1,000...	(X)	103	105	97	83	66	63	70
Station wagon (truck chassis)	1,000...	(X)	86	138	138	112	110	201	321
Minipassenger carrier	1,000...	(X)	301	692	688	750	706	840	1,002
6,000 to 10,000 pounds [11]	1,000...	975	1,280	1,333	1,297	1,097	876	1,021	1,232
Utility	1,000...	108	108	90	93	68	37	51	60
Van	1,000...	172	261	302	289	254	203	241	279
Pickup, conventional	1,000...	546	628	666	663	568	476	524	647
Station wagon (truck chassis)	1,000...	39	95	104	100	85	55	80	60
10,001 pounds and over	1,000...	271	295	349	331	298	242	275	330

NA Not available.   X Not applicable.   [1] Based on data from U.S. Dept. of Commerce.   [2] Includes other countries, not shown separately.   [3] Source: Motorcycle Industry Council, Inc., Irvine, CA. Data from U.S. Dept. of Commerce. Excludes mopeds/motorized bicycles and all-terrain vehicles. Excludes moped imports (motorcycle imports less than 51 cc's) from all countries (except Japan).   [4] Represents c.i.f. value.   [5] Covers assembled and unassembled vehicles.   [6] Includes rubber tires and tubes and used vehicles.   [7] Includes domestic models produced in Canada and Mexico.   [8] Excludes domestic models produced in Canada.   [9] Excludes motorcoaches and light-duty imports from foreign manufactures. Includes imports sold by franchised dealers of U.S. manufacturers. Starting in 1988, includes sales of trucks over 10,000 lbs. GVW by foreign manufacturers.   [10] Gross vehicle weight (fully loaded vehicle).   [11] Includes vehicles, not shown separately.

No. 1025. Motor Vehicles in Use: 1980 to 1993

ITEM	Unit	1980	1985	1988	1989	1990	1991	1992	1993
Cars in use, total	**Million..**	**104.6**	**114.7**	**121.5**	**122.8**	**123.3**	**123.3**	**120.3**	**121.1**
Under 5 years	Million..	52.3	48.7	55.5	57.6	56.5	54.6	50.4	48.5
6-8 years	Million..	25.2	27.8	21.6	20.7	22.6	25.5	27.5	27.8
9-11 years	Million..	14.6	17.2	22.4	21.1	19.1	16.7	16.0	18.1
12 years and over	Million..	12.5	21.0	22.0	23.4	25.1	26.6	26.4	26.6
Average age	Years...	6.6	7.6	7.6	7.6	7.8	7.9	8.1	8.3
Cars retired from use [1]	1,000...	8,405	7,729	8,754	8,981	8,897	8,565	11,194	7,366
Trucks in use, total	**Million..**	**35.2**	**42.4**	**50.2**	**53.2**	**56.0**	**58.2**	**61.2**	**65.3**
Under 3 years	Million..	8.8	9.0	12.5	12.5	12.8	12.0	11.3	12.1
3-5 years	Million..	8.1	6.3	10.3	12.6	13.2	14.0	14.0	13.9
6-8 years	Million..	7.4	10.2	5.9	6.3	8.0	9.9	11.9	12.7
9-11 years	Million..	4.4	6.2	8.9	7.9	6.6	5.3	5.6	7.2
12 years and over	Million..	6.5	10.7	12.6	14.0	15.5	17.0	18.3	19.3
Average age	Years...	7.1	8.1	7.9	7.9	8.0	8.1	8.4	8.6
Trucks retired from use [1]	1,000...	1,732	2,100	2,251	2,189	2,177	2,284	1,587	1,048

[1] For years ending June 30. Represents vehicles failing to re-register.

Source of tables 1024 and 1025: Except as noted, American Automobile Manufacturers Association Inc., Detroit, MI, *Motor Vehicle Facts and Figures*, annual (copyright); and *World Motor Vehicle Data*, annual (copyright).

No. 1026. Motor Vehicle Registrations: 1980 to 1993

[In thousands]

ITEM	1980	1985	1988	1989	1990	1991	1992	1993
Total [1]	155,796	171,654	184,397	187,261	188,798	188,136	190,362	194,063
Automobiles	121,601	131,864	141,252	143,081	143,550	142,569	144,213	146,314
Buses	529	593	616	625	627	631	645	654
Private and commercial:								
Commercial	107	109	112	113	114	114	114	115
School and other	147	157	160	162	161	161	161	161
Publicly owned:								
Federal	4	4	5	4	5	5	5	5
School	271	323	339	346	347	352	365	374
Private and commercial trailers, total	14,372	15,008	15,707	16,115	16,098	16,269	16,715	17,498
Motorcycles	5,694	5,444	4,584	4,434	4,259	4,177	4,065	4,065
Truck tractors	1,402	1,150	1,183	1,237	1,240	1,236	1,279	1,289
Light trucks [2]	(NA)	32,146	35,320	36,530	37,380	37,728	38,257	39,786

NA Not available.　[1] Components may not add to total because of double counting.　[2] Excludes farm trucks.

Source: U.S. Federal Highway Administration, *Highway Statistics*, annual.

No. 1027. Motor Vehicle Tires and Batteries: 1980 to 1993

[In millions]

ITEM	1980	1985	1988	1989	1990	1991	1992	1993
Tires, passenger car, total [1]	145.9	200.9	218.8	214.8	213.6	214.5	228.6	235.0
Radials	83.5	164.7	200.2	200.4	202.1	205.7	221.4	227.4
Replacement	106.9	141.5	155.3	151.2	152.3	155.4	165.8	165.1
Tires, truck and bus, total [1]	31.1	41.1	46.0	46.9	46.9	42.4	45.0	48.4
Radials	3.8	19.7	29.4	30.6	32.5	32.4	36.1	40.3
Replacement	24.4	32.1	33.9	35.2	36.6	32.9	33.7	35.7
Batteries, total [2]	61.7	74.4	80.1	80.3	79.7	79.8	(NA)	(NA)
Replacement automobile batteries	50.1	58.7	63.5	64.4	65.2	66.6	(NA)	(NA)

NA Not available.　[1] Includes original equipment. Also includes exports, not shown separately.　[2] Source: Battery Council International, Chicago, IL, and U.S. Bureau of the Census.

Source: Except as noted, The Rubber Manufacturers Association, Inc., Washington, DC, *RMA Monthly Tire Report*.

No. 1028. Automobile Output and Trade in National Income Accounts: 1980 to 1994

[**In billions of dollars**. Vehicle output equals final dollar sales value of new vehicles, plus net dollar value of used vehicle sales adjusted for changes in inventories and net balance of vehicle exports and imports]

ITEM	CURRENT DOLLARS					CONSTANT (**1982**) DOLLARS				
	1980	1990	1992	1993	1994	1980	1990	1992	1993	1994
Auto output, total	59.2	129.2	133.3	144.5	158.5	79.1	121.4	117.6	121.6	130.1
Final sales	60.1	132.3	133.2	142.2	154.3	80.5	125.3	117.2	121.1	127.1
Personal consumption expenditures	57.2	129.8	125.9	139.3	153.1	80.9	124.5	112.8	119.3	125.5
Producers' durable equipment	14.3	35.6	38.0	38.8	44.0	16.8	33.4	33.2	34.4	38.5
Net exports	−12.8	−35.4	−32.8	−37.7	−44.8	−19.2	−34.7	−30.5	34.2	−38.5
Government purchases	1.4	2.3	2.0	1.9	2.0	2.0	2.1	1.8	1.6	1.6
Change in business inventories	−0.9	−3.1	0.1	2.2	4.2	−1.5	−3.9	0.4	0.5	2.9
New	−0.1	−2.3	0.5	1.9	3.2	−0.1	−3.2	0.7	0.6	2.1
Used	−0.8	−0.8	−0.4	0.3	1.0	−1.3	−0.8	−0.3	−0.1	0.8

Source: U.S. Bureau of Economic Analysis, *The National Income and Product Accounts of the United States: Volume 2, 1959-88*, and *Survey of Current Business*, July 1992, August 1993, and March 1994.

No. 1029. Recreational Vehicles—Number and Retail Value of Shipments: 1970 to 1993

ITEM	1970	1975	1980	1985	1986	1987	1988	1989	1990	1991	1992	1993
NUMBER (1,000)												
Total	380.3	339.6	181.4	351.7	371.7	393.6	420.0	388.3	347.3	293.7	382.7	420.2
Motorized homes	30.3	96.6	99.9	233.3	249.6	255.7	277.1	261.6	226.5	172.6	226.3	(NA)
Travel trailers	138.0	150.6	52.0	75.4	78.2	86.2	89.6	82.9	80.4	77.6	102.5	113.6
Folding camping trailers	116.1	48.1	24.5	35.9	36.5	41.6	42.3	33.9	30.7	33.9	43.3	(NA)
Truck campers	95.9	44.3	5.0	6.9	7.4	10.1	11.0	9.9	9.7	9.6	10.6	(NA)
RETAIL VALUE (mil. dol.)												
Total	1,122	2,320	1,952	6,904	7,434	8,288	9,061	9,019	8,101	6,623	8,774	9,518
Motorized homes	318	1,251	1,381	5,724	6,155	6,826	7,543	7,420	6,660	5,284	6,963	(NA)
Travel trailers	445	856	485	997	1,083	1,219	1,254	1,252	1,220	1,107	1,523	1,644
Folding camping trailers	175	101	69	137	144	167	175	147	134	146	189	(NA)
Truck campers	183	112	17	46	53	76	88	81	86	87	99	(NA)

NA Not available.

Source: Recreation Vehicle Industry Association, Reston, VA, *RV's ... A Year-End Report/1989*. Data also in American Automobile Manufacturers Association of the United States, Inc., Detroit, MI, *Motor Vehicle Facts and Figures*, annual.

No. 1030. Transportation to Work: 1990

[In thousands, except as indicated. Based on workers 16 years old or older]

REGION, DIVISION, AND STATE	MEANS OF TRANSPORTATION TO WORK			Worked at home	Average travel time to work [1] (minutes)	HOUSEHOLDS WITH VEHICLES AVAILABLE		
	Car, truck, van		Percent using public transport-ation			None	One vehicle	Two or more vehicles
	Drove alone	Car-pooled						
United States	84,215	15,378	5.3	3,406	22.4	10,602	31,039	50,306
Northeast.	15,902	2,771	12.8	630	24.5	3,603	6,408	8,862
New England	4,892	749	5.1	191	21.5	568	1,699	2,676
Maine	424	80	0.9	24	19.0	40	159	266
New Hampshire.	443	70	0.7	20	21.9	26	132	254
Vermont	200	36	0.7	17	18.0	17	72	122
Massachusetts	2,148	318	8.3	75	22.7	321	819	1,107
Rhode Island	376	58	2.5	10	19.2	40	132	206
Connecticut	1,301	187	3.9	45	21.1	124	386	721
Middle Atlantic	11,010	2,023	15.7	438	25.7	3,035	4,709	6,186
New York	4,461	861	24.8	213	28.6	1,994	2,153	2,492
New Jersey	2,731	472	8.8	80	25.3	360	966	1,468
Pennsylvania	3,818	690	6.4	145	21.6	681	1,589	2,226
Midwest.	21,091	3,207	3.5	987	20.7	2,238	7,365	12,714
East North Central	14,749	2,206	4.3	551	21.7	1,693	5,230	8,674
Ohio	3,889	521	2.5	119	20.7	416	1,351	2,320
Indiana	2,040	332	1.3	73	20.4	175	670	1,221
Illinois	3,742	653	10.1	144	25.1	588	1,476	2,138
Michigan	3,328	429	1.6	100	21.2	344	1,133	1,943
Wisconsin	1,751	270	2.5	114	18.3	170	600	1,052
West North Central	6,342	1,002	1.9	436	18.4	545	2,135	4,040
Minnesota	1,593	247	3.6	116	19.1	142	517	988
Iowa	971	157	1.2	89	16.2	75	332	657
Missouri	1,816	312	2.0	84	21.6	191	652	1,118
North Dakota	210	31	0.6	24	13.0	16	73	152
South Dakota	233	33	0.3	31	13.8	17	76	166
Nebraska	590	87	1.2	44	15.8	43	182	377
Kansas	929	136	0.6	49	17.2	60	302	583
South	29,495	5,886	2.6	936	22.0	3,208	10,987	17,627
South Atlantic	15,481	3,156	3.4	501	22.5	1,725	5,725	9,053
Delaware	258	43	2.4	8	20.0	20	80	147
Maryland	1,733	376	8.1	65	27.0	216	554	979
District of Columbia	107	37	36.6	9	27.1	93	103	53
Virginia	2,281	500	4.0	103	24.0	205	717	1,370
West Virginia	493	107	1.1	16	21.0	94	247	347
North Carolina	2,528	530	1.0	71	19.8	242	786	1,489
South Carolina	1,235	277	1.1	31	20.5	137	402	720
Georgia	2,379	468	2.8	65	22.7	244	730	1,393
Florida	4,468	819	2.0	132	21.8	474	2,106	2,555
East South Central	5,110	1,005	1.2	149	21.1	607	1,814	3,231
Kentucky	1,195	229	1.6	47	20.7	159	447	773
Tennessee	1,763	324	1.3	52	21.5	181	593	1,079
Alabama	1,374	267	0.8	31	21.2	156	466	885
Mississippi	777	184	0.8	19	20.6	111	307	494
West South Central	8,904	1,725	2.0	286	21.6	876	3,448	5,343
Arkansas	765	153	0.5	28	19.0	88	303	501
Louisiana	1,239	247	3.0	31	22.3	209	542	749
Oklahoma	1,079	191	0.6	41	19.3	91	414	701
Texas	5,821	1,134	2.2	185	22.2	489	2,190	3,392
West	17,727	3,513	4.1	854	22.7	1,553	6,279	11,103
Mountain	4,586	873	2.1	229	19.7	343	1,697	2,993
Montana	250	41	0.6	22	14.8	20	91	194
Idaho	330	53	1.9	21	17.3	17	101	243
Wyoming	154	28	1.4	9	15.4	8	48	113
Colorado	1,217	210	2.9	67	20.7	89	412	781
New Mexico	472	96	1.0	24	19.1	38	185	320
Arizona	1,178	239	2.1	48	21.6	107	532	730
Utah	541	111	2.3	26	18.9	29	153	355
Nevada	444	94	2.7	12	19.8	36	174	256
Pacific	13,141	2,640	4.8	625	23.8	1,210	4,582	8,111
Washington	1,701	282	4.5	86	22.0	141	582	1,149
Oregon	949	165	3.4	56	19.6	88	355	660
California	9,982	2,036	4.9	453	24.6	923	3,452	6,006
Alaska	165	40	2.4	11	16.7	23	64	102
Hawaii	344	116	7.4	19	23.8	35	129	193

[1] Excludes persons who worked at home.

Source: U.S. Bureau of the Census, *Census of Population and Housing, 1990.*

No. 1031. National Personal Transportation Survey (NPTS)—Summary of Travel Trends: 1969 to 1990

[Data obtained by collecting information on all trips taken by the respondent on a specific day (known as travel day), combined with longer trips taken over a 2-week period (known as travel period). Contains data from previous NPTS surveys. For compatibility with previous survey data, all data are based only on trips taken during travel day. Be aware that terminology changes from survey to survey. See source for details]

CHARACTERISTICS	Unit	1969	1977	1983	1990	Percent change, 1969-90	Annual percent change, 1969-90
Households, total	1,000	62,504	75,412	85,371	93,347	49.0	1.9
1 person	1,000	10,980	16,214	19,354	22,999	109.0	3.6
2 persons	1,000	18,448	22,925	27,169	30,114	63.0	2.4
3 persons	1,000	10,746	13,046	14,756	16,128	50.0	2.0
4 persons or more	1,000	22,330	23,227	24,092	24,106	8.0	0.4
Persons, total	1,000	197,213	213,141	229,453	[1]239,416	21.0	0.9
Under 16 yrs. old	1,000	60,100	54,958	53,682	54,303	-10.0	-0.5
16-19 yrs. old	1,000	14,598	16,552	15,268	13,851	-5.0	-0.2
20-34 yrs. old	1,000	40,060	52,252	60,788	59,517	49.0	1.9
35-64 yrs. old	1,000	62,982	66,988	75,353	82,480	31.0	1.3
65 yrs. old and over	1,000	19,473	22,391	24,362	26,955	38.0	1.6
5 yrs. old and over	1,000	(NA)	198,434	212,932	222,101	12.0	0.9
Males	1,000	94,465	102,521	111,514	114,441	21.0	0.8
16 yrs. old and over	1,000	66,652	74,542	83,645	86,432	30.0	1.1
Females	1,000	102,748	110,620	117,939	124,975	22.0	0.8
16 yrs. old and over	1,000	73,526	83,721	92,080	96,371	31.0	1.1
Licensed drivers	1,000	102,986	127,552	147,015	163,025	58.0	2.2
Male	1,000	57,981	66,199	75,639	80,289	38.0	1.6
Female	1,000	45,005	61,353	71,376	82,707	84.0	2.9
Workers	1,000	75,758	93,019	103,244	118,343	56.0	2.1
Male	1,000	48,487	55,625	58,849	63,996	32.0	1.3
Female	1,000	27,271	37,394	44,395	54,334	99.0	3.3
Households with—							
No vehicle	1,000	12,876	11,538	11,548	8,573	-33.0	-1.9
One vehicle	1,000	30,252	26,092	28,780	30,654	1.0	0.1
Two vehicles	1,000	16,501	25,942	28,632	35,872	117.0	3.8
Three or more vehicles	1,000	2,875	11,840	16,411	18,248	535.0	9.2
All vehicles available	1,000	72,500	120,098	143,714	165,221	128.0	4.0
Vehicle trips	Millions	87,284	108,826	126,874	158,927	82.0	2.9
Vehicle miles of travel (VMT)	Millions	775,940	907,603	1,002,139	1,409,600	82.0	2.9
Person trips	Millions	145,146	211,778	224,385	249,562	72.0	2.6
Person miles of travel	Millions	1,404,137	1,879,215	1,946,662	2,315,300	65.0	2.4
Ratios:							
Persons per household	Number	[2]3.16	2.83	2.69	2.56	(NA)	(NA)
Vehicles per household	Number	[2]1.16	1.59	1.68	1.77	(NA)	(NA)
Licensed drivers per household	Number	[2]1.65	1.69	1.72	1.75	(NA)	(NA)
Vehicles per licensed driver	Number	[2]0.70	0.94	0.98	1.01	(NA)	(NA)
Workers per household	Number	[2]1.21	1.23	1.21	1.27	(NA)	(NA)
Vehicles per worker	Number	[2]0.96	1.29	1.39	1.40	(NA)	(NA)
Daily vehicle trips per household	Number	[2]3.83	3.95	4.07	4.66	(NA)	(NA)
Daily VMT per household	Number	[2]34.01	32.97	32.16	41.37	(NA)	(NA)
Average vehicle trip length (miles)	Number	[2]8.89	8.34	7.90	8.87	(NA)	(NA)
Average annual VMT	Miles	12,423	12,036	11,739	15,100	22.0	(NA)
Home to work	Miles	4,183	3,815	3,538	4,853	16.0	(NA)
Shopping	Miles	929	1,336	1,567	1,743	88.0	(NA)
Other family or personal business	Miles	1,270	1,444	1,816	3,014	137.0	(NA)
Social and recreational	Miles	4,094	3,286	3,534	4,060	-1.0	(NA)
Average annual vehicle trips	Number	1,396	1,442	1,486	1,702	22.0	(NA)
Home to work	Number	445	423	414	448	0.7	(NA)
Shopping	Number	213	268	297	345	62.0	(NA)
Other family or personal business	Number	195	215	272	411	111.0	(NA)
Social and recreational	Number	312	320	335	349	12.0	(NA)
Average vehicle trip length	Miles	8.9	8.4	7.9	9.0	1.0	(NA)
Home to work	Miles	9.4	9.1	8.5	11.0	17.0	(NA)
Shopping	Miles	4.4	5.0	5.3	5.1	16.0	(NA)
Other family or personal business	Miles	6.5	6.8	6.7	7.4	14.0	(NA)
Social and recreational	Miles	13.1	10.3	10.5	11.8	-10.0	(NA)
Average vehicle occupancy [3]	Persons	(NA)	1.9	1.7	1.6	[4]-1.3	(NA)
Home to work	Persons	(NA)	1.3	1.3	1.1	[4]-1.3	(NA)
Shopping	Persons	(NA)	2.1	1.8	1.7	[4]-1.6	(NA)
Other family or personal business	Persons	(NA)	2.0	1.8	1.8	[4]-0.8	(NA)
Social and recreational	Persons	(NA)	2.4	2.1	2.1	[4]-1.0	(NA)
Journey-to-work trip mode	Percent	100.0	100.0	100.0	100.0	(NS)	(NS)
Auto	Percent	82.7	80.5	77.6	91.4	(NS)	(NS)
Truck [5]	Percent	8.1	12.5	14.8	(NA)	(NS)	(NS)
Public transit	Percent	8.4	4.7	5.8	5.5	(NS)	(NS)
Other	Percent	0.8	2.3	1.8	3.1	(NS)	(NS)

NA Not available.   NS Percent change irrelevant.   [1] Includes "don't know" and "refusals."   [2] Excludes pickups and other light-trucks as household vehicles.   [3] Includes other purposes not shown separately.   [4] Change from 1977.   [5] Household based trucks, primarily pickups.

Source: Federal Highway Administration, *National Personal Transportation Survey, Summary of Travel Trends, 1969, 1977, 1983,* and *1990.*

No. 1032. Roadway Congestion: 1991

[Various Federal, State, and local information sources were used to develop the data base with the primary source being the Federal Highway Administration's Highway Performance Monitoring System]

URBANIZED AREAS	DAILY VEHICLE MILES OF TRAVEL		VEHICLE HOURS OF DELAY		CONGESTION COST		Delay and fuel cost (mil. dol.)
	Total miles (1,000)	Per lane-mile of freeway	Total hours	Per 1,000 persons	Per reg. vehicle (dol.)	Per capita (dol.)	
Total, average	25,740	1,840	207,170	80	480	340	880
Northeastern cities	41,260	3,070	432,060	90	720	380	1,840
Baltimore, MD	25,820	2,010	130,470	60	530	270	550
Boston, MA	34,900	2,450	356,220	120	920	510	1,520
Hartford, CT.	10,050	930	30,260	50	250	210	130
New York, NY.	133,650	9,530	1,544,140	90	1,090	390	6,620
Philadelphia, PA	29,620	2,440	272,760	60	410	270	1,140
Pittsburgh, PA	13,280	1,630	115,340	60	390	260	480
Washington, DC	41,470	2,460	575,280	180	1,440	740	2,430
Midwestern cities	23,580	1,920	120,860	40	300	190	510
Chicago, IL	62,760	3,920	555,790	70	580	310	2,360
Cincinnati, OH	18,680	1,470	44,440	40	210	160	190
Cleveland, OH	22,490	1,840	49,780	30	140	120	220
Columbus, OH	13,690	1,300	41,570	50	240	200	180
Detroit, MI	38,160	2,870	383,690	100	560	400	1,610
Indianapolis, IN	13,120	1,230	17,130	20	130	80	70
Kansas City, MO.	20,150	2,190	28,390	20	160	100	120
Louisville, KY	10,060	950	21,470	30	190	110	90
Milwaukee, WI	12,570	970	47,960	40	380	170	200
Minneapolis-St. Paul, MN	29,320	2,410	105,880	50	270	220	450
Oklahoma City, OK	11,310	1,170	22,070	30	190	130	90
St. Louis, MO.	30,670	2,730	132,170	70	540	280	550
Southern cities.	11,530	930	87,620	80	400	330	370
Atlanta, GA	40,200	2,770	239,490	130	640	530	1,010
Charlotte, NC.	4,010	480	36,550	80	410	340	150
Ft. Lauderdale, FL	11,480	970	71,040	60	290	230	300
Jacksonville, FL	8,810	720	55,100	70	390	310	230
Memphis, TN	7,080	630	21,600	20	150	110	90
Miami, FL	14,140	990	228,860	120	670	510	950
Nashville, TN	8,390	810	40,090	70	330	290	170
New Orleans, LA	8,110	590	69,730	60	330	270	290
Norfolk, VA	8,960	760	78,150	80	400	350	330
Orlando, FL	9,730	970	74,330	80	420	360	310
Tampa, FL.	5,880	490	48,840	70	320	290	210
Southwestern cities.	16,560	1,300	116,140	70	390	300	500
Albuquerque, NM	3,990	350	19,840	40	200	150	80
Austin, TX	8,860	730	49,020	90	410	400	210
Corpus Christi, TX.	2,580	300	3,470	10	70	50	10
Dallas, TX	38,480	2,760	274,030	130	780	570	1,180
Denver, CO	18,390	1,440	146,110	90	450	390	620
El Paso, TX	5,460	570	9,670	20	120	80	40
Fort Worth, TX	19,800	1,660	105,680	90	450	380	450
Houston, TX.	47,500	3,240	409,970	140	780	600	1,750
Phoenix, AZ.	13,140	1,030	179,060	90	600	390	750
Salt Lake City, UT	8,830	830	17,850	20	110	90	80
San Antonio, TX	15,090	1,340	62,910	50	310	230	270
Western cities	45,140	2,560	404,710	130	770	550	1,730
Honolulu, HI.	7,570	550	57,640	90	500	380	250
Los Angeles, CA.	177,550	8,410	1,834,240	160	1,000	660	7,790
Portland, OR	12,110	900	87,280	80	550	360	380
Sacramento, CA	15,520	1,220	82,020	70	280	300	350
San Bernardino-River, CA.	24,100	1,460	249,720	200	1,340	870	1,070
San Diego, CA.	44,600	2,780	159,710	70	490	300	690
San Francisco-Oakland, CA . . .	67,620	3,850	658,550	180	930	760	2,830
San Jose, CA.	26,600	1,890	236,310	160	990	670	1,010
Seattle-Everett, WA.	30,590	1,960	276,930	150	890	660	1,190

Source: Texas Transportation Institute, College Station, Texas; *Roadway Congestion in Major Urban Areas,* annual (copyright).

No. 1033. Motor Vehicle Accidents—Number and Deaths: 1972 to 1993

[See also *Historical Statistics, Colonial Times to 1970,* series Q 208 and Q 224-232]

ITEM	Unit	1972 [1]	1980	1985	1988	1989	1990	1991	1992	1993
Motor vehicle accidents [2]	Million	17.0	17.9	19.3	20.6	12.8	11.5	11.3	(NA)	11.9
Cars	Million	24.5	22.8	25.6	28.2	15.3	14.3	13.7	(NA)	14.1
Trucks	Million	3.5	5.5	6.1	6.8	6.5	4.4	4.7	(NA)	5.9
Motorcycles	1,000	343	560	480	370	211	180	239	(NA)	187
Motor vehicle deaths within 1 yr. [3]	1,000	56.3	53.2	45.9	49.1	47.6	46.8	43.5	40.8	42.0
Noncollision accidents	1,000	15.8	14.7	12.6	5.3	4.9	4.9	4.7	4.4	4.5
Collision accidents:										
With other motor vehicles	1,000	23.9	23.0	19.9	20.9	20.3	19.9	18.2	17.2	17.9
With pedestrians	1,000	10.3	9.7	8.5	7.7	7.8	7.3	6.6	6.5	6.2
With fixed objects	1,000	3.9	3.7	3.2	13.4	12.9	13.1	12.6	11.5	11.9
Deaths within 30 days [4]	1,000	54.6	51.1	43.8	47.1	45.6	44.6	41.5	39.3	40.1
Vehicle occupants	1,000	41.4	36.8	31.5	35.5	34.9	33.9	31.9	30.5	31.1
Pedestrians	1,000	9.2	8.1	6.8	6.9	6.6	6.5	5.8	5.5	5.6
Motorcyclists [5]	1,000	3.0	5.1	4.6	3.7	3.1	3.2	2.8	2.4	2.4
Bicyclists	1,000	1.0	1.0	0.9	0.9	0.8	0.9	0.8	0.7	0.8
Traffic death rates: [4] [6]										
Per 100,000 resident population	Rate	26.2	22.5	18.4	19.2	18.4	17.9	16.5	15.4	15.6
Per 100,000 registered vehicles	Rate	44.5	34.8	24.8	24.9	23.6	23.1	21.6	21.2	21.3
Per 100 million vehicle miles	Rate	4.3	3.3	2.5	2.3	2.2	2.1	1.9	1.8	1.8
Per 100,000 licensed drivers	Rate	46.1	35.2	27.9	28.9	27.6	26.7	24.6	22.7	22.8
Motor vehicle accidents [7]	Million	24.9	24.1	32.5	34.2	34.4	33.4	31.3	31.8	32.8
Injuries [7]	1,000	5,190	5,230	5,044	5,500	5,560	5,560	5,285	5,445	5,675
Economic loss [7] [8]	Bil. dol.	28.7	57.1	76.0	89.0	93.9	95.9	93.8	98.1	104.1

NA Not available.   [1] Represents peak year for deaths from motor vehicle accidents.   [2] Covers only accidents occurring on the road.   [3] Deaths that occur within 1 year of accident. Includes collision categories not shown separately.   [4] Within 30 days of accident. Source: U.S. National Highway Traffic Safety Administration, unpublished data from Fatal Accident Reporting System.   [5] Includes motor scooters and motorized bicycles (mopeds).   [6] Based on 30-day definition of traffic deaths. [7] Source: Insurance Information Institute, New York, NY, *Insurance Facts.* Estimates based on official reports from a representative cross-section of States. Includes all motor vehicle accidents on and off the road and all injuries regardless of length of disability. [8] Wage loss; legal, medical, hospital, and funeral expenses; insurance administrative costs; and property damage.

Source: Except as noted, National Safety Council, Itasca, IL, *Accident Facts,* annual (copyright).

No. 1034. Motor Vehicle Deaths, by State: 1985 to 1993

[Includes both traffic and nontraffic motor vehicle deaths. See source for definitions]

REGION DIVISION STATE	1985	1990	1992	1993	MILEAGE RATE [1] 1985	MILEAGE RATE [1] 1993	REGION DIVISION STATE	1985	1990	1992	1993	MILEAGE RATE [1] 1985	MILEAGE RATE [1] 1993
U.S.	45,901	47,151	40,800	42,000	2.6	1.8	DC	96	91	(NA)	(NA)	3.0	(NA)
							VA	1,021	1,091	839	875	2.1	1.3
Northeast	6,797	6,610	5,403	5,382	(NA)	(NA)	WV	461	502	420	429	3.6	2.5
N.E.	1,873	1,617	1,292	1,310	(NA)	(NA)	NC	1,553	1,489	1,262	1,384	3.1	2.0
ME	224	215	213	186	2.4	1.5	SC	943	987	807	845	3.5	2.4
NH	198	154	123	122	2.6	1.2	GA	1,462	1,659	1,323	1,406	2.7	1.8
VT	117	94	96	112	2.5	1.8	FL	2,968	3,049	2,480	2,693	3.4	2.3
MA	761	655	485	474	1.9	1.0	E.S.C	3,664	4,259	3,579	3,880	(NA)	(NA)
RI	124	104	79	74	2.1	0.9	KY	749	850	819	876	2.5	2.2
CT	449	395	296	342	2.0	1.3	TN	1,219	1,312	1,155	1,175	2.4	2.3
M.A.	4,924	4,993	4,111	4,072	(NA)	(NA)	AL	1,005	1,234	1,001	1,016	2.0	2.2
NY	2,121	2,318	1,800	1,756	2.3	1.6	MS	691	863	604	813	2.9	3.0
NJ	986	908	766	787	1.9	1.3	W.S.C.	6,197	5,713	5,134	5,173	(NA)	(NA)
PA	1,817	1,767	1,545	1,529	2.4	1.7	AR	580	625	587	583	2.9	2.5
Midwest	9,760	10,248	8,565	8,714	(NA)	(NA)	LA	1,011	1,023	871	881	2.7	2.5
E.N.C.	6,602	6,913	5,656	5,879	(NA)	(NA)	OK	781	684	619	672	2.1	1.9
OH	1,581	1,708	1,440	1,484	2.1	1.5	TX	3,825	3,381	3,057	3,037	2.1	1.8
IN	1,045	1,097	902	891	2.6	1.5	West	10,352	10,561	8,026	8,248	(NA)	(NA)
IL	1,594	1,650	1,375	1,392	2.3	1.6	Mt	3,409	3,379	2,861	2,910	(NA)	(NA)
MI	1,605	1,633	1,295	1,409	2.4	1.6	MT	233	225	190	194	2.7	2.2
WI	777	825	644	703	2.1	1.4	ID	268	259	243	233	2.6	2.1
W.N.C.	3,158	3,335	2,909	2,835	(NA)	(NA)	WY	145	130	118	120	2.2	1.9
MN	657	644	581	538	2.0	1.3	CO	628	583	519	561	2.1	1.9
IA	478	481	437	437	2.4	1.8	NM	561	534	461	433	3.3	2.3
MO	1,005	1,174	985	949	2.6	1.7	AZ	942	947	810	803	2.7	2.2
ND	117	128	88	89	2.2	1.4	UT	335	296	269	303	4.0	1.8
SD	142	166	161	140	2.3	1.9	NV	297	405	251	263	3.9	2.4
NE	259	289	270	254	2.1	1.7	Pac	6,943	7,182	5,165	5,338	(NA)	(NA)
KS	500	453	387	428	2.6	1.7	WA	786	875	651	662	2.3	1.3
South	19,250	19,732	16,648	17,470	(NA)	(NA)	OR	605	608	464	522	2.8	1.8
S.A.	9,389	9,760	7,935	8,417	(NA)	(NA)	CA	5,294	5,411	3,816	3,903	2.6	1.5
DE	119	151	140	113	2.2	1.6	AK	124	102	106	117	3.2	3.0
MD	766	741	664	672	2.3	1.6	HI	134	186	128	134	2.0	1.6

NA Not available.   [1] Deaths per 100 million vehicle miles.

Source: 1985: National Center for Health Statistics; thereafter, National Safety Council, Itasca, IL, *Accident Facts,* annual (copyright).

No. 1035. Fatal Motor Vehicle Accidents—National Summary: 1980 to 1993

[Based on data from the Fatal Accident Reporting System (FARS). FARS gathers data on accidents that result in loss of human life. FARS is operated and maintained by National Highway Traffic Safety Administration's (NHTSA) National Center for Statistics and Analysis (NCSA). FARS data are gathered on motor vehicle accidents that occurred on a roadway customarily open to the public, resulting in the death of a person within 30 days of the accident. Collection of these data depend on the use of police, hospital, medical examiner/coroner, and Emergency Medical Services reports; State vehicle registration, driver licensing, and highway department files; and vital statistics documents and death certificates. See source for further detail]

ITEM	1980	1985	1988	1989	1990	1991	1992	1993
Fatal accidents, total	**45,284**	**39,196**	**42,130**	**40,741**	**39,836**	**36,937**	**34,942**	**35,747**
One vehicle involved	28,306	22,875	24,716	23,742	23,445	21,910	20,388	20,562
Two or more vehicles involved	16,978	16,321	17,414	16,999	16,391	15,027	14,554	15,185
Persons killed in fatal accidents	**51,091**	**43,825**	**47,087**	**45,582**	**44,599**	**41,508**	**39,250**	**40,115**
Occupants [1]	41,927	36,043	39,170	38,087	37,134	34,740	32,880	33,553
Drivers	28,816	25,337	27,253	26,389	25,750	23,930	22,584	23,132
Passengers	12,972	10,619	11,805	11,624	11,276	10,688	10,211	10,350
Nonmotorists [1]	9,164	7,782	7,917	7,495	7,465	6,768	6,370	6,562
Pedestrians	8,070	6,808	6,870	6,556	6,482	5,801	5,549	5,638
Pedalcyclists	965	890	911	832	859	843	723	814
Occupant fatalities by type								
of vehicle, total	**41,927**	**36,043**	**39,170**	**38,087**	**37,134**	**34,740**	**32,880**	**33,553**
Passenger cars [1]	27,449	23,212	25,808	25,063	24,092	22,385	21,387	21,494
Mini-compact	3,141	3,571	3,813	3,812	3,556	3,039	2,714	2,614
Subcompact	4,158	4,422	4,975	4,928	4,753	4,655	4,314	4,238
Compact	927	2,635	4,764	5,099	5,310	5,338	5,354	5,608
Intermediate	3,878	4,391	5,016	5,055	4,849	4,681	4,418	4,424
Full size	4,831	2,974	2,840	2,641	2,386	2,073	2,120	2,061
Largest size	6,746	3,612	2,904	2,610	2,249	1,967	1,676	1,602
Motorcycles	4,961	4,417	3,492	3,036	3,129	2,703	2,291	2,331
Other motorized cycles	183	147	170	105	115	103	104	113
Multipurpose vehicles	895	855	1,040	1,135	1,214	1,476	1,335	1,519
Light trucks	6,591	5,834	7,266	7,416	7,387	6,915	6,763	6,968
Pickup	5,483	4,640	5,880	5,870	5,979	5,671	5,385	5,524
Van	1,000	791	1,001	1,214	1,154	1,154	1,292	1,358
Medium trucks	285	157	125	128	134	115	99	96
Heavy trucks	977	820	786	730	571	546	486	514
Buses	46	57	54	50	32	31	28	18
Persons involved in fatal accidents	**113,269**	**104,045**	**112,958**	**109,866**	**107,777**	**99,369**	**95,691**	**97,449**
Occupants [1]	103,049	95,482	104,086	101,401	99,297	91,707	88,367	90,031
Drivers	62,957	57,883	62,253	6,435	58,893	54,391	51,901	53,343
Passengers	39,892	37,477	41,656	40,816	40,229	37,108	36,330	36,538
Nonoccupants	10,240	8,563	8,872	8,465	8,480	7,662	7,324	7,418
Vehicle miles traveled (VMT) (100 million)	15,273	17,742	20,256	21,070	21,444	21,721	22,471	22,966
Licensed drivers (1,000)	145,295	156,868	162,853	165,555	167,015	168,995	173,125	175,878
Registered vehicles (1,000)	161,490	177,098	188,981	191,694	192,915	192,314	194,427	198,041
Fatalities by road type [1]	(NA)	(NA)	47,087	45,582	44,599	41,508	39,250	40,115
Interstate	4,427	4,148	5,142	4,971	4,993	4,574	4,350	4,191
Federal-aid primary	(NA)	14,526	15,185	14,732	14,203	13,158	12,052	11,256
Federal-aid secondary	(NA)	6,429	6,919	6,769	6,892	6,249	5,849	4,896
Federal-aid urban	(NA)	8,116	8,534	8,398	8,432	7,511	6,582	6,069
Non-Federal-aid	(NA)	10,408	10,844	10,579	10,039	9,924	8,826	8,495
Fatal accidents by the highest blood alcohol concentration (BAC) in accident:								
0.00 percent	(NA)	48.5	50.1	51.1	50.6	52.1	54.5	56.5
0.01 to 0.09 percent	(NA)	10.3	10.2	9.8	9.7	9.4	9.1	8.5
0.10 percent and over	(NA)	41.2	39.7	39.1	39.7	38.5	36.4	35.0
Fatality rate by age group:								
Under 5 years old	6.9	5.2	5.4	5.4	4.9	4.6	4.5	4.5
5 years to 15 years old	8.7	7.4	7.4	7.0	6.4	6.1	5.9	5.8
16 years to 24 years old	46.0	37.1	40.0	36.7	35.2	33.0	29.5	22.2
25 years to 44 years old	24.6	19.6	20.3	20.0	19.7	17.7	16.6	12.2
45 years to 64 years old	17.2	14.5	15.0	15.0	14.9	13.5	13.1	8.8
65 years to 79 years old	19.6	18.0	19.5	19.1	18.8	18.0	17.9	17.9
80 years old and over	25.3	25.1	29.1	28.8	26.8	26.9	26.0	27.9
Fatalities per 100 million VMT	3.3	2.5	2.3	2.2	2.1	1.9	1.8	1.8
Fatalities per 100,000 licensed drivers	35.2	27.9	28.9	27.5	26.7	24.6	22.7	22.8
Licensed driver per person	0.6	0.7	0.7	0.7	0.7	0.7	0.7	0.7
VMT per registered vehicle	9,458	10,018	10,718	10,936	11,107	11,294	11,558	12,149
Fatalities per 100,000 registered vehicles	31.6	24.8	24.9	23.8	23.1	21.6	20.2	21.3
Fatal crashes per 100 million VMT	2.9	2.2	2.1	1.9	1.9	1.7	1.6	1.6
Involved vehicles per fatal crash	1.4	1.5	1.5	1.5	1.5	1.5	1.5	1.5
Fatalities per fatal crash	1.2	1.1	1.1	1.1	1.1	1.1	1.1	1.1
Average occupants per fatal crash	2.3	2.4	2.5	2.5	2.5	2.5	2.5	2.5
Fatalities per 100,000 population	22.5	18.4	19.2	18.4	17.9	16.5	15.4	15.6

NA Not available.

Source: National Highway Traffic Safety Administration, *Fatal Accident Reporting System,* annual.

No. 1036. Highway Mileage, Vehicle Miles of Travel, Accidents, and Fatalities, 1980 to 1993, and by Type of Highway System, 1993

YEAR AND TYPE OF SYSTEM	Highway mileage (1,000)	Vehicle miles of travel (bil.)	Daily vehicle miles per mile	FATAL ACCIDENTS		NONFATAL INJURY ACCIDENTS		FATALITIES [2]	
				Number	Rate [1]	Number (1,000)	Rate [1]	Number	Rate [1]
1980	3,857	1,527	1,082	45,284	2.96	2,008	131	51,091	3.35
1985	3,862	1,774	1,259	39,168	2.21	2,219	125	43,825	2.47
1986	3,880	1,835	1,298	41,062	2.23	2,254	123	46,087	2.51
1987	3,874	1,921	1,361	41,434	2.15	2,294	119	46,390	2.41
1988	3,871	2,026	1,430	42,119	2.08	2,302	114	47,087	2.32
1989	3,877	2,096	1,489	40,718	1.93	2,384	113	45,582	2.16
1990	3,880	2,148	1,516	39,779	1.85	2,501	116	44,529	2.07
1991	3,889	2,172	1,530	36,895	1.70	2,210	102	41,462	
1992	3,902	2,240	1,568	34,928	1.56	2,216	98.93	39,235	1.75
1993, total	**3,905**	**2,297**	**1,611**	**35,750**	**1.56**	**(NA)**	**(NA)**	**40,115**	**1.75**
Urban.	803	1,410	4,811	15,612	1.11	(NA)	(NA)	16,915	1.20
Rural	3,102	887	783	20,138	2.27	(NA)	(NA)	23,200	2.62
Interstate	46	524	31,209	3,916	0.75	(NA)	(NA)	4,535	0.87
Urban.	13	316	67,193	1,747	0.55	(NA)	(NA)	1,936	0.61
Rural	33	208	17,454	2,169	1.04	(NA)	(NA)	2,599	1.25
Noninterstate.	3,859	1,773	1,258	31,834	1.80	(NA)	(NA)	35,580	2.01
Urban.	790	1,094	3,792	13,865	1.27	(NA)	(NA)	14,979	1.37
Rural	3,069	679	606	17,969	2.65	(NA)	(NA)	20,601	3.03

NA Not available.   [1] Rate per 100 million vehicle miles of travel.   [2] Represents fatalities occurring within 30 days of accident. Excludes nontraffic accidents which, for example, occur outside the rights-of-way or other boundaries of roads that are open for public use.

Source: U.S. Federal Highway Administration, *Fatal and Injury Accident Rates on Public Roads in the United States,* annual.

No. 1037. Motor Vehicle Safety Defect Recalls, by Domestic and Foreign Manufacturers: 1980 to 1994

[Covers manufacturers reporting to U.S. National Highway Traffic Administration under section 151 of National Traffic and Motor Vehicle Safety Act of 1966, as amended]

MANUFACTURER	Unit	1980	1985	1987	1988	1989	1990	1991	1992	1993	1994
Motor vehicles:											
Total recall campaigns [1]	**Number**	**167**	**173**	**199**	**197**	**237**	**208**	**220**	**187**	**221**	**244**
Domestic	Number.	129	137	150	152	182	159	168	142	178	179
Foreign.	Number.	38	36	49	45	55	49	52	45	43	65
Total vehicles recalled	**1,000** ..	**4,868**	**5,629**	**9,091**	**4,486**	**7,137**	**5,985**	**8,279**	**10,122**	**10,938**	**6,495**
Domestic	1,000 ..	3,943	4,995	7,298	3,171	6,173	4,070	6,646	6,545	7,671	4,713
Vehicles recalled by four leading auto manufacturers	1,000 ..	3,735	4,811	6,946	[2]2,900	5,855	3,926	6,303	5,880	7,345	4,608
Foreign.	1,000 ..	925	634	1,793	1,315	964	1,915	1,633	3,577	3,267	1,782
Motor vehicle tires:											
Recall campaigns [1] . . .	Number.	24	19	16	12	11	13	12	7	5	5
Tires recalled	1,000 ..	7,070	28	42	215	115	172	153	8	6	93

[1] A recall campaign is the notification to the Secretary of the U.S. Dept. of Transportation and to owners, purchasers, and dealers of motor vehicles and motor vehicle equipment.   [2] Three leading automobile manufacturers.

Source: U.S. National Highway Traffic Safety Administration, *Motor Vehicles Recall Campaigns,* annual.

No. 1038. Cost of Owning and Operating an Automobile: 1980 to 1993

ITEM	Unit	1980	1985	1988	1989	1990	1991	1992	1993
Cost per mile [1]	Cents	27.95	27.20	33.40	38.20	40.96	43.64	45.77	45.14
Cost per 10,000 miles [1] . . .	Dollars. . . .	2,795	2,720	3,341	3,820	4,096	4,364	4,577	4,514
Variable cost	Cents/mile .	7.62	8.04	7.60	7.90	8.40	9.80	9.10	9.30
Gas and oil	Cents/mile .	5.86	6.16	5.20	5.20	5.40	6.70	6.00	6.00
Maintenance.	Cents/mile .	1.12	1.23	1.60	1.90	2.10	2.20	2.20	2.40
Tires	Cents/mile .	0.64	0.65	0.80	0.80	0.90	0.90	0.90	0.90
Fixed cost	Dollars. . . .	2,033	2,441	3,061	3,534	3,877	4,217	4,538	4,486
Insurance.	Dollars. . . .	490	503	573	663	675	726	747	724
License and registration	Dollars. . . .	82	115	139	151	165	169	179	183
Depreciation.	Dollars. . . .	1,038	1,253	1,784	2,094	2,357	2,543	2,780	2,883
Finance charge	Dollars. . . .	423	570	565	626	680	779	832	696

[1] Beginning 1985, not comparable to previous data.

Source: American Automobile Manufacturers Association Inc., Detroit, MI, *Motor Vehicle Facts and Figures,* annual (copyright).

No. 1039. State Legislation—Alcohol and Road Safety Laws: Various Years

REGION, DIVISION, AND STATE	ALCOHOL LEGISLATION			MANDATORY BELT USE LAW			Child safety seat law date [5]	Motor-cycle helmet law [6]	65 SPEED LIMIT	
	21 year drinking age since [1]	Open container law [2]	BAC limit [3]	Effective date	Enforcement [4]	Seating positions			Effective date [7]	Applicable vehicles
Northeast:										
N.E:										
ME	1985	no	0.08	none	(X)	(X)	9/83	[8][9]15	6/87	all
NH	1985	yes	0.08	none	(X)	(X)	7/89	18	4/87	all
VT	1986	no	0.08	1/94	2	all	7/84	yes	4/87	all
MA	1985	yes	0.10	2/94	2	all	1/82	yes	12/91	all
RI	1984	no	[10]0.10	7/91	2	all	7/87	([11])	none	(X)
CT	1985	no	0.10	1/86	1	front	1982	18	none	(X)
M.A:										
NY	1985	no	0.10	12/84	1	front	4/82	yes	none	(X)
NJ	1982	yes	0.10	3/85	2	front	4/83	yes	none	(X)
PA	1935	no	0.10	11/87	2	front	11/83	yes	none	(X)
Midwest:										
E.N.C:										
OH	1987	yes	[10]0.10	5/86	2	front	6/83	[9]18	7/87	some
IN	1935	no	0.10	7/87	2	front	1/84	18	6/87	some
IL	1980	yes	0.10	7/85	2	front	7/83	no	4/87	some
MI	1978	yes	0.10	7/85	2	all	3/82	yes	12/87	some
WI	1986	yes	[10]0.10	12/87	2	front	4/84	[8]18	6/87	all
W.N.C:										
MN	1986	yes	0.10	8/86	2	front	8/83	[8]18	6/87	all
IA	1986	yes	0.10	7/86	1	front	1/85	no	5/87	all
MO	1945	no	0.10	9/85	2	front	1/84	yes	4/87	some
ND	1936	yes	0.10	none	(X)	(X)	1/84	18	4/87	all
SD	1987	yes	0.10	none	(X)	(X)	7/84	18	4/87	all
NE	1985	no	0.10	1/93	2	front	8/83	yes	4/87	all
KS	1985	yes	0.08	7/86	2	front	7/81	18	5/87	some
South:										
S.A:										
DE	1983	yes	0.10	1992	2	front	6/82	[8][12]19	none	(X)
MD	1982	no	0.10	7/86	2	[13]front	1/84	yes	none	(X)
DC	1986	no	0.10	12/85	2	[13]front	7/83	yes	none	(X)
VA	1986	no	0.10	1/88	2	front	1/83	yes	7/88	some
WV	1986	no	0.10	9/93	2	front	7/81	yes	5/87	all
NC	1986	yes	0.08	10/85	1	front	7/85	yes	4/87	all
SC	1986	yes	0.10	7/89	2	front	1/89	21	7/87	all
GA	1986	yes	0.10	9/88	2	front	7/84	yes	2/88	all
FL	1985	yes	0.08	7/86	2	front	7/83	yes	4/87	all
E.S.C:										
KY	1938	no	0.10	none	(X)	(X)	7/82	yes	6/87	all
TN	1984	no	0.10	4/86	2	front	1/78	yes	5/87	all
AL	1985	no	0.10	7/92	2	front	1982	yes	1987	all
MS	1986	no	0.10	3/90	2	front	7/83	yes	4/87	all
W.S.C:										
AR	1967	no	0.10	7/91	2	front	8/83	yes	4/87	all
LA	1987	no	0.10	7/86	2	front	1/85	yes	4/87	all
OK	1983	yes	0.10	2/87	2	front	11/83	18	4/87	all
TX	1985	no	[10]0.10	9/85	1	front	1/85	yes	5/87	some
West:										
Mountain:										
MT	1987	[14]no	0.10	10/87	2	all	10/83	18	4/87	all
ID	1987	[14]Yes	0.10	7/86	2	front	1/85	18	5/87	all
WY	1988	no	0.10	6/89	2	front	4/85	18	5/87	all
CO	1987	no	0.10	7/87	2	front	1/84	no	4/87	all
NM	1934	yes	0.08	1/86	1	front	5/83	18	4/87	all
AZ	1984	no	0.10	1/91	2	front	1984	18	4/87	all
UT	1935	yes	0.08	4/86	2	front	4/83	18	5/87	all
NV	1933	yes	0.10	7/87	2	all	7/83	yes	4/87	all
Pacfic:										
WA	1934	yes	0.10	6/86	2	all	1/84	yes	4/87	some
OR	1935	yes	[10]0.08	12/90	1	all	1/84	yes	10/87	some
CA	1933	yes	[10]0.08	1/86	1	all	1/83	yes	5/87	some
AK	1983	yes	0.10	9/90	2	all	6/85	18	8/92	all
HI	1986	Yes	0.10	12/85	1	front	1983	18	none	(X)

X Not applicable.   [1] Year in which original law became effective, not when grandfather clauses expired.   [2] Law prohibiting open liquor containers in motor vehicles.   [3] Percent blood alcohol concentration (BAC) which constitutes the threshold of legal intoxication.   [4] "1" indicates primary enforcement (law can be enforced on its own), "2" indicates secondary enforcement. (Law enforced only if vehicle stopped for a separate offense.)   [5] Effective date of original law, not of subsequent revisions.   [6] Presence of law or age below which riders are required to wear helmet.   [7] Includes administrative action as well as legislation.   [8] Plus instruction permit holders.   [9] Plus novice license holders.   [10] Different legal limit for minors; repeat offenders (WI only).   [11] Operators under 21 for first year; passengers.   [12] Possession of helmet required by all.   [13] Excluding front center seat.   [14] Does not include beer.

Source: National Safety Council, Itasca, IL, *Accident Facts*, annual.

No. 1040. Estimated Arrests for Driving Under the Influence, by Age: 1980 and 1989

[Total drivers and arrests in thousands. Represents licensed drivers and arrests for those 16 years old and over]

AGE	1980			1989			Percent change in rate, 1980-89
	Drivers	Arrests	Arrests per 100,000 drivers	Drivers	Arrests	Arrests per 100,000 drivers	
Total	145,207	1,425	981	165,518	1,735	1,048	6.9
Percent distribution.	100.0	100.0	(X)	100.0	100.0	(X)	(X)
16 to 17 years old. . . .	3.2	2.2	668	2.3	1.1	503	−24.7
18 to 24 years old. . . .	7.2	12.9	1,757	5.4	8.3	1,607	−8.5
25 to 29 years old. . . .	13.0	17.9	1,347	12.4	22.2	1,869	38.8
30 to 34 years old. . . .	12.0	13.1	1,076	12.4	17.6	1,486	38.1
35 to 39 years old. . . .	9.4	9.6	996	11.2	12.0	1,123	12.8
40 to 44 years old. . . .	7.7	7.4	944	9.7	8.1	872	−7.6
45 to 49 years old. . . .	6.9	5.9	837	7.6	5.3	725	−13.4
50 to 54 years old. . . .	6.9	4.9	686	6.2	3.3	558	−18.7
55 to 59 years old. . . .	6.7	3.5	509	5.7	2.2	400	−21.4
60 to 64 years old. . . .	5.7	1.9	335	5.6	1.4	262	−21.8
65 years old and over .	10.7	1.5	140	13.0	1.2	100	−28.6

X Not applicable.

Source: U.S. Bureau of Justice Statistics, *Drunk Driving, Special Report.*

No. 1041. Police-Reported Traffic Accidents, by Age Group: 1993

[Based on probability sample of police-reported accidents. See source for details]

ITEM	Total	15 yrs. and under	16 to 20 yrs.	21 to 24 yrs.	25 to 34 yrs.	35 to 44 yrs.	45 to 54 yrs.	55 to 64 yrs.	65 yrs. and older
Crash-involved.	10,668,000	74,000	1,665,000	1,342,000	2,866,000	2,068,000	1,181,000	692,000	780,000
Percent male	62	63	61	63	63	60	61	65	63
Percent female.	38	37	39	37	37	40	39	35	37
Percent alcohol-involved.	4	5	2	5	5	4	3	2	1
Passengers injured or killed	1,003,000	291,000	189,000	99,000	159,000	93,000	60,000	47,000	64,000
Percent male	40	45	46	47	43	33	28	16	20
Percent female.	60	55	54	53	57	67	72	84	80
Pedestrians injured or killed	92,000	31,000	8,000	7,000	14,000	12,000	8,000	4,000	8,000
Percent during day	65	74	63	43	57	58	63	75	75
Percent at night	35	26	37	57	43	42	37	25	25
Pedalcyclists injured or killed	65,000	31,000	7,000	6,000	9,000	7,000	3,000	1,000	1,000

Source: U.S. National Highway Traffic Safety Administration, *General Estimates System,* annual; and unpublished data.

No. 1042. Domestic Motor Fuel Consumption, by Type of Vehicle: 1970 to 1993

[Comprises all fuel types used for propulsion of vehicles under State motor fuels laws. Excludes Federal purchases for military use. Minus sign (-) indicates decrease. See also *Historical Statistics, Colonial Times to 1970,* series Q 156-162]

YEAR	FUEL CONSUMPTION					AVG. FUEL CONSUMPTION PER VEHICLE (gal.)			AVG. MILES PER GALLON		
	All vehicles (bil. gal.)	Avg. annual percent change [1]	Cars [2] (bil. gal.)	Buses [3] (bil. gal.)	Trucks [4] (bil. gal.)	Cars [2]	Buses [3]	Trucks [4]	Cars [2]	Buses [3]	Trucks [4]
1970 . .	92.3	5.4	67.8	0.8	23.6	760	2,172	1,257	13.52	5.54	7.85
1975 . .	109.0	2.5	76.4	1.1	31.4	716	2,279	1,217	13.52	5.75	8.99
1980 . .	115.0	−5.9	71.9	1.0	41.9	591	1,926	1,243	15.46	5.95	9.54
1981 . .	114.5	−0.4	71.0	1.1	42.2	576	1,938	1,219	15.94	5.92	9.59
1982 . .	113.4	−0.9	70.1	1.0	42.1	566	1,756	1,191	16.65	5.93	9.80
1983 . .	116.1	2.4	69.9	0.9	45.1	553	1,507	1,229	17.14	5.92	9.77
1984 . .	118.7	2.3	68.7	0.8	49.0	536	1,359	1,308	17.83	5.85	9.83
1985 . .	121.3	2.2	69.3	0.8	51.0	525	1,407	1,302	18.20	5.84	9.79
1986 . .	125.2	3.2	71.4	0.9	52.9	526	1,463	1,320	18.27	5.84	9.81
1987 . .	127.5	1.8	70.6	0.9	55.8	514	1,500	1,357	19.20	5.89	9.87
1988 . .	130.1	2.0	71.9	0.9	57.2	509	1,496	1,345	19.95	5.93	10.16
1989 . .	131.8	1.3	72.7	0.9	57.9	509	1,518	1,328	20.40	5.96	10.41
1990 . .	130.8	−0.8	72.0	0.9	57.7	502	1,428	1,290	21.02	6.39	10.67
1991 . .	128.6	−1.7	70.7	0.9	56.8	496	1,369	1,264	21.69	6.65	10.97
1992 . .	132.9	3.2	73.9	0.9	58.0	512	1,360	1,275	21.68	6.57	10.88
1993 . .	137.2	3.1	75.1	0.9	61.0	513	1,447	1,295	21.64	6.46	10.77

[1] From prior year, except 1970, change from 1965.   [2] Includes taxicabs.   [3] Includes school buses.   [4] Includes combinations.

Source: U.S. Federal Highway Administration, *Highway Statistics Summary to 1985,* and *Highway Statistics,* annual.

No. 1043. U.S. Vehicle, by Model Year and Vehicle Fuel Efficiency: 1991

[For composition of regions, see table 27]

1990 HOUSEHOLD CHARACTERISTICS	U.S. VEHICLES (mil.)					U.S. VEHICLE FUEL EFFICIENCY (mpg)				
	All model years	Model year				All model years	Model year			
		1991 to 1992	1990	1989	1986 to 1988		1991 to 1992	1990	1989	1986 to 1988
Total	151.2	5.5	10.5	12.5	39.0	19.3	21.8	21.5	21.8	22.0
Urban	114.3	4.5	8.5	10.2	30.8	19.8	21.8	21.9	22.1	22.2
Rural	36.9	1.0	2.0	2.4	8.2	18.0	21.6	19.6	20.6	21.5
Household size:										
One person	22.1	0.7	1.4	1.5	4.9	19.1	(S)	21.0	21.7	23.4
Two persons.	49.9	1.9	3.7	4.0	13.1	19.3	20.9	21.1	22.1	21.3
Three persons.	30.3	1.1	2.0	2.8	8.5	20.1	22.5	22.3	21.8	22.9
Four persons	29.3	1.3	2.0	2.9	7.7	19.4	21.7	21.7	21.6	22.2
Five persons.	13.6	0.4	0.9	0.9	3.5	18.9	(S)	21.4	21.8	21.4
Six persons or more.	6.0	(S)	(S)	(S)	1.2	17.6	(S)	(S)	(S)	19.3
Households with children	65.1	2.5	4.5	5.5	16.8	19.4	21.9	21.8	22.0	22.0
Households without children	86.2	3.0	6.0	7.0	22.2	19.3	21.7	21.2	21.7	22.0
One adult.	22.1	0.7	1.4	1.5	4.9	19.1	(S)	21.0	21.7	23.4
Two or more adults	64.0	2.3	4.5	5.5	17.2	19.4	21.3	21.2	21.7	21.7
White	135.3	5.1	9.4	11.1	35.8	19.3	21.8	21.4	21.6	21.9
Black	12.8	(S)	0.7	1.1	2.5	19.4	(S)	(S)	24.3	23.5
Other	3.1	(S)	(S)	(S)	0.6	19.3	(S)	(S)	(S)	(S)
Hispanic descent:										
Yes	9.4	(S)	(S)	(S)	2.3	18.3	(S)	(S)	(S)	20.1
No	141.8	5.3	10.0	12.0	36.6	19.4	21.8	21.4	21.8	22.1

S Figure does not meet publications standards.

Source: U.S. Energy Information Administration, *Household Vehicles Energy Consumption, 1991.*

No. 1044. Household Vehicles—Annual Mileage, Fuel Consumption, and Fuel Expenditures: 1991

1990 HOUSEHOLD CHARACTERISTICS	VEHICLES		VEHICLE MILES TRAVELED		CONSUMPTION			EXPENDITURES	
	Total (mil.)	Percent	Total (bil.)	Percent	Total (bil. gal.)	Gallon (percent)	Btu. (quadril- lion)	Total (bil. dol.)	Percent
Total	151.2	100.0	1,602	100.0	82.8	100.0	10.3	98.2	100.0
Households with children	65.1	43.0	753	47.0	38.9	46.9	4.8	46.1	46.9
Households without children . . .	86.2	57.0	849	53.0	44.0	53.1	5.5	52.2	53.1
One adult.	22.1	14.6	198	12.4	10.4	12.5	1.3	12.3	12.5
Two or more adults	64.0	42.3	651	40.6	33.6	40.6	4.2	39.9	40.6
White	135.3	89.5	1,429	89.2	73.9	89.2	9.1	87.5	89.1
Black	12.8	8.4	143	8.9	7.4	8.9	0.9	8.9	9.0
Other	3.1	2.1	30	1.9	1.6	1.9	0.2	1.8	1.9
Hispanic descent:									
Yes	9.4	6.2	95	5.9	5.2	6.3	0.6	6.1	6.3
No	141.8	93.8	1,507	94.1	77.6	93.7	9.6	92.1	93.7
Eligible for Federal assistance . .	29.8	19.7	279	17.4	15.6	18.8	1.9	18.3	18.6
Number of drivers (fall 1990):									
One.	34.6	22.9	321	20.0	16.8	20.3	2.1	20.0	20.3
Two.	86.7	57.3	934	58.3	48.5	58.6	6.0	57.5	58.6
Three	22.0	14.5	258	16.1	13.0	15.7	1.6	15.5	15.8
Four or more.	7.2	4.7	84	5.2	4.2	5.1	0.5	4.9	5.0
Average number of vehicles per household during the year:									
Part-year vehicle	2.1	1.4	21	1.3	1.1	1.3	0.1	1.3	1.4
Only 1	27.5	18.2	269	16.8	13.4	16.2	1.7	16.0	16.3
Between 1 and 2	14.1	9.3	152	9.5	7.9	9.5	1.0	9.4	9.5
Only 2	49.4	32.6	534	33.3	27.1	32.7	3.4	32.3	32.9
Between 2 and 3	19.3	12.8	219	13.7	11.6	14.1	1.4	13.7	14.0
Only 3	17.6	11.6	187	11.7	9.8	11.8	1.2	11.6	11.8
Between 3 and 4	10.6	7.0	112	7.0	6.0	7.2	0.7	7.0	7.1
4 or more	10.8	7.2	108	6.8	5.9	7.1	0.7	7.0	7.1

Source: U.S. Energy Information Administration, *Household Vehicles Energy Consumption, 1991.*

No. 1045. Motor Vehicle Travel, by Type of Vehicle and by Speed: 1970 to 1993

[Travel in billions of vehicle-miles, except as indicated. Travel estimates based on automatic traffic recorder data. Speed trend data for 1970-1975 were collected by several State highway agencies, normally during summer months; beginning Oct. 1975 all States have monitored speeds at locations on several highway systems Monitoring Program. See also *Historical Statistics, Colonial Times to 1970,* series Q 199-207]

| YEAR | VEHICLE-MILES OF TRAVEL (bil.) | | | | AVG. MILES PER VEHICLE (1,000) | | | MOTOR VEHICLE SPEED ON RURAL INTERSTATE | | | | |
| | Total | Cars [1] | Buses | Trucks | Passenger vehicles | | Trucks | Citations recorded (1,000) [2] | Avg. speed (miles per hour) | Percent of vehicles exceeding— | | |
					Cars [1]	Buses				55 mph	60 mph	65 mph
1970	1,110	917	4.5	186	10.3	12.0	9.9	200	63.8	87	69	44
1980	1,527	1,111	6.1	399	9.1	11.5	11.9	667	57.5	66	25	7
1985	1,774	1,261	4.9	500	9.6	8.2	12.7	8,449	59.5	75	44	17
1986	1,835	1,301	5.1	519	9.6	8.5	13.0	8,549	59.7	76	46	18
1987	1,921	1,355	5.3	551	9.9	8.8	13.4	7,992	59.7	74	46	19
1988	2,026	1,430	5.5	581	10.1	8.9	13.7	7,566	59.5	74	46	19
1989	2,096	1,478	5.7	603	10.3	9.0	13.8	7,488	60.1	77	49	22
1990	2,144	1,513	5.7	616	10.5	9.1	13.8	7,511	60.4	78	50	23
1991	2,172	1,543	5.7	624	10.8	9.1	13.9	7,594	59.9	76	48	21
1992	2,247	1,601	5.8	631	11.1	8.9	13.9	7,004	61.2	81	56	28
1993	2,297	1,624	6.1	657	11.1	9.4	13.9	6,433	60.8	78	51	24

[1] Includes motorcycles.　　[2] Citations issued for 55 mph violations.

Source: U.S. Federal Highway Administration, *Highway Statistics Summary,* annual.

No. 1046. Passenger Transit Industry—Summary: 1985 to 1993

[Includes Puerto Rico. Includes aggregate information for all transit systems in the United States. Excludes nontransit services such as taxicab, school bus, unregulated jitney, sightseeing bus, intercity bus, and special application mass transportation systems (e.g., amusement parks, airports, island, and urban park ferries) Includes active vehicles only]

ITEM	Unit	1985	1988	1989	1990	1991	1992	1993, prel.
Operating systems	Number. . .	4,972	5,036	5,046	5,078	5,084	5,086	5,088
Motor bus systems [1] . . .	Number. . .	2,631	2,671	2,665	2,688	2,689	2,693	2,694
Publicly owned systems [1] . .	Number. . .	1,435	(NA)	(NA)	1,580	(NA)	(NA)	(NA)
Passenger vehicles owned [2] .	Number. . .	94,368	97,209	92,293	92,961	96,399	102,251	106,664
Motor bus	Number. . .	64,258	62,572	58,919	58,714	60,377	63,080	64,648
Trolley bus.	Number. . .	676	710	725	832	752	907	851
Heavy rail	Number. . .	9,326	10,539	10,506	10,419	10,331	10,245	10,261
Light rail	Number. . .	717	831	755	913	1,095	1,058	1,025
Commuter rail	Number. . .	4,035	4,649	4,472	4,415	4,370	4,413	4,494
Demand response.	Number. . .	14,490	16,812	15,856	16,471	17,879	20,695	23,105
Total revenue	Mil. dol	12,195	14,537	14,985	16,053	16,533	16,915	17,093
Passenger revenue	Mil. dol . .	4,575	5,225	5,420	5,891	6,037	6,152	6,320
Other operating revenue [3] .	Mil. dol . .	702	841	837	895	767	646	1,060
Operating assistance.	Mil. dol . .	6,918	8,471	8,728	9,267	9,729	10,117	9,713
Federal	Mil. dol . .	940	901	937	970	956	969	1,042
Local [4].	Mil. dol . .	5,979	4,893	4,995	5,327	5,573	5,268	4,963
State [4].	Mil. dol . .	(NA)	2,677	2,796	2,970	3,200	3,898	3,708
Total expense	Mil. dol . .	14,077	16,442	17,169	17,979	19,332	20,034	20,866
Operating expense	Mil. dol . .	12,381	14,287	14,972	15,742	16,541	16,781	17,506
Transportation.	Mil. dol . .	5,655	6,052	6,275	6,654	6,727	7,660	8,053
Maintenance.	Mil. dol . .	3,672	4,313	4,493	4,631	4,597	4,831	4,739
Administration.	Mil. dol . .	2,505	3,078	3,251	3,450	3,585	2,674	2,773
Reconciling expense	Mil. dol . .	1,696	2,155	2,196	2,237	2,791	3,253	3,360
Capital expenditure, Federal. .	Mil. dol	2,510	2,521	2,590	2,380	2,396	2,613	3,465
Vehicle-miles operated [2]	Million. . . .	2,791	3,157	3,203	3,242	3,306	3,355	3,387
Motor bus	Million. . . .	1,863	2,097	2,109	2,130	2,167	2,178	2,205
Trolley bus.	Million. . . .	16	15	15	14	14	14	14
Heavy rail	Million. . . .	451	517	532	537	527	525	525
Light rail	Million. . . .	17	21	21	24	28	29	28
Commuter rail	Million. . . .	183	202	210	213	215	219	224
Demand response.	Million. . . .	247	289	300	306	335	364	360
Passengers carried [2]	Million. . . .	8,636	8,666	8,931	8,799	8,575	8,501	8,362
Motor bus	Million. . . .	5,675	5,590	5,620	5,677	5,624	5,517	5,371
Trolley bus.	Million. . . .	142	136	130	126	125	126	121
Heavy rail	Million. . . .	2,290	2,308	2,542	2,346	2,172	2,207	2,209
Light rail	Million. . . .	132	154	162	175	184	188	188
Commuter rail	Million. . . .	275	325	330	328	318	314	322
Demand response.	Million. . . .	59	73	70	68	71	72	75
Avg. revenue per passenger. .	Cents	53.0	60.3	60.7	66.9	70.4	72.4	75.6
Employees, number (avg.) [5]. .	1,000	270	276	272	273	276	279	303
Payroll, employee.	Mil. dol . . .	5,843	6,675	6,898	7,226	7,395	7,671	7,936
Fringe benefits, employee . . .	Mil. dol . . .	2,868	3,529	3,737	3,986	3,998	4,319	4,392

NA Not available.　　[1] Includes systems with combined services including motor buses, heavy rail cars, light rail cars, trolley coaches, cable cars, and inclined plane cars. Combined services also include commuter rail cars, urban ferry boats, vanpools, aerial tramways, automated guideways, and demand response vehicles.　　[2] Includes other not shown separately.　　[3] Includes other operating revenue, nonoperating revenue, and auxiliary income.　　[4] For 1985, State and local combined.　　[5] Thru 1992, represents employee equivalents of 2,080 hours = one employee; beginning 1993, equals actual employees.

Source: American Public Transit Association, Washington, DC, *Transit Fact Book,* annual.

No. 1047. Transportation Industry Summary: 1992

[Includes only establishments with payroll. N.e.c. = Not elsewhere classified]

KIND OF BUSINESS	SIC [1] code	Establish-ments (number)	Revenue ($1,000)	Annual payroll ($1,000)	First-quarter payroll	Paid employees for pay period including March 12 (number)
Total transportation, except U.S. Post Office		(NA)	327,623	92,211	(NA)	3,356,872
Railroad transportation	40	(NA)	28,349	8,753	(NA)	197,421
Passenger transportation	41	17,805	12,649	5,191	1,246	354,913
Local and suburban passenger transportation	411	8,275	5,968	2,624	613	153,278
Local and suburban transit	4111	1,135	1,364	838	199	37,653
Other local passenger transportation	4119	7,140	4,604	1,786	414	115,625
Sightseeing bus	4119 pt	277	342	104	22	5,565
Limousine service	4119 pt	2,430	964	278	64	20,739
Ambulance or rescue service, except by air . .	4119 pt	3,070	2,507	1,104	256	66,885
Other local passenger transportation, n.e.c . . .	4119 pt	1,363	791	300	72	22,436
Taxicabs.	412	3,337	992	306	75	26,338
Other bus transportation and terminal service	413, 4, 5, 7	6,193	5,689	2,261	558	175,297
Intercity and rural bus service	413	607	1,092	483	116	20,404
Charter bus service.	414	1,307	1,269	394	86	24,604
Local charter bus	4141	429	375	125	29	7,699
Charter bus, except local	4142	878	894	269	58	16,905
School buses.	415	4,260	3,315	1,380	355	130,093
Bus terminal and service facilities	417	19	12	4	1	196
Motor freight transportation and warehousing	42	110,908	143,794	39,896	9,196	1,580,095
Trucking and courier services, except air	421	101,169	135,437	37,760	8,691	1,484,655
Local trucking without storage.	4212	49,870	33,554	8,043	1,799	354,742
Household goods moving	4212 pt	2,566	661	196	43	13,237
General freight	4212 pt	12,186	8,404	2,250	522	97,594
Garbage and trash collection.	4212 pt	7,405	10,985	2,473	577	94,054
Dump trucking	4212 pt	13,383	6,807	1,418	277	66,956
Other local trucking without storage	4212 pt	14,330	6,698	1,707	380	82,901
Hazardous materials.	4212 pt	1,279	885	238	57	9,270
Agricultural products.	4212 pt	6,203	2,188	478	106	26,897
Other local trucking without storage, n.e.c . .	4212 pt	6,848	3,625	990	218	46,734
Trucking, except local	4213	40,821	78,358	20,974	4,808	758,435
Household goods moving	4213 pt	3,248	7,433	1,354	302	61,592
General freight trucking	4213 pt	25,014	55,257	15,880	3,650	553,202
Other trucking, except local.	4213 pt	12,559	15,668	3,741	856	143,641
Hazardous products	4213 pt	1,666	2,759	720	170	25,617
Agricultural products.	4213 pt	4,483	3,304	665	146	30,518
Other trucking, except storage, n.e.c	4213 pt	6,410	9,605	2,356	540	87,506
Local trucking with storage.	4214	4,512	4,191	1,346	303	64,417
Household goods moving	4214 pt	2,641	2,175	703	155	36,483
Other local trucking with storage	4214 pt	1,871	2,016	643	149	27,934
Courier services, except by air	4215	5,966	19,334	7,396	1,780	307,061
Public warehousing and storage	422	9,718	8,330	2,127	504	95,145
Farm products warehousing and storage	4221	584	656	130	31	6,497
Refrigerated warehousing and storage	4222	929	1,745	464	111	18,963
General warehousing and storage	4225	6,753	3,919	983	233	49,091
General goods warehousing	4225 pt	2,251	2,641	832	196	37,814
Self-service or miniwarehousing.	4225 pt	4,502	1,279	151	37	11,277
Special warehousing and storage, n.e.c	4226	1,452	2,009	551	129	20,594
Trucking terminal facilities	423	21	27	8	2	295
Pipelines, except natural gas.	46	844	7,063	821	203	16,779
Refined petroleum pipelines.	4613	358	2,010	252	61	5,578
Other pipelines.	4612, 9	486	5,053	569	142	11,201
Crude petroleum pipelines	4612	405	4,409	531	132	10,355
Pipelines, n.e.c.	4619	81	644	38	10	846
Transportation services	47	46,593	23,890	7,850	1,854	329,202
Arrangement of passenger transportation	472	31,793	10,573	3,921	931	192,981
Travel agencies	4724	27,688	6,964	2,836	673	149,140
Other arrangement of passenger transportation . .	4725,9	4,105	3,608	1,086	258	43,841
Tour operators	4725	3,008	1,865	690	155	30,519
Arrangement of passenger transportation, n.e.c	4729	1,097	1,744	396	102	13,322
Freight shipping services.	473	12,553	9,159	3,233	761	106,979
Freight forwarding.	4731 pt	5,308	4,156	1,437	335	48,903
Arrangement of freight and cargo, n.e.c	4731 pt	7,245	5,002	1,796	426	58,076
Other transportation services	474, 8	2,247	4,158	696	162	29,242
Rental of railroad cars	474	125	1,881	85	23	1,926
Miscellaneous services incidental to transportation	478	2,122	2,277	612	140	27,316
Packing and crating.	4783	835	522	155	33	8,123
Fixed facilities, inspection and weighing services	4785	263	221	65	15	2,810
Transportation services, n.e.c	4789	1,024	1,534	392	91	16,383

NA Not available.   [1]Standard Industrial Classification.

Source: U.S. Bureau of the Census, *1992 Census of Transportation, Communications, and Utilities.*

No. 1048. Class I Intercity Motor Carriers of Passengers: 1980 to 1992

[Carriers subject to ICC regulations. See text, section 21. Minus sign (-) indicates deficit. See also *Historical Statistics, Colonial Times to 1970*, series Q 69-75]

ITEM	Unit	1980	1983	1984	1985	1986	1987	1988	1989	1990	1991	1992
Carriers reporting [1]	Number.	48	45	43	43	29	32	21	20	21	21	21
Number of employees, average. . . .	1,000 . .	31	25	25	24	20	(NA)	(NA)	(NA)	(NA)	(NA)	(NA)
Compensation of employees.	Mil. dol .	599	570	551	518	443	(NA)	(NA)	(NA)	(NA)	(NA)	(NA)
Operating revenue . . . [2]	Mil. dol .	1,397	1,276	1,255	1,233	1,117	1,079	1,122	1,205	943	980	938
Passenger revenue [2]	Mil. dol .	947	876	861	836	765	751	825	890	738	793	755
Special bus revenue and other . .	Mil. dol .	215	180	180	184	155	165	155	165	90	187	183
Operating expenses	*Mil. dol* .	*1,318*	*1,283*	*1,254*	*1,168*	*1,082*	*1,081*	*1,059*	*1,133*	*1,015*	*967*	*874*
Net operating revenue	Mil. dol .	79	-7	1	65	35	-2	63	72	-72	13	64
Ordinary income:												
Before income taxes	Mil. dol .	107	16	53	65	50	-11	(NA)	(NA)	(NA)	(NA)	(NA)
After income taxes.	Mil. dol .	90	26	43	53	36	-21	(NA)	12	-180	162	21
Passenger vehicles in service [2]	1,000 . .	8.6	7.3	7.0	8.4	8.3	(NA)	(NA)	(NA)	(NA)	(NA)	(NA)
Vehicle-miles, passenger	Million. .	781	591	585	567	495	(NA)	(NA)	(NA)	(NA)	(NA)	(NA)
Revenue passengers carried	Million. .	134	94	89	88	74	82	55	54	43	42	41
Expense per vehicle-mile.	Dollar . .	1.69	2.17	2.14	2.06	2.18	(NA)	(NA)	(NA)	(NA)	(NA)	(NA)

NA Not available.   [1] Excludes carriers preponderantly in local or suburban service and carriers engaged in transportation of both property and passengers.   [2] Regular route, intercity, and local.

Source: U.S. Interstate Commerce Commission, *Transport Statistics in the United States,* part 2, annual.

No. 1049. Bus Profile: 1960 to 1991

BUS PROFILE	Unit	1960	1970	1980	1990	1991
School bus expenditures	$1,000 . . .	486	1,219	3,833	7,605	7,879
Intercity bus:						
Operating revenue.	$1,000 . . .	559.0	799.0	1,709.0	1,750.0	1,875.0
Operating expenses.	$1,000 . . .	494.8	812.2	1,810.9	2,041.1	1,979.3
Operating companies	Number . .	1,150	1,000	1,283	3,925	4,204
Miles of highway served	Miles	265,000	267,000	279,000	213,000	(NA)
Revenue passenger miles.	Mil.	19,300	25,300	27,400	23,000	23,500
Revenue passengers	1,000	366,000	401,000	370,000	334,000	337,000
Average passenger trip length	Miles	78.3	63.2	74.1	71.4	69.7
Average miles traveled per vehicle:						
All buses	Miles	16,004	12,035	11,458	9,121	9,097
Commercial	Miles	37,789	32,591	32,765	38,499	39,038
School and nonrevenue bus	Miles	7,556	7,274	7,592	10,000	12,286
Fuel consumed:						
All buses	Mil. gal. . .	827	820	1,018	895	864
Commercial	Mil. gal. . .	618	644	696	723	738
School and nonrevenue bus	Mil. gal. . .	209	300	380	472	533
Average miles per gallon:						
All buses	Mpg.	5.3	5.5	6.0	6.4	6.6
Commercial	Mpg.	4.7	4.6	5.0	4.4	4.4
School and nonrevenue bus	Mpg.	7.1	7.0	7.6	8.1	8.1
Average revenue per passenger mile	Cents. . . .	2.7	3.6	7.3	11.6	11.3

NA Not available.

Source: U.S. Bureau of Transportation Statistics, *National Transportation Statistics, Historical Compendium, 1960-1992.*

No. 1050. Warehousing Services—Revenues, Expenses, and Payroll: 1991 and 1992

[In millions of dollars]

KIND OF BUSINESS	SIC [1] code	OPERATING REVENUE		OPERATING EXPENSES		ANNUAL PAYROLL	
		1991	1992	1991	1992	1991	1992
Motor frgt. transport. and warehousing services [2] .	42	123,724	132,231	114,934	123,230	38,969	41,019
Trucking and courier services, except by air [3]. . . .	421	117,048	124,742	109,220	116,887	37,179	39,009
Public warehousing and storage	422	6,516	7,256	5,559	6,121	1,757	1,963
Local trucking without storage	4212	27,297	29,318	24,000	26,363	7,328	7,837
Trucking, except local	4213	68,516	72,618	65,642	69,601	20,724	21,726
Local trucking with storage	4214	3,992	4,159	3,805	3,900	1,349	1,372
Courier services, except by air.	4215	17,243	18,647	15,773	17,023	7,778	8,074
Farm product warehousing and storage.	4211	500	567	440	490	131	142
Refrigerated warehousing.	4222	1,490	1,657	1,264	1,412	441	484
General warehousing and storage	4225	3,248	3,567	2,750	2,951	816	906
Special warehousing and storage [4].	4226	1,278	1,465	1,105	1,268	369	431

[1] Standard Industrial Classification.   [2] Includes terminal and joint terminal maintenance facilities for motor carrier transportation (SIC 4231) not shown separately.   [3] Excludes private motor carriers that operate as auxiliary establishments to nontransportation companies and independent owner-operators with no paid employees.   [4] Includes household goods warehousing.

Source: U.S. Bureau of the Census, *Current Business Reports, 1992 Motor Freight Transportation and Warehousing Survey.*

No. 1051. Trucking and Courier Services—Operating Revenue, Operating Expenses, and Equipment, by Type of Carrier: 1990 to 1992

[In millions of dollars, except as indicated. Data cover SIC group 421. Excludes private motor carriers that operate as auxiliary establishments to nontransportation companies and independent owner-operators with no paid employees. Some unpublished estimates can be derived from this table by subtracting published data from their respective totals. However, the figures obtained by such subtraction are subject to these same limitations. These unpublished data are for internal use only]

ITEM	ALL CARRIERS			SPECIALTY CARRIERS			GENERAL CARRIERS		
	1990	1991	1992	1990	1991	1992	1990	1991	1992
Operating revenues:									
Total [1]	117,511	117,048	124,742	32,835	31,918	33,324	84,676	85,130	91,418
Motor carrier	107,997	108,604	116,974	28,302	27,905	29,616	79,695	80,699	87,358
Local trucking	25,246	24,582	27,803	13,183	13,077	14,345	12,063	11,505	13,458
Long-distance trucking	82,751	84,022	89,171	15,119	14,828	15,271	67,632	69,194	73,900
Operating expenses:									
Total	109,074	109,220	116,887	28,977	28,507	29,991	80,097	80,713	86,896
Annual payroll	36,490	37,179	39,009	8,242	8,123	8,397	28,248	29,056	30,612
Employer contrib. to Soc. Sec. and other benefits	9,365	9,721	10,486	1,937	1,881	1,980	7,428	7,840	8,506
Purchased fuels	8,647	8,719	9,712	1,653	1,667	1,855	6,994	7,052	7,857
Purchased transportation	19,630	19,321	21,054	5,701	5,384	5,797	13,929	13,937	15,257
Lease and rental	2,168	2,161	2,168	631	631	623	1,537	1,530	1,545
Insurance	3,898	3,998	4,152	1,108	1,161	1,220	2,790	2,837	2,932
Maintenance and repair	6,133	6,133	6,861	1,867	1,843	2,006	4,266	4,290	4,855
Depreciation	5,603	5,632	5,987	1,623	1,596	1,648	3,980	4,036	4,339
Taxes and licenses	2,325	2,439	2,762	518	510	584	1,807	1,929	2,178
Drug and alcohol testing and rehabilitation programs	27	35	46	7	10	13	20	25	33
Other operating expenses	14,788	13,882	14,650	5,690	5,701	5,868	9,098	8,181	8,782
Equipment (1,000 units): [2]									
Trucks	226	231	242	100	100	109	126	131	133
Truck-tractors	525	524	562	111	108	110	414	416	452
Trailers (full and semi)	1,179	1,191	1,244	214	205	203	965	986	1,041

[1] Includes other revenue not shown separately. [2] Represents revenue generating equipment as of December 31. Includes owned and leased equipment.

Source: U.S. Bureau of the Census, *Current Business Reports, 1992 Motor Freight Transportation and Warehousing Survey.*

No. 1052. Class I Intercity Motor Carriers of Property, by Carrier: 1980 to 1992

[See headnote, table 1048. Common carriers are carriers offering regular scheduled service. Contract carriers provide service at request of user. Minus sign (-) indicates loss]

ITEM	Unit	1980	1990	1991	1992	1980	1990	1991	1992
		COMMON CARRIER, GENERAL FREIGHT				COMMON CARRIER OTHER THAN GENERAL FREIGHT			
Carriers reporting	Number	298	191	201	208	441	322	295	330
Number of employees, average	1,000	413	465	474	490	101	87	74	88
Compensation of employees	Mil. dol.	9,803	13,556	14,032	14,967	1,931	2,236	1,920	2,358
Operating revenues	Mil. dol.	19,725	29,682	31,619	34,594	8,792	9,042	7,761	9,367
Intercity freight	Mil. dol.	19,480	29,517	19,698	21,654	8,339	8,762	7,480	8,960
Operating expenses	Mil. dol.	18,870	28,340	30,269	32,977	8,426	8,702	7,509	8,942
Ordinary income before taxes	Mil. dol.	701	1,146	1,180	1,453	230	198	122	309
Net income	Mil. dol.	−72	746	749	878	14	153	85	221
Total power units, intercity service	1,000	102	(NA)	(NA)	(NA)	95	(NA)	(NA)	(NA)
Trucks, tractors owned in operation, avg.	1,000	73	(NA)	(NA)	(NA)	33	(NA)	(NA)	(NA)
Intercity vehicle-miles	Million	6,547	6,804	7,615	8,674	6,889	6,566	5,372	6,696
Tons of intercity revenue freight carried	Million	178	157	169	196	324	302	253	298
		CONTRACT CARRIER OTHER THAN GENERAL FREIGHT				CARRIERS OF HOUSEHOLD GOODS			
Carriers reporting	Number	69	87	83	113	28	36	36	32
Number of employees, average	1,000	14	34	34	42	10	13	12	12
Compensation of employees	Mil. dol.	336	1,082	989	1,325	157	296	298	291
Operating revenues	Mil. dol.	1,272	3,486	3,644	4,501	1,824	3,152	3,026	3,180
Intercity freight	Mil. dol.	1,172	3,209	3,449	4,104	1,676	2,702	2,318	2,787
Operating expenses	Mil. dol.	1,207	3,422	3,547	4,333	1,781	3,129	2,973	3,159
Ordinary income before taxes	Mil. dol.	48	3	53	127	74	12	27	−1
Net income	Mil. dol.	28	−13	20	80	42	8	17	8
Total power units, intercity service	1,000	13	(NA)	(NA)	(NA)	25	(NA)	(NA)	(NA)
Trucks, tractors owned in operation, avg.	1,000	7	(NA)	(NA)	(NA)	1	(NA)	(NA)	(NA)
Intercity vehicle-miles	Million	934	2,044	2,339	2,933	969	1,366	1,086	1,136
Tons of intercity revenue freight carried	Million	37	80	76	110	5	8	7	9

NA Not available.

Source: U.S. Interstate Commerce Commission, *Transport Statistics in the United States,* part 2, annual.

No. 1053. Trucks—Percent Distribution, Operational Characteristics: 1982 to 1992

[See headnote, table 1054]

CHARACTERISTIC	1982	1987	1992	CHARACTERISTIC	1982	1987	1992
Total	100.0	100.0	100.0	Purchased used	51.5	50.1	51.4
				Leased [5]	2.8	2.6	3.1
Major use:				Fleet size: 1 [6]	77.8	65.1	(NA)
Agriculture [1]	12.2	8.5	6.4	2 to 5	10.9	24.9	(NA)
Construction	11.2	10.0	8.4	6 to 19	5.3	5.4	(NA)
Manufacturing	1.6	1.3	1.3	20 or more	6.0	4.6	(NA)
Wholesale and retail trade	6.8	5.6	5.2	Truck-type:			
Personal transportation	56.7	65.7	68.3	Single-unit	95.7	96.3	96.5
All other	11.4	8.8	10.4	Combination	4.3	3.7	3.5
Body type:				Annual miles:			
Pickup and panel [2]	85.8	89.0	91.4	Less than 5,000	26.0	25.3	20.8
Platform and cattlerack	5.1	3.7	2.7	5,000 to 9,999	25.5	23.4	20.7
Van [3]	3.8	3.2	2.5	10,000 to 19,999	35.0	34.5	38.3
All other	5.2	4.0	3.4	20,000 to 29,999	8.4	10.7	12.7
Vehicle size: [4] Light	89.3	91.9	93.2	30,000 miles or more	5.0	6.1	7.6
Medium	3.5	2.3	2.1	Range of operation: [7]			
Light-heavy	2.4	1.7	1.2	Local	76.6	75.6	73.8
Heavy-heavy	4.8	4.1	3.4	Short-range	10.3	14.8	15.0
Year model:				Long-range	3.1	4.5	4.9
1 to 2 years old	8.9	17.2	14.9	Off-the-road [5]	10.0	5.1	6.3
3 to 4 years old	16.5	16.5	15.7	Fuel type:			
4 years or more	74.6	66.3	69.4	Gasoline	94.3	93.7	92.9
Vehicle acquisition:				Diesel and LPG	5.5	6.2	6.8
Purchased new	45.7	47.3	45.6	Not reported	0.2	0.1	0.3

NA Not available.　[1] Includes forestry and lumbering.　[2] Also includes walk-in, minivan, station wagon, and utility trucks.　[3] Includes multi-stop or walk-in.　[4] See footnote 6, table 1054.　[5] Includes not reported.　[6] See footnote 8, table 1054.　[7] See footnote 9, table 1054.

No. 1054. Trucks and Truck-Miles, by Vehicle and Operational Characteristics: 1992

[Data are based on a stratified probability sample of trucks drawn from current registrations on file with motor vehicle departments in the 50 States and DC]

ITEM	TRUCKS (1,000) Total	TRUCKS (1,000) Excl. pickups, panels [1]	TRUCK-MILES (bil.)	ITEM	TRUCKS (1,000) Total	TRUCKS (1,000) Excl. pickups, panels [1]	TRUCK-MILES (bil.)
Total	59,201	5,112	786.3	25 to 99	1,246	558	31.0
Major use:				100 or more	1,524	860	49.3
Agriculture [2]	3,819	999	45.6	Not reported	28,875	547	332.0
Construction	4,986	1,015	78.2	Truck type:			
Manufacturing	787	258	17.4	Single-unit	57,157	3,684	703.9
Wholesale and retail trade	3,087	873	60.9	Combination	2,044	1,428	82.3
Personal transportation	40,442	231	464.0	Range of operation: [9]			
All other	6,080	1,736	120.2	Local	43,700	2,968	520.1
Body type:				Short-range	8,862	1,038	158.7
Pickup and panel [3]	54,088	(X)	669.7	Long-range	2,886	561	81.3
Platform [4]	1,617	1,617	24.3	Off-the-road [7]	3,752	546	26.2
Van [5]	1,502	1,502	58.5	Products carried:			
All other	1,993	1,993	33.8	Farm products	1,350	615	18.0
Vehicle size: [6] Light	55,193	1,326	681.3	Building materials	1,288	649	21.4
Medium	1,259	1,038	14.0	Mixed cargoes	597	257	17.1
Light-heavy	732	732	8.1	Craftsman's equipment	2,895	323	45.5
Heavy-heavy	2,017	2,016	82.8	Personal transportation	40,443	231	464.0
Year model:				All other	12,628	3,038	220.3
1 to 2 years old	8,840	412	136.6	Types of hazardous material: [10]			
3 to 4 years old	9,275	579	166.5	Flammable liquids	182	182	2.6
4 years or more	41,086	4,121	483.2	Combustible liquids	110	110	1.1
Vehicle acquisition:				Corrosive liquids	129	129	1.5
Purchased new	26,967	2,091	393.6	Flammable solids	67	67	0.3
Purchased used	30,417	2,601	352.1	Oxidizers	82	82	0.5
Leased [7]	1,397	374	35.8	Flammable gas	104	104	1.6
	419	47	4.7	Nonflammable gas	75	75	0.7
Fleet size: 1 [7] [8]	16,390	724	210.3	Corrosive solids	393	4,201	2.1
2 to 5	8,272	1,395	109.5	Not reported	27	27	1.3
6 to 9	1,385	448	23.0				
10 to 24	1,509	582	31.2				

X Not applicable.　[1] Also excludes minivans, utilities, and station wagons.　[2] Includes forestry and lumbering.　[3] Also includes, minivans, station wagon, and utilities, and station wagon.　[4] Includes livestock truck.　[5] Includes multi-stop or walk-in.　[6] Average vehicle weight (empty-weight of the vehicle plus the average weight of load carried). Light=10,000 lbs. or less; medium=10,001-19,500 lbs.; light-heavy=19,501-26,000 lbs.; and heavy-heavy=26,001 lbs. or more.　[7] Includes not reported.　[8] Includes "No load carried" and "not in use."　[9] Area in which usually operated. Local=less than 50 miles; short-range=50 to 200 miles; long-range=more than 200 miles.　[10] Detail does not add to totals because items were not applicable or multiple responses were possible.

Source of tables 1053 and 1054: U.S. Bureau of the Census, *1992 Census of Transportation, TC92-T-52.*

No. 1055. Railroads, Class I—Summary: 1980 to 1993

[As of **Dec. 31,** or **calendar year** data, except as noted. Compiled from annual reports of class I railroads only except where noted. Beginning 1985, financial data are not comparable with earlier years due to change in method of accounting for track and related structures. Minus sign (-) indicates deficit. See also *Historical Statistics, Colonial Times to 1970,* series Q 284-312, Q 319, Q 330, Q 356-378, and Q 400-401]

ITEM	Unit	1980	1985	1987	1988	1989	1990	1991	1992	1993
Class I line-hauling companies [1]	Number.	40	23	18	17	15	14	14	13	13
Employees [2]	1,000	458	302	249	236	228	216	206	197	193
Compensation	Mil. dol	11,318	10,563	9,373	9,301	9,043	8,654	8,695	8,753	8,732
Average per hour	Dollars	10.2	14.3	15.1	15.6	15.8	15.8	16.8	17.8	17.9
Average per year	Dollars	24,695	34,991	37,716	39,431	39,742	39,987	42,131	44,336	45,354
Mileage:										
Railroad line owned [3]	1,000	178	162	158	150	149	146	143	139	137
Railroad track owned [4]	1,000	292	269	261	251	250	244	241	234	231
Equipment:										
Locomotives in service	Number.	28,094	22,548	19,647	19,364	19,015	18,835	18,344	18,004	18,161
Average horsepower	1,000 lb	2,302	2,469	2,549	2,579	2,624	2,665	2,714	2,750	2,777
Cars in service:										
Passenger train	Number.	4,347	2,502	2,350	2,332	(NA)	(NA)	(NA)	(NA)	(NA)
Freight train [5]	1,000	1,711	1,422	1,288	1,239	1,224	1,212	1,190	1,173	1,173
Freight cars [6]	1,000	1,168	867	749	725	682	659	633	605	587
Income and expenses:										
Operating revenues	Mil. dol.	28,258	27,586	26,622	27,934	27,956	28,370	27,845	28,349	28,825
Operating expenses	Mil. dol.	26,355	25,225	23,878	24,811	25,038	24,652	28,061	25,325	24,517
Net revenue from operations	*Mil. dol*	*1,902*	*2,361*	*2,744*	*3,123*	*2,918*	*3,718*	*-216*	*3,024*	*4,308*
Income before fixed charges	Mil. dol.	2,897	3,393	3,932	4,460	4,162	4,627	928	4,127	4,990
Provision for taxes [7]	Mil. dol.	592	660	1,051	1,162	1,040	1,088	-156	1,092	1,810
Ordinary income	Mil. dol.	1,129	1,788	1,965	2,286	2,009	1,961	-91	2,055	2,258
Net income	Mil. dol.	1,129	1,882	2,055	2,382	2,203	1,977	-281	1,800	2,240
Net railway operating income	Mil. dol.	1,339	1,746	1,756	1,980	1,894	2,648	-37	1,955	2,517
Total taxes [8]	Mil. dol.	2,585	3,169	3,553	3,871	3,742	3,780	2,649	3,732	4,343
Indus. return on net investment.	Percent.	4.2	4.6	4.8	6.7	6.3	8.1	1.3	6.3	7.1
Gross capital expenditures	Mil. dol.	3,238	4,485	3,076	3,546	3,865	3,591	3,439	3,680	4,504
Balance sheet:										
Total property investment	Mil. dol.	43,923	64,241	66,760	68,550	67,661	70,348	71,622	72,677	75,217
Accrued depreciation and amortization	Mil. dol.	10,706	19,756	21,070	21,497	21,481	22,222	23,057	23,378	23,892
Net investment	Mil. dol.	33,419	46,237	45,690	47,053	47,370	48,126	48,565	49,299	51,325
Shareholder's equity	Mil. dol.	19,860	27,605	25,616	26,467	25,753	23,662	22,603	23,115	24,658
Net working capital	Mil. dol.	922	1,084	34	-190	-2119	-3505	-3,988	-4,372	-3,295
Cash dividends	Mil. dol.	610	1,444	1,252	1,814	1,910	2,074	915	830	1,054
AMTRAK passenger traffic:										
Passenger revenue	Mil. dol.	(NA)	604.9	681.1	784.2	893.0	941.9	962.3	933.2	924.4
Revenue passengers carried	1,000	21,303	20,945	20,727	21,490	21,394	22,382	21,693	21,678	21,841
Revenue passenger miles	Million.	4,645	4,977	5,368	5,686	5,912	6,125	6,249	6,181	6,064
Averages:										
Revenue per passenger	Dollars	(NA)	28.9	32.9	36.5	41.8	42.1	44.4	43.0	42.3
Revenue per passenger mile	Cents	(NA)	12.2	12.7	13.8	15.1	15.4	15.4	15.1	15.2
Trip per passenger	Miles	218.1	237.6	259.0	264.6	276.3	273.7	288.0	285.1	277.7
Freight service:										
Freight revenue	Mil. dol.	26,200	26,688	25,797	27,092	27,059	24,471	26,949	27,508	27,991
Per ton-mile	Cents	2.8	3.0	2.7	2.7	2.7	2.7	2.6	2.6	2.5
Per ton originated	Dollar	17.7	20.2	18.8	19.0	19.3	19.3	19.5	19.7	20.0
Revenue-tons originated	Million.	1,492	1,320	1,372	1,430	1,402	1,425	1,383	1,399	1,397
Revenue-tons carried	Million.	2,434	1,985	1,984	2,045	1,988	2,024	1,987	2,022	2,047
Tons carried one mile	Billion.	919	877	944	996	1,014	1,034	1,039	1,067	1,109
Average miles of road operated	1,000	179	161	147	141	138	133	130	126	124
Revenue ton-miles per mile of road	1,000	5,133	5,446	6,395	7,052	7,373	7,763	8,001	8,451	8,965
Revenue per ton-mile	Cents	3	3	3	3	3	3	3	3	3
Train miles	Million.	428	347	361	379	383	380	375	390	405
Net ton-miles per train-mile [9]	Number.	2,175	2,574	2,644	2,662	2,683	2,755	2,796	2,759	2,759
Net ton-miles per loaded car-mile [9]	Number.	63.5	62.7	64.0	65.5	67.0	69.1	71.6	70.9	71.6
Train-miles per train-hour	Miles	18.2	21.9	22.2	21.5	23.0	23.7	23.7	23.7	23.1
Haul per ton, U.S. as a system	Miles	616	664	688	697	723	726	751	763	794
Accident: [10]										
All railroads	Number.	63,663	35,340	27,198	28,253	28,039	26,440	24,662	22,553	20,400
Persons killed	Number.	1,417	1,036	1,165	1,199	1,324	1,297	1,194	1,170	1,279
Persons injured	Number.	62,246	34,304	26,033	27,054	26,715	25,143	23,468	21,383	19,121
Class I railroads	Number.	57,755	29,388	21,852	22,093	21,809	20,450	18,728	17,055	15,058
Persons killed	Number.	1,344	955	1,074	1,076	1,195	1,166	1,069	1,047	1,124
Persons injured	Number.	56,411	28,433	20,778	21,017	20,614	19,284	17,659	16,008	13,934

NA Not available. [1] See text, section 21, for definition of Class I. [2] Average midmonth count. [3] Represents the aggregate length of roadway of all line-haul railroads. Excludes yard tracks, sidings, and parallel lines. (Includes estimate for class II and III railroads). [4] Includes multiple main tracks, yard tracks, and sidings owned by both line-haul and switching and terminal. (Includes estimate for class II and III railroads). [5] Includes cars owned by all railroads, private car companies, and shippers. [6] Class I railroads only. [7] Includes State income taxes. [8] Includes payroll, income, and other taxes. [9] Revenue and nonrevenue freight. [10] Includes highway grade crossing casualties.

Source: Association of American Railroads, Washington, DC, *Railroad Facts, Statistics of Railroads of Class I,* annual, and *Analysis of Class I Railroads,* annual. Accident data: U.S. Federal Railroad Administration, *Accident Bulletin,* annual.

No. 1056. Railroads, Class I-Cars of Revenue Freight Loaded, 1970 to 1993, and by Commodity Group, 1992 and 1993

[**In thousands.** Figures are 52-week totals. N.e.c.= Not elsewhere classified]

YEAR	CARLOADS		COMMODITY GROUP	CARLOADS		COMMODITY GROUP	CARLOADS	
	Total	Piggy-back		1992	1993		1992	1993
1970 ..	27,160	1,450	Coal	6,178	5,942	Metals and products	457	508
1975 ..	23,217	1,308	Metallic ores	486	440	Stone, clay, and glass products . .	454	465
1980 ..	22,598	1,661	Chemicals, allied products. . . .	1,412	1,441	Crushed stone, gravel, sand	571	596
1985 ..	19,574	2,863	Grain.	1,421	1,417	Nonmetalic minerals, n.e.c	440	431
1989 ..	16,030	(NA)	Motor vehicles and equipment .	913	1,015	Waste and scrap materials	417	470
1990 ..	16,177	(NA)	Pulp, paper, allied products . . .	482	484	Lumber, wood products, n.e.c. [1]..	276	270
1991 ..	15,533	(NA)	Primary forest products	380	372	Coke.	270	283
1992 ..	15,798	(NA)	Food and kindred prod., n.e.c. .	463	464	Petroleum product	271	261
1993 ..	15,781	(NA)	Grain mill products	515	529	All other carloads	394	392

NA Not available.　　[1] Excludes furniture.

Source: Association of American Railroads, Washington, DC, *Weekly Railroad Traffic*, annual.

No. 1057. Railroads, Class I Line-Haul-Revenue Freight Originated, by Commodity Group: 1980 to 1993

[See *Historical Statistics, Colonial Times to 1970*, series Q 332, for total carloads originated]

COMMODITY GROUP	1980	1985	1987	1988	1989	1990	1991	1992	1993
Carloads (1,000) [1]	**22,223**	**19,501**	**20,602**	**21,600**	**21,226**	**21,401**	**20,868**	**21,205**	**21,683**
Coal.	5,789	5,684	5,430	5,621	5,672	5,912	5,683	5,572	5,310
Farm products	1,866	1,494	1,907	1,977	1,781	1,689	1,605	1,646	1,636
Chemicals, allied products	1,322	1,296	1,410	1,497	1,486	1,531	1,556	1,568	1,606
Food and kindred products	1,767	1,224	1,326	1,318	1,284	1,307	1,316	1,352	1,380
Nonmetallic minerals [2]	1,474	1,196	1,188	1,290	1,254	1,202	1,075	1,029	1,044
Transportation equipment [3]	1,004	1,202	1,085	1,160	1,141	1,091	1,068	1,181	1,355
Lumber and wood products [3]	1,384	948	986	910	843	780	716	726	710
Pulp, paper, allied products	954	703	561	646	615	611	616	618	620
Petroleum and coal products	596	491	520	568	561	573	533	583	584
Stone, clay, and glass products. . .	776	551	559	577	565	539	479	483	487
Metallic ores	1,258	511	494	582	523	508	499	489	443
Primary metal products	756	449	428	479	452	477	469	481	528
Waste and scrap materials.	632	429	440	471	444	439	433	487	558
Machinery, exc. electrical.	77	35	33	40	38	39	39	39	37
Fabricated metal products [4]	72	31	24	26	27	31	34	32	37
Tons (mil.) [1]	**1,492**	**1,320**	**1,372**	**1,429**	**1,403**	**1,425**	**1,383**	**1,399**	**1,397**
Coal.	522	538	523	543	551	579	560	554	534
Farm products	156	127	163	170	154	147	144	149	147
Chemicals, allied products	108	106	116	123	123	126	127	130	134
Nonmetallic minerals [2]	125	108	109	115	111	109	99	94	96
Food and kindred products	92	74	81	81	79	81	83	86	88
Lumber and wood products [3]	86	63	67	62	57	53	48	50	49
Metallic ores	105	47	45	52	47	47	45	45	41
Stone, clay, and glass products. . .	54	44	44	46	47	44	39	40	40
Petroleum and coal products	38	33	35	39	39	40	37	41	41
Primary metal products	53	34	33	38	36	38	37	39	43
Pulp, paper, allied products	42	36	36	35	34	33	33	34	34
Waste and scrap materials.	34	26	28	30	28	28	27	30	35
Transportation equipment	24	27	24	25	24	23	22	25	29
Machinery, exc. electrical.	2	1	1	1	1	1	1	1	1
Fabricated metal products [4]	2	1	1	1	1	1	1	1	1
Gross revenue (mil. dol.) [1]. . .	**26,938**	**28,225**	**27,657**	**29,529**	**29,328**	**29,775**	**29,319**	**29,777**	**30,376**
Coal.	4,956	6,556	6,097	6,430	6,581	6,954	6,903	6,717	6,481
Chemicals, allied products	2,946	3,342	3,477	3,795	3,788	3,933	4,043	4,123	4,277
Transportation equipment	1,917	3,110	2,866	3,218	3,269	3,100	2,633	2,753	3,021
Farm products	2,801	1,977	2,246	2,534	2,444	2,422	2,332	2,454	2,528
Food and kindred products	2,837	2,256	2,171	2,198	2,128	2,188	2,254	2,308	2,336
Pulp, paper, allied products	1,652	1,641	1,542	1,540	1,514	1,486	1,502	1,508	1,511
Lumber and wood products [3]	1,543	1,525	1,660	1,626	1,500	1,390	1,282	1,342	1,324
Primary metal products	1,332	872	863	1,013	972	979	977	970	1,021
Stone, clay, and glass products. . .	1,025	960	914	965	960	931	878	911	944
Petroleum and coal products	865	861	809	903	917	918	888	943	929
Nonmetallic minerals [2]	948	949	854	890	868	885	824	812	818
Waste and scrap materials.	513	446	474	526	492	504	515	558	613
Metallic ores	597	403	348	415	397	408	400	409	385
Machinery, exc. electrical.	176	72	57	63	66	67	62	61	59
Fabricated metal products [4]	110	48	37	38	38	42	48	45	50

[1] Includes commodity groups and small packaged freight shipments, not shown separately.　　[2] Except fuels.　　[3] Except furniture.　　[4] Except ordnance, machinery, and transport.

Source: Association of American Railroads, Washington, DC, *Freight Commodity Statistics*, annual.

No. 1058. Railroad Freight—Producer Price Indexes: 1980 to 1994

[**Dec. 1984=100.** Reflects prices for shipping a fixed set of commodities under specified and unchanging conditions]

COMMODITY	1980	1985	1987	1988	1989	1990	1991	1992	1993	1994
Total railroad freight	75.9	99.9	100.1	104.8	106.4	107.5	109.3	109.9	110.9	111.8
Coal.	75.8	100.0	100.1	104.3	105.3	104.2	105.2	105.9	106.6	107.5
Farm products	75.6	99.0	99.3	105.5	108.5	110.4	111.4	111.1	113.7	114.5
Food products	75.2	100.0	98.6	103.1	103.9	105.4	108.1	108.7	109.0	111.0
Metallic ores	74.5	100.2	99.0	103.9	105.8	106.5	106.7	106.6	106.7	104.6
Chemicals or allied products	75.6	100.1	100.8	106.9	110.0	111.7	113.5	115.6	116.2	117.6
Nonmetallic minerals	72.2	100.1	101.1	106.1	108.3	111.7	115.9	117.6	119.3	119.7
Wood or lumber products	72.7	100.0	100.4	105.3	105.9	107.5	108.6	108.8	109.7	110.0
Transportation equipment	81.7	100.0	99.3	103.4	106.4	107.5	109.7	110.8	113.1	115.3
Pulp, paper, or allied products	76.7	100.0	100.6	104.0	105.1	108.0	111.5	111.8	112.6	111.1
Primary metal products	77.8	99.7	99.7	108.8	112.3	113.1	116.1	117.5	116.3	115.6
Clay, concrete, glass, or stone products .	74.2	100.0	102.2	107.5	110.5	114.1	117.1	116.5	117.9	120.1

Source: U.S. Bureau of Labor Statistics, *Producer Price Indexes,* monthly and annual.

No. 1059. Petroleum Pipeline Companies—Characteristics: 1980 to 1993

[Covers pipeline companies operating in interstate commerce and subject to jurisdiction of Federal Energy Regulatory Commission]

ITEM	Unit	1980	1985	1987	1988	1989	1990	1991	1992	1993
Miles of pipeline, total	1,000.	173	171	168	171	169	168	172	164	164
Gathering lines	1,000.	36	35	35	34	33	32	31	29	29
Trunk lines	1,000.	136	136	133	136	135	136	141	136	135
Total deliveries	Mil. bbl. . . .	10,600	10,745	11,194	11,484	11,281	11,378	11,496	11,447	12,219
Crude oil	Mil. bbl. . . .	6,405	6,239	6,278	6,509	6,435	6,563	6,685	6,541	6,708
Products	Mil. bbl. . . .	4,195	4,506	4,917	4,974	4,847	4,816	4,811	4,906	5,511
Total trunk line traffic	Bil. bbl-miles .	3,405	3,342	3,524	3,619	3,505	3,500	3,470	3,428	3,051
Crude oil	Bil. bbl-miles .	1,948	1,842	1,932	1,970	1,918	1,891	1,899	1,853	1,382
Products	Bil. bbl-miles .	1,458	1,500	1,592	1,649	1,587	1,609	1,571	1,575	1,669
Carrier property value	Mil. dol. . . .	19,752	21,605	21,353	24,332	24,638	25,828	26,943	27,106	31,625
Operating revenues.	Mil. dol. . . .	6,356	7,461	7,057	6,861	6,512	7,149	6,798	7,154	6,931
Net income	Mil. dol. . . .	1,912	2,431	2,475	2,505	2,227	2,340	1,788	2,061	1,763

Source: PennWell Publishing Co., Tulsa, OK, *Oil & Gas Journal,* annual (copyright).

No. 1060. Major Interstate Natural Gas Pipeline Companies—Summary: 1985 to 1991

[The classification of A and B interstate natural gas pipeline companies changed to major companies and nonmajor companies. Major natural gas pipeline companies are those whose combined sales for resale and natural gas transported or stored for a fee exceed 50 billion cubic feet. They account for more than 85 percent of all interstate natural gas]

ITEM	Unit	1985	1986	1987	1988	1989	1990	1991
Sales.	Tril. cu. ft . .	11.3	7.8	6.5	6.4	5.6	4.5	3.9
Residential.	Tril. cu. ft . .	0.3	0.2	0.2	0.3	0.1	0.2	0.2
Commercial, industrial	Tril. cu. ft . .	1.1	0.5	0.4	0.5	0.5	0.4	0.3
For resale	Tril. cu. ft . .	9.9	7.1	5.8	5.9	5.6	3.9	3.3
Operating revenues	Mil. dol . . .	49,106	33,859	27,565	27,501	25,695	22,574	21,420
From sales [1]	Mil. dol . . .	44,996	29,508	22,942	22,512	19,786	15,981	14,135
Residential.	Mil. dol . . .	1,879	1,122	1,094	1,553	819	912	1,081
Commercial, industrial	Mil. dol . . .	4,466	1,909	1,464	1,544	1,452	1,272	1,086
For resale	Mil. dol . . .	38,545	26,413	20,351	19,420	17,505	13,791	11,967
From transportation of gas of others. . . .	Mil. dol . . .	2,272	3,027	3,622	4,059	4,959	5,505	6,117
Other	Mil. dol . . .	1,838	1,325	1,002	929	950	1,088	1,167
Operation, maintenance expenses.	Mil. dol . . .	42,528	27,460	21,794	22,742	20,829	17,446	17,335
Production.	Mil. dol . . .	36,739	22,208	16,955	17,625	15,257	12,124	11,663
Storage.	Mil. dol . . .	418	420	409	436	458	417	460
Transmission	Mil. dol . . .	3,409	2,984	2,598	2,589	2,589	2,720	2,880
Distribution	Mil. dol . . .	132	80	80	127	94	112	133
Administrative, general, and other	Mil. dol . . .	1,830	1,768	1,752	1,966	2,430	2,074	2,048
Pipeline mileage.	1,000	230.2	217.3	249.5	246.9	253.2	230.2	249.5
Transmission lines	1,000	189.7	184.6	181.2	191.6	194.1	195.5	146.8
Field lines	1,000	69.6	64.5	62.9	55.5	55.1	54.0	50.7
Storage.	1,000	4.8	4.6	4.6	4.3	4.8	4.8	4.7

[1] Includes other ultimate customers not shown separately.

Source: U.S. Energy Information Administration, *Statistics of Interstate Natural Gas Pipeline Companies,* annual.

Figure 22.1
**Revenue Passengers Enplaned—
Top 10 Airports: 1993**

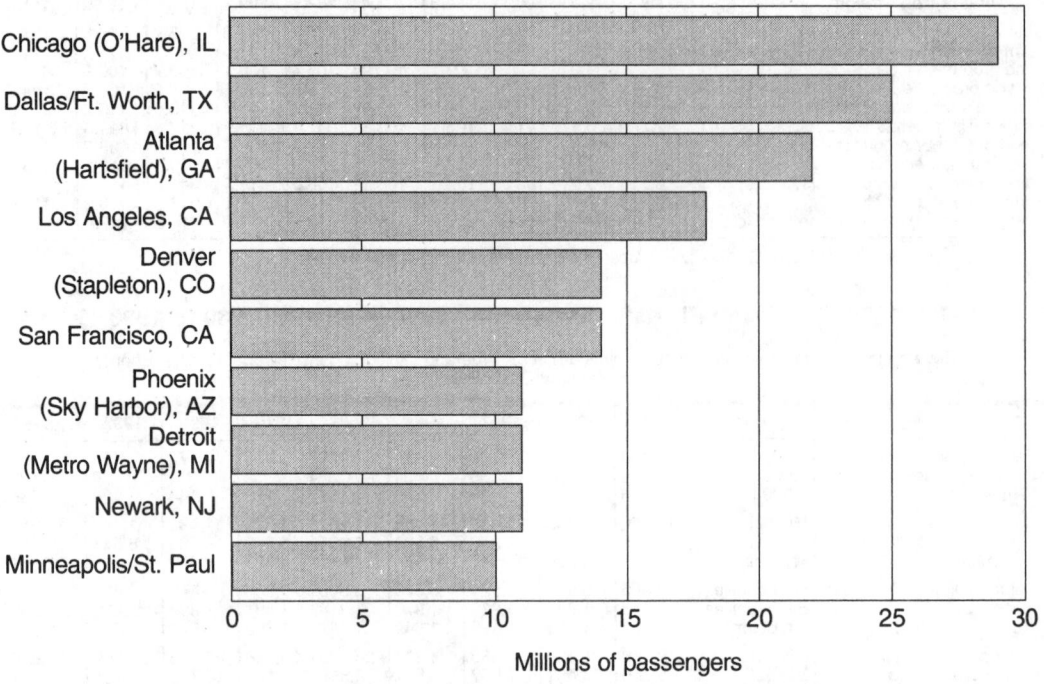

Source: Chart prepared by U.S. Bureau of the Census. For data, see table 1064.

Figure 22.2
**Consumer Complaints Against
U.S. Airlines: 1986 to 1994**

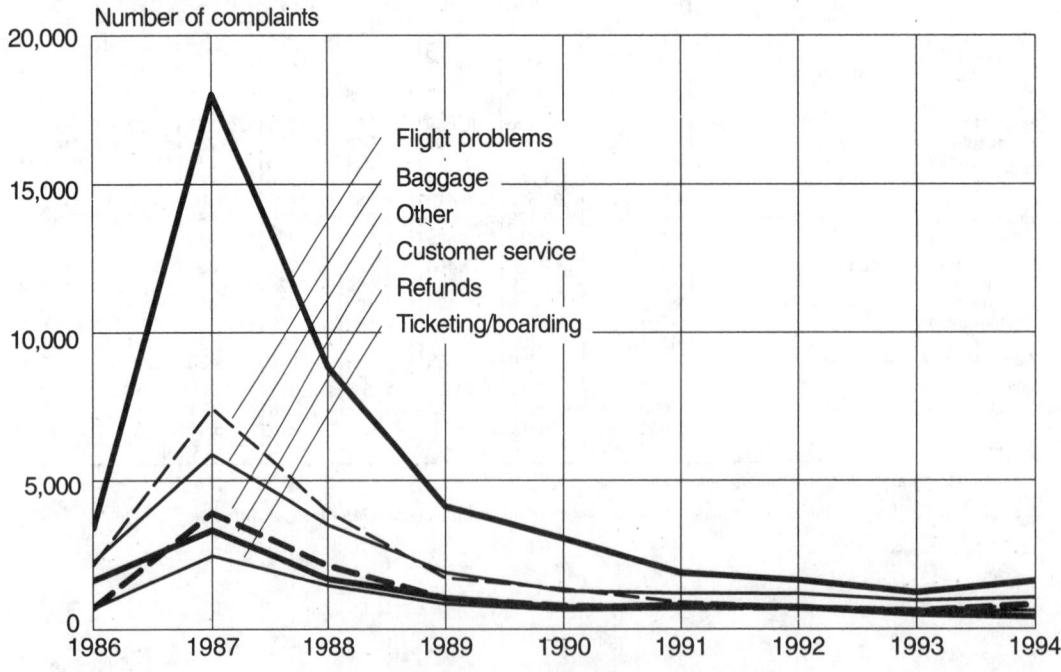

Source: Chart prepared by U.S. Bureau of the Census. For data, see table 1070.

Transportation— Air and Water

This section presents data on civil air transportation, both passenger and cargo, and on water transportation, including inland waterways, oceanborne commerce, the merchant marine, cargo and vessel tonnages, and shipbuilding. Comparative data on various types of transportation carriers are presented in section 21.

Principal sources of these data are the annual *FAA Statistical Handbook of Aviation* issued by the Federal Aviation Administration (FAA); the annual *Waterborne Commerce of the United States* issued by the Corps of Engineers of the Department of the Army; the monthly and annual issues of *U.S. Waterborne Exports and General Imports,* and the annual *Vessel Entrances and Clearances,* and the monthly *Highlights of U.S. Export and Import Trade,* issued by the Bureau of the Census. In addition, the Bureau of the Census in its commodity transportation survey (part of the census of transportation, taken every 5 years, for years ending in "2" and "7") provides data on the type, weight, and value of commodities shipped by manufacturing establishments in the United States, by means of transportation, origin, and destination.

Air transportation data are also presented annually by the Air Transport Association of America, Washington, DC in *Air Transport Facts and Figures.* Additional sources of data on water transportation include *Merchant Fleets of the World* issued periodically by the U.S. Maritime Administration; *The Bulletin,* issued monthly by the American Bureau of Shipping, New York, NY; and *World Fleet Statistics* and the *Register Book,* published by Lloyd's Register of Shipping, London, England.

Civil aviation.—Federal promotion and regulation of civil aviation have been carried out by the FAA and the Civil Aeronautics Board (CAB). The CAB promoted and regulated the civil air transportation industry within the United States and between the United States and foreign

In Brief

SCHEDULED AIR CARRIERS

Revenue passengers enplaned:

1985	*382 million*
1993	*487 million*

Net profit:

1985	*+$863 million*
1993	*-$2,138 million*

countries. The Board granted licenses to provide air transportation service, approved or disapproved proposed rates and fares, and approved or disapproved proposed agreements and corporate relationships involving air carriers. In December 1984, the CAB ceased to exist as an agency. Some of its functions were transferred to the Department of Transportation (DOT), as outlined below. The responsibility for investigation of aviation accidents resides with the National Transportation Safety Board.

The Office of the Secretary, DOT aviation activities include the following: negotiation of international air transportation rights, selection of U.S. air carriers to serve capacity controlled international markets, oversight of international rates and fares, maintenance of essential air service to small communities, and consumer affairs. DOT's Research and Special Programs Administration (RSPA) handles aviation information functions formerly assigned to CAB.

The principal activities of the FAA include the promotion of air safety, controlling the use of navigable airspace, prescribing regulations dealing with the competency of airmen, airworthiness of aircraft, and air traffic control, operation of air route traffic control centers, airport traffic control towers, and flight service stations, the design, construction, maintenance, and inspection of navigation, traffic control, and communications equipment, and the development of general aviation.

The CAB published monthly and quarterly financial and traffic statistical data for the certificated route air carriers. RSPA continues these publications, including both certificated and noncertificated (commuter) air carriers. The FAA publishes data annually on the use of airway facilities; data related to the location of airmen, aircraft, and airports; the volume of activity in the field of nonair carrier (general aviation) flying; and aircraft production and registration.

General aviation comprises all civil flying (including such commercial operations as small demand air taxis, agriculture application, powerline patrol, etc.) but excludes certificated route air carriers, supplemental operators, large-aircraft commercial operators and commuter airlines.

Air carriers and service.—The CAB previously issued "certificates of public convenience and necessity" under Section 401 of the Federal Aviation Act of 1958 for scheduled and nonscheduled (charter) passenger services and cargo services. It also issued certificates under Section 418 of the Act to cargo air carriers for domestic all-cargo service only. The DOT Office of the Secretary now issues the certificates under a "fit, willing, and able" test of air carrier operations. Carriers operating only 60 seat or less aircraft are given exemption authority to carry passengers, cargo, and mail in scheduled and nonscheduled service under Part 298 of the DOT (formerly CAB) regulations. Exemption authority carriers who offer scheduled passenger service to an essential air service point must meet the "fit, willing, and able" test.

Vessel shipments, entrances, and clearances.—Shipments by dry cargo vessels comprise shipments on all types of watercraft, except tanker vessels; shipments by tanker vessels comprise all types of cargo, liquid and dry, carried by tanker vessels.

A vessel is reported as entered only at the first port which it enters in the United States, whether or not cargo is unloaded at that port. A vessel is reported as cleared only at the last port at which clearance is made to a foreign port, whether or not it takes on cargo. Army and Navy vessels entering or clearing without commercial cargo are not included in the figures.

Units of measurement.—Cargo (or freight) tonnage and shipping weight both represent the gross weight of the cargo including the weight of containers, wrappings, crates, etc. However, shipping weight excludes lift and cargo vans and similar substantial outer containers. Other tonnage figures generally refer to stowing capacity of vessels, 100 cubic feet being called 1 ton. Gross tonnage comprises the space within the frames and the ceiling of the hull, together with those closed-in spaces above deck available for cargo, stores, passengers, or crew, with certain minor exceptions. Net or registered tonnage is the gross tonnage less the spaces occupied by the propelling machinery, fuel, crew quarters, master's cabin, and navigation spaces. Substantially, it represents space available for cargo and passengers. The net tonnage capacity of a ship may bear little relation to weight of cargo. Deadweight tonnage is the weight in long tons required to depress a vessel from light water line (that is, with only the machinery and equipment on board) to load line. It is, therefore, the weight of the cargo, fuel, etc., which a vessel is designed to carry with safety.

Historical statistics.—Tabular headnotes provide cross-references, where applicable, to *Historical Statistics of the United States, Colonial Times to 1970*. See Appendix IV.

No. 1061. Air and Water Transportation Industries—Summary: 1992

[For establishments with payroll]

INDUSTRY	1987 SIC [1] Code	Establish- ments	Revenue (mil. dol.)	Annual payroll (mil. dol.)	Paid employees [2]
Air transportation	45	(NA)	82,670	24,530	707
Air transportation, including air courier services	451,2	(NA)	76,503	22,734	627
Scheduled and air courier services	451	(NA)	73,070	22,026	604
Scheduled	4512	(NA)	62,057	19,090	505
Air courier services	4513	2,639	11,013	2,935	99
Nonscheduled	452	1,791	3,433	708	23
Airport terminal services	458	3,252	6,168	1,796	80
Water transportation	44	8,147	29,207	5,170	171
Water transportation of freight	441,2,3,4	836	14,704	1,523	37
Deep sea foreign and domestic freight	441, 2	615	11,948	1,148	27
Deep sea foreign freight	4412	334	8,490	629	13
Deep sea domestic freight	4424	281	3,458	519	13
Other water transportation of freight	443,4	221	2,756	375	10
Great Lakes-St. Lawrence Seaway freight	4432	26	559	81	1
Water transportation of freight, n.e.c. [3]	4449	195	2,197	293	9
Water transportation of passengers	448	1,033	4,133	508	23
Ferries	4482	118	155	51	2
Water transportation of passengers, except ferry	4481,9	915	3,978	457	22
Deep sea transportation, except by ferry	4481	72	3,268	275	13
Water transportation of passengers, n.e.c. [3]	4489	843	710	182	9
Services incidental to water transportation	449	6,278	10,370	3,140	111
Marinas	4493	3,348	1,651	346	18
Other services incidental to water transportation	4491,2,9	2,930	8,719	2,794	93
Marine cargo handling	4491	871	5,066	1,841	59
Towing and tugboat services	4492	941	2,682	689	25
Water transportation services, n.e.c. [3]	4499	1,118	971	263	9

NA Not available. [1] 1987 Standard Industrial Classification code; see text, section 13. [2] For the pay period including March 12. [3] N.e.c. means not elsewhere classified.

Source: U.S. Bureau of the Census, *Census of Transportation, Communications, and Utilities* UC92-A-1.

No. 1062. U. S. Scheduled Airline Industry—Summary: 1985 to 1993

[**For calendar years or Dec. 31.** For domestic and international operations. Covers carriers certificated under Section 401 of the Federal Aviation Act. Minus sign (-) indicates loss]

ITEM	Unit	1985	1987	1988	1989	1990	1991	1992	1993
SCHEDULED SERVICE									
Revenue passengers enplaned	Mil.	382.0	447.7	454.6	453.7	465.6	452.3	475.1	487.2
Revenue passenger miles	Bil.	336.4	404.5	423.3	432.7	457.9	448.0	478.6	489.1
Available seat miles	Bil.	547.8	648.7	676.8	684.4	733.4	715.2	752.8	770.8
Revenue passenger load factor	Percent	61.4	62.3	62.5	63.2	62.4	62.6	63.6	63.5
Mean passenger trip length [1]	Miles	881	903	931	954	984	990	1,007	1,004
Freight and express ton miles	Mil.	6,030.5	8,260.3	9,632.2	10,275.0	10,546.3	10,225.2	11,129.7	11,914.8
Aircraft departures	1,000	5,835.5	6,581.3	6,699.6	6,622.1	6,923.6	6,782.8	7,050.6	7,230.3
FINANCES									
Total operating revenue [2]	Mil. dol.	46,664	56,986	63,749	69,316	76,142	75,159	78,140	83,792
Passenger revenue	Mil. dol.	39,236	44,940	50,296	53,802	58,453	57,092	59,829	63,951
Freight and express revenue	Mil. dol.	2,681	6,398	7,478	6,893	5,432	5,509	5,916	6,321
Mail revenue	Mil. dol.	890	923	972	955	970	957	1,184	1,242
Charter revenue	Mil. dol.	1,280	1,612	1,698	2,052	2,877	3,717	2,801	3,045
Total operating expense	Mil. dol.	45,238	54,517	60,312	67,505	78,054	76,943	80,585	82,358
Operating profit	Mil. dol.	1,426	2,469	3,437	1,811	-1,912	-1,785	-2,445	1,434
Interest expense	Mil. dol.	1,588	1,695	1,846	1,944	1,978	1,177	1,743	2,024
Net profit	Mil. dol.	863	593	1,686	128	-3,921	-1,940	-4,791	-2,138
Revenue per passenger mile	Cents	11.7	11.1	11.9	12.4	12.8	12.7	12.5	13.1
Rate of return on investment	Percent	9.6	7.2	10.8	6.3	-6.0	-0.5	-9.3	-0.4
Operating profit margin	Percent	3.1	4.3	5.4	2.6	-2.5	-2.3	-3.1	1.7
Net profit margin	Percent	1.8	1.0	2.6	0.2	-5.1	-2.6	-6.1	-2.6
EMPLOYEES									
Total	1,000	355	457	481	507	546	534	540	537
Pilots, copilots, and other flight personnel	1,000	40	51	52	52	56	56	59	60
Flight attendants	1,000	63	73	76	78	83	82	86	85
Mechanics	1,000	43	51	55	57	61	59	59	58
Aircraft and traffic servicing personnel	1,000	101	199	212	225	252	237	243	243
Other	1,000	108	84	86	95	94	98	93	92

[1] For definition of mean, see Guide to Tabular Presentation. [2] Includes other types of revenues, not shown separately.

Source: Air Transport Association of America, Washington, DC, *Air Transport*, annual, and *Air Transport, Facts and Figures*, annual.

No. 1063. Airline Cost Indexes: 1980 to 1993

[Covers U.S. major and national service carriers. Major carriers have operating revenues of $1 billion or more; nationals have operating revenues from $75 million to $1 billion. Minus sign (-) indicates decrease]

ITEM	INDEX (1982=100)								PERCENT DISTRIBUTION OF CASH OPERATING EXPENSES [1]			
	1980	1985	1988	1989	1990	1991	1992	1993	1980	1985	1990	1993
INDEX												
Composite	86.3	103.1	102.4	109.0	117.0	119.8	122.0	124.8	100.0	100.0	100.0	100.0
Labor.	84.8	111.1	115.0	118.4	121.1	127.6	134.4	144.2	35.1	34.9	32.6	35.6
Interest [2]	88.7	105.5	99.6	111.5	107.3	88.3	84.8	85.3	2.9	3.5	2.5	2.7
Fuel.	91.6	81.4	54.2	61.2	78.7	68.9	64.1	59.7	29.7	22.3	17.6	12.3
Passenger food	94.3	102.0	111.9	122.8	132.6	141.4	144.1	127.8	2.9	3.2	3.6	3.4
Advertising and promotion	69.5	99.8	96.9	105.0	107.6	97.9	89.8	90.4	1.7	2.3	2.1	1.8
Landing fees	90.0	101.2	129.1	137.1	148.1	161.9	179.5	176.6	1.7	1.7	1.9	2.1
Passenger traffic commissions	77.3	117.6	148.3	163.4	176.8	193.5	192.2	196.6	4.8	7.4	9.8	10.8
All other	85.6	112.7	123.9	129.4	134.7	140.6	144.6	149.1	21.3	24.6	29.9	31.2
PERCENT CHANGE [3]												
Composite	23.3	0.3	4.1	6.4	7.3	2.4	1.8	2.3	(X)	(X)	(X)	(X)
Labor.	10.0	2.9	4.4	3.0	2.3	5.4	5.3	7.3	(X)	(X)	(X)	(X)
Interest [2]	16.9	-3.2	2.2	11.9	-3.8	-17.7	-4.0	0.6	(X)	(X)	(X)	(X)
Fuel.	55.8	-5.7	-4.6	12.9	28.6	-12.5	-7.0	-6.9	(X)	(X)	(X)	(X)
Passenger food	11.9	-4.2	6.0	9.7	8.0	6.6	1.9	-11.3	(X)	(X)	(X)	(X)
Advertising and promotion	24.3	-0.2	6.6	8.4	2.5	-9.0	-8.3	0.7	(X)	(X)	(X)	(X)
Landing fees	9.6	-0.2	6.3	6.2	8.0	9.3	10.8	-1.6	(X)	(X)	(X)	(X)
Passenger traffic commissions	40.0	0.8	15.1	10.2	8.2	9.4	-0.7	2.3	(X)	(X)	(X)	(X)
All other	9.3	3.7	3.9	4.4	4.1	4.4	2.9	3.1	(X)	(X)	(X)	(X)

X Not applicable. [1] Total operating expenses plus interest on long term debt, less depreciation and amortization.
[2] Interest on debt. [3] Change from immediate prior year.
Source: Air Transport Association of America, Washington, DC, *Air Transport,* annual; and unpublished data.

No. 1064. Top 10 Airports—Traffic Summary: 1993

[**In thousands, except percent change.** For **calendar year.** Airports ranked by revenue passengers enplaned. For scheduled carriers only; excludes charter-only carriers]

AIRPORT	Rank	AIRCRAFT DEPARTURES		REVENUE PASSENGERS ENPLANED		ENPLANED REVENUE TONS		
		Total [1]	Completed scheduled	Total	Percent change, 1980-1993	Total	Freight	U.S. mail
All airports [2]	(X)	7,194	6,931	468,313	67.9	8,203	6,384	1,819
Atlanta, Hartsfield International . . .	3	273	268	22,295	11.5	291	178	113
Chicago, O'Hare	1	384	378	29,134	51.5	465	315	150
Dallas/Ft. Worth International	2	357	349	24,656	136.3	295	191	104
Denver, Stapleton International . . .	5	183	178	14,328	49.0	145	95	50
Detroit, Metro Wayne	8	146	142	11,027	119.4	113	68	45
Los Angeles International.	4	192	187	18,457	30.4	450	375	75
Minneapolis/St. Paul	10	137	132	10,378	136.7	151	96	55
Newark International	9	141	136	10,965	160.7	279	230	49
Phoenix, Sky Harbor International .	7	148	144	11,295	234.2	92	62	30
San Francisco International	6	152	151	14,003	48.9	263	198	65

X Not applicable. [1] Includes completed scheduled and unscheduled. [2] Includes other airports, not shown separately.
Source: U.S. Federal Aviation Administration and Research and Special Programs Administration, *Airport Activity Statistics,* annual.

No. 1065. Domestic Airline Markets: 1993

[**For calendar year.** Data are for the 30 top markets and include all commercial airports in each metro area. Data do not include connecting passengers]

MARKET	Passengers	MARKET	Passengers
New York to—from Los Angeles	2,735,140	Chicago to—from Detroit	1,357,100
New York to—from Chicago	2,483,940	Los Angeles to—from Oakland	1,295,530
New York to—from Boston	2,473,660	Los Angeles to—from Honolulu	1,276,860
Honolulu to—from Kahului, Maui	2,427,790	Honolulu to—from Lihue, Kauai	1,269,600
New York to—from Miami.	2,357,870	Honolulu to—from Kona, Hawaii	1,225,650
New York to—from Washington	2,285,290	New York to—from West Palm Beach. . . .	1,138,870
Dallas/Ft. Worth to—from Houston	2,186,940	Chicago to—from Los Angeles	1,137,200
Los Angeles to—from San Francisco	2,037,710	Honolulu to—from Hilo, Hawaii	1,134,910
New York to—from San Francisco	1,903,390	San Francisco to—from San Diego	1,045,680
New York to—from Orlando	1,879,430	Boston to—from Washington	1,037,640
New York to—from Ft. Lauderdale	1,763,910	San Francisco to—from Honolulu.	1,013,640
New York to—from San Juan	1,589,570	Chicago to—from St. Louis.	1,007,120
New York to—from Atlanta	1,581,160	New York to—from Dallas/Ft. Worth	970,000
Los Angeles to—from Las Vegas	1,457,300	Los Angeles to—from Seattle	926,460
Los Angeles to—from Phoenix	1,359,650	Chicago to—from Minneapolis.	919,450

Source: Air Transport Association of America, Washington, DC, *Air Transport 1994.*

No. 1066. Worldwide Airline Fatalities: 1970 to 1993

[For scheduled air transport operations]

YEAR	Fatal accidents	Passenger deaths	Death rate [1]	YEAR	Fatal accidents	Passenger deaths	Death rate [1]
1970	29	700	0.29	1986 [2]	22	546	0.06
1975	20	467	0.13	1987 [2]	26	901	0.09
1980	22	814	0.14	1988 [2]	28	729	0.07
1981	21	362	0.06	1989 [2]	27	817	0.05
1982	26	764	0.13	1990 [2]	25	495	0.03
1983	20	809	0.13	1991 [2]	30	653	0.04
1984	16	223	0.03	1992 [2] [3]	29	1,097	0.06
1985	22	1,066	0.15	1993 [2] [3]	34	936	0.05

[1] Rate per 100 million passenger miles flown.   [2] Includes former USSR which began reporting in 1986.   [3] Preliminary.
Source: International Civil Aviation Organization, Montreal, Canada, *Civil Aviation Statistics of the World,* annual.

No. 1067. Airline Passenger Screening Results: 1980 to 1993

[Calendar year data]

YEAR	Passengers screened (mil.)	WEAPONS DETECTED				PERSONS ARRESTED	
		Firearms		Other	Explosive/ incendiary devices	Carrying firearms/ explosives	Giving false information
		Handguns	Long guns				
1980	585	1,878	36	108	8	1,031	32
1981	599	2,124	44	87	11	1,187	49
1982	630	2,559	57	60	1	1,314	27
1983	709	2,634	67	83	4	1,282	34
1984	776	2,766	98	91	6	1,285	27
1985	993	2,823	90	74	12	1,310	42
1986	1,055	2,981	146	114	11	1,415	89
1987	1,096	3,012	99	141	14	1,581	81
1988	1,055	2,591	74	108	11	1,493	222
1989	1,113	2,397	92	390	26	1,436	83
1990	1,145	2,490	59	304	15	1,336	18
1991	1,015	1,597	47	275	94	893	28
1992	1,111	2,503	105	[1]2,341	167	1,282	13
1993	1,150	2,707	91	[1]3,867	251	1,354	31

[1] Though 1991, includes other firearms; beginning 1992, includes stunning guns, chemical agents, martial arts equipment, knives, bludgeons, and other designated items.
Source: U.S. Federal Aviation Administration, *Annual Report to Congress on Civil Aviation Security.*

No. 1068. Aircraft Accidents and Hijackings: 1975 to 1993

[For years ending December 31]

ITEM	Unit	1975	1980	1985	1990	1991	1992	1993
Aircraft accidents: [1] General aviation [2]	Number . . .	3,995	3,590	2,738	2,214	2,170	2,074	2,022
Fatal	Number . . .	633	618	498	442	431	447	385
Rate per 100,000 aircraft hours flown	Rate	2.20	1.69	1.75	1.55	1.58	1.87	1.67
Fatalities	Number . . .	1,252	1,239	955	766	781	862	715
Air carrier, all services [3]	Number . . .	(NA)	19	22	24	26	18	23
Fatal	Number . . .	(NA)	1	7	6	4	4	1
Rate per 1,000,000 aircraft miles flown	Rate	(X)	-	0.002	0.001	0.001	0.001	-
Fatalities	Number . . .	(NA)	1	526	39	62	33	1
Air carrier, scheduled services	Number . . .	29	15	17	22	25	16	23
Fatal	Number . . .	2	-	4	6	4	4	1
Rate per 1,000,000 aircraft miles flown . . .	Rate	0.001	-	0.001	0.001	0.001	0.001	-
Fatalities	Number . . .	122	-	197	39	62	33	1
Commuter air carriers [4]	Number . . .	48	38	21	15	22	23	16
Fatal	Number . . .	12	8	7	3	8	7	4
Rate per 1,000,000 aircraft miles flown	Rate	0.07	0.04	0.02	0.01	0.02	0.02	0.01
Fatalities	Number . . .	28	37	37	6	99	21	24
Air taxis [5]	Number . . .	152	171	154	106	87	76	71
Fatal	Number . . .	24	46	35	28	27	24	19
Rate per 100,000 aircraft hours flown	Rate	0.95	1.27	1.36	1.24	1.20	1.19	0.90
Fatalities	Number . . .	69	105	76	50	70	70	42
Hijacking incidents, worldwide	Number . . .	19	39	26	40	24	12	31
U.S. registered aircraft	Number . . .	6	21	4	1	1	-	-
Successful [6]	Number . . .	4	13	2	(NA)	(NA)	-	-
Foreign-registered aircraft	Number . . .	13	18	22	39	23	12	31
Successful [6]	Number . . .	3	9	18	(NA)	(NA)	(NA)	(NA)
Bomb threats:								
U.S. airports	Number . . .	449	268	256	448	498	188	(NA)
Explosions	Number . . .	4	1	-	-	-	-	(NA)
U.S. worldwide and foreign aircraft in U.S	Number . . .	1,853	1,179	372	338	388	215	(NA)
Explosions	Number . . .	2	1	1	-	-	-	(NA)

- Represents or rounds to zero.   NA Not available.   X Not applicable.   [1] Data from National Transportation Safety Board.   [2] See text, section 22.   [3] U.S. air carriers operating under 14 CFR 121.   [4] All scheduled service of U.S. air carriers operating under 14 CFR 135.   [5] All nonscheduled service of U.S. air carriers operating under 14 CFR 135.   [6] Hijacker controls flight and reaches destination or objective.
Source: U.S. Federal Aviation Administration, *FAA Statistical Handbook of Aviation,* annual; and unpublished data. Includes data from U.S. Department of Transportation, Research and Special Programs Administration.

No. 1069. On-Time Flight Arrivals and Departures at Major U.S. Airports: 1994

[In percent. Quarterly, based on gate arrival and departure times for domestic scheduled operations in the 48 contiguous States of major U.S. airlines, per DOT reporting rule effective September 1987. All U.S. airlines with 1 percent or more of total U.S. domestic scheduled airline passenger revenues are required to report on-time data. A flight is considered on time if it operated less than 15 minutes after the scheduled time shown in the carrier's computerized reservation system. Cancelled and diverted flights are considered late. Excludes flight operations delayed/cancelled due to aircraft mechanical problems reported on FAA maintenance records (4-5 percent of the reporting airlines' scheduled operations). See source for data on individual airlines]

AIRPORT	ON-TIME ARRIVALS				ON-TIME DEPARTURES			
	1st. qtr.	2d. qtr.	3rd. qtr.	4th. qtr.	1st. qtr.	2d. qtr.	3rd. qtr.	4th. qtr.
Total, all airports	75.7	84.2	83.7	82.0	80.3	88.8	88.2	86.1
Total major airports	74.4	83.6	83.3	81.9	78.4	87.7	87.0	85.2
Atlanta, Hartsfield International	75.2	81.0	78.2	79.6	81.2	86.5	85.6	85.8
Boston, Logan International	59.0	76.7	75.1	82.1	66.4	84.6	83.3	87.8
Charlotte, Douglas	78.7	87.0	82.2	84.3	74.9	82.6	79.2	82.5
Chicago, O'Hare	73.8	86.3	85.9	87.9	76.8	89.9	88.9	88.4
Cincinnati International	77.7	85.1	83.7	88.9	80.0	89.4	87.5	90.0
Dallas/Ft. Worth International	77.5	82.3	84.9	77.7	81.6	87.2	88.3	78.6
Denver, Stapleton International	71.9	80.8	86.8	82.8	77.4	85.7	89.6	84.7
Detroit, Metro Wayne	80.3	87.9	86.9	88.2	78.6	87.6	86.9	88.2
Houston Intercontinental	77.1	84.1	85.9	81.4	81.7	87.8	89.5	85.5
Las Vegas, McCarran International	79.5	86.2	84.1	79.2	82.6	88.9	87.2	82.5
Los Angeles International	75.0	81.6	83.7	75.2	82.6	89.1	88.8	81.8
Miami International	73.3	83.6	78.7	81.4	82.8	90.9	87.4	88.9
Minneapolis/St. Paul International	81.4	88.7	87.0	87.4	83.3	91.5	90.2	88.8
Nashville Airport	84.2	88.6	88.8	89.2	84.2	89.8	89.4	90.0
Newark International	53.5	73.4	74.3	78.8	63.5	80.1	81.1	85.3
New York, Kennedy International	67.0	75.9	70.2	80.7	71.4	85.6	79.5	85.4
New York, LaGuardia	70.3	81.1	77.9	83.6	74.8	87.9	84.5	85.9
Orlando International	72.8	83.2	80.2	83.9	81.7	89.9	87.0	90.7
Philadelphia International	70.0	82.5	77.3	82.6	70.4	85.8	82.6	87.7
Phoenix, Sky Harbor International	80.7	87.1	87.4	77.7	82.2	87.7	87.9	80.4
Pittsburgh, Greater International	69.9	83.6	82.0	85.1	65.2	80.9	78.2	83.5
Raleigh/Durham	82.0	89.9	87.2	88.6	81.1	92.6	90.6	90.4
St. Louis, Lambert	79.0	86.3	89.9	78.7	80.5	88.9	91.8	81.9
Salt Lake City International	82.3	88.7	86.0	80.6	84.9	92.8	88.9	82.6
San Diego International, Lindbergh	78.5	86.5	87.5	78.8	84.3	91.5	92.0	85.2
San Francisco International	71.4	81.3	84.3	77.1	81.5	89.7	90.2	84.2
Seattle-Tacoma International	72.9	83.5	84.4	75.8	86.1	92.3	90.2	85.8
Tampa International	72.5	83.9	78.6	81.8	80.2	90.5	87.7	89.2
Washington National	72.4	82.4	81.6	85.8	76.4	87.4	87.6	90.5

Source: U.S. Department of Transportation, Office of Consumer Affairs, *Air Travel Consumer Report*, monthly.

No. 1070. Consumer Complaints Against U.S. Airlines: 1987 to 1994

[**Calendar year data.** See source for data on individual airlines]

COMPLAINT CATEGORY	1987	1988	1989	1990	1991	1992	1993	1994
Total	40,985	21,493	10,553	7,703	6,106	5,639	4,438	5,179
Flight problems [1]	18,019	8,831	4,111	3,034	1,877	1,624	1,211	1,586
Customer service [2]	3,888	2,120	1,002	758	714	695	599	805
Baggage	7,438	3,938	1,702	1,329	883	752	627	761
Ticketing/boarding [3]	2,458	1,445	821	624	659	680	577	598
Refunds	3,313	1,667	1,023	701	783	721	482	393
Oversales [4]	2,122	1,353	607	399	301	265	257	301
Fares [5]	937	455	341	312	388	573	398	267
Tours	90	37	22	29	23	12	16	127
Advertising	344	141	89	96	96	54	51	94
Smoking	888	546	232	74	30	25	30	20
Credit	101	35	.19	5	10	10	4	2
Other	1,387	925	584	342	342	228	186	225

[1] Cancellations, delays, etc. from schedule. [2] Unhelpful employees, inadequate meals or cabin service, treatment of delayed passengers. [3] Errors in reservations and ticketing; problems in making reservations and obtaining tickets. [4] All bumping problems, whether or not airline complied with DOT regulations. [5] Incorrect or incomplete information about fares, discount fare conditions, and availability, etc.

Source: U.S. Dept. of Transportation, Office of Consumer Affairs, *Air Travel Consumer Report*, monthly.

No. 1071. Commuter/Regional Airline Operations—Summary: 1980 to 1993

[**Calendar year data.** Commuter/regional airlines operate primarily aircraft of predominately 75 passengers or less and 18,000 pounds of payload capacity serving short haul and small community markets. Represents operations within all North America by U.S. Regional Carriers. Averages are means. For definition of mean, see Guide to Tabular Presentation]

ITEM	Unit	1980	1985	1988	1989	1990	1991	1992	1993
Passenger carriers operating	Number.	214	179	163	151	150	144	127	130
Passengers enplaned	Millions .	14.8	[1]26.0	35.2	37.4	42.1	42.0	48.9	527
Average passengers enplaned per carrier. .	1,000 . .	69.2	152.4	213.9	247.4	277.5	291.4	385.0	405.2
Revenue passenger miles (RPM)	Billions .	1.92	[1]4.41	6.04	6.77	7.61	7.80	9.46	10.61
Average RPM's per carrier.	Millions .	8.97	[1]24.64	37.05	44.84	50.75	54.18	74.50	81.59
Airports served	Number.	732	854	861	817	811	811	802	829
Average trip length	Miles. . .	129	173	173	181	183	186	194	201
Passenger aircraft operated	Number.	1,339	1,745	1,801	1,907	1,917	1,992	2,103	2,208
Average seating capacity (seats).	Number.	13.9	19.2	20.5	21.8	22.1	22.8	23.4	23.0
Fleet flying hours	1,000 .	1,740	2,854	3,078	3,266	3,447	3,671	4,259	4,490
Average annual utilization aircraft	Hours . .	1,299	1,635	1,709	1,712	1,798	1,843	2,025	2,033

[1] Adjusted to exclude a merger in 1986.

Source: Regional Airline Association, Washington, DC, Annual Report of the Regional Airline Industry (copyright).

No. 1072. Civil Flying—Summary: 1970 to 1993

[As of **Dec. 31** or for years ending **Dec. 31**, except as noted. See also *Historical Statistics, Colonial Times to 1970*, series Q 604-623]

ITEM	Unit	1970	1980	1985	1990	1991	1992	1993
Airports in operation [1]	Number. . .	11,261	15,161	16,318	17,490	17,581	17,846	18,317
Heliports	Number. . .	790	2,336	3,120	4,085	4,199	4,323	4,569
Public.	Number. . .	4,260	4,814	5,861	5,078	5,090	5,116	5,157
Private	Number. . .	7,001	10,347	10,457	12,412	12,491	12,730	13,160
Airports with runway lights	Number. . .	3,554	4,738	4,941	4,822	4,811	4,831	4,842
Airports with paved runways.	Number. . .	3,805	5,833	6,721	7,694	7,822	7,936	8,186
Airport Improvement Program [2]	Mil. dol. . . .	50.5	639.0	842.1	1,244.7	1,621.6	1,765.0	1,830.0
Total civil aircraft	1,000 . . .	154.5	259.4	274.9	275.9	275.5	277.0	279.0
Active aircraft [3]	1,000 . . .	134.5	214.8	215.4	218.9	204.6	191.7	183.3
Air carriers, total [4]	1,000 . . .	2.8	3.8	4.7	6.7	6.1	7.3	7.3
General aviation aircraft [5]	1,000 . . .	131.7	211.0	210.7	212.2	198.5	184.4	176.0
Fixed-wing aircraft: Multi-engine . . .	1,000 . . .	18.4	31.7	33.6	32.7	30.5	27.3	24.6
Single-engine	1,000 . . .	109.5	168.4	164.4	165.1	154.2	143.5	130.7
Rotorcraft [6]	1,000 . . .	2.2	6.0	6.4	7.4	6.3	5.8	4.5
Balloons, blimps, gliders, etc	1,000 . . .	1.6	5.0	6.3	7.0	7.6	7.8	5.2
Airman certificates held	1,000 . . .	1,002	1,195	1,105	1,195	1,210	1,224	1,225
Pilot [7]	1,000 . . .	733	827	710	703	692	683	665
Held by women	Percent . . .	4.0	6.4	6.1	5.8	5.9	5.9	5.9
Airline transport.	1,000 . . .	34	70	83	108	112	116	117
Commercial	1,000 . . .	187	183	152	149	148	146	143
Private.	1,000 . . .	304	357	311	299	293	288	284
Student	1,000 . . .	196	200	147	128	120	115	104
Nonpilot [8]	1,000 . . .	269	368	395	492	517	541	560
Ground technicians [9]	1,000 . . .	241	321	341	421	444	478	485
FAA employees: Total	Number. . .	53,125	55,340	47,245	51,269	54,119	53,871	52,680
Air traffic control specialists [10]	Number. . .	(NA)	27,190	23,580	24,339	25,741	24,983	24,630
Full performance [11]	Number. . .	(NA)	16,317	11,672	12,985	13,480	14,377	14,931
Developmental [11]	Number. . .	(NA)	4,387	4,304	5,042	5,080	3,759	3,040
Assistants [11]	Number. . .	(X)	(X)	1,465	1,153	928	792	632
Traffic management coordinators [12] . .	Number. . .	(X)	(X)	(X)	370	448	471	482
Electronic technicians	Number. . .	(NA)	8,871	6,856	6,458	6,641	6,572	6,262
Aviation safety inspectors	Number. . .	(NA)	2,038	1,897	2,984	3,101	3,017	2,920
Engineers	Number. . .	(NA)	2,436	2,457	2,745	3,073	3,208	3,198
Other	Number. . .	(NA)	14,805	12,455	14,743	15,563	16,091	15,670
General aviation: [5]								
Hours flown	Million	26.0	41.0	34.1	34.8	30.1	26.5	24.3
Fuel consumed: [13]								
Gasoline	Mil. gal. . . .	362	520	420	353	354	314	268
Jet fuel [14]	Mil. gal. . . .	415	766	691	663	577	494	454

NA Not available.   X Not applicable.   [1] Existing airports, heliports, seaplane bases, etc. recorded with FAA. Includes military airports with joint civil and military use. Includes U.S. outlying areas. Airport-type definitions: Public—publicly owned and under control of a public agency; private—owned by a private individual or corporation. May or may not be open for public use. [2] Fiscal year data. Does not include System Planning Grants. Includes U.S. outlying areas. 1970-1980 data are obligated Federal funds for the Airport Development Aid Program. Thereafter, data are appropriated Federal funds under the Airport and Airway Improvement Act of 1982. [3] Registered aircraft that flew 1 or more hours during the year. [4] Includes helicopters. [5] See text, section 22. Beginning 1993, excludes commuters and includes experimental aircraft, not shown separately. Prior to 1993, experimental aircraft were included in the appropriate type. [6] Includes autogyros; excludes air carrier helicopters. [7] Includes all active pilots. An active pilot is one with a pilot certificate and a valid medical certificate. Also includes pilots who hold only a helicopter, glider, or lighter than air certificate, not shown separately. [8] Includes dispatchers, flight navigators and engineers, and ground technicians—mechanics, parachute riggers, and ground instructors. [9] No medical examinations are required, therefore, data represent all certificates on record and include retired or otherwise inactive technicians. [10] Includes all air traffic control specialists (staff positions, managers, supervisors, and for 1970-1985 traffic management coordinators, not shown separately) and air traffic assistants. [11] Serving in-flight service stations, towers, and centers. [12] Prior to 1990, included in total air traffic control specialists. [13] Source: 1970, U.S. Bureau of Mines; thereafter, FAA General Aviation Activity and Avionics Survey. [14] Includes kerosene-type and naphtha-type jet fuels.

Source: Except as noted, U.S. Federal Aviation Administration, *FAA Statistical Handbook of Aviation*, annual; and unpublished data. Includes data from U.S. Department of Transportation, Research and Special Programs Administration.

No. 1073. Net Orders Booked for U.S. Civil Jet Transport Aircraft: 1985 to 1994

[Value in millions of dollars. 1985-1992 are net new firm orders; beginning 1993, net announced orders. Minus sign (-) indicates net cancellations]

TYPE OF AIRCRAFT AND CUSTOMER	1985	1989	1990	1991	1992	1993	1994
Total number [1]	468	1,015	670	280	231	31	79
U.S. customers	242	507	259	36	82	44	12
Foreign customers	226	508	411	244	149	-13	67
Boeing 737, total	253	397	189	75	91	-34	49
U.S. customers	146	216	38	-8	43	-29	9
Foreign customers	107	181	151	83	48	-5	40
Boeing 747, total	37	57	153	48	41	-25	-5
U.S. customers	13	4	24	-5	-	-25	-1
Foreign customers	24	53	129	53	41	-	-4
Boeing 757, total	51	190	66	80	7	20	5
U.S. customers	39	137	33	42	29	46	-1
Foreign customers	12	53	33	38	-22	-26	6
Boeing 767, total	10	138	60	58	20	43	27
U.S. customers	4	40	23	28	10	41	11
Foreign customers	6	98	37	30	10	2	16
Boeing 777, total	-	-	34	52	36	29	-
U.S. customers	-	-	34	-	-	5	-
Foreign customers	-	-	-	52	36	24	-
McDonnell Douglas MD-11, total	-	38	52	-31	1	-1	2
U.S. customers	-	17	16	-26	4	-	2
Foreign customers	-	21	36	-5	-3	-1	-
McDonnell Douglas MD-80/90, total	114	195	116	-2	35	-1	1
U.S. customers	37	93	91	5	-4	6	-8
Foreign customers	77	102	25	-7	39	-7	9
Total value	14,811	47,470	45,485	23,351	16,640	(NA)	(NA)
U.S. customers	7,869	20,304	14,828	2,144	3,200	(NA)	(NA)
Foreign customers	6,942	27,166	30,657	21,207	13,440	(NA)	(NA)

- Represents zero.　NA Not available　[1] Includes types of aircraft not shown separately.
Source: Aerospace Industries Association of America, Washington, DC, Research Center, Statistical Series 23.

No. 1074. U.S. Aircraft Shipments With Projections: 1970 to 1994

[Value in millions of dollars]

YEAR	TOTAL		CIVIL						MILITARY	
	Units	Value	Large transports		General Aviation [1]		Helicopters		Units	Value
			Units	Value	Units	Value	Units	Value		
1970	11,632	7,511	311	3,158	7,292	337	495	49	3,534	3,967
1975	16,958	9,355	285	4,006	14,056	1,033	838	266	1,779	4,050
1980	14,660	18,845	383	9,793	11,877	2,486	1,353	674	1,047	5,892
1985	3,597	29,312	273	9,375	2,029	1,431	376	505	919	18,001
1986	3,261	35,622	329	11,120	1,495	1,262	330	288	1,107	22,952
1987	2,995	37,317	255	11,900	1,160	1,320	270	320	1,210	23,777
1988	3,285	33,840	380	13,000	1,270	1,420	330	400	1,305	19,020
1989	3,675	34,228	398	15,074	1,535	1,803	515	251	1,227	17,100
1990	3,486	39,206	521	22,215	1,144	2,007	603	254	1,218	14,730
1991	2,934	40,776	589	26,856	1,021	1,968	571	211	753	11,741
1992	2,507	41,832	610	30,268	941	1,840	324	142	632	9,582
1993 [2]	2,282	37,108	408	26,456	964	2,144	260	122	650	8,386
1994 [3]	2,146	30,589	306	20,437	960	2,150	260	82	620	7,920

[1] Excludes off-the-shelf military aircraft.　[2] Estimated.　[3] Forecast.
Source: U.S. Department of Commerce, International Trade Administration, U.S. Industrial Outlook, 1994; and unpublished data.

No. 1075. Employment and Earnings in Aircraft Industries: 1985 to 1994

[Annual averages of monthly figures. See headnote, table 666]

ITEM	1987 SIC [1] code	Unit	1985	1990	1992	1993	1994
Employment: Total	(X)	1,000	794	898	758	666	588
Aircraft	3721	1,000	326	381	332	30;	270
Aircraft engines and engine parts	3724	1,000	148	152	127	110	96
Aircraft equipment, n.e.c. [2]	3728	1,000	143	180	153	131	114
Guided missiles, space vehicles, and parts	376	1,000	177	185	146	124	108
Average weekly earnings: [3]							
Aircraft	3721	Dollars	(NA)	(NA)	(NA)	(NA)	(NA)
Aircraft engines and parts	3724	Dollars	542	637	689	715	753
Guided missiles, space vehicles, and parts	376	Dollars	515	612	652	696	738
Average hourly earnings: [3]							
Aircraft [4]	3721	Dollars	13.18	15.66	17.70	18.43	19.50
Aircraft engines and parts	3724	Dollars	12.85	14.84	16.28	16.70	17.31
Guided missiles, space vehicles, and parts	376	Dollars	12.14	14.39	15.99	16.80	17.48

NA Not available.　X Not applicable.　[1] 1987 Standard Industrial Classification; see text, section 13.　[2] N.e.c. means not elsewhere classified.　[3] For production workers.　[4] Excludes lump-sum payments. Earnings which include proration of lump-sum payments were: $13.40 in 1985; $16.32 in 1990; $18.18 in 1992; $19.00 in 1993; and $19.57 in 1994.
Source: U.S. Bureau of Labor Statistics, Bulletin 2445; and Employment and Earnings, monthly, March and June issues.

No. 1076. Aerospace—Sales, New Orders, and Backlog: 1980 to 1993

[**In billions of dollars, except as indicated.** Reported by establishments in which the principal business is the development and/or production of aerospace products]

ITEM	1980	1985	1986	1987	1988	1989 [1]	1990 [1]	1991 [1]	1992 [1]	1993 [1]
Net sales	58.4	100.5	105.6	110.3	113.5	122.1	136.6	123.9	118.7	105.4
Percent U.S. Government	45.6	63.2	61.9	62.2	60.0	58.0	54.0	48.9	50.0	48.4
Complete aircraft and parts [2]	22.6	34.2	38.0	37.0	35.7	38.4	49.9	52.9	54.0	45.8
Aircraft engines and parts	6.9	9.7	9.8	12.0	15.0	15.4	16.4	15.6	13.7	12.1
Missiles and space vehicles, parts	8.4	16.7	17.5	20.7	21.5	22.6	22.0	23.3	21.3	19.8
Other products, services	20.5	39.8	40.3	40.5	41.3	45.7	48.3	32.0	29.7	27.8
Net, new orders	70.4	111.0	110.8	121.2	147.1	173.6	146.0	122.5	100.3	73.3
Backlog, Dec. 31	90.5	143.0	148.2	158.7	191.5	252.4	250.1	245.2	236.1	205.4

[1] Data beginning 1989 are not comparable with earlier years. Data are being reported which were previously not available. The extent of this noncomparability is not known.   [2] Except engines sold separately.

Source: U.S. Bureau of the Census, *Current Industrial Reports,* series MA-37D.

No. 1077. Aerospace Industry Sales, by Product Group and Customer: 1985 to 1995

[**In billions of dollars.** Due to reporting practices and tabulating methods, figures may differ from those in table 1076]

ITEM	CURRENT DOLLARS					CONSTANT (1987) DOLLARS [3]				
	1985	1990	1993	1994 [1]	1995 [2]	1985	1990	1993	1994 [1]	1995 [2]
Total sales	96.6	134.4	124.2	112.8	109.4	97.8	121.6	102.8	92.4	86.9
PRODUCT GROUP										
Aircraft, total	50.5	71.4	66.5	58.2	56.7	51.1	64.6	55.1	47.7	45.1
Civil [4]	13.7	31.4	33.8	26.3	25.8	13.9	28.4	27.9	21.5	20.5
Military	36.8	40.1	32.8	32.0	30.9	37.2	36.3	27.1	26.2	24.6
Missiles	11.4	14.2	8.1	7.3	6.6	11.6	12.8	6.7	6.0	5.2
Space	18.6	26.4	28.9	28.5	27.8	18.8	23.9	23.9	23.3	22.1
Related products and services [5]	16.1	22.4	20.7	18.8	18.2	16.3	20.3	17.1	15.4	14.5
CUSTOMER GROUP										
Aerospace, total	80.5	112.0	103.5	94.0	91.2	81.5	101.3	85.7	77.0	72.4
DOD [6]	53.2	60.5	47.1	44.6	41.9	53.9	54.8	39.0	36.5	33.3
NASA [7] and other agencies	6.3	11.1	12.3	12.2	12.0	6.3	10.0	10.2	10.0	9.5
Other customers [8]	21.0	40.4	44.1	37.2	37.2	21.3	36.5	36.5	30.5	29.6
Related products and services [5]	16.1	22.4	20.7	18.8	18.2	16.3	20.3	17.1	15.4	14.5

[1] Preliminary.   [2] Estimate.   [3] Based on AIA's aerospace composite price deflator.   [4] All civil sales of aircraft (domestic and export sales of jet transports, commuters, business, and personal aircraft and helicopters).   [5] Electronics, software, and ground support equipment, plus sales of non-aerospace products which are produced by aerospace-manufacturing use technology, processes, and materials derived from aerospace products.   [6] Department of Defense.   [7] National Aeronautics and Space Administration.   [8] Includes civil aircraft sales (see footnote 4), commercial space sales, all exports of military aircraft and missiles and related propulsion and parts.

Source: Aerospace Industries Association of America, Inc., Washington, DC, *1994 Year-end Review and Forecast.*

No. 1078. Aerospace Industry—Net Profits After Taxes: 1980 to 1994

[**For calendar year.** Minus sign (-) indicates loss]

YEAR	AEROSPACE INDUSTRY PROFITS				ALL MANUFACTURING CORPORATIONS PROFITS AS A PERCENT OF—		
	Total (mil. dol.)	As percent of—			Sales	Assets	Equity
		Sales	Assets	Equity			
1980	2,588	4.3	5.2	16.0	4.8	6.9	13.9
1981	2,966	4.4	5.2	16.0	4.7	6.7	13.6
1982	2,193	3.3	3.7	12.0	3.5	4.5	9.2
1983	2,829	3.5	4.1	12.1	4.1	5.1	10.5
1984	3,639	4.1	4.7	14.1	4.6	6.0	12.5
1985	3,274	3.1	3.6	11.1	3.8	4.6	10.1
1986	3,093	2.8	3.1	9.4	3.7	4.2	9.5
1987	4,582	4.1	4.4	14.6	4.9	5.6	12.8
1988	4,883	4.3	4.4	14.9	6.0	6.9	16.2
1989	3,866	3.3	3.3	10.7	5.0	5.6	13.7
1990	4,487	3.4	3.4	11.5	4.0	4.3	10.7
1991	[1]2,484	1.8	1.9	6.1	2.5	2.6	6.4
1992	[1]-1,836	-1.4	-1.2	-5.2	1.0	1.0	2.6
1993	4,621	3.6	3.5	13.2	2.8	2.9	8.1
1994, prel.	5,233	4.7	4.3	15.2	5.2	5.5	15.0

[1] Reflects unusually large nonoperating expenses totalling $3.4 billion in 1991 and $8.7 billion in 1992 due to the initial implementation of a change in accounting for future retirement benefit costs and defense-downsizing restructuring charges. Many large aercspace corporations chose to write off against first quarter earnings amounts required to comply with FASB 106.

Source: Aerospace Industries Association of America, Washington, DC, *1994 Year-end Review and Forecast.*

No. 1079. U.S. Exports of Aerospace Vehicles and Equipment: 1990 to 1993

ITEM	NUMBER OF UNITS				VALUE (mil. dol.)			
	1990	1991	1992	1993 [1]	1990	1991	1992	1993 [1]
Aerospace vehicles and equipment .	(NA)	(NA)	(NA)	(NA)	39,083	43,796	45,030	39,426
Civilian aircraft	3,779	3,329	2,086	1,758	18,148	22,388	24,337	19,845
Under 4,536 kg. unladen weight, new .	1,134	911	586	555	324	311	297	234
4,536-15,000 kg. unladen weight, new.	79	69	60	58	245	279	295	324
Over 15,000 kg. unladen weight, new .	306	385	387	276	16,691	20,881	22,379	18,146
Rotocraft, new.	349	318	212	175	161	168	118	120
Nonpowered aircraft, new	(NA)	(NA)	(NA)	(NA)	15	15	7	9
Used or rebuilt.	1,911	1,646	841	694	712	734	1,241	1,012
Military aircraft, new and used	445	490	428	632	1,481	1,784	2,083	1,460
Aircraft engines and parts.	(NA)	(NA)	(NA)	(NA)	6,883	7,049	6,699	6,278
Piston engines and parts	(NA)	(NA)	(NA)	(NA)	421	417	315	294
Complete engines, new and used . .	6,411	7,812	7,278	7,613	110	111	104	123
Engine parts	(NA)	(NA)	(NA)	(NA)	311	306	211	172
Turbine engines and parts	(NA)	(NA)	(NA)	(NA)	6,462	6,632	6,384	5,984
Complete engines, new and used . .	24,687	17,565	18,540	17,088	1,856	2,229	2,484	2,409
Engine parts	(NA)	(NA)	(NA)	(NA)	4,606	4,403	3,900	3,575
Propellers, rotors, and parts	(NA)	(NA)	(NA)	(NA)	343	317	289	308
Landing gear and parts	(NA)	(NA)	(NA)	(NA)	276	333	362	338
Aircraft parts and accessories, n.e.c. [2] . .	(NA)	(NA)	(NA)	(NA)	8,982	9,386	8,496	8,574
Guided missiles and parts.	(NA)	(NA)	(NA)	(NA)	1,306	1,204	1,428	1,231
Flight simulators	(NA)	(NA)	(NA)	(NA)	255	245	205	197
Space vehicles and parts	(NA)	(NA)	(NA)	(NA)	660	308	336	548
Avionics.	(NA)	(NA)	(NA)	(NA)	747	780	795	646

NA Not available.   [1] Estimated.   [2] N.e.c.=Not elsewhere classified.
Source: U.S. Dept. of Commerce, International Trade Administration, *U.S. Industrial Outlook, 1994*; and unpublished data.

No. 1080. International Transportation Transactions of the United States, by Type: 1980 to 1994

[**In millions of dollars.** Data are international transportation transactions recorded for balance of payment purposes (see table 1319). Receipts include freight on exports carried by U.S.-operated carriers and foreign carrier expenditures in U.S. ports. Payments include freight on imports carried by foreign carriers and U.S. carrier port expenditures abroad. Freight on exports carried by foreign carriers is excluded since such payments are directly or indirectly for foreign account. Similarly, freight on U.S. imports carried by U.S. carriers is a domestic rather than an international transaction. Minus sign (-) indicates excess of payments over receipts. See *Historical Statistics, Colonial Times to 1970*, series U 3 and U 10, for totals]

ITEM	1980	1985	1988	1989	1990	1991	1992	1993	1994 [1]
Total receipts	**14,208**	**19,085**	**28,432**	**31,190**	**37,252**	**38,203**	**39,676**	**39,701**	**42,357**
Ocean passenger fares	(Z)	60	128	132	154	156	173	237	236
Other ocean transportation	7,757	8,846	11,218	11,704	12,141	12,281	12,457	12,565	13,367
Freight	3,229	3,440	3,750	3,896	4,104	4,000	3,931	3,983	4,321
Port expenditures	4,435	5,274	7,315	7,609	7,815	8,041	8,267	8,335	8,792
Charter hire	93	132	153	199	222	240	259	247	254
Air passenger fares [2]	2,591	4,351	8,848	10,525	15,144	15,698	16,799	16,313	17,388
Other air transportation	3,355	5,347	6,792	7,310	8,174	8,556	8,505	8,854	9,549
Freight	742	706	1,385	1,719	2,432	2,722	2,589	2,856	3,236
Port expenditures	2,613	4,641	5,407	5,591	5,742	5,834	5,916	5,998	6,313
Miscellaneous receipts.	505	481	1,446	1,519	1,639	1,512	1,742	1,732	1,817
Total payments.	**15,397**	**22,087**	**27,263**	**28,908**	**33,932**	**33,309**	**34,068**	**35,918**	**38,277**
Ocean passenger fares	268	154	164	193	248	279	301	341	341
Other ocean transportation	8,179	10,698	12,180	12,227	13,078	12,303	11,921	12,790	13,737
Import freight	5,809	8,114	9,372	9,391	10,290	9,593	9,269	10,028	10,645
Port expenditures	1,905	2,048	2,244	2,228	2,174	2,093	2,029	2,143	2,477
Charter hire	465	536	564	608	614	617	623	619	615
Air passenger fares [2]	3,339	6,290	7,565	8,056	10,283	9,733	10,307	11,075	12,217
Other air transportation	3,366	4,719	6,981	8,080	9,881	10,513	11,032	11,177	11,395
Import freight	562	1,666	2,226	2,197	2,207	2,257	2,375	2,580	2,914
Port expenditures	2,804	3,053	4,755	5,883	7,674	8,256	8,657	8,597	8,481
Miscellaneous payments	245	226	373	352	442	481	507	535	587
Balance.	**-1,189**	**-3,002**	**1,169**	**2,282**	**3,320**	**4,894**	**5,608**	**3,783**	**4,080**

Z Less than $500,000.   [1] Preliminary.   [2] Beginning 1990, includes interairline settlements.
Source: U.S. Bureau of Economic Analysis, *Survey of Current Business*, June issues; and unpublished data.

No. 1081. Exports and Imports, by Method of Transport: 1980 to 1994

[Exports are free alongside ship (f.a.s.) value (see text, section 28) for all years; imports are f.a.s. value for 1980 and customs value for other years. Export data include both domestic and foreign; import data for general imports only. For details, see source]

ITEM	Unit	EXPORTS					IMPORTS				
		1980	1985	1990	1993	1994	1980	1985	1990	1993	1994
All methods [1]	Bil. dol.	220.7	213.1	393.0	464.9	512.4	240.8	345.3	495.3	580.5	663.4
Vessel.	Bil. dol.	120.9	91.7	150.8	166.6	177.6	165.1	208.4	283.4	310.4	339.4
Air	Bil. dol.	46.1	52.3	110.5	135.1	150.3	28.0	51.3	90.9	119.7	143.0
Shipping weight: Vessel . . .	Bil. kg .	363.7	317.7	372.4	349.5	334.5	443.1	361.5	496.3	531.0	586.9
Air	Bil. kg .	1.0	0.8	1.5	1.7	2	0.6	1.3	1.7	1.9	2.2

[1] Includes types other than vessel and air and revisions that are not distributed by method of transport.
Source: U.S. Bureau of the Census, *Highlights of U.S. Export and Import Trade*, through 1985, FT 990, monthly; thereafter, *U.S. Merchandise Trade: Selected Highlights*, FT-920, monthly.

No. 1082. Federal Expenditures for Civil Functions of the Corps of Engineers, United States Army: 1965 to 1993

[In millions of dollars. **For fiscal years ending in year shown,** see text, section 9. These expenditures represent the work of the Corps of Engineers to plan, design, construct, operate, and maintain civil works projects and activities, particularly in the management and improvement of rivers, harbors, and waterways for navigation, flood control, and multiple purposes. The amounts listed below do not include the expenditure of funds contributed, advanced, or reimbursed by other government agencies or local interests. Includes Puerto Rico and outlying areas]

FISCAL YEAR	Total program [1]	Navigation	Flood control	Multiple purpose	FISCAL YEAR	Total program [1]	Navigation	Flood control	Multiple purpose
1965	1,169	426	447	283	1986	3,163	1,345	1,300	402
1970	1,128	398	379	331	1987	2,937	1,135	1,272	411
1975	2,070	694	904	439	1988	3,086	1,271	1,271	423
1980	3,061	1,225	1,228	551	1989	3,252	1,395	1,253	462
1982	2,940	1,331	1,083	453	1990	3,297	1,391	1,397	375
1983	2,959	1,290	1,088	482	1991	3,511	1,473	1,447	443
1984	3,085	1,383	1,154	445	1992	3,675	1,562	1,469	469
1985	2,956	1,234	1,187	419	1993	3,335	1,461	1,243	464

[1] Includes expenditures which are not associated with a specific purpose (e.g., headquarters staff supervision, management and administration activities, and some research and development activities).

Source: U.S. Army Corps of Engineers, *Report of Civil Works Expenditures by State and Fiscal Year,* annual.

No. 1083. Freight Carried on Inland Waterways, by System: 1960 to 1989

[In billions of ton-miles. Excludes Alaska and Hawaii, except as noted. Includes waterways, canals, and connecting channels]

ITEM	1960	1970	1980	1982	1983	1984	1985	1986	1987	1988	1989
Total..............	220.3	318.6	406.9	351.2	359.0	399.0	381.7	392.6	410.7	438.2	448.7
Atlantic coast waterways......	28.6	28.6	30.4	25.4	22.5	24.7	24.8	25.7	25.9	28.1	28.2
Gulf coast waterways........	16.9	28.6	36.6	31.8	32.4	36.7	36.5	39.0	37.9	44.6	42.5
Pacific coast waterways [1]....	6.0	8.4	14.9	12.8	13.2	20.5	19.9	20.8	22.8	24.5	24.0
Mississippi River system [2]....	69.3	138.5	228.9	218.0	223.0	234.6	224.7	239.3	251.6	257.8	268.1
Great Lakes System [3].......	99.5	114.5	96.0	63.2	67.9	82.5	75.8	67.9	72.5	83.1	85.8

[1] Includes Alaskan waterways.   [2] Comprises main channels and all tributaries of the Mississippi, Illinois, Missouri, and Ohio Rivers.   [3] Does not include traffic between foreign ports.

Source: U.S. Army Corps of Engineers, *Waterborne Commerce of the United States,* annual.

No. 1084. Waterborne Commerce, by Type of Commodity: 1980 to 1993

[In millions of short tons. Domestic trade includes all commercial movements between United States ports and on inland rivers, Great Lakes, canals, and connecting channels of the United States, Puerto Rico, and Virgin Islands.]

COMMODITY	1980 Total	1980 Domestic	1985 Total	1985 Domestic	1990 Total	1990 Domestic	1993 Total	1993 Domestic
Net total	1,998.9	1,077.5	1,788.4	1,014.1	2,163.9	1,122.3	2,128.2	1,068.2
Petroleum products [1] ...	423.2	339.2	368.8	259.0	437.5	281.4	428.3	273.4
Gasoline	87.3	81.0	94.0	78.0	116.8	96.4	112.3	95.1
Distillate fuel oil	74.6	72.1	70.0	55.0	77.3	58.3	83.2	58.5
Residual fuel oil	188.0	141.3	130.0	83.7	145.1	90.4	123.1	81.3
Crude petroleum	480.2	174.2	357.7	194.7	485.7	176.2	505.6	147.4
Coal and lignite	256.4	164.1	273.9	179.9	333.7	222.5	292.3	209.5
Nonmetallic minerals [1][2] .	157.1	111.6	150.7	108.5	167.5	119.0	167.3	116.7
Sand and gravel [3]	65.1	60.8	66.4	62.0	62.8	57.4	65.4	56.1
Limestone	34.2	23.9	24.5	21.9	43.0	38.1	45.9	38.9
Phosphate rock	23.7	9.5	19.4	8.4	14.5	6.7	9.9	5.4
Iron and concentrates ...	98.4	64.9	72.7	50.0	86.1	62.8	82.2	60.7
Farm products [1]	216.8	63.4	172.8	60.0	215.5	78.7	208.1	75.3
Corn............	98.6	30.8	76.3	29.0	96.1	39.6	78.8	35.3
Wheat...........	53.4	14.3	38.0	10.6	44.4	13.3	52.5	13.2
Soybeans	39.6	16.1	32.9	14.9	32.2	15.9	37.7	17.7
Chemicals and allied products	91.9	49.4	108.5	53.3	123.7	67.3	136.1	71.4
Food and kindred products	54.8	20.4	52.5	17.6	56.7	17.3	62.6	22.3
Lumber and wood products [4]	52.0	22.7	47.2	18.8	57.9	22.4	49.9	20.3
Primary metal products ..	28.9	9.0	33.4	8.5	28.3	8.1	32.1	9.2
Waste and scrap	31.1	18.8	37.4	23.9	60.6	31.9	53.9	26.9
Other.............	108.1	39.8	112.8	40.0	110.7	35.7	109.8	35.1

[1] Includes categories not shown separately.   [2] Excludes fuels.   [3] Includes crushed rock.   [4] Excludes furniture.

Source: U.S. Army Corps of Engineers, *Waterborne Commerce of the United States,* annual.

No. 1085. Waterborne Imports and Exports, by Coastal District: 1980 to 1993

[Exports are free alongside ship (f.a.s.) value for all years; imports are f.a.s. value for 1980 and customs value for other years, see text, section 28. Includes commodities classified for security reasons as "Special Category" (exports only) and exports by Dept. of Defense (grant-aid shipments), and merchandise shipped in transit through the United States. See Appendix III]

DISTRICT	CARGO TONNAGE (mil. sh. tons)						VALUE (bil. dol.)					
	1980	1985	1990	1991	1992	1993	1980	1985	1990	1991	1992	1993
Imports:												
Atlantic	183	190	207	176	185	197	71.5	94.4	110.8	101.1	108.2	117.7
Gulf	243	141	225	217	232	267	56.4	32.8	41.0	36.4	36.3	38.7
Pacific.	56	51	55	49	55	58	45.0	90.4	143.3	143.7	156.6	168.8
Great Lakes	16	17	16	13	14	16	1.9	2.8	7.6	8.4	9.2	10.3
Exports:												
Atlantic	117	93	101	107	102	83	51.0	35.2	62.4	70.1	78.2	75.4
Gulf	163	144	148	167	165	155	41.5	31.8	41.2	44.2	45.0	39.9
Pacific.	78	81	100	102	101	96	25.2	25.8	53.7	56.6	60.4	59.9
Great Lakes	45	34	26	18	24	21	4.6	2.4	1.7	1.2	1.6	1.5

Source: U.S. Bureau of the Census, *U.S. Waterborne Exports and General Imports,* through 1985, FT 985, annual; thereafter TM 985, monthly.

No. 1086. Vessels Entered and Cleared in Foreign Trade, Net Registered Tonnage: 1966 to 1993

[**In millions of net registered tons, except as indicated.** Includes Puerto Rico and Virgin Islands. Seaports comprise all ports except Great Lakes ports. See also *Historical Statistics, Colonial Times to 1970,* series Q 507-517]

YEARLY AVERAGE OR YEAR	Number of vessels	ALL PORTS			SEAPORTS					
		Tonnage, all vessels			Tonnage, all vessels			Tonnage, with cargo		
		Total	U.S.	Foreign	Total	U.S.	Foreign	Total	U.S.	Foreign
Entered:										
1966-70	53,459	232	29	203	206	27	180	157	18	139
1971-75	53,760	319	30	290	292	28	264	220	24	196
1976-80	53,700	458	40	418	425	38	387	316	30	286
1981-85	50,124	452	57	395	424	55	369	277	36	241
1986-90	61,978	548	46	502	521	45	476	346	30	315
1970.	53,293	254	26	226	227	24	202	171	19	152
1975.	51,443	355	32	323	326	30	297	240	26	215
1980.	53,645	492	52	440	460	50	410	310	34	276
1985.	53,531	451	53	398	426	52	374	283	34	249
1989.	64,946	587	44	543	558	42	516	367	31	335
1990.	66,424	589	41	548	564	40	524	367	30	337
1991.	57,254	516	39	476	494	38	455	311	28	283
1992.	55,056	515	37	478	493	36	457	312	28	284
1993.	54,834	515	35	480	493	33	460	329	26	303
Cleared:										
1966-70	52,415	232	30	202	206	27	179	122	23	99
1971-75	53,039	324	31	293	296	29	267	149	21	127
1976-80	52,931	453	41	412	420	38	382	203	26	177
1981-85	50,291	460	57	403	432	55	377	251	34	217
1986-90	60,249	551	47	504	524	46	478	284	31	253
1970.	52,195	253	27	226	226	25	201	132	20	112
1975.	51,017	363	34	329	334	31	303	168	23	144
1980.	52,928	487	54	433	456	51	405	246	33	213
1985.	53,095	461	55	406	435	53	382	253	36	217
1989.	63,042	590	45	545	561	44	517	304	30	274
1990.	63,648	592	43	550	566	41	525	304	29	275
1991.	55,100	521	40	480	498	39	459	282	28	253
1992.	54,127	519	38	481	496	37	460	276	28	248
1993.	53,637	519	36	483	497	35	462	262	28	234

Source: U.S. Bureau of the Census, *Vessel Entrances and Clearances,* through 1989, FT 975, annual; thereafter TA 987, annual.

No. 1087. Domestic Merchant Vessels Completed by U.S. Shipyards: 1970 to 1992

[**Vessels of 1,000 gross tons and over.** See also *Historical Statistics, Colonial Times to 1970,* series Q 438-48]

TYPE	Unit	1970	1975	1980	1983	1984	1985	1986	1987	1988	1992
Merchant vessels	Number. . .	13	15	10	13	5	8	5	4	4	1
Gross tons.	1,000	342	452	375	376	118	172	215	153	153	32
Cargo.	Number. . .	6	3	6	6	-	4	2	3	3	1
Gross tons.	1,000	120	65	105	228	-	113	66	58	58	32
Deadweight tons.	1,000	134	71	114	219	-	97	53	63	63	29
Tankers	Number. . .	7	12	4	7	5	4	3	1	1	-
Gross tons.	1,000	222	387	270	148	118	59	149	95	95	-
Deadweight tons.	1,000	427	742	354	277	210	92	271	209	209	-

- Represents zero.

Source: U.S. Maritime Administration, *New Ship Construction,* annual.

No. 1088. United States Flag Merchant Vessels: 1994

[**As of January.** Covers ocean-going vessels of 1,000 gross tons and over engaged in foreign and domestic trade, and inactive vessels. Excludes vessels operating exclusively on Great Lakes, inland waterways, and those owned by the United States Army and Navy, and special types such as cable ships, tugs, etc. See also Historical Statistics, Colonial Times to 1970, series Q 487-502]

VESSEL TYPE	NUMBER						DEADWEIGHT TONS (1,000)					
	Total	Passenger [1]	Cargo [2]	Intercoastal	Bulk carrier [3]	Tanker [4]	Total	Passenger [1]	Cargo [2]	Intercoastal	Bulk carrier [3]	Tanker [4]
Total	564	12	145	176	21	210	21,126	104	2,097	4,928	949	13,048
Active vessels.	359	7	30	132	20	170	16,358	56	494	3,896	886	11,026
Privately owned.	345	2	26	128	20	169	16,198	14	444	3,845	886	11,009
U.S. foreign trade	134	-	18	68	17	31	5,479	-	282	2,355	803	2,039
Foreign-to-foreign	28	-	1	10	1	16	1,753	-	15	299	37	1,402
Domestic trade.	134	2	-	24	2	106	7,727	14	-	520	46	7,147
Coastal	62	-	-	1	2	59	2,235	-	-	14	46	2,175
Noncontiguous	72	2	-	23	-	47	5,492	14	-	506	-	4,972
Military Sea Lift Command .	49	-	7	26	-	16	1,239	-	147	671	-	421
Government owned	14	5	4	4	-	1	160	42	50	51	-	17
Ready reserve force	3	1	2	-	-	-	37	9	28	-	-	-
Other Custody	1	-	-	1	-	-	16	-	-	16	-	-
Other Reserve	7	3	1	3	-	-	68	22	11	35	-	-
Non-Retention	3	1	1	-	-	1	39	11	11	-	-	17
Inactive vessels	205	5	115	44	1	40	4,768	48	1,603	1,032	63	2,022
Privately owned.	22	-	4	3	1	14	1,355	-	58	55	63	1,179
Temporarily inactive	4	-	-	2	1	1	137	-	-	36	63	38
Laid-up.	16	-	4	1	-	11	1,150	-	58	19	-	1,073
Laid-up (MARAD Custody) [5]	2	-	-	-	-	2	68	-	-	-	-	68
Government owned (MARAD Custody) [5]	183	5	111	41	-	26	3,413	48	1,545	977	-	843
National defense reserve fleet	147	1	82	41	-	23	2,958	10	1,213	977	-	758
Ready reserve fleet	94	-	54	27	-	13	1,857	-	756	697	-	404
Other reserve	53	1	28	14	-	10	1,101	10	457	280	-	354
Nonretention [6]	36	4	29	-	-	3	455	38	332	-	-	85

- Represents zero. [1] Includes combination passenger and cargo vessels. [2] General cargo. [3] Includes tug barges. [4] Includes tanker barges and liquified natural gas vessels. [5] In the custody of the Maritime Administration. [6] Vessels not actively maintained.

Source: U.S. Maritime Administration, *Employment Report of the United States Flag Merchant Fleet Ocean-Going Vessels 1,000 Gross Tons and Over,* annual.

No. 1089. Private Shipyards—Summary: 1980 to 1993

[**For calendar year, unless noted.** See also *Historical Statistics, Colonial Times to 1970,* series Q 449-458 and series Q 467-472]

ITEM	Unit	1980	1985	1987	1988	1989	1990	1991	1992	1993
Employment [1]	1,000. . .	177.3	130.3	120.4	121.0	123.4	121.8	127.2	123.5	111.0
Production workers	1,000. . .	141.8	99.0	90.8	90.9	88.6	86.4	95.5	93.3	84.3
Value of work done.	Mil. dol. .	9,269	9,358	8,531	(NA)	(NA)	(NA)	(NA)	(NA)	(NA)
On ships only.	Mil. dol. .	8,889	9,483	8,377	(NA)	(NA)	(NA)	(NA)	(NA)	(NA)
Value added	Mil. dol. .	5,338	5,740	5,227	(NA)	(NA)	(NA)	(NA)	(NA)	(NA)
Building activity: [2]										
Merchant vessels: [2]										
Under construction [3]	Number .	69	10	6	-	-	-	3	3	1
Ordered	Number .	7	-	-	-	-	3	-	1	-
Delivered	Number .	23	3	4	-	-	-	-	3	-
Cancelled	Number .	4	-	2	-	-	-	-	-	-
Under contract [4]	Number .	49	7	-	-	-	3	3	1	1
Naval vessels: [2]										
Under construction [3]	Number .	99	100	79	83	105	98	91	90	82
Ordered	Number .	11	11	20	32	16	8	13	10	12
Delivered	Number .	19	26	16	10	23	15	14	18	19
Under contract [4][5]	Number .	91	85	83	105	98	91	90	82	73
Repairs/conversions:										
Commercial ships	Mil. dol. .	1,335	852	806	202	279	373	380	226	292
Naval ships	Mil. dol. .	1,134	2,311	1,930	1,238	1,091	1,119	993	526	573
Unfinished work: [3]										
Commercial ships	Mil. dol. .	2,070	450	53	-	-	-	99	32	42
Naval ships	Mil. dol. .	7,107	12,091	8,265	10,500	16,010	15,450	14,151	12,286	(NA)

- Represents zero. NA Not available. [1] Annual average of monthly data. [2] Vessels of 1,000 tons or larger. [3] As of Jan. 1. [4] As of Dec. 31. [5] Two ships were cancelled in August 1993.

Source: Shipbuilders Council of America, Arlington, VA., *Annual Report,* through 1980; thereafter, unpublished data.

No. 1090. Employees in Government and Private Shipyards: 1960 to 1994

[**In thousands.** Annual average employment in establishments primarily engaged in building and repairing all types of ships, barges, canal boats, and lighters of 5 gross tons and over, whether propelled by sail or motor power or towed by other craft. Includes all full- and part-time employees]

YEAR	Total	Private yards	Navy yards	YEAR	Total	Private yards	Navy yards	YEAR	Total	Private yards	Navy yards
1960	208	112	96	1985	219	138	80	1990	198	130	68
1970	216	134	83	1986	206	131	75	1991	193	131	62
1975	217	154	65	1987	200	124	75	1992	183	124	59
1980	250	178	72	1988	197	124	73	1993	164	113	51
1984	229	146	83	1989	196	126	71	1994	150	107	43

Source: U.S. Bureau of Labor Statistics, Bulletin 2445; *Employment and Earnings*, monthly, March and June issues; and unpublished data.

No. 1091. Employment on U.S. Flag Merchant Vessels, 1970 to 1994, and Basic Monthly Wage Scale for Able-Bodied Seamen, 1970 to 1995

[**Employment in thousands.** See also *Historical Statistics, Colonial Times to 1970*, series Q 414-416]

YEAR	Employment [1]	YEAR	Employment [1]	YEAR	East coast wage rate [2]	West coast wage rate [2]	YEAR	East coast wage rate [2]	West coast wage rate [2]
1970	37.6	1989	9.9	1970	$470	$652	1990	$1,505	$2,218
1975	20.5	1990	11.1	1975	612	900	1991	1,581	2,329
1980	19.6	1991	11.7	1980	967	1,414	1992	1,655	2,438
1985	13.1	1992	9.2	1985	1,419	2,029	1993	1,721	2,438
1987	10.4	1993	9.3	1988	1,419	2,175	1994	1,790	2,536
1988	10.7	1994	9.1	1989	1,448	2,218	1995	1,853	2,536

[1] As of June 30, except beginning 1980, as of Sept. 30. Estimates of personnel employed on merchant ships, 1,000 gross tons and over. Excludes vessels on inland waterways, Great Lakes, and those owned by, or operated for, U.S. Army and Navy, and special types such as cable ships, tugs, etc.　　[2] As of January. Basic monthly wage, over and above subsistence (board and room); excludes overtime and fringe pay benefits. West coast incorporates extra pay for Saturdays and Sundays at sea into base wages but east coast does not.

Source: U.S. Maritime Administration, *U.S. Merchant Marine Data Sheet,* monthly; and unpublished data.

No. 1092. Worldwide Tanker Casualties: 1975 to 1994

[Data for **1975** and **1980** covers tankers, ore/oil carriers and bulk/oil vessels of 6,000 deadweight tons and over; beginning **1985**, 10,000 deadweight tons and over; excludes liquid gas carriers. Incident is counted in the year it is reported. Based on data from "Lloyd's List" published by Lloyd's of London. "Casualties" include weather damage, strandings, collisions and other contact, fires and explosions, machinery damage, and other mishaps]

ITEM	Unit	1975	1980	1985	1988	1989	1990	1991	1992	1993	1994
Casualties.	Number	906	(NA)	340	456	528	541	507	396	314	270
Total losses [1]	Number	22	15	12	3	8	10	10	11	9	11
Deaths	Number	90	132	53	63	74	119	205	86	26	88
Oil spills	Number	45	32	9	13	31	31	26	17	24	29
Amount	1,000 tons	188	136	80	178	188	61	439	152	120	110
Amount	Mil. gallons	58	42	25	55	58	19	136	47	37	33

NA Not available.　　[1] Excludes losses due to hostilities.

Source: Tanker Advisory Center, Inc., New York, NY, "Worldwide Tanker Casualty Returns," quarterly.

No. 1093. Merchant Vessels—World and United States: 1960 to 1993

[**Through 1992, as of mid-year; thereafter for year-end.** For propelled sea-going merchant ships of not less than 100 gross tonnage. See also Historical Statistics, Colonial Times to 1970, series Q 473-480]

YEAR	WORLD: COMPLETED		WORLD: OWNED		U.S.: COMPLETED		U.S.: REGISTERED	
	Number	Gross tonnage (1,000)	Number	Gross tonnage (1,000)	Number	Gross tonnage (1,000)	Number	Gross tonnage (1,000)
1960	2,005	8,382	36,311	129,770	49	379	4,059	24,837
1970	2,814	20,980	52,444	227,490	156	375	2,983	18,463
1980	2,412	13,101	73,832	419,911	205	555	5,579	18,464
1985	1,964	18,157	76,395	416,269	66	180	6,447	19,518
1989	1,593	13,236	76,100	410,481	10	4	6,375	20,588
1990	1,672	15,885	78,336	423,627	16	15	6,348	21,328
1991	1,574	16,095	80,030	436,027	17	9	6,222	20,291
1992	1,506	18,633	79,845	444,305	27	54	5,737	18,228
1993	1,505	20,025	80,655	457,915	30	14	5,646	14,087

Source: Through 1992, Lloyd's Register of Shipping, London, England, *Statistical Tables*, annual; and *Annual Summary of Merchant Ships Completed in the World;* thereafter, *World Fleet Statistics,* annual.

No. 1094. Merchant Vessels—Ships and Tonnage Lost Worldwide: 1980 to 1993

[**For merchant vessels of 100 gross tonnage and above.** Excludes ships which have been declared constructive losses but have undergone repair during the year. Loss counted in the year the casualty occurred, providing that information was available at time of relevant publication]

TYPE OF SHIP	SHIPS LOST					GROSS TONNAGE LOST (1,000)				
	1980	1985	1990	1992	1993	1980	1985	1990	1992	1993
Total [1]	**387**	**307**	**188**	**213**	**219**	**1,804**	**1,651**	**1,126**	**1,223**	**778**
Tankers	24	19	8	7	12	707	776	138	332	198
Ore/bulk carriers [2]	21	22	15	13	7	458	405	687	576	160
General cargo	211	155	87	81	96	478	363	202	174	310
Container ships	2	5	-	4	1	6	41	-	40	5
Passenger [3]	9	-	-	1	1	112	-	-	13	4
Fishing	96	66	50	77	74	30	26	20	31	39

- Represents zero.   [1] Includes types not shown separately.   [2] Includes ore/bulk/oil carriers.   [3] Includes passenger cargo ships.

Source: Lloyd's Register of Shipping, London, England, *Casualty Return,* annual.

No. 1095. Merchant Fleets of the World: 1980 to 1993

[**Vessels of 1,000 gross tons and over.** As of **Jan. 1** of the following year. Specified countries have 100 or more ships]

YEAR AND COUNTRY OF REGISTRY, 1993	TOTAL		PASSENGER/ CARGO COMB.		FREIGHTERS		BULK CARRIERS [1]		TANKERS	
	Number	Average age (yr.)	Number	Average age (yr.)	Number	Average age (yr.)	Number	Average age (yr.)	Number	Average age (yr.)
1980, world total	**24,867**	**13**	**468**	**24**	**14,242**	**14**	**4,798**	**10**	**5,359**	**12**
United States	864	23	65	34	471	23	20	22	308	20
Foreign	24,003	13	403	22	13,771	13	4,778	10	5,051	11
1985, world total	**25,555**	**14**	**375**	**25**	**13,937**	**15**	**5,787**	**11**	**5,456**	**13**
United States	737	23	37	38	417	25	25	9	258	19
Foreign	24,818	14	338	23	13,520	15	5,762	11	5,198	13
1993, world total	**24,331**	**(NA)**	**374**	**(NA)**	**12,685**	**(NA)**	**5,388**	**(NA)**	**5,884**	**(NA)**
United States	564	(NA)	12	(NA)	321	(NA)	21	17	210	(NA)
Privately owned	367	20	2	44	161	18	21	17	183	22
Government owned	197	33	10	47	160	32	-	(NA)	27	36
Foreign	23,767	(NA)	362	(NA)	12,364	(NA)	5,367	(NA)	5,674	(NA)
Antigua and Barbuda	198	13	-	-	178	12	6	17	14	18
Bahamas	863	14	54	21	414	14	155	15	240	14
Brazil	212	16	1	33	59	18	66	14	86	16
Bulgaria	117	19	2	26	59	21	37	17	19	14
China: Mainland	1,311	18	28	22	788	19	307	18	188	17
Cyprus	1,373	17	13	30	635	16	565	18	160	16
Denmark (DIS) [2]	306	9	-	-	208	9	12	8	86	9
Egypt	127	20	1	43	100	21	14	11	12	23
Germany	376	8	6	11	308	8	18	12	44	8
Greece	970	18	22	35	192	21	483	17	273	18
Honduras	233	27	4	31	189	27	10	25	30	25
Hong Kong	214	12	-	-	68	14	118	11	28	15
India	288	14	2	25	89	15	118	14	79	13
Indonesia	385	19	7	20	267	19	16	15	95	19
Iran	128	18	-	-	44	20	50	15	34	20
Italy	431	17	19	18	146	17	47	15	219	18
Japan	881	10	16	12	320	9	219	12	326	8
Latvia	114	19	-	-	72	20	-	-	42	17
Liberia	1,515	13	29	15	384	13	470	15	632	13
Malaysia	183	17	-	-	102	21	24	11	57	11
Malta	852	19	6	44	366	19	287	19	193	20
Netherlands	366	11	6	18	291	10	13	15	56	10
Norway (NIS) [2]	665	14	14	13	199	16	156	13	296	13
Panama	3,323	15	31	28	1,794	15	745	14	753	13
Philippines	522	15	5	36	225	18	244	10	48	23
Poland	177	16	2	14	96	17	74	15	5	20
Romania	238	16	-	-	179	15	48	18	11	14
Russia	1,443	19	13	25	1,133	20	89	16	208	17
Saint Vincent	524	21	4	28	348	21	100	20	72	24
Singapore	526	14	-	-	229	16	93	11	204	14
South Korea	408	15	-	-	213	16	120	15	75	15
Spain	165	17	1	21	100	17	20	17	44	18
Sweden	152	16	4	9	79	15	9	21	60	16
Taiwan	206	12	-	-	134	14	55	9	17	8
Thailand	200	23	1	33	125	24	15	19	59	23
Turkey	380	18	4	44	195	16	124	18	57	21
Ukraine	448	19	14	24	348	20	55	16	31	14
United Kingdom	145	17	17	17	56	16	13	14	59	18
Vanuatu	122	13	-	-	58	13	53	14	11	14
All others	2,680	(NA)	36	(NA)	1574	(NA)	319	(NA)	751	(NA)

NA Not available.   - Represents zero.   [1] Includes bulk/oil, ore/oil, and ore/bulk/oil carriers.   [2] International Shipping Registry which is an open registry under which the ship flies the flag of the specified nation but is exempt from certain taxation and other regulations.

Source: U.S. Maritime Administration, *Merchant Fleets of the World,* summary report, annual; and unpublished data.

Figure 23.1
**Consumer Expenditures for Farm Foods:
1980, 1990, and 1993**

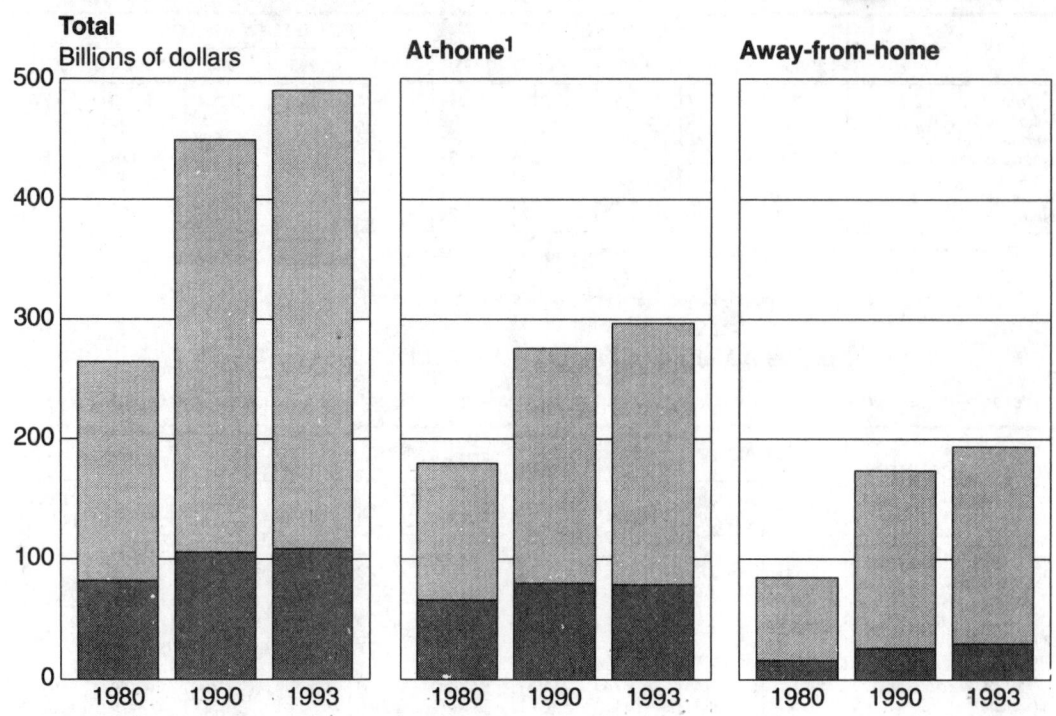

[1]Food purchased from retail food stores for use at home.
Source: Chart prepared by U.S. Bureau of the Census. For data, see table 1118.

Figure 23.2
**Corn, Soybeans, and Wheat—
U.S. Production and Exports: 1994**

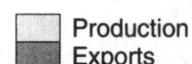

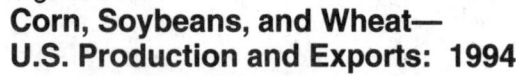

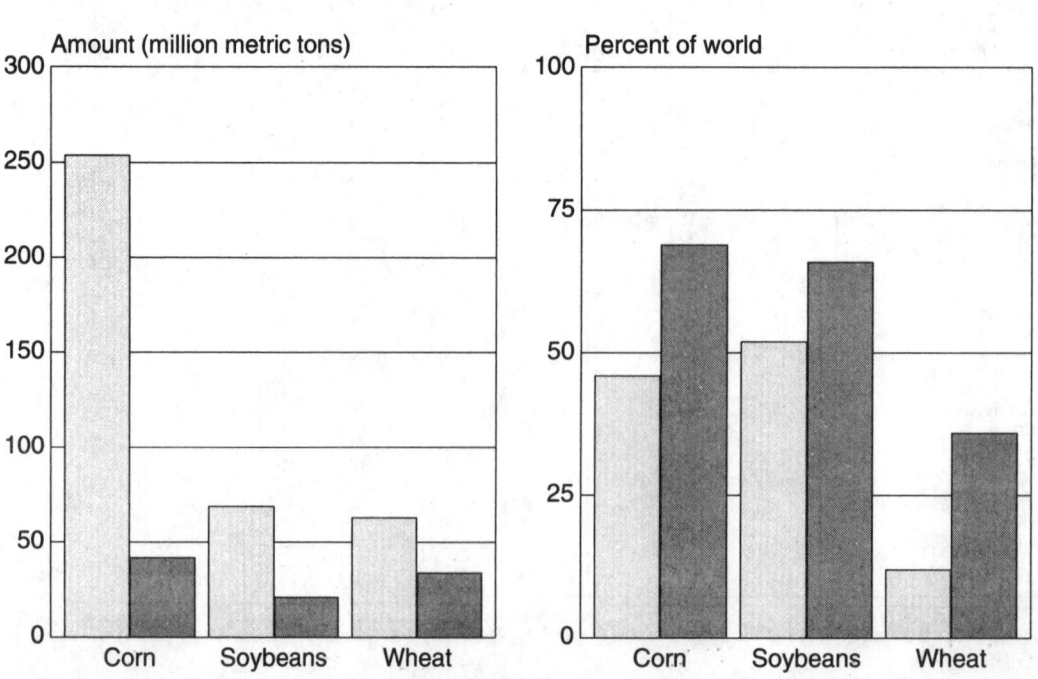

Source: Chart prepared by U.S. Bureau of the Census. For data, see table 1129.

Agriculture

This section presents statistics on farms and farm population; land use and irrigation; farm cooperatives; farm income, expenditures, and debt; farm output, productivity, and marketings; foreign trade in agricultural products; specific crops; and livestock, poultry, and their products.

The principal sources are the reports issued by the U.S. Bureau of the Census and by the National Agricultural Statistics Service (NASS) and the Economic Research Service (ERS) of the U.S. Department of Agriculture. The 1992 Census of Agriculture is the 24th taken by the Bureau of the Census. The information is available in printed form in the volume 1, Geographic Area Series, and in electronic format on CD-ROM. The Department of Agriculture publishes annually *Agricultural Statistics*, a general reference book on agricultural production, supplies, consumption, facilities, costs, and returns. The Economic Research Service publishes a series of annual reports, *Economic Indicators of the Farm Sector*. This series comprises four reports: *National Financial Summary, State Financial Summary, Production and Efficiency Statistics*, and *Costs of Production—Major Field Crops & Livestock and Dairy*. Sources of current data on agricultural exports and imports include *Foreign Agricultural Trade of the United States*, published by the ERS, and the reports of the Bureau of the Census, particularly *U.S. Imports for Consumption and General Imports—HTSUSA Commodity by Country of Origin* (FT247), *U.S. Exports, Harmonized Schedule B, Commodity by Country* (FT447) and *U.S. Merchandise Trade: Exports, General Imports, and Imports for Consumption* (FT925).

The 45 field offices of the NASS collect data on crops, livestock and products, agricultural prices, farm employment, and other related subjects mainly through sample surveys. Information is obtained on some 75 crops and 50 livestock items as well as scores of items pertaining to agricultural production and marketing. State estimates and supporting information are sent to the Agricultural Statistics Board of NASS which

In Brief

Number of farms, 1994: 2.0 million
  Leading States—

Texas	*185,000*
Missouri	*104,000*
Iowa	*100,000*

Farm marketings cash receipts, 1993: $175 billion
  Leading commodities—

Cattle, calves	*$40 billion*
Dairy products	*$19 billion*
Corn	*$14 billion*

reviews the estimates and issues reports containing State and national data. Among these reports are annual summaries such as *Crop Production, Crop Values, Agricultural Prices*, and *Livestock Production, Disposition and Income*. For more information about concepts and methods underlying USDA's statistical series, see *Major Statistical Series of the U.S. Department of Agriculture* (Agricultural Handbook No. 671), a 12-volume set of publications.

Farms and farmland.—The Bureau of the Census has used varying definitions of a farm. Since 1850, when minimum criteria defining a farm for census purposes first were established, the farm definition has been changed nine times. The current definition, first used for the 1974 census, is any place from which $1,000 or more of agricultural products were produced and sold, or normally would have been sold, during the census year.

Acreage designated as "land in farms" consists primarily of agricultural land used for crops, pasture, or grazing. It also includes woodland and wasteland not actually under cultivation or used for pasture or grazing, provided it was part of the farm operator's total operation. Land in farms includes acres set aside under annual commodity acreage programs as well as acres in the Conservation Reserve and Wetlands Reserve Programs for places meeting the farm definition. Land in farms is an operating unit concept and includes land owned and operated as well as land rented from others. All grazing land, except land used under government permits on a per-head basis, was included as "land in farms" provided it was part of a farm or ranch.

Coverage estimates for 1982 and 1987 indicate about 9.1 and 7.2 percent of all farms, respectively, were not included in census totals. Farms undercounted in these censuses were usually small and accounted for approximately 1 percent of the total value of agricultural products sold and approximately 2 percent of the land in farms. For more explanation about mail list compilation and census coverage, see Appendixes A and C, *1992 Census of Agriculture*, volume 1 reports and *Coverage Evaluation*, Volume 2, Part 2.

Farm income.—Gross farm income comprises cash receipts from farm marketings of crops and livestock, Federal government payments made directly to farmers for farm–related activities, rental value of farm homes, value of farm products consumed in farm homes, and other farm–related income such as machine hire and custom work. Farm marketings represent quantities of agricultural products sold by farmers multiplied by prices received per unit of production at the local market. Information on prices received for farm products is generally obtained by the NASS Agricultural Statistics Board from surveys of firms (such as grain elevators, packers, and processors) purchasing agricultural commodities directly from producers. In some cases, the price information is obtained directly from the producers.

Crops.—Estimates of crop acreage and production by the NASS are based on current sample survey data obtained from individual producers and objective yield counts, reports of carlot shipments, market records, personal field observations by field statisticians, and reports

from other sources. Prices received by farmers are marketing year averages. These averages are based on U.S.. monthly prices weighted by monthly marketings during specific periods. U.S. monthly prices are State average prices weighted by marketings during the month. Marketing year average prices do not include allowances for outstanding loans, government purchases, deficiency payments or disaster payments.

All State prices are based on individual State marketing years, while U.S. marketing year averages are based on standard marketing years for each crop. For a listing of the crop marketing years and the participating States in the monthly program, see *Crop Values*, January 1992. Value of production is computed by multiplying State prices by each State's production. The U.S. value of production is the sum of State values for all States. Value of production figures shown in tables 1131, 1133–1135, 1137, and 1138 should not be confused with cash receipts from farm marketings which relate to sales during a calendar year, irrespective of the year of production.

Livestock.—Annual inventory numbers of livestock and estimates of livestock, dairy, and poultry production prepared by the Department of Agriculture are based on information from farmers and ranchers obtained by probability survey sampling methods.

Statistical reliability.—For a discussion of statistical collection and estimation, sampling procedures, and measures of statistical reliability pertaining to Census Bureau and Department of Agriculture data, see Appendix III.

Historical statistics.—Tabular headnotes provide cross–references, where applicable, to *Historical Statistics of the United States, Colonial Times to 1970*. See Appendix IV.

No. 1096. Farms—Number and Acreage, by Size of Farm: 1982 to 1992

[See also *Historical Statistics, Colonial Times to 1970*, series K 162-173]

SIZE OF FARM	NUMBER OF FARMS (1,000)			LAND IN FARMS (mil. acres)			CROPLAND HARVESTED (mil. acres)			PERCENT DISTRIBUTION, 1992		
	1982	1987	1992	1982	1987	1992	1982	1987	1992	Number of farms	All land in farms	Cropland harvested
Total	**2,241**	**2,088**	**1,925**	**986.8**	**964.5**	**945.5**	**326.3**	**282.2**	**295.9**	**100.0**	**100.0**	**100.0**
Under 10 acres	188	183	166	0.7	0.7	0.7	0.3	0.2	0.2	8.6	0.1	0.1
10 to 49 acres	449	412	388	12.1	11.1	10.3	4.5	3.9	3.5	20.1	1.1	1.2
50 to 99 acres	344	311	283	24.8	22.5	20.4	9.5	7.9	7.2	14.7	2.2	2.4
100 to 179 acres	368	334	301	49.9	45.3	40.7	21.2	17.1	15.4	15.6	4.3	5.2
180 to 259 acres	211	192	172	45.7	41.5	37.2	21.7	17.2	15.5	8.9	3.9	5.2
260 to 499 acres	315	286	255	113.0	103.0	91.7	60.5	47.3	43.6	13.3	9.7	14.7
500 to 999 acres	204	200	186	140.5	138.5	129.3	77.6	67.4	68.6	9.7	13.7	23.2
1,000 to 1,999 acres . .	97	102	102	132.4	138.8	139.0	64.5	61.1	69.3	5.3	14.7	23.4
2,000 acres and over . .	65	67	71	467.5	463.2	476.3	66.6	60.2	72.5	3.7	50.4	24.5

No. 1097. Farms—Number and Acreage, by Tenure of Operator: 1978 to 1992

[*Full owners* own all the land they operate. *Part owners* own a part and rent from others the rest of the land they operate. See also *Historical Statistics, Colonial Times to 1970*, series K 109-113 and 142-146]

ITEM AND YEAR	Unit	Total	Full owner	Part owner	Tenant	PERCENT DISTRIBUTION			
						Total	Full owner	Part owner	Tenant
NUMBER OF FARMS									
1978	1,000	2,258	1,298	681	279	100.0	57.5	30.1	12.4
1982	1,000	2,241	1,326	656	259	100.0	59.2	29.3	11.5
1987	1,000	2,088	1,239	609	240	100.0	59.3	29.2	11.5
1992	1,000	1,925	1,112	597	217	100.0	57.7	31.0	11.3
Under 50 acres	1,000	554	444	58	52	100.0	80.1	10.5	9.4
50 to 179 acres	1,000	584	395	130	59	100.0	67.6	22.3	10.1
180 to 499 acres	1,000	428	190	183	55	100.0	44.4	42.8	12.8
500 to 999 acres	1,000	186	48	111	27	100.0	25.8	59.7	14.5
1,000 acres or more	1,000	173	35	114	24	100.0	20.2	65.9	13.9
LAND IN FARMS									
1978	Mil. acres .	1,015	332	561	122	100.0	32.7	55.3	12.0
1982	Mil. acres .	987	342	531	114	100.0	34.7	53.8	11.6
1987	Mil. acres .	964	318	520	127	100.0	32.9	53.9	13.2
1992	Mil. acres .	946	296	527	123	100.0	31.3	55.7	13.0

No. 1098. Farm Operators—Tenure and Characteristics: 1987 and 1992

[In thousands, except as indicated. See also *Historical Statistics, Colonial Times to 1970*, series K 82-113]

CHARACTERISTIC	ALL FARMS		FARMS WITH SALES OF $10,000 AND OVER		CHARACTERISTIC	ALL FARMS		FARMS WITH SALES OF $10,000 AND OVER	
	1987	1992	1987	1992		1987	1992	1987	1992
Total operators	**2,088**	**1,925**	**1,060**	**1,019**	Tenant	240	217	161	148
White	2,043	1,882	1,046	1,003					
Black	23	19	4	5	Principal occupation:				
American Indian, Eskimo, and					Farming	1,138	1,053	811	754
Aleut	7	8	2	3	Other	950	872	248	265
Asian or Pacific Islander	8	8	5	5	Place of residence: [2]				
Other	7	8	2	3	On farm operated	1,488	1,379	776	736
Operators of Hispanic origin [1] .	17	21	6	8	Not on farm operated	443	409	215	215
Female	132	145	42	50	Years on present farm: [2]				
					2 years or less	114	95	49	41
Under 25 years old	36	28	21	17	3 to 4 years	135	133	56	58
25 to 34 years old	243	179	147	112	5 to 9 years	304	259	138	121
35 to 44 years old	411	382	212	217	10 years or more	1,163	1,113	653	648
45 to 54 years old	455	429	228	223					
55 to 64 years old	496	430	263	229	Days worked off farm: [2]				
65 years old and over	447	478	188	220	None	844	802	561	536
Average age (years)	52.0	53.3	50.6	51.9	Less than 100 days	200	165	124	104
					100 to 199 days	178	162	80	76
Full owner	1,239	1,112	445	422	200 days or more	737	666	219	226
Part owner	609	597	454	448					

[1] Operators of Hispanic origin may be of any race.   [2] Excludes not reported.

Source of tables 1096-1098: U.S. Bureau of the Census, *Census of Agriculture: 1987*, vol. 1; and *1992*, vol. 1.

No. 1099. Farms—Number, Acreage, and Value, by Type of Organization: 1987 and 1992

ITEM	Unit	Total [1]	Individual or family	Partner-ship	Corpo-ration	PERCENT DISTRIBUTION			
						Total [1]	Individual or family	Partner-ship	Corpo-ration
ALL FARMS									
Number of farms: 1987	1,000	2,088	1,809	200	67	100.0	86.7	9.6	3.2
1992	1,000	1,925	1,653	187	73	100.0	85.9	9.7	3.8
Land in farms: 1987	Mil. acres.	964	628	153	119	100.0	65.1	15.9	12.4
1992	Mil. acres.	946	604	153	123	100.0	63.9	16.2	13.0
Value of land and buildings: [2] 1987	Bil. dol.	604	424	95	69	100.0	70.1	15.7	11.4
1992	Bil. dol.	687	474	109	85	100.0	69.0	15.8	12.4
Value of farm products sold: 1987	Bil. dol.	136	77	23	35	100.0	56.3	17.1	25.6
1992	Bil. dol.	163	88	29	44	100.0	54.1	18.0	27.2
FARMS WITH SALES OF $10,000 AND OVER									
Number of farms: 1987	1,000	1,060	861	136	56	100.0	81.3	12.8	5.3
1992	1,000	1,019	820	131	61	100.0	80.5	12.8	6.0
Land in farms: 1987	Mil. acres.	829	525	143	116	100.0	63.3	17.3	14.0
1992	Mil. acres.	822	512	143	119	100.0	62.2	17.4	14.4

[1] Includes other types, not shown separately.   [2] Based on a sample of farms.

No. 1100. Corporate Farms—Characteristics, by Type: 1992

ITEM	Unit	All corpora-tions	FAMILY HELD CORPORATIONS			OTHER CORPORATIONS		
			Total	1-10 stock-holders	11 or more stock-holders	Total	1-10 stock-holders	11 or more stock-holders
Farms	Number	72,567	64,528	62,755	1,773	8,039	6,914	1,125
Percent distribution	Percent	100.0	88.9	86.5	2.4	11.1	9.5	1.6
Land in farms	Mil. acres.	122.8	110.8	100.9	9.9	11.9	8.0	4.0
Average per farm	Acres	1,692	1,718	1,608	5,597	1,484	1,152	3,524
Value of—								
Land and buildings [1]	Bil. dol.	85.1	72.5	66.5	6.0	12.5	8.1	4.4
Average per farm	$1,000	1,172	1,131	1,068	3,385	1,484	1,105	3,950
Farm products sold	Bil. dol.	44.2	34.4	29.7	4.7	9.8	6.5	3.3
Average per farm	$1,000	609	533	474	2,626	1,218	941	2,915

[1] Based on a sample of farms.

No. 1101. Farms—Number, Acreage, and Value of Sales, by Size of Sales: 1992

VALUE OF PRODUCTS SOLD	Farms (1,000)	ACREAGE		VALUE OF SALES		PERCENT DISTRIBUTION		
		Total (mil.)	Average per farm	Total (mil. dol.)	Average per farm (dol.)	Farms	Acreage	Value of sales
Total	1,925	945.5	491	162,608	84,459	100.0	100.0	100.0
Less than $10,000	907	123.5	136	3,043	3,357	47.1	13.1	1.9
Less than $2,500	423	55.7	132	411	972	22.0	5.9	0.3
$2,500-$4,999	232	26.9	116	836	3,605	12.1	2.8	0.5
$5,000-$9,999	252	40.9	162	1,797	7,132	13.1	4.3	1.1
$10,000 or more	1,019	822.0	807	159,565	156,623	52.9	86.9	98.1
$10,000-$24,999	302	81.8	271	4,841	16,039	15.7	8.7	3.0
$25,000-$49,999	195	91.4	477	6,967	35,662	10.1	9.7	4.3
$50,000-$99,999	188	133.9	713	13,517	71,990	9.8	14.2	8.3
$100,000-$249,999	208	228.0	1,094	32,711	156,958	10.8	24.1	20.1
$250,000-$499,999	79	130.9	1,666	26,914	342,653	4.1	13.8	16.6
$500,000-$999,999	31	80.6	2,598	20,953	675,368	1.6	8.5	12.9
$1,000,000 or more	16	75.5	4,751	53,663	3,377,175	0.8	8.0	33.0

Source of tables 1099-1101: U.S. Bureau of the Census, *1992 Census of Agriculture*, vol. 1.

No. 1102. Farms—Number, Acreage, and Value, by State: 1987 and 1992

[See also *Historical Statistics, Colonial Times to 1970*, series K 17-18]

REGION, DIVISION, AND STATE	ALL FARMS								FARMS WITH SALES OF $10,000 OR MORE, 1992			
	Number of farms (1,000)		Land in farms (mil. acres)		Average size of farm (acres)		Total value [1] (mil. dol.)		Number of farms (1,000)	Land in farms (mil. acres)	Average size of farm (acres)	Total value [1] (mil. dol.)
	1987	1992	1987	1992	1987	1992	1987	1992				
U.S.	2,088	1,925	964.5	945.5	462	491	604,168	687,432	1,019	822.0	807	555,056
Northeast ...	123	109	21.4	19.4	174	177	32,045	38,305	56	14.7	261	27,504
N.E.	25	23	4.2	3.9	169	168	7,866	8,834	10	2.7	257	5,449
ME	6	6	1.3	1.3	214	218	1,321	1,396	3	0.9	340	842
NH	2	2	0.4	0.4	169	158	900	836	1	0.2	257	418
VT	6	5	1.4	1.3	240	235	1,521	1,730	3	1.0	328	1,219
MA	6	5	0.6	0.5	99	100	2,154	2,421	2	0.3	145	1,478
RI	1	1	0.1	0.1	84	76	295	313	(Z)	(Z)	118	194
CT	4	3	0.4	0.4	111	105	1,674	2,138	1	0.2	173	1,299
M.A	98	86	17.2	15.5	175	180	24,179	29,472	46	12.0	261	22,055
NY	38	32	8.4	7.5	223	231	8,263	9,130	18	6.0	332	7,012
NJ	9	9	0.9	0.8	99	93	3,579	5,590	4	0.6	179	3,734
PA	51	45	7.9	7.2	153	160	12,337	14,752	24	5.4	221	11,309
Midwest	862	777	350.5	343.6	407	442	228,073	263,320	514	310.8	605	235,102
E.N.C	365	326	86.6	82.7	237	254	96,291	110,003	200	73.7	368	96,755
OH	79	71	15.0	14.2	189	201	18,023	20,626	38	11.9	314	16,799
IN	70	63	16.2	15.6	229	249	18,716	21,732	37	14.1	384	19,151
IL	89	78	28.5	27.3	321	351	35,779	41,844	56	26.0	464	39,607
MI	51	47	10.3	10.1	202	217	10,034	11,517	24	8.3	352	8,999
WI	75	68	16.6	15.5	221	228	13,740	14,285	46	13.4	290	12,199
W.N.C	497	451	263.8	260.9	531	578	131,782	153,317	313	237.2	757	138,347
MN	85	75	26.6	25.7	312	342	18,616	23,319	53	23.2	438	21,005
IA	105	97	31.6	31.3	301	325	29,830	38,063	77	29.9	388	36,345
MO	106	98	29.2	28.5	275	291	18,634	22,070	47	22.5	477	16,771
ND	35	31	40.3	39.4	1,143	1,267	12,934	13,163	25	36.8	1,449	12,194
SD	36	34	44.2	44.8	1,214	1,316	11,871	12,264	27	39.0	1,452	10,955
NE	60	53	45.3	44.7	749	839	20,828	22,713	42	42.6	1,007	21,640
KS	69	63	46.6	46.7	680	738	19,068	21,725	41	43.2	1,041	19,438
South.	824	775	281.2	277.0	341	357	207,777	222,294	315	222.2	706	158,473
S.A.	240	223	51.2	48.6	214	218	64,886	76,544	93	36.5	393	54,951
DE	3	3	0.6	0.6	205	224	1,096	1,351	2	0.5	309	1,184
MD	15	13	2.4	2.2	162	171	5,419	6,570	7	1.8	282	4,862
VA	45	42	8.7	8.3	194	197	10,409	13,534	17	6.0	355	9,100
WV	17	17	3.4	3.3	196	192	2,255	2,810	4	1.5	394	1,229
NC	59	52	9.4	8.9	159	172	11,845	13,950	25	7.0	281	10,118
SC	20	20	4.8	4.5	232	221	4,127	5,093	7	3.0	452	2,986
GA	44	41	10.7	10.0	247	246	9,852	11,437	17	7.5	431	7,547
FL	37	35	11.2	10.8	306	306	19,884	21,801	15	9.2	614	17,924
E.S.C	250	235	45.6	43.5	183	185	38,811	45,055	90	30.4	337	29,328
KY	92	90	14.0	13.7	152	151	12,545	14,775	41	10.0	248	10,603
TN	80	75	11.7	11.2	147	149	11,648	13,977	24	7.3	298	8,007
AL.	43	38	9.1	8.5	211	223	7,284	8,350	14	5.7	410	5,152
MS	34	32	10.7	10.2	315	318	7,333	7,952	12	7.5	640	5,566
W.S.C	335	317	184.4	185.0	551	583	104,079	100,695	131	155.2	1,181	74,195
AR	48	44	14.4	14.1	298	322	10,884	12,407	21	11.3	536	9,668
LA	27	26	8.0	7.8	293	306	7,348	7,474	11	6.4	604	5,645
OK	70	67	31.5	32.1	449	480	15,102	15,754	30	26.3	889	11,851
TX.	189	181	130.5	130.9	691	725	70,746	65,060	70	111.2	1,586	47,031
West	278	264	311.3	305.6	1,118	1,158	136,274	163,513	134	274.3	2,046	133,977
Mountain. .	124	118	244.1	240.7	1,965	2,035	62,906	69,720	65	217.3	3,362	58,517
MT	25	23	60.2	59.6	2,451	2,613	12,418	13,578	15	53.6	3,612	11,658
ID	24	22	13.9	13.5	577	609	8,126	9,077	13	11.6	909	7,829
WY	9	9	33.6	32.9	3,650	3,772	4,909	5,242	6	29.7	5,376	4,516
CO	27	27	34.0	34.0	1,248	1,252	12,519	14,568	15	30.7	2,029	11,932
NM	14	14	46.0	46.8	3,230	3,281	8,291	9,220	6	42.4	7,273	7,298
AZ.	8	7	36.3	35.0	4,732	5,173	10,111	10,984	3	32.7	10,260	9,837
UT	14	14	10.0	9.6	710	712	4,259	4,704	6	8.2	1,372	3,546
NV	3	3	10.0	9.3	3,300	3,205	2,272	2,347	1	8.3	6,081	1,902
Pacific ...	154	146	67.3	64.8	466	445	73,367	93,793	69	57.0	821	75,461
WA	34	30	16.1	15.7	480	520	11,948	14,178	15	13.5	915	11,060
OR	32	32	17.8	17.6	556	552	9,597	11,824	12	15.6	1,289	8,534
CA	83	78	30.6	29.0	368	373	48,567	63,689	40	25.8	639	52,685
AK	1	1	1.0	0.9	1,789	1,803	317	249	(Z)	0.6	3,788	138
HI	5	5	1.7	1.6	353	298	2,938	3,854	2	1.5	729	3,044

Z Less than 500 farms or 50,000 acres. [1] Value of land and buildings. Based on reports for a sample of farms.

Source: U.S. Bureau of the Census, *1992 Census of Agriculture,* vol. 1.

No. 1103. Irrigated Farms and Acreage, by State: 1987 and 1992

[See also *Historical Statistics, Colonial Times to 1970*, series J 85-91]

STATE	IRRIGATED FARMS				LAND IN IRRIGATED FARMS				IRRIGATED LAND			
	Number (1,000)		Percent of all farms		Acreage (1,000)		Percent of all land in farms		Acreage (1,000)		Percent of all land in farms	
	1987	1992	1987	1992	1987	1992	1987	1992	1987	1992	1987	1992
U.S. [1]	291.6	279.4	13.9	14.5	241,069	231,853	24.9	24.5	46,386	49,404	4.8	5.2
California	58.9	56.5	70.7	72.8	17,567	16,444	57.4	54.9	7,596	7,571	24.8	26.1
Colorado.	14.9	15.2	54.6	56.0	16,729	16,648	49.1	49.0	3,014	3,170	8.9	9.3
Florida	12.0	13.5	32.7	38.3	4,670	4,937	41.7	45.9	1,623	1,783	14.5	16.6
Idaho.	16.6	15.5	68.8	70.0	9,053	8,579	64.9	63.7	3,219	3,260	23.1	24.2
Kansas.	7.4	6.5	10.7	10.3	10,654	10,519	22.8	22.5	2,463	2,680	5.3	5.7
Montana	9.5	8.9	38.7	38.9	23,259	22,024	38.6	36.9	1,997	1,978	3.3	3.3
Nebraska	22.6	19.3	37.3	36.5	22,499	22,027	49.6	49.6	5,682	6,312	12.5	14.2
Oregon.	14.4	15.0	45.0	47.0	11,340	10,419	63.6	59.2	1,648	1,622	9.3	9.2
Texas.	19.8	18.8	10.4	10.4	20,270	19,353	15.5	14.8	4,271	4,912	3.3	3.8
Washington. . . .	15.4	14.1	45.9	46.5	5,468	5,101	33.9	32.4	1,519	1,641	9.4	10.4
Wyoming	5.2	5.1	56.7	58.2	18,207	17,955	54.1	54.6	1,518	1,465	4.5	4.5

[1] Includes other States not shown separately.
Source: U.S. Bureau of the Census, *1992 Census of Agriculture*, vol. 1.

No. 1104. Farms—Number and Acreage: 1980 to 1994

[As of **June 1**. Based on 1974 census definition; for definition of farms and farmland, see text, section 23. Data for census years (indicated by italics) have been adjusted for underenumeration and are used as reference points along with data from acreage and livestock surveys in estimating data for other years. Minus sign (-) indicates decrease. See also *Historical Statistics, Colonial Times to 1970*, series K 4-7]

YEAR	FARMS		LAND IN FARMS		YEAR	FARMS		LAND IN FARMS	
	Number (1,000)	Annual change [1] (1,000)	Total (mil. acres)	Average per farm (acres)		Number (1,000)	Annual change [1] (1,000)	Total (mil. acres)	Average per farm (acres)
1980	2,440	3	1,039	426	1990	2,140	-31	987	461
1985	2,293	-41	1,012	441	1991	2,105	-35	983	467
1986	2,250	-43	1,005	447	1992	2,094	-11	980	468
1987	*2,213*	*-37*	*999*	*451*	1993	2,064	-30	978	474
1988	2,197	-16	995	453	1994	2,040	-24	975	478
1989	2,171	-26	991	457					

[1] Annual change from preceding year shown.

No. 1105. Farms—Number and Acreage, by State: 1990 and 1994

[See headnote, table 1104]

STATE	FARMS (1,000)		ACREAGE (mil.)		ACREAGE PER FARM		STATE	FARMS (1,000)		ACREAGE (mil.)		ACREAGE PER FARM	
	1990	1994	1990	1994	1990	1994		1990	1994	1990	1994	1990	1994
U.S.	2,140	2,040	987	975	461	478	Missouri	108	104	30	30	281	288
							Montana	25	23	61	60	2,449	2,584
Alabama	47	46	10	10	215	217	Nebraska	57	55	47	47	826	856
Alaska	1	1	1	1	1,724	1,788	Nevada.	3	2	9	9	3,560	3,708
Arizona.	8	8	36	36	4,615	4,557	New Hampshire	3	3	(Z)	(Z)	169	180
Arkansas.	47	44	16	15	330	350	New Jersey . . .	8	9	1	1	107	101
California.	85	76	31	30	362	388	New Mexico. . .	14	14	45	44	3,296	3,274
Colorado.	27	25	33	33	1,249	1,292	New York	39	37	8	8	218	216
Connecticut . . .	4	4	(Z)	(Z)	108	108	North Carolina .	62	58	10	9	156	160
Delaware	3	3	1	1	197	220	North Dakota . .	34	32	41	40	1,191	1,263
Florida	41	39	11	10	266	264	Ohio.	84	75	16	15	187	203
Georgia	48	43	13	12	260	281	Oklahoma	70	70	33	34	471	486
Hawaii	5	4	2	2	372	389	Oregon	37	38	18	18	488	467
Idaho	22	21	14	14	628	659	Pennsylvania . .	53	51	8	8	153	153
Illinois.	83	77	29	28	343	368	Rhode Island . .	1	1	(Z)	(Z)	95	87
Indiana	68	63	16	16	240	254	South Carolina .	25	24	5	5	208	213
Iowa.	104	100	34	33	322	332	South Dakota . .	35	34	44	44	1,266	1,300
Kansas.	69	65	48	48	694	735	Tennessee. . . .	89	84	12	12	139	146
Kentucky	93	89	14	14	152	158	Texas.	186	185	132	129	710	699
Louisiana	32	28	9	8	278	300	Utah.	13	13	11	11	856	854
Maine.	7	7	1	1	201	201	Vermont	7	6	2	1	216	230
Maryland	15	15	2	2	148	152	Virginia	46	43	9	9	193	200
Massachusetts .	7	6	1	1	99	102	Washington. . . .	37	36	16	16	432	445
Michigan	54	52	11	11	200	206	West Virginia . .	21	20	4	4	180	185
Minnesota	89	85	30	30	337	349	Wisconsin	80	78	18	17	220	217
Mississippi	40	39	13	13	325	326	Wyoming.	9	9	35	35	3,910	3,772

Z Less than 500,000 acres.
Source of tables 1104 and 1105: U.S. Dept. of Agriculture, National Agricultural Statistics Service, *Farm Numbers, 1975-80; Farms and Land in Farms, Final Estimates by States, 1979-1987; Crop Production* (August 1988-89); and *Farm Numbers and Land In Farms*, July releases.

No. 1106. Farm Real Estate—Summary: 1980 to 1994

[1980 and 1986-89, value data as of Feb. 1; 1985, as of April 1; 1990-94, as of January 1. Excludes Alaska and Hawaii. Total value of land and buildings is estimated by multiplying the number of acres of farmland by the average value per acre of land and buildings. Per acre values are based on data from the census of agriculture. For intercensal years, estimates are based on surveys conducted by the U.S. Dept. of Agriculture]

ITEM	Unit	1980	1985	1986	1987	1988	1989	1990	1991	1992	1993	1994
Total value	Bil. dol	763.3	719.4	641.1	597.1	626.9	653.5	658.2	667.7	668.0	682.0	725.7
Average value per acre.	Dollars.	737	713	640	599	632	661	668	681	684	700	744
Average value, operating unit. . .	$1,000.	313.5	314.5	285.6	270.5	286.0	301.8	308.2	318.0	319.6	330.6	351.7

No. 1107. Farm Real Estate—Value of Land and Buildings, by State: 1990 to 1994

[See headnote, table 1106. See also *Historical Statistics, Colonial Times to 1970*, series K 16]

STATE	VALUE OF LAND AND BUILDINGS (mil. dol.)			AVERAGE VALUE OF LAND AND BUILDINGS, PER ACRE			STATE	VALUE OF LAND AND BUILDINGS (mil. dol.)			AVERAGE VALUE OF LAND AND BUILDINGS, PER ACRE		
	1990	1993	1994	1990	1993	1994		1990	1993	1994	1990	1993	1994
U.S..	658,187	682,039	725,711	$668	$700	$744	MT	14,399	16,189	18,115	238	270	302
							NE	25,905	27,326	29,894	550	580	635
AL	8,474	8,628	9,637	839	863	964	NV	1,727	1,917	2,036	194	215	229
AZ	9,468	10,966	11,295	263	305	314	NH	1,096	1,024	1,116	2,237	2,178	2,374
AR	11,625	11,693	12,312	750	759	800	NJ	4,032	3,946	4,210	4,634	4,536	4,840
CA	52,483	51,153	51,153	1,704	1,722	1,722	NM	8,722	9,925	10,630	196	225	240
CO	11,850	12,548	14,104	358	383	430	NY	8,182	9,178	10,261	974	1,119	1,251
CT	1,855	1,763	1,921	4,417	4,299	4,686	NC	12,251	12,394	12,679	1,263	1,319	1,349
DE	1,288	1,299	1,452	2,259	2,362	2,641	ND	13,770	15,679	16,541	340	388	409
FL	22,727	21,364	22,709	2,085	2,074	2,205	OH	18,903	19,257	21,067	1,204	1,267	1,386
GA	12,650	11,660	11,893	1,012	964	983	OK	16,401	17,411	18,143	497	512	534
ID. . . .	9,056	9,328	10,587	661	691	784	OR	10,164	11,496	12,956	571	657	740
IL	39,587	42,545	46,544	1,389	1,503	1,645	PA	14,637	13,805	15,088	1,807	1,747	1,910
IN. . . .	20,277	21,864	23,569	1,244	1,366	1,473	RI. . . .	352	308	336	5,028	4,894	5,334
IA. . . .	36,917	41,474	43,838	1,102	1,245	1,316	SC	4,727	4,487	4,751	909	871	923
KS	22,130	23,616	25,647	462	494	537	SD	14,543	16,339	17,139	328	370	388
KY	13,832	15,286	16,127	981	1,084	1,144	TN	12,350	13,013	13,066	996	1,049	1,054
LA	8,144	8,130	8,366	915	945	973	TX	65,340	61,266	64,146	495	471	493
ME. . . .	1,478	1,408	1,535	1,019	992	1,081	UT	4,396	5,201	5,685	389	464	508
MD. . . .	5,445	5,545	6,305	2,420	2,521	2,866	VT	1,797	1,748	1,906	1,190	1,158	1,262
MA. . . .	2,559	2,380	2,595	3,763	3,662	3,992	VA	13,492	11,139	11,506	1,516	1,295	1,338
MI	10,854	12,087	12,969	1,005	1,130	1,212	WA	12,464	12,507	14,370	779	782	898
MN. . . .	24,150	26,616	26,722	805	896	900	WV	2,268	2,576	2,638	613	696	713
MS. . . .	9,464	9,838	10,585	728	757	814	WI	14,133	15,929	16,678	803	932	975
MO. . . .	20,642	21,591	23,016	679	715	762	WY. . . .	5,185	5,200	5,871	149	149	169

Source of tables 1106 and 1107: U.S. Dept. of Agriculture, Economic Research Service, *Agricultural Resources, Agricultural Land Values and Markets, Situation and Outlook Report*, annual.

No. 1108. Balance Sheet of the Farming Sector: 1980 to 1993

[In billions of dollars, except as indicated. As of December 31. See *Historical Statistics, Colonial Times to 1970*, series K 204-219, for data before revisions]

ITEM	1980	1984	1985	1986	1987	1988	1989	1990	1991	1992	1993
CURRENT DOLLARS											
Assets	983.2	857.0	772.7	724.4	772.6	801.1	829.7	848.3	842.4	860.8	888.0
Real estate.	782.8	661.8	586.2	542.3	578.9	595.5	615.7	628.2	623.2	633.1	656.3
Nonreal estate.	173.7	162.7	153.3	147.6	158.6	170.2	177.2	181.8	178.6	184.7	185.5
Livestock and poultry	60.6	49.5	46.3	47.8	58.0	62.2	66.2	70.9	68.1	71.0	72.8
Machinery, motor vehicles . . .	80.3	85.0	82.9	81.5	80.0	81.2	85.1	85.4	85.8	85.6	85.2
Crops stored	32.7	26.1	22.9	16.3	17.5	23.3	23.4	22.8	22.0	24.1	23.4
Purchased inputs	(NA)	2.0	1.2	2.1	3.2	3.5	2.6	2.8	2.7	3.9	4.2
Financial assets.	26.7	32.6	33.3	34.5	35.1	35.4	36.8	38.3	40.6	43.1	46.1
Investment in cooperatives. . .	19.3	24.3	24.3	24.4	25.3	25.1	26.3	27.5	28.7	29.4	30.8
Other financial assets	7.4	8.3	9.0	10.0	9.9	10.3	10.5	10.9	11.8	13.6	15.3
Claims	983.2	857.0	772.7	724.4	772.6	801.1	829.7	848.3	842.4	860.8	888.0
Debt	166.8	193.8	177.6	157.0	144.4	139.4	137.2	137.4	138.8	138.6	141.9
Real estate debt.	89.7	106.7	100.1	90.4	82.4	77.6	75.4	74.1	74.5	75.0	76.0
Nonreal estate debt	77.1	87.1	77.5	66.6	62.0	61.7	61.9	63.2	64.3	63.6	65.9
Equity	816.4	663.3	595.1	567.5	628.2	661.7	692.4	710.9	703.6	722.2	746.1
Farm debt/asset ratio (percent).	**17.0**	**22.6**	**23.0**	**21.7**	**18.7**	**17.4**	**16.5**	**16.2**	**16.5**	**16.1**	**16.0**
CONSTANT (1987) DOLLARS [1]											
Assets	1,371.2	941.8	818.6	747.6	772.6	771.0	764.7	748.7	716.3	712.0	719.0
Debt	232.7	213.0	188.1	162.0	144.4	134.1	126.5	121.2	118.0	114.7	114.9
Equity	1,138.6	728.9	630.4	585.6	628.2	636.9	638.2	627.5	598.3	597.3	604.1

NA Not available. [1] Constant dollar figures are based on gross domestic product implicit price deflators for year.

Source: U.S. Dept. of Agriculture, Economic Research Service, *Economic Indicators of the Farm Sector: National Financial Summary, 1993.*

Agriculture

No. 1109. Gross Farm Product—Summary: 1980 to 1993

[**In billions of dollars**. For definition of gross product, see text, section 14. Minus sign (-) indicates decrease]

ITEM	1980	1984	1985	1986	1987	1988	1989	1990	1991	1992	1993
CURRENT DOLLARS											
Farm output, total [1]	142.9	160.0	152.7	144.0	152.1	158.2	178.7	186.4	181.7	188.6	184.5
Cash receipts from farm marketings	140.3	144.6	136.3	135.2	147.7	159.3	166.5	172.6	171.4	172.5	178.4
Farm housing	5.1	5.1	5.0	4.9	4.9	4.9	5.0	5.2	5.3	5.4	5.6
Other farm income	2.4	3.5	4.6	4.4	5.1	4.6	5.0	4.9	5.0	4.5	4.8
Change in farm inventories	-6.1	5.7	5.8	-1.5	-6.4	-11.3	1.5	3.1	-0.6	5.7	-4.7
Less: Intermediate goods and services purchased [2]	86.8	91.4	85.6	81.1	86.1	90.6	97.6	101.3	103.0	103.1	109.2
Equals: **Gross farm product**	56.1	68.5	67.1	62.9	66.0	67.6	81.1	85.1	78.6	85.6	75.3
Less: Consumption of fixed capital	19.4	23.2	22.9	22.5	22.0	21.6	21.9	21.6	21.5	21.9	21.5
Indirect business tax [3]	3.0	3.1	3.3	3.3	3.6	3.6	3.8	4.2	4.2	4.4	4.4
Plus: Subsidies to operators	1.0	7.0	6.3	9.5	13.9	11.8	9.3	8.1	7.4	8.2	11.8
Equals: **Farm national income**	34.7	49.2	47.2	46.6	54.3	54.2	64.7	67.4	60.3	67.5	61.2
CONSTANT (1987) DOLLARS											
Farm output, total [1]	137.1	139.0	146.0	146.4	152.1	146.5	151.1	158.7	158.9	169.9	163.5
Cash receipts from farm marketings	130.7	127.8	133.1	137.9	147.7	143.9	141.9	146.8	149.2	156.4	157.7
Farm housing	6.3	5.4	5.3	5.1	4.9	4.7	4.6	4.5	4.5	4.4	4.2
Other farm income	2.3	3.1	4.3	4.6	5.1	4.1	4.2	4.4	4.4	4.1	4.4
Change in farm inventories	-3.4	1.7	2.4	-2.1	-6.4	-7.0	-0.1	2.5	0.2	4.5	-3.2
Less: Intermediate goods and services purchased [2]	86.1	83.9	81.8	82.2	86.1	83.3	84.9	87.1	88.2	89.1	92.5
Equals: **Gross farm product**	51.0	55.1	64.2	64.3	66.0	63.2	66.2	71.6	70.7	80.8	71.0
Less: Consumption of fixed capital	26.7	25.1	24.3	23.1	22.0	21.1	20.5	19.5	18.9	18.8	17.9
Indirect business tax [3]	2.8	3.0	3.5	3.5	3.6	3.5	3.6	3.9	3.9	4.4	3.9
Plus: Subsidies to operators	11.9	10.7	11.4	12.3	13.9	12.9	12.7	13.5	13.6	14.7	14.8
Equals: **Farm national income**	33.4	37.7	47.8	49.9	54.3	51.6	54.8	61.6	61.6	72.3	64.0

[1] Includes farm products consumed in farm households where raised, not shown separately. [2] Includes rent paid to nonoperator landlords. [3] Includes nontax liability.

Source: U.S. Bureau of Economic Analysis, *Survey of Current Business*, July 1992, August 1993, and July 1994; and *National Income and Product Accounts of the United States: Volume 2, 1959-88*.

No. 1110. Farm Income and Expenses: 1980 to 1993

[**In billions of dollars**. See also *Historical Statistics, Colonial Times to 1970*, series K 192, K 259-260, K 264-285, and K 326]

ITEM	1980	1983	1984	1985	1986	1987	1988	1989	1990	1991	1992	1993
Gross farm income	149.3	153.9	168.0	161.2	156.1	168.5	175.8	192.8	198.2	192.3	200.2	201.4
Cash income	143.3	151.1	156.1	157.9	152.9	165.2	172.9	179.8	186.8	184.9	188.2	197.2
Farm marketings	139.7	136.8	142.8	144.1	135.4	141.8	151.2	161.1	170.0	168.8	171.2	175.1
Crops	71.7	67.2	69.9	74.3	63.8	65.9	71.7	77.0	80.1	82.1	84.9	84.5
Livestock and products	68.0	69.6	72.9	69.8	71.6	76.0	79.4	84.1	89.8	86.7	86.4	90.6
Government payments	1.3	9.3	8.4	7.7	11.8	16.7	14.5	10.9	9.3	8.2	9.2	13.4
Other farm income [1]	2.3	5.1	4.9	6.0	5.7	6.6	7.3	7.8	7.6	7.8	7.8	8.8
Value of home consumption	1.2	1.0	1.0	0.9	0.9	0.7	0.7	0.7	0.7	0.6	0.6	0.5
Rental value of dwellings [2]	11.0	12.6	4.9	4.7	4.6	4.9	5.6	7.5	7.3	7.1	7.2	7.3
Value of inventory adjustment [3]	-6.3	-10.9	6.0	-2.3	-2.2	-2.3	-3.4	4.8	3.4	-0.3	4.3	-3.6
Expenses of farm production	133.1	139.6	141.9	132.4	125.1	128.8	137.8	144.9	151.3	151.2	150.1	158.0
Intermediate products	76.1	75.8	78.0	72.3	70.6	74.8	82.4	86.9	90.8	92.4	91.3	98.0
Farm origin	34.9	32.1	32.3	29.3	30.4	32.6	37.1	38.3	39.7	38.7	38.9	41.5
Feed purchased	21.0	20.6	19.4	16.9	17.5	17.5	20.2	20.7	20.4	19.3	20.1	21.4
Livestock, poultry purchased	10.7	8.8	9.5	9.2	9.8	11.8	12.8	13.1	14.8	14.3	13.9	14.9
Seed purchased [4]	3.2	2.7	3.4	3.1	3.2	3.3	4.1	4.4	4.5	5.1	4.9	5.2
Manufactured inputs	22.4	20.1	22.4	20.2	18.2	18.1	19.0	20.6	22.0	23.2	22.7	23.2
Fertilizer and lime	9.5	7.1	8.4	7.5	6.8	6.5	7.7	8.2	8.2	8.7	8.3	8.4
Pesticides	3.5	3.9	4.7	4.3	4.3	4.5	4.1	5.0	5.4	6.3	6.5	6.7
Fuel and oil	7.9	7.2	7.3	6.4	5.3	5.0	4.8	4.8	5.8	5.6	5.3	5.4
Electricity	1.5	2.0	2.1	1.9	1.8	2.2	2.4	2.6	2.6	2.6	2.6	2.7
Repairs and maintenance [5]	7.1	6.5	6.4	6.4	6.4	6.8	7.7	8.4	8.6	8.6	8.5	9.2
Other [6]	11.8	17.1	16.9	16.5	15.5	17.4	18.6	19.6	20.5	21.8	21.2	24.1
Interest	16.3	21.4	21.1	18.6	16.5	15.0	14.3	13.9	13.4	12.1	11.2	10.8
Real estate	7.5	10.8	10.7	9.9	9.1	8.2	7.6	7.2	6.7	6.0	5.8	5.5
Nonreal estate	8.7	10.6	10.4	8.7	7.4	6.8	6.7	6.7	6.7	6.1	5.4	5.3
Contract, hired labor expenses [7]	9.3	8.9	9.4	10.0	9.5	10.0	10.9	12.0	14.1	14.0	14.0	15.0
Net rent to nonoperator landlords [8]	6.1	5.2	8.2	7.7	6.1	7.1	7.6	8.7	9.0	8.9	9.5	9.6
Capital consumption [9]	21.5	23.8	20.8	19.3	17.8	17.1	17.6	18.2	18.3	18.2	18.3	18.4
Property taxes	3.9	4.5	4.3	4.5	4.6	4.9	5.0	5.2	5.7	5.6	5.8	6.3
Net farm income	16.1	14.2	26.1	28.8	31.1	39.7	38.0	47.9	46.9	41.1	50.1	43.4

[1] Includes forest product sales. [2] Data for 1980 and 1983 are not comparable with later data. [3] Minus sign (-) indicates decrease in inventories. [4] Includes bulbs, plants, and trees. [5] Expenditures for repairs and maintenance of farm buildings, motor vehicles, and machinery. [6] Includes machine hire and customwork expenses; marketing, storage, and transportation expenses and miscellaneous expenses. [7] Includes Social Security payments and perquisites. [8] Data for years 1980 and 1983 are based on different sources from those for 1984 and later, creating potential inconsistencies in estimates among these periods. Includes landlord capital consumption. [9] Depreciation and accidental damage.

Source: U.S. Dept. of Agriculture, Economic Research Service, *Economic Indicators of the Farm Sector: National Financial Summary*, annual.

No. 1111. Farm Income—Cash Receipts From Farm Marketings: 1990 to 1993

[**In millions of dollars.** Represents gross receipts from commercial market sales as well as net Commodity Credit Corporation loans. See also *Historical Statistics, Colonial Times to 1970*, series K 286-302]

COMMODITY	1990	1991	1992	1993	COMMODITY	1990	1991	1992	1993
Total	**169,974**	**168,795**	**171,202**	**175,052**	Fruits, tree nuts [2] . . .	9,420	9,909	10,123	9,927
					Apples	1,086	1,651	1,661	1,364
All crops [1]	80,131	82,060	84,853	84,497	Avocados	245	204	180	133
Barley	823	813	847	724	Cherries	156	229	233	221
Corn	13,340	14,405	14,458	14,012	Grapefruit	355	425	373	256
Cotton lint, seed	5,489	5,236	5,192	5,015	Grapes	1,677	1,736	1,846	2,000
Hay	3,280	2,973	3,000	3,244	Lemons	306	280	240	178
Oats	221	142	174	143	Oranges	1,718	1,398	1,409	1,337
Peanuts	1,258	1,392	1,286	1,004	Peaches	372	394	379	398
Rice	1,076	1,099	1,243	828	Pears	261	272	276	247
Sorghum	1,002	1,152	1,298	1,205	Plums and prunes .	295	256	254	264
Soybean	10,756	10,975	11,607	11,622	Strawberries	590	634	686	747
Sunflower/safflower . .	217	294	345	377	Almonds	598	564	691	911
Tobacco	2,741	2,886	2,961	2,949	Pecans	248	307	241	214
Wheat	6,426	6,300	7,195	7,376	Walnuts	236	280	286	364
					Sugar beets	1,178	1,084	1,205	1,083
Vegetables [2]	11,449	11,561	11,767	12,656	Sugarcane	820	868	877	850
Dry beans	692	519	494	499	Mushrooms	667	661	668	685
Snap beans	205	205	254	291	Greenhouse, nursery .	8,530	8,904	9,150	9,293
Broccoli	268	242	284	279					
Carrots	273	309	364	301	All livestock and				
Celery	215	206	237	285	products [1]	89,843	86,735	86,350	90,555
Sweet corn	468	497	471	489	Cattle and calves . . .	39,945	39,644	37,958	39,986
Cucumbers	231	231	280	273	Dairy products	20,149	18,037	19,835	19,316
Lettuce	844	818	1,172	1,474	Hogs	11,552	11,045	10,046	10,889
Onions	535	608	540	799	Broilers	8,365	8,383	9,173	10,407
Green peppers . . .	150	207	380	402	Eggs	4,010	3,909	3,387	3,771
Potatoes	2,448	2,141	1,977	2,320	Turkeys	2,379	2,345	2,388	2,504
Tomatoes	1,626	1,801	1,877	1,696	Sheep and lambs . . .	414	400	463	489
Cantaloups	195	100	242	283	Horses and mules . . .	490	466	433	441
					Aquaculture	541	495	571	594

[1] Includes other commodities not shown separately.   [2] Melons included with vegetables.

Source: U.S. Dept. of Agriculture, Economic Research Service, *Economic Indicators of the Farm Sector: National Financial Summary*, annual.

No. 1112. Indexes of Prices Received and Paid by Farmers: 1990 to 1994

[**1990-92=100, except as noted**. See also *Historical Statistics, Colonial Times to 1970*, series K 344-353]

ITEM	1990	1992	1993	1994, prel.	ITEM	1990	1992	1993	1994, prel.
Prices received,					Prices paid, total [3]	99	101	103	106
all products	**104**	**98**	**101**	**100**	Production	99	101	103	106
					Feed	103	99	99	105
Crops [1]	103	101	102	105	Livestock & poultry	102	96	104	95
Food grains	100	113	105	118	Seed	102	99	105	109
Feed grains and hay	105	98	98	106	Fertilizer	97	100	97	106
Cotton	107	88	89	109	Agricultural chemicals . . .	95	103	107	112
Tobacco	97	101	101	101	Fuels	100	96	92	84
Oil-bearing crops	105	100	108	110	Supplies & repairs	96	104	107	110
Fruits	97	99	92	89	Autos and trucks	101	100	103	107
Commercial vegetables [2] .	102	111	116	107	Farm machinery	96	104	106	110
Potatoes & dry beans . . .	133	88	106	111	Building materials	99	101	105	109
					Farm services	97	104	109	112
Livestock and products	105	97	100	95	Interest	107	93	87	97
Meat animals	105	96	100	90	Taxes	95	104	107	112
Dairy products	105	100	98	100	Wage rates	96	105	108	111
Poultry and eggs	105	97	105	106	Parity ratio (1910-14=100) [4] . . .	51	47	47	46

[1] Includes other items not shown separately.   [2] Excludes potatoes and dry beans.   [3] Includes production items, interest, taxes, wage rates, and a family living component. The family living component is the Consumer Price Index for all urban consumers from the Bureau of Labor Statistics. See text, section 15, and table 761.   [4] Ratio of prices received by farmers to prices paid.

Source: U.S. Dept. of Agriculture, National Agricultural Statistics Service, *Agricultural Prices: Annual Summary*.

No. 1113. Commodity Credit Corporation—Net Outlays, by Commodity and Function: 1990 to 1994

[In millions of dollars. For fiscal year ending in year shown; see text, section 9. Excludes value of commodity certificates which may also be issued to farmers in lieu of cash under certain programs. Minus sign (-) indicates a net receipt (excess of repayments or other receipts over gross outlays of funds)]

COMMODITY	1990	1992	1993	1994	FUNCTION	1990	1992	1993	1994
Total	6,471	9,738	16,047	10,336	Total.	6,471	9,738	16,047	10,336
Feed grains	2,693	2,510	5,765	972	Price support loans [4]	–399	584	2,065	559
Wheat	796	1,719	2,185	1,731	Direct payments [5]	4,370	5,847	9,143	5,061
Cotton, upland	–79	1,443	2,239	1,539	Deficiency payments. . . .	4,178	5,491	8,607	4,395
Dairy	505	232	253	158					
Rice	667	715	887	837					
Wool	104	191	179	211	1988/93 crop disaster	[3]5	960	872	2,461
Honey	47	17	22	-	Emergency livestock/forage				
Peanuts	1	41	–13	37	assistance	156	94	72	105
Sugar	15	–19	–35	–24	Purchases [6]	–48	321	525	293
Tobacco	–307	29	235	693	Producer storage payments	185	14	9	12
Soybeans	5	–29	109	–183	Processing, storage and				
Operating expense [1]	618	6	6	6	transportation	278	185	136	112
Interest expenditure	632	532	129	–17	Operating expense [1]	618	6	6	6
Export programs [2]	–34	1,459	2,193	1,950	Interest expenditure	632	532	129	–17
1988/93 disaster/livestock					Export programs [2]	–34	1,459	2,193	1,950
assistance	[3]161	1,054	944	2,566	Other.	708	–264	897	–206
Other	647	–162	949	–140					

- Represents zero. [1] Excludes CCC transfers to the general sales manager. [2] Covers the direct export credit sales program, the export guarantee program, transfers to the general sales manager, market promotion program (beginning 1991), and beginning 1992, the export guarantee program-credit reform, export enhancement program, dairy export incentive program, and technical assistance to emerging democracies. [3] Approximately $1.5 billion in benefits to farmers under the Disaster Assistance Act of 1989 were paid in generic certificates and were not recorded directly as disaster assistance outlays. [4] Price support loans made less loans repaid. [5] Includes dairy termination program and loan deficiency payments. Cash payments only. Excludes generic certificates. [6] Purchases less sales proceeds.

Source: U.S. Agricultural Stabilization and Conservation Service, *Commodity Credit Corporation Report of Financial Condition and Operations*, annual, and *Agricultural Outlook*, monthly.

No. 1114. Net Cash Income and Net Cash Flow From Farming: 1980 to 1993

[In billions of dollars. Net cash income measures the cash income from a farm operator's farm business and net cash flow measures the cash flow within the agricultural sector. Minus sign (-) indicates net loan redemption or decrease]

ITEM	1980	1983	1984	1985	1986	1987	1988	1989	1990	1991	1992	1993
Net cash income.	34.2	38.4	37.4	47.1	47.9	55.8	53.9	54.2	55.1	53.2	57.4	58.5
Gross cash income	143.3	151.1	156.1	157.9	152.9	165.2	172.9	179.8	186.8	184.9	188.2	197.2
Cash expenses	109.1	112.8	118.7	110.7	105.0	109.4	119.0	125.6	131.8	131.7	130.8	138.7
Change in loans outstanding. .	15.3	2.3	2.7	–16.2	–20.6	–12.6	–5.0	–2.1	0.1	1.4	–0.1	3.3
Real estate loans.	10.0	1.4	3.5	–6.6	–9.7	–8.0	–4.8	–2.3	–1.2	0.4	0.5	1.0
Nonreal estate loans [1]	5.3	0.9	–0.8	–9.6	–11.0	–4.6	–0.3	0.1	1.3	1.0	–0.6	2.3
Net change in other financial												
assets.	0.1	0.3	0.2	0.7	1.1	–0.2	0.5	0.1	0.4	1.0	1.8	1.7
Net rent received by												
nonoperator landlords [2]	6.1	5.2	8.2	7.7	6.1	7.1	9.0	10.0	10.4	10.3	10.9	10.9
Capital expenditures	18.0	12.7	12.5	9.2	8.5	11.2	11.5	13.1	14.1	13.2	12.7	14.0
Net cash flow [3]	37.6	33.4	36.0	30.1	26.0	39.0	46.8	49.1	51.9	52.7	57.3	60.4

[1] Excludes Commodity Credit Corporation loans. [2] Beginning 1988, excludes landlord capital consumption. [3] Net cash income plus change in loans outstanding plus net change in other financial assets plus net rent received by nonoperator landlords minus capital expenditures.

Source: U.S. Dept. of Agriculture, Economic Research Service, *Economic Indicators of the Farm Sector: National Financial Summary*, annual.

No. 1115. Average Income to Farm Operator Households: 1989 to 1993

[In dollars per operator household. Data for 1989 and 1990 are expanded to represent only the farm operator households surveyed in USDA's Farm Costs and Returns Survey; beginning 1991 data represent the total number of farms and ranches in the contiguous United States]

ITEM	1989	1990	1991	1992	1993
Farm income to household [1]	5,796	5,742	5,810	7,180	4,815
Self-employment farm income	4,723	4,973	4,458	5,172	3,623
Other farm income to household	1,073	769	1,352	2,008	1,192
Plus: Total off-farm income.	26,223	33,265	31,638	35,731	35,408
Income from wages, salaries, and nonfarm businesses.	19,467	24,778	23,551	27,022	25,215
Income from interest, dividends, transfer payments, etc.	6,756	8,487	8,086	8,709	10,194
Equals: Farm operator household income	32,019	39,007	37,447	42,911	40,223

[1] Farm income to the household equals self-employment income plus amounts that operators pay themselves and family members to work on the farm, income from renting out acreage (1990-92), and net income from a farm business other than the one being surveyed. In 1993, income from renting out acreage is included in income from interest, dividends, transfer payments, etc.

Source: U.S. Dept. of Agriculture, Economic Research Service, *Agricultural Income and Finance Situation and Outlook*, June 1995.

No. 1116. Farm Assets, Debt, and Income, by State: 1992 and 1993

[**Assets and debt**, as of **December 31**. Farm income data are after inventory adjustment and include income and expenses related to the farm operator's dwelling]

DIVISION AND STATE	ASSETS (mil. dol.)		DEBT (mil. dol.)		DEBT/ASSET RATIO (percent)		GROSS FARM INCOME (mil. dol.)		NET FARM INCOME (mil. dol.)	
	1992	1993	1992	1993	1992	1993	1992	1993	1992	1993
United States........	860,822	887,996	138,645	141,900	16.1	16.0	200,213	201,431	50,074	43,401
New England:										
Maine..........	1,899	2,021	287	303	15.1	15.0	567	571	158	154
New Hampshire	1,226	1,298	67	71	5.5	5.5	211	201	71	58
Vermont	2,341	2,462	317	334	13.5	13.6	556	517	162	114
Massachusetts.........	3,642	3,685	299	298	8.2	8.1	573	560	212	191
Rhode Island	389	413	38	38	9.7	9.2	83	87	38	40
Connecticut	2,950	3,120	199	188	6.7	6.0	558	565	217	216
Middle Atlantic:										
New York	12,443	13,106	2,085	2,083	16.7	15.9	3,185	3,051	649	494
New Jersey	7,290	6,894	455	471	6.2	6.8	782	813	223	242
Pennsylvania	17,448	18,026	2,378	2,434	13.6	13.5	4,065	4,039	875	816
East North Central:										
Ohio...............	24,032	24,778	3,138	3,147	13.0	12.7	4,970	5,139	1,158	1,183
Indiana	26,417	27,543	4,521	4,538	17.1	16.5	5,503	5,770	750	832
Illinois...........	50,762	53,960	7,363	7,449	14.5	13.8	9,373	9,161	1,694	1,342
Michigan...........	15,581	15,829	2,602	2,578	16.7	16.3	3,809	4,062	595	624
Wisconsin	23,942	23,776	4,688	4,777	19.6	20.1	6,034	5,778	922	474
West North Central:										
Minnesota	35,494	34,826	6,708	6,850	18.9	19.7	8,096	7,105	1,527	193
Iowa.............	53,945	54,776	9,949	10,369	18.4	18.9	12,007	10,221	2,212	462
Missouri	27,738	28,800	4,565	4,660	16.4	16.2	5,223	4,907	978	564
North Dakota	21,613	22,459	3,262	3,314	15.1	14.8	3,864	3,540	1,133	690
South Dakota	21,883	22,443	3,424	3,534	15.7	15.8	3,942	3,909	1,361	1,179
Nebraska	36,106	38,249	6,856	7,148	19.0	18.7	10,006	9,872	2,696	2,092
Kansas...........	30,675	32,087	5,566	5,747	18.1	17.9	8,640	8,605	1,806	1,623
South Atlantic:										
Delaware...........	1,472	1,543	327	334	22.2	21.6	692	684	126	107
Maryland..........	6,242	6,748	962	990	15.4	14.7	1,585	1,551	368	313
Virginia	13,083	13,427	1,910	1,897	14.5	14.1	2,496	2,373	659	465
West Virginia	2,949	3,022	404	409	13.7	13.6	456	514	99	105
North Carolina	14,796	15,108	2,623	2,700	17.7	17.9	6,175	6,472	2,497	2,490
South Carolina	5,802	5,916	876	860	15.1	14.5	1,408	1,418	372	288
Georgia............	14,335	14,466	2,779	2,731	19.4	18.9	4,765	4,876	1,725	1,532
Florida	24,436	25,298	3,622	3,822	14.8	15.1	6,345	6,070	2,837	2,224
East South Central:										
Kentucky..........	18,085	19,026	2,676	2,689	14.8	14.1	3,871	3,778	1,357	1,135
Tennessee..........	15,644	15,682	1,977	2,007	12.6	12.8	2,767	2,659	739	549
Alabama..........	10,069	11,085	1,466	1,510	14.6	13.6	3,398	3,491	1,148	1,093
Mississippi..........	11,597	12,320	2,413	2,470	20.7	20.0	3,417	3,230	808	368
West South Central:										
Arkansas..........	14,583	15,072	3,106	3,193	21.1	21.2	5,588	5,457	1,494	1,051
Louisiana	8,310	8,023	1,704	1,679	20.4	20.9	2,407	2,246	579	335
Oklahoma	21,928	22,296	3,588	3,746	16.3	16.8	4,395	4,666	1,104	1,250
Texas..............	74,437	76,331	9,300	9,674	12.5	12.7	14,181	15,725	3,200	4,098
Mountain:										
Montana	19,356	21,206	2,448	2,510	12.6	11.8	2,101	2,511	472	765
Idaho	11,763	12,860	2,467	2,524	20.9	19.6	3,020	3,314	923	1,072
Wyoming...........	6,567	7,257	832	899	12.7	12.4	934	1,002	247	262
Colorado..........	15,839	17,277	2,785	2,898	17.6	16.8	4,225	4,689	765	996
New Mexico..........	11,187	11,840	1,048	1,073	9.4	9.1	1,680	1,835	505	565
Arizona...........	11,311	11,346	1,172	1,197	10.4	10.6	1,984	2,100	601	638
Utah..............	5,857	6,119	651	655	11.1	10.7	922	946	306	291
Nevada............	2,784	2,621	238	236	8.5	9.0	272	311	60	80
Pacific:										
Washington	15,198	16,651	2,805	2,878	18.4	17.3	5,181	5,568	1,532	1,572
Oregon	13,307	14,358	2,298	2,174	17.2	15.1	3,048	3,389	725	905
California..........	68,001	66,491	13,063	13,502	19.2	20.3	20,282	21,533	5,344	5,235
Alaska	596	614	48	47	8.0	7.7	34	35	8	7
Hawaii	3,474	3,444	295	272	8.5	7.9	542	519	37	29

Source: U.S. Dept. of Agriculture, Economic Research Service, *Economic Indicators of the Farm Sector: State Financial Summary, 1993*; and unpublished data.

No. 1117. Farm Income—Farm Marketings, 1992 and 1993, Government Payments, 1993, and Principal Commodities, 1993, by State

[In millions of dollars. Cattle include calves; sheep include lambs; and greenhouse includes nursery]

DIVISION AND STATE	1992 Farm marketings			1993 Farm marketings			Government payments	State rank for total farm marketings and four principal commodities in order of marketing receipts
	Total	Crops	Livestock and products	Total	Crops	Livestock and products		
U.S..	171,202	84,853	86,350	175,052	84,497	90,555	13,402	Cattle, dairy products, corn, soybeans
N.E.	**2,129**	**1,031**	**1,098**	**2,217**	**1,083**	**1,134**	**32**	(X)
ME . .	457	204	253	472	198	274	20	45-Eggs, potatoes, dairy products, aquaculture
NH . . .	145	81	65	163	99	65	2	48-Dairy products, greenhouse, Christmas trees, apples
VT . . .	460	72	388	484	81	403	3	44-Dairy products, cattle, greenhouse, Christmas trees
MA . . .	487	361	126	497	375	122	4	42-Greenhouse, cranberries, dairy products, eggs
RI	73	60	13	79	67	12	(Z)	49-Greenhouse, eggs, dairy products, potatoes
CT . . .	506	253	254	521	263	258	3	41-Greenhouse, eggs, dairy products, aquaculture
M.A	**7,169**	**2,518**	**4,651**	**7,236**	**2,528**	**4,708**	**125**	(X)
NY . . .	2,917	1,010	1,907	2,817	930	1,888	72	26-Dairy products, greenhouse, cattle, apples
NJ. . .	654	463	190	706	508	199	7	39-Greenhouse, dairy products, eggs, blueberries
PA. . .	3,599	1,045	2,554	3,712	1,091	2,622	45	19-Dairy products, cattle, greenhouse, mushrooms
E.N.C . . .	**24,908**	**13,659**	**11,249**	**26,211**	**14,818**	**11,393**	**2,047**	(X)
OH . . .	4,108	2,559	1,550	4,393	2,720	1,673	265	13-Soybeans, corn, dairy products, greenhouse
IN . . .	4,463	2,639	1,824	5,118	3,186	1,932	379	11-Corn, soybeans, hogs, cattle
IL . . .	7,648	5,395	2,253	8,082	5,835	2,248	851	5-Corn, soybeans, hogs, cattle
MI. . .	3,220	1,910	1,311	3,367	1,991	1,376	241	21-Dairy products, corn, greenhouse, soybeans
WI. . .	5,469	1,158	4,312	5,250	1,086	4,164	310	10-Dairy products, cattle, corn, hogs
W.N.C . . .	**43,699**	**19,136**	**24,563**	**43,154**	**17,690**	**25,464**	**5,095**	(X)
MN . . .	7,023	3,413	3,610	6,574	2,800	3,774	823	7-Dairy products, cattle, hogs, corn
IA . . .	10,409	4,810	5,600	10,001	4,173	5,829	1,230	3-Hogs, corn, cattle, soybeans
MO . . .	4,174	1,987	2,186	4,053	1,783	2,270	455	17-Cattle, soybeans, hogs, corn
ND . . .	2,984	2,234	749	2,933	2,227	707	565	23-Wheat, cattle, barley, sugar beets
SD . . .	3,157	1,198	1,960	3,320	1,147	2,173	432	22-Cattle, wheat, hogs, corn
NE . . .	8,783	3,107	5,675	8,909	3,067	5,842	806	4-Cattle, corn, hogs, soybeans
KS . . .	7,170	2,387	4,783	7,363	2,493	4,870	784	6-Cattle, wheat, corn, soybeans
S.A.	**21,030**	**11,353**	**9,678**	**21,098**	**10,539**	**10,559**	**656**	(X)
DE . . .	628	177	451	622	159	463	6	40-Broilers, soybeans, corn, greenhouse
MD . . .	1,365	576	789	1,366	560	806	26	35-Broilers, greenhouse, dairy products, soybeans
VA. . .	2,141	779	1,362	2,068	683	1,385	46	29-Broilers, cattle, dairy products, tobacco
WV . . .	343	76	267	405	77	328	6	46-Cattle, broilers, dairy products, turkeys
NC . . .	5,177	2,379	2,799	5,457	2,256	3,201	132	9-Tobacco, broilers, hogs, turkeys
SC . . .	1,197	652	545	1,221	618	603	103	36-Tobacco, broilers, cattle, greenhouse
GA . . .	4,087	1,781	2,306	4,211	1,639	2,572	226	15-Broilers, peanuts, cattle, eggs
FL. . .	6,092	4,932	1,160	5,750	4,548	1,202	111	8-Greenhouse, oranges, tomatoes, sugar
E.S.C . . .	**10,776**	**4,674**	**6,102**	**10,930**	**4,438**	**6,493**	**778**	(X)
KY . . .	3,204	1,563	1,641	3,376	1,656	1,720	97	20-Tobacco, cattle, horses, dairy products
TN . . .	2,122	1,063	1,058	2,039	1,027	1,012	161	30-Cattle, dairy products, tobacco, soybeans
AL. . .	2,816	769	2,048	2,910	727	2,184	137	24-Broilers, cattle, eggs, greenhouse
MS . . .	2,635	1,280	1,355	2,605	1,028	1,577	384	27-Broilers, cotton, soybeans, aquaculture
W.S.C . . .	**21,697**	**8,298**	**13,399**	**22,625**	**7,932**	**14,693**	**2,817**	(X)
AR . . .	4,660	1,950	2,710	4,382	1,480	2,902	705	14-Broilers, soybeans, cotton, cattle
LA. . . .	1,911	1,299	612	1,757	1,069	688	367	33-Cotton, sugar, cattle, soybeans
OK . . .	3,665	1,113	2,553	3,869	1,108	2,762	324	18-Cattle, wheat, greenhouse, broilers
TX . . .	11,461	3,937	7,524	12,617	4,275	8,342	1,421	2-Cattle, cotton, dairy products, greenhouse
Mountain. . . .	**13,456**	**5,342**	**8,114**	**14,163**	**5,689**	**8,473**	**1,025**	(X)
MT . . .	1,706	808	898	1,781	843	938	338	32-Cattle, wheat, barley, hay
ID. . . .	2,775	1,601	1,173	2,847	1,680	1,167	159	25-Cattle, potatoes, dairy products, wheat
WY . . .	776	170	607	817	160	657	43	37-Cattle, sugar beets, hay, sheep
CO . . .	3,801	1,055	2,746	4,083	1,204	2,879	250	16-Cattle, wheat, corn, dairy products
NM . . .	1,530	492	1,039	1,621	486	1,135	76	34-Cattle, dairy products, hay, greenhouse
AZ . . .	1,839	947	893	1,922	1,037	885	114	31-Cattle, cotton, dairy products, hay
UT . . .	753	195	558	804	177	626	37	38-Cattle, dairy products, hay, turkeys
NV . . .	276	75	202	289	102	187	7	47-Cattle, hay, dairy products, potatoes
Pacific . .	**26,338**	**18,842**	**7,496**	**27,418**	**19,780**	**7,638**	**827**	(X)
WA . . .	4,437	2,889	1,548	4,574	3,013	1,561	207	12-Cattle, apples, dairy products, wheat
OR . . .	2,460	1,662	798	2,476	1,737	739	93	28-Cattle, greenhouse, dairy products, wheat
CA . . .	18,896	13,841	5,056	19,850	14,604	5,246	522	1-Dairy products, greenhouse, grapes, cattle
AK . . .	26	20	6	27	21	6	2	50-Greenhouse, dairy products, potatoes, hay
HI. . . .	520	431	89	492	406	85	3	43-Sugar, pineapples, greenhouse, nuts

X Not applicable.　Z Less than $500,000.

Source: U.S. Dept. of Agriculture, Economic Research Service, *Economic Indicators of the Farm Sector: State Financial Summary, 1993.*

No. 1118. Civilian Consumer Expenditures for Farm Foods—Farm Value and Marketing Bill: 1980 to 1993

[In billions of dollars, except percent. Excludes imported and nonfarm foods, such as coffee and seafood, as well as food consumed by the military, or exported. See *Historical Statistics, Colonial Times to 1970*, series K 358-360 for data before revisions]

ITEM	1980	1984	1985	1986	1987	1988	1989	1990	1991	1992	1993
Consumer expenditures, total	**264.4**	**332.0**	**345.4**	**359.6**	**375.5**	**398.8**	**419.4**	**449.8**	**465.1**	**474.5**	**491.3**
Farm value, total	81.7	89.8	86.4	88.8	90.4	96.8	103.8	106.2	101.6	105.1	109.2
Marketing bill, total [1]	182.7	242.2	259.0	270.8	285.1	301.9	315.6	343.6	363.5	369.4	382.1
Percent of total consumer expenditures	69.1	73.0	75.0	75.3	75.9	75.7	75.3	76.4	78.2	77.9	77.8
At-home expenditures [2]	180.1	213.1	220.8	226.0	230.2	242.1	255.5	276.2	286.1	289.6	297.0
Farm value	65.9	69.5	66.6	67.6	67.5	72.5	77.9	80.2	76.7	76.9	78.9
Marketing bill [1]	114.2	143.6	154.2	158.4	162.7	169.6	177.6	196.0	209.4	212.7	218.1
Percent of at-home expenditures	63.4	67.4	69.8	70.1	70.7	70.1	69.5	71.0	73.2	73.4	73.4
Away-from-home expenditures	84.3	118.9	124.6	133.6	145.3	156.7	163.9	173.6	179.0	184.9	194.3
Farm value	15.8	20.3	19.8	21.2	22.9	24.3	25.9	26.0	24.9	28.2	30.3
Marketing bill [1]	68.5	98.6	104.8	112.4	122.4	132.4	138.0	147.6	154.1	156.7	164.0
Percent of away-from-home expenditures	81.3	82.9	84.1	84.1	84.2	84.5	84.2	85.0	86.1	84.7	84.4
Marketing bill cost components:											
Labor cost [3]	81.5	109.3	115.6	122.9	130.0	137.9	145.1	154.0	160.9	168.4	177.6
Packaging materials	21.0	26.2	26.9	27.7	29.9	32.6	35.2	36.5	38.1	39.2	40.5
Rail and truck transport [4]	13.0	15.9	16.5	16.8	17.2	17.8	18.6	19.8	20.4	20.6	21.1
Corporate profits before taxes	9.9	9.6	10.4	10.3	11.1	12.0	12.9	14.8	15.9	15.7	15.3
Fuels and electricity	9.0	12.5	13.1	13.2	13.6	14.1	14.8	15.2	16.3	16.7	17.3
Other [5]	48.3	68.7	76.5	79.9	83.3	87.5	89.0	103.3	111.9	108.8	110.3
Processing	66.3	80.8	88.4	91.0	93.9	99.7	103.8	113.4	120.5	122.6	126.3
Wholesaling	20.4	28.6	29.8	30.5	31.8	33.8	35.2	39.0	39.9	40.5	41.7
Transportation	13.0	16.0	16.6	16.8	17.6	17.7	18.6	19.6	20.5	20.5	21.1
Retailing and food service	83.0	116.8	124.2	132.5	141.8	150.8	158.0	171.6	182.6	185.8	193.0
SELECTED FOOD COMMODITY GROUPS											
Meat products:											
Total expenditures	83.3	101.7	103.2	106.3	110.0	117.6	121.5	128.4	133.4	135.5	139.3
Farm value	30.8	32.4	30.5	30.9	32.7	33.5	34.0	36.9	34.7	34.4	35.3
Percent of total	37.0	31.9	29.6	29.1	29.7	28.5	28.0	28.7	26.0	25.4	25.3
Marketing bill [1]	52.5	69.3	72.7	75.4	77.3	84.1	87.5	91.5	98.7	101.1	104.0
Poultry and eggs:											
Total expenditures	18.3	24.2	26.0	27.6	29.4	31.3	33.9	36.6	37.7	38.0	39.2
Farm value	8.4	11.0	10.2	11.5	10.3	12.1	14.2	13.9	13.9	14.3	15.7
Percent of total	45.9	45.5	39.2	41.7	35.0	38.7	41.9	38.0	36.9	37.6	40.1
Marketing bill [1]	9.9	13.2	15.8	16.1	19.1	19.2	19.7	22.7	23.8	23.7	23.5
Dairy products:											
Total expenditures	37.8	47.4	49.4	51.4	54.0	55.8	58.1	62.5	63.0	63.5	65.5
Farm value	16.0	18.1	17.7	17.8	18.2	17.9	19.6	20.5	18.4	20.1	20.1
Percent of total	42.3	38.2	35.8	34.6	33.7	32.1	33.7	32.8	29.2	31.7	30.7
Marketing bill [1]	21.8	29.3	31.7	33.6	35.8	37.9	38.5	42.0	44.6	43.4	45.4
Fruits and vegetables:											
Total expenditures	55.5	74.7	78.5	81.6	84.7	89.3	96.0	103.7	107.9	111.7	116.5
Farm value	11.7	13.5	13.3	14.6	14.3	16.2	17.8	16.5	17.0	17.7	18.4
Percent of total	21.1	18.1	16.9	17.9	16.9	18.1	18.5	15.9	15.8	15.8	15.8
Marketing bill [1]	43.8	61.2	65.2	67.0	70.4	73.1	78.2	87.2	90.9	94.0	98.1
Bakery, grain mill products:											
Total expenditures	35.2	43.3	45.5	48.3	49.9	54.7	57.7	63.3	66.0	67.9	70.9
Farm value	5.1	5.1	4.7	4.0	3.8	4.9	5.9	5.1	4.6	5.1	5.2
Percent of total	14.5	11.8	10.3	8.3	7.6	9.0	10.2	8.1	7.0	7.5	7.3
Marketing bill [1]	30.1	38.2	40.8	44.3	46.1	49.8	51.8	58.2	61.4	62.8	65.7

[1] The difference between expenditures for domestic farm-originated food products and the farm value or payment farmers received for the equivalent farm products.   [2] Food primarily purchased from retail food stores for use at home.   [3] Covers employee wages and salaries, and their health and welfare benefits. Also includes imputed earnings of proprietors, partners, and family workers not receiving stated remuneration.   [4] Excludes local hauling.   [5] Represents advertising, rent, depreciation, interest on borrowed capital, taxes other than income, and other costs.

Source: U.S. Dept. of Agriculture, Economic Research Service, *Food Cost Review, 1993*, AER-696, August 1994; *Food Review*, periodic; and *Agricultural Statistics*, annual.

No. 1119. Selected Indexes of Farm Inputs: 1970 to 1991

[1982=100. Inputs based on physical quantities of resources used in production. See *Historical Statistics, Colonial Times to 1970*, series K 486-495 for data before revisions]

INPUT	1970	1980	1983	1984	1985	1986	1987	1988	1989	1990	1991
Total	**93**	**106**	**96**	**98**	**95**	**92**	**89**	**87**	**87**	**89**	**89**
Farm labor	119	108	95	97	89	87	84	86	82	87	88
Farm real estate	94	101	92	97	97	94	91	90	91	90	89
Durable equipment	78	102	95	91	86	80	74	70	67	65	63
Energy	92	110	97	100	90	84	93	93	91	90	89
Agricultural chemicals [1]	76	131	93	106	101	111	100	90	93	90	94
Feed, seed, and livestock purchases [2]	87	102	99	101	106	105	101	98	99	105	104
Other purchased inputs [3]	90	116	107	108	99	89	92	90	96	97	100

[1] Includes fertilizer, lime, and pesticides.   [2] Includes nonfarm portion of feed, seed, and livestock purchases.   [3] Includes purchased services and miscellaneous inputs.

Source: U.S. Dept. of Agriculture, Economic Research Service, *Agricultural Outlook*, monthly. Also published in the U.S. Council of Economic Advisers, *Economic Report of the President*, annual.

No. 1120. Farm Machinery and Equipment: 1980 to 1993

[See also *Historical Statistics, Colonial Times to 1970*, series K 184-191]

ITEM	Unit	1980	1983	1984	1985	1986	1987	1988	1989	1990	1991	1992	1993
Value of farm implements and machinery [1]	Bil. dol. . .	80.3	85.8	85.0	82.9	81.5	80.0	81.2	85.1	85.4	85.8	85.6	85.2
Farmers' expenditures:													
Motor vehicles [2]	Mil. dol. .	5,813	4,724	4,583	3,699	3,227	4,275	4,912	5,484	5,750	4,993	5,126	5,151
Tractors	Mil. dol. .	3,683	2,606	2,539	1,937	1,513	2,104	2,540	2,903	3,119	2,593	2,826	2,655
Machinery, equipment	Mil. dol. .	6,956	4,735	4,682	3,232	3,094	4,297	4,222	5,087	5,589	5,410	5,132	5,526
Repair and maintenance	Mil. dol. .	5,205	4,793	4,908	4,834	4,825	5,017	5,869	6,607	6,311	6,414	5,966	6,472
Tractors, machinery and equipment	Mil. dol. .	3,746	3,616	3,592	3,442	3,428	3,540	4,022	4,506	4,366	4,485	4,196	4,508
Autos and trucks	Mil. dol. .	1,459	1,178	1,316	1,392	1,397	1,477	1,847	2,101	1,945	1,929	1,770	1,964
Retail sales: [3]													
Tractors, total [4]	1,000. . .	119.3	71.3	66.7	58.5	47.1	48.3	52.0	59.7	66.3	58.1	52.8	57.8
Two-wheel drive	1,000. . .	108.4	66.2	62.7	55.5	45.1	46.6	49.3	55.5	61.2	54.0	50.1	54.5
Four-wheel drive	1,000. . .	10.9	5.1	4.1	3.0	2.0	1.7	2.7	4.2	5.1	4.1	2.7	3.3
Combines	1,000. . .	25.7	12.8	11.4	8.4	7.7	7.2	6.0	9.1	10.4	9.7	7.7	7.9

[1] Farm inventory valuations as of December 31.　[2] For farm business use.　[3] Source: Equipment Manufacturers Institute, Chicago, IL, unpublished data.　[4] Covers tractors over 40 hp. only.

Source: Except as noted, U.S. Dept. of Agriculture, Economic Research Service, *Economic Indicators of the Farm Sector: National Financial Summary*, annual. Also in *Agricultural Statistics*, annual.

No. 1121. Hired Farmworkers—Workers and Weekly Earnings: 1990 and 1993

[Represents average number of persons 15 years old and over in the civilian noninstitutional population who were employed at hired farmwork at any time during the year. Based on Current Population Survey; see text, section 1, and Appendix III. For definition of median, see Guide to Tabular Presentation]

CHARACTERISTIC	WORKERS (1,000)		MEDIAN WEEKLY EARNINGS [1]		CHARACTERISTIC	WORKERS (1,000)		MEDIAN WEEKLY EARNINGS [1]	
	1990	1993	1990	1993		1990	1993	1990	1993
All workers	**886**	**803**	**$200**	**$220**	White [2]	540	462	201	225
					Black and other races [2]	85	71	175	200
15 to 19 years old	144	112	100	125	Hispanic	260	270	213	225
20 to 24 years old	135	106	206	210					
25 to 34 years old	251	236	240	250	Educational attainment: [3]				
35 to 44 years old	170	175	250	250	Less than 5th grade	98	132	204	210
45 to 54 years old	90	97	200	250	5th to 8th grade	191	140	200	200
55 years old and over	95	77	200	200	9th to 12th grade (no diploma)	202	175	168	200
					High school diploma	278	217	240	240
Male	735	680	216	225	Beyond high school	116	139	260	270
Female	151	123	175	192					

[1] The weekly earnings the farmworker usually earns at his farmwork job before deductions and includes any overtime pay or commissions.　[2] Excludes persons of Hispanic origin.　[3] Data for 1990 reflect years of school completed rather than degrees or diplomas received.

Source: U.S. Dept. of Agriculture, Economic Research Service, unpublished data.

No. 1122. Farm Output Indexes: 1970 to 1991

[**1982=100**. See also *Historical Statistics, Colonial Times to 1970*, series K 414-429]

ITEM	1970	1980	1981	1983	1984	1985	1986	1987	1988	1989	1990	1991
Farm output [1]	**72**	**90**	**100**	**84**	**101**	**105**	**102**	**104**	**97**	**108**	**112**	**112**
Per unit of total input	**78**	**85**	**97**	**88**	**103**	**111**	**111**	**117**	**112**	**124**	**127**	**126**
Gross production:												
Livestock and products [2]	90	99	101	102	100	103	103	106	108	110	112	114
Meat animals	100	104	104	102	100	99	99	100	102	102	102	105
Dairy products	86	95	98	103	99	105	106	105	107	106	109	109
Poultry and eggs	76	96	100	100	103	108	112	122	125	130	138	144
Crops [3]	59	83	100	71	100	106	99	101	88	105	112	109
Feed crops	49	64	102	31	108	125	119	101	63	116	113	113
Food grains	50	86	102	84	93	87	77	77	70	77	99	76
Oil crops	53	80	89	75	87	96	88	88	71	87	87	92
Cotton and cottonseed	92	95	135	68	111	113	83	127	133	103	138	140
Tobacco	98	90	106	75	89	77	58	61	69	71	83	85
Vegetables and melons	76	94	96	97	103	109	110	117	111	114	123	122
Fruits and nuts	71	103	101	100	100	99	95	109	117	111	113	105
Other crops	65	94	98	101	110	111	120	132	137	141	141	148

[1] Annual production available for eventual human use.　[2] Includes livestock products not shown separately and excludes horses and mules.　[3] Includes crops not shown separately.

Source: U.S. Dept. of Agriculture, Economic Research Service, *Agricultural Outlook*, monthly.

No. 1123. Agricultural Exports and Imports—Volume, by Principal Commodities: 1980 to 1993

[In thousands of metric tons]

EXPORTS	1980	1990	1992	1993	IMPORTS	1980	1990	1992	1993
Animal products [1]	2,575	2,737	3,627	3,823	Fruits, nuts, vegetables ...	2,325	4,573	4,502	5,113
Wheat and products [2]	37,130	28,282	34,655	36,728	Bananas	2,352	3,094	3,531	3,513
Feed grains and products	72,970	61,397	52,958	48,286	Green coffee	1,089	1,174	1,300	1,081
Rice	3,075	2,509	2,181	2,776	Cocoa and products	325	765	755	801
Feeds and fodders	6,888	10,979	11,336	11,728	Meat and products [5]	931	1,165	1,119	1,153
Protein meal [3]	7,427	5,138	7,020	6,344					
Oilseeds and products [3]	23,631	15,778	20,511	20,028	Vegetable oils	704	1,183	1,420	1,419
Vegetable oils	1,837	1,204	1,722	1,708	Rubber, crude natural	931	840	931	1,000
Fruits, nuts, vegetables [4]	4,147	5,552	6,148	6,172	Sugar	3,744	1,856	1,648	1,617
Cotton and linters	1,880	1,733	1,449	1,184	Spices	86	129	155	144
Tobacco, unmanufactured	272	223	261	208	Tobacco, unmanufactured .	392	187	398	461

[1] Includes meat and products, poultry meats, dairy products, and fats, oils and greases. Excludes live animals, hides, skins, and eggs. [2] Includes flour and bulgur. [3] Includes soybeans, sunflowerseeds, peanuts, cottonseed, safflowerseed, flaxseed, and nondefatted soybean flour. [4] Excludes fruit juices. [5] Excludes poultry.

Source: U.S. Dept. of Agriculture, Economic Research Service, *Foreign Agricultural Trade of the United States*, Jan./Feb. 1994, and calendar year supplements.

No. 1124. Agricultural Exports and Imports—Value: 1980 to 1993

[**In billions of dollars, except percent**. Includes Puerto Rico. Excludes forest products and distilled liquors; includes crude rubber and similar gums (now mainly plantation products). Includes shipments under foreign aid programs. See also *Historical Statistics, Colonial Times to 1970*, series K 251-255]

YEAR	Trade balance	Exports, domestic products	Percent of all exports	Imports for consumption	Percent of all imports	YEAR	Trade balance	Exports, domestic products	Percent of all exports	Imports for consumption	Percent of all imports
1980	23.9	41.2	18	17.4	7	1988	16.1	37.1	12	21.0	5
1983	19.5	36.1	18	16.6	7	1989	18.2	39.9	11	21.7	5
1984	18.5	37.8	17	19.3	6	1990	16.6	39.4	10	22.8	5
1985	9.1	29.0	13	20.0	6	1991	16.5	39.2	10	22.7	5
1986	4.8	26.2	13	21.5	6	1992	18.3	42.9	10	24.6	5
1987	8.3	28.7	12	20.4	5	1993	17.6	42.6	10	25.0	4

Source: U.S. Dept. of Agriculture, Economic Research Service, *Foreign Agricultural Trade of the United States*, Jan.-Feb. issues, and calendar year supplements. Also in *Agricultural Statistics*, annual.

No. 1125. Agricultural Exports and Imports—Leading Trading Partners: 1993

[**In billions of dollars**. For year ending **Sept. 30**. Minus sign (-) denotes an excess of imports over exports]

TRADING PARTNER	Exports	Imports	Trade balance	MAJOR COMMODITIES Exported by United States	MAJOR COMMODITIES Imported by United States
Japan	8.7	0.3	8.5	Corn, beef, soybeans	Vegetables and preps., beverages, seeds
European Union	6.8	4.8	2.1	Soybeans, animal feeds, nuts and preps.	Wine and beer, vegetables and preps., cheese
Taiwan [1]	2.0	0.1	1.9	Corn, soybeans, wheat	Vegetables and preps., noodles, biscuits/wafers
Korea, South	1.9	0.1	1.9	Cattle hides, cotton, soybeans	Vegetables and preps., noodles, fruit and preps.
Soviet Union (former) .	1.8	(Z)	1.7	Corn, wheat, soymeal	Casein, furskins, cheese
Mexico	3.6	2.7	0.9	Soybeans, grain sorghum, vegetables and preps.	Vegetables and preps., cattle, fruit and preps.
Hong Kong	0.9	0.1	0.8	Fruit and preps., chicken, vegetables and preps.	Vegetables and preps., biscuits/wafers, noodles
Canada	5.3	4.6	0.7	Vegetables and preps., fruit and preps., beef	Cattle, pork, beef
Egypt	0.7	(Z)	0.6	Wheat, corn, wheat flour	Essential oils, vegetables and preps., fibers (ex. cotton)
Turkey	0.4	0.3	(Z)	Tobacco, corn oil, rice	Tobacco, fruits and preps., nuts and preps.
Philippines	0.5	0.4	(Z)	Wheat, soymeal, vegetables and preps.	Coconut oil, fruit and preps., sugar
China [1]	0.4	0.5	-0.1	Wheat, soybeans, chicken	Vegetables and preps., tobacco, feathers
Guatemala	0.2	0.5	-0.3	Wheat, corn, cotton	Coffee, bananas, sugar
Costa Rica	0.1	0.6	-0.4	Corn, soybeans, wheat	Bananas, fruit and preps., beef
Thailand	0.3	0.7	-0.4	Wheat, tobacco, animal feeds	Rubber, fruit and preps., tobacco
Indonesia	0.3	0.8	-0.5	Cotton, soybeans, animal feeds	Rubber, cocoa, coffee
Colombia	0.2	0.8	-0.6	Corn, wheat, soymeal	Coffee, cut flowers, bananas
New Zealand	0.1	0.8	-0.7	Beverages, fruit and preps., soymeal	Beef, casein, fruit and preps.
Australia	0.3	1.1	-0.7	Beverages, vegetables and preps., soymeal	Beef, wool, sugar
Brazil	0.2	1.4	-1.2	Cotton, wheat, vegetables and preps.	Tobacco, coffee, orange juice

Z Less than $100 million.   [1] See text, section 30.

Source: U.S. Dept. of Agriculture, Economic Research Service, *Foreign Agricultural Trade of the United States*, calendar year supplement.

No. 1126. Agricultural Exports—Value, by Principal Commodities and Selected Countries of Destination: 1980 to 1993

[See headnote, table 1124. Data by country of destination for 1980 are not adjusted for transshipments]

COMMODITY AND COUNTRY	VALUE (mil. dol.)								PERCENT		
	1980	1985	1988	1989	1990	1991	1992	1993	1980	1990	1993
Total agricultural exports [1]	41,234	29,041	37,080	39,909	39,363	39,204	42,930	42,609	100.0	100.0	100.0
Grains and feeds [2]	19,126	11,882	13,994	17,155	14,378	12,746	14,174	13,980	46.4	36.5	32.8
Feed grains and products	9,852	6,112	5,973	7,870	7,151	5,869	5,881	5,174	23.9	18.2	12.1
Corn	8,492	5,206	5,043	6,580	6,027	4,922	4,708	4,220	20.6	15.3	9.9
Wheat and products	6,660	3,898	5,126	6,136	4,033	3,511	4,675	4,909	16.2	10.2	11.5
Rice	1,289	665	809	971	800	751	725	770	3.2	2.0	1.8
Oilseeds and products [2]	9,394	5,794	7,695	6,345	5,710	6,397	7,197	7,270	22.8	14.5	17.1
Soybeans	5,880	3,732	4,863	3,942	3,551	3,957	4,387	4,599	14.3	9.0	10.8
Soybean oilcake and meal	1,666	870	1,580	1,181	992	1,157	1,242	1,071	4.1	2.5	2.5
Vegetable oils and waxes	1,216	870	983	872	808	768	1,018	1,056	3.0	2.1	2.5
Animals and animal products [2]	3,768	4,150	6,422	6,378	6,712	7,007	7,925	7,931	9.2	17.1	18.6
Hides and skins, incl. furskins	1,046	1,295	1,829	1,717	1,747	1,371	1,346	1,285	2.6	4.4	3.0
Cattle hides	637	1,007	1,513	1,383	1,428	1,137	1,132	1,079	1.6	3.6	2.5
Meats and meat products	890	905	1,974	2,348	2,558	2,853	3,339	3,325	2.2	6.5	7.8
Beef and veal	249	467	1,109	1,420	1,579	1,757	2,043	1,995	0.6	4.0	4.7
Fats, oils, and greases	769	619	577	512	424	442	525	504	1.9	1.1	1.2
Poultry and poultry products	603	384	689	713	954	1,094	1,211	1,376	1.5	2.4	3.2
Cotton, excluding linters	2,864	1,633	1,975	2,250	2,783	2,480	1,999	1,528	7.0	7.1	3.6
Tobacco, unmanufactured	1,334	1,521	1,253	1,301	1,441	1,428	1,651	1,306	3.3	3.7	3.1
Fruits and preparations	1,335	1,186	1,762	1,835	2,359	2,498	2,732	2,764	3.3	6.0	6.5
Fresh fruits	739	743	1,093	1,133	1,486	1,561	1,683	1,707	1.8	3.8	4.0
Vegetables and preparations	1,188	930	1,361	1,601	2,302	2,615	2,872	3,277	2.9	5.8	7.7
Nuts and preparations	757	683	884	846	976	1,020	1,139	1,182	1.9	2.5	2.8
Other	1,468	1,262	1,734	2,198	2,702	3,013	3,241	3,371	3.6	6.9	7.9
Asia [1]	15,046	11,191	16,858	18,828	17,640	16,450	17,924	18,074	36.5	44.8	42.4
Japan	6,133	5,409	7,640	8,162	8,104	7,729	8,437	8,739	14.9	20.6	20.5
Korea, South	1,797	1,413	2,274	2,593	2,644	2,104	2,222	1,932	4.4	6.7	4.5
Taiwan [3]	1,095	1,231	1,661	1,754	1,661	1,899	1,900	2,043	2.7	4.2	4.8
Hong Kong	437	389	489	611	701	771	862	875	1.1	1.8	2.1
Western Europe [1][4]	12,917	7,002	7,911	7,070	7,353	7,467	7,805	7,324	31.4	18.7	17.2
European Union [5]	12,177	6,542	7,370	6,577	6,850	6,916	7,291	6,839	29.6	17.4	16.1
Netherlands	3,476	1,869	2,059	1,722	1,581	1,698	1,853	1,702	8.5	4.0	4.0
Germany	2,373	1,009	1,248	1,075	1,158	1,076	1,163	1,071	5.8	2.9	2.5
Spain [6]	1,488	837	883	820	937	928	936	782	3.6	2.4	1.8
United Kingdom	996	604	835	703	829	831	910	945	2.5	2.1	2.2
Italy	1,203	669	699	637	710	674	670	600	3.0	1.8	1.4
France	765	403	534	458	528	581	595	593	1.9	1.3	1.4
Latin America [1]	6,154	4,224	4,935	5,337	5,092	5,684	6,668	6,794	15.0	13.0	15.9
Mexico	2,469	1,439	2,234	2,724	2,553	2,999	3,791	3,603	6.0	6.5	8.5
Venezuela	703	638	683	448	351	316	440	489	1.7	0.9	1.1
Canada	1,908	1,622	2,019	2,221	4,197	4,554	4,902	5,271	4.7	10.7	12.4
Soviet Union (former)	1,138	1,923	2,252	3,597	2,271	2,508	2,346	1,758	2.8	5.8	4.1
Eastern Europe	1,644	414	464	327	537	234	317	432	4.0	1.4	1.0
Africa [1]	2,237	2,488	2,387	2,260	1,935	1,908	2,570	2,485	5.5	4.9	5.8
Algeria	195	227	596	504	513	483	437	516	0.5	1.3	1.2
Egypt	774	891	841	989	693	687	766	661	1.9	1.8	1.6

[1] Includes areas not shown separately. [2] Includes commodities not shown separately. [3] See text, section 30. [4] Includes Canary Islands and Madeira Islands for all years. [5] Includes Belgium, Luxembourg, Denmark, Greece, Ireland, and Portugal, not shown separately. As of Jan. 1, 1981, Greece became a member of the European Union. As of Jan. 1, 1986, Spain and Portugal became members of the European Union. For consistency, data for all years are shown on same basis. [6] As of Jan. 1, 1984, includes Canary Islands and Spanish Africa, not elsewhere classified.

Source: U.S. Dept. of Agriculture, Economic Research Service, *Foreign Agricultural Trade of the United States*, Jan./Feb. 1994, and calendar year supplements. Also in *Agricultural Statistics*, annual.

No. 1127. Spices—Imports, by Type of Spice: 1980 to 1993

[In millions of pounds. Data shown are **annual averages**. The United States produces only three major spices - capsicum (red pepper), paprika, and mustard - in any profitable degree. Unground or unprocessed spices enter duty-free. Most spices imported into the United States are unground or unprocessed, generally ensuring better quality]

SPICE	1980-84	1985-89	1990-93	1992	1993	SPICE	1980-84	1985-89	1990-93	1992	1993
Total [1]	351.3	398.9	492.7	515.0	498.3	Mace	0.6	0.6	0.5	0.5	0.5
						Mustard seed	79.5	94.5	139.5	140.9	140.0
Anise seed	1.4	2.2	2.5	2.3	3.0	Nutmeg	4.8	4.2	3.9	3.7	4.1
Capsicum	13.9	23.8	48.4	59.3	51.8	Paprika	10.5	13.1	8.4	6.8	9.1
Caraway seed	7.5	7.7	7.7	7.2	8.6	Pepper, black and white	72.5	79.4	95.2	103.0	92.8
Cassia and cinnamon	23.4	29.4	30.8	34.3	31.8	Pimento	1.7	1.9	2.3	1.9	2.5
Celery seed	4.7	5.4	5.9	5.9	6.9	Poppy seed	7.2	8.8	9.6	10.8	11.4
Cloves	2.1	2.5	3.0	2.5	2.7	Sage	3.7	4.4	4.5	5.3	4.1
Coriander seed	10.4	7.7	5.0	5.1	4.8	Sesame seed	80.4	81.1	83.4	77.3	81.4
Cumin seed	8.8	9.2	11.2	14.2	11.5	Turmeric	3.7	4.4	4.5	5.7	4.4
Fennel seed	3.4	4.8	6.2	7.0	6.0	Vanilla beans	1.6	2.4	2.7	2.8	2.9
Ginger root	9.5	11.4	17.6	18.5	18.1						

[1] The United States also imports limited amounts of other spices which are not included in the total.

Source: U.S. Dept. of Agriculture, Economic Research Service, *Foreign Agricultural Trade of the United States*, calendar year supplement, and U.S. Bureau of the Census, *U.S. Imports for Consumption*, series FT247, annual.

No. 1128. Agricultural Imports—Value, by Selected Commodity, 1980 to 1993, and by Leading Countries of Origin, 1993

[In millions of dollars]

COMMODITY	1980	1985	1989	1990	1991	1992	1993	Leading countries of origin, 1993
Total	17,366	19,968	21,749	22,770	22,719	24,624	24,981	**Canada, Mexico, Brazil**
Competitive products	10,374	13,067	15,610	17,202	17,139	18,946	19,362	Canada, Mexico, Australia
Cattle, live	237	307	662	978	952	1,245	1,341	Canada, Mexico, Japan
Beef and veal	1,780	1,276	1,662	1,872	1,964	1,891	1,938	Australia, New Zealand, Canada
Pork	486	861	754	938	795	620	694	Canada, Denmark, Hungary
Dairy products	488	765	828	867	772	857	873	New Zealand, Ireland, Italy
Fruits and preparations. .	564	1,738	1,820	2,219	2,131	2,216	2,037	Mexico, Chile, Brazil
Vegetables and preparations	864	1,385	2,047	2,266	2,211	2,184	2,450	Mexico, Canada, Spain
Wine	692	998	930	917	915	1,087	976	France, Italy, Spain
Malt beverages	367	633	855	923	825	864	941	Netherlands, Mexico, Canada
Grains and feeds	371	623	1,219	1,189	1,321	1,586	1,813	Canada, Thailand, Italy
Sugar and related products	2,205	1,190	956	1,172	1,065	1,139	1,065	Canada, Dominican Republic, Guatemala
Oilseeds and products . .	599	756	916	949	974	1,219	1,193	Canada, Italy, Philippines
Noncompetitive products . .	6,992	6,902	6,139	5,568	5,580	5,678	5,618	Indonesia, Colombia, Brazil
Coffee and products. . . .	4,186	3,322	2,432	1,915	1,859	1,706	1,522	Colombia, Brazil, Mexico
Rubber, crude natural. . .	817	654	958	707	663	770	852	Indonesia, Thailand, Malaysia
Cocoa and products. . . .	920	1,351	991	1,094	1,092	1,080	1,062	Canada, Brazil, Ivory Coast
Bananas and plantains . .	430	763	872	939	1,006	1,097	1,071	Costa Rica, Ecuador, Colombia

Source: U.S. Dept. of Agriculture, Economic Research Service, *Foreign Agricultural Trade of the United States*, calendar year supplement.

No. 1129. Selected Farm Products—United States and World Production and Exports: 1992 to 1994

[**In metric tons, except as indicated**. Metric ton=1.102 short tons or .984 long tons]

ITEM	Unit	AMOUNT						UNITED STATES AS PERCENT OF WORLD		
		United States			World			1992	1993	1994
		1992	1993	1994	1992	1993	1994			
PRODUCTION [1]										
Wheat	Million	67	65	63	561	559	527	11.9	11.6	11.9
Corn for grain	Million	241	161	254	529	467	556	45.6	34.4	45.6
Soybeans	Million	60	51	69	117	117	133	51.2	43.6	51.8
Rice, milled	Million	5.7	5.0	6.2	351	350	353	1.6	1.4	1.7
Tobacco, unmanufactured [2] . .	1,000	781	732	674	8,325	8,345	7,775	9.4	8.8	7.8
Cotton [3]	Million bales [4] . .	17.6	16.2	16.1	96.0	82.8	76.8	18.3	19.6	21.0
EXPORTS [5]										
Wheat [6]	Million	37.0	33.1	34.0	109.4	99.5	95.6	33.8	33.2	35.6
Corn	Million	41.8	32.8	41.5	60.1	54.9	60.5	69.6	59.7	68.6
Soybeans	Million	20.9	16.0	21.0	29.5	27.7	31.9	70.1	57.8	65.8
Rice, milled basis . . . . [7]	Million	2.1	2.6	2.7	14.0	15.5	15.1	15.0	16.8	17.9
Tobacco, unmanufactured [7] . .	1,000	261	208	200	1,752	1,814	1,712	14.9	11.5	11.7
Cotton [3]	Million bales [4] . .	6.7	5.2	6.9	28.3	25.4	26.9	23.7	20.5	25.7

[1] Production years vary by commodity. In most cases, includes harvests from July 1 of the year shown through June 30 of the following year. [2] Farm sales weight basis. [3] For production and trade years ending in year shown. [4] Bales of 480 lb. net weight. [5] Trade years may vary by commodity. [6] Includes wheat flour on a grain equivalent. [7] Dried weight basis.

Source: U.S. Department of Agriculture, Foreign Agricultural Service, *Foreign Agricultural Commodity Circular Series*, periodic.

No. 1130. Cropland Used for Crops and Acreages of Crops Harvested: 1980 to 1994

[**In millions of acres**, except as indicated. See also *Historical Statistics, Colonial Times to 1970*, series K 496-501]

ITEM	1980	1985	1987	1988	1989	1990	1991	1992, prel.	1993, prel.	1994, prel.
Cropland used for crops	382	372	331	327	341	341	337	340	332	340
Index (1977=100)	101	98	88	87	90	90	89	90	88	90
Cropland harvested [1]	342	334	293	287	306	310	306	308	299	311
Crop failure	10	7	6	10	8	6	7	9	11	7
Cultivated summer fallow	30	31	32	30	27	25	24	23	22	22
Acres of crops harvested [2] . . .	352	342	302	298	318	322	318	320	309	322

[1] Land supporting one or more harvested crops. [2] Area in principal crops harvested as reported by Crop Reporting Board plus acreages in fruits, vegetables for sale, tree nuts, and farm gardens.

Source: U.S. Dept. of Agriculture, Economic Research Service, *Economic Indicators of the Farm Sector: Production and Efficiency Statistics*, annual. Also in *Agricultural Statistics*, annual. Beginning 1991 data from *Agricultural Resources: Cropland, Water, and Conservation Situation and Outlook Report*.

No. 1131. Principal Crops—Production, Supply, and Disappearance: 1990 to 1994

[Marketing year beginning May 1 for hay, June 1 for wheat, August 1 for cotton and rice, September 1 for soybeans, corn, and sorghum. Acreage, production, and yield of all crops periodically revised on basis of census data. See also *Historical Statistics, Colonial Times to 1970*, series K 506-563]

CROP AND YEAR	ACREAGE (mil.)—			Yield per acre	Pro-duction	Farm price[2]	Farm value (mil. dol.)	Total sup-ply[3]	DISAPPEAR-ANCE		Ending stocks
	Set aside[1]	Plant-ed	Har-vested						Total[4]	Ex-ports	
Corn for grain:				Bu.	Mil. bu.	$/bu.			Mil. bu.		
1990......	10.7	74.2	67.0	118.5	7,934	2.28	18,192	9,282	7,761	1,725	1,521
1991......	7.4	76.0	68.8	108.6	7,475	2.37	17,864	9,016	7,915	1,584	1,100
1992......	5.3	79.3	72.1	131.5	9,477	2.07	19,723	10,584	8,471	1,663	2,113
1993......	10.9	73.2	62.9	100.7	6,336	2.50	16,032	8,470	7,620	1,328	850
1994, prel....	2.4	79.2	72.9	138.6	10,103	2.20	22,158	10,963	9,375	2,025	1,588
Soybeans:				Bu.	Mil. bu.	$/bu.			Mil. bu.		
1990......	-	57.8	56.5	34.1	1,926	5.74	11,042	2,168	1,839	557	329
1991......	-	59.2	58.0	34.2	1,987	5.58	11,092	2,319	2,041	684	278
1992......	-	59.2	58.2	37.6	2,190	5.56	12,168	2,471	2,179	770	292
1993......	-	60.1	57.3	32.6	1,871	6.40	11,950	2,170	1,961	589	209
1994, prel....	-	61.9	61.1	41.9	2,558	5.35	13,785	2,775	2,340	800	435
Hay:				Sh. tons	Mil. sh. tons	$/ton			Mil. sh. tons		
1990......	-	(NA)	61.4	2.39	147	[5][6]80.60	10,462	174	147	(NA)	27
1991......	-	(NA)	62.5	2.45	153	[5][6]71.20	10,006	180	152	(NA)	29
1992......	-	(NA)	59.6	2.50	149	[5][6]74.30	10,436	178	157	(NA)	21
1993......	-	(NA)	60.4	2.46	149	[5][6]84.70	10,957	170	147	(NA)	23
1994, prel....	-	(NA)	60.3	2.55	154	[5][6]86.50	11,198	175	(NA)	(NA)	(NA)
Wheat:				Bu.	Mil. bu.	$/bu.			Mil. bu.		
1990......	7.5	77.0	69.1	39.5	2,730	2.61	7,184	3,303	2,435	1,069	868
1991......	15.9	69.9	57.8	34.3	1,980	3.00	5,957	2,889	2,414	1,282	475
1992......	7.3	72.2	62.8	39.3	2,467	3.24	8,010	3,012	2,481	1,354	531
1993......	5.7	72.2	62.7	38.2	2,396	3.26	7,645	3,036	2,467	1,228	568
1994, prel....	5.2	70.4	61.8	37.6	2,321	3.50	8,233	2,979	2,488	1,250	491
Cotton:				Lb.	Mil. bales[7]	cents/lb.			Mil. bales[7]		
1990......	2.0	12.3	11.7	634	[8]15.5	67.1	5,076	18.5	16.5	7.8	[9]2.3
1991......	1.2	14.1	13.0	652	[8]17.6	56.8	4,913	20.0	16.3	6.7	[9]3.7
1992......	1.7	13.2	11.1	700	[8]16.2	54.9	4,274	19.9	15.5	5.2	[9]4.7
1993......	1.4	13.4	12.8	606	[8]16.1	58.4	4,521	20.8	17.3	6.9	[9]3.5
1994, prel....	1.7	13.7	13.3	708	[8]19.7	67.7	6,413	23.2	21.3	10.0	[9]2.0
Tobacco:[10]				Lb.	Mil. lb.	$/lb.			Mil. lb.		
1990......	(NA)	(NA)	0.7	2,218	1,626	[6]1.74	2,827	4,026	1,794	631	[11]2,232
1991......	(NA)	(NA)	0.8	2,179	1,664	[6]1.77	2,951	3,896	1,616	640	[11]2,280
1992......	(NA)	(NA)	0.8	2,195	1,722	[6]1.78	3,059	4,002	1,590	630	[11]2,412
1993......	(NA)	(NA)	0.7	2,159	1,614	[6]1.75	2,831	4,026	1,438	538	[11]2,588
1994, prel....	(NA)	(NA)	0.7	2,345	1,582	[6]1.78	2,840	4,170	(NA)	(NA)	(NA)
Potatoes:				Cwt.	Mil. cwt.	$/cwt.			Mil. cwt.		
1990......	(NA)	1.4	1.4	293	402	6.08	2,431	582	[12]319	[13]17	(NA)
1991......	(NA)	1.4	1.4	304	418	4.96	2,043	618	[12]330	[13]19	(NA)
1992......	(NA)	1.3	1.3	323	425	5.52	2,336	640	[12]339	[13]23	(NA)
1993......	(NA)	1.4	1.3	326	429	6.18	2,641	642	[12]345	[13]24	(NA)
1994, prel....	(NA)	1.4	1.4	334	459	5.36	2,449	(NA)	(NA)	(NA)	(NA)
Sorghum for grain:				Bu.	Mil. bu.	$/bu.			Mil. bu.		
1990......	3.3	10.5	9.1	63.1	573	2.12	1,221	793	651	232	143
1991......	2.5	11.1	9.9	59.3	585	2.25	1,331	727	674	292	53
1992......	2.0	13.2	12.1	72.6	875	1.89	1,667	928	753	277	175
1993......	2.3	9.9	8.9	59.9	534	2.31	1,235	709	662	202	48
1994, prel....	1.6	9.8	9.0	73.0	655	2.05	1,331	703	617	210	86
Rice, rough:				Lb.	Mil. cwt.	$/cwt.			Mil. cwt.		
1990......	1.0	2.9	2.8	5,529	156	6.70	1,047	187	163	71	25
1991......	0.9	2.9	2.8	5,731	159	7.58	1,201	189	162	66	27
1992......	0.4	3.2	3.1	5,736	180	5.89	1,057	213	174	77	39
1993......	0.7	2.9	2.8	5,510	156	7.98	1,247	203	177	78	26
1994, prel....	0.3	3.4	3.3	5,964	198	6.25	1,218	232	191	83	40

- Represents zero.   NA Not available.   [1] Acreage set aside under diversion, PIK (payment-in-kind) and acreage reduction programs.   [2] Except as noted, marketing year average price. U.S. prices are computed by weighting U.S. monthly prices by estimated monthly marketings and do not include an allowance for outstanding loans and government purchases and payments. [3] Comprises production, imports, and beginning stocks.   [4] Includes feed, residual, and other domestic uses not shown separately.   [5] Prices are for hay sold baled.   [6] Season average prices received by farmers. U.S. prices are computed by weighting State prices by estimated sales and include an allowance for outstanding loans and government purchases, if any, for crops under government programs.   [7] Bales of 480 pounds, net weight.   [8] State production figures, which conform with U.S. Bureau of the Census annual ginning enumeration with allowance for cross-State ginnings, rounded to thousands and added for U.S. totals.   [9] Stock estimates based on Census Bureau data which results in an unaccounted difference between supply and use estimates and changes in ending stocks.   [10] Flue-cured and cigar wrapper, crop year July-June; all other types October-September. Farm-sales-weight basis.   [11] Includes tobacco carried over on farms.   [12] Covers potatoes used for table use, frozen and canned products, chips, and dehydration.   [13] Covers fresh potatoes, chips, frozen and dehydrated products.

Source: Production—U.S. Dept. of Agriculture, National Agricultural Statistics Service. In *Crop Production*, annual; and *Crop Values*, annual. Supply and disappearance—U.S. Dept. of Agriculture, Economic Research Service, *Feed Situation*, quarterly; *Fats and Oils Situation*, quarterly; *Wheat Situation*, quarterly; *Tobacco Situation*, quarterly; *Cotton and Wool Outlook Statistics*, periodic; and *Agricultural Supply and Demand Estimates*, periodic. All data are also in *Agricultural Statistics*, annual; and *Agricultural Outlook*, monthly.

No. 1132. Crops—Acreage and Value, by State: 1990 to 1994

| STATE | ACREAGE HARVESTED (1,000) | | | | FARM VALUE (mil. dol.) | | | 1994, prel. | |
	1990	1992	1993	1994, prel.	1990	1992	1993	Value	Rank
U.S.[1]	304,574	306,652[2]	295,529[2]	308,474[2]	80,855	87,450	84,129	94,953	(X)
AL	2,334	2,105	2,116	2,170	464	613	561	669	34
AZ	830	736	695	744	894	828	966	995	31
AR	7,603	8,110	8,305	8,160	1,648	1,948	1,782	2,115	16
CA	4,892	4,444	4,402	4,674	10,642	11,364	12,720	12,445	1
CO	5,677	5,544	5,661	5,632	1,194	1,159	1,421	1,342	25
CT	127	125	111	123	111	85	84	96	46
DE	537	515	499	494	139	135	122	135	44
FL	1,128	1,088	1,077	1,048	2,768	3,907	3,546	3,390	9
GA	4,200	3,693	3,551	3,874	1,273	1,619	1,426	1,939	20
HI	81	68	70	67	411	341	326	332	37
ID	4,226	4,006	4,322	4,244	1,735	1,815	1,870	1,910	21
IL	22,977	23,237	22,241	23,393	5,812	6,432	6,535	6,901	3
IN	11,631	11,759	11,768	12,071	3,023	3,311	3,585	3,441	8
IA	24,097	23,716	22,001	23,967	5,818	6,362	4,226	7,037	2
KS	18,794	20,237	20,485	21,724	2,610	2,953	2,930	3,496	7
KY	5,487	5,335	5,375	5,353	1,721	2,045	1,915	1,954	19
LA	4,075	4,069	3,811	3,810	1,184	1,185	1,119	1,350	24
ME	364	377	364	339	180	188	195	165	42
MD	1,601	1,619	1,569	1,506	386	421	360	394	36
MA	136	135	133	135	147	173	163	175	41
MI	6,360	6,714	6,554	6,815	1,839	1,886	2,094	2,033	18
MN	18,652	19,301	16,940	19,534	4,177	4,058	2,757	4,691	4
MS	4,611	4,855	4,709	4,813	1,149	1,274	1,035	1,426	22
MO	13,249	12,826	11,483	12,466	2,083	2,547	2,069	2,522	13
MT	9,225	8,459	8,816	8,988	881	1,023	1,264	1,183	28
NE	17,450	18,104	17,718	18,619	3,621	3,721	3,435	4,344	6
NV	554	403	527	491	154	103	150	150	43
NH	84	103	107	96	29	35	30	35	48
NJ	378	391	413	410	170	264	278	313	38
NM	967	1,051	986	985	395	395	380	407	35
NY	3,560	3,085	3,101	3,071	916	891	960	999	30
NC	4,492	4,519	4,168	4,489	1,981	2,083	1,894	2,266	14
ND	20,520	21,091	19,832	20,719	2,082	2,658	2,386	2,807	10
OH	10,339	10,037	10,009	10,277	2,597	2,695	2,629	2,779	11
OK	9,396	9,372	8,780	8,788	1,142	1,070	1,025	1,108	29
OR	2,337	2,147	2,240	2,240	1,035	1,098	1,170	1,226	27
PA	4,198	4,048	4,035	4,063	1,358	1,388	1,305	1,350	23
RI	12	13	13	12	5	7	7	8	49
SC	2,280	1,885	1,602	1,926	517	565	498	698	33
SD	14,896	15,658	14,073	15,714	1,638	1,812	1,651	2,167	15
TN	4,569	4,316	4,458	4,396	954	1,147	1,039	1,232	26
TX	16,690	18,769	18,108	17,529	4,023	3,884	4,182	4,419	5
UT	983	995	1,032	1,050	257	228	255	280	40
VT	422	433	404	409	77	98	71	76	47
VA	2,767	2,745	2,682	2,749	846	901	727	865	32
WA	3,876	3,957	4,227	3,922	2,529	2,577	2,937	2,770	12
WV	664	639	621	636	114	128	132	124	45
WI	8,615	8,096	7,511	8,074	1,830	1,754	1,606	2,105	17
WY	1,628	1,668	1,806	1,637	294	274	311	290	39

X Not applicable.   [1] Excludes Alaska.   [2] Includes sunflower and sugarbeet acreage unallocated by State.

Source: U.S. Dept. of Agriculture, National Agricultural Statistics Service, *Crop Production*, annual; and *Crop Values*, annual.

No. 1133. Corn—Acreage, Production, and Value, by Leading States: 1992 to 1994

[One bushel of corn=56 pounds. See also *Historical Statistics, Colonial Times to 1970*, series K 502-508]

| STATE | ACREAGE HARVESTED (1,000 acres) | | | YIELD PER ACRE (bu.) | | | PRODUCTION (mil. bu.) | | | PRICE ($/bu.) | | | FARM VALUE (mil. dol.) | | |
	1992	1993	1994	1992	1993	1994	1992	1993	1994	1992	1993	1994	1992	1993	1994
U.S.[1]	72,077	62,921	72,917	132	101	139	9,477	6,336	10,103	2.07	2.50	2.20	19,723	16,032	22,158
IA	12,950	11,000	12,700	147	80	152	1,904	880	1,930	2.00	2.44	2.15	3,807	2,147	4,150
IL	11,050	10,000	11,450	149	130	156	1,646	1,300	1,786	2.11	2.57	2.20	3,474	3,341	3,930
NE	7,900	7,550	8,300	135	104	139	1,067	785	1,154	2.09	2.52	2.25	2,229	1,979	2,596
MN	6,500	4,600	6,450	114	70	142	741	322	916	1.91	2.26	2.10	1,415	728	1,923
IN	5,970	5,400	5,960	147	132	144	878	713	858	2.09	2.51	2.15	1,834	1,789	1,845
OH	3,550	3,280	3,500	143	110	139	508	361	487	2.06	2.57	2.10	1,046	927	1,022
WI	2,950	2,350	3,100	104	92	141	307	216	437	2.12	2.46	2.15	650	532	940
SD	3,300	2,550	3,400	84	63	108	277	161	367	1.84	2.27	1.90	510	365	698
KS	1,730	1,800	2,130	150	120	143	260	216	305	2.15	2.61	2.35	558	564	716
MO	2,400	1,850	2,300	135	90	119	324	167	274	2.11	2.58	2.25	684	430	616
MI	2,300	2,050	2,230	105	110	117	242	226	261	1.95	2.46	2.15	471	555	561
TX	1,620	1,850	2,040	125	115	117	203	213	239	2.41	2.61	2.55	488	555	609
KY	1,300	1,220	1,220	132	104	128	172	127	156	2.23	2.58	2.25	383	327	351

[1] Includes other States, not shown separately.

Source: U.S. Dept. of Agriculture, National Agricultural Statistics Service, *Crop Production*, annual; and *Crop Values*, annual.

No. 1134. Soybeans—Acreage, Production, and Value, by Leading States: 1992 to 1994

[One bushel of soybeans=60 pounds. See also *Historical Statistics, Colonial Times to 1970*, series K 520-522]

STATE	ACREAGE HARVESTED (1,000 acres)			YIELD PER ACRE (bu.)			PRODUCTION (mil. bu.)			PRICE ($/bu.)			FARM VALUE (mil. dol.)		
	1992	1993	1994	1992	1993	1994	1992	1993	1994	1992	1993	1994	1992	1993	1994
U.S. [1] .	58,233	57,347	61,129	38	33	42	2,190	1,871	2,558	5.56	6.40	5.35	12,168	11,950	13,785
IA.....	8,170	8,300	8,770	44	31	51	359	257	447	5.54	6.34	5.35	1,992	1,631	2,393
IL.....	9,430	9,000	9,530	43	43	46	405	387	438	5.69	6.49	5.50	2,307	2,512	2,411
MN....	5,400	5,000	5,600	32	23	41	173	115	230	5.52	6.18	5.35	954	711	1,228
IN.....	4,520	4,850	4,680	43	46	47	194	223	220	5.61	6.31	5.40	1,090	1,408	1,188
OH....	3,680	4,110	3,990	40	38	44	147	156	176	5.65	6.42	5.35	832	1,003	939
MO....	4,250	3,600	4,560	38	33	38	162	119	173	5.45	6.36	5.30	880	756	918
NE....	2,460	2,500	2,860	42	36	48	103	90	137	5.37	6.20	5.15	555	558	707
AR....	3,160	3,550	3,400	33	26	34	104	92	116	5.64	6.65	5.75	588	614	665
SD....	2,250	1,750	2,420	28	22	39	63	39	94	5.18	6.03	5.00	326	232	472
KS....	1,850	1,900	2,100	37	28	36	68	53	76	5.42	6.41	5.30	371	341	401
MS....	1,750	1,950	1,920	34	22	31	60	43	60	5.69	6.53	5.55	339	280	330
MI	1,440	1,440	1,540	33	38	38	48	55	59	5.53	6.32	5.45	263	346	319

[1] Includes other States, not shown separately.
Source: U.S. Dept. of Agriculture, National Agricultural Statistics Service, *Crop Production*, annual; and *Crop Values*, annual.

No. 1135. Wheat—Acreage, Production, and Value, by Leading States: 1992 to 1994

[One bushel of wheat= 60 pounds. See also *Historical Statistics, Colonial Times to 1970*, series K 506-508]

STATE	ACREAGE HARVESTED (1,000 acres)			YIELD PER ACRE (bu.)			PRODUCTION (mil. bu.)			PRICE ($/bu.)			FARM VALUE (mil. dol.)		
	1992	1993	1994	1992	1993	1994	1992	1993	1994	1992	1993	1994	1992	1993	1994
U.S. [1] .	62,761	62,712	61,771	39.3	38.2	37.6	2,467	2,396	2,321	3.24	3.26	3.50	8,010	7,645	8,233
KS.....	10,700	11,100	11,400	34.0	35.0	38.0	364	389	433	3.13	3.00	3.40	1,139	1,166	1,473
ND.....	11,500	10,850	11,238	41.1	31.0	31.7	473	337	356	3.14	4.04	4.00	1,490	1,329	1,400
MT.....	4,947	5,264	5,378	30.1	39.2	31.7	149	206	171	3.42	3.50	3.80	509	715	646
OK.....	5,900	5,400	5,300	28.5	29.0	27.0	168	157	143	3.19	2.94	3.45	536	460	494
WA.....	2,420	2,790	2,545	49.4	63.6	52.7	120	178	134	3.80	3.24	4.10	453	574	551
ID.....	1,440	1,390	1,410	69.5	79.4	71.1	100	110	100	3.48	2.88	3.80	348	319	380
SD.....	3,733	3,488	3,353	32.0	32.0	28.4	120	112	95	3.21	3.35	3.65	385	377	347
CO.....	2,397	2,583	2,592	30.9	37.5	30.8	74	97	80	3.15	3.21	3.50	233	310	279
TX.....	3,800	3,700	2,900	34.0	32.0	26.0	129	118	75	3.18	2.86	3.20	411	339	241
MN.....	2,805	2,298	2,572	49.9	31.0	28.0	140	71	72	3.17	3.31	3.60	443	235	259
NE.....	1,850	2,100	2,100	30.0	35.0	34.0	56	74	71	3.16	3.04	3.50	175	223	250

[1] Includes other States, not shown separately.
Source: U.S. Dept. of Agriculture, National Agricultural Statistics Service, *Crop Production*, annual; and *Crop Values*, annual.

No. 1136. Greenhouse and Nursery Crops—Summary, by Type of Product: 1990 to 1994

[**In millions of dollars, except per capita**. Based on a survey of 36 commercial floriculture States and estimates by source]

ITEM	Total	Cut flowers	Potted flowering plants	Foliage plants	Bedding plants	Cut cultivated greens	Other [1]
Domestic production: [2]							
1990..................	8,531	529	747	608	1,124	121	5,402
1991..................	8,904	533	815	576	1,284	124	5,572
1992..................	9,129	519	823	624	1,391	126	5,646
1993..................	9,262	474	805	662	1,605	131	5,585
1994..................	9,500	481	812	672	1,681	136	5,718
Imports:							
1990..................	526	326	18	25	(NA)	14	143
1991..................	533	322	22	27	(NA)	13	149
1992..................	586	352	27	30	(NA)	15	162
1993..................	638	382	27	37	(NA)	20	172
1994..................	643	380	27	37	(NA)	19	180
RETAIL CONSUMER EXPENDITURES [3]							
Total:							
1990..................	33,668	4,955	1,692	1,346	2,530	659	22,486
1991..................	34,784	4,931	1,848	1,277	2,890	685	23,153
1992..................	35,575	5,032	1,872	1,390	3,130	684	23,467
1993..................	35,787	4,937	1,832	1,485	3,611	741	23,181
1994..................	36,583	4,961	1,848	1,509	3,783	755	23,727
Per capita (dol.): [4]							
1990..................	135	20	7	5	10	3	90
1994..................	140	19	7	6	14	3	91

NA Not available. [1] Includes turfgrass (sod), bulbs, nursery stock, groundcovers, and other greenhouse and nursery products except the following: seeds, cut Christmas trees, and food crops grown under cover. [2] Equivalent wholesale values. [3] Excludes services such as landscaping, installation, and maintenance. [4] Based on U.S. Bureau of the Census estimated resident population as of July 1.
Source: U.S. Dept. of Agriculture, Economic Research Service, unpublished data.

No. 1137. Commercial Vegetable and Other Specified Crops—Area, Production, and Value, 1992 to 1994, and Leading Producing States, 1994

[Except as noted, relates to commercial production for fresh market and processing combined. Includes market garden areas but excludes minor producing acreage in minor producing States. Excludes production for home use in farm and nonfarm gardens. Value is for season or crop year and should not be confused with calendar-year income]

CROP	AREA [1] (1,000 acres)			PRODUCTION [2] (1,000 short tons)			VALUE [3] (mil. dol.)			Leading States in order of production, 1994
	1992	1993	1994	1992	1993	1994	1992	1993	1994	
Beans, snap.....	278	281	302	843	857	1,011	251	270	285	WI, OR, MI [4]
Beans, dry edible..	1,530	1,622	1,845	1,131	1,096	1,459	457	540	628	ND, MI, NE
Broccoli........	111	107	111	622	540	569	284	278	336	CA, AZ, OR
Cabbage.......	87	85	81	1,329	1,403	1,467	213	290	244	NY,TX,CA [5]
Cantaloups.....	109	108	103	906	954	947	251	297	308	CA, AZ, TX
Carrots.......	107	103	106	1,640	1,584	1,525	353	296	310	CA, WA, MI
Corn, sweet	708	682	741	4,175	3,663	4,787	480	532	630	(NA)
Fresh market...	221	210	225	924	942	1,056	271	335	374	FL, CA, NY
Processed.....	486	472	516	3,252	2,721	3,731	210	197	256	WI, MN, WA
Cucumbers.....	151	167	173	1,016	1,059	1,085	292	296	282	MI, NC, TX [4]
Lettuce, head	215	208	196	3,541	3,391	3,143	882	1,087	819	CA, AZ, FL
Mushrooms [6] ...	142	(NA)	(NA)	373	388	377	670	686	721	(NA)
Onions........	142	151	160	2,737	2,853	3,152	629	813	602	CA, OR, WA
Peppers, green ...	67	65	64	721	725	793	386	437	468	FL, CA, NJ
Potatoes	1,315	1,317	1,377	21,268	21,435	22,967	2,336	2,641	2,449	ID, WA, CO
Strawberries	49	51	49	657	724	813	684	671	824	CA, FL, OR
Tomatoes.......	406	442	469	10,729	11,452	13,321	1,906	1,708	1,683	(NA)
Fresh market...	132	135	129	1,952	1,775	1,779	1,397	1,126	966	CA, FL, VA
Processed.....	274	307	340	8,777	9,677	11,542	509	582	717	CA, OH, IN
Watermelons....	230	205	208	1,889	1,889	1,999	223	262	256	FL, TX, CA

NA Not available.   [1] Area of crops for harvest for fresh market, including any partially harvested or not harvested because of low prices or other factors, plus area harvested for processing.   [2] Excludes some quantities not marketed.   [3] Fresh market vegetables valued at f.o.b. shipping point. Processing vegetables are equivalent returns at packinghouse door.   [4] Processing only.   [5] Fresh market only.   [6] Area is shown in million square feet. All data are for marketing year ending June 30.

Source: U.S. Dept. of Agriculture, National Agricultural Statistics Service, *Vegetables*, annual summary. Also in *Agricultural Statistics*, annual.

No. 1138. Fruits and Nuts—Utilized Production and Value, 1992 to 1994, and Leading Producing States, 1994

FRUIT OR NUT	UTILIZED PRODUCTION [1]				FARM VALUE (mil. dol.)			Leading States in order of production, 1994
	Unit	1992	1993	1994	1992	1993	1994	
Apples (36 States) [2]	Mil. lb	10,474	10,605	10,733	1,431	1,370	1,323	WA, NY, MI
Apricots	1,000 tons ..	106	97	145	38	39	51	CA, WA, UT
Avocados	1,000 tons ..	185	292	144	196	118	255	CA, FL, HI
Bananas	Mil. lb	12	12	13	5	4	5	HI
Cherries, sweet	1,000 tons ..	192	161	193	176	191	200	WA, OR, CA
Cherries, tart	Mil. lb	313	257	280	55	30	(NA)	MI, UT, NY
Cranberries	1,000 bbl. [3]	4,160	3,919	4,529	215	197	(NA)	MA, WI, NJ
Dates (CA)	1,000 tons ..	21	25	25	22	25	30	CA
Figs (fresh) (CA)...........	1,000 tons ..	47	61	49	19	24	21	CA
Grapefruit (4 States)	Mil. boxes [4]	55	68	65	428	311	327	FL, CA, AZ
Grapes (13 States)	1,000 tons ..	6,032	6,018	5,923	1,848	2,010	1,801	CA, WA, NY
Kiwifruit (CA)	1,000 tons ..	48	45	38	14	17	(NA)	CA
Lemons (2 States)	Mil. boxes [5]	20	25	26	257	240	238	CA, AZ
Limes (FL)...............	Mil. boxes [6]	2	1	(Z)	23	7	4	FL
Nectarines (CA)	1,000 tons ..	236	205	242	74	102	68	CA
Olives (CA)	1,000 tons ..	165	122	84	91	57	40	CA
Oranges and tangerines (4 States) .	Mil. boxes [7]	216	262	247	1,649	1,573	1,676	FL, CA, AZ
Papayas	Mil. lb	71	64	58	14	14	13	HI
Peaches (31 States)	Mil. lb	2,480	2,487	2,352	379	398	313	CA, GA, SC
Pears	1,000 tons ..	924	948	1,036	273	232	220	CA, WA, OR
Pineapples	1,000 tons ..	550	370	365	102	80	79	HI
Plums and prunes (fresh)	1,000 tons ..	828	522	812	261	239	(NA)	CA, WA, MI
Tangelos (FL).............	Mil. boxes [8]	3	3	3	24	16	18	FL
Temples (FL)	Mil. boxes [8]	2	3	2	20	12	12	FL
Almonds (shelled basis) (CA)	Mil. lb	548	490	660	691	911	776	CA
Hazelnuts (in the shell)	1,000 tons ..	28	41	20	15	26	17	OR, WA
Macadamia nuts	Mil. lb	48	49	50	33	33	35	HI
Pecans (in the shell) (11 States) ...	Mil. lb	166	365	175	240	214	184	GA, TX, NM
Pistachios	Mil. lb	147	152	128	151	163	118	CA
Walnuts, English (in the shell)	1,000 tons ..	203	260	228	286	361	(NA)	CA

NA Not available.   Z Less than 500,000 boxes.   [1] Excludes quantities not harvested or not marketed.   [2] Production in commercial orchards with 100 or more bearing age trees.   [3] Barrels of 100 pounds.   [4] Approximate average, net weight, is 65 lb. in AZ and CA through 1993 and 67 starting in 1994; 85 in FL; and 80 in TX.   [5] About 76 lb. net.   [6] Approximate net weight is 88 lb.   [7] Net contents of box varies. In CA and AZ approximate average for oranges and tangerines is 75 lb.; FL oranges, 90 lb.; TX oranges, 85 lb.; and FL tangerines, 95 lb.   [8] Approximate net weight is 90 lb.

Source: U.S. Dept. of Agriculture, National Agricultural Statistics Service, *Noncitrus Fruits and Nuts*, annual; and *Citrus Fruits*, annual.

Agriculture

No. 1139. Red Meats—Slaughter, Supply, and Use: 1980 to 1994

[**Quantities in millions of pounds** (carcass weight equivalent), except as noted. Carcass weight equivalent is the weight of the animal minus entrails, head, hide, and internal organs; includes fat, and bone. Covers Federal and State inspected, and farm slaughter. See also *Historical Statistics, Colonial Times to 1970*, series K 583-594]

YEAR AND TYPE OF MEAT	Animals slaughtered (mil. head)	Production	Imports	Supply,[1] total	Consumption[2]	Exports	Ending stocks
All red meats:							
1980....................	139.7	38,978	2,668	42,481	41,170	429	882
1990....................	126.3	38,787	3,295	42,741	40,784	1,250	707
1991....................	128.6	39,585	3,222	43,514	41,214	1,481	820
1992....................	135.3	40,978	3,135	44,933	42,436	1,739	758
1993.[3].................	133.5	40,759	3,195	44,712	42,092	1,718	900
1994 [3].................	136.3	42,683	3,163	46,746	43,592	2,151	1,003
Beef:							
1980....................	34.1	21,643	2,064	24,166	23,560	173	432
1990....................	33.4	22,743	2,356	25,434	24,031	1,006	397
1991....................	32.9	22,917	2,406	25,720	24,113	1,188	419
1992....................	33.1	23,086	2,440	25,945	24,261	1,324	360
1993.[3].................	33.5	23,049	2,401	25,810	24,006	1,275	529
1994 [3].................	34.3	24,386	2,371	27,286	25,127	1,611	548
Pork:							
1980....................	97.2	16,617	550	17,521	16,838	252	431
1990....................	85.4	15,354	898	16,565	16,031	238	296
1991....................	88.4	15,999	775	17,070	16,399	283	388
1992....................	95.2	17,234	645	18,267	17,475	407	385
1993.[3].................	93.3	17,088	740	18,213	17,419	435	359
1994 [3].................	95.8	17,696	743	18,798	17,829	531	438
Veal:							
1980....................	2.7	400	21	432	420	2	9
1990....................	1.8	327	(NA)	331	325	(NA)	6
1991....................	1.5	306	(NA)	312	305	(NA)	7
1992....................	1.4	310	(NA)	317	312	(NA)	5
1993.[3].................	1.2	285	(NA)	290	286	(NA)	4
1994 [3].................	1.2	293	(NA)	297	291	(NA)	6
Lamb and mutton:							
1980....................	5.7	318	33	362	351	1	9
1990....................	5.7	363	41	411	397	6	8
1991....................	5.8	363	41	412	397	10	6
1992....................	5.6	348	50	404	388	8	8
1993.[3].................	5.3	337	54	399	381	8	8
1994 [3].................	5.0	308	49	365	345	9	11

NA Not available. [1] Total supply equals production plus imports plus ending stocks of previous year. [2] Includes shipments to territories. [3] Forecast.

Source: U.S. Dept. of Agriculture, Economic Research Service, *Livestock and Meat Statistics*, quarterly. Also published in *Agricultural Outlook*, monthly.

No. 1140. Livestock Inventory and Production: 1980 to 1995

[**Production in live weight**; includes animals for slaughter market, younger animals shipped to other States for feeding or breeding purposes, farm slaughter and custom slaughter consumed on farms where produced, minus livestock shipped into States for feeding or breeding with an adjustment for changes in inventory. See also *Historical Statistics, Colonial Times to 1970*, series K 564-569 and 575-582]

TYPE OF LIVESTOCK	Unit	1980	1985	1987	1988	1989	1990	1991	1992	1993	1994	1995
ALL CATTLE [1]												
Inventory: [2] Number on farms.....	Mil....	111.2	109.6	102.1	99.6	96.7	95.8	96.4	97.6	99.2	101.0	103.3
Total value..........	Bil. dol..	55.8	44.0	41.6	52.1	56.2	59.0	63.1	61.5	64.4	66.5	63.6
Value per head.......	Dol....	502	402	407	523	581	616	655	630	649	659	616
Production: Quantity.....	Bil. lb..	40.3	40.1	40.5	39.7	38.9	39.2	39.8	40.3	40.9	42.7	(NA)
Beef, price per 100 lb..	Dol....	62.40	53.70	61.10	66.60	69.50	74.60	72.70	71.30	72.60	66.70	(NA)
Calves, price per 100 lb.	Dol....	76.80	62.10	78.50	89.20	90.80	95.60	98.00	89.00	91.20	87.20	(NA)
Value of production....	Bil. dol..	25.5	21.2	24.8	26.6	27.1	29.3	29.4	28.6	30.3	28.7	(NA)
HOGS AND PIGS												
Inventory: [3] Number on farms.....	Mil....	67.3	54.1	51.0	54.4	55.5	53.8	54.4	57.6	58.2	57.9	59.6
Total value..........	Bil. dol..	3.8	4.1	4.7	4.1	3.7	4.3	4.6	4.0	4.2	4.3	3.2
Value per head.......	Dol....	56.00	75.00	91.90	76.00	66.30	79.10	85.40	68.80	71.20	74.90	53.20
Production: Quantity......	Bil. lb..	23.4	20.2	20.4	21.7	21.9	21.3	22.7	23.9	23.7	24.5	(NA)
Price per 100 lb......	Dol....	38.00	44.00	51.20	42.30	42.50	53.70	49.10	41.60	45.20	39.90	(NA)
Value of production....	Bil. dol..	8.9	8.9	10.4	9.2	9.3	11.3	11.1	9.9	10.6	9.7	(NA)
SHEEP AND LAMBS												
Inventory: [2] Number on farms.....	Mil....	12.7	10.7	10.6	10.9	10.9	11.4	11.2	10.8	10.2	9.7	8.9
Total value..........	Mil. dol	993	654	799	985	894	901	732	661	714	681	664
Value per head.......	Dol....	78.20	61.10	75.70	90.00	82.40	79.30	65.60	61.20	70.00	69.90	74.70
Production: Quantity..........	Mil. lb..	746	704	733	731	811	781	796	746	689	626	(NA)
Sheep, price per 100 lb..	Dol....	21.30	23.90	29.50	25.60	24.40	23.20	19.70	25.80	28.60	30.90	(NA)
Lambs, price per 100 lb.	Dol....	63.60	67.70	77.60	69.10	66.10	55.50	52.20	59.50	64.40	65.60	(NA)
Value of production....	Mil. dol	403	434	503	434	468	374	357	394	394	373	(NA)

NA Not available. [1] Includes milk cows. [2] As of Jan. 1. [3] As of Dec. 1 of preceding year.

Source: U.S. Dept. of Agriculture, National Agricultural Statistics Service, *Meat Animals—Production, Disposition, and Income*, annual; and annual livestock summaries. Also in *Agricultural Statistics*, annual.

No. 1141. Cattle and Calves; and Hogs and Pigs—Number, Production, and Value, by State: 1991 to 1994

[See headnote, table 1140]

STATE	NUMBER ON FARMS [1] (1,000)			QUANTITY PRODUCED (mil. lb.)			VALUE OF PRODUCTION (mil. dol.)			COMMERCIAL SLAUGHTER [2] (mil. lb.)		
	1992	1993	1994	1992	1993	1994	1992	1993	1994	1991	1992	1993
CATTLE AND CALVES [3]												
U.S. [4]	97,556	99,176	100,988	40,253	40,875	42,721	28,633	30,330	28,702	38,029	38,417	38,686
CA	4,550	4,600	4,550	1,909	1,838	1,997	1,143	1,215	1,162	1,338	1,116	1,050
CO	2,900	2,950	3,000	1,895	1,938	1,924	1,411	1,498	1,336	2,634	2,938	2,915
ID	1,720	1,680	1,700	836	795	865	542	546	536	([5])	([5])	([5])
IA	4,300	4,200	4,100	2,108	2,052	1,961	1,467	1,468	1,284	1,952	1,952	1,953
KS	5,650	5,900	6,000	3,245	3,173	3,652	2,429	2,438	2,549	6,937	7,027	7,191
MN	2,700	2,750	2,700	1,190	1,187	1,205	795	798	720	1,344	1,262	1,319
MO	4,450	4,550	4,750	1,232	1,278	1,179	952	1,034	863	299	263	218
MT	2,550	2,500	2,550	1,020	1,048	1,061	705	809	774	21	22	23
NE	5,800	5,900	6,150	3,776	3,788	3,905	2,783	2,847	2,694	7,424	7,808	7,811
OK	5,300	5,200	5,100	1,824	1,895	2,092	1,349	1,533	1,559	44	46	42
SD	3,550	3,750	3,750	1,445	1,425	1,475	1,088	1,120	1,041	625	482	292
TX	13,400	14,100	14,800	6,391	6,768	7,271	4,722	5,131	4,972	6,158	6,264	6,591
WI	4,000	3,950	3,850	1,158	1,037	1,095	752	687	651	1,347	1,584	1,716
HOGS AND PIGS												
U.S. [4]	57,649	58,202	57,904	23,947	23,693	24,459	9,854	10,628	9,691	22,200	23,952	23,611
IL	5,900	5,900	5,450	2,484	2,435	2,385	1,024	1,072	924	2,221	2,239	2,041
IN	4,600	4,550	4,300	1,801	1,728	1,719	711	757	657	901	1,148	1,012
IA	15,000	14,900	15,000	6,303	6,000	6,100	2,656	2,716	2,427	7,121	7,636	7,488
MN	4,900	4,700	4,750	1,941	1,955	1,976	827	909	810	1,827	2,093	2,029
NE	4,500	4,600	4,300	1,833	1,784	1,782	763	816	728	1,355	1,443	1,398
NC	3,650	4,500	5,400	1,823	2,074	2,592	756	954	1,053	([5])	([5])	([5])

[1] Cattle and calves, as of January 1; hogs and pigs as of December 1 of preceding year. [2] Data for cattle and calves cover cattle only. Includes slaughter in federally inspected and other slaughter plants; excludes animals slaughtered on farms. [3] Includes milk cows. [4] Includes other States not shown separately. [5] Included in U.S. total. Not printed to avoid disclosing individual operation.

Source: U.S. Dept. of Agriculture, National Agricultural Statistics Service, *Meat Animals-Production, Disposition and Income*, annual.

No. 1142. Milk Production and Commercial Use: 1980 to 1994

[In billions of pounds milkfat basis]

YEAR	Production	Farm use	COMMERCIAL		Imports	Commercial supply, total	CCC net removals [1]	COMMERCIAL		Milk price per 100 lb. [2] (dol.)
			Farm marketings	Beginning stock				Ending stock	Disappearance	
1980	128.4	2.3	126.1	5.3	2.1	133.5	9.0	5.6	118.8	13.1
1990	147.7	2.0	145.7	4.1	2.7	152.5	9.0	5.1	138.3	13.7
1991	147.7	2.0	145.7	5.1	2.6	153.4	10.4	4.5	138.6	12.2
1992	150.9	1.9	149.0	4.5	2.5	155.9	9.9	4.7	141.3	13.1
1993	150.6	1.9	148.7	4.7	2.8	156.2	6.7	4.6	145.0	12.9
1994	153.6	1.9	151.7	4.6	3.0	159.1	4.8	4.3	150.1	13.1

[1] Removals from commercial supply by Commodity Credit Corporation. [2] Wholesale price received by farmers for all milk delivered to plants and dealers.

Source: U.S. Dept. of Agriculture, *Agricultural Outlook*, monthly.

No. 1143. Milk Cows—Number, Production, and Value, by State: 1992 to 1994

STATE	NUMBER ON FARMS [1] (1,000)			MILK PRODUCED ON FARMS (mil. lb.)			VALUE OF PRODUCTION [2] (mil. dol.)		
	1992	1993	1994	1992	1993	1994	1992	1993	1994
United States [3]	9,688	9,589	9,525	150,885	150,582	153,622	19,994	19,484	20,167
California	1,180	1,210	1,235	22,092	22,927	25,019	2,615	2,667	2,951
Iowa	268	264	265	4,006	4,054	3,962	521	519	511
Michigan	333	330	328	5,435	5,435	5,545	726	715	746
Minnesota	653	635	609	9,858	9,693	9,342	1,267	1,241	1,208
New York	735	727	718	11,557	11,415	11,420	1,553	1,488	1,523
Ohio	313	305	294	4,695	4,620	4,520	629	601	601
Pennsylvania	646	640	639	10,368	10,181	10,230	1,500	1,424	1,460
Texas	386	394	402	5,590	5,910	6,225	770	786	834
Washington	249	257	261	4,836	4,980	5,203	648	639	681
Wisconsin	1,618	1,543	1,494	23,844	22,844	22,412	3,140	2,945	2,912

[1] Average number during year. Represents cows and heifers that have calved, kept for milk; excluding heifers not yet fresh. [2] Valued at average returns per 100 pounds of milk in combined marketings of milk and cream. Includes value of milk fed to calves. [3] Includes other States not shown separately.

Source: U.S. Dept. of Agriculture, National Agricultural Statistics Service, *Dairy Products*, annual; and *Milk: Production, Disposition, and Income*, annual.

No. 1144. Milk Production and Manufactured Dairy Products: 1980 to 1994

[See also *Historical Statistics, Colonial Times to 1970*, series K 595-601]

ITEM	Unit	1980	1985	1988	1989	1990	1991	1992	1993	1994
Number of farms with milk cows	1,000	334	269	216	203	193	181	171	159	150
Cows and heifers that have calved, kept for milk	Mil. head	10.8	11.0	10.2	10.0	10.0	9.8	9.7	9.6	9.5
Milk produced on farms	Bil. lb	128	143	145	144	148	148	151	151	154
Production per cow	1,000 lb	11.9	13.0	14.2	14.3	14.8	15.0	15.6	15.7	16.1
Whole milk sold from farms [1]	Bil. lb	126	141	143	142	146	146	149	149	152
Sales to plants and dealers	Bil. lb	125	139	142	141	145	145	148	148	151
Value of milk produced	Bil. dol.	16.9	18.4	17.9	19.6	20.4	18.3	20.0	19.5	20.2
Gross farm income, dairy products	Bil. dol.	16.7	18.1	17.7	19.4	20.2	18.1	19.8	19.3	20.0
Cash receipts from marketing of milk and cream [1]	Bil. dol.	16.6	18.1	17.6	19.4	20.1	18.0	19.7	19.2	19.9
Sales to plants and dealers	Bil. dol.	16.3	17.8	17.4	19.1	19.9	17.8	19.5	19.0	19.6
Number of dairy manufacturing plants	Number	2,257	2,061	1,846	1,754	1,723	1,680	1,603	1,534	1,531
Manufactured dairy products:										
Butter (incl. whey butter)	Mil. lb	1,145	1,248	1,208	1,295	1,302	1,336	1,365	1,315	1,296
Cheese, total [2]	Mil. lb	3,984	5,081	5,572	5,615	6,059	6,055	6,488	6,528	6,730
American (excl. full-skim American)	Mil. lb	2,376	2,855	2,757	2,674	2,894	2,769	2,937	2,957	2,977
Cream and Neufchatel	Mil. lb	229	294	376	401	431	447	517	540	573
All Italian varieties	Mil. lb	983	1,491	1,937	2,043	2,207	2,329	2,509	2,495	2,622
Cottage cheese: Creamed [3]	Mil. lb	825	716	647	572	531	498	457	431	410
Curd, pot, and bakers	Mil. lb	667	599	557	527	493	491	502	471	463
Condensed bulk milk	Mil. lb	952	1,232	1,364	1,417	1,426	1,530	1,624	1,605	1,504
Evaporated and condensed canned milk	Mil. lb	740	656	612	545	615	543	853	557	565
Nonfat dry milk [4]	Mil. lb	1,168	1,398	998	893	902	885	872	964	1,227
Dry whey [5]	Mil. lb	690	987	1,137	1,069	1,143	1,167	1,237	1,196	1,164
Ice cream of all kinds	Mil. gal	830	901	882	831	824	863	875	866	876
Ice milk	Mil. gal	293	301	355	377	352	345	329	325	360

[1] Comprises sales to plants and dealers, and retail sales by farmers direct to consumers.　[2] Includes varieties not shown separately.　[3] Includes partially creamed (low fat).　[4] Includes dry skim milk for animal feed.　[5] Includes animal but excludes modified whey production.

Source: U.S. Dept. of Agriculture, National Agricultural Statistics Service, *Dairy Products*, annual; and *Milk: Production, Disposition, and Income*, annual.

No. 1145. Broiler, Turkey, and Egg Production: 1980 to 1994

[**For year ending November 30**. See also *Historical Statistics, Colonial Times to 1970*, series K 614-623]

ITEM	Unit	1980	1985	1986	1987	1988	1989	1990	1991	1992	1993	1994
Broilers:[1]												
Number	Million	3,963	4,470	4,649	5,004	5,238	5,517	5,864	6,137	6,402	6,694	7,018
Weight	Bil. lb.	15.5	18.9	19.7	21.5	22.5	24.0	25.6	27.2	28.8	30.6	32.5
Price per lb	Cents	27.7	30.1	34.5	28.7	33.1	36.6	32.6	30.8	31.8	34.0	35.0
Production value	Mil. dol.	4,303	5,668	6,784	6,177	7,435	8,778	8,366	8,383	9,174	10,417	11,374
Turkeys:												
Number	Million	165	185	207	240	242	261	282	285	289	288	289
Weight	Bil. lb.	3.1	3.7	4.1	4.9	5.1	5.5	6.0	6.1	6.3	6.4	6.6
Price per lb	Cents	41.3	49.1	47.1	34.8	38.6	40.9	39.4	38.0	37.7	39.0	40.4
Production value	Mil. dol.	1,272	1,820	1,951	1,703	1,951	2,235	2,393	2,353	2,396	2,509	2,672
Eggs:												
Number	Billion	69.7	68.4	69.1	70.4	69.7	67.2	67.9	69.0	70.5	71.9	73.9
Price per dozen	Cents	56.3	57.2	61.5	54.7	52.8	68.9	70.9	67.8	57.6	63.4	61.4
Production value	Mil. dol.	3,268	3,262	3,543	3,209	3,073	3,877	4,021	3,915	3,397	3,800	3,777

[1] Young chickens of the heavy breeds and other meat-type birds, to be marketed at 2-5 lbs. live weight and from which no pullets are kept for egg production.

Source: U.S. Dept. of Agriculture, National Agricultural Statistics Service, *Poultry—Production and Value*, annual; *Turkeys*, annual; and *Layers and Egg Production*, annual.

No. 1146. Poultry—Production, by State: 1992 to 1994

[**In millions of pounds, liveweight production**. See *Historical Statistics, Colonial Times to 1970*, series K 614 and 621 for U.S. totals]

STATE	BROILERS			TURKEYS			STATE	BROILERS			TURKEYS		
	1992	1993	1994	1992	1993	1994		1992	1993	1994	1992	1993	1994
U.S. [1]	28,829	30,618	32,529	6,334	6,433	6,610	MS	2,145	2,430	2,712	(NA)	(NA)	(NA)
AL	3,855	3,970	4,184	(NA)	(NA)	(NA)	MO	542	580	658	431	447	478
AR	4,499	4,615	4,854	518	513	510	NC	2,852	3,138	3,218	1,321	1,366	1,362
CA	1,188	1,102	1,131	509	486	449	OH	117	137	166	145	158	176
DE	1,256	1,295	1,369	(NA)	(NA)	(NA)	OK	600	666	799	(NA)	(NA)	(NA)
FL	541	552	571	(NA)	(NA)	(NA)	PA	572	547	597	178	169	202
GA	4,026	4,416	4,724	61	44	42	SC	447	514	589	196	195	173
IN	(NA)	(NA)	(NA)	350	334	336	TN	509	552	549	(NA)	(NA)	(NA)
IA	92	90	83	232	231	250	TX	1,582	1,623	1,670	(NA)	(NA)	(NA)
KY	173	174	237	(NA)	(NA)	(NA)	VA	1,048	1,124	1,188	363	393	409
MD	1,262	1,332	1,311	3	4	3	WA	169	180	200	(NA)	(NA)	(NA)
MN	231	238	249	800	815	847	WV	177	303	384	77	80	104

NA Not available.　[1] Includes other States not shown separately.

Source: U.S. Dept. of Agriculture, National Agricultural Statistics Service, *Poultry—Production and Value*, annual; and *Turkeys*, annual.

Natural Resources

This section presents data on the area, ownership, production, trade, reserves and disposition of natural resources. Natural resources is defined here as including forestry, fisheries, and mining and mineral products.

Forestry.—Presents data on the area, ownership, and timber resource of commercial timberland; forestry statistics covering the National Forests and Forest Service cooperative programs; product data for lumber, pulpwood, woodpulp, paper and paperboard, and similar data.

The principal sources of data relating to forests and forest products are: An Analysis of the Timber Situation in the United States, 1989—2040, 1990; Forest Resources of the United States, 1992, 1993; U.S. Timber Production, Trade, Consumption, and Price Statistics; Land Areas of the National Forest System, issued annually by the Forest Service of the Department of Agriculture; Agricultural Statistics issued by the Department of Agriculture; and reports of the census of manufactures (taken every 5 years) and the annual Current Industrial Reports, issued by the Bureau of the Census. Additional information is published in the monthly Survey of Current Business of the Bureau of Economic Analysis; and the annual Wood Pulp and Fiber Statistics and The Statistics of Paper, Paperboard, and Wood Pulp of the American Forest and Paper Association, Washington, DC.

The completeness and reliability of statistics on forests and forest products vary considerably. The data for forest land area and stand volumes are much more reliable for areas which have been recently surveyed than for those for which only estimates are available. In general, more data are available for lumber and other manufactured products such as particle board and softwood panels, etc., than for the primary forest products such as poles and piling and fuelwood.

Fisheries.—The principal source of data relating to fisheries is Fisheries of the United States, issued annually by the National Marine Fisheries Service (NMFS), National Oceanic and Atmospheric Administration (NOAA).

In Brief

	1994
Paper and board production	90.5 mil. sh. tns.
Recovered paper consumption	30.0 mil. sh. tns.

Petroleum balance, 1993:
Products supplied	6.3 billion barrels
Net imports	2.4 billion barrels
Stocks	1.6 billion barrels

The NMFS collects and disseminates data on commercial landings of fish and shellfish. Annual reports include quantity and value of commercial landings of fish and shellfish disposition of landings, number of fishermen, and number and kinds of fishing vessels and fishing gear. Reports for the fish-processing industry include annual output for the wholesaling and fish processing establishments, annual and seasonal employment. The Magnuson Fishery Conservation and Management Act of 1976 (Magnuson Act), Public Law 94-265 as amended, provides for the conservation and management of all fishery resources within the U.S. Exclusive Economic Zone (EEZ), and gives the Federal Government exclusive authority over domestic and foreign fisheries within 200 nautical miles of U.S. shores and over certain living marine resources beyond the EEZ. Within the EEZ, the total allowable level of foreign fishing, if any, is that portion of the "optimum yield" not harvested by U.S. vessels. Adjustments in the "optimum yield" level may occur periodically. For details, see Fisheries of the United States, 1993. The NMFS collects and disseminates data on catches by foreign fishing vessels in the EEZ.

Mining and mineral products.—Presents data relating to mineral industries and their products, general summary measures of production and employment, and more detailed data on production, prices, imports and exports, consumption, and distribution for specific industries and products. Data on mining and mineral products may also be found in sections 26 and 30 of this Abstract; data on mining employment may be found in section 13.

Mining comprises the extraction of minerals occurring naturally (coal, ores, crude petroleum, natural gas) and quarrying, well operation, milling, refining and processing and other preparation customarily done at the mine or well site or as a part of extraction activity. (Mineral preparation plants are usually operated together with mines or quarries.) Exploration for minerals is included as is the development of mineral properties.

The principal governmental sources of these data are the Minerals Yearbook, published by the Bureau of Mines, Department of the Interior, and various monthly and annual publications of the Energy Information Administration, Department of Energy. See text, section 19 for list of Department of Energy publications. In addition, the Bureau of the Census conducts a census of mineral industries every 5 years. Non-government sources include the Annual Statistical Report of the American Iron and Steel Institute, Washington, DC; Metals Week and the monthly Engineering and Mining Journal, issued by the McGraw-Hill Publishing Co., New York, NY; The Iron Age, issued weekly by the Chilton Co., Philadelphia, PA; and the Joint Association Survey of the U.S. Oil and Gas Industry, conducted jointly by the American Petroleum Institute, Independent Petroleum Association of America, and Mid-Continent Oil and Gas Association.

Mineral statistics, with principal emphasis on commodity detail, have been collected by the Geological Survey or by the Bureau of Mines since 1880. Current data in Bureau of Mines publications include quantity and value of nonfuel minerals produced, sold or used by producers, or shipped; quantity of minerals stocked; crude materials treated and prepared minerals recovered; and consumption of mineral raw materials. The U.S. Mine Safety and Health Administration also collects and publishes data on workhours, employment, accidents, and injuries in the mineral industries, except petroleum and natural gas. In October 1977, mineral fuel data collection activities of the Bureau of Mines were transferred to the Energy Information Administration.

Censuses of mineral industries have been conducted by the Bureau of the Census at various intervals since 1840. Beginning with the 1967 census, legislation provides for a census to be conducted every 5th year for years ending in "2" and "7." The censuses provide, for the various types of mineral establishments, information on operating costs, capital expenditures, labor, equipment, and energy requirements in relation to their value of shipments and other receipts. Commodity statistics on many manufactured mineral products are also collected by the Bureau at monthly, quarterly, or annual intervals and issued in its Current Industrial Reports series.

In general, figures shown in the individual commodity tables include data for outlying areas and may therefore not agree with summary tables. Except for crude petroleum and refined products, the export and import figures include foreign trade passing through the customs districts of United States and Puerto Rico, but exclude shipments between U.S. territories and the customs districts.

Historical statistics.—Tabular headnotes provide cross-references, where applicable, to *Historical Statistics of the United States, Colonial Times to 1970.* See Appendix IV.

No. 1147. National Forest System—Summary: 1970 to 1993

[**For fiscal years ending in year shown;** see text, section 9. Includes Alaska and Puerto Rico, except as noted. See *Historical Statistics, Colonial Times to 1970*, series J 33-34, for similar grazing data, and L 15-31]

ITEM	Unit	1970	1980	1985	1988	1989	1990	1991	1992	1993
Timber cut, total value	Mil. dol	309	737	725	1,243	1,313	1,191	1,012	938	918
Commercial and cost sales: [1]										
Volume	Mil. bd.	11,527	9,178	10,941	12,649	11,951	10,500	8,475	7,290	5,917
Value	Mil. dol	308	730	721	1,240	1,310	1,188	1,009	935	914.6
Free use:										
Volume	Mil. bd.	179	2,070	399	223	214	151	121	80	80
Value [2]	Mil. dol	0.3	5.7	2.2	1.2	1.2	1.0	1.0	0.8	0.8
Misc. forest products:										
Value	Mil. dol	0.7	1.1	1.7	2.0	2.2	2.6	2.7	2.7	2.8
Livestock grazing: [3]										
Cattle and horses [4]	1,000 .	1,607	1,521	1,565	1,313	1,526	1,236	1,265	1,216	(NA)
Sheep and goats	1,000 .	2,105	1,328	1,183	1,067	972	958	1,029	1,017	(NA)
Roads and trails:										
Road construction [5]	Miles . .	942	925	1,903	1,352	866	857	910	853	816
Trail construction [5][6]	Miles . .	278	2,419	987	1,834	1,944	1,635	1,921	1,976	1976
Receipts, total	Mil. dol	300	703	636	980	1,051	971	772	614	503
Timber use	Mil. dol	284	625	515	888	910	849	667	520	425
Grazing use	Mil. dol	4	16	9	9	11	10	11	11	11
Special land use, etc	Mil. dol	11	62	112	83	130	112	93	84	67
Payments to local govt. [7]	Mil. dol	73	240	229	325	368	368	335	322	323
25-percent fund [8]	Mil. dol	72	234	212	317	354	358	327	(NA)	(NA)
Other [9]	Mil. dol	1	7	17	8	15	10	8	(NA)	(NA)
Allotments to Forest Service [10] . . .	Mil. dol	30	73	60	104	111	106	88	(NA)	(NA)
Roads and trails	Mil. dol	29	65	55	92	96	91	73	(NA)	(NA)
Other	Mil. dol	1	8	5	12	15	14	16	(NA)	(NA)

NA Not available. [1] Includes land exchanges. [2] Includes some free use timber not reducible to board feet. [3] For 1970, data for livestock permitted to graze; thereafter, for number actually grazed. Calendar-year data, prior to 1980. Excludes Puerto Rico. [4] Excludes animals under 6 months of age. 1970 includes swine. Beginning 1980, includes burros. [5] Includes reconstruction. [6] Beginning 1980, includes work accomplished by Human Resource Programs and volunteers. [7] Payments made in following year. [8] Includes Tongass Alaska suspense account. [9] Includes Arizona and New Mexico School Fund (through 1980), State of Minnesota, and receipts paid to counties under Bankhead-Jones Farm Tenant Act. [10] For use in following year.

Source: U.S. Forest Service. In *Agricultural Statistics*, annual; and unpublished data.

No. 1148. Forest and Timberland Area, Sawtimber and Stock: 1970 to 1992

[As of **Jan. 1**]

YEAR AND REGION	Total forest land (mil. acres)	TIMBERLAND, OWNERSHIP [1]				SAWTIMBER, NET VOLUME [3]		GROWING STOCK, NET VOLUME [4]	
		All owner-ships (mil. acres)	Federally owned or managed [2] (mil. acres)	State, county, and municipal (mil. acres)	Private (mil. acres)	Total (bil. bd. ft.)	Softwood (bil. bd. ft.)	Total (bil. cu. ft.)	Softwood (bil. cu. ft.)
United States, 1970 .	754	504	116	29	360	2,587	2,035	694	458
North	(NA)	154	11	18	126	295	81	146	39
South	(NA)	203	15	3	185	569	302	191	87
Rocky Mountains	(NA)	65	42	2	20	398	384	101	95
Pacific Coast	(NA)	82	47	5	29	1,325	1,268	257	238
United States, 1987 .	731	485	97	34	354	2,853	2,040	766	453
North	165	154	11	19	124	459	126	190	48
South	203	197	16	4	177	781	388	245	106
Rocky Mountains	142	61	39	3	20	411	394	108	100
Pacific Coast	220	72	31	8	32	1,202	1,132	223	199
United States, 1992 .	737	490	97	35	358	2,992	2,047	786	450
North	168	158	11	19	127	540	137	207	51
South	212	199	16	4	179	842	389	251	103
Rocky Mountains	140	63	40	3	20	415	397	110	101
Pacific Coast	217	70	30	8	32	1,196	1,124	218	195

NA Not available. [1] Timberland is forest land that is producing or is capable of crops of industrial wood and not withdrawn from timber utilization by statute or administrative regulation. Areas qualifying as timberland have the capability of producing in excess of 20 cubic feet per acre per year of industrial wood in natural stands. Currently inaccessible and inoperable areas are included. [2] Includes Indian lands. [3] Sawtimber is timber suitable for sawing into lumber. Live trees of commercial species containing at least one 12-foot sawlog or two noncontiguous 8-foot logs, and meeting regional specifications for freedom from defect. Softwood trees must be at least 9.0-inches diameter, and hardwood trees must be at least 11.0-inches diameter at 4 1/2 feet above ground. International 1/4-inch rule. [4] Live trees of commercial species meeting specified standards of quality or vigor. Cull trees are excluded. Includes only trees 5.0-inches diameter or larger at 4 1/2 feet above ground.

Source: U.S. Forest Service, *Forest Resources of the United States, 1992.*

No. 1149. National Forest System Land—States and Other Areas: 1990 and 1992

[In thousands of acres. As of **Sept. 30.** See also *Historical Statistics, Colonial Times to 1970,* series L 10-11]

STATE	GROSS AREA WITHIN UNIT BOUNDARIES [1]		NATIONAL FOREST SYSTEM LAND [2]		OTHER LANDS WITHIN UNIT BOUNDARIES	
	1990	1992	1990	1992	1990	1992
United States.	231,443	231,502	191,324	191,453	40,119	40,049
Alabama.	1,280	1,288	658	659	622	629
Alaska.	24,345	24,345	22,220	22,193	2,126	2,152
Arizona.	11,880	11,887	11,239	11,247	642	641
Arkansas	3,490	3,490	2,509	2,529	981	961
California	24,401	24,401	20,619	20,616	3,782	3,785
Colorado.	16,039	16,037	14,462	14,467	1,577	1,570
Connecticut.	-	(Z)	-	(Z)	-	-
Delaware	-	-	-	-	-	-
Florida	1,246	1,254	1,128	1,135	118	119
Georgia	1,846	1,846	859	860	987	986
Hawaii	-	(Z)	-	(Z)	-	-
Idaho.	21,674	21,674	20,438	20,441	1,236	1,233
Illinois	840	840	266	268	573	572
Indiana.	644	644	188	189	456	455
Iowa	-	-	-	-	-	-
Kansas.	116	116	108	108	8	8
Kentucky	2,102	2,102	670	673	1,431	1,428
Louisiana	1,022	1,022	601	601	422	421
Maine.	93	93	53	53	40	40
Maryland	-	-	-	-	-	-
Massachusetts.	-	-	-	-	-	-
Michigan.	4,885	4,895	2,816	2,849	2,069	2,046
Minnesota.	5,467	5,467	2,810	2,815	2,657	2,652
Mississippi	2,310	2,310	1,150	1,153	1,160	1,157
Missouri	3,082	3,082	1,475	1,478	1,606	1,603
Montana.	19,101	19,102	16,806	16,806	2,295	2,296
Nebraska	442	442	352	352	90	90
Nevada	6,275	6,275	5,797	5,801	478	474
New Hampshire	825	825	720	721	105	104
New Jersey.	-	-	-	-	-	-
New Mexico	10,367	10,367	9,321	9,321	1,046	1,045
New York	13	13	13	13	-	-
North Carolina.	3,165	3,165	1,232	1,234	1,934	1,932
North Dakota.	1,106	1,106	1,106	1,106	-	(Z)
Ohio	833	833	203	212	630	622
Oklahoma.	461	465	297	301	165	164
Oregon.	17,502	17,504	15,651	15,655	1,851	1,849
Pennsylvania.	744	744	513	513	231	231
Rhode Island.	-	-	-	-	-	-
South Carolina.	1,376	1,376	607	609	768	767
South Dakota	2,344	2,352	1,996	2,013	349	339
Tennessee	1,212	1,212	628	628	585	585
Texas.	1,994	1,994	753	755	1,241	1,240
Utah	9,186	9,186	8,099	8,099	1,087	1,087
Vermont	815	816	340	345	475	471
Virginia.	3,223	3,223	1,645	1,648	1,578	1,575
Washington.	10,050	10,061	9,151	9,160	899	901
West Virginia.	1,863	1,863	1,025	1,025	838	838
Wisconsin.	2,023	2,023	1,517	1,518	506	505
Wyoming	9,704	9,704	9,255	9,255	449	449

- Represents zero.   Z Less than half the unit of measure.   [1] Comprises all publicly and privately owned land within authorized boundaries of national forests, purchase units, national grasslands, land utilization projects, research and experimental areas, and other areas.   [2] Federally owned land within the "gross area within unit boundaries."

Source: U.S. Forest Service, *Land Areas of the National Forest System,* annual.

No. 1150. Public Lands—Disposal: 1980 to 1993

[For fiscal year ending in year shown: see text, section 9. Period figures are totals, not annual averages.
See also *Historical Statistics, Colonial Times to 1970,* series J 10-15 and J 28-32]

ITEM	Unit	1980	1985	1987	1988	1989	1990	1991	1992	1993
Applications, entries, and selections allowed [1] . . .	1,000 acres	1,167	1,404	1	1	1	7	1	1	-
Applications, entries, and selections approved [1] . .	1,000 acres	175	6,491	1,812	1,387	579	238	436	1,219	819
Patents and certificates [1] . .	1,000 acres	2,495	4,217	3,000	5,419	780	1,052	476	1,585	1,460
Mineral class, total	Number. . .	106,125	119,419	89,789	82,585	83,762	81,355	83,358	72,337	59,631
Leases [2]	Number. . .	105,963	119,101	89,546	82,450	83,656	81,248	83,259	72,192	59,523
Permits [2]	Number. . .	132	316	231	121	96	96	88	121	84
Licenses . . . . . [3] . .	Number. . .	30	2	12	14	10	11	11	24	24
Grazing Leases [3]	Number. . .	7,700	7,387	7,164	7,197	7,263	7,105	7,185	7,036	6,994
Permits [4]	Number. . .	14,741	12,493	12,368	12,537	12,362	12,153	12,312	12,128	12,069

- Represents or rounds to zero.   [1] Excludes Indian fee and reissue trust and corrective patents.   [2] Excludes free-use permits for disposition of mineral materials.   [3] Beginning 1985, as of September 30.   [4] Licenses and permits within grazing districts.
Source: U.S. Bureau of Land Management, *Public Land Statistics,* annual.

No. 1151. Timber-Based Industries—Summary of Manufactures: 1991 and 1992

[Data based on *1987 Standard Industrial Classification Manual,* published by the Office of Management and Budget, see text, section 26. N.e.c. = Not elsewhere classified]

INDUSTRY	SIC [1] code	1991			1992		
		All employees		Value of ship-ments (bil. dol.)	All employees		Value of ship-ments (bil. dol.)
		Num-ber (1,000)	Payroll (mil. dol.)		Num-ber (1,000)	Payroll (mil. dol.)	
Logging and sawmills	241/242	207.6	4,307	28.9	221.7	4,739	31.3
Logging	2411	78.1	1,561	11.4	83.6	1,693	13.8
Sawmills and planing mills, general	2421	129.5	2,747	17.5	138.1	3,046	17.5
Hardwood dimension and flooring mills.	2426	26.1	462	1.7	28.5	502	2.0
Special product sawmills, n.e.c.	2429	2.0	36	0.2	1.8	31	0.1
Millwork and veneer [2]	243	209.9	4,487	21.4	224.6	5,027	24.9
Millwork	2431	84.9	1,836	9.0	85.9	1,973	9.6
Wood kitchen cabinets	2434	57.1	1,139	4.2	63.0	1,311	5.0
Hardwood veneer and plywood.	2435	17.3	320	1.9	20.2	400	2.3
Softwood veneer and plywood	2436	31.7	810	4.6	313	828	5.5
Structural wood members, n.e.c.	2439	18.9	382	1.8	24.3	516	2.5
Wood containers	244	39.8	634	2.9	40.0	639	2.9
Nailed and lock corner wood boxes	2441	6.2	100	0.4	5.9	101	0.4
Wood pallets and skids	2448	27.1	413	2.0	28.6	448	2.1
Wood containers, n.e.c	2449	6.5	120	0.4	5.5	90	0.3
Wood buildings, mobile homes	245	54.1	1,106	6.0	56.2	1,230	6.6
Mobile homes	2451	35.1	714	3.9	37.1	813	4.5
Prefabricated wood buildings and components	2452	19.0	392	2.0	19.1	416	2.1
Miscellaneous wood products	249	90.9	1,706	9.5	84.9	1,740	10.3
Wood preserving	2491	11.7	233	2.6	11.0	237	2.7
Reconstituted wood products	2493	21.0	537	3.0	22.9	613	3.9
Wood products, n.e.c	2499	58.1	936	3.8	51.0	890	3.7
Pulp mills	261	16.8	697	5.3	15.9	688	5.5
Paper mills	262	130.3	5,224	33.3	130.7	5,425	32.8
Paperboard mills	263	50.6	2,027	15.0	51.5	2,135	16.1
Paperboard containers and boxes	265	198.6	5,392	30.6	199.0	5,710	32.6
Setup paperboard boxes	2652	8.7	150	0.6	6.6	129	0.4
Corrugated and solid fiber boxes.	2653	108.7	3,047	18.0	111.0	3,247	19.7
Fiber cans, tubes, drums, & similar prods.	2655	12.9	341	1.9	12.4	337	1.9
Sanitary food containers, except folding	2656	17.6	411	2.7	15.4	386	2.5
Folding paperboard boxes, incl. sanitary	2657	50.7	1,443	7.4	53.6	1,610	8.0
Converted paper and paperboard products [3]	267	224.3	6,043	44.6	229.2	6,521	46.0
Packaging paper & plastics film, coated & laminated.	2671	15.4	492	3.1	18.2	560	3.7
Coated and laminated paper, n.e.c	2672	34.2	992	7.4	32.3	1,032	7.6
Plastics, foil, and coated paper bags	2673	35.4	875	5.1	38.4	979	5.7
Uncoated paper and multiwall bags	2674	17.9	398	2.7	18.7	440	2.8
Die-cut paper and paperboard and cardboard	2675	17.0	408	2.3	15.6	373	2.0
Sanitary paper products	2676	38.8	1,343	15.6	40.5	1,451	15.5
Envelopes	2677	24.5	616	2.7	24.9	672	2.8
Stationery, tablets, and related products	2678	10.1	209	1.4	9.3	218	1.4
Converted paper and paperboard products, n.e.c. . .	2679	30.9	711	4.3	31.2	795	4.4

[1] Standard Industrial Classification code; see text, section 13.   [2] Includes plywood and structural members.   [3] Except containers and boxes.
Source: U.S. Bureau of the Census, *Census of Manufactures, 1987 Final Industry Series,* MC87-I-24A-D and MC87-I-26A-C, and *Annual Survey of Manufactures.*

No. 1152. Timber Products—Production, Foreign Trade, and Consumption, by Type of Product: 1970 to 1988

[In millions of cubic feet, roundwood equivalent. See also *Historical Statistics, Colonial Times to 1970,* series L 72-97]

ITEM	Unit	1970	1975	1980	1983	1984	1985	1986	1987	1988, prel.
Industrial roundwood:										
Domestic production	Mil. cu. ft..	11,105	10,575	12,120	12,065	12,725	12,515	13,845	14,670	14,985
Imports	Mil. cu. ft..	2,430	2,215	3,250	3,710	4,165	4,340	4,375	4,575	4,445
Exports	Mil. cu. ft..	1,540	1,685	2,350	2,110	2,060	2,070	2,300	2,650	3,200
Consumption.	Mil. cu. ft..	11,995	11,105	13,020	13,665	14,830	14,785	15,920	16,595	16,230
Lumber:										
Domestic production	Mil. cu. ft..	5,215	4,890	5,300	5,370	5,770	5,665	6,545	6,990	6,920
Plywood and veneer:										
Domestic production	Mil. cu. ft..	1,020	1,165	1,175	1,365	1,400	1,420	1,505	1,650	1,630
Pulp products:										
Domestic production	Mil. cu. ft..	3,835	3,485	4,390	4,165	4,355	4,165	4,545	4,670	4,885
Logs:										
Imports	Mil. cu. ft..	25	15	25	30	30	20	15	15	15
Pulpwood chips, exports.	Mil. cu. ft..	145	195	275	155	145	145	150	160	215
Fuelwood consumption.	Mil. cu. ft..	540	570	3,105	3,235	3,620	3,450	3,115	3,150	3,360
Timber products, per capita .	Cu. ft	61.1	54.0	70.8	72.0	77.9	76.2	78.8	81.0	79.5
Industrial roundwood	Cu. ft	58.5	51.4	57.2	58.2	62.6	61.8	65.9	68.0	65.9
Fuelwood.	Cu. ft	2.6	2.6	13.6	13.8	15.3	14.4	12.9	12.9	13.6
Lumber	Bd. ft . . .	193.0	171.0	188.0	190.0	205.0	207.0	224.0	233.0	221.0
Plywood and veneer	Bd. ft . . .	34.0	32.0	30.0	34.0	34.0	35.0	37.0	39.0	37.0
Pulp products	Cords (128 cu. ft.)	0.3	0.2	0.3	0.3	0.3	0.3	0.3	0.3	0.3

Source: U.S. Forest Service, *U.S. Timber Production, Trade, Consumption, and Price Statistics, 1960-88,* annual.

No. 1153. Lumber Consumption, by Species Group and End Use: 1970 to 1992

[In million board feet, except per capita in board feet. Per capita consumption based on estimated resident population as of **July 1**]

ITEM	1970	1986	1991	1992	END-USE	1970	1976	1986	1991
Total	39.9	57.0	54.8	56.0	New housing	13.3	17.0	19.3	15.0
					Residential upkeep and improvements	4.7	5.7	10.1	11.6
Per capita	194	237	217	219	New nonresidential construction [1]	4.7	4.5	5.3	5.4
Species group:					Manufacturing.	4.7	4.9	4.8	5.6
Softwoods	32.0	48.0	44.0	45.7	Shipping	5.7	5.9	6.8	8.2
Hardwoods	7.9	9.0	10.8	10.3	Other [2]	6.8	6.7	10.9	8.8

[1] In addition to new construction, includes railroad ties laid as replacements in existing track and lumber used by railroads for railcar repair.   [2] Includes upkeep and improvement of nonresidential buildings and structures; made-at-home projects, such as furniture, boats, and picnic tables; made-on-the-job items such as advertising and display structures; and miscellaneous products and uses.

Source: U.S. Forest Service. *The 1993 RPA Timber Assessment Update,* forthcoming.

No. 1154. Selected Timber Products—Producer Price Indexes: 1980 to 1994

[See also *Historical Statistics, Colonial Times to 1970,* series L 206-210]

PRODUCT	Unit	1980	1985	1990	1992	1993	1994
Lumber and wood products, except furniture . . .	Dec. 1984=100 . .	(NA)	100.3	117.0	129.7	148.3	154.4
Logging camps and logging contractors	Dec. 1981=100 . .	(NA)	94.8	135.6	151.3	186.4	192.6
Sawmills and planing mills	Dec. 1984=100 . .	(NA)	99.7	113.7	131.3	161.8	165.2
Millwork, veneer, and plywood [1]	Dec. 1984=100 . .	(NA)	99.9	115.4	128.4	142.8	148.7
Softwood plywood	Dec. 1980=100 . .	91.4	90.0	102.5	124.2	145.4	153.1
Wood containers	June 1985=100 . .	(NA)	(NA)	113.9	123.5	141.7	147.4
Wood buildings and mobile homes	Dec. 1984=100 . .	(NA)	100.6	115.5	121.5	129.5	139.8
Particleboard.	Dec. 1982=100 . .	92.1	110.0	117.1	120.7	138.6	156.2
Paper and allied products	Dec. 1984=100 . .	(NA)	98.8	121.9	121.2	120.2	123.6
Pulp mills	Dec. 1982=100 . .	105.5	100.9	153.8	118.5	105.8	117.2
Paper mill products; except building paper. . .	June 1981=100 . .	93.5	109.5	134.0	126.6	126.6	128.4
Paperboard mills.	Dec. 1982=100 . .	97.3	112.0	146.0	142.6	138.3	152.2
Converted paper and paperboard products [2] .	June 1993=100 . .	(NA)	(NA)	(NA)	(NA)	(NA)	100.6
Paperboard containers and boxes	Dec. 1984=100 . .	(NA)	98.4	117.7	118.5	118.0	123.7

NA Not available.   [1] Includes structural wood members.   [2] Excludes containers and boxes.

Source: U.S. Bureau of Labor Statistics, *Producer Price Indexes,* monthly.

No. 1155. Selected Species—Stumpage Prices In Current and Constant (1982) Dollars: 1980 to 1993

[**In dollars per 1,000 board feet.** Stumpage prices are based on sales of sawtimber from National Forests. See also *Historical Statistics, Colonial Times to 1970*, series L 199-205]

SPECIES	1980	1983	1984	1985	1986	1987	1988	1989	1990	1991	1992	1993
CURRENT DOLLARS												
Softwoods:												
Douglas fir [1]	432	162	133	126	161	190	256	390	466	395	477	318
Southern pine [2]	155	141	139	91	104	136	142	131	127	166	198	217
Sugar pine [3]	667	138	84	110	170	288	260	289	285	241	492	598
Ponderosa pine [3][4]	206	104	123	101	157	209	182	292	252	238	292	535
Western hemlock [5]	213	62	62	51	75	105	163	223	203	164	165	364
Hardwoods:												
All eastern hardwoods [6]	52	60	90	65	70	88	151	136	146	160	167	264
Oak, white, red, and black [6]	66	88	145	95	108	147	146	179	188	164	211	195
Maple, sugar [7]	70	55	81	70	66	81	108	129	135	121	145	220
CONSTANT (1982) DOLLARS [8]												
Softwoods:												
Douglas fir [1]	481	160	128	122	160	185	240	347	401	339	407	270
Southern pine [2]	173	139	134	88	103	132	133	117	109	143	169	184
Sugar pine [3]	742	136	81	106	169	280	244	258	245	207	419	508
Ponderosa pine [3][4]	230	103	118	98	156	204	170	260	217	204	249	455
Western hemlock [5]	237	61	60	49	75	103	152	199	175	141	140	309
Hardwoods:												
All eastern hardwoods [6]	58	59	87	63	70	86	142	121	126	137	142	224
Oak, white, red, and black [6]	73	87	140	92	108	143	137	159	162	140	180	166
Maple, sugar [7]	78	54	78	68	66	78	101	115	116	104	123	187

[1] Western Washington and western Oregon.   [2] Southern region.   [3] Pacific Southwest region (formerly California region).
[4] Includes Jeffrey pine.   [5] Pacific Northwest region.   [6] Eastern and Southern regions.   [7] Eastern region.   [8] Deflated by the producer price index, all commodities.

Source: U.S. Forest Service, *U.S. Timber Production, Trade, Consumption, and Price Statistics*, annual.

No. 1156. Lumber Production and Consumption, by Kind of Wood: 1988 to 1993

[**In millions of board feet, except as indicated.** Based on sample survey; see source for sampling variability. See also *Historical Statistics, Colonial Times to 1970*, series L 98-112 and L 122-137]

ITEM	1988	1989	1990 [1]	1991 [1]	1992	1993
Total production	**44,576**	**43,576**	**43,466**	**40,031**	**(NA)**	**(NA)**
Softwoods [2]	36,845	36,040	36,224	33,250	(NA)	(NA)
Hardwoods [2]	7,731	7,536	7,242	6,781	(NA)	(NA)
Domestic consumption	**58,834**	**58,847**	**54,482**	**51,134**	**(NA)**	**(NA)**
Percent net imports [3]	16.5	16.7	15.7	15.5	(NA)	(NA)
Softwoods	48,513	47,975	45,003	41,998	(NA)	(NA)
Hardwoods	10,321	10,872	9,480	9,136	(NA)	(NA)
United States	**50,300**	**49,960**	**48,451**	**44,794**	**46,635**	**45,247**
North	6,814	6,797	6,917	6,620	6,750	6,767
South	19,751	19,695	20,110	18,885	20,893	21,239
West	23,735	23,468	21,423	19,290	18,992	17,242

NA Not available.   [1] New sample, based on the new MA-24T sample.   [2] Includes types not shown separately.   [3] Imports minus exports.

Source: U.S. Bureau of the Census, *Current Industrial Reports*, series MA-24T, annual.

No. 1157. Wood Products—Production: 1980 to 1990

ITEM	Unit	1980	1981	1982	1983	1984	1985	1986	1987	1988	1989	1990, prel.
Hardwood flooring	Mil. bd. ft	78	83	75	98	110	122	145	174	193	206	205
Softwood plywood	Bil. sq. ft, 3/8"	15.5	15.5	15.1	18.3	18.9	19.3	20.4	21.1	22.9	21.4	20.7
Insulation boards [1]	1,000 short tons	1,051	845	593	713	785	735	732	605	529	460	474
Hardboard [1]	Mil. sq. ft, 1/8"	6,140	6,104	5,587	7,303	6,837	6,300	5,822	5,458	5,118	5,196	5,025
Particleboard	Mil. sq. ft, 3/4"	2,950	2,869	2,393	3,009	3,196	3,331	3,603	3,706	3,829	3,858	3,806

[1] Beginning 1982, data are for shipments.

Source: U.S. Dept. of Commerce, International Trade Administration, *Forest Products Review*, monthly (discontinued April 1983); and unpublished data. Based on reports of U.S. Bureau of the Census, National Oak Flooring Manufacturers Association and National Particleboard Association.

No. 1158. Paper and Paperboard—Production, New Supply, and Ratio of New Supply to Real GDP: 1990 to 1993

[In thousands of short tons. See also *Historical Statistics, Colonial Times to 1970*, series L 172, L 174, and L 178-191]

ITEM	PRODUCTION				NEW SUPPLY				RATIO OF NEW SUPPLY TO REAL GDP [1]			
	1990	1991	1992	1993	1990	1991	1992	1993	1990	1991	1992	1993
Total paper	39,361	39,084	40,973	41,745	49,494	47,379	49,424	51,244	10.106	9.734	9.926	9.980
Total paperboard	39,423	40,416	41,985	43,213	36,406	36,826	38,543	40,045	7.434	7.566	7.741	7.799
Unbleached Kraft	20,357	20,950	21,658	21,447	17,780	17,794	18,515	18,456	3.631	3.656	3.718	3.595
Semichemical	5,640	5,552	5,762	5,672	5,609	5,482	5,730	5,774	1.145	1.126	1.151	1.125
Bleached Kraft	4,399	4,572	4,503	4,583	3,638	3,781	3,690	3,788	0.743	0.777	0.741	0.738
Recycled	9,026	9,332	10,063	11,510	9,378	9,768	10,608	12,026	1.915	2.007	2.130	2.342

[1] GDP = Gross domestic product.

Source: American Forest and Paper Association, Washington, DC, *Monthly Statistical Summary of Paper, Paperboard and Woodpulp.*

No. 1159. Newsprint—Production, Stocks, Consumption, and Price Index: 1970 to 1992

[In thousands of metric tons, except price index. See also *Historical Statistics, Colonial Times to 1970*, series L 192-198]

COUNTRY AND ITEM	1970	1980	1985	1987	1988	1989	1990	1991	1992
Canada: Production	7,808	8,625	8,890	9,630	9,840	9,640	9,068	8,977	8,931
Shipments from mills	7,795	8,622	8,899	9,718	9,740	9,606	9,074	8,728	9,143
Stocks at mills, end of year	236	165	288	189	288	321	315	564	351
United States:									
Consumption, estimate	6,468	10,088	11,507	12,303	12,245	12,241	12,125	11,381	11,634
Production	3,142	4,239	4,924	5,300	5,427	5,523	5,997	6,206	6,424
Shipments from mills	3,136	4,234	4,927	5,310	5,415	5,515	6,007	6,152	6,464
Stocks, end of year: At mills . . .	33	21	57	36	48	56	46	98	59
At and in transit to publishers .	749	732	910	900	932	749	801	932	938
Producer price index (1982=100)	34.1	[1]88.5	105.3	112.3	127.6	122.5	119.5	120.9	109.9

[1] Average for 11 months.

Source: U.S. Bureau of Economic Analysis, *Survey of Current Business*, monthly. Data from American Forest and Paper Association, Washington, DC, and Canadian Pulp & Paper Association.

No. 1160. Recovered Paper Utilization and Recovery Rates: 1970 to 1994

[In millions of short tons, except percent. Recovery rate is ratio of total recovered paper to new supply. Recovered paper utilization is the ratio of recovered paper consumption at paper and board mills to paper and board production. See *Historical Statistics, Colonial Times to 1970*, series L 175, for U.S. wastepaper consumption]

ITEM	1970	1980	1985	1988	1989	1990	1991	1992	1993	1994
Paper and board, production [1]	51.7	63.6	68.7	78.1	78.4	80.3	81.1	84.6	86.6	90.5
Recovered paper consumption	11.8	14.9	16.4	19.7	20.2	21.7	23.7	26.2	28.0	30.0
Recovered paper utilization rate (percent) . .	22.8	23.5	23.8	25.2	25.8	27.1	29.2	31.0	32.4	33.1
Other recovered paper uses [2]	0.42	0.47	0.53	0.70	0.72	1.00	1.08	1.10	1.15	1.20
Recovered paper exports	0.41	2.64	3.56	5.95	6.31	6.51	6.60	6.45	5.89	7.71
Total paper recovered	12.6	17.9	20.4	26.2	27.1	29.1	31.2	33.6	34.9	38.6
Paper and board, new supply [3]	56.0	67.2	76.1	85.5	85.2	86.7	84.9	88.1	91.4	95.4
Recovery rate (percent)	22.4	26.7	26.8	30.6	31.8	33.6	36.8	38.1	38.2	40.5

[1] Excludes hard pressed board; includes construction paper and board, and wet machine board.   [2] Estimated.   [3] Excludes production of hard pressed board.

Source: American Forest and Paper Association, Washington, DC, *Statistics of Paper, Paperboard, and Woodpulp*, annual; and unpublished data.

No. 1161. Selected Wood Products—Production and Consumption: 1970 to 1989

[See also *Historical Statistics, Colonial Times to 1970*, series L 151-170]

ITEM	Unit	1970	1975	1980	1984	1985	1986	1987	1988	1989
PULPWOOD										
Receipts, total	Mil. cords [1]	68.9	65.4	81.0	88.0	85.4	90.6	93.9	95.1	97.0
Softwood	Mil. cords [1]	52.4	49.3	60.2	62.9	60.2	63.3	65.3	65.8	67.1
Hardwood	Mil. cords [1]	16.5	16.2	20.8	25.2	25.1	27.3	28.6	29.3	29.9
Consumption, total	Mil. cords [1]	67.6	65.4	79.7	87.0	84.8	91.1	92.4	95.3	96.1
Softwood	Mil. cords [1]	51.3	48.9	58.8	62.0	59.7	63.1	64.2	65.9	66.3
Hardwood	Mil. cords [1]	16.3	16.5	20.9	24.9	25.1	28.1	28.2	29.4	29.7
Inventories [2]	Mil. cords [1]	6.6	6.6	6.7	5.2	5.1	4.7	5.6	5.3	5.8
WOODPULP										
Production	Mil. short tons	43.9	43.1	53.0	57.8	57.7	60.6	62.4	64.1	64.6
Consumption, [3] total	Mil. short tons	43.2	42.4	52.4	57.5	56.6	60.0	61.2	62.8	62.7
Own pulp	Mil. short tons	38.9	38.5	46.6	50.3	49.7	52.6	53.8	54.9	54.9
Purchased pulp	Mil. short tons	4.3	3.9	5.9	7.2	7.0	7.5	7.4	7.9	7.8
PLYWOOD										
Softwood:										
Production	Mil. sq. ft. [4]	14,149	15,706	15,483	18,865	19,341	20,363	22,312	22,233	20,919
Consumption, total	Mil. sq. ft. [4]	(NA)	(NA)	15,145	18,526	19,122	19,880	21,503	22,277	20,904
Value	Mil. dol.	949	(NA)	2,582	2,995	3,080	3,237	3,483	3,513	3,734
Hardwood:										
Production	Mil. sq. ft. [5]	1,904	1,280	1,311	1,185	1,016	1,088	1,256	1,217	1,213
Consumption, total	Mil. sq. ft. [5]	5,772	4,970	3,416	3,831	4,311	4,884	4,918	4,193	(NA)
Value	Mil. dol.	516	586	977	1,199	1,192	1,320	1,471	1,405	1,392

- Represents or rounds to zero. NA Not available. [1] Standard cords. 128 cubic feet roughwood bases. [2] As of Dec. 31. [3] In the manufacture of paper and board. [4] 3/8" basis. [5] Surface measure.
Source: U.S. Bureau of the Census, *Current Industrial Reports*, series MA26-A, MA24-H, and MA24-F.

No. 1162. Selected Timber Products—Imports and Exports: 1970 to 1993

ITEM	Unit	1970	1980	1985	1988	1989	1990	1991	1992	1993, prel.
IMPORTS [1]										
Lumber, total [2]	Mil. bd. ft	6,114	9,866	14,996	14,226	15,277	12,159	11,756	13,474	15,625
From Canada	Percent	96.0	97.5	97.6	97.5	91.3	98.5	98.3	98.3	97.6
Softwoods	Mil. bd. ft	5,778	9,573	14,632	13,841	14,928	11,927	11,545	13,214	15,260
Value	Mil. dol	434	1,826	2,898	2,939	2,875	2,534	2,507	3,310	4,787
Hardwoods	Mil. bd. ft	337	293	364	386	349	232	210	260	335
Value	Mil. dol	62	152	180	238	152	141	142	176	224
Logs, total	Mil. bd. ft. [3]	144	128	99	68	42	28	15	46	94
From Canada	Percent	79.6	97.4	81.8	91.9	61.5	67.5	74.5	88.9	77.7
Softwoods	Mil. bd. ft. [3]	107	114	71	56	24	18	9	40	86
Value	Mil. dol	9	17	17	15	12	7	6	20	41
Hardwoods	Mil. bd. ft. [3]	38	13	28	12	18	10	6	7	8
Value	Mil. dol	5	3	4	3	17	10	6	6	9
Paper and board [4]	1,000 tons	7,115	8,780	11,522	13,110	13,100	13,148	12,167	12,543	13,971
Value	Mil. dol	1,039	3,418	5,698	8,002	8,330	8,427	7,929	7,899	8,527
Woodpulp	1,000 tons	3,518	4,051	4,466	4,938	5,105	4,893	4,997	5,029	5,413
Value	Mil. dol	483	1,684	1,521	2,608	3,037	2,831	2,132	2,094	1,860
Plywood	Mil. sq. ft. [5]	2,049	1,235	1,817	1,698	1,955	1,687	1,457	1,776	1,798
Value	Mil. dol	208	409	463	577	516	537	457	574	677
EXPORTS										
Lumber, total [2]	Mil. bd. ft	1,243	2,494	1,945	4,527	4,243	3,802	3,997	3,603	3,385
To: Canada	Percent	21.7	25.3	23.7	17.6	15.6	18.1	15.1	17.3	17.4
Japan	Percent	30.8	26.0	32.1	34.5	38.1	33.5	30.5	30.9	36.3
Europe	Percent	24.1	23.8	15.1	20.5	16.6	19.1	19.6	21.2	15.9
Softwoods	Mil. bd. ft	1,115	2,007	1,518	3,266	3,379	2,941	3,055	2,613	2,376
Value	Mil. dol	163	789	497	1,143	1,404	1,336	1,358	1,363	1,372
Hardwoods	Mil. bd. ft	128	487	427	1,261	863	861	942	990	1,008
Value	Mil. dol	31	272	263	683	659	818	879	988	1,077
Logs, total	Mil. bd. ft. [3]	2,741	3,261	3,843	4,798	4,745	4,262	3,816	3,316	2,877
To: Canada	Percent	10.6	9.7	11.6	7.9	5.8	9.3	11.2	12.6	13.6
Japan	Percent	86.3	78.0	49.4	50.3	63.5	62.5	56.7	62.1	65.4
China: Mainland	Percent	(NA)	2.7	27.8	23.4	9.6	8.5	9.7	7.1	4.6
Softwoods	Mil. bd. ft. [3]	2,672	3,109	3,732	4,594	4,532	4,044	3,532	3,092	2,640
Value	Mil. dol	320	1,452	1,169	2,090	2,176	2,170	1,870	1,925	2,237
Hardwoods	Mil. bd. ft. [3]	69	152	111	204	214	218	283	224	237
Value	Mil. dol	36	129	91	160	223	251	234	238	253
Paper and board [4]	1,000 tons	2,817	5,214	4,071	5,691	6,300	6,796	8,331	8,971	9,126
Value	Mil. dol	602	2,773	2,266	3,753	4,261	5,035	6,006	6,392	6,541
Woodpulp	1,000 tons	3,095	3,806	3,796	5,528	6,231	5,906	6,337	7,222	6,499
Value	Mil. dol	464	1,652	1,354	2,915	3,513	3,156	2,800	3,114	2,389
Plywood	Mil. sq. ft. [5]	172	413	358	1,093	1,562	1,767	1,552	1,759	1,648
Value	Mil. dol	16	108	86	247	292	338	295	366	401

NA Not available. [1] Customs value of imports; see text, section 29. [2] Includes railroad ties. [3] Log scale. [4] Includes paper and board products. Excludes hardboard. [5] 3/8 inch basis.
Source: U.S. Foreign Agricultural Service, *Trade, Consumption, and Price Statistics: 1960-89*, forthcoming, and unpublished data.

No. 1163. Fishery Products—Domestic Catch and Imports, Summary: 1970 to 1993

[Live weight, in millions of pounds, except percent. 1979-1993 preliminary. For data on commercial catch for selected countries, see table 1404, section 30. See *Historical Statistics, Colonial Times to 1970,* series L 224-226, for domestic catch]

ITEM	1970	1980	1984	1985	1986	1987	1988	1989	1990	1991	1992	1993
Total	**11,474**	**11,357**	**12,552**	**15,150**	**14,368**	**15,744**	**14,628**	**15,485**	**16,349**	**16,364**	**16,106**	**20,334**
For human food	6,213	8,006	8,498	9,337	9,620	10,561	10,505	12,268	12,662	13,020	13,242	13,821
Finfish	(NA)	6,139	6,303	6,991	7,087	7,919	7,786	9,735	10,120	10,186	10,297	10,796
Shellfish [1]	(NA)	1,867	2,195	2,346	2,533	2,642	2,719	2,533	2,542	2,834	2,945	3,025
For industrial use	5,261	3,351	4,054	5,813	4,748	5,183	4,123	3,217	3,687	3,344	2,864	6,513
Domestic catch	**4,917**	**6,482**	**6,438**	**6,258**	**6,031**	**6,896**	**7,192**	**8,463**	**9,404**	**9,484**	**9,637**	**10,467**
Percent of total	42.8	57.1	51.3	41.3	42.0	43.8	.49.2	54.7	57.5	58.0	59.8	51.5
For human food	2,537	3,654	3,320	3,294	3,393	3,946	4,588	6,204	7,041	7,031	7,618	8,214
Finfish	(NA)	2,516	2,348	2,273	2,240	2,769	3,306	4,897	5,747	5,564	6,182	6,746
Shellfish [1]	(NA)	1,138	972	1,021	1,153	1,177	1,282	1,307	1,294	1,467	1,436	1,468
For industrial use	2,380	2,828	3,118	2,964	2,638	2,950	2,604	2,259	2,363	2,453	2,019	2,253
Imports [2]	**6,557**	**4,875**	**6,114**	**8,892**	**8,337**	**8,848**	**7,436**	**7,022**	**6,945**	**6,879**	**6,469**	**9,867**
Percent of total	57.2	42.9	48.7	58.7	58.0	56.2	50.8	45.3	42.5	42.0	40.2	48.5
For human food	3,676	4,352	5,178	6,043	6,227	6,615	5,917	6,064	5,621	5,989	5,624	5,607
Finfish	(NA)	3,623	3,955	4,718	4,847	5,150	4,480	4,838	4,373	4,622	4,115	4,026
Shellfish [1]	(NA)	729	1,223	1,325	1,380	1,465	1,437	1,226	1,248	1,367	1,509	1,581
For industrial use [3] . . .	2,881	523	936	2,849	2,110	2,233	1,519	958	1,324	890	845	4,260

NA Not available.   [1] For univalve and bivalve mollusks (conchs, clams, oysters, scallops, etc.), the weight of meats, excluding the shell, is reported.   [2] Excludes imports of edible fishery products consumed in Puerto Rico; includes landings of tuna caught by foreign vessels in American Samoa.   [3] Fish meal and sea herring.

Source: U.S. National Oceanic and Atmospheric Administration, National Marine Fisheries Service, *Fishery Statistics of the United States,* annual; and *Fisheries of the United States,* annual.

No. 1164. Fisheries—Employment, Fishing Craft, and Establishments: 1970 to 1992

[In thousands. As of Dec. 31. 1979-92 preliminary. Data for employment and establishments exclude Alaska. See also *Historical Statistics, Colonial Times to 1970,* series L 254-261]

ITEM	1970	1980	1983	1984	1985	1986	1987	1988	1989 [1]	1990 [1]	1991 [1]	1992 [1]
Persons employed in U.S.	**227**	**296**	**333**	**340**	**351**	**347**	**359**	**364**	**(NA)**	**(NA)**	**(NA)**	**(NA)**
Fishermen	140	193	223	230	239	247	256	274	(NA)	(NA)	(NA)	(NA)
Shore workers [2]	87	103	110	110	112	100	103	90	73	72	73	72
Craft used	**88**	**113**	**127**	**127**	**130**	**128**	**[3]93**	**[3]110**	**111**	**95**	**(NA)**	**(NA)**
Vessels, 5 net tons and over .	14	19	21	24	24	38	[3]23	[3]32	36	32	(NA)	(NA)
Motorboats	72	93	105	102	104	88	[3]68	[3]78	75	63	(NA)	(NA)
Other boats	2	1	1	1	2	2	[3]2	(NA)	(NA)	(NA)	(NA)	(NA)
Fishery shore establishments.	**3.7**	**3.6**	**3.9**	**4.0**	**4.0**	**4.0**	**4.2**	**4.6**	**4.5**	**4.6**	**4.6**	**4.9**

NA Not available.   [1] Estimated and excludes Mississippi River. Maryland and Virginia represent only Federal collected data.   [2] Seasonal average for processors and wholesaling plants.   [3] Excludes Maryland and Virginia.

Source: U.S. National Oceanic and Atmospheric Administration, National Marine Fisheries Service, *Fishery Statistics of the United States,* annual; and *Fisheries of the United States,* annual.

No. 1165. Fisheries—Quantity and Value of Domestic Catch: 1970 to 1993

[1979-1993 preliminary. See also *Historical Statistics, Colonial Times to 1970,* series L 224-226, L 229, and L 310]

YEAR	QUANTITY (mil. lb. [1])			Value (mil. dol.)	Average price per lb. (cents)	YEAR	QUANTITY (mil. lb. [1])			Value (mil. dol.)	Average price per lb. (cents)
	Total	For human food	For indus-trial prod-ucts [2]				Total	For human food	For indus-trial prod-ucts [2]		
1970	4,917	2,537	2,380	613	12.5	1982	6,367	3,285	3,082	2,390	37.5
1971	5,018	2,441	2,577	651	13.0	1983	6,439	3,238	3,201	2,355	36.6
1972	4,806	2,435	2,371	748	15.6	1984	6,438	3,320	3,118	2,350	36.5
1973	4,858	2,398	2,460	937	19.3	1985	6,258	3,294	2,964	2,326	37.2
1974	4,967	2,496	2,471	932	18.7	1986	6,031	3,393	2,638	2,763	45.8
1975	4,877	2,465	2,412	977	20.0	1987	6,896	3,946	2,950	3,115	45.2
1976	5,388	2,775	2,613	1,349	25.0	1988	7,192	4,588	2,604	3,520	48.9
1977	5,271	2,952	2,319	1,554	29.5	1989	8,463	6,204	2,259	3,238	38.3
1978	6,028	3,177	2,851	1,854	30.7	1990	9,404	7,041	2,363	3,522	37.5
1979	6,267	3,318	2,949	2,234	35.6	1991	9,484	7,031	2,453	3,308	34.9
1980	6,482	3,654	2,828	2,237	34.5	1992	9,637	7,618	2,019	3,678	38.2
1981	5,977	3,547	2,430	2,388	40.0	1993	10,467	8,214	2,253	3,471	33.2

[1] Live weight.   [2] Meal, oil, fish solubles, homogenized condensed fish, shell products, bait, and animal food.

Source: U.S. National Oceanic and Atmospheric Administration, National Marine Fisheries Service, *Fishery Statistics of the United States,* annual; and *Fisheries of the United States,* annual.

No. 1166. Domestic Fisheries—Catch, by Selected Ports: 1985 to 1993

[See *Historical Statistics, Colonial Times to 1970*, series L 236-253, for data on quantity and value of catch]

PORT	CATCH (mil. lb.)					VALUE (mil. dol.)				
	1985	1990	1991	1992	1993	1985	1990	1991	1992	1993
New Bedford, MA	90.6	114.8	106.4	103.3	82.1	103.2	160.4	157.7	151.8	107.5
Dutch Harbor-Unalaska, AK	106.3	509.9	731.7	736.0	793.9	21.3	126.2	130.6	194.0	161.2
Kodiak, AK	96.1	272.5	287.3	274.0	374.2	65.8	101.7	96.9	90.0	81.5
Dulac-Chauvin, LA	398.6	164.4	166.8	65.0	142.4	59.9	52.7	50.1	52.1	48.0
Empire-Venice, LA	224.5	244.2	309.4	269.1	335.4	34.3	46.3	50.2	50.1	52.3
Gloucester, MA	116.5	126.2	107.2	101.7	67.6	37.1	40.5	40.0	34.1	31.3
Petersburg, AK	(NA)	67.5	90.3	81.0	110.2	(NA)	39.4	34.6	33.0	32.8
Cordova, AK	(NA)	70.8	47.5	30.0	18.1	(NA)	36.8	19.5	17.0	10.7
Cape May-Wildwood, NJ	30.3	69.2	93.1	93.9	95.0	18.1	34.4	40.1	34.9	36.2
Point Judith, RI	56.8	58.7	64.7	66.7	60.4	28.0	32.2	37.5	36.6	35.2
Portland, ME	36.1	48.9	63.4	59.2	86.1	17.2	31.7	44.1	43.6	49.1
Ketchikan, AK	(NA)	52.6	68.5	70.0	100.6	(NA)	28.3	21.9	27.0	27.0
Beaufort-Morehead City, NC	133.2	102.0	137.0	78.7	88.4	22.7	23.0	23.0	16.2	15.6
Cameron, LA	673.6	232.6	288.4	246.0	323.1	29.9	20.6	26.3	26.5	27.4
Morgan City-Berwick, LA	7.7	146.5	112.3	130.8	147.5	(NA)	19.7	9.4	14.3	13.0
Pascagoula-Moss Point, MS	423.2	303.9	227.3	177.0	169.7	18.4	18.8	15.1	12.4	10.7
Los Angeles, CA	150.3	158.5	141.5	94.9	99.8	32.5	21.3	17.4	14.6	13.7
Astoria, OR	25.5	41.2	53.0	67.0	68.0	9.5	16.2	17.0	19.0	19.0
Port Hueneme-Oxnard-Ventura, CA	19.9	39.4	52.0	18.7	39.9	5.4	12.5	14.0	10.7	10.3
Intercoastal City, LA	(NA)	173.0	211.4	175.9	202.7	(NA)	7.6	12.0	10.4	11.0

NA Not available.

Source: U.S. National Oceanic and Atmospheric Administration, National Marine Fisheries Service, *Fisheries of the United States,* annual.

No. 1167. Domestic Fish and Shellfish Catch and Value, by Species: 1985 to 1993

SPECIES	QUANTITY (1,000 lb.)				VALUE ($1,000)		
	1988-92 5-year average	1985	1990	1993	1985	1990	1993
Total	(X)	6,257,642	9,403,571	10,466,895	2,326,237	3,521,995	3,471,460
Fish, total [1]	(X)	5,214,363	8,091,068	8,999,142	1,193,427	1,900,097	1,884,121
Cod: Atlantic	80,859	82,823	95,881	50,503	35,140	61,329	44,956
Pacific	453,996	120,275	526,396	482,799	18,556	91,384	116,172
Flounder	347,282	195,718	254,519	599,180	129,121	112,921	135,598
Herring, sea; Atlantic	104,642	57,133	113,095	109,645	2,968	5,746	6,511
Herring, sea; Pacific	128,219	142,074	108,120	106,572	47,025	32,178	18,711
Menhaden	1,931,671	2,739,401	1,962,160	1,983,319	100,680	93,896	103,258
Pollock, Alaska	2,506,943	92,833	3,108,031	3,257,990	5,409	268,344	358,378
Salmon	724,855	726,946	733,146	888,134	439,795	612,367	423,530
Shellfish, total [1]	(X)	1,043,279	1,312,503	1,467,753	1,132,810	1,621,898	1,587,339
Clams	137,159	150,551	139,198	147,752	128,349	130,194	138,030
Crabs	537,548	337,632	499,416	604,437	203,044	483,837	510,494
Lobsters: American	56,353	46,152	61,017	56,513	114,895	154,677	151,746
Oysters	31,805	44,173	29,193	33,575	70,053	93,718[2]	86,698
Scallops: Calico	19,583	12,513	1,135	[2]12,524	1,281		105,603
Sea	35,412	15,829	39,917	18,116	74,562	153,696	
Shrimp	337,347	333,691	346,494	292,887	472,850	491,433	412,896
Squid: Atlantic	65,250	7,157	59,809	90,809	7,256	21,178	38,323
Pacific	55,219	22,276	36,082	71,550	4,047	2,636	8,079

X Not applicable.   [1] Includes other types of fish and shellfish, not shown separately.

Source: U.S. National Oceanic and Atmospheric Administration, National Marine Fisheries Service, *Fisheries of the United States,* annual.

No. 1168. Disposition of U.S. Domestic Catch: 1970 to 1993

[**Live weight catch in millions of pounds.** 1980-93 preliminary. In addition to whole fish, a large portion of waste (400-500 million lb.) derived from canning, filleting, and dressing fish and shellfish utilized in production of fish meal and oil in each year shown. See *Historical Statistics, Colonial Times to 1970*, series L 305-310, for similar but not entirely comparable data]

DISPOSITION	1970	1975	1980	1985	1986	1987	1988	1989	1990	1991	1992	1993
Total	4,917	4,877	6,482	6,258	6,031	6,896	7,192	8,463	9,404	9,484	9,637	10,467
Fresh and frozen	1,595	1,744	2,621	2,242	2,487	3,157	3,813	5,585	6,501	6,541	7,288	7,744
Canned	1,150	907	1,161	1,232	1,134	1,009	1,017	798	751	674	543	649
Cured	71	55	96	70	60	89	86	128	126	119	100	115
Reduced to meal, oil, etc.	2,101	2,171	2,604	2,714	2,350	2,641	2,276	1,952	2,026	2,150	1,696	1,959

Source: U.S. National Oceanic and Atmospheric Administration, National Marine Fisheries Service, *Fishery Statistics of the United States,* annual; and *Fisheries of the United States,* annual.

No. 1169. U.S. Private Aquaculture—Trout and Catfish Production and Value: 1988 to 1994

[Periods are from Sept. 1 of the previous year to Aug. 31 of stated year. Data are for foodsize fish, those over 12 inches long]

ITEM	Unit	1988	1989	1990	1991	1992	1993	1994
TROUT								
Number sold	Mil	70.5	67.4	67.8	67.7	64.5	60.9	58.3
Total weight	Mil. lb	56.0	55.5	56.8	58.9	55.2	54.6	52.1
Total value of sales	Mil. dol	57.9	60.0	64.6	58.3	51.0	54.3	52.7
Average price received	$/lb	1.03	1.08	1.14	0.99	0.92	0.99	1.01
Average weight	Lb	0.8	0.8	0.8	0.9	0.9	0.9	0.9
CATFISH								
Fish sold to processors	Mil. lb	295.1	341.9	360.4	390.9	457.4	459.0	(NA)
Avg. price paid by processors	Cents/lb	76.4	71.7	75.8	63.1	59.8	71.0	(NA)
Value	Mil. dol	225.5	245.1	273.2	246.7	273.5	325.9	(NA)
Processor sales	Mil. lb	149.6	176.3	183.1	199.8	231.3	233.5	(NA)
Avg. price received by processors	Cents/lb	220.8	211.2	224.0	208.6	200.3	218.7	(NA)
Value	Mil. dol	330.3	372.3	410.1	416.8	463.3	510.7	(NA)
Inventory (Jan. 1)	Mil. lb	5.3	8.8	8.1	9.4	9.6	11.6	9.5

NA Not available.

Source: U.S. Dept. of Agriculture, National Agricultural Statistics Service, USDA.

No. 1170. Supply of Selected Fishery Items: 1980 to 1993

[In millions of pounds. Totals available for U.S. consumption are supply minus exports plus imports. Round weight is the complete or full weight as caught. Data are preliminary]

ITEM	Unit	1980	1984	1985	1987	1988	1989	1990	1991	1992	1993
Tuna, canned	Canned weight	666	777	759	866	843	1,028	856	933	922	835
Shrimp	Heads-off weight	425	584	633	773	767	743	734	744	820	840
Clams	Meat weight	102	144	164	151	145	150	152	144	155	156
Salmon, canned	Canned weight	126	150	113	76	59	159	148	131	73	114
American lobster	Round weight	69	100	108	116	121	85	95	107	95	92
Spiny lobster	Round weight	127	153	154	151	139	89	89	85	81	76
Scallops	Meat weight	51	87	72	79	74	79	74	62	69	66
Sardines, canned	Canned weight	69	58	76	77	63	61	61	52	41	41
Oysters	Meat weight	71	84	90	92	78	66	56	47	50	48
Crab meat, canned	Canned weight	9	7	8	8	8	8	9	11	9	9
Snow crab	Round weight	54	23	45	29	30	58	37	60	88	66
King crab	Round weight	133	13	11	14	10	18	19	20	15	8

Source: U.S. National Oceanic and Atmospheric Administration, National Marine Fisheries Service, *Fisheries of the United States,* annual.

No. 1171. Canned, Fresh, and Frozen Fishery Products: 1980 to 1993

[Fresh fishery products exclude Alaska and Hawaii. Canned fishery products data are for natural pack only. See also *Historical Statistics, Colonial Times to 1970,* series L 338-357 (production data in cases) and L 358]

PRODUCT	PRODUCTION (mil. lb.)						VALUE (mil. dol.)					
	1980	1985	1990	1991	1992	1993	1980	1985	1990	1991	1992	1993
Canned, [1]	1,516	1,161	1,178	1,386	1,343	1615	1,928	1,360	1,562	1,644	1,577	1,626
Tuna	602	545	581	593	609	619	1,144	821	902	877	888	904
Salmon	200	159	196	196	152	199	376	228	366	413	293	307
Clam products	77	117	110	129	126	116	66	109	76	84	88	90
Mackerel [2]	38	15	23	9	5	(NA)	12	7	11	3	2	(NA)
Sardines, Maine	20	20	13	14	17	14	32	38	17	19	25	25
Shrimp	16	4	1	1	1	1	80	19	3	4	4	4
Crabs	5	1	1	(Z)	(Z)	(Z)	19	2	4	(Z)	1	1
Oysters [3]	(Z)	2	1	1	(NA)	(Z)	(Z)	2	1	2	(NA)	(Z)
Fish fillets and steaks [4]	202	246	441	473	449	409	261	440	843	1,021	912	829
Cod	31	57	65	71	65	54	43	89	132	180	158	131
Flounder	49	69	54	48	46	35	87	157	154	147	120	100
Haddock	17	8	7	8	5	4	29	19	24	30	19	17
Ocean perch, Atlantic	7	2	1	1	1	1	9	3	1	1	3	2
Rockfish	14	18	33	22	19	18	13	25	53	36	30	28
Pollock, Atlantic	9	15	12	8	9	8	9	17	21	18	19	18
Pollock, Alaska	(NA)	11	164	152	165	154	(NA)	24	174	206	205	179
Other	74	66	105	163	139	135	71	106	284	403	358	354

NA Not available. Z Less than 500,000 pounds or $500,000. [1] Includes other products, not shown separately. [2] Includes Jack and a small amount of Pacific mackerel. [3] Includes oyster specialties. [4] Fresh and frozen.

Source: U.S. National Oceanic and Atmospheric Administration, National Marine Fisheries Service, *Fisheries of the United States,* annual.

No. 1172. Summary of Mineral Operations: 1963 to 1992

[Represents mineral operations only. Beginning 1967, excludes single unit establishments without paid employees. See also *Historical Statistics, Colonial Times to 1970*, series M 1-11]

ITEM	Unit	1963	1967	1972	1977	1982	1987	1992
Establishments	Number .	38,651	28,579	25,269	31,359	42,241	33,617	30,828
With 20 or more employees	Number .	5,499	5,682	5,312	6,632	(NA)	6,299	5,581
Including all operations in manufactures	Number .	40,532	29,688	26,178	31,967	42,585	34,041	(NA)
Excluding oil and gas extraction	Number .	19,290	13,330	11,680	13,520	12,267	10,707	9,951
Employees, total	1,000. . .	616	567	595	799	1,114	698	637
Production workers [1]	1,000. . .	482	433	443	593	762	451	414
All other	1,000. . .	134	134	152	206	352	247	223
Worker-hours, production workers [1]	Million .	973	892	909	1,183	1,578	942	873
Worker-hours per production workers	1,000. . .	2.0	2.1	2.1	2.0	2.1	2.1	2.1
Payroll, total	Mil. dol. .	3,743	4,187	6,226	13,167	28,637	21,739	24,303
Wages, production workers [1]	Mil. dol. .	2,680	2,888	4,250	9,082	18,030	12,443	13,874
Salaries, all other employees	Mil. dol. .	1,063	1,299	1,976	4,085	10,607	9,296	10,429
Cost of supplies, etc. [2]	Mil. dol. .	8,974	10,576	14,884	46,079	109,697	62,423	64,602
Value added in mining	Mil. dol. .	15,910	19,330	26,471	68,013	188,056	110,959	113,780
Metal mining	Mil. dol. .	1,418	1,557	2,382	3,504	3,215	4,610	7,180
Coal mining	Mil. dol. .	1,727	2,091	3,754	11,266	18,631	17,068	17,283
Oil and gas extraction	Mil. dol. .	11,020	13,394	17,612	48,587	159,937	80,049	79,700
Nonmetallic minerals mining	Mil. dol. .	1,745	2,288	2,723	4,656	6,273	9,233	9,619
Value of shipments and receipts [3]	Mil. dol. .	18,804	22,784	36,319	96,375	250,000	157,964	162,339
Capital expenditures	Mil. dol. .	3,264	4,058	5,036	17,718	47,753	15,418	16,043

NA Not available.   [1] See footnote 4, table 1176.   [2] Includes purchased machinery installed.   [3] See footnote 6, table 1176.

Source: U.S. Bureau of the Census, *Census of Mineral Industries, 1972, 1977, 1982, 1987,* and *1992.*

No. 1173. Gross Domestic Product (GDP) in Mining: 1980 to 1992

[**In millions of dollars, except percent.** For definition of gross national product, see text, section 14. For 1947-86, based on 1972 Standard Industrial Classification (SIC); for 1987, estimates are shown first based on the 1972 SIC and then on the 1987 SIC. Estimates thereafter based on 1987 SIC]

MINING INDUSTRY	1980	1985	1986	1987	1988	1989	1990	1991	1992
Current dollars, total	112.6	130.6	82.7	83.0	87.9	84.2	103.1	92.0	85.2
Metal mining	4.4	2.5	2.5	2.6	4.8	5.2	6.2	6.3	6.3
Coal mining	13.6	13.8	14.0	12.5	12.5	12.9	12.7	12.4	13.1
Oil and gas extraction	89.1	108.4	59.5	60.8	63.2	58.8	76.9	66.1	58.5
Nonmetallic minerals, exc. fuels	5.5	5.9	6.7	7.2	7.3	7.4	7.2	7.1	7.3
Constant (1987) dollars, total	79.9	83.3	83.0	83.0	94.2	83.3	91.8	92.3	89.0
Metal mining	1.6	2.5	2.9	2.6	4.3	5.0	6.6	7.7	8.0
Coal mining	10.1	11.3	13.0	12.5	13.8	14.8	15.3	15.5	16.7
Oil and gas extraction	61.8	63.2	60.2	60.8	69.0	56.2	62.9	62.2	57.2
Nonmetallic minerals, exc. fuels	6.4	6.3	6.9	7.2	7.1	7.3	7.0	6.9	7.1

Source: U.S. Bureau of Economic Analysis, *Survey of Current Business,* October 1994.

No. 1174. Mining and Primary Metal Production Indexes: 1970 to 1994

[1987=100. See also *Historical Statistics, Colonial Times to 1970*, series M 68-71]

INDUSTRY GROUP	1970	1980	1985	1986	1988	1989	1990	1991	1992	1993	1994
Mining	100.4	110.0	109.0	101.0	101.3	100.0	102.0	100.2	98.9	98.2	99.8
Coal	67.2	90.2	96.3	97.1	103.1	107.0	112.2	108.2	108.2	102.9	112.0
Anthracite	274.1	169.6	132.8	120.8	115.6	96.3	103.2	72.7	66.1	(NA)	(NA)
Bituminous	66.0	89.7	96.1	96.9	105.0	105.8	113.3	109.4	105.8	(NA)	(NA)
Oil and gas extraction	104.8	112.1	111.9	102.0	99.7	96.0	96.8	95.9	93.2	93.0	92.9
Metal mining	129.5	108.8	91.3	95.2	120.3	140.5	153.1	153.7	163.8	162.4	159.4
Iron ore	194.4	149.4	104.9	84.4	119.4	122.5	117.9	118.3	116.3	115.7	122.5
Nonferrous ores	111.5	95.0	86.4	99.1	120.5	144.1	160.2	160.8	173.3	171.7	166.4
Copper ore	123.2	93.1	86.9	91.2	113.7	120.0	126.8	131.1	141.9	143.3	145.4
Primary metals, manufacturing	115.2	110.8	101.8	93.7	108.7	107.2	106.5	98.7	101.9	106.9	114.5
Nonferrous metals	77.1	92.5	98.5	97.3	103.1	101.7	99.5	96.1	97.6	101.0	109.3
Copper	135.2	94.7	99.8	99.1	100.1	98.9	102.2	110.0	124.8	135.3	137.5
Aluminum	107.8	138.7	104.7	90.9	117.6	120.5	121.0	123.2	120.5	110.5	98.6
Iron and steel	148.2	126.0	104.5	90.8	112.7	111.2	111.5	100.5	105.1	111.4	118.3

NA Not available.

Source: Board of Governors of the Federal Reserve System, *Federal Reserve Bulletin,* monthly.

No. 1175. Mineral Production, 1990 to 1994,

[Data represent production as measured by mine shipments, mine sales, or marketable production,

	MINERAL	Unit	PRODUCTION QUANTITY			
			1990	1992	1993	1994
1	Total mineral production	(X)	(X)	(X)	(X)	(X)
2	**Mineral fuels.**	**(X)**	**(X)**	**(X)**	**(X)**	**(X)**
3	Coal: Bituminous and lignite.	Mil. sh. tons	1,026	998	945	(NA)
4	Pennsylvania anthracite.	Mil. sh. tons	4	3	4	(NA)
5	Natural gas (wet)	Tril. cu. ft.	18.6	18.7	19.3	19.7
6	Petroleum (crude)	Mil. bbl. [1]	2,685	2,625	2,499	(NA)
7	Uranium [2]	Mil. lb.	8.9	5.6	3.1	(NA)
8	**Industrial minerals**	**(X)**	**(X)**	**(X)**	**(X)**	**(X)**
9	Abrasive stone [3]	Metric tons	3,709	1,732	(Z)	(NA)
10	Asbestos (sales)	1,000 metric tons . .	(D)	15.6	13.0	10.0
11	Asphalt and related bitumens (native) [4] . . .	Mil. metric tons . . .	25	25	(NA)	(NA)
12	Barite, primary, sold/used by producers	1,000 metric tons . .	430	326	315	340
13	Boron minerals, sold or used by producers. .	1,000 metric tons . .	1,094	1,009	1,055	560
14	Bromine, sold or used by producers	1,000 metric tons . .	177	171	177	197
15	Calcium chloride (natural)	1,000 sh. tons . . .	(D)	(D)	–	–
16	Carbon dioxide, natural (estimate).	Mil. cu. ft.	–	–	–	–
17	Cement: Portland.	Mil. sh. tons	75.6	72.8	78.9	83.6
18	Masonry	Mil. sh. tons	3.3	2.9	3.0	4.0
19	Clays	1,000 metric tons . .	42,904	40,237	41,074	42,300
20	Diatomite [6]	1,000 metric tons . .	631	595	599	596
21	Feldspar [6]	1,000 metric tons . .	630	726	770	740
22	Fluorspar, finished shipments.	1,000 metric tons . .	64	51	60	50
23	Garnet (abrasive).	1,000 metric tons . .	47.0	54.1	44.0	46.5
24	Gemstones (estimate).	(X)	(NA)	(NA)	(NA)	(NA)
25	Gypsum, crude	Mil. sh. tons	16.4	16.3	17.4	19.1
26	Helium [7]	Mil. cu. meters . . .	87	94	96	96
27	Lime, sold or used by producers.	Mil. sh. tons	17.5	16.1	18.7	19.1
28	Mica, scrap & flake, sold/used by producers .	1,000 metric tons . .	109	85	88	96
29	Peat, sales by producers.	1,000 sh. tons . . .	795	719	675	750
30	Perlite, processed, sold or used	1,000 metric tons . .	576	541	569	610
31	Phosphate rock (marketable)	Mil. metric tons . . .	46.3	47.0	35.0	41.0
32	Potash (K_2O equivalent) sales	1,000 metric tons . .	1,713	1,705	1,506	1,425
33	Pumice & pumicite, producer sales	1,000 metric tons . .	443	481	469	485
34	Pyrites	1,000 metric tons . .	(D)	(D)	(D)	(D)
35	Salt, common, sold/used by producers . . .	Mil. metric tons . . .	36.9	34.8	38.7	38.6
36	Sand & gravel, sold/used by producer	Mil. metric tons . . .	852	858	895	949
37	Construction	Mil. metric tons . . .	829	834	869	922
38	Industrial	Mil. metric tons . . .	26	25	26	27
39	Sodium carbonate (natural) (soda ash) . . .	1,000 metric tons . .	9,156	9,379	8,959	9,100
40	Sodium sulfate (natural)	1,000 metric tons . .	349	337	322	300
41	Stone [8]	Mil. metric tons . . .	1,110	1,055	1,167	1,196
42	Crushed and broken.	Mil. metric tons . . .	1,109	1,054	1,116	1,195
43	Dimension	1,000 metric tons . .	1,118	1,061	1,235	1,070
44	Sulfur: Frasch mines (shipments)	1,000 metric tons . .	3,676	2,600	1,904	2,700
45	Talc, and pyrophyllite, crude [9]	1,000 metric tons . .	1,267	997	(D)	972
46	Tripoli	1,000 metric tons . .	94	85	94	(NA)
47	Vermiculite concentrate.	1,000 metric tons . .	209	190	190	190
48	Industrial minerals, undistributed.	(X)	(X)	(X)	(X)	(X)
49	**Metals**	**(X)**	**(X)**	**(X)**	**(X)**	**(X)**
50	Antimony ore and concentrate [10]	Metric tons	(D)	(D)	(D)	(D)
51	Bauxite (dried).	1,000 metric tons . .	(D)	(D)	(D)	(D)
52	Copper [2]	1,000 metric tons . .	1,590	1,760	1,800	1,840
53	Gold [2]	Metric tons	294	330	331	330
54	Iron ore, [14] [15]	Mil. metric tons . . .	57.0	55.6	56.3	57.0
55	Lead [2]	1,000 metric tons . .	497	407	362	365
56	Magnesium metal [16]	1,000 metric tons . .	139	137	132	135
57	Manganiferous ore [15] [17]	1,000 metric tons . .	(D)	(D)	(D)	(D)
58	Mercury [18]	Metric tons	562	64	(D)	(D)
59	Molybdenum [19]	1,000 metric tons . .	62	50	37	40
60	Nickel [20]	1,000 metric tons . .	0.3	6.7	2.5	(NA)
61	Palladium metal	Kilograms	5,930	6,470	6,500	6,500
62	Platinum metal	Kilograms	1,810	1,840	1,800	1,800
63	Silver [2]	Metric tons	2,121	1,804	1,645	1,400
64	Titanium concentrate: Ilmenite [15]	1,000 metric tons . .	(D)	(D)	(D)	(D)
65	Tungsten ore and concentrate [20]	Metric tons	(D)	(D)	(D)	(D)
66	Vanadium [2]	Metric tons	(D)	(D)	(D)	(D)
67	Zinc mine production [2]	1,000 metric tons . .	515	523	488	540
68	Metals, undistributed	(X)	(X)	(X)	(X)	(X)

- Represents zero.   D Withheld to avoid disclosing individual company data.   NA Not available.   X Not applicable.
Z Less than half the unit of measure.   [1] 42 gal. bbl.   [2] Recoverable content of ores, etc.   [3] Includes grindstones, oilstones, whetstones, and deburring media. Excludes grinding pebbles, and tubemill liners.   [4] Contains bituminous limestone and sandstone, and gilsonite. Includes road oil, 1989-92.   [5] Value included in "Industrial minerals, undistributed."   [6] Includes aplite, 1992-93.   [7] 1980, crude and refined; thereafter, refined only.   [8] Excludes abrasive stone, bituminous limestone and sandstone, and ground soapstone, all included elsewhere in table; 1993 excludes dimension stone. State ranks based on publishable data. Includes calcareous marl and slate.

and Principal Producing States, 1994

Value in millions of dollars. See *Historical Statistics, Colonial Times to 1970*, series M 13-37 for selected values]

PRODUCTION VALUE (mil. dol.)				Principal producing States ranked by quantity, 1993	
1990	1992	1993	1994		
141,741	(NA)	(NA)	(NA)	(X)	1
108,422	(NA)	(NA)	(NA)	(X)	2
22,274	(NA)	(NA)	(NA)	(NA)	3
133	(NA)	(NA)	(NA)	(NA)	4
31,658	32,571	(NA)	(NA)	(NA)	5
53,772	(NA)	(NA)	(NA)	(NA)	6
140	(NA)	(Z)	(NA)	(NA)	7
21,022	20,496	(NA)	(NA)	(NA)	8
(Z)	(Z)	(Z)	(NA)	(NA)	9
(5)	6	6	5	CA, VT	10
3,480	2,794	(NA)	(NA)	NV, GA, MO	11
16	20	19	13	NV, GA, MO	12
436	339	373	370	CA	13
173	170	123	157	AR, MI	14
(5)	(5)	(X)	(X)	(NA)	15
-	-	(X)	(X)	(NA)	16
3,683	3,500	3,916	4,155	CA, TX, PA	17
225	195	229	264	FL, IN, TX	18
1,620	1,482	1,488	1,597	GA, AL, TX	19
138	141	150	162	CA, NV, OR	20
28	29	31	30	NC, VA, OK	21
(5)	(5)	(5)	(5)	IL, VT	22
7	5	4	5	ID, NY	23
53	66	58	52	(NA)	24
100	101	107	118	OK, IA, TX	25
113	187	189	191	KS, WY	26
902	950	977	996	OH, MO, AL	27
6	5	4	5	NC, GA, NM	28
19	17	17	18	FL, MI, MN	29
17	16	17	19	NM, AZ, CA	30
1,075	1,058	759	902	FL, NC, ID	31
303	334	286	274	NM	32
11	15	12	14	OR, NM, CA	33
(5)	(5)	(5)	(5)	(NA)	34
827	803	894	906	LA, TX, NY	35
3,686	3,766	3,988	4,293	(NA)	36
3,249	3,341	3,534	3,835	CA, MI, OH	37
436	425	454	458	IL, NJ, CA	38
836	836	734	650	WY, CA	39
34	26	(D)	25	CA, UT	40
5,822	5,775	5,987	6,731	(NA)	41
5,591	5,594	5,770	6,731	TX, PA, FL	42
231	181	217	(8)	GA, WI, MA	43
335	159	101	135	LA, TX	44
31	31	(D)	32	MT, TX, VT	45
3	3	4	(NA)	(NA)	46
19	15	15	(D)	SC, VA	47
504	478	212	136	(NA)	48
12,442	11,537	11,876	(NA)	(NA)	49
(12)	(12)	(12)	(12)	ID	50
(12)	(12)	(12)	(12)	AL, GA	51
4,311	4,179	3,636	4,382	AZ, UT, NM	52
3,650	3,662	3,841	3,843	NV, CA, UT	53
1,741	1,732	1,643	1,700	MN, MI	54
491	308	249	286	MO, AL, ID	55
433	360	377	(D)	(NA)	56
(12)	(12)	(12)	(12)	SC	57
(12)	0.4	(D)	(D)	NV	58
348	209	165	215	AZ, CO, TX	59
(NA)	(12)	(12)	(NA)	(NA)	60
22	18	25	25	MT	61
27	21	21	21	MT	62
329	229	227	192	NV, AZ, ID	63
(12)	(12)	(12)	(12)	FL, CA	64
(12)	(12)	(12)	(12)	CA	65
(12)	(12)	(12)	(12)	ID	66
847	674	497	549	AL, TN, NY	67
242	156	306	113	(NA)	68

[9] For 1991-92, production quantity, talc only; 1989-92 [10] Comprises value of items that cannot be disclosed. [11] Antimony content. [12] Included with "Metals, undistributed. [13] Dried equivalent. [14] Represents shipments; includes byproduct ores. [15] Gross weight. [16] For 1980-85, magnesium chloride for magnesium metal included in "Metals undistributed," canvass for magnesium chloride for magnesium metal discontinued in 1986. [17] 5 to 35 percent manganiferous ore. [18] 1986-89, mercury produced as the primary product only; thereafter, mercury produced as a byproduct of gold ores only. [19] Content of concentrate. [20] Content of ore and concentrate. [21] Tungsten content.

Source: U.S. Bureau of Mines, *Minerals Yearbook* thru 1991; *Annual Reports* and *Mineral Commodities Summaries,* annual. U.S. Energy Information Administration, *Annual Energy Review; Uranium Industry Annual; Petroleum Supply Annual,* vol. 1; *Natural Gas Annual; and Quarterly Coal Report.*

No. 1176. Mineral Industries—Summary: 1987 and 1992

["N.e.c." means not elsewhere classified. See also *Historical Statistics, Colonial Times to 1970*, series M1-12]

MINERAL INDUSTRY	1987 Establishments, total	1987 All employees Number [1] (1,000)	1987 All employees Payroll [2] (mil. dol.)	1987 Production workers [3] Number [1] (1,000)	1987 Production workers [3] Wages (mil. dol.)	1987 Value added in mining [4] (mil. dol.)	1987 Value of shipments and receipts [5] (mil. dol.)	1992 Establishments Total	1992 Establishments With 20 or more employees	1992 All employees Number [1] (1,000)	1992 All employees Payroll [2] (mil. dol.)	1992 Production workers [3] Number [1] (1,000)	1992 Production workers [3] Hours [6] (mil.)	1992 Production workers [3] Wages (mil. dol.)	1992 Value added in mining [4] (mil. dol.)	1992 Value of shipments and receipts [5] (mil. dol.)	1992 Capital expenditures (mil. dol.)
All industries	33,617	698	21,739	451	12,443	110,959	157,964	30,828	5,581	637	24,303	414	873	13,874	113,780	162,339	16,043
Metal mining	1,027	44	1,354	34	952	4,610	6,852	1,063	273	53	2,113	42	89	1,542	7,180	10,327	1,574
Iron ores	51	7	224	6	166	768	1,362	40	18	9	348	7	15	274	985	1,715	53
Copper ores	61	14	405	11	283	1,301	2,150	62	35	15	550	12	25	405	1,730	2,935	516
Lead and zinc ores	39	2	58	1	40	176	268	44	24	3	113	2	5	86	287	472	22
Gold and silver ores	372	13	423	10	305	1,814	2,261	428	116	19	827	16	33	601	3,641	4,453	(D)
Ferroalloy ores, except vanadium	58	1	46	1	24	61	110	(NA)	(NA)	(NA)	(NA)	(NA)	(NA)	(NA)	(NA)	(NA)	(NA)
Metal mining services	268	3	81	2	60	176	251	303	38	3	120	3	6	92	263	357	(D)
Miscellaneous metal ores	236	5	162	4	99	374	559	186	42	4	155	3	5	84	274	396	58
Coal mining	3,905	163	5,567	129	4,251	17,068	25,955	3,086	1,239	134	5,438	108	227	4,197	17,283	26,984	1,899
Bituminous coal and lignite mining	3,507	158	5,410	124	4,125	16,679	25347	2,642	1,155	128	5,247	103	216	4,051	16,792	26,269	1,869
Anthracite mining	107	2	41	2	32	109	206	76	19	2	47	1	2	30	97	161	4
Coal mining services	291	4	116	3	94	280	402	368	65	5	145	4	9	116	394	554	26
Oil and gas extraction	22,910	378	11,961	206	5,283	80,049	112,363	20,877	2,686	344	13,526	187	391	5,992	79,700	111,518	11,423
Crude petroleum and natural gas	10,203	199	7,510	69	2,154	67,955	76,518	9,388	1,017	174	8,409	64	131	2,601	66,297	72,298	9,850
Natural gas liquids	714	13	433	10	320	4,025	24,750	591	197	13	532	9	18	360	4,246	27,206	619
Oil and gas field services	11,993	167	4,018	127	2,809	8,069	11,095	10,898	1,472	157	4,585	114	242	3,031	9,156	12,014	955
Drilling oil and gas wells	2,591	55	1,318	46	1,012	2,549	3,626	2,129	450	48	1,371	38	81	982	2,516	3,584	289
Oil, gas exploration services	1,917	17	452	13	311	771	1,096	1,489	85	14	462	14	19	238	742	980	182
Oil, gas field services, n.e.c	7,485	95	2,248	69	1,486	4,748	6,373	7,280	937	96	2,753	68	143	1,811	5,899	7,451	484
Nonmetallic mining	5,775	113	2,858	83	1,956	9,233	12,795	5,802	1,383	106	3,226	77	166	2,144	9,619	13,510	1,147
Dimension stone [7]	149	1	25	1	18	65	86	171	17	1	31	1	2	22	79	101	5
Crushed and broken stone [8]	2,002	44	1,082	33	754	3,465	4,768	2,142	664	42	1,222	31	68	840	3,670	5,071	430
Sand and gravel [8]	2,750	33	772	24	551	2,320	3,139	2,678	440	30	889	21	47	594	2,321	3,160	262
Clay and related minerals [8]	197	10	272	7	165	827	1,249	200	100	10	320	8	17	211	935	1,400	87
Chemical and fertilizer minerals	148	16	501	12	336	1,999	2,772	156	76	15	564	10	22	347	2,071	3,017	308
Nonmetallic minerals, services	177	2	45	1	32	119	165	175	14	2	47	1	3	35	128	170	14
Miscellaneous [8]	352	7	162	5	101	438	616	280	72	5	154	4	8	96	415	590	42

D Withheld to avoid disclosure. NA Not available. [1] Excludes proprietors and firm members of unincorporated concerns. [2] Gross earnings paid to all employees on payroll. [3] Represents employees up through the working foreman level engaged in manual work. Includes development and exploration workers. [4] Computed by subtracting cost of supplies, minerals received for preparation, purchased fuel and electric energy, contract work, and purchased machinery from the value of shipments and capital expenditures. [5] Represents value of shipments of primary and secondary products of the industry and amount received for services performed for other establishments on a contract, fee, or other basis. [6] Excludes paid vacations, holidays, and sick leave; includes actual overtime hours (not straight-time equivalent). [7] Excludes data for dimension stone quarries operated in conjunction with dressing plants. [8] Excludes data for mining included in establishments classified in manufacturing industries.

Source: U.S. Bureau of the Census, *Census of Mineral Industries: 1987*, and *1992*, final industry series reports.

No. 1177. Nonfuel Mineral Commodities—Summary: 1994

[Preliminary estimates. Average price in dollars per metric tons except as noted]

MINERAL	Unit	MINERAL DISPOSITION				Average price per unit (dollars)	Employ-ment (number)
		Production	Exports	Net import reliance [1] (percent)	Consump-tion, apparent		
Aluminum	1,000 metric tons	5,000	1,300	31	7,300	[2]0.65	21,100
Antimony (contained)	Metric tons	[3]37,000	4,000	62	45,000	[21]1.60	100
Arsenic	Metric tons	-	100	100	19,400	[2]0.50	(NA)
Asbestos	1,000 metric tons	10	21	95	28	[4]531	(NA)
Barite	1,000 metric tons	340	10	82	1,450	[4]38	350
Bauxite and alumina	1,000 metric tons	(D)	1,150	99	3,500	[4]15-18	35
Beryllium (contained)	Metric tons	200	20	(5)	191	[2][6]225	425
Bismuth (contained)	Metric tons	(D)	140	(D)	[1]1,500	[2]3.25	30
Boron (B$_2$O$_3$ content)	1,000 metric tons	560	550	(5)	362	[4][8]324	900
Bromine (contained)	1,000 metric tons	197	20	-	287	[9]36.2	1,600
Cadmium (contained)	Metric tons	[3]1,000	490	50	2,020	[2][10]1.03	140
Cement	1,000 short tons	80,007	599	12	90,492	56.22	18,000
Chromium	1,000 metric tons	[11]91	28	75	387	[4][12]110	(NA)
Clays	1,000 metric tons	42,300	4,400	(5)	37,900	(NA)	11,000
Cobalt (contained)	Metric tons	[11]1,600	1,300	79	7,800	[2]25.00	(NA)
Columbium (contained)	Metric tons	-	160	100	3,700	[2][13]2.60	(NA)
Copper (Mine, contained)	1,000 metric tons	2,380	680	14	2,800	[2]1.08	13,500
Diamond (industrial)	Million carats	149.1	110	17	181	[14]0.62	(NA)
Diatomite	1,000 metric tons	596	104	(5)	494	[4]272	1,000
Feldspar	1,000 metric tons	740	12	(5)	738	[4]41.00	400
Fluorspar	1,000 metric tons	170	20	88	455	(NA)	180
Gallium (contained)	Kilograms	-	(NA)	(NA)	[1]11,500	395	20
Garnet (industrial)	Metric tons	46,500	10,000	(5)	50,400	100-2000	160
Gemstones	Million dollars	66.3	1,550	98	3,536	(NA)	1,000
Germanium (contained)	Kilograms	[3]10,000	(NA)	(NA)	[1]25,000	[15]1,060	100
Gold (contained)	Metric tons	330	140	(5)	310	[16]389.00	13,500
Graphite (crude)	1,000 metric tons	-	19	100	40	[4][17]603	[18]6,700
Gypsum (crude)	1,000 short tons	17,300	100	30	2,600	[4]6.80	(NA)
Indium	Metric tons	-	(NA)	(NA)	[1]40	[19]135.00	(NA)
Iodine	Metric tons	2,000	1,000	58	4,800	[20]7.13	35
Iron ore (usable)	Million metric tons	57.0	4.0	18	69.3	[21]72.5-74.0	7,000
Iron and steel scrap (metal)	Million metric tons	76.4	8.3	(5)	69.6	[4][22]125.00	40,000
Iron and steel slag (metal)	1,000 metric tons	19,000	4	1	[1]19,000	[4]6.70	2,500
Lead (contained)	1,000 metric tons	365	30	17	1,500	[23]36.3	1,500
Lime	1,000 short tons	17,300	80	(1)	17,400	[4]57.50	5,500
Magnesium compounds	1,000 metric tons	380	50	37	600	(NA)	600
Magnesium metal	1,000 metric tons	194	48	(5)	152	[24]1.48-1.53	1,400
Manganese (gross weight)	1,000 metric tons	-	23	100	695	[25][26]2.40	(NA)
Mercury	Metric tons	[27]400	400	(D)	[1]550	[28]180.00	(NA)
Mica, scrap and flake	1,000 metric tons	96	6	14	111	[4]51	80
Molybdenum (contained)	Metric tons	40,000	30,000	(5)	18,000	[29]7.70	700
Nickel (contained)	Metric tons	-	7,570	66	131,000	[30]6,089	2
Nitrogen (fixed)-ammonia	1,000 metric tons	13,050	200	18	16,000	[4][31]215	2,500
Nonrenewable organics	Million metric tons	(NA)	(NA)	(NA)	(NA)	(NA)	(NA)
Peat	1,000 short tons	660	23	49	1,300	[4]26.00	650
Perlite	1,000 metric tons	610	24	8	660	[4]31.15	125
Phosphate rock	1,000 metric tons	41,000	3,400	2	42,000	[4]22.00	5,200
Platinum-group metals	Kilograms	8,300	90,000	91	127,000	[32]400	400
Potash (K$_2$O equivalent)	1,000 metric tons	1,425	400	74	5,390	[4][33]128	1,655
Pumice and pumicite	1,000 metric tons	485	18	24	637	[4]28.22	55
Salt	1,000 metric tons	39,500	700	19	47,400	[4]3[4] 112.00	4,150
Silicon (contained)	1,000 metric tons	390	30	39	640	[35]44.1	(NA)
Silver (contained)	Metric tons	1,400	1,600	(NA)	4,000	[16]5.30	1,000
Sodium carbonate (soda ash)	1,000 metric tons	9,100	2,900	(5)	6,314	[4][36]98.00	2,800
Sodium sulfate	1,000 metric tons	610	85	14	712	[37]114.00	240
Stone (crushed)	Million short tons	1,195	5	-	1,198	[4]5.47	77,000
Sulfur (all forms)	1,000 metric tons	11,300	850	16	13,450	[4][38]45.00	3,100
Talc	1,000 metric tons	972	165	(5)	944	[4]7-350	800
Thallium (contained)	Kilograms	-	(NA)	100	[1]800	285	-
Tin (contained)	Metric tons	[11]11,900	2,700	84	46,000	[2]2.46	5
Titanium dioxide	1,000 metric tons	1,250	344	(5)	1,110	[2][39]10.95	4,600
Tungsten (contained)	Metric tons	(D)	-	94	[7]4,000	[40]45	20
Vermiculite	1,000 metric tons	190	5	12	215	(D)	230
Zinc (contained)	1,000 metric tons	540	390	41	[41]1,350	[23]46.4	2,200
Zirconium (Z$_r$O2) content	Metric tons	(D)	18,587	(D)	(D)	[42]200	(NA)

- Represents or rounds to zero.   D Withheld to avoid disclosure.   NA Not available.   [1] Calculated as a percent of apparent consumption.   [2] Price per pound.   [3] Refinery production.   [4] Price per metric ton.   [5] Net exporter.   [6] Metal, vacuum-cast ingot.   [7] Estimated consumption.   [8] Granulated pentahydrate borax in bulk, f.o.b mine.   [9] Cents per kilogram, bulk, purified bromine.   [10] 1- to 5-short ton lots.   [11] Secondary production.   [12] Turkish, chromite price.   [13] Columbite price.   [14] Value of imports per carat.   [15] Zone refined, first reduction quality.   [16] Price per troy ounce.   [17] Price of flake imports.   [18] Includes employment at calcining plants.   [19] 99.97% indium, per kilogram.   [20] O.i.f. value, crude, per kilogram.   [21] Lake Superior pellets. Cents per long ton unit of iron.   [22] Delivered, No. 1 Heavy Melting composite price.   [23] Cents per pound.   [24] Year-end price, per pound.   [25] Estimated manganese content.   [26] 46%-48% Mn metallurgical ore, per unit contained Mn, c.i.f. U.S. ports.   [27] Secondary industrial production.   [28] Price per 76-pound flask.   [29] Price per kilogram.   [30] London Metal Exchange cash price.   [31] F.o.b. gulf coast.   [32] Dealer price of platinum. Per troy ounce, palladium price was $140 for 1994 and $120 for 1993; rhodium price was $810 for 1994 and $1,066 for 1993.   [33] Price of K20, muriate.   [34] Vacuum and open pan, bulk, pellets and packaged, f.o.b. mine and plant.   [35] Ferrosilicon, 50% Si.   [36] Quoted year-end price, dense, bulk, f.o.b. Green River, WY.   [37] Quoted price, bulk, f.o.b. works, East, per short ton.   [38] Elemental sulfur, f.o.b. mine and/or plant.   [39] Rutile, list, year-end.   [40] Price per unit W03 (7.93 kilograms of contained tungsten per unit).   [41] All forms.   [42] Price for imported zircon, f.o.b. U.S. east coast.

Source: U.S. Bureau of Mines, *Mineral Commodity Summaries,* annual.

No. 1178. Value of Domestic Nonfuel Mineral Production: 1980 to 1994

[In millions of dollars]

AREA	1980	1990	1992	1993	1994	Principal minerals in order of value
U.S. [1] .	25,140	33,452	32,012	[1] 31,912	[1] 34,209	(X)
Northeast..	1,581	2,479	2,308	2,451	2,536	(X)
N.E	268	446	423	424	427	(X)
ME . . .	37	55	56	60	58	Sand and gravel (construction), cement (portland), and stone (crushed and broken).
NH . . .	25	36	42	37	40	Sand and gravel (construction), stone (crushed and broken), and stone dimension).
VT . . .	43	87 [2]	60 [2]	53 [2]	48	Stone (dimension), stone (crushed and broken), and sand and gravel (construction).
MA . . .	91	128	147	160	157	Stone (crushed and broken), sand and gravel (construction), and stone (dimension).
RI	6	18	21 [2]	23 [2]	27	Sand and gravel (construction), stone (crushed and broken), and sand and gravel (industrial).
CT . . .	66	122	97	91	97	Stone, sand, and gravel (construction), & sand and gravel (industrial).
M.A	1,313	2,033	1,885	2,027	2,109	(X)
NY . . .	496	773	766	852	871	Salt, Stone (crushed and broken), and sand and gravel (construction).
NJ . . .	149	229	240	262	274	Stone (crushed and broken), sand and gravel (construction), and sand and gravel (industrial).
PA . . .	668	1,031	879	913	964	Stone (crushed and broken), cement (portland), and lime.
Midwest...	6,610	7,163	7,261	7,357	7,906	(X)
E.N.C. . .	2,930	3,483	3,762	3,875	4,145	(X)
OH . . .	562	733	742	851	893	Stone (crushed and broken), sand and gravel (construction), and salt.
IN	288	428	477	473	517	Stone (crushed and broken), cement (portland), and sand and gravel (construction).
IL	443	667	734	734	770	Stone (crushed and broken), sand and gravel (construction), and cement (portland).
MI	1,485	1,440	1,587	1,504	1,621	Iron ore (usable), cement (portland), & sand and gravel (construction).
WI . . .	152	215	222	313	344	Stone (crushed & broken), sand & gravel (construction), & copper.
W.N.C. . .	3,680	3,680	3,499	3,482	3,761	(X)
MN . . .	1,782	1,482	1,364	1,299	1,352	Iron ore (usable), sand and gravel (construction), and stone (crushed and broken).
IA	252	310	391	398	426	Stone (crushed and broken), cement (portland), and sand and gravel (construction).
MO . . .	1,054	1,105	897	855	1,003	Stone (crushed and broken), cement (portland), and lead.
ND . . .	22	25	26	25	26	Sand and gravel (construction), lime, and sand and gravel (industrial).
SD . . .	228	319	301	337	322	Gold (lode), cement (portland), and sand and gravel (construction).
NE . . .	80	90	115	126	137	Cement (portland), stone (crushed and broken), and sand and gravel (construction).
KS . . .	262	349	405	442	495	Stone (crushed and broken), salt, and Helium (Grade-A).
South	7,320	9,291	8,560	8,578	9,309	(X)
S.A . . .	3,454	5,132	4,651	4,689	5,146	(X)
DE [2] . .	2	10	9	[2]10	[2]9	Magnesium compounds, sand and gravel (construction).
MD . . .	186	368	339	314	324	Stone (crushed and broken), cement (portland), and sand and gravel (construction).
VA . . .	305	507	462	465	514	Stone (crushed and broken), cement (portland), and lime.
WV . . .	106	133	112	149	176	Stone (crushed and broken), cement (portland), and sand and gravel (industrial).
NC . . .	380	586	596	617	705	Stone (crushed and broken), phosphate rock, and sand and gravel (construction).
SC . . .	195	450	247	391	415	Stone (crushed and broken), cement (portland), and gold (lode).
GA . . .	771	1,504	1,346	1,432	1,535	Clay, stone (crushed and broken), and cement (portland).
FL . . .	1,509	1,574	1,440	1,311	1,468	Phosphate rock, stone (crushed and broken), and cement (portland).
E.S.C . . .	1,030	1,692	1,640	1,564	1,696	(X)
KY . . .	204	359	401	388	431	Stone (crushed and broken), lime and cement (portland).
TN . . .	394	663	576	510	577	Stone (crushed and broken), zinc, and cement (portland).
AL . . .	328	559	543	562	576	Stone (crushed and broken), cement (portland), and lime.
MS . . .	104	111	120	104	112	Sand and gravel (construction), clay, and cement (portland).
W.S.C . . .	2,836	2,467	2,269	2,325	2,467	(X)
AR . . .	293	381	404	347	392	Bromine, stone (crushed & broken), & sand & gravel (construction).
LA . . .	584	368	309	232	328	Salt, sulfur (Frasch), and sand and gravel (construction).
OK . . .	224	259	253	298	338	Stone (crushed and broken), cement (portland), and sand and gravel (construction).
TX . . .	1,735	1,459	1,303	1,448	1,409	Cement (portland), stone (crushed and broken), and magnesium metal.
West	9,629	14,512	13,858	13,424	14,354	(X)
Mt	7,223	10,380	10,154	9,736	10,482	(X)
MT . . .	280	573	539	484	492	Gold (lode), copper, and cement (portland).
ID . . .	522	375	306	274	343	Phosphate rock, gold (lode), and sand and gravel (construction).
WY . . .	761	911	951	856	781	Soda ash, clay, and helium (Grade-A).
CO . . .	1,265	377	385	399	440	Sand and gravel (construction), cement (portland), and gold (lode).
NM . . .	766	1,103	871	804	914	Copper, potash, and sand and gravel (construction).
AZ . . .	2,471	3,085	3,166	2,776	3,323	Copper, sand and gravel (construction), and cement (portland).
UT . . .	764	1,335	1,348	1,314	1,428	Copper, gold (lode), and magnesium metal.
NV . . .	394	2,621	2,588	2,829	2,761	Gold (lode), sand and gravel (construction), and diatomite.
Pac . . .	2,406	4,132	3,704	3,688	3,872	(X)
WA . . .	207	483	469	505	556	Sand and gravel (construction), magnesium metal, and stone (crushed and broken).
OR . . .	152	205	214	226	253	Stone (crushed and broken), sand and gravel (construction), and cement (portland).
CA . . .	1,872	2,771	2,346	2,440	2,497	Cement (portland), sand and gravel (construction), and gold (lode).
AK . . .	115	577	526	378	429	Zinc, gold (lode), and sand and gravel (construction).
HI	60	106	149	139	137	Stone (crushed and broken), cement (portland), and sand and gravel (construction).

X Not applicable.   [1] Includes undistributed not shown separately.   [2] Partial data only.
Source: U.S. Bureau of Mines, *Annual Reports, and Mineral Commodities Summary*, annual.

No. 1179. Mineral Industries—Gross Assets and Capital Expenditures: 1977 to 1992

[In millions of dollars]

INDUSTRY AND YEAR	END OF YEAR GROSS VALUE OF DEPRECIABLE ASSETS					CAPITAL EXPENDITURES					
	Total [1]	Buildings and other structures	Machinery and equipment	Mineral exploration and development [1]	Mineral land and rights [1]	Total [1]	New buildings and other structures	New machinery and equipment	Used buildings and other structures	Used machinery and equipment	Mineral exploration and development [1]
Mineral industries: [2]											
1977.........	44,664	6,099	33,068	2,625	2,871	6,802	785	5,068	30	399	520
1982.........	94,613	10,228	73,419	5,036	5,930	13,472	1,229	10,551	78	937	677
1987.........	84,286	9,314	64,143	5,034	5,795	4,869	349	3,234	88	797	401
1992.........	(NA)	(NA)	(NA)	(NA)	(NA)	6,193	(NA)	(NA)	(NA)	(NA)	(NA)
Crude oil, nat. gas:											
1977.........	94,414	(NA)	(NA)	(NA)	(NA)	10,916	571	2,269	14	93	7,969
1982.........	233,052	(NA)	(NA)	(NA)	(NA)	34,281	1,967	5,550	20	215	26,529
1987.........	(NA)	(NA)	(NA)	(NA)	(NA)	10,549	590	3,176	18	218	6,548
1992.........	(NA)	(NA)	(NA)	(NA)	(NA)	9,850	(NA)	(NA)	(NA)	(NA)	(NA)

NA Not available. [1] Excludes data for mineral exploration and development, and mineral land and rights portions for mining service industries and natural gas liquids industry. [2] Excludes crude petroleum and natural gas.

Source: U.S. Bureau of the Census, *Census of Mineral Industries, 1987* and preliminary summary for 1992.

No. 1180. Mineral Industries—Employment, Hours, and Earnings: 1992 to 1994

ITEM	Unit	1992	1993	1994	ITEM	Unit	1992	1993	1994
All mining:					Avg. weekly hours	No ..	43.8	43.8	44.1
All employees.........	1,000 .	635	611	605	Avg. weekly earnings ..	Dol .	614	619	622
Production workers	1,000 .	448	432	431	Metal mining:				
Avg. weekly hours	No ...	43.9	44.3	44.7	All employees.........	1,000 .	53	50	51
Avg. weekly earnings ..	Dol ...	638	647	666	Production workers	1,000 .	42	40	41
Coal mining:					Avg. weekly hours	No ...	42.9	43.1	43.6
All employees.........	1,000 .	127	109	114	Avg. weekly earnings ..	Dol ...	655	659	703
Production workers	1,000 .	103	87	92	Nonmetallic minerals,				
Avg. weekly hours	No ...	44.0	44.4	45.2	except fuels:				
Avg. weekly earnings ..	Dol ...	755	766	802	All employees.........	1,000 .	102	101	101
Oil and gas extraction:					Production workers	1,000 .	76	76	76
All employees.........	1,000 .	353	351	339	Avg. weekly hours	No ...	44.9	46.1	46.5
Production workers	1,000 .	228	229	222	Avg. weekly earnings ..	Dol ...	551	585	608

Source: U.S. Bureau of Labor Statistics, *Bulletin 2370* and *Employment and Earnings,* March and June issues.

No. 1181. Selected Mineral Products—Average Prices: 1970 to 1994

[Excludes Alaska and Hawaii, except as noted. See *Historical Statistics, Colonial Times to 1970,* series M 96, M 139, M 209, M 248, and M 262, for bituminous coal, crude petroleum, iron ore, lead, and aluminum, respectively]

YEAR	Tantalum (dol. per lb.) [1]	Copper, electrolytic [2] (cents per lb.)	Platinum [3] (dol./ troy oz.)	Gold (dol./ fine oz.)	Silver (dol./ fine oz.)	Lead [4] (cents per lb.)	Tin (New York) [5] (cents per lb.)	Zinc [6] (cents per lb.)	Sulfur, crude [7] (dol./ metric ton)	Bituminous coal [8] (dol./ short ton)	Crude petroleum [8] (dol./ bbl.)	Natural gas [8] (dol./ 1,000 cu. ft.)
1970	9.15	58	133	36	1.77	16	174	15	[9]22.41	6.26	3.18	0.17
1975	18.32	64	164	161	4.42	22	340	39	[9]44.20	19.23	7.67	0.44
1980	126.37	101	677	613	20.63	43	846	37	89.06	24.52	21.59	1.59
1981	99.51	84	446	460	10.52	37	733	45	111.48	26.29	31.77	1.98
1982	49.95	73	327	376	7.95	26	654	39	108.27	27.14	28.52	2.46
1983	30.60	77	424	424	11.44	22	655	41	87.24	25.85	26.19	2.59
1984	37.44	67	357	361	8.14	26	624	49	94.31	25.51	25.88	2.66
1985	33.68	67	291	318	6.14	19	596	40	106.46	25.10	24.09	2.51
1986	23.74	66	461	368	5.47	22	383	38	105.22	23.70	12.51	1.94
1987	27.08	83	553	478	7.01	36	419	42	89.78	23.00	15.40	1.67
1988	47.37	121	523	438	6.53	37	441	60	85.95	22.00	12.58	1.69
1989	44.93	131	507	383	5.50	39	520	82	86.62	21.76	15.86	1.69
1990	38.06	123	467	385	4.82	46	386	75	80.14	21.71	20.03	1.71
1991	36.70	109	371	363	4.04	34	363	53	71.45	21.45	16.54	1.64
1992	34.42	107	356	345	3.94	35	402	58	48.14	20.98	15.99	1.74
1993	(NA)	92	370	361	4.30	32	350	46	31.86	20.56	14.24	1.97
1994, prel.	(NA)	108	400	389	5.30	36	358	46	45.00	(NA)	(NA)	(NA)

NA Not available. [1] Dollars per pound of tantalum content. [2] Domestic market prices for wirebar, 1970, 1975-77; prices for cathode thereafter. [3] Average annual dealer prices. [4] 1970, New York prices; beginning 1975, nationwide delivered basis. [5] Straits tin through 1975; thereafter, composite price. [6] Prime western. Beginning 1975, delivered price. [7] F.o.b. works. [8] Average value at the point of production. Source: U.S. Energy Information Administration, *Annual Energy Review.*

Source: Except as noted, U.S. Bureau of Mines, *Mineral Facts and Problems,* 1980 edition; and *Mineral Commodity Summaries,* annual.

No. 1182. Principal Fuels, Nonmetals, and Metals—U.S. Production, as Percent of World Production: 1980 to 1993

MINERAL	Unit	WORLD PRODUCTION				PERCENT U.S. OF WORLD			
		1980	1985	1990	1993	1980	1985	1990	1993
Fuels: [1]									
Coal	Bil. sh. ton	4.2	4.8	5.2	(NA)	20	18	20	(NA)
Petroleum (crude)	Bil. bbl	21.7	19.6	22	(NA)	14	17	12	(NA)
Natural gas (dry, marketable)	Tril. cu. ft	53.1	62	74.3	(NA)	37	26	24	(NA)
Natural gas plant liquids	Bil. bbl	1.4	1.5	1.8	(NA)	43	38	32	(NA)
Nonmetals:									
Asbestos	1,000 metric tons	4,699	4,249	4,003	2,775	2	1	(D)	(NA)
Barite	1,000 metric tons	7,495	6,067	5,633	4,890	27	11	8	6
Feldspar	1,000 metric tons	3,202	4,039	5,456	6,009	20	16	12	13
Fluorspar	1,000 metric tons	5,006	4,979	5,131	4,031	2	1	1	1
Gypsum	Mil. metric tons	78	87	100	103	14	15	15	15
Mica (incl. scrap)	1,000 metric tons	228	255	215	190	46	49	51	46
Nitrogen, (fixed) - ammonia	Mil. metric tons	74	91	97	91	20	14	13	14
Phosphate rock, gross wt.	Mil. metric tons	144	149	162	132	38	34	29	27
Potash (k$_2$O equivalent)	Mil. metric tons	28	29	28	(NA)	8	4	6	(NA)
Sulfur, elemental	Mil. metric tons	55	54	58	52	22	22	20	21
Metals, mine basis:									
Bauxite	Mil. metric tons	89	84	109	106	2	1	(D)	(NA)
Columbian concentrates (Nb content)	1,000 metric tons	15	15	15	31	(NA)	-	(NA)	-
Copper	1,000 metric tons	7,405	7,988	9,017	9,352	16	14	18	19
Gold	Metric tons	1,219	1,532	2,133	2,330	2	5	14	14
Iron ore	Mil. metric tons	891	861	982	989	8	6	6	6
Lead [2]	1,000 metric tons	3,470	3,431	3,353	2,926	17	12	15	12
Mercury	Metric tons	6,806	6,136	4,523	2,563	16	9	12	(NA)
Molybdenum	1,000 metric tons	111	98	128	95	62	50	48	39
Nickel [2]	1,000 metric tons	779	813	965	899	2	1	(Z)	(NA)
Silver	1,000 metric tons	11	13	16	14	9	9	13	12
Tantalum concentrates (ta content)	Metric tons	544	315	400	(NA)	(NA)	-	(NA)	(NA)
Titanium concentrates:									
Ilmenite	1,000 metric tons	3,726	3,457	4,072	3,579	14	(D)	(D)	(NA)
Rutile	1,000 metric tons	436	373	481	464	(D)	(D)	(D)	(NA)
Tungsten [2]	1,000 metric tons	52	47	43	30	5	2	14	(NA)
Vanadium [2]	1,000 metric tons	37	30	31	29	12	(D)	(D)	10
Zinc [2]	1,000 metric tons	5,954	6,758	7,184	6,895	6	4	8	7
Metals, smelter basis:									
Aluminum	1,000 metric tons	15,383	15,398	19,292	19,816	30	23	21	19
Cadmium	1,000 metric tons	18	19	20	19	9	8	8	6
Copper	1,000 metric tons	7,649	8,630	9,472	9,352	14	14	15	19
Iron, pig	Mil. metric tons	514	499	532	989	12	9	9	6
Lead [3]	1,000 metric tons	5,430	5,641	5,763	2,926	23	20	23	12
Magnesium [4]	1,000 metric tons	316	325	354	284	49	42	39	47
Raw Steel	Mil. metric tons	717	718	771	725	14	11	12	12
Tin [5]	1,000 metric tons	251	193	223	193	1	2	-	(NA)
Zinc	1,000 metric tons	6,049	6,786	7,060	7,177	6	5	5	5

- Represents or rounds to zero.   D Withheld to avoid disclosing company data.   NA Not available.   Z Less than half the unit of measure.   [1] Source: Energy Information Administration, *International Energy Annual.*   [2] Content of ore and concentrate.   [3] Refinery production.   [4] Primary production; no smelter processing necessary.   [5] Production from primary sources only.

Source: Except as noted, U.S. Bureau of Mines, *Annual Reports,* and *Mineral Commodity Summaries,* annual.

No. 1183. Federal Strategic and Critical Materials Inventory: 1980 to 1994

[As of **Dec. 31.** Covers strategic and critical materials essential to military and industrial requirements in time of national emergency]

MINERAL	Unit	QUANTITY [1]				VALUE (mil. dol.) [2]			
		1980	1985	1990	1994	1980	1985	1990	1994
Tin	1,000 metric ton	200	185	169	145	3,158	2,324	962	684
Silver	1,000 troy oz	139,500	136,006	92,151	59,507	2,288	801	374	158
Cobalt	Mil. lb	41	53	53	52	1,020	590	443	561
Bauxite [3]	1,000 lg. ton	14,333	17,957	18,033	16,549	583	871	888	191
Manganese [4]	1,000 sh. ton	5,130	4,470	4,017	2,792	599	520	962	468
Tungsten [5]	Mil. lb	97	87	82	82	817	369	253	178
Zinc	1,000 sh. ton	380	378	379	360	317	268	483	307
Titanium	1,000 sh. ton	43	48	37	37	432	405	402	221
Platinum	1,000 troy oz	466	466	453	453	215	154	186	131
Chromium [6]	1,000 sh. ton	804	854	1,074	1,149	773	836	917	837
Diamonds: Stones	Carat 1,000	19,224	12,549	7,777	6,457	349	336	267	533
Industrial, bort	Carat 1,000	23,693	22,001	17,353	4,012	73	39	16	3

[1] Consists of stockpile and nonstockpile grades and reflects uncommitted balances.   [2] Market values are estimated trade values of similar materials and not necessarily amounts that would be realized at time of sale.   [3] Consists of abrasive grade, metallic grade Jamaica, metallic grade Suriname, and refractory.   [4] Consists of chemical grade, dioxide battery natural, dioxide battery synthetic, electrolytic, ferro-high carbon, ferro-med. carbon, ferro-silicon, and metal.   [5] Consists of carbide powder, ferro, metal powder, and ores and concentrates.   [6] Consists of ferro-high carbon, ferro-low carbon, ferro-silicon, and metal.

Source: U.S. Defense Logistics Agency, *Statistical Supplement, Stockpile Report to the Congress* (AP-3).

No. 1184. Federal Strategic and Critical Materials—Summary: 1990 to 1994

ITEM	Unit	Tin	Silver	Cobalt	Bauxite	Manganese	Tungsten	Zinc	Titanium	Platinum	Chromium	DIAMONDS Stones	DIAMONDS Industrial bort
Production:													
1990	1,000 metric tons	[1]13.2	[1]2.1	1.2	(D)	-	(D)	263	24.7	[2]7,740	[1]101	-	[3][4]90.0
1992	1,000 metric tons	18.8	[1]1.8	1.6	(D)	-	(D)	272	(D)	[2]8,310	[1]102	-	[3][4]95.0
1993	1,000 metric tons	17.2	[1]1.6	1.6	(D)	-	(D)	240	(D)	[2]8,300	192	-	[3][4]105.0
1994	1,000 metric tons	7.4	1.4	1.6	(D)	-	(D)	240	(D)	8,300	91	-	108.0
Imports:													
1990	1,000 metric tons	33.8	3.4	6.4	12,987	307	6.4	723	1.1	[2]125,354	346	[4]11.0	[4]85.4
1992	1,000 metric tons	27.3	5.0	5.8	11,372	247	2.5	740	0.7	[2]132,006	324	[4]9.8	[4]97.3
1993	1,000 metric tons	33.7	3.8	5.9	11,936	232	1.7	805	2.2	[2]153,165	330	[4]5.2	[4]133.0
1994	1,000 metric tons	34.0	3.6	7.3	11,200	280	3.6	800	5.0	160,000	281	3.0	140.0
Export:													
1990	1,000 metric tons	0.7	1.8	1.3	64	70	0.1	128	[5]15.8	[2]55,044	16	[4]1.7	[4]71.0
1992	1,000 metric tons	1.9	1.8	1.4	68	13	(6)	120	[5]8.0	[2]57,830	18	[4]5.6	[4]83.6
1993	1,000 metric tons	2.6	1.7	0.8	92	16	(6)	52	57.9	[2]78,521	21	[4]3.4	[4]107.0
1994	1,000 metric tons	2.7	1.6	1.3	150	12	(6)	50	9.0	90,000	28	1.0	110.0
Consumption:													
1990	1,000 metric tons	[7]45.5	4.4	7.6	[8]4,570	497	8.4	992	[9]23.2	[2]117,043	445	[4]9.8	[4]112.7
1992	1,000 metric tons	[7]43.6	4.1	6.5	[8]4,863	438	7.1	1,035	[9]14.2	[2]110,900	422	[4]4.3	[4]121.9
1993	1,000 metric tons	[7]44.2	3.3	6.5	[8]4,633	389	7.1	1,148	[9]15.1	[2]122,700	470	[4]1.9	[4]146.0
1994	1,000 metric tons	46.0	4.0	7.2	3,500	430	8.4	1,220	16.0	127,000	387	2.0	181.0
Net Import reliance:													
1990	Percent	71.0	(10)	84.0	98	100	81.0	41	(11)	88	71	95.0	13.0
1992	Percent	80.0	(10)	75.0	100	100	86.0	30	(D)	87	76	98.0	19.0
1993	Percent	84.0	(10)	79.0	100	100	82.0	45	(D)	89	74	95.0	18.0
1994	Percent	84.0	(10)	79.0	99	100	94.0	41	(D)	91	75	95.0	17.0
Stocks, end of year:													
1990	1,000 metric tons	17.3	9.2	3.2	2,300	379	1.1	87	3.3	[2]30,324	126	(NA)	(NA)
1992	1,000 metric tons	10.7	10.1	1.8	2,300	276	0.7	75	1.9	[2]25,338	118	(NA)	(NA)
1993	1,000 metric tons	10.9	11.2	1.5	1,000	302	0.6	78	2.9	[2]20,782	104	(NA)	(NA)
1994	1,000 metric tons	10.0	8.4	3.1	2,200	325	0.4	75	4.0	20,000	100	(NA)	(NA)
World production:													
1990	1,000 metric tons	218.1	16.5	42.4	109,042	26,108	51.8	7,158	100.8	[2]291,015	12,959	(12)	[4]58.5
1992	1,000 metric tons	178.4	14.7	27.1	101,145	21,608	37.5	7,227	38.6	[2]281,438	10,993	(12)	[4]48.8
1993	1,000 metric tons	178.2	14.1	22.2	105,550	21,757	29.5	6,895	37.0	[2]250,718	10,001	(12)	[4]50.4
1994	1,000 metric tons	180.0	14.0	22.0	110,000	21,000	21.0	6,700	31.0	250,000	9,400	(12)	50.0

- Represents or rounds to zero. D Withheld to avoid disclosure of individual company data. NA Not available. [1] Production from scrap or secondary production. [2] Kilograms. [3] Manufactured diamond bort, grit, and powder and dust. [4] Million carats. [5] All metal forms. [6] Less than 50 metric tons. [7] Apparent demand. [8] Includes alumina. [9] Reported consumption. [10] Net importer; however, changes in unreported investor stocks preclude calculation of a meaningful net import reliance. [11] Net exporter. [12] Included with bort production; data not separable.

Source: U.S. Bureau of Mines, *Annual Reports*, and *Mineral Commodity Summaries*, annual.

No. 1185. Selected Mineral and Metal Products—Quantity and Value of Imports and Exports: 1990 to 1993

[Imports represent imports for consumption. Exports include shipments under foreign aid programs. Import and export data are not necessarily comparable to prior data due to change in tariff schedule to Harmonized System]

PRODUCT	Unit	QUANTITY				VALUE (mil. dol.)			
		1990	1991	1992	1993	1990	1991	1992	1993
IMPORTS									
Petroleum (crude) [1]	Mil. bbls	2,222	2,124	(NA)	(NA)	43,833	37,123	(NA)	(NA)
Gem stones: Diamonds	Mil. carats	7.5	8.5	9.4	11.5	3,955	3,992	4,144	5,096
Ores and concentrates:									
Chromium (Cr_2O_3 content)	1,000 metric tons	134	94	99	123	22	15	15	17
Copper	1,000 metric tons	91.5	60.8	102.1	37	131	69	125	46
Iron	Mil. metric tons	18.1	13.3	12.5	14	560	437	396	421
Tungsten	1,000 metric tons	6.4	7.8	2.5	1.7	31	43	16	8
Metals:									
Aluminum	1,000 metric tons	960	1,025	1,156	1,836	1,597	1,428	1,501	2,147
Cobalt [2]	1,000 metric tons	6.0	6.4	5.3	5.4	107	158	246	166
Copper refined ingots, etc	1,000 metric tons	262	289	289	343	675	685	660	669
Gold (refined bullion)	Metric tons	65	147	141	130	795	1,722	1,568	1,495
Iron and steel products (major)	Mil. metric tons	17.8	16.2	17.4	20.0	11,612	11,962	10,977	(NA)
Platinum group [3]	Metric tons	125	126	132	153	1,906	1,743	1,484	1,311
Silver (refined bullion)	Metric tons	2,698	2,525	2,662	2,183	437	339	341	297
Zinc: Blocks, pigs, slabs	1,000 metric tons	632	549	644	724	992	620	784	699
EXPORTS									
Fuels: [1]									
Bituminous coal	Mil. sh. tons	95.3	98.4	(NA)	(NA)	4,464	4,588	(NA)	(NA)
Petroleum (crude)	Mil. bbls	8.0	2.7	(NA)	(NA)	198.6	54.1	(NA)	(NA)
Nonmetallic minerals:									
Gem stones: Diamonds	Mil. carats	1.2	1.8	1.9	1.6	1,433	1,383	1,362	1,499
Nitrogen compounds (maj.)	Mil. metric tons	11.9	13.9	12.8	11.5	(NA)	(NA)	(NA)	(NA)
Phosphatic fertilizers [4]	Mil. metric tons	9.2	11.5	10.3	9.2	1,515	1,974	(NA)	(NA)
Metals:									
Aluminum: Ingots, slabs, crude	1,000 metric tons	684	793	604	400	1,169	1,274	843	541
Plates, sheets, bars, etc	1,000 metric tons	419	489	534	571	1,278	1,384	1,416	1,346
Gold (refined bullion)	Metric tons	141	174	257	658	1,719	2,039	2,877	7,611
Iron and steel products (major)	Mil. metric tons	4.7	6.6	4.7	4.5	4,665	5,753	5,374	4,848
Magnesium [5]	1,000 metric tons	51.8	55.2	52	39	164	150	132	103
Molybdenum [6]	Metric tons	180	88	74	52	2	1	1	1
Silver (refined bullion)	Metric tons	736	787	911	705	120	115	126	100
Scrap exports:									
Aluminum	1,000 metric tons	537	461	295	212	719	542	300	211
Iron and steel	Mil. metric tons	11.7	9.5	9.4	10	1,653	1,253	1,113	1,341

NA Not available.   [1] Source: U.S. Bureau of the Census, *U.S. Imports for Consumption* and *General Imports, TSUSA Commodity and Country,* FT 246, annual; and *U.S. Exports, Schedule B Commodity and Country,* FT 446, annual; 1989 and 1990, *U.S. Exports of Merchandise* and *U.S. Imports of Merchandise* compact discs, December issues.   [2] Includes unwrought metal, waste and scrap.   [3] Unwrought and semimanufactured.   [4] Superphosphates and ammonium phosphates.   [5] Metal and alloys, scrap, semimanufactured forms.   [6] Metals and alloys, crude and scrap.

Source: Except as noted, U.S. Bureau of Mines, *Minerals Yearbook,* and *Annual Reports.*

No. 1186. Mineral Industries—Lost Workday Injuries and Fatalities: 1993

[Excludes office workers. Lost workday injuries are nonfatal occurrences that result in days away from work, days of restricted work activity or a permanent disability. Data for all years includes injuries to independent contractors at mine sites. Rates for the noncoal industries are based only on employment and hours worked by mine employees. See also *Historical Statistics, Colonial Times to 1970,* series M 271-286]

ITEM	Coal mining	Quarrying; related industries [1]	Metal mining [2]	Sand and gravel mining	Nonmetal mining
Injuries, total	8,375	3,208	1,741	1,126	965
Fatal	47	19	14	13	5
Rate per million work-hours:					
Fatal	0.20	0.15	0.16	0.23	0.10
Nonfatal	36.0	24.9	19.9	19.9	19.1
Fatalities per 1,000 employed [3]	0.35	0.30	0.32	0.40	0.19

[1] Includes cement.   [2] Nonmetal mines exclude extraction of Frasch process sulfur.   [3] Average number of persons at work each day mines were active.

Source: U.S. Mine Safety and Health Administration, Denver, CO, unpublished data.

No. 1187. Net U.S. Imports of Selected Minerals and Metals as Percent of Apparent Consumption, 1980 to 1994, and by Major Foreign Sources

[**Percent,** based on net imports which equal the difference between imports and exports plus or minus Government stockpile and industry stock changes]

MINERAL	1980	1990	1992	1993	1994	Rank of major foreign sources, 1990-93
Columbium	100	100	100	100	100	Brazil, 66%; Canada, 25%; Germany 4%
Manganese. . . .	98	100	100	100	100	Rep. of So. Africa, 24%; France, 13%; Brazil, 12%
Mica (sheet) . . .	100	100	100	100	100	India, 64%; Belgium, 18%; China, 3%
Strontium	100	100	100	100	100	Mexico, 92%; Germany, 6%
Bauxite [1]	94	98	100	100	99	Australia, 36%; Jamaica, 20%; Guinea, 18%
Asbestos	78	90	95	95	95	Canada, 98%; Rep. of South Africa, 1%
Platinum group .	87	88	87	89	91	Rep. of So. Africa, 47%; Russia, 15%; U.K., 14%.
Tantalum	90	86	85	85	86	Germany, 27%; Australia, 21%; Canada, 8%
Cobalt	93	84	75	79	79	Zambia, 26%; Zaire, 19%; Canada, 16%
Chromium.	91	71	76	74	75	Rep. of So. Africa, 43%; Turkey, 15%; Zimbabwe, 9%
Tungsten	53	81	86	82	84	China, 45%; Bolivia, 9%; Peru, 7%
Nickel.	76	64	59	63	66	Canada, 51%; Norway, 15%; Australia, 10%
Tin.	79	71	80	84	84	Brazil, 25%; Bolivia, 24%; China, 23%
Barite.	44	71	52	70	82	China, 72%; India, 19%; Mexico, 5%.
Potash	65	68	68	72	74	Canada, 91%; Israel, 3%; former U.S.S.R., 3%
Antimony	47	51	60	62	62	China, 60%; Mexico, 10%; Rep. of So. Africa, 10%
Cadmium	55	46	52	61	50	Canada, 37%; Mexico, 18%; Australia, 8%
Selenium	59	46	48	39	39	Canada, 41%; Japan, 14%; Philippines, 13%
Zinc.	60	[2]41	[2]30	[2]45	41	Canada, 60%; Mexico, 13%; Peru, 6%
Gypsum	35	36	31	31	30	Canada, 71%; Mexico, 22%; Spain, 5%.
Iron ore	25	21	12	14	18	Canada, 53%; Brazil, 21%; Venezuela, 21%
Iron and steel . .	13	13	13	15	21	EEC [3], 31%; Canada, 21%; Japan, 15%
Sulfur.	14	15	20	12	16	Canada, 61%; Mexico, 31%.
Copper.	16	3	2	7	14	Canada, 41%; Chile, 15%; Mexico, 13%
Aluminum	(4)	(4)	1	19	31	Canada, 75%; Russia, 6%; Venezuela, 5%
Silver	7	(NA)	(NA)	(NA)	(NA)	Mexico, 29%; Canada, 25%; Peru, 10%
Mercury	27	(D)	(NA)	(D)	(D)	Canada, 78%; Germany, 20%
Titanium	32	(4)	(D)	(4)	(4)	Japan, 43%; former U.S.S.R., 36%; China, 14%
Vanadium	35	(D)	(D)	(D)	(D)	Canada, 24%; EC, 20%; So. Amer.& Mexico, 16%

D Withheld to avoid disclosure.   NA Not available.   [1] Includes alumina.   [2] Effect of sharp rise in exports of concentrates. If calculated on a refined zinc-only basis, reliance would be about the same as pre-1990 level; 1990, 64%; 1991, 61%; and 1992, 64%.   [3] European Economic Community.   [4] Net exports.

Source: U.S. Bureau of Mines, *Mineral Commodity Summaries;* import and export data from U.S. Bureau of the Census.

No. 1188. Federal Offshore Leasing, Exploration, Production, and Revenue: 1980 to 1993

[See source for explanation of terms and for reliability statement]

ITEM	Unit	1980	1985	1987	1988	1989	1990	1991	1992	1993
Tracts offered	Number. .	483	15,754	10,926	33,376	11,013	10,459	16,800	9,618	10,164
Tracts leased.	Number. .	218	667	640	1,856	1,049	825	676	204	336
Acres offered.	1,000 . . .	2,563	87,029	59,762	85,366	60,096	56,788	80,288	52,380	55,070
Acres leased.	1,000 . . .	1,134	3,512	45,075	10,040	5,580	4,263	3,416	1,021	1,714
Bonus paid for leased tracts	Bil. dol. . .	4.2	1.5	0.5	1.2	0.6	0.6	0.4	0.1	0.1
New wells being drilled:										
Active.	Number. .	191	195	142	116	123	120	64	104	129
Suspended	Number. .	739	348	265	289	361	266	249	180	133
Wells completed.	Number. .	9,638	12,285	12,736	12,827	12,938	13,167	13,184	13,209	13,181
Wells plugged and abandoned.	Number. .	8,057	10,487	12,373	13,164	13,846	14,677	15,430	16,348	16,709
Revenue, total [1]	Bil. dol. . .	6.4	5.2	2.9	3.4	2.8	3.3	2.8	2.5	2.6
Bonuses	Bil. dol. . .	4.2	1.5	0.5	1.2	0.6	0.6	0.4	0.1	0.1
Oil and gas royalties [1]	Bil. dol. . .	2.1	3.6	2.3	2.1	2.1	2.6	2.3	2.3	2.5
Rentals	Bil. dol. . .	(Z)	0.1	0.1	0.1	0.1	0.1	0.1	0.1	(Z)
Production, value [2]	Bil. dol. . .	13.1	22.2	14.6	12.9	13.0	16.5	14.2	14.5	15.8
Crude oil	Bil. dol. . .	4.8	9.6	5.6	4.2	4.4	5.9	5.2	5.3	4.9
Condensate	Bil. dol. . .	0.4	1.0	0.7	0.7	0.8	1.1	1.1	1.0	1.0
Natural gas	Bil. dol. . .	7.9	11.5	8.1	7.9	7.8	9.5	7.9	8.2	9.9
Production: [2]										
Crude oil	Mil. bbls. .	259	352	325	279	260	274	263	301	307
Condensate	Mil. bbls. .	19	37	41	41	45	51	52	52	55
Natural gas	Bil. cu. . . .	4,641	4,000	4,425	4,310	4,200	5,093	4,516	4,685	4,533

Z Less than $50 million.   [1] Includes condensate royalties.   [2] Production value is value at time of production, not current value.

Source: U.S. Dept. of the Interior, Minerals Management Service, *Federal Offshore Statistics,* annual.

No. 1189. Petroleum Industry—Summary: 1980 to 1993

[Includes all costs incurred for drilling and equipping wells to point of completion as productive wells or abandonment after drilling becomes unproductive. Based on sample of operators of different size drilling establishments]

ITEM	Unit	1980	1985	1987	1988	1989	1990	1991	1992	1993
Crude oil producing wells (Dec. 31).	1,000...	548	647	620	612	603	602	614	594	584
Daily output per well	Bbl.	15.9	13.9	13.5	13.5	12.6	12.2	12.1	12.1	11.7
Completed wells drilled, total	1,000...	56.93	57.88	28.71	25.58	22.82	26.23	24.56	19.82	20.85
Crude oil.	1,000...	30.50	33.14	15.33	12.53	9.76	11.53	11.36	8.22	7.70
Gas.	1,000...	15.13	12.97	7.08	7.58	8.57	9.86	8.67	7.59	8.65
Dry	1,000...	11.30	11.76	6.30	5.48	4.49	4.83	4.53	4.01	4.49
Average depth per well [1].	Feet . . .	4,773	4,637	4,762	5,051	4,925	5,043	5,100	5,445	5,668
Average cost per well [1]	$1,000. .	368	349	280	355	362	384	421	383	427
Offshore	$1,000. .	3,024	4,073	2,896	3,112	3,197	3,112	3,550	3,223	3,250
Average cost per foot [1]	Dollars. .	77.02	75.35	58.71	70.23	73.55	76.07	82.64	70.27	75.30
Crude oil production, total	Mil. bbl. .	3,146	3,275	3,047	2,979	2,785	2,685	2,707	2,625	2,499
Value at wells	Bil. dol. .	67.9	78.9	46.9	37.5	44.1	53.8	44.7	42.0	35.5
Average price per barrel	Dollars. .	21.59	24.09	15.40	12.58	15.86	20.03	16.54	15.99	14.24
Refinery input of crude oil	Mil. bbl. .	4,934	4,381	4,692	4,848	4,891	4,895	4,855	4,909	4,969
Imports: Crude oil	Mil. bbl. .	1,926	1,168	1,706	1,869	2,133	2,151	2,111	2,223	2,472
Refined petroleum products	Mil. bbl. .	603	681	731	840	809	775	500	471	(NA)
Import value	Bil. dol. .	78.7	53.5	43.5	42.6	51.9	63.8	53.5	54.8	55.0
Export value	Bil. dol. .	7.9	9.9	7.5	7.1	7.5	9.2	9.7	9.1	7.6
Operable refineries.	Number .	319	223	219	213	204	205	202	199	187
Capacity (Jan. 1)	Mil. bbl. .	6,566	5,716	5,683	5,811	5,712	5,683	5,723	5,731	5,519
Output	Mil. bbl. .	5,352	5,019	5,339	5,498	5,539	5,570	5,933	6,050	(NA)
Utilization rate	Percent .	75.4	77.6	83.1	84.7	86.6	87.1	86.0	87.9	91.4
Proved reserves	Bil. bbl. .	29.8	28.4	27.3	26.8	26.5	26.3	24.7	23.7	23.0

NA Not available.   [1] Source: American Petroleum Institute, *Joint Association Survey on Drilling Costs,* annual.

Source: Except as noted, U.S. Energy Information Administration, *Annual Energy Review, Petroleum Supply Annual;* U.S. *Crude Oil, Natural Gas,* and *Natural Gas Liquids Reserves.*

No. 1190. Natural Gas—Financial Performance Measures: 1985 to 1993

[LT = Long term. S&P = Standard & Poor's]

ITEM	1985	1986	1987	1988	1989	1990	1991	1992	1993
Producer segment, majors:									
Average adjusted stock price	28.24	34.82	37.01	41.64	51.79	49.20	50.01	48.50	57.50
S&P bond rating	AA-	A+	A	AA-	AA	AA	AA	AA	AA
LT debt as a percent of invested capital.	32.06	31.51	28.33	30.54	30.35	27.76	29.19	30.10	28.85
Times interest earned ratio	5.09	3.41	3.76	4.42	4.32	5.07	4.04	3.93	4.80
Rate of return on common equity (%) . .	14.30	10.34	10.64	17.67	18.56	17.78	12.54	9.05	13.74
Price/earnings ratio	7.35	10.47	11.69	9.11	10.65	9.98	15.15	15.14	16.40
Market/book value ratio	1.18	1.31	1.69	1.65	1.99	1.92	2.01	2.07	2.38
Producer segment, independents:									
Average adjusted stock price	14.66	14.52	12.33	12.84	17.34	15.14	12.01	11.93	14.53
S&P bond rating	A-	BBB+	BBB	BBB-	BBB-	BBB-	BB+		BB+
LT debt as a percent of invested capital.	47.39	59.03	61.13	73.47	68.00	63.00	55.87	53.93	52.21
Times interest earned ratio	0.36	−0.56	0.52	0.91	1.59	1.46	1.21	1.46	1.23
Rate of return on common equity (%) . .	−10.39	−15.08	−7.85	−1.69	6.51	1.93	−1.17	1.99	1.21
Price/earnings ratio	6.78	22.07	15.70	17.96	16.45	23.75	31.28	21.50	29.61
Market/book value ratio	1.23	1.45	1.96	1.84	2.32	2.63	2.05	1.85	2.18
Pipeline segment, w/Columbia:									
Average adjusted stock price	19.68	19.97	17.96	20.52	27.84	23.76	20.10	23.49	26.26
S&P bond rating	BBB-	BBB-	BBB-	BBB	BBB	BBB	BBB-	BB+	BB+
LT debt as a percent of invested capital.	53.35	57.20	52.92	52.29	52.99	53.24	55.91	54.61	50.39
Times interest earned ratio	1.89	0.83	1.75	1.44	1.79	1.65	1.00	1.74	2.33
Rate of return on common equity (%) . .	6.32	−3.93	7.97	6.18	8.63	7.47	1.01	6.23	10.97
Price/earnings ratio	10.94	13.00	12.04	13.42	14.66	16.00	17.36	13.18	16.57
Market/book value ratio	1.11	1.30	1.31	1.28	1.51	1.55	1.52	1.53	1.86
Average adjusted stock price	17.69	19.94	18.84	18.66	23.29	21.21	20.53	22.78	26.06
S&P bond rating	BBB+	BBB+	A	A	A	A	A	A	A
LT debt as a percent of invested capital . .	44.21	45.04	44.27	47.30	46.31	47.28	48.62	48.83	46.46
Times interest earned ratio	2.81	2.67	3.01	2.51	2.49	2.04	1.95	2.42	3.07
Rate of return on common equity (%) . . .	8.55	11.41	12.19	10.35	12.35	9.17	7.17	4.09	11.07
Price/earnings ratio	8.42	12.74	11.96	10.16	12.01	12.69	15.15	14.38	14.48
Market/book value ratio	1.29	1.48	1.48	1.36	1.49	1.51	1.47	1.56	1.75

Source: U.S. Energy Information Administration, *Natural Gas 1994: Issues and Trends.*

No. 1191. World Crude Oil Production: 1980 to 1993

[In thousands of barrels]

COUNTRY	1980	1985	1988	1989	1990	1991	1992	1993
Total [1]	59,599	53,981	58,662	59,773	60,471	60,105	60,255	60,070
Algeria	1,106	1,037	1,040	1,095	1,175	1,230	1,217	1,190
Kuwait.	1,656	1,023	1,492	1,783	1,175	190	1,029	1,872
Libya	1,787	1,059	1,175	1,150	1,375	1,483	1,483	1,377
Saudi Arabia	9,900	3,388	5,086	5,064	6,410	8,115	8,438	8,198
United Arab Emirates	1,709	1,193	1,565	1,860	2,117	2,386	2,325	2,241
Indonesia.	1,577	1,325	1,342	1,409	1,462	1,592	1,566	1,507
Iran	1,662	2,250	2,240	2,810	3,088	3,312	3,429	3,650
Nigeria	2,055	1,495	1,450	1,716	1,810	1,892	1,982	2,050
Venezuela	2,168	1,677	1,903	1,907	2,137	2,375	2,334	2,377
Canada	1,435	1,471	1,616	1,560	1,553	1,548	1,598	1,678
Mexico	1,936	2,745	2,512	2,520	2,553	2,680	2,668	2,671
United Kingdom	1,622	2,530	2,232	1,802	1,820	1,797	1,825	1,909
United States	8,597	8,971	8,140	7,613	7,355	7,417	7,171	6,847
China	2,114	2,505	2,730	2,757	2,774	2,835	2,838	2,911
U.S.S.R. (former)	11,706	11,585	11,978	11,625	10,880	9,887	8,388	7,297

[1] Includes countries not shown separately.

Source: U.S. Energy Information Administration, *Monthly Energy Review*.

No. 1192. World Natural Gas Production: 1984 to 1992

[In quadrillion Btu's]

REGION AND COUNTRY	1984	1985	1986	1987	1988	1989	1990	1991	1992 [1]
World total.	58.33	60.62	61.89	64.93	68.07	70.56	72.00	73.96	74.27
North America	21.54	20.80	20.13	20.88	21.87	22.34	22.99	23.37	23.76
Canada	2.61	2.98	2.77	3.00	3.47	3.67	3.72	4.18	4.56
United States	17.93	16.91	16.47	17.05	17.52	17.78	18.36	18.28	18.31
Central and South America.	1.78	1.84	1.86	1.82	2.04	2.21	2.22	2.22	2.21
Western Europe	6.03	6.25	6.26	6.59	6.28	6.47	6.47	7.56	7.60
Eastern Europe	21.31	23.11	24.54	25.61	27.08	27.96	28.34	28.04	26.85
Middle East	2.10	2.50	2.76	3.18	3.53	3.87	3.89	3.89	4.31
Africa	1.91	1.97	1.99	2.23	2.32	2.53	2.60	2.82	2.92
Far East and Oceania	3.66	4.16	4.35	4.63	4.96	5.18	5.48	6.06	6.62

[1] Preliminary.

Source: U.S. Energy Information Administration, *International Energy Annual*.

No. 1193. Domestic Motor Gasoline Supply: 1980 to 1994

[In 1,000 barrels per day, except as noted]

ITEM	1980	1985	1986	1987	1988	1989	1990	1991	1992	1993	1994
Supply [1]	6,579	6,831	7,034	7,206	7,336	7,328	7,235	7,188	7,268	7,476	7,592
Production	6,506	6,419	6,752	6,841	6,956	6,963	6,959	6,975	7,058	7,360	7,291
Net imports	140	381	326	384	405	369	342	297	294	247	354
Stocks (mil. bbl.) [2] . .	261	223	233	226	228	213	220	219	216	226	211

NA Not available. [1] Production plus net imports less net increase in primary stocks. [2] End of year, includes motor gasoline blending components.

Source: U.S. Energy Information Administration, *Monthly Energy Review*.

No. 1194. Natural Gas Plant Liquids—Production and Value: 1970 to 1993

[Barrels of 42 gallons. See also *Historical Statistics, Colonial Times to 1970*, series M 143-146]

ITEM	Unit	1970	1980	1985	1987	1988	1989	1990	1991	1992	1993
Field production [1]	Mil. bbl . . .	606	576	587	582	595	564	566	606	621	634
Pentanes plus	Mil. bbl . . .	197	126	103	106	111	113	112	118	121	122
Liquefied petroleum gases .	Mil. bbl . . .	400	441	479	474	483	451	454	488	500	512
Natural gas processed	Tril. cu. ft. .	19	15	13	13	13	13	15	16	16	16

[1] Includes other finished petroleum products, not shown separately.

Source: Through 1975, U.S. Bureau of Mines, *Minerals Yearbook;* thereafter, U.S. Energy Information Administration, *Energy Data Reports, Petroleum Statement Annual, Petroleum Supply Annual,* and *Natural Gas Annual*.

No. 1195. U.S. Petroleum Balance: 1980 to 1993

[In millions of barrels]

ITEM	1980	1985	1988	1989	1990	1991	1992	1993
Petroleum products supplied	**6,242**	**5,740**	**6,308**	**6,324**	**6,201**	**6,101**	**6,234**	**6,291**
New supply of products	6,249	5,676	6,290	6,270	6,259	6,110	6,206	6,316
Production of products	5,765	5,363	5,849	5,874	5,934	5,933	6,050	6,182
Crude input to refineries	4,934	4,381	4,835	4,891	4,894	4,855	4,909	4,969
Oil, field production	3,146	3,275	2,979	2,779	2,685	2,707	2,625	2,499
Alaska	592	666	738	684	647	656	627	577
Lower 48 States	2,555	2,608	2,241	2,095	2,037	2,050	1,997	1,922
Net imports	1,821	1,094	1,807	2,081	2,112	2,068	2,194	2,441
Imports (gross excluding SPR) [1]	1,910	1,125	1,845	2,112	2,142	2,111	2,223	2,472
SPR [1] imports	16	43	19	20	10	-	4	5
Exports	−105	75	57	52	40	42	32	36
Other sources	33	12	57	32	98	80	90	28
Natural gas plant liquids (NGPL), supply	577	604	593	563	574	613	628	664
Other liquids	253	378	418	420	465	466	513	550
Net imports of refined products	484	313	441	396	326	177	156	134
Imports	578	523	681	656	598	500	471	461
Exports	94	210	240	260	272	323	315	327
Stock withdrawal, refined products	−7	64	17	53	−59	−10	28	−24
Ending stocks, all oils	1,392	1,519	1,597	1,581	1,621	1,617	1,592	1,647
Crude oil and lease condensate	358	321	330	341	323	325	318	335
Strategic Petroleum Reserve (SPR) [1]	108	493	560	580	586	569	575	587
Unfinished oils	124	107	100	(NA)	(NA)	(NA)	(NA)	(NA)
Gasoline blending components	17	33	39	(NA)	(NA)	(NA)	(NA)	(NA)
Pentanes plus	(NA)	8	7	(NA)	(NA)	(NA)	(NA)	(NA)
Finished refined products	785	557	562	580	712	724	(NA)	(NA)
PRODUCT TYPE SUPPLIED								
Total products	**6,242**	**5,740**	**6,326**	**6,324**	**6,201**	**6,101**	**6,234**	**6,291**
Finished motor gasoline	2,407	2,493	2,678	2,675	2,641	2,623	2,660	2,729
Distillate fuel oil	1,049	1,047	1,140	1,152	1,103	1,066	1,090	1,110
Residual fuel oil	918	439	5,030	500	449	423	401	394
Liquefied petroleum gases [2]	414	584	604	609	568	616	642	633
Pentanes plus, other liquids, etc.	1,454	1,155	1,369	1,378	1,431	1,365	70	72
Crude oil	(NA)	22	15	10	9	7	5	4

- Represents zero.   NA Not available.   [1] SPR=Strategic Petroleum Reserve. (See table 956.)   [2] Includes ethane.

Source: U.S. Energy Information Administration, *Petroleum Supply Annual*.

No. 1196. Crude Petroleum and Natural Gas—Production, by State: 1985 to 1993

[See also *Historical Statistics, Colonial Times to 1970*, series M 138, M 142, and M 147-161]

STATE	CRUDE PETROLEUM						NATURAL GAS MARKETED PRODUCTION [1]					
	Quantity (mil. bbl.)			Value (mil. dol.)			Quantity (bil. cu. ft.)			Value (mil. dol.)		
	1985	1990	1993	1985	1990	1993	1985	1990	1993	1985	1990	1993
Total [2]	3,274	2,685	2,499	78,884	53,772	35,611	17,270	18,594	19,305	43,343	31,658	39,185
AL	22	18	19	579	387	308	107	135	388	398	373	956
AK	666	658	577	10,655	10,086	8,141	321	403	430	236	554	611
AR	19	10	10	443	222	150	155	175	196	393	360	551
CA	424	322	293	8,386	5,732	3,548	491	363	316	1,653	857	753
CO	30	31	29	758	722	481	178	243	401	517	377	646
FL	11	6	6	(NA)	(NA)	(NA)	11	6	7	26	15	15
IL	30	20	17	795	467	288	1	1	(Z)	4	1	1
IN	5	3	3	134	73	51	(Z)	(Z)	(Z)	1	1	(Z)
KS	75	59	50	1,939	1,359	798	528	574	686	671	893	1,238
KY	8	5	6	201	124	99	73	75	87	174	169	198
LA	508	148	139	5,387	3,409	2,349	5,014	5,242	5,166	13,355	9,587	11,052
MI	27	20	14	726	458	235	132	140	205	475	420	487
MS	31	30	23	796	630	336	144	95	81	456	167	139
MT	30	20	17	734	429	250	52	50	55	125	90	84
NE	7	5	5	163	119	75	2	1	2	6	2	4
NM	79	66	68	2,028	1,472	1,118	905	965	1,409	2,370	1,629	2,512
NY	1	(Z)	(Z)	25	9	-	32	25	21	106	55	51
ND	51	39	31	1,307	849	478	73	52	60	138	93	110
OH	15	8	8	361	196	140	182	155	137	560	393	337
OK	163	117	97	4,256	2,690	1,598	1,936	2,258	2,050	4,930	3,548	3,859
PA	5	2	2	114	54	35	150	178	132	474	417	359
TX	889	674	619	23	15,060	10,022	6,053	6,343	6,250	14,097	9,939	13,059
UT	41	23	22	773	524	385	83	146	225	293	249	398
WV	4	2	2	86	43	34	145	178	176	558	568	467
WY	129	103	88	3,061	2,169	1,284	417	736	779	1,252	856	1,549

NA Not available.   Z Less than 500 million cubic feet or less than $500,000.   [1] Excludes nonhydrocarbon gases.   [2] Includes other States not shown separately. State production does not include State offshore production.

Source: U.S. Energy Information Administration, *Energy Data Reports, Petroleum Supply Annual, Natural Gas Annual,* and *Natural Gas Monthly*.

No. 1197. Natural Gas—Supply, Consumption, Reserves, and Marketed Production: 1970 to 1993

[See also *Historical Statistics, Colonial Times to 1970*, series M 147-161]

ITEM	Unit	1970	1975	1980	1985	1987	1988	1989	1990	1991	1992	1993
Producing wells (year-end)	1,000	117	130	182	243	249	257	262	270	277	276	286
Production value at wells	Bil. dol	3.7	8.9	32.1	43.2	29.0	30.3	30.6	31.8	30.3	32.6	39.2
Avg. per 1,000 cu. ft . .	Dollars . . .	0.17	0.44	1.59	2.51	1.67	1.69	1.69	1.71	1.64	1.74	2.03
Proved reserves [1]	Tril. cu. ft . .	291	228	199	193	187	168	167	169	167	165	165
Marketed production [2]	Tril. cu. ft . .	21.9	20.1	20.2	17.3	17.4	17.9	18.1	18.6	18.5	18.7	19.3
Drawn from storage	Tril. cu. ft . .	1.5	1.8	2.0	2.4	1.9	2.3	2.9	2.0	2.8	2.8	2.8
Imports [3]	Tril. cu. ft . .	0.8	1.0	1.0	1.0	1.0	1.3	1.4	1.5	1.8	2.1	2.3
Consumption, total	Tril. cu. ft . .	21.1	19.5	19.9	17.3	17.2	18.0	18.8	18.7	19.0	19.5	20.2
Residential.	Tril. cu. ft . .	4.8	4.9	4.8	4.4	4.3	4.6	4.8	4.4	4.6	4.7	5.0
Commercial [4]	Tril. cu. ft . .	2.4	2.5	2.6	2.4	2.4	2.7	2.7	2.6	2.7	2.8	2.9
Industrial	Tril. cu. ft . .	9.3	8.4	8.2	6.9	7.1	7.5	7.9	8.3	8.4	8.7	9.0
Lease and plant fuel	Tril. cu. ft . .	1.4	1.4	1.0	1.0	1.1	1.1	1.1	1.2	1.1	1.2	1.2
Other industrial . . .	Tril. cu. ft . .	7.9	7.0	7.2	5.9	6.0	6.4	6.8	7.0	7.2	7.5	7.8
Electric utilities	Tril. cu. ft . .	3.9	3.2	3.7	3.0	2.8	2.6	2.8	2.8	2.8	2.8	2.7
Transportation [5]	Tril. cu. ft . .	0.7	0.6	0.6	0.5	0.5	0.6	0.6	0.7	0.6	0.6	0.6
Extraction losses [6]	Tril. cu. ft . .	0.9	0.9	0.8	0.8	0.8	0.8	0.8	0.8	0.8	0.9	(NA)
Exports	Tril. cu. ft . .	0.1	0.1	0.1	0.1	0.1	0.1	0.1	0.1	0.1	0.2	1.0
Additions to storage [7]	Tril. cu. ft . .	1.9	2.1	2.0	2.2	1.9	2.2	2.5	2.5	2.7	2.6	2.9
World production (dry) . . .	Tril. cu. ft . .	(NA)	44.1	53.1	62.0	66.2	69.8	71.9	74.3	74.8	(NA)	(NA)
U.S. production (dry) . .	Tril. cu. ft . .	21.0	19.2	19.4	16.4	16.5	17.0	17.3	17.8	17.8	17.7	17.8
Percent U.S. of world	Percent . . .	56.0	43.6	36.5	26.4	25.0	24.4	24.0	24.0	23.7	(NA)	(NA)

NA Not available.   [1] Estimated, end of year. Source: 1970-1976; American Gas Association, Arlington, VA, (copyright); thereafter, U.S. Energy Information Administration, *U.S. Crude Oil, Natural Gas,* and *Natural Gas Liquids Reserves, annual.* [2] Marketed production includes gross withdrawals from reservoirs less quantities used for reservoir repressuring and quantities vented or flared. For 1980 and thereafter, it excludes the nonhydrocarbon gases subsequently removed.   [3] Includes imports of liquefied natural gas.   [4] Includes deliveries to municipalities and public authorities for institutional heating and other purposes. [5] Pipeline fuel and vehicle fuel.   [6] Volumetric reduction in natural gas resulting from the extraction of natural gas constituents at natural gas processing plants.   [7] Beginning with 1980, includes liquefied natural gas (LNG) storage in above ground tanks.

Source: Except as noted, U.S. Energy Information Administration, *Annual Energy Review, International Energy Annual, Natural Gas Annual,* Volume I and II and *Monthly Energy Review.*

No. 1198. Liquefied Petroleum Gases—Summary: 1980 to 1993

[In millions of **42-gallon barrels.** Includes ethane]

ITEM	1980	1990	1992	1993	ITEM	1980	1990	1992	1993
Production	561	638	720	850	**Consumption.**	538	568	629	633
At natural gas plants.	441	456	500	634	Ethane [1]	164	186	209	217
At refineries	121	182	222	216	Propane [1][2]	298	335	378	367
Imports	79	68	57	70	Butane (incl. isobutane) [2] .	76	47	42	49
Refinery input	85	107	172	179	Stocks, Dec. 31	116	98	98	117
Exports	9	14	18	16					

[1] Reported consumption of ethane-propane mixtures have been allocated 70 percent ethane and 30 percent propane. [2] Reported consumption of butane-propane mixtures have been allocated 60 percent butane and 40 percent propane.

Source: U.S. Energy Information Administration, *Petroleum Supply Annual.*

No. 1199. World Coal Trade: 1980 to 1991

[In millions of short tons]

COUNTRIES	1980	1982	1983	1984	1985	1986	1987	1988	1989	1990	1991
Exporting countries, total [1]	**277.2**	**292.0**	**284.5**	**332.9**	**370.2**	**376.3**	**383.0**	**415.0**	**423.5**	**440.2**	**434.6**
United States	88.7	106.5	78.2	82.0	93.2	85.5	79.6	94.9	100.8	105.8	109
Australia	46.6	48.8	62.3	82.2	96.6	101.3	111.9	109.8	108.5	116.9	132.5
South Africa	30.7	30.5	32.7	40.9	49.8	50.1	46.9	47.4	51.6	54.5	52.7
Soviet Union	26.2	23.0	22.8	22.8	26.5	36.9	39.1	46.0	43.9	42.7	31
Germany [2]	13.8	11.2	11.5	12.4	10.5	7.9	6.9	5.5	5.9	6.0	3.9
Canada	16.1	16.6	18.6	26.8	30.3	28.6	29.5	35.0	36.1	34.2	37.6
Poland	34.6	30.6	38.7	47.2	39.7	37.9	34.2	35.5	31.8	61.8	19.8
China.	4.2	5.1	6.8	7.7	8.6	10.9	14.4	16.2	16.9	19.1	20.7
Importing countries, total [1]	**277.2**	**292.0**	**284.5**	**332.9**	**370.2**	**376.3**	**383.0**	**415.0**	**423.5**	**440.2**	**434.6**
Western Europe/Mediterranean.	126.9	126.5	112.9	132.4	152.3	149.0	145.6	146.2	154.7	172.1	180.6
Japan	75.6	86.5	82.8	96.2	103.0	99.6	100.2	111.6	111.7	113.9	123.5
Eastern Europe	34.8	37.0	39.7	39.9	39.1	45.4	44.9	45.1	39.6	30.6	21.9
Canada	17.4	17.3	16.7	20.3	16.1	14.7	15.8	19.3	15.1	15.7	13.7

[1] Includes areas not shown separately.   [2] Represents United Germany beginning, 1990.

Source: U.S. Energy Information Administration, 1975-84, *Outlook for U.S. Coal Imports;* thereafter, *Annual Prospects for World Coal Trade.*

Natural Resources

No. 1200. Coal and Coke—Summary: 1970 to 1993

[Includes coal consumed at mines. Demonstrated coal reserve base for United States on Jan. 1, 1992, was an estimated 476 billion tons. Recoverability varies between 40 and 90 percent for individual deposits; 50 percent or more of overall U.S. coal reserve base is believed to be recoverable. See also *Historical Statistics, Colonial Times to 1970*, series M 93-126]

ITEM	Unit	1970	1980	1985	1989	1990	1991	1992	1993
Coal production, total [1]	**Mil. sh. tons**	**613**	**830**	**884**	**981**	**1,029**	**996**	**998**	**945**
Value	Mil. dol.	3,882	20,453	22,277	21,330	(NA)	(NA)	(NA)	(NA)
Anthracite production	Mil. sh. tons	9.7	6.1	4.7	3.3	3.5	3.4	3.5	3.6
Bituminous coal and lignite: [2]									
Number of mines	Number	5,601	5,598	4,547	3,429	3,243	2,846	2,746	2,475
Production	Mil. sh. tons	603	824	879	977	1,026	993	995	945
Value, total	Mil. dol.	3,774	20,196	22,061	21,260	22,274	21,598	(NA)	(NA)
Average per ton	Dollars	6.26	24.52	25.10	21.76	21.71	21.75	21.03	19.85
Exports	Mil. sh. tons	72	92	93	101	106	109	103	75
Value	Mil. dol.	961	4,627	4,465	4,287	4,510	4,619	(NA)	(NA)
Imports	1,000 sh. tons	36	1,194	1,952	2,851	2,699	3,390	3,803	(NA)
Method of mining:									
Underground	Mil. sh. tons	339	337	350	394	425	407	407	351
Surface	Mil. sh. tons	264	487	529	587	605	589	590	594
Percent of total prod.	Percent	43.8	59.1	60.2	59.8	58.7	59.1	59.1	(NA)
Value	Mil. dol.	(Z)	30	70	(NA)	(NA)	(NA)	(NA)	(NA)
Consumption [3]	Mil. sh. tons	523	703	818	890	896	888	892	928
Electric power utilities	Mil. sh. tons	320	569	694	767	774	772	780	814
Industrial	Mil. sh. tons	184	126	116	76	76	75	74	75
Productivity average: [4]									
Daily employment	1,000	140	225	169	131	131	121	110	101
Days worked	Number	228	210	204	269	271	274	280	280
Tons per worker:									
Per day	Sh. tons	18.84	16.32	23.13	31.75	32.90	35.18	37.71	(NA)
Per year	Sh. tons	4,296	3,427	4,719	6,795	7,106	7,880	(NA)	(NA)
Production, by State:									
Alabama	Mil. sh. tons	21	26	28	28	29	27	26	25
Illinois	Mil. sh. tons	65	63	59	59	60	60	60	41
Indiana	Mil. sh. tons	22	31	33	34	36	32	31	29
Kentucky	Mil. sh. tons	125	150	152	167	173	159	161	156
Montana	Mil. sh. tons	3	30	33	38	38	38	39	36
Ohio	Mil. sh. tons	55	39	36	34	35	31	30	29
Pennsylvania	Mil. sh. tons	90	93	71	71	71	65	68	60
Virginia	Mil. sh. tons	35	41	41	43	47	42	43	39
West Virginia	Mil. sh. tons	144	122	128	154	169	167	162	131
Wyoming	Mil. sh. tons	7	95	141	172	184	194	190	210
Other States	Mil. sh. tons	44	140	161	182	187	181	189	(NA)
World production	Mil. sh. tons	3,295	4,103	4,779	5,252	5,214	4,952	4,975	(NA)
Coke production [5]	**Mil. sh. tons**	**66.5**	**46.1**	**28.4**	**28.1**	**27.6**	**24.1**	**23.4**	**23.2**
Oven coke [6]	Mil. sh. tons	65.7	46.1	28.7	33.0	27.6	24.0	23.0	(NA)
Value of product at plant	Mil. dol.	2,193	6,029	(NA)	(NA)	(NA)	(NA)	(NA)	(NA)
Coke and breeze	Mil. dol.	1,899	4,784	(NA)	(NA)	(NA)	(NA)	(NA)	(NA)
Avg. market value per ton	Dollars	28	103	103	(NA)	(NA)	(NA)	(NA)	(NA)
Coal carbonized	Mil. sh. tons	96.5	66.7	41.1	41.4	38.9	33.9	32.4	31.6
Average value per ton	Dollars	12.47	56.26	54.30	47.50	47.73	48.88	47.9	47.4
Yield of coke from coal	Percent	69.1	69.2	69.8	79.8	71.0	71.0	(NA)	(NA)

NA Not available.   Z Less than $500,000.   [1] Includes bituminous coal, lignite, and anthracite.   [2] All domestic production data for 1970 are for mines producing 1,000 short tons or more per year; thereafter, data are for all mines.   [3] Includes some categories not shown separately.   [4] Data for 1970 are for mines producing 1,000 short tons or more per year; thereafter, for mines producing 10,000 short tons more. Beginning 1985, includes anthracite.   [5] Includes beehive coke.   [6] Prior to 1980, excludes screenings or breeze; thereafter, includes beehive and other nonrecoverable coke-oven operations.

Source: 1970, U.S. Bureau of Mines, *Minerals Yearbook*; thereafter, U.S. Energy Information Administration, *Coal Industry*, annual; *Annual Energy Review*, and *Quarterly Coal Report*, and unpublished data.

No. 1201. Uranium Concentrate (U_3O_8) Industry—Summary: 1980 to 1993

[Middle demand case. See table 969. See also *Historical Statistics, Colonial Times to 1970*, series M 266-267]

ITEM	Unit	1980	1985	1986	1987	1988	1989	1990	1991	1992	1993
Production	1,000 sh. tons	21.9	5.6	6.8	6.5	6.5	6.9	4.4	4.0	2.8	3.1
Net imports (U_3O_8)	1,000 sh. tons	-1.1	3.2	6.4	7.5	6.4	5.6	12.1	9.8	12.3	(NA)
Utility and Suppliers inventories (U_3O_8 equivalent)	1,000 sh. tons	54.4	[1]68.3	[1]66.2	[1]64.5	[1]59.1	[1]54.9	45.6	36.70	(NA)	(NA)
Price (1988 dol./lb. U_3O_8):											
Long-term contract price	Dollars	41.4	24.7	19.3	18.5	(NA)	(NA)	(NA)	(NA)	(NA)	(NA)
Spot market price	Dollars	45.0	17.0	18.1	17.3	14.5	14.2	(NA)	(NA)	(NA)	(NA)
Delivered price	Dollars	39.9	[2]33.6	[2]31.9	[2]19.6	[2]25.7	[2]27.8	(NA)	(NA)	(NA)	(NA)
Capital expenditures (1988 dollars)	Mil. dol.	1,107	37	29	63	36	35	(NA)	(NA)	(NA)	(NA)
Employment	1,000	19.9	2.4	2.1	2.0	2.10	1.6	1.3	1.0	0.7	0.4

NA Not available.   [1] Includes natural U_3O_8 (uranium oxide), natural UF_6 (uranium hexafluoride), natural UF_6 under usage agreement, UF_6 at enrichment suppliers, enriched UF_6 and fabricated fuel.   [2] Average U.S. contract prices and market price settlements.

Source: U.S. Department of Energy, *Domestic Uranium Mining and Milling Industry*, annual, and *Uranium Industry*, annual.

Construction and Housing

This section presents data on the construction industry and on various indicators of its activity and costs; on housing units and their characteristics and occupants; and on the characteristics and vacancy rates for commercial buildings. There are new data on commercial building from the Energy Information Administration for the first time in three years. Also, there are new data from the 1992 Census of Construction Industries for the first time in 5 years.

The principal source of these data is the U.S. Bureau of the Census, which issues a variety of current publications. Construction statistics compiled by the Bureau appear in its monthly *Current Construction Reports* series with various quarterly or annual supplements; *Housing Starts* and *Housing Completions* present data by type of structure and by four major census regions; *New One-Family Houses Sold and For Sale* also provides statistics annually on physical and financial characteristics for all new housing by the four major census regions; *Price Index of New One-Family Houses Sold* presents quarterly figures and annual regional data; and *Housing Units Authorized by Building Permits* covers approximately 17,000 permit-issuing jurisdictions in the United States (this changes to 19,000 places beginning 1995). Statistics on expenditures by owners of residential properties are issued quarterly and annually in *Expenditures for Residential Upkeep and Improvements. Value of New Construction Put in Place* presents data on all types of construction and includes monthly composite cost indexes. Reports of the censuses of construction industries (see below) are also issued on various topics.

Other Census Bureau publications include the *Current Housing Reports* series, which comprises the quarterly *Housing Vacancies,* the quarterly *Market Absorption of Apartments,* the American Housing Survey (formerly Annual Housing Survey) and reports of the censuses of housing and of construction industries. *Construction Review,* published quarterly by the International Trade Administration, U.S. Department of Commerce, contains many of the

In Brief

New housing starts reached 1.46 million in 1994, the highest number since 1988.

U.S. home ownership rate in 1994 of 64.0 percent unchanged from rate in 1984.

The Nation's office vacancy rate declined to 16.2 percent at yearend 1994, the lowest rate since 1984.

census series and other construction statistics series from the Federal Government and private agencies.

Other sources include the monthly *Dodge Construction Potentials* of F. W. Dodge Division, McGraw-Hill Information Systems Company, New York, NY, which presents national and State data on construction contracts; the National Association of Home Builders with –State-level data on housing starts; the NATIONAL ASSOCIATION OF REALTORS, which presents data on existing home sales; the Society of Industrial and Office Realtors and Oncor International on commercial office space; the Bureau of Economic Analysis, which presents data on residential capital and gross housing product; and the U.S. Energy Information Administration, which provides data on commercial buildings through its periodic sample surveys.

Censuses and surveys.—Censuses of the construction industry were first conducted by the Bureau of the Census for 1929, 1935, and 1939; beginning in 1967, a census has been taken every five years (for years ending in "2" and "7"). The latest reports are for 1992.

The 1992 Census of Construction Industries, in accordance with the 1987 *Standard Industrial Classification Manual* (see text, section 13), covers all employer establishments primarily engaged in (1) building construction by general contractors or operative builders; (2) heavy (non-building) construction by general contractors; and (3) construction by special trade contractors.

From 1850 through 1930, the Bureau of the Census collected some housing data as part of its censuses of population and agriculture. Beginning in 1940, separate censuses of housing have been taken at 10-year intervals. For the 1970 and 1980 censuses, data on year-round housing units were collected and issued on occupancy and structural characteristics, plumbing facilities, value, and rent; for 1990 such characteristics were presented for all housing units.

The American Housing Survey (*Current Housing Reports* series H-150 and H-170), which began in 1973, provided an annual and ongoing series of data on selected housing and demographic characteristics until 1983. In 1984 the name of the survey was changed from the Annual Housing Survey. It is currently based on a biennial national sample and on 11 annual MSA samples. All samples represent a cross section of the housing stock in their respective areas. Estimates are subject to both sampling and nonsampling errors; caution should therefore, be used in making comparisons with 1970 and 1980 census data.

Data on residential mortgages were collected continuously from 1890 to 1970, except 1930, as part of the decennial census by the Bureau of the Census. Since 1973, mortgage status data, limited to single family homes on less than ten acres with no business on the property, have been presented in the American Housing Survey. Data on mortgage activity are covered in section 16.

Housing units.—In general, a housing unit is a group of rooms or a single room occupied or intended for occupancy as separate living quarters; that is, the occupants do not live and eat with any other persons in the structure and there is direct access from the outside or through a common hall. Transient accommodations, barracks for workers, and institutional-type quarters are not counted as housing units.

Statistical reliability.—For a discussion of statistical collection and estimation, sampling procedures, and measures of statistical reliability applicable to Census Bureau data, see Appendix III.

Historical statistics.—Tabular headnotes provide cross-references, where applicable, to *Historical Statistics of the United States, Colonial Times to 1970*. See Appendix IV.

No. 1202. Construction Industries—Summary, by Industry: 1992

[Based on a probability sample of about 160,000 construction establishments with payroll in 1987; see Appendix III. N.e.c.= Not elsewhere classified]

INDUSTRY	SIC[1] code	Establishments with payroll (1,000)	EMPLOYEES (1,000)		PAYROLL (mil. dol.)		VALUE OF CONSTRUCTION WORK (mil. dol.)		Value added[3] (mil. dol.)
			Total	Construction workers	Total	Construction workers	Total	Net[2]	
All industries, total	(X)	573.3	4,674	3,596	117,772	82,937	529,277	391,638	235,231
General building contractors	15	168.2	1,092	754	27,154	16,133	216,298	114,839	63,743
Single-family houses	1521	107.1	404	296	7,300	4,886	48,652	33,664	17,193
Other residential buildings	1522	6.5	49	35	1,175	719	7,934	4,328	2,573
Operative builders	1531	17.0	113	49	3,404	1,049	45,073	27,094	15,480
Industrial buildings and warehouses	1541	7.7	123	92	3,497	2,322	20,818	10,993	6,487
Nonresidential buildings, n.e.c	1542	29.5	398	279	11,638	7,066	92,701	38,081	21,659
Heavy construction contractors	16	37.3	803	650	23,667	17,517	95,821	77,694	49,066
Highway and street construction	1611	10.1	255	208	7,303	5,412	35,174	27,746	15,600
Bridge, tunnel, and elevated highway	1622	1.1	46	38	1,523	1,134	7,615	5,441	3,133
Water, sewer, and utility lines	1623	10.2	194	160	5,573	4,200	20,021	17,444	11,716
Heavy construction, n.e.c	1629	15.8	305	241	9,155	6,691	32,507	26,615	18,336
Special trade contractors	17	367.8	2,779	2,192	66,951	49,287	217,158	199,105	122,422
Plumbing, heating, air-conditioning	1711	75.3	613	456	16,563	11,746	56,989	50,830	29,476
Painting and paperhanging	1721	32.1	165	138	3,198	2,497	8,818	8,208	5,903
Electrical work	1731	53.8	485	378	13,490	9,946	39,924	38,231	23,327
Masonry and other stonework	1741	22.6	148	130	2,876	2,364	8,524	8,005	5,171
Plastering, drywall, insulation	1742	18.6	207	174	4,908	3,826	14,078	12,851	8,152
Terrazzo, tile, marble, and mosaic work	1743	6.5	33	26	762	559	2,408	2,297	1,345
Carpentry	1751	38.0	176	144	3,448	2,654	12,772	11,252	6,716
Floorlaying and other floor work	1752	10.2	49	36	1,065	724	4,468	4,072	2,181
Roofing, siding, and sheet metal work	1761	27.6	216	170	4,638	3,235	16,856	15,652	8,958
Concrete work	1771	26.0	193	161	4,059	3,103	14,490	13,225	7,721
Water well drilling	1781	3.8	20	15	453	327	1,756	1,712	1,031
Structural steel erection	1791	4.0	59	48	1,651	1,240	5,015	4,560	3,088
Glass and glazing work	1793	4.6	33	22	819	505	2,800	2,716	1,463
Excavation work	1794	13.7	75	61	1,771	1,366	6,675	5,969	4,225
Wrecking and demolition work	1795	1.0	12	10	278	200	985	862	745
Installing building equipment, n.e.c	1796	3.9	74	56	2,218	1,645	6,066	5,545	4,145
Special trade contractors, n.e.c	1799	25.4	208	159	4,477	3,141	13,601	12,263	8,233

X Not applicable. [1] Standard Industrial Classification; see text, section 13. [2] Value of construction work less payments for construction work subcontracted to others, not shown separately. [3] Dollar value of business done less (a) payments for materials, components, and supplies, and (b) payments for construction work subcontracted to others, not shown separately.
Source: U.S. Bureau of the Census, *Census of Construction Industries, 1992,* series CC92-I-1(P) through CC92-I-27(P).

No. 1203. Construction Materials—Producer Price Indexes: 1980 to 1994

[1982=100, except as noted. For discussion of producer price index, see text, section 15. This index, more formally known as the special commodity grouping index for construction materials, covers materials incorporated as integral part of a building or normally installed during construction and not readily removable. Excludes consumer durables such as kitchen ranges, refrigerators, etc. This index is not the same as the stage-of-processing index of intermediate materials and components for construction. See *Historical Statistics, Colonial Times to 1970,* series N 140-155 for similar data]

COMMODITY	1980	1985	1987	1988	1989	1990	1991	1992	1993	1994
Construction materials	**92.5**	**107.6**	**109.5**	**115.7**	**119.5**	**119.6**	**120.4**	**122.5**	**128.6**	**133.8**
Interior solvent based paint	91.3	107.3	111.6	120.3	128.8	133.0	140.2	141.7	142.9	148.1
Plastic construction products	103.9	108.6	108.4	121.1	120.1	117.2	115.1	112.7	116.6	122.7
Douglas fir, dressed	132.6	126.5	125.1	135.7	151.6	138.4	139.6	169.5	237.6	236.4
Southern pine, dressed	104.0	105.2	114.1	112.4	108.0	111.2	111.0	130.6	168.8	182.5
Millwork	93.2	111.7	117.7	121.9	127.3	130.4	135.5	143.3	156.6	162.4
Softwood plywood	109.5	107.4	109.8	109.1	124.2	119.6	120.8	147.2	169.7	176.8
Hardwood plywood and related products	97.5	89.9	92.9	94.2	99.8	102.7	102.8	106.9	115.4	122.3
Softwood plywood veneer, ex. reinforced/backed	126.0	100.1	108.4	117.3	142.1	142.3	138.5	168.3	216.0	207.8
Building paper and building board mill products	86.1	107.4	111.2	113.3	115.6	112.2	111.8	119.6	132.9	144.1
Tube, drawn, 6000 alloy series	85.6	109.7	111.2	128.9	131.0	127.1	124.1	123.4	(NA)	(NA)
Builders hardware	84.9	113.5	117.4	122.5	127.8	133.0	138.1	141.4	144.9	147.9
Plumbing fixtures and brass fittings	88.5	111.9	119.7	128.7	137.7	144.3	149.7	153.1	155.9	159.7
Heating equipment	87.0	109.5	115.5	119.2	125.1	131.6	134.1	137.3	140.4	142.5
Metal doors, sash, and trim	87.8	107.3	112.0	122.4	130.0	131.4	134.6	135.0	136.6	142.0
Incandescent outdoor lighting fixtures	82.7	109.2	117.2	122.4	128.0	137.3	136.5	139.1	138.5	141.0
Bright nails	90.9	100.2	101.2	104.7	110.4	(NA)	(NA)	115.1	115.9	117.9
Welded steel wire fabric for concrete reinforcing	98.9	101.3	98.3	109.2	108.6	109.7	100.0	101.3	104.5	108.4
Elevators, escalators, and other lifts	87.3	97.7	100.4	103.6	107.1	110.1	108.7	109.4	110.7	112.4
Stamped metal outlet box	82.7	119.7	160.1	168.7	171.7	179.4	179.7	187.2	195.7	(NA)
Concrete ingredients and related products	88.4	108.5	110.4	112.0	113.2	115.3	118.4	119.4	123.4	128.7
Concrete products	92.0	107.5	109.4	110.0	111.2	113.5	116.6	117.2	120.2	124.5
Clay construction products exc. refractories	88.8	113.5	121.4	124.9	127.0	129.9	130.2	132.0	135.1	138.3
Prep. asphalt and tar roofing and siding products	105.5	100.5	91.9	94.4	95.6	97.1	96.2	94.3	94.9	92.8
Gypsum products	100.1	132.3	125.2	112.9	110.0	105.2	99.3	99.9	108.3	136.0
Insulation materials	80.7	105.2	105.0	105.8	106.7	108.4	110.8	102.3	105.8	111.9
Paving mixtures and blocks	83.7	111.6	100.8	102.7	101.0	101.2	103.2	100.2	102.0	103.2

NA Not available.
Source: U.S. Bureau of Labor Statistics, *Producer Price Indexes,* monthly and annual.

No. 1204. Price and Cost Indexes for Construction: 1980 to 1994

[**1987=100.** Excludes Alaska and Hawaii. Indexes of certain sources are published on bases different from those shown here. See *Historical Statistics, Colonial Times to 1970,* series N 118-137, for construction cost indexes on a 1947-49 base]

NAME OF INDEX	1980	1985	1988	1989	1990	1991	1992	1993	1994
Bureau of the Census:									
Composite fixed-weighted [1]	77.6	93.1	103.8	107.4	110.3	111.2	112.4	116.2	120.3
Implicit price deflator [2]	79.1	93.9	104.1	108.3	111.2	111.8	112.7	117.2	122.0
Bureau of the Census houses under construction: [3]									
Fixed-weighted	75.6	91.0	103.6	107.0	110.2	110.6	112.9	117.2	121.0
Price deflator	77.9	92.0	104.1	108.4	111.5	111.7	113.7	118.9	123.7
Federal Highway Administration, composite [4]	97.2	102.0	106.6	107.7	108.5	107.5	105.1	108.3	115.1
Bureau of Reclamation composite [5]	81	98	103	107	111	114	116	119	123
Turner Construction Co.: Building construction [6]	69	94	104	107	111	113	113	116	119
E. H. Boeckh, building cost index: [7]									
Residences	(NA)	96.2	102.5	106.3	109.9	113.0	116.7	121.3	125.3
Apartments, hotels, and office buildings	(NA)	96.3	102.7	106.2	109.0	112.0	114.9	118.1	121.3
Commercial and factory buildings	(NA)	96.7	103.0	107.2	110.8	114.2	117.4	120.5	124.1
Engineering News-Record: [8]									
Buildings	76.5	95.5	102.2	103.6	106.3	108.3	111.5	117.9	122.4
Construction	73.5	95.2	102.6	104.7	107.4	109.7	113.1	118.2	122.7
Handy-Whitman public utility: [9]									
Buildings	83	96	104	107	108	105	107	113	119
Electric [10]	80	98	107	111	115	116	118	122	126
Gas	79	100	106	111	114	116	118	121	128
Water [11]	81	97	103	106	108	108	110	115	120
C. A. Turner Telephone Plant [12]	102	101	101	110	113	114	114	115	117

NA Not available.   [1] Weighted average of the various indexes used to deflate the Construction Put in Place series. In calculating the index, the weights (i.e., the composition of current dollar estimates in 1987 by category) are held constant. [2] Derived ratio of total current to constant dollar Construction Put in Place (multiplied by 100).   [3] Excludes value of site.   [4] Based on average contract unit bid prices for composite mile (involving specific average amounts of excavation, paving, reinforcing steel, structural steel, and structural concrete).   [5] Derived from the four quarterly indexes which are weighted averages of costs of labor, materials, and equipment for the construction of dams and reclamation projects.   [6] Based on firm's cost experience with respect to labor rates, materials prices, competitive conditions, efficiency of plant and management, and productivity.   [7] Average of 20 cities for types shown. Weights based on surveys of building costs.   [8] Building index computed on the basis of a hypothetical unit of construction requiring 6 bbl. of portland cement, 1,088 M bd. ft. of 2" x 4" lumber, 2,500 lb. of structural steel, and 68.38 hours of skilled labor. Construction index based on same materials components combined with 200 hours of common labor.   [9] Based on data covering public utility construction costs in six geographic regions. Covers skilled and common labor. [10] As derived by U.S. Bureau of the Census. Covers steam generation plants only.   [11] As derived by U.S. Bureau of the Census. Reflects costs for structures and improvements at water pumping and treatment plants.   [12] Computed by the Census Bureau by averaging the weighted component indexes published for six geographic regions.

Source: U.S. Bureau of the Census. In U.S. Department of Commerce, International Trade Administration, *Construction Review,* bimonthly.

No. 1205. Value of New Construction Put in Place: 1964 to 1994

[**In millions of dollars.** Represents value of construction put in place during year; differs from building permit and construction contract data in timing and coverage. Includes installed cost of normal building service equipment and selected types of industrial production equipment (largely site fabricated). Excludes cost of shipbuilding, land, and most types of machinery and equipment. For methodology, see Appendix III. See also *Historical Statistics, Colonial Times to 1970,* series N 1-29 and N 66-69]

YEAR	CURRENT DOLLARS					CONSTANT (**1987**) DOLLARS				
		Private					Private			
	Total	Total	Residential buildings	Nonresidential buildings	Public	Total	Total	Residential buildings	Nonresidential buildings	Public
1964	72,124	51,921	30,526	14,412	20,203	294,569	211,627	124,768	60,892	82,942
1970	100,727	72,819	35,863	23,008	27,908	309,244	225,168	114,138	71,796	84,077
1971	117,311	87,612	48,514	24,204	29,699	337,451	254,502	145,554	69,621	82,949
1972	133,318	103,288	60,693	26,568	30,030	360,780	281,593	170,190	71,490	79,187
1973	146,826	114,477	65,085	30,683	32,348	364,938	285,937	166,249	76,259	79,001
1974	147,476	109,344	55,967	32,195	38,132	319,362	242,274	130,126	70,029	77,089
1975	145,623	102,330	51,581	28,397	43,293	290,137	208,991	109,920	58,990	81,147
1976	165,441	121,462	68,273	27,936	43,979	315,865	235,338	136,685	55,617	80,527
1977	193,126	150,044	92,004	30,871	43,083	340,833	266,393	165,926	57,134	74,440
1978	230,178	180,032	109,838	39,135	50,146	362,862	285,880	174,695	65,343	76,982
1979	259,839	203,194	116,444	51,732	56,646	364,554	288,789	165,116	77,359	75,766
1980	259,746	196,100	100,381	58,290	63,646	328,435	252,645	128,926	78,972	75,790
1981	271,950	207,259	99,241	68,450	64,691	320,950	247,427	118,343	85,091	73,523
1982	260,594	197,531	84,676	73,953	63,064	297,759	226,510	97,595	87,505	71,249
1983	294,945	231,494	125,521	70,438	63,450	332,625	261,398	143,108	80,888	71,227
1984	348,838	278,600	153,849	87,493	70,238	382,447	306,152	170,732	96,664	76,296
1985	377,358	299,543	158,474	103,455	77,815	401,940	321,706	172,338	111,262	80,234
1986	407,682	323,100	187,148	98,674	84,582	421,341	335,709	195,377	102,596	85,632
1987	419,386	328,738	194,656	100,933	90,648	419,372	328,637	194,622	100,877	90,735
1988	432,251	337,516	198,101	106,994	94,735	415,036	324,404	190,292	103,037	90,632
1989	443,651	345,477	196,551	113,988	98,174	409,723	318,717	181,321	105,711	91,006
1990	442,161	334,682	182,856	117,971	107,478	397,658	300,101	163,980	106,067	97,557
1991	403,645	293,536	157,835	97,841	110,109	360,892	262,023	141,300	87,608	98,869
1992	435,357	316,115	187,869	87,241	119,243	385,818	277,833	165,079	77,081	107,985
1993	466,365	341,101	210,454	90,065	125,264	398,051	288,289	176,969	76,893	109,762
1994	506,944	377,784	237,944	97,795	129,160	415,697	307,055	192,150	80,372	108,643

Source: U.S. Bureau of the Census, *Current Construction Reports,* series C30, and press release, CB-93-14.

No. 1206. Value of New Construction Put in Place in Current and Constant (1987) Dollars: 1990 to 1994

[In millions of dollars. Represents value of construction put in place during year; differs from building permit and construction contract data in timing and coverage. Includes installed cost of normal building service equipment and selected types of industrial production equipment (largely site fabricated). Excludes cost of shipbuilding, land, and most types of machinery and equipment. For details on derivation of constant values and description of revised series, see source. For description of nature of revisions and deflators used, see *Construction Reports*, series C30-9005. For methodology, see Appendix III. See also *Historical Statistics, Colonial Times to 1970*, series N 1-29 and N 66-69]

TYPE OF CONSTRUCTION	CURRENT DOLLARS					CONSTANT (1987) DOLLARS				
	1990	1991	1992	1993	1994	1990	1991	1992	1993	1994
Total new construction .	442,161	403,645	435,357	466,365	506,944	397,658	360,892	385,818	398,051	415,697
Private construction	334,682	293,536	316,115	341,101	[1]377,784	300,101	262,023	277,833	288,289	[1]307,055
Residential buildings	182,856	157,835	187,869	210,454	237,944	163,980	141,300	165,079	176,969	192,150
New housing units	127,987	110,592	129,600	144,070	167,413	114,784	99,002	113,901	121,139	135,195
1 unit	108,737	95,444	116,505	133,282	153,651	97,518	85,435	102,372	112,062	124,096
2 or more units	19,250	15,148	13,094	10,788	13,762	17,266	13,567	11,529	9,077	11,099
Improvements	54,869	47,243	58,269	66,384	(NA)	49,196	42,297	51,178	55,829	(NA)
Nonresidential buildings . . .	117,971	97,841	87,241	90,065	97,795	106,067	87,608	77,081	76,893	80,372
Industrial	23,848	22,280	20,719	19,531	21,599	21,441	19,951	18,312	16,682	17,749
Office	28,722	23,010	17,241	15,414	16,727	25,829	20,604	15,246	13,166	13,750
Hotels, motels	9,673	6,286	3,507	4,286	4,095	8,699	5,630	3,097	3,659	3,369
Other commercial	34,140	25,470	24,283	27,211	31,539	30,693	22,805	21,440	23,220	25,908
Religious	3,390	3,415	3,382	3,636	3,689	3,046	3,058	2,986	3,104	3,031
Educational	4,219	3,929	4,254	4,229	4,447	3,792	3,518	3,760	3,610	3,658
Hospital and institutional .	9,450	9,189	10,110	11,001	10,418	8,494	8,228	8,931	9,395	8,565
Miscellaneous [2]	4,528	4,260	3,746	4,756	5,281	4,072	3,814	3,309	4,057	4,342
Farm nonresidential	2,670	2,563	2,211	2,344	(NA)	2,400	2,295	1,953	2,001	(NA)
Public utilities	28,228	32,354	35,225	34,958	(NA)	24,967	28,195	30,482	29,535	(NA)
Telecommunications	9,803	9,203	9,301	9,586	10,383	8,709	8,102	8,203	8,308	8,924
Other public utilities	18,425	23,151	25,924	25,372	(NA)	16,258	20,093	22,280	21,226	(NA)
Railroads	2,600	2,406	2,928	3,629	(NA)	2,362	2,145	2,653	3,189	(NA)
Electric light and power .	10,594	14,440	15,246	14,347	(NA)	9,290	12,523	13,071	11,903	(NA)
Gas	4,820	5,555	6,901	6,410	(NA)	4,243	4,780	5,837	5,318	(NA)
Petroleum pipelines	411	750	849	986	(NA)	362	645	718	817	(NA)
All other private [3]	2,957	2,943	3,570	3,281	2,890	2,688	2,626	3,238	2,892	2,450
Public construction	107,478	110,109	119,243	125,264	129,160	97,557	98,869	107,985	109,762	108,643
Buildings	43,615	47,406	50,198	51,457	52,025	39,195	42,443	44,340	43,879	42,700
Housing and development	3,808	3,587	3,825	4,036	4,585	3,414	3,212	3,366	3,395	3,703
Industrial	1,433	1,823	1,793	1,718	1,458	1,289	1,633	1,583	1,467	1,200
Educational	16,055	19,202	20,735	22,065	22,793	14,427	17,189	18,318	18,832	18,731
Hospital	2,860	2,829	3,271	3,684	3,805	2,573	2,533	2,890	3,146	3,130
Other [4]	19,458	19,965	20,574	19,954	19,383	17,492	17,876	18,183	17,038	15,936
Highways and streets	32,104	32,041	34,899	37,355	40,186	29,605	29,142	33,347	34,507	35,294
Military facilities	2,665	1,837	2,502	2,453	2,337	2,427	1,660	2,298	2,182	1,990
Conservation and development	4,686	5,011	6,021	5,977	6,245	4,206	4,384	5,194	5,018	5,091
Sewer systems	10,276	10,039	10,179	10,433	11,115	9,214	8,783	8,784	8,761	9,062
Water supply facilities	4,909	4,981	5,171	6,021	6,097	4,529	4,615	4,702	5,236	5,059
Miscellaneous public [5]	9,223	8,793	10,272	11,568	11,155	8,381	7,843	9,320	10,179	9,447

NA Not available. [1] Includes estimates for types of construction indicated as (NA). [2] Includes amusement and recreational buildings, bus and airline terminals, animal hospitals and shelters, etc. [3] Includes privately owned streets and bridges, parking areas, sewer and water facilities, parks and playgrounds, golf courses, airfields, etc. [4] Includes federal administrative buildings, prisons, police and fire stations, courthouses, civic centers, passenger terminals, space facilities, postal facilities, etc. [5] Includes open amusement and recreational facilities, power generating facilities, transit systems, airfields, open parking facilities, etc.

Source: U.S. Bureau of the Census, *Current Construction Reports,* series C30, monthly.

No. 1207. Value of Privately Owned Nonresidential Building Projects, by Construction Status, 1986 to 1994, and by Type of Project, 1994

[In billions of dollars]

CONSTRUCTION STATUS	1986	1987	1988	1989	1990	1991	1992	1993	1994				
									Total	Industrial	Office building	Other commercial	Other[1]
Value of projects—													
Started	97.1	95.7	107.7	109.9	89.5	72.9	81.3	81.3	91.8	16.3	17.2	32.0	26.2
Completed	107.5	91.4	101.6	107.7	114.0	109.5	100.1	94.8	103.5	23.9	18.2	31.7	29.6

[1] Privately owned hotels and motels, religious, educational, hospital and institutional, and miscellaneous nonresidential building projects.

Source: U.S. Bureau of the Census, *Current Construction Reports,* series C30.

No. 1208. Construction Contracts—Value of Construction and Floor Space of Buildings, by Class of Construction: 1980 to 1994

[Includes new structures and additions, and major alterations to existing structures which affect only valuation, since no additional floor area is created by "alteration." See also *Historical Statistics, Colonial Times to 1970*, series N 78-100]

YEAR	Total	Resi-dential build-ings	NONRESIDENTIAL BUILDINGS									Non-build-ing con-struc-tion
			Total	Com-mer-cial [1]	Manu-fac-turing	Educa-tional [2]	Hos-pital	Public build-ings	Reli-gious	Social and recrea-tional	Mis-cella-neous	
VALUE (bil. dol.)												
1980	151.8	60.4	56.9	27.7	9.2	7.4	5.4	1.6	1.2	2.7	1.7	34.5
1981	157.3	56.3	65.5	35.2	9.3	6.6	6.4	1.4	1.2	3.4	2.0	35.4
1982	157.1	55.0	64.6	32.3	9.6	6.8	8.0	1.9	1.2	2.8	2.0	37.5
1983	194.1	88.4	67.9	38.3	5.4	7.1	8.5	2.1	1.5	2.9	2.1	37.8
1984	214.3	95.3	82.1	48.2	7.9	8.5	7.4	2.7	1.7	3.3	2.4	36.9
1985	235.6	102.1	92.1	54.6	8.1	10.0	7.8	3.1	2.0	4.0	2.5	41.4
1986	249.3	115.6	91.6	52.4	7.3	11.7	7.9	3.2	2.1	4.2	2.8	42.1
1987	259.0	114.1	98.8	53.7	8.6	13.2	9.0	4.7	2.1	4.3	3.2	46.1
1988	262.2	116.2	97.9	51.6	9.5	14.1	8.2	4.4	2.2	4.7	3.2	48.1
1989	271.3	116.2	106.1	53.6	12.7	15.9	8.8	5.2	2.0	5.0	2.9	49.0
1990	246.0	100.9	95.4	44.8	8.4	16.6	9.2	5.7	2.2	5.3	3.1	49.7
1991	230.9	94.5	86.2	32.7	8.3	19.0	9.6	6.2	2.4	5.1	3.0	50.2
1992	252.2	110.6	87.0	32.8	8.9	17.7	10.8	5.8	2.5	5.5	3.1	54.6
1993	271.3	123.8	88.6	34.2	8.9	19.3	10.5	4.0	2.4	6.8	2.6	58.8
1994	293.8	133.0	99.8	40.5	10.0	20.8	10.5	6.2	2.5	6.4	2.9	60.9
FLOOR SPACE (mil. sq. ft.)												
1980	3,102	1,839	1,263	738	220	103	55	18	28	49	52	(X)
1981	2,805	1,562	1,243	787	188	83	60	14	25	46	41	(X)
1982	2,455	1,440	1,015	631	119	82	71	19	25	38	30	(X)
1983	3,387	2,276	1,111	716	112	84	84	20	29	36	31	(X)
1984	3,661	2,311	1,350	901	157	100	70	23	29	37	34	(X)
1985	3,853	2,324	1,529	1,039	165	111	73	28	32	44	38	(X)
1986	3,935	2,481	1,454	960	148	129	73	30	32	44	39	(X)
1987	3,756	2,288	1,469	933	160	139	78	42	32	46	38	(X)
1988	3,594	2,181	1,413	883	162	142	71	38	32	49	37	(X)
1989	3,516	2,115	1,400	867	158	151	72	41	27	48	35	(X)
1990	3,020	1,817	1,203	694	128	152	69	47	29	51	32	(X)
1991	2,635	1,654	981	476	100	177	72	50	29	45	33	(X)
1992	2,800	1,864	936	462	95	157	77	41	30	42	32	(X)
1993	3,061	2,090	971	481	110	166	75	30	30	51	29	(X)
1994	3,384	2,254	1,130	596	135	172	72	46	31	50	29	(X)

X Not applicable.   [1] Includes nonindustrial warehouses.   [2] Includes science.

No. 1209. Construction Contracts—Value, by State: 1990 to 1994

[**In millions of dollars.** See headnote, table 1208. Represents value of construction in States in which work was actually done]

STATE	1990	1992	1993	1994 Total (incl. non-bldg.)	1994 Resi-den-tial	1994 Non-resi-den-tial	STATE	1990	1992	1993	1994 Total (incl. non-bldg.)	1994 Resi-den-tial	1994 Non-resi-den-tial
U.S	**246,022**	**252,191**	**271,284**	**293,757**	**133,030**	**99,784**	MO	3,833	4,397	5,150	5,589	2,622	1,980
							MT	332	603	765	770	348	236
AL	2,939	3,245	3,830	4,165	1,861	1,432	NE	1,318	1,535	1,591	1,826	660	663
AK	1,919	1,918	927	883	226	299	NV	3,334	3,999	3,823	4,690	2,285	1,632
AZ	4,553	5,319	6,478	7,981	5,281	1,811	NH	1,021	1,007	923	1,092	483	385
AR	1,438	2,021	2,171	2,735	1,228	829	NJ	6,141	5,509	6,273	6,452	2,252	2,653
CA	37,318	27,302	28,221	30,412	12,275	10,914	NM	1,124	1,355	1,665	1,928	845	659
CO	3,235	5,744	6,067	6,415	3,893	1,548	NY	14,137	14,132	12,792	13,179	3,464	5,936
CT	3,058	2,902	3,231	3,027	1,175	1,052	NC	6,614	8,051	8,954	10,040	5,384	3,212
DE	787	786	700	705	339	228	ND	506	587	641	850	226	326
DC	795	752	1,132	859	49	575	OH	9,885	10,773	11,162	11,935	5,147	4,349
FL	16,975	16,744	19,082	21,927	11,596	6,582	OK	2,164	2,488	2,427	2,990	1,265	999
GA	7,120	8,159	9,463	10,623	5,868	3,023	OR	3,101	2,835	3,581	4,137	2,114	962
HI	2,831	2,878	2,243	2,156	908	823	PA	10,117	9,987	10,372	9,620	3,746	3,828
ID	986	1,277	1,746	1,790	1,043	494	RI	594	643	1,289	673	278	235
IL	10,796	10,413	11,318	11,916	5,165	3,735	SC	3,664	3,439	4,158	4,182	2,223	1,341
IN	6,350	6,533	7,148	7,629	3,792	2,614	SD	468	586	756	851	267	298
IA	2,034	2,177	2,379	2,705	944	972	TN	4,388	5,204	5,604	6,314	3,181	2,140
KS	2,193	2,535	2,685	3,146	1,401	936	TX	13,197	16,659	19,146	20,713	9,704	6,981
KY	3,174	3,856	4,321	4,262	2,095	1,329	UT	1,884	2,113	3,126	3,364	1,684	1,199
LA	3,191	3,015	3,597	4,065	1,325	1,728	VT	515	580	512	553	255	208
ME	897	1,163	959	1,056	463	297	VA	7,180	7,366	7,577	8,459	4,126	2,413
MD	6,056	5,243	5,257	6,077	2,725	1,955	WA	6,185	7,582	6,996	7,823	3,790	2,506
MA	5,135	5,719	6,329	6,366	2,478	2,597	WV	1,253	1,091	1,167	1,205	244	513
MI	7,646	7,476	7,994	9,592	4,085	3,378	WI	4,654	5,068	5,169	5,442	2,565	1,875
MN	4,953	5,238	5,329	5,478	2,598	1,999	WY	462	468	679	560	174	118
MS	1,569	1,720	2,379	2,546	885	983							

Source of tables 1208 and 1209: F. W. Dodge, McGraw-Hill, Inc., New York, NY. Figures reported currently in *Dodge Construction Potentials*.

No. 1210. New Privately-Owned Housing Units Authorized, by State: 1993 and 1994

[Based on about 17,000 places in United States having building permit systems]

STATE	HOUSING UNITS (1,000) 1993	HOUSING UNITS (1,000) 1994 Total	HOUSING UNITS (1,000) 1994 1 unit	VALUATION (mil. dol.) 1993	VALUATION (mil. dol.) 1994 Total	VALUATION (mil. dol.) 1994 1 unit
U.S.	1,199.1	1,371.6	1,068.5	106,801	123,278	109,294
AL	16.1	19.1	14.4	1,147	1,357	1,168
AK	1.7	2.1	1.5	228	230	199
AZ	38.7	51.8	42.1	3,778	5,075	4,560
AR	10.0	12.4	7.8	644	795	648
CA	84.3	97.0	77.8	10,195	11,937	10,569
CO	29.9	37.2	29.3	3,096	3,906	3,422
CT	9.2	9.5	8.1	930	1,030	965
DE	4.9	5.0	4.7	313	337	326
DC	0.3	0.2	0.1	21	18	13
FL	115.1	128.6	96.3	9,658	11,076	9,230
GA	53.9	64.9	52.5	4,302	5,095	4,627
HI	6.6	7.3	4.5	679	801	603
ID	11.6	12.6	9.3	929	1,043	898
IL	44.7	49.3	38.5	4,487	5,012	4,442
IN	30.8	34.4	28.5	2,896	3,324	3,095
IA	10.6	12.5	7.9	882	998	811
KS	11.0	13.0	10.2	1,028	1,177	1,078
KY	15.9	18.6	14.2	1,173	1,370	1,236
LA	11.2	14.8	12.8	859	1,141	1,072
ME	3.8	4.6	4.3	309	377	367
MD	30.0	29.0	25.0	2,309	2,395	2,236
MA	17.5	18.1	16.5	1,891	2,046	1,966
MI	39.8	46.5	38.5	3,390	4,149	3,814
MN	27.3	25.6	21.3	2,672	2,558	2,329
MS	8.1	10.9	8.0	495	660	572
MO	21.7	26.4	20.9	1,750	2,149	1,945
MT	2.9	3.0	2.1	212	233	186
NE	7.8	7.9	5.4	551	574	489
NV	23.3	31.1	22.9	1,637	2,185	1,818
NH	4.2	4.7	4.1	381	454	421
NJ	25.2	25.4	22.4	2,087	2,318	2,189
NM	8.9	11.5	9.2	775	969	870
NY	28.6	31.1	22.2	2,621	2,787	2,348
NC	53.3	62.9	49.1	4,431	5,277	4,774
ND	2.9	3.4	1.6	190	211	153
OH	44.2	47.2	35.6	4,319	4,799	4,318
OK	8.7	9.5	8.2	809	903	847
OR	20.5	24.1	16.1	1,956	2,276	1,906
PA	40.1	40.2	37.0	3,547	3,728	3,577
RI	2.6	2.5	2.3	235	233	224
SC	21.1	24.6	20.0	1,694	2,019	1,798
SD	3.7	4.6	2.4	242	288	202
TN	27.0	31.9	26.8	2,171	2,539	2,368
TX	77.8	102.6	70.4	6,896	8,098	7,008
UT	17.3	18.6	14.7	1,508	1,717	1,524
VT	2.3	2.4	2.0	202	220	203
VA	45.0	46.8	39.5	3,700	3,965	3,700
WA	41.3	44.0	31.5	3,629	4,018	3,330
WV	2.6	3.9	3.3	185	283	265
WI	32.1	34.6	22.8	2,624	2,917	2,389
WY	1.2	2.0	1.7	136	210	196

Source: U.S. Bureau of the Census, Construction Reports, series C40, annual.

No. 1211. Valuation of Construction Authorized by Permit, by Type of Construction and State: 1994

[In millions of dollars]

STATE	Total [1]	Residential	NONRESIDENTIAL Total [2]	NONRESIDENTIAL Industrial	NONRESIDENTIAL Office	NONRESIDENTIAL Stores
U.S.	208,326	123,278	37,166	6,457	7,247	14,388
AL	2,577	1,357	696	69	175	302
AK	382	230	69	9	11	36
AZ	6,369	5,075	621	133	121	268
AR	1,491	795	437	97	114	138
CA	21,345	11,937	3,156	589	501	1,432
CO	5,343	3,906	546	96	133	225
CT	2,199	1,030	417	26	70	84
DE	626	337	104	7	28	37
DC	178	18	61	-	52	5
FL	16,254	11,076	2,226	212	426	915
GA	7,787	5,095	1,434	290	229	629
HI	1,442	801	273	7	150	67
ID	1,610	1,043	291	105	62	68
IL	9,483	5,012	2,099	693	308	629
IN	5,594	3,324	1,252	363	191	535
IA	1,937	998	495	120	160	130
KS	1,917	1,177	370	68	85	137
KY	2,235	1,370	497	180	56	196
LA	2,187	1,141	551	73	94	223
ME	755	377	150	21	31	51
MD	3,643	2,395	379	51	59	152
MA	4,002	2,046	523	43	90	206
MI	7,439	4,149	1,502	345	267	493
MN	4,587	2,558	626	142	149	213
MS	1,421	660	424	62	55	148
MO	3,961	2,149	824	102	126	333
MT	506	233	136	9	34	56
NE	1,118	574	255	44	67	88
NV	3,522	2,185	568	45	137	141
NH	861	454	167	38	21	35
NJ	4,794	2,318	578	46	129	135
NM	1,421	969	226	29	47	109
NY	6,138	2,787	1,170	142	144	566
NC	8,286	5,277	1,475	216	363	562
ND	413	211	106	20	25	44
OH	8,420	4,799	1,573	264	406	626
OK	1,578	903	367	79	53	170
OR	3,686	2,276	650	172	81	168
PA	6,960	3,728	1,444	207	241	546
RI	440	233	42	3	1	30
SC	3,446	2,019	757	163	120	298
SD	570	288	116	12	34	43
TN	4,366	2,539	899	145	203	348
TX	13,550	8,098	2,737	280	457	1,355
UT	2,621	1,717	529	114	116	205
VT	462	220	151	33	27	60
VA	6.006	3,965	818	114	200	303
WA	6,380	4,018	1,122	113	332	470
WV	708	283	293	24	48	72
WI	4,973	2,917	916	236	211	284
WY	330	210	44	6	6	21

- Represents zero. [1] Includes residential and nonresidential additions and alterations, residential nonhousekeeping buildings, and residential garages and carports, not shown separately. [2] Includes other types of construction not shown separately.

Source: U.S. Bureau of the Census, unpublished data.

No. 1212. New Privately-Owned Housing Units Started—Selected Characteristics: 1970 to 1994

[In thousands. For composition of regions, see table 27. See also *Historical Statistics, Colonial Times to 1970*, series N 156-163 and 170]

YEAR	Total units	STRUCTURES WITH—			REGION				CONDOMINIUM UNITS [1]		
		One unit	2 to 4 units	5 or more units	North-east	Mid-west	South	West	Total	Single-family	Multi-family
1970	1,434	813	85	536	218	294	612	311	(NA)	(NA)	(NA)
1971	2,052	1,151	120	781	264	434	869	486	(NA)	(NA)	(NA)
1972	2,357	1,309	141	906	330	443	1,057	527	(NA)	(NA)	(NA)
1973	2,045	1,132	118	795	277	440	899	429	241	69	172
1974	1,338	888	68	382	183	317	553	285	175	46	130
1975	1,160	892	64	204	149	294	442	275	65	20	45
1976	1,538	1,162	86	289	169	400	569	400	95	30	64
1977	1,987	1,451	122	414	202	465	783	538	118	41	77
1978	2,020	1,433	125	462	200	451	824	545	156	42	114
1979	1,745	1,194	122	429	178	349	748	470	198	43	156
1980	1,292	852	110	331	125	218	643	306	186	35	150
1981	1,084	705	91	288	117	165	562	240	181	36	145
1982	1,062	663	80	320	117	149	591	205	170	40	130
1983	1,703	1,068	113	522	168	218	935	382	276	77	199
1984	1,750	1,084	121	544	204	243	866	436	291	96	194
1985	1,742	1,072	93	576	252	240	782	468	225	79	146
1986	1,805	1,179	84	542	294	296	733	483	214	80	134
1987	1,620	1,146	65	409	269	298	634	420	196	73	123
1988	1,488	1,081	59	348	235	274	575	404	148	53	95
1989	1,376	1,003	55	318	179	266	536	396	118	37	82
1990	1,193	895	37	260	131	253	479	329	75	22	53
1991	1,014	840	36	138	113	233	414	254	60	21	39
1992	1,200	1,030	31	139	127	288	497	288	74	35	40
1993	1,288	1,126	29	133	126	298	562	302	86	45	41
1994	1,457	1,198	35	224	138	329	639	351	96	48	48

NA Not available.   [1] Type of ownership under which the owners of the individual housing units are also joint owners of the common areas of the building or community. Includes a small number of cooperatively-owned units.

Source: U.S. Bureau of the Census, *Current Construction Reports*, series C20, monthly.

No. 1213. New Privately-Owned Housing Units Started, by State: 1991 to 1994

[In thousands of units]

REGION, DIVISION, AND STATE	1991	1992	1993	1994 Total units	1994 Single-family units	REGION, DIVISION, AND STATE	1991	1992	1993	1994 Total units	1994 Single-family units
U.S.	1,014.0	1,200.0	1,288.0	1,457.0	1,199.0	DC	0.3	0.3	0.4	0.3	0.1
						VA	34.8	41.4	47.4	50.0	43.4
Northeast . .	113.0	129.0	125.0	135.0	120.0	WV	3.4	4.0	4.4	5.5	5.0
N.E.	33.8	39.7	39.0	40.7	38.1	NC	41.3	54.1	61.7	70.0	57.8
ME	4.3	5.1	4.3	4.4	4.2	SC	20.1	22.1	23.8	27.7	23.4
NH	3.9	4.1	4.2	4.3	4.0	GA	39.4	50.1	58.4	62.4	53.4
VT	2.4	2.5	2.5	2.2	2.0	FL	99.9	105.8	115.3	130.8	102.1
MA	13.2	16.2	16.7	17.8	16.9	E.S.C.	59.3	74.8	88.4	97.7	82.0
RI	2.5	2.7	2.5	2.6	2.5	KY	14.5	18.5	20.9	22.5	18.5
CT	7.5	9.1	8.7	9.4	8.5	TN	23.1	29.3	34.0	37.2	33.1
M.A.	79.1	88.9	86.1	94.7	82.3	AL	14.9	18.4	22.2	24.1	19.4
NY	27.7	29.7	25.2	28.3	20.3	MS	6.8	8.6	11.2	13.9	11.0
NJ	15.6	19.8	22.3	29.8	27.6	W.S.C . . .	84.8	108.9	131.8	153.3	118.5
PA	35.7	39.5	38.7	36.6	34.4	AR	9.2	10.7	13.5	14.7	11.3
Midwest . . .	233.0	289.0	298.0	323.0	265.0	LA	8.7	12.2	14.6	15.5	14.5
E.N.C.	163.9	200.0	205.0	225.0	186.9	OK	8.3	11.1	13.1	14.1	12.2
OH	39.5	47.3	48.5	54.3	44.7	TX	58.6	74.9	90.7	109.1	80.4
IN	27.4	35.3	35.6	41.4	36.7	West	254.0	282.0	294.0	341.0	277.0
IL	36.0	41.8	46.1	48.2	39.1	Mountain .	82.1	108.5	133.2	160.4	131.9
MI	34.3	42.3	42.2	48.1	41.6	MT	2.2	3.3	3.7	3.9	3.1
WI	26.7	33.4	33.0	33.4	24.7	ID	7.5	12.1	13.3	14.2	11.2
W.N.C . . .	69.4	88.5	92.2	97.5	78.3	WY	1.1	2.0	2.1	2.8	2.5
MN	20.8	27.3	26.2	24.5	21.0	CO	14.7	25.5	32.6	38.2	31.8
IA	9.5	12.4	12.3	13.6	9.7	NM	4.8	6.4	7.8	10.5	8.6
MO	17.6	22.5	25.0	28.1	23.9	AZ	24.0	32.9	38.7	51.8	43.9
ND	2.5	2.9	3.4	3.8	2.2	UT	9.5	15.2	19.2	20.0	16.0
SD	2.7	3.7	4.3	4.7	3.1	NV	18.4	17.3	23.6	29.5	23.5
NE	7.2	8.2	8.6	8.9	7.0	Pacific . . .	171.5	173.1	160.4	181.0	145.3
KS	9.0	11.5	12.5	13.8	11.3	WA	35.0	40.2	40.8	45.1	35.0
South	414.0	497.0	569.0	636.0	520.0	OR	16.8	19.9	21.6	24.8	18.4
S.A	270.0	313.6	348.7	385.3	319.2	CA	110.6	104.7	89.9	101.2	84.9
DE	4.9	5.5	5.8	6.2	5.9	AK	1.3	1.6	2.1	2.2	1.8
MD	26.0	30.5	31.4	32.5	28.1	HI	7.7	6.7	6.0	7.8	5.1

Source: National Association of Home Builders, Economics, Mortgage Finance and Housing Policy Division, *Forecast of Housing Activity*.

No. 1214. Characteristics of New Privately Owned One-Family Houses Completed: 1970 to 1994

[Percent distribution, except as indicated. Data beginning 1980 show percent distribution of characteristics for all houses completed (includes new houses completed, houses built for sale completed, contractor-built and owner-built houses completed, and houses completed for rent). Data for 1970 cover contractor-built, owner-built, and houses for rent for year construction started and houses sold for year of sale. Percents exclude houses for which characteristics specified were not reported]

CHARACTERISTIC	1970	1980	1990	1993	1994	CHARACTERISTIC	1970	1980	1990	1993	1994
Total houses (1,000)....	793	957	966	1,039	1,160	Bedrooms...........	100	100	100	100	100
						2 or less...........	13	17	15	12	12
Financing...........	100	100	100	100	100	3.............	63	63	57	58	58
Mortgage..........	84	82	82	87	89	4 or more.........	24	20	29	30	30
FHA-insured......	30	16	14	9	8	Bathrooms...........	100	100	100	100	100
VA-guaranteed.....	7	8	4	6	5	1 1/2 or less........	52	27	13	12	11
Conventional.....	47	55	62	72	74	2.............	32	48	42	40	40
Farmers Home						2 1/2 or more.......	16	25	45	48	49
Administration	(1)	3	2	1	1	Heating fuel.........	100	100	100	100	100
Cash or equivalent....	16	18	18	13	11	Electricity.........	28	50	33	29	29
						Gas.............	62	41	59	66	67
Floor area...........	100	100	100	100	100	Oil.............	8	3	5	3	3
Under 1,200 sq. ft	36	21	11	9	9	Other...........	1	5	3	2	1
1,200 to 1,599 sq. ft...	28	29	22	21	21	Heating system.....	100	100	100	100	100
1,600 to 1,999 sq. ft...	16	22	22	23	24	Warm air furnace....	71	57	65	67	67
2,000 to 2,399 sq. ft...	21	13	17	18	18	Electric heat pump....	(NA)	24	23	24	24
2,400 sq. ft. and over ..	(2)	15	29	29	29	Other...........	29	19	12	10	9
Average (sq. ft.)......	1,500	1,740	2,080	2,095	2,100	Central air-conditioning .	100	100	100	100	100
Median (sq. ft.)	1,385	1,595	1,905	1,945	1,940	With.............	34	63	76	78	79
						Without..........	66	37	24	22	21
Number of stories	100	100	100	100	100	Fireplaces...........	100	100	100	100	100
1..............	74	60	46	48	49	No fireplace	65	43	34	37	36
2 or more..........	17	31	49	48	47	1 or more.........	35	56	66	63	64
Split level	10	8	4	4	3	Parking facilities	100	100	100	100	100
Foundation..........	100	100	100	100	100	Garage	58	69	82	84	86
Full or partial basement.	37	36	38	40	39	Carport	17	7	2	2	2
Slab	36	45	40	40	41	No garage or carport ..	25	24	16	14	13
Crawl space	27	19	21	20	20						

NA Not available.   1 Included with "Conventional" financing.   2 Included with floor area of 2,000 to 2,399 square feet.
Source: U.S. Bureau of the Census and U.S. Dept. of Housing and Urban Development, *Current Construction Reports*, series C25, *Characteristics of New Housing,* annual.

No. 1215. New Privately Owned One-Family Houses Sold, by Region and Type of Financing, 1970 to 1994, and by Sales-Price Group, 1994

[In thousands. Based on a national probability sample of monthly interviews with builders or owners of one-family houses for which building permits have been issued or, for nonpermit areas, on which construction has started. For details, see source. For composition of regions, see table 27]

YEAR AND SALES-PRICE GROUP	Total sales	REGION				FINANCING TYPE			
		North-east	Midwest	South	West	Conven-tional	FHA and VA	Farmers Home Admin.	Cash
1970	485	61	100	203	121	1213	244	(1)	27
1971	656	82	127	270	176	1314	314	(1)	28
1972	718	96	130	305	187	1447	242	(1)	30
1973	634	95	120	257	161	1465	134	(1)	34
1974	519	69	103	207	139	1378	112	(1)	28
1975	549	71	106	222	150	363	122	43	22
1976	646	72	128	247	199	458	134	23	31
1977	819	86	162	317	255	592	166	24	38
1978	817	78	145	331	262	575	174	26	43
1979	709	67	112	304	225	469	186	18	36
1980	545	50	81	267	145	302	196	14	32
1981	436	46	60	219	112	244	142	14	36
1982	412	47	48	219	99	193	173	11	34
1983	623	76	71	323	152	350	217	8	49
1984	639	94	76	309	160	423	149	9	58
1985	688	112	82	323	170	403	208	11	64
1986	750	136	96	322	196	411	268	12	59
1987	671	117	97	271	186	408	190	8	64
1988	676	101	97	276	202	437	171	6	62
1989	650	86	102	260	202	416	162	14	58
1990	534	71	89	225	149	337	138	10	50
1991	509	57	93	215	144	329	128	9	43
1992	610	65	116	259	170	428	134	7	41
1993	666	60	123	295	188	476	147	6	37
1994.	**670**	**61**	**123**	**295**	**191**	**490**	**130**	**9**	**41**
Under $80,000.	72	2	10	52	8	30	29	8	4
$80,000 to $119,999 ...	201	10	37	101	53	122	65	(B)	14
$120,000 to $149,999 ...	140	11	28	54	47	108	25	(B)	7
$150,000 to $199,999 ...	129	17	25	46	41	111	10	(B)	9
$200,000 and over ...	127	21	22	41	42	119	(B)	(B)	7

B Withheld because estimate did not meet publication standards on the basis of sample size.   1 Houses financed by Farmers Home Administration included under conventional financing.
Source: U.S. Bureau of the Census and U.S. Dept. of Housing and Urban Development, *Current Construction Reports,* series C25, *Characteristics of New Housing,* annual; and *New One-Family Houses Sold,* monthly.

No. 1216. Median Sales Price of New Privately Owned One-Family Houses Sold, by Region: 1970 to 1994

[**In dollars.** For definition of median, see Guide to Tabular Presentation. For composition of regions, see table 27]

YEAR	U.S.	North-east	Midwest	South	West	YEAR	U.S.	North-east	Midwest	South	West
1970	23,400	30,300	24,400	20,300	24,000	1983	75,300	82,200	79,500	70,900	80,100
1971	25,200	30,600	27,200	22,500	25,500	1984	79,900	88,600	85,400	72,000	87,300
1972	27,600	31,400	29,300	25,800	27,500	1985	84,300	103,300	80,300	75,000	92,600
1973	32,500	37,100	32,900	30,900	32,400	1986	92,000	125,000	88,300	80,200	95,700
1974	35,900	40,100	36,100	34,500	35,800	1987	104,500	140,000	95,000	88,000	111,000
1975	39,300	44,000	39,600	37,300	40,600	1988	112,500	149,000	101,600	92,000	126,500
1976	44,200	47,300	44,800	40,500	47,200	1989	120,000	159,600	108,800	96,400	139,000
1977	48,800	51,600	51,500	44,100	53,500	1990	122,900	159,000	107,900	99,000	147,500
1978	55,700	58,100	59,200	50,300	61,300	1991	120,000	155,900	110,000	100,000	141,100
1979	62,900	65,500	63,900	57,300	69,600	1992	121,500	169,000	115,600	105,500	130,400
1980	64,600	69,500	63,400	59,600	72,300	1993	126,500	162,600	125,000	115,000	135,000
1981	68,900	76,000	65,900	64,400	77,800	1994	130,000	169,000	132,900	116,900	140,400
1982	69,300	78,200	68,900	66,100	75,000						

Source: U.S. Bureau of the Census and U.S. Dept. of Housing and Urban Development, *Current Construction Reports*, series C25, *Characteristics of New Housing*, annual; and *New One-Family Houses Sold*, monthly.

No. 1217. New Mobile Homes Placed for Residential Use and Average Sales Price, by Region: 1980 to 1994

[A mobile home is a moveable dwelling, 10 feet or more wide and 35 feet or more long, designed to be towed on its own chassis and without need of a permanent foundation. Excluded are travel trailers, motor homes, and modular housing. Data are based on a probability sample and subject to sampling variability; see source. For composition of regions, see table 27]

YEAR	UNITS PLACED (1,000)					AVERAGE SALES PRICE (dol.)				
	Total	Northeast	Midwest	South	West	U.S.	Northeast	Midwest	South	West
1980	233.7	12.3	32.3	140.3	48.7	19,800	18,500	18,600	18,200	25,400
1981	229.2	12.0	30.1	143.5	43.6	19,900	19,000	18,900	18,400	25,600
1982	234.1	12.4	25.6	161.1	35.0	19,700	19,800	20,000	18,500	24,700
1983	278.1	16.3	34.3	186.0	41.4	21,000	21,400	20,400	19,700	27,000
1984	287.9	19.8	35.2	193.4	39.4	21,500	22,200	21,100	20,200	27,400
1985	283.4	20.2	38.6	187.6	36.9	21,800	22,700	21,500	20,400	28,700
1986	256.1	21.2	37.2	162.3	35.4	22,400	24,400	21,800	20,700	29,900
1987	239.2	23.6	40.0	145.5	30.1	23,700	25,600	23,700	21,900	31,000
1988	224.3	22.7	39.1	130.7	31.8	25,100	27,000	24,600	22,700	33,900
1989	202.8	20.2	39.1	112.8	30.6	27,200	30,200	26,700	24,100	37,800
1990	195.4	18.8	37.7	108.4	30.6	27,800	30,000	27,000	24,500	39,300
1991	174.3	14.3	35.4	97.6	27.0	27,700	30,400	27,600	24,500	38,600
1992	212.0	15.0	42.2	124.4	30.4	28,400	30,900	28,800	25,400	39,000
1993	242.5	15.4	44.5	146.7	35.9	30,500	32,000	31,400	27,700	40,500
1994	285.3	16.1	52.8	174.1	42.3	33,500	33,700	34,700	30,500	44,600

Source: U.S. Bureau of the Census, *Current Construction Reports*, series C20.

No. 1218. Existing One-Family Houses Sold and Price, by Region: 1970 to 1994

[Based on data (adjusted and aggregated to regional and national totals) reported by participating real estate multiple listing services. For definition of median, see Guide to Tabular Presentation. For composition of regions, see table 27]

YEAR	HOUSES SOLD (1,000)					MEDIAN SALES PRICE (dol.)				
	Total	Northeast	Midwest	South	West	Total	Northeast	Midwest	South	West
1970	1,612	251	501	568	292	23,000	25,200	20,100	22,200	24,300
1971	2,018	311	583	735	389	24,800	27,100	22,100	24,300	26,500
1972	2,252	361	630	788	473	26,700	29,800	23,900	26,400	28,400
1973	2,334	367	674	847	446	28,900	32,800	25,300	29,000	31,000
1974	2,272	354	645	839	434	32,000	35,800	27,700	32,300	34,800
1975	2,476	370	701	862	543	35,300	39,300	30,100	34,800	39,600
1976	3,064	439	881	1,033	712	38,100	41,800	32,900	36,500	46,100
1977	3,650	515	1,101	1,231	803	42,900	44,400	36,700	39,800	57,300
1978	3,986	516	1,144	1,416	911	48,700	47,900	42,200	45,100	66,700
1979	3,827	526	1,061	1,353	887	55,700	53,600	47,800	51,300	77,400
1980	2,973	403	806	1,092	672	62,200	60,800	51,900	58,300	89,300
1981	2,419	353	632	917	516	66,400	63,700	54,300	64,400	96,200
1982	1,990	354	490	780	366	67,800	63,500	55,100	67,100	98,900
1983	2,719	493	709	1,035	481	70,300	72,200	56,600	69,200	94,900
1984	2,868	511	755	1,073	529	72,400	78,700	57,100	71,300	95,800
1985	3,214	622	866	1,172	554	75,500	88,900	58,900	75,200	95,400
1986	3,565	703	991	1,261	610	80,300	104,800	63,500	78,200	100,900
1987	3,526	685	959	1,282	600	85,600	133,300	66,000	80,400	113,200
1988	3,594	673	929	1,350	642	89,300	143,000	68,400	82,200	124,900
1989	3,346	531	855	1,185	775	93,100	145,200	71,300	84,500	139,900
1990	3,211	469	831	1,202	709	95,500	141,200	74,000	85,900	139,600
1991	3,220	479	840	1,199	702	100,300	141,900	77,800	88,900	147,200
1992	3,520	534	939	1,292	755	103,700	140,000	81,700	92,100	143,800
1993	3,802	571	1,007	1,416	808	106,800	139,500	85,200	95,000	142,600
1994	3,946	592	1,027	1,464	863	109,800	139,100	87,900	96,000	146,700

Source: National Association of REALTORS, Washington, DC, *Real Estate Outlook: Market Trends & Insights* (copyright).

No. 1219. Median Sales Price of Existing One-Family Homes, by Selected Metropolitan Area: 1990 to 1994

[**In thousands of dollars.** Areas are metropolitan statistical areas (MSA's) except as indicated; for definitions and components, see Appendix II]

METROPOLITAN AREA	1990	1992	1993	1994	METROPOLITAN AREA	1990	1992	1993	1994
U.S., all areas	**95.5**	**103.7**	**106.8**	**109.8**	Louisville, KY-IN	60.8	69.5	74.5	80.5
					Memphis, TN-AR-MS	78.1	85.3	87.0	86.3
Albany-Schenectady-Troy, NY	106.9	111.4	112.3	112.0	Miami-Hialeah, FL PMSA	89.3	97.1	98.8	103.2
Anaheim-Santa Ana, CA MSA	242.4	230.9	217.2	211.0	Milwaukee, WI PMSA	84.4	97.0	104.1	109.0
Atlanta, GA	(NA)	89.5	91.8	93.6	Minneapolis-St. Paul, MN-WI	88.7	94.2	98.2	101.5
Baltimore, MD	105.9	113.4	115.7	115.4	Nashville, TN	81.8	88.8	90.4	96.5
Birmingham, AL	80.8	90.9	96.5	100.2	New Orleans, LA	67.8	73.6	76.8	76.9
Boston, MA PMSA	174.1	171.1	173.2	(NA)	New York-Northern New Jersey-				
Buffalo-Niagara Falls,					Long Island, NY-NJ-CT CMSA	174.9	172.7	173.2	173.2
NY CMSA	77.2	81.7	83.5	82.3	Oklahoma City, OK	53.2	61.6	64.9	66.7
Charlotte-Gastonia-Rock Hill,					Orlando, FL	82.8	87.6	90.1	90.7
NC-SC	93.1	102.2	106.1	106.5	Philadelphia, PA-NJ PMSA	108.7	117.0	118.0	119.5
Chicago, IL PMSA	116.8	136.8	142.0	144.1	Phoenix, AZ	84.0	86.8	89.1	91.4
Cincinnati, OH-KY-IN PMSA	79.8	88.6	91.4	96.5	Pittsburgh, PA PMSA	70.1	78.6	82.2	80.7
Cleveland, OH PMSA	80.6	90.7	95.0	98.5	Portland, OR PMSA	79.5	97.7	106.0	116.9
Columbus, OH	81.6	91.0	91.8	94.8	Richmond-Petersburg, VA	87.5	93.9	94.1	95.4
Dallas, TX PMSA	89.5	91.3	94.5	95.0	Riverside/San Bernardino, CA				
Denver, CO PMSA	86.4	96.2	104.7	116.8	PMSA	132.1	136.2	134.4	129.1
Detroit, MI PMSA	76.7	81.3	86.0	87.0	Rochester, NY	79.8	84.7	84.8	85.6
Ft. Lauderdale-Hollywood-					St. Louis, MO-IL	76.7	83.2	84.8	85.0
Pompano Beach, FL PMSA	92.6	99.1	103.1	103.1	Sacramento, CA	137.5	134.0	129.2	124.5
Ft. Worth-Arlington, TX PMSA	76.7	80.2	82.9	82.5	Salt Lake City-Ogden, UT	69.4	76.5	84.9	98.0
Hartford, CT PMSA	157.3	141.1	135.3	133.4	San Antonio, TX	63.6	70.4	77.0	78.2
Honolulu, HI	352.0	349.0	358.5	360.0	San Diego, CA	183.2	183.1	176.9	176.0
Houston, TX PMSA	70.7	80.3	80.9	80.5	San Francisco, CA PMSA	259.3	259.3	254.4	255.6
Indianapolis, IN	74.8	83.7	86.6	90.7	Seattle-Tacoma, WA CMSA	142.0	145.7	150.2	155.9
Jacksonville, FL	72.4	76.8	77.1	81.9	Tampa-St. Petersburg-				
Kansas City, MO-KS	74.1	79.5	83.6	87.1	Clearwater, FL	71.4	72.6	75.0	76.2
Las Vegas, NV	93.0	104.3	108.2	110.5	Washington, DC-MD-VA	150.5	157.8	158.3	157.9
Los Angeles-Long Beach, CA					West Palm Beach-Boca Raton-				
PMSA	212.1	213.1	197.9	(NA)	Delray Beach, FL	108.0	114.1	114.6	117.6

NA Not available.

Source: National Association of REALTORS, Washington, DC, *Real Estate Outlook: Market Trends & Insights* (copyright).

No. 1220. Existing Home Sales, by State: 1990 to 1994

[In thousands]

STATE	1990	1991	1992	1993	1994	STATE	1990	1991	1992	1993	1994
United States [1]	**3,211**	**3,220**	**3,520**	**3,802**	**3,946**	Missouri	84.1	82.7	98.8	106.4	110.2
Alabama	61.1	64.0	72.5	77.9	77.4	Montana	12.7	13.9	16.6	16.2	15.6
Alaska	(NA)	(NA)	(NA)	(NA)	(NA)	Nebraska	19.3	19.9	22.4	23.2	23.3
Arizona	86.3	79.7	89.8	107.9	123.8	Nevada	26.2	25.6	25.6	30.5	32.9
Arkansas	44.8	43.4	47.8	52.8	52.3	New Hampshire	7.9	9.3	12.0	13.6	16.2
California [2]	452.1	425.4	427.3	436.8	482.8	New Jersey	114.8	118.8	132.1	139.0	145.4
Colorado	54.2	59.6	71.4	82.1	80.6	New Mexico	23.6	24.4	29.2	31.0	30.4
Connecticut	34.3	37.6	40.0	45.9	49.8	New York	125.5	127.2	136.3	143.0	156.3
Delaware	9.7	10.4	10.0	9.4	10.4	North Carolina	135.9	139.9	160.2	185.0	204.1
District of Columbia	13.1	12.5	12.4	12.3	12.3	North Dakota	10.4	10.3	11.9	11.8	10.9
Florida	183.3	176.0	179.2	208.9	229.7	Ohio	151.6	149.8	167.4	179.1	186.4
Georgia	73.2	70.7	(NA)	(NA)	(NA)	Oklahoma	53.4	52.5	57.6	61.5	59.7
Hawaii	19.2	12.2	11.6	12.5	13.1	Oregon	56.6	48.1	52.5	58.8	58.1
Idaho	18.1	19.0	21.6	23.4	23.1	Pennsylvania	182.7	179.2	204.4	216.1	216.4
Illinois	160.9	168.1	186.2	193.9	188.4	Rhode Island	7.8	7.8	10.0	11.0	11.6
Indiana	80.1	76.0	84.8	100.8	103.3	South Carolina	57.8	53.9	58.9	62.2	67.3
Iowa	51.9	54.1	53.1	53.5	54.3	South Dakota	11.6	11.3	12.7	13.7	13.2
Kansas	38.8	37.1	46.2	53.7	55.7	Tennessee	92.7	92.0	102.2	120.5	129.8
Kentucky	66.4	67.8	78.7	83.3	81.1	Texas	240.0	242.0	242.7	258.8	266.9
Louisiana	41.6	47.1	47.0	49.3	51.4	Utah	22.1	26.3	31.5	31.2	32.4
Maine	(NA)	(NA)	10.3	11.6	13.0	Vermont	6.1	8.1	9.5	11.0	10.9
Maryland	67.1	66.8	69.0	73.4	69.5	Virginia	96.9	90.3	101.3	104.2	99.5
Massachusetts	44.0	49.6	57.6	66.0	68.7	Washington	87.7	86.9	91.3	97.0	101.2
Michigan	145.0	145.0	157.3	170.6	184.2	West Virginia	42.0	43.3	46.8	45.7	45.8
Minnesota	64.8	66.3	75.7	81.8	82.0	Wisconsin	71.7	82.8	91.5	94.6	94.3
Mississippi	34.7	35.2	39.2	43.6	43.5	Wyoming	7.4	8.2	9.9	10.9	11.0

NA Not available.   [1] U.S. totals are derived independently and therefore are not equal to the sum of the States.   [2] Provided by the California Association of Realtors.

Source: National Association of REALTORS, Washington, DC, *Real Estate Outlook: Market Trends & Insights* (copyright).

No. 1221. New Apartments Completed and Rented in 3 Months, by Region: 1980 to 1993

[Structures with five or more units, privately financed, nonsubsidized, unfurnished apartments. Based on sample and subject to sampling variability. For composition of regions, see table 27]

YEAR AND RENT	NUMBER (1,000)					PERCENT RENTED IN 3 MONTHS				
	U.S.	Northeast	Midwest	South	West	U.S.	Northeast	Midwest	South	West
1980	196.1	14.2	43.8	91.5	46.6	75	77	77	74	75
1981	135.3	4.9	36.9	68.4	25.1	80	85	86	78	75
1982	117.0	4.6	21.9	66.8	23.7	72	74	79	70	72
1983	191.5	3.5	41.1	115.1	31.8	69	73	86	63	69
1984	313.2	3.8	41.2	194.4	73.9	67	64	79	63	70
1985	365.2	8.1	54.0	166.1	137.0	65	69	72	59	68
1986	407.6	16.9	64.5	171.7	154.5	66	70	70	62	67
1987	345.6	11.3	66.0	124.5	143.9	63	73	65	59	64
1988	284.5	8.7	60.4	91.7	123.8	66	52	73	58	69
1989	247.8	13.4	45.8	86.3	102.3	70	74	74	68	69
1990	214.3	12.7	44.3	77.2	80.0	67	66	75	64	65
1991	165.3	6.8	37.9	63.6	57.0	70	83	78	65	68
1992	110.2	10.9	34.0	37.4	28.0	74	75	80	72	70
1993	**77.2**	**3.7**	**25.3**	**27.7**	**20.5**	**75**	**37**	**81**	**76**	**73**
Less than $350	4.9	(Z)	2.0	2.6	.2	96	(Z)	98	95	79
$350-$549	30.4	1.3	15.3	7.5	6.3	74	11	75	74	83
$350-$449	11.9	0.3	7.0	3.0	1.6	67	43	65	61	86
$450-$549	18.5	1.0	8.3	4.5	4.7	79	1	84	82	83
$550-$749	22.6	1.5	6.4	9.3	5.5	79	39	86	80	82
$550-$649	13.8	1.1	5.1	4.8	2.8	80	26	86	84	81
$650-$749	8.9	0.4	1.3	4.5	2.7	79	75	86	75	83
$750 or more	19.3	0.9	1.6	8.2	8.5	66	67	91	68	58
Median asking rent	573	599	493	625	687	(X)	(X)	(X)	(X)	(X)

X Not applicable.   Z Less than 50 units.

Source: U.S. Bureau of the Census, *Current Housing Reports*, series H130 and H131, and unpublished data.

No. 1222. Gross Housing Product—Summary: 1980 to 1993

[**In billions of dollars.** For definition of current and constant dollars, see Guide to Tabular Presentation]

ITEM	CURRENT DOLLARS					CONSTANT (**1987**) DOLLARS				
	1980	1990	1991	1992	1993	1980	1990	1991	1992	1993
Housing output [1]	245.3	525.7	552.7	577.5	604.0	383.1	456.6	462.5	468.5	475.6
Nonfarm housing	240.2	520.6	547.4	572.1	598.5	376.9	452.1	458.0	464.1	471.4
Owner-occupied	178.4	379.5	399.3	417.6	438.3	278.7	326.6	330.8	334.6	340.3
Tenant-occupied	61.8	141.1	148.2	154.6	160.2	98.2	125.5	127.2	129.5	131.2
Farm housing	5.1	5.2	5.3	5.4	5.6	6.3	4.5	4.5	4.4	4.2
Less: Intermediate goods and services consumed	35.8	71.6	74.2	71.2	76.6	55.9	62.3	63.0	65.1	61.1
Equals: **Gross housing product**	209.5	454.1	478.5	506.3	527.4	327.2	394.4	399.5	403.3	414.5

[1] Equals personal consumption expenditures (see text, section 14) for housing, less expenditures for transient hotels, motels, clubs, schools, and other group housing.

Source: U.S. Bureau of Economic Analysis, *Survey of Current Business*, August 1993 and July 1994 issues, and *National Income and Product Accounts of the United States: Volume 2, 1959-88.*

No. 1223. Residential Capital—Year-End Stocks and Average Age: 1970 to 1993

[As of **Dec. 31.** Data based on fixed residential capital formation components of the gross national product. For definition of current and constant dollars, see Guide to Tabular Presentation]

ITEM	CURRENT DOLLARS (bil. dol.)				CONSTANT (**1987**) DOLLARS (bil. dol.)				AVERAGE AGE [1] (years)			
	1970	1980	1990	1993	1970	1980	1990	1993	1970	1980	1990	1993
Gross stocks [2]	**1,244**	**4,391**	**7,563**	**8,798**	**3,961**	**5,443**	**6,916**	**7,312**	**24.8**	**23.2**	**23.6**	**24.0**
Private nonfarm:												
1 to 4 units	1,001	3,502	6,074	7,164	3,208	4,356	5,556	5,916	25.3	23.9	24.2	24.4
5 or more units	131	522	933	1,015	421	647	853	878	17.7	17.8	19.8	21.4
Farm (1 to 4 units)	55	136	163	172	176	170	150	143	43.9	42.8	43.2	43.2
Other nonfarm structures [3]	10	24	32	34	32	29	29	28	14.6	19.3	23.7	25.1
Mobile homes	15	79	124	147	31	88	112	110	5.1	7.7	10.7	11.1
Public: Federal, State, and local	25	99	176	198	80	122	162	173	14.9	17.2	19.5	20.3
Net stocks [2][4]	**813**	**2,910**	**4,913**	**5,650**	**2,590**	**3,607**	**4,491**	**4,696**	**16.2**	**15.8**	**16.8**	**17.3**
Private nonfarm:												
1 to 4 units	656	2,334	3,991	4,672	2,102	2,902	3,649	3,856	16.8	16.3	17.2	17.6
5 or more units	93	371	629	656	301	459	575	568	11.0	12.8	15.2	16.9
Farm (1 to 4 units)	24	58	68	72	76	73	62	59	28.7	26.4	26.6	26.7
Other nonfarm structures [3]	6	12	14	14	21	15	12	11	9.0	16.0	18.4	19.1
Mobile homes	11	48	62	71	23	54	55	54	3.8	6.0	7.5	7.6
Public: Federal, State, and local	18	70	99	129	60	87	107	113	12.7	13.5	14.6	14.9

[1] Constant-dollar stocks.   [2] Includes equipment, not shown separately.   [3] Consists of dormitories, fraternity and sorority houses, nurses' homes, etc.   [4] Based on straight-line depreciation.

Source: U.S. Bureau of Economic Analysis, *Fixed Reproducible Tangible Wealth in the United States, 1925-89,* and *Survey of Current Business,* January 1992, September 1993, and August 1994 issues.

No. 1224. Housing Units—Historical Trends for Selected Characteristics: 1950 to 1993

[As of **April 1, except 1993,** as of **fall.** Based on the Census of Population and Housing and American Housing Survey; see Appendix III]

CHARACTERISTIC	NUMBER OF UNITS						PERCENT DISTRIBUTION					
	1950	1960	1970	1980	1990	1993	1950	1960	1970	1980	1990	1993
UNITS IN STRUCTURE												
All housing units [1]	**45,983**	**58,315**	**67,699**	**86,759**	**102,264**	**106,611**	**100.0**	**100.0**	**100.0**	**100.0**	**100.0**	**100.0**
1 detached	29,116	40,103	44,801	53,596	60,383	64,283	63.3	68.8	66.2	61.8	59.0	60.3
1 attached	[2]2,799	3,655	1,990	3,587	5,378	6,079	[2]6.1	6.3	2.9	4.1	5.3	5.7
2	5,302	4,464	5,444	5,309	4,948	([3])	11.5	7.7	8.0	6.1	4.8	([3])
3 or 4	3,374	3,088	3,563	4,373	4,928	[3] 10,732	7.3	5.3	5.3	5.0	4.8	[3]10.1
5 or more	5,078	6,238	9,829	15,478	18,105	18,444	11.0	10.7	14.5	17.8	17.7	17.3
Mobile home or trailer	315	767	2,073	4,416	7,400	7,072	0.7	1.3	3.1	5.1	7.2	6.6
Other	(NA)	(NA)	(NA)	(NA)	1,121	(NA)	(NA)	(NA)	(NA)	(NA)	1.1	(NA)
PLUMBING FACILITIES												
All housing units [1]	**44,502**	**58,315**	**67,657**	**86,693**	**102,264**	**106,611**	**100.0**	**100.0**	**100.0**	**100.0**	**100.0**	**100.0**
Complete plumbing facilities	28,729	48,537	62,984	84,359	101,162	104,302	64.6	83.2	93.1	97.3	98.9	97.8
Lacking complete plumbing facilities	15,773	9,778	4,672	2,334	1,102	1,854	35.4	16.8	6.9	2.7	1.1	1.7
Not reported	1,481	(NA)	(NA)	(NA)	(NA)	(NA)	(X)	(NA)	(NA)	(NA)	(NA)	(NA)
TELEPHONE IN HOUSING UNIT [4]												
Occupied housing units	**41,829**	**53,024**	**63,450**	**80,390**	**91,947**	**94,724**	**(NA)**	**100.0**	**100.0**	**100.0**	**100.0**	**100.0**
With telephone	(NA)	41,618	55,177	74,720	87,130	88,442	(NA)	78.5	87.0	92.9	94.8	93.4
No telephone	(NA)	11,406	8,273	5,670	4,817	6,282	(NA)	21.5	13.0	7.1	5.2	6.6

NA Not available.   X Not applicable.   [1] Data for 1970 and 1980 are "Year-round housing units," which exclude seasonal and migratory vacant units.   [2] Includes 1,588,902 units classified as "1 and 2 dwelling unit."   [3] Structures with "2 units" included with units of "3 or 4."   [4] Beginning 1980, data are not completely comparable with earlier years due to change in question asked.

Source: U.S. Bureau of the Census, *1990 Census of Housing,* series CH-1, and earlier census reports; and *Current Housing Reports,* series H150/93, American Housing Survey in the United States.

No. 1225. Occupied Housing Units—Tenure, by Race of Householder: 1920 to 1993

[**In thousands, except as indicated.** As of **April 1, except 1991,** as of **fall.** Prior to **1960,** excludes Alaska and Hawaii. Statistics on the number of occupied units are essentially comparable although identified by various terms. See also *Historical Statistics, Colonial Times to 1970,* series N 238-245]

RACE AND TENURE	1920	1930	1940	1950	1960	1970	1980	1990	1993
ALL RACES									
Occupied units, total	**24,352**	**29,905**	**34,855**	**42,826**	**53,024**	**63,445**	**80,390**	**91,947**	**94,724**
Owner occupied	11,114	14,280	15,196	23,560	32,797	39,886	51,795	59,025	61,252
Percent of occupied	45.6	47.8	43.6	55.0	61.9	62.9	64.4	64.2	64.7
Renter occupied	13,238	15,624	19,659	19,266	20,227	23,560	28,595	32,923	33,472
WHITE									
Occupied units, total	**21,826**	**26,983**	**31,561**	**39,044**	**47,880**	**56,606**	**68,810**	**76,880**	**80,029**
Owner occupied	10,511	13,544	14,418	22,241	30,823	37,005	46,671	52,433	54,878
Percent of occupied	48.2	50.2	45.7	57.0	64.4	65.4	67.8	68.2	68.6
Renter occupied	11,315	13,439	17,143	16,803	17,057	19,601	22,139	24,447	25,151
BLACK AND OTHER									
Occupied units, total	**2,526**	**2,922**	**3,293**	**3,783**	**5,144**	**6,839**	**11,580**	**15,067**	**14,695**
Owner occupied	603	737	778	1,319	1,974	2,881	5,124	6,592	6,374
Percent of occupied	23.9	25.2	23.6	34.9	38.4	42.1	44.2	43.8	43.4
Renter occupied	1,923	2,185	2,516	2,464	3,170	3,959	6,456	8,475	8,321

Source: U.S. Bureau of the Census, *Census of Housing: 1960,* vol. 1, *1970,* vol. 1; *1980 Census of Housing,* vol. 1, chapter A (HC80-1-A); and *1990 Census of Housing, General Housing Characteristics,* series CH-90-1; 1993 data, *Current Housing Reports,* series H150/93, American Housing Survey in the United States.

No. 1226. Occupied Housing Units—Tenure, by Race and Hispanic Origin of Householder: 1980 and 1990

[As of **April 1.** Based on the Census of Population and Housing; see Appendix III]

RACE AND HISPANIC ORIGIN OF HOUSEHOLDER	ALL HOUSEHOLDS			OWNER OCCUPIED		PERCENT OWNER OCCUPIED		RENTER OCCUPIED	
	1980	1990	Percent change, 1980-1990	1980	1990	1980	1990	1980	1990
Total units	**80,389,673**	**91,947,410**	**14.4**	**51,794,545**	**59,024,811**	**64.4**	**64.2**	**28,595,128**	**32,922,599**
White	68,810,123	76,880,105	11.7	46,670,775	52,432,648	67.8	68.2	22,139,348	24,447,457
Black	8,381,668	9,976,161	19.0	3,724,251	4,327,265	44.4	43.4	4,657,417	5,648,896
American Indian, Eskimo, or Aleut	397,252	591,372	48.9	212,209	318,001	53.4	53.8	185,043	273,371
Asian or Pacific Islander	993,458	2,013,735	102.7	521,230	1,050,182	52.5	52.2	472,228	963,553
Other race	1,807,172	2,486,037	37.6	666,080	896,715	36.9	36.1	1,141,092	1,589,322
Hispanic origin [1]	4,007,896	6,001,718	49.7	1,738,920	2,545,584	43.4	42.4	2,268,976	3,456,134

[1] Persons of Hispanic origin may be of any race.

U.S. Bureau of the Census, *1980 Census of Housing,* vol. 1, chapter A (HC80-1-A); and *1990 Census of Housing, General Housing Characteristics,* series CH-90-1.

No. 1227. Housing Units—

[In thousands of units, except as indicated. As of April.

STATE	Total housing units (1,000)	YEAR STRUCTURE BUILT				LACKING COMPLETE PLUMBING		PERCENT OF UNITS WITH—	
		Percent			Median year built	Total units (1,000)	Percent of total housing units	Public water system or private company	Public sewer
		1939 or earlier	1970 to 1979	1980 to March 1990					
United States ..	**102,263.7**	**18.4**	**21.8**	**20.7**	**1965**	**1,101.7**	**1.1**	**84.2**	**74.8**
Alabama	1,670.4	9.3	25.5	23.5	1970	27.5	1.6	87.1	54.5
Alaska..........	232.6	3.0	32.7	38.0	1976	29.0	12.5	65.6	62.3
Arizona	1,659.4	3.2	30.7	37.8	1976	31.5	1.9	94.5	81.3
Arkansas........	1,000.7	9.4	27.8	24.2	1971	18.4	1.8	81.5	60.1
California........	11,182.9	10.7	21.7	22.9	1967	69.4	0.6	95.4	89.6
Colorado	1,477.3	13.0	28.9	24.7	1971	11.8	0.8	91.0	86.9
Connecticut	1,320.9	25.5	15.7	15.7	1959	5.7	0.4	77.7	70.8
Delaware	289.9	14.3	20.2	24.3	1967	1.7	0.6	76.2	73.4
District of Columbia .	278.5	37.7	8.4	5.5	1947	2.3	0.8	99.9	99.3
Florida..........	6,100.3	3.7	29.3	35.0	1975	28.0	0.5	86.9	73.8
Georgia	2,638.4	8.1	24.5	32.1	1973	28.5	1.1	81.3	62.1
Hawaii	389.8	6.7	30.5	20.8	1970	4.3	1.1	97.6	80.2
Idaho	413.3	15.9	32.4	18.0	1970	6.0	1.5	70.0	64.0
Illinois	4,506.3	27.1	18.4	11.7	1958	29.3	0.7	89.8	86.2
Indiana	2,246.0	24.2	20.2	14.5	1961	16.2	0.7	74.1	67.9
Iowa	1,143.7	35.0	20.2	10.0	1956	9.8	0.9	81.1	76.0
Kansas	1,044.1	24.5	20.3	17.0	1961	7.9	0.8	89.5	81.2
Kentucky	1,506.8	15.9	25.0	20.0	1967	44.2	2.9	80.6	56.4
Louisiana........	1,716.2	10.6	25.3	22.1	1969	21.9	1.3	89.0	72.6
Maine	587.0	34.9	19.8	20.7	1960	20.8	3.5	53.2	45.4
Maryland	1,891.9	15.5	19.6	21.6	1965	12.7	0.7	82.8	81.1
Massachusetts	2,472.7	38.9	14.1	13.8	1953	12.4	0.5	91.6	72.9
Michigan	3,847.9	20.8	20.4	13.6	1960	32.5	0.8	70.5	70.8
Minnesota	1,848.4	24.5	22.1	18.5	1963	24.4	1.3	73.0	73.4
Mississippi	1,010.4	8.6	27.5	24.1	1971	21.9	2.2	87.3	57.9
Missouri.........	2,199.1	20.4	21.5	18.3	1964	26.8	1.2	83.6	73.6
Montana	361.2	21.8	26.6	17.5	1966	7.0	1.9	65.5	60.5
Nebraska	660.6	30.7	22.1	12.9	1960	5.2	0.8	83.0	80.9
Nevada	518.9	2.9	30.5	40.1	1977	2.7	0.5	92.5	87.9
New Hampshire ...	503.9	27.1	20.5	27.7	1968	5.9	1.2	60.3	49.6
New Jersey	3,075.3	24.6	14.9	14.8	1959	15.6	0.5	89.6	87.9
New Mexico......	632.1	8.1	26.5	27.5	1972	20.0	3.2	83.1	71.7
New York.......	7,226.9	35.7	11.9	9.4	1952	67.3	0.9	87.6	79.1
North Carolina	2,818.2	9.9	24.3	28.6	1971	43.0	1.5	65.4	49.8
North Dakota	276.3	24.7	26.6	16.6	1965	5.6	2.0	79.0	73.9
Ohio	4,371.9	25.8	18.6	12.2	1959	32.9	0.8	82.4	77.6
Oklahoma	1,406.5	12.4	25.4	22.1	1969	13.8	1.0	87.0	73.1
Oregon	1,193.6	16.8	28.7	16.6	1967	10.4	0.9	80.7	70.0
Pennsylvania	4,938.1	35.1	15.8	12.4	1954	47.1	1.0	78.1	74.3
Rhode Island	414.6	34.0	14.7	15.1	1955	2.3	0.5	88.8	70.9
South Carolina	1,424.2	8.5	26.3	29.0	1972	20.2	1.4	77.2	58.0
South Dakota	292.4	30.4	24.6	14.8	1961	5.9	2.0	81.4	71.1
Tennessee	2,026.1	10.2	24.8	24.2	1970	32.4	1.6	85.7	59.9
Texas	7,009.0	7.1	25.9	29.7	1972	85.1	1.2	91.6	81.2
Utah	598.4	13.5	28.1	24.4	1971	5.9	1.0	95.8	88.4
Vermont.........	271.2	36.5	19.6	22.4	1963	6.1	2.3	50.9	42.5
Virginia	2,496.3	11.0	23.6	26.3	1970	46.1	1.8	76.1	69.7
Washington	2,032.4	15.7	24.6	23.1	1969	18.6	0.9	85.7	68.3
West Virginia	781.3	23.7	22.8	17.7	1962	25.1	3.2	72.1	54.8
Wisconsin	2,055.8	28.5	21.1	14.5	1960	29.8	1.4	66.5	70.0
Wyoming	203.4	15.6	31.1	21.4	1971	3.2	1.6	77.6	74.2

Selected Characteristics: 1990

Based on the Census of Population and Housing; see Appendix III]

Occupied housing units (1,000)	Percent owner occupied	Percent condominium	PERCENT WITH—						Median value (dol.)	Gross rent (dol.)	STATE
			Vehicles available		No telephone in unit	Major house heating fuels					
			None	2 or more		Utility gas	Electricity	Fuel oil, kerosene			
91,947.4	**64.2**	**4.4**	**11.5**	**54.7**	**5.2**	**51.0**	**25.8**	**12.2**	**79,100**	**447**	**United States**
1,506.8	70.5	1.1	10.3	58.7	8.7	42.8	34.6	1.2	53,700	325	Alabama
188.9	56.1	5.3	11.9	54.0	8.3	42.8	11.8	32.3	94,400	559	Alaska
1,368.8	64.2	6.0	7.8	53.3	8.5	39.5	51.4	0.2	80,100	438	Arizona
891.2	69.6	0.7	9.8	56.2	10.9	52.8	22.7	0.2	46,300	328	Arkansas
10,381.2	55.6	7.4	8.9	57.9	3.0	73.2	19.2	0.3	195,500	620	California
1,282.5	62.3	7.3	6.9	60.9	4.2	77.0	12.9	0.3	82,700	418	Colorado
1,230.5	65.6	8.7	10.0	58.6	2.6	26.3	15.1	54.4	177,800	598	Connecticut
247.5	70.3	2.6	8.2	59.3	3.1	30.5	21.8	38.5	100,100	495	Delaware
249.6	38.9	10.4	37.4	21.2	4.2	63.5	20.5	12.5	123,900	479	District of Columbia
5,134.9	67.2	12.9	9.2	49.8	5.3	7.5	78.8	4.1	77,100	481	Florida
2,366.6	64.9	2.6	10.3	58.8	8.3	53.3	27.2	1.5	71,300	433	Georgia
356.3	53.9	18.4	9.9	54.1	2.6	3.3	37.9	0.2	245,300	650	Hawaii
360.7	70.1	1.2	4.6	67.3	5.8	28.2	39.8	9.0	58,200	330	Idaho
4,202.2	64.2	5.4	14.0	50.9	4.6	80.3	11.2	1.8	80,900	445	Illinois
2,065.4	70.2	1.4	8.5	59.1	5.9	63.1	19.3	6.2	53,900	374	Indiana
1,064.3	70.0	1.1	7.1	61.7	3.4	65.6	10.5	5.5	45,900	336	Iowa
944.7	67.9	1.7	6.4	61.7	4.4	75.9	11.8	0.3	52,200	372	Kansas
1,379.8	69.6	1.3	11.5	56.0	10.2	45.6	30.0	4.8	50,500	319	Kentucky
1,499.3	65.9	1.6	13.9	49.9	8.3	55.1	36.2	0.3	58,500	352	Louisiana
465.3	70.5	1.6	8.7	57.1	3.7	1.8	11.6	69.5	87,400	419	Maine
1,749.0	65.0	5.5	12.3	56.0	3.2	43.2	29.6	22.1	116,500	548	Maryland
2,247.1	59.3	6.1	14.3	49.3	2.1	38.0	13.5	44.0	162,800	580	Massachusetts
3,419.3	71.0	2.7	10.1	56.8	4.1	76.9	5.4	6.9	60,600	423	Michigan
1,647.9	71.8	3.1	8.6	60.0	2.5	62.9	10.5	11.9	74,000	422	Minnesota
911.4	71.5	0.6	12.1	54.2	12.6	40.8	30.6	0.5	45,600	309	Mississippi
1,961.2	68.8	2.0	9.8	57.0	5.2	60.4	18.1	1.5	59,800	368	Missouri
306.2	67.3	1.2	6.7	63.5	6.9	54.2	17.9	4.1	56,600	311	Montana
602.4	66.5	1.2	7.2	62.5	3.6	70.2	13.6	2.5	50,400	348	Nebraska
466.3	54.8	6.7	7.8	54.8	5.4	47.7	39.3	3.7	95,700	509	Nevada
411.2	68.2	5.8	6.3	61.7	3.4	15.2	12.4	55.8	129,400	549	New Hampshire
2,794.7	64.9	6.7	12.9	52.5	3.1	57.5	10.0	29.2	162,300	592	New Jersey
542.7	67.4	1.5	6.9	59.0	12.4	70.1	9.1	0.3	70,100	372	New Mexico
6,639.3	52.2	4.6	30.0	37.5	5.0	45.7	8.5	39.6	131,600	486	New York
2,517.0	68.0	2.5	9.6	59.2	7.1	18.6	42.0	22.5	65,800	382	North Carolina
240.9	65.6	2.3	6.5	63.2	3.5	39.6	26.2	15.7	50,800	313	North Dakota
4,087.5	67.5	2.5	10.2	56.8	4.7	68.2	16.8	7.5	63,500	379	Ohio
1,206.1	68.1	1.5	7.5	58.1	8.8	64.4	20.5	0.1	48,100	340	Oklahoma
1,103.3	63.1	1.7	8.0	59.9	4.5	24.7	44.6	11.4	67,100	408	Oregon
4496.0	70.7	2.0	15.2	49.5	2.6	49.5	14.8	27.9	69,700	404	Pennsylvania
378.0	59.5	2.8	10.6	54.5	3.1	40.7	7.9	47.0	133,500	489	Rhode Island
1,258.0	69.9	2.3	10.9	57.2	9.1	24.6	46.9	13.2	61,100	376	South Carolina
259.0	66.1	0.8	6.5	64.1	6.0	43.0	17.8	13.6	45,200	306	South Dakota
1,853.7	68.0	2.0	9.8	58.2	7.1	30.0	50.5	3.8	58,400	357	Tennessee
6,070.9	60.9	2.7	8.1	55.9	8.6	50.4	40.2	0.1	59,600	395	Texas
537.3	68.1	4.6	5.4	66.1	4.0	81.9	9.5	1.3	68,900	369	Utah
210.7	69.0	3.1	8.0	58.0	4.5	8.0	9.1	54.3	95,500	446	Vermont
2,291.8	66.3	4.8	9.0	59.8	5.4	28.9	40.1	20.2	91,000	495	Virginia
1,872.4	62.6	3.0	7.5	61.4	3.5	22.4	55.1	9.9	93,400	445	Washington
688.6	74.1	0.6	13.7	50.4	10.3	50.7	25.3	7.8	47,900	303	West Virginia
1,822.1	66.7	1.6	9.3	57.8	2.8	61.0	9.3	14.6	62,500	399	Wisconsin
168.8	67.8	1.2	4.7	66.9	5.6	62.9	16.5	0.7	61,600	333	Wyoming

Source: U.S. Bureau of the Census, *1990 Census of Housing, Detailed Housing Characteristics*, series CH-2, and *Census of Population and Housing, 1990: Summary Tape File 3C on CD-ROM.*

No. 1228. Homeownership Rates, by Age of Householder: 1984 to 1994

[In percent. Represents the proportion of households that are owners or the number of owner occupied households divided by the total number of households]

AGE	1984	1985	1986	1987	1988	1989	1990	1991	1992	1993[1]	1994
United States	64.5	63.9	63.8	64.0	63.8	63.9	63.9	64.1	64.1	64.0	64.0
Less than 25 yrs. old	17.9	17.2	17.2	16.0	15.8	16.6	15.7	15.3	14.9	14.8	14.9
25 to 29 yrs. old	38.6	37.7	36.7	36.4	35.9	35.3	35.2	33.8	33.6	33.6	34.1
30 to 34 yrs. old	54.8	54.0	53.6	53.5	53.2	53.2	51.8	51.2	50.5	50.8	50.6
35 to 39 yrs. old	66.1	65.4	64.8	64.1	63.6	63.4	63.0	62.2	61.4	61.8	61.2
40 to 44 yrs. old	72.3	71.4	70.5	70.8	70.7	70.2	69.8	69.5	69.1	68.6	68.2
45 to 49 yrs. old	74.6	74.3	74.1	74.6	74.4	74.1	73.9	73.7	74.2	73.7	73.8
50 to 54 yrs. old	78.4	77.5	78.1	77.8	77.1	77.2	76.8	76.1	76.2	77.2	76.8
55 to 59 yrs. old	80.1	79.2	80.0	80.0	79.3	79.1	78.8	79.5	79.3	78.9	78.4
60 to 64 yrs. old	79.9	79.9	79.8	80.4	79.8	80.1	79.8	80.5	81.2	80.9	80.1
65 to 69 yrs. old	79.3	79.5	79.4	79.5	80.0	80.0	80.0	81.4	80.8	80.7	80.6
70 to 74 yrs. old	75.5	76.8	77.2	77.7	77.7	77.8	78.4	78.8	79.0	79.9	80.1
75 yrs. old and over	71.5	69.8	70.0	70.8	70.8	71.2	72.3	73.1	73.3	73.4	73.5

[1] Based on 1990 census controls.

Source: Bureau of the Census, *Current Housing Reports*, series H111/94.

No. 1229. Homeownership Rates, by State: 1984 to 1994

[In percent]

STATE	1984	1990	1992	1993	1994	STATE	1984	1990	1992	1993	1994
United States	64.5	64.1	64.1	64.0	64.0	Missouri	69.5	64.2	65.2	66.4	68.4
Alabama	73.7	69.9	70.3	70.2	68.5	Montana	66.4	69.6	69.9	69.7	68.8
Alaska	57.6	57.1	55.5	55.4	58.8	Nebraska	69.3	67.5	68.4	67.7	68.0
Arizona	65.2	66.3	69.3	69.1	67.7	Nevada	58.9	55.8	55.1	55.8	55.8
Arkansas	65.9	68.6	70.3	70.5	68.1	New Hampshire	67.1	66.8	66.6	65.4	65.1
California	53.7	54.5	55.3	56.0	55.5	New Jersey	63.4	64.8	64.6	64.5	64.1
Colorado	64.7	59.8	60.9	61.8	62.9	New Mexico	68.0	69.5	70.5	69.1	66.8
Connecticut	67.8	65.5	66.1	64.5	63.8	New York	51.1	52.6	53.3	52.8	52.5
Delaware	70.4	70.2	73.8	74.1	70.5	North Carolina	68.8	69.3	68.6	68.8	68.7
Dist. of Columbia	37.3	35.1	35.0	35.7	37.8	North Dakota	70.1	65.4	63.7	62.7	63.3
Florida	66.5	66.1	66.0	65.5	65.7	Ohio	67.7	68.7	69.1	68.5	67.4
Georgia	63.6	65.7	66.9	66.5	63.4	Oklahoma	71.0	69.2	68.9	70.3	68.5
Hawaii	50.7	55.2	53.8	52.8	52.3	Oregon	61.9	65.2	64.3	63.8	63.9
Idaho	69.7	68.4	70.3	72.1	70.7	Pennsylvania	71.1	74.0	73.1	72.0	71.8
Illinois	62.4	63.0	62.4	61.8	64.2	Rhode Island	60.9	58.2	56.8	57.6	56.5
Indiana	69.9	66.1	67.6	68.7	68.4	South Carolina	69.1	73.1	71.0	71.1	72.0
Iowa	71.3	68.4	66.3	68.2	70.1	South Dakota	69.6	66.1	66.5	65.6	66.4
Kansas	72.7	69.7	69.8	68.9	69.0	Tennessee	67.6	68.0	67.4	64.1	65.2
Kentucky	70.2	67.2	69.0	68.8	70.6	Texas	62.5	59.0	58.3	58.7	59.7
Louisiana	70.1	68.9	66.7	65.4	65.8	Utah	69.9	70.7	70.0	68.9	69.3
Maine	74.1	72.0	72.0	71.9	72.6	Vermont	66.9	70.8	70.8	68.5	69.4
Maryland	67.8	63.8	64.8	65.5	64.1	Virginia	68.3	68.9	67.8	68.5	69.3
Massachusetts	61.7	60.2	61.8	60.7	60.6	Washington	65.7	61.8	62.5	63.1	62.4
Michigan	72.7	70.6	70.6	72.3	72.0	West Virginia	72.0	72.4	73.3	73.3	73.7
Minnesota	72.6	68.9	66.7	65.8	68.9	Wisconsin	65.2	68.9	69.4	65.7	64.2
Mississippi	72.3	71.8	70.4	69.7	69.2	Wyoming	68.8	68.7	67.9	67.1	65.8

Source: U.S. Bureau of the Census, *Current Housing Reports*, series H111/94-A.

No. 1230. Housing Units—Summary of Characteristics and Equipment, by Tenure and Region: 1993

[In thousands of units, except as indicated. Based on the American Housing Survey; see Appendix III. For composition of regions, see table 27]

ITEM	Total housing units	Sea-sonal	YEAR-ROUND UNITS							Vacant
			Occupied							
			Total	Owner	Renter	North-east	Mid-west	South	West	
Total units	**106,611**	**3,088**	**94,724**	**61,252**	**33,472**	**18,906**	**23,031**	**32,936**	**19,850**	**8,799**
Percent distribution	100.0	2.9	88.9	57.5	31.4	17.7	21.6	30.9	18.6	8.3
Units in structure:										
Single family detached	64,283	1,808	58,918	50,490	8,428	9,749	15,411	21,668	12,091	3,557
Single family attached	6,079	114	5,375	2,824	2,550	1,535	970	1,779	1,091	591
2 to 4 units	10,732	127	9,279	1,774	7,505	3,099	2,353	2,073	1,754	1,327
5 to 9 units	5,521	76	4,724	409	4,315	923	1,054	1,605	1,142	721
10 to 19 units	5,025	102	4,190	359	3,831	735	846	1,597	1,011	733
20 to 49 units	3,826	107	3,154	335	2,819	886	611	755	902	566
50 or more units	4,072	93	3,429	579	2,850	1,432	676	692	628	551
Mobile home or trailer	7,072	663	5,655	4,482	1,173	547	1,110	2,766	1,232	754
Stories in structure: [1]										
One story	2,807	32	2,424	266	2,158	82	387	1,156	799	350
2 stories	10,742	173	9,101	976	8,125	1,009	1,328	3,627	3,137	1,469
3 stories	8,373	166	7,137	1,204	5,934	2,432	2,564	1,204	937	1,070
4 to 6 stories	4,543	61	3,829	595	3,234	2,125	895	407	402	652
7 or more stories	2,721	72	2,294	420	1,873	1,429	366	330	169	356
Foundation: [2]										
Full or partial basement	31,516	344	29,910	26,280	3,630	9,662	12,478	4,902	2,869	1,262
Crawlspace	18,774	761	16,564	13,026	3,538	625	2,218	8,946	4,775	1,449
Concrete slab	18,453	498	16,697	13,196	3,501	894	1,492	8,982	5,329	1,257
Other	1,619	319	1,121	811	310	102	193	618	208	179
Year structure built: [3]										
1939 and earlier	22,676	502	19,886	11,290	8,596	7,357	6,406	3,766	2,358	2,290
1940 to 1949	8,529	252	7,539	4,696	2,843	1,635	1,791	2,554	1,559	737
1950 to 1959	13,633	406	12,360	8,855	3,505	2,521	3,212	3,959	2,667	867
1960 to 1969	16,070	538	14,405	9,482	4,923	2,421	3,389	5,266	3,329	1,127
1970 to 1979	23,474	859	20,818	13,290	7,528	2,629	4,622	8,475	5,092	1,797
1980 or later	22,228	532	19,716	13,637	6,079	2,342	3,612	8,916	4,846	1,979
Median year	1965	1967	1965	1966	1964	1952	1960	1971	1970	1964
Main heating equipment:										
Warm-air furnace	55,763	818	51,248	36,603	14,645	6,525	17,074	16,918	10,730	3,697
Electric heat pump	9,697	348	8,422	6,078	2,344	422	593	6,190	1,218	927
Steam or hot water system	14,896	75	13,657	7,338	6,320	9,548	2,549	830	729	1,164
Floor, wall, or pipeless furnace	5,625	214	4,746	2,070	2,676	184	435	1,533	2,594	665
Built-in electric units	8,084	460	6,722	2,891	3,831	1,325	1,327	1,934	2,136	903
Room heaters with flue	2,163	168	1,766	984	782	249	219	965	333	229
Room heaters without flue	1,893	53	1,597	919	677	42	52	1,422	81	244
Stoves	3,477	354	2,831	2,091	740	412	425	1,298	697	292
Fireplaces	1,076	138	884	740	143	36	97	419	332	54
None	1,644	361	911	366	545	38	46	355	472	372
Portable elec. heaters	833	61	682	330	352	4	14	431	233	90
Other	1,459	38	1,257	840	417	121	200	641	295	163
Air conditioning:										
Central	46,277	762	42,183	30,560	11,622	3,397	10,430	21,764	6,592	3,332
Percent of total units	43.4	24.7	44.5	49.9	34.7	18.0	45.3	66.1	33.2	37.9
One or more room units	27,968	434	26,090	15,620	10,470	8,251	6,540	8,543	2,756	1,444
Source of water:										
Public system or private company	90,327	1,659	81,028	50,064	30,963	15,990	19,110	28,007	17,921	7,640
Percent of total units	84.7	53.7	85.5	81.7	92.5	84.6	83.0	85.0	90.3	86.8
Well serving 1 to 5 units	13,880	936	11,967	10,140	1,826	2,698	3,674	4,396	1,198	978
Other	2,404	494	1,730	1,047	683	218	247	534	732	181
Means of sewage disposal:										
Public sewer	80,830	1,226	72,797	42,722	30,075	14,684	18,088	23,175	16,849	6,807
Percent of total units	75.8	39.7	76.9	69.7	89.9	77.7	78.5	70.4	84.9	77.4
Septic tank, cesspool, chemical toilet	25,221	1,550	21,807	18,444	3,362	4,214	4,927	9,672	2,994	1,864
Other	559	312	121	85	35	8	16	90	7	127

[1] Limited to multiunit structures.   [2] Limited to single-family units.   [3] For mobile home, oldest category is 1939 or earlier.

Source: U.S. Bureau of the Census, *Current Housing Reports*, series H-150/93, American Housing Survey in the United States.

No. 1231. Occupied Housing Units—Housing Value and Gross Rent, by Region: 1993

[Based on the American Housing Survey; see Appendix III. For composition of regions, see table 27]

CATEGORY	NUMBER (1,000)					PERCENT DISTRIBUTION				
	Total units	North-east	Midwest	South	West	Total units	North-east	Midwest	South	West
VALUE										
Owner occupied units.	**61,252**	**11,751**	**15,617**	**21,841**	**12,043**	**100.0**	**100.0**	**100.0**	**100.0**	**100.0**
Less than $10,000	1,856	192	445	969	251	3.0	1.6	2.8	4.4	2.1
$10,000 to $19,999	2,391	282	704	1,102	303	3.9	2.4	4.5	5.0	2.5
$20,000 to $29,999	2,685	348	810	1,236	292	4.4	3.0	5.2	5.7	2.4
$30,000 to $39,999	3,353	355	1,173	1,613	212	5.5	3.0	7.5	7.4	1.8
$40,000 to $49,999	4,148	394	1,517	1,895	342	6.8	3.4	9.7	8.7	2.8
$50,000 to $59,999	4,101	471	1,331	1,915	384	6.7	4.0	8.5	8.8	3.2
$60,000 to $69,999	4,802	590	1,564	2,117	532	7.8	5.0	10.0	9.7	4.4
$70,000 to $79,999	4,666	730	1,393	1,971	572	7.6	6.2	8.9	9.0	4.7
$80,000 to $99,999	8,034	1,582	2,256	2,840	1,356	13.1	13.5	14.4	13.0	11.3
$100,000 to $119,999	5,171	1,158	1,316	1,622	1,075	8.4	9.9	8.4	7.4	8.9
$120,000 to $149,999	5,922	1,586	1,253	1,619	1,463	9.7	13.5	8.0	7.4	12.1
$150,000 to $199,999	6,284	1,943	939	1,440	1,963	10.3	16.5	6.0	6.6	16.3
$200,000 to $249,999	2,999	899	405	551	1,144	4.9	7.7	2.6	2.5	9.5
$250,000 to $299,999	1,734	474	195	365	700	2.8	4.0	1.2	1.7	5.8
$300,000 or more	3,104	748	315	586	1,455	5.1	6.4	2.0	2.7	12.1
Median value (dol.)	86,529	116,102	71,898	70,376	134,430	(X)	(X)	(X)	(X)	(X)
GROSS RENT										
Renter occupied units.	**33,472**	**7,155**	**7,415**	**11,096**	**7,808**	**100.0**	**100.0**	**100.0**	**100.0**	**100.0**
Less than $100	551	82	165	242	63	1.6	1.1	2.2	2.2	0.8
$100 to $199	2,079	465	552	764	298	6.2	6.5	7.4	6.9	3.8
$200 to $249	1,424	258	426	530	210	4.3	3.6	5.7	4.8	2.7
$250 to $299	1,728	293	527	685	223	5.2	4.1	7.1	6.2	2.9
$300 to $349	2,071	335	616	758	363	6.2	4.7	8.3	6.8	4.6
$350 to $399	2,741	420	769	1,102	451	8.2	5.9	10.4	9.9	5.8
$400 to $449	2,850	453	833	1,048	516	8.5	6.3	11.2	9.4	6.6
$450 to $499	2,851	513	694	1,026	618	8.5	7.2	9.4	9.2	7.9
$500 to $599	4,817	1,084	1,040	1,499	1,194	14.4	15.2	14.0	13.5	15.3
$600 to $699	3,683	1,036	668	947	1,032	11.0	14.5	9.0	8.5	13.2
$700 to $799	2,382	678	287	607	810	7.1	9.5	3.9	5.5	10.4
$800 to $999	2,257	692	208	514	843	6.7	9.7	2.8	4.6	10.8
$1,000 to $1,249	971	251	72	201	447	2.9	3.5	1.0	1.8	5.7
$1,250 to $1,499	379	91	32	65	191	1.1	1.3	0.4	0.6	2.4
$1,500 or more	275	95	14	46	120	0.8	1.3	0.2	0.4	1.5
No cash rent	2,414	408	514	1,062	430	7.2	5.7	6.9	9.6	5.5
Median gross rent (dol.) . . .	487	551	424	445	579	(X)	(X)	(X)	(X)	(X)

X Not applicable.
Source: U.S. Bureau of the Census, *Current Housing Reports,* series H-150/93, American Housing Survey in the United States.

No. 1232. Heating Equipment and Fuels for Occupied Units: 1950 to 1993

[As of **April 1, except 1993**, as of **fall.** Based on the Census of Population and Housing and American Housing Survey; see Appendix III]

ITEM	NUMBER (1,000)					PERCENT DISTRIBUTION				
	1950	1960	1970	1980	1993	1950	1960	1970	1980	1993
Occupied units, total	**42,826**	**53,024**	**63,445**	**80,390**	**94,724**	**100.0**	**100.0**	**100.0**	**100.0**	**100.0**
Heating equipment:										
Warm air furnace	[1]11,508	17,378	27,515	39,279	51,248	[1]26.9	32.8	43.4	48.9	54.1
Heat pumps.	(NA)	(NA)	(NA)	2,835	8,422	(NA)	(NA)	(NA)	3.5	8.9
Steam or hot water	10,071	11,990	13,211	13,859	13,657	23.5	22.6	20.8	17.2	14.4
Floor, wall, or pipeless furnace .	([1])	6,088	5,552	4,693	4,746	([1])	11.5	8.8	5.8	5.0
Built-in electric units	-	664	3,236	6,370	6,722	-	1.3	5.1	7.9	7.1
Room heaters with flue	[2]15,399	[2]11,183	7,209	6,098	1,766	[2]36.0	[2]21.1	11.4	7.6	1.9
Room heaters without flue	5,268	5,218	3,558	2,736	1,597	12.3	9.8	5.6	3.4	1.7
Fireplaces, stoves, portable										
heaters or other	([2])	([2])	2,766	3,977	5,654	([2])	([2])	4.4	4.9	6.0
None	581	503	398	541	911	1.4	0.9	0.6	0.7	1.0
House heating fuel:										
Utility gas	11,387	22,851	35,014	42,658	47,669	26.6	43.1	55.2	53.1	50.3
Fuel oil, kerosene, etc	9,686	17,158	16,473	14,655	12,189	22.6	32.4	26.0	18.2	12.9
Electricity.	283	933	4,876	14,768	25,107	0.7	1.8	7.7	18.3	26.5
Bottled, tank, or LP gas	787	2,686	3,807	4,535	3,922	1.8	5.1	6.0	5.6	4.1
Wood and other fuel	4,855	2,460	1,060	2,729	4,630	11.3	4.6	1.7	3.4	4.9
Coal or coke	14,828	6,456	1,821	504	297	34.6	12.2	2.9	0.6	0.3
None	999	478	395	541	910	2.3	0.9	0.6	0.7	1.0
Cooking fuel:										
Electricity.	6,403	16,351	25,768	41,906	55,887	15.0	30.8	40.6	52.1	59.0
Gas [3]	25,501	33,787	36,558	37,944	37,996	59.6	63.7	57.6	47.2	40.1
Other fuel	10,796	2,603	908	398	479	25.2	4.9	1.4	0.5	0.5
None	124	280	213	142	362	0.3	0.5	0.3	0.2	0.4

- Represents zero.   NA Not available.   [1] "Floor, wall, or pipeless furnace" included in "Warm air furnace."   [2] "Fireplaces, stoves, or portable heaters" included in "Room heaters with flue."   [3] Includes utility, bottled, tank, and LP gas.
Source: U.S. Bureau of the Census, *Census of Housing, 1960,* vol. 1; *1970 and 1980,* vol. 1; and *1990 Census of Housing, Detailed Housing Characteristics,* series CH-2, and *Current Housing Reports,* series H-150/93, American Housing Survey in the United States.

No. 1233. Appliances Used by Households, by Region and Family Income: 1990

[In millions, except percent. As of November. Represents appliances possessed and generally used by the household. Based on the Residential Energy Consumption Survey; see Appendix III. For composition of regions, see table 27]

TYPE OF APPLIANCE	HOUSEHOLDS USING APPLIANCE		REGION				FAMILY INCOME IN 1990			
	Number	Percent of total	North-east	Midwest	South	West	Under $15,000	$15,000 -$24,999	$25,000 -$34,999	$35,000 and over
Total households . .	94.0	100.0	19.2	23.1	32.3	19.4	27.3	17.4	15.3	34.0
Air conditioners: Room . .	29.1	31.0	8.1	8.0	10.3	2.8	9.7	5.5	4.9	9.0
Central system [1]	36.6	38.9	3.2	9.2	19.0	5.2	6.0	6.0	6.0	18.7
Clothes washer	71.7	76.3	14.4	17.7	25.6	14.0	16.3	12.3	12.3	30.7
Clothes dryer	64.7	68.8	12.4	16.9	22.7	12.8	12.7	10.6	11.4	29.9
Dehumidifier	11.3	12.0	3.5	5.3	2.0	0.5	1.5	1.7	1.7	6.4
Dishwasher	42.7	45.4	8.0	9.3	15.3	10.0	5.2	5.9	7.5	23.9
Evaporative cooler [2]	3.8	4.0	(B)	(B)	(B)	2.9	1.3	0.8	0.9	0.8
Freezer	32.4	34.5	5.0	9.1	12.3	5.9	7.9	5.7	5.4	13.4
Microwave oven [3]	74.1	78.8	13.6	19.4	25.7	15.3	16.9	13.4	12.8	31.0
Outdoor gas grill	24.9	26.4	6.8	7.1	7.0	4.0	2.4	3.2	4.1	15.1
Outdoor gas light	1.0	1.1	0.3	0.3	0.3	(B)	0.2	0.2	0.1	0.5
Oven: Electric	55.3	58.9	9.3	12.7	22.1	11.2	13.7	9.7	9.8	22.2
Gas	38.4	40.8	9.8	10.5	10.1	8.0	13.3	7.7	5.5	11.9
Personal computer	14.8	15.7	3.0	3.2	4.8	3.7	1.4	1.3	2.0	10.1
Portable electric heater . .	13.5	14.4	2.2	2.8	5.4	3.1	3.9	2.8	2.0	4.8
Portable kerosene heater .	4.6	4.9	0.9	1.3	2.2	0.2	1.3	0.9	1.1	1.3
Range: Electric	54.3	57.8	9.1	12.6	21.8	10.8	16.4	9.7	9.8	21.3
Gas	39.6	42.1	10.0	10.6	10.5	8.6	13.6	7.8	5.5	12.6
Refrigerator: Frost-free . .	75.0	79.8	15.0	18.2	27.0	14.8	18.3	13.2	12.5	31.0
Nonfrost-free [5]	24.8	26.4	5.5	7.1	6.6	5.6	9.8	5.3	3.7	5.9
Television set: Color	90.3	96.1	18.6	22.3	30.8	18.6	25.0	16.9	14.8	33.5
Black and white	28.7	30.6	5.9	8.2	10.4	4.2	8.4	5.3	4.6	10.3
Water heater: [6] Gas	44.6	47.4	7.2	13.3	12.6	11.4	11.5	7.7	6.9	18.5
Electric	33.5	35.6	4.2	6.9	17.2	5.3	9.9	6.9	5.8	10.9
Other fuel	2.0	2.1	1.9	(B)	0.1	(B)	0.4	0.2	0.3	1.1
Whole house cooling fan .	9.4	10.1	2.1	2.1	4.0	1.2	1.5	1.4	1.5	5.1
Window or ceiling fan . . .	47.9	51.0	9.0	12.0	20.3	6.6	11.0	8.7	8.1	20.2

B Base figure too small to meet statistical standards for reliability.   [1] Includes the .9 million households with both central air conditioning and window or wall air conditioning units.   [2] An air-cooling unit used in dry climates that turns air into moist, cool air by saturating the air with water vapor.   [3] Microwave is first or second most used oven.   [4] All motorized vehicles used by U.S. households for personal transportation excluding motorcycles, mopeds, large trucks, and buses.   [5] Includes refrigerators without freezer compartments.   [6] Excludes water heaters that serve more than one household.
Source: U.S. Energy Information Administration, *Housing Characteristics: 1990.*

No. 1234. Expenditures by Residential Property Owners for Improvements and Maintenance and Repairs, by Type of Property and Activity: 1970 to 1994

[In millions of dollars]

YEAR AND TYPE OF EXPENDITURE	Total	1-unit properties with owner occupant	Other properties	ADDITIONS AND ALTERATIONS				Major replacements	Maintenance and repairs
				Total	To structures		To property outside of structures		
					Additions	Alterations			
1970	14,770	9,469	5,301	6,246	1,411	3,539	1,296	2,629	5,895
1975	25,239	15,684	9,556	10,997	1,971	6,844	2,182	4,484	9,758
1980	46,338	31,481	14,857	21,336	4,183	11,193	5,960	9,816	15,187
1981	46,351	30,201	16,150	20,414	3,164	11,947	5,303	9,915	16,022
1982	45,291	29,779	15,512	18,774	2,641	10,711	5,423	9,707	16,810
1983	49,295	32,524	16,771	20,271	4,739	11,673	3,859	10,895	18,128
1984	69,784	43,781	26,003	27,822	6,007	14,486	7,329	13,067	28,894
1985	80,267	47,742	32,525	28,775	3,966	17,599	7,211	16,134	35,358
1986	91,274	54,298	36,976	38,608	7,377	21,192	10,040	16,695	35,971
1987	94,082	54,791	39,291	39,978	9,557	21,641	8,779	15,875	38,229
1988	101,117	60,822	40,295	43,339	11,333	22,703	9,303	16,893	40,885
1989	100,891	59,858	41,033	39,786	6,828	23,129	9,828	18,415	42,689
1990	106,773	59,683	47,090	37,253	8,561	21,920	6,771	18,215	51,305
1991	97,528	58,083	39,445	30,944	14,868	16,076	6,954	16,744	49,840
1992, total [1]	103,734	67,316	36,418	40,186	6,783	22,700	10,704	18,393	45,154
Heating and air conditioning [2] .	6,952	5,302	1,650	1,103	(NA)	1,103	(NA)	3,546	2,303
Plumbing	9,549	5,653	3,896	1,540	(NA)	1,540	(NA)	3,104	4,905
Roofing	10,714	5,327	5,387	(NA)	(NA)	(NA)	(NA)	6,257	4,457
Painting	11,147	5,867	5,280	(NA)	(NA)	(NA)	(NA)	(NA)	11,147
1993, total [1]	108,305	70,746	37,559	45,797	12,757	24,781	8,259	20,809	41,699
Heating and air conditioning [2] .	7,918	5,814	2,103	1,259	(NA)	1,259	(NA)	4,040	2,618
Plumbing	8,700	4,488	4,212	1,597	(NA)	1,597	(NA)	2,990	4,114
Roofing	8,943	5,559	3,385	(NA)	(NA)	(NA)	(NA)	4,821	4,122
Painting	12,566	6,567	5,998	(NA)	(NA)	(NA)	(NA)	(NA)	12,566
1994, total [1]	115,030	77,270	37,760	48,828	9,647	28,672	10,509	23,248	42,953
Heating and air conditioning [2] .	8,581	5,712	2,869	2,060	(NA)	2,060	(NA)	3,904	2,617
Plumbing	8,941	5,222	3,719	1,677	(NA)	1,677	(NA)	2,836	4,428
Roofing	11,406	6,371	5,034	(NA)	(NA)	(NA)	(NA)	7,008	4,398
Painting	11,446	6,439	5,007	(NA)	(NA)	(NA)	(NA)	(NA)	11,446

NA Not available.   [1] Includes types of expenditures not separately specified.   [2] Central air-conditioning.
Source: U.S. Bureau of the Census, *Current Construction Reports,* series C50.

No. 1235. Expenditures for Improvements and Repairs to Nonresidential Buildings, by Ownership and Selected Building Characteristic: 1992

[In millions of dollars. Based on data collected as a supplement to the U.S. Department of Energy's Commercial Buildings Energy Consumption Survey. Excludes buildings of 1,000 square feet or smaller and all industrial and agricultural buildings. Also excludes all building either owned by the Federal government or by privately owned public utilities]

BUILDING CHARACTERISTIC	ALL BUILDINGS			PRIVATE NONRESIDENTIAL BUILDINGS			STATE AND LOCAL GOVERNMENT NONRESIDENTIAL BUILDINGS		
	Total	Improve-ments	Repairs	Total	Improve-ments	Repairs	Total	Improve-ments	Repairs
All buildings	**91,163**	**55,059**	**36,104**	**63,194**	**37,212**	**25,982**	**27,969**	**17,847**	**10,122**
PRINCIPAL ACTIVITY									
Office	25,605	16,250	9,355	22,546	14,252	8,294	3,059	1,998	1,061
Educational	17,577	10,512	7,065	1,815	951	864	15,762	9,561	6,201
Health care	10,763	6,885	3,878	7,496	4,428	3,068	3,267	2,457	810
Mercantile/service (nonfood)	11,228	7,100	4,128	11,228	7,100	4,128	(NA)	(NA)	(NA)
Food sales/service	3,550	1,516	2,034	3,550	1,516	2,034	(NA)	(NA)	(NA)
Warehouse	4,416	2,588	1,828	4,416	2,588	1,828	(NA)	(NA)	(NA)
Religious	3,064	1,902	1,162	3,064	1,902	1,162	(NA)	(NA)	(NA)
Public order and safety	1,217	698	519	(NA)	(NA)	(NA)	1,217	698	519
Lodging	4,687	2,085	2,602	4,687	2,085	2,602	(NA)	(NA)	(NA)
Other	7,165	4,645	2,520	2,675	1,570	1,105	4,490	3,075	141
Vacant	1,890	878	1,012	1,717	820	897	173	58	115
YEAR CONSTRUCTED									
1919 or before	6,622	4,175	2,447	4,957	3,161	1,796	1,665	1,014	651
1920 to 1945	10,035	6,011	4,024	7,105	4,176	2,929	2,930	1,835	1,095
1946 to 1959	11,133	5,990	5,143	6,900	3,881	3,019	4,233	2,109	2,124
1960 to 1969	19,705	13,193	6,512	10,747	6,774	3,973	8,958	6,419	2,539
1970 to 1979	22,898	14,219	8,679	15,514	9,204	6,310	7,384	5,015	2,369
1980 to 1989	16,587	9,393	7,194	15,072	8,706	6,366	1,515	687	828
1990 to 1992	3,147	1,735	1,412	1,933	996	937	1,214	739	475
Not reported	1,036	345	691	966	315	651	70	30	40
REGION									
Northeast	20,086	12,138	7,948	13,547	8,034	5,513	6,539	4,104	2,435
Midwest	23,414	14,538	8,876	13,539	8,399	5,140	9,875	6,139	3,736
South	28,350	17,899	10,451	22,578	14,408	8,170	5,772	3,491	2,281
West	19,313	10,484	8,829	13,530	6,371	7,159	5,783	4,113	1,670
BUILDING SIZE (sq. ft.)									
1,001 to 10,000	16,109	9,030	7,079	13,381	7,363	6,018	2,728	1,667	1,061
10,001 to 25,000	10,317	6,011	4,306	7,171	3,512	3,659	3,146	2,499	647
25,001 to 50,000	11,233	6,558	4,675	8,080	4,348	3,732	3,153	2,210	943
50,001 to 100,000	11,543	7,070	4,473	6,579	3,734	2,845	4,964	3,336	1,628
100,001 to 200,000	14,542	9,707	4,835	9,970	6,583	3,387	4,572	3,124	1,448
200,001 to 500,000	15,404	8,591	6,813	7,981	4,790	3,191	7,423	3,801	3,622
Over 500,000	12,013	8,092	3,921	10,030	6,881	3,149	1,983	1,211	772

NA Not available.
Source: U.S Bureau of the Census, *Expenditures for Nonresidential Improvements and Repairs: 1992*, series CSS/92.

No. 1236. Vacancy Rates for Housing Units—Characteristics: 1990 to 1994

[In percent. Annual averages. Based on Current Population Survey and Quarterly Household Survey. Rate is relationship between vacant housing for rent or for sale and the total rental and homeowner supply, which comprises occupied units, units rented or sold and awaiting occupancy, and vacant units available for rent or sale. For composition of regions, see table 27. See also *Historical Statistics, Colonial Times to 1970*, series N 249-2]

CHARACTERISTIC	RENTAL UNITS					HOMEOWNER UNITS				
	1990	1991	1992	1993 [1]	1994	1990	1991	1992	1993 [1]	1994
Total units	**7.2**	**7.4**	**7.4**	**7.3**	**7.4**	**1.7**	**1.7**	**1.5**	**1.4**	**1.5**
Inside MSA's	7.1	7.5	7.4	7.5	7.3	1.7	1.7	1.6	1.4	1.5
Outside MSA's	7.6	7.3	7.0	6.5	7.7	1.8	1.8	1.5	1.5	1.5
Northeast	6.1	6.9	6.9	7.0	7.1	1.6	1.5	1.3	1.3	1.5
Midwest	6.4	6.7	6.7	6.6	6.8	1.3	1.3	1.2	1.1	1.1
South	8.8	8.9	8.2	7.9	8	2.1	2.2	1.7	1.7	1.7
West	6.6	6.5	7.1	7.4	7.1	1.3	1.7	1.9	1.4	1.6
Units in structure:										
1 unit	4.0	3.9	3.8	3.7	4.5	1.4	1.4	1.3	1.2	1.3
2 units or more	9.0	9.4	9.4	9.4	9.1	7.1	6.8	5.8	5.3	4.9
5 units or more	9.6	10.4	10.0	10.2	9.8	8.4	7.9	7.4	6.8	5.6
Units with—										
3 rooms or less	10.3	10.8	11.4	10.7	11.0	10.2	10.5	8.6	6.9	9.0
4 rooms	8.0	8.1	7.9	8.1	7.9	3.2	3.0	2.6	2.5	2.9
5 rooms	5.7	5.9	5.3	5.7	5.6	2.0	1.9	1.9	1.7	1.7
6 rooms or more	3.0	3.1	3.1	3.2	3.4	1.1	1.2	1.1	1.0	1.0

[1] Beginning 1993, based on 1990 population census controls.
Source: U.S. Bureau of the Census, *Current Housing Reports,* series H111/94, and prior reports.

No. 1237. Recent Home Buyers—General Characteristics: 1976 to 1994

[As of **October**. Based on a sample survey; subject to sampling variability]

ITEM	Unit	1976	1980	1985	1989	1990	1991	1992	1993	1994
Median purchase price . .	Dollars . .	43,340	68,714	90,400	129,800	131,200	134,300	141,000	141,900	145,400
First-time buyers	Dollars . .	37,670	61,450	75,100	105,200	106,000	118,700	122,400	121,100	125,000
Repeat buyers [1]	Dollars . .	50,090	75,750	106,200	144,700	149,400	152,500	158,000	159,600	163,500
Average monthly mortgage										
payment	Dollars . .	329	599	896	1,054	1,127	1,144	1,064	1,015	1,028
Percent of income	Percent . .	24.0	32.4	30.0	31.8	33.8	34.0	33.2	31.5	31.4
Percent buying—										
New houses	Percent . .	15.1	22.4	23.8	21.8	21.2	19.7	20.5	22.3	22.0
Existing houses	Percent . .	84.9	77.6	76.2	78.2	78.8	80.3	79.5	77.7	78.0
Single-family houses . .	Percent . .	88.8	82.4	87.0	84.8	83.8	85.3	85.0	84.2	83.9
Condominiums [2]	Percent . .	11.2	17.6	10.6	13.5	13.1	11.5	13.1	12.8	12.1
For the first time	Percent . .	44.8	32.9	36.6	40.2	41.9	45.1	47.7	46.0	47.1
Average age:										
First-time buyers	Years . . .	28.1	28.3	28.4	29.6	30.5	30.7	31.0	31.6	31.6
Repeat buyers [1]	Years . . .	35.9	36.4	38.4	39.4	39.1	39.8	40.8	41.0	41.7
Downpayment/sales price	Percent . .	25.2	28.0	24.8	24.4	23.3	22.6	21.4	20.2	20.2
First-time buyers	Percent . .	18.0	20.5	11.4	15.8	15.7	14.7	14.3	14.0	13.7
Repeat buyers [1]	Percent . .	30.8	32.7	32.7	30.3	28.9	29.1	28.0	25.4	26.1

[1] Buyers who previously owned a home.   [2] Includes multiple-family houses.
Source: Chicago Title Insurance Company, Chicago, IL, *The Guarantor*, bimonthly (copyright).

No. 1238. Low-Income Public Housing Units, by Progress Stage: 1970 to 1993

[**In thousands**. As of **Dec. 31**. Housing for the elderly intended for persons 62 years old or over, disabled, or handicapped. Includes Puerto Rico and Virgin Islands. Covers units subsidized by HUD under annual contributions contracts. See also *Historical Statistics, Colonial Times to 1970*, series N 186-191]

YEAR	Total[1]	Occupied units[2]	Under construction	YEAR	Total[1]	Occupied units[2]	Under construction
1970	1,155.3	893.5	126.8	1990	1,305.3	1,028.1	7.6
Elderly	249.4	143.4	65.7	Elderly	(NA)	342.2	(NA)
1980	1,321.1	1,195.6	20.9	1992	1,323.3	1,199.4	7.2
Elderly	358.3	317.7	11.5	Elderly	(NA)	513.5	(NA)
1985	1,378.0	1,344.6	9.6	1993	1,324.7	1,207.6	(NA)
Elderly	373.5	361.1	2.1	Elderly	(NA)	507.5	(NA)

NA Not available. [1] Includes units to be constructed or to go directly "under management" because no rehabilitation needed not shown separately. [2] Under management or available for occupancy.
Source: U.S. Dept. of Housing and Urban Development, unpublished data based on the Field Office Report Monitoring System.

No. 1239. Office Buildings—Vacancy Rates for Major Cities, 1980 to 1994, and Status of Supply, 1994

[**As of December**. Excludes government owned and occupied, owner-occupied, and medical office buildings]

CITY	VACANCY RATE FOR EXISTING SPACE (percent)									SUPPLY STATUS, December 1994 (mil. sq. ft.)		
										Existing space		Space under construction
	1980	1985	1988	1989	1990	1991	1992	1993	1994	Total	Available for lease	
Total [1]	4.6	16.9	18.6	19.5	20.0	20.2	20.5	19.4	16.2	(NA)	(NA)	(NA)
Atlanta, GA	10.0	21.0	18.3	19.9	19.1	19.5	19.4	16.8	13.0	87.4	11.4	(Z)
Baltimore, MD	7.2	11.5	13.4	16.4	20.0	21.0	20.6	17.3	15.5	41.1	6.4	-
Boston, MA	3.8	13.1	14.1	15.3	19.6	19.1	17.5	17.7	13.3	137.0	18.3	(Z)
Charlotte, NC	(NA)	16.7	16.5	14.3	16.5	19.4	(NA)	(NA)	10.0	20.4	2.0	0.3
Chicago, IL	7.0	16.5	15.9	17.0	18.6	20.0	22.1	21.4	18.7	186.5	34.8	(NA)
Dallas, TX	8.6	23.0	29.7	26.9	25.8	26.0	31.3	29.5	21.7	116.3	25.3	(NA)
Denver, CO	6.6	24.7	27.6	26.1	24.8	23.0	21.5	15.9	12.8	68.5	8.8	(NA)
Detroit, MI	(NA)	(NA)	(NA)	(NA)	(NA)	(NA)	(NA)	21.4	19.7	59.0	11.6	(NA)
Houston, TX	4.0	27.6	29.2	27.5	24.9	27.3	27.0	25.1	24.7	140.9	34.8	(NA)
Indianapolis, IN . . .	(NA)	(NA)	21.3	20.0	21.2	21.4	22.4	18.8	18.4	22.3	4.1	(NA)
Kansas City, MO. . .	4.2	16.2	19.9	15.8	14.1	16.9	15.2	13.9	11.5	32.6	3.7	(Z)
Los Angeles, CA. . .	0.9	15.3	15.8	19.7	16.8	20.2	21.2	21.0	19.6	189.0	37.1	0.1
Miami, FL	2.4	20.9	24.0	22.0	23.4	22.6	18.5	19.0	15.4	29.4	4.5	(NA)
Milwaukee, WI	(NA)	(NA)	19.3	20.4	22.9	19.5	18.4	21.0	17.6	24.1	4.3	(NA)
New Orleans, LA . . .	(NA)	21.8	25.6	25.7	29.0	25.0	(NA)	(NA)	(NA)	(NA)	(NA)	(NA)
New York, NY [2] . . .	3.1	7.9	11.5	15.1	16.0	18.8	18.3	17.9	16.3	318.8	51.8	(NA)
Philadelphia, PA . . .	6.3	14.5	15.8	16.3	18.2	17.3	19.0	17.8	16.3	70.4	11.5	(NA)
Pittsburgh, PA	1.2	(NA)	17.6	16.3	16.3	14.2	(NA)	17.0	15.8	36.3	5.7	(Z)
San Diego, CA. . . .	(NA)	24.7	20.1	17.6	19.5	23.7	23.8	22.1	18.8	37.6	7.1	(NA)
San Francisco, CA .	0.4	13.7	15.5	15.7	14.7	13.3	12.5	13.7	11.7	53.9	6.3	(NA)
Seattle, WA	(NA)	(NA)	13.2	16.4	12.3	12.8	15.9	17.6	14.7	30.8	4.5	(NA)
St. Louis, MO. . . .	(NA)	(NA)	18.4	22.6	21.0	20.5	21.8	19.1	18.1	32.5	5.9	(NA)
Washington, DC . . .	2.5	9.0	13.2	14.4	19.0	17.6	15.4	14.1	13.4	222.3	29.9	2.2

- Represents zero.   NA Not available.   Z Less than 50,000 sq. ft.   [1] Includes other cities not shown separately. In 1993, 51 cities were covered.   [2] Refers to Manhattan.
Source: ONCOR International, Houston, TX, 1980-1985, *National Office Market Report*, semi-annual; 1986-1990, *International Office Market Report*, semi-annual; thereafter, *Office Market Data Book* (copyright).

Construction and Housing

No. 1240. Commercial Office Space—Inventory and Vacancy Rates for the Largest Metropolitan Areas: 1994

[As of **December 31, except population as of July 1.** Data based on responses from individuals knowledgeable in the local markets. Represents primarily the metropolitan area as indicated, but in many cases may exclude outlying countries beyond the central portion]

METROPOLITAN AREAS	Resident population, 1992 (1,000)	Inventory (1,000 sq. ft.)	Vacant space (1,000 sq. ft.)	Vacancy rate (percent)	Construction (1,000 sq. ft.)	Absorption (1,000 sq. ft.)
Albany-Schenectady-Troy, NY MSA	872	13,043	976	7.5	246	437
Atlanta, GA MSA	3,143	98,145	11,571	11.8	360	2,540
Austin-San Marcos, TX MSA	901	19,999	2,382	11.9	-	4,713
Baltimore, MD PMSA	2,433	23,701	4,033	17.0	-	140
Birmingham, AL MSA	859	15,360	1,579	10.3	180	410
Boston, MA-NH PMSA	3,211	87,822	11,791	13.4	-	1,237
Buffalo-Niagara Falls, NY MSA	1,194	7,491	995	13.3	50	416
Charlotte, NC MSA	1,212	19,593	1,850	9.4	247	769
Chicago, IL PMSA	7,561	147,637	25,429	17.2	-	3,443
Cincinnati, OH PMSA	1,560	21,887	2,958	13.5	-	338
Cleveland-Lorain-Elyria, OH PMSA	2,221	35,646	6,775	19.0	-	47
Columbus, OH MSA	1,394	25,155	775	3.1	1,500	745
Dallas, TX PMSA	4,215	116,348	26,479	22.8	-	3,494
Dayton, OH MSA	962	6,717	1,118	16.6	(NA)	−44
Denver, CO PMSA [1]	1,715	55,207	6,608	12.0	-	1,705
Detroit, MI PMSA	4,308	55,651	8,476	15.2	565	746
Fort Lauderdale, FL PMSA	1,301	16,035	2,147	13.4	-	490
Fort Worth, TX PMSA	1,419	18,038	3,457	19.1	-	−411
Fresno, CA MSA	805	11,875	1,337	11.3	29	596
Grand Rapids-Muskegon-Holland, MI MSA	964	7,963	1,626	20.4	75	596
Greensboro-Winston Salem-High Point, NC MSA	1,078	21,707	2,073	9.5	1,196	612
Greenville-Spartanburg-Anderson, SC MSA	853	4,064	726	17.9	-	19
Hartford, CT MSA	1,156	20,877	3,152	15.1	-	102
Honolulu, HI MSA	863	14,582	2,317	15.9	637	42
Houston, TX PMSA	3,530	111,802	19,485	17.4	-	−1,022
Indianapolis, IN MSA	1,424	18,425	3,293	17.9	-	603
Jacksonville, FL MSA	953	19,272	2,473	12.8	80	(NA)
Kansas City, MO-KS MSA	1,617	34,226	4,289	12.5	234	610
Las Vegas, NV MSA	971	6,346	468	7.4	318	695
Los Angeles, CA PMSA	9,054	143,379	27,969	19.5	-	1,041
Louisville, KY MSA	968	13,730	2,140	15.6	48	411
Memphis, TN MSA	1,034	18,408	1,766	9.6	150	1,388
Miami, FL PMSA	2,008	21,941	3,584	16.3	(NA)	−5,363
Milwaukee-Waukesha, WI PMSA	1,450	24,724	2,764	11.2	250	391
Minneapolis-St. Paul, MN-WI MSA	2,618	46,308	5,811	12.5	-	1,968
Nashville, TN MSA	1,023	12,454	1,163	9.3	45	252
New Jersey-Central/Northern [2]	3,897	151,094	25,603	16.9	500	1,466
New Orleans, LA MSA	1,303	21,737	5,603	25.8	-	−17
New York City, NY PMSA [3]	9,705	450,422	74,436	16.5	1,851	−2,377
Nassau-Suffolk, NY PMSA	2,640	35,872	4,057	11.3	100	2,303
Norfolk-Virginia Beach-Newport News, VA MSA	1,497	16,434	2,334	14.2	122	496
Oakland, CA PMSA	2,148	42,337	5,905	13.9	-	1,051
Oklahoma City, OK MSA	984	15,460	4,050	26.2	-	−400
Orange County, CA PMSA	2,485	54,436	9,708	17.8	-	603
Orlando, FL MSA	1,305	20,932	2,328	11.1	300	316
Philadelphia, PA PMSA [4]	4,944	82,888	13,990	16.9	-	3,851
Pheonix, AZ MSA	2,330	22,907	3,026	13.2	-	1,264
Pittsburgh, PA MSA	2,406	28,463	3,808	13.4	(NA)	516
Portland-Vancouver, OR PMSA	1,897	16,430	1,298	7.9	180	188
Providence, RI MSA	1,131	6,102	1,194	19.6	-	−117
Raleigh-Durham-Chapel Hill, NC MSA	909	16,919	1,026	6.1	300	963
Richmond-Petersburg, VA MSA	896	19,377	1,835	9.5	-	963
Sacramento-Yolo, CA MSA	1,563	25,993	2,971	11.4	360	890
St. Louis, MO MSA	2,519	38,842	4,505	11.6	200	1,777
Salt Lake City-Ogden, UT MSA	1,128	10,647	645	6.1	328	676
San Antonio, TX MSA [5]	1,379	15,804	2,348	14.9	-	189
San Diego, CA MSA	2,601	42,506	6,161	14.5	-	1,248
San Francisco, CA PMSA	2,523	90,055	8,448	26.7	290	1,657
San Jose, CA PMSA	1,528	34,500	3,125	9.1	(NA)	(NA)
Seattle, WA PMSA [6]	2,124	29,562	4,291	14.5	-	416
Syracuse, NY MSA	752	8,195	958	11.7	-	81
Tampa-St. Petersburg-Clearwater, FL MSA [7]	2,107	19,714	3,292	16.7	-	70
Tulsa OK MSA	732	12,074	1,725	14.3	-	637
Washington, DC-MD-VA-WV PMSA [8]	4,630	168,215	23,782	14.1	2,652	1,597
West Palm Beach-Boca Raton, FL MSA	901	6,707	902	13.4	-	412
Wichita, KS MSA	501	5,800	1,115	19.2	(NA)	−140

- Represents zero.   NA Not available.   [1] Represents only the suburban portion of the metropolitan area.   [2] Data are for area identified by source as New Jersey-Central/Northern with a market area of Bergen, Essex, Hudson, Morris, and Passaic, Hunterdon, Mercer, Middlesex, Monmouth, Somerset, and Union counties.   [3] Represents primarily Brooklyn, Manhattan, Queens, Rockland, and Westchester counties.   [4] Represents only the Pennsylvania portion of the metropolitan area.   [5] Represents only Bexar County.   [6] Represents only the central business district portion of Seattle.   [7] Represents only Pinnellas and Hillsborough counties.   [8] Excludes the Maryland portion of the metropolitan area and some outlying counties in Virginia.

Source: Resident population, U.S. Bureau of the Census. Office data, Society of Industrial and Office REALTORS, Washington, DC, *Comparative Statistics of Industrial and Office Real Estate Markets*, (copyright).

No. 1241. Commercial Buildings—Selected Characteristics, by Square Footage of Floorspace: 1992

[Excludes buildings 1,000 square feet or smaller. Building type based on predominant activity in which the occupants were engaged. Based on a sample survey of building representatives conducted between August and December 1992; therefore, subject to sampling variability. For composition of regions, see table 27]

CHARACTERISTIC	Number of build-ings (1,000)	FLOORSPACE (mil. sq. ft.)							Mean sq. ft. per building (1,000)	Median sq. ft. per building (1,000)
		Total	Within all buildings having square footage of—							
			5,000 or less	5,001 to 10,000	10,001 to 25,000	25,001 to 50,000	50,001 to 100,000	100,001 and over		
All buildings	**4,806**	**67,876**	**7,327**	**7,199**	**10,375**	**10,069**	**8,062**	**24,845**	**14.1**	**4.5**
Region:										
Northeast	771	13,400	1,074	1,337	1,663	1,976	1,752	5,597	17.4	5.2
Midwest	1,202	17,280	1,889	1,763	2,689	2,353	2,097	6,488	14.4	4.5
South	1,963	24,577	3,155	2,723	3,782	3,696	2,842	8,379	12.5	4.0
West.	870	12,619	1,208	1,376	2,241	2,043	1,371	4,380	14.5	5.0
Year constructed:										
1899 or before	169	1,721	251	397	297	431	(S)	(S)	10.2	5.5
1900 to 1919	255	3,608	336	523	503	522	319	(S)	14.1	5.0
1920 to 1945	724	8,712	1,150	1,106	1,507	1,267	927	1,934	12.0	4.2
1946 to 1959	880	10,421	1,352	1,255	1,775	1,792	1,236	2,531	11.8	4.2
1960 to 1969	783	12,612	1,167	986	1,892	1,856	1,625	5,085	16.1	4.5
1970 to 1979	982	14,014	1,536	1,505	1,902	2,216	1,776	5,079	14.3	4.5
1980 to 1989	884	14,287	1,339	1,251	2,189	1,658	1,717	6,132	16.2	4.8
1990 to 1992	128	2,502	197	176	309	327	268	1,224	19.6	4.8
Principal activity within building:										
Public assembly [1]	644	8,303	1,002	1,056	1,742	1,278	378	418	12.9	(NA)
Education	301	8,470	292	307	997	1,551	2,045	3,262	28.2	9.0
Food sales	130	757	286	(S)	(S)	(S)	(S)	(S)	5.8	2.6
Food service	260	1,491	485	343	325	(S)	(S)	(S)	5.7	3.4
Health care	63	1,763	108	(S)	(S)	(S)	(S)	1,286	27.9	4.3
Lodging.	154	2,891	159	294	412	711	420	758	18.8	8.0
Mercantile/services	1,272	12,402	2,203	1,987	2,003	1,369	1,268	3,570	9.7	4.0
Office	749	12,319	1,018	1,248	1,656	1,823	1,355	5,218	16.4	5.0
Parking garage.	24	1,652	(S)	(S)	(S)	(S)	(S)	694	69.9	6.0
Public order and safety . . .	60	820	91	(S)	(S)	(S)	(S)	(S)	13.7	5.0
Warehouse	761	11,484	1,089	1,106	2,066	1,631	1,250	4,343	15.1	5.0
Other	69	1,130	99	(S)	110	(S)	(S)	(S)	16.4	4.0
Vacant	319	4,396	473	459	635	768	503	821	13.8	4.2
Government owned.	599	15,124	689	848	1,735	1,953	2,241	7,659	25.2	6.7
Nongovernment owned . . .	4,206	52,752	6,638	6,351	8,640	8,116	5,821	17,186	12.5	4.3
Fuels used alone or in combination:										
Electricity.	4,616	66,549	6,996	7,057	10,097	9,856	7,936	24,607	14.4	4.7
Natural gas	2,665	45,097	3,761	4,266	6,865	6,510	5,735	17,959	16.9	5.1
Fuel oil	559	13,218	829	925	978	1,377	1,539	7,570	23.7	5.0
Propane	337	3,393	573	466	456	501	411	500	10.1	3.5
District heat	95	5,339	56	73	450	545	653	3,562	56.0	17.0
District chilled water	28	2,066	(S)	(S)	115	311	(S)	1,504	72.6	26.5
Any other	163	1,551	250	311	(S)	(S)	(S)	(S)	9.5	3.6
Workers:										
Fewer than 5	2,718	17,944	5,095	3,329	3,053	2,107	910	(S)	6.6	3.0
5 to 9	895	7,524	1,554	1,612	1,801	1,348	595	(S)	8.4	4.8
10 to 19	561	8,077	537	1,446	2,323	1,538	643	(S)	14.4	8.0
20 to 49	405	10,556	120	757	2,608	3,049	1,899	(S)	26.1	16.3
50 to 99	130	7,763	(S)	(S)	450	1,445	2,151	(S)	59.7	38.5
100 to 249.	64	7,378	(S)	(S)	(S)	517	1,303	5,433	114.6	79.0
250 or more.	31	8,633	(S)	(S)	(S)	(S)	561	7,992	274.4	150.0
Weekly operating hours:										
39 or less	1,039	8,246	1,797	1,341	1,592	1,309	1,007	(S)	7.9	3.5
40 to 48	1,278	14,998	1,904	2,186	2,994	2,553	1,698	3,662	11.7	4.9
49 to 60	1,004	14,046	1,430	1,610	2,549	2,536	1,440	4,482	14.0	5.0
61 to 84	645	12,062	926	1,098	1,408	1,443	1,769	5,418	18.7	5.0
85 to 167	478	8,467	772	492	1,022	1,151	1,132	3,897	17.7	4.0
168 (open continuously). . .	362	10,057	498	472	810	1,077	1,015	6,185	27.8	5.0

NA Not available.   S Figure does not meet publication standards.   [1] Includes religious worship.

Source: U.S. Energy Information Administration, *Commercial Buildings Characteristics, 1992.*

Construction and Housing

No. 1242. Commercial Buildings—Number and Square Footage of Floorspace, by Type of Building and Characteristic: 1992

[For composition of regions, see table 27]

BUILDING CHARACTERISTICS	All build-ings [1]	Public as-sembly[2]	Educa-tion	Food sales	Food service	Health care	Lodg-ing	Mer-cantile/serv-ices	Offices	Public order and safety	Ware-house
NUMBER (1,000)											
All buildings	**4,806**	**644**	**301**	**130**	**260**	**63**	**154**	**1,272**	**749**	**60**	**761**
Region:											
Northeast	771	70	38	(S)	54	12	31	246	126	16	109
Midwest	1,202	162	46	29	73	14	26	329	170	(S)	233
South	1,963	314	112	57	83	15	56	510	299	24	316
West	870	99	104	32	50	23	41	187	154	(S)	103
Year constructed:											
1899 or before	169	(S)	(S)	(S)	(S)	(S)	(S)	34	31	(NA)	(S)
1900 to 1919	255	48	12	(S)	(S)	(S)	(S)	59	38	(S)	27
1920 to 1945	724	98	28	(S)	43	7	14	210	108	(S)	112
1946 to 1959	880	131	76	(S)	51	10	24	235	136	(S)	117
1960 to 1969	783	111	72	(S)	33	15	38	208	102	(S)	107
1970 to 1979	982	107	46	28	73	14	27	247	163	16	185
1980 to 1986	671	69	37	(S)	23	9	22	200	113	(S)	125
1987 to 1989	212	(S)	12	(S)	(S)	(S)	(S)	47	42	(S)	50
1990 to 1992	128	(S)	17	(S)	(S)	(S)	4	32	15	(S)	21
Government owned	599	65	201	(NA)	10	13	15	63	69	49	59
Nongovernment owned	4,206	578	99	130	250	51	139	1,210	680	(S)	702
FLOORSPACE (mil. sq. ft.)											
All buildings	**67,876**	**8,303**	**8,470**	**757**	**1,491**	**1,763**	**2,891**	**12,402**	**12,319**	**820**	**11,484**
Region:											
Northeast	13,400	1,229	1,968	(S)	445	386	616	2,798	2,525	269	1,763
Midwest	17,280	1,998	2,386	182	432	487	577	3,156	2,804	(S)	3,108
South	24,577	3,635	2,620	245	407	597	1,043	4,233	4,152	238	4,964
West	12,619	1,441	1,496	209	208	292	654	2,214	2,838	(S)	1,649
Year constructed:											
1899 or before	1,721	(S)	(S)	(S)	(S)	(S)	(S)	239	435	(NA)	(S)
1900 to 1919	3,608	575	441	(S)	(S)	(S)	(S)	422	716	(S)	269
1920 to 1945	8,712	850	1,077	(S)	246	227	410	1,381	1,389	(S)	1,853
1946 to 1959	10,421	1,434	1,903	(S)	283	152	328	1,883	1,400	(S)	1,805
1960 to 1969	12,612	1,180	2,405	(S)	187	492	482	2,680	2,187	(S)	1,815
1970 to 1979	14,014	1,601	1,728	155	365	544	579	2,607	2,283	168	2,397
1980 to 1986	10,149	819	480	(S)	103	240	550	2,109	2,419	(S)	2,233
1987 to 1989	4,138	(S)	173	(S)	(S)	(S)	(S)	535	899	(S)	610
1990 to 1992	2,502	(S)	253	(S)	(S)	(S)	97	545	590	(S)	377
Government owned	15,124	(S)	6,961	(NA)	157	521	370	1,082	1,654	767	599
Nongovernment owned	52,752	6,945	1,508	757	1,334	1,242	2,520	11,319	10,665	(S)	10,885

NA Not available. S Figure does not meet publication standards. [1] Includes parking garages, vacant, and other commercial buildings, not shown separately. [2] Includes religious worship.

Source: U.S. Energy Information Administration, *Commercial Buildings Characteristics, 1992.*

No. 1243. Commercial Buildings and Workers—Selected Building Characteristics, by Floorspace: 1992

[See headnote, table 1241]

BUILDING CHARACTERISTICS	NUMBER OF BUILDINGS (1,000)							WORKERS		
		Square footage of—								
	Total	5,000 or less	5,001 to 10,000	10,001 to 25,000	25,001 to 50,000	50,001 to 100,000	100,001 and over	Number (1,000)	Average sq. ft. per worker	Median sq. ft. per worker
All buildings	**4,806**	**2,681**	**975**	**647**	**280**	**116**	**106**	**71,236**	**953**	**1,013**
Region:										
Northeast	771	383	180	109	54	25	19	18,570	722	1,050
Midwest	1,202	676	241	163	66	29	27	14,872	1,162	1,225
South	1,963	1,171	370	239	106	41	36	23,220	1,058	1,013
West	870	451	184	136	56	20	24	14,574	866	800
Principal activity within building:										
Public assembly [1]	644	339	143	111	34	6	(S)	5,050	1,644	(NA)
Education	301	112	43	57	40	30	(S)	6,872	1,232	960
Food sales	130	103	(S)	(S)	(S)	(S)	(NA)	842	899	1,000
Food service	260	179	51	21	(S)	(S)	(NA)	2,244	665	613
Health care	63	39	(S)	(S)	(S)	(S)	5	3,385	521	500
Lodging	154	56	39	26	21	7	(S)	2,022	1,429	1,700
Mercantile/services	1,272	807	265	127	40	18	14	15,979	776	1,077
Office	749	387	168	102	51	20	21	27,161	454	500
Parking garage	24	(S)	(S)	(S)	(S)	(S)	(S)	215	7668	3000
Public order and safety	60	30	(S)	(S)	(S)	(S)	(S)	801	1,023	1,050
Warehouse and storage	761	402	149	129	43	17	20	4,451	2,580	1,925
Other	69	(S)	(S)	(S)	(S)	(S)	(S)	1,232	918	1,273
Vacant	319	177	64	42	23	7	(S)	981	4,481	2,000
Nongovernment owned	4,206	2,423	861	540	228	82	73	52,310	1,008	1,025
Government owned	599	258	114	108	53	34	33	18,926	799	1,000

NA Not available.   S Figure does not meet publication standards.   [1] Includes religious worship.

Source: U.S. Energy Information Administration, *Commercial Buildings Characteristics, 1992.*

Manufactures

This section presents summary data for manufacturing as a whole and more detailed information for major industry groups and selected products. The types of measures shown at the different levels include data for establishments; employment and wages; raw materials, fuels, and electricity consumed; plant and equipment expenditures; value and quantity of production and shipments; value added by manufacture; inventories; and various indicators of financial status.

The principal sources of these data are Bureau of the Census reports of the censuses of manufactures conducted every 5 years; the *Annual Survey of Manufactures;* and the *Current Industrial Reports* series, which presents monthly, quarterly, or annual data on production, shipments, and stocks for particular commodities. Indexes of industrial production are presented monthly in the Federal Reserve Board's *Federal Reserve Bulletin.* Reports on current activities of industries, or current movements of individual commodities, are compiled by such government agencies as the Bureau of Labor Statistics; the Economic Research Service of the Department of Agriculture; the International Trade Administration; and by private research or trade associations such as The Conference Board, Inc., New York, NY and the American Iron and Steel Institute, Washington, DC.

Data on financial aspects of manufacturing industries are collected by the Bureau of Economic Analysis (BEA) and the Bureau of the Census. Industry aggregates in the form of balance sheets, profit and loss statements, analyses of sales and expenses, lists of subsidiaries, and types and amounts of security issues are published for leading manufacturing corporations registered with the Securities and Exchange Commission. The BEA issues data on capital in manufacturing industries and capacity utilization rates in manufacturing. See also section 17, Business Enterprise.

Censuses and annual surveys.—The first census of manufactures covered the year 1809. Between 1809 and 1963, a census was conducted at periodic intervals. Since 1967 it has been taken every

In Brief

Personal computer shipments topped 14.8 million units in 1993.

1-megabit DRAM chips:

	1993
Revenue (millions)	*$2,031*
Shipments (mil. units)	*601*

5 years (for years ending in "2" and "7"). Census data, either direct reports or estimates from administrative records, are obtained for every manufacturing plant with one paid employee or more.

The *Annual Survey of Manufactures (ASM),* conducted for the first time in 1949, collects data for the years between censuses for the more general measures of manufacturing activity covered in detail by the censuses. The annual survey data are estimates derived from a scientifically selected sample of establishments. The 1991 annual survey is based on a sample of about 55,000 establishments of an approximate total of 200,000. These establishments represent all manufacturing establishments of multiunit companies and all single-establishment manufacturing companies mailed schedules in the 1987 Census of Manufactures. The 1989 through 1993 ASM sample is similar to the previous sample. For the current panel, all establishments of companies with 1987 shipments in manufacturing in excess of $500 million were included in the survey with certainty. For the remaining portion of the mail survey, the establishment was defined as the sampling unit. For this portion, all establishments with 250 employees or more and establishments with a very large value of shipments also were included. Therefore, of the 55,000 establishments included in the ASM panel, approximately 28,000 are selected with certainty. These establishments account for approximately 80 percent of total value of shipments in the 1987 census. Smaller establishments in the remaining portion of the mail survey were selected by sample.

The basic statistical measures of manufacturing activity, such as employment, payrolls, value added, etc., are defined in essentially the same way for both the annual surveys and the census of manufactures. However, the bases for computing average employment vary for different years. For example, beginning with 1949, average employment was calculated from the figures reported for the pay periods ending nearest the 15th of March, May, August, and November; whereas, for 1947 such averages were based on 12 monthly employment figures. In 1967, the average employment calculation was revised to the pay periods which include the 12th of March, May, August, and November to provide data more comparable with other statistical series.

Establishments and classification.— The censuses of manufactures for 1947 through 1987 cover operating manufacturing establishments as defined in the *Standard Industrial Classification Manual (SIC),* issued by the U.S. Office of Management and Budget (see text, section 13). The *Manual* is also used for classifying establishments in the annual surveys. The comparability of manufactures data over time is affected by changes in the official definitions of industries as presented in the *Manual.* It is important to note, therefore, that the 1987 edition of the *Manual* was used for the 1987 census; and the 1972 edition of the *Manual* and the *1977 Supplement* were used for the 1972 through 1982 censuses. For the censuses from 1947 to 1963, reports were required from all establishments employing one or more persons at any time during the census year. Beginning with the 1967 census, an effort was made to relieve the very small establishments from the necessity of filing a census report. Approximately 150,000 small single-unit manufacturing firms identified as having less than 20 employees (cutoff varied by industry) benefited from this procedure. Data for these single-unit companies were estimated on the basis of government administrative records and industry averages. Each of the establishments tabulated was classified in one of the approximately 459

manufacturing industries as defined by the *SIC Manual* in 1987. The *Manual* defines an industry as a number of establishments producing a single product or a closely related group of products. In the main, an establishment is classified in a particular industry if its production of a product or product group exceeds in value added its production of any other product group. While some establishments produce only the products of the industry in which they are classified, few within an industry specialize to that extent. The statistics on employment, payrolls, value added, inventories, and expenditures, therefore, reflect both the primary and secondary activities of the establishments in that industry. For this reason, care should be exercised in relating such statistics to the total shipments figures of products primary to the industry.

The censuses for 1947 through 1987 were conducted on an establishment basis. The term "establishment" signifies a single physical plant site or factory. It is not necessarily identical to the business unit or company, which may consist of one or more establishments. A company operating establishments at more than one location is required to submit a separate report for each location. An establishment engaged in distinctly different lines of activity and maintaining separate payroll and inventory records is also required to submit separate reports.

Durable goods.—Items with a normal life expectancy of 3 years or more. Automobiles, furniture, household appliances, and mobile homes are common examples.

Nondurable goods.—Items which generally last for only a short time (3 years or less). Food, beverages, clothing, shoes, and gasoline are common examples.

Statistical reliability.—For a discussion of statistical collection and estimation, sampling procedures and measures of statistical reliability applicable to Census Bureau data, see Appendix III.

Historical statistics.—Tabular headnotes provide cross-references, where applicable, to *Historical Statistics of the United States, Colonial Times to 1970.* See Appendix IV.

No. 1244. Gross Domestic Product in Manufacturing: 1980 to 1992

[In billions of dollars. 1980 through 1986 data are shown on the basis of the 1972 Standard Industrial Classification (SIC). 1987 through 1992 data are based on the 1987 SIC. Data include nonfactor charges (capital consumption allowances, indirect business taxes, etc.) as well as factor charges against gross product; corporate profits and capital consumption allowances have been shifted from a company to an establishment basis]

ITEM	1980	1985	1987	1988	1989	1990	1991	1992
CURRENT DOLLARS								
Gross domestic product	2,708	4,039	4,540	4,900	5,251	1,025	5,725	6,020
Manufacturing	588	798	878	961	1,005	1,025	1,033	1,063
Durable goods	349	472	502	541	563	564	554	568
Lumber and wood products	19	24	31	32	33	31	29	31
Furniture and fixtures	8	14	15	16	16	16	16	17
Stone, clay, and glass products	18	24	24	24	25	25	23	25
Primary metal industries	44	36	36	43	46	44	42	40
Fabricated metal products	45	57	59	63	67	67	65	70
Machinery, exc. electrical	77	87	(X)	(X)	(X)	(X)	(X)	(X)
Industrial machinery and equipment	(X)	(X)	88	100	106	109	101	103
Electric and electronic equipment	55	84	(X)	(X)	(X)	(X)	(X)	(X)
Electronic and other electric equipment	(X)	(X)	77	81	87	86	88	86
Motor vehicles and equipment	27	58	59	59	53	46	45	57
Other transportation equipment	26	48	57	56	60	65	66	61
Instruments and related products	20	27	40	50	52	56	59	60
Misc. manufacturing industries	10	14	15	17	18	19	19	20
Nondurable goods	239	327	376	420	442	461	478	495
Food and kindred products	52	72	79	83	88	97	102	104
Tobacco manufactures	7	11	13	14	14	16	17	19
Textile mill products	15	17	20	20	21	22	22	24
Apparel and other textile products	17	21	23	24	25	25	26	27
Paper and allied products	23	33	39	44	47	46	46	46
Printing and publishing	33	52	61	65	71	72	74	77
Chemicals and allied products	48	67	82	94	100	104	107	111
Petroleum and coal products	24	24	26	41	38	40	44	43
Rubber and misc. plastics products	17	26	30	31	34	35	36	39
Leather and leather products	4	4	3	4	4	4	4	5
CONSTANT (1987) DOLLARS								
Gross domestic product	3,776	4,280	4,540	4,719	4,838	4,897	4,868	4,979
Manufacturing	725	811	878	924	932	929	911	925
Durable goods	424	468	502	536	543	537	526	534
Lumber and wood products	22	25	31	30	29	28	26	25
Furniture and fixtures	12	14	15	15	15	14	14	15
Stone, clay, and glass products	24	25	24	25	26	26	23	25
Primary metal industries	49	35	36	34	33	35	38	36
Fabricated metal products	55	58	59	62	61	60	57	60
Machinery, exc. electrical	81	78	(X)	(X)	(X)	(X)	(X)	(X)
Industrial machinery and equipment	(X)	(X)	88	97	102	102	101	108
Electric and electronic equipment	70	83	(X)	(X)	(X)	(X)	(X)	(X)
Electronic and other electric equipment	(X)	(X)	77	85	91	91	94	93
Motor vehicles and equipment	40	63	59	63	57	49	44	51
Other transportation equipment	38	47	57	58	61	64	61	54
Instruments and related products	24	27	40	50	50	50	51	50
Misc. manufacturing industries	10	14	15	17	17	17	17	17
Nondurable goods	301	342	376	387	389	392	385	391
Food and kindred products	64	75	79	82	79	84	83	83
Tobacco manufactures	20	14	13	12	10	9	9	8
Textile mill products	17	18	20	20	21	21	21	23
Apparel and other textile products	20	21	23	24	25	24	24	25
Paper and allied products	31	36	39	40	39	42	42	44
Printing and publishing	53	59	61	63	64	62	59	58
Chemicals and allied products	58	67	82	83	84	88	86	88
Petroleum and coal products	15	23	26	30	31	26	25	25
Rubber and misc. plastic products	19	26	30	30	32	32	33	35
Leather and leather products	5	4	4	4	4	4	4	4

X Not applicable.

Source: U.S. Bureau of Economic Analysis, *Survey of Current Business,* May and November 1993.

No. 1245. Manufactures—Summary: 1967 to 1992

[For establishment coverage, see text, section 27. For composition of regions, see table 26. See also, *Historical Statistics, Colonial Times to 1970*, series P 1-12]

ITEM	Unit	1967	1972	1977	1982	1987	1991 [1]	1992
ALL ESTABLISHMENTS								
Number of establishments [2]	1,000	311	321	360	358	369	(NA)	382
With 20 or more employees	1,000	110	114	119	123	126	(NA)	125
Employee size-class:								
Establishments [3]	1,000	306	313	351	348	359	(NA)	(NA)
Under 20	1,000	199	203	237	230	238	(NA)	(NA)
20 to 99	1,000	74	76	78	84	86	(NA)	(NA)
100 to 249	1,000	20	21	22	21	22	(NA)	(NA)
250 to 999	1,000	11	11	12	11	11	(NA)	(NA)
1,000 and over	1,000	3	3	2	2	2	(NA)	(NA)
Form of organization:								
Corporate	1,000	153.9	233.2	284.2	283.2	287.4	(NA)	(NA)
Noncorporate [4]	1,000	33.2	87.5	75.7	74.0	81.5	(NA)	(NA)
Individual proprietorship	1,000	24.9	42.5	52.3	45.6	35.4	(NA)	(NA)
Partnership	1,000	6.7	17.7	18.3	15.0	13.2	(NA)	(NA)
All employees: [5]								
Annual average [6]	Million	19.3	19.0	19.6	19.1	18.9	18.1	18.3
Payroll	Bil. dol.	132	174	264	380	476	529	560
Payroll per employee	$1,000	6.8	9.2	13.5	19.9	25.2	29.3	30.7
Production workers:								
Annual average	Million	14.0	13.5	13.7	12.4	12.2	11.5	11.7
Percent of all employees	Percent	72.5	71.1	69.9	64.9	64.6	63.7	63.8
Hours	Billion	27.8	26.7	26.7	23.5	24.3	23.2	23.6
Hours per worker	1,000	2.0	2.0	1.9	1.9	2.0	2.0	2.0
Wages	Bil. dol.	81	106	157	205	251	266	282
Percent of payroll for all employees	Percent	61.4	60.9	59.5	53.9	52.8	50.0	50.3
Wages per worker	$1,000	5.8	7.9	11.5	16.5	20.6	23.1	24.2
Wages per worker hour	Dollar	2.91	3.97	5.89	8.72	10.35	11.49	11.94
Value added by manufacture [7]	Bil. dol.	262	354	585	824	1,166	1,314	1,429
Per production worker	$1,000	18.7	26.2	42.7	66.5	95.5	114.1	122.6
Per production worker hour	Dollar	9.42	13.26	21.91	35.06	47.97	56.70	60.56
Per dollar of workers' wages	Dollar	3.23	3.34	3.73	4.02	4.64	4.93	5.07
Value added, percent distribution:								
Northeast	Percent	29.1	26.3	23.7	23.7	23.7	20.5	19.9
North Central	Percent	35.0	34.9	34.4	29.8	29.8	29.9	30.2
South	Percent	22.7	25.5	27.4	29.5	29.5	32.2	32.1
West	Percent	13.0	13.4	14.5	17.0	17.0	17.4	17.8
Cost of materials	Bil. dol.	299	407	782	1,130	1,320	1,504	1,571
Value of shipments [8]	Bil. dol.	557	757	1,359	1,960	2,476	2,826	3,006
Per production worker	$1,000	39.8	56.1	99.2	158.1	203.0	245.5	258.0
End-of-year inventories	Bil. dol.	84	108	188	307	333	380	(NA)
New capital expenditures [9]	Bil. dol.	21.5	24.1	47.5	75.0	78.6	99.0	104.0
Gross book value of depreciable assets	Bil. dol.	218	301	439	692	868	(NA)	(NA)
Machinery and equipment	Bil. dol.	157	218	328	527	671	(NA)	(NA)
Assets per employee	$1,000	11.3	16.4	22.4	36.2	48.6	(NA)	(NA)
Ratios:								
Value added to shipments	Ratio	47.0	46.7	42.9	42.0	47.1	(NA)	(NA)
Inventories to shipments	Ratio	15.0	14.2	13.8	15.7	13.4	(NA)	(NA)
Payroll to value added	Ratio	50.3	49.1	45.2	46.1	40.8	(NA)	(NA)
MULTIUNIT COMPANIES								
Establishments	1,000	51.7	70.2	81.2	81.7	80.9	(NA)	(NA)
Employees	Million	13.3	14.3	15.0	14.3	13.8	(NA)	(NA)
Production workers	Million	9.8	9.8	10.1	8.8	8.5	(NA)	(NA)
Payroll	Bil. dol.	93.8	138.8	214.2	307.5	377.3	(NA)	(NA)
Wages, production workers	Bil. dol.	60.9	81.9	124.9	159.1	191.8	(NA)	(NA)
Value added by manufacture	Bil. dol.	206.4	286.1	485.0	678.4	953.6	(NA)	(NA)
New capital expenditures	Bil. dol.	18.6	20.0	41.0	65.2	66.5	(NA)	(NA)
SINGLE-UNIT COMPANIES [10]								
Establishments	1,000	254.0	250.5	278.7	276.3	288.0	(NA)	(NA)
Employees	Million	5.2	4.8	4.6	4.8	5.1	(NA)	(NA)
Payroll	Bil. dol.	28.5	35.4	49.8	72.1	98.3	(NA)	(NA)
Value added by manufacture	Bil. dol.	55.5	67.9	100.1	145.7	212.1	(NA)	(NA)

NA Not available. [1] Estimated data based on *Annual Survey of Manufactures;* see text, section 27. [2] Includes administrative and auxiliary units. [3] Excludes administrative offices and auxiliary units. [4] Includes forms of organization not shown separately. [5] Includes data for employees of manufacturing establishments engaged in distribution and construction work. [6] Data are based on pay periods ending nearest 15th of March, May, August, and November. [7] Adjusted value added; takes into account (a) value added by merchandising operations (that is, difference between the sales value and cost of merchandise sold without further manufacture, processing, or assembly), plus (b) net change in finished goods and work-in-process inventories between beginning and end of year. [8] Includes extensive and unmeasurable duplication from shipments between establishments in the same industry classification. [9] Includes plants under construction and not yet in operation. [10] Beginning 1967, includes data obtained from Federal administrative records.

Source: Except as noted, U.S. Bureau of the Census, *Census of Manufactures, 1967, 1972, 1977, 1982, 1987* and *1992* and *Annual Survey of Manufactures.*

No. 1246. Manufactures—Summary, by Industry: 1982, 1987, and 1992

[Data based on various editions of the *Standard Industrial Classification (SIC) Manual*, published by the Office of Management and Budget; see text, section 26. N.e.c.=Not elsewhere classified. See also *Historical Statistics, Colonial Times to 1970*, series P 58-67]

INDUSTRY	SIC code	1982 Establish-ments	1982 All employees Number (1,000)	1982 Payroll (mil. dol.)	1982 Value of shipments (mil. dol.)	1987 Establish-ments	1987 All employees Number (1,000)	1987 Payroll (mil. dol.)	1987 Value of shipments (mil. dol.)	1992 All employees Number (1,000)	1992 Payroll (mil. dol.)	1992 Production workers	1992 Value added by manufacture (mil. dol.)	1992 Value of shipments (mil. dol.)
All manufacturing establishments	(X)	358,061	19,094	379,627	1,960,206	368,897	18,950	475,651	2,475,901	18,253	560,485	11,654	1,428,707	3,006,275
Food and kindred products	20	22,130	1,488	26,088	280,529	20,624	1,449	30,268	329,725	1,505	36,821	1,100	156,843	403,836
Meat products	201	3,623	318	4,993	67,602	3,267	341	5,701	77,002	400	7,542	342	18,950	93,466
Dairy products	202	2,724	140	2,553	38,771	2,366	142	3,217	44,755	137	3,776	86	16,066	54,096
Preserved fruits and vegetables	203	(NA)	(NA)	(NA)	(NA)	1,912	209	3,784	36,343	212	4,713	176	22,004	45,192
Grain mill products	204	2,745	108	2,197	31,386	2,610	102	2,704	36,737	108	3,395	74	21,183	49,169
Bakery products	205	(NA)	(NA)	(NA)	(NA)	2,850	217	4,761	23,677	216	5,610	134	17,932	28,629
Sugar and confectionery products	206	1,033	96	1,661	15,576	1,094	90	1,991	18,887	91	2,403	72	10,951	22,718
Fats and oils	207	724	39	774	16,752	595	30	702	15,881	30	812	21	3,806	19,340
Beverages	208	2,584	194	4,244	38,801	2,214	161	4,521	47,327	145	4,822	75	29,665	56,983
Miscellaneous foods and kindred products	209	3,941	158	2,300	23,959	3,716	158	2,887	29,116	166	3,748	122	16,888	34,244
Tobacco products	21	163	58	1,324	16,061	138	45	1,486	20,757	38	1,537	27	27,167	35,137
Cigarettes	211	14	42	1,094	12,127	11	32	1,486	17,372	25	1,205	18	24,802	29,746
Cigars	212	60	5	59	254	20	3	36	192	3	67	2	171	275
Chewing and smoking tobacco	213	29	3	52	665	29	3	77	1,114	3	92	2	1,213	1,608
Tobacco stemming and redrying	214	60	8	120	3,015	78	7	139	2,079	7	173	5	982	3,508
Textile mill products	22	6,630	717	9,046	47,515	6,412	672	11,410	62,786	615	12,352	527	29,862	70,694
Broadwoven fabric mills, cotton	221	269	77	965	3,972	301	72	1,260	5,508	56	1,148	50	2,484	5,907
Broadwoven fabric mills, manmade	222	523	141	1,815	8,191	441	88	1,596	8,049	87	1,849	76	3,993	8,680
Broadwoven fabric mills, wool	223	131	13	176	763	119	14	236	1,051	14	280	12	676	1,606
Narrow fabric mills	224	281	18	216	852	277	19	296	1,136	17	325	14	720	1,319
Knitting mills	225	(NA)	(NA)	(NA)	(NA)	2,130	203	2,988	13,531	194	3,357	169	8,030	17,053
Textile finishing, except wool	226	753	58	834	4,972	971	56	1,036	7,042	51	1,153	42	2,779	7,057
Carpets and rugs	227	505	42	603	5,808	477	53	1,039	9,795	49	1,084	39	3,491	9,812
Yarn and thread mills	228	714	109	98	7,036	610	114	1,850	10,277	93	1,758	84	4,184	11,476
Miscellaneous textile goods	229	(NA)	(NA)	(NA)	(NA)	1,086	53	1,109	6,398	54	1,399	41	3,506	7,784
Apparel and other textile products	23	24,391	1,189	12,129	53,388	22,872	1,081	13,904	64,243	986	15,367	824	36,357	71,617
Men's and boys' suits and coats	231	529	75	878	3,062	347	55	779	2,863	44	723	38	1,366	2,426
Men's and boys' furnishings	232	2,544	299	2,837	12,727	2,195	280	3,246	15,441	263	3,680	230	9,874	17,926
Women's and misses' outerwear	233	10,838	419	4,110	18,225	10,290	349	4,297	19,389	305	4,602	254	10,788	21,610
Women's and children's undergarments	234	755	82	783	3,323	557	68	8,439	3,738	54	797	45	2,153	3,934

See footnotes at end of table.

No. 1246. Manufactures—Summary, by Industry: 1982, 1987, and 1992—Continued

[See headnote, page 749]

INDUSTRY	SIC code	1982 Establish-ments	1982 All employees Number[1] (1,000)	1982 All employees Payroll (mil. dol.)	1982 Value of shipments (mil. dol.)	1987 Establish-ments	1987 All employees Number[1] (1,000)	1987 All employees Payroll (mil. dol.)	1987 Value of shipments (mil. dol.)	1992 All employees Number[1] (1,000)	1992 All employees Payroll (mil. dol.)	1992 Produc-tion workers	1992 Value added by manufac-ture (mil. dol.)	1992 Value of shipments (mil. dol.)
Apparel, other textile products—Con.														
Hats, caps, and millinery	235	419	16	157	522	461	17	204	663	19	280	16	581	978
Girls' and children's outerwear	236	968	71	671	2,711	834	72	826	3,753	54	780	44	1,642	3,144
Fur goods	237	504	3	60	419	380	2	48	423	1	24	1	81	205
Miscellaneous apparel and accessories	238	1,223	50	513	2,118	986	41	518	2,229	36	556	29	1,227	2,321
Miscellaneous fabricated textile products	239	6,611	174	2,120	10,281	6,822	198	3,143	15,744	211	3,926	168	8,644	19,074
Lumber and wood products	**24**	**32,984**	**576**	**8,445**	**42,935**	**33,982**	**698**	**12,707**	**69,747**	**658**	**13,916**	**542**	**33,352**	**81,798**
Logging	241	11,658	81	1,208	8,274	11,952	86	1,518	10,938	84	1,697	70	5,113	8,773
Sawmills and planing mills	242	7,403	158	2,306	11,132	6,696	180	3,297	19,220	169	3,584	144	8,847	23,210
Millwork, plywood, and structural members	243	6,545	165	2,596	11,683	7,930	240	4,658	22,614	225	5,027	182	10,952	24,865
Wood containers	244	2,250	36	391	1,635	2,216	37	483	2,069	40	639	33	1,315	2,922
Wood buildings and mobile homes	245	1,163	60	880	4,955	1,077	65	1,215	6,575	56	1,230	44	2,511	6,634
Miscellaneous Wood Products	249	3,965	77	1,064	5,255	4,104	90	1,536	8,330	85	1,740	69	4,615	10,324
Furniture and fixtures [2]	**25**	**10,003**	**436**	**6,084**	**24,129**	**11,613**	**511**	**9,082**	**37,462**	**473**	**10,216**	**374**	**22,821**	**43,688**
Household furniture	251	5,475	263	3,162	12,776	5,606	284	4,452	18,559	257	4,861	216	10,602	20,707
Office Furniture	252	700	59	1,051	4,150	986	81	1,790	7,538	68	1,866	50	4,634	8,002
Public building and related furniture	253	413	19	295	1,103	484	22	397	2,088	29	679	22	1,609	4,140
Partitions and fixtures	254	2,148	60	1,025	3,710	2,455	74	1,552	5,537	74	1,813	54	3,617	6,569
Miscellaneous furniture and fixtures	259	1,267	36	551	2,390	2,084	50	892	3,740	45	998	31	2,359	4,270
Paper and allied products	**26**	**(NA)**	**(NA)**	**(NA)**	**(NA)**	**6,342**	**611**	**16,860**	**108,989**	**626**	**20,479**	**479**	**59,923**	**132,954**
Pulp mills	261	43	17	468	3,110	39	14	535	4,314	16	688	12	2,549	5,457
Paper mills	262	299	129	3,431	20,995	281	129	4,597	28,918	131	5,425	101	14,872	32,817
Paperboard mills	263	222	56	1,502	9,531	199	52	1,859	13,730	52	2,135	39	8,187	16,126
Paperboard containers and boxes	265	2,781	188	3,517	19,192	2,796	194	4,618	25,863	199	5,710	151	12,387	32,577
Miscellaneous converted paper products	267	3,006	213	3,961	26,701	3,027	222	5,251	36,165	229	6,521	176	21,927	45,977
Printing and publishing	**27**	**53,406**	**1,292**	**22,707**	**85,797**	**61,774**	**1,494**	**33,440**	**136,196**	**1,506**	**41,471**	**790**	**113,244**	**167,284**
Newspapers	271	8,846	402	6,555	21,276	9,079	434	9,022	31,850	416	10,506	136	27,264	34,203
Periodicals	272	3,328	94	1,986	11,478	4,017	110	2,983	17,329	117	4,076	21	15,763	21,976
Books	273	2,811	112	2,090	10,132	2,856	114	2,821	15,876	135	4,242	58	14,717	21,854
Miscellaneous publishing	274	2,057	45	706	2,871	2,376	70	1,513	7,810	66	1,741	24	8,535	11,000
Commercial printing	275	(NA)	(NA)	(NA)	(NA)	36,103	553	12,301	44,786	570	15,357	409	31,963	56,415
Manifold business forms	276	810	50	934	5,059	853	53	1,281	7,397	48	1,338	34	3,903	7,415
Greeting cards	277	154	21	344	1,894	162	22	471	2,911	23	585	12	3,394	4,196
Blankbooks and bookbinding	278	1,487	61	903	2,803	1,545	69	1,265	4,080	66	1,478	52	3,640	5,060
Printing trade services	279	(NA)	(NA)	(NA)	(NA)	4,783	69	1,784	4,157	65	2,147	46	4,067	5,166

See footnotes at end of table.

INDUSTRY	SIC code	1982 Establish-ments	1982 All employees Number[1] (1,000)	1982 All employees Payroll (mil. dol.)	1982 Value of shipments (mil. dol.)	1987 Establish-ments	1987 All employees Number[1] (1,000)	1987 All employees Payroll (mil. dol.)	1987 Value of shipments (mil. dol.)	1992 All employees Number[1] (1,000)	1992 All employees Payroll (mil. dol.)	1992 Produc-tion workers	1992 Value added by manufac-ture (mil. dol.)	1992 Value of shipments (mil. dol.)
Chemicals and allied products	**28**	**11,901**	**873**	**20,836**	**170,737**	**12,109**	**814**	**25,016**	**229,546**	**850**	**32,503**	**479**	**165,135**	**305,761**
Industrial inorganic chemicals	281	1,365	108	2,795	17,280	1,405	94	3,099	19,774	103	4,219	55	16,687	27,167
Plastics materials and synthetics	282	606	141	3,451	28,428	680	123	4,013	40,851	128	5,111	86	21,270	48,535
Drugs	283	1,281	166	3,966	24,695	1,356	172	5,304	39,263	196	7,859	93	48,736	67,969
Soap, cleaners, and toilet goods	284	2,379	127	2,581	26,031	2,399	119	3,099	34,748	124	3,943	75	26,526	43,404
Paints and allied products	285	1,441	54	1,158	9,162	1,431	55	1,492	12,702	51	1,710	26	7,153	14,970
Industrial organic chemicals	286	969	144	4,005	38,157	961	126	4,541	51,158	125	5,519	73	26,193	64,525
Agricultural chemicals	287	1,127	51	1,156	14,653	973	40	1,171	14,267	40	1,451	25	8,628	18,802
Miscellaneous chemical products	289	2,733	82	1,725	12,330	2,904	85	2,298	16,782	83	2,690	48	9,942	20,389
Petroleum and coal products	**29**	**2,322**	**152**	**4,339**	**208,919**	**2,254**	**116**	**3,996**	**130,414**	**114**	**4,966**	**74**	**23,797**	**149,961**
Petroleum refining	291	(NA)	(NA)	(NA)	(NA)	331	75	2,845	118,186	75	3,637	48	19,104	136,265
Asphalt paving and roofing materials	295	1,307	30	629	5,948	1,367	28	786	7,749	26	844	18	2,962	7,737
Miscellaneous petroleum and coal products	299	582	14	312	3,614	556	13	365	4,479	14	486	8	1,731	5,958
Rubber and misc. plastics products	**30**	**13,449**	**682**	**11,597**	**55,416**	**14,515**	**831**	**17,581**	**86,634**	**907**	**23,144**	**697**	**58,477**	**113,544**
Tires and inner tubes	301	164	70	1,734	9,340	164	65	2,070	10,427	65	2,498	53	6,478	11,824
Rubber and plastics footwear	302	65	18	197	706	66	11	153	557	14	216	11	468	907
Hose and belting and plastics and packing	305	635	55	999	3,612	693	52	1,159	4,648	52	1,416	38	3,316	5,994
Fabricated rubber products, n.e.c	306	(NA)	(NA)	(NA)	(NA)	1,573	104	2,245	9,227	106	2,607	79	5,919	11,363
Miscellaneous plastics products, n.e.c.	308	(NA)	(NA)	(NA)	(NA)	12,019	599	11,955	61,775	671	16,407	515	42,296	83,456
Leather and leather products	**31**	**2,735**	**200**	**2,219**	**9,719**	**2,193**	**129**	**1,831**	**9,082**	**101**	**1,795**	**83**	**4,517**	**9,677**
Leather tanning and finishing	311	384	20	311	1,753	344	15	292	2,219	17	420	13	886	2,910
Footwear cut stock	313	161	7	81	368	128	5	70	324	4	63	3	154	323
Footwear, except rubber	314	751	121	1,250	5,269	479	71	913	4,073	49	762	41	2,072	3,907
Leather gloves and mittens	315	96	4	37	178	77	3	34	185	3	36	2	69	137
Luggage	316	292	16	194	789	241	11	196	929	10	182	7	495	944
Handbags and personal leather goods	317	636	25	271	1,035	529	17	232	942	11	201	9	547	890
Leather goods, n.e.c.	319	415	7	76	327	395	7	95	411	8	131	6	294	565

See footnotes at end of table.

No. 1246. Manufactures—Summary, by Industry: 1982, 1987, and 1992—Continued

[See headnote, page 749]

INDUSTRY	SIC code	1982				1987				1992				
		Establishments	All employees Number [1] (1,000)	All employees Payroll (mil. dol.)	Value of shipments (mil. dol.)	Establishments	All employees Number [1] (1,000)	All employees Payroll (mil. dol.)	Value of shipments (mil. dol.)	All employees Number [1] (1,000)	All employees Payroll (mil. dol.)	Production workers	Value added by manufacture (mil. dol.)	Value of shipments (mil. dol.)
Stone, clay, and glass products	**32**	16,545	532	10,097	45,181	16,166	524	12,349	61,477	470	13,128	357	34,558	62,479
Flat glass	321	69	15	414	1,666	81	15	507	2,549	12	440	10	1,315	2,082
Glass and glassware, pressed or blown	322	459	97	2,032	7,941	522	77	1,959	8,339	66	2,080	56	5,922	9,055
Products of purchased glass	323	1,337	41	696	2,977	1,432	51	1,060	5,429	56	1,387	43	3,809	6,955
Cement, hydraulic	324	237	25	636	3,542	215	19	599	4,335	17	592	13	2,136	4,035
Structural clay products	325	628	30	491	1,868	598	35	689	2,915	31	737	24	1,698	2,864
Pottery and related products	326	910	37	598	1,762	1,006	38	762	2,416	36	842	28	1,954	2,752
Concrete, gypsum, and plaster products	327	9,933	167	2,995	14,947	9,814	203	4,632	24,427	174	4,748	126	10,983	23,053
Cut stone and stone products	328	711	11	156	555	745	13	243	841	12	283	9	607	1,007
Miscellaneous nonmetallic mineral products	329	(NA)	(NA)	(NA)	(NA)	1,753	73	1,898	10,226	66	2,018	49	6,134	10,677
Primary metal industries [2]	**33**	7,061	854	20,603	104,667	6,771	701	19,777	120,248	663	22,187	508	51,816	138,333
Blast furnace and basic steel products	331	1,068	366	267	46,720	1,241	253	8,166	51,815	241	9,243	184	22,290	58,713
Iron and steel foundries	332	1,438	157	3,113	9,642	1,231	130	3,426	10,628	123	3,754	100	6,916	11,914
Primary nonferrous metals	333	161	44	1,307	11,321	397	32	996	10,869	34	1,284	25	3,275	14,142
Secondary nonferrous metals	334	458	19	402	4,852	169	13	312	4,431	14	414	10	1,272	5,921
Nonferrous rolling and drawing	335	1,022	167	3,636	25,463	1,066	163	4,298	33,282	148	4,640	109	12,124	39,906
Nonferrous foundries (castings)	336	(NA)	(NA)	(NA)	(NA)	1,687	80	1,805	6,315	74	1,923	59	3,864	6,923
Fabricated metal products	**34**	35,560	1,460	28,283	119,444	36,105	1,458	35,000	147,366	1,370	39,166	999	83,871	167,015
Metal cans and shipping containers	341	566	59	1,533	12,172	538	48	1,527	12,114	40	1,463	33	3,725	13,247
Cutlery, handtools, and hardware	342	2,238	141	2,585	10,082	2,327	145	3,389	13,481	134	3,633	99	8,959	15,338
Plumbing and heating, except electric	343	1,177	48	821	4,003	828	46	1,005	5,283	42	1,150	29	3,108	5,840
Fabricated structural metal products	344	12,681	422	7,897	34,904	12,579	407	9,042	40,416	392	10,451	277	21,403	45,252
Screw machine products, bolts, etc.	345	2,690	94	1,727	5,834	2,569	95	2,270	7,890	90	2,619	68	5,268	9,013
Metal forgings and stampings	346	4,019	236	5,110	20,057	4,062	255	7,235	28,410	234	7,738	185	14,929	30,668
Metal services, n.e.c.	347	5,070	97	1,518	5,125	5,251	113	2,167	7,790	109	2,669	84	5,634	10,042
Ordnance and accessories, n.e.c.	348	349	79	1,780	4,993	374	88	2,458	7,644	65	2,251	38	4,671	6,996
Miscellaneous fabricated metal products	349	6,770	284	5,312	22,274	7,577	262	5,906	24,340	264	7,193	186	16,175	30,620
Industrial machinery and equipment	**35**	52,912	2,189	46,911	187,896	52,135	1,844	50,553	217,670	1,742	57,253	1,088	132,144	258,273
Engines and turbines	351	341	112	2,850	13,040	356	87	2,906	14,570	83	3,145	52	7,506	17,402
Farm and garden machinery	352	2,078	114	2,386	13,018	1,804	82	1,917	11,474	87	2,374	63	7,377	14,897
Construction and related machinery	353	3,952	326	7,332	32,038	3,467	188	5,272	24,622	181	5,810	111	12,668	27,675
Metalworking machinery	354	(NA)	(NA)	(NA)	(NA)	11,470	268	7,301	22,004	256	8,604	179	16,508	26,589
Special industry machinery	355	(NA)	(NA)	(NA)	(NA)	4,550	169	4,588	17,096	160	5,446	90	11,514	21,263
General industrial machinery	356	(NA)	(NA)	(NA)	(NA)	3,929	240	6,203	24,121	247	7,798	155	17,954	31,686
Computer and office equipment	357	(NA)	(NA)	(NA)	(NA)	2,134	328	10,668	60,627	249	10,062	88	28,711	66,149
Refrigeration and service machinery	358	1,937	172	3,344	16,450	2,129	190	4,752	23,235	177	5,230	124	13,374	27,253
Industrial machinery, n.e.c	359	(NA)	(NA)	(NA)	(NA)	22,296	292	6,946	19,921	303	8,785	226	16,532	25,359

See footnotes at end of table.

INDUSTRY	SIC code	1982 Establishments	1982 Number (1,000)	1982 Payroll (mil. dol.)	1982 Value of shipments (mil. dol.)	1987 Establishments	1987 Number (1,000)	1987 Payroll (mil. dol.)	1987 Value of shipments (mil. dol.)	1992 Number (1,000)	1992 Payroll (mil. dol.)	1992 Production workers	1992 Value added by manufacture (mil. dol.)	1992 Value of shipments (mil. dol.)
Electronics; other electric equip.	**36**	(NA)	(NA)	(NA)	(NA)	15,962	1,565	38,738	171,286	1,444	44,504	914	121,950	217,906
Electric distribution equipment	361	(NA)	(NA)	(NA)	(NA)	766	77	1,791	8,197	68	1,932	48	5,245	9,620
Electrical industrial apparatus	362	(NA)	(NA)	(NA)	(NA)	2,213	166	3,882	15,266	157	4,379	106	10,427	18,949
Household appliances	363	(NA)	(NA)	(NA)	(NA)	480	117	2,642	16,498	103	2,588	83	7,817	18,480
Electric lighting and wiring equipment	364	1,993	159	2,718	12,048	1,986	167	3,732	18,004	148	3,989	108	11,186	19,655
Household audio and video equipment	365	(NA)	(NA)	(NA)	(NA)	854	44	850	7,833	48	1,140	35	3,541	10,766
Communications equipment	366	(NA)	(NA)	(NA)	(NA)	1,437	260	7,537	34,001	241	9,247	115	26,993	43,557
Electronic components and accessories	367	(NA)	(NA)	(NA)	(NA)	5,911	546	13,623	50,258	530	16,776	317	45,297	74,604
Misc. electrical equipment and supplies	369	(NA)	(NA)	(NA)	(NA)	2,315	188	4,682	21,230	150	4,454	101	11,445	22,275
Transportation equipment	**37**	9,443	1,596	40,812	201,346	10,500	1,817	58,790	332,936	1,646	62,584	1,079	161,058	401,214
Motor vehicles and equipment	371	3,867	616	15,393	112,270	4,422	751	23,910	205,923	703	26,171	564	80,525	240,110
Aircraft and parts	372	1,471	539	14,718	52,027	1,618	596	20,590	77,304	546	22,481	280	49,279	104,730
Ship and boat building and repairing	373	2,566	205	4,326	13,326	2,766	177	4,266	13,857	164	4,659	122	8,594	15,330
Railroad equipment	374	200	35	790	3,457	173	22	631	2,471	28	886	20	1,956	4,574
Motorcycles, bicycles, and parts	375	273	13	225	1,341	246	7	158	1,063	12	315	9	779	1,967
Guided missiles, space vehicles, parts	376	105	146	4,481	14,398	156	214	8,114	26,285	149	6,903	52	16,886	27,302
Miscellaneous transportation equipment	379	961	43	879	4,528	1,119	49	1,122	6,033	45	1,168	32	3,040	7,203
Instruments and related products	**38**	(NA)	(NA)	(NA)	(NA)	10,326	982	28,778	107,325	910	33,240	461	89,806	135,479
Search and navigation equipment	381	(NA)	(NA)	(NA)	(NA)	1,137	369	12,368	36,267	260	11,318	106	25,213	36,185
Measuring and controlling devices	382	(NA)	(NA)	(NA)	(NA)	4,240	285	7,807	26,042	273	9,501	137	21,394	34,173
Medical instruments and supplies	384	2,973	189	3,559	15,133	3,443	204	5,027	22,865	263	8,489	154	25,957	39,365
Ophthalmic goods	385	410	26	409	1,273	494	24	475	1,689	29	693	19	1,905	2,633
Photographic equipment and supplies	386	795	119	3,193	17,038	791	88	2,878	19,241	77	3,062	39	14,843	22,093
Watches, clocks, watchcases and parts	387	237	17	248	1,188	221	12	223	1,221	8	176	6	493	1,032
Misc. manufacturing industries	**39**	15,871	383	5,647	26,891	16,544	374	6,884	32,012	365	8,411	254	22,010	39,626
Jewelry, silverware, and plated ware	391	2,882	50	770	4,379	2,978	50	941	5,554	46	1,071	31	2,479	5,742
Musical instruments	393	452	18	258	916	425	12	218	814	12	273	9	595	988
Toys and sporting goods	394	2,570	99	1,389	8,256	2,711	89	1,512	8,798	96	2,088	70	6,768	12,012
Pens, pencils, office, and art supplies	395	1,026	32	485	2,372	1,013	29	540	2,536	30	668	21	2,003	3,415
Costume jewelry and notions	396	(NA)	(NA)	(NA)	(NA)	1,020	32	498	2,062	28	557	19	1,371	2,318
Miscellaneous manufactures[3]	399	(NA)	(NA)	(NA)	(NA)	8,397	163	3,174	12,248	154	3,753	104	8,794	15,152
Administrative and auxiliary[3]	(X)	9,676	1,276	38,220	-	9,480	1,234	47,202	-	1,263	65,448	(X)	(X)	(X)

- Represents zero.   NA Not applicable.   X Not applicable.   [1] Represents the average of production workers plus all other employees for the payroll period ended nearest the 15th of March.   [2] Includes other industries not shown separately.   [3] Manufacturing concerns often report separately for central offices or auxiliaries which serve the manufacturing establishment of a company, rather than the general public. Separate reports were obtained from such units if at a different location or if they serviced more than one establishment.

Source: U.S. Bureau of the Census, *1992 Census of Manufactures and Annual Survey of Manufactures.*

No. 1247. Manufactures—Summary, by Industry; Selected Based on Value Added: 1982, 1987, and 1992

[Data based on various editions of the *Standard Industrial Classification (SIC) Manual*, published by the Office of Management and Budget; see text, section 26. N.e.c.=Not elsewhere classified. See also *Historical Statistics, Colonial Times to 1970*, series P 58-67]

INDUSTRY	SIC code	1982 Establishments	1982 All employees Number (1,000)	1982 All employees Payroll (mil. dol.)	1982 Value of shipments (mil. dol.)	1987 Establishments	1987 All employees Number (1,000)	1987 All employees Payroll (mil. dol.)	1987 Value of shipments (mil. dol.)	1992 All employees Number (1,000)	1992 All employees Payroll (mil. dol.)	1992 Production workers	1992 Value added by manufacture (mil. dol.)	1992 Value of shipments (mil. dol.)
Meat packing plants	2011	1,780	134.4	2,549	44,854	1,434	113.2	2,141	44,991	120.6	2,423	103.7	6,852	49,679
Sausages and other prepared meats	2013	1,311	65.5	1,206	12,278	1,344	79.1	1,619	16,623	85.0	2,027	65.7	5,551	20,043
Poultry slaughtering and processing	2015	532	117.7	1,237	10,471	463	147.7	1,919	14,912	193.5	3,092	172.5	6,547	23,744
Fluid milk	2026	1,190	78.2	1,469	18,736	946	72.4	1,681	20,591	63.4	1,844	32.5	5,983	21,920
Canned fruits and vegetables	2033	715	70.5	1,040	9,283	647	65.6	1,163	11,890	63.9	1,475	53.4	6,972	14,876
Frozen specialties, n.e.c.	2038	(NA)	(NA)	(NA)	(NA)	288	37.5	669.1	5,624.8	46.7	971	38.3	4,100	7,838
Cereal breakfast foods	2043	52	15.6	435	4,132	53	16.0	599	6,566	16.1	745	13.1	7,338	9,799
Bread, cake, and related products	2051	2,305	170.7	3,254	13,143	2,357	161.6	3,556	16,202	155.0	4,062	88.2	11,431	18,121
Cookies and crackers	2052	358	45.6	797	4,665	380	45.4	1,010	6,309	47.2	1,250	35.1	5,542	8,755
Candy and other confectionery products	2064	(NA)	(NA)	(NA)	(NA)	134	45.8	900	6,980	51.6	1,265	41.1	6,350	10,219
Malt beverages	2082	109	43.0	1,308	11,183	685	31.9	1,355	13,619	34.5	1,567	25.1	10,600	17,328
Bottled and canned soft drinks	2086	1,626	113.8	2,146	16,808	1,190	95.6	2,277	22,006	77.1	2,163	30.4	10,017	25,485
Flavoring extracts and syrups, n.e.c.	2087	(NA)	11.6	237	4,237	280	9.1	258	4,665	11.4	379	6.6	4,470	6,196
Food preparations, n.e.c.	2099	(NA)	(NA)	(NA)	(NA)	1,658	57.9	1,110	9,787	62.5	1,442	44.6	6,245	12,247
Cigarettes	2111	14	41.5	1,094	12,127	12	32.0	1,234	17,372	25.4	1,205	18.1	24,802	29,746
Logging	2411	11,658	80.8	1,208	8,274	11,936	85.7	1,516	10,880	83.8	1,697	69.5	5,113	13,844
Sawmills and planing mills, general	2421	6,316	131.9	2,020	10,065	5,742	148.2	2,817	7,357	138.6	3,053	118.3	7,795	21,045
Wood household furniture	2511	2,607	125.6	1,403	5,057	2,948	135.8	2,017	7,980	121.2	2,176	105.4	4,742	8,762
Paper mills	2621	299	129.0	3,431	20,995	282	129.1	4,597	28,916	130.7	5,425	100.5	14,872	32,817
Paperboard mills	2631	222	55.6	1,502	9,531	205	52.3	1,859	13,730	51.5	2,135	39.3	8,187	16,126
Corrugated and solid fiber boxes	2653	1,492	94.4	1,862	10,558	1,601	105.8	2,610	16,107	111.0	3,247	80.2	6,687	19,681
Sanitary paper products	2676	138	36.7	863	9,086	133	38.4	1,155	11,698	40.5	1,451	32.7	8,038	15,468
Newspapers	2711	8,846	401.5	6,555	21,276	9,091	434.6	9,025	31,849	415.8	10,506	135.5	27,264	34,203
Periodicals	2721	3,328	94.0	1,986	11,478	4,020	110.0	2,983	17,329	116.7	4,076	20.5	15,763	21,976
Book publishing	2731	2,130	67.1	1,327	7,740	2,298	70.1	1,860	12,620	83.8	2,869	19.0	8,535	17,126
Miscellaneous publishing	2741	2,057	45.3	706	2,871	2,369	69.4	1,513	7,810	66.4	1,742	24.2		11,000
Commercial printing, lithographic	2752	17,842	311.9	5,746	19,442	24,980	403.0	9,132	32,698	441.1	12,043	317.5	24,885	43,651
Commercial printing, n.e.c.	2759	(NA)	(NA)	(NA)	(NA)	10,796	126.2	2,490	8,973	106.9	2,587	73.6	5,382	9,194
Manifold business forms	2761	810	49.5	934	5,059	853	53.2	1,276	7,359	47.7	1,338	33.5	3,903	7,415
Industrial inorganic chemicals, n.e.c.	2819	645	81.7	2,134	12,060	662	72.2	2,425	13,212	60.9	2,677	39.4	11,171	17,979
Plastics materials and resins	2821	440	54.7	1,434	15,769	480	56.3	2,006	26,246	44.4	1,545	36.3	12,971	31,478
Organic fibers, noncellulosic	2824	70	60.2	1,382	8,263	72	45.7		10,112				5,613	11,114
Pharmaceutical preparations	2834	683	124.4	3,053	18,998	732	131.6	4,168		125.0	4,995	63.2	37,435	50,745
Soap and other detergents	2841	723	35.4	827	9,167	764	31.7	956	11,559	33.0	1,177	20.0	7,858	14,888
Polishes and sanitation goods	2842	(NA)	23.0	444	4,614	726	20.6	500	5,594	22.0	663	13.4	4,383	6,892
Toilet preparations	2844	639	60.4	1,102	10,183	694	58.5	1,353	14,593	60.5	1,782	37.5	13,109	18,751
Paints and allied products	2851	1,441	54.1	1,158	9,162	1,426	55.2	1,491	12,701	51.1	1,710	25.6	7,153	14,970
Industrial organic chemicals, n.e.c.	2869	(NA)	(NA)	(NA)	(NA)	699	100.3	3,696	42,189	100.3	4,517	57.4	22,489	54,222
Agricultural chemicals, n.e.c.	2879	330	16.5	404	5,436	277	16.1	518	6,300	16.8	669	9.6	5,513	9,129
Chemical preparations, n.e.c.	2899	1,443	39.7	837	6,344	1,529	37.9	1,021	8,024	36.4	1,193	20.9	5,003	9,780

See footnotes at end of table.

INDUSTRY	SIC code	1982				1987				1992				
		Establish-ments	All employees Number[1] (1,000)	Payroll (mil. dol.)	Value of shipments (mil. dol.)	Establish-ments	All employees Number[1] (1,000)	Payroll (mil. dol.)	Value of shipments (mil. dol.)	All employees Number[1] (1,000)	Payroll (mil. dol.)	Produc-tion workers	Value added by manufac-ture (mil. dol.)	Value of shipments (mil. dol.)
Petroleum refining	2911	(NA)	(NA)	(NA)	(NA)	309	74.6	2,846	118,216	74.8	3,637	47.9	19,104	136,265
Tires and inner tubes	3011	164	70.3	1,734	9,340	163	65.4	2,070	10,427	64.6	2,498	52.8	6,478	11,824
Unsupported plastics film and sheet	3081	(NA)	(NA)	(NA)	(NA)	594	48.4	1,256	8,140	57.2	1,763	40.6	5,375	11,607
Plastics products, n.e.c.	3089	(NA)	(NA)	(NA)	(NA)	8,571	384.7	7,286	33,774	23.0	667	15.3	1,777	4,331
Ready-mixed concrete	3273	5,379	81.4	1,475	8,163	5,321	96.9	2,289	12,975	83.1	2,313	61.2	5,389	12,089
Blast furnaces and steel mills	3312	301	295.8	8,678	36,824	342	188.9	6,451	38,663	171.7	7,070	132.2	16,633	42,278
Nonferrous wiredrawing and insulating	3357	440	67.6	1,270	8,217	487	64.9	1,504	10,827	60.8	1,729	44.9	4,764	13,021
Hardware, n.e.c.	3429	1,185	80.1	1,521	5,741	1,240	85.6	2,056	8,175	75.1	2,057	56.0	4,783	8,754
Fabricated structural metal	3441	2,740	103.6	1,990	8,853	2,454	80.9	1,881	8,667	72.3	1,970	51.0	3,971	8,940
Fabricated plate work (boiler shops)	3443	1,929	102.9	2,180	8,225	1,740	74.6	1,842	6,795	79.0	2,339	55.9	4,868	9,085
Sheet metal work	3444	3,795	81.1	1,495	6,854	4,297	100.3	2,237	9,700	104.0	2,843	75.4	5,725	11,467
Automotive stampings	3465	668	90.5	2,293	8,777	713	119.8	3,977	15,252	104.3	4,069	86.4	7,184	15,711
Metal stampings, n.e.c.	3469	2,843	100.4	1,783	6,438	2,815	95.5	2,132	8,331	93.2	2,501	71.1	5,211	9,735
Internal combustion engines, n.e.c.	3519	253	79.6	1,979	9,363	278	64.0	2,043	11,123	56.9	2,082	38.1	4,900	11,945
Farm machinery and equipment	3523	1,903	96.1	2,067	10,743	1,634	57.0	1,416	6,880	62.4	1,807	43.2	5,226	9,727
Construction machinery	3531	939	115.5	2,653	11,658	955	81.2	2,429	12,773	77.9	2,596	50.2	5,874	13,603
Special dies, tools, jigs, and fixtures	3544	7,255	1.0	2,293	5,375	7,317	114.4	3,164	7,550	111.6	3,904	85.4	6,656	9,334
Special industry machinery, n.e.c.	3559	(NA)	(NA)	(NA)	(NA)	2,531	83.3	2,286	8,275	81.8	2,902	43.9	6,225	11,289
Electronic computers	3571	(NA)	(NA)	(NA)	(NA)	974	151.9	4,953	33,627	109.5	4,805	30.6	15,691	37,765
Refrigeration and heating equipment	3585	865	120.5	2,393	12,390	892	133.3	3,355	17,027	120.7	3,594	89.1	9,350	19,677
Industrial machinery, n.e.c.	3599	(NA)	(NA)	(NA)	(NA)	21,545	228.4	5,119	13,692	247.7	7,006	188.5	12,845	19,017
Motors and generators	3621	472	84.2	1,546	6,060	462	74.6	1,664	6,753	67.8	1,763	51.9	4,169	8,032
Relays and industrial controls	3625	(NA)	(NA)	(NA)	(NA)	1,168	66.6	1,631	6,101	61.0	1,831	34.9	4,475	7,529
Telephone and telegraph apparatus	3661	(NA)	(NA)	(NA)	(NA)	469	112.3	3,178	17,583	93.3	3,810	45.7	12,964	21,117
Radio and TV communications equip.	3663	(NA)	(NA)	(NA)	(NA)	655	126.0	3,776	14,229	124.4	4,780	58.8	12,270	19,510
Semiconductors and related devices	3674	766	166.5	3,785	12,430	853	184.6	5,495	19,795	172.2	6,893	84.8	23,296	33,178
Electronic components, n.e.c.	3679	(NA)	(NA)	(NA)	(NA)	2,900	162.6	3,891	15,439	180.4	5,120	108.1	11,775	23,524
Motor vehicles and car bodies	3711	355	240.1	6,822	70,740	413	284.4	10,376	133,346	220.3	10,162	186.3	44,632	152,152
Motor vehicle parts and accessories	3714	2,420	321.4	7,614	36,293	2,807	389.1	11,947	62,007	406.3	14,174	318.7	32,262	76,761
Aircraft	3721	165	275.1	7,744	28,024	155	268.2	9,680	39,093	264.7	11,495	122.1	25,173	63,134
Aircraft engines and engine parts	3724	340	130.7	3,544	13,809	453	139.6	4,814	20,262	116.7	4,851	64.2	11,384	21,870
Aircraft parts and equipment, n.e.c.	3728	966	132.8	3,429	10,193	1,013	187.7	6,088	17,923	164.7	6,134	93.3	12,723	19,726
Ship building and repairing	3731	689	166.7	3,738	10,967	590	120.2	3,218	8,504	118.7	3,636	87.4	6,566	10,645
Guided missiles and space vehicles	3761	29	99.6	3,159	10,219	40	166.7	6,415	21,566	91.7	4,315	29.3	11,855	18,219
Search and navigation equipment	3812	(NA)	(NA)	(NA)	(NA)	1,084	369.4	12,373	36,267	260.0	11,318	105.7	25,213	36,185
Instruments to measure electricity	3825	749	89.7	1,888	6,094	930	85.2	2,477	7,703	68.4	2,536	32.0	5,694	8,828
Surgical and medical instruments	3841	859	56.9	1,000	4,085	1,136	73.1	1,786	7,780	98.6	3,106	58.7	9,428	13,428
Surgical appliances and supplies	3842	1,367	68.8	1,211	5,667	1,500	78.5	1,786	8,533	96.5	2,855	61.4	8,893	13,789
Photographic equipment and supplies	3861	795	119.3	3,193	17,038	787	88.0	2,878	19,241	77.2	3,062	39.2	14,843	22,093

NA Not available.   [1] Represents the average of production workers plus all other employees for the payroll period ended nearest the 15th of the month.

Source: U.S. Bureau of the Census, 1987 Census of Manufactures and Annual Survey of Manufactures.

No. 1248. Manufactures Summary: 1982 and 1987

[Sum of State totals may not add to U.S. total because U.S. and State figures were independently derived]

REGION, DIVISION AND STATE	1982				1987				
	Establishments[1]	All employees[2]		Value of shipments[3] (mil. dol.)	Establishments[1]	All employees[2]		Value added by manufacture[4] (mil. dol.)	Value of shipments[3] (mil. dol.)
		Number (1,000)	Payroll (mil. dol.)			Number (1,000)	Payroll (mil. dol.)		
U.S.	358,061	19,094	379,627	1,960,206	368,897	18,950	475,651	1,165,917	2,475,902
Northeast	91,102	4,798	95,919	400,767	88,287	4,357	112,222	259,074	483,748
N.E.	25,659	1,445	27,603	105,938	26,393	1,350	34,455	78,908	136,989
ME	2,009	110	1,775	8,649	2,172	102	2,192	5,271	10,662
NH	1,981	107	1,792	7,636	2,328	108	2,509	8,189	12,214
VT	1,104	47	863	3,730	1,262	49	1,140	2,543	4,753
MA	11,017	643	12,353	48,204	11,006	591	15,211	35,770	62,794
RI	2,855	114	1,760	7,652	2,878	112	2,292	4,788	9,166
CT	6,693	424	9,060	30,067	6,747	389	11,111	22,349	37,400
M.A.	65,443	3,353	68,316	294,829	61,894	3,007	77,767	180,165	346,759
NY	32,651	1,419	29,156	121,469	29,608	1,279	33,916	80,033	145,657
NJ	15,126	754	15,845	70,420	14,442	691	18,550	42,527	82,451
PA	17,666	1,180	23,315	102,940	17,844	1,038	25,302	57,605	118,651
Midwest	91,318	5,609	117,830	596,245	94,269	5,508	148,994	351,139	787,123
E.N.C.	67,378	4,337	92,400	440,702	69,756	4,186	116,148	266,248	590,487
OH	16,960	1,102	24,740	112,278	17,544	1,100	30,765	71,707	158,560
IN	7,960	585	12,559	63,332	8,641	602	15,757	39,279	83,788
IL	18,618	1,069	22,681	112,929	18,404	990	26,235	63,350	132,204
MI	15,158	884	22,223	99,715	16,010	980	30,628	60,259	146,339
WI	8,682	497	10,197	52,448	9,157	514	12,763	31,653	69,596
W.N.C.	23,940	1,272	25,430	155,543	24,513	1,322	32,846	84,891	196,637
MN	6,775	350	7,423	35,321	7,112	374	10,142	23,152	47,604
IA	3,598	213	4,403	31,397	3,569	206	4,971	14,469	35,409
MO	7,069	406	8,013	41,459	7,290	419	10,390	25,917	59,889
ND	587	15	246	2,465	627	15	310	979	2,574
SD	748	25	398	3,005	764	28	498	1,476	3,859
NE	1,928	92	1,624	15,143	1,876	91	1,938	5,819	16,076
KS	3,235	171	3,323	26,753	3,275	189	4,597	12,909	31,056
South	99,304	5,819	101,293	647,918	104,500	5,839	128,278	354,380	800,875
S.A.	48,855	2,930	48,588	256,625	53,478	3,104	66,893	179,075	373,181
DE	632	68	1,743	8,383	673	67	2,091	3,866	10,730
MD	3,883	234	4,859	21,282	4,244	230	5,956	14,020	28,009
DC	514	17	394	1,537	486	17	494	1,525	2,128
VA	5,568	391	6,649	36,803	6,137	429	9,740	26,857	51,902
WV	1,662	96	2,007	9,869	1,619	84	2,108	5,404	11,561
NC	10,133	799	11,717	64,176	10,995	842	16,293	47,007	95,317
SC	4,206	368	5,540	27,836	4,534	366	7,324	19,112	41,212
GA	8,534	503	7,906	48,056	9,187	570	11,933	33,708	75,709
FL	13,723	454	7,773	38,683	15,603	499	10,954	27,574	56,613
E.S.C.	18,573	1,241	20,132	119,698	19,718	1,303	26,524	74,296	164,862
KY	3,502	247	4,639	29,639	3,693	252	5,865	18,092	41,827
TN	6,417	462	7,378	40,777	6,864	485	9,869	27,050	57,753
AL	5,528	330	5,234	29,794	5,843	347	6,963	18,652	40,901
MS	3,126	202	2,881	19,488	3,318	219	3,827	10,503	24,381
W.S.C.	31,876	1,648	32,573	271,595	31,304	1,432	34,861	101,009	262,832
AR	3,313	190	2,824	19,747	3,390	206	3,815	10,827	25,308
LA	4,107	202	4,304	57,058	3,816	161	4,176	16,426	50,700
OK	4,168	197	4,010	23,116	3,728	151	3,629	9,857	24,074
TX	20,288	1,059	21,435	171,674	20,370	914	23,241	63,899	162,751
West	76,337	3,074	64,587	315,277	81,841	3,246	86,158	201,325	404,325
Mountain	14,854	556	10,863	56,997	16,479	596	14,689	35,822	73,554
MT	1,090	20	379	3,668	1,239	20	426	1,112	3,498
ID	1,404	48	865	5,370	1,491	53	1,149	3,057	7,005
WY	511	10	183	2,558	500	8	180	493	2,074
CO	4,406	192	3,983	17,963	4,718	184	4,958	12,046	23,236
NM	1,223	33	521	3,815	1,322	35	713	1,653	4,226
AZ	3,407	150	3,037	12,907	4,151	184	4,669	11,299	20,758
UT	1,962	83	1,539	8,960	2,083	89	2,073	4,883	10,287
NV	851	20	356	1,756	975	24	521	1,279	2,470
Pacific	61,483	2,518	53,724	258,280	65,362	2,650	71,469	165,503	330,771
WA	6,788	291	6,681	34,665	7,630	310	8,842	19,016	46,532
OR	5,659	185	3,783	17,897	6,353	203	4,767	11,610	25,352
CA	47,625	2,005	42,630	199,695	49,930	2,104	57,148	132,638	252,729
AK	445	13	270	2,580	427	11	272	834	2,711
HI	966	24	360	3,443	1,022	22	440	1,405	3,448

[1] Includes central administrative offices and auxiliary units. [2] Includes employment and payroll at administrative offices and auxiliary units. All employees represents the average of production workers plus all other employees for the payroll period ended nearest the 12th of March. Production workers represents the average of the employment for the payroll periods ended nearest the 12th of March, May, August, and November. [3] Includes extensive and unmeasurable duplication from shipments between establishments in the same industry classification. [4] Adjusted value added; takes into account (a) value added by merchandising operations (that is, difference between the sales value and cost of merchandise sold without further manufacture, processing, or assembly), plus (b) net change in finished goods and work-in-process inventories between beginning and end of year.

Source: U.S. Bureau of the Census, *1982* and *1987 Census of Manufactures.*

No. 1249. Manufactures Summary, by State: 1992

[Sum of State totals may not add to U.S. total because U.S. and State figures were independently derived]

REGION, DIVISION, AND STATE	Estab-lish-ments [1]	ALL EMPLOYEES [2]		Produc-tion workers (1,000)	Value added by manu-facture [3] (mil. dol.)	Value of ship-ments [4] (mil. dol.)
		Number (1,000)	Payroll (mil. dol.)			
United States................	381,870	18,253	560,485	11,654	1,428,707	3,006,275
Northeast................	82,967	3,699	122,862	2,162	283,865	525,662
New England	24,967	1,124	37,791	660	81,692	145,315
Maine................	2,200	91	2,447	67	5,458	11,611
New Hampshire	2,332	94	2,820	60	6,493	11,260
Vermont................	1,343	45	1,289	30	3,379	6,386
Massachusetts	10,145	480	16,421	273	36,519	65,702
Rhode Island	2,664	88	2,403	59	5,166	9,578
Connecticut	6,283	326	12,411	171	24,677	40,778
Middle Atlantic	58,000	2,575	85,071	1,502	202,173	380,347
New York................	26,617	1,049	35,225	592	86,349	154,211
New Jersey	13,281	574	20,616	301	46,091	86,885
Pennsylvania	18,102	952	29,230	609	69,733	139,251
Midwest................	73,020	5,470	175,883	3,525	432,051	942,160
East North Central	72,979	4,098	135,913	2,646	323,581	697,113
Ohio................	18,292	1,046	34,904	681	86,161	184,637
Indiana................	9,285	619	19,114	435	49,662	104,871
Illinois................	18,784	970	31,605	588	74,860	158,129
Michigan................	16,531	917	34,207	574	71,724	161,409
Wisconsin................	10,087	546	16,083	368	41,174	88,067
West North Central	26,740	1,372	39,970	879	108,470	245,047
Minnesota................	7,934	394	12,664	225	27,175	57,324
Iowa................	3,913	227	6,484	158	20,502	46,432
Missouri................	7,846	408	11,868	260	33,995	73,746
North Dakota	666	19	438	13	1,423	3,678
South Dakota	889	35	739	25	2,267	5,956
Nebraska................	2,028	100	2,516	72	7,952	21,816
Kansas................	3,464	189	5,261	126	15,156	36,095
South................	112,543	5,908	158,853	4,095	458,531	1,019,572
South Atlantic................	56,717	2,989	80,393	2,052	228,773	461,046
Delaware................	736	67	2,770	31	4,881	13,000
Maryland................	4,337	195	6,291	114	15,588	31,047
District of Columbia	458	13	553	4	1,570	2,008
Virginia................	6,521	408	11,265	283	35,933	65,860
West Virginia	1,786	78	2,337	56	6,511	13,217
North Carolina	11,877	831	20,456	609	65,446	128,599
South Carolina	4,839	367	9,425	272	24,725	51,996
Georgia................	9,767	556	14,278	394	41,038	90,999
Florida................	16,396	474	13,018	289	33,081	64,320
East South Central	22,123	1,399	34,389	1,045	98,705	221,601
Kentucky................	4,310	277	7,524	203	25,265	60,029
Tennessee................	7,610	504	12,618	370	35,799	76,209
Alabama................	6,436	380	9,217	284	23,653	52,708
Mississippi................	3,767	238	5,030	188	13,988	32,655
West South Central................	33,703	1,520	44,071	998	131,053	336,925
Arkansas................	3,913	227	4,878	179	14,204	34,050
Louisiana................	4,048	179	5,460	126	20,509	60,940
Oklahoma................	4,064	157	4,282	109	13,808	30,287
Texas................	21,678	957	29,451	584	82,532	211,648
West................	86,641	3,183	102,889	1,873	254,261	518,884
Mountain................	19,211	631	18,453	387	50,939	100,596
Montana................	1,375	22	544	16	1,421	4,137
Idaho................	1,838	66	1,769	46	4,465	10,557
Wyoming................	577	9	225	6	856	2,385
Colorado................	5,295	184	5,926	107	15,300	29,220
New Mexico	1,594	39	965	27	4,946	9,492
Arizona................	4,758	177	5,420	99	14,960	25,767
Utah................	2,525	106	2,860	68	7,271	15,750
Nevada................	1,249	28	744	18	1,720	3,288
Pacific................	67,430	2,552	84,436	1,486	203,322	418,288
Washington................	8,521	342	11,612	200	27,765	72,800
Oregon................	6,865	213	6,076	144	14,444	32,215
California................	50,513	1,960	65,766	1,117	158,240	305,805
Alaska................	513	16	426	12	1,347	3,678
Hawaii................	1,018	21	556	13	1,526	3,790

[1] Includes central administrative offices and auxiliary units. [2] Includes employment and payroll at administrative offices and auxiliary units. All employees represents the average of production workers plus all other employees for the payroll period ended nearest the 12th of March. Production workers represents the average of the employment for the payroll periods ended nearest the 12th of March, May, August, and November. [3] Adjusted value added; takes into account (a) value added by merchandising operations (that is, difference between the sales value and cost of merchandise sold without further manufacture, processing, or assembly), plus (b) net change in finished goods and work-in-process inventories between beginning and end of year. [4] Includes extensive and unmeasurable duplication from shipments between establishments in the same industry classification.

Source: U.S. Bureau of the Census, *1992 Census of Manufactures.*

Manufactures

No. 1250. Average Hourly Earnings of Production Workers in Manufacturing Industries, by State: 1980 to 1994

[In dollars]

DIVISION AND STATE	1980	1985	1988	1989	1990	1991	1992	1993	1994
United States.	7.27	9.54	10.19	10.48	10.83	11.18	11.46	11.74	12.06
New England:									
Maine	6.00	8.40	9.31	9.92	10.59	11.08	11.40	11.63	(NA)
New Hampshire	5.87	8.39	9.97	10.37	10.83	10.84	11.22	11.62	11.73
Vermont	6.14	8.41	9.47	9.99	10.52	11.00	11.52	11.82	11.54
Massachusetts	6.51	9.00	10.40	10.87	11.39	11.81	12.15	12.36	12.59
Rhode Island	5.59	7.59	8.64	9.06	9.45	9.73	9.92	10.20	10.35
Connecticut	7.08	9.57	10.78	11.21	11.53	11.99	12.46	13.01	13.53
Middle Atlantic:									
New York	7.18	9.67	10.43	10.67	11.11	11.43	11.72	11.97	12.19
New Jersey	7.31	9.86	10.86	11.17	11.76	12.17	12.57	12.98	13.38
Pennsylvania	7.59	9.57	10.33	10.66	11.04	11.46	11.78	12.11	12.49
East North Central:									
Ohio	8.57	11.38	12.00	12.26	12.64	13.12	13.49	14.05	14.38
Indiana	8.49	(NA)	(NA)	11.70	12.03	12.43	12.79	13.17	13.56
Illinois	8.02	10.37	10.98	11.21	11.44	11.68	11.84	12.04	12.26
Michigan	9.52	12.64	13.31	13.51	13.86	14.52	14.81	15.36	16.13
Wisconsin	8.03	10.26	10.61	10.77	11.11	11.47	11.85	12.17	12.41
West North Central:									
Minnesota	7.61	10.05	10.59	10.95	11.23	11.52	11.92	12.23	12.60
Iowa	8.67	10.32	10.56	10.82	11.27	11.62	11.92	12.22	12.47
Missouri	7.26	9.57	10.24	10.49	10.74	10.86	11.24	11.55	11.78
North Dakota	6.56	8.05	8.36	8.80	9.27	9.25	9.60	9.86	10.19
South Dakota	6.50	7.43	8.09	8.30	8.48	8.79	8.84	8.89	9.19
Nebraska	7.38	9.02	9.38	9.53	9.66	9.84	10.22	10.46	10.94
Kansas	7.37	9.45	10.24	10.68	10.94	11.24	11.60	11.99	12.14
South Atlantic:									
Delaware	7.58	9.86	11.49	12.36	12.39	12.20	12.35	13.29	13.90
Maryland	7.61	9.73	10.71	11.19	11.57	11.92	12.50	12.83	13.15
District of Columbia	8.46	10.48	11.10	11.79	12.51	13.05	13.17	13.18	13.46
Virginia	6.22	8.51	9.37	9.69	10.07	10.43	10.62	10.85	11.25
West Virginia	8.08	10.24	10.81	11.17	11.53	11.77	12.11	12.27	12.60
North Carolina	5.37	7.29	8.12	8.42	8.79	9.19	9.49	9.81	10.19
South Carolina	5.59	7.61	8.30	8.54	8.84	9.17	9.48	9.80	9.99
Georgia	5.77	8.10	8.65	8.87	9.17	9.56	9.86	10.09	10.35
Florida	5.98	7.86	8.39	8.67	8.98	9.30	9.59	9.76	9.97
East South Central:									
Kentucky	7.34	9.53	10.16	10.37	10.70	11.00	11.28	11.47	11.82
Tennessee	6.08	8.29	8.96	9.22	9.55	9.92	10.13	10.33	10.51
Alabama	6.49	8.48	8.95	9.10	9.39	9.72	9.99	10.35	10.75
Mississippi	5.44	7.22	7.83	8.03	8.37	8.67	8.91	9.16	9.40
West South Central:									
Arkansas	5.71	7.57	8.07	8.26	8.51	8.81	9.05	9.36	9.65
Louisiana	7.74	10.43	10.94	11.13	11.61	11.86	12.19	12.66	13.13
Oklahoma	7.36	9.86	10.35	10.48	10.73	11.09	11.38	11.42	11.41
Texas	7.15	9.41	9.97	10.25	10.47	10.84	10.92	11.02	11.14
Mountain:									
Montana	8.78	10.95	10.68	11.15	11.51	11.57	12.18	12.40	12.50
Idaho	7.55	9.41	10.00	10.21	10.60	11.11	11.42	11.88	11.88
Wyoming	7.01	9.64	10.27	10.58	10.83	10.98	11.10	11.53	11.81
Colorado	7.63	9.52	10.38	10.44	10.94	11.33	11.32	12.01	12.27
New Mexico	5.79	8.41	8.87	8.74	9.04	9.40	9.68	9.74	10.14
Arizona	7.29	9.48	9.85	9.92	10.21	10.70	10.96	11.06	11.17
Utah	7.02	9.64	10.11	10.14	10.32	10.77	11.09	11.10	11.26
Nevada	7.72	9.15	10.08	10.33	11.05	11.04	11.55	11.65	11.83
Pacific:									
Washington	(NA)	11.63	11.90	12.12	12.61	13.13	13.59	14.01	14.42
Oregon	8.65	10.50	10.60	10.81	11.15	11.53	11.97	12.18	12.31
California	7.70	10.12	10.80	11.16	11.48	11.87	12.19	12.38	12.44
Alaska	10.22	12.19	11.98	12.01	12.46	11.40	10.75	11.14	10.96
Hawaii	6.83	8.65	9.84	10.37	10.99	11.39	11.61	11.98	12.22

NA Not available.

Source: U.S. Bureau of Labor Statistics, *Employment and Earnings,* monthly.

No. 1251. Industrial Production Indexes, by Industry: 1970 to 1994

[1987=100. Beginning 1988, data based on 1987 Standard Industrial Classification (SIC), earlier years based on 1977 SIC; see text, section 26. See also *Historical Statistics, Colonial Times to 1970,* series P 13 and P 18-39]

INDUSTRY	SIC code	1970	1975	1980	1985	1988	1989	1990	1991	1992	1993	1994
Total index	(X)	61.4	66.3	84.1	94.4	95.3	104.4	106.0	106.0	104.3	107.6	112.0
Manufacturing	(X)	56.4	61.1	78.8	91.6	94.3	104.7	106.4	106.1	103.9	108.0	112.9
Durable goods	(X)	53.3	56.7	75.7	91.8	93.9	106.6	108.6	107.4	104.2	109.3	116.1
Lumber and products	24	66.7	66.5	76.9	88.0	95.1	100.1	99.4	97.1	90.5	95.8	100.2
Furniture and fixtures	25	55.6	59.4	78.5	88.1	92.5	100.3	101.6	100.1	93.9	99.1	105.0
Stone, clay, and glass products	32	71.1	77.8	92.0	93.6	97.1	102.6	102.5	100.3	92.5	95.3	99.2
Primary metals	33	115.2	107.2	110.8	101.8	93.7	108.7	107.2	106.5	98.7	101.9	106.9
Fabricated metal products	34	75.9	76.7	92.5	94.5	93.8	104.2	102.8	99.5	95.3	98.8	103.7
Industrial, commercial machinery[1]	35	32.8	38.1	60.6	86.8	90.3	113.0	117.3	117.6	115.0	124.6	141.1
Electrical machinery	36	40.5	45.1	73.3	93.1	94.3	108.5	111.0	111.4	113.4	121.9	139.3
Transportation equipment	37	55.5	59.7	72.3	91.8	96.9	105.2	109.6	107.0	101.3	105.1	105.5
Instruments	38	38.8	52.4	78.8	95.7	95.1	103.6	104.6	104.9	106.3	106.3	106.2
Nondurable goods	(X)	61.1	67.7	83.1	91.5	94.9	102.3	103.7	104.4	103.6	106.5	109.3
Foods	20	64.0	71.4	84.6	94.9	97.4	101.5	102.5	103.7	105.3	107.0	109.4
Tobacco products	21	90.6	97.8	103.6	97.3	95.8	101.8	100.7	100.8	94.6	96.5	88.7
Textile mill products	22	74.4	77.7	92.1	89.7	93.9	98.6	100.3	97.1	96.6	103.9	105.7
Paper and products	26	62.9	65.9	83.1	92.2	97.1	103.1	105.0	105.6	106.5	108.9	113.8
Printing and publishing	27	52.7	53.7	70.3	87.6	90.6	100.9	101.1	100.8	97.0	97.2	99.3
Chemicals and products	28	55.9	69.1	87.8	91.4	94.6	106.0	109.2	111.8	111.1	114.7	119.1
Petroleum products	29	83.9	91.5	99.0	92.6	98.9	101.9	102.3	103.3	101.3	102.1	104.5
Rubber and plastics products	30	37.6	47.4	61.7	85.8	90.8	102.6	106.0	107.2	105.4	115.6	123.1
Leather and products	31	208.0	182.5	161.7	112.5	102.6	99.8	99.6	96.0	86.4	89.0	87.3
Mining	(X)	100.4	98.0	110.0	109.0	101.0	101.3	100.0	102.0	100.2	98.9	98.2
Utilities	(X)	72.9	84.3	95.9	99.5	96.3	105.0	108.7	109.9	112.3	111.9	116.2

X Not applicable.   [1] Includes computer equipment.
Source: Board of Governors of the Federal Reserve System, *Federal Reserve Bulletin,* monthly.

No. 1252. Index of Manufacturing Capacity: 1950 to 1994

[1987 output=100. Annual figures are averages of quarterly data. Capacity represents estimated quantity of output relative to output in 1967 which the *current* stock of plant and equipment in manufacturing industries was capable of producing. Primary processing industries comprise textiles, lumber, paper and pulp, petroleum, rubber, stone, clay, glass, primary metals, fabricated metals, and a portion of chemicals. Advanced processing industries comprise chemical products, food, beverages, tobacco, apparel, furniture, printing and publishing, leather, machinery, transportation equipment, instruments, ordnance, and miscellaneous industry groups]

YEAR	Index of capacity	RELATION OF OUTPUT TO CAPACITY (percent)			YEAR	Index of capacity	RELATION OF OUTPUT TO CAPACITY (percent)		
		All manu-facturing	Primary processing	Advanced processing			All manu-facturing	Primary processing	Advanced processing
1950	29	83	88	80	1985	115	80	80	79
1955	36	87	92	84	1986	119	79	81	78
1960	44	80	80	80	1987	123	82	85	80
1965	54	90	91	89	1988	125	84	87	82
1970	71	80	80	79	1989	128	83	86	82
1975	84	73	73	74	1990	131	81	84	80
1980	98	80	78	81	1991	133	78	80	77
1981	102	79	78	79	1992	136	79	82	78
1982	105	73	69	75	1993	140	81	85	79
1983	108	75	75	75	1994	144	83	88	82
1984	111	80	80	79					

Source: Board of Governors of the Federal Reserve System, *Capacity Utilization In Manufacturing, Mining, Utilities, and Industrial Materials,* G.3., monthly. (Based on data from Federal Reserve Board, Commerce, U.S. Bureau of Labor Statistics, and McGraw-Hill Information Systems Company, New York, NY, and other sources.)

No. 1253. Finances of Manufacturing Corporations: 1970 to 1994

[In billions of dollars. Beginning 1986, data exclude estimates for corporations with less than $250,000 in assets at time of sample selection. Prior years include estimates for corporations in this size category. See table 890 for individual industry data]

ITEM	1970	1980	1984	1985	1986	1987	1988	1989	1990	1991	1992	1993	1994
Net sales	709	1,897	2,335	2,331	2,221	2,378	2,596	2,745	2,811	2,761	2,890	3,015	3,261
Net operating profit	50	129	159	138	125	159	190	182	173	133	151	180	241
Net profit:													
Before taxes	48	145	166	137	129	173	216	189	160	100	33	119	244
After taxes	29	92	108	88	83	116	155	136	112	68	23	84	175
Cash dividends	15	36	45	46	46	50	57	65	62	60	63	67	70
Net income retained in business	14	58	63	42	37	66	98	71	49	7	-40	17	105

Source: Through 1980, U.S. Federal Trade Commission; thereafter, U.S. Bureau of the Census, *Quarterly Financial Report for Manufacturing, Mining, and Trade Corporations.*

No. 1254. Capital in Manufacturing Establishments: 1980 to 1993

[In billions of dollars, except percent. Data refer to privately owned manufacturing establishments and are based on the capital expenditures data from the Census of Manufactures, the *Annual Survey of Manufactures*, and the inventory investment component of GNP. For details, see source]

ITEM	CURRENT DOLLARS						CONSTANT (1987) DOLLARS					
	1980	1985	1990	1991	1992	1993	1980	1985	1990	1991	1992	1993
Purchases of equipment and structures	80	98	128	126	121	135	103	102	118	115	111	126
Percent equipment	71	65	66	68	69	73	69	65	67	68	70	76
Depreciation (straight line) [1] .	54	78	101	106	109	113	72	83	93	96	98	102
Percent equipment	76	74	73	73	73	73	76	74	74	74	74	74
Net investment [2]	26	20	27	20	12	22	31	19	25	19	12	25
Net stock, end of year [1] . . .	976	1,238	1,576	1,591	1,615	1,665	1,222	1,285	1,403	1,417	1,421	1,447
Equipment and structures	666	898	1,153	1,184	1,219	1,270	860	950	1,026	1,047	1,061	1,087
Percent equipment . . .	62	58	57	57	56	56	61	58	57	56	56	57
Inventories	310	340	424	407	397	395	361	336	377	371	360	360

[1] Depreciation and net stock estimates for equipment and structures are derived using the perpetual inventory method and the straight-line depreciation formula. [2] Represents the difference between purchases and depreciation.

Source: U.S. Bureau of Economic Analysis, *The National Income and Product Accounts of the United States,* volume 2, 1959-88, *Fixed Reproducible Tangible Wealth in the United States, 1925-89,* and *Survey of Current Business,* January 1992, August and September 1994, July and August 1994 issues.

No. 1255. U.S. Exports of Manufactures; Origin of World Exports of Manufacture: 1970 to 1994

[In millions of dollars, except percents]

ITEM	1970-74	1975-79	1980-84	1985-89	1990	1991	1992	1993	1994
Manufactures export value	40	88	143	185	281	305	327	339	381
Machinery & transport equipment . .	25	56	91	120	174	190	203	211	233
Chemicals	5	12	21	28	39	40	44	45	52
Other	10	20	31	38	68	75	80	83	97
Origin of world exports of manu. (percent):									
United States	13.1	12.4	12.8	10.7	11.3	12.0	11.8	12.7	(NA)
Machinery & transport equipment.	18.1	16.9	17.3	14.2	14.4	15.1	14.9	(NA)	(NA)
Chemicals.	14.6	13.8	15.2	13.0	13.1	13.3	13.1	(NA)	(NA)
Other	7.5	6.9	6.9	5.6	7.0	7.6	7.4	(NA)	(NA)
Germany [2]	15.9	15.4	13.7	14.4	14.6	14.2	14.0	12.5	(NA)
Japan	10.0	10.9	12.8	13.0	11.2	11.9	11.8	13.0	(NA)
Other G-7 countries [3]	23.6	23.5	22.1	21.3	22.0	21.6	21.0	20.8	(NA)
East Asian NIC's [4]	2.8	4.1	6.0	7.7	7.6	8.2	8.1	9.3	(NA)

NA Not available. [1] U.S. exports are domestic exports only. [2] Prior to 1991, data for are for former West Germany only. [3] Other Group of Seven (G-7) Countries: Canada, France, Italy, United Kingdom. [4] East Asian newly industrialized countries (NIC's): Hong Kong, S. Korea, Singapore, Taiwan.

Source: U.S. Dept. of Commerce, International Trade Administration, Office of Trade and Economic Analysis. Based on United Nations Commodity Trade Statistics, *Statistical Yearbook of the Republic of China,* and unpublished data.

No. 1256. Foreign Direct Investment Position in the United States—Manufacturing: 1992 and 1993

[In millions of dollars. Book value at year end. Covers U.S. firms in which foreign interest or ownership was 10% or more. Minus sign (-) indicates a negative position]

AREA OR COUNTRY	TOTAL [1]		FOOD AND KINDRED PRODUCTS		CHEMICALS AND ALLIED PRODUCTS		PRIMARY AND FABRICATED METALS		MACHINERY	
	1992	1993	1992	1993	1992	1993	1992	1993	1992	1993
All countries [2]	163,354	166,698	25,587	25,376	53,681	57,693	12,911	12,969	29,156	29,748
Canada	17,005	16,600	(D)	(D)	(D)	(D)	2,446	2,321	2,643	2,363
Europe [2]	117,617	122,590	17,111	17,099	47,481	51,429	7,886	8,356	20,658	21,210
France	17,563	16,937	1,561	1,601	7,416	7,516	2,316	2,642	3,078	2,949
Germany	15,376	17,852	–106	–122	8,780	10,449	976	977	3,154	3,974
United Kingdom	40,777	42,543	8,269	8,480	15,339	17,530	1,845	1,953	3,168	2,983
Sweden	4,909	5,384	1	-	895	1,074	179	233	2,403	2,549
Switzerland	11,088	11,299	2,408	2,494	3,957	4,522	557	521	2,484	2,274
Latin America	6,636	5,219	111	246	1,412	1,247	76	45	–116	–69
Asia and Pacific [2]	21,768	21,618	(D)	(D)	(D)	(D)	2,518	2,260	5,932	5,873
Japan	18,321	17,746	946	986	3,231	3,308	1,554	1,508	5,023	4,768

- Represents or rounds to zero. D Data withheld to avoid disclosure of individual companies. [1] Includes other manufacturing industries not shown separately. [2] Includes other countries not shown separately.

Source: U.S. Bureau of Economic Analysis, *Survey of Current Business,* July 1993.

No. 1257. Employment Related to Manufactured Exports, by Industry: 1985 to 1991

[Total employment related to manufactured exports is the sum of employment directly calculated for the plants shipping the exported product, the supplying industries and service organizations, and the central offices and auxiliaries. For manufacturing industries, employment is limited to paid employees in manufacturing plants, while for nonmanufacturing it includes an estimate for working proprietors and partners]

| INDUSTRY | EMPLOYMENT RELATED TO MANUFACTURED EXPORTS | | | | | | CIVILIAN EMPLOYMENT (1,000) | | |
| | Employees (1,000) | | | Percent of civilian employment | | | | | |
	1985	1990	1991	1985	1990	1991	1985	1990	1991
Total	**4,413**	**5,729**	**6,092**	**4.0**	**4.8**	**5.1**	**110,136**	**119,943**	**120,040**
Manufacturing	2,295	3,212	3,363	12.2	17.1	18.6	18,788	18,840	18,062
Nonmanufacturing	2,118	2,516	2,730	2.3	2.5	2.7	91,348	101,103	101,978
Trade	949	1,211	1,427	4.3	5.1	6.0	21,999	23,718	23,780
Business services	227	256	268	1.1	1.0	1.0	21,139	25,611	26,206
Transportation [1]	282	401	397	4.6	6.2	6.0	6,155	6,500	6,641
Agriculture	127	139	139	3.7	4.1	4.0	3,423	3,382	3,470
Mining	50	68	78	4.9	9.2	10.2	1,016	738	767
Other	483	442	421	1.3	1.1	1.0	37,616	41,154	41,114

[1] Includes communications and utilities.

No. 1258. Manufacturing Establishments—Export-Related Shipments and Employment, 1977 to 1990, and by Industry, 1991

[The export-related employment data do not include the jobs involved in the export of nonmanufactured goods and various services sold to foreign buyers. Thus, jobs in the manufacturing sector that relate to the export of nonmanufactured goods are excluded from the estimates. In addition, all of the indirect exports being reported are domestically produced; that is, they exclude imports. See source for further details on methodology]

| INDUSTRY | SIC code[1] | MANUFACTURER'S SHIPMENT VALUE | | | | MANUFACTURING EMPLOYMENT | | | |
| | | Total [2] (bil. dol.) | Export related | | Export related as percent of shipments | Total (1,000) | Export related | | Export related as percent of total employment |
			Total (bil. dol.)	Direct exports [3] (bil. dol.)			Total (1,000)	Direct exports [4] (1,000)	
1977	(X)	1,358.4	142.4	85.8	10.4	19,590	1,990	1,106	10.2
1980	(X)	1,852.7	249.8	151.2	13.5	20,647	2,639	1,486	12.8
1981	(X)	2,017.5	271.7	164.3	13.4	20,264	2,604	1,486	12.9
1983	(X)	2,055.3	246.4	141.6	12.0	18,737	2,173	1,118	11.6
1984	(X)	2,253.8	268.3	151.0	11.9	19,141	2,179	1,083	11.4
1985	(X)	2,278.9	286.7	156.9	12.6	18,788	2,295	1,083	12.2
1986	(X)	2,260.3	294.3	159.4	13.0	18,371	2,318	1,061	12.6
1987	(X)	2,475.9	378.8	193.6	15.3	18,900	2,771	1,185	14.7
1988	(X)	2,684.7	395.3	242.9	14.7	19,147	2,638	1,412	13.8
1989	(X)	2,793.0	460.5	287.4	16.5	19,042	2,948	1,610	15.5
1990	(X)	2,873.5	515.0	293.7	17.9	18,840	3,214	1,614	17.1
1991, total	(X)	**2,826.2**	**546.9**	**314.1**	**19.4**	**18,062**	**3,363**	**1,697**	**18.6**
Food and kindred products	20	387.6	26.5	17.6	6.8	1,475	91	63	6.2
Tobacco products	21	32.0	6.5	4.7	20.2	40	9	7	23.1
Textile mill products	22	65.7	10.0	4.2	15.2	598	85	32	14.3
Apparel, other textile products . . .	23	65.3	4.8	3.6	7.4	960	61	45	6.3
Lumber and wood products	24	70.6	14.1	6.2	20.0	631	105	41	16.6
Furniture and fixtures	25	40.0	2.1	1.4	5.3	466	24	16	5.2
Paper and allied products	26	128.4	19.8	8.0	15.4	621	87	31	14.0
Printing and publishing	27	156.7	13.0	3.1	8.3	1,488	123	23	8.3
Chemical and allied products . . .	28	292.3	76.2	38.6	26.1	846	221	117	26.2
Petroleum and coal products . . .	29	158.1	15.7	5.7	9.9	113	11	5	10.1
Rubber, misc. plastics products . .	30	100.7	19.4	6.8	19.3	840	160	53	19.0
Leather, leather products	31	9.1	1.9	1.5	20.9	106	15	11	13.7
Stone, clay, glass products . . .	32	59.6	6.8	3.0	11.5	476	51	22	10.7
Primary metal industries	33	132.8	39.5	10.5	29.8	677	198	43	29.3
Fabricated metal products	34	157.1	28.5	9.9	18.2	1,359	256	83	18.8
Machinery, except electric	35	243.5	79.2	53.9	32.5	1,774	512	323	28.8
Electric, electronic equipment . . .	36	197.9	61.2	39.5	30.9	1,427	484	321	33.9
Transportation equipment	37	364.0	89.7	72.2	24.6	1,634	377	293	23.1
Instruments and related products .	38	127.2	26.3	19.7	20.7	901	183	137	20.3
Misc. manufacturing	39	37.1	5.6	3.9	15.0	363	49	33	13.6
Administrative and auxiliary	(X)	(X)	(X)	(X)	(X)	1,269	261	(X)	20.5

X Not applicable.   [1] Standard Industrial Classification; see text, section 13.   [2] Includes total domestic and export shipments for all manufacturing establishments.   [3] Includes only the value of manufactured products exported by the producing plants.   [4] Employment is limited to paid employees in manufacturing plants producing the export product. The number of employees related to export shipments was calculated for each establishment, aggregated by industry and by States, and inflated to a level comparable to the plant value of exports reported in the official foreign trade statistics at port value.

Source of tables 1257 and 1258: U.S. Bureau of the Census, *1987* and *1992 Census of Manufactures* and *Annual Survey of Manufactures.*

No. 1259. Export-Related Shipments and Employment of Manufacturing Establishments, by State: 1991

[Export-related figures exclude jobs in the manufacturing sector that are involved in the export of nonmanufactured goods and various services sold to foreign buyers. In addition, all of the indirect exports being reported are domestically produced, that is they exclude imports. Includes central administration and auxiliary office employees]

REGION, DIVISION, AND STATE	MANUFACTURES SHIPMENT VALUE					MANUFACTURING EMPLOYMENT				
	Total (bil. dol.)	Export related			Export related shipments, percent of total	Total (1,000)	Export related			Export related employment, percent of total
		Total (bil. dol.)	Direct exports (bil. dol.)	Supporting exports (bil. dol.)			Total (1,000)	Direct exports (1,000)	Supporting exports (1,000)	
United States	2,826.2	546.9	314.1	232.8	19.4	18,061.7	3,362.5	1,697.2	1,665.3	18.6
Northeast	506.8	95.7	54.5	41.2	18.9	3,757.2	715.4	352.9	362.5	18.8
New England	138.6	32.5	20.6	11.9	23.4	1,150.3	254.1	141.5	112.6	22.1
Maine	11.6	2.4	1.3	1.2	20.9	98.8	17.9	9.7	8.2	18.1
New Hampshire	9.8	2.2	1.3	0.9	22.1	85.8	18.2	9.0	9.2	21.2
Vermont	5.8	1.2	0.5	0.7	20.6	42.8	7.9	3.7	4.2	18.5
Massachusetts..........	61.9	14.4	9.5	4.9	23.4	489.7	111.0	63.9	47.1	22.7
Rhode Island..........	9.6	1.9	1.0	0.9	19.4	94.6	17.0	8.2	8.8	18.0
Connecticut...........	40.0	10.4	7.0	3.3	25.9	338.6	82.1	47.0	35.1	24.2
Middle Atlantic..........	368.1	63.2	33.9	29.3	17.1	2,606.9	461.3	211.4	249.9	17.7
New York	148.4	27.6	16.5	11.1	18.6	1,054.0	189.5	98.8	90.7	18.0
New Jersey...........	85.7	13.0	6.4	6.5	15.2	590.9	102.0	39.0	63.0	17.3
Pennsylvania..........	134.0	22.6	10.9	11.7	16.8	962.0	169.8	73.6	96.2	17.7
Midwest	877.2	155.4	86.2	69.4	17.7	5,351.7	979.3	450.5	528.8	18.3
East North Central	647.2	121.1	67.1	53.9	18.7	4,006.8	764.8	348.7	416.1	19.1
Ohio................	174.9	35.9	20.4	15.5	20.5	1,045.4	209.5	96.4	113.1	20.0
Indiana..............	97.3	17.6	8.9	8.7	18.1	594.1	105.9	47.9	58.0	17.8
Illinois..............	151.9	27.4	14.4	12.9	18.0	976.1	181.9	80.9	101.0	18.6
Michigan.............	143.1	27.3	16.5	10.8	19.1	858.2	175.4	81.9	93.5	20.4
Wisconsin............	80.0	12.9	6.9	6.0	16.2	533.0	92.1	41.6	50.5	17.3
West North Central........	230.0	34.3	19.1	15.5	14.9	1,344.9	214.5	101.8	112.7	16.1
Minnesota............	53.3	8.8	4.9	3.9	16.4	384.5	69.4	32.9	36.5	18.0
Iowa................	45.0	6.6	3.6	3.0	14.6	224.0	33.3	16.6	16.7	14.9
Missouri	66.4	10.0	5.5	4.6	15.1	401.4	61.6	27.5	34.1	15.3
North Dakota..........	3.1	0.4	0.3	0.2	14.4	17.2	2.1	1.1	1.0	12.2
South Dakota..........	4.5	0.6	0.3	0.3	13.7	30.3	5.0	2.6	2.4	16.5
Nebraska	21.0	2.7	1.6	1.2	13.1	100.5	13.8	6.6	7.2	13.7
Kansas..............	36.7	5.2	2.9	2.3	14.3	187.0	29.3	14.5	14.8	15.7
South.................	955.1	177.1	92.6	84.4	18.5	5,788.2	988.7	492.5	496.2	17.1
South Atlantic	425.5	76.8	41.9	34.8	18.0	2,935.5	469.2	218.8	250.4	16.0
Delaware	11.9	2.0	1.2	0.9	17.1	62.4	12.4	3.3	9.1	19.9
Maryland............	29.6	4.9	2.8	2.1	16.7	200.6	31.3	14.4	16.9	15.6
District of Columbia........	2.1	0.2	0.1	0.1	10.4	13.3	1.2	0.2	1.0	9.0
Virginia..............	61.6	10.6	6.1	4.5	17.2	408.4	57.2	26.3	30.9	14.0
West Virginia..........	12.5	3.3	1.4	1.9	26.2	78.1	15.8	5.5	10.3	20.2
North Carolina.........	118.2	20.7	10.6	10.1	17.5	801.9	122.2	54.9	67.3	15.2
South Carolina.........	47.5	10.2	5.2	4.9	21.4	352.6	63.4	27.8	35.6	18.0
Georgia	82.8	13.0	6.8	6.2	15.7	545.1	80.9	37.7	43.2	14.8
Florida..............	59.3	11.9	7.7	4.1	20.0	473.1	84.8	48.7	36.1	17.9
East South Central.........	202.7	35.8	18.0	17.7	17.7	1,366.4	209.7	98.6	111.1	15.4
Kentucky.............	53.5	9.3	5.0	4.3	17.4	272.9	45.2	22.0	23.2	16.6
Tennessee	69.5	12.0	6.1	5.8	17.2	493.0	77.5	37.2	40.3	15.7
Alabama.............	48.5	9.3	4.1	5.2	19.1	363.3	56.5	24.1	32.4	15.6
Mississippi	31.2	5.2	2.8	2.4	16.6	237.2	30.5	15.3	15.2	12.9
West South Central	326.9	64.5	32.7	31.9	19.7	1,486.3	309.8	175.1	134.7	20.8
Arkansas	31.1	5.0	2.4	2.6	16.0	220.2	32.3	15.2	17.1	14.7
Louisiana............	63.4	12.2	5.5	6.6	19.2	174.8	29.8	13.7	16.1	17.0
Oklahoma............	28.4	4.2	2.0	2.3	14.9	168.6	26.9	12.3	14.6	16.0
Texas...............	204.0	43.1	22.8	20.4	21.1	922.7	220.8	133.9	86.9	23.9
West	487.1	118.9	80.7	38.0	24.4	3,165.1	679.2	401.4	277.8	21.5
Mountain...............	91.4	18.2	10.0	8.0	19.9	607.4	113.4	57.4	56.0	18.7
Montana.............	3.8	0.6	0.1	0.4	15.1	19.8	2.8	0.6	2.2	14.1
Idaho...............	9.8	2.8	2.0	0.8	28.8	60.5	13.3	7.7	5.6	22.0
Wyoming............	2.7	0.4	0.1	0.3	13.3	9.8	1.4	0.4	1.0	14.3
Colorado............	26.8	4.5	2.6	1.9	16.9	176.3	32.0	17.3	14.7	18.2
New Mexico	8.0	1.7	0.6	1.0	20.7	40.7	5.9	2.5	3.4	14.5
Arizona.............	23.0	5.3	3.1	2.2	23.0	173.5	36.1	17.7	18.4	20.8
Utah................	14.5	2.5	1.3	1.2	17.2	101.8	18.0	9.4	8.6	17.7
Nevada..............	2.8	0.4	0.2	0.2	15.6	25.6	3.9	1.8	2.1	15.2
Pacific................	395.7	100.7	70.7	30.0	25.4	2,557.7	565.8	344.0	221.8	22.1
Washington	68.0	29.6	25.3	4.3	43.6	353.8	110.4	81.2	29.2	31.2
Oregon..............	30.7	7.1	4.1	3.0	23.1	208.4	43.6	24.0	19.6	20.9
California............	289.6	61.6	39.3	22.3	21.3	1,961.8	402.0	230.7	171.3	20.5
Alaska..............	3.6	1.8	1.6	0.2	49.7	14.4	7.1	6.3	0.8	49.3
Hawaii	3.8	0.6	0.4	0.2	16.3	19.3	2.7	1.8	0.9	14.0

Source: U.S. Bureau of the Census, *Exports from Manufacturing Establishments* AR91-1.

No. 1260. Manufacturing Technology—Percent of Establishments Using and Planning to Use: 1993

ESTABLISHMENT CHARACTERISTIC	ESTABLISHMENTS USING SELECTED TECHNOLOGIES							PLANNING TO USE WITHIN 2 YEARS						
	Computer aided design (CAD) or computer aided engineering	Numerically controlled machines	Automated storage and retrieval	Automated sensor based inspection or testing	Programmable controllers	Computer control on factory floor	Inter-company computer network	Computer aided design (CAD) or computer aided engineering	Numerically controlled machines	Automated storage and retrieval	Automated sensor based inspection or testing	Programmable controllers	Computer control on factory floor	Inter-company computer network
Major SIC¹ group:														
34, Fabricated metal products	46.5	40.4	1.2	9.6	30.2	20.2	16.7	5.1	2.5	0.9	4.1	3.2	9.2	8.0
35, Industrial mach. and equip.	64.1	61.9	2.3	10.6	29.0	28.1	15.4	4.1	2.1	0.9	4.0	4.3	9.1	7.5
36, Electronic and other	64.2	34.5	3.8	17.5	30.7	33.2	21.9	4.2	2.4	1.7	5.1	3.5	9.9	9.8
37, Transportation equip.	53.9	44.1	3.8	16.2	30.7	26.8	23.4	5.3	2.9	0.8	4.4	3.2	8.2	7.0
38, Instruments, related prod.	65.5	35.1	4.8	14.7	29.8	29.0	15.3	3.3	2.3	1.6	4.4	4.4	8.7	10.2
Employment size:														
20 to 99	49.5	41.4	0.6	7.9	20.5	18.8	12.0	4.7	2.4	0.4	3.8	3.6	9.0	6.7
100 to 499	76.4	56.5	4.1	20.0	49.1	41.8	28.4	4.5	2.1	2.5	5.7	4.5	10.1	12.4
500 and over	87.2	67.1	23.6	38.8	69.8	62.8	47.1	1.0	2.3	3.1	4.5	2.4	5.6	11.1
Age of plant (years):														
Less than 5	63.5	38.4	2.5	11.0	25.6	27.5	15.0	5.7	3.8	1.5	6.7	4.6	13.1	9.7
5 to 15	62.0	47.9	2.5	13.3	30.4	28.2	18.0	5.2	2.5	1.0	4.6	4.1	10.7	8.9
16 to 30	64.4	53.7	2.5	13.3	33.1	29.4	20.5	4.8	2.9	1.0	4.5	3.6	8.9	9.4
Over 30	63.1	57.3	4.0	15.6	39.1	30.7	22.0	4.1	6.5	1.3	3.7	4.3	8.2	8.3
Manufacturing process:														
Fabrication/machining	51.5	57.1	2.1	13.1	29.5	26.6	16.3	4.5	3.4	0.6	5.2	3.4	10.0	7.7
Assembly	67.3	14.6	1.8	15.7	25.1	28.5	20.7	4.4	1.9	1.8	4.3	3.8	9.4	9.9
Both	69.0	62.7	2.8	13.5	36.0	30.8	20.5	5.3	2.7	1.0	4.9	4.6	10.6	9.5
Neither	29.3	12.8	1.1	10.5	29.8	20.9	12.3	3.4	0.7	1.4	2.2	1.3	4.9	6.2
Market for most products:														
Consumer	48.2	33.9	2.7	12.6	35.3	25.2	20.6	4.8	2.6	1.4	4.6	3.6	10.8	9.8
Commercial	66.3	44.4	3.0	11.6	30.2	32.2	18.7	2.8	1.9	1.8	4.2	5.2	10.4	10.8
Industrial	64.3	55.6	2.4	12.2	32.2	27.4	18.2	5.4	2.8	0.9	3.8	4.0	9.5	9.0
Transportation	74.1	54.9	3.5	21.1	44.3	34.2	32.2	6.2	2.4	0.7	7.8	3.6	11.4	6.8
Government	63.7	62.9	6.3	18.4	29.3	33.6	15.7	1.4	1.5	1.0	5.7	4.2	9.4	7.8
Other		42.2	2.4	12.7	24.1	26.9	13.6	5.8	3.2	1.3	5.8	3.3	8.2	8.6
Market price for most products:														
Less than $5	46.3	39.4	2.1	18.1	45.1	30.4	26.1	7.4	3.4	1.4	7.5	3.5	10.9	11.3
$5 to $100	53.6	51.1	1.9	13.3	36.1	29.8	22.3	5.4	2.9	1.5	4.9	4.6	10.9	10.2
$101 to $1,000	63.6	54.6	3.0	13.8	30.6	28.1	16.4	4.1	2.0	0.7	4.7	4.0	10.3	8.4
$1,001 to $2,000	68.3	43.7	3.9	13.6	23.5	26.3	16.2	3.7	3.2	1.6	3.5	3.8	8.7	6.2
$2,001 to $10,000	73.5	54.9	2.5	9.7	24.5	27.3	14.9	5.8	1.5	1.1	4.3	4.5	10.0	6.9
Over $10,000	83.3	54.2	4.8	12.7	30.0	30.1	18.5	2.9	2.6	1.2	3.2	4.0	8.8	8.8

¹ Standard Industrial Classification; see text, section 13.

Source: U.S. Bureau of the Census, *Current Industrial Reports, Manufacturing Technology; Prevalence and Plans for Use 1993.*

No. 1261. Alcoholic Beverages—Summary: 1980 to 1992

[For 1980-1985, stocks on hand for years ending June 30; later data for years ending September 30. All other items for fiscal years ending in year shown; see text, section 9. Includes Puerto Rico. Excludes imports. See *Historical Statistics, Colonial Times to 1970*, series P 235 for beer and P 236a for distilled spirits]

ITEM	Unit	1980	1985	1987	1988	1989	1990	1991	1992
BEER									
Breweries operated	Number	86	103	245	286	333	392	480	619
Production[1]	Mil. bbl.[2]	193	194	198	202	204	202	202	203
Value of shipments[3]	Mil. dol.	9,362	12,216	14,321	15,186	15,925	17,328	(NA)	(NA)
Tax-paid withdrawals	Mil. bbl.[2]	172	175	179	182	183	182	180	180
Stocks on hand	Mil. bbl.[2]	15	14	14	14	14	13.4	13.7	13.4
DISTILLED SPIRITS									
Production facilities operated	Number	143	117	140	143	145	143	132	150
Warehouses operated	Number	200	214	260	243	224	236	235	230
Production[1 4]	Mil. tax gal.[5]	236	117	135	122	129	110	111	99
Tax-paid withdrawals[6]	Mil. tax gal.[5]	330	306	251	251	242	246	240	229
Stocks on hand[4]	Mil. tax gal.[5]	696	588	456	451	459	365	420	410
Bottled for consumption	Mil. wine gal.[7]	392	371	312	306	299	304	306	300
Whisky:　Production[1]	Mil. tax gal.[5]	87	65	75	77	75	62	59	59
Stocks on hand	Mil. tax gal.[5]	566	467	361	365	368	309	361	354
Bottled for consumption	Mil. wine gal.[7]	165	138	109	106	100	101	99	95
STILL WINES									
Production[1]	Mil. wine gal.[7]	982	622	611	577	478	484	417	438
Distilling materials	Mil. wine gal.[7]	184	148	122	103	108	134	98	113
Tax-paid withdrawals[8]	Mil. wine gal.[7]	340	414	464	468	387	387	354	356
Stocks on hand[9]	Mil. wine gal.[7]	486	602	558	562	539	525	520	477
EFFERVESCENT WINES[10]									
Production[1]	Mil. wine gal.[7]	26.8	32.0	30.9	26.9	22.8	24.7	27.7	23.7
Tax-paid withdrawals	Mil. wine gal.[7]	24.1	30.9	27.0	26.2	24.6	24.1	24.4	23.7
Stocks on hand	Mil. wine gal.[7]	11.9	21.3	19.4	22.1	20.4	18.8	19.5	16.5

NA Not available.　[1] Production represents total amount removed from fermenters, including distilling material, and includes increase after fermentation (by amelioration, sweetening, and addition of wine spirits).　[2] Barrels of 31 wine gallons.　[3] Source: U.S. Bureau of the Census, *Census of Manufactures,* and *Annual Survey of Manufactures.*　[4] Excludes alcohol produced for industrial use.　[5] For spirits of 100 proof or over, a tax gallon is equivalent to the proof gallon; for spirits of less than 100 proof, the tax gallon is equivalent to the wine gallon. A proof gallon is the alcoholic equivalent of a U.S. gallon at 60 degrees F, containing 50 percent of ethyl alcohol by volume.　[6] Includes ethyl alcohol.　[7] A wine gallon is the U.S. gallon equivalent to the volume of 231 cubic inches.　[8] Includes special natural wines.　[9] Excludes distilling materials.　[10] Includes champagne, other effervescent wines, and artificially carbonated wines.

Source: Except as noted, U.S. Bureau of Alcohol, Tobacco, and Firearms, *Alcohol and Tobacco Summary Statistics,* annual.

No. 1262. Tobacco Products—Production, Consumption, and Expenditures: 1970 to 1992

[Production data are for calendar years. Excludes cigars produced in customs bonded manufacturing warehouses. See also *Historical Statistics, Colonial Times to 1970*, series P 239-241]

ITEM	Unit	1970	1980	1983	1984	1985	1986	1987	1988	1989	1990	1991	1992
PRODUCTION													
Cigarettes	Billions	583	714	667	669	665	658	689	695	677	710	695	719
Nonfilter tip	Billions	116	54	43	39	36	33	30	28	24	23	19	18
Regular	Billions	54	23	19	18	16	15	14	12	11	11	9	9
King	Billions	62	30	24	21	20	18	16	16	13	12	10	9
Filter tip	Billions	467	661	625	630	629	625	660	667	654	687	675	701
Long and king	Billions	362	439	384	380	378	373	397	400	392	417	423	430
Extra long	Billions	105	222	241	251	252	252	263	267	261	270	253	271
Cigars	Billions	8	4	4	4	3	3	2	2	2	2	2	2
Tobacco[1]	Mil. lb.	165	163	162	163	158	147	143	142	141	142	142	141
CONSUMPTION PER PERSON[2]													
Total	Lb.[3]	10	8	7	7	7	7	6	6	6	6	5	5
Cigarettes	1,000	4	4	4	3	3	3	3	3	3	3	3	3
Cigars[4]	Number	60	24	21	20	18	17	15	14	14	13	12	12
CONSUMER EXPENDITURES													
Total	Mil. dol.	11.5	21.0	28.7	30.7	32.2	33.7	35.4	37.8	40.9	43.8	47.4	48.4
Cigarettes	Mil. dol.	10.4	19.4	26.8	28.8	30.3	31.8	33.6	35.9	38.3	41.6	45.2	45.8
Cigars	Mil. dol.	0.7	0.7	0.7	0.7	0.7	0.7	0.6	0.6	0.7	0.7	0.7	0.6
Other	Mil. dol.	0.4	0.9	1.2	1.2	1.2	1.2	1.3	1.4	1.4	1.5	1.8	2.0

[1] Smoking and chewing tobaccos and snuff output.　[2] Based on estimated population 18 years old and over, as of July 1, including Armed Forces abroad.　[3] Unstemmed processing weight equivalent.　[4] Weighing over 3 pounds per 1,000.

Source: U.S. Dept. of Agriculture, Economic Research Service, *Tobacco Situation and Outlook,* quarterly.

No. 1263. Cotton, Wool, and Manmade Fibers—Consumption, by End-Use: 1990 to 1993

[Represents products manufactured by U.S. mills. Excludes glass fiber]

YEAR	Total (mil. lb.)	COTTON		WOOL		MAN-MADE FIBERS					
						Total (mil. lb.)	Percent of end-use	Cellulosic [1]		Noncellulosic [2]	
		Total (mil. lb.)	Percent of end-use	Total (mil. lb.)	Percent of end-use			Total (mil. lb.)	Percent of end-use	Total (mil. lb.)	Percent of end-use
Total:											
1990	14,011	4,699	33.5	185	1.3	9,127	65.2	599	4.3	8,528	60.9
1991	14,421	5,033	34.8	213	1.5	9,175	63.7	557	3.9	8,618	59.8
1992	15,481	5,424	35.0	218	1.4	9,839	63.6	557	3.6	9,282	60.0
1993	16,177	5,656	34.9	236	1.5	10,285	63.6	594	3.7	9,691	59.9
Apparel:											
1990	5,204	2,897	55.7	118	2.3	2,189	42.0	287	5.5	1,902	36.5
1991	5,434	3,086	56.8	142	2.6	2,206	40.6	270	5.0	1,936	35.6
1992	5,967	3,375	56.5	144	2.4	2,448	41.1	272	4.6	2,176	36.5
1993	6,193	3,489	56.4	151	2.4	2,553	41.2	287	4.6	2,266	36.6
Home furnishings:											
1990	2,235	1,325	59.3	14	0.6	896	40.1	104	4.7	792	35.4
1991	2,340	1,442	61.3	11	0.5	887	37.9	97	4.1	790	34.8
1992	2,465	1,543	62.6	11	0.4	911	37.0	96	3.9	815	33.1
1993	2,606	1,632	62.6	16	0.6	958	36.8	104	4.0	854	32.8
Floor coverings:											
1990	3,075	18	0.6	21	0.7	3,036	98.7	-	-	3,036	98.7
1991	2,995	22	0.8	25	0.8	2,948	98.4	-	-	2,948	98.4
1992	3,296	19	0.6	26	0.8	3,251	98.6	-	-	3,251	98.6
1993	3,508	24	0.6	30	0.9	3,454	98.5	-	-	3,454	98.5
Exports of domestic products:											
1990	532	146	27.4	22	4.1	364	68.5	29	5.5	335	63.0
1991	572	155	27.1	23	4.0	394	68.9	32	5.6	362	63.3
1992	614	164	26.8	24	3.9	426	69.3	34	5.5	392	63.8
1993	657	174	26.5	24	3.7	459	69.8	37	5.6	422	64.2
Industrial: [3]											
1990	2,965	313	10.6	10	0.3	2,642	88.1	179	6.0	2,463	83.1
1991	3,080	328	10.7	12	0.4	2,740	88.9	158	5.1	2,582	83.8
1992	3,139	323	10.3	13	0.4	2,803	89.3	155	4.9	2,648	84.4
1993	3,213	337	10.4	15	0.5	2,861	89.1	166	5.2	2,695	83.9

- Represents or rounds to zero.   [1] Rayon and acetate.   [2] Nylon, polyester, acrylic, and olefin.   [3] Includes consumer-type products.

Source: Fiber Economics Bureau, Inc., Roseland, NJ, *Textile Organon,* monthly, (copyright).

No. 1264. Textiles and Apparel Products—U.S. Exports and Imports: 1992 to 1994

[**In millions of dollars.** Excludes glass fibers, rubber and leather apparel, and clothing donated for charity. Minus sign (-) indicates deficit]

PRODUCT	EXPORTS			GENERAL IMPORTS			MERCHANDISE TRADE BALANCE		
	1992	1993	1994	1992	1993	1994	1992	1993	1994
Total	**10,120**	**10,977**	**12,208**	**39,070**	**42,225**	**45,952**	**−28,950**	**−31,248**	**−33,744**
Textile yarn fabrics	5,911	6,025	6,592	7,844	8,438	9,208	−1,933	−2,413	−2,616
Textile yarn	1,179	1,045	1,213	955	1,146	1,335	224	−101	−122
Cotton fabric, woven	591	641	725	1,493	1,552	1,498	−902	−911	−773
Woven fabric of manmade textiles . .	825	883	925	1,206	1,261	1,291	−381	−378	−366
Woven fabric of textile material	185	210	236	666	662	695	−481	−452	−459
Special yarns	1,335	1,418	1,588	797	878	977	538	540	611
Other	1,796	1,828	1,905	2,727	2,939	3,412	−931	−1,111	−1,507
Apparel	4,209	4,952	5,616	31,226	33,787	36,744	−27,017	−28,835	−31,128

Source: U.S. Bureau of the Census, *U.S. Merchandise Trade: Exports, General Imports, and Imports for Consumption,* Report FT925, monthly.

No. 1265. Iron and Steel Industry—Summary: 1980 to 1994

[For financial data, the universe in 1992 consists of the companies that produced 68 percent of the total reported raw steel production. The financial data represent the operations of the steel segment of the companies. Minus sign (-) indicates net loss]

ITEM	Unit	1980	1985	1987	1988	1989	1990	1991	1992	1993	1994
Steel mill products, apparent supply . . .	Mil. tons [1] . .	95.2	96.4	95.9	102.7	96.8	97.8	88.3	95.0	104.6	121.3
Net shipments	Mil. tons [1] . .	83.9	73.0	76.7	83.8	84.1	85.0	78.8	82.2	89.0	95.1
Exports	Mil. tons [1] . .	4.1	1.0	1.1	2.1	4.6	4.3	6.3	4.3	4.0	3.8
Imports	Mil. tons [1] . .	15.5	24.3	20.4	20.9	17.3	17.2	15.8	17.1	19.5	30.1
Scrap consumed	Mil. tons [1] . .	66.6	53.2	51.7	56.3	51.7	50.1	50.5	51.9	58.5	(NA)
Scrap inventory	Mil. tons [1] . .	6.9	4.0	3.8	3.5	3.5	3.6	3.7	3.3	3.6	(NA)
Iron and steel products: Exports	Mil. tons [1] . .	5.1	1.6	1.7	2.8	5.4	5.3	7.4	5.3	4.7	4.9
Imports	Mil. tons [1] . .	17.9	27.6	23.8	25.7	22.1	21.9	20.2	21.9	21.8	32.7
Capacity by steelmaking process	Mil. net tons	153.7	133.6	112.2	112.0	115.9	116.7	117.6	113.1	109.9	108.2
Revenue	Bil. dol.	37.7	28.4	27.1	32.7	31.8	30.9	27.1	26.9	29.8	(NA)
Net income	Bil. dol.	0.7	–1.8	1.0	–0.6	1.6	0.1	–2.0	–4.1	1.9	(NA)
Stockholders' equity	Bil. dol.	14.5	6.9	3.0	2.2	2.1	4.3	2.8	–0.6	3.7	(NA)
Total assets	Bil. dol.	30.8	24.0	21.9	24.2	24.6	28.3	27.4	28.8	30.7	(NA)
Capital expenditures	Bil. dol.	2.7	1.6	1.2	1.8	2.3	2.6	2.3	1.8	1.5	(NA)
Working capital ratio [2]	Ratio	1.6	1.3	1.5	1.7	1.6	1.6	1.4	1.4	1.4	(NA)
Inventories	Bil. dol.	4.7	3.5	3.4	3.8	4.0	4.7	4.4	4.5	4.6	(NA)
Average employment	1,000	399	208	163	169	169	164	146	140	127	(NA)
Hours worked	Million	758	419	354	363	360	350	304	293	274	(NA)
Producer price indexes: [3]											
Iron and steel, total	1982=100 . .	90.0	104.8	104.6	115.7	119.1	117.2	114.1	116.0	121.9	(NA)
Steel mill products	1982=100 . .	86.6	104.7	102.3	110.7	114.5	112.1	109.5	108.2	113.4	(NA)
Blast and electric furnace products . . .	1982=100 . .	97.1	95.6	97.1	119.6	129.4	120.1	116.9	115.7	116.6	(NA)
Iron ore	1982=100 . .	87.8	97.5	84.2	82.8	82.8	83.3	83.6	82.7	82.8	(NA)
Scrap, iron and steel	1982=100 . .	140.9	112.6	128.4	177.1	173.7	166.0	147.6	172.5	192.5	(NA)
Foundry and forge shop products . . .	1982=100 . .	89.7	105.2	105.7	109.6	114.6	117.2	119.0	121.3	123.8	(NA)

NA Not available. [1] In millions of short tons. [2] Current assets to current liabilities. [3] Source: U.S. Bureau of Labor Statistics, *Producer Price Indexes,* monthly and annual.

No. 1266. Raw Steel, Pig Iron, and Ferroalloys Production: 1970 to 1994

[**In millions, except percent.** *See also Historical Statistics, Colonial Times to 1970,* series P 265-269]

ITEM	1970	1980	1985	1987	1988	1989	1990	1991	1992	1993	1994
Raw steel (net tons):											
World production	654.2	790.4	792.9	811.1	859.2	865.3	848.8	811.1	810.2	814.6	(NA)
U.S. production	131.5	111.8	88.3	89.2	99.9	97.9	98.9	87.9	92.9	97.9	100.6
Percent of world	20	14	11	11	12	11	12	11	12	12	(NA)
Basic oxygen process . .	63.3	67.6	51.9	52.5	58.0	58.3	58.5	52.7	57.6	59.3	61.0
Electric	20.2	31.2	29.9	34.0	36.8	35.2	36.9	33.8	35.3	38.5	39.6
Open hearth	48.0	13.0	6.4	2.7	5.1	4.4	3.5	1.4	-	-	-
Carbon	117.4	94.7	76.7	78.0	86.8	86.2	86.6	77.9	82.5	86.9	89.5
Alloy and stainless	14.1	17.1	11.6	11.2	13.1	11.7	12.3	10.0	10.4	11.0	11.1
Pig iron and ferroalloys, production (sh. tons) [1]	93.5	68.7	50.4	48.4	55.7	55.9	54.8	48.6	52.2	53.1	54.4

- Represents or rounds to zero. NA Not available. [1] For 1970, excludes blast furnace ferroalloys.

No. 1267. Steel Products—Net Shipments, by Market Classes: 1970 to 1993

[**In thousands of short tons.** Comprises carbon, alloy, and stainless steel]

MARKET CLASS	1970	1980	1985	1988	1989	1990	1991	1992	1993
Total [1]	90,798	83,853	73,043	83,840	84,100	84,981	78,846	82,241	89,022
Automotive	14,475	12,124	12,950	12,555	11,763	11,100	10,015	11,092	12,719
Steel service centers, distributors	16,025	16,172	18,439	21,037	20,769	21,111	19,464	21,328	23,714
Construction, incl. maintenance	8,913	8,742	7,900	8,607	8,318	9,245	9,161	9,536	13,429
Containers, packaging, shipping	7,775	5,551	4,089	4,421	4,459	4,474	4,278	3,974	4,355
Machinery, industrial equipment, tools . .	5,169	4,543	2,271	2,798	2,409	2,388	1,982	1,951	2,191
Steel for converting and processing . . .	3,443	4,117	5,484	8,492	8,235	9,441	8,265	9,226	9,451
Rail transportation	3,098	3,155	1,061	1,146	1,229	1,080	999	1,052	1,223
Contractors' products	4,440	3,148	3,330	3,495	3,182	2,870	2,306	2,694	2,913
Oil and gas industries	3,550	5,371	2,044	1,477	1,203	1,892	1,425	1,454	1,526
Electrical equipment	2,694	2,441	1,869	2,459	2,449	2,453	2,102	2,136	2,213
Appliances, utensils, and cutlery	2,160	1,725	1,466	1,638	1,721	1,540	1,388	1,503	1,592

[1] Includes nonclassified shipments and other classes not shown separately.

Source of tables 1265-1267: American Iron and Steel Institute, Washington, DC, *Annual Statistical Report,* (copyright).

No. 1268. Computer Shipments and Revenues: 1991 to 1993

[Revenue is in if-sold, end-user dollars]

ITEM	FACTORY REVENUE (mil. dol.)			SHIPMENTS (units)		
	1991	1992	1993	1991	1992	1993
United States:						
Supercomputer	876	938	701	558	571	405
Mainframe	9,713	7,453	4,643	3,227	2,421	1,929
Midrange	7,967	8,534	6,705	151,574	124,745	107,034
Workstation	3,458	3,719	4,375	210,541	237,730	262,869
Personal computer	24,589	25,858	29,695	10,903,000	12,544,374	14,775,000
Canada:						
Supercomputer	22	37	38	17	26	29
Mainframe	671	623	243	204	156	123
Midrange	485	618	509	10,117	9,094	6,794
Workstation	188	185	181	8,017	11,806	10,687
Personal computer	2,077	2,405	2,730	926,000	1,175,000	1,415,000
Western Europe:						
Supercomputer	529	479	448	241	269	213
Mainframe	9,629	7,490	5,782	4,088	2,455	1,963
Midrange	9,699	6,727	7,157	198,780	155,142	145,353
Workstation	2,540	2,604	2,828	154,581	175,762	171,744
Personal computer	17,517	18,872	17,999	8,406,937	9,495,441	10,323,974
Japan:						
Supercomputer	494	450	558	140	108	122
Mainframe	6,252	5,367	5,569	5,631	3,630	4,191
Midrange	5,673	4,916	4,808	286,626	233,967	194,385
Workstation	1,885	1,883	2,143	124,712	124,073	133,750
Personal computer	4,586	4,750	5,885	2,354,300	2,223,810	2,464,093
Asia/Pacific:						
Supercomputer	54	83	82	44	63	58
Mainframe	544	642	568	257	238	265
Midrange	263	522	784	3,978	8,757	12,883
Workstation	256	327	351	15,871	23,842	20,374
Personal computer	4,574	5,219	7,053	2,235,000	3,031,398	3,935,135
Rest of World:						
Supercomputer	16	67	31	13	50	18
Mainframe	382	584	473	158	200	246
Midrange	476	506	625	15,063	13,209	18,862
Workstation	373	340	408	15,808	24,038	24,006
Personal computer	4,237	6,991	10,256	2,140,763	3,940,777	5,929,798

No. 1269. Microcontrollers and Chip Shipments: 1990 to 1993

ITEM	REVENUE (mil. dol.)				SHIPMENTS (millions of units)			
	1990	1991	1992	1993	1990	1991	1992	1993
Microcontrollers, worldwide	3,667	4,519	4,613	5,813	1,365	1,562	1,895	2,155
8-bit	2,079	2,618	(NA)	3,612	567	729	844	1,096
4-bit	1,394	1,598	(NA)	1,705	781	801	1,003	999
16-bit	194	303	(NA)	496	17	32	48	60
32-bit processors	1,402	2,456	4,363	8,427	26	44	61	77
RISC [1]	175	270	305	642	1	1	3	7
CISC [2]	1,227	2,186	4,057	7,785	25	42	27	70
256K DRAM [3] chips	1,322	622	270	162	620	299	193	105
1-Megabit DRAM chips	4,229	3,776	2,644	2,031	665	835	821	601

NA Not available.   [1] RISC=Reduced Instruction Set Computer.   [2] CISC=Complex Instruction Set Computer.
[3] DRAM=Dynamic Random Access Memory.

Source of tables 1268 and 1269: Dataquest, Inc., San Jose, CA, Consolidate Data Base, January 1994, and unpublished data.

No. 1270. Computers and Industrial Electronics—Shipments: 1984 to 1992

[In millions of dollars]

ITEM	1984	1985	1986	1987	1988	1989	1990	1991	1992
Total	**41,795**	**43,993**	**43,404**	**48,275**	**49,797**	**51,339**	**50,793**	**50,121**	**51,335**
Computer and peripheral equipment:									
Computers	18,933	21,107	21,209	24,410	24,354	25,610	25,973	26,691	27,655
Peripheral equipment	22,863	22,887	22,195	23,865	25,443	25,729	24,820	23,430	23,680
Total	20,388	20,121	20,286	21,325	22,100	24,799	26,183	26,126	25,797
Industrial electronics:									
Controlling, processing equipment	8,683	8,719	8,924	9,193	9,861	11,992	12,728	12,633	12,844
Testing, measuring equipment	6,279	6,008	5,736	6,009	5,807	5,953	6,859	7,492	7,273
Nuclear electronic equipment	480	519	560	601	616	606	567	571	581
Robots, accessories, and components	281	345	346	284	229	256	275	294	(NA)
Other electronic equipment	4,665	4,530	4,720	5,238	5,588	5,992	5,754	5,137	5,098

NA Not available.

Source: Electronic Industries Association, Washington, DC, *Electronic Market Data Book,* annual (copyright).

No. 1271. Factory Sales of Consumer Electronics (including imports), and Electronic Components in the United States: 1985 to 1993

[In millions of dollars]

CATEGORY	1985	1986	1987	1988	1989	1990	1991	1992	1993
Total	22,815	26,570	28,984	32,046	33,350	35,016	35,145	37,152	40,199
Television sets:									
Direct-view color TV	5,514	5,844	6,282	6,247	6,490	6,197	5,979	6,591	7,316
LCD color TV	7	14	21	30	40	50	56	60	60
Projection TV	488	530	527	529	478	626	683	714	841
TV/VCR combinations	(NA)	(NA)	(NA)	(NA)	(NA)	178	265	375	599
Monochrome TV	308	333	328	196	116	99	61	47	40
LCD monochrome TV	(NA)	(NA)	(NA)	40	40	33	31	32	33
Other video:									
VCR decks	4,173	3,978	3,442	2,848	2,625	2,439	2,454	2,947	2,851
Camcorders	793	1,338	1,651	1,972	2,007	2,260	2,013	1,841	1,958
Laserdisc players	23	26	26	34	50	72	81	93	123
Home satellite earth stations	(NA)	256	304	331	365	421	408	375	395
Videocassette players	(NA)	(NA)	(NA)	57	63	65	71	49	61
Audio:									
Audio systems	1,372	1,370	1,048	1,225	1,217	1,270	1,264	1,371	1,464
Separate audio components	1,132	1,358	1,715	1,854	1,871	1,935	1,805	1,586	1,635
Home radios	379	408	409	377	379	360	310	324	307
Portable audio equipment	1,140	1,389	1,469	1,547	1,595	1,645	1,780	2,096	2,187
Aftermarket autosound equipment .	961	1,035	1,023	1,187	1,125	1,192	1,232	1,467	1,604
Factory installed autosound	1,800	2,100	2,500	2,750	3,000	3,100	2,875	2,990	3,199
Home information:									
Cordless telephones	280	295	435	681	830	842	1,125	1,091	1,046
Corded telephones	630	561	461	441	532	638	605	575	617
Telephone answering devices	325	464	607	755	838	827	1,000	934	1,026
Cellular telephones	115	266	267	430	653	1,133	962	1,146	1,257
Home computers	2,050	2,890	2,920	3,150	3,500	3,795	4,160	4,524	4,861
Personal wordprocessors	(NA)	580	620	650	688	656	600	555	558
Home fax machines	(NA)	(NA)	(NA)	(NA)	188	219	220	247	332
Home security systems	(NA)	(NA)	800	900	1,000	1,150	1,250	1,250	1,315
Blank media:									
Blank audio cassettes	270	300	375	354	367	376	373	376	362
Blank videocassettes	1,055	1,235	1,006	936	923	948	980	872	779
Blank floppy diskettes	(NA)	(NA)	(NA)	258	297	314	357	371	400
Accessories:									
Electronic accessories	(NA)	(NA)	748	847	829	793	721	715	759
Total primary batteries	(NA)	(NA)	(NA)	1,420	1,244	1,383	1,424	1,538	2,215
U.S. electronic component ship. .	44,064	43,755	49,971	55,287	59,121	61,313	61,762	62,750	72,891
Electron tubes	2,068	2,135	2,192	2,299	2,586	2,646	2,586	2,655	(NA)
Solid State products	14,650	14,410	16,820	19,790	22,246	23,553	26,302	25,813	(NA)
Passive and other components	27,346	27,210	30,959	33,198	34,289	35,114	32,874	34,282	(NA)

NA Not available.

Source: Electronic Industries Association, Washington, DC, *Electronic Market Data Book*, annual (copyright).

No. 1272. Semiconductors and Related Devices: 1980 to 1993

[In millions of dollars, except percent. Semiconductors and related devices represent SIC 3674]

ITEM	1980	1985	1988	1989	1990	1991	1992	1993
Consumption, North American market [1]	6,053	9,420	15,844	17,070	16,540	16,990	20,426	27,998
Revenues (North American companies)	8,062	11,051	18,586	19,515	21,047	22,940	27,105	37,453
Capital expenditures (North America) [2]	1,438	2,629	3,434	3,642	3,855	4,077	4,296	5,809
Percent of sales	17.8	23.8	18.5	18.7	18.3	17.8	15.9	15.5
Japan capital expend. as a percent of revenues	11.0	11.4	14.9	15.5	20.5	20.4	22.2	16.2
R&D (North America)	423	1,159	3,873	4,269	5,172	5,652	6,122	5,587
Imports, total [3]	2,223	4,870	9,502	10,758	(NA)	(NA)	(NA)	(NA)
Shipments [4]	9,455	15,253	20,332	23,488	23,978	26,302	25,964	30,425
Integrated microcircuits	6,768	10,872	14,857	16,682	16,372	19,151	20,065	24,084
Semiconductor devices, n.e.c. [5]	1,398	2,569	3,337	4,875	5,584	5,761	5,899	6,341
Assets, beginning of year	4,014	12,200	(NA)	(NA)	(NA)	(NA)	(NA)	(NA)

NA Not available.   [1] Source: Dataquest Inc., San Jose, CA, unpublished data. Revenue from shipments by all companies into Canada and the United States.   [2] Capital expenditures by all companies in Canada and the United States.   [3] Imports for consumption. Includes imports not shown separately.   [4] Includes items not shown separately.   [5] N.e.c. = Not elsewhere classified.

Source: Except as noted, U.S. Bureau of the Census, *Current Industrial Reports*, series MA-36Q; *U.S. Imports, FT 210, 1980-1988; Import CD-ROM Disc 1989;* and *Annual Survey of Manufactures.*

No. 1273. Machine Tools—New Orders and Shipments: 1970 to 1994

[**In millions of dollars.** Data represents total industry volume based on reports from over 200 manufacturers]

YEAR	METAL CUTTING TOOLS					METAL FORMING TOOLS				
	New orders (net)		Shipments		Order backlog, end of period	New orders (net)		Shipments		Order backlog, end of period
	Total	Domestic	Total	Domestic		Total	Domestic	Total	Domestic	
1970	651	507	993	827	471	261	227	450	412	235
1971	609	524	672	554	408	252	223	326	286	162
1972	1,009	877	714	627	702	403	368	304	267	260
1973	1,825	1,550	1,074	935	1,454	787	717	427	388	621
1974	2,017	1,716	1,445	1,241	2,025	566	470	585	522	600
1975	916	781	1,879	1,548	1,062	361	284	573	485	388
1976	1,662	1,477	1,482	1,270	1,243	541	485	578	474	351
1977	2,202	1,981	1,651	1,470	1,794	793	729	630	560	515
1978	3,373	3,043	2,189	1,960	2,981	973	901	825	729	663
1979	4,495	3,866	2,930	2,606	4,546	1,126	991	947	860	843
1980	3,885	3,496	3,681	3,206	4,750	870	744	1,011	879	701
1981	2,228	1,946	4,105	3,552	2,873	717	617	991	824	427
1982	1,064	890	2,895	2,599	1,043	433	372	710	600	151
1983	1,152	1,069	1,372	1,200	823	545	489	474	430	222
1984	1,916	1,700	1,607	1,484	1,132	1,000	932	679	609	542
1985	1,853	1,652	1,742	1,549	1,243	675	610	803	743	414
1986	1,544	1,377	1,890	1,685	897	581	507	688	621	307
1987	1,451	1,294	1,677	1,499	672	667	536	647	538	327
1988	2,708	2,316	1,575	1,400	1,806	883	749	825	702	386
1989	1,977	1,723	2,359	2,059	1,423	832	719	837	704	380
1990	2,070	1,772	2,330	2,004	1,164	894	761	970	851	304
1991	1,894	1,549	1,872	1,595	1,186	748	546	802	625	251
1992	1,756	1,532	1,918	1,605	1,025	726	609	678	547	299
1993	2,322	2,177	2,160	1,955	1,187	971	825	1,044	881	225
1994	2,914	2,775	2,515	2,333	1,587	1,527	1,382	1,184	1,038	568

Source: The Association For Manufacturing Technology, McLean, VA, *The Economic Handbook of The Machine Tool Industry,* annual, (copyright), thereafter, *Survey of Current Business,* monthly.

No. 1274. Manufacturers' Shipments, Inventories, and Orders: 1950 to 1994

[**In billions of dollars, except ratio.** See also *Historical Statistics, Colonial Times to 1970,* series P 74-92]

YEAR	Shipments	Inventories (Dec. 31) [1]	Ratio of inventories to shipments [2]	New orders	Unfilled orders (Dec. 31)	YEAR	Shipments	Inventories (Dec. 31) [1]	Ratio of inventories to shipments [2]	New orders	Unfilled orders (Dec. 31)
1950	224	32	1.41	242	41	1973	875	124	1.63	913	158
1951	261	39	1.78	287	67	1974	1,018	158	1.86	1,047	187
1952	270	42	1.71	279	76	1975	1,039	160	1.77	1,023	171
1953	298	44	1.90	283	60	1976	1,186	175	1.66	1,194	180
1954	280	42	1.71	268	48	1977	1,358	188	1.58	1,381	202
1955	318	45	1.63	330	60	1978	1,523	209	1.55	1,580	259
1956	333	51	1.74	340	68	1979	1,727	239	1.61	1,771	303
1957	345	52	1.90	331	53	1980	1,853	262	1.61	1,876	326
1958	327	50	1.75	324	47	1981	2,018	280	1.74	2,015	323
1959	363	53	1.68	369	52	1982	1,960	307	1.91	1,947	309
1960	371	54	1.79	363	45	1983	2,071	308	1.80	2,105	343
1961	371	55	1.67	373	47	1984	2,288	334	1.78	2,315	370
1962	400	58	1.76	401	48	1985	2,334	330	1.72	2,348	384
1963	421	60	1.66	426	53	1986	2,336	318	1.66	2,342	390
1964	448	63	1.62	460	65	1987	2,476	333	1.64	2,513	427
1965	492	68	1.58	505	79	1988	2,682	361	1.64	2,724	469
1966	538	78	1.70	557	97	1989	2,793	380	1.66	2,831	507
1967	558	84	1.71	565	104	1990	2,874	392	1.66	2,888	522
1968	603	90	1.76	608	110	1991	2,826	380	1.64	2,812	508
1969	642	98	1.81	647	115	1992	2,934	373	1.55	2,899	472
1970	634	101	1.91	625	106	1993	3,102	370	1.46	3,068	438
1971	671	102	1.76	672	107	1994	3,370	384	1.40	3,383	452
1972	756	108	1.58	770	12031)						

[1] Beginning in 1982, inventories are stated at current cost and are not comparable to the book value estimates for prior years.   [2] Ratio based on December seasonally adjusted data.

Source: U.S. Bureau of the Census, Current Industrial Reports, *Manufacturers' Shipments, Inventories, and Orders: 1982-1992,* series M3; and monthly press releases.

No. 1275. Value of Manufactures Shipments and Inventories, by Industry: 1980 to 1994

[**In billions of dollars.** Based on 1987 Standard Industrial Classification (SIC). See also *Historical Statistics, Colonial Times to 1970*, series P 74-79]

INDUSTRY	SIC code	1980	1985	1990	1991	1992	1993	1994
Shipments	(X)	1,853	2,335	2,874	2,826	2,934	3,102	3,370
Durable goods [1]	(X)	929	1,215	1,469	1,430	1,507	1,632	1,813
Stone, clay, and glass products	32	45	56	64	60	67	706	803
Primary metals	33	134	112	146	133	136	138	157
Fabricated metal products	34	116	143	163	157	161	170	182
Industrial machinery and equipment	35	181	218	256	244	253	288	330
Engines and turbines	351	14	15	17	17	17	19	22
Construction, mining [2]	353	34	28	31	28	25	30	33
Computer and office equipment	357	30	60	64	59	66	77	89
Electronic and other	36	113	164	195	198	209	233	274
Elec. transmission and distribution	361-2	20	24	28	27	28	29	31
Household appliances	363	13	16	18	18	18	20	23
Household audio and video equipment	365	9	12	9	10	11	11	13
Communications equipment	366	21	35	39	38	42	48	62
Electronic components	367	27	42	61	65	70	81	97
Transportation equipment [1]	37	187	307	368	364	391	425	463
Motor vehicles and parts	371	105	193	215	206	236	282	329
Aircraft, missiles, and parts	372, 6	59	91	125	131	128	113	102
Instruments and related products [1]	38	60	96	124	127	127	129	132
Measuring and controlling devices	382	16	26	32	32	34	35	39
Nondurable goods [1]	(X)	924	1,119	1,405	1,396	1,428	1,471	1,557
Food and kindred products [1]	20	256	309	384	388	395	414	430
Beverages	208	33	44	52	55	57	59	63
Tobacco products	21	12	19	30	32	33	31	33
Textile mill products	22	47	55	66	66	70	70	74
Paper and allied products [1]	26	73	95	131	129	131	129	138
Paper, pulp, paperboard mill products	261-3,6	32	39	58	54	54	52	55
Paperboard containers and boxes	265	17	23	31	31	33	32	36
Chemicals and allied products [1]	28	168	205	288	292	302	314	342
Industrial chemicals	281,2,6,8	102	115	157	154	156	161	180
Drugs, soaps, toiletries	283-4	42	61	95	103	110	117	122
Petroleum and coal products	29	193	177	173	158	155	147	144
Rubber and plastics products	30	49	76	101	101	103	104	114
Inventories (Dec. 31)	(X)	262	330	393	380	373	370	384
Durable goods [1]	(X)	172	214	255	244	233	231	242
Stone, clay, and glass products	32	6	7	8	8	8	7	8
Primary metals	33	23	20	22	20	19	19	21
Fabricated metal products	34	19	23	24	23	23	23	24
Industrial machinery and equipment	35	40	46	48	47	44	45	48
Engines and turbines	351	3	3	3	3	3	3	4
Construction, mining [2]	353	9	8	7	6	6	6	6
Computer and office equipment	357	8	12	10	10	10	11	10
Electronic and other	36	21	30	32	31	30	33	39
Elec. transmission and distrib.	361-2	4	5	5	4	4	4	5
Household appliances	363	2	3	3	2	2	2	3
Household audio and video equipment	365	1	1	1	1	1	1	1
Communications equipment	366	5	8	7	7	7	9	12
Electronic components	367	5	8	8	10	10	11	12
Transportation equipment [1]	37	35	52	75	72	65	60	57
Motor vehicles and parts	371	10	12	13	13	11	12	12
Aircraft, missiles, and parts	372, 6	22	36	58	55	50	45	41
Instruments and related products [1]	38	13	21	25	24	23	21	21
Measuring and controlling devices	382	4	6	7	7	7	6	7
Nondurable goods [1]	(X)	90	116	138	136	140	140	142
Food and kindred products [1]	20	22	24	29	30	30	31	31
Beverages	208	4	5	5	5	5	5	5
Tobacco products	21	4	6	6	7	7	7	6
Textile mill products	22	7	7	8	8	9	9	9
Paper and allied products [1]	26	8	10	13	13	13	13	13
Paper, pulp, paperboard mill products	261-3,6	3	4	5	6	6	6	5
Paperboard containers and boxes	265	2	3	3	3	3	3	4
Chemicals and allied products [1]	28	20	26	33	34	35	34	34
Industrial chemicals	281,2,6,8	11	14	18	17	17	17	17
Drugs, soaps, toiletries	283-4	6	8	11	12	13	13	13
Petroleum and coal products	29	10	14	13	11	11	10	10
Rubber and plastics products	30	6	9	12	11	12	12	13

X Not applicable.   [1] Includes industries not shown separately.   [2] Also includes material handling industries.

Source: U.S. Bureau of the Census, Current Industrial Reports, *Manufactures' Shipments, Inventories, and Orders: 1982-1994,* and monthly press releases.

No. 1276. Fiber, Rugs, Carpeting, and Sheets—Shipments: 1988 to 1994

PRODUCT	Unit	1988	1989	1990	1991	1992	1993	1994
All fibers [1]	Mil. lbs..	730	743	812	837	926	1,008	1030
Raw wool [2][3]	Mil. lbs..	133	135	133	152	151	157	153
Noils, and fiber [4]	Mil. lbs..	24	24	20	21	21	23	19
Other fibers	Mil. lbs..	573	584	659	664	754	829	858
Knit fabric production	Mil. lbs..	1,662	1,935	1,901	1,963	2,179	2,185	(NA)
Rugs, carpet and carpeting	Mil. dol.	8,417	8,431	8,527	7,980	8,749	9,318	(NA)
Sheets	1,000 doz	15,505	15,663	15,408	14,001	15,198	16,734	(NA)
Pillow cases	1,000 doz	12,564	13,089	12,665	11,301	12,523	11,928	(NA)
Terry towels	1,000 doz	47,179	62,741	42,376	43,158	48,789	48,517	(NA)

NA Not available.   [1] Includes man-made fiber top converted from tow without combing. A number of companies were added for 1990 based on information in the 1987 Census of Manufactures. Data were received from these companies for 1990; therefore, the information shown for years prior to 1990 may not be directly comparable. These changes represent approximately 20 percent of the total fibers consumed on the woolen system and worsted combing.   [2] Data are shown on a scoured basis for greasy wool. [3] Shorn and pulled wool of sheep excludes raw wool consumed in cotton system spinning to avoid disclosing figures for individual companies.   [4] Includes reprocessed and reused wool, mohair, alpaca, vicuna, and other specialty fibers as well as tops and noils consumed in woolen spinning and mohair consumed in worsted combing. Does not include wool tops consumed in cotton system spinning.

Source: U.S. Bureau of the Census, *Current Industrial Reports,* MA22K, MA22Q, and MQ23X, annual.

No. 1277. Glass Containers, Clay Construction Products, and Refractories— Shipments: 1986 to 1992

[In millions of dollars]

PRODUCT	1986	1987	1988	1989	1990	1991	1992
Glass container shipments	282	280	286	285	279	283	290
Brick shipments [1]	(NA)	(NA)	1,088	1,014	883	920	1,006
Clay tile shipments [2]	(NA)	(NA)	698	687	639	646	701
Clay pipe and fittings shipments	(NA)	(NA)	63	60	51	38	32
Refractory shipments	1,682	1,950	2,011	2,003	1,947	1,956	1,912
Clay	740	814	823	771	784	786	749
Nonclay	943	1,136	1,188	1,232	1,163	1,170	1,163

NA Not available.   [1] Building or common and face bricks.   [2] Floor and wall tile including quarry tile.

Source: U.S. Bureau of the Census, *Current Industrial Reports,* M32G, MQ32D, and MA32C, annual.

No. 1278. Mining and Mineral Processing Equipment—Shipments: 1992 and 1993

PRODUCT	Product code	Number of companies 1993	QUANTITY (units)		VALUE (mil. dol.)	
			1992	1993	1992	1993
Portable crushing, screening, washing, and combination plants	3531K	16	468	933	65	150
Underground mining machinery [1]	35325	34	1,293	2,958	248	303
Mineral processing and beneficiation equip. [1]	35326	(NA)	5,310	(NA)	70	(NA)
Crushing/pulverizing/screening machinery [2]	35327	47	2,469	2,879	135	173
Drills, mining machinery, n.e.c. [1][3]	35328	27	12,749	10,742	162	218
Portable drilling rigs and parts	3533A	30	(X)	(X)	255	339

NA Not available.   X Not applicable.   [1] Excludes parts.   [2] Excludes portables and parts.   [3] N.e.c. = Not elsewhere classified.

Source: U.S. Bureau of the Census, *Current Industrial Reports,* MA35F, annual.

No. 1279. Inorganic Materials and Pharmaceutical Preparations: 1990 to 1993

PRODUCT	Product code	Unit	1990	1991	1992	1993
INORGANIC FERTILIZERS						
Ammonia, synthetic anhydrous:	28731 31					
Total production		1,000 sh. tons	17,003	17,169	17,924	16,858
Shipments		1,000 sh. tons	10,382	10,002	10,642	10,072
Shipments value		Mil. dol..	1,072	1,036	1,095	1,134
Ammonium nitrate, original solution:	28731 50					
Total production		1,000 sh. tons	7,714	7,819	7,981	8,255
Ammonium sulfate:	28731 57					
Total production		1,000 sh. tons	2,519	2,243	2,391	2,424
Shipments		1,000 sh. tons	2,529	2,251	2,239	2,415
Shipments value		Mil. dol..	130	130	140	150
Urea (100%):	28732					
Total production		1,000 sh. tons	8,217	8,133	8,766	8,286
Shipments		1,000 sh. tons	5,362	5,432	5,343	5,215
Shipments value		Mil. dol..	640	723	696	621
Nitric acid (100%):	28731 11					
Total production		1,000 sh. tons	7,931	7,927	8,136	8,254
Shipments		1,000 sh. tons	647	623	672	668
Shipments value		Mil. dol..	81	82	85	88
Phosphoric acid (100% P2O5):	28741 81					
Total production	28741 85	1,000 sh. tons	12,035	12,109	12,826	11,515
Shipments		1,000 sh. tons	4,170	4,398	4,375	3,688
Shipments value		Mil. dol..	1,226	1,282	1,182	969
Sulfuric acid, gross (100%):	28193					
Total production		1,000 sh. tons	44,337	43,466	44,524	39,348
Shipments		1,000 sh. tons	11,879	11,536	10,950	11,408
Shipments value		Mil. dol..	589	587	529	480
Superphosphates and other fertilizer materials (100% P2O5):	28742					
Total production		1,000 sh. tons	8,982	9,044	9,696	8,645
Shipments		1,000 sh. tons	9,016	9,017	9,666	8,666
Shipments value		Mil. dol..	2,711	2,832	2,530	2,043
INORGANIC CHEMICAL SHIPMENTS						
Alkalies and chlorine	2812	Mil. dol..	3,187	3,029	2,761	2,295
Chlorine (100% Cl).	28121	Mil. dol..	478	260	194	561
Sodium hydroxide (caustic soda)	28123	Mil. dol..	2,341	2,387	2,206	1,365
Other alkalies	28125	Mil. dol..	361	375	353	363
Alkalies and chlorine n.s.k.	28120 00	Mil. dol..	7	7	7	7
Inorganic color pigments	2816	Mil. dol..	2,261	2,065	2,428	2,391
Titanium dioxide (composite and pure) (commodity weight)	28161 00	Mil. dol..	2,131	1,949	2,316	2,253
Inorganic chemicals n.e.c.	2819	Mil. dol..	13,612	12,817	12,838	12,212
Sulfuric acid, gross (new and fortified)	28193	Mil. dol..	589	587	529	480
Inorganic acids, except nitric, phosphoric and sulfuric	28194	Mil. dol..	603	559	505	455
Aluminum oxide, except natural alumina	28195	Mil. dol..	1,499	1,081	947	920
Aluminum compounds	28196	Mil. dol..	665	662	595	576
Potassium and sodium compounds (except bleaches, alkalies, and alums)	28197	Mil. dol..	1,956	1,892	1,932	1,869
Chemical catalytic preparations	28198	Mil. dol..	1,221	1,238	1,350	1,405
Other inorganic chemicals n.e.c..	28199	Mil. dol..	6,846	6,567	6,533	6,107
Industrial inorganic chemicals n.s.k.	28190 00	Mil. dol..	232	232	220	199
Household bleaching compounds	28422 00	Mil. dol..	724	826	920	888
PHARMACEUTICAL PREP. SHIPMENTS						
Affecting neoplasms, endocrine systems, and metabolic disease	28341	Mil. dol..	2,743	2,877	3,179	(NA)
Acting on the central nervous system and sense organs	28342	Mil. dol..	7,219	7,431	8,103	(NA)
Acting on the cardiovascular system	28343	Mil. dol..	4,815	4,810	4,877	(NA)
Acting on the respiratory system.	28344	Mil. dol..	3,724	4,260	5,024	(NA)
Acting on the digestive system.	28345	Mil. dol..	4,840	5,625	7,050	(NA)
Acting on the skin	28346	Mil. dol..	1,558	1,579	1,687	(NA)
Vitamin, nutrient, and hematinic preps.	28347	Mil. dol..	2,588	2,787	2,998	(NA)
Affecting parasitic and infective disease	28348	Mil. dol..	5,411	6,006	7,060	(NA)
Pharmaceutical preps. for veterinary use	28349	Mil. dol..	1,057	1,462	1,350	(NA)

NA Not available.

Source: U.S. Bureau of the Census, *Current Industrial Reports,* MA28A, MA28B, and MA28G, annual.

No. 1280. Engines, Refrigeration and Heating Equipment, and Pumps and Compressors: 1991 to 1993

PRODUCT	Product code	Unit	1991	1992	1993
Internal combustion engines produced	(X)	1,000	16,791	18,868	21,342
Gasoline (except outboard, aircraft, and auto).	35191	1,000	16,220	18,217	20,538
Nonautomotive diesel (except aircraft).	35193	1,000	184	178	191
Automotive diesel	35194	1,000	383	469	608
Natural gas and LPG	35196	1,000	4	4	5
Air-conditioning, heating equipment shipments:					
Heat transfer equipment	35851	Mil. dol. . . .	3,925	4,118	4,705
Unitary air-conditioners.	35852	Mil. dol. . . .	3,533	3,913	3,977
Commercial refrigeration equipment	35853 pt	Mil. dol. . . .	148	(D)	183
Compressors and compressor units	35854	Mil. dol. . . .	2,317	2,931	3,101
Condensing units, refrigeration (complete)	35855	Mil. dol. . . .	210	203	206
Room air-conditioners and dehumidifiers	35856	Mil. dol. . . .	812	774	821
Nonelectric warm air furnaces and humidifiers	3585C pt	Mil. dol. . . .	957	1,216	1,323
Pumps and compressors [1]	(X)	Mil. dol. . . .	5,119	5,916	6,140
Industrial pumps	35611	Mil. dol. . . .	2,263	2,465	2,499
Hydraulic fluid power pumps and motors	35617,8	Mil. dol. . . .	−2	(NA)	(NA)
Domestic water systems	35613	Mil. dol. . . .	273	331	330
Oil well, oilfield, and other pumps					
(including laboratory pumps)	35615	Mil. dol. . . .	597	805	911
Compressors and vacuum pumps	35631	Mil. dol. . . .	1,993	2,315	2,403

D Data withheld to avoid disclosure of company data.   NA Not available.   X Not applicable.   [1] Excludes hand pumps, automotive circulating pumps, compressors for icemaking and refrigeration equipment, air conditioning units, and replacements and repair parts for pumps and compressors.

Source: U.S. Bureau of the Census, *Current Industrial Reports,* MA35L, MA35M, and MA35P, annual.

No. 1281. Computers and Office and Accounting Machines—Shipments: 1992 and 1993

PRODUCT	Product code	Number of companies, 1992	QUANTITY (number)		VALUE (mil. dol.)	
			1992	1993	1992	1993
Electronic computers (automatic data processors) .	3571	192	(X)	(X)	28,571	28,447
Large-scale processing equipment [1]	35713	27	23	31	5,267	4,095
Medium- and small-scale processing equipment [2]	35714	43	181	190	3,347	2,426
Personal computers and workstations	35715	76	9,104	13,383	17,060	17,782
Portable computers	35716	25	1,590	2,694	1,644	2,575
Computer storage devices and equipment	35721	103	4,490	12,537	6,202	7,017
Parts for computer storage devices and						
subassemblies	35722	29	(X)	(X)	1,357	1,394
Computer terminals	35751	73	3,851	4,360	1,708	1,531
Parts for computer terminals	35752	18	(X)	(X)	192	276
Computer peripheral equipment, n.e.c.	35771	265	(X)	(X)	8,506	10,007
Calculating and accounting machines	35784	15	(X)	(X)	967	1,029
Automatic typing and word processing machines. .	35792	5	2,323	1,717	465	343
Mailing, letter handling, addressing machines	35795	30	906	1,258	1,152	1,268
Other office machines, n.e.c.	35799	48	(X)	(X)	(D)	(D)
Magnetic and optical recording media	36950	64	(X)	(X)	4,337	4,293

NA Not available.   X Not applicable.   [1] 64 megabytes in MINIMUM main memory configuration.   [2] Up to 64 megabytes in MINIMUM main memory configuration.

Source: U.S. Bureau of the Census, *Current Industrial Report,* MA35R, annual.

No. 1282. Metalworking Machinery—Shipments: 1987 to 1993

[In millions of dollars]

PRODUCT	Product code	1987	1988	1989	1990	1991	1992	1993
Metalworking machinery	(X)	2,669	2,858	3,514	3,426	3,172	3,074	3,222
Metal cutting type	(X)	1,781	1,735	2,429	2,371	2,139	2,000	2,085
Machining centers [1]	3541A	218	334	442	437	362	378	485
Station type machines	3541B	300	225	563	502	450	435	375
Other metal cutting machine tools [2]	3541C	174	165	174	142	196	167	166
Metal forming type.	(X)	888	1,123	1,086	1,065	1,033	1,074	1,140

X Not applicable.   [1] Multi-function numerically controlled machines.   [2] Excludes those designed primarily for home workshops, labs, etc.

Source: U.S. Bureau of the Census, *Current Industrial Reports,* MQ35W, annual.

No. 1283. Switchgear, Switchboard Apparatus, Relays, and Industrial Controls—Shipments: 1988 to 1993

[In millions of dollars]

PRODUCT	Product code	Companies, 1992 (number)	1988	1989	1990	1991	1992	1993
Power circuit breakers	36132	23	386	393	388	368	481	516
Low volt panelboards & dist. boards [1] . . .	36133	117	1,664	1,747	1,722	1,643	1,531	1,620
Fuses and fuse equipment [2]	36134	19	390	419	419	409	413	478
Molded case circuit breakers, 1,000 volts and under	36135	37	948	952	959	917	955	1,017
Duct [3]	36136	24	152	188	194	184	189	200
Switchgear, except ducts	36139	121	1,100	1,319	1,324	1,398	1,615	1,459
General purpose and other relays	36251	117	873	835	805	772	782	703
Specific purpose industrial controls. . . .	36252	196	1,808	1,928	2,020	1,993	1,916	2,124
General purpose industrial controls	36253	255	2,655	2,971	2,912	2,879	2,778	2,999
Motor controller accessories [4]	36254	122	459	503	452	434	448	444

[1] Includes other switching and interruption devices, 1,000 volts and below. [2] Under 2,300 volts, except power distribution cutouts. [3] Includes plug-in units and accessories, 1,000 volts and under, consisting of enclosed sectionalized prefabricated bus bars rated 20 amperes or more, associated structures and fittings. [4] Includes parts for industrial controls.

Source: U.S. Bureau of the Census, *Current Industrial Reports*, MA36A, annual.

No. 1284. Selected Industrial Air Pollution Control Equipment—Shipments: 1993

[Quantity in number of units, value in millions of dollars]

PRODUCT	Product code	Number of companies	NEW ORDERS		SHIPMENTS		BACKLOG (Dec. 31)	
			Quantity	Value	Quantity	Value	Quantity	Value
Selected industrial air pollution control equipment.	35646	107	66,504	667,138	65,737	761,246	6,202	573,256
Particulate emissions collectors	(X)	85	54,876	447,899	54,343	466,801	5,480	212,457
Electrostatic precipitators	35646 51	18	469	129,798	441	171,771	143	84,012
Fabric filters	35646 54	53	48,248	217,365	47,463	207,073	4,482	59,626
Mechanical collectors	35646 55	38	5,016	57,535	5,196	47,852	608	28,019
Wet scrubbers	35646 58	30	1,143	43,201	1,243	40,105	247	40,800
Gaseous emissions control devices	(X)	35	1,000	152,740	1,012	226,530	266	329,044
Catalytic oxidation systems	35646 70	11	96	18,202	117	20,249	38	8,250
Thermal and direct oxidation systems .	35646 72	15	270	32,990	294	32,499	22	8,665
Scrubbers (gas absorber)	35646 73	11	577	12,004	528	11,110	152	3,719
Dry flue gas desulfurization systems . .	35646 75	9	(D)	(D)	(D)	(D)	(D)	(D)
Gas absorbers	35646 76	8	34	5,927	(D)	(D)	(D)	(D)
Other types of industrial air pollution control equipment	35646 79	22	10,628	66,499	10,382	67,915	456	31,755

D Data withheld to avoid disclosure of company data.   X Not applicable.

Source: U.S. Bureau of the Census, *Current Industrial Reports*, MA35J, annual.

No. 1285. Fluid Power Products—Shipments: 1988 to 1993

[In millions of dollars. Includes aerospace]

PRODUCT	Product code	1988	1989	1990	1991	1992	1993
Fluid power products, incl. aerospace. . .		6,785	6,915	7,207	6,475	6,330	6,490
Hydraulic valves, nonaerospace type	34921	615	629	663	606	583	649
Pneumatic valves, nonaerospace type	34922	445	463	458	434	458	503
Aerospace type hydraulic & pneumatic valves.	34923	400	451	498	527	443	357
Fittings for metal and plastic tubing [1]	34924	460	505	500	471	516	557
Hydraulic and pneumatic fittings and couplings for hose (nonaerospace)	34925	649	625	620	552	630	663
Hydraulic and pneumatic hose or tube end fitting and assemblies (aerospace)	34926	327	336	394	386	354	302
Parts for hydraulic & pneumatic valves	34927	219	206	209	161	151	125
Filters for hydraulic and pneumatic fluid power systems	35692	310	352	385	409	395	434
Hydraulic and pneumatic cylinders etc.:							
Nonaerospace.	35931	907	909	941	800	864	975
Aerospace	35932	636	646	636	510	479	457
Parts for hydraulic and pneumatic cylinders [2] .	35933	291	281	264	269	171	168
Hydraulic fluid power pumps and motors	35941	1,178	1,180	1,240	997	974	1,014
Parts for pumps and motors	35942	348	333	399	354	312	285

[1] Used in fluid and power transfer systems (nonaerospace). [2] Includes parts for actuators, accumulators, cushions, and nonvehicular shock absorbers.

Source: U.S. Bureau of the Census, *Current Industrial Reports*, MA35N, annual.

No. 1286. Selected Instruments and Related Products—Shipments: 1987 to 1993

[In millions of dollars]

PRODUCT	Product code	1987	1988	1989	1990	1991	1992	1993
Automatic regulating and control valves	34918	1,221	1,262	1,331	1,418	1,537	1,579	1,586
Solenoid-operated valves (except nuclear and fluid power transfer)	34919	327	338	374	346	360	405	408
Aeronautical, nautical, and navigational instruments	38121	2,270	2,365	2,521	2,518	2,672	2,519	2,146
Search & detection, navigation & guidance systems and equipment	38122	30,911	31,145	30,840	32,420	31,774	31,311	28,678
Laboratory apparatus and laboratory furniture [1]	38210	1,549	1,565	1,698	1,675	1,612	1,715	1,587
Controls for monitoring residential and commercial environments and appliance	38220	2,093	2,207	2,224	1,982	1,982	2,197	2,270
Process control instruments	38230	4,084	4,348	4,743	5,224	5,230	5,731	5,918
Integrating and totalizing meters for gas and liquids.	38242	589	610	647	725	698	727	739
Counting devices	38243	198	193	206	210	226	273	290
Motor vehicle instruments [2]	38244	232	682	637	1,457	1,330	1,576	1,702
Integrating instruments, electrical	38251	401	388	401	396	390	439	461
Test equipment for testing electrical, radio and communication circuits, and motors	38252	6,144	6,248	6,134	6,156	6,525	6,493	6,626
Instruments to measure electricity	38253	647	663	620	586	584	558	526
Analytical, scientific instruments (except optical).	38260	3,046	3,442	4,042	4,412	4,519	4,886	4,999
Sighting, tracking, and fire-control equipment, optical type	38271	726	609	595	581	547	771	731
Optical instruments and lenses [3]	38274	1,215	1,270	1,274	1,252	1,292	1,322	1,318
Aircraft engine instruments (except flight)	38291	520	505	508	579	682	590	554
Physical properties and kinematic testing equip..	38292	859	894	946	1,012	1,024	1,149	1,171
Nuclear radiation detection and monitoring instruments	38294	637	654	606	567	570	533	520
Commercial, geophysical, meteorological, and general purpose instruments	38295	358	1,072	1,035	1,140	1,335	1,361	1,215
Surveying and drafting instruments	38296	247	270	270	274	235	255	304

[1] Beginning 1987, includes laboratory furniture. Prior to 1987, laboratory furniture was included in product class 38296. [2] Beginning 1990, includes some data previously classified in product class 37149, "Other motor vehicle parts and accessories, new, n.e.c." [3] Beginning 1992, product classes 38272, "Binoculars and astronomical instruments," and 38273, "Other optical instruments and lenses" were combined into product class 38274; prior years have been restated to reflect revision.

Source: U.S. Bureau of the Census, *Current Industrial Reports*, MA38B, annual.

No. 1287. Robots—Shipments: 1987 to 1989

[Based on a survey of all known manufacturers of robots, robot accessories, and components. Shipment value represents the net sales price, f.o.b. plant, to the customer or branch to which the products are shipped, net of discounts, allowances, freight charges and returns. A robot is a reprogrammable multifunctional manipulator designed to move materials, parts, tools, or specialized devices through variable programmed motions for the performance of a variety of tasks]

ROBOTS, ACCESSORIES, AND COMPONENTS	QUANTITY (number)			VALUE (mil. dol.)		
	1987	1988	1989	1987	1988	1989
Robots, robot accessories, and components	(X)	(X)	(X)	284	238	256
Robots, complete.	6,037	4,603	2,217	220	164	151
Servo-controlled robots	2,677	2,072	1,840	203	138	136
Point-to-point type:						
Welding, etc	675	304	273	65	32	29
Foundry, forging, and/or heat treating [1]	28	31	34	3	3	9
Assembly for nonelectronic/elec. prods.	535	296	238	20	8	8
Material handling and/or parts transfer	726	247	162	48	27	26
Continuous-path type:						
Welding, etc.	110	79	31	9	4	2
Spraying, painting, gluing, and/or sealing	297	292	254	41	30	35
Fettling/grinding/polishing, and/or deburring [2]	306	823	848	17	33	26
Nonservo-controlled robots.	215	336	377	8	17	15
Other robots	3,145	2,195	([3])	9	9	([3])
Robot accessories, subassemblies, etc	(X)	(X)	(X)	65	74	105
Miscellaneous receipts	(X)	(X)	(X)	8	6	3

X Not applicable.   [1] Includes all point-to-point robots, except assembly, material handling, and/or parts transfer. [2] Includes other continuous-path type, not elsewhere classified.   [3] Beginning 1989, data no longer available for other robots which included education hobby, experimental, and nonindustrial robots.

Source: U.S. Bureau of the Census, *Current Industrial Reports*, MA35X(89-1).

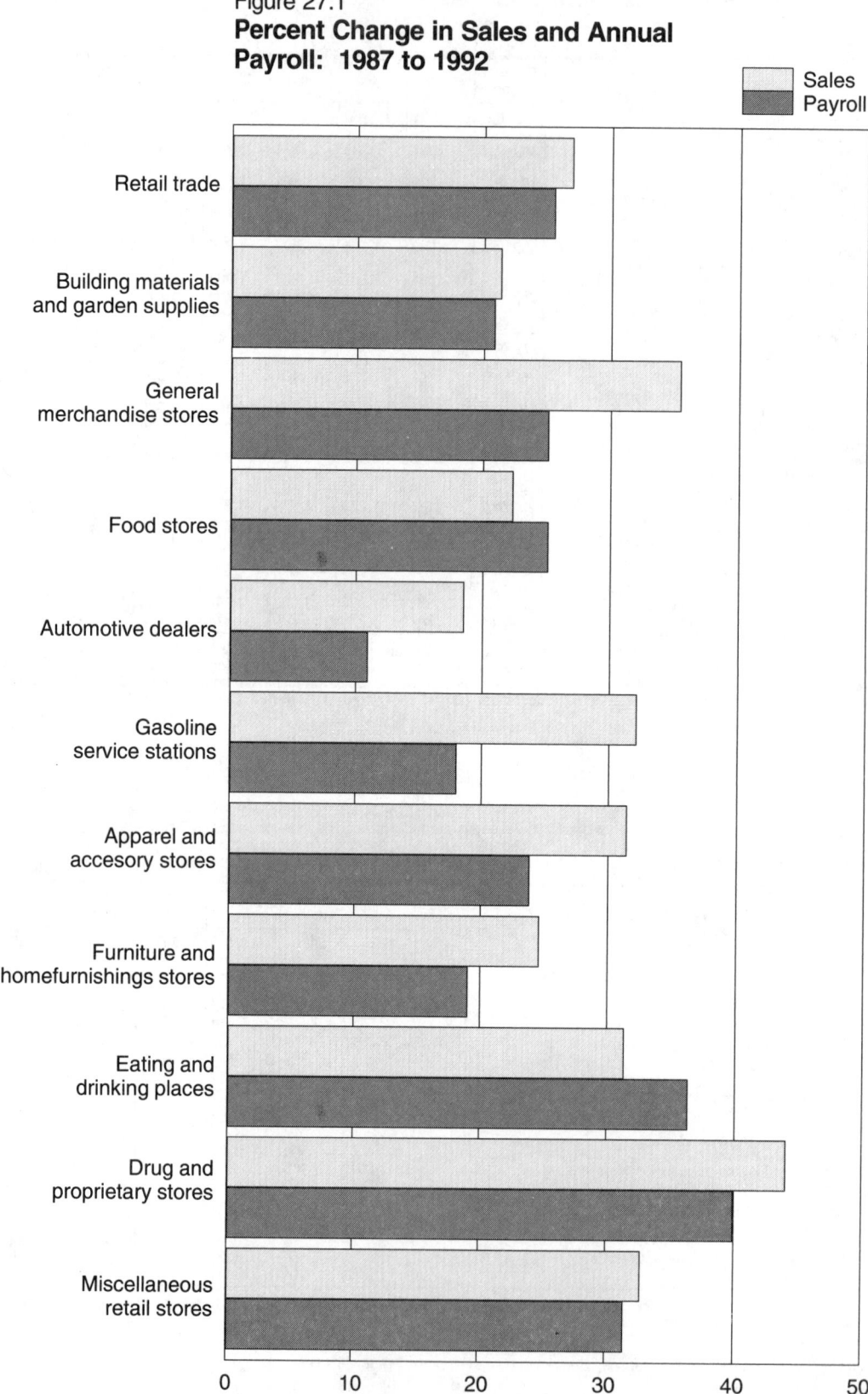

Figure 27.1
**Percent Change in Sales and Annual
Payroll: 1987 to 1992**

Sales
Payroll

Retail trade

Building materials
and garden supplies

General
merchandise stores

Food stores

Automotive dealers

Gasoline
service stations

Apparel and
accesory stores

Furniture and
homefurnishings stores

Eating and
drinking places

Drug and
proprietary stores

Miscellaneous
retail stores

0   10   20   30   40   50

Source: Chart prepared by U.S. Bureau of the Census. For data, see table 1291.

Domestic Trade and Services

This section presents statistics relating to the distributive trades and service industries. Data shown for the trades, classified by kind of business, and for the various categories of services (e.g., personal, business, repair, hotel) cover sales or receipts, establishments, employees, payrolls, and other items. The principal sources of these data are census reports and survey reports of the Bureau of the Census. Data on gross product in trade and service industries usually appear in the *Survey of Current Business*, issued by the U.S. Bureau of Economic Analysis. Financial data for firms engaged in retail, wholesale, or service activities appear in the annual *Statistics of Income*, published by the Internal Revenue Service.

Censuses.—Censuses of retail trade and wholesale trade have been taken at various intervals since 1929. Limited coverage of the service industries started in 1933. Beginning with the 1967 census, legislation provides for a census of each area to be conducted every 5 years (for years ending in "2" and "7"). The industries covered in the censuses and surveys of business are those classified in three divisions defined in the *Standard Industrial Classification Manual* (see text, section 13). *Retail trade* refers to places of business primarily engaged in selling merchandise for personal or household consumption; *wholesale trade,* to establishments primarily engaged in selling goods to dealers and distributors for resale or to purchasers who buy for business and farm uses; and *services,* to establishments primarily engaged in providing a wide range of services for individuals and for businesses.

Beginning with the 1954 Censuses of Retail Trade and Service Industries, data for nonemployer establishments are included and published separately. The census of wholesale trade excludes establishments with no paid employees. Beginning in 1977, sales taxes and finance charges are excluded from sales (or receipt) figures of the three censuses. In 1982 and prior censuses, the count of establishments represented the number

---

In Brief

Retail sales, 1994:

Total	$2.2 trillion
Automotive dealers	$.5 trillion
Food stores	$.4 trillion

Annual receipts of taxable service firms ($ billions):

	1990	1993
Business services	278	336
Health services	247	304

---

in business at the end of the year. Beginning 1987, the count of establishments represents those in business at any time during the year.

For the 1987 and 1992 Censuses of Service Industries hospitals operated by governmental organizations are included. Government-operated facilities in other service kind-of-business classifications are excluded from the census. In 1987 and 1992, data were not collected for elementary and secondary schools, colleges and universities, labor unions and similar organizations, and political organizations.

The census of retail trade beginning in 1977, excludes nonemployer direct sellers. Beginning 1982, the census treated each leased department in a store as a separate establishment and classified it according to the kind of business it conducted. In prior years, data for leased departments were consolidated with the data for stores in which they were located.

Current surveys.—Current sample surveys conducted by the Bureau of the Census cover various aspects of the retail and wholesale trade and selected service industries. Its *Monthly Retail Trade Report* contains monthly estimates of sales, inventories, inventory/sales ratios, and sales of organizations operating 11 or more retail stores, for the United States, by kind of business. In addition, monthly retail sales data for census regions and divisions, large States, metropolitan areas, and cities are included.

Annual figures on sales, year-end inventories, and sales/inventory ratios, by kind of business, appear in the *Combined Annual and Revised Monthly Retail Trade Report.*

Statistics from the Bureau's monthly wholesale trade survey include national estimates of merchant wholesalers' sales, inventories, and stock-sales ratios by major summary groups—durable and nondurable—and selected kinds of business. Merchant wholesalers are those wholesalers who take title to the goods they sell (e.g., jobbers, exporters, importers, major distributors). These data, based on reports submitted by a sample of firms, appear in the *Monthly Wholesale Trade Report.* Annual figures on sales, sales-inventory ratios, and year-end inventories appear in the *Combined Annual and Revised Monthly Wholesale Trade Report.* The *Service Annual Survey* provides annual estimates of receipts for selected service kinds of business for the United States as a whole.

For the current sample survey programs, retail trade coverage is the same as for the census; wholesale trade coverage is limited to merchant wholesalers; and selected services coverage is less inclusive than the census.

Estimates obtained from annual and monthly surveys are based on sample data and are not expected to agree exactly with results that would be obtained from a complete census of all establishments. Data include estimates for sampling units not reporting.

Statistical reliability.—For a discussion of statistical collection and estimation, sampling procedures, and measures of statistical reliability applicable to Census Bureau data, see Appendix III.

Historical statistics.—Tabular headnotes provide cross-references, where applicable, to *Historical Statistics of the United States, Colonial Times to 1970.* See Appendix IV.

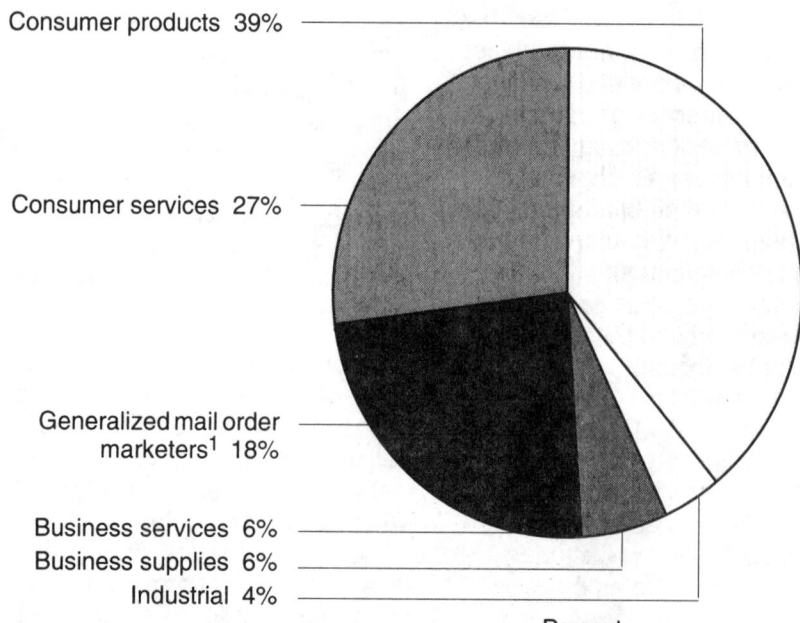

Figure 27.2
U.S. Mail Order Sales, by Kind of Business: 1992

1992 Mail Order Sales: $168.1 Billion

Consumer products 39%

Consumer services 27%

Generalized mail order marketers[1] 18%

Business services 6%
Business supplies 6%
Industrial 4%

Percent

[1]Mail order as part of the overall selling channel mix of multichannel industrial marketers not specializing in mail order selling.

Source: Chart prepared by U.S. Bureau of the Census. For data, see table 1301.

No. 1288. Gross Domestic Product in Domestic Trade and Service Industries in Current and Constant (1987) Dollars: 1987 to 1992

[**In billions of dollars, except percent**. For definition of gross domestic product, see text, section 14. Based on 1987 Standard Industrial Classification]

INDUSTRY	CURRENT DOLLARS				CONSTANT (1987) DOLLARS			
	1987	1990	1991	1992	1987	1990	1991	1992
Wholesale and retail trade	**744.8**	**878.7**	**905.3**	**951.9**	**744.8**	**797.6**	**797.7**	**827.6**
Percent of gross domestic product	16.4	15.8	15.8	15.8	16.4	16.3	16.4	16.6
Wholesale trade.	303.1	363.0	373.4	394.4	303.1	319.5	324.5	340.9
Retail trade	441.8	515.7	531.9	557.5	441.8	478.1	473.2	486.7
Services.	**782.5**	**1,040.0**	**1,093.3**	**1,182.7**	**782.5**	**869.4**	**871.4**	**889.9**
Percent of gross domestic product	17.2	18.8	19.1	19.6	17.2	17.8	17.9	17.9
Hotels and other lodging places	42.6	49.9	52.4	53.9	42.6	45.0	45.5	46.0
Personal services.	31.0	36.3	36.8	39.0	31.0	31.0	29.9	30.4
Business services.	141.6	198.2	199.2	220.5	141.6	172.6	167.9	173.7
Auto repair, services, and garages	38.2	46.2	48.1	48.8	38.2	38.9	38.9	37.1
Miscellaneous repair services.	13.7	17.1	16.2	16.9	13.7	15.9	14.6	13.9
Motion pictures	13.7	18.6	18.3	19.3	13.7	15.5	14.6	14.6
Amusement and recreation services	28.1	40.2	44.8	51.1	28.1	34.6	36.8	40.8
Health services	228.9	304.4	335.2	364.4	228.9	241.4	248.0	252.0
Legal services.	61.1	79.6	82.3	88.7	61.1	66.1	64.7	66.0
Educational services.	30.3	38.1	43.4	45.6	30.3	32.1	34.8	35.1
Social services, membership organizations	45.7	60.6	65.0	70.2	45.7	55.0	57.5	59.6
Other services	100.0	141.3	142.4	154.1	100.0	112.3	110.0	112.2
Private households.	7.7	9.4	9.2	10.1	7.7	8.9	8.2	8.8

Source: U.S. Bureau of Economic Analysis, *Survey of Current Business*, November 1993 and October 1994.

No. 1289. Retail Trade—Summary: 1963 to 1992

[1972 through 1982 based on 1972 Standard Industrial Classification (SIC) code; beginning 1987 based on 1987 SIC code. Prior years based on earlier editions of SIC. Comparability of data over time is affected by changes in the SIC code. See also *Historical Statistics, Colonial Times to 1970*, series T 43-47 and T 79-91]

ITEM	Unit	1963	1967	1972	1977	1982	1987	1992
Firms, total [1]	1,000	1,532	1,577	1,665	1,567	1,573	1,992	2,212
Multiunit establishments [1][2].	1,000	240	234	301	343	415	498	528
Establishments, total [1]	1,000	1,708	1,763	1,780	1,855	1,923	2,420	2,672
With payroll	1,000	1,206	1,192	1,265	1,304	1,324	1,504	1,526
With sales of $1,000,000 or more	1,000	(NA)	(NA)	74	119	193	259	326
Consumer Price Index: [3]								
All items	1982-84=100 . .	30.6	33.4	41.8	60.6	96.5	113.6	140.3
All commodities.	1982-84=100 . .	34.4	36.8	44.5	64.2	97.0	107.7	129.1
Sales	Bil. dol.	244	310	457	723	1,066	1,540	1,949
By establishments with payroll	Bil. dol.	233	295	440	700	1,039	1,493	1,895
By multiunit establishments [2]	Bil. dol.	90	124	202	341	567	844	1,137
Percent of total sales.	Percent	36.6	39.8	44.0	47.1	53.2	56.5	60.0
Percent of multiunit sales by 100-or-more establishment multiunits [2][4]	Percent	43.1	46.7	55.8	55.8	54.5	54.6	57.0
In 1987 dollars [5]	Bil. dol.	712	843	1,042	1,170	1,175	1,540	1,669
Percent of sales by corporations	Percent	61.9	67.4	76.4	79.8	84.6	88.9	89.9
Per capita sales: [6]								
Current dollars	Dollars	1,296	1,571	2,186	3,291	4,601	6,357	7,643
Constant (1987) dollars [5]	Dollars	3,777	4,269	4,978	5,325	5,073	6,357	6,544
Sales as percent of personal income	Percent	51.3	48.0	46.6	45.2	39.6	40.5	37.9
Payroll, entire year [7]	Bil. dol.	27.6	36.2	55.4	85.9	123.6	177.5	222.9
Percent of sales [7]	Percent	11.9	12.3	12.6	12.3	11.9	11.9	11.8
Paid employees, March 12 pay period [8]	1,000	8,410	9,381	11,211	13,040	14,468	17,780	18,407

NA Not available.   [1] Through 1982, represents the number of establishments and firms in business at the end of the year. Beginning 1987, represents the number of establishments and firms in business at any time during year.   [2] Establishments operated by firms which operate at two or more locations.   [3] Source: U.S. Bureau of Labor Statistics, *Monthly Labor Review*. Beginning 1982, CPI-U annual averages, see text, section 14.   [4] Prior to 1982, data provided for percent of multiunit sales by 101-or-more establishment units.   [5] Based on implicit price deflators for retail sales supplied by U.S. Bureau of Economic Analysis.   [6] Based on estimated resident population as of July 1.   [7] Covers only establishments with payroll.   [8] For 1963 week including November 15.

Source: Except as noted, U.S. Bureau of the Census, *U.S. Census of Business: 1963*, vol. I; *1967*, vol. I; and *Census of Retail Trade, 1972*, RC72-S-1; *1977*, RC77-52; *1982*, RC82-A-52 and RC82-I-1; *1987*, RC87-A-52, RC87-N-1, and RC87-S-1; and *1992*, RC92-A-52, RC92-N-1, and RC92-S-1.

Domestic Trade and Services

No. 1290. Retail Trade—Establishments, Employees, and Payroll: 1990 and 1992

[Excludes government employees, railroad employees, self-employed persons, etc. For statement on methodology, see Appendix III]

KIND OF BUSINESS	1987 SIC code [1]	ESTABLISHMENTS (1,000)		EMPLOYEES (1,000)		PAYROLL (bil. dol.)	
		1990	1992	1990	1992	1990	1992
Retail trade, total	(G)	**1,529.7**	**1,564.2**	**19,815**	**19,672**	**241.7**	**258.6**
Building materials and garden supplies [2]	52	71.9	69.6	703	685	11.9	12.2
Lumber and other building materials	521	27.5	25.5	403	395	7.5	7.7
Paint, glass, and wallpaper stores	523	10.2	10.1	54	50	0.9	0.9
Hardware stores	525	19.0	19.0	143	143	1.9	2.0
Retail nurseries and garden stores	526	10.1	10.3	76	71	1.0	1.0
Mobile home dealers	527	4.2	4.1	23	23	0.4	0.5
General merchandise stores [2]	53	36.6	36.3	2,135	2,059	22.9	24.4
Department stores	531	10.1	10.1	1,710	1,614	18.3	19.1
Variety stores	533	10.0	9.8	109	96	1.0	0.9
Misc. general merchandise stores	539	15.0	15.4	310	344	3.6	4.3
Food stores [2]	54	186.1	190.3	3,124	3,090	35.8	38.8
Grocery stores	541	132.5	136.4	2,757	2,728	32.4	35.0
Meat and fish markets	542	9.3	9.2	54	52	0.6	0.7
Fruit and vegetable markets	543	2.9	3.3	19	20	0.2	0.3
Candy, nut, confectionery stores	544	5.4	5.5	29	30	0.2	0.3
Retail bakeries	546	19.9	21.3	176	177	1.5	1.7
Automotive dealers and service stations [2]	55	207.3	202.8	2,104	1,982	40.0	41.0
New and used car dealers	551	26.1	25.5	917	859	23.9	24.5
Used car dealers	552	14.3	16.9	56	61	1.0	1.1
Auto and home supply stores	553	43.4	44.8	305	308	5.1	5.5
Gasoline service stations	554	104.8	100.1	701	649	7.5	7.6
Boat dealers	555	4.6	4.6	34	27	0.6	0.6
Recreational vehicle dealers	556	2.7	2.8	24	22	0.5	0.5
Motorcycle dealers	557	3.4	3.5	22	23	0.4	0.4
Apparel and accessory stores [2]	56	150.2	146.6	1,193	1,168	12.2	12.6
Men's and boys' clothing stores	561	14.7	14.1	108	96	1.5	1.4
Women's clothing stores	562	50.2	49.5	439	439	4.0	4.1
Women's accessory and specialty stores	563	7.7	8.6	46	45	0.5	0.5
Children's and infants' wear stores	564	5.6	5.6	36	39	0.3	0.3
Family clothing stores	565	17.8	19.4	283	295	3.0	3.3
Shoe stores	566	37.4	35.9	206	187	2.2	2.2
Misc. apparel and accessory stores	569	9.1	9.1	47	47	0.5	0.5
Furniture and homefurnishings stores [2]	57	108.1	113.1	749	800	12.3	14.0
Furniture and homefurnishings stores [2]	571	61.1	63.5	430	413	7.2	7.3
Furniture stores	5712	30.8	31.5	245	233	4.3	4.4
Floor covering stores	5713	13.2	13.7	77	73	1.5	1.5
Drapery and upholstery stores	5714	3.4	3.2	16	14	0.2	0.2
Misc. homefurnishings stores	5719	13.3	14.6	92	91	1.1	1.2
Household appliance stores	572	10.0	10.7	63	114	1.1	2.0
Radio, television, and computer stores [2]	573	34.2	37.4	245	266	3.9	4.5
Radio, TV, and electronic stores	5731	16.5	17.2	120	127	2.1	2.2
Computer and software stores	5734	5.1	7.0	33	46	0.8	1.1
Record and prerecorded tape stores	5735	7.1	7.9	60	63	0.6	0.6
Eating and drinking places [2]	58	402.6	430.1	6,461	6,571	49.6	54.3
Eating places	5812	286.8	324.9	5,700	5,719	43.8	47.5
Drinking places	5813	43.8	51.0	267	284	2.0	2.2
Miscellaneous retail [2]	59	349.0	359.2	2,487	2,496	33.2	36.0
Drug stores and proprietary stores	591	50.0	48.7	593	611	8.3	9.6
Liquor stores	592	30.8	30.3	141	134	1.6	1.6
Used merchandise stores	593	15.0	19.1	79	96	0.9	1.2
Sporting goods and bicycle shops	5941	21.4	24.1	139	148	1.6	1.9
Book stores	5942	11.7	13.1	86	99	0.8	1.0
Stationery stores	5943	4.8	5.5	34	44	0.4	0.6
Jewelry stores	5944	26.6	26.8	161	148	2.3	2.2
Hobby, toy, and game shops	5945	9.4	10.5	83	90	1.0	1.0
Camera, photo supply stores	5946	3.6	3.5	22	22	0.4	0.4
Gift, novelty, and souvenir shops	5947	29.5	34.8	164	172	1.4	1.6
Sewing, needlework, and piece goods	5949	8.2	8.3	68	67	0.5	0.5
Catalog and mail-order houses	5961	7.2	7.4	141	139	2.6	2.9
Merchandising machine operators	5962	5.1	5.8	76	73	1.3	1.3
Direct selling establishments	5963	8.8	10.0	107	99	1.7	1.6
Fuel dealers	598	12.0	11.8	100	92	2.2	2.2
Florists	5992	25.8	27.1	131	125	1.2	1.3
Optical goods stores	5995	13.2	13.9	66	67	1.1	1.2
Administrative and auxiliary	(X)	18.0	16.2	860	822	23.7	25.4

X Not applicable. [1] Based on 1987 Standard Industrial Classification; see text, section 13. [2] Includes kinds of business not shown separately.

Source: U.S. Bureau of the Census, *County Business Patterns*, annual.

No. 1291. Retail Trade Establishments—Number, Sales, Payroll, and Employees, by Kind of Business: 1987 and 1992

[Each kind-of-business classification includes leased departments classified in that kind of business as if they were separate establishments. See *Historical Statistics, Colonial Times to 1970*, series T 79-196 for similar but not comparable data]

KIND OF BUSINESS	1987 SIC code [1]	ALL ESTABLISHMENTS				ESTABLISHMENTS WITH PAYROLL		
		Number [2] (1,000)		Sales (mil. dol.)		Annual payroll, 1992 (mil. dol.)	Paid employees [3] (1,000)	
		1987	1992	1987	1992		1987	1992
Retail trade, total [4]	(G)	2,420	2,672	1,540,263	1,949,193	222,868	17,780	18,407
Building materials & garden supplies	52	107	105	83,454	100,837	11,790	668	666
Building materials, supply stores	521, 3	51	51	61,302	75,358	8,423	432	435
Lumber and other building materials	521	(NA)	36	(NA)	68,930	7,519	380	386
Paint, glass, and wallpaper stores	523	(NA)	15	(NA)	6,428	903	52	49
Hardware stores	525	27	25	11,036	12,729	1,871	138	136
Retail nurseries and garden stores	526	21	22	5,809	6,773	1,018	71	71
Mobile home dealers	527	8	7	5,307	5,978	478	27	23
General merchandise stores	53	57	63	181,971	246,420	24,503	2,003	2,079
Department stores (incl. leased depts.) [5]	531	10	11	153,679	190,785	(NA)	(NA)	(NA)
Department stores (excl. leased depts.) [5]	531	10	11	144,017	186,423	20,136	1,651	1,719
Variety stores	533	21	23	7,134	9,516	1,088	121	116
Misc. general merchandise stores	539	26	29	30,819	50,481	3,279	231	243
Food stores [6]	54	290	278	309,460	377,098	37,228	2,855	2,969
Grocery stores	541	197	186	290,979	358,148	34,425	2,502	2,682
Meat and fish markets	542	[7]11	[7]9	[7]5,616	[7]5,041	556	59	45
Retail bakeries	546	31	31	5,194	5,732	1,407	185	157
Automotive dealers [6]	55 ex. 554	194	207	342,896	406,936	31,807	1,373	1,268
New and used car dealers	551	28	24	280,529	333,801	24,421	940	860
Used car dealers	552	75	92	18,295	25,511	1,132	55	63
Auto and home supply stores	553	67	63	26,622	29,817	4,683	286	269
Boat dealers	555	[7]5	[7]5	[7]6,824	[7]5,537	558	35	27
Recreational vehicle dealers	556	[7]3	[7]3	[7]5,538	[7]6,314	514	25	22
Motorcycle dealers	557	[7]4	[7]4	[7]3,475	[7]4,163	427	27	22
Gasoline service stations	554	137	120	104,769	136,950	7,569	702	675
Apparel and accessory stores [6]	56	197	221	79,322	104,211	12,039	1,121	1,145
Men's and boys' clothing stores	561	19	19	9,017	10,197	1,440	115	105
Women's clothing, specialty stores	562, 3	77	87	29,208	35,749	4,170	455	467
Women's clothing stores	562	64	65	26,366	31,828	3,690	419	423
Family clothing stores	565	27	33	21,472	33,222	3,469	268	310
Shoe stores	566	43	42	14,594	18,122	2,185	205	184
Furniture and homefurnishings stores	57	180	189	78,072	96,947	11,869	703	702
Furniture stores	5712	46	48	26,740	31,216	4,355	247	233
Homefurnishings stores	5713, 4, 9	63	64	17,737	21,132	2,835	176	181
Floor covering stores	5713	[7]14	[7]14	[7]9,226	[7]9,616	1,382	75	69
Household appliance stores	572	17	16	8,642	8,407	965	65	54
Radio, television, computer stores	573	54	61	24,953	36,192	3,714	215	235
Radio, TV, and electronic stores	5731	(NA)	28	(NA)	20,275	2,112	123	121
Computer and software stores	5734	8	15	2,799	7,120	607	22	30
Record and prerecorded tape stores	5735	[7]6	[7]8	[7]3,930	[7]5,860	593	44	60
Eating and drinking places	58	490	558	153,462	200,163	52,570	6,100	6,548
Eating places [6]	5812	402	474	142,627	187,758	50,307	5,787	6,244
Restaurants and lunchrooms	5812 pt.	[7]155	[7]170	[7]66,364	[7]85,178	25,369	2,822	2,989
Refreshment places	5812 pt.	[7]138	[7]164	[7]56,870	[7]77,686	18,808	2,352	2,652
Cafeterias	5812 pt.	[7]7	[7]6	[7]3,778	[7]3,619	1,037	138	109
Drinking places	5813	88	84	10,834	12,406	2,263	313	304
Drug stores and proprietary stores	591	56	51	54,142	77,788	9,060	574	588
Miscellaneous retail stores [4][6]	59 ex. 591	710	881	152,716	201,842	24,434	1,682	1,769
Liquor stores	592	45	40	19,826	21,698	1,523	157	133
Used merchandise stores	593	89	124	5,217	8,219	1,124	69	93
Misc. shopping goods stores [6]	594	263	311	53,777	71,650	8,563	706	750
Sporting goods, bicycle shops	5941	50	55	11,256	15,617	1,733	121	137
Book stores	5942	19	23	5,338	8,329	928	72	92
Jewelry stores	5944	50	55	12,925	15,259	2,224	163	148
Hobby, toy, and game shops	5945	28	38	7,451	11,298	992	76	95
Gift, novelty, souvenir shops	5947	79	104	8,446	12,036	1,467	151	164
Nonstore retailers [4]	596	66	116	34,878	52,790	6,280	318	339
Catalog and mail-order houses	5961	31	66	20,765	35,538	3,079	123	150
Merchandising machine operators	5962	24	36	6,258	7,082	1,232	74	70
Direct selling establishments [4]	5963	11	14	7,855	10,170	1,969	121	119
Fuel dealers	598	17	15	14,503	14,202	1,928	99	82
Florists	5992	50	55	5,441	6,433	1,207	125	122
Optical goods stores	5995	15	16	3,480	4,917	1,114	54	65

NA Not available. [1] Based on 1987 Standard Industrial Classification; see text, section 13. [2] Represents the number of establishments in business at any time during year. [3] For pay period including March 12. [4] Excludes nonemployer direct sellers, SIC 5963. [5] Includes sales from catalog order desks. [6] Includes other kinds of businesses, not shown separately. [7] Covers only establishments with payroll.

Source: U.S. Bureau of the Census, *1987* and *1992 Census of Retail Trade*, RC87-N-1, RC92-A-52, and RC92-N-1.

No. 1292. Retail Trade Sales—Summary: 1980 to 1994

[Sales and inventories for leased departments and concessions are tabulated in the kind-of-business category of the leased department or concession. Based on Current Business Survey, see Appendix III. Minus sign (-) indicates decrease. See also *Historical Statistics, Colonial Times to 1970*, series T 245, 246, and 255]

YEAR	CURRENT DOLLARS							CONSTANT (1987) DOLLARS [4]		
	Total sales (bil. dol.)	Annual percent change [1]	Per capita [2] (dol.)	Index of sales (1982= 100)	Durable goods (bil. dol.)	Nondurable goods (bil. dol.)		Total sales (bil. dol.)	Annual percent change [1]	Per capita [2] (dol.)
						Total	Dept. stores [3]			
1980	957	6.7	4,213	89.5	299	658	86	1,193	-3.8	5,252
1981	1,039	8.5	4,527	97.1	325	714	96	1,201	0.6	5,232
1982	1,069	3.0	4,616	100.0	336	733	100	1,189	-1.0	5,130
1983	1,170	9.4	5,005	109.4	391	779	109	1,272	7.0	5,440
1984	1,287	10.0	5,457	120.3	454	832	120	1,360	6.9	5,767
1985	1,375	6.8	5,779	128.6	498	877	126	1,420	4.4	5,969
1986	1,450	5.4	6,037	135.6	541	909	134	1,498	5.5	6,240
1987	1,541	6.3	6,361	144.2	576	965	144	1,539	2.7	6,351
1988	1,656	7.5	6,774	154.9	629	1,027	152	1,599	3.9	6,539
1989	1,759	6.2	7,127	164.5	657	1,102	161	1,641	2.7	6,650
1990	1,845	4.9	7,396	172.5	669	1,176	166	1,653	0.7	6,627
1991	1,856	0.6	7,361	173.6	650	1,206	173	1,619	-2.1	6,421
1992	1,952	5.2	7,652	182.5	704	1,248	186	1,671	3.2	6,552
1993	2,074	6.3	8,047	194.0	778	1,297	200	1,758	5.2	6,822
1994	2,237	7.9	8,592	209.2	880	1,357	218	1,866	6.1	7,168

[1] Change from immediate prior year. [2] Based on Bureau of the Census estimates of resident population as of July 1. [3] Excludes leased departments. [4] Source: U.S. Bureau of Economic Analysis, *Survey of Current Business*, monthly; and unpublished data.

No. 1293. Retail Trade—Sales, by Kind of Business: 1980 to 1994

[**In billions of dollars**. See headnote, table 1292. Based on Current Business Survey, see Appendix III. See also *Historical Statistics, Colonial Times to 1970*, series T 245-271]

KIND OF BUSINESS	1987 SIC code [1]	1980	1985	1989	1990	1991	1992	1993	1994
Retail trade, total.		957.4	1,375.0	1,759.0	1,844.6	1,855.9	1,951.6	2,074.5	2,237.0
Durable goods stores, total [2]		299.2	498.1	657.2	668.8	650.0	703.6	777.5	880.4
Building materials and garden supplies	52	50.8	71.2	92.4	94.6	91.5	100.8	109.6	122.5
Building materials, supply stores	521,3	35.0	50.8	67.5	70.3	68.2	75.4	82.4	92.8
Hardware stores	525	8.3	10.5	12.6	12.5	12.1	12.7	13.2	14.2
Automotive dealers	55 exc. 554	164.1	303.2	386.0	387.6	372.6	406.9	456.9	526.3
Motor vehicle, misc. automotive dealers. . .	551,2,5,6,7,9	146.2	278.0	356.5	356.8	343.0	377.1	426.1	493.5
Motor vehicle dealers	551,2	137.7	263.1	337.7	338.7	325.2	359.3	405.7	466.1
Motor vehicle dealers, franchised. . . .	551	130.5	251.6	311.6	316.0	301.3	333.8	377.2	434.1
Auto and home supply stores	553	18.0	25.2	29.5	30.8	29.6	29.8	30.8	32.8
Furniture and homefurnishings stores [2] . . .	57	44.2	68.3	91.3	91.5	91.7	97.0	105.7	119.6
Furniture, homefurnishings stores	571	26.3	38.3	51.2	50.5	49.5	52.3	55.7	60.2
Furniture stores	5712	(NA)	23.9	31.9	30.8	30.2	31.2	33.4	35.6
Floor covering stores	5713	(NA)	7.9	10.7	10.7	10.1	10.4	10.6	11.8
Household appliance, radio, TV, and computer stores	5722,31,34	14.0	25.1	32.7	33.0	33.6	35.8	40.7	48.9
Household appliance stores	5722	(NA)	8.4	9.3	8.8	8.3	8.4	9.0	9.5
Radio, TV, and computer stores	5731,34	(NA)	16.7	23.4	24.3	25.3	27.4	31.7	39.4
Sporting goods and bicycle shops	5941	(NA)	8.7	14.2	15.0	15.1	15.6	17.1	19.2
Book stores	5942	(NA)	4.5	6.5	7.4	7.7	8.3	9.0	9.6
Jewelry stores	5944	(NA)	11.2	14.4	15.2	14.7	15.3	16.5	16.9
Nondurable goods stores, total [2]		658.1	876.9	1,101.8	1,175.8	1,206.0	1,248.0	1,297.0	1,356.5
General merchandise stores	53	109.0	158.6	206.3	215.5	226.7	246.4	264.6	282.5
Department stores [3]	531	85.5	126.4	160.5	165.8	172.9	186.4	200.5	218.1
Variety stores	533	7.8	8.5	7.9	8.3	8.3	9.5	9.0	7.9
Misc. general merchandise stores.	539	15.7	23.8	37.8	41.4	45.5	50.5	55.1	56.6
Food stores	54	220.2	285.1	347.0	368.3	374.5	377.1	385.4	397.8
Grocery stores	541	205.6	269.5	328.1	348.2	354.3	358.1	365.7	376.3
Gasoline service stations . . . . [2]	554	94.1	113.3	122.9	138.5	137.3	137.0	138.3	142.2
Apparel and accessory stores [2]	56	49.3	70.2	92.3	95.8	97.4	104.2	107.2	109.6
Men's and boys' clothing stores	561	7.7	8.5	10.5	10.5	10.4	10.2	10.3	12.2
Women's clothing specialty stores	562,3	17.6	26.1	32.2	32.8	32.9	35.8	36.8	34.9
Women's clothing stores	562	15.9	23.6	29.0	29.8	29.9	31.8	33.0	31.5
Family clothing stores.	565	10.8	17.8	26.4	28.4	30.5	33.2	34.9	37.1
Shoe stores	566	10.5	13.1	17.3	18.0	17.5	18.1	18.2	18.3
Eating and drinking places	58	90.1	127.9	177.8	190.1	194.4	200.2	213.7	228.4
Eating places	5812	80.4	117.6	167.2	178.7	182.6	187.8	201.4	215.5
Restaurants, lunchrooms, cafeterias . . .	5812 pt	(NA)	68.2	92.9	99.9	102.4	103.6	110.1	117.0
Refreshment places	5812 pt	(NA)	48.1	71.5	75.7	77.2	81.5	88.4	95.4
Drinking places	5813	(NA)	10.3	10.7	11.5	11.8	12.4	12.3	12.8
Drug stores and proprietary stores	591	31.0	47.0	63.3	70.6	75.5	77.8	79.6	81.5
Liquor stores	592	16.9	19.5	20.1	21.7	22.5	21.7	21.6	21.8
Nonstore retailers	596	22.8	28.3	43.6	45.6	49.1	55.2	57.9	63.9
Catalog and mail-order houses	5961	(NA)	15.8	26.2	26.6	30.0	35.5	38.8	46.0
Fuel dealers.	598	(NA)	16.8	14.7	15.6	14.6	14.2	13.9	13.2

NA Not available. [1] Based on 1987 Standard Industrial Classification code; see text, section 13. [2] Includes kinds of business, not shown separately. [3] Excludes leased departments.

Source of tables 1292 and 1293: Except as noted, U.S. Bureau of the Census, *Current Business Reports, Combined Annual and Revised Monthly Retail Trade, January 1985 Through December 1994*, (BR/94-RV) and prior issues.

No. 1294. Retail Trade—Sales of Multiunit Organizations, by Kind of Business: 1980 to 1994

[Data based on sales of companies which had 11 or more retail establishments according to the most recent update of multiestablishment files selected with certainty (i.e., their sales size exceeded specified dollar volume cutoffs which varied by kind of business). For details, see source. See also *Historical Statistics, Colonial Times to 1970*, series T 197-219]

KIND OF BUSINESS	1987 SIC code [1]	SALES (bil. dol.)						PERCENT OF TOTAL RETAIL SALES		
		1980	1990	1991	1992	1993	1994	1980	1990	1994
Total		**361.3**	**733.4**	**758.8**	**804.8**	**847.1**	**898.1**	**37.3**	**39.8**	**40.1**
Durable goods stores		35.2	96.5	99.4	109.5	120.5	137.8	11.4	14.4	15.7
Auto and home supply stores [2]	553	4.7	9.6	9.7	10.3	11.0	11.9	26.2	31.1	36.3
Nondurable goods stores [2]		326.0	636.9	659.4	695.3	726.5	760.3	49.1	54.2	56.0
General merchandise stores	53	101.6	205.1	214.5	233.5	252.1	271.1	90.6	95.2	95.9
Department stores	531	83.2	162.8	170.1	183.7	198.0	215.8	96.1	98.2	98.9
Variety stores	533	6.3	5.5	5.3	6.5	6.2	5.3	80.9	66.6	67.8
Misc. general merchandise stores	539	12.1	36.8	39.1	43.4	47.9	50.0	58.1	88.9	88.4
Food stores	54	119.8	217.2	223.7	226.4	230.5	237.2	54.4	59.0	59.6
Grocery stores	541	118.1	214.1	220.3	223.3	227.5	234.1	57.4	61.5	62.2
Apparel and accessory stores [2]	56	21.1	58.0	61.0	65.5	68.8	71.7	42.7	60.5	65.4
Women's clothing specialty stores	562,3	8.3	19.5	20.3	22.0	22.9	21.7	47.1	59.5	62.1
Family clothing	565	(NA)	21.0	23.0	25.2	26.9	29.4	(NA)	74.0	79.4
Shoe stores	566	5.3	11.8	11.5	12.2	12.6	12.7	50.8	65.6	69.3
Eating places	5812	22.6	45.7	45.1	47.3	50.0	52.0	28.1	25.6	24.1
Drug stores and proprietary stores	591	16.8	42.6	45.8	48.1	49.4	51.7	54.3	60.4	63.4

NA Not available.   [1] Based on 1987 Standard Industrial Classification code; see text, section 13.   [2] Includes kinds of business not shown separately.

No. 1295. Retail Trade—Merchandise Inventories and Inventory/Sales Ratios, by Kind of Business: 1990 to 1994

[As of **Dec. 31**. Includes warehouses. Adjusted for seasonal variations. Sales data also adjusted for holiday, and trading-day differences. See headnote, table 1292]

KIND OF BUSINESS	1987 SIC code [1]	INVENTORIES AT COST [2] (bil. dol.)				INVENTORY/SALES RATIOS			
		1990	1992	1993	1994	1990	1992	1993	1994
Total		**239.8**	**252.0**	**267.7**	**290.0**	**1.57**	**1.50**	**1.49**	**1.51**
Excluding automotive group		*176.7*	*188.0*	*198.4*	*212.3*	*1.45*	*1.42*	*1.44*	*1.44*
Durable goods stores [3]		121.1	122.9	133.7	149.1	2.27	2.00	1.91	1.98
Building materials and garden supplies	52	17.0	17.3	18.5	20.9	2.28	1.97	1.85	2.00
Automotive dealers	55 exc. 554	63.1	64.0	69.2	77.7	2.05	1.80	1.65	1.74
Furniture and homefurnishings stores	57	17.4	17.9	19.9	23.0	2.36	2.12	2.15	2.15
Nondurable goods stores [3]		118.7	129.0	134.0	140.9	1.19	1.21	1.22	1.21
General merchandise stores	53	42.4	48.7	52.4	56.1	2.34	2.31	2.32	2.30
Department stores	531	33.4	38.1	41.2	44.5	2.40	2.38	2.39	2.34
Food stores	54	25.0	25.8	26.1	26.8	0.81	0.81	0.80	0.78
Apparel and accessory stores	56	19.7	22.2	22.8	23.5	2.50	2.48	2.52	2.56

[1] Based on 1987 Standard Industrial Classification code; see text, section 13.   [2] Excludes supplies and equipment used in store and warehouse operations that are not for resale.   [3] Includes kinds of business not shown separately.

Source of tables 1294 and 1295: U.S. Bureau of the Census, *Current Business Reports, Combined Annual and Revised Monthly Retail Trade, January 1985 Through December 1994* (BR/94-RV).

No. 1296. Motor Vehicle Factory Sales and Retail Sales: 1980 to 1993

[**In thousands**. See also *Historical Statistics, Colonial Times to 1970*, series Q 148 and 150]

YEAR	1980	1984	1985	1986	1987	1988	1989	1990	1991	1992	1993
Factory sales, total	**8,067**	**10,696**	**11,359**	**10,909**	**10,907**	**11,225**	**10,869**	**9,769**	**8,783**	**9,747**	**10,856**
Passenger cars	6,400	7,621	8,002	7,516	7,085	7,105	6,807	6,050	5,407	5,685	5,960
Trucks and buses	1,667	3,075	3,357	3,393	3,821	4,121	4,062	3,719	3,375	4,062	4,895
Retail sales, total	**11,466**	**14,483**	**15,724**	**16,323**	**15,189**	**15,679**	**14,713**	**14,146**	**12,539**	**13,116**	**14,199**
Passenger cars (new), total	8,979	10,390	11,042	11,460	10,277	10,530	9,772	9,300	8,175	8,213	8,518
Domestic	6,581	7,952	8,205	8,215	7,081	7,526	7,073	6,897	6,137	6,277	6,734
Imports	2,398	2,439	2,838	3,245	3,196	3,004	2,699	2,403	2,038	1,937	1,783
Trucks (new), total	2,487	4,093	4,682	4,863	4,912	5,149	4,941	4,846	4,365	4,903	5,681
Domestic	2,001	3,475	3,902	3,921	4,055	4,508	4,403	4,215	3,813	4,481	5,287
Imports	486	618	780	942	857	641	538	631	551	422	394

Source: American Automobile Manufacturers Association, Detroit, MI, *AAMA Motor Vehicle Facts and Figures*, annual (copyright).

No. 1297. Franchised New Car Dealerships—Summary: 1980 to 1993

ITEM	Unit	1980	1985	1986	1987	1988	1989	1990	1991	1992	1993
Dealerships [1]	Number	27,900	24,725	24,825	25,150	25,025	25,000	24,825	24,200	23,500	22,950
Sales	Bil. dol.	130.5	251.6	270.4	280.5	302.6	310.3	313.8	298.4	328.9	375.1
New cars	1,000	8,979	11,046	11,463	10,225	10,595	9,830	9,296	8,176	8,211	8,518
Used vehicles	1,000	9,717	13,360	13,540	13,260	14,600	14,610	14,180	14,270	15,140	16,300
Employment	1,000	745.2	856.9	896.7	926.0	960.1	956.4	926.4	886.4	876.0	907.4
Annual payroll	Bil. dol.	11.0	20.1	21.7	22.6	24.7	24.4	24.1	23.3	23.9	25.7
Advertising expenses	Bil. dol.	1.2	2.8	3.2	3.7	4.0	3.9	3.6	3.4	3.7	4.1
Dealer pretax profits as a percentage of sales	Percent	0.6	2.2	2.2	1.9	1.7	1.0	1.0	1.0	1.4	1.6
Inventory: [2] Domestic: [3]											
Total	1,000	1,506	1,510	1,687	1,710	1,549	1,677	1,450	1,263	1,196	1,310
Days' supply	Days	71	58	63	74	65	72	66	64	62	61
Imported: [3]											
Total	1,000	458	271	392	567	647	648	597	584	539	456
Days' supply	Days	55	30	37	55	65	70	74	86	83	71

[1] At beginning of year. [2] Annual average. [3] Classification based on where automobiles are produced (i.e., automobiles manufactured by foreign companies but produced in the United States are classified as domestic).
Source: National Automobile Dealers Association, McLean, VA, *NADA Data*, annual.

No. 1298. Retail Foodstores—Number and Sales, by Type: 1980 to 1993

TYPE OF FOODSTORE	NUMBER [1] (1,000)					SALES [2] (bil. dol.)					PERCENT DISTRIBUTION			
											Number		Sales	
	1980	1990	1991	1992	1993	1980	1990	1991	1992	1993	1980	1993	1980	1993
Total	253.4	253.3	252.1	250.8	249.6	220.2	368.3	374.5	377.1	385.4	100.0	100.0	100.0	100.0
Grocery stores	178.3	170.2	168.0	165.9	163.8	205.6	348.2	354.3	358.1	365.7	70.4	65.6	93.4	94.9
Supermarkets [3]	26.8	25.0	24.9	24.6	24.5	157.0	260.1	268.9	274.3	281.0	10.6	9.8	71.3	72.9
Conventional	21.5	13.7	12.8	12.5	12.2	114.7	90.7	81.8	84.7	78.6	8.5	4.9	52.1	20.4
Superstore [4]	3.2	5.8	5.9	6.0	6.3	27.8	87.6	91.1	93.3	100.6	1.2	2.5	12.6	26.1
Warehouse [5]	1.7	3.4	3.5	3.4	3.1	6.6	33.1	35.3	33.1	31.9	0.7	1.3	3.0	8.3
Combination food and drug [6]	0.5	1.6	2.1	2.1	2.2	6.3	34.8	46.0	42.3	45.8	0.2	0.9	2.9	11.9
Superwarehouse [7]	(Z)	0.3	0.5	0.5	0.5	1.6	12.6	13.8	13.9	15.3	(Z)	0.2	0.7	4.0
Hypermarket [8]	(Z)	0.1	0.1	0.1	0.2	(NA)	1.3	0.9	7.0	8.8	(Z)	0.1	(NA)	2.3
Convenience stores [9]	35.8	51.7	50.7	49.9	49.5	18.9	47.7	48.5	49.8	50.8	14.1	19.8	8.6	13.2
Superette [10]	115.7	93.5	92.4	91.4	89.8	29.7	40.4	36.9	34.1	33.9	45.7	36.0	13.5	8.8
Specialized food stores [11]	75.0	83.2	84.0	84.9	85.8	14.6	20.1	20.2	19.0	19.7	29.6	34.4	6.6	5.1

NA Not available. Z Less than 50 or 0.05 percent. [1] Estimated. [2] Includes nonfood items. [3] A grocery store, primarily self-service in operation, providing a full range of departments, and having at least $2.5 million in annual sales in 1985 dollars. [4] Contains greater variety of products than conventional supermarkets, including specialty and service departments, and considerable nonfood (general merchandise) products. [5] Contains limited product variety and fewer services provided, incorporating case lot stocking and shelving practices. [6] Contains a pharmacy, a nonprescription drug department, and a greater variety of health and beauty aids than that carried by conventional supermarkets. [7] A larger warehouse store that offers expanded product variety and often service meat, deli, or seafood departments. [8] A very large store offering a greater variety of general merchandise—like clothes, hardware, and seasonal goods—and personal care products than other grocery stores. [9] A small grocery store selling a limited variety of food and nonfood products, typically open extended hours. [10] A grocery store, primarily self-service in operation, selling a wide variety of food and nonfood products with annual sales below $2.5 million (1985 dollars). [11] Primarily engaged in the retail sale of a single food category such as meat and seafood stores and retail bakeries.
Source: U.S. Dept. of Agriculture, Economic Research Service, *Food Marketing Review*, annual.

No. 1299. Percent of Supermarkets Offering Selected Services and Product Lines: 1990 and 1993

[In percent. Based on a sample survey of chain and independent supermarkets and subject to sampling variability; for details, see source]

SERVICE OR PRODUCT LINE OFFERED	TOTAL		CHAINS		INDEPENDENTS	
	1990	1993	1990	1993	1990	1993
Service delicatessen	73	79	76	81	69	77
Service bakery	60	62	66	66	53	55
Hot takeout food	55	55	59	57	49	52
Chilled prepared food	50	46	55	50	42	40
Service meat	42	47	45	47	37	46
Self-service delicatessen	38	50	38	52	39	46
Service fish	33	37	43	47	20	21
Separate cheese department	33	34	43	44	19	20
Salad bar	18	19	22	23	13	13
Plastic grocery bags	88	94	94	97	79	89
Reusable grocery bags	58	61	68	65	44	54
Carryout services	82	82	81	79	84	86
Scanning checkouts	71	85	79	91	61	75
Automated teller machines (ATM's)	20	38	28	46	10	25
Accept credit cards	19	51	23	55	13	44
Accept debit cards	(NA)	31	(NA)	36	(NA)	23
Pharmacy	15	20	22	28	6	8
Home delivery	(NA)	16	(NA)	10	(NA)	25

NA Not available.
Source: Maclean Hunter Media Inc., Stamford, CT, *Progressive Grocer, 61st Annual Report of the Grocery Industry* (copyright).

No. 1300. Commercial and Institutional Groups—Food and Drink Sales: 1980 to 1995

[Excludes military. Data refer to sales to consumers of food and alcoholic beverages. Sales are estimated. For details, see source]

TYPE OF GROUP	Number, 1992	SALES (mil. dol.)							
		1980	1985	1990	1991	1992	1993 [1]	1994 [1]	1995 [1]
Total	737,611	119,004	172,787	237,700	245,417	253,997	263,553	276,647	288,579
Commercial foodservice [2][3]	561,897	101,529	151,762	211,083	217,983	226,141	234,462	246,114	258,004
Eating places [2]	350,305	72,276	111,657	154,227	159,272	166,044	173,848	182,488	191,694
Full-service restaurants	167,262	39,307	57,939	76,072	78,355	80,313	83,102	85,290	87,799
Limited-service restaurants [4]	156,454	28,699	47,477	69,458	71,889	76,346	80,927	87,082	93,352
Bars and taverns [5]	37,227	7,785	8,338	9,212	9,442	9,131	8,875	9,106	9,352
Food contractors [2]	15,739	6,818	9,460	14,149	14,829	15,400	15,740	16,358	17,111
Manufacturing and industrial plants	(NA)	2,121	2,721	3,856	3,918	4,040	3,894	4,275	4,463
Colleges and universities	(NA)	1,140	1,738	2,788	3,072	3,238	3,527	3,505	3,646
Lodging places [2]	27,405	6,768	10,557	14,272	14,601	15,053	15,065	16,219	16,933
Hotel restaurants	17,283	4,964	8,986	12,907	13,281	13,733	13,791	14,917	15,638
Motel restaurants	8,482	1,151	975	820	790	788	753	775	766
Retail hosts [2][6]	110,700	3,264	5,254	9,888	10,380	10,828	11,010	11,779	12,328
Department store restaurants	4,980	857	865	950	980	1,047	(NA)	(NA)	(NA)
Grocery store restaurants [6]	44,966	830	2,074	5,733	6,013	6,214	(NA)	(NA)	(NA)
Gasoline service stations	36,481	492	1,052	1,681	1,824	1,985	(NA)	(NA)	(NA)
Recreation and sports	14,627	1,452	1,972	2,916	2,949	3,085	3,146	3,291	3,411
Institutional foodservice [2]	175,714	17,475	21,025	26,617	27,435	27,857	29,090	29,533	30,575
Employee foodservice	7,525	1,635	1,971	1,985	1,913	1,835	1,778	1,753	1,787
Industrial, commercial organizations	2,922	1,377	1,682	1,603	1,535	1,457	(NA)	(NA)	(NA)
Educational foodservice	96,444	4,610	5,978	7,671	8,223	8,548	8,977	9,077	9,375
Elementary and secondary schools	93,586	2,312	2,919	3,700	3,878	4,012	4,123	4,239	4,386
Hospitals	6,510	6,668	7,104	8,968	9,018	8,988	9,344	9,582	9,916
Miscellaneous [2]	31,568	1,521	2,077	2,845	2,993	3,053	3,386	3,376	3,528
Clubs	10,310	1,056	1,537	1,993	2,039	2,010	(NA)	2,339	2,410

NA Not available.　[1] Projection.　[2] Includes other types of groups, not shown separately.　[3] Data for establishments with payroll.　[4] Fast-food restaurants.　[5] For establishments serving food.　[6] Beginning 1990, a portion of delicatessen sales in grocery stores are considered foodservice.

Source: National Restaurant Association, Washington, DC, *Foodservice Numbers: A Statistical Digest for the Foodservice Industry*, 1992; *Foodservice Industry in Review*, annual; and *National Restaurant Association Foodservice Industry Forecast*, December 1994, (copyright).

No. 1301. U.S. Mail Order Sales, by Kind of Business: 1981 to 1992

[**In millions of dollars**. Mail order sales represent orders placed by mail, phone, or electronically without the person ordering coming to the point of sale to place the order, or the seller coming to the office or home of the orderer to take the order or using an agent to collect the order. Excludes orders placed at catalog desks or elsewhere in stores even in response to a catalog but does include products or services delivered in the store as long as the order was placed by mail, phone, or electronically. Statistics are generated independently each year and are not adjusted for any discontinuities of available data]

KIND OF BUSINESS	1981	1985	1986	1987	1988	1989	1990	1991	1992
Total mail order sales	50,705	93,780	99,540	111,240	122,720	137,390	151,640	162,050	168,050
Consumer, total	30,945	58,690	61,900	69,670	77,160	87,000	98,190	107,970	110,740
Products	24,325	38,470	39,750	43,380	48,380	54,490	57,500	64,940	65,210
Specialty [1]	15,330	26,770	28,720	34,370	38,370	41,990	44,520	50,010	50,560
Apparel	1,165	2,360	2,540	2,980	3,760	3,640	4,250	4,410	4,820
Books	1,775	2,080	2,150	2,230	2,500	2,520	2,760	2,770	3,120
Collectibles	980	1,410	1,240	1,460	1,580	1,510	1,690	1,810	2,000
Computer software & hardware	(NA)	(NA)	740	760	840	920	1,000	1,330	2,160
Health products	535	1,090	1,180	1,860	2,510	2,530	2,480	2,770	2,940
Magazines	2,890	4,310	4,660	4,900	5,320	6,360	6,020	6,580	6,340
Multi-products	1,775	2,610	3,020	4,700	5,400	7,020	7,410	8,440	6,860
Newspapers	(NA)	2,600	2,600	3,020	3,020	3,020	3,020	3,020	3,020
Sporting goods	825	1,310	1,670	2,010	2,380	2,750	3,460	3,910	3,650
General merchandise	8,995	11,700	11,030	9,010	10,010	12,500	12,980	14,930	14,650
Services	6,620	20,220	22,150	26,290	28,780	32,510	40,690	43,030	45,530
Non-financial	(NA)	10,710	12,030	13,690	16,180	19,390	21,660	25,740	26,620
Financial	(NA)	9,510	10,120	12,600	12,600	13,120	19,030	17,290	18,910
Business products and services	19,760	35,090	37,640	41,570	45,560	50,390	53,450	54,080	57,310
Business supplies [1]	(NA)	3,660	4,760	4,520	5,820	6,800	7,160	9,180	10,060
Data processing-oriented supplies	(NA)	750	950	1,020	1,300	1,520	1,520	2,060	2,320
Computer hardware	(NA)	(NA)	730	540	590	650	700	1,800	2,400
Business services [1]	(NA)	4,890	5,210	7,420	7,200	7,690	8,900	8,940	10,410
Communications	(NA)	1,850	2,150	3,700	3,420	3,450	4,240	4,140	5,580
Information	(NA)	1,600	1,900	1,970	2,200	2,460	2,500	2,500	2,500
Industrial	(NA)	1,340	1,440	1,580	2,160	3,640	5,390	5,560	6,440
Generalized mail order marketers [2]	(NA)	25,200	26,460	28,050	30,290	32,260	32,000	30,400	30,400

NA Not available.　[1] Includes other kinds of business not shown separately.　[2] Mail order as part of the overall selling channel mix of multichannel industrial marketers not specializing in mail order selling.

Source: Fishman, Arnold L., *Portable Mail Order Industry Statistics, 1993 Edition*, Richard D. Irwin, Inc., Burr Ridge, IL, 1994 (copyright). Data are extracted from *Annual Guides to Mail Order Sales, 1981-1993*, Marketing Logistics Inc., Highland Park, IL, 60035 (copyright).

No. 1302. Shopping Centers—Number, Gross Leasable Area, and Retail Sales, by Gross Leasable Area: 1990 to 1994

[As of **December 31**. A shopping center is a group of architecturally unified commercial establishments built on a site that is planned, developed, owned, and managed as an operating unit related in its location, size, and type of shops to the trade area that the unit serves. The unit provides on-site parking in definite relationship to the types and total size of the stores. The data base attempts to include all centers with three or more stores. Estimates are based on a sample of data available on shopping center properties; for details, contact source]

YEAR	Total	GROSS LEASABLE AREA (sq. ft.)					
		Less than 100,001	100,001- 200,000	200,001- 400,000	400,001- 800,000	800,001- 1,000,000	More than 1 million
NUMBER							
1990	36,515	23,231	8,756	2,781	1,102	288	357
1992	38,966	24,578	9,467	3,086	1,170	294	371
1993	39,633	24,993	9,611	3,166	1,194	295	374
1994	40,368	25,450	9,784	3,251	1,210	297	376
Percent distribution	100.0	63.0	24.2	8.1	3.0	0.7	0.9
Percent change, 1993-94	1.9	1.8	1.8	2.7	1.3	0.7	0.5
GROSS LEASABLE AREA							
1990 (mil. sq. ft.)	4,390	1,125	1,197	734	618	259	457
1992 (mil. sq. ft.)	4,679	1,190	1,289	807	653	264	475
1993 (mil. sq. ft.)	4,771	1,214	1,312	834	666	265	479
1994 (mil. sq. ft.)	4,861	1,239	1,339	859	675	267	482
Percent distribution	100.0	25.5	27.5	17.7	13.9	5.5	9.9
Percent change, 1993-94	1.9	2.0	2.0	3.0	1.4	0.8	0.6
RETAIL SALES							
1990 (bil. dol.)	706.4	205.1	179.5	108.0	91.7	45.1	77.0
1992 (bil. dol.)	768.2	223.3	195.3	117.2	99.6	49.0	83.8
1993 (bil. dol.)	806.6	234.4	205.0	123.1	104.6	51.5	88.1
1994 (bil. dol.)	851.3	247.3	216.3	129.9	110.3	54.3	93.1
Percent distribution	100.0	29.1	25.4	15.3	13.0	6.4	10.9
Percent change, 1993-94	5.5	5.5	5.5	5.6	5.5	5.5	5.6

No. 1303. Shopping Centers—Number, Gross Leasable Area, and Retail Sales, by State: 1994

[See headnote, table 1302. Minus sign (-) indicates decrease]

DIVISION AND STATE	Number	Gross leas- able area (mil. sq. ft.)	Retail sales (bil. dol.)	PERCENT CHANGE, 1993-94			DIVISION AND STATE	Number	Gross leas- able area (mil. sq. ft.)	Retail sales (bil. dol.)	PERCENT CHANGE, 1993-94		
				Num- ber	Gross leas- able area	Retail sales per sq. ft.					Num- ber	Gross leas- able area	Retail sales per sq. ft.
U.S ..	40,368	4,861	851.3	1.9	1.9	3.6	VA	1,162	151	25.8	2.1	2.7	3.1
							WV....	155	21	3.2	-	-	4.2
N.E	2,347	253	44.5	2.2	2.4	4.0	NC	1,412	147	24.1	1.9	1.1	4.2
ME	196	17	3.2	3.7	5.9	1.1	SC	760	73	13.1	1.5	0.8	4.2
NH	206	22	3.3	2.0	2.4	5.6	GA	1,418	150	26.3	1.5	2.4	2.7
VT	106	7	1.3	2.9	2.0	4.6	FL	3,086	390	75.1	1.4	1.3	4.9
MA	925	104	18.9	2.0	2.7	3.3	**E.S.C ..**	2,749	297	51.0	1.3	1.3	3.6
RI	187	17	3.1	1.6	2.0	3.5	KY	593	64	11.7	1.4	0.9	4.0
CT	727	86	14.7	2.3	1.4	5.2	TN	1,137	125	19.1	1.4	1.3	4.0
M.A	4,170	580	92.8	2.5	2.1	3.5	AL	601	70	13.2	1.3	1.4	3.2
NY	1,598	219	37.0	2.2	2.3	3.0	MS	418	39	7.2	1.0	1.8	2.1
NJ	1,051	144	22.7	3.9	2.9	3.3	**W.S.C....**	4,395	501	106.1	1.3	1.4	3.6
PA	1,521	216	33.1	1.9	1.4	4.1	AR	339	32	6.4	1.8	1.7	2.7
							LA	676	79	15.6	1.5	2.3	2.8
E.N.C	5,923	766	119.8	1.6	1.6	3.7	OK	556	58	11.4	1.3	1.9	2.2
OH	1,559	221	34.8	1.3	1.3	3.8	TX	2,824	331	72.7	1.2	1.1	4.1
IN	848	112	18.0	1.6	1.3	3.7							
IL	1,961	235	34.1	2.3	2.2	3.6	**Mountain .**	2,681	320	60.5	1.9	1.5	4.1
MI	967	127	21.0	0.9	1.5	3.8	MT	91	9	1.7	-	-	5.5
WI	588	72	12.0	1.0	1.4	4.2	ID	140	16	2.8	2.2	0.6	4.0
W.N.C. ...	2,385	301	54.0	1.8	1.3	3.9	WY....	53	6	1.2	-	-	4.8
MN	436	62	11.5	1.9	0.3	5.2	CO	674	87	18.5	0.9	0.8	5.3
IA	277	37	6.3	1.8	1.8	3.3	NM	288	27	5.4	2.1	1.2	3.7
MO	834	103	18.9	1.6	1.6	3.6	AZ	933	110	20.1	1.6	1.7	4.0
ND	84	9	1.8	5.0	3.1	2.3	UT	210	29	5.5	1.4	0.9	3.7
SD	51	7	1.1	-	-	5.1	NV	292	34	5.4	5.8	4.5	1.5
NE	245	32	4.8	2.1	1.2	3.9							
KS	458	51	9.7	1.6	1.6	3.5	**Pacific ...**	6,691	769	129.5	2.5	3.3	2.2
							WA	672	87	14.5	3.2	3.2	2.5
S.A	9,027	1,074	193.1	1.6	1.5	4.2	OR	441	50	7.6	1.6	1.8	4.1
DE	126	19	3.4	1.6	1.3	5.3	CA	5,350	607	102.8	2.5	3.4	2.0
MD	837	114	20.6	1.3	0.8	4.7	AK	63	8	1.6	5.0	0.6	6.3
DC	71	9	1.4	7.6	3.8	1.6	HI	165	17	3.1	3.1	5.8	2.3

- Represents zero.

Source of tables 1302 and 1303: National Research Bureau, Chicago, IL. Data for 1990 published by Monitor Publishing, Clearwater, FL, in *Monitor Magazine*, November/December 1991, (copyright). Data for 1992 published by Communication Channels, Inc., Atlanta, GA, in *Shopping Center World*, March 1993, (copyright). Data for 1993 and 1994 published by International Council of Shopping Centers in *Shopping Centers Today*, April 1994 and 1995, (copyright—Blackburn Marketing Services (U.S.), Inc.).

No. 1304. Retail Trade—Summary of Establishments, by State: 1992

[Kind-of-business classification based on 1987 Standard Industrial Classification code; see text, section 13]

DIVISION AND STATE	NUMBER OF ESTABLISHMENTS (1,000)				SALES (mil. dol.)				Annual payroll (mil. dol.)	Paid employees[3] (1,000)
	Total[1]	Establishments with payroll			Total[1]	Establishments with payroll				
		Total[2]	Food stores	Automotive dealers		Total[2]	Food stores	Automotive dealers		
U.S. . . .	2,671.7	1,526.2	180.6	96.4	1,949,193	1,894,880	369,199	395,148	222,868	18,407
N.E	151.2	88.9	10.7	4.5	111,407	108,272	22,178	19,100	13,234	1,011
ME. . . .	17.2	9.3	1.4	0.6	10,594	10,287	2,327	1,742	1,120	90
NH. . . .	14.8	8.6	1.1	0.5	11,389	11,099	2,409	2,052	1,261	97
VT. . . .	9.0	5.2	0.8	0.3	4,882	4,735	1,119	887	564	46
MA. . . .	63.7	38.5	4.5	1.7	49,042	47,663	9,443	8,339	5,986	470
RI	11.1	6.4	0.8	0.3	6,986	6,734	1,418	1,061	839	67
CT	35.4	21.0	2.3	1.1	28,515	27,754	5,463	5,019	3,464	241
M.A. . . .	394.2	231.1	31.3	11.1	278,202	269,783	54,904	49,806	32,523	2,472
NY	185.6	110.8	16.5	4.5	122,649	118,886	24,359	18,972	14,867	1,088
NJ	80.4	48.6	6.4	2.3	64,945	63,109	13,044	12,994	7,613	522
PA	128.2	71.7	8.4	4.3	90,607	87,788	17,501	17,841	10,043	862
E.N.C.	416.3	248.4	27.0	15.2	323,893	317,044	55,355	68,769	36,642	3,238
OH. . . .	106.1	63.7	7.5	4.0	80,699	79,031	15,048	16,660	9,257	838
IN	58.8	33.4	3.0	2.5	43,365	42,373	7,319	8,840	4,772	442
IL	107.2	64.8	6.7	3.6	87,595	85,766	14,934	18,389	10,076	846
MI	89.7	54.5	7.2	3.3	73,039	71,523	11,168	16,588	8,187	707
WI	54.5	32.0	2.7	1.9	39,195	38,351	6,886	8,292	4,350	405
W.N.C	202.4	117.6	11.5	8.1	135,772	132,394	24,275	28,849	15,205	1,417
MN. . . .	46.9	27.7	2.7	1.6	36,411	35,622	6,066	7,369	4,069	372
IA	34.0	19.7	1.8	1.4	20,477	19,960	4,084	4,417	2,304	226
MO	56.6	32.2	3.3	2.4	38,936	37,918	6,916	8,430	4,411	392
ND. . . .	7.7	4.8	0.5	0.3	4,816	4,697	783	1,124	514	52
SD. . . .	9.4	5.6	0.5	0.4	5,260	5,108	903	1,189	576	57
NE	19.2	11.4	1.1	0.8	11,837	11,522	2,156	2,368	1,308	132
KS	28.6	16.3	1.5	1.2	18,034	17,567	3,367	3,953	2,022	186
S.A.	475.8	280.1	33.0	19.2	359,143	349,935	67,503	77,842	40,784	3,444
DE	7.6	4.9	0.5	0.2	6,623	6,492	1,173	1,243	763	60
MD. . . .	46.3	28.0	3.2	1.4	38,436	37,625	7,730	7,677	4,801	367
DC. . . .	5.1	3.8	0.4	(Z)	3,637	3,587	640	126	642	47
VA	60.8	37.4	4.9	2.5	48,979	48,049	9,885	9,707	5,753	475
WV	18.6	10.5	1.5	0.8	11,540	11,194	2,541	2,349	1,208	112
NC	78.0	44.2	5.3	3.5	51,214	49,564	9,829	10,681	5,687	508
SC	40.9	22.8	2.7	1.8	25,618	24,743	5,179	5,083	2,845	264
GA	68.9	40.9	4.7	2.9	51,306	49,940	9,331	10,947	5,809	509
FL	149.6	87.7	9.7	6.0	121,789	118,742	21,195	30,029	13,276	1,102
E.S.C.	168.3	92.0	12.6	7.7	109,360	105,291	21,417	23,044	11,619	1,050
KY	40.8	22.1	3.0	1.8	26,241	25,268	5,280	4,927	2,803	261
TN	56.9	30.6	4.0	2.4	38,785	37,508	7,032	8,838	4,231	368
AL	43.4	24.1	3.1	2.2	28,845	27,734	5,682	6,175	2,989	270
MS	27.2	15.3	2.5	1.3	15,489	14,781	3,423	3,104	1,597	151
W.S.C . . .	294.1	155.4	20.7	11.6	202,205	195,631	39,775	44,836	21,709	1,883
AR	27.9	14.9	1.9	1.3	16,661	15,925	3,063	3,750	1,633	152
LA	39.6	22.6	3.7	1.5	28,635	27,806	6,166	5,842	3,096	289
OK. . . .	37.3	19.4	2.5	1.5	22,071	21,213	4,184	5,262	2,305	211
TX	189.3	98.4	12.6	7.2	134,837	130,686	26,363	29,982	14,676	1,230
Mountain . .	154.4	87.8	8.0	5.9	113,406	110,625	22,661	23,756	12,983	1,085
MT	11.5	6.8	0.7	0.4	6,449	6,247	1,282	1,380	697	64
ID	12.6	7.0	0.7	0.6	7,937	7,727	1,635	1,926	846	74
WY. . . .	6.4	3.7	0.3	0.3	3,651	3,554	674	737	413	37
CO. . . .	40.5	22.9	1.8	1.3	29,274	28,533	5,603	6,019	3,488	283
NM. . . .	17.0	9.3	0.9	0.7	11,596	11,279	2,202	2,305	1,294	112
AZ	37.0	21.4	2.2	1.4	29,999	29,366	6,176	6,379	3,437	288
UT	16.2	9.2	0.8	0.7	12,709	12,373	2,730	2,733	1,385	126
NV	13.1	7.5	0.8	0.5	11,791	11,546	2,359	2,276	1,422	99
Pacific	415.1	224.9	25.7	13.1	315,805	305,905	61,131	59,147	38,169	2,808
WA. . . .	53.4	31.7	3.6	2.2	41,720	40,910	8,193	8,086	5,081	381
OR. . . .	33.8	19.6	2.4	1.3	24,828	24,170	4,353	5,256	2,872	227
CA. . . .	307.9	162.1	18.5	9.1	232,647	224,593	45,350	43,531	28,064	2,051
AK	6.7	3.7	0.4	0.2	5,101	4,982	1,156	784	671	39
HI	13.2	7.8	0.9	0.3	11,510	11,250	2,079	1,490	1,481	110

Z Less than 50.   [1] Includes establishments without payroll.   [2] Includes other kinds of business not shown separately.   [3] For pay period including March 12.

Source: U.S. Bureau of the Census, *1992 Census of Retail Trade*, Geographic Area Series, RC92-A-1 to 52; and Nonemployer Statistics Series, RC92-N-1.

No. 1305. Retail Sales, by Type of Store and State: 1992 and 1993

[In millions of dollars, except as indicated. Kind-of-business classification based on 1987 Standard Industrial Classification code; see text, section 13. Data are estimates]

REGION, DIVISION, AND STATE	ALL STORES [1]				FOOD STORES				GENERAL MERCHANDISE STORES			
	1992, total	1993 Total	1993 Sales per household [2]		Total		Supermarkets		Total		Department stores	
			Amount (dol.)	Percent change, 1992-93	1992	1993	1992	1993	1992	1993	1992	1993
U.S. . . .	1,964,022	2,079,201	21,683	4.7	384,574	392,206	360,319	367,100	247,448	266,511	197,069	212,802
Northeast . .	399,627	405,976	21,263	1.3	82,080	80,469	74,671	73,131	39,905	42,894	32,791	35,400
N.E.	112,745	114,720	23,082	1.9	24,136	24,270	22,060	22,152	11,340	12,687	8,994	10,069
ME . . .	11,450	11,992	25,407	4.2	2,746	2,844	2,593	2,681	1,013	1,170	706	822
NH . . .	11,978	12,566	30,056	8.0	2,688	2,775	2,555	2,633	1,356	1,554	970	1,111
VT . . .	5,096	5,090	23,382	-0.8	1,220	1,206	1,145	1,130	357	392	249	275
MA . . .	47,451	48,498	21,505	2.0	9,810	9,906	8,785	8,857	4,889	5,498	3,887	4,379
RI . . .	7,357	7,593	19,970	3.3	1,564	1,595	1,362	1,387	835	947	659	749
CT . . .	29,412	28,980	23,621	-1.4	6,106	5,945	5,621	5,465	2,891	3,125	2,524	2,732
M.A . . .	286,883	291,257	20,622	1.1	57,944	56,199	52,611	50,979	28,564	30,207	23,797	25,331
NY . . .	126,079	127,516	19,079	1.0	25,546	24,728	22,757	22,002	12,166	12,843	9,839	10,476
NJ . . .	67,702	67,277	23,626	-1.5	13,658	12,950	12,555	11,889	6,292	6,500	5,384	5,594
PA . . .	93,102	96,464	21,007	3.0	18,739	18,520	17,300	17,088	10,106	10,864	8,574	9,261
Midwest . . .	471,615	510,728	22,215	7.3	83,217	87,222	78,006	81,674	63,346	68,330	52,384	56,557
E.N.C .	330,386	355,228	22,131	6.5	56,972	58,816	53,068	54,729	44,105	47,589	37,122	40,092
OH . . .	81,163	92,428	21,970	12.9	15,347	16,739	14,395	15,676	11,258	12,836	9,277	10,610
IN . . .	41,526	45,787	21,346	8.7	6,950	7,348	6,621	6,991	5,329	5,874	4,255	4,682
IL . . .	94,705	95,828	22,274	0.4	15,741	15,276	14,609	14,160	11,579	11,767	9,875	10,040
MI . . .	73,197	79,236	22,624	7.5	11,951	12,392	10,912	11,307	10,857	11,741	9,645	10,449
WI . . .	39,795	41,949	22,140	4.2	6,982	7,061	6,532	6,596	5,083	5,370	4,071	4,311
W.N.C .	141,229	155,500	22,410	9.1	26,246	28,406	24,938	26,945	19,240	20,741	15,262	16,465
MN . . .	35,686	39,583	23,020	9.8	6,084	6,630	5,749	6,256	5,019	5,466	3,623	3,936
IA . . .	22,000	24,293	22,324	9.7	4,531	4,919	4,343	4,709	2,881	3,111	2,275	2,467
MO . . .	41,238	44,823	22,154	7.5	7,543	8,061	7,222	7,706	5,807	6,175	4,931	5,255
ND . . .	5,312	5,921	24,294	10.6	922	1,011	885	968	725	787	571	623
SD . . .	5,608	6,276	23,330	10.5	1,062	1,171	1,018	1,121	603	661	463	509
NE . . .	12,112	13,266	21,424	8.7	2,300	2,477	2,052	2,199	1,576	1,695	1,282	1,382
KS . . .	19,273	21,338	21,861	9.9	3,803	4,137	3,668	3,986	2,630	2,846	2,117	2,293
South	666,419	714,817	21,283	5.6	135,470	136,330	128,969	129,601	88,602	96,761	69,814	76,481
S.A. . . .	357,145	388,230	22,175	7.1	69,557	71,631	65,989	67,867	43,779	48,478	34,785	38,622
DE . . .	6,299	6,860	26,263	7.3	1,117	1,148	1,033	1,061	954	1,060	834	932
MD . . .	38,205	40,364	22,091	4.6	7,184	7,175	6,729	6,713	4,845	5,216	3,874	4,192
DC . . .	3,553	3,740	15,839	7.3	583	589	522	527	345	376	301	330
VA. . . .	53,335	58,251	24,096	7.5	10,879	11,267	10,474	10,832	6,409	7,148	4,999	5,581
WV . . .	10,651	11,586	16,484	7.7	2,488	2,576	2,333	2,411	1,661	1,841	1,127	1,248
NC . . .	50,741	55,206	20,621	6.7	10,019	10,331	9,659	9,946	5,599	6,206	4,182	4,657
SC . . .	25,440	27,914	20,955	7.9	5,375	5,603	5,180	5,393	2,883	3,227	2,221	2,497
GA . . .	49,628	54,313	21,250	6.6	9,404	9,770	9,045	9,384	6,545	7,286	5,324	5,923
FL . . .	119,291	129,996	23,648	7.9	22,510	23,172	21,013	21,600	14,540	16,118	11,923	13,262
E.S.C . . .	105,676	114,507	19,407	6.6	23,652	23,304	22,487	22,123	15,507	17,245	12,103	13,491
KY . . .	25,585	27,507	19,267	6.3	5,988	5,877	5,702	5,588	3,776	4,180	2,930	3,246
TN . . .	38,140	41,884	21,399	7.4	7,885	7,863	7,479	7,446	5,641	6,336	4,491	5,057
AL. . . .	27,625	29,779	18,911	6.2	6,141	6,015	5,834	5,705	3,833	4,237	3,110	3,447
MS . . .	14,325	15,336	16,306	5.6	3,638	3,549	3,472	3,384	2,258	2,492	1,573	1,740
W.S.C . . .	203,599	212,081	20,835	2.4	42,261	41,396	40,493	39,610	29,316	31,038	22,927	24,368
AR . . .	15,741	16,998	18,295	6.4	3,136	3,182	3,021	3,061	2,503	2,742	2,088	2,288
LA. . . .	30,736	31,410	20,457	1.5	7,251	7,011	6,907	6,669	4,714	4,918	3,550	3,718
OK . . .	19,879	20,818	16,740	3.5	4,142	4,082	3,948	3,885	2,793	2,972	2,268	2,420
TX. . . .	137,243	142,855	22,076	1.9	27,732	27,121	26,617	25,995	19,307	20,406	15,021	15,942
West	426,360	447,679	22,138	3.7	83,806	88,185	78,673	82,694	55,595	58,527	42,080	44,364
Mountain.	109,569	124,102	22,395	9.6	24,748	26,776	23,806	25,719	13,596	15,397	10,389	11,785
MT . . .	6,334	7,220	22,354	12.2	1,538	1,680	1,483	1,617	664	757	516	591
ID . . .	7,064	8,147	20,256	10.0	1,695	1,871	1,640	1,808	750	865	573	661
WY . . .	3,199	3,531	20,098	8.8	702	743	685	724	361	402	273	305
CO . . .	29,137	33,261	23,437	9.9	6,196	6,742	5,965	6,482	3,815	4,350	3,041	3,473
NM . . .	10,934	12,337	21,099	10.3	2,361	2,547	2,246	2,419	1,392	1,571	1,002	1,138
AZ. . . .	30,290	33,825	22,441	8.6	7,159	7,634	6,910	7,357	3,728	4,166	2,640	2,941
UT . . .	11,623	13,390	22,995	11.7	2,704	2,982	2,588	2,849	1,526	1,754	1,187	1,369
NV . . .	10,988	12,390	22,643	7.5	2,392	2,575	2,289	2,461	1,360	1,531	1,157	1,307
Pacific . . .	316,791	323,577	22,042	1.6	59,058	61,409	54,867	56,976	41,999	43,130	31,690	32,579
WA . . .	40,691	43,370	21,332	3.7	8,436	9,143	8,051	8,716	5,343	5,724	4,015	4,304
OR . . .	25,235	27,767	23,336	7.0	4,529	5,056	4,248	4,735	4,018	4,422	2,858	3,142
CA . . .	233,688	233,725	21,515	0.2	42,653	43,358	39,352	39,931	29,864	29,940	22,654	22,752
AK . . .	5,090	5,471	26,088	5.1	1,247	1,378	1,206	1,331	781	842	571	617
HI	12,086	13,244	34,454	7.6	2,194	2,474	2,009	2,263	1,994	2,203	1,593	1,764

See footnotes at end of table.

No. 1305. Retail Sales, by Type of Store and State: 1992 and 1993—Continued

[See headnote, page 788]

REGION, DIVISION, AND STATE	AUTOMOTIVE DEALERS		EATING AND DRINKING PLACES		GASOLINE SERVICE STATIONS		BUILDING MATERIALS DEALERS [3]		APPAREL AND ACCESSORIES STORES		FURNITURE AND APPLIANCE STORES [4]	
	1992	1993	1992	1993	1992	1993	1992	1993	1992	1993	1992	1993
U.S. . . .	398,768	453,308	202,079	208,023	133,727	135,802	103,134	112,997	105,050	105,961	104,906	114,345
Northeast . . .	70,997	77,677	41,823	39,817	23,749	22,606	19,000	21,090	27,680	26,956	19,130	20,553
N.E	18,570	19,393	13,065	12,467	6,924	6,763	6,382	7,010	6,667	6,984	4,608	4,889
ME	1,869	2,009	1,143	1,124	744	747	771	872	469	509	341	374
NH	2,202	2,361	1,156	1,130	614	616	858	967	558	600	536	585
VT	850	873	568	534	347	334	413	446	233	241	179	188
MA	7,678	8,060	6,171	5,923	2,716	2,672	2,279	2,516	3,090	3,261	1,964	2,097
RI	1,091	1,156	936	905	508	503	384	427	438	466	245	265
CT	4,879	4,934	3,091	2,852	1,996	1,891	1,678	1,782	1,879	1,907	1,342	1,380
M.A.	52,427	58,284	28,757	27,349	16,824	15,843	12,617	14,081	21,013	19,971	14,522	15,664
NY	20,631	22,929	13,565	12,880	6,405	6,015	5,429	6,050	10,174	9,674	6,706	7,235
NJ	13,564	14,731	6,263	5,823	4,186	3,851	2,850	3,105	5,311	4,943	3,802	4,017
PA	18,232	20,624	8,930	8,646	6,234	5,977	4,338	4,926	5,527	5,355	4,013	4,412
Midwest	102,872	120,040	48,637	53,217	34,631	35,103	24,392	27,176	22,042	22,230	23,371	26,656
E.N.C	71,246	82,326	35,164	38,661	21,980	22,563	16,870	18,450	15,955	16,163	17,320	19,446
OH	17,745	21,688	8,804	10,254	5,611	6,086	3,940	4,561	3,331	3,588	4,027	4,795
IN	9,394	11,100	4,243	4,782	2,951	3,101	2,368	2,650	1,714	1,796	1,932	2,226
IL	19,319	21,025	10,174	10,548	5,649	5,454	4,414	4,546	5,583	5,367	5,203	5,522
MI	16,664	19,310	7,474	8,250	4,824	4,964	3,893	4,274	3,781	3,867	4,011	4,536
WI	8,125	9,202	4,469	4,827	2,944	2,958	2,253	2,418	1,546	1,545	2,146	2,367
W.N.C	31,625	37,714	13,473	14,556	12,651	12,540	7,523	8,726	6,087	6,067	6,051	7,211
MN . . .	7,368	8,868	3,343	3,638	2,923	2,914	2,108	2,462	1,603	1,621	1,685	2,024
IA	5,025	6,013	2,000	2,168	2,099	2,081	1,135	1,319	934	941	857	1,027
MO . . .	9,642	11,334	4,081	4,351	3,744	3,671	2,101	2,408	1,740	1,715	1,648	1,931
ND. . . .	1,259	1,523	485	530	530	532	307	361	238	241	182	219
SD. . . .	1,301	1,577	513	564	588	594	306	361	235	240	211	256
NE. . . .	2,601	3,082	1,224	1,318	1,122	1,103	576	664	530	531	611	725
KS. . . .	4,429	5,316	1,828	1,988	1,643	1,645	989	1,151	806	778	857	1,029
South	141,428	163,441	64,421	68,262	47,572	49,247	36,989	39,360	33,546	35,043	36,683	39,758
S.A.	74,681	88,008	36,136	38,573	24,364	24,816	21,932	23,455	18,725	19,882	20,622	22,893
DE. . . .	1,242	1,469	568	607	360	365	415	445	300	319	366	407
MD. . . .	8,027	9,197	3,693	3,828	2,533	2,503	1,939	2,016	2,285	2,355	2,287	2,468
DC. . . .	151	176	856	899	131	131	74	77	357	373	213	233
VA. . . .	11,209	13,252	4,990	5,355	3,844	3,944	3,071	3,291	2,749	2,938	3,174	3,540
WV	2,040	2,413	880	942	826	845	732	786	421	449	442	491
NC. . . .	10,528	12,432	5,042	5,391	3,535	3,602	3,961	4,239	2,645	2,813	3,109	3,453
SC. . . .	4,956	5,915	2,496	2,696	1,988	2,048	1,888	2,041	1,470	1,584	1,401	1,574
GA. . . .	10,135	12,021	5,004	5,376	3,698	3,794	3,235	3,489	2,512	2,682	2,721	3,042
FL. . . .	26,393	31,135	12,607	13,479	7,449	7,584	6,617	7,072	5,985	6,371	6,909	7,684
E.S.C	20,339	24,015	9,436	10,207	8,225	8,925	6,222	6,751	4,353	4,643	5,731	6,197
KY. . . .	4,327	5,081	2,428	2,611	2,145	2,318	1,545	1,667	894	949	1,337	1,437
TN. . . .	7,703	9,193	3,526	3,856	3,060	3,358	2,222	2,439	1,587	1,712	2,275	2,484
AL. . . .	5,696	6,684	2,366	2,543	2,021	2,176	1,641	1,770	1,335	1,415	1,459	1,569
MS	2,613	3,057	1,116	1,198	999	1,073	814	875	537	568	660	708
W.S.C	46,409	51,418	18,850	19,482	14,983	15,506	8,835	9,154	10,468	10,518	10,330	10,668
AR. . . .	3,730	4,276	1,145	1,224	1,285	1,375	1,005	1,077	646	671	684	732
LA. . . .	5,939	6,472	2,754	2,799	2,214	2,257	1,377	1,403	1,460	1,441	1,495	1,517
OK. . . .	4,768	5,300	1,871	1,944	1,478	1,535	872	908	1,042	1,051	970	1,005
TX. . . .	31,972	35,370	13,081	13,516	10,006	10,339	5,580	5,766	7,321	7,354	7,182	7,415
West.	83,471	92,150	47,198	46,728	27,775	28,847	22,753	25,372	21,781	21,732	25,722	27,378
Mountain . .	20,994	25,000	12,004	13,903	7,811	7,910	6,255	7,674	4,538	4,556	5,910	7,397
MT. . . .	1,167	1,403	728	851	534	547	407	504	246	249	293	369
ID	1,450	1,761	689	814	576	596	466	582	277	282	353	449
WY . . .	589	689	360	409	352	348	177	212	133	131	118	145
CO	5,401	6,473	3,466	4,042	1,943	1,974	1,522	1,879	1,241	1,254	1,658	2,090
NM	2,155	2,556	1,238	1,428	825	832	700	855	463	462	511	637
AZ. . . .	5,956	6,990	3,221	3,673	1,984	1,983	1,634	1,981	1,149	1,137	1,723	2,123
UT. . . .	2,210	2,679	1,097	1,294	888	916	651	812	552	563	720	917
NV. . . .	2,066	2,449	1,206	1,391	708	713	698	849	477	477	535	667
Pacific. . . .	62,476	67,150	35,194	32,825	19,964	20,937	16,498	17,697	17,244	17,176	19,812	19,982
WA	7,531	8,465	4,342	4,203	2,738	3,000	2,392	2,689	2,044	2,103	2,291	2,414
OR	5,369	6,216	2,533	2,537	1,670	1,881	1,298	1,497	1,159	1,241	1,326	1,448
CA. . . .	47,236	49,765	25,727	23,487	14,606	14,982	12,182	12,786	12,866	12,572	15,544	15,411
AK. . . .	667	756	643	632	253	281	263	299	275	288	176	188
HI	1,673	1,947	1,949	1,966	698	792	364	426	899	971	475	521

[1] Includes other types of stores, not shown separately. [2] Based on number of households as of July 1 as estimated by source. Minus sign (-) indicates decrease. [3] Includes hardware dealers. [4] Includes homefurnishings stores.

Source: Market Statistics, New York, NY, *The Survey of Buying Power Data Service*, annual (copyright).

No. 1306. Retail Trade—Sales, by Metropolitan Area: 1992

[Covers only establishments with payroll. Areas as defined by U.S. Office of Management and Budget, June 30, 1993. CMSA=consolidated metropolitan statistical area. MSA=metropolitan statistical area. For definition, see Appendix II]

METROPOLITAN AREAS RANKED BY VOLUME OF SALES	Total sales (mil. dol.)	Sales per capita (dol.)	METROPOLITAN AREAS RANKED BY VOLUME OF SALES	Total sales (mil. dol.)	Sales per capita (dol.)
New York-Northern New Jersey-Long Island, NY-NJ-CT-PA CMSA	140,681	(NA)	Atlanta, GA MSA	26,525	8,461
Los Angeles-Riverside-Orange County, CA CMSA	107,567	7,141	Seattle-Tacoma-Bremerton, WA CMSA	26,436	8,440
Chicago-Gary-Kenosha, IL-IN-WI CMSA	64,858	7,721	Minneapolis-St. Paul, MN-WI MSA	22,603	8,637
Washington-Baltimore, DC-MD-VA-WV CMSA	54,251	7,849	Cleveland-Akron, OH CMSA	20,840	7,218
San Francisco-Oakland-San Jose, CA CMSA	52,731	8,226	San Diego, CA MSA	19,216	7,386
Philadelphia-Wilmington-Atlantic City, PA-NJ-DE-MD CMSA	46,633	7,867	St. Louis, MO-IL MSA	19,145	7,609
Boston-Worcester-Lawrence, MA-NH-ME-CT CMSA	44,532	(NA)	Phoenix-Mesa, AZ MSA	18,724	8,027
Detroit-Ann Arbor-Flint, MI CMSA	41,636	7,952	Tampa-St. Petersburg-Clearwater, FL MSA	18,487	8,734
Dallas-Fort Worth, TX CMSA	35,359	8,406	Denver-Boulder-Greeley, CO CMSA	17,743	8,499
Miami-Fort Lauderdale, FL CMSA	32,182	9,702	Pittsburgh, PA MSA	17,575	7,309
Houston-Galveston-Brazoria, TX CMSA	30,576	7,740	Portland-Salem, OR-WA CMSA	15,542	8,183
			Cincinnati-Hamilton, OH-KY-IN CMSA	13,739	7,379
			Milwaukee-Racine, WI CMSA	12,747	7,825
			Kansas City, MO-KS MSA	12,655	7,840
			Indianapolis, IN MSA	12,352	8,671
			Orlando, FL MSA	12,343	9,470
			Columbus, OH MSA	12,224	8,787

NA Not available.
Source: U.S. Bureau of the Census, *1992 Census of Retail Trade*, RC92-A-52.

No. 1307. Wholesale Trade—Summary: 1963 to 1992

[Data prior to 1972 based on earlier editions of Standard Industrial Classification (SIC) code. Comparability of data over time is affected by changes in the SIC code; for details, see source. See also *Historical Statistics, Colonial Times to 1970*, series T 43-47, and T 274-279]

ITEM	Unit	1963	1967	1972 [1]	1977 [1]	1982 [1]	1987 [1]	1987 [2]	1992 [2]
Firms, total [3]	1,000	232	233	276	289	335	(NA)	364	387
Establishments, total [3]	1,000	308	311	370	383	435	467	470	495
With sales of $1,000,000 or more	1,000	62	75	103	152	(NA)	(NA)	222	285
Sales, all establishments	Bil. dol.	358	459	695	1,258	1,998	2,524	[4]2,525	[4]3,239
Merchant wholesalers	Bil. dol.	157	206	354	678	1,159	1,477	[4]1,478	[4]1,847
Inventories, end of year	Bil. dol.	20.1	28.1	45.7	82.3	130.7	(NA)	165.1	213.4
Payroll, entire year	Bil. dol.	18.1	23.9	36.9	58.3	95.2	133.2	133.4	173.3
Paid employees, Mar. 12 workweek [5]	1,000	3,089	3,519	4,026	4,397	4,985	5,581	5,596	5,791

NA Not available.   [1] Based on 1972 SIC code.   [2] Based on 1987 SIC code.   [3] Through 1977 number of firms and establishments in business at end of year; beginning 1982 number of firms and establishments in business at any time during year.   [4] Revised since publication of reports.   [5] 1963 data for workweek including Nov. 15.

No. 1308. Wholesale Trade, by Kind of Business: 1987 and 1992

[Based on 1987 Standard Industrial Classification code; see text, section 13. See *Historical Statistics, Colonial Times to 1970*, series T 274-287 and T 352-369 for similar but not comparable data]

KIND OF BUSINESS	ESTABLISH-MENTS [1] (1,000)		SALES[2] (mil. dol.)		ANNUAL PAYROLL (mil. dol.)		PAID EMPLOYEES [3] (1,000)	
	1987	1992	1987	1992	1987	1992	1987	1992
Wholesale trade	**469.5**	**495.5**	**2,524,727**	**3,238,520**	**133,359**	**173,272**	**5,596**	**5,791**
Merchant wholesalers	391.0	414.8	1,478,169	1,847,274	100,416	127,987	4,476	4,588
Other operating types	78.6	80.6	1,046,557	1,391,247	32,944	45,285	1,120	1,203
Durable goods	**297.3**	**313.5**	**1,278,771**	**1,593,874**	**82,770**	**105,155**	**3,332**	**3,349**
Motor vehicles, parts, and supplies	45.8	47.3	326,625	394,104	9,872	12,065	483	489
Furniture and home furnishings	14.5	16.5	48,123	58,927	3,652	4,612	153	161
Lumber and construction materials	19.1	19.5	79,946	89,764	5,476	6,060	231	211
Professional & commercial equipment	44.2	46.8	175,149	262,974	19,728	26,380	698	685
Metals and minerals, except petroleum	11.1	11.2	114,528	118,322	4,038	4,684	143	138
Electrical goods	33.5	39.3	173,174	227,784	11,526	15,070	421	436
Hardware, plumbing, heating equipment	23.1	24.7	57,126	76,088	5,610	7,106	235	241
Machinery, equipment, supplies	73.6	73.9	185,446	230,004	17,308	21,267	702	690
Miscellaneous durable goods	32.3	34.3	118,654	135,906	5,558	7,912	266	299
Nondurable goods	**172.2**	**182.0**	**1,245,956**	**1,644,647**	**50,589**	**68,117**	**2,264**	**2,442**
Paper and paper products	16.8	19.7	83,173	106,580	5,202	6,939	228	269
Drugs, proprietaries, and sundries	4.9	6.1	64,280	129,306	2,968	5,368	120	158
Apparel, piece goods, and notions	16.9	19.6	81,476	109,203	4,661	6,522	181	196
Groceries and related products	42.1	42.9	380,945	504,567	16,729	21,723	763	812
Farm-product raw materials	12.6	11.6	117,606	136,869	1,847	2,100	117	109
Chemicals and allied products	12.7	14.2	94,620	132,471	3,847	5,596	131	147
Petroleum and petroleum products	16.7	16.1	234,874	281,585	3,658	4,447	175	169
Beer, wine, and distilled beverages	5.8	5.3	49,433	59,487	3,849	4,670	146	142
Misc. nondurable goods	43.7	46.8	139,550	184,577	7,828	10,754	404	441

[1] Number of establishments in business at any time during the year.   [2] Revised since publication of reports.   [3] For pay period including March 12.

Source of tables 1307 and 1308: U.S. Bureau of the Census, *U.S. Census of Business: 1963*, vol. IV; *1967*, vol. III; and *Census of Wholesale Trade: 1972*, vol. I; *1977*, WC77-A-52; *1982*, WC82-A-52; *1987*, WC87-A-52; and *1992*, WC92-A-52.

No. 1309. Merchant Wholesalers—Summary: 1989 to 1994

[**Inventories and stock/sales ratios**, as of **December, seasonally adjusted**. Data reflect latest revision. Based on Current Business Survey; see Appendix III. See *Historical Statistics, Colonial Times to 1970*, series T 280-371, for related sales data]

KIND OF BUSINESS	1987 SIC code [1]	1989	1990	1991	1992	1993	1994
SALES (bil. dol.)							
Merchant wholesalers		**1,728.1**	**1,793.8**	**1,779.6**	**1,843.7**	**1,940.8**	**2,072.5**
Durable goods	**50**	**853.3**	**881.2**	**859.9**	**906.0**	**987.4**	**1,089.5**
Motor vehicles, parts, and supplies	501	167.7	173.9	166.4	170.3	179.5	201.2
Furniture and homefurnishings	502	31.9	33.9	32.3	33.1	34.9	36.0
Lumber and construction materials	503	62.9	63.6	58.2	63.7	71.7	76.8
Professional and commercial equipment	504	109.7	114.3	124.0	139.2	159.1	165.2
Metals and minerals, except petroleum	505	80.0	77.8	76.0	76.6	80.3	95.5
Electrical goods	506	113.6	116.5	113.3	115.0	131.7	147.4
Hardware, plumbing and heating equipment	507	48.9	52.7	49.9	52.9	55.5	63.3
Machinery, equipment and supplies	508	149.2	157.0	146.5	148.8	160.7	180.4
Miscellaneous durable goods	509	89.3	91.4	93.2	106.3	113.9	123.8
Nondurable goods	**51**	**874.8**	**912.6**	**919.7**	**937.7**	**953.5**	**983.0**
Paper and paper products	511	50.6	51.6	52.1	54.6	59.2	64.9
Drugs, proprietaries, and sundries	512	45.3	51.5	59.6	66.8	72.2	78.4
Apparel, piece goods, and notions	513	61.5	64.9	64.6	67.7	70.3	73.4
Groceries and related products	514	259.5	272.5	277.2	278.3	285.7	286.5
Farm-product raw materials	515	119.9	107.6	104.7	105.9	96.0	95.8
Chemicals and allied products	516	33.3	35.7	37.1	39.0	39.2	42.2
Petroleum and petroleum products	517	136.5	148.5	140.0	142.1	139.5	138.3
Beer, wine, and distilled beverages	518	45.4	49.3	51.6	50.2	51.2	53.0
Miscellaneous nondurable goods	519	123.0	131.0	133.0	133.1	140.4	150.4
INVENTORIES (bil. dol.)							
Merchant wholesalers		**187.0**	**195.6**	**200.1**	**207.7**	**215.9**	**234.7**
Durable goods	**50**	**122.2**	**126.2**	**127.1**	**131.1**	**135.6**	**149.2**
Motor vehicles, parts, and supplies	501	21.9	23.5	24.1	24.1	24.4	24.5
Furniture and homefurnishings	502	4.7	4.6	4.6	4.8	4.8	4.9
Lumber and construction materials	503	6.1	6.0	5.8	6.3	6.7	6.9
Professional and commercial equipment	504	14.8	15.8	16.8	17.0	17.9	20.2
Metals and minerals, except petroleum	505	10.9	10.7	10.0	10.0	11.1	13.2
Electrical goods	506	15.5	15.9	16.1	17.2	17.5	19.9
Hardware, plumbing and heating equipment	507	8.2	8.5	8.4	8.8	9.3	10.6
Machinery, equipment and supplies	508	30.0	31.5	29.7	30.0	29.2	33.2
Miscellaneous durable goods	509	10.2	9.8	11.4	12.8	14.6	15.8
Nondurable goods	**51**	**64.8**	**69.4**	**73.0**	**76.6**	**80.2**	**85.5**
Paper and paper products	511	4.5	4.9	5.2	5.6	6.3	7.3
Drugs, proprietaries, and sundries	512	5.9	6.5	7.7	9.0	10.4	11.0
Apparel, piece goods, and notions	513	9.6	9.8	9.5	10.6	11.4	11.9
Groceries and related products	514	14.1	14.7	15.6	16.0	15.7	16.3
Farm-product raw materials	515	8.2	8.8	9.1	9.0	10.0	10.9
Chemicals and allied products	516	2.6	3.1	3.1	3.2	3.7	4.1
Petroleum and petroleum products	517	3.8	4.4	4.5	4.4	4.0	4.6
Beer, wine, and distilled beverages	518	4.2	4.4	4.7	4.3	4.5	4.5
Miscellaneous nondurable goods	519	11.9	12.7	13.6	14.4	14.2	15.0
STOCK/SALES RATIO							
Merchant wholesalers		**1.27**	**1.31**	**1.34**	**1.33**	**1.33**	**1.28**
Durable goods	**50**	**1.71**	**1.75**	**1.77**	**1.67**	**1.60**	**1.53**
Motor vehicles, parts, and supplies	501	1.67	1.66	1.75	1.64	1.61	1.41
Furniture and homefurnishings	502	1.75	1.71	1.78	1.62	1.68	1.49
Lumber and construction materials	503	1.22	1.33	1.22	1.12	1.02	1.01
Professional and commercial equipment	504	1.52	1.58	1.54	1.39	1.35	1.35
Metals and minerals, except petroleum	505	1.78	1.60	1.58	1.55	1.60	1.51
Electrical goods	506	1.55	1.71	1.72	1.72	1.52	1.51
Hardware, plumbing and heating equipment	507	1.94	1.90	2.01	2.01	1.93	1.84
Machinery, equipment and supplies	508	2.38	2.49	2.47	2.34	2.10	2.03
Miscellaneous durable goods	509	1.30	1.27	1.45	1.37	1.53	1.46
Nondurable goods	**51**	**0.85**	**0.90**	**0.94**	**0.98**	**1.04**	**1.00**
Paper and paper products	511	1.05	1.16	1.17	1.20	1.23	1.21
Drugs, proprietaries, and sundries	512	1.44	1.49	1.43	1.51	1.70	1.65
Apparel, piece goods, and notions	513	1.72	1.77	1.83	1.80	2.09	1.98
Groceries and related products	514	0.63	0.66	0.67	0.68	0.67	0.65
Farm-product raw materials	515	0.90	1.04	1.08	1.01	1.21	1.26
Chemicals and allied products	516	0.92	0.97	0.98	0.97	1.14	1.08
Petroleum and petroleum products	517	0.29	0.33	0.38	0.39	0.40	0.39
Beer, wine, and distilled beverages	518	1.07	0.95	1.04	1.06	1.07	1.02
Miscellaneous nondurable goods	519	1.09	1.17	1.21	1.41	1.24	1.14

[1] Based on 1987 Standard Industrial Classification code; see text, section 13.

Source: U.S. Bureau of the Census, *Current Business Reports, Combined Annual and Revised Monthly Wholesale Trade, January 1987 Through January 1995*, (BW/94-RV).

No. 1310. Wholesale Trade—Summary, by State: 1992

[Kind-of-business classification based on 1987 Standard Industrial Classification code; see text, section 13]

DIVISION AND STATE	Estab-lish-ments [1]	Sales (bil. dol.)	Paid employ-ees [2] (1,000)	Annual payroll (mil. dol.)	DIVISION AND STATE	Estab-lish-ments [1]	Sales (bil. dol.)	Paid employ-ees [2] (1,000)	Annual payroll (mil. dol.)
U.S. . .	**495,457**	**3,249.9**	**5,791.4**	**173,272**	VA	9,290	51.5	115.8	3,268
					WV	2,427	7.8	24.5	575
N.E	**24,173**	**190.8**	**291.8**	**10,269**	NC	13,351	76.4	151.1	4,167
ME	1,974	6.5	21.9	541	SC	5,564	21.3	56.7	1,457
NH	2,104	8.2	20.5	635	GA	14,608	113.8	179.4	5,329
VT	1,112	4.5	11.4	307	FL	30,137	132.6	280.9	7,485
MA	10,950	86.7	141.5	5,035	**E.S.C. . . . .**	**26,206**	**139.0**	**305.7**	**7,630**
RI	1,771	6.6	19.5	551	KY	5,931	31.6	70.3	1,701
CT	6,262	78.3	77.1	3,200	TN	9,341	59.7	115.4	3,064
M.A	**79,608**	**590.1**	**950.8**	**32,334**	AL	7,066	32.0	80.1	1,951
NY	40,934	287.7	433.6	15,220	MS	3,868	15.8	39.9	914
NJ	18,444	176.0	262.7	9,629	**W.S.C. . . . .**	**54,247**	**363.0**	**592.0**	**16,180**
PA	20,230	126.4	254.4	7,485	AR	4,296	18.1	43.9	989
E.N.C.	**79,106**	**572.4**	**1,010.6**	**30,448**	LA	7,347	37.3	81.3	1,994
OH	19,305	127.3	260.1	7,283	OK	5,993	26.4	57.9	1,398
IN	10,264	52.4	115.7	3,052	TX	36,611	281.3	408.9	11,800
IL	24,637	219.4	331.9	10,931	**Mountain .**	**27,021**	**121.5**	**285.2**	**7,476**
MI	15,517	125.7	185.2	5,960	MT	1,853	5.9	16.4	343
WI	9,383	47.6	117.6	3,223	ID	2,288	8.9	24.9	528
W.N.C. . . .	**42,210**	**251.7**	**465.8**	**12,467**	WY	987	2.5	7.0	165
MN	10,219	72.5	123.1	3,819	CO	7,554	46.9	84.0	2,478
IA	6,971	29.4	69.4	1,639	NM	2,515	6.3	22.6	513
MO	11,236	68.4	129.6	3,553	AZ	6,518	28.0	68.8	1,837
ND	2,086	7.6	18.5	406	UT	3,231	15.3	39.6	1,005
SD	1,809	6.5	16.4	335	NV	2,075	7.8	21.8	607
NE	4,035	32.5	47.1	1,076	**Pacific . . .**	**78,734**	**549.4**	**958.1**	**30,101**
KS	5,854	34.9	61.8	1,638	WA	10,732	62.5	122.5	3,628
S.A	**84,152**	**471.8**	**931.5**	**26,366**	OR	6,455	42.4	72.1	2,021
DE	1,088	12.3	16.1	674	CA	58,437	432.9	731.6	23,537
MD	7,188	52.9	100.5	3,180	AK	908	3.6	8.5	290
DC	499	3.3	6.6	231	HI	2,202	8.0	23.3	625

[1] Number of establishments in business at any time during the year.　[2] For the pay period including March 12.

Source: U.S. Bureau of the Census, *1992 Census of Wholesale Trade*, Geographic Area Series, WC92-A-1 to 52.

No. 1311. Wholesale Trade—Establishments and Sales by Selected Metropolitan Areas: 1992

[Kind-of-business classification based on 1987 Standard Industrial Classification code; see text, section 13. Metropolitan statistical areas (MSA's) and consolidated metropolitan statistical areas (CMSA's) are as defined by the U.S. Office of Management and Budget as of June 30, 1993; see Appendix II for definitions and components]

METROPOLITAN AREA	ALL ESTABLISHMENTS [1]			MERCHANT WHOLESALERS	
	Estab-lish-ments	Sales		Estab-lish-ments	Sales (bil. dol.)
		Amount (bil. dol.)	Rank		
New York-Northern New Jersey-Long Island, NY-NJ-CT-PA CMSA	50,178	457.8	1	43,048	301.4
Los Angeles-Riverside-Orange County, CA CMSA	31,250	248.9	2	26,744	162.9
Chicago-Gary-Kenosha, IL-IN-WI CMSA	18,573	188.5	3	14,244	87.2
San Francisco-Oakland-San Jose, CA CMSA	13,550	125.4	4	11,054	61.2
Houston-Galveston-Brazoria, TX CMSA	9,046	117.3	5	7,408	64.3
Dallas-Fort Worth, TX CMSA	10,567	98.8	6	7,906	37.3
Detroit-Ann Arbor-Flint, MI CMSA	9,068	95.7	7	6,864	31.3
Atlanta, GA MSA	9,070	93.4	8	6,546	34.4
Philadelphia-Wilmington-Atlantic City, PA-NJ-DE-MD CMSA	11,229	90.6	9	8,966	39.9
Boston-Worcester-Lawrence, MA-NH-ME-CT CMSA	10,733	88.0	10	8,478	46.4
Washington-Baltimore, DC-MD-VA-WV CMSA	9,294	71.5	11	7,521	36.3
Minneapolis-St. Paul, MN-WI MSA	6,436	58.2	12	4,817	28.4
Seattle-Tacoma-Bremerton, WA CMSA	7,101	48.9	13	5,597	28.3
Miami-Fort Lauderdale, FL CMSA	12,024	48.6	14	10,556	35.0
Denver-Boulder-Greeley, CO CMSA	5,353	41.9	15	4,069	18.2
Cleveland-Akron, OH CMSA	6,069	40.0	16	4,653	18.3
St. Louis, MO-IL MSA	5,302	38.7	17	4,075	20.9
Kansas City, MO-KS MSA	4,016	38.2	18	3,036	18.5
Portland-Salem, OR-WA CMSA	4,615	38.1	19	3,723	26.2
Cincinnati-Hamilton, OH-KY-IN CMSA	3,546	37.6	20	2,579	13.3

[1] Includes other types of operations, not shown separately.

Source: U.S. Bureau of the Census, *1992 Census of Wholesale Trade*, Geographic Area Series, WC92-A-52.

No. 1312. Selected Service Industries—Summary: 1987 and 1992

[For establishments with payroll]

KIND OF BUSINESS	1987 SIC code [1]	ESTABLISH-MENTS [2] (1,000)		RECEIPTS OR EXPENSES [3] (mil. dol.)		PAID EMPLOYEES [4] (1,000)	
		1987	1992	1987	1992	1987	1992
Firms subject to Federal income tax [5]	(X)	**1,626**	**1,825**	**772,194**	**1,202,613**	**16,055**	**19,290**
Hotels and other lodging places [6]	70 ex. 704	47	49	51,865	69,204	1,411	1,489
Personal services	72	185	197	31,491	43,280	1,105	1,218
Business services	73	252	307	166,322	274,892	4,414	5,542
Automotive repair, services, and parking	75	151	172	51,423	70,033	785	864
Miscellaneous repair services	76	66	72	20,838	30,732	346	428
Amusement and recreation services and museums [7]	78, 79, 84	99	115	57,638	92,915	1,094	1,382
Health services	80	407	442	182,289	299,067	3,592	4,453
Legal services	81	138	152	66,998	101,114	808	924
Social services	83	43	59	7,330	13,349	357	505
Engineering and management services [8]	87 ex. 8733	205	233	127,344	192,819	1,969	2,271
Firms exempt from Federal income tax [5]	(X)	**176**	**209**	**253,284**	**423,900**	**6,737**	**8,109**
Selected health services	8011 pt.; 8021 pt 805, 6, 8, 9	19	24	184,920	312,050	4,648	5,565
Social services	83	63	82	26,884	47,170	1,110	1,407
Selected membership organizations	861, 2, 4, 9	68	72	22,028	33,795	539	603
Research, testing, and consulting services [9]	873, 4 ex. 8744	4	6	8,837	14,314	121	147

X Not applicable.   [1] Based on 1987 Standard Industrial Classification; see text, section 13.   [2] Number of establishments in business at any time during the year.   [3] Receipts refer to establishments subject to Federal income tax. Expenses refer to establishments exempt from Federal income tax.   [4] For pay period including March 12.   [5] Includes other kinds of business, not shown separately.   [6] Excludes membership lodging.   [7] Includes motion pictures.   [8] Except noncommercial research organizations.   [9] Excludes facilities support management services.

Source: U.S. Bureau of the Census, *1992 Census of Service Industries*, Geographic Area Series, SC92-A-52.

No. 1313. Selected Service Industries—Revenue and Expenses for Tax-Exempt Firms: 1990 to 1993

[**In billions of dollars**. Estimated from a sample of employer firms only]

KIND OF BUSINESS	1987 SIC code [1]	REVENUE			EXPENSES		
		1990	1992	1993	1990	1992	1993
Selected amusement and recreation services [2]	792, 7991, 7997, 7999	8.2	9.6	10.6	8.2	9.6	10.6
Offices and clinics of doctors of medicine	801	12.0	15.4	17.8	11.7	15.0	17.4
Nursing and personal care facilities	805	9.4	11.8	13.0	9.3	11.6	12.7
Hospitals	806	251.9	302.1	317.4	226.7	270.8	287.7
Home health care services	808	3.2	4.8	5.7	3.1	4.5	5.5
Health and allied services, n.e.c.	809	4.6	6.2	6.9	4.6	6.0	6.8
Social services	83	45.0	53.4	58.4	40.1	48.0	52.8
Individual and family social services	8322	12.9	15.9	17.4	12.3	15.1	16.5
Job training and related services	8331	5.1	6.1	6.7	4.8	5.9	6.5
Child day care services	8351	2.9	3.8	4.2	3.0	3.7	4.0
Residential care	8361	8.6	10.1	11.5	8.4	10.0	11.2
Selected membership organizations [3]	86 (pt)	34.3	39.4	41.8	29.6	34.6	36.9
Research and testing services	873	12.1	14.7	15.5	11.4	14.0	15.0

[1] Standard Industrial Classification; see text, section 13.   [2] Covers theatrical producers, bands, orchestras, and entertainers (SIC 792); physical fitness facilities (SIC 7991); membership sports and recreation clubs (SIC 7997); and amusement and recreation services, not elsewhere classified (SIC 7999).   [3] Includes business associations (SIC 861); professional membership organizations (SIC 862); civic, social, and fraternal organizations (SIC 864); and other membership organizations, except labor unions and political and religious organizations (SIC 869).

Source: U.S. Bureau of the Census, *Current Business Reports, Service Annual Survey: 1993* (BS/93).

No. 1314. National Nonprofit Associations—Number, by Type: 1980 to 1994

[Data compiled during last few months of year previous to year shown and the beginning months of year shown]

TYPE	1980	1985	1990	1994	TYPE	1980	1985	1990	1994
Total	**14,726**	**19,121**	**22,289**	**22,512**	Fraternal, foreign interest, nationality, ethnic	435	492	573	548
Trade, business, commercial	3,118	3,719	3,918	3,768	Religious	797	953	1,172	1,227
Agriculture	677	882	940	1,119	Veteran, hereditary, patriotic	208	281	462	577
Legal, governmental, public admin., military	529	658	792	781	Hobby, avocational	910	1,311	1,475	1,555
Scientific, engineering, tech	1,039	1,270	1,417	1,347	Athletic sports	504	737	840	838
Educational	[1]2,376	[1]2,822	1,291	1,289	Labor unions	235	252	253	245
Cultural	([1])	([1])	1,886	1,904	Chambers of Commerce [2]	105	142	168	169
Social welfare	994	1,450	1,705	1,852	Greek and non-Greek letter societies	318	331	340	335
Health, medical	1,413	1,886	2,227	2,331	Fan clubs	(NA)	(NA)	581	458
Public affairs	1,068	1,935	2,249	2,169					

NA Not available.   [1] Data for cultural associations included with educational associations.   [2] National and binational.

Source: Gale Research Inc., Detroit, MI. Compiled from *Encyclopedia of Associations*, annual (copyright).

No. 1315. Service Industries—Summary of Establishments, by Tax Status: 1992

[See *Historical Statistics, Colonial Times to 1970*, series T 391-443, for similar but not comparable data]

KIND OF BUSINESS	1987 SIC code [1]	ALL ESTABLISHMENTS		ESTABLISHMENTS WITH PAYROLL			
		Establishments [2] (1,000)	Receipts or revenues [3] (mil. dol.)	Establishments [2] (1,000)	Receipts or revenues [3] (mil. dol.)	Annual payroll (mil. dol.)	Paid employees [4] (1,000)
Firms subject to Federal income tax [5] . . .	(X)	8,593.5	1,345,146	1,825.4	1,202,613	452,697	19,290
Hotels and other lodging places [5][6]	70 ex. 704	92.9	71,038	48.6	69,204	19,633	1,489
Hotels and motels	701	69.1	68,508	41.7	67,193	19,187	1,456
Personal services [5]	72	1,320.9	59,598	197.1	43,280	14,379	1,218
Laundry, cleaning, and garment services	721	124.4	18,805	55.8	17,140	5,588	426
Beauty and barber shops	723, 4	471.6	15,951	87.7	10,347	4,428	402
Funeral service and crematories	726	25.2	7,588	15.6	7,145	1,856	88
Business services [5]	73	2,056.2	309,439	306.6	274,892	109,299	5,542
Advertising [5]	731	91.6	22,673	19.0	19,456	7,223	196
Advertising agencies	7311	(NA)	(NA)	13.9	13,608	5,649	132
Credit reporting and collection	732	14.6	6,377	7.5	6,151	2,163	98
Mailing, reproduction, stenographic [5]	733	154.5	20,990	32.1	18,339	5,522	235
Direct mail advertising services	7331	(NA)	(NA)	3.9	6,434	1,777	79
Services to dwellings and other buildings . . .	734	460.5	23,586	57.6	19,003	9,164	818
Miscellaneous equipment rental and leasing . .	735	52.4	22,782	24.8	21,778	4,905	200
Personnel supply services [5]	736	54.1	38,709	31.2	38,163	26,436	1,975
Help supply services	7363	(NA)	(NA)	19.0	33,587	24,075	1,842
Computer and data processing services [5] . . .	737	223.6	104,650	59.1	101,073	35,598	886
Computer programming services	7371	(NA)	(NA)	23.3	23,548	10,890	243
Prepackaged software	7372	(NA)	(NA)	7.1	20,802	6,614	131
Computer integrated systems design	7373	(NA)	(NA)	5.0	14,805	4,151	98
Data processing and preparation	7374	(NA)	(NA)	7.3	20,200	6,796	230
Computer maintenance and repair	7378	(NA)	(NA)	5.0	7,353	2,300	63
Detective and armored car services	7381	(NA)	(NA)	11.6	9,193	5,794	482
Auto repair, services, and parking [5]	75	454.3	78,512	172.0	70,033	15,550	864
Automotive rentals, no drivers [5]	751	22.2	20,906	10.6	20,574	2,757	132
Truck rental and leasing, no drivers	7513	(NA)	(NA)	4.3	7,445	1,029	42
Passenger car rental	7514	(NA)	(NA)	4.9	10,280	1,475	81
Automotive repair shops [5]	753	334.5	46,200	128.7	39,746	10,337	520
Top and body repair and paint shops	7532	(NA)	(NA)	35.0	12,262	3,445	166
General automotive repair shops	7538	(NA)	(NA)	64.8	17,773	4,406	230
Automotive services, except repair	754	85.8	7,661	22.5	6,047	1,776	160
Miscellaneous repair services [5]	76	269.8	35,237	71.6	30,732	9,695	428
Electrical repair shops	762	71.6	11,875	21.2	10,667	3,707	162
Amusement and recreation services [5][7] . . .	78, 79, 84	691.7	103,556	114.8	92,915	25,357	1,382
Motion picture prod., distribution, services	781, 2	54.1	34,289	13.0	33,062	8,084	249
Producers, orchestras, entertainers [8]	792	288.6	13,054	10.1	8,625	2,895	69
Commercial sports	794	71.6	9,010	3.8	7,594	4,022	90
Health services [5]	80	1,005.5	321,650	441.7	299,067	129,093	4,453
Offices and clinics of doctors of medicine	801	328.9	151,824	197.7	141,429	68,732	1,357
Offices and clinics of dentists	802	138.5	36,939	108.8	35,523	13,039	555
Offices, clinics of other health practitioners . . .	804	243.0	23,892	74.7	18,926	6,150	283
Nursing and personal care facilities	805	51.8	34,742	15.0	33,990	15,954	1,135
Hospitals [5]	806	(NA)	(NA)	1.4	31,083	10,556	428
General medical and surgical hospitals	8062	(NA)	(NA)	0.7	24,162	8,013	323
Medical and dental laboratories [5]	807	29.4	15,172	16.0	14,460	4,804	178
Medical laboratories	8071	(NA)	(NA)	8.4	12,511	3,980	139
Home health care services	808	(NA)	(NA)	8.0	10,414	4,853	342
Legal services	81	326.9	108,443	151.7	101,114	39,328	924
Selected educational services	823, 4, 9	240.7	9,158	14.7	7,242	2,457	133
Social services	83	617.4	18,201	59.1	13,349	5,466	505
Engineering and architectural services [5]	871	225.4	83,033	68.1	78,770	32,745	825
Engineering services	8711	131.3	67,716	41.8	65,245	27,247	658
Architectural services	8712	71.6	12,682	17.9	11,244	4,408	122
Accounting, auditing, and bookkeeping	872	325.5	37,191	79.1	34,038	14,001	521
Research and testing services [9]	873 ex. 8733	30.4	22,910	13.5	22,690	9,227	282
Management and public relations [5]	874	735.8	72,490	72.1	57,321	23,371	644
Management services	8741	111.0	23,774	19.7	21,728	8,516	278
Management consulting services	8742	(NA)	(NA)	33.8	22,629	9,620	212
Firms exempt from Federal income tax [5] . .	(X)	(NA)	(NA)	208.9	446,256	186,672	8,109
Nursing and personal care facilities	805	(NA)	(NA)	5.9	15,220	7,591	498
Hospitals	806	(NA)	(NA)	5.7	279,735	126,202	4,566
Hospitals, excluding government	806	(NA)	(NA)	3.6	203,360	87,062	3,252
Social services [5]	83	(NA)	(NA)	81.7	53,672	19,331	1,407
Individual and family social services	832	(NA)	(NA)	28.9	16,046	6,381	434
Residential care	836	(NA)	(NA)	15.0	10,615	4,830	319
Business associations	861	(NA)	(NA)	14.3	11,068	3,157	102
Civic, social, and fraternal associations	864	(NA)	(NA)	41.8	13,176	3,657	355
Research and testing services	873	(NA)	(NA)	3.8	12,535	4,511	126

NA Not available. [1] Based on 1987 Standard Industrial Classification; see text, section 13. [2] Represents the number of establishments in business at any time during year. [3] Receipts refer to establishments subject to Federal income tax. Revenues refer to establishments exempt from Federal income tax. [4] For pay period including March 12. [5] Includes other kinds of business, not shown separately. [6] Excludes membership lodging. [7] Includes motion pictures and museums. [8] Excludes motion picture producers. [9] Excludes noncommercial research organizations.

Source: U.S. Bureau of the Census, *1992 Census of Service Industries*, SC92-A-52 and SC92-N-1.

No. 1316. Services—Establishments, Employees, and Payroll: 1990 and 1992

[Covers establishments with payroll. Excludes government employees, railroad employees, self-employed persons, etc. For statement on methodology, see Appendix III]

KIND OF BUSINESS	1987 SIC code [1]	ESTABLISHMENTS (1,000)		EMPLOYEES (1,000)		PAYROLL (bil. dol.)	
		1990	1992	1990	1992	1990	1992
Services, total [2]	(I)	**2,059.3**	**2,217.7**	**28,800**	**30,654**	**599.4**	**703.6**
Hotels and other lodging places	70	50.6	53.3	1,529	1,502	19.1	20.2
Hotels and motels	701	39.2	42.7	1,463	1,445	18.3	19.4
Personal services [2]	72	186.1	198.1	1,196	1,233	13.5	14.9
Laundry, cleaning, and garment services	721	50.4	54.9	418	425	5.2	5.7
Drycleaning plants, except rug	7216	17.6	18.7	148	144	1.6	1.7
Beauty shops	723	76.1	80.8	371	380	3.9	4.2
Barber shops	724	5.1	5.0	16	16	0.2	0.2
Funeral service and crematories	726	14.9	15.2	85	89	1.7	1.9
Business services [2]	73	292.3	306.5	5,119	5,346	98.1	110.4
Advertising	731	19.1	19.8	204	193	7.3	7.5
Advertising agencies	7311	11.1	11.9	137	127	5.4	5.4
Credit reporting and collection	732	6.6	7.2	94	101	2.0	2.3
Mailing, reproduction, stenographic [2]	733	26.2	30.6	233	240	5.1	5.6
Direct mail advertising services	7331	3.5	3.9	84	81	1.7	1.8
Commercial art and graphic design	7336	9.0	11.2	52	50	1.5	1.5
Services to buildings	734	48.5	56.2	802	820	8.3	9.5
Misc. equipment rental and leasing	735	22.6	23.3	209	198	4.9	4.9
Personnel supply services	736	27.0	29.4	1,518	1,687	20.6	24.8
Help supply services	7363	13.3	16.1	1,210	1,405	15.6	20.2
Computer and data processing services [2]	737	40.5	54.7	773	834	28.5	33.5
Computer programming services	7371	12.4	18.4	217	228	8.9	10.2
Prepackaged software	7372	3.8	5.0	76	100	3.5	5.0
Computer integrated systems design	7373	3.3	4.2	82	94	3.5	4.2
Data processing and preparation	7374	6.8	7.0	229	222	6.4	6.9
Computer maintenance and repair	7378	3.3	4.3	53	56	1.9	2.0
Miscellaneous business services	738	62.7	70.8	1,093	1,160	17.2	19.5
Detective and armored car services [2]	7381	9.4	11.1	467	462	5.2	5.8
Automotive repair, services, and parking [2]	75	156.6	167.3	877	861	15.2	15.7
Automotive rentals, no drivers [2]	751	10.5	10.6	147	137	2.9	2.9
Truck rental and leasing, no drivers	7513	4.0	4.1	51	45	1.2	1.1
Passenger car rental [2]	7514	4.5	4.6	78	79	1.3	1.5
Automotive repair shops [2]	753	112.7	121.2	507	495	9.6	10.0
Top and body repair and paint shops	7532	30.5	32.6	164	155	3.2	3.2
General automotive repair shops	7538	54.8	60.1	214	215	3.8	4.1
Automotive services, except repair	754	18.1	21.0	145	153	1.5	1.8
Miscellaneous repair services	76	67.4	68.0	403	384	8.7	9.0
Electrical repair shops	762	17.2	19.1	115	115	2.6	2.9
Motion pictures [2]	78	35.4	40.7	430	463	8.6	9.6
Motion picture production and services	781	9.2	10.7	189	219	5.9	6.8
Motion picture distribution and services	782	1.0	1.1	24	16	0.9	0.8
Motion picture theaters	783	7.0	6.9	107	107	0.8	0.9
Video tape rental	784	16.4	20.4	103	115	0.8	1.0
Amusement and recreation services [2]	79	75.2	84.3	1,032	1,125	16.1	19.2
Producers, orchestras, entertainers	792	9.7	12.1	126	133	3.3	3.7
Commercial sports	794	3.3	3.8	79	89	3.0	4.0
Amusement parks	7996	0.7	0.8	69	81	1.1	1.3
Membership sports and recreation clubs	7997	13.1	13.8	242	254	3.4	3.9
Health services [2]	80	436.7	464.9	8,811	9,727	213.8	266.7
Offices and clinics of medical doctors	801	193.6	199.5	1,387	1,535	63.0	72.8
Offices and clinics of dentists	802	104.7	108.5	533	565	11.6	13.4
Offices of other health practitioners	804	62.5	73.9	250	300	5.0	6.5
Offices and clinics of chiropractors	8041	22.9	26.6	73	83	1.3	1.6
Nursing and personal care facilities	805	19.1	21.2	1,461	1,593	18.6	23.2
Hospitals	806	6.3	6.9	4,325	4,708	99.2	128.8
Medical and dental laboratories	807	14.4	15.6	158	175	3.8	4.8
Medical laboratories	8071	7.1	8.1	118	135	3.0	3.9
Home health care services	808	7.7	9.5	351	467	4.8	7.5
Legal services	81	142.4	153.6	932	952	36.0	39.9
Elementary and secondary schools	821	14.3	16.6	451	525	6.6	8.3
Colleges and universities	822	3.0	3.5	1,082	1,172	19.2	22.6
Vocational schools	824	4.6	5.0	97	78	1.8	1.7
Social services [2]	83	115.6	139.4	1,750	1,954	20.9	25.7
Child day care services	835	39.0	43.8	405	423	3.4	4.1
Residential care	836	21.0	26.1	417	486	5.4	6.8
Museums, botanical, zoological gardens	84	3.2	3.8	64	70	1.1	1.3
Business associations	861	12.7	14.0	99	102	2.7	3.0
Civic and social associations	864	40.0	44.3	366	392	3.7	4.3
Engineering and management services [2]	87	201.1	235.3	2,473	2,619	79.8	91.7
Engineering services	8711	33.1	39.2	652	663	24.9	27.7
Architectural services	8712	15.7	17.3	140	124	4.8	4.6
Accounting, auditing, and bookkeeping	872	67.9	78.7	524	574	13.8	16.0
Research and testing services	873	14.9	17.9	393	421	12.3	14.3
Management services	8741	15.3	18.1	286	320	7.7	10.0
Management consulting services	8742	24.5	31.4	226	248	8.6	10.5
Facilities support services	8744	0.7	1.1	70	82	2.2	2.6

[1] Based on 1987 Standard Industrial Classification; see text, section 13.   [2] Includes kinds of business not shown separately.

Source: U.S. Bureau of the Census, *County Business Patterns*, annual.

No. 1317. Service Industries—Annual Receipts of Taxable Firms: 1985 to 1993

[**In billions of dollars**. Covers employer and nonemployer firms except as noted. Estimated]

KIND OF BUSINESS	1987 SIC code [1]	1985	1988	1989	1990	1991	1992	1993
Hotels and other lodging places [2]	70	45.4	57.6	59.0	60.3	59.8	63.8	67.0
Hotels and motels	701	43.5	55.3	56.6	58.1	57.7	61.4	64.3
Personal services [3]	72	36.7	48.4	52.1	53.8	53.7	58.5	60.3
Laundry, cleaning, and garment services	721	12.8	15.5	16.3	16.7	16.8	17.7	18.0
Drycleaning plants, except rug cleaning	7216	3.8	4.6	4.6	4.2	4.3	5.1	5.1
Beauty shops	723	9.0	11.4	12.3	12.5	12.7	13.8	14.0
Barber shops	7241	1.2	1.5	1.5	1.6	1.6	1.8	1.7
Funeral service and crematories	726	5.2	6.2	6.5	7.0	7.4	7.9	8.5
Business services [3]	73	155.9	222.2	249.0	278.2	284.9	306.8	335.8
Advertising	731	14.9	18.7	20.0	21.9	21.2	22.5	23.7
Advertising agencies	7311	11.1	13.8	15.1	16.5	15.8	16.6	17.7
Credit reporting and collection	732	3.7	4.6	4.9	5.1	5.2	5.5	6.1
Mailing, reproduction, stenographic [3]	733	14.5	19.0	20.2	20.3	19.7	20.1	21.8
Direct mail advertising services	7331	3.8	5.7	6.2	7.3	7.0	7.3	8.3
Commercial art and graphic design	7336	(NA)	(NA)	(NA)	6.1	6.2	6.3	6.4
Services to dwellings and other buildings	734	13.3	17.3	19.7	21.8	21.6	22.5	22.9
Miscellaneous equipment rental and leasing	735	(NA)	(NA)	(NA)	21.5	20.9	21.0	22.7
Personnel supply services	736	14.7	24.3	26.3	29.4	28.9	32.0	35.5
Help supply services	7363	(NA)	(NA)	(NA)	21.7	21.5	24.1	26.7
Computer and data processing services [3]	737	45.1	67.7	77.2	86.9	92.4	102.0	114.0
Computer programming services	7371	(NA)	(NA)	(NA)	19.9	21.8	23.2	26.1
Prepackaged software	7372	(NA)	(NA)	(NA)	11.3	12.5	14.4	16.7
Computer integrated systems design	7373	(NA)	(NA)	(NA)	18.6	19.8	21.9	24.6
Data processing and preparation	7374	(NA)	(NA)	(NA)	17.8	18.8	20.6	22.8
Computer maintenance and repair	7378	(NA)	(NA)	(NA)	4.1	4.1	4.5	4.4
Miscellaneous business services [3]	738	(NA)	(NA)	(NA)	71.4	74.9	81.3	89.2
Detective and armored car services	7381	(NA)	(NA)	(NA)	9.6	10.2	10.3	10.8
Automotive repair, services, and parking [3]	75	51.7	66.4	71.7	75.4	73.1	79.6	85.5
Automotive rentals, no drivers [3]	751	14.6	19.5	21.1	23.3	22.9	23.6	25.2
Truck rental and leasing, without drivers	7513	5.5	7.7	8.2	9.0	8.5	8.4	8.5
Passenger car rental	7514	(NA)	(NA)	(NA)	9.7	10.2	11.2	12.2
Automotive repair shops [3]	753	30.5	38.6	42.9	43.8	41.5	46.3	49.8
Top & body repair & paint shops	7532	(NA)	(NA)	(NA)	13.3	12.6	13.6	14.6
General automotive repair shops	7538	(NA)	(NA)	(NA)	18.4	16.6	19.8	21.3
Automotive services, except repair	754	(NA)	(NA)	(NA)	6.1	6.3	7.2	7.9
Miscellaneous repair services	76	20.7	27.8	30.4	32.9	32.4	35.3	36.3
Electrical repair shops	762	(NA)	(NA)	(NA)	11.1	11.1	11.5	11.9
Motion pictures	78	21.5	31.2	35.0	38.3	41.0	43.6	48.1
Motion picture produc., distribution, allied services	781,2	15.0	22.6	24.7	26.6	29.0	31.1	34.7
Motion picture theaters	783	3.8	4.6	5.5	6.3	6.5	6.2	6.5
Video tape rental	784	(NA)	(NA)	(NA)	5.4	5.6	6.3	6.9
Amusement and recreation services [3]	79	31.2	40.2	42.2	48.0	48.7	53.7	59.4
Producers, orchestras, entertainers	792	6.4	8.4	8.0	10.0	10.6	11.6	14.0
Commercial sports	794	5.0	6.9	7.9	9.3	9.7	10.6	10.9
Amusement parks	7996	2.6	4.0	4.4	4.7	4.5	4.9	5.2
Membership sports and recreation clubs	7997	3.5	4.1	4.1	4.3	4.5	4.6	5.1
Health services [3][4]	80	147.4	203.8	220.1	247.3	266.4	289.6	304.1
Offices and clinics of doctors of medicine	801	72.1	101.0	107.9	117.7	125.5	136.4	139.4
Offices and clinics of dentists	802	20.6	25.7	27.3	29.1	30.4	33.4	35.4
Offices of other health practitioners	804	7.9	12.2	13.0	15.1	16.0	17.8	19.3
Offices and clinics of chiropractors	8041	2.7	4.0	4.5	4.9	5.1	6.0	6.5
Nursing and personal care facilities	805	17.5	21.5	23.7	27.0	29.4	31.3	33.8
Hospitals	806	15.7	22.7	24.8	28.8	31.2	33.6	35.3
Medical and dental laboratories	807	5.4	8.1	8.9	10.0	10.7	11.3	12.2
Medical laboratories	8071	3.9	6.6	7.4	8.3	9.0	9.5	10.3
Home health care services	808	(NA)	(NA)	(NA)	6.4	7.7	9.4	10.9
Legal services [4]	81	52.8	75.5	82.0	89.3	91.0	98.1	101.1
Vocational schools [4]	824	2.6	4.0	4.5	4.8	4.5	4.7	4.8
Social services [4]	83	(NA)	(NA)	(NA)	12.6	13.6	15.1	16.5
Child day care services	8351	2.6	3.6	3.8	4.3	4.3	4.9	5.3
Residential care	8361	(NA)	(NA)	(NA)	4.8	5.4	5.7	6.3
Museums, botanical, zoological gardens [4]	84	(NA)	(NA)	(NA)	0.1	0.1	0.2	0.2
Engineering and management services [3]	87	(NA)	(NA)	(NA)	196.2	200.8	213.9	223.7
Engineering services	8711	(NA)	(NA)	(NA)	58.5	59.4	61.2	61.3
Architectural services	8712	(NA)	(NA)	(NA)	12.8	12.0	12.4	13.2
Accounting, auditing, & bookkeeping	8721	21.2	29.3	32.4	32.8	34.0	37.6	40.6
Research and testing services [5]	873, ex. 8733	(NA)	(NA)	(NA)	22.5	23.0	25.0	27.4
Management services	8741	(NA)	(NA)	(NA)	19.9	21.0	22.8	23.8
Management consulting services	8742	(NA)	(NA)	(NA)	29.5	30.5	32.8	34.7
Facilities support services	8744	(NA)	(NA)	(NA)	5.6	6.0	6.0	5.8
Arrangement of passenger transportation [4]	472	6.3	8.1	8.9	9.3	8.8	9.3	9.7
Real estate agents and managers [4]	653	31.3	42.6	45.0	45.5	45.6	52.8	59.0

NA Not available.　[1] Standard Industrial Classification; see text, section 13.　[2] Excludes those on membership basis.　[3] Includes other kinds of businesses, not shown separately.　[4] Covers employer firms only.　[5] Excludes noncommercial research organizations.

Source: U.S. Bureau of the Census, *Current Business Reports, Service Annual Survey: 1993* (BS/93); and unpublished data.

No. 1318. Service Industries—Summary of Establishments, by State: 1992

[Based on 1987 Standard Industrial Classification code; see text, section 13]

DIVISION AND STATE	FIRMS SUBJECT TO FEDERAL INCOME TAX						TAX-EXEMPT FIRMS			
	All establishments		Establishments with payroll				Establishments with payroll			
	Establishments [1] (1,000)	Receipts (mil. dol.)	Establishments [1] (1,000)	Receipts (mil. dol.)	Payroll (mil. dol.)	Paid employees [2] (1,000)	Establishments [1] (1,000)	Revenues (mil. dol.)	Payroll (mil. dol.)	Paid employees [2] (1,000)
U.S	8,593.5	1,345,146	1,825.4	1,202,613	452,697	19,290	208.9	446,256	186,672	8,109
N.E. . . .	524.0	81,419	104.9	71,871	27,908	1,070	15.9	31,225	14,154	573
ME . .	46.7	4,246	9.0	3,597	1,367	68	1.7	2,068	956	45
NH . .	46.7	5,413	9.2	4,612	1,840	83	1.4	1,933	767	36
VT . .	27.7	2,325	5.0	1,946	633	37	1.1	1,021	449	22
MA . .	246.2	43,676	46.6	38,949	15,103	545	7.2	16,940	7,698	302
RI . .	33.3	4,196	7.6	3,664	1,413	64	1.1	2,217	1,003	43
CT . .	123.4	21,562	27.4	19,102	7,551	273	3.4	7,046	3,280	125
M.A . . .	1,227.9	227,191	277.4	202,649	75,238	2,812	33.6	89,401	40,752	1,631
NY . .	617.1	115,939	133.7	103,025	38,012	1,344	16.3	49,030	22,980	871
NJ . .	265.2	55,842	65.9	50,242	18,485	671	4.8	13,855	6,282	245
PA . .	345.6	55,409	77.8	49,383	18,741	797	12.4	26,516	11,490	514
E.N.C . .	1,273.3	185,044	277.5	167,019	65,455	2,946	35.7	77,872	32,219	1,482
OH . .	321.5	45,210	69.9	40,844	16,137	758	9.3	20,111	8,361	394
IN . . .	164.6	19,610	34.5	17,548	6,742	355	5.2	9,009	3,649	180
IL . . .	370.7	63,955	79.8	57,927	22,077	902	9.0	23,341	9,521	417
MI . . .	278.3	39,049	61.3	35,124	14,203	614	7.5	16,757	7,154	306
WI . .	138.1	17,220	32.0	15,577	6,295	317	4.8	8,654	3,534	185
W.N.C . .	636.2	72,240	122.4	64,468	24,808	1,235	20.9	32,693	14,274	738
MN . .	176.5	21,146	31.0	18,764	7,544	349	5.6	9,718	4,346	208
IA . . .	95.3	8,755	17.8	7,711	2,899	163	3.7	4,656	2,065	121
MO . .	166.6	22,388	36.4	20,339	7,699	374	4.4	9,484	3,996	195
ND . .	22.2	1,795	4.2	1,576	616	33	1.1	1,312	585	37
SD . .	25.2	2,076	4.8	1,790	592	34	1.1	1,258	552	33
NE . .	59.3	6,492	11.3	5,828	2,290	120	1.9	2,572	1,118	59
KS . .	91.0	9,589	16.9	8,460	3,168	162	3.0	3,693	1,611	86
S.A. . . .	1,460.4	239,872	335.5	217,306	82,773	3,637	32.6	75,442	29,708	1,261
DE . .	21.2	3,142	5.3	2,823	1,170	54	0.6	1,324	588	26
MD . .	179.1	29,822	36.8	26,937	10,765	419	3.9	9,853	3,925	163
DC . .	26.0	11,752	7.4	11,238	4,299	121	2.6	9,782	3,118	96
VA . .	200.8	36,436	45.9	33,606	13,138	526	4.7	10,782	4,191	176
WV . .	44.0	4,951	9.5	4,466	1,575	84	1.6	2,718	1,138	57
NC . .	196.1	24,631	42.2	22,155	8,410	425	4.8	9,777	4,152	185
SC . .	90.0	12,169	21.5	10,930	4,349	233	2.1	4,200	1,694	76
GA . .	207.7	34,081	46.9	30,802	11,409	502	3.8	9,122	3,706	163
FL . .	495.6	82,890	120.0	74,347	27,658	1,274	8.4	17,885	7,195	318
E.S.C . .	406.6	55,607	88.7	49,925	18,598	930	10.2	20,583	8,317	398
KY . .	103.8	11,685	21.0	10,378	3,864	211	2.6	4,753	1,922	99
TN . .	148.3	22,712	32.0	20,410	7,581	362	3.5	7,549	3,028	139
AL . .	98.7	14,933	23.0	13,649	5,162	248	2.4	5,319	2,148	99
MS . .	55.9	6,277	12.8	5,487	1,991	108	1.6	2,961	1,219	61
W.S.C . .	894.1	130,736	185.9	116,445	44,205	2,057	17.9	34,160	13,778	655
AR . .	67.8	6,902	14.0	6,007	2,250	133	1.9	2,946	1,206	64
LA . .	117.1	17,943	27.1	16,067	5,912	296	2.6	5,587	2,338	110
OK . .	112.1	11,169	21.2	9,607	3,641	196	2.5	3,935	1,620	83
TX . .	597.2	94,721	123.6	84,763	32,402	1,430	10.9	21,692	8,614	398
Mt	558.2	80,847	113.0	72,714	26,295	1,258	12.1	19,276	7,667	360
MT . .	34.3	2,629	6.9	2,197	722	44	1.4	1,243	524	29
ID . . .	38.3	3,918	7.3	3,440	1,305	64	0.9	1,089	447	22
WY . .	19.2	1,612	4.1	1,384	436	26	0.7	561	257	15
CO . .	168.2	21,229	32.9	18,810	7,183	319	3.3	6,301	2,401	104
NM . .	53.2	6,880	10.7	6,191	2,332	111	1.5	1,899	849	43
AZ . .	132.4	18,648	28.7	16,616	6,220	299	2.6	5,386	2,075	94
UT . .	65.4	8,389	11.7	7,491	2,667	139	1.0	1,784	732	35
NV . .	47.2	17,541	10.8	16,585	5,431	256	0.7	1,013	382	16
Pac . . .	1,612.8	272,189	320.2	240,217	87,418	3,346	30.1	65,604	25,804	1,011
WA . .	185.1	24,125	39.5	21,448	8,091	355	5.0	8,837	3,778	162
OR . .	118.9	12,382	23.3	10,663	3,963	195	3.1	4,479	1,857	87
CA . .	1,243.0	224,885	244.5	198,432	71,824	2,646	20.1	49,179	18,799	707
AK . .	24.2	2,770	4.5	2,382	884	32	0.9	1,028	445	17
HI . . .	41.6	8,027	8.5	7,291	2,654	118	1.0	2,081	924	37

[1] Number of establishments in business at any time during year.   [2] For the pay period including March 12.

Source: U.S. Bureau of the Census, *1992 Census of Service Industries*, Geographic Area Series, SC92-A-1 to 52 and Nonemployer Statistics Series, SC92-N-1.

Figure 28.1
U.S. International Transaction Balances: 1960 to 1994

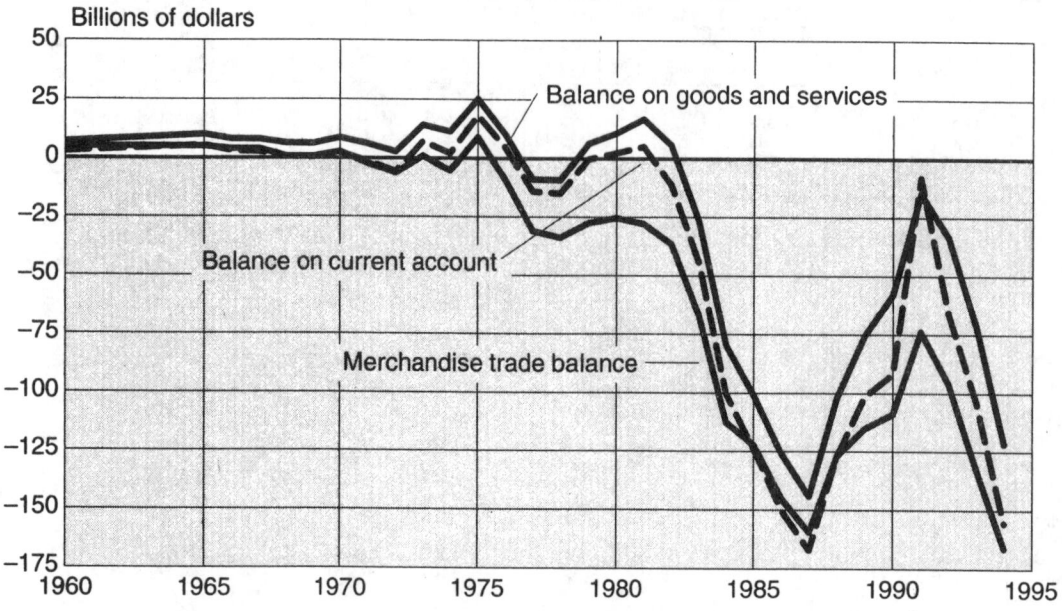

Source: Chart prepared by U.S. Bureau of the Census. For data, see table 1319.

Figure 28.2
Top Purchasers of U.S. Exports and Suppliers of U.S. General Imports: 1994

Total U.S. Exports $513 billion

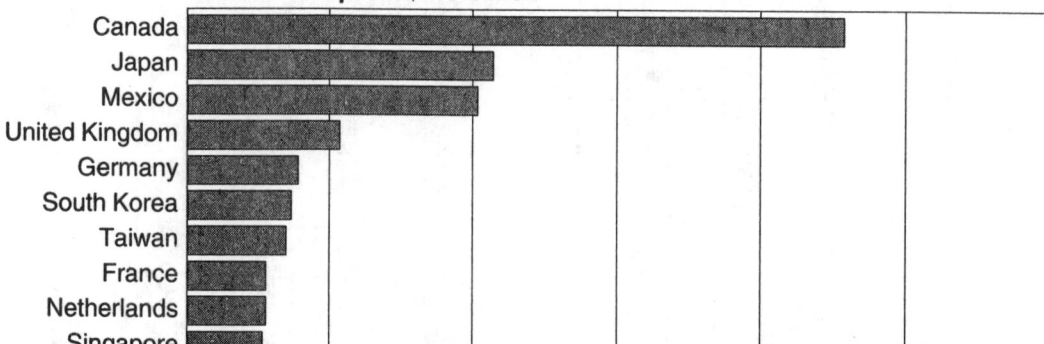

Total U.S. General Imports $664 billion

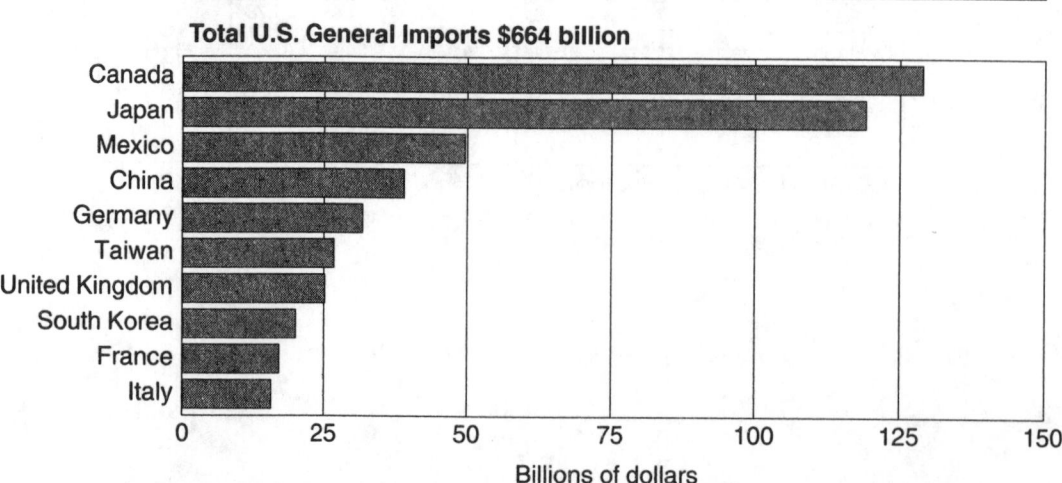

Billions of dollars

Source: Chart prepared by U.S. Bureau of the Census. For data, see table 1341.

Foreign Commerce and Aid

This section presents data on the flow of goods, services, and capital between the United States and other countries; changes in official reserve assets of the United States; international investments; foreign assistance programs; and import duties.

The Bureau of Economic Analysis publishes current figures on U.S. international transactions and the U.S. international investment position in its monthly *Survey of Current Business.* Statistics for the foreign aid programs are presented by the Agency for International Development (AID) in its annual *U.S. Overseas Loans and Grants and Assistance from International Organizations;* and by the Department of Agriculture in its *Foreign Agricultural Trade of the United States.*

The principal source of merchandise import and export data is the Bureau of the Census. Current data are presented monthly in *U.S. Merchandise Trade,* (beginning 1994, retitled *U.S. International Trade in Goods and Services*) report series FT900, and *U.S. Merchandise Trade: Exports, General Imports, and Imports for Consumption,* report series FT925. The *Bureau of the Census Catalog* and the *Guide to Foreign Trade Statistics* lists the Bureau's monthly and annual reports in this field. In addition, the International Trade Administration and the Bureau of Economic Analysis present summary as well as selected commodity and country data for U.S. foreign trade in the *Overseas Business Reports* and the *Survey of Current Business,* respectively. The merchandise trade data in the latter source include balance of payments adjustments to the Census data. The Treasury Department's *Monthly Treasury Statement of Receipts and Outlays of the United States Government* contains information on import duties.

International accounts.—The international transactions tables (Nos. 1319 to 1321) show, for given time periods, the transfer of goods, services, grants, and financial assets and liabilities between the United States and the rest of the world. The international investment

In Brief

The U.S. international trade in goods and services saw the deficit increase from $75.5 billion in 1993 to $108.1 billion in 1994.

U.S. trade in advanced technology products showed a $22.4 billion surplus in 1994, led by surpluses in aerospace and information and communication products.

position table (No. 1322) presents, for specific dates, the value of U.S. investments abroad and of foreign investments in the United States. The movement of foreign and U.S. capital as presented in the balance of payments is not the only factor affecting the total value of foreign investments. Among the other factors are changes in the valuation of assets or liabilities, including changes in prices of securities, defaults, expropriations, and write-offs.

Direct investment abroad means the ownership or control, directly or indirectly, by one person of 10 percent or more of the voting securities of an incorporated business enterprise or an equivalent interest in an unincorporated business enterprise. Direct investment position is the value of U.S. parents' claims on the equity of, and receivables due from, foreign affiliates, less foreign affiliates' receivables due from their U.S. parents. Income consists of parents' shares in the earnings of their affiliates plus net interest received by parents on intercompany accounts, less withholding taxes on dividends and interest.

Foreign aid.—Foreign assistance is divided into three major categories—grants (military supplies and services and other grants), credits, and other assistance (through net accumulation of foreign currency claims from the sale of agricultural commodities). *Grants* are transfers for which no payment is expected (other than a limited percentage of the foreign currency "counterpart" funds generated by the grant), or which at most involve an obligation on the part of the receiver to extend aid to the United States or other countries to achieve a common objective. *Credits* are loan disbursements or transfers under other agreements which give rise to specific obligations to repay, over a period of years, usually with interest. All known returns to the U.S. Government stemming from grants and credits (reverse grants, returns of grants, and payments of principal) are taken into account in net grants and net credits, but no allowance is made for interest or commissions. *Other assistance* represents the transfer of U.S. farm products in exchange for foreign currencies (plus, since enactment of Public Law 87-128, currency claims from principal and interest collected on credits extended under the farm products program), *less* the Government's disbursements of the currencies as grants, credits, or for purchases. The net acquisition of currencies represents net transfers of resources to foreign countries under the agricultural programs, in addition to those classified as grants or credits.

The basic instrument for extending military aid to friendly nations has been the Mutual Defense Assistance Program authorized by the Congress in 1949. Prior to 1952, economic and technical aid was authorized in the Foreign Assistance Act of 1948, the 1950 Act for International Development, and other legislation which set up programs for specific countries. In 1952, these economic, technical, and military aid programs were combined under the Mutual Security Act, which in turn was followed by the Foreign Assistance Act passed in 1961. Appropriations to provide military assistance were also made in the Department of Defense Appropriation Act (rather than the Foreign Assistance Appropriation Act) beginning in 1966 for certain countries in Southeast Asia and in other legislation concerning program for specific countries (such as Israel). Figures on activity under the Foreign Assistance Act as reported in the *Foreign Grants and Credits* series differ from data published by AID or its immediate predecessors, due largely to differences in reporting, timing, and treatment of particular items.

Exports.—The Bureau of the Census compiles export data primarily from Shipper's Export Declarations required to be filed with customs officials for shipments leaving the United States. They include U.S. exports under mutual security programs and exclude shipments to U.S. Armed Forces for their own use.

The value reported in the export statistics is generally equivalent to a free alongside ship (f.a.s.) value at the U.S. port of export, based on the transaction price, including inland freight, insurance, and other charges incurred in placing the merchandise alongside the carrier at the U.S. port of exportation. This value, as defined, excludes the cost of loading merchandise aboard the exporting carrier and also excludes freight, insurance, and any other charges or transportation and other costs beyond the U.S. port of exportation. The country of destination is defined as the country of ultimate destination or country where the merchandise is to be consumed, further processed, or manufactured, as known to the shipper at the time of exportation. When ultimate destination is not known, the shipment is statistically credited to the last country to which the shipper knows the merchandise will be shipped in the same form as exported.

For certain "low-valued" shipments, the export statistics include estimates based upon selected samples of such shipments. The dollar value of the "low-valued" shipments has varied. For instance, effective January 1987 through September 1989, data are estimated for shipments valued under $1,501; from October 1989 through December 1989, data are estimated for shipments valued under $2,501 to all countries.

Effective January 1990, the United States began substituting Canadian import statistics for U.S. exports to Canada. As a result of the data exchange between the United States and Canada, the United States has adopted the Canadian import exemption level for its export statistics based on shipments to Canada.

Data are estimated for shipments valued under $2,501 to all countries, except Canada, using factors based on the ratios of low-valued shipments to individual country totals. These shipments represent slightly less than 2.5 percent of the monthly value of U.S. exports to those countries. Data are estimated for shipments reported on Canadian import documents which total less than $900 (Canadian). Such shipments represent 2 percent of the monthly value of U.S. exports to Canada.

Prior to 1989, exports were based on Schedule B, Statistical Classification of Domestic and Foreign Commodities Exported from the United States. These statistics were retabulated and published using Schedule E, Standard International Trade Classification, Revision 2. Beginning in 1989, Schedule B classifications were based on the Harmonized System and made to coincide with the Standard International Trade Classification, Revision 3. This revision will affect the comparability of most export series beginning with the 1989 data for commodities.

Imports.—The Bureau of the Census compiles import data from various customs forms required to be filed with customs officials. Data on import values are presented on two bases in this section: the c.i.f. (cost, insurance, and freight) and the customs import value (as appraised by the U.S. Customs Service in accordance with legal requirements of the Tariff Act of 1930, as amended). This latter valuation, primarily used for collection of import duties, frequently does not reflect the actual transaction value. Country of origin is defined as country where the merchandise was grown, mined, or manufactured. If country of origin is unknown, country of shipment is reported.

Imports are classified either as "General imports" or "Imports for consumption." *General imports* are a combination of entries for immediate consumption, entries into customs bonded warehouses, and entries into U.S. Foreign Trade Zones, thus generally reflecting total arrivals of merchandise. *Imports for consumption* are a combination of entries for immediate

consumption, withdrawals from warehouses for consumption, and entries of merchandise into U.S. customs territory from U.S. Foreign Trade Zones, thus generally reflecting the total of the commodities entered into U.S. consumption channels.

Since July 1953, the import statistics include estimates, not classified by commodity, for certain low-valued shipments. For instance, from January 1985 through September 1989, import statistics include estimates for shipments valued under $1,001. Effective October 1989, import statistics are fully compiled on shipments valued over $1,250 or, under certain textile programs, for any article which must be reported on a formal entry. Value data for shipments valued under $1,251 and not required to be reported on formal entries are estimated for individual countries using factors based on the ratios of low-valued shipments to individual country totals for past periods. The estimated low-valued shipments generally amount to slightly less than 4 percent of the import total.

Prior to 1989, imports were based on the Tariff Schedule of the United States Annotated. The statistics were retabulated and published using Schedule A, Standard International Trade Classification, Revision 2. Beginning in 1989, the statistics are based on the Harmonized Tariff Schedule of the United States, which coincides with the Standard International Trade Classification, Revision 3. This revision will affect the comparability of most import commodity series beginning with the 1989 data.

Area coverage.—Except as noted, the geographic area covered by the export and import trade statistics is the United States Customs area (includes the 50 States, the District of Columbia and Puerto Rico), the U.S. Virgin Islands (effective January 1981), and U.S. Foreign Trade Zones (effective July 1982). Data for selected tables and total values for 1980, have been revised to reflect the U.S. Virgin Islands' trade with foreign countries, where possible.

No. 1319. U.S. International Transactions, by Type of Transaction: 1980 to 1994

[In millions of dollars. Minus sign (-) indicates debits. See also *Historical Statistics, Colonial Times to 1970*, series U 1-25]

TYPE OF TRANSACTION	1980	1985	1986	1987	1988	1989	1990	1991	1992	1993	1994
Exports of goods and services [1]	**344,440**	**381,572**	**400,337**	**447,262**	**557,630**	**641,471**	**696,841**	**717,041**	**731,373**	**755,533**	**832,871**
Merchandise, excl. military [2][3]	224,250	215,915	223,344	250,208	320,230	362,116	389,303	416,913	440,361	456,866	502,729
Foods, feeds, and beverages	36,278	24,566	23,522	25,229	33,770	37,428	35,118	35,829	40,334	40,692	42,084
Industrial supplies and materials	72,088	61,159	64,720	70,052	90,019	99,909	105,682	109,826	109,593	111,871	121,466
Capital goods, except automotive	76,283	79,322	82,815	92,707	119,103	139,562	153,278	166,453	176,073	182,218	205,550
Automotive vehicles and parts [4]	17,443	24,945	25,097	27,583	33,397	34,940	36,503	40,008	47,028	52,406	57,174
Consumer goods (nonfood) [5]	17,751	14,593	16,730	20,307	26,981	36,565	42,779	46,858	51,424	54,655	59,990
Services	47,584	72,896	86,135	97,816	109,986	126,838	147,239	163,215	176,563	184,811	195,287
Transfers under U.S. military agency sales contracts	9,029	8,718	8,549	11,106	9,289	8,587	9,964	10,924	10,828	11,413	10,845
Travel	10,588	17,762	20,385	23,563	29,434	36,205	43,007	48,385	54,284	57,621	60,001
Passenger fares	2,591	4,411	5,582	7,003	8,976	10,657	15,298	15,854	16,972	16,550	17,651
Other transportation	11,618	14,674	15,784	17,334	19,456	20,533	21,954	22,349	22,704	23,151	24,733
Royalties and license fees	7,085	6,550	7,927	9,914	11,802	13,818	16,634	18,107	19,922	20,398	22,823
Other private services	6,276	19,904	27,312 [6]	28,369	30,366	36,450	39,713	46,906	50,992	54,870	58,453
U.S. Government misc. services	398	878	595	526	664	587	668	690	861	808	782
Income on U.S. assets abroad	72,606	92,760	90,858	99,239	127,414	152,517	160,300	136,914	114,449	113,856	134,855
Direct investment	37,146	29,630	30,850	38,080	50,436	55,368	58,740	52,124	49,889	57,515	66,585
Other private receipts	32,898	57,631	53,596	55,848	70,275	91,496	91,048	76,766	57,447	51,272	64,232
U.S. Government receipts	2,562	5,499	6,413	5,311	6,703	5,653	10,512	8,023	7,114	5,070	4,038
Imports of goods, services and income	**-333,774**	**-483,994**	**-527,363**	**-591,307**	**-660,847**	**-718,157**	**-754,926**	**-730,680**	**-767,217**	**-827,312**	**-954,422**
Merchandise, excl. military [2][3]	-249,750	-338,088	-368,425	-409,765	-447,189	-477,365	-498,336	-490,981	-536,458	-589,441	-669,093
Foods, feeds, and beverages	-18,564	-21,850	-24,376	-24,809	-24,928	-25,077	-26,⬤3	-26,205	-27,609	-27,866	-30,958
Industrial supplies and materials	-132,472	-114,008	-104,210	-113,746	-122,684	-135,112	-144,831	-132,963	-140,590	-152,435	-164,815
Capital goods, except automotive	-31,576	-61,287	-71,990	-85,128	-102,202	-112,454	-116,041	-120,802	-134,252	-152,366	-184,538
Automotive vehicles and parts [4]	-28,257	-64,905	-78,061	-85,174	-87,947	-87,379	-88,472	-85,696	-91,788	-102,421	-118,636
Consumer goods (nonfood) [5]	-34,268	-66,336	-79,355	-88,824	-96,425	-103,453	-105,293	-107,777	-122,657	-134,015	-146,304
Services	-41,491	-72,818	-79,842	-90,240	-97,851	-101,934	-117,016	-117,618	-120,850	-127,961	-135,293
Direct defense expenditures	-10,851	-13,108	-13,730	-14,950	-15,604	-15,313	-17,531	-16,409	-13,862	-12,176	-10,577
Travel	-10,397	-24,558	-25,913	-29,310	-32,114	-33,416	-37,349	-35,322	-39,007	-40,564	-43,059
Passenger fares	-3,607	-6,444	-6,505	-7,283	-7,729	-8,249	-10,531	-10,608	-10,608	-11,416	-12,558
Other transportation	-11,790	-15,643	-16,715	-17,788	-19,534	-20,659	-23,401	-23,297	-23,460	-24,502	-25,718
Royalties and license fees	-724	-1,165	-1,392	-1,844	-2,585	-2,528	-3,135	-4,076	-4,987	-4,840	-5,926
Other private services	-2,909	-10,166	-13,901 [6]	-17,172	-18,365	-19,898	-23,150	-26,387	-26,625	-32,119	-34,791
U.S. Government miscellaneous services	-1,214	-1,735	-1,686	-1,893	-1,921	-1,871	-1,919	-2,116	-2,301	-2,344	-2,663
Income on foreign assets in the United States	-42,532	-73,087	-79,095	-91,302	-115,806	-138,858	-139,574	-122,081	-109,909	-109,910	-150,036
Direct investment	-8,635	-7,213	-7,058	-7,425	-11,693	-6,507	-2,871	3,244	-2,176	-5,110	-25,188
Other private payments	-21,214	-42,745	-47,412	-57,659	-72,398	-93,987	-95,661	-83,796	-67,253	-63,239	-77,829
U.S. Government payments	-12,684	-23,129	-24,625	-26,218	-31,715	-38,364	-41,042	-41,529	-40,480	-41,561	-47,019
Unilateral transfers (excl. military grants), net	**-8,349**	**-22,950**	**-24,176**	**-23,052**	**-24,977**	**-26,134**	**-33,663**	**6,687**	**-32,042**	**-32,117**	**-34,121**
U.S. Government grants	-5,486	-11,268	-11,867	-10,287	-10,518	-10,918	-17,685	23,959	-15,010	-14,620	-14,532
U.S. Government pensions	-1,818	-2,138	-2,197	-2,221	-2,501	-2,516	-2,934	-3,461	-3,735	-3,785	-4,246
Private remittances and other transfers	-1,044	-9,545	-10,112	-10,544	-11,958	-12,700	-13,043	-13,811	-13,297	-13,712	-15,343

TYPE OF TRANSACTION	1980	1985	1986	1987	1988	1989	1990	1991	1992	1993	1994
U.S. assets abroad, net (increase/capital outflow (-))	**-86,967**	**-39,225**	**-104,818**	**-71,443**	**-99,360**	**-168,744**	**-70,363**	**-51,512**	**-61,510**	**-147,898**	**-125,687**
U.S. official reserve assets, net	-8,155	-3,858	312	9,149	-3,912	-25,293	-2,158	5,763	3,901	-1,379	5,346
Special drawing rights	-16	-897	-246	-509	127	-535	-192	-177	2,316	-537	-441
Reserve position in the International Monetary Fund	-1,667	908	1,501	2,070	1,025	471	731	-367	-2,692	-44	494
Foreign currencies	-6,472	-3,869	-942	7,588	-5,064	-25,229	-2,697	6,307	4,277	-797	5,293
U.S. Govt. assets, other than official reserve assets, net	-5,162	-2,821	-2,022	1,006	2,967	1,259	2,307	2,900	-1,652	-306	-278
U.S. credits and other long-term assets	-9,860	-7,657	-9,084	-6,506	-7,680	-5,590	-8,430	-12,874	-7,392	-6,024	-5,156
Repayments on U.S. credits and other long-term assets [7]	4,456	4,719	6,089	7,625	10,370	6,723	10,867	16,776	5,805	6,026	4,923
U.S. foreign currency holdings and U.S. short-term assets, net	242	117	973	-113	277	125	-130	-1,002	-65	-308	-45
U.S. private assets, net	-73,651	-32,547	-103,109	-81,597	-98,414	-144,710	-70,512	-60,175	-63,759	-146,213	-130,755
Direct investments abroad	-19,222	-13,401	-17,090	-27,181	-15,448	-36,834	-29,950	-31,295	-41,004	-57,870	-58,422
Foreign securities	-3,568	-7,481	-4,271	-5,251	-7,846	-22,070	-28,765	-44,740	-45,114	-119,983	-60,621
U.S. claims on unaffiliated foreigners reported by U.S. nonbanking concerns	-4,023	-10,342	-21,773	-7,046	-21,193	-27,646	-27,824	11,097	45	-598	-9,679
U.S. claims reported by U.S. banks, n.i.e. [8]	-46,838	-1,323	-59,975	-42,119	-53,927	-58,160	16,027	4,763	22,314	32,238	-2,033
Foreign assets in the U.S., net (increase/capital inflow (+))	**58,112**	**141,183**	**226,111**	**242,983**	**240,265**	**218,490**	**122,192**	**98,134**	**146,504**	**230,698**	**314,614**
Foreign official assets in the U.S., net	15,497	-1,119	35,648	45,387	39,758	8,503	33,910	17,199	40,858	71,681	38,912
U.S. Government securities	11,895	-1,139	33,150	44,802	43,050	1,532	30,243	16,147	22,403	52,764	36,429
U.S. Treasury securities	9,708	-838	34,364	43,238	41,741	149	29,576	14,846	18,454	48,702	30,441
Other	2,187	-301	-1,214	1,564	1,309	1,383	667	1,301	3,949	4,062	5,988
Other U.S. Government liabilities	615	844	2,195	-2,326	-467	160	1,868	1,177	2,572	1,666	2,514
U.S. liabilities reported by U.S. banks, n.i.e. [8]	-159	645	1,187	3,918	-319	4,976	3,385	-1,484	16,571	14,666	2,317
Other foreign official assets	3,145	-1,469	-884	-1,007	-2,506	1,835	-1,586	1,359	-688	2,585	-2,348
Other foreign assets in the United States, net	42,615	142,301	190,463	197,596	200,507	209,987	88,282	80,935	105,646	159,017	275,702
Direct investments in the United States	16,918	20,010	35,623	58,219	57,278	67,736	47,915	26,086	9,888	21,366	60,071
U.S. Treasury securities	2,645	20,433	3,809	-7,643	20,239	29,618	-2,534	18,826	36,857	24,849	32,925
U.S. securities other than U.S. Treasury securities	5,457	50,962	70,969	42,120	26,353	38,767	1,592	35,144	29,867	80,068	58,562
U.S. liabilities to unaffiliated foreigners reported by U.S. nonbanking concerns	6,852	9,851	3,325	18,363	32,893	22,086	45,133	-3,115	13,573	14,282	17,955
U.S. liabilities reported by U.S. banks, n.i.e. [8]	10,743	41,045	76,737	86,537	63,744	51,780	-3,824	3,994	15,461	18,452	106,189
Allocations of special drawing rights	**1,152**	**(X)**	**(X)**	**(X)**	**(X)**	**(X)**	**(X)**	**(X)**	**(X)**	**(X)**	**(X)**
Statistical discrepancy	25,386	23,415	29,908	-4,443	-12,712	53,075	39,919	-39,670	-17,108	21,096	-33,255
Balance on merchandise trade	-25,500	-122,173	-145,081	-159,557	-126,959	-115,249	-109,033	-74,068	-96,097	-132,575	-166,364
Balance on services	6,093	78	6,292	7,576	12,135	24,904	30,223	45,596	55,713	56,850	59,994
Balance on investment income	30,073	19,673	11,763	7,937	11,607	13,659	20,725	14,833	4,540	3,946	-15,181
Balance on goods, services, and income	10,666	-102,422	-127,026	-144,045	-103,217	-76,686	-58,085	-13,639	-35,844	-71,779	-121,551
Unilateral transfers, net	-8,349	-22,950	-24,176	-23,052	-24,977	-26,134	-33,663	6,687	-32,042	-32,117	-34,121
Balance on current account	2,317	-125,372	-151,201	-167,097	-128,194	-102,820	-91,748	-6,952	-67,886	-103,896	-155,673

X Not applicable.   [1] Excludes transfers of goods and services under U.S. military grant programs.   [2] Excludes exports of goods and services under U.S. military agency sales contracts identified in Bureau of the Census export documents, excludes imports of goods under direct defense expenditures identified in Census import documents, and reflects various other adjustments (for valuation, coverage, and timing) of Census statistics to a balance of payments basis.   [3] Includes other end-use items, not shown separately.   [4] Includes engines.   [5] Excludes automotive.   [6] Break in series due to inclusion of new data. See Technical Note in *Survey of Current Business,* June 1979.   [7] Includes sales of foreign obligations to foreigners.   [8] Not included elsewhere.

Source: U.S. Bureau of Economic Analysis, *Survey of Current Business,* March 1995.

No. 1320. U.S. Balances on International Transactions, by Area and Selected Country: 1992 to 1994

[In millions of dollars. Minus sign (-) indicates debits]

AREA OR COUNTRY	1992, BALANCE ON—			1993, BALANCE ON—			1994, BALANCE ON—		
	Merchandise trade [1]	Goods, services, and income	Current account	Merchandise trade [1]	Goods, services, and income	Current account	Merchandise trade [1]	Goods, services, and income	Current account
All areas	**-96,097**	**-35,844**	**-67,886**	**-132,575**	**-71,779**	**-103,896**	**-166,364**	**-121,551**	**-155,673**
Western Europe	3,068	4,656	5,060	-9,690	-13,039	-12,222	-17,560	-29,182	-28,321
European Economic	6,640	6,170	7,785	-7,246	-11,423	-9,478	-11,915	-23,635	-21,956
United Kingdom	2,459	-9,385	-8,077	4,165	-7,586	-6,111	1,040	-18,150	-16,866
Eastern Europe	3,654	3,358	1,928	2,658	3,190	1,444	-486	-108	-2,977
Canada	-9,503	3,634	3,348	-12,116	1,703	1,391	-16,527	-4,554	-4,922
Latin America, other Western Hemisphere	6,207	16,552	7,895	3,025	17,045	8,330	3,554	16,222	8,002
Australia	5,015	9,125	9,045	4,812	9,248	9,174	6,356	11,738	11,649
Japan [2]	-50,525	-42,969	-43,135	-60,544	-54,097	-54,279	-67,317	-65,846	-65,996
Other Asia and Africa	-54,101	-39,238	-53,127	-60,944	-45,200	-58,949	-74,474	-59,513	-73,046
International and unallocated	88	9,038	1,102	224	9,371	1,216	90	9,691	-61

[1] Adjusted to balance of payments basis; excludes exports under U.S. military sales contracts and imports under direct defense expenditures.   [2] Includes Ryukyu Islands.

Source: U.S. Bureau of Economic Analysis, *Survey of Current Business,* June 1994 and March 1995.

No. 1321. Private Services Transaction, by Type of Service and Country: 1990 to 1993

[In millions of dollars]

TYPE OF SERVICE AND COUNTRY	EXPORTS				IMPORTS			
	1990	1991	1992	1993	1990	1991	1992	1993
Total private services	**136,606**	**151,602**	**164,874**	**172,590**	**97,566**	**99,093**	**104,688**	**113,441**
Travel	43,007	48,385	54,284	57,621	37,349	35,322	39,007	40,564
Overseas	30,806	34,518	40,406	45,044	28,929	26,506	30,294	31,740
Canada	7,093	8,500	8,182	7,458	3,541	3,705	3,554	3,692
Mexico	5,108	5,367	5,696	5,119	4,879	5,111	5,159	5,132
Passenger fares	15,298	15,854	16,972	16,550	10,531	10,012	10,608	11,416
Other transportation	21,954	22,349	22,704	23,151	23,401	23,297	23,460	24,502
Freight	7,272	7,334	7,230	7,559	12,586	11,947	11,725	12,700
Port services	13,662	13,979	14,294	14,467	9,920	10,421	10,762	10,817
Other	1,020	1,036	1,180	1,125	895	929	974	985
Royalties and license fees	16,634	18,107	19,922	20,398	3,135	4,076	4,987	4,840
Affiliated services	13,250	14,395	15,927	15,974	2,206	2,996	3,259	3,479
Unaffiliated services	3,384	3,712	3,994	4,424	931	1,080	1,728	1,360
Other private services	39,713	46,906	50,992	54,870	23,150	26,387	26,625	32,119
Affiliated services	13,622	14,343	16,115	15,981	9,117	9,602	9,970	10,594
Unaffiliated services	26,091	32,564	34,878	38,888	14,033	16,785	16,655	21,525
Education	5,126	5,683	6,210	6,830	658	699	723	764
Financial services	4,417	4,976	5,466	6,518	2,475	2,668	3,524	5,606
Insurance, net	751	1,046	1,173	1,519	1,910	2,467	1,333	2,913
Telecommunications	2,735	3,291	3,019	3,224	5,583	6,608	6,061	6,538
Business, professional, and technical services	6,951	11,249	12,110	13,289	1,891	2,785	3,389	3,928
Advertising	130	274	323	313	243	301	484	612
Computer and data processing services	1,031	1,738	1,823	2,142	44	116	126	289
Data base and other information services	283	442	648	735	54	51	84	88
Research, development, and testing services	384	602	662	610	210	241	251	255
Management, consulting, and public relations services	354	870	729	761	135	271	246	291
Legal services	451	1,309	1,397	1,453	111	244	314	326
Construction, engineering, architectural, and mining services	867	1,478	1,923	2,347	170	315	279	297
Other services	947	1,578	1,565	1,586	135	679	831	846
Canada	15,532	17,412	17,099	16,352	7,515	7,962	8,016	8,585
Europe	48,644	54,020	62,076	63,518	39,849	39,236	42,262	47,480
Western Europe	47,641	52,841	60,837	61,826	39,050	38,183	40,851	46,449
European Union [1]	39,476	44,496	51,667	52,865	33,417	32,883	35,290	39,800
Belgium-Luxembourg	1,756	1,977	2,333	2,315	1,018	957	946	1,018
France	5,565	6,175	7,103	6,916	4,168	3,924	4,723	5,051
Germany	7,478	8,924	11,057	11,236	6,823	6,434	6,673	7,381
Italy	3,321	3,720	4,360	4,132	3,474	3,256	3,571	3,553
Netherlands	3,279	3,595	3,798	4,037	1,939	2,197	2,345	2,204
United Kingdom	13,027	14,188	16,054	17,432	11,567	12,107	11,990	15,838
Other	5,050	5,917	6,962	6,797	4,428	4,008	5,042	4,755
Other Western Europe	8,165	8,345	9,170	8,961	5,633	5,300	5,561	6,649
Eastern Europe	1,003	1,179	1,239	1,692	799	1,053	1,411	1,031
Latin America and other Western Hemisphere	21,226	24,010	25,218	27,709	19,401	20,374	20,650	21,501
Mexico	7,387	8,235	8,651	8,426	7,388	7,754	7,999	8,331
Venezuela	1,045	1,224	1,357	1,640	719	601	642	711
Other	12,794	14,551	15,210	17,643	11,294	12,019	12,009	12,459
Other countries	45,881	51,779	55,793	60,267	28,095	29,379	31,496	34,069
Australia	3,299	3,252	3,426	3,593	2,293	2,381	2,241	2,139
Japan	21,402	24,160	25,419	26,901	10,547	11,720	11,580	12,885
Other	21,180	24,367	26,948	29,773	15,255	15,278	17,675	19,045
Int'l organizations and unallocated	5,325	4,383	4,690	4,746	2,706	2,143	2,265	1,808

[1] Formerly European Community (EC12), comprises Belgium, Denmark, France, Germany, Greece, Ireland, Italy, Luxembourg, Netherlands, Portugal, Spain, and the United Kingdom.

Source: U.S. Bureau of Economic Analysis, *Survey of Current Business,* September 1994.

No. 1322. International Investment Position: 1980 to 1993

[**In millions of dollars.** Estimates for end of year; subject to considerable error due to nature of basic data. See *Historical Statistics, Colonial Times to 1970,* series U 26-39, for similar data]

TYPE OF INVESTMENT	1980	1985	1988	1989	1990	1991	1992	1993
U.S. net international investment position:								
Current cost	**392,547**	**125,268**	**−144,817**	**−251,413**	**−251,441**	**−349,541**	**−507,943**	**−555,735**
Market value	(NA)	128,523	910	−91,806	−224,062	−368,716	−590,008	−507,659
U.S. assets abroad:								
Current cost	**936,275**	**1,296,388**	**1,772,958**	**1,978,956**	**2,066,885**	**2,136,988**	**2,149,589**	**2,370,427**
Market value	(NA)	1,288,313	1,935,870	2,236,700	2,165,720	2,300,154	2,267,311	2,647,415
U.S. official reserve assets	171,412	117,930	144,179	168,714	174,664	159,223	147,435	164,945
Gold	155,816	85,834	107,434	105,164	102,406	92,561	87,168	102,556
Special drawing rights	2,610	7,293	9,637	9,951	10,989	11,240	8,503	9,039
Reserve position in IMF	2,852	11,947	9,745	9,048	9,076	9,488	11,759	11,818
Foreign currencies	10,134	12,856	17,363	44,551	52,193	45,934	40,005	41,532
U.S. Government assets, other	63,865	87,752	86,117	84,489	81,993	78,984	80,635	80,882
U.S. loans and other long-term assets	62,023	85,814	85,388	83,903	81,365	77,426	79,011	78,987
U.S. foreign currency holdings and short-term assets	1,842	1,938	729	586	628	1,558	1,624	1,895
U.S. private assets:								
Current cost	700,998	1,090,706	1,542,662	1,725,753	1,810,228	1,898,781	1,921,519	2,124,600
Market value	(NA)	1,082,631	1,705,574	1,983,497	1,909,063	2,061,947	2,039,241	2,401,588
Direct investments abroad:								
Current cost	396,249	387,183	515,702	560,017	620,533	650,591	668,181	716,163
Market value	(NA)	379,108	678,614	817,761	719,368	813,757	785,903	993,151
Foreign securities	62,454	114,288	175,976	217,612	228,693	301,493	331,445	518,481
U.S. claims on unaffiliated foreigners [1]	38,429	141,872	197,757	234,307	265,315	256,295	253,870	254,502
U.S. claims reported by U.S. banks [2]	203,866	447,363	653,227	713,817	695,687	690,402	668,023	635,454
Foreign assets in the U.S.								
Current cost	**543,728**	**1,171,120**	**1,917,775**	**2,230,369**	**2,318,326**	**2,486,529**	**2,657,532**	**2,926,162**
Market value	(NA)	1,159,790	1,934,960	2,328,506	2,389,782	2,668,870	2,857,319	3,155,074
Foreign official assets in the U.S.	176,062	202,482	322,036	341,859	375,337	401,487	442,943	516,874
U.S. Government securities	118,189	145,063	260,934	263,725	295,005	315,932	335,695	388,528
Other U.S. Government liabilities	13,367	15,803	15,200	15,374	17,241	18,419	20,991	22,657
U.S. liabilities reported by U.S. banks [2]	30,381	26,734	31,520	36,495	39,880	38,396	54,967	69,633
Other foreign official assets	14,125	14,882	14,382	26,265	23,211	28,740	31,290	36,056
Other foreign assets in the U.S:								
Current cost	367,666	968,638	1,595,739	1,888,510	1,942,989	2,085,042	2,214,589	2,409,288
Market value	(NA)	957,308	1,612,924	1,986,647	2,014,445	2,267,383	2,414,376	2,638,200
Direct investments:								
Current cost	125,944	231,326	374,345	436,597	468,145	491,877	497,059	516,724
Market value	(NA)	219,996	391,530	534,734	539,601	674,218	696,846	745,636
U.S. securities other than U.S. Treasury securities	74,114	207,868	392,292	482,864	467,437	559,180	620,972	733,172
U.S. liabilities to unaffiliated foreigners [1]	30,426	86,993	144,548	167,093	213,406	208,908	220,692	233,299
U.S. liabilities reported by U.S. banks [2]	121,069	354,497	583,677	635,467	631,597	635,571	651,031	672,011
U.S. Treasury securities	16,113	87,954	100,877	166,489	162,404	189,506	224,835	254,082

NA Not available.   [1] Reported by U.S. nonbanking concerns.   [2] Not included elsewhere.

Source: U.S. Bureau of Economic Analysis, *Survey of Current Business,* June 1994.

No. 1323. U.S. Reserve Assets: 1980 to 1994

[**In billions of dollars.** As of **end of year,** except as indicated]

TYPE	1980	1985	1986	1987	1988	1989	1990	1991	1992	1993	1994
Total	26.8	43.2	48.5	45.8	47.8	74.6	83.3	77.7	71.3	73.4	74.3
Gold stock [1]	11.2	11.1	11.1	11.1	11.1	11.1	11.1	11.1	11.1	11.1	11.1
Special drawing rights	2.6	7.3	8.4	10.3	9.6	10.0	11.0	11.2	8.5	9.0	10.0
Foreign currencies	10.1	12.9	17.3	13.1	17.4	44.6	52.2	45.9	40.0	41.5	41.2
Reserve position in IMF [2]	2.9	11.9	11.7	11.3	9.7	9.0	9.1	9.5	11.8	11.8	12.0

[1] Includes gold in Exchange Stabilization Fund; excludes gold held under earmark at Federal Reserve banks for foreign and international accounts. Beginning 1975, gold assets were valued at $42.22 pursuant to the amending of Section 2 of the Par Value Modification Act, PL-93-110, approved September 21, 1973.   [2] International Monetary Fund.

Source: Board of Governors of the Federal Reserve System, *Federal Reserve Bulletin,* monthly; and Department of the Treasury, *Treasury Bulletin,* monthly.

No. 1324. Foreign Direct Investment Position in the U.S. on a Historical Cost Basis—Value, by Area and Industry: 1980 to 1993

[In millions of dollars. Book value at year end. Covers U.S. firms, including real estate investments in which foreign interest or ownership was 10 percent or more. Minus sign (-) indicates a negative position. See also *Historical Statistics, Colonial Times to 1970*, series U 47-74]

AREA AND INDUSTRY	1980	1985	1986	1987	1988	1989	1990	1991	1992	1993,prel.
All areas [1]	**83,046**	**184,615**	**220,414**	**263,394**	**314,754**	**368,924**	**394,911**	**418,780**	**425,636**	**445,268**
Petroleum	12,200	28,270	29,094	37,815	36,006	40,345	42,882	37,222	34,347	32,647
Manufacturing	32,993	59,584	71,963	93,865	122,582	150,949	152,805	158,559	163,354	166,698
Finance and insurance	12,027	27,429	34,978	39,455	44,010	59,597	35,482	50,621	51,948	65,696
Trade, wholesale and retail	15,210	35,873	42,920	42,920	45,399	53,590	54,005	60,152	67,216	69,005	69,720
Canada	**12,162**	**17,131**	**20,318**	**24,684**	**26,566**	**30,370**	**29,544**	**36,341**	**37,845**	**38,408**
Petroleum	1,817	1,589	1,432	1,088	1,181	1,141	1,373	1,511	1,649	1,991
Manufacturing	5,227	4,607	6,108	8,085	9,730	9,766	9,201	15,440	17,005	16,600
Finance and insurance	1,612	4,008	4,283	5,797	5,769	7,356	6,033	7,088	5,155	7,684
Europe	**54,688**	**121,413**	**144,181**	**181,006**	**208,942**	**239,190**	**247,320**	**252,692**	**251,206**	**270,767**
Petroleum	10,137	25,636	26,139	35,700	33,499	32,649	34,284	28,790	26,006	24,979
Manufacturing	21,953	45,841	56,016	74,300	95,641	118,129	115,831	116,039	117,617	122,590
Finance and insurance	8,673	17,022	21,787	26,336	27,121	33,157	21,310	26,696	27,855	38,542
United Kingdom	14,105	43,555	55,935	75,519	95,698	103,458	98,676	98,236	89,073	95,415
Petroleum	-257	12,155	11,758	17,950	19,522	16,666	15,900	13,980	10,901	9,367
Manufacturing	6,159	11,687	16,500	30,372	41,708	50,166	42,365	40,838	40,777	42,543
Finance and insurance	3,350	6,483	10,163	9,801	11,256	12,790	11,609	12,249	10,851	16,919
Netherlands	19,140	37,056	40,717	46,636	48,128	56,734	64,671	59,776	65,323	68,477
Petroleum	9,265	11,481	(D)	(D)	9,045	10,061	13,267	12,422	11,783	12,424
Manufacturing	4,777	13,351	13,293	15,615	17,843	23,090	24,734	18,889	22,994	22,856
Switzerland	5,070	10,568	12,058	13,772	14,372	18,746	17,674	20,155	20,635	21,384
Manufacturing	3,116	6,881	7,520	6,921	7,613	11,798	10,651	11,331	11,088	11,299
Finance and insurance	1,033	5,425	2,517	3,211	3,506	4,492	4,833	5,549	5,428	5,478
Germany [2]	7,596	14,816	17,250	21,905	25,250	28,386	28,232	28,602	29,603	34,667
Manufacturing	3,875	6,015	7,426	10,298	13,980	15,560	15,718	15,394	15,376	17,852
Finance and insurance	1,248	(D)	1,962	3,442	2,683	3,139	1,652	1,212	2,066	4,542
Other Europe [3]	8,777	15,417	18,221	23,174	25,494	31,866	38,067	45,923	46,572	50,824
Petroleum	991	(D)	(D)	(D)	4,580	4,786	4,835	2,107	2,606	(D)
Manufacturing	4,026	7,907	11,277	11,094	14,497	17,515	22,363	29,587	27,382	28,040
Finance and insurance	1,193	(D)	(D)	2,189	406	2,519	-1,817	-368	-18	1,896
Japan	**4,723**	**19,313**	**26,824**	**34,421**	**51,126**	**67,268**	**83,091**	**93,787**	**97,537**	**96,213**
Other areas	**11,472**	**26,758**	**29,091**	**23,283**	**28,120**	**32,096**	**34,956**	**35,960**	**39,047**	**38,879**

D Withheld to avoid disclosure of data of individual companies.   [1] Area totals include industries not shown separately.
[2] For 1989, includes only the Federal Republic of Germany. For 1990, also includes the former German Democratic Republic (GDR). This change has no effect on the data because, prior to 1990, there were no U.S. affiliates of the former GDR.   [3] Direct investments in 1993 (in millions of dollars): Belgium and Luxembourg, 5,579; France, 28,470; Italy, 1,229; and Sweden, 8,077.
Source: U.S. Bureau of Economic Analysis, *Survey of Current Business,* August 1994, and earlier issues.

No. 1325. U.S. Affiliates of Foreign Companies—Assets, Sales, Employment, Land, Exports, and Imports: 1992

[A U.S. affiliate is a U.S. business enterprise in which one foreign owner (individual, branch, partnership, association, trust, corporation, or government) has a direct or indirect voting interest of 10 percent or more. Universe estimates based on a sample survey of nonbank affiliates with assets, sales, or net income of $10 million or more]

INDUSTRY	Total assets (mil. dol.)	Sales [1] (mil. dol.)	Employ-ment [2] (1,000)	Employee compen-sation (mil. dol.)	GROSS BOOK VALUE (mil. dol.) Plant and equip-ment [3]	Land	Land owned (1,000 acres)	Merchan-dise exports [4] (mil. dol.)	Mer-chandise imports [4] (mil. dol.)
Total	**1,809,950**	**1,222,651**	**4,705.5**	**181,709**	**595,727**	**65,090**	**14,836**	**100,615**	**182,152**
Petroleum	95,634	111,868	122.2	6,544	95,822	2,708	492	3,221	17,167
Manufacturing	473,047	427,022	2,231.7	97,621	249,780	17,193	4,573	39,700	50,919
Chemicals and allied products	161,181	123,479	515.3	26,891	97,592	9,837	1,023	12,497	11,805
Wholesale trade [5]	187,346	374,047	443.7	19,451	50,792	2,844	453	53,443	109,833
Motor vehicles and auto parts and supplies	58,223	97,944	78.0	4,115	22,829	806	27	6,479	34,524
Farm-product raw materials	9,055	35,848	19.1	605	2,388	89	38	13,118	2,496
Retail trade	41,621	81,704	707.1	12,782	21,337	2,412	72	1,257	2,800
Finance, except banking	385,693	30,119	55.1	5,724	5,482	744	51	5	2
Insurance	342,648	75,667	152.5	7,249	18,289	1,459	88	-	1
Real estate	106,732	14,385	37.9	1,229	66,213	24,001	2,320	8	3
Services	97,996	45,854	600.8	16,148	38,843	7,599	203	413	369
Other	79,233	61,984	354.7	14,961	49,109	6,130	6,583	2,569	1,058

- Represents zero.   [1] Excludes returns, discounts, allowances, and sales and excise taxes.   [2] Average number of full-time and part-time employees.   [3] Includes other property, value of mineral rights owned and capitalized value of mineral rights leased.   [4] F.a.s. value at port of exportation.   [5] Includes industries not shown separately.
Source: U.S. Bureau of Economic Analysis, *Survey of Current Business,* July 1994, and *Foreign Direct Investment in the United States, Operations of U.S. Affiliates of Foreign Companies,* Revised 1991 Estimates and *Foreign Direct Investment in the United States, 1992 Benchmark Survey,* Preliminary Results.

No. 1326. Foreign Direct Investment in the United States—Gross Book Value and Employment of U.S. Affiliates of Foreign Companies, by State: 1981 to 1992

[A U.S. affiliate is a U.S. business enterprise in which one foreign owner (individual, branch, partnership, association, trust corporation, or government) has a direct or indirect voting interest of 10 percent or more. Universe estimates based on a sample survey of nonbank affiliates with assets, sales, or net income of $10 million or more]

DIVISION, STATE, AND OTHER AREA	GROSS BOOK VALUE OF PROPERTY, PLANT, AND EQUIPMENT (mil. dol.)				TOTAL EMPLOYMENT			1992	
	1981	1990	1991	1992	1981	1990	1991	Total (1,000)	Percent of all businesses
Total	187,956	578,355	640,140	660,817	2,416.6	4,734.5	4,871.9	4,705.5	(X)
United States	178,003	552,902	612,807	631,952	2,402.3	4,704.4	4,838.2	4,670.5	5.0
New England	5,686	19,524	104,875	107,963	143.9	280.6	1,113.3	1,038.5	5.4
Maine	1,637	2,080	22,636	23,180	17.7	26.6	286.1	266.9	5.0
New Hampshire	409	1,446	2,254	2,427	13.9	25.9	26.6	24.1	5.6
Vermont	315	631	1,741	1,843	6.0	7.7	28.4	27.7	6.5
Massachusetts	1,712	8,890	669	817	55.6	131.2	7.2	7.5	3.5
Rhode Island	359	1,120	10,452	9,793	9.9	13.3	128.6	113.6	4.5
Connecticut	1,254	5,357	1,375	1,815	40.8	75.9	14.0	12.3	3.3
Middle Atlantic	20,216	71,619	6,145	6,485	480.2	796.1	81.3	81.7	6.0
New York	7,892	36,424	82,239	84,783	210.3	347.5	827.2	771.6	5.5
New Jersey	6,552	18,608	42,992	43,184	134.9	227.0	371.8	340.0	5.2
Pennsylvania	5,772	16,587	20,862	21,888	135.0	221.6	229.6	216.3	7.3
East North Central	19,215	74,495	18,385	19,711	388.6	812.8	225.8	215.3	4.8
Ohio	5,178	20,549	112,136	115,619	99.9	219.1	1,085.6	1,065.8	4.5
Indiana	1,883	13,426	81,565	87,477	47.0	126.9	818.9	807.4	4.9
Illinois	5,646	23,420	22,540	24,536	113.6	245.8	220.8	212.6	5.0
Michigan	4,188	12,012	14,057	14,748	65.9	139.6	124.8	126.2	5.7
Wisconsin	2,320	5,088	25,657	27,680	62.2	81.4	250.4	246.4	5.4
West North Central	8,400	28,155	13,707	14,531	112.2	248.4	138.9	140.4	4.1
Minnesota	2,902	11,972	5,604	5,982	33.0	89.8	84.0	81.8	4.0
Iowa	1,032	2,712	30,571	28,142	21.6	32.8	266.7	258.4	3.7
Missouri	1,894	5,757	12,746	12,741	32.6	73.7	94.5	94.1	5.0
North Dakota	1,155	1,251	3,270	3,360	3.5	3.1	33.7	32.6	3.1
South Dakota	299	553	6,471	6,555	1.3	4.5	77.6	77.2	3.8
Nebraska	241	776	1,273	1,276	5.6	14.9	4.2	5.3	2.4
Kansas	877	5,134	589	662	14.6	29.6	4.9	5.8	2.3
South Atlantic	33,271	94,766	899	863	476.0	934.7	16.8	16.0	2.6
Delaware	1,869	5,818	5,323	2,685	36.0	43.1	35.0	27.4	3.0
Maryland	2,103	5,713	228,642	237,930	45.1	79.6	1,678.2	1,662.6	5.4
District of Columbia	547	3,869	105,059	109,878	3.2	11.4	948.4	925.9	5.6
Virginia	3,046	10,702	6,142	6,229	49.8	113.3	41.5	35.8	11.9
West Virginia	3,992	7,975	6,645	6,342	35.4	34.9	77.1	74.8	4.3
North Carolina	5,543	15,234	4,301	4,389	89.0	181.0	11.1	9.7	2.4
South Carolina	5,318	10,067	12,420	12,429	65.1	104.7	119.1	119.9	5.2
Georgia	4,558	16,729	8,321	8,667	78.5	161.0	34.7	34.1	6.7
Florida	6,295	18,659	16,546	19,023	73.9	205.7	181.0	191.3	7.1
East South Central	9,802	29,798	10,889	11,925	121.7	261.9	110.1	111.1	8.8
Kentucky	1,848	9,229	18,830	19,116	26.0	65.7	162.6	154.3	6.1
Tennessee	3,747	10,280	20,965	21,758	57.4	116.9	211.2	194.9	4.2
Alabama	2,776	7,300	35,121	37,282	27.0	55.7	280.3	275.6	5.2
Mississippi	1,431	2,989	10,735	11,905	11.3	23.6	71.3	69.4	5.5
West South Central	34,651	82,904	12,523	13,030	268.5	433.7	120.4	121.7	6.3
Arkansas	636	2,344	8,540	9,020	17.5	29.2	65.0	60.7	4.4
Louisiana	7,872	17,432	3,323	3,327	47.0	61.4	23.6	23.8	3.1
Oklahoma	2,760	6,049	88,462	90,770	25.0	43.6	449.5	461.1	5.0
Texas	23,383	57,079	2,515	2,820	179.0	299.5	30.4	30.8	3.8
Mountain	12,353	33,197	19,076	20,757	97.9	197.1	62.2	62.1	4.7
Montana	1,235	2,181	5,736	5,852	3.0	5.1	44.0	43.8	4.5
Idaho	312	776	61,135	61,341	3.8	11.7	312.9	324.4	5.3
Wyoming	2,144	2,782	167,156	170,441	4.2	5.8	961.1	903.5	4.7
Colorado	2,369	6,544	36,494	35,218	24.7	56.3	206.6	197.3	3.9
New Mexico	997	4,312	2,244	2,131	7.9	17.4	5.5	5.4	2.1
Arizona	2,949	7,234	1,035	787	30.6	57.1	12.9	13.5	3.9
Utah	1,791	3,918	2,910	3,029	16.8	21.0	5.6	5.5	3.6
Nevada	556	5,450	7,141	6,868	6.9	22.7	62.0	61.0	4.5
Pacific	34,409	118,445	4,571	4,159	313.3	738.7	14.8	13.6	2.9
Washington	2,430	7,985	7,913	7,199	26.0	77.5	56.7	52.6	4.1
Oregon	845	3,427	4,361	4,362	13.1	39.1	24.0	22.7	3.6
California	20,404	75,768	6,319	6,683	248.4	555.9	25.1	23.0	4.0
Alaska	(D)	19,435	130,662	135,223	8.8	13.2	754.5	706.2	5.0
Hawaii	(D)	11,830	9,673	9,958	17.0	53.0	82.1	78.7	4.2
Puerto Rico	413	1,499	1,798	2,046	9.5	16.1	19.3	19.8	(X)
Other territories and offshore	7,496	18,484	18,513	17,371	3.1	9.0	10.0	10.0	(X)
Foreign	2,044	5,470	7,022	9,448	1.6	5.0	4.3	5.2	(X)

D Withheld to avoid disclosure of data of individual companies.   X Not applicable.

Source: U.S. Bureau of Economic Analysis, *Survey of Current Business,* July 1994, and *Foreign Direct Investment in the United States, Operations of U.S. Affiliates of Foreign Companies,* Revised 1991 Estimates; and *Foreign Direct Investment in the United States, 1992 Benchmark Survey.*

No. 1327. U.S. Businesses Acquired or Established by Foreign Direct Investors— Investment Outlays, by Industry of U.S. Business Enterprise and Country of Ultimate Beneficial Owner: 1987 to 1993

[In millions of dollars. Foreign direct investment is the ownership or control, directly or indirectly, by one foreign individual branch, partnership, association, trust, corporation, or government of 10 percent or more of the voting securities of a U.S. business enterprise or an equivalent interest in an unincorporated one. Data represent full cost of acquisitions of existing U.S. business enterprises, including business segments or operating units of existing U.S. business enterprises and establishments of new enterprises. Investments may be made by the foreign direct investor itself, or indirectly by an existing U.S. affiliate of the foreign direct investor. Covers investments in U.S. business enterprises with assets of over $1 million, or ownership of 200 acres of U.S. land]

INDUSTRY AND COUNTRY	1987	1988	1989	1990	1991	1992	1993, prel.
Total	40,310	72,692	71,163	65,932	25,538	15,333	26,182
Petroleum	1,107	4,740	1,189	1,141	702	463	774
Manufacturing	19,751	36,136	35,958	23,898	11,461	6,014	12,418
Wholesale trade	1,271	2,454	2,634	1,676	623	698	758
Retail trade	1,212	8,022	1,861	1,250	1,605	256	1,560
Banking [1]	924	1,800	349	897	482	529	1,071
Finance, except banking [1]	1,604	972	4,186	2,121	2,199	797	1,166
Insurance	165	5,855	1,901	2,093	2,102	291	921
Real estate	4,765	3,518	6,438	7,771	3,823	2,161	1,610
Services	7,630	5,597	10,058	19,369	2,256	2,023	3,934
Other [2]	1,881	3,597	6,587	5,716	284	2,101	1,971
Canada	1,276	11,360	4,403	3,430	3,454	1,351	3,999
Europe	25,517	37,173	40,724	36,011	13,994	8,344	17,127
France [3]	2,044	4,199	3,469	10,217	4,976	406	1,078
Germany [3]	4,664	2,090	2,435	2,363	1,922	1,964	3,140
Netherlands	391	2,214	3,629	2,247	1,661	1,331	1,528
United Kingdom	15,142	22,559	23,047	13,096	2,169	2,255	9,031
Latin America and other Western Hemisphere	1,483	(D)	1,084	796	375	1,438	779
South and Central America	355	(D)	650	399	108	1,152	545
Other Western Hemisphere	1,128	187	434	397	267	286	234
Africa	(D)	296	(D)	(D)	(D)	(D)	(D)
Middle East	925	1,613	243	472	1,006	238	1,369
Asia and Pacific	10,928	21,819	24,530	23,170	6,560	3,716	2,744
Australia	2,691	4,556	4,574	1,412	251	164	125
Japan	7,006	16,188	17,410	19,933	5,357	2,921	1,848
Other Asia and Pacific	1,231	1,075	2,546	1,825	952	631	771

D Data witheld to avoid disclosure of data of individual companies.   [1] Beginning 1992, savings institutions and credit unions are included with "Banking" instead of "Finance, except banking."   [2] Includes agriculture, forestry, and fishing; mining; construction; transportation; and communication and public utilities.   [3] Beginning 1990, Germany included the former German Democratic Republic.

Source: U.S. Bureau of Economic Analysis, *Survey of Current Business,* May 1994 issue.

No. 1328. U.S. Businesses Acquired by Foreign Direct Investors—Assets, Sales, and Employment, by Industry of U.S. Business Enterprise: 1992 and 1993

[See headnote, table 1327. Minus sign (-) indicates loss]

INDUSTRY	1992					1993, prel.				
	Total assets (mil. dol.)	Sales (mil. dol.)	Net income (mil. dol.)	Employment (1,000)	Acres of land owned (1,000)	Total assets (mil. dol.)	Sales (mil. dol.)	Net income (mil. dol.)	Employment (1,000)	Acres of land owned (1,000)
Total	24,728	21,498	–316	121	131	88,701	51,635	–1,910	306	297
Petroleum	1,001	(D)	80	1	-	(D)	(D)	(D)	(D)	1
Manufacturing	5,894	7,509	–254	55	6	15,192	14,219	–26	87	(D)
Wholesale trade	962	1,816	22	6	-	1,074	2,209	16	7	1
Retail trade	964	2,629	–254	28	-	(D)	4,306	42	34	(D)
Banking	7,450	(D)	69	3	(D)	10,595	829	–48	4	(D)
Finance, except banking .	885	145	8	1	(D)	4,141	660	8	(D)	(D)
Insurance	(D)	196	5	1	-	(D)	(D)	(D)	2	(D)
Real estate	(D)	77	–64	-	(D)	(D)	(D)	10	(D)	(D)
Services	1,795	1,214	–43	13	1	(D)	14,575	46	78	1
Other [1]	(D)	4,306	116	12	(D)	10,481	9,994	(D)	68	(D)

- Represents zero.   D Withheld to avoid disclosure of data of individual companies.   [1] Includes agriculture, forestry, and fishing; mining; construction; transportation; and communication and public utilities.

Source: U.S. Bureau of Economic Analysis, *Survey of Current Business,* May 1994; and unpublished data.

No. 1329. U.S. Direct Investment Position Abroad, by Country: 1980 to 1993

[**In millions of dollars.** Direct investments represent private enterprises in one country owned or controlled by investors in another country or in the management of which foreign investors have an important role. Negative position occurs when U.S. parent company's liabilities to the foreign affiliate are greater than its equity in, and loans to the foreign affiliate. See also *Historical Statistics, Colonial Times to 1970,* series U 41-46]

COUNTRY	1980	1985	1990	1991	1992	1993			
						Total [1]	Manu-facturing	Petro-leum	Finance [2]
All countries	215,375	230,250	430,521	467,844	498,991	548,644	199,457	62,409	155,597
Canada	45,119	46,909	69,508	70,711	68,832	70,395	34,062	8,840	12,242
Europe [3]	96,287	105,171	214,739	235,163	246,228	269,156	96,752	24,203	85,111
Austria	524	493	1,113	1,268	1,378	1,384	578	210	110
Belgium	6,259	5,038	9,464	10,611	11,115	11,552	5,557	249	2,794
Denmark	1,266	1,281	1,726	1,940	1,676	1,797	206	(D)	363
Finland	188	258	544	386	364	336	127	(D)	1
France	9,347	7,643	19,164	21,569	24,709	23,565	13,257	973	2,374
Germany [4]	15,415	16,764	27,609	32,411	33,578	37,524	22,283	2,468	5,107
Greece	347	210	282	306	372	424	125	(D)	34
Ireland	2,319	3,693	5,894	6,471	7,686	9,575	5,122	(D)	3,389
Italy	5,397	5,906	14,063	15,085	13,899	13,920	8,745	352	1,816
Luxembourg	652	690	1,697	1,734	1,783	2,314	1,289	30	753
Netherlands	8,039	7,129	19,120	20,293	20,142	19,887	7,775	1,055	5,199
Norway	1,679	3,215	4,209	4,318	3,824	4,353	584	3,136	141
Portugal	257	237	897	1,034	1,225	1,162	340	(D)	127
Spain	2,678	2,281	7,868	8,088	8,345	6,437	3,481	140	160
Sweden	1,474	933	1,787	2,323	1,887	1,802	1,166	1	167
Switzerland	11,280	15,766	25,099	25,682	29,190	32,901	1,923	629	17,823
Turkey	207	234	522	545	674	1,023	606	(D)	(Z)
United Kingdom	28,460	33,024	72,707	79,819	82,641	96,430	22,855	13,802	44,401
Japan	6,225	9,235	22,599	25,403	26,590	31,393	13,610	5,429	4,780
Australia	7,654	8,772	15,110	16,072	16,885	18,437	7,076	2,579	2,060
New Zealand	579	576	3,156	2,949	3,206	3,037	778	339	198
South Africa	2,350	1,394	775	868	879	925	544	(D)	(D)
Latin America [3]	39,581	28,758	71,413	77,677	90,671	101,936	29,641	5,506	46,496
South America [3]	16,342	17,623	22,933	24,607	28,360	30,921	17,135	3,074	4,227
Argentina	2,540	2,705	2,531	2,831	3,399	4,355	1,993	566	578
Brazil	7,704	8,893	14,384	14,997	16,343	16,908	12,574	738	1,946
Chile	536	88	1,896	2,069	2,655	2,869	229	(D)	1,185
Colombia	1,012	2,148	1,677	1,876	2,436	2,542	769	758	335
Ecuador	322	361	280	321	294	511	97	355	-
Peru	1,665	1,243	599	492	620	631	20	(D)	-
Venezuela	1,908	1,588	1,087	1,427	1,977	2,295	1,371	198	156
Central America [3]	11,013	10,155	20,415	23,939	25,863	28,966	11,569	1,132	11,873
Costa Rica	303	113	251	417	275	385	339	2	-
Guatemala	229	213	130	107	115	138	102	28	7
Honduras	288	171	262	255	239	223	144	(D)	23
Mexico	5,986	5,088	10,313	12,501	13,723	15,413	10,802	(D)	912
Panama	3,170	3,959	9,289	10,484	11,329	12,575	169	724	10,926
Other W. Hemisphere [3]	12,226	980	28,065	29,131	36,448	42,049	937	1,300	30,396
Bahamas, The	2,712	3,795	4,004	3,864	4,733	4,194	(D)	471	817
Barbados	40	81	252	291	494	644	7	95	88
Bermuda	11,045	13,116	20,169	22,262	25,668	28,153	(D)	(D)	26,826
Dominican Republic	316	212	529	661	779	1,020	237	(D)	3
Jamaica	407	122	625	763	892	1,077	168	(D)	8
Netherlands Antilles	-4,336	-20,499	-4,501	-5,072	-2,072	20	21	(D)	-23
Trinidad and Tobago	951	484	485	510	565	693	(D)	469	(D)
U.K. Islands, Caribbean	979	3,490	5,929	5,397	5,315	6,054	171	30	2,648
Other Africa [3]	3,778	4,497	3,650	4,427	4,440	5,297	1,064	2,958	577
Egypt	1,038	1,926	1,231	1,246	1,337	1,374	81	1,087	(D)
Nigeria	18	44	-401	529	301	527	50	(D)	2
Middle East [3]	2,163	4,606	3,959	4,963	5,644	6,459	2,091	2,225	1,185
Israel	379	717	746	826	1,358	1,660	(D)	(D)	202
Saudi Arabia	1,037	2,442	1,899	2,303	2,351	2,567	(D)	(D)	(D)
United Arab Emirates	384	792	409	416	429	537	(Z)	291	(D)
Other Asia and Pacific [3]	8,505	15,400	64,718	72,219	79,984	92,269	35,846	17,328	9,987
China	-6	311	354	426	516	877	461	223	-2
Hong Kong	2,078	3,295	6,055	6,656	8,730	10,457	2,660	496	1,562
India	398	383	372	415	485	759	395	(D)	(D)
Indonesia	1,314	4,475	3,207	3,826	4,472	5,031	160	4,552	(D)
Korea, South	575	743	2,695	2,900	2,850	3,001	1,236	74	169
Malaysia	632	1,140	1,466	1,774	1,598	1,928	1,079	303	332
Philippines	1,259	1,032	1,355	1,395	1,724	1,770	960	(D)	(D)
Singapore	1,204	1,874	3,975	5,363	6,728	8,782	4,632	1,937	356
Taiwan	498	750	2,226	2,666	2,910	3,096	1,896	(D)	144
Thailand	361	1,074	1,790	2,025	2,595	2,893	863	1,011	(D)
International	3,955	5,428	2,535	2,684	3,193	3,132	-	1,348	-
Addendum: OPEC [5]	6,090	10,383	7,145	9,729	10,779	11,853	2,461	6,422	1,133

- Represents zero.   D Suppressed to avoid disclosure of data of individual companies.   Z Less than $500,000.   [1] Includes industries not shown separately.   [2] Includes insurance.   [3] Includes countries not shown separately.   [4] Prior to 1991, West Germany only.   [5] OPEC=Organization of Petroleum Exporting Countries. Includes Algeria, Ecuador, Gabon, Indonesia, Iran, Iraq, Kuwait, Libya, Nigeria, Qatar, Saudi Arabia, the United Arab Emirates, and Venezuela. Prior to 1993, Ecuador was also a member and was included in this line.

Source: U.S. Bureau of Economic Analysis, *Survey of Current Business,* August 1994.

No. 1330. U.S. Government Foreign Grants and Credits, by Type and Country: 1946 to 1992

[In millions of dollars. See text, section 28. Negative figures (-) occur when the total of grant returns, principal repayments, and/or foreign currencies disbursed by the U.S. Government exceeds new grants and new credits utilized and/or acquisitions of foreign currencies through new sales of farm products. See also *Historical Statistics, Colonial Times to 1970,* series U 75-186]

TYPE AND COUNTRY	1946-1955, total	1956-1965, total	1966-1975, total	1976-1985, total	1988	1989	1990	1991	1992, prel.
Total, net	51,509	49,723	70,368	104,188	8,081	10,041	14,297	-31,897	16,624
Investment in financial institutions ...	635	655	2,719	10,432	1,314	1,173	1,301	1,498	1,419
African Development Bank	-	-	-	54	9	7	19	(Z)	9
African Development Fund	-	-	-	125	40	34	75	78	131
Asian Development Bank	-	-	110	602	111	160	127	146	86
Inter-American Development Bank ...	-	300	1,321	2,770	124	97	90	74	128
Special Facility For Sub-Saharan Africa	-	-	-	-	48	-	-	-	-
International Bank for Reconstruction and Development	635	-	13	353	95	23	61	72	94
International Development Association.	-	320	1,275	6,417	826	852	842	1,051	835
International Finance Corporation	-	35	-	111	25	-	75	40	25
Inter-American Investment Corporation	-	-	-	-	13	-	13	(Z)	12
Multilateral Investment Guarantee Agency	-	-	-	-	22	-	-	-	-
European Bank for Reconstruction and Development	-	-	-	-	-	-	-	36	99
Under assistance programs	50,875	49,067	67,649	93,756	6,768	8,868	12,996	-33,395	15,206
Developed Countries	35,150	5,834	616	757	-131	63	193	-14,288	1,173
Developing Countries	15,725	43,233	67,033	92,998	6,899	8,805	12,804	-19,107	14,032
Western Europe.	33,067	6,752	1,004	1,626	121	-247	-58	-5,859	553
Austria.	1,001	193	-19	34	-9	-11	-10	-19	-1
Belgium and Luxembourg	1,570	305	17	-46	-9	-9	-9	-3	-
Denmark	596	276	64	-58	-	-	-	-	-
Finland	86	-26	-19	21	6	7	-8	-5	-5
France.	8,661	-171	-93	-222	-14	-14	-15	-8	-2
Germany	3,881	10	-117	-117	-	-1	-338	-6,117	-
Iceland.	34	33	-8	-12	-4	(Z)	(Z)	-	-
Ireland	146	-16	-51	7	-6	-7	2	-6	-6
Italy.	3,851	1,435	85	133	-28	-28	-30	-14	(Z)
Netherlands	1,716	322	116	-180	-	-	-	-	-
Norway	697	362	379	-257	-	-	-	-1	-15
Portugal	248	241	34	1,003	69	71	56	44	158
Spain.	258	1,203	607	965	-113	-474	-122	-76	-123
Sweden	107	-20	17	-1	-3	-2	-	-	-
United Kingdom.	7,458	105	-546	-964	-105	-109	-111	-113	-115
Yugoslavia	1,356	1,151	84	174	-2	11	-39	-55	-21
Other [1] and unspecified	1,399	1,351	454	1,146	338	320	566	514	682
Eastern Europe	823	501	226	1,029	-121	419	954	898	577
Albania	9	-	-	-	-	-	-	12	29
Armenia	(X)	(X)	(X)	(X)	(X)	(X)	(X)	(X)	16
Belarus	(X)	(X)	(X)	(X)	(X)	(X)	(X)	(X)	22
Bulgaria	-	-	-	-	-	-	-	34	29
Czechoslovakia	136	-	-	-5	-	-	(Z)	32	46
Estonia	(X)	(X)	(X)	(X)	(X)	(X)	(X)	(X)	24
Hungary.	18	5	-5	6	-	-	1	37	38
Latvia	(X)	(X)	(X)	(X)	(X)	(X)	(X)	(X)	25
Lithuania	(X)	(X)	(X)	(X)	(X)	(X)	(X)	(X)	25
Poland.	350	555	-75	1,017	-53	524	919	714	112
Romania	-	-	92	55	-1	-59	64	48	25
Russia.	(X)	(X)	(X)	(X)	(X)	(X)	(X)	(X)	47
Soviet Union	292	-59	214	-44	-66	-46	-30	3	(X)
Other and unspecified.	17	(Z)	-	-	-	-	-	11	140
Near East and South Asia.	4,944	16,828	17,195	50,793	2,128	4,442	6,674	-24,589	7,241
Afghanistan	31	227	185	56	30	76	57	59	70
Bangladesh	-	-	701	1,670	170	138	175	188	136
Cyprus.	-	19	20	138	14	19	16	18	10
Egypt.	41	1,009	271	13,600	3,490	2,085	4,976	2,508	2,539
Greece	2,026	1,281	905	362	488	306	282	-181	388
India	370	4,890	3,810	1,021	139	73	-8	100	17
Iran.	314	1,061	914	-847	-19	-	-	-23	-
Iraq.	13	81	-5	5	29	-16	-7	336	9
Israel.	390	483	3,760	25,417	-1,826	1,902	4,454	2,029	4,746
Jordan.	26	495	618	1,320	-231	161	139	67	118
Kuwait.	-	-	-	-	-	-	-2,506	-13,550	-2
Lebanon.	15	78	90	233	-7	(Z)	8	5	11
Nepal	3	86	105	177	19	15	20	16	19
Oman	-	-	(Z)	79	9	8	4	3	13
Pakistan	189	3,092	2,048	1,971	389	-387	524	346	89
Saudi Arabia	12	35	23	-20	-	-	-1,614	-13,913	-1,328
Sri Lanka	(Z)	89	153	512	43	43	72	109	53
Syria	1	57	15	262	(Z)	-	(Z)	-	-
Turkey.	1,295	3,020	2,703	3,760	-720	-91	367	865	231
United Arab Emirates	-	-	-	-	(Z)	-	-361	-3,709	-
Yemen (Sanaa)	-	40	24	216	33	42	14	(X)	(X)

See footnotes at end of table.

No. 1330. U.S. Government Foreign Grants and Credits, by Type and Country: 1946 to 1992—Continued

[In millions of dollars. See headnote, p. 810]

COUNTRY	1946-1955, total	1956-1965, total	1966-1975, total	1976-1985, total	1988	1989	1990	1991	1992, prel.
Near East and South Asia—Continued									
Yemen [2]	-	-	-	-	-	-	28	19	14
UNRWA [2]	131	274	296	596	54	39	7	76	69
Other and unspecified	85	510	559	264	26	29	27	43	40
Africa	**147**	**2,272**	**3,610**	**11,074**	**1,257**	**982**	**1,841**	**1,485**	**1,396**
Algeria	1	135	263	345	-58	-77	59	-42	-13
Angola	-	-	6	115	2	-13	-15	-4	-30
Benin	-	7	12	44	5	12	5	10	16
Botswana	-	-	35	169	20	15	17	11	8
Burkina	-	5	40	287	18	14	15	32	14
Burundi	-	4	5	62	5	3	18	6	16
Cameroon	-	16	50	150	24	18	42	57	34
Cape Verde	-	-	1	68	6	4	6	7	8
Chad	(Z)	5	20	145	38	15	24	26	32
Ethiopia	13	200	297	310	71	37	54	123	62
Ghana	(Z)	64	203	152	17	46	14	32	28
Guinea	-	58	68	74	19	5	15	22	16
Ivory Coast	-	14	57	57	27	2	25	58	46
Kenya	(Z)	34	76	549	47	56	110	88	75
Lesotho	-	(Z)	27	197	23	19	15	11	14
Liberia	24	139	86	459	27	13	31	64	19
Madagascar	-	7	13	86	21	7	33	31	12
Malawi	-	5	30	56	34	44	34	51	38
Mali	-	12	58	199	50	27	31	44	31
Mauritania	-	1	20	161	11	14	11	6	2
Morocco	7	464	413	948	181	-5	95	98	13
Mozambique	-	-	1	175	56	48	80	89	61
Niger	-	5	64	223	25	34	33	44	34
Nigeria	(Z)	87	284	267	169	44	156	34	31
Rwanda	-	2	13	91	16	9	13	27	7
Senegal	-	18	48	361	45	46	60	40	37
Sierra Leone	(Z)	22	36	85	8	12	2	11	14
Somalia	(Z)	42	47	582	62	38	77	11	307
Sudan	-	86	52	1,358	110	118	145	113	11
Swaziland	-	(Z)	8	58	12	11	14	13	12
Tanzania	2	34	123	259	16	16	40	42	28
Togo	-	9	18	60	9	15	10	19	11
Tunisia	2	407	376	563	-175	56	38	5	16
Uganda	-	12	33	40	21	20	43	39	22
Zaire	(Z)	258	342	938	142	72	241	48	33
Zambia	-	1	35	331	18	21	63	50	76
Zimbabwe	-	(Z)	(Z)	271	6	12	10	28	72
Other and unspecified	96	118	350	781	133	157	176	141	185
Far East and Pacific	**9,678**	**16,199**	**34,780**	**9,635**	**304**	**408**	**-124**	**-9,152**	**583**
Australia	-9	-	276	-12	-26	-18	-34	-26	-18
Burma	25	134	43	31	9	1	1	-3	(Z)
Cambodia	28	327	1,771	-	-	-	-	-	-
China	-	-	-	49	48	35	71	55	31
Taiwan	1,267	2,681	1,523	648	-8	-7	-7	-8	-7
Hong Kong	3	35	41	11	-8	-8	-8	-	-
Indonesia	246	501	1,390	1,661	-3	36	46	23	81
Japan and Ryukyu Islands	3,267	1,318	-345	-210	-4	-1	-635	-9,377	-30
Korea, South	1,420	4,744	5,426	3,518	-383	-132	-192	-331	-132
Laos	37	647	1,868	-	-	-	-	-	-
Malaysia	1	30	86	39	-9	-36	-1	-2	(Z)
New Zealand	3	2	95	-68	-4	-4	-2	-2	-1
Pacific Islands, Trust Territory of the [3]	28	89	488	1,260	138	156	52	16	1
Philippines	1,028	554	729	1,466	418	338	566	391	503
Singapore	-	-	78	110	1	1	2	3	3
Thailand	192	727	996	733	72	12	-19	49	43
Vietnam [2]	244	3,566	19,721	-	-	-	-	-	-
Other and unspecified	1,898	844	595	400	65	36	39	59	111
Western Hemisphere	**1,248**	**5,181**	**6,816**	**9,860**	**1,448**	**1,194**	**2,034**	**1,976**	**2,244**
Argentina	86	342	34	21	16	-6	64	87	90
Bolivia	77	288	270	413	82	131	116	197	174
Brazil	509	1,400	1,518	399	(Z)	-202	260	-21	494
Canada	-1	4	272	317	-50	-30	-41	-50	-38
Chile	100	740	724	-565	11	-46	-32	-40	-56
Colombia	43	446	846	298	-23	29	-29	19	-77
Costa Rica	15	83	103	687	107	143	108	63	23
Dominican Republic	2	184	360	550	52	52	28	25	3
Ecuador	32	131	144	153	47	24	62	26	26
El Salvador	3	56	93	1,681	405	406	303	309	288
Guatemala	23	146	160	270	142	161	96	82	105
Guyana	(Z)	7	71	36	5	8	42	11	9
Haiti	27	75	42	370	41	76	53	69	40
Honduras	6	53	113	801	194	133	223	194	126
Jamaica	16	3	120	643	95	148	108	111	83

See footnotes at end of table.

No. 1330. U.S. Government Foreign Grants and Credits, by Type and Country: 1946 to 1992—Continued

[In millions of dollars. See headnote, p. 810]

COUNTRY	1946-1955, total	1956-1965, total	1966-1975, total	1976-1985, total	1988	1989	1990	1991	1992, prel.
Western Hemisphere—Continued									
Mexico	225	178	305	1,162	62	−100	141	38	−172
Nicaragua	8	67	150	197	(Z)	(Z)	100	395	205
Panama	10	103	210	205	13	8	102	152	193
Paraguay	4	67	86	22	(Z)	1	(Z)	1	(Z)
Peru	55	304	274	757	67	36	87	139	607
Trinidad and Tobago	-	35	21	151	−11	16	5	5	−10
Uruguay	8	90	116	−9	9	−6	−4	−5	−3
Venezuela	6	156	115	−35	−28	−21	−18	−14	−3
Central American Bank for Economic Integration	-	6	121	36	−3	−1	−5	−5	3
Caribbean Development Bank	-	-	8	108	−2	−2	−2	−6	−7
Other [4] and unspecified	−6	218	543	1,193	219	233	268	195	138
Other international organizations and unspecified areas	969	1,335	4,018	9,739	1,629	1,668	1,675	1,846	2,612

- Represents zero.   Z Less than $500,000.   X Not applicable.   [1] Includes European Atomic Energy Community, European Coal and Steel Community, European Payments Union, European Productivity Agency, North Atlantic Treaty Organization, and Organization for European Economic Cooperation.   [2] United Nations Relief and Works Agency for Palestine refugees. [3] Excludes transactions after October 1986, with Commonwealth of the Northern Mariana Islands; includes transactions with Federated States of Micronesia, Republic of the Marshall Islands, and Republic of Palau.   [4] Includes Andean Development Corporation, Eastern Caribbean Central Bank, Inter-American Institute of Agricultural Sciences, Organization of American States, and Pan American Health Organization.

Source: U.S. Bureau of Economic Analysis, press releases; and unpublished data.

No. 1331. U.S. Foreign Economic and Military Aid Programs: 1946 to 1993

[In millions of dollars. For years ending June 30 except, beginning 1977, ending Sept. 30. Economic aid shown here represents U.S. economic aid—not just aid under the Foreign Assistance Act. Major components in recent years include AID, Food for Peace, Peace Corps, and paid-in subscriptions to international financial institutions, such as IBRD, and IDB. Cumulative totals for 1946-1993 are true totals net of deobligation; annual figures however, are gross unadjusted program figures. Military aid includes Military Assistance Program (MAP) grants, foreign military credit sales, service-funded programs, and excess defense articles]

PERIOD OR YEAR AND REGION	Total economic and military aid	ECONOMIC AID			MILITARY AID		
		Total	Loans	Grants	Total	Loans	Grants
1946-1993, total	**439,565**	**287,850**	**63,253**	**224,598**	**151,715**	**39,877**	**111,837**
1946 to 1952	41,661	31,116	8,518	22,598	10,545	-	10,545
1953 to 1961	43,358	24,053	5,850	18,203	19,305	161	19,144
1962 to 1969	50,254	33,392	15,421	17,972	16,862	1,620	15,242
1970 to 1979	87,986	49,174	17,659	31,515	38,812	14,180	24,631
1980 to 1989	140,130	92,082	13,740	78,342	48,048	21,884	26,164
1970	6,568	3,676	1,389	2,288	2,892	70	2,822
1975	6,916	4,908	1,679	3,229	2,009	750	1,259
1976	6,412	3,878	1,759	2,119	2,535	1,442	1,093
1976, TQ [1]	2,603	1,931	840	1,091	672	494	178
1977	7,784	5,594	2,083	3,511	2,190	1,411	779
1978	9,014	6,661	2,530	4,131	2,353	1,601	752
1979	13,845	7,120	1,900	5,220	6,725	5,173	1,552
1980	9,695	7,573	1,993	5,580	2,122	1,450	672
1981	10,550	7,305	1,460	5,845	3,245	2,546	699
1982	12,324	8,129	1,454	6,675	4,195	3,084	1,111
1983	14,202	8,603	1,619	6,984	5,599	3,932	1,667
1984	15,524	9,038	1,621	7,417	6,486	4,401	2,085
1985	18,128	12,327	1,579	10,748	5,801	2,365	3,436
1986	16,739	10,900	1,330	9,570	5,839	1,980	3,859
1987	14,488	9,386	1,138	8,248	5,102	953	4,149
1988	13,792	8,961	852	8,109	4,831	763	4,068
1989	14,688	9,860	694	9,166	4,828	410	4,418
1990	15,727	10,834	756	10,078	4,893	404	4,489
1991	16,663	11,904	354	11,550	4,760	428	4,332
1992	15,589	11,242	494	10,748	4,347	345	4,002
1993	**28,196**	**24,054**	**462**	**23,592**	**4,143**	**855**	**3,288**
Near East and South Asia	5,373	2,215	61	2,154	3,158	-	3,158
East Asia	842	821	70	751	22	-	22
Europe	1,534	671	72	599	863	855	8
New Independent States [2]	1,007	1,005	148	857	1	-	1
Latin America	1,392	1,318	96	1,223	74	-	74
Africa	1,553	1,529	15	1,514	24	-	24
Oceania and other	32	32	-	32	-	-	-
Nonregional	16,462	16,462	-	16,462	1	-	1

- Represents zero.   [1] Transition quarter, July-Sept.   [2] Former republics of the Soviet Union.

Source: U.S. Agency for International Development, *U.S. Overseas Loans and Grants and Assistance from International Organizations,* annual.

No. 1332. U.S. Foreign Military Aid, by Region and Selected Countries: 1985 to 1993

[**In millions of dollars.** For years ending **Sept. 30.** Military aid data include Military Assistance Program (MAP) grants, foreign military credit sales, International Military Education and Training, and excess defense articles]

REGION AND COUNTRY	1985	1990	1991	1992	1993	REGION AND COUNTRY	1985	1990	1991	1992	1993
Total	5,801	4,894	4,760	4,348	4,143	Philippines	42	143	203	28	18
Europe	1,736	939	1,007	960	863	South Korea	232	1	1	1	-
Greece	501	349	351	350	315	Thailand	102	5	1	-	2
Portugal	128	87	101	102	91	Africa [1]	279	39	38	17	24
Spain	403	2	2	1	-	Kenya	22	11	1	1	1
Turkey	704	501	554	504	453	Liberia	13	-	-	-	-
South Asia	2,833	3,236	3,182	3,158	3,158	Somalia	34	1	-	-	-
Egypt	1,177	1,296	1,302	1,302	1,302	Sudan	46	1	-	-	-
Israel	1,400	1,792	1,800	1,800	1,800	Latin America [1]	269	234	237	124	74
Jordan	92	70	21	21	10	Colombia	1	73	50	49	29
Morocco	50	44	44	23	41	Costa Rica	11	-	-	-	-
Oman	40	-	3	1	1	El Salvador	136	81	67	23	11
Tunisia	67	31	12	11	3	Honduras	67	21	34	6	3
East Asia	416	383	233	32	22	Panama	11	-	-	-	-
Indonesia	34	2	27	2	-	Peru	9	2	25	-	-
Pakistan	326	230	-	-	-	Nonregional	58	63	61	56	1

- Represents zero.   [1] Includes countries not shown separately.

No. 1333. U.S. Foreign Aid—Commitments for Economic Assistance, by Region and Selected Countries: 1985 to 1993

[**In millions of dollars.** For years ending **Sept. 30.** Falls under economic portion of the Foreign Assistance Act. Data cover commitments for economic and technical assistance by AID. See text, section 28]

REGION AND COUNTRY	1985	1990	1991	1992	1993	REGION AND COUNTRY	1985	1990	1991	1992	1993
Total	8,132	6,964	7,668	6,819	7,059	Guinea	4	15	31	27	24
						Kenya	40	36	25	20	16
Europe [1]	284	160	606	514	469	Liberia	60	-	-	1	-
Portugal	80	39	43	40	-	Madagascar	5	17	11	42	44
Turkey	175	14	250	1	200	Malawi	25	23	57	28	55
East European Regional	(X)	97	294	411	249	Mali	32	21	37	36	34
New Independent States [2]	(X)	(X)	(X)	130	487	Mozambique	13	50	60	69	54
						Niger	28	20	28	29	17
Near East [1]	3,270	2,199	2,754	2,205	2,124	Rwanda	19	12	40	21	6
Egypt	1,065	901	783	893	748	Senegal	44	37	25	34	22
Israel	1,950	1,195	1,850	1,200	1,200	Somalia	51	1	1	11	28
Jordan	100	4	31	-	65	South Africa	-	33	50	80	80
Lebanon	20	8	9	9	10	Sudan	149	8	2	3	-
Morocco	38	31	50	41	33	Tanzania	(Z)	9	39	17	23
Oman	20	13	16	30	-	Uganda	9	43	45	42	39
Tunisia	23	14	4	4	5	Zaire	36	31	22	-	-
West Bank/Gaza	-	-	-	6	30	Zambia	42	17	35	40	26
Yemen Arab Republic	28	23	3	3	4	Zimbabwe	41	28	43	41	49
Regional	23	12	8	17	28	Regional	96	73	92	98	97
Asia [1]	781	873	749	511	375	Latin America [1]	1,506	1,486	1,075	855	780
Bangladesh	76	56	49	57	35	Belize	23	6	7	5	5
India	89	23	30	48	25	Bolivia	18	58	100	127	86
Indonesia	72	48	60	43	48	Costa Rica	196	78	42	24	9
Kampuchea	-	-	-	-	57	Dominican Rep.	126	18	14	16	20
Nepal	18	17	24	17	21	Ecuador	33	17	16	22	13
Pakistan	250	276	96	-	6	El Salvador	376	200	180	234	172
Philippines	183	314	328	201	83	Guatemala	76	86	60	34	33
Sri Lanka	35	21	28	20	17	Haiti	31	42	51	31	47
Thailand	36	14	3	2	8	Honduras	205	167	99	65	33
Regional	7	106	118	105	42	Jamaica	115	28	27	38	43
Sub-Saharan Africa [1]	839	621	865	891	783	Nicaragua	-	220	215	43	128
Burundi	4	20	15	15	17	Panama	74	396	40	15	6
Cameroon	24	22	20	22	10	Peru	38	22	69	24	41
Gambia, The	6	5	15	46	38	ROCAP [3]	107	30	21	12	17
Ghana	2	15	29	31	40	Regional	30	88	96	134	59
						South Pacific Regional	6	18	20	21	23
						Nonregional	1,453	1,607	1,598	1,693	2,018

- Represents zero.   Z Less than $500,000.   [1] Includes countries not shown separately.   [2] Former republics of the Soviet Union.   [3] Regional programs covering Costa Rica, El Salvador, Guatemala, Honduras, Nicaragua, and Panama.

Source of tables 1332 and 1333: U.S. Agency for International Development, *U.S. Overseas Loans and Grants and Assistance from International Organizations,* annual; and unpublished data.

No. 1334. U.S. International Trade in Goods and Services: 1992 to 1994

[**In millions of dollars**. Data presented on a balance of payments basis and will not agree with the following merchandise trade tables 1335 to 1344]

CATEGORY	EXPORTS			IMPORTS			TRADE BALANCE		
	1992	1993	1994	1992	1993	1994	1992	1993	1994
Total	616,924	641,677	696,430	657,308	717,402	804,539	−40,384	−75,725	−108,109
Goods	440,361	456,866	502,804	536,458	589,441	669,091	−96,097	−132,575	−166,287
Services	176,563	184,811	193,626	120,850	127,961	135,448	55,713	56,850	58,178
Travel	54,284	57,621	59,152	39,007	40,564	43,150	15,277	17,057	16,002
Passenger fares	16,972	16,550	17,147	10,608	11,416	12,592	6,364	5,134	4,555
Other transportation	22,704	23,151	24,537	23,460	24,502	25,735	−756	−1,351	−1,198
Royalties and license fees	19,922	20,398	22,502	4,987	4,840	6,002	14,935	15,558	16,500
Other private services	50,992	54,870	58,438	26,625	32,119	34,806	24,367	22,751	23,632
Direct defense expenditures	10,828	11,413	11,117	13,862	12,176	10,561	−3,034	−763	556
U.S. Government miscellaneous services	861	808	733	2,301	2,344	2,602	−1,440	−1,536	−1,869

Source: U.S. Bureau of the Census, *U.S. International Trade in Goods and Services*, series FT-900(94).

No. 1335. U.S. Exports and Imports of Merchandise: 1970 to 1994

[**In billions of dollars, except percent**. Includes silver ore and bullion; beginning 1974, includes shipments of nonmonetary gold. Data may differ from those shown in other tables due to revisions and inclusion of the Virgin Islands since 1974. For basis of dollar values, see text, section 28. See also *Historical Statistics, Colonial Times to 1970*, series U 190-195 and U 207-21]

YEAR	Merchandise trade balance	EXPORTS [1]					GENERAL IMPORTS [4]				AVERAGE ANNUAL PERCENT CHANGE [5]	
		Total [2]	Domestic				Total [3]	Petroleum	Machinery	Transport equipment	Domestic exports	General imports
			Total [3]	Agricultural	Machinery	Transport equipment						
1970	2.7	42.7	42.0	7.2	11.4	6.5	40.0	2.8	5.3	5.9	14.1	10.8
1971	−2.0	43.5	42.9	7.7	11.6	7.9	45.6	3.3	6.0	7.9	1.9	14.0
1972	−6.4	49.2	48.4	9.4	13.2	8.3	55.6	4.3	7.8	9.6	13.1	21.9
1973	1.3	70.8	69.7	17.7	17.1	10.7	69.5	7.6	10.0	11.1	43.9	25.0
1974	−4.5	98.1	96.5	22.0	23.7	14.5	102.6	24.3	11.6	12.5	38.6	47.6
1975	9.1	107.7	106.1	21.9	28.5	17.2	98.5	24.8	12.0	12.2	9.8	−4.0
1976	−8.3	115.2	113.5	23.0	31.3	18.2	123.5	31.8	15.2	14.6	7.0	25.4
1977	−29.2	121.2	118.9	23.7	32.5	18.5	150.4	41.5	17.7	17.8	5.2	21.8
1978	−31.1	143.7	141.0	29.4	37.0	22.3	174.8	39.1	24.4	23.2	18.6	16.2
1979	−27.6	181.9	178.6	34.8	44.7	25.8	209.5	56.0	28.0	25.6	26.6	19.9
1980	−24.2	220.6	216.5	41.3	55.8	28.8	244.9	77.6	31.9	28.6	21.3	16.9
1981	−27.3	233.7	228.9	43.3	62.9	32.8	261.0	75.6	38.2	31.4	5.9	6.6
1982	−31.8	212.3	207.1	36.6	60.3	23.6	244.0	59.4	39.7	33.6	−9.2	−6.5
1983	−57.5	200.5	196.0	36.1	54.3	28.3	258.0	52.3	47.0	39.2	−5.6	5.7
1984	−107.9	217.9	212.1	37.8	60.3	29.7	325.7	55.9	68.4	50.8	8.7	26.2
1985	−132.1	213.1	206.9	29.2	59.5	34.8	345.3	49.6	75.3	62.0	−2.2	6.0
1986	−152.7	217.3	206.4	26.1	60.4	34.9	370.0	34.1	87.5	74.0	2.0	7.2
1987	−152.1	254.1	243.9	28.6	69.6	39.0	406.2	41.5	99.4	78.4	16.9	9.8
1988	−118.6	322.4	310.0	37.0	88.4	46.7	441.0	38.8	117.3	79.8	26.9	8.6
1989	−109.6	363.8	349.4	40.0	98.3	50.5	473.4	49.1	126.8	79.0	12.8	7.3
1990	−101.7	393.6	375.1	38.7	122.4	32.1	495.3	60.5	134.8	72.4	8.2	4.6
1991	−65.4	421.7	401.1	38.5	139.7	34.9	487.1	50.1	131.8	70.6	7.1	−1.7
1992	−84.5	448.2	425.7	42.2	126.6	36.9	532.7	50.4	148.3	75.5	6.3	9.4
1993	−115.6	465.1	439.3	41.9	136.4	36.6	580.7	49.7	168.7	83.3	3.8	9.0
1994	−151.1	512.7	472.3	45.0	156.7	44.9	663.8	49.6	204.6	95.1	7.5	15.3

[1] Includes "Special Category" items and beginning 1974, includes trade of Virgin Islands with foreign countries. F.a.s. value basis.   [2] Domestic and foreign exports excluding M.A.P. Grant-Aid shipments, through 1985; 1986 through 1988 include Grant-Aid shipments.   [3] Includes commodity groups not shown separately.   [4] 1970-73, 1982-91, customs value basis; 1974-81, f.a.s. value basis. Beginning 1974, includes trade of Virgin Islands with foreign countries.   [5] 1970, change from 1965; thereafter, from previous year. For explanation of average annual percent change, see Guide to Tabular Presentation.

Source: U.S. Bureau of the Census, 1970-88, *Highlights of U.S. Export and Import Trade*, FT 990, monthly; beginning 1989, *U.S. Merchandise Trade: Export, General Imports, and Imports for Consumption*, series FT 925, monthly.

No. 1336. U.S. Exports and Imports for Consumption of Merchandise, by Major Customs District: 1980 to 1994

[**In billions of dollars.** Exports are f.a.s. (free alongside ship) value all years; imports are on customs value basis. See also *Historical Statistics, Colonial Times to 1970,* series U 264-273]

CUSTOMS DISTRICT	EXPORTS						IMPORTS FOR CONSUMPTION					
	1980	1990	1991	1992	1993	1994	1980	1990	1991	1992	1993	1994
Total [1]	220.8	393.0	421.9	447.5	464.9	512.4	244.0	490.6	483.0	525.1	574.9	663.8
Anchorage, AK	1.0	3.7	4.6	5.1	4.8	5.3	0.2	0.7	0.9	1.3	2.0	7.0
Baltimore, MD	9.0	6.7	8.0	7.7	7.7	8.2	6.0	11.2	10.1	10.8	11.7	11.8
Boston, MA	0.8	5.6	4.3	4.4	4.4	4.7	5.0	12.2	11.8	12.0	11.7	7.3
Buffalo, NY	6.3	15.8	15.7	18.0	19.5	21.3	7.4	19.2	18.7	21.2	24.2	26.4
Charleston, SC [2]	3.1	6.7	7.2	7.3	7.3	7.9	1.8	6.8	6.3	6.6	7.5	9.4
Chicago, IL	4.2	10.2	11.3	11.9	13.2	15.2	4.1	18.3	19.4	22.5	25.1	18.8
Cleveland, OH	1.8	4.0	4.0	4.1	4.4	5.4	1.5	11.3	11.8	13.8	15.5	6.4
Dallas/Fort Worth, TX	0.5	3.4	2.6	3.9	4.2	4.1	1.2	4.8	4.9	5.3	6.3	2.8
Detroit, MI	14.6	35.6	36.0	37.4	44.3	53.7	12.7	37.8	37.6	42.0	47.5	55.4
Duluth, MN	1.5	0.8	0.8	0.9	0.9	1.1	3.0	3.9	3.3	3.6	4.1	4.9
El Paso, TX	1.8	3.9	4.7	6.1	6.5	7.4	1.4	5.0	5.5	6.5	8.1	11.0
Great Falls, MT	1.8	2.4	3.3	3.1	3.5	3.2	3.2	4.7	4.6	4.9	5.7	5.3
Honolulu, HI	0.2	0.5	0.6	0.6	1.1	1.0	1.8	2.1	1.9	2.1	2.2	3.2
Houston/Galveston, TX . . .	15.7	17.6	20.5	20.2	19.8	21.2	20.1	21.6	19.2	18.7	19.7	21.1
Laredo, TX	8.3	15.2	18.2	21.7	22.7	28.3	2.7	10.0	10.4	11.8	13.7	18.7
Los Angeles, CA	14.8	42.1	46.0	49.4	48.3	55.8	20.0	64.1	66.4	71.9	79.5	130.5
Miami, FL	6.9	11.2	13.4	16.0	17.1	19.5	2.6	7.1	7.3	8.4	9.4	12.7
Milwaukee, WI	0.4	0.1	0.1	0.1	0.1	0.1	0.4	1.1	1.1	1.2	1.2	0.5
Minneapolis, MN	0.1	0.9	0.9	1.1	1.1	1.3	0.3	2.0	2.2	2.7	2.5	1.0
Mobile, AL [2]	2.6	1.9	2.2	2.2	2.1	2.7	3.0	3.4	3.3	3.2	3.1	3.3
New Orleans, LA	19.5	18.0	18.8	20.1	19.7	20.7	22.5	24.1	22.3	23.3	24.7	24.3
New York, NY	38.9	50.9	54.6	53.4	58.5	56.5	43.4	68.0	67.4	72.8	75.7	78.4
Nogales, AZ	0.8	2.1	2.2	2.8	3.0	4.1	1.2	4.2	4.4	4.6	5.7	5.3
Norfolk, VA [2]	8.0	11.7	11.5	11.9	11.0	12.4	4.7	7.4	7.4	7.5	7.3	10.5
Ogdensburg, NY	3.8	7.9	7.5	7.9	7.8	9.1	4.6	9.8	9.9	10.0	11.4	12.5
Pembina, ND	2.3	3.4	4.3	4.3	4.8	5.9	3.0	4.1	4.1	4.5	5.3	6.2
Philadelphia, PA	3.2	4.0	4.4	4.4	4.4	5.0	15.6	18.3	16.1	16.4	16.1	13.4
Port Arthur, TX	2.0	0.9	0.7	0.8	0.9	0.9	9.4	3.2	2.8	3.1	3.8	4.0
Portland, ME	4.3	1.7	2.1	1.8	2.2	1.9	1.6	4.3	3.8	4.0	4.0	4.1
Portland, OR	3.8	5.8	6.0	7.2	7.4	8.1	2.6	5.6	5.3	5.1	5.7	5.8
Providence, RI	2.7	(Z)	(Z)	(Z)	0.1	0.1	1.5	1.3	1.1	1.1	1.1	0.6
San Diego, CA	1.4	3.4	3.9	4.6	4.6	5.6	1.0	4.3	4.7	5.5	6.2	7.0
San Francisco, CA	10.6	23.1	23.9	27.1	29.5	34.2	8.3	28.0	29.2	33.2	38.8	47.4
San Juan, PR	0.9	2.5	2.4	2.5	2.7	2.6	3.7	5.4	4.8	5.0	4.9	4.6
Savannah, GA	2.4	7.4	8.4	8.7	8.7	9.3	2.2	9.8	10.1	11.3	12.8	11.3
Seattle, WA	12.0	32.6	35.0	35.5	35.2	33.1	9.2	20.9	18.9	20.5	21.8	45.4
St. Albans, VT	0.7	4.0	4.1	4.0	3.8	4.1	1.6	5.2	5.2	5.3	5.5	6.2
St. Louis, MO	0.2	0.3	0.4	0.7	0.3	0.3	0.9	3.0	2.8	3.4	3.9	0.9
Tampa, FL	2.8	4.3	5.2	5.2	4.7	5.6	3.7	7.0	6.8	7.0	7.3	8.5
Virgin Islands of the U.S. . . .	0.1	0.2	0.3	0.1	0.2	0.2	4.1	2.1	1.7	1.8	1.6	2.1
Washington, DC	0.3	1.1	1.6	1.6	1.9	2.0	0.4	0.8	0.7	0.8	0.8	1.3
Wilmington, NC	1.3	3.0	2.8	3.9	3.0	3.9	1.1	3.3	3.4	4.6	5.6	1.9

Z Less than $50 million.   [1] Totals shown for exports reflect the value of estimated parcel post and Special Category shipments, and beginning 1990, adjustments for undocumented exports to Canada which are not distributed by customs district. Beginning 1990, the value of bituminous coal exported through Norfolk, VA; Charleston, SC; and Mobile, AL is reflected in the total but not distributed by district.   [2] Beginning 1990, excludes exports of bituminous coal.

Source: U.S. Bureau of the Census, 1980, *Highlights of U.S. Export and Import Trade,* FT 990; beginning 1990, *U.S. Merchandise Trade: Selected Highlights,* series FT 920, monthly.

No. 1337. Export and Import Unit Value Indexes—Selected Countries: 1991 to 1994

[**Indexes in U.S. dollars, 1990=100.** A unit value is an implicit price derived from value and quantity data]

COUNTRY	EXPORT UNIT VALUE				IMPORT UNIT VALUE			
	1991	1992	1993	1994	1991	1992	1993	1994
United States	**100.9**	**101.0**	**101.4**	**103.6**	**100.0**	**100.8**	**100.1**	**101.8**
Australia	91.2	87.7	82.3	86.0	100.8	99.3	99.4	105.1
Austria	94.2	98.0	88.6	(NA)	97.6	102.2	93.4	(NA)
Belgium-Luxembourg	96.0	100.5	(NA)	(NA)	96.5	99.2	(NA)	(NA)
Canada	98.2	95.3	94.4	(NA)	100.4	99.2	98.6	(NA)
Denmark	96.9	101.6	91.4	(NA)	97.3	99.7	89.2	(NA)
France	96.2	99.6	90.1	(NA)	95.5	97.9	87.0	(NA)
Germany	96.8	102.1	92.0	(NA)	99.0	102.0	91.1	(NA)
Italy	99.4	100.8	87.9	(NA)	95.8	95.9	(NA)	(NA)
Japan	107.2	114.0	124.5	(NA)	97.4	96.3	97.0	(NA)
Netherlands	95.8	98.6	90.9	(NA)	97.0	100.7	90.8	(NA)
Norway	92.4	88.7	78.1	(NA)	95.0	97.2	85.8	(NA)
Sweden	98.7	98.9	81.2	(NA)	97.3	98.4	80.9	(NA)
United Kingdom	100.4	101.7	96.7	100.6	100.3	100.8	93.4	98.6

NA Not available.

Source: International Monetary Fund, Washington, DC, *International Financial Statistics,* monthly.

Foreign Commerce and Aid

No. 1338. U.S. Exports, by State of Origin: 1990 to 1994

[In millions of dollars. Exports are on a f.a.s. value basis]

STATE AND OTHER AREAS	1990	1993	1994 Total	1994 Rank
Total	394,045	464,767	512,670	(X)
U.S.	315,065	391,925	429,808	(X)
AL	2,834	3,440	3,895	26
AK	2,850	2,512	2,456	31
AZ	3,729	5,436	6,467	20
AR	920	1,353	1,672	35
CA	44,520	57,198	66,292	1
CO	2,274	3,065	3,802	27
CT	4,356	5,519	5,664	22
DE	1,344	1,318	1,498	38
DC	320	464	546	(X)
FL	11,634	14,239	16,287	8
GA	5,763	6,823	8,237	16
HI	179	260	297	49
ID	898	1,122	1,466	39
IL	12,965	16,424	19,097	6
IN	5,273	7,188	8,256	15
IA	2,189	2,779	3,214	29
KS	2,113	2,668	3,028	30
KY	3,175	4,212	4,803	25
LA	14,199	14,372	14,549	9
ME	870	1,027	1,090	41
MD	2,592	4,376	4,874	24
MA	9,501	10,426	11,199	12
MI	18,474	23,198	25,830	4
MN	5,091	6,228	6,621	19
MS	1,605	1,687	1,846	34
MO	3,130	3,528	3,541	28
MT	229	272	328	48
NE	693	1,355	1,573	37
NV	394	539	621	44
NH	973	904	1,000	42
NJ	7,633	9,286	10,519	13
NM	249	434	526	45
NY	22,072	28,370	25,912	3
NC	8,010	9,889	11,863	10
ND	360	408	458	46
OH	13,378	17,306	19,007	7
OK	1,646	2,101	2,110	33
OR	4,065	5,273	6,103	21
PA	8,491	10,463	11,650	11
RI	595	893	923	43
SC	3,116	4515	5,236	23
SD	205	254	295	50
TN	3,746	5,597	6,749	18
TX	32,931	45,290	51,818	2
UT	1,596	2,367	2,355	32
VT	1,154	1,342	1,371	40
VA	9,333	9,052	9,573	14
WA	24,432	26,624	23,629	5
WV	1,550	1,423	1,586	36
WI	5,158	6,769	7,722	17
WY	264	337	360	47
PR	3,600	4,073	4,473	(X)
VI	51	150	139	(X)
Other [1]	75,328	68,619	78,250	(X)

X Not applicable.   [1] Includes unreported, not specified, special category, estimated shipments, foreign trade zone, re-exports, and any timing adjustments.

Source: U.S. Bureau of the Census, *U.S. Merchandise Trade,* series FT 900, December issues.

No. 1339. U.S. Trade in Advanced Technology Products: 1990 to 1994

[In billions of dollars. Exports are f.a.s. value basis and imports are on customs value basis]

PRODUCT CATEGORY	EXPORTS 1990	1991	1992	1993	1994	GENERAL IMPORTS 1990	1991	1992	1993	1994
Total	93.4	100.0	105.1	108.4	120.8	59.3	63.1	71.8	81.2	98.4
Advanced materials [1]	6.4	6.2	0.6	0.7	0.9	1.0	1.1	0.4	0.5	0.6
Aerospace	37.0	41.9	42.5	37.4	35.0	10.7	12.1	12.8	11.6	11.4
Biotechnology [2]	0.6	0.7	0.7	0.8	1.0	(Z)	(Z)	(Z)	0.1	0.1
Electronics.................	7.5	8.9	16.5	19.6	25.8	11.0	12.4	15.4	19.4	25.9
Flexible manufacturing [3]	3.1	3.3	3.4	4.0	5.2	1.7	1.8	1.7	2.2	2.9
Information and communications ..	31.4	30.7	32.5	36.7	42.9	30.2	29.2	33.9	40.1	49.9
Life science	4.9	5.5	5.8	6.1	6.8	3.4	4.3	4.8	4.7	4.8
Nuclear technology	1.3	1.3	1.5	1.4	1.6	(Z)	(Z)	(Z)	(Z)	(Z)
Opto-electronics [4]	0.5	0.6	0.6	0.7	0.9	1.1	2.0	2.6	2.5	2.5
Weapons.................	0.7	0.9	0.8	0.7	0.7	0.1	0.2	(Z)	0.2	0.1

Z Less than $50 million.   [1] Encompasses recent advances in the development of materials that allow for further development and application of other advanced technologies. Examples are semiconductor materials, optical fiber cable and video discs. [2] Biotechnology is the medical and industrial application of advanced scientific discoveries in genetics to the creation of new drugs, hormones and other therapeutic items for both agricultural and human use.   [3] Encompasses advances in robotics, numerically—controlled machine tools, and similar products involving industrial automation that allow for greater flexibility to the manufacturing process and reduce the amount of human intervention. Includes robots, numerically controlled machine tools and semiconductor production and assembly machines.   [4] Encompasses electronic products and components that involve the emitting and/or detection of light. Examples of products included are optical scanners, optical disc players, solar cells, photo-sensitive semiconductors and laser printers.

Source: U. S. Bureau of the Census, *U. S. Merchandise Trade,* series FT 900, December issues.

No. 1340. U.S. Exports and General Imports of Major SITC Commodity Groups—Value, by Area: 1994

[In millions of dollars. SITC=Standard International Trade Classification. Includes nonmonetary gold. Exports are f.a.s. (free alongside ship) transaction value basis; imports are customs value basis]

COMMODITY GROUPS	Total [1]	WESTERN HEMISPHERE		WESTERN EUROPE				ASIA	
		Canada	Mexico	United Kingdom	Germany	France	Italy	Japan	Korea, South
Exports, total [1]	**512,416**	**114,255**	**50,840**	**26,833**	**19,237**	**13,622**	**7,193**	**53,481**	**18,028**
Meat and meat preparations	5,208	622	713	17	15	26	3	2,201	280
Fish (except marine mammal) crustaceans, etc., preparations	3,153	447	68	97	24	73	30	1,886	115
Cereals and cereal preparations	11,281	573	1,107	59	32	23	76	2,465	496
Vegetables and fruit	7,295	2,320	373	269	301	134	86	1,441	135
Feeding stuff for animals not including unmilled cereal	3,458	487	271	160	84	78	53	551	18
Miscellaneous edible products and preparations	2,218	583	179	42	24	11	7	175	44
Tobacco and tobacco manufactures	6,741	23	42	50	224	10	28	1,805	132
Hides, skins, and furskins, raw	1,551	101	104	3	8	13	55	235	632
Oil seeds and oleaginous fruits	4,725	82	610	55	237	49	128	874	231
Cork and wood	5,581	813	227	89	158	41	177	2,968	235
Pulp and waste paper	3,839	385	389	182	216	151	258	572	432
Textile fibers & their wastes (excluding wool tops, etc)	3,989	220	311	78	64	9	58	387	358
Crude fertilizers & crude minerals [2]	1,553	291	78	49	84	15	45	302	73
Metalliferous ores and metal scrap	3,773	1,219	137	128	74	9	27	495	461
Crude animal and vegetable materials, n.e.s.	1,201	240	152	47	68	26	23	124	25
Coal, coke and briquettes	2,964	386	28	153	15	127	324	392	143
Petroleum, petroleum products, and related materials	5,432	714	799	42	40	66	126	333	432
Organic chemicals	13,064	1,557	1,031	435	364	329	260	1,070	745
Inorganic chemicals	4,153	595	296	123	249	79	41	1,120	194
Dyeing, tanning and coloring materials	2,353	750	248	102	47	27	15	119	86
Medicinal and pharmaceutical products	6,184	970	188	411	474	370	262	843	67
Essential oils, etc; toilet, polishing, preparations	3,644	898	309	189	100	90	45	387	75
Fertilizers [3]	2,706	203	147	1	29	18	11	174	70
Plastics in primary forms	8,721	2,008	962	253	239	77	65	494	294
Plastics in nonprimary forms	3,864	1,039	704	187	142	92	40	219	105
Chemical materials and products, n.e.s.	7,763	1,647	523	360	496	358	140	901	238
Rubber manufactures, n.e.s.	3,096	1,422	412	94	95	28	22	303	39
Cork and wood manufactures other than furniture	1,609	415	187	145	176	13	28	146	81
Paper, paperboard and articles	7,522	2,010	1,316	241	151	77	91	672	153
Textile yarn, fabrics, made-up articles, n.e.s.	6,592	1,857	972	303	205	92	79	251	148
Nonmetallic mineral manufactures, n.e.s.	5,975	1,459	432	216	131	109	38	437	130
Iron and steel	3,903	1,793	719	100	51	31	37	100	61
Nonferrous metals	5,382	1,771	759	210	111	99	49	728	193
Manufactures of metals, n.e.s.	9,066	3,343	1,901	373	348	126	62	427	166
Power generating machinery and equipment	20,870	5,793	1,785	1,321	711	2,159	253	1,143	591
Machinery specialized for particular industries	20,669	4,133	1,632	933	723	675	249	1,060	798
Metalworking machinery	4,112	975	351	211	188	103	85	243	252
General industrial machinery, equipment, parts	22,563	6,849	2,456	907	704	505	273	955	999
Office machines and automatic data processing machines	35,396	5,945	2,074	3,605	2,612	1,609	518	3,789	777
Telecommunications, sound recording, reproduction apparatus and equipment	17,129	2,610	2,140	1,010	496	287	190	1,524	956
Electrical machinery, apparatus, and appliances, n.e.s.	52,921	10,732	7,484	3,325	1,928	1,056	584	3,960	2,340
Road vehicles (incl. air-cushion vehicles)	46,305	24,595	5,493	805	1,618	255	114	2,852	422
Transport equipment, n.e.s.	32,377	1,556	666	3,042	1,039	1,233	908	3,500	1,729
Furniture, bedding, mattresses, etc.	3,275	1,488	707	96	48	37	10	228	22
Articles of apparel and clothing accessories	5,616	480	1,176	83	90	60	40	783	18
Professional scientific and control instruments and apparatus	17,207	2,900	1,440	1,087	1,218	836	399	2,228	722
Photo apparatus, equipment and optical goods n.e.s.; watch and clocks	4,681	868	340	401	278	194	73	620	76
Miscellaneous manufactured articles	26,539	5,607	2,576	1,747	1,295	699	345	2,679	678
Special transactions and commodities not classified by kind	4,975	1,847	161	237	211	37	23	336	91
Gold, nonmonetary (excluding ores and concentrates)	5,677	446	157	1,611	235	440	7	30	28
Shipments under $10,000 and under $1,500 documented exports	11,700	1,913	1,906	819	514	384	172	651	189

See footnotes at end of table.

No. 1340. U.S. Exports and General Imports of Major SITC Commodity Groups— Value, by Area: 1994—Continued

[In millions of dollars. See headnote, page 817]

COMMODITY GROUPS	Total [1]	WESTERN HEMISPHERE		WESTERN EUROPE				ASIA	
		Canada	Mexico	United Kingdom	Germany	France	Italy	Japan	Korea, South
Imports, total [1]	**663,830**	**128,947**	**49,493**	**25,063**	**31,749**	**16,775**	**13,216**	**119,149**	**19,658**
Meat and meat preparations	2,636	808	4	-	1	4	7	4	-
Fish (except marine mammal) crustaceans, etc., preps	6,593	1,133	354	18	6	24	2	151	88
Vegetables and fruit	6,074	414	1,623	7	87	28	35	43	14
Coffee, tea, cocoa, spices manufactures thereof	3,976	250	360	32	97	34	23	5	1
Beverages	4,307	652	334	689	174	962	326	29	8
Cork and wood	6,683	5,970	178	2	3	1	2	-	-
Pulp and waste paper	2,315	1,992	2	5	4	-	-	-	-
Metalliferous ores and metal scrap	3,252	1,078	248	60	28	20	2	18	7
Petroleum, petroleum products, and related materials	49,325	6,638	4,994	3,265	123	296	349	34	135
Gas, natural and manufactured	5,481	4,878	98	34	1	25	6	1	9
Organic chemicals	10,799	1,070	275	1,374	1,212	583	406	1,507	4
Inorganic chemicals	4,104	1,237	244	196	328	266	53	296	31
Medicinal and pharmaceutical products	4,680	309	30	792	500	276	335	453	15
Chemical materials and products, n.e.s.	3,238	457	74	269	441	222	47	591	10
Rubber manufactures, n.e.s.	4,783	1,366	128	116	226	163	94	1,330	8
Cork and wood manufactures other than furniture	3,471	1,485	122	12	38	52	46	9	70
Paper, paperboard and articles	9,065	6,378	161	250	304	158	56	257	609
Textile yarn, fabrics, made-up articles, n.e.s.	9,208	914	468	317	414	235	506	653	62
Nonmetallic mineral manufactures, n.e.s.	13,313	1,025	637	579	529	360	559	859	567
Iron and steel	14,218	2,440	638	547	1,081	741	437	1,940	18
Nonferrous metals	11,565	4,745	485	264	473	158	38	318	538
Manufactures of metals, n.e.s.	12,084	1,991	946	340	753	315	254	1,912	109
Power generating machinery and equipment	19,561	3,083	2,338	2,095	1,832	2,220	248	5,642	166
Machinery specialized for particular industries	16,755	1,812	235	1,201	3,354	773	925	4,592	60
Metalworking machinery	4,614	374	13	209	712	46	129	1,830	371
General industrial machinery, equipment, parts	21,337	3,572	1,791	1,095	2,757	541	773	5,155	2,539
Office machines and automatic data processing machines	52,118	3,326	1,780	1,415	743	341	300	18,057	1,958
Telecommunications, sound recording, reproduction apparatus and equipment	32,456	1,621	5,473	369	209	95	36	9,179	4,927
Electrical machinery, apparatus and appliances, n.e.s.	57,672	3,656	8,119	1,391	2,436	995	379	15,531	1,656
Road vehicles (incl. air-cushion vehicles)	95,128	37,823	7,152	1,527	6,659	840	463	33,931	61
Transport equipment, n.e.s.	8,601	2,698	39	1,028	313	2,176	717	626	47
Furniture, bedding, mattresses, etc.	7,567	2,020	1,107	111	126	55	426	176	252
Travel goods, handbags and similar containers	3,080	20	73	5	17	98	177	6	2,221
Articles of apparel and clothing accessories	36,744	713	1,889	190	117	183	870	104	681
Footwear	11,716	97	206	88	60	56	760	6	98
Professional scientific and control instruments and apparatus	9,964	896	1,528	805	1,226	270	97	2,391	181
Photo apparatus, equipment and optical goods, n.e.s.; watch and clocks	9,213	346	172	338	384	206	324	3,655	1,170
Miscellaneous manufactured articles	33,602	2,272	1,442	1,617	1,061	1,048	1,837	4,096	136
Special transactions and commodities not classified by kind	16,312	5,406	1,599	1,132	830	569	173	1,031	-
Estimate of low valued import transactions	4,568	1,253	343	261	384	139	109	786	-

- Represents zero or rounds to zero.   [1] Includes countries and commodities not shown separately.   [2] Other than fertilizers covered in SITC division 56 (Fertilizers).   [3] Other than crude fertilizers covered in SITC division 272.

Source: U.S. Bureau of the Census, *U.S. Merchandise Trade: Exports, General Imports, and Imports for Consumption*, series FT 927.

No. 1341. U.S. Exports, Imports, and Merchandise Trade Balance, by Country: 1990 to 1994

[In millions of dollars. Includes silver ore and bullion. Country totals include exports of special category commodities, if any. Data include nonmonetary gold and includes trade of Virgin Islands with foreign countries, see footnote 2 for exception. Minus sign (-) denotes an excess of imports over exports. See Historical Statistics, Colonial Times to 1970, series U 317-352, for selected countries]

COUNTRY	EXPORTS, DOMESTIC AND FOREIGN					GENERAL IMPORTS [1]					MERCHANDISE TRADE BALANCE				
	1990	1991	1992	1993	1994	1990	1991	1992	1993	1994	1990	1991	1992	1993	1994
Total [2]	393,592	421,730	448,164	464,767	512,670	495,311	487,129	532,665	580,511	663,768	-101,718	-65,399	-84,501	-115,744	-151,098
Afghanistan	4	3	4	10	5	5	5	2	3	6	-1	-2	2	7	-1
Albania	10	18	36	34	16	2	3	5	7	6	8	15	31	27	10
Algeria	951	727	688	938	1,191	2,626	2,103	1,586	1,583	1,525	-1,674	-1,376	-898	-645	-334
Andorra	40	17	16	15	5	(Z)	(Z)	(Z)	(Z)	(Z)	40	17	16	15	5
Angola	152	186	158	174	197	1,904	1,775	2,303	2,092	2,061	-1,752	-1,589	-2,145	-1,918	-1,864
Anguilla	15	11	68	14	13	(Z)	(Z)	(Z)	(Z)	(Z)	15	10	11	14	13
Antigua	69	74	68	73	65	4	4	5	15	6	65	70	63	58	59
Argentina	1,179	2,045	3,223	3,776	4,466	1,511	1,287	1,256	1,206	1,725	-333	758	1,967	2,570	2,741
Armenia	(X)	(X)	25	78	274	(X)	(X)	1	1	1	(X)	(X)	23	77	73
Aruba	202	235	288	266	274	1	100	212	457	462	201	135	76	-191	-188
Australia	8,538	8,404	8,876	8,277	9,781	4,447	3,988	3,688	3,297	3,200	4,091	4,416	5,188	4,979	6,581
Austria	875	1,056	1,256	1,326	1,373	1,318	1,264	1,306	1,411	1,749	-444	-208	-50	-85	-377
Azerbaijan	(X)	(X)	(Z)	37	27	(X)	(X)	(Z)	(Z)	(Z)	(X)	(X)	(Z)	36	27
Bahamas, The	800	721	712	704	685	509	470	605	328	203	291	252	107	376	482
Bahrain	721	500	489	636	443	81	87	61	97	155	640	413	428	539	288
Bangladesh	181	179	188	255	234	539	524	831	887	1,080	-357	-345	-643	-632	-846
Barbados	161	166	128	146	161	31	31	31	35	35	130	135	97	111	127
Byelarus	(X)	(X)	25	92	47	(X)	(X)	25	34	53	(X)	(X)	(Z)	58	-7
Belgium	10,318	10,572	9,775	8,878	10,944	4,375	3,929	4,476	5,149	6,342	5,942	6,643	5,299	3,729	4,602
Belize	105	114	117	136	115	47	45	59	54	51	58	69	58	82	64
Benin	24	26	27	22	26	18	23	10	15	10	6	4	17	7	16
Bermuda	255	233	242	265	300	12	8	7	15	9	242	225	236	250	291
Bolivia	138	192	222	218	186	203	209	162	191	260	-65	-17	60	27	-74
Bosnia-Hercegovina [3]	(X)	(X)	5	25	39	(X)	(X)	10	7	5	(X)	(X)	-4	18	35
Botswana	19	31	47	25	23	13	13	12	8	14	6	18	34	17	9
Brazil	5,048	6,148	5,751	6,058	8,118	7,898	6,717	7,609	7,479	8,708	-2,850	-569	-1,858	-1,421	-590
British Virgin Islands	60	45	44	46	47	2	2	3	14	15	58	43	41	32	32
Brunei	143	162	453	473	376	96	27	30	30	46	47	136	424	442	330
Bulgaria	84	142	85	115	110	47	56	79	159	212	37	86	7	-44	-102
Burkina	15	24	13	18	7	1	1	(Z)	1	(Z)	14	23	13	17	7
Cameroon	47	45	57	49	54	147	127	84	101	55	-100	-82	-27	-53	-2
Canada	83,674	85,150	90,594	100,444	114,441	91,380	91,064	98,630	111,216	128,948	-7,707	-5,914	-8,036	-10,772	-14,506
Cayman Islands	183	117	282	164	202	21	18	10	35	53	162	99	272	130	150
Chad	8	14	5	8	8	(Z)	(Z)	(Z)	(Z)	2	8	14	5	8	6
Chile	1,664	1,839	2,466	2,599	2,776	1,313	1,302	1,388	1,462	1,822	351	537	1,078	1,137	954
China	4,806	6,278	7,418	8,763	9,287	15,237	18,969	25,728	31,540	38,781	-10,431	-12,691	-18,309	-22,777	-29,494
Colombia	2,029	1,952	3,286	3,235	4,070	3,168	2,736	2,837	3,032	3,172	-1,139	-784	449	203	899
Congo (Brazzaville)	90	43	59	27	38	414	410	510	500	403	-324	-367	-451	-473	-365
Costa Rica [3]	986	1,034	1,357	1,542	1,867	1,005	1,154	1,411	1,541	1,646	-19	-120	-54	1	-220
Croatia [3]	(X)	(X)	91	103	147	(X)	(X)	43	106	115	(X)	(X)	48	-3	32
Cyprus	129	119	166	138	209	18	12	11	16	18	111	107	155	122	191
Czechoslovakia	91	123	413	(X)	(X)	87	145	242	(X)	(X)	4	-22	171	(X)	(X)
Czech Republic	(X)	(X)	(X)	267	297	(X)	(X)	(X)	277	316	(X)	(X)	(X)	-10	-18
Denmark	1,311	1,574	1,473	1,092	1,215	1,678	1,661	1,667	1,664	2,122	-367	-87	-194	-572	-907

See footnotes at end of table.

No. 1341. U.S. Exports, Imports, and Merchandise Trade Balance, by Country: 1990 to 1994—Continued

[See headnote, page 819]

COUNTRY	EXPORTS, DOMESTIC AND FOREIGN					GENERAL IMPORTS [1]					MERCHANDISE TRADE BALANCE				
	1990	1991	1992	1993	1994	1990	1991	1992	1993	1994	1990	1991	1992	1993	1994
Djibouti	7	10	11	13	7	(Z)	(Z)	(Z)	(Z)	-	7	10	11	13	7
Dominica	31	42	34	27	26	9	5	5	6	7	22	37	29	22	19
Dominican Republic	1,656	1,743	2,100	2,350	2,800	1,752	2,008	2,372	2,672	3,094	-96	-265	-273	-322	-294
East Germany [4]	62	(X)	(X)	(X)	(X)	85	(X)	(X)	(X)	(X)	-23	(X)	(X)	(X)	(X)
Ecuador	678	948	999	1,100	1,196	1,376	1,327	1,343	1,399	1,727	-697	-379	-344	-299	-531
Egypt	2,249	2,720	3,088	2,768	2,844	398	206	435	613	548	1,851	2,514	2,654	2,155	2,295
El Salvador	554	534	742	873	932	238	303	384	488	609	316	231	358	385	323
Equatorial Guinea	(Z)	13	11	3	2	(Z)	(Z)	(Z)	(Z)	(Z)	(Z)	13	11	3	2
Estonia	(X)	(X)	59	54	33	(X)	(X)	13	20	29	(X)	(X)	46	34	4
Ethiopia	157	210	250	139	143	40	15	9	22	34	117	196	241	117	109
Federated States of Micronesia	25	(X)	32	25	25	(X)	6	13	14	13	(X)	(X)	19	11	11
Fiji	25	18	59	27	118	34	43	67	69	97	-9	-25	-8	-42	21
Finland	1,126	952	785	848	1,069	1,262	1,085	1,185	1,608	1,803	-136	-133	-400	-761	-734
France	13,665	15,346	14,593	13,267	13,622	13,153	13,333	14,797	15,279	16,775	511	2,013	-205	-2,013	-3,152
French Guiana	271	150	82	323	196	2	(Z)	4	2	3	269	150	78	321	193
French Polynesia	70	80	82	102	72	10	13	11	8	14	60	68	71	94	58
Gabon	49	85	55	48	40	701	712	921	961	1,155	-652	-627	-866	-913	-1,114
Gambia	9	11	10	10	4	2	2	(Z)	9	2	7	9	10	1	2
Georgia	(X)	(X)	16	48	79	(X)	(X)	7	21	2	(X)	(X)	9	27	77
Germany [4]	18,760	21,302	21,249	18,932	19,237	28,162	26,137	28,820	28,562	31,749	-9,402	-4,835	-7,572	-9,630	-12,512
Ghana	140	142	124	215	125	169	152	96	216	199	-29	-10	27	-1	-74
Gibraltar	32	10	11	8	23	1	1	2	3	4	31	9	9	5	19
Greece	763	1,039	901	880	830	509	429	370	348	455	255	610	531	533	375
Greenland	6	4	3	3	3	1	4	11	13	9	5	-	-8	-10	-6
Grenada	35	31	24	24	24	8	8	8	8	8	27	23	16	16	16
Guadeloupe	53	83	60	49	51	1	2	2	5	2	52	81	59	44	49
Guatemala	764	945	1,205	1,312	1,355	794	899	1,081	1,194	1,283	-31	46	124	118	72
Guinea	43	88	61	59	50	141	138	103	117	92	-98	-50	-42	-58	-42
Guyana	76	86	118	122	110	53	83	102	91	98	23	3	17	32	12
Haiti	477	395	209	229	211	343	284	107	154	59	134	111	102	74	152
Honduras	564	625	811	899	1,012	491	557	783	914	1,097	73	68	28	-15	-86
Hong Kong	6,817	8,137	9,077	9,874	11,445	9,622	9,279	9,793	9,554	9,698	-2,805	-1,142	-716	319	1,748
Hungary	156	256	295	435	309	348	367	347	401	470	-191	-111	-52	34	-161
Iceland	232	156	119	147	112	163	209	165	233	249	69	-53	-46	-86	-137
India	2,486	1,999	1,917	2,778	2,296	3,197	3,193	3,780	4,554	5,302	-711	-1,194	-1,863	-1,776	-3,005
Indonesia	1,897	1,892	2,780	2,770	2,811	3,341	3,241	4,530	5,435	6,523	-1,444	-1,349	-1,750	-2,665	-3,712
Iran	163	528	748	616	329	7	231	1	(Z)	1	156	297	747	616	328
Iraq	732	(Z)	-	7	1	3,008	6	-	(Z)	-	-2,276	-6	-	7	1
Ireland	2,540	2,681	2,862	2,728	3,416	1,755	1,948	2,262	2,519	2,890	784	733	600	209	525
Israel	3,203	3,911	4,077	4,429	5,006	3,313	3,484	3,816	4,420	5,223	-110	427	261	9	-217
Italy	7,992	8,570	8,721	6,464	7,193	12,751	11,764	12,314	13,216	14,711	-4,760	-3,194	-3,593	-6,752	-7,518
Ivory Coast	79	81	87	89	111	200	223	188	178	185	-121	-142	-100	-90	-74
Jamaica	943	961	939	1,116	1,066	569	576	599	720	747	374	385	340	397	320
Japan	48,580	48,125	47,813	47,892	53,481	89,684	91,511	97,414	107,246	119,149	-41,105	-43,386	-49,601	-59,355	-65,669
Jordan	309	219	258	361	288	11	6	18	19	29	298	213	240	342	259
Kazakhstan	(X)	(X)	15	68	131	(X)	(X)	21	41	60	(X)	(X)	-6	27	71
Kenya	116	91	124	131	170	58	69	73	92	109	58	22	51	39	61

See footnotes at end of table.

COUNTRY	EXPORTS, DOMESTIC AND FOREIGN					GENERAL IMPORTS [1]					MERCHANDISE TRADE BALANCE				
	1990	1991	1992	1993	1994	1990	1991	1992	1993	1994	1990	1991	1992	1993	1994
Kiribati	19	27	35	31	23	(Z)	1	(Z)	2	1	19	26	35	29	23
Korea	14,404	15,505	14,639	14,782	18,028	18,485	17,019	16,682	17,118	19,658	-4,081	-1,514	-2,043	-2,336	-1,629
Kuwait	403	1,228	1,337	999	1,175	569	36	281	1,819	1,445	-166	1,192	1,055	-819	-270
Kyrgyzstan	(X)	(X)	2	18	6	(X)	(X)	2	2	8	(X)	(X)	(X)	16	-2
Latvia	(X)	(X)	55	90	101	(X)	27	11	22	51	(X)	(X)	44	67	51
Lebanon	98	165	311	377	443	24	27	28	26	25	74	138	283	351	418
Lesotho	3	4	3	8	3	25	28	53	56	63	-22	-24	-50	-48	-60
Liberia	44	50	31	39	46	49	9	13	3	3	-5	41	18	36	43
Liechtenstein	12	10	12	11	14	15	21	35	100	96	-3	-11	-23	-89	-82
Lithuania	(X)	(X)	44	57	41	(X)	(X)	5	16	15	(X)	(X)	39	41	26
Luxembourg	134	217	272	560	228	210	188	227	253	288	-76	29	45	307	-59
Macao [3]	8	10	19	28	21	736	581	721	669	791	-728	-571	-702	-641	-770
Macedonia [3]	(X)	(X)	4	11	14	(X)	(X)	46	111	82	(X)	(X)	-42	-100	-68
Madagascar	11	14	6	11	48	41	47	53	43	57	-30	-33	-47	-32	-9
Malawi	14	55	14	26	19	50	73	60	58	57	-36	-18	-46	-32	-38
Malaysia	3,425	3,900	4,363	6,064	6,965	5,272	6,102	8,294	10,563	13,977	-1,847	-2,202	-3,931	-4,499	-7,012
Mali	9	18	11	33	19	3	2	1	1	4	6	16	10	32	15
Malta	45	57	58	172	88	53	65	91	104	96	-8	-8	-33	68	-8
Marshall Islands	27	38	34	36	33	2	3	8	12	8	25	35	26	24	25
Martinique	34	36	33	33	31	1	1	2	2	3	33	35	31	31	28
Mauritania	15	22	59	20	14	24	11	8	7	3	-9	11	51	13	11
Mauritius	13	15	22	18	24	159	132	136	198	217	-146	-117	-113	-180	-193
Mexico	28,279	33,277	40,592	41,581	50,840	30,157	31,130	35,211	39,917	49,493	-1,878	2,147	5,381	1,664	1,348
Moldova	(X)	(X)	9	6	6	(X)	(X)	13	16	18	(X)	(X)	9	31	20
Monaco	10	7	31	31	23	13	14	37	41	35	-3	-7	-6	-10	-12
Morocco	495	403	496	600	405	109	154	178	185	192	386	249	318	415	213
Mozambique	50	101	150	59	39	29	23	20	9	15	21	78	130	50	24
Namibia	44	33	34	22	16	33	35	23	23	28	11	-2	11	-1	-12
Netherlands	13,022	13,511	13,752	12,839	13,591	4,952	4,811	5,300	5,443	6,015	8,071	8,700	8,452	7,395	7,576
Netherlands Antilles	543	627	478	519	520	429	647	644	397	425	114	-20	-166	123	96
New Caledonia	34	44	36	23	27	27	20	15	24	21	7	24	21	-2	5
New Zealand	1,135	1,006	1,307	1,249	1,508	1,197	1,209	1,219	1,208	1,421	-62	-203	88	41	88
Nicaragua	68	150	185	150	186	15	60	69	128	167	52	91	117	22	19
Niger	12	10	13	16	12	46	5	3	3	2	-34	5	10	13	10
Nigeria	553	831	1,001	895	509	5,982	5,168	5,103	5,301	4,430	-5,429	-4,337	-4,102	-4,407	-3,921
Norway	1,281	1,489	1,279	1,212	1,268	1,830	1,624	1,969	1,958	2,373	-549	-135	-690	-745	-1,105
Oman	163	202	257	251	219	292	115	186	277	459	-129	87	71	-26	-240
Pakistan	1,143	950	881	811	719	610	663	865	897	1,012	533	288	16	-86	-293
Panama	869	978	1,103	1,187	1,276	234	269	254	280	323	635	709	850	908	954
Papua New Guinea	54	96	72	50	65	22	34	64	98	108	32	62	8	-48	-43
Paraguay	307	374	415	521	794	51	43	35	50	80	256	331	380	472	713
Peru	772	840	1,005	1,072	1,408	802	776	739	754	840	-30	64	267	318	568
Philippines	2,471	2,265	2,759	3,529	3,888	3,384	3,471	4,355	4,894	5,720	-913	-1,206	-1,597	-1,364	-1,832
Poland	406	459	641	912	625	408	357	375	454	651	-2	102	266	458	-26
Portugal	922	792	1,024	727	1,055	832	695	664	785	898	90	97	360	-59	156
Qatar	115	147	189	166	162	53	30	70	65	81	62	117	119	101	81
Romania	369	209	248	324	337	231	69	87	69	195	138	140	161	254	142

See footnotes at end of table.

No. 1341. U.S. Exports, Imports, and Merchandise Trade Balance, by Country: 1990 to 1994—Continued

[See headnote, page 819]

COUNTRY	EXPORTS, DOMESTIC AND FOREIGN					GENERAL IMPORTS [1]					MERCHANDISE TRADE BALANCE				
	1990	1991	1992	1993	1994	1990	1991	1992	1993	1994	1990	1991	1992	1993	1994
Russia	(X)	(X)	2,112	2,970	2,579	(X)	(X)	481	1,743	3,235	(X)	(X)	1,631	1,227	-656
Saudi Arabia	4,049	6,557	7,167	6,661	6,011	10,021	10,900	10,371	7,708	7,687	-5,971	-4,343	-3,204	-1,047	-1,676
Senegal	52	76	80	70	43	6	10	10	8	11	46	66	70	63	31
Sierra Leone	27	25	28	22	24	46	48	61	47	51	-19	-23	-33	-25	-27
Singapore	8,023	8,804	9,626	11,678	13,022	9,800	9,957	11,313	12,798	15,361	-1,778	-1,153	-1,687	-1,120	-2,339
Slovakia	(X)	(X)	(X)	34	43	(X)	(X)	2	65	129	(X)	(X)	(X)	-31	-86
Somalia	12	7	21	46	30	(Z)	3	2	(Z)	(Z)	12	4	18	46	30
South Africa	1,732	2,113	2,434	2,188	2,173	1,698	1,728	1,727	1,845	2,030	34	385	707	344	142
Spain	5,213	5,474	5,537	4,168	4,625	3,311	2,848	3,002	2,992	3,554	1,901	2,626	2,535	1,176	1,071
Sri Lanka	137	121	178	203	198	538	604	789	1,002	1,093	-401	-483	-612	-799	-895
Sudan	42	92	53	59	55	16	16	11	12	35	26	76	42	47	19
Suriname	156	134	142	114	122	50	52	46	58	43	106	82	96	56	79
Sweden	3,405	3,287	2,844	2,354	2,520	4,937	4,525	4,716	4,534	5,044	-1,533	-1,238	-1,872	-2,180	-2,524
Switzerland	4,943	5,557	4,540	6,807	5,614	5,587	5,576	5,645	5,973	6,376	-645	-19	-1,105	834	-762
Syria	150	209	165	187	199	52	25	42	130	64	98	184	123	56	134
Taiwan	11,491	13,182	15,250	16,168	17,078	22,666	23,023	24,596	25,102	26,711	-11,175	-9,841	-9,346	-8,934	-9,633
Tajikistan	(X)	(X)	9	12	15	(X)	(X)	11	18	60	(X)	(X)	-7	-6	-44
Tanzania	48	35	34	33	49	16	15	11	15	15	33	20	23	21	34
Thailand	2,995	3,753	3,989	3,766	4,861	5,289	6,122	7,529	8,542	10,307	-2,293	-2,369	-3,540	-4,775	-5,446
Togo	31	24	20	13	13	4	2	6	3	4	27	22	13	9	8
Trinidad and Tobago	428	468	447	529	541	1,020	866	848	803	1,109	-592	-398	-401	-274	-569
Tunisia	177	172	233	232	327	40	25	48	41	54	137	147	184	192	273
Turkey	2,243	2,468	2,735	3,429	2,754	1,183	1,006	1,110	1,198	1,575	1,061	1,462	1,625	2,231	1,178
Turkmenistan	(X)	(X)	35	46	137	(X)	(X)	1	2	2	(X)	(X)	34	44	136
Turks and Caicos Islands	39	40	38	22	29	4	4	6	4	4	36	36	32	18	25
Uganda	26	13	15	21	28	15	18	12	10	35	11	-5	3	11	-7
Ukraine	(X)	(X)	307	310	181	(X)	(X)	89	166	327	(X)	(X)	218	145	-146
United Arab Emirates	1,004	1,455	1,553	1,811	1,593	889	713	812	727	449	114	742	741	1,084	1,144
United Kingdom	23,490	22,046	22,800	26,438	26,833	20,188	18,413	20,093	21,730	25,063	3,302	3,633	2,707	4,708	1,770
Uruguay	144	216	231	254	311	206	237	266	266	168	-62	-21	-35	-12	143
U.S.S.R. (former)	3,087	3,579	1,036	(X)	(X)	1,059	802	187	(X)	(X)	2,028	2,777	849	(X)	(X)
Uzbekistan	(X)	(X)	51	73	90	(X)	(X)	(Z)	7	3	(X)	(X)	51	66	87
Venezuela	3,108	4,656	5,444	4,590	4,042	9,480	8,179	8,181	8,140	8,378	-6,371	-3,523	-2,737	-3,550	-4,337
Vietnam	7	4	5	7	172	-	1	(Z)	-	51	7	4	5	7	122
Western Samoa	5	7	73	10	7	-	1	(Z)	1	(Z)	5	6	72	9	7
Yemen	110	192	321	322	178	391	152	41	98	183	-281	40	281	224	-5
Yugoslavia (former) [3]	565	371	167	2	1	776	674	225	(Z)	(X)	-211	-303	-58	2	-
Yugoslavia, Fed. Rep. of	(X)	(X)	6	2	(X)	(X)	(X)	39	(Z)	(X)	(X)	(X)	-33	-33	(X)
Zaire	138	62	33	35	40	325	294	250	238	188	-187	-232	-218	-203	-148
Zambia	80	24	68	42	33	29	42	70	41	64	52	-18	-2	2	-31
Zimbabwe	135	53	144	84	93	119	90	106	110	102	16	-37	38	-26	-10

- Represents zero.   Z Less than $500,000.   X Not applicable.   [1] Imports are on a customs value basis. Exports are f.a.s. value.   [2] Includes revisions not carried to area values; therefore, area values will not add to total.   [3] Beginning June 1992 trade data were reported for the following countries which were formerly part of Yugoslavia — Croatia, Slovenia, Bosnia-Hercegovina, and Macedonia. The Federal Republic of Yugoslavia, which now includes only Serbia and Montenegro, will continue to be shown as "Yugoslavia." "Yugoslavia (former)" reflects data for the former country and includes data for the period of January through May 1992.   [4] Effective October 3, 1990, East Germany ceased to exist as a sovereign state and became a part of West Germany. Accordingly, trade statistics for East Germany reflect trade for January through September 1990. Trade statistics for 1990 for former West Germany reflect this unification beginning with October 1990. Data for Germany reflect the consolidation of the two countries for 1991.

Source: U.S. Bureau of the Census, *U.S. Merchandise Trade*, series FT 900, monthly.

No. 1342. U.S. Exports and General Imports, by Selected Commodity Groups: 1991 to 1994

[In millions of dollars. N.e.s.=Not elsewhere specified]

COMMODITY GROUP	EXPORTS [1]				GENERAL IMPORTS [2]			
	1991	1992	1993	1994	1991	1992	1993	1994
Total	421,730	448,164	465,091	512,521	487,129	532,665	580,659	663,829
Agricultural commodities	38,510	42,238	41,938	44,951	22,140	23,375	23,641	25,949
Animal feeds	3,192	3,550	3,464	3,348	312	337	368	436
Bulbs	113	112	107	112	178	201	217	238
Cereal flour	813	924	1,099	1,164	641	724	802	970
Cocoa	23	31	39	34	823	774	739	698
Coffee	10	18	32	53	1,738	1,563	1,383	2,270
Corn	5,146	4,966	4,504	4,187	39	69	61	85
Cotton, raw and linters	2,514	2,015	1,575	2,676	16	11	12	21
Dairy products; eggs	455	711	820	717	452	506	544	583
Furskins, raw	107	95	98	131	57	61	59	78
Grains, unmilled	701	894	683	694	112	122	157	181
Hides and skins	1,276	1,253	1,187	1,392	110	124	119	126
Live animals	688	609	519	587	1,172	1,437	1,536	1,392
Meat and preparations	3,630	4,208	4,353	5,191	2,908	2,712	2,792	2,629
Oils/fats, animal	447	497	472	567	29	18	21	22
Oils/fats, vegetable	596	725	734	962	735	955	859	1,051
Plants	99	135	112	117	105	102	92	105
Rice	754	726	791	1,008	80	92	106	130
Seeds	274	302	294	315	132	153	154	152
Soybeans	3,995	4,463	4,580	4,353	27	16	22	46
Sugar	12	6	2	5	713	662	606	551
Tobacco, unmanufactured	1,430	1,649	1,299	1,303	989	951	942	698
Vegetables and fruit	5,342	5,736	6,008	6,752	5,391	5,698	5,665	6,074
Wheat	3,350	4,503	4,679	4,057	66	191	213	286
Other agricultural	3,546	4,112	4,489	5,227	5,313	5,898	6,172	7,128
Manufactured goods	325,978	347,494	364,849	402,106	392,433	434,349	479,898	557,871
ADP equipment, office machinery . . .	25,979	27,000	27,177	30,879	30,019	36,377	43,193	52,118
Airplanes	24,335	26,286	21,270	18,824	3,347	3,860	3,805	3,805
Airplane parts	10,284	9,366	9,487	9,841	4,046	3,358	2,613	2,743
Aluminum	3,128	2,667	2,310	2,776	2,409	2,540	3,277	4,947
Artwork/antiques	1,239	1,076	951	1,185	1,979	2,087	2,673	2,427
Basketware, etc	1,290	1,522	1,644	1,817	1,911	2,189	2,392	2,590
Chemicals, cosmetics	2,361	2,632	3,047	3,536	1,415	1,711	1,808	1,995
Chemicals, dyeing	1,649	1,871	2,014	2,323	1,416	1,623	1,700	1,868
Chemicals, fertilizers	2,977	2,371	1,798	2,699	918	952	1,136	1,296
Chemicals, inorganic	4,083	4,123	3,810	4,068	3,297	3,305	3,284	4,105
Chemicals, medicinal	4,609	5,357	5,751	6,093	3,047	3,810	4,135	4,680
Chemicals, organic	10,898	10,993	11,076	12,826	8,133	9,406	9,279	10,799
Chemicals, plastics	10,316	10,258	10,743	12,486	3,784	4,292	4,848	5,933
Chemicals, n.e.s.	6,019	6,265	6,835	7,570	2,122	2,622	2,941	3,238
Clothing	3,215	4,092	4,815	5,464	26,202	31,227	33,780	36,744
Copper	1,328	1,172	1,200	1,268	1,573	1,642	1,733	2,296
Electrical machinery	30,050	32,172	36,817	44,309	35,067	39,710	46,735	57,672
Footwear	543	603	605	647	9,554	10,163	11,173	11,716
Furniture and parts	2,120	2,553	2,948	3,127	4,936	5,503	6,249	7,567
Gem diamonds	209	369	153	183	4,002	4,148	5,103	5,740
General industrial machinery	17,153	18,480	19,515	21,783	14,396	15,520	17,082	21,337
Glass	1,145	1,213	1,341	1,459	770	850	1,004	1,351
Glassware	449	496	502	560	937	1,015	1,031	1,157
Gold, nonmonetary	3,279	4,109	9,115	5,644	1,922	1,899	2,014	1,932
Iron and steel mill products	4,211	3,606	3,330	3,548	8,301	8,328	9,027	12,876
Lighting, plumbing	877	977	1,097	1,252	1,246	1,547	1,762	2,024
Metal manufactures, n.e.s.	5,189	5,513	5,975	7,012	6,372	6,727	7,647	8,848
Metalworking machinery	2,709	3,034	3,256	3,899	3,605	3,187	3,683	4,614
Motorcycles, bicycles	1,308	1,439	1,433	1,518	1,636	1,913	2,161	2,323
Nickel	219	196	199	209	1,061	797	686	735
Optical goods	713	766	797	965	1,484	1,645	1,683	1,816
Paper and paperboard	5,965	6,348	6,463	7,450	8,021	7,998	8,640	9,065
Photographic equipment	2,926	2,950	2,932	3,017	3,641	3,844	4,267	4,678
Plastic articles, n.e.s.	2,240	2,777	2,988	3,573	3,114	3,572	3,937	4,513
Platinum	311	292	339	304	1,659	1,429	1,255	1,324
Pottery	87	103	110	105	1,242	1,404	1,436	1,556
Power generating machinery	16,960	17,995	19,167	20,270	14,195	15,888	17,125	19,561
Printed materials	3,589	3,803	3,995	3,973	1,702	1,875	2,026	2,232
Records/magnetic media	4,267	4,846	5,317	5,867	2,788	3,106	3,443	3,611
Rubber articles, n.e.s.	579	622	679	785	705	878	1,014	1,251
Rubber tires and tubes	1,274	1,409	1,465	1,614	2,309	2,512	2,736	3,035

See footnotes at end of table.

No. 1342. U.S. Exports and General Imports, by Selected SITC Commodity Groups: 1991 to 1994—Continued

[In millions of dollars]

COMMODITY GROUP	EXPORTS [1]				GENERAL IMPORTS [2]			
	1991	1992	1993	1994	1991	1992	1993	1994
Manufactured goods—Continued								
Scientific instruments	13,499	14,375	15,223	16,463	6,733	7,602	8,457	9,964
Ships, boats	1,155	1,421	976	1,166	249	319	969	806
Silver and bullion	237	209	203	247	363	449	390	488
Spacecraft	257	270	393	444	-	92	-	219
Specialized industrial machinery	16,686	16,689	17,626	19,695	10,864	11,814	13,565	16,755
Telecommunications equipment	9,999	11,248	13,122	15,845	23,446	25,803	27,297	32,457
Textile yarn, fabric	5,482	5,778	5,895	6,429	6,981	7,844	8,438	9,208
Toys/games/sporting goods	2,087	2,437	2,707	3,086	8,821	10,749	11,637	11,824
Travel goods	159	194	199	233	2,346	2,509	2,653	3,080
Vehicles/new cars, Canada	6,195	5,931	6,350	7,420	13,518	13,890	17,654	22,081
Vehicles/new cars, Japan	496	694	982	1,724	20,422	20,801	21,581	23,973
Vehicles/new cars, Other	3,070	5,095	4,914	5,287	10,813	11,561	12,022	14,559
Vehicles/trucks	3,879	3,706	4,144	5,126	8,293	9,772	10,109	10,348
Vehicles/chassis/bodies	241	310	370	428	352	338	406	428
Vehicles/parts	14,371	16,753	19,307	21,163	14,067	15,838	17,653	19,610
Watches/clocks/parts	225	208	236	277	2,285	2,320	2,546	2,643
Wood manufactures	1,251	1,389	1,475	1,543	1,907	2,410	2,869	3,387
Zinc	40	38	40	47	652	855	736	787
Other manufactured goods	24,570	27,031	26,220	28,758	30,042	32,924	35,397	41,135
Mineral fuel	**12,081**	**11,254**	**9,756**	**8,895**	**54,056**	**55,256**	**55,900**	**56,412**
Coal	4,776	4,427	3,197	2,962	310	419	514	646
Crude oil	33	32	20	44	36,902	38,553	38,469	38,464
Petroleum preparations	4,399	4,011	3,920	3,161	12,312	11,277	10,789	10,242
Liquified propane/butane	253	257	229	195	859	707	951	873
Natural gas	308	353	241	254	2,482	3,030	3,678	4,014
Electricity	44	63	102	30	487	590	662	960
Other mineral fuels	2,268	2,111	2,046	2,248	704	680	836	1,213
Selected commodities:								
Fish and preparations	3,063	3,383	2,991	3,033	5,638	5,657	5,820	6,593
Cork, wood, lumber	5,114	5,314	5,786	5,554	3,057	3,970	5,633	6,683
Pulp and waste paper	3,600	3,859	2,978	3,793	2,163	2,129	1,886	2,315
Metal ores; scrap	4,039	3,470	3,227	3,734	3,561	3,340	3,030	3,253
Crude fertilizers	1,385	1,388	1,345	1,445	982	894	936	1,027
Cigarettes	4,238	4,193	3,919	4,965	130	271	491	71
Alcoholic bev. distilled	279	344	343	356	1,595	1,827	1,737	1,826
All other	2,822	2,801	2,716	3,243	1,375	1,597	1,687	1,829
Re-exports	20,621	22,427	25,244	30,529	(X)	(X)	(X)	(X)
Agricultural commodities	857	893	889	1,068	(X)	(X)	(X)	(X)
Manufactured goods	19,153	20,977	23,832	28,926	(X)	(X)	(X)	(X)
Mineral fuels	206	76	107	78	(X)	(X)	(X)	(X)
Other, re-exports	405	481	416	457	(X)	(X)	(X)	(X)
Timing adjustment	(X)	(X)	(X)	68	(X)	(X)	(X)	-62

- Represents zero.   X Not applicable.   [1] F.A.S. basis.   [2] Customs value basis.
Source: U.S. Bureau of the Census, *U.S. Merchandise Trade*, series FT 900, Final Reports.

No. 1343. Imports for Consumption—Values and Duties: 1970 to 1994

[Imports are on customs value basis. Beginning 1970, includes silver ores and bullion, and beginning 1980, includes trade of Virgin Islands with foreign countries. For basis of dollar values and for area coverage, see text, section 28. See also *Historical Statistics, Colonial Times to 1970*, series U 207-212]

YEAR	VALUES				Duties calculated [1] (mil. dol.)	RATIO OF DUTIES TO VALUES		Duties per capita [2] (dollar)
	Total (mil. dol.)	Free (mil. dol.)	Dutiable (mil. dol.)	Percent free		Total imports (percent)	Dutiable imports (percent)	
1970	39,756	13,870	25,886	35	2,584	6.5	10.0	12.60
1975	96,516	31,030	65,486	32	3,780	3.9	5.8	17.50
1980	[3]244,007	106,992	132,951	45	7,535	3.1	5.7	33.09
1981	259,012	76,338	182,674	29	8,893	3.4	4.9	38.67
1982	242,340	75,856	166,484	31	8,688	3.6	5.2	37.40
1983	256,679	83,397	173,283	32	9,430	3.7	5.4	40.21
1984	322,989	102,977	220,012	32	12,042	3.7	5.5	50.90
1985	343,553	106,035	237,518	31	13,067	3.8	5.5	54.73
1986	368,657	121,742	246,915	33	13,312	3.6	5.4	55.10
1987	402,066	132,152	269,914	33	13,923	3.5	5.2	57.08
1988	437,140	151,693	285,447	35	15,054	3.4	5.3	61.12
1989	468,012	156,365	311,647	33	16,096	3.4	5.2	64.70
1990	490,554	161,108	329,446	33	16,339	3.3	5.0	65.38
1991	483,028	167,641	315,386	35	16,197	3.4	5.1	64.10
1992	525,091	194,583	330,508	37	17,164	3.3	5.2	67.12
1993	574,863	236,007	338,856	41	18,334	3.2	5.4	70.99
1994	657,885	292,257	365,628	44	19,846	3.0	5.6	73.64

[1] Customs duties (including import excise taxes) calculated on the basis of reports of quantity and value of imports of merchandise entered directly for consumption or withdrawn from bonded customs warehouses.   [2] Based on estimated population including Armed Forces abroad as of July 1.   [3] Total includes revisions not carried to free and dutiable values.
Source: U.S. Bureau of the Census, 1970-1988, *Highlights of U.S. Export and Import Trade*, series FT 990, monthly; beginning 1989, *U.S. Merchandise Trade: Selected Highlights*, series FT 920, and unpublished data.

No. 1344. Domestic Exports and Imports for Consumption of Merchandise, by Selected SIC-Based Product Category: 1985 to 1994

[In millions of dollars. Includes nonmonetary gold]

SIC-BASED PRODUCT CATEGORY	SIC [1] code	1985	1989	1990	1991	1992	1993	1994
Domestic exports, total [2]	(X)	212,961	349,433	374,537	400,842	425,377	439,282	482,141
Agricultural, forestry and fishery products.	(X)	20,074	27,198	26,225	25,052	26,785	25,324	26,102
Agricultural products	01	19,199	24,142	22,597	21,075	22,633	21,615	22,189
Livestock and livestock products	02	735	821	829	970	871	836	973
Forestry products	08	122	270	281	306	324	276	263
Fish, fresh or chilled; and other marine products [3]	09	18	1,965	2,518	2,701	2,959	2,596	2,677
Mineral commodities	(X)	6,394	7,030	7,335	7,442	7,210	5,584	5,650
Metallic ores and concentrates	10	686	1,247	1,137	1,014	1,084	799	1,018
Bituminous, lignite and anthracite coal	11,12	4,465	4,287	4,513	4,623	4,241	3,090	2,858
Crude petroleum and natural gas	13	476	490	638	675	737	588	576
Nonmetallic minerals, exc. fuels	14	767	1,006	1,047	1,130	1,148	1,107	1,199
Manufactured commodities	(X)	175,752	290,536	330,403	359,635	383,082	400,721	441,501
Food and kindred products	20	10,055	15,205	16,160	17,492	19,761	20,509	23,094
Tobacco manufactures	21	1,268	3,632	5,040	4,574	4,509	4,253	5,367
Textile mill products	22	1,462	2,794	3,635	4,108	4,473	4,687	5,151
Apparel and related products	23	1,019	2,349	2,848	3,679	4,599	5,433	6,145
Lumber and related products	24	2,668	6,050	6,523	6,477	6,802	7,361	7,252
Furniture and fixtures	25	483	1,011	1,589	2,086	2,518	2,818	3,030
Paper and allied products	26	3,886	8,126	8,631	9,214	9,969	9,457	11,000
Printing and publishing	27	1,250	2,598	3,150	3,590	3,808	4,057	4,070
Chemicals and allied products	28	21,797	35,825	37,806	41,483	41,953	42,742	48,950
Petroleum and coal products	29	5,433	5,019	6,794	7,026	6,403	6,163	5,510
Rubber and misc. plastics products	30	2,765	5,010	6,398	7,049	7,872	8,554	9,942
Leather and leather products	31	478	1,131	1,388	1,413	1,541	1,536	1,539
Stone, clay, and glass products	32	1,792	2,638	3,295	3,533	3,855	3,844	4,215
Primary metal products	33	4,747	12,110	13,116	15,243	15,105	18,669	16,327
Fabricated metal products	34	5,765	9,117	11,138	11,962	13,265	13,497	13,395
Machinery, except electrical	35	37,478	55,524	61,229	65,300	68,554	72,279	82,120
Electric and electronic machinery	36	18,908	32,718	39,807	42,330	45,992	52,947	63,839
Transportation equipment	37	38,024	56,875	68,113	76,172	82,862	80,196	85,068
Instruments and related products	38	8,623	17,327	19,524	21,699	22,815	24,699	26,560
Misc. manufactured commodities	39	1,773	4,553	4,296	4,621	5,446	5,288	5,813
Imports for consumption, total [2]	(X)	343,553	468,012	490,554	483,028	525,091	574,863	657,884
Agricultural, forestry and fishery products.	(X)	12,805	13,251	12,750	13,148	14,216	15,866	17,427
Agricultural products	01	7,483	6,109	5,925	6,107	6,716	7,839	8,657
Livestock and livestock products	02	933	1,290	1,453	1,501	1,873	2,161	2,047
Forestry products	08	830	1,235	1,015	978	1,088	1,068	1,208
Fish, fresh or chilled; and other marine products [3]	09	3,559	4,617	4,357	4,562	4,540	4,798	5,515
Mineral commodities	(X)	39,011	41,264	51,391	44,581	44,823	45,965	47,300
Metallic ores and concentrates	10	1,265	1,425	1,500	1,244	1,167	1,108	1,283
Bituminous, lignite and anthracite coal	11,12	70	97	93	112	127	218	229
Crude petroleum and natural gas	13	35,872	38,842	48,917	42,415	42,796	43,871	44,949
Nonmetallic minerals, exc. fuels	14	1,804	900	881	810	734	767	839
Manufactured commodities	(X)	280,089	396,903	407,043	406,550	445,127	490,289	567,052
Food and kindred products	20	12,521	15,122	16,564	16,298	17,445	16,090	17,342
Tobacco manufactures	21	78	88	94	199	285	467	163
Textile mill products	22	3,616	7,294	6,807	7,132	7,808	6,161	6,534
Apparel and related products	23	15,710	22,841	24,644	25,497	30,533	35,475	38,561
Lumber and related products	24	5,105	5,848	5,446	5,229	6,700	8,901	10,528
Furniture and fixtures	25	3,220	5,148	5,235	5,130	5,601	6,242	7,522
Paper and allied products	26	7,493	11,880	11,669	10,431	10,382	10,891	11,772
Printing and publishing	27	1,200	1,807	1,849	1,878	2,046	2,211	2,422
Chemicals and allied products	28	12,790	20,118	21,611	22,999	25,849	27,259	31,697
Petroleum and coal products	29	18,282	11,979	14,472	11,097	10,410	9,906	9,504
Rubber and misc. plastics products	30	4,721	9,488	9,731	9,855	11,287	13,053	14,393
Leather and leather products	31	7,724	9,837	10,944	10,714	11,342	11,692	12,977
Stone, clay, and glass products	32	4,296	5,775	5,845	5,558	5,951	6,431	7,594
Primary metal products	33	20,439	25,563	23,232	22,262	22,891	22,772	30,106
Fabricated metal products	34	7,754	11,568	11,608	11,396	12,436	12,941	14,664
Machinery, except electrical	35	31,310	54,051	55,021	55,578	62,274	73,370	89,705
Electric and electronic machinery	36	37,951	55,316	55,736	58,610	65,596	76,869	94,332
Transportation equipment	37	65,944	87,972	89,599	88,004	92,930	102,259	115,998
Instruments and related products	38	8,805	15,364	16,846	18,668	20,338	22,080	24,410
Misc. manufactured commodities	39	11,130	19,844	20,090	20,015	23,025	25,219	26,830

X Not applicable. [1] Standard Industrial Classification. [2] Includes scrap and waste, used or secondhand merchandise, manufactured commodities not identified by kind, and timing adjustments. [3] Includes frozen and packaged fish.

Source: U.S. Bureau of the Census, 1985 and 1988, *Highlights of U.S. Export and Import Trade*, series FT 990; beginning 1989, *U.S. Merchandise Trade*, series FT 900.

Figure 29.1
Selected Outlying Areas of the United States

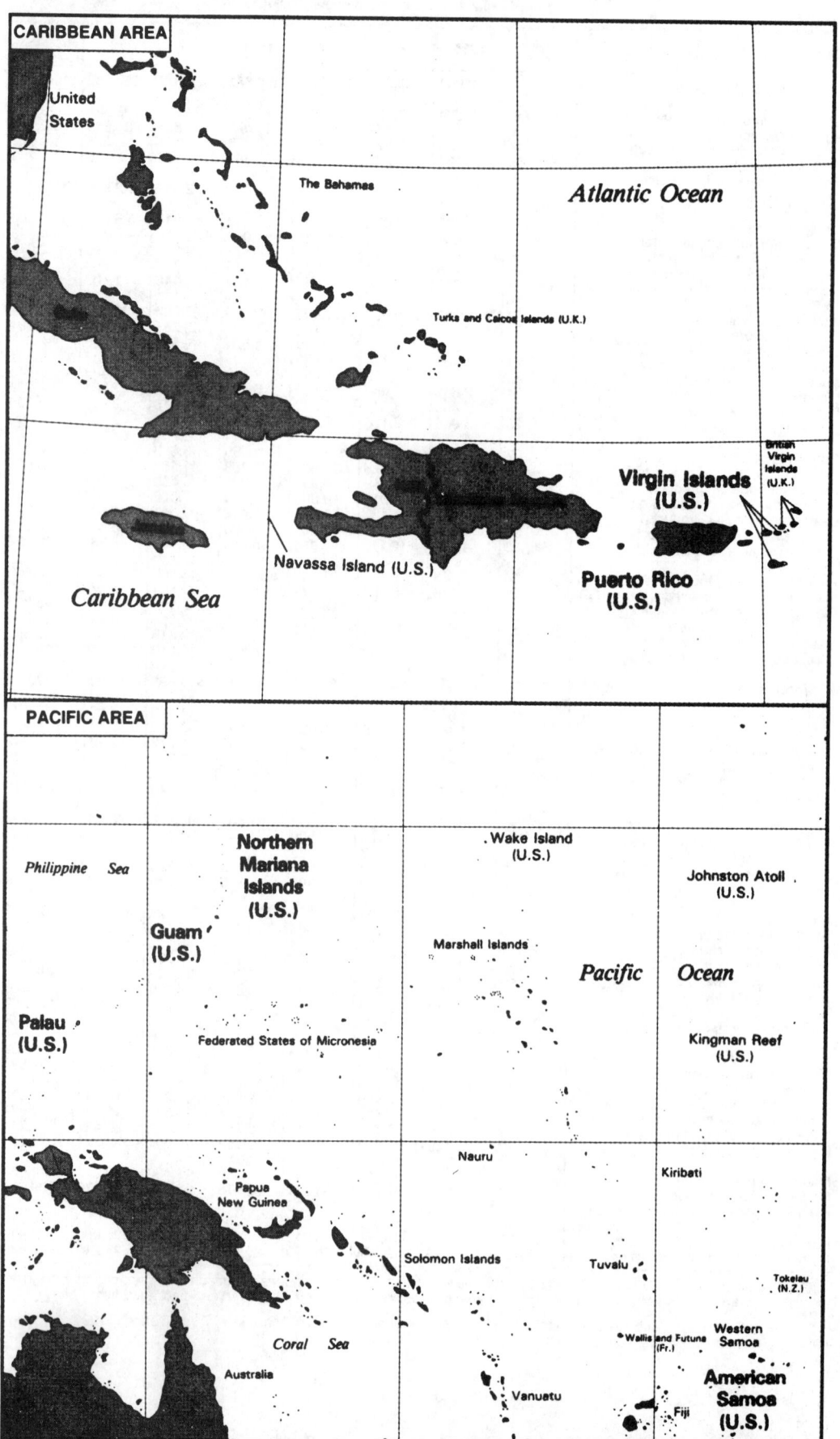

Outlying Areas

This section presents summary economic and social statistics for Puerto Rico, Virgin Islands, Guam, American Samoa, and the Northern Mariana Islands.

Primary sources are the decennial censuses of population and housing, and the censuses of agriculture, business, manufactures, and construction (taken every 5 years) conducted by the Bureau of the Census; the annual *Vital Statistics of the United States,* issued by the National Center for Health Statistics; and the annual *Income and Product* of the Puerto Rico Planning Board, San Juan.

Jurisdiction.—The United States gained jurisdiction over these areas as follows:

The islands of *Puerto Rico* and *Guam,* surrendered by Spain to the United States in October 1898, were ceded to the United States by the Treaty of Paris, ratified in 1899. Puerto Rico became a Commonwealth on July 25, 1952, thereby achieving a high degree of local autonomy under its own constitution. The *Virgin Islands,* comprising 50 islands and cays, was purchased by the United States from Denmark in 1917. *American Samoa,* a group of seven islands, was acquired by the United States in accordance with a convention among the United States, Great Britain, and Germany, ratified in 1900 (Swains Island was annexed in 1925).

By an agreement approved by the Security Council and the United States, the Northern Mariana Islands, previously under Japanese mandate, was administered by the United States between 1947 and 1986 under the United Nations trusteeship system. The Northern Mariana Islands became a Commonwealth in 1986.

For a brief summary of U.S. territorial development, see table 362.

Censuses.—Because characteristics of the outlying areas differ, the presentation of census data for them is not uniform. The 1960 Census of Population covered all of the places listed above except the

In Brief

Persons per household, 1990:

Puerto Rico	*3.3*
Virgin Islands	*3.1*
Guam	*4.0*
American Samoa	*7.0*
Northern Mariana Islands	*4.6*

Northern Mariana Islands (their census was conducted in April 1958 by the Office of the High Commissioner), while the 1960 Census of Housing also excluded American Samoa. The 1970, 1980 and 1990 Censuses of Population and Housing covered all five areas. The 1959, 1969, and 1978 Censuses of Agriculture covered Puerto Rico, American Samoa, Guam, and the Virgin Islands; the 1964, 1974, and 1982 censuses covered the same areas except American Samoa; and the 1969, 1978, 1987, and 1992 censuses included the Northern Mariana Islands. Beginning in 1967, Congress authorized the economic censuses, to be taken at 5-year intervals, for years ending in "2" and "7." Prior economic censuses were conducted in Puerto Rico for 1949, 1954, 1958, and 1963 and in Guam and the Virgin Islands for 1958 and 1963. In 1967, the census of construction industries was added for the first time in Puerto Rico; in 1972, Virgin Islands and Guam were covered. For 1982, 1987, and 1992 the economic censuses covered the Northern Mariana Islands.

Information in other sections.—In addition to the statistics presented in this section, other data are included as integral parts of many tables showing distribution by States in various sections of the *Abstract.* See "Outlying areas of the United States" in the index. For definition and explanation of terms used, see section 1, Population; section 4, Education; section 23, Agriculture; section 25, Construction and Housing; section 26, Manufactures; and section 27, Domestic Trade and Services.

No. 1345. Estimated Resident Population With Projections: 1960 to 2020

[In thousands. Population data generally are de facto figures for the present territory. Population estimates were derived from information available as of early 1995. See text, section 30, for general comments regarding the data. For details of methodology, coverage, and reliability, see source]

AREA	1960	1970	1980	1990	1994	1995	2000, proj.	2010, proj.	2020, proj.
Puerto Rico	2,358	2,716	3,206	3,605	3,807	3,813	3,850	4,017	4,227
American Samoa	20	27	32	47	55	57	69	85	86
Guam	67	86	107	134	150	153	171	202	230
Virgin Islands	33	63	98	101	98	97	99	107	111
Northern Mariana Islands	9	12	17	44	50	51	57	71	86

Source: U.S. Bureau of the Census, International Data Base.

No. 1346. Vital Statistics—Specified Areas: 1960 to 1992

[Births, deaths, and infant deaths by place of residence; marriages and divorces by place of occurrence. Rates for 1960, 1970, 1980, and 1990 based on population enumerated as of **April 1**; for other years, on population estimated as of **July 1**]

AREA AND YEAR	BIRTHS		DEATHS		INFANT DEATHS		MARRIAGES		DIVORCES [3]	
	Number	Rate [1]	Number	Rate [1]	Number	Rate [2]	Number	Rate [1]	Number	Rate [1]
Puerto Rico: 1960	76,314	32.5	15,791	6.7	3,307	43.3	[4]20,212	[4]8.6	5,218	2.2
1970	67,628	24.8	18,080	6.7	1,930	28.6	29,905	11.0	9,688	3.6
1980	72,986	22.8	20,413	6.4	1,351	18.5	33,167	10.4	15,276	4.8
1985	63,547	19.4	23,071	7.0	944	14.9	30,355	9.2	14,686	4.5
1990	66,417	18.9	25,957	7.4	888	13.4	(NA)	(NA)	(NA)	(NA)
1992	64,344	18.0	(NA)	(NA)	(NA)	(NA)	(NA)	(NA)	(NA)	(NA)
Guam: 1965	2,523	32.8	336	4.4	82	32.5	471	6.2	53	0.7
1970	2,842	28.8	355	5.8	62	21.6	874	9.9	84	1.0
1980	2,945	27.8	393	3.7	43	14.6	(NA)	(NA)	(NA)	(NA)
1985	3,049	24.6	415	3.4	35	11.5	(NA)	(NA)	(NA)	(NA)
1990	3,839	28.8	520	3.9	31	8.1	(NA)	(NA)	(NA)	(NA)
1992	4,206	(NA)	(NA)	(NA)	(NA)	(NA)	(NA)	(NA)	(NA)	(NA)
Virgin Islands: 1960	1,180	36.8	332	10.3	42	35.6	359	11.1	135	4.2
1970	2,898	46.8	469	7.9	72	24.6	1,149	18.4	270	4.3
1980	2,504	25.9	504	5.2	61	24.4	1,112	11.5	478	4.9
1985	2,375	21.4	506	4.6	42	17.7	1,448	13.1	363	3.3
1990	2,267	22.3	480	4.7	33	14.6	(NA)	(NA)	(NA)	(NA)
1992	2,515	(NA)	(NA)	(NA)	(NA)	(NA)	(NA)	(NA)	(NA)	(NA)

NA Not available. [1] Per 1,000 population. [2] Per 1,000 live births. [3] Includes reported annulments. [4] Data are incomplete.

Source: U.S. National Center for Health Statistics, *Vital Statistics of the United States,* annual.

No. 1347. Land Area and Population Characteristics, by Area: 1990

[As of **April 1**. See also table 362 for gross area (land and water). For definition of median, see Guide to Tabular Presentation]

ITEM	United States	Puerto Rico	Virgin Islands	Guam	American Samoa	Northern Mariana Islands
Land area (sq. miles)	3,536,338	3,427	134	210	77	179
Total resident population	248,709,873	3,522,037	101,809	133,152	46,773	43,345
Per square mile	70.3	1,027.9	760.9	634.1	607.4	242.2
Percent increase, 1980-90	9.8	10.2	5.4	25.6	44.8	158.3
Urban	187,053,487	2,508,346	37,885	50,801	15,599	12,151
Rural	61,656,386	1,013,691	63,924	82,351	31,174	31,194
Male	121,239,418	1,705,642	49,210	70,945	24,023	22,802
Female	127,470,455	1,816,395	52,599	62,207	22,750	20,543
Males per 100 females	95.1	93.9	93.6	114.0	105.6	111.0
Median age (years)	32.9	28.4	28.2	25.0	20.9	27.4
Male (years)	31.7	27.2	27.1	25.2	20.6	29.9
Female (years)	34.1	29.6	29.2	24.9	21.2	24.9
Marital status, persons 15 years old and over	195,142,002	2,563,818	72,365	93,200	28,952	33,030
Never married	52,559,853	711,470	27,539	30,759	11,412	13,810
Married [1]	111,498,578	1,499,449	35,199	54,717	15,958	17,869
Widowed or divorced	31,083,571	352,899	9,627	7,724	1,582	1,351
Households and families:						
Households	91,947,410	1,054,924	32,020	31,373	6,607	6,873
Persons in households	242,012,129	3,487,667	100,488	124,596	46,267	31,856
Persons per household	2.63	3.31	3.14	3.97	7.00	4.63
Families	64,517,947	886,339	23,012	27,313	6,301	5,312
Husband-wife families	50,708,322	634,872	13,197	21,342	5,153	3,947
Children ever born per 1,000 females 15 to 44 years	1,223	1,512	1,662	1,523	1,757	1,226

[1] For Puerto Rico, includes consensually married couples and for all areas, includes separated couples.

Source: U.S. Bureau of the Census, *1990 Census of Population,* CP-1 parts 1, (United States), 53 (Puerto Rico), 55 (Virgin Islands); *1990 Census of Population and Housing,* CPH-1, parts 53A and 55; CPH-6, parts G (Guam), AS (American Samoa), and CNMI (Commonwealth of the Northern Mariana Islands); and Summary Tape File, parts 3C, (United States), 3A (Puerto Rico), and 3 (Virgin Islands).

No. 1348. Selected Social and Economic Characteristics, by Area: 1990

[As of **April 1**]

CHARACTERISTIC	United States	Puerto Rico	Virgin Islands	Guam	American Samoa	Northern Mariana Islands
EDUCATIONAL ATTAINMENT						
Persons 25 years and over	158,868,436	1,952,297	55,639	66,700	19,570	24,633
Less than 9th grade.	16,502,211	691,835	12,908	9,238	3,664	4,285
9th to 12th grade, no diploma	22,841,507	290,173	11,278	8,602	5,239	4,016
High school graduate.	47,642,763	410,559	14,021	22,220	6,253	8,659
Some college or associate degree	39,571,702	281,248	9,011	14,984	3,062	3,818
Bachelor's degree or higher	32,310,253	278,482	8,421	11,656	1,352	3,855
EMPLOYMENT STATUS						
Total persons, 16 years old and over ..	191,829,271	2,497,078	70,323	90,990	27,991	32,522
In labor force	125,182,378	1,180,162	47,553	66,138	14,198	26,589
Percent of total..............	65.3	47.3	67.6	72.7	50.7	81.8
Armed forces	1,708,928	5,486	110	11,952	11	8
Civilian labor force	123,473,450	1,174,676	47,443	54,186	14,187	26,581
Employed	115,681,202	934,736	44,267	52,144	13,461	25,965
Unemployed	7,792,248	239,940	3,176	2,042	726	616
Percent of civilian labor force...	6.3	20.4	6.7	3.8	5.1	2.3
Not in labor force	66,646,893	1,316,916	22,770	24,852	13,793	5,933
FAMILY INCOME IN 1989						
Families, census year.	65,049,428	889,998	23,012	27,313	6,301	5,312
Percent distribution by income class	100.0	100.0	100.0	100.0	100.0	100.0
Less than $5,000.............	4.0	25.1	8.8	4.0	11.0	8.2
$5,000 to $9,999	5.6	24.9	9.5	4.7	19.2	13.9
$10,000 to $14,999	7.2	16.5	12.8	8.3	17.0	13.1
$15,000 to $24,999	16.4	17.5	20.6	21.1	23.6	21.6
$25,000 or more	66.9	16.0	48.3	61.9	29.1	43.2
Median income (dollars)	35,225	9,988	24,036	31,178	15,979	21,275
RESIDENCE IN 1985						
Persons 5 years and over	230,445,777	3,219,765	92,579	118,055	39,821	39,206
Same house.................	122,796,970	2,190,479	56,098	54,665	30,759	11,479
Different house in this area	102,540,097	879,691	25,003	24,763	2,763	6,870
Outside area	5,108,710	149,595	11,478	38,627	6,299	20,857
LANGUAGE SPOKEN AT HOME						
Persons 5 years and over	230,445,777	3,219,765	92,579	118,055	39,821	39,206
Speak only English at home	198,600,798	(NA)	70,442	44,048	1,203	1,878

NA Not available.

Source: U.S. Bureau of the Census, *1990 Census of Population and Housing,* Summary Tape File, parts 3C, (United States), 3A, and unpublished data, (Puerto Rico), and 3 (Virgin Islands); CPH-L-98, *The Foreign Born Population in the United States: 1990; 1990 Census of Population and Housing,* CPH-6, parts G (Guam), AS (American Samoa), and CNMI (Commonwealth of the Northern Mariana Islands).

No. 1349. Federal Direct Payments for Individuals: 1993 and 1994

[**In thousands of dollars.** For fiscal years ending **September 30**]

PROGRAM PAYMENTS	1993				1994			
	Puerto Rico	Guam	Virgin Islands	American Samoa	Puerto Rico	Guam	Virgin Islands	American Samoa
Total	**4,483,643**	**136,608**	**124,703**	**18,249**	**4,743,891**	**146,208**	**137,337**	**23,846**
Pell Grants	297,048	1,019	674	377	352,878	1,411	1,279	1,114
Medicare: Hospital Insurance ..	275,526	3,351	7,335	-	330,739	4,022	8,805	-
Supplemental medical insurance	257,239	2,734	4,569	-	291,071	3,094	5,170	-
Social Security:								
Disability insurance	704,821	4,678	7,996	3,385	764,742	5,335	9,163	4,070
Retirement insurance......	1,321,392	25,784	40,483	5,283	1,386,927	28,422	43,532	5,724
Survivors insurance	575,940	14,525	14,058	5,382	610,065	15,652	14,807	5,803
Veterans:								
Pension and disability......	335,243	4,633	3,027	1,781	358,035	4,932	1,902	2,010
Education assistance	2,270	84	22	20	2,468	78	23	29
Federal retirement and disability	158,151	49,355	6,987	1,903	162,788	52,644	7,291	1,839
Food Stamps...........	[1]1,018,582	17,316	19,328	-	[1]1,083,040	21,815	22,547	-
Other	556,013	13,129	20,224	118	484,178	8,803	22,818	3,257

- Represents or rounds to zero.   [1] Food stamp program in Puerto Rico was replaced by the Nutritional Assistance Grant Program. Figures shown represent grants to State and local governments, not included in totals.

Source: U.S. Bureau of the Census, *Federal Expenditures by State for Fiscal Year,* annual.

No. 1350. Public Elementary and Secondary Schools, by Areas: 1993

[For school year ending in year shown, unless otherwise indicated]

ITEM	Puerto Rico	Guam	Virgin Islands	American Samoa	ITEM	Puerto Rico	Guam	Virgin Islands	American Samoa
PUBLIC EL/SEC					Teachers	38,381	1,628	1,595	725
Enrollment, fall	637,034	30,057	22,887	13,994	Other support				
Elementary (kindergarten-grade 8)	469,764	22,408	16,804	10,582	services staff.	20,576	1,287	704	288
Secondary (grades 9-12 and post graduates)	167,270	7,649	6,083	3,412	Current expenditures [1] ($1,000)	1,359,567	148,899	128,678	29,165
Staff, fall	67,643	3,506	3,353	1,350	Per pupil [2] (dol.) . . .	2,134	4,954	5,622	2,084
School district staff .	1,727	147	411	107	HIGHER EDUCATION				
School staff	45,340	2,072	2,238	955	Enrollment, fall	158,120	4,845	2,856	1,295

[1] Public elementary and secondary day schools. [2] Annual expenditures per pupil enrolled.

Source: U.S. National Center for Education Statistics, unpublished data.

No. 1351. Puerto Rico—Summary: 1970 to 1994

ITEM	Unit	1970	1980	1985	1990	1991	1992	1993	1994
POPULATION									
Total [1]	1,000	2,722	3,184	3,378	3,528	3,549	3,580	3,622	3,685
Persons per family	Number . . .	4.6	4.3	3.9	3.7	3.7	3.6	3.6	3.6
EDUCATION [2]									
Enrollment, total.	1,000	922.6	1,090.9	1,107.9	(NA)	(NA)	(NA)	(NA)	(NA)
Public day school	1,000	672.3	716.1	692.9	651.2	644.7	642.7	(NA)	(NA)
Other public	1,000	103.9	149.5	152.0	(NA)	(NA)	(NA)	(NA)	(NA)
Private schools.	1,000	89.1	95.2	107.3	145.8	134.2	(NA)	(NA)	(NA)
College and university	1,000	57.3	130.1	155.7	156.1	157.5	157.1	(NA)	(NA)
Expenses	Mil. dol. . . .	288.8	825.0	1,171.8	1,686.4	1,759.7	2,039.0	(NA)	(NA)
As percent of GNP	Percent . . .	6.2	7.5	7.8	7.8	7.7	8.6	(NA)	(NA)
Public.	Mil. dol. . . .	254.6	612.2	810.2	1,054.2	1,081.9	1,328.0	(NA)	(NA)
Private	Mil. dol. . . .	34.2	212.8	361.6	644.2	677.8	711.0	(NA)	(NA)
LABOR FORCE [3]									
Total [4]	1,000	765	907	985	1,124	1,152	1,170	1,201	1,205
Employed [5]	1,000	686	753	774	963	977	977	999	1,011
Agriculture [6]	1,000	68	38	39	36	35	34	34	34
Manufacturing.	1,000	132	143	141	168	164	164	168	166
Trade	1,000	128	138	150	185	195	193	201	201
Government	1,000	106	184	183	222	217	219	217	224
Unemployed	1,000	79	154	211	161	175	193	202	194
Unemployment rate [7]	Rate	10	17	21	14	15	17	17	16
Compensation of employees	Mil. dol. . . .	2,800	7,200	9,442	13,639	14,277	14,997	16,042	16,804
Avg. compensation	Dollar . . .	4,082	9,563	12,456	14,854	14,613	15,350	16,058	16,621
Salary and wages	Mil. dol. . . .	2,555	6,290	8,137	11,681	12,193	12,831	13,734	14,389
INCOME [8]									
Personal income:									
Current dollars	Mil. dol. . . .	3,753	11,002	14,588	21,105	21,884	22,911	24,608	25,745
Constant (1954) dollars	Mil. dol. . . .	2,654	3,985	4,274	5,551	5,514	5,694	6,054	6,241
Disposable personal income:									
Current dollars	Mil. dol. . . .	3,565	10,403	13,760	19,914	20,632	21,537	23,191	24,127
Constant (1954) dollars	Mil. dol. . . .	2,521	3,768	4,032	5,238	5,198	5,352	5,705	5,849
Average family income:									
Current dollars	Dollar	6,366	14,858	16,914	22,231	22,883	23,142	24,606	25,368
Constant (1954) dollars	Dollar	4,503	5,381	4,957	5,847	5,765	5,751	6,053	6,150
BANKING [9]									
Assets	Mil. dol. . . .	3,322	10,223	21,209	27,902	27,946	31,564	31,635	32,778
TOURISM [8]									
Number of visitors	1,000	1,225.0	2,140.0	2,061.6	3,425.8	3,504.3	3,730.0	3,869.0	4,022.6
Visitor expenditures	Mil. dol. . . .	235.4	618.7	757.7	1,366.4	1,435.7	1,519.7	1,628.1	1,736.6
Average per visitor	Dollar . . .	192	289	368	399	410	407	421	432
Net income from tourism	Mil. dol. . . .	89.8	202.2	223.1	383.3	400.8	429.6	465.0	482.0

NA Not available. [1] 1970, 1980, and 1990 enumerated as of April 1; all other years estimated as of July 1. [2] Enrollment for the first school month. Expenses for school year ending in year shown. [3] Annual average of monthly figures. For fiscal years. [4] Beginning 1980, for population 16 years old and over; 1970, for population 14 years and over. [5] Includes other employment not shown separately. [6] Includes forestry and fisheries. [7] Percent unemployed of the labor force. [8] For fiscal years. [9] As of June 30.

Source: Puerto Rico Planning Board, San Juan, PR, *Income and Product,* annual; and *Socioeconomics Statistics,* annual.

No. 1352. Puerto Rico—Gross Product and Net Income: 1980 to 1994

[In millions of dollars. For fiscal years ending June 30. Data for 1994 are preliminary]

ITEM	1980	1985	1989	1990	1991	1992	1993	1994
Gross product	**11,065**	**15,002**	**19,954**	**21,619**	**22,809**	**23,696**	**25,234**	**26,647**
Agriculture	380	357	443	434	449	420	408	411
Manufacturing	5,306	7,909	11,133	12,126	12,661	14,183	15,239	16,309
Contract construction and mining [1]	369	334	662	720	770	798	836	850
Transportation [2]	1,279	1,709	2,315	2,468	2,671	2,828	2,992	3,089
Trade	2,273	3,160	4,376	4,728	4,832	4,990	5,344	5,676
Finance, insurance, real estate	1,486	2,547	3,750	3,896	4,308	4,596	4,791	5,085
Services	1,279	1,837	2,699	3,015	3,322	3,582	3,927	4,249
Government	1,897	2,346	3,187	3,337	3,522	3,672	3,887	4,071
Commonwealth	1,574	1,996	2,745	2,884	3,044	3,154	3,327	3,476
Municipalities	323	350	442	453	478	518	555	596
Rest of the world	−3,372	−5,287	−8,313	−8,985	−9,478	−10,934	−11,613	−12,618
Statistical discrepancy	166	91	−298	−121	−248	−439	−570	−476
Net income	**9,007**	**12,182**	**16,662**	**17,941**	**18,927**	**19,631**	**21,087**	**22,021**
Agriculture	435	410	494	486	503	476	466	467
Manufacturing	4,756	7,117	10,299	11,277	11,732	13,215	14,277	15,301
Mining	9	10	24	26	26	28	30	29
Contract construction	337	309	624	679	728	753	788	803
Transportation [2]	1,022	1,248	1,681	1,777	1,900	1,943	2,103	2,117
Trade	1,609	2,285	3,154	3,420	3,485	3,538	3,776	3,953
Finance, insurance, and real estate	1,200	2,141	3,136	3,280	3,609	3,814	3,968	4,214
Services	1,114	1,606	2,377	2,643	2,901	3,125	3,411	3,686
Commonwealth government [3]	1,897	2,346	3,187	3,337	3,522	3,672	3,881	4,071
Rest of the world	−3,372	−5,287	−8,313	−8,985	−9,478	−10,934	−11,613	−12,618

[1] Mining includes only quarries. [2] Includes other public utilities, and radio and television broadcasting. [3] Includes public enterprises not elsewhere classified.
Source: Puerto Rico Planning Board, San Juan, PR, *Economic Report of the Governor, 1993-94.*

No. 1353. Puerto Rico—Transfer Payments: 1985 to 1994

[**In millions of dollars**. Data represent transfer payments between Federal and State governments and other nonresidents. See headnote, table 1352]

ITEM	1985	1989	1990	1991	1992	1993	1994
Total receipts	**3,531**	**4,289**	**4,871**	**4,973**	**5,108**	**5,595**	**6,151**
Federal government	3,348	4,082	4,649	4,708	4,903	5,396	5,755
Transfers to individuals [1]	3,283	4,014	4,577	4,633	4,818	5,303	5,728
Veterans benefits	317	337	349	370	383	409	446
Medicare	220	320	368	415	487	517	570
Old age, disability, survivors	1,581	1,940	2,055	2,243	2,315	2,659	2,932
Nutritional assistance	780	853	880	916	957	975	995
Industry subsidies	65	68	72	75	86	93	95
U.S. State governments	17	17	18	18	29	33	23
Other nonresidents	166	191	205	246	175	166	305
Total payments	**1,180**	**1,664**	**1,801**	**1,857**	**1,981**	**2,105**	**2,291**
Federal government	1,145	1,651	1,756	1,840	1,912	2,036	2,140
Transfers from individuals	508	766	817	864	916	986	1,040
Contribution to Medicare	44	89	97	101	108	122	138
Employee contribution for Social Security	463	675	720	762	808	864	902
Transfers from industries	13	15	16	19	24	26	32
Unemployment insurance	189	237	247	243	209	208	211
Employer contribution for Social Security	435	633	675	714	760	815	856
Other nonresidents	35	13	45	17	69	69	156
Net balance	**2,351**	**2,625**	**3,070**	**3,116**	**3,127**	**3,490**	**3,855**
Federal government	2,203	2,431	2,893	2,869	2,992	3,360	3,683
U.S. State governments	14	14	16	15	25	27	16
Other nonresidents	134	180	162	232	110	104	155

[1] Includes other receipts and payments not shown separately.
Source: Puerto Rico Planning Board, San Juan, PR, *Economic Report of the Governor, 1993-94.*

No. 1354. Puerto Rico—Merchandise Imports and Exports: 1980 to 1992

[**In millions of dollars**. Imports are imports for consumption; see text, section 28]

ITEM	1980	1982	1983	1984	1985	1986	1987	1988	1989	1990	1991	1992
Imports	9,018	8,167	8,708	10,116	10,162	10,321	11,308	13,096	15,010	16,200	15,079	16,476
From U.S.	5,345	5,300	5,162	5,738	6,130	6,467	7,307	8,788	10,193	10,792	10,306	11,463
From other	3,673	2,867	3,546	4,378	4,032	3,854	4,001	4,308	4,817	5,408	4,773	5,013
Exports	6,576	8,888	8,242	9,426	11,087	11,854	12,508	14,436	17,455	20,402	21,128	20,455
To U.S.	5,643	7,624	6,936	8,074	9,873	10,524	11,153	12,756	15,334	17,915	18,729	17,990
To other	933	1,264	1,306	1,352	1,214	1,330	1,355	1,680	2,121	2,487	2,399	2,465

Source: U.S. Bureau of the Census, *Foreign Commerce and Navigation of the United States,* annual; *U.S. Trade with Puerto Rico and U.S. Possessions, FT 895;* and, through 1988, *Highlights of U.S. Export and Import Trade, FT990;* thereafter, FT990 supplement.

Outlying Areas

No. 1355. Puerto Rico—Economic Summary, by Industry: 1992

[Excludes employees of establishments totally exempt from the Federal Insurance Contributions Act: government workers, railroad employment jointly covered by Social Security and railroad retirement programs, self-employed persons, domestic service, agriculture production employees, and employees on oceanborne vessels or in foreign countries]

INDUSTRY	1987 SIC code [1]	Total establishments	Employment-size class					Employees [2]	Annual payroll (mil. dol.)
			1 to 4	5 to 9	10 to 19	20 to 49	50 or more		
Total [3]	(X)	**36,271**	**21,490**	**5,981**	**3,996**	**2,956**	**1,848**	**565,600**	**8,000.2**
Agricultural services, forestry, and fishing	A	89	64	14	7	4	-	422	2.8
Mining	B	38	7	11	6	10	4	905	10.3
Nonmetallic minerals, except fuels	14	30	5	9	5	9	2	516	7.2
Construction [3]	C	951	397	140	110	134	170	38,364	425.3
General contractors and operative builders	15	379	128	45	39	60	107	23,965	249.4
Special trade contractors	17	497	249	86	59	61	42	9,599	116.4
Manufacturing [3]	D	1,614	361	162	259	297	535	144,771	2,568.0
Food and kindred products	20	227	53	33	41	41	59	18,557	325.1
Textile mill products	22	15	3	-	2	3	7	2,954	34.9
Apparel and other textile products	23	237	43	15	20	39	120	29,393	294.6
Furniture and fixtures	25	82	24	16	17	17	8	1,831	18.8
Paper and allied products	26	42	3	4	12	11	12	1,844	32.3
Printing and publishing	27	159	75	22	33	19	10	3,826	68.5
Chemicals and allied products	28	151	19	10	15	25	82	27,528	797.6
Petroleum and coal products	29	13	1	-	3	4	5	1,219	36.9
Rubber and misc. plastic products	30	82	7	4	18	28	25	5,820	98.7
Leather and leather products	31	26	3	2	3	1	17	5,990	67.4
Stone, clay, and glass products	32	105	17	12	35	30	11	3,390	66.6
Fabricated metal products	34	110	30	13	19	22	26	3,736	55.0
Industrial machinery and equip	35	74	28	8	9	12	17	3,704	68.5
Electronic and other electronic equip	36	88	8	4	5	5	66	15,178	251.9
Instruments and related products	38	69	7	2	3	11	46	13,608	244.7
Transportation and public utilities [3]	E	930	534	161	95	79	61	24,430	493.4
Trucking and warehousing	42	304	170	66	31	25	12	3,122	55.1
Water transportation	44	56	22	4	9	7	14	5,552	86.1
Air transportation	45	66	21	13	8	14	10	1,774	41.1
Transportation services	47	318	247	40	15	9	7	2,104	32.5
Communication	48	105	26	21	23	21	14	11,023	266.1
Electric, gas, and sanitary services	49	17	9	2	1	1	4	540	9.5
Wholesale trade [3]	F	1,878	757	372	329	256	164	33,553	646.8
Durable goods	50	963	374	206	186	136	61	14,332	269.6
Nondurable goods	51	898	382	160	141	114	101	18,787	365.4
Retail trade [3]	G	9,650	5,073	2,024	1,280	921	352	106,864	1,039.8
Building materials, garden supplies	52	576	325	126	68	49	8	4,710	53.3
General merchandise stores	53	403	154	51	71	66	61	13,054	132.6
Food stores	54	1,252	696	175	132	110	139	22,370	190.5
Automotive dealers and service stations	55	1,460	948	313	117	67	15	8,679	101.0
Apparel and accessory stores	56	1,462	537	444	326	143	12	13,882	117.9
Furniture and home furnishings	57	748	400	222	74	48	4	4,838	58.1
Eating and drinking places	58	1,819	918	270	260	304	67	22,421	174.5
Finance, insurance, and real estate [3]	H	1,777	812	349	302	213	101	36,211	672.5
Depository institutions	60	319	59	51	117	68	24	14,324	282.9
Nondepository institutions	61	378	89	108	80	70	31	7,878	121.6
Insurance carriers	63	79	23	9	9	24	14	3,866	87.5
Insurance agents, brokers, and service	64	232	121	43	35	18	15	3,690	78.2
Real estate	65	715	486	130	57	29	13	5,558	63.9
Services [3]	I	7,899	5,188	1,062	702	486	461	126,916	1,591.1
Personal services	72	555	372	96	53	29	5	3,411	32.2
Business services	73	702	301	102	96	77	126	31,817	368.2
Auto repair, services, and parking	75	568	402	96	44	18	8	3,179	36.4
Motion pictures	78	86	34	17	19	13	3	998	13.1
Amusement and recreation services	79	137	76	20	22	13	6	1,714	17.6
Health services	80	2,915	2,308	335	125	61	86	30,929	363.8
Legal services	81	737	612	42	59	15	9	3,302	59.8
Education services	82	444	102	57	68	114	103	21,439	262.4
Social services	83	241	113	45	37	19	27	5,198	49.1
Membership organizations	86	510	311	87	47	42	23	5,821	55.6
Engineering and management services	87	611	361	103	67	46	34	7,061	132.6

- Represents or rounds to zero.   X Not applicable.   [1] 1987 Standard Industrial Classification (SIC) code; see text, section 13.   [2] For the pay period including March 12.   [3] Includes other establishments not shown separately.

Source: U.S. Bureau of the Census, *County Business Patterns,* 1992.

No. 1356. Puerto Rico—Agriculture: 1987 and 1992

[1 cuerda=.97 acre]

ITEM	1987	1992	ITEM	1987	1992
Farms	20,245	22,350	Tenants	84.0	63.4
Percent—			SALES ($1,000)		
Less than 10 cuerdas	48.7	46.6	Sugarcane	26,643	24,739
10 to 19 cuerdas	19.5	20.0	Coffee	41,786	56,802
20 to 49 cuerdas	16.7	17.7	Pineapples	15,495	11,254
50 to 99 cuerdas	6.7	7.7	Plantains	(NA)	23,227
100 to 174 cuerdas	3.7	3.7	Bananas	(NA)	5,695
175 or more cuerdas	4.7	4.3	Grains	7,263	9,767
Cuerdas in farms	886,846	826,893	Fruits/nuts [1]	20,645	11,277
Tenure of operator:			Vegetables and melons [2]	8,236	16,214
Percent—			Horticulture specialities	14,489	28,364
Full-owners	79.8	79.5	Cattle and calves	30,206	51,616
Part-owners	13.1	9.9	Poultry	70,560	98,939
Tenants	7.1	10.6	Dairy products	157,864	197,703
Avg. farm size—cuerdas:			Hogs and pigs	9,525	11,633
Full-owners	33.4	26.6	Sheep and goats	437	522
Part-owners	85.7	92.3	Fish and aquaculture	(NA)	628

NA Not available.   [1] 1987 data include plantains and bananas.   [2] 1987 data exclude melons.

Source: U.S. Bureau of the Census, *1992 Census of Agriculture*, vol. 1, part 52.

No. 1357. Virgin Islands—Agriculture: 1987 and 1992

[1 cuerda=.97 acre]

ITEM	1987	1992	ITEM	1987	1992
Farms	267	202	Tenants	8.6	15.3
Percent—			SALES ($1,000)		
Less than 3 acres	30.0	35.1	Vegetables	355	429
3 to 9 acres	30.3	29.7	Fruits and nuts	147	142
10 to 19 acres	12.0	13.9	Horticulture specialities	241	1,093
20 or more acres	27.7	21.3	Cattle and calves	613	501
Acres in farms	17,785	13,666	Hogs and pigs	125	291
Tenure of operator:			Livestock	839	844
Percent—			Poultry	3	9
Full-owners	77.9	60.9	Chicken eggs	14	23
Part-owners	13.5	23.8	Milk	1,043	780

Source: U.S. Bureau of the Census, *1992 Census of Agriculture*, vol. 1, part 54.

No. 1358. Guam, Virgin Islands, and Northern Mariana Islands—Economic Summary: 1992

[Sales and payroll in millions of dollars]

ITEM	Guam	Virgin Islands	No. Mariana Islands	ITEM	Guam	Virgin Islands	No. Mariana Islands
Total:				Wholesale trade:			
Establishments	1,955	2,932	1,266	Establishments	154	114	60
Sales	3,018	2,281	1,132	Sales	428	414	132
Annual payroll	567	338	161	Annual payroll	32	21	6
Paid employees [1]	33,057	20,968	20,105	Paid employees [1]	1,715	1,030	534
Unpaid family workers [2]	337	330	268	Unpaid family workers [2]	4	1	3
Construction:				Retail trade:			
Establishments	240	147	103	Establishments	886	1,339	616
Sales	709	169	88	Sales	1,114	881	384
Annual payroll	178	44	18	Annual payroll	141	120	38
Paid employees [1]	9,131	2,224	3,036	Paid employees [1]	9,565	8,859	4,715
Unpaid family workers [2]	17	3	20	Unpaid family workers [2]	237	239	157
Manufacturing:				Services:			
Establishments	48	78	73	Establishments	627	1,254	414
Sales	110	134	264	Sales	656	682	264
Annual payroll	23	23	49	Annual payroll	193	130	51
Paid employees [1]	1,130	1,196	6,267	Paid employees [1]	11,516	7,659	5,553
Unpaid family workers [2]	8	3	4	Unpaid family workers [2]	71	84	84

[1] For pay period including March 12.   [2] Includes those who worked 15 hours or more during the week including March 12.

Source: U.S. Bureau of the Census, *1992 Economic Census of Outlying Areas*, OA92-E-5 to OA92-E-7.

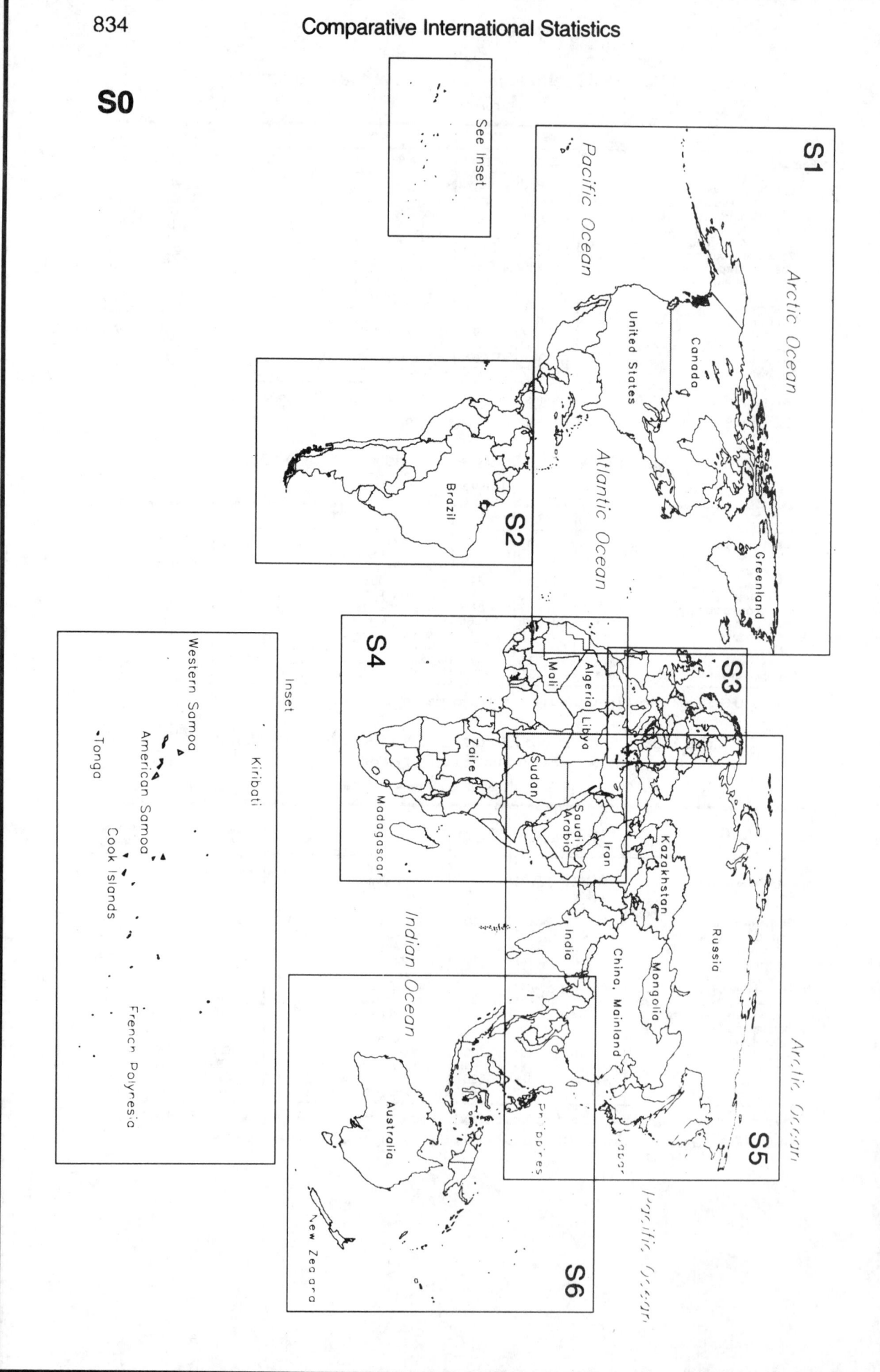

Comparative International Statistics

This section presents statistics for the world as a whole and for many countries on a comparative basis with the United States. Data are shown for population, births and deaths, social and industrial indicators, finances, agriculture, communication, and military affairs.

Statistics of the individual nations may be found primarily in official national publications, generally in the form of yearbooks, issued by most of the nations at various intervals in their own national languages and expressed in their own or customary units of measure. (For a listing of selected publications, see Guide to Sources.) For handier reference, especially for international comparisons, the Statistical Office of the United Nations compiles data as submitted by member countries and issues a number of international summary publications, generally in English and French. Among these are the *Statistical Yearbook;* the *Demographic Yearbook;* the *Yearbook of International Trade Statistics;* the *Yearbook of National Accounts Statistics: Vol. II, International Tables; Population and Vital Statistics Reports* (quarterly); the *Monthly Bulletin of Statistics;* and the *Energy Statistics Yearbook.* Specialized agencies of the United Nations also issue international summary publications on agricultural, labor, health, and education statistics. Among these are the *Production Yearbook* and *Trade Yearbook* issued by the Food and Agriculture Organization, the *Yearbook of Labour Statistics* issued by the International Labour Office, the *World Health Statistics* issued by the World Health Organization, and the *Statistical Yearbook* issued by the Educational, Scientific, and Cultural Organization.

The Bureau of the Census presents estimates of basic demographic measures for countries and regions of the world in the *World Population Profile* series. The *International Population Statistics Reports,* P90 and P91 series, also present population figures for many foreign countries. Detailed population statistics are also available from the Bureau of the Census' International Data Base.

In Brief	
Ten most populous countries in 1995: (million persons)	
China	1,203
India	937
United States	264
Indonesia	204
Brazil	161
Russia	150
Pakistan	132
Bangladesh	128
Japan	126
Nigeria	101

The U.S. Arms Control and Disarmament Agency and the International Monetary Fund (IMF) also compile data on international statistics. In its annual *World Military Expenditures and Arms Transfers,* the Arms Control and Disarmament Agency presents data on various economic indicators, as well as basic military data. Among the topics presented have been military expenditures, gross national product, imports and exports, and armed forces. The IMF publishes a series of reports relating to financial data. These include *International Financial Statistics, Direction of Trade,* and *Balance of Payments Yearbook,* published in English, French, and Spanish.

Statistical coverage, country names, and classifications.— Problems of space and availability of data limit the number of countries and the extent of statistical coverage shown. The list of countries included and the spelling of country names are based almost entirely on the list of sovereign nations, dependencies, and areas of special sovereignty provided by the U.S. Department of State.

In recent years, several important changes took place in the status of the world's nations. In 1990, a unified Germany was formed from the Federal Republic of Germany (West) and the German Democratic Republic (East). The Republic of Yemen was formed by union of the Yemen Arab Republic and the People's Democratic Republic of Yemen. Also in 1990, Namibia, once a United Nations mandate, realized its independence from South Africa.

In 1991 the Soviet Union broke up into fifteen independent countries: Armenia, Azerbaijan, Belarus, Estonia, Georgia, Kazakhstan, Kyrgyzstan, Latvia, Lithuania, Moldova, Russia, Tajikistan, Turkmenistan, Ukraine, and Uzbekistan.

In 1992, the Socialist Federal Republic of Yugoslavia dissolved; none of the successor states has been recognized as its continuation. The United States recognizes Bosnia and Herzegovina, Croatia, Slovenia, and The Former Yugoslav Republic of Macedonia as independent countries. Serbia and Montenegro have asserted the formation of a joint independent state, but this entity has not been formally recognized as a state by the United States.

On January 1, 1993, Czechoslovakia was succeeded by two independent countries: the Czech Republic and Slovakia. Eritrea announced its independence from Ethiopia in April 1993, and was subsequently recognized as an independent nation by the United States.

The population estimates and projections used in tables 1361–1363 were prepared by the Census Bureau. For each country, the data on population, by age and sex, fertility, mortality, and international migration were evaluated and, where necessary, adjusted for inconsistencies and errors in the data. In most instances, comprehensive projections were made by the component method, resulting in distributions of the population by age and sex, and requiring an assessment of probable future trends of fertility, mortality, and international migration.

Economic associations.—The Organization for European Economic Co- operation (OEEC), a regional grouping of Western European countries established in 1948 for the purpose of harmonizing national economic policies and conditions, was succeeded on September 30, 1961, by the Organization for Economic Cooperation and Development (OECD). The member nations of the OECD are Australia, Austria, Belgium, Canada, Denmark, Finland, France, Germany, Greece, Iceland, Ireland, Italy, Japan, Luxembourg, Mexico, the Netherlands, New Zealand, Norway, Portugal, Spain, Sweden, Switzerland,

Turkey, the United Kingdom, and the United States.

Quality and comparability of the data.— The quality and comparability of the data presented here are affected by a number of factors:

(1) The year for which data are presented may not be the same for all subjects for a particular country, or for a given subject for different countries, though the data shown are the most recent available. All such variations have been noted. The data shown are for calendar years except as otherwise specified.

(2) The bases, methods of estimating, methods of data collection, extent of coverage, precision of definition, scope of territory, and margins of error may vary for different items within a particular country, and for like items for different countries.

Footnotes and headnotes to the tables give a few of the major time-period and coverage qualifications attached to the figures; considerably more detail is presented in the source publications. Many of the measures shown are, at best, merely rough indicators of magnitude.

(3) Figures shown in this section for the United States may not always agree with figures shown in the preceding sections. Disagreements may be attributable to the use of differing original sources, a difference in the definition of geographic limits (the 50 States, conterminous United States only, or the United States including certain outlying areas and possessions), or to possible adjustments made in the United States figures by the United Nations or other sources in order to make them more comparable with figures from other countries.

International comparisons of national accounts data.—In order to compare national accounts data for different countries, it is necessary to convert each country's data into a common unit of currency, usually the U.S. dollar. The market exchange rates which are often used in converting national currencies do not necessarily reflect the relative purchasing power in the various countries. It is necessary that the goods and services produced in different countries be valued consistently if the differences observed are meant to reflect real differences in the volumes of goods and services produced. The use of purchasing power parities (see table 1374) instead of exchange rates is intended to achieve this objective.

The method used to present the data shown in table 1374 is to construct volume measures directly by revaluing the goods and services sold in different countries at a common set of international prices. By dividing the ratio of the gross domestic products of two countries expressed in their own national currencies by the corresponding ratio calculated at constant international prices, it is possible to derive the implied purchasing power parity (PPP) between the two currencies concerned. PPP's show how many units of currency are needed in one country to buy the same amount of goods and services which one unit of currency will buy in the other country. For further information, see *National Accounts, Main Aggregates*, volume I, issued annually by the Organization for Economic Cooperation and Development, Paris, France.

International Standard Industrial Classification.—The original version of the International Standard Industrial Classification of All Economic Activities (ISIC) was adopted in 1948. Wide use has been made both nationally and internationally in classifying data according to kind of economic activity in the fields of production, employment, national income, and other economic statistics. A number of countries have utilized the ISIC as the basis for devising their industrial classification scheme.

Substantial comparability has been attained between the industrial classifications of many other countries, including the United States, and the ISIC by ensuring, as far as practicable, that the categories at detailed levels of classification in national schemes fitted into only one category of the ISIC. For more detail, see Bureau of the Census, The *International Standard Industrial Classification and the U.S. Standard Industrial Classification*, Technical Paper No. 14 and text, section 27. The United Nations, the International Labour Organisation, the Food and Agriculture Organization, and other international bodies have utilized the ISIC in publishing and analyzing statistical data. Revisions of the ISIC were issued in 1958, 1968, and 1989.

International maps. A series of regional world maps is provided on pages 834 and 838–843. References are included in table 1361 for easy location of individual countries on the maps. The Robinson map projection is used for this series of maps. A map projection is used to portray all or part of the round Earth on a flat surface, but this cannot be done without some distortion. For the Robinson projection, distortion is very low along the Equator and within 45 degrees of the center but is greatest near the poles. For additional information on map projections and maps, please contact the Earth Science Information Center, U.S. Geological Survey, 507 National Center, Reston, VA 22092.

S1

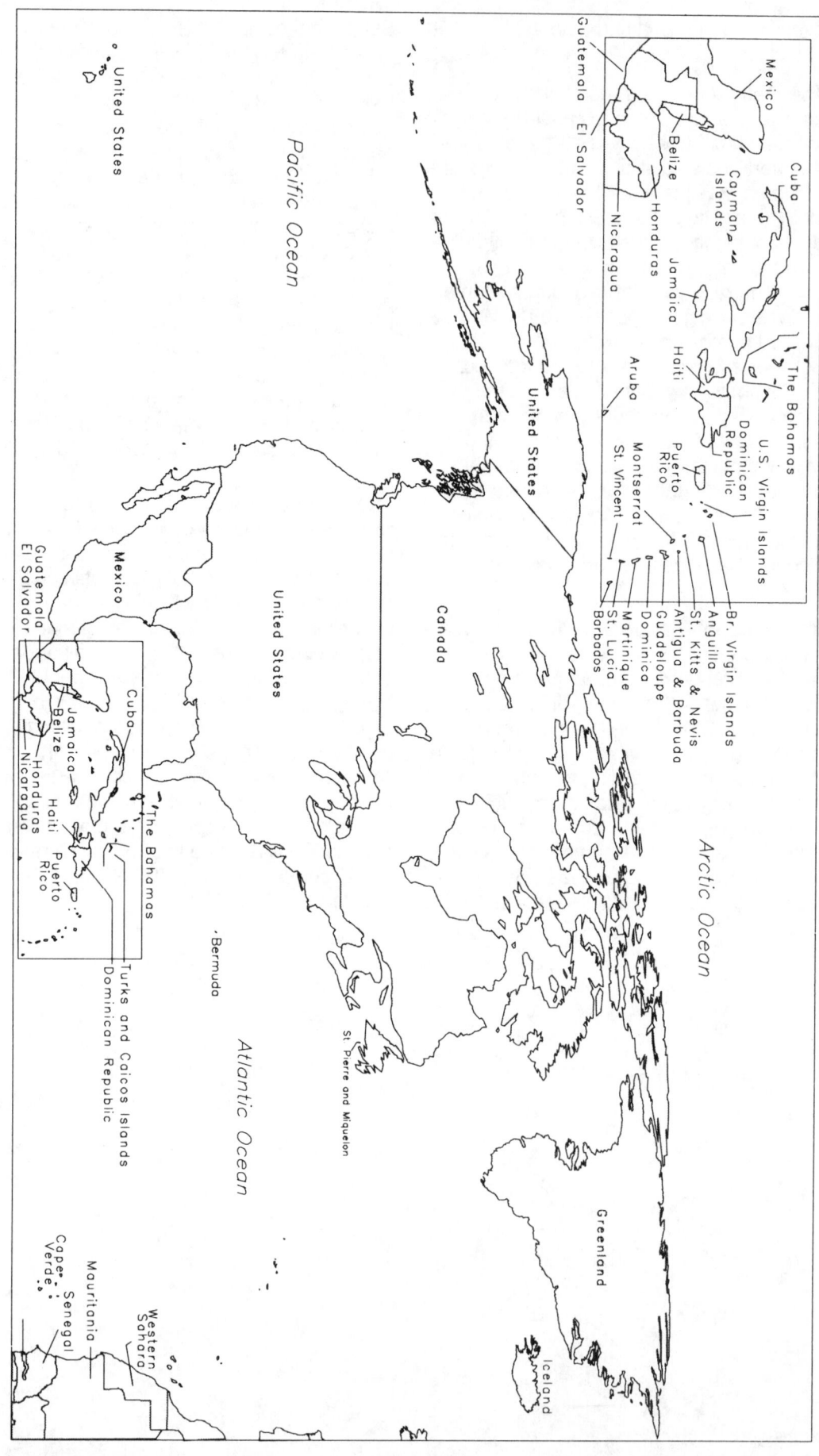

Pacific Ocean

United States

Mexico

Guatemala
El Salvador

Belize
Honduras
Nicaragua

Cuba

Cayman
Islands

Jamaica

Haiti

The Bahamas

Aruba

Dominican
Republic

Puerto
Rico

Montserrat
St. Vincent

U.S. Virgin Islands

Br. Virgin Islands
Anguilla
St. Kitts & Nevis
Antigua & Barbuda
Guadeloupe
Dominica
Martinique
St. Lucia
Barbados

Arctic Ocean

United States

Canada

Mexico

Guatemala
El Salvador

Belize
Honduras
Nicaragua

Jamaica

Haiti

Cuba

Puerto
Rico

The Bahamas

Turks and Caicos Islands
Dominican Republic

Bermuda

St. Pierre and Miquelon

Atlantic Ocean

Greenland

Iceland

Mauritania
Western
Sahara

Cape
Verde

Senegal

S2

Nicaragua

Costa
Rica

Panama

Netherlands
Antilles

Grenada

Trinidad & Tobago

Venezuela

Guyana

Suriname

French Guiana

Colombia

Ecuador

Peru

Brazil

Bolivia

Paraguay

Chile

Pacific Ocean

Argentina

Uruguay

Atlantic Ocean

Arctic Ocean

Faroe Islands

Norway

Sweden

Finland

Russia

Denmark

Estonia

Russia

Latvia

Lithuania

Russia

Netherlands

Germany

Poland

Belarus

Ireland

United Kingdom

Isle of Man

Ukraine

Guernsey

Jersey

France

Romania

San Marino

Serbia

Italy

Monaco

Andorra

Montenegro

Bulgaria

Spain

Albania

The Former Yugoslav Republic of Macedonia

Greece

Portugal

Gibraltar

Atlantic Ocean

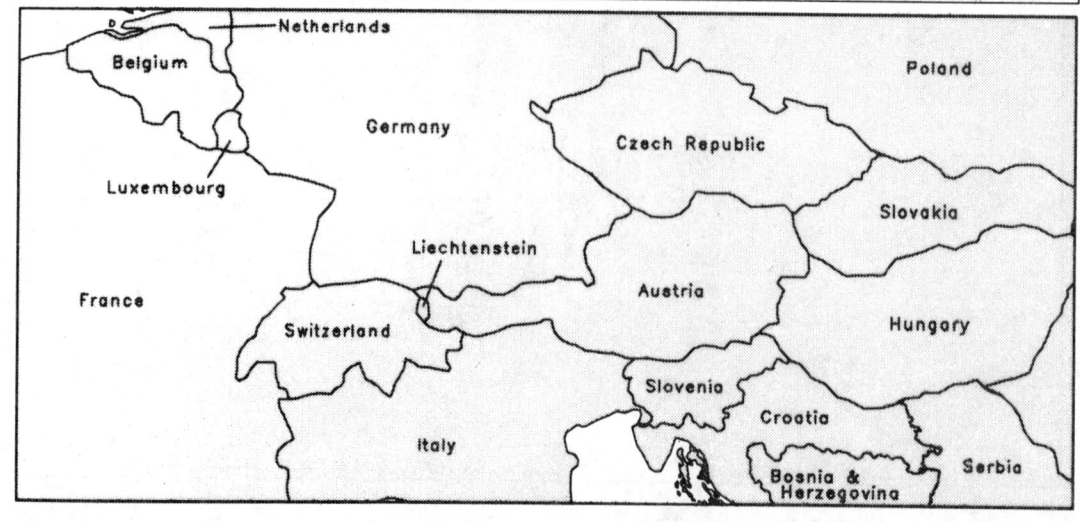

Netherlands

Belgium

Poland

Germany

Czech Republic

Luxembourg

Slovakia

Liechtenstein

Austria

Hungary

France

Switzerland

Slovenia

Italy

Croatia

Bosnia & Herzegovina

Serbia

S4

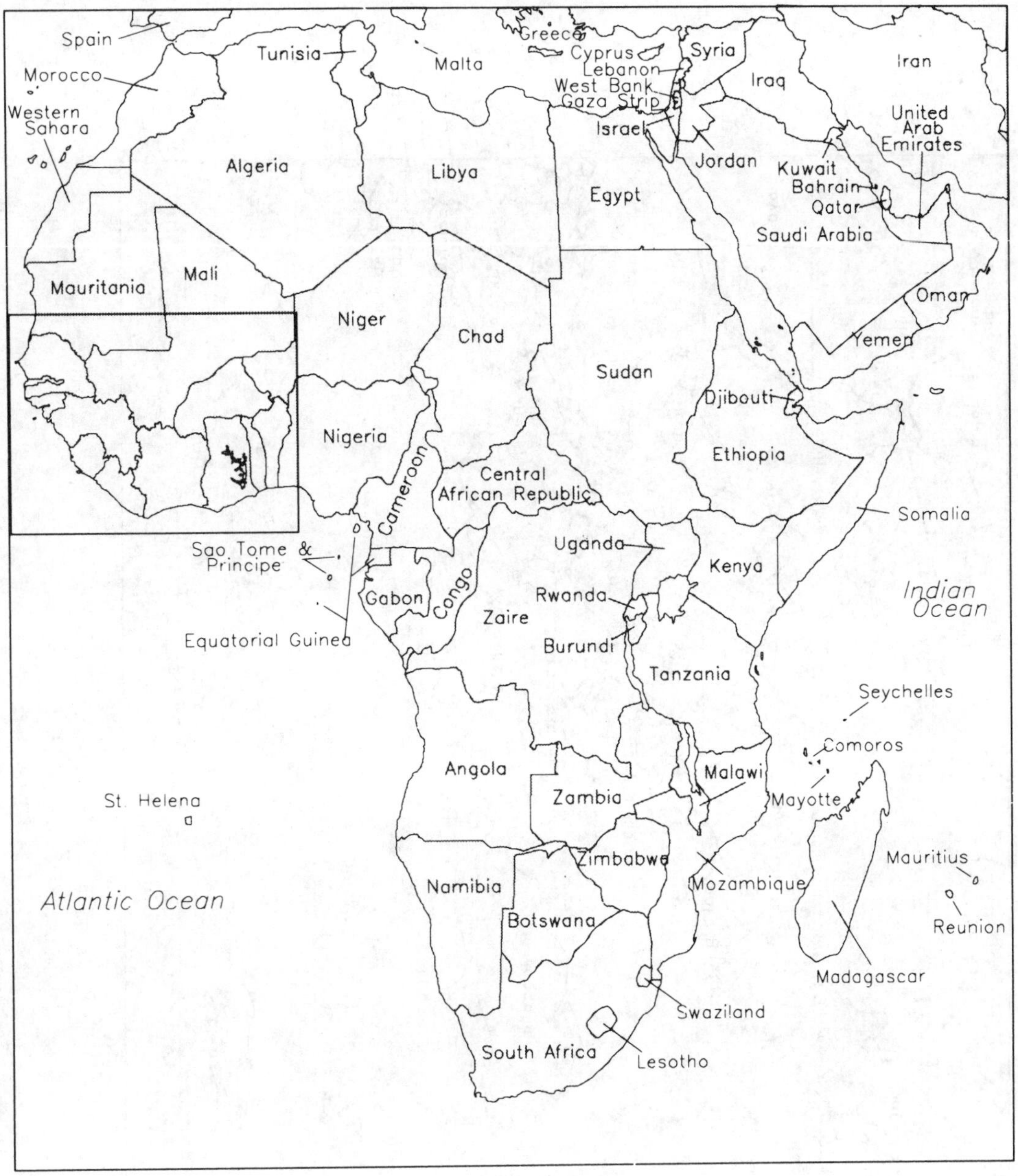

Spain
Morocco
Western Sahara
Tunisia
Malta
Greece
Cyprus
Lebanon
West Bank
Gaza Strip
Israel
Syria
Iraq
Iran
United Arab Emirates
Algeria
Libya
Egypt
Jordan
Kuwait
Bahrain
Qatar
Saudi Arabia
Oman
Mauritania
Mali
Niger
Chad
Sudan
Yemen
Djibouti
Nigeria
Cameroon
Central African Republic
Ethiopia
Somalia
Sao Tome & Principe
Gabon
Congo
Zaire
Uganda
Rwanda
Burundi
Kenya
Indian Ocean
Equatorial Guinea
Tanzania
Seychelles
Comoros
Mayotte
Angola
Zambia
Malawi
St. Helena
Atlantic Ocean
Namibia
Zimbabwe
Botswana
Mozambique
Mauritius
Reunion
Madagascar
Swaziland
South Africa
Lesotho

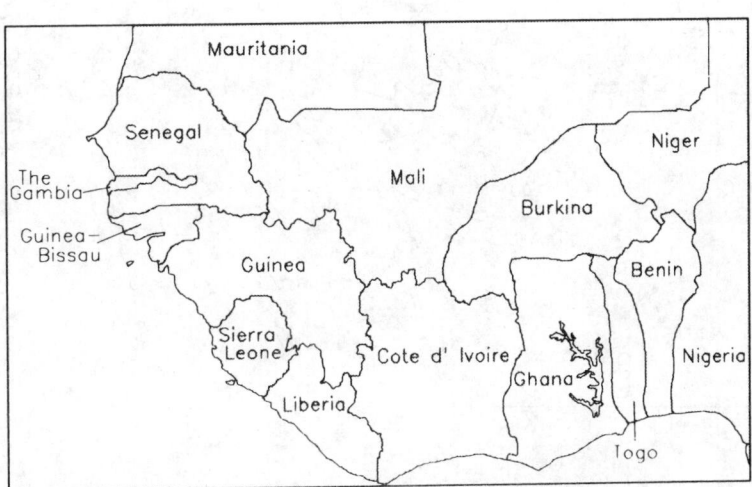

Mauritania
Senegal
The Gambia
Guinea-Bissau
Mali
Niger
Burkina
Benin
Guinea
Sierra Leone
Cote d' Ivoire
Ghana
Nigeria
Liberia
Togo

S5

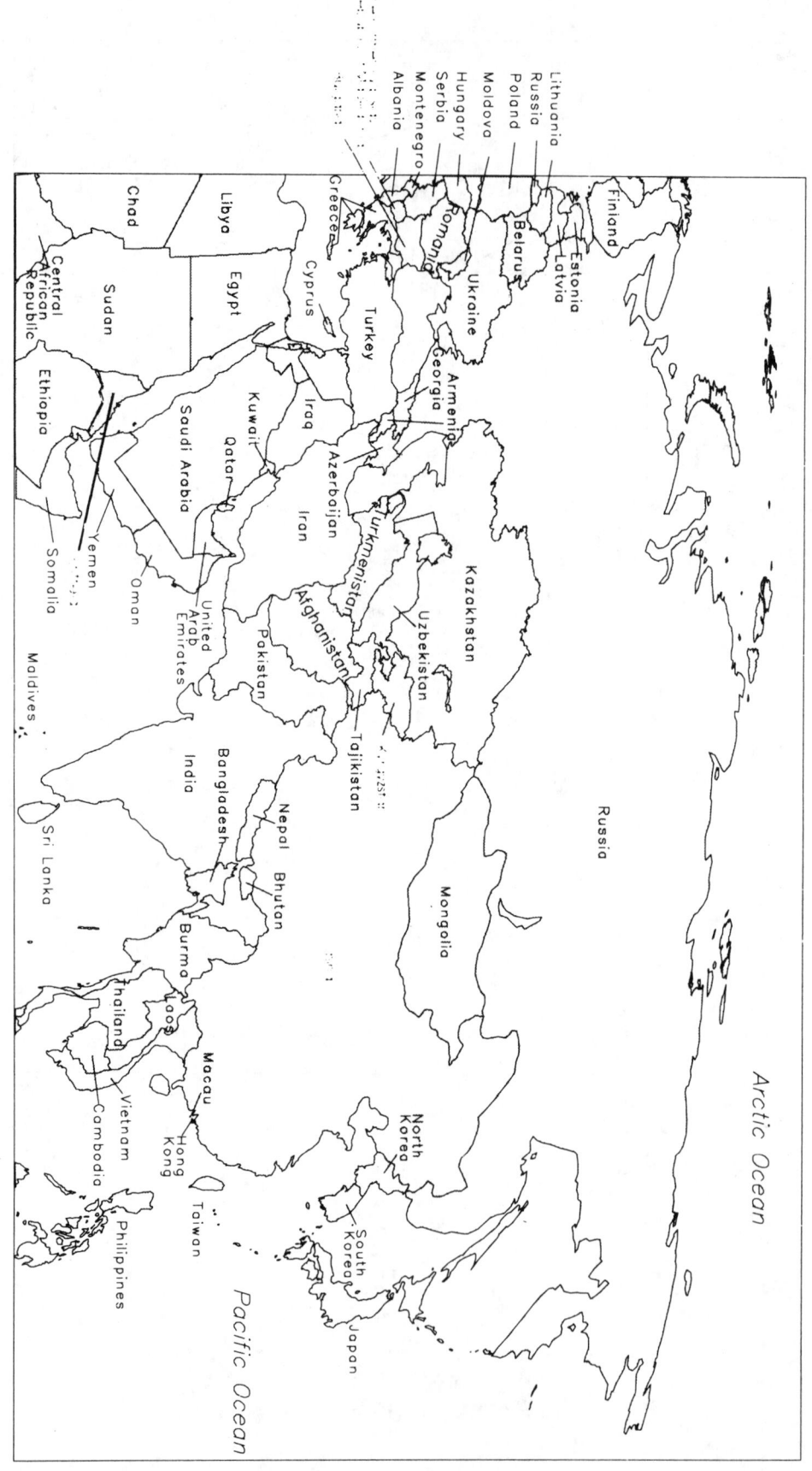

S6

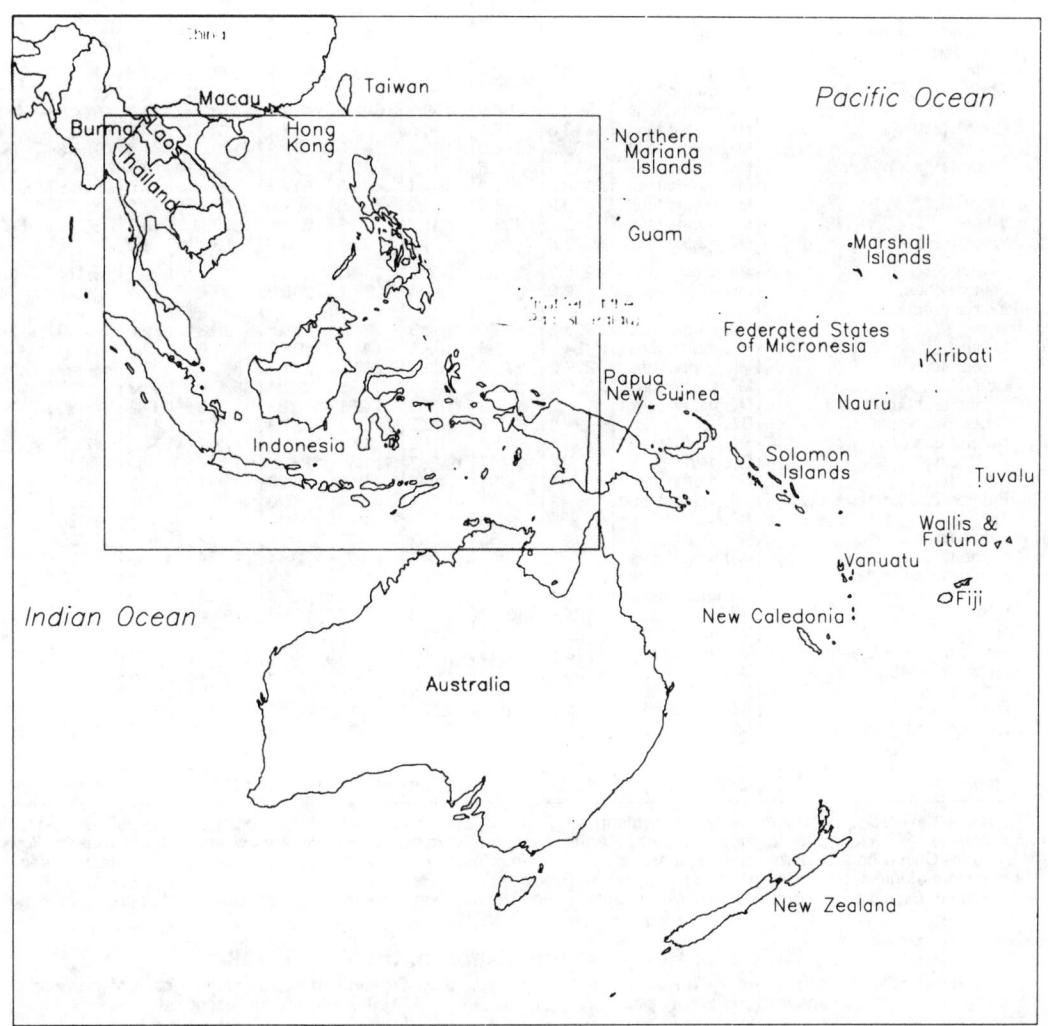

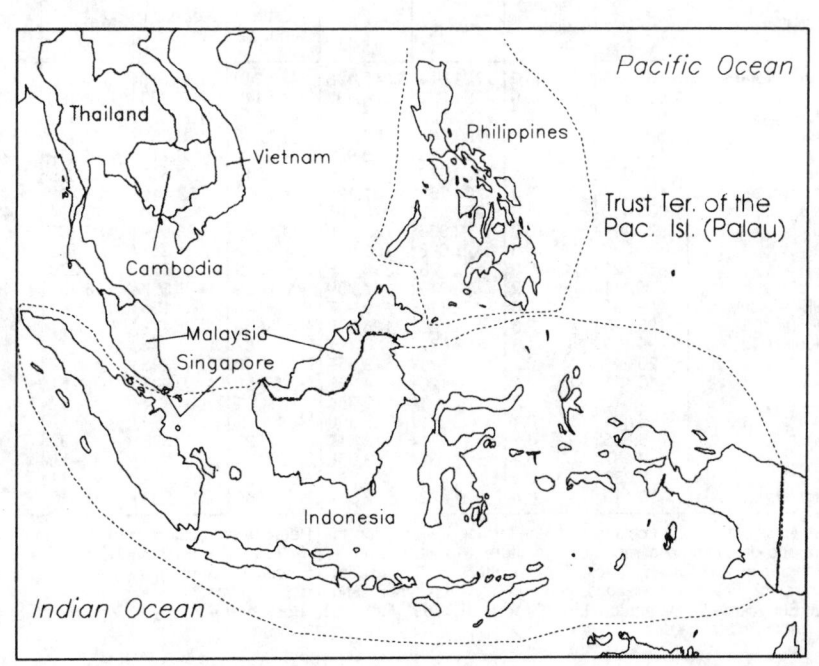

Comparative International Statistics

No. 1359. World Summary: 1980 to 1993

[See text, section 30, for general comments concerning quality of the data]

ITEM	Unit	1980	1985	1987	1988	1989	1990	1991	1992	1993
Population.	Millions	4,453	4,850	5,024	5,112	5,202	5,292	5,385	5,480	5,572
Agriculture, forestry, fishing production: [1]										
Barley	Mil. metric tons .	156.7	172.7	175.5	163.3	164.2	177.8	168.6	165.5	166.9
Coffee	Mil. metric tons .	4.8	5.8	6.4	5.7	6.0	6.1	6.1	5.8	5.7
Corn	Mil. metric tons .	397.5	486.9	450.9	398.5	472.8	476.7	487.9	524.0	461.5
Cotton (lint)	Mil. metric tons .	13.8	17.4	16.6	18.3	17.1	18.5	20.7	18.2	17.7
Meats	Mil. metric tons .	135.9	152.9	163.0	169.8	172.9	178.2	181.5	184.3	(NA)
Peanuts (groundnuts).	Mil. metric tons .	16.9	20.8	21.7	25.4	23.1	23.1	23.4	24.2	(NA)
Rice	Mil. metric tons .	398.9	471.0	464.1	490.8	517.4	520.5	517.8	526.6	518.9
Tobacco.	Mil. metric tons .	5.3	7.0	6.2	6.8	7.0	7.0	7.5	8.0	8.0
Wheat	Mil. metric tons .	440.1	499.6	504.9	500.8	538.6	592.9	546.7	565.0	563.6
Wool, greasy	Mil. metric tons .	2.8	3.0	3.1	3.1	3.0	3.1	3.0	2.9	2.7
Roundwood	Mil. cubic meters	2,932	3,178	3,342	3,404	3,464	3,511	3,422	3,477	(NA)
Fish catches.	Mil. metric tons .	72.0	86.3	94.4	99.1	100.3	97.6	97.1	98.1	(NA)
Industrial production:										
Wine [1]	Mil. metric tons .	35.3	29.5	32.3	27.3	28.5	28.3	29.0	27.0	(NA)
Sugar [1]	Mil. metric tons .	84.4	98.6	102.5	104.4	105.9	111.8	112.3	117.4	110.3
Wheat flour [1]	Mil. metric tons .	237.2	270.0	280.4	288.4	291.7	300.1	305.3	305.9	(NA)
Coal	Mil. metric tons .	2,728	3,161	3,411	3,488	3,584	3,517	3,463	3,527	3,655
Lignite and brown coal	Mil. metric tons .	1,042	1,202	1,250	1,261	1,282	1,218	1,081	1,033	944
Crude petroleum [2]	Bil. bbl.	21.8	19.7	21.5	21.4	21.8	22.1	21.9	22.0	(NA)
Natural gas (dry) [2]	Trl. cu. ft	53.1	61.8	66.3	69.7	72.1	73.7	74.8	75.0	76.0
Electricity	Bil. kWh.	8,247	9,747	10,587	11,059	11,505	11,774	11,989	12,027	12,003
Iron ore	Mil. metric tons .	841	862	890	916	920	921	922	930	940
Pig iron and ferroalloys.	Mil. metric tons .	542	507	503	504	570	543	505	530	535
Tin [3]	1,000 metric tons	231	196	194	210	242	237	214	230	220
Crude steel	Mil. metric tons .	699	685	682	685	777	762	687	700	710
Cement	Mil. metric tons .	872	949	1,045	1,109	1,144	1,154	1,148	1,160	1,180
Non-cellulosic fibers [3]	Mil. metric tons .	10.0	11.5	12.4	13.2	13.3	13.3	12.6	11.2	11.3
Sawnwood	Mil. cubic meters	451	468	506	508	508	506	458	(NA)	(NA)
Woodpulp	Mil. metric tons .	125.8	135.7	146.8	151.7	155.9	154.4	154.6	153.7	(NA)
Newsprint.	Mil. metric tons .	25.4	28.2	30.4	31.7	32.0	32.8	32.5	32.0	(NA)
Merchant vessels, launched [3]	Mil. gross tons .	13.9	17.3	9.6	11.8	12.7	14.7	16.7	20.5	18.7
Motor vehicles	Millions	38.9	44.8	45.9	48.1	48.9	48.1	46.4	47.4	(NA)
External trade:										
Imports, c.i.f	Bil. U.S. dollars.	2,047	2,028	2,560	2,915	3,162	3,567	3,546	3,805	3,717
Exports, f.o.b	Bil. U.S. dollars.	1,998	1,927	2,491	2,827	3,044	3,437	3,421	3,656	3,632
Transport:										
Civil aviation, kilometers flown [4]	Millions	9,362	10,565	12,208	13,020	13,570	14,350	14,240	15,310	(NA)

NA Not available.   [1] Source: U.S. Department of Agriculture, Economic Research Service, *World Agriculture-Trends and Indicators.*   [2] Source: U.S. Energy Information Administration, *International Energy Annual* and *Annual Energy Review.*
[3] Excludes China. Tin and merchant vessels exclude Soviet Republics. For other exclusions, see source.   [4] Scheduled services of members of International Civil Aviation Organization. Excludes Soviet Republics.
Source: Except as noted, Statistical Division of the United Nations, New York, NY, *Monthly Bulletin of Statistics,* (copyright).

No. 1360. Religious Population of the World: 1994

[**In thousands, except percent**. Refers to adherents of all religions as defined and enumerated for each of the world's countries in *World Encyclopedia (1982),* projected to mid-1994, adjusted for recent data]

RELIGION	Total	Percent distri- bution	Africa	Asia	Latin America	Northern America	Europe	Eurasia [1]	Oceania
Total population. . .	**5,661,525**	**100.0**	**722,814**	**3,345,498**	**474,240**	**288,788**	**514,655**	**287,164**	**28,366**
Christians	1,901,148	33.6	351,682	304,887	442,140	247,293	422,159	109,747	23,240
Roman Catholics	1,058,069	18.7	132,102	132,053	411,514	100,386	267,972	5,615	8,427
Protestants	391,143	6.9	93,865	87,051	17,513	99,652	75,441	9,903	7,718
Orthodox	174,184	3.1	30,685	3,904	1,789	6,217	36,869	94,129	591
Anglicans	78,038	1.4	28,873	755	1,319	7,593	33,625	1	5,872
Other Christians	199,707	3.5	66,158	81,125	10,004	33,445	8,252	100	623
Muslims	1,033,453	18.3	293,993	675,297	1,395	5,500	13,194	43,967	107
Nonreligious [2]	923,104	16.3	2,936	733,740	19,327	22,910	58,199	82,236	3,756
Hindus	764,000	13.5	1,608	759,059	912	1,315	725	2	379
Buddhists	338,621	6.0	23	336,755	559	578	279	401	26
Atheists	239,111	4.2	344	167,739	3,329	1,367	16,362	49,407	563
Chinese folk-religionists [3] .	149,336	2.6	14	149,037	76	126	61	1	21
New-religionists [4]	128,975	2.3	23	126,869	548	1,473	51	1	10
Tribal religionists	99,150	1.8	69,872	28,197	967	42	1	-	71
Sikhs	20,204	0.4	29	19,557	8	363	237	1	9
Jews	13,451	0.2	128	4,289	458	5,907	1,761	813	95
Shamanists.	11,010	0.2	1	10,754	1	1	2	250	1
Confucians	6,334	0.1	1	6,300	2	26	2	2	1
Baha'is.	5,835	0.1	1,631	2,817	827	379	93	7	81
Jains	3,987	0.1	57	3,906	4	4	15	-	1
Shintoists	3,387	0.1	-	3,383	1	1	1	-	1
Other religionists	20,419	0.4	472	12,912	3,686	1,503	1,513	329	4

- Represents zero.   [1] Source's term for the former Soviet Union.   [2] Persons professing no religion, nonbelievers, agnostics, freethinkers, and dereligionized secularists indifferent to all religion.   [3] Followers of traditional Chinese religion (local deities, ancestor veneration, Confucian ethics, Taoism, etc.).   [4] Followers of Asiatic 20th-century New Religions, New Religious movements, radical new crisis religions, and non-Christian syncretistic mass religions.
Source: Encyclopedia Britannica, Inc., Chacgo, IL, *1995 Britannica Book of the Year.* (Reprinted with permission). © 1995 by Encyclopedia Britannica, Inc.

No. 1361. Population, by Country: 1980 to 2000

[Population data generally are de facto figures for the present territory. Population estimates were derived from information available as of late 1994. See text, section 31, for general comments concerning the data. For details of methodology, coverage, and reliability, see source. Minus sign (-) indicates decrease]

COUNTRY OR AREA	Map reference	MIDYEAR POPULATION (1,000)				Population rank, 1995	ANNUAL RATE OF GROWTH [1] (percent)		Population per sq. mile, 1995
		1980	1990	1995	2000, proj.		1980-1990	1990-2000	
World	S0	4,457,463	5,296,327	5,734,106	6,169,794	(X)	1.7	1.5	113
Afghanistan................	S5	14,985	15,647	21,252	29,263	44	0.4	6.3	85
Albania.................	S3	2,673	3,249	3,414	3,610	125	2.0	1.1	323
Algeria.................	S4	18,862	25,352	28,539	31,788	36	3.0	2.3	31
Andorra.................	S3	34	53	66	73	202	4.5	3.3	378
Angola.................	S4	6,794	8,430	10,070	11,513	75	2.2	3.1	21
Antigua and Barbuda	S1	69	64	65	68	203	-0.7	0.7	384
Argentina................	S2	28,237	32,386	34,293	36,202	31	1.4	1.1	32
Armenia.................	S5	3,115	3,363	3,557	3,685	122	0.8	0.9	309
Australia................	S6	14,616	17,071	18,322	19,386	51	1.6	1.3	6
Austria.................	S3	7,549	7,718	7,987	8,108	85	0.2	0.5	250
Azerbaijan................	S5	6,173	7,216	7,790	8,243	88	1.6	1.3	233
Bahamas, The.............	S1	210	241	257	269	177	1.4	1.1	66
Bahrain.................	S4	348	502	576	642	161	3.7	2.5	2,410
Bangladesh................	S5	88,077	114,023	128,095	143,548	8	2.6	2.3	2,478
Barbados................	S1	252	254	256	260	178	0.1	0.2	1,544
Belarus.................	S3	9,644	10,248	10,437	10,576	69	0.6	0.3	130
Belgium.................	S3	9,847	9,962	10,082	10,144	74	0.1	0.2	864
Belize.................	S1	144	190	214	242	181	2.7	2.4	24
Benin.................	S4	3,444	4,676	5,523	6,517	99	3.1	3.3	129
Bhutan.................	S5	1,281	1,585	1,781	1,996	144	2.1	2.3	98
Bolivia.................	S2	5,470	7,029	7,896	8,801	87	2.5	2.2	19
Bosnia and Herzegovina	S3	4,092	4,360	3,202	3,376	129	0.6	-2.6	162
Botswana................	S4	903	1,224	1,392	1,554	148	3.0	2.4	6
Brazil.................	S2	122,830	150,062	160,737	169,543	5	2.0	1.2	49
Brunei.................	S6	185	254	292	331	174	3.2	2.6	144
Bulgaria................	S3	8,844	8,966	8,775	8,742	83	0.1	-0.3	206
Burkina.................	S4	6,939	9,042	10,423	11,871	71	2.6	2.7	99
Burma.................	S5	33,578	41,044	45,104	49,300	25	2.0	1.8	178
Burundi................	S4	4,138	5,558	6,262	6,939	93	3.0	2.2	632
Cambodia................	S5	6,499	8,731	10,561	12,098	68	3.0	3.3	155
Cameroon................	S4	8,756	11,697	13,521	15,677	61	2.9	2.9	75
Canada.................	S1	24,070	26,620	28,435	29,867	37	1.0	1.2	8
Cape Verde................	S1	296	375	436	503	165	2.4	2.9	280
Central African Republic	S4	2,269	2,866	3,210	3,511	128	2.3	2.0	13
Chad.................	S4	4,024	5,024	5,587	6,221	97	2.2	2.1	11
Chile.................	S2	11,094	13,108	14,161	15,207	59	1.7	1.5	49
China [2].................	S5	984,736	1,136,626	1,203,097	1,260,154	1	1.4	1.0	334
Colombia................	S2	26,580	32,983	36,200	39,172	30	2.2	1.7	90
Comoros.................	S4	334	460	549	656	162	3.2	3.5	656
Congo.................	S4	1,620	2,215	2,505	2,784	136	3.1	2.3	19
Costa Rica................	S2	2,307	3,031	3,419	3,797	124	2.7	2.3	175
Cote d'Ivoire.............	S4	8,418	12,399	14,791	17,371	57	3.9	3.4	120
Croatia.................	S3	4,593	4,754	4,666	4,727	110	0.3	-0.1	214
Cuba.................	S1	9,653	10,544	10,938	11,227	64	0.9	0.7	256
Cyprus.................	S5	627	702	737	768	157	1.1	0.9	206
Czech Republic.............	S3	10,289	10,363	10,433	10,607	70	0.1	0.2	215
Denmark................	S3	5,123	5,141	5,199	5,255	104	(Z)	0.2	318
Djibouti.................	S4	279	370	421	454	167	2.8	2.0	50
Dominica................	S1	75	81	83	84	197	0.7	0.4	285
Dominican Republic...........	S1	5,697	7,213	7,948	8,635	86	2.4	1.8	425
Ecuador................	S2	8,123	9,806	10,891	11,945	65	1.9	2.0	102
Egypt.................	S4	42,441	56,106	62,360	68,437	17	2.8	2.0	162
El Salvador...............	S1	4,655	5,303	5,870	6,459	95	1.3	2.0	734
Equatorial Guinea	S4	256	369	420	478	168	3.7	2.6	39
Eritrea.................	S4	2,555	2,896	3,579	4,537	121	1.3	4.5	76
Estonia.................	S3	1,482	1,583	1,625	1,670	146	0.7	0.5	93
Ethiopia................	S4	36,413	48,293	55,979	64,835	22	2.8	2.9	129
Fiji.................	S6	635	738	773	823	155	1.5	1.1	110
Finland.................	S3	4,780	4,986	5,085	5,153	106	0.4	0.3	43
France.................	S3	53,870	56,720	58,109	59,354	21	0.5	0.5	276
Gabon.................	S4	808	1,078	1,156	1,244	150	2.9	1.4	12
Gambia, The................	S4	644	848	989	1,154	153	2.8	3.1	256
Georgia.................	S5	5,048	5,484	5,726	5,925	96	0.8	0.8	213
Germany................	S3	78,298	79,357	81,338	82,239	12	0.1	0.4	601
Ghana.................	S4	10,777	15,195	17,763	20,608	53	3.4	3.0	200
Greece.................	S3	9,643	10,123	10,648	10,878	66	0.5	0.7	211
Grenada................	S2	90	94	94	98	195	0.4	0.4	722
Guatemala	S1	7,232	9,633	10,999	12,408	63	2.9	2.5	263
Guinea.................	S4	4,320	5,930	6,549	7,372	91	3.2	2.2	69
Guinea-Bissau.............	S4	789	998	1,125	1,263	152	2.3	2.4	104
Guyana.................	S2	759	748	724	710	158	-0.2	-0.5	10
Haiti.................	S1	5,068	6,027	6,518	6,997	92	1.7	1.5	613
Honduras................	S1	3,625	4,741	5,460	6,192	100	2.7	2.7	126
Hungary................	S3	10,711	10,365	10,319	10,372	73	-0.3	(Z)	289
Iceland.................	S1	228	255	266	277	175	1.1	0.8	7
India.................	S5	692,394	852,656	936,546	1,018,105	2	2.1	1.8	816
Indonesia................	S6	154,936	187,728	203,584	219,496	4	1.9	1.6	289
Iran.................	S5	39,274	56,946	64,625	71,879	15	3.7	2.3	102

See footnotes at end of table.

No. 1361. Population, by Country: 1980 to 2000—Continued

[See headnote, page 845]

COUNTRY OR AREA	Map refer-ence	MIDYEAR POPULATION (1,000)				Popu-lation rank, 1995	ANNUAL RATE OF GROWTH [1] (percent)		Popula-tion per sq. mile, 1995
		1980	1990	1995	2000, proj.		1980-1990	1990-2000	
Iraq	S5	13,233	18,425	20,644	24,731	46	3.3	2.9	123
Ireland	S3	3,401	3,508	3,550	3,627	123	0.3	0.3	133
Israel	S4	3,737	4,303	5,143	5,507	105	1.4	2.5	655
Italy	S3	56,451	57,661	58,262	58,865	20	0.2	0.2	513
Jamaica	S1	2,229	2,466	2,574	2,664	135	1.0	0.8	616
Japan	S5	116,807	123,540	125,506	127,554	9	0.6	0.3	823
Jordan	S4	2,168	3,277	4,101	4,704	116	4.1	3.6	116
Kazakhstan	S5	14,994	16,749	17,377	17,886	54	1.1	0.7	17
Kenya	S4	16,681	24,229	28,817	32,479	34	3.7	2.9	131
Kiribati	S6	58	72	79	87	198	2.1	1.9	287
Korea, North	S5	17,999	21,412	23,487	25,491	39	1.7	1.7	505
Korea, South	S5	38,124	43,237	45,554	47,861	24	1.3	1.0	1,202
Kuwait	S5	1,370	2,128	1,817	2,420	143	4.4	1.3	264
Kyrgyzstan	S5	3,623	4,392	4,770	5,119	108	1.9	1.5	62
Laos	S5	3,293	4,191	4,837	5,557	107	2.4	2.8	54
Latvia	S3	2,525	2,693	2,763	2,833	133	0.6	0.5	111
Lebanon	S4	3,137	3,367	3,696	4,115	120	0.7	2.0	936
Lesotho	S4	1,347	1,755	1,993	2,242	142	2.6	2.4	170
Liberia	S4	1,900	2,311	3,073	3,620	130	2.0	4.5	83
Libya	S4	3,119	4,355	5,248	6,294	103	3.3	3.7	8
Liechtenstein	S3	25	29	31	32	215	1.3	1.2	493
Lithuania	S5	3,436	3,727	3,876	4,007	118	0.8	0.7	154
Luxembourg	S3	364	382	405	415	169	0.5	0.8	405
Macedonia, The Former Yugoslav Republic of [3]	S3	1,893	2,031	2,160	2,246	139	0.7	1.0	218
Madagascar	S4	8,700	11,811	13,862	16,232	60	3.1	3.2	62
Malawi	S4	6,128	9,289	9,808	11,045	76	4.2	1.7	270
Malaysia	S6	13,764	17,556	19,724	21,953	47	2.4	2.2	155
Maldives	S5	154	218	261	310	176	3.5	3.5	2,256
Mali	S4	6,728	8,234	9,375	10,911	78	2.0	2.8	20
Malta	S4	364	354	370	382	173	-0.3	0.8	2,982
Marshall Islands	S6	31	46	56	68	208	4.1	3.9	804
Mauritania	S4	1,456	1,935	2,263	2,653	138	2.8	3.2	6
Mauritius	S4	964	1,074	1,127	1,194	151	1.1	1.1	1,579
Mexico	S1	68,686	85,121	93,986	102,912	11	2.1	1.9	127
Micronesia, Federated States of	S6	77	109	123	133	190	3.4	2.0	454
Moldova	S5	3,996	4,389	4,490	4,565	111	0.9	0.4	345
Monaco	S3	27	30	32	32	214	1.2	0.7	40,812
Mongolia	S5	1,662	2,186	2,494	2,826	137	2.7	2.6	4
Montenegro [3]	S3	579	616	708	729	159	0.6	1.7	133
Morocco	S4	20,457	26,164	29,169	32,229	33	2.5	2.1	169
Mozambique	S4	12,103	14,438	18,115	20,868	52	1.8	3.7	60
Namibia	S4	967	1,387	1,652	1,957	145	3.6	3.4	5
Nauru	S6	8	9	10	11	223	2.0	1.3	1,252
Nepal	S5	15,001	19,104	21,561	24,364	42	2.4	2.4	408
Netherlands	S3	14,144	14,952	15,453	15,801	55	0.6	0.6	1,179
New Zealand	S6	3,113	3,300	3,407	3,476	126	0.6	0.5	33
Nicaragua	S2	2,776	3,617	4,206	4,759	115	2.6	2.7	91
Niger	S4	5,661	7,868	9,280	10,985	79	3.3	3.3	19
Nigeria	S4	65,699	86,551	101,232	118,620	10	2.8	3.2	288
Norway	S3	4,086	4,242	4,331	4,387	113	0.4	0.3	36
Oman	S5	1,164	1,752	2,125	2,549	140	4.1	3.8	26
Pakistan	S5	85,219	114,842	131,542	148,540	7	3.0	2.6	438
Palau	S6	13	15	17	18	218	1.3	1.7	94
Panama	S2	1,956	2,427	2,681	2,934	134	2.2	1.9	91
Papua New Guinea	S6	2,991	3,823	4,295	4,812	114	2.5	2.3	25
Paraguay	S2	3,379	4,651	5,358	6,104	102	3.2	2.7	35
Peru	S2	17,295	21,879	24,087	26,258	38	2.4	1.8	49
Philippines	S6	51,092	65,168	73,266	81,594	14	2.4	2.2	636
Poland	S3	35,578	38,112	38,792	39,531	29	0.7	0.4	330
Portugal	S3	9,778	10,365	10,562	10,744	67	0.6	0.4	299
Qatar	S5	231	452	534	587	163	6.7	2.6	126
Romania	S5	22,201	23,191	23,198	23,383	40	0.4	0.1	261
Russia	S5	139,045	148,124	149,909	151,460	6	0.6	0.2	23
Rwanda	S4	5,170	7,415	8,605	9,715	84	3.6	2.7	893
St. Kitts and Nevis	S1	44	40	41	43	211	-1.0	0.8	295
St. Lucia	S1	122	146	156	165	186	1.8	1.2	661
St. Vincent and the Grenadines	S1	98	113	118	121	191	1.4	0.7	898
San Marino	S3	21	23	24	25	216	0.8	0.9	1,050
Sao Tome and Principe	S4	94	123	140	159	189	2.7	2.6	379
Saudi Arabia	S4	9,949	15,871	18,730	22,246	49	4.7	3.4	23
Senegal	S4	5,731	7,715	9,007	10,533	80	3.0	3.1	122
Serbia [3]	S3	9,262	9,705	10,394	10,617	72	0.5	0.9	305
Seychelles	S4	65	70	73	75	200	0.6	0.8	413
Sierra Leone	S4	3,315	4,230	4,753	5,421	109	2.4	2.5	172
Singapore	S6	2,414	2,720	2,890	3,025	132	1.2	1.1	11,997
Slovakia	S3	4,966	5,298	5,432	5,585	101	0.6	0.5	112
Slovenia	S3	1,885	1,969	2,052	2,071	141	0.4	0.5	262
Solomon Islands	S6	233	336	399	470	171	3.7	3.4	38
Somalia	S4	5,799	6,753	7,348	9,176	89	1.5	3.1	30

See footnotes at end of table.

No. 1361. Population, by Country: 1980 to 2000—Continued

[See headnote, page 845]

COUNTRY OR AREA	Map refer- ence	MIDYEAR POPULATION (1,000)				Popu- lation rank, 1995	ANNUAL RATE OF GROWTH [1] (percent)		Popula- tion per sq. mile, 1995
		1980	1990	1995	2000, proj.		1980- 1990	1990- 2000	
South Africa	S4	30,270	39,535	45,095	51,334	26	2.7	2.6	96
Spain	S3	37,488	38,964	39,404	39,972	28	0.4	0.3	204
Sri Lanka	S5	14,900	17,227	18,343	19,377	50	1.5	1.2	734
Sudan	S4	19,064	26,542	30,120	35,236	32	3.3	2.8	33
Suriname	S2	355	398	430	465	166	1.2	1.6	7
Swaziland	S4	607	853	967	1,137	154	3.4	2.9	146
Sweden	S3	8,310	8,559	8,822	8,994	82	0.3	0.5	56
Switzerland	S3	6,385	6,779	7,085	7,268	90	0.6	0.7	461
Syria	S4	8,692	12,762	15,452	18,519	56	3.8	3.7	217
Taiwan [2]	S5	17,848	20,436	21,501	22,448	43	1.4	0.9	1,726
Tajikistan	S5	3,969	5,346	6,155	6,956	94	3.0	2.6	111
Tanzania	S4	18,695	25,155	28,701	32,254	35	3.0	2.5	84
Thailand	S5	47,026	56,220	60,271	63,620	18	1.8	1.2	305
Togo	S4	2,596	3,680	4,410	5,263	112	3.5	3.6	210
Tonga	S0	93	101	106	110	192	0.9	0.8	381
Trinidad and Tobago	S2	1,091	1,256	1,271	1,273	149	1.4	0.1	642
Tunisia	S4	6,452	8,084	8,880	9,615	81	2.3	1.7	148
Turkey	S5	45,121	57,130	63,406	69,624	16	2.4	2.0	213
Turkmenistan	S5	2,875	3,660	4,075	4,474	117	2.4	2.0	22
Tuvalu	S6	7	9	10	11	224	2.0	1.6	995
Uganda	S4	12,252	16,927	19,573	21,358	48	3.2	2.3	254
Ukraine	S5	50,047	51,674	51,868	51,931	23	0.3	(Z)	223
United Arab Emirates	S5	1,000	2,252	2,925	3,582	131	8.1	4.6	91
United Kingdom	S3	56,314	57,418	58,295	58,951	19	0.2	0.3	625
United States	S1	227,726	249,908	263,814	276,621	3	0.9	1.0	75
Uruguay	S2	2,920	3,106	3,223	3,344	127	0.6	0.7	48
Uzbekistan	S5	16,000	20,615	23,089	25,467	41	2.5	2.1	134
Vanuatu	S6	117	154	174	193	185	2.8	2.2	30
Venezuela	S2	14,452	18,776	21,005	23,196	45	2.6	2.1	62
Vietnam	S5	54,234	67,718	74,393	80,533	13	2.2	1.7	592
Western Samoa	S0	155	186	209	235	182	1.8	2.3	190
Yemen	S5	8,007	11,588	14,728	18,022	58	3.7	4.4	72
Zaire	S4	27,954	37,903	44,061	51,413	27	3.0	3.0	50
Zambia	S4	5,638	8,233	9,446	10,625	77	3.8	2.6	33
Zimbabwe	S4	7,298	10,187	11,140	12,013	62	3.3	1.6	75
AREAS OF SPECIAL SOVER- EIGNTY AND DEPENDENCIES									
American Samoa	S0	32	47	57	69	207	3.8	3.8	747
Anguilla	S1	7	7	7	7	225	0.5	0.7	202
Aruba	S1	60	64	66	68	201	0.6	0.6	885
Bermuda	S1	55	59	62	64	205	0.8	0.8	3,258
Cayman Islands	S1	17	27	33	41	212	4.4	4.3	331
Cook Islands	S0	18	18	19	20	217	0.1	1.1	208
Faroe Islands	S3	43	47	49	51	210	0.9	0.7	90
French Guiana	S2	68	116	145	173	188	5.4	4.0	4
French Polynesia	S0	151	196	220	245	179	2.6	2.2	156
Gaza Strip	S4	454	633	757	898	156	3.3	3.5	5,149
Gibraltar	S3	29	31	32	33	213	0.6	0.5	13,759
Greenland	S1	50	56	58	60	206	1.0	0.8	(Z)
Guadeloupe	S1	337	378	403	426	170	1.1	1.2	592
Guam	S6	107	134	153	171	187	2.3	2.4	734
Guernsey	S3	53	61	64	67	204	1.4	1.0	859
Hong Kong	S5	5,063	5,558	5,543	5,587	98	0.9	0.1	14,516
Jersey	S3	76	84	87	89	196	1.0	0.7	1,918
Macau	S6	318	456	491	516	164	3.6	1.2	79,465
Man, Isle of	S3	64	69	73	76	199	0.7	1.0	320
Martinique	S1	339	374	395	416	172	1.0	1.1	966
Mayotte	S4	52	80	97	117	194	4.3	3.8	669
Montserrat	S1	12	13	13	13	222	0.6	0.3	330
Netherlands Antilles	S2	170	195	207	217	183	1.4	1.1	557
New Caledonia	S6	139	168	185	200	184	1.9	1.7	25
Northern Mariana Islands	S6	17	44	51	57	209	9.7	2.6	277
Puerto Rico	S1	3,206	3,605	3,813	3,850	119	1.2	0.7	1,102
Reunion	S4	507	600	666	730	160	1.7	2.0	690
St. Helena	S4	6	7	7	7	226	0.3	0.3	43
St. Pierre and Miquelon	S1	6	6	7	7	227	0.8	0.8	73
Turks and Caicos Islands	S1	7	12	14	15	220	4.5	2.7	84
Virgin Islands	S1	98	101	97	99	193	0.4	-0.2	719
Virgin Islands, British	S1	11	12	13	14	221	1.1	1.3	225
Wallis and Futuna	S6	11	14	14	15	219	2.4	1.1	137
West Bank	S4	916	1,275	1,481	1,661	147	3.3	2.6	680
Western Sahara	S4	126	191	217	245	180	4.2	2.5	2

X Not applicable. Z Less than .05 percent or one person per square mile. [1] Computed by the exponential method. For explanation of average annual percent change, see Guide to Tabular Presentation. [2] With the establishment of diplomatic relations with China on January 1, 1979, the U.S. government recognized the People's Republic of China as the sole legal government of China and acknowledged the Chinese position that there is only one China and that Taiwan is part of China. [3] The U.S. view is that the Socialist Federal Republic of Yugoslavia has dissolved and no successor state represents its continuation. Macedonia has proclaimed independent statehood, but has not been recognized as a state by the United States. Serbia and Montenegro have asserted the formation of a joint independent state, but this entity has not been recognized by the United States.

Source: U.S. Bureau of the Census, unpublished data.

Comparative International Statistics

No. 1362. Age Distribution, by Country: 1995 and 2000

[**In percent.** Covers countries with 10 million or more population in 1995]

COUNTRY OR AREA	1995 Under 5 years old	1995 5 to 14 years old	1995 15 to 64 years old	1995 65 years old and over	2000, proj. Under 5 years old	2000, proj. 5 to 14 years old	2000, proj. 15 to 64 years old	2000, proj. 65 years old and over
World	**11.1**	**20.5**	**62.0**	**6.4**	**10.5**	**20.0**	**62.7**	**6.8**
Afghanistan	16.6	25.0	55.8	2.6	16.1	25.4	55.8	2.7
Algeria	13.6	26.9	55.8	3.7	12.5	23.9	59.7	3.9
Angola	17.9	26.6	52.9	2.6	17.4	27.4	52.4	2.8
Argentina	9.3	18.7	62.3	9.7	9.1	17.6	63.3	10.0
Australia	7.2	14.5	66.6	11.8	6.8	14.2	67.0	12.0
Bangladesh	14.6	25.6	56.8	3.0	14.1	23.8	59.1	3.1
Belarus	6.5	15.4	65.0	13.0	6.2	14.0	65.4	14.5
Belgium	5.9	11.9	66.1	16.1	5.4	11.8	65.6	17.2
Brazil	9.8	21.4	64.2	4.6	9.3	19.2	66.4	5.2
Burkina	19.3	28.7	48.8	3.2	18.7	29.4	49.0	3.0
Burma	12.8	23.2	59.6	4.4	12.1	22.2	61.1	4.6
Cambodia	18.3	27.2	51.4	3.1	17.2	27.7	52.1	3.0
Cameroon	17.2	27.1	52.4	3.4	17.1	26.5	52.9	3.4
Canada	7.1	13.6	67.0	12.3	6.4	13.6	67.2	12.8
Chile	10.0	19.1	64.3	6.7	9.3	18.3	65.1	7.3
China [1]	8.6	17.9	67.4	6.1	7.7	17.3	68.2	6.8
Colombia	10.9	21.4	63.2	4.4	9.6	20.3	65.2	5.0
Cote d'Ivoire	19.2	28.4	50.3	2.1	18.7	29.2	49.9	2.3
Cuba	7.4	15.0	68.4	9.2	6.9	15.0	68.3	9.8
Czech Republic	6.4	12.9	67.7	13.0	6.7	12.4	67.4	13.4
Ecuador	12.2	23.8	59.8	4.2	10.9	22.0	62.5	4.5
Egypt	13.1	24.2	59.2	3.5	12.1	23.1	61.1	3.7
Ethiopia	18.5	27.2	51.6	2.7	18.3	27.7	51.3	2.7
France	6.5	12.6	65.2	15.6	6.2	12.8	64.5	16.4
Germany	5.5	11.0	68.0	15.6	5.2	11.1	67.2	16.5
Ghana	18.6	27.0	51.4	3.0	17.7	28.4	50.9	3.0
Greece	5.2	12.2	67.3	15.3	5.3	10.8	66.8	17.1
Guatemala	15.9	27.3	53.4	3.4	14.6	26.6	55.2	3.7
Hungary	6.1	12.1	67.6	14.2	6.4	11.9	66.8	14.9
India	12.6	22.5	60.9	4.0	11.5	21.8	62.3	4.4
Indonesia	11.0	21.4	64.0	3.6	10.5	19.7	65.6	4.3
Iran	16.3	28.7	51.1	3.8	14.1	27.6	54.1	4.2
Iraq	19.0	28.8	49.2	3.1	18.2	28.8	50.2	2.9
Italy	5.2	10.2	68.4	16.2	5.4	10.1	67.0	17.5
Japan	5.1	11.3	69.5	14.2	5.5	10.2	67.8	16.5
Kazakhstan	9.5	20.7	62.7	7.0	8.8	19.2	64.6	7.3
Kenya	18.2	29.7	49.8	2.3	16.9	29.3	51.4	2.4
Korea, North	11.1	18.4	66.3	4.1	10.2	19.2	65.9	4.7
Korea, South	7.5	16.5	70.6	5.4	7.3	14.4	71.8	6.5
Madagascar	18.9	28.0	50.0	3.2	18.3	28.3	50.4	3.0
Malaysia	13.3	23.4	59.4	3.8	12.4	23.0	60.6	4.0
Mexico	12.8	24.0	58.8	4.3	11.9	22.8	60.5	4.8
Morocco	13.1	25.1	57.5	4.2	12.1	23.3	60.1	4.6
Mozambique	17.9	27.0	52.5	2.5	17.4	27.4	52.6	2.6
Nepal	16.0	26.6	54.6	2.9	15.5	25.7	55.7	3.0
Netherlands	6.3	12.0	68.3	13.4	5.8	12.3	67.8	14.1
Nigeria	18.1	26.9	52.2	2.9	17.8	26.9	52.3	2.9
Pakistan	17.3	26.6	52.1	3.9	16.8	26.9	52.5	3.9
Peru	11.8	23.3	60.9	4.1	10.8	21.3	63.4	4.5
Philippines	14.2	24.1	58.0	3.7	13.2	23.7	59.2	3.9
Poland	6.7	16.3	65.9	11.2	6.5	13.9	67.3	12.3
Portugal	5.7	12.7	67.4	14.1	5.8	11.5	67.7	15.1
Romania	6.6	14.7	66.7	12.0	6.6	13.8	65.9	13.6
Russia	6.3	15.7	66.0	12.0	6.1	14.0	67.2	12.6
Saudi Arabia	17.2	25.6	55.0	2.2	16.6	26.3	54.4	2.6
Serbia [2]	7.0	14.8	66.5	11.6	6.7	13.9	65.6	13.8
South Africa	15.0	24.7	56.2	4.1	14.7	24.7	56.5	4.1
Spain	5.3	11.6	68.1	15.0	5.7	10.5	67.4	16.4
Sri Lanka	9.0	20.0	65.1	5.9	8.3	17.3	67.8	6.6
Sudan	18.0	28.2	51.6	2.2	16.9	27.7	53.1	2.3
Syria	19.2	29.1	48.8	2.8	18.4	29.1	49.7	2.8
Taiwan [1]	7.8	16.5	68.3	7.5	7.2	14.6	69.8	8.4
Tanzania	18.4	28.2	50.5	2.8	18.1	28.6	50.5	2.8
Thailand	9.3	19.5	66.2	4.9	8.4	17.8	68.0	5.7
Turkey	12.0	22.7	60.1	5.2	11.0	21.5	61.8	5.8
Uganda	19.6	29.6	48.6	2.2	18.6	31.1	48.1	2.3
Ukraine	6.1	14.4	65.4	14.2	6.0	13.1	66.4	14.5
United Kingdom	6.7	12.9	64.6	15.8	6.2	13.2	64.7	15.9
United States	7.6	14.4	65.2	12.8	7.0	14.6	65.6	12.8
Uzbekistan	14.0	25.9	55.4	4.7	12.7	25.1	57.4	4.9
Venezuela	12.2	23.2	60.3	4.3	11.2	21.7	62.4	4.7
Vietnam	12.7	23.8	58.6	4.9	11.2	22.7	60.9	5.2
Yemen	20.4	29.3	47.6	2.6	19.0	30.3	48.0	2.7
Zaire	19.4	28.4	49.6	2.7	19.2	29.0	49.3	2.6
Zimbabwe	16.5	30.2	50.6	2.6	15.0	29.2	53.0	2.7

[1] See footnote 2, table 1361.   [2] Serbia and Montenegro have asserted the formation of a joint independent state, but this entity has not been recognized by the United States. Data in this table are for Serbia alone.

Source: U.S. Bureau of the Census, unpublished data.

No. 1363. Vital Statistics, by Country: 1995 and 2000

[Covers countries with 5 million or more population in 1995]

COUNTRY OR AREA	CRUDE BIRTH RATE [1]		CRUDE DEATH RATE [2]		EXPECTATION OF LIFE AT BIRTH (years)		INFANT MORTALITY RATE [3]		TOTAL FERTILITY RATE [4]	
	1995	2000, proj.	1995	2000, proj.	1995	2000, proj.	1995	2000, proj.	1995	2000, proj.
United States.....	15.3	14.2	8.4	8.5	76.0	76.4	7.9	6.6	2.08	2.09
Afghanistan.........	42.7	40.8	18.5	16.5	45.4	47.8	152.8	137.5	6.21	5.87
Algeria.............	29.0	26.5	6.1	5.4	68.0	69.6	50.3	42.2	3.70	3.16
Angola.............	45.1	42.6	18.1	15.9	46.3	48.9	142.1	125.9	6.42	6.05
Argentina..........	19.5	19.1	8.6	8.6	71.5	72.3	28.8	26.1	2.65	2.50
Australia...........	14.1	13.2	7.4	7.4	77.8	78.7	7.1	6.4	1.82	1.80
Austria............	11.2	10.1	10.3	10.0	76.9	78.0	6.9	6.2	1.48	1.50
Azerbaijan..........	22.1	18.5	6.6	6.5	71.1	72.5	33.9	28.7	2.64	2.39
Bangladesh.........	34.6	32.5	11.4	10.3	55.5	57.5	104.6	93.0	4.39	4.00
Belarus............	13.0	12.6	11.2	11.3	71.0	72.2	18.6	16.4	1.87	1.83
Belgium............	11.5	10.4	10.2	10.2	77.2	78.2	7.0	6.3	1.62	1.60
Benin..............	47.3	44.9	13.9	12.0	52.2	54.6	107.6	95.3	6.72	6.32
Bolivia.............	31.6	28.8	8.1	7.1	63.9	66.3	70.6	57.2	4.10	3.63
Brazil.............	21.2	19.2	9.0	10.1	61.8	60.9	57.2	47.8	2.39	2.14
Bulgaria...........	11.8	11.7	11.3	10.9	73.7	75.5	11.4	9.4	1.71	1.70
Burkina...........	48.1	45.6	18.2	20.3	46.6	41.6	116.9	112.8	6.88	6.48
Burma.............	28.0	25.9	9.6	8.7	60.5	62.8	61.6	52.4	3.58	3.29
Burundi............	43.4	40.9	21.5	21.3	39.9	39.1	111.9	102.2	6.63	6.25
Cambodia..........	44.4	41.0	16.2	14.3	49.5	51.5	109.6	100.5	5.81	5.81
Cameroon..........	40.4	40.1	11.2	10.2	57.5	59.4	75.4	67.5	5.80	5.61
Canada............	13.7	12.3	7.4	7.7	78.3	79.1	6.8	6.2	1.83	1.80
Chad..............	42.1	39.7	20.3	18.4	41.2	43.3	129.7	118.6	5.33	5.05
Chile..............	20.3	19.0	5.4	5.3	74.9	76.4	14.3	11.4	2.49	2.43
China.............	17.8	15.0	7.4	7.0	68.1	70.2	52.1	38.7	1.84	1.80
Colombia...........	21.9	19.0	4.7	4.6	72.5	74.2	26.9	21.3	2.40	2.17
Cote d'Ivoire........	46.2	43.9	15.0	14.7	48.9	48.5	93.1	83.8	6.61	6.21
Cuba..............	14.5	13.8	6.5	6.7	77.1	77.8	8.1	7.5	1.63	1.80
Czech Republic......	13.5	13.6	10.9	9.9	73.5	75.4	8.9	7.5	1.84	1.80
Denmark...........	12.4	11.7	11.1	10.7	76.1	77.4	6.8	6.1	1.69	1.70
Dominican Republic	24.1	21.1	5.7	5.4	68.7	70.4	49.5	40.8	2.72	2.42
Ecuador...........	25.1	22.5	5.6	5.2	70.4	72.0	37.7	31.1	2.97	2.59
Egypt.............	28.7	26.2	8.9	8.1	61.1	62.7	74.5	65.7	3.67	3.24
El Salvador.........	32.4	29.5	6.2	5.5	67.5	69.7	38.9	30.9	3.69	3.30
Ethiopia...........	46.7	44.6	15.8	14.5	50.0	51.5	120.6	112.0	7.07	6.75
Finland............	12.2	11.4	9.8	9.7	76.2	77.5	5.2	4.9	1.79	1.80
France............	13.0	12.3	9.3	9.3	78.4	79.2	6.5	5.9	1.80	1.80
Georgia............	15.8	14.4	8.7	8.9	73.1	74.5	22.6	18.6	2.16	2.05
Germany...........	11.0	9.8	10.8	10.5	76.6	77.8	6.3	5.7	1.50	1.53
Ghana.............	43.6	40.5	12.0	10.8	55.9	57.5	81.7	74.8	6.09	5.76
Greece............	10.6	10.6	9.3	9.5	77.9	78.8	8.3	7.3	1.46	1.50
Guatemala.........	34.7	31.2	7.3	6.5	64.9	66.9	52.2	44.6	4.63	4.00
Guinea............	43.4	39.9	19.1	16.9	44.6	47.0	136.6	123.7	5.79	5.46
Haiti..............	38.6	34.9	18.7	18.3	44.8	43.9	107.5	102.2	5.82	5.16
Honduras..........	34.1	30.3	6.0	5.2	68.0	70.0	43.4	35.4	4.55	3.83
Hong Kong.........	12.0	11.2	6.0	6.8	80.2	80.6	5.8	5.5	1.39	1.50
Hungary...........	12.7	12.9	12.4	11.4	71.9	74.1	11.9	9.7	1.82	1.80
India.............	27.8	24.7	10.1	9.1	59.0	61.4	76.3	65.8	3.40	3.04
Indonesia..........	24.1	22.5	8.5	8.1	61.2	63.4	65.0	55.4	2.74	2.53
Iran..............	34.9	29.2	6.9	5.8	67.0	69.1	54.6	45.1	4.93	3.90
Iraq..............	43.6	40.8	6.8	5.6	66.5	68.7	62.4	50.1	6.56	5.81
Israel.............	20.4	19.7	6.4	6.3	78.1	78.9	8.4	7.5	2.81	2.66
Italy..............	10.9	10.9	9.8	10.0	77.9	78.7	7.4	6.6	1.41	1.50
Japan.............	10.7	11.4	7.5	8.3	79.4	80.0	4.3	4.1	1.56	1.60
Kazakhstan.........	19.3	18.3	7.9	7.9	68.3	69.6	40.0	34.6	2.43	2.32
Kenya	41.7	37.5	12.0	15.2	52.4	46.4	73.5	72.3	5.76	4.97
Korea, North.......	23.3	19.9	5.5	5.4	70.1	71.5	26.8	22.2	2.34	2.21
Korea, South........	15.6	14.8	6.2	6.4	70.9	72.3	20.9	17.7	1.66	1.70
Libya	44.9	42.6	7.9	6.9	64.3	66.2	61.4	52.1	6.32	6.00
Madagascar	44.8	42.7	13.0	11.3	54.5	56.7	86.9	77.1	6.62	6.25
Malawi	49.8	46.9	23.5	25.7	39.0	35.2	140.2	134.2	7.36	6.94
Malaysia..........	28.0	25.6	5.6	5.2	69.5	71.0	24.7	20.9	3.47	3.31
Mali..............	51.9	49.3	19.9	17.5	46.4	48.8	104.5	95.6	7.33	6.91
Mexico............	26.6	24.3	4.6	4.4	73.3	75.0	26.0	20.7	3.09	2.79
Morocco...........	27.9	25.1	6.0	5.1	69.0	71.8	45.8	32.9	3.69	3.13
Mozambique........	44.6	42.1	15.9	14.1	49.0	51.3	126.0	112.8	6.19	5.84
Nepal.............	37.3	35.6	12.9	11.2	53.1	55.9	81.2	70.1	5.15	4.68
Netherlands........	12.4	10.9	8.5	8.6	78.0	78.8	6.0	5.5	1.56	1.50
Niger.............	54.8	51.7	20.8	18.1	45.1	47.5	109.3	100.3	7.35	7.00
Nigeria............	43.3	41.6	12.0	10.1	56.0	59.1	72.6	61.4	6.31	5.95
Pakistan...........	41.8	39.7	12.1	10.8	57.9	59.7	99.5	90.3	6.35	5.94
Paraguay..........	31.5	29.1	4.4	4.1	73.6	74.9	24.1	19.6	4.22	3.86
Peru	24.9	22.7	6.8	6.3	66.1	68.1	52.1	42.9	3.00	2.63
Philippines.........	30.4	28.4	7.0	6.6	65.7	66.9	49.6	44.4	3.81	3.53
Poland............	13.3	13.2	9.2	8.7	73.1	75.0	12.4	10.0	1.92	1.80
Portugal...........	11.7	11.7	9.7	9.5	75.5	76.9	9.1	7.8	1.47	1.50
Romania...........	13.7	13.5	9.9	9.5	72.2	74.4	18.7	14.3	1.82	1.80
Russia............	12.6	12.7	11.4	11.2	69.1	70.5	26.4	22.6	1.82	1.80
Rwanda...........	48.5	45.9	21.8	23.8	39.3	35.7	118.1	110.2	8.12	7.64
Saudi Arabia	38.8	37.2	5.5	4.7	68.5	71.1	48.9	36.3	6.48	6.30
Senegal	42.9	41.3	11.6	10.0	57.2	59.9	73.6	63.5	6.03	5.71
Serbia [5]	14.2	13.3	8.7	8.6	73.9	75.7	18.6	15.1	2.00	1.90

See footnotes at end of table.

No. 1363. Vital Statistics, by Country: 1995 and 2000—Continued

[See headnote, page 849]

COUNTRY OR AREA	CRUDE BIRTH RATE [1]		CRUDE DEATH RATE [2]		EXPECTATION OF LIFE AT BIRTH (years)		INFANT MORTALITY RATE [3]		TOTAL FERTILITY RATE [4]	
	1995	2000, proj.	1995	2000, proj.	1995	2000, proj.	1995	2000, proj.	1995	2000, proj.
Slovakia	14.5	14.1	9.1	8.5	73.2	75.1	10.0	8.4	1.93	1.80
Somalia	45.5	42.4	13.3	9.8	55.7	61.1	119.5	87.1	7.13	6.53
South Africa	33.4	32.3	7.4	6.9	65.4	67.0	45.8	39.8	4.35	4.23
Spain	11.2	11.6	8.9	9.2	77.9	78.8	6.7	6.1	1.41	1.50
Sri Lanka	18.1	16.9	5.8	5.9	72.1	73.2	21.3	18.7	2.08	1.95
Sudan	41.3	38.8	11.7	10.3	54.7	56.8	77.7	69.2	6.00	5.47
Sweden	13.2	11.5	10.8	10.6	78.4	79.2	5.6	5.2	1.97	1.80
Switzerland	12.0	10.8	9.2	9.1	78.4	79.1	6.3	5.8	1.60	1.60
Syria	43.2	40.5	6.1	5.3	66.8	68.4	41.1	35.2	6.55	6.00
Taiwan	15.3	14.5	5.7	6.1	75.5	76.4	5.6	5.3	1.81	1.80
Tajikistan	34.1	30.4	6.6	6.0	69.0	70.5	60.4	52.1	4.55	4.10
Tanzania	45.3	43.6	19.8	22.4	42.5	38.4	109.0	104.3	6.15	5.85
Thailand	18.9	17.2	6.5	8.1	68.4	65.9	35.7	34.3	2.04	1.91
Tunisia	22.5	20.2	4.9	4.7	73.3	74.8	32.3	25.3	2.73	2.33
Turkey	25.3	22.8	5.6	5.1	71.5	73.8	45.6	33.3	3.12	2.78
Uganda	48.0	43.7	24.4	26.3	36.6	33.6	112.2	106.8	6.70	6.24
Ukraine	12.3	12.2	12.7	12.6	70.1	71.2	20.5	18.1	1.81	1.79
United Kingdom	13.2	11.9	10.7	10.3	77.0	78.1	7.0	6.3	1.82	1.80
Uzbekistan	29.5	26.8	6.4	6.0	68.8	70.1	52.0	45.1	3.67	3.37
Venezuela	25.1	22.9	4.6	4.5	73.3	74.4	26.5	22.6	2.97	2.68
Vietnam	26.3	22.9	7.6	7.0	65.7	67.1	44.6	39.9	3.21	2.80
Yemen	44.9	43.1	8.0	5.6	62.5	67.7	58.2	37.3	7.15	6.56
Zaire	48.3	46.1	16.6	15.5	47.5	48.4	108.7	97.9	6.70	6.39
Zambia	45.5	43.2	18.4	23.0	42.9	36.5	86.0	85.3	6.62	6.28
Zimbabwe	36.4	32.3	18.5	20.0	41.4	39.6	72.7	65.9	4.93	4.11

[1] Number of births during 1 year per 1,000 persons (based on midyear population).   [2] Number of deaths during 1 year per 1,000 persons (based on midyear population).   [3] Number of deaths of children under 1 year of age per 1,000 live births in a calendar year.   [4] Average number of children that would be born if all women lived to the end of their childbearing years and, at each year of age, they experienced the birth rates occurring in the specified year.   [5] Serbia and Montenegro have asserted the formation of a joint independent state, but this entity has not been recognized by the United States. Data in this table are for Serbia alone.

Source: U.S. Bureau of the Census, unpublished data.

No. 1364. Foreign or Immigrant Population, 1982 and 1993, and Foreign Labor Force, 1991, by Country

[In Australia, Canada, and the United States the data refer to people present in the country who are foreign born. In the European countries and Japan they generally refer to foreigners and represent the nationalities of residents; as a result, persons born in these countries may be counted among the foreign population, whereas others, who are foreign-born, may have acquired the host-country nationality. Except as noted, data are from population registers. Data for foreign labor in European Community (EC) countries are taken from the EC labor force survey. For the other European countries data are based on population registers]

COUNTRY	FOREIGNERS				FOREIGN LABOR FORCE, 1991	
	Number (1,000)		Percent of total population		Number (1,000)	Percent of total labor force
	1982	1993	1982	1993		
United States [1]	[2]14,080	[3]19,767	[2]4.7	[3]7.9	[3]11,636	[3]9.3
Australia [4]	3,004	[5]4,125	20.6	[5]22.7	[5]2,164	[5]24.8
Austria	303	[6]562	4.0	[6]7.1	[6]296	[6]8.9
Belgium	891	[6]909	9.0	[6]9.0	297	7.4
Canada [1]	3,843	4,343	16.1	15.6	[6]2,681	[6]18.5
Denmark	103	189	2.0	3.6	74	2.5
Finland	14	56	0.3	1.1	(NA)	(NA)
France [1]	3,714	[3]3,597	6.8	[3]6.3	1,505	6.2
Germany	4,667	[7]6,878	7.6	8.5	[7]2,703	8.9
Italy	359	987	0.6	1.7	(NA)	(NA)
Japan [8]	802	1,321	0.7	1.1	[6]590	[6]0.9
Luxembourg	96	[6]120	26.2	[6]30.3	55	33.3
Netherlands	547	[6]757	3.8	[6]5.0	269	3.9
Norway	91	162	2.2	3.8	[6][9]47	[6]4.4
Spain	200	[6]393	0.5	[6]1.0	59	0.4
Sweden	406	[6]499	4.9	[6]5.7	[6]244	[6]5.5
Switzerland	926	1,260	14.4	18.1	[6]717	[6]20.1
United Kingdom [4]	1,601	2,001	2.8	3.5	960	3.3

NA Not available.   [1] Census data.   [2] 1980 data.   [3] 1990 data.   [4] Labor force survey.   [5] 1994 data.   [6] 1992 data.   [7] Western Germany only.   [8] Residence permits.   [9] Excludes unemployed.

Source: Organization for Economic Cooperation and Development, Paris, France, The OECD Observer, No. 192, February/March 1995 (copyright).

No. 1365. Percent Distribution of Households, by Type and Country

YEAR	Total	MARRIED COUPLE [1]			Single parent [2]	One person	Other [3]
		Total	With children [2]	Without children [2]			
United States:							
1960.	100	74	44	30	4	13	8
1970.	100	71	40	30	5	17	7
1980.	100	61	31	30	8	23	9
1990.	100	56	26	30	8	25	11
1992.	100	55	26	29	9	25	11
1993.	100	55	26	29	9	25	11
Canada:							
1961.	100	[4]78	[4]51	[4]27	[4]4	9	[4]9
1971.	100	74	47	28	5	13	8
1981.	100	67	36	31	5	20	8
1991.	100	63	30	33	6	23	9
Japan:							
1960.	100	65	49	16	3	17	14
1970.	100	64	45	20	2	20	13
1980.	100	68	43	26	2	20	10
1990.	100	65	33	32	2	23	10
Denmark: [5]							
1976.	100	45	24	21	5	(NA)	(NA)
1983.	100	44	23	21	5	(NA)	(NA)
1990.	100	40	19	21	5	(NA)	(NA)
1992.	100	39	18	21	4	50	7
1993.	100	39	18	21	4	50	7
France:							
1968.	100	70	44	27	4	20	5
1975.	100	69	42	27	4	22	5
1982.	100	67	40	27	4	25	4
1990.	100	65	39	26	7	26	2
1992.	100	64	37	27	7	27	2
1993.	100	64	37	27	7	27	2
Germany:							
1961.	100	67	44	22	11	21	2
1970.	100	65	42	23	6	27	3
1980.	100	61	37	24	7	30	3
1990.	100	54	31	23	6	35	4
1992 [6].	100	55	31	24	7	34	4
1993.	100	54	31	24	7	34	4
Netherlands:							
1961.	100	78	55	22	6	12	5
1971.	100	74	52	22	5	17	4
1981.	100	67	44	23	6	21	6
1985.	100	60	39	22	7	28	5
1990 [7].	100	64	36	28	5	30	1
1992.	100	63	34	29	5	31	1
1993.	100	63	33	30	5	31	1
Sweden:							
1960.	100	66	36	31	4	20	10
1970.	100	64	30	34	3	25	7
1980.	100	58	25	33	3	33	6
1985.	100	55	22	33	3	36	6
1990.	100	52	20	32	3	40	5
United Kingdom: [8]							
1961.	100	74	38	36	2	12	12
1971.	100	70	34	35	3	18	9
1981.	100	64	31	34	5	22	9
1990.	100	61	25	36	6	26	7
1992.	100	60	24	36	6	27	7
1993.	100	60	25	35	7	27	6

NA Not available.   [1] May include unmarried cohabiting couples. Such couples are explicitly included under married couples in Canada (beginning in 1981) and France. For Sweden, beginning in 1980, all cohabitants are included as married couples, and the figures for 1970 have been adjusted to include all cohabitants. For Denmark, beginning 1983, persons reported separately as living in consensual unions with joint children have been classified here as married couples. In other countries, some unmarried cohabitants are included as married couples, while some are classified under "other households," depending on responses to surveys and censuses.   [2] Children are defined as unmarried children living at home according to the following age limits: under 18 years old in the United States, Canada, Japan, Denmark, and the United Kingdom, except that the United Kingdom includes 16- and 17-year-olds only if they are in full-time education; under 25 years old in France; under 16 years old in Sweden; and children of all ages in the Netherlands and Germany.   [3] Includes both family and nonfamily households not elsewhere classified. These households comprise, for example, siblings residing together, other households composed of relatives, and households made up of roommates. Some unmarried cohabiting couples may also be included in the "other" group. See footnote 1.   [4] Estimated by the U.S. Bureau of Labor Statistics.   [5] From family-based statistics. However, one person living alone constitutes a family in Denmark. In this respect, the Danish data are closer to household statistics.   [6] Prior to 1992, data are for former West Germany.   [7] Beginning 1990, data are not strictly comparable with prior years due to change in source of data.   [8] Great Britain only (excludes Northern Ireland).

Source: U.S. Bureau of Labor Statistics, *Monthly Labor Review,* March 1990; and unpublished data.

No. 1366. Marriage and Divorce Rates, by Country: 1970 to 1992

COUNTRY	MARRIAGE RATE PER 1,000 POPULATION, 15 TO 64 YEARS OLD						DIVORCE RATE PER 1,000 MARRIED WOMEN					
	1970	1980	1989	1990	1991	1992	1970	1980	1989	1990	1991	1992
United States [1]	17	16	15	15	14	14	15	23	21	21	21	21
Canada................	14	12	11	10	10	(NA)	6	10	12	11	11	11
Denmark..............	12	8	9	9	9	9	8	11	14	13	12	13
France	12	10	8	8	7	7	3	6	8	8	9	(NA)
Germany [2].............	12	9	9	9	8	8	5	6	9	8	7	7
Italy	11	9	8	8	8	8	1	1	2	2	2	2
Japan	14	10	8	8	9	(NA)	4	5	5	5	6	(NA)
Netherlands	15	10	9	9	9	9	3	8	8	8	8	9
Sweden..............	8	7	[3]20	7	7	6	7	11	12	12	12	12
United Kingdom	14	12	11	10	8	(NA)	[4]5	[4]12	13	13	13	12

NA Not available. [1] Beginning 1980, includes unlicensed marriages registered in California. [2] Prior to 1991, data are for former West Germany. [3] Increase due to change in inheritance laws which caused many cohabiting couples to marry. [4] England and Wales only.

No. 1367. Births to Unmarried Women, by Country: 1970 to 1992

[For U.S. figures, beginning 1980, marital status is inferred from a comparison of the child's and parents' surnames on the birth certificate for those States that do not report on marital status. No estimates are included for misstatements on birth records or failures to register births]

COUNTRY	1970		1980		1990		1992	
	Total live births (1,000)	Percent born to unmarried women	Total live births (1,000)	Percent born to unmarried women	Total live births (1,000)	Percent born to unmarried women	Total live births (1,000)	Percent born to unmarried women
United States	3,731	11	3,612	18	4,158	28	4,065	30
Canada [1]	372	10	360	13	398	24	399	(NA)
Denmark........	71	11	57	33	63	46	68	46
France	850	7	800	11	762	30	743	33
Germany [2]	811	6	621	8	727	11	809	15
Italy	902	2	640	4	554	6	561	7
Japan	1,932	1	1,616	1	1,240	1	1,228	1
Netherlands	239	2	181	4	198	11	197	12
Sweden	110	18	97	40	124	47	123	50
United Kingdom	904	8	754	12	799	28	781	31

NA Not available. [1] 1980 through 1990 data exclude Newfoundland. [2] Prior to 1991, data are for former West Germany.
Source of tables 1366 and 1367: U.S. Bureau of Labor Statistics, *Monthly Labor Review*, 1990; and unpublished data.

No. 1368. Death Rates, by Cause and Country

[**Age-standardized death rate per 100,000 population**. For explanation of age-adjustment, see text, section 2. The standard population for this table is the old European standard; see source for details. Deaths classified to ninth revision of *International Classification of Diseases*; see text, section 2]

COUNTRY	Year	Ischemic heart disease	Cerebrovascular disease	CANCER OF —			Bronchitis, [1] emphysema, asthma	Chronic liver disease and cirrhosis	Motor vehicle traffic accidents	Suicide and self-inflicted injury
				Lung, trachea, bronchus	Stomach	Female breast				
United States	1990	176.0	50.0	57.8	5.4	32.1	9.0	11.2	17.7	12.3
Australia	1992	173.0	65.1	37.5	7.1	27.4	11.8	6.6	10.4	11.9
Austria	1992	150.7	89.0	33.8	15.9	31.3	15.5	27.6	14.0	20.6
Bulgaria	1992	218.8	231.3	32.8	22.4	22.5	11.9	16.5	12.3	16.6
Canada..........	1991	155.6	48.5	54.4	7.3	32.5	7.8	8.8	12.3	12.9
Czech Republic......	1992	283.7	174.9	54.7	17.3	30.5	20.4	18.4	13.9	18.8
Denmark	1992	190.3	72.0	51.1	7.8	40.6	36.5	13.5	10.2	20.4
Finland	1992	228.5	91.9	34.5	11.8	23.8	16.2	11.3	10.8	27.8
France	1991	61.1	54.6	34.9	8.5	28.2	9.4	16.5	15.7	18.9
Germany [2]........	1991	158.5	91.2	35.9	15.9	32.0	21.7	21.7	12.8	15.5
Hungary	1992	249.5	172.4	64.4	23.7	33.9	40.2	68.4	21.8	37.0
Italy	1990	94.1	91.6	42.7	18.6	29.4	24.1	22.6	14.4	6.8
Japan	1992	34.7	80.6	27.5	33.4	9.0	10.3	12.2	10.9	15.5
Netherlands	1989	134.9	67.8	54.6	13.4	39.0	18.2	5.5	8.9	10.0
New Zealand	1991	202.0	77.4	41.5	9.4	36.6	12.7	4.4	18.4	13.9
Norway..........	1991	176.8	78.3	29.6	11.9	25.7	11.8	4.3	7.0	15.5
Poland	1992	123.3	79.6	50.8	19.9	22.7	20.1	12.4	19.7	15.6
Portugal	1992	80.2	199.3	20.5	25.3	26.6	10.8	26.2	26.5	8.2
Spain	1990	73.7	89.7	32.8	15.3	24.2	9.0	19.3	19.3	7.1
Sweden..........	1990	185.8	69.3	23.5	9.7	25.3	12.3	6.6	8.2	15.9
Switzerland	1992	106.4	51.5	35.0	9.6	35.0	17.8	9.0	10.2	19.1
United Kingdom:										
England and Wales .	1992	199.7	82.3	51.0	11.7	39.5	10.9	5.5	7.4	7.4
Scotland.........	1992	246.4	108.1	68.6	12.6	37.9	7.6	8.4	8.6	10.8

[1] Chronic and unspecified. [2] Former West Germany.
Source: World Health Organization, Geneva, Switzerland, *World Health Statistics Annual*.

No. 1369. Health Expenditures, by Country: 1980 to 1993

[G.D.P.=gross domestic product; for explanation, see text, section 14. For explanation of purchasing power parities, see text, section 30]

COUNTRY	TOTAL HEALTH EXPENDITURES							PUBLIC HEALTH EXPENDITURES		
	Percent of gross domestic product					Per capita on basis of G.D.P. purchasing power parities		Percent of gross domestic product		
	1980	1985	1990	1991	1993	1991	1993	1980	1991	1993
United States	9.2	10.5	12.4	13.4	14.1	2,867	3,299	3.9	5.9	6.2
Australia	7.3	7.7	8.2	8.6	8.5	1,411	1,494	4.6	5.8	5.8
Austria	7.9	8.1	8.4	8.6	9.2	1,492	1,777	5.4	5.7	6.0
Belgium	6.6	7.4	7.6	7.9	8.3	1,354	1,601	5.5	7.0	7.3
Canada	7.4	8.5	9.5	10.0	10.2	1,917	1,971	5.5	7.2	7.4
Denmark.	6.8	6.3	6.3	6.5	6.7	1,151	1,296	5.8	5.4	5.5
Finland.	6.5	7.3	8.0	9.1	8.8	1,420	1,363	5.1	7.4	7.0
France	7.6	8.5	8.9	9.1	9.8	1,656	1,835	6.0	6.8	7.3
Germany [1]	8.4	8.7	8.3	8.4	8.6	1,663	1,814	6.3	6.0[2]	6.0
Greece.	4.3	4.9	5.4	5.2	5.7	404	500	3.6	4.1[2]	4.3
Iceland	6.4	7.1	8.3	8.4	8.3	1,476	1,564	5.7	7.2	6.9
Ireland	9.2	8.2	7.0	7.3	6.7	844	923	7.5	5.6	5.1
Italy	6.9	7.0	8.1	8.3	8.5	1,408	1,523	5.6	6.5	6.2
Japan	6.6	6.5	6.7	6.8	7.3	1,307	1,495	4.6	4.8	5.2
Luxembourg	6.8	6.8	7.2	7.3	6.9	1,476	1,993	6.3	6.6[2]	6.3
Mexico	(NA)	(NA)	(NA)	(NA)	4.9[3]	(NA)	340[3]	(NA)	(NA)	2.9[3]
Netherlands	8.0	8.0	8.2	8.4	8.7	1,366	1,532	6.0	6.1	6.8
New Zealand.	7.2	6.5	7.3	7.7	7.7	1,047	1,179	6.0	6.1	5.9
Norway.	6.6	6.4	7.4	7.6	8.2	1,305	1,592	6.5	7.3	7.6
Portugal	5.9	7.0	6.7	6.8	7.3	624	866	4.3	4.1[2]	4.1
Spain.	5.6	5.7	6.6	6.7	7.3	848	972	4.5	5.5	5.7
Sweden	9.4	8.8	8.6	8.6	7.5	1,443	1,266	8.7	6.7	6.2
Switzerland.	7.3	7.6	7.8	7.9	9.9	1,730	2,283	4.9	5.4[2]	6.8
Turkey	4.0	2.8	4.0	4.0	2.7	142	146	1.1	1.4[2]	(NA)
United Kingdom	5.8	6.0	6.2	6.6	7.1	1,033	1,213	5.2	5.5	5.9

NA Not available.　[1] Former West Germany.　[2] 1990 data.　[3] 1992 data.

Source: Organization for Economic Cooperation and Development, Paris, France, *OECD Health Data*, 1995; *OECD Health Systems: Facts and Trends*, 1993; and unpublished data.

No. 1370. Education Expenditures, by Country: 1992

[Includes both current and capital expenditures. Public expenditure refers to the spending of public authorities at all levels and includes subsidies to private sector. Private expenditure refers to the spending of private sources- mainly households, private nonprofit institutions, and firms and businesses. Expenditure per student based on full-time equivalent students enrolled in public schools. Purchasing power parities (PPP's) are the rates of currency conversion that equalize the purchasing power of different currencies. This means that a given sum of money, when converted into different currencies at the PPP rates, will buy the same basket of goods and services in all countries. Thus, PPP's are the rates of currency conversion that eliminate differences in price levels between countries. Educational program levels classified according to the International Standard Classification for Education developed by United Nations Educational, Scientific, and Cultural Organization]

COUNTRY	EXPENDITURES AS PERCENT OF GROSS DOMESTIC PRODUCT			Public expenditure for education as percent of total public expenditures	EXPENDITURES PER STUDENT USING PURCHASING POWER PARITIES (U.S. dollars)				
	Total	Public sources	Private sources		Early childhood education [1]	Primary and secondary			Higher education
						Total	Primary	Secondary [2]	
OECD, total . . .	6.5	5.1	(NA)	12.0	3,000	4,700	4,170	5,170	10,030
Australia	6.2	5.5	0.7	14.0	(NA)	(NA)	(NA)	(NA)	6,600
Austria	(NA)	5.8	(NA)	11.3	3,280	5,490	4,010	6,420	5,820
Belgium [3]	(NA)	6.0	(NA)	10.5	1,860	3,840	2,390	5,150	6,850
Canada.	7.6	7.2	0.2	14.0	(NA)	(NA)	(NA)	(NA)	12,350
Denmark	7.8	7.6	0.2	12.5	6,300	4,660	4,220	4,940	6,710
Finland	(NA)	8.3	(NA)	13.9	6,280	4,350	3,850	4,820	8,650
France [3]	6.2	5.5	0.4	10.6	2,580	4,380	2,900	5,430	5,760
Germany [4]	(NA)	4.1	(NA)	8.5	3,350	5,230	2,980	6,210	6,550
Ireland	6.0	5.6	0.4	13.7	1,750	2,240	1,770	2,770	7,270
Italy	(NA)	5.1	(NA)	9.5	3,280	4,470	4,050	4,700	5,850
Japan	4.8	3.6	1.1	11.3	3,020	3,710	3,530	3,900	7,140[5]
Netherlands [3]	5.8	5.6	(NA)	9.5	2,230	2,990	2,560	3,310	8,720
New Zealand	(NA)	6.5	(NA)	(NA)	1,900	2,340	2,030	2,620	6,080
Norway	(NA)	7.6	(NA)	14.0[6]	7,350	5,420	4,480	6,200	8,720
Spain [3]	5.8	4.6	0.7	10.4	2,090	2,500	2,030	2,790	3,770[7]
Sweden.	7.8	7.7	0.1	11.7	6,070	5,450	4,840	6,050	7,120
Switzerland	(NA)	5.7	(NA)	16.5	1,890	(NA)	3,560	(NA)	12,900
United Kingdom . . .	(NA)	5.2	(NA)	11.9	1,860	3,780	3,120	4,390	10,370[3]
United States	7.2	5.4	1.6	14.2	3,210	6,010	5,600	6,470	13,890[5]

NA Not available.　[1] Covers young children participating in a program intended to foster learning, and emotional and social development.　[2] Includes general, technical, or vocational education for students. It may either be "terminal" (i.e., preparing students for entry directly into working life) and/or "preparatory" (i.e., preparing students for higher education).　[3] Expenditures per student include government-dependent private schools.　[4] Data for former West Germany.　[5] Public and private schools.　[6] Direct expenditures only.　[7] Public schools only.

Source: Organization for Economic Cooperation and Development, Paris, France, *Eduation at a Glance*, annual, (copyright).

No. 1371. Ratio of Students to Teachers, by Country: 1992

[Public and private education. Educational program levels classified according to the International Standard Classification for Education developed by United Nations Educational, Scientific, and Cultural Organization]

COUNTRY	Early childhood education [1]	Primary	SECONDARY [2]		
			Total	Lower	Upper
Australia....................	(NA)	18.4	12.9	(NA)	(NA)
Austria.....................	18.3	12.2	9.4	7.7	11.6
Belgium....................	18.4	13.7	7.8	(NA)	(NA)
Denmark...................	10.7	10.9	9.7	9.1	10.4
Finland....................	12.5	19.0	(NA)	(NA)	(NA)
France.....................	26.0	20.4	14.3	(NA)	(NA)
Germany [3]...............	23.9	19.6	16.2	14.6	19.0
Ireland....................	27.2	25.6	17.1	(NA)	(NA)
Italy......................	13.3	10.9	8.9	9.0	8.8
Japan.....................	18.5	19.8	16.6	16.8	16.4
Netherlands...............	25.9	23.6	18.8	(NA)	(NA)
New Zealand..............	8.8	18.5	17.7	(NA)	(NA)
Spain.....................	23.4	21.2	16.6	17.6	15.9
Sweden...................	(NA)	11.9	13.0	10.6	16.0
Turkey....................	16.6	29.3	23.4	47.5	13.2
United Kingdom............	38.1	20.8	15.2	15.9	14.8
United States.............	**(NA)**	**(NA)**	**15.9**	**16.8**	**15.0**

NA Not available.   [1] Covers young children participating in a program intended to foster learning, and emotional and social development.   [2] Includes general, technical, or vocational education for students. It may either be "terminal" (i.e., preparing students for entry directly into working life) and/or "preparatory" (i.e., preparing students for higher education).   [3] Data for former West Germany.

Source: Organization for Economic Cooperation and Development, Paris, France, *Education at a Glance,* annual, (copyright).

No. 1372. Educational Attainment, by Country: 1992

[Percent of persons 25 to 64 years old]

COUNTRY	Total	Early childhood, primary, and lower secondary education only	Upper secondary education only	Nonuniversity tertiary education only	University education only
Australia....................	100	47	30	11	12
Austria.....................	100	32	61	([1])	[1]7
Belgium....................	100	55	25	11	9
Canada....................	100	29	30	26	15
Denmark...................	100	41	40	6	13
Finland....................	100	39	43	8	10
France.....................	100	48	36	6	10
Germany...................	100	18	60	10	12
Greece....................	100	66	21	3	10
Ireland....................	100	58	25	9	8
Italy......................	100	72	22	([1])	[1]6
Netherlands...............	100	42	37	([1])	[1]21
New Zealand..............	100	43	33	13	11
Norway....................	100	21	54	13	12
Portugal...................	100	86	7	2	5
Spain.....................	100	77	10	3	10
Sweden...................	100	30	46	12	12
Switzerland................	100	19	60	13	8
Turkey....................	100	86	9	([1])	[1]5
United Kingdom............	100	32	49	8	11
United States.............	**100**	**16**	**53**	**7**	**24**

[1] Nonuniversity tertiary education included in University education only.

Source: Organization for Economic Cooperation and Development, Paris, France, *Education at a Glance*, annual, (copyright).

No. 1373. Gross National Product, by Country: 1985 to 1993

[**In billions of dollars, except per capita.** For most countries, data for GNP are based on local currencies which are deflated to constant 1993 local currency values before conversion to U.S. dollar equivalents. In general, rates used for conversion are the 1993 average par/market exchange rates as supplied by the International Bank for Reconstruction and Development]

COUNTRY	CURRENT DOLLARS				CONSTANT (1993) DOLLARS				Per capita (dollars)		
	1985	1990	1992	1993	1985	1990	1992	1993	1985	1990	1993
United States	**4,054**	**5,568**	**6,026**	**6,348**	**5,304**	**6,071**	**6,157**	**6,348**	**22,240**	**24,290**	**24,580**
Algeria	34	41	44	45	45	45	45	45	2,033	1,776	1,646
Argentina	144	179	232	252	188	195	237	252	6,179	6,019	7,505
Australia	172	236	264	282	225	257	270	282	14,270	15,050	15,810
Austria	114	159	177	180	150	173	181	180	19,790	22,400	22,790
Bangladesh	14	20	23	24	18	22	23	24	175	190	200
Belgium	131	184	204	205	172	200	208	205	17,410	20,110	20,420
Brazil	352	474	511	553	461	517	522	553	3,367	3,444	3,528
Bulgaria	41	[1]45	32	32	54	[1]49	33	32	6,030	[1]5,508	3,573
Burma	35	37	43	(NA)	45	41	44	(NA)	1,218	991	(NA)
Canada	345	475	502	526	452	518	513	526	17,940	19,450	18,940
Chile	17	30	38	42	23	33	39	42	1,889	2,536	3,067
China	777	1,351	1,769	2,047	1,016	1,473	1,808	2,047	964	1,296	1,738
Colombia	25	38	43	47	33	41	44	47	1,118	1,245	1,339
Cuba [1]	30	34	24	21	39	37	24	21	3,830	3,459	1,959
Denmark	89	115	126	131	117	125	129	131	22,860	24,370	25,300
Egypt	24	33	38	39	31	36	39	39	633	647	651
El Salvador	5	6	7	8	6	7	7	8	1,242	1,236	1,342
Ethiopia	2	3	3	3	3	4	3	3	70	73	66
Finland	60	85	79	78	79	92	81	78	16,030	18,480	15,480
France	812	1,130	1,224	1,239	1,063	1,232	1,251	1,239	19,260	21,720	21,530
Germany [2]	1,003	1,404	1,704	1,698	1,312	1,531	1,741	1,698	21,500	24,260	21,020
Ghana	3	4	5	5	4	5	5	5	291	311	325
Greece	50	65	72	74	65	71	74	74	6,550	6,975	7,021
Hungary	53	[1]63	64	64	69	[1]68	65	64	6,460	[1]6,585	6,233
India	133	215	242	255	174	234	248	255	226	275	282
Indonesia	62	102	124	136	82	112	127	136	475	594	689
Iran	85	106	133	138	111	115	136	138	2,400	2,022	2,229
Iraq [1]	31	24	16	(NA)	41	26	16	(NA)	2,617	1,400	(NA)
Israel	35	52	65	69	46	57	66	69	11,580	13,230	14,020
Italy	639	885	957	975	836	965	978	975	14,620	16,730	16,800
Japan	2,459	3,688	4,160	4,260	3,217	4,021	4,250	4,260	26,640	32,550	34,160
Kenya	3	5	5	5	4	5	5	5	198	214	189
Korea, North [1]	26	30	22	(NA)	34	32	22	(NA)	1,756	1,513	(NA)
Korea, South	126	249	305	329	165	272	311	329	4,040	6,285	7,368
Kuwait [3]	26	25	23	27	34	27	24	27	19,840	12,640	15,640
Madagascar	2	3	3	3	3	3	3	3	287	280	249
Malaysia	26	45	55	61	34	49	56	61	2,172	2,767	3,255
Mexico	218	285	325	333	285	311	332	333	3,720	3,651	3,679
Morocco	16	23	25	26	20	26	26	26	882	976	939
Mozambique	1	1	1	1	[1]1	1	1	1	[1]61	70	74
Nepal	2	2	3	3	2	3	3	3	122	136	139
Netherlands	189	264	291	299	248	288	298	299	17,100	19,240	19,570
Nigeria	16	25	30	32	21	28	31	32	277	318	340
Norway	66	86	96	103	87	94	98	103	20,940	22,080	23,900
Pakistan	25	39	46	48	33	43	47	48	331	372	386
Peru	30	34	36	39	39	37	37	39	1,976	1,670	1,699
Philippines	31	49	53	55	41	53	54	55	710	818	791
Poland	144	[1]163	181	193	189	[1]178	185	193	5,077	[1]4,672	5,000
Portugal	42	66	73	74	55	72	75	74	5,418	6,991	7,071
Romania	99	[1]105	64	66	130	[1]114	66	66	5,721	[1]4,933	2,858
Saudi Arabia	93	111	127	130	122	121	130	130	9,025	7,452	7,359
South Africa	78	100	105	109	101	109	107	109	2,927	2,767	2,540
Spain	285	427	467	472	373	465	477	472	9,688	11,940	12,030
Sri Lanka	6	8	9	10	7	9	10	10	465	512	578
Sudan	3	4	5	[1]6	4	5	5	[1]6	175	174	[1]196
Sweden	131	175	180	179	171	191	184	179	20,480	22,270	20,550
Switzerland	166	226	240	244	217	246	245	244	33,240	36,290	34,940
Syria	25	30	(NA)	(NA)	33	33	(NA)	(NA)	3,090	2,587	(NA)
Taiwan	91	168	204	221	120	183	208	221	6,181	8,954	10,460
Tanzania	1	2	2	2	2	2	2	2	78	85	86
Thailand	45	89	110	122	59	97	112	122	1,136	1,731	2,077
Turkey	61	98	112	123	80	107	114	123	1,562	1,866	2,014
Uganda	2	3	4	4	3	3	4	4	188	205	214
United Kingdom	617	861	902	938	807	938	922	938	14,250	16,340	16,180
Venezuela	33	45	57	57	43	49	58	57	2,603	2,625	2,852
Zaire	6	8	(NA)	(NA)	8	9	(NA)	(NA)	259	235	(NA)

NA Not available.   [1] Estimated.   [2] Prior to 1992, data are for former West Germany.   [3] Constant dollars are estimated.

Source: U.S. Arms Control and Disarmament Agency, *World Military Expenditures and Arms Transfers,* annual. Data from International Bank for Reconstruction and Development and U.S. Central Intelligence Agency.

No. 1374. Gross Domestic Product, by Country: 1980 to 1993

COUNTRY	PURCHASING POWER PARITY BASIS [1]												CONSTANT (1990) PRICE LEVELS AND EXCHANGE RATES [2]								
	Amount (bil. dol.)						Per capita (dollars)						Amount (bil. dol.)						Annual growth rate [3] (percent)		
	1980	1985	1990	1991	1992	1993	1980	1985	1990	1991	1992	1993	1980	1985	1990	1991	1992	1993	1991	1992	1993
OECD, total [4]	7,341	10,738	14,989	15,680	16,766	17,239	8,464	11,888	15,946	16,537	17,526	17,889	12,718	14,289	16,754	16,948	17,209	17,398	1.2	1.5	1.1
OECD Europe	3,062	4,318	6,065	6,367	6,857	6,889	7,455	10,274	14,035	14,639	15,662	15,646	5,669	6,128	7,182	7,288	7,367	7,348	1.5	1.1	-0.3
European Community [4]	2,666	3,731	5,232	5,508	5,950	5,939	7,969	11,040	15,248	15,974	17,175	17,089	4,891	5,257	6,170	6,281	6,353	6,328	1.8	1.1	-0.4
Australia	127	194	272	278	285	302	8,665	12,284	15,946	16,085	16,281	17,103	214	251	295	290	298	309	-1.4	2.6	3.8
Austria	67	93	128	136	148	153	8,850	12,278	16,623	17,342	18,744	19,128	128	137	158	163	166	166	2.9	1.9	-0.1
Belgium	87	118	163	172	190	195	8,827	11,943	16,333	17,160	18,889	19,517	159	166	192	197	200	197	2.3	1.9	-1.7
Canada	246	370	509	517	531	554	10,020	14,262	18,304	18,395	18,657	19,278	427	493	568	557	561	574	-1.9	0.7	2.3
Denmark	45	67	85	90	94	100	8,746	12,997	16,548	17,439	18,245	19,335	106	120	129	130	132	134	-1.0	1.3	1.4
Finland	38	57	81	78	76	79	8,004	11,682	16,193	15,460	15,018	15,530	99	114	135	125	121	118	-7.1	-3.6	-2.0
France	507	712	984	1,036	1,101	1,079	9,414	12,872	17,347	18,156	19,189	18,709	957	1,031	1,195	1,203	1,217	1,205	0.6	1.2	-1.0
Germany	646	889	1,252	1,359	1,503	1,503	8,249	11,458	15,779	16,993	18,649	18,510	1,296	1,372	1,618	1,700	1,737	1,718	5.0	2.2	-1.1
Greece	42	58	75	79	88	91	4,325	5,838	7,424	7,764	8,556	8,797	58	61	67	69	69	69	3.3	0.9	-0.5
Iceland	2	3	4	5	5	5	9,496	13,105	17,267	17,916	18,643	19,212	5	5	6	6	6	6	1.3	-3.2	0.8
Ireland	18	26	39	42	48	49	5,172	7,333	11,206	11,966	13,379	13,856	31	35	45	46	48	50	2.9	5.0	4.0
Italy	478	666	923	974	1,041	1,018	8,464	11,756	16,274	17,167	18,310	17,830	880	943	1,095	1,108	1,117	1,109	1.2	0.7	-0.7
Japan	936	1,463	2,174	2,348	2,503	2,559	8,011	12,112	17,596	18,951	20,131	20,523	1,960	2,354	2,932	3,057	3,092	3,094	4.3	1.1	0.1
Luxembourg	4	6	9	10	11	11	11,074	16,179	23,398	24,695	27,048	28,368	7	8	11	11	11	11	3.0	1.8	0.4
Mexico	237	340	435	467	604	621	3,406	4,361	5,044	5,312	6,747	6,808	207	228	244	253	260	262	3.6	2.8	0.6
Netherlands	126	172	239	248	266	269	8,881	11,861	15,950	16,427	17,531	17,593	232	244	284	290	294	295	2.3	1.3	0.4
New Zealand	24	37	45	47	50	54	7,726	11,206	13,514	13,642	14,470	15,493	36	42	44	43	44	47	-1.4	3.0	5.3
Norway	34	53	68	72	80	84	8,391	12,669	16,006	16,765	18,551	19,476	83	98	106	107	111	114	1.6	3.4	3.3
Portugal	44	60	93	103	113	118	4,550	6,100	9,363	10,404	11,499	11,953	50	52	67	69	69	69	2.1	1.1	-1.2
Spain	219	308	458	496	519	521	5,868	8,000	11,755	12,705	13,278	13,311	366	395	492	503	506	501	2.2	0.7	-1.1
Sweden	77	109	146	145	149	147	9,250	13,057	17,004	16,839	17,139	16,831	188	205	230	227	224	218	-1.1	-1.4	-2.6
Switzerland	75	104	143	148	158	161	11,720	15,969	21,283	21,758	22,999	23,195	184	197	226	226	225	223	(Z)	-0.3	-0.9
Turkey	102	169	264	276	293	322	2,284	3,327	4,660	4,811	5,410	5,410	91	115	151	152	161	173	0.9	6.0	7.5
United Kingdom	451	649	912	901	976	985	8,011	11,462	15,888	15,580	16,824	17,036	749	828	976	956	951	971	-2.0	-0.5	2.0
United States	2,708	4,017	5,490	5,656	5,937	6,260	11,891	16,786	21,965	22,385	23,228	24,302	4,205	4,793	5,490	5,459	5,587	5,765	-0.6	2.3	3.2

[1] The goods and services produced in different countries should be valued consistently if the differences observed are meant to reflect real differences in the volumes of goods and services produced. The use of purchasing power parities (PPP) instead of exchange rates is intended to achieve this objective. PPP's show how many units of currency are needed in one country to buy the same amount of goods and services which one unit of currency will buy in the other country. See text, section 30. [2] Based on constant (1990) price data converted to U.S. dollars using 1990 exchange rates. [3] Percent change from immediate prior year. Minus sign (-) indicates decrease. [4] For countries, see text, section 30.

Source: Organization for Economic Cooperation and Development, Paris, France, *National Accounts of OECD Countries*, vol. I, annual.

No. 1375. Selected International Economic Indicators, by Country: 1980 to 1994

[Data cover gross domestic product (GDP) at market prices. Gross fixed capital formation covers private and government sectors except military. Savings data are calculated by deducting outlays—such as personal consumption expenditures, interest paid, and transfer payments to foreigners—from disposable personal income]

YEAR	United States	France	Germany	Italy	Nether-lands	United Kingdom	Japan	Canada
Ratio of gross fixed capital formation to GDP (current prices):								
1980	20.4	23.0	(NA)	24.3	21.6	17.9	31.6	23.3
1990	16.8	21.4	(NA)	20.3	20.9	19.5	32.2	21.1
1991	15.4	21.2	23.0	19.7	20.4	17.0	31.8	19.7
1992	15.3	20.0	23.2	19.1	20.3	15.7	30.7	18.6
1993	15.9	18.6	22.2	17.1	19.7	15.0	29.8	17.8
1994	16.8	18.1	22.4	(NA)	(NA)	14.8	28.6	18.2
Ratio of savings to disposable personal income:								
1980	7.9	17.6	(NA)	21.6	11.0	13.4	17.9	13.3
1990	4.2	12.5	(NA)	19.4	15.8	8.4	14.1	9.5
1991	5.0	13.2	12.7	19.5	12.7	10.5	15.1	9.5
1992	5.5	13.7	12.9	19.1	13.0	12.8	14.3	9.6
1993	4.1	13.8	12.3	16.8	12.3	11.7	14.6	9.1
1994	4.1	13.4	11.0	(NA)	(NA)	10.4	(NA)	7.6

NA Not available.

Source: U.S. Dept. of Commerce, International Trade Administration, Office of Trade and Economic Analysis, based on official statistics of listed countries.

No. 1376. Percent of Households Owning Selected Appliances, by Country: 1991

APPLIANCE	United States [1,2]	Bel-gium	Den-mark	France	Ger-many [3]	Italy	Nether-lands	Spain	Sweden	Swit-zerland	United King-dom
Cassette recorder	(NA)	75	82	76	74	64	81	67	88	82	[4]88
Clothes washer	75	88	[2]74	88	88	96	89	87	72	78	87
Dishwasher	44	26	[2]36	33	34	18	11	11	31	32	11
Food processor	(NA)	91	83	83	92	48	84	50	77	91	80
Microwave oven	81	21	[2]31	25	36	6	22	9	37	15	48
Radio	(NA)	90	98	98	84	92	99	95	93	99	90
Television set, color/mono	95	97	98	94	97	98	95	98	97	93	[4]98
Tumbledrier	69	39	[2]30	12	17	10	27	5	18	27	32
Vacuum cleaner	(NA)	92	96	89	96	56	98	29	97	93	98
Video recorder	(NA)	42	[2]63	35	42	25	50	40	48	41	[4]69

NA Not available. [1] Represents appliances possessed and generally used by the household (as of November). Source: U.S. Energy Information Administration, *Annual Energy Review*. [2] 1993 data. [3] Former West Germany. [4] 1992 data.

Source: Except as noted, Euromonitor Publications Limited, London, England, *European Marketing Data and Statistics*, annual, (copyright).

No. 1377. Motor Vehicle Registrations, by Country: 1992

COUNTRY	All vehicles Number (mil.)	All vehicles Persons per vehicle	Passenger cars Number (mil.)	Passenger cars Persons per car	COUNTRY	All vehicles Number (mil.)	All vehicles Persons per vehicle	Passenger cars Number (mil.)	Passenger cars Persons per car
Argentina	6.0	6	4.4	7	Israel	1.1	4	0.9	5
Australia	10.0	2	7.9	2	Italy	32.3	2	29.5	2
Austria	4.0	2	3.2	2	Japan	61.7	2	39.0	3
Belgium	4.5	2	4.0	3	Kuwait	0.4	3	0.3	4
Bulgaria	1.5	6	1.4	7	Netherlands	6.3	2	5.7	3
Canada	17.0	2	13.3	2	New Zealand	1.9	2	1.6	2
Chile	1.2	11	1.0	13	Norway	2.0	2	1.6	3
Costa Rica	0.3	12	0.1	22	Panama	0.2	11	0.2	17
Denmark	1.9	3	1.6	3	Paraguay	0.1	41	0.1	62
Dominican					Poland	7.9	5	6.5	6
Republic	0.3	29	0.2	50	Portugal	2.7	4	2.0	5
Ecuador	0.3	41	0.1	113	Puerto Rico	1.6	2	1.4	3
Finland	2.2	2	2.0	3	Singapore	0.4	7	0.3	10
France	29.1	2	24.0	2	Sweden	3.9	2	3.6	2
Germany	42.0	2	39.1	2	Switzerland	3.4	2	3.1	2
Greece	2.6	4	1.8	6	Syria	0.3	51	0.1	117
Hong Kong	0.5	13	0.3	21	Thailand	3.0	19	0.9	65
Hungary	2.3	4	2.1	5	United States	190.4	1	144.2	2
Ireland	1.0	4	0.9	4	Uruguay	0.4	9	0.2	14

Source: American Automobile Manufactures Association, *AAMA Motor Vehicle Facts & Figures*, annual, (copyright).

No. 1378. Food and Beverage Expenditures, by Country

[Percent of total private consumption expenditures]

COUNTRY	Year	Food [1]	Alcoholic beverages	COUNTRY	Year	Food [1]	Alcoholic beverages
United States	**1991**	**8.3**	**1.3**	Israel	1991	21.3	0.7
				Netherlands.	1991	11.7	1.5
Austria	1991	16.8	2.1	Norway.	1991	19.0	3.2
Belgium	1991	15.2	1.3	Philippines.	1991	52.6	(NA)
Canada.	1991	10.8	2.8	Portugal	1990	26.3	1.5
Colombia.	1990	27.3	4.1	Singapore	1991	17.5	1.9
Denmark.	1991	15.5	3.2	South Africa.	1991	27.9	6.1
Finland	1991	15.4	4.4	Spain	1991	20.1	1.2
France	1991	16.3	1.9	Sweden	1991	15.3	3.0
Germany.	1991	[2]19.1	(NA)	Switzerland	1990	19.4	(NA)
Greece	1991	33.4	3.1	Thailand	1991	23.0	4.1
India.	1990	53.1	0.8	United Kingdom . . .	1991	11.5	6.6
Ireland	1990	20.5	11.6	Venezuela.	1991	34.3	1.9

NA Not available.   [1] Includes nonalcoholic beverages.   [2] Includes all beverages.

Source: U.S. Dept. of Agriculture, Economic Research Service. Based on data from the United Nations, New York, NY, *National Accounts Statistics,* annual.

No. 1379. Time Spent to Earn the Retail Value of Selected Food Items, by Country: 1993

[**Except as noted, in hours and minutes per pound** (e.g., residents of metropolitan Washington DC had to work an average of 2 hours and 35 minutes to buy the selection of items in the market basket.) The data represent a ratio of a country's average wages to the retail cost of a market basket of food in the capital. The extent to which a country taxes wages and supplements personal income also affects the affordability of food. Wages are an average across industries in each country and are used as proxies for wages in the capital. Wage data for most countries are from the International Monetary Fund and the International Labor Organization]

ITEM IN MARKET BASKET	Bonn, Germany	Brasilia, Brazil	London, United Kingdom	Mexico City, Mexico	Ottawa, Canada	Paris, France	Pretoria, South Africa	Rome, Italy	Tokyo, Japan	Metro. Washington, DC, U.S.A.
Total	**2:42**	**12:37**	**3:52**	**7:19**	**2:31**	**5:20**	**7:53**	**4:42**	**4:57**	**2:35**
Sirloin steak, boneless. .	0:27	1:04	0:37	0:53	0:19	0:51	0:43	0:42	1:14	0:21
Pork roast, boneless . . .	0:14	1:16	0:25	0:55	0:15	0:30	0:26	0:24	0:21	0:24
Broilers, whole	0:05	0:29	0:08	0:17	0:05	0:23	0:17	0:14	0:09	0:04
Large eggs, dozen	0:05	0:30	0:13	0:19	0:05	0:14	0:18	0:14	0:05	0:05
Butter.	0:09	0:47	0:11	0:27	0:12	0:18	0:31	0:21	0:14	0:09
Cheddar cheese, Emmenthaler	0:18	1:08	0:18	0:57	0:23	0:23	0:43	0:27	0:22	0:18
Whole milk (quart).	0:03	0:31	0:05	0:10	0:06	0:08	0:14	0:08	0:05	0:04
Cooking oil (quart)	0:05	0:39	0:10	0:17	0:10	0:19	0:27	0:08	0:09	0:07
Potatoes	0:02	0:32	0:04	0:23	0:03	0:07	0:11	0:05	0:08	0:04
Apples	0:07	1:21	0:11	0:23	0:08	0:10	0:22	0:10	0:10	0:08
Oranges	0:08	0:12	0:12	0:11	0:08	0:12	0:09	0:13	0:12	0:07
Flour	0:02	0:25	0:05	0:09	0:04	0:10	0:14	0:04	0:05	0:03
Rice.	0:11	0:28	0:10	0:18	0:08	0:18	0:20	0:15	0:09	0:06
Sugar	0:05	0:24	0:06	0:11	0:02	0:11	0:13	0:08	0:06	0:05
Coffee	0:40	2:49	0:58	1:27	0:24	1:07	2:45	1:09	1:28	0:30

Source: U.S. Dept. of Agriculture, Economic Research Service, *Food Review,* September-December 1994.

No. 1380. Per Capita Consumption of Meat and Poultry: 1994

[**Preliminary. In pounds per capita.** Beef, veal, and pork quantities are as of September and in carcass-weight equivalents; poultry quantities are as of July and are on ready-to-cook basis]

COUNTRY	PORK Quantity	PORK Rank	COUNTRY	POULTRY Quantity	POULTRY Rank	COUNTRY	BEEF AND VEAL Quantity	BEEF AND VEAL Rank
Denmark.	147	1	Israel	98	1	Uruguay	189	1
Spain.	118	2	**United States . . . .**	**92**	**2**	Argentina	144	2
Belgium-Luxembourg	116	3	Hong Kong	90	3	**United States . . . .**	**98**	**3**
Austria	113	4	Singapore	85	4	Australia	82	4
Germany	107	5	Canada.	69	5	Canada.	78	5
Netherlands	103	6	Saudi Arabia	67	6	New Zealand	64	6
Taiwan	89	7	Taiwan	61	7	France	61	7
Switzerland	86	8	Australia	59	8	Italy	58	8
France	85	9	Spain	53	9	Brazil	56	9
Singapore	84	10	United Kingdom . . .	51	10	Kazakhstan	54	10
United States	**68**	**18**						

Source: U.S. Department of Agriculture, Foreign Agricultural Service, *World Poultry Situation* and *World Livestock Situation,* annual.

No. 1381. Telephones, Newspapers, Television, and Radio, by Country

[See text, section 30, for general comments about the data. For data qualifications for countries, see source]

COUNTRY	Telephone main lines per 100 people, [1] 1994	Cellular telephone subscribers per 100,000 people, [1] 1992	Daily newspaper circulation per 1,000 people, [2] 1990	Television receivers per 1,000 people, [3] 1991	Radio receivers per 1,000 people, [4] 1991
Algeria	4	18	51	74	234
Argentina	14	136	124	220	676
Australia	50	2,510	246	480	1,268
Austria	47	2,188	351	478	617
Belgium	45	615	301	451	769
Brazil	7	20	54	207	386
Bulgaria	34	-	452	252	442
Canada	58	3,727	[5]228	639	1,029
Chile	11	474	455	209	344
China	2	15	[6]37	31	182
Colombia	9	25	62	116	177
Costa Rica	13	-	[7]101	140	258
Cuba	3	2	172	163	345
Cyprus	45	1,353	110	144	292
Czech Republic	21	(NA)	(NA)	(NA)	(NA)
Denmark	60	3,993	352	536	1,031
Dominican Republic	8	94	32	84	171
Ecuador	5	-	87	84	317
Egypt	4	13	57	116	326
Finland	55	7,028	558	501	997
France	55	568	208	407	888
Germany	48	958	593	556	876
Greece	48	-	[8]139	197	421
Guatemala	2	(NA)	21	52	66
Honduras	2	-	39	73	386
Hong Kong	54	4,023	110	278	667
Hungary	17	226	233	412	596
Iceland	56	5,866	[6]467	319	786
India	1	-	[6]26	35	79
Indonesia	1	19	28	59	146
Iran	7	-	26	63	231
Iraq	3	-	36	72	215
Ireland	33	1,239	169	301	630
Israel	37	696	258	269	470
Italy	43	1,355	108	421	791
Jamaica	10	320	64	131	420
Japan	48	1,260	587	613	907
Korea, South	40	623	277	208	1,001
Kuwait	23	2,589	210	283	343
Lebanon	9	134	117	325	833
Luxembourg	54	287	383	267	632
Malaysia	15	442	140	149	430
Mexico	9	298	133	148	255
Morocco	4	12	13	74	210
Netherlands	51	1,097	[5]647	485	907
New Zealand	47	2,938	324	443	929
Norway	55	6,527	610	423	794
Pakistan	1	12	15	18	90
Panama	11	-	70	166	224
Paraguay	3	33	39	50	171
Peru	4	121	79	98	253
Philippines	2	17	54	44	138
Poland	13	7	128	295	433
Portugal	35	378	39	187	228
Puerto Rico	33	1,428	129	264	710
Russia	16	4	(NA)	(NA)	(NA)
Romania	12	-	[5]158	196	199
Saudi Arabia	10	99	40	266	304
Singapore	47	4,270	282	378	646
South Africa	9	31	35	98	302
Spain	37	461	[8]82	400	310
Sweden	68	7,558	525	468	877
Switzerland	60	3,231	456	406	842
Syria	5	-	23	60	255
Taiwan	40	1,850	[9]174	(NA)	(NA)
Thailand	4	431	73	114	191
Trinidad and Tobago	16	101	77	315	492
Tunisia	5	22	37	79	199
Turkey	20	104	71	175	161
United Kingdom	47	2,595	[8]394	434	1,143
United States	**59**	**4,326**	**249**	**814**	**2,118**
Uruguay	17	55	233	231	604
Venezuela	11	101	145	162	447

- Represents or rounds to zero.   NA Not available.   [1] As of December 31.   [2] Publications containing general news and appearing at least 4 times a week; may range in size from a single sheet to 50 or more pages. Circulation data refer to average circulation per issue or number of printed copies per issue and include copies sold outside the country.   [3] Estimated number of sets in use.   [4] Data cover estimated number of receivers in use and apply to all types of receivers for radio broadcasts to the public, including receivers connected to a radio "redistribution system" but excluding television sets.   [5] For 1989.   [6] For 1985.   [7] For 1991.   [8] For 1988.   [9] Source: U.S. Bureau of the Census. Data from Republic of China publications.

Source: Except as noted, International Telecommunications Union, Geneva, Switzerland, *World Telecom Indicators,* (copyright); and United Nations Educational, Scientific, and Cultural Organization, Paris, France, *Statistical Yearbook,* (copyright).

No. 1382. Tax Revenues, by Country: 1980 to 1992

[Covers national and local taxes and Social Security contributions]

COUNTRY	TAX REVENUES, 1992		PERCENT CHANGE IN TOTAL TAX REVENUE AS EXPRESSED IN NATIONAL CURRENCY [1]					TAX REVENUES AS PERCENT OF GROSS DOMESTIC PRODUCT				
	Total (bil. dol.)	Per capita (dol.)	1988	1989	1990	1991	1992	1980	1985	1990	1991	1992
Australia	84.9	4,845	12.1	8.8	3.0	−3.4	2.8	28.4	30.1	30.6	28.9	28.5
Austria	80.6	10,224	4.9	4.3	8.4	8.5	9.8	41.2	43.1	41.3	42.0	43.5
Belgium	99.4	9,910	3.5	4.6	7.2	4.6	6.0	44.4	47.9	44.9	44.9	45.4
Canada	209.2	7,623	7.0	9.9	5.2	3.6	0.5	31.6	33.1	36.3	37.0	36.5
Denmark	69.8	13,498	4.8	2.8	0.2	3.8	4.2	45.5	49.0	48.7	48.9	49.3
Finland	49.9	9,889	20.9	12.4	10.7	−1.7	−2.9	36.9	40.8	45.4	46.9	47.0
France	576.9	10,056	6.0	7.1	5.7	4.6	2.6	41.7	44.5	43.7	44.0	43.6
Germany [2]	766.8	11,825	4.5	7.7	4.5	22.4	10.0	38.2	38.1	36.8	38.6	39.6
Greece	31.5	3,060	13.4	15.0	28.9	25.7	21.8	29.4	35.1	37.2	38.5	40.5
Iceland	2.2	8,520	34.1	23.6	14.3	8.9	2.7	30.2	28.6	32.3	32.4	33.4
Ireland	18.5	5,204	12.3	1.7	6.3	5.6	7.3	33.8	36.4	35.5	36.2	36.6
Italy	518.0	8,947	12.9	12.8	13.6	10.4	12.6	30.2	34.5	39.1	39.7	42.4
Japan	1,081.0	8,694	8.6	8.4	9.9	3.4	−2.6	25.4	27.6	31.4	30.8	29.4
Luxembourg	5.1	13,088	8.0	10.4	7.7	5.4	6.1	46.0	50.1	48.8	48.5	48.4
Netherlands	150.3	9,900	4.2	−0.2	5.9	11.1	3.2	44.7	44.1	44.6	47.2	46.9
New Zealand	14.9	4,358	6.0	14.2	−1.1	−3.6	5.0	32.9	33.5	37.2	36.0	35.9
Norway	52.6	12,278	3.6	2.5	7.1	5.7	1.2	47.1	47.6	46.3	47.1	46.6
Portugal	31.7	3,219	27.7	20.7	18.7	19.3	20.5	28.7	31.6	30.7	31.4	33.0
Spain	205.9	5,268	11.8	18.5	10.7	10.6	10.5	24.1	28.8	34.4	34.8	35.8
Sweden	123.5	14,234	7.7	12.0	10.6	0.8	−5.6	48.8	50.0	55.6	52.7	50.0
Switzerland	77.2	11,175	7.1	5.4	7.3	4.4	5.1	30.8	32.0	31.5	31.2	32.0
Turkey	35.7	607	63.6	84.6	85.4	68.0	85.4	18.1	15.3	20.1	21.4	23.1
United Kingdom . .	368.5	6,371	11.1	8.0	7.4	2.3	1.0	35.3	37.9	36.9	36.2	35.2
United States . . .	**1,723.2**	**6,757**	**6.7**	**8.2**	**5.0**	**3.6**	**4.1**	**29.3**	**28.7**	**29.4**	**29.5**	**29.4**

[1] Change from previous year.   [2] Prior to 1991, data are for former West Germany.

Source: Organization for Economic Cooperation and Development, Paris, France, *Revenue Statistics of OECD Member Countries,* annual.

No. 1383. Percent Distribution of Tax Receipts, by Country: 1980 to 1992

COUNTRY	Total [1]	INCOME AND PROFITS TAXES [2]			SOCIAL SECURITY CONTRIBUTIONS			TAXES ON GOODS AND SERVICES [5]		
		Total [3]	Individual	Corporate	Total [4]	Employees	Employers	Total [3]	General consumption taxes [6]	Taxes on specific goods, services [7]
United States: 1980	100.0	47.0	36.9	10.2	26.2	10.0	15.5	16.6	6.6	7.8
1990	100.0	43.2	35.8	7.4	29.5	11.6	16.6	16.5	7.6	6.8
1992	100.0	41.5	34.3	7.2	29.9	11.8	16.8	17.1	7.6	7.4
Canada: 1980	100.0	46.6	34.1	11.6	10.5	3.7	6.6	32.6	11.5	13.0
1990	100.0	48.8	41.1	7.2	14.4	4.4	9.7	26.0	14.5	9.6
1992	100.0	45.0	39.6	4.8	16.5	5.3	10.9	26,1	14.3	10.0
France: 1980	100.0	18.1	12.9	5.1	42.7	11.1	28.4	30.4	21.1	8.4
1990	100.0	17.2	11.8	5.3	44.1	13.2	27.2	28.4	18.8	8.7
1992	100.0	17.3	13.8	3.5	44.6	13.4	27.5	26.8	17.6	8.2
Germany [8]: 1980	100.0	35.1	29.6	5.5	34.3	15.3	18.4	27.1	16.6	9.3
1990	100.0	32.4	27.6	4.8	37.5	16.2	19.1	26.7	16.6	9.2
1992	100.0	32.0	28.0	4.0	38.4	16.9	19.5	26.9	16.5	9.3
Italy: 1980	100.0	31.1	23.1	7.8	38.0	6.9	28.4	26.5	15.6	9.7
1990	100.0	36.5	26.3	10.0	32.9	6.3	23.6	28.0	14.7	10.6
1992	100.0	39.1	27.2	11.6	31.3	6.2	21.8	26.9	13.2	10.7
Japan: 1980	100.0	46.1	24.3	21.8	29.1	10.2	14.8	16.3	-	14.1
1990	100.0	48.3	26.8	21.5	29.2	10.9	15.2	13.2	4.2	7.3
1992	100.0	42.4	25.3	17.1	32.8	12.7	16.8	14.0	4.8	7.5
Netherlands: 1980	100.0	32.8	26.3	6.6	38.1	15.7	17.8	25.2	15.8	7.3
1990	100.0	32.2	24.7	7.5	37.4	23.1	7.5	26.4	16.5	7.5
1992	100.0	31.4	24.8	6.6	38.8	24.5	7.3	25.8	15.4	8.1
Sweden: 1980	100.0	43.5	41.0	2.5	28.8	0.1	27.6	24.0	13.4	9.2
1990	100.0	41.6	38.5	3.1	27.2	0.1	26.0	25.0	14.9	9.2
1992	100.0	38.5	36.0	2.4	28.8	0.2	27.7	26.5	15.9	9.6
United Kingdom: 1980	100.0	38.2	29.8	8.3	16.6	6.7	9.5	29.2	14.4	13.1
1990	100.0	39.5	28.6	10.9	17.1	6.5	9.9	30.5	16.5	12.6
1992	100.0	36.1	28.4	7.6	17.8	6.7	10.5	34.4	19.7	13.3

- Represents zero.   [1] Includes property taxes, employer payroll taxes other than Social Security contributions, and miscellaneous taxes, not shown separately.   [2] Includes taxes on capital gains.   [3] Includes other taxes not shown separately. [4] Includes contributions of self-employed not shown separately.   [5] Taxes on the production, sales, transfer, leasing, and delivery of goods and services and rendering of services.   [6] Primary value-added and sales taxes.   [7] For example, excise taxes on alcohol, tobacco, and gasoline.   [8] Prior to 1990, data are for former West Germany.

Source: Organization for Economic Cooperation and Development, Paris, France, *Revenue Statistics of OECD Member Countries,* annual.

No. 1384. Employee-Employer Payroll Tax Rates for Social Security Programs, by Country: 1981 to 1993

[In percent. Covers old-age, disability and survivors insurance, public health or sickness insurance, workers' compensation, unemployment insurance, and family allowance programs]

COUNTRY	ALL SOCIAL SECURITY PROGRAMS					OLD-AGE, DISABILITY, SURVIVORS INSURANCE				
	1981	1991	1993			1981	1991	1993		
			Total	Employer	Employee			Total	Employer	Employee
United States . . .	**17.60**	**20.50**	**20.50**	**12.85**	**7.65**	**10.70**	**12.40**	**12.40**	**6.20**	**6.20**
Austria	35.80	[1]39.40	[1]41.00	24.55	16.45	21.10	22.80	22.80	12.55	10.25
Belgium	34.70	39.33	39.33	[2]26.86	13.07	15.11	16.36	16.36	8.85	7.50
Canada.	[3]7.92	[3]10.00	[3]13.70	8.20	5.50	3.60	4.60	5.00	2.50	2.50
France	47.55	54.41	49.88	31.61	[4]18.27	13.00	17.00	17.25	8.20	[4]9.05
Germany [5]	34.80	36.16	38.19	19.79	18.40	18.50	17.70	17.50	8.75	8.75
Ireland	14.95	21.70	21.20	13.45	[6]7.75	12.00	18.70	18.70	12.20	[6]6.50
Italy	54.30	55.72	55.59	[7]46.45	9.14	24.46	27.42	28.27	[7]20.13	8.14
Japan.	21.41	[8]24.86	[8]24.62	13.39	11.23	10.60	14.50	14.50	7.25	7.25
Luxembourg . . .	34.25	[1]31.78	[1]32.20	[2]14.70	17.50	16.00	16.00	16.00	8.00	8.00
Netherlands.	54.85	43.73	46.50	12.94	[9]33.56	32.45	20.25	21.82	-	[9]21.82
Sweden	32.65	34.11	32.31	31.36	0.95	21.15	20.95	19.89	19.89	-
Switzerland	11.90	12.00	12.69	6.89	5.80	9.40	9.60	9.60	4.80	4.80
United Kingdom . .	21.45	21.45	21.40	[10]10.40	[11]11.00	(NA)	(NA)	(NA)	(NA)	(NA)

- Represents zero. NA Not available. [1] Sickness and maternity refers to wage earners. [2] Work-injury refers to wage earners. [3] Excludes work-injury. [4] Includes 2.4 percent employee tax on all sources of income. [5] Prior to 1991, data are for former West Germany. [6] Includes 1 percent tax to finance employment training for youth. [7] OASDI, work injury, and unemployment refers to industrial workers. [8] OASDI rate refers to male employees and contributions for employee pension insurance only. [9] The employed persons' Supplementary Disability Pension Program has been adjusted downward to avoid the distortions that would otherwise occur from taxing only a very narrow band of earnings. [10] 4.6 to 10.4 percent. Covers all programs. [11] 2 percent on first 46 pounds per week plus 9 percent of earnings between 46 and 350 pounds. Covers all programs.

Source: U.S. Social Security Administration, Office of Research and Statistics, *Social Security Programs Throughout the World*, biennial.

No. 1385. Annual Percent Change in Consumer Prices, by Country: 1990 to 1994

[Change from previous year. See text, section 30, for general comments concerning the data. For additional qualifications of the data for individual countries, see source. Minus sign (-) indicates decrease]

COUNTRY	1990	1991	1992	1993	1994	COUNTRY	1990	1991	1992	1993	1994
United States . .	**5**	**4**	**3**	**3**	**3**	Italy	6	6	5	5	(NA)
Argentina	2,314	172	25	11	4	Japan.	3	3	2	1	1
Australia	7	3	1	2	2	Korea, South. . .	9	9	6	5	6
Austria	3	3	4	4	3	Mexico.	27	23	16	10	7
Belgium	3	3	2	3	2	Netherlands . . .	3	3	3	3	3
Brazil.	2,938	441	1,009	2,148	2,669	Norway.	4	3	2	2	1
Canada	5	6	2	2	-	Peru	7,482	410	74	49	24
Chile	26	22	15	13	11	Philippines	14	19	9	8	9
France	3	3	2	2	2	Portugal	13	11	9	7	5
Germany [1]	3	4	4	4	3	South Africa . . .	14	15	14	10	9
Greece.	20	20	16	14	11	Spain.	7	6	6	5	5
Guatemala	41	33	10	12	(NA)	Sweden	11	9	2	5	2
India	9	14	12	6	10	Switzerland	5	6	4	3	1
Indonesia	8	9	8	9	9	Turkey	60	66	70	66	106
Iran	8	17	26	21	32	United Kingdom .	10	6	4	2	3
Israel	17	19	12	11	12	Venezuela.	41	34	31	38	61

- Represents zero. NA Not available. [1] Prior to July 1990, data for former West Germany.

Source: International Monetary Fund, Washington, DC, *International Financial Statistics*, monthly.

No. 1386. Civilian Employment-Population Ratio and Females as Percent of Total Civilian Employment, by Country: 1980 to 1993

[See headnote, table 1387]

COUNTRY	CIVILIAN EMPLOYMENT-POPULATION RATIO [1]								CIVILIAN EMPLOYMENT, PERCENT FEMALE			
	Women				Men							
	1980	1990	1992	1993	1980	1990	1992	1993	1980	1990	1992	1993
Australia	41.9	49.3	47.7	47.5	75.1	71.3	66.6	66.0	36.4	41.3	42.1	42.3
Canada	46.2	53.7	51.6	51.4	73.0	69.8	65.0	64.7	39.7	44.7	45.5	45.5
France	40.3	41.5	41.4	[2]40.6	68.6	61.3	59.4	[2]58.3	39.5	43.0	43.7	[2]43.6
Germany [3]	38.9	[4]40.9	[2]42.2	[2]41.4	69.9	65.6	[2]64.1	[2]62.2	39.2	[2]41.0	[2]42.0	[2]42.3
Italy	27.9	29.2	[2]30.3	[2][4]29.5	66.0	[4]60.1	[2]61.1	[2][4]59.3	31.7	34.7	35.3	35.4
Japan.	45.7	48.0	48.7	48.3	77.9	75.4	76.1	75.9	38.4	40.3	40.5	40.3
Netherlands . . .	31.0	(NA)	(NA)	(NA)	74.1	(NA)	(NA)	(NA)	30.2	(NA)	(NA)	(NA)
Sweden	58.0	61.5	[2]58.1	[2]55.3	73.6	70.2	[2]65.3	[2]61.3	45.2	47.8	48.3	48.7
United Kingdom .	44.8	49.7	[2]48.8	[2]48.8	72.8	70.1	[2]65.0	[2]64.1	40.4	[2]43.5	[2]44.9	[2]45.2

NA Not available. [1] Civilian employment as a percent of the civilian working age population. [2] Preliminary. [3] Former West Germany. [4] Break in series.

Source: U.S. Bureau of Labor Statistics, *Comparative Labor Force Statistics for Ten Countries, 1959-1993*, August 1994.

No. 1387. Civilian Labor Force, Employment, and Unemployment, by Country: 1980 to 1993

[Data based on U.S. labor force definitions (see source) except that minimum age for population base varies as follows: United States, France, Sweden, and United Kingdom, 16 years; Australia, Canada, Japan, Netherlands, Germany, and Italy, (beginning 1993), 15 years; Italy and prior to 1993, 14 years]

YEAR	United States	Australia	Canada	France	Germany [1]	Italy	Japan	Netherlands	Sweden	United Kingdom
Civilian labor force (mil.):										
1980	106.9	6.7	11.6	22.9	27.3	21.1	55.7	5.9	4.3	26.5
1985	115.5	7.3	12.5	23.6	28.0	21.8	58.8	6.2	4.4	27.2
1990	124.8	8.5	13.7	24.3	29.4	22.7	63.0	6.8	4.6	28.5
1991	125.3	8.5	13.8	24.5	[2]28.0	[3]22.9	64.3	6.9	4.6	28.4
1992	127.0	8.6	13.8	24.6	[2]30.0	[2]22.9	65.0	[2]7.0	4.5	28.2
1993	128.0	8.7	13.9	24.6	[2]30.0	[2,3]22.6	65.5	[2]7.1	4.4	[2]28.2
Labor force participation rate: [4]										
1980	63.9	62.1	64.1	57.5	54.7	48.2	62.6	55.4	66.9	62.5
1985	64.8	61.6	65.3	56.9	54.7	47.2	62.3	55.5	66.9	62.2
1990	66.4	64.7	67.0	55.6	55.0	47.2	62.6	56.8	66.9	63.9
1991	66.0	64.3	66.3	55.6	[2]55.4	[3]48.6	63.2	57.5	66.4	[2]63.4
1992	66.3	64.0	65.5	55.7	[2]55.1	[2]48.5	63.4	[2]57.9	[2]65.0	[2]62.8
1993	66.2	63.6	65.2	[2]55.6	[2]54.5	[2,3]48.8	63.3	[2]58.6	[2]63.3	[2]62.6
Civilian employment (mil.):										
1980	99.3	6.3	10.7	21.4	26.5	20.2	54.6	5.5	4.2	24.7
1985	107.2	6.7	11.2	21.2	26.0	20.5	57.3	5.6	4.3	24.2
1990	117.9	7.9	12.6	22.1	28.0	21.1	61.7	6.3	4.5	26.6
1991	116.9	7.7	12.3	22.1	[2]28.5	[3]21.4	62.9	6.4	4.4	25.9
1992	117.6	7.7	12.2	22.0	[2]28.7	[2]21.2	63.6	[2]6.5	4.3	[2]25.4
1993	119.3	7.7	12.4	21.7	[2]28.2	[2,3]20.2	63.8	[2]6.5	4.0	[2]25.2
Employment-population ratio: [5]										
1980	59.2	58.3	59.3	53.8	53.1	46.1	61.3	52.1	65.6	58.1
1985	60.1	56.5	58.5	51.0	50.7	44.4	60.6	50.1	65.0	55.2
1990	62.7	60.2	61.5	50.5	52.2	43.9	61.3	52.5	65.8	59.5
1991	61.6	58.1	59.5	50.3	[2]53.0	[3]45.3	61.8	53.4	64.5	[2]57.8
1992	61.4	57.1	58.1	49.9	[2]52.6	[2]44.9	62.0	[2]53.8	[2]61.7	[2]56.5
1993	61.6	56.7	57.9	[2]49.0	[2]51.3	[2,3]43.7	61.7	[2]53.4	[2]58.2	[2]56.1
Unemployment rate:										
1980	7.1	6.1	7.5	6.5	2.8	4.4	2.0	6.0	2.0	7.0
1985	7.2	8.3	10.5	10.5	7.2	6.0	2.6	9.6	2.8	11.2
1990	5.5	6.9	8.1	[6]9.1	[6]5.0	7.0	2.1	7.5	1.7	[6]6.9
1991	6.7	9.6	10.3	[6]9.6	[2,6]4.3	[3]6.9	2.1	7.1	2.9	[6]8.8
1992	7.4	10.8	11.3	[6]10.4	[2]4.6	[2]7.3	2.2	[2]7.2	5.2	[6]10.0
1993	6.8	10.9	11.2	[6]11.8	[2]5.8	[2,3]10.5	2.5	[2]8.8	8.1	[2,6]10.4
Under 25 years old	13.3	18.8	17.7	24.8	(NA)	(NA)	5.2	(NA)	18.7	17.3
Teenagers [7]	19.0	23.9	19.9	26.7	(NA)	(NA)	7.2	(NA)	19.8	19.2
20 to 24 years old	10.5	15.7	16.4	24.6	(NA)	(NA)	4.7	(NA)	18.4	16.4
25 years old and over	5.6	8.7	9.9	9.7	(NA)	(NA)	2.1	(NA)	6.7	8.7

NA Not available. [1] Former West Germany. [2] Preliminary. [3] Break in series. [4] Civilian labor force as a percent of the civilian working age population. Germany and Japan include the institutionalized population as part of the working age population. [5] Civilian employment as a percent of the civilian working age population. Germany and Japan include the institutionalized population as part of the working age population. [6] French data are for March; German data are for April; United Kingdom data are for the Spring quarter. [7] 16 to 19 years old in the United States, France, Sweden, and the United Kingdom; 15 to 19 years old in Canada, Australia, and Japan.

Source: U.S. Bureau of Labor Statistics, *Comparative Labor Force Statistics for Ten Countries, 1959-1993*, August 1994, and *Monthly Labor Review*.

No. 1388. Female Labor Force Participation Rates, by Country: 1983 and 1993

[**In percent**. Female labor force of all ages divided by female population 15-64 years old]

COUNTRY	1983	1993	COUNTRY	1983	1993
United States	61.7	69.1	Italy	40.3	[1]46.5
Australia	52.7	62.3	Japan	57.2	[1]61.7
Austria	49.7	[1]58.0	Luxembourg	41.7	[3]44.7
Belgium	48.7	[1]54.1	Netherlands	40.3	[1]55.5
Canada	60.0	65.3	New Zealand	45.7	[1]63.2
Denmark	74.2	78.3	Norway	65.5	[1]70.9
Finland	72.7	70.0	Portugal	56.7	59.4
France	54.3	59.0	Spain	33.2	42.8
Germany	[2]52.5	[1]61.3	Sweden	76.6	75.8
Greece	40.4	43.6	Switzerland	55.2	[1]58.5
Iceland	62.2	[3]80.5	Turkey	(NA)	33.2
Ireland	37.8	[3]39.9	United Kingdom	57.2	[1]64.8

NA Not available. [1] 1992 data. [2] Former West Germany. [3] 1991 data.

Source: Organization for Economic Cooperation and Development, Paris, France, *OECD in Figures, Statistics on the Member Countries,* annual.

No. 1389. Civilian Employment, by Industry and Country: 1980 and 1991

[Data based on U.S. labor force definitions except that minimum age for population base varies as follows: United States, France, Sweden, and United Kingdom, 16 years; Australia, Canada, Germany, Japan, and Netherlands, 15 years; Italy, 14 years. Industries based on International Standard Industrial Classification; see text, section 31]

INDUSTRY	United States	Australia	Canada	France	Germany[1]	Italy	Japan	Netherlands	Sweden	United Kingdom
TOTAL EMPLOYMENT (1,000)										
1980, total	**99,303**	**6,284**	**10,708**	**21,443**	**26,486**	**20,195**	**54,600**	**5,520**	**4,214**	**25,004**
Agriculture, forestry, fishing	3,529	408	583	1,821	1,373	2,870	5,510	285	237	654
Industry[2]	29,136	1,818	2,931	7,523	11,373	[3]7,694	19,180	1,642	1,327	9,059
Manufacturing	21,942	1,248	2,111	5,530	8,998	5,433	13,630	1,176	1,025	7,081
Services	66,638	4,058	7,194	12,099	13,740	9,631	29,910	3,593	2,650	15,291
Public utilities	1,179	130	124	190	215	(3)	300	50	36	353
Wholesale and retail trade, restaurants and hotels	21,339	1,467	2,411	3,440	4,079	3,765	12,980	985	582	4,818
Transport and communication . .	5,619	461	782	1,329	1,572	1,124	3,500	328	295	1,580
Finance, insurance, real estate, and business	8,351	518	1,018	1,603	1,540	518	3,170	435	283	1,837
Community, social, personal[4] . .	30,148	1,452	2,859	5,536	6,335	4,224	9,920	1,794	1,454	6,703
1991, total	**116,877**	**7,713**	**12,340**	**22,142**	**28,501**	**21,364**	**62,910**	**6,444**	**4,493**	**26,008**
Agriculture, forestry, fishing	3,390	432	554	1,196	927	1,807	3,990	295	164	607
Industry[2]	28,254	1,763	2,734	6,331	10,928	[3]6,913	21,520	1,613	1,227	7,060
Manufacturing	20,434	1,117	1,865	4,639	8,894	4,728	15,460	1,178	900	5,155
Services	85,233	5,518	9,052	14,615	16,646	12,646	37,400	4,536	3,102	18,341
Public utilities	1,303	105	136	207	256	(3)	300	44	37	(NA)
Wholesale and retail trade, restaurants and hotels	25,868	1,838	2,934	3,860	4,750	4,653	15,080	1,146	637	(NA)
Transport and communication . .	6,348	539	780	1,436	1,686	1,147	3,810	406	321	(NA)
Finance, insurance, real estate, and business	13,170	1,009	1,471	2,274	2,426	1,002	5,280	687	410	(NA)
Community, social, personal[4] . .	38,543	2,028	3,730	6,838	7,527	5,843	12,950	2,252	1,696	(NA)
PERCENT DISTRIBUTION										
1980, total	**100**	**100**	**100**	**100**	**100**	**100**	**100**	**100**	**100**	**100**
Agriculture, forestry, fishing	4	7	5	9	5	14	10	5	6	3
Industry[2]	29	29	27	35	43	[3]38	35	30	32	36
Services	67	65	67	56	52	48	55	65	63	61
1991, total	**100**	**100**	**100**	**100**	**100**	**100**	**100**	**100**	**100**	**100**
Agriculture, forestry, fishing	3	6	5	5	3	9	6	5	4	2
Industry[2]	24	23	22	29	38	[3]32	34	25	27	27
Services	73	72	73	66	58	59	60	70	69	71

Not available.   [1] 1980 data for former West Germany.   [2] Includes mining and construction.   [3] Public utilities included in industry.   [4] Includes public administration, education, health, and recreation services.

Source: U.S. Bureau of Labor Statistics, Office of Productivity and Technology, *Monthly Labor Review,* October 1993 and unpublished data.

No. 1390. Index of Industrial Production, by Country: 1980 to 1993

[Industrial production index measures output in the manufacturing, mining, and electric and gas utilities industries. Minus sign (-) indicates decrease]

COUNTRY	INDEX (1990=100)							ANNUAL PERCENT CHANGE					
	1980	1985	1989	1990	1991	1992	1993	1980-81	1985-86	1989-90	1990-91	1991-92	1992-93
OECD, total	**78.9**	**86.3**	**98.5**	**100.0**	**99.6**	**99.2**	**98.9**	**0.3**	**1.2**	**1.5**	**-0.4**	**-0.4**	**-0.3**
Australia[1]	73.7	86.9	98.9	100.0	98.9	99.5	104.0	3.1	-0.2	1.1	-1.1	0.6	4.5
Austria	76.1	82.5	93.2	100.0	101.9	100.8	99.0	-1.6	1.1	7.3	1.9	-1.1	-1.8
Belgium[2]	82.1	85.5	96.4	100.0	98.0	98.0	92.8	-2.7	0.8	3.7	-2.0	-	-5.3
Canada[2]	81.5	94.5	103.4	100.0	95.9	96.8	101.5	2.0	-0.7	-3.3	-4.1	0.9	4.9
Finland	75.3	87.8	99.6	100.0	90.3	92.4	96.9	2.5	1.6	0.4	-9.7	2.3	4.9
France	89.2	87.6	98.1	100.0	99.9	98.8	95.1	-1.0	0.8	1.9	-0.1	-1.1	-3.7
Germany[3]	82.9	85.6	95.1	100.0	102.9	101.0	93.6	-1.8	1.8	5.2	2.9	-1.8	-7.3
Greece	90.8	98.2	102.4	100.0	98.6	97.4	95.4	0.9	-1.0	-2.3	-1.4	-1.2	-2.1
Ireland	54.2	69.5	95.5	100.0	103.3	112.7	119.0	5.4	2.3	4.7	3.3	9.1	5.6
Italy	87.5	84.8	100.7	100.0	99.1	97.8	95.7	-2.2	4.1	-0.7	-0.9	-1.3	-2.1
Japan	67.3	79.8	95.9	100.0	101.9	96.0	92.0	1.0	-0.3	4.3	1.9	-5.8	-4.2
Luxembourg	69.7	84.7	100.5	100.0	100.5	99.6	96.6	-5.6	1.9	-0.5	0.5	-0.9	-3.0
Netherlands	86.8	91.7	97.7	100.0	103.8	104.0	102.9	-1.8	0.2	2.4	3.8	0.2	-1.1
Norway	58.3	79.0	98.1	100.0	102.1	108.6	112.8	-0.9	3.3	1.9	2.1	6.4	3.9
Portugal	62.8	73.9	91.7	100.0	100.0	97.7	95.2	2.2	7.3	9.1	-	-2.3	-2.6
Spain	83.3	86.1	100.0	100.0	99.3	96.5	91.9	-1.1	3.1	-	-0.7	-2.8	-4.8
Sweden[4]	82.5	91.5	98.9	100.0	94.4	90.7	93.5	-1.7	0.4	1.1	-5.6	-3.9	3.1
Switzerland[5]	82.0	85.0	97.0	100.0	101.0	100.0	100.0	-	3.5	3.1	1.0	-1.0	-
United Kingdom	81.6	88.2	100.4	100.0	96.1	95.8	98.0	-3.1	2.4	-0.4	-1.7	-0.3	2.3
United States	**79.3**	**89.0**	**100.0**	**100.0**	**98.3**	**101.5**	**105.7**	**1.9**	**1.0**	**-**	**-1.7**	**3.3**	**4.1**

- Represents or rounds to zero.   [1] Index of Real Gross Product in industry.   [2] Gross domestic product in industry at factor cost and 1986 prices.   [3] Former West Germany.   [4] Mining and manufacturing.   [5] Excludes mining and quarrying.

Source: Organization for Economic Cooperation and Development, Paris, France, *Main Economic Indicators,* monthly.

No. 1391. International Economic Composite Indexes, by Country: 1980 to 1994

[Average annual percent change from previous year; derived from indexes with base 1980=100. The coincident index changes are for calendar years and the leading index changes are for years ending June 30 because they lead the coincident indexes by about 6 months, on average. The G-7 countries are United States, Canada, France, Germany, Italy, United Kingdom, and Japan. Minus sign (-) indicates decrease]

COUNTRY	1980	1984	1985	1986	1987	1988	1989	1990	1991	1992	1993	1994
LEADING INDEX												
Total, 11 countries	2.4	9.1	3.1	2.0	4.3	8.0	5.0	2.3	-1.1	0.7	0.9	5.2
10 countries, excluding U.S.	6.6	5.9	4.4	1.6	5.2	8.2	5.9	3.3	-0.9	-2.1	-1.9	3.2
G-7 countries	2.3	9.1	2.9	1.9	4.2	7.8	4.9	2.3	-1.1	0.5	0.7	5.0
North America	-2.8	13.7	1.3	2.7	3.2	7.3	3.5	0.7	-1.6	4.6	5.0	7.7
United States	-3.3	13.9	1.0	2.7	3.2	7.5	3.7	0.9	-1.3	4.8	5.0	7.7
Canada	3.2	11.3	4.3	3.0	2.7	6.1	1.0	-2.5	-5.2	1.6	5.0	7.8
Four European countries	2.8	4.0	2.3	2.2	3.6	3.1	4.2	1.5	1.1	0.8	-	3.8
France	4.5	3.9	2.6	1.9	6.1	5.1	6.0	0.5	1.2	2.6	0.3	4.9
Germany [1]	2.4	6.1	2.0	3.0	1.6	3.4	5.2	4.7	4.2	0.3	-1.9	3.8
Italy	3.0	0.9	2.7	4.0	4.3	0.6	2.1	0.3	-1.3	0.2	1.2	3.3
United Kingdom	1.0	3.4	2.2	0.2	3.4	1.9	2.4	-0.9	-2.0	-0.3	2.0	3.2
Five Pacific region countries	14.4	8.4	7.8	0.6	7.9	16.1	8.6	6.1	-2.7	-6.2	-5.5	1.7
Australia	5.2	12.9	6.5	2.1	3.2	7.6	5.2	-3.3	-3.9	3.4	5.4	6.2
Japan	17.2	7.9	8.3	-0.4	7.6	17.6	8.9	7.2	-3.2	-8.7	-8.2	-0.1
Korea, South	-2.6	9.3	4.7	9.8	17.2	13.7	10.0	4.5	3.7	5.2	4.0	11.7
New Zealand	1.8	6.4	5.4	-1.2	2.8	-1.5	0.8	1.2	-2.8	2.5	3.5	2.7
Taiwan	4.7	11.9	6.5	8.1	13.6	14.9	12.3	7.0	1.2	7.9	5.8	8.5
COINCIDENT INDEX												
Total, 11 countries	0.3	5.9	3.7	3.2	4.1	6.1	4.8	3.6	0.3	0.7	0.2	3.4
10 countries, excluding U.S.	2.5	3.6	4.0	3.5	4.5	6.9	6.4	5.8	2.7	0.5	-1.3	1.9
G-7 countries	0.2	5.8	3.6	2.9	4.0	6.0	4.6	3.6	0.3	0.7	0.1	3.1
North America	-2.4	9.3	3.6	2.6	3.8	4.8	2.4	-0.1	-3.7	1.0	3.0	5.8
United States	-2.8	9.6	3.4	2.5	3.7	4.7	2.3	-	-3.7	1.0	3.1	6.0
Canada	2.0	6.3	5.3	3.5	4.8	5.8	2.8	-	-3.9	0.4	2.4	4.6
Four European countries	1.4	2.2	2.9	3.7	3.8	6.1	6.0	5.6	2.0	-0.1	-2.7	1.5
France	1.3	0.5	1.4	3.9	5.0	8.0	8.7	7.1	2.5	0.9	-1.2	5.1
Germany [1]	2.5	2.7	3.5	4.3	3.0	3.6	5.4	7.2	5.7	0.4	-4.5	-1.5
Italy	5.2	3.4	2.5	1.7	1.5	5.3	2.0	4.7	2.1	-1.1	-8.0	-2.2
United Kingdom	-2.1	2.6	4.3	3.6	5.2	8.0	5.9	2.3	-4.4	-1.5	1.2	3.8
Five Pacific region countries	4.2	5.4	5.0	3.5	5.2	8.2	7.5	6.8	4.6	1.5	-	2.1
Australia	4.8	9.3	7.6	4.9	4.3	8.5	9.9	0.9	-7.4	-0.9	2.3	10.1
Japan	4.5	4.6	4.7	2.6	4.6	8.3	7.3	7.6	5.8	1.4	-0.8	0.5
Korea, South	-4.3	9.0	5.5	11.7	13.5	10.6	6.2	9.5	7.9	4.4	3.7	8.9
New Zealand	1.9	4.2	1.8	1.5	1.4	-0.8	-0.7	1.2	-1.1	1.4	3.3	5.3
Taiwan	7.1	12.6	3.7	10.1	11.9	8.0	7.3	2.8	5.8	6.0	5.0	5.7

- Represents or rounds to zero.　[1] Former West Germany.

Source: Center for International Business Cycle Research, Columbia Business School, New York, NY, *International Economic Indicators*, monthly.

No. 1392. Patents, by Country: 1993

[Includes only U.S. patents granted to residents of areas outside of the United States and its territories]

COUNTRY	Total[1]	Inventions	Designs	COUNTRY	Total[1]	Inventions	Designs
Total	48,652	45,107	3,214	Netherlands	945	801	78
				Korea, South	830	779	50
Japan	23,398	22,292	1,037	Sweden	741	635	102
Germany	7,183	6,890	228	Australia	470	378	88
France	3,154	2,908	215	Belgium	377	350	25
United Kingdom	2,520	2,294	197	Israel	358	314	22
Canada	2,229	1,943	275	Austria	341	313	26
Taiwan	1,510	1,189	320	Finland	311	293	17
Italy	1,454	1,286	165	Denmark	261	197	60
Switzerland	1,197	1,126	69	Other countries	1,373	1,119	240

[1] Includes patents for botanical plants and reissues not shown separately.

Source: U.S. Patent and Trademark Office, Technology Assessment and Forecast Data Base.

No. 1393. World's 500 Largest Corporations, by Country: 1994

[**For company's fiscal year ended on or before March 31, 1995.** All companies on the list must publish financial data and report part or all of their figures to a government agency. Includes revenues from discontinued operations and consolidated subsidiaries; excludes excise taxes. Profits are shown after taxes, after extraordinary credits or charges, and after cumulative effects of accounting changes]

COUNTRY	Number of companies	Revenues ($bil.)	Profits ($bil.)	COUNTRY	Number of companies	Revenues ($bil.)	Profits ($bil.)	COUNTRY	Number of companies	Revenues ($bil.)	Profits ($bil.)
Total [1]	500	10,245	282	Switzerland	14	245	13	Spain	6	77	2
Japan	149	3,806	26	Italy	11	228	2	Canada	5	52	3
U.S.	151	2,939	142	Netherlands	8	142	7	Sweden	3	45	3
Germany	44	896	12	Britain/Netherlands				China	3	41	1
France	40	742	3	lands	2	140	9	Belgium	4	41	1
U.K.	33	454	36	Korea, South	8	134	4	Mexico	2	37	3

[1] Includes other countries not shown separately.

Source: Time Warner, New York, NY, *Fortune*, August 7, 1995, (copyright).

No. 1394. Indexes of Hourly Compensation Costs for Production Workers in Manufacturing, by Country: 1980 to 1994

[United States=100. Compensation costs include all pay made directly to the worker—pay for time worked and not worked (e.g., leave, except sick leave), other direct pay, employer expenditures for legally required insurance programs and contractual and private benefit plans, and for some countries, other labor taxes. Data adjusted for exchange rates. Area averages are trade-weighted to account for difference in countries' relative importance to U.S. trade in manufactured goods. The trade weights used are the sum of U.S. imports of manufactured products for consumption (customs value) and U.S. domestic exports of manufactured products (f.a.s. value) in 1992; see source for detail]

AREA OR COUNTRY	1980	1990	1991	1992	1993	1994	AREA OR COUNTRY	1980	1990	1991	1992	1993	1994
United States	**100**	**100**	**100**	**100**	**100**	**100**	Austria [6]	90	119	116	126	122	127
Total [1]	67	83	86	88	86	88	Belgium.	133	129	127	138	129	134
OECD [2]	77	94	97	99	96	99	Denmark.	110	120	117	124	114	120
Europe	102	118	117	123	112	115	Finland [7]	83	141	136	123	99	110
Asian newly industrial-							France	91	102	98	105	97	100
izing economies [3] . . .	12	25	28	30	31	34	Germany [6][8].	125	147	146	157	154	160
Canada.	88	106	110	105	98	92	Greece	38	45	44	46	41	(NA)
Mexico	22	11	12	14	15	15	Ireland	60	79	78	83	73	(NA)
Australia [4]	86	88	87	81	75	80	Italy	83	119	119	121	96	95
Hong Kong [5]	15	21	23	24	26	28	Luxembourg.	121	110	108	117	111	(NA)
Israel	38	57	56	56	53	53	Netherlands	122	123	117	126	119	122
Japan	56	86	94	101	114	125	Norway	117	144	139	143	121	122
Korea, South	10	25	30	32	33	37	Portugal	21	25	27	32	27	27
New Zealand	54	56	54	49	48	52	Spain	60	76	78	83	69	67
Singapore	15	25	28	31	31	37	Sweden.	127	140	142	152	106	110
Sri Lanka.	2	2	3	2	3	(NA)	Switzerland	112	140	139	144	135	145
Taiwan	10	26	28	32	31	32	United Kingdom	77	85	88	89	76	80

NA Not available.   [1] The 24 foreign economies for which 1994 data are available.   [2] Canada, Mexico, Australia, Japan, New Zealand, and the European countries.   [3] Hong Kong, South Korea, Singapore, and Taiwan.   [4] Includes non-production workers, except in managerial, executive, professional, and higher supervisory positions.   [5] Average of selected manufacturing industries.   [6] Excludes workers in establishments considered handicraft manufactures (including all printing and publishing and miscellaneous manufacturing in Austria).   [7] Includes workers in mining and electrical power plants.   [8] Former West Germany.

Source: U.S. Bureau of Labor Statistics, *International Comparisons of Hourly Compensation Costs for Production Workers in Manufacturing, 1975-1994,* June 1995.

No. 1395. Structure of Manufacturing Industry, by Country: 1975 to 1990

[In percent. Contribution of each industry group to total manufacturing production. Based on International Standard Industrial Classification; see text, section 30, and source. Numbers in parentheses refer to ISIC codes]

COUNTRY	Food [1] (3100)	Textile [2] (3200)	Wood [3] (3300)	Paper [4] (3400)	Chemi-cal [5] (3500)	Non-metal [6] (3600)	Basic metal [7] (3700)	Machin-ery [8] (3800)	Other (3900)
United States: 1975 . .	16.7	6.7	2.8	7.8	18.4	2.7	7.6	35.9	1.3
1980	14.5	5.6	2.8	7.7	22.2	2.5	6.8	36.6	1.3
1985	14.1	5.3	2.9	9.1	19.9	2.4	4.5	40.8	1.1
1990	14.5	4.9	3.1	9.9	19.9	2.3	4.7	39.5	1.2
Japan: 1975	13.5	6.9	3.8	6.0	17.6	3.5	15.4	32.1	1.2
1980	11.3	5.4	3.6	6.2	19.3	3.9	11.4	37.7	1.2
1985	11.0	4.9	2.4	6.1	16.7	3.3	8.5	45.7	1.4
1990	10.2	4.2	2.5	6.6	14.2	3.3	7.4	50.2	1.4
France: 1975	19.5	8.4	2.8	5.3	19.1	2.9	8.8	32.0	1.1
1980	17.0	6.9	3.1	5.6	21.4	3.5	8.4	32.6	1.3
1985	17.6	6.9	2.5	6.5	21.6	3.0	7.3	33.3	1.3
1990	16.5	5.9	2.8	7.4	18.4	3.4	6.5	37.9	1.3
Italy: 1975	13.2	10.7	2.3	4.7	20.7	4.7	10.9	32.1	0.7
1980	12.2	11.4	3.2	4.6	19.7	5.6	10.1	32.5	0.8
1985	12.6	13.5	2.9	5.4	22.5	4.8	9.6	27.8	0.8
1988	12.2	13.4	3.2	5.7	20.1	4.9	8.1	31.8	0.7
Portugal: 1975	26.1	18.9	5.5	6.9	16.9	5.5	3.1	16.8	0.3
1980	18.2	18.9	6.0	6.3	24.5	6.1	2.2	17.6	0.2
1985	19.5	18.5	3.6	6.8	28.5	4.8	3.3	15.0	0.2
1987	20.4	20.8	4.2	8.0	22.0	5.5	2.9	15.9	0.2
Sweden: 1975	13.3	3.7	7.5	13.8	10.4	2.7	8.7	39.5	0.4
1980	13.3	2.6	8.1	13.5	15.3	2.6	8.5	35.8	0.4
1985	13.9	2.1	6.4	13.9	15.5	2.1	7.9	37.9	0.3
1989	13.5	1.7	7.2	15.4	12.6	2.3	8.3	38.8	0.3
United Kingdom: 1975 .	18.5	7.5	2.9	6.2	18.5	3.1	7.8	34.4	1.1
1980	18.6	5.9	2.9	6.8	20.6	3.6	6.8	33.9	0.9
1985	18.7	5.6	2.7	7.5	21.1	3.5	5.8	34.2	0.9
1990	15.8	5.0	3.1	8.7	18.9	3.9	5.4	38.2	1.0
West Germany: 1975 . .	13.3	7.0	3.3	4.4	18.7	3.5	10.8	38.6	0.5
1980	12.4	5.4	3.4	4.1	22.9	3.4	7.6	40.3	0.5
1985	12.2	4.8	2.4	4.2	23.7	2.7	6.6	43.1	0.4
1990	11.7	4.4	2.8	(NA)	(NA)	2.8	5.5	47.5	0.5

NA Not available.   [1] Manufacture of food, beverages, and tobacco.   [2] Textile, apparel, and leather.   [3] Wood products and furniture.   [4] Paper, paper products and printing.   [5] Chemical products, petroleum, coal, rubber, and plastic products.   [6] Nonmetallic mineral products, except petroleum and coal products.   [7] Basic metal industries, including iron, steel, and nonferrous metal.   [8] Fabricated metal products, machinery and equipment.

Source: Organization for Economic Cooperation and Development, Paris, France, *OECD Industrial Structure Statistics, 1988;* and unpublished data.

No. 1396. Selected Indexes of Manufacturing Activity, by Country: 1970 to 1993

[1982=100. Data relate to all employed persons in the United States, Canada, France, Germany, Japan, and Sweden; all employees (wage and salary workers) in other countries. Minus sign (-) indicates decrease. For an explanation of average annual percent change, see Guide to Tabular Presentation]

INDEX	United States	Bel- gium	Cana- da	Den- mark	France	Ger- many [1]	Italy	Japan	Neth- erlands	Swe- den	United King- dom
Output per hour:											
1970	(NA)	44.0	76.9	57.2	58.6	66.4	54.6	50.3	52.9	69.0	72.1
1980	92.9	86.9	99.9	98.0	90.8	98.5	95.5	91.1	93.9	96.7	91.0
1985	106.7	119.6	119.8	105.0	107.9	113.4	122.3	114.9	118.7	113.6	116.4
1990	122.1	134.1	122.0	105.5	127.6	125.6	139.3	149.1	130.1	125.0	140.1
1992	127.5	142.2	128.0	107.7	130.9	128.0	150.8	156.8	132.2	132.8	152.4
1993	131.6	146.4	130.9	113.9	132.3	130.0	159.2	157.3	133.8	141.5	159.7
Average annual percent change:											
1979-85	2.0	6.6	2.4	2.1	3.0	2.1	5.0	4.6	4.2	3.0	4.1
1985-93	2.7	2.6	1.1	1.0	2.6	1.7	3.4	4.0	1.5	2.8	4.0
1992-93	3.2	2.9	2.3	5.7	1.1	1.6	5.6	0.3	1.2	6.6	4.8
Compensation per hour, national currency basis: [2]											
1970	(NA)	23.2	28.7	22.3	18.5	34.5	11.6	25.0	27.8	24.4	14.7
1980	83.3	86.3	78.6	83.4	72.7	89.2	70.2	89.0	88.5	84.5	78.9
1985	111.3	122.0	116.8	120.6	129.6	116.3	150.9	110.1	115.5	131.8	125.1
1990	134.7	147.5	143.0	156.5	161.3	147.9	210.8	138.3	123.3	197.5	180.6
1992	147.9	164.9	158.1	167.2	174.1	165.6	249.7	153.0	136.6	225.0	219.7
1993	152.8	171.2	159.0	171.4	179.8	177.8	266.1	157.1	140.5	221.6	236.1
Average annual percent change:											
1979-85	6.9	7.8	8.7	8.1	12.7	5.9	16.7	4.7	4.8	9.6	11.5
1985-93	4.0	4.3	3.9	4.5	4.2	5.4	7.4	4.5	2.9	6.7	8.3
1992-93	3.3	3.8	0.5	2.5	3.3	7.4	6.6	2.7	2.9	-1.5	7.5
Real hourly compensation: [2][3]											
1970	(NA)	55.1	77.4	70.1	59.4	62.6	60.3	63.6	63.9	72.6	65.3
1980	97.5	101.0	97.9	102.6	92.2	99.9	96.0	96.0	100.0	103.0	96.1
1985	99.8	101.6	101.8	101.4	103.9	107.9	109.3	103.6	102.7	102.6	107.3
1990	99.5	110.6	100.1	108.6	111.2	128.6	115.9	121.7	109.2	114.4	116.1
1992	101.7	116.9	103.3	110.9	113.4	133.7	122.3	128.2	112.3	117.1	128.6
1993	102.0	118.1	102.0	112.3	114.8	138.3	125.0	129.8	113.2	112.0	136.1
Average annual percent change:											
1979-85	0.1	0.8	0.7	-0.5	2.2	1.8	1.5	1.1	0.3	-0.5	2.3
1985-93	0.3	1.9	(Z)	1.3	1.3	3.2	1.7	2.9	1.2	1.1	3.0
1992-93	0.3	1.0	-1.3	1.3	1.2	3.4	2.3	1.3	0.8	-4.4	5.8
Unit labor costs, national currency:											
1970	(NA)	52.6	37.3	39.0	31.5	51.9	21.3	49.7	52.7	35.4	20.4
1980	89.7	99.4	78.7	85.1	80.1	90.6	73.5	97.8	94.2	87.4	86.7
1985	104.2	102.0	97.6	114.9	120.2	102.6	123.4	95.8	93.9	116.1	107.5
1990	110.4	110.0	117.2	148.3	126.4	117.8	151.3	92.7	94.7	158.0	128.9
1992	116.0	115.9	123.5	155.1	133.0	129.4	165.6	97.5	103.3	169.5	144.2
1993	116.1	117.0	121.4	150.5	135.9	136.8	167.2	99.9	105.1	156.6	147.8
Average annual percent change:											
1979-85	4.9	1.1	6.1	5.9	9.5	3.8	11.1	0.1	0.6	6.4	7.1
1985-93	1.4	1.7	2.8	3.4	1.6	3.7	3.9	0.5	1.4	3.8	4.1
1992-93	0.1	0.9	-1.7	-3.0	2.2	5.7	0.9	2.4	1.7	-7.6	2.5
Unit labor costs, U.S. dollar basis: [4]											
1970	(NA)	48.5	44.1	43.4	37.5	34.6	46.0	34.6	38.9	42.8	28.0
1980	89.7	155.8	83.1	126.2	124.9	121.1	116.3	107.9	126.8	129.8	115.4
1985	104.2	78.7	88.2	90.4	88.0	84.7	87.5	100.1	75.6	84.8	79.8
1990	110.4	150.7	124.0	200.0	152.7	176.9	170.9	159.3	138.9	167.6	131.6
1992	116.0	165.1	126.2	214.4	165.3	201.2	182.0	191.6	157.0	182.8	145.7
1993	116.1	154.8	116.2	193.6	157.8	200.8	143.8	223.9	151.0	126.3	127.0
Average annual percent change:											
1979-85	4.9	-10.1	3.4	-5.8	-3.4	-4.1	-3.3	-1.4	-7.5	-5.2	-1.3
1985-93	1.4	8.8	3.5	10.0	7.6	11.4	6.4	10.6	9.0	5.1	6.0
1992-93	0.1	-6.2	-7.9	-9.7	-4.5	-0.2	-21.0	16.9	-3.8	-30.9	-12.8
Employment:											
1970	102.6	137.7	96.3	119.6	106.9	116.7	97.6	102.8	135.4	114.9	140.3
1980	107.8	109.9	108.4	103.9	104.9	104.9	107.8	99.5	108.1	106.9	116.7
1985	102.4	95.1	103.6	112.4	92.6	97.4	89.8	104.6	96.5	99.6	92.5
1990	101.9	92.9	109.4	111.7	88.5	103.0	91.0	108.6	103.2	95.7	90.9
1992	96.6	88.6	97.2	108.8	84.4	102.7	85.2	113.5	101.7	81.7	80.0
1993	96.3	83.8	97.8	104.4	81.1	96.6	80.6	111.1	98.0	75.7	77.9
Average annual percent change:											
1979-85	-1.4	-2.7	-0.8	1.0	-2.3	-1.1	-2.9	1.2	-2.1	-1.2	-4.6
1985-93	-0.8	-1.6	-0.7	-0.9	-1.7	-0.1	-1.3	0.8	0.2	-3.4	-2.1
1992-93	-0.3	-5.4	0.6	-4.1	-3.9	-5.9	-5.4	-2.1	-3.6	-7.3	-2.6
Aggregate hours:											
1970	106.5	159.9	102.1	132.3	123.9	131.1	107.0	109.6	152.0	132.0	153.3
1980	109.8	110.1	110.8	103.7	110.8	106.3	108.0	100.5	108.1	105.9	117.3
1985	106.8	93.5	106.0	109.8	91.8	95.6	89.0	105.5	93.6	101.9	93.5
1990	107.0	94.3	112.2	106.6	88.1	96.9	95.0	107.7	99.4	99.4	92.0
1992	102.0	88.4	100.3	104.4	83.8	96.3	87.8	106.9	97.6	85.4	79.5
1993	102.9	82.3	102.9	99.4	80.3	87.6	81.4	102.2	94.0	81.4	76.9
Average annual percent change:											
1979-85	-1.2	-3.3	-0.9	0.8	-3.3	-1.8	-3.1	1.1	-2.5	-0.8	-5.0
1985-93	-0.5	-1.6	-0.4	-1.2	-1.7	-1.1	-1.1	-0.4	0.1	-2.8	-2.4
1992-93	0.8	-6.9	2.6	-4.8	-4.2	-9.1	-7.3	-4.4	-3.6	-4.7	-3.3

NA Not available.   Z Less than .05 percent.   [1] Former West Germany.   [2] Compensation includes, but real hourly compensation excludes, adjustments for payroll and employment taxes that are not compensation to employees, but are labor costs to employers.   [3] Index of hourly compensation divided by the index of consumer prices to adjust for changes in purchasing power.   [4] Indexes in national currency adjusted for changes in prevailing exchange rates.

Source: U.S. Bureau of Labor Statistics, *Monthly Labor Review*, February 1995.

No. 1397. Crude Steel Production, by Country: 1980 to 1993

[In million metric tons. Covers both ingots and steel for castings and excludes wrought (puddled) iron]

COUNTRY	1980	1985	1986	1987	1988	1989	1990	1991	1992	1993
World	718.2	727.1	721.2	741.2	783.3	785.0	767.0	736.4	722.4	725.1
United States [1]	101.5	80.1	74.0	80.9	91.8	[2]88.9	[2]89.7	79.7	84.3	88.8
Argentina [3]	2.6	2.8	3.1	3.5	3.5	3.9	[2]3.6	[2]3.0	2.9	3.0
Australia [3]	7.9	6.3	6.8	6.2	6.1	6.7	6.7	6.0	6.9	7.7
Austria	4.6	4.7	4.3	4.3	4.4	4.7	[2]4.3	4.2	3.9	3.9
Belgium	12.3	10.8	9.8	9.8	11.3	11.0	11.4	11.3	10.3	10.3
Brazil	15.3	20.5	21.2	22.1	24.6	25.1	20.5	22.6	24.0	25.0
Bulgaria	2.6	2.9	3.0	3.0	2.9	2.9	2.2	1.6	1.6	1.4
Canada	15.9	13.5	14.1	14.7	14.8	[2]15.5	[2]12.3	13.0	13.9	14.4
China	39.0	49.5	54.8	58.9	62.1	61.2	66.1	71.0	80.0	88.7
Czechoslovakia (former)	15.2	15.0	15.1	15.4	15.4	15.5	14.8	12.1	10.5	[4]7.5
Finland	2.5	2.5	2.6	2.7	2.8	2.9	2.9	2.9	3.1	3.1
France	23.2	18.8	17.9	17.7	19.1	19.3	19.0	18.4	18.0	17.2
Germany	51.1	48.4	45.1	44.4	49.1	48.9	44.0	42.2	39.7	37.6
Greece	1.1	1.0	1.0	0.9	1.0	1.0	1.0	1.0	0.9	0.9
Hungary	3.8	3.5	3.6	3.5	3.5	3.4	3.0	1.9	1.6	1.6
India . . . . . [5]	9.4	11.2	11.4	12.3	13.0	12.8	15.3	17.5	18.5	18.5
Indonesia [5]	0.4	1.2	1.5	1.5	[2]2.0	[2]2.4	[2]2.9	3.3	3.2	3.2
Italy	26.5	23.9	22.9	22.9	23.9	25.2	25.4	25.0	24.9	25.7
Japan . . . . . [2][5]	111.4	105.3	98.3	98.5	105.7	107.9	110.3	109.6	98.1	99.6
Korea, North [2][5]	5.8	6.5	6.5	6.5	8.0	7.3	8.0	8.0	8.1	8.1
Korea, South	14.4	18.6	18.8	19.5	21.3	21.9	23.1	26.0	28.1	33.0
Luxembourg	4.6	3.9	3.7	3.3	3.7	3.7	3.6	3.4	3.1	3.1
Mexico	7.0	7.2	7.0	7.2	7.3	7.9	8.7	7.9	8.4	9.2
Netherlands	5.3	5.5	5.3	5.1	5.5	5.7	5.4	5.2	5.4	6.0
Poland	18.6	15.4	16.3	16.3	15.9	15.1	13.6	10.4	9.9	9.9
Romania	10.7	14.6	15.0	14.6	15.1	14.4	9.8	7.1	5.4	5.0
Russia	(NA)	(NA)	(NA)	(NA)	(NA)	(NA)	(NA)	(NA)	67.0	58.0
South Africa	9.1	8.6	8.1	9.1	8.8	9.3	8.6	9.4	9.1	8.6
Spain	12.6	14.7	[2]12.1	[2]11.6	[2]11.7	[2]12.8	[2]12.7	12.9	12.3	12.8
Sweden	4.2	4.9	4.7	4.7	4.8	4.7	[2]4.5	4.3	4.4	4.3
Turkey	1.7	4.7	6.0	7.0	8.0	7.9	9.3	9.3	10.3	11.4
United Kingdom	11.3	15.7	14.7	17.4	19.0	18.8	17.9	16.5	16.1	16.0
Venezuela	1.8	3.1	3.4	3.7	3.7	2.9	3.2	3.1	3.2	3.3

NA Not available.   [1] Excludes steel for castings made in foundries operated by companies not producing ingots. [2] Estimated.   [3] For year ending June 30.   [4] Czech Republic only.   [5] Source: U.S. Bureau of Mines.

Source: Except as noted, Statistical Office of the United Nations, New York, NY, *Statistical Yearbook* and *Industrial Commodity Statistics Yearbook,* annuals (copyright).

No. 1398. World Production of Major Mineral Commodities: 1990 to 1994

COUNTRY	Unit	1990	1992	1993, est.	1994, est.	Leading producers, 1993
MINERAL FUELS [1]						
Coal	Mil. metric tons .	4,856	4,546	4,446	(NA)	China, United States, Russia
Dry natural gas	Tril. cu. ft. . . .	73.7	74.5	76.0	(NA)	Russia, United States, Canada
Natural gas plant liquids [2] . . .	Mil. barrels [3] . . .	1,690	1,808	1,882	(NA)	United States, Saudi Arabia, Canada
Petroleum, crude	Mil. barrels [3] . . .	22,107	21,978	22,134	(NA)	Saudi Arabia, Russia, United States
Petroleum, refined	Mil. barrels [3] . . .	23,791	23,959	(NA)	(NA)	United States, Russia, Japan (for 1992)
NONMETALLIC MINERALS						
Cement, hydraulic	Mil. metric tons .	1,148	1,254	1,300	1,300	China, Japan, United States
Diamond, gem and industrial .	1,000 carats . . .	110,919	105,521	107,620	(NA)	Australia, Botswana, Zaire
Nitrogen in ammonia	Mil. metric tons .	97.1	92.5	92.0	92.0	United States, India, Canada
Phosphate rock	Mil. metric tons .	162	144	120	130	United States, China, Morocco
Potash, marketable	Mil. metric tons .	27.8	24.3	21.0	22.0	Canada, Germany, Russia
Salt	Mil. metric tons .	184	185	190	190	United States, China, Germany
Sulfur, elemental basis	Mil. metric tons .	58.1	52.4	52.0	52.0	United States, Canada, China
METALS						
Aluminum [4]	Mil. metric tons .	19.3	19.2	20.0	19.0	United States, Russia, Canada
Bauxite, gross weight	Mil. metric tons .	108.6	103.6	110.0	110.0	Australia, Guinea, Jamaica
Chromite, gross weight [2]	1,000 metric tons .	12,968	10,993	10,001	10,000	Kazakhstan, South Africa, India
Copper, metal content [5]	1,000 metric tons	9,017	9,290	9,400	9,300	Chile, United States, Canada
Gold, metal content	Metric tons	2,133	2,248	2,300	2,300	South Africa, United States, Australia
Iron ore, gross weight [6]	Mil. metric tons .	982	930	1,000	1,000	China, Brazil, Australia
Lead, metal content [5]	1,000 metric tons	3,353	3,242	2,900	2,900	Australia, United States, China
Manganese ore, gross weight .	Mil. metric tons .	25.3	21.6	21.8	21.0	Ukraine, China, South Africa
Nickel, metal content [5]	1,000 metric tons	965	922	900	850	Russia, Canada, New Caledonia
Steel, crude	Mil. metric tons .	771	721	730	720	Japan, United States, China
Tin, metal content [5]	1,000 metric tons	222	179	180	180	China, Brazil, Indonesia
Zinc, metal content [5]	1,000 metric tons	7,184	7,137	6,900	6,700	Canada, Australia, China

NA Not available.   [1] Source: Energy Information Administration, *International Energy Annual.* 1993 data preliminary. [2] Excludes China.   [3] 42-gallon barrels.   [4] Unalloyed ingot metal.   [5] Mine output.   [6] Includes iron ore concentrates and iron ore agglomerates.

Source: Except as noted, U.S. Bureau of Mines, *Minerals Yearbook, 1993; Annual Reports, 1993;* and *Mineral Commodity Summaries, 1995.*

No. 1399. Energy Consumption and Production, by Country: 1990 and 1992

[See text, section 30, for general comments about the data. For data qualifications for countries, see source]

COUNTRY	ENERGY CONSUMED [1] (coal equiv.)				ELECTRIC ENERGY PRODUCTION [2] (bil. kWh)		CRUDE PETROLEUM PRODUCTION [3] (mil. metric tons)		COAL PRODUCTION [4] (mil. metric tons)	
	Total (mil. metric tons)		Per capita (kilograms)							
	1990	1992	1990	1992	1990	1992	1990	1992	1990	1992
World	10,826	10,948	2,004	1,993	11,774	12,027	3,003	2,992	3,517	3,527
United States	2,687	2,740	10,749	10,737	[5]3,012	[5]3,075	371	363	854	823
Algeria	40	42	1,586	1,594	16	18	37	36	[6](Z)	(Z)
Argentina	61	66	1,895	1,994	51	56	25	29	(Z)	(Z)
Australia	127	130	7,442	7,376	155	159	25	25	159	175
Austria	32	32	4,128	4,171	50	51	1	1	-	-
Bahrain	8	8	16,231	14,780	3	4	2	2	(NA)	(NA)
Bangladesh [7]	8	10	75	84	8	10	[6](Z)	(Z)	(NA)	(NA)
Belgium	67	69	6,686	6,872	71	72	(X)	(X)	[8]1	(Z)
Brazil	117	125	785	810	223	241	32	31	5	5
Bulgaria	37	28	4,170	3,139	42	36	(Z)	(Z)	[6](Z)	(Z)
Burma [9]	2	2	59	53	3	3	[6]1	1	[6](Z)	(Z)
Canada	292	300	10,957	10,965	482	521	76	79	38	32
Chile	17	18	1,328	1,305	18	22	1	1	2	2
China	893	973	788	833	621	754	138	142	[10]1,080	1,116
Colombia	27	29	821	854	35	36	22	22	20	24
Cuba	15	12	1,391	1,152	15	12	[6]1	1	(X)	(X)
Czechoslovakia	96	(NA)	6,149	(NA)	87	(X)	(Z)	(Z)	[6][8]22	(X)
Denmark	24	24	4,642	4,655	26	31	6	8	(X)	(X)
Ecuador	8	9	728	770	6	7	15	17	(X)	(X)
Egypt	37	39	697	704	39	45	44	46	(X)	(X)
Ethiopia	1	2	30	29	1	1	(X)	(X)	(NA)	(NA)
Finland	34	33	6,877	6,566	[5]54	[5]57	4	3	(X)	(X)
France [11]	295	311	5,191	5,434	[5]420	[5]462	(Z)	(X)	[8]10	9
Germany [12]	383	473	6,241	5,890	452	537	[13]4	(X)	[6]77	72
Greece	31	33	3,085	3,241	35	37	[13]1	1	(X)	(X)
Hong Kong	10	13	1,769	2,285	29	35	(NA)	(NA)	(X)	(X)
Hungary	39	35	3,670	3,339	28	32	2	2	[8]2	1
India [9]	269	308	318	350	289	328	33	27	202	238
Indonesia	58	73	312	383	44	46	72	74	7	21
Iran [14]	93	102	1,596	1,661	51	53	159	172	[6]1	2
Iraq	16	24	887	1,247	29	25	101	26	(NA)	(NA)
Ireland	13	14	3,755	3,997	15	16	(X)	(X)	(Z)	(Z)
Israel	15	17	3,149	3,268	21	24	(Z)	(Z)	(X)	(X)
Italy [15]	224	232	3,878	4,019	217	226	5	4	(Z)	(Z)
Japan	564	589	4,567	4,735	857	895	1	1	8	8
Korea, North	94	96	4,322	4,256	54	38	(X)	(X)	[6]68	70
Korea, South	119	141	2,743	3,188	119	148	(X)	(X)	17	12
Kuwait [16]	15	8	6,895	4,038	19	11	60	54	(NA)	(NA)
Libya	16	17	3,508	3,458	17	17	67	69	(X)	(X)
Malaysia	27	34	1,490	1,801	23	32	30	31	(Z)	(Z)
Mexico	157	167	1,863	1,891	[5]122	[5]122	132	139	[6]7	7
Morocco	9	11	378	405	10	10	(Z)	(Z)	1	1
Netherlands	109	108	7,286	7,122	1	1	(X)	(X)	-	-
New Zealand [17]	18	21	5,411	5,935	30	31	2	2	2	3
Nigeria	23	24	212	207	12	12	86	92	[6](Z)	(Z)
Norway [18]	29	29	6,803	6,713	122	118	80	104	(Z)	(Z)
Pakistan [7]	34	37	292	299	44	52	3	4	3	3
Peru	11	11	495	484	14	13	7	6	[6](Z)	(Z)
Philippines	25	26	398	404	26	22	(Z)	(Z)	1	2
Poland	137	134	3,590	3,484	136	133	(Z)	(Z)	[6]148	132
Portugal	19	21	1,947	2,111	29	30	(X)	(X)	(Z)	(Z)
Romania	80	63	3,445	2,702	64	54	8	7	[6]4	4
Saudi Arabia [16]	87	97	5,859	6,097	47	49	320	416	(NA)	(NA)
South Africa [19]	112	113	2,608	2,488	167	169	(X)	(X)	176	175
Soviet Union (former)	1,919	(X)	6,631	(X)	1,764	(X)	553	(X)	474	(X)
Spain	115	122	2,961	3,109	152	159	1	1	[8]15	15
Sudan	2	2	64	61	1	1	(X)	(X)	(NA)	(NA)
Sweden	57	60	6,707	6,937	146	146	(Z)	(Z)	(Z)	(Z)
Switzerland [20]	32	33	4,765	4,877	56	59	(X)	(X)	(X)	(X)
Syria	15	17	1,227	1,291	11	13	23	26	(NA)	(NA)
Taiwan [21]	67	(NA)	3,285	3,644	90	(NA)	(Z)	(Z)	(Z)	(NA)
Tanzania	1	1	39	35	1	1	(X)	(X)	[6](Z)	(Z)
Thailand	42	50	765	888	46	60	1	1	-	(Z)
Trinidad and Tobago	10	11	7,946	8,422	4	4	8	7	(NA)	(NA)
Tunisia	6	6	791	733	6	6	5	5	(X)	(X)
Turkey	59	61	1,052	1,045	58	67	4	4	3	3
United Arab Emirates	35	44	21,980	26,072	17	17	102	104	(NA)	(NA)

See footnotes at end of table.

No. 1399. Energy Consumption and Production, by Country: 1990 and 1992—Continued

[See text, section 30, for general comments about the data. For additional data qualifications for countries, see source]

COUNTRY	ENERGY CONSUMED [1] (coal equiv.)				ELECTRIC ENERGY PRODUCTION [2] (bil. kWh)		CRUDE PETROLEUM PRODUCTION [3] (mil. metric tons)		COAL PRODUCTION [4] (mil. metric tons)	
	Total (mil. metric tons)		Per capita (kilograms)							
	1990	1992	1990	1992	1990	1992	1990	1992	1990	1992
United Kingdom	307	313	5,335	5,400	319	327	88	89	[8]94	85
Venezuela	65	65	3,352	3,214	60	69	112	124	2	2
Vietnam	9	8	137	120	9	10	[3]3	5	5	5
Zaire	2	3	66	64	6	6	[6]1	1	[6](Z)	(Z)
Zambia	2	2	209	201	8	8	(X)	(X)	(Z)	(Z)

- Represents zero.   NA Not available.   X Not applicable.   Z Less than 500,000 metric tons.   [1] Based on apparent consumption of coal, lignite, petroleum products, natural gas, and hydro, nuclear, and geothermal electricity.   [2] Comprises production by utilities generating primarily for public use, and production by industrial establishments generating primarily for own use. Relates to production at generating centers, including station use and transmission losses.   [3] Includes shale oil, but excludes natural gasoline.   [4] Excludes lignite and brown coal, except as noted.   [5] Net production, i.e. excluding station use.   [6] Provisional.   [7] For year ending June of year shown.   [8] Includes recovered slurries.   [9] For year ending April of year shown.   [10] Includes lignite.   [11] Includes Monaco.   [12] Prior to 1991, data for former West Germany.   [13] Includes inputs other than crude petroleum and natural gas liquids.   [14] For year ending March 20 of year shown.   [15] Includes San Marino.   [16] Includes share of production and consumption in the Neutral Zone.   [17] For year ending March 31 for year shown.   [18] Includes Svalbard and Jan Mayen Islands.   [19] Includes Botswana, Lesotho, Namibia, and Swaziland.   [20] Includes Liechtenstein.   [21] Source: U.S. Bureau of the Census. Data from Republic of China publications.

Source: Except as noted, Statistical Office of the United Nations, New York, NY, *Energy Statistics Yearbook*, annual (copyright).

No. 1400. Selected Petroleum Product Prices, by Country: 1994

[As of January. Includes taxes]

COUNTRY	AUTOMOTIVE FUELS (U.S. dollars per gallon)		RESIDENTIAL (U.S. dollars per gallon)			INDUSTRIAL (U.S. dollars per barrel)	
	Premium gasoline	Diesel fuel	Light fuel oil	Kerosene	Liquified petroleum gases	Light fuel oil	Heavy fuel oil
United States [1]	**1.24**	**0.96**	**0.90**	**0.80**	**0.55**	**25.87**	**13.65**
Argentina	2.65	(NA)	1.02	1.02	(NA)	(NA)	(NA)
Australia [1]	1.74	1.70	(NA)	(NA)	(NA)	32.74	14.24
Austria	3.13	2.03	1.30	(NA)	(NA)	27.31	15.99
Belgium [1]	3.15	2.14	0.78	(NA)	(NA)	51.41	(NA)
Bolivia	2.28	1.30	1.22	0.80	0.53	19.29	10.07
Brazil	1.88	1.09	(NA)	1.49	0.62	24.14	17.74
Canada [1]	1.57	1.47	1.09	(NA)	(NA)	(NA)	20.38
Chile	1.46	1.16	(NA)	1.01	(NA)	38.77	18.52
Denmark [1]	3.00	1.74	2.25	(NA)	0.62	38.53	19.27
El Salvador	1.75	0.88	(NA)	0.92	0.62	38.25	20.14
Finland [1]	3.12	2.15	1.11	(NA)	(NA)	38.51	19.34
France [1]	3.31	2.10	1.34	(NA)	(NA)	34.15	16.10
Germany [1]	3.34	2.16	0.93	(NA)	(NA)	48.20	21.80
Greece [1]	2.78	1.66	1.35	(NA)	0.66	28.08	25.29
India	2.28	0.74	(NA)	0.31	0.72	18.06	18.06
Indonesia	1.26	0.68	0.43	(NA)	(NA)	42.08	18.44
Ireland [1]	2.96	2.89	1.31	(NA)	(NA)	97.59	20.63
Italy [1]	3.46	2.31	2.76	1.83	(NA)	45.53	29.69
Japan	4.14	2.48	1.71	(NA)	(NA)	30.10	15.37
Korea, South	2.90	0.99	(NA)	(NA)	0.90	(NA)	17.15
Lebanon	1.19	(NA)	0.85	0.90	(NA)	31.66	15.43
Luxembourg [1]	2.36	1.81	0.84	(NA)	(NA)	43.03	9.25
Mexico [1]	1.60	1.02	(NA)	(NA)	(NA)	(NA)	22.91
Netherlands [1]	3.66	2.61	1.06	(NA)	(NA)	35.09	29.51
New Zealand	1.88	0.97	(NA)	(NA)	(NA)	52.29	45.90
Norway [1]	3.79	2.68	1.52	(NA)	1.10	25.47	14.13
Pakistan	1.79	0.77	0.61	0.75	0.83	(NA)	29.93
Panama	1.43	0.99	(NA)	0.97	(NA)	42.30	19.69
Peru	2.03	1.18	(NA)	1.18	0.72	(NA)	15.21
Philippines	1.37	0.96	(NA)	0.96	(NA)	90.26	21.62
Portugal [1]	3.12	2.15	2.26	(NA)	(NA)	(NA)	5.10
Russia	0.41	0.45	(NA)	(NA)	(NA)	43.19	17.11
Spain [1]	2.75	1.91	1.18	(NA)	(NA)	33.21	21.61
Sweden [1]	3.44	2.44	1.78	(NA)	(NA)	26.17	20.75
Switzerland [1]	2.93	3.17	0.71	(NA)	(NA)	32.26	20.90
Taiwan [1]	2.23	1.59	(NA)	(NA)	(NA)	(NA)	19.93
Turkey [1]	2.39	1.58	1.69	(NA)	(NA)	26.65	14.67
United Kingdom [1]	2.86	2.46	0.71	(NA)	(NA)	(NA)	5.06
Venezuela	0.18	0.16	(NA)	0.12	(NA)	(NA)	5.06

NA Not available.   [1] Average for January.

Source: Energy Information Administration, *International Energy Annual*.

No. 1401. Indices of Food Production, by Country: 1980 to 1993

[1979-1981=100. For explanation of average annual percent change, see Guide to Tabular Presentation. Minus sign (-) indicates decrease]

REGION AND COUNTRY	TOTAL FOOD PRODUCTION						PER CAPITA FOOD PRODUCTION					
	1980	1990	1992	1993	Average annual percent change		1980	1990	1992	1993	Average annual percent change	
					1980-1993	1992-1993					1980-1993	1992-1993
World	**99.2**	**125.7**	**128.4**	**127.3**	**2.2**	**-0.8**	**99.2**	**105.6**	**104.2**	**101.6**	**0.2**	**-2.5**
Developed countries	98.8	110.9	108.8	105.2	0.5	-3.3	98.8	103.5	100.3	96.3	-0.2	-4.0
United States	95.7	105.6	114.0	105.9	0.8	-7.2	95.6	96.2	101.8	93.6	-0.2	-8.1
Canada	99.3	127.1	124.3	122.2	1.8	-1.6	99.3	114.8	109.0	106.2	0.5	-2.6
Europe	101.0	108.9	105.8	104.4	0.3	-1.4	101.0	105.3	101.7	100.0	-0.1	-1.7
Japan	94.5	100.9	99.4	89.4	-0.4	-10.0	94.5	95.4	93.4	83.6	-0.9	-10.6
Oceania	94.7	110.9	120.8	116.5	1.8	-3.5	94.7	95.2	100.2	95.3	(Z)	-5.0
South Africa	96.5	103.6	81.2	101.5	0.4	25.0	96.6	80.7	60.3	73.6	-1.8	22.1
Soviet Union (former) . . .	99.5	121.1	101.4	99.1	(-Z)	-2.3	99.5	111.4	92.0	89.3	-0.8	-2.9
Developing countries	99.6	140.9	148.4	149.9	3.9	1.1	99.6	114.3	115.6	114.5	1.1	-1.0
Africa	99.8	132.7	134.9	138.9	3.0	2.9	99.8	98.4	94.1	93.9	-0.5	-0.1
China	99.3	156.1	167.7	168.0	5.3	0.1	99.3	134.8	140.7	138.8	3.1	-1.3
Near East	100.3	133.4	142.5	143.0	3.3	0.3	100.4	100.0	100.7	98.1	-0.2	-2.6
Far East	99.5	148.2	157.1	159.1	4.6	1.3	99.5	123.1	125.9	125.3	2.0	-0.5
India	98.1	148.9	156.9	161.0	4.9	2.6	98.1	121.3	123.0	123.8	2.0	0.7
Latin America	99.4	127.1	132.5	132.1	2.5	-0.3	99.4	103.5	103.9	101.8	0.2	-2.1
Mexico	100.0	125.9	134.4	128.2	2.2	-4.6	100.0	100.0	102.3	95.6	-0.3	-6.5
Brazil	103.4	132.9	146.4	148.5	3.4	1.4	103.4	108.2	115.2	115.0	0.9	-0.2
Argentina	95.3	109.9	116.8	113.1	1.4	-3.2	95.2	96.0	99.6	95.3	(Z)	-4.3

Z Less than .05 percent.

Source: Food and Agriculture Organization of the United Nations, Rome, Italy, FAO AGRISTAT Database.

No. 1402. Wheat, Rice, and Corn—Exports and Imports of 10 Leading Countries: 1980 to 1992

[**In millions of dollars.** Countries listed are the ten leading exporters or importers in 1992]

LEADING EXPORTERS	EXPORTS			LEADING IMPORTERS	IMPORTS		
	1980	1990	1992		1980	1990	1992
WHEAT				**WHEAT**			
United States	**6,376**	**3,887**	**4,499**	Soviet Union (former) . . .	2,891	2,490	3,420
Canada	3,302	2,863	3,871	China	2,582	2,157	1,663
France	2,110	3,296	3,302	Italy	773	1,217	1,651
Australia	2,425	1,971	1,161	Japan	1,236	1,019	1,177
Germany	198	504	883	Brazil	1,051	331	750
United Kingdom	260	760	776	Egypt	839	853	725
Argentina	816	871	716	India	108	(NA)	600
Turkey	52	4	341	Korea, South	367	419	544
Greece	27	156	262	Belgium-Luxembourg . . .	360	384	535
Saudi Arabia	-	211	210	Indonesia	162	282	402
RICE				**RICE**			
Thailand	953	1,086	1,426	Iran	209	225	375
United States	**1,285**	**804**	**735**	Saudi Arabia	230	153	320
Italy	289	357	452	Soviet Union (former) . . .	265	119	275
Pakistan	422	242	412	France	154	216	258
India	173	258	370	United Kingdom	98	209	232
Vietnam	10	305	285	Iraq	217	124	220
China	510	84	233	Germany	(NA)	(NA)	207
Australia	145	143	188	Indonesia	690	(NA)	172
Spain	22	108	162	Hong Kong	158	150	169
Belgium-Luxembourg . . .	91	168	159	Brazil	99	144	158
CORN				**CORN**			
United States	**8,571**	**6,206**	**4,951**	Japan	2,011	2,295	2,251
France	869	1,854	1,911	Soviet Union (former) . . .	1,508	1,690	980
China	17	404	1,220	Korea, South	376	837	847
Argentina	513	329	637	China	716	750	717
Hungary	27	51	220	Netherlands	626	538	517
Greece	-	32	157	United Kingdom	547	396	417
South Africa	541	176	92	South Africa	4	(NA)	413
Germany	(NA)	71	79	Germany	(NA)	486	402
Yugoslavia	86	(NA)	60	Spain	668	307	289
Canada	113	28	51	Italy	450	363	287

- Represents or rounds to zero.   NA Not available.

Source: Food and Agriculture Organization of the United Nations, Rome, Italy, FAO AGRISTAT database.

No. 1403. Wheat, Rice, and Corn Production, by Country: 1990 to 1993

[In thousands of metric tons. Rice data cover paddy. Data for each country pertain to the calendar year in which all or most of the crop was harvested. See text, section 30, for general comments concerning quality of the data]

COUNTRY	WHEAT			RICE			CORN		
	1990	1992	1993	1990	1992	1993	1990	1992	1993
World	592,811	566,282	564,349	520,549	526,360	518,808	479,008	530,067	477,538
Argentina	11,014	9,685	10,000	428	695	502	5,047	10,699	11,300
Australia	15,066	16,184	15,328	846	1,128	961	219	210	250
Austria	1,404	1,325	1,318	(X)	(X)	(X)	1,620	1,118	1,352
Belgium-Luxembourg	1,347	1,428	1,526	(X)	(X)	(X)	56	86	77
Brazil	3,094	2,796	2,340	7,421	9,962	10,376	21,348	30,557	29,422
Burma	124	143	144	13,969	14,915	16,943	187	206	282
Canada	32,098	29,871	28,151	(X)	(X)	(X)	7,066	4,883	6,852
China	98,232	101,594	103,005	191,589	188,290	181,600	97,158	95,760	93,380
Egypt	4,268	4,618	4,786	3,167	3,910	3,800	4,799	5,069	5,300
France	33,313	32,508	29,613	125	122	120	9,291	14,886	14,318
Germany	15,242	15,542	15,520	(X)	(X)	(X)	1,552	2,139	2,730
Greece	1,938	2,385	2,350	99	101	110	2,131	2,048	1,600
Hungary	6,198	3,444	3,032	39	15	15	4,500	4,417	6,000
India	49,850	55,087	56,855	111,517	108,011	112,511	8,962	10,400	9,920
Indonesia	(X)	(X)	(X)	45,179	47,700	47,690	6,734	7,996	6,513
Iran	8,012	10,350	10,900	1,981	2,500	2,646	130	200	210
Iraq	1,196	1,006	1,187	229	180	206	172	260	280
Italy	8,109	8,943	8,400	1,291	1,284	1,300	5,864	7,679	7,000
Japan	952	759	770	13,124	13,216	10,540	1	1	1
Korea, South	1	1	-	7,722	7,835	6,466	7,722	7,835	6,466
Mexico	3,935	3,626	3,600	394	361	350	14,640	17,003	16,500
Pakistan	14,316	15,684	16,273	4,891	4,674	4,780	1,185	1,178	1,279
Soviet Union (former)	101,891	90,037	87,000	2,166	1,969	2,054	9,886	7,319	10,281
Sweden	2,243	1,411	1,770	(X)	(X)	(X)	(X)	(X)	(X)
Thailand	-	1	1	17,193	19,935	17,375	3,722	3,672	3,724
United Kingdom	14,033	14,092	12,400	(X)	(X)	(X)	-	-	-
United States	74,473	66,920	65,904	7,080	8,123	7,496	201,532	240,774	176,839
Yugoslavia	6,359	4,100	3,100	28	43	43	6,724	7,025	5,500

- Represents or rounds to zero.   X Not applicable.

Source: Food and Agriculture Organization of the United Nations, Rome, Italy, FAO AGRISTAT database.

No. 1404. Fisheries—Commercial Catch, by Selected Country: 1989 to 1992

[In thousands of metric tons, live weight. Catch of fish, crustaceans, mollusks (including weight of shells). Does not include marine mammals and aquatic plants. Countries shown had a commercial catch of 1,000,000 metric tons or more in 1992]

COUNTRY	1989	1990	1991	1992	COUNTRY	1989	1990	1991	1992
World total [1]	100,311	97,556	97,051	98,112	Korea, South	2,840	2,843	2,521	2,695
Canada	1,572	1,624	1,534	1,251	Mexico	1,469	1,400	1,453	1,247
Chile	6,454	5,195	6,002	6,501	Norway	1,908	1,711	2,095	2,549
China	11,219	12,095	13,134	15,007	Peru	6,853	6,875	6,949	6,842
Denmark	1,929	1,518	1,795	1,995	Philippines	2,098	2,208	2,311	2,271
Iceland	1,502	1,508	1,050	1,577	Russia	(X)	(X)	6,894	5,611
India	3,640	3,794	4,044	4,175	Spain (est.)	1,560	1,400	1,320	1,330
Indonesia	2,948	3,044	3,251	3,357	Thailand	2,699	2,786	2,967	2,855
Japan	11,173	10,354	9,301	8,460	**United States**	5,778	5,870	5,488	5,602
Korea, North (est.)	1,700	1,750	1,700	1,750	Vietnam	930	960	1,020	1,080

X Not applicable.   [1] Includes other countries, not shown separately.

Source: U.S. National Oceanic and Atmospheric Administration, National Marine Fisheries Service, *Fisheries of the United States,* annual. Data from Food and Agricultural Organization of the United Nations, Rome, Italy.

No. 1405. Meat Production, by Country: 1990 to 1993

[In thousands of metric tons, carcass weight. Covers beef and veal (incl. buffalo meat), pork (incl. bacon and ham), mutton and lamb (incl. goat meat), horsemeat, and poultry. Refers to meat from animals slaughtered within the national boundaries irrespective of origin of animals, and relates to commercial and farm slaughter. Excludes lard, tallow, and edible offals. See text, section 30, for general comments concerning the data]

COUNTRY	1990	1992	1993	COUNTRY	1990	1992	1993
World	178,169	184,323	185,917	Italy	3,950	3,988	3,936
				Japan	3,503	3,398	3,378
Argentina	3,383	3,540	3,617	Mexico	3,478	3,563	3,628
Brazil	6,439	7,343	7,545	Soviet Union (former)	19,996	16,297	15,566
France	5,765	6,188	6,085	Spain	3,466	3,681	3,701
Germany	7,292	6,204	5,947	United Kingdom	3,357	3,365	2,340
India	3,723	3,899	3,992	**United States**	28,632	30,780	31,350

Source: Food and Agriculture Organization of the United Nations, Rome, Italy, FAO AGRISTAT database.

No. 1406. United States and Foreign Stock Markets—Market Capitalization and Value of Shares Traded: 1985 to 1993

[In millions of U.S. dollars. Market capitalization is the total amount of the various securities (bonds, debentures, and stock) issued by corporations]

COUNTRY	MARKET CAPITALIZATION				VALUE OF SHARES TRADED			
	1985	1990	1992	1993	1985	1990	1992	1993
United States	**2,324,646**	**3,089,651**	**4,757,879**	**5,223,768**	**997,189**	**1,815,476**	**2,678,523**	**3,507,223**
Argentina	2,037	3,268	18,633	43,967	631	852	15,679	10,339
Australia	60,163	107,611	135,451	203,964	15,736	39,333	45,005	67,711
Austria	4,602	11,476	21,750	28,437	686	18,609	4,931	6,561
Belgium	20,871	65,449	64,172	78,067	1,876	6,425	8,030	11,199
Brazil	42,768	16,354	45,261	99,430	21,484	5,598	20,525	57,409
Canada	147,000	241,920	243,018	326,524	39,905	71,278	83,448	142,222
Chile	2,012	13,645	29,644	44,622	57	783	2,029	2,797
Colombia	416	1,416	5,681	9,237	30	71	554	732
Denmark	15,096	39,063	32,635	41,785	1,274	11,105	15,806	20,989
Finland	5,855	22,721	12,202	23,562	502	3,933	2,292	8,112
France	79,000	314,384	350,858	456,111	14,672	116,893	121,842	174,283
Germany	183,765	355,073	348,138	463,476	71,572	501,805	446,019	302,985
Greece	765	15,228	9,489	12,319	17	3,924	1,605	2,713
Hong Kong	34,504	83,397	172,106	385,247	9,732	34,633	78,598	131,550
India	14,364	38,567	65,119	97,976	4,959	21,918	20,597	21,879
Indonesia	117	8,081	12,038	32,953	3	3,992	3,903	9,158
Italy	58,502	148,766	129,191	136,153	13,782	42,566	28,100	65,770
Japan	978,663	2,917,679	2,399,004	2,999,756	329,970	1,602,388	635,261	954,341
Korea, South	7,381	110,594	107,448	139,420	4,162	75,949	116,101	211,710
Luxembourg	12,658	10,456	11,936	19,337	36	87	118	1,104
Malaysia	16,229	48,611	94,004	220,328	2,335	10,871	21,730	153,661
Mexico	3,815	32,725	139,061	200,671	2,360	12,212	44,582	62,454
Netherlands	59,363	119,825	134,594	181,876	16,864	40,199	45,511	67,185
New Zealand	8,761	8,835	15,348	25,597	935	1,933	3,168	6,785
Norway	10,063	26,130	17,821	27,380	1,877	13,996	10,151	8,751
Pakistan	1,370	2,850	8,028	11,602	236	231	980	1,844
Philippines	669	5,927	13,794	40,327	111	1,216	3,104	6,785
Portugal	192	9,201	9,213	12,417	5	1,687	3,455	4,835
Spain	19,000	111,404	98,969	119,264	3,382	40,967	39,987	47,156
Sweden	37,296	92,102	76,622	107,376	9,644	15,718	28,395	43,593
Switzerland	90,000	160,044	195,285	271,713	(NA)	(NA)	75,407	167,880
Taiwan	10,432	100,710	101,124	195,198	4,899	715,005	240,667	346,487
Thailand	1,856	23,896	58,259	130,510	568	22,894	72,060	86,934
Turkey	(NA)	19,065	9,931	37,496	(NA)	5,841	8,191	23,242
United Kingdom	328,000	848,866	927,129	1,151,646	68,417	278,740	382,996	423,526

NA Not available.

Source: International Finance Corporation, Washington, DC, *Emerging Stock Markets Factbook, 1994*, (copyright).

No. 1407. Dow-Jones World Stock Index, by Country and Industry: 1992 to 1994

[Index figures shown are as of **December 31**. Indexes based on **June 30, 1982=100** for United States; **December 31, 1991=100** for World. Based on share prices denominated in U.S. dollars. Stocks in countries that impose significant restrictions on foreign ownership are included in the world index in the same proportion that shares are available to foreign investors]

INDUSTRY	1992	1993	1994	INDUSTRY	1992	1993	1994
World, total	**92.83**	**111.08**	**113.94**	Asia/Pacific	79.42	106.76	119.48
Americas	104.37	112.18	108.53	Australia	84.66	113.29	114.89
United States	413.29	442.19	433.07	Hong Kong	125.44	270.36	183.94
Canada	84.65	100.36	95.23	Indonesia	112.32	233.92	175.71
Mexico	123.13	182.88	107.06	Japan	76.89	95.71	116.21
Europe	93.66	116.08	115.70	Malaysia	128.80	269.99	216.69
Austria	81.30	104.82	104.36	New Zealand	95.89	151.52	155.86
Belgium	90.06	111.55	115.75	Singapore	103.07	179.22	178.06
Denmark	71.95	95.73	98.16	Thailand	116.82	243.90	207.66
Finland	79.59	138.67	205.91				
France	97.86	117.78	109.17	Basic materials	91.88	109.04	124.39
Germany	88.76	118.94	122.57	Conglomerate	93.90	129.80	127.60
Ireland	80.72	111.95	122.59	Consumer, cyclical	98.88	123.24	124.31
Italy	77.92	99.11	109.54	Consumer, noncyclical	92.51	93.01	98.64
Netherlands	98.07	125.74	133.88	Energy	93.28	107.82	110.24
Norway	78.47	103.28	122.60	Financial services	90.75	114.97	112.78
Spain	78.10	94.89	89.33	Industrial	86.34	106.00	112.26
Sweden	83.07	104.06	119.42	Technology	94.63	114.61	134.95
Switzerland	111.46	158.28	162.99	Utilities	92.52	114.42	101.20
United Kingdom	94.32	112.30	107.34				

Source: Dow Jones & Company, Inc., New York, NY, *Wall Street Journal*, January 3, 1995, (copyright).

No. 1408. Foreign Stock Market Activity—Morgan Stanley Capital International Indexes: 1990 to 1994

[Index figures shown are as of **December 31. January 1, 1970=100, except as noted**. Based on share prices denominated in U.S. dollars. EMG=Emerging Markets Global. GDP=Gross Domestic Product]

INDEX AND COUNTRY	INDEX			PERCENT CHANGE [1]		INDEX AND COUNTRY	INDEX			PERCENT CHANGE [1]	
	1990	1993	1994	1993	1994		1990	1993	1994	1993	1994
All Country World index [2]	114.3	152.3	157.2	22.6	3.2	Sweden	915	1,163	1,363	35.6	17.3
Combined Far East Free index [3]	88.9	108.3	120.2	36.8	11.0	Switzerland	567	1,076	1,102	44.1	2.4
						United Kingdom	514	641	611	20.6	-4.7
DEVELOPED MARKETS						Hong Kong	1,547	5,907	4,076	109.9	-31.0
						Japan	2,638	2,773	3,347	24.6	20.7
World index [4]	462	598	619	20.4	3.4	Singapore	1,166	2,472	2,604	65.5	5.4
EAFE index [5]	789	977	1,038	30.5	6.2						
Europe index	479	616	617	26.4	0.1	EMERGING MARKETS					
Pacific index	1,735	2,075	2,321	34.4	11.8	EMG Far East index	168.2	294.8	294.5	76.7	-0.1
						India [7]	(NA)	133.0	145.1	33.0	9.1
GDP-weighted indexes:						Indonesia	610.8	647.6	472.8	102.2	-27.0
World index	540	711	739	22.5	4.0	Korea, South	139.4	149.2	182.3	29.1	22.1
EAFE index [5]	817	1,035	1,100	31.6	6.3	Malaysia	170.4	421.0	333.8	107.3	-20.7
						Pakistan [7]	(NA)	161.4	148.2	61.4	-8.2
United States	306.9	435.0	431.3	7.0	-0.9	Philippines	94.1	521.5	523.2	130.2	0.3
Canada	341.9	365.7	347.9	15.1	-4.9	Sri Lanka [7]	(NA)	163.2	156.9	63.2	-3.9
						Taiwan	177.7	272.9	326.7	82.3	19.7
Australia	184.6	273.0	281.0	32.0	2.9	Thailand	205.0	624.3	554.7	97.8	-11.1
New Zealand [6]	53.0	92.0	97.4	62.6	5.8						
						EMG Latin America	236.7	979.9	928.3	49.1	-5.3
Austria	1,052	1,017	945	26.7	-7.1	Argentina	318	1,520	1,140	55.9	-25.0
Belgium	568	702	736	19.4	4.9	Brazil	89.2	448.4	734.5	75.3	63.8
Denmark	867	933	958	31.7	2.6	Chile	214	682	962	31.4	41.2
Finland [6]	66.3	82.4	124.6	81.3	51.3	Colombia [7]	(NA)	128.3	152.6	28.3	18.9
France	461	642	599	19.0	-6.6	Mexico	424	1,742	969	44.0	-44.4
Germany	551	690	713	33.6	3.3	Peru [7]	(NA)	125.4	181.3	25.4	44.5
Ireland [6]	138.4	161.5	180.7	38.9	11.9	Venezuela [7]	(NA)	86.8	56.4	-13.2	-35.0
Italy	205.2	189.4	209.1	26.7	10.4	Greece [6]	321.9	220.4	213.3	36.4	-3.2
Netherlands	594	881	959	31.5	8.9	Jordan	55.3	100.3	91.2	17.8	-9.1
Norway	896	801	978	40.3	22.1	Portugal [6]	66.8	64.8	70.1	29.5	8.2
Spain	132.0	139.1	128.9	25.7	-7.4	Turkey	195.2	231.0	109.6	207.7	-52.6

NA Not available.   [1] Percent change during calendar year (e.g. December 31, 1992, through December 31, 1993). Adjusted for foreign exchange fluctuations relative to U.S. dollar.   [2] Comprises World index, all emerging markets, and Luxembourg.   [3] Comprises Hong Kong, Japan, Singapore, and EMG Far East.   [4] Includes South African gold mines quoted in London.   [5] Europe, Australia, Far East Index. Comprises all European and Far East countries listed under developed markets plus Australia and New Zealand.   [6] January 1, 1988=100.   [7] December 1992=100.

Source: Morgan Stanley Capital International, New York, NY, unpublished data, (copyright).

No. 1409. 500 Largest Banks in the World—Number and Deposits, by Location of Bank: 1980 to 1993

[**Deposits in billions of dollars, except percent**. Data cover U.S. commercial banks and foreign banks that conduct a commercial banking business; beginning 1985, includes U.S. and foreign savings banks. Beginning 1985, covers top 500 banks in assets available. Number of banks includes banks more than 50 percent owned by other banks. To avoid double-counting of deposits, banks more than 50 percent owned by other banks are excluded from deposit totals if their parent bank consolidates their deposits]

LOCATION OF BANK	1980	1985	1986	1987	1988	1989	1990	1991	1992	1993	PERCENT		
											1980	1990	1993
NUMBER													
U.S. banks	93	110	102	90	107	108	96	91	88	102	19	19	20
Foreign banks	407	390	398	410	393	392	404	409	412	398	81	81	80
Japan	78	96	108	111	111	108	106	110	118	117	16	21	23
United Kingdom	34	22	20	18	18	20	22	20	18	15	7	4	3
Germany	38	39	38	42	38	37	39	41	43	42	8	8	8
France	28	20	23	23	20	20	20	18	17	17	6	4	3
Italy	27	29	31	32	29	28	31	31	29	26	5	6	5
DEPOSITS													
Total	4,994	7,022	9,220	12,090	12,837	13,565	15,854	16,479	17,001	18,113	100	100	100
U.S. banks	754	1,014	1,084	1,108	1,347	1,352	1,329	1,311	1,313	1,437	15	8	8
Foreign banks	4,240	6,008	8,136	10,982	11,489	12,214	14,525	15,168	15,688	16,676	85	92	92
Japan	1,131	2,179	3,350	4,936	5,333	5,236	5,888	6,213	7,097	7,927	24	37	44
United Kingdom	349	403	458	588	646	673	822	880	800	748	7	5	4
Germany	603	684	912	1,208	1,151	1,309	1,692	1,909	1,907	2,103	12	11	12
France	483	502	650	836	822	970	1,175	1,101	1,032	1,061	10	7	6
Italy	290	395	527	647	606	708	870	1,008	873	782	6	5	4

Source: American Banker-Bond Buyer, New York, NY, *American Banker Ranking The Banks*, annual, (copyright).

874 Comparative International Statistics

No. 1410. Central Bank Discount Rates, Money Market Rates, and Government Bond Yields, by Country: 1980 to 1995

[In percent per annum. Central bank discount rates refer to the rate at which the monetary authority lends or discounts eligible paper for deposit money banks. **Money market rates** refer to the rate at which short-term borrowings are effected between financial institutions. **Government bond yields** refer to one or more series representing average yields to maturity of government bonds or other bonds that would be indicative of longer term rates]

NATIONAL INTEREST RATE AND YEAR	United States	Canada	Japan	France	Germany [1]	Italy	Netherlands	Sweden	Switzerland	United Kingdom
Central bank discount rates: [2]										
1980	13.00	17.26	7.25	9.50	7.50	16.50	8.00	10.00	3.00	14.00
1985	7.50	9.49	5.00	9.50	4.00	15.00	5.00	10.50	4.00	([3])
1990	6.50	11.78	6.00	9.50	6.00	12.50	7.25	11.50	6.00	([3])
1991	3.50	7.67	4.50	9.50	8.00	12.00	8.50	8.00	7.00	([3])
1992	3.00	7.36	3.25	9.50	8.25	12.00	7.75	[4]10.00	6.00	([3])
1993	3.00	4.11	1.75	9.50	5.75	8.00	5.00	5.00	4.00	([3])
1994	4.75	7.00	1.75	9.50	4.50	7.50	(NA)	7.00	3.50	([3])
1995, February	5.25	8.00	1.75	9.50	4.50	(NA)	(NA)	7.00	3.50	([3])
Money market rates: [5]										
1980	13.36	13.28	10.93	11.85	9.10	17.17	10.13	12.17	2.29	15.62
1985	8.10	9.57	6.46	9.93	5.20	15.25	6.30	13.85	3.75	10.78
1990	8.10	11.62	7.24	9.85	7.92	12.38	8.29	13.45	8.33	14.68
1991	5.70	7.40	7.46	9.49	8.84	12.18	9.01	11.81	7.73	11.75
1992	3.52	6.79	4.58	10.35	9.42	13.97	9.27	18.42	7.47	9.55
1993	3.02	3.79	[4]3.06	8.75	7.49	10.20	7.10	9.08	4.94	5.63
1994	4.20	5.54	2.20	5.69	5.35	(NA)	5.14	7.36	3.85	4.76
1995, February	5.92	8.02	2.22	5.34	4.99	(NA)	4.92	7.65	3.26	5.63
Government bond yields:										
1980	11.46	12.48	9.22	13.03	8.50	16.11	10.21	11.74	4.77	13.79
1985	10.62	11.04	6.34	10.94	6.87	13.00	7.34	13.09	4.78	10.62
1990	8.55	10.85	7.36	9.96	8.88	11.51	8.92	13.08	[4]6.68	11.08
1991	7.86	9.76	6.53	9.05	8.63	[4]13.18	8.74	10.69	6.35	9.92
1992	7.01	8.77	4.94	8.60	7.96	13.27	8.10	10.02	5.48	9.15
1993	5.82	7.85	3.69	6.91	6.28	11.31	6.51	8.54	4.05	7.87
1994	7.11	8.63	3.71	7.35	6.67	10.56	7.20	[4]9.41	5.23	8.05
1995, February	7.47	8.86	(NA)	8.05	7.27	(NA)	7.74	(NA)	5.23	8.52

NA Not available. [1] Prior to July 1990, data are for former West Germany. [2] End of period. [3] Minimum lending rate suspended as of August 20, 1981. [4] Beginning in year shown, data not comparable with previous years. [5] Period averages.

Source: International Monetary Fund, Washington, DC, *International Financial Statistics,* monthly.

No. 1411. External Debt of Eastern European Countries: 1980 to 1993

[In billions of dollars. **Gross debt:** total amount owed. **Commercial debt:** money owed to private institutions or individuals. **Official debt:** money owed to or guaranteed by a foreign government]

ITEM	1980	1985	1987	1988	1989	1990	1991	1992	1993
Bulgaria: Gross debt	3.5	3.7	6.1	8.9	10.2	10.6	12.7	10.9	(NA)
Commercial debt	3.2	3.1	5.3	7.0	8.5	8.6	9.8	8.7	(NA)
Official debt	0.3	0.6	0.9	1.9	1.7	2.0	2.9	2.2	(NA)
Czech Republic: Gross debt	(X)	(X)	(X)	(X)	(X)	(X)	(X)	3.9	8.7
Commercial debt	(X)	(X)	(X)	(X)	(X)	(X)	(X)	2.8	6.3
Official debt	(X)	(X)	(X)	(X)	(X)	(X)	(X)	0.8	1.7
Multilateral institutions	(X)	(X)	(X)	(X)	(X)	(X)	(X)	0.3	0.7
Hungary: Gross debt	9.1	11.8	17.8	19.6	20.4	21.3	22.7	21.4	24.7
Commercial debt	8.8	9.8	15.0	16.6	17.3	18.2	18.1	15.7	18.6
Official debt	0.3	0.8	1.0	1.2	1.4	1.4	2.8	2.4	2.7
Multilateral institutions	-	1.2	1.8	1.8	1.7	1.7	1.7	3.3	3.4
Poland: Gross debt	25.0	29.3	39.2	39.2	40.8	48.5	48.4	47.0	48.4
Commercial debt	14.9	10.6	12.8	15.4	15.3	14.4	16.4	12.1	12.7
Official debt	10.1	18.7	26.4	23.2	24.9	32.8	30.2	30.9	29.6
Multilateral institutions	-	-	-	0.6	0.6	1.3	1.8	4.0	6.1
Romania: Gross debt	9.4	6.6	5.1	2.2	0.1	0.9	2.1	3.8	(NA)
Commercial debt	6.5	2.9	1.7	0.4	0.1	0.4	0.6	0.7	(NA)
Official debt	1.7	1.1	0.8	0.6	-	0.1	0.6	0.9	(NA)
Multilateral institutions	1.2	2.6	2.6	1.2	-	0.4	0.9	2.2	(NA)
Russia: [1] Gross debt	20.5	29.0	40.8	42.4	50.8	53.6	61.0	74.0	(NA)
Commercial debt	11.0	19.5	30.1	33.7	40.5	35.6	31.8	38.0	(NA)
Official debt	9.5	9.5	10.7	8.7	10.2	18.0	29.2	36.0	(NA)
Slovakia: Gross debt	(X)	(X)	(X)	(X)	(X)	(X)	(X)	1.9	3.1
Commercial debt	(X)	(X)	(X)	(X)	(X)	(X)	(X)	1.4	2.3
Official debt	(X)	(X)	(X)	(X)	(X)	(X)	(X)	0.4	0.6
Multilateral institutions	(X)	(X)	(X)	(X)	(X)	(X)	(X)	0.1	0.2

- Represents zero. NA Not available. X Not applicable. [1] The debt of the former Soviet Union was assumed by Russia.

Source: U.S. Central Intelligence Agency, *Handbook of International Economic Statistics, 1993;* and unpublished data.

No. 1412. External Public Debt, by Country: 1990 to 1993

[External public debt is defined as debt repayable to external creditors in foreign currency, goods, or services, with an original or extended maturity of more than 1 year, which is a direct obligation of, or has repayment guaranteed by, a public body in the borrowing country. Excludes undisbursed debt (amounts not yet drawn by recipient) and unguaranteed private debt, which for some countries is substantial. Debt contracted for the purchase of military equipment is not usually reported. **Debt service payments** represent the sum of interest payments and repayments of principal on external public debt]

COUNTRY	TOTAL EXTERNAL PUBLIC DEBT (mil. dol.)			1993 Total [1]	1993 Bilateral official	1993 Banks	1993 International organizations	DEBT SERVICE PAYMENTS (mil. dol.) 1990	1992	1993	DEBT SERVICE RATIO [2] (percent) 1990	1992	1993
	1990	1991	1992										
Argentina	46,905	47,568	47,036	55,415	8,520	204	7,128	4,812	3,320	6,521	32	21	39
Bangladesh	11,452	11,961	12,244	13,048	4,907	-	7,996	516	430	427	19	13	11
Bolivia	3,690	3,534	3,671	3,687	1,601	19	1,987	275	224	413	28	28	50
Brazil	83,761	81,477	86,204	86,650	16,843	44,686	9,374	6,345	6,254	4,979	17	15	11
Bulgaria	9,817	9,990	9,957	9,746	1,141	6,645	1,115	1,324	265	238	29	6	5
Cameroon	4,704	4,913	5,417	5,436	3,230	253	1,389	244	180	271	11	8	14
Chile	10,426	10,071	9,578	8,868	777	3,554	4,327	1,612	1,438	1,574	15	11	13
China	45,397	49,342	58,341	70,023	13,649	20,776	10,690	5,866	7,912	9,296	10	9	10
Colombia	14,671	14,469	13,238	12,861	1,563	3,720	5,679	3,115	3,452	2,760	33	33	25
Congo	4,183	4,022	3,857	4,097	2,323	917	532	475	127	95	32	10	8
Costa Rica	3,076	3,320	3,207	3,139	1,289	10	1,219	432	476	451	21	18	15
Cote d'Ivoire	10,014	10,635	10,669	10,550	5,117	2,408	2,841	492	502	441	14	15	14
Croatia	(X)	(X)	(X)	870	204	54	561	(X)	(X)	170	(X)	(X)	(NA)
Dominican Republic	3,434	3,751	3,725	3,763	1,965	796	889	145	269	274	6	11	9
Ecuador	9,867	9,951	9,831	9,935	2,191	4,831	2,342	874	812	762	27	22	21
Egypt	34,337	36,111	35,809	36,603	29,860	414	3,463	2,738	2,010	2,058	21	12	13
Ethiopia	3,628	3,976	4,185	4,530	2,227	79	1,817	203	99	63	24	13	8
Gabon	3,135	3,180	3,002	2,889	1,897	172	401	102	334	61	4	13	2
Ghana	2,701	2,987	3,123	3,341	787	-	2,386	180	189	167	18	17	14
Guatemala	2,240	2,234	2,106	2,301	1,127	149	836	164	449	224	10	21	10
Honduras	3,416	3,083	3,211	3,479	1,275	97	1,953	307	349	329	29	32	29
Hungary	18,006	18,931	17,843	20,357	688	5,130	3,218	3,750	4,350	3,895	33	34	36
India [3]	70,828	73,431	78,992	83,254	27,988	18,911	26,130	6,234	6,720	8,170	24	26	26
Indonesia	55,224	61,610	65,698	68,865	26,523	2,837	17,825	8,492	10,753	12,458	28	28	31
Jamaica	3,931	3,806	3,686	3,604	1,988	250	1,163	497	564	377	20	19	14
Jordan	7,023	7,447	6,914	6,825	3,765	595	907	532	641	516	17	18	13
Kenya	4,850	4,992	4,978	5,121	1,395	894	2,660	529	456	429	24	21	18
Korea, South	18,787	22,481	24,051	24,566	6,230	3,350	3,202	4,770	4,592	6,213	6	5	6
Macedonia, The Former Yugoslav Republic of	(X)	(X)	(X)	528	111	104	226	(X)	(X)	8	(X)	(X)	(NA)
Madagascar	3,782	3,972	3,909	3,920	2,213	46	1,466	193	75	51	36	15	10
Malaysia	12,684	14,014	13,468	13,863	2,902	2,354	1,626	2,827	2,545	3,331	8	5	6
Mali	2,345	2,455	2,470	2,506	1,393	2	1,110	40	33	14	7	6	3
Mexico	77,557	79,119	72,264	74,450	10,098	7,368	16,059	7,983	15,326	10,360	15	25	16
Morocco	22,142	20,301	20,510	20,310	10,019	3,215	5,608	1,432	1,894	2,376	17	21	28
Nicaragua	8,245	8,762	8,991	8,773	5,714	1,299	1,162	9	77	110	2	24	28
Oman	2,399	2,472	2,340	2,319	421	1,312	163	714	493	583	12	8	(NA)
Pakistan	16,410	17,620	18,455	20,306	9,132	842	9,908	1,387	1,766	1,911	17	18	19
Panama	3,988	3,918	3,771	3,709	682	2,162	625	141	632	217	6	27	9
Papua New Guinea	1,502	1,592	1,534	1,515	380	153	845	274	196	265	18	9	10
Peru	13,634	15,301	15,417	16,123	9,314	3,126	2,742	179	760	1,711	4	17	39
Philippines	24,073	25,063	25,605	27,471	13,541	619	7,645	2,899	3,788	4,243	22	22	22
Poland	39,263	45,049	42,941	41,426	31,010	8,743	1,471	841	1,283	1,315	5	8	8
Portugal	17,133	19,543	21,433	25,173	1,292	9,624	3,673	4,390	4,870	4,799	16	16	13
Senegal	2,939	2,863	2,961	3,011	1,246	68	1,657	211	131	68	13	9	5
Slovenia	(X)	(X)	(X)	1,256	259	497	463	(X)	(X)	187	(X)	(X)	(NA)
Sri Lanka	4,938	5,654	5,618	5,936	3,091	233	2,359	285	378	372	10	10	9
Sudan	9,155	9,220	8,984	8,994	5,582	1,449	1,959	23	25	17	3	5	3
Syria	14,917	16,353	15,912	16,234	14,222	-	835	1,191	207	174	22	4	3
Tanzania	6,298	6,483	6,579	6,734	3,976	84	2,378	191	292	144	31	44	23
Thailand	12,630	13,418	13,426	14,562	6,302	2,563	3,039	3,270	2,155	2,165	10	5	4
Tunisia	6,662	7,109	7,202	7,424	3,144	552	3,111	1,220	1,214	1,219	21	18	18
Turkey	38,512	39,041	39,513	43,321	7,413	11,149	9,302	6,467	7,387	6,909	26	26	23
Uganda	2,234	2,359	2,521	2,617	780	30	1,739	79	69	287	36	34	115
Uruguay	4,524	4,356	4,498	4,629	234	269	1,091	797	549	621	33	21	38
Venezuela	24,509	24,939	25,830	26,856	938	290	2,884	4,167	1,829	2,301	20	11	13
Yemen [4]	5,154	5,256	5,253	5,341	2,518	80	1,108	108	103	99	4	7	6
Yugoslavia [4]	12,986	11,641	11,015	8,199	2,470	4,121	1,600	2,719	968	14	9	8	·
Zaire	9,006	9,271	8,948	8,769	5,722	511	2,211	137	56	12	6	3	1
Zambia	4,852	4,991	4,719	4,666	2,577	73	1,757	173	245	217	13	21	20
Zimbabwe	2,464	2,611	2,787	3,021	1,002	98	1,307	370	470	483	18	25	25

- Represents or rounds to zero.   NA Not available.   X Not applicable.   [1] Includes other types of creditors not shown separately.   [2] Debt service payments as percent of exports.   [3] Fiscal year basis.   [4] The bulk of the debt of Yugoslovian enterprises is reported as nonguaranteed.

Source: The World Bank, Washington, DC, *World Debt Tables,* periodic.

Comparative International Statistics

No. 1413. Net Flow of Financial Resources to Developing Countries: 1980 to 1993

[In billions of U.S. dollars. Net flow covers loans, grants, and grant-like flows minus amortization on loans. Military flows are excluded. Developing countries cover countries designated by Development Assistance Committee (DAC) as developing. Official development assistance covers all flows to developing countries and multilateral institutions provided by official agencies, including State and local governments, or by their executive agencies, which are administered with the promotion of economic development and welfare of developing countries as their main objective and whose financial terms are intended to be concessional in character with grant element of at least 25 percent. Other official flows cover export credits and portfolio investment from the official sector]

ORIGIN AND TYPE OF RESOURCE	1980	1985	1986	1987	1988	1989	1990	1991	1992	1993
DAC countries [1]	75.4	45.2	68.8	66.4	85.6	84.4	76.4	94.7	115.8	(NA)
Official development assistance .	27.3	29.4	36.7	41.6	48.1	45.7	53.0	56.7	60.9	56.0
Bilateral grants [2]	14.1	17.8	21.1	23.4	26.0	25.9	30.8	34.6	32.9	33.1
Bilateral loans	4.0	4.1	5.2	6.6	7.1	7.1	6.4	6.6	8.3	5.9
Multilateral contributions [3]	9.2	7.5	10.4	11.6	15.0	12.8	15.8	15.4	19.6	17.0
Other official flows	5.3	3.4	2.1	2.0	4.9	5.8	8.6	7.1	8.9	7.5
Private flows at market terms...	40.4	9.4	26.7	18.8	28.3	28.8	9.8	25.5	40.1	62.0
Direct investment	10.1	6.5	11.0	21.0	25.1	30.1	26.3	22.6	28.1	34.9
Private export credits	11.5	0.8	-1.7	-2.4	-1.3	5.7	-0.4	1.1	0.6	1.4
Portfolio investment	18.7	2.1	17.4	0.3	4.4	-7.0	-16.2	1.8	11.2	25.7
Private voluntary agencies.....	2.4	2.9	3.3	4.0	4.2	4.0	5.1	5.4	6.0	5.6
OPEC [4]	10.8	4.1	(NA)	(NA)	(NA)	(NA)	(NA)	(NA)	(NA)	(NA)
Official development assistance .	9.7	3.6	4.7	3.3	2.4	1.7	6.0	2.7	1.2	(NA)
Other official flows	1.1	0.5	(NA)	(NA)	(NA)	(NA)	(NA)	(NA)	(NA)	(NA)
Total net flow to developing countries, by DAC country [1]	75.4	45.2	68.8	66.4	85.6	84.4	76.4	94.7	115.8	(NA)
United States	13.9	1.8	18.2	13.8	17.5	16.4	11.1	20.8	33.5	58.3
Official development assistance	7.1	9.4	9.6	8.9	10.1	7.7	11.4	11.3	11.7	10.1
Bilateral grants [2]	3.0	7.3	7.0	6.7	6.5	6.8	8.5	12.1	8.7	8.5
Bilateral loans	1.4	0.9	0.6	0.3	0.3	(Z)	-0.2	-2.7	-0.8	-1.2
Multilateral contributions [3]	2.8	1.2	2.0	1.9	3.4	0.9	3.0	1.9	3.9	2.8
Other official flows	1.1	0.2	-0.6	-1.8	1.9	-0.5	-0.4	-0.8	1.3	0.1
Private flows at market terms .	4.3	-9.3	7.5	4.4	3.2	7.3	-2.4	7.6	17.7	45.4
Direct investment	3.4	0.9	3.1	8.0	4.2	7.1	7.8	10.5	14.0	20.6
Private export credits and portfolio investment	0.9	-10.2	4.4	-3.6	-1.0	-0.3	-10.1	-2.9	3.7	24.8
Private voluntary agencies ...	1.3	1.5	1.7	1.6	2.3	1.9	2.5	2.7	2.8	2.6
Australia	0.9	1.2	1.1	0.9	3.6	1.5	1.5	-2.1	4.2	2.1
Austria	0.3	0.2	0.1	0.2	0.3	0.2	0.6	0.7	0.8	0.7
Belgium	2.9	1.3	-0.8	-0.3	1.8	1.5	0.1	1.5	2.2	(NA)
Canada	3.2	1.7	1.6	2.5	3.0	2.7	3.5	4.0	4.2	5.3
Denmark	0.8	0.4	0.5	0.9	0.7	0.9	1.1	1.1	1.6	1.4
Finland	0.2	0.3	0.4	0.6	0.8	0.9	1.0	1.0	0.8	0.3
France	11.6	8.9	9.2	8.7	5.4	5.3	5.7	6.5	10.8	(NA)
Germany [5]	10.6	5.8	7.9	8.8	11.8	12.1	13.6	13.1	8.9	15.3
Ireland	(Z)	0.1	0.1	0.1	0.1	0.1	0.2	0.1	0.2	0.1
Italy	4.0	2.2	2.6	2.0	5.1	5.8	3.2	7.5	6.2	2.4
Japan	6.8	11.6	14.6	20.3	18.9	22.0	17.2	24.5	16.2	15.9
Luxembourg	(NA)	(NA)	(NA)	(NA)	(NA)	(NA)	(NA)	(Z)	5.9	(NA)
Netherlands	2.4	2.6	2.8	3.2	2.7	2.5	4.0	4.4	3.4	5.6
New Zealand	0.1	0.1	0.1	0.1	0.1	0.1	0.1	0.1	0.1	0.1
Norway	0.9	0.6	0.7	0.9	0.9	0.9	1.2	1.4	1.4	1.2
Portugal	(NA)	(NA)	(NA)	(NA)	0.1	0.1	0.3	0.2	0.4	0.3
Spain	(NA)	(NA)	0.2	1.2	0.6	0.4	1.0	1.3	1.6	1.3
Sweden	1.9	1.4	1.7	1.8	2.3	2.3	2.8	1.8	3.0	2.5
Switzerland	2.7	2.5	1.4	1.6	1.4	1.8	3.4	3.0	3.1	0.9
United Kingdom	12.2	2.5	6.7	3.5	4.3	9.5	6.5	5.6	9.3	8.8

NA Not available.   Z Less than $50 million.   [1] Includes flows to OPEC countries (see footnote 4). DAC countries listed below. Country totals may not add to DAC total because debt forgiveness of non-official development assistance claims is not included in DAC totals.   [2] Includes "grant-like" flows (i.e., loans repayable in recipients' currencies).   [3] Includes capital subscriptions to multilateral organizations in the form of demand instruments as of date of issue.   [4] Organization of Petroleum Exporting Countries: Algeria, Ecuador, Gabon, Iran, Iraq, Kuwait, Libya, Nigeria, Qatar, Saudi Arabia, United Arab Emirates, and Venezuela.   [5] Former West Germany.

No. 1414. Per Capita Public and Private Aid to Developing Countries: 1990 to 1993

[In dollars. See headnote, table 1413. Private aid figures exclude government subsidies to voluntary agencies]

COUNTRY	OFFICIAL DEVELOPMENT ASSISTANCE			PRIVATE VOLUNTARY AID			COUNTRY	OFFICIAL DEVELOPMENT ASSISTANCE			PRIVATE VOLUNTARY AID		
	1990	1992	1993	1990	1992	1993		1990	1992	1993	1990	1992	1993
Australia	56	58	54	3	4	5	Luxembourg	(NA)	98	129	(NA)	10	13
Austria	51	71	68	4	10	9	Netherlands	170	181	165	16	17	18
Belgium	89	87	80	6	3	13	New Zealand	28	28	28	4	3	4
Canada	93	92	83	10	10	10	Norway	284	296	234	31	30	30
Denmark	228	270	258	6	9	9	Portugal	14	30	25	(NA)	(Z)	(NA)
Finland	170	127	70	7	2	1	Spain	25	39	30	2	2	2
France	127	144	137	3	5	3	Sweden	235	283	203	16	15	15
Germany [1]	100	94	86	12	11	10	Switzerland	111	165	115	17	24	21
Ireland	16	20	23	7	8	7	United Kingdom	46	56	50	6	8	8
Italy	59	71	52	(NA)	2	1							
Japan	73	90	90	1	2	1	United States	45	46	38	10	11	10

NA Not available.   Z Less than 50 cents.   [1] Former West Germany.
Source of tables 1413 and 1414: Organization for Economic Cooperation and Development, Paris, France, unpublished data.

No. 1415. Reserve Assets and International Transaction Balances, by Country: 1990 to 1994

[**In millions of U.S. dollars.** Assets include holdings of convertible foreign currencies, special drawing rights, and reserve position in International Monetary Fund and exclude gold holdings. Minus sign (-) indicates decrease]

COUNTRY	TOTAL RESERVE ASSETS		1994		CURRENT ACCOUNT BALANCE			MERCHANDISE TRADE BALANCE		
	1990	1993	Total	Currency holdings [1]	1990	1993	1994	1990	1993	1994
United States	**72,260**	**62,350**	**63,280**	**41,220**	**−91,740**	**−103,930**	**−155,680**	**−109,020**	**−132,570**	**−166,360**
Algeria	725	1,475	2,674	2,651	1,420	(NA)	(NA)	4,187	(NA)	(NA)
Argentina	4,592	13,791	14,327	13,764	4,552	−7,452	(NA)	8,628	−2,428	(NA)
Australia	16,265	11,102	11,285	10,706	−14,849	−10,369	(NA)	368	−123	(NA)
Austria	9,376	14,611	16,822	16,008	1,174	−875	(NA)	−7,012	−7,825	−9,210
Bangladesh	629	2,411	3,139	3,103	−398	197	(NA)	−1,587	−1,283	(NA)
Belgium	12,151	11,415	13,876	12,884	4,950	12,588	(NA)	590	3,933	(NA)
Brazil	7,441	30,604	37,070	37,069	−3,788	−637	(NA)	10,747	13,072	(NA)
Burma	313	303	(NA)	(NA)	(NA)	(NA)	(NA)	(NA)	(NA)	(NA)
Cameroon	26	2	2	2	−467	−742	(NA)	778	217	(NA)
Canada	17,845	12,481	12,286	10,219	−21,548	−23,869	−18,171	8,330	7,612	12,787
Chile	6,069	9,640	13,088	13,087	−648	−2,093	(NA)	1,273	−979	(NA)
China	29,586	22,387	52,914	51,620	11,997	−11,609	(NA)	9,165	−10,654	(NA)
Colombia	4,212	7,552	7,750	7,453	542	(NA)	(NA)	1,971	(NA)	(NA)
Cote d'Ivoire	4	2	185	185	−1,210	−1,229	(NA)	1,327	1,072	(NA)
Denmark	10,591	10,301	9,056	8,444	1,372	4,711	(NA)	4,875	7,812	(NA)
Ecuador	839	1,380	1,841	1,812	−166	−360	(NA)	1,003	578	(NA)
Egypt	2,684	12,904	13,481	13,316	185	2,299	(NA)	−6,699	−6,680	(NA)
Finland	9,644	5,411	10,662	10,051	−6,961	−980	1,068	725	6,392	7,660
France [2]	36,778	22,649	26,257	23,520	−15,236	10,201	4,899	−13,671	6,997	8,660
Germany [2]	67,902	77,640	77,363	72,219	46	−15	−23	71	45	56
Ghana	219	410	584	554	−229	(NA)	(NA)	−308	(NA)	(NA)
Greece	3,412	7,790	14,488	14,322	−3,537	−747	(NA)	−10,178	−10,557	(NA)
Hungary	1,070	6,771	(NA)	(NA)	379	−4,262	(NA)	534	−4,021	(NA)
India	1,521	10,199	19,698	19,386	−7,037	(NA)	(NA)	−5,151	(NA)	(NA)
Indonesia	7,459	11,263	12,133	11,820	−2,988	−2,016	(NA)	5,352	8,231	(NA)
Ireland	5,223	5,925	6,115	5,745	45	3,646	(NA)	3,969	8,172	(NA)
Israel	6,275	6,383	6,792	6,792	558	−1,373	−2,757	−2,981	−5,607	−6,096
Italy	62,927	27,545	32,265	30,107	−16,827	11,176	(NA)	1,373	32,278	(NA)
Japan	78,501	98,524	125,860	115,146	35,870	131,150	(NA)	63,580	141,570	(NA)
Kenya	205	406	558	539	−520	153	(NA)	−995	−307	(NA)
Korea, South	14,793	20,228	25,639	25,032	−2,172	384	(NA)	−2,004	1,860	(NA)
Kuwait	1,952	4,214	3,501	3,212	4,164	6,344	(NA)	3,578	4,373	(NA)
Libya	5,839	(NA)	(NA)	(NA)	2,201	(NA)	(NA)	3,777	(NA)	(NA)
Malaysia	9,754	27,249	(NA)	(NA)	−918	−2,466	(NA)	2,622	3,183	(NA)
Mexico	9,863	25,110	6,278	6,101	−7,451	−23,391	(NA)	−4,433	−18,891	(NA)
Morocco	2,066	3,655	4,352	4,281	−200	−525	(NA)	−2,071	−2,380	(NA)
Nepal	295	640	694	685	−289	−223	(NA)	−449	−462	(NA)
Netherlands	17,484	31,344	34,532	32,716	8,930	9,371	(NA)	10,330	12,915	(NA)
Nigeria	3,864	1,372	1,386	1,386	4,988	(NA)	(NA)	8,653	(NA)	(NA)
Norway	15,332	19,622	19,026	17,992	4,023	2,453	(NA)	7,761	8,016	(NA)
Pakistan	296	1,197	2,929	2,929	−1,654	−2,936	(NA)	−2,714	−2,552	(NA)
Peru	1,040	3,408	(NA)	(NA)	−901	−1,800	(NA)	339	−580	(NA)
Philippines	924	4,676	6,017	5,866	−2,695	−3,289	(NA)	−4,020	−6,222	(NA)
Poland	4,492	4,092	5,842	5,728	3,067	−5,788	(NA)	3,589	−3,505	(NA)
Portugal	14,485	15,840	(NA)	(NA)	−181	947	(NA)	−6,831	−6,886	(NA)
Romania	373	995	2,086	2,031	−3,254	−1,162	(NA)	−3,344	−1,128	(NA)
Saudi Arabia	11,668	7,428	7,378	5,888	−4,117	−14,218	(NA)	22,756	19,020	(NA)
Singapore	27,748	48,361	58,177	57,890	2,094	2,039	(NA)	−4,718	−8,065	(NA)
South Africa	1,008	1,020	1,685	1,684	2,077	1,805	(NA)	6,783	5,781	(NA)
Spain	51,228	41,045	41,569	40,205	−16,819	−4,640	−5,173	−29,566	−15,718	−15,335
Sri Lanka	423	1,629	2,046	2,016	−298	−381	(NA)	−473	−742	(NA)
Sudan	11	38	(NA)	(NA)	−372	(NA)	(NA)	−322	(NA)	(NA)
Sweden	17,988	19,050	23,254	22,527	−6,693	−4,057	(NA)	3,402	7,669	(NA)
Switzerland	29,223	32,635	34,729	33,554	6,942	16,696	(NA)	−6,391	2,237	(NA)
Syria	(NA)	(NA)	(NA)	(NA)	1,762	−607	(NA)	2,094	−322	(NA)
Thailand	13,305	24,473	29,332	28,884	−7,282	−6,928	(NA)	−6,751	−4,146	(NA)
Trinidad and Tobago	492	206	352	352	440	102	(NA)	988	524	(NA)
Turkey	6,050	6,272	7,169	7,121	−2,625	−6,380	(NA)	−9,555	−14,162	(NA)
United Kingdom	35,850	36,780	41,010	38,530	−33,037	−16,842	(NA)	−32,742	−19,869	(NA)
Venezuela	8,321	9,216	8,067	7,393	8,279	−2,223	(NA)	10,637	2,902	(NA)
Zaire	219	46	121	121	−643	(NA)	(NA)	600	(NA)	(NA)

NA Not available.   [1] Holdings of convertible foreign currencies.   [2] Prior to July 1990, data for former West Germany.

Source: International Monetary Fund, Washington, DC, *International Financial Statistics*, monthly.

No. 1416. Foreign Trade—Source of Imports and Destination of Exports, by Country: 1993

[**In billions of dollars.** All exports are f.o.b. (free on board) and all imports are c.i.f. (cost insurance freight) except for United States, Australian, and Canadian imports, which are f.o.b.]

COUNTRY	Total [1]	O.E.C.D. [2]		C.E.E.C. [4]	China, Vietnam, North Korea	O.P.E.C. [5]	Other developing countries [6]	Africa	America [7]	Middle East [8]	Far East [9]
		Total	E.C. [3]								
IMPORTS											
Value (Bil. dol.):											
Australia	42.4	30.0	8.2	0.1	2.2	1.9	8.1	0.2	0.4	1.3	9.2
Austria	48.6	40.6	32.5	3.3	0.7	1.0	2.9	1.0	0.4	0.4	2.5
Belgium-Luxembourg	105.4	92.4	76.7	2.0	0.5	1.2	9.3	3.8	1.3	1.1	4.5
Canada	131.4	114.1	11.4	0.5	2.4	2.1	9.8	1.1	2.1	0.8	10.1
France	202.3	161.6	118.6	4.9	4.0	8.5	20.5	9.4	3.6	5.5	13.4
Germany	329.7	253.1	152.7	21.7	8.7	8.4	37.6	8.6	7.1	3.9	31.6
Italy	137.4	103.2	76.2	7.2	2.4	9.0	15.3	10.1	3.2	3.9	7.7
Japan	240.7	115.7	30.3	3.5	21.9	37.5	62.1	3.8	6.9	27.0	82.5
Netherlands	112.7	89.2	64.5	2.9	1.5	6.6	12.5	2.8	2.9	4.8	9.9
Spain	83.0	66.3	50.9	1.6	1.4	4.8	8.2	4.7	2.5	2.2	4.7
Sweden	42.8	37.0	23.6	1.3	0.8	0.8	2.8	0.2	0.7	0.7	2.8
Switzerland	60.8	55.0	44.1	0.7	0.7	-	4.4	0.8	0.8	0.5	2.9
United Kingdom	206.1	161.1	94.1	3.2	2.0	5.0	27.0	4.4	3.6	4.3	20.8
United States	580.5	377.6	98.0	3.5	31.5	33.1	134.6	14.8	34.5	15.4	133.8
Percent distribution:											
Australia	100.0	70.8	19.3	0.2	5.2	4.5	19.1	0.5	0.9	3.1	21.7
Austria	100.0	83.5	66.9	6.8	1.4	2.1	6.0	2.1	0.8	0.8	5.1
Belgium-Luxembourg	100.0	87.7	72.8	1.9	0.5	1.1	8.8	3.6	1.2	1.0	4.3
Canada	100.0	86.8	8.7	0.4	1.8	1.6	7.5	0.8	1.6	0.6	7.7
France	100.0	79.9	58.6	2.4	2.0	4.2	10.1	4.6	1.8	2.7	6.6
Germany	100.0	76.8	46.3	6.6	2.6	2.5	11.4	2.6	2.2	1.2	9.6
Italy	100.0	75.1	55.5	5.2	1.7	6.6	11.1	7.4	2.3	2.8	5.6
Japan	100.0	48.1	12.6	1.5	9.1	15.6	25.8	1.6	2.9	11.2	34.3
Netherlands	100.0	79.1	57.2	2.6	1.3	5.9	11.1	2.5	2.6	4.3	8.8
Spain	100.0	79.9	61.3	1.9	1.7	5.8	9.9	5.7	3.0	2.7	5.7
Sweden	100.0	86.4	55.1	3.0	1.9	1.9	6.5	0.5	1.6	1.6	6.5
Switzerland	100.0	90.5	72.5	1.2	1.2	-	7.2	1.3	1.3	0.8	4.8
United Kingdom	100.0	78.2	45.7	1.6	1.0	2.4	13.1	2.1	1.7	2.1	10.1
United States	100.0	65.0	16.9	0.6	5.4	5.7	23.2	2.5	5.9	2.7	23.0
EXPORTS											
Value (Bil. dol.):											
Australia	42.4	22.8	4.8	0.2	1.6	2.1	14.6	0.6	0.5	1.1	14.9
Austria	40.2	31.8	25.5	4.2	0.3	1.1	2.8	0.6	0.3	0.8	1.6
Belgium-Luxembourg	117.7	100.3	85.1	2.1	0.7	2.5	11.4	2.7	1.0	4.3	6.5
Canada	144.7	134.5	8.3	0.6	1.3	1.8	6.4	0.8	2.2	0.9	5.5
France	207.8	162.5	124.7	4.5	1.9	8.7	30.1	13.6	7.0	6.1	11.8
Germany	365.3	282.5	175.1	25.8	6.0	11.2	39.0	8.7	6.6	10.0	27.1
Italy	156.9	117.0	83.7	6.3	2.4	7.7	22.7	6.5	4.8	7.2	10.8
Japan	360.9	190.6	56.6	2.3	18.1	17.2	132.7	7.3	11.9	12.0	135.6
Netherlands	127.3	108.8	91.6	3.5	0.7	3.2	10.0	2.8	1.9	2.6	5.9
Spain	63.0	51.4	43.2	0.9	0.6	2.2	7.6	3.1	2.7	1.3	2.5
Sweden	49.9	41.9	26.6	1.4	0.6	1.3	4.6	1.0	0.8	1.2	3.3
Switzerland	63.1	49.6	35.8	1.4	0.7	2.4	9.1	1.2	1.4	2.9	6.3
United Kingdom	181.4	136.4	88.0	3.2	1.1	8.5	24.4	6.1	2.8	8.8	15.2
United States	464.9	312.4	97.0	6.1	8.8	20.6	116.7	9.3	36.8	16.8	82.1
Percent distribution:											
Australia	100.0	53.8	11.3	0.5	3.8	5.0	34.4	1.4	1.2	2.6	35.1
Austria	100.0	79.1	63.4	10.4	0.7	2.7	7.0	1.5	0.7	2.0	4.0
Belgium-Luxembourg	100.0	85.2	72.3	1.8	0.6	2.1	9.7	2.3	0.8	3.7	5.5
Canada	100.0	93.0	5.7	0.4	0.9	1.2	4.4	0.6	1.5	0.6	3.8
France	100.0	78.2	60.0	2.2	0.9	4.2	14.5	6.5	3.4	2.9	5.7
Germany	100.0	77.3	47.9	7.1	1.6	3.1	10.7	2.4	1.8	2.7	7.4
Italy	100.0	74.6	53.3	4.0	1.5	4.9	14.5	4.1	3.1	4.6	6.9
Japan	100.0	52.8	15.7	0.6	5.0	4.8	36.8	2.0	3.3	3.3	37.6
Netherlands	100.0	85.5	72.0	2.7	0.5	2.5	7.9	2.2	1.5	2.0	4.6
Spain	100.0	81.6	68.6	1.4	1.0	3.5	12.1	4.9	4.3	2.1	4.0
Sweden	100.0	84.0	53.3	2.8	1.2	2.6	9.2	2.0	1.6	2.4	6.6
Switzerland	100.0	78.6	56.7	2.2	1.1	3.8	14.4	1.9	2.2	4.6	10.0
United Kingdom	100.0	75.2	48.5	1.8	0.6	4.7	13.5	3.4	1.5	4.9	8.4
United States	100.0	67.2	20.9	1.3	1.9	4.4	25.1	2.0	7.9	3.6	17.7

- Represents or rounds to zero. [1] Includes other areas not shown separately. [2] Organization for Economic Cooperation and Development. For member countries, see text, section 30. [3] European Community comprises Belgium-Luxembourg, Denmark, France, Germany, Greece, Ireland, Italy, Netherlands, Portugal, Spain, and United Kingdom. [4] Central and Eastern European countries comprises Albania, the Baltic States (Estonia, Latvia, Lithuania), Bulgaria, Czech Republic, Hungary, new independent states of the ex-Soviet Union, Poland, Romania, and Slovakia. [5] Organization of Petroleum Exporting Countries comprises Algeria, Ecuador, Gabon, Iran, Iraq, Kuwait, Libya, Nigeria, Qatar, Saudi Arabia, United Arab Emirates, and Venezuela. [6] Comprises trade with all countries other than China, North Korea, Vietnam, South Africa, Eastern Europe, and members of OPEC and OECD. [7] All countries comprising the continent except Canada and the United States. [8] Comprises Syria, Lebanon, Israel, Gaza Strip, Jordan, Iraq, Saudi Arabia, Yemen, Kuwait, Bahrain, United Arab Emirates, Qatar, Oman, and Iran. [9] All countries comprising the continent of Asia except Japan, China, North Korea, Vietnam, and those countries listed under Middle East.

Source: Organization for Economic Cooperation and Development, Paris, France. Data derived from *Monthly Statistics of Foreign Trade*.

No. 1417. Foreign Exchange Rates: 1980 to 1994

[National currency units per dollar, except as noted. Data are averages of certified noon buying rates for cable transfers]

YEAR	Australia [1] (dollar)	Austria (schilling)	Belgium (franc)	Canada (dollar)	Taiwan (dollar)	Denmark (krone)	France (franc)	Greece (drachma)	Hong Kong (dollar)
1980	114.00	12.945	29.237	1.1693	36.015	5.6345	4.2250	42.62	4.9760
1981	114.95	15.948	37.194	1.1990	36.849	7.1350	5.4396	55.41	5.5678
1982	101.65	17.060	45.780	1.2344	39.124	8.3443	6.5793	66.87	6.0697
1983	90.14	17.968	51.121	1.2325	40.065	9.1483	7.6203	87.90	7.2569
1984	87.94	20.005	57.749	1.2953	39.633	10.3540	8.7355	112.73	7.8188
1985	70.03	20.676	59.336	1.3658	39.889	10.5980	8.9799	138.40	7.7911
1986	67.09	15.260	44.662	1.3896	37.837	8.0954	6.9256	139.93	7.8037
1987	70.14	12.649	37.357	1.3259	31.756	6.8477	6.0121	135.47	7.7985
1988	78.41	12.357	36.783	1.2306	28.636	6.7411	5.9594	142.00	7.8071
1989	79.19	13.236	39.409	1.1842	26.407	7.3210	6.3802	162.60	7.8008
1990	78.07	11.331	33.424	1.1668	26.918	6.1899	5.4467	158.59	7.7899
1991	75.93	11.686	34.195	1.1460	26.759	6.4038	5.6468	182.63	7.7712
1992	73.52	10.992	32.148	1.2085	25.160	6.0372	5.2935	190.81	7.7402
1993	67.99	11.639	34.581	1.2902	26.416	6.4863	5.6669	229.64	7.7357
1994	73.16	11.409	33.426	1.3664	26.465	6.3561	5.5459	242.50	7.7290

YEAR	India (rupee)	Ireland [1] (pound)	Italy (lira)	Japan (yen)	Malaysia (ringgit)	Netherlands (guilder)	New Zealand [1] (dollar)	Norway (krone)	Portugal (escudo)
1980	7.887	205.77	856.20	226.63	2.1767	1.9875	97.34	4.9381	50.08
1981	8.681	161.32	1,138.60	220.63	2.3048	2.4998	86.85	5.7430	61.74
1982	9.485	142.05	1,354.00	249.06	2.3395	2.6719	75.10	6.4567	80.10
1983	10.104	124.81	1,519.30	237.55	2.3204	2.8543	66.79	7.3012	111.61
1984	11.348	108.64	1,756.10	237.45	2.3448	3.2083	57.84	8.1596	147.70
1985	12.332	106.62	1,908.90	238.47	2.4806	3.3184	49.75	8.5933	172.07
1986	12.597	134.14	1,491.16	168.35	2.5830	2.4484	52.46	7.3984	149.80
1987	12.943	148.79	1,297.03	144.60	2.5185	2.0263	59.33	6.7408	141.20
1988	13.899	152.49	1,302.39	128.17	2.6189	1.9778	65.56	6.5242	144.26
1989	16.213	141.80	1,372.28	138.07	2.7079	2.1219	59.35	6.9131	157.53
1990	17.492	165.76	1,198.27	145.00	2.7057	1.8215	59.62	6.2541	142.70
1991	22.712	174.70	1,241.28	134.59	2.7503	1.8720	54.03	6.4912	144.77
1992	28.156	170.42	1,232.17	126.78	2.5463	1.7587	53.79	6.2142	135.07
1993	31.291	146.47	1,573.41	111.08	2.5738	1.8585	54.13	7.0979	161.08
1994	31.394	149.69	1,611.49	102.18	2.6237	1.8190	59.36	7.0553	165.93

YEAR	Singapore (dollar)	South Africa (rand)	Korea, South (won)	Spain (peseta)	Sweden (krona)	Switzerland (franc)	Thailand (baht)	United Kingdom [1] (pound)	Germany (deutsche mark)
1980	2.1412	0.7796	607.43	71.76	4.2309	1.6772	20.476	232.43	1.8175
1981	2.1053	0.8787	681.03	92.40	5.0659	1.9674	21.731	202.43	2.2632
1982	2.1406	1.0876	731.93	110.09	6.2838	2.0327	23.014	174.80	2.4281
1983	2.1136	1.1146	776.04	143.50	7.6717	2.1006	22.991	151.59	2.5539
1984	2.1325	1.4761	807.91	160.78	8.2706	2.3500	23.582	133.66	2.8455
1985	2.2008	2.2344	861.89	169.98	8.6031	2.4551	27.193	129.74	2.9420
1986	2.1782	2.2919	884.61	140.04	7.1272	1.7979	26.314	146.77	2.1705
1987	2.1059	2.0385	825.93	123.54	6.3468	1.4918	25.774	163.98	1.7981
1988	2.0132	2.2770	734.51	116.52	6.1369	1.4642	25.312	178.13	1.7570
1989	1.9511	2.6214	674.29	118.44	6.4559	1.6369	25.725	163.82	1.8808
1990	1.8134	2.5885	710.64	101.96	5.9231	1.3901	25.609	178.41	1.6166
1991	1.7283	2.7633	736.73	104.01	6.0521	1.4356	25.528	176.74	1.6610
1992	1.6294	2.8524	784.58	102.38	5.8258	1.4064	25.411	176.63	1.5618
1993	1.6158	3.2729	805.75	127.48	7.7956	1.4781	25.333	150.16	1.6545
1994	1.5275	3.5526	806.93	133.88	7.7161	1.3667	25.161	153.19	1.6216

[1] Value is U.S. cents per unit of foreign currency.

Source: Board of Governors of the Federal Reserve System, *Federal Reserve Bulletin*, monthly.

No. 1418. Exchange Rates—Indexes of Value of Foreign Currency Relative to U.S. Dollar: 1980 to 1994

[1982=100]

YEAR	United States	Canada	France	Germany [1]	Hong Kong	Italy	Japan	Korea, South	Mexico	Singapore	Taiwan	United Kingdom
1980	100.0	105.6	155.9	133.8	122.0	158.3	110.4	120.4	245.5	100.0	108.6	133.0
1985	100.0	90.3	73.3	82.5	77.9	70.9	104.4	84.0	22.0	97.3	98.2	74.2
1986	100.0	88.8	95.0	111.9	77.8	90.8	147.9	82.9	9.2	98.3	103.4	84.0
1987	100.0	93.1	109.4	135.0	77.8	104.4	172.3	88.9	4.1	101.6	122.9	93.8
1988	100.0	100.2	110.4	138.2	77.8	104.0	194.3	99.9	2.5	106.4	136.8	101.9
1989	100.0	104.2	103.1	129.1	77.8	98.7	180.4	108.9	2.3	109.7	148.1	93.7
1990	100.0	105.7	120.8	150.2	77.9	113.0	171.8	103.3	2.0	118.0	145.3	102.1
1991	100.0	107.7	116.5	146.2	78.1	109.1	185.1	99.7	1.9	123.8	146.2	101.1
1992	100.0	102.1	124.3	155.4	78.4	109.9	196.5	93.7	1.8	131.4	155.5	101.0
1993	100.0	95.7	116.1	146.7	78.5	86.1	224.2	91.1	1.8	132.4	148.1	85.9
1994	100.0	90.3	118.6	149.7	78.5	84.0	243.7	91.0	1.7	140.1	147.8	87.6

[1] Prior to 1991, data for former West Germany.

Source: U.S. Bureau of Labor Statistics, *Report 893*, June 1995.

Comparative International Statistics

No. 1419. Military Expenditures, by Country: 1980 to 1993

[**In millions of dollars,** except as indicated. See also table 557. For most countries, data for expenditures and for GNP were based on local currencies which were deflated to constant 1993 local currency values before conversion to U.S. dollar equivalents. In general, the rates used for conversion are the 1993 average par/market exchange rates as supplied by the International Bank for Reconstruction and Development]

COUNTRY	CURRENT DOLLARS				CONSTANT (1993) DOLLARS					
								1993		
	1980	1990	1992	1993	1980	1990	1992	Total	Per capita (dollars)	Percent of GNP
United States	144,000	306,200	305,100	297,600	212,100	333,900	311,800	297,600	1,153	5
Algeria [1]	940	845	910	1,360	1,385	922	930	1,360	50	3
Argentina	1,559	3,386	4,447	4,251	2,296	3,692	4,544	4,251	127	2
Australia	3,226	5,489	6,616	7,441	4,753	5,986	6,760	7,441	417	3
Austria	820	1,704	1,702	1,730	1,208	1,858	1,739	1,730	219	1
Belgium	2,951	4,492	3,863	3,746	4,348	4,899	3,947	3,746	373	2
Brazil	1,899	8,084	5,653	5,852	2,799	8,816	5,776	5,852	37	1
Bulgaria [1]	3,993	3,887	935	1,010	5,883	4,239	955	1,010	114	3
Canada	5,176	9,990	10,020	10,300	7,626	10,890	10,240	10,300	371	2
Chile [2]	449	[1]999	992	1,002	662	[1]1,090	1,013	1,002	[1]73	[1]2
China	16,370	49,620	53,700	56,170	24,120	54,110	54,870	56,170	48	3
Cuba [2]	1,140	1,400	500	426	1,680	1,527	511	426	39	2
Denmark	1,454	2,464	2,629	2,682	2,143	2,687	2,686	2,682	518	2
Egypt [1]	2,923	1,541	1,578	1,670	4,306	1,680	1,612	1,670	28	4
El Salvador [1]	120	197	120	100	177	215	122	100	18	1
Finland	909	1,376	1,758	1,710	1,339	1,500	1,796	1,710	339	2
France [3]	21,230	40,490	42,230	42,590	31,270	44,150	43,150	42,590	740	3
Germany [3]	22,400	[1]39,370	39,890	36,650	33,000	[1]42,930	40,760	36,650	[1]454	[1]2
Greece	1,779	3,776	4,071	4,070	2,621	4,118	4,159	4,070	389	6
Hungary [1]	2,832	1,277	1,387	1,261	4,173	1,393	1,417	1,261	122	2
India	3,608	6,398	7,500	8,471	5,316	6,977	7,663	8,471	9	3
Indonesia	1,093	1,657	1,833	2,031	1,611	1,807	1,872	2,031	10	2
Iran [1]	2,624	6,308	3,853	4,857	3,867	6,878	3,937	4,857	78	4
Iraq [1]	(NA)	11,340	(NA)	(NA)	(NA)	12,370	(NA)	(NA)	(NA)	(NA)
Israel	6,654	6,562	6,493	6,290	9,805	7,155	6,634	6,290	1,279	9
Italy	10,110	19,110	19,950	20,570	14,900	20,840	20,380	20,570	354	2
Japan	12,330	35,880	40,450	41,730	18,170	39,130	41,330	41,730	335	1
Korea, North [1]	4,380	5,940	5,500	(NA)	6,454	6,477	5,620	(NA)	(NA)	23
Korea, South	3,821	10,390	11,390	11,930	5,629	11,330	11,640	11,930	267	4
Kuwait	892	[1]13,020	18,780	3,545	1,314	[1]14,200	19,190	3,545	2,088	13
Malaysia	664	1,189	2,403	2,642	978	1,297	2,456	2,642	140	4
Mexico	456	[1]1,329	1,629	1,656	671	1,450	1,664	1,656	18	1
Morocco [1]	763	1,251	1,514	1,193	1,124	1,364	1,547	1,193	43	5
Netherlands	4,048	6,917	7,206	7,055	5,965	7,543	7,363	7,055	462	2
Nicaragua [1]	53	(NA)	42	37	78	(NA)	43	37	9	3
Nigeria	447	214	189	210	658	233	193	210	2	1
Norway	1,320	2,837	3,335	3,232	1,945	3,094	3,407	3,232	752	3
Oman	1,059	1,707	1,767	1,638	1,560	1,861	1,806	1,638	997	22
Pakistan	777	2,716	2,867	3,111	1,145	2,962	2,929	3,111	25	6
Peru [1]	1,457	664	675	696	2,147	724	689	696	30	2
Philippines	501	1,058	1,012	1,200	738	1,153	1,034	1,200	17	2
Poland [1]	9,644	8,752	4,152	4,334	14,210	9,544	4,242	4,334	113	2
Portugal	858	2,099	2,214	2,192	1,265	2,289	2,262	2,192	209	3
Romania [1]	4,587	3,869	2,824	1,676	6,759	4,219	2,885	1,676	72	3
Russia	(NA)	(NA)	142,300	113,800	(NA)	(NA)	145,400	113,800	762	15
Saudi Arabia	14,990	[1]22,870	34,550	20,480	22,090	[1]24,930	35,310	20,480	[1]1,163	[1]16
Singapore	533	1,766	2,543	2,700	785	1,926	2,599	2,700	955	5
South Africa	2,563	[1]4,446	3,236	2,896	3,777	[1]4,848	3,306	2,896	[1]68	[1]3
Spain	4,560	7,924	7,458	8,289	6,719	8,641	7,621	8,289	211	2
Sweden	3,257	4,661	4,708	5,011	4,799	5,083	4,810	5,011	574	3
Switzerland	2,461	4,674	4,224	4,061	3,626	5,097	4,316	4,061	581	2
Syria [1] [2]	1,936	4,435	(NA)	(NA)	2,852	4,836	(NA)	(NA)	(NA)	(NA)
Taiwan	3,222	9,052	10,450	10,420	4,748	[1]9,870	10,680	10,420	[1]494	[1]5
Thailand	1,011	2,197	2,907	3,511	1,489	2,396	2,971	3,511	60	3
Turkey	1,635	4,866	6,094	7,075	2,409	5,306	6,227	7,075	116	6
United Arab Emirates	1,724	[1]2,590	2,098	1,771	2,541	[1]2,824	2,143	1,771	[1]666	[1]5
United Kingdom	22,080	35,240	34,680	34,020	32,530	38,420	35,430	34,020	587	4
Venezuela	317	927	1,475	1,029	467	[1]1,011	1,507	1,029	[1]51	[1]2

NA Not available. [1] Estimated. [2] Data probably omit a major share of total military expenditures, probably including most arms acquisitions. [3] Prior to 1991, data for former West Germany.

Source: U.S. Arms Control and Disarmament Agency, *World Military Expenditures and Arms Transfers*, annual.

No. 1420. Armed Forces Personnel, by Country: 1980 to 1993

[**Personnel data as of July.** Armed Forces refer to active-duty military personnel, including paramilitary forces where those forces resemble regular units in their organization, equipment, training, or mission. Reserve forces are not included]

COUNTRY	ARMED FORCES PERSONNEL (1,000)						ARMED FORCES PER 1,000 POPULATION					
	1980	1985	1990	1991	1992	1993	1980	1985	1990	1991	1992	1993
United States	**2,050**	**2,244**	**2,181**	**2,115**	**1.919**	**1,815**	**9.0**	**9.4**	**8.7**	**8.4**	**7.5**	**7.0**
Algeria	101	170	126	126	9	139	5.4	7.7	5.0	4.8	5.2	5.1
Argentina	155	129	85	70	65	65	5.5	4.2	2.6	2.1	2.0	1.9
Australia	71	70	68	66	68	68	4.9	4.4	4.0	3.9	3.9	3.8
Austria	40	40	43	44	52	(NA)	5.3	5.3	5.6	5.6	6.6	(NA)
Belgium	108	107	106	101	79	70	11.0	10.9	10.6	10.1	7.9	7.0
Brazil	450	496	295	295	296	296	3.7	3.6	2.0	1.9	1.9	1.9
Bulgaria	188	189	129	107	99	52	21.2	21.2	14.4	12.0	11.2	5.9
Canada	82	83	87	86	82	76	3.4	3.3	3.3	3.2	3.0	2.7
Chile	116	124	95	90	92	92	10.5	10.3	7.2	6.8	6.8	6.7
China	4,650	4,100	3,500	3,200	3,160	3,031	4.7	3.9	3.1	2.8	2.7	2.6
Cuba	220	297	297	297	175	175	22.8	29.4	27.9	27.6	16.1	16.0
Denmark	33	29	31	30	28	27	6.4	5.7	6.0	5.8	5.4	5.2
Egypt	447	466	434	434	424	424	10.7	9.5	7.8	7.6	7.3	7.1
El Salvador	16	48	55	60	49	49	3.4	10.0	10.4	11.1	8.9	8.7
Finland	36	40	31	32	33	31	7.5	8.2	6.2	6.4	6.5	6.1
France	575	563	550	542	522	506	10.7	10.2	9.7	9.5	9.1	8.8
Germany [1]	490	495	[2]545	[2]457	442	398	8.0	8.1	8.6	5.7	5.5	4.9
Greece	186	201	201	205	208	213	19.3	20.2	19.9	20.0	20.1	20.3
Honduras	14	21	18	17	17	17	3.9	5.0	3.8	3.5	3.4	3.3
Hungary	120	117	94	87	78	(NA)	11.2	11.0	9.1	8.4	7.5	(NA)
India	1,104	1,260	1,262	1,265	1,265	1,265	1.6	1.6	1.5	1.5	1.4	1.4
Indonesia	250	278	283	278	283	271	1.6	1.6	1.5	1.5	1.5	1.4
Iran	305	345	440	465	528	528	7.8	7.5	7.7	7.9	8.7	8.5
Iraq	430	788	1,390	475	407	407	32.5	50.2	75.4	26.5	22.0	21.2
Israel	196	195	190	190	181	181	52.4	49.6	44.2	41.9	38.1	36.8
Italy	500	504	493	473	471	450	8.9	8.8	8.5	8.2	8.1	7.8
Japan	242	241	250	250	242	242	2.1	2.0	2.0	2.0	1.9	1.9
Korea, North	700	784	1,200	1,200	1,200	1,200	38.9	40.0	56.0	55.0	54.0	53.0
Korea, South	600	600	650	750	750	750	15.7	14.7	15.0	17.2	17.0	16.8
Kuwait	12	16	7	10	12	12	8.8	9.3	3.3	11.9	8.7	7.1
Malaysia	83	110	130	128	128	115	6.0	[2]7.1	7.4	7.1	7.0	6.1
Mexico	120	140	175	175	175	175	1.7	1.8	2.1	2.0	2.0	1.9
Morocco	117	165	195	195	195	195	5.7	7.1	7.5	7.3	7.1	7.0
Netherlands	107	103	104	104	90	86	7.6	7.1	7.0	6.9	5.9	5.6
Nicaragua	24	74	28	20	15	15	8.6	23.5	7.7	5.3	3.9	3.8
Nigeria	150	134	94	94	76	76	1.7	1.8	1.1	1.1	0.8	0.8
Norway	40	36	51	41	42	42	8.7	8.7	12.0	9.6	9.8	9.8
Oman	15	25	32	29	35	35	15.2	20.2	21.6	18.9	22.0	21.3
Pakistan	467	483	550	565	580	580	5.5	4.9	4.8	4.8	4.8	4.6
Peru	151	128	125	123	112	112	8.7	6.5	5.7	5.5	4.9	4.8
Philippines	155	115	109	107	107	107	3.0	2.0	1.7	1.6	1.6	1.5
Poland	408	439	313	305	270	180	11.5	11.8	8.2	8.0	7.0	4.7
Portugal	88	102	87	86	80	68	9.0	10.0	8.4	8.3	7.7	6.5
Qatar	6	7	11	11	8	8	26.0	[2]20.3	24.4	23.5	16.5	16.0
Romania	211	237	126	201	172	167	9.5	10.4	5.4	8.7	7.4	7.2
Russia	(NA)	(NA)	(NA)	(NA)	2,030	2,250	(NA)	(NA)	(NA)	(NA)	13.6	15.1
Saudi Arabia	79	80	146	191	172	172	7.8	[2]5.9	9.0	11.6	10.1	9.8
Singapore	50	56	56	56	56	56	20.7	21.9	20.6	20.3	20.1	19.8
South Africa	70	95	85	80	72	72	2.3	2.7	2.1	2.0	1.7	1.7
Spain	356	314	263	246	198	204	9.5	8.2	6.7	6.3	5.1	5.2
Sweden	70	69	65	63	45	44	8.4	[2]8.3	7.6	7.3	5.2	5.0
Switzerland	23	23	22	22	31	31	3.6	[2]3.5	3.2	3.2	4.5	4.4
Syria	250	402	408	408	408	408	28.8	38.2	32.0	30.7	29.5	28.5
Taiwan	465	444	370	370	360	442	26.1	23.0	18.1	17.9	17.2	21.0
Thailand	234	235	283	283	283	295	5.0	4.5	5.0	5.0	4.9	5.0
Turkey	717	814	769	804	704	686	15.9	16.0	13.5	13.8	11.8	11.3
United Arab Emirates . . .	44	44	66	66	55	55	44.0	28.0	29.3	27.6	21.8	20.7
United Kingdom	330	334	308	301	293	271	5.9	5.9	5.4	5.2	5.1	4.7
Venezuela	55	71	75	73	75	75	3.7	4.3	4.0	3.8	3.8	3.7
Vietnam	900	1,027	1,052	1,041	857	857	16.9	16.9	15.5	15.1	12.2	11.9

NA Not available.   [1] Prior to 1991, data for former West Germany.   [2] Estimated.

Source: U.S. Arms Control and Disarmament Agency, *World Military Expenditures and Arms Transfers*, annual.

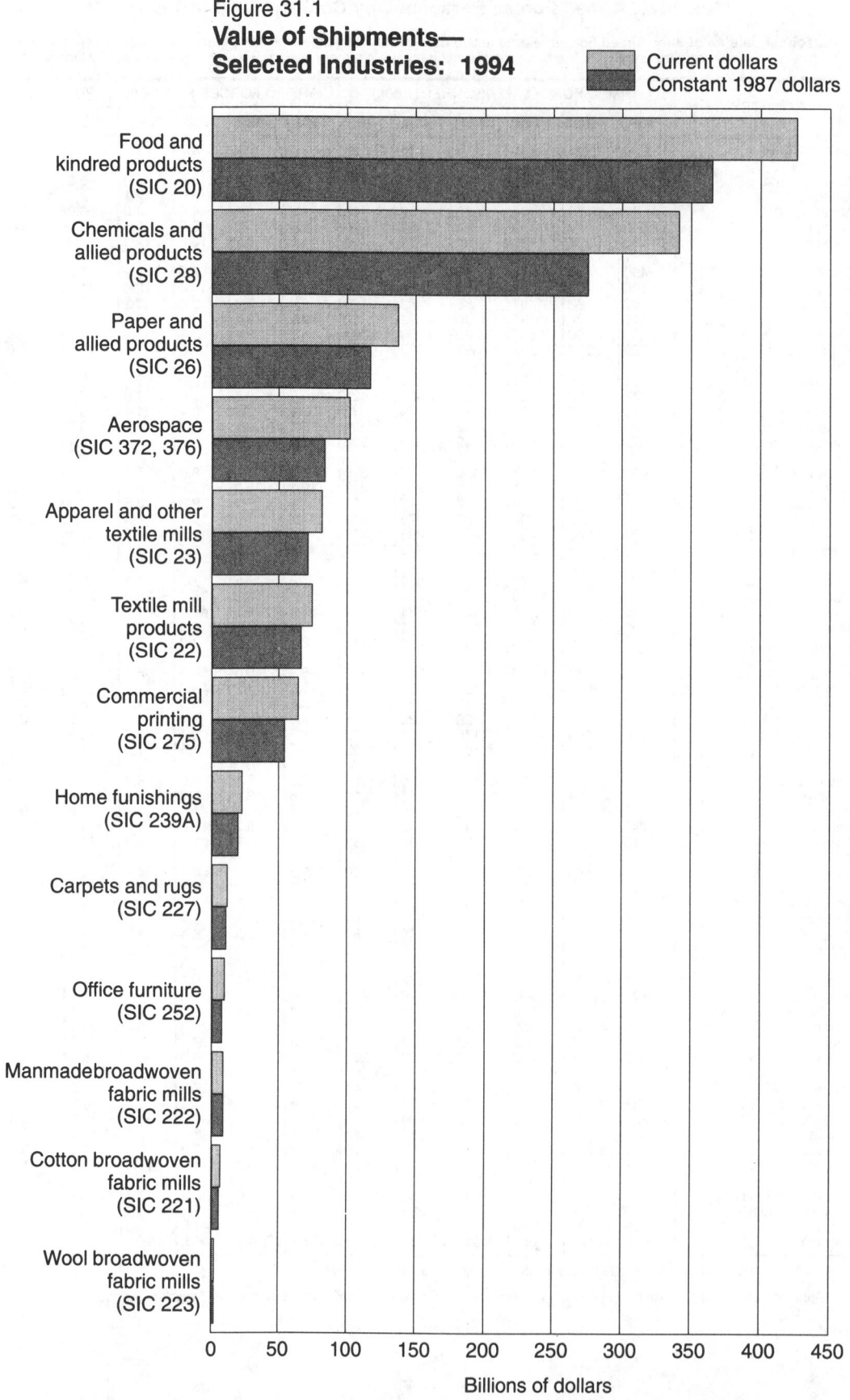

Figure 31.1
**Value of Shipments—
Selected Industries: 1994**

Current dollars
Constant 1987 dollars

Food and kindred products (SIC 20)

Chemicals and allied products (SIC 28)

Paper and allied products (SIC 26)

Aerospace (SIC 372, 376)

Apparel and other textile mills (SIC 23)

Textile mill products (SIC 22)

Commercial printing (SIC 275)

Home funishings (SIC 239A)

Carpets and rugs (SIC 227)

Office furniture (SIC 252)

Manmadebroadwoven fabric mills (SIC 222)

Cotton broadwoven fabric mills (SIC 221)

Wool broadwoven fabric mills (SIC 223)

0   50   100   150   200   250   300   350   400   450

Billions of dollars

Source: Chart prepared by U.S. Bureau of the Census. For data, see section 31.

Industrial Outlook

This new section presents statistics for major manufacturing groups and selected products. The 199 industries covered were among those featured in the *U.S. Industrial Outlook* published by the Department of Commerce's International Trade Administration (ITA) for many years. The 1994 edition of the *U.S. Industrial Outlook* was the last volume published in that series of publications.

The 92 tables combine industry and product shipments data from the *1992 Census of Manufactures* and estimates for 1993 and 1994 by ITA's analysts. The estimates were prepared in the spring of 1995 prior to the release of *1993 Annual Survey of Manufacture*s results. The tables also contain employment, wages, capital expenditures, import and export data.

The value of shipments shown in these tables are expressed both in "current" and "constant" dollars. Current dollars show the value of the goods produced in the particular year referred to. Constant dollars, or sometimes referred to as changes in real dollars, show the value of a year's output in the prices of a base year so you can accurately compare real changes in output levels over time. In these tables the base year was 1987. ITA uses the Producer Price Index (for more information, see text, section 15) from the Bureau of Labor Statistics at the product level to deflate the current dollar shipments.

The tables distinguish between industry and product shipments. Shipments data are collected separately for individual factories, or establishments, and not at the company level. Most factories make a variety of products. For statistical purposes, each is an establishment classified in the industry identified with its major product. For instance, the total output of a plant may consist of 80 percent tires and 20 percent hose and belting. In this case, the total output of the plant would be credited to the tire industry. The total output of all plants so classified would make up the "industry shipments" of the tire industry in this case. The value of all tires shipped by all establishments is aggregated to derive "product shipments."

Trade data shown in the tables were tabulated following the Bureau of the Census' trade concordance, as adjusted by the ITA's analyst, to approximate the Standard Industrial Classification (SIC) industry grouping. The trade figures reflect final 1993 estimates and preliminary 1994 data. Exports are limited to domestic exports and are valued "free alongside ship" or f.a.s. Imports are restricted to goods imported for consumption and are on a customs value basis.

No. 1421. Recent Trends in Food and Kindred Products (SIC 20): 1988 to 1994

ITEM	Unit	1988	1989	1990	1991	1992	1993 [1]	1994 [1]
INDUSTRY DATA								
Value of shipments [2]	Mil. dol.	351,515	364,403	384,009	387,601	403,836	414,423	425,612
Value of shipments (1987 dollars)	Mil. dol.	337,265	333,011	339,697	344,351	358,837	359,279	364,916
Total employment	1,000.	1,465	1,459	1,470	1,475	1,505	1,487	1,502
Production workers	1,000.	1,045	1,049	1,061	1,070	1,100	1,092	1,107
Average hourly earnings	Dollar	9.52	9.68	9.82	10.10	10.38	10.59	10.83
Capital expenditures	Mil. dol.	7,493	8,330	8,858	9,362	9,932	(NA)	(NA)
PRODUCT DATA								
Value of shipments [3]	Mil. dol.	326,728	340,733	359,713	363,943	379,263	392,665	403,911
Value of shipments (1987 dollars)	Mil. dol.	313,412	311,497	318,608	323,763	337,643	340,373	346,272
TRADE DATA								
Value of imports	Mil. dol.	(NA)	18,744	19,834	19,779	20,869	20,859	22,802
Value of exports	Mil. dol.	(NA)	17,070	18,473	19,918	22,504	22,937	25,587

NA Not available. [1] Estimate, except exports and imports. [2] Value of all products and services sold by establishments in the food and kindred products industry. [3] Value of products classified in the food and kindred products industry produced by all industries.

Source: U.S. Department of Commerce: Bureau of the Census, International Trade Administration (ITA). Estimates by ITA.

No. 1422. Recent Trends in Higher Value Added Foods and Beverages and Lower Value Foods and Feeds: 1988 to 1994

ITEM	Unit	1988	1989	1990	1991	1992	1993 [1]	1994 [1]
HIGHER VALUE ADDED FOODS AND BEVERAGES [2]								
Industry data:								
Value of shipments [3]	Mil. dol.	170,018	176,415	185,953	192,654	199,877	207,100	213,520
Value of shipments (1987 dollars)	Mil. dol.	165,588	163,879	167,010	169,621	173,444	175,807	178,379
Total employment	1,000.	831	820	816	814	828	809	820
Production workers	1,000.	559	558	556	557	571	559	567
Average hourly earnings	Dollar	10.48	10.71	10.95	11.27	11.60	11.87	12.14
Capital expenditures	Mil. dol.	4,770	5,236	5,474	5,969	6,424	(NA)	(NA)
Product data:								
Value of shipments [4]	Mil. dol.	160,287	167,143	175,899	182,570	188,967	197,366	203,485
Value of shipments (1987 dollars)	Mil. dol.	156,310	155,482	158,189	161,032	164,480	167,543	169,996
Trade data:								
Value of imports	Mil. dol.	(NA)	8,430	9,075	8,719	9,724	9,456	10,356
Value of exports	Mil. dol.	(NA)	4,044	4,852	5,725	6,660	7,501	8,632
LOWER VALUE FOODS AND FEEDS [5]								
Industry data:								
Value of shipments [3]	Mil. dol.	181,497	187,988	198,056	194,947	203,959	207,323	212,092
Value of shipments (1987 dollars)	Mil. dol.	171,677	169,131	172,688	174,730	185,393	183,472	186,537
Total employment	1,000.	634	639	654	662	677	678	682
Production workers	1,000.	486	491	505	513	529	533	540
Average hourly earnings	Dollar	8.47	8.56	8.63	8.86	9.23	9.48	9.78
Capital expenditures	Mil. dol.	2,722	3,094	3,384	3,393	3,508	(NA)	(NA)
Product data:								
Value of shipments [4]	Mil. dol.	166,440	173,590	183,814	181,373	190,296	195,298	200,426
Value of shipments (1987 dollars)	Mil. dol.	157,103	156,015	160,419	162,731	173,163	172,830	176,276
Trade data:								
Value of imports	Mil. dol.	(NA)	10,314	10,759	11,060	11,145	11,403	12,446
Value of exports	Mil. dol.	(NA)	13,025	13,621	14,193	15,844	15,436	16,956

NA Not available. [1] Estimate, except exports and imports. [2] SIC's 2023, 24, 32-38, 43, 45, 47, 51-53, 64-68, 82, 84-86, 95, 96, 98, and 99. This aggregation includes those industries defined as higher value added. [3] Value of all products and services sold by establishments in this industry. [4] Value of products classified in this industry produced by all industries. [5] SIC 20 excluding 2023, 24, 32-38, 43, 45, 47, 51-53, 64-68, 82, 84-86, 95, 96, 98, and 99. This aggregation includes those industries defined as lower value added.

Source: U.S. Department of Commerce: Bureau of the Census, International Trade Administration (ITA). Estimates by ITA.

No. 1423. Recent Trends in Red Meat and Poultry Slaughtering and Processing: 1988 to 1994

ITEM	Unit	1988	1989	1990	1991	1992	1993 [1]	1994 [1]
RED MEAT (SIC 2011, 2013)								
Industry data:								
Value of shipments [2]	Mil. dol.	64,591	64,058	69,849	67,687	69,722	72,319	72,496
Value of shipments (1987 dollars)	Mil. dol.	64,372	60,313	59,350	59,573	64,799	64,701	67,936
Total employment	1,000.	199	199	200	200	206	208	207
Production workers	1,000.	160	160	161	162	169	171	171
Average hourly earnings	Dollar	8.52	8.44	8.58	8.68	8.98	9.08	9.24
Capital expenditures	Mil. dol.	533	670	758	749	718	(NA)	(NA)
Product data:								
Value of shipments [3]	Mil. dol.	58,206	58,343	64,079	62,676	64,367	66,729	66,892
Value of shipments (1987 dollars)	Mil. dol.	57,992	54,894	54,400	55,134	59,790	59,700	62,685
Trade data:								
Value of imports	Mil. dol.	(NA)	2,775	3,162	3,138	2,924	3,067	2,979
Value of exports	Mil. dol.	(NA)	4,078	4,364	4,348	4,807	4,698	5,273
POULTRY SLAUGHTERING AND PROCESSING (SIC 2015)								
Industry data:								
Value of shipments [2]	Mil. dol.	16,598	20,283	20,928	21,703	23,744	25,998	28,621
Value of shipments (1987 dollars)	Mil. dol.	15,512	17,425	18,888	20,284	22,506	23,917	25,600
Total employment	1,000.	156	164	177	190	194	200	205
Production workers	1,000.	139	147	158	168	173	178	181
Average hourly earnings	Dollar	6.37	6.53	6.63	6.96	7.39	7.59	7.87
Capital expenditures	Mil. dol.	348	500	498	587	466	(NA)	(NA)
Product data:								
Value of shipments [3]	Mil. dol.	15,963	19,718	20,353	21,246	23,390	25,611	28,194
Value of shipments (1987 dollars)	Mil. dol.	14,918	16,940	18,369	19,856	22,171	23,561	25,218
Trade data:								
Value of imports	Mil. dol.	(NA)	42.7	31.8	37.3	27.4	31.8	27.2
Value of exports	Mil. dol.	(NA)	555	717	879	990	1,157	1,633

NA Not available. [1] Estimate, except exports and imports. [2] Value of all products and services sold by establishments in this industry. [3] Value of products classified in this industry produced by all industries.
Source: U.S. Department of Commerce: Bureau of the Census, International Trade Administration (ITA). Estimates by ITA.

No. 1424. Recent Trends in Alcoholic Beverages (SIC 2082, 2084, 2085): 1988 to 1994

ITEM	Unit	1988	1989	1990	1991	1992	1993 [1]	1994 [1]
INDUSTRY DATA								
Value of shipments [2]	Mil. dol.	20,868	21,462	22,318	23,167	24,743	25,794	25,971
2082 Malt beverages	Mil. dol.	13,871	14,321	15,186	15,925	17,328	18,194	18,376
2084 Wines & brandy	Mil. dol.	3,528	3,539	3,658	3,586	3,917	4,074	3,951
2085 Distilled liquor	Mil. dol.	3,469	3,602	3,474	3,656	3,499	3,526	3,644
Value of shipments (1987 dollars)	Mil. dol.	20,617	20,591	21,055	20,723	21,782	22,751	23,227
2082 Malt beverages	Mil. dol.	13,774	13,945	14,787	14,732	15,752	16,676	17,190
2084 Wines & brandy	Mil. dol.	3,439	3,301	3,243	3,081	3,292	3,387	3,295
2085 Distilled liquor	Mil. dol.	3,404	3,344	3,026	2,911	2,738	2,688	2,742
Total employment	1,000.	55.0	53.4	54.4	53.7	55.6	55.7	55.8
2082 Malt beverages	1,000.	32.4	32.0	32.6	32.4	34.5	34.5	33.8
2084 Wines & brandy	1,000.	14.3	13.9	14.4	13.9	14.0	14.0	14.3
2085 Distilled liquor	1,000.	8.3	7.5	7.4	7.4	7.1	7.2	7.7
Production workers	1,000.	36.5	35.7	35.8	35.5	36.7	37.0	38.1
2082 Malt beverages	1,000.	23.2	23.3	23.5	23.5	25.1	25.6	25.8
2084 Wines & brandy	1,000.	7.4	7.1	7.1	6.8	6.5	6.5	6.9
2085 Distilled liquor	1,000.	5.9	5.3	5.2	5.2	5.1	4.9	5.4
Average hourly earnings	Dollar	18.00	18.26	18.33	19.06	18.44	18.71	19.26
2082 Malt beverages	Dollar	21.20	21.26	21.34	22.30	20.60	20.91	21.44
2084 Wines & brandy	Dollar	11.69	11.97	11.95	12.13	12.58	12.76	13.22
2085 Distilled liquor	Dollar	13.55	13.74	13.78	14.23	15.05	15.27	17.72
Capital expenditures	Mil. dol.	708.0	763.0	687.0	805.0	736.0	(NA)	(NA)
2082 Malt beverages	Mil. dol.	570.0	602.0	543.0	649.0	565.0	(NA)	(NA)
2084 Wines & brandy	Mil. dol.	104.0	123.0	108.0	96.9	115.0	(NA)	(NA)
2085 Distilled liquor	Mil. dol.	33.4	37.6	36.4	59.1	56.3	(NA)	(NA)
PRODUCT DATA								
Value of shipments [3]	Mil. dol.	20,409	20,961	21,864	22,758	24,308	25,288	25,388
2082 Malt beverages	Mil. dol.	13,693	14,195	15,111	15,887	17,289	18,103	18,210
2084 Wines & brandy	Mil. dol.	3,523	3,301	3,505	3,467	3,666	3,870	3,753
2085 Distilled liquor	Mil. dol.	3,194	3,465	3,248	3,404	3,353	3,314	3,425
Value of shipments (1987 dollars)	Mil. dol.	20,165	20,119	20,650	20,385	21,422	22,336	22,742
2082 Malt beverages	Mil. dol.	13,598	13,822	14,714	14,696	15,717	16,593	17,035
2084 Wines & brandy	Mil. dol.	3,433	3,079	3,107	2,978	3,081	3,217	3,130
2085 Distilled liquor	Mil. dol.	3,134	3,218	2,829	2,710	2,624	2,526	2,577
TRADE DATA								
Value of imports	Mil. dol.	(NA)	3,165	3,374	3,065	3,527	3,387	3,668
2082 Malt beverages	Mil. dol.	(NA)	870	939	840	881	961	1,072
2084 Wines & brandy	Mil. dol.	(NA)	1,130	1,129	1,094	1,347	1,152	1,268
2085 Distilled liquor	Mil. dol.	(NA)	1,165	1,305	1,131	1,299	1,274	1,328
Value of exports	Mil. dol.	(NA)	516	585	661	751	777	983
2082 Malt beverages	Mil. dol.	(NA)	174	178	207	221	234	391
2084 Wines & brandy	Mil. dol.	(NA)	104	134	155	182	184	201
2085 Distilled liquor	Mil. dol.	(NA)	238	273	300	347	359	390

NA Not available. [1] Estimate, except exports and imports. [2] Value of all products and services sold by establishments in the alcoholic beverages industry. [3] Value of products classified in the alcoholic beverages industry industry produced by all industries.
Source: U.S. Department of Commerce: Bureau of the Census, International Trade Administration (ITA). Estimates by ITA.

No. 1425. Recent Trends in Textile Mill Products (SIC 22): 1988 to 1994

ITEM	Unit	1988	1989	1990	1991	1992	1993 [1]	1994 [1]
INDUSTRY DATA								
Value of shipments [2]	Mil. dol. . .	64,768	67,321	65,951	65,706	70,694	72,272	74,241
Value of shipments (1987 dollars)	Mil. dol. . .	62,251	63,311	60,870	60,172	64,260	65,103	65,688
Total employment	1,000. . .	668	653	633	598	615	616	613
Production workers	1,000. . . .	572	566	548	515	527	524	521
Average hourly earnings	Dollar . . .	7.62	7.93	7.93	8.08	8.59	8.89	9.14
PRODUCT DATA								
Value of shipments [3]	Mil. dol. . .	63,610	65,747	64,986	65,266	69,747	71,322	73,141
Value of shipments (1987 dollars)	Mil. dol. . .	61,137	61,826	59,935	59,659	63,314	64,247	64,715
TRADE DATA								
Value of imports	Mil. dol. . .	(NA)	4,786	4,888	5,375	5,843	6,161	6,534
Value of exports	Mil. dol. . .	(NA)	2,803	3,636	4,101	4,467	4,687	5,151

NA Not available.   [1] Estimate, except exports and imports.   [2] Value of all products and services sold by establishments in the textile mill products industry.   [3] Value of products classified in the textile mill products industry produced by all industries.

Source: U.S. Department of Commerce: Bureau of the Census, International Trade Administration (ITA). Estimates by ITA.

No. 1426. Recent Trends in Cotton, Manmade, and Wool Broadwoven Fabric Mills: 1988 to 1994

ITEM	Unit	1988	1989	1990	1991	1992	1993 [1]	1994 [1]
COTTON BROADWOVEN FABRIC MILLS (SIC 221)								
Industry data:								
Value of shipments [2]	Mil. dol. . .	5,665	5,457	5,325	5,695	5,907	5,674	5,721
Value of shipments (1987 dollars)	Mil. dol. . .	5,436	5,313	5,110	5,398	5,434	5,210	5,173
Total employment	1,000. . .	72.3	67.2	62.5	65.9	56.1	55.2	54.5
Production workers	1,000. . . .	64.8	60.3	55.6	58.8	50.1	49.4	48.8
Average hourly earnings	Dollar . . .	7.91	8.17	8.19	8.35	8.91	9.25	9.53
Product data:								
Value of shipments [3]	Mil. dol. . .	5,350	5,337	5,286	5,498	5,782	5,538	5,591
Value of shipments (1987 dollars)	Mil. dol. . .	5,134	5,197	5,073	5,211	5,320	5,085	5,055
Trade data:								
Value of imports	Mil. dol. . .	(NA)	1,063	1,120	1,277	1,475	1,525	1,482
Value of exports	Mil. dol. . .	(NA)	369	503	542	579	621	704
MANMADE BROADWOVEN FABRIC MILLS (SIC 222)								
Industry data:								
Value of shipments [2]	Mil. dol. . .	8,463	8,690	8,578	8,315	8,680	8,547	8,277
Value of shipments (1987 dollars)	Mil. dol. . .	8,090	8,160	7,928	7,735	7,898	7,951	7,928
Total employment	1,000. . .	90.4	88.4	85.3	78.3	87.0	87.6	88.5
Production workers	1,000. . . .	78.8	77.6	74.6	68.5	76.4	75.3	74.6
Average hourly earnings	Dollar . . .	8.10	8.45	8.55	8.68	9.20	9.64	10.02
Product data:								
Value of shipments [3]	Mil. dol. . .	8,332	8,434	8,133	7,898	8,367	8,253	8,002
Value of shipments (1987 dollars)	Mil. dol. . .	7,966	7,919	7,517	7,347	7,613	7,677	7,665
Trade data:								
Value of imports	Mil. dol. . .	(NA)	1,247	1,241	1,381	1,468	1,541	1,586
Value of exports	Mil. dol. . .	(NA)	658	756	790	891	974	1,049
WOOL BROADWOVEN FABRIC MILLS (SIC 223)								
Industry data:								
Value of shipments [2]	Mil. dol. . .	1,928	2,068	1,798	1,804	1,606	1,638	1,605
Value of shipments (1987 dollars)	Mil. dol. . .	1,807	1,771	1,562	1,634	1,500	1,559	1,535
Total employment	1,000. . .	16.9	17.2	15.7	15.3	13.8	13.7	13.8
Production workers	1,000. . . .	14.6	14.8	13.5	13.2	11.9	11.9	12.1
Average hourly earnings	Dollar . . .	7.65	8.19	8.09	8.03	8.53	8.78	8.97
Product data:								
Value of shipments [3]	Mil. dol. . .	1,626	1,658	1,443	1,492	1,390	1,388	1,330
Value of shipments (1987 dollars)	Mil. dol. . .	1,524	1,420	1,253	1,351	1,299	1,321	1,372
Trade data:								
Value of imports	Mil. dol. . .	(NA)	237	241	247	240	230	242
Value of exports	Mil. dol. . .	(NA)	39.2	49.0	62.4	99.3	84.6	87.2

NA Not available.   [1] Estimate, except exports and imports.   [2] Value of all products and services sold by establishments in this industry.   [3] Value of products classified in this industry produced by all industries.

Source: U.S. Department of Commerce: Bureau of the Census, International Trade Administration (ITA). Estimates by ITA.

No. 1427. Recent Trends in Broadwoven Fabric Mills (SIC 221, 222, 223): 1988 to 1994

ITEM	Unit	1988	1989	1990	1991	1992	1993 [1]	1994 [1]
INDUSTRY DATA								
Value of shipments [2]	Mil. dol. . .	16,056	16,215	15,701	15,814	16,193	15,859	15,603
Value of shipments (1987 dollars)	Mil. dol. . .	15,334	15,244	14,600	14,767	14,833	14,720	14,636
Total employment	1,000. . . .	180	173	164	160	157	156	155
Production workers	1,000. . . .	158	153	144	141	138	137	136
Average hourly earnings	Dollar . . .	7.98	8.31	8.37	8.48	9.04	9.46	9.87
PRODUCT DATA								
Value of shipments [3]	Mil. dol. . .	15,308	15,429	14,862	14,888	15,539	15,179	14,923
Value of shipments (1987 dollars)	Mil. dol. . .	14,624	14,536	13,844	13,909	14,232	14,083	14,092
TRADE DATA								
Value of imports	Mil. dol. . .	(NA)	2,547	2,602	2,905	3,183	3,295	3,310
Value of exports	Mil. dol. . .	(NA)	1,066	1.308	1,395	1,569	1,680	1,840

NA Not available.   [1] Estimate, except exports and imports.   [2] Value of all products and services sold by establishments in the food and kindred products industry.   [3] Value of products classified in the food and kindred products industry produced by all industries.

Source: U.S. Department of Commerce: Bureau of the Census, International Trade Administration (ITA). Estimates by ITA.

No. 1428. Recent Trends in Carpets and Rugs, Weft, Lace, and Knit, and Yarn Spinning Mills: 1988 to 1994

ITEM	Unit	1988	1989	1990	1991	1992	1993 [1]	1994 [1]
CARPETS AND RUGS (SIC 227)								
Industry data:								
Value of shipments [2]	Mil. dol. . .	10,256	10,220	10,038	8,988	9,812	10,392	10,932
Value of shipments (1987 dollars)	Mil. dol. . .	9,938	9,733	9,452	8,408	9,213	9,762	10,226
Total employment	1,000. . . .	54.6	54.5	51.8	48.5	49.3	50.3	52.5
Production workers	1,000. . . .	42.6	43.4	41.0	37.8	38.8	39.3	41.6
Average hourly earnings	Dollar . . .	7.83	7.97	7.95	8.26	8.83	9.16	9.41
Product data:								
Value of shipments [3]	Mil. dol. . .	9,759	9,826	9,611	8,555	9,514	9,992	10,507
Value of shipments (1987 dollars)	Mil. dol. . .	9,456	9,358	9,049	8,003	8,933	9,387	9,828
Trade data:								
Value of imports	Mil. dol. . .	(NA)	604	590	584	700	660	736
Value of exports	Mil. dol. . .	(NA)	366	534	683	705	698	667
WEFT, LACE, AND WARP KNIT FABRIC MILLS (SIC 2257, 2258)								
Industry data:								
Value of shipments [2]	Mil. dol. . .	5,246	6,576	5,887	6,399	7,310	7,047	7,237
Value of shipments (1987 dollars)	Mil. dol. . .	5,075	6,205	5,459	5,925	6,788	6,513	6,670
Total employment	1,000. . . .	53.5	56.0	53.0	53.2	62.4	63.9	65.4
Production workers	1,000. . . .	44.9	47.8	44.7	44.8	52.4	53.8	53.8
Average hourly earnings	Dollar . . .	7.84	8.22	8.09	8.08	8.41	8.70	8.91
Product data:								
Value of shipments [3]	Mil. dol. . .	5,492	6,575	5,923	6,542	7,492	7,172	7,382
Value of shipments (1987 dollars)	Mil. dol. . .	5,310	6,203	5,490	6,048	6,951	6,628	6,804
Trade data:								
Value of imports	Mil. dol. . .	(NA)	139	164	200	233	302	354
Value of exports	Mil. dol. . .	(NA)	153	253	334	377	375	400
YARN SPINNING MILLS (SIC 2281)								
Industry data:								
Value of shipments [2]	Mil. dol. . .	7,279	7,327	7,259	7,265	7,798	7,678	7,825
Value of shipments (1987 dollars)	Mil. dol. . .	7,060	7,169	6,973	6,880	7,398	7,602	7,679
Total employment	1,000. . . .	83.8	77.2	75.0	69.8	69.3	67.7	65.6
Production workers	1,000. . . .	76.5	71.0	68.8	63.6	63.3	62.1	60.1
Average hourly earnings	Dollar . . .	7.43	7.93	8.02	8.28	8.44	8.72	8.99
Product data:								
Value of shipments [3]	Mil. dol. . .	7,626	7,662	7,551	7,519	7,903	7,903	8,068
Value of shipments (1987 dollars)	Mil. dol. . .	7,396	7,497	7,254	7,120	7,498	7,825	7,918
Trade data:								
Value of imports	Mil. dol. . .	(NA)	291	234	264	321	337	388
Value of exports	Mil. dol. . .	(NA)	126	175	202	169	146	209

NA Not available.   [1] Estimate, except exports and imports.   [2] Value of all products and services sold by establishments in this industry.   [3] Value of products classified in this industry produced by all industries.

Source: U.S. Department of Commerce: Bureau of the Census, International Trade Administration (ITA). Estimates by ITA.

No. 1429. Recent Trends in Apparel and Other Textile Products (SIC 23): 1988 to 1994

ITEM	Unit	1988	1989	1990	1991	1992	1993 [1]	1994 [1]
INDUSTRY DATA								
Value of shipments [2]	Mil. dol.	65,032	63,398	64,414	65,345	71,617	75,986	81,305
Value of shipments (1987 dollars)	Mil. dol.	63,119	60,174	59,489	59,025	63,642	66,858	71,245
Total employment	1,000.	1,066	1,018	993	960	985	963	933
Production workers	1,000.	895	865	845	815	824	806	780
Average hourly earnings	Dollar	6.34	6.46	6.54	6.73	7.15	7.29	7.54
PRODUCT DATA								
Value of shipments [3]	Mil. dol.	62,750	61,447	61,962	62,649	68,455	73,093	78,210
Value of shipments (1987 dollars)	Mil. dol.	60,929	58,337	57,242	56,638	60,825	64,313	68,533
TRADE DATA								
Value of imports	Mil. dol.	(NA)	25,372	26,602	27,230	32,462	35,278	38,343
Value of exports	Mil. dol.	(NA)	2,362	2,864	3,708	4,625	5,405	6,117

NA Not available. [1] Estimate, except exports and imports. [2] Value of all products and services sold by establishments in the apparel and other textile products industry. [3] Value of products classified in the apparel and other textile products industry produced by all industries.

Source: U.S. Department of Commerce: Bureau of the Census, International Trade Administration (ITA). Estimates by ITA.

No. 1430. Recent Trends in Selected Men's and Boys' Apparel (SIC 231, 2321, –3, –5, –6): 1988 to 1994

ITEM	Unit	1988	1989	1990	1991	1992	1993 [1]	1994 [1]
INDUSTRY DATA								
Value of shipments [2]	Mil. dol.	15,101	14,772	14,484	15,386	17,035	18,140	19,498
2311 Men/boys' suits/coats	Mil. dol.	3,169	2,918	2,622	2,467	2,426	2,645	2,888
2321 Men's and boys' shirts	Mil. dol.	4,031	3,873	4,243	4,494	5,894	5,866	6,244
2323 Men's and boys' neckwear	Mil. dol.	500	534	500	532	655	572	617
2325 Men/boys' trousers	Mil. dol.	5,767	5,983	5,657	6,467	6,488	7,186	7,719
2326 Men/boys' work clothing	Mil. dol.	1,633	1,464	1,462	1,426	1,572	1,871	2,029
Value of shipments (1987 dollars)	Mil. dol.	14,508	13,720	13,076	13,562	14,519	15,387	16,521
2311 Men/boys' suits/coats	Mil. dol.	3,010	2,596	2,239	2,057	1,990	2,189	2,359
2321 Men's and boys' shirts	Mil. dol.	3,876	3,613	3,836	3,939	4,966	4,925	5,252
2323 Men's and boys' neckwear	Mil. dol.	490	496	447	465	563	485	517
2325 Men/boys' trousers	Mil. dol.	5,562	5,655	5,229	5,847	5,632	6,200	6,695
2326 Men/boys' work clothing	Mil. dol.	1,570	1,361	1,325	1,254	1,368	1,587	1,698
Total employment	1,000.	270.0	258.0	239.0	230.0	247.0	240.0	229.4
2311 Men/boys' suits/coats	1,000.	60.0	54.5	48.4	43.6	44.2	42.0	40.1
2321 Men's and boys' shirts	1,000.	77.4	73.7	69.7	68.8	84.2	81.3	75.5
2323 Men's and boys' neckwear	1,000.	7.5	8.0	7.4	6.4	7.5	7.4	7.1
2325 Men/boys' trousers	1,000.	91.9	88.0	81.7	80.5	78.3	76.3	74.2
2326 Men/boys' work clothing	1,000.	33.3	34.0	31.5	30.8	32.5	33.0	32.5
Production workers	1,000.	236.0	225.0	208.0	201.0	215.0	209.1	199.1
2311 Men/boys' suits/coats	1,000.	51.7	47.0	41.3	36.5	37.5	35.4	33.7
2321 Men's and boys' shirts	1,000.	68.0	65.1	61.7	60.9	74.1	71.7	66.3
2323 Men's and boys' neckwear	1,000.	6.2	6.6	6.0	5.1	5.8	5.7	5.5
2325 Men/boys' trousers	1,000.	80.8	76.7	71.6	70.8	69.2	67.5	65.2
2326 Men/boys' work clothing	1,000.	29.5	30.0	27.8	27.2	28.3	28.8	28.4
Average hourly earnings	Dollar	6.18	6.42	6.61	6.79	6.93	7.10	7.38
2311 Men/boys' suits/coats	Dollar	7.09	7.58	7.84	8.14	7.92	8.10	8.27
2321 Men's and boys' shirts	Dollar	5.77	6.29	6.46	6.87	6.84	7.03	7.28
2323 Men's/boys' neckwear	Dollar	7.15	7.04	7.28	8.02	7.48	7.69	7.92
2325 Men/boys' trousers	Dollar	6.26	6.17	6.43	6.36	6.87	7.04	7.39
2326 Men/boys' work clothing	Dollar	5.17	5.41	5.46	5.68	5.91	6.03	6.24
PRODUCT DATA								
Value of shipments [3]	Mil. dol.	14,174	14,383	13,771	14,143	15,785	17,173	18,464
2311 Men/boys' suits/coats	Mil. dol.	2,977	2,915	2,633	2,450	2,370	2,656	2,900
2321 Men's and boys' shirts	Mil. dol.	3,728	3,681	3,740	3,915	5,308	5,170	5,504
2323 Men's and boys' neckwear	Mil. dol.	457	526	498	525	544	570	614
2325 Men/boys' trousers	Mil. dol.	5,475	5,889	5,544	5,911	6,048	7,043	7,565
2326 Men/boys' work clothing	Mil. dol.	1,537	1,372	1,355	1,341	1,515	1,734	1,881
Value of shipments (1987 dollars)	Mil. dol.	13,617	13,357	12,428	12,458	13,452	14,570	15,648
2311 Men/boys' suits/coats	Mil. dol.	2,827	2,593	2,248	2,043	1,945	2,198	2,369
2321 Men's and boys' shirts	Mil. dol.	3,584	3,433	3,382	3,431	4,472	4,341	4,629
2323 Men's and boys' neckwear	Mil. dol.	448	489	445	459	467	483	515
2325 Men/boys' trousers	Mil. dol.	5,279	5,566	5,124	5,345	5,250	6,076	6,561
2326 Men/boys' work clothing	Mil. dol.	1,478	1,275	1,229	1,180	1,318	1,471	1,574
TRADE DATA								
Value of imports	Mil. dol.	(NA)	5,566	5,716	6,167	7,624	8,281	9,178
2311 Men/boys' suits/coats	Mil. dol.	(NA)	745	650	678	789	824	954
2321 Men's and boys' shirts	Mil. dol.	(NA)	2,749	2,792	3,039	4,028	4,519	4,917
2323 Men's and boys' neckwear	Mil. dol.	(NA)	100	110	140	151	158	156
2325 Men/boys' trousers	Mil. dol.	(NA)	1,971	2,164	2,310	2,657	2,780	3,151
2326 Men/boys' work clothing	Mil. dol.	(NA)	-	-	-	-	-	-
Value of exports	Mil. dol.	(NA)	713	906	1,140	1,478	1,795	2,036
2311 Men/boys' suits/coats	Mil. dol.	(NA)	84	129	161	197	237	292
2321 Men's and boys' shirts	Mil. dol.	(NA)	217	268	333	457	595	721
2323 Men's and boys' neckwear	Mil. dol.	(NA)	10.1	9.8	14.5	15.5	21.1	17.9
2325 Men/boys' trousers	Mil. dol.	(NA)	402	500	631	809	942	1,005
2326 Men/boys' work clothing	Mil. dol.	(NA)	-	-	-	-	-	-

- Represents or rounds to zero. NA Not available. [1] Estimate, except exports and imports. [2] Value of all products and services sold by establishments in the selected men's and boys' apparel industry. [3] Value of products classified in the selected men's and boys' apparel industry produced by all industries.

Source: U.S. Department of Commerce: Bureau of the Census, International Trade Administration (ITA). Estimates by ITA.

No. 1431. Recent Trends in Men's and Boys' Underwear and Nightwear (SIC 2322): 1988 to 1994

ITEM	Unit	1988	1989	1990	1991	1992	1993 [1]	1994 [1]
INDUSTRY DATA								
Value of shipments [2]	Mil. dol. . .	1,045	828	725	710	749	798	878
Value of shipments (1987 dollars)	Mil. dol. . .	1,014	786	675	660	685	705	802
Total employment	1,000. . . .	17.1	16.2	15.3	11.8	12.8	13.1	13.4
Production workers	1,000. . . .	16.1	15.3	14.4	10.9	11.8	13.1	13.4
Average hourly earnings	Dollar . . .	6.20	6.21	6.07	7.42	6.66	6.91	7.16
PRODUCT DATA								
Value of shipments [3]	Mil. dol. . .	1,001	779	738	744	804	812	894
Value of shipments (1987 dollars)	Mil. dol. . .	971	739	687	692	735	718	816
TRADE DATA								
Value of imports	Mil. dol. . .	(NA)	226	251	289	396	528	652
Value of exports	Mil. dol. . .	(NA)	53	95	157	218	314	331

NA Not available. [1] Estimate, except exports and imports. [2] Value of all products and services sold by establishments in the men's and boys' underwear and nightwear industry. [3] Value of products classified in the men's and boys' underwear and nightwear industry produced by all industries.

Source: U.S. Department of Commerce: Bureau of the Census, International Trade Administration (ITA). Estimates by ITA.

No. 1432. Recent Trends in Selected Women's Outerwear (SIC 2331, 2335, 2337): 1988 to 1994

ITEM	Unit	1988	1989	1990	1991	1992	1993 [1]	1994 [1]
INDUSTRY DATA								
Value of shipments [2]	Mil. dol. . .	14,316	13,009	13,810	13,790	13,881	15,729	16,684
2331 Women's/misses' blouses	Mil. dol. . .	3,574	3,402	3,733	3,801	4,051	4,137	4,400
2335 Women's/misses' dresses	Mil. dol. . .	6,037	5,366	5,915	5,665	5,405	6,795	7,217
2337 Women's suits and coats	Mil. dol. . .	4,705	4,241	4,163	4,324	4,425	4,797	5,067
Value of shipments (1987 dollars)	Mil. dol. . .	13,808	12,264	12,688	12,354	12,267	13,626	15,438
2331 Women's/misses' blouses	Mil. dol. . .	3,463	3,207	3,375	3,325	3,439	3,489	4,527
2335 Women's/misses' dresses	Mil. dol. . .	5,856	4,968	5,314	4,960	4,704	5,860	6,271
2337 Women's suits and coats	Mil. dol. . .	4,489	4,089	3,999	4,068	4,124	4,277	4,640
Total employment	1,000. . . .	235.0	215.0	217.0	210.0	189.0	176.8	159.1
2331 Women's/misses' blouses	1,000. . . .	67.0	64.6	64.4	59.5	57.0	51.1	47.3
2335 Women's/misses' dresses	1,000. . . .	115.0	105.0	106.0	102.0	83.4	75.4	68.8
2337 Women's suits and coats	1,000. . . .	53.3	46.1	45.9	47.9	48.9	50.3	43.0
Production workers	1,000. . . .	191	180	184	178	157	145	129
2331 Women's/misses' blouses	1,000. . . .	56.7	55.2	54.3	49.4	48.0	42.6	39.2
2335 Women's/misses' dresses	1,000. . . .	91.8	89.2	93.3	89.6	70.8	63.0	57.3
2337 Women's suits and coats	1,000. . . .	42.2	36.0	36.6	39.3	38.3	39.0	32.4
Average hourly earnings	Dollar . . .	6.20	6.16	6.13	6.38	7.01	7.27	7.55
2331 Women's/misses' blouses	Dollar . . .	5.65	5.70	5.85	5.93	6.68	6.97	7.21
2335 Women's/misses' dresses	Dollar . . .	6.40	6.10	5.93	6.30	6.87	7.13	7.36
2337 Women's suits and coats	Dollar . . .	6.57	7.02	7.00	7.09	7.68	7.73	8.09
PRODUCT DATA								
Value of shipments [3]	Mil. dol. . .	13,927	12,500	12,817	12,805	13,523	14,586	15,475
2331 Women's/misses' blouses	Mil. dol. . .	3,983	3,635	3,660	3,618	4,239	4,056	4,314
2335 Women's/misses' dresses	Mil. dol. . .	5,810	5,245	5,746	5,443	5,219	6,601	7,011
2337 Women's suits and coats	Mil. dol. . .	4,134	3,620	3,410	3,745	4,065	3,930	4,150
Value of shipments (1987 dollars)	Mil. dol. . .	13,439	11,773	11,748	11,454	11,929	12,617	14,331
2331 Women's/misses' blouses	Mil. dol. . .	3,859	3,426	3,309	3,165	3,598	3,421	4,438
2335 Women's/misses' dresses	Mil. dol. . .	5,636	4,856	5,163	4,766	4,542	5,692	6,091
2337 Women's suits and coats	Mil. dol. . .	3,944	3,491	3,276	3,523	3,788	3,504	3,801
TRADE DATA								
Value of imports	Mil. dol. . .	(NA)	5,881	6,190	6,119	7,073	7,718	7,960
2331 Women's/misses' blouses	Mil. dol. . .	(NA)	2,983	3,005	2,923	3,501	3,864	3,948
2335 Women's/misses' dresses	Mil. dol. . .	(NA)	937	1,028	981	1,054	1,130	1,339
2337 Women's suits and coats	Mil. dol. . .	(NA)	1,962	2,157	2,215	2,518	2,724	2,673
Value of exports	Mil. dol. . .	(NA)	235	291	362	519	590	591
2331 Women's/misses' blouses	Mil. dol. . .	(NA)	77.2	80.6	100	171	213	243
2335 Women's/misses' dresses	Mil. dol. . .	(NA)	42.3	50.9	65.0	98.3	105	103
2337 Women's suits and coats	Mil. dol. . .	(NA)	116	159	197	250	272	245

NA Not available. [1] Estimate, except exports and imports. [2] Value of all products and services sold by establishments in the selected women's outerwear industry. [3] Value of products classified in the selected women's outerwear industry produced by all industries.

Source: U.S. Department of Commerce: Bureau of the Census, International Trade Administration (ITA). Estimates by ITA.

No. 1433. Recent Trends in Women's and Children's Undergarments (SIC 234): 1988 to 1994

ITEM	Unit	1988	1989	1990	1991	1992	1993 [1]	1994 [1]
INDUSTRY DATA								
Value of shipments [2]	Mil. dol. . .	3,884	3,366	3,424	3,683	3,934	3,871	4,175
2341 Women/child's underwear	Mil. dol. . .	2,621	2,301	2,337	2,386	2,350	2,627	2,832
2342 Bras and allied garments	Mil. dol. . .	1,263	1,064	1,087	1,297	1,583	1,244	1,343
Value of shipments (1987 dollars)	Mil. dol. . .	3,764	3,190	3,199	3,385	3,528	3,397	3,631
2341 Women/child's underwear	Mil. dol. . .	2,543	2,189	2,180	2,193	2,104	2,302	2,467
2342 Bras and allied garments	Mil. dol. . .	1,221	1,000	1,019	1,192	1,424	1,094	1,164
Total employment	1,000. . .	66.8	61.2	60.3	57.5	53.5	49.8	49.1
2341 Women/child's underwear	1,000. . .	53.9	49.4	48.7	46.9	41.4	37.6	36.5
2342 Bras and allied garments	1,000. . .	12.9	11.8	11.6	10.6	12.1	12.2	12.6
Production workers	1,000. . .	56.0	51.6	50.8	48.5	45.4	42.6	42.2
2341 Women/child's underwear	1,000. . .	46.7	43.2	42.3	40.7	35.7	32.7	32.0
2342 Bras and allied garments	1,000. . .	9.3	8.4	8.5	7.8	9.7	9.9	10.2
Average hourly earnings	Dollar . . .	5.87	5.75	6.02	6.24	6.74	6.96	7.20
2341 Women/child's underwear	Dollar . . .	5.83	5.68	5.96	6.10	6.47	6.61	6.75
2342 Bras + allied garments	Dollar . . .	6.03	6.16	6.34	7.01	7.79	8.00	7.89
PRODUCT DATA								
Value of shipments [3]	Mil. dol. . .	3,644	3,365	3,322	3,660	3,806	3,759	4,054
2341 Women/child's underwear	Mil. dol. . .	2,513	2,303	2,119	2,260	2,214	2,382	2,568
2342 Bras and allied garments	Mil. dol. . .	1,131	1,062	1,203	1,400	1,592	1,377	1,486
Value of shipments (1987 dollars)	Mil. dol. . .	3,531	3,189	3,104	3,364	3,413	3,299	3,525
2341 Women/child's underwear	Mil. dol. . .	2,438	2,191	1,976	2,077	1,982	2,088	2,237
2342 Bras and allied garments	Mil. dol. . .	1,094	998	1,127	1,287	1,431	1,211	1,288
TRADE DATA								
Value of imports	Mil. dol. . .	(NA)	928	1,079	1,256	1,519	1,787	2,067
2341 Women/child's underwear	Mil. dol. . .	(NA)	601	727	829	985	1,168	1,342
2342 Bras and allied garments	Mil. dol. . .	(NA)	327	352	427	534	619	725
Value of exports	Mil. dol. . .	(NA)	254	266	355	407	466	521
2341 Women/child's underwear	Mil. dol. . .	(NA)	88	96	136	155	186	222
2342 Bras and allied garments	Mil. dol. . .	(NA)	165	170	219	252	280	299

NA Not available.   [1] Estimate, except exports and imports.   [2] Value of all products and services sold by establishments in the women's and children's undergarments industry.   [3] Value of products classified in the women's and children's undergarments industry produced by all industries.

Source: U.S. Department of Commerce: Bureau of the Census, International Trade Administration (ITA). Estimates by ITA.

No. 1434. Recent Trends in Girls' and Children's Outerwear (SIC 236): 1988 to 1994

ITEM	Unit	1988	1989	1990	1991	1992	1993 [1]	1994 [1]
INDUSTRY DATA								
Value of shipments [2]	Mil. dol. . .	3,673	3,691	3,698	3,579	3,144	3,751	4,473
2361 Child's dresses/blouses	Mil. dol. . .	1,604	1,671	1,725	1,800	1,635	1,720	2,047
2369 Children's outerwear n.e.c.	Mil. dol. . .	2,070	2,020	1,973	1,779	1,509	2,031	2,426
Value of shipments (1987 dollars)	Mil. dol. . .	3,629	3,564	3,398	3,214	2,790	3,320	3,973
2361 Child's dresses/blouses	Mil. dol. . .	1,569	1,585	1,568	1,601	1,430	1,513	1,808
2369 Children's outerwear n.e.c.	Mil. dol. . .	2,060	1,979	1,830	1,613	1,359	1,807	2,164
Total employment	1,000. . .	68.9	66.7	60.9	58.8	53.7	51.3	47.1
2361 Child's dresses/blouses	1,000. . .	28.9	30.6	29.0	30.2	24.4	24.4	22.5
2369 Children's outerwear n.e.c.	1,000. . .	40.0	36.1	31.9	28.6	29.3	26.9	24.6
Production workers	1,000. . .	57.6	56.5	50.7	49.7	44.0	41.8	39.0
2361 Child's dresses/blouses	1,000. . .	23.7	25.6	24.2	25.6	19.6	19.3	17.6
2369 Children's outerwear n.e.c.	1,000. . .	33.9	30.9	26.5	24.1	24.4	22.5	21.4
Average hourly earnings	Dollar . . .	55.5	5.65	5.52	5.72	6.44	6.50	6.69
2361 Child's dresses/blouses	Dollar . . .	5.70	5.64	5.80	5.94	6.67	6.79	6.94
2369 Children's outerwear n.e.c.	Dollar . . .	5.44	5.65	5.31	5.51	6.26	6.35	6.47
PRODUCT DATA								
Value of shipments [3]	Mil. dol. . .	3,533	3,607	3,648	3,592	3,490	3,697	4,408
2361 Child's dresses/blouses	Mil. dol. . .	1,622	1,765	1,812	1,812	1,720	1,808	2,151
2369 Children's outerwear n.e.c.	Mil. dol. . .	1,912	1,842	1,835	1,780	1,770	1,889	2,257
Value of shipments (1987 dollars)	Mil. dol. . .	3,489	3,478	3,350	3,226	3,100	3,270	3,913
2361 Child's dresses/blouses	Mil. dol. . .	1,587	1,674	1,647	1,612	1,505	1,590	1,900
2369 Children's outerwear n.e.c.	Mil. dol. . .	1,902	1,804	1,703	1,614	1,595	1,681	2,013
TRADE DATA								
Value of imports	Mil. dol. . .	(NA)	6,360	6,487	6,694	8,016	8,196	8,926
2361 Child's dresses/blouses	Mil. dol. . .	(NA)	-	-	-	-	-	-
2369 Children's outerwear n.e.c.	Mil. dol. . .	(NA)	6,360	6,487	6,694	8,016	8,196	8,926
Value of exports	Mil. dol. . .	(NA)	282	341	458	625	703	920
2361 Child's dresses/blouses	Mil. dol. . .	(NA)	-	-	-	-	-	-
2369 Children's outerwear n.e.c.	Mil. dol. . .	(NA)	282	341	458	625	703	920

- Represents of rounds to zero.   NA Not available.   [1] Estimate, except exports and imports.   [2] Value of all products and services sold by establishments in the girls' and children's outerwear industry.   [3] Value of products classified in the girls' and children's outerwear industry produced by all industries.

Source: U.S. Department of Commerce: Bureau of the Census, International Trade Administration (ITA). Estimates by ITA.

No. 1435. Recent Trends in Misc. Fabricated Textile Products (SIC 239): 1988 to 1994

ITEM	Unit	1988	1989	1990	1991	1992	1993 [1]	1994 [1]
INDUSTRY DATA								
Value of shipments [2]	Mil. dol.	15,833	16,339	17,086	16,894	19,074	20,212	21,810
239A Homefurnishings	Mil. dol.	6,122	6,168	6,371	6,483	7,013	7,427	8,065
239B Misc. textile products	Mil. dol.	9,711	10,171	10,715	10,411	12,062	12,786	13,745
Value of shipments (1987 dollars)	Mil. dol.	15,445	15,675	15,965	15,470	17,281	18,238	19,398
239A Homefurnishings	Mil. dol.	5,956	5,893	5,931	5,870	6,280	6,632	7,096
239B Misc. textile products	Mil. dol.	9,489	9,782	10,033	9,600	11,001	11,606	12,302
Total employment	1,000	197.0	188.0	190.0	186.0	211.0	202.4	207.8
239A Homefurnishings	1,000	76.8	69.6	68.2	67.1	74.8	74.4	75.1
239B Misc. textile products	1,000	121.0	119.0	121.0	119.0	136.0	128.0	132.7
Production workers	1,000	161.0	155.0	155.0	152.0	168.0	165.5	169.5
239A Homefurnishings	1,000	63.6	57.6	56.2	55.3	61.6	61.1	61.5
239B Misc. textile products	1,000	97.3	97.1	98.7	96.4	107.0	104.4	108.0
Average hourly earnings	Dollar	7.62	7.92	8.06	8.19	8.39	8.40	8.62
239A Homefurnishings	Dollar	6.16	6.36	6.43	6.64	7.34	7.54	7.79
239B Misc. textile products	Dollar	8.58	8.90	9.04	9.12	9.01	8.83	9.02
PRODUCT DATA								
Value of shipments [3]	Mil. dol.	15,261	15,703	16,397	16,207	18,131	19,212	20,730
239A Homefurnishings	Mil. dol.	5,932	5,892	6,013	6,100	6,628	7,019	7,623
239B Misc. textile products	Mil. dol.	9,329	9,811	10,385	10,107	11,503	12,193	13,108
Value of shipments (1987 dollars)	Mil. dol.	14,896	15,095	15,347	14,873	16,427	17,336	18,439
239A Homefurnishings	Mil. dol.	5,772	5,629	5,596	5,521	5,937	6,269	6,708
239B Misc. textile products	Mil. dol.	9,125	9,466	9,750	9,352	10,490	11,067	11,731
TRADE DATA								
Value of imports	Mil. dol.	(NA)	1,854	2,138	2,316	2,698	3,116	3,428
239A Homefurnishings	Mil. dol.	(NA)	922	976	1,000	1,178	1,334	1,553
239B Misc. textile products	Mil. dol.	(NA)	932	1,162	1,315	1,520	1,782	1,875
Value of exports	Mil. dol.	(NA)	520	622	780	862	971	1,079
239A Homefurnishings	Mil. dol.	(NA)	202	245	317	338	349	362
239B Misc. textile products	Mil. dol.	(NA)	318	377	463	523	623	718

NA Not available.   [1] Estimate, except exports and imports.   [2] Value of all products and services sold by establishments in the misc. fabricated textile products industry. The designation 239A represents SIC's 2391 and 2392; 239B represents SIC 239 less SIC's 2391 and 2392.   [3] Value of products classified in the misc. fabricated textile products industry produced by all industries.

Source: U.S. Department of Commerce: Bureau of the Census, International Trade Administration (ITA). Estimates by ITA.

No. 1436. Recent Trends in Logging and Sawmills and Planing Mills, General: 1988 to 1994

ITEM	Unit	1988	1989	1990	1991	1992	1993 [1]	1994 [1]
LOGGING (SIC 2411)								
Industry data:								
Value of shipments [2]	Mil. dol.	11,664	12,017	12,229	11,434	13,844	16,165	16,852
Value of shipments (1987 dollars)	Mil. dol.	10,405	9,940	9,569	8,912	9,902	9,803	9,901
Total employment	1,000	86.9	81.7	83.4	78.1	83.8	(NA)	(NA)
Production workers	1,000	73.0	68.0	68.9	65.4	69.5	(NA)	(NA)
Average hourly earnings	Dollar	9.09	9.50	9.55	9.80	9.96	(NA)	(NA)
Capital expenditures	Mil. dol.	222	354	406	293	375	(NA)	(NA)
Product data:								
Value of shipments [3]	Mil. dol.	11,087	11,360	11,572	10,728	13,351	15,591	16,254
Value of shipments (1987 dollars)	Mil. dol.	9,890	9,396	9,054	8,362	9,550	9,455	9,550
Trade data:								
Value of imports	Mil. dol.	(NA)	248	210	199	219	265	273
Value of exports	Mil. dol.	(NA)	2,836	2,930	2,715	2,749	3,077	2,915
SAWMILLS AND PLANING MILLS, GENERAL (SIC 2421)								
Industry data:								
Value of shipments [2]	Mil. dol.	18,260	18,479	17,923	17,485	21,045	25,604	26,307
Value of shipments (1987 dollars)	Mil. dol.	17,711	17,190	16,973	16,341	17,151	16,979	17,149
Total employment	1,000	152	144	139	130	139	138	140
Production workers	1,000	132	126	125	116	118	118	120
Average hourly earnings	Dollar	8.75	8.94	9.23	9.33	9.63	(NA)	(NA)
Capital expenditures	Mil. dol.	581	573	522	464	459	(NA)	(NA)
Product data:								
Value of shipments [3]	Mil. dol.	18,198	18,439	17,862	17,515	20,430	24,858	25,540
Value of shipments (1987 dollars)	Mil. dol.	17,650	17,152	16,915	16,369	16,650	16,484	16,649
Trade data:								
Value of imports	Mil. dol.	(NA)	3,016	2,659	2,638	3,472	5,022	6,039
Value of exports	Mil. dol.	(NA)	2,034	2,128	2,203	2,322	2,450	2,428

NA Not available.   [1] Estimate, except exports and imports.   [2] Value of all products and services sold by establishments in this industry.   [3] Value of products classified in this industry produced by all industries.

Source: U.S. Department of Commerce: Bureau of the Census, International Trade Administration (ITA). Estimates by ITA.

No. 1437. Recent Trends in Hardwood Veneer and Softwood Veneer: 1988 to 1994

ITEM	Unit	1988	1989	1990	1991	1992	1993 [1]	1994 [1]
HARDWOOD VENEER AND PLYWOOD (SIC 2435)								
Industry data:								
Value of shipments [1]	Mil. dol.	2,100	2,185	2,052	1,897	2,257	2,467	2,770
Value of shipments (1987 dollars)	Mil. dol.	2,033	2,044	1,845	1,727	1,971	2,001	2,121
Total employment	1,000	20.6	20.1	18.7	17.3	20.2	21.2	22.0
Production workers	1,000	17.3	17.0	15.7	14.8	17.0	18.0	18.7
Average hourly earnings	Dollar	7.20	7.58	7.83	8.03	8.18	(NA)	(NA)
Capital expenditures	Mil. dol.	37.2	47.2	40.8	45.5	46.6	(NA)	(NA)
Product data:								
Value of shipments [3]	Mil. dol.	1,827	1,937	1,879	1,743	2,085	(NA)	(NA)
Value of shipments (1987 dollars)	Mil. dol.	1,768	1,812	1,690	1,587	1,821	(NA)	(NA)
Trade data:								
Value of imports	Mil. dol.	(NA)	660	688	588	729	857	890
Value of exports	Mil. dol.	(NA)	181	230	248	278	297	348
SOFTWOOD VENEER AND PLYWOOD (SIC 2436)								
Industry data:								
Value of shipments [2]	Mil. dol.	4,848	5,310	5,030	4,592	5,516	5,826	6,313
Value of shipments (1987 dollars)	Mil. dol.	4,735	5,076	4,684	4,320	4,756	4,756	4,830
Total employment	1,000	38.4	36.5	35.6	31.7	31.3	32.0	32.3
Production workers	1,000	34.7	32.9	32.2	28.6	28.1	28.9	28.9
Average hourly earnings	Dollar	10.09	10.34	10.44	10.78	11.09	(NA)	(NA)
Capital expenditures	Mil. dol.	126	140	103	86.7	98.8	(NA)	(NA)
Product data:								
Value of shipments [3]	Mil. dol.	4,324	4,605	4,412	3,972	4,742	(NA)	(NA)
Value of shipments (1987 dollars)	Mil. dol.	4,222	4,402	4,108	3,737	4,088	(NA)	(NA)
Trade data:								
Value of imports	Mil. dol.	(NA)	52.5	44.3	35.5	59.0	76.9	96.4
Value of exports	Mil. dol.	(NA)	292	326	275	336	369	323

NA Not available. [1] Estimate, except exports and imports. [2] Value of all products and services sold by establishments in this industry. [3] Value of products classified in this industry produced by all industries.

Source: U.S. Department of Commerce: Bureau of the Census, International Trade Administration (ITA). Estimates by ITA.

No. 1438. Recent Trends in Reconstituted Wood Products (SIC 2493): 1988 to 1994

ITEM	Unit	1988	1989	1990	1991	1992	1993 [1]	1994 [1]
INDUSTRY DATA								
Value of shipments [2]	Mil. dol.	2,971	3,199	3,043	3,041	3,944	4,556	5,163
Value of shipments (1987 dollars)	Mil. dol.	2,907	3,064	3,001	2,981	3,700	3,848	4,002
Total employment	1,000	22.8	22.2	22.3	21.0	22.9	(NA)	(NA)
Production workers	1,000	18.3	18.2	18.2	17.1	18.6	(NA)	(NA)
Average hourly earnings	Dollar	10.16	10.15	10.41	10.73	11.44	(NA)	(NA)
Capital expenditures	Mil. dol.	216	133	130	187	142	(NA)	(NA)
PRODUCT DATA								
Value of shipments [3]	Mil. dol.	2,996	3,240	3,050	3,046	3,939	(NA)	(NA)
Value of shipments (1987 dollars)	Mil. dol.	2,931	3,103	3,008	2,986	3,695	(NA)	(NA)
TRADE DATA								
Value of imports	Mil. dol.	(NA)	298	262	234	402	581	834
Value of exports	Mil. dol.	(NA)	169	214	225	244	256	292

NA Not available. [1] Estimate, except exports and imports. [2] Value of all products and services sold by establishments in the reconstituted wood products industry. [3] Value of products classified in the reconstituted wood products industry produced by all industries.

Source: U.S. Department of Commerce: Bureau of the Census, International Trade Administration (ITA). Estimates by ITA.

No. 1439. Recent Trends in Household Furniture (SIC 251): 1988 to 1994

ITEM	Unit	1988	1989	1990	1991	1992	1993 [1]	1994 [1]
INDUSTRY DATA								
Value of shipments [2]	Mil. dol.	19,131	19,955	19,913	19,499	20,707	22,706	24,985
2511 Wood furniture, house	Mil. dol.	8,275	8,461	8,303	7,980	8,762	9,679	10,745
2512 Upholstered furniture, house	Mil. dol.	5,409	5,618	5,815	5,859	6,221	7,065	7,801
2514 Metal furniture, house.	Mil. dol.	2,225	2,229	2,184	2,090	2,116	2,202	2,318
2515 Mattresses and bedsprings	Mil. dol.	2,457	2,893	2,905	2,923	2,843	2,959	3,279
2517 Wood TV & radio cabinets	Mil. dol.	341	281	247	235	309	302	314
2519 Other furniture	Mil. dol.	424	473	459	412	452	499	529
Value of shipments (1987 dollars)	Mil. dol.	18,370	18,531	18,033	17,276	18,068	19,381	20,586
2511 Wood furniture, house	Mil. dol.	7,911	7,776	7,400	6,921	7,412	7,896	8,401
2512 Upholstered furniture, house	Mil. dol.	5,176	5,246	5,335	5,246	5,530	6,131	6,499
2514 Metal furniture, house.	Mil. dol.	2,162	2,081	1,987	1,868	1,856	1,930	2,028
2515 Mattresses and bedsprings	Mil. dol.	2,367	2,689	2,636	2,633	2,549	2,680	2,888
2517 Wood TV & radio cabinets	Mil. dol.	343	284	243	229	300	309	317
2519 Other furniture	Mil. dol.	411	455	432	379	421	435	453
Total employment	1,000	283	280	275	259	257	261	265
Production workers	1,000	241	236	231	217	216	222	225
Average hourly earnings	Dollar	7.33	7.46	7.58	7.96	8.33	8.53	8.82
Capital expenditures	Mil. dol.	373	414	347	297	354	(NA)	(NA)
2511 Wood furniture, house	Mil. dol.	212	264	185	166	197	(NA)	(NA)
2512 Upholstered furniture, house	Mil. dol.	84.8	56.3	73.0	49.9	73.8	(NA)	(NA)
2514 Metal furniture, house.	Mil. dol.	27.9	33.6	35.7	34.1	36.9	(NA)	(NA)
2515 Mattresses and bedsprings	Mil. dol.	20.2	30.6	28.2	35.5	31.2	(NA)	(NA)
2517 Wood TV & radio cabinets	Mil. dol.	6.7	10.3	6.2	3.8	3.5	(NA)	(NA)
2519 Other furniture	Mil. dol.	20.9	19.7	18.8	7.6	10.8	(NA)	(NA)
PRODUCT DATA								
Value of shipments [3]	Mil. dol.	18,372	19,208	19,232	18,842	19,676	21,602	23,772
2511 Wood furniture, house	Mil. dol.	7,710	7,853	7,847	7,592	8,001	8,832	9,803
2512 Upholstered furniture, house	Mil. dol.	5,049	5,324	5,392	5,402	5,780	6,555	7,240
2514 Metal furniture, house.	Mil. dol.	2,034	2,049	2,054	1,982	1,954	2,031	2,138
2515 Mattresses and bedsprings	Mil. dol.	2,747	3,135	3,185	3,182	3,092	3,304	3,660
2517 Wood TV & radio cabinets	Mil. dol.	365	353	313	292	365	376	392
2519 Other furniture	Mil. dol.	467	494	442	393	484	504	539
Value of shipments (1987 dollars)	Mil. dol.	17,645	17,846	17,421	16,703	17,192	18,408	19,547
2511 Wood furniture, house	Mil. dol.	7,371	7,218	6,994	6,584	6,769	7,210	7,672
2512 Upholstered furniture, house	Mil. dol.	4,832	4,971	4,946	4,836	5,138	5,696	6,039
2514 Metal furniture, house.	Mil. dol.	1,977	1,913	1,869	1,771	1,714	1,782	1,872
2515 Mattresses and bedsprings	Mil. dol.	2,646	2,913	2,890	2,866	2,773	2,916	3,141
2517 Wood TV & radio cabinets	Mil. dol.	363	349	302	281	381	349	352
2519 Other furniture	Mil. dol.	456	482	419	365	417	455	471
TRADE DATA								
Value of imports	Mil. dol.	(NA)	2,742	2,738	2,729	2,995	3,397	3,965
Value of exports	Mil. dol.	(NA)	471	756	955	1,113	1,183	1,307

NA Not available. [1] Estimate, except exports and imports. [2] Value of all products and services sold by establishments in the household furniture industry. [3] Value of products classified in the household furniture industry produced by all industries.

Source: U.S. Department of Commerce: Bureau of the Census, International Trade Administration (ITA). Estimates by ITA.

No. 1440. Recent Trends in Office Furniture (SIC 252): 1988 to 1994

ITEM	Unit	1988	1989	1990	1991	1992	1993 [1]	1994 [1]
INDUSTRY DATA								
Value of shipments [2]	Mil. dol.	7,779	8,257	8,030	7,263	8,002	8,427	9,015
Value of shipments (1987 dollars)	Mil. dol.	7,276	7,450	6,976	6,172	6,819	7,101	7,423
Total employment	1,000	80.6	79.6	74.9	66.1	68.1	67.2	69.1
Production workers	1,000	60.9	59.4	55.5	47.8	50.4	49.0	49.5
Average hourly earnings	Dollar	10.24	10.49	10.69	10.91	10.83	11.25	11.63
Capital expenditures	Mil. dol.	306	302	292	173	206	(NA)	(NA)
PRODUCT DATA								
Value of shipments [3]	Mil. dol.	7,561	8,051	7,880	7,130	7,691	8,095	8,671
Value of shipments (1987 dollars)	Mil. dol.	7,075	7,276	6,861	6,068	6,556	6,827	7,137
TRADE DATA								
Value of imports	Mil. dol.	(NA)	627	631	609	652	777	953
Value of exports	Mil. dol.	(NA)	286	365	419	509	567	637

NA Not available. [1] Estimate, except exports and imports. [2] Value of all products and services sold by establishments in the office furniture industry. [3] Value of products classified in the office furniture industry produced by all industries.

Source: U.S. Department of Commerce: Bureau of the Census, International Trade Administration (ITA). Estimates by ITA.

No. 1441. Recent Trends in Household Consumer Durables (SIC 251, 3524, 363, 3651): 1988 to 1994

ITEM	Unit	1988	1989	1990	1991	1992	1993 [1]	1994 [1]
INDUSTRY DATA								
Value of shipments [2]	Mil. dol.	47,618	50,227	50,412	50,004	53,241	57,782	62,304
Value of shipments (1987 dollars)	Mil. dol.	46,857	48,087	47,446	46,502	49,301	52,956	56,217
Total employment	1,000	459	453	441	419	416	424	434
Production workers	1,000	379	372	361	341	342	348	357
Average hourly earnings	Dollar	8.42	8.46	8.64	8.96	9.33	9.51	9.84
Capital expenditures	Mil. dol.	1,067	1,166	1,075	1,162	1,293	(NA)	(NA)
PRODUCT DATA								
Value of shipments [3]	Mil. dol.	44,856	47,080	47,167	46,353	48,458	52,564	56,723
Value of shipments (1987 dollars)	Mil. dol.	44,132	45,109	44,420	43,107	44,909	48,145	51,110
TRADE DATA								
Value of imports	Mil. dol.	(NA)	19,458	18,406	19,365	21,202	22,747	25,043
Value of exports	Mil. dol.	(NA)	4,127	5,129	5,890	6,521	7,130	7,833

NA Not available.   [1] Estimate, except exports and imports.   [2] Value of all products and services sold by establishments in the household consumer durables industry.   [3] Value of products classified in the household consumer durables industry produced by all industries.

Source: U.S. Department of Commerce: Bureau of the Census, International Trade Administration (ITA). Estimates by ITA.

No. 1442. Recent Trends in Paper and Allied Products (SIC 26): 1988 to 1994

ITEM	Unit	1988	1989	1990	1991	1992	1993 [1]	1994 [1]
INDUSTRY DATA								
Value of shipments [2]	Mil. dol.	122,556	131,366	131,444	128,824	132,954	129,407	137,431
Value of shipments (1987 dollars)	Mil. dol.	112,208	113,352	113,364	113,398	118,037	113,315	117,281
Total employment	1,000	619	630	628	621	626	622	624
Production workers	1,000	476	484	480	477	478	477	478
Average hourly earnings	Dollar	12.33	12.65	12.93	13.34	13.79	13.83	13.87
Capital expenditures	Mil. dol.	7,211	10,067	10,809	9,009	7,814	(NA)	(NA)
PRODUCT DATA								
Value of shipments [3]	Mil. dol.	118,725	127,266	127,528	124,658	128,657	125,225	132,989
Value of shipments (1987 dollars)	Mil. dol.	108,555	109,559	109,873	109,813	114,236	109,667	113,505
TRADE DATA								
Value of imports	Mil. dol.	(NA)	11,894	11,702	10,473	10,424	10,948	11,842
Value of exports	Mil. dol.	(NA)	8,193	8,726	9,332	10,122	9,547	11,100

NA Not available.   [1] Estimate, except exports and imports.   [2] Value of all products and services sold by establishments in the paper and allied products industry.   [3] Value of products classified in the paper and allied products produced by all industries.

Source: U.S. Department of Commerce: Bureau of the Census, International Trade Administration (ITA). Estimates by ITA.

No. 1443. Recent Trends in Pulp Mills and Paper and Paperboard Mills: 1988 to 1994

ITEM	Unit	1988	1989	1990	1991	1992	1993 [1]	1994 [1]
PULP MILLS (SIC 2611)								
Industry data:								
Value of shipments [2]	Mil. dol.	5,260	6,416	6,239	5,329	5,457	4,797	5,300
Value of shipments (1987 dollars)	Mil. dol.	4,280	4,443	4,502	4,898	5,124	5,180	5,258
Total employment	1,000	14.4	15.2	16.1	16.8	15.9	16.0	16.2
Production workers	1,000	11.2	11.7	12.3	12.8	12.1	12.1	12.2
Average hourly earnings	Dollar	17.28	17.43	17.48	18.36	18.97	19.12	19.30
Capital expenditures	Mil. dol.	309	697	1,054	991	727	(NA)	(NA)
Product data:								
Value of shipments [3]	Mil. dol.	6,686	7,719	6,917	5,741	6,095	5,358	5,920
Value of shipments (1987 dollars)	Mil. dol.	5,440	5,345	4,991	5,277	5,723	5,786	5,873
Trade data:								
Value of imports	Mil. dol.	(NA)	3,051	2,851	2,142	2,104	1,868	2,285
Value of exports	Mil. dol.	(NA)	3,643	3,288	2,920	3,236	2,482	2,954
PAPER AND PAPERBOARD MILLS (SIC 262, 263)								
Industry data:								
Value of shipments [2]	Mil. dol.	49,640	51,706	51,241	48,357	48,943	49,731	53,475
Value of shipments (1987 dollars)	Mil. dol.	44,679	44,190	44,388	43,135	44,435	45,501	47,549
Total employment	1,000	184	182	183	181	182	182	183
Production workers	1,000	142	141	139	138	140	139	140
Average hourly earnings	Dollar	16.29	16.75	17.13	17.55	17.95	18.15	18.25
Capital expenditures	Mil. dol.	4,817	6,890	7,254	5,790	4,842	(NA)	(NA)
Product data:								
Value of shipments [3]	Mil. dol.	47,420	49,756	49,701	47,148	47,291	48,011	51,625
Value of shipments (1987 dollars)	Mil. dol.	42,679	42,511	43,055	42,072	42,898	43,927	45,904
Trade data:								
Value of imports	Mil. dol.	(NA)	7,377	7,411	6,949	6,774	7,269	7,418
Value of exports	Mil. dol.	(NA)	3,082	3,523	4,135	4,349	4,284	4,917

NA Not available.   [1] Estimate, except exports and imports.   [2] Value of all products and services sold by establishments in this industry.   [3] Value of products classified in this industry produced by all industries.

Source: U.S. Department of Commerce: Bureau of the Census, International Trade Administration (ITA). Estimates by ITA.

No. 1444. Recent Trends in Printing and Publishing (SIC 27): 1988 to 1994

ITEM	Unit	1988	1989	1990	1991	1992	1993 [1]	1994 [1]
INDUSTRY DATA								
Value of shipments [2]	Mil. dol.	143,907	149,912	157,060	156,685	167,284	176,518	187,550
2711 Newspapers	Mil. dol.	32,927	34,146	34,642	33,702	34,203	35,489	37,853
2721 Periodicals	Mil. dol.	18,612	19,787	20,397	20,345	21,976	22,855	24,249
2731 Book publishing	Mil. dol.	13,571	14,074	15,318	16,596	17,126	18,246	19,414
2732 Book printing	Mil. dol.	3,566	3,839	4,132	4,140	4,728	4,955	5,284
2741 Misc publishing	Mil. dol.	8,154	8,021	8,875	9,762	11,000	12,110	13,212
275 Commercial printing	Mil. dol.	47,460	50,312	52,904	51,948	56,415	59,983	63,644
2761 Manifold business forms	Mil. dol.	7,781	7,553	7,808	7,234	7,415	7,652	7,712
2771 Greeting cards	Mil. dol.	3,082	3,449	3,721	3,810	4,196	4,603	5,086
2782 Blankbooks and binders	Mil. dol.	3,058	3,058	3,186	3,243	3,671	3,860	4,084
2789 Bookbinding	Mil. dol.	1,218	1,240	1,363	1,328	1,389	1,417	1,481
2791 Typesetting	Mil. dol.	1,920	1,776	1,957	1,813	1,679	1,615	1,525
2796 Platemaking services	Mil. dol.	2,559	2,657	2,758	2,764	3,487	3,733	4,006
Value of shipments (1987 dollars)	Mil. dol.	136,941	135,281	136,044	130,577	135,804	138,868	143,802
2711 Newspapers	Mil. dol.	30,859	30,031	28,653	26,126	25,094	24,957	25,715
2721 Periodicals	Mil. dol.	17,525	17,449	16,815	15,735	16,076	16,407	16,969
2731 Book publishing	Mil. dol.	12,803	12,455	12,872	13,341	13,370	13,878	14,211
2732 Book printing	Mil. dol.	3,409	3,480	3,647	3,594	3,825	3,982	4,173
2741 Misc publishing	Mil. dol.	7,707	7,246	7,670	7,975	8,614	9,096	9,469
275 Commercial printing	Mil. dol.	46,065	46,653	47,782	46,129	49,814	51,707	54,215
2761 Manifold business forms	Mil. dol.	7,218	6,726	6,971	6,470	6,771	6,297	6,105
2771 Greeting cards	Mil. dol.	2,885	3,136	3,241	3,151	3,359	3,477	3,616
2782 Blankbooks and binders	Mil. dol.	2,929	2,716	2,714	2,609	2,890	2,936	3,012
2789 Bookbinding	Mil. dol.	1,175	1,155	1,241	1,181	1,229	1,245	1,274
2791 Typesetting	Mil. dol.	1,864	1,675	1,831	1,666	1,523	1,439	1,344
2796 Platemaking services	Mil. dol.	2,501	2,559	2,607	2,600	3,238	3,447	3,699

[1] Estimate.   [2] Value of all products and services sold by establishments in the printing and publishing industry.
Source: U.S. Department of Commerce: Bureau of the Census, International Trade Administration (ITA). Estimates by ITA.

No. 1445. Recent Trends in Periodicals, Book Publishing, and Commercial Printing: 1988 to 1994

ITEM	Unit	1988	1989	1990	1991	1992	1993 [1]	1994 [1]
PERIODICALS (SIC 2721)								
Industry data:								
Value of shipments [2]	Mil. dol.	18,612	19,787	20,397	20,345	21,976	22,855	24,249
Value of shipments (1987 dollars)	Mil. dol.	17,525	17,449	16,815	15,735	16,076	16,407	16,969
Total employment	1,000	111	116	115	111	117	120	122
Production workers	1,000	19.1	20.7	21.6	20.7	20.5	20.8	20.3
Average hourly earnings	Dollar	11.99	12.45	13.09	13.21	13.72	14.32	14.58
Capital expenditures	Mil. dol.	246	272	275	223	269	(NA)	(NA)
Product data:								
Value of shipments [3]	Mil. dol.	17,664	18,748	19,256	19,424	20,792	21,624	22,943
Value of shipments (1987 dollars)	Mil. dol.	16,632	16,533	15,874	15,022	15,210	15,523	16,055
Trade data:								
Value of imports	Mil. dol.	(NA)	140	122	121	136	195	212
Value of exports	Mil. dol.	(NA)	448	666	705	731	737	788
BOOK PUBLISHING (SIC 2731)								
Industry data:								
Value of shipments [2]	Mil. dol.	13,571	14,074	15,318	16,596	17,126	18,246	19,414
Value of shipments (1987 dollars)	Mil. dol.	12,803	12,455	12,872	13,341	13,370	13,878	14,211
Total employment	1,000	70.2	73.9	73.5	77.3	83.8	84.8	87.4
Production workers	1,000	16.5	17.1	17.3	17.1	19.0	18.5	18.6
Average hourly earnings	Dollar	10.76	11.56	11.68	12.72	12.49	12.81	13.18
Capital expenditures	Mil. dol.	302	319	329	331	342	(NA)	(NA)
Product data:								
Value of shipments [3]	Mil. dol.	12,156	12,981	14,267	15,215	15,436	16,362	17,311
Value of shipments (1987-100)	Mil. dol.	11,468	11,487	11,989	12,230	12,050	12,436	12,685
Trade data:								
Value of imports	Mil. dol.	(NA)	746	845	878	990	1,007	1,093
Value of exports	Mil. dol.	(NA)	1,123	1,428	1,498	1,636	1,659	1,697
COMMERCIAL PRINTING (SIC 275)								
Industry data:								
Value of shipments [2]	Mil. dol.	47,460	50,312	52,904	51,948	56,415	59,983	63,644
Value of shipments (1987 dollars)	Mil. dol.	46,065	46,653	47,782	46,129	49,814	51,707	54,215
Total employment	1,000	557	569	580	556	570	564	588
Production workers	1,000	402	414	421	401	409	403	421
Average hourly earnings	Dollar	10.01	10.34	10.47	10.75	11.45	11.63	11.81
Capital expenditures	Mil. dol.	1,898	2,135	2,220	2,051	2,206	(NA)	(NA)
Product data:								
Value of shipments [3]	Mil. dol.	46,597	49,621	52,572	51,761	54,953	57,756	60,817
Value of shipments (1987 dollars)	Mil. dol.	45,215	45,997	47,466	45,949	48,515	49,922	51,919
Trade data:								
Value of imports	Mil. dol.	(NA)	371	393	420	442	505	584
Value of exports	Mil. dol.	(NA)	811	772	1,026	1,056	1,201	1,061

NA Not available.   [1] Estimate, except exports and imports.   [2] Value of all products and services sold by establishments in this industry.   [3] Value of products classified in this industry produced by all industries.
Source: U.S. Department of Commerce: Bureau of the Census, International Trade Administration (ITA). Estimates by ITA.

No. 1446. Recent Trends in Chemicals and Allied Products (SIC 28): 1988 to 1994

ITEM	Unit	1988	1989	1990	1991	1992	1993 [1]	1994 [1]
INDUSTRY DATA								
Value of shipments [2]	Mil. dol.	259,699	278,085	288,184	292,326	305,761	313,752	341,293
Value of shipments (1987 dollars)	Mil. dol.	239,529	242,930	248,952	245,187	254,463	258,247	275,084
Total employment	1,000.	830	848	853	846	850	847	842
Production workers	1,000.	475	484	484	477	479	478	477
Average hourly earnings	Dollar	13.21	13.82	14.40	14.98	15.25	15.86	15.96
Capital expenditures	Mil. dol.	10,858	13,480	15,202	16,009	16,526	(NA)	(NA)
PRODUCT DATA								
Value of shipments [3]	Mil. dol.	244,515	260,649	268,505	268,934	283,239	290,641	316,154
Value of shipments (1987 dollars)	Mil. dol.	225,097	227,632	232,379	226,554	236,516	240,033	255,682
TRADE DATA [4]								
Value of imports	Mil. dol.	(NA)	20,519	22,173	23,808	27,214	28,502	33,407
Value of exports	Mil. dol.	(NA)	36,489	38,989	42,974	43,964	45,066	51,599

NA Not available. [1] Estimate, except exports and imports. [2] Value of all products and services sold by establishments in the products industry. [3] Value of products classified in the chemicals and allied products industry produced by all industries. [4] Trade data corresponds to SITC 5 (Standard International Trade Classification, rev. 3) rather than SIC 28.

Source: U.S. Department of Commerce: Bureau of the Census, International Trade Administration (ITA). Estimates by ITA.

No. 1447. Recent Trends in Industrial Inorganic Chemicals, Except Pigments (SIC 2812, 2813, 2819): 1988 to 1994

ITEM	Unit	1988	1989	1990	1991	1992	1993 [1]	1994 [1]
INDUSTRY DATA								
Value of shipments [2]	Mil. dol.	19,345	21,085	23,487	23,572	23,862	25,583	28,001
Value of shipments (1987 dollars)	Mil. dol.	18,238	18,585	20,096	19,781	20,417	21,206	22,969
Total employment	1,000.	86.8	88.4	92.4	95.6	94.5	94.2	94.1
Production workers	1,000.	46.8	48.4	49.5	51.1	48.9	48.7	48.6
Average hourly earnings	Dollar	13.73	15.21	15.75	16.14	16.60	17.06	17.59
PRODUCT DATA								
Value of shipments [3]	Mil. dol.	16,476	17,700	19,448	19,083	18,419	19,745	21,561
Value of shipments (1987 dollars)	Mil. dol.	15,463	15,449	16,461	15,825	15,678	16,367	17,686
TRADE DATA								
Value of imports	Mil. dol.	(NA)	4,229	4,324	4,284	4,166	4,039	4,707
Value of exports	Mil. dol.	(NA)	4,801	4,662	4,990	5,130	4,822	5,215

NA Not available. [1] Estimate, except exports and imports. [2] Value of all products and services sold by establishments in the industrial inorganic chemicals, except pigments industry. [3] Value of products classified in the industrial inorganic chemicals, except pigments industry produced by all industries.

Source: U.S. Department of Commerce: Bureau of the Census, International Trade Administration (ITA). Estimates by ITA.

No. 1448. Recent Trends in Petrochemicals (SIC 2821, 2822, 2824, 2843, 2865, 2869, 2873): 1988 to 1994

ITEM	Unit	1988	1989	1990	1991	1992	1993 [1]	1994 [1]
INDUSTRY DATA								
Value of shipments [2]	Mil. dol.	113,216	120,851	118,989	115,600	117,231	125,368	139,290
Value of shipments (1987 dollars)	Mil. dol.	101,036	103,187	103,738	99,477	101,869	105,233	113,557
Total employment	1,000.	254	260	264	262	257	254	253
Production workers	1,000.	159	164	165	162	158	156	155
Average hourly earnings	Dollar	15.39	15.89	16.50	17.05	17.58	18.09	18.63
Capital expenditures	Mil. dol.	5,926	7,294	9,065	9,104	7,973	(NA)	(NA)
PRODUCT DATA								
Value of shipments [3]	Mil. dol.	111,244	117,634	115,972	112,464	113,582	121,891	135,294
Value of shipments (1987 dollars)	Mil. dol.	98,979	100,255	101,007	97,082	99,043	102,314	110,299
TRADE DATA								
Value of imports	Mil. dol.	(NA)	8,927	9,667	9,942	11,084	12,099	14,599
Value of exports	Mil. dol.	(NA)	20,601	21,173	23,103	22,150	22,047	26,555

NA Not available. [1] Estimate, except exports and imports. [2] Value of all products and services sold by establishments in the petrochemicals industry. [3] Value of products classified in the petrochemicals industry produced by all industries.

Source: U.S. Department of Commerce: Bureau of the Census, International Trade Administration (ITA). Estimates by ITA.

No. 1449. Recent Trends in Plastics Materials and Resins and Synthetic Rubber: 1988 to 1994

ITEM	Unit	1988	1989	1990	1991	1992	1993 [1]	1994 [1]
PLASTIC MATERIALS AND RESINS (SIC 2821)								
Industry data:								
Value of shipments [2]	Mil. dol.	32,110	33,257	31,326	29,566	31,478	32,885	35,119
Value of shipments (1987 dollars)	Mil. dol.	26,893	27,622	27,870	27,100	29,753	30,400	31,842
Total employment	1,000.	58.3	62.0	62.4	60.5	60.9	58.8	57.7
Production workers	1,000.	36.0	37.8	37.9	36.7	36.3	36.0	36.3
Average hourly earnings	Dollars	15.37	15.92	16.88	17.25	18.49	19.59	20.78
Capital expenditures	Mil. dol.	1,606	1,966	2,437	2,252	1,715	(NA)	(NA)
Product data:								
Value of shipments [3]	Mil. dol.	34,235	34,692	33,038	31,723	32,809	33,641	36,954
Value of shipments (1987 dollars)	Mil. dol.	28,673	28,814	29,393	29,077	31,010	31,676	33,178
Trade data:								
Value of imports	Mil. dol.	(NA)	1,554	1,811	1,776	2,063	2,520	3,281
Value of exports	Mil. dol.	(NA)	5,590	6,316	7,447	7,052	7,225	8,478
SYNTHETIC RUBBER (SIC 2822)								
Industry data:								
Value of shipments [2]	Mil. dol.	3,996	4,008	4,210	4,088	4,195	4,305	4,728
Value of shipments (1987 dollars)	Mil. dol.	3,609	3,630	3,696	3,771	3,895	3,903	4,210
Total employment	1,000.	11.3	11.2	11.4	11.5	11.7	(NA)	(NA)
Production workers	1,000.	7.1	7.1	7.2	7.4	7.5	(NA)	(NA)
Average hourly earnings	Dollar	16.36	16.78	17.91	17.79	18.69	(NA)	(NA)
Capital expenditures	Mil. dol.	216	266	379	360	318	(NA)	(NA)
Product data:								
Value of shipments [3]	Mil. dol.	3,916	4,070	4,219	3,939	4,303	(NA)	(NA)
Value of shipments (1987 dollars)	Mil. dol.	3,537	3,686	3,704	3,634	3,995	(NA)	(NA)
Trade data:								
Value of imports	Mil. dol.	(NA)	514	514	466	530	555	624
Value of exports	Mil. dol.	(NA)	869	885	900	1,010	947	1,081

NA Not available.   [1] Estimate, except exports and imports.   [2] Value of all products and services sold by establishments in this industry.   [3] Value of products classified in this industry produced by all industries.

Source: U.S. Department of Commerce: Bureau of the Census, International Trade Administration (ITA). Estimates by ITA.

No. 1450. Recent Trends in Man-Made Fibers (SIC 2823, 2824): 1988 to 1994

ITEM	Unit	1988	1989	1990	1991	1992	1993 [1]	1994 [1]
INDUSTRY DATA								
Value of shipments [2]	Mil. dol.	12,283	13,266	12,884	12,581	12,862	13,046	13,708
Value of shipments (1987 dollars)	Mil. dol.	11,772	12,066	11,480	11,016	11,237	11,265	11,702
Total employment	1,000.	56.0	58.1	57.8	57.4	55.4	53.0	51.1
Production workers	1,000.	42.3	43.9	43.3	42.7	41.7	41.8	42.8
Average hourly earnings	Dollar	12.83	13.45	13.62	14.46	14.22	14.46	14.75
PRODUCT DATA								
Value of shipments [3]	Mil. dol.	10,858	11,687	11,191	10,930	10,883	10,887	11,236
Value of shipments (1987 dollars)	Mil. dol.	10,404	10,621	9,959	9,555	9,495	9,400	9,592
TRADE DATA								
Value of imports	Mil. dol.	(NA)	584	703	784	907	1,127	1,302
Value of exports	Mil. dol.	(NA)	1,455	1,627	1,694	1,473	1,407	1,594

NA Not available.   [1] Estimate, except exports and imports.   [2] Value of all products and services sold by establishments in the man-made fibers industry.   [3] Value of products classified in the man-made fibers industry produced by all industries.

Source: U.S. Department of Commerce: Bureau of the Census, International Trade Administration (ITA). Estimates by ITA.

No. 1451. Recent Trends in Drugs (SIC 283): 1988 to 1994

ITEM	Unit	1988	1989	1990	1991	1992	1993 [1]	1994 [1]
INDUSTRY DATA								
Value of shipments [2]	Mil. dol.	43,987	49,114	53,720	60,835	67,969	69,722	76,739
2833 Medicinals and botanicals	Mil. dol.	4,150	4,753	4,919	6,308	6,420	6,586	7,176
2834 Pharmaceutical preps.	Mil. dol.	35,825	40,028	44,182	47,376	50,745	52,051	57,643
2835 Diagnostic substances	Mil. dol.	2,261	2,325	2,462	4,746	6,848	7,025	7,535
2836 Bio. prod. ex. diagnostic	Mil. dol.	1,750	2,008	2,156	2,406	3,957	4,060	4,385
Value of shipments (1987 dollars)	Mil. dol.	40,942	41,998	42,773	45,470	48,570	47,910	51,298
2833 Medicinals and botanicals	Mil. dol.	3,960	4,213	4,274	5,141	5,123	4,846	5,075
2834 Pharmaceutical preps.	Mil. dol.	32,988	33,581	34,144	33,767	33,785	33,281	35,626
2835 Diagnostic substances	Mil. dol.	2,237	2,275	2,282	4,280	6,055	6,151	6,639
2836 Bio. prod. ex. diagnostic	Mil. dol.	1,757	1,929	2,073	2,282	3,607	3,631	3,958
Total employment	1,000	175.0	184.0	183.0	184.0	196.0	(NA)	(NA)
2833 Medicinals and botanicals	1,000	11.3	11.4	10.9	12.5	12.8	(NA)	(NA)
2834 Pharmaceutical preps.	1,000	133.0	142.0	144.0	129.0	125.0	128.0	128.0
2835 Diagnostic substances	1,000	16.2	16.1	14.9	30.5	39.8	(NA)	(NA)
2836 Bio. prod. ex. diagnostic	1,000	13.7	14.5	13.3	12.1	18.3	(NA)	(NA)
Production workers	1,000	81.0	82.8	81.4	82.7	93.1	(NA)	(NA)
2833 Medicinals and botanicals	1,000	6.2	6.6	6.5	7.2	7.3	(NA)	(NA)
2834 Pharmaceutical preps.	1,000	60.8	62.4	61.5	59.2	63.2	65.3	68.2
2835 Diagnostic substances	1,000	7.5	6.8	6.6	9.9	14.6	(NA)	(NA)
2836 Bio. prod. ex. diagnostic	1,000	6.5	7.0	6.8	6.4	8.0	(NA)	(NA)
Average hourly earnings	Dollar	12.67	13.48	14.22	15.36	14.76	(NA)	(NA)
2833 Medicinals and botanicals	Dollar	16.09	16.29	17.35	20.06	19.16	(NA)	(NA)
2834 Pharmaceutical preps.	Dollar	12.93	13.83	14.71	14.77	14.69	(NA)	(NA)
2835 Diagnostic substances	Dollar	10.93	11.54	11.80	18.17	14.03	(NA)	(NA)
2836 Bio. prod. ex. diagnostic	Dollar	9.13	9.30	9.15	11.00	12.47	(NA)	(NA)
Capital expenditures	Mil. dol.	2,058	2,392	2,280	2,669	3,873	(NA)	(NA)
2833 Medicinals and botanicals	Mil. dol.	151	219	195	487	549	(NA)	(NA)
2834 Pharmaceutical preps.	Mil. dol.	1,725	1,933	1,809	1,772	2,461	(NA)	(NA)
2835 Diagnostic substances	Mil. dol.	93.3	117.0	147.0	302.0	570.0	(NA)	(NA)
2836 Bio. prod. ex. diagnostic	Mil. dol.	89.1	124.0	130.0	108.0	294.0	(NA)	(NA)
PRODUCT DATA								
Value of shipments [3]	Mil. dol.	39,532	43,796	47,832	51,880	61,316	62,897	69,182
2833 Medicinals and botanicals	Mil. dol.	4,948	5,393	5,789	6,647	6,947	7,126	7,765
2834 Pharmaceutical preps.	Mil. dol.	29,555	32,713	35,280	37,416	43,743	44,869	49,689
2835 Diagnostic substances	Mil. dol.	3,063	3,471	4,234	4,973	6,160	6,319	6,778
2836 Bio. prod. ex. diagnostic	Mil. dol.	1,966	2,220	2,529	2,844	4,467	4,583	4,950
Value of shipments (1987 dollars)	Mil. dol.	36,939	37,753	38,649	39,269	44,185	43,566	46,641
2833 Medicinals and botanicals	Mil. dol.	4,721	4,781	5,030	5,417	5,544	5,244	5,492
2834 Pharmaceutical preps.	Mil. dol.	27,214	27,443	27,264	26,668	29,123	28,689	30,710
2835 Diagnostic substances	Mil. dol.	3,030	3,396	3,924	4,484	5,446	5,533	5,971
2836 Bio. prod. ex. diagnostic	Mil. dol.	1,974	2,132	2,431	2,699	4,072	4,100	4,468
TRADE DATA								
Value of imports	Mil. dol.	(NA)	3,531	3,884	4,812	5,958	6,094	6,966
2833 Medicinals and botanicals	Mil. dol.	(NA)	2,354	2,303	2,854	3,277	3,101	3,366
2834 Pharmaceutical preps.	Mil. dol.	(NA)	868	1,103	1,442	1,859	2,096	2,517
2835 Diagnostic substances	Mil. dol.	(NA)	118	207	191	336	379	530
2836 Bio. prod. ex. diagnostic	Mil. dol.	(NA)	191	271	325	486	518	553
Value of exports	Mil. dol.	(NA)	4,345	5,050	5,731	6,774	7,222	7,565
2833 Medicinals and botanicals	Mil. dol.	(NA)	1,794	1,908	2,064	2,444	2,401	2,281
2834 Pharmaceutical preps.	Mil. dol.	(NA)	974	1,258	1,478	1,818	2,027	2,315
2835 Diagnostic substances	Mil. dol.	(NA)	739	909	1,160	1,370	1,485	1,507
2836 Bio. prod. ex. diagnostic	Mil. dol.	(NA)	839	974	1,028	1,142	1,309	1,462

NA Not available.   [1] Estimate, except exports and imports.   [2] Value of all products and services sold by establishments in the drugs industry.   [3] Value of products classified in the drugs industry produced by all industries.

Source: U.S. Department of Commerce: Bureau of the Census, International Trade Administration (ITA). Estimates by ITA.

No. 1452. Recent Trends in Soap, Cleaners, and Toilet Goods (SIC 284): 1988 to 1994

ITEM	Unit	1988	1989	1990	1991	1992	1993 [1]	1994 [1]
INDUSTRY DATA								
Value of shipments [2]	Mil. dol.	37,856	38,869	41,438	41,854	43,404	44,518	48,426
2841 Soap and other detergents	Mil. dol.	12,306	13,281	15,373	15,299	14,888	15,280	16,621
2842 Polishes/sanitation goods	Mil. dol.	5,858	5,987	5,848	6,172	6,892	7,059	7,679
2843 Surface active agents	Mil. dol.	3,399	2,959	3,168	3,299	2,873	2,946	3,205
2844 Toilet preparations	Mil. dol.	16,294	16,642	17,048	17,085	18,751	19,233	20,921
Value of shipments (1987 dollars)	Mil. dol.	36,427	35,970	38,016	37,718	38,359	38,713	42,052
2841 Soap and other detergents	Mil. dol.	11,776	12,207	14,422	14,338	13,609	13,778	15,032
2842 Polishes/sanitation goods	Mil. dol.	5,611	5,418	5,157	5,325	5,860	5,952	6,392
2843 Surface active agents	Mil. dol.	3,081	2,480	2,549	2,565	2,222	2,244	2,402
2844 Toilet preparations	Mil. dol.	15,958	15,865	15,889	15,490	16,667	16,739	18,226
Total employment	1,000	128.0	129.0	126.0	123.0	124.0	(NA)	(NA)
2841 Soap and other detergents	1,000	33.3	34.8	36.3	36.6	33.0	34.5	32.8
2842 Polishes/sanitation goods	1,000	20.5	21.2	19.6	19.6	22.0	(NA)	(NA)
2843 Surface active agents	1,000	9.0	9.0	9.1	9.3	8.2	8.3	8.4
2844 Toilet preparations	1,000	64.9	63.8	61.1	57.4	60.5	60.5	58.2
Production workers	1,000	79.7	79.4	77.8	75.7	75.1	(NA)	(NA)
2841 Soap and other detergents	1,000	21.0	22.0	22.8	23.1	20.0	20.2	18.4
2842 Polishes/sanitation goods	1,000	13.4	13.4	12.3	12.2	13.4	(NA)	(NA)
2843 Surface active agents	1,000	4.8	4.6	4.6	4.8	4.2	4.4	4.6
2844 Toilet preparations	1,000	40.5	39.4	38.1	35.6	37.5	38.1	38.0
Average hourly earnings	Dollars	10.81	11.25	11.73	12.25	12.34	(NA)	(NA)
2841 Soap and other detergents	Dollars	13.85	14.36	14.65	14.67	14.87	(NA)	(NA)
2842 Polishes/sanitation goods	Dollars	10.06	10.24	10.63	11.09	11.81	(NA)	(NA)
2843 Surface active agents	Dollars	13.70	13.32	13.71	14.28	15.11	(NA)	(NA)
2844 Toilet preparations	Dollars	9.08	9.69	10.14	10.81	10.83	(NA)	(NA)
Capital expenditures	Mil. dol.	924	980	1,016	1,225	1,302	(NA)	(NA)
2841 Soap and other detergents	Mil. dol.	368	396	476	631	575	(NA)	(NA)
2842 Polishes/sanitation goods	Mil. dol.	72	141	95	137	124	(NA)	(NA)
2843 Surface active agents	Mil. dol.	192	129	165	157	93	(NA)	(NA)
2844 Toilet preparations	Mil. dol.	293	314	280	300	510	(NA)	(NA)
PRODUCT DATA								
Value of shipments [3]	Mil. dol.	34,753	36,764	38,634	38,695	40,859	(NA)	(NA)
2841 Soap and other detergents	Mil. dol.	9,961	10,916	11,860	11,785	11,185	(NA)	(NA)
2842 Polishes/sanitation goods	Mil. dol.	5,191	5,306	5,531	5,546	6,740	(NA)	(NA)
2843 Surface active agents	Mil. dol.	3,193	3,671	3,877	3,975	4,174	(NA)	(NA)
2844 Toilet preparations	Mil. dol.	16,409	16,872	17,366	17,390	18,761	(NA)	(NA)
Value of shipments (1987 dollars)	Mil. dol.	33,470	33,995	35,307	34,686	35,859	(NA)	(NA)
2841 Soap and other detergents	Mil. dol.	9,532	10,033	11,126	11,045	10,224	(NA)	(NA)
2842 Polishes/sanitation goods	Mil. dol.	4,972	4,802	4,877	4,785	5,731	(NA)	(NA)
2843 Surface active agents	Mil. dol.	2,894	3,077	3,119	3,091	3,228	(NA)	(NA)
2844 Toilet preparations	Mil. dol.	16,072	16,084	16,185	15,766	16,676	(NA)	(NA)
TRADE DATA								
Value of imports	Mil. dol.	(NA)	893	1,000	1,076	1,308	1,463	1,689
2841 Soap and other detergents	Mil. dol.	(NA)	148	196	178	213	254	335
2842 Polishes/sanitation goods	Mil. dol.	(NA)	30.9	36.6	33.5	46.0	49.8	56.3
2843 Surface active agents	Mil. dol.	(NA)	120	134	152	158	204	263
2844 Toilet preparations	Mil. dol.	(NA)	594	634	712	892	956	1,035
Value of exports	Mil. dol.	(NA)	1,421	1,853	2,235	2,529	2,853	3,358
2841 Soap and other detergents	Mil. dol.	(NA)	271	390	510	583	644	716
2842 Polishes/sanitation goods	Mil. dol.	(NA)	77	112	130	144	170	174
2843 Surface active agents	Mil. dol.	(NA)	379	465	477	548	604	734
2844 Toilet preparations	Mil. dol.	(NA)	694	886	1,118	1,254	1,437	1,733

NA Not available.   [1] Estimate, except exports and imports.   [2] Value of all products and services sold by establishments in the soap, cleaners, and toilet goods industry.   [3] Value of products classified in the soap, cleaners, and toilet goods industry produced by all industries.

Source: U.S. Department of Commerce: Bureau of the Census, International Trade Administration (ITA). Estimates by ITA.

No. 1453. Recent Trends in Paints and Allied Products (SIC 2851): 1988 to 1994

ITEM	Unit	1988	1989	1990	1991	1992	1993 [1]	1994 [1]
INDUSTRY DATA								
Value of shipments [2]	Mil. dol.	13,532	13,656	14,239	14,255	14,970	15,361	16,710
Value of shipments (1987 dollars)	Mil. dol.	12,986	12,292	12,233	11,742	12,151	12,309	13,154
Total employment	1,000.	56.9	55.0	53.9	51.1	51.1	(NA)	(NA)
Production workers	1,000.	28.3	27.7	27.2	25.2	25.6	(NA)	(NA)
Average hourly earnings	Dollar	11.20	11.69	11.89	12.09	12.70	(NA)	(NA)
Capital expenditures	Mil. dol.	253	241	271	256	299	(NA)	(NA)
PRODUCT DATA								
Value of shipments [3]	Mil. dol.	12,851	13,185	13,681	13,722	14,396	(NA)	(NA)
Value of shipments (1987 dollars)	Mil. dol.	12,333	11,867	11,753	11,303	11,685	(NA)	(NA)
TRADE DATA								
Value of imports	Mil. dol.	(NA)	106	137	141	184	197	261
Value of exports	Mil. dol.	(NA)	422	570	686	754	811	936

NA Not available. [1] Estimate, except exports and imports. [2] Value of all products and services sold by establishments in the paints and allied products industry. [3] Value of products classified in the paints and allied products industry produced by all industries.

Source: U.S. Department of Commerce: Bureau of the Census, International Trade Administration (ITA). Estimates by ITA.

No. 1454. Recent Trends in Organic Chemicals, Except Gum and Wood (SIC 2865, 2869): 1988 to 1994

ITEM	Unit	1988	1989	1990	1991	1992	1993 [1]	1994 [1]
INDUSTRY DATA								
Value of shipments [2]	Mil. dol.	59,406	65,324	65,053	63,721	63,791	68,199	73,983
Value of shipments (1987 dollars)	Mil. dol.	53,963	55,566	55,993	52,973	52,919	54,503	57,787
Total employment	1,000.	121	121	123	125	123	121	115
Production workers	1,000.	70.8	72.2	72.7	72.5	70.6	73.4	74.3
Average hourly earnings	Dollar	16.50	17.01	17.73	18.29	18.70	18.89	18.99
Capital expenditures	Mil. dol.	3,182	4,069	5,111	5,252	4,889	(NA)	(NA)
PRODUCT DATA								
Value of shipments [3]	Mil. dol.	56,492	61,187	61,044	59,326	58,873	62,941	68,290
Value of shipments (1987-100)	Mil. dol.	51,300	51,992	52,466	49,492	49,048	50,301	53,340
TRADE DATA								
Value of imports	Mil. dol.	(NA)	5,815	6,272	6,584	7,242	7,330	8,654
Value of exports	Mil. dol.	(NA)	9,834	9,738	10,063	10,036	10,409	12,336

NA Not available. [1] Estimate, except exports and imports. [2] Value of all products and services sold by establishments in the organic chemicals, except gum and wood industry. [3] Value of products classified in the organic chemicals, except gum and wood industry produced by all industries.

Source: U.S. Department of Commerce: Bureau of the Census, International Trade Administration (ITA). Estimates by ITA.

No. 1455. Recent Trends in Nitrogenous Fertilizers, and Phosphatic Fertilizers: 1988 to 1994

ITEM	Unit	1988	1989	1990	1991	1992	1993 [1]	1994 [1]
NITROGENOUS FERTILIZERS (SIC 2873)								
Industry data:								
Value of shipments [2]	Mil. dol.	2,761	2,866	3,113	3,238	3,173	3,467	4,077
Value of shipments (1987 dollars)	Mil. dol.	2,362	2,402	2,654	2,605	2,649	2,785	2,912
Total employment	1,000.	7.2	7.0	7.5	7.3	7.0	7.1	7.4
Production workers	1,000.	4.4	4.4	4.8	4.7	4.7	4.7	4.9
Average hourly earnings	Dollar	12.96	14.03	13.80	14.77	15.64	15.64	15.64
Capital expenditures	Mil. dol.	48.1	123.0	99.4	220.0	209.0	(NA)	(NA)
Product data:								
Value of shipments [3]	Mil. dol.	3,281	3,147	3,357	3,438	3,625	3,960	4,658
Value of shipments (1987 dollars)	Mil. dol.	2,806	2,638	2,861	2,766	3,026	3,181	3,327
PHOSPHATIC FERTILIZERS (SIC 2874)								
Industry data:								
Value of shipments [2]	Mil. dol.	4,474	4,187	4,636	4,984	4,306	3,931	4,796
Value of shipments (1987 dollars)	Mil. dol.	3,942	3,892	4,622	4,829	4,774	4,810	4,833
Total employment	1,000.	10.4	10.8	10.5	10.3	9.5	9.3	10.1
Production workers	1,000.	7.1	7.4	7.5	7.3	6.7	6.6	7.1
Average hourly earnings	Dollar	13.10	13.55	13.70	14.65	13.86	13.92	14.22
Capital expenditures	Mil. dol.	134.0	132.0	138.0	197.0	308.0	(NA)	(NA)
Product data:								
Value of shipments [3]	Mil. dol.	4,150	4,285	4,462	4,572	4,048	3,696	4,509
Value of shipments (1987 dollars)	Mil. dol.	3,656	3,982	4,449	4,430	4,488	4,522	4,543

NA Not available [1] Estimate. [2] Value of all products and services sold by establishments in this industry. [3] Value of products classified in this industry produced by all industries.

Source: U.S. Department of Commerce: Bureau of the Census, International Trade Administration (ITA). Estimates by ITA.

No. 1456. Recent Trends in Agricultural Chemicals, n.e.c. (SIC 2879): 1988 to 1994

ITEM	Unit	1988	1989	1990	1991	1992	1993 [1]	1994 [1]
INDUSTRY DATA								
Value of shipments [2]	Mil. dol.	6,978	8,327	8,539	8,346	9,129	9,550	9,953
Value of shipments (1987 dollars)	Mil. dol.	6,716	7,455	7,355	6,869	7,321	7,382	7,391
Total employment	1,000	15.9	17.4	17.7	16.4	16.8	16.4	16.3
Production workers	1,000	8.9	9.8	10.2	9.1	9.6	9.3	9.2
Average hourly earnings	Dollar	13.98	15.08	16.27	15.15	15.54	15.57	15.63
Capital expenditures	Mil. dol.	332	503	558	481	428	(NA)	(NA)
PRODUCT DATA								
Value of shipments [3]	Mil. dol.	6,360	7,277	7,280	7,448	8,219	8,605	8,950
Value of shipments (1987 dollars)	Mil. dol.	6,121	6,515	6,271	6,130	6,591	6,651	6,646

NA Not available   [1] Estimate.   [2] Value of all products and services sold by establishments in the agricultural chemicals, n.e.c. industry.   [3] Value of products classified in the agricultural chemicals, n.e.c. industry produced by all industries.

Source: U.S. Department of Commerce: Bureau of the Census, International Trade Administration (ITA). Estimates by ITA.

No. 1457. Recent Trends in Adhesives and Sealants (SIC 2891): 1988 to 1994

ITEM	Unit	1988	1989	1990	1991	1992	1993 [1]	1994 [1]
INDUSTRY DATA								
Value of shipments [2]	Mil. dol.	4,860	5,286	5,485	5,483	5,663	5,811	6,321
Value of shipments (1987 dollars)	Mil. dol.	4,496	4,557	4,729	4,539	4,653	4,649	4,905
Total employment	1,000	21.2	21.9	21.4	20.9	21.1	(NA)	(NA)
Production workers	1,000	11.8	12.3	11.9	11.7	11.6	(NA)	(NA)
Average hourly earnings	Dollar	11.05	11.02	11.50	11.43	12.42	(NA)	(NA)
Capital expenditures	Mil. dol.	118	136	127	139	196	(NA)	(NA)
PRODUCT DATA								
Value of shipments [3]	Mil. dol.	4,845	5,134	5,403	5,382	5,396	(NA)	(NA)
Value of shipments (1987 dollars)	Mil. dol.	4,482	4,426	4,657	4,455	4,434	(NA)	(NA)
TRADE DATA								
Value of imports	Mil. dol.	(NA)	70	90	94	112	119	135
Value of exports	Mil. dol.	(NA)	123	159	169	202	241	283

NA Not available.   [1] Estimate, except exports and imports.   [2] Value of all products and services sold by establishments in the adhesives and sealants industry.   [3] Value of products classified in the adhesives and sealants industry produced by all industries.

Source: U.S. Department of Commerce: Bureau of the Census, International Trade Administration (ITA). Estimates by ITA.

No. 1458. Recent Trends in Petroleum Refining (SIC 2911): 1988 to 1994

ITEM	Unit	1988	1989	1990	1991	1992	1993 [1]	1994 [1]
INDUSTRY DATA								
Value of shipments [2]	Mil. dol.	118,830	131,192	159,411	145,392	136,265	132,062	127,219
Value of shipments (1987 dollars)	Mil. dol.	124,169	122,153	121,410	123,213	119,846	121,269	122,798
Total employment	1,000	73.2	72.4	71.9	73.9	74.8	(NA)	(NA)
Production workers	1,000	49.5	47.9	47.3	47.6	47.9	(NA)	(NA)
Average hourly earnings	Dollar	17.80	17.77	18.56	19.46	19.72	(NA)	(NA)
Capital expenditures	Mil. dol.	2,327	2,987	3,819	5,601	6,263	(NA)	(NA)
PRODUCT DATA								
Value of shipments [3]	Mil. dol.	112,989	124,452	151,559	138,322	131,439	127,620	122,951
Value of shipments (1987 dollars)	Mil. dol.	118,066	115,877	115,429	117,222	115,602	116,975	118,450
TRADE DATA								
Value of imports	Mil. dol.	(NA)	11,797	14,269	10,890	10,185	9,742	9,274
Value of exports	Mil. dol.	(NA)	4,318	5,988	6,356	5,759	5,641	4,958

NA Not available.   [1] Estimate, except exports and imports.   [2] Value of all products and services sold by establishments in the petroleum refining industry.   [3] Value of products classified in the petroleum refining industry produced by all industries.

Source: U.S. Department of Commerce, Bureau of the Census; U.S. Department of Energy, Energy Information Administration (EIA). Estimates by EIA.

No. 1459. Recent Trends in Tires and Inner Tubes (SIC 3011): 1988 to 1994

ITEM	Unit	1988	1989	1990	1991	1992	1993 [1]	1994 [1]
INDUSTRY DATA								
Value of shipments [2]	Mil. dol...	11,240	11,680	11,861	11,883	11,824	12,133	13,198
Value of shipments (1987 dollars)	Mil. dol...	10,850	10,947	11,168	11,043	10,878	11,172	12,140
Total employment	1,000...	67.8	68.0	67.7	65.5	64.6	(NA)	(NA)
Production workers	1,000...	54.6	54.6	54.7	52.4	52.8	(NA)	(NA)
Average hourly earnings	Dollar...	15.52	16.57	16.84	17.70	18.54	(NA)	(NA)
Capital expenditures	Mil. dol...	418	785	652	506	507	(NA)	(NA)
PRODUCT DATA								
Value of shipments [3]	Mil. dol...	10,841	11,256	11,340	11,303	11,328	(NA)	(NA)
Value of shipments (1987 dollars)	Mil. dol...	10,464	10,549	10,678	10,504	10,421	(NA)	(NA)
TRADE DATA								
Value of imports	Mil. dol...	(NA)	2,667	2,553	2,271	2,463	2,680	2,979
Value of exports	Mil. dol...	(NA)	854	1,140	1,262	1,395	1,453	1,598

NA Not available. [1] Estimate, except exports and imports. [2] Value of all products and services sold by establishments in the tires and inner tubes industry. [3] Value of products classified in the tires and inner tubes industry produced by all industries.

Source: U.S. Department of Commerce: Bureau of the Census, International Trade Administration (ITA). Estimates by ITA.

No. 1460. Recent Trends in Fabricated Rubber Products, n.e.c. (SIC 3069): 1988 to 1994

ITEM	Unit	1988	1989	1990	1991	1992	1993 [1]	1994 [1]
INDUSTRY DATA								
Value of shipments [2]	Mil. dol...	6,124	6,343	6,629	6,644	6,742	7,180	7,526
Value of shipments (1987 dollars)	Mil. dol...	5,940	5,934	6,043	5,875	5,929	6,200	6,365
Total employment	1,000...	57.2	57.1	56.6	55.8	56.4	(NA)	(NA)
Production workers	1,000...	43.2	44.0	43.6	42.6	41.5	(NA)	(NA)
Average hourly earnings	Dollar...	9.28	9.15	9.30	9.84	10.06	(NA)	(NA)
Capital expenditures	Mil. dol...	167	212	182	160	204	(NA)	(NA)
PRODUCT DATA								
Value of shipments [3]	Mil. dol...	5,839	6,157	6,423	6,432	6,517	(NA)	(NA)
Value of shipments (1987 dollars)	Mil. dol...	5,663	5,760	5,855	5,687	5,732	(NA)	(NA)
TRADE DATA								
Value of imports	Mil. dol...	(NA)	755	733	847	1,090	1,303	1,528
Value of exports	Mil. dol...	(NA)	483	660	716	735	786	930

NA Not available. [1] Estimate, except exports and imports. [2] Value of all products and services sold by establishments in the fabricated rubber products, n.e.c. industry. [3] Value of products classified in the fabricated rubber products, not elsewhere classified industry produced by all industries.

Source: U.S. Department of Commerce: Bureau of the Census, International Trade Administration (ITA). Estimates by ITA.

No. 1461. Recent Trends in Miscellaneous Plastic Products Excluding Bottles and Plumbing (SIC 3081-4, –6, –7, –9): 1988 to 1994

ITEM	Unit	1988	1989	1990	1991	1992	1993 [1]	1994 [1]
INDUSTRY DATA								
Value of shipments [2]	Mil. dol...	63,019	65,746	68,064	67,545	77,990	79,550	84,323
Value of shipments (1987 dollars)	Mil. dol...	59,117	60,877	62,370	61,711	71,561	72,394	75,378
Total employment	1,000...	584	597	595	575	628	606	595
Production workers	1,000...	452	460	457	440	480	476	480
Average hourly earnings	Dollar...	8.56	8.74	9.22	9.54	9.97	10.43	11.06
Capital expenditures	Mil. dol...	2,452	2,929	2,891	3,012	3,479	(NA)	(NA)
PRODUCT DATA								
Value of shipments [3]	Mil. dol...	62,260	65,219	67,410	66,669	75,564	77,076	81,700
Value of shipments (1987 dollars)	Mil. dol...	58,390	60,360	61,762	60,882	69,304	70,111	73,709
TRADE DATA								
Value of imports	Mil. dol...	(NA)	3,535	3,677	3,751	4,330	4,693	5,300
Value of exports	Mil. dol...	(NA)	2,837	3,519	3,858	4,471	5,029	5,933

NA Not available. [1] Estimate, except exports and imports. [2] Value of all products and services sold by establishments in the miscellaneous plastic products excluding bottles and plumbing industry. [3] Value of products classified in the miscellaneous plastic products excluding bottles and plumbing industry produced by all industries.

Source: U.S. Department of Commerce: Bureau of the Census, International Trade Administration (ITA). Estimates by ITA.

No. 1462. Recent Trends in Plumbing Parts (SIC 3088, 3261, 3431, 3432): 1988 to 1994

ITEM	Unit	1988	1989	1990	1991	1992	1993 [1]	1994 [1]
INDUSTRY DATA								
Value of shipments [2]	Mil. dol.	5,376	5,678	5,520	5,180	5,540	6,541	7,228
3088 Plastics plumbing fix	Mil. dol.	927	1,023	965	879	1,097	1,350	1,528
3261 Vitreous plumbing fix	Mil. dol.	941	871	825	742	902	1,055	1,148
3431 Metal sanitary ware	Mil. dol.	946	1,052	980	904	838	914	980
3432 Plumbing fittings	Mil. dol.	2,563	2,733	2,750	2,655	2,702	3,222	3,571
Value of shipments (1987 dollars)	Mil. dol.	4,962	5,032	4,797	4,430	4,826	5,583	6,025
3088 Plastics plumbing fix	Mil. dol.	809	965	997	972	1,312	1,548	1,700
3261 Vitreous plumbing fix	Mil. dol.	917	829	771	685	829	975	1,045
3431 Metal sanitary ware	Mil. dol.	904	955	865	766	703	760	800
3432 Plumbing fittings	Mil. dol.	2,332	2,283	2,164	2,007	1,981	2,300	2,480
Total employment	1,000	46.1	44.2	43.4	39.8	43.2	45.4	47.3
3088 Plastics plumbing fix	1,000	9.4	9.3	9.1	7.7	10.9	11.6	12.3
3261 Vitreous plumbing fix	1,000	11.1	9.4	9.3	8.4	8.4	9.1	9.6
3431 Metal sanitary ware	1,000	7.7	7.8	7.7	7.3	6.5	7.2	7.6
3432 Plumbing fittings	1,000	17.9	17.7	17.3	16.4	17.4	17.5	17.8
Production workers	1,000	36.4	34.6	33.4	30.5	33.7	35.2	36.6
3088 Plastics plumbing fix	1,000	7.1	7.0	6.8	5.9	8.3	8.7	8.9
3261 Vitreous plumbing fix	1,000	9.4	7.9	7.8	7.0	7.1	7.6	8.1
3431 Metal sanitary ware	1,000	6.0	6.0	5.9	5.5	5.0	5.5	5.9
3432 Plumbing fittings	1,000	13.9	13.7	12.9	12.1	13.3	13.4	13.7
Average hourly earnings	Dollar	9.55	10.11	10.44	10.97	10.97	(NA)	(NA)
3088 Plastics plumbing fix	Dollar	8.15	8.16	8.53	8.98	8.84	(NA)	(NA)
3261 Vitreous plumbing fix	Dollar	10.42	12.10	11.96	12.44	12.47	(NA)	(NA)
3431 Metal sanitary ware	Dollar	11.21	10.98	10.93	11.48	13.05	(NA)	(NA)
3432 Plumbing fittings	Dollar	8.97	9.51	10.25	10.83	10.68	(NA)	(NA)
Capital expenditures	Mil. dol.	125.0	193.0	203.0	178.0	138.0	(NA)	(NA)
3088 Plastics plumbing fix	Mil. dol.	18.9	68.5	110.0	91.1	31.3	(NA)	(NA)
3261 Vitreous plumbing fix	Mil. dol.	17.3	22.8	16.3	17.9	14.3	(NA)	(NA)
3431 Metal sanitary ware	Mil. dol.	21.3	36.0	33.9	28.0	18.5	(NA)	(NA)
3432 Plumbing fittings	Mil. dol.	67.0	65.5	42.5	40.5	74.2	(NA)	(NA)
PRODUCT DATA								
Value of shipments [3]	Mil. dol.	5,452	5,404	5,282	4,979	5,306	6,273	6,989
3088 Plastics plumbing fix	Mil. dol.	1,302	989	939	888	1,171	1,441	1,681
3261 Vitreous plumbing fix	Mil. dol.	811	773	741	675	829	974	1,055
3431 Metal sanitary ware	Mil. dol.	849	921	865	815	754	817	876
3432 Plumbing fittings	Mil. dol.	2,491	2,721	2,737	2,601	2,553	3,040	3,377
Value of shipments (1987 dollars)	Mil. dol.	5,004	4,778	4,579	4,262	4,666	5,403	5,890
3088 Plastics plumbing fix	Mil. dol.	1,136	933	970	982	1,401	1,653	1,870
3261 Vitreous plumbing fix	Mil. dol.	791	735	693	624	762	900	960
3431 Metal sanitary ware	Mil. dol.	811	836	763	690	632	680	715
3432 Plumbing fittings	Mil. dol.	2,266	2,273	2,153	1,966	1,872	2,170	2,345
TRADE DATA								
Value of imports	Mil. dol.	(NA)	330	319	303	375	422	524
3088 Plastics plumbing fix	Mil. dol.	(NA)	24.4	21.2	24.1	31.7	45.5	53.7
3261 Vitreous plumbing fix	Mil. dol.	(NA)	72.6	71.9	64.4	81.8	99.4	137
3431 Metal sanitary ware	Mil. dol.	(NA)	107	101	91.5	100	105	112
3432 Plumbing fittings	Mil. dol.	(NA)	126	125	123	161	172	221
Value of exports	Mil. dol.	(NA)	155	200	211	259	265	263
3088 Plastics plumbing fix	Mil. dol.	(NA)	18.5	29.1	31.0	41.4	44.3	38.4
3261 Vitreous plumbing fix	Mil. dol.	(NA)	41.1	54.1	46.1	55.5	75.4	77.9
3431 Metal sanitary ware	Mil. dol.	(NA)	50.9	71.1	72.1	79.7	89.6	75.0
3432 Plumbing fittings	Mil. dol.	(NA)	44.7	45.3	62.0	82.7	55.6	72.2

NA Not available.   [1] Estimate, except exports and imports.   [2] Value of all products and services sold by establishments in the plumbing parts industry.   [3] Value of products classified in the plumbing parts industry produced by all industries.

Source: U.S. Department of Commerce: Bureau of the Census, International Trade Administration (ITA). Estimates by ITA.

No. 1463. Recent Trends in Footwear, Except Rubber (SIC 314): 1988 to 1994

ITEM	Unit	1988	1989	1990	1991	1992	1993 [1]	1994 [1]
INDUSTRY DATA								
Value of shipments [2]	Mil. dol. . .	4,258	4,262	4,232	3,775	3,907	4,340	4,130
3142 House slippers	Mil. dol. . .	244	287	276	277	273	361	299
3143 Men's footwear	Mil. dol. . .	2,168	2,228	2,149	2,064	2,210	2,518	2,348
3144 Women's footwear	Mil. dol. . .	1,374	1,351	1,393	1,154	1,116	1,173	1,221
3149 Footwear n.e.c.	Mil. dol. . .	472	396	414	280	309	288	262
Value of shipments (1987 dollars)	Mil. dol. . .	4,038	3,852	3,676	3,199	3,221	3,525	3,320
3142 House slippers	Mil. dol. . .	228	257	248	251	253	345	279
3143 Men's footwear	Mil. dol. . .	2,028	1,970	1,809	1,686	1,755	1,961	1,806
3144 Women's footwear	Mil. dol. . .	1,333	1,276	1,265	1,028	960	987	1,026
3149 Footwear n.e.c.	Mil. dol. . .	448	348	354	233	252	232	209
Total employment	1,000. . . .	70.4	66.0	62.1	53.1	49.0	47.9	46.4
Production workers	1,000. . . .	61.6	57.5	53.5	46.0	41.4	40.1	38.3
Average hourly earnings	Dollar	6.07	6.38	6.50	6.83	7.28	7.53	7.76
Capital expenditures	Mil. dol. . .	39.0	40.7	42.1	31.5	51.1	(NA)	(NA)
3142 House slippers	Mil. dol. . .	4.1	3.8	3.3	2.4	2.1	(NA)	(NA)
3143 Men's footwear	Mil. dol. . .	17.4	21.2	22.8	18.1	32.8	(NA)	(NA)
3144 Women's footwear	Mil. dol. . .	12.4	11.1	13.4	9.1	10.4	(NA)	(NA)
3149 Footwear n.e.c.	Mil. dol. . .	5.1	4.6	2.6	1.9	5.8	(NA)	(NA)
PRODUCT DATA								
Value of shipments [3]	Mil. dol. . .	4,032	3,908	3,780	3,495	3,617	4,028	3,823
3142 House slippers	Mil. dol. . .	215	233	257	256	247	326	270
3143 Men's footwear	Mil. dol. . .	1,914	1,940	1,839	1,763	1,807	2,089	1,920
3144 Women's footwear	Mil. dol. . .	1,459	1,339	1,311	1,186	1,252	1,320	1,370
3149 Footwear n.e.c.	Mil. dol. . .	444	396	373	289	312	293	263
Value of shipments (1987 dollars)	Mil. dol. . .	3,829	3,537	3,288	2,971	2,996	3,285	3,090
3142 House slippers	Mil. dol. . .	201	209	231	232	229	312	252
3143 Men's footwear	Mil. dol. . .	1,791	1,716	1,548	1,441	1,435	1,627	1,477
3144 Women's footwear	Mil. dol. . .	1,417	1,264	1,190	1,057	1,077	1,110	1,151
3149 Footwear n.e.c.	Mil. dol. . .	421	348	319	241	255	236	210
TRADE DATA								
Value of imports	Mil. dol. . .	(NA)	7,401	8,408	8,312	8,588	9,256	9,657
Value of exports	Mil. dol. . .	(NA)	179	254	306	342	331	379

NA Not available.   [1] Estimate, except exports and imports.   [2] Value of all products and services sold by establishments in the footwear, except rubber industry.   [3] Value of products classified in the footwear, except rubber industry produced by all industries.

Source: U.S. Department of Commerce: Bureau of the Census, International Trade Administration (ITA). Estimates by ITA.

No. 1464. Recent Trends in Leather Tanning and Finishing (SIC 3111): 1988 to 1994

ITEM	Unit	1988	1989	1990	1991	1992	1993 [1]	1994 [1]
INDUSTRY DATA								
Value of shipments [2]	Mil. dol. . .	2,488	2,501	2,411	2,183	2,910	3,509	3,940
Value of shipments (1987 dollars)	Mil. dol. . .	2,150	2,125	1,958	1,847	2,471	2,888	3,090
Total employment	1,000. . . .	15.1	12.3	12.1	11.5	16.6	16.5	16.0
Production workers	1,000. . . .	12.5	10.6	10.3	9.8	13.3	13.3	13.0
Average hourly earnings	Dollar . . .	8.89	9.67	9.58	10.62	10.52	10.84	11.16
Capital expenditures	Mil. dol. . .	34.6	47.9	39.0	41.4	48.5	(NA)	(NA)
PRODUCT DATA								
Value of shipments [3]	Mil. dol. . .	2,425	2,525	2,458	2,226	2,930	3,533	3,967
Value of shipments (1987 dollars)	Mil. dol. . .	2,096	2,146	1,997	1,883	2,487	2,908	3,111
TRADE DATA								
Value of imports	Mil. dol. . .	(NA)	744	683	571	631	736	960
Value of exports	Mil. dol. . .	(NA)	625	751	680	705	764	812

NA Not available.   [1] Estimate, except exports and imports.   [2] Value of all products and services sold by establishments in the leather tanning and finishing industry.   [3] Value of products classified in the leather tanning and finishing industry produced by all industries.

Source: U.S. Department of Commerce: Bureau of the Census, International Trade Administration (ITA). Estimates by ITA.

No. 1465. Recent Trends in Luggage and Personal Leather Goods
(SIC 2386, 315, 316, 317): 1988 to 1994

ITEM	Unit	1988	1989	1990	1991	1992	1993 [1]	1994 [1]
INDUSTRY DATA								
Value of shipments [2]	Mil. dol.	2,348	2,340	2,403	2,354	2,180	2,248	2,286
2386 Leather and sheep-lined clothing	Mil. dol.	221	163	167	159	209	229	231
3151 Leather gloves/mittens	Mil. dol.	192	149	155	141	137	144	146
3161 Luggage	Mil. dol.	957	1,121	1,169	1,148	944	1,004	1,048
3171 Women's handbags/purses	Mil. dol.	563	544	547	545	463	455	449
3172 Personal leather goods	Mil. dol.	416	363	365	362	428	416	412
Value of shipments (1987 dollars)	Mil. dol.	2,218	2,134	2,106	2,011	1,834	1,870	1,892
2386 Leather and sheep-lined clothing	Mil. dol.	207	147	147	139	183	201	210
3151 Leather gloves/mittens	Mil. dol.	176	131	130	118	113	118	115
3161 Luggage	Mil. dol.	906	1,013	1,013	968	778	820	853
3171 Women's handbags/purses	Mil. dol.	538	512	497	483	406	393	381
3172 Personal leather goods	Mil. dol.	391	330	319	304	353	338	333
Total employment	1,000	33.2	31.7	31.9	29.3	26.2	26.4	26.2
Production workers	1,000	26.4	24.8	25.3	23.0	20.7	20.8	20.8
Average hourly earnings	Dollar	6.57	6.60	7.23	7.34	7.39	7.46	7.56
Capital expenditures	Mil. dol.	21.3	28.2	24.4	18.2	26.8	(NA)	(NA)
2386 Leather and sheep-lined clothing	Mil. dol.	0.5	0.8	0.4	0.3	1.6	(NA)	(NA)
3151 Leather gloves/mittens	Mil. dol.	0.6	0.5	0.5	0.2	0.5	(NA)	(NA)
3161 Luggage	Mil. dol.	9.2	15.0	11.5	9.6	14.5	(NA)	(NA)
3171 Women's handbags/purses	Mil. dol.	8.1	6.3	6.8	3.1	3.4	(NA)	(NA)
3172 Personal leather goods	Mil. dol.	2.9	5.6	5.2	5.0	6.8	(NA)	(NA)
PRODUCT DATA								
Value of shipments [3]	Mil. dol.	2,176	2,126	2,170	2,164	2,112	2,169	2,203
2386 Leather and sheep-lined clothing	Mil. dol.	192	158	161	201	199	218	220
3151 Leather gloves/mittens	Mil. dol.	152	117	113	127	108	114	116
3161 Luggage	Mil. dol.	871	1,001	1,064	1,028	847	901	941
3171 Women's handbags/purses	Mil. dol.	537	462	453	432	455	447	441
3172 Personal leather goods	Mil. dol.	424	388	379	375	504	489	485
Value of shipments (1987 dollars)	Mil. dol.	2,057	1,938	1,902	1,848	1,776	1,804	1,823
2386 Leather and sheep-lined clothing	Mil. dol.	180	143	142	176	174	191	200
3151 Leather gloves/mittens	Mil. dol.	140	103	95	106	89	94	91
3161 Luggage	Mil. dol.	825	904	922	867	698	736	766
3171 Women's handbags/purses	Mil. dol.	512	435	412	383	399	386	374
3172 Personal leather goods	Mil. dol.	400	353	331	316	416	397	392
TRADE DATA								
Value of imports	Mil. dol.	(NA)	3,410	3,545	3,499	3,819	3,990	4,460
2386 Leather and sheep-lined clothing	Mil. dol.	(NA)	1,173	1,209	1,079	1,229	1,221	1,238
3151 Leather gloves/mittens	Mil. dol.	(NA)	170	181	158	171	214	261
3161 Luggage	Mil. dol.	(NA)	977	1,058	1,103	1,247	1,367	1,649
3171 Women's handbags/purses	Mil. dol.	(NA)	832	842	893	883	902	949
3172 Personal leather goods	Mil. dol.	(NA)	258	255	266	289	286	363
Value of exports	Mil. dol.	(NA)	163	204	235	278	290	321
2386 Leather and sheep-lined clothing	Mil. dol.	(NA)	45.8	51.9	57.3	65.5	69.5	64.9
3151 Leather gloves/mittens	Mil. dol.	(NA)	11.5	14.0	13.1	12.2	14.0	13.8
3161 Luggage	Mil. dol.	(NA)	68.4	95.2	115.0	143.0	146.0	177.0
3171 Women's handbags/purses	Mil. dol.	(NA)	25.4	25.0	28.1	34.4	40.3	41.2
3172 Personal leather goods	Mil. dol.	(NA)	11.5	17.8	21.3	22.8	20.0	23.9

Not available.   [1] Estimate, except exports and imports.   [2] Value of all products and services sold by establishments in the luggage and personal leather goods industry.   [3] Value of products classified in the luggage and personal leather goods industry produced by all industries.

Source: U.S. Department of Commerce: Bureau of the Census, International Trade Administration (ITA). Estimates by ITA.

No. 1466. Recent Trends in Flat Glass (SIC 3211): 1988 to 1994

ITEM	Unit	1988	1989	1990	1991	1992	1993 [1]	1994 [1]
INDUSTRY DATA								
Value of shipments [2]	Mil. dol.	2,442	2,477	2,279	2,104	2,082	2,297	2,612
Value of shipments (1987 dollars)	Mil. dol.	2,385	2,460	2,354	2,248	2,234	2,413	2,558
Total employment	1,000	13.8	15.0	14.6	13.2	11.9	(NA)	(NA)
Production workers	1,000	11.2	12.1	11.9	10.7	9.7	(NA)	(NA)
Average hourly earnings	Dollar	16.18	16.47	16.19	16.77	16.80	(NA)	(NA)
Capital expenditures	Mil. dol.	151	144	127	112	148	(NA)	(NA)
PRODUCT DATA								
Value of shipments [3]	Mil. dol.	3,413	3,405	3,180	2,944	2,003	2,210	2,512
Value of shipments (1987 dollars)	Mil. dol.	3,333	3,381	3,285	3,146	2,149	2,321	2,460
TRADE DATA								
Value of imports	Mil. dol.	(NA)	481	328	324	319	392	488
Value of exports	Mil. dol.	(NA)	497	665	692	723	833	895

NA Not available.   [1] Estimate, except exports and imports.   [2] Value of all products and services sold by establishments in the flat glass industry.   [3] Value of products classified in the flat glass industry produced by all industries.

Source: U.S. Department of Commerce: Bureau of the Census, International Trade Administration (ITA). Estimates by ITA.

No. 1467. Recent Trends in Cement and Hydraulic, Ceramic Tile, and Gypsum Products: 1988 to 1994

ITEM	Unit	1988	1989	1990	1991	1992	1993 [1]	1994 [1]
CEMENT, HYDRAULIC (SIC 3241)								
Industry data:								
Value of shipments [2]	Mil. dol. . .	4,234	4,129	4,251	3,778	4,035	4,422	4,963
Value of shipments (1987 dollars) . . .	Mil. dol. . .	4,222	4,121	4,180	3,605	3,865	4,031	4,235
Total employment	1,000. . . .	18.6	16.9	17.6	16.4	17.0	17.8	18.3
Production workers	1,000. . . .	14.2	13.0	13.4	12.2	12.8	13.2	13.6
Average hourly earnings	Dollar . . .	13.97	14.53	15.16	14.86	15.08	(NA)	(NA)
Capital expenditures	Mil. dol. . .	193	263	265	225	226	(NA)	(NA)
Product data:								
Value of shipments [3]	Mil. dol. . .	4,023	3,898	4,113	3,701	3,911	4,286	4,811
Value of shipments (1987 dollars) . . .	Mil. dol. . .	4,011	3,890	4,044	3,531	3,746	3,907	4,105
Trade data:								
Value of imports	Mil. dol. . .	(NA)	492	444	333	250	283	443
Value of exports	Mil. dol. . .	(NA)	25.4	38.3	45.8	48.7	47.8	45.2
CERAMIC WALL AND FLOOR TILE (SIC 3253)								
Industry data:								
Value of shipments [2]	Mil. dol. . .	756	793	845	751	734	840	914
Value of shipments (1987 dollars) . . .	Mil. dol. . .	732	749	785	705	681	774	830
Total employment	1,000. . . .	9.8	10.0	9.8	9.5	9.0	9.5	9.9
Production workers	1,000. . . .	8.1	8.4	8.1	7.7	7.3	7.8	8.2
Average hourly earnings	Dollar . . .	9.50	8.98	9.57	8.94	9.45	(NA)	(NA)
Capital expenditures	Mil. dol. . .	71.9	32.3	68.8	22.1	49.0	(NA)	(NA)
Product data:								
Value of shipments [3]	Mil. dol. . .	675	681	696	683	693	792	860
Value of shipments (1987 dollars) . . .	Mil. dol. . .	654	644	647	641	643	730	781
Trade data:								
Value of imports	Mil. dol. . .	(NA)	431	421	365	419	472	519
Value of exports	Mil. dol. . .	(NA)	17.9	20.5	21.0	19.3	22.6	23.5
GYPSUM PRODUCTS (SIC 3275)								
Industry data:								
Value of shipments [2]	Mil. dol. . .	2,379	2,408	2,375	2,008	2,136	2,662	3,541
Value of shipments (1987 dollars) . . .	Mil. dol. . .	2,721	2,863	2,999	2,744	2,925	3,295	3,530
Total employment	1,000. . . .	11.4	11.3	11.5	10.3	10.8	11.4	11.8
Production workers	1,000. . . .	9.2	9.0	9.1	8.1	8.6	9.1	9.3
Average hourly earnings	Dollar . . .	11.00	12.00	12.27	12.83	12.63	(NA)	(NA)
Capital expenditures	Mil. dol. . .	57.0	53.6	68.1	34.2	45.1	(NA)	(NA)
Product data:								
Value of shipments [3]	Mil. dol. . .	2,270	2,238	2,258	1,899	2,000	2,497	3,320
Value of shipments (1987 dollars) . . .	Mil. dol. . .	2,597	2,661	2,851	2,594	2,740	3,090	3,310
Trade data:								
Value of imports	Mil. dol. . .	(NA)	32.2	25.8	12.8	13.2	24.5	50.6
Value of exports	Mil. dol. . .	(NA)	51.5	67.0	65.6	71.2	55.3	50.5

NA Not available.   [1] Estimate, except exports and imports.   [2] Value of all products and services sold by establishments in this industry.   [3] Value of products classified in this industry produced by all industries.

Source: U.S. Department of Commerce: Bureau of the Census, International Trade Administration (ITA). Estimates by ITA.

No. 1468. Recent Trends in Steel Mill Products (SIC 3312, 3315, 3316, 3317): 1988 to 1994

ITEM	Unit	1988	1989	1990	1991	1992	1993 [1]	1994 [1]
INDUSTRY DATA								
Value of shipments [2]	Mil. dol. . .	62,783	63,054	60,941	55,182	57,449	63,414	71,311
Value of shipments (1987 dollars)	Mil. dol. . .	57,998	56,464	55,595	51,234	54,468	59,100	63,500
Total employment	1,000. . . .	261	256	254	241	236	(NA)	(NA)
Production workers	1,000. . . .	201	199	196	184	181	(NA)	(NA)
Capital expenditures	Mil. dol. . .	2,222	2,961	3,011	3,337	2,572	(NA)	(NA)
PRODUCT DATA								
Value of shipments [3]	Mil. dol. . .	61,715	62,105	60,065	53,968	56,478	62,449	70,188
Value of shipments (1987 dollars)	Mil. dol. . .	57,056	55,631	54,791	50,133	53,560	58,200	62,500
TRADE DATA								
Value of imports	Mil. dol. . .	(NA)	9,599	8,911	8,339	8,499	9,290	13,431
Value of exports	Mil. dol. . .	(NA)	2,953	2,921	3,819	3,167	2,953	3,170

NA Not available.   [1] Estimate, except exports and imports.   [2] Value of all products and services sold by establishments in the steel mill products industry.   [3] Value of products classified in the steel mill products industry produced by all industries.

Source: U.S. Department of Commerce: Bureau of the Census, International Trade Administration (ITA). Estimates by ITA.

No. 1469. Recent Trends in General Components (SIC 345, 3491, 3494, 3562): 1988 to 1994

[The code 349A in the table represents an aggregation of SIC's 3491 and 3494]

ITEM	Unit	1988	1989	1990	1991	1992	1993 [1]	1994 [1]
INDUSTRY DATA								
Value of shipments [2]	Mil. dol.	20,447	21,130	21,699	21,310	22,024	22,712	23,726
3451 Screw machine products	Mil. dol.	3,159	3,124	3,034	2,975	3,828	4,214	4,947
3452 Industrial fasteners	Mil. dol.	5,484	5,606	5,689	5,509	5,185	5,381	5,655
349A Valves and pipe fittings	Mil. dol.	7,660	8,073	8,669	8,776	8,724	8,541	8,299
3562 Ball and roller bearings	Mil. dol.	4,144	4,327	4,306	4,051	4,288	4,576	4,825
Value of shipments (1987 dollars)	Mil. dol.	19,508	18,801	18,422	17,530	18,057	18,337	18,824
3451 Screw machine products	Mil. dol.	3,043	2,866	2,712	2,619	3,355	3,664	4,250
3452 Industrial fasteners	Mil. dol.	5,334	5,171	5,048	4,803	4,508	4,643	4,829
349A Valves and pipe fittings	Mil. dol.	7,214	7,004	7,104	6,919	6,875	6,545	6,152
3562 Ball and roller bearings	Mil. dol.	3,917	3,760	3,559	3,190	3,319	3,485	3,593
Total employment	1,000	211.0	212.0	207.0	198.0	193.0	(NA)	(NA)
3451 Screw machine products	1,000	43.7	44.8	42.4	40.6	46.3	47.7	50.7
3452 Industrial fasteners	1,000	54.3	54.9	52.8	50.0	44.1	43.9	44.6
349A Valves and pipe fittings	1,000	74.4	73.3	72.4	70.9	67.8	(NA)	(NA)
3562 Ball and roller bearings	1,000	38.8	39.1	39.0	36.6	34.9	33.4	32.8
Production workers	1,000	157.0	158.0	154.0	146.0	142.0	(NA)	(NA)
3451 Screw machine products	1,000	34.7	35.8	34.3	32.3	36.4	37.4	39.8
3452 Industrial fasteners	1,000	40.4	40.7	39.0	36.3	31.8	32.0	33.4
349A Valves and pipe fittings	1,000	50.7	49.2	49.0	47.7	45.6	(NA)	(NA)
3562 Ball and roller bearings	1,000	31.4	32.1	32.1	29.8	28.2	27.0	26.6
Average hourly earnings	Dollar	10.82	11.19	11.53	11.92	12.54	(NA)	(NA)
3451 Screw machine products	Dollar	9.43	9.77	10.13	10.23	11.22	(NA)	(NA)
3452 Industrial fasteners	Dollar	11.11	11.34	11.39	11.83	12.77	(NA)	(NA)
349A Valves and pipe fittings	Dollar	10.69	11.13	11.66	12.08	12.35	(NA)	(NA)
3562 Ball and roller bearings	Dollar	12.18	12.70	13.14	13.85	14.34	(NA)	(NA)
Capital expenditures	Mil. dol.	618	808	949	828	751	(NA)	(NA)
3451 Screw machine products	Mil. dol.	82	129	125	101	135	(NA)	(NA)
3452 Industrial fasteners	Mil. dol.	156	181	167	175	151	(NA)	(NA)
349A Valves and pipe fittings	Mil. dol.	184	226	293	247	258	(NA)	(NA)
3562 Ball and roller bearings	Mil. dol.	196	271	364	306	207	(NA)	(NA)
PRODUCT DATA								
Value of shipments [3]	Mil. dol.	19,507	20,326	21,106	20,407	20,658	21,225	22,197
3451 Screw machine products	Mil. dol.	3,114	3,130	3,034	2,926	3,640	4,005	4,703
3452 Industrial fasteners	Mil. dol.	5,226	5,391	5,529	5,275	4,833	5,016	5,271
349A Valves and pipe fittings	Mil. dol.	7,178	7,644	8,301	8,313	8,053	7,793	7,573
3562 Ball and roller bearings	Mil. dol.	3,989	4,161	4,242	3,893	4,133	4,410	4,651
Value of shipments (1987 dollars)	Mil. dol.	18,612	18,076	17,909	16,779	16,931	17,142	17,618
3451 Screw machine products	Mil. dol.	3,000	2,871	2,711	2,576	3,190	3,483	4,040
3452 Industrial fasteners	Mil. dol.	5,083	4,973	4,906	4,599	4,202	4,328	4,501
349A Valves and pipe fittings	Mil. dol.	6,759	6,617	6,786	6,540	6,340	5,972	5,614
3562 Ball and roller bearings	Mil. dol.	3,770	3,615	3,506	3,065	3,199	3,359	3,463
TRADE DATA								
Value of imports	Mil. dol.	(NA)	3,816	3,922	3,863	4,221	4,630	5,490
3451 Screw machine products	Mil. dol.	(NA)	-	-	-	-	-	-
3452 Industrial fasteners	Mil. dol.	(NA)	1,234	1,213	1,121	1,231	1,386	1,666
349A Valves and pipe fittings	Mil. dol.	(NA)	1,651	1,836	1,931	2,096	2,240	2,652
3562 Ball and roller bearings	Mil. dol.	(NA)	932	873	812	895	1,004	1,171
Value of exports	Mil. dol.	(NA)	1,989	2,794	2,970	3,149	3,327	3,842
3451 Screw machine products	Mil. dol.	(NA)	-	-	-	-	-	-
3452 Industrial fasteners	Mil. dol.	(NA)	357	621	634	685	710	905
349A Valves and pipe fittings	Mil. dol.	(NA)	1,158	1,485	1,662	1,805	1,960	2,204
3562 Ball and roller bearings	Mil. dol.	(NA)	474	689	674	659	658	733

- Represents or rounds to zero. NA Not available. [1] Estimate, except exports and imports. [2] Value of all products and services sold by establishments in the general components industry. [3] Value of products classified in the general components industry produced by all industries.

Source: U.S. Department of Commerce: Bureau of the Census, International Trade Administration (ITA). Estimates by ITA.

No. 1470. Recent Trends in Automotive Parts and Accessories (SIC 3465, 3592, 3647, 3691, 3694, 3714): 1988 to 1994

ITEM	Unit	1988	1989	1990	1991	1992	1993 [1]	1994 [1]
INDUSTRY DATA								
Value of shipments [2]	Mil. dol.	101,358	97,629	93,020	90,711	107,410	99,996	112,639
Value of shipments (1987 dollars)	Mil. dol.	100,046	94,672	88,897	86,124	101,561	92,854	104,275
Total employment	1,000.	647	630	604	567	615	656	697
Production workers	1,000.	521	506	482	448	487	524	559
Average hourly earnings	Dollar	14.72	14.99	15.35	15.70	15.89	14.66	15.07
Capital expenditures	Mil. dol.	3,389	4,334	4,874	4,548	4,645	(NA)	(NA)
PRODUCT DATA								
Value of shipments [3]	Mil. dol.	96,629	94,379	89,444	88,768	103,868	108,798	115,567
Value of shipments (1987 dollars)	Mil. dol.	95,365	91,538	85,479	84,312	98,245	101,027	106,986
TRADE DATA [4]								
Value of imports [5]	Mil. dol.	30,966	31,992	31,681	29,835	33,524	38,304	44,852
Value of exports [6]	Mil. dol.	17,418	17,457	22,856	24,130	28,484	33,457	37,135

NA Not available.   [1] Estimate, except exports and imports.   [2] Value of all products and services sold by establishments in the automotive parts and accessories industry.   [3] Value of products classified in the automotive parts and accessories industry produced by all industries.   [4] Trade data encompasses more than is indicated by the SIC's cited.   [5] General imports, customs value.   [6] Total exports, f.a.s. value.

Source: U.S. Department of Commerce: Bureau of the Census, International Trade Administration (ITA). Estimates by ITA.

No. 1471. Recent Trends in Farm Machinery and Equipment (SIC 3523): 1988 to 1994

ITEM	Unit	1988	1989	1990	1991	1992	1993 [1]	1994 [1]
INDUSTRY DATA								
Value of shipments [2]	Mil. dol.	8,732	10,419	11,546	10,347	9,727	10,894	11,874
Value of shipments (1987 dollars)	Mil. dol.	8,519	9,783	10,487	9,116	8,342	9,151	9,792
Total employment	1,000.	62.4	67.8	69.6	65.1	62.4	65.7	68.9
Production workers	1,000.	43.6	48.9	49.9	45.4	43.2	45.8	49.2
Average hourly earnings	Dollar	11.38	11.90	12.31	12.65	13.12	13.50	13.78
Capital expenditures	Mil. dol.	180	183	210	205	204	(NA)	(NA)
PRODUCT DATA								
Value of shipments [3]	Mil. dol.	7,902	9,578	10,871	9,724	9,038	10,123	11,034
Value of shipments (1987 dollars)	Mil. dol.	7,709	8,993	9,874	8,567	7,751	8,503	9,098
TRADE DATA								
Value of imports	Mil. dol.	(NA)	2,222	2,475	1,911	2,022	2,148	2,917
Value of exports	Mil. dol.	(NA)	2,219	2,298	2,130	2,176	2,473	2,647

NA Not available.   [1] Estimate, except exports and imports.   [2] Value of all products and services sold by establishments in the farm machinery and equipment industry.   [3] Value of products classified in the farm machinery and equipment industry produced by all industries.

Source: U.S. Department of Commerce: Bureau of the Census, International Trade Administration (ITA). Estimates by ITA.

No. 1472. Recent Trends in Lawn and Garden Equipment (SIC 3524): 1988 to 1994

ITEM	Unit	1988	1989	1990	1991	1992	1993 [1]	1994 [1]
INDUSTRY DATA								
Value of shipments [2]	Mil. dol.	4,828	4,578	4,910	4,820	5,170	5,791	6,203
Value of shipments (1987 dollars)	Mil. dol.	4,752	4,286	4,447	4,276	4,551	5,061	5,329
Total employment	1,000.	26.1	25.7	24.5	24.4	24.8	26.0	27.5
Production workers	1,000.	19.9	19.4	18.3	18.9	19.8	21.0	22.6
Average hourly earnings	Dollar	9.55	8.86	9.82	9.88	11.65	12.21	12.63
Capital expenditures	Mil. dol.	97.4	127	82.2	91.3	126	(NA)	(NA)
PRODUCT DATA								
Value of shipments [3]	Mil. dol.	4,175	4,044	4,343	4,267	4,303	4,820	5,164
Value of shipments (1987 dollars)	Mil. dol.	4,109	3,786	3,934	3,786	3,788	4,213	4,436
TRADE DATA								
Value of imports	Mil. dol.	(NA)	174	177	118	134	162	175
Value of exports	Mil. dol.	(NA)	457	495	562	612	686	740

NA Not available.   [1] Estimate, except exports and imports.   [2] Value of all products and services sold by establishments in the lawn and garden equipment industry.   [3] Value of products classified in the lawn and garden equipment industry produced by all industries.

Source: U.S. Department of Commerce: Bureau of the Census, International Trade Administration (ITA). Estimates by ITA.

No. 1473. Recent Trends in Construction Machinery (SIC 3531): 1988 to 1994

ITEM	Unit	1988	1989	1990	1991	1992	1993 [1]	1994 [1]
INDUSTRY DATA								
Value of shipments [2]	Mil. dol. . .	14,477	15,349	16,070	13,351	13,603	15,018	15,573
Value of shipments (1987 dollars)	Mil. dol. . .	14,138	14,345	14,516	11,722	11,636	12,567	12,881
Total employment	1,000. . . .	85.2	87.7	89.9	81.0	77.9	82.7	81.4
Production workers	1,000. . . .	57.7	60.6	60.7	52.8	50.2	55.1	57.9
Average hourly earnings	Dollar . . .	14.18	14.46	14.96	15.21	15.37	(NA)	(NA)
Capital expenditures	Mil. dol. . .	463	633	638	462	430	(NA)	(NA)
PRODUCT DATA								
Value of shipments [3]	Mil. dol. . .	13,407	14,206	14,888	12,297	12,710	13,903	14,417
Value of shipments (1987 dollars)	Mil. dol. . .	13,093	13,276	13,449	10,797	10,873	11,634	11,925
TRADE DATA								
Value of imports	Mil. dol. . .	(NA)	2,958	3,071	2,102	2,571	3,397	4,277
Value of exports	Mil. dol. . .	(NA)	3,992	4,546	4,379	4,246	4,328	5,179

NA Not available.   [1] Estimate, except exports and imports.   [2] Value of all products and services sold by establishments in the construction machinery industry.   [3] Value of products classified in the construction machinery industry produced by all industries.

Source: U.S. Department of Commerce: Bureau of the Census, International Trade Administration (ITA). Estimates by ITA.

No. 1474. Recent Trends in Mining Machinery (SIC 3532): 1988 to 1994

ITEM	Unit	1988	1989	1990	1991	1992	1993 [1]	1994 [1]
INDUSTRY DATA								
Value of shipments [2]	Mil. dol. . .	1,569	1,806	1,866	1,643	1,560	1,685	1,769
Value of shipments (1987 dollars)	Mil. dol. . .	1,517	1,654	1,642	1,401	1,308	1,373	1,407
Total employment	1,000. . .	13.6	15.7	15.5	14.5	12.6	12.0	11.8
Production workers	1,000. . .	8.5	9.8	9.7	8.5	7.4	7.0	6.9
Average hourly earnings	Dollar . . .	11.25	11.05	10.92	10.90	11.87	(NA)	(NA)
Capital expenditures	Mil. dol. . .	29.7	31.9	38.2	32.5	32.9	(NA)	(NA)
PRODUCT DATA								
Value of shipments [3]	Mil. dol. . .	1,478	1,677	1,754	1,584	1,442	1,557	1,656
Value of shipments (1987 dollars)	Mil. dol. . .	1,430	1,536	1,544	1,350	1,210	1,271	1,303
TRADE DATA								
Value of imports	Mil. dol. . .	(NA)	399	361	328	275	316	384
Value of exports	Mil. dol. . .	(NA)	594	741	782	832	864	1,004

NA Not available.   [1] Estimate, except exports and imports.   [2] Value of all products and services sold by establishments in the mining machinery industry.   [3] Value of products classified in the mining machinery industry produced by all industries.

Source: U.S. Department of Commerce: Bureau of the Census, International Trade Administration (ITA). Estimates by ITA.

No. 1475. Recent Trends in Oil and Gas Field Machinery (SIC 3533): 1988 to 1994

ITEM	Unit	1988	1989	1990	1991	1992	1993 [1]	1994 [1]
INDUSTRY DATA								
Value of shipments [2]	Mil. dol. . .	3,401	3,314	3,635	4,073	3,952	3,792	3,798
Value of shipments (1987 dollars)	Mil. dol. . .	3,279	3,147	3,381	3,598	3,561	3,450	3,346
Total employment	1,000. . . .	27.0	26.1	27.2	28.7	27.5	26.7	26.0
Production workers	1,000. . . .	15.5	14.7	15.3	16.0	15.5	15.4	15.4
Average hourly earnings	Dollar . . .	13.11	12.99	13.11	13.51	13.62	(NA)	(NA)
Capital expenditures	Mil. dol. . .	46.9	77.1	72.2	99.7	105.0	(NA)	(NA)
PRODUCT DATA								
Value of shipments [3]	Mil. dol. . .	2,848	2,829	3,013	3,400	2,991	2,753	2,701
Value of shipments (1987 dollars)	Mil. dol. . .	2,746	2,687	2,802	3,003	2,695	2,505	2,380
TRADE DATA								
Value of imports	Mil. dol. . .	(NA)	35.5	52.4	64.4	36.2	47.8	67.9
Value of exports	Mil. dol. . .	(NA)	2,409	2,709	3,946	4,000	3,761	3,560

NA Not available.   [1] Estimate, except exports and imports.   [2] Value of all products and services sold by establishments in the oil and gas field machinery industry.   [3] Value of products classified in the oil and gas field machinery industry produced by all industries.

Source: U.S. Department of Commerce: Bureau of the Census, International Trade Administration (ITA). Estimates by ITA.

No. 1476. Recent Trends in Machine Tools (SIC 3541, 3542): 1988 to 1994

ITEM	Unit	1988	1989	1990	1991	1992	1993 [1]	1994 [1]
INDUSTRY DATA								
Value of shipments [2]	Mil. dol.	4,891	5,353	5,260	4,875	5,010	5,760	7,193
3541 Metal cutting machines	Mil. dol.	3,138	3,623	3,607	3,370	3,556	4,009	4,904
3542 Metal forming machines	Mil. dol.	1,753	1,730	1,653	1,506	1,454	1,751	2,289
Value of shipments (1987 dollars)	Mil. dol.	4,712	4,930	4,597	4,105	4,103	4,652	5,714
3541 Metal cutting machines	Mil. dol.	3,006	3,303	3,134	2,817	2,884	3,212	3,877
3542 Metal forming machines	Mil. dol.	1,707	1,627	1,464	1,288	1,220	1,440	1,837
Total employment	1,000.	44.5	46.0	44.9	41.5	39.2	38.1	39.2
3541 Metal cutting machines	1,000.	29.9	31.0	30.3	28.0	26.9	25.8	26.5
3542 Metal forming machines	1,000.	14.6	15.0	14.6	13.5	12.3	12.3	12.7
Production workers	1,000.	27.1	28.0	27.5	25.0	23.0	22.4	23.3
3541 Metal cutting machines	1,000.	17.7	18.4	18.2	16.5	15.2	14.4	14.9
3542 Metal forming machines	1,000.	9.4	9.6	9.3	8.5	7.8	8.0	8.4
Average hourly earnings	Dollar	13.50	13.97	14.19	14.44	15.30	(NA)	(NA)
3541 Metal cutting machines	Dollar	13.52	14.06	14.13	14.51	15.49	(NA)	(NA)
3542 Metal forming machines	Dollar	13.46	13.82	14.30	14.30	14.94	(NA)	(NA)
Capital expenditures	Mil. dol.	101.0	134.0	118.0	98.0	122.0	(NA)	(NA)
3541 Metal cutting machines	Mil. dol.	64.5	94.6	84.2	66.4	81.7	(NA)	(NA)
3542 Metal forming machines	Mil. dol.	36.5	39.4	33.3	31.6	40.4	(NA)	(NA)
PRODUCT DATA								
Value of shipments [3]	Mil. dol.	4,314	4,857	4,806	4,291	4,412	5,083	6,361
3541 Metal cutting machines	Mil. dol.	2,612	3,172	3,249	2,838	3,013	3,398	4,158
3542 Metal forming machines	Mil. dol.	1,703	1,685	1,557	1,453	1,399	1,685	2,203
Value of shipments (1987 dollars)	Mil. dol.	4,159	4,476	4,202	3,616	3,617	4,108	5,055
3541 Metal cutting machines	Mil. dol.	2,501	2,891	2,823	2,373	2,444	2,723	3,287
3542 Metal forming machines	Mil. dol.	1,658	1,585	1,379	1,243	1,174	1,385	1,768
TRADE DATA								
Value of imports	Mil. dol.	(NA)	3,003	2,801	2,596	2,319	2,599	3,403
3541 Metal cutting machines	Mil. dol.	(NA)	2,246	2,062	1,935	1,689	1,885	2,398
3542 Metal forming machines	Mil. dol.	(NA)	757	740	661	630	714	1,004
Value of exports	Mil. dol.	(NA)	1,574	1,600	1,555	1,836	1,744	2,179
3541 Metal cutting machines	Mil. dol.	(NA)	893	913	877	1,017	975	1,353
3542 Metal forming machines	Mil. dol.	(NA)	680	687	677	819	769	825

NA Not available.   [1] Estimate, except exports and imports.   [2] Value of all products and services sold by establishments in the machine tools industry.   [3] Value of products classified in the machine tools industry produced by all industries.

Source: U.S. Department of Commerce: Bureau of the Census, International Trade Administration (ITA). Estimates by ITA.

No. 1477. Recent Trends in Special Dies, Tools, Jigs and Fixtures (SIC 3544): 1988 to 1994

ITEM	Unit	1988	1989	1990	1991	1992	1993 [1]	1994 [1]
INDUSTRY DATA								
Value of shipments [2]	Mil. dol.	8,078	9,236	9,487	8,890	9,334	10,242	12,080
Value of shipments (1987 dollars)	Mil. dol.	7,943	8,839	8,809	7,931	8,202	8,776	10,092
Total employment	1,000.	116	122	120	114	112	116	120
Production workers	1,000.	89.7	94.7	92.2	87.5	85.4	89.1	92.4
Average hourly earnings	Dollar	12.58	13.20	13.56	13.59	14.57	(NA)	(NA)
Capital expenditures	Mil. dol.	273	386	413	386	378	(NA)	(NA)
PRODUCT DATA								
Value of shipments [3]	Mil. dol.	8,790	9,911	10,055	9,692	10,212	(NA)	(NA)
Value of shipments (1987 dollars)	Mil. dol.	8,643	9,484	9,336	8,645	8,974	(NA)	(NA)
TRADE DATA								
Value of imports	Mil. dol.	(NA)	952	852	1,325	1,039	1,632	2,375
Value of exports	Mil. dol.	(NA)	455	542	543	667	1,082	1,144

NA Not available.   [1] Estimate, except exports and imports.   [2] Value of all products and services sold by establishments in the special dies, tools, jigs and fixtures industry.   [3] Value of products classified in the special dies, tools, jigs and fixtures industry produced by all industries.

Source: U.S. Department of Commerce: Bureau of the Census, International Trade Administration (ITA). Estimates by ITA.

No. 1478. Recent Trends in Power-Driven Handtools and Welding Apparatus: 1988 to 1994

ITEM	Unit	1988	1989	1990	1991	1992	1993 [1]	1994 [1]
POWER-DRIVEN HANDTOOLS (SIC 3546)								
Industry data:								
Value of shipments [2]	Mil. dol.	2,505	2,618	2,806	2,581	2,871	3,067	3,305
Value of shipments (1987 dollars)	Mil. dol.	2,446	2,451	2,532	2,260	2,450	2,560	2,693
Total employment	1,000	17.1	17.5	18.3	17.5	16.1	16.4	16.5
Production workers	1,000	12.0	12.3	12.6	11.4	10.6	10.8	11.0
Average hourly earnings	Dollar	9.69	10.03	10.18	10.86	11.08	(NA)	(NA)
Capital expenditures	Mil. dol.	59.0	66.2	98.4	74.7	72.3	(NA)	(NA)
Product data:								
Value of shipments [3]	Mil. dol.	2,155	2,281	2,365	2,239	2,413	2,572	2,782
Value of shipments (1987 dollars)	Mil. dol.	2,105	2,136	2,135	1,960	2,059	2,152	2,271
Trade data:								
Value of imports	Mil. dol.	(NA)	780	716	689	766	823	952
Value of exports	Mil. dol.	(NA)	476	521	550	568	600	699
WELDING APPARATUS (SIC 3548)								
Industry data:								
Value of shipments [2]	Mil. dol.	2,498	2,521	2,684	2,651	2,761	2,905	3,096
Value of shipments (1987 dollars)	Mil. dol.	2,356	2,279	2,336	2,215	2,227	2,254	2,317
Total employment	1,000	19.7	19.0	19.2	19.5	19.8	20.0	26.3
Production workers	1,000	12.3	11.6	12.0	11.8	11.8	11.9	12.0
Average hourly earnings	Dollar	12.45	12.67	13.15	13.07	13.93	(NA)	(NA)
Capital expenditures	Mil. dol.	49.3	59.1	67.7	50.5	65.7	(NA)	(NA)
Product data:								
Value of shipments [3]	Mil. dol.	2,263	2,298	2,475	2,434	2,416	2,524	2,677
Value of shipments (1987 dollars)	Mil. dol.	2,135	2,077	2,154	2,034	1,948	1,958	2,004
Trade data:								
Value of imports	Mil. dol.	(NA)	480	365	478	381	533	528
Value of exports	Mil. dol.	(NA)	491	566	597	621	651	681

NA Not available.   [1] Estimate, except exports and imports.   [2] Value of all products and services sold by establishments in this industry.   [3] Value of products classified in this industry produced by all industries.

Source: U.S. Department of Commerce: Bureau of the Census, International Trade Administration (ITA). Estimates by ITA.

No. 1479. Recent Trends in Textile Machinery and Paper Industries Machinery: 1988 to 1994

ITEM	Unit	1988	1989	1990	1991	1992	1993 [1]	1994 [1]
TEXTILE MACHINERY (SIC 3552)								
Industry data:								
Value of shipments [2]	Mil. dol.	1,487	1,561	1,505	1,396	1,563	1,651	1,796
Value of shipments (1987 dollars)	Mil. dol.	1,434	1,452	1,340	1,188	1,289	1,308	1,413
Total employment	1,000	17.1	16.4	16.0	14.9	15.0	15.3	15.2
Production workers	1,000	11.7	11.5	11.0	10.1	9.6	9.8	9.6
Average hourly earnings	Dollar	9.87	10.26	10.85	11.42	11.03	(NA)	(NA)
Capital expenditures	Mil. dol.	40.6	37.4	46.6	32.9	39.4	(NA)	(NA)
Product data:								
Value of shipments [3]	Mil. dol.	1,312	1,338	1,325	1,235	1,325	1,400	1,523
Value of shipments (1987 dollars)	Mil. dol.	1,265	1,245	1,180	1,051	1,093	1,109	1,198
Trade data:								
Value of imports	Mil. dol.	(NA)	1,388	1,449	1,165	1,464	1,781	1,772
Value of exports	Mil. dol.	(NA)	514	580	534	547	553	567
PAPER INDUSTRIES MACHINERY (SIC 3554)								
Industry data:								
Value of shipments [2]	Mil. dol.	2,012	2,580	2,770	2,206	2,512	2,389	2,588
Value of shipments (1987 dollars)	Mil. dol.	1,940	2,314	2,403	1,865	2,085	1,965	2,092
Total employment	1,000	17.3	19.9	20.3	17.8	18.2	18.0	18.4
Production workers	1,000	10.4	11.7	12.2	9.6	10.1	10.0	10.3
Average hourly earnings	Dollar	12.68	13.74	13.19	14.83	14.77	(NA)	(NA)
Capital expenditures	Mil. dol.	60.0	84.6	72.0	62.6	65.2	(NA)	(NA)
Product data:								
Value of shipments [3]	Mil. dol.	1,832	2,238	2,453	2,061	2,196	2,111	2,276
Value of shipments (1987 dollars)	Mil. dol.	1,767	2,007	2,128	1,742	1,823	1,736	1,840
Trade data:								
Value of imports	Mil. dol.	(NA)	962	880	694	637	709	907
Value of exports	Mil. dol.	(NA)	494	599	637	583	652	653

NA Not available.   [1] Estimate, except exports and imports.   [2] Value of all products and services sold by establishments in this industry.   [3] Value of products classified in this industry produced by all industries.

Source: U.S. Department of Commerce: Bureau of the Census, International Trade Administration (ITA). Estimates by ITA.

No. 1480. Recent Trends in Printing Trades Machinery, Food Products Machinery, and Packaging Machinery: 1988 to 1994

ITEM	Unit	1988	1989	1990	1991	1992	1993 [1]	1994 [1]
PRINTING TRADES MACHINERY (SIC 3555)								
Industry data:								
Value of shipments [2]	Mil. dol. . .	3,313	3,692	3,538	3,538	2,600	2,768	2,924
Value of shipments (1987 dollars) . . .	Mil. dol. . .	3,161	3,403	3,205	3,156	2,309	2,403	2,510
Total employment	1,000. . .	25.6	26.4	25.0	24.0	18.9	17.8	17.3
Production workers	1,000. . .	13.1	13.6	12.9	12.1	10.4	10.0	9.8
Average hourly earnings	Dollar . . .	12.81	12.77	13.07	13.29	13.60	13.65	13.78
Capital expenditures	Mil. dol. . .	86.3	99.5	89.6	74.7	60.2	(NA)	(NA)
Product data:								
Value of shipments [3]	Mil. dol. . .	2,783	3,303	3,141	3,171	2,290	2,742	2,798
Value of shipments (1987 dollars) . . .	Mil. dol. . .	2,656	3,044	2,845	2,829	2,033	2,380	2,402
Trade data:								
Value of imports	Mil. dol. . .	(NA)	1,177	1,127	1,146	1,220	1,350	1,558
Value of exports	Mil. dol. . .	(NA)	845	1,081	1,072	1,054	1,064	1,029
FOOD PRODUCTS MACHINERY (SIC 3556)								
Industry data:								
Value of shipments [2]	Mil. dol. . .	2,092	2,126	2,261	2,193	2,399	2,456	2,602
Value of shipments (1987 dollars) . . .	Mil. dol. . .	2,004	1,927	1,966	1,825	1,935	1,932	2,001
Total employment	1,000. . .	20.0	19.0	19.0	17.9	18.7	18.9	19.3
Production workers	1,000. . .	12.2	11.1	11.2	10.5	11.0	11.2	11.8
Average hourly earnings	Dollar . . .	11.41	11.50	12.07	12.70	13.07	(NA)	(NA)
Capital expenditures	Mil. dol. . .	33.7	63.6	45.8	42.1	46.4	(NA)	(NA)
Product data:								
Value of shipments [3]	Mil. dol. . .	1,780	1,881	1,954	1,970	2,067	2,193	2,303
Value of shipments (1987 dollars) . . .	Mil. dol. . .	1,705	1,706	1,699	1,639	1,667	1,725	1,770
Trade data:								
Value of imports	Mil. dol. . .	(NA)	374	452	427	474	439	481
Value of exports	Mil. dol. . .	(NA)	523	551	621	687	696	734
PACKAGING MACHINERY (SIC 3565)								
Industry data:								
Value of shipments [2]	Mil. dol. . .	2,186	2,498	2,762	2,880	3,127	3,171	3,394
Value of shipments (1987 dollars) . . .	Mil. dol. . .	2,135	2,334	2,491	2,528	2,686	2,649	2,743
Total employment	1,000. . .	21.7	23.5	23.5	23.9	26.3	(NA)	(NA)
Production workers	1,000. . .	12.5	14.0	13.3	13.7	15.4	(NA)	(NA)
Average hourly earnings	Dollar . . .	12.60	12.65	13.61	13.99	13.82	(NA)	(NA)
Capital expenditures	Mil. dol. . .	39.4	67.1	73.5	68.4	70.1	(NA)	(NA)
Product data:								
Value of shipments [3]	Mil. dol. . .	2,153	2,343	2,680	2,767	2,834	3,079	3,295
Value of shipments (1987 dollars) . . .	Mil. dol. . .	2,103	2,189	2,417	2,429	2,435	2,489	2,663
Trade data:								
Value of imports	Mil. dol. . .	(NA)	597	621	643	699	719	842
Value of exports	Mil. dol. . .	(NA)	486	579	611	606	672	792

NA Not available.   [1] Estimate, except exports and imports.   [2] Value of all products and services sold by establishments in this industry.   [3] Value of products classified in this industry produced by all industries.

Source: U.S. Department of Commerce: Bureau of the Census, International Trade Administration (ITA). Estimates by ITA.

No. 1481. Recent Trends in Computers and Peripherals (SIC 3571,2,5,7): 1988 to 1994

[Census reclassified some parts for electronic computers (3571) to component industries (367) for 1989-1990]

ITEM	Unit	1988	1989	1990	1991	1992	1993 [1]	1994 [1]
INDUSTRY DATA								
Value of shipments [2]	Mil. dol. . .	62,773	59,758	58,981	54,703	61,385	65,900	70,500
Total employment	1,000. . . .	290	263	248	227	219	201	191
Production workers	1,000. . . .	105.0	96.8	89.6	76.2	73.3	68.0	67.0
Average hourly earnings	Dollar . . .	10.93	11.68	11.72	12.52	12.47	12.59	13.01
Capital expenditures	Mil. dol. . .	2,213	2,148	1,993	1,813	2,123	(NA)	(NA)
PRODUCT DATA								
Value of shipments [3]	Mil. dol. . .	53,230	54,891	52,628	49,144	54,342	58,700	62,900
TRADE DATA								
Value of imports	Mil. dol. . .	(NA)	21,714	23,323	26,424	32,137	38,636	46,833
Value of exports	Mil. dol. . .	(NA)	22,360	24,138	25,182	26,304	26,696	30,393

NA Not available.   [1] Estimate, except exports and imports.   [2] Value of all products and services sold by establishments in the computers and peripherals industry.   [3] Value of products classified in the computers and peripherals industry produced by all industries.

Source: U.S. Department of Commerce: Bureau of the Census, International Trade Administration (ITA). Estimates by ITA.

No. 1482. Recent Trends in Electrical Equipment (SIC 361, 3621, 3625): 1988 to 1994

ITEM	Unit	1988	1989	1990	1991	1992	1993 [1]	1994 [1]
INDUSTRY DATA								
Value of shipments (1987 dollars)	Mil. dol. . .	22,764	22,724	22,237	20,831	21,380	22,040	22,748
3612 Transformers	Mil. dol. . .	3,764	3,704	3,658	3,363	3,554	3,571	3,642
3613 Switchgear and apparatus.	Mil. dol. . .	5,264	4,979	4,839	4,498	4,636	4,552	4,706
3621 Motors and generators	Mil. dol. . .	7,246	7,273	6,695	6,610	6,847	7,257	7,474
3625 Relays and controls	Mil. dol. . .	6,490	6,769	7,044	6,361	6,343	ʃ 660	6,926

[1] Estimate.

Source: U.S. Department of Commerce: Bureau of the Census, International Trade Administration (ITA). Estimates by ITA.

No. 1483. Recent Trends in Transformers, except Electronic (SIC 3612): 1988 to 1994

ITEM	Unit	1988	1989	1990	1991	1992	1993 [1]	1994 [1]
INDUSTRY DATA								
Value of shipments [2]	Mil. dol. . .	3,670	3,934	4,178	3,995	4,094	4,017	4,094
Value of shipments (1987 dollars)	Mil. dol. . .	3,764	3,704	3,658	3,363	3,554	3,571	3,642
Total employment	1,000. . . .	32.9	33.5	32.8	30.6	29.0	28.6	28.4
Production workers	1,000. . . .	25.1	25.8	24.8	23.2	22.0	21.9	22.5
Average hourly earnings.	Dollar . . .	10.11	10.16	10.89	11.17	11.64	(NA)	(NA)
Capital expenditures	Mil. dol. . .	66.8	78.0	109.0	115.0	85.9	(NA)	(NA)
PRODUCT DATA								
Value of shipments [3]	Mil. dol. . .	3,496	3,811	4,032	3,956	4,036	3,960	4,036
Value of shipments (1987 dollars)	Mil. dol. . .	3,586	3,588	3,531	3,330	3,504	3,521	3,591
TRADE DATA								
Value of imports	Mil. dol. . .	(NA)	290	359	435	500	608	592
Value of exports	Mil. dol. . .	(NA)	234	261	301	338	359	384

NA Not available.   [1] Estimate, except exports and imports.   [2] Value of all products and services sold by establishments in the transformers, except electronic industry.   [3] Value of products classified in the transformers, except electronic industry produced by all industries.

Source: U.S. Department of Commerce: Bureau of the Census, International Trade Administration (ITA). Estimates by ITA.

No. 1484. Recent Trends in Household Appliances (SIC 363): 1988 to 1994

ITEM	Unit	1988	1989	1990	1991	1992	1993 [1]	1994 [1]
INDUSTRY DATA								
Value of shipments [2]	Mil. dol. . .	17,332	18,335	18,069	17,692	18,479	19,889	21,110
3631 Household cooking equipment . .	Mil. dol. . .	3,699	3,095	2,994	2,891	2,950	3,155	3,375
3632 Household refrigerators	Mil. dol. . .	3,902	4,015	3,800	3,721	4,232	4,516	4,836
3633 Household laundry equipment . .	Mil. dol. . .	3,118	3,104	3,234	3,206	3,329	3,525	3,636
3634 Electric housewares and fans . .	Mil. dol. . .	2,828	3,078	3,056	3,112	2,895	2,921	3,007
3635 Household vacuums	Mil. dol. . .	1,473	1,605	1,860	1,805	1,905	2,017	2,246
3639 Home appliances, n.e.c.	Mil. dol. . .	2,312	3,438	3,125	2,958	3,169	3,755	4,010
Value of shipments (1987 dollars)	Mil. dol. . .	17,265	17,820	17,268	16,826	17,523	18,603	19,747
3631 Household cooking equipment . .	Mil. dol. . .	3,771	3,138	3,009	2,914	2,970	3,112	3,345
3632 Household refrigerators	Mil. dol. . .	3,886	3,887	3,696	3,688	4,195	4,441	4,707
3633 Household laundry equipment . .	Mil. dol. . .	3,121	3,043	3,086	3,059	3,213	3,418	3,551
3634 Electric housewares and fans . .	Mil. dol. . .	2,784	2,957	2,891	2,892	2,656	2,661	2,769
3635 Household vacuums	Mil. dol. . .	1,450	1,533	1,724	1,615	1,715	1,776	1,940
3639 Home appliances, n.e.c.	Mil. dol. . .	2,253	3,262	2,862	2,658	2,775	3,195	3,435
Total employment	1,000. . . .	117	114	110	104	103	106	110
Production workers	1,000. . . .	93.3	91.8	88.3	83.8	83.2	83.5	86.3
Average hourly earnings.	Dollar . . .	10.97	10.92	11.09	11.20	11.34	11.29	11.74
Capital expenditures	Mil. dol. . .	469	485	390	496	556	(NA)	(NA)
PRODUCT DATA								
Value of shipments [3]	Mil. dol. . .	16,210	16,688	16,500	16,089	16,664	17,875	18,982
3631 Household cooking equipment . .	Mil. dol. . .	3,311	3,136	3,027	2,942	3,008	3,217	3,441
3632 Household refrigerators	Mil. dol. . .	3,683	3,895	3,711	3,621	4,045	4,316	4,622
3633 Household laundry equipment . .	Mil. dol. . .	2,841	2,913	2,906	2,860	2,994	3,171	3,271
3634 Electric housewares and fans . .	Mil. dol. . .	2,675	2,847	2,684	2,608	2,520	2,543	2,618
3635 Household vacuums	Mil. dol. . .	1,461	1,626	1,876	1,834	1,809	1,916	2,134
3639 Home appliances, n.e.c.	Mil. dol. . .	2,239	2,271	2,296	2,224	2,289	2,712	2,896
Value of shipments (1987 dollars)	Mil. dol. . .	16,140	16,250	15,805	15,348	15,872	16,803	17,839
3631 Household cooking equipment . .	Mil. dol. . .	3,375	3,180	3,042	2,966	3,029	3,174	3,412
3632 Household refrigerators	Mil. dol. . .	3,668	3,771	3,610	3,589	4,009	4,244	4,499
3633 Household laundry equipment . .	Mil. dol. . .	2,844	2,856	2,772	2,729	2,890	3,075	3,195
3634 Electric housewares and fans . .	Mil. dol. . .	2,633	2,735	2,539	2,424	2,312	2,317	2,411
3635 Household vacuums	Mil. dol. . .	1,438	1,553	1,739	1,642	1,628	1,686	1,842
3639 Home appliances, n.e.c.	Mil. dol. . .	2,182	2,155	2,103	1,998	2,004	2,307	2,480
TRADE DATA								
Value of imports	Mil. dol. . .	(NA)	3,009	2,975	3,258	3,830	4,021	4,842
Value of exports	Mil. dol. . .	(NA)	1,560	1,833	2,139	2,365	2,570	2,670

NA Not available.   [1] Estimate, except exports and imports.   [2] Value of all products and services sold by establishments in the household appliances industry.   [3] Value of products classified in the household appliances industry produced by all industries.

Source: U.S. Department of Commerce: Bureau of the Census, International Trade Administration (ITA). Estimates by ITA.

No. 1485. Recent Trends in Lighting Fixtures and Wiring Devices: 1988 to 1994

ITEM	Unit	1988	1989	1990	1991	1992	1993 [1]	1994 [1]
LIGHTING FIXTURES (SIC 3645, 3646, 3648)								
Industry data:								
Value of shipments [2].............	Mil. dol...	6,469	6,699	6,620	6,212	6,686	7,220	7,436
Value of shipments (1987 dollars)...	Mil. dol...	6,265	6,163	5,903	5,445	5,810	6,332	6,522
Total employment..............	1,000...	58.3	59.0	55.3	52.1	51.5	(NA)	(NA)
Production workers.............	1,000...	41.5	41.6	38.8	36.5	35.7	(NA)	(NA)
Average hourly earnings........	Dollar...	8.67	8.58	8.84	9.11	9.35	(NA)	(NA)
Product data:								
Value of shipments [3].............	Mil. dol...	6,423	6,687	6,621	6,194	6,688	(NA)	(NA)
3645 Residential lighting fixtures...	Mil. dol...	1,795	1,777	1,586	1,409	1,677	(NA)	(NA)
3646 Commercial lighting fixtures..	Mil. dol...	2,762	3,056	3,196	2,955	3,071	(NA)	(NA)
3648 Lighting equipment, n.e.c....	Mil. dol...	1,866	1,854	1,838	1,830	1,941	(NA)	(NA)
Value of shipments (1987 dollars)...	Mil. dol...	6,221	6,151	5,903	5,429	5,811	(NA)	(NA)
3645 Residential lighting fixtures...	Mil. dol...	1,726	1,608	1,383	1,217	1,434	(NA)	(NA)
3646 Commercial lighting fixtures..	Mil. dol...	2,664	2,817	2,839	2,560	2,636	(NA)	(NA)
3648 Lighting equipment, n.e.c....	Mil. dol...	1,831	1,726	1,682	1,651	1,741	(NA)	(NA)
WIRING DEVICES (SIC 3643, 3644)								
Industry data:								
Value of shipments (1987 dollars)...	Mil. dol...	7,233	7,201	7,039	6,357	7,070	7,422	7,792
3643 Wiring devices, current.....	Mil. dol...	4,159	4,235	4,147	3,930	4,334	4,550	4,777
3644 Wiring goods, noncurrent....	Mil. dol...	3,075	2,966	2,892	2,427	2,736	2,872	3,015

NA Not available.　[1] Estimate.　[2] Value of all products and services sold by establishments in this industry.　[3] Value of products classified in this industry produced by all industries.

Source: U.S. Department of Commerce: Bureau of the Census, International Trade Administration (ITA). Estimates by ITA.

No. 1486. Recent Trends in Household Audio and Video Equipment (SIC 3651): 1988 to 1994

ITEM	Unit	1988	1989	1990	1991	1992	1993 [1]	1994 [1]
INDUSTRY DATA								
Value of shipments [2]............	Mil. dol...	6,327	7,360	7,521	7,994	8,884	9,396	10,006
Value of shipments (1987 dollars).....	Mil. dol...	6,469	7,450	7,698	8,124	9,159	9,911	10,555
Total employment...............	1,000....	31.6	33.2	30.8	31.1	31.5	31.1	31.9
Production workers..............	1,000....	24.2	24.9	22.5	21.7	22.6	21.9	22.6
Average hourly earnings..........	Dollar...	8.54	8.54	9.00	9.36	9.58	9.86	10.16
Capital expenditures.............	Mil. dol...	128	139	256	278	257	(NA)	(NA)
PRODUCT DATA								
Value of shipments [3]............	Mil. dol...	6,100	7,141	7,092	7,154	7,815	8,267	8,805
Value of shipments (1987 dollars).....	Mil. dol...	6,238	7,227	7,259	7,271	8,057	8,721	9,288
TRADE DATA								
Value of imports.................	Mil. dol...	(NA)	13,533	12,515	13,260	14,243	15,166	16,060
Value of exports.................	Mil. dol...	(NA)	1,640	2,045	2,235	2,430	2,691	3,116

NA Not available.　[1] Estimate, except exports and imports.　[2] Value of all products and services sold by establishments in the household audio and video equipment industry.　[3] Value of products classified in the household audio and video equipment industry produced by all industries.

Source: U.S. Department of Commerce: Bureau of the Census, International Trade Administration (ITA). Estimates by ITA.

No. 1487. Recent Trends in Telecommunications Equipment (SIC 3661, 3663): 1988 to 1994

ITEM	Unit	1988	1989	1990	1991	1992	1993 [1]	1994 [1]
INDUSTRY DATA								
Value of shipments [2]............	Mil. dol...	33,594	32,754	36,057	35,590	40,627	44,529	48,501
Value of shipments (1987 dollars).....	Mil. dol...	33,898	32,843	36,408	35,528	40,174	43,384	46,980
Total employment...............	1,000....	241	232	228	218	218	(NA)	(NA)
Production workers..............	1,000....	116	111	109	101	105	(NA)	(NA)
Average hourly earnings..........	Dollar...	12.43	13.13	12.99	13.39	14.28	11.76	12.28
Capital expenditures.............	Mil. dol...	1,330	1,271	1,345	1,051	1,312	(NA)	(NA)
PRODUCT DATA								
Value of shipments [3]............	Mil. dol...	32,130	31,014	33,772	32,531	36,630	41,179	44,846
Value of shipments (1987 dollars).....	Mil. dol...	32,404	31,101	34,092	32,436	36,209	40,038	43,345
TRADE DATA [4]								
Value of imports.................	Mil. dol...	(NA)	7,016	7,126	7,231	8,323	9,111	11,343
Value of exports.................	Mil. dol...	(NA)	5,081	6,374	6,717	7,827	9,689	12,260

NA Not available.　[1] Estimate, except exports and imports.　[2] Value of all products and services sold by establishments in the telecommunications equipment industry.　[3] Value of products classified in the telecommunications equipment industry produced by all industries.　[4] Data deviates from the SIC's cited: includes coaxial and fiber optic cable; excludes CB radios, low power radio transceivers and TV cameras.

Source: U.S. Department of Commerce: Bureau of the Census, International Trade Administration (ITA). Estimates by ITA.

No. 1488. Recent Trends in Telephone and Telegraph Apparatus, and Radio and TV Communications Equipment: 1988 to 1994

ITEM	Unit	1988	1989	1990	1991	1992	1993 [1]	1994 [1]
TELEPHONE AND TELEGRAPH APPARATUS (SIC 3661)								
Industry data:								
Value of shipments [2]	Mil. dol.	17,901	15,467	17,297	17,425	21,117	23,696	25,793
Value of shipments (1987 dollars)	Mil. dol.	18,360	15,995	17,981	17,927	21,837	24,130	26,186
Total employment	1,000	112	96	93	94	93	93	91
Production workers	1,000	57.2	49.0	46.5	46.9	45.7	46.1	44.6
Average hourly earnings	Dollar	13.37	14.51	14.48	14.47	14.92	(NA)	(NA)
Capital expenditures	Mil. dol.	625	573	593	459	624	(NA)	(NA)
Product data:								
Value of shipments [3]	Mil. dol.	16,668	14,679	16,037	15,284	18,900	21,035	22,890
Value of shipments (1987 dollars)	Mil. dol.	17,096	15,180	16,671	15,724	19,545	21,421	23,239
Trade data:								
Value of imports	Mil. dol.	(NA)	4,289	4,108	4,550	5,171	5,633	6,647
Value of exports	Mil. dol.	(NA)	2,072	2,361	2,535	3,270	4,003	4,789
RADIO AND TV COMMUNICATIONS EQUIPMENT (SIC 3663)								
Industry data:								
Value of shipments [2]	Mil. dol.	15,693	17,287	18,759	18,165	19,510	20,833	22,707
Value of shipments (1987 dollars)	Mil. dol.	15,538	16,848	18,428	17,602	18,337	19,254	20,794
Total employment	1,000	129	135	135	123	124	(NA)	(NA)
Production workers	1,000	58.5	62.1	62.4	53.7	58.8	(NA)	(NA)
Average hourly earnings	Dollar	11.55	12.10	11.90	12.51	13.81	(NA)	(NA)
Capital expenditures	Mil. dol.	705	698	752	592	688	(NA)	(NA)
Product data:								
Value of shipments [3]	Mil. dol.	15,462	16,335	17,735	17,247	17,730	20,144	21,956
Value of shipments (1987 dollars)	Mil. dol.	15,309	15,921	17,422	16,712	16,663	18,617	20,106

NA Not available.   [1] Estimate, except exports and imports.   [2] Value of all products and services sold by establishments in this industry.   [3] Value of products classified in this industry produced by all industries.
Source: U.S. Department of Commerce: Bureau of the Census, International Trade Administration (ITA). Estimates by ITA.

No. 1489. Recent Trends in Electronic Components and Accessories (SIC 367): 1988 to 1994

ITEM	Unit	1988	1989	1990	1991	1992	1993 [1]	1994 [1]
INDUSTRY DATA								
Value of shipments [2]	Mil. dol.	56,999	59,913	60,844	65,233	74,604	87,975	105,559
Value of shipments (1987 dollars)	Mil. dol.	56,075	58,502	60,514	65,849	76,710	91,685	111,438
Total employment	1,000	552	551	536	519	530	532	542
Production workers	1,000	337	339	325	314	317	317	326
Average hourly earnings	Dollar	9.78	9.96	10.22	10.34	10.84	11.20	11.25
PRODUCT DATA								
Value of shipments [3]	Mil. dol.	52,688	57,009	59,307	62,766	72,103	84,889	102,565
Value of shipments (1987 dollars)	Mil. dol.	51,853	55,666	58,843	63,174	73,683	87,870	107,389
TRADE DATA								
Value of imports	Mil. dol.	(NA)	18,342	19,111	20,409	22,842	27,532	36,092
Value of exports	Mil. dol.	(NA)	12,630	15,581	15,498	16,192	18,867	24,525

NA Not available.   [1] Estimate, except exports and imports.   [2] Value of all products and services sold by establishments in the electronic components and accessories industry.   [3] Value of products classified in the electronic components and accessories industry produced by all industries.
Source: U.S. Department of Commerce: Bureau of the Census, International Trade Administration (ITA). Estimates by ITA.

No. 1490. Recent Trends in Electron Tubes (SIC 3671): 1988 to 1994

ITEM	Unit	1988	1989	1990	1991	1992	1993 [1]	1994 [1]
INDUSTRY DATA								
Value of shipments [2]	Mil. dol.	2,943	3,039	2,570	2,568	3,144	3,427	3,838
Value of shipments (1987 dollars)	Mil. dol.	2,702	2,677	2,241	2,208	2,746	2,993	3,352
Total employment	1,000	27.4	27.8	23.4	22.1	22.2	20.5	20.4
Production workers	1,000	19.4	20.0	17.5	16.3	16.8	15.7	15.5
Average hourly earnings	Dollar	13.64	12.53	12.58	12.90	13.21	13.47	13.79
Capital expenditures	Mil. dol.	194	202	170	77	62	(NA)	(NA)
PRODUCT DATA								
Value of shipments [3]	Mil. dol.	2,465	2,638	2,650	2,659	3,356	3,692	4,172
Value of shipments (1987 dollars)	Mil. dol.	2,263	2,324	2,310	2,286	2,931	3,224	3,643
TRADE DATA								
Value of imports	Mil. dol.	(NA)	818	782	817	928	990	1,218
Value of exports	Mil. dol.	(NA)	537	640	759	771	929	1,232

NA Not available.   [1] Estimate, except exports and imports.   [2] Value of all products and services sold by establishments in the electron tubes industry.   [3] Value of products classified in the electron tubes industry produced by all industries.
Source: U.S. Department of Commerce: Bureau of the Census, International Trade Administration (ITA). Estimates by ITA.

No. 1491. Recent Trends in Printed Circuit Boards and Semiconductors and Related Devices: 1988 to 1994

ITEM	Unit	1988	1989	1990	1991	1992	1993 [1]	1994 [1]
PRINTED CIRCUIT BOARDS (SIC 3672)								
Industry data:								
Value of shipments [2]	Mil. dol.	7,961	7,354	7,844	6,353	7,392	7,724	8,319
Value of shipments (1987 dollars)	Mil. dol.	7,744	7,058	7,572	6,150	7,205	7,709	8,480
Total employment	1,000	80.9	79.0	76.7	69.9	76.2	78.0	80.0
Production workers	1,000	53.9	52.4	51.0	47.1	51.1	53.0	55.0
Average hourly earnings	Dollar	9.12	9.44	9.68	9.92	10.19	10.40	10.75
Capital expenditures	Mil. dol.	337	373	405	311	320	(NA)	(NA)
Product data:								
Value of shipments [3]	Mil. dol.	7,359	7,338	7,617	5,899	6,437	6,601	7,238
Value of shipments (1987 dollars)	Mil. dol.	7,158	7,042	7,352	5,711	6,274	6,588	7,378
Trade data:								
Value of imports	Mil. dol.	(NA)	1,751	2,601	2,712	2,097	2,141	2,384
Value of exports	Mil. dol.	(NA)	799	1,818	1,374	1,092	973	1,377
SEMICONDUCTORS AND RELATED DEVICES (SIC 3674)								
Industry data:								
Value of shipments [2]	Mil. dol.	22,597	25,708	25,977	29,668	33,178	43,463	57,371
Value of shipments (1987 dollars)	Mil. dol.	22,574	25,837	27,665	32,782	38,624	50,597	66,789
Total employment	1,000	179	184	182	175	172	170	176
Production workers	1,000	86.5	90.5	87.7	86.2	84.8	85.6	91.5
Average hourly earnings	Dollar	11.38	12.02	12.58	12.69	13.54	14.55	14.25
Product data:								
Value of shipments [3]	Mil. dol.	20,332	23,488	23,978	27,438	30,363	39,776	52,504
Value of shipments (1987 dollars)	Mil. dol.	20,312	23,606	25,535	30,318	35,347	46,305	61,122
Trade data:								
Value of imports	Mil. dol.	(NA)	12,172	12,023	12,928	15,275	19,244	25,670
Value of exports	Mil. dol.	(NA)	9,531	10,710	10,831	11,465	13,744	17,991

NA Not available.   [1] Estimate, except exports and imports.   [2] Value of all products and services sold by establishments in this industry.   [3] Value of products classified in this industry produced by all industries.
Source: U.S. Department of Commerce: Bureau of the Census, International Trade Administration (ITA). Estimates by ITA.

No. 1492. Recent Trends in Passive Components (SIC 3675-9): 1988 to 1994

ITEM	Unit	1988	1989	1990	1991	1992	1993 [1]	1994 [1]
INDUSTRY DATA								
Value of shipments [2]	Mil. dol.	23,500	23,813	24,452	26,644	30,890	33,361	36,030
Value of shipments (1987 dollars)	Mil. dol.	23,055	22,930	23,036	24,708	28,135	30,386	32,817
Total employment	1,000	264	260	254	252	260	263	266
Production workers	1,000	177	176	169	164	165	163	164
Average hourly earnings	Dollar	8.78	8.77	8.93	8.99	9.47	9.90	10.15
Capital expenditures	Mil. dol.	742	826	789	794	984	(NA)	(NA)
PRODUCT DATA								
Value of shipments [3]	Mil. dol.	22,533	23,545	25,063	26,771	31,946	34,821	38,651
Value of shipments (1987 dollars)	Mil. dol.	22,120	22,693	23,645	24,860	29,131	31,753	35,246
TRADE DATA								
Value of imports	Mil. dol.	(NA)	3,602	3,705	3,952	4,543	5,157	6,820
Value of exports	Mil. dol.	(NA)	1,763	2,413	2,534	2,863	3,221	3,926

NA Not available.   [1] Estimate, except exports and imports.   [2] Value of all products and services sold by establishments in the passive components industry.   [3] Value of products classified in the passive components industry produced by all industries.
Source: U.S. Department of Commerce: Bureau of the Census, International Trade Administration (ITA). Estimates by ITA.

No. 1493. Recent Trends in Motor Vehicles and Car Bodies (SIC 3711): 1988 to 1994

ITEM	Unit	1988	1989	1990	1991	1992	1993 [1]	1994 [1]
INDUSTRY DATA								
Value of shipments [2]	Mil. dol.	142,060	149,315	140,417	133,861	152,152	165,815	185,111
Value of shipments (1987 dollars)	Mil. dol.	140,237	143,572	132,594	120,922	133,117	140,402	151,358
Total employment	1,000	250	250	240	218	220	223	237
Production workers	1,000	214	213	200	179	186	187	198
Average hourly earnings	Dollar	18.68	19.40	20.31	21.32	21.74	23.07	24.57
Capital expenditures	Mil. dol.	1,137	2,374	3,004	3,262	2,774	(NA)	(NA)
PRODUCT DATA								
Value of shipments [3]	Mil. dol.	139,864	144,448	135,741	128,754	147,470	161,847	181,801
Value of shipments (1987 dollars)	Mil. dol.	138,069	138,892	128,178	116,309	129,020	137,042	148,652
TRADE DATA								
Value of imports [4]	Mil. dol.	(NA)	54,460	55,836	55,268	57,086	62,992	72,596
Value of exports [5]	Mil. dol.	(NA)	13,302	13,848	16,545	18,791	19,367	22,038

NA Not available.   [1] Estimate, except exports and imports.   [2] Value of all products and services sold by establishments in the motor vehicles and car bodies industry.   [3] Value of products classified in the motor vehicles and car bodies industry produced by all industries.   [4] General imports, Customs value basis.   [5] Total exports, F.A.S. value.
Source: U.S. Department of Commerce: Bureau of the Census, International Trade Administration (ITA). Estimates by ITA.

No. 1494. Recent Trends in Aerospace (SIC 372, 376): 1988 to 1994

ITEM	Unit	1988	1989	1990	1991	1992	1993 [1]	1994 [1]
INDUSTRY DATA								
Value of shipments [2]	Mil. dol.	107,746	113,477	125,194	131,345	132,031	112,770	101,500
Value of shipments (1987 dollars)	Mil. dol.	105,605	107,690	114,557	115,068	111,300	93,700	83,017
Total employment	1,000.	820	823	816	746	695	617	552
Production workers	1,000.	399	400	396	362	332	295	264
Average hourly earnings	Dollar	15.35	15.84	16.36	16.73	18.60	(NA)	(NA)
Capital expenditures	Mil. dol.	3,388	3,921	3,490	3,407	3,854	(NA)	(NA)
PRODUCT DATA								
Value of shipments [3]	Mil. dol.	102,242	106,320	118,141	124,109	124,612	105,961	95,454
Value of shipments (1987 dollars)	Mil. dol.	100,046	100,637	107,578	108,221	104,960	87,765	77,700
TRADE DATA								
Value of imports [4]	Mil. dol.	(NA)	9,646	10,985	12,422	12,914	11,527	11,642
Value of exports	Mil. dol.	(NA)	30,688	37,304	42,343	43,562	37,901	35,761

NA Not available.   [1] Estimate, except exports and imports.   [2] Value of all products and services sold by establishments in the aerospace industry.   [3] Value of products classified in the aerospace industry produced by all industries.   [4] 1989 import data for SIC 3728 contains unpublished corrections.
Source: U.S. Department of Commerce: Bureau of the Census, International Trade Administration (ITA). Estimates by ITA.

No. 1495. Recent Trends in Aircraft and Aircraft Engines and Engine Parts: 1988 to 1994

ITEM	Unit	1988	1989	1990	1991	1992	1993 [1]	1994 [1]
AIRCRAFT (SIC 3721)								
Industry data:								
Value of shipments [2]	Mil. dol.	41,494	43,339	51,370	58,090	63,134	50,400	42,500
Value of shipments (1987 dollars)	Mil. dol.	40,760	40,166	45,180	48,449	50,669	39,585	32,692
Total employment	1,000.	274	278	289	258	265	240	215
Production workers	1,000.	140	140	140	125	122	109	97
Average hourly earnings	Dollar	16.16	16.40	17.02	17.82	20.00	20.80	22.05
Capital expenditures	Mil. dol.	1,030	1,270	1,021	1,046	1,661	(NA)	(NA)
Product data:								
Value of shipments [3]	Mil. dol.	37,765	39,531	46,885	52,514	56,582	45,152	38,075
Value of shipments (1987 dollars)	Mil. dol.	37,097	36,637	41,236	43,798	45,411	35,463	29,288
Trade data:								
Value of imports	Mil. dol.	(NA)	2,805	2,838	3,438	3,921	3,738	3,809
Value of exports	Mil. dol.	(NA)	14,339	19,631	24,173	26,419	21,306	18,831
AIRCRAFT ENGINES AND ENGINE PARTS (SIC 3724)								
Industry data:								
Value of shipments [2]	Mil. dol.	20,339	21,566	22,813	22,746	21,870	17,900	16,500
Value of shipments (1987 dollars)	Mil. dol.	19,613	20,193	20,278	19,211	17,524	14,078	12,771
Total employment	1,000.	141	132	129	122	117	107	100
Production workers	1,000.	76.8	76.2	72.6	67.3	64.2	59.0	54.5
Average hourly earnings	Dollar	14.29	14.81	15.68	15.56	16.97	17.40	17.98
Capital expenditures	Mil. dol.	693	718	785	771	590	(NA)	(NA)
Product data:								
Value of shipments [3]	Mil. dol.	18,867	19,904	21,580	21,315	20,468	16,750	15,440
Value of shipments (1987 dollars)	Mil. dol.	18,194	18,637	19,182	18,002	16,401	13,174	11,950
Trade data:								
Value of imports	Mil. dol.	(NA)	3,897	4,739	4,990	5,752	5,245	5,270
Value of exports	Mil. dol.	(NA)	6,578	6,833	6,994	6,642	6,209	6,423

NA Not available.   [1] Estimate, except exports and imports.   [2] Value of all products and services sold by establishments in this industry.   [3] Value of products classified in this industry produced by all industries.
Source: U.S. Department of Commerce: Bureau of the Census, International Trade Administration (ITA). Estimates by ITA.

No. 1496. Recent Trends in Aircraft Parts and Equipment, n.e.c. (SIC 3728): 1988 to 1994

ITEM	Unit	1988	1989	1990	1991	1992	1993 [1]	1994 [1]
INDUSTRY DATA								
Value of shipments [2]	Mil. dol.	17,720	19,075	20,458	21,544	19,726	17,600	16,900
Value of shipments (1987 dollars)	Mil. dol.	16,973	17,678	18,497	18,865	16,549	14,413	13,080
Total employment	1,000.	181	193	198	187	165	142	125
Production workers	1,000.	98	103	111	108	93	80	70
Average hourly earnings	Dollar	13.85	14.55	14.89	15.05	16.44	17.38	17.76
Capital expenditures	Mil. dol.	640	813	815	1,006	1,130	(NA)	(NA)
PRODUCT DATA								
Value of shipments [3]	Mil. dol.	20,545	21,295	23,082	25,288	21,997	19,620	18,650
Value of shipments (1987 dollars)	Mil. dol.	19,680	19,735	20,870	22,144	18,454	16,067	14,435
TRADE DATA								
Value of imports [4]	Mil. dol.	(NA)	2,825	3,324	3,888	3,132	2,437	2,476
Value of exports	Mil. dol.	(NA)	8,708	9,517	9,953	9,050	9,133	9,472

NA Not available.   [1] Estimate, except exports and imports.   [2] Value of all products and services sold by establishments in the aircraft parts and equipment, n.e.c. industry.   [3] Value of products classified in the aircraft parts and equipment, n.e.c. industry produced by all industries.   [4] 1989 import data contains unpublished corrections.
Source: U.S. Department of Commerce: Bureau of the Census, International Trade Administration (ITA). Estimates by ITA.

No. 1497. Recent Trends in Ship Building and Repairing (SIC 3731): 1988 to 1994

ITEM	Unit	1988	1989	1990	1991	1992	1993 [1]	1994 [1]
INDUSTRY DATA								
Value of shipments [2]	Mil. dol.	8,793	9,640	10,856	10,849	10,645	10,876	10,940
Value of shipments (1987 dollars)	Mil. dol.	8,562	9,052	9,887	9,652	9,362	9,011	8,731
Total employment	1,000	120	119	121	121	119	107	102
Production workers	1,000	89.5	87.9	91.0	90.1	87.4	79.7	74.2
Average hourly earnings	Dollar	12.30	12.31	12.59	12.97	12.98	(NA)	(NA)
Capital expenditures [3]	Mil. dol.	238	193	227	228	215	161	168
PRODUCT DATA								
Value of shipments [4]	Mil. dol.	8,630	9,530	10,741	10,700	10,157	10,378	10,439
Value of shipments (1987 dollars)	Mil. dol.	8,403	8,948	9,782	9,519	8,933	8,598	8,331
TRADE DATA								
Value of imports	Mil. dol.	(NA)	145	15	14	51	517	12
Value of exports	Mil. dol.	(NA)	313	434	321	652	379	595

NA Not available. [1] Estimate, except exports and imports. [2] Value of all products and services sold by establishments in the ship building and repairing industry. [3] Capital expenditures, 1991 and 1992, supplied by U.S. Department of Transportation. [4] Value of products classified in the ship building and repairing industry produced by all industries.

Source: U.S. Department of Commerce: Bureau of the Census, International Trade Administration (ITA). Estimates by U.S. Department of Transportation

No. 1498. Recent Trends in Boat Building and Repairing (SIC 3732): 1988 to 1994

ITEM	Unit	1988	1989	1990	1991	1992	1993 [1]	1994 [1]
INDUSTRY DATA								
Value of shipments [2]	Mil. dol.	5,935	5,739	4,998	3,676	4,685	5,075	5,975
Value of shipments (1987 dollars)	Mil. dol.	5,762	5,334	4,455	3,177	3,950	4,194	4,858
Total employment	1,000	62.8	60.4	54.1	40.8	44.9	45.9	50.7
Production workers	1,000	51.9	49.2	42.7	31.7	34.7	35.7	40.3
Average hourly earnings	Dollar	8.22	8.44	8.68	9.17	9.69	9.93	9.95
Capital expenditures	Mil. dol.	141	120	83	39	64	(NA)	(NA)
PRODUCT DATA								
Value of shipments [3]	Mil. dol.	5,896	5,613	4,877	3,518	4,397	4,760	5,605
Value of shipments (1987 dollars)	Mil. dol.	5,724	5,217	4,347	3,040	3,707	3,934	4,557
TRADE DATA								
Value of imports	Mil. dol.	(NA)	404	279	207	257	425	564
Value of exports	Mil. dol.	(NA)	615	793	774	714	534	507

NA Not available. [1] Estimate, except exports and imports. [2] Value of all products and services sold by establishments in the boat building and repairing industry. [3] Value of products classified in the boat building and repairing industry produced by all industries.

Source: U.S. Department of Commerce: Bureau of the Census, International Trade Administration (ITA). Estimates by ITA.

No. 1499. Recent Trends in Motorcycles, Bicycles, and Parts (SIC 3751): 1988 to 1994

ITEM	Unit	1988	1989	1990	1991	1992	1993 [1]	1994 [1]
INDUSTRY DATA								
Value of shipments [2]	Mil. dol.	1,057	1,370	1,476	1,914	1,967	2,145	2,203
Value of shipments (1987 dollars)	Mil. dol.	1,019	1,271	1,337	1,701	1,714	1,827	1,845
Total employment	1,000	7.5	8.4	9.4	10.8	12.3	12.9	13.0
Production workers	1,000	5.8	6.7	7.6	8.5	9.4	9.9	10.0
Average hourly earnings	Dollar	9.62	10.13	10.26	11.69	11.42	11.50	11.55
Capital expenditures	Mil. dol.	16.7	25.9	24.0	61.5	47.1	(NA)	(NA)
PRODUCT DATA								
Value of shipments [3][4]	Mil. dol.	1,191	1,515	1,799	2,112	2,110	2,300	2,365
37511 Bicycles and parts	Mil. dol.	531	686	863	1,110	1,012	1,103	1,081
37512 Motorcycles and parts	Mil. dol.	530	697	715	776	837	927	1,006
Value of shipments (1987 dollars)[4]	Mil. dol.	1,149	1,405	1,629	1,877	1,838	1,959	1,981
37511 Bicycles and parts	Mil. dol.	500	619	765	981	991	1,091	1,069
37512 Motorcycles and parts	Mil. dol.	523	665	665	695	661	702	739
TRADE DATA								
Value of imports	Mil. dol.	(NA)	1,318	1,199	1,329	1,537	1,717	1,763
Bicycles and parts	Mil. dol.	(NA)	681	750	745	734	841	825
Motorcycles and parts	Mil. dol.	(NA)	637	449	584	803	877	937
Value of exports	Mil. dol.	(NA)	245	420	615	671	703	711
Bicycles and parts	Mil. dol.	(NA)	46	114	174	175	197	200
Motorcycles and parts	Mil. dol.	(NA)	199	306	441	497	506	511

NA Not available. [1] Estimate, except exports and imports. [2] Value of all products and services sold by establishments in the motorcycles, bicycles, and parts industry. [3] Value of products classified in the motorcycles, bicycles, and parts industry produced by all industries. [4] Includes other products, not shown separately.

Source: U.S. Department of Commerce: Bureau of the Census, International Trade Administration (ITA). Estimates by ITA.

No. 1500. Recent Trends in Guided Missiles and Space Vehicles and Space Propulsion Units and Parts: 1988 to 1994

ITEM	Unit	1988	1989	1990	1991	1992	1993 [1]	1994 [1]
GUIDED MISSILES AND SPACE VEHICLES (SIC 3761)								
Industry data:								
Value of shipments [2]	Mil. dol. . .	22,513	23,983	25,083	23,399	18,219	18,150	17,200
Value of shipments (1987 dollars)	Mil. dol. . .	22,649	24,225	25,439	23,446	18,292	18,141	17,269
Total employment	1,000. . . .	169	173	156	136	92	77	66
Production workers	1,000. . . .	61.3	60.1	54.2	45.0	29.3	25.2	22.0
Average hourly earnings	Dollar . . .	17.19	17.53	18.25	19.07	22.67	23.60	24.78
Capital expenditures	Mil. dol. . .	758	795	659	450	288	(NA)	(NA)
Product data:								
Value of shipments [3]	Mil. dol. . .	17,459	17,049	16,907	16,075	15,234	14,750	14,010
Value of shipments (1987 dollars)	Mil. dol. . .	17,565	17,221	17,147	16,107	15,295	14,743	14,066
Trade data:								
Value of imports	Mil. dol. . .	(NA)	6.9	4.2	1.8	4.1	5.2	1.6
Value of exports	Mil. dol. . .	(NA)	396	568	318	599	507	364
SPACE PROPULSION UNITS AND PARTS (SIC 3764)								
Industry data:								
Value of shipments [2]	Mil. dol. . .	3,881	3,747	3,756	3,658	5,904	5,750	5,600
Value of shipments (1987 dollars)	Mil. dol. . .	3,831	3,688	3,543	3,347	5,382	4,923	4,794
Total employment	1,000. . . .	35.3	30.0	29.7	27.7	35.2	31.7	29.5
Production workers	1,000. . . .	12.6	10.6	10.6	9.5	13.6	13.0	12.6
Average hourly earnings	Dollar . . .	17.08	19.51	18.87	19.05	23.88	(NA)	(NA)
Capital expenditures	Mil. dol. . .	209	262	182	102	140	(NA)	(NA)
Product data:								
Value of shipments [3]	Mil. dol. . .	3,785	4,584	4,662	4,530	5,978	5,679	5,508
Value of shipments (1987 dollars)	Mil. dol. . .	3,737	4,512	4,398	4,145	5,449	4,862	4,716
Trade data:								
Value of imports	Mil. dol. . .	(NA)	1.2	0.1	0.5	0.4	0.2	-
Value of exports	Mil. dol. . .	(NA)	11.0	30.7	6.7	12.6	1.1	1.6

- Represents or rounds to zero.   NA Not available.   [1] Estimate, except exports and imports.   [2] Value of all products and services sold by establishments in this industry.   [3] Value of products classified in this industry produced by all industries.
Source: U.S. Department of Commerce: Bureau of the Census, International Trade Administration (ITA). Estimates by ITA.

No. 1501. Recent Trends in Space Vehicle Equipment, n.e.c. (SIC 3769): 1988 to 1994

ITEM	Unit	1988	1989	1990	1991	1992	1993 [1]	1994 [1]
INDUSTRY DATA								
Value of shipments [2]	Mil. dol. . .	1,800	1,768	1,716	1,907	3,179	2,970	2,800
Value of shipments (1987 dollars)	Mil. dol. . .	1,778	1,740	1,620	1,750	2,885	2,560	2,410
Total employment	1,000. . . .	19.4	18.4	14.4	14.2	22.4	18.8	16.4
Production workers	1,000. . . .	9.5	9.1	8.0	7.7	9.5	8.6	8.0
Average hourly earnings	Dollar . . .	15.47	16.56	16.61	18.36	17.88	(NA)	(NA)
Capital expenditures	Mil. dol. . .	59.8	64.2	28.0	31.4	45.1	(NA)	(NA)
PRODUCT DATA								
Value of shipments [3]	Mil. dol. . .	3,820	3,958	5,024	4,387	4,354	4,010	3,770
Value of shipments (1987 dollars)	Mil. dol. . .	3,775	3,896	4,744	4,025	3,951	3,456	3,244
TRADE DATA								
Value of imports	Mil. dol. . .	(NA)	110	79	103	104	102	86
Value of exports	Mil. dol. . .	(NA)	656	724	899	839	745	669

NA Not available.   [1] Estimate, except exports and imports.   [2] Value of all products and services sold by establishments in the space vehicle equipment, n.e.c. industry.   [3] Value of products classified in the space vehicle equipment, not elsewhere classified industry produced by all industries.
Source: U.S. Department of Commerce: Bureau of the Census, International Trade Administration (ITA). Estimates by ITA.

No. 1502. Recent Trends in Search and Navigation Equipment (SIC 3812): 1988 to 1994

ITEM	Unit	1988	1989	1990	1991	1992	1993 [1]	1994 [1]
INDUSTRY DATA								
Value of shipments [2]	Mil. dol. . .	36,597	35,295	36,734	36,213	36,185	35,824	36,540
Value of shipments (1987 dollars)	Mil. dol. . .	36,198	33,938	34,076	32,951	32,308	31,900	31,857
Total employment	1,000. . . .	361	340	314	280	260	234	208
Production workers	1,000. . . .	155	141	130	112	106	94	81
Average hourly earnings	Dollar . . .	14.99	14.99	14.49	14.08	17.64	18.31	18.99
Capital expenditures	Mil. dol. . .	1,369	1,367	1,125	830	811	(NA)	(NA)
PRODUCT DATA								
Value of shipments [3]	Mil. dol. . .	35,004	33,608	35,250	34,173	34,587	31,474	32,103
Value of shipments (1987 dollars)	Mil. dol. . .	34,623	32,316	32,699	31,095	30,881	28,027	27,988
TRADE DATA								
Value of imports	Mil. dol. . .	(NA)	766	781	858	881	750	863
Value of exports	Mil. dol. . .	(NA)	2,106	2,159	2,241	2,133	2,105	2,031

NA Not available.   [1] Estimate, except exports and imports.   [2] Value of all products and services sold by establishments in the search and navigation equipment industry.   [3] Value of products classified in the search and navigation equipment industry produced by all industries.
Source: U.S. Department of Commerce: Bureau of the Census, International Trade Administration (ITA). Estimates by ITA.

No. 1503. Recent Trends in Laboratory Instruments (SIC 3821, 3826, 3827): 1988 to 1994

ITEM	Unit	1988	1989	1990	1991	1992	1993 [1]	1994 [1]
INDUSTRY DATA								
Value of shipments [2]	Mil. dol.	7,933	8,193	9,041	9,234	9,275	9,211	9,157
3821 Lab apparatus and furniture	Mil. dol.	2,069	1,970	1,917	1,783	2,114	1,966	1,877
3826 Analytical instruments	Mil. dol.	3,863	4,306	4,906	5,071	5,243	5,364	5,577
3827 Optical instruments	Mil. dol.	2,001	1,918	2,218	2,380	1,919	1,881	1,703
Value of shipments (1987 dollars)	Mil. dol.	7,759	7,772	8,256	8,241	8,054	7,872	7,923
3821 Lab apparatus and furniture	Mil. dol.	1,985	1,807	1,714	1,564	1,769	1,577	1,480
3826 Analytical instruments	Mil. dol.	3,776	4,101	4,547	4,580	4,640	4,697	4,829
3827 Optical instruments	Mil. dol.	1,997	1,863	1,994	2,097	1,645	1,598	1,614
Total employment	1,000	72.8	75.2	77.6	74.2	74.8	(NA)	(NA)
3821 Lab apparatus and furniture	1,000	19.3	18.2	17.8	14.8	17.6	(NA)	(NA)
3826 Analytical instruments	1,000	32.2	35.9	37.8	37.0	40.0	38.8	38.6
3827 Optical instruments	1,000	21.3	21.1	22.0	22.4	17.2	(NA)	(NA)
Production workers	1,000	36.5	37.0	36.8	32.7	33.5	(NA)	(NA)
3821 Lab apparatus and furniture	1,000	11.2	9.8	9.1	6.9	8.9	(NA)	(NA)
3826 Analytical instruments	1,000	13.6	15.3	15.1	14.7	15.4	(NA)	(NA)
3827 Optical instruments	1,000	11.7	11.9	12.6	11.1	9.2	(NA)	(NA)
Average hourly earnings	Dollar	11.25	11.51	11.86	12.38	12.73	(NA)	(NA)
3821 Lab apparatus and furniture	Dollar	10.14	10.57	10.80	11.41	11.62	(NA)	(NA)
3826 Analytical instruments	Dollar	11.53	11.51	11.79	12.30	13.33	(NA)	(NA)
3827 Optical instruments	Dollar	12.04	12.34	12.71	13.10	12.84	(NA)	(NA)
Capital expenditures	Mil. dol.	316.0	294.0	289.0	326.0	350.0	(NA)	(NA)
3821 Lab apparatus and furniture	Mil. dol.	66.1	58.1	59.5	52.7	55.8	(NA)	(NA)
3826 Analytical instruments	Mil. dol.	167.0	163.0	152.0	195.0	232.0	(NA)	(NA)
3827 Optical instruments	Mil. dol.	83.3	72.4	77.2	77.6	61.9	(NA)	(NA)
PRODUCT DATA								
Value of shipments [3]	Mil. dol.	7,159	7,790	8,251	8,464	9,090	9,036	8,977
3821 Lab apparatus and furniture	Mil. dol.	1,691	1,794	1,779	1,673	1,879	1,747	1,668
3826 Analytical instruments	Mil. dol.	3,373	4,020	4,461	4,763	5,163	5,282	5,492
3827 Optical instruments	Mil. dol.	2,095	1,977	2,011	2,029	2,048	2,007	1,817
Value of shipments (1987 dollars)	Mil. dol.	7,010	7,395	7,534	7,557	7,898	7,73?	7,794
3821 Lab apparatus and furniture	Mil. dol.	1,623	1,646	1,592	1,468	1,572	1,401	1,315
3826 Analytical instruments	Mil. dol.	3,297	3,828	4,134	4,302	4,569	4,625	4,756
3827 Optical instruments	Mil. dol.	2,091	1,921	1,808	1,787	1,757	1,705	1,723
TRADE DATA								
Value of imports	Mil. dol.	(NA)	1,631	1,730	1,838	1,998	2,063	2,317
3821 Lab apparatus and furniture	Mil. dol.	(NA)	124	121	121	116	126	148
3826 Analytical instruments	Mil. dol.	(NA)	669	755	794	891	890	988
3827 Optical instruments	Mil. dol.	(NA)	839	855	922	992	1,047	1,181
Value of exports	Mil. dol.	(NA)	2,333	2,493	2,793	2,939	3,036	3,327
3821 Lab apparatus and furniture	Mil. dol.	(NA)	215	215	186	170	195	243
3826 Analytical instruments	Mil. dol.	(NA)	1,424	1,594	1,779	1,923	2,090	2,223
3827 Optical instruments	Mil. dol.	(NA)	694	684	828	846	750	861

NA Not available.   [1] Estimate, except exports and imports.   [2] Value of all products and services sold by establishments in the laboratory instruments industry.   [3] Value of products classified in the laboratory instruments industry produced by all industries.

Source: U.S. Department of Commerce: Bureau of the Census, International Trade Administration (ITA). Estimates by ITA.

No. 1504. Recent Trends in Measuring and Controlling Instruments (SIC 3822, 3823, 3824, 3829): 1988 to 1994

ITEM	Unit	1988	1989	1990	1991	1992	1993 [1]	1994 [1]
INDUSTRY DATA								
Value of shipments [2]	Mil. dol.	12,898	13,515	14,026	14,789	16,069	16,367	17,197
3822 Environmental controls	Mil. dol.	2,291	2,336	2,396	2,244	2,642	2,721	2,884
3823 Process controls	Mil. dol.	5,249	5,693	5,924	5,904	6,347	6,537	6,929
3824 Fluid meters and devices	Mil. dol.	1,659	1,657	1,666	2,247	2,668	2,828	3,026
3829 Instruments, n.e.c.	Mil. dol.	3,699	3,829	4,040	4,395	4,413	4,281	4,358
Value of shipments (1987 dollars)	Mil. dol.	12,570	12,751	12,772	13,063	13,880	13,773	13,958
3822 Environmental controls	Mil. dol.	2,251	2,240	2,246	2,047	2,369	2,268	2,234
3823 Process controls	Mil. dol.	5,076	5,301	5,327	5,165	5,425	5,461	5,656
3824 Fluid meters and devices	Mil. dol.	1,628	1,581	1,520	1,940	2,255	2,382	2,397
3829 Instruments, n.e.c.	Mil. dol.	3,615	3,629	3,679	3,910	3,830	3,662	3,671
Total employment	1,000	131.0	130.0	128.0	124.0	130.0	(NA)	(NA)
3822 Environmental controls	1,000	27.1	25.4	26.1	22.5	25.2	24.6	24.9
3823 Process controls	1,000	53.7	55.0	54.7	50.4	50.0	48.8	48.0
3824 Fluid meters and devices	1,000	10.9	10.7	10.4	12.8	16.7	(NA)	(NA)
3829 Instruments, n.e.c.	1,000	38.8	38.4	36.3	38.7	38.2	(NA)	(NA)
Production workers	1,000	74.3	73.4	69.0	66.4	71.8	(NA)	(NA)
3822 Environmental controls	1,000	19.5	18.2	18.2	14.9	17.0	16.0	16.1
3823 Process controls	1,000	26.8	28.0	26.1	23.7	24.0	22.9	22.5
3824 Fluid meters and devices	1,000	7.3	6.8	6.6	8.3	11.5	(NA)	(NA)
3829 Instruments, n.e.c.	1,000	20.7	20.4	18.1	19.5	19.3	(NA)	(NA)
Average hourly earnings	Dollar	10.40	10.76	11.20	11.75	12.61	(NA)	(NA)
3822 Environmental controls	Dollar	10.09	10.21	10.42	11.29	11.10	(NA)	(NA)
3823 Process controls	Dollar	10.49	11.18	11.38	11.39	12.35	(NA)	(NA)
3824 Fluid meters and devices	Dollar	10.41	10.43	10.74	13.13	15.25	(NA)	(NA)
3829 Instruments, n.e.c.	Dollar	10.59	10.78	11.86	11.95	12.67	(NA)	(NA)
Capital expenditures	Mil. dol.	344	388	396	616	496	(NA)	(NA)
3822 Environmental controls	Mil. dol.	57.0	66.3	61.2	56.0	81.6	(NA)	(NA)
3823 Process controls	Mil. dol.	130	136	151	347	158	(NA)	(NA)
3824 Fluid meters and devices	Mil. dol.	40.4	38.2	57.0	81.8	75.6	(NA)	(NA)
3829 Instruments, n.e.c.	Mil. dol.	117	147	127	132	181	(NA)	(NA)
PRODUCT DATA								
Value of shipments [3]	Mil. dol.	12,242	12,912	14,221	14,121	15,407	15,687	16,479
3822 Environmental controls	Mil. dol.	2,255	2,353	2,312	2,164	2,437	2,510	2,661
3823 Process controls	Mil. dol.	4,749	5,218	5,515	5,304	5,915	6,092	6,458
3824 Fluid meters and devices	Mil. dol.	1,637	1,563	2,470	2,300	2,685	2,846	3,045
3829 Instruments, n.e.c.	Mil. dol.	3,601	3,778	3,924	4,353	4,370	4,239	4,315
Value of shipments (1987 dollars)	Mil. dol.	11,934	12,187	12,953	12,474	13,304	13,205	13,525
3822 Environmental controls	Mil. dol.	2,215	2,256	2,167	1,975	2,186	2,092	2,061
3823 Process controls	Mil. dol.	4,592	4,859	4,960	4,641	5,055	5,089	5,272
3824 Fluid meters and devices	Mil. dol.	1,607	1,491	2,254	1,986	2,270	2,398	2,557
3829 Instruments, n.e.c.	Mil. dol.	3,520	3,581	3,574	3,873	3,794	3,626	3,635
TRADE DATA								
Value of imports	Mil. dol.	(NA)	1,772	1,904	2,044	2,372	2,772	3,696
3822 Environmental controls	Mil. dol.	(NA)	317	378	399	511	611	897
3823 Process controls	Mil. dol.	(NA)	716	683	755	856	866	966
3824 Fluid meters and devices	Mil. dol.	(NA)	159	196	208	296	554	954
3829 Instruments, n.e.c.	Mil. dol.	(NA)	580	647	682	708	742	878
Value of exports	Mil. dol.	(NA)	2,960	3,519	3,919	4,007	4,607	5,108
3822 Environmental controls	Mil. dol.	(NA)	240	397	447	488	718	905
3823 Process controls	Mil. dol.	(NA)	1,086	1,363	1,557	1,610	1,748	1,811
3824 Fluid meters and devices	Mil. dol.	(NA)	116	136	159	170	272	427
3829 Instruments, n.e.c.	Mil. dol.	(NA)	1,518	1,622	1,757	1,738	1,869	1,964

NA Not available. [1] Estimate, except exports and imports. [2] Value of all products and services sold by establishments in the measuring and controlling instruments industry. [3] Value of products classified in the measuring and controlling instruments industry produced by all industries.

Source: U.S. Department of Commerce: Bureau of the Census, International Trade Administration (ITA). Estimates by ITA.

No. 1505. Recent Trends in Instruments to Measure Electricity (SIC 3825): 1988 to 1994

ITEM	Unit	1988	1989	1990	1991	1992	1993 [1]	1994 [1]
INDUSTRY DATA								
Value of shipments [2]	Mil. dol. . .	7,984	7,920	8,390	8,240	8,828	9,777	11,139
Value of shipments (1987 dollars)	Mil. dol. . .	7,882	7,528	7,531	7,159	7,481	8,154	9,138
Total employment	1,000. . . .	82.9	78.4	78.4	69.3	68.4	64.9	62.6
Production workers	1,000. . . .	42.1	39.6	38.7	34.0	32.0	29.7	28.0
Average hourly earnings	Dollar . . .	11.70	12.24	12.88	12.47	14.14	15.40	15.70
Capital expenditures	Mil. dol. . .	215	305	293	257	324	(NA)	(NA)
PRODUCT DATA								
Value of shipments [3]	Mil. dol. . .	7,683	7,623	7,943	7,804	8,024	8,887	10,209
Value of shipments (1987 dollars)	Mil. dol. . .	7,584	7,246	7,130	6,780	6,800	7,412	8,375
TRADE DATA								
Value of imports	Mil. dol. . .	(NA)	555	587	633	651	751	868
Value of exports	Mil. dol. . .	(NA)	2,237	2,186	2,400	2,568	2,640	2,944

NA Not available.　[1] Estimate, except exports and imports.　[2] Value of all products and services sold by establishments in the instruments to measure electricity industry.　[3] Value of products classified in the instruments to measure electricity industry produced by all industries.

Source: U.S. Department of Commerce: Bureau of the Census, International Trade Administration (ITA). Estimates by ITA.

No. 1506. Recent Trends in Surgical and Medical Instruments and Surgical Appliances and Supplies: 1988 to 1994

ITEM	Unit	1988	1989	1990	1991	1992	1993 [1]	1994 [1]
SURGICAL AND MEDICAL INSTRUMENTS (SIC 3841)								
Industry data:								
Value of shipments [2]	Mil. dol. . .	8,259	8,972	10,262	10,710	13,428	14,896	15,794
Value of shipments (1987 dollars)	Mil. dol. . .	8,161	8,553	9,546	9,817	12,033	13,101	13,794
Total employment	1,000. . . .	75.7	83.9	88.9	87.7	98.6	101.0	100.0
Production workers	1,000. . . .	46.7	50.7	53.8	53.1	58.7	60.7	60.5
Average hourly earnings	Dollar . . .	9.57	9.58	9.81	10.59	10.86	(NA)	(NA)
Capital expenditures	Mil. dol. . .	385	403	469	536	691	(NA)	(NA)
Product data:								
Value of shipments [3]	Mil. dol. . .	7,959	8,655	9,857	10,474	13,124	14,489	15,306
Value of shipments (1987 dollars)	Mil. dol. . .	7,865	8,251	9,169	9,600	11,760	12,743	13,368
Trade data:								
Value of imports	Mil. dol. . .	(NA)	654	800	996	1,111	1,307	1,349
Value of exports	Mil. dol. . .	(NA)	1,497	1,854	2,173	2,445	2,539	2,487
SURGICAL APPLIANCES AND SUPPLIES (SIC 3842)								
Industry data:								
Value of shipments [2]	Mil. dol. . .	9,828	10,187	11,128	12,555	13,789	15,405	16,768
Value of shipments (1987 dollars)	Mil. dol. . .	9,654	9,656	10,088	10,984	11,706	12,617	13,287
Total employment	1,000. . . .	82.1	84.4	86.6	93.3	96.5	96.5	95.1
Production workers	1,000. . . .	52.8	54.3	55.8	60.6	61.4	60.2	58.8
Average hourly earnings	Dollar . . .	8.98	9.35	9.60	10.12	10.83	(NA)	(NA)
Capital expenditures	Mil. dol. . .	220	240	266	425	503	(NA)	(NA)
Product data:								
Value of shipments [3]	Mil. dol. . .	8,895	9,474	10,355	11,514	12,514	14,089	15,298
Value of shipments (1987 dollars)	Mil. dol. . .	8,738	8,980	9,388	10,074	10,623	11,539	12,122
Trade data:								
Value of imports	Mil. dol. . .	(NA)	394	554	645	892	899	1,004
Value of exports	Mil. dol. . .	(NA)	965	1,226	1,450	1,693	1,834	2,030

NA Not available.　[1] Estimate, except exports and imports.　[2] Value of all products and services sold by establishments in this industry.　[3] Value of products classified in this industry produced by all industries.

Source: U.S. Department of Commerce: Bureau of the Census, International Trade Administration (ITA). Estimates by ITA.

No. 1507. Recent Trends in Dental Equipment and Supplies (SIC 3843): 1988 to 1994

ITEM	Unit	1988	1989	1990	1991	1992	1993 [1]	1994 [1]
INDUSTRY DATA								
Value of shipments [2]	Mil. dol. . .	1,473	1,277	1,365	1,576	1,910	2,148	2,332
Value of shipments (1987 dollars)	Mil. dol. . .	1,503	1,334	1,410	1,723	2,090	2,235	2,327
Total employment	1,000. . . .	14.9	12.9	12.9	13.8	15.1	(NA)	(NA)
Production workers	1,000. . . .	8.9	8.4	8.4	8.6	8.9	(NA)	(NA)
Average hourly earnings	Dollar . . .	9.45	10.31	11.34	11.23	11.50	(NA)	(NA)
Capital expenditures	Mil. dol. . .	30.0	27.3	24.4	32.2	48.6	(NA)	(NA)
PRODUCT DATA								
Value of shipments [3]	Mil. dol. . .	1,227	1,177	1,265	1,397	1,619	1,805	1,967
Value of shipments (1987 dollars)	Mil. dol. . .	1,252	1,230	1,307	1,527	1,771	1,878	1,963
TRADE DATA								
Value of imports	Mil. dol. . .	(NA)	138	168	183	230	226	221
Value of exports	Mil. dol. . .	(NA)	265	312	376	448	498	512

NA Not available.　[1] Estimate, except exports and imports.　[2] Value of all products and services sold by establishments in the dental equipment and supplies industry.　[3] Value of products classified in the dental equipment and supplies industry produced by all industries.

Source: U.S. Department of Commerce: Bureau of the Census, International Trade Administration (ITA). Estimates by ITA.

No. 1508. Recent Trends in X-Ray Apparatus and Tubes and Electromedical Equipment: 1988 to 1994

ITEM	Unit	1988	1989	1990	1991	1992	1993 [1]	1994 [1]
X-RAY APPARATUS AND TUBES (SIC 3844)								
Industry data:								
Value of shipments [2]	Mil. dol...	1,615	1,926	2,577	3,011	3,235	3,394	3,156
Value of shipments (1987 dollars)	Mil. dol...	1,551	1,801	2,501	2,812	2,990	3,119	2,931
Total employment	1,000...	9.4	9.4	12.6	13.0	14.3	(NA)	(NA)
Production workers	1,000...	5.4	5.5	6.8	6.6	7.1	(NA)	(NA)
Average hourly earnings	Dollar...	12.47	12.93	13.79	14.37	14.79	(NA)	(NA)
Capital expenditures	Mil. dol...	41.8	56.9	91.5	65.3	63.6	(NA)	(NA)
Product data:								
Value of shipments [3]	Mil. dol...	1,649	1,690	1,854	2,201	2,502	2,625	2,441
Value of shipments (1987 dollars)	Mil. dol...	1,584	1,581	1,800	2,055	2,312	2,411	2,266
Trade data:								
Value of imports	Mil. dol...	(NA)	878	997	1,117	1,155	1,236	1,131
Value of exports	Mil. dol...	(NA)	527	605	753	791	850	987
ELECTROMEDICAL EQUIPMENT (SIC 3845)								
Industry data:								
Value of shipments [2]	Mil. dol...	4,155	4,821	5,604	5,743	7,002	6,904	6,490
Value of shipments (1987 dollars)	Mil. dol...	4,151	4,793	5,532	5,625	6,752	6,664	6,371
Total employment	1,000...	31.4	31.8	33.6	33.2	38.9	(NA)	(NA)
Production workers	1,000...	14.4	14.1	13.8	14.5	17.5	(NA)	(NA)
Average hourly earnings	Dollar...	10.21	10.91	11.49	11.74	11.79	(NA)	(NA)
Capital expenditures	Mil. dol...	126	174	174	181	277	(NA)	(NA)
Product data:								
Value of shipments [3]	Mil. dol...	4,031	4,658	4,808	5,194	6,158	6,072	5,707
Value of shipments (1987 dollars)	Mil. dol...	4,027	4,630	4,746	5,087	5,938	5,860	5,602
Trade data:								
Value of imports	Mil. dol...	(NA)	978	1,156	1,286	1,277	1,303	1,308
Value of exports	Mil. dol...	(NA)	1,610	1,796	2,043	2,255	2,396	2,820

NA Not available. [1] Estimate, except exports and imports. [2] Value of all products and services sold by establishments in this industry. [3] Value of products classified in this industry produced by all industries.
Source: U.S. Department of Commerce: Bureau of the Census, International Trade Administration (ITA). Estimates by ITA.

No. 1509. Recent Trends in Photographic Equipment and Supplies (SIC 3861): 1988 to 1994

ITEM	Unit	1988	1989	1990	1991	1992	1993 [1]	1994 [1]
INDUSTRY DATA								
Value of shipments [2]	Mil. dol...	20,546	22,738	21,018	21,398	22,093	22,045	22,179
Value of shipments (1987 dollars)	Mil. dol...	20,484	20,356	18,245	20,359	21,243	22,200	23,200
Total employment	1,000...	87.5	87.0	79.3	78.0	77.2	74.5	70.5
Production workers	1,000...	43.9	43.9	41.2	40.0	39.2	37.5	36.5
Average hourly earnings	Dollar...	13.11	13.41	13.69	14.73	14.66	14.79	15.11
Capital expenditures	Mil. dol...	810	1,008	1,009	1,089	809	(NA)	(NA)
PRODUCT DATA								
Value of shipments [3]	Mil. dol...	16,630	17,894	17,854	18,518	18,634	18,668	18,833
Value of shipments (1987 dollars)	Mil. dol...	16,580	16,020	15,498	17,619	17,917	18,800	19,700
TRADE DATA								
Value of imports	Mil. dol...	(NA)	5,562	5,444	5,818	6,425	7,042	7,726
Value of exports	Mil. dol...	(NA)	3,050	3,464	3,794	3,771	3,655	3,721

NA Not available. [1] Estimate, except exports and imports. [2] Value of all products and services sold by establishments in the photographic equipment and supplies industry. [3] Value of products classified in the photographic equipment and supplies industry produced by all industries.
Source: U.S. Department of Commerce: Bureau of the Census, International Trade Administration (ITA). Estimates by ITA.

No. 1510. Recent Trends in Jewelry, Precious Metal (SIC 3911): 1988 to 1994

ITEM	Unit	1988	1989	1990	1991	1992	1993 [1]	1994 [1]
INDUSTRY DATA								
Value of shipments [2]	Mil. dol...	4,273	4,227	4,180	3,733	4,138	4,377	4,522
Value of shipments (1987 dollars)	Mil. dol...	4,145	4,073	3,870	3,422	3,803	3,955	4,035
Total employment	1,000...	37.1	35.5	35.6	32.6	32.5	33.5	34.0
Production workers	1,000...	25.6	24.1	24.6	22.2	22.1	22.8	22.6
Average hourly earnings	Dollar...	7.54	8.39	8.80	8.76	9.70	9.81	10.03
Capital expenditures	Mil. dol...	26.4	29.8	43.2	40.5	36.1	(NA)	(NA)
PRODUCT DATA								
Value of shipments [3]	Mil. dol...	4,001	3,988	3,959	3,502	3,658	3,868	3,994
Value of shipments (1987 dollars)	Mil. dol...	3,880	3,842	3,666	3,210	3,362	3,496	3,565
TRADE DATA								
Value of imports	Mil. dol...	(NA)	2,567	2,455	2,461	2,724	3,153	3,453
Value of exports	Mil. dol...	(NA)	398	407	414	476	388	366

NA Not available. [1] Estimate, except exports and imports. [2] Value of all products and services sold by establishments in the jewelry, precious metal industry. [3] Value of products classified in the jewelry, precious metal industry produced by all industries.
Source: U.S. Department of Commerce: Bureau of the Census, International Trade Administration (ITA). Estimates by ITA.

No. 1511. Recent Trends in Dolls, Toys, and Games (SIC 3942, 3944): 1988 to 1994

ITEM	Unit	1988	1989	1990	1991	1992	1993 [1]	1994 [1]
INDUSTRY DATA								
Value of shipments [2]	Mil. dol.	4,223	4,125	4,003	4,307	4,386	4,485	4,743
3942 Dolls and stuffed toys	Mil. dol.	272	323	380	420	253	269	282
3944 Games and toys	Mil. dol.	3,951	3,803	3,623	3,887	4,133	4,216	4,461
Value of shipments (1987 dollars)	Mil. dol.	4,093	3,827	3,654	3,888	3,901	3,980	4,178
3942 Dolls and stuffed toys	Mil. dol.	264	309	342	367	217	223	232
3944 Games and toys	Mil. dol.	3,828	3,518	3,312	3,521	3,684	3,757	3,946
Total employment	1,000	38.0	36.5	32.8	32.0	33.9	34.1	33.8
3942 Dolls and stuffed toys	1,000	3.9	4.4	4.9	5.0	3.6	3.7	3.7
3944 Games and toys	1,000	34.1	32.1	27.9	27.0	30.3	30.4	30.1
Production workers	1,000	29.6	27.8	23.7	23.2	25.5	25.0	23.8
3942 Dolls and stuffed toys	1,000	3.1	3.4	3.8	3.8	2.8	2.7	2.6
3944 Games and toys	1,000	26.5	24.4	19.9	19.4	22.7	22.3	21.2
Average hourly earnings	Dollar	7.27	7.22	7.71	8.31	8.55	8.83	9.17
Capital expenditures	Mil. dol.	98.3	128.0	90.5	104.0	140.0	(NA)	(NA)
3942 Dolls and stuffed toys	Mil. dol.	2.3	10.4	11.8	11.4	3.0	(NA)	(NA)
3944 Games and toys	Mil. dol.	96.0	118.0	78.7	92.1	137.0	(NA)	(NA)
PRODUCT DATA								
Value of shipments [3]	Mil. dol.	3,765	3,732	3,666	3,840	3,844	3,934	4,158
3942 Dolls and stuffed toys	Mil. dol.	334	313	395	399	272	291	304
3944 Games and toys	Mil. dol.	3,431	3,419	3,271	3,440	3,572	3,643	3,854
Value of shipments (1987 dollars)	Mil. dol.	3,649	3,463	3,345	3,465	3,418	3,487	3,659
3942 Dolls and stuffed toys	Mil. dol.	324	300	355	349	234	241	250
3944 Games and toys	Mil. dol.	3,325	3,163	2,990	3,116	3,183	3,246	3,409
TRADE DATA								
Value of imports	Mil. dol.	(NA)	5,486	6,115	5,652	6,978	7,743	7,246
3942 Dolls and stuffed toys	Mil. dol.	(NA)	1,193	1,384	1,466	1,661	1,687	1,711
3944 Games and toys	Mil. dol.	(NA)	4,293	4,731	4,186	5,317	6,056	5,535
Value of exports	Mil. dol.	(NA)	386	527	549	692	720	844
3942 Dolls and stuffed toys	Mil. dol.	(NA)	31.5	33.9	39.3	54.5	45.1	56.1
3944 Games and toys	Mil. dol.	(NA)	354	493	510	637	675	788

NA Not available. [1] Estimate, except exports and imports. [2] Value of all products and services sold by establishments in the dolls, toys, and games industry. [3] Value of products classified in the dolls, toys, and games industry produced by all industries.

Source: U.S. Department of Commerce: Bureau of the Census, International Trade Administration (ITA). Estimates by ITA.

No. 1512. Recent Trends in Sporting and Athletic Goods, n.e.c. and Costume Jewelry: 1988 to 1994

ITEM	Unit	1988	1989	1990	1991	1992	1993 [1]	1994 [1]
SPORTING AND ATHLETIC GOODS, n.e.c. (SIC 3949)								
Industry data:								
Value of shipments [2]	Mil. dol.	5,747	6,510	7,040	7,036	7,626	8,006	8,500
Value of shipments (1987 dollars)	Mil. dol.	5,580	6,112	6,441	6,260	6,591	6,878	7,203
Total employment	1,000	55.7	59.3	65.8	61.3	61.7	62.9	64.1
Production workers	1,000	41.7	45.4	49.5	45.4	44.2	44.6	45.8
Average hourly earnings	Dollar	7.70	8.26	8.20	8.20	8.57	8.76	8.96
Capital expenditures	Mil. dol.	120	166	170	138	176	(NA)	(NA)
Product data:								
Value of shipments [3]	Mil. dol.	4,883	5,640	6,202	6,504	6,900	7,248	7,694
Value of shipments (1987 dollars)	Mil. dol.	4,741	5,296	5,674	5,787	5,964	6,227	6,520
Trade data:								
Value of imports	Mil. dol.	(NA)	1,868	1,933	2,111	2,554	2,587	3,188
Value of exports	Mil. dol.	(NA)	943	1,025	1,152	1,293	1,496	1,741
COSTUME JEWELRY (SIC 3961)								
Industry data:								
Value of shipments [2]	Mil. dol.	1,389	1,306	1,416	1,371	1,450	1,490	1,485
Value of shipments (1987 dollars)	Mil. dol.	1,357	1,224	1,293	1,213	1,256	1,280	1,267
Total employment	1,000	23.7	19.2	19.2	17.6	17.5	17.1	16.8
Production workers	1,000	16.0	13.5	13.1	12.4	12.6	12.9	12.5
Average hourly earnings	Dollar	6.06	6.37	6.65	6.93	7.25	7.39	7.33
Capital expenditures	Mil. dol.	14.7	13.2	11.5	9.4	12.8	(NA)	(NA)
Product data:								
Value of shipments [3]	Mil. dol.	1,292	1,315	1,417	1,399	1,509	1,552	1,547
Value of shipments (1987 dollars)	Mil. dol.	1,263	1,232	1,294	1,238	1,308	1,334	1,321
Trade data:								
Value of imports	Mil. dol.	(NA)	443	465	493	535	546	569
Value of exports	Mil. dol.	(NA)	92	115	128	121	135	148

NA Not available. [1] Estimate, except exports and imports. [2] Value of all products and services sold by establishments in this industry. [3] Value of products classified in this industry produced by all industries.

Source: U.S. Department of Commerce: Bureau of the Census, International Trade Administration (ITA). Estimates by ITA.

Guide to—Sources of Statistics, State Statistical Abstracts, and Foreign Statistical Abstracts

Alphabetically arranged by subject, this guide contains references to the important primary sources of statistical information for the United States published since 1990. Secondary sources have been included if the information contained in them is presented in a particularly convenient form or if primary sources are not readily available. Nonrecurrent publications presenting compilations or estimates for years later than 1990 or types of data not available in regular series are also included.

Much valuable information may also be found in State reports (see pp. 954-957) and foreign statistical abstracts (see pp. 958 and 959) and in reports for particular commodities, industries, or similar segments of our economic and social structures, many of which are not included here.

Publications listed under each subject are divided into two main groups: "U.S. Government" and "Other." The location of the publisher of each report is given except for Federal agencies located in Washington, DC. Most Federal publications may be purchased from the Superintendent of Documents, U.S. Government Printing Office, Washington, DC 20402, tel. 202-512-1800, or from Government Printing Office bookstores in certain major cities. In some cases, Federal publications may be obtained from the issuing agency.

Major reports, such as the Census of Population, which consist of many volumes, are listed by their general, all-inclusive titles.

Bureau of the Census Publications

In most cases, separate reports of the most recent censuses are available for each State, subject, industry, etc. Complete information on publications of all the censuses and current surveys conducted by the Bureau of the Census appears in the *Bureau of the Census Catalog,* published annually and available from the Superintendent of Documents.

Abortions—*see* Vital Statistics.

Accidents —*see also* Health; Insurance; and Vital Statistics

  U.S. Government

    Bureau of Labor Statistics

      Evaluating Your Firm's Injury and Illness Record, Construction Industries, Report 776 (1990).

      Heatburn Injuries, Bulletin 2358 (1990).

      Occupational Injuries and Illnesses in the United States by Industry. Annual.

    Department of Transportation

      Transportation Safety Information Report. Quarterly.

    Federal Railroad Administration

      Accident/Incident Bulletin. Summary, statistics, and analysis of accidents on railroads in the United States. Annual.

      Rail-Highway Crossing Accident/Incident and Inventory Bulletin. Annual.

Accidents —Con.

  U.S. Government —Con.

    Mine Safety and Health Administration

      Informational Reports by Mining Industry: Coal; Metallic Minerals; Nonmetallic Minerals (except stone and coal); Stone, Sand, and Gravel. Annual.

      Mine Injuries and Worktime. (Some preliminary data.) Quarterly.

    National Center for Health Statistics

      Vital Statistics of the United States. Annual.

        Volume I, Natality

        Volume II, Mortality

        Volume III, Marriage and Divorce

    National Transportation Safety Board

      Accidents; Air Carriers. Annual.

Air Force —*see* National Defense.

Air Pollution —*see* Environment.

Aliens —*see* Immigration.

American Samoa —*see* Outlying Areas.

Area —*see* Geography.

Army— *see* National Defense.

Aviation— *see* Transportation.

Banks and Banking— *see* Money.

Births— *see* Vital Statistics.

Broadcasting— *see* Communications.

Building Permits— *see* Construction.

Business —*see also* Economic Indexes; Investments; Manufactures; Retail and Wholesale Trade; Science Resources; *and* Service Establishments

U.S. Government

Administrative Office of the United States Courts

Annual Report of the Director.

Board of Governors of the Federal Reserve System

Annual Statistical Digest.

Federal Reserve Bulletin. Monthly.

Bureau of the Census

Census of Finance, Insurance, and Real Estate Industries. Quinquennial. (1992, most recent.)

Census of Retail Trade. Quinquennial. (1992, most recent.)

Census of Service Industries. Quinquennial. (1992, most recent.)

Census of Transportation, Communications, and Utilities. Quinquennial. (1992, most recent.)

Census of Wholesale Trade. Quinquennial. (1992, most recent.)

County Business Patterns. Annual.

Current Business Reports. Retail Trade, Sales, and Inventories, BR; and Wholesale Trade, Sales, and Inventories, BW.

Minority-Owned Businesses. Quinquennial. (1992, most recent.)

Quarterly Financial Report for Manufacturing, Mining, and Trade Corporations.

Bureau of Economic Analysis

Business Statistics, 1963-91. 1992. (Discontinued)

The Detailed Input-Output Structure of the U.S. Economy, 1982. 1991.

Fixed Reproducible Tangible Wealth in the United States, 1925-89. 1993.

The National Income and Product Accounts of the United States, 1929-1988: Statistical Tables. Volume I, 1993 and Volume II, 1992.

Summary Input-Output Tables of the U.S. Economy: 1966-87, 1992.

Survey of Current Business. Monthly.

U.S. Direct Investment Abroad: 1989 Benchmark Survey, 1992.

Business —Con.

U.S. Government —Con.

U.S. Direct Investment Abroad: Operations of U.S. Parent Companies and their Foreign Affiliates, Annual.

Council of Economic Advisers

Economic Indicators. Monthly.

Economic Report of the President. Annual.

Internal Revenue Service

Statistics of Income.

Corporation Income Tax Returns. Annual.

Statistics of Income Bulletin. Quarterly.

International Trade Administration

U.S. Industrial Outlook. Annual. (Discontinued after 1994 edition)

Patent and Trademark Office

Commissioner of Patents and Trademarks Annual Report.

Technology Assessment and Forecast Report - "All Technologies." Annual.

Securities and Exchange Commission

Annual Report.

Small Business Administration

Annual Report.

Other

The Dun & Bradstreet Corporation, Wilton, CT.

The Business Failure Record. Annual.

Monthly Business Failure Report.

Monthly New Business Incorporations Report.

Quarterly Survey of Business Expectations.

Fortune (Time Warner), New York, NY

The Fortune Directory of the 500 Largest Industrial Corporations.

The Fortune Directory of the 500 Global Industrial Corporations.

Child Welfare —*see* Education; *and* Social Insurance.

City Government —*see* State and Local Government.

Civil Service —*see* Federal Government; *and* State and Local Government.

Climate —*see also* Agriculture

U.S. Government

National Oceanic and Atmospheric Administration

Climatography of the United States, No. 20, Supplement No. 1, Freeze/Frost Data.

Climatography of the United States, No. 81: Monthly Normals of Temperature, Precipitation, and Heating and Cooling Degree Days 1961-90. 1992. Issued by State.

Climatological Data. Issued in sections for States and outlying areas. Monthly with annual summary.

Education —Con.
  U.S. Government —Con.
      Residence and Migration of College
        Students. (1992, most recent.)
      Revenues and Expenditures for Public
        Elementary and Secondary Education.
        Annual.
    National Science Foundation
      Academic Research Equipment and
        Equipment Needs in Selected
        Science/Engineering Fields: 1989-90.
      Academic Science and Engineering:
        Graduate Enrollment and Support.
        Detailed Statistical Tables. Annual.
      Academic Science/Engineering: R&D
        Expenditures. Detailed Statistical
        Tables. Annual.
      Blacks in Undergraduate Science and
        Engineering Education, April 1992.
        Special Report (NSF (92-305.)
      Characteristics of Doctoral Scientists and
        Engineers in the United States. Detailed
        Statistical Tables. Biennial.
      Characteristics of Recent
        Science/Engineering Graduates.
        Detailed Statistical Tables. Biennial.
      Characteristics of Science/Engineering
        Equipment in Academic Settings:
        1989-90. Report.
      Federal Support to Universities, Colleges,
        and Nonprofit Institutions. A report to
        the President and Congress. Detailed
        Statistical Tables. Annual.
      International Science and Technology
        Data Update. Report. Annual.
      National Patterns of R&D Resources.
        Report. Annual.
      Science and Engineering Degrees.
        A Source Book. Detailed Statistical
        Tables. Annual.
      Science and Engineering Degrees,
        by Race/Ethnicity of Recipients:
        1977-90. Detailed Statistical Tables.
        Biennial.
      Science and Engineering Doctorates.
        Detailed Statistical Tables. Annual.
      Science and Engineering Indicators.
        Report. Biennial.
      Science and Engineering Personnel: A
        National Overview. Report. Biennial.
      Science and Technology Pocket Data
        Book. Report. Annual.
      Scientific and Engineering Research
        Facilities at Universities and Colleges.
        Report. Biennial.
      Undergraduate Origins of Recent Science
        and Engineering Doctorate Recipients.
        Special Report (NSF 92-332.)
      U.S. Universities and Colleges Report a
        9-percent Net Increase in Research
        Space Since 1988, the Majority of it
        Within Doctorate-Granting Institutions
        (NSF 92-333.)

Education —Con.
  U.S. Government —Con.
      Women and Minorities in Science
        and Engineering. Report.
        Biennial.
  Other
    American Council on Education,
      Washington, DC
        A Fact Book on Higher Education.
          Quarterly.
        National Norms for Entering College
          Freshmen. Annual.
    Bowker (R.R.) Company, New Providence,
      NJ
        American Library Directory. Annual.
        Bowker Annual Library and Book Trade
          Almanac.
    Chronicle of Higher Education, Inc.,
      Washington, DC
        Almanac. Annual.
    College Entrance Examination Board,
      New York, NY
        National Report on College-Bound
          Seniors. Annual.
    National Catholic Educational Association,
      Washington, DC
        Catholic Schools in America. Annual.
        United States Catholic Elementary
          and Secondary Schools. Staffing and
          Enrollment. Annual.
        U.S. Catholic Elementary Schools and
          their Finances. Biennial.
        U.S. Catholic Secondary Schools and
          their Finances. Biennial.
    National Education Association,
      Washington, DC
        Estimates of School Statistics. Annual.
        Rankings of the States. Annual.
        Status of the American Public School
          Teacher, 1990-91. Quinquennial.
    Research Associates of Washington,
      Washington, DC
        Inflation Measures for Schools, Colleges,
          and Libraries. Annual.
        State Profiles: Financing Public Higher
          Education. Annual.

Elections
  U.S. Government
    Bureau of the Census
      Congressional District Data:
        1990 Census of Population
          and Housing, 1990 CPH-4,
          Congressional Districts of the
          103rd Congress.
      Current Population Reports. (Series P20,
        Voting and Registration in the Election
        of November 19—. Biennial survey; and
        P25, Projections of the Population of
        Voting Age for States: November 19—,
        Biennial projection.)

Health and Medical Care —Con.
  U.S. Government —Con.
      Employee Benefits in State and Local
        Governments. Biennial.
      Monthly Labor Review.
    Centers for Disease Control and Prevention,
    Atlanta, GA
      Morbidity and Mortality Weekly Report.
        (HHS Pub. No. CDC 90-8017.)
    Department of Agriculture, Food and
    Nutrition Service
      Annual Historical Review:
    Food and Nutrition Service Programs.
      Food Program Update. Monthly.
    Department of Health and Human Services
      Annual Report.
    Department of Veterans Affairs
      Annual Report of The Secretary of Veter-
        ans Affairs.
      Summary of Medical Programs. Quarterly.
    Drug Enforcement Administration
      Drug Abuse and Law Enforcement Statis-
        tics. Irregular.
    Health Care Financing Administration
      Health Care Financing Program Statistics.
        Medicare and Medicaid data. Annual.
      Health Care Financing Research Reports.
        Occasional.
      Health Care Financing Review. Quarterly.
    National Center for Health Statistics
      Health: United States. Annual. (DHHS
        Pub. No. PHS year-1232.)
      Vital and Health Statistics. (A series of
        statistical reports covering health-
        related topics.)
          Series 10: Health Interview Survey
            Statistics. Irregular.
              Current Estimates from the Health
                Interview Survey. Annual.
          Series 11: Health and Nutrition
            Examination Survey Statistics.
            Irregular.
          Series 13: Health Resources Utiliza-
            tion Statistics. Irregular.
              National Hospital Discharge Sur-
                vey: Annual Summary. Annual.
          Series 14: Health Resources: Man-
            power and Facilities Statistics.
            Irregular.
    National Institute on Drug Abuse
      High School Senior Survey. 1975-1991.
    Substance Abuse and Mental Health
    Services Administration
      Drug Abuse Warning Network. Advance
        Reports, Annual Report, latest year
        available 1992.
      National Drug and Alcoholism Treatment
        Unit Survey, latest year available 1992.
      National Household Survey on Drug
        Abuse. Advance Reports, Main Find-
        ings, Population Estimates, latest year
        available 1993.

Health and Medical Care —Con.
  U.S. Government —Con.
    Social Security Administration
      Social Security Bulletin. Quarterly with
        annual statistical supplement.
  Other
    American Dental Association, Chicago, IL
      Dental Statistics Handbook. Triennial.
      Dental Students' Register. Annual.
      Distribution of Dentists in the United
        States by Region and State. Triennial.
      Survey of Dental Practice. Annual.
    American Hospital Association, Chicago, IL
      Hospital Statistics. Annual.
    American Medical Association, Chicago, IL
      Physician Characteristics and Distribution
        in the U.S. Annual.
      Socioeconomic Characteristics of Medical
        Practice. 1994.
      U.S. Medical Licensure Statistics, and
        License Requirements. Annual.
    American Osteopathic Association, Chicago,
    IL
      Yearbook and Directory of Osteopathic
        Physicians. Annual.
    Medical Economics, Montvale, NJ
      Physicians' Earnings and Expenses. Pub-
        lished annually in Medical Economics
        magazine.
    Metropolitan Life Insurance Company,
    New York, NY
      Health and Safety Education.
      Statistical Bulletin. Quarterly.
Hospitals —*see* Health.
Hotels —*see* Service Establishments.
Household Appliances —*see* Construction, Hous-
  ing, and Real Estate. Housing—*see* Construction.
Immigration and Naturalization
  U.S. Government
    Department of State, Bureau of Consular
    Affairs
      Report of the Visa Office. Annual. (Dept.
        of State Pub. 8810.)
    Department of Transportation
      Report of Passenger Travel Between the
        United States and Foreign Countries.
        Annual, semiannual, quarterly, monthly.
    Immigration and Naturalization Service
      I&N Reporter. Quarterly.
      Statistical Yearbook of the Immigration
        and Naturalization Service. Annual.
    National Science Foundation
      Immigrant Scientists and Engineers.
        Detailed Statistical Tables. Annual.
      Science and Engineering Doctoral
        Awards Reached Record Highs in
        1990. SRS Data Brief. (NSF 91-308.)
      Survey of Direct U.S. Private Capital
        Investment in Research and Develop-
        ment Facilities in Japan. (NSF 91-312)
      Science and Engineering Doctorates.
        Detailed Statistical Tables. Annual.

International Accounts and Aid —Con.
  Other —Con.
      World Debt Tables. 1994-95.
      World Development Report. 1994.
      World Tables: 1994.
International Statistics —*see also* International Accounts
  U.S. Government
    Bureau of the Census
      Country Demographic Profiles. (Series ISP-30.)
      International Population Reports. Irregular. (Series P-91.)
      World Population Profile: 1994 (most recent).
    Bureau of Labor Statistics
      International Comparisons of Hourly Compensation Costs for Production Workers in Manufacturing. Quarterly.
      International Comparisons of Manufacturing Productivity and Labor Cost Trends. Annual.
      Monthly Labor Review.
    Energy Information Administration
      International Energy Annual.
    Internal Revenue Service
      Statistics of Income Bulletin. Quarterly. (Includes periodic reports on international income and taxes.)
    National Science Foundation
      International Science and Technology Data Update. Report. Annual.
      National Patterns of R&D Resources. Report. Annual.
      Science and Engineering Indicators. Report. Biennial.
      Science and Technology Pocket Data Book. Report. Annual.
      Survey of Direct U.S. Private Capital Investment in Research and Development Facilities in Japan. Report. (NSH 91-312.)
  Other
    American Automobile Manufacturers Association, Detroit MI.
      Motor Vehicle Facts and Figures. Annual
      World Motor Vehicle Data. Annual.
    Euromonitor London, England
      Consumer Asia 1995.
      Consumer China. 1994.
      Consumer Eastern Europe. 1994.
      Consumer Europe. Annual.
      Consumer International. 1995.
      Consumer Japan 1993.
      Consumer Latin America 1995.
      Consumer Southern Europe 1993.
      Consumer USA
      European Marketing Data and Statistics. Annual.
      International Marketing Data and Statistics. Annual.

International Statistics —Con.
  Other —Con.
    Food and Agriculture Organization of the United Nations, Rome, Italy
      Production Yearbook.
      Trade Yearbook.
      Yearbook of Fishery Statistics.
      Yearbook of Forest Products.
    Inter-American Development Bank, Washington, DC
      Annual Report.
      Economic and Social Progress in Latin America. Annual Survey.
    The International Institute for Strategic Studies, London, England
      The Military Balance. Annual.
    International Labour Office, Geneva, Switzerland
    Yearbook of Labour Statistics. 49th issue. 1989-1990.
    International Monetary Fund, Washington, DC
      International Financial Statistics. Monthly with annual yearbook.
    Jane's Information Group, Coulsdon, UK and Alexandria, VA
      Jane's Air-Launched Weapons. (Binder-4 monthly update.)
      Jane's All the World's Aircraft. Annual.
      Jane's Armour and Artillery. Annual.
      Jane's Avionics. Annual.
      Jane's Fighting Ships. Annual.
      Jane's Infantry Weapons. Annual.
      Jane's Merchant Ships. Annual.
      Jane's Military Communications. Annual.
      Jane's Military Logistics. Annual.
      Jane's Military Training Systems. Annual.
      Jane's NATO Handbook. Annual.
      Jane's Spaceflight Directory. Annual.
    Organization for Economic Cooperation and Development, Paris, France
      Annual Oil Market Report.
      Coal Information. Annual.
      Demographic Trends 1950-1990.
      Energy Balances of OECD Countries. Annual.
      Energy Prices and Taxes. Quarterly.
      Energy Statistics. Annual.
      Financial Market Trends. Triennial.
      Food Consumption Statistics. Irregular.
      Geographical Distribution of Financial Flows to Developing Countries.
      Historical Statistics of Foreign Trade Series A. Annual.
      Indicators of Industrial Activity. Quarterly.
      Industrial Structure Statistics. Annual.
      The Iron and Steel Industry. Annual.
      Labour Force Statistics. Annual.
      Latest Information on National Accounts of Developing Countries. Annual.

Labor —Con.
  U.S. Government —Con.
    Department of Labor

      Annual Report of the Secretary.

    Employment and Training Administration

      Employment and Training Report of the President. Annual.

      Unemployment Insurance Claims. Weekly.

    Interstate Commerce Commission

      Monthly Report of Class I Railroad Employees, by Group. (Statement No. 350.)

      Wage Statistics of Class I Railroads in the United States. Annual. (Statement No. 300.)

    Maritime Administration

      Employment Report of United States Flag Merchant Fleet Ocean-going Vessels 1,000 Gross Tons and Over. Annual. (Monthly and quarterly data available from source.)

      Seafaring Wage Rates. Biennial.

    National Science Foundation

      Characteristics of Doctoral Scientists and Engineers in the United States. Detailed Statistical Tables. Biennial.

      Characteristics of Recent Science and Engineering Graduates. Detailed Statistical Tables. Biennial.

      Immigrant Scientists and Engineers. Detailed Statistical Tables. Annual.

      U.S. Scientists and Engineers. Detailed Statistical Tables. Biennial.

      Woman and Minorities in Science and Engineering. Report. Biennial.

    Office of Personnel Management

      Demographic Profile of the Federal Workforce. Biennial. (Even years.)

      Occupations of Federal White-Collar and Blue-Collar Workers. Biennial. (Odd years.)

    Women's Bureau

      Handbook on Women Workers. Periodic.

  Other

    Aerospace Industries Association of America, Washington, DC

      Employment in the Aerospace Industry. Monthly.

      Survey of Aerospace Employment. Annual.

    The Bureau of National Affairs, Inc., Washington, DC

      Basic Patterns in Union Contracts. Annual.

      BNA's Employment Outlook. Quarterly.

      BNA's Job Absence and Turnover. Quarterly.

      Briefing Sessions on Employee Relations Workbook. Annual.

      Calendar of Negotiations. Annual.

Labor —Con.
  Other —Con.

      Directory of U.S. Labor Organizations. Annual.

      National Labor Relations Board Election Statistics. Annual.

      NLRB Representation and Decertification Elections Statistics. Quarterly.

      101 Key Statistics on Work and Family for the 1990's. (The BNA Special Report Series on Work and Family. Special Report No. 21, September 21, 1989.)

      PPF Survey (Personnel Policies Forum.) Three times a year.

Law Enforcement, Courts, and Prisons
  U.S. Government

    Administrative Office of the United States Courts

      Annual Report of the Director ... with, as issued, Reports of the Proceedings of the Judicial Conference of the United States. Includes statistics on Federal Courts.

      Calendar Year Reports on Authorized Wiretaps. (State and Federal.)

      Federal Court Management Statistics. Annual.

      Federal Judicial Workload Statistics. Quarterly.

    Bureau of the Census

      Census of Population. Decennial. (1990, most recent.)

    Bureau of Justice Statistics

      American Response to Crime: An Overview of Criminal Justice Systems. December 1983.

      Black Victims. April 1990.

      Capital Punishment. Annual.

      Census of Local Jails, 1988. February 1990.

      Census of State and Federal correctional facilities 1990, June 1992.

      Compendium of Federal justice statistics: 1989, May 1992.

      Correctional Populations in the United States. Annual.

      Crime and the Nation's households, 1990. July 1992.

      Criminal Victimization in the United States. Annual.

      Drug enforcement and treatment in prisons 1990, July 1992.

      Drug enforcement by police and sheriffs' departments, 1990. May 1992.

      Drugs and crime facts: 1994.

      Drugs and jail inmates. August 1991.

      Drunk driving: 1989 Survey of Inmates of Local Jails. September 1992.

      Elderly Victims. October 1992.

      Expenditure and Employment Data for the Criminal Justice System. Annual.

Recreation —Con.
  U.S. Government —Con.
    Bureau of Economic Analysis

      The National Income and Product
        Accounts of the United States,
      1929-82: Statistical Tables. 1986.
      Survey of Current Business. Monthly.

    Department of Transportation

      U.S. International Air Travel Statistics.
        Annual.

    Fish and Wildlife Service

      Federal Aid in Fish and Wildlife Restora-
        tion. Annual.
      National Survey of Fishing, Hunting, and
        Wildlife-Associated Recreation. Quin-
        quennial. (1991, most recent.)

    National Park Service

      Federal Recreation Fee Report. Annual.
      National Park Statistical Abstract. Annual.

  Other

    Association of Racing Commissioners Inter-
      national, Inc., Lexington, KY

      Statistical Reports on Greyhound Racing
        in the United States. Annual.
      Statistical Reports on Horse Racing in the
        United States. Annual.
      Statistical Reports on Jai Alai in the
        United States. Annual.

    National Golf Foundation, Jupiter, FL

      Americans' Attitudes Toward Golf in Their
        Community.
      An Operational Profile of Canadian Golf
        Facilities.
      Commercial Golf Ranges in the U.S.
      Golf Consumer Spending and Facility
        Fees.
      Golf Course Operations.
      Golf Facilities in Canada.
      Golf Facilities in the United States. 1994.
      Golf Participation in Canada.
      Golf Participation in the United States.
        1994.
      Golf Travel in the United States.
      Trends in the Golf Industry 1989-1993.
      Women in Golf.

    National Marine Manufacturers Association,
      Chicago, IL

      Boating. (A Statistical Report on
        America's Top Family Sport.) Annual.
      State Boat Registration. Annual.

    National Sporting Goods Association, Mt.
      Prospect, IL

      The Sporting Goods Market in 1993.
        Annual.
      Sports Participation in 1992. Annual.

Religious Bodies

  Other

    American Jewish Committee. New York, NY

      American Jewish Year Book.

Religious Bodies —Con.
  Other —Con.
    Glenmary Research Center, Atlanta, GA

      Churches and Church Membership in the
        United States 1990 by M. Bradley;
        N. Green, Jr.; D. Jones; M. Lynn; and
        L. McNeil. 1992.

    National Council of the Churches of Christ in
      the U.S.A., New York, NY

      Yearbook of American and Canadian
        Churches. Annual.

Research and Development —*see* Science
  Resources.

Retail and Wholesale Trade —*see also* Commodity Prices; Economic Indexes; *and* Service Establishments

  U.S. Government

    Board of Governors of the Federal Reserve
      System

      Annual Statistical Digest
      Federal Reserve Bulletin. Monthly.

    Bureau of the Census

      Combined Annual and Revised Monthly
        Retail Trade.
      Combined Annual and Revised Monthly
        Wholesale Trade.
      Census of Retail Trade. Quinquennial.
        (1992, most recent.)
      Census of Wholesale Trade. Quinquen-
        nial. (1992, most recent.)
      County Business Patterns. Annual.
      Merchant Wholesalers Measures of Value
        Produced, Capital Expenditures, Depre-
        ciable Assets, and Operating Expenses.
        (1987, most recent.)
      Monthly Retail Trade Report. Sales and
        Inventories.
      Monthly Wholesale Trade Report. Sales
        and Inventories.
      Selected Characteristics of Retail Trade-
        Measures of Value Produced, Capital
        Expenditures, Depreciable Assets, and
        Operating Expenses. (1987, most
        recent.)

    Bureau of Economic Analysis

      Business Statistics, 1963-91. 1992.
      Survey of Current Business. Monthly.

    Bureau of Labor Statistics

      Compensation and Working Conditions.
        Monthly
      CPI Detailed Report. Monthly.
      Employment and Earnings. Monthly, with
        annual supplement.
      Employment, Hours, and Earnings,
        United States, 1909-94. 1994. (Bulletin
        No. 2445.)
      Monthly Labor Review.
      Occupational Employment in Selected
        Nonmanufacturing Industries. 1990.
        (Bulletin No. 2348.)
      Occupational Injuries and Illnesses in the
        United States by Industry. Annual.

Retail and Wholesale Trade —Con.

U.S. Government —Con.

Producer Price Indexes. Monthly, with annual supplement.

Productivity Measures for Selected Industries and Government Services. Annual.

Technology and Labor in Three Service Industries: Utilities, Retail Trade, and Lodging. 1990. (Bulletin 2367.)

Other

Dealerscope Merchandising, Philadelphia, PA

Merchandising. Annual.

Lebhar-Friedman, Inc., New York, NY

Accounting Today. Biweekly.

Apparel Merchandising. Monthly.

Market Statistics, New York, NY

The Survey of Buying Power Data Service. Annual.

National Restaurant Association, Washington, DC

Foodservice Industry Forecast. Annual.

Foodservice Industry in Review. Annual.

Foodservice Market Measure. Monthly in Restaurants USA.

Foodservice Numbers: A Statistical Digest for the Foodservice Industry. 1992.

Restaurant Industry Operations Report. Annual.

Restaurants USA. Monthly.

Survey of Wage Rates for Hourly Employees. Biennial.

Compensation for Salaried Personnel in Foodservice. Triennial.

Roads —*see* Transportation.

Sales —*see* Retail and Wholesale Trade.

Savings Institutions —*see* Money.

Science Resources

U.S. Government

Bureau of the Census

Current Industrial Reports, MA37D. Annual.

Energy Research and Development Administration

The Nuclear Industry. Annual.

National Aeronautics and Space Administration

Annual Procurement Report.

The Civil Service Work Force.

Pocket Statistics. Annual.

National Science Foundation

Academic Research Equipment and Equipment needs in Selected Science/Engineering Fields: 1989-90.

Academic Research and Equipment Needs in the Physical Sciences: 1989.

Academic Science and Engineering: Graduate Enrollment and Support. Detailed Statistical Tables. Annual.

Science Resources —Con.

U.S. Government —Con.

Academic Science and Engineering: R&D Expenditures. Detailed Statistical Tables. Annual.

Blacks in Undergraduate Science and Engineering Education, April 1992. Special Report. (NSF 92-305.)

Characteristics of Doctoral Scientists and Engineers in the United States. Detailed Statistical Tables. Biennial.

Characteristics of Recent Grads.

Characteristics of Recent Scientists and Engineers. Detailed Statistical Tables. Biennial.

Characteristics of Science and Engineering Equipment in Academic Settings: 1989-90.

Federal R&D Funding by Budget Function. Report. Annual.

Federal Funds for Research and Development. Detailed Statistical Tables. Annual.

Federal Academic R&D Support Increased by 6 Percent Between FY's 1989 and 1990. (NSF 92-328.)

Federal Support to Universities, Colleges, and Nonprofit Institutions. Detailed Statistical Tables. Annual.

Immigrant Scientists and Engineers. Detailed Statistical Tables. Annual.

International Science and Technology Data Update. Report. Annual.

National Patterns of R&D Resources. Report. Annual.

Planned R&D Expenditures of Major U.S. firms: 1990-91. Special Report. (NSF 91-306.)

Research and Development Expenditures of State Government Agencies: Fiscal Years 1987 and 1988. Special Report. (NSF 90-309.)

Research and Development in Industry. Detailed Statistical Tables. Annual.

Science and Engineering Degrees. Detailed Statistical Tables. Annual.

Science and Engineering Degrees, by Race/Ethnicity of Recipients: 1977-90. Detailed Statistical Tables. Annual.

Science and Engineering Doctorates. Detailed Statistical Tables. Annual.

Science and Engineering Indicators. Report. Biennial.

Science and Engineering Personnel: A National Overview. Report. Biennial.

Science and Technology Pocket Data Book. Report. Annual.

Scientific and Engineering Research Facilities at Universities and Colleges. Report. Biennial.

Social Insurance and Human Services —Con.
  U.S. Government —Con.
        Finances of Selected Public Employee
        Retirement Systems. Quarterly. (GR
        Nos. 1-4.)

      Bureau of Labor Statistics

        Employee Benefits in Medium and Large
        Firms. Biennial.

        Employee Benefits in State and Local
        Governments. Biennial.

      Department of Health and Human Services
      Annual Report.

      Department of Labor

        Annual Report of the Secretary.

      Department of Veterans Affairs

        Annual Report of The Secretary of Veter-
        ans Affairs.

        Government Life Insurance Programs for
        Veterans and Members of the Services.
        Annual.

      Employment and Training Administration

        Unemployment Insurance Claims.
        Weekly.

      Family Support Administration

        Quarterly Public Assistance Statistics.
        Annual.

      Health Care Financing Administration

        Health Care Financing Program Statistics.
        Medicare and Medicaid data. Annual.

        Health Care Financing Review. Quarterly.

      Office of Personnel Management

        Civil Service Retirement and Disability
        Fund Annual Report. (P.L. 95-595.)

        Employment and Trends. Bimonthly.
        (Odd Months.)

        Statistical Abstract for the Federal
        Employee Benefit Programs. Annual.

      Rehabilitation Services Administration.
      Annual Report.

        Caseload Statistics of State Vocational
        Rehabilitation Agencies in Fiscal Year.
        Annual.

      Railroad Retirement Board, Chicago, IL

        Annual Report.

        Monthly Benefit Statistics.

        Statistical Supplement to the Annual
        Report.

      Social Security Administration

        Benefits and Beneficiaries Under Public
        Employee Retirement Systems, Fiscal
        Year 1991, Social Security Bulletin,
        Spring 1995.

        Income and Resources of the Population
        55 and over, 1992. 1994.

        Private Social Welfare Expenditures,
        1972-91, Social Security Bulletin, Fall
        1992. Social Security Bulletin, Spring
        1994.

        Public Social Welfare Expenditures,
        Fiscal Year 1991. Social Security
        Bulletin, Spring 1994.

Social Insurance and Human Services —Con.
  U.S. Government —Con.
        Social Security Beneficiaries by State and
        County. Annual.

        Social Security Bulletin. Quarterly with
        annual statistical supplement. (Data on
        OASDHI, Supplemental Security
        Income, Aid to Families with Dependent
        Children, Medicaid, Low Income Home
        Energy Assistance, Food Stamps, black
        lung benefits, and other programs.)

        Social Security Programs in the United
        States, Social Security Bulletin, Winter
        1993.

        SSA's 1982 New Beneficiary Survey:
        Compilation of Reports, 1993.

        State Assistance Programs for SSI
        Recipients. January 1994.

        Statistical Notes from the New Benefi-
        ciary Data System, Social Security
        Bulletin, Spring 1994.

        Supplemental Security Income, State and
        County Data. Annual.

        Workers' Compensation Coverage,
        Benefits, and Costs, 1990-1991, Social
        Security Bulletin, Fall 1993.

        Workers' Compensation: 1984-88
        Benchmark Revisions, Social Security
        Bulletin, Fall 1992.

  Other

    AAFRC Trust For Philanthropy, New York,
    NY

      Giving USA. Annual.

    American Red Cross, Washington, DC

      Annual Report.

    The Foundation Center, New York, NY

      The Foundation Grants Index, 1995.
      Edition 23. 1994.

      Guide to U.S. Foundations, Their Trust-
      ees, Officers, and Donors, Vol. 1, 1994
      edition.

    Girl Scouts of the U.S.A., New York, NY

      Annual Report.

    United Way of America, Alexandria, VA

      Annual Directory.

Soil Conservation —*see* Agriculture.

Sports —*see* Recreation.

State and Local Government —*see also* Federal
Government

  U.S. Government

    Bureau of the Census

      Census of Governments. Quinquennial.
      (1992, most recent.)

      City Employment. Annual. (GE No. 2.)

      City Government Finances. Annual.
      (GF No. 4.)

      County Government Employment. Annual.
      (GE No. 4.)

      County Government Finances. Annual.
      (GF No. 8.)

      Federal Expenditures by State. Annual.

State and Local Government —Con.

U.S. Government —Con.

Finances of Employee-Retirement Systems of State and Local Governments. Annual. (GF No. 2.)

Finances of Public School Systems. Annual. (GF No. 10.)

Finances of Selected Public Employee Retirement Systems. Quarterly. (GR Nos. 1-4.)

Government Finances. Annual. Covers Federal, State, and local governments. (GF No. 5.)

Local Government Employment in Major County Areas. Annual. (GE No. 3.)

Local Government Finances in Major County Areas. Annual. (GF No. 6.)

Public Employment. Annual. (GE No. 1.)

Quarterly Summary of Federal, State, and Local Tax Revenue. (GT Nos. 1-4.)

State Government Finances. Annual. (GF No. 3.)

State Government Tax Collections. Annual. (GF No. 1.)

Bureau of Labor Statistics

Employee Benefits in State and Local Governments. Biennial.

Employment and Earnings. Monthly.

Employment, Hours, and Earnings, United States, 1909-94. 1994. (Bulletin No. 2445.)

Occupational Employment in Transportation, Communications, Utilities, and Trade. 1990. (Bulletin No. 2348.)

Federal Highway Administration

Highway Statistics. Annual.

Office of Management and Budget

The Budget of the United States Government. Annual.

Social Security Administration

Benefits and Beneficiaries Under Public Employee Retirement Systems, Fiscal Year 1990, Social Security Bulletin, Fall 1993.

Other

Advisory Commission on Intergovernmental Relations, Washington, DC

1991: State Revenue Capacity and Effort.

Significant Features of Fiscal Federalism. Annual.

The Council of State Governments, Lexington, KY

The Book of the States. Biennial.

State Administrative Officials Classified by Function. Biennial.

International City Management Association, Washington, DC

Baseline Data Reports. Bimonthly.

Compensation: An Annual Report on Local Government Executive Salaries and Fringe Benefits.

State and Local Government —Con.

Other —Con.

Municipal Year Book. Annual.

Special Data Issues. Periodical.

National Governors' Association, Washington, DC

Directory of Governors of the American States, Commonwealths & Territories. Annual.

Governors' Staff Directory. Biannual.

National Governors' Association and National Association of State Budget Officers, Washington, DC

The Fiscal Survey of States. Biannual.

Tax Foundation, Washington, DC

Facts and Figures on Government Finance. Annual.

Stocks and Bonds —*see* Investments.

Stores —*see* Retail and Wholesale Trade *and* Service Establishments.

Tax Collections —*see* Federal Government; *and* State and Local Government.

Telephone and Telegraph Systems —*see* Communications.

Television —*see* Communications.

Trade —*see* Foreign Commerce; Retail and Wholesale Trade; *and* Service Establishments.

Transportation —*see also* Foreign Commerce

U.S. Government

Army, Corps of Engineers

Waterborne Commerce of the United States (in five parts). Annual.

Bureau of the Census

Census of Transportation, Communications and Utilities. Quinquennial. (1992, most recent.)

Commodity Flow Survey. 1993. (Forthcoming.)

Motor Freight Transportation and Warehousing Survey. Annual.

Truck Inventory and Use Survey. Quinquennial. (1992, most recent.)

Bureau of Economic Analysis

Business Statistics, 1963-91. 1992. (Discontinued.)

Survey of Current Business. Monthly.

Coast Guard

Annual Report of the Secretary of Transportation.

Marine Casualty Statistics. Annual.

Polluting Incidents In And Around U.S. Waters. Annual.

Department of State, Bureau of Consular Affairs

Summary of Passport Statistics. Annual.

Department of Transportation

National Transportation Statistics. Annual.

Transportation Safety Information Report. Quarterly.

U.S. International Air Travel Statistics. Annual.

Transportation —Con.
   U.S. Government —Con.
      Federal Aviation Administration
         Census of U.S. Civil Aircraft. Annual.
         FAA Air Traffic Activity. Annual, for fiscal years.
         FAA Aviation Forecasts. Annual.
         FAA Statistical Handbook of Aviation. Annual.
         General Aviation Activity and Avionics Survey. Annual.
         U.S. Civil Airman Statistics. Annual.
      Federal Aviation Administration and Research and Special Programs Administration
         Airport Activity Statistics of Certificated Route Air Carriers. Annual.
      Federal Highway Administration
         Drivers Licenses. Annual.
         Highway Statistics. Annual.
         Highway Statistics, Summary to 1985. (Published every 10 years.)
         Selected Highway Statistics and Charts. Annual.
      Interstate Commerce Commission
         Class I Freight Railroads Selected Earnings Data. Quarterly.
         Large Class I Household Goods Carriers Selected Earnings Data. Quarterly.
         Large Class I Motor Carriers of Passengers Selected Earnings Data. Quarterly.
         Large Class I Motor Carriers of Property Selected Earnings Data. Quarterly.
         Quarterly Report.
         Transport Statistics in the United States. Issued annually in two separate parts:
            Part 1: Railroads
            Part 2: Motor Carriers
      Maritime Administration
         Annual Report.
         Employment Report of United States Flag Merchant Fleet Ocean-going Vessels 1,000 Gross Tons and Over. Annual. (Monthly and quarterly data available from source.)
         Foreign Flag Merchant Ships Owned by U.S. Parent Companies. Annual.
         Maritime Manpower Report. Monthly.
         United States Oceanborne Foreign Trade Routes. Annual.
      Research and Special Programs Administration
         Air Carrier Financial Statistics. Quarterly.
         Air Carrier Industry Scheduled Service Traffic Statistics. Quarterly.
         Air Carrier Traffic Statistics. Monthly.
   Other
      Aerospace Industries Association of America, Washington, DC

Transportation —Con.
   Other —Con.
         Aerospace Facts and Figures. Annual.
         Commercial Helicopter Shipments. Quarterly.
      Air Transport Association of America, Washington, DC
         Air Transport Facts and Figures. Annual.
      American Automobile Manufacturers Association, Detroit, MI.
         Motor Vehicle Facts and Figures. Annual.
         World Motor Vehicle Data. Annual.
      American Bureau of Shipping, Paramus, NJ
         The Record. Annual with one supplement.
      American Public Transit Association, Washington, DC
         Transit Fact Book. Annual.
      Association of American Railroads, Washington, DC
         Analysis of Class I Railroads. Annual.
         Cars of Revenue Freight Loaded. Weekly with annual summary.
         Freight Commodity Statistics, Class I Railroads in the United States. Annual.
         Yearbook of Railroad Facts.
      ENO Transportation Foundation, Leesburg, VA
         Transportation in America. mid-year, annually with periodic supplements.
      General Aviation Manufacturers Association, Washington, DC
         Shipment Report. Quarterly and Annual.
         Statistical Databook. Annual.
      Lake Carriers' Association, Cleveland, OH
         Annual Report.
         Monthly Bulk Commodities Report.
      Lloyd's Register of Shipping, London, England
         Casualty Return. (Annual statistical summary of all merchant ships totally lost or reported broken up during year.)
         Merchant Shipbuilding Returns. (Quarterly Statistical summary of world shipbuilding.)
         World Fleet Statistics. (An end-year analysis of world merchant fleet.)
      National Air Carrier Association, Washington, DC
         Annual Report.
      Regional Airline Association, Washington, DC
         Statistical Reports.
      Shipbuilders Council of America, Arlington, VA
         Annual Report.
      Tanker Advisory Center, Inc., New York, NY
         Worldwide Tanker Casualty Returns. Annual.

Travel —*see* Recreation *and* Transportation.

Unemployment Insurance —*see* Labor; *and* Social Insurance.

Guide to State Statistical Abstracts

This bibliography includes the most recent statistical abstracts for States and Puerto Rico published since 1985 plus those that will be issued in late 1995 or early 1996. For some States, a near equivalent has been listed in substitution for, or in addition to, a statistical abstract. All sources contain statistical tables on a variety of subjects for the State as a whole, its component parts, or both. The page counts given for publications are approximate.

Alabama

University of Alabama, Center for Business and Economic Research, Box 870221, Tuscaloosa 35487
205-348-6191

*Economic Abstract of Alabama.*1994. 600 pp.

Alaska

Department of Commerce and Economic Development, Division of Economic Development, P.O. Box 110804, Juneau 99811
907-465-2017

The Alaska Economy Performance Report. 1994

Arizona

University of Arizona, Economic and Business Research, College of Business and Public Administration, McClelland Hall 204 Tucson, Arizona 85721-0001
520-621-2155 FAX 520-621-2150

Arizona Statistical Abstract: A 1993 Data Handbook. 616 pp.

Arizona Economic Indicators. 52 pp. Biennial.

Arizona's Economy. 20 pp. (Quarterly newsletter and data.)

Arkansas

University of Arkansas at Little Rock, Institute for Economic Advancement, Library 512, Little Rock 72204

Arkansas State and County Economic Data. 9 pp. (Revised annually.)

University of Arkansas at Little Rock, Institute for Economic Advancement, Library 508, Little Rock 72204
501-569-8530

Arkansas Statistical Abstract. 650 pp. (Revised biennially.)

California

Department of Finance, 915 L Street, 8th Floor, Sacramento 95814
916-322-2263

California Statistical Abstract, 1995.

Pacific Data Resources, P.O. Box 1922, Santa Barbara, CA 93116-1922
800-422-2546

California Almanac, 6th ed. Biennial. 275 pp.

Colorado

University of Colorado, Business Research Division, Campus Box 420, Boulder 80309
303-492-8227

Statistical Abstract of Colorado, 1987. 600 pp.

Connecticut

Connecticut Department of Economic Development, 865 Brook St., Rocky Hill 06067-3405
1-800-392-2122

Connecticut Market Data. 1995, 140 pp. (Diskette also available.)

Connecticut Town Profiles. 400 pp.

Delaware

Delaware Economic Development Office, P.O. Box 1401, Kings Highway, Dover 19903
302-739-4271

Delaware Statistical Overview, 1995. 141 pp.

University of Delaware Bureau of Economic Research, College of Business and Economics, Newark 19716-2730
302-831-8401

Delaware Economic Report 1994-95. 200 pp. Annual

District of Columbia

Office of Planning, Data Management Division, Presidential Bldg., Suite 500, 415 12th St., N.W. Washington 20004
202-727-6533

1990 Census, Population and Housing for the District of Columbia 72 pp.

1990 Census: Social, Economic and Housing Characteristics. (44 pp. for each of nine volumes).

Socio-Economic Indicators by Census Tract. 221 pp.

Socio-Economic Indicators of Change by Census Tract, 1980-1990. 146 pp.

Office of Policy and Evaluation, Executive Office of the Mayor, 1 Judiciary Square, Suite 1000, 441 4th St., N.W., Washington 20001
202-727-6979

Indices—A Statistical Index to DC Services, Dec. 1995. 370 pp.

Florida

University of Florida, Bureau of Economic and Business Research, Box 117145, Gainesville 32611-7145
904-392-0171

Florida Statistical Abstract, 1995. 29th ed. 800 pp. Also available on diskette.

1994 County Perspective. One profile for each county. Annual.

Georgia

University of Georgia, Selig Center for
Economic Growth, Terry College of Business,
Athens 30602-6269   706-542-4085

Georgia Statistical Abstract, 1994-95. 1994.
521 pp. 1996-1997 edition will be released
in December 1996.

University of Georgia, College of Agricultural
and Environmental Sciences,
Cooperative Extension Service, Athens, GA
30602-4356
706-542-8938 FAX 706-542-8934

The Georgia County Guide. 1995. 14th ed.
Annual. 200 pp.

Office of Planning and Budget,
254 Washington St., S.W.,
Atlanta 30334-8501   404-656-0911

Georgia Descriptions in Data. 1990-91.
249 pp.

Hawaii

Hawaii State Department of Business, and
Economic Development & Tourism,
Research and Economic Analysis Division,
Statistics Branch P.O. Box 2359,
Honolulu 96804. Inquiries 808-586-2481;
Copies 808-586-2424

*The State of Hawaii Data Book 1993-94: A
Statistical Abstract.* 27th ed. 1994. 571 pp.

Idaho

Department of Commerce,
700 West State St., Boise 83720
208-334-2470

County Profiles of Idaho, 1994

Idaho Community Profiles, 1995.

Idaho Facts, 1994.

Idaho Facts Data Book, 1995.

Profile of Rural Idaho 1993.

Illinois

University of Illinois, Bureau of Economic and
Business Research, 428 Commerce West,
1206 South 6th Street, Champaign 61820
217-333-2332

Illinois Statistical Abstract. 1994. 850 pages

Indiana

Indiana University, Indiana Business Research
Center, School of Business,
801 W. Michigan BS4015
Indianapolis 46202-5151
317-274-2204

Indiana Factbook, 1994-95. 413 pages.

Iowa

Public Interest Institute cø Iowa Wesleyan
College, 600 N. Jackson Street,
Mount Pleasant, IA 52641
319-385-3462

1995 Statistical Profile of Iowa.

Kansas

University of Kansas, Institute for Public Policy
and Business Research, 607 Blake Hall,
Lawrence 66045-2960 913-864-3701

Kansas Statistical Abstract, 1993-94. 29th
ed. 1995.

Kentucky

Kentucky Cabinet for Economic Development,
Division of Research, 500 Mcro Street,
Capital Plaza Tower, Frankfort 40601
502-564-4886

Kentucky Deskbook of Economic Statistics.
31st ed. 1995.

Louisiana

University of New Orleans, Division of Business
and Economic Research, New Orleans 70148
504-286-6248

Statistical Abstract of Louisiana. 9th ed.
1994.

Maine

Maine Department of Economic and Community Development, State House Station 59,
Augusta 04333
207-287-2656

Maine: A Statistical Summary. (Updated
periodically.)

Maryland

Department of Business and Economic
Development, 217 E. Redwood St.,
Baltimore 21202
Inquiries 410-333-6953

Maryland Statistical Abstract. 1993-94.
274 pp.

Massachusetts

Massachusetts Institute for Social and
Economic Research, 128 Thompson Hall,
University of Massachusetts at Amherst
01003
413-545-3460 FAX 413-545-3686

*Projected Total Population and Age
Distribution for 2000 and 2005: Massachusetts Cities and Towns.* Dec. 1994.

*Projection of the Population, Mass., Cities
and Towns, Years 2000-2010.*

Michigan

Wayne State University, Bureau of Business
Research, School of Business Administration,
Detroit 48202

Michigan Statistical Abstract. 20th ed. 1986-
87. 629 pp. (Out of print.)

Minnesota

Department of Trade and Economic Development, Business and Community Development
Division, 500 Metro Square Building,
St. Paul 55101
612-296-8283

*Compare Minnesota: An Economic and Sta-
tistical Factbook, 1994-95.* 165 pp.

*Economic Report to the Governor: State of
Minnesota, 1992.*148 pp.

Office of State Demographer, Minnesota
Planning, 300 Centennial Bldg.,
St. Paul 55155
612-296-2557

*Minnesota Population and Household Esti-
mates, 1993.* . Available diskette in Lotus,
dBase or ASCII formats. Summary analysis
available in printed form.

Mississippi

Mississippi State University, College of Business and Industry, Division of Research, Mississippi State 39762.
601-325-3817

Mississippi Statistical Abstract. 1994. 820 pp.

Missouri

University of Missouri, Business and Public Administration Research Center, Columbia 65211.
314-882-4805

Statistical Abstract for Missouri, 1993 Biennial. 280 pp.

Montana

Montana Department of Commerce, Census and Economic Information Center, 1424 9th Ave., Helena 59620
406-444-2896

Statistical Reports from the Montana County Database. (Separate county and State reports; available by subject section as well as complete reports by county and State, updated periodically.)

Nebraska

Department of Economic Development, Division of Research, Box 94666, Lincoln 68509.   402-471-3784

Nebraska Statistical Handbook. 1995-1996. 300+ pp.

Nevada

Department of Administration, Budget and Planning Division, Capitol Complex, Carson City 89710
702-687-4065

Nevada Statistical Abstract. 1994. Biennial. 225 pp.

New Hampshire

Office of State Planning, 2 1/2 Beacon St., Concord 03301
603-271-2155

Current Estimates and Trends in New Hampshire's Housing Supply. Update: 1993. 32 pp.

1992 Population Estimates for New Hampshire Cities and Towns, New Hampshire Population Projections for Cities and Towns 1990-2015.

New Jersey

New Jersey State Data Center, NJ Department of Labor, CN 388, Trenton 08625-0388
609-984-2593

New Jersey Source Book, 1993. 156 pp.

New Mexico

University of New Mexico, Bureau of Business and Economic Research, 1920 Lomas N.E. Albuquerque 87131-6021
505-277-2216   FAX 505-277-2773

County Profiles. *1994. 72 pp. The County Profiles are available from the Bureau of Business and Economic Research (hard copy format.) They can also be accessed on line by dialing 1-800-283-2638 and entering ONESTOP.*

New York

Nelson Rockefeller Institute of Government, 411 State Street, Albany 12203-1003
518-443-5522

New York State Statistical Yearbook, 1995. 20th ed. 590 pp.

North Carolina

Office of Governor Office of State Planning, 116 West Jones Street, Raleigh 27603-8003
919-733-4131

Statistical Abstract of North Carolina Counties, 1991. 6th edition. (No longer being published.)

North Dakota

University of North Dakota, Bureau of Business and Economic Research, Grand Forks 58202.
701-777-2637

The Statistical Abstract of North Dakota. 1988. 700 pp.

Ohio

Ohio Department of Development, Office of Strategic Research, P.O. Box 1001, Columbus 43216-1001
614-466-2115

Value-added Census Products. (Updated continuously.)

The Ohio State University, School of Public Policy and Management, 1775 College Road, Columbus 43210-1399
614-292-8696

Benchmark Ohio, 1991. Biennial. 300 pp.

Oklahoma

University of Oklahoma, Center for Economic and Management Research, 307 West Brooks Street, Room 4, Norman 73019
405-325-2931

Statistical Abstract of Oklahoma, 1994. Annual. 513 pp.

Oregon

Secretary of State, Room 136, State Capitol, Salem 97310

Oregon Blue Book. 1995-1996. Biennial. 441 pp. $12.

Pennsylvania

Pennsylvania State Data Center, Institute of State and Regional Affairs, Penn State Harrisburg, 777 West Harrisburg Pike, Middleton Pennsylvania 17057-4898.
717-948-6336

Pennsylvania Statistical Abstract, 1994. 31st ed. 1994. 249 pp.

Rhode Island

Department of Economic Development, 7 Jackson Walkway, Providence, RI 02903
401-277-2601 FAX 401-277-2102

Rhode Island 1990 Census of Population and Housing Summary. 1990.

The Rhode Island Economy. May 1994.

Monthly Economic Trends.

South Carolina

Budget and Control Board, Office of Research
and Statistical Services,
R. C. Dennis Building, Room 425,
Columbia, SC 29201.
803-734-3780

South Carolina Statistical Abstract: 1995.
430 pp.

South Dakota

University of South Dakota,
State Data Center, Vermillion 57069
605-677-5287

*Selected Social and Economic
Characteristics.* 550 pp.

1995 South Dakota Community Abstracts.
400 pp.

Tennessee

University of Tennessee, Center for Business
and Economic Research,
Knoxville 37996-4170
615-974-5441

Tennessee Statistical Abstract, 1994-95.
15th ed. 800 pp. Annual.

Texas

Dallas Morning News, Communications Center,
P.O. Box 655237,
Dallas 75265
214-977-8261

Texas Almanac, 1994-1995. 1993. 672 pp.
and Texas Almanac, 1996-97. 1995.
672 pp. (Available Oct. 1, 1995)

University of Texas, Bureau of Business
Research, Austin 78712.
512-471-5180

Texas Fact Book, 1989. 6th ed. 250 pp.

Utah

University of Utah, Bureau of Economic and
Business Research,
401 Kendall D. Garff Building,
Salt Lake City 84112.
801-581-6333

Statistical Abstract of Utah. 1993. (Triennial.)

Utah Foundation, 10 West 100 South,
Suite 323, Salt Lake City 84101-1544
801-364-1837

*Statistical Review of Government in
Utah.*1995. 160 pp.

Vermont

Department of Employment and Training,
Montpelier 05601
802-828-4202

Demographic and Economic Profiles. Annual

Virginia

University of Virginia, Weldon Cooper Center
for Public Service, 918 Emmet Street,
Suite 300, 2015 Ivy Road,
Charlottesville 22903
804-924-3921

Virginia Statistical Abstract, 1996-97.
Biennial. 950 pp.

Washington

Washington State Office of Financial
Management, Forecasting Division
P.O. Box 43113 Olympia,
WA 98504-3113
206-753-5617

Washington State Data Book, 1993.
Biennial. 306 pp.

Population Trends for Washington State.
Annual. 48 pages.

West Virginia

West Virginia Chamber of Commerce,
P.O. Box 2789, Charleston 25330
304-342-1115

*West Virginia: Economic-Statistical Profile,
1994.* Biennial. 750 pp.

West Virginia Research League, Inc.,
405 Capitol Street,Suite 414,
Charleston 25301
304-346-9451

Economic Indicators. 1995. 110 pp.

The 1994 Statistical Handbook. 94 pp.

Wisconsin

Wisconsin Legislative Reference Bureau,
P.O. Box 2037,
Madison 53701-2037
608-266-0341

1993-1994 Wisconsin Blue Book.
1,000 pp. Biennial.
1995-96 edition will be published
September/October 1995.

Wyoming

Department of Administration and Information,
Division of Economic Analysis,
327 E. Emerson Building,
Cheyenne 82002
307-777-7504

The Equality State Almanac 1994.
139 pp.

Puerto Rico

Planning Board, Area of Economic
and Social Planning, Bureau of Economic
Analysis and Bureau of Statistics,
Santurce 00940
809-722-2070

Monthly Economic Indicators.
December 1993.

*Historic Series of Employment,
Unemployment and Labor Force,
1992.*

Social Statistics Abstract. 1990.

*Socioeconomic Statistics of Puerto Rico.
1992.*

Guide to Foreign Statistical Abstracts

This bibliography presents recent statistical abstracts for Mexico, Russia, and member nations of the Organization for Economic Cooperation and Development. All sources contain statistical tables on a variety of subjects for the individual countries. Many of the following publications provide text in English as well as in the national language(s). For further information on these publications, contact the named statistical agency which is responsible for editing the publication.

Austria

Osterreichisches Statistisches Zentralamt, P.O. Box 9000, A-1033 Vienna

Statistisches Jahrbuch for die Republik Osterreich. Annual. 1994 587 pp. (In German.)

Australia

Australian Bureau of Statistics, Canberra

Yearbook Australia. Annual. 1995 836 pp. (In English.)

Belgium

Institut National de Statistique, 44 rue de Louvain, 1000 Brussels

Annuaire statistique de la Belgique. Annual. 1991 792 pp. (In French and Dutch.)

Canada

Statistics Canada, Ottawa, Ontario, KIA OT6

Canada Yearbook: A review of economic, social and political developments in Canada. 1994 707 pp. Irregular. (In English and French.)

Croatia

Republika Hrvatska, Republicki Zavod Za Statistiku

Statisticki ljetopis 1992 601 pp. (In English and Serbo-Croatian.)

Czech Republic

Czech Statistical Office, Sokolovska 142, 186 04 Praha 8

Statisticka Rocenka Ceske Rpubliky 1994 502 pp. (In English and Czech.)

Denmark

Danmarks Statistik, Postboks 2550 Sejrogade 11, DK 2100, Copenhagen

Statistical Yearbook. 1994. Annual. 559 pp. (In Danish with English translations of table headings.)

Finland

Central Statistical Office of Finland, Box 504 SF-00101 Helsinki

Statistical Yearbook of Finland. Annual. 1994 648 pp. (In English, Finnish, and Swedish.)

France

Institut National de la Statistique et des Etudes Economiques, Paris 18, Bld. Adolphe Pinard, 75675 Paris (Cedex 14)

Annuaire Statistique de la France. Annual. 1994 872 pp. (In French.)

Greece

National Statistical Office, 14-16 Lycourgou St., 101-66 Athens

Concise Statistical Yearbook 1992 251 pp. (In English.)

Statistical Yearbook of Greece. Annual. 1990-1991 567 pp. (plus 7 pages of diagrams). (In English and Greek.)

Iceland

Hagstofa Islands/Statistical Bureau, Hverfisgata 8-10, Reykjavik.

Statistical Abstract of Iceland. 1994. Irregular. 303 pp. (In English and Icelandic.)

Ireland

Central Statistics Office, Earlsfort Terrace, Dublin 2

Statistical Abstract. Annual. 1994 424 pp. (In English.)

Italy

ISTAT (Istituto Centrale di Statistica), Via Cesare Balbo 16, 00100 Rome

Annuario Statistico Italiano. Annual. 1993 565 pp. (In Italian.)

Japan

Statistics Bureau, Management & Coordination Agency, 19-1 Wakamatsucho, Shinjuku Tokyo 162

Japan Statistical Yearbook. Annual. 1994/95 873 pp. (In English and Japanese.)

Luxembourg

STATEC (Service Central de la Statistique et des Etudes), P.O. Box 304, L-2013, Luxembourg

Annuaire Statistique. Annual. 1994 529 pp. (In French.)

Mexico

Instituto Nacional de Estadistica Geografia e Informatica, Avda. Insurgentes Sur No. 795-PH Col. Napoles, Del. Benito Juarez 03810 Mexico, D.F.

Anuario estadistico de los Estados Unidos Mexicanos. Annual. 1993 610 pp. Also on disc. (In Spanish.)

Netherlands

Centraal Bureau voor de Statistiek. 428 Prinses Beatrixlaan P.O. Box 959, 2270 AZ Voorburg

Statistisch Yearbook 1994. 577 pp. (In Dutch.)

New Zealand

Department of Statistics, Wellington

New Zealand Official Yearbook. Annual. 1992 484 pp. (In English.)

Norway

Central Bureau of Statistics, Skippergate 15, P.B. 8131 Dep. N-Oslo 1

Statistical Yearbook. Annual. 1993 495 pp. (In English and Norwegian.)

Portugal

INE (Instituto Nacional de Estatistica), Avenida Antonio Jose de Almeida, P-1078 Lisbon Codex

Anuario Estatistico: de Portugal. 1993 358 pp. (In Portugese.)

Russia

State Committee of Statistics of Russia, Moscow

Russian Federation in the Year 1993. Statistical Yearbook. 1993 383 pp. (In Russian.)

Slovakia

Statistical Office of the Slovak Republic, Mileticova 3, 824 67 Bratislava

Statisticka Rocenka Slovensak 1991. 514 pp. (In English and Slovak)

Slovenia

Statistical Office of the Republic of Slovenia, Vozarski Pot 12, 61000 Ljubljana

Statisticni Letopis Republike Slovenije 1992. 530 pp. (In Slovenian.)

Spain

INE (Instituto Nacional de Estadistica), Paseo de la Castellana, 183, Madrid 16

Anuario Estadistico de Espana. Annual. 1993 902 pp. (In Spanish.)

Anuario Estadistico. 1988. (Edicion Manual.) 976 pp.

Sweden

Statistics Sweden, S-11581 Stockholm

Statistical Yearbook of Sweden. Annual. 1995 573 pp. (In English and Swedish.)

Switzerland

Bundesamt fur Statistik, Hallwylstrasse 15, CH-3003, Bern

Statistisches Jahrbuch der Schweiz. Annual. 1995 448 pp. (In French and German.)

Turkey

State Institute of Statistics, Prime Ministry, 114 Necatibey Caddesi, Bakanliklar, Yenisehir, Ankara

Statistical Yearbook of Turkey. Published on odd numbered years. 1993 716 pp. (In English and Turkish.)

Statistical Pocketbook of Turkey. Published on even numbered years. 1990 312 pp. (In English and Turkish.)

United Kingdom

Central Statistical Office, Great George Street, London SW1P 3AQ

Annual Abstract of Statistics. Annual. 1991 349 pp. (In English.)

West Germany

Statistische Bundesamt, Postfach 5528, 6200 Wiesbaden

Statistisches Jahrbuch fur die Bundesrepublic Deutschland. Annual. 1994 792 pp. (In German.)

Statistisches Jahrbuch fur das Ausland. 1994. 393 pp.

Metropolitan Areas: Concepts, Components, and Population

Statistics for metropolitan areas (MA's) shown in the *Statistical Abstract* represent areas designated by the U.S. Office of Management and Budget (OMB) as metropolitan statistical areas (MSA's), consolidated metropolitan statistical areas (CMSA's), and primary metropolitan statistical areas (PMSA's).

The general concept of an MA is that of a core area containing a large population nucleus, together with adjacent communities having a high degree of economic and social integration with that core. Currently defined MA's are based on application of 1990 standards (which appeared in the *Federal Register* on March 30, 1990) to 1990 decennial census data. These MA definitions were announced by OMB effective June 30, 1993.

In this appendix, tables A, B, and C present historical summary information for MA's and nonmetropolitan areas as defined on certain dates. Table E presents geographic components and 1992 populations for each MSA, CMSA, and PMSA. As of the June 1993 OMB announcement, there were 250 MSA's, and 18 CMSA's comprising 73 PMSA's in the United States. (In addition, there were 3 MSA's, 1 CMSA, and 3 PMSA's in Puerto Rico; MA's in Puerto Rico do not appear in these tables.) Table D presents definitions and data for New England county metropolitan areas (NECMA's), the county-based alternative metropolitan areas for the city- and town-based MSA's and CMSA's of the six New England States.

Standard definitions of metropolitan areas were first issued in 1949 by the then Bureau of the Budget (predecessor of OMB), under the designation "standard metropolitan area" (SMA). The term was changed to "standard metropolitan statistical area" (SMSA) in 1959, and to "metropolitan statistical area" (MSA) in 1983. The current collective term "metropolitan area" (MA) became effective in 1990. OMB has been responsible for the official metropolitan areas since they were first defined, except for the period 1977 to 1981, when they were the responsibility of the Office of Federal Statistical Policy and Standards, Department of Commerce.

The standards for defining metropolitan areas were modified in 1958, 1971, 1975, 1980, and 1990.

Defining MSA's, CMSA's, and PMSA's. The current standards provide that each MSA must include at least: (a) One city with 50,000 or more inhabitants, or (b) A Census Bureau-defined urbanized area (of at least 50,000 inhabitants) and a total metropolitan population of at least 100,000 (75,000 in New England).

Under the standards the county (or counties) that contains the largest city becomes the central county (counties), along with any adjacent counties that have at least 50 percent of their population in the urbanized area surrounding the largest city. Additional "outlying counties" are included in the MSA if they meet specified requirements of commuting to the central counties and other selected requirements of metropolitan character (such as population density and percent urban). In New England, the MSA's are defined in terms of cities and towns rather than counties.

An area that meets these requirements for recognition as an MSA and also has a population of one million or more may be recognized as a CMSA if: 1) separate component areas can be identified within the entire area by meeting statistical criteria specified in the standards, and 2) local opinion indicates there is support for the component areas. If recognized, the component areas are designated PMSA's, and the entire area becomes a CMSA. (PMSA's, like the CMSA's that contain them, are composed of individual or groups of counties outside New England, and cities and towns within New England.) If no PMSA's are recognized, the entire area is designated as an MSA.

The largest city in each MSA/CMSA is designated a "central city," and additional cities qualify if specified requirements are met concerning population size and commuting patterns. The title of each MSA consists of the names of up to three of its central cities and the name of each State into which the MSA extends. However, a central city with less than one-third the population of the area's largest city is not included in an MSA title unless local opinion desires its inclusion. Titles of PMSA's also typically are based on central city names but in certain cases consist of county names. Generally, titles of CMSA's are based on the names of their component PMSA's.

A 1990 census list, CPH-L-145, showing 1990 and 1980 populations for current MA's and their component counties or New England subcounty areas is available through the Statistical Information Office, Population Division, (301) 457-2422. A 1990 census Supplementary Report, 1990 CPH-S-1-1, *Metropolitan Areas as Defined by the Office of Management and Budget, June 30, 1993,* contains extensive population and housing statistics for the current MA's and is available from the U.S. Government Printing Office (GPO) (stock number 003-024-08738-3). Also available from the GPO is the Census Bureau's wall map for the 1993 MA's (stock number 003-024-08740-5).

Defining NECMA's. The OMB defines NECMA's as a county-based alternative for the city- and town-based New England MSA's and CMSA's. The NECMA for an MSA or CMSA includes: 1) the county containing the first-named city in that MSA/CMSA title (this county may include the first-named cities of other MSA's/CMSA's as well), and 2) each additional county having at least half its population in the MSA's/CMSA's whose first-named cities are in the previously identified county. NECMA's are not identified for individual PMSA's. There are twelve NECMA's, including one for the Boston-Worcester-Lawrence CMSA and one for the portion of the New York-Northern New Jersey-Long Island CMSA in Connecticut.

Central cities of a NECMA are those cities in the NECMA that qualify as central cities of an MSA or a CMSA. NECMA titles derive from names of central cities of MSA's/CMSA's.

Changes in MA definitions over time. Changes in the definitions of MA's since the 1950 census have consisted chiefly of (1) the recognition of new areas as they reached the minimum required city or area population;

and (2) the addition of counties or New England cities and towns to existing areas as new census data showed them to qualify. Also, former separate MA's have been merged with other areas, and occasionally territory has been transferred from one MA to another or from an MA to nonmetropolitan territory. The large majority of changes have taken place on the basis of decennial census data, although the MA standards specify the bases for intercensal updates.

Because of these changes in definition, users must be cautious in comparing MA data from different dates. For some purposes, comparisons of data for MA's as defined at given dates may be appropriate. To facilitate constant-area comparisons, data for earlier dates have been revised in tables where possible to reflect the MA boundaries of the more recent date.

In tables A, B, and C below, data are given for MA's as defined for specific dates, thereby indicating the extent of change in population and land area resulting from revisions in definitions.

Table A. Number, Population, and Land Area of MA's as Defined at Specified Dates From 1960 to 1993

[The differences in population shown here for each year within each column of the table result entirely from net expansion of metropolitan territory through changes in the MA definitions. The differences in population over time shown for each MA definition (on the successive lines of the table) result entirely from population changes within that territory, unaffected by changes in MA definitions. The changes in 1990 land area result entirely from net change in MA territory. All data include Alaska and Hawaii and exclude Puerto Rico. Subtraction of any line of the table from the line below will show the net effect of change in population and land area undergone by the MA's as the result of changes in definitions between the specified dates. Such changes may have occurred throughout the period, not on any single date, and may have included reductions in, as well as additions to, MA territory. Census population data through 1980 include corrections made since publication. The area data for the 1960, 1970, and 1980 census definitions of MA's differ from the data published in those censuses because of subsequent remeasurement of land areas and changes in inland water area occurring for the 1990 census]

| MA DEFINITION AS OF— | Number of MA's | POPULATION | | | | | Land area, 1990 (sq. mi.) |
		1960 (April 1)	1970 (April 1)	1980 (April 1)	1990 (April 1)	1992 (July 1)	
1960 census (Nov. 1960)	212	[1]112,885,139	130,982,661	140,793,427	155,088,626	(NA)	308,742
1964 (Aug. 31) [2]	217	115,876,343	134,700,911	145,503,863	160,500,956	(NA)	348,400
1968 (Jan. 31) [3]	230	118,413,604	137,976,252	149,811,057	165,707,672	(NA)	377,042
1970 census (Feb. 28, 1971). . .	243	[4]119,593,498	[5]139,479,806	151,662,221	167,896,646	(NA)	386,241
1974 (Apr. 30) [6]	265	[7]126,613,710	148,198,993	162,753,335	181,125,276	(NA)	490,551
1977 (Dec. 31) [8]	277	127,674,818	149,482,664	164,383,496	182,989,860	(NA)	509,841
1980 census (June 30, 1981) [9] .	318	131,318,714	153,693,767	169,430,623	188,759,597	(NA)	565,288
1983 (June 30)	[10]275	132,633,988	155,411,328	171,776,970	191,634,355	(NA)	559,752
1984 (June 30)	[10]277	132,707,748	155,519,340	171,955,900	191,903,497	(NA)	563,796
1985 (June 30)	[10]280	132,887,134	155,700,823	172,169,456	192,135,964	(NA)	569,816
1986 (June 30)	[10]281	132,977,580	155,805,452	172,304,016	192,314,367	(NA)	571,745
1987 (June 30) [11]	[10]281	133,003,445	155,832,688	172,334,547	192,345,395	(NA)	572,284
1988 (June 30) [12]	[10]282	133,088,400	155,937,275	172,454,948	192,476,951	(NA)	573,560
1989 (June 30) [12]	[10]283	133,233,777	156,084,580	172,601,873	192,618,846	(NA)	574,622
1990 census (June 30, 1990) [12] .	[10]284	133,275,412	156,137,337	172,679,870	192,725,741	(NA)	580,136
1992 (Dec. 31) [12]	[10]268	(NA)	(NA)	176,662,797	197,466,567	202,903,519	669,927
1993 (June 30) [12] [13]	[10]268	(NA)	(NA)	176,892,735	197,724,892	203,172,185	673,057

NA Not available.   [1] Corresponds to total MA population for 1960 published in 1960 census (112,885,178), corrected by subtracting population (39) erroneously included in Franklin County, Ohio (Columbus metropolitan area).   [2] MA's as defined for the 1963 economic censuses.   [3] MA's as defined for the 1967 economic censuses.   [4] Corresponds to total 1960 population for 1970 MA's published in 1970 census (119,594,754), corrected by subtracting 1,256 population from Lawrence-Haverhill metropolitan area; this represented an addition to the 1960 population of Andover town made subsequent to the original census tabulations, and therefore not reflected in State or national totals.   [5] Corresponds to total MA population for 1970 published in 1970 census (139,418,811), plus net corrections made subsequent to publication.   [6] MA's as defined for the 1972 economic censuses.   [7] Includes 1960 population (82,833) of Anchorage Census Division, as defined in 1970.   [8] MA's as defined for the 1977 economic censuses.   [9] MA's as defined for the 1982 economic censuses.   [10] MSA's and CMSA's.   [11] MA's as defined for the 1987 economic censuses.   [12] Data exclude the portion of Sullivan city in Crawford County, MO (1990 population 1,116) added to the St. Louis, MO-IL MSA by congressional action effective Dec. 22, 1987.   [13] MA's as defined for the 1992 economic censuses.

Source: U.S. Bureau of the Census, 1960-70, *U.S. Census of Population*, vol. 1; *1980 Census of Population*, vol. 1, chapters A and B and *Supplementary Report, Metropolitan Statistical Areas* (PC80-S1-18); *1990 Census of Population and Housing Data Paper Listing* (CPH-L-10 and CPH-L-118); *1990 Census of Population and Housing, Supplementary Reports, Metropolitan Areas as Defined by the Office of Management and Budget, June 30, 1993*, (1990 CPH-S-1-1); and *Population Paper Listing* (PPL-2).

Table B. Nonmetropolitan Population and Land Area as Defined at Specified Dates From 1960 to 1993

[See headnote for table A. Nonmetropolitan population and land area are equivalent to that portion of the total national population and land area not included within MA's at the dates specified]

METROPOLITAN AREA DEFINITION AS OF—	POPULATION					Land area, 1990 (sq. mi.)
	1960 (April 1)	1970 (April 1)	1980 (April 1)	1990 (April 1)	1992 (July 1)	
1960 census (Nov. 1960)	66,438,036	72,319,370	85,752,378	93,621,247	(NA)	3,231,027
1964 (Aug. 31).	63,446,832	68,601,120	81,041,942	88,208,917	(NA)	3,191,368
1968 (Jan. 31).	60,909,571	65,325,779	76,734,748	83,002,201	(NA)	3,162,726
1970 census (Feb. 28, 1971)	59,729,677	63,822,225	74,883,584	80,813,227	(NA)	3,153,527
1974 (Apr. 30).	52,709,465	55,103,038	63,792,470	67,584,597	(NA)	3,049,218
1977 (Dec. 31).	51,648,357	53,819,367	62,162,309	65,720,013	(NA)	3,029,928
1980 census (June 30, 1981)	48,004,461	49,608,264	57,115,182	59,950,276	(NA)	2,974,481
1983 (June 30).	46,689,187	47,890,703	54,768,835	57,075,518	(NA)	2,980,016
1984 (June 30).	46,615,427	47,782,691	54,589,905	56,806,376	(NA)	2,975,972
1985 (June 30).	46,436,041	47,601,208	54,376,349	56,573,909	(NA)	2,969,952
1986 (June 30).	46,345,595	47,496,579	54,241,789	56,395,506	(NA)	2,968,023
1987 (June 30).	46,319,730	47,469,343	54,211,258	56,364,478	(NA)	2,967,484
1988 (June 30).	46,234,775	47,364,756	54,090,857	56,232,922	(NA)	2,966,208
1989 (June 30).	46,089,398	47,217,451	53,943,932	56,091,027	(NA)	2,965,146
1990 census (June 30, 1990)	46,047,763	47,164,694	53,865,935	55,984,132	(NA)	2,959,632
1992 (Dec. 31).	(NA)	(NA)	49,883,008	51,243,306	52,174,017	2,866,411
1993 (June 30).	(NA)	(NA)	49,649,464	50,984,981	51,905,351	2,863,281

NA Not available.

Table C. Percent of Total U.S. Population and Percent of Land Area Inside MA's as Defined at Specified Dates From 1960 to 1993

[See headnote for table A]

METROPOLITAN AREA DEFINITION AS OF—	PERCENT OF POPULATION					Percent of land area, 1990
	1960 (April 1)	1970 (April 1)	1980 (April 1)	1990 (April 1)	1992 (July 1)	
1960 census (Nov. 1960)	63.0	64.4	62.1	62.4	(NA)	8.7
1964 (Aug. 31).	64.6	66.3	64.2	64.5	(NA)	9.8
1968 (Jan. 31).	66.0	67.9	66.1	66.6	(NA)	10.7
1970 census (Feb. 28, 1971)	66.7	68.6	66.9	67.5	(NA)	10.9
1974 (Apr. 30)	70.6	72.9	71.8	72.8	(NA)	13.9
1977 (Dec. 31)	71.2	73.5	72.6	73.6	(NA)	14.4
1980 census (June 30, 1981)	73.2	75.6	74.8	75.9	(NA)	16.0
1983 (June 30).	74.0	76.4	75.8	77.1	(NA)	15.8
1984 (June 30).	74.0	76.5	75.9	77.2	(NA)	15.9
1985 (June 30).	74.1	76.6	76.0	77.3	(NA)	16.1
1986 (June 30).	74.2	76.6	76.1	77.3	(NA)	16.2
1987 (June 30).	74.2	76.7	76.1	77.3	(NA)	16.2
1988 (June 30).	74.2	76.7	76.1	77.4	(NA)	16.2
1989 (June 30).	74.3	76.8	76.2	77.4	(NA)	16.2
1990 census (June 30, 1990)	74.3	76.8	76.2	77.5	(NA)	16.4
1992 (Dec. 31).	(NA)	(NA)	78.0	79.4	79.5	18.9
1993 (June 30).	(NA)	(NA)	78.1	79.5	79.7	19.0

NA Not available.

Source: U.S. Bureau of the Census, 1960-70, *U.S. Census of Population*, vol. 1; *1980 Census of Population*, vol. 1, chapters A and B and *Supplementary Report, Metropolitan Statistical Areas* (PC80-S1-18); *1990 Census of Population and Housing Data Paper Listing* (CPH-L-10 and CPH-L-118); *1990 Census of Population and Housing, Supplementary Reports, Metropolitan Areas as Defined by the Office of Management and Budget, June 30, 1993*, (1990 CPH-S-1-1); and *Population Paper Listing* (PPL-2).

Table D. New England County Metropolitan Areas (NECMA's)

[In thousands. As of July 1]

NECMA	Popu-lation, 1994	NECMA	Popu-lation, 1994	NECMA	Popu-lation, 1994
Bangor, ME	146	**Burlington, VT**	186	**New London-Norwich, CT** . . .	250
Penobscot County.	146	Chittenden County	138	New London County	250
		Franklin County	43	
Barnstable-Yarmouth, MA . . .	196	Grand Isle County.	6	**Pittsfield, MA**	136
Barnstable County.	196			Berkshire County	136
		Hartford, CT	1,117	
Boston-Worcester-Lawrence-		Hartford County	840	**Portland, ME**	248
Lowell-Brockton, MA-NH . . .	5,730	Middlesex County	147	Cumberland County.	248
Bristol County, MA	510	Tolland County	131	
Essex County, MA.	678			**Providence-Warwick-**	
Middlesex County, MA.	1,403	**Lewiston-Auburn, ME**	104	**Pawtucket, RI**	912
Norfolk County, MA	631	Androscoggin County.	104	Bristol County.	49
Plymouth County, MA	450			Kent County.	163
Suffolk County, MA	633	**New Haven-Bridgeport-**		Providence County	585
Worcester County, MA	717	**Stamford-Waterbury-**		Washington County	116
Hillsborough County, NH . . .	347	**Danbury, CT**	1,626	
Rockingham County, NH . . .	254	Fairfield County	830	**Springfield, MA**	596
Strafford County, NH	106	New Haven County	796	Hampden County	446
				Hampshire County	149

Source: U.S. Bureau of the Census, unpublished data.

Table E. Metropolitan Areas and Their Components as of June 30, 1993

[Population estimated as of **July 1, 1992**. All metropolitan areas are arranged alphabetically. For relationship of PMSA's to their CMSA's, see CMSA entry. At the time we went to press the 1994 population estimates for counties were available; however the 1994 estimates for cities and towns were not ready. Since New England CMSA's and MSA's are defined in terms of cities and towns, 1992 data are the latest figures for all CMSA's and MSA's. For 1994 estimates for CMSA's and MSA's outside New England, see table 43]

	Population, 1992 (1,000)
Abilene, TX MSA	**121**
Taylor County	121
Akron, OH PMSA	**669**
Portage County	146
Summit County	523
Albany, GA MSA	**115**
Dougherty County	98
Lee County	17
Albany-Schenectady-Troy, NY MSA	**872**
Albany County	293
Montgomery County	52
Rensselaer County	156
Saratoga County	188
Schenectady County	150
Schoharie County	32
Albuquerque, NM MSA	**616**
Bernalillo County	499
Sandoval County	69
Valencia County	48
Alexandria, LA MSA	**131**
Rapides Parish	131
Allentown-Bethlehem-Easton, PA MSA	**606**
Carbon County	58
Lehigh County	296
Northampton County	252
Altoona, PA MSA	**131**
Blair County	131
Amarillo, TX MSA	**192**
Potter County	100
Randall County	92
Anchorage, AK MSA	**246**
Anchorage Borough	246
Ann Arbor, MI PMSA	**505**
Lenawee County	94
Livingston County	123
Washtenaw County	288
Anniston, AL MSA	**116**
Calhoun County	116
Appleton-Oshkosh-Neenah, WI MSA	**324**
Calumet County	35
Outagamie County	144
Winnebago County	145
Asheville, NC MSA	**197**
Buncombe County	180
Madison County	17
Athens, GA MSA	**129**
Clarke County	88
Madison County	22
Oconee County	19
Atlanta, GA MSA	**3,143**
Barrow County	32
Bartow County	60
Carroll County	74
Cherokee County	102
Clayton County	189
Cobb County	479
Coweta County	60
De Kalb County	564
Douglas County	75
Fayette County	70
Forsyth County	50
Fulton County	666
Gwinnett County	392
Henry County	68
Newton County	45
Paulding County	47
Pickens County	15
Rockdale County	59
Spalding County	56
Walton County	41
Atlantic-Cape May, NJ PMSA	**326**
Atlantic County	229
Cape May County	97
Augusta-Aiken, GA-SC MSA	**444**
Columbia County, GA	73
McDuffie County, GA	21
Richmond County, GA	202
Aiken County, SC	129
Edgefield County, SC	19
Austin-San Marcos, TX MSA	**901**
Bastrop County	40
Caldwell County	27
Hays County	68
Travis County	613
Williamson County	153
Bakersfield, CA MSA	**588**
Kern County	588
Baltimore, MD PMSA	**2,434**
Anne Arundel County	441
Baltimore County	705
Carroll County	130
Harford County	195
Howard County	200
Queen Anne's County	35
Baltimore city	726
Bangor, ME MSA	**90**
Penobscot County (pt.)	87
Waldo County (pt.)	3
Barnstable-Yarmouth, MA MSA	**137**
Barnstable County (pt.)	137
Baton Rouge, LA MSA	**546**
Ascension Parish	61
East Baton Rouge Parish	392
Livingston Parish	74
West Baton Rouge Parish	20
Beaumont-Port Arthur, TX MSA	**370**
Hardin County	43
Jefferson County	243
Orange County	83
Bellingham, WA MSA	**138**
Whatcom County	138
Benton Harbor, MI MSA	**161**
Berrien County	161
Bergen-Passaic, NJ PMSA	**1,291**
Bergen County	835
Passaic County	456
Billings, MT MSA	**118**
Yellowstone County	118
Biloxi-Gulfport-Pascagoula, MS MSA	**324**
Hancock County	33
Harrison County	170
Jackson County	121
Binghamton, NY MSA	**266**
Broome County	212
Tioga County	53
Birmingham, AL MSA	**859**
Blount County	40
Jefferson County	658
St. Clair County	53
Shelby County	107
Bismarck, ND MSA	**86**
Burleigh County	62
Morton County	24
Bloomington, IN MSA	**111**
Monroe County	111
Bloomington-Normal, IL MSA	**133**
McLean County	133
Boise City, ID MSA	**320**
Ada County	223
Canyon County	96
Boston, MA-NH PMSA	**3,211**
Bristol County, MA (pt.)	94
Essex County, MA (pt.)	430
Middlesex County, MA (pt.)	1,118
Norfolk County, MA (pt.)	616
Plymouth County, MA (pt.)	224
Suffolk County, MA	639
Worcester County, MA (pt.)	82
Rockingham County, NH (pt.)	7
Boston-Worcester-Lawrence, MA-NH-ME-CT CMSA	**5,439**
Boston, MA-NH PMSA	3,211
Brockton, MA PMSA	236
Fitchburg-Leominster, MA PMSA	137
Lawrence, MA-NH PMSA	357
Lowell, MA-NH PMSA	283
Manchester, NH PMSA	175
Nashua, NH PMSA	171
New Bedford, MA PMSA	173
Portsmouth-Rochester, NH-ME PMSA	219
Worcester, MA-CT PMSA	477
Boulder-Longmont, CO PMSA	**238**
Boulder County	238
Brazoria, TX PMSA	**204**
Brazoria County	204
Bremerton, WA PMSA	**211**
Kitsap County	211

	Population, 1992 (1,000)		Population, 1992 (1,000)		Population, 1992 (1,000)
Bridgeport, CT PMSA	**443**	Lake County	541	**Cumberland, MD-WV MSA** . .	**102**
Fairfield County (pt.)	334	McHenry County	200	Allegany County, MD	75
New Haven County (pt.) . .	109	Will County	376	Mineral County, WV	27
Brockton, MA PMSA	**236**	**Chicago-Gary-Kenosha,**		**Dallas, TX PMSA**	**2,795**
Bristol County (pt.)	30	**IL-IN-WI CMSA**	**8,410**	Collin County	291
Norfolk County, (pt.)	5	Chicago, IL PMSA	7,561	Dallas County	1,913
Plymouth County, (pt.)	201	Gary, IN PMSA	617	Denton County	295
		Kankakee, IL PMSA	99	Ellis County	88
Brownsville-Harlingen, TX		Kenosha, WI PMSA	134	Henderson County	60
MSA	**279**			Hunt County	65
Cameron County	279	**Chico-Paradise, CA MSA** . . .	**188**	Kaufman County	54
		Butte County	188	Rockwall County	29
Bryan-College Station, TX				
MSA	**125**	**Cincinnati, OH-KY-IN**		**Dallas-Fort Worth, TX**	
Brazos County	125	**PMSA**	**1,560**	**CMSA**	**4,215**
		Brown County, OH	36	Dallas, TX PMSA	2,795
Buffalo-Niagara Falls, NY		Clermont County, OH	158	Fort Worth-Arlington, TX	
MSA	**1,194**	Hamilton County, OH	872	PMSA	1,419
Erie County	972	Warren County, OH	120		
Niagara County	222	Boone County, KY	63	**Danbury, CT PMSA**	**196**
				Fairfield County (pt.)	165
Burlington, VT MSA	**154**	Campbell County, KY	85	Litchfield County (pt.)	32
Chittenden County (pt.) . . .	127	Gallatin County, KY	6		
Franklin County (pt.)	25	Grant County, KY	17	**Danville, VA MSA**	**109**
Grand Isle County (pt.) . . .	3	Kenton County, KY	144	Pittsylvania County	56
		Pendleton County, KY	13	Danville city	54
Canton-Massillon, OH MSA .	**399**	Dearborn County, IN	41		
Carroll County	27	Ohio County, IN	5	**Davenport-Moline-**	
Stark County	372			**Rock Island, IA-IL MSA** . . .	**356**
		Cincinnati-Hamilton, OH-		Scott County, IA	155
Casper, WY MSA	**63**	**KY-IN CMSA**	**1,865**	Henry County, IL	51
Natrona County	63	Cincinnati, OH-KY-IN		Rock Island County, IL	150
		PMSA	1,560		
Cedar Rapids, IA MSA	**173**	Hamilton-Middletown, OH		**Dayton-Springfield, OH**	
Linn County	173	PMSA	305	**MSA**	**962**
				Clark County	148
Champaign-Urbana,		**Clarksville-Hopkinsville,**		Greene County	140
IL MSA	**175**	**TN-KY MSA**	**178**	Miami County	95
Champaign County	175	Montgomery County, TN . .	110	Montgomery County	579
		Christian County, KY	68		
Charleston, WV MSA	**253**			**Daytona Beach, FL MSA** . . .	**422**
Kanawha County	208	**Cleveland-Akron, OH**		Flagler County	34
Putnam County	45	**CMSA**	**2,890**	Volusia County	388
		Akron, OH PMSA	669		
Charleston-North Charleston,		Cleveland-Lorain-Elyria, OH		**Decatur, AL MSA**	**136**
SC MSA	**529**	PMSA	2,221	Lawrence County	32
Berkeley County	136			Morgan County	104
Charleston County	305	**Cleveland-Lorain-Elyria, OH**			
Dorchester County	88	**PMSA**	**2,221**	**Decatur, IL MSA**	**118**
		Ashtabula County	101	Macon County	118
Charlotte-Gastonia-Rock		Cuyahoga County	1,411		
Hill, NC-SC MSA	**1,212**	Geauga County	83	**Denver, CO PMSA**	**1,715**
Cabarrus County, NC	104	Lake County	220	Adams County	282
Gaston County, NC	179	Lorain County	277	Arapahoe County	421
Lincoln County, NC	53	Medina County	129	Denver County	484
Mecklenburg County, NC . .	538			Douglas County	73
Rowan County, NC	113	**Colorado Springs, CO MSA** .	**421**	Jefferson County	456
Union County, NC	89	El Paso County	421		
York County, SC	137			**Denver-Boulder-Greeley, CO**	
		Columbia, MO MSA	**117**	**CMSA**	**2,089**
Charlottesville, VA MSA . . .	**134**	Boone County	117	Boulder-Longmont, CO	
Albemarle County	68			PMSA	238
Fluvanna County	14	**Columbia, SC MSA**	**472**	Denver, CO PMSA	1,715
Greene County	12	Lexington County	178	Greeley, CO PMSA	136
Charlottesville city	41	Richland County	294		
				Des Moines, IA MSA	**406**
Chattanooga, TN-GA MSA . .	**431**	**Columbus, GA-AL MSA**	**270**	Dallas County	31
Hamilton County, TN	289	Chattahoochee County, GA.	16	Polk County	338
Marion County, TN	25	Harris County, GA.	18	Warren County	37
Catoosa County, GA	44	Muscogee County, GA. . . .	186		
Dade County, GA	13	Russell County, AL	49	**Detroit, MI PMSA**	**4,308**
Walker County, GA	59			Lapeer County	79
		Columbus, OH MSA	**1,394**	Macomb County	728
Cheyenne, WY MSA	**75**	Delaware County	71	Monroe County	136
Laramie County	75	Fairfield County	109	Oakland County	1,119
		Franklin County	992	St. Clair County	150
Chicago, IL PMSA	**7,561**	Licking County	132	Wayne County	2,096
Cook County	5,139	Madison County	39		
DeKalb County	80	Pickaway County	50	**Detroit-Ann Arbor-Flint, MI**	
Du Page County	816			**CMSA**	**5,246**
Grundy County	34	**Corpus Christi, TX MSA** . . .	**361**	Ann Arbor, MI PMSA	505
Kane County	334	Nueces County	301	Detroit, MI PMSA	4,308
Kendall County	41	San Patricio County	61	Flint, MI PMSA	434

	Popu- lation, **1992** (1,000)
Dothan, AL MSA	133
Dale County	50
Houston County	83
Dover, DE MSA	116
Kent County	116
Dubuque, IA MSA	87
Dubuque County	87
Duluth, MN-WI MSA	241
St. Louis County, MN	199
Douglas County, WI	42
Dutchess County, NY PMSA.	263
Dutchess County	263
Eau Claire, WI MSA	140
Chippewa County	53
Eau Claire County	87
El Paso, TX MSA.	628
El Paso County	628
Elkhart-Goshen, IN MSA	159
Elkhart County	159
Elmira, NY MSA	95
Chemung County	95
Enid, OK MSA.	56
Garfield County	56
Erie, PA MSA	280
Erie County	280
Eugene-Springfield, OR MSA	291
Lane County	291
Evansville-Henderson, IN-KY MSA	283
Posey County, IN	26
Vanderburgh County, IN.	166
Warrick County, IN	47
Henderson County, KY	44
Fargo-Moorhead, ND-MN MSA	158
Cass County, ND	107
Clay County, MN.	51
Fayetteville, NC MSA	277
Cumberland County	277
Fayetteville-Springdale-Rogers, AR MSA	226
Benton County	106
Washington County	120
Fitchburg-Leominster, MA PMSA	137
Middlesex County (pt.)	3
Worcester County (pt.)	134
Flint, MI PMSA	434
Genesee County	434
Florence, AL MSA	134
Colbert County	52
Lauderdale County	82
Florence, SC MSA.	119
Florence County	119
Fort Collins-Loveland, CO MSA	198
Larimer County	198
Fort Lauderdale, FL PMSA	1,301
Broward County	1,301
Fort Myers-Cape Coral, FL MSA	352
Lee County	352

	Popu- lation, **1992** (1,000)
Fort Pierce-Port St. Lucie, FL MSA.	265
Martin County	104
St. Lucie County	161
Fort Smith, AR-OK MSA	181
Crawford County, AR	44
Sebastian County, AR	101
Sequoyah County, OK	35
Fort Walton Beach, FL MSA	153
Okaloosa County	153
Fort Wayne, IN MSA	463
Adams County	31
Allen County	305
De Kalb County	37
Huntington County	36
Wells County	26
Whitley County	28
Fort Worth-Arlington, TX PMSA	1,419
Hood County	31
Johnson County	100
Parker County	68
Tarrant County	1,220
Fresno, CA MSA	805
Fresno County	706
Madera County	99
Gadsden, AL MSA.	100
Etowah County	100
Gainesville, FL MSA	189
Alachua County	189
Galveston-Texas City, TX PMSA.	228
Galveston County	228
Gary, IN PMSA	617
Lake County	482
Porter County	135
Glens Falls, NY MSA	121
Warren County	60
Washington County	60
Goldsboro, NC MSA	108
Wayne County	108
Grand Forks, ND-MN MSA	103
Grand Forks County, ND	71
Polk County, MN	32
Grand Rapids-Muskegon-Holland, MI MSA	964
Allegan County	93
Kent County	512
Muskegon County	162
Ottawa County	197
Great Falls, MT MSA	79
Cascade County	79
Greeley, CO PMSA	136
Weld County	136
Green Bay, WI MSA.	201
Brown County	201
Greensboro-Winston-Salem-High Point, NC MSA	1,078
Alamance County	111
Davidson County	130
Davie County	28
Forsyth County	271
Guilford County	358
Randolph County	110
Stokes County	39
Yadkin County	31

	Popu- lation, **1992** (1,000)
Greenville, NC MSA	112
Pitt County	112
Greenville-Spartanburg-Anderson, SC MSA	853
Anderson County	148
Cherokee County	46
Greenville County	328
Pickens County	99
Spartanburg County	233
Hagerstown, MD PMSA	125
Washington County	125
Hamilton-Middletown, OH PMSA	305
Butler County	305
Harrisburg-Lebanon-Carlisle, PA MSA	601
Cumberland County	201
Dauphin County	242
Lebanon County	116
Perry County	42
Hartford, CT MSA	1,156
Hartford County (pt.)	845
Litchfield County (pt.)	38
Middlesex County (pt.)	98
New London County (pt.)	18
Tolland County (pt.)	129
Windham County (pt.)	28
Hickory-Morganton, NC MSA	299
Alexander County	28
Burke County	77
Caldwell County	72
Catawba County	122
Honolulu, HI MSA	863
Honolulu County	863
Houma, LA MSA	187
Lafourche Parish	87
Terrebonne Parish	100
Houston, TX PMSA	3,530
Chambers County	21
Fort Bend County	256
Harris County	2,972
Liberty County	55
Montgomery County	204
Waller County	24
Houston-Galveston-Brazoria, TX CMSA	3,962
Brazoria, TX PMSA	204
Galveston-Texas City, TX PMSA	228
Houston, TX PMSA	3,530
Huntington-Ashland, WV-KY-OH MSA	315
Cabell County, WV	96
Wayne County, WV	42
Boyd County, KY	51
Carter County, KY	25
Greenup County, KY	37
Lawrence County, OH	63
Huntsville, AL MSA	308
Limestone County	57
Madison County	251
Indianapolis, IN MSA	1,424
Boone County	38
Hamilton County	121
Hancock County	48
Hendricks County	79
Johnson County	93
Madison County	132
Marion County	813
Morgan County	59
Shelby County	41

	Popu-lation, 1992 (1,000)
Iowa City, IA MSA	98
Johnson County	98
Jackson, MI MSA	152
Jackson County	152
Jackson, MS MSA	405
Hinds County	255
Madison County	58
Rankin County	92
Jackson, TN MSA	80
Madison County	80
Jacksonville, FL MSA	953
Clay County	114
Duval County	701
Nassau County	47
St. Johns County	90
Jacksonville, NC MSA	145
Onslow County	145
Jamestown, NY MSA	142
Chautauqua County	142
Janesville-Beloit, WI MSA	143
Rock County	143
Jersey City, NJ PMSA	555
Hudson County	555
Johnson City-Kingsport-Bristol, TN-VA MSA	445
Carter County, TN	52
Hawkins County, TN	46
Sullivan County, TN	147
Unicoi County, TN	17
Washington County, TN	95
Scott County, VA	23
Washington County, VA	47
Bristol city, VA	18
Johnstown, PA MSA	241
Cambria County	162
Somerset County	79
Joplin, MO MSA	138
Jasper County	92
Newton County	46
Kalamazoo-Battle Creek, MI MSA	436
Calhoun County	138
Kalamazoo County	226
Van Buren County	72
Kankakee, IL PMSA	99
Kankakee County	99
Kansas City, MO-KS MSA	1,617
Cass County, MO	67
Clay County, MO	159
Clinton County, MO	17
Jackson County, MO	634
Lafayette County, MO	31
Platte County, MO	62
Ray County, MO	22
Johnson County, KS	375
Leavenworth County, KS	67
Miami County, KS	24
Wyandotte County, KS	159
Kenosha, WI PMSA	134
Kenosha County	134
Killeen-Temple, TX MSA	255
Bell County	191
Coryell County	64
Knoxville, TN MSA	610
Anderson County	71
Blount County	90
Knox County	348
Loudon County	33

	Popu-lation, 1992 (1,000)
Sevier County	55
Union County	14
Kokomo, IN MSA	99
Howard County	82
Tipton County	16
La Crosse, WI-MN MSA	118
La Crosse County, WI	99
Houston County, MN	19
Lafayette, IN MSA	165
Clinton County	32
Tippecanoe County	133
Lafayette, LA MSA	353
Acadia Parish	56
Lafayette Parish	171
St. Landry Parish	81
St. Martin Parish	45
Lake Charles, LA MSA	172
Calcasieu Parish	172
Lakeland-Winter Haven, FL MSA	419
Polk County	419
Lancaster, PA MSA	434
Lancaster County	434
Lansing-East Lansing, MI MSA	436
Clinton County	59
Eaton County	95
Ingham County	282
Laredo, TX MSA	148
Webb County	148
Las Cruces, NM MSA	147
Dona Ana County	147
Las Vegas, NV-AZ MSA	971
Clark County, NV	846
Nye County, NV	20
Mohave County, AZ	106
Lawrence, KS MSA	85
Douglas County	85
Lawrence, MA-NH PMSA	357
Essex County, MA (pt.)	240
Rockingham County, NH (pt.)	117
Lawton, OK MSA	120
Comanche County	120
Lewiston-Auburn, ME MSA	92
Androscoggin County (pt.)	92
Lexington, KY MSA	420
Bourbon County	19
Clark County	30
Fayette County	233
Jessamine County	32
Madison County	60
Scott County	25
Woodford County	21
Lima, OH MSA	156
Allen County	110
Auglaize County	46
Lincoln, NE MSA	220
Lancaster County	220
Little Rock-North Little Rock, AR MSA	526
Faulkner County	64
Lonoke County	41
Pulaski County	353
Saline County	67

	Popu-lation, 1992 (1,000)
Longview-Marshall, TX MSA	197
Gregg County	108
Harrison County	57
Upshur County	32
Los Angeles-Long Beach, CA PMSA	9,054
Los Angeles County	9,054
Los Angeles-Riverside-Orange County, CA CMSA	15,048
Los Angeles-Long Beach, CA PMSA	9,054
Orange County, CA PMSA	2,485
Riverside-San Bernardino, CA PMSA	2,823
Ventura, CA PMSA	687
Louisville, KY-IN MSA	968
Bullitt County, KY	51
Jefferson County, KY	671
Oldham County, KY	36
Clark County, IN	90
Floyd County, IN	67
Harrison County, IN	31
Scott County, IN	22
Lowell, MA-NH PMSA	283
Middlesex County, MA (pt.)	273
Hillsborough County, NH (pt.)	10
Lubbock, TX MSA	225
Lubbock County	225
Lynchburg, VA MSA	198
Amherst County	29
Bedford County	48
Campbell County	49
Bedford city	6
Lynchburg city	66
Macon, GA MSA	299
Bibb County	152
Houston County	94
Jones County	21
Peach County	22
Twiggs County	10
Madison, WI MSA	380
Dane County	380
Manchester, NH PMSA	175
Hillsborough County (pt.)	133
Merrimack County (pt.)	13
Rockingham County (pt.)	28
Mansfield, OH MSA	175
Crawford County	48
Richland County	128
McAllen-Edinburg-Mission, TX MSA	421
Hidalgo County	421
Medford-Ashland, OR MSA	154
Jackson County	154
Melbourne-Titusville-Palm Bay, FL MSA	426
Brevard County	426
Memphis, TN-AR-MS MSA	1,034
Fayette County, TN	26
Shelby County, TN	845
Tipton County, TN	39
Crittenden County, AR	50
De Soto County, MS	74
Merced, CA MSA	189
Merced County	189
Miami, FL PMSA	2,008
Dade County	2,008

	Popu- lation, **1992** (1,000)		Popu- lation, **1992** (1,000)		Popu- lation, **1992** (1,000)
Miami-Fort Lauderdale, FL CMSA	**3,309**	**New Haven-Meriden, CT PMSA**	**527**	**Ocala, FL MSA**	**208**
Fort Lauderdale, FL PMSA	1,301	Middlesex County (pt.)	18	Marion County	208
Miami, FL PMSA	2,008	New Haven County (pt.)	509		
				Odessa-Midland, TX MSA	**234**
Middlesex-Somerset-Hunterdon, NJ PMSA	**1,047**	**New London-Norwich, CT-RI MSA**	**284**	Ector County	122
Hunterdon County	112	Middlesex County, CT (pt.)	10	Midland County	111
Middlesex County	684	New London County, CT (pt.)	226		
Somerset County	250	Windham County, CT (pt.)	19	**Oklahoma City, OK MSA**	**984**
		Washington County, RI (pt.)	29	Canadian County	77
Milwaukee-Racine, WI CMSA	**1,629**			Cleveland County	181
Milwaukee-Waukesha, WI PMSA	1,450	**New Orleans, LA MSA**	**1,303**	Logan County	29
Racine, WI PMSA	180	Jefferson Parish	458	McClain County	23
		Orleans Parish	490	Oklahoma County	613
Milwaukee-Waukesha, WI PMSA	**1,450**	Plaquemines Parish	26	Pottawatomie County	59
Milwaukee County	952	St. Bernard Parish	67		
Ozaukee County	76	St. Charles Parish	44	**Olympia, WA PMSA**	**177**
Washington County	102	St. James Parish	21	Thurston County	177
Waukesha County	320	St. John the Baptist Parish	41		
		St. Tammany Parish	156	**Omaha, NE-IA MSA**	**656**
Minneapolis-St. Paul, MN-WI MSA	**2,618**			Cass County, NE	22
Anoka County, MN	259	**New York, NY PMSA**	**8,552**	Douglas County, NE	426
Carver County, MN	52	Bronx County	1,195	Sarpy County, NE	107
Chisago County, MN	32	Kings County	2,286	Washington County, NE	17
Dakota County, MN	296	New York County	1,489	Pottawattamie County, IA	84
Hennepin County, MN	1,041	Putnam County	87		
Isanti County, MN	27	Queens County	1,951	**Orange County, CA PMSA**	**2,485**
Ramsey County, MN	486	Richmond County	391	Orange County	2,485
Scott County, MN	62	Rockland County	271		
Sherburne County, MN	46	Westchester County	882	**Orlando, FL MSA**	**1,305**
Washington County, MN	158			Lake County	161
Wright County, MN	72	**New York-Northern New Jersey-Long Island, NY-NJ-CT-PA CMSA**	**19,670**	Orange County	715
Pierce County, WI	33	Bergen-Passaic, NJ PMSA	1,291	Osceola County	119
St. Croix County, WI	52	Bridgeport, CT PMSA	443	Seminole County	310
		Danbury, CT PMSA	196		
Mobile, AL MSA	**496**	Dutchess County, NY PMSA	263	**Owensboro, KY MSA**	**89**
Baldwin County	106	Jersey City, NJ PMSA	555	Daviess County	89
Mobile County	389	Middlesex-Somerset-Hunterdon, NJ PMSA	1,047		
		Monmouth-Ocean, NJ PMSA	1,004	**Panama City, FL MSA**	**134**
Modesto, CA MSA	**395**	Nassau-Suffolk, NY PMSA	2,640	Bay County	134
Stanislaus County	395	New Haven-Meriden, CT PMSA	527		
		New York, NY PMSA	8,552	**Parkersburg-Marietta, WV-OH MSA**	**150**
Monmouth-Ocean, NJ PMSA	**1,004**	Newark, NJ PMSA	1,923	Wood County, WV	87
Monmouth County	566	Newburgh, NY-PA PMSA	348	Washington County, OH	63
Ocean County	438	Stamford-Norwalk, CT PMSA	331		
		Trenton, NJ PMSA	328	**Pensacola, FL MSA**	**361**
Monroe, LA MSA	**145**	Waterbury, CT PMSA	222	Escambia County	271
Ouachita Parish	145			Santa Rosa County	90
		Newark, NJ PMSA	**1,923**		
Montgomery, AL MSA	**304**	Essex County	773	**Peoria-Pekin, IL MSA**	**343**
Autauga County	36	Morris County	428	Peoria County	184
Elmore County	53	Sussex County	135	Tazewell County	126
Montgomery County	215	Union County	493	Woodford County	33
		Warren County	94		
Muncie, IN MSA	**120**			**Philadelphia, PA-NJ PMSA**	**4,944**
Delaware County	120	**Newburgh, NY-PA PMSA**	**348**	Bucks County, PA	556
		Orange County, NY	316	Chester County, PA	388
Myrtle Beach, SC MSA	**152**	Pike County, PA	33	Delaware County, PA	550
Horry County	152			Montgomery County, PA	690
		Norfolk-Virginia Beach-Newport News, VA-NC MSA	**1,497**	Philadelphia County, PA	1,553
Naples, FL MSA	**165**	Gloucester County, VA	31	Burlington County, NJ	398
Collier County	165	Isle of Wight County, VA	26	Camden County, NJ	508
		James City County, VA	37	Gloucester County, NJ	237
Nashua, NH PMSA	**171**	Mathews County, VA	8	Salem County, NJ	65
Hillsborough County (pt.)	171	York County, VA	47		
		Chesapeake city, VA	166	**Philadelphia-Wilmington-Atlantic City, PA-NJ-DE-MD CMSA**	**5,939**
Nashville, TN MSA	**1,023**	Hampton city, VA	137	Atlantic-Cape May, NJ PMSA	326
Cheatham County	29	Newport News city, VA	177	Philadelphia, PA-NJ PMSA	4,944
Davidson County	518	Norfolk city, VA	254	Vineland-Millville-Bridgeton, NJ PMSA	138
Dickson County	37	Poquoson city, VA	11	Wilmington-Newark, DE-MD PMSA	530
Robertson County	44	Portsmouth city, VA	104		
Rutherford County	129	Suffolk city, VA	53	**Phoenix-Mesa, AZ MSA**	**2,330**
Sumner County	108	Virginia Beach city, VA	417	Maricopa County	2,210
Williamson County	89	Williamsburg city, VA	12	Pinal County	121
Wilson County	71	Currituck County, NC	15		
				Pine Bluff, AR MSA	**85**
Nassau-Suffolk, NY PMSA	**2,640**	**Oakland, CA PMSA**	**2,148**	Jefferson County	85
Nassau County	1,302	Alameda County	1,308		
Suffolk County	1,338	Contra Costa County	841	**Pittsburgh, PA MSA**	**2,406**
				Allegheny County	1,334
New Bedford, MA PMSA	**173**			Beaver County	189
Bristol County (pt.)	159			Butler County	157
Plymouth County (pt.)	14			

	Population, 1992 (1,000)
Fayette County	146
Washington County	206
Westmoreland County	374
Pittsfield, MA MSA	**87**
Berkshire County (pt.)	87
Portland, ME MSA	**222**
Cumberland County (pt.)	202
York County (pt.)	20
Portland-Salem, OR-WA CMSA	**1,897**
Portland-Vancouver, OR-WA PMSA	1,605
Salem, OR PMSA	292
Portland-Vancouver, OR-WA PMSA	**1,605**
Clackamas County, OR	297
Columbia County, OR	39
Multnomah County, OR	601
Washington County, OR	338
Yamhill County, OR	69
Clark County, WA	261
Portsmouth-Rochester, NH-ME PMSA	**219**
Rockingham County, NH (pt.)	84
Strafford County, NH (pt.)	98
York County, ME (pt.)	37
Providence-Fall River-Warwick, RI-MA MSA	**1,131**
Bristol County, RI	49
Kent County, RI	162
Newport County, RI (pt.)	23
Providence County, RI	591
Washington County, RI (pt.)	82
Bristol County, MA (pt.)	224
Provo-Orem, UT MSA	**275**
Utah County	275
Pueblo, CO MSA	**124**
Pueblo County	124
Punta Gorda, FL MSA	**119**
Charlotte County	119
Racine, WI PMSA	**180**
Racine County	180
Raleigh-Durham-Chapel Hill, NC MSA	**909**
Chatham County	40
Durham County	188
Franklin County	38
Johnston County	86
Orange County	100
Wake County	457
Rapid City, SD MSA	**85**
Pennington County	85
Reading, PA MSA	**343**
Berks County	343
Redding, CA MSA	**158**
Shasta County	158
Reno, NV MSA	**269**
Washoe County	269
Richland-Kennewick-Pasco, WA MSA	**161**
Benton County	120
Franklin County	41
Richmond-Petersburg, VA MSA	**896**
Charles City County	6
Chesterfield County	225

	Population, 1992 (1,000)
Dinwiddie County	20
Goochland County	15
Hanover County	68
Henrico County	223
New Kent County	11
Powhatan County	17
Prince George County	28
Colonial Heights city	16
Hopewell city	24
Petersburg city	40
Richmond city	202
Riverside-San Bernardino, CA PMSA	**2,823**
Riverside County	1,288
San Bernardino County	1,534
Roanoke, VA MSA	**226**
Botetourt County	26
Roanoke County	80
Roanoke city	97
Salem city	24
Rochester, MN MSA	**110**
Olmsted County	110
Rochester, NY MSA	**1,081**
Genesee County	61
Livingston County	63
Monroe County	724
Ontario County	98
Orleans County	44
Wayne County	91
Rockford, IL MSA	**340**
Boone County	33
Ogle County	47
Winnebago County	259
Rocky Mount, NC MSA	**137**
Edgecombe County	56
Nash County	81
Sacramento, CA PMSA	**1,419**
El Dorado County	138
Placer County	187
Sacramento County	1,093
Sacramento-Yolo, CA CMSA	**1,563**
Sacramento, CA PMSA	1,419
Yolo, CA PMSA	145
Saginaw-Bay City-Midland, MI MSA	**403**
Bay County	112
Midland County	78
Saginaw County	212
St. Cloud, MN MSA	**153**
Benton County	31
Stearns County	121
St. Joseph, MO MSA	**98**
Andrew County	15
Buchanan County	83
St. Louis, MO-IL MSA	**2,519**
Franklin County, MO	84
Jefferson County, MO	178
Lincoln County, MO	30
St. Charles County, MO	226
St. Louis County, MO	1,001
Warren County, MO	21
St. Louis city, MO	384
Clinton County, IL	34
Jersey County, IL	21
Madison County, IL	253
Monroe County, IL	23
St. Clair County, IL	263
Salem, OR PMSA	**292**
Marion County	239
Polk County	53

	Population, 1992 (1,000)
Salinas, CA MSA	**368**
Monterey County	368
Salt Lake City-Ogden, UT MSA	**1,128**
Davis County	200
Salt Lake County	764
Weber County	165
San Angelo, TX MSA	**99**
Tom Green County	99
San Antonio, TX MSA	**1,379**
Bexar County	1,233
Comal County	55
Guadalupe County	67
Wilson County	24
San Diego, CA MSA	**2,601**
San Diego County	2,601
San Francisco, CA PMSA	**1,626**
Marin County	234
San Francisco County	729
San Mateo County	664
San Francisco-Oakland-San Jose, CA CMSA	**6,410**
Oakland, CA PMSA	2,148
San Francisco, CA PMSA	1,626
San Jose, CA PMSA	1,529
Santa Cruz-Watsonville, CA PMSA	231
Santa Rosa, CA PMSA	401
Vallejo-Fairfield-Napa, CA PMSA	475
San Jose, CA PMSA	**1,529**
Santa Clara County	1,529
San Luis Obispo-Atascadero-Paso Robles, CA MSA	**221**
San Luis Obispo County	221
Santa Barbara-Santa Maria-Lompoc, CA MSA	**376**
Santa Barbara County	376
Santa Cruz-Watsonville, CA PMSA	**231**
Santa Cruz County	231
Santa Fe, NM MSA	**123**
Los Alamos County	18
Santa Fe County	105
Santa Rosa, CA PMSA	**401**
Sonoma County	401
Sarasota-Bradenton, FL MSA	**499**
Manatee County	217
Sarasota County	282
Savannah, GA MSA	**267**
Bryan County	18
Chatham County	222
Effingham County	27
Scranton-Wilkes-Barre-Hazleton, PA MSA	**639**
Columbia County	63
Lackawanna County	217
Luzerne County	329
Wyoming County	29
Seattle-Bellevue-Everett, WA PMSA	**2,124**
Island County	65
King County	1,558
Snohomish County	501
Seattle-Tacoma-Bremerton, WA CMSA	**3,131**
Bremerton, WA PMSA	211
Olympia, WA PMSA	177

	Popu-lation, **1992** (1,000)
Seattle-Bellevue-Everett, WA	
PMSA	2,124
Tacoma, WA PMSA	620
Sharon, PA MSA	**122**
Mercer County	122
Sheboygan, WI MSA	**105**
Sheboygan County	105
Sherman-Denison, TX	
MSA	**95**
Grayson County	95
Shreveport-Bossier City, LA	
MSA	**374**
Bossier Parish	86
Caddo Parish	246
Webster Parish	41
Sioux City, IA-NE MSA	**117**
Woodbury County, IA.	100
Dakota County, NE	17
Sioux Falls, SD MSA	**146**
Lincoln County	16
Minnehaha County	130
South Bend, IN MSA	**251**
St. Joseph County.	251
Spokane, WA MSA	**381**
Spokane County	381
Springfield, IL MSA.	**193**
Menard County.	11
Sangamon County	181
Springfield, MA MSA.	**584**
Franklin County (pt.)	3
Hampden County (pt.) . . .	441
Hampshire County (pt.) . . .	140
Springfield, MO MSA.	**276**
Christian County	36
Greene County.	215
Webster County	24
Stamford-Norwalk, CT PMSA	**331**
Fairfield County (pt.)	331
State College, PA MSA	**127**
Centre County	127
Steubenville-Weirton, OH-	
WV MSA	**142**
Jefferson County, OH	80
Brooke County, WV.	27
Hancock County, WV.	35
Stockton-Lodi, CA MSA. . . .	**504**
San Joaquin County	504
Sumter, SC MSA.	**105**
Sumter County	105
Syracuse, NY MSA	**752**
Cayuga County.	83
Madison County	71
Onondaga County	474
Oswego County	125
Tacoma, WA PMSA	**620**
Pierce County.	620
Tallahassee, FL MSA.	**245**
Gadsden County	42
Leon County.	203
Tampa-St. Petersburg-	
Clearwater, FL MSA.	**2,107**
Hernando County	110
Hillsborough County	859
Pasco County.	284
Pinellas County.	855

	Popu-lation, **1992** (1,000)
Terre Haute, IN MSA	**149**
Clay County	25
Vermillion County	17
Vigo County	107
Texarkana, TX-Texarkana,	
AR MSA	**121**
Bowie County, TX	82
Miller County, AR	39
Toledo, OH MSA	**615**
Fulton County.	40
Lucas County.	462
Wood County	114
Topeka, KS MSA	**163**
Shawnee County	163
Trenton, NJ PMSA	**328**
Mercer County	328
Tucson, AZ MSA	**690**
Pima County	690
Tulsa, OK MSA	**732**
Creek County	62
Osage County	42
Rogers County	58
Tulsa County	520
Wagoner County	50
Tuscaloosa, AL MSA	**154**
Tuscaloosa County	154
Tyler, TX MSA	**154**
Smith County	154
Utica-Rome, NY MSA	**318**
Herkimer County	66
Oneida County	252
Vallejo-Fairfield-Napa, CA	
PMSA	**475**
Napa County	113
Solano County	362
Ventura, CA PMSA	**687**
Ventura County.	687
Victoria, TX MSA.	**77**
Victoria County	77
Vineland-Millville-Bridgeton,	
NJ PMSA	**138**
Cumberland County	138
Visalia-Tulare-Porterville,	
CA MSA	**331**
Tulare County.	331
Waco, TX MSA	**192**
McLennan County.	192
Washington, DC-MD-VA-WV	
PMSA	**4,360**
District of Columbia.	585
Calvert County, MD.	57
Charles County, MD	106
Frederick County, MD . . .	160
Montgomery County, MD . .	781
Prince George's County,	
MD	751
Arlington County, VA	172
Clarke County, VA.	12
Culpeper County, VA	29
Fairfax County, VA	857
Fauquier County, VA	51
King George County, VA . .	14
Loudoun County, VA	94
Prince William County,	
VA.	230
Spotsylvania County, VA . .	61
Stafford County, VA	71
Warren County, VA	28

	Popu-lation, **1992** (1,000)
Alexandria city, VA	113
Fairfax city, VA	21
Falls Church city, VA . . .	9
Fredericksburg city, VA . . .	21
Manassas city, VA.	30
Manassas Park city, VA . . .	7
Berkeley County, WV	63
Jefferson County, WV	38
Washington-Baltimore, DC-MD-	
VA-WV CMSA	**6,920**
Baltimore, MD PMSA	2,434
Hagerstown, MD PMSA . . .	125
Washington, DC-MD-VA-WV	
PMSA	4,360
Waterbury, CT PMSA.	**222**
Litchfield County (pt.)	39
New Haven County (pt.) . .	183
Waterloo-Cedar Falls, IA	
MSA.	**125**
Black Hawk County.	125
Wausau, WI MSA	**118**
Marathon County	118
West Palm Beach-Boca	
Raton, FL MSA	**901**
Palm Beach County	901
Wheeling, WV-OH MSA	**158**
Marshall County, WV . . .	37
Ohio County, WV	50
Belmont County, OH	71
Wichita, KS MSA.	**501**
Butler County	54
Harvey County	31
Sedgwick County	417
Wichita Falls, TX MSA.	**128**
Archer County	8
Wichita County	120
Williamsport, PA MSA	**120**
Lycoming County	120
Wilmington, NC MSA	**182**
Brunswick County	54
New Hanover County	128
Wilmington-Newark, DE-MD	
PMSA	**530**
New Castle County, DE . . .	455
Cecil County, MD	75
Worcester, MA-CT PMSA. . .	**477**
Hampden County, MA (pt.). .	2
Worcester County, MA (pt.). .	466
Windham County, CT (pt.) . .	9
Yakima, WA MSA	**198**
Yakima County	198
Yolo, CA PMSA.	**145**
Yolo County	145
York, PA MSA	**350**
York County	350
Youngstown-Warren, OH	
MSA	**606**
Columbiana County	110
Mahoning County	266
Trumbull County	230
Yuba City, CA MSA	**130**
Sutter County	69
Yuba County	61
Yuma, AZ MSA	**118**
Yuma County	118

Limitations of the Data

Introduction.—The data presented in this *Statistical Abstract* came from many sources. The sources include not only Federal statistical bureaus and other organizations that collect and issue statistics as their principal activity, but also governmental administrative and regulatory agencies, private research bodies, trade associations, insurance companies, health associations, and private organizations such as the National Education Association and philanthropic foundations. Consequently, the data vary considerably as to reference periods, definitions of terms and, for ongoing series, the number and frequency of time periods for which data are available.

The statistics presented were obtained and tabulated by various means. Some statistics are based on complete enumerations or censuses while others are based on samples. Some information is extracted from records kept for administrative or regulatory purposes (school enrollment, hospital records, securities registration, financial accounts, social security records, income tax returns, etc.), while other information is obtained explicitly for statistical purposes through interviews or by mail. The estimation procedures used vary from highly sophisticated scientific techniques, to crude "informed guesses."

Each set of data relates to a group of individuals or units of interest referred to as the *target universe* or *target population,* or simply as the *universe* or *population.* Prior to data collection the target universe should be clearly defined. For example, if data are to be collected for the universe of households in the United States, it is necessary to define a "household." The target universe may not be completely tractable. Cost and other considerations may restrict data collection to a *survey universe* based on some available list, such list may be inaccurate and out of date. This list is called a *survey frame* or *sampling frame.*

The data in many tables are based on data obtained for all population units, *a census,* or on data obtained for only a portion, or *sample,* of the population units. When the data presented are based on a sample, the sample is usually a scientifically selected *probability sample.* This is a sample selected from a list or sampling frame in such a way that every possible sample has a known chance of selection and usually each unit selected can be assigned a number, greater than zero and less than or equal to one, representing its likelihood or probability of selection.

For large-scale sample surveys, the probability sample of units is often selected as a multistage sample. The first stage of a multistage sample is the selection of a probability sample of large groups of population members, referred to as primary sampling units (PSU's). For example, in a national multistage household sample, PSU's are often counties or groups of counties. The second stage of a multistage sample is the selection, within each PSU selected at the first stage, of smaller groups of population units, referred to as secondary sampling units. In subsequent stages of selection, smaller and smaller nested groups are chosen until the ultimate sample of population units is obtained. To qualify a multistage sample as a probability sample, all stages of sampling must be carried out using probability sampling methods.

Prior to selection at each stage of a multistage (or a single stage) sample, a list of the sampling units or sampling frame for that stage must be obtained. For example, for the first stage of selection of a national household sample, a list of the counties and county groups that form the PSU's must be obtained. For the final stage of selection, lists of households, and sometimes persons within the households, have to be compiled in the field. For surveys of economic entities and for the economic census, the Census Bureau generally uses a frame constructed from the Bureau's Standard Statistical Establishment List (SSEL). The SSEL contains all establishments with payroll in the United States including small single establishment firms as well as large multi-establishment firms.

Wherever the quantities in a table refer to an entire universe, but are constructed from data collected in a sample survey, the table quantities are referred to as *sample estimates.* In constructing a sample estimate, an attempt is made to come as close as is feasible to the corresponding universe quantity that would be obtained from a complete census of the universe. Estimates based on a sample will, however, generally differ from the hypothetical census figures. Two classifications of errors are associated with estimates based on sample surveys: (1) *sampling error*—the error arising from the use of a sample, rather than a census, to estimate population quantities and (2) *nonsampling error*—those errors arising from nonsampling sources. As discussed below, the magnitude of the sampling error for an estimate can usually be estimated from the sample data. However, the magnitude of the nonsampling error for an estimate can rarely be estimated. Consequently, actual error in an estimate exceeds the error that can be estimated.

The particular sample used in a survey is only one of a large number of possible samples of the same size which could have been selected using the same sampling procedure. Estimates derived from the different samples would, in general, differ from each other. The *standard error* (SE) is a measure of the variation among the estimates derived from all possible samples. The standard error is the most commonly used measure of the sampling error of an estimate. Valid estimates of the standard errors of survey estimates can usually be calculated from the data collected in a probability sample. For convenience, the standard error is sometimes expressed as a percent of the estimate and is called the relative standard error or *coefficient of variation* (CV). For example, an estimate of 200 units with an estimated standard error of 10 units has an estimated CV of 5 percent.

A sample estimate and an estimate of its standard error or CV can be used to construct interval estimates that have a prescribed confidence that the interval includes the average of the estimates derived from all possible samples with a known probability. To illustrate, if all possible samples were selected under essentially the same general conditions, and using the same sample design, and if an estimate and its estimated standard error were calculated from each sample, then: 1) Approximately 68 percent of the intervals from one standard error below the estimate to one standard error above the estimate would include the average estimate derived from all possible samples; 2) approximately 90 percent of the intervals from 1.6 standard errors below the estimate to 1.6 standard errors above the estimate would include the average estimate derived from all possible samples; and 3) approximately 95 percent of the intervals from two standard errors below the estimate to two standard errors above the estimate would include the average estimate derived from all possible samples.

Thus, for a particular sample, one can say with the appropriate level of confidence (e.g., 90 percent or 95 percent) that the average of all possible samples is included in the constructed interval. Example of a confidence interval: An estimate is 200 units with a standard error of 10 units. An approximately 90 percent confidence interval (plus or minus 1.6 standard errors) is from 184 to 216.

All surveys and censuses are subject to nonsampling errors. Nonsampling errors are of two kinds—*random* and *nonrandom.* Random nonsampling errors arise because of the varying interpretation of questions (by respondents or interviewers) and varying actions of coders, keyers, and other processors. Some randomness is also introduced when respondents must estimate values. These same errors usually have a nonrandom component. Nonrandom nonsampling errors result from total nonresponse (no usable data obtained for a sampled unit), partial or item nonresponse (only a portion of a response may be usable), inability or unwillingness on the part of respondents to provide correct information, difficulty interpreting questions, mistakes in recording or keying data, errors of collection or processing, and coverage problems (overcoverage and undercoverage of the target universe). Random nonresponse errors usually, but not always, result in an understatement of sampling errors and thus an overstatement of the precision of survey estimates. Estimating the magnitude of nonsampling errors would require special experiments or access to independent data and, consequently, the magnitudes are seldom available.

Nearly all types of nonsampling errors that affect surveys also occur in complete censuses. Since surveys can be conducted on a smaller scale than censuses, nonsampling errors can presumably be controlled more tightly. Relatively more funds and effort can perhaps be expended toward eliciting responses, detecting and correcting response error, and reducing processing errors. As a result, survey results can sometimes be more accurate than census results.

To compensate for suspected nonrandom errors, adjustments of the sample estimates are often made. For example, adjustments are frequently made for nonresponse, both total and partial. Adjustments made for either type of nonresponse are often referred to as *imputations.* Imputation for total nonresponse is usually made by substituting for the questionnaire responses of the nonrespondents the "average" questionnaire responses of the respondents. These imputations usually are made separately within various groups of sample members, formed by attempting to place respondents and nonrespondents together that have "similar" design or ancillary characteristics. Imputation for item nonresponse is usually made by substituting for a missing item the response to that item of a respondent having characteristics that are "similar" to those of the nonrespondent.

For an estimate calculated from a sample survey, the *total error* in the estimate is composed of the sampling error, which can usually be estimated from the sample, and the nonsampling error, which usually cannot be estimated from the sample. The total error present in a population quantity obtained from a complete census is composed of only nonsampling errors. Ideally, estimates of the total error associated with data given in the *Statistical Abstract* tables should be given. However, due to the unavailability of estimates of nonsampling errors, only estimates of the levels of sampling errors, in terms of estimated standard errors or coefficients of variation, are available. To obtain estimates of the estimated standard errors from the sample of interest, obtain a copy of the referenced report which appears at the end of each table.

Principal data bases.—Beginning below are brief descriptions of 35 of the sample surveys and censuses that provide a substantial portion of the data contained in this *Abstract.*

SECTION 1. POPULATION

Source and Title: Bureau of the Census, *Census of Population*

Tables: See tables citing *Census of Population* in section 1 and also in sections 2, 4, 6, 8, 13, 14, 21, 25, and 29.

Universe, Frequency, and Types of Data: Complete count of U.S. population conducted every 10 years since 1790. Data obtained on number and characteristics of inhabitants.

Type of Data Collection Operation: In 1970, 1980, and 1990 complete census for some items—age, sex, race, marital status, and relationship to household head. In 1970, other items collected from a 5% and a 15% probability (systematic) sample of the population. In 1980, approximately 19% of the housing units were included in the sample; in 1990, approximately 17%.

Data Collection and Imputation Procedures: In 1970, extensive use of mail questionnaires in urban areas; personal interviews in most rural areas. In 1980 and 1990, mail questionnaires were used in even more areas than in 1970, with personal interviews in the remainder. Extensive telephone and personal followup for nonrespondents was done in the censuses. Imputations were made for missing characteristics.

Estimates of Sampling Error: Sampling errors for data are estimated for all items collected by sample and vary by characteristic and geographic area. The CV's for national and State estimates are generally very small.

Other (nonsampling) Errors: Since 1950, evaluation programs have been conducted to provide information on the magnitude of some sources of nonsampling errors such as response bias and undercoverage in each census. Results from the evaluation program for the 1990 census indicate that the net under coverage amounted to about 1.5 to 2 percent of the total resident population.

Sources of Additional Material: U.S. Bureau of the Census, *The Coverage of Population in the 1980 Census,* PHC80-E4; *Content Reinterview Study: Accuracy of Data for Selected Population and Housing Characteristics as Measured by Reinterview,* PHC80-E2; *1980 Census of Population,* vol. 1., (PC80-1), appendixes B, C, and D.

Source and Title: U.S. Bureau of the Census, *Current Population Survey (CPS)*

Tables: See tables citing *Current Population Reports* primarily in section 1, but also in sections 2, 3, 4, 8, 12, 13, 14, 18, 23, and 29. Many Bureau of Labor Statistics' (BLS) tables in section 13 are CPS based.

Universe, Frequency, and Types of Data: Nationwide monthly sample survey of civilian noninstitutional population, 15 years old or over, to obtain data on employment, unemployment, and a number of other characteristics.

Type of Data Collection Operation: Multistage probability sample of about 60,000 households in 729 PSU's in 1993. Oversampling in some States and the largest MSA's to improve reliability for those areas of employment data on annual average basis. A continual sample rotation system is used. Households are in sample 4 months, out for 8 months, and in for 4 more. Month-to-month overlap is 75%; year-to-year overlap is 50%.

Data Collection and Imputation Procedures: For first and fifth months that a household is in sample, personal interviews; other months, approximately, 85% of the data collected by phone. Imputation is done for both item and total nonresponse. Adjustment for total nonresponse is done by a predefined cluster of units, by MSA size and residence; for item nonresponse imputation varies by subject matter.

Estimates of Sampling Error: Estimated CV's on national annual averages for labor force, total employment, and nonagricultural employment, 0.2%; for total unemployment and agricultural employment, 1.0% to 2.5%. The estimated CV's for family income and poverty rate for all persons in 1986 are 0.5% and 1.5%, respectively. CV's for subnational areas, such as States, would be larger and would vary by area.

Other (nonsampling) Errors: Estimates of response bias on unemployment are not available, but estimates of unemployment are usually 5% to 9% lower than estimates from reinterviews. Four to 5.0% of sample households unavailable for interviews.

Sources of Additional Material: U.S. Bureau of the Census and Bureau of Labor Statistics, *Concepts and Methods Used in Labor Force Statistics from Current Population Survey* (Census series P-23, No. 62; BLS Report No. 463) and Bureau of the Census, *Current Population Survey* (Tech. Paper 40) and Bureau of Labor Statistics, *Employment and Earnings,* monthly, Explanatory Notes and Estimates of Error, tables 1-A through 1-H and *BLS Handbook of Methods,* Chapter 1 (Bulletin 2414.)

SECTION 2. VITAL STATISTICS

Source and Title: U.S. National Center for Health Statistics (NCHS), *Vital Registration System*

Tables: See tables citing *Vital Statistics of the United States;* 314 in section 5; and 1346 in section 29.

Universe, Frequency, and Types of Data: Annual data on births and deaths in the United States.

Type of Data Collection Operation: Mortality data based on complete file of death records, except 1972, based on 50% sample. Natality statistics 1951-71, based on 50% sample of birth certificates, except a 20% to 50% in 1967, received by NCHS. Beginning 1972, data from some States received through Vital Statistics Cooperative Program (VSCP) and complete file used; data from other States based on 50% sample. Beginning 1986, all reporting areas participated in the VSCP.

Data Collection and Imputation Procedures: Reports based on records from registration offices of all States, District of Columbia, New York City, Puerto Rico, Virgin Islands, and Guam.

Estimates of Sampling Error: For recent years, CV's for births are small due to large portion of total file in sample (except for very small estimated totals).

Other (nonsampling) Errors: Data on births and deaths believed to be at least 99% complete.

Sources of Additional Material: U.S. National Center for Health Statistics, *Vital Statistics of the United States,* vol. I and vol. II, annual, and *Monthly Vital Statistics Report.*
(See section 1 above for information pertaining to tables 99-104.)

SECTION 3. HEALTH AND NUTRITION

Source and Title: U.S. National Center for Health Statistics, *National Health Interview Survey (NHIS)*

Tables: 178, 179, 204, 207, 208, 210, 214, 215, 219, 221 and 222.

Universe, Frequency, and Types of Data: Continuous data collection covering the civilian noninstitutional population to obtain information on personal and demographic characteristics, illnesses, injuries, impairments, and other health topics.

Type of Data Collection Operation: Multistage probability sample of 42,000 households (in 376 PSU's) selected in groups of about four adjacent households.

Data Collection and Imputation Procedures: Personal household interviews with extensive followup of nonrespondents. Data are adjusted for nonresponse by imputation procedure based on "average" characteristics of persons in interviewed households in the same geographic area.

Estimates of Sampling Error: Estimated CV's: For physician visits by males, 1.5%; for workdays lost by males, 3.5%; for persons injured at home, 4.7%.

Other (nonsampling) Errors: Response rate was 95.7% in 1985 for the NHIS.

Sources of Additional Material: U.S. National Center for Health Statistics, "Current Estimates from the National Health Interview Survey, U.S., 1983," Vital and Health Statistics, series 10.
(See section 13 for information pertaining to table 173, section 15 for table 167, and section 27 for table 174.)

SECTION 4. EDUCATION

Source and Title: U.S. Department of Education, National Center for Education Statistics, *Higher Education General Information Survey (HEGIS), Fall Enrollment in Institutions of Higher Education;* beginning 1986, *Integrated Postsecondary Education Data Survey (IPEDS), Fall Enrollment*

Tables: 277, 278, 281 and 282.

Universe, Frequency, and Types of Data: Annual survey of all institutions and branches listed in the *Directory* to obtain data on total enrollment by sex, level of enrollment, type of program, racial/ethnic characteristics (in alternate years) and attendance status of student, and on first-time students.

Type of Data Collection Operation: Complete census.

Data Collection and Imputation Procedures: Survey package is usually mailed in the spring with surveys due at varying dates in the summer and fall; mail and phone followup procedures for nonrespondents. Missing data are imputed by using data of similar institutions.

Estimates of Sampling Error: Not applicable.

Other (nonsampling) Errors: Approximately 87% response rate.

Sources of Additional Material: U.S. Department of Education, National Center for Education Statistics, *Fall Enrollment in Higher Education,* annual.

Source and Title: U.S. Department of Education, National Center for Education Statistics, *Higher Education General Information Survey (HEGIS), Financial Statistics of Institutions of Higher Education;* beginning 1986, *Integrated Postsecondary Education Data Survey (IPEDS), Financial Statistics of Institutions of Higher Education*

Tables: 229, 232, 281, and 284.

Universe, Frequency, and Types of Data: Annual survey of all institutions and branches listed in the *Education Directory, Colleges and Universities* to obtain data on financial status and operations, including current funds revenues, current funds expenditures, and physical plant assets.

Type of Data Collection Operation: Complete census.

Data Collection and Imputation Procedures: Survey package is usually mailed in the spring with surveys due at varying dates in the summer and fall; mail and phone followup procedures for nonrespondents. Missing data are imputed by using data of similar institutions.

Estimates of Sampling Error: Not applicable.

Other (nonsampling) Errors: For 1990, a 87% response rate. Imputed expenditures amounted to about 2.8% of total expenditures.

Sources of Additional Material: U.S. Department of Education, National Center for Education Statistics, *Financial Statistics of Institutions of Higher Education,* annual.

Source and Title: U.S. Department of Education, National Center for Education Statistics, *Higher Education General Information Survey (HEGIS), Degrees and Other Formal Awards Conferred.* Beginning 1986, *Integrated Postsecondary Education Data Survey (IPEDS), Degrees and Other Formal Awards Conferred.*

Tables: 298-303.

Universe, Frequency, and Types of Data: Annual survey of all institutions and branches listed in the *Education Directory, Colleges and Universities* to obtain data on earned degrees and other formal awards, conferred by field of study, level of degree, sex, and by racial/ethnic characteristics (in alternate years).

Type of Data Collection Operation: Complete census.

Data Collection and Imputation Procedures: Survey package is usually mailed in the spring with surveys due at varying dates in the summer and fall; mail and phone followup procedures for nonrespondents. Missing data are imputed by using data of similar institutions.

Estimates of Sampling Error: Not applicable.

Other (nonsampling) Errors: For 1989-90, approximately 92.3% response rate.

Sources of Additional Material: U.S. Department of Education, National Center for Education Statistics, *Earned Degrees Conferred,* annual.

(See sections 1 and 9 for information pertaining to the Bureau of the Census and section 3 above for the National Center for Health Statistics.)

SECTION 5. LAW ENFORCEMENT, COURTS, AND PRISONS

Source and Title: U.S. Federal Bureau of Investigation, *Uniform Crime Reporting (UCR) Program*

Tables: 308-313, 315, 316, 322-324, and 326.

Universe, Frequency, and Types of Data: Monthly reports on the number of criminal offenses that become known to law enforcement agencies. Data are collected on crimes cleared by arrest, by age, sex, and race of offender, and on assaults on law enforcement officers.

Type of Data Collection Operation: Crime statistics are based on reports of crime data submitted either directly to the FBI by contributing law enforcement agencies or through cooperating State UCR programs.

Data Collection and Imputation Procedures: States with UCR programs collect data directly from individual law enforcement agencies and forward reports, prepared in accordance with UCR standards, to FBI. Accuracy and consistency edits are performed by FBI.

Estimates of Sampling Error: Not applicable.

Other (nonsampling) Errors: Coverage of 97% of the population (96.6% in MSA's, 85.8% in "other cities," and 85.6% in rural areas) by UCR program, though varying number of agencies report. Some error may be present through incorrect reporting.

Sources of Additional Material: U.S. Federal Bureau of Investigation, *Crime in the United States.*

Source and Title: U.S. Bureau of Justice Statistics (BJS), *National Crime Victimization Survey*

Tables: 317-321.

Universe, Frequency, and Types of Data: Monthly survey of individuals and households in the United States to obtain data on criminal victimization of those units for compilation of annual estimates.

Type of Data Collection Operation: National probability sample survey of about 50,000 interviewed households in 376 PSU's selected from a list of addresses from the 1980 census, supplemented by new construction permits and an area sample where permits are not required.

Data Collection and Imputation Procedures: Interviews are conducted every 6 months for 3 years for each household in the sample; 8,000 households are interviewed monthly. Personal interviews are used in the first and fifth interviews; the intervening interviews are conducted by telephone whenever possible.

Estimates of Sampling Error: CV's in 1985: 2.2% for crimes of violence; 14.8% for estimate of rape counts; 5.5% for robbery counts; 2.5% for assault counts; 1.4% for personal larceny counts; 2.2% for burglary counts; 1.8% for household larceny; 1.3% for all household crimes; and 4.8% for motor vehicle theft counts.

Other (nonsampling) Errors: Respondent recall errors which may include reporting incidents for other than the reference period; interviewer coding and processing errors; and possible mistaken reporting or classifying of events. Adjustment is made for a household noninterview rate of about 4% and for a smaller within-household non-interview rate.

Sources of Additional Material: U.S. Bureau of Justice Statistics, *Criminal Victimization in the United States,* annual. *(See section 2 for details on table 314 and section 9 for details on table 333.)*

SECTION 7. PARKS AND RECREATION

(See section 27 for details on table 405 and 427.)

SECTION 8. ELECTIONS

(See section 1 above for information pertaining to tables 459 and 460 and section 9 for information pertaining to tables 452 and 454.)

SECTION 9. STATE AND LOCAL GOVERNMENT FINANCES AND EMPLOYMENT

Source and Title: U.S. Bureau of the Census, *Census of Governments*

Tables: See tables in section 9 citing *Census of Governments* and tables 452 and 454 in section 8.

Universe, Frequency, and Types of Data: Survey of all governmental units in the United States conducted every 5 years to obtain data on government revenue, expenditures, debt, assets, employment and employee retirement systems, property values, public school systems, and number, size, and structure of governments.

Type of Data Collection Operation: Complete census. List of units derived through classification of government units recently authorized in each State and identification, counting, and classification of existing local governments and public school systems.

Data Collection and Imputation Procedures: Data collected through field and office compilation of financial data from official records and reports for States and large local governments; mail canvass of selected data items, like State tax revenue and employee retirement systems; and collection of local government statistics through central collection arrangements with State governments.

Estimates of Sampling Error: Not applicable.

Other (nonsampling) Errors: Some non-sampling errors may arise due to possible inaccuracies in classification, response, and processing.

Sources of Additional Material: U.S. Bureau of the Census, *Census of Governments, 1987,* various reports, and *State Government Finances in 1990,* GF 90, No. 3.

Source and Title: U.S. Bureau of the Census, *Annual Surveys of State and Local Government*

Tables: See tables citing *Public Employment* and *Governmental Finances* in section 9; table 256 in section 4; table 333 in section 5; and table 598 in section 12.

Universe, Frequency, and Types of Data: Sample survey conducted annually to obtain data on revenue, expenditure, debt, and employment of State and local governments. Universe is all governmental units in the United States (about 83,000).

Type of Data Collection Operation: Sample of about 22,000 units includes all State governments, county governments with 50,000+ population, municipalities and townships with 25,000+ population, all school districts with 10,000+ enrollment in October 1986, and other governments meeting certain criteria; probability sample for remaining units.

Data Collection and Imputation Procedures: Field and office compilation of data from official records and reports for States and large local governments; central collection of local governmental financial data through cooperative agreements with a number of State governments; mail canvass of other units with mail and telephone followups of nonrespondents. Data for nonresponses are imputed from previous year data or obtained from secondary sources, if available.

Estimates of Sampling Error: CV's for estimates of major employment and financial items are generally less than 2% for most States and less than 1.2% for the majority of States.

Other (nonsampling) Errors: Nonresponse rate is less than 15% for number of units. Other possible errors may result from undetected inaccuracies in classification, response, and processing.

Sources of Additional Material: U.S. Bureau of the Census, *Public Employment in 1990,* GE 90, No. 1, *Governmental Finances in 1989-90,* GF 90, No. 5, and *Census of Governments, 1987,* various reports.

SECTION 10. FEDERAL GOVERNMENT

Source and Title: U.S. Internal Revenue Service, *Statistics of Income, Individual Income Tax Returns*

Tables: 533-527.

Universe, Frequency, and Types of Data: Annual study of unaudited individual income tax returns, forms 1040, 1040A, and 1040EZ, filed by U.S. citizens and residents. Data provided on various financial characteristics by size of adjusted gross income, marital status, and by taxable and nontaxable returns. Data by State, based on 100% file, also include returns from 1040NR, filed by nonresident aliens plus certain self-employment tax returns.

Type of Data Collection Operation: Annual stratified probability sample of approximately 125,000 returns broken into sample strata based on the larger of total income or total loss amounts as well as the size of business plus farm receipts. Sampling rates for sample strata varied from .025% to 100%.

Data Collection and Imputation Procedures: Computer selection of sample of tax return records. Data adjusted during editing for incorrect, missing, or inconsistent entries to ensure consistency with other entries on return.

Estimates of Sampling Error: Estimated CV's for tax year 1987: Adjusted gross income less deficit .13%; salaries and wages .20%; and tax-exempt interest received 4.51%. (State data not subject to sampling error.)

Other (nonsampling) Errors: Processing errors and errors arising from the use of tolerance checks for the data.

Sources of Additional Material: U.S. Internal Revenue Service, *Statistics of Income, Individual Income Tax Returns,* annual.

SECTION 12. SOCIAL INSURANCE AND HUMAN SERVICES

Source and Title: U.S. Social Security Administration, *Benefit Data*

Tables: 594 and 595.

Universe, Frequency, and Types of Data: All persons receiving monthly benefits under Title II of Social Security Act. Data on number and amount of benefits paid by type and State.

Type of Data Collection Operation: Data based on administrative records. Data based on 100% files, as well as 10% and 1% sample files.

Data Collection and Imputation Procedures: Records used consist of actions pursuant to applications for benefits, updated by subsequent post-entitlement actions.

Estimates of Sampling Error: Varies by size of estimate and sample file size.

Other (nonsampling) Errors: Processing errors, which are believed to be small.

Sources of Additional Material: U.S. Social Security Administration, *Annual Statistical Supplement to the Social Security Bulletin.*

Source and Title: U.S. Social Security Administration, *Supplemental Security Income (SSI) Program*

Tables: 609-612.

Universe, Frequency, and Types of Data: All eligible aged, blind, or disabled persons receiving SSI benefit payments under SSI program. Data include number of persons receiving federally administered SSI, amounts paid, and State administered supplementation.

Type of Data Collection Operation: Data based on administrative records.

Data Collection and Imputation Procedures: Data adjusted to reflect returned checks and overpayment refunds. For federally administered payments, actual adjusted amounts are used.

Estimates of Sampling Error: Not applicable.

Other (nonsampling) Errors: Processing errors, which are believed to be small.

Sources of Additional Material: U.S. Social Security Administration, *Annual Statistical Supplement to the Social Security Bulletin.* *(See section 1 above for information pertaining to the Current Population Survey, section 3 for information pertaining to the National Center for Health Statistics, and section 9 for information pertaining to Annual Surveys of State and Local Government.)*

SECTION 13. LABOR FORCE, EMPLOYMENT, AND EARNINGS

Source and Title: U.S. Bureau of Labor Statistics (BLS), *Current Employment Statistics (CES)* Program

Tables: 666-668, 673; in section 3, table 173; in section 21, table 1008; and in section 22, table 1075.

Universe, Frequency, and Types of Data: Monthly survey covering about 6 million nonagricultural establishments to obtain data on employment, hours, and earnings, by industry.

Type of Data Collection Operation: Sample survey of over 390,000 establishments in March 1993.

Data Collection and Imputation Procedures: Cooperating State agencies mail questionnaires to sample establishments to develop State and local estimates; information is forwarded to BLS where national estimates are prepared.

Estimates of Sampling Error: Estimated CV's for employment, 0.1%, for average weekly hours paid, 0.4% and for average hourly earnings, 0.3%.

Other (nonsampling) Errors: Estimates of employment adjusted annually to reflect complete universe. Average adjustment is 0.2%.

Sources of Additional Material: U.S. Bureau of Labor Statistics, *Employment and Earnings,* monthly, Explanatory Notes and Estimates of Error, tables 2-A through 2-G and *BLS Handbook of Methods,* Chapter 2, Bulletin 2414 (Sept. 1992). *(See section 1 above for information pertaining to the Current Population Survey.)*

SECTION 14. INCOME, EXPENDITURES, AND WEALTH

(See·section 1 above for information pertaining to the Bureau of the Census.)

SECTION 15. PRICES

Source and Title: U.S. Bureau of Labor Statistics (BLS), *Consumer Price Index (CPI)*

Tables: 760-764, 777, 778, and in section 3, table 167.

Universe, Frequency, and Types of Data: Monthly survey of price changes of all types of consumer goods and services purchased by urban wage earners and clerical workers prior to 1978, and urban consumers thereafter. Both indexes continue to be published.

Type of Data Collection Operation: Prior to 1978, sample of various consumer items in 56 urban areas; thereafter, in 85 PSU's, except from January 1987 through March 1988, when 91 areas were sampled.

Data Collection and Imputation Procedures: Prices of consumer items are obtained from about 57,000 housing units, and 19,000 other reporters in 85 areas. Prices of food, fuel, and a few other items are obtained monthly; prices of most other commodities and services are collected every month in the five largest geographic areas and every other month in others.

Estimates of Sampling Error: Estimates of standard errors are not available at present.

Other (nonsampling) Errors: Errors result from inaccurate reporting, difficulties in defining concepts and their operational implementation, and introduction of product quality changes and new products.

Sources of Additional Material: U.S. Bureau of Labor Statistics, *The Consumer Price Index:* 1987 Revision, Report 736, and *BLS Handbook of Methods,* Chapter 19, Bulletin 2414.

Source and Title: U.S. Bureau of Labor Statistics, *Producer Price Index (PPI)*

Tables: 760, 767-769, and in section 21, table 1058; in section 24, table 1154; and in section 25, table 1203.

Universe, Frequency, and Types of Data: Monthly survey of producing companies to determine price changes of all commodities produced in the United States for sale in commercial transactions. Data on agriculture, forestry, fishing, manufacturing, mining, gas, electricity, public utilities, and a few services.

Type of Data Collection Operation: Probability sample of approximately 3,100 commodities and about 75,000 quotations per month.

Data Collection and Imputation Procedures: Data are collected by mail. If transaction prices are not supplied, list prices are used. Some prices are obtained from trade publications, organized exchanges, and government agencies. To calculate index, price changes are multiplied by their relative weights based on total net selling value of all commodities in 1982.

Estimates of Sampling Error: Not applicable.

Other (nonsampling) Errors: Not available at present.

Sources of Additional Material: U.S. Bureau of Labor Statistics, *BLS Handbook of Methods,* Chapter 16, Bulletin 2414.

SECTION 17. BUSINESS ENTERPRISE

Source and Title: U.S. Internal Revenue Service, *Statistics of Income, Sole Proprietorship Returns* and *Statistics of Income Bulletin*

Tables: 846-849.

Universe, Frequency, and Types of Data: Annual study of unaudited income tax returns of nonfarm sole proprietorships, form 1040 with business schedules. Data provided on various financial characteristics by industry.

Type of Data Collection Operation: Stratified probability sample of approximately 31,000 sole proprietorships for tax year 1990. The sample is classified based on presence or absence of certain business schedules; the larger of total income or loss; and size of business plus farm receipts. Sampling rates vary from .043% to 100%.

Data Collection and Imputation Procedures: Computer selection of sample of tax return records. Data adjusted during editing for incorrect, missing, or inconsistent entries to ensure consistency with other entries on return.

Estimates of Sampling Error: Estimated CV's for tax year 1990 are not available; for 1987 (the latest available): For sole proprietorships, business receipts, 1.66%; net income, (less loss), 1.33%; depreciation 2.17%; interest expense 2.80%; and employee benefit programs 7.55%.

Other (nonsampling) Errors: Processing errors and errors arising from the use of tolerance checks for the data.

Sources of Additional Material: U.S. Internal Revenue Service, *Statistics of Income, Sole Proprietorship Returns* (for years through 1980) and *Statistics of Income Bulletin,* vol. 10, No. 1 (summer 1990).

Source and Title: U.S. Internal Revenue Service, *Statistics of Income, Partnership Returns* and *Statistics of Income Bulletin*

Tables: 846-848, 850, and 851.

Universe, Frequency, and Types of Data: Annual study of unaudited income tax returns of partnerships, Form 1065. Data provided on various financial characteristics by industry.

Type of Data Collection Operation: Stratified probability sample of approximately 28,000 partnership returns from a population of 1,660,000 filed during calendar year 1990. The sample is classified based on combinations of gross receipts, net income or loss, and total assets, and on industry. Sampling rates vary from .04% to 100%.

Data Collection and Imputation Procedures: Computer selection of sample of tax return records. Data are adjusted during editing for incorrect, missing, or inconsistent entries to ensure consistency with other entries on return. Data not available due to regulations are not imputed.

Estimates of Sampling Error: Estimated CV's for tax year 1988 (latest available): For number of partnerships, .51%; business receipts, .78%; net income, 3.03%; net loss, 2.21% and total assets, 1.22%.

Other (nonsampling) Errors: Processing errors and errors arising from the use of tolerance checks for the data.

Sources of Additional Material: U.S. Internal Revenue Service, *Statistics of Income, Partnership Returns* and *Statistics of Income Bulletin,* vol. 10, No. 1 (summer 1990).

Source and Title: U.S. Internal Revenue Service, *Corporation Income Tax Returns*

Tables: 846-848 and 854-856.

Universe, Frequency, and Types of Data: Annual study of unaudited corporation income tax returns, Forms 1120 and 1120 (A, F, L, PC, REIT, RIC, and S), filed by corporations or businesses legally defined as corporations. Data provided on various financial characteristics by industry and size of total assets, and business receipts.

Type of Data Collection Operation: Stratified probability sample of approximately 85,000 returns for 1987, distributed by sample classes generally based on type of return, size of total assets, size of net income or deficit, and selected business activity. Sampling rates for sample strata varied from .25% to 100%.

Data Collection and Imputation Procedures: Computer selection of sample of tax return records. Data adjusted during editing for incorrect, missing, or inconsistent entries to ensure consistency with other entries on return and to achieve statistical definitions.

Estimates of Sampling Error: Estimated CV's for 1988: Number of returns in subgroups ranged from 1.4% with assets under $100,000, to 0% with assets over $100 mil.; for amount of net income and amount of income tax, .18%

Other (nonsampling) Errors: Processing errors and errors arising from the use of tolerance checks for the data.

Sources of Additional Material: U.S. Internal Revenue Service, *Statistics of Income, Corporation Income Tax Returns,* annual.

SECTION 18. COMMUNICATIONS

(See section 1 for information pertaining to table 904, and section 26 for table 916.)

SECTION 19. ENERGY

Source and Title: U.S. Energy Information Administration, *Residential Energy Consumption Survey*

Tables: 943, 944 and table 1233 in section 25.

Universe, Frequency, and Types of Data: Triennial survey of households and fuel suppliers. Data are obtained on energy-related household characteristics, housing unit characteristics, use of fuels, and energy consumption and expenditures by fuel type.

Type of Data Collection Operation: Probability sample of 7,183 eligible units in 129 PSU's. For responding units, fuel consumption and expenditure data obtained from fuel suppliers to those households.

Data Collection and Imputation Procedures: Personal interviews. Extensive followup of nonrespondents including mail questionnaires for some households. Adjustments for nonrespondents were made in weighting for respondents. Most item nonresponses were imputed.

Estimates of Sampling Error: Estimated CV's for household averages: For consumption, 1.3%; for expenditures, 1.0%; for various fuels, values ranged from 1.4% for electricity to 5.9% for LPG.

Other (nonsampling) Errors: Household response rate of 86.7%. Nonconsumption data were mostly imputed for mail respondents (5.2% of eligible units). Usable responses from fuel suppliers for various fuels ranged from 82.8% for electricity to 55.7% for fuel oil.

Sources of Additional Material: U.S. Energy Information Administration, *Household Energy Consumption and Expenditures, 1990* and *Housing Characteristics, 1990.*

SECTION 21. TRANSPORTATION—LAND

(See section 1 for information pertaining to table 1030, section 13 for table 1008, and section 15 for table 1058 and section 27 for table 1010.)

SECTION 22. TRANSPORTATION—AIR AND WATER

Source and Title: U.S. Bureau of the Census, *Foreign Trade—Export Statistics*

Tables: See Bureau of the Census citations for export statistics in source notes in sections 22 and 28 and also table 1185 in section 24; and 1354 in section 29.

Universe, Frequency, and Types of Data: The export declarations collected by Customs are processed each month to obtain data on the movement of U.S. merchandise exports to foreign countries. Data obtained include value, quantity, and shipping weight of exports by commodity, country of destination, Customs district of exportation, and mode of transportation.

Type of Data Collection Operation: Shipper's Export Declarations are required to be filed for the exportation of merchandise valued over $1,500. Customs officials collect and transmit the documents to the Bureau of the Census on a flow basis for data compilation. Value data for shipments valued under $1,501 are estimated, based on established percentages of individual country totals.

Data Collection and Imputation Procedures: Statistical copies of Shipper's Export Declarations are received on a daily basis from Customs ports throughout the country and subjected to a monthly processing cycle. They are fully processed to the extent they reflect items valued over $1,500. Estimates for shipments valued at $1,500 or less are made, based on established percentages of individual country totals.

Estimates of Sampling Error: Not applicable.

Other (nonsampling) Errors: Clerical and complex computer checks intercept most processing errors and minimize otherwise significant reporting errors; other nonsampling errors are caused by undercounting of exports to Canada due to the nonreceipt of some Shipper's Export Declarations.

Sources of Additional Material: U.S. Bureau of the Census, *U.S. Merchandise Trade: Exports, General Imports, and Imports for Consumption, SITC, Commodity by Country,* FT 925.

Source and Title: U.S. Bureau of the Census, *Foreign Trade—Import Statistics*

Tables: See Bureau of the Census citations for import statistics in source notes in sections 22 and 28 and also table 1185 in section 24; and 1354 in section 29.

Universe, Frequency, and Types of Data: The import entry documents collected by Customs are processed each month to obtain data on the movement of merchandise imported into the United States. Data obtained include value, quantity, and shipping weight by commodity, country of origin, Customs district of entry, and mode of transportation.

Type of Data Collection Operation: Import entry documents are required to be filed for the importation of goods into the United States valued over $1,000 or for articles which must be reported on formal entries. Customs officials collect and transmit statistical copies of the documents to the Bureau of the Census on a flow basis for data compilation. Estimates for shipments valued under $1,001 and not reported on formal entries are based on established percentages of individual country totals.

Data Collection and Imputation Procedures: Statistical copies of import entry documents, received on a daily basis from Customs ports of entry throughout the country, are subjected to a monthly processing cycle. They are fully processed to the extent they reflect items valued at $1,001 and over or items which must be reported on formal entries.

Estimates of Sampling Error: Not applicable.

Other (nonsampling) Errors: Verification of statistical data reporting by Customs officials prior to transmittal and a subsequent program of clerical and computer checks are utilized to hold nonsampling errors arising from reporting and/or processing errors to a minimum.

Sources of Additional Material: U.S. Bureau of the Census, *U.S. Merchandise Trade: Exports, General Imports and Imports for Consumption, SITC, Commodity by Country, FT 925.*

(See section 13 for information pertaining to table 1075.)

SECTION 23. AGRICULTURE

Source and Title: U.S. Bureau of the Census, *Census of Agriculture.*

Tables: 1096-1103.

Universe, Frequency, and Types of Data: Complete count of U.S. farms and ranches conducted once every five years with data at the national, state, and county level. Data published on farm numbers and related items/characteristics.

Type of Data Collection Operation: Complete census for— number of farms; land in farms; estimated market value of land and buildings, machinery and equipment, agriculture products sold; total cropland; irrigated land; total farm production expenses; farm operator characteristics; livestock and poultry inventory and sales; and selected crops harvested.

Data Collection and Imputation Procedures: Data collection is by mailing questionnaires to all farmers and ranchers. Nonrespondents are conducted by telephone and correspondence followups. Imputations were made for all nonresponse item/characteristics.

Estimates of Sampling Error: Variability in the estimates is due to the sample selection and estimation for items collected by sample and census nonresponse estimation procedures. The CV's for national and state estimates are generally very small. Approximately 85% response rate.

Other (nonsampling) Errors: Nonsampling errors are due to incompleteness of the census mailing list, duplications on the list, respondent reporting errors, errors in editing reported data, and in imputation for missing data. Evaluation studies are conducted to measure certain nonsampling errors such as list coverage and classification error. Results from the evaluation program for the 1987 census indicate the net under coverage amounted to about 7.2% of the nations total farms.

Sources of Additional Material: U.S. Bureau of the Census, *1992 Census of Agriculture,* Volume 2, Subject Series— Part 1, *Agriculture Atlas of the U.S.,* Part 2, *Coverage Evaluation,* Part 3, *Rankings of States and Counties,* Part 4, *History,* Part 5, *ZIP Code Tabulation of Selected Items,* ; and Volume 4 *Farm and Ranch Irrigation Survey.*

Source and Title: U.S. Department of Agriculture, National Agricultural Statistics Service (NASS), *Basic Area Frame Sample*

Tables: See tables citing NASS in source notes in section 23, which pertain to this or the following two surveys.

Universe, Frequency, and Types of Data: Two annual area sample surveys of U.S. farm operators: June agricultural survey collects data on planted acreage and livestock inventories; and a February Farm Costs and Returns survey that collects data on total farm production, expenses and specific commodity costs of production.

Type of Data Collection Operation: Stratified probability sample of about 16,000 land area units of about 1 sq. mile (range from 0.1 sq. mile in cities to several sq. miles in open grazing areas). Sample includes 60,000 parcels of agricultural land. About 20% of the sample replaced annually.

Data Collection and Imputation Procedures: Data collection is by personal enumeration. Imputation is based on enumerator observation or data reported by respondents having similar agricultural characteristics.

Estimates of Sampling Error: Estimated CV's range from 1% to 2% for regional estimates to 3% to 6% for State estimates of livestock inventories.

Other (nonsampling) Errors: Minimized through rigid quality controls on the collection process and careful review of all reported data.

Sources of Additional Material: U.S. Department of Agriculture, SRS, *Scope and Methods of the Statistical Reporting Service,* (name changed to National Agricultural Statistics Service), Miscellaneous Publication No. 1308, September 1983 (revised).

Source and Title: U.S. Department of Agriculture, National Agricultural Statistics Service (NASS), *Multiple Frame Surveys*

Tables: See tables citing NASS in source notes in section 23, which pertain to this or the following survey.

Universe, Frequency, and Types of Data: Surveys of U.S. farm operators to obtain data on major livestock inventories, selected crop acreages and production, grain stocks, and farm labor characteristics; and to obtain farm economic data for price indexing.

Type of Data Collection Operation: Primary frame is obtained from general or special purpose lists, supplemented by a probability sample of land areas used to estimate for list incompleteness.

Data Collection and Imputation Procedures: Mail, telephone, or personal interviews used for initial data collection. Mail nonrespondent followup by phone and personal interviews. Imputation based on average of respondents.

Estimates of Sampling Error: Estimated CV for number of hired farm workers is about 3%. Estimated CV's range from 1% to 2% for regional estimates to 3% to 6% for State estimates of livestock inventories.

Other (nonsampling) Errors: In addition to above, replicated sampling procedures used to monitor effects of changes in survey procedures.

Sources of Additional Material: U.S. Department of Agriculture, SRS, *Scope and Methods of the Statistical Reporting Service,* (name changed to National Agricultural Statistics Service), Miscellaneous Publication No. 1308, September 1983 (revised).

Source and Title: U.S. Department of Agriculture, National Agricultural Statistics Service (NASS), *Objective Yield Surveys*

Tables: See tables citing NASS in source notes in section 23, which pertain to this or the preceding survey.

Universe, Frequency, and Types of Data: Surveys for data on corn, cotton, potatoes, soybeans, wheat, and rice to forecast and estimate yields.

Type of Data Collection Operation: Random location of plots in probability sample of fields. Fields selected in June from Basic Area Frame Sample (see above).

Data Collection and Imputation Procedures: Enumerators count and measure plant characteristics in sample fields. Production measured from plots at harvest. Harvest loss measured from post harvest gleanings.

Estimates of Sampling Error: CV's for national estimates of production are about 2-3%.

Other (nonsampling) Errors: In addition to above, replicated sampling procedures used to monitor effects of changes in survey procedures.

Sources of Additional Material: U.S. Department of Agriculture, SRS, *Scope and Methods of the Statistical Reporting Service,* (name changed to National Agricultural Statistics Service), Miscellaneous Publication No. 1308, September 1983 (revised).

(See section 1 above for information pertaining to the Census of Population and Current Population Survey.)

SECTION 24. NATURAL RESOURCES

(See section 15 for table 1154, and section 22 for table 1185.)

SECTION 25. CONSTRUCTION AND HOUSING

Source and Title: U.S. Bureau of the Census, *Monthly Survey of Construction*

Tables: 1212 and 1214-1216.

Universe, Frequency, and Types of Data: Survey conducted monthly of newly constructed housing units (excluding mobile homes). Data are collected on the start, completion, and sale of housing. (Annual figures are aggregates of monthly estimates.)

Type of Data Collection Operation: Probability sample of housing units obtained from building permits selected from 17,000 places. For nonpermit places, multistage probability sample of new housing units selected in 169 PSU's. In those areas, all roads are canvassed in selected enumeration districts.

Data Collection and Imputation Procedures: Data are obtained by telephone inquiry and field visit.

Estimates of Sampling Error: Estimated CV of 3% to 4% for estimates of national totals, but are as high as 20% for estimated totals of more detailed characteristics, such as housing units in multiunit structures.

Other (nonsampling) Errors: Response rate is over 90% for most items. Nonsampling errors are attributed to definitional problems, differences in interpretation of questions, incorrect reporting, inability to obtain information about all cases in the sample, and processing errors.

Sources of Additional Material: U.S. Bureau of the Census, *Construction Reports,* series C20, *Housing Starts;* C22, *Housing Completions; and* C25, *New One-Family Houses Sold and For Sale.*

Source and Title: U.S. Bureau of the Census, *Value of New Construction Put in Place*

Tables: 1205-1207.

Universe, Frequency, and Types of Data:
Survey conducted monthly on total value of
all construction put in place in the current
month, both public and private projects.
Construction values include costs of materials and labor, contractors' profits, overhead
costs, cost of architectural and engineering
work, and miscellaneous project costs.
(Annual figures are aggregates of monthly
estimates.)

Type of Data Collection Operation: Varies
by type of activity: Total cost of private one-
family houses started each month is distributed into value put in place using fixed
patterns of monthly construction progress;
using a multistage probability sample, data
for private multifamily housing are obtained
by mail from owners of multiunit projects.
Data for residential additions and alterations
are obtained in a quarterly survey measuring expenditures; monthly estimates are
interpolated from quarterly data. Estimates
of value of private nonresidential buildings,
and State and local government construction are obtained by mail from owners (or
agents) for a probability sample of projects.
Estimates of farm nonresidential construction expenditures are based on U.S.
Department of Agriculture annual estimates
of construction; public utility estimates are
obtained from reports submitted to Federal
regulatory agencies and from private utility
companies; estimates for all other private
construction (nonbuilding) are obtained by
phasing F. W. Dodge contract award data;
estimates of Federal construction are based
on monthly data supplied by Federal agencies.

**Data Collection and Imputation Proce-
dures:** See "Type of Data Collection
Operation." Imputation accounts for
approximately 20% of estimated value of
construction each month.

Estimates of Sampling Error: CV estimates
for private nonresidential building construction range from 3% for estimated value of
industrial buildings to 9% for religious buildings. CV is approximately 2% for total new
private nonresidential buildings.

Other (nonsampling) Errors: For directly
measured data series based on samples,
some nonsampling errors may arise from
processing errors, imputations, and misun-
derstanding of questions. Indirect data
series are dependent on the validity of the
underlying assumptions and procedures.

Sources of Additional Material: U.S.
Bureau of the Census, *Construction
Reports,* series C30, *Value of New
Construction Put in Place.*

Source and Title: U.S. Bureau of the
Census, *Census of Housing*

Tables: See tables citing *Census of Housing*
in source notes in section 25.

Universe, Frequency, and Types of Data:
Census of all occupied and vacant housing,
excluding group quarters, conducted every
10 years as part of the decennial census
(see section 1 above) to determine characteristics of U.S. housing.

Type of Data Collection Operation: For
1970, 1980, and 1990, a complete count of
some housing items (e.g. Owned or rented,
and value). In 1970, other items collected
from 5% and 15% probability samples
selected from two sets of detailed questions
on housing (these two sets having some
common items). In 1980, approximately
19% of the housing units were included in
the sample; in 1990, approximately 17%.

**Data Collection and Imputation Proce-
dures:** In 1970, a self-enumeration census
using a mail-out/mail-back procedure was
used in most areas. In 1980 and 1990, mail
questionnaires were used in even more
areas than in 1970, with personal interviews
in the remainder. Followup for nonrespondents and identification of vacant units done
by phone and personal visit.

Estimates of Sampling Error: Sampling
errors for data are estimated for all items
collected by sample and vary by characteristic and geographic area.

Other (nonsampling) Errors: Evaluation
studies for 1980 estimated the underenumeration of occupied housing units at 1.5%.
The missed rate in 1980 for all units was
2.6% or approximately 2.3 million units, 1
million of which were vacant housing units.

Sources of Additional Material: U.S.
Bureau of the Census, *1980 Census of
Population and Housing, The Coverage of
Housing in the 1980 Census,* PHC80-E1,
July 1985.

Source and Title: U.S. Bureau of the Census, *American Housing Survey*

Tables: See tables citing *American Housing
Survey* in source notes.

Universe, Frequency, and Types of Data:
Conducted nationally in the fall in odd numbered years to obtain data on the approximately 103 million occupied or vacant
housing units in the United States (group
quarters are excluded). Data include characteristics of occupied housing units, vacant
units, new housing and mobile home units,
financial characteristics, recent mover
households, housing and neighborhood
quality indicators, and energy characteristics.

Type of Data Collection Operation: The national sample was a multistage probability sample with about 51,300 units eligible for interview in 1987. Sample units, selected within 394 PSU's, were surveyed over a 5-month period.

Data Collection and Imputation Procedures: For 1987, the survey was conducted by personal interviews. The interviewers obtained the information from the occupants or, if the unit was vacant, from informed persons such as landlords, rental agents, or knowledgeable neighbors.

Estimates of Sampling Error: For the national sample, illustrations of the S.E. of the estimates are provided in the appendix B of the 1987 report. As an example, the estimated CV is about 0.5% for the estimated percentage of owner occupied units with two persons.

Other (nonsampling) Errors: Response rate was about 97%. Nonsampling errors may result from incorrect or incomplete responses, errors in coding and recording, and processing errors. For the 1985 national sample, approximately 6% of the total housing inventory was not adequately represented by the AHS sample.

Sources of Additional Material: U.S. Bureau of the Census, *Current Housing Reports,* series H-150 and H-170, *American Housing Survey.*

(See section 1 above for information pertaining to the Census of Population, section 15 pertaining to table 1203, and section 19 for table 1233.)

Section 26. MANUFACTURES

Source and Title: U.S. Bureau of the Census, *Census of Manufactures*

Tables: See tables citing *Census of Manufactures* in source notes in section 26 and also table 916 in section 18 and table 1358 in section 29.

Universe, Frequency, and Types of Data: Conducted every 5 years to obtain information on labor, materials, capital input and output characteristics, plant location, and legal form of organization for all plants in the United States with one or more paid employees. Universe was 350,000 manufacturing establishments in 1987.

Type of Data Collection Operation: Complete enumeration of data items obtained from 200,000 firms. Administrative records from Internal Revenue Service and Social Security Administration are used for 150,000 smaller single-location firms, which were determined by various cutoffs based on size and industry.

Data Collection and Imputation Procedures: Five mail and telephone followups for larger nonrespondents. Data for small single-location firms (generally those with fewer than 10 employees) not mailed census questionnaires were estimated from administrative records of IRS and SSA. Data for nonrespondents were imputed from related responses or administrative records from IRS and SSA. Approximately 8% of total value of shipments was represented by fully imputed records in 1987.

Estimates of Sampling Error: Not applicable.

Other (nonsampling) Errors: Based on evaluation studies, estimates of nonsampling errors for 1972 were about 1.3% for estimated total payroll; 2% for total employment; and 1% for value of shipments. Estimates for later years are not available.

Sources of Additional Material: U.S. Bureau of the Census, *1987 Census of Manufactures, Industry Series, Geographic Area Series, and Subject Series.*

Source and Title: U.S. Bureau of the Census, *Annual Survey of Manufactures*

Tables: See tables citing *Annual Survey of Manufactures* in source notes.

Universe, Frequency, and Types of Data: Conducted annually to provide basic measures of manufacturing activity for intercensal years for all manufacturing establishments having one or more paid employees.

Type of Data Collection Operation: Sampling frame is 350,000 establishments in the 1987 Census of Manufactures (see above), supplemented by Social Security Administration lists of new manufacturers and new manufacturing establishments of multi-establishment companies identified annually by the Census Bureau's Company Organization Survey. A probability sample of about 55,000 establishments is selected. All establishments of companies with more than $500 million of manufacturing shipments in 1987 are included with certainty. All establishments with 250+ employees are also included with certainty along with a probability sample of smaller establishments.

Data Collection and Imputation Procedures: Survey is conducted by mail with phone and mail followups of nonrespondents. Imputation (for all nonresponse items) is based on previous year reports, or for new establishments in survey, on industry averages.

Estimates of Sampling Error: Estimated standard errors for number of employees, new expenditure, and for value added totals are given in annual publications. For U.S. level industry statistics, most estimated standard errors are 2% or less, but vary considerably for detailed characteristics.

Other (nonsampling) Errors: Response rate is about 85%. Nonsampling errors include those due to collection, reporting, and transcription errors, many of which are corrected through computer and clerical checks.

Sources of Additional Material: U.S. Bureau of the Census, *Annual Survey of Manufactures,* and Technical Paper 24.

Section 27. DOMESTIC TRADE AND SERVICES

Source and Title: U.S. Bureau of the Census, *Census of Wholesale Trade, Census of Retail Trade, Census of Service Industries*

Tables: See tables citing the above censuses in source notes in section 27 and table 1358 in section 29.

Universe, Frequency, and Types of Data: Conducted every 5 years to obtain data on number of establishments, number of employees, total payroll size, total sales, and other industry-specific statistics. In 1992, the universe was all employer establishments primarily engaged in wholesale trade, and employer and nonemployer establishments in retail trade or service industries.

Type of Data Collection Operation: All wholesale firms with paid employees surveyed; all retail and service large employer firms surveyed (i.e. all employer firms above the payroll size cutoff established to separate large from small employers) plus a 10-percent sample of smaller employer firms. Firms with no employees were not required to file a census return.

Data Collection and Imputation Procedures: Mail questionnaire is utilized with both mail and telephone followups for nonrespondents. Data for nonrespondents and "nonselected" small employer firms in retail trade and service industries are obtained from administrative records of IRS and the Social Security Administration.

Estimates of Sampling Error: Not applicable.

Other (nonsampling) Errors: Response rate in 1992 of 88% for single establishment firms; 89% for multi-establishment firms. Item response ranged from 60% to 90% with higher rates for less detailed questions.

Sources of Additional Material: U.S. Bureau of the Census, Appendix A of *Census of Retail Trade; Census of Service Industries; Census of Wholesale Trade;* and *History of the 1987 Economic Censuses,* April 1992.

Source and Title: U.S. Bureau of the Census, *Current Business Surveys*

Tables: 1292-1295, 1309, 1313, 1317, and table 174 in section 3, tables 405 and 427 in section 7, and table 1010 in section 21.

Universe, Frequency, and Types of Data: Provides monthly estimates of retail sales by kind of business and geographic area, and end-of-month inventories of retail stores; monthly wholesale sales and end-of-month inventories; and annual receipts of selected service industries.

Type of Data Collection Operation: Probability sample of all firms from a list frame and, additionally, (before August 1993) for retail and service an area frame. The list frame is the Bureau's Standard Statistical Establishment List (SSEL) updated quarterly for recent birth Employer Identification (EIN) Numbers issued by the Internal Revenue Service and assigned a kind-of-business code by the Social Security Administration. The largest firms are included monthly; a sample of others is included every three months on a rotating basis. Prior to August 1993, an area sample was used to account for employer births and nonemployers in retail trade. To account for sales and inventories for employer births and nonemployers, a benchmarking operation was initiated.

Data Collection and Imputation Procedures: Data are collected by mail questionnaire with telephone followups for nonrespondents. Imputation made for each nonresponse item and each item failing edit checks.

Estimates of Sampling Error: For the 1995 monthly surveys, CV's are about 0.7% for estimated total retail sales, 1.3% for wholesale sales, 1.8% for wholesale inventories. For dollar volume of receipts, CV's from the *Service Annual Survey* vary by kind of business and range between 1.5% to 15.0%. Sampling errors are shown in monthly publications.

Other (nonsampling) Errors: Imputation rates are about 18% to 23% for monthly retail sales, 27% to 32% for retail inventories, 23% to 28% for wholesale sales, about 25% to 30% for monthly wholesale inventories and 14% for the *Service Annual Survey.*

Sources of Additional Material: U.S. Bureau of the Census, *Current Business Reports, Monthly Retail Trade, Monthly Wholesale Trade,* and *Service Annual Survey.*

Section 29. OUTLYING AREAS

(See section 1 for information pertaining to tables 1347 and 1348, section 2 for table 1346, section 22 for table 1354, sections 26 and 27 for table 1358.)

Index to Tables Having Historical Statistics, Colonial Times to 1970 Series

[The most recent historical supplement to the *Statistical Abstract* is the bicentennial edition, *Historical Statistics of the United States, Colonial Times to 1970* (see inside back cover). Listed below are statistical time series (identified by number) appearing in this edition, for which tables in the *Statistical Abstract* present comparable figures. Historical series are listed only where related or comparable data are available for one or more years later than 1970. In a few instances, it may be necessary to combine figures shown in the *Abstract* to obtain totals comparable to the series shown in *Historical Statistics*]

Historical Statistics series	1995 Abstract table number	Historical Statistics series	1995 Abstract table number	Historical Statistics series	1995 Abstract table number	Historical Statistics series	1995 Abstract table number
M—Con.		**Q—Con.**		**T—Con.**		**X—Con.**	
M 93-126	1200	Q 284-312 . . .	1055	T 245-271 . . .	1293	X 454-455 . . .	819
M 127-128 . . .	952	Q 319, 330. . .	1055	T 274-287 . . .	1308	X 474-491 . . .	823
M 143-146 . . .	1194	Q 332.	1057	T 280-371 . . .	1309	X 492-498 . . .	821
M 147-161 . . .	1197	Q 356-378 . . .	1055	T 391-443 . . .	1315	X 517-530 . . .	828
M 266-267 . . .	1201	Q 400-401 . . .	1055	T 444-471 . . .	929	X 536-539 . . .	837
M 271-286 . . .	1186	Q 414-416 . . .	1091	T 472-484 . . .	928	X 551-560 . . .	810
		Q 438-448 . . .	1087			X 588-609 . . .	794
N		Q 449-458 . . .	1089			X 716-724 . . .	792
N 1-29	1206	Q 473-480 . . .	1093	**U**		X 741, 748 . . .	793
N 66-69	1206	Q 487-502 . . .	1088	U 1-25	1319	X 756, 761 . . .	793
N 78-100	1208	Q 507-517 . . .	1086	U 26-39	1322	X 821; 835 . . .	784
N 118-137 . . .	1204	Q 604-623 . . .	1072	U 41-46	1329	X 864-878 . . .	800
N 140-155 . . .	1203			U 47-74	1324	X 879-889 . . .	843
N 156-163 . . .	1212	**R**		U 75-186	1330	X 890-917 . . .	845
N 170.	1212	R 1-12	903	U 190-195 . . .	1335		
N 186-191 . . .	1238	R 31-45	903	U 207-212 . . .	1343		
N 238-245 . . .	1225	R 46-70	901	U 264-273 . . .	1336	**Y**	
N 249-258 . . .	1236	R 75-88	901	U 317-352 . . .	1341	Y 79-83	433
N 273, 276. . .	804	R 106-109 . . .	929			Y 84-134	436
		R 123-126 . . .	929			Y 135-186 . . .	437
		R 140-148 . . .	906	**V**		Y 189-198 . . .	445
P		R 163-171 . . .	924	V 1-12	846	Y 199-203 . . .	446
P 1-12	1245	R 172-186 . . .	925	V 20-30	860	Y 204-210 . . .	441
P 13.	1251	R 188-191 . . .	926	V 42-53	848	Y 211-214. . . .	439
P 18-39	1251	R 191-216 . . .	921	V 167-183 . . .	856	Y 272-307 . . .	506
P 58-67	1246	R 224-231 . . .	918	V 193-196 . . .	856	Y 308-317 . . .	542
P 74-92	1274	R 232-243 . . .	917	V 197-212 . . .	971	Y 318-331 . . .	541
P 93-106	891					Y 339-342 . . .	517
P 235, 236a . .	1261			**W**		Y 343-351 . . .	518
P 239-241 . . .	1262	**S**		W 14, 17, 19 .	669	Y 358-373 . . .	532
P 265-269 . . .	1266	S 1-14	934	W 22-25	670	Y 381-392 . . .	854
		S 32-52	962	W 30-54.	669	Y 393-411. . . .	533
Q		S 78-82	962	W 62-65	669	Y 412-439 . . .	538
Q 36-42	1008	S 86-107	962	W 82-95	908	Y 458-460 . . .	550
Q 50-51, 55 . .	1012	S 133-146 . . .	971	W 96-108 . . .	871	Y 472-487 . . .	518
Q 69-75	1048	S 160-175 . . .	973	W 109-125 . . .	981	Y 505-637 . . .	474
Q 90-94	1016	S 190-204 . . .	977	W 126	984	Y 638-651 . . .	479
Q 136-147 . . .	1019	S 205-218 . . .	976	W 142	983	Y 652-848 . . .	474
Q 148; 150. . .	1296			W 167	992	Y 710-782 . . .	490
Q 156-162 . . .	1042	**T**				Y 787-788 . . .	476
Q 199-207 . . .	1045	T 43-47	1289	**X**		Y 794.	485
Q 208.	1033	T 79-196	1291	X 114-147 . . .	787	Y 856-903 . . .	569
Q 224-232 . . .	1033	T 197-219 . . .	1294	X 192, 229. . .	784	Y 904-916 . . .	564
Q 233-234 . . .	1018	T 245-246 . . .	1292	X 410-417 . . .	815	Y 943-956 . . .	577
Q 238-250 . . .	1046			X 444-453 . . .	820	Y 998-999 . . .	580

Tables Deleted From the 1994 Edition of the Statistical Abstract

Entire section new, consisting of 92 tables.

Index

NOTE: Index citations refer to table numbers, not page numbers.

NOTE: Index citations refer to table numbers, not page numbers.

NOTE: Index citations refer to table numbers, not page numbers.

NOTE: Index citations refer to table numbers, not page numbers.

NOTE: Index citations refer to table numbers, not page numbers.

NOTE: Index citations refer to table numbers, not page numbers.

NOTE: Index citations refer to table numbers, not page numbers.

NOTE: Index citations refer to table numbers, not page numbers.

NOTE: Index citations refer to table numbers, not page numbers.

NOTE: Index citations refer to table numbers, not page numbers.

NOTE: Index citations refer to table numbers, not page numbers.

1004   Index

NOTE: Index citations refer to table numbers, not page numbers.

NOTE: Index citations refer to table numbers, not page numbers.

NOTE: Index citations refer to table numbers, not page numbers.

NOTE: Index citations refer to table numbers, not page numbers.

NOTE: Index citations refer to table numbers, not page numbers.

NOTE: Index citations refer to table numbers, not page numbers.

NOTE: Index citations refer to table numbers, not page numbers.

NOTE: Index citations refer to table numbers, not page numbers.

NOTE: Index citations refer to table numbers, not page numbers.

Table

NOTE: Index citations refer to table numbers, not page numbers.

NOTE: Index citations refer to table numbers, not page numbers.

NOTE: Index citations refer to table numbers, not page numbers.

NOTE: Index citations refer to table numbers, not page numbers.

NOTE: Index citations refer to table numbers, not page numbers.

NOTE: Index citations refer to table numbers, not page numbers.

NOTE: Index citations refer to table numbers, not page numbers.

NOTE: Index citations refer to table numbers, not page numbers.

Table

NOTE: Index citations refer to table numbers, not page numbers.

NOTE: Index citations refer to table numbers, not page numbers.

Table

NOTE: Index citations refer to table numbers, not page numbers.

Index

NOTE: Index citations refer to table numbers, not page numbers.

NOTE: Index citations refer to table numbers, not page numbers.

NOTE: Index citations refer to table numbers, not page numbers.

NOTE: Index citations refer to table numbers, not page numbers.

NOTE: Index citations refer to table numbers, not page numbers.

NOTE: Index citations refer to table numbers, not page numbers.

NOTE: Index citations refer to table numbers, not page numbers.

NOTE: Index citations refer to table numbers, not page numbers.

NOTE: Index citations refer to table numbers, not page numbers.

NOTE: Index citations refer to table numbers, not page numbers.

NOTE: Index citations refer to table numbers, not page numbers.

NOTE: Index citations refer to table numbers, not page numbers.

NOTE: Index citations refer to table numbers, not page numbers.

NOTE: Index citations refer to table numbers, not page numbers.

NOTE: Index citations refer to table numbers, not page numbers.

NOTE: Index citations refer to table numbers, not page numbers.

NOTE: Index citations refer to table numbers, not page numbers.

Table   **Table**

NOTE: Index citations refer to table numbers, not page numbers.

NOTE: Index citations refer to table numbers, not page numbers.

NOTE: Index citations refer to table numbers, not page numbers.

NOTE: Index citations refer to table numbers, not page numbers.

Index

NOTE: Index citations refer to table numbers, not page numbers.